"What does THE BIBLE say about..."

"What does THE BIBLE say about..."

THE ULTIMATE BIBLE ANSWER BOOK

BRIAN RIDOLFI

Advancing the Ministries of the Gospel

AMG Publishers

God's Word to you is our highest calling.

Library of Congress Cataloging-in-Publication Data

Bible. English. Authorized. Selections. 2005.
  What does the Bible say about-- : the ultimate Bible answer book / [compiled by] Brian Ridolfi.
    p. cm.
  Summary: "Serves as a topical reference Bible, a concordance, and a question and answer book all in one volume. With more than 400 categories and 3000 subcategories, it is a useful reference tool for studying the King James Version of the Bible"--Provided by publisher.
  ISBN-13: 978-0-89957-379-3 (hardcover : alk. paper)
  ISBN-10: 0-89957-379-7 (hardcover : alk. paper)
  1. Bible--Concordances, English. I. Ridolfi, Brian, 1973- II. Title.
  BS425.B53 2005
  220.5'2033--dc22
                                        2005016694

Printed in the United States of America
11 10 09 08 07 06   –R– 8 7 6 5 4 3 2

I wish to extend special thanks to my parents Dewey and Adrienne—their support was vital. This book could not have been done without their help.

To God, my Lord and Savior, without Him nothing is possible.

Contents

Aa

B*b*

Cc

D*d*

Ee

F*f*

G g

H*h*

I*i*

Jj

M*m*

N*n*

Oo

Pp

Qq

Rr

S*s*

T*t*

Uu

Yy

Preface

The Holy Bible is the world's all time bestseller; nevertheless, its size intimidates readers. **What Does The Bible Say About . . .** makes delving into the Bible easier and less overwhelming by providing readers easy access to biblical truths. Use the book as a reference tool, a study aid, a sermon or lesson planner, a witnessing tool, or a help-hand within a Bible study group. It is also a quality assurance manual of sorts to check out Biblical passages and teachings that might be misconstrued or misquoted by laymen and pastors alike. This book battles false doctrine by presenting readers unbiased quotes straight from the biblical record without private interpretation from anyone. Versatility lends it to many uses.

How to Use What Does the Bible Say About . . .

What Does the Bible Say About . . . functions like a dictionary or encyclopedia. It isn't meant to be read from cover to cover like a Bible commentary, but rather as a reference tool for finding quick information.

First, find the subject or category of interest within the table of contents.

Next, search through the subcategories underneath the major subject, and then locate the subcategory that interests you.

Finally, note the page number and look it up in the body of the text.

Oftentimes passages are found in various subject categories as well as a number of subject subcategories. For example John 3:16 says, "For God so loved the world, that he gave his only begotten Son, that whosoever believeth in him should not perish, but have everlasting life." You will be able to find this well known verse under these subject categories: **Belief, Eternal Life, Jesus Christ, Love, Perishing, Salvation,** and **Sending and Those Sent.**

The words *believeth, everlasting life, begotten Son, loved,* and *perish* are key words which will help you locate this passage in the table of contents. The words *salvation* and *sending* are not mentioned in the text, even though the John 3:16 text is found under **Salvation** and **Sending and Those Sent** because it affirms God sent His Son to save us from our sins.

If you want to know who shall receive eternal life, look up **Eternal Life** in the table of contents, searching through the subcategory **Who Shall Receive Eternal Life** and there you will see a page number to find John 3:16 as well as other verses that answer the question who shall receive eternal life.

It is our hope that this unique reference book will be a blessing to you in your study of God's Word.

Who Shall Abide In The Lord's Tabernacle

Psalm 15:1-5 "¹LORD, who shall abide in thy tabernacle? who shall dwell in thy holy hill? ²He that walketh uprightly, and worketh righteousness, and speaketh the truth in his heart. ³He that backbiteth not with his tongue, nor doeth evil to his neighbour, nor taketh up a reproach against his neighbour. ⁴In whose eyes a vile person is contemned; but he honoureth them that fear the LORD. He that sweareth to his own hurt, and changeth not. ⁵He that putteth not out his money to usury, nor taketh reward against the innocent. He that doeth these things shall never be moved."

Psalm 61:1-4 "¹Hear my cry, O God; attend unto my prayer. ²From the end of the earth will I cry unto thee, when my heart is overwhelmed: lead me to the rock that is higher than I. ³For thou hast been a shelter for me, and a strong tower from the enemy. ⁴I will abide in thy tabernacle for ever: I will trust in the covert of thy wings. Selah."

Who Shall Abide Under
The Shadow Of The Almighty

Psalm 61:1-4 "¹Hear my cry, O God; attend unto my prayer. ²From the end of the earth will I cry unto thee, when my heart is overwhelmed: lead me to the rock that is higher than I. ³For thou hast been a shelter for me, and a strong tower from the enemy. ⁴I will abide in thy tabernacle for ever: I will trust in the covert of thy wings. Selah."

Psalm 91:1 "He that dwelleth in the secret place of the most High shall abide under the shadow of the Almighty."

ABODES

Who God The Father And Jesus Christ
Make Their Abode With

John 14:22-23 "²²Judas saith unto him, not Iscariot, Lord, how is it that thou wilt manifest thyself unto us, and not unto the world? ²³Jesus answered and said unto him, If a man love me, he will keep my words: and my Father will love him, and we will come unto him, and make our abode with him."

ABOMINATION

The Abomination That Makes Desolate

Jeremiah 32:32-36 "³²Because of all the evil of the children of Israel and of the children of Judah, which they have done to provoke me to anger, they, their kings, their princes, their priests, and their prophets, and the men of Judah, and the inhabitants of Jerusalem. ³³And they have turned unto me the back, and not the face: though I taught them, rising up early and teaching them, yet they have not hearkened to receive instruction. ³⁴But they set their abominations in the house, which is called by my name, to defile it. ³⁵And they built the high places of Baal, which are in the valley of the son of Hinnom, to cause their sons and their daughters to pass through the fire unto Molech; which I commanded them not, neither came it into my mind, that they should do this abomination, to cause Judah to sin. ³⁶And now therefore thus saith the LORD, the God of Israel, concerning this city, whereof ye say, It shall be delivered into the hand of the king of Babylon by the sword, and by the famine, and by the pestilence."

Ezekiel 8:5-6 "⁵Then said he unto me, Son of man, lift up thine eyes now the way toward the north. So I lifted up mine eyes the way toward the north, and behold northward at the gate of the altar this image of jealousy in the entry. ⁶He said furthermore unto me, Son of man, seest thou what they do? even the great abominations that the house of Israel committeth here, that I should go far off from my sanctuary? but turn thee yet again, and thou shalt see greater abominations."

Daniel 8:8-14 "⁸Therefore the he goat waxed very great: and when he was strong, the great horn was broken; and for it came up four notable ones toward the four winds of heaven. ⁹And out of one of them came forth a little horn, which waxed exceeding great, toward the south, and toward the east, and toward the pleasant land. ¹⁰And it waxed great, even to the host of heaven; and it cast down some of the host and of the stars to the ground, and stamped upon them. ¹¹Yea, he magnified himself even to the prince of the host, and by him the daily sacrifice was taken away, and the place of his sanctuary was cast down. ¹²And an host was given him against the daily sacrifice by reason of transgression, and it cast down the truth to the ground; and it practised, and prospered. ¹³Then I heard one saint speaking, and another saint said unto that certain saint which spake, How long shall be the vision concerning the daily sacrifice, and the transgression of desolation, to give both the sanctuary and the host to be trodden under foot? ¹⁴And he said unto me, Unto two thousand and three hundred days; then shall the sanctuary be cleansed."

Daniel 9:24-27 "²⁴Seventy weeks are determined upon thy people and upon thy holy city, to finish the transgression, and to make an end of sins, and to make reconciliation for iniquity, and to bring in everlasting righteousness, and to seal up the vision and prophecy, and to anoint the most Holy. ²⁵Know therefore and understand, that from the going forth of the commandment to restore and to build Jerusalem unto the Messiah the Prince shall be seven weeks, and threescore and two weeks: the street shall be built again, and the wall, even in troublous times. ²⁶And after threescore and two weeks shall Messiah be cut off, but not for himself: and the people of the prince that shall come shall destroy the city and the sanctuary; and the end thereof shall be with a flood, and unto the end of the war desolations are determined. ²⁷And he shall confirm the covenant with many for one week: and in the midst of the week he shall cause the sacrifice and the oblation to cease, and for the overspreading of abominations he shall make it desolate, even until the consummation, and that determined shall be poured upon the desolate."

Daniel 11:20-31 "²⁰Then shall stand up in his estate a raiser of taxes in the glory of the kingdom: but within few days he shall be destroyed, neither in anger, nor in battle. ²¹And in his estate shall stand up a vile person, to whom they shall not give the honour of the kingdom: but he shall come in peaceably, and obtain the kingdom by flatteries. ²²And with the arms of a flood shall they be overflown from before him, and shall be broken; yea, also the prince of the covenant. ²³And after the league made with him he shall work deceitfully: for he shall come up, and shall become strong with a small people. ²⁴He shall enter peaceably even upon the fattest places of the province; and he shall do that which his fathers have not done, nor his fathers' fathers; he shall scatter among them the prey, and spoil, and riches: yea, and he shall forecast his devices against the strong holds, even for a time. ²⁵And he shall stir up his power and his courage against the king of the south with a great army; and the king of the south shall be

stirred up to battle with a very great and mighty army; but he shall not stand: for they shall forecast devices against him. ²⁶Yea, they that feed of the portion of his meat shall destroy him, and his army shall overflow: and many shall fall down slain. ²⁷And both these kings' hearts shall be to do mischief, and they shall speak lies at one table; but it shall not prosper: for yet the end shall be at the time appointed. ²⁸Then shall he return into his land with great riches; and his heart shall be against the holy covenant; and he shall do exploits, and return to his own land. ²⁹At the time appointed he shall return, and come toward the south; but it shall not be as the former, or as the latter. ³⁰For the ships of Chittim shall come against him: therefore he shall be grieved, and return, and have indignation against the holy covenant: so shall he do; he shall even return, and have intelligence with them that forsake the holy covenant. ³¹And arms shall stand on his part, and they shall pollute the sanctuary of strength, and shall take away the daily sacrifice, and they shall place the abomination that maketh desolate."

Daniel 12:5-11 "⁵Then I Daniel looked, and, behold, there stood other two, the one on this side of the bank of the river, and the other on that side of the bank of the river. ⁶And one said to the man clothed in linen, which was upon the waters of the river, How long shall it be to the end of these wonders? ⁷And I heard the man clothed in linen, which was upon the waters of the river, when he held up his right hand and his left hand unto heaven, and sware by him that liveth for ever that it shall be for a time, times, and an half; and when he shall have accomplished to scatter the power of the holy people, all these things shall be finished. ⁸And I heard, but I understood not: then said I, O my Lord, what shall be the end of these things? ⁹And he said, Go thy way, Daniel: for the words are closed up and sealed till the time of the end. ¹⁰Many shall be purified, and made white, and tried; but the wicked shall do wickedly: and none of the wicked shall understand; but the wise shall understand. ¹¹And from the time that the daily sacrifice shall be taken away, and the abomination that maketh desolate set up, there shall be a thousand two hundred and ninety days."

Matthew 24:15-18 "¹⁵When ye therefore shall see the abomination of desolation, spoken of by Daniel the prophet, stand in the holy place, (whoso readeth, let him understand:) [16]Then let them which be in Judaea flee into the mountains: [17]Let him which is on the housetop not come down to take any thing out of his house: [18]Neither let him which is in the field return back to take his clothes."

Mark 13:14-16 "[14]But when ye shall see the abomination of desolation, spoken of by Daniel the prophet, standing where it ought not, (let him that readeth understand,) then let them that be in Judaea flee to the mountains: [15]And let him that is on the housetop not go down into the house, neither enter therein, to take any thing out of his house: [16]And let him that is in the field not turn back again for to take up his garment."

What Is An Abomination

Leviticus 11:2-23 "[2]Speak unto the children of Israel, saying, These are the beasts which ye shall eat among all the beasts that are on the earth. [3]Whatsoever parteth the hoof, and is clovenfooted, and cheweth the cud, among the beasts, that shall ye eat. [4]Nevertheless these shall ye not eat of them that chew the cud, or of them that divide the hoof: as the camel, because he cheweth the cud, but divideth not the hoof; he is unclean unto you. [5]And the coney, because he cheweth the cud, but divideth not the hoof; he is unclean unto you. [6]And the hare, because he cheweth the cud, but divideth not the hoof; he is unclean unto you. [7]And the swine, though he divide the hoof, and be clovenfooted, yet he cheweth not the cud; he is unclean to you. [8]Of their flesh shall ye not eat, and their carcase shall ye not touch; they are unclean to you. [9]These shall ye eat of all that are in the waters: whatsoever hath fins and scales in the waters, in the seas, and in the rivers, them shall ye eat. [10]And all that have not fins and scales in the seas, and in the rivers, of all that move in the waters, and of any living thing which is in the waters, they shall be an abomination unto you: [11]They shall be even an abomination unto you; ye shall not eat of their flesh, but ye shall have their carcases in abomination. [12]Whatsoever hath no fins nor scales in the waters, that shall be an abomination unto you. [13]And these are they which ye shall have in abomination among the fowls; they shall not be eaten, they are an abomination: the eagle, and the ossifrage, and the ospray, [14]And the vulture, and the kite after his kind; [15]Every raven after

his kind; [16]And the owl, and the night hawk, and the cuckow, and the hawk after his kind, [17]And the little owl, and the cormorant, and the great owl, [18]And the swan, and the pelican, and the gier eagle, [19]And the stork, the heron after her kind, and the lapwing, and the bat. [20]All fowls that creep, going upon all four, shall be an abomination unto you. [21]Yet these may ye eat of every flying creeping thing that goeth upon all four, which have legs above their feet, to leap withal upon the earth; [22]Even these of them ye may eat; the locust after his kind, and the bald locust after his kind, and the beetle after his kind, and the grasshopper after his kind. [23]But all other flying creeping things, which have four feet, shall be an abomination unto you."

Leviticus 11:41-43 "[41]And every creeping thing that creepeth upon the earth shall be an abomination; it shall not be eaten. [42]Whatsoever goeth upon the belly, and whatsoever goeth upon all four, or whatsoever hath more feet among all creeping things that creep upon the earth, them ye shall not eat; for they are an abomination. [43]Ye shall not make yourselves abominable with any creeping thing that creepeth, neither shall ye make yourselves unclean with them, that ye should be defiled thereby."

Leviticus 18:22 "Thou shalt not lie with mankind, as with womankind: it is abomination."

Leviticus 20:13 "If a man also lie with mankind, as he lieth with a woman, both of them have committed an abomination: they shall surely be put to death; their blood shall be upon them."

Deuteronomy 7:25 "The graven images of their gods shall ye burn with fire: thou shalt not desire the silver or gold that is on them, nor take it unto thee, lest thou be snared therein: for it is an abomination to the LORD thy God."

Deuteronomy 12:31 "Thou shalt not do so unto the LORD thy God: for every abomination to the LORD, which he hateth, have they done unto their gods; for even their sons and their daughters they have burnt in the fire to their gods."

Deuteronomy 18:9-12 "[9]When thou art come into the land which the LORD thy God giveth thee, thou shalt not learn to do after the abominations of those nations. [10]There shall not be found among you any one that maketh his son or his daughter to pass through the fire, or that useth divination, or an observer of times, or an enchanter, or a witch, [11]Or a charmer, or a consulter with familiar spirits, or a wizard, or a necromancer. [12]For all that do these things are an abomination unto the LORD: and because of these abominations the LORD thy God doth drive them out from before thee."

Deuteronomy 22:5 "The woman shall not wear that which pertaineth unto a man, neither shall a man put on a woman's garment: for all that do so are abomination unto the LORD thy God."

Deuteronomy 23:17-18 "[17]There shall be no whore of the daughters of Israel, nor a sodomite of the sons of Israel. [18]Thou shalt not bring the hire of a whore, or the price of a dog, into the house of the LORD thy God for any vow: for even both these are abomination unto the LORD thy God."

Deuteronomy 24:1-4 "[1]When a man hath taken a wife, and married her, and it come to pass that she find no favour in his eyes, because he hath found some uncleanness in her: then let him write her a bill of divorcement, and give it in her hand, and send her out of his house. [2]And when she is departed out of his house, she may go and be another man's wife. [3]And if the latter husband hate her, and write her a bill of divorcement, and giveth it in her hand, and sendeth her out of his house; or if the latter husband die, which took her to be his wife; [4]Her former husband, which sent her away, may not take her again to be his wife, after that she is defiled; for that is abomination before the LORD: and thou shalt not cause the land to sin, which the LORD thy God giveth thee for an inheritance."

Deuteronomy 27:15 "Cursed be the man that maketh any graven or molten image, an abomination unto the LORD, the work of the hands of the craftsman, and putteth it in a secret place. And all the people shall answer and say, Amen."

Proverbs 3:32 "For the froward is abomination to the LORD: but his secret is with the righteous."

Proverbs 6:16-19 "[16]These six things doth the LORD hate: yea, seven are an abomination unto him: [17]A proud look, a lying tongue, and hands

that shed innocent blood, [18]An heart that deviseth wicked imaginations, feet that be swift in running to mischief, [19]A false witness that speaketh lies, and he that soweth discord among brethren."

Proverbs 11:1 "A false balance is abomination to the LORD: but a just weight is his delight."

Proverbs 11:20 "They that are of a froward heart are abomination to the LORD: but such as are upright in their way are his delight."

Proverbs 12:22 "Lying lips are abomination to the LORD: but they that deal truly are his delight."

Proverbs 15:8-9 "[8]The sacrifice of the wicked is an abomination to the LORD: but the prayer of the upright is his delight. [9]The way of the wicked is an abomination unto the LORD: but he loveth him that followeth after righteousness."

Proverbs 15:26 "The thoughts of the wicked are an abomination to the LORD: but the words of the pure are pleasant words."

Proverbs 16:5 "Every one that is proud in heart is an abomination to the LORD: though hand join in hand, he shall not be unpunished."

Proverbs 16:12 "It is an abomination to kings to commit wickedness: for the throne is established by righteousness."

Proverbs 17:15 "He that justifieth the wicked, and he that condemneth the just, even they both are abomination to the LORD."

Proverbs 20:10 "Divers weights, and divers measures, both of them are alike abomination to the LORD."

Proverbs 20:23 "Divers weights are an abomination unto the LORD; and a false balance is not good."

Proverbs 21:27 "The sacrifice of the wicked is abomination: how much more, when he bringeth it with a wicked mind?"

Proverbs 28:9 "He that turneth away his ear from hearing the law, even his prayer shall be abomination."

Isaiah 1:10-14 "[10]Hear the word of the LORD, ye rulers of Sodom; give ear unto the law of our God, ye people of Gomorrah. [11]To what purpose is the multitude of your sacrifices unto me? saith the LORD: I am full of the burnt offerings of rams, and the fat of fed beasts; and I delight not in the blood of bullocks, or of lambs, or of he goats. [12]When ye come to appear before me, who hath required this at your hand, to tread my courts? [13]Bring no more vain oblations; incense is an abomination unto me; the new moons and sabbaths, the calling of assemblies, I cannot away with; it is iniquity, even the solemn meeting. [14]Your new moons and your appointed feasts my soul hateth: they are a trouble unto me; I am weary to bear them."

Luke 16:15 "And he said unto them, Ye are they which justify yourselves before men; but God knoweth your hearts: for that which is highly esteemed among men is abomination in the sight of God."

ABUNDANCE/BOUNTY

The Lord Dealing Bountifully
Psalm 13:6 "I will sing unto the LORD, because he hath dealt bountifully with me."

Psalm 23:5-6 "[5]Thou preparest a table before me in the presence of mine enemies: thou anointest my head with oil; my cup runneth over. [6]Surely goodness and mercy shall follow me all the days of my life: and I will dwell in the house of the LORD for ever."

2 Corinthians 9:8-9 "[8]And God is able to make all grace abound toward you; that ye, always having all sufficiency in all things, may abound to every good work: [9](As it is written, He hath dispersed abroad; he hath given to the poor: his righteousness remaineth for ever."

James 1:5 "If any of you lack wisdom, let him ask of God, that giveth to all men liberally, and upbraideth not; and it shall be given him."

Those That Have A Bountiful Eye
Proverbs 22:9 "He that hath a bountiful eye shall be blessed; for he giveth of his bread to the poor."

Who The Lord Plentifully Rewards
Psalm 31:23 "O love the LORD, all ye his saints: for the LORD preserveth the faithful, and plentifully rewardeth the proud doer."

ACCOUNTABILITY

Everyone Giving Account
Of Themselves To God
Matthew 12:36-37 "[36]But I say unto you, That every idle word that men shall speak, they shall give account thereof in the day of judgment. [37]For by thy words thou shalt be justified, and by thy words thou shalt be condemned."

Romans 14:10-12 "[10]But why dost thou judge thy brother? or why dost thou set at nought thy brother? for we shall all stand before the judgment seat of Christ. [11]For it is written, As I live, saith the Lord, every knee shall bow to me, and every tongue shall confess to God. [12]So then every one of us shall give account of himself to God."

ACKNOWLEDGMENT

The Reward For Acknowledging Sin
Psalm 32:5 "I acknowledged my sin unto thee, and mine iniquity have I not hid. I said, I will confess my transgressions unto the LORD; and thou forgavest the iniquity of my sin. Selah."

The Reward For Acknowledging The Lord
Proverbs 3:5-6 "[5]Trust in the LORD with all thine heart; and lean not unto thine own understanding. [6]In all thy ways acknowledge him, and he shall direct thy paths."

Those That Acknowledge Christ
1 John 2:23 "Whosoever denieth the Son, the same hath not the Father: (but) he that acknowledgeth the Son hath the Father also."

ADMONITION

Admonishing One Another
Romans 15:14 "And I myself also am persuaded of you, my brethren, that ye also are full of goodness, filled with all knowledge, able also to admonish one another."

Colossians 3:16 "Let the word of Christ dwell in you richly in all wisdom; teaching and admonishing one another in psalms and hymns and spiritual songs, singing with grace in your hearts to the Lord."

Who Should Be Admonished

2 Thessalonians 3:14-15 "[14]And if any man obey not our word by this epistle, note that man, and have no company with him, that he may be ashamed. [15]Yet count him not as an enemy, but admonish him as a brother."

ADULTERY

Adulterers And Adulteresses

Leviticus 20:10 "And the man that committeth adultery with another man's wife, even he that committeth adultery with his neighbour's wife, the adulterer and the adulteress shall surely be put to death."

Deuteronomy 22:22 "If a man be found lying with a woman married to an husband, then they shall both of them die, both the man that lay with the woman, and the woman: so shalt thou put away evil from Israel."

Proverbs 6:24-34 "[24]To keep thee from the evil woman, from the flattery of the tongue of a strange woman. [25] Lust not after her beauty in thine heart; neither let her take thee with her eyelids. [26] For by means of a whorish woman a man is brought to a piece of bread: and the adulteress will hunt for the precious life. [27] Can a man take fire in his bosom, and his clothes not be burned? [28] Can one go upon hot coals, and his feet not be burned? [29] So he that goeth in to his neighbour's wife; whosoever toucheth her shall not be innocent. [30] Men do not despise a thief, if he steal to satisfy his soul when he is hungry; [31] But if he be found, he shall restore sevenfold; he shall give all the substance of his house. [32] But whoso committeth adultery with a woman lacketh understanding: he that doeth it destroyeth his own soul. [33] A wound and dishonour shall he get; and his reproach shall not be wiped away. [34] For jealousy is the rage of a man: therefore he will not spare in the day of vengeance."

Proverbs 30:18-20 "[18]There be three things which are too wonderful for me, yea, four which I know not: [19] The way of an eagle in the air; the way of a serpent upon a rock; the way of a ship in the midst of the sea; and the way of a man with a maid. [20] Such is the way of an adulterous woman; she eateth, and wipeth her mouth, and saith, I have done no wickedness."

John 8:3-5 "[3]And the scribes and Pharisees brought unto him a woman taken in adultery; and when they had set her in the midst, [4] They say unto him, Master, this woman was taken in adultery, in the very act. [5] Now Moses in the law commanded us, that such should be stoned: but what sayest thou?"

Hebrews 13:4 "Marriage is honourable in all, and the bed undefiled: but whoremongers and adulterers God will judge."

James 4:4 "Ye adulterers and adulteresses, know ye not that the friendship of the world is enmity with God? whosoever therefore will be a friend of the world is the enemy of God."

Revelation 2:18-22 "[18]And unto the angel of the church in Thyatira write; These things saith the Son of God, who hath his eyes like unto a flame of fire, and his feet are like fine brass; [19] I know thy works, and charity, and service, and faith, and thy patience, and thy works; and the last to be more than the first. [20] Notwithstanding I have a few things against thee, because thou sufferest that woman Jezebel, which calleth herself a prophetess, to teach and to seduce my servants to commit fornication, and to eat things sacrificed unto idols. [21] And I gave her space to repent of her fornication; and she repented not. [22] Behold, I will cast her into a bed, and them that commit adultery with her into great tribulation, except they repent of their deeds."

Not Committing Adultery

Exodus 20:14 "Thou shalt not commit adultery."

Leviticus 18:20 "Moreover thou shalt not lie carnally with thy neighbour's wife, to defile thyself with her."

Deuteronomy 5:18 "Neither shalt thou commit adultery."

Matthew 19:18 "He saith unto him, Which? Jesus said, Thou shalt do no murder, Thou shalt not commit adultery, Thou shalt not steal, Thou shalt not bear false witness."

Romans 13:8-9 "[8]Owe no man any thing, but to love one another: for he that loveth another hath fulfilled the law. [9]For this, Thou shalt not commit adultery, Thou shalt not kill, Thou shalt not steal, Thou shalt not bear false witness, Thou shalt not covet; and if there be any other commandment, it is briefly comprehended in this saying, namely, Thou shalt love thy neighbour as thyself."

James 2:11 "For he that said, Do not commit adultery, said also, Do not kill. Now if thou commit no adultery, yet if thou kill, thou art become a transgressor of the law."

The Reward For Committing Adultery
Hosea 4:1-3 "¹Hear the word of the LORD, ye children of Israel: for the LORD hath a controversy with the inhabitants of the land, because there is no truth, nor mercy, nor knowledge of God in the land. ²By swearing, and lying, and killing, and stealing, and committing adultery, they break out, and blood toucheth blood. ³Therefore shall the land mourn, and every one that dwelleth therein shall languish, with the beasts of the field, and with the fowls of heaven; yea, the fishes of the sea also shall be taken away."

Who Commits Adultery
Matthew 5:31-32 "³¹It hath been said, Whosoever shall put away his wife, let him give her a writing of divorcement: ³²But I say unto you, That whosoever shall put away his wife, saving for the cause of fornication, causeth her to commit adultery: and whosoever shall marry her that is divorced committeth adultery."

Matthew 19:9 "And I say unto you, Whosoever shall put away his wife, except it be for fornication, and shall marry another, committeth adultery: and whoso marrieth her which is put away doth commit adultery."

Mark 10:11-12 "¹¹And he saith unto them, Whosoever shall put away his wife, and marry another, committeth adultery against her. ¹²And if a woman shall put away her husband, and be married to another, she committeth adultery."

Luke 16:18 "Whosoever putteth away his wife, and marrieth another, committeth adultery: and whosoever marrieth her that is put away from her husband committeth adultery."

Romans 7:1-3 "¹Know ye not, brethren, (for I speak to them that know the law,) how that the law hath dominion over a man as long as he liveth? ²For the woman which hath an husband is bound by the law to her husband so long as he liveth; but if the husband be dead, she is loosed from the law of her husband. ³So then if, while her husband liveth, she be married to another man, she shall be called an adulteress: but if her husband be dead, she is free from that law; so that she is no adulteress, though she be married to another man."

Who Commits Adultery In Their Heart
Matthew 5:28 "But I say unto you, That whosoever looketh on a woman to lust after her hath committed adultery with her already in his heart."

Who Does Not Commit Adultery
Romans 7:2-3 "²For the woman which hath an husband is bound by the law to her husband so long as he liveth; but if the husband be dead, she is loosed from the law of her husband. ³So then if, while her husband liveth, she be married to another man, she shall be called an adulteress: but if her husband be dead, she is free from that law; so that she is no adulteress, though she be married to another man."

AFFLICTION

Christians Being Afflicted
Matthew 10:16-18 "¹⁶Behold, I send you forth as sheep in the midst of wolves: be ye therefore wise as serpents, and harmless as doves. ¹⁷ But beware of men: for they will deliver you up to the councils, and they will scourge you in their synagogues; ¹⁸ And ye shall be brought before governors and kings for my sake, for a testimony against them and the Gentiles."

Matthew 24:8-13 "⁸All these are the beginning of sorrows. ⁹ Then shall they deliver you up to be afflicted, and shall kill you: and ye shall be hated of all nations for my name's sake. ¹⁰ And then shall many be offended, and shall betray one another, and shall hate one another. ¹¹ And many false prophets shall rise, and shall deceive many. ¹² And because iniquity shall abound, the love of many shall wax cold. ¹³ But he that shall endure unto the end, the same shall be saved."

Enduring Afflictions
2 Timothy 4:5 "But watch thou in all things, endure afflictions, do the work of an evangelist, make full proof of thy ministry."

The Afflicted
Exodus 22:22-23 "²²Ye shall not afflict any widow, or fatherless child. ²³ If thou afflict them in any

wise, and they cry at all unto me, I will surely hear their cry."

2 Samuel 22:21-28 "²¹The LORD rewarded me according to my righteousness: according to the cleanness of my hands hath he recompensed me. ²² For I have kept the ways of the LORD, and have not wickedly departed from my God. ²³ For all his judgments were before me: and as for his statutes, I did not depart from them. ²⁴ I was also upright before him, and have kept myself from mine iniquity. ²⁵ Therefore the LORD hath recompensed me according to my righteousness; according to my cleanness in his eye sight. ²⁶ With the merciful thou wilt shew thyself merciful, and with the upright man thou wilt shew thyself upright. ²⁷ With the pure thou wilt shew thyself pure; and with the froward thou wilt shew thyself unsavoury. ²⁸ And the afflicted people thou wilt save: but thine eyes are upon the haughty, that thou mayest bring them down."

Job 34:23-28 "²³For he will not lay upon man more than right; that he should enter into judgment with God. ²⁴ He shall break in pieces mighty men without number, and set others in their stead. ²⁵ Therefore he knoweth their works, and he overturneth them in the night, so that they are destroyed. ²⁶ He striketh them as wicked men in the open sight of others; ²⁷ Because they turned back from him, and would not consider any of his ways: ²⁸ So that they cause the cry of the poor to come unto him, and he heareth the cry of the afflicted."

Psalm 140:12 "I know that the LORD will maintain the cause of the afflicted, and the right of the poor."

Proverbs 15:15 "All the days of the afflicted are evil: but he that is of a merry heart hath a continual feast."

Proverbs 22:22-23 "²²Rob not the poor, because he is poor: neither oppress the afflicted in the gate: ²³ For the LORD will plead their cause, and spoil the soul of those that spoiled them."

The Afflictions Of The Righteous

Psalm 34:19 "Many are the afflictions of the righteous: but the LORD delivereth him out of them all."

The Lord Not Afflicting

Job 37:23 "Touching the Almighty, we cannot find him out: he is excellent in power, and in judgment, and in plenty of justice: he will not afflict."

Lamentations 3:31-39 "³¹For the Lord will not cast off for ever: ³²But though he cause grief, yet will he have compassion according to the multitude of his mercies. ³³For he doth not afflict willingly nor grieve the children of men. ³⁴To crush under his feet all the prisoners of the earth, ³⁵To turn aside the right of a man before the face of the most High, ³⁶To subvert a man in his cause, the Lord approveth not. ³⁷Who is he that saith, and it cometh to pass, when the Lord commandeth it not? ³⁸Out of the mouth of the most High proceedeth not evil and good? ³⁹Wherefore doth a living man complain, a man for the punishment of his sins?"

The Servant Of The Lord Being Afflicted

Isaiah 53:1-12 "¹Who hath believed our report? and to whom is the arm of the LORD revealed? ²For he shall grow up before him as a tender plant, and as a root out of a dry ground: he hath no form nor comeliness; and when we shall see him, there is no beauty that we should desire him. ³He is despised and rejected of men; a man of sorrows, and acquainted with grief: and we hid as it were our faces from him; he was despised, and we esteemed him not. ⁴Surely he hath borne our griefs, and carried our sorrows: yet we did esteem him stricken, smitten of God, and afflicted. ⁵But he was wounded for our transgressions, he was bruised for our iniquities: the chastisement of our peace was upon him; and with his stripes we are healed. ⁶All we like sheep have gone astray; we have turned every one to his own way; and the LORD hath laid on him the iniquity of us all. ⁷He was oppressed, and he was afflicted, yet he opened not his mouth: he is brought as a lamb to the slaughter, and as a sheep before her shearers is dumb, so he openeth not his mouth. ⁸He was taken from prison and from judgment: and who shall declare his generation? for he was cut off out of the land of the living: for the transgression of my people was he stricken. ⁹And he made his grave with the wicked, and with the rich in his death; because he had done no violence, neither was any deceit in his mouth. ¹⁰Yet it pleased the

LORD to bruise him; he hath put him to grief: when thou shalt make his soul an offering for sin, he shall see his seed, he shall prolong his days, and the pleasure of the LORD shall prosper in his hand. [11]He shall see of the travail of his soul, and shall be satisfied: by his knowledge shall my righteous servant justify many; for he shall bear their iniquities. [12]Therefore will I divide him a portion with the great, and he shall divide the spoil with the strong; because he hath poured out his soul unto death: and he was numbered with the transgressors; and he bare the sin of many, and made intercession for the transgressors."

What Affliction Is For

2 Corinthians 1:6 "And whether we be afflicted, it is for your consolation and salvation, which is effectual in the enduring of the same sufferings which we also suffer: or whether we be comforted, it is for your consolation and salvation."

What Comes Out Of Affliction

2 Corinthians 4:17-18 "[17]For our light affliction, which is but for a moment, worketh for us a far more exceeding and eternal weight of glory; [18]While we look not at the things which are seen, but at the things which are not seen: for the things which are seen are temporal; but the things which are not seen are eternal."

Who Is Afflicted

Psalm 107:17 "Fools because of their transgression, and because of their iniquities, are afflicted."

ALERTNESS

Being Aware

Exodus 34:12 "Take heed to thyself, lest thou make a covenant with the inhabitants of the land whither thou goest, lest it be for a snare in the midst of thee."

Deuteronomy 4:15-16 "[15]Take ye therefore good heed unto yourselves; for ye saw no manner of similitude on the day that the LORD spake unto you in Horeb out of the midst of the fire: [16]Lest ye corrupt yourselves, and make you a graven image, the similitude of any figure, the likeness of male or female."

Deuteronomy 4:23-25 "[23]Take heed unto yourselves, lest ye forget the covenant of the LORD your God, which he made with you, and make you a graven image, or the likeness of any thing, which the LORD thy God hath forbidden thee. [24]For the LORD thy God is a consuming fire, even a jealous God. [25]When thou shalt beget children, and children's children, and ye shall have remained long in the land, and shall corrupt yourselves, and make a graven image, or the likeness of any thing, and shall do evil in the sight of the LORD thy God, to provoke him to anger."

Deuteronomy 8:11 "Beware that thou forget not the LORD thy God, in not keeping his commandments, and his judgments, and his statutes, which I command thee this day."

Deuteronomy 11:16 "Take heed to yourselves, that your heart be not deceived, and ye turn aside, and serve other gods, and worship them."

Proverbs 4:25-27 "[25]Let thine eyes look right on, and let thine eyelids look straight before thee. [26]Ponder the path of thy feet, and let all thy ways be established. [27]Turn not to the right hand nor to the left: remove thy foot from evil."

Proverbs 5:1-2 "[1]My son, attend unto my wisdom, and bow thine ear to my understanding: [2]That thou mayest regard discretion, and that thy lips may keep knowledge."

Matthew 24:42-44 "[42]Watch therefore: for ye know not what hour your Lord doth come. [43]But know this, that if the goodman of the house had known in what watch the thief would come, he would have watched, and would not have suffered his house to be broken up. [44]Therefore be ye also ready: for in such an hour as ye think not the Son of man cometh."

Matthew 25:13 "Watch therefore, for ye know neither the day nor the hour wherein the Son of man cometh."

Matthew 26:41 "Watch and pray, that ye enter not into temptation: the spirit indeed is willing, but the flesh is weak."

Mark 13:34-37 "[34]For the Son of man is as a man taking a far journey, who left his house, and gave authority to his servants, and to every man his work, and commanded the porter to watch. [35]Watch ye therefore: for ye know not when the master of the house cometh, at even, or at midnight, or at the cockcrowing, or in the morning: ³⁶Lest coming suddenly he find you sleeping. ³⁷And what I say unto you I say unto all, Watch."

Mark 14:38 "Watch ye and pray, lest ye enter into temptation. The spirit truly is ready, but the flesh is weak."

Luke 12:40 "Be ye therefore ready also: for the Son of man cometh at an hour when ye think not."

Luke 21:33-36 "³³Heaven and earth shall pass away: but my words shall not pass away. ³⁴And take heed to yourselves, lest at any time your hearts be overcharged with surfeiting, and drunkenness, and cares of this life, and so that day come upon you unawares. ³⁵For as a snare shall it come on all them that dwell on the face of the whole earth. ³⁶Watch ye therefore, and pray always, that ye may be accounted worthy to escape all these things that shall come to pass, and to stand before the Son of man."

1 Corinthians 16:13 "Watch ye, stand fast in the faith, quit you like men, be strong."

Colossians 2:8 "Beware lest any man spoil you through philosophy and vain deceit, after the tradition of men, after the rudiments of the world, and not after Christ."

1 Thessalonians 5:1-8 "¹But of the times and the seasons, brethren, ye have no need that I write unto you. ²For yourselves know perfectly that the day of the Lord so cometh as a thief in the night. ³For when they shall say, Peace and safety; then sudden destruction cometh upon them, as travail upon a woman with child; and they shall not escape. ⁴But ye, brethren, are not in darkness, that that day should overtake you as a thief. ⁵Ye are all the children of light, and the children of the day: we are not of the night, nor of darkness. ⁶Therefore let us not sleep, as do others; but let us watch and be sober. ⁷For they that sleep sleep in the night; and they that be drunken are drunken in the night. ⁸But let us, who are of the day, be sober, putting on the breastplate of faith and love; and for an helmet, the hope of salvation."

2 Timothy 4:5 "But watch thou in all things, endure afflictions, do the work of an evangelist, make full proof of thy ministry."

Hebrews 2:1 "Therefore we ought to give the more earnest heed to the things which we have heard, lest at any time we should let them slip."

1 Peter 5:8 "Be sober, be vigilant; because your adversary the devil, as a roaring lion, walketh about, seeking whom he may devour."

Revelation 3:1-2 "¹And unto the angel of the church in Sardis write; These things saith he that hath the seven Spirits of God, and the seven stars; I know thy works, that thou hast a name that thou livest, and art dead. ²Be watchful, and strengthen the things which remain, that are ready to die: for I have not found thy works perfect before God."

The Reward For Not Being Aware
Revelation 3:1-3 "¹And unto the angel of the church in Sardis write; These things saith he that hath the seven Spirits of God, and the seven stars; I know thy works, that thou hast a name that thou livest, and art dead. ²Be watchful, and strengthen the things which remain, that are ready to die: for I have not found thy works perfect before God. ³Remember therefore how thou hast received and heard, and hold fast, and repent. If therefore thou shalt not watch, I will come on thee as a thief, and thou shalt not know what hour I will come upon thee."

Those That Watch
Revelation 16:15 "Behold, I come as a thief. Blessed is he that watcheth, and keepeth his garments, lest he walk naked, and they see his shame."

What To Be Aware Of
Jeremiah 9:4-6 "⁴Take ye heed every one of his neighbour, and trust ye not in any brother: for every brother will utterly supplant, and every neighbour will walk with slanders. ⁵And they will deceive every one his neighbour, and will not speak the truth: they have taught their tongue to speak lies, and weary themselves to commit iniquity. ⁶Thine habitation is in the midst of deceit; through deceit they refuse to know me, saith the LORD."

Matthew 7:15 "Beware of false prophets, which come to you in sheep's clothing, but inwardly they are ravening wolves."

Matthew 10:16-18 "¹⁶Behold, I send you forth as sheep in the midst of wolves: be ye therefore wise as serpents, and harmless as doves. [17]But beware of men: for they will deliver you up to the councils, and they will scourge you in their synagogues; [18]And ye shall be brought before governors and kings for my sake, for a testimony against them and the Gentiles."

Luke 12:13-21 "[13]And one of the company said unto him, Master, speak to my brother, that he divide the inheritance with me. [14]And he said unto him, Man, who made me a judge or a divider over you? [15]And he said unto them, Take heed, and beware of covetousness: for a man's life consisteth not in the abundance of the things which he possesseth. [16]And he spake a parable unto them, saying, The ground of a certain rich man brought forth plentifully: [7]And he thought within himself, saying, What shall I do, because I have no room where to bestow my fruits? [18]And he said, This will I do: I will pull down my barns, and build greater; and there will I bestow all my fruits and my goods. [19]And I will say to my soul, Soul, thou hast much goods laid up for many years; take thine ease, eat, drink, and be merry. [20]But God said unto him, Thou fool, this night thy soul shall be required of thee: then whose shall those things be, which thou hast provided? [21]So is he that layeth up treasure for himself, and is not rich toward God."

Philippians 3:2 "Beware of dogs, beware of evil workers, beware of the concision."

Who Watches In Vain
Psalm 127:1 "Except the LORD build the house, they labour in vain that build it: except the LORD keep the city, the watchman waketh but in vain."

ANGELS

The Angels Accompanying Christ When He Returns
Matthew 16:27 "For the Son of man shall come in the glory of his Father with his angels; and then he shall reward every man according to his works."

Matthew 25:31 "When the Son of man shall come in his glory, and all the holy angels with him, then shall he sit upon the throne of his glory."

Mark 8:38 "Whosoever therefore shall be ashamed of me and of my words in this adulterous and sinful generation; of him also shall the Son of man be ashamed, when he cometh in the glory of his Father with the holy angels."

2 Thessalonians 1:7 "And to you who are troubled rest with us, when the Lord Jesus shall be revealed from heaven with his mighty angels."

The Lord Creating The Angels
Psalm 104:1-4 "[1]Bless the LORD, O my soul. O LORD my God, thou art very great; thou art clothed with honour and majesty. [2]Who coverest thyself with light as with a garment: who stretchest out the heavens like a curtain: [3]Who layeth the beams of his chambers in the waters: who maketh the clouds his chariot: who walketh upon the wings of the wind: [4]Who maketh his angels spirits; his ministers a flaming fire."

Hebrews 1:6-7 "[6]And again, when he bringeth in the firstbegotten into the world, he saith, And let all the angels of God worship him. [7]And of the angels he saith, Who maketh his angels spirits, and his ministers a flame of fire."

Who Are As Angels
Matthew 22:29-32 "[29]Jesus answered and said unto them, Ye do err, not knowing the scriptures, nor the power of God. [30]For in the resurrection they neither marry, nor are given in marriage, but are as the angels of God in heaven. [31]But as touching the resurrection of the dead, have ye not read that which was spoken unto you by God, saying, [32]I am the God of Abraham, and the God of Isaac, and the God of Jacob? God is not the God of the dead, but of the living."

Mark 12:24-27 "[24]And Jesus answering said unto them, Do ye not therefore err, because ye know not the scriptures, neither the power of God? [25]For when they shall rise from the dead, they neither marry, nor are given in marriage; but are as the angels which are in heaven. [26]And as touching the dead, that they rise: have ye not read in the book of Moses, how in the bush God spake unto him, saying, I am the God of Abraham, and the God of Isaac, and the God of Jacob? [27]He is not the God of the dead, but the God of the living: ye therefore do greatly err."

Luke 20:34-38 "[34]And Jesus answering said unto them, The children of this world marry, and are given in marriage: ³⁵But they which shall be accounted worthy to obtain that world, and the resurrection from the dead, neither marry, nor are given in marriage: ³⁶Neither can they die any more: for they are equal unto the angels; and are the children of God, being the children of the resurrection. ³⁷Now that the dead are raised, even Moses shewed at the bush, when he calleth the Lord the God of Abraham, and the God of Isaac, and the God of Jacob. ³⁸For he is not a God of the dead, but of the living: for all live unto him."

Who The Angels Guard
Psalm 34:6-7 "⁶This poor man cried, and the LORD heard him, and saved him out of all his troubles. ⁷The angel of the LORD encampeth round about them that fear him, and delivereth them."

Psalm 91:9-12 "⁹Because thou hast made the LORD, which is my refuge, even the most High, thy habitation; ¹⁰There shall no evil befall thee, neither shall any plague come nigh thy dwelling. ¹¹For he shall give his angels charge over thee, to keep thee in all thy ways. ¹²They shall bear thee up in their hands, lest thou dash thy foot against a stone."

ANGER

Angry Countenances
Proverbs 25:23 "The north wind driveth away rain: so doth an angry countenance a backbiting tongue."

Angry People
Proverbs 14:17 "He that is soon angry dealeth foolishly: and a man of wicked devices is hated."

Proverbs 15:18 "A wrathful man stirreth up strife: but he that is slow to anger appeaseth strife."

Proverbs 29:22 "An angry man stirreth up strife, and a furious man aboundeth in transgression."

Not Being Angry
Psalm 37:8 "Cease from anger, and forsake wrath: fret not thyself in any wise to do evil."

Ecclesiastes 7:9 "Be not hasty in thy spirit to be angry: for anger resteth in the bosom of fools."

Ephesians 4:26 "Be ye angry, and sin not: let not the sun go down upon your wrath."

Ephesians 4:31 "Let all bitterness, and wrath, and anger, and clamour, and evil speaking, be put away from you, with all malice."

James 1:19 "Wherefore, my beloved brethren, let every man be swift to hear, slow to speak, slow to wrath."

The Anger Of The Lord
Psalm 30:4-5 "⁴Sing unto the LORD, O ye saints of his, and give thanks at the remembrance of his holiness. ⁵For his anger endureth but a moment; in his favour is life: weeping may endure for a night, but joy cometh in the morning."

Psalm 103:8-9 "⁸The LORD is merciful and gracious, slow to anger, and plenteous in mercy. ⁹He will not always chide: neither will he keep his anger for ever."

Isaiah 9:19-21 "¹⁹Through the wrath of the LORD of hosts is the land darkened, and the people shall be as the fuel of the fire: no man shall spare his brother. ²⁰And he shall snatch on the right hand, and be hungry; and he shall eat on the left hand, and they shall not be satisfied: they shall eat every man the flesh of his own arm: ²¹Manasseh, Ephraim; and Ephraim, Manasseh: and they together shall be against Judah. For all this his anger is not turned away, but his hand is stretched out still."

Isaiah 12:1 "And in that day thou shalt say, O LORD, I will praise thee: though thou wast angry with me, thine anger is turned away, and thou comfortedst me."

Jeremiah 3:11-12 "¹¹And the LORD said unto me, The backsliding Israel hath justified herself more than treacherous Judah. ¹²Go and proclaim these words toward the north, and say, Return, thou backsliding Israel, saith the LORD; and I will not cause mine anger to fall upon you: for I am merciful, saith the LORD, and I will not keep anger for ever."

Jeremiah 10:10 "But the LORD is the true God, he is the living God, and an everlasting king: at his wrath the earth shall tremble, and the nations shall not be able to abide his indignation."

Jeremiah 23:18-20 "¹⁸For who hath stood in the counsel of the LORD, and hath perceived and heard his word? who hath marked his word, and heard it? [19]Behold, a whirlwind of the LORD is gone forth in fury, even a grievous whirlwind: it shall fall grievously upon the head of the wicked. [20] The anger of the LORD shall not return, until he have executed, and till he have performed the thoughts of his heart: in the latter days ye shall consider it perfectly."

Jeremiah 30:23-24 "[23]Behold, the whirlwind of the LORD goeth forth with fury, a continuing whirlwind: it shall fall with pain upon the head of the wicked. [24]The fierce anger of the LORD shall not return, until he have done it, and until he have performed the intents of his heart: in the latter days ye shall consider it."

Micah 7:18-20 "[18]Who is a God like unto thee, that pardoneth iniquity, and passeth by the transgression of the remnant of his heritage? he retaineth not his anger for ever, because he delighteth in mercy. [19]He will turn again, he will have compassion upon us; he will subdue our iniquities; and thou wilt cast all their sins into the depths of the sea. [20]Thou wilt perform the truth to Jacob, and the mercy to Abraham, which thou hast sworn unto our fathers from the days of old."

The Lord Being Slow To Anger
Psalm 103:8-9 "[8]The LORD is merciful and gracious, slow to anger, and plenteous in mercy. [9]He will not always chide: neither will he keep his anger for ever."

Psalm 145:8 "The LORD is gracious, and full of compassion; slow to anger, and of great mercy."

Joel 2:12-13 "[12]Therefore also now, saith the LORD, turn ye even to me with all your heart, and with fasting, and with weeping, and with mourning: [13]And rend your heart, and not your garments, and turn unto the LORD your God: for he is gracious and merciful, slow to anger, and of great kindness, and repenteth him of the evil."

Nahum 1:3 "The LORD is slow to anger, and great in power, and will not at all acquit the wicked: the LORD hath his way in the whirlwind and in the storm, and the clouds are the dust of his feet."

Those That Are Slow To Anger
Proverbs 14:29 "He that is slow to wrath is of great understanding: but he that is hasty of spirit exalteth folly."

Proverbs 15:18 "A wrathful man stirreth up strife: but he that is slow to anger appeaseth strife."

Proverbs 16:32 "He that is slow to anger is better than the mighty; and he that ruleth his spirit than he that taketh a city."

What Anger Is
Proverbs 27:4 "Wrath is cruel, and anger is outrageous; but who is able to stand before envy?"

What Defers Anger
Proverbs 19:11 "The discretion of a man deferreth his anger; and it is his glory to pass over a transgression."

What Pacifies Anger
Proverbs 21:14 "A gift in secret pacifieth anger: and a reward in the bosom strong wrath."

What Stirs Up Anger
Proverbs 15:1 "A soft answer turneth away wrath: but grievous words stir up anger."

Where Anger Rests
Ecclesiastes 7:9 "Be not hasty in thy spirit to be angry: for anger resteth in the bosom of fools."

Who God Is Angry With
Psalm 7:11 "God judgeth the righteous, and God is angry with the wicked every day."

ANOINTING

God The Father Anointing Jesus Christ
Isaiah 61:1-3 "[1]The Spirit of the Lord GOD is upon me; because the LORD hath anointed me to preach good tidings unto the meek; he hath sent me to bind up the brokenhearted, to proclaim liberty to the captives, and the opening of the prison to them that are bound; [2]To proclaim the acceptable year of the LORD, and the day of vengeance of our God; to comfort all that mourn; [3]To appoint unto them that mourn in Zion, to give unto them beauty for ashes, the oil of joy for mourning, the garment of praise for the spirit of heaviness; that they might be called trees of righteousness, the planting of the LORD, that he might be glorified."

Luke 4:14-19 "[14]And Jesus returned in the power of the Spirit into Galilee: and there went out a fame of him through all the region round about. [15]And he taught in their synagogues, being glorified of all. [16]And he came to Nazareth, where he had been brought up: and, as his custom was, he went into the synagogue on the sabbath day, and stood up for to read. [17]And there was delivered unto him the book of the prophet Esaias. And when he had opened the book, he found the place where it was written, [18]The Spirit of the Lord is upon me, because he hath anointed me to preach the gospel to the poor; he hath sent me to heal the brokenhearted, to preach deliverance to the captives, and recovering of sight to the blind, to set at liberty them that are bruised, [19]To preach the acceptable year of the Lord."

Acts 4:24-27 "[24]And when they heard that, they lifted up their voice to God with one accord, and said, Lord, thou art God, which hast made heaven, and earth, and the sea, and all that in them is: [25]Who by the mouth of thy servant David hast said, Why did the heathen rage, and the people imagine vain things? [26]The kings of the earth stood up, and the rulers were gathered together against the Lord, and against his Christ. [27]For of a truth against thy holy child Jesus, whom thou hast anointed, both Herod, and Pontius Pilate, with the Gentiles, and the people of Israel, were gathered together."

Acts 10:37-38 "[37]That word, I say, ye know, which was published throughout all Judaea, and began from Galilee, after the baptism which John preached; [38]How God anointed Jesus of Nazareth with the Holy Ghost and with power: who went about doing good, and healing all that were oppressed of the devil; for God was with him."

Hebrews 1:8-9 "[8]But unto the Son he saith, Thy throne, O God, is for ever and ever: a sceptre of righteousness is the sceptre of thy kingdom. [9]Thou hast loved righteousness, and hated iniquity; therefore God, even thy God, hath anointed thee with the oil of gladness above thy fellows."

The Anointed Of The Lord
1 Samuel 2:10 "The adversaries of the LORD shall be broken to pieces; out of heaven shall he thunder upon them: the LORD shall judge the ends of the earth; and he shall give strength unto his king, and exalt the horn of his anointed."

2 Samuel 22:50-51 "[50]Therefore I will give thanks unto thee, O LORD, among the heathen, and I will sing praises unto thy name. [51]He is the tower of salvation for his king: and sheweth mercy to his anointed, unto David, and to his seed for evermore."

Psalm 20:6-7 "[6]Now know I that the LORD saveth his anointed; he will hear him from his holy heaven with the saving strength of his right hand. [7]Some trust in chariots, and some in horses: but we will remember the name of the LORD our God."

Psalm 28:7-8 "[7]The LORD is my strength and my shield; my heart trusted in him, and I am helped: therefore my heart greatly rejoiceth; and with my song will I praise him. [8]The LORD is their strength, and he is the saving strength of his anointed."

The Anointing Of The Lord
1 John 2:24-29 "[24]Let that therefore abide in you, which ye have heard from the beginning. If that which ye have heard from the beginning shall remain in you, ye also shall continue in the Son, and in the Father. [25]And this is the promise that he hath promised us, even eternal life. [26]These things have I written unto you concerning them that seduce you. [27]But the anointing which ye have received of him abideth in you, and ye need not that any man teach you: but as the same anointing teacheth you of all things, and is truth, and is no lie, and even as it hath taught you, ye shall abide in him. [28]And now, little children, abide in him; that, when he shall appear, we may have confidence, and not be ashamed before him at his coming. [29]If ye know that he is righteous, ye know that every one that doeth righteousness is born of him."

The Lord Anointing
Psalm 23:5-6 "[5]Thou preparest a table before me in the presence of mine enemies: thou anointest my head with oil; my cup runneth over. [6]Surely goodness and mercy shall follow me all the days of my life: and I will dwell in the house of the LORD for ever."

Who Has An Unction From The Holy One
1 John 2:20-21 "[20]But ye have an unction from the Holy One, and ye know all things. [21]I have not written unto you because ye know not the truth, but because ye know it, and that no lie is of the truth."

ANTICHRIST

The Coming Of Antichrist

John 14:23-30 "²³Jesus answered and said unto him, If a man love me, he will keep my words: and my Father will love him, and we will come unto him, and make our abode with him. ²⁴He that loveth me not keepeth not my sayings: and the word which ye hear is not mine, but the Father's which sent me. ²⁵These things have I spoken unto you, being yet present with you. ²⁶But the Comforter, which is the Holy Ghost, whom the Father will send in my name, he shall teach you all things, and bring all things to your remembrance, whatsoever I have said unto you. ²⁷Peace I leave with you, my peace I give unto you: not as the world giveth, give I unto you. Let not your heart be troubled, neither let it be afraid. ²⁸Ye have heard how I said unto you, I go away, and come again unto you. If ye loved me, ye would rejoice, because I said, I go unto the Father: for my Father is greater than I. ²⁹And now I have told you before it come to pass, that, when it is come to pass, ye might believe. ³⁰Hereafter I will not talk much with you: for the prince of this world cometh, and hath nothing in me."

2 Thessalonians 2:1-12 "¹Now we beseech you, brethren, by the coming of our Lord Jesus Christ, and by our gathering together unto him, ²That ye be not soon shaken in mind, or be troubled, neither by spirit, nor by word, nor by letter as from us, as that the day of Christ is at hand. ³Let no man deceive you by any means: for that day shall not come, except there come a falling away first, and that man of sin be revealed, the son of perdition; ⁴Who opposeth and exalteth himself above all that is called God, or that is worshipped; so that he as God sitteth in the temple of God, shewing himself that he is God. ⁵Remember ye not, that, when I was yet with you, I told you these things? ⁶And now ye know what withholdeth that he might be revealed in his time. ⁷For the mystery of iniquity doth already work: only he who now letteth will let, until he be taken out of the way. ⁸And then shall that Wicked be revealed, whom the Lord shall consume with the spirit of his mouth, and shall destroy with the brightness of his coming: ⁹Even him, whose coming is after the working of Satan with all power and signs and lying wonders, ¹⁰And with all deceivableness of unrighteousness in them that perish; because they received not the love of the truth, that they might be saved. ¹¹And for this cause God shall send them strong delusion, that they should believe a lie: ¹²That they all might be damned who believed not the truth, but had pleasure in unrighteousness."

1 John 2:18-19 "¹⁸Little children, it is the last time: and as ye have heard that antichrist shall come, even now are there many antichrists; whereby we know that it is the last time. ¹⁹They went out from us, but they were not of us; for if they had been of us, they would no doubt have continued with us: but they went out, that they might be made manifest that they were not all of us."

1 John 4:1-3 "¹Beloved, believe not every spirit, but try the spirits whether they are of God: because many false prophets are gone out into the world. ²Hereby know ye the Spirit of God: Every spirit that confesseth that Jesus Christ is come in the flesh is of God: ³And every spirit that confesseth not that Jesus Christ is come in the flesh is not of God: and this is that spirit of antichrist, whereof ye have heard that it should come; and even now already is it in the world."

Who Is An Antichrist

1 John 2:22 "Who is a liar but he that denieth that Jesus is the Christ? He is antichrist, that denieth the Father and the Son."

1 John 4:1-3 "¹Beloved, believe not every spirit, but try the spirits whether they are of God: because many false prophets are gone out into the world. ²Hereby know ye the Spirit of God: Every spirit that confesseth that Jesus Christ is come in the flesh is of God: ³And every spirit that confesseth not that Jesus Christ is come in the flesh is not of God: and this is that spirit of antichrist, whereof ye have heard that it should come; and even now already is it in the world."

2 John 7 "For many deceivers are entered into the world, who confess not that Jesus Christ is come in the flesh. This is a deceiver and an antichrist."

ANXIETY

Not Being Anxious

Psalm 37:1 "Fret not thyself because of evildoers, neither be thou envious against the workers of iniquity."

Psalm 37:7 "Rest in the LORD, and wait patiently for him: fret not thyself because of him who prospereth in his way, because of the man who bringeth wicked devices to pass."

Proverbs 24:19 "Fret not thyself because of evil men, neither be thou envious at the wicked."

Matthew 6:25 "Therefore I say unto you, Take no thought for your life, what ye shall eat, or what ye shall drink; nor yet for your body, what ye shall put on. Is not the life more than meat, and the body than raiment?"

Matthew 6:31 "Therefore take no thought, saying, What shall we eat? or, What shall we drink? or, Wherewithal shall we be clothed?"

Matthew 6:34 "Take therefore no thought for the morrow: for the morrow shall take thought for the things of itself. Sufficient unto the day is the evil thereof."

Luke 12:22 "And he said unto his disciples, Therefore I say unto you, Take no thought for your life, what ye shall eat; neither for the body, what ye shall put on."

Philippians 4:6 "Be careful for nothing; but in every thing by prayer and supplication with thanksgiving let your requests be made known unto God."

Why You Should Not Be Anxious
Psalm 37:1-2 "¹Fret not thyself because of evildoers, neither be thou envious against the workers of iniquity. ²For they shall soon be cut down like the grass, and wither as the green herb."

Proverbs 24:19-20 "¹⁹Fret not thyself because of evil men, neither be thou envious at the wicked; ²⁰For there shall be no reward to the evil man; the candle of the wicked shall be put out."

Matthew 6:25-34 "²⁵Therefore I say unto you, Take no thought for your life, what ye shall eat, or what ye shall drink; nor yet for your body, what ye shall put on. Is not the life more than meat, and the body than raiment? ²⁶Behold the fowls of the air: for they sow not, neither do they reap, nor gather into barns; yet your heavenly Father feedeth them. Are ye not much better than they? ²⁷Which of you by taking thought can add one cubit unto his stature? ²⁸And why take ye thought for raiment? Consider the lilies of the field, how they grow; they toil not, neither do they spin: ²⁹And yet I say unto you, That even Solomon in all his glory was not arrayed like one of these. ³⁰Wherefore, if God so clothe the grass of the field, which to day is, and to morrow is cast into the oven, shall he not much more clothe you, O ye of little faith? ³¹Therefore take no thought, saying, What shall we eat? or, What shall we drink? or, Wherewithal shall we be clothed? ³² (For after all these things do the Gentiles seek:) for your heavenly Father knoweth that ye have need of all these things. ³³But seek ye first the kingdom of God, and his righteousness; and all these things shall be added unto you. ³⁴Take therefore no thought for the morrow: for the morrow shall take thought for the things of itself. Sufficient unto the day is the evil thereof."

Luke 12:22-34 "²²And he said unto his disciples, Therefore I say unto you, Take no thought for your life, what ye shall eat; neither for the body, what ye shall put on. ²³The life is more than meat, and the body is more than raiment. ²⁴Consider the ravens: for they neither sow nor reap; which neither have storehouse nor barn; and God feedeth them: how much more are ye better than the fowls? ²⁵And which of you with taking thought can add to his stature one cubit? ²⁶If ye then be not able to do that thing which is least, why take ye thought for the rest? ²⁷Consider the lilies how they grow: they toil not, they spin not; and yet I say unto you, that Solomon in all his glory was not arrayed like one of these. ²⁸If then God so clothe the grass, which is to day in the field, and to morrow is cast into the oven; how much more will he clothe you, O ye of little faith? ²⁹And seek not ye what ye shall eat, or what ye shall drink, neither be ye of doubtful mind. ³⁰For all these things do the nations of the world seek after: and your Father knoweth that ye have need of these things. ³¹But rather seek ye the kingdom of God; and all these things shall be added unto you. ³²Fear not, little flock; for it is your Father's good pleasure to give you the kingdom. ³³Sell that ye have, and give alms; provide yourselves bags which wax not old, a treasure in the heavens that faileth not, where no thief approacheth, neither moth corrupteth. ³⁴For where your treasure is, there will your heart be also."

ARMOR

The Lord Armoring Himself With Righteousness And Salvation

Isaiah 59:15-17 "¹⁵Yea, truth faileth; and he that departeth from evil maketh himself a prey: and the LORD saw it, and it displeased him that there was no judgment. ¹⁶And he saw that there was no man, and wondered that there was no intercessor: therefore his arm brought salvation unto him; and his righteousness, it sustained him. ¹⁷For he put on righteousness as a breastplate, and an helmet of salvation upon his head; and he put on the garments of vengeance for clothing, and was clad with zeal as a cloke."

What Armor To Put On

Romans 13:11-12 "¹¹And that, knowing the time, that now it is high time to awake out of sleep: for now is our salvation nearer than when we believed. ¹²The night is far spent, the day is at hand: let us therefore cast off the works of darkness, and let us put on the armour of light."

Ephesians 6:10-17 "¹⁰Finally, my brethren, be strong in the Lord, and in the power of his might. ¹¹Put on the whole armour of God, that ye may be able to stand against the wiles of the devil. ¹²For we wrestle not against flesh and blood, but against principalities, against powers, against the rulers of the darkness of this world, against spiritual wickedness in high places. ¹³Wherefore take unto you the whole armour of God, that ye may be able to withstand in the evil day, and having done all, to stand. ¹⁴Stand therefore, having your loins girt about with truth, and having on the breastplate of righteousness; ¹⁵And your feet shod with the preparation of the gospel of peace; ¹⁶Above all, taking the shield of faith, wherewith ye shall be able to quench all the fiery darts of the wicked. ¹⁷And take the helmet of salvation, and the sword of the Spirit, which is the word of God."

1 Thessalonians 5:8 "But let us, who are of the day, be sober, putting on the breastplate of faith and love; and for an helmet, the hope of salvation."

ATONEMENT

Blood Making An Atonement For The Soul

Exodus 30:10 "And Aaron shall make an atonement upon the horns of it once in a year with the blood of the sin offering of atonements: once in the year shall he make atonement upon it throughout your generations: it is most holy unto the LORD."

Leviticus 5:6 "And he shall bring his trespass offering unto the LORD for his sin which he hath sinned, a female from the flock, a lamb or a kid of the goats, for a sin offering; and the priest shall make an atonement for him concerning his sin."

Leviticus 12:6-7 "⁶And when the days of her purifying are fulfilled, for a son, or for a daughter, she shall bring a lamb of the first year for a burnt offering, and a young pigeon, or a turtledove, for a sin offering, unto the door of the tabernacle of the congregation, unto the priest: ⁷Who shall offer it before the LORD, and make an atonement for her; and she shall be cleansed from the issue of her blood. This is the law for her that hath born a male or a female."

Leviticus 14:19-20 "¹⁹And the priest shall offer the sin offering, and make an atonement for him that is to be cleansed from his uncleanness; and afterward he shall kill the burnt offering: ²⁰And the priest shall offer the burnt offering and the meat offering upon the altar: and the priest shall make an atonement for him, and he shall be clean."

Leviticus 16:11 "And Aaron shall bring the bullock of the sin offering, which is for himself, and shall make an atonement for himself, and for his house, and shall kill the bullock of the sin offering which is for himself."

Leviticus 17:11 "For the life of the flesh is in the blood: and I have given it to you upon the altar to make an atonement for your souls: for it is the blood that maketh an atonement for the soul."

2 Chronicles 29:24 "And the priests killed them, and they made reconciliation with their blood upon the altar, to make an atonement for all Israel:

for the king commanded that the burnt offering and the sin offering should be made for all Israel."

Matthew 26:26-28 "²⁶And as they were eating, Jesus took bread, and blessed it, and brake it, and gave it to the disciples, and said, Take, eat; this is my body. ²⁷And he took the cup, and gave thanks, and gave it to them, saying, Drink ye all of it; ²⁸For this is my blood of the new testament, which is shed for many for the remission of sins."

Mark 14:22-24 "²²And as they did eat, Jesus took bread, and blessed, and brake it, and gave to them, and said, Take, eat: this is my body. ²³And he took the cup, and when he had given thanks, he gave it to them: and they all drank of it. ²⁴And he said unto them, This is my blood of the new testament, which is shed for many."

Luke 22:19-20 "¹⁹And he took bread, and gave thanks, and brake it, and gave unto them, saying, This is my body which is given for you: this do in remembrance of me. ²⁰Likewise also the cup after supper, saying, This cup is the new testament in my blood, which is shed for you."

Romans 5:8-11 "⁸But God commendeth his love toward us, in that, while we were yet sinners, Christ died for us. ⁹Much more then, being now justified by his blood, we shall be saved from wrath through him. ¹⁰For if, when we were enemies, we were reconciled to God by the death of his Son, much more, being reconciled, we shall be saved by his life. ¹¹And not only so, but we also joy in God through our Lord Jesus Christ, by whom we have now received the atonement."

Ephesians 2:13-15 "¹³But now in Christ Jesus ye who sometimes were far off are made nigh by the blood of Christ. ¹⁴For he is our peace, who hath made both one, and hath broken down the middle wall of partition between us; ¹⁵Having abolished in his flesh the enmity, even the law of command-ments contained in ordinances; for to make in himself of twain one new man, so making peace."

Colossians 1:12-22 "¹²Giving thanks unto the Father, which hath made us meet to be partakers of the inheritance of the saints in light: ¹³Who hath delivered us from the power of darkness, and hath translated us into the kingdom of his dear Son: ¹⁴In whom we have redemption through his blood, even the forgiveness of sins: ¹⁵Who is the image of the invisible God, the firstborn of every creature: ¹⁶For by him were all things created, that are in heaven, and that are in earth, visible and invisible, whether they be thrones, or dominions, or principalities, or powers: all things were created by him, and for him: ¹⁷And he is before all things, and by him all things consist. ¹⁸And he is the head of the body, the church: who is the beginning, the first-born from the dead; that in all things he might have the preeminence. ¹⁹For it pleased the Father that in him should all fulness dwell; ²⁰And, having made peace through the blood of his cross, by him to rec-oncile all things unto himself; by him, I say, whether they be things in earth, or things in heaven. ²¹And you, that were sometime alienated and enemies in your mind by wicked works, yet now hath he rec-onciled ²²In the body of his flesh through death, to present you holy and unblameable and unreprove-able in his sight."

1 John 1:7 "But if we walk in the light, as he is in the light, we have fellowship one with another, and the blood of Jesus Christ his Son cleanseth us from all sin."

The Day Of Atonement

Leviticus 16:29-30 "²⁹And this shall be a statute for ever unto you: that in the seventh month, on the tenth day of the month, ye shall afflict your souls, and do no work at all, whether it be one of your own country, or a stranger that sojourneth among you: ³⁰For on that day shall the priest make an atonement for you, to cleanse you, that ye may be clean from all your sins before the LORD."

Leviticus 23:27 "Also on the tenth day of this sev-enth month there shall be a day of atonement: it shall be an holy convocation unto you; and ye shall afflict your souls, and offer an offering made by fire unto the LORD."

Numbers 29:7-8 "⁷And ye shall have on the tenth day of this seventh month an holy convocation; and ye shall afflict your souls: ye shall not do any work therein: ⁸But ye shall offer a burnt offering unto the LORD for a sweet savour; one young bul-lock, one ram, and seven lambs of the first year; they shall be unto you without blemish."

AVAIL

What Avails

Galatians 5:6 "For in Jesus Christ neither circumcision availeth anything, nor uncircumcision; but faith which worketh by love."

Galatians 6:15 "For in Christ Jesus neither circumcision availeth anything, nor uncircumcision, but a new creature."

James 5:16 "Confess your faults one to another, and pray one for another, that ye may be healed. The effectual fervent prayer of a righteous man availeth much."

Bb

BACKSLIDING

The Backslider In Heart
Proverbs 14:14 "The backslider in heart shall be filled with his own ways: and a good man shall be satisfied from himself."

What Backslidings Do
Jeremiah 2:19 "Thine own wickedness shall correct thee, and thy backslidings shall reprove thee: know therefore and see that it is an evil thing and bitter, that thou hast forsaken the LORD thy God, and that my fear is not in thee, saith the Lord GOD of hosts."

BAPTISM

Baptism Saving
1 Peter 3:20-21 "20Which sometime were disobedient, when once the longsuffering of God waited in the days of Noah, while the ark was a preparing, wherein few, that is, eight souls were saved by water. 21The like figure whereunto even baptism doth also now save us (not the putting away of the filth of the flesh, but the answer of a good conscience toward God,) by the resurrection of Jesus Christ."

Baptizing All Nations
Matthew 28:18-20 "18And Jesus came and spake unto them, saying, All power is given unto me in heaven and in earth. 19Go ye therefore, and teach all nations, baptizing them in the name of the Father, and of the Son, and of the Holy Ghost: 20Teaching them to observe all things whatsoever I have commanded you: and, lo, I am with you alway, even unto the end of the world. Amen."

Jesus Christ Baptizing With The Holy Spirit
Matthew 3:11-14 "11I indeed baptize you with water unto repentance: but he that cometh after me is mightier than I, whose shoes I am not worthy to bear: he shall baptize you with the Holy Ghost, and with fire: 12Whose fan is in his hand, and he will throughly purge his floor, and gather his wheat into the garner; but he will burn up the chaff with unquenchable fire. 13Then cometh Jesus from Galilee to Jordan unto John, to be baptized of him. 14But John forbad him, saying, I have need to be baptized of thee, and comest thou to me?"

Mark 1:7-9 "7And preached, saying, There cometh one mightier than I after me, the latchet of whose shoes I am not worthy to stoop down and unloose. 8I indeed have baptized you with water: but he shall baptize you with the Holy Ghost. 9And it came to pass in those days, that Jesus came from Nazareth of Galilee, and was baptized of John in Jordan."

Luke 3:15-21 "15And as the people were in expectation, and all men mused in their hearts of John, whether he were the Christ, or not; 16John answered, saying unto them all, I indeed baptize you with water; but one mightier than I cometh, the latchet of whose shoes I am not worthy to unloose: he shall baptize you with the Holy Ghost and with fire: 17Whose fan is in his hand, and he will throughly purge his floor, and will gather the wheat into his garner; but the chaff he will burn with fire unquenchable. 18And many other things in his exhortation preached he unto the people. 19But Herod the tetrarch, being reproved by him for Herodias his brother Philip's wife, and for all the evils which Herod had done, 20Added yet this above all, that he shut up John in prison. 21Now when all the people were baptized, it came to pass, that Jesus also being baptized, and praying, the heaven was opened."

John 1:29-34 "29The next day John seeth Jesus coming unto him, and saith, Behold the Lamb of God, which taketh away the sin of the world. 30This is he of whom I said, After me cometh a man which is preferred before me: for he was before me. 31And I knew him not: but that he should be made manifest to Israel, therefore am I come baptizing with water. 32And John bare record, saying, I saw the Spirit descending from heaven like a dove, and it abode upon him. 33And I knew him not: but he that sent me to baptize with water, the same said unto me, Upon whom thou shalt see the Spirit descending, and remaining on him, the same is he which baptizeth with the Holy Ghost. 34And I saw, and bare record that this is the Son of God."

Acts 1:5 "For John truly baptized with water; but ye shall be baptized with the Holy Ghost not many days hence."

Acts 11:16 "Then remembered I the word of the Lord, how that he said, John indeed baptized with water; but ye shall be baptized with the Holy Ghost."

Acts 19:4-6 "⁴Then said Paul, John verily baptized with the baptism of repentance, saying unto the people, that they should believe on him which should come after him, that is, on Christ Jesus. ⁵When they heard this, they were baptized in the name of the Lord Jesus. ⁶And when Paul had laid his hands upon them, the Holy Ghost came on them; and they spake with tongues, and prophesied."

The Reward For Being Baptized In The Name Of Jesus Christ

Acts 2:38 "Then Peter said unto them, Repent, and be baptized every one of you in the name of Jesus Christ for the remission of sins, and ye shall receive the gift of the Holy Ghost."

There Being One Baptism

Ephesians 4:4-6 "⁴There is one body, and one Spirit, even as ye are called in one hope of your calling; ⁵One Lord, one faith, one baptism, ⁶One God and Father of all, who is above all, and through all, and in you all."

Those That Believe And Are Baptized

Mark 16:16-19 "¹⁶He that believeth and is baptized shall be saved; but he that believeth not shall be damned. ¹⁷And these signs shall follow them that believe; In my name shall they cast out devils; they shall speak with new tongues; ¹⁸They shall take up serpents; and if they drink any deadly thing, it shall not hurt them; they shall lay hands on the sick, and they shall recover. ¹⁹So then after the Lord had spoken unto them, he was received up into heaven, and sat on the right hand of God."

Those That Have Been Baptized Into Christ

Galatians 3:27-29 "²⁷For as many of you as have been baptized into Christ have put on Christ. ²⁸There is neither Jew nor Greek, there is neither bond nor free, there is neither male nor female: for ye are all one in Christ Jesus. ²⁹And if ye be Christ's, then are ye Abraham's seed, and heirs according to the promise."

What John The Baptist Baptized With

Matthew 3:1-11 "¹In those days came John the Baptist, preaching in the wilderness of Judaea, ²And saying, Repent ye: for the kingdom of heaven is at hand. ³For this is he that was spoken of by the prophet Esaias, saying, The voice of one crying in the wilderness, Prepare ye the way of the Lord, make his paths straight. ⁴And the same John had his raiment of camel's hair, and a leathern girdle about his loins; and his meat was locusts and wild honey. ⁵Then went out to him Jerusalem, and all Judaea, and all the region round about Jordan, ⁶And were baptized of him in Jordan, confessing their sins. ⁷But when he saw many of the Pharisees and Sadducees come to his baptism, he said unto them, O generation of vipers, who hath warned you to flee from the wrath to come? ⁸Bring forth therefore fruits meet for repentance: ⁹And think not to say within yourselves, We have Abraham to our father: for I say unto you, that God is able of these stones to raise up children unto Abraham. ¹⁰And now also the axe is laid unto the root of the trees: therefore every tree which bringeth not forth good fruit is hewn down, and cast into the fire. ¹¹I indeed baptize you with water unto repentance: but he that cometh after me is mightier than I, whose shoes I am not worthy to bear: he shall baptize you with the Holy Ghost, and with fire."

Mark 1:7-8 "⁷And preached, saying, There cometh one mightier than I after me, the latchet of whose shoes I am not worthy to stoop down and unloose. ⁸I indeed have baptized you with water: but he shall baptize you with the Holy Ghost."

Luke 3:16 "John answered, saying unto them all, I indeed baptize you with water; but one mightier than I cometh, the latchet of whose shoes I am not worthy to unloose: he shall baptize you with the Holy Ghost and with fire."

John 1:26-34 "²⁶John answered them, saying, I baptize with water: but there standeth one among you, whom ye know not; ²⁷He it is, who coming after me is preferred before me, whose shoe's latchet I am not worthy to unloose. ²⁸These things were done in Bethabara beyond Jordan, where John was baptizing. ²⁹The next day John seeth Jesus coming unto him, and saith, Behold the Lamb of God, which taketh away the sin of the world. ³⁰This is he of whom I said, After me cometh a man which is preferred before me: for he was before me. ³¹And I knew him not: but that he should be made manifest to Israel, therefore am I come baptizing with water. [32]And John bare record, saying, I saw the Spirit descending from heaven like a dove, and it abode upon him. [33]And I knew him not: but he that sent me to baptize with water, the same said unto me, Upon whom thou shalt see the Spirit descending, and remaining on him, the same is he which baptizeth with the Holy Ghost. [34]And I saw, and bare record that this is the Son of God."

Acts 1:5 "For John truly baptized with water; but ye shall be baptized with the Holy Ghost not many days hence."

Acts 11:16 "Then remembered I the word of the Lord, how that he said, John indeed baptized with water; but ye shall be baptized with the Holy Ghost."

Acts 19:4 "Then said Paul, John verily baptized with the baptism of repentance, saying unto the people, that they should believe on him which should come after him, that is, on Christ Jesus."

BEARING FRUIT

Being Fruitful
Genesis 1:27-28 "[27]So God created man in his own image, in the image of God created he him; male and female created he them. [28]And God blessed them, and God said unto them, Be fruitful, and multiply, and replenish the earth, and subdue it: and have dominion over the fish of the sea, and over the fowl of the air, and over every living thing that moveth upon the earth."

Genesis 9:1 "And God blessed Noah and his sons, and said unto them, Be fruitful, and multiply, and replenish the earth."

Genesis 9:7 "And you, be ye fruitful, and multiply; bring forth abundantly in the earth, and multiply therein."

Everything Being Known By The Fruit It Bears
Proverbs 20:11 "Even a child is known by his doings, whether his work be pure, and whether it be right."

Matthew 7:15-16 "[15]Beware of false prophets, which come to you in sheep's clothing, but inwardly they are ravening wolves. [16]Ye shall know them by their fruits. Do men gather grapes of thorns, or figs of thistles?"

Matthew 12:33 "Either make the tree good, and his fruit good; or else make the tree corrupt, and his fruit corrupt: for the tree is known by his fruit."

Luke 6:43-45 "[43]For a good tree bringeth not forth corrupt fruit; neither doth a corrupt tree bring forth good fruit. [44]For every tree is known by his own fruit. For of thorns men do not gather figs, nor of a bramble bush gather they grapes. [45]A good man out of the good treasure of his heart bringeth forth that which is good; and an evil man out of the evil treasure of his heart bringeth forth that which is evil: for of the abundance of the heart his mouth speaketh."

Every Tree That
Does Not Bring Forth Good Fruit
Matthew 3:10 "And now also the axe is laid unto the root of the trees: therefore every tree which bringeth not forth good fruit is hewn down, and cast into the fire."

Matthew 7:19 "Every tree that bringeth not forth good fruit is hewn down, and cast into the fire."

Matthew 15:12-13 "[12]Then came his disciples, and said unto him, Knowest thou that the Pharisees were offended, after they heard this saying? [13]But he answered and said, Every plant, which my heavenly Father hath not planted, shall be rooted up."

Luke 3:9 "And now also the axe is laid unto the root of the trees: every tree therefore which bringeth not forth good fruit is hewn down, and cast into the fire."

John 15:1-6 "[1]I am the true vine, and my Father is the husbandman. [2]Every branch in me that beareth not fruit he taketh away: and every branch that beareth fruit, he purgeth it, that it may bring forth more fruit. [3]Now ye are clean through the word which I have spoken unto you. [4]Abide in me, and I in you. As the branch cannot bear fruit of itself, except it abide in the vine; no more can ye, except ye abide in me. [5]I am the vine, ye are the branches: He that abideth in me, and I in him, the same bringeth forth much fruit: for without me ye can do nothing. [6]If a man abide not in me, he is cast forth as a branch, and is withered; and men gather them, and cast them into the fire, and they are burned."

God Giving The Increase

1 Corinthians 3:3-9 "³For ye are yet carnal: for whereas there is among you envying, and strife, and divisions, are ye not carnal, and walk as men? ⁴For while one saith, I am of Paul; and another, I am of Apollos; are ye not carnal? ⁵Who then is Paul, and who is Apollos, but ministers by whom ye believed, even as the Lord gave to every man? ⁶I have planted, Apollos watered; but God gave the increase. ⁷So then neither is he that planteth any thing, neither he that watereth; but God that giveth the increase. ⁸Now he that planteth and he that watereth are one: and every man shall receive his own reward according to his own labour. ⁹For we are labourers together with God: ye are God's husbandry, ye are God's building."

Jesus Christ Being The True Vine
And God The Father Being The Husbandman

John 15:1-8 "¹I am the true vine, and my Father is the husbandman. ²Every branch in me that beareth not fruit he taketh away: and every branch that beareth fruit, he purgeth it, that it may bring forth more fruit. ³Now ye are clean through the word which I have spoken unto you. ⁴Abide in me, and I in you. As the branch cannot bear fruit of itself, except it abide in the vine; no more can ye, except ye abide in me. ⁵I am the vine, ye are the branches: He that abideth in me, and I in him, the same bringeth forth much fruit: for without me ye can do nothing. ⁶If a man abide not in me, he is cast forth as a branch, and is withered; and men gather them, and cast them into the fire, and they are burned. ⁷If ye abide in me, and my words abide in you, ye shall ask what ye will, and it shall be done unto you. ⁸Herein is my Father glorified, that ye bear much fruit; so shall ye be my disciples."

Reaping What You Sow

Isaiah 3:10-11 "¹⁰Say ye to the righteous, that it shall be well with him: for they shall eat the fruit of their doings. ¹¹Woe unto the wicked! it shall be ill with him: for the reward of his hands shall be given him."

Hosea 10:12-13 "¹²Sow to yourselves in righteousness, reap in mercy; break up your fallow ground: for it is time to seek the LORD, till he come and rain righteousness upon you. ¹³Ye have plowed wickedness, ye have reaped iniquity; ye have eaten the fruit of lies: because thou didst trust in thy way, in the multitude of thy mighty men."

Obadiah 15-16 "¹⁵For the day of the LORD is near upon all the heathen: as thou hast done, it shall be done unto thee: thy reward shall return upon thine own head. ¹⁶For as ye have drunk upon my holy mountain, so shall all the heathen drink continually, yea, they shall drink, and they shall swallow down, and they shall be as though they had not been."

Galatians 6:7-8 "⁷Be not deceived; God is not mocked: for whatsoever a man soweth, that shall he also reap. ⁸For he that soweth to his flesh shall of the flesh reap corruption; but he that soweth to the Spirit shall of the Spirit reap life everlasting."

Ephesians 6:8 "Knowing that whatsoever good thing any man doeth, the same shall he receive of the Lord, whether he be bond or free."

The Fruit Of The Spirit

Galatians 5:22-24 "²²But the fruit of the Spirit is love, joy, peace, longsuffering, gentleness, goodness, faith, ²³Meekness, temperance: against such there is no law. ²⁴And they that are Christ's have crucified the flesh with the affections and lusts."

Ephesians 5:9-10 "⁹(For the fruit of the Spirit is in all goodness and righteousness and truth;) ¹⁰Proving what is acceptable unto the Lord."

The Fruit Of The Wicked

Proverbs 10:16 "The labour of the righteous tendeth to life: the fruit of the wicked to sin."

The Fruit Of Wisdom

Proverbs 8:12-19 "¹²I wisdom dwell with prudence, and find out knowledge of witty inventions. ¹³The fear of the LORD is to hate evil: pride, and arrogancy, and the evil way, and the froward mouth, do I hate. ¹⁴Counsel is mine, and sound wisdom: I am understanding; I have strength. ¹⁵By me kings reign, and princes decree justice. ¹⁶By me princes rule, and nobles, even all the judges of the earth. ¹⁷I love them that love me; and those that seek me early shall find me. ¹⁸Riches and honour are with me; yea, durable riches and righteousness. ¹⁹My fruit is better than gold, yea, than fine gold; and my revenue than choice silver."

The Sowing Of God's Word

Matthew 13:3-9 "³And he spake many things unto them in parables, saying, Behold, a sower went forth to sow; ⁴And when he sowed, some seeds fell by the way side, and the fowls came and devoured them up: [5]Some fell upon stony places, where they had not much earth: and forthwith they sprung up, because they had no deepness of earth: [6]And when the sun was up, they were scorched; and because they had no root, they withered away. [7]And some fell among thorns; and the thorns sprung up, and choked them: [8]But other fell into good ground, and brought forth fruit, some an hundredfold, some sixtyfold, some thirtyfold. [9]Who hath ears to hear, let him hear."

Matthew 13:18-23 "[18]Hear ye therefore the parable of the sower. [19]When any one heareth the word of the kingdom, and understandeth it not, then cometh the wicked one, and catcheth away that which was sown in his heart. This is he which received seed by the way side. [20]But he that received the seed into stony places, the same is he that heareth the word, and anon with joy receiveth it; [21]Yet hath he not root in himself, but dureth for a while: for when tribulation or persecution ariseth because of the word, by and by he is offended. [22]He also that received seed among the thorns is he that heareth the word; and the care of this world, and the deceitfulness of riches, choke the word, and he becometh unfruitful. [23]But he that received seed into the good ground is he that heareth the word, and understandeth it; which also beareth fruit, and bringeth forth, some an hundredfold, some sixty, some thirty."

Mark 4:1-20 "[1]And he began again to teach by the sea side: and there was gathered unto him a great multitude, so that he entered into a ship, and sat in the sea; and the whole multitude was by the sea on the land. [2]And he taught them many things by parables, and said unto them in his doctrine, [3]Hearken; Behold, there went out a sower to sow: [4]And it came to pass, as he sowed, some fell by the way side, and the fowls of the air came and devoured it up. [5]And some fell on stony ground, where it had not much earth; and immediately it sprang up, because it had no depth of earth: [6]But when the sun was up, it was scorched; and because it had no root, it withered away. [7]And some fell among thorns, and the thorns grew up, and choked it, and it yielded no fruit. [8]And other fell on good ground, and did yield fruit that sprang up and increased; and brought forth, some thirty,

and some sixty, and some an hundred. [9]And he said unto them, He that hath ears to hear, let him hear. [10]And when he was alone, they that were about him with the twelve asked of him the parable. [11]And he said unto them, Unto you it is given to know the mystery of the kingdom of God: but unto them that are without, all these things are done in parables: [12]That seeing they may see, and not perceive; and hearing they may hear, and not understand; lest at any time they should be converted, and their sins should be forgiven them. [13]And he said unto them, Know ye not this parable? and how then will ye know all parables? [14]The sower soweth the word. [15]And these are they by the way side, where the word is sown; but when they have heard, Satan cometh immediately, and taketh away the word that was sown in their hearts. [16]And these are they likewise which are sown on stony ground; who, when they have heard the word, immediately receive it with gladness; [17]And have no root in themselves, and so endure but for a time: afterward, when affliction or persecution ariseth for the word's sake, immediately they are offended. [18]And these are they which are sown among thorns; such as hear the word, [19]And the cares of this world, and the deceitfulness of riches, and the lusts of other things entering in, choke the word, and it becometh unfruitful. [20]And these are they which are sown on good ground; such as hear the word, and receive it, and bring forth fruit, some thirtyfold, some sixty, and some an hundred."

Luke 8:4-15 "[4]And when much people were gathered together, and were come to him out of every city, he spake by a parable: [5]A sower went out to sow his seed: and as he sowed, some fell by the way side; and it was trodden down, and the fowls of the air devoured it. [6]And some fell upon a rock; and as soon as it was sprung up, it withered away, because it lacked moisture. [7]And some fell among thorns; and the thorns sprang up with it, and choked it. [8]And other fell on good ground, and sprang up, and bare fruit an hundredfold. And when he had said these things, he cried, He that hath ears to hear, let him hear. [9]And his disciples asked him, saying, What might this parable be? [10]And he said, Unto you it is given to know the mysteries of the kingdom of God: but to others in parables; that seeing they might not see, and hearing they might not understand. [11]Now the parable is this: The seed is the word of God. [12]Those by the way side are they that hear; then cometh the devil, and taketh away the word out of their hearts, lest they should believe and be saved. [13]They on the rock are they, which, when they hear, receive the word with joy; and these have no root, which for a while believe, and in time of temptation fall away. [14]And that which fell among thorns are they, which, when they have heard, go forth, and are choked with cares and riches and pleasures of this life, and bring no fruit to perfection. [15]But that on the good ground are they, which in an honest and good heart, having heard the word, keep it, and bring forth fruit with patience."

Those That Are Rooted In The Lord
Psalm 92:13 "Those that be planted in the house of the LORD shall flourish in the courts of our God."

John 15:1-8 "[1]I am the true vine, and my Father is the husbandman. [2]Every branch in me that beareth not fruit he taketh away: and every branch that beareth fruit, he purgeth it, that it may bring forth more fruit. [3]Now ye are clean through the word which I have spoken unto you. [4]Abide in me, and I in you. As the branch cannot bear fruit of itself, except it abide in the vine; no more can ye, except ye abide in me. [5]I am the vine, ye are the branches: He that abideth in me, and I in him, the same bringeth forth much fruit: for without me ye can do nothing. [6]If a man abide not in me, he is cast forth as a branch, and is withered; and men gather them, and cast them into the fire, and they are burned. [7]If ye abide in me, and my words abide in you, ye shall ask what ye will, and it shall be done unto you. [8]Herein is my Father glorified, that ye bear much fruit; so shall ye be my disciples."

Those That Sow Bountifully
2 Corinthians 9:6-7 "[6]But this I say, He which soweth sparingly shall reap also sparingly; and he which soweth bountifully shall reap also bountifully. [7]Every man according as he purposeth in his heart, so let him give; not grudgingly, or of necessity: for God loveth a cheerful giver."

Those That Sow Iniquity
Job 4:8 "Even as I have seen, they that plow iniquity, and sow wickedness, reap the same."

Proverbs 22:8 "He that soweth iniquity shall reap vanity: and the rod of his anger shall fail."

Colossians 3:25 "But he that doeth wrong shall receive for the wrong which he hath done: and there is no respect of persons."

Those That Sow Righteousness
Proverbs 11:18 "The wicked worketh a deceitful work: but to him that soweth righteousness shall be a sure reward."

Those That Sow Sparingly
2 Corinthians 9:6-7 "[6]But this I say, He which soweth sparingly shall reap also sparingly; and he which soweth bountifully shall reap also bountifully. [7]Every man according as he purposeth in his heart, so let him give; not grudgingly, or of necessity: for God loveth a cheerful giver."

Those That Sow To Their Flesh
Galatians 6:8 "For he that soweth to his flesh shall of the flesh reap corruption; but he that soweth to the Spirit shall of the Spirit reap life everlasting."

Those That Sow To The Spirit
Galatians 6:8 "For he that soweth to his flesh shall of the flesh reap corruption; but he that soweth to the Spirit shall of the Spirit reap life everlasting."

What Brings Forth Evil Fruit
Matthew 7:17-20 "[17]Even so every good tree bringeth forth good fruit; but a corrupt tree bringeth forth evil fruit. [18]A good tree cannot bring forth evil fruit, neither can a corrupt tree bring forth good fruit. [19]Every tree that bringeth not forth good fruit is hewn down, and cast into the fire. [20]Wherefore by their fruits ye shall know them."

Matthew 12:35 "A good man out of the good treasure of the heart bringeth forth good things: and an evil man out of the evil treasure bringeth forth evil things."

Luke 6:43-45 "[43]For a good tree bringeth not forth corrupt fruit; neither doth a corrupt tree bring forth good fruit. [44]For every tree is known by his own fruit. For of thorns men do not gather figs, nor of a bramble bush gather they grapes. [45]A good man out of the good treasure of his heart bringeth forth that which is good; and an evil man out of the evil treasure of his heart bringeth forth that which is evil: for of the abundance of the heart his mouth speaketh."

What Brings Forth Good Fruit

Matthew 7:17-20 "¹⁷Even so every good tree bringeth forth good fruit; but a corrupt tree bringeth forth evil fruit. ¹⁸A good tree cannot bring forth evil fruit, neither can a corrupt tree bring forth good fruit. ¹⁹Every tree that bringeth not forth good fruit is hewn down, and cast into the fire. ²⁰Wherefore by their fruits ye shall know them."

Matthew 12:35 "A good man out of the good treasure of the heart bringeth forth good things: and an evil man out of the evil treasure bringeth forth evil things."

Luke 6:43-45 "⁴³For a good tree bringeth not forth corrupt fruit; neither doth a corrupt tree bring forth good fruit. ⁴⁴For every tree is known by his own fruit. For of thorns men do not gather figs, nor of a bramble bush gather they grapes. ⁴⁵A good man out of the good treasure of his heart bringeth forth that which is good; and an evil man out of the evil treasure of his heart bringeth forth that which is evil: for of the abundance of the heart his mouth speaketh."

Colossians 1:5-6 "⁵For the hope which is laid up for you in heaven, whereof ye heard before in the word of the truth of the gospel; ⁶Which is come unto you, as it is in all the world; and bringeth forth fruit, as it doth also in you, since the day ye heard of it, and knew the grace of God in truth."

What Brings Forth Much Fruit

John 12:23-24 "²³And Jesus answered them, saying, The hour is come, that the Son of man should be glorified. ²⁴Verily, verily, I say unto you, Except a corn of wheat fall into the ground and die, it abideth alone: but if it die, it bringeth forth much fruit."

What Fruit To Bring Forth

Matthew 3:8 "Bring forth therefore fruits meet for repentance."

Luke 3:8 "Bring forth therefore fruits worthy of repentance, and begin not to say within yourselves, We have Abraham to our father: for I say unto you, That God is able of these stones to raise up children unto Abraham."

What Is Full Of Good Fruits

James 3:17 "But the wisdom that is from above is first pure, then peaceable, gentle, and easy to be intreated, full of mercy and good fruits, without partiality, and without hypocrisy."

Who Is Planted Firmly

Psalm 1:1-3 "¹Blessed is the man that walketh not in the counsel of the ungodly, nor standeth in the way of sinners, nor sitteth in the seat of the scornful. ²But his delight is in the law of the LORD; and in his law doth he meditate day and night. ³And he shall be like a tree planted by the rivers of water, that bringeth forth his fruit in his season; his leaf also shall not wither; and whatsoever he doeth shall prosper."

Psalm 52:8 "But I am like a green olive tree in the house of God: I trust in the mercy of God for ever and ever."

Psalm 92:12-13 "¹²The righteous shall flourish like the palm tree: he shall grow like a cedar in Lebanon. ¹³Those that be planted in the house of the LORD shall flourish in the courts of our God."

Proverbs 11:28 "He that trusteth in his riches shall fall: but the righteous shall flourish as a branch."

Proverbs 12:3 "A man shall not be established by wickedness: but the root of the righteous shall not be moved."

Jeremiah 17:7-8 "⁷Blessed is the man that trusteth in the LORD, and whose hope the LORD is. ⁸For he shall be as a tree planted by the waters, and that spreadeth out her roots by the river, and shall not see when heat cometh, but her leaf shall be green; and shall not be careful in the year of drought, neither shall cease from yielding fruit."

Matthew 13:30 "Let both grow together until the harvest: and in the time of harvest I will say to the reapers, Gather ye together first the tares, and bind them in bundles to burn them: but gather the wheat into my barn."

Who Shall Be Rooted Up

I Kings 14:15-16 "¹⁵For the LORD shall smite Israel, as a reed is shaken in the water, and he shall root up Israel out of this good land, which he gave to their fathers, and shall scatter them beyond the river, because they have made their groves, provoking the LORD to anger. ¹⁶And he shall give Israel up because of the sins of Jeroboam, who did sin, and who made Israel to sin."

Job 8:11-17 "[11]Can the rush grow up without mire? can the flag grow without water? [12]Whilst it is yet in his greenness, and not cut down, it withereth before any other herb. [13]So are the paths of all that forget God; and the hypocrite's hope shall perish: [14]Whose hope shall be cut off, and whose trust shall be a spider's web. [15]He shall lean upon his house, but it shall not stand: he shall hold it fast, but it shall not endure. [16]He is green before the sun, and his branch shooteth forth in his garden. [17]His roots are wrapped about the heap, and seeth the place of stones."

Job 18:5-16 "[5]Yea, the light of the wicked shall be put out, and the spark of his fire shall not shine. [6]The light shall be dark in his tabernacle, and his candle shall be put out with him. [7]The steps of his strength shall be straitened, and his own counsel shall cast him down. [8]For he is cast into a net by his own feet, and he walketh upon a snare. [9]The gin shall take him by the heel, and the robber shall prevail against him. [10]The snare is laid for him in the ground, and a trap for him in the way. [11]Terrors shall make him afraid on every side, and shall drive him to his feet. [12]His strength shall be hungerbitten, and destruction shall be ready at his side. [13]It shall devour the strength of his skin: even the firstborn of death shall devour his strength. [14]His confidence shall be rooted out of his tabernacle, and it shall bring him to the king of terrors. [15]It shall dwell in his tabernacle, because it is none of his: brimstone shall be scattered upon his habitation. [16]His roots shall be dried up beneath, and above shall his branch be cut off."

Job 24:13-24 "[13]They are of those that rebel against the light; they know not the ways thereof, nor abide in the paths thereof. [14]The murderer rising with the light killeth the poor and needy, and in the night is as a thief. [15]The eye also of the adulterer waiteth for the twilight, saying, No eye shall see me: and disguiseth his face. [16]In the dark they dig through houses, which they had marked for themselves in the daytime: they know not the light. [17]For the morning is to them even as the shadow of death: if one know them, they are in the terrors of the shadow of death. [18]He is swift as the waters; their portion is cursed in the earth: he beholdeth not the way of the vineyards. [19]Drought and heat consume the snow waters: so doth the grave those which have sinned. [20]The womb shall forget him; the worm shall feed sweetly on him; he shall be no more remembered; and wickedness shall be broken as a tree. [21]He evil entreateth the barren that beareth not: and doeth not good to the widow. [22]He draweth also the mighty with his power: he riseth up, and no man is sure of life. [23]Though it be given him to be in safety, whereon he resteth; yet his eyes are upon their ways. [24]They are exalted for a little while, but are gone and brought low; they are taken out of the way as all other, and cut off as the tops of the ears of corn."

Psalm 37:1-2 "[1]Fret not thyself because of evildoers, neither be thou envious against the workers of iniquity. [2]For they shall soon be cut down like the grass, and wither as the green herb."

Psalm 52:1-7 "[1]Why boastest thou thyself in mischief, O mighty man? the goodness of God endureth continually. [2]Thy tongue deviseth mischiefs; like a sharp rasor, working deceitfully. [3]Thou lovest evil more than good; and lying rather than to speak righteousness. Selah. [4]Thou lovest all devouring words, O thou deceitful tongue. [5]God shall likewise destroy thee for ever, he shall take thee away, and pluck thee out of thy dwelling place, and root thee out of the land of the living. Selah. [6]The righteous also shall see, and fear, and shall laugh at him: [7]Lo, this is the man that made not God his strength; but trusted in the abundance of his riches, and strengthened himself in his wickedness."

Proverbs 2:21-22 "[21]For the upright shall dwell in the land, and the perfect shall remain in it. [22]But the wicked shall be cut off from the earth, and the transgressors shall be rooted out of it."

Isaiah 5:24 "Therefore as the fire devoureth the stubble, and the flame consumeth the chaff, so their root shall be as rottenness, and their blossom shall go up as dust: because they have cast away the law of the LORD of hosts, and despised the word of the Holy One of Israel."

Joel 3:12-14 "[12]Let the heathen be wakened, and come up to the valley of Jehoshaphat: for there will I sit to judge all the heathen round about. [13]Put ye in the sickle, for the harvest is ripe: come, get you down; for the press is full, the fats overflow; for their wickedness is great. [14]Multitudes, multitudes in the valley of decision: for the day of the LORD is near in the valley of decision."

Zephaniah 2:4-5 "4For Gaza shall be forsaken, and Ashkelon a desolation: they shall drive out Ashdod at the noon day, and Ekron shall be rooted up. 5Woe unto the inhabitants of the sea coast, the nation of the Cherethites! the word of the LORD is against you; O Canaan, the land of the Philistines, I will even destroy thee, that there shall be no inhabitant."

Matthew 3:10 "And now also the axe is laid unto the root of the trees: therefore every tree which bringeth not forth good fruit is hewn down, and cast into the fire."

Matthew 7:19 "Every tree that bringeth not forth good fruit is hewn down, and cast into the fire."

Matthew 13:30 "Let both grow together until the harvest: and in the time of harvest I will say to the reapers, Gather ye together first the tares, and bind them in bundles to burn them: but gather the wheat into my barn."

Matthew 15:12-13 "12Then came his disciples, and said unto him, Knowest thou that the Pharisees were offended, after they heard this saying? 13But he answered and said, Every plant, which my heavenly Father hath not planted, shall be rooted up."

Luke 3:9 "And now also the axe is laid unto the root of the trees: every tree therefore which bringeth not forth good fruit is hewn down, and cast into the fire."

John 15:1-6 "1I am the true vine, and my Father is the husbandman. 2Every branch in me that beareth not fruit he taketh away: and every branch that beareth fruit, he purgeth it, that it may bring forth more fruit. 3Now ye are clean through the word which I have spoken unto you. 4Abide in me, and I in you. As the branch cannot bear fruit of itself, except it abide in the vine; no more can ye, except ye abide in me. 5I am the vine, ye are the branches: He that abideth in me, and I in him, the same bringeth forth much fruit: for without me ye can do nothing. 6If a man abide not in me, he is cast forth as a branch, and is withered; and men gather them, and cast them into the fire, and they are burned."

Jude 7-12 "7Even as Sodom and Gomorrha, and the cities about them in like manner, giving themselves over to fornication, and going after strange flesh, are set forth for an example, suffering the vengeance of eternal fire. 8Likewise also these filthy dreamers defile the flesh, despise dominion, and speak evil of dignities. 9Yet Michael the archangel, when contending with the devil he disputed about the body of Moses, durst not bring against him a railing accusation, but said, The Lord rebuke thee. 10But these speak evil of those things which they know not: but what they know naturally, as brute beasts, in those things they corrupt themselves. 11Woe unto them! for they have gone in the way of Cain, and ran greedily after the error of Balaam for reward, and perished in the gainsaying of Core. 12These are spots in your feasts of charity, when they feast with you, feeding themselves without fear: clouds they are without water, carried about of winds; trees whose fruit withereth, without fruit, twice dead, plucked up by the roots."

Who Shall Not Sow And Reap

Ecclesiastes 11:1-4 "1Cast thy bread upon the waters: for thou shalt find it after many days. 2Give a portion to seven, and also to eight; for thou knowest not what evil shall be upon the earth. 3If the clouds be full of rain, they empty themselves upon the earth: and if the tree fall toward the south, or toward the north, in the place where the tree falleth, there it shall be. 4He that observeth the wind shall not sow; and he that regardeth the clouds shall not reap."

Who Shall Yield Fruit

Psalm 1:1-3 "1Blessed is the man that walketh not in the counsel of the ungodly, nor standeth in the way of sinners, nor sitteth in the seat of the scornful. 2But his delight is in the law of the LORD; and in his law doth he meditate day and night. 3And he shall be like a tree planted by the rivers of water, that bringeth forth his fruit in his season; his leaf also shall not wither; and whatsoever he doeth shall prosper."

Proverbs 12:12 "The wicked desireth the net of evil men: but the root of the righteous yieldeth fruit."

Jeremiah 17:7-8 "7Blessed is the man that trusteth in the LORD, and whose hope the LORD is. 8For he shall be as a tree planted by the waters, and that spreadeth out her roots by the river, and shall not see when heat cometh, but her leaf shall be green;

and shall not be careful in the year of drought, neither shall cease from yielding fruit."

Matthew 13:23 "But he that received seed into the good ground is he that heareth the word, and understandeth it; which also beareth fruit, and bringeth forth, some an hundredfold, some sixty, some thirty."

Mark 4:20 "And these are they which are sown on good ground; such as hear the word, and receive it, and bring forth fruit, some thirtyfold, some sixty, and some an hundred."

Luke 8:15 "But that on the good ground are they, which in an honest and good heart, having heard the word, keep it, and bring forth fruit with patience."

John 15:1-16 "¹I am the true vine, and my Father is the husbandman. ²Every branch in me that beareth not fruit he taketh away: and every branch that beareth fruit, he purgeth it, that it may bring forth more fruit. ³Now ye are clean through the word which I have spoken unto you. ⁴Abide in me, and I in you. As the branch cannot bear fruit of itself, except it abide in the vine; no more can ye, except ye abide in me. ⁵I am the vine, ye are the branches: He that abideth in me, and I in him, the same bringeth forth much fruit: for without me ye can do nothing. ⁶If a man abide not in me, he is cast forth as a branch, and is withered; and men gather them, and cast them into the fire, and they are burned. ⁷If ye abide in me, and my words abide in you, ye shall ask what ye will, and it shall be done unto you. ⁸Herein is my Father glorified, that ye bear much fruit; so shall ye be my disciples. ⁹As the Father hath loved me, so have I loved you: continue ye in my love. ¹⁰If ye keep my commandments, ye shall abide in my love; even as I have kept my Father's commandments, and abide in his love. ¹¹These things have I spoken unto you, that my joy might remain in you, and that your joy might be full. ¹²This is my commandment, That ye love one another, as I have loved you. ¹³Greater love hath no man than this, that a man lay down his life for his friends. ¹⁴Ye are my friends, if ye do whatsoever I command you. ¹⁵Henceforth I call you not servants; for the servant knoweth not what his lord doeth: but I have called you friends; for all things that I

have heard of my Father I have made known unto you. ¹⁶Ye have not chosen me, but I have chosen you, and ordained you, that ye should go and bring forth fruit, and that your fruit should remain: that whatsoever ye shall ask of the Father in my name, he may give it you."

Galatians 6:9 "And let us not be weary in well doing: for in due season we shall reap, if we faint not."

BELIEF

Believing In Christ
John 6:29 "Jesus answered and said unto them, This is the work of God, that ye believe on him whom he hath sent."

John 14:1-2 "¹Let not your heart be troubled: ye believe in God, believe also in me. ²In my Father's house are many mansions: if it were not so, I would have told you. I go to prepare a place for you."

Acts 19:4 "Then said Paul, John verily baptized with the baptism of repentance, saying unto the people, that they should believe on him which should come after him, that is, on Christ Jesus."

Philippians 1:29 "For unto you it is given in the behalf of Christ, not only to believe on him, but also to suffer for his sake."

1 John 3:23 "And this is his commandment, That we should believe on the name of his Son Jesus Christ, and love one another, as he gave us commandment."

Believing The Gospel
Mark 1:15 "And saying, The time is fulfilled, and the kingdom of God is at hand: repent ye, and believe the gospel."

Devils Believing In God
James 2:19 "Thou believest that there is one God; thou doest well: the devils also believe, and tremble."

The Reward For Believing In The Lord
Genesis 15:6 "And he believed in the LORD; and he counted it to him for righteousness."

2 Chronicles 20:20 "And they rose early in the morning, and went forth into the wilderness of

Tekoa: and as they went forth, Jehoshaphat stood and said, Hear me, O Judah, and ye inhabitants of Jerusalem; Believe in the LORD your God, so shall ye be established; believe his prophets, so shall ye prosper."

Psalm 91:9-13 "⁹Because thou hast made the LORD, which is my refuge, even the most High, thy habitation; ¹⁰There shall no evil befall thee, neither shall any plague come nigh thy dwelling. ¹¹For he shall give his angels charge over thee, to keep thee in all thy ways. ¹²They shall bear thee up in their hands, lest thou dash thy foot against a stone. ¹³Thou shalt tread upon the lion and adder: the young lion and the dragon shalt thou trample under feet."

Daniel 6:23 "Then was the king exceeding glad for him, and commanded that they should take Daniel up out of the den. So Daniel was taken up out of the den, and no manner of hurt was found upon him, because he believed in his God."

Matthew 17:20 "And Jesus said unto them, Because of your unbelief: for verily I say unto you, If ye have faith as a grain of mustard seed, ye shall say unto this mountain, Remove hence to yonder place; and it shall remove; and nothing shall be impossible unto you."

Matthew 21:21-22 "²¹Jesus answered and said unto them, Verily I say unto you, If ye have faith, and doubt not, ye shall not only do this which is done to the fig tree, but also if ye shall say unto this mountain, Be thou removed, and be thou cast into the sea; it shall be done. ²²And all things, whatsoever ye shall ask in prayer, believing, ye shall receive."

Mark 9:23 "Jesus said unto him, If thou canst believe, all things are possible to him that believeth."

Mark 11:23-24 "²³For verily I say unto you, That whosoever shall say unto this mountain, Be thou removed, and be thou cast into the sea; and shall not doubt in his heart, but shall believe that those things which he saith shall come to pass; he shall have whatsoever he saith. ²⁴Therefore I say unto you, What things soever ye desire, when ye pray, believe that ye receive them, and ye shall have them."

Luke 8:50 "But when Jesus heard it, he answered him, saying, Fear not: believe only, and she shall be made whole."

John 11:40 "Jesus saith unto her, Said I not unto thee, that, if thou wouldest believe, thou shouldest see the glory of God?"

John 12:35-36 "³⁵Then Jesus said unto them, Yet a little while is the light with you. Walk while ye have the light, lest darkness come upon you: for he that walketh in darkness knoweth not whither he goeth. ³⁶While ye have light, believe in the light, that ye may be the children of light. These things spake Jesus, and departed, and did hide himself from them."

John 16:19-27 "¹⁹Now Jesus knew that they were desirous to ask him, and said unto them, Do ye inquire among yourselves of that I said, A little while, and ye shall not see me: and again, a little while, and ye shall see me? ²⁰Verily, verily, I say unto you, That ye shall weep and lament, but the world shall rejoice: and ye shall be sorrowful, but your sorrow shall be turned into joy. ²¹A woman when she is in travail hath sorrow, because her hour is come: but as soon as she is delivered of the child, she remembereth no more the anguish, for joy that a man is born into the world. ²²And ye now therefore have sorrow: but I will see you again, and your heart shall rejoice, and your joy no man taketh from you. ²³And in that day ye shall ask me nothing. Verily, verily, I say unto you, Whatsoever ye shall ask the Father in my name, he will give it you. ²⁴Hitherto have ye asked nothing in my name: ask, and ye shall receive, that your joy may be full. ²⁵These things have I spoken unto you in proverbs: but the time cometh, when I shall no more speak unto you in proverbs, but I shall shew you plainly of the Father. ²⁶At that day ye shall ask in my name: and I say not unto you, that I will pray the Father for you: ²⁷For the Father himself loveth you, because ye have loved me, and have believed that I came out from God."

John 20:31 "But these are written, that ye might believe that Jesus is the Christ, the Son of God; and that believing ye might have life through his name."

Acts 16:31 "And they said, Believe on the Lord Jesus Christ, and thou shalt be saved, and thy house."

Romans 4:3 "For what saith the scripture? Abraham believed God, and it was counted unto him for righteousness."

Romans 10:9 "That if thou shalt confess with thy mouth the Lord Jesus, and shalt believe in thine heart that God hath raised him from the dead, thou shalt be saved."

Galatians 3:6 "Even as Abraham believed God, and it was accounted to him for righteousness."

James 2:23 "And the scripture was fulfilled which saith, Abraham believed God, and it was imputed unto him for righteousness: and he was called the Friend of God."

Those That Believe In The Lord
Isaiah 28:16 "Therefore thus saith the Lord GOD, Behold, I lay in Zion for a foundation a stone, a tried stone, a precious corner stone, a sure foundation: he that believeth shall not make haste."

Mark 9:23 "Jesus said unto him, If thou canst believe, all things are possible to him that believeth."

Mark 16:16-19 "[16]He that believeth and is baptized shall be saved; but he that believeth not shall be damned. [17]And these signs shall follow them that believe; In my name shall they cast out devils; they shall speak with new tongues; [18]They shall take up serpents; and if they drink any deadly thing, it shall not hurt them; they shall lay hands on the sick, and they shall recover. [19]So then after the Lord had spoken unto them, he was received up into heaven, and sat on the right hand of God."

John 1:1-12 "[1]In the beginning was the Word, and the Word was with God, and the Word was God. [2]The same was in the beginning with God. [3]All things were made by him; and without him was not any thing made that was made. [4]In him was life; and the life was the light of men. [5]And the light shineth in darkness; and the darkness comprehended it not. [6]There was a man sent from God, whose name was John. [7]The same came for a witness, to bear witness of the Light, that all men through him might believe. [8]He was not that Light, but was sent to bear witness of that Light. [9]That was the true Light, which lighteth every man that cometh into the world. [10]He was in the world, and the world was made by him, and the world knew him not. [11]He came unto his own, and his own received him not. [12]But as many as received him, to them gave he

power to become the sons of God, even to them that believe on his name."

John 3:14-18 "[14]And as Moses lifted up the serpent in the wilderness, even so must the Son of man be lifted up: [15]That whosoever believeth in him should not perish, but have eternal life. [16]For God so loved the world, that he gave his only begotten Son, that whosoever believeth in him should not perish, but have everlasting life. [17]For God sent not his Son into the world to condemn the world; but that the world through him might be saved. [18]He that believeth on him is not condemned: but he that believeth not is condemned already, because he hath not believed in the name of the only begotten Son of God."

John 3:36 "He that believeth on the Son hath everlasting life: and he that believeth not the Son shall not see life; but the wrath of God abideth on him."

John 6:35-40 "[35]And Jesus said unto them, I am the bread of life: he that cometh to me shall never hunger; and he that believeth on me shall never thirst. [36]But I said unto you, That ye also have seen me, and believe not. [37]All that the Father giveth me shall come to me; and him that cometh to me I will in no wise cast out. [38]For I came down from heaven, not to do mine own will, but the will of him that sent me. [39]And this is the Father's will which hath sent me, that of all which he hath given me I should lose nothing, but should raise it up again at the last day. [40]And this is the will of him that sent me, that every one which seeth the Son, and believeth on him, may have everlasting life: and I will raise him up at the last day."

John 6:43-47 "[43]Jesus therefore answered and said unto them, Murmur not among yourselves. [44]No man can come to me, except the Father which hath sent me draw him: and I will raise him up at the last day. [45]It is written in the prophets, And they shall be all taught of God. Every man therefore that hath heard, and hath learned of the Father, cometh unto me. [46]Not that any man hath seen the Father, save he which is of God, he hath seen the Father. [47]Verily, verily, I say unto you, He that believeth on me hath everlasting life."

John 7:37-39 "[37]In the last day, that great day of the feast, Jesus stood and cried, saying, If any man thirst, let him come unto me, and drink. [38]He that believeth on me, as the scripture hath said, out of his belly shall flow rivers of living water. [39](But this spake he of the Spirit, which they that believe on him should receive: for the Holy Ghost was not yet given; because that Jesus was not yet glorified.)"

John 8:31 "Then said Jesus to those Jews which believed on him, If ye continue in my word, then are ye my disciples indeed."

John 11:25-26 "[25]Jesus said unto her, I am the resurrection, and the life: he that believeth in me, though he were dead, yet shall he live: [26]And whosoever liveth and believeth in me shall never die. Believest thou this?"

John 12:44-46 "[44]Jesus cried and said, He that believeth on me, believeth not on me, but on him that sent me. [45]And he that seeth me seeth him that sent me. [46]I am come a light into the world, that whosoever believeth on me should not abide in darkness."

John 14:9-12 "[9]Jesus saith unto him, Have I been so long time with you, and yet hast thou not known me, Philip? he that hath seen me hath seen the Father; and how sayest thou then, Shew us the Father? [10]Believest thou not that I am in the Father, and the Father in me? the words that I speak unto you I speak not of myself: but the Father that dwelleth in me, he doeth the works. [11]Believe me that I am in the Father, and the Father in me: or else believe me for the very works' sake. [12]Verily, verily, I say unto you, He that believeth on me, the works that I do shall he do also; and greater works than these shall he do; because I go unto my Father."

John 17:1-26 "[1]These words spake Jesus, and lifted up his eyes to heaven, and said, Father, the hour is come; glorify thy Son, that thy Son also may glorify thee: [2]As thou hast given him power over all flesh, that he should give eternal life to as many as thou hast given him. [3]And this is life eternal, that they might know thee the only true God, and Jesus Christ, whom thou hast sent. [4]I have glorified thee on the earth: I have finished the work which thou gavest me to do. [5]And now, O Father, glorify thou me with thine own self with the glory which I had with thee before the world was. [6]I have manifested thy name unto the men which thou gavest me out of the world: thine they were,

and thou gavest them me; and they have kept thy word. [7]Now they have known that all things whatsoever thou hast given me are of thee. [8]For I have given unto them the words which thou gavest me; and they have received them, and have known surely that I came out from thee, and they have believed that thou didst send me. [9]I pray for them: I pray not for the world, but for them which thou hast given me; for they are thine. [10]And all mine are thine, and thine are mine; and I am glorified in them. [11]And now I am no more in the world, but these are in the world, and I come to thee. Holy Father, keep through thine own name those whom thou hast given me, that they may be one, as we are. [12]While I was with them in the world, I kept them in thy name: those that thou gavest me I have kept, and none of them is lost, but the son of perdition; that the scripture might be fulfilled. [13]And now come I to thee; and these things I speak in the world, that they might have my joy fulfilled in themselves. [14]I have given them thy word; and the world hath hated them, because they are not of the world, even as I am not of the world. [15]I pray not that thou shouldest take them out of the world, but that thou shouldest keep them from the evil. [16]They are not of the world, even as I am not of the world. [17]Sanctify them through thy truth: thy word is truth. [18]As thou hast sent me into the world, even so have I also sent them into the world. [19]And for their sakes I sanctify myself, that they also might be sanctified through the truth. [20]Neither pray I for these alone, but for them also which shall believe on me through their word; [21]That they all may be one; as thou, Father, art in me, and I in thee, that they also may be one in us: that the world may believe that thou hast sent me. [22]And the glory which thou gavest me I have given them; that they may be one, even as we are one: [23]I in them, and thou in me, that they may be made perfect in one; and that the world may know that thou hast sent me, and hast loved them, as thou hast loved me. [24]Father, I will that they also, whom thou hast given me, be with me where I am; that they may behold my glory, which thou hast given me: for thou lovedst me before the foundation of the world. [25]O righteous Father, the world hath not known thee: but I have known thee, and these have known that thou hast sent me. [26]And I have declared unto them thy name, and will declare it:

that the love wherewith thou hast loved me may be in them, and I in them."

Acts 10:37-43 "³⁷That word, I say, ye know, which was published throughout all Judaea, and began from Galilee, after the baptism which John preached; ³⁸How God anointed Jesus of Nazareth with the Holy Ghost and with power: who went about doing good, and healing all that were oppressed of the devil; for God was with him. ³⁹And we are witnesses of all things which he did both in the land of the Jews, and in Jerusalem; whom they slew and hanged on a tree: ⁴⁰Him God raised up the third day, and shewed him openly; ⁴¹Not to all the people, but unto witnesses chosen before of God, even to us, who did eat and drink with him after he rose from the dead. ⁴²And he commanded us to preach unto the people, and to testify that it is he which was ordained of God to be the Judge of quick and dead. ⁴³To him give all the prophets witness, that through his name whosoever believeth in him shall receive remission of sins."

Acts 13:33-39 "³³God hath fulfilled the same unto us their children, in that he hath raised up Jesus again; as it is also written in the second psalm, Thou art my Son, this day have I begotten thee. ³⁴And as concerning that he raised him up from the dead, now no more to return to corruption, he said on this wise, I will give you the sure mercies of David. ³⁵Wherefore he saith also in another psalm, Thou shalt not suffer thine Holy One to see corruption. ³⁶For David, after he had served his own generation by the will of God, fell on sleep, and was laid unto his fathers, and saw corruption: ³⁷But he, whom God raised again, saw no corruption. ³⁸Be it known unto you therefore, men and brethren, that through this man is preached unto you the forgiveness of sins: ³⁹And by him all that believe are justified from all things, from which ye could not be justified by the law of Moses."

Romans 1:16 "For I am not ashamed of the gospel of Christ: for it is the power of God unto salvation to every one that believeth; to the Jew first, and also to the Greek."

Romans 3:22 "Even the righteousness of God which is by faith of Jesus Christ unto all and upon all them that believe: for there is no difference."

Romans 9:33 "As it is written, Behold, I lay in Sion a stumblingstone and rock of offence: and whosoever believeth on him shall not be ashamed."

Romans 10:4 "For Christ is the end of the law for righteousness to every one that believeth."

Romans 10:9-11 "⁹That if thou shalt confess with thy mouth the Lord Jesus, and shalt believe in thine heart that God hath raised him from the dead, thou shalt be saved. ¹⁰For with the heart man believeth unto righteousness; and with the mouth confession is made unto salvation. ¹¹For the scripture saith, Whosoever believeth on him shall not be ashamed."

1 Corinthians 14:22 "Wherefore tongues are for a sign, not to them that believe, but to them that believe not: but prophesying serveth not for them that believe not, but for them which believe."

Galatians 3:22 "But the scripture hath concluded all under sin, that the promise by faith of Jesus Christ might be given to them that believe."

1 Thessalonians 2:13 "For this cause also thank we God without ceasing, because, when ye received the word of God which ye heard of us, ye received it not as the word of men, but as it is in truth, the word of God, which effectually worketh also in you that believe."

2 Thessalonians 1:7-10 "⁷And to you who are troubled rest with us, when the Lord Jesus shall be revealed from heaven with his mighty angels, ⁸In flaming fire taking vengeance on them that know not God, and that obey not the gospel of our Lord Jesus Christ: ⁹Who shall be punished with everlasting destruction from the presence of the Lord, and from the glory of his power; ¹⁰When he shall come to be glorified in his saints, and to be admired in all them that believe (because our testimony among you was believed) in that day."

Titus 3:8 "This is a faithful saying, and these things I will that thou affirm constantly, that they which have believed in God might be careful to maintain good works. These things are good and profitable unto men."

1 Peter 2:6-7 "⁶Wherefore also it is contained in the scripture, Behold, I lay in Sion a chief corner stone, elect, precious: and he that believeth on him shall not be confounded. [7]Unto you therefore which believe he is precious: but unto them which be disobedient, the stone which the builders disallowed, the same is made the head of the corner."

1 John 5:1 "Whosoever believeth that Jesus is the Christ is born of God: and every one that loveth him that begat loveth him also that is begotten of him."

1 John 5:5 "Who is he that overcometh the world, but he that believeth that Jesus is the Son of God?"

1 John 5:10 "He that believeth on the Son of God hath the witness in himself: he that believeth not God hath made him a liar; because he believeth not the record that God gave of his Son."

1 John 5:13 "These things have I written unto you that believe on the name of the Son of God; that ye may know that ye have eternal life, and that ye may believe on the name of the Son of God."

Those That Have Not Seen
And Yet Have Believed In Jesus Christ
John 20:29 "Jesus saith unto him, Thomas, because thou hast seen me, thou hast believed: blessed are they that have not seen, and yet have believed."

1 Peter 1:7-9 "[7]That the trial of your faith, being much more precious than of gold that perisheth, though it be tried with fire, might be found unto praise and honour and glory at the appearing of Jesus Christ: [8]Whom having not seen, ye love; in whom, though now ye see him not, yet believing, ye rejoice with joy unspeakable and full of glory: [9]Receiving the end of your faith, even the salvation of your souls."

Who Must Believe God
Hebrews 11:6 "But without faith it is impossible to please him: for he that cometh to God must believe that he is, and that he is a rewarder of them that diligently seek him."

Why You Should Believe Jesus Christ
John 5:44-47 "[44]How can ye believe, which receive honour one of another, and seek not the honour that cometh from God only? [45]Do not think that I will accuse you to the Father: there is one that accuseth you, even Moses, in whom ye trust. [46]For had ye believed Moses, ye would have believed me: for he wrote of me. [47]But if ye believe not his writings, how shall ye believe my words?"

John 10:34-38 "[34]Jesus answered them, Is it not written in your law, I said, Ye are gods? [35]If he called them gods, unto whom the word of God came, and the scripture cannot be broken; [36]Say ye of him, whom the Father hath sanctified, and sent into the world, Thou blasphemest; because I said, I am the Son of God? [37]If I do not the works of my Father, believe me not. [38]But if I do, though ye believe not me, believe the works: that ye may know, and believe, that the Father is in me, and I in him."

John 14:9-11 "[9]Jesus saith unto him, Have I been so long time with you, and yet hast thou not known me, Philip? he that hath seen me hath seen the Father; and how sayest thou then, Shew us the Father? [10]Believest thou not that I am in the Father, and the Father in me? the words that I speak unto you I speak not of myself: but the Father that dwelleth in me, he doeth the works. [11]Believe me that I am in the Father, and the Father in me: or else believe me for the very works' sake."

BELONGING

What And Who Belongs To The Lord
Genesis 14:19 "And he blessed him, and said, Blessed be Abram of the most high God, possessor of heaven and earth."

Exodus 19:3-5 "[3]And Moses went up unto God, and the LORD called unto him out of the mountain, saying, Thus shalt thou say to the house of Jacob, and tell the children of Israel; [4]Ye have seen what I did unto the Egyptians, and how I bare you on eagles' wings, and brought you unto myself. [5]Now therefore, if ye will obey my voice indeed, and keep my covenant, then ye shall be a peculiar treasure unto me above all people: for all the earth is mine."

Leviticus 27:30 "And all the tithe of the land, whether of the seed of the land, or of the fruit of the tree, is the LORD's: it is holy unto the LORD."

Deuteronomy 1:17 "Ye shall not respect persons in judgment; but ye shall hear the small as well as the great; ye shall not be afraid of the face of man; for the judgment is God's: and the cause that is too hard for you, bring it unto me, and I will hear it."

Deuteronomy 10:14 "Behold, the heaven and the heaven of heavens is the LORD's thy God, the earth also, with all that therein is."

Deuteronomy 29:29 "The secret things belong unto the LORD our God: but those things which are revealed belong unto us and to our children for ever, that we may do all the words of this law."

Deuteronomy 32:35-36 "^{35}To me belongeth vengeance, and recompence; their foot shall slide in due time: for the day of their calamity is at hand, and the things that shall come upon them make haste. ^{36}For the LORD shall judge his people, and repent himself for his servants, when he seeth that their power is gone, and there is none shut up, or left."

1 Samuel 2:8 "He raiseth up the poor out of the dust, and lifteth up the beggar from the dunghill, to set them among princes, and to make them inherit the throne of glory: for the pillars of the earth are the LORD's, and he hath set the world upon them."

1 Chronicles 29:11-12 "^{11}Thine, O LORD, is the greatness, and the power, and the glory, and the victory, and the majesty: for all that is in the heaven and in the earth is thine; thine is the kingdom, O LORD, and thou art exalted as head above all. ^{12}Both riches and honour come of thee, and thou reignest over all; and in thine hand is power and might; and in thine hand it is to make great, and to give strength unto all."

Psalm 3:8 "Salvation belongeth unto the LORD: thy blessing is upon thy people. Selah."

Psalm 22:28 "For the kingdom is the LORD's: and he is the governor among the nations."

Psalm 24:1 "The earth is the LORD's, and the fulness thereof; the world, and they that dwell therein."

Psalm 47:7-9 "^{7}For God is the King of all the earth: sing ye praises with understanding. ^{8}God reigneth over the heathen: God sitteth upon the throne of his holiness. ^{9}The princes of the people are gathered together, even the people of the God of Abraham: for the shields of the earth belong unto God: he is greatly exalted."

Psalm 50:7-12 "^{7}Hear, O my people, and I will speak; O Israel, and I will testify against thee: I am God, even thy God. ^{8}I will not reprove thee

for thy sacrifices or thy burnt offerings, to have been continually before me. ^{9}I will take no bullock out of thy house, nor he goats out of thy folds. ^{10}For every beast of the forest is mine, and the cattle upon a thousand hills. ^{11}I know all the fowls of the mountains: and the wild beasts of the field are mine. ^{12}If I were hungry, I would not tell thee: for the world is mine, and the fulness thereof."

Psalm 62:11-12 "^{11}God hath spoken once; twice have I heard this; that power belongeth unto God. ^{12}Also unto thee, O Lord, belongeth mercy: for thou renderest to every man according to his work."

Psalm 89:8-11 "^{8}O LORD God of hosts, who is a strong LORD like unto thee? or to thy faithfulness round about thee? ^{9}Thou rulest the raging of the sea: when the waves thereof arise, thou stillest them. ^{10}Thou hast broken Rahab in pieces, as one that is slain; thou hast scattered thine enemies with thy strong arm. ^{11}The heavens are thine, the earth also is thine: as for the world and the fulness thereof, thou hast founded them."

Psalm 94:1 "O LORD God, to whom vengeance belongeth; O God, to whom vengeance belongeth, shew thyself."

Psalm 95:3-5 "^{3}For the LORD is a great God, and a great King above all gods. ^{4}In his hand are the deep places of the earth: the strength of the hills is his also. ^{5}The sea is his, and he made it: and his hands formed the dry land."

Psalm 115:16 "The heaven, even the heavens, are the LORD's: but the earth hath he given to the children of men."

Proverbs 16:11 "A just weight and balance are the LORD's: all the weights of the bag are his work."

Ezekiel 18:3-4 "^{3}As I live, saith the Lord GOD, ye shall not have occasion any more to use this proverb in Israel. ^{4}Behold, all souls are mine; as the soul of the father, so also the soul of the son is mine: the soul that sinneth, it shall die."

Daniel 2:20 "Daniel answered and said, Blessed be the name of God for ever and ever: for wisdom and might are his."

Daniel 9:7-9 "^{7}O Lord, righteousness belongeth unto thee, but unto us confusion of faces, as at this day; to the men of Judah, and to the inhabitants of Jerusalem, and unto all Israel, that are near, and that are far off, through all the countries whither thou hast driven them, because of their trespass that they have trespassed against thee. ⁸O Lord, to us belongeth confusion of face, to our kings, to our princes, and to our fathers, because we have sinned against thee. ⁹To the Lord our God belong mercies and forgivenesses, though we have rebelled against him."

Mark 9:40-41 "⁴⁰For he that is not against us is on our part. ⁴¹For whosoever shall give you a cup of water to drink in my name, because ye belong to Christ, verily I say unto you, he shall not lose his reward."

John 17:1-10 "¹These words spake Jesus, and lifted up his eyes to heaven, and said, Father, the hour is come; glorify thy Son, that thy Son also may glorify thee: ²As thou hast given him power over all flesh, that he should give eternal life to as many as thou hast given him. ³And this is life eternal, that they might know thee the only true God, and Jesus Christ, whom thou hast sent. ⁴I have glorified thee on the earth: I have finished the work which thou gavest me to do. ⁵And now, O Father, glorify thou me with thine own self with the glory which I had with thee before the world was. ⁶I have manifested thy name unto the men which thou gavest me out of the world: thine they were, and thou gavest them me; and they have kept thy word. ⁷Now they have known that all things whatsoever thou hast given me are of thee. ⁸For I have given unto them the words which thou gavest me; and they have received them, and have known surely that I came out from thee, and they have believed that thou didst send me. ⁹I pray for them: I pray not for the world, but for them which thou hast given me; for they are thine. ¹⁰And all mine are thine, and thine are mine; and I am glorified in them."

Romans 12:19 "Dearly beloved, avenge not yourselves, but rather give place unto wrath: for it is written, Vengeance is mine; I will repay, saith the Lord."

Romans 14:7-8 "⁷For none of us liveth to himself, and no man dieth to himself. ⁸For whether we live, we live unto the Lord; and whether we die, we die unto the Lord: whether we live therefore, or die, we are the Lord's."

1 Corinthians 3:23 "And ye are Christ's; and Christ is God's."

1 Corinthians 6:19-20 "¹⁹What? know ye not that your body is the temple of the Holy Ghost which is in you, which ye have of God, and ye are not your own? ²⁰For ye are bought with a price: therefore glorify God in your body, and in your spirit, which are God's."

1 Corinthians 10:26-28 "²⁶For the earth is the Lord's, and the fulness thereof. ²⁷If any of them that believe not bid you to a feast, and ye be disposed to go; whatsoever is set before you, eat, asking no question for conscience sake. ²⁸But if any man say unto you, This is offered in sacrifice unto idols, eat not for his sake that shewed it, and for conscience sake: for the earth is the Lord's, and the fulness thereof."

Hebrews 10:30 "For we know him that hath said, Vengeance belongeth unto me, I will recompense, saith the Lord. And again, The Lord shall judge his people."

BISHOP

The Duties Of A Bishop
1 Timothy 3:1-7 "¹This is a true saying, If a man desire the office of a bishop, he desireth a good work. ²A bishop then must be blameless, the husband of one wife, vigilant, sober, of good behaviour, given to hospitality, apt to teach; ³Not given to wine, no striker, not greedy of filthy lucre; but patient, not a brawler, not covetous; ⁴One that ruleth well his own house, having his children in subjection with all gravity; ⁵(For if a man know not how to rule his own house, how shall he take care of the church of God?) ⁶Not a novice, lest being lifted up with pride he fall into the condemnation of the devil. ⁷Moreover he must have a good report of them which are without; lest he fall into reproach and the snare of the devil."

BLASPHEMY

Those That Blaspheme Against The Holy Spirit
Matthew 12:31-32 "³¹Wherefore I say unto you, All manner of sin and blasphemy shall be forgiven unto men: but the blasphemy against the Holy

Ghost shall not be forgiven unto men. [32] And whosoever speaketh a word against the Son of man, it shall be forgiven him: but whosoever speaketh against the Holy Ghost, it shall not be forgiven him, neither in this world, neither in the world to come."

Mark 3:28-29 "[28] Verily I say unto you, All sins shall be forgiven unto the sons of men, and blasphemies wherewith soever they shall blaspheme: [29] But he that shall blaspheme against the Holy Ghost hath never forgiveness, but is in danger of eternal damnation."

Luke 12:10 "And whosoever shall speak a word against the Son of man, it shall be forgiven him: but unto him that blasphemeth against the Holy Ghost it shall not be forgiven."

Those That Blaspheme
The Name Of The Lord
Leviticus 24:16 "And he that blasphemeth the name of the LORD, he shall surely be put to death, and all the congregation shall certainly stone him: as well the stranger, as he that is born in the land, when he blasphemeth the name of the LORD, shall be put to death."

Who Blasphemies The Name
Of The Lord
2 Samuel 12:13-14 "[13] And David said unto Nathan, I have sinned against the LORD. And Nathan said unto David, The LORD also hath put away thy sin; thou shalt not die. [14] Howbeit, because by this deed thou hast given great occasion to the enemies of the LORD to blaspheme, the child also that is born unto thee shall surely die."

Psalm 74:18 "Remember this, that the enemy hath reproached, O LORD, and that the foolish people have blasphemed thy name."

Romans 2:21-24 "[21] Thou therefore which teachest another, teachest thou not thyself? thou that preachest a man should not steal, dost thou steal? [22] Thou that sayest a man should not commit adultery, dost thou commit adultery? thou that abhorrest idols, dost thou commit sacrilege? [23] Thou that makest thy boast of the law, through breaking the law dishonourest thou God? [24] For the name of God is blasphemed among the Gentiles through you, as it is written."

BLESSINGS

The Blessing Of The Lord
Psalm 3:8 "Salvation belongeth unto the LORD: thy blessing is upon thy people. Selah."

Proverbs 10:22 "The blessing of the LORD, it maketh rich, and he addeth no sorrow with it."

Isaiah 44:2-3 "[2] Thus saith the LORD that made thee, and formed thee from the womb, which will help thee; Fear not, O Jacob, my servant; and thou, Jesurun, whom I have chosen. [3] For I will pour water upon him that is thirsty, and floods upon the dry ground: I will pour my spirit upon thy seed, and my blessing upon thine offspring."

The Blessing Of The Upright
Proverbs 11:11 "By the blessing of the upright the city is exalted: but it is overthrown by the mouth of the wicked."

The Lord Being Blessed
Genesis 14:19-20 "[19] And he blessed him, and said, Blessed be Abram of the most high God, possessor of heaven and earth: [20] And blessed be the most high God, which hath delivered thine enemies into thy hand. And he gave him tithes of all."

Exodus 18:10 "And Jethro said, Blessed be the LORD, who hath delivered you out of the hand of the Egyptians, and out of the hand of Pharaoh, who hath delivered the people from under the hand of the Egyptians."

2 Samuel 22:47 "The LORD liveth; and blessed be my rock; and exalted be the God of the rock of my salvation."

1 Chronicles 16:36 "Blessed be the LORD God of Israel for ever and ever. And all the people said, Amen, and praised the LORD."

1 Chronicles 29:10 "Wherefore David blessed the LORD before all the congregation: and David said, Blessed be thou, LORD God of Israel our father, for ever and ever."

Job 1:20-21 "[20] Then Job arose, and rent his mantle, and shaved his head, and fell down upon the ground, and worshipped, [21] And said, Naked came I out of my mother's womb, and naked shall I return thither: the LORD gave, and the LORD hath taken away; blessed be the name of the LORD."

Psalm 18:46 "The LORD liveth; and blessed be my rock; and let the God of my salvation be exalted."

Psalm 28:6 "Blessed be the LORD, because he hath heard the voice of my supplications."

Psalm 66:20 "Blessed be God, which hath not turned away my prayer, nor his mercy from me."

Psalm 68:19 "Blessed be the Lord, who daily loadeth us with benefits, even the God of our salvation. Selah."

Psalm 68:35 "O God, thou art terrible out of thy holy places: the God of Israel is he that giveth strength and power unto his people. Blessed be God."

Psalm 72:18-19 "18Blessed be the LORD God, the God of Israel, who only doeth wondrous things. 19And blessed be his glorious name for ever: and let the whole earth be filled with his glory; Amen, and Amen."

Psalm 106:48 "Blessed be the Lord God of Israel from everlasting to everlasting: and let all the people say, Amen. Praise ye the LORD."

Psalm 118:26-27 "26Blessed be he that cometh in the name of the LORD: we have blessed you out of the house of the LORD. 27God is the LORD, which hath shewed us light: bind the sacrifice with cords, even unto the horns of the altar."

Psalm 144:1 "Blessed be the LORD my strength, which teacheth my hands to war, and my fingers to fight."

Daniel 2:20 "Daniel answered and said, Blessed be the name of God for ever and ever: for wisdom and might are his."

Daniel 3:28 "Then Nebuchadnezzar spake, and said, Blessed be the God of Shadrach, Meshach, and Abed-nego, who hath sent his angel, and delivered his servants that trusted in him, and have changed the king's word, and yielded their bodies, that they might not serve nor worship any god, except their own God."

Matthew 21:9-11 "9And the multitudes that went before, and that followed, cried, saying, Hosanna to the Son of David: Blessed is he that cometh in the name of the Lord; Hosanna in the highest. 10And when he was come into Jerusalem, all the city was moved, saying, Who is this? 11And the multitude said, This is Jesus the prophet of Nazareth of Galilee."

Mark 11:9-11 "9And they that went before, and they that followed, cried, saying, Hosanna; Blessed is he that cometh in the name of the Lord: 10Blessed be the kingdom of our father David, that cometh in the name of the Lord: Hosanna in the highest. 11And Jesus entered into Jerusalem, and into the temple: and when he had looked round about upon all things, and now the eventide was come, he went out unto Bethany with the twelve."

Luke 1:68 "Blessed be the Lord God of Israel; for he hath visited and redeemed his people."

Luke 13:35 Blessed is he that cometh in the name of the Lord."

Luke 19:35-38 "35And they brought him to Jesus: and they cast their garments upon the colt, and they set Jesus thereon. 36And as he went, they spread their clothes in the way. 37And when he was come nigh, even now at the descent of the mount of Olives, the whole multitude of the disciples began to rejoice and praise God with a loud voice for all the mighty works that they had seen; 38Saying, Blessed be the King that cometh in the name of the Lord: peace in heaven, and glory in the highest."

John 12:12-13 "12On the next day much people that were come to the feast, when they heard that Jesus was coming to Jerusalem, 13Took branches of palm trees, and went forth to meet him, and cried, Hosanna: Blessed is the King of Israel that cometh in the name of the Lord."

Romans 1:25 "Who changed the truth of God into a lie, and worshipped and served the creature more than the Creator, who is blessed for ever. Amen."

2 Corinthians 1:3 "Blessed be God, even the Father of our Lord Jesus Christ, the Father of mercies, and the God of all comfort."

Ephesians 1:3 "Blessed be the God and Father of our Lord Jesus Christ, who hath blessed us with all spiritual blessings in heavenly places in Christ."

1 Peter 1:3 "Blessed be the God and Father of our Lord Jesus Christ, which according to his abundant mercy hath begotten us again unto a lively hope by the resurrection of Jesus Christ from the dead."

Those That Are Blessed Of The Lord

Psalm 37:20-22 "20But the wicked shall perish, and the enemies of the LORD shall be as the fat of lambs: they shall consume; into smoke shall they consume away. [21]The wicked borroweth, and payeth not again: but the righteous sheweth mercy, and giveth. [22]For such as be blessed of him shall inherit the earth; and they that be cursed of him shall be cut off."

What Shall Not Be Blessed
Proverbs 20:21 "An inheritance may be gotten hastily at the beginning; but the end thereof shall not be blessed."

Who All Nations Are Blessed In
Genesis 12:1-3 "[1]Now the LORD had said unto Abram, Get thee out of thy country, and from thy kindred, and from thy father's house, unto a land that I will shew thee: [2]And I will make of thee a great nation, and I will bless thee, and make thy name great; and thou shalt be a blessing: [3]And I will bless them that bless thee, and curse him that curseth thee: and in thee shall all families of the earth be blessed."

Genesis 18:18 "Seeing that Abraham shall surely become a great and mighty nation, and all the nations of the earth shall be blessed in him?"

Genesis 22:15-18 "[15]And the angel of the LORD called unto Abraham out of heaven the second time, [16]And said, By myself have I sworn, saith the LORD, for because thou hast done this thing, and hast not withheld thy son, thine only son: [17]That in blessing I will bless thee, and in multiplying I will multiply thy seed as the stars of the heaven, and as the sand which is upon the sea shore; and thy seed shall possess the gate of his enemies; [18]And in thy seed shall all the nations of the earth be blessed; because thou hast obeyed my voice."

Genesis 26:3-4 "[3]Sojourn in this land, and I will be with thee, and will bless thee; for unto thee, and unto thy seed, I will give all these countries, and I will perform the oath which I sware unto Abraham thy father; [4]And I will make thy seed to multiply as the stars of heaven, and will give unto thy seed all these countries; and in thy seed shall all the nations of the earth be blessed."

Acts 3:25 "Ye are the children of the prophets, and of the covenant which God made with our fathers, saying unto Abraham, And in thy seed shall all the kindreds of the earth be blessed."

Galatians 3:6-8 "[6]Even as Abraham believed God, and it was accounted to him for righteousness. [7]Know ye therefore that they which are of faith, the same are the children of Abraham. [8]And the scripture, foreseeing that God would justify the heathen through faith, preached before the gospel unto Abraham, saying, In thee shall all nations be blessed."

Who Is Blessed
Genesis 5:1-2 "[1]This is the book of the generations of Adam. In the day that God created man, in the likeness of God made he him; [2]Male and female created he them; and blessed them, and called their name Adam, in the day when they were created."

Genesis 12:1-3 "[1]Now the LORD had said unto Abram, Get thee out of thy country, and from thy kindred, and from thy father's house, unto a land that I will shew thee: [2]And I will make of thee a great nation, and I will bless thee, and make thy name great; and thou shalt be a blessing: [3]And I will bless them that bless thee, and curse him that curseth thee: and in thee shall all families of the earth be blessed."

Genesis 14:19-20 "[19]And he blessed him, and said, Blessed be Abram of the most high God, possessor of heaven and earth: [20]And blessed be the most high God, which hath delivered thine enemies into thy hand. And he gave him tithes of all."

Genesis 17:15-16 "[15]And God said unto Abraham, As for Sarai thy wife, thou shalt not call her name Sarai, but Sarah shall her name be. [16]And I will bless her, and give thee a son also of her: yea, I will bless her, and she shall be a mother of nations; kings of people shall be of her."

Genesis 17:20 "And as for Ishmael, I have heard thee: Behold, I have blessed him, and will make him fruitful, and will multiply him exceedingly; twelve princes shall he beget, and I will make him a great nation."

Exodus 23:25 "And ye shall serve the LORD your God, and he shall bless thy bread, and thy water; and I will take sickness away from the midst of thee."

Numbers 24:5-9 "[5]How goodly are thy tents, O Jacob, and thy tabernacles, O Israel! [6]As the valleys are they spread forth, as gardens by the river's side, as the trees of lign aloes which the LORD hath planted, and as cedar trees beside the waters. 7He shall pour the water out of his buckets, and his seed shall be in many waters, and his king shall be higher than Agag, and his kingdom shall be exalted. 8God brought him forth out of Egypt; he hath as it were the strength of an unicorn: he shall eat up the nations his enemies, and shall break their bones, and pierce them through with his arrows. 9He couched, he lay down as a lion, and as a great lion: who shall stir him up? Blessed is he that blesseth thee, and cursed is he that curseth thee."

Deuteronomy 7:6-14 "6For thou art an holy people unto the LORD thy God: the LORD thy God hath chosen thee to be a special people unto himself, above all people that are upon the face of the earth. 7The LORD did not set his love upon you, nor choose you, because ye were more in number than any people; for ye were the fewest of all people: 8But because the LORD loved you, and because he would keep the oath which he had sworn unto your fathers, hath the LORD brought you out with a mighty hand, and redeemed you out of the house of bondmen, from the hand of Pharaoh king of Egypt. 9Know therefore that the LORD thy God, he is God, the faithful God, which keepeth covenant and mercy with them that love him and keep his commandments to a thousand generations; 10And repayeth them that hate him to their face, to destroy them: he will not be slack to him that hateth him, he will repay him to his face. 11Thou shalt therefore keep the commandments, and the statutes, and the judgments, which I command thee this day, to do them. 12Wherefore it shall come to pass, if ye hearken to these judgments, and keep, and do them, that the LORD thy God shall keep unto thee the covenant and the mercy which he sware unto thy fathers: 13And he will love thee, and bless thee, and multiply thee: he will also bless the fruit of thy womb, and the fruit of thy land, thy corn, and thy wine, and thine oil, the increase of thy kine, and the flocks of thy sheep, in the land which he sware unto thy fathers to give thee. 14Thou shalt be blessed above all people: there shall not be male or female barren among you, or among your cattle."

Deuteronomy 11:26-28 "26Behold, I set before you this day a blessing and a curse; 27A blessing, if ye obey the commandments of the LORD your God, which I command you this day: 28And a curse, if ye will not obey the commandments of the LORD your God, but turn aside out of the way which I command you this day, to go after other gods, which ye have not known."

Deuteronomy 15:1-6 "1At the end of every seven years thou shalt make a release. 2And this is the manner of the release: Every creditor that lendeth ought unto his neighbour shall release it; he shall not exact it of his neighbour, or of his brother; because it is called the LORD's release. 3Of a foreigner thou mayest exact it again: but that which is thine with thy brother thine hand shall release; 4Save when there shall be no poor among you; for the LORD shall greatly bless thee in the land which the LORD thy God giveth thee for an inheritance to possess it: 5Only if thou carefully hearken unto the voice of the LORD thy God, to observe to do all these commandments which I command thee this day. 6For the LORD thy God blesseth thee, as he promised thee: and thou shalt lend unto many nations, but thou shalt not borrow; and thou shalt reign over many nations, but they shall not reign over thee."

Deuteronomy 28:1-12 "1And it shall come to pass, if thou shalt hearken diligently unto the voice of the LORD thy God, to observe and to do all his commandments which I command thee this day, that the LORD thy God will set thee on high above all nations of the earth: 2And all these blessings shall come on thee, and overtake thee, if thou shalt hearken unto the voice of the LORD thy God. 3Blessed shalt thou be in the city, and blessed shalt thou be in the field. 4Blessed shall be the fruit of thy body, and the fruit of thy ground, and the fruit of thy cattle, the increase of thy kine, and the flocks of thy sheep. 5Blessed shall be thy basket and thy store. 6Blessed shalt thou be when thou comest in, and blessed shalt thou be when thou goest out. 7The LORD shall cause thine enemies that rise up against thee to be smitten before thy face: they shall come out against thee one way, and flee before thee seven ways. 8The LORD shall command the blessing upon thee in thy storehouses, and in all that thou settest thine hand unto; and he shall bless thee in the land which the LORD thy God giveth thee. 9The LORD shall establish thee an holy people unto himself, as he hath sworn unto thee, if thou shalt keep the commandments of the LORD thy God, and walk in his ways. 10And all people of the earth shall see that thou art called by the name of the LORD; and they shall be afraid of thee. [11]And the LORD shall make thee plenteous in goods, in the fruit of thy body, and in the fruit of thy cattle, and in the fruit of thy ground, in the land which the LORD sware unto thy fathers to give thee. [12]The LORD shall open unto thee his good treasure, the heaven to give the rain unto thy land in his season, and to bless all the work of thine hand: and thou shalt lend unto many nations, and thou shalt not borrow."

Deuteronomy 30:15-16 "[15]See, I have set before thee this day life and good, and death and evil; [16]In that I command thee this day to love the LORD thy God, to walk in his ways, and to keep his commandments and his statutes and his judgments, that thou mayest live and multiply: and the LORD thy God shall bless thee in the land whither thou goest to possess it."

Job 1:6-10 "[6]Now there was a day when the sons of God came to present themselves before the LORD, and Satan came also among them. [7]And the LORD said unto Satan, Whence comest thou? Then Satan answered the LORD, and said, From going to and fro in the earth, and from walking up and down in it. [8]And the LORD said unto Satan, Hast thou considered my servant Job, that there is none like him in the earth, a perfect and an upright man, one that feareth God, and escheweth evil? [9]Then Satan answered the LORD, and said, Doth Job fear God for nought? [10]Hast not thou made an hedge about him, and about his house, and about all that he hath on every side? thou hast blessed the work of his hands, and his substance is increased in the land."

Psalm 1:1 "Blessed is the man that walketh not in the counsel of the ungodly, nor standeth in the way of sinners, nor sitteth in the seat of the scornful."

Psalm 2:11-12 "[11]Serve the LORD with fear, and rejoice with trembling. [12]Kiss the Son, lest he be angry, and ye perish from the way, when his wrath is kindled but a little. Blessed are all they that put their trust in him."

Psalm 5:12 "For thou, LORD, wilt bless the righteous; with favour wilt thou compass him as with a shield."

Psalm 29:11 "The LORD will give strength unto his people; the LORD will bless his people with peace."

Psalm 32:1-2 "[1]Blessed is he whose transgression is forgiven, whose sin is covered. [2]Blessed is the man unto whom the LORD imputeth not iniquity, and in whose spirit there is no guile."

Psalm 33:12 "Blessed is the nation whose God is the LORD: and the people whom he hath chosen for his own inheritance."

Psalm 34:8 "O taste and see that the LORD is good: blessed is the man that trusteth in him."

Psalm 40:4 "Blessed is that man that maketh the LORD his trust, and respecteth not the proud, nor such as turn aside to lies."

Psalm 41:1 "Blessed is he that considereth the poor: the LORD will deliver him in time of trouble."

Psalm 65:1-4 "[1]Praise waiteth for thee, O God, in Sion: and unto thee shall the vow be performed. [2]O thou that hearest prayer, unto thee shall all flesh come. [3]Iniquities prevail against me: as for our transgressions, thou shalt purge them away. [4]Blessed is the man whom thou choosest, and causest to approach unto thee, that he may dwell in thy courts: we shall be satisfied with the goodness of thy house, even of thy holy temple."

Psalm 67:4-7 "[4]O let the nations be glad and sing for joy: for thou shalt judge the people righteously, and govern the nations upon earth. Selah. [5]Let the people praise thee, O God; let all the people praise thee. [6]Then shall the earth yield her increase; and God, even our own God, shall bless us. [7]God shall bless us; and all the ends of the earth shall fear him."

Psalm 84:12 "O LORD of hosts, blessed is the man that trusteth in thee."

Psalm 89:15-16 "[15]Blessed is the people that know the joyful sound: they shall walk, O LORD, in the light of thy countenance. [16]In thy name shall they rejoice all the day: and in thy righteousness shall they be exalted."

Psalm 94:12 "Blessed is the man whom thou chastenest, O LORD, and teachest him out of thy law."

Psalm 106:3 "Blessed are they that keep judgment, and he that doeth righteousness at all times."

Psalm 112:1-2 "[1]Praise ye the LORD. Blessed is the man that feareth the LORD, that delighteth greatly in his commandments. [2]His seed shall be mighty upon earth: the generation of the upright shall be blessed."

Psalm 115:11-15 "[11]Ye that fear the LORD, trust in the LORD: he is their help and their shield. [12]The LORD hath been mindful of us: he will bless us; he will bless the house of Israel; he will bless the house of Aaron. [13]He will bless them that fear the LORD, both small and great. [14]The LORD shall increase you more and more, you and your children. [15]Ye are blessed of the LORD which made heaven and earth."

Psalm 119:1-3 "[1]Blessed are the undefiled in the way, who walk in the law of the LORD. [2]Blessed are they that keep his testimonies, and that seek him with the whole heart. [3]They also do no iniquity: they walk in his ways."

Psalm 128:1-5 "[1]Blessed is every one that feareth the LORD; that walketh in his ways. [2]For thou shalt eat the labour of thine hands: happy shalt thou be, and it shall be well with thee. [3]Thy wife shall be as a fruitful vine by the sides of thine house: thy children like olive plants round about thy table. [4]Behold, that thus shall the man be blessed that feareth the LORD. [5]The LORD shall bless thee out of Zion: and thou shalt see the good of Jerusalem all the days of thy life."

Psalm 132:13-15 "[13]For the LORD hath chosen Zion; he hath desired it for his habitation. [14]This is my rest for ever: here will I dwell; for I have desired it. [15]I will abundantly bless her provision: I will satisfy her poor with bread."

Proverbs 3:33 "The curse of the LORD is in the house of the wicked: but he blesseth the habitation of the just."

Proverbs 8:32-35 "[32]Now therefore hearken unto me, O ye children: for blessed are they that keep my ways. [33]Hear instruction, and be wise, and refuse it not. [34]Blessed is the man that heareth me, watching daily at my gates, waiting at the posts of my doors. [35]For whoso findeth me findeth life, and shall obtain favour of the LORD."

Proverbs 10:6-7 "[6]Blessings are upon the head of the just: but violence covereth the mouth of the wicked. [7]The memory of the just is blessed: but the name of the wicked shall rot."

Proverbs 20:7 "The just man walketh in his integrity: his children are blessed after him."

Proverbs 22:9 "He that hath a bountiful eye shall be blessed; for he giveth of his bread to the poor."

Proverbs 24:24-25 "[24]He that saith unto the wicked, Thou are righteous; him shall the people curse, nations shall abhor him: [25]But to them that rebuke him shall be delight, and a good blessing shall come upon them."

Proverbs 28:20 "A faithful man shall abound with blessings: but he that maketh haste to be rich shall not be innocent."

Ecclesiastes 10:17 "Blessed art thou, O land, when thy king is the son of nobles, and thy princes eat in due season, for strength, and not for drunkenness!"

Isaiah 30:18 "And therefore will the LORD wait, that he may be gracious unto you, and therefore will he be exalted, that he may have mercy upon you: for the LORD is a God of judgment: blessed are all they that wait for him."

Isaiah 51:1-2 "[1]Hearken to me, ye that follow after righteousness, ye that seek the LORD: look unto the rock whence ye are hewn, and to the hole of the pit whence ye are digged. [2]Look unto Abraham your father, and unto Sarah that bare you: for I called him alone, and blessed him, and increased him."

Isaiah 56:1-2 "[1]Thus saith the LORD, Keep ye judgment, and do justice: for my salvation is near to come, and my righteousness to be revealed. [2]Blessed is the man that doeth this, and the son of man that layeth hold on it; that keepeth the sabbath from polluting it, and keepeth his hand from doing any evil."

Isaiah 61:1-9 "[1]The Spirit of the Lord GOD is upon me; because the LORD hath anointed me to preach good tidings unto the meek; he hath sent me to bind up the brokenhearted, to proclaim liberty to the captives, and the opening of the prison to them that are bound; [2]To proclaim the acceptable year of the LORD, and the day of vengeance of our God; to comfort all that mourn; [3]To appoint unto them that mourn in Zion, to give unto them beauty for ashes, the oil of joy for mourning, the garment of praise for the spirit of heaviness; that they might be called trees of righteousness, the planting of the LORD, that he might be glorified. 4And they shall build the old wastes, they shall raise up the former desolations, and they shall repair the waste cities, the desolations of many generations. 5And strangers shall stand and feed your flocks, and the sons of the alien shall be your plowmen and your vinedressers. 6But ye shall be named the Priests of the LORD: men shall call you the Ministers of our God: ye shall eat the riches of the Gentiles, and in their glory shall ye boast yourselves. 7For your shame ye shall have double; and for confusion they shall rejoice in their portion: therefore in their land they shall possess the double: everlasting joy shall be unto them. 8For I the LORD love judgment, I hate robbery for burnt offering; and I will direct their work in truth, and I will make an everlasting covenant with them. 9And their seed shall be known among the Gentiles, and their offspring among the people: all that see them shall acknowledge them, that they are the seed which the LORD hath blessed."

Isaiah 65:22-23 "22They shall not build, and another inhabit; they shall not plant, and another eat: for as the days of a tree are the days of my people, and mine elect shall long enjoy the work of their hands. 23They shall not labour in vain, nor bring forth for trouble; for they are the seed of the blessed of the LORD, and their offspring with them."

Jeremiah 17:7-8 "7Blessed is the man that trusteth in the LORD, and whose hope the LORD is. 8For he shall be as a tree planted by the waters, and that spreadeth out her roots by the river, and shall not see when heat cometh, but her leaf shall be green; and shall not be careful in the year of drought, neither shall cease from yielding fruit."

Daniel 12:11-13 "11And from the time that the daily sacrifice shall be taken away, and the abomination that maketh desolate set up, there shall be a thousand two hundred and ninety days. 12Blessed is he that waiteth, and cometh to the thousand three hundred and five and thirty days. 13But go thou thy way till the end be: for thou shalt rest, and stand in thy lot at the end of the days."

Matthew 5:3-11 "3Blessed are the poor in spirit: for theirs is the kingdom of heaven. 4Blessed are they that mourn: for they shall be comforted. 5Blessed are the meek: for they shall inherit the earth. 6Blessed are they which do hunger and thirst after righteousness: for they shall be filled. 7Blessed are the merciful: for they shall obtain mercy. 8Blessed are the pure in heart: for they shall see God. 9Blessed are the peacemakers: for they shall be called the children of God. 10Blessed are they which are persecuted for righteousness' sake: for theirs is the kingdom of heaven. 11Blessed are ye, when men shall revile you, and persecute you, and shall say all manner of evil against you falsely, for my sake."

Matthew 11:4-6 "4Jesus answered and said unto them, Go and shew John again those things which ye do hear and see: 5The blind receive their sight, and the lame walk, the lepers are cleansed, and the deaf hear, the dead are raised up, and the poor have the gospel preached to them. 6And blessed is he, whosoever shall not be offended in me."

Matthew 13:16-17 "16But blessed are your eyes, for they see: and your ears, for they hear. 17For verily I say unto you, That many prophets and righteous men have desired to see those things which ye see, and have not seen them; and to hear those things which ye hear, and have not heard them."

Matthew 16:13-18 "13When Jesus came into the coasts of Caesarea Philippi, he asked his disciples, saying, Whom do men say that I the Son of man am? 14And they said, Some say that thou art John the Baptist: some, Elias; and others, Jeremias, or one of the prophets. 15He saith unto them, But whom say ye that I am? 16And Simon Peter answered and said, Thou art the Christ, the Son of the living God. 17And Jesus answered and said unto him, Blessed art thou, Simon Barjona: for flesh and blood hath not revealed it unto thee, but my Father which is in heaven. 18And I say also unto thee, That thou art Peter, and upon this rock I will build my church; and the gates of hell shall not prevail against it."

Matthew 24:45-47 "45Who then is a faithful and wise servant, whom his lord hath made ruler over his household, to give them meat in due season? 46Blessed is that servant, whom his lord when he cometh shall find so doing. 47Verily I say unto you, That he shall make him ruler over all his goods."

Luke 1:27-28 "27To a virgin espoused to a man whose name was Joseph, of the house of David; and the virgin's name was Mary. 28And the angel came in unto her, and said, Hail, thou that art highly favoured, the Lord is with thee: blessed art thou among women."

Luke 6:20-23 "20And he lifted up his eyes on his disciples, and said, Blessed be ye poor: for yours is the kingdom of God. 21Blessed are ye that hunger now: for ye shall be filled. Blessed are ye that weep now: for ye shall laugh. 22Blessed are ye, when men shall hate you, and when they shall separate you from their company, and shall reproach you, and cast out your name as evil, for the Son of man's sake. 23Rejoice ye in that day, and leap for joy: for, behold, your reward is great in heaven: for in the like manner did their fathers unto the prophets."

Luke 7:22-23 "22Then Jesus answering said unto them, Go your way, and tell John what things ye have seen and heard; how that the blind see, the lame walk, the lepers are cleansed, the deaf hear, the dead are raised, to the poor the gospel is preached. 23And blessed is he, whosoever shall not be offended in me."

Luke 11:27-28 "27And it came to pass, as he spake these things, a certain woman of the company lifted up her voice, and said unto him, Blessed is the womb that bare thee, and the paps which thou hast sucked. 28But he said, Yea rather, blessed are they that hear the word of God, and keep it."

Luke 12:36-38 "36And ye yourselves like unto men that wait for their lord, when he will return from the wedding; that when he cometh and knocketh, they may open unto him immediately. 37Blessed are those servants, whom the lord when he cometh shall find watching: verily I say unto you, that he shall gird himself, and make them to sit down to meat, and will come forth and serve them. 38And if he shall come in the second watch, or come in the third watch, and find them so, blessed are those servants."

Luke 14:12-15 "12Then said he also to him that bade him, When thou makest a dinner or a supper, call not thy friends, nor thy brethren, neither thy kinsmen, nor thy rich neighbours; lest they also bid thee again, and a recompence be made thee. 13But when thou makest a feast, call the poor, the maimed, the lame, the blind: 14And thou shalt be blessed; for they cannot recompense thee: for thou shalt be recompensed at the resurrection of the just. 15And when one of them that sat at meat with him heard these things, he said unto

him, Blessed is he that shall eat bread in the kingdom of God."

John 20:29 "Jesus saith unto him, Thomas, because thou hast seen me, thou hast believed: blessed are they that have not seen, and yet have believed."

Romans 4:6-7 "6Even as David also describeth the blessedness of the man, unto whom God imputeth righteousness without works, 7Saying, Blessed are they whose iniquities are forgiven, and whose sins are covered."

Galatians 3:8-9 "8And the scripture, foreseeing that God would justify the heathen through faith, preached before the gospel unto Abraham, saying, In thee shall all nations be blessed. 9So then they which be of faith are blessed with faithful Abraham."

Ephesians 1:3-5 "3Blessed be the God and Father of our Lord Jesus Christ, who hath blessed us with all spiritual blessings in heavenly places in Christ: 4According as he hath chosen us in him before the foundation of the world, that we should be holy and without blame before him in love: 5Having predestinated us unto the adoption of children by Jesus Christ to himself, according to the good pleasure of his will."

Hebrews 6:7 "For the earth which drinketh in the rain that cometh oft upon it, and bringeth forth herbs meet for them by whom it is dressed, receiveth blessing from God."

James 1:25 "But whoso looketh into the perfect law of liberty, and continueth therein, he being not a forgetful hearer, but a doer of the work, this man shall be blessed in his deed."

1 Peter 3:8-9 "8Finally, be ye all of one mind, having compassion one of another, love as brethren, be pitiful, be courteous: 9Not rendering evil for evil, or railing for railing: but contrariwise blessing; knowing that ye are thereunto called, that ye should inherit a blessing."

Revelation 1:1-3 "1The Revelation of Jesus Christ, which God gave unto him, to shew unto his servants things which must shortly come to pass; and he sent and signified it by his angel unto his servant John: 2Who bare record of the word of God, and of the testimony of Jesus Christ, and of all things that he saw. 3Blessed is he that readeth, and they that hear the words of this prophecy, and keep those things which are written therein: for the time is at hand."

Revelation 14:13 "And I heard a voice from heaven saying unto me, Write, Blessed are the dead which die in the Lord from henceforth: Yea, saith the Spirit, that they may rest from their labours; and their works do follow them."

Revelation 16:15 "Behold, I come as a thief. Blessed is he that watcheth, and keepeth his garments, lest he walk naked, and they see his shame."

Revelation 19:9 "And he saith unto me, Write, Blessed are they which are called unto the marriage supper of the Lamb. And he saith unto me, These are the true sayings of God."

Revelation 20:6 "Blessed and holy is he that hath part in the first resurrection: on such the second death hath no power, but they shall be priests of God and of Christ, and shall reign with him a thousand years."

Revelation 22:7 "Behold, I come quickly: blessed is he that keepeth the sayings of the prophecy of this book."

Revelation 22:13-14 "13I am Alpha and Omega, the beginning and the end, the first and the last. 14Blessed are they that do his commandments, that they may have right to the tree of life, and may enter in through the gates into the city."

Who To Bless

Matthew 5:43-45 "43Ye have heard that it hath been said, Thou shalt love thy neighbour, and hate thine enemy. 44But I say unto you, Love your enemies, bless them that curse you, do good to them that hate you, and pray for them which despitefully use you, and persecute you; 45That ye may be the children of your Father which is in heaven: for he maketh his sun to rise on the evil and on the good, and sendeth rain on the just and on the unjust."

Luke 6:27-28 "27But I say unto you which hear, Love your enemies, do good to them which hate you, 28Bless them that curse you, and pray for them which despitefully use you."

Romans 12:14 "Bless them which persecute you: bless, and curse not."

BLINDNESS

Blind Guides

Isaiah 56:9-12 "9All ye beasts of the field, come to devour, yea, all ye beasts in the forest. 10His watchmen are blind: they are all ignorant, they are all dumb dogs, they cannot bark; sleeping, lying down, loving to slumber. 11Yea, they are greedy dogs which can never have enough, and they are shepherds that cannot understand: they all look to their own way, every one for his gain, from his quarter. 12Come ye, say they, I will fetch wine, and we will fill ourselves with strong drink; and to morrow shall be as this day, and much more abundant."

Matthew 15:12-14 "12Then came his disciples, and said unto him, Knowest thou that the Pharisees were offended, after they heard this saying? 13But he answered and said, Every plant, which my heavenly Father hath not planted, shall be rooted up. 14Let them alone: they be blind leaders of the blind. And if the blind lead the blind, both shall fall into the ditch."

Matthew 23:16-26 "16Woe unto you, ye blind guides, which say, Whosoever shall swear by the temple, it is nothing; but whosoever shall swear by the gold of the temple, he is a debtor! 17Ye fools and blind: for whether is greater, the gold, or the temple that sanctifieth the gold? 18And, Whosoever shall swear by the altar, it is nothing; but whosoever sweareth by the gift that is upon it, he is guilty. 19Ye fools and blind: for whether is greater, the gift, or the altar that sanctifieth the gift? 20Whoso therefore shall swear by the altar, sweareth by it, and by all things thereon. 21And whoso shall swear by the temple, sweareth by it, and by him that dwelleth therein. 22And he that shall swear by heaven, sweareth by the throne of God, and by him that sitteth thereon. 23Woe unto you, scribes and Pharisees, hypocrites! for ye pay tithe of mint and anise and cummin, and have omitted the weightier matters of the law, judgment, mercy, and faith: these ought ye to have done, and not to leave the other undone. 24Ye blind guides, which strain at a gnat, and swallow a camel. 25Woe unto you, scribes and Pharisees, hypocrites! for ye make clean the outside of the cup and of the platter, but within they are full of extortion and excess. 26Thou blind Pharisee, cleanse first that which is within the cup and platter, that the outside of them may be clean also."

Luke 6:39 "And he spake a parable unto them, Can the blind lead the blind? shall they not both fall into the ditch?"

If The Blind Lead The Blind
Matthew 15:12-14 "[12]Then came his disciples, and said unto him, Knowest thou that the Pharisees were offended, after they heard this saying? [13]But he answered and said, Every plant, which my heavenly Father hath not planted, shall be rooted up. [14]Let them alone: they be blind leaders of the blind. And if the blind lead the blind, both shall fall into the ditch."

Luke 6:39 "And he spake a parable unto them, Can the blind lead the blind? shall they not both fall into the ditch?"

The Lord Opening The Eyes Of The Blind
Psalm 146:8 "The LORD openeth the eyes of the blind: the LORD raiseth them that are bowed down: the LORD loveth the righteous."

Isaiah 42:5-7 "[5]Thus saith God the LORD, he that created the heavens, and stretched them out; he that spread forth the earth, and that which cometh out of it; he that giveth breath unto the people upon it, and spirit to them that walk therein: [6]I the LORD have called thee in righteousness, and will hold thine hand, and will keep thee, and give thee for a covenant of the people, for a light of the Gentiles; [7]To open the blind eyes, to bring out the prisoners from the prison, and them that sit in darkness out of the prison house."

Matthew 11:4-5 "[4]Jesus answered and said unto them, Go and shew John again those things which ye do hear and see: [5]The blind receive their sight, and the lame walk, the lepers are cleansed, and the deaf hear, the dead are raised up, and the poor have the gospel preached to them."

Luke 7:22 "Then Jesus answering said unto them, Go your way, and tell John what things ye have seen and heard; how that the blind see, the lame walk, the lepers are cleansed, the deaf hear, the dead are raised, to the poor the gospel is preached."

Luke 24:44-47 "[44]And he said unto them, These are the words which I spake unto you, while I was yet with you, that all things must be fulfilled, which were written in the law of Moses, and in the prophets, and in the psalms, concerning me. [45]Then opened he their understanding, that they might understand the scriptures, [46]And said unto them, Thus it is written, and thus it behoved Christ to suffer, and to rise from the dead the third day: [47]And that repentance and remission of sins should be preached in his name among all nations, beginning at Jerusalem."

John 9:39 "And Jesus said, For judgment I am come into this world, that they which see not might see; and that they which see might be made blind."

2 Corinthians 3:14-16 "[14]But their minds were blinded: for until this day remaineth the same vail untaken away in the reading of the old testament; which vail is done away in Christ. [15]But even unto this day, when Moses is read, the vail is upon their heart. [16]Nevertheless when it shall turn to the Lord, the vail shall be taken away."

The Place Where There Is No Vision
Proverbs 29:18 "Where there is no vision, the people perish: but he that keepeth the law, happy is he."

Those That Walk In Darkness
John 11:9-10 "[9]Jesus answered, Are there not twelve hours in the day? If any man walk in the day, he stumbleth not, because he seeth the light of this world. [10]But if a man walk in the night, he stumbleth, because there is no light in him."

John 12:35-36 "[35]Then Jesus said unto them, Yet a little while is the light with you. Walk while ye have the light, lest darkness come upon you: for he that walketh in darkness knoweth not whither he goeth. [36]While ye have light, believe in the light, that ye may be the children of light. These things spake Jesus, and departed, and did hide himself from them."

Ephesians 4:17-18 "[17]This I say therefore, and testify in the Lord, that ye henceforth walk not as other Gentiles walk, in the vanity of their mind, [18]Having the understanding darkened, being alienated from the life of God through the ignorance that is in them, because of the blindness of their heart."

1 John 1:5-6 "[5]This then is the message which we have heard of him, and declare unto you, that God is light, and in him is no darkness at all. [6]If we say that we have fellowship with him, and walk in darkness, we lie, and do not the truth."

1 John 2:11 "But he that hateth his brother is in darkness, and walketh in darkness, and knoweth not whither he goeth, because that darkness hath blinded his eyes."

What Blinds People

Exodus 23:8 "And thou shalt take no gift: for the gift blindeth the wise, and perverteth the words of the righteous."

Deuteronomy 16:19 "Thou shalt not wrest judgment; thou shalt not respect persons, neither take a gift: for a gift doth blind the eyes of the wise, and pervert the words of the righteous."

1 John 2:11 "But he that hateth his brother is in darkness, and walketh in darkness, and knoweth not whither he goeth, because that darkness hath blinded his eyes."

Who Blinds The Minds Of Unbelievers

2 Corinthians 4:3-4 "³But if our gospel be hid, it is hid to them that are lost: ⁴In whom the god of this world hath blinded the minds of them which believe not, lest the light of the glorious gospel of Christ, who is the image of God, should shine unto them."

Revelation 12:9 "And the great dragon was cast out, that old serpent, called the Devil, and Satan, which deceiveth the whole world: he was cast out into the earth, and his angels were cast out with him."

Who Is Blind

2 Corinthians 3:13-15 "¹³And not as Moses, which put a vail over his face, that the children of Israel could not stedfastly look to the end of that which is abolished: ¹⁴But their minds were blinded: for until this day remaineth the same vail untaken away in the reading of the old testament; which vail is done away in Christ. ¹⁵But even unto this day, when Moses is read, the vail is upon their heart."

Ephesians 4:17-18 "¹⁷This I say therefore, and testify in the Lord, that ye henceforth walk not as other Gentiles walk, in the vanity of their mind, ¹⁸Having the understanding darkened, being alienated from the life of God through the ignorance that is in them, because of the blindness of their heart."

2 Peter 1:1-9 "¹Simon Peter, a servant and an apostle of Jesus Christ, to them that have obtained like precious faith with us through the righteousness of God and our Saviour Jesus Christ: ²Grace and peace be multiplied unto you through the knowledge of God, and of Jesus our Lord, ³According as his divine power hath given unto us all things that pertain unto life and godliness, through the knowledge of him that hath called us to glory and virtue: ⁴Whereby are given unto us exceeding great and precious promises: that by these ye might be partakers of the divine nature, having escaped the corruption that is in the world through lust. ⁵And beside this, giving all diligence, add to your faith virtue; and to virtue knowledge; ⁶And to knowledge temperance; and to temperance patience; and to patience godliness; ⁷And to godliness brotherly kindness; and to brotherly kindness charity. ⁸For if these things be in you, and abound, they make you that ye shall neither be barren nor unfruitful in the knowledge of our Lord Jesus Christ. ⁹But he that lacketh these things is blind, and cannot see afar off, and hath forgotten that he was purged from his old sins."

BLOOD

Blood Making An Atonement For The Soul

Exodus 30:10 "And Aaron shall make an atonement upon the horns of it once in a year with the blood of the sin offering of atonements: once in the year shall he make atonement upon it throughout your generations: it is most holy unto the LORD."

Leviticus 5:6 "And he shall bring his trespass offering unto the LORD for his sin which he hath sinned, a female from the flock, a lamb or a kid of the goats, for a sin offering; and the priest shall make an atonement for him concerning his sin."

Leviticus 12:6-7 "⁶And when the days of her purifying are fulfilled, for a son, or for a daughter, she shall bring a lamb of the first year for a burnt offering, and a young pigeon, or a turtledove, for a sin offering, unto the door of the tabernacle of the congregation, unto the priest: ⁷Who shall offer it before the LORD, and make an atonement for her; and she shall be cleansed from the issue of her blood. This is the law for her that hath born a male or a female."

Leviticus 14:19-20 "¹⁹And the priest shall offer the sin offering, and make an atonement for him that is to be cleansed from his uncleanness; and afterward he shall kill the burnt offering: 20And the priest shall offer the burnt offering and the meat offering upon the altar: and the priest shall make an atonement for him, and he shall be clean."

Leviticus 16:11 "And Aaron shall bring the bullock of the sin offering, which is for himself, and shall make an atonement for himself, and for his house, and shall kill the bullock of the sin offering which is for himself."

Leviticus 17:11 "For the life of the flesh is in the blood: and I have given it to you upon the altar to make an atonement for your souls: for it is the blood that maketh an atonement for the soul."

2 Chronicles 29:24 "And the priests killed them, and they made reconciliation with their blood upon the altar, to make an atonement for all Israel: for the king commanded that the burnt offering and the sin offering should be made for all Israel."

Matthew 26:26-28 "26And as they were eating, Jesus took bread, and blessed it, and brake it, and gave it to the disciples, and said, Take, eat; this is my body. 27And he took the cup, and gave thanks, and gave it to them, saying, Drink ye all of it; 28For this is my blood of the new testament, which is shed for many for the remission of sins."

Mark 14:22-24 "22And as they did eat, Jesus took bread, and blessed, and brake it, and gave to them, and said, Take, eat: this is my body. 23And he took the cup, and when he had given thanks, he gave it to them: and they all drank of it. 24And he said unto them, This is my blood of the new testament, which is shed for many."

Luke 22:19-20 "19And he took bread, and gave thanks, and brake it, and gave unto them, saying, This is my body which is given for you: this do in remembrance of me. 20Likewise also the cup after supper, saying, This cup is the new testament in my blood, which is shed for you."

Romans 5:8-11 "8But God commendeth his love toward us, in that, while we were yet sinners, Christ died for us. 9Much more then, being now justified by his blood, we shall be saved from wrath through him. 10For if, when we were enemies, we were reconciled to God by the death of his Son, much more, being reconciled, we shall be saved by his life. 11And not only so, but we also joy

in God through our Lord Jesus Christ, by whom we have now received the atonement."

Ephesians 2:13-15 "13But now in Christ Jesus ye who sometimes were far off are made nigh by the blood of Christ. 14For he is our peace, who hath made both one, and hath broken down the middle wall of partition between us; 15Having abolished in his flesh the enmity, even the law of commandments contained in ordinances; for to make in himself of twain one new man, so making peace."

Colossians 1:12-22 "12Giving thanks unto the Father, which hath made us meet to be partakers of the inheritance of the saints in light: 13Who hath delivered us from the power of darkness, and hath translated us into the kingdom of his dear Son: 14In whom we have redemption through his blood, even the forgiveness of sins: 15Who is the image of the invisible God, the firstborn of every creature: 16For by him were all things created, that are in heaven, and that are in earth, visible and invisible, whether they be thrones, or dominions, or principalities, or powers: all things were created by him, and for him: 17And he is before all things, and by him all things consist. 18And he is the head of the body, the church: who is the beginning, the firstborn from the dead; that in all things he might have the preeminence. 19For it pleased the Father that in him should all fulness dwell; 20And, having made peace through the blood of his cross, by him to reconcile all things unto himself; by him, I say, whether they be things in earth, or things in heaven. 21And you, that were sometime alienated and enemies in your mind by wicked works, yet now hath he reconciled 22In the body of his flesh through death, to present you holy and unblameable and unreproveable in his sight."

1 John 1:7 "But if we walk in the light, as he is in the light, we have fellowship one with another, and the blood of Jesus Christ his Son cleanseth us from all sin."

Jesus Christ's Blood
Matthew 26:26-28 "26And as they were eating, Jesus took bread, and blessed it, and brake it, and gave it to the disciples, and said, Take, eat; this is my body. 27And he took the cup, and gave thanks, and gave it to them, saying, Drink ye all of it; 28For this is my blood of the new testament, which is shed for many for the remission of sins."

Mark 14:22-24 "²²And as they did eat, Jesus took bread, and blessed, and brake it, and gave to them, and said, Take, eat: this is my body. ²³And he took the cup, and when he had given thanks, he gave it to them: and they all drank of it. ²⁴And he said unto them, This is my blood of the new testament, which is shed for many."

Luke 22:19-22 "¹⁹And he took bread, and gave thanks, and brake it, and gave unto them, saying, This is my body which is given for you: this do in remembrance of me. ²⁰Likewise also the cup after supper, saying, This cup is the new testament in my blood, which is shed for you. ²¹But, behold, the hand of him that betrayeth me is with me on the table. ²²And truly the Son of man goeth, as it was determined: but woe unto that man by whom he is betrayed!"

John 6:53-55 "⁵³Then Jesus said unto them, Verily, verily, I say unto you, Except ye eat the flesh of the Son of man, and drink his blood, ye have no life in you. ⁵⁴Whoso eateth my flesh, and drinketh my blood, hath eternal life; and I will raise him up at the last day. ⁵⁵For my flesh is meat indeed, and my blood is drink indeed."

1 Corinthians 11:23-25 "²³For I have received of the Lord that which also I delivered unto you, That the Lord Jesus the same night in which he was betrayed took bread: ²⁴And when he had given thanks, he brake it, and said, Take, eat: this is my body, which is broken for you: this do in remembrance of me. ²⁵After the same manner also he took the cup, when he had supped, saying, This cup is the new testament in my blood: this do ye, as oft as ye drink it, in remembrance of me."

Ephesians 2:13 "But now in Christ Jesus ye who sometimes were far off are made nigh by the blood of Christ."

1 John 1:7 "But if we walk in the light, as he is in the light, we have fellowship one with another, and the blood of Jesus Christ his Son cleanseth us from all sin."

Not Consuming Blood
Genesis 9:3-4 "³Every moving thing that liveth shall be meat for you; even as the green herb have I given you all things. ⁴But flesh with the life thereof, which is the blood thereof, shall ye not eat."

Leviticus 17:12 "Therefore I said unto the children of Israel, No soul of you shall eat blood, neither shall any stranger that sojourneth among you eat blood."

Leviticus 19:26 "Ye shall not eat any thing with the blood: neither shall ye use enchantment, nor observe times."

Those That Drink The Blood Of Jesus Christ
John 6:53-56 "⁵³Then Jesus said unto them, Verily, verily, I say unto you, Except ye eat the flesh of the Son of man, and drink his blood, ye have no life in you. ⁵⁴Whoso eateth my flesh, and drinketh my blood, hath eternal life; and I will raise him up at the last day. ⁵⁵For my flesh is meat indeed, and my blood is drink indeed. ⁵⁶He that eateth my flesh, and drinketh my blood, dwelleth in me, and I in him."

1 Corinthians 11:25-26 "²⁵After the same manner also he took the cup, when he had supped, saying, This cup is the new testament in my blood: this do ye, as oft as ye drink it, in remembrance of me. ²⁶For as often as ye eat this bread, and drink this cup, ye do shew the Lord's death till he come."

Those That Drink The Blood Of Jesus Christ Unworthily
1 Corinthians 11:27-29 "²⁷Wherefore whosoever shall eat this bread, and drink this cup of the Lord, unworthily, shall be guilty of the body and blood of the Lord. ²⁸But let a man examine himself, and so let him eat of that bread, and drink of that cup. ²⁹For he that eateth and drinketh unworthily, eateth and drinketh damnation to himself, not discerning the Lord's body."

What Blood Is
Genesis 9:3-4 "³Every moving thing that liveth shall be meat for you; even as the green herb have I given you all things. ⁴But flesh with the life thereof, which is the blood thereof, shall ye not eat."

Leviticus 17:11 "For the life of the flesh is in the blood: and I have given it to you upon the altar to make an atonement for your souls: for it is the blood that maketh an atonement for the soul."

BOASTING

Boasting In God
Psalm 44:8 "In God we boast all the day long, and praise thy name for ever. Selah."

Those That Boast Of A False Gift
Proverbs 25:14 "Whoso boasteth himself of a false gift is like clouds and wind without rain."

What Not To Boast Of
Proverbs 27:1 "Boast not thyself of to morrow; for thou knowest not what a day may bring forth."

James 4:13-16 "[13]Go to now, ye that say, To day or to morrow we will go into such a city, and continue there a year, and buy and sell, and get gain: [14]Whereas ye know not what shall be on the morrow. For what is your life? It is even a vapour, that appeareth for a little time, and then vanisheth away. [15]For that ye ought to say, If the Lord will, we shall live, and do this, or that. [16]But now ye rejoice in your boastings: all such rejoicing is evil."

Who Boasts Of Their Heart's Desire
Psalm 10:3 "For the wicked boasteth of his heart's desire, and blesseth the covetous, whom the LORD abhorreth."

BODY

Christ Being Magnified In Your Body
Philippians 1:20 "According to my earnest expectation and my hope, that in nothing I shall be ashamed, but that with all boldness, as always, so now also Christ shall be magnified in my body, whether it be by life, or by death."

**Jesus Christ Being The
Head Of The Body (The Church)**
Ephesians 1:19-23 "[19]And what is the exceeding greatness of his power to usward who believe, according to the working of his mighty power, [20]Which he wrought in Christ, when he raised him from the dead, and set him at his own right hand in the heavenly places, [21]Far above all principality, and power, and might, and dominion, and every name that is named, not only in this world, but also in that which is to come: [22]And hath put all things under his feet, and gave him to be the head over all things to the church, [23]Which is his body, the fulness of him that filleth all in all."

Ephesians 5:22-23 "[22]Wives, submit yourselves unto your own husbands, as unto the Lord. [23]For the husband is the head of the wife, even as Christ is the head of the church: and he is the saviour of the body."

Colossians 1:12-20 "[12]Giving thanks unto the Father, which hath made us meet to be partakers of the inheritance of the saints in light: [13]Who hath delivered us from the power of darkness, and hath translated us into the kingdom of his dear Son: [14]In whom we have redemption through his blood, even the forgiveness of sins: [15]Who is the image of the invisible God, the firstborn of every creature: [16]For by him were all things created, that are in heaven, and that are in earth, visible and invisible, whether they be thrones, or dominions, or principalities, or powers: all things were created by him, and for him: [17]And he is before all things, and by him all things consist. [18]And he is the head of the body, the church: who is the beginning, the firstborn from the dead; that in all things he might have the preeminence. [19]For it pleased the Father that in him should all fulness dwell; [20]And, having made peace through the blood of his cross, by him to reconcile all things unto himself; by him, I say, whether they be things in earth, or things in heaven."

Jesus Christ Changing Your Body
Philippians 3:20-21 "[20]For our conversation is in heaven; from whence also we look for the Saviour, the Lord Jesus Christ: [21]Who shall change our vile body, that it may be fashioned like unto his glorious body, according to the working whereby he is able even to subdue all things unto himself."

Jesus Christ's Body
Matthew 26:26 "And as they were eating, Jesus took bread, and blessed it, and brake it, and gave it to the disciples, and said, Take, eat; this is my body."

Mark 14:22 "And as they did eat, Jesus took bread, and blessed, and brake it, and gave to them, and said, Take, eat: this is my body."

Luke 22:19-22 "[19]And he took bread, and gave thanks, and brake it, and gave unto them, saying, This is my body which is given for you: this do in remembrance of me. [20]Likewise also the cup after supper, saying, This cup is the new testament in my blood, which is shed for you. [21]But, behold, the hand of him that betrayeth me is with me on the table. [22]And truly the Son of man goeth, as it was determined: but woe unto that man by whom he is betrayed!"

John 6:53-55 "[53]Then Jesus said unto them, Verily, verily, I say unto you, Except ye eat the flesh of the

Son of man, and drink his blood, ye have no life in you. ⁵⁴Whoso eateth my flesh, and drinketh my blood, hath eternal life; and I will raise him up at the last day. ⁵⁵For my flesh is meat indeed, and my blood is drink indeed."

1 Corinthians 11:23-24 "²³For I have received of the Lord that which also I delivered unto you, That the Lord Jesus the same night in which he was betrayed took bread: ²⁴And when he had given thanks, he brake it, and said, Take, eat: this is my body, which is broken for you: this do in remembrance of me."

The Body Belonging To God
1 Corinthians 6:20 "For ye are bought with a price: therefore glorify God in your body, and in your spirit, which are God's."

The Body Of Christ
Romans 12:4-8 "⁴For as we have many members in one body, and all members have not the same office: ⁵So we, being many, are one body in Christ, and every one members one of another. ⁶Having then gifts differing according to the grace that is given to us, whether prophecy, let us prophesy according to the proportion of faith; ⁷Or ministry, let us wait on our ministering: or he that teacheth, on teaching; ⁸Or he that exhorteth, on exhortation: he that giveth, let him do it with simplicity; he that ruleth, with diligence; he that sheweth mercy, with cheerfulness."

1 Corinthians 6:15-17 "¹⁵Know ye not that your bodies are the members of Christ? shall I then take the members of Christ, and make them the members of an harlot? God forbid. ¹⁶What? know ye not that he which is joined to an harlot is one body? for two, saith he, shall be one flesh. ¹⁷But he that is joined unto the Lord is one spirit."

1 Corinthians 10:16-17 "¹⁶The cup of blessing which we bless, is it not the communion of the blood of Christ? The bread which we break, is it not the communion of the body of Christ? ¹⁷For we being many are one bread, and one body: for we are all partakers of that one bread."

1 Corinthians 12:12-31 "¹²For as the body is one, and hath many members, and all the members of that one body, being many, are one body: so also is Christ. ¹³For by one Spirit are we all baptized into one body, whether we be Jews or Gentiles, whether we be bond or free; and have been all made to drink into one Spirit. ¹⁴For the body is not one member, but many. ¹⁵If the foot shall say, Because I am not the hand, I am not of the body; is it therefore not of the body? ¹⁶And if the ear shall say, Because I am not the eye, I am not of the body; is it therefore not of the body? ¹⁷If the whole body were an eye, where were the hearing? If the whole were hearing, where were the smelling? ¹⁸But now hath God set the members every one of them in the body, as it hath pleased him. ¹⁹And if they were all one member, where were the body? ²⁰But now are they many members, yet but one body. ²¹And the eye cannot say unto the hand, I have no need of thee: nor again the head to the feet, I have no need of you. ²²Nay, much more those members of the body, which seem to be more feeble, are necessary: ²³And those members of the body, which we think to be less honourable, upon these we bestow more abundant honour; and our uncomely parts have more abundant comeliness. ²⁴For our comely parts have no need: but God hath tempered the body together, having given more abundant honour to that part which lacked: ²⁵That there should be no schism in the body; but that the members should have the same care one for another. ²⁶And whether one member suffer, all the members suffer with it; or one member be honoured, all the members rejoice with it. ²⁷Now ye are the body of Christ, and members in particular. ²⁸And God hath set some in the church, first apostles, secondarily prophets, thirdly teachers, after that miracles, then gifts of healings, helps, governments, diversities of tongues. ²⁹Are all apostles? are all prophets? are all teachers? are all workers of miracles? ³⁰Have all the gifts of healing? do all speak with tongues? do all interpret? ³¹But covet earnestly the best gifts: and yet shew I unto you a more excellent way."

Ephesians 1:19-23 "¹⁹And what is the exceeding greatness of his power to usward who believe, according to the working of his mighty power, ²⁰Which he wrought in Christ, when he raised him from the dead, and set him at his own right hand in the heavenly places, ²¹Far above all principality, and power, and might, and dominion, and every name that is named, not only in this world, but also in that which is to come: ²²And hath put all things under his feet, and gave him to be the head over all things to the church, ²³Which is his body, the fulness of him that filleth all in all."

Ephesians 4:1-16 "¹I therefore, the prisoner of the Lord, beseech you that ye walk worthy of the vocation wherewith ye are called, ²With all lowliness and meekness, with longsuffering, forbearing one another in love; ³Endeavouring to keep the unity of the Spirit in the bond of peace. ⁴There is one body, and one Spirit, even as ye are called in one hope of your calling; ⁵One Lord, one faith, one baptism, ⁶One God and Father of all, who is above all, and through all, and in you all. ⁷But unto every one of us is given grace according to the measure of the gift of Christ. ⁸Wherefore he saith, When he ascended up on high, he led captivity captive, and gave gifts unto men. ⁹(Now that he ascended, what is it but that he also descended first into the lower parts of the earth? ¹⁰He that descended is the same also that ascended up far above all heavens, that he might fill all things.) ¹¹And he gave some, apostles; and some, prophets; and some, evangelists; and some, pastors and teachers; ¹²For the perfecting of the saints, for the work of the ministry, for the edifying of the body of Christ: ¹³Till we all come in the unity of the faith, and of the knowledge of the Son of God, unto a perfect man, unto the measure of the stature of the fulness of Christ: ¹⁴That we henceforth be no more children, tossed to and fro, and carried about with every wind of doctrine, by the sleight of men, and cunning craftiness, whereby they lie in wait to deceive; ¹⁵But speaking the truth in love, may grow up into him in all things, which is the head, even Christ: ¹⁶From whom the whole body fitly joined together and compacted by that which every joint supplieth, according to the effectual working in the measure of every part, maketh increase of the body unto the edifying of itself in love."

Ephesians 4:22-25 "²²That ye put off concerning the former conversation the old man, which is corrupt according to the deceitful lusts; ²³And be renewed in the spirit of your mind; ²⁴And that ye put on the new man, which after God is created in righteousness and true holiness. ²⁵Wherefore putting away lying, speak every man truth with his neighbour: for we are members one of another."

Ephesians 5:22-33 "²²Wives, submit yourselves unto your own husbands, as unto the Lord. ²³For the husband is the head of the wife, even as Christ is the head of the church: and he is the saviour of the body. ²⁴Therefore as the church is subject unto Christ, so let the wives be to their own husbands in every thing. ²⁵Husbands, love your wives, even as Christ also loved the church, and gave himself for it; ²⁶That he might sanctify and cleanse it with the washing of water by the word, ²⁷That he might present it to himself a glorious church, not having spot, or wrinkle, or any such thing; but that it should be holy and without blemish. ²⁸So ought men to love their wives as their own bodies. He that loveth his wife loveth himself. ²⁹For no man ever yet hated his own flesh; but nourisheth and cherisheth it, even as the Lord the church: ³⁰For we are members of his body, of his flesh, and of his bones. ³¹For this cause shall a man leave his father and mother, and shall be joined unto his wife, and they two shall be one flesh. ³²This is a great mystery: but I speak concerning Christ and the church. ³³Nevertheless let every one of you in particular so love his wife even as himself; and the wife see that she reverence her husband."

Colossians 1:24 "Who now rejoice in my sufferings for you, and fill up that which is behind of the afflictions of Christ in my flesh for his body's sake, which is the church."

Colossians 3:15 "And let the peace of God rule in your hearts, to the which also ye are called in one body; and be ye thankful."

The Light Of The Body
Luke 11:33-36 "³³No man, when he hath lighted a candle, putteth it in a secret place, neither under a bushel, but on a candlestick, that they which come in may see the light. ³⁴The light of the body is the eye: therefore when thine eye is single, thy whole body also is full of light; but when thine eye is evil, thy body also is full of darkness. ³⁵Take heed therefore that the light which is in thee be not darkness. ³⁶If thy whole body therefore be full of light, having no part dark, the whole shall be full of light, as when the bright shining of a candle doth give thee light."

The Time When You Are At Home In The Body
2 Corinthians 5:6-9 "⁶Therefore we are always confident, knowing that, whilst we are at home in the

body, we are absent from the Lord: [7](For we walk by faith, not by sight:) [8]We are confident, I say, and willing rather to be absent from the body, and to be present with the Lord. [9]Wherefore we labour, that, whether present or absent, we may be accepted of him."

Those That Eat The Body Of Christ
John 6:53-58 "[53]Then Jesus said unto them, Verily, verily, I say unto you, Except ye eat the flesh of the Son of man, and drink his blood, ye have no life in you. [54]Whoso eateth my flesh, and drinketh my blood, hath eternal life; and I will raise him up at the last day. [55]For my flesh is meat indeed, and my blood is drink indeed. [56]He that eateth my flesh, and drinketh my blood, dwelleth in me, and I in him. [57]As the living Father hath sent me, and I live by the Father: so he that eateth me, even he shall live by me. [58]This is that bread which came down from heaven: not as your fathers did eat manna, and are dead: he that eateth of this bread shall live for ever."

1 Corinthians 11:25-26 "[25]After the same manner also he took the cup, when he had supped, saying, This cup is the new testament in my blood: this do ye, as oft as ye drink it, in remembrance of me. [26]For as often as ye eat this bread, and drink this cup, ye do shew the Lord's death till he come."

Those That Eat The Body Of Christ Unworthily
1 Corinthians 11:27-29 "[27]Wherefore whosoever shall eat this bread, and drink this cup of the Lord, unworthily, shall be guilty of the body and blood of the Lord. [28]But let a man examine himself, and so let him eat of that bread, and drink of that cup. [29]For he that eateth and drinketh unworthily, eateth and drinketh damnation to himself, not discerning the Lord's body."

What The Body Is
1 Corinthians 3:16-17 "[16]Know ye not that ye are the temple of God, and that the Spirit of God dwelleth in you? [17]If any man defile the temple of God, him shall God destroy; for the temple of God is holy, which temple ye are."

1 Corinthians 6:15-16 "[15]Know ye not that your bodies are the members of Christ? shall I then take the members of Christ, and make them the members of an harlot? God forbid. [16]What? know ye not that he which is joined to an harlot is one body? for two, saith he, shall be one flesh."

1 Corinthians 6:19-20 "[19]What? know ye not that your body is the temple of the Holy Ghost which is in you, which ye have of God, and ye are not your own? [20]For ye are bought with a price: therefore glorify God in your body, and in your spirit, which are God's."

2 Corinthians 6:16 "And what agreement hath the temple of God with idols? for ye are the temple of the living God; as God hath said, I will dwell in them, and walk in them; and I will be their God, and they shall be my people."

What The Body Is For
1 Corinthians 6:13 "Meats for the belly, and the belly for meats: but God shall destroy both it and them. Now the body is not for fornication, but for the Lord; and the Lord for the body."

What The Body Is Not For
1 Corinthians 6:13 "Meats for the belly, and the belly for meats: but God shall destroy both it and them. Now the body is not for fornication, but for the Lord; and the Lord for the body."

What Type Of Bodies There Are
1 Corinthians 15:35-50 "[35]But some man will say, How are the dead raised up? and with what body do they come? [36]Thou fool, that which thou sowest is not quickened, except it die: [37]And that which thou sowest, thou sowest not that body that shall be, but bare grain, it may chance of wheat, or of some other grain: [38]But God giveth it a body as it hath pleased him, and to every seed his own body. [39]All flesh is not the same flesh: but there is one kind of flesh of men, another flesh of beasts, another of fishes, and another of birds. [40]There are also celestial bodies, and bodies terrestrial: but the glory of the celestial is one, and the glory of the terrestrial is another. [41]There is one glory of the sun, and another glory of the moon, and another glory of the stars: for one star differeth from another star in glory. [42]So also is the resurrection of the dead. It is sown in corruption; it is raised in incorruption: [43]It is sown in dishonour; it is raised in glory: it is sown in weakness; it is raised in power: [44]It is sown a natural body; it is raised a spiritual body. There is a natural body, and there is a spiritual body. [45]And so it is written, The first man Adam was made a living soul; the last Adam was made a quickening spirit. [46]Howbeit that was not first which is

spiritual, but that which is natural; and afterward that which is spiritual. [47]The first man is of the earth, earthy: the second man is the Lord from heaven. [48]As is the earthy, such are they also that are earthy: and as is the heavenly, such are they also that are heavenly. [49]And as we have borne the image of the earthy, we shall also bear the image of the heavenly. [50]Now this I say, brethren, that flesh and blood cannot inherit the kingdom of God; neither doth corruption inherit incorruption."

BOLDNESS

Who Is Bold
Proverbs 28:1 "The wicked flee when no man pursueth: but the righteous are bold as a lion."

Why You Can Be Bold
Ephesians 3:10-12 "[10]To the intent that now unto the principalities and powers in heavenly places might be known by the church the manifold wisdom of God, [11]According to the eternal purpose which he purposed in Christ Jesus our Lord: [12]In whom we have boldness and access with confidence by the faith of him."

BORROWING

Borrowers
Proverbs 22:7 "The rich ruleth over the poor, and the borrower is servant to the lender."

Not Withholding What You Borrowed
Proverbs 3:27-28 "[27]Withhold not good from them to whom it is due, when it is in the power of thine hand to do it. [28]Say not unto thy neighbour, Go, and come again, and to morrow I will give; when thou hast it by thee."

Who Borrows, And Does Not Pay Back
Psalm 37:21 "The wicked borroweth, and payeth not again: but the righteous sheweth mercy, and giveth."

BOWING

Bowing Before The Lord
Psalm 95:6 "O come, let us worship and bow down: let us kneel before the LORD our maker."

Everyone Bowing Before The Lord
Psalm 22:28-29 "[28]For the kingdom is the LORD's: and he is the governor among the nations. [29]All they that be fat upon earth shall eat and worship: all they that go down to the dust shall bow before him: and none can keep alive his own soul."

Isaiah 45:22-23 "[22]Look unto me, and be ye saved, all the ends of the earth: for I am God, and there is none else. [23]I have sworn by myself, the word is gone out of my mouth in righteousness, and shall not return, That unto me every knee shall bow, every tongue shall swear."

Romans 14:11 "For it is written, As I live, saith the Lord, every knee shall bow to me, and every tongue shall confess to God."

Philippians 2:9-11 "[9]Wherefore God also hath highly exalted him, and given him a name which is above every name: [10]That at the name of Jesus every knee should bow, of things in heaven, and things in earth, and things under the earth; [11]And that every tongue should confess that Jesus Christ is Lord, to the glory of God the Father."

What Not To Bow Down Before
Exodus 20:2-5 "[2]I am the LORD thy God, which have brought thee out of the land of Egypt, out of the house of bondage. [3]Thou shalt have no other gods before me. [4]Thou shalt not make unto thee any graven image, or any likeness of any thing that is in heaven above, or that is in the earth beneath, or that is in the water under the earth: [5]Thou shalt not bow down thyself to them, nor serve them: for I the LORD thy God am a jealous God, visiting the iniquity of the fathers upon the children unto the third and fourth generation of them that hate me."

Exodus 23:24 "Thou shalt not bow down to their gods, nor serve them, nor do after their works: but thou shalt utterly overthrow them, and quite break down their images."

Leviticus 26:1 "Ye shall make you no idols nor graven image, neither rear you up a standing image, neither shall ye set up any image of stone in your land, to bow down unto it: for I am the LORD your God."

Deuteronomy 5:6-9 "[6]I am the LORD thy God, which brought thee out of the land of Egypt, from the house of bondage. [7]Thou shalt have none other gods before me. [8]Thou shalt not make thee any graven image, or any likeness of any thing that is in heaven above, or that is in the earth beneath, or that is in the waters beneath the earth: [9]Thou shalt not bow down thyself unto them, nor serve them: for I the LORD thy God am a jealous God, visiting the iniquity of the fathers upon the children unto the third and fourth generation of them that hate me."

Joshua 23:6-7 "[6]Be ye therefore very courageous to keep and to do all that is written in the book of the law of Moses, that ye turn not aside therefrom to the right hand or to the left; [7]That ye come not among these nations, these that remain among you; neither make mention of the name of their gods, nor cause to swear by them, neither serve them, nor bow yourselves unto them."

Who Bows Before The Good
Proverbs 14:19 "The evil bow before the good; and the wicked at the gates of the righteous."

Why You Should Bow Down To God The Father
Ephesians 3:14-16 "[14]For this cause I bow my knees unto the Father of our Lord Jesus Christ, [15]Of whom the whole family in heaven and earth is named, [16]That he would grant you, according to the riches of his glory, to be strengthened with might by his Spirit in the inner man."

BRANCH OF JESSE

The Coming Of The Branch Of Jesse
Isaiah 4:2-6 "[2]In that day shall the branch of the LORD be beautiful and glorious, and the fruit of the earth shall be excellent and comely for them that are escaped of Israel. [3]And it shall come to pass, that he that is left in Zion, and he that remaineth in Jerusalem, shall be called holy, even every one that is written among the living in Jerusalem [4]When the Lord shall have washed away the filth of the daughters of Zion, and shall have purged the blood of Jerusalem from the midst thereof by the spirit of judgment, and by the spirit of burning. [5]And the LORD will create upon every dwelling place of mount Zion, and upon her assemblies, a cloud and smoke by day, and the shining of a flaming fire by night: for upon all the glory shall be a defence. [6]And there shall be a tabernacle for a shadow in the daytime from the heat, and for a place of refuge, and for a covert from storm and from rain."

Isaiah 11:1-16 "[1]And there shall come forth a rod out of the stem of Jesse, and a Branch shall grow out of his roots [2]And the spirit of the LORD shall rest upon him, the spirit of wisdom and understanding, the spirit of counsel and might, the spirit of knowledge and of the fear of the LORD; [3]And shall make him of quick understanding in the fear of the LORD: and he shall not judge after the sight of his eyes, neither reprove after the hearing of his ears [4]But with righteousness shall he judge the poor, and reprove with equity for the meek of the earth: and he shall smite the earth with the rod of his mouth, and with the breath of his lips shall he slay the wicked. [5]And righteousness shall be the girdle of his loins, and faithfulness the girdle of his reins. [6]The wolf also shall dwell with the lamb, and the leopard shall lie down with the kid; and the calf and the young lion and the fatling together; and a little child shall lead them. [7]And the cow and the bear shall feed; their young ones shall lie down together: and the lion shall eat straw like the ox. [8]And the sucking child shall play on the hole of the asp, and the weaned child shall put his hand on the cockatrice' den. [9]They shall not hurt nor destroy in all my holy mountain: for the earth shall be full of the knowledge of the LORD, as the waters cover the sea. [10]And in that day there shall be a root of Jesse, which shall stand for an ensign of the people; to it shall the Gentiles seek: and his rest shall be glorious. [11]And it shall come to pass in that day, that the Lord shall set his hand again the second time to recover the remnant of his people, which shall be left, from Assyria, and from Egypt, and from Pathros, and from Cush, and from Elam, and from Shinar, and from Hamath, and from the islands of the sea. [12]And he shall set up an ensign for the nations, and shall assemble the outcasts of Israel, and gather together the dispersed of Judah from the four corners of the earth. [13]The envy also of Ephraim shall depart, and the adversaries of Judah shall be cut off: Ephraim shall not envy Judah, and Judah shall not vex Ephraim. [14]But they shall fly upon the shoulders of the Philistines toward the west; they shall spoil them of the east together: they shall lay their hand upon Edom and Moab; and the children of Ammon shall obey them. 15 And the LORD shall utterly destroy the tongue of the Egyptian sea; and with his mighty wind shall he shake his hand over the river, and shall smite it in the seven streams, and make men go over dryshod. 16 And there shall be an highway for the remnant of his people, which shall be left, from Assyria; like as it was to Israel in the day that he came up out of the land of Egypt."

Isaiah 53:1-12 "1Who hath believed our report? and to whom is the arm of the LORD revealed? 2 For he shall grow up before him as a tender plant, and as a root out of a dry ground: he hath no form nor comeliness; and when we shall see him, there is no beauty that we should desire him. 3 He is despised and rejected of men; a man of sorrows, and acquainted with grief: and we hid as it were our faces from him; he was despised, and we esteemed him not. 4 Surely he hath borne our griefs, and carried our sorrows: yet we did esteem him stricken, smitten of God, and afflicted. 5 But he was wounded for our transgressions, he was bruised for our iniquities: the chastisement of our peace was upon him; and with his stripes we are healed. 6 All we like sheep have gone astray; we have turned every one to his own way; and the LORD hath laid on him the iniquity of us all. 7 He was oppressed, and he was afflicted, yet he opened not his mouth: he is brought as a lamb to the slaughter, and as a sheep before her shearers is dumb, so he openeth not his mouth. 8 He was taken from prison and from judgment: and who shall declare his generation? for he was cut off out of the land of the living: for the transgression of my people was he stricken. 9 And he made his grave with the wicked, and with the rich in his death; because he had done no violence, neither was any deceit in his mouth. 10 Yet it pleased the LORD to bruise him; he hath put him to grief: when thou shalt make his soul an offering for sin, he shall see his seed, he shall prolong his days, and the pleasure of the LORD shall prosper in his hand. 11 He shall see of the travail of his soul, and shall be satisfied: by his knowledge shall my righteous servant justify many; for he shall bear their iniquities. 12 Therefore will I divide him a portion with the great, and he shall divide the spoil with the strong; because he hath poured out his soul unto

death: and he was numbered with the transgressors; and he bare the sin of many, and made intercession for the transgressors."

Jeremiah 23:5-8 "5Behold, the days come, saith the LORD, that I will raise unto David a righteous Branch, and a King shall reign and prosper, and shall execute judgment and justice in the earth. 6 In his days Judah shall be saved, and Israel shall dwell safely: and this is his name whereby he shall be called, THE LORD OUR RIGHTEOUSNESS. 7 Therefore, behold, the days come, saith the LORD, that they shall no more say, The LORD liveth, which brought up the children of Israel out of the land of Egypt; 8 But, The LORD liveth, which brought up and which led the seed of the house of Israel out of the north country, and from all countries whither I had driven them; and they shall dwell in their own land."

Jeremiah 33:14-17 "14Behold, the days come, saith the LORD, that I will perform that good thing which I have promised unto the house of Israel and to the house of Judah. 15 In those days, and at that time, will I cause the Branch of righteousness to grow up unto David; and he shall execute judgment and righteousness in the land. 16 In those days shall Judah be saved, and Jerusalem shall dwell safely: and this is the name wherewith she shall be called, The LORD our righteousness. 17 For thus saith the LORD; David shall never want a man to sit upon the throne of the house of Israel."

Zechariah 6:12 "And speak unto him, saying, Thus speaketh the LORD of hosts, saying, Behold the man whose name is The BRANCH; and he shall grow up out of his place, and he shall build the temple of the LORD."

The Gentiles Trusting In The Branch Of Jesse
Isaiah 11:1 "And there shall come forth a rod out of the stem of Jesse, and a Branch shall grow out of his roots."

Isaiah 11:10 "And in that day there shall be a root of Jesse, which shall stand for an ensign of the people; to it shall the Gentiles seek: and his rest shall be glorious."

Zechariah 6:12 "And speak unto him, saying, Thus speaketh the LORD of hosts, saying, Behold the man whose name is The BRANCH; and he shall grow up out of his place, and he shall build the temple of the LORD."

Romans 15:8-12 "⁸Now I say that Jesus Christ was a minister of the circumcision for the truth of God, to confirm the promises made unto the fathers ⁹And that the Gentiles might glorify God for his mercy; as it is written, For this cause I will confess to thee among the Gentiles, and sing unto thy name. ¹⁰And again he saith, Rejoice, ye Gentiles, with his people. ¹¹And again, Praise the Lord, all ye Gentiles; and laud him, all ye people. ¹²And again, Esaias saith, There shall be a root of Jesse, and he that shall rise to reign over the Gentiles; in him shall the Gentiles trust."

The Root Of David Prevailing
Revelation 5:5 "And one of the elders saith unto me, Weep not: behold, the Lion of the tribe of Juda, the Root of David, hath prevailed to open the book, and to loose the seven seals thereof."

BRIBERY

Not Taking Gifts (Bribes)
Exodus 23:8 "And thou shalt take no gift: for the gift blindeth the wise, and perverteth the words of the righteous."

Deuteronomy 16:19 "Thou shalt not wrest judgment; thou shalt not respect persons, neither take a gift: for a gift doth blind the eyes of the wise, and pervert the words of the righteous."

2 Chronicles 19:7 "Wherefore now let the fear of the LORD be upon you; take heed and do it: for there is no iniquity with the LORD our God, nor respect of persons, nor taking of gifts."

The Tabernacles Of Bribery
Job 15:34 "For the congregation of hypocrites shall be desolate, and fire shall consume the tabernacles of bribery."

Those That Do Not Receive Bribes
Isaiah 33:15-16 "¹⁵He that walketh righteously, and speaketh uprightly; he that despiseth the gain of oppressions, that shaketh his hands from holding of bribes, that stoppeth his ears from hearing of blood, and shutteth his eyes from seeing evil; ¹⁶He shall dwell on high: his place of defence shall be the munitions of rocks: bread shall be given him; his waters shall be sure."

Those That Hate Gifts (Bribes)
Proverbs 15:27 "He that is greedy of gain troubleth his own house; but he that hateth gifts shall live."

Those That Receive Gifts (Bribes)
Proverbs 29:4 "The king by judgment establisheth the land: but he that receiveth gifts overthroweth it."

What Gifts (Bribes) Do
Exodus 23:8 "And thou shalt take no gift: for the gift blindeth the wise, and perverteth the words of the righteous."

Deuteronomy 16:19 "Thou shalt not wrest judgment; thou shalt not respect persons, neither take a gift: for a gift doth blind the eyes of the wise, and pervert the words of the righteous."

Proverbs 18:16 "A man's gift maketh room for him, and bringeth him before great men."

Ecclesiastes 7:7 "Surely oppression maketh a wise man mad; and a gift destroyeth the heart."

BURDEN

Bearing The Burdens Of Others
Acts 20:35 "I have shewed you all things, how that so labouring ye ought to support the weak, and to remember the words of the Lord Jesus, how he said, It is more blessed to give than to receive."

Galatians 6:1-2 "¹Brethren, if a man be overtaken in a fault, ye which are spiritual, restore such an one in the spirit of meekness; considering thyself, lest thou also be tempted. ²Bear ye one another's burdens, and so fulfil the law of Christ."

Hebrews 13:1-3 "¹Let brotherly love continue. ²Be not forgetful to entertain strangers: for thereby some have entertained angels unawares. ³Remember them that are in bonds, as bound with them; and them which suffer adversity, as being yourselves also in the body."

The Burden Of Jesus Christ
Matthew 11:28-30 "²⁸Come unto me, all ye that labour and are heavy laden, and I will give you rest. ²⁹Take my yoke upon you, and learn of me; for I am meek and lowly in heart: and ye shall find rest unto your souls. ³⁰For my yoke is easy, and my burden is light."

The Reward For Casting
Your Burden Upon The Lord
Psalm 55:22 "Cast thy burden upon the LORD, and he shall sustain thee: he shall never suffer the righteous to be moved."

Who Should Bear The Burdens Of The Weak
Romans 15:1-3 "¹We then that are strong ought to bear the infirmities of the weak, and not to please ourselves. ²Let every one of us please his neighbour for his good to edification. ³For even Christ pleased not himself; but, as it is written, The reproaches of them that reproached thee fell on me."

Cc

CALLING

Calling On The Lord

1 Chronicles 16:8-9 "⁸Give thanks unto the LORD, call upon his name, make known his deeds among the people. ⁹Sing unto him, sing psalms unto him, talk ye of all his wondrous works."

Psalm 105:1-2 "¹O give thanks unto the LORD; call upon his name: make known his deeds among the people. ²Sing unto him, sing psalms unto him: talk ye of all his wondrous works."

Isaiah 12:4-6 "⁴And in that day shall ye say, Praise the LORD, call upon his name, declare his doings among the people, make mention that his name is exalted. ⁵Sing unto the LORD; for he hath done excellent things: this is known in all the earth. ⁶Cry out and shout, thou inhabitant of Zion: for great is the Holy One of Israel in the midst of thee."

Isaiah 55:6 "Seek ye the LORD while he may be found, call ye upon him while he is near."

Jeremiah 33:2-3 "²Thus saith the LORD the maker thereof, the LORD that formed it, to establish it; the LORD is his name; ³Call unto me, and I will answer thee, and shew thee great and mighty things, which thou knowest not."

Many Being Called

Matthew 20:16 "So the last shall be first, and the first last: for many be called, but few chosen."

Matthew 22:14 "For many are called, but few are chosen."

Not Many Noble Or Mighty Men Being Called

1 Corinthians 1:26 "For ye see your calling, brethren, how that not many wise men after the flesh, not many mighty, not many noble, are called."

The Calling Of God

Romans 11:29 "For the gifts and calling of God are without repentance."

The Lord Calling

Isaiah 49:1-5 "¹Listen, O isles, unto me; and hearken, ye people, from far; The LORD hath called me from the womb; from the bowels of my mother hath he made mention of my name. ²And he hath made my mouth like a sharp sword; in the shadow of his hand hath he hid me, and made me a polished shaft; in his quiver hath he hid me; ³And said unto me, Thou art my servant, O Israel, in whom I will be glorified. ⁴Then I said, I have laboured in vain, I have spent my strength for nought, and in vain: yet surely my judgment is with the LORD, and my work with my God. ⁵And now, saith the LORD that formed me from the womb to be his servant, to bring Jacob again to him, Though Israel be not gathered, yet shall I be glorious in the eyes of the LORD, and my God shall be my strength."

Jeremiah 1:4-5 "⁴Then the word of the LORD came unto me, saying, ⁵Before I formed thee in the belly I knew thee; and before thou camest forth out of the womb I sanctified thee, and I ordained thee a prophet unto the nations."

1 Corinthians 1:9 "God is faithful, by whom ye were called unto the fellowship of his Son Jesus Christ our Lord."

1 Corinthians 7:17-21 "¹⁷But as God hath distributed to every man, as the Lord hath called every one, so let him walk. And so ordain I in all churches. ¹⁸Is any man called being circumcised? let him not become uncircumcised. Is any called in uncircumcision? let him not be circumcised. ¹⁹Circumcision is nothing, and uncircumcision is nothing, but the keeping of the commandments of God. ²⁰Let every man abide in the same calling wherein he was called. ²¹Art thou called being a servant? care not for it: but if thou mayest be made free, use it rather."

Galatians 1:15-16 "¹⁵But when it pleased God, who separated me from my mother's womb, and called me by his grace, ¹⁶To reveal his Son in me, that I might preach him among the heathen; immediately I conferred not with flesh and blood."

1 Thessalonians 4:7 "For God hath not called us unto uncleanness, but unto holiness."

1 Thessalonians 5:23-24 "²³And the very God of peace sanctify you wholly; and I pray God your whole spirit and soul and body be preserved blameless unto the coming of our Lord Jesus Christ. ²⁴Faithful is he that calleth you, who also will do it."

1 Peter 5:10 "But the God of all grace, who hath called us unto his eternal glory by Christ Jesus, after that ye have suffered a while, make you perfect, stablish, strengthen, settle you."

2 Peter 1:1-3 "¹Simon Peter, a servant and an apostle of Jesus Christ, to them that have obtained like precious faith with us through the righteousness of God and our Saviour Jesus Christ: ²Grace and peace be multiplied unto you through the knowledge of God, and of Jesus our Lord, ³According as his divine power hath given unto us all things that pertain unto life and godliness, through the knowledge of him that hath called us to glory and virtue."

The Reward For Calling On The Lord

Judges 10:11-12 "¹¹And the LORD said unto the children of Israel, Did not I deliver you from the Egyptians, and from the Amorites, from the children of Ammon, and from the Philistines? ¹²The Zidonians also, and the Amalekites, and the Maonites, did oppress you; and ye cried to me, and I delivered you out of their hand."

2 Samuel 22:4-7 "⁴I will call on the LORD, who is worthy to be praised: so shall I be saved from mine enemies. ⁵When the waves of death compassed me, the floods of ungodly men made me afraid; ⁶The sorrows of hell compassed me about; the snares of death prevented me; ⁷In my distress I called upon the LORD, and cried to my God: and he did hear my voice out of his temple, and my cry did enter into his ears."

1 Chronicles 4:10 "And Jabez called on the God of Israel, saying, Oh that thou wouldest bless me indeed, and enlarge my coast, and that thine hand might be with me, and that thou wouldest keep me from evil, that it may not grieve me! And God granted him that which he requested."

Psalm 18:3 "I will call upon the LORD, who is worthy to be praised: so shall I be saved from mine enemies."

Psalm 34:4 "I sought the LORD, and he heard me, and delivered me from all my fears."

Psalm 34:6 "This poor man cried, and the LORD heard him, and saved him out of all his troubles."

Psalm 34:17 "The righteous cry, and the LORD heareth, and delivereth them out of all their troubles."

Psalm 50:14-15 "¹⁴Offer unto God thanksgiving; and pay thy vows unto the most High: ¹⁵And call upon me in the day of trouble: I will deliver thee, and thou shalt glorify me."

Psalm 55:16-19 "¹⁶As for me, I will call upon God; and the LORD shall save me. ¹⁷Evening, and morning, and at noon, will I pray, and cry aloud: and he shall hear my voice. ¹⁸He hath delivered my soul in peace from the battle that was against me: for there were many with me. ¹⁹God shall hear, and afflict them, even he that abideth of old. Selah. Because they have no changes, therefore they fear not God."

Psalm 86:6-7 "⁶Give ear, O LORD, unto my prayer; and attend to the voice of my supplications. ⁷In the day of my trouble I will call upon thee: for thou wilt answer me."

Psalm 91:9-15 "⁹Because thou hast made the LORD, which is my refuge, even the most High, thy habitation; ¹⁰There shall no evil befall thee, neither shall any plague come nigh thy dwelling. ¹¹For he shall give his angels charge over thee, to keep thee in all thy ways. ¹²They shall bear thee up in their hands, lest thou dash thy foot against a stone. ¹³Thou shalt tread upon the lion and adder: the young lion and the dragon shalt thou trample under feet. ¹⁴Because he hath set his love upon me, therefore will I deliver him: I will set him on high, because he hath known my name. ¹⁵He shall call upon me, and I will answer him: I will be with him in trouble; I will deliver him, and honour him."

Psalm 99:6 "Moses and Aaron among his priests, and Samuel among them that call upon his name; they called upon the LORD, and he answered them."

Psalm 107:8-14 "⁸Oh that men would praise the LORD for his goodness, and for his wonderful works to the children of men! ⁹For he satisfieth the longing soul, and filleth the hungry soul with goodness. ¹⁰Such as sit in darkness and in the shadow of death, being bound in affliction and iron; ¹¹Because they rebelled against the words of God, and contemned the counsel of the most High: ¹²Therefore he brought down their heart with labour; they fell down, and there was none to help. ¹³Then they cried unto the LORD in their trouble, and he saved them out of their distresses. ¹⁴He brought them out of darkness and the shadow of death, and brake their bands in sunder."

Psalm 116:3-8 "³The sorrows of death compassed me, and the pains of hell gat hold upon me: I found trouble and sorrow. ⁴Then called I upon the name of the LORD; O LORD, I beseech thee, deliver my soul. ⁵Gracious is the LORD, and righteous; yea, our God is merciful. ⁶The LORD preserveth the simple: I was brought low, and he helped me. ⁷Return unto thy rest, O my soul; for the LORD hath dealt bountifully with thee. ⁸For thou hast delivered my soul from death, mine eyes from tears, and my feet from falling."

Psalm 118:5 "I called upon the LORD in distress: the LORD answered me, and set me in a large place."

Psalm 138:3-4 "³In the day when I cried thou answeredst me, and strengthenedst me with strength in my soul. ⁴All the kings of the earth shall praise thee, O LORD, when they hear the words of thy mouth."

Isaiah 58:8-9 "⁸Then shall thy light break forth as the morning, and thine health shall spring forth speedily: and thy righteousness shall go before thee; the glory of the LORD shall be thy rereward. ⁹Then shalt thou call, and the LORD shall answer; thou shalt cry, and he shall say, Here I am. If thou take away from the midst of thee the yoke, the putting forth of the finger, and speaking vanity."

Jeremiah 33:2-3 "²Thus saith the LORD the maker thereof, the LORD that formed it, to establish it; the LORD is his name; ³ Call unto me, and I will answer thee, and shew thee great and mighty things, which thou knowest not."

Zechariah 13:9 "And I will bring the third part through the fire, and will refine them as silver is refined, and will try them as gold is tried: they shall call on my name, and I will hear them: I will say, It is my people: and they shall say, The LORD is my God."

The Reward For
Not Answering The Calls Of The Lord
Isaiah 65:11-15 "¹¹But ye are they that forsake the LORD, that forget my holy mountain, that prepare a table for that troop, and that furnish the drink offering unto that number. ¹²Therefore will I number you to the sword, and ye shall all bow down to the slaughter: because when I called, ye did not answer; when I spake, ye did not hear; but

did evil before mine eyes, and did choose that wherein I delighted not. ¹³Therefore thus saith the Lord GOD, Behold, my servants shall eat, but ye shall be hungry: behold, my servants shall drink, but ye shall be thirsty: behold, my servants shall rejoice, but ye shall be ashamed: ¹⁴Behold, my servants shall sing for joy of heart, but ye shall cry for sorrow of heart, and shall howl for vexation of spirit. ¹⁵And ye shall leave your name for a curse unto my chosen: for the Lord GOD shall slay thee, and call his servants by another name."

Isaiah 66:1-4 "¹Thus saith the LORD, The heaven is my throne, and the earth is my footstool: where is the house that ye build unto me? and where is the place of my rest? ²For all those things hath mine hand made, and those things have been, saith the LORD: but to this man will I look, even to him that is poor and of a contrite spirit, and trembleth at my word. ³He that killeth an ox is as if he slew a man; he that sacrificeth a lamb, as if he cut off a dog's neck; he that offereth an oblation, as if he offered swine's blood; he that burneth incense, as if he blessed an idol. Yea, they have chosen their own ways, and their soul delighteth in their abominations. ⁴I also will choose their delusions, and will bring their fears upon them; because when I called, none did answer; when I spake, they did not hear: but they did evil before mine eyes, and chose that in which I delighted not."

Jeremiah 35:17 "Therefore thus saith the LORD God of hosts, the God of Israel; Behold, I will bring upon Judah and upon all the inhabitants of Jerusalem all the evil that I have pronounced against them: because I have spoken unto them, but they have not heard; and I have called unto them, but they have not answered."

The Reward For
Not Answering The Calls Of Wisdom
Proverbs 1:20-32 "²⁰Wisdom crieth without; she uttereth her voice in the streets: ²¹She crieth in the chief place of concourse, in the openings of the gates: in the city she uttereth her words, saying, ²²How long, ye simple ones, will ye love simplicity? and the scorners delight in their scorning, and fools hate knowledge? ²³Turn you at my reproof: behold, I will pour out my spirit unto you, I will make known my words unto you. ²⁴Because I have called, and ye refused; I have stretched out my hand, and no man regarded; ²⁵But ye have set at nought all my

counsel, and would none of my reproof: 26I also will laugh at your calamity; I will mock when your fear cometh; 27When your fear cometh as desolation, and your destruction cometh as a whirlwind; when distress and anguish cometh upon you. 28Then shall they call upon me, but I will not answer; they shall seek me early, but they shall not find me: 29For that they hated knowledge, and did not choose the fear of the LORD: 30They would none of my counsel: they despised all my reproof. 31Therefore shall they eat of the fruit of their own way, and be filled with their own devices. 32For the turning away of the simple shall slay them, and the prosperity of fools shall destroy them."

The Reward For Not Calling On The Lord

Isaiah 43:16-28 "16Thus saith the LORD, which maketh a way in the sea, and a path in the mighty waters; 17Which bringeth forth the chariot and horse, the army and the power; they shall lie down together, they shall not rise: they are extinct, they are quenched as tow. 18Remember ye not the former things, neither consider the things of old. 19Behold, I will do a new thing; now it shall spring forth; shall ye not know it? I will even make a way in the wilderness, and rivers in the desert. 20The beast of the field shall honour me, the dragons and the owls: because I give waters in the wilderness, and rivers in the desert, to give drink to my people, my chosen. 21This people have I formed for myself; they shall shew forth my praise. 22But thou hast not called upon me, O Jacob; but thou hast been weary of me, O Israel. 23Thou hast not brought me the small cattle of thy burnt offerings; neither hast thou honoured me with thy sacrifices. I have not caused thee to serve with an offering, nor wearied thee with incense. 24Thou hast bought me no sweet cane with money, neither hast thou filled me with the fat of thy sacrifices: but thou hast made me to serve with thy sins, thou hast wearied me with thine iniquities. 25I, even I, am he that blotteth out thy transgressions for mine own sake, and will not remember thy sins. 26Put me in remembrance: let us plead together: declare thou, that thou mayest be justified. 27Thy first father hath sinned, and thy teachers have transgressed against me. 28Therefore I have profaned the princes of the sanctuary, and have given Jacob to the curse, and Israel to reproaches."

Those That Are Called By God

Romans 8:28-30 "28And we know that all things work together for good to them that love God, to them who are the called according to his purpose. 29For whom he did foreknow, he also did predestinate to be conformed to the image of his Son, that he might be the firstborn among many brethren. 30Moreover whom he did predestinate, them he also called: and whom he called, them he also justified: and whom he justified, them he also glorified."

Romans 9:20-26 "20Nay but, O man, who art thou that repliest against God? Shall the thing formed say to him that formed it, Why hast thou made me thus? 21Hath not the potter power over the clay, of the same lump to make one vessel unto honour, and another unto dishonour? 22What if God, willing to shew his wrath, and to make his power known, endured with much longsuffering the vessels of wrath fitted to destruction: 23And that he might make known the riches of his glory on the vessels of mercy, which he had afore prepared unto glory, 24Even us, whom he hath called, not of the Jews only, but also of the Gentiles? 25As he saith also in Osee, I will call them my people, which were not my people; and her beloved, which was not beloved. 26And it shall come to pass, that in the place where it was said unto them, Ye are not my people; there shall they be called the children of the living God."

1 Corinthians 1:23-24 "23But we preach Christ crucified, unto the Jews a stumblingblock, and unto the Greeks foolishness; 24But unto them which are called, both Jews and Greeks, Christ the power of God, and the wisdom of God."

1 Corinthians 7:22-24 "22For he that is called in the Lord, being a servant, is the Lord's freeman: likewise also he that is called, being free, is Christ's servant. 23Ye are bought with a price; be not ye the servants of men. 24Brethren, let every man, wherein he is called, therein abide with God."

Revelation 19:9 "And he saith unto me, Write, Blessed are they which are called unto the marriage supper of the Lamb. And he saith unto me, These are the true sayings of God."

Those That Call On The Lord

Psalm 86:5 "For thou, Lord, art good, and ready to forgive; and plenteous in mercy unto all them that call upon thee."

Psalm 145:18 "The LORD is nigh unto all them that call upon him, to all that call upon him in truth."

Jeremiah 29:10-13 "10For thus saith the LORD, That after seventy years be accomplished at Babylon I will visit you, and perform my good word toward you, in causing you to return to this place. 11For I know the thoughts that I think toward you, saith the LORD, thoughts of peace, and not of evil, to give you an expected end. 12Then shall ye call upon me, and ye shall go and pray unto me, and I will hearken unto you. 13And ye shall seek me, and find me, when ye shall search for me with all your heart."

Joel 2:32 "And it shall come to pass, that whosoever shall call on the name of the LORD shall be delivered: for in mount Zion and in Jerusalem shall be deliverance, as the LORD hath said, and in the remnant whom the LORD shall call."

Acts 2:21 "And it shall come to pass, that whosoever shall call on the name of the Lord shall be saved."

Romans 10:12-13 "12For there is no difference between the Jew and the Greek: for the same Lord over all is rich unto all that call upon him. 13For whosoever shall call upon the name of the Lord shall be saved."

What Not To Call Someone

Matthew 23:8-10 "8But be not ye called Rabbi: for one is your Master, even Christ; and all ye are brethren. 9And call no man your father upon the earth: for one is your Father, which is in heaven. 10Neither be ye called masters: for one is your Master, even Christ."

Acts 10:28 "And he said unto them, Ye know how that it is an unlawful thing for a man that is a Jew to keep company, or come unto one of another nation; but God hath shewed me that I should not call any man common or unclean."

Who Does Not Call On The Lord

Psalm 14:4 "Have all the workers of iniquity no knowledge? who eat up my people as they eat bread, and call not upon the LORD."

Who Is Called By The Lord

Deuteronomy 28:1-10 "1And it shall come to pass, if thou shalt hearken diligently unto the voice of the LORD thy God, to observe and to do all his commandments which I command thee this day, that the LORD thy God will set thee on high above all nations of the earth: 2And all these blessings shall come on thee, and overtake thee, if thou shalt hearken unto the voice of the LORD thy God. 3Blessed shalt thou be in the city, and blessed shalt thou be in the field. 4Blessed shall be the fruit of thy body, and the fruit of thy ground, and the fruit of thy cattle, the increase of thy kine, and the flocks of thy sheep. 5Blessed shall be thy basket and thy store. 6Blessed shalt thou be when thou comest in, and blessed shalt thou be when thou goest out. 7The LORD shall cause thine enemies that rise up against thee to be smitten before thy face: they shall come out against thee one way, and flee before thee seven ways. 8The LORD shall command the blessing upon thee in thy storehouses, and in all that thou settest thine hand unto; and he shall bless thee in the land which the LORD thy God giveth thee. 9The LORD shall establish thee an holy people unto himself, as he hath sworn unto thee, if thou shalt keep the commandments of the LORD thy God, and walk in his ways. 10And all people of the earth shall see that thou art called by the name of the LORD; and they shall be afraid of thee."

2 Chronicles 7:12-14 "12And the LORD appeared to Solomon by night, and said unto him, I have heard thy prayer, and have chosen this place to myself for an house of sacrifice. 13If I shut up heaven that there be no rain, or if I command the locusts to devour the land, or if I send pestilence among my people; 14If my people, which are called by my name, shall humble themselves, and pray, and seek my face, and turn from their wicked ways; then will I hear from heaven, and will forgive their sin, and will heal their land."

Isaiah 41:8-10 "8But thou, Israel, art my servant, Jacob whom I have chosen, the seed of Abraham my friend. 9Thou whom I have taken from the ends of the earth, and called thee from the chief men thereof, and said unto thee, Thou art my servant; I have chosen thee, and not cast thee away. 10Fear thou not; for I am with thee: be not dismayed; for I am thy God: I will strengthen thee; yea, I will help thee; yea, I will uphold thee with the right hand of my righteousness."

Isaiah 45:3-4 "³And I will give thee the treasures of darkness, and hidden riches of secret places, that thou mayest know that I, the LORD, which call thee by thy name, am the God of Israel. ⁴For Jacob my servant's sake, and Israel mine elect, I have even called thee by thy name: I have sur-named thee, though thou hast not known me."

Isaiah 48:12 "Hearken unto me, O Jacob and Israel, my called; I am he; I am the first, I also am the last."

Isaiah 51:1-2 "¹Hearken to me, ye that follow after righteousness, ye that seek the LORD: look unto the rock whence ye are hewn, and to the hole of the pit whence ye are digged. ²Look unto Abra-ham your father, and unto Sarah that bare you: for I called him alone, and blessed him, and increased him."

Isaiah 54:5-6 "⁵For thy Maker is thine husband; the LORD of hosts is his name; and thy Redeemer the Holy One of Israel; The God of the whole earth shall he be called. ⁶For the LORD hath called thee as a woman forsaken and grieved in spirit, and a wife of youth, when thou wast refused, saith thy God."

Romans 8:28-30 "²⁸And we know that all things work together for good to them that love God, to them who are the called according to his purpose. ²⁹For whom he did foreknow, he also did predes-tinate to be conformed to the image of his Son, that he might be the firstborn among many brethren. ³⁰Moreover whom he did predestinate, them he also called: and whom he called, them he also justified: and whom he justified, them he also glorified."

1 Corinthians 1:2-9 "²Unto the church of God which is at Corinth, to them that are sanctified in Christ Jesus, called to be saints, with all that in every place call upon the name of Jesus Christ our Lord, both theirs and ours: ³Grace be unto you, and peace, from God our Father, and from the Lord Jesus Christ. ⁴I thank my God always on your behalf, for the grace of God which is given you by Jesus Christ; ⁵That in every thing ye are enriched by him, in all utterance, and in all

knowledge; ⁶Even as the testimony of Christ was confirmed in you: ⁷So that ye come behind in no gift; waiting for the coming of our Lord Jesus Christ: ⁸Who shall also confirm you unto the end, that ye may be blameless in the day of our Lord Jesus Christ. ⁹God is faithful, by whom ye were called unto the fellowship of his Son Jesus Christ our Lord."

Ephesians 4:1-5 "¹I therefore, the prisoner of the Lord, beseech you that ye walk worthy of the vocation wherewith ye are called, ²With all lowli-ness and meekness, with longsuffering, forbearing one another in love; ³Endeavouring to keep the unity of the Spirit in the bond of peace. ⁴There is one body, and one Spirit, even as ye are called in one hope of your calling; ⁵One Lord, one faith, one baptism."

Colossians 3:8-15 "⁸But now ye also put off all these; anger, wrath, malice, blasphemy, filthy com-munication out of your mouth. ⁹Lie not one to another, seeing that ye have put off the old man with his deeds; ¹⁰And have put on the new man, which is renewed in knowledge after the image of him that created him: ¹¹Where there is neither Greek nor Jew, circumcision nor uncircumcision, Barbarian, Scythian, bond nor free: but Christ is all, and in all. ¹²Put on therefore, as the elect of God, holy and beloved, bowels of mercies, kind-ness, humbleness of mind, meekness, longsuffer-ing; ¹³Forbearing one another, and forgiving one another, if any man have a quarrel against any: even as Christ forgave you, so also do ye. ¹⁴And above all these things put on charity, which is the bond of perfectness. ¹⁵And let the peace of God rule in your hearts, to the which also ye are called in one body; and be ye thankful."

1 Peter 2:4-10 "⁴To whom coming, as unto a living stone, disallowed indeed of men, but chosen of God, and precious, ⁵Ye also, as lively stones, are built up a spiritual house, an holy priesthood, to offer up spiritual sacrifices, acceptable to God by Jesus Christ. ⁶Wherefore also it is contained in the scripture, Behold, I lay in Sion a chief corner stone, elect, precious: and he that believeth on him shall not be confounded. ⁷Unto you therefore which believe he is precious: but unto them which be disobedient, the stone which the builders disal-lowed, the same is made the head of the corner,

[8]And a stone of stumbling, and a rock of offence, even to them which stumble at the word, being disobedient: whereunto also they were appointed. [9]But ye are a chosen generation, a royal priesthood, an holy nation, a peculiar people; that ye should shew forth the praises of him who hath called you out of darkness into his marvellous light: [10]Which in time past were not a people, but are now the people of God: which had not obtained mercy, but now have obtained mercy."

1 Peter 5:8-10 "[8]Be sober, be vigilant; because your adversary the devil, as a roaring lion, walketh about, seeking whom he may devour: [9]Whom resist stedfast in the faith, knowing that the same afflictions are accomplished in your brethren that are in the world. [10]But the God of all grace, who hath called us unto his eternal glory by Christ Jesus, after that ye have suffered a while, make you perfect, stablish, strengthen, settle you."

Revelation 17:14 "These shall make war with the Lamb, and the Lamb shall overcome them: for he is Lord of lords, and King of kings: and they that are with him are called, and chosen, and faithful."

Who Only Calls Upon God
When They Are In Trouble
Job 27:8-10 "[8]For what is the hope of the hypocrite, though he hath gained, when God taketh away his soul? [9]Will God hear his cry when trouble cometh upon him? [10]Will he delight himself in the Almighty? will he always call upon God?"

CARNALITY

The Carnal Mind
Romans 8:6-7 "[6]For to be carnally minded is death; but to be spiritually minded is life and peace. [7]Because the carnal mind is enmity against God: for it is not subject to the law of God, neither indeed can be."

Who Is Carnal
Romans 7:11-14 "[11]For sin, taking occasion by the commandment, deceived me, and by it slew me. [12]Wherefore the law is holy, and the commandment holy, and just, and good. [13]Was then that which is good made death unto me? God forbid. But sin, that it might appear sin, working death in me by that which is good; that sin by the commandment might become exceeding sinful. [14]For

we know that the law is spiritual: but I am carnal, sold under sin."

1 Corinthians 3:1-4 "[1]And I, brethren, could not speak unto you as unto spiritual, but as unto carnal, even as unto babes in Christ. [2]I have fed you with milk, and not with meat: for hitherto ye were not able to bear it, neither yet now are ye able. [3]For ye are yet carnal: for whereas there is among you envying, and strife, and divisions, are ye not carnal, and walk as men? [4]For while one saith, I am of Paul; and another, I am of Apollos; are ye not carnal?"

CHANGE

The Lord Changing Believers
1 Corinthians 15:50-57 "[50]Now this I say, brethren, that flesh and blood cannot inherit the kingdom of God; neither doth corruption inherit incorruption. [51]Behold, I shew you a mystery; We shall not all sleep, but we shall all be changed, [52]In a moment, in the twinkling of an eye, at the last trump: for the trumpet shall sound, and the dead shall be raised incorruptible, and we shall be changed. [53]For this corruptible must put on incorruption, and this mortal must put on immortality. [54]So when this corruptible shall have put on incorruption, and this mortal shall have put on immortality, then shall be brought to pass the saying that is written, Death is swallowed up in victory. [55]O death, where is thy sting? O grave, where is thy victory? [56]The sting of death is sin; and the strength of sin is the law. [57]But thanks be to God, which giveth us the victory through our Lord Jesus Christ."

2 Corinthians 3:17-18 "[17]Now the Lord is that Spirit: and where the Spirit of the Lord is, there is liberty. [18]But we all, with open face beholding as in a glass the glory of the Lord, are changed into the same image from glory to glory, even as by the Spirit of the Lord."

Philippians 3:20-21 "[20]For our conversation is in heaven; from whence also we look for the Saviour, the Lord Jesus Christ: [21]Who shall change our vile body, that it may be fashioned like unto his glorious body, according to the working whereby he is able even to subdue all things unto himself."

The Lord Never Changing
Psalm 90:2 "Before the mountains were brought forth, or ever thou hadst formed the earth and the

world, even from everlasting to everlasting, thou art God."

Psalm 102:24-27 "24I said, O my God, take me not away in the midst of my days: thy years are throughout all generations. 25Of old hast thou laid the foundation of the earth: and the heavens are the work of thy hands. 26They shall perish, but thou shalt endure: yea, all of them shall wax old like a garment; as a vesture shalt thou change them, and they shall be changed: 27But thou art the same, and thy years shall have no end."

Daniel 6:26 "I make a decree, That in every dominion of my kingdom men tremble and fear before the God of Daniel: for he is the living God, and stedfast for ever, and his kingdom that which shall not be destroyed, and his dominion shall be even unto the end."

Malachi 3:6 "For I am the LORD, I change not; therefore ye sons of Jacob are not consumed."

Hebrews 1:10-12 "10And, Thou, Lord, in the beginning hast laid the foundation of the earth; and the heavens are the works of thine hands: 11They shall perish; but thou remainest; and they all shall wax old as doth a garment; 12And as a vesture shalt thou fold them up, and they shall be changed: but thou art the same, and thy years shall not fail."

Hebrews 13:8 "Jesus Christ the same yesterday, and today, and for ever."

James 1:17 "Every good gift and every perfect gift is from above, and cometh down from the Father of lights, with whom is no variableness, neither shadow of turning."

What Shall Be Changed
Psalm 102:24-26 "24I said, O my God, take me not away in the midst of my days: thy years are throughout all generations. 25Of old hast thou laid the foundation of the earth: and the heavens are the work of thy hands. 26They shall perish, but thou shalt endure: yea, all of them shall wax old like a garment; as a vesture shalt thou change them, and they shall be changed."

Hebrews 1:10-12 "10And, Thou, Lord, in the beginning hast laid the foundation of the earth; and the heavens are the works of thine hands: 11They shall perish; but thou remainest; and they all shall

wax old as doth a garment; 12And as a vesture shalt thou fold them up, and they shall be changed: but thou art the same, and thy years shall not fail."

CHARITY

Following After Charity
1 Corinthians 14:1 "Follow after charity, and desire spiritual gifts, but rather that ye may prophesy."

Giving
Acts 20:35 "I have shewed you all things, how that so labouring ye ought to support the weak, and to remember the words of the Lord Jesus, how he said, It is more blessed to give than to receive."

How Not To Give
Matthew 6:1-2 "1Take heed that ye do not your alms before men, to be seen of them: otherwise ye have no reward of your Father which is in heaven. 2Therefore when thou doest thine alms, do not sound a trumpet before thee, as the hypocrites do in the synagogues and in the streets, that they may have glory of men. Verily I say unto you, They have their reward."

2 Corinthians 9:6-7 "6But this I say, He which soweth sparingly shall reap also sparingly; and he which soweth bountifully shall reap also bountifully. 7Every man according as he purposeth in his heart, so let him give; not grudgingly, or of necessity: for God loveth a cheerful giver."

How To Give
Matthew 6:3-4 "3But when thou doest alms, let not thy left hand know what thy right hand doeth: 4That thine alms may be in secret: and thy Father which seeth in secret himself shall reward thee openly."

Romans 12:4-8 "4For as we have many members in one body, and all members have not the same office: 5So we, being many, are one body in Christ, and every one members one of another. 6Having then gifts differing according to the grace that is given to us, whether prophecy, let us prophesy according to the proportion of faith; 7Or ministry, let us wait on our ministering: or he that teacheth, on teaching; 8Or he that exhorteth, on exhortation: he that giveth, let him do it with simplicity; he that ruleth, with diligence; he that sheweth mercy, with cheerfulness."

The Attributes Of Charity

1 Corinthians 8:1 "Now as touching things offered unto idols, we know that we all have knowledge. Knowledge puffeth up, but charity edifieth."

1 Corinthians 13:4-13 "⁴Charity suffereth long, and is kind; charity envieth not; charity vaunteth not itself, is not puffed up, ⁵Doth not behave itself unseemly, seeketh not her own, is not easily provoked, thinketh no evil; ⁶Rejoiceth not in iniquity, but rejoiceth in the truth; ⁷Beareth all things, believeth all things, hopeth all things, endureth all things. ⁸Charity never faileth: but whether there be prophecies, they shall fail; whether there be tongues, they shall cease; whether there be knowledge, it shall vanish away. ⁹For we know in part, and we prophesy in part. ¹⁰But when that which is perfect is come, then that which is in part shall be done away. ¹¹When I was a child, I spake as a child, I understood as a child, I thought as a child: but when I became a man, I put away childish things. ¹²For now we see through a glass, darkly; but then face to face: now I know in part; but then shall I know even as also I am known. ¹³And now abideth faith, hope, charity, these three; but the greatest of these is charity."

1 Peter 4:7-9 "⁷But the end of all things is at hand: be ye therefore sober, and watch unto prayer. ⁸And above all things have fervent charity among yourselves: for charity shall cover the multitude of sins. ⁹Use hospitality one to another without grudging."

The Reward For Being Charitable

Deuteronomy 15:7-11 "⁷If there be among you a poor man of one of thy brethren within any of thy gates in thy land which the LORD thy God giveth thee, thou shalt not harden thine heart, nor shut thine hand from thy poor brother: ⁸But thou shalt open thine hand wide unto him, and shalt surely lend him sufficient for his need, in that which he wanteth. ⁹Beware that there be not a thought in thy wicked heart, saying, The seventh year, the year of release, is at hand; and thine eye be evil against thy poor brother, and thou givest him nought; and he cry unto the LORD against thee, and it be sin unto thee. ¹⁰Thou shalt surely give him, and thine heart shall not be grieved when thou givest unto him: because that for this thing the LORD thy God shall bless thee in all thy works, and in all that thou puttest thine hand unto. ¹¹For the poor shall never cease out of the land: therefore I command thee, saying, Thou shalt open thine hand wide unto thy brother, to thy poor, and to thy needy, in thy land."

Isaiah 58:10-11 "¹⁰And if thou draw out thy soul to the hungry, and satisfy the afflicted soul; then shall thy light rise in obscurity, and thy darkness be as the noonday: ¹¹And the LORD shall guide thee continually, and satisfy thy soul in drought, and make fat thy bones: and thou shalt be like a watered garden, and like a spring of water, whose waters fail not."

Matthew 19:21 "Jesus said unto him, If thou wilt be perfect, go and sell that thou hast, and give to the poor, and thou shalt have treasure in heaven: and come and follow me."

Luke 6:35 "But love ye your enemies, and do good, and lend, hoping for nothing again; and your reward shall be great, and ye shall be the children of the Highest: for he is kind unto the unthankful and to the evil."

Luke 14:12-14 "¹²Then said he also to him that bade him, When thou makest a dinner or a supper, call not thy friends, nor thy brethren, neither thy kinsmen, nor thy rich neighbours; lest they also bid thee again, and a recompence be made thee. ¹³But when thou makest a feast, call the poor, the maimed, the lame, the blind: ¹⁴And thou shalt be blessed; for they cannot recompense thee: for thou shalt be recompensed at the resurrection of the just."

Those That Are Charitable

Psalm 41:1 "Blessed is he that considereth the poor: the LORD will deliver him in time of trouble."

Proverbs 11:24-26 "²⁴There is that scattereth, and yet increaseth; and there is that withholdeth more than is meet, but it tendeth to poverty. ²⁵The liberal soul shall be made fat: and he that watereth shall be watered also himself. ²⁶He that withholdeth corn, the people shall curse him: but blessing shall be upon the head of him that selleth it."

Proverbs 19:17 "He that hath pity upon the poor lendeth unto the LORD; and that which he hath given will he pay him again."

Proverbs 28:27 "He that giveth unto the poor shall not lack: but he that hideth his eyes shall have many a curse."

Ezekiel 18:5-9 "⁵But if a man be just, and do that which is lawful and right, ⁶And hath not eaten upon the mountains, neither hath lifted up his eyes to the idols of the house of Israel, neither hath defiled his neighbour's wife, neither hath come near to a menstruous woman, ⁷And hath not oppressed any, but hath restored to the debtor his pledge, hath spoiled none by violence, hath given his bread to the hungry, and hath covered the naked with a garment; ⁸He that hath not given forth upon usury, neither hath taken any increase, that hath withdrawn his hand from iniquity, hath executed true judgment between man and man, ⁹Hath walked in my statutes, and hath kept my judgments, to deal truly; he is just, he shall surely live, saith the Lord GOD."

Mark 9:41 "For whosoever shall give you a cup of water to drink in my name, because ye belong to Christ, verily I say unto you, he shall not lose his reward."

2 Corinthians 9:6-7 "⁶But this I say, He which soweth sparingly shall reap also sparingly; and he which soweth bountifully shall reap also bountifully. ⁷Every man according as he purposeth in his heart, so let him give; not grudgingly, or of necessity: for God loveth a cheerful giver."

2 Peter 1:1-11 "¹Simon Peter, a servant and an apostle of Jesus Christ, to them that have obtained like precious faith with us through the righteousness of God and our Saviour Jesus Christ: ²Grace and peace be multiplied unto you through the knowledge of God, and of Jesus our Lord, ³According as his divine power hath given unto us all things that pertain unto life and godliness, through the knowledge of him that hath called us to glory and virtue: ⁴Whereby are given unto us exceeding great and precious promises: that by these ye might be partakers of the divine nature, having escaped the corruption that is in the world through lust. ⁵And beside this, giving all diligence, add to your faith virtue; and to virtue knowledge; ⁶And to knowledge temperance; and to temperance patience; and to patience godliness; ⁷And to godliness brotherly kindness; and to brotherly kindness charity. ⁸For if these things be in you, and abound, they make you that ye shall neither be barren nor unfruitful in the knowledge of our Lord Jesus Christ. ⁹But he that lacketh these things is blind, and cannot see afar off, and hath forgotten that he was purged from his old sins. ¹⁰Wherefore the rather, brethren, give diligence to make your calling and election sure: for if ye do these things, ye shall never fall: ¹¹For so an entrance shall be ministered unto you abundantly into the everlasting kingdom of our Lord and Saviour Jesus Christ."

Those That Are Not Charitable

Proverbs 28:27 "He that giveth unto the poor shall not lack: but he that hideth his eyes shall have many a curse."

2 Peter 1:1-9 "¹Simon Peter, a servant and an apostle of Jesus Christ, to them that have obtained like precious faith with us through the righteousness of God and our Saviour Jesus Christ: ²Grace and peace be multiplied unto you through the knowledge of God, and of Jesus our Lord, ³According as his divine power hath given unto us all things that pertain unto life and godliness, through the knowledge of him that hath called us to glory and virtue: ⁴Whereby are given unto us exceeding great and precious promises: that by these ye might be partakers of the divine nature, having escaped the corruption that is in the world through lust. ⁵And beside this, giving all diligence, add to your faith virtue; and to virtue knowledge; ⁶And to knowledge temperance; and to temperance patience; and to patience godliness; ⁷And to godliness brotherly kindness; and to brotherly kindness charity. ⁸For if these things be in you, and abound, they make you that ye shall neither be barren nor unfruitful in the knowledge of our Lord Jesus Christ. ⁹But he that lacketh these things is blind, and cannot see afar off, and hath forgotten that he was purged from his old sins."

1 John 3:17 "But whoso hath this world's good, and seeth his brother have need, and shutteth up his bowels of compassion from him, how dwelleth the love of God in him?"

What Charity Is

Colossians 3:14 "And above all these things put on charity, which is the bond of perfectness."

1 Timothy 1:5 "Now the end of the commandment is charity out of a pure heart, and of a good conscience, and of faith unfeigned."

Who Is Charitable

Psalm 112:5 "A good man sheweth favour, and lendeth: he will guide his affairs with discretion."

Proverbs 22:9 "He that hath a bountiful eye shall be blessed; for he giveth of his bread to the poor."

Proverbs 31:10-20 "¹⁰Who can find a virtuous woman? for her price is far above rubies. ¹¹The heart of her husband doth safely trust in her, so that he shall have no need of spoil. ¹²She will do him good and not evil all the days of her life. ¹³She seeketh wool, and flax, and worketh willingly with her hands. ¹⁴She is like the merchants' ships; she bringeth her food from afar. ¹⁵She riseth also while it is yet night, and giveth meat to her household, and a portion to her maidens. ¹⁶She considereth a field, and buyeth it: with the fruit of her hands she planteth a vineyard. ¹⁷She girdeth her loins with strength, and strengtheneth her arms. ¹⁸She perceiveth that her merchandise is good: her candle goeth not out by night. ¹⁹She layeth her hands to the spindle, and her hands hold the distaff. ²⁰She stretcheth out her hand to the poor; yea, she reacheth forth her hands to the needy."

Luke 21:1-4 "¹And he looked up, and saw the rich men casting their gifts into the treasury. ²And he saw also a certain poor widow casting in thither two mites. ³And he said, Of a truth I say unto you, that this poor widow hath cast in more than they all: ⁴For all these have of their abundance cast in unto the offerings of God: but she of her penury hath cast in all the living that she had."

CHASTISEMENT

Chastening Your Children
Proverbs 19:18 "Chasten thy son while there is hope, and let not thy soul spare for his crying."

Proverbs 23:13 "Withhold not correction from the child: for if thou beatest him with the rod, he shall not die."

Proverbs 29:17 "Correct thy son, and he shall give thee rest; yea, he shall give delight unto thy soul."

The Lord Chastening
Deuteronomy 8:5 "Thou shalt also consider in thine heart, that, as a man chasteneth his son, so the LORD thy God chasteneth thee."

Psalm 94:10-11 "¹⁰He that chastiseth the heathen, shall not he correct? he that teacheth man knowledge, shall not he know? ¹¹The LORD knoweth the thoughts of man, that they are vanity."

Psalm 118:18 "The LORD hath chastened me sore: but he hath not given me over unto death."

Jeremiah 10:24 "O LORD, correct me, but with judgment; not in thine anger, lest thou bring me to nothing."

Hebrews 12:7-10 "⁷If ye endure chastening, God dealeth with you as with sons; for what son is he whom the father chasteneth not? ⁸But if ye be without chastisement, whereof all are partakers, then are ye bastards, and not sons. ⁹Furthermore we have had fathers of our flesh which corrected us, and we gave them reverence: shall we not much rather be in subjection unto the Father of spirits, and live? ¹⁰For they verily for a few days chastened us after their own pleasure; but he for our profit, that we might be partakers of his holiness."

The Reward For Correcting Your Child
Proverbs 23:13-14 "¹³Withhold not correction from the child: for if thou beatest him with the rod, he shall not die. ¹⁴Thou shalt beat him with the rod, and shalt deliver his soul from hell."

Proverbs 29:17 "Correct thy son, and he shall give thee rest; yea, he shall give delight unto thy soul."

The Reward For Enduring The Chastening Of The Lord
Hebrews 12:7 "If ye endure chastening, God dealeth with you as with sons; for what son is he whom the father chasteneth not?"

The Reward For Not Receiving Correction
Zephaniah 3:1-2 "¹Woe to her that is filthy and polluted, to the oppressing city! ²She obeyed not the voice; she received not correction; she trusted not in the LORD; she drew not near to her God."

Those That Spare Their Rod
Proverbs 13:24 "He that spareth his rod hateth his son: but he that loveth him chasteneth him betimes."

Those Whom The Lord Chastens
Job 5:17 "Behold, happy is the man whom God correcteth: therefore despise not thou the chastening of the Almighty."

Psalm 94:12 "Blessed is the man whom thou chastenest, O LORD, and teachest him out of thy law."

What Chastening Does

Proverbs 20:30 "The blueness of a wound cleanseth away evil: so do stripes the inward parts of the belly."

Proverbs 22:15 "Foolishness is bound in the heart of a child; but the rod of correction shall drive it far from him."

Proverbs 29:15 "The rod and reproof give wisdom: but a child left to himself bringeth his mother to shame."

Hebrews 12:11 "Now no chastening for the present seemeth to be joyous, but grievous: nevertheless afterward it yieldeth the peaceable fruit of righteousness unto them which are exercised thereby."

Who Chastening Is For

Proverbs 10:13 "In the lips of him that hath understanding wisdom is found: but a rod is for the back of him that is void of understanding."

Proverbs 19:29 "Judgments are prepared for scorners, and stripes for the back of fools."

Proverbs 26:3 "A whip for the horse, a bridle for the ass, and a rod for the fool's back."

Who Chastens Their Children

Proverbs 13:24 "He that spareth his rod hateth his son: but he that loveth him chasteneth him betimes."

Who Correction Is Grievous To

Proverbs 15:10 "Correction is grievous unto him that forsaketh the way: and he that hateth reproof shall die."

Who The Lord Chastens

Leviticus 26:13-28 "[13]I am the LORD your God, which brought you forth out of the land of Egypt, that ye should not be their bondmen; and I have broken the bands of your yoke, and made you go upright. [14]But if ye will not hearken unto me, and will not do all these commandments; [15]And if ye shall despise my statutes, or if your soul abhor my judgments, so that ye will not do all my commandments, but that ye break my covenant: [16]I also will do this unto you; I will even appoint over you terror, consumption, and the burning ague, that shall consume the eyes, and cause sorrow of heart: and ye shall sow your seed in vain, for your enemies shall eat it. [17]And I will set my face against you, and ye shall be slain before your enemies: they that hate you shall reign over you; and ye shall flee when none pursueth you. [18]And if ye will not yet for all this hearken unto me, then I will punish you seven times more for your sins. [19]And I will break the pride of your power; and I will make your heaven as iron, and your earth as brass: [20]And your strength shall be spent in vain: for your land shall not yield her increase, neither shall the trees of the land yield their fruits. [21]And if ye walk contrary unto me, and will not hearken unto me; I will bring seven times more plagues upon you according to your sins. [22]I will also send wild beasts among you, which shall rob you of your children, and destroy your cattle, and make you few in number; and your highways shall be desolate. [23]And if ye will not be reformed by me by these things, but will walk contrary unto me; [24]Then will I also walk contrary unto you, and will punish you yet seven times for your sins. [25]And I will bring a sword upon you, that shall avenge the quarrel of my covenant: and when ye are gathered together within your cities, I will send the pestilence among you; and ye shall be delivered into the hand of the enemy. [26]And when I have broken the staff of your bread, ten women shall bake your bread in one oven, and they shall deliver you your bread again by weight: and ye shall eat, and not be satisfied. [27]And if ye will not for all this hearken unto me, but walk contrary unto me; [28]Then I will walk contrary unto you also in fury; and I, even I, will chastise you seven times for your sins."

Proverbs 3:11-12 "[11]My son, despise not the chastening of the LORD; neither be weary of his correction: [12]For whom the LORD loveth he correcteth; even as a father the son in whom he delighteth."

Hebrews 12:5-6 "[5]And ye have forgotten the exhortation which speaketh unto you as unto children, My son, despise not thou the chastening of the Lord, nor faint when thou art rebuked of him: [6]For whom the Lord loveth he chasteneth, and scourgeth every son whom he receiveth."

Revelation 3:14-21 "[14]And unto the angel of the church of the Laodiceans write; These things saith the Amen, the faithful and true witness, the beginning of the creation of God; [15]I know thy works, that thou art neither cold nor hot: I would thou wert cold or hot. [16]So then because thou art lukewarm, and neither cold nor hot, I will spue thee out of my mouth. [17]Because thou sayest, I am rich, and increased with goods, and have need of nothing; and knowest not that thou art wretched, and miserable, and poor, and blind, and naked: [18]I counsel thee to buy of me gold tried in the fire, that thou mayest be rich; and white raiment, that thou mayest be clothed, and that the shame of thy nakedness do not appear; and anoint thine eyes with eyesalve, that thou mayest see. [19]As many as I love, I rebuke and chasten: be zealous therefore, and repent. [20]Behold, I stand at the door, and knock: if any man hear my voice, and open the door, I will come in to him, and will sup with him, and he with me. [21]To him that overcometh will I grant to sit with me in my throne, even as I also overcame, and am set down with my Father in his throne."

Why The Lord Chastens People
1 Corinthians 11:31-32 "[31]For if we would judge ourselves, we should not be judged. [32]But when we are judged, we are chastened of the Lord, that we should not be condemned with the world."

Hebrews 12:7-10 "[7]If ye endure chastening, God dealeth with you as with sons; for what son is he whom the father chasteneth not? [8]But if ye be without chastisement, whereof all are partakers, then are ye bastards, and not sons. [9]Furthermore we have had fathers of our flesh which corrected us, and we gave them reverence: shall we not much rather be in subjection unto the Father of spirits, and live? [10]For they verily for a few days chastened us after their own pleasure; but he for our profit, that we might be partakers of his holiness."

CHILDREN

Children Left To Themselves
Proverbs 29:15 "The rod and reproof give wisdom: but a child left to himself bringeth his mother to shame."

Children That Cause Shame
Proverbs 17:2 "A wise servant shall have rule over a son that causeth shame, and shall have part of the inheritance among the brethren."

Foolish Children
Proverbs 10:1 "The proverbs of Solomon. A wise son maketh a glad father: but a foolish son is the heaviness of his mother."

Proverbs 15:20 "A wise son maketh a glad father: but a foolish man despiseth his mother."

Proverbs 17:25 "A foolish son is a grief to his father, and bitterness to her that bare him."

Proverbs 19:13 "A foolish son is the calamity of his father: and the contentions of a wife are a continual dropping."

Rebellious Children
Ecclesiastes 11:9 "Rejoice, O young man, in thy youth; and let thy heart cheer thee in the days of thy youth, and walk in the ways of thine heart, and in the sight of thine eyes: but know thou, that for all these things God will bring thee into judgment."

Isaiah 30:1 "Woe to the rebellious children, saith the LORD, that take counsel, but not of me; and that cover with a covering, but not of my spirit, that they may add sin to sin."

Strange Children
Psalm 144:7-11 "[7]Send thine hand from above; rid me, and deliver me out of great waters, from the hand of strange children; [8]Whose mouth speaketh vanity, and their right hand is a right hand of falsehood. [9]I will sing a new song unto thee, O God: upon a psaltery and an instrument of ten strings will I sing praises unto thee. [10]It is he that giveth salvation unto kings: who delivereth David his servant from the hurtful sword. [11]Rid me, and deliver me from the hand of strange children, whose mouth speaketh vanity, and their right hand is a right hand of falsehood."

The Children Of The Lord
Proverbs 14:26 "In the fear of the LORD is strong confidence: and his children shall have a place of refuge."

1 John 3:9-10 "[9]Whosoever is born of God doth not commit sin; for his seed remaineth in him: and he cannot sin, because he is born of God. [10]In this the children of God are manifest, and the children of the devil: whosoever doeth not righteousness is not of God, neither he that loveth not his brother."

The Glory Of Children
Proverbs 17:6 "Children's children are the crown of old men; and the glory of children are their fathers."

What Childhood And Youth Are
Ecclesiastes 11:9-10 "⁹Rejoice, O young man, in thy youth; and let thy heart cheer thee in the days of thy youth, and walk in the ways of thine heart, and in the sight of thine eyes: but know thou, that for all these things God will bring thee into judgment. ¹⁰Therefore remove sorrow from thy heart, and put away evil from thy flesh: for childhood and youth are vanity."

What Children Are
Psalm 127:3-4 "³Lo, children are an heritage of the LORD: and the fruit of the womb is his reward. ⁴As arrows are in the hand of a mighty man; so are children of the youth."

What Children Should Do
Proverbs 6:20-21 "²⁰My son, keep thy father's commandment, and forsake not the law of thy mother: ²¹Bind them continually upon thine heart, and tie them about thy neck."

Proverbs 23:22 "Hearken unto thy father that begat thee, and despise not thy mother when she is old."

Ephesians 6:1 "Children, obey your parents in the Lord: for this is right."

Colossians 3:20 "Children, obey your parents in all things: for this is well pleasing unto the Lord."

What Is Bound In The Heart Of A Child
Proverbs 22:15 "Foolishness is bound in the heart of a child; but the rod of correction shall drive it far from him."

Who Are The Children Of God
Matthew 5:9 "Blessed are the peacemakers: for they shall be called the children of God."

Matthew 5:44-45 "⁴⁴But I say unto you, Love your enemies, bless them that curse you, do good to them that hate you, and pray for them which despitefully use you, and persecute you; ⁴⁵That ye may be the children of your Father which is in heaven: for he maketh his sun to rise on the evil and on the good, and sendeth rain on the just and on the unjust."

Luke 6:35 "But love ye your enemies, and do good, and lend, hoping for nothing again; and your reward shall be great, and ye shall be the children of the Highest: for he is kind unto the unthankful and to the evil."

Acts 17:23-29 "²³For as I passed by, and beheld your devotions, I found an altar with this inscription, TO THE UNKNOWN GOD. Whom therefore ye ignorantly worship, him declare I unto you. ²⁴God that made the world and all things therein, seeing that he is Lord of heaven and earth, dwelleth not in temples made with hands; ²⁵Neither is worshipped with men's hands, as though he needed any thing, seeing he giveth to all life, and breath, and all things; ²⁶And hath made of one blood all nations of men for to dwell on all the face of the earth, and hath determined the times before appointed, and the bounds of their habitation; ²⁷That they should seek the Lord, if haply they might feel after him, and find him, though he be not far from every one of us: ²⁸For in him we live, and move, and have our being; as certain also of your own poets have said, For we are also his offspring. ²⁹Forasmuch then as we are the offspring of God, we ought not to think that the Godhead is like unto gold, or silver, or stone, graven by art and man's device."

Romans 8:14-17 "¹⁴For as many as are led by the Spirit of God, they are the sons of God. ¹⁵For ye have not received the spirit of bondage again to fear; but ye have received the Spirit of adoption, whereby we cry, Abba, Father. ¹⁶The Spirit itself beareth witness with our spirit, that we are the children of God: ¹⁷And if children, then heirs; heirs of God, and joint-heirs with Christ; if so be that we suffer with him, that we may be also glorified together."

Romans 9:20-26 "²⁰Nay but, O man, who art thou that repliest against God? Shall the thing formed say to him that formed it, Why hast thou made me thus? ²¹Hath not the potter power over the clay, of the same lump to make one vessel unto honour, and another unto dishonour? ²²What if God, willing to shew his wrath, and to make his power known, endured with much longsuffering the vessels of wrath fitted to destruction: ²³And that he might make known the riches of his glory on the vessels of mercy, which he had afore prepared unto glory, ²⁴Even us, whom he hath called, not of the Jews only, but also of the Gentiles? ²⁵As he saith also in Osee, I will call them my people, which were not my people; and her beloved, which was not beloved. [26]And it shall come to pass, that in the place where it was said unto them, Ye are not my people; there shall they be called the children of the living God."

2 Corinthians 6:14-18 "[14]Be ye not unequally yoked together with unbelievers: for what fellowship hath righteousness with unrighteousness? and what communion hath light with darkness? [15]And what concord hath Christ with Belial? or what part hath he that believeth with an infidel? [16]And what agreement hath the temple of God with idols? for ye are the temple of the living God; as God hath said, I will dwell in them, and walk in them; and I will be their God, and they shall be my people. [17]Wherefore come out from among them, and be ye separate, saith the Lord, and touch not the unclean thing; and I will receive you, [18]And will be a Father unto you, and ye shall be my sons and daughters, saith the Lord Almighty."

Philippians 2:14-15 "[14]Do all things without murmurings and disputings: [15]That ye may be blameless and harmless, the sons of God, without rebuke, in the midst of a crooked and perverse nation, among whom ye shine as lights in the world."

1 John 3:1-2 "[1]Behold, what manner of love the Father hath bestowed upon us, that we should be called the sons of God: therefore the world knoweth us not, because it knew him not. [2]Beloved, now are we the sons of God, and it doth not yet appear what we shall be: but we know that, when he shall appear, we shall be like him; for we shall see him as he is."

Revelation 21:7 "He that overcometh shall inherit all things; and I will be his God, and he shall be my son."

Who Is A Child That Causes Shame
Proverbs 10:5 "He that gathereth in summer is a wise son: but he that sleepeth in harvest is a son that causeth shame."

Proverbs 19:26 "He that wasteth his father, and chaseth away his mother, is a son that causeth shame, and bringeth reproach."

Proverbs 28:7 "Whoso keepeth the law is a wise son: but he that is a companion of riotous men shameth his father."

Who Is A Wise Child
Proverbs 10:5 "He that gathereth in summer is a wise son: but he that sleepeth in harvest is a son that causeth shame."

Proverbs 28:7 "Whoso keepeth the law is a wise son: but he that is a companion of riotous men shameth his father."

Wise Children
Proverbs 10:1 "The proverbs of Solomon. A wise son maketh a glad father: but a foolish son is the heaviness of his mother."

Proverbs 13:1 "A wise son heareth his father's instruction: but a scorner heareth not rebuke."

Proverbs 15:20 "A wise son maketh a glad father: but a foolish man despiseth his mother."

Proverbs 29:3 "Whoso loveth wisdom rejoiceth his father: but he that keepeth company with harlots spendeth his substance."

Ecclesiastes 4:13-14 "[13]Better is a poor and a wise child than an old and foolish king, who will no more be admonished. [14]For out of prison he cometh to reign; whereas also he that is born in his kingdom becometh poor."

CHOOSING/CHOSEN

Few Being Chosen
Matthew 20:16 "So the last shall be first, and the first last: for many be called, but few chosen."

Matthew 22:14 "For many are called, but few are chosen."

The Reward For Choosing Life
Deuteronomy 30:15-20 "[15]See, I have set before thee this day life and good, and death and evil; [16]In that I command thee this day to love the LORD thy God, to walk in his ways, and to keep his commandments and his statutes and his judgments, that thou mayest live and multiply: and the LORD thy God shall bless thee in the land whither thou goest to possess it. [17]But if thine heart turn away, so that thou wilt not hear, but shalt be drawn away, and worship other gods, and serve them; [18]I denounce unto you this day, that ye shall surely perish, and that ye shall not prolong your days upon the land, whither thou

passest over Jordan to go to possess it. [19]I call heaven and earth to record this day against you, that I have set before you life and death, blessing and cursing: therefore choose life, that both thou and thy seed may live: [20]That thou mayest love the LORD thy God, and that thou mayest obey his voice, and that thou mayest cleave unto him: for he is thy life, and the length of thy days: that thou mayest dwell in the land which the LORD sware unto thy fathers, to Abraham, to Isaac, and to Jacob, to give them."

Those That Are Chosen Of The Lord

Psalm 33:12 "Blessed is the nation whose God is the LORD: and the people whom he hath chosen for his own inheritance."

Psalm 65:1-4 "[1]Praise waiteth for thee, O God, in Sion: and unto thee shall the vow be performed. [2]O thou that hearest prayer, unto thee shall all flesh come. [3]Iniquities prevail against me: as for our transgressions, thou shalt purge them away. [4]Blessed is the man whom thou choosest, and causest to approach unto thee, that he may dwell in thy courts: we shall be satisfied with the goodness of thy house, even of thy holy temple."

John 13:13-18 "[13]Ye call me Master and Lord: and ye say well; for so I am. [14]If I then, your Lord and Master, have washed your feet; ye also ought to wash one another's feet. [15]For I have given you an example, that ye should do as I have done to you. [16]Verily, verily, I say unto you, The servant is not greater than his lord; neither he that is sent greater than he that sent him. [17]If ye know these things, happy are ye if ye do them. [18]I speak not of you all: I know whom I have chosen: but that the scripture may be fulfilled, He that eateth bread with me hath lifted up his heel against me."

What The Lord Has Chosen

Deuteronomy 12:11 "Then there shall be a place which the LORD your God shall choose to cause his name to dwell there; thither shall ye bring all that I command you; your burnt offerings, and your sacrifices, your tithes, and the heave offering of your hand, and all your choice vows which ye vow unto the LORD."

I Kings 8:38-48 "[38]What prayer and supplication soever be made by any man, or by all thy people Israel, which shall know every man the plague of his own heart, and spread forth his hands toward this house: [39]Then hear thou in heaven thy dwelling place, and forgive, and do, and give to every man according to his ways, whose heart thou knowest; (for thou, even thou only, knowest the hearts of all the children of men;) [40]That they may fear thee all the days that they live in the land which thou gavest unto our fathers. [41]Moreover concerning a stranger, that is not of thy people Israel, but cometh out of a far country for thy name's sake; [42](For they shall hear of thy great name, and of thy strong hand, and of thy stretched out arm;) when he shall come and pray toward this house; [43]Hear thou in heaven thy dwelling place, and do according to all that the stranger calleth to thee for: that all people of the earth may know thy name, to fear thee, as do thy people Israel; and that they may know that this house, which I have builded, is called by thy name. [44]If thy people go out to battle against their enemy, whithersoever thou shalt send them, and shall pray unto the LORD toward the city which thou hast chosen, and toward the house that I have built for thy name: [45]Then hear thou in heaven their prayer and their supplication, and maintain their cause. [46]If they sin against thee, (for there is no man that sinneth not,) and thou be angry with them, and deliver them to the enemy, so that they carry them away captives unto the land of the enemy, far or near; [47]Yet if they shall bethink themselves in the land whither they were carried captives, and repent, and make supplication unto thee in the land of them that carried them captives, saying, We have sinned, and have done perversely, we have committed wickedness; [48]And so return unto thee with all their heart, and with all their soul, in the land of their enemies, which led them away captive, and pray unto thee toward their land, which thou gavest unto their fathers, the city which thou hast chosen, and the house which I have built for thy name."

I Kings 11:31-36 "[31]And he said to Jeroboam, Take thee ten pieces: for thus saith the LORD, the God of Israel, Behold, I will rend the kingdom out of the hand of Solomon, and will give ten tribes to thee: [32](But he shall have one tribe for my servant David's sake, and for Jerusalem's sake, the city which I have chosen out of all the tribes of Israel:) [33]Because that they have forsaken me, and have worshipped Ashtoreth the goddess of the Zidonians, Chemosh the god of the Moabites, and Milcom the god of the children of Ammon, and have not walked in my ways, to do that which is right in mine eyes, and to keep my statutes and my judgments, as did David his father. 34Howbeit I will not take the whole kingdom out of his hand: but I will make him prince all the days of his life for David my servant's sake, whom I chose, because he kept my commandments and my statutes: 35But I will take the kingdom out of his son's hand, and will give it unto thee, even ten tribes. 36And unto his son will I give one tribe, that David my servant may have a light alway before me in Jerusalem, the city which I have chosen me to put my name there."

2 Kings 21:7 "And he set a graven image of the grove that he had made in the house, of which the LORD said to David, and to Solomon his son, In this house, and in Jerusalem, which I have chosen out of all tribes of Israel, will I put my name for ever."

2 Chronicles 6:19-40 "19Have respect therefore to the prayer of thy servant, and to his supplication, O LORD my God, to hearken unto the cry and the prayer which thy servant prayeth before thee: 20That thine eyes may be open upon this house day and night, upon the place whereof thou hast said that thou wouldest put thy name there; to hearken unto the prayer which thy servant prayeth toward this place. 21Hearken therefore unto the supplications of thy servant, and of thy people Israel, which they shall make toward this place: hear thou from thy dwelling place, even from heaven; and when thou hearest, forgive. 22If a man sin against his neighbour, and an oath be laid upon him to make him swear, and the oath come before thine altar in this house; 23Then hear thou from heaven, and do, and judge thy servants, by requiting the wicked, by recompensing his way upon his own head; and by justifying the righteous, by giving him according to his righteousness. 24And if thy people Israel be put to the worse before the enemy, because they have sinned against thee; and shall return and confess thy name, and pray and make supplication before thee in this house; 25Then hear thou from the heavens, and forgive the sin of thy people Israel, and bring them again unto the land which thou gavest to them and to their fathers. 26When the heaven is shut up, and there is no rain, because they have sinned against thee; yet if they pray toward this place, and confess thy name, and turn from their sin, when thou dost afflict them; 27Then hear thou from heaven, and forgive the sin of thy servants, and of thy people Israel, when thou hast taught them the good way, wherein they should walk; and send rain upon thy land, which thou hast given unto thy people for an inheritance. 28If there be dearth in the land, if there be pestilence, if there be blasting, or mildew, locusts, or caterpillers; if their enemies besiege them in the cities of their land; whatsoever sore or whatsoever sickness there be: 29Then what prayer or what supplication soever shall be made of any man, or of all thy people Israel, when every one shall know his own sore and his own grief, and shall spread forth his hands in this house: 30Then hear thou from heaven thy dwelling place, and forgive, and render unto every man according unto all his ways, whose heart thou knowest; (for thou only knowest the hearts of the children of men:) 31That they may fear thee, to walk in thy ways, so long as they live in the land which thou gavest unto our fathers. 32Moreover concerning the stranger, which is not of thy people Israel, but is come from a far country for thy great name's sake, and thy mighty hand, and thy stretched out arm; if they come and pray in this house; 33Then hear thou from the heavens, even from thy dwelling place, and do according to all that the stranger calleth to thee for; that all people of the earth may know thy name, and fear thee, as doth thy people Israel, and may know that this house which I have built is called by thy name. 34If thy people go out to war against their enemies by the way that thou shalt send them, and they pray unto thee toward this city which thou hast chosen, and the house which I have built for thy name; 35Then hear thou from the heavens their prayer and their supplication, and maintain their cause. 36If they sin against thee, (for there is no man which sinneth not,) and thou be angry with them, and deliver them over before their enemies, and they carry them away captives unto a land far off or near; 37Yet if they bethink themselves in the land whither they are carried captive, and turn and pray unto thee in the land of their captivity, saying, We have sinned, we have done amiss, and have dealt wickedly; 38If they return to thee with all their heart and with all their soul in the land of their captivity, whither they have carried them captives, and pray toward their land, which thou gavest unto their fathers, and toward the city which thou hast chosen, and toward the house which I have built for thy name: [39]Then hear thou from the heavens, even from thy dwelling place, their prayer and their supplications, and maintain their cause, and forgive thy people which have sinned against thee. [40]Now, my God, let, I beseech thee, thine eyes be open, and let thine ears be attent unto the prayer that is made in this place."

2 Chronicles 7:11-12 "[11]Thus Solomon finished the house of the LORD, and the king's house: and all that came into Solomon's heart to make in the house of the LORD, and in his own house, he prosperously effected. [12]And the LORD appeared to Solomon by night, and said unto him, I have heard thy prayer, and have chosen this place to myself for an house of sacrifice."

2 Chronicles 33:7 "And he set a carved image, the idol which he had made, in the house of God, of which God had said to David and to Solomon his son, In this house, and in Jerusalem, which I have chosen before all the tribes of Israel, will I put my name for ever."

Nehemiah 1:2-9 "[2]That Hanani, one of my brethren, came, he and certain men of Judah; and I asked them concerning the Jews that had escaped, which were left of the captivity, and concerning Jerusalem. [3]And they said unto me, The remnant that are left of the captivity there in the province are in great affliction and reproach: the wall of Jerusalem also is broken down, and the gates thereof are burned with fire. [4]And it came to pass, when I heard these words, that I sat down and wept, and mourned certain days, and fasted, and prayed before the God of heaven, [5]And said, I beseech thee, O LORD God of heaven, the great and terrible God, that keepeth covenant and mercy for them that love him and observe his commandments: [6]Let thine ear now be attentive, and thine eyes open, that thou mayest hear the prayer of thy servant, which I pray before thee now, day and night, for the children of Israel thy servants, and confess the sins of the children of Israel, which we have sinned against thee: both I and my father's house have sinned. [7]We have dealt very corruptly against thee, and have not kept the commandments, nor the statutes, nor the judgments, which

thou commandedst thy servant Moses. [8]Remember, I beseech thee, the word that thou commandedst thy servant Moses, saying, If ye transgress, I will scatter you abroad among the nations: [9]But if ye turn unto me, and keep my commandments, and do them; though there were of you cast out unto the uttermost part of the heaven, yet will I gather them from thence, and will bring them unto the place that I have chosen to set my name there."

Psalm 132:13-15 "[13]For the LORD hath chosen Zion; he hath desired it for his habitation. [14]This is my rest for ever: here will I dwell; for I have desired it. [15]I will abundantly bless her provision: I will satisfy her poor with bread."

Zechariah 2:10-13 "[10]Sing and rejoice, O daughter of Zion: for, lo, I come, and I will dwell in the midst of thee, saith the LORD. [11]And many nations shall be joined to the LORD in that day, and shall be my people: and I will dwell in the midst of thee, and thou shalt know that the LORD of hosts hath sent me unto thee. [12]And the LORD shall inherit Judah his portion in the holy land, and shall choose Jerusalem again. [13]Be silent, O all flesh, before the LORD: for he is raised up out of his holy habitation."

1 Corinthians 1:27-28 "[27]But God hath chosen the foolish things of the world to confound the wise; and God hath chosen the weak things of the world to confound the things which are mighty; [28]And base things of the world, and things which are despised, hath God chosen, yea, and things which are not, to bring to nought things that are."

Who The Lord Has Chosen
Deuteronomy 4:35-38 "[35]Unto thee it was shewed, that thou mightest know that the LORD he is God; there is none else beside him. [36]Out of heaven he made thee to hear his voice, that he might instruct thee: and upon earth he shewed thee his great fire; and thou heardest his words out of the midst of the fire. [37]And because he loved thy fathers, therefore he chose their seed after them, and brought thee out in his sight with his mighty power out of Egypt; [38]To drive out nations from before thee greater and mightier than thou art, to bring thee in, to give thee their land for an inheritance, as it is this day."

Deuteronomy 7:6-8 "[6]For thou art an holy people unto the LORD thy God: the LORD thy God hath chosen thee to be a special people unto himself, above all people that are upon the face of the earth. [7]The LORD did not set his love upon you, nor choose you, because ye were more in number than any people; for ye were the fewest of all people: [8]But because the LORD loved you, and because he would keep the oath which he had sworn unto your fathers, hath the LORD brought you out with a mighty hand, and redeemed you out of the house of bondmen, from the hand of Pharaoh king of Egypt."

I Kings 11:31-34 "[31]And he said to Jeroboam, Take thee ten pieces: for thus saith the LORD, the God of Israel, Behold, I will rend the kingdom out of the hand of Solomon, and will give ten tribes to thee: [32](But he shall have one tribe for my servant David's sake, and for Jerusalem's sake, the city which I have chosen out of all the tribes of Israel:) [33]Because that they have forsaken me, and have worshipped Ashtoreth the goddess of the Zidonians, Chemosh the god of the Moabites, and Milcom the god of the children of Ammon, and have not walked in my ways, to do that which is right in mine eyes, and to keep my statutes and my judgments, as did David his father. [34]Howbeit I will not take the whole kingdom out of his hand: but I will make him prince all the days of his life for David my servant's sake, whom I chose, because he kept my commandments and my statutes."

1 Chronicles 16:11-13 "[11]Seek the LORD and his strength, seek his face continually. [12]Remember his marvellous works that he hath done, his wonders, and the judgments of his mouth; [13]O ye seed of Israel his servant, ye children of Jacob, his chosen ones."

1 Chronicles 28:2-7 "[2]Then David the king stood up upon his feet, and said, Hear me, my brethren, and my people: As for me, I had in mine heart to build an house of rest for the ark of the covenant of the LORD, and for the footstool of our God, and had made ready for the building: [3]But God said unto me, Thou shalt not build an house for my name, because thou hast been a man of war, and hast shed blood. [4]Howbeit the LORD God of Israel chose me before all the house of my father to be king over Israel for ever: for he hath chosen Judah to be the ruler; and of the house of Judah, the house of my father; and among the sons of my father he liked me to make me king over all

Israel: [5]And of all my sons, (for the LORD hath given me many sons,) he hath chosen Solomon my son to sit upon the throne of the kingdom of the LORD over Israel. [6]And he said unto me, Solomon thy son, he shall build my house and my courts: for I have chosen him to be my son, and I will be his father. [7]Moreover I will establish his kingdom for ever, if he be constant to do my commandments and my judgments, as at this day."

Nehemiah 9:7-8 "[7]Thou art the LORD the God, who didst choose Abram, and broughtest him forth out of Ur of the Chaldees, and gavest him the name of Abraham; [8]And foundest his heart faithful before thee, and madest a covenant with him to give the land of the Canaanites, the Hittites, the Amorites, and the Perizzites, and the Jebusites, and the Girgashites, to give it, I say, to his seed, and hast performed thy words; for thou art righteous."

Psalm 105:4-6 "[4]Seek the LORD, and his strength: seek his face evermore. [5]Remember his marvellous works that he hath done; his wonders, and the judgments of his mouth; [6]O ye seed of Abraham his servant, ye children of Jacob his chosen."

Isaiah 14:1 "For the LORD will have mercy on Jacob, and will yet choose Israel, and set them in their own land: and the strangers shall be joined with them, and they shall cleave to the house of Jacob."

Isaiah 41:8-10 "[8]But thou, Israel, art my servant, Jacob whom I have chosen, the seed of Abraham my friend. [9]Thou whom I have taken from the ends of the earth, and called thee from the chief men thereof, and said unto thee, Thou art my servant; I have chosen thee, and not cast thee away. [10]Fear thou not; for I am with thee: be not dismayed; for I am thy God: I will strengthen thee; yea, I will help thee; yea, I will uphold thee with the right hand of my righteousness."

Isaiah 43:3-10 "[3]For I am the LORD thy God, the Holy One of Israel, thy Saviour: I gave Egypt for thy ransom, Ethiopia and Seba for thee. [4]Since thou wast precious in my sight, thou hast been honourable, and I have loved thee: therefore will I give men for thee, and people for thy life. [5]Fear not: for I am with thee: I will bring thy seed from the east, and gather thee from the west; [6]I will say to the north, Give up; and to the south, Keep not back: bring my sons from far, and my daughters from the ends of the earth; ⁷Even every one that is called by my name: for I have created him for my glory, I have formed him; yea, I have made him. ⁸Bring forth the blind people that have eyes, and the deaf that have ears. ⁹Let all the nations be gathered together, and let the people be assembled: who among them can declare this, and shew us former things? let them bring forth their witnesses, that they may be justified: or let them hear, and say, It is truth. ¹⁰Ye are my witnesses, saith the LORD, and my servant whom I have chosen: that ye may know and believe me, and understand that I am he: before me there was no God formed, neither shall there be after me."

Isaiah 43:16-21 "¹⁶Thus saith the LORD, which maketh a way in the sea, and a path in the mighty waters; ¹⁷Which bringeth forth the chariot and horse, the army and the power; they shall lie down together, they shall not rise: they are extinct, they are quenched as tow. ¹⁸Remember ye not the former things, neither consider the things of old. ¹⁹Behold, I will do a new thing; now it shall spring forth; shall ye not know it? I will even make a way in the wilderness, and rivers in the desert. ²⁰The beast of the field shall honour me, the dragons and the owls: because I give waters in the wilderness, and rivers in the desert, to give drink to my people, my chosen. ²¹This people have I formed for myself; they shall shew forth my praise."

Isaiah 44:1-2 "¹Yet now hear, O Jacob my servant; and Israel, whom I have chosen: ²Thus saith the LORD that made thee, and formed thee from the womb, which will help thee; Fear not, O Jacob, my servant; and thou, Jesurun, whom I have chosen."

Isaiah 49:7 "Thus saith the LORD, the Redeemer of Israel, and his Holy One, to him whom man despiseth, to him whom the nation abhorreth, to a servant of rulers, Kings shall see and arise, princes also shall worship, because of the LORD that is faithful, and the Holy One of Israel, and he shall choose thee."

Jeremiah 1:1-5 "¹The words of Jeremiah the son of Hilkiah, of the priests that were in Anathoth in the land of Benjamin: ²To whom the word of the LORD came in the days of Josiah the son of Amon king of Judah, in the thirteenth year of his reign. ³It came also in the days of Jehoiakim the son of Josiah king of Judah, unto the end of the eleventh year of Zedekiah the son of Josiah king of Judah, unto the carrying away of Jerusalem captive in the fifth month. ⁴Then the word of the LORD came unto me, saying, ⁵Before I formed thee in the belly I knew thee; and before thou camest forth out of the womb I sanctified thee, and I ordained thee a prophet unto the nations."

John 6:70 "Jesus answered them, Have not I chosen you twelve, and one of you is a devil?"

John 15:1-19 "¹I am the true vine, and my Father is the husbandman. ²Every branch in me that beareth not fruit he taketh away: and every branch that beareth fruit, he purgeth it, that it may bring forth more fruit. ³Now ye are clean through the word which I have spoken unto you. ⁴Abide in me, and I in you. As the branch cannot bear fruit of itself, except it abide in the vine; no more can ye, except ye abide in me. ⁵I am the vine, ye are the branches: He that abideth in me, and I in him, the same bringeth forth much fruit: for without me ye can do nothing. ⁶If a man abide not in me, he is cast forth as a branch, and is withered; and men gather them, and cast them into the fire, and they are burned. ⁷If ye abide in me, and my words abide in you, ye shall ask what ye will, and it shall be done unto you. ⁸Herein is my Father glorified, that ye bear much fruit; so shall ye be my disciples. ⁹As the Father hath loved me, so have I loved you: continue ye in my love. ¹⁰If ye keep my commandments, ye shall abide in my love; even as I have kept my Father's commandments, and abide in his love. ¹¹These things have I spoken unto you, that my joy might remain in you, and that your joy might be full. ¹²This is my commandment, That ye love one another, as I have loved you. ¹³Greater love hath no man than this, that a man lay down his life for his friends. ¹⁴Ye are my friends, if ye do whatsoever I command you. ¹⁵Henceforth I call you not servants; for the servant knoweth not what his lord doeth: but I have called you friends; for all things that I have heard of my Father I have made known unto you. ¹⁶Ye have not chosen me, but I have chosen you, and ordained you, that ye should go and bring forth fruit, and that your fruit should remain: that whatsoever ye shall ask of the Father in my name, he may give it you.

¹⁷These things I command you, that ye love one another. ¹⁸If the world hate you, ye know that it hated me before it hated you. ¹⁹If ye were of the world, the world would love his own: but because ye are not of the world, but I have chosen you out of the world, therefore the world hateth you."

Acts 1:1-2 "¹The former treatise have I made, O Theophilus, of all that Jesus began both to do and teach, ²Until the day in which he was taken up, after that he through the Holy Ghost had given commandments unto the apostles whom he had chosen."

Acts 9:11-15 "¹¹And the Lord said unto him, Arise, and go into the street which is called Straight, and inquire in the house of Judas for one called Saul, of Tarsus: for, behold, he prayeth, ¹²And hath seen in a vision a man named Ananias coming in, and putting his hand on him, that he might receive his sight. ¹³Then Ananias answered, Lord, I have heard by many of this man, how much evil he hath done to thy saints at Jerusalem: ¹⁴And here he hath authority from the chief priests to bind all that call on thy name. ¹⁵But the Lord said unto him, Go thy way: for he is a chosen vessel unto me, to bear my name before the Gentiles, and kings, and the children of Israel."

Acts 10:37-41 "³⁷That word, I say, ye know, which was published throughout all Judaea, and began from Galilee, after the baptism which John preached; ³⁸How God anointed Jesus of Nazareth with the Holy Ghost and with power: who went about doing good, and healing all that were oppressed of the devil; for God was with him. ³⁹And we are witnesses of all things which he did both in the land of the Jews, and in Jerusalem; whom they slew and hanged on a tree: ⁴⁰Him God raised up the third day, and shewed him openly; ⁴¹Not to all the people, but unto witnesses chosen before of God, even to us, who did eat and drink with him after he rose from the dead."

Ephesians 1:3-5 "³Blessed be the God and Father of our Lord Jesus Christ, who hath blessed us with all spiritual blessings in heavenly places in Christ: ⁴According as he hath chosen us in him before the foundation of the world, that we should be holy and without blame before him in love: ⁵Having predestinated us unto the adoption of children by Jesus Christ to himself, according to the good pleasure of his will."

James 2:5 "Hearken, my beloved brethren, Hath not God chosen the poor of this world rich in faith, and heirs of the kingdom which he hath promised to them that love him?"

1 Peter 2:4-10 "⁴To whom coming, as unto a living stone, disallowed indeed of men, but chosen of God, and precious, ⁵Ye also, as lively stones, are built up a spiritual house, an holy priesthood, to offer up spiritual sacrifices, acceptable to God by Jesus Christ. ⁶Wherefore also it is contained in the scripture, Behold, I lay in Sion a chief corner stone, elect, precious: and he that believeth on him shall not be confounded. ⁷Unto you therefore which believe he is precious: but unto them which be disobedient, the stone which the builders disallowed, the same is made the head of the corner, ⁸And a stone of stumbling, and a rock of offence, even to them which stumble at the word, being disobedient: whereunto also they were appointed. ⁹But ye are a chosen generation, a royal priesthood, an holy nation, a peculiar people; that ye should shew forth the praises of him who hath called you out of darkness into his marvellous light: ¹⁰Which in time past were not a people, but are now the people of God: which had not obtained mercy, but now have obtained mercy."

Revelation 17:14 "These shall make war with the Lamb, and the Lamb shall overcome them: for he is Lord of lords, and King of kings: and they that are with him are called, and chosen, and faithful."

CIRCUMCISION

Jesus Christ Being A
Minister Of The Circumcision
Romans 15:8-9 "⁸Now I say that Jesus Christ was a minister of the circumcision for the truth of God, to confirm the promises made unto the fathers: ⁹And that the Gentiles might glorify God for his mercy; as it is written, For this cause I will confess to thee among the Gentiles, and sing unto thy name."

Colossians 2:8-15 "⁸Beware lest any man spoil you through philosophy and vain deceit, after the tradition of men, after the rudiments of the world, and not after Christ. ⁹For in him dwelleth all the fulness of the Godhead bodily. [10]And ye are complete in him, which is the head of all principality and power: [11]In whom also ye are circumcised with the circumcision made without hands, in putting off the body of the sins of the flesh by the circumcision of Christ: [12]Buried with him in baptism, wherein also ye are risen with him through the faith of the operation of God, who hath raised him from the dead. [13]And you, being dead in your sins and the uncircumcision of your flesh, hath he quickened together with him, having forgiven you all trespasses; [14]Blotting out the handwriting of ordinances that was against us, which was contrary to us, and took it out of the way, nailing it to his cross; [15]And having spoiled principalities and powers, he made a shew of them openly, triumphing over them in it."

The Covenant Of Circumcision
Genesis 17:1-14 "[1]And when Abram was ninety years old and nine, the LORD appeared to Abram, and said unto him, I am the Almighty God; walk before me, and be thou perfect. [2]And I will make my covenant between me and thee, and will multiply thee exceedingly. [3]And Abram fell on his face: and God talked with him, saying, [4]As for me, behold, my covenant is with thee, and thou shalt be a father of many nations. [5]Neither shall thy name any more be called Abram, but thy name shall be Abraham; for a father of many nations have I made thee. [6]And I will make thee exceeding fruitful, and I will make nations of thee, and kings shall come out of thee. [7]And I will establish my covenant between me and thee and thy seed after thee in their generations for an everlasting covenant, to be a God unto thee, and to thy seed after thee. [8]And I will give unto thee, and to thy seed after thee, the land wherein thou art a stranger, all the land of Canaan, for an everlasting possession; and I will be their God. [9]And God said unto Abraham, Thou shalt keep my covenant therefore, thou, and thy seed after thee in their generations. [10]This is my covenant, which ye shall keep, between me and you and thy seed after thee; Every man child among you shall be circumcised. [11]And ye shall circumcise the flesh of your foreskin; and it shall be a token of the covenant betwixt me and you. [12]And he that is eight days old shall be circumcised among you, every man child in your generations, he that is born in the house, or bought with money of any stranger, which is not of thy seed. [13]He that is born in thy house, and he that

is bought with thy money, must needs be circumcised: and my covenant shall be in your flesh for an everlasting covenant. [14]And the uncircumcised man child whose flesh of his foreskin is not circumcised, that soul shall be cut off from his people; he hath broken my covenant."

The Lord Circumcising The Heart Of Israel
Deuteronomy 30:1-6 "[1]And it shall come to pass, when all these things are come upon thee, the blessing and the curse, which I have set before thee, and thou shalt call them to mind among all the nations, whither the LORD thy God hath driven thee, [2]And shalt return unto the LORD thy God, and shalt obey his voice according to all that I command thee this day, thou and thy children, with all thine heart, and with all thy soul; [3]That then the LORD thy God will turn thy captivity, and have compassion upon thee, and will return and gather thee from all the nations, whither the LORD thy God hath scattered thee. [4]If any of thine be driven out unto the outmost parts of heaven, from thence will the LORD thy God gather thee, and from thence will he fetch thee: [5]And the LORD thy God will bring thee into the land which thy fathers possessed, and thou shalt possess it; and he will do thee good, and multiply thee above thy fathers. [6]And the LORD thy God will circumcise thine heart, and the heart of thy seed, to love the LORD thy God with all thine heart, and with all thy soul, that thou mayest live."

What Is More Important Than Circumcision
1 Corinthians 7:19 "Circumcision is nothing, and uncircumcision is nothing, but the keeping of the commandments of God."

Galatians 5:6 "For in Jesus Christ neither circumcision availeth anything, nor uncircumcision; but faith which worketh by love."

Galatians 6:15 "For in Christ Jesus neither circumcision availeth anything, nor uncircumcision, but a new creature."

Who Are The Circumcision
Romans 2:28-29 "[28]For he is not a Jew, which is one outwardly; neither is that circumcision, which is outward in the flesh: [29]But he is a Jew, which is one inwardly; and circumcision is that of the heart, in the spirit, and not in the letter; whose praise is not of men, but of God."

Philippians 3:3 "For we are the circumcision, which worship God in the spirit, and rejoice in Christ Jesus, and have no confidence in the flesh."

Whose Circumcision Is Made Uncircumcision

Romans 2:25-27 "²⁵For circumcision verily profiteth, if thou keep the law: but if thou be a breaker of the law, thy circumcision is made uncircumcision. ²⁶Therefore if the uncircumcision keep the righteousness of the law, shall not his uncircumcision be counted for circumcision? ²⁷And shall not uncircumcision which is by nature, if it fulfil the law, judge thee, who by the letter and circumcision dost transgress the law?"

CLEANNESS

Being Clean

Isaiah 1:16 "Wash you, make you clean; put away the evil of your doings from before mine eyes; cease to do evil."

Isaiah 52:11 "Depart ye, depart ye, go ye out from thence, touch no unclean thing; go ye out of the midst of her; be ye clean, that bear the vessels of the Lord."

James 4:8 "Draw nigh to God, and he will draw nigh to you. Cleanse your hands, ye sinners; and purify your hearts, ye double minded."

The Lord Cleansing

Isaiah 4:2-4 "²In that day shall the branch of the Lord be beautiful and glorious, and the fruit of the earth shall be excellent and comely for them that are escaped of Israel. ³And it shall come to pass, that he that is left in Zion, and he that remaineth in Jerusalem, shall be called holy, even every one that is written among the living in Jerusalem: ⁴When the Lord shall have washed away the filth of the daughters of Zion, and shall have purged the blood of Jerusalem from the midst thereof by the spirit of judgment, and by the spirit of burning."

Jeremiah 33:4-8 "⁴For thus saith the Lord, the God of Israel, concerning the houses of this city, and concerning the houses of the kings of Judah, which are thrown down by the mounts, and by the sword; ⁵They come to fight with the Chaldeans, but it is to fill them with the dead bodies of men, whom I have slain in mine anger and in my fury, and for all whose wickedness I have hid my face from this city. ⁶Behold, I will bring it health and cure, and I will cure them, and will reveal unto them the abundance of peace and truth. ⁷And I will cause the captivity of Judah and the captivity of Israel to return, and will build them, as at the first. ⁸And I will cleanse them from all their iniquity, whereby they have sinned against me; and I will pardon all their iniquities, whereby they have sinned, and whereby they have transgressed against me."

Ezekiel 36:22-29 "²²Therefore say unto the house of Israel, Thus saith the Lord God; I do not this for your sakes, O house of Israel, but for mine holy name's sake, which ye have profaned among the heathen, whither ye went. ²³And I will sanctify my great name, which was profaned among the heathen, which ye have profaned in the midst of them; and the heathen shall know that I am the Lord, saith the Lord God, when I shall be sanctified in you before their eyes. ²⁴For I will take you from among the heathen, and gather you out of all countries, and will bring you into your own land. ²⁵Then will I sprinkle clean water upon you, and ye shall be clean: from all your filthiness, and from all your idols, will I cleanse you. ²⁶A new heart also will I give you, and a new spirit will I put within you: and I will take away the stony heart out of your flesh, and I will give you an heart of flesh. ²⁷And I will put my spirit within you, and cause you to walk in my statutes, and ye shall keep my judgments, and do them. ²⁸And ye shall dwell in the land that I gave to your fathers; and ye shall be my people, and I will be your God. ²⁹I will also save you from all your uncleannesses: and I will call for the corn, and will increase it, and lay no famine upon you."

Joel 3:21 "For I will cleanse their blood that I have not cleansed: for the Lord dwelleth in Zion."

Zechariah 13:1-6 "¹In that day there shall be a fountain opened to the house of David and to the inhabitants of Jerusalem for sin and for uncleanness. ²And it shall come to pass in that day, saith the Lord of hosts, that I will cut off the names of the idols out of the land, and they shall no more be remembered: and also I will cause the prophets and the unclean spirit to pass out of the land. ³And it shall come to pass, that when any shall yet prophesy, then his father and his mother that begat him shall say unto him, Thou shalt not live; for thou speakest lies in the name of the LORD: and his father and his mother that begat him shall thrust him through when he prophesieth. ⁴And it shall come to pass in that day, that the prophets shall be ashamed every one of his vision, when he hath prophesied; neither shall they wear a rough garment to deceive: ⁵But he shall say, I am no prophet, I am an husbandman; for man taught me to keep cattle from my youth. ⁶And one shall say unto him, What are these wounds in thine hands? Then he shall answer, Those with which I was wounded in the house of my friends."

Matthew 11:4-5 "⁴Jesus answered and said unto them, Go and shew John again those things which ye do hear and see: ⁵The blind receive their sight, and the lame walk, the lepers are cleansed, and the deaf hear, the dead are raised up, and the poor have the gospel preached to them."

Luke 7:22 "Then Jesus answering said unto them, Go your way, and tell John what things ye have seen and heard; how that the blind see, the lame walk, the lepers are cleansed, the deaf hear, the dead are raised, to the poor the gospel is preached."

Ephesians 5:24-26 "²⁴Therefore as the church is subject unto Christ, so let the wives be to their own husbands in every thing. ²⁵Husbands, love your wives, even as Christ also loved the church, and gave himself for it; ²⁶That he might sanctify and cleanse it with the washing of water by the word."

1 John 1:7-9 "⁷But if we walk in the light, as he is in the light, we have fellowship one with another, and the blood of Jesus Christ his Son cleanseth us from all sin. ⁸If we say that we have no sin, we deceive ourselves, and the truth is not in us. ⁹If we confess our sins, he is faithful and just to forgive us our sins, and to cleanse us from all unrighteousness."

Revelation 1:4-5 "⁴John to the seven churches which are in Asia: Grace be unto you, and peace, from him which is, and which was, and which is to come; and from the seven Spirits which are before his throne; ⁵And from Jesus Christ, who is the faithful witness, and the first begotten of the dead, and the prince of the kings of the earth. Unto him that loved us, and washed us from our sins in his own blood."

What Animals Are Clean

Leviticus 11:2-3 "²Speak unto the children of Israel, saying, These are the beasts which ye shall eat among all the beasts that are on the earth. ³Whatsoever parteth the hoof, and is clovenfooted, and cheweth the cud, among the beasts, that shall ye eat."

Leviticus 11:9 "These shall ye eat of all that are in the waters: whatsoever hath fins and scales in the waters, in the seas, and in the rivers, them shall ye eat."

Leviticus 11:21-22 "²¹Yet these may ye eat of every flying creeping thing that goeth upon all four, which have legs above their feet, to leap withal upon the earth; ²²Even these of them ye may eat; the locust after his kind, and the bald locust after his kind, and the beetle after his kind, and the grasshopper after his kind."

Deuteronomy 14:3-6 "³Thou shalt not eat any abominable thing. ⁴These are the beasts which ye shall eat: the ox, the sheep, and the goat, ⁵The hart, and the roebuck, and the fallow deer, and the wild goat, and the pygarg, and the wild ox, and the chamois. ⁶And every beast that parteth the hoof, and cleaveth the cleft into two claws, and cheweth the cud among the beasts, that ye shall eat."

Deuteronomy 14:9 "These ye shall eat of all that are in the waters: all that have fins and scales shall ye eat."

What Cleanses

Proverbs 20:30 "The blueness of a wound cleanseth away evil: so do stripes the inward parts of the belly."

John 15:1-3 "¹I am the true vine, and my Father is the husbandman. ²Every branch in me that beareth not fruit he taketh away: and every branch that beareth fruit, he purgeth it, that it may bring forth more fruit. ³Now ye are clean through the word which I have spoken unto you."

1 Corinthians 6:9-11 "⁹Know ye not that the unrighteous shall not inherit the kingdom of God? Be not deceived: neither fornicators, nor idolaters, nor adulterers, nor effeminate, nor abusers of themselves with mankind, [10]Nor thieves, nor covetous, nor drunkards, nor revilers, nor extortioners, shall inherit the kingdom of God. [11]And such were some of you: but ye are washed, but ye are sanctified, but ye are justified in the name of the Lord Jesus, and by the Spirit of our God."

Ephesians 5:24-26 "[24]Therefore as the church is subject unto Christ, so let the wives be to their own husbands in every thing. [25]Husbands, love your wives, even as Christ also loved the church, and gave himself for it; [26]That he might sanctify and cleanse it with the washing of water by the word."

1 John 1:7 "But if we walk in the light, as he is in the light, we have fellowship one with another, and the blood of Jesus Christ his Son cleanseth us from all sin."

What Is Clean
Psalm 19:9 "The fear of the LORD is clean, enduring for ever: the judgments of the LORD are true and righteous altogether."

What To Cleanse
Matthew 23:25-26 "[25]Woe unto you, scribes and Pharisees, hypocrites! for ye make clean the outside of the cup and of the platter, but within they are full of extortion and excess. [26]Thou blind Pharisee, cleanse first that which is within the cup and platter, that the outside of them may be clean also."

James 4:8 "Draw nigh to God, and he will draw nigh to you. Cleanse your hands, ye sinners; and purify your hearts, ye double minded."

What To Cleanse Yourself From
2 Corinthians 7:1 "Having therefore these promises, dearly beloved, let us cleanse ourselves from all filthiness of the flesh and spirit, perfecting holiness in the fear of God."

Who Cleanses The Outside
Of The Cup, But Not The Inside
Matthew 23:25-28 "[25]Woe unto you, scribes and Pharisees, hypocrites! for ye make clean the outside of the cup and of the platter, but within they are full of extortion and excess. [26]Thou blind Pharisee, cleanse first that which is within the cup and platter, that the outside of them may be clean also. [27]Woe unto you, scribes and Pharisees, hypocrites! for ye

are like unto whited sepulchres, which indeed appear beautiful outward, but are within full of dead men's bones, and of all uncleanness. [28]Even so ye also outwardly appear righteous unto men, but within ye are full of hypocrisy and iniquity."

Mark 7:3-4 "[3]For the Pharisees, and all the Jews, except they wash their hands oft, eat not, holding the tradition of the elders. [4]And when they come from the market, except they wash, they eat not. And many other things there be, which they have received to hold, as the washing of cups, and pots, brasen vessels, and of tables."

Luke 11:39-42 "[39]And the Lord said unto him, Now do ye Pharisees make clean the outside of the cup and the platter; but your inward part is full of ravening and wickedness. [40]Ye fools, did not he that made that which is without make that which is within also? [41]But rather give alms of such things as ye have; and, behold, all things are clean unto you. [42]But woe unto you, Pharisees! for ye tithe mint and rue and all manner of herbs, and pass over judgment and the love of God: these ought ye to have done, and not to leave the other undone."

Who Will Be Cleansed From Sin
1 John 1:7-9 "[7]But if we walk in the light, as he is in the light, we have fellowship one with another, and the blood of Jesus Christ his Son cleanseth us from all sin. [8]If we say that we have no sin, we deceive ourselves, and the truth is not in us. [9]If we confess our sins, he is faithful and just to forgive us our sins, and to cleanse us from all unrighteousness."

CLEAVING

Cleaving To The Lord
Deuteronomy 10:20 "Thou shalt fear the LORD thy God; him shalt thou serve, and to him shalt thou cleave, and swear by his name."

Deuteronomy 13:4 "Ye shall walk after the LORD your God, and fear him, and keep his commandments, and obey his voice, and ye shall serve him, and cleave unto him."

Deuteronomy 30:19-20 "[19]I call heaven and earth to record this day against you, that I have set before you life and death, blessing and cursing: therefore choose life, that both thou and thy seed may live:

[20]That thou mayest love the Lord thy God, and that thou mayest obey his voice, and that thou mayest cleave unto him: for he is thy life, and the length of thy days: that thou mayest dwell in the land which the Lord sware unto thy fathers, to Abraham, to Isaac, and to Jacob, to give them."

Joshua 22:5 "But take diligent heed to do the commandment and the law, which Moses the servant of the Lord charged you, to love the Lord your God, and to walk in all his ways, and to keep his commandments, and to cleave unto him, and to serve him with all your heart and with all your soul."

Joshua 23:8 "But cleave unto the Lord your God, as ye have done unto this day."

The Reward For Cleaving To The Lord
Deuteronomy 11:22-23 "[22]For if ye shall diligently keep all these commandments which I command you, to do them, to love the Lord your God, to walk in all his ways, and to cleave unto him; [23]Then will the Lord drive out all these nations from before you, and ye shall possess greater nations and mightier than yourselves."

Those That Cleave To The Lord
Deuteronomy 4:4 "But ye that did cleave unto the Lord your God are alive every one of you this day."

2 Kings 18:5-8 "[5]He trusted in the Lord God of Israel; so that after him was none like him among all the kings of Judah, nor any that were before him. [6]For he clave to the Lord, and departed not from following him, but kept his commandments, which the Lord commanded Moses. [7]And the Lord was with him; and he prospered whithersoever he went forth: and he rebelled against the king of Assyria, and served him not. [8]He smote the Philistines, even unto Gaza, and the borders thereof, from the tower of the watchmen to the fenced city."

What To Cleave To
Romans 12:9 "Let love be without dissimulation. Abhor that which is evil; cleave to that which is good."

CLOSENESS

Drawing Near To God
Psalm 73:28 "But it is good for me to draw near to God: I have put my trust in the Lord God, that I may declare all thy works."

The Lord Being Near
Psalm 16:8 "I have set the Lord always before me: because he is at my right hand, I shall not be moved."

Psalm 119:151 "Thou art near, O Lord; and all thy commandments are truth."

Proverbs 18:24 "A man that hath friends must shew himself friendly: and there is a friend that sticketh closer than a brother."

Isaiah 50:7-8 "[7]For the Lord God will help me; therefore shall I not be confounded: therefore have I set my face like a flint, and I know that I shall not be ashamed. [8]He is near that justifieth me; who will contend with me? let us stand together: who is mine adversary? let him come near to me."

Jeremiah 23:23 "Am I a God at hand, saith the Lord, and not a God afar off?"

Acts 17:27 "That they should seek the Lord, if haply they might feel after him, and find him, though he be not far from every one of us."

The Reward For Drawing Near To God
James 4:8 "Draw nigh to God, and he will draw nigh to you. Cleanse your hands, ye sinners; and purify your hearts, ye double minded."

The Reward For Not Drawing Near To God
Zephaniah 3:1-2 "[1]Woe to her that is filthy and polluted, to the oppressing city! [2]She obeyed not the voice; she received not correction; she trusted not in the Lord; she drew not near to her God."

Those That Are Close To The Lord
1 Chronicles 11:9 "So David waxed greater and greater: for the Lord of hosts was with him."

Who The Lord Is Near To
1 Chronicles 11:9 "So David waxed greater and greater: for the Lord of hosts was with him."

Psalm 34:18 "The Lord is nigh unto them that are of a broken heart; and saveth such as be of a contrite spirit."

Psalm 145:18 "The Lord is nigh unto all them that call upon him, to all that call upon him in truth."

Amos 5:14 "Seek good, and not evil, that ye may live: and so the Lord, the God of hosts, shall be with you, as ye have spoken."

2 Corinthians 13:11 "Finally, brethren, farewell. Be perfect, be of good comfort, be of one mind, live in peace; and the God of love and peace shall be with you."

James 4:8 "Draw nigh to God, and he will draw nigh to you. Cleanse your hands, ye sinners; and purify your hearts, ye double minded."

COMFORT

Being Of Good Comfort
2 Corinthians 13:11 "Finally, brethren, farewell. Be perfect, be of good comfort, be of one mind, live in peace; and the God of love and peace shall be with you."

Comforting One Another
1 Thessalonians 5:11 "Wherefore comfort yourselves together, and edify one another, even as also ye do."

God Being The God Of All Comfort
2 Corinthians 1:3 "Blessed be God, even the Father of our Lord Jesus Christ, the Father of mercies, and the God of all comfort."

The Comforter
John 14:16-18 "16And I will pray the Father, and he shall give you another Comforter, that he may abide with you for ever; 17Even the Spirit of truth; whom the world cannot receive, because it seeth him not, neither knoweth him: but ye know him; for he dwelleth with you, and shall be in you. 18I will not leave you comfortless: I will come to you."

John 14:23-26 "23Jesus answered and said unto him, If a man love me, he will keep my words: and my Father will love him, and we will come unto him, and make our abode with him. 24He that loveth me not keepeth not my sayings: and the word which ye hear is not mine, but the Father's which sent me. 25These things have I spoken unto you, being yet present with you. 26But the Comforter, which is the Holy Ghost, whom the Father will send in my name, he shall teach you all things, and bring all things to your remembrance, whatsoever I have said unto you."

John 15:1-26 "1I am the true vine, and my Father is the husbandman. 2Every branch in me that beareth not fruit he taketh away: and every branch that beareth fruit, he purgeth it, that it may bring forth more fruit. 3Now ye are clean through the word which I have spoken unto you. 4Abide in me, and I in you. As the branch cannot bear fruit of itself, except it abide in the vine; no more can ye, except ye abide in me. 5I am the vine, ye are the branches: He that abideth in me, and I in him, the same bringeth forth much fruit: for without me ye can do nothing. 6If a man abide not in me, he is cast forth as a branch, and is withered; and men gather them, and cast them into the fire, and they are burned. 7If ye abide in me, and my words abide in you, ye shall ask what ye will, and it shall be done unto you. 8Herein is my Father glorified, that ye bear much fruit; so shall ye be my disciples. 9As the Father hath loved me, so have I loved you: continue ye in my love. 10If ye keep my commandments, ye shall abide in my love; even as I have kept my Father's commandments, and abide in his love. 11These things have I spoken unto you, that my joy might remain in you, and that your joy might be full. 12This is my commandment, That ye love one another, as I have loved you. 13Greater love hath no man than this, that a man lay down his life for his friends. 14Ye are my friends, if ye do whatsoever I command you. 15Henceforth I call you not servants; for the servant knoweth not what his lord doeth: but I have called you friends; for all things that I have heard of my Father I have made known unto you. 16Ye have not chosen me, but I have chosen you, and ordained you, that ye should go and bring forth fruit, and that your fruit should remain: that whatsoever ye shall ask of the Father in my name, he may give it you. 17These things I command you, that ye love one another. 18If the world hate you, ye know that it hated me before it hated you. 19If ye were of the world, the world would love his own: but because ye are not of the world, but I have chosen you out of the world, therefore the world hateth you. 20Remember the word that I said unto you, The servant is not greater than his lord. If they have persecuted me, they will also persecute you; if they have kept my saying, they will keep yours also. 21But all these things will they do unto you for my name's sake, because they know not him that sent me. 22If I had not come and spoken unto them, they had not had sin: but now they have no cloke for their sin. 23He that hateth me hateth my Father also. 24If I had not done among them the works which none other man did, they had not had sin: but now have they both seen and hated both me and my Father. 25But this cometh to pass, that the word might be fulfilled that is written in their law, They hated me without a cause. 26But when the Comforter is come, whom I will send unto you from the Father, even the Spirit of truth, which proceedeth from the Father, he shall testify of me."

John 16:5-15 "5But now I go my way to him that sent me; and none of you asketh me, Whither goest thou? 6But because I have said these things unto you, sorrow hath filled your heart. 7Nevertheless I tell you the truth; It is expedient for you that I go away: for if I go not away, the Comforter will not come unto you; but if I depart, I will send him unto you. 8And when he is come, he will reprove the world of sin, and of righteousness, and of judgment: 9Of sin, because they believe not on me; 10Of righteousness, because I go to my Father, and ye see me no more; 11Of judgment, because the prince of this world is judged. 12I have yet many things to say unto you, but ye cannot bear them now. 13Howbeit when he, the Spirit of truth, is come, he will guide you into all truth: for he shall not speak of himself; but whatsoever he shall hear, that shall he speak: and he will shew you things to come. 14He shall glorify me: for he shall receive of mine, and shall shew it unto you. 15All things that the Father hath are mine: therefore said I, that he shall take of mine, and shall shew it unto you."

The Lord Comforting

Psalm 23:1-4 "1The LORD is my shepherd; I shall not want. 2He maketh me to lie down in green pastures: he leadeth me beside the still waters. 3He restoreth my soul: he leadeth me in the paths of righteousness for his name's sake. 4Yea, though I walk through the valley of the shadow of death, I will fear no evil: for thou art with me; thy rod and thy staff they comfort me."

Psalm 138:6-7 "6Though the LORD be high, yet hath he respect unto the lowly: but the proud he knoweth afar off. 7Though I walk in the midst of trouble, thou wilt revive me: thou shalt stretch forth thine hand against the wrath of mine enemies, and thy right hand shall save me."

Isaiah 12:1 "And in that day thou shalt say, O LORD, I will praise thee: though thou wast angry with me, thine anger is turned away, and thou comfortedst me."

Jeremiah 31:10-14 "10Hear the word of the LORD, O ye nations, and declare it in the isles afar off, and say, He that scattered Israel will gather him, and keep him, as a shepherd doth his flock. 11For the LORD hath redeemed Jacob, and ransomed him from the hand of him that was stronger than he. 12Therefore they shall come and sing in the height of Zion, and shall flow together to the goodness of the LORD, for wheat, and for wine, and for oil, and for the young of the flock and of the herd: and their soul shall be as a watered garden; and they shall not sorrow any more at all. 13Then shall the virgin rejoice in the dance, both young men and old together: for I will turn their mourning into joy, and will comfort them, and make them rejoice from their sorrow. 14And I will satiate the soul of the priests with fatness, and my people shall be satisfied with my goodness, saith the LORD."

2 Corinthians 1:3-4 "3Blessed be God, even the Father of our Lord Jesus Christ, the Father of mercies, and the God of all comfort; 4Who comforteth us in all our tribulation, that we may be able to comfort them which are in any trouble, by the comfort wherewith we ourselves are comforted of God."

Who Shall Be Comforted

Isaiah 51:3 "For the LORD shall comfort Zion: he will comfort all her waste places; and he will make her wilderness like Eden, and her desert like the garden of the LORD; joy and gladness shall be found therein, thanksgiving, and the voice of melody."

Isaiah 61:1-2 "1The Spirit of the Lord GOD is upon me; because the LORD hath anointed me to preach good tidings unto the meek; he hath sent me to bind up the brokenhearted, to proclaim liberty to the captives, and the opening of the prison to them that are bound; 2To proclaim the acceptable year of the LORD, and the day of vengeance of our God; to comfort all that mourn."

Matthew 5:4 "Blessed are they that mourn: for they shall be comforted."

Who To Comfort

1 Thessalonians 5:14 "Now we exhort you, brethren, warn them that are unruly, comfort the feebleminded, support the weak, be patient toward all men."

Why God Comforts You
When You Are In Trouble
2 Corinthians 1:3-6 "³Blessed be God, even the Father of our Lord Jesus Christ, the Father of mercies, and the God of all comfort; ⁴Who comforteth us in all our tribulation, that we may be able to comfort them which are in any trouble, by the comfort wherewith we ourselves are comforted of God. ⁵For as the sufferings of Christ abound in us, so our consolation also aboundeth by Christ. ⁶And whether we be afflicted, it is for your consolation and salvation, which is effectual in the enduring of the same sufferings which we also suffer: or whether we be comforted, it is for your consolation and salvation."

COMING

Coming To The Lord
Isaiah 55:1-3 "¹Ho, every one that thirsteth, come ye to the waters, and he that hath no money; come ye, buy, and eat; yea, come, buy wine and milk without money and without price. ²Wherefore do ye spend money for that which is not bread? and your labour for that which satisfieth not? hearken diligently unto me, and eat ye that which is good, and let your soul delight itself in fatness. ³Incline your ear, and come unto me: hear, and your soul shall live; and I will make an everlasting covenant with you, even the sure mercies of David."

John 7:37-38 "³⁷In the last day, that great day of the feast, Jesus stood and cried, saying, If any man thirst, let him come unto me, and drink. ³⁸He that believeth on me, as the scripture hath said, out of his belly shall flow rivers of living water."

Revelation 22:16-17 "¹⁶I Jesus have sent mine angel to testify unto you these things in the churches. I am the root and the offspring of David, and the bright and morning star. ¹⁷And the Spirit and the bride say, Come. And let him that heareth say, Come. And let him that is athirst come. And whosoever will, let him take the water of life freely."

No One Coming To God The Father,
Except They Go Through Jesus Christ
John 14:6 "Jesus saith unto him, I am the way, the truth, and the life: no man cometh unto the Father, but by me."

Those That Come To The Lord
John 6:35-37 "³⁵And Jesus said unto them, I am the bread of life: he that cometh to me shall never hunger; and he that believeth on me shall never thirst. ³⁶But I said unto you, That ye also have seen me, and believe not. ³⁷All that the Father giveth me shall come to me; and him that cometh to me I will in no wise cast out."

John 6:43-44 "⁴³Jesus therefore answered and said unto them, Murmur not among yourselves. ⁴⁴No man can come to me, except the Father which hath sent me draw him: and I will raise him up at the last day."

Hebrews 11:6 "But without faith it is impossible to please him: for he that cometh to God must believe that he is, and that he is a rewarder of them that diligently seek him."

Who Comes To Jesus Christ
John 6:35-37 "³⁵And Jesus said unto them, I am the bread of life: he that cometh to me shall never hunger; and he that believeth on me shall never thirst. ³⁶But I said unto you, That ye also have seen me, and believe not. ³⁷All that the Father giveth me shall come to me; and him that cometh to me I will in no wise cast out."

John 6:43-46 "⁴³Jesus therefore answered and said unto them, Murmur not among yourselves. ⁴⁴No man can come to me, except the Father which hath sent me draw him: and I will raise him up at the last day. ⁴⁵It is written in the prophets, And they shall be all taught of God. Every man therefore that hath heard, and hath learned of the Father, cometh unto me. ⁴⁶Not that any man hath seen the Father, save he which is of God, he hath seen the Father."

John 6:64-65 "⁶⁴But there are some of you that believe not. For Jesus knew from the beginning who they were that believed not, and who should betray him. ⁶⁵And he said, Therefore said I unto you, that no man can come unto me, except it were given unto him of my Father."

Who God The Father
And Jesus Christ Come To
John 14:21-23 "²¹He that hath my commandments, and keepeth them, he it is that loveth me: and he that loveth me shall be loved of my Father, and I will love him, and will manifest myself to him. ²²Judas saith unto him, not Iscariot, Lord, how is it that thou wilt manifest thyself unto us, and not

unto the world? [23]Jesus answered and said unto him, If a man love me, he will keep my words: and my Father will love him, and we will come unto him, and make our abode with him."

Revelation 3:14-20 "[14]And unto the angel of the church of the Laodiceans write; These things saith the Amen, the faithful and true witness, the beginning of the creation of God; [15]I know thy works, that thou art neither cold nor hot: I would thou wert cold or hot. [16]So then because thou art lukewarm, and neither cold nor hot, I will spue thee out of my mouth. [17]Because thou sayest, I am rich, and increased with goods, and have need of nothing; and knowest not that thou art wretched, and miserable, and poor, and blind, and naked: [18]I counsel thee to buy of me gold tried in the fire, that thou mayest be rich; and white raiment, that thou mayest be clothed, and that the shame of thy nakedness do not appear; and anoint thine eyes with eyesalve, that thou mayest see. [19]As many as I love, I rebuke and chasten: be zealous therefore, and repent. [20]Behold, I stand at the door, and knock: if any man hear my voice, and open the door, I will come in to him, and will sup with him, and he with me."

Who Should Come To Christ
Isaiah 55:1 "Ho, every one that thirsteth, come ye to the waters, and he that hath no money; come ye, buy, and eat; yea, come, buy wine and milk without money and without price."

John 7:37-38 "[37]In the last day, that great day of the feast, Jesus stood and cried, saying, If any man thirst, let him come unto me, and drink. [38]He that believeth on me, as the scripture hath said, out of his belly shall flow rivers of living water."

Revelation 22:16-17 "[16]I Jesus have sent mine angel to testify unto you these things in the churches. I am the root and the offspring of David, and the bright and morning star. [17]And the Spirit and the bride say, Come. And let him that heareth say, Come. And let him that is athirst come. And whosoever will, let him take the water of life freely."

COMING OF THE LORD JESUS CHRIST

Being Patient For The Coming Of The Lord
2 Thessalonians 2:1-3 "[1]Now we beseech you, brethren, by the coming of our Lord Jesus Christ,

and by our gathering together unto him, [2] That ye be not soon shaken in mind, or be troubled, neither by spirit, nor by word, nor by letter as from us, as that the day of Christ is at hand. [3] Let no man deceive you by any means: for that day shall not come, except there come a falling away first, and that man of sin be revealed, the son of perdition."

James 5:7-8 "[7]Be patient therefore, brethren, unto the coming of the Lord. Behold, the husbandman waiteth for the precious fruit of the earth, and hath long patience for it, until he receive the early and latter rain. [8] Be ye also patient; stablish your hearts: for the coming of the Lord draweth nigh."

How The Lord Will Come
Isaiah 66:15-17 "[15]For, behold, the LORD will come with fire, and with his chariots like a whirlwind, to render his anger with fury, and his rebuke with flames of fire. [16]For by fire and by his sword will the LORD plead with all flesh: and the slain of the LORD shall be many. [17]They that sanctify themselves, and purify themselves in the gardens behind one tree in the midst, eating swine's flesh, and the abomination, and the mouse, shall be consumed together, saith the LORD."

Daniel 7:13-14 "[13]I saw in the night visions, and, behold, one like the Son of man came with the clouds of heaven, and came to the Ancient of days, and they brought him near before him. [14]And there was given him dominion, and glory, and a kingdom, that all people, nations, and languages, should serve him: his dominion is an everlasting dominion, which shall not pass away, and his kingdom that which shall not be destroyed."

Matthew 16:27-28 "[27]For the Son of man shall come in the glory of his Father with his angels; and then he shall reward every man according to his works. [28]Verily I say unto you, There be some standing here, which shall not taste of death, till they see the Son of man coming in his kingdom."

Matthew 24:26-30 "[26]Wherefore if they shall say unto you, Behold, he is in the desert; go not forth: behold, he is in the secret chambers; believe it not. [27]For as the lightning cometh out of the east, and shineth even unto the west; so shall also the coming of the Son of man be. [28]For wheresoever the carcase is, there will the eagles be gathered together. [29]Immediately after the tribulation of those days shall the sun be darkened, and the moon shall not give her light, and the stars shall fall from heaven, and the powers of the heavens shall be shaken: ³⁰And then shall appear the sign of the Son of man in heaven: and then shall all the tribes of the earth mourn, and they shall see the Son of man coming in the clouds of heaven with power and great glory."

Mark 8:38 "Whosoever therefore shall be ashamed of me and of my words in this adulterous and sinful generation; of him also shall the Son of man be ashamed, when he cometh in the glory of his Father with the holy angels."

Mark 13:24-26 "²⁴But in those days, after that tribulation, the sun shall be darkened, and the moon shall not give her light, ²⁵And the stars of heaven shall fall, and the powers that are in heaven shall be shaken. ²⁶And then shall they see the Son of man coming in the clouds with great power and glory."

Mark 14:60-62 "⁶⁰And the high priest stood up in the midst, and asked Jesus, saying, Answerest thou nothing? what is it which these witness against thee? ⁶¹But he held his peace, and answered nothing. Again the high priest asked him, and said unto him, Art thou the Christ, the Son of the Blessed? ⁶²And Jesus said, I am: and ye shall see the Son of man sitting on the right hand of power, and coming in the clouds of heaven."

Luke 17:20-25 "²⁰And when he was demanded of the Pharisees, when the kingdom of God should come, he answered them and said, The kingdom of God cometh not with observation: ²¹Neither shall they say, Lo here! or, lo there! for, behold, the kingdom of God is within you. ²²And he said unto the disciples, The days will come, when ye shall desire to see one of the days of the Son of man, and ye shall not see it. ²³And they shall say to you, See here; or, see there: go not after them, nor follow them. ²⁴For as the lightning, that lighteneth out of the one part under heaven, shineth unto the other part under heaven; so shall also the Son of man be in his day. ²⁵But first must he suffer many things, and be rejected of this generation."

Luke 21:25-36 "²⁵And there shall be signs in the sun, and in the moon, and in the stars; and upon the earth distress of nations, with perplexity; the sea and the waves roaring; ²⁶Men's hearts failing them for fear, and for looking after those things which are coming on the earth: for the powers of heaven shall be shaken. ²⁷And then shall they see the Son of man coming in a cloud with power and great glory. ²⁸And when these things begin to come to pass, then look up, and lift up your heads; for your redemption draweth nigh. ²⁹And he spake to them a parable; Behold the fig tree, and all the trees; ³⁰When they now shoot forth, ye see and know of your own selves that summer is now nigh at hand. ³¹So likewise ye, when ye see these things come to pass, know ye that the kingdom of God is nigh at hand. ³²Verily I say unto you, This generation shall not pass away, till all be fulfilled. ³³Heaven and earth shall pass away: but my words shall not pass away. ³⁴And take heed to yourselves, lest at any time your hearts be overcharged with surfeiting, and drunkenness, and cares of this life, and so that day come upon you unawares. ³⁵For as a snare shall it come on all them that dwell on the face of the whole earth. ³⁶Watch ye therefore, and pray always, that ye may be accounted worthy to escape all these things that shall come to pass, and to stand before the Son of man."

Acts 1:6-11 "⁶When they therefore were come together, they asked of him, saying, Lord, wilt thou at this time restore again the kingdom to Israel? ⁷And he said unto them, It is not for you to know the times or the seasons, which the Father hath put in his own power. ⁸But ye shall receive power, after that the Holy Ghost is come upon you: and ye shall be witnesses unto me both in Jerusalem, and in all Judaea, and in Samaria, and unto the uttermost part of the earth. ⁹And when he had spoken these things, while they beheld, he was taken up; and a cloud received him out of their sight. ¹⁰And while they looked stedfastly toward heaven as he went up, behold, two men stood by them in white apparel; ¹¹Which also said, Ye men of Galilee, why stand ye gazing up into heaven? this same Jesus, which is taken up from you into heaven, shall so come in like manner as ye have seen him go into heaven."

1 Thessalonians 4:16 "For the Lord himself shall descend from heaven with a shout, with the voice of the archangel, and with the trump of God: and the dead in Christ shall rise first."

Revelation 1:4-7 "⁴John to the seven churches which are in Asia: Grace be unto you, and peace, from him which is, and which was, and which is to come; and from the seven Spirits which are before his throne; 5And from Jesus Christ, who is the faithful witness, and the first begotten of the dead, and the prince of the kings of the earth. Unto him that loved us, and washed us from our sins in his own blood, 6And hath made us kings and priests unto God and his Father; to him be glory and dominion for ever and ever. Amen. 7Behold, he cometh with clouds; and every eye shall see him, and they also which pierced him: and all kindreds of the earth shall wail because of him. Even so, Amen."

Revelation 3:1-3 "1And unto the angel of the church in Sardis write; These things saith he that hath the seven Spirits of God, and the seven stars; I know thy works, that thou hast a name that thou livest, and art dead. 2Be watchful, and strengthen the things which remain, that are ready to die: for I have not found thy works perfect before God. 3Remember therefore how thou hast received and heard, and hold fast, and repent. If therefore thou shalt not watch, I will come on thee as a thief, and thou shalt not know what hour I will come upon thee."

Revelation 16:12-15 "12And the sixth angel poured out his vial upon the great river Euphrates; and the water thereof was dried up, that the way of the kings of the east might be prepared. 13And I saw three unclean spirits like frogs come out of the mouth of the dragon, and out of the mouth of the beast, and out of the mouth of the false prophet. 14For they are the spirits of devils, working miracles, which go forth unto the kings of the earth and of the whole world, to gather them to the battle of that great day of God Almighty. 15Behold, I come as a thief. Blessed is he that watcheth, and keepeth his garments, lest he walk naked, and they see his shame."

Revelation 22:1-12 "1And he shewed me a pure river of water of life, clear as crystal, proceeding out of the throne of God and of the Lamb. 2In the midst of the street of it, and on either side of the river, was there the tree of life, which bare twelve manner of fruits, and yielded her fruit every month: and the leaves of the tree were for the healing of the nations. 3And there shall be no more curse: but the throne of God and of the Lamb shall be in it; and his servants shall serve him: 4And they shall see his face; and his name

shall be in their foreheads. 5And there shall be no night there; and they need no candle, neither light of the sun; for the Lord God giveth them light: and they shall reign for ever and ever. 6And he said unto me, These sayings are faithful and true: and the Lord God of the holy prophets sent his angel to shew unto his servants the things which must shortly be done. 7Behold, I come quickly: blessed is he that keepeth the sayings of the prophecy of this book. 8And I John saw these things, and heard them. And when I had heard and seen, I fell down to worship before the feet of the angel which shewed me these things. 9Then saith he unto me, See thou do it not: for I am thy fellowservant, and of thy brethren the prophets, and of them which keep the sayings of this book: worship God. 10And he saith unto me, Seal not the sayings of the prophecy of this book: for the time is at hand. 11He that is unjust, let him be unjust still: and he which is filthy, let him be filthy still: and he that is righteous, let him be righteous still: and he that is holy, let him be holy still. 12And, behold, I come quickly; and my reward is with me, to give every man according as his work shall be."

Revelation 22:20 "He which testifieth these things saith, Surely I come quickly. Amen. Even so, come, Lord Jesus."

Nobody Other Than God The Father Knowing Exactly When The Lord Will Come

Matthew 24:29-36 "29Immediately after the tribulation of those days shall the sun be darkened, and the moon shall not give her light, and the stars shall fall from heaven, and the powers of the heavens shall be shaken: 30And then shall appear the sign of the Son of man in heaven: and then shall all the tribes of the earth mourn, and they shall see the Son of man coming in the clouds of heaven with power and great glory. 31And he shall send his angels with a great sound of a trumpet, and they shall gather together his elect from the four winds, from one end of heaven to the other. 32Now learn a parable of the fig tree; When his branch is yet tender, and putteth forth leaves, ye know that summer is nigh: 33So likewise ye, when ye shall see all these things, know that it is near, even at the doors. 34Verily I say unto you, This generation shall not pass, till all these things be fulfilled. 35Heaven and earth shall pass away, but my words shall not pass away. 36But of that day and hour knoweth no man, no, not the angels of heaven, but my Father only."

Matthew 24:42 "Watch therefore: for ye know not what hour your Lord doth come."

Matthew 25:13 "Watch therefore, for ye know neither the day nor the hour wherein the Son of man cometh."

Mark 13:28-37 "28Now learn a parable of the fig tree; When her branch is yet tender, and putteth forth leaves, ye know that summer is near: 29So ye in like manner, when ye shall see these things come to pass, know that it is nigh, even at the doors. 30Verily I say unto you, that this generation shall not pass, till all these things be done. 31Heaven and earth shall pass away: but my words shall not pass away. 32But of that day and that hour knoweth no man, no, not the angels which are in heaven, neither the Son, but the Father. 33Take ye heed, watch and pray: for ye know not when the time is. 34For the Son of man is as a man taking a far journey, who left his house, and gave authority to his servants, and to every man his work, and commanded the porter to watch. 35Watch ye therefore: for ye know not when the master of the house cometh, at even, or at midnight, or at the cockcrowing, or in the morning: 36Lest coming suddenly he find you sleeping. 37And what I say unto you I say unto all, Watch."

Revelation 3:1-3 "1And unto the angel of the church in Sardis write; These things saith he that hath the seven Spirits of God, and the seven stars; I know thy works, that thou hast a name that thou livest, and art dead. 2Be watchful, and strengthen the things which remain, that are ready to die: for I have not found thy works perfect before God. 3Remember therefore how thou hast received and heard, and hold fast, and repent. If therefore thou shalt not watch, I will come on thee as a thief, and thou shalt not know what hour I will come upon thee."

People Scoffing At The Coming Of The Lord

2 Peter 3:1-7 "1This second epistle, beloved, I now write unto you; in both which I stir up your pure minds by way of remembrance: 2That ye may be mindful of the words which were spoken before by the holy prophets, and of the commandment of us the apostles of the Lord and Saviour: 3Knowing

this first, that there shall come in the last days scoffers, walking after their own lusts, 4And saying, Where is the promise of his coming? for since the fathers fell asleep, all things continue as they were from the beginning of the creation. 5For this they willingly are ignorant of, that by the word of God the heavens were of old, and the earth standing out of the water and in the water: 6Whereby the world that then was, being overflowed with water, perished: 7But the heavens and the earth, which are now, by the same word are kept in store, reserved unto fire against the day of judgment and perdition of ungodly men."

The Lord Going Away Only To Return Later

Mark 13:34-35 "34For the Son of man is as a man taking a far journey, who left his house, and gave authority to his servants, and to every man his work, and commanded the porter to watch. 35Watch ye therefore: for ye know not when the master of the house cometh, at even, or at midnight, or at the cockcrowing, or in the morning."

John 14:1-6 "1Let not your heart be troubled: ye believe in God, believe also in me. 2In my Father's house are many mansions: if it were not so, I would have told you. I go to prepare a place for you. 3And if I go and prepare a place for you, I will come again, and receive you unto myself; that where I am, there ye may be also. 4And whither I go ye know, and the way ye know. 5Thomas saith unto him, Lord, we know not whither thou goest; and how can we know the way? 6Jesus saith unto him, I am the way, the truth, and the life: no man cometh unto the Father, but by me."

John 14:23-28 "23Jesus answered and said unto him, If a man love me, he will keep my words: and my Father will love him, and we will come unto him, and make our abode with him. 24He that loveth me not keepeth not my sayings: and the word which ye hear is not mine, but the Father's which sent me. 25These things have I spoken unto you, being yet present with you. 26But the Comforter, which is the Holy Ghost, whom the Father will send in my name, he shall teach you all things, and bring all things to your remembrance, whatsoever I have said unto you. 27Peace I leave with you, my peace I give unto you: not as the world giveth, give I unto you. Let not your heart be troubled, neither let it be afraid.

[28]Ye have heard how I said unto you, I go away, and come again unto you. If ye loved me, ye would rejoice, because I said, I go unto the Father: for my Father is greater than I."

John 16:19-22 "[19]Now Jesus knew that they were desirous to ask him, and said unto them, Do ye inquire among yourselves of that I said, A little while, and ye shall not see me: and again, a little while, and ye shall see me? [20]Verily, verily, I say unto you, That ye shall weep and lament, but the world shall rejoice: and ye shall be sorrowful, but your sorrow shall be turned into joy. [21]A woman when she is in travail hath sorrow, because her hour is come: but as soon as she is delivered of the child, she remembereth no more the anguish, for joy that a man is born into the world. [22]And ye now therefore have sorrow: but I will see you again, and your heart shall rejoice, and your joy no man taketh from you."

What Shall Come To Pass
Before The Coming Of The Lord

Matthew 24:1-44 "[1]And Jesus went out, and departed from the temple: and his disciples came to him for to shew him the buildings of the temple. [2]And Jesus said unto them, See ye not all these things? verily I say unto you, There shall not be left here one stone upon another, that shall not be thrown down. [3]And as he sat upon the mount of Olives, the disciples came unto him privately, saying, Tell us, when shall these things be? and what shall be the sign of thy coming, and of the end of the world? [4]And Jesus answered and said unto them, Take heed that no man deceive you. [5]For many shall come in my name, saying, I am Christ; and shall deceive many. [6]And ye shall hear of wars and rumours of wars: see that ye be not troubled: for all these things must come to pass, but the end is not yet. [7]For nation shall rise against nation, and kingdom against kingdom: and there shall be famines, and pestilences, and earthquakes, in divers places. [8]All these are the beginning of sorrows. [9]Then shall they deliver you up to be afflicted, and shall kill you: and ye shall be hated of all nations for my name's sake. [10]And then shall many be offended, and shall betray one another, and shall hate one another. [11]And many false prophets shall rise, and shall deceive many. [12]And because iniquity shall abound, the love of many shall wax cold. [13]But he that shall endure unto the end, the same shall be saved. [14]And this gospel of the kingdom shall be preached in all the world for a witness unto all nations; and then shall the end come. [15]When ye therefore shall see the abomination of desolation, spoken of by Daniel the prophet, stand in the holy place, (whoso readeth, let him understand:) [16]Then let them which be in Judaea flee into the mountains: [17]Let him which is on the housetop not come down to take any thing out of his house: [18]Neither let him which is in the field return back to take his clothes. [19]And woe unto them that are with child, and to them that give suck in those days! [20]But pray ye that your flight be not in the winter, neither on the sabbath day: [21]For then shall be great tribulation, such as was not since the beginning of the world to this time, no, nor ever shall be. [22]And except those days should be shortened, there should no flesh be saved: but for the elect's sake those days shall be shortened. [23]Then if any man shall say unto you, Lo, here is Christ, or there; believe it not. [24]For there shall arise false Christs, and false prophets, and shall shew great signs and wonders; insomuch that, if it were possible, they shall deceive the very elect. [25]Behold, I have told you before. [26]Wherefore if they shall say unto you, Behold, he is in the desert; go not forth: behold, he is in the secret chambers; believe it not. [27]For as the lightning cometh out of the east, and shineth even unto the west; so shall also the coming of the Son of man be. [28]For wheresoever the carcase is, there will the eagles be gathered together. [29]Immediately after the tribulation of those days shall the sun be darkened, and the moon shall not give her light, and the stars shall fall from heaven, and the powers of the heavens shall be shaken: [30]And then shall appear the sign of the Son of man in heaven: and then shall all the tribes of the earth mourn, and they shall see the Son of man coming in the clouds of heaven with power and great glory. [31]And he shall send his angels with a great sound of a trumpet, and they shall gather together his elect from the four winds, from one end of heaven to the other. [32]Now learn a parable of the fig tree; When his branch is yet tender, and putteth forth leaves, ye know that summer is nigh: [33]So likewise ye, when ye shall see all these things, know that it is near, even at the doors. [34]Verily I say unto you, This generation shall not pass, till all these things be fulfilled. [35]Heaven and earth shall pass away, but my words shall not pass away. [36]But of that day and hour knoweth no man, no, not the angels of heaven, but my Father only. [37]But as the days of Noe were, so shall also the coming of the Son of man be. [38]For as in the days that were before the flood they were eating and drinking, marrying and giving in marriage, until the day that Noe entered into the ark, [39]And knew not until the flood came, and took them all away; so shall also the coming of the Son of man be. [40]Then shall two be in the field; the one shall be taken, and the other left. [41]Two women shall be grinding at the mill; the one shall be taken, and the other left. [42]Watch therefore: for ye know not what hour your Lord doth come. [43]But know this, that if the goodman of the house had known in what watch the thief would come, he would have watched, and would not have suffered his house to be broken up. [44]Therefore be ye also ready: for in such an hour as ye think not the Son of man cometh."

Mark 13:1-30 "[1]And as he went out of the temple, one of his disciples saith unto him, Master, see what manner of stones and what buildings are here! [2]And Jesus answering said unto him, Seest thou these great buildings? there shall not be left one stone upon another, that shall not be thrown down. [3]And as he sat upon the mount of Olives over against the temple, Peter and James and John and Andrew asked him privately, [4]Tell us, when shall these things be? and what shall be the sign when all these things shall be fulfilled? [5]And Jesus answering them began to say, Take heed lest any man deceive you: [6]For many shall come in my name, saying, I am Christ; and shall deceive many. [7]And when ye shall hear of wars and rumours of wars, be ye not troubled: for such things must needs be; but the end shall not be yet. [8]For nation shall rise against nation, and kingdom against kingdom: and there shall be earthquakes in divers places, and there shall be famines and troubles: these are the beginnings of sorrows. [9]But take heed to yourselves: for they shall deliver you up to councils; and in the synagogues ye shall be beaten: and ye shall be brought before rulers and kings for my sake, for a testimony against them. [10]And the gospel must first be published among all nations. [11]But when they shall lead you, and deliver you up, take no thought beforehand what

ye shall speak, neither do ye premeditate: but whatsoever shall be given you in that hour, that speak ye: for it is not ye that speak, but the Holy Ghost. [12]Now the brother shall betray the brother to death, and the father the son; and children shall rise up against their parents, and shall cause them to be put to death. [13]And ye shall be hated of all men for my name's sake: but he that shall endure unto the end, the same shall be saved. [14]But when ye shall see the abomination of desolation, spoken of by Daniel the prophet, standing where it ought not, (let him that readeth understand,) then let them that be in Judaea flee to the mountains: [15]And let him that is on the housetop not go down into the house, neither enter therein, to take any thing out of his house: [16]And let him that is in the field not turn back again for to take up his garment. [17]But woe to them that are with child, and to them that give suck in those days! [18]And pray ye that your flight be not in the winter. [19]For in those days shall be affliction, such as was not from the beginning of the creation which God created unto this time, neither shall be. [20]And except that the Lord had shortened those days, no flesh should be saved: but for the elect's sake, whom he hath chosen, he hath shortened the days. [21]And then if any man shall say to you, Lo, here is Christ; or, lo, he is there; believe him not: [22]For false Christs and false prophets shall rise, and shall shew signs and wonders, to seduce, if it were possible, even the elect. [23]But take ye heed: behold, I have foretold you all things. [24]But in those days, after that tribulation, the sun shall be darkened, and the moon shall not give her light, [25]And the stars of heaven shall fall, and the powers that are in heaven shall be shaken. [26]And then shall they see the Son of man coming in the clouds with great power and glory. [27]And then shall he send his angels, and shall gather together his elect from the four winds, from the uttermost part of the earth to the uttermost part of heaven. [28]Now learn a parable of the fig tree; When her branch is yet tender, and putteth forth leaves, ye know that summer is near: [29]So ye in like manner, when ye shall see these things come to pass, know that it is nigh, even at the doors. [30]Verily I say unto you, that this generation shall not pass, till all these things be done."

Luke 21:5-36 "[5]And as some spake of the temple, how it was adorned with goodly stones and gifts, he said, 6As for these things which ye behold, the days will come, in the which there shall not be left one stone upon another, that shall not be thrown down. 7And they asked him, saying, Master, but when shall these things be? and what sign will there be when these things shall come to pass? 8And he said, Take heed that ye be not deceived: for many shall come in my name, saying, I am Christ; and the time draweth near: go ye not therefore after them. 9But when ye shall hear of wars and commotions, be not terrified: for these things must first come to pass; but the end is not by and by. 10Then said he unto them, Nation shall rise against nation, and kingdom against kingdom: 11And great earthquakes shall be in divers places, and famines, and pestilences; and fearful sights and great signs shall there be from heaven. 12But before all these, they shall lay their hands on you, and persecute you, delivering you up to the synagogues, and into prisons, being brought before kings and rulers for my name's sake. 13And it shall turn to you for a testimony. 14Settle it therefore in your hearts, not to meditate before what ye shall answer: 15For I will give you a mouth and wisdom, which all your adversaries shall not be able to gainsay nor resist. 16And ye shall be betrayed both by parents, and brethren, and kinsfolks, and friends; and some of you shall they cause to be put to death. 17And ye shall be hated of all men for my name's sake. 18But there shall not an hair of your head perish. 19In your patience possess ye your souls. 20And when ye shall see Jerusalem compassed with armies, then know that the desolation thereof is nigh. 21Then let them which are in Judaea flee to the mountains; and let them which are in the midst of it depart out; and let not them that are in the countries enter thereinto. 22For these be the days of vengeance, that all things which are written may be fulfilled. 23But woe unto them that are with child, and to them that give suck, in those days! for there shall be great distress in the land, and wrath upon this people. 24And they shall fall by the edge of the sword, and shall be led away captive into all nations: and Jerusalem shall be trodden down of the Gentiles, until the times of the Gentiles be fulfilled. 25And there shall be signs in the sun, and in the moon, and in the stars; and upon the earth distress of nations, with perplexity; the sea and the waves roaring; 26Men's hearts failing them for fear, and

for looking after those things which are coming on the earth: for the powers of heaven shall be shaken. 27And then shall they see the Son of man coming in a cloud with power and great glory. 28And when these things begin to come to pass, then look up, and lift up your heads; for your redemption draweth nigh. 29And he spake to them a parable; Behold the fig tree, and all the trees; 30When they now shoot forth, ye see and know of your own selves that summer is now nigh at hand. 31So likewise ye, when ye see these things come to pass, know ye that the kingdom of God is nigh at hand. 32Verily I say unto you, This generation shall not pass away, till all be fulfilled. 33Heaven and earth shall pass away: but my words shall not pass away. 34And take heed to yourselves, lest at any time your hearts be overcharged with surfeiting, and drunkenness, and cares of this life, and so that day come upon you unawares. 35For as a snare shall it come on all them that dwell on the face of the whole earth. 36Watch ye therefore, and pray always, that ye may be accounted worthy to escape all these things that shall come to pass, and to stand before the Son of man."

2 Thessalonians 2:1-12 "1Now we beseech you, brethren, by the coming of our Lord Jesus Christ, and by our gathering together unto him, 2That ye be not soon shaken in mind, or be troubled, neither by spirit, nor by word, nor by letter as from us, as that the day of Christ is at hand. 3Let no man deceive you by any means: for that day shall not come, except there come a falling away first, and that man of sin be revealed, the son of perdition; 4Who opposeth and exalteth himself above all that is called God, or that is worshipped; so that he as God sitteth in the temple of God, shewing himself that he is God. 5Remember ye not, that, when I was yet with you, I told you these things? 6And now ye know what withholdeth that he might be revealed in his time. 7For the mystery of iniquity doth already work: only he who now letteth will let, until he be taken out of the way. 8And then shall that Wicked be revealed, whom the Lord shall consume with the spirit of his mouth, and shall destroy with the brightness of his coming: 9Even him, whose coming is after the working of Satan with all power and signs and lying wonders, 10And with all deceivableness of unrighteousness in them that perish; because they received not the love of the truth, that they might be saved. [11]And for this cause God shall send them strong delusion, that they should believe a lie: [12]That they all might be damned who believed not the truth, but had pleasure in unrighteousness."

What Shall Come To Pass
When The Lord Comes

Psalm 50:1-6 "[1]The mighty God, even the LORD, hath spoken, and called the earth from the rising of the sun unto the going down thereof. [2]Out of Zion, the perfection of beauty, God hath shined. [3]Our God shall come, and shall not keep silence: a fire shall devour before him, and it shall be very tempestuous round about him. [4]He shall call to the heavens from above, and to the earth, that he may judge his people. [5]Gather my saints together unto me; those that have made a covenant with me by sacrifice. [6]And the heavens shall declare his righteousness: for God is judge himself. Selah."

Zechariah 14:1-5 "[1]Behold, the day of the LORD cometh, and thy spoil shall be divided in the midst of thee. [2]For I will gather all nations against Jerusalem to battle; and the city shall be taken, and the houses rifled, and the women ravished; and half of the city shall go forth into captivity, and the residue of the people shall not be cut off from the city. [3]Then shall the LORD go forth, and fight against those nations, as when he fought in the day of battle. [4]And his feet shall stand in that day upon the mount of Olives, which is before Jerusalem on the east, and the mount of Olives shall cleave in the midst thereof toward the east and toward the west, and there shall be a very great valley; and half of the mountain shall remove toward the north, and half of it toward the south. [5]And ye shall flee to the valley of the mountains; for the valley of the mountains shall reach unto Azal: yea, ye shall flee, like as ye fled from before the earthquake in the days of Uzziah king of Judah: and the LORD my God shall come, and all the saints with thee."

Malachi 3:1-5 "[1]Behold, I will send my messenger, and he shall prepare the way before me: and the Lord, whom ye seek, shall suddenly come to his temple, even the messenger of the covenant, whom ye delight in: behold, he shall come, saith the LORD of hosts. [2]But who may abide the day of his coming? and who shall stand when he appeareth? for he is like a refiner's fire, and like fullers' soap: [3]And he shall sit as a refiner and purifer of silver: and he shall purify the sons of Levi, and purge them as gold and silver, that they may offer unto the LORD an offering in righteousness. [4]Then shall the offering of Judah and Jerusalem be pleasant unto the LORD, as in the days of old, and as in former years. [5]And I will come near to you to judgment; and I will be a swift witness against the sorcerers, and against the adulterers, and against false swearers, and against those that oppress the hireling in his wages, the widow, and the fatherless, and that turn aside the stranger from his right, and fear not me, saith the LORD of hosts."

Matthew 16:27 "For the Son of man shall come in the glory of his Father with his angels; and then he shall reward every man according to his works."

Matthew 24:29-31 "[29]Immediately after the tribulation of those days shall the sun be darkened, and the moon shall not give her light, and the stars shall fall from heaven, and the powers of the heavens shall be shaken: [30]And then shall appear the sign of the Son of man in heaven: and then shall all the tribes of the earth mourn, and they shall see the Son of man coming in the clouds of heaven with power and great glory. [31]And he shall send his angels with a great sound of a trumpet, and they shall gather together his elect from the four winds, from one end of heaven to the other."

Matthew 25:31-46 "[31]When the Son of man shall come in his glory, and all the holy angels with him, then shall he sit upon the throne of his glory: [32]And before him shall be gathered all nations: and he shall separate them one from another, as a shepherd divideth his sheep from the goats: [33]And he shall set the sheep on his right hand, but the goats on the left. [34]Then shall the King say unto them on his right hand, Come, ye blessed of my Father, inherit the kingdom prepared for you from the foundation of the world: [35]For I was an hungred, and ye gave me meat: I was thirsty, and ye gave me drink: I was a stranger, and ye took me in: [36]Naked, and ye clothed me: I was sick, and ye visited me: I was in prison, and ye came unto me. [37]Then shall the righteous answer him, saying, Lord, when saw we thee an hungred, and fed thee? or thirsty, and gave thee drink? [38]When saw we thee a stranger, and took thee in? or naked, and clothed thee? [39]Or when saw we thee sick, or in prison, and came unto thee? [40]And the King shall answer and say unto them, Verily I say unto you, Inasmuch as ye have done it unto one of the least of these my brethren, ye have done it unto me. [41]Then shall he say also unto them on the left hand, Depart from me, ye cursed, into everlasting fire, prepared for the devil and his angels: [42]For I was an hungred, and ye gave me no meat: I was thirsty, and ye gave me no drink: [43]I was a stranger, and ye took me not in: naked, and ye clothed me not: sick, and in prison, and ye visited me not. [44]Then shall they also answer him, saying, Lord, when saw we thee an hungred, or athirst, or a stranger, or naked, or sick, or in prison, and did not minister unto thee? [45]Then shall he answer them, saying, Verily I say unto you, Inasmuch as ye did it not to one of the least of these, ye did it not to me. [46]And these shall go away into everlasting punishment: but the righteous into life eternal."

Mark 13:24-27 "[24]But in those days, after that tribulation, the sun shall be darkened, and the moon shall not give her light, [25]And the stars of heaven shall fall, and the powers that are in heaven shall be shaken. [26]And then shall they see the Son of man coming in the clouds with great power and glory. [27]And then shall he send his angels, and shall gather together his elect from the four winds, from the uttermost part of the earth to the uttermost part of heaven."

John 14:1-4 "[1]Let not your heart be troubled: ye believe in God, believe also in me. [2]In my Father's house are many mansions: if it were not so, I would have told you. I go to prepare a place for you. [3]And if I go and prepare a place for you, I will come again, and receive you unto myself; that where I am, there ye may be also. [4]And whither I go ye know, and the way ye know."

1 Corinthians 4:3-5 "[3]But with me it is a very small thing that I should be judged of you, or of man's judgment: yea, I judge not mine own self. [4]For I know nothing by myself; yet am I not hereby justified: but he that judgeth me is the Lord. [5]Therefore judge nothing before the time, until the Lord come, who both will bring to light the hidden things of darkness, and will make manifest the counsels of the hearts: and then shall every man have praise of God."

1 Corinthians 15:20-28 "[20]But now is Christ risen from the dead, and become the firstfruits of them that slept. [21]For since by man came death, by man came also the resurrection of the dead. [22]For as in Adam all die, even so in Christ shall all be made alive. [23]But every man in his own order: Christ the firstfruits; afterward they that are Christ's at his coming. [24]Then cometh the end, when he shall have delivered up the kingdom to God, even the Father; when he shall have put down all rule and all authority and power. [25]For he must reign, till he hath put all enemies under his feet. [26]The last enemy that shall be destroyed is death. [27]For he hath put all things under his feet. But when he saith, all things are put under him, it is manifest that he is excepted, which did put all things under him. [28]And when all things shall be subdued unto him, then shall the Son also himself be subject unto him that put all things under him, that God may be all in all."

2 Thessalonians 1:7-10 "[7]And to you who are troubled rest with us, when the Lord Jesus shall be revealed from heaven with his mighty angels, [8]In flaming fire taking vengeance on them that know not God, and that obey not the gospel of our Lord Jesus Christ: [9]Who shall be punished with everlasting destruction from the presence of the Lord, and from the glory of his power [10]When he shall come to be glorified in his saints, and to be admired in all them that believe (because our testimony among you was believed) in that day."

2 Timothy 4:1 "I charge thee therefore before God, and the Lord Jesus Christ, who shall judge the quick and the dead at his appearing and his kingdom."

1 John 3:1-2 "[1]Behold, what manner of love the Father hath bestowed upon us, that we should be called the sons of God: therefore the world knoweth us not, because it knew him not. [2]Beloved, now are we the sons of God, and it doth not yet appear what we shall be: but we know that, when he shall appear, we shall be like him; for we shall see him as he is."

What The Coming Of The Lord Is Likened To

Matthew 25:1-13 "¹Then shall the kingdom of heaven be likened unto ten virgins, which took their lamps, and went forth to meet the bridegroom. ²And five of them were wise, and five were foolish. ³They that were foolish took their lamps, and took no oil with them: ⁴But the wise took oil in their vessels with their lamps. ⁵While the bridegroom tarried, they all slumbered and slept. ⁶And at midnight there was a cry made, Behold, the bridegroom cometh; go ye out to meet him. ⁷Then all those virgins arose, and trimmed their lamps. ⁸And the foolish said unto the wise, Give us of your oil; for our lamps are gone out. ⁹But the wise answered, saying, Not so; lest there be not enough for us and you: but go ye rather to them that sell, and buy for yourselves. ¹⁰And while they went to buy, the bridegroom came; and they that were ready went in with him to the marriage: and the door was shut. ¹¹Afterward came also the other virgins, saying, Lord, Lord, open to us. ¹²But he answered and said, Verily I say unto you, I know you not. ¹³Watch therefore, for ye know neither the day nor the hour wherein the Son of man cometh."

Mark 13:33-37 "³³Take ye heed, watch and pray: for ye know not when the time is. ³⁴For the Son of man is as a man taking a far journey, who left his house, and gave authority to his servants, and to every man his work, and commanded the porter to watch. ³⁵Watch ye therefore: for ye know not when the master of the house cometh, at even, or at midnight, or at the cockcrowing, or in the morning: ³⁶Lest coming suddenly he find you sleeping. ³⁷And what I say unto you I say unto all, Watch."

Luke 12:35-40 "³⁵Let your loins be girded about, and your lights burning; ³⁶And ye yourselves like unto men that wait for their lord, when he will return from the wedding; that when he cometh and knocketh, they may open unto him immediately. ³⁷Blessed are those servants, whom the lord when he cometh shall find watching: verily I say unto you, that he shall gird himself, and make them to sit down to meat, and will come forth and serve them. ³⁸And if he shall come in the second watch, or come in the third watch, and find them so, blessed are those servants. ³⁹And this know, that if the goodman of the house had known what hour the thief would come, he would have watched, and not have suffered his house to be broken through. ⁴⁰Be ye therefore ready also: for the Son of man cometh at an hour when ye think not."

Luke 19:11-27 "¹¹And as they heard these things, he added and spake a parable, because he was nigh to Jerusalem, and because they thought that the kingdom of God should immediately appear. ¹²He said therefore, A certain nobleman went into a far country to receive for himself a kingdom, and to return. ¹³And he called his ten servants, and delivered them ten pounds, and said unto them, Occupy till I come. ¹⁴But his citizens hated him, and sent a message after him, saying, We will not have this man to reign over us. ¹⁵And it came to pass, that when he was returned, having received the kingdom, then he commanded these servants to be called unto him, to whom he had given the money, that he might know how much every man had gained by trading. ¹⁶Then came the first, saying, Lord, thy pound hath gained ten pounds. ¹⁷And he said unto him, Well, thou good servant: because thou hast been faithful in a very little, have thou authority over ten cities. ¹⁸And the second came, saying, Lord, thy pound hath gained five pounds. ¹⁹And he said likewise to him, Be thou also over five cities. ²⁰And another came, saying, Lord, behold, here is thy pound, which I have kept laid up in a napkin: ²¹For I feared thee, because thou art an austere man: thou takest up that thou layedst not down, and reapest that thou didst not sow. ²²And he saith unto him, Out of thine own mouth will I judge thee, thou wicked servant. Thou knewest that I was an austere man, taking up that I laid not down, and reaping that I did not sow: ²³Wherefore then gavest not thou my money into the bank, that at my coming I might have required mine own with usury? ²⁴And he said unto them that stood by, Take from him the pound, and give it to him that hath ten pounds. ²⁵(And they said unto him, Lord, he hath ten pounds.) ²⁶For I say unto you, That unto every one which hath shall be given; and from him that hath not, even that he hath shall be taken away from him. ²⁷But those mine enemies, which would not that I should reign over them, bring hither, and slay them before me."

Luke 21:29-36 "²⁹And he spake to them a parable; Behold the fig tree, and all the trees; ³⁰When they now shoot forth, ye see and know of your own selves that summer is now nigh at hand. ³¹So likewise ye, when ye see these things come to pass, know ye that the kingdom of God is nigh at hand. ³²Verily I say unto you, This generation shall not pass away, till all be fulfilled. ³³Heaven and earth shall pass away: but my words shall not pass away. ³⁴And take heed to yourselves, lest at any time your hearts be overcharged with surfeiting, and drunkenness, and cares of this life, and so that day come upon you unawares. ³⁵For as a snare shall it come on all them that dwell on the face of the whole earth. ³⁶Watch ye therefore, and pray always, that ye may be accounted worthy to escape all these things that shall come to pass, and to stand before the Son of man."

What The Days Will Be Like When The Lord Comes

Matthew 24:37-51 "³⁷But as the days of Noe were, so shall also the coming of the Son of man be. ³⁸For as in the days that were before the flood they were eating and drinking, marrying and giving in marriage, until the day that Noe entered into the ark, ³⁹And knew not until the flood came, and took them all away; so shall also the coming of the Son of man be. ⁴⁰Then shall two be in the field; the one shall be taken, and the other left. ⁴¹Two women shall be grinding at the mill; the one shall be taken, and the other left. ⁴²Watch therefore: for ye know not what hour your Lord doth come. ⁴³But know this, that if the goodman of the house had known in what watch the thief would come, he would have watched, and would not have suffered his house to be broken up. ⁴⁴Therefore be ye also ready: for in such an hour as ye think not the Son of man cometh. ⁴⁵Who then is a faithful and wise servant, whom his lord hath made ruler over his household, to give them meat in due season? ⁴⁶Blessed is that servant, whom his lord when he cometh shall find so doing. ⁴⁷Verily I say unto you, That he shall make him ruler over all his goods. ⁴⁸But and if that evil servant shall say in his heart, My lord delayeth his coming; ⁴⁹And shall begin to smite his fellowservants, and to eat and drink with the drunken; ⁵⁰The lord of that servant shall come in a day when he looketh not for him, and in an hour that he is not aware of, ⁵¹And shall cut him asunder, and appoint him his portion with the hypocrites: there shall be weeping and gnashing of teeth."

Luke 17:26-37 "²⁶And as it was in the days of Noe, so shall it be also in the days of the Son of man. ²⁷They did eat, they drank, they married wives, they were given in marriage, until the day that Noe entered into the ark, and the flood came, and destroyed them all. ²⁸Likewise also as it was in the days of Lot; they did eat, they drank, they bought, they sold, they planted, they builded; ²⁹But the same day that Lot went out of Sodom it rained fire and brimstone from heaven, and destroyed them all. ³⁰Even thus shall it be in the day when the Son of man is revealed. ³¹In that day, he which shall be upon the housetop, and his stuff in the house, let him not come down to take it away: and he that is in the field, let him likewise not return back. ³²Remember Lot's wife. ³³Whosoever shall seek to save his life shall lose it; and whosoever shall lose his life shall preserve it. ³⁴I tell you, in that night there shall be two men in one bed; the one shall be taken, and the other shall be left. ³⁵Two women shall be grinding together; the one shall be taken, and the other left. ³⁶Two men shall be in the field; the one shall be taken, and the other left. ³⁷And they answered and said unto him, Where, Lord? And he said unto them, Wheresoever the body is, thither will the eagles be gathered together."

When The Lord Will Come

Matthew 24:42-51 "⁴²Watch therefore: for ye know not what hour your Lord doth come. ⁴³But know this, that if the goodman of the house had known in what watch the thief would come, he would have watched, and would not have suffered his house to be broken up. ⁴⁴Therefore be ye also ready: for in such an hour as ye think not the Son of man cometh. ⁴⁵Who then is a faithful and wise servant, whom his lord hath made ruler over his household, to give them meat in due season? ⁴⁶Blessed is that servant, whom his lord when he cometh shall find so doing. ⁴⁷Verily I say unto you, That he shall make him ruler over all his goods. ⁴⁸But and if that evil servant shall say in his heart, My lord delayeth his coming; ⁴⁹And shall begin to smite his fellowservants, and to eat and drink with the drunken; ⁵⁰The lord of that servant shall come in a day when he looketh not for him, and in an hour that he is not aware of, ⁵¹And shall cut him asunder, and appoint him his portion with the hypocrites: there shall be weeping and gnashing of teeth."

Luke 12:40 "Be ye therefore ready also: for the Son of man cometh at an hour when ye think not."

Revelation 3:1-3 "[1]And unto the angel of the church in Sardis write; These things saith he that hath the seven Spirits of God, and the seven stars; I know thy works, that thou hast a name that thou livest, and art dead. [2]Be watchful, and strengthen the things which remain, that are ready to die: for I have not found thy works perfect before God. [3]Remember therefore how thou hast received and heard, and hold fast, and repent. If therefore thou shalt not watch, I will come on thee as a thief, and thou shalt not know what hour I will come upon thee."

Who Christ Will Appear
To The Second Time

Hebrews 9:28 "So Christ was once offered to bear the sins of many; and unto them that look for him shall he appear the second time without sin unto salvation."

Who Shall Be Blameless
When The Lord Comes

1 Corinthians 1:2-9 "[2]Unto the church of God which is at Corinth, to them that are sanctified in Christ Jesus, called to be saints, with all that in every place call upon the name of Jesus Christ our Lord, both theirs and ours: [3]Grace be unto you, and peace, from God our Father, and from the Lord Jesus Christ. [4]I thank my God always on your behalf, for the grace of God which is given you by Jesus Christ; [5]That in every thing ye are enriched by him, in all utterance, and in all knowledge; [6]Even as the testimony of Christ was confirmed in you: [7]So that ye come behind in no gift; waiting for the coming of our Lord Jesus Christ: [8]Who shall also confirm you unto the end, that ye may be blameless in the day of our Lord Jesus Christ. [9]God is faithful, by whom ye were called unto the fellowship of his Son Jesus Christ our Lord."

Who Shall Be Gathered Together
When The Lord Comes

Psalm 50:1-5 "[1]The mighty God, even the LORD, hath spoken, and called the earth from the rising of the sun unto the going down thereof. [2]Out of Zion, the perfection of beauty, God hath shined. [3]Our God shall come, and shall not keep silence: a fire shall devour before him, and it shall be very tempestuous round about him. [4]He shall call to the heavens from above, and to the earth, that he may judge his people. [5]Gather my saints together unto me; those that have made a covenant with me by sacrifice."

Matthew 24:29-31 "[29]Immediately after the tribulation of those days shall the sun be darkened, and the moon shall not give her light, and the stars shall fall from heaven, and the powers of the heavens shall be shaken: [30]And then shall appear the sign of the Son of man in heaven: and then shall all the tribes of the earth mourn, and they shall see the Son of man coming in the clouds of heaven with power and great glory. [31]And he shall send his angels with a great sound of a trumpet, and they shall gather together his elect from the four winds, from one end of heaven to the other."

Mark 13:24-27 "[24]But in those days, after that tribulation, the sun shall be darkened, and the moon shall not give her light, [25]And the stars of heaven shall fall, and the powers that are in heaven shall be shaken. [26]And then shall they see the Son of man coming in the clouds with great power and glory. [27]And then shall he send his angels, and shall gather together his elect from the four winds, from the uttermost part of the earth to the uttermost part of heaven."

Ephesians 1:3-11 "[3]Blessed be the God and Father of our Lord Jesus Christ, who hath blessed us with all spiritual blessings in heavenly places in Christ: [4]According as he hath chosen us in him before the foundation of the world, that we should be holy and without blame before him in love: [5]Having predestinated us unto the adoption of children by Jesus Christ to himself, according to the good pleasure of his will, [6]To the praise of the glory of his grace, wherein he hath made us accepted in the beloved. [7]In whom we have redemption through his blood, the forgiveness of sins, according to the riches of his grace; [8]Wherein he hath abounded toward us in all wisdom and prudence; [9]Having made known unto us the mystery of his will, according to his good pleasure which he hath purposed in himself: [10]That in the dispensation of the fulness of times he might gather together in one all things in Christ, both which are in heaven, and which are on earth; even in him: [11]In whom also we have obtained an inheritance, being predestinated according to the purpose of him who worketh all things after the counsel of his own will."

1 Thessalonians 4:13-18 "¹³But I would not have you to be ignorant, brethren, concerning them which are asleep, that ye sorrow not, even as others which have no hope. ¹⁴For if we believe that Jesus died and rose again, even so them also which sleep in Jesus will God bring with him. ¹⁵For this we say unto you by the word of the Lord, that we which are alive and remain unto the coming of the Lord shall not prevent them which are asleep. ¹⁶For the Lord himself shall descend from heaven with a shout, with the voice of the archangel, and with the trump of God: and the dead in Christ shall rise first: ¹⁷Then we which are alive and remain shall be caught up together with them in the clouds, to meet the Lord in the air: and so shall we ever be with the Lord. ¹⁸Wherefore comfort one another with these words."

1 Thessalonians 5:1-11 "¹But of the times and the seasons, brethren, ye have no need that I write unto you. ²For yourselves know perfectly that the day of the Lord so cometh as a thief in the night. ³For when they shall say, Peace and safety; then sudden destruction cometh upon them, as travail upon a woman with child; and they shall not escape. ⁴But ye, brethren, are not in darkness, that that day should overtake you as a thief. ⁵Ye are all the children of light, and the children of the day: we are not of the night, nor of darkness. ⁶Therefore let us not sleep, as do others; but let us watch and be sober. ⁷For they that sleep sleep in the night; and they that be drunken are drunken in the night. ⁸But let us, who are of the day, be sober, putting on the breastplate of faith and love; and for an helmet, the hope of salvation. ⁹For God hath not appointed us to wrath, but to obtain salvation by our Lord Jesus Christ, ¹⁰Who died for us, that, whether we wake or sleep, we should live together with him. ¹¹Wherefore comfort yourselves together, and edify one another, even as also ye do."

2 Thessalonians 2:1-2 "¹Now we beseech you, brethren, by the coming of our Lord Jesus Christ, and by our gathering together unto him, ²That ye be not soon shaken in mind, or be troubled, neither by spirit, nor by word, nor by letter as from us, as that the day of Christ is at hand."

Who Shall Be Resurrected
When The Lord Comes

1 Corinthians 15:20-23 "²⁰But now is Christ risen from the dead, and become the firstfruits of them that slept. ²¹For since by man came death, by man came also the resurrection of the dead. ²²For as in Adam all die, even so in Christ shall all be made alive. ²³But every man in his own order: Christ the firstfruits; afterward they that are Christ's at his coming."

Colossians 3:1-4 "¹If ye then be risen with Christ, seek those things which are above, where Christ sitteth on the right hand of God. ²Set your affection on things above, not on things on the earth. ³For ye are dead, and your life is hid with Christ in God. ⁴When Christ, who is our life, shall appear, then shall ye also appear with him in glory."

1 Thessalonians 4:13-18 "¹³But I would not have you to be ignorant, brethren, concerning them which are asleep, that ye sorrow not, even as others which have no hope. ¹⁴For if we believe that Jesus died and rose again, even so them also which sleep in Jesus will God bring with him. ¹⁵For this we say unto you by the word of the Lord, that we which are alive and remain unto the coming of the Lord shall not prevent them which are asleep. ¹⁶For the Lord himself shall descend from heaven with a shout, with the voice of the archangel, and with the trump of God: and the dead in Christ shall rise first: ¹⁷Then we which are alive and remain shall be caught up together with them in the clouds, to meet the Lord in the air: and so shall we ever be with the Lord. ¹⁸Wherefore comfort one another with these words."

Who Shall Have Confidence
When The Lord Comes

1 John 2:22-28 "²²Who is a liar but he that denieth that Jesus is the Christ? He is antichrist, that denieth the Father and the Son. ²³Whosoever denieth the Son, the same hath not the Father: (but) he that acknowledgeth the Son hath the Father also. ²⁴Let that therefore abide in you, which ye have heard from the beginning. If that which ye have heard from the beginning shall remain in you, ye also shall continue in the Son, and in the Father. ²⁵And this is the promise that he hath promised us, even eternal life. ²⁶These things have I written unto you concerning them that seduce you. ²⁷But the anointing which ye have received of him abideth in you, and ye need not that any man teach you: but as the same anointing teacheth you of all things, and is truth, and is no lie, and even as it hath taught you, ye shall abide in him. ²⁸And now, little children, abide in him; that, when he shall appear, we may have confidence, and not be ashamed before him at his coming."

Who The Lord Will Come With

Zechariah 14:4-5 "⁴And his feet shall stand in that day upon the mount of Olives, which is before Jerusalem on the east, and the mount of Olives shall cleave in the midst thereof toward the east and toward the west, and there shall be a very great valley; and half of the mountain shall remove toward the north, and half of it toward the south. ⁵And ye shall flee to the valley of the mountains; for the valley of the mountains shall reach unto Azal: yea, ye shall flee, like as ye fled from before the earthquake in the days of Uzziah king of Judah: and the LORD my God shall come, and all the saints with thee."

Matthew 16:27 "For the Son of man shall come in the glory of his Father with his angels; and then he shall reward every man according to his works."

Matthew 24:29-31 "²⁹Immediately after the tribulation of those days shall the sun be darkened, and the moon shall not give her light, and the stars shall fall from heaven, and the powers of the heavens shall be shaken: ³⁰And then shall appear the sign of the Son of man in heaven: and then shall all the tribes of the earth mourn, and they shall see the Son of man coming in the clouds of heaven with power and great glory. ³¹And he shall send his angels with a great sound of a trumpet, and they shall gather together his elect from the four winds, from one end of heaven to the other."

Matthew 25:31 "When the Son of man shall come in his glory, and all the holy angels with him, then shall he sit upon the throne of his glory."

Mark 8:38 "Whosoever therefore shall be ashamed of me and of my words in this adulterous and sinful generation; of him also shall the Son of man be ashamed, when he cometh in the glory of his Father with the holy angels."

Mark 13:24-27 "²⁴But in those days, after that tribulation, the sun shall be darkened, and the moon shall not give her light, ²⁵And the stars of heaven shall fall, and the powers that are in heaven shall be shaken. ²⁶And then shall they see the Son of man coming in the clouds with great power and glory. ²⁷And then shall he send his angels, and shall gather together his elect from the four winds, from the uttermost part of the earth to the uttermost part of heaven."

1 Thessalonians 4:13-18 "¹³But I would not have you to be ignorant, brethren, concerning them which are asleep, that ye sorrow not, even as others which have no hope. ¹⁴For if we believe that Jesus died and rose again, even so them also which sleep in Jesus will God bring with him. ¹⁵For this we say unto you by the word of the Lord, that we which are alive and remain unto the coming of the Lord shall not prevent them which are asleep. ¹⁶For the Lord himself shall descend from heaven with a shout, with the voice of the archangel, and with the trump of God: and the dead in Christ shall rise first: ¹⁷Then we which are alive and remain shall be caught up together with them in the clouds, to meet the Lord in the air: and so shall we ever be with the Lord. ¹⁸Wherefore comfort one another with these words."

2 Thessalonians 1:7 "And to you who are troubled rest with us, when the Lord Jesus shall be revealed from heaven with his mighty angels."

Jude 14 "And Enoch also, the seventh from Adam, prophesied of these, saying, Behold, the Lord cometh with ten thousands of his saints."

Revelation 19:11-14 "¹¹And I saw heaven opened, and behold a white horse; and he that sat upon him was called Faithful and True, and in righteousness he doth judge and make war. ¹²His eyes were as a flame of fire, and on his head were many crowns; and he had a name written, that no man knew, but he himself. ¹³And he was clothed with a vesture dipped in blood: and his name is called The Word of God. ¹⁴And the armies which were in heaven followed him upon white horses, clothed in fine linen, white and clean."

COMMANDMENT

Not Adding To Or Diminishing From The Commandments Of The Lord

Deuteronomy 4:2 "Ye shall not add unto the word which I command you, neither shall ye diminish ought from it, that ye may keep the commandments of the LORD your God which I command you."

Deuteronomy 12:31-32 "³¹Thou shalt not do so unto the LORD thy God: for every abomination to the

LORD, which he hateth, have they done unto their gods; for even their sons and their daughters they have burnt in the fire to their gods. [32]What thing soever I command you, observe to do it: thou shalt not add thereto, nor diminish from it."

Proverbs 30:5-6 "[5]Every word of God is pure: he is a shield unto them that put their trust in him. [6]Add thou not unto his words, lest he reprove thee, and thou be found a liar."

The Commandments
Of The Lord
Psalm 19:8 "The statutes of the LORD are right, rejoicing the heart: the commandment of the LORD is pure, enlightening the eyes."

Psalm 111:4-8 "[4]He hath made his wonderful works to be remembered: the LORD is gracious and full of compassion. [5]He hath given meat unto them that fear him: he will ever be mindful of his covenant. [6]He hath shewed his people the power of his works, that he may give them the heritage of the heathen. [7]The works of his hands are verity and judgment; all his commandments are sure. [8]They stand fast for ever and ever, and are done in truth and uprightness."

Psalm 119:89-96 "[89]For ever, O LORD, thy word is settled in heaven. [90]Thy faithfulness is unto all generations: thou hast established the earth, and it abideth. [91]They continue this day according to thine ordinances: for all are thy servants. [92]Unless thy law had been my delights, I should then have perished in mine affliction. [93]I will never forget thy precepts: for with them thou hast quickened me. [94]I am thine, save me; for I have sought thy precepts. [95]The wicked have waited for me to destroy me: but I will consider thy testimonies. [96]I have seen an end of all perfection: but thy commandment is exceeding broad."

Psalm 119:151 "Thou art near, O LORD; and all thy commandments are truth."

John 12:49-50 "[49]For I have not spoken of myself; but the Father which sent me, he gave me a commandment, what I should say, and what I should speak. [50]And I know that his commandment is life everlasting: whatsoever I speak therefore, even as the Father said unto me, so I speak."

Romans 7:12 "Wherefore the law is holy, and the commandment holy, and just, and good."

1 John 5:3 "For this is the love of God, that we keep his commandments: and his commandments are not grievous."

The Commandments Of Your Parents
Proverbs 6:20-23 "[20]My son, keep thy father's commandment, and forsake not the law of thy mother: [21]Bind them continually upon thine heart, and tie them about thy neck. [22]When thou goest, it shall lead thee; when thou sleepest, it shall keep thee; and when thou awakest, it shall talk with thee. [23]For the commandment is a lamp; and the law is light; and reproofs of instruction are the way of life."

The End Of Commandment
1 Timothy 1:5 "Now the end of the commandment is charity out of a pure heart, and of a good conscience, and of faith unfeigned."

The Great Commandment
Leviticus 19:17-18 "[17]Thou shalt not hate thy brother in thine heart: thou shalt in any wise rebuke thy neighbour, and not suffer sin upon him. [18]Thou shalt not avenge, nor bear any grudge against the children of thy people, but thou shalt love thy neighbour as thyself: I am the LORD."

Matthew 22:36-40 "[36]Master, which is the great commandment in the law? [37]Jesus said unto him, Thou shalt love the Lord thy God with all thy heart, and with all thy soul, and with all thy mind. [38]This is the first and great commandment. [39]And the second is like unto it, Thou shalt love thy neighbour as thyself. [40]On these two commandments hang all the law and the prophets."

Mark 12:28-33 "[28]And one of the scribes came, and having heard them reasoning together, and perceiving that he had answered them well, asked him, Which is the first commandment of all? [29]And Jesus answered him, The first of all the commandments is, Hear, O Israel; The Lord our God is one Lord: [30]And thou shalt love the Lord thy God with all thy heart, and with all thy soul, and with all thy mind, and with all thy strength: this is the first commandment. [31]And the second is like, namely this, Thou shalt love thy neighbour as thyself. There is none other commandment greater than these. [32]And the scribe said unto him, Well, Master, thou hast said the truth: for there is one God; and there is none other but he: [33]And to love him with all the heart, and with all the understanding, and with all the soul, and with all the strength, and to love his neighbour as himself, is more than all whole burnt offerings and sacrifices."

Luke 10:25-28 "25And, behold, a certain lawyer stood up, and tempted him, saying, Master, what shall I do to inherit eternal life? 26He said unto him, What is written in the law? how readest thou? 27And he answering said, Thou shalt love the Lord thy God with all thy heart, and with all thy soul, and with all thy strength, and with all thy mind; and thy neighbour as thyself. 28And he said unto him, Thou hast answered right: this do, and thou shalt live."

John 13:31-35 "31Therefore, when he was gone out, Jesus said, Now is the Son of man glorified, and God is glorified in him. 32If God be glorified in him, God shall also glorify him in himself, and shall straightway glorify him. 33Little children, yet a little while I am with you. Ye shall seek me: and as I said unto the Jews, Whither I go, ye cannot come; so now I say to you. 34A new commandment I give unto you, That ye love one another; as I have loved you, that ye also love one another. 35By this shall all men know that ye are my disciples, if ye have love one to another."

John 15:12-13 "12This is my commandment, That ye love one another, as I have loved you. 13Greater love hath no man than this, that a man lay down his life for his friends."

John 15:17 "These things I command you, that ye love one another."

Romans 13:8-9 "8Owe no man any thing, but to love one another: for he that loveth another hath fulfilled the law. 9For this, Thou shalt not commit adultery, Thou shalt not kill, Thou shalt not steal, Thou shalt not bear false witness, Thou shalt not covet; and if there be any other commandment, it is briefly comprehended in this saying, namely, Thou shalt love thy neighbour as thyself."

1 John 2:7-11 "7Brethren, I write no new commandment unto you, but an old commandment which ye had from the beginning. The old commandment is the word which ye have heard from the beginning. 8Again, a new commandment I write unto you, which thing is true in him and in you: because the darkness is past, and the true light now shineth. 9He that saith he is in the light, and hateth his brother, is in darkness even until now. 10He that loveth his brother abideth in the light, and there is none occasion of stumbling in him. 11But he that hateth his brother is in darkness, and walketh in darkness, and knoweth not whither he goeth, because that darkness hath blinded his eyes."

1 John 3:23 "And this is his commandment, That we should believe on the name of his Son Jesus Christ, and love one another, as he gave us commandment."

1 John 4:21 "And this commandment have we from him, That he who loveth God love his brother also."

2 John 3-6 "3Grace be with you, mercy, and peace, from God the Father, and from the Lord Jesus Christ, the Son of the Father, in truth and love. 4I rejoiced greatly that I found of thy children walking in truth, as we have received a commandment from the Father. 5And now I beseech thee, lady, not as though I wrote a new commandment unto thee, but that which we had from the beginning, that we love one another. 6And this is love, that we walk after his commandments. This is the commandment, That, as ye have heard from the beginning, ye should walk in it."

The Ten Commandments

Exodus 20:1-17 "1And God spake all these words, saying, 2I am the LORD thy God, which have brought thee out of the land of Egypt, out of the house of bondage. 3Thou shalt have no other gods before me. 4Thou shalt not make unto thee any graven image, or any likeness of any thing that is in heaven above, or that is in the earth beneath, or that is in the water under the earth: 5Thou shalt not bow down thyself to them, nor serve them: for I the LORD thy God am a jealous God, visiting the iniquity of the fathers upon the children unto the third and fourth generation of them that hate me; 6And shewing mercy unto thousands of them that love me, and keep my commandments. 7Thou shalt not take the name of the LORD thy God in vain; for the LORD will not hold him guiltless that taketh his name in vain. 8Remember the sabbath day, to keep it holy. 9Six days shalt thou labour, and do all thy work: 10But the seventh day is the sabbath of the LORD thy God: in it thou shalt not do any work, thou, nor thy son, nor thy daughter, thy manservant, nor thy maidservant, nor thy cattle, nor thy stranger that is within thy gates: [11]For in six days the LORD made heaven and earth, the sea, and all that in them is, and rested the seventh day: wherefore the LORD blessed the sabbath day, and hallowed it. [12]Honour thy father and thy mother: that thy days may be long upon the land which the LORD thy God giveth thee. [13]Thou shalt not kill. [14]Thou shalt not commit adultery. [15]Thou shalt not steal. [16]Thou shalt not bear false witness against thy neighbour. [17]Thou shalt not covet thy neighbour's house, thou shalt not covet thy neighbour's wife, nor his manservant, nor his maidservant, nor his ox, nor his ass, nor any thing that is thy neighbour's."

Deuteronomy 5:6-21 "[6]I am the LORD thy God, which brought thee out of the land of Egypt, from the house of bondage. [7]Thou shalt have none other gods before me. [8]Thou shalt not make thee any graven image, or any likeness of any thing that is in heaven above, or that is in the earth beneath, or that is in the waters beneath the earth: [9]Thou shalt not bow down thyself unto them, nor serve them: for I the LORD thy God am a jealous God, visiting the iniquity of the fathers upon the children unto the third and fourth generation of them that hate me, [10]And shewing mercy unto thousands of them that love me and keep my commandments. [11]Thou shalt not take the name of the LORD thy God in vain: for the LORD will not hold him guiltless that taketh his name in vain. [12]Keep the sabbath day to sanctify it, as the LORD thy God hath commanded thee. [13]Six days thou shalt labour, and do all thy work: [14]But the seventh day is the sabbath of the LORD thy God: in it thou shalt not do any work, thou, nor thy son, nor thy daughter, nor thy manservant, nor thy maidservant, nor thine ox, nor thine ass, nor any of thy cattle, nor thy stranger that is within thy gates; that thy manservant and thy maidservant may rest as well as thou. [15]And remember that thou wast a servant in the land of Egypt, and that the LORD thy God brought thee out thence through a mighty hand and by a stretched out arm: therefore the LORD thy God commanded thee to keep the sabbath day. [16]Honour thy father and thy mother, as the LORD thy God hath commanded thee; that thy days may be prolonged, and that it may go well with thee, in the land which the LORD thy God giveth thee. [17]Thou shalt not kill. [18]Neither shalt thou commit adultery. [19]Neither shalt thou steal. [20]Neither shalt thou bear false witness against thy neighbour. [21]Neither shalt thou desire thy neighbour's wife, neither shalt thou covet thy neighbour's house, his field, or his manservant, or his maidservant, his ox, or his ass, or any thing that is thy neighbour's."

COMMENDING

How A Man Shall Be Commended
Proverbs 12:8 "A man shall be commended according to his wisdom: but he that is of a perverse heart shall be despised."

Those That Commend Themselves
2 Corinthians 10:18 "For not he that commendeth himself is approved, but whom the Lord commendeth."

Those Whom The Lord Commends
2 Corinthians 10:18 "For not he that commendeth himself is approved, but whom the Lord commendeth."

COMMITMENT

The Reward For Committing To The Lord
Psalm 37:5-6 "[5]Commit thy way unto the LORD; trust also in him; and he shall bring it to pass. [6]And he shall bring forth thy righteousness as the light, and thy judgment as the noonday."

Proverbs 16:3 "Commit thy works unto the LORD, and thy thoughts shall be established."

COMMUNION

Those That Are Joined To The Lord
1 Corinthians 6:15-17 "[15]Know ye not that your bodies are the members of Christ? shall I then take the members of Christ, and make them the members of an harlot? God forbid. [16]What? know ye not that he which is joined to an harlot is one body? for two, saith he, shall be one flesh. [17]But he that is joined unto the Lord is one spirit."

What Cannot Have Communion Together
1 Corinthiaĺns 10:20-21 "[20]But I say, that the things which the Gentiles sacrifice, they sacrifice

to devils, and not to God: and I would not that ye should have fellowship with devils. ²¹Ye cannot drink the cup of the Lord, and the cup of devils: ye cannot be partakers of the Lord's table, and of the table of devils."

2 Corinthians 6:14-16 "¹⁴Be ye not unequally yoked together with unbelievers: for what fellowship hath righteousness with unrighteousness? and what communion hath light with darkness? ¹⁵And what concord hath Christ with Belial? or what part hath he that believeth with an infidel? ¹⁶And what agreement hath the temple of God with idols? for ye are the temple of the living God; as God hath said, I will dwell in them, and walk in them; and I will be their God, and they shall be my people."

COMPANY

The Companion Of Fools
Proverbs 13:20 "He that walketh with wise men shall be wise: but a companion of fools shall be destroyed."

The Companion Of Riotous Men
Proverbs 28:7 "Whoso keepeth the law is a wise son: but he that is a companion of riotous men shameth his father."

Those That Have No Companionship
Ecclesiastes 4:7-12 "⁷Then I returned, and I saw vanity under the sun. ⁸There is one alone, and there is not a second; yea, he hath neither child nor brother: yet is there no end of all his labour; neither is his eye satisfied with riches; neither saith he, For whom do I labour, and bereave my soul of good? This is also vanity, yea, it is a sore travail. ⁹Two are better than one; because they have a good reward for their labour. ¹⁰For if they fall, the one will lift up his fellow: but woe to him that is alone when he falleth; for he hath not another to help him up. ¹¹Again, if two lie together, then they have heat: but how can one be warm alone? ¹²And if one prevail against him, two shall withstand him; and a threefold cord is not quickly broken."

Those That Keep Company With Harlots
Proverbs 29:3 "Whoso loveth wisdom rejoiceth his father: but he that keepeth company with harlots spendeth his substance."

Those That Walk With Wise Men
Proverbs 13:20 "He that walketh with wise men shall be wise: but a companion of fools shall be destroyed."

Who Is The Companion Of A Destroyer
Proverbs 28:24 "Whoso robbeth his father or his mother, and saith, It is no transgression; the same is the companion of a destroyer."

Who Not To Have Company With
Proverbs 22:24-25 "²⁴Make no friendship with an angry man; and with a furious man thou shalt not go: ²⁵Lest thou learn his ways, and get a snare to thy soul."

Proverbs 23:20-21 "²⁰Be not among winebibbers; among riotous eaters of flesh: ²¹For the drunkard and the glutton shall come to poverty: and drowsiness shall clothe a man with rags."

Proverbs 24:1-2 "¹Be not thou envious against evil men, neither desire to be with them. ²For their heart studieth destruction, and their lips talk of mischief."

1 Corinthians 5:9-13 "⁹I wrote unto you in an epistle not to company with fornicators: ¹⁰Yet not altogether with the fornicators of this world, or with the covetous, or extortioners, or with idolaters; for then must ye needs go out of the world. ¹¹But now I have written unto you not to keep company, if any man that is called a brother be a fornicator, or covetous, or an idolater, or a railer, or a drunkard, or an extortioner; with such an one no not to eat. ¹²For what have I to do to judge them also that are without? do not ye judge them that are within? ¹³But them that are without God judgeth. Therefore put away from among yourselves that wicked person."

1 Timothy 6:3-5 "³If any man teach otherwise, and consent not to wholesome words, even the words of our Lord Jesus Christ, and to the doctrine which is according to godliness; ⁴He is proud, knowing nothing, but doting about questions and strifes of words, whereof cometh envy, strife, railings, evil surmisings, ⁵Perverse disputings of men of corrupt minds, and destitute of the truth, supposing that gain is godliness: from such withdraw thyself."

2 Thessalonians 3:6 "Now we command you, brethren, in the name of our Lord Jesus Christ, that ye withdraw yourselves from every brother that walketh disorderly, and not after the tradition which he received of us."

2 Thessalonians 3:14-15 "14And if any man obey not our word by this epistle, note that man, and have no company with him, that he may be ashamed. 15Yet count him not as an enemy, but admonish him as a brother."

2 John 9-11 "9Whosoever transgresseth, and abideth not in the doctrine of Christ, hath not God. He that abideth in the doctrine of Christ, he hath both the Father and the Son. 10If there come any unto you, and bring not this doctrine, receive him not into your house, neither bid him God speed: 11For he that biddeth him God speed is partaker of his evil deeds."

COMPASSION

Being Compassionate
Zechariah 7:9 "Thus speaketh the LORD of hosts, saying, Execute true judgment, and shew mercy and compassions every man to his brother."

1 Peter 3:8 "Finally, be ye all of one mind, having compassion one of another, love as brethren, be pitiful, be courteous."

Jude 20-23 "20But ye, beloved, building up yourselves on your most holy faith, praying in the Holy Ghost, 21Keep yourselves in the love of God, looking for the mercy of our Lord Jesus Christ unto eternal life. 22And of some have compassion, making a difference: 23And others save with fear, pulling them out of the fire; hating even the garment spotted by the flesh."

The Compassions Of The Lord
Lamentations 3:22-23 "22It is of the LORD's mercies that we are not consumed, because his compassions fail not. 23They are new every morning: great is thy faithfulness."

The Lord Being Compassionate
Deuteronomy 30:3 "That then the LORD thy God will turn thy captivity, and have compassion upon thee, and will return and gather thee from all the nations, whither the LORD thy God hath scattered thee."

Psalm 78:32-38 "32For all this they sinned still, and believed not for his wondrous works. 33Therefore their days did he consume in vanity, and their

years in trouble. 34When he slew them, then they sought him: and they returned and inquired early after God. 35And they remembered that God was their rock, and the high God their redeemer. 36Nevertheless they did flatter him with their mouth, and they lied unto him with their tongues. 37For their heart was not right with him, neither were they stedfast in his covenant. 38But he, being full of compassion, forgave their iniquity, and destroyed them not: yea, many a time turned he his anger away, and did not stir up all his wrath."

Psalm 86:15 "But thou, O Lord, art a God full of compassion, and gracious, longsuffering, and plenteous in mercy and truth."

Psalm 111:4 "He hath made his wonderful works to be remembered: the LORD is gracious and full of compassion."

Psalm 145:8 "The LORD is gracious, and full of compassion; slow to anger, and of great mercy."

Jeremiah 12:14-15 "14Thus saith the LORD against all mine evil neighbours, that touch the inheritance which I have caused my people Israel to inherit; Behold, I will pluck them out of their land, and pluck out the house of Judah from among them. 15And it shall come to pass, after that I have plucked them out I will return, and have compassion on them, and will bring them again, every man to his heritage, and every man to his land."

Lamentations 3:31-36 "31For the Lord will not cast off for ever: 32But though he cause grief, yet will he have compassion according to the multitude of his mercies. 33For he doth not afflict willingly nor grieve the children of men. 34To crush under his feet all the prisoners of the earth, 35To turn aside the right of a man before the face of the most High, 36To subvert a man in his cause, the Lord approveth not."

Micah 7:18-20 "18Who is a God like unto thee, that pardoneth iniquity, and passeth by the transgression of the remnant of his heritage? he retaineth not his anger for ever, because he delighteth in mercy. 19He will turn again, he will have compassion upon us; he will subdue our iniquities; and thou wilt cast all their sins into the depths of the sea. 20Thou wilt perform the truth to Jacob, and the mercy to Abraham, which thou hast sworn unto our fathers from the days of old."

Those That Are Not Compassionate
1 John 3:17 "But whoso hath this world's good, and seeth his brother have need, and shutteth up his bowels of compassion from him, how dwelleth the love of God in him?"

COMPLAINING

The Reward For Complaining
Numbers 11:1 "And when the people complained, it displeased the LORD: and the LORD heard it; and his anger was kindled; and the fire of the LORD burnt among them, and consumed them that were in the uttermost parts of the camp."

What To Do Instead Of Complaining
Lamentations 3:39-40 "³⁹Wherefore doth a living man complain, a man for the punishment of his sins? ⁴⁰Let us search and try our ways, and turn again to the LORD."

Who Are Complainers
Jude 7-16 "⁷Even as Sodom and Gomorrha, and the cities about them in like manner, giving themselves over to fornication, and going after strange flesh, are set forth for an example, suffering the vengeance of eternal fire. ⁸Likewise also these filthy dreamers defile the flesh, despise dominion, and speak evil of dignities. ⁹Yet Michael the archangel, when contending with the devil he disputed about the body of Moses, durst not bring against him a railing accusation, but said, The Lord rebuke thee. ¹⁰But these speak evil of those things which they know not: but what they know naturally, as brute beasts, in those things they corrupt themselves. ¹¹Woe unto them! for they have gone in the way of Cain, and ran greedily after the error of Balaam for reward, and perished in the gainsaying of Core. ¹²These are spots in your feasts of charity, when they feast with you, feeding themselves without fear: clouds they are without water, carried about of winds; trees whose fruit withereth, without fruit, twice dead, plucked up by the roots; ¹³Raging waves of the sea, foaming out their own shame; wandering stars, to whom is reserved the blackness of darkness for ever. ¹⁴And Enoch also, the seventh from Adam, prophesied of these, saying, Behold, the Lord cometh with ten thousands of his saints, ¹⁵To execute judgment upon all, and to convince all that are ungodly among them of all their ungodly deeds which they have ungodly committed, and of all their hard speeches which ungodly sinners have spoken against him. ¹⁶These are murmurers, complainers, walking after their own lusts; and their mouth speaketh great swelling words, having men's persons in admiration because of advantage."

CONDEMNATION

How Condemnation Came Upon Man
Romans 5:18-19 "¹⁸Therefore as by the offence of one judgment came upon all men to condemnation; even so by the righteousness of one the free gift came upon all men unto justification of life. ¹⁹For as by one man's disobedience many were made sinners, so by the obedience of one shall many be made righteous."

If Your Heart Does Not Condemn You
1 John 3:21 "Beloved, if our heart condemn us not, then have we confidence toward God."

Jesus Christ Condemning Sin
Romans 8:3 "For what the law could not do, in that it was weak through the flesh, God sending his own Son in the likeness of sinful flesh, and for sin, condemned sin in the flesh."

Those That Condemn The Just
Proverbs 17:15 "He that justifieth the wicked, and he that condemneth the just, even they both are abomination to the LORD."

What Condemnation Is Based Upon
John 3:17-21 "¹⁷For God sent not his Son into the world to condemn the world; but that the world through him might be saved. ¹⁸He that believeth on him is not condemned: but he that believeth not is condemned already, because he hath not believed in the name of the only begotten Son of God. ¹⁹And this is the condemnation, that light is come into the world, and men loved darkness rather than light, because their deeds were evil. ²⁰For every one that doeth evil hateth the light, neither cometh to the light, lest his deeds should be reproved. ²¹But he that doeth truth cometh to the light, that his deeds may be made manifest, that they are wrought in God."

What You Are Condemned By

Matthew 12:36-37 "36But I say unto you, That every idle word that men shall speak, they shall give account thereof in the day of judgment. 37For by thy words thou shalt be justified, and by thy words thou shalt be condemned."

Who Is Condemned

Proverbs 12:2 "A good man obtaineth favour of the LORD: but a man of wicked devices will he condemn."

John 3:17-18 "17For God sent not his Son into the world to condemn the world; but that the world through him might be saved. 18He that believeth on him is not condemned: but he that believeth not is condemned already, because he hath not believed in the name of the only begotten Son of God."

Who Is Not Condemned

Luke 6:37 "Judge not, and ye shall not be judged: condemn not, and ye shall not be condemned: forgive, and ye shall be forgiven."

John 3:17-18 "17For God sent not his Son into the world to condemn the world; but that the world through him might be saved. 18He that believeth on him is not condemned: but he that believeth not is condemned already, because he hath not believed in the name of the only begotten Son of God."

John 5:24-25 "24Verily, verily, I say unto you, He that heareth my word, and believeth on him that sent me, hath everlasting life, and shall not come into condemnation; but is passed from death unto life. 25Verily, verily, I say unto you, The hour is coming, and now is, when the dead shall hear the voice of the Son of God: and they that hear shall live."

Romans 8:1-2 "1There is therefore now no condemnation to them which are in Christ Jesus, who walk not after the flesh, but after the Spirit. 2For the law of the Spirit of life in Christ Jesus hath made me free from the law of sin and death."

1 Corinthians 11:31-32 "31For if we would judge ourselves, we should not be judged. 32But when we are judged, we are chastened of the Lord, that we should not be condemned with the world."

CONDUCT

Christian Conduct

Titus 2:1-15 "1But speak thou the things which become sound doctrine: 2That the aged men be sober, grave, temperate, sound in faith, in charity, in patience. 3The aged women likewise, that they be in behaviour as becometh holiness, not false accusers, not given to much wine, teachers of good things; 4That they may teach the young women to be sober, to love their husbands, to love their children, 5To be discreet, chaste, keepers at home, good, obedient to their own husbands, that the word of God be not blasphemed. 6Young men likewise exhort to be sober minded. 7In all things shewing thyself a pattern of good works: in doctrine shewing uncorruptness, gravity, sincerity, 8Sound speech, that cannot be condemned; that he that is of the contrary part may be ashamed, having no evil thing to say of you. 9Exhort servants to be obedient unto their own masters, and to please them well in all things; not answering again; 10Not purloining, but shewing all good fidelity; that they may adorn the doctrine of God our Saviour in all things. 11For the grace of God that bringeth salvation hath appeared to all men, 12Teaching us that, denying ungodliness and worldly lusts, we should live soberly, righteously, and godly, in this present world; 13Looking for that blessed hope, and the glorious appearing of the great God and our Saviour Jesus Christ; 14Who gave himself for us, that he might redeem us from all iniquity, and purify unto himself a peculiar people, zealous of good works. 15These things speak, and exhort, and rebuke with all authority. Let no man despise thee."

1 Peter 3:8-12 "8Finally, be ye all of one mind, having compassion one of another, love as brethren, be pitiful, be courteous: 9Not rendering evil for evil, or railing for railing: but contrariwise blessing; knowing that ye are thereunto called, that ye should inherit a blessing. 10For he that will love life, and see good days, let him refrain his tongue from evil, and his lips that they speak no guile: 11Let him eschew evil, and do good; let him seek peace, and ensue it. 12For the eyes of the Lord are over the righteous, and his ears are open unto their prayers: but the face of the Lord is against them that do evil."

CONFESSION

Confessing Your Sins

Numbers 5:5-7 "⁵And the LORD spake unto Moses, saying, ⁶Speak unto the children of Israel, When a man or woman shall commit any sin that men commit, to do a trespass against the LORD, and that person be guilty; ⁷Then they shall confess their sin which they have done: and he shall recompense his trespass with the principal thereof, and add unto it the fifth part thereof, and give it unto him against whom he hath trespassed."

Psalm 38:18 "For I will declare mine iniquity; I will be sorry for my sin."

Jeremiah 3:13 "Only acknowledge thine iniquity, that thou hast transgressed against the LORD thy God, and hast scattered thy ways to the strangers under every green tree, and ye have not obeyed my voice, saith the LORD."

James 5:16 "Confess your faults one to another, and pray one for another, that ye may be healed. The effectual fervent prayer of a righteous man availeth much."

Every Tongue Confessing The Lord

Isaiah 45:22-23 "²²Look unto me, and be ye saved, all the ends of the earth: for I am God, and there is none else. ²³I have sworn by myself, the word is gone out of my mouth in righteousness, and shall not return, That unto me every knee shall bow, every tongue shall swear."

Romans 14:11 "For it is written, As I live, saith the Lord, every knee shall bow to me, and every tongue shall confess to God."

Philippians 2:9-11 "⁹Wherefore God also hath highly exalted him, and given him a name which is above every name: ¹⁰That at the name of Jesus every knee should bow, of things in heaven, and things in earth, and things under the earth; ¹¹And that every tongue should confess that Jesus Christ is Lord, to the glory of God the Father."

The Reward For Confessing Sin

Leviticus 26:40-45 "⁴⁰If they shall confess their iniquity, and the iniquity of their fathers, with their trespass which they trespassed against me, and that also they have walked contrary unto me; ⁴¹And that I also have walked contrary unto them, and have brought them into the land of their enemies; if then their uncircumcised hearts be humbled, and they then accept of the punishment of their iniquity: ⁴²Then will I remember my covenant with Jacob, and also my covenant with Isaac, and also my covenant with Abraham will I remember; and I will remember the land. ⁴³The land also shall be left of them, and shall enjoy her sabbaths, while she lieth desolate without them: and they shall accept of the punishment of their iniquity: because, even because they despised my judgments, and because their soul abhorred my statutes. ⁴⁴And yet for all that, when they be in the land of their enemies, I will not cast them away, neither will I abhor them, to destroy them utterly, and to break my covenant with them: for I am the LORD their God. ⁴⁵But I will for their sakes remember the covenant of their ancestors, whom I brought forth out of the land of Egypt in the sight of the heathen, that I might be their God: I am the LORD."

Psalm 32:5 "I acknowledged my sin unto thee, and mine iniquity have I not hid. I said, I will confess my transgressions unto the LORD; and thou forgavest the iniquity of my sin. Selah."

James 5:16 "Confess your faults one to another, and pray one for another, that ye may be healed. The effectual fervent prayer of a righteous man availeth much."

1 John 1:5-9 "⁵This then is the message which we have heard of him, and declare unto you, that God is light, and in him is no darkness at all. ⁶If we say that we have fellowship with him, and walk in darkness, we lie, and do not the truth: ⁷But if we walk in the light, as he is in the light, we have fellowship one with another, and the blood of Jesus Christ his Son cleanseth us from all sin. ⁸If we say that we have no sin, we deceive ourselves, and the truth is not in us. ⁹If we confess our sins, he is faithful and just to forgive us our sins, and to cleanse us from all unrighteousness."

The Reward For Confessing The Lord

I Kings 8:33-36 "³³When thy people Israel be smitten down before the enemy, because they have sinned against thee, and shall turn again to thee, and confess thy name, and pray, and make supplication unto thee in this house: ³⁴Then hear thou in heaven, and forgive the sin of thy people Israel, and bring them again unto the land which thou gavest unto their fathers. [35]When heaven is shut up, and there is no rain, because they have sinned against thee; if they pray toward this place, and confess thy name, and turn from their sin, when thou afflictest them: [36]Then hear thou in heaven, and forgive the sin of thy servants, and of thy people Israel, that thou teach them the good way wherein they should walk, and give rain upon thy land, which thou hast given to thy people for an inheritance."

2 Chronicles 6:24-25 "[24]And if thy people Israel be put to the worse before the enemy, because they have sinned against thee; and shall return and confess thy name, and pray and make supplication before thee in this house; [25]Then hear thou from the heavens, and forgive the sin of thy people Israel, and bring them again unto the land which thou gavest to them and to their fathers."

Proverbs 3:5-6 "[5]Trust in the LORD with all thine heart; and lean not unto thine own understanding. [6]In all thy ways acknowledge him, and he shall direct thy paths."

Those That Confess Jesus Christ
Matthew 10:32 "Whosoever therefore shall confess me before men, him will I confess also before my Father which is in heaven."

Luke 12:8 "Also I say unto you, Whosoever shall confess me before men, him shall the Son of man also confess before the angels of God."

Romans 10:9-11 "[9]That if thou shalt confess with thy mouth the Lord Jesus, and shalt believe in thine heart that God hath raised him from the dead, thou shalt be saved. [10]For with the heart man believeth unto righteousness; and with the mouth confession is made unto salvation. [11]For the scripture saith, Whosoever believeth on him shall not be ashamed."

1 John 2:23 "Whosoever denieth the Son, the same hath not the Father: (but) he that acknowledgeth the Son hath the Father also."

1 John 4:2 "Hereby know ye the Spirit of God: Every spirit that confesseth that Jesus Christ is come in the flesh is of God."

1 John 4:15 "Whosoever shall confess that Jesus is the Son of God, God dwelleth in him, and he in God."

Those That Confess Their Sins
Proverbs 28:13 "He that covereth his sins shall not prosper: but whoso confesseth and forsaketh them shall have mercy."

Those That Do Not Confess Jesus Christ
1 John 4:3 "And every spirit that confesseth not that Jesus Christ is come in the flesh is not of God: and this is that spirit of antichrist, whereof ye have heard that it should come; and even now already is it in the world."

2 John 7 "For many deceivers are entered into the world, who confess not that Jesus Christ is come in the flesh. This is a deceiver and an antichrist."

Who Jesus Christ Will Confess
Matthew 10:32 "Whosoever therefore shall confess me before men, him will I confess also before my Father which is in heaven."

Luke 12:8 "Also I say unto you, Whosoever shall confess me before men, him shall the Son of man also confess before the angels of God."

Revelation 3:1-5 "[1]And unto the angel of the church in Sardis write; These things saith he that hath the seven Spirits of God, and the seven stars; I know thy works, that thou hast a name that thou livest, and art dead. [2]Be watchful, and strengthen the things which remain, that are ready to die: for I have not found thy works perfect before God. [3]Remember therefore how thou hast received and heard, and hold fast, and repent. If therefore thou shalt not watch, I will come on thee as a thief, and thou shalt not know what hour I will come upon thee. [4]Thou hast a few names even in Sardis which have not defiled their garments; and they shall walk with me in white: for they are worthy. [5]He that overcometh, the same shall be clothed in white raiment; and I will not blot out his name out of the book of life, but I will confess his name before my Father, and before his angels."

CONFIDENCE

Confidence In An Unfaithful Man
Proverbs 25:19 "Confidence in an unfaithful man in time of trouble is like a broken tooth, and a foot out of joint."

The Lord Being Your Confidence
Proverbs 3:25-26 "[25]Be not afraid of sudden fear, neither of the desolation of the wicked, when it

cometh. [26]For the Lord shall be thy confidence, and shall keep thy foot from being taken."

What You Can Be Confident In
1 John 5:13-15 "[13]These things have I written unto you that believe on the name of the Son of God; that ye may know that ye have eternal life, and that ye may believe on the name of the Son of God. [14]And this is the confidence that we have in him, that, if we ask any thing according to his will, he heareth us: [15]And if we know that he hear us, whatsoever we ask, we know that we have the petitions that we desired of him."

Where Strong Confidence Is
Proverbs 14:26 "In the fear of the Lord is strong confidence: and his children shall have a place of refuge."

Who Has No Confidence In The Flesh
Philippians 3:3-4 "[3]For we are the circumcision, which worship God in the spirit, and rejoice in Christ Jesus, and have no confidence in the flesh. [4]Though I might also have confidence in the flesh. If any other man thinketh that he hath whereof he might trust in the flesh, I more."

Who Is Confident
2 Corinthians 5:5-9 "[5]Now he that hath wrought us for the selfsame thing is God, who also hath given unto us the earnest of the Spirit. [6]Therefore we are always confident, knowing that, whilst we are at home in the body, we are absent from the Lord: [7](For we walk by faith, not by sight:) [8]We are confident, I say, and willing rather to be absent from the body, and to be present with the Lord. [9]Wherefore we labour, that, whether present or absent, we may be accepted of him."

1 John 2:22-28 "[22]Who is a liar but he that denieth that Jesus is the Christ? He is antichrist, that denieth the Father and the Son. [23]Whosoever denieth the Son, the same hath not the Father: (but) he that acknowledgeth the Son hath the Father also. [24]Let that therefore abide in you, which ye have heard from the beginning. If that which ye have heard from the beginning shall remain in you, ye also shall continue in the Son, and in the Father. [25]And this is the promise that he hath promised us, even eternal life. [26]These things have I written unto you concerning them that seduce you. [27]But the anointing which ye have received of him abideth in you, and ye need not that any man

teach you: but as the same anointing teacheth you of all things, and is truth, and is no lie, and even as it hath taught you, ye shall abide in him. [28]And now, little children, abide in him; that, when he shall appear, we may have confidence, and not be ashamed before him at his coming."

1 John 3:21 "Beloved, if our heart condemn us not, then have we confidence toward God."

Who Not To Put
Your Confidence In
Psalm 118:8-9 "[8]It is better to trust in the Lord than to put confidence in man. [9]It is better to trust in the Lord than to put confidence in princes."

CONFORMITY

What Not To Be Conformed To
Romans 12:1-2 "[1]I beseech you therefore, brethren, by the mercies of God, that ye present your bodies a living sacrifice, holy, acceptable unto God, which is your reasonable service. [2]And be not conformed to this world: but be ye transformed by the renewing of your mind, that ye may prove what is that good, and acceptable, and perfect, will of God."

Who Is Predestined To Be
Conformed To The Image Of Jesus Christ
Romans 8:28-29 "[28]And we know that all things work together for good to them that love God, to them who are the called according to his purpose. [29]For whom he did foreknow, he also did predestinate to be conformed to the image of his Son, that he might be the firstborn among many brethren."

CONFUSION

God Not Being The Author Of Confusion
1 Corinthians 14:33 "For God is not the author of confusion, but of peace, as in all churches of the saints."

What Is Confusion
Leviticus 18:22-23 "[22]Thou shalt not lie with mankind, as with womankind: it is abomination. [23]Neither shalt thou lie with any beast to defile thyself therewith: neither shall any woman stand before a beast to lie down thereto: it is confusion."

Isaiah 41:29 "Behold, they are all vanity; their works are nothing: their molten images are wind and confusion."

Where Confusion Is
James 3:13-16 "13Who is a wise man and endued with knowledge among you? let him shew out of a good conversation his works with meekness of wisdom. 14But if ye have bitter envying and strife in your hearts, glory not, and lie not against the truth. 15This wisdom descendeth not from above, but is earthly, sensual, devilish. 16For where envying and strife is, there is confusion and every evil work."

Who Has Wrought Confusion
Leviticus 20:11-12 "11And the man that lieth with his father's wife hath uncovered his father's nakedness: both of them shall surely be put to death; their blood shall be upon them. 12And if a man lie with his daughter in law, both of them shall surely be put to death: they have wrought confusion; their blood shall be upon them."

CONSCIENCE

The Conscience Witnessing
Romans 2:14-15 "14For when the Gentiles, which have not the law, do by nature the things contained in the law, these, having not the law, are a law unto themselves: 15Which shew the work of the law written in their hearts, their conscience also bearing witness, and their thoughts the mean while accusing or else excusing one another;)"

Whose Conscience Is Defiled
Titus 1:10-15 "10For there are many unruly and vain talkers and deceivers, specially they of the circumcision: 11Whose mouths must be stopped, who subvert whole houses, teaching things which they ought not, for filthy lucre's sake. 12One of themselves, even a prophet of their own, said, The Cretians are alway liars, evil beasts, slow bellies. 13This witness is true. Wherefore rebuke them sharply, that they may be sound in the faith; 14Not giving heed to Jewish fables, and commandments of men, that turn from the truth. 15Unto the pure all things are pure: but unto them that are defiled and unbelieving is nothing pure; but even their mind and conscience is defiled."

CONSIDERATION

Considering Others
Hebrews 10:23-24 "23Let us hold fast the profession of our faith without wavering; (for he is faithful that promised;) 24And let us consider one another to provoke unto love and to good works."

Those That Consider The Poor
Psalm 41:1 "Blessed is he that considereth the poor: the LORD will deliver him in time of trouble."

What To Consider
Proverbs 23:1-8 "1When thou sittest to eat with a ruler, consider diligently what is before thee: 2And put a knife to thy throat, if thou be a man given to appetite. 3Be not desirous of his dainties: for they are deceitful meat. 4Labour not to be rich: cease from thine own wisdom. 5Wilt thou set thine eyes upon that which is not? for riches certainly make themselves wings; they fly away as an eagle toward heaven. 6Eat thou not the bread of him that hath an evil eye, neither desire thou his dainty meats: 7For as he thinketh in his heart, so is he: Eat and drink, saith he to thee; but his heart is not with thee. 8The morsel which thou hast eaten shalt thou vomit up, and lose thy sweet words."

Who Considers The Poor
Proverbs 29:6-7 "6In the transgression of an evil man there is a snare: but the righteous doth sing and rejoice. 7The righteous considereth the cause of the poor: but the wicked regardeth not to know it."

Who Does Not Consider The Lord
Job 34:23-27 "23For he will not lay upon man more than right; that he should enter into judgment with God. 24He shall break in pieces mighty men without number, and set others in their stead. 25Therefore he knoweth their works, and he overturneth them in the night, so that they are destroyed. 26He striketh them as wicked men in the open sight of others; 27Because they turned back from him, and would not consider any of his ways."

Isaiah 5:11-12 "11Woe unto them that rise up early in the morning, that they may follow strong drink; that continue until night, till wine inflame them! 12And the harp, and the viol, the tabret, and pipe, and wine, are in their feasts: but they regard not the work of the LORD, neither consider the operation of his hands."

CONTEMPT

Some Awaking To Everlasting Contempt
Daniel 12:1-2 "1And at that time shall Michael stand up, the great prince which standeth for the

children of thy people: and there shall be a time of trouble, such as never was since there was a nation even to that same time: and at that time thy people shall be delivered, every one that shall be found written in the book. ²And many of them that sleep in the dust of the earth shall awake, some to everlasting life, and some to shame and everlasting contempt."

John 5:26-29 "²⁶For as the Father hath life in himself; so hath he given to the Son to have life in himself; ²⁷And hath given him authority to execute judgment also, because he is the Son of man. ²⁸Marvel not at this: for the hour is coming, in the which all that are in the graves shall hear his voice, ²⁹And shall come forth; they that have done good, unto the resurrection of life; and they that have done evil, unto the resurrection of damnation."

When Contempt Comes
Proverbs 18:3 "When the wicked cometh, then cometh also contempt, and with ignominy reproach."

Who The Lord Made Contemptible
Malachi 2:7-9 "⁷For the priest's lips should keep knowledge, and they should seek the law at his mouth: for he is the messenger of the LORD of hosts. ⁸But ye are departed out of the way; ye have caused many to stumble at the law; ye have corrupted the covenant of Levi, saith the LORD of hosts. ⁹Therefore have I also made you contemptible and base before all the people, according as ye have not kept my ways, but have been partial in the law."

CONTENTION

Contentious People
Proverbs 19:13 "A foolish son is the calamity of his father: and the contentions of a wife are a continual dropping."

Proverbs 21:9 "It is better to dwell in a corner of the housetop, than with a brawling woman in a wide house."

Proverbs 21:19 "It is better to dwell in the wilderness, than with a contentious and an angry woman."

Proverbs 25:24 "It is better to dwell in the corner of the housetop, than with a brawling woman and in a wide house."

Proverbs 26:21 "As coals are to burning coals, and wood to fire; so is a contentious man to kindle strife."

Proverbs 27:15-16 "¹⁵A continual dropping in a very rainy day and a contentious woman are alike. ¹⁶Whosoever hideth her hideth the wind, and the ointment of his right hand, which bewrayeth itself."

Romans 2:8 "But unto them that are contentious, and do not obey the truth, but obey unrighteousness, indignation and wrath."

How To Get Rid Of Contention
Proverbs 22:10 "Cast out the scorner, and contention shall go out; yea, strife and reproach shall cease."

If A Wise Man Contends With A Foolish Man
Proverbs 29:9 "If a wise man contendeth with a foolish man, whether he rage or laugh, there is no rest."

Those That Strive With Their Maker
Isaiah 45:9 "Woe unto him that striveth with his Maker! Let the potsherd strive with the potsherds of the earth. Shall the clay say to him that fashioneth it, What makest thou? or thy work, He hath no hands?"

What Brings Contention
Proverbs 13:10 "Only by pride cometh contention: but with the well advised is wisdom."

What Causes Contentions To Cease
Proverbs 18:18 "The lot causeth contentions to cease, and parteth between the mighty."

Where Contention Ceases
Proverbs 26:20 "Where no wood is, there the fire goeth out: so where there is no talebearer, the strife ceaseth."

Who Contends With The Wicked
Proverbs 28:4 "They that forsake the law praise the wicked: but such as keep the law contend with them."

Who Has Contentions
Proverbs 23:29-30 "²⁹Who hath woe? who hath sorrow? who hath contentions? who hath babbling? who hath wounds without cause? who hath redness of eyes? ³⁰They that tarry long at the wine; they that go to seek mixed wine."

Who The Lord Contends With

Isaiah 49:14-25 "[14]But Zion said, The LORD hath forsaken me, and my Lord hath forgotten me. [15]Can a woman forget her sucking child, that she should not have compassion on the son of her womb? yea, they may forget, yet will I not forget thee. [16]Behold, I have graven thee upon the palms of my hands; thy walls are continually before me. [17]Thy children shall make haste; thy destroyers and they that made thee waste shall go forth of thee. [18]Lift up thine eyes round about, and behold: all these gather themselves together, and come to thee. As I live, saith the LORD, thou shalt surely clothe thee with them all, as with an ornament, and bind them on thee, as a bride doeth. [19]For thy waste and thy desolate places, and the land of thy destruction, shall even now be too narrow by reason of the inhabitants, and they that swallowed thee up shall be far away. [20]The children which thou shalt have, after thou hast lost the other, shall say again in thine ears, The place is too strait for me: give place to me that I may dwell. [21]Then shalt thou say in thine heart, Who hath begotten me these, seeing I have lost my children, and am desolate, a captive, and removing to and fro? and who hath brought up these? Behold, I was left alone; these, where had they been? [22]Thus saith the Lord GOD, Behold, I will lift up mine hand to the Gentiles, and set up my standard to the people: and they shall bring thy sons in their arms, and thy daughters shall be carried upon their shoulders. [23]And kings shall be thy nursing fathers, and their queens thy nursing mothers: they shall bow down to thee with their face toward the earth, and lick up the dust of thy feet; and thou shalt know that I am the LORD: for they shall not be ashamed that wait for me. [24]Shall the prey be taken from the mighty, or the lawful captive delivered? [25]But thus saith the LORD, Even the captives of the mighty shall be taken away, and the prey of the terrible shall be delivered: for I will contend with him that contendeth with thee, and I will save thy children."

Whose Lips Enter Into Contention

Proverbs 18:6-7 "[6]A fool's lips enter into contention, and his mouth calleth for strokes. [7]A fool's mouth is his destruction, and his lips are the snare of his soul."

CONTENTMENT

Being Content With What You Have

Luke 3:14 "And the soldiers likewise demanded of him, saying, And what shall we do? And he said unto them, Do violence to no man, neither accuse any falsely; and be content with your wages."

1 Timothy 6:7-8 "[7]For we brought nothing into this world, and it is certain we can carry nothing out. [8]And having food and raiment let us be therewith content."

Hebrews 13:5 "Let your conversation be without covetousness; and be content with such things as ye have: for he hath said, I will never leave thee, nor forsake thee."

Godliness With Contentment

1 Timothy 6:6 "But godliness with contentment is great gain."

CONTROVERSY

What Happens When
The Lord Has A Controversy

Jeremiah 25:30-38 "[30]Therefore prophesy thou against them all these words, and say unto them, The LORD shall roar from on high, and utter his voice from his holy habitation; he shall mightily roar upon his habitation; he shall give a shout, as they that tread the grapes, against all the inhabitants of the earth. [31]A noise shall come even to the ends of the earth; for the LORD hath a controversy with the nations, he will plead with all flesh; he will give them that are wicked to the sword, saith the LORD. [32]Thus saith the LORD of hosts, Behold, evil shall go forth from nation to nation, and a great whirlwind shall be raised up from the coasts of the earth. [33]And the slain of the LORD shall be at that day from one end of the earth even unto the other end of the earth: they shall not be lamented, neither gathered, nor buried; they shall be dung upon the ground. [34]Howl, ye shepherds, and cry; and wallow yourselves in the ashes, ye principal of the flock: for the days of your slaughter and of your dispersions are accomplished; and ye shall fall like a pleasant vessel. [35]And the shepherds shall have no way to flee, nor the principal of the flock to escape. [36]A voice of the cry of the shepherds, and an howling of the principal of the flock, shall be heard: for the LORD hath spoiled their pasture. 37And the peaceable habitations are cut down because of the fierce anger of the LORD. 38He hath forsaken his covert, as the lion: for their land is desolate because of the fierceness of the oppressor, and because of his fierce anger."

Why The Lord Has Controversies
Hosea 4:1 "Hear the word of the LORD, ye children of Israel: for the LORD hath a controversy with the inhabitants of the land, because there is no truth, nor mercy, nor knowledge of God in the land."

CONVERSION

Being Converted
Acts 3:19 "Repent ye therefore, and be converted, that your sins may be blotted out, when the times of refreshing shall come from the presence of the Lord."

Those That Are Not Converted
Matthew 18:1-3 "1At the same time came the disciples unto Jesus, saying, Who is the greatest in the kingdom of heaven? 2And Jesus called a little child unto him, and set him in the midst of them, 3And said, Verily I say unto you, Except ye be converted, and become as little children, ye shall not enter into the kingdom of heaven."

Those That Convert Sinners
James 5:20 "Let him know, that he which converteth the sinner from the error of his way shall save a soul from death, and shall hide a multitude of sins."

What Converts The Soul
Psalm 19:7 "The law of the LORD is perfect, converting the soul: the testimony of the LORD is sure, making wise the simple."

CORRUPTION

Corrupt Trees
Matthew 7:17-18 "17Even so every good tree bringeth forth good fruit; but a corrupt tree bringeth forth evil fruit. 18A good tree cannot bring forth evil fruit, neither can a corrupt tree bring forth good fruit."

Matthew 12:33 "Either make the tree good, and his fruit good; or else make the tree corrupt, and his fruit corrupt: for the tree is known by his fruit."

Luke 6:43-45 "43For a good tree bringeth not forth corrupt fruit; neither doth a corrupt tree bring forth good fruit. 44For every tree is known by his own fruit. For of thorns men do not gather figs, nor of a bramble bush gather they grapes. 45A good man out of the good treasure of his heart bringeth forth that which is good; and an evil man out of the evil treasure of his heart bringeth forth that which is evil: for of the abundance of the heart his mouth speaketh."

The Reward For Corrupting The Earth
Genesis 6:11-13 "11The earth also was corrupt before God, and the earth was filled with violence. 12And God looked upon the earth, and, behold, it was corrupt; for all flesh had corrupted his way upon the earth. 13And God said unto Noah, The end of all flesh is come before me; for the earth is filled with violence through them; and, behold, I will destroy them with the earth."

What Corruption Cannot Inherit
1 Corinthians 15:50 "Now this I say, brethren, that flesh and blood cannot inherit the kingdom of God; neither doth corruption inherit incorruption."

What Corrupts Good Manners
1 Corinthians 15:33 "Be not deceived: evil communications corrupt good manners."

What Is Corrupt
Proverbs 25:26 "A righteous man falling down before the wicked is as a troubled fountain, and a corrupt spring."

Ephesians 4:22 "That ye put off concerning the former conversation the old man, which is corrupt according to the deceitful lusts."

Who Are The Servants of Corruption
2 Peter 2:1-19 "1But there were false prophets also among the people, even as there shall be false teachers among you, who privily shall bring in damnable heresies, even denying the Lord that bought them, and bring upon themselves swift destruction. 2And many shall follow their pernicious ways; by reason of whom the way of truth shall be evil spoken of. 3And through covetousness shall they with feigned words make merchandise of you: whose judgment now of a long time lingereth

not, and their damnation slumbereth not. [4]For if God spared not the angels that sinned, but cast them down to hell, and delivered them into chains of darkness, to be reserved unto judgment; [5]And spared not the old world, but saved Noah the eighth person, a preacher of righteousness, bringing in the flood upon the world of the ungodly; [6]And turning the cities of Sodom and Gomorrha into ashes condemned them with an overthrow, making them an ensample unto those that after should live ungodly; [7]And delivered just Lot, vexed with the filthy conversation of the wicked: [8](For that righteous man dwelling among them, in seeing and hearing, vexed his righteous soul from day to day with their unlawful deeds;) [9]The Lord knoweth how to deliver the godly out of temptations, and to reserve the unjust unto the day of judgment to be punished: [10]But chiefly them that walk after the flesh in the lust of uncleanness, and despise government. Presumptuous are they, selfwilled, they are not afraid to speak evil of dignities. [11]Whereas angels, which are greater in power and might, bring not railing accusation against them before the Lord. [12]But these, as natural brute beasts, made to be taken and destroyed, speak evil of the things that they understand not; and shall utterly perish in their own corruption; [13]And shall receive the reward of unrighteousness, as they that count it pleasure to riot in the day time. Spots they are and blemishes, sporting themselves with their own deceivings while they feast with you; [14]Having eyes full of adultery, and that cannot cease from sin; beguiling unstable souls: an heart they have exercised with covetous practices; cursed children: [15]Which have forsaken the right way, and are gone astray, following the way of Balaam the son of Bosor, who loved the wages of unrighteousness; [16]But was rebuked for his iniquity: the dumb ass speaking with man's voice forbad the madness of the prophet. [17]These are wells without water, clouds that are carried with a tempest; to whom the mist of darkness is reserved for ever. [18]For when they speak great swelling words of vanity, they allure through the lusts of the flesh, through much wantonness, those that were clean escaped from them who live in error. [19]While they promise them liberty, they themselves are the servants of corruption: for of whom a man is overcome, of the same is he brought in bondage."

Who Corrupted The Covenant Of Levi

Malachi 2:1-8 "[1]And now, O ye priests, this commandment is for you. [2]If ye will not hear, and if ye will not lay it to heart, to give glory unto my name, saith the LORD of hosts, I will even send a curse upon you, and I will curse your blessings: yea, I have cursed them already, because ye do not lay it to heart. [3]Behold, I will corrupt your seed, and spread dung upon your faces, even the dung of your solemn feasts; and one shall take you away with it. [4]And ye shall know that I have sent this commandment unto you, that my covenant might be with Levi, saith the LORD of hosts. [5]My covenant was with him of life and peace; and I gave them to him for the fear wherewith he feared me, and was afraid before my name. [6]The law of truth was in his mouth, and iniquity was not found in his lips: he walked with me in peace and equity, and did turn many away from iniquity. [7]For the priest's lips should keep knowledge, and they should seek the law at his mouth: for he is the messenger of the LORD of hosts. [8]But ye are departed out of the way; ye have caused many to stumble at the law; ye have corrupted the covenant of Levi, saith the LORD of hosts."

Who Is Corrupt

Exodus 32:7-8 "[7]And the LORD said unto Moses, Go, get thee down; for thy people, which thou broughtest out of the land of Egypt, have corrupted themselves: [8]They have turned aside quickly out of the way which I commanded them: they have made them a molten calf, and have worshipped it, and have sacrificed thereunto, and said, These be thy gods, O Israel, which have brought thee up out of the land of Egypt."

Judges 2:19 "And it came to pass, when the judge was dead, that they returned, and corrupted themselves more than their fathers, in following other gods to serve them, and to bow down unto them; they ceased not from their own doings, nor from their stubborn way."

Psalm 14:1 "The fool hath said in his heart, There is no God. They are corrupt, they have done abominable works, there is none that doeth good."

Psalm 53:1 "The fool hath said in his heart, There is no God. Corrupt are they, and have done abominable iniquity: there is none that doeth good."

Hosea 9:1-9 "¹Rejoice not, O Israel, for joy, as other people: for thou hast gone a whoring from thy God, thou hast loved a reward upon every cornfloor. ²The floor and the winepress shall not feed them, and the new wine shall fail in her. ³They shall not dwell in the LORD's land; but Ephraim shall return to Egypt, and they shall eat unclean things in Assyria. ⁴They shall not offer wine offerings to the LORD, neither shall they be pleasing unto him: their sacrifices shall be unto them as the bread of mourners; all that eat thereof shall be polluted: for their bread for their soul shall not come into the house of the LORD. ⁵What will ye do in the solemn day, and in the day of the feast of the LORD? ⁶For, lo, they are gone because of destruction: Egypt shall gather them up, Memphis shall bury them: the pleasant places for their silver, nettles shall possess them: thorns shall be in their tabernacles. ⁷The days of visitation are come, the days of recompence are come; Israel shall know it: the prophet is a fool, the spiritual man is mad, for the multitude of thine iniquity, and the great hatred. ⁸The watchman of Ephraim was with my God: but the prophet is a snare of a fowler in all his ways, and hatred in the house of his God. ⁹They have deeply corrupted themselves, as in the days of Gibeah: therefore he will remember their iniquity, he will visit their sins."

2 Timothy 3:6-8 "⁶For of this sort are they which creep into houses, and lead captive silly women laden with sins, led away with divers lusts, ⁷Ever learning, and never able to come to the knowledge of the truth. ⁸Now as Jannes and Jambres withstood Moses, so do these also resist the truth: men of corrupt minds, reprobate concerning the faith."

Jude 7-10 "⁷Even as Sodom and Gomorrha, and the cities about them in like manner, giving themselves over to fornication, and going after strange flesh, are set forth for an example, suffering the vengeance of eternal fire. ⁸Likewise also these filthy dreamers defile the flesh, despise dominion, and speak evil of dignities. ⁹Yet Michael the archangel, when contending with the devil he disputed about the body of Moses, durst not bring against him a railing accusation, but said, The Lord rebuke thee. ¹⁰But these speak evil of those things which they know not: but what they know naturally, as brute beasts, in those things they corrupt themselves."

Who Shall Be Delivered From Corruption
Romans 8:20-21 "²⁰For the creature was made subject to vanity, not willingly, but by reason of him who hath subjected the same in hope, ²¹Because the creature itself also shall be delivered from the bondage of corruption into the glorious liberty of the children of God."

1 Corinthians 15:50-57 "⁵⁰Now this I say, brethren, that flesh and blood cannot inherit the kingdom of God; neither doth corruption inherit incorruption. ⁵¹Behold, I shew you a mystery; We shall not all sleep, but we shall all be changed, ⁵²In a moment, in the twinkling of an eye, at the last trump: for the trumpet shall sound, and the dead shall be raised incorruptible, and we shall be changed. ⁵³For this corruptible must put on incorruption, and this mortal must put on immortality. ⁵⁴So when this corruptible shall have put on incorruption, and this mortal shall have put on immortality, then shall be brought to pass the saying that is written, Death is swallowed up in victory. ⁵⁵O death, where is thy sting? O grave, where is thy victory? ⁵⁶The sting of death is sin; and the strength of sin is the law. ⁵⁷But thanks be to God, which giveth us the victory through our Lord Jesus Christ."

Who Shall Reap Corruption
Galatians 6:8 "For he that soweth to his flesh shall of the flesh reap corruption; but he that soweth to the Spirit shall of the Spirit reap life everlasting."

COUNSEL

Counsel In The Heart Of Man
Proverbs 20:5 "Counsel in the heart of man is like deep water; but a man of understanding will draw it out."

Hearing Counsel
Proverbs 19:20 "Hear counsel, and receive instruction, that thou mayest be wise in thy latter end."

Hearty Counsel
Proverbs 27:9 "Ointment and perfume rejoice the heart: so doth the sweetness of a man's friend by hearty counsel."

The Counsel Of The Froward
Job 5:13 "He taketh the wise in their own craftiness: and the counsel of the froward is carried headlong."

The Counsel Of The Heathen
Psalm 33:10 "The LORD bringeth the counsel of the heathen to nought: he maketh the devices of the people of none effect."

The Counsel(s) Of The Lord
Psalm 33:11 "The counsel of the LORD standeth for ever, the thoughts of his heart to all generations."

Proverbs 19:21 "There are many devices in a man's heart; nevertheless the counsel of the LORD, that shall stand."

Isaiah 25:1 "O LORD, thou art my God; I will exalt thee, I will praise thy name; for thou hast done wonderful things; thy counsels of old are faithfulness and truth."

Isaiah 46:9-10 "⁹Remember the former things of old: for I am God, and there is none else; I am God, and there is none like me, ¹⁰Declaring the end from the beginning, and from ancient times the things that are not yet done, saying, My counsel shall stand, and I will do all my pleasure."

The Counselors Of Peace
Proverbs 12:20 "Deceit is in the heart of them that imagine evil: but to the counsellers of peace is joy."

The Counsels Of The Wicked
Proverbs 12:5 "The thoughts of the righteous are right: but the counsels of the wicked are deceit."

The Lord Giving Counsel
Psalm 16:7 "I will bless the LORD, who hath given me counsel: my reins also instruct me in the night seasons."

The Multitude Of Counselors
Proverbs 11:14 "Where no counsel is, the people fall: but in the multitude of counsellers there is safety."

Proverbs 15:22 "Without counsel purposes are disappointed: but in the multitude of counsellers they are established."

Proverbs 24:6 "For by wise counsel thou shalt make thy war: and in multitude of counsellers there is safety."

The Place Where There Is No Counsel
Proverbs 11:14 "Where no counsel is, the people fall: but in the multitude of counsellers there is safety."

Proverbs 15:22 "Without counsel purposes are disappointed: but in the multitude of counsellers they are established."

The Reward For Seeking Counsel Other Than That Of The Lord
1 Chronicles 10:13-14 "¹³So Saul died for his transgression which he committed against the LORD, even against the word of the LORD, which he kept not, and also for asking counsel of one that had a familiar spirit, to inquire of it; ¹⁴And inquired not of the LORD: therefore he slew him, and turned the kingdom unto David the son of Jesse."

Isaiah 30:1 "Woe to the rebellious children, saith the LORD, that take counsel, but not of me; and that cover with a covering, but not of my spirit, that they may add sin to sin."

There Being No Counsel Against The Lord
Proverbs 21:30 "There is no wisdom nor understanding nor counsel against the LORD."

Those That Consult Pagans
Leviticus 20:1-6 "¹And the LORD spake unto Moses, saying, ²Again, thou shalt say to the children of Israel, Whosoever he be of the children of Israel, or of the strangers that sojourn in Israel, that giveth any of his seed unto Molech; he shall surely be put to death: the people of the land shall stone him with stones. ³And I will set my face against that man, and will cut him off from among his people; because he hath given of his seed unto Molech, to defile my sanctuary, and to profane my holy name. ⁴And if the people of the land do any ways hide their eyes from the man, when he giveth of his seed unto Molech, and kill him not: ⁵Then I will set my face against that man, and against his family, and will cut him off, and all that go a whoring after him, to commit whoredom with Molech, from among their people. ⁶And the soul that turneth after such as have familiar spirits, and after wizards, to go a whoring after them, I will even set my face against that soul, and will cut him off from among his people."

Those That Do Not Walk
In The Counsel Of The Ungodly
Psalm 1:1 "Blessed is the man that walketh not in the counsel of the ungodly, nor standeth in the way of sinners, nor sitteth in the seat of the scornful."

Those That Listen To Counsel
Proverbs 12:15 "The way of a fool is right in his own eyes: but he that hearkeneth unto counsel is wise."

Those That Take Counsel
Together Against The Lord
Psalm 2:1-6 "¹Why do the heathen rage, and the people imagine a vain thing? ²The kings of the earth set themselves, and the rulers take counsel together, against the LORD, and against his anointed, saying, ³Let us break their bands asunder, and cast away their cords from us. ⁴He that sitteth in the heavens shall laugh: the Lord shall have them in derision. ⁵Then shall he speak unto them in his wrath, and vex them in his sore displeasure. ⁶Yet have I set my king upon my holy hill of Zion."

What Is Established By Counsel
Proverbs 20:18 "Every purpose is established by counsel: and with good advice make war."

Proverbs 24:6 "For by wise counsel thou shalt make thy war: and in multitude of counsellers there is safety."

Whose Counsel Should Not Be Heeded
Proverbs 14:7 "Go from the presence of a foolish man, when thou perceivest not in him the lips of knowledge."

COUNTENANCE

An Angry Countenance
Proverbs 25:23 "The north wind driveth away rain: so doth an angry countenance a backbiting tongue."

People Sharpening The
Countenance Of Their Friends
Proverbs 27:17 "Iron sharpeneth iron; so a man sharpeneth the countenance of his friend."

The Countenance Of The Lord
Psalm 11:7 "For the righteous LORD loveth righteousness; his countenance doth behold the upright."

God Being The Health Of Your Countenance
Psalm 42:11 "Why art thou cast down, O my soul? and why art thou disquieted within me? hope thou in God: for I shall yet praise him, who is the health of my countenance, and my God."

Psalm 43:5 "Why art thou cast down, O my soul? and why art thou disquieted within me? hope in God: for I shall yet praise him, who is the health of my countenance, and my God."

What Makes A Cheerful Countenance
Proverbs 15:13 "A merry heart maketh a cheerful countenance: but by sorrow of the heart the spirit is broken."

Who Shall Walk In The Light
Of The Lord's Countenance
Psalm 89:15 "Blessed is the people that know the joyful sound: they shall walk, O LORD, in the light of thy countenance."

COURAGE

Being Courageous
Deuteronomy 31:6-8 "⁶Be strong and of a good courage, fear not, nor be afraid of them: for the LORD thy God, he it is that doth go with thee; he will not fail thee, nor forsake thee. ⁷And Moses called unto Joshua, and said unto him in the sight of all Israel, Be strong and of a good courage: for thou must go with this people unto the land which the LORD hath sworn unto their fathers to give them; and thou shalt cause them to inherit it. ⁸And the LORD, he it is that doth go before thee; he will be with thee, he will not fail thee, neither forsake thee: fear not, neither be dismayed."

Joshua 1:6-9 "⁶Be strong and of a good courage: for unto this people shalt thou divide for an inheritance the land, which I sware unto their fathers to give them. ⁷Only be thou strong and very courageous, that thou mayest observe to do according to all the law, which Moses my servant commanded thee: turn not from it to the right hand or to the left, that thou mayest prosper whithersoever thou goest. ⁸This book of the law shall not depart out of thy mouth; but thou shalt meditate therein day and night, that thou mayest observe to do according to all that is written therein: for then thou shalt make thy way prosperous, and then thou shalt have good success. [9]Have not I commanded thee? Be strong and of a good courage; be not afraid, neither be thou dismayed: for the LORD thy God is with thee whithersoever thou goest."

Joshua 23:6 "Be ye therefore very courageous to keep and to do all that is written in the book of the law of Moses, that ye turn not aside therefrom to the right hand or to the left."

1 Chronicles 22:13 "Then shalt thou prosper, if thou takest heed to fulfil the statutes and judgments which the LORD charged Moses with concerning Israel: be strong, and of good courage; dread not, nor be dismayed."

2 Chronicles 32:7-8 "[7]Be strong and courageous, be not afraid nor dismayed for the king of Assyria, nor for all the multitude that is with him: for there be more with us than with him: [8]With him is an arm of flesh; but with us is the LORD our God to help us, and to fight our battles. And the people rested themselves upon the words of Hezekiah king of Judah."

Psalm 27:14 "Wait on the LORD: be of good courage, and he shall strengthen thine heart: wait, I say, on the LORD."

Psalm 31:24 "Be of good courage, and he shall strengthen your heart, all ye that hope in the LORD."

COVENANT

Being Mindful Of The Lord's Covenant
Deuteronomy 4:23 "Take heed unto yourselves, lest ye forget the covenant of the LORD your God, which he made with you, and make you a graven image, or the likeness of any thing, which the LORD thy God hath forbidden thee."

1 Chronicles 16:14-15 "[14]He is the LORD our God; his judgments are in all the earth. [15]Be ye mindful always of his covenant; the word which he commanded to a thousand generations."

The Covenant Of Peace
Isaiah 54:10 "For the mountains shall depart, and the hills be removed; but my kindness shall not depart from thee, neither shall the covenant of my peace be removed, saith the LORD that hath mercy on thee."

Ezekiel 34:25-31 "[25]And I will make with them a covenant of peace, and will cause the evil beasts to cease out of the land: and they shall dwell safely in the wilderness, and sleep in the woods. [26]And I will make them and the places round about my hill a blessing; and I will cause the shower to come down in his season; there shall be showers of blessing. [27]And the tree of the field shall yield her fruit, and the earth shall yield her increase, and they shall be safe in their land, and shall know that I am the LORD, when I have broken the bands of their yoke, and delivered them out of the hand of those that served themselves of them. [28]And they shall no more be a prey to the heathen, neither shall the beast of the land devour them; but they shall dwell safely, and none shall make them afraid. [29]And I will raise up for them a plant of renown, and they shall be no more consumed with hunger in the land, neither bear the shame of the heathen any more. [30]Thus shall they know that I the LORD their God am with them, and that they, even the house of Israel, are my people, saith the Lord GOD. [31]And ye my flock, the flock of my pasture, are men, and I am your God, saith the Lord GOD."

The Covenant With Abraham
Genesis 17:1-22 "[1]And when Abram was ninety years old and nine, the LORD appeared to Abram, and said unto him, I am the Almighty God; walk before me, and be thou perfect. [2]And I will make my covenant between me and thee, and will multiply thee exceedingly. [3]And Abram fell on his face: and God talked with him, saying, [4]As for me, behold, my covenant is with thee, and thou shalt be a father of many nations. [5]Neither shall thy name any more be called Abram, but thy name shall be Abraham; for a father of many nations have I made thee. [6]And I will make thee exceeding fruitful, and I will make nations of thee, and kings shall come out of thee. [7]And I will establish my covenant between me and thee and thy seed after thee in their generations for an everlasting covenant, to be a God unto thee, and to thy seed after thee. [8]And I will give unto thee, and to thy seed after thee, the land wherein thou art a stranger, all the land of Canaan, for an everlasting possession; and I will be their God. [9]And God said unto Abraham, Thou shalt keep my covenant therefore, thou, and thy seed after thee in their

generations. [10]This is my covenant, which ye shall keep, between me and you and thy seed after thee; Every man child among you shall be circumcised. [11]And ye shall circumcise the flesh of your foreskin; and it shall be a token of the covenant betwixt me and you. [12]And he that is eight days old shall be circumcised among you, every man child in your generations, he that is born in the house, or bought with money of any stranger, which is not of thy seed. [13]He that is born in thy house, and he that is bought with thy money, must needs be circumcised: and my covenant shall be in your flesh for an everlasting covenant. [14]And the uncircumcised man child whose flesh of his foreskin is not circumcised, that soul shall be cut off from his people; he hath broken my covenant. [15]And God said unto Abraham, As for Sarai thy wife, thou shalt not call her name Sarai, but Sarah shall her name be. [16]And I will bless her, and give thee a son also of her: yea, I will bless her, and she shall be a mother of nations; kings of people shall be of her. [17]Then Abraham fell upon his face, and laughed, and said in his heart, Shall a child be born unto him that is an hundred years old? and shall Sarah, that is ninety years old, bear? [18]And Abraham said unto God, O that Ishmael might live before thee! [19]And God said, Sarah thy wife shall bear thee a son indeed; and thou shalt call his name Isaac: and I will establish my covenant with him for an everlasting covenant, and with his seed after him. [20]And as for Ishmael, I have heard thee: Behold, I have blessed him, and will make him fruitful, and will multiply him exceedingly; twelve princes shall he beget, and I will make him a great nation. [21]But my covenant will I establish with Isaac, which Sarah shall bear unto thee at this set time in the next year. [22]And he left off talking with him, and God went up from Abraham."

Nehemiah 9:7-8 "[7]Thou art the LORD the God, who didst choose Abram, and broughtest him forth out of Ur of the Chaldees, and gavest him the name of Abraham; [8]And foundest his heart faithful before thee, and madest a covenant with him to give the land of the Canaanites, the Hittites, the Amorites, and the Perizzites, and the Jebusites, and the Girgashites, to give it, I say, to his seed, and hast performed thy words; for thou art righteous."

Psalm 105:7-10 "[7]He is the LORD our God: his judgments are in all the earth. [8]He hath remembered his covenant for ever, the word which he commanded to a thousand generations. [9]Which covenant he made with Abraham, and his oath unto Isaac; [10]And confirmed the same unto Jacob for a law, and to Israel for an everlasting covenant."

The Covenant With Noah

Genesis 6:18-22 "[18]But with thee will I establish my covenant; and thou shalt come into the ark, thou, and thy sons, and thy wife, and thy sons' wives with thee. [19]And of every living thing of all flesh, two of every sort shalt thou bring into the ark, to keep them alive with thee; they shall be male and female. [20]Of fowls after their kind, and of cattle after their kind, of every creeping thing of the earth after his kind, two of every sort shall come unto thee, to keep them alive. [21]And take thou unto thee of all food that is eaten, and thou shalt gather it to thee; and it shall be for food for thee, and for them. [22]Thus did Noah; according to all that God commanded him, so did he."

Genesis 8:21 "And the LORD smelled a sweet savour; and the LORD said in his heart, I will not again curse the ground any more for man's sake; for the imagination of man's heart is evil from his youth; neither will I again smite any more every thing living, as I have done."

Genesis 9:8-17 "[8]And God spake unto Noah, and to his sons with him, saying, [9]And I, behold, I establish my covenant with you, and with your seed after you; [10]And with every living creature that is with you, of the fowl, of the cattle, and of every beast of the earth with you; from all that go out of the ark, to every beast of the earth. [11]And I will establish my covenant with you; neither shall all flesh be cut off any more by the waters of a flood; neither shall there any more be a flood to destroy the earth. [12]And God said, This is the token of the covenant which I make between me and you and every living creature that is with you, for perpetual generations: [13]I do set my bow in the cloud, and it shall be for a token of a covenant between me and the earth. [14]And it shall come to pass, when I bring a cloud over the earth, that the bow shall be seen in the cloud: [15]And I will remember my covenant, which is between me and you and every living creature of all flesh; and the waters shall no more become a flood to destroy all flesh. [16]And the bow shall be in the cloud; and I will look upon it, that I may remember the everlasting covenant between God and every living creature of all flesh that is upon the earth. [17]And God said unto Noah, This is the token of the covenant, which I have established between me and all flesh that is upon the earth."

Isaiah 54:9 "For this is as the waters of Noah unto me: for as I have sworn that the waters of Noah should no more go over the earth; so have I sworn that I would not be wroth with thee, nor rebuke thee."

The Lord Being Mindful Of His Covenant
Genesis 9:12-16 "[12]And God said, This is the token of the covenant which I make between me and you and every living creature that is with you, for perpetual generations: [13]I do set my bow in the cloud, and it shall be for a token of a covenant between me and the earth. [14]And it shall come to pass, when I bring a cloud over the earth, that the bow shall be seen in the cloud: [15]And I will remember my covenant, which is between me and you and every living creature of all flesh; and the waters shall no more become a flood to destroy all flesh. [16]And the bow shall be in the cloud; and I will look upon it, that I may remember the everlasting covenant between God and every living creature of all flesh that is upon the earth."

Deuteronomy 4:31 "(For the LORD thy God is a merciful God;) he will not forsake thee, neither destroy thee, nor forget the covenant of thy fathers which he sware unto them."

Deuteronomy 7:6-8 "[6]For thou art an holy people unto the LORD thy God: the LORD thy God hath chosen thee to be a special people unto himself, above all people that are upon the face of the earth. [7]The LORD did not set his love upon you, nor choose you, because ye were more in number than any people; for ye were the fewest of all people: [8]But because the LORD loved you, and because he would keep the oath which he had sworn unto your fathers, hath the LORD brought you out with a mighty hand, and redeemed you out of the house of bondmen, from the hand of Pharaoh king of Egypt."

Judges 2:1 "And an angel of the LORD came up from Gilgal to Bochim, and said, I made you to go up out of Egypt, and have brought you unto the land which I sware unto your fathers; and I said, I will never break my covenant with you."

Psalm 89:26-34 "[26]He shall cry unto me, Thou art my father, my God, and the rock of my salvation. [27]Also I will make him my firstborn, higher than the kings of the earth. [28]My mercy will I keep for him for evermore, and my covenant shall stand fast with him. [29]His seed also will I make to endure for ever, and his throne as the days of heaven. [30]If his children forsake my law, and walk not in my judgments; [31]If they break my statutes, and keep not my commandments; [32]Then will I visit their transgression with the rod, and their iniquity with stripes. [33]Nevertheless my lovingkindness will I not utterly take from him, nor suffer my faithfulness to fail. [34]My covenant will I not break, nor alter the thing that is gone out of my lips."

Psalm 105:7-8 "[7]He is the LORD our God: his judgments are in all the earth. [8]He hath remembered his covenant for ever, the word which he commanded to a thousand generations."

Psalm 111:2-9 "[2]The works of the LORD are great, sought out of all them that have pleasure therein. [3]His work is honourable and glorious: and his righteousness endureth for ever. [4]He hath made his wonderful works to be remembered: the LORD is gracious and full of compassion. [5]He hath given meat unto them that fear him: he will ever be mindful of his covenant. [6]He hath shewed his people the power of his works, that he may give them the heritage of the heathen. [7]The works of his hands are verity and judgment; all his commandments are sure. [8]They stand fast for ever and ever, and are done in truth and uprightness. [9]He sent redemption unto his people: he hath commanded his covenant for ever: holy and reverend is his name."

The Lord Making A Covenant With Israel
Deuteronomy 5:1-3 "[1]And Moses called all Israel, and said unto them, Hear, O Israel, the statutes and judgments which I speak in your ears this day, that ye may learn them, and keep, and do them. [2]The LORD our God made a covenant with us in Horeb. [3]The LORD made not this covenant with our fathers, but with us, even us, who are all of us

here alive this day."

Psalm 105:7-10 "[7]He is the LORD our God: his judgments are in all the earth. [8]He hath remembered his covenant for ever, the word which he commanded to a thousand generations. [9]Which covenant he made with Abraham, and his oath unto Isaac; [10]And confirmed the same unto Jacob for a law, and to Israel for an everlasting covenant."

Isaiah 61:1-9 "[1]The Spirit of the Lord GOD is upon me; because the LORD hath anointed me to preach good tidings unto the meek; he hath sent me to bind up the brokenhearted, to proclaim liberty to the captives, and the opening of the prison to them that are bound; [2]To proclaim the acceptable year of the LORD, and the day of vengeance of our God; to comfort all that mourn; [3]To appoint unto them that mourn in Zion, to give unto them beauty for ashes, the oil of joy for mourning, the garment of praise for the spirit of heaviness; that they might be called trees of righteousness, the planting of the LORD, that he might be glorified. [4]And they shall build the old wastes, they shall raise up the former desolations, and they shall repair the waste cities, the desolations of many generations. [5]And strangers shall stand and feed your flocks, and the sons of the alien shall be your plowmen and your vinedressers. [6]But ye shall be named the Priests of the LORD: men shall call you the Ministers of our God: ye shall eat the riches of the Gentiles, and in their glory shall ye boast yourselves. [7]For your shame ye shall have double; and for confusion they shall rejoice in their portion: therefore in their land they shall possess the double: everlasting joy shall be unto them. [8]For I the LORD love judgment, I hate robbery for burnt offering; and I will direct their work in truth, and I will make an everlasting covenant with them. [9]And their seed shall be known among the Gentiles, and their offspring among the people: all that see them shall acknowledge them, that they are the seed which the LORD hath blessed."

Jeremiah 11:3-5 "[3]And say thou unto them, Thus saith the LORD God of Israel; Cursed be the man that obeyeth not the words of this covenant, [4]Which I commanded your fathers in the day that I brought them forth out of the land of Egypt, from the iron furnace, saying, Obey my voice, and do them, according to all which I command you: so shall ye be my people, and I will be your God:

[5]That I may perform the oath which I have sworn unto your fathers, to give them a land flowing with milk and honey, as it is this day. Then answered I, and said, So be it, O LORD."

The New Covenant With The Lord

Deuteronomy 6:5-6 "[5]And thou shalt love the LORD thy God with all thine heart, and with all thy soul, and with all thy might. [6]And these words, which I command thee this day, shall be in thine heart."

Deuteronomy 30:1-6 "[1]And it shall come to pass, when all these things are come upon thee, the blessing and the curse, which I have set before thee, and thou shalt call them to mind among all the nations, whither the LORD thy God hath driven thee, [2]And shalt return unto the LORD thy God, and shalt obey his voice according to all that I command thee this day, thou and thy children, with all thine heart, and with all thy soul; [3]That then the LORD thy God will turn thy captivity, and have compassion upon thee, and will return and gather thee from all the nations, whither the LORD thy God hath scattered thee. [4]If any of thine be driven out unto the outmost parts of heaven, from thence will the LORD thy God gather thee, and from thence will he fetch thee: [5]And the LORD thy God will bring thee into the land which thy fathers possessed, and thou shalt possess it; and he will do thee good, and multiply thee above thy fathers. [6]And the LORD thy God will circumcise thine heart, and the heart of thy seed, to love the LORD thy God with all thine heart, and with all thy soul, that thou mayest live."

Psalm 37:31 "The law of his God is in his heart; none of his steps shall slide."

Psalm 40:8 "I delight to do thy will, O my God: yea, thy law is within my heart."

Isaiah 51:3-7 "[3]For the LORD shall comfort Zion: he will comfort all her waste places; and he will make her wilderness like Eden, and her desert like the garden of the LORD; joy and gladness shall be found therein, thanksgiving, and the voice of melody. [4]Hearken unto me, my people; and give ear unto me, O my nation: for a law shall proceed from me, and I will make my judgment to rest for a light of the people. [5]My righteousness is near; my salvation is gone forth, and mine arms shall judge the people; the isles shall wait upon me, and on mine arm shall they trust. 6Lift up your eyes to the heavens, and look upon the earth beneath: for the heavens shall vanish away like smoke, and the earth shall wax old like a garment, and they that dwell therein shall die in like manner: but my salvation shall be for ever, and my righteousness shall not be abolished. 7Hearken unto me, ye that know righteousness, the people in whose heart is my law; fear ye not the reproach of men, neither be ye afraid of their revilings."

Isaiah 55:1-3 "1Ho, every one that thirsteth, come ye to the waters, and he that hath no money; come ye, buy, and eat; yea, come, buy wine and milk without money and without price. 2Wherefore do ye spend money for that which is not bread? and your labour for that which satisfieth not? hearken diligently unto me, and eat ye that which is good, and let your soul delight itself in fatness. 3Incline your ear, and come unto me: hear, and your soul shall live; and I will make an everlasting covenant with you, even the sure mercies of David."

Isaiah 59:21 "As for me, this is my covenant with them, saith the LORD; My spirit that is upon thee, and my words which I have put in thy mouth, shall not depart out of thy mouth, nor out of the mouth of thy seed, nor out of the mouth of thy seed's seed, saith the LORD, from henceforth and for ever."

Jeremiah 3:14-18 "14Turn, O backsliding children, saith the LORD; for I am married unto you: and I will take you one of a city, and two of a family, and I will bring you to Zion: 15And I will give you pastors according to mine heart, which shall feed you with knowledge and understanding. 16And it shall come to pass, when ye be multiplied and increased in the land, in those days, saith the LORD, they shall say no more, The ark of the covenant of the LORD: neither shall it come to mind: neither shall they remember it; neither shall they visit it; neither shall that be done any more. 17At that time they shall call Jerusalem the throne of the LORD; and all the nations shall be gathered unto it, to the name of the LORD, to Jerusalem: neither shall they walk any more after the imagination of their evil heart. 18In those days the house of Judah shall walk with the house of Israel, and they shall come together out of the land of the north to the land that I have given for an inheritance unto your fathers."

Jeremiah 24:1-7 "1The LORD shewed me, and, behold, two baskets of figs were set before the temple of the LORD, after that Nebuchadrezzar king of Babylon had carried away captive Jeconiah the son of Jehoiakim king of Judah, and the princes of Judah, with the carpenters and smiths, from Jerusalem, and had brought them to Babylon. 2One basket had very good figs, even like the figs that are first ripe: and the other basket had very naughty figs, which could not be eaten, they were so bad. 3Then said the LORD unto me, What seest thou, Jeremiah? And I said, Figs; the good figs, very good; and the evil, very evil, that cannot be eaten, they are so evil. 4Again the word of the LORD came unto me, saying, 5Thus saith the LORD, the God of Israel; Like these good figs, so will I acknowledge them that are carried away captive of Judah, whom I have sent out of this place into the land of the Chaldeans for their good. 6For I will set mine eyes upon them for good, and I will bring them again to this land: and I will build them, and not pull them down; and I will plant them, and not pluck them up. 7And I will give them an heart to know me, that I am the LORD: and they shall be my people, and I will be their God: for they shall return unto me with their whole heart."

Jeremiah 31:31-34 "31Behold, the days come, saith the LORD, that I will make a new covenant with the house of Israel, and with the house of Judah: 32Not according to the covenant that I made with their fathers in the day that I took them by the hand to bring them out of the land of Egypt; which my covenant they brake, although I was an husband unto them, saith the LORD: 33But this shall be the covenant that I will make with the house of Israel; After those days, saith the LORD, I will put my law in their inward parts, and write it in their hearts; and will be their God, and they shall be my people. 34And they shall teach no more every man his neighbour, and every man his brother, saying, Know the LORD: for they shall all know me, from the least of them unto the greatest of them, saith the LORD; for I will forgive their iniquity, and I will remember their sin no more."

Jeremiah 32:37-40 "37Behold, I will gather them out of all countries, whither I have driven them in mine anger, and in my fury, and in great wrath; and I will bring them again unto this place, and I will cause them to dwell safely: ³⁸And they shall be my people, and I will be their God: ³⁹And I will give them one heart, and one way, that they may fear me for ever, for the good of them, and of their children after them: ⁴⁰And I will make an everlasting covenant with them, that I will not turn away from them, to do them good; but I will put my fear in their hearts, that they shall not depart from me."

Ezekiel 11:16-21 "¹⁶Therefore say, Thus saith the Lord GOD; Although I have cast them far off among the heathen, and although I have scattered them among the countries, yet will I be to them as a little sanctuary in the countries where they shall come. ¹⁷Therefore say, Thus saith the Lord GOD; I will even gather you from the people, and assemble you out of the countries where ye have been scattered, and I will give you the land of Israel. ¹⁸And they shall come thither, and they shall take away all the detestable things thereof and all the abominations thereof from thence. ¹⁹And I will give them one heart, and I will put a new spirit within you; and I will take the stony heart out of their flesh, and will give them an heart of flesh: ²⁰That they may walk in my statutes, and keep mine ordinances, and do them: and they shall be my people, and I will be their God. ²¹But as for them whose heart walketh after the heart of their detestable things and their abominations, I will recompense their way upon their own heads, saith the Lord GOD."

Ezekiel 36:22-27 "²²Therefore say unto the house of Israel, Thus saith the Lord GOD; I do not this for your sakes, O house of Israel, but for mine holy name's sake, which ye have profaned among the heathen, whither ye went. ²³And I will sanctify my great name, which was profaned among the heathen, which ye have profaned in the midst of them; and the heathen shall know that I am the LORD, saith the Lord GOD, when I shall be sanctified in you before their eyes. ²⁴For I will take you from among the heathen, and gather you out of all countries, and will bring you into your own land. ²⁵Then will I sprinkle clean water upon you, and ye shall be clean: from all your filthiness, and from all your idols, will I cleanse you. ²⁶A new heart also will I give you, and a new spirit will I put within you: and I will take away the stony heart out of your flesh, and

I will give you an heart of flesh. ²⁷And I will put my spirit within you, and cause you to walk in my statutes, and ye shall keep my judgments, and do them."

Romans 11:26-27 "²⁶And so all Israel shall be saved: as it is written, There shall come out of Sion the Deliverer, and shall turn away ungodliness from Jacob: ²⁷For this is my covenant unto them, when I shall take away their sins."

Hebrews 8:6-13 "⁶But now hath he obtained a more excellent ministry, by how much also he is the mediator of a better covenant, which was established upon better promises. ⁷For if that first covenant had been faultless, then should no place have been sought for the second. ⁸For finding fault with them, he saith, Behold, the days come, saith the Lord, when I will make a new covenant with the house of Israel and with the house of Judah: ⁹Not according to the covenant that I made with their fathers in the day when I took them by the hand to lead them out of the land of Egypt; because they continued not in my covenant, and I regarded them not, saith the Lord. ¹⁰For this is the covenant that I will make with the house of Israel after those days, saith the Lord; I will put my laws into their mind, and write them in their hearts: and I will be to them a God, and they shall be to me a people: ¹¹And they shall not teach every man his neighbour, and every man his brother, saying, Know the Lord: for all shall know me, from the least to the greatest. ¹²For I will be merciful to their unrighteousness, and their sins and their iniquities will I remember no more. ¹³In that he saith, A new covenant, he hath made the first old. Now that which decayeth and waxeth old is ready to vanish away."

Hebrews 10:16-18 "¹⁶This is the covenant that I will make with them after those days, saith the Lord, I will put my laws into their hearts, and in their minds will I write them; ¹⁷And their sins and iniquities will I remember no more. ¹⁸Now where remission of these is, there is no more offering for sin."

Revelation 21:1-4 "¹And I saw a new heaven and a new earth: for the first heaven and the first earth were passed away; and there was no more sea. ²And I John saw the holy city, new Jerusalem, coming down from God out of heaven, prepared as a bride adorned for her husband. ³And I heard a great voice out of heaven saying, Behold, the tabernacle of God is with men, and he will dwell with them, and they shall be his people, and God himself shall be with them, and be their God. ⁴And God shall wipe away all tears from their eyes; and there shall be no more death, neither sorrow, nor crying, neither shall there be any more pain: for the former things are passed away."

The Reward For Transgressing
The Covenant Of The Lord

Deuteronomy 29:19-25 "¹⁹And it come to pass, when he heareth the words of this curse, that he bless himself in his heart, saying, I shall have peace, though I walk in the imagination of mine heart, to add drunkenness to thirst: ²⁰The LORD will not spare him, but then the anger of the LORD and his jealousy shall smoke against that man, and all the curses that are written in this book shall lie upon him, and the LORD shall blot out his name from under heaven. ²¹And the LORD shall separate him unto evil out of all the tribes of Israel, according to all the curses of the covenant that are written in this book of the law: ²²So that the generation to come of your children that shall rise up after you, and the stranger that shall come from a far land, shall say, when they see the plagues of that land, and the sicknesses which the LORD hath laid upon it; ²³And that the whole land thereof is brimstone, and salt, and burning, that it is not sown, nor beareth, nor any grass groweth therein, like the overthrow of Sodom, and Gomorrah, Admah, and Zeboim, which the LORD overthrew in his anger, and in his wrath: ²⁴Even all nations shall say, Wherefore hath the LORD done thus unto this land? what meaneth the heat of this great anger? ²⁵Then men shall say, Because they have forsaken the covenant of the LORD God of their fathers, which he made with them when he brought them forth out of the land of Egypt."

Deuteronomy 31:16-17 "¹⁶And the LORD said unto Moses, Behold, thou shalt sleep with thy fathers; and this people will rise up, and go a whoring after the gods of the strangers of the land, whither they go to be among them, and will forsake me, and break my covenant which I have made with them. ¹⁷Then my anger shall be kindled against them in that day, and I will forsake them, and I will hide my face from them, and they shall be devoured, and many evils and troubles shall befall them; so that

they will say in that day, Are not these evils come upon us, because our God is not among us?"

Joshua 23:15-16 "¹⁵Therefore it shall come to pass, that as all good things are come upon you, which the LORD your God promised you; so shall the LORD bring upon you all evil things, until he have destroyed you from off this good land which the LORD your God hath given you. ¹⁶When ye have transgressed the covenant of the LORD your God, which he commanded you, and have gone and served other gods, and bowed yourselves to them; then shall the anger of the LORD be kindled against you, and ye shall perish quickly from off the good land which he hath given unto you."

Judges 2:20-23 "²⁰And the anger of the LORD was hot against Israel; and he said, Because that this people hath transgressed my covenant which I commanded their fathers, and have not hearkened unto my voice; ²¹I also will not henceforth drive out any from before them of the nations which Joshua left when he died: ²²That through them I may prove Israel, whether they will keep the way of the LORD to walk therein, as their fathers did keep it, or not. ²³Therefore the LORD left those nations, without driving them out hastily; neither delivered he them into the hand of Joshua."

2 Kings 18:11-12 "¹¹And the king of Assyria did carry away Israel unto Assyria, and put them in Halah and in Habor by the river of Gozan, and in the cities of the Medes: ¹²Because they obeyed not the voice of the LORD their God, but transgressed his covenant, and all that Moses the servant of the LORD commanded, and would not hear them, nor do them."

Those That Keep The Covenant Of The Lord

Psalm 25:10 "All the paths of the LORD are mercy and truth unto such as keep his covenant and his testimonies."

Psalm 103:17-18 "¹⁷But the mercy of the LORD is from everlasting to everlasting upon them that fear him, and his righteousness unto children's children; ¹⁸To such as keep his covenant, and to those that remember his commandments to do them."

Isaiah 56:4-7 "⁴For thus saith the LORD unto the eunuchs that keep my sabbaths, and choose the things that please me, and take hold of my covenant; ⁵Even unto them will I give in mine house and within my walls a place and a name better than of sons and of daughters: I will give them an everlasting name, that shall not be cut off. ⁶Also the sons of the stranger, that join themselves to the LORD, to serve him, and to love the name of the LORD, to be his servants, every one that keepeth the sabbath from polluting it, and taketh hold of my covenant; ⁷Even them will I bring to my holy mountain, and make them joyful in my house of prayer: their burnt offerings and their sacrifices shall be accepted upon mine altar; for mine house shall be called an house of prayer for all people."

Who Made A Covenant With Death
Isaiah 28:14-15 "¹⁴Wherefore hear the word of the LORD, ye scornful men, that rule this people which is in Jerusalem. ¹⁵Because ye have said, We have made a covenant with death, and with hell are we at agreement; when the overflowing scourge shall pass through, it shall not come unto us: for we have made lies our refuge, and under falsehood have we hid ourselves."

Who Not To Make A Covenant With
Exodus 23:31-32 "³¹And I will set thy bounds from the Red sea even unto the sea of the Philistines, and from the desert unto the river: for I will deliver the inhabitants of the land into your hand; and thou shalt drive them out before thee. ³²Thou shalt make no covenant with them, nor with their gods."

Exodus 34:11-16 "¹¹Observe thou that which I command thee this day: behold, I drive out before thee the Amorite, and the Canaanite, and the Hittite, and the Perizzite, and the Hivite, and the Jebusite. ¹²Take heed to thyself, lest thou make a covenant with the inhabitants of the land whither thou goest, lest it be for a snare in the midst of thee: ¹³But ye shall destroy their altars, break their images, and cut down their groves: ¹⁴For thou shalt worship no other god: for the LORD, whose name is Jealous, is a jealous God: ¹⁵Lest thou make a covenant with the inhabitants of the land, and they go a whoring after their gods, and do sacrifice unto their gods, and one call thee, and thou eat of his sacrifice; ¹⁶And thou take of their

daughters unto thy sons, and their daughters go a whoring after their gods, and make thy sons go a whoring after their gods."

Deuteronomy 7:1-2 "¹When the LORD thy God shall bring thee into the land whither thou goest to possess it, and hath cast out many nations before thee, the Hittites, and the Girgashites, and the Amorites, and the Canaanites, and the Perizzites, and the Hivites, and the Jebusites, seven nations greater and mightier than thou; ²And when the LORD thy God shall deliver them before thee; thou shalt smite them, and utterly destroy them; thou shalt make no covenant with them, nor shew mercy unto them."

Who The Lord Keeps Covenant With
Leviticus 26:1-9 "¹Ye shall make you no idols nor graven image, neither rear you up a standing image, neither shall ye set up any image of stone in your land, to bow down unto it: for I am the LORD your God. ²Ye shall keep my sabbaths, and reverence my sanctuary: I am the LORD. ³If ye walk in my statutes, and keep my commandments, and do them; ⁴Then I will give you rain in due season, and the land shall yield her increase, and the trees of the field shall yield their fruit. ⁵And your threshing shall reach unto the vintage, and the vintage shall reach unto the sowing time: and ye shall eat your bread to the full, and dwell in your land safely. ⁶And I will give peace in the land, and ye shall lie down, and none shall make you afraid: and I will rid evil beasts out of the land, neither shall the sword go through your land. ⁷And ye shall chase your enemies, and they shall fall before you by the sword. ⁸And five of you shall chase an hundred, and an hundred of you shall put ten thousand to flight: and your enemies shall fall before you by the sword. ⁹For I will have respect unto you, and make you fruitful, and multiply you, and establish my covenant with you."

Deuteronomy 7:6-9 "⁶For thou art an holy people unto the LORD thy God: the LORD thy God hath chosen thee to be a special people unto himself, above all people that are upon the face of the earth. ⁷The LORD did not set his love upon you, nor choose you, because ye were more in number than any people; for ye were the fewest of all people: ⁸But because the LORD loved you, and because he would keep the oath which he had sworn unto your fathers, hath the LORD brought you out with a mighty hand, and redeemed you out of the house of bondmen, from the hand of Pharaoh king of Egypt. ⁹Know therefore that the LORD thy God, he is God, the faithful God, which keepeth covenant and mercy with them that love him and keep his commandments to a thousand generations."

Deuteronomy 7:11-12 "¹¹Thou shalt therefore keep the commandments, and the statutes, and the judgments, which I command thee this day, to do them. ¹²Wherefore it shall come to pass, if ye hearken to these judgments, and keep, and do them, that the LORD thy God shall keep unto thee the covenant and the mercy which he sware unto thy fathers."

1 Kings 8:23 "And he said, LORD God of Israel, there is no God like thee, in heaven above, or on earth beneath, who keepest covenant and mercy with thy servants that walk before thee with all their heart."

2 Chronicles 6:14 "And said, O LORD God of Israel, there is no God like thee in the heaven, nor in the earth; which keepest covenant, and shewest mercy unto thy servants, that walk before thee with all their hearts."

Nehemiah 1:5 "And said, I beseech thee, O LORD God of heaven, the great and terrible God, that keepeth covenant and mercy for them that love him and observe his commandments."

Isaiah 55:1-5 "¹Ho, every one that thirsteth, come ye to the waters, and he that hath no money; come ye, buy, and eat; yea, come, buy wine and milk without money and without price. ²Wherefore do ye spend money for that which is not bread? and your labour for that which satisfieth not? hearken diligently unto me, and eat ye that which is good, and let your soul delight itself in fatness. ³Incline your ear, and come unto me: hear, and your soul shall live; and I will make an everlasting covenant with you, even the sure mercies of David. ⁴Behold, I have given him for a witness to the people, a leader and commander to the people. ⁵Behold, thou shalt call a nation that thou knowest not, and nations that knew not thee shall run unto thee because of the LORD thy God,

and for the Holy One of Israel; for he hath glorified thee."

Daniel 9:4 "And I prayed unto the LORD my God, and made my confession, and said, O Lord, the great and dreadful God, keeping the covenant and mercy to them that love him, and to them that keep his commandments."

Who The Lord Will Show His Covenant To
Psalm 25:14 "The secret of the LORD is with them that fear him; and he will shew them his covenant."

COVETOUSNESS

Being Aware Of Covetousness
Luke 12:13-15 "¹³And one of the company said unto him, Master, speak to my brother, that he divide the inheritance with me. ¹⁴And he said unto him, Man, who made me a judge or a divider over you? ¹⁵And he said unto them, Take heed, and beware of covetousness: for a man's life consisteth not in the abundance of the things which he possesseth."

Covetous People
Luke 12:13-21 "¹³And one of the company said unto him, Master, speak to my brother, that he divide the inheritance with me. ¹⁴And he said unto him, Man, who made me a judge or a divider over you? ¹⁵And he said unto them, Take heed, and beware of covetousness: for a man's life consisteth not in the abundance of the things which he possesseth. ¹⁶And he spake a parable unto them, saying, The ground of a certain rich man brought forth plentifully: ¹⁷And he thought within himself, saying, What shall I do, because I have no room where to bestow my fruits? ¹⁸And he said, This will I do: I will pull down my barns, and build greater; and there will I bestow all my fruits and my goods. ¹⁹And I will say to my soul, Soul, thou hast much goods laid up for many years; take thine ease, eat, drink, and be merry. ²⁰But God said unto him, Thou fool, this night thy soul shall be required of thee: then whose shall those things be, which thou hast provided? ²¹So is he that layeth up treasure for himself, and is not rich toward God."

Ephesians 5:5 "For this ye know, that no whoremonger, nor unclean person, nor covetous man, who is an idolater, hath any inheritance in the kingdom of Christ and of God."

Not Coveting
Exodus 20:17 "Thou shalt not covet thy neighbour's house, thou shalt not covet thy neighbour's wife, nor his manservant, nor his maidservant, nor his ox, nor his ass, nor any thing that is thy neighbour's."

Deuteronomy 5:21 "Neither shalt thou desire thy neighbour's wife, neither shalt thou covet thy neighbour's house, his field, or his manservant, or his maidservant, his ox, or his ass, or any thing that is thy neighbour's."

Romans 13:8-9 "8Owe no man any thing, but to love one another: for he that loveth another hath fulfilled the law. 9For this, Thou shalt not commit adultery, Thou shalt not kill, Thou shalt not steal, Thou shalt not bear false witness, Thou shalt not covet; and if there be any other commandment, it is briefly comprehended in this saying, namely, Thou shalt love thy neighbour as thyself."

Ephesians 5:3 "But fornication, and all uncleanness, or covetousness, let it not be once named among you, as becometh saints."

Hebrews 13:5 "Let your conversation be without covetousness; and be content with such things as ye have: for he hath said, I will never leave thee, nor forsake thee."

The Reward For Covetousness
Ephesians 5:5-6 "5For this ye know, that no whoremonger, nor unclean person, nor covetous man, who is an idolater, hath any inheritance in the kingdom of Christ and of God. 6Let no man deceive you with vain words: for because of these things cometh the wrath of God upon the children of disobedience."

Colossians 3:5-6 "5Mortify therefore your members which are upon the earth; fornication, uncleanness, inordinate affection, evil concupiscence, and covetousness, which is idolatry: 6For which things' sake the wrath of God cometh on the children of disobedience."

Those That Hate Covetousness
Proverbs 28:16 "The prince that wanteth understanding is also a great oppressor: but he that hateth covetousness shall prolong his days."

What Covetousness Is
Ephesians 5:5 "For this ye know, that no whoremonger, nor unclean person, nor covetous man, who is an idolater, hath any inheritance in the kingdom of Christ and of God."

Colossians 3:5 "Mortify therefore your members which are upon the earth; fornication, uncleanness, inordinate affection, evil concupiscence, and covetousness, which is idolatry."

What To Covet
1 Corinthians 12:27-31 "27Now ye are the body of Christ, and members in particular. 28And God hath set some in the church, first apostles, secondarily prophets, thirdly teachers, after that miracles, then gifts of healings, helps, governments, diversities of tongues. 29Are all apostles? are all prophets? are all teachers? are all workers of miracles? 30Have all the gifts of healing? do all speak with tongues? do all interpret? 31But covet earnestly the best gifts: and yet shew I unto you a more excellent way."

1 Corinthians 14:1 "Follow after charity, and desire spiritual gifts, but rather that ye may prophesy."

1 Corinthians 14:39 "Wherefore, brethren, covet to prophesy, and forbid not to speak with tongues."

Who Is Covetous
Ezekiel 33:30-31 "30Also, thou son of man, the children of thy people still are talking against thee by the walls and in the doors of the houses, and speak one to another, every one to his brother, saying, Come, I pray you, and hear what is the word that cometh forth from the LORD. 31And they come unto thee as the people cometh, and they sit before thee as my people, and they hear thy words, but they will not do them: for with their mouth they shew much love, but their heart goeth after their covetousness."

Luke 16:14-15 "14And the Pharisees also, who were covetous, heard all these things: and they derided him. 15And he said unto them, Ye are they which justify yourselves before men; but God knoweth your hearts: for that which is highly esteemed among men is abomination in the sight of God."

CRAFTINESS

Who Does Not Walk In Craftiness

2 Corinthians 4:1-2 "¹Therefore seeing we have this ministry, as we have received mercy, we faint not; ²But have renounced the hidden things of dishonesty, not walking in craftiness, nor handling the word of God deceitfully; but by manifestation of the truth commending ourselves to every man's conscience in the sight of God."

Who The Lord Takes In Their Own Craftiness

Job 5:8-13 "⁸I would seek unto God, and unto God would I commit my cause: ⁹Which doeth great things and unsearchable; marvellous things without number: ¹⁰Who giveth rain upon the earth, and sendeth waters upon the fields: ¹¹To set up on high those that be low; that those which mourn may be exalted to safety. ¹²He disappointeth the devices of the crafty, so that their hands cannot perform their enterprise. ¹³He taketh the wise in their own craftiness: and the counsel of the froward is carried headlong."

1 Corinthians 3:18-19 "¹⁸Let no man deceive himself. If any man among you seemeth to be wise in this world, let him become a fool, that he may be wise. ¹⁹For the wisdom of this world is foolishness with God. For it is written, He taketh the wise in their own craftiness."

CREATION

Everything Being Created
By The Word Of God (Jesus Christ)

Psalm 33:6 "By the word of the Lord were the heavens made; and all the host of them by the breath of his mouth."

John 1:1-10 "¹In the beginning was the Word, and the Word was with God, and the Word was God. ²The same was in the beginning with God. ³All things were made by him; and without him was not any thing made that was made. ⁴In him was life; and the life was the light of men. ⁵And the light shineth in darkness; and the darkness comprehended it not. ⁶There was a man sent from God, whose name was John. ⁷The same came for a witness, to bear witness of the Light, that all men through him might believe. ⁸He was not that Light, but was sent to bear witness of that Light. ⁹That was the true Light, which lighteth every man that cometh into the world. ¹⁰He was in the world, and the world was made by him, and the world knew him not."

1 Corinthians 8:6 "But to us there is but one God, the Father, of whom are all things, and we in him; and one Lord Jesus Christ, by whom are all things, and we by him."

Ephesians 3:9 "And to make all men see what is the fellowship of the mystery, which from the beginning of the world hath been hid in God, who created all things by Jesus Christ."

Colossians 1:12-17 "¹²Giving thanks unto the Father, which hath made us meet to be partakers of the inheritance of the saints in light: ¹³Who hath delivered us from the power of darkness, and hath translated us into the kingdom of his dear Son: ¹⁴In whom we have redemption through his blood, even the forgiveness of sins: ¹⁵Who is the image of the invisible God, the firstborn of every creature: ¹⁶For by him were all things created, that are in heaven, and that are in earth, visible and invisible, whether they be thrones, or dominions, or principalities, or powers: all things were created by him, and for him: ¹⁷And he is before all things, and by him all things consist."

Hebrews 1:1-2 "¹God, who at sundry times and in divers manners spake in time past unto the fathers by the prophets, ²Hath in these last days spoken unto us by his Son, whom he hath appointed heir of all things, by whom also he made the worlds."

Hebrews 11:3 "Through faith we understand that the worlds were framed by the word of God, so that things which are seen were not made of things which do appear."

2 Peter 3:5-7 "⁵For this they willingly are ignorant of, that by the word of God the heavens were of old, and the earth standing out of the water and in the water: ⁶Whereby the world that then was, being overflowed with water, perished: ⁷But the heavens and the earth, which are now, by the same word are kept in store, reserved unto fire against the day of judgment and perdition of ungodly men."

Revelation 3:14 "And unto the angel of the church of the Laodiceans write; These things saith the

Amen, the faithful and true witness, the beginning of the creation of God."

The Lord Creating Everything

Genesis 1:1-31 "¹In the beginning God created the Heaven and the earth. ²And the earth was without form, and void; and darkness was upon the face of the deep. And the Spirit of God moved upon the face of the waters. ³And God said, Let there be light: and there was light. ⁴And God saw the light, that it was good: and God divided the light from the darkness. ⁵And God called the light Day, and the darkness he called Night. And the evening and the morning were the first day. ⁶And God said, Let there be a firmament in the midst of the waters, and let it divide the waters from the waters. ⁷And God made the firmament, and divided the waters which were under the firmament from the waters which were above the firmament: and it was so. ⁸And God called the firmament Heaven. And the evening and the morning were the second day. ⁹And God said, Let the waters under the heaven be gathered together unto one place, and let the dry land appear: and it was so. ¹⁰And God called the dry land Earth; and the gathering together of the waters called he Seas: and God saw that it was good. ¹¹And God said, Let the earth bring forth grass, the herb yielding seed, and the fruit tree yielding fruit after his kind, whose seed is in itself, upon the earth: and it was so. ¹²And the earth brought forth grass, and herb yielding seed after his kind, and the tree yielding fruit, whose seed was in itself, after his kind: and God saw that it was good. ¹³And the evening and the morning were the third day. ¹⁴And God said, Let there be lights in the firmament of the heaven to divide the day from the night; and let them be for signs, and for seasons, and for days, and years: ¹⁵And let them be for lights in the firmament of the heaven to give light upon the earth: and it was so. ¹⁶And God made two great lights; the greater light to rule the day, and the lesser light to rule the night: he made the stars also. ¹⁷And God set them in the firmament of the heaven to give light upon the earth, ¹⁸And to rule over the day and over the night, and to divide the light from the darkness: and God saw that it was good. ¹⁹And the evening and the morning were the fourth day. ²⁰And God said, Let the waters bring forth abundantly the moving creature that hath life, and fowl that may fly above the earth in the open firmament of heaven. ²¹And God created great whales, and every living creature that moveth, which the waters brought forth abundantly, after their kind, and every winged fowl after his kind: and God saw that it was good. ²²And God blessed them, saying, Be fruitful, and multiply, and fill the waters in the seas, and let fowl multiply in the earth. ²³And the evening and the morning were the fifth day. ²⁴And God said, Let the earth bring forth the living creature after his kind, cattle, and creeping thing, and beast of the earth after his kind: and it was so. ²⁵And God made the beast of the earth after his kind, and cattle after their kind, and every thing that creepeth upon the earth after his kind: and God saw that it was good. ²⁶And God said, Let us make man in our image, after our likeness: and let them have dominion over the fish of the sea, and over the fowl of the air, and over the cattle, and over all the earth, and over every creeping thing that creepeth upon the earth. ²⁷So God created man in his own image, in the image of God created he him; male and female created he them. ²⁸And God blessed them, and God said unto them, Be fruitful, and multiply, and replenish the earth, and subdue it: and have dominion over the fish of the sea, and over the fowl of the air, and over every living thing that moveth upon the earth. ²⁹And God said, Behold, I have given you every herb bearing seed, which is upon the face of all the earth, and every tree, in the which is the fruit of a tree yielding seed; to you it shall be for meat. ³⁰And to every beast of the earth, and to every fowl of the air, and to every thing that creepeth upon the earth, wherein there is life, I have given every green herb for meat: and it was so. ³¹And God saw every thing that he had made, and, behold, it was very good. And the evening and the morning were the sixth day."

Genesis 2:4-7 "⁴These are the generations of the heavens and of the earth when they were created, in the day that the LORD God made the earth and the heavens, ⁵And every plant of the field before it was in the earth, and every herb of the field before it grew: for the LORD God had not caused it to rain upon the earth, and there was not a man to till the ground. ⁶But there went up a mist from the earth, and watered the whole face of the ground. 7And the LORD God formed man of the dust of the ground, and breathed into his nostrils the breath of life; and man became a living soul."

Genesis 2:18-22 "18And the LORD God said, It is not good that the man should be alone; I will make him an help meet for him. 19And out of the ground the LORD God formed every beast of the field, and every fowl of the air; and brought them unto Adam to see what he would call them: and whatsoever Adam called every living creature, that was the name thereof. 20And Adam gave names to all cattle, and to the fowl of the air, and to every beast of the field; but for Adam there was not found an help meet for him. 21And the LORD God caused a deep sleep to fall upon Adam and he slept: and he took one of his ribs, and closed up the flesh instead thereof; 22And the rib, which the LORD God had taken from man, made he a woman, and brought her unto the man."

Genesis 5:1-2 "1This is the book of the generations of Adam. In the day that God created man, in the likeness of God made he him; 2Male and female created he them; and blessed them, and called their name Adam, in the day when they were created."

Exodus 20:11 "For in six days the LORD made heaven and earth, the sea, and all that in them is, and rested the seventh day: wherefore the LORD blessed the sabbath day, and hallowed it."

Exodus 31:17 "It is a sign between me and the children of Israel for ever: for in six days the LORD made heaven and earth, and on the seventh day he rested, and was refreshed."

Deuteronomy 32:18 "Of the Rock that begat thee thou art unmindful, and hast forgotten God that formed thee."

2 Kings 19:15 "And Hezekiah prayed before the LORD, and said, O LORD God of Israel, which dwellest between the cherubims, thou art the God, even thou alone, of all the kingdoms of the earth: thou hast made heaven and earth."

1 Chronicles 16:26 "For all the gods of the people are idols: but the LORD made the heavens."

Nehemiah 9:6 "Thou, even thou, art LORD alone; thou hast made heaven, the heaven of heavens,

with all their host, the earth, and all things that are therein, the seas, and all that is therein, and thou preservest them all; and the host of heaven worshippeth thee."

Job 33:4-6 "4The Spirit of God hath made me, and the breath of the Almighty hath given me life. 5If thou canst answer me, set thy words in order before me, stand up. 6Behold, I am according to thy wish in God's stead: I also am formed out of the clay."

Job 34:12-19 "12Yea, surely God will not do wickedly, neither will the Almighty pervert judgment. 13Who hath given him a charge over the earth? or who hath disposed the whole world? 14If he set his heart upon man, if he gather unto himself his spirit and his breath; 15All flesh shall perish together, and man shall turn again unto dust. 16If now thou hast understanding, hear this: hearken to the voice of my words. 17Shall even he that hateth right govern? and wilt thou condemn him that is most just? 18Is it fit to say to a king, Thou art wicked? and to princes, Ye are ungodly? 19How much less to him that accepteth not the persons of princes, nor regardeth the rich more than the poor? for they all are the work of his hands."

Job 35:10 "But none saith, Where is God my maker, who giveth songs in the night."

Psalm 8:1-3 "1O LORD our Lord, how excellent is thy name in all the earth! who hast set thy glory above the heavens. 2Out of the mouth of babes and sucklings hast thou ordained strength because of thine enemies, that thou mightest still the enemy and the avenger. 3When I consider thy heavens, the work of thy fingers, the moon and the stars, which thou hast ordained."

Psalm 33:6 "By the word of the LORD were the heavens made; and all the host of them by the breath of his mouth."

Psalm 89:8-11 "8O LORD God of hosts, who is a strong LORD like unto thee? or to thy faithfulness round about thee? 9Thou rulest the raging of the sea: when the waves thereof arise, thou stillest them. 10Thou hast broken Rahab in pieces, as one that is slain; thou hast scattered thine enemies with thy strong arm. 11The heavens are thine, the earth also is thine: as for the world and the fulness thereof, thou hast founded them."

Psalm 90:2 "Before the mountains were brought forth, or ever thou hadst formed the earth and the world, even from everlasting to everlasting, thou art God."

Psalm 95:3-5 "³For the LORD is a great God, and a great King above all gods. ⁴In his hand are the deep places of the earth: the strength of the hills is his also. ⁵The sea is his, and he made it: and his hands formed the dry land."

Psalm 96:5 "For all the gods of the nations are idols: but the LORD made the heavens."

Psalm 100:3 "Know ye that the LORD he is God: it is he that hath made us, and not we ourselves; we are his people, and the sheep of his pasture."

Psalm 102:24-25 "²⁴I said, O my God, take me not away in the midst of my days: thy years are throughout all generations. ²⁵Of old hast thou laid the foundation of the earth: and the heavens are the work of thy hands."

Psalm 104:1-13 "¹Bless the LORD, O my soul. O LORD my God, thou art very great; thou art clothed with honour and majesty. ²Who coverest thyself with light as with a garment: who stretchest out the heavens like a curtain: ³Who layeth the beams of his chambers in the waters: who maketh the clouds his chariot: who walketh upon the wings of the wind: ⁴Who maketh his angels spirits; his ministers a flaming fire: ⁵Who laid the foundations of the earth, that it should not be removed for ever. ⁶Thou coveredst it with the deep as with a garment: the waters stood above the mountains. ⁷At thy rebuke they fled; at the voice of thy thunder they hasted away. ⁸They go up by the mountains; they go down by the valleys unto the place which thou hast founded for them. ⁹Thou hast set a bound that they may not pass over; that they turn not again to cover the earth. ¹⁰He sendeth the springs into the valleys, which run among the hills. ¹¹They give drink to every beast of the field: the wild asses quench their thirst. ¹²By them shall the fowls of the heaven have their habitation, which sing among the branches. ¹³He watereth the hills from his chambers: the earth is satisfied with the fruit of thy works."

Psalm 104:24-25 "²⁴O LORD, how manifold are thy works! in wisdom hast thou made them all: the earth is full of thy riches. ²⁵So is this great and wide sea, wherein are things creeping innumerable, both small and great beasts."

Psalm 115:15 "Ye are blessed of the LORD which made heaven and earth."

Psalm 119:73-75 "⁷³Thy hands have made me and fashioned me: give me understanding, that I may learn thy commandments. ⁷⁴They that fear thee will be glad when they see me; because I have hoped in thy word. ⁷⁵I know, O LORD, that thy judgments are right, and that thou in faithfulness hast afflicted me."

Psalm 119:89-90 "⁸⁹For ever, O LORD, thy word is settled in heaven. ⁹⁰Thy faithfulness is unto all generations: thou hast established the earth, and it abideth."

Psalm 121:2 "My help cometh from the LORD, which made heaven and earth."

Psalm 124:8 "Our help is in the name of the LORD, who made heaven and earth."

Psalm 136:1-9 "¹O give thanks unto the LORD; for he is good: for his mercy endureth for ever. ²O give thanks unto the God of gods: for his mercy endureth for ever. ³O give thanks to the Lord of lords: for his mercy endureth for ever. ⁴To him who alone doeth great wonders: for his mercy endureth for ever. ⁵To him that by wisdom made the heavens: for his mercy endureth for ever. ⁶To him that stretched out the earth above the waters: for his mercy endureth for ever. ⁷To him that made great lights: for his mercy endureth for ever: ⁸The sun to rule by day: for his mercy endureth for ever: ⁹The moon and stars to rule by night: for his mercy endureth for ever."

Psalm 139:13-17 "¹³For thou hast possessed my reins: thou hast covered me in my mother's womb. ¹⁴I will praise thee; for I am fearfully and wonderfully made: marvellous are thy works; and that my soul knoweth right well. ¹⁵My substance was not hid from thee, when I was made in secret, and curiously wrought in the lowest parts of the earth. ¹⁶Thine eyes did see my substance, yet being unperfect; and in thy book all my members were written, which in continuance were fashioned, when as yet there was none of them. ¹⁷How precious also are thy thoughts unto me, O God! how great is the sum of them!"

Psalm 146:5-6 "⁵Happy is he that hath the God of Jacob for his help, whose hope is in the LORD his God: ⁶Which made heaven, and earth, the sea, and all that therein is: which keepeth truth for ever."

Psalm 148:1-6 "¹Praise ye the LORD. Praise ye the LORD from the heavens: praise him in the heights. ²Praise ye him, all his angels: praise ye him, all his hosts. ³Praise ye him, sun and moon: praise him, all ye stars of light. ⁴Praise him, ye heavens of heavens, and ye waters that be above the heavens. ⁵Let them praise the name of the LORD: for he commanded, and they were created. ⁶He hath also stablished them for ever and ever: he hath made a decree which shall not pass."

Proverbs 3:19 "The LORD by wisdom hath founded the earth; by understanding hath he established the heavens."

Proverbs 8:22-31 "²²The LORD possessed me in the beginning of his way, before his works of old. ²³I was set up from everlasting, from the beginning, or ever the earth was. ²⁴When there were no depths, I was brought forth; when there were no fountains abounding with water. ²⁵Before the mountains were settled, before the hills was I brought forth: ²⁶While as yet he had not made the earth, nor the fields, nor the highest part of the dust of the world. ²⁷When he prepared the heavens, I was there: when he set a compass upon the face of the depth: ²⁸When he established the clouds above: when he strengthened the fountains of the deep: ²⁹When he gave to the sea his decree, that the waters should not pass his commandment: when he appointed the foundations of the earth: ³⁰Then I was by him, as one brought up with him: and I was daily his delight, rejoicing always before him; ³¹Rejoicing in the habitable part of his earth; and my delights were with the sons of men."

Proverbs 16:4 "The LORD hath made all things for himself: yea, even the wicked for the day of evil."

Proverbs 20:12 "The hearing ear, and the seeing eye, the LORD hath made even both of them."

Proverbs 22:2 "The rich and poor meet together: the LORD is the maker of them all."

Proverbs 26:10 "The great God that formed all things both rewardeth the fool, and rewardeth transgressors."

Proverbs 30:4-5 "⁴Who hath ascended up into heaven, or descended? who hath gathered the wind in his fists? who hath bound the waters in a garment? who hath established all the ends of the earth? what is his name, and what is his son's name, if thou canst tell? ⁵Every word of God is pure: he is a shield unto them that put their trust in him."

Ecclesiastes 11:5 "As thou knowest not what is the way of the spirit, nor how the bones do grow in the womb of her that is with child: even so thou knowest not the works of God who maketh all."

Isaiah 37:16 "O LORD of hosts, God of Israel, that dwellest between the cherubims, thou art the God, even thou alone, of all the kingdoms of the earth: thou hast made heaven and earth."

Isaiah 40:28 "Hast thou not known? hast thou not heard, that the everlasting God, the LORD, the Creator of the ends of the earth, fainteth not, neither is weary? there is no searching of his understanding."

Isaiah 42:5 "Thus saith God the LORD, he that created the heavens, and stretched them out; he that spread forth the earth, and that which cometh out of it; he that giveth breath unto the people upon it, and spirit to them that walk therein."

Isaiah 43:1 "But now thus saith the LORD that created thee, O Jacob, and he that formed thee, O Israel, Fear not: for I have redeemed thee, I have called thee by thy name; thou art mine."

Isaiah 43:3-7 "³For I am the LORD thy God, the Holy One of Israel, thy Saviour: I gave Egypt for thy ransom, Ethiopia and Seba for thee. ⁴Since thou wast precious in my sight, thou hast been honourable, and I have loved thee: therefore will I give men for thee, and people for thy life. ⁵Fear not: for I am with thee: I will bring thy seed from the east, and gather thee from the west; ⁶I will say to the north, Give up; and to the south, Keep not back: bring my sons from far, and my daughters from the ends of the earth; 7Even every one that is called by my name: for I have created him for my glory, I have formed him; yea, I have made him."

Isaiah 43:14-15 "14Thus saith the LORD, your redeemer, the Holy One of Israel; For your sake I have sent to Babylon, and have brought down all their nobles, and the Chaldeans, whose cry is in the ships. 15I am the LORD, your Holy One, the creator of Israel, your King."

Isaiah 44:2 "Thus saith the LORD that made thee, and formed thee from the womb, which will help thee; Fear not, O Jacob, my servant; and thou, Jesurun, whom I have chosen."

Isaiah 44:24 "Thus saith the LORD, thy redeemer, and he that formed thee from the womb, I am the LORD that maketh all things; that stretcheth forth the heavens alone; that spreadeth abroad the earth by myself."

Isaiah 45:7-8 "7I form the light, and create darkness: I make peace, and create evil: I the LORD do all these things. 8Drop down, ye heavens, from above, and let the skies pour down righteousness: let the earth open, and let them bring forth salvation, and let righteousness spring up together; I the LORD have created it."

Isaiah 45:11-12 "11Thus saith the LORD, the Holy One of Israel, and his Maker, Ask me of things to come concerning my sons, and concerning the work of my hands command ye me. 12I have made the earth, and created man upon it: I, even my hands, have stretched out the heavens, and all their host have I commanded."

Isaiah 45:18 "For thus saith the LORD that created the heavens; God himself that formed the earth and made it; he hath established it, he created it not in vain, he formed it to be inhabited: I am the LORD; and there is none else."

Isaiah 48:12-13 "12Hearken unto me, O Jacob and Israel, my called; I am he; I am the first, I also am the last. 13Mine hand also hath laid the foundation of the earth, and my right hand hath spanned the heavens: when I call unto them, they stand up together."

Isaiah 51:13-16 "13And forgettest the LORD thy maker, that hath stretched forth the heavens, and laid the foundations of the earth; and hast feared continually every day because of the fury of the oppressor, as if he were ready to destroy? and where is the fury of the oppressor? 14The captive exile hasteneth that he may be loosed, and that he should not die in the pit, nor that his bread should fail. 15But I am the LORD thy God, that divided the sea, whose waves roared: The LORD of hosts is his name. 16And I have put my words in thy mouth, and I have covered thee in the shadow of mine hand, that I may plant the heavens, and lay the foundations of the earth, and say unto Zion, Thou art my people."

Isaiah 54:5 "For thy Maker is thine husband; the LORD of hosts is his name; and thy Redeemer the Holy One of Israel; The God of the whole earth shall he be called."

Isaiah 54:13-16 "13And all thy children shall be taught of the LORD; and great shall be the peace of thy children. 14In righteousness shalt thou be established: thou shalt be far from oppression; for thou shalt not fear: and from terror; for it shall not come near thee. 15Behold, they shall surely gather together, but not by me: whosoever shall gather together against thee shall fall for thy sake. 16Behold, I have created the smith that bloweth the coals in the fire, and that bringeth forth an instrument for his work; and I have created the waster to destroy."

Isaiah 57:15-19 "15For thus saith the high and lofty One that inhabiteth eternity, whose name is Holy; I dwell in the high and holy place, with him also that is of a contrite and humble spirit, to revive the spirit of the humble, and to revive the heart of the contrite ones. 16For I will not contend for ever, neither will I be always wroth: for the spirit should fail before me, and the souls which I have made. 17For the iniquity of his covetousness was I wroth, and smote him: I hid me, and was wroth, and he went on frowardly in the way of his heart. 18I have seen his ways, and will heal him: I will lead him also, and restore comforts unto him and to his mourners. 19I create the fruit of the lips; Peace, peace to him that is far off, and to him that is near, saith the LORD; and I will heal him."

Isaiah 64:8 "But now, O LORD, thou art our father; we are the clay, and thou our potter; and we all are the work of thy hand."

Isaiah 66:1-2 "¹Thus saith the LORD, The heaven is my throne, and the earth is my footstool: where is the house that ye build unto me? and where is the place of my rest? ²For all those things hath mine hand made, and those things have been, saith the LORD: but to this man will I look, even to him that is poor and of a contrite spirit, and trembleth at my word."

Jeremiah 10:10-12 "¹⁰But the LORD is the true God, he is the living God, and an everlasting king: at his wrath the earth shall tremble, and the nations shall not be able to abide his indignation. ¹¹Thus shall ye say unto them, The gods that have not made the heavens and the earth, even they shall perish from the earth, and from under these heavens. ¹²He hath made the earth by his power, he hath established the world by his wisdom, and hath stretched out the heavens by his discretion."

Jeremiah 14:22 "Are there any among the vanities of the Gentiles that can cause rain? or can the heavens give showers? art not thou he, O LORD our God? therefore we will wait upon thee: for thou hast made all these things."

Jeremiah 27:4-5 "⁴And command them to say unto their masters, Thus saith the LORD of hosts, the God of Israel; Thus shall ye say unto your masters; ⁵I have made the earth, the man and the beast that are upon the ground, by my great power and by my outstretched arm, and have given it unto whom it seemed meet unto me."

Jeremiah 32:17 "Ah Lord GOD! behold, thou hast made the heaven and the earth by thy great power and stretched out arm, and there is nothing too hard for thee."

Jeremiah 33:2 "Thus saith the LORD the maker thereof, the LORD that formed it, to establish it; the LORD is his name."

Amos 4:13 "For, lo, he that formeth the mountains, and createth the wind, and declareth unto man what is his thought, that maketh the morning darkness, and treadeth upon the high places of the earth, The LORD, The God of hosts, is his name."

Amos 5:8 "Seek him that maketh the seven stars and Orion, and turneth the shadow of death into the morning, and maketh the day dark with night: that calleth for the waters of the sea, and poureth them out upon the face of the earth: The LORD is his name."

Jonah 1:9 "And he said unto them, I am an Hebrew; and I fear the LORD, the God of heaven, which hath made the sea and the dry land."

Zechariah 12:1 "The burden of the word of the LORD for Israel, saith the LORD, which stretcheth forth the heavens, and layeth the foundation of the earth, and formeth the spirit of man within him."

Malachi 2:10 "Have we not all one father? hath not one God created us? why do we deal treacherously every man against his brother, by profaning the covenant of our fathers?"

Matthew 19:4-6 "⁴And he answered and said unto them, Have ye not read, that he which made them at the beginning made them male and female, ⁵And said, For this cause shall a man leave father and mother, and shall cleave to his wife: and they twain shall be one flesh? ⁶Wherefore they are no more twain, but one flesh. What therefore God hath joined together, let not man put asunder."

Mark 10:6 "But from the beginning of the creation God made them male and female."

Mark 13:19 "For in those days shall be affliction, such as was not from the beginning of the creation which God created unto this time, neither shall be."

John 1:1-10 "¹In the beginning was the Word, and the Word was with God, and the Word was God. ²The same was in the beginning with God. ³All things were made by him; and without him was not any thing made that was made. ⁴In him was life; and the life was the light of men. ⁵And the light shineth in darkness; and the darkness comprehended it not. ⁶There was a man sent from God, whose name was John. ⁷The same came for a witness, to bear witness of the Light, that all men through him might believe. ⁸He was not that Light, but was sent to bear witness of that Light.

[9]That was the true Light, which lighteth every man that cometh into the world. [10]He was in the world, and the world was made by him, and the world knew him not."

Acts 4:24 "And when they heard that, they lifted up their voice to God with one accord, and said, Lord, thou art God, which hast made heaven, and earth, and the sea, and all that in them is."

Acts 14:15 "And saying, Sirs, why do ye these things? We also are men of like passions with you, and preach unto you that ye should turn from these vanities unto the living God, which made heaven, and earth, and the sea, and all things that are therein."

Acts 17:23-25 "[23]For as I passed by, and beheld your devotions, I found an altar with this inscription, TO THE UNKNOWN GOD. Whom therefore ye ignorantly worship, him declare I unto you. [24]God that made the world and all things therein, seeing that he is Lord of heaven and earth, dwelleth not in temples made with hands; [25]Neither is worshipped with men's hands, as though he needed any thing, seeing he giveth to all life, and breath, and all things."

1 Corinthians 8:6 "But to us there is but one God, the Father, of whom are all things, and we in him; and one Lord Jesus Christ, by whom are all things, and we by him."

Ephesians 3:9 "And to make all men see what is the fellowship of the mystery, which from the beginning of the world hath been hid in God, who created all things by Jesus Christ."

Colossians 1:12-17 "[12]Giving thanks unto the Father, which hath made us meet to be partakers of the inheritance of the saints in light: [13]Who hath delivered us from the power of darkness, and hath translated us into the kingdom of his dear Son: [14]In whom we have redemption through his blood, even the forgiveness of sins: [15]Who is the image of the invisible God, the firstborn of every creature: [16]For by him were all things created, that are in heaven, and that are in earth, visible and invisible, whether they be thrones, or dominions, or principalities, or powers: all things were created by him, and for him: [17]And he is before all things, and by him all things consist."

Colossians 3:1-10 "[1]If ye then be risen with Christ, seek those things which are above, where Christ sitteth on the right hand of God. [2]Set your affection on things above, not on things on the earth. [3]For ye are dead, and your life is hid with Christ in God. [4]When Christ, who is our life, shall appear, then shall ye also appear with him in glory. [5]Mortify therefore your members which are upon the earth; fornication, uncleanness, inordinate affection, evil concupiscence, and covetousness, which is idolatry: [6]For which things' sake the wrath of God cometh on the children of disobedience: [7]In the which ye also walked some time, when ye lived in them. [8]But now ye also put off all these; anger, wrath, malice, blasphemy, filthy communication out of your mouth. [9]Lie not one to another, seeing that ye have put off the old man with his deeds; [10]And have put on the new man, which is renewed in knowledge after the image of him that created him."

Hebrews 1:1-2 "[1]God, who at sundry times and in divers manners spake in time past unto the fathers by the prophets, [2]Hath in these last days spoken unto us by his Son, whom he hath appointed heir of all things, by whom also he made the worlds."

Hebrews 1:5-7 "[5]For unto which of the angels said he at any time, Thou art my Son, this day have I begotten thee? And again, I will be to him a Father, and he shall be to me a Son? [6]And again, when he bringeth in the firstbegotten into the world, he saith, And let all the angels of God worship him. [7]And of the angels he saith, Who maketh his angels spirits, and his ministers a flame of fire."

Hebrews 1:10-12 "[10]And, Thou, Lord, in the beginning hast laid the foundation of the earth; and the heavens are the works of thine hands: [11]They shall perish; but thou remainest; and they all shall wax old as doth a garment; [12]And as a vesture shalt thou fold them up, and they shall be changed: but thou art the same, and thy years shall not fail."

Hebrews 3:4 "For every house is builded by some man; but he that built all things is God."

Hebrews 11:3 "Through faith we understand that the worlds were framed by the word of God, so that things which are seen were not made of things which do appear."

James 3:9 "Therewith bless we God, even the Father; and therewith curse we men, which are made after the similitude of God."

2 Peter 3:5-7 "⁵For this they willingly are ignorant of, that by the word of God the heavens were of old, and the earth standing out of the water and in the water: ⁶Whereby the world that then was, being overflowed with water, perished: ⁷But the heavens and the earth, which are now, by the same word are kept in store, reserved unto fire against the day of judgment and perdition of ungodly men."

Revelation 4:11 "Thou art worthy, O Lord, to receive glory and honour and power: for thou hast created all things, and for thy pleasure they are and were created."

Revelation 10:5-6 "⁵And the angel which I saw stand upon the sea and upon the earth lifted up his hand to heaven, ⁶And sware by him that liveth for ever and ever, who created heaven, and the things that therein are, and the earth, and the things that therein are, and the sea, and the things which are therein, that there should be time no longer."

Revelation 14:7 "Saying with a loud voice, Fear God, and give glory to him; for the hour of his judgment is come: and worship him that made heaven, and earth, and the sea, and the fountains of waters."

CRITICISM

The Reward For Criticizing One Another
Galatians 5:15 "But if ye bite and devour one another, take heed that ye be not consumed one of another."

CROOKEDNESS

The Crooked
Isaiah 40:1-4 "¹Comfort ye, comfort ye my people, saith your God. ²Speak ye comfortably to Jerusalem, and cry unto her, that her warfare is accomplished, that her iniquity is pardoned: for she hath received of the LORD's hand double for all her sins. ³The voice of him that crieth in the wilderness, Prepare ye the way of the LORD, make

straight in the desert a highway for our God. ⁴Every valley shall be exalted, and every mountain and hill shall be made low: and the crooked shall be made straight, and the rough places plain."

Luke 3:4-6 "⁴As it is written in the book of the words of Esaias the prophet, saying, The voice of one crying in the wilderness, Prepare ye the way of the Lord, make his paths straight. ⁵Every valley shall be filled, and every mountain and hill shall be brought low; and the crooked shall be made straight, and the rough ways shall be made smooth; ⁶And all flesh shall see the salvation of God."

Those That Make Crooked Paths
Isaiah 59:7-8 "⁷Their feet run to evil, and they make haste to shed innocent blood: their thoughts are thoughts of iniquity; wasting and destruction are in their paths. ⁸The way of peace they know not; and there is no judgment in their goings: they have made them crooked paths: whosoever goeth therein shall not know peace."

Whose Ways Are Crooked
Proverbs 2:11-15 "¹¹Discretion shall preserve thee, understanding shall keep thee: ¹²To deliver thee from the way of the evil man, from the man that speaketh froward things; ¹³Who leave the paths of uprightness, to walk in the ways of darkness; ¹⁴Who rejoice to do evil, and delight in the frowardness of the wicked; ¹⁵Whose ways are crooked, and they froward in their paths."

CURSES

The Curse Causeless
Proverbs 26:2 "As the bird by wandering, as the swallow by flying, so the curse causeless shall not come."

The Curse Of The Lord
Proverbs 3:33 "The curse of the LORD is in the house of the wicked: but he blesseth the habitation of the just."

Those That Are Cursed
Psalm 37:20-22 "²⁰But the wicked shall perish, and the enemies of the LORD shall be as the fat of lambs: they shall consume; into smoke shall they

consume away. [21]The wicked borroweth, and payeth not again: but the righteous sheweth mercy, and giveth. [22]For such as be blessed of him shall inherit the earth; and they that be cursed of him shall be cut off."

Jeremiah 17:5-6 "[5]Thus saith the LORD; Cursed be the man that trusteth in man, and maketh flesh his arm, and whose heart departeth from the LORD. [6]For he shall be like the heath in the desert, and shall not see when good cometh; but shall inhabit the parched places in the wilderness, in a salt land and not inhabited."

Matthew 25:41 "Then shall he say also unto them on the left hand, Depart from me, ye cursed, into everlasting fire, prepared for the devil and his angels."

Those That Curse Their Parents

Exodus 21:17 "And he that curseth his father, or his mother, shall surely be put to death."

Leviticus 20:9 "For every one that curseth his father or his mother shall be surely put to death: he hath cursed his father or his mother; his blood shall be upon him."

Proverbs 20:20 "Whoso curseth his father or his mother, his lamp shall be put out in obscure darkness."

Mark 7:10 "For Moses said, Honour thy father and thy mother; and, Whoso curseth father or mother, let him die the death."

Who Is Cursed

Genesis 3:14-19 "[14]And the LORD God said unto the serpent, Because thou hast done this, thou art cursed above all cattle, and above every beast of the field; upon thy belly shalt thou go, and dust shalt thou eat all the days of thy life: [15]And I will put enmity between thee and the woman, and between thy seed and her seed; it shall bruise thy head, and thou shalt bruise his heel. [16]Unto the woman he said, I will greatly multiply thy sorrow and thy conception; in sorrow thou shalt bring forth children; and thy desire shall be to thy husband, and he shall rule over thee. [17]And unto Adam he said, Because thou hast hearkened unto the voice of thy wife, and hast eaten of the tree, of which I commanded thee, saying, Thou shalt not eat of it: cursed is the ground for thy sake; in sor-row shalt thou eat of it all the days of thy life; [18]Thorns also and thistles shall it bring forth to thee; and thou shalt eat the herb of the field; [19]In the sweat of thy face shalt thou eat bread, till thou return unto the ground; for out of it wast thou taken: for dust thou art, and unto dust shalt thou return."

Genesis 12:1-3 "[1]Now the LORD had said unto Abram, Get thee out of thy country, and from thy kindred, and from thy father's house, unto a land that I will shew thee: [2]And I will make of thee a great nation, and I will bless thee, and make thy name great; and thou shalt be a blessing: [3]And I will bless them that bless thee, and curse him that curseth thee: and in thee shall all families of the earth be blessed."

Numbers 24:5-9 "[5]How goodly are thy tents, O Jacob, and thy tabernacles, O Israel! [6]As the valleys are they spread forth, as gardens by the river's side, as the trees of lign aloes which the LORD hath planted, and as cedar trees beside the waters. [7]He shall pour the water out of his buckets, and his seed shall be in many waters, and his king shall be higher than Agag, and his kingdom shall be exalted. [8]God brought him forth out of Egypt; he hath as it were the strength of an unicorn: he shall eat up the nations his enemies, and shall break their bones, and pierce them through with his arrows. [9]He couched, he lay down as a lion, and as a great lion: who shall stir him up? Blessed is he that bles-seth thee, and cursed is he that curseth thee."

Deuteronomy 11:26-28 "[26]Behold, I set before you this day a blessing and a curse; [27]A blessing, if ye obey the commandments of the LORD your God, which I command you this day: [28]And a curse, if ye will not obey the commandments of the LORD your God, but turn aside out of the way which I command you this day, to go after other gods, which ye have not known."

Deuteronomy 21:22-23 "[22]And if a man have com-mitted a sin worthy of death, and he be to be put to death, and thou hang him on a tree: [23]His body shall not remain all night upon the tree, but thou shalt in any wise bury him that day; (for he that is hanged is accursed of God;) that thy land be not defiled, which the LORD thy God giveth thee for an inheritance."

Deuteronomy 27:15-26 "15Cursed be the man that maketh any graven or molten image, an abomination unto the LORD, the work of the hands of the craftsman, and putteth it in a secret place. And all the people shall answer and say, Amen. 16Cursed be he that setteth light by his father or his mother. And all the people shall say, Amen. 17Cursed be he that removeth his neighbour's landmark. And all the people shall say, Amen. 18Cursed be he that maketh the blind to wander out of the way. And all the people shall say, Amen. 19Cursed be he that perverteth the judgment of the stranger, fatherless, and widow. And all the people shall say, Amen. 20Cursed be he that lieth with his father's wife; because he uncovereth his father's skirt. And all the people shall say, Amen. 21Cursed be he that lieth with any manner of beast. And all the people shall say, Amen. 22Cursed be he that lieth with his sister, the daughter of his father, or the daughter of his mother. And all the people shall say, Amen. 23Cursed be he that lieth with his mother in law. And all the people shall say, Amen. 24Cursed be he that smiteth his neighbour secretly. And all the people shall say, Amen. 25Cursed be he that taketh reward to slay an innocent person. And all the people shall say, Amen. 26Cursed be he that confirmeth not all the words of this law to do them. And all the people shall say, Amen."

Deuteronomy 28:15-20 "15But it shall come to pass, if thou wilt not hearken unto the voice of the LORD thy God, to observe to do all his commandments and his statutes which I command thee this day; that all these curses shall come upon thee, and overtake thee: 16Cursed shalt thou be in the city, and cursed shalt thou be in the field. 17Cursed shall be thy basket and thy store. 18Cursed shall be the fruit of thy body, and the fruit of thy land, the increase of thy kine, and the flocks of thy sheep. 19Cursed shalt thou be when thou comest in, and cursed shalt thou be when thou goest out. 20The LORD shall send upon thee cursing, vexation, and rebuke, in all that thou settest thine hand unto for to do, until thou be destroyed, and until thou perish quickly; because of the wickedness of thy doings, whereby thou hast forsaken me."

Deuteronomy 28:45-47 "45Moreover all these curses shall come upon thee, and shall pursue thee, and overtake thee, till thou be destroyed; because thou hearkenedst not unto the voice of the LORD thy

God, to keep his commandments and his statutes which he commanded thee: 46And they shall be upon thee for a sign and for a wonder, and upon thy seed for ever. 47Because thou servedst not the LORD thy God with joyfulness, and with gladness of heart, for the abundance of all things."

Deuteronomy 29:19-27 "19And it come to pass, when he heareth the words of this curse, that he bless himself in his heart, saying, I shall have peace, though I walk in the imagination of mine heart, to add drunkenness to thirst: 20The LORD will not spare him, but then the anger of the LORD and his jealousy shall smoke against that man, and all the curses that are written in this book shall lie upon him, and the LORD shall blot out his name from under heaven. 21And the LORD shall separate him unto evil out of all the tribes of Israel, according to all the curses of the covenant that are written in this book of the law: 22So that the generation to come of your children that shall rise up after you, and the stranger that shall come from a far land, shall say, when they see the plagues of that land, and the sicknesses which the LORD hath laid upon it; 23And that the whole land thereof is brimstone, and salt, and burning, that it is not sown, nor beareth, nor any grass groweth therein, like the overthrow of Sodom, and Gomorrah, Admah, and Zeboim, which the LORD overthrew in his anger, and in his wrath: 24Even all nations shall say, Wherefore hath the LORD done thus unto this land? what meaneth the heat of this great anger? 25Then men shall say, Because they have forsaken the covenant of the LORD God of their fathers, which he made with them when he brought them forth out of the land of Egypt: 26For they went and served other gods, and worshipped them, gods whom they knew not, and whom he had not given unto them: 27And the anger of the LORD was kindled against this land, to bring upon it all the curses that are written in this book."

Proverbs 24:24 "He that saith unto the wicked, Thou are righteous; him shall the people curse, nations shall abhor him."

Proverbs 28:27 "He that giveth unto the poor shall not lack: but he that hideth his eyes shall have many a curse."

Isaiah 24:5-6 "⁵The earth also is defiled under the inhabitants thereof; because they have transgressed the laws, changed the ordinance, broken the everlasting covenant. ⁶Therefore hath the curse devoured the earth, and they that dwell therein are desolate: therefore the inhabitants of the earth are burned, and few men left."

Isaiah 43:16-28 "¹⁶Thus saith the LORD, which maketh a way in the sea, and a path in the mighty waters; ¹⁷Which bringeth forth the chariot and horse, the army and the power; they shall lie down together, they shall not rise: they are extinct, they are quenched as tow. ¹⁸Remember ye not the former things, neither consider the things of old. ¹⁹Behold, I will do a new thing; now it shall spring forth; shall ye not know it? I will even make a way in the wilderness, and rivers in the desert. ²⁰The beast of the field shall honour me, the dragons and the owls: because I give waters in the wilderness, and rivers in the desert, to give drink to my people, my chosen. ²¹This people have I formed for myself; they shall shew forth my praise. ²²But thou hast not called upon me, O Jacob; but thou hast been weary of me, O Israel. ²³Thou hast not brought me the small cattle of thy burnt offerings; neither hast thou honoured me with thy sacrifices. I have not caused thee to serve with an offering, nor wearied thee with incense. ²⁴Thou hast bought me no sweet cane with money, neither hast thou filled me with the fat of thy sacrifices: but thou hast made me to serve with thy sins, thou hast wearied me with thine iniquities. ²⁵I, even I, am he that blotteth out thy transgressions for mine own sake, and will not remember thy sins. ²⁶Put me in remembrance: let us plead together: declare thou, that thou mayest be justified. ²⁷Thy first father hath sinned, and thy teachers have transgressed against me. ²⁸Therefore I have profaned the princes of the sanctuary, and have given Jacob to the curse, and Israel to reproaches."

Jeremiah 11:3 "And say thou unto them, Thus saith the LORD God of Israel; Cursed be the man that obeyeth not the words of this covenant."

Jeremiah 17:5-6 "⁵Thus saith the LORD; Cursed be the man that trusteth in man, and maketh flesh his arm, and whose heart departeth from the LORD. ⁶For he shall be like the heath in the desert, and shall not see when good cometh; but shall inhabit the parched places in the wilderness, in a salt land and not inhabited."

Jeremiah 48:10 "Cursed be he that doeth the work of the LORD deceitfully, and cursed be he that keepeth back his sword from blood."

Daniel 9:10-14 "¹⁰Neither have we obeyed the voice of the LORD our God, to walk in his laws, which he set before us by his servants the prophets. ¹¹Yea, all Israel have transgressed thy law, even by departing, that they might not obey thy voice; therefore the curse is poured upon us, and the oath that is written in the law of Moses the servant of God, because we have sinned against him. ¹²And he hath confirmed his words, which he spake against us, and against our judges that judged us, by bringing upon us a great evil: for under the whole heaven hath not been done as hath been done upon Jerusalem. ¹³As it is written in the law of Moses, all this evil is come upon us: yet made we not our prayer before the LORD our God, that we might turn from our iniquities, and understand thy truth. ¹⁴Therefore hath the LORD watched upon the evil, and brought it upon us: for the LORD our God is righteous in all his works which he doeth: for we obeyed not his voice."

Malachi 1:14 "But cursed be the deceiver, which hath in his flock a male, and voweth, and sacrificeth unto the LORD a corrupt thing: for I am a great King, saith the LORD of hosts, and my name is dreadful among the heathen."

Malachi 2:1-2 "¹And now, O ye priests, this commandment is for you. ²If ye will not hear, and if ye will not lay it to heart, to give glory unto my name, saith the LORD of hosts, I will even send a curse upon you, and I will curse your blessings: yea, I have cursed them already, because ye do not lay it to heart."

Galatians 3:8-10 "⁸And the scripture, foreseeing that God would justify the heathen through faith, preached before the gospel unto Abraham, saying, In thee shall all nations be blessed. ⁹So then they which be of faith are blessed with faithful Abraham. ¹⁰For as many as are of the works of the law are under the curse: for it is written, Cursed is every one that continueth not in all things which are written in the book of the law to do them."

Galatians 3:13 "Christ hath redeemed us from the curse of the law, being made a curse for us: for it is written, Cursed is every one that hangeth on a tree."

Hebrews 6:7-8 "⁷For the earth which drinketh in the rain that cometh oft upon it, and bringeth forth herbs meet for them by whom it is dressed, receiveth blessing from God: ⁸But that which beareth thorns and briers is rejected, and is nigh unto cursing; whose end is to be burned."

Who Not To Curse
Exodus 22:28 "Thou shalt not revile the gods, nor curse the ruler of thy people."

Leviticus 19:14 "Thou shalt not curse the deaf, nor put a stumblingblock before the blind, but shalt fear thy God: I am the LORD."

Ecclesiastes 10:20 "Curse not the king, no not in thy thought; and curse not the rich in thy bedchamber: for a bird of the air shall carry the voice, and that which hath wings shall tell the matter."

Romans 12:14 "Bless them which persecute you: bless, and curse not."

Dd

DAMNATION

Who Shall Receive Damnation

Matthew 25:41-46 "⁴¹Then shall he say also unto them on the left hand, Depart from me, ye cursed, into everlasting fire, prepared for the devil and his angels: ⁴²For I was an hungred, and ye gave me no meat: I was thirsty, and ye gave me no drink: ⁴³I was a stranger, and ye took me not in: naked, and ye clothed me not: sick, and in prison, and ye visited me not. ⁴⁴Then shall they also answer him, saying, Lord, when saw we thee an hungred, or athirst, or a stranger, or naked, or sick, or in prison, and did not minister unto thee? ⁴⁵Then shall he answer them, saying, Verily I say unto you, Inasmuch as ye did it not to one of the least of these, ye did it not to me. ⁴⁶And these shall go away into everlasting punishment: but the righteous into life eternal."

Mark 3:28-29 "²⁸Verily I say unto you, All sins shall be forgiven unto the sons of men, and blasphemies wherewith soever they shall blaspheme: ²⁹But he that shall blaspheme against the Holy Ghost hath never forgiveness, but is in danger of eternal damnation."

Mark 16:16-19 "¹⁶He that believeth and is baptized shall be saved; but he that believeth not shall be damned. ¹⁷And these signs shall follow them that believe; In my name shall they cast out devils; they shall speak with new tongues; ¹⁸They shall take up serpents; and if they drink any deadly thing, it shall not hurt them; they shall lay hands on the sick, and they shall recover. ¹⁹So then after the Lord had spoken unto them, he was received up into heaven, and sat on the right hand of God."

Luke 16:19-31 "¹⁹There was a certain rich man, which was clothed in purple and fine linen, and fared sumptuously every day: ²⁰And there was a certain beggar named Lazarus, which was laid at his gate, full of sores, ²¹And desiring to be fed with the crumbs which fell from the rich man's table: moreover the dogs came and licked his sores. ²²And it came to pass, that the beggar died, and was carried by the angels into Abraham's bosom: the rich man also died, and was buried; ²³And in hell he lift up his eyes, being in torments, and seeth Abraham afar off, and Lazarus in his bosom. ²⁴And he cried and said, Father Abraham, have mercy on me, and send Lazarus, that he may dip the tip of his finger in water, and cool my tongue; for I am tormented in this flame. ²⁵But Abraham said, Son, remember that thou in thy lifetime receivedst thy good things, and likewise Lazarus evil things: but now he is comforted, and thou art tormented. ²⁶And beside all this, between us and you there is a great gulf fixed: so that they which would pass from hence to you cannot; neither can they pass to us, that would come from thence. ²⁷Then he said, I pray thee therefore, father, that thou wouldest send him to my father's house: ²⁸For I have five brethren; that he may testify unto them, lest they also come into this place of torment. ²⁹Abraham saith unto him, They have Moses and the prophets; let them hear them. ³⁰And he said, Nay, father Abraham: but if one went unto them from the dead, they will repent. ³¹And he said unto him, If they hear not Moses and the prophets, neither will they be persuaded, though one rose from the dead."

Luke 20:46-47 "⁴⁶Beware of the scribes, which desire to walk in long robes, and love greetings in the markets, and the highest seats in the synagogues, and the chief rooms at feasts; ⁴⁷Which devour widows' houses, and for a shew make long prayers: the same shall receive greater damnation."

John 5:24-29 "²⁴Verily, verily, I say unto you, He that heareth my word, and believeth on him that sent me, hath everlasting life, and shall not come into condemnation; but is passed from death unto life. ²⁵Verily, verily, I say unto you, The hour is coming, and now is, when the dead shall hear the voice of the Son of God: and they that hear shall live. ²⁶For as the Father hath life in himself; so hath he given to the Son to have life in himself; ²⁷And hath given him authority to execute judgment also, because he is the Son of man. ²⁸Marvel not at this: for the hour is coming, in the which all that are in the graves shall hear his voice, ²⁹And shall come forth; they that have done good, unto the resurrection of life; and they that have done evil, unto the resurrection of damnation."

Romans 13:1-2 "Let every soul be subject unto the higher powers. For there is no power but of God: the powers that be are ordained of God. ²Whosoever therefore resisteth the power, resisteth the ordinance of God: and they that resist shall receive to themselves damnation."

Romans 14:20-23 "²⁰For meat destroy not the work of God. All things indeed are pure; but it is evil for that man who eateth with offence. ²¹It is good neither to eat flesh, nor to drink wine, nor any thing whereby thy brother stumbleth, or is offended, or is made weak. ²²Hast thou faith? have it to thyself before God. Happy is he that condemneth not himself in that thing which he alloweth. ²³And he that doubteth is damned if he eat, because he eateth not of faith: for whatsoever is not of faith is sin."

1 Corinthians 11:27-29 "²⁷Wherefore whosoever shall eat this bread, and drink this cup of the Lord, unworthily, shall be guilty of the body and blood of the Lord. ²⁸But let a man examine himself, and so let him eat of that bread, and drink of that cup. ²⁹For he that eateth and drinketh unworthily, eateth and drinketh damnation to himself, not discerning the Lord's body."

2 Thessalonians 2:8-12 "⁸And then shall that Wicked be revealed, whom the Lord shall consume with the spirit of his mouth, and shall destroy with the brightness of his coming: ⁹Even him, whose coming is after the working of Satan with all power and signs and lying wonders, ¹⁰And with all deceivableness of unrighteousness in them that perish; because they received not the love of the truth, that they might be saved. ¹¹And for this cause God shall send them strong delusion, that they should believe a lie: ¹²That they all might be damned who believed not the truth, but had pleasure in unrighteousness."

DARKNESS

Casting Off The Works Of Darkness
Romans 13:11-12 "¹¹And that, knowing the time, that now it is high time to awake out of sleep: for now is our salvation nearer than when we believed. ¹²The night is far spent, the day is at hand: let us therefore cast off the works of darkness, and let us put on the armour of light."

The Lord Creating Darkness
Isaiah 45:7 "I form the light, and create darkness: I make peace, and create evil: I the LORD do all these things."

There Being No Darkness In God
1 John 1:5 "This then is the message which we have heard of him, and declare unto you, that God is light, and in him is no darkness at all."

Those That Put Darkness For Light, And Light For Darkness
Isaiah 5:20 "Woe unto them that call evil good, and good evil; that put darkness for light, and light for darkness; that put bitter for sweet, and sweet for bitter!"

Those That Walk In Darkness
John 11:9-10 "⁹Jesus answered, Are there not twelve hours in the day? If any man walk in the day, he stumbleth not, because he seeth the light of this world. ¹⁰But if a man walk in the night, he stumbleth, because there is no light in him."

John 12:35-36 "³⁵Then Jesus said unto them, Yet a little while is the light with you. Walk while ye have the light, lest darkness come upon you: for he that walketh in darkness knoweth not whither he goeth. ³⁶While ye have light, believe in the light, that ye may be the children of light. These things spake Jesus, and departed, and did hide himself from them."

Ephesians 4:17-18 "¹⁷This I say therefore, and testify in the Lord, that ye henceforth walk not as other Gentiles walk, in the vanity of their mind, ¹⁸Having the understanding darkened, being alienated from the life of God through the ignorance that is in them, because of the blindness of their heart."

1 John 1:5-6 "⁵This then is the message which we have heard of him, and declare unto you, that God is light, and in him is no darkness at all. ⁶If we say that we have fellowship with him, and walk in darkness, we lie, and do not the truth."

1 John 2:11 "But he that hateth his brother is in darkness, and walketh in darkness, and knoweth not whither he goeth, because that darkness hath blinded his eyes."

What Came Out Of Darkness
Genesis 1:2-3 "²And the earth was without form, and void; and darkness was upon the face of the deep. And the Spirit of God moved upon the face of the waters. ³And God said, Let there be light: and there was light."

2 Corinthians 4:6 "For God, who commanded the light to shine out of darkness, hath shined in our hearts, to give the light of the knowledge of the glory of God in the face of Jesus Christ."

What Happens In The Night
1 Thessalonians 5:7 "For they that sleep sleep in the night; and they that be drunken are drunken in the night."

What Is As Darkness
Proverbs 4:19 "The way of the wicked is as darkness: they know not at what they stumble."

When Your Body Is Full Of Darkness
Luke 11:34-35 "³⁴The light of the body is the eye: therefore when thine eye is single, thy whole body also is full of light; but when thine eye is evil, thy body also is full of darkness. ³⁵Take heed therefore that the light which is in thee be not darkness."

Who Is In Darkness
Job 24:13-16 "¹³They are of those that rebel against the light; they know not the ways thereof, nor abide in the paths thereof. ¹⁴The murderer rising with the light killeth the poor and needy, and in the night is as a thief. ¹⁵The eye also of the adulterer waiteth for the twilight, saying, No eye shall see me: and disguiseth his face. ¹⁶In the dark they dig through houses, which they had marked for themselves in the daytime: they know not the light."

Proverbs 2:11-15 "¹¹Discretion shall preserve thee, understanding shall keep thee: ¹²To deliver thee from the way of the evil man, from the man that speaketh froward things; ¹³Who leave the paths of uprightness, to walk in the ways of darkness; ¹⁴Who rejoice to do evil, and delight in the frowardness of the wicked; ¹⁵Whose ways are crooked, and they froward in their paths."

Ecclesiastes 2:14 "The wise man's eyes are in his head; but the fool walketh in darkness: and I myself perceived also that one event happeneth to them all."

1 John 2:9-11 "⁹He that saith he is in the light, and hateth his brother, is in darkness even until now. ¹⁰He that loveth his brother abideth in the light, and there is none occasion of stumbling in him. ¹¹But he that hateth his brother is in darkness, and walketh in darkness, and knoweth not whither he goeth, because that darkness hath blinded his eyes."

Who Is Not In Darkness
1 Thessalonians 5:4-5 "⁴But ye, brethren, are not in darkness, that that day should overtake you as a thief. ⁵Ye are all the children of light, and the children of the day: we are not of the night, nor of darkness."

DAY OF THE LORD

How The Day Of The Lord Will Come
Isaiah 13:6-9 "⁶Howl ye; for the day of the LORD is at hand; it shall come as a destruction from the Almighty. ⁷Therefore shall all hands be faint, and every man's heart shall melt: ⁸And they shall be afraid: pangs and sorrows shall take hold of them; they shall be in pain as a woman that travaileth: they shall be amazed one at another; their faces shall be as flames. ⁹Behold, the day of the LORD cometh, cruel both with wrath and fierce anger, to lay the land desolate: and he shall destroy the sinners thereof out of it."

1 Thessalonians 5:1-4 "¹But of the times and the seasons, brethren, ye have no need that I write unto you. ²For yourselves know perfectly that the day of the Lord so cometh as a thief in the night. ³For when they shall say, Peace and safety; then sudden destruction cometh upon them, as travail upon a woman with child; and they shall not escape. ⁴But ye, brethren, are not in darkness, that that day should overtake you as a thief."

2 Peter 3:10-12 "¹⁰But the day of the Lord will come as a thief in the night; in the which the heavens shall pass away with a great noise, and the elements shall melt with fervent heat, the earth also and the works that are therein shall be burned up. [11]Seeing then that all these things shall be dissolved, what manner of persons ought ye to be in all holy conversation and godliness, [12]Looking for and hasting unto the coming of the day of God, wherein the heavens being on fire shall be dissolved, and the elements shall melt with fervent heat?"

The Coming Day Of The Lord

Isaiah 13:6-9 "[6]Howl ye; for the day of the LORD is at hand; it shall come as a destruction from the Almighty. [7]Therefore shall all hands be faint, and every man's heart shall melt: [8]And they shall be afraid: pangs and sorrows shall take hold of them; they shall be in pain as a woman that travaileth: they shall be amazed one at another; their faces shall be as flames. [9]Behold, the day of the LORD cometh, cruel both with wrath and fierce anger, to lay the land desolate: and he shall destroy the sinners thereof out of it."

Joel 3:13-14 "[13]Put ye in the sickle, for the harvest is ripe: come, get you down; for the press is full, the fats overflow; for their wickedness is great. [14]Multitudes, multitudes in the valley of decision: for the day of the LORD is near in the valley of decision."

Obadiah 15 "For the day of the LORD is near upon all the heathen: as thou hast done, it shall be done unto thee: thy reward shall return upon thine own head."

Zechariah 14:1 "Behold, the day of the LORD cometh, and thy spoil shall be divided in the midst of thee."

Malachi 4:1 "For, behold, the day cometh, that shall burn as an oven; and all the proud, yea, and all that do wickedly, shall be stubble: and the day that cometh shall burn them up, saith the LORD of hosts, that it shall leave them neither root nor branch."

What Is Kept In Store
For The Day Of Judgment

2 Peter 3:5-7 "[5]For this they willingly are ignorant of, that by the word of God the heavens were of old, and the earth standing out of the water and in the water: [6]Whereby the world that then was, being overflowed with water, perished: [7]But the heavens and the earth, which are now, by the same word are kept in store, reserved unto fire against the day of judgment and perdition of ungodly men."

What Shall Come To Pass
Before The Day Of The Lord

Joel 2:27-32 "[27]And ye shall know that I am in the midst of Israel, and that I am the LORD your God, and none else: and my people shall never be ashamed. [28]And it shall come to pass afterward, that I will pour out my spirit upon all flesh; and your sons and your daughters shall prophesy, your old men shall dream dreams, your young men shall see visions: [29]And also upon the servants and upon the handmaids in those days will I pour out my spirit. [30]And I will shew wonders in the heavens and in the earth, blood, and fire, and pillars of smoke. [31]The sun shall be turned into darkness, and the moon into blood, before the great and the terrible day of the LORD come. [32]And it shall come to pass, that whosoever shall call on the name of the LORD shall be delivered: for in mount Zion and in Jerusalem shall be deliverance, as the LORD hath said, and in the remnant whom the LORD shall call."

Acts 2:17-22 "[17]And it shall come to pass in the last days, saith God, I will pour out of my Spirit upon all flesh: and your sons and your daughters shall prophesy, and your young men shall see visions, and your old men shall dream dreams: [18]And on my servants and on my handmaidens I will pour out in those days of my Spirit; and they shall prophesy: [19]And I will shew wonders in heaven above, and signs in the earth beneath; blood, and fire, and vapour of smoke: [20]The sun shall be turned into darkness, and the moon into blood, before that great and notable day of the Lord come: [21]And it shall come to pass, that whosoever shall call on the name of the Lord shall be saved. [22]Ye men of Israel, hear these words; Jesus of Nazareth, a man approved of God among you by miracles and wonders and signs, which God did by him in the midst of you, as ye yourselves also know."

What Shall Come To Pass
In The Day Of The Lord

Psalm 110:5-7 "[5]The Lord at thy right hand shall strike through kings in the day of his wrath. [6]He shall judge among the heathen, he shall fill the places with the dead bodies; he shall wound the heads over many countries. [7]He shall drink of the brook in the way: therefore shall he lift up the head."

Isaiah 2:10-21 "[10]Enter into the rock, and hide thee in the dust, for fear of the LORD, and for the glory of his majesty. [11]The lofty looks of man shall be humbled, and the haughtiness of men shall be bowed down, and the LORD alone shall be exalted in that day. [12]For the day of the LORD of hosts shall be upon every one that is proud and lofty, and upon every one that is lifted up; and he shall be brought low: [13]And upon all the cedars of Lebanon, that are high and lifted up, and upon all the oaks of Bashan, [14]And upon all the high mountains, and upon all the hills that are lifted up, [15]And upon every high tower, and upon every fenced wall, [16]And upon all the ships of Tarshish, and upon all pleasant pictures. [17]And the loftiness of man shall be bowed down, and the haughtiness of men shall be made low: and the LORD alone shall be exalted in that day. [18]And the idols he shall utterly abolish. [19]And they shall go into the holes of the rocks, and into the caves of the earth, for fear of the LORD, and for the glory of his majesty, when he ariseth to shake terribly the earth. [20]In that day a man shall cast his idols of silver, and his idols of gold, which they made each one for himself to worship, to the moles and to the bats; [21]To go into the clefts of the rocks, and into the tops of the ragged rocks, for fear of the LORD, and for the glory of his majesty, when he ariseth to shake terribly the earth."

Isaiah 13:6-16 "[6]Howl ye; for the day of the LORD is at hand; it shall come as a destruction from the Almighty. [7]Therefore shall all hands be faint, and every man's heart shall melt: [8]And they shall be afraid: pangs and sorrows shall take hold of them; they shall be in pain as a woman that travaileth: they shall be amazed one at another; their faces shall be as flames. [9]Behold, the day of the LORD cometh, cruel both with wrath and fierce anger, to lay the land desolate: and he shall destroy the sinners thereof out of it. [10]For the stars of heaven and the constellations thereof shall not give their light: the sun shall be darkened in his going forth, and the moon shall not cause her light to shine. [11]And

I will punish the world for their evil, and the wicked for their iniquity; and I will cause the arrogancy of the proud to cease, and will lay low the haughtiness of the terrible. [12]I will make a man more precious than fine gold; even a man than the golden wedge of Ophir. [13]Therefore I will shake the heavens, and the earth shall remove out of her place, in the wrath of the LORD of hosts, and in the day of his fierce anger. [14]And it shall be as the chased roe, and as a sheep that no man taketh up: they shall every man turn to his own people, and flee every one into his own land. [15]Every one that is found shall be thrust through; and every one that is joined unto them shall fall by the sword. [16]Their children also shall be dashed to pieces before their eyes; their houses shall be spoiled, and their wives ravished."

Isaiah 34:1-4 "[1]Come near, ye nations, to hear; and hearken, ye people: let the earth hear, and all that is therein; the world, and all things that come forth of it. [2]For the indignation of the LORD is upon all nations, and his fury upon all their armies: he hath utterly destroyed them, he hath delivered them to the slaughter. [3]Their slain also shall be cast out, and their stink shall come up out of their carcases, and the mountains shall be melted with their blood. [4]And all the host of heaven shall be dissolved, and the heavens shall be rolled together as a scroll: and all their host shall fall down, as the leaf falleth off from the vine, and as a falling fig from the fig tree."

Isaiah 63:3-6 "[3]I have trodden the winepress alone; and of the people there was none with me: for I will tread them in mine anger, and trample them in my fury; and their blood shall be sprinkled upon my garments, and I will stain all my raiment. [4]For the day of vengeance is in mine heart, and the year of my redeemed is come. [5]And I looked, and there was none to help; and I wondered that there was none to uphold: therefore mine own arm brought salvation unto me; and my fury, it upheld me. [6]And I will tread down the people in mine anger, and make them drunk in my fury, and I will bring down their strength to the earth."

Jeremiah 25:30-38 "[30]Therefore prophesy thou against them all these words, and say unto them, The LORD shall roar from on high, and utter his voice from his holy habitation; he shall mightily roar upon his habitation; he shall give a shout, as they that tread the grapes, against all the inhabitants of the earth. ³¹A noise shall come even to the ends of the earth; for the LORD hath a controversy with the nations, he will plead with all flesh; he will give them that are wicked to the sword, saith the LORD. ³²Thus saith the LORD of hosts, Behold, evil shall go forth from nation to nation, and a great whirlwind shall be raised up from the coasts of the earth. ³³And the slain of the LORD shall be at that day from one end of the earth even unto the other end of the earth: they shall not be lamented, neither gathered, nor buried; they shall be dung upon the ground. ³⁴Howl, ye shepherds, and cry; and wallow yourselves in the ashes, ye principal of the flock: for the days of your slaughter and of your dispersions are accomplished; and ye shall fall like a pleasant vessel. ³⁵And the shepherds shall have no way to flee, nor the principal of the flock to escape. ³⁶A voice of the cry of the shepherds, and an howling of the principal of the flock, shall be heard: for the LORD hath spoiled their pasture. ³⁷And the peaceable habitations are cut down because of the fierce anger of the LORD. ³⁸He hath forsaken his covert, as the lion: for their land is desolate because of the fierceness of the oppressor, and because of his fierce anger."

Joel 3:1-16 "¹For, behold, in those days, and in that time, when I shall bring again the captivity of Judah and Jerusalem, ²I will also gather all nations, and will bring them down into the valley of Jehoshaphat, and will plead with them there for my people and for my heritage Israel, whom they have scattered among the nations, and parted my land. ³And they have cast lots for my people; and have given a boy for an harlot, and sold a girl for wine, that they might drink. ⁴Yea, and what have ye to do with me, O Tyre, and Zidon, and all the coasts of Palestine? will ye render me a recompence? and if ye recompence me, swiftly and speedily will I return your recompence upon your own head; ⁵Because ye have taken my silver and my gold, and have carried into your temples my goodly pleasant things: ⁶The children also of Judah and the children of Jerusalem have ye sold unto the Grecians, that ye might remove them far from their border. ⁷Behold, I will raise them out of the place whither ye have sold them, and will return your recompence upon your own head: ⁸And I will sell your sons and your daughters into the hand of the children of Judah, and they shall sell them to the Sabeans, to a people far off: for the LORD hath spoken it. ⁹Proclaim ye this among the Gentiles; Prepare war, wake up the mighty men, let all the men of war draw near; let them come up: ¹⁰Beat your plowshares into swords, and your pruninghooks into spears: let the weak say, I am strong. ¹¹Assemble yourselves, and come, all ye heathen, and gather yourselves together round about: thither cause thy mighty ones to come down, O LORD. ¹²Let the heathen be wakened, and come up to the valley of Jehoshaphat: for there will I sit to judge all the heathen round about. ¹³Put ye in the sickle, for the harvest is ripe: come, get you down; for the press is full, the fats overflow; for their wickedness is great. ¹⁴Multitudes, multitudes in the valley of decision: for the day of the LORD is near in the valley of decision. ¹⁵The sun and the moon shall be darkened, and the stars shall withdraw their shining. ¹⁶The LORD also shall roar out of Zion, and utter his voice from Jerusalem; and the heavens and the earth shall shake: but the LORD will be the hope of his people, and the strength of the children of Israel."

Zephaniah 1:14-18 "¹⁴The great day of the LORD is near, it is near, and hasteth greatly, even the voice of the day of the LORD: the mighty man shall cry there bitterly. ¹⁵That day is a day of wrath, a day of trouble and distress, a day of wasteness and desolation, a day of darkness and gloominess, a day of clouds and thick darkness, ¹⁶A day of the trumpet and alarm against the fenced cities, and against the high towers. ¹⁷And I will bring distress upon men, that they shall walk like blind men, because they have sinned against the LORD: and their blood shall be poured out as dust, and their flesh as the dung. ¹⁸Neither their silver nor their gold shall be able to deliver them in the day of the LORD's wrath; but the whole land shall be devoured by the fire of his jealousy: for he shall make even a speedy riddance of all them that dwell in the land."

Zephaniah 3:8 "Therefore wait ye upon me, saith the LORD, until the day that I rise up to the prey: for my determination is to gather the nations, that I may assemble the kingdoms, to pour upon them mine indignation, even all my fierce anger: for all the earth shall be devoured with the fire of my jealousy."

Zechariah 14:1-21 "¹Behold, the day of the LORD cometh, and thy spoil shall be divided in the midst of thee. ²For I will gather all nations against Jerusalem to battle; and the city shall be taken, and the houses rifled, and the women ravished; and half of the city shall go forth into captivity, and the residue of the people shall not be cut off from the city. ³Then shall the LORD go forth, and fight against those nations, as when he fought in the day of battle. ⁴And his feet shall stand in that day upon the mount of Olives, which is before Jerusalem on the east, and the mount of Olives shall cleave in the midst thereof toward the east and toward the west, and there shall be a very great valley; and half of the mountain shall remove toward the north, and half of it toward the south. ⁵And ye shall flee to the valley of the mountains; for the valley of the mountains shall reach unto Azal: yea, ye shall flee, like as ye fled from before the earthquake in the days of Uzziah king of Judah: and the LORD my God shall come, and all the saints with thee. ⁶And it shall come to pass in that day, that the light shall not be clear, nor dark: ⁷But it shall be one day which shall be known to the LORD, not day, nor night: but it shall come to pass, that at evening time it shall be light. ⁸And it shall be in that day, that living waters shall go out from Jerusalem; half of them toward the former sea, and half of them toward the hinder sea: in summer and in winter shall it be. ⁹And the LORD shall be king over all the earth: in that day shall there be one LORD, and his name one. ¹⁰All the land shall be turned as a plain from Geba to Rimmon south of Jerusalem: and it shall be lifted up, and inhabited in her place, from Benjamin's gate unto the place of the first gate, unto the corner gate, and from the tower of Hananeel unto the king's winepresses. ¹¹And men shall dwell in it, and there shall be no more utter destruction; but Jerusalem shall be safely inhabited. ¹²And this shall be the plague wherewith the LORD will smite all the people that have fought against Jerusalem; Their flesh shall consume away while they stand upon their feet, and their eyes shall consume away in their holes, and their tongue shall consume away in their mouth. ¹³And it shall come to pass in that day, that a great tumult from the LORD shall be among them; and they shall lay hold every one on the hand of his neighbour, and his hand shall rise up against the hand of his neighbour. ¹⁴And Judah also shall fight at Jerusalem; and the wealth of all the heathen round about shall be gathered together, gold, and silver, and apparel, in great abundance. ¹⁵And so shall be the plague of the horse, of the mule, of the camel, and of the ass, and of all the beasts that shall be in these tents, as this plague. ¹⁶And it shall come to pass, that every one that is left of all the nations which came against Jerusalem shall even go up from year to year to worship the King, the LORD of hosts, and to keep the feast of tabernacles. ¹⁷And it shall be, that whoso will not come up of all the families of the earth unto Jerusalem to worship the King, the LORD of hosts, even upon them shall be no rain. ¹⁸And if the family of Egypt go not up, and come not, that have no rain; there shall be the plague, wherewith the LORD will smite the heathen that come not up to keep the feast of tabernacles. ¹⁹This shall be the punishment of Egypt, and the punishment of all nations that come not up to keep the feast of tabernacles. ²⁰In that day shall there be upon the bells of the horses, HOLINESS UNTO THE LORD; and the pots in the LORD's house shall be like the bowl's before the altar. ²¹Yea, every pot in Jerusalem and in Judah shall be holiness unto the LORD of hosts: and all they that sacrifice shall come and take of them, and see the therein: and in that day there shall be no more the Canaanite in the house of the LORD of hosts."

Malachi 4:1-3 "¹For, behold, the day cometh, that shall burn as an oven; and all the proud, yea, and all that do wickedly, shall be stubble: and the day that cometh shall burn them up, saith the LORD of hosts, that it shall leave them neither root nor branch. ²But unto you that fear my name shall the Sun of righteousness arise with healing in his wings; and ye shall go forth, and grow up as calves of the stall. ³And ye shall tread down the wicked; for they shall be ashes under the soles of your feet in the day that I shall do this, saith the LORD of hosts."

1 Thessalonians 5:1-3 "¹But of the times and the seasons, brethren, ye have no need that I write unto you. ²For yourselves know perfectly that the day of the Lord so cometh as a thief in the night. [3]For when they shall say, Peace and safety; then sudden destruction cometh upon them, as travail upon a woman with child; and they shall not escape."

2 Peter 3:10-12 "[10]But the day of the Lord will come as a thief in the night; in the which the heavens shall pass away with a great noise, and the elements shall melt with fervent heat, the earth also and the works that are therein shall be burned up. [11]Seeing then that all these things shall be dissolved, what manner of persons ought ye to be in all holy conversation and godliness, [12]Looking for and hasting unto the coming of the day of God, wherein the heavens being on fire shall be dissolved, and the elements shall melt with fervent heat?"

Revelation 6:1-17 "[1]And I saw when the Lamb opened one of the seals, and I heard, as it were the noise of thunder, one of the four beasts saying, Come and see. [2]And I saw, and behold a white horse: and he that sat on him had a bow; and a crown was given unto him: and he went forth conquering, and to conquer. [3]And when he had opened the second seal, I heard the second beast say, Come and see. [4]And there went out another horse that was red: and power was given to him that sat thereon to take peace from the earth, and that they should kill one another: and there was given unto him a great sword. [5]And when he had opened the third seal, I heard the third beast say, Come and see. And I beheld, and lo a black horse; and he that sat on him had a pair of balances in his hand. [6]And I heard a voice in the midst of the four beasts say, A measure of wheat for a penny, and three measures of barley for a penny; and see thou hurt not the oil and the wine. [7]And when he had opened the fourth seal, I heard the voice of the fourth beast say, Come and see. [8]And I looked, and behold a pale horse: and his name that sat on him was Death, and Hell followed with him. And power was given unto them over the fourth part of the earth, to kill with sword, and with hunger, and with death, and with the beasts of the earth. [9]And when he had opened the fifth seal, I saw under the altar the souls of them that were slain for the word of God, and for the testimony which they held: [10]And they cried with a loud voice, saying, How long, O Lord, holy and true, dost thou not judge and avenge our blood on them that dwell on the earth? [11]And white robes were given unto every one of them; and it was said unto them, that they should rest yet for a little season, until their fellowservants also and their brethren, that should be killed as they were, should be fulfilled. [12]And I beheld when he had opened the sixth seal, and, lo, there was a great earthquake; and the sun became black as sackcloth of hair, and the moon became as blood; [13]And the stars of heaven fell unto the earth, even as a fig tree casteth her untimely figs, when she is shaken of a mighty wind. [14]And the heaven departed as a scroll when it is rolled together; and every mountain and island were moved out of their places. [15]And the kings of the earth, and the great men, and the rich men, and the chief captains, and the mighty men, and every bondman, and every free man, hid themselves in the dens and in the rocks of the mountains; [16]And said to the mountains and rocks, Fall on us, and hide us from the face of him that sitteth on the throne, and from the wrath of the Lamb: [17]For the great day of his wrath is come; and who shall be able to stand?"

Revelation 14:15-20 "[15]And another angel came out of the temple, crying with a loud voice to him that sat on the cloud, Thrust in thy sickle, and reap: for the time is come for thee to reap; for the harvest of the earth is ripe. [16]And he that sat on the cloud thrust in his sickle on the earth; and the earth was reaped. [17]And another angel came out of the temple which is in heaven, he also having a sharp sickle. [18]And another angel came out from the altar, which had power over fire; and cried with a loud cry to him that had the sharp sickle, saying, Thrust in thy sharp sickle, and gather the clusters of the vine of the earth; for her grapes are fully ripe. [19]And the angel thrust in his sickle into the earth, and gathered the vine of the earth, and cast it into the great winepress of the wrath of God. [20]And the winepress was trodden without the city, and blood came out of the winepress, even unto the horse bridles, by the space of a thousand and six hundred furlongs."

Revelation 16:12-21 "[12]And the sixth angel poured out his vial upon the great river Euphrates; and the water thereof was dried up, that the way of the kings of the east might be prepared. [13]And I saw three unclean spirits like frogs come out of the mouth of the dragon, and out of the mouth of the beast, and out of the mouth of the false prophet. [14]For they are the spirits of devils, working miracles, which go forth unto the kings of the earth and of the whole world, to gather them to the battle of that great day of God Almighty. [15]Behold, I come as a thief. Blessed is he that watcheth, and keepeth his garments, lest he walk naked, and they see his shame. [16]And he gathered them together into a place called in the Hebrew tongue Armageddon. [17]And the seventh angel poured out his vial into the air; and there came a great voice out of the temple of heaven, from the throne, saying, It is done. [18]And there were voices, and thunders, and lightnings; and there was a great earthquake, such as was not since men were upon the earth, so mighty an earthquake, and so great. [19]And the great city was divided into three parts, and the cities of the nations fell: and great Babylon came in remembrance before God, to give unto her the cup of the wine of the fierceness of his wrath. [20]And every island fled away, and the mountains were not found. [21]And there fell upon men a great hail out of heaven, every stone about the weight of a talent: and men blasphemed God because of the plague of the hail; for the plague thereof was exceeding great."

What Shall Not Profit
In The Day Of The Lord's Wrath
Proverbs 11:4 "Riches profit not in the day of wrath: but righteousness delivereth from death."

Zephaniah 1:18 "Neither their silver nor their gold shall be able to deliver them in the day of the LORD's wrath; but the whole land shall be devoured by the fire of his jealousy: for he shall make even a speedy riddance of all them that dwell in the land."

Who The Day Of The Lord Shall Be Upon
Isaiah 2:12-17 "[12]For the day of the LORD of hosts shall be upon every one that is proud and lofty, and upon every one that is lifted up; and he shall be brought low: [13]And upon all the cedars of Lebanon, that are high and lifted up, and upon all the oaks of Bashan, [14]And upon all the high mountains, and upon all the hills that are lifted up, [15]And upon every high tower, and upon every fenced wall, [16]And upon all the ships of Tarshish, and upon all pleasant pictures. [17]And the loftiness of man shall be bowed down, and the haughtiness of men shall be made low: and the LORD alone shall be exalted in that day."

Isaiah 13:9-11 "[9]Behold, the day of the LORD cometh, cruel both with wrath and fierce anger, to lay the land desolate: and he shall destroy the sinners thereof out of it. [10]For the stars of heaven and the constellations thereof shall not give their light: the sun shall be darkened in his going forth, and the moon shall not cause her light to shine. [11]And I will punish the world for their evil, and the wicked for their iniquity; and I will cause the arrogancy of the proud to cease, and will lay low the haughtiness of the terrible."

Obadiah 15-16 "[15]For the day of the LORD is near upon all the heathen: as thou hast done, it shall be done unto thee: thy reward shall return upon thine own head. [16]For as ye have drunk upon my holy mountain, so shall all the heathen drink continually, yea, they shall drink, and they shall swallow down, and they shall be as though they had not been."

Zephaniah 2:1-2 "[1]Gather yourselves together, yea, gather together, O nation not desired; [2]Before the decree bring forth, before the day pass as the chaff, before the fierce anger of the LORD come upon you, before the day of the LORD's anger come upon you."

Malachi 4:1-3 "[1]For, behold, the day cometh, that shall burn as an oven; and all the proud, yea, and all that do wickedly, shall be stubble: and the day that cometh shall burn them up, saith the LORD of hosts, that it shall leave them neither root nor branch. [2]But unto you that fear my name shall the Sun of righteousness arise with healing in his wings; and ye shall go forth, and grow up as calves of the stall. [3]And ye shall tread down the wicked; for they shall be ashes under the soles of your feet in the day that I shall do this, saith the LORD of hosts."

Matthew 10:5-15 "[5]These twelve Jesus sent forth, and commanded them, saying, Go not into the way of the Gentiles, and into any city of the Samaritans enter ye not: [6]But go rather to the lost sheep of the house of Israel. [7]And as ye go, preach, saying, The kingdom of heaven is at hand. [8]Heal the sick, cleanse the lepers, raise the dead, cast out devils: freely ye have received, freely give. [9]Provide neither gold, nor silver, nor brass in your purses, [10]Nor scrip for your journey, neither two coats, neither shoes, nor yet staves: for the workman is worthy of his meat. [11]And into whatsoever city or town ye shall enter, inquire who in it is worthy; and there abide till ye go thence. [12]And when ye come into an house, salute it. [13]And if the house be worthy, let your peace come upon it: but if it be not worthy, let your peace return to you. [14]And whosoever shall not receive you, nor hear your words, when ye depart out of that house or city, shake off the dust of your feet. [15]Verily I say unto you, It shall be more tolerable for the land of Sodom and Gomorrha in the day of judgment, than for that city."

Mark 6:7-11 "[7]And he called unto him the twelve, and began to send them forth by two and two; and gave them power over unclean spirits; [8]And commanded them that they should take nothing for their journey, save a staff only; no scrip, no bread, no money in their purse: [9]But be shod with sandals; and not put on two coats. [10]And he said unto them, In what place soever ye enter into an house, there abide till ye depart from that place. [11]And whosoever shall not receive you, nor hear you, when ye depart thence, shake off the dust under your feet for a testimony against them. Verily I say unto you, It shall be more tolerable for Sodom and Gomorrha in the day of judgment, than for that city."

2 Peter 2:9 "The Lord knoweth how to deliver the godly out of temptations, and to reserve the unjust unto the day of judgment to be punished."

Who The Day Of The Lord Shall Not Be Upon
Zephaniah 2:3 "Seek ye the LORD, all ye meek of the earth, which have wrought his judgment; seek righteousness, seek meekness: it may be ye shall be hid in the day of the LORD's anger."

DEACONS

The Duties Of A Deacon
1 Timothy 3:8-13 "[8]Likewise must the deacons be grave, not doubletongued, not given to much wine, not greedy of filthy lucre; [9]Holding the mystery of the faith in a pure conscience. [10]And let these also first be proved; then let them use the

office of a deacon, being found blameless. [11]Even so must their wives be grave, not slanderers, sober, faithful in all things. [12]Let the deacons be the husbands of one wife, ruling their children and their own houses well. [13]For they that have used the office of a deacon well purchase to themselves a good degree, and great boldness in the faith which is in Christ Jesus."

DEATH

Everyone Dying Alike
Job 21:23-26 "[23]One dieth in his full strength, being wholly at ease and quiet. [24]His breasts are full of milk, and his bones are moistened with marrow. [25]And another dieth in the bitterness of his soul, and never eateth with pleasure. [26]They shall lie down alike in the dust, and the worms shall cover them."

How Death Entered Into The World
Romans 5:12-21 "[12]Wherefore, as by one man sin entered into the world, and death by sin; and so death passed upon all men, for that all have sinned: [13](For until the law sin was in the world: but sin is not imputed when there is no law. [14]Nevertheless death reigned from Adam to Moses, even over them that had not sinned after the similitude of Adam's transgression, who is the figure of him that was to come. [15]But not as the offence, so also is the free gift. For if through the offence of one many be dead, much more the grace of God, and the gift by grace, which is by one man, Jesus Christ, hath abounded unto many. [16] And not as it was by one that sinned, so is the gift: for the judgment was by one to condemnation, but the free gift is of many offences unto justification. [17]For if by one man's offence death reigned by one; much more they which receive abundance of grace and of the gift of righteousness shall reign in life by one, Jesus Christ.) [18]Therefore as by the offence of one judgment came upon all men to condemnation; even so by the righteousness of one the free gift came upon all men unto justification of life. [19]For as by one man's disobedience many were made sinners, so by the obedience of one shall many be made righteous. [20]Moreover the law entered, that the offence might abound. But where sin abounded, grace did much more abound: [21]That as sin hath reigned

unto death, even so might grace reign through righteousness unto eternal life by Jesus Christ our Lord."

1 Corinthians 15:20-23 "²⁰But now is Christ risen from the dead, and become the firstfruits of them that slept. ²¹For since by man came death, by man came also the resurrection of the dead. ²²For as in Adam all die, even so in Christ shall all be made alive. ²³But every man in his own order: Christ the firstfruits; afterward they that are Christ's at his coming."

Jesus Christ Having The Keys Of Death
Revelation 1:18 "I am he that liveth, and was dead; and, behold, I am alive for evermore, Amen; and have the keys of hell and of death."

Men Being Appointed To Die Once
Hebrews 9:27 "And as it is appointed unto men once to die, but after this the judgment."

No Man Having Power Over Death
Psalm 22:28-29 "²⁸For the kingdom is the LORD's: and he is the governor among the nations. ²⁹All they that be fat upon earth shall eat and worship: all they that go down to the dust shall bow before him: and none can keep alive his own soul."

Ecclesiastes 8:8 "There is no man that hath power over the spirit to retain the spirit; neither hath he power in the day of death: and there is no discharge in that war; neither shall wickedness deliver those that are given to it."

Romans 14:7-8 "⁷For none of us liveth to himself, and no man dieth to himself. ⁸For whether we live, we live unto the Lord; and whether we die, we die unto the Lord: whether we live therefore, or die, we are the Lord's."

The Day Of Death
Ecclesiastes 7:1 "A good name is better than precious ointment; and the day of death than the day of one's birth."

The Dead
Psalm 115:17 "The dead praise not the LORD, neither any that go down into silence."

Ecclesiastes 9:5-6 "⁵For the living know that they shall die: but the dead know not any thing, neither have they any more a reward; for the memory of them is forgotten. ⁶Also their love, and

their hatred, and their envy, is now perished; neither have they any more a portion for ever in any thing that is done under the sun."

Isaiah 38:18 "For the grave cannot praise thee, death can not celebrate thee: they that go down into the pit cannot hope for thy truth."

Romans 6:7 "For he that is dead is freed from sin."

1 Corinthians 15:50-52 "⁵⁰Now this I say, brethren, that flesh and blood cannot inherit the kingdom of God; neither doth corruption inherit incorruption. ⁵¹Behold, I shew you a mystery; We shall not all sleep, but we shall all be changed, ⁵²In a moment, in the twinkling of an eye, at the last trump: for the trumpet shall sound, and the dead shall be raised incorruptible, and we shall be changed."

Revelation 14:13 "And I heard a voice from heaven saying unto me, Write, Blessed are the dead which die in the Lord from henceforth: Yea, saith the Spirit, that they may rest from their labours; and their works do follow them."

The Death Of The Wicked
Proverbs 11:7 "When a wicked man dieth, his expectation shall perish: and the hope of unjust men perisheth."

Ezekiel 18:21-23 "²¹But if the wicked will turn from all his sins that he hath committed, and keep all my statutes, and do that which is lawful and right, he shall surely live, he shall not die. ²²All his transgressions that he hath committed, they shall not be mentioned unto him: in his righteousness that he hath done he shall live. ²³Have I any pleasure at all that the wicked should die? saith the Lord GOD: and not that he should return from his ways, and live?"

Ezekiel 18:31-32 "³¹Cast away from you all your transgressions, whereby ye have transgressed; and make you a new heart and a new spirit: for why will ye die, O house of Israel? ³²For I have no pleasure in the death of him that dieth, saith the Lord GOD: wherefore turn yourselves, and live ye."

Ezekiel 33:11 "Say unto them, As I live, saith the Lord GOD, I have no pleasure in the death of the wicked; but that the wicked turn from his way and live: turn ye, turn ye from your evil ways; for why will ye die, O house of Israel?"

The Lord Destroying Death

Isaiah 25:8-9 "⁸He will swallow up death in victory; and the Lord GOD will wipe away tears from off all faces; and the rebuke of his people shall he take away from off all the earth: for the LORD hath spoken it. ⁹And it shall be said in that day, Lo, this is our God; we have waited for him, and he will save us: this is the LORD; we have waited for him, we will be glad and rejoice in his salvation."

1 Corinthians 15:25-28 "²⁵For he must reign, till he hath put all enemies under his feet. ²⁶The last enemy that shall be destroyed is death. ²⁷For he hath put all things under his feet. But when he saith, all things are put under him, it is manifest that he is excepted, which did put all things under him. ²⁸And when all things shall be subdued unto him, then shall the Son also himself be subject unto him that put all things under him, that God may be all in all."

1 Corinthians 15:50-56 "⁵⁰Now this I say, brethren, that flesh and blood cannot inherit the kingdom of God; neither doth corruption inherit incorruption. ⁵¹Behold, I shew you a mystery; We shall not all sleep, but we shall all be changed, ⁵²In a moment, in the twinkling of an eye, at the last trump: for the trumpet shall sound, and the dead shall be raised incorruptible, and we shall be changed. ⁵³For this corruptible must put on incorruption, and this mortal must put on immortality. ⁵⁴So when this corruptible shall have put on incorruption, and this mortal shall have put on immortality, then shall be brought to pass the saying that is written, Death is swallowed up in victory. ⁵⁵O death, where is thy sting? O grave, where is thy victory? ⁵⁶The sting of death is sin; and the strength of sin is the law."

Hebrews 2:9-14 "⁹But we see Jesus, who was made a little lower than the angels for the suffering of death, crowned with glory and honour; that he by the grace of God should taste death for every man. ¹⁰For it became him, for whom are all things, and by whom are all things, in bringing many sons unto glory, to make the captain of their salvation perfect through sufferings. ¹¹For both he that sanctifieth and they who are sanctified are all of one: for which cause he is not ashamed to call them brethren, ¹²Saying, I will declare thy name unto my brethren, in the midst of the church will I sing praise unto thee. ¹³And again, I will put my trust in him. And again, Behold I and the children which God hath given me. ¹⁴Forasmuch then as the children are partakers of flesh and blood, he also himself likewise took part of the same; that through death he might destroy him that had the power of death, that is, the devil."

The Second Death

Revelation 2:11 "He that hath an ear, let him hear what the Spirit saith unto the churches; He that overcometh shall not be hurt of the second death."

Revelation 20:6 "Blessed and holy is he that hath part in the first resurrection: on such the second death hath no power, but they shall be priests of God and of Christ, and shall reign with him a thousand years."

Revelation 20:12-15 "¹²And I saw the dead, small and great, stand before God; and the books were opened: and another book was opened, which is the book of life: and the dead were judged out of those things which were written in the books, according to their works. ¹³And the sea gave up the dead which were in it; and death and hell delivered up the dead which were in them: and they were judged every man according to their works. ¹⁴And death and hell were cast into the lake of fire. This is the second death. ¹⁵And whosoever was not found written in the book of life was cast into the lake of fire."

Revelation 21:8 "But the fearful, and unbelieving, and the abominable, and murderers, and whoremongers, and sorcerers, and idolaters, and all liars, shall have their part in the lake which burneth with fire and brimstone: which is the second death."

The Sting Of Death

1 Corinthians 15:56 "The sting of death is sin; and the strength of sin is the law."

What Brings Forth Death

James 1:15 "Then when lust hath conceived, it bringeth forth sin: and sin, when it is finished, bringeth forth death."

What Ends In Death

Proverbs 14:12 "There is a way which seemeth right unto a man, but the end thereof are the ways of death."

Proverbs 16:25 "There is a way that seemeth right unto a man, but the end thereof are the ways of death."

What Frees You From Death

Proverbs 11:4 "Riches profit not in the day of wrath: but righteousness delivereth from death."

Romans 8:1-4 "[1]There is therefore now no condemnation to them which are in Christ Jesus, who walk not after the flesh, but after the Spirit. [2]For the law of the Spirit of life in Christ Jesus hath made me free from the law of sin and death. [3]For what the law could not do, in that it was weak through the flesh, God sending his own Son in the likeness of sinful flesh, and for sin, condemned sin in the flesh: [4]That the righteousness of the law might be fulfilled in us, who walk not after the flesh, but after the Spirit."

What Is Death

Romans 6:20-21 "[20]For when ye were the servants of sin, ye were free from righteousness. [21]What fruit had ye then in those things whereof ye are now ashamed? for the end of those things is death."

Romans 6:23 "For the wages of sin is death; but the gift of God is eternal life through Jesus Christ our Lord."

Romans 8:6 "For to be carnally minded is death; but to be spiritually minded is life and peace."

What Works Death

2 Corinthians 7:10 "For godly sorrow worketh repentance to salvation not to be repented of: but the sorrow of the world worketh death."

Where There Is No Death

Proverbs 12:28 "In the way of righteousness is life; and in the pathway thereof there is no death."

Who Has Hope In Their Death

Proverbs 14:32 "The wicked is driven away in his wickedness: but the righteous hath hope in his death."

Philippians 1:20-21 "[20]According to my earnest expectation and my hope, that in nothing I shall be ashamed, but that with all boldness, as always, so now also Christ shall be magnified in my body, whether it be by life, or by death. [21]For to me to live is Christ, and to die is gain."

Who Loves Death

Proverbs 8:32-36 "[32]Now therefore hearken unto me, O ye children: for blessed are they that keep my ways. [33]Hear instruction, and be wise, and refuse it not. [34]Blessed is the man that heareth me, watching daily at my gates, waiting at the posts of my doors. [35]For whoso findeth me findeth life, and shall obtain favour of the LORD. [36]But he that sinneth against me wrongeth his own soul: all they that hate me love death."

Who Pursues Death

Proverbs 11:19 "As righteousness tendeth to life: so he that pursueth evil pursueth it to his own death."

Who Shall Die

Job 34:16-20 "[16]If now thou hast understanding, hear this: hearken to the voice of my words. [17]Shall even he that hateth right govern? and wilt thou condemn him that is most just? [18]Is it fit to say to a king, Thou art wicked? and to princes, Ye are ungodly? [19]How much less to him that accepteth not the persons of princes, nor regardeth the rich more than the poor? for they all are the work of his hands. [20]In a moment shall they die, and the people shall be troubled at midnight, and pass away: and the mighty shall be taken away without hand."

Job 36:5-12 "[5]Behold, God is mighty, and despiseth not any: he is mighty in strength and wisdom. [6]He preserveth not the life of the wicked: but giveth right to the poor. [7]He withdraweth not his eyes from the righteous: but with kings are they on the throne; yea, he doth establish them for ever, and they are exalted. [8]And if they be bound in fetters, and be holden in cords of affliction; [9]Then he sheweth them their work, and their transgressions that they have exceeded. [10]He openeth also their ear to discipline, and commandeth that they return from iniquity. [11]If they obey and serve him, they shall spend their days in prosperity, and their years in pleasures. [12]But if they obey not, they shall perish by the sword, and they shall die without knowledge."

Proverbs 5:21-23 "²¹For the ways of man are before the eyes of the LORD, and he pondereth all his goings. ²²His own iniquities shall take the wicked himself, and he shall be holden with the cords of his sins. ²³He shall die without instruction; and in the greatness of his folly he shall go astray."

Proverbs 15:10 "Correction is grievous unto him that forsaketh the way: and he that hateth reproof shall die."

Proverbs 19:16 "He that keepeth the commandment keepeth his own soul; but he that despiseth his ways shall die."

Proverbs 21:16 "The man that wandereth out of the way of understanding shall remain in the congregation of the dead."

Ezekiel 3:18-20 "¹⁸When I say unto the wicked, Thou shalt surely die; and thou givest him not warning, nor speakest to warn the wicked from his wicked way, to save his life; the same wicked man shall die in his iniquity; but his blood will I require at thine hand. ¹⁹Yet if thou warn the wicked, and he turn not from his wickedness, nor from his wicked way, he shall die in his iniquity; but thou hast delivered thy soul. ²⁰Again, When a righteous man doth turn from his righteousness, and commit iniquity, and I lay a stumblingblock before him, he shall die: because thou hast not given him warning, he shall die in his sin, and his righteousness which he hath done shall not be remembered; but his blood will I require at thine hand."

Ezekiel 18:4 "Behold, all souls are mine; as the soul of the father, so also the soul of the son is mine: the soul that sinneth, it shall die."

Ezekiel 18:10-13 "¹⁰If he beget a son that is a robber, a shedder of blood, and that doeth the like to any one of these things, ¹¹And that doeth not any of those duties, but even hath eaten upon the mountains, and defiled his neighbour's wife, ¹²Hath oppressed the poor and needy, hath spoiled by violence, hath not restored the pledge, and hath lifted up his eyes to the idols, hath committed abomination, ¹³Hath given forth upon usury, and hath taken increase: shall he then live? he shall not live: he hath done all these abominations; he shall surely die; his blood shall be upon him."

Ezekiel 18:18 "As for his father, because he cruelly oppressed, spoiled his brother by violence, and did that which is not good among his people, lo, even he shall die in his iniquity."

Ezekiel 18:20 "The soul that sinneth, it shall die. The son shall not bear the iniquity of the father, neither shall the father bear the iniquity of the son: the righteousness of the righteous shall be upon him, and the wickedness of the wicked shall be upon him."

Ezekiel 18:24-26 "²⁴But when the righteous turneth away from his righteousness, and committeth iniquity, and doeth according to all the abominations that the wicked man doeth, shall he live? All his righteousness that he hath done shall not be mentioned: in his trespass that he hath trespassed, and in his sin that he hath sinned, in them shall he die. ²⁵Yet ye say, The way of the Lord is not equal. Hear now, O house of Israel; Is not my way equal? are not your ways unequal? ²⁶When a righteous man turneth away from his righteousness, and committeth iniquity, and dieth in them; for his iniquity that he hath done shall he die."

Ezekiel 33:8 "When I say unto the wicked, O wicked man, thou shalt surely die; if thou dost not speak to warn the wicked from his way, that wicked man shall die in his iniquity; but his blood will I require at thine hand."

Ezekiel 33:12-13 "¹²Therefore, thou son of man, say unto the children of thy people, The righteousness of the righteous shall not deliver him in the day of his transgression: as for the wickedness of the wicked, he shall not fall thereby in the day that he turneth from his wickedness; neither shall the righteous be able to live for his righteousness in the day that he sinneth. ¹³When I shall say to the righteous, that he shall surely live; if he trust to his own righteousness, and commit iniquity, all his righteousnesses shall not be remembered; but for his iniquity that he hath committed, he shall die for it."

Ezekiel 33:18 "When the righteous turneth from his righteousness, and committeth iniquity, he shall even die thereby."

John 8:21-24 "²¹Then said Jesus again unto them, I go my way, and ye shall seek me, and shall die in your sins: whither I go, ye cannot come. ²²Then said the Jews, Will he kill himself? because he saith, Whither I go, ye cannot come. 23And he said unto them, Ye are from beneath; I am from above: ye are of this world; I am not of this world. 24I said therefore unto you, that ye shall die in your sins: for if ye believe not that I am he, ye shall die in your sins."

Romans 8:13 "For if ye live after the flesh, ye shall die: but if ye through the Spirit do mortify the deeds of the body, ye shall live."

1 John 3:14 "We know that we have passed from death unto life, because we love the brethren. He that loveth not his brother abideth in death."

Who Shall Not Die
Ezekiel 18:14-17 "14Now, lo, if he beget a son, that seeth all his father's sins which he hath done, and considereth, and doeth not such like, 15That hath not eaten upon the mountains, neither hath lifted up his eyes to the idols of the house of Israel, hath not defiled his neighbour's wife, 16Neither hath oppressed any, hath not withholden the pledge, neither hath spoiled by violence, but hath given his bread to the hungry, and hath covered the naked with a garment, 17That hath taken off his hand from the poor, that hath not received usury nor increase, hath executed my judgments, hath walked in my statutes; he shall not die for the iniquity of his father, he shall surely live."

Ezekiel 18:21 "But if the wicked will turn from all his sins that he hath committed, and keep all my statutes, and do that which is lawful and right, he shall surely live, he shall not die."

Ezekiel 18:27-28 "27Again, when the wicked man turneth away from his wickedness that he hath committed, and doeth that which is lawful and right, he shall save his soul alive. 28Because he considereth, and turneth away from all his transgressions that he hath committed, he shall surely live, he shall not die."

Ezekiel 33:14-15 "14Again, when I say unto the wicked, Thou shalt surely die; if he turn from his sin, and do that which is lawful and right; 15If the wicked restore the pledge, give again that he had robbed, walk in the statutes of life, without committing iniquity; he shall surely live, he shall not die."

John 8:49-51 "49Jesus answered, I have not a devil; but I honour my Father, and ye do dishonour me. 50And I seek not mine own glory: there is one that seeketh and judgeth. 51Verily, verily, I say unto you, If a man keep my saying, he shall never see death."

John 11:25-26 "25Jesus said unto her, I am the resurrection, and the life: he that believeth in me, though he were dead, yet shall he live: 26And whosoever liveth and believeth in me shall never die. Believest thou this?"

Romans 8:13 "For if ye live after the flesh, ye shall die: but if ye through the Spirit do mortify the deeds of the body, ye shall live."

Revelation 2:11 "He that hath an ear, let him hear what the Spirit saith unto the churches; He that overcometh shall not be hurt of the second death."

Revelation 20:6 "Blessed and holy is he that hath part in the first resurrection: on such the second death hath no power, but they shall be priests of God and of Christ, and shall reign with him a thousand years."

Why The Body Dies
Romans 8:10-11 "10And if Christ be in you, the body is dead because of sin; but the Spirit is life because of righteousness. 11But if the Spirit of him that raised up Jesus from the dead dwell in you, he that raised up Christ from the dead shall also quicken your mortal bodies by his Spirit that dwelleth in you."

1 Corinthians 15:35-38 "35But some man will say, How are the dead raised up? and with what body do they come? 36Thou fool, that which thou sowest is not quickened, except it die: 37And that which thou sowest, thou sowest not that body that shall be, but bare grain, it may chance of wheat, or of some other grain: 38But God giveth it a body as it hath pleased him, and to every seed his own body."

DECEPTION

Bread Of Deceit
Proverbs 20:17 "Bread of deceit is sweet to a man; but afterwards his mouth shall be filled with gravel."

Deceivers
Psalm 5:6 "Thou shalt destroy them that speak leasing: the LORD will abhor the bloody and deceitful man."

Psalm 55:23 "But thou, O God, shalt bring them down into the pit of destruction: bloody and deceitful men shall not live out half their days; but I will trust in thee."

Proverbs 14:25 "A true witness delivereth souls: but a deceitful witness speaketh lies."

Proverbs 26:18-19 "18As a mad man who casteth firebrands, arrows, and death, 19So is the man that deceiveth his neighbour, and saith, Am not I in sport?"

Proverbs 26:24-26 "24He that hateth dissembleth with his lips, and layeth up deceit within him; 25When he speaketh fair, believe him not: for there are seven abominations in his heart. 26Whose hatred is covered by deceit, his wickedness shall be shewed before the whole congregation."

Proverbs 29:13 "The poor and the deceitful man meet together: the LORD lighteneth both their eyes."

Jeremiah 48:10 "Cursed be he that doeth the work of the LORD deceitfully, and cursed be he that keepeth back his sword from blood."

Malachi 1:14 "But cursed be the deceiver, which hath in his flock a male, and voweth, and sacrificeth unto the LORD a corrupt thing: for I am a great King, saith the LORD of hosts, and my name is dreadful among the heathen."

2 John 7 "For many deceivers are entered into the world, who confess not that Jesus Christ is come in the flesh. This is a deceiver and an antichrist."

Not Being Deceitful
Proverbs 24:28 "Be not a witness against thy neighbour without cause; and deceive not with thy lips."

Not Letting Anyone Deceive You
1 Corinthians 15:33 "Be not deceived: evil communications corrupt good manners."

Ephesians 5:6 "Let no man deceive you with vain words: for because of these things cometh the wrath of God upon the children of disobedience."

2 Thessalonians 2:1-3 "1Now we beseech you, brethren, by the coming of our Lord Jesus Christ, and by our gathering together unto him, 2That ye be not soon shaken in mind, or be troubled, neither by spirit, nor by word, nor by letter as from us, as that the day of Christ is at hand. 3Let no man deceive you by any means: for that day shall not come, except there come a falling away first, and that man of sin be revealed, the son of perdition."

1 John 3:2 "Little children, let no man deceive you: he that doeth righteousness is righteous, even as he is righteous."

What Is Deceit/Deceitful
Proverbs 12:5 "The thoughts of the righteous are right: but the counsels of the wicked are deceit."

Proverbs 14:8 "The wisdom of the prudent is to understand his way: but the folly of fools is deceit."

Proverbs 27:6 "Faithful are the wounds of a friend; but the kisses of an enemy are deceitful."

Proverbs 31:30 "Favour is deceitful, and beauty is vain: but a woman that feareth the LORD, she shall be praised."

Jeremiah 17:9-10 "9The heart is deceitful above all things, and desperately wicked: who can know it? 10I the LORD search the heart, I try the reins, even to give every man according to his ways, and according to the fruit of his doings."

Who Deceives Themselves
Galatians 6:3-4 "3For if a man think himself to be something, when he is nothing, he deceiveth himself. 4But let every man prove his own work, and then shall he have rejoicing in himself alone, and not in another."

James 1:22-26 "22But be ye doers of the word, and not hearers only, deceiving your own selves. 23For if any be a hearer of the word, and not a doer, he is like unto a man beholding his natural face in a glass: 24For he beholdeth himself, and goeth his way, and straightway forgetteth what manner of man he was. 25But whoso looketh into the perfect law of liberty, and continueth therein, he being not a forgetful hearer, but a doer of the work, this man shall be blessed in his deed. 26If any man among you seem to be religious, and bridleth not his tongue, but deceiveth his own heart, this man's religion is vain."

1 John 1:8 "If we say that we have no sin, we deceive ourselves, and the truth is not in us."

Who Is A Deceiver

Psalm 50:16-19 "16But unto the wicked God saith, What hast thou to do to declare my statutes, or that thou shouldest take my covenant in thy mouth? 17Seeing thou hatest instruction, and castest my words behind thee. 18When thou sawest a thief, then thou consentedst with him, and hast been partaker with adulterers. 19Thou givest thy mouth to evil, and thy tongue frameth deceit."

Proverbs 11:18 "The wicked worketh a deceitful work: but to him that soweth righteousness shall be a sure reward."

Proverbs 12:17 "He that speaketh truth sheweth forth righteousness: but a false witness deceit."

Proverbs 12:20 "Deceit is in the heart of them that imagine evil: but to the counsellers of peace is joy."

Proverbs 26:24 "He that hateth dissembleth with his lips, and layeth up deceit within him."

Jeremiah 5:26-27 "26For among my people are found wicked men: they lay wait, as he that setteth snares; they set a trap, they catch men. 27As a cage is full of birds, so are their houses full of deceit: therefore they are become great, and waxen rich."

Jeremiah 14:13-14 "13Then said I, Ah, Lord GOD! behold, the prophets say unto them, Ye shall not see the sword, neither shall ye have famine; but I will give you assured peace in this place. 14Then the LORD said unto me, The prophets prophesy lies in my name: I sent them not, neither have I commanded them, neither spake unto them: they prophesy unto you a false vision and divination, and a thing of nought, and the deceit of their heart."

Jeremiah 23:25-26 "25I have heard what the prophets said, that prophesy lies in my name, saying, I have dreamed, I have dreamed. 26How long shall this be in the heart of the prophets that prophesy lies? yea, they are prophets of the deceit of their own heart."

Micah 6:10-12 "10Are there yet the treasures of wickedness in the house of the wicked, and the scant measure that is abominable? 11Shall I count them pure with the wicked balances, and with the bag of deceitful weights? 12For the rich men thereof are full of violence, and the inhabitants thereof have spoken lies, and their tongue is deceitful in their mouth."

Matthew 24:5 "For many shall come in my name, saying, I am Christ; and shall deceive many."

Matthew 24:11 "And many false prophets shall rise, and shall deceive many."

Matthew 24:23-24 "23Then if any man shall say unto you, Lo, here is Christ, or there; believe it not. 24For there shall arise false Christs, and false prophets, and shall shew great signs and wonders; insomuch that, if it were possible, they shall deceive the very elect."

Mark 13:6 "For many shall come in my name, saying, I am Christ; and shall deceive many."

Mark 13:22 "For false Christs and false prophets shall rise, and shall shew signs and wonders, to seduce, if it were possible, even the elect."

Luke 21:8 "And he said, Take heed that ye be not deceived: for many shall come in my name, saying, I am Christ; and the time draweth near: go ye not therefore after them."

2 Corinthians 11:3-15 "3But I fear, lest by any means, as the serpent beguiled Eve through his subtilty, so your minds should be corrupted from the simplicity that is in Christ. 4For if he that cometh preacheth another Jesus, whom we have not preached, or if ye receive another spirit, which ye have not received, or another gospel, which ye have not accepted, ye might well bear with him. 5For I suppose I was not a whit behind the very chiefest apostles. 6But though I be rude in speech, yet not in knowledge; but we have been throughly made manifest among you in all things. 7Have I committed an offence in abasing myself that ye might be exalted, because I have preached to you the gospel of God freely? 8I robbed other churches, taking wages of them, to do you service. 9And when I was present with you, and wanted, I was chargeable to no man: for that which was lacking to me the brethren which came from Macedonia supplied: and in all things I have kept myself from being burdensome unto you, and so will I keep myself. 10As the truth of Christ is in me, no man shall stop me of this boasting in the regions of Achaia. 11Wherefore? because I love you not? God knoweth. [12]But what I do, that I will do, that I may cut off occasion from them which desire occasion; that wherein they glory, they may be found even as we. [13]For such are false apostles, deceitful workers, transforming themselves into the apostles of Christ. [14]And no marvel; for Satan himself is transformed into an angel of light. [15]Therefore it is no great thing if his ministers also be transformed as the ministers of righteousness; whose end shall be according to their works."

2 Timothy 3:13 "But evil men and seducers shall wax worse and worse, deceiving, and being deceived."

2 John 7 "For many deceivers are entered into the world, who confess not that Jesus Christ is come in the flesh. This is a deceiver and an antichrist."

Revelation 12:9 "And the great dragon was cast out, that old serpent, called the Devil, and Satan, which deceiveth the whole world: he was cast out into the earth, and his angels were cast out with him."

Revelation 19:19-20 "[19]And I saw the beast, and the kings of the earth, and their armies, gathered together to make war against him that sat on the horse, and against his army. [20]And the beast was taken, and with him the false prophet that wrought miracles before him, with which he deceived them that had received the mark of the beast, and them that worshipped his image. These both were cast alive into a lake of fire burning with brimstone."

Revelation 20:7-10 "[7]And when the thousand years are expired, Satan shall be loosed out of his prison, [8]And shall go out to deceive the nations which are in the four quarters of the earth, Gog and Magog, to gather them together to battle: the number of whom is as the sand of the sea. [9]And they went up on the breadth of the earth, and compassed the camp of the saints about, and the beloved city: and fire came down from God out of heaven, and devoured them. [10]And the devil that deceived them was cast into the lake of fire and brimstone, where the beast and the false prophet are, and shall be tormented day and night for ever and ever."

Who Shall Not Be Deceitful
Zephaniah 3:13 "The remnant of Israel shall not do iniquity, nor speak lies; neither shall a deceitful tongue be found in their mouth: for they shall feed and lie down, and none shall make them afraid."

DECLARATION

All Men Declaring The Work Of God
Psalm 64:9 "And all men shall fear, and shall declare the work of God; for they shall wisely consider of his doing."

Declaring The Lord And His Works
Deuteronomy 32:1-4 "[1]Give ear, O ye heavens, and I will speak; and hear, O earth, the words of my mouth. [2]My doctrine shall drop as the rain, my speech shall distil as the dew, as the small rain upon the tender herb, and as the showers upon the grass: [3]Because I will publish the name of the LORD: ascribe ye greatness unto our God. [4]He is the Rock, his work is perfect: for all his ways are judgment: a God of truth and without iniquity, just and right is he."

1 Chronicles 16:8-9 "[8]Give thanks unto the LORD, call upon his name, make known his deeds among the people. [9]Sing unto him, sing psalms unto him, talk ye of all his wondrous works."

1 Chronicles 16:23-24 "[23]Sing unto the LORD, all the earth; shew forth from day to day his salvation. [24]Declare his glory among the heathen; his marvellous works among all nations."

Psalm 71:17 "O God, thou hast taught me from my youth: and hitherto have I declared thy wondrous works."

Psalm 73:28 "But it is good for me to draw near to God: I have put my trust in the Lord GOD, that I may declare all thy works."

Psalm 105:1-2 "[1]O give thanks unto the LORD; call upon his name: make known his deeds among the people. [2]Sing unto him, sing psalms unto him: talk ye of all his wondrous works."

Psalm 107:21-22 "[21]Oh that men would praise the LORD for his goodness, and for his wonderful works to the children of men! [22]And let them sacrifice the sacrifices of thanksgiving, and declare his works with rejoicing."

Psalm 118:17 "I shall not die, but live, and declare the works of the LORD."

Isaiah 12:4-6 "⁴And in that day shall ye say, Praise the LORD, call upon his name, declare his doings among the people, make mention that his name is exalted. ⁵Sing unto the LORD; for he hath done excellent things: this is known in all the earth. ⁶Cry out and shout, thou inhabitant of Zion: for great is the Holy One of Israel in the midst of thee."

Jeremiah 51:10 "The LORD hath brought forth our righteousness: come, and let us declare in Zion the work of the LORD our God."

Hebrews 2:9-12 "⁹But we see Jesus, who was made a little lower than the angels for the suffering of death, crowned with glory and honour; that he by the grace of God should taste death for every man. ¹⁰For it became him, for whom are all things, and by whom are all things, in bringing many sons unto glory, to make the captain of their salvation perfect through sufferings. ¹¹For both he that sanctifieth and they who are sanctified are all of one: for which cause he is not ashamed to call them brethren, ¹²Saying, I will declare thy name unto my brethren, in the midst of the church will I sing praise unto thee."

Jesus Christ Declaring God The Father

Psalm 22:22-23 "²²I will declare thy name unto my brethren: in the midst of the congregation will I praise thee. ²³Ye that fear the LORD, praise him; all ye the seed of Jacob, glorify him; and fear him, all ye the seed of Israel."

John 1:18 "No man hath seen God at any time; the only begotten Son, which is in the bosom of the Father, he hath declared him."

John 17:1-26 "¹These words spake Jesus, and lifted up his eyes to heaven, and said, Father, the hour is come; glorify thy Son, that thy Son also may glorify thee: ²As thou hast given him power over all flesh, that he should give eternal life to as many as thou hast given him. ³And this is life eternal, that they might know thee the only true God, and Jesus Christ, whom thou hast sent. ⁴I have glorified thee on the earth: I have finished the work which thou gavest me to do. ⁵And now, O Father, glorify thou me with thine own self with the glory which I had with thee before the world was. ⁶I have manifested thy name unto the men which thou gavest me out of the world: thine they were, and thou gavest them me; and they have kept thy word. ⁷Now they have known that all things whatsoever thou hast given me are of thee. ⁸For I have given unto them the words which thou gavest me; and they have received them, and have known surely that I came out from thee, and they have believed that thou didst send me. ⁹I pray for them: I pray not for the world, but for them which thou hast given me; for they are thine. ¹⁰And all mine are thine, and thine are mine; and I am glorified in them. ¹¹And now I am no more in the world, but these are in the world, and I come to thee. Holy Father, keep through thine own name those whom thou hast given me, that they may be one, as we are. ¹²While I was with them in the world, I kept them in thy name: those that thou gavest me I have kept, and none of them is lost, but the son of perdition; that the scripture might be fulfilled. ¹³And now come I to thee; and these things I speak in the world, that they might have my joy fulfilled in themselves. ¹⁴I have given them thy word; and the world hath hated them, because they are not of the world, even as I am not of the world. ¹⁵I pray not that thou shouldest take them out of the world, but that thou shouldest keep them from the evil. ¹⁶They are not of the world, even as I am not of the world. ¹⁷Sanctify them through thy truth: thy word is truth. ¹⁸As thou hast sent me into the world, even so have I also sent them into the world. ¹⁹And for their sakes I sanctify myself, that they also might be sanctified through the truth. ²⁰Neither pray I for these alone, but for them also which shall believe on me through their word; ²¹That they all may be one; as thou, Father, art in me, and I in thee, that they also may be one in us: that the world may believe that thou hast sent me. ²²And the glory which thou gavest me I have given them; that they may be one, even as we are one: ²³I in them, and thou in me, that they may be made perfect in one; and that the world may know that thou hast sent me, and hast loved them, as thou hast loved me. ²⁴Father, I will that they also, whom thou hast given me, be with me where I am; that they may behold my glory, which thou hast given me: for thou lovedst me before the foundation of the world. ²⁵O righteous Father, the world hath not known thee: but I have known thee, and these have known that thou hast sent me. ²⁶And I have declared unto them thy name, and will declare it: that the love wherewith thou hast loved me may be in them, and I in them."

Hebrews 2:9-12 "⁹But we see Jesus, who was made a little lower than the angels for the suffering of death, crowned with glory and honour; that he by the grace of God should taste death for every man. ¹⁰For it became him, for whom are all things, and by whom are all things, in bringing many sons unto glory, to make the captain of their salvation perfect through sufferings. ¹¹For both he that sanctifieth and they who are sanctified are all of one: for which cause he is not ashamed to call them brethren, ¹²Saying, I will declare thy name unto my brethren, in the midst of the church will I sing praise unto thee."

Those That Declare Their Sin
Isaiah 3:9 "The shew of their countenance doth witness against them; and they declare their sin as Sodom, they hide it not. Woe unto their soul! for they have rewarded evil unto themselves."

What The Lord Declares
Isaiah 45:19 "I have not spoken in secret, in a dark place of the earth: I said not unto the seed of Jacob, Seek ye me in vain: I the LORD speak righteousness, I declare things that are right."

Isaiah 48:2-3 "²For they call themselves of the holy city, and stay themselves upon the God of Israel; The LORD of hosts is his name. ³I have declared the former things from the beginning; and they went forth out of my mouth, and I shewed them; I did them suddenly, and they came to pass."

Who Shall Declare The Lord's Glory Among The Gentiles
Isaiah 66:15-19 "¹⁵For, behold, the LORD will come with fire, and with his chariots like a whirlwind, to render his anger with fury, and his rebuke with flames of fire. ¹⁶For by fire and by his sword will the LORD plead with all flesh: and the slain of the LORD shall be many. ¹⁷They that sanctify themselves, and purify themselves in the gardens behind one tree in the midst, eating swine's flesh, and the

abomination, and the mouse, shall be consumed together, saith the LORD. ¹⁸For I know their works and their thoughts: it shall come, that I will gather all nations and tongues; and they shall come, and see my glory. ¹⁹And I will set a sign among them, and I will send those that escape of them unto the nations, to Tarshish, Pul, and Lud, that draw the bow, to Tubal, and Javan, to the isles afar off, that have not heard my fame, neither have seen my glory; and they shall declare my glory among the Gentiles."

DEEDS

Doing All Things Decently And In Order
1 Corinthians 14:40 "Let all things be done decently and in order."

Doing All Things In The Name Of The Lord Jesus Christ
Ephesians 6:5-8 "⁵Servants, be obedient to them that are your masters according to the flesh, with fear and trembling, in singleness of your heart, as unto Christ; ⁶Not with eyeservice, as menpleasers; but as the servants of Christ, doing the will of God from the heart; ⁷With good will doing service, as to the Lord, and not to men: ⁸Knowing that whatsoever good thing any man doeth, the same shall he receive of the Lord, whether he be bond or free."

Colossians 3:17 "And whatsoever ye do in word or deed, do all in the name of the Lord Jesus, giving thanks to God and the Father by him."

Colossians 3:22-24 "²²Servants, obey in all things your masters according to the flesh; not with eyeservice, as menpleasers; but in singleness of heart, fearing God: ²³And whatsoever ye do, do it heartily, as to the Lord, and not unto men; ²⁴Knowing that of the Lord ye shall receive the reward of the inheritance: for ye serve the Lord Christ."

Doing All Things With Might
Ecclesiastes 9:7-10 "⁷Go thy way, eat thy bread with joy, and drink thy wine with a merry heart; for God now accepteth thy works. ⁸Let thy garments be always white; and let thy head lack no ointment. ⁹Live joyfully with the wife whom thou lovest all the days of the life of thy vanity, which he hath given thee under the sun, all the days of thy vanity: for that is thy portion in this life, and in thy

labour which thou takest under the sun. [10]Whatsoever thy hand findeth to do, do it with thy might; for there is no work, nor device, nor knowledge, nor wisdom, in the grave, whither thou goest."

The Deeds Of The Law
Romans 3:19-20 "[19]Now we know that what things soever the law saith, it saith to them who are under the law: that every mouth may be stopped, and all the world may become guilty before God. [20]Therefore by the deeds of the law there shall no flesh be justified in his sight: for by the law is the knowledge of sin."

Romans 3:28-31 "[28]Therefore we conclude that a man is justified by faith without the deeds of the law. [29]Is he the God of the Jews only? is he not also of the Gentiles? Yes, of the Gentiles also: [30]Seeing it is one God, which shall justify the circumcision by faith, and uncircumcision through faith. [31]Do we then make void the law through faith? God forbid: yea, we establish the law."

What Can Be Done By And Through The Lord
2 Samuel 22:30 "For by thee I have run through a troop: by my God have I leaped over a wall."

Psalm 18:29-33 "[29]For by thee I have run through a troop; and by my God have I leaped over a wall. [30]As for God, his way is perfect: the word of the LORD is tried: he is a buckler to all those that trust in him. [31]For who is God save the LORD? or who is a rock save our God? [32]It is God that girdeth me with strength, and maketh my way perfect. [33]He maketh my feet like hinds' feet, and setteth me upon my high places."

Psalm 60:11-12 "[11]Give us help from trouble: for vain is the help of man. [12]Through God we shall do valiantly: for he it is that shall tread down our enemies."

Psalm 108:12-13 "[12]Give us help from trouble: for vain is the help of man. [13]Through God we shall do valiantly: for he it is that shall tread down our enemies."

Habakkuk 3:19 "The LORD God is my strength, and he will make my feet like hinds' feet, and he will make me to walk upon mine high places. To the chief singer on my stringed instruments."

Philippians 4:13 "I can do all things through Christ which strengtheneth me."

What Not To Do
Leviticus 18:1-3 "[1]And the LORD spake unto Moses, saying, [2]Speak unto the children of Israel, and say unto them, I am the LORD your God. [3]After the doings of the land of Egypt, wherein ye dwelt, shall ye not do: and after the doings of the land of Canaan, whither I bring you, shall ye not do: neither shall ye walk in their ordinances."

Deuteronomy 12:8 "Ye shall not do after all the things that we do here this day, every man whatsoever is right in his own eyes."

Philippians 2:3 "Let nothing be done through strife or vainglory; but in lowliness of mind let each esteem other better than themselves."

What To Do
Zechariah 8:16-17 "[16]These are the things that ye shall do; Speak ye every man the truth to his neighbour; execute the judgment of truth and peace in your gates: [17]And let none of you imagine evil in your hearts against his neighbour; and love no false oath: for all these are things that I hate, saith the LORD."

Luke 3:8-14 "[8]Bring forth therefore fruits worthy of repentance, and begin not to say within yourselves, We have Abraham to our father: for I say unto you, That God is able of these stones to raise up children unto Abraham. [9]And now also the axe is laid unto the root of the trees: every tree therefore which bringeth not forth good fruit is hewn down, and cast into the fire. [10]And the people asked him, saying, What shall we do then? [11]He answereth and saith unto them, He that hath two coats, let him impart to him that hath none; and he that hath meat, let him do likewise. [12]Then came also publicans to be baptized, and said unto him, Master, what shall we do? [13]And he said unto them, Exact no more than that which is appointed you. [14]And the soldiers likewise demanded of him, saying, And what shall we do? And he said unto them, Do violence to no man, neither accuse any falsely; and be content with your wages."

Acts 2:37-38 "[37]Now when they heard this, they were pricked in their heart, and said unto Peter and to the rest of the apostles, Men and brethren, what shall we do? [38]Then Peter said unto them, Repent, and be baptized every one of you in the name of Jesus Christ for the remission of sins, and ye shall receive the gift of the Holy Ghost."

What You Should Do To Others

Matthew 7:12 "Therefore all things whatsoever ye would that men should do to you, do ye even so to them: for this is the law and the prophets."

Luke 6:31 "And as ye would that men should do to you, do ye also to them likewise."

Luke 10:29-37 "29But he, willing to justify himself, said unto Jesus, And who is my neighbour? 30And Jesus answering said, A certain man went down from Jerusalem to Jericho, and fell among thieves, which stripped him of his raiment, and wounded him, and departed, leaving him half dead. 31And by chance there came down a certain priest that way: and when he saw him, he passed by on the other side. 32And likewise a Levite, when he was at the place, came and looked on him, and passed by on the other side. 33But a certain Samaritan, as he journeyed, came where he was: and when he saw him, he had compassion on him, 34And went to him, and bound up his wounds, pouring in oil and wine, and set him on his own beast, and brought him to an inn, and took care of him. 35And on the morrow when he departed, he took out two pence, and gave them to the host, and said unto him, Take care of him; and whatsoever thou spendest more, when I come again, I will repay thee. 36Which now of these three, thinkest thou, was neighbour unto him that fell among the thieves? 37And he said, He that shewed mercy on him. Then said Jesus unto him, Go, and do thou likewise."

John 13:13-15 "13Ye call me Master and Lord: and ye say well; for so I am. 14If I then, your Lord and Master, have washed your feet; ye also ought to wash one another's feet. 15For I have given you an example, that ye should do as I have done to you."

DEFENSE

The Lord Being Your Defense

2 Samuel 22:3 "The God of my rock; in him will I trust: he is my shield, and the horn of my salvation, my high tower, and my refuge, my saviour; thou savest me from violence."

2 Samuel 22:31 "As for God, his way is perfect; the word of the LORD is tried: he is a buckler to all them that trust in him."

Job 22:25 "Yea, the Almighty shall be thy defence, and thou shalt have plenty of silver."

Psalm 3:3 "But thou, O LORD, art a shield for me; my glory, and the lifter up of mine head."

Psalm 7:10 "My defence is of God, which saveth the upright in heart."

Psalm 18:2 "The LORD is my rock, and my fortress, and my deliverer; my God, my strength, in whom I will trust; my buckler, and the horn of my salvation, and my high tower."

Psalm 18:30 "As for God, his way is perfect: the word of the LORD is tried: he is a buckler to all those that trust in him."

Psalm 28:7-8 "7The LORD is my strength and my shield; my heart trusted in him, and I am helped: therefore my heart greatly rejoiceth; and with my song will I praise him. 8The LORD is their strength, and he is the saving strength of his anointed."

Psalm 32:5-7 "5I acknowledged my sin unto thee, and mine iniquity have I not hid. I said, I will confess my transgressions unto the LORD; and thou forgavest the iniquity of my sin. Selah. 6For this shall every one that is godly pray unto thee in a time when thou mayest be found: surely in the floods of great waters they shall not come nigh unto him. 7Thou art my hiding place; thou shalt preserve me from trouble; thou shalt compass me about with songs of deliverance. Selah."

Psalm 33:20 "Our soul waiteth for the LORD: he is our help and our shield."

Psalm 59:9 "Because of his strength will I wait upon thee: for God is my defence."

Psalm 59:16-17 "16But I will sing of thy power; yea, I will sing aloud of thy mercy in the morning: for thou hast been my defence and refuge in the day of my trouble. 17Unto thee, O my strength, will I sing: for God is my defence, and the God of my mercy."

Psalm 61:1-3 "1Hear my cry, O God; attend unto my prayer. 2From the end of the earth will I cry unto thee, when my heart is overwhelmed: lead me to the rock that is higher than I. 3For thou hast been a shelter for me, and a strong tower from the enemy."

Psalm 62:1-2 "¹Truly my soul waiteth upon God: from him cometh my salvation. ²He only is my rock and my salvation; he is my defence; I shall not be greatly moved."

Psalm 62:6-7 "⁶He only is my rock and my salvation: he is my defence; I shall not be moved. ⁷In God is my salvation and my glory: the rock of my strength, and my refuge, is in God."

Psalm 84:11 "For the LORD God is a sun and shield: the LORD will give grace and glory: no good thing will he withhold from them that walk uprightly."

Psalm 89:18 "For the LORD is our defence; and the Holy One of Israel is our king."

Psalm 91:2-4 "²I will say of the LORD, He is my refuge and my fortress: my God; in him will I trust. ³Surely he shall deliver thee from the snare of the fowler, and from the noisome pestilence. ⁴He shall cover thee with his feathers, and under his wings shalt thou trust: his truth shall be thy shield and buckler."

Psalm 94:22 "But the LORD is my defence; and my God is the rock of my refuge."

Psalm 115:9-11 "⁹O Israel, trust thou in the LORD: he is their help and their shield. ¹⁰O house of Aaron, trust in the LORD: he is their help and their shield. ¹¹Ye that fear the LORD, trust in the LORD: he is their help and their shield."

Psalm 119:113-115 "¹¹³I hate vain thoughts: but thy law do I love. ¹¹⁴Thou art my hiding place and my shield: I hope in thy word. ¹¹⁵Depart from me, ye evildoers: for I will keep the commandments of my God."

Psalm 144:1-2 "¹Blessed be the LORD my strength, which teacheth my hands to war, and my fingers to fight: ²My goodness, and my fortress; my high tower, and my deliverer; my shield, and he in whom I trust; who subdueth my people under me."

Proverbs 2:6-7 "⁶For the LORD giveth wisdom: out of his mouth cometh knowledge and understanding. ⁷He layeth up sound wisdom for the righteous: he is a buckler to them that walk uprightly."

Proverbs 3:25-26 "²⁵Be not afraid of sudden fear, neither of the desolation of the wicked, when it cometh. ²⁶For the LORD shall be thy confidence, and shall keep thy foot from being taken."

Proverbs 30:5 "Every word of God is pure: he is a shield unto them that put their trust in him."

Ezekiel 11:16 "Therefore say, Thus saith the Lord GOD; Although I have cast them far off among the heathen, and although I have scattered them among the countries, yet will I be to them as a little sanctuary in the countries where they shall come."

Nahum 1:7 "The LORD is good, a strong hold in the day of trouble; and he knoweth them that trust in him."

Zechariah 2:4-5 "⁴And said unto him, Run, speak to this young man, saying, Jerusalem shall be inhabited as towns without walls for the multitude of men and cattle therein: ⁵For I, saith the LORD, will be unto her a wall of fire round about, and will be the glory in the midst of her."

2 Thessalonians 3:3 "But the Lord is faithful, who shall stablish you, and keep you from evil."

What Is A Defense
Psalm 91:2-4 "²I will say of the LORD, He is my refuge and my fortress: my God; in him will I trust. ³Surely he shall deliver thee from the snare of the fowler, and from the noisome pestilence. ⁴He shall cover thee with his feathers, and under his wings shalt thou trust: his truth shall be thy shield and buckler."

Ecclesiastes 7:12 "For wisdom is a defence, and money is a defence: but the excellency of knowledge is, that wisdom giveth life to them that have it."

Who The Lord Defends
1 Samuel 2:6-9 "⁶The LORD killeth, and maketh alive: he bringeth down to the grave, and bringeth up. ⁷The LORD maketh poor, and maketh rich: he bringeth low, and lifteth up. ⁸He raiseth up the poor out of the dust, and lifteth up the beggar from the dunghill, to set them among princes, and to make them inherit the throne of glory: for the pillars of the earth are the LORD's, and he hath set the world upon them. ⁹He will keep the feet of his saints, and the wicked shall be

silent in darkness; for by strength shall no man prevail."

2 Samuel 22:31 "As for God, his way is perfect; the word of the LORD is tried: he is a buckler to all them that trust in him."

Job 1:6-10 "⁶Now there was a day when the sons of God came to present themselves before the LORD, and Satan came also among them. ⁷And the LORD said unto Satan, Whence comest thou? Then Satan answered the LORD, and said, From going to and fro in the earth, and from walking up and down in it. ⁸And the LORD said unto Satan, Hast thou considered my servant Job, that there is none like him in the earth, a perfect and an upright man, one that feareth God, and escheweth evil? ⁹Then Satan answered the LORD, and said, Doth Job fear God for nought? ¹⁰Hast not thou made an hedge about him, and about his house, and about all that he hath on every side? thou hast blessed the work of his hands, and his substance is increased in the land."

Psalm 5:12 "For thou, LORD, wilt bless the righteous; with favour wilt thou compass him as with a shield."

Psalm 18:30 "As for God, his way is perfect: the word of the LORD is tried: he is a buckler to all those that trust in him."

Psalm 28:7-8 "⁷The LORD is my strength and my shield; my heart trusted in him, and I am helped: therefore my heart greatly rejoiceth; and with my song will I praise him. ⁸The LORD is their strength, and he is the saving strength of his anointed."

Psalm 84:11 "For the LORD God is a sun and shield: the LORD will give grace and glory: no good thing will he withhold from them that walk uprightly."

Psalm 125:2 "As the mountains are round about Jerusalem, so the LORD is round about his people from henceforth even for ever."

Proverbs 2:6-7 "⁶For the LORD giveth wisdom: out of his mouth cometh knowledge and understanding. ⁷He layeth up sound wisdom for the righteous: he is a buckler to them that walk uprightly."

Proverbs 30:5 "Every word of God is pure: he is a shield unto them that put their trust in him."

DEFILEMENT

Not Defiling The Land
Leviticus 18:24-30 "²⁴Defile not ye yourselves in any of these things: for in all these the nations are defiled which I cast out before you: ²⁵And the land is defiled: therefore I do visit the iniquity thereof upon it, and the land itself vomiteth out her inhabitants. ²⁶Ye shall therefore keep my statutes and my judgments, and shall not commit any of these abominations; neither any of your own nation, nor any stranger that sojourneth among you: ²⁷(For all these abominations have the men of the land done, which were before you, and the land is defiled;) ²⁸That the land spue not you out also, when ye defile it, as it spued out the nations that were before you. ²⁹For whosoever shall commit any of these abominations, even the souls that commit them shall be cut off from among their people. ³⁰Therefore shall ye keep mine ordinance, that ye commit not any one of these abominable customs, which were committed before you, and that ye defile not yourselves therein: I am the LORD your God."

Numbers 35:33-34 "³³So ye shall not pollute the land wherein ye are: for blood it defileth the land: and the land cannot be cleansed of the blood that is shed therein, but by the blood of him that shed it. ³⁴Defile not therefore the land which ye shall inhabit, wherein I dwell: for I the LORD dwell among the children of Israel."

Those That Are Defiled
Titus 1:15-16 "¹⁵Unto the pure all things are pure: but unto them that are defiled and unbelieving is nothing pure; but even their mind and conscience is defiled. ¹⁶They profess that they know God; but in works they deny him, being abominable, and disobedient, and unto every good work reprobate."

Those That Defile The Temple Of God
1 Corinthians 3:16-17 "¹⁶Know ye not that ye are the temple of God, and that the Spirit of God dwelleth in you? ¹⁷If any man defile the temple of God, him shall God destroy; for the temple of God is holy, which temple ye are."

Those That Defile Themselves

Leviticus 18:24-29 "²⁴Defile not ye yourselves in any of these things: for in all these the nations are defiled which I cast out before you: ²⁵And the land is defiled: therefore I do visit the iniquity thereof upon it, and the land itself vomiteth out her inhabitants. ²⁶Ye shall therefore keep my statutes and my judgments, and shall not commit any of these abominations; neither any of your own nation, nor any stranger that sojourneth among you: ²⁷(For all these abominations have the men of the land done, which were before you, and the land is defiled;) ²⁸That the land spue not you out also, when ye defile it, as it spued out the nations that were before you. ²⁹For whosoever shall commit any of these abominations, even the souls that commit them shall be cut off from among their people."

What Defiles A Man

Leviticus 18:20 "Moreover thou shalt not lie carnally with thy neighbour's wife, to defile thyself with her."

Matthew 15:10-11 "¹⁰And he called the multitude, and said unto them, Hear, and understand: ¹¹Not that which goeth into the mouth defileth a man; but that which cometh out of the mouth, this defileth a man."

Matthew 15:15-20 "¹⁵Then answered Peter and said unto him, Declare unto us this parable. ¹⁶And Jesus said, Are ye also yet without understanding? ¹⁷Do not ye yet understand, that whatsoever entereth in at the mouth goeth into the belly, and is cast out into the draught? ¹⁸But those things which proceed out of the mouth come forth from the heart; and they defile the man. ¹⁹For out of the heart proceed evil thoughts, murders, adulteries, fornications, thefts, false witness, blasphemies: ²⁰These are the things which defile a man: but to eat with unwashen hands defileth not a man."

Mark 7:14-23 "¹⁴And when he had called all the people unto him, he said unto them, Hearken unto me every one of you, and understand: ¹⁵There is nothing from without a man, that entering into him can defile him: but the things which come out of him, those are they that defile the man. ¹⁶If any man have ears to hear, let him hear. ¹⁷And when he was entered into the house from the people, his disciples asked him concerning the parable. ¹⁸And he saith unto them, Are ye so without understanding also? Do ye not perceive, that whatsoever thing from without entereth into the man, it cannot defile him; ¹⁹Because it entereth not into his heart, but into the belly, and goeth out into the draught, purging all meats? ²⁰And he said, That which cometh out of the man, that defileth the man. ²¹For from within, out of the heart of men, proceed evil thoughts, adulteries, fornications, murders, ²²Thefts, covetousness, wickedness, deceit, lasciviousness, an evil eye, blasphemy, pride, foolishness: ²³All these evil things come from within, and defile the man."

James 3:6 "And the tongue is a fire, a world of iniquity: so is the tongue among our members, that it defileth the whole body, and setteth on fire the course of nature; and it is set on fire of hell."

What Defiles The House Of God

Jeremiah 19:12-13 "¹²Thus will I do unto this place, saith the LORD, and to the inhabitants thereof, and even make this city as Tophet: ¹³And the houses of Jerusalem, and the houses of the kings of Judah, shall be defiled as the place of Tophet, because of all the houses upon whose roofs they have burned incense unto all the host of heaven, and have poured out drink offerings unto other gods."

Jeremiah 32:34-36 "³⁴But they set their abominations in the house, which is called by my name, to defile it. ³⁵And they built the high places of Baal, which are in the valley of the son of Hinnom, to cause their sons and their daughters to pass through the fire unto Molech; which I commanded them not, neither came it into my mind, that they should do this abomination, to cause Judah to sin. ³⁶And now therefore thus saith the LORD, the God of Israel, concerning this city, whereof ye say, It shall be delivered into the hand of the king of Babylon by the sword, and by the famine, and by the pestilence."

Who Defiles The Flesh

Jude 7-8 "⁷Even as Sodom and Gomorrha, and the cities about them in like manner, giving themselves over to fornication, and going after strange flesh, are set forth for an example, suffering the vengeance of eternal fire. ⁸Likewise also these filthy dreamers defile the flesh, despise dominion, and speak evil of dignities."

Who Defiles The Land

Genesis 6:11-13 "11The earth also was corrupt before God, and the earth was filled with violence. 12And God looked upon the earth, and, behold, it was corrupt; for all flesh had corrupted his way upon the earth. 13And God said unto Noah, The end of all flesh is come before me; for the earth is filled with violence through them; and, behold, I will destroy them with the earth."

Numbers 35:30-33 "30Whoso killeth any person, the murderer shall be put to death by the mouth of witnesses: but one witness shall not testify against any person to cause him to die. 31Moreover ye shall take no satisfaction for the life of a murderer, which is guilty of death: but he shall be surely put to death. 32And ye shall take no satisfaction for him that is fled to the city of his refuge, that he should come again to dwell in the land, until the death of the priest. 33So ye shall not pollute the land wherein ye are: for blood it defileth the land: and the land cannot be cleansed of the blood that is shed therein, but by the blood of him that shed it."

Psalm 106:37-39 "37Yea, they sacrificed their sons and their daughters unto devils, 38And shed innocent blood, even the blood of their sons and of their daughters, whom they sacrificed unto the idols of Canaan: and the land was polluted with blood. 39Thus were they defiled with their own works, and went a whoring with their own inventions."

Isaiah 24:5 "The earth also is defiled under the inhabitants thereof; because they have transgressed the laws, changed the ordinance, broken the everlasting covenant."

Jeremiah 16:16-21 "16Behold, I will send for many fishers, saith the LORD, and they shall fish them; and after will I send for many hunters, and they shall hunt them from every mountain, and from every hill, and out of the holes of the rocks. 17For mine eyes are upon all their ways: they are not hid from my face, neither is their iniquity hid from mine eyes. 18And first I will recompense their iniquity and their sin double; because they have defiled my land, they have filled mine inheritance with the carcases of their detestable and abominable things. 19O LORD, my strength,

and my fortress, and my refuge in the day of affliction, the Gentiles shall come unto thee from the ends of the earth, and shall say, Surely our fathers have inherited lies, vanity, and things wherein there is no profit. 20Shall a man make gods unto himself, and they are no gods? 21Therefore, behold, I will this once cause them to know, I will cause them to know mine hand and my might; and they shall know that my name is The LORD."

Ezekiel 36:16-18 "16Moreover the word of the LORD came unto me, saying, 17Son of man, when the house of Israel dwelt in their own land, they defiled it by their own way and by their doings: their way was before me as the uncleanness of a removed woman. 18Wherefore I poured my fury upon them for the blood that they had shed upon the land, and for their idols wherewith they had polluted it."

DEFRAUDING

Not Defrauding Others

Leviticus 19:13 "Thou shalt not defraud thy neighbour, neither rob him: the wages of him that is hired shall not abide with thee all night until the morning."

1 Corinthians 7:1-5 "1Now concerning the things whereof ye wrote unto me: It is good for a man not to touch a woman. 2Nevertheless, to avoid fornication, let every man have his own wife, and let every woman have her own husband. 3Let the husband render unto the wife due benevolence: and likewise also the wife unto the husband. 4The wife hath not power of her own body, but the husband: and likewise also the husband hath not power of his own body, but the wife. 5Defraud ye not one the other, except it be with consent for a time, that ye may give yourselves to fasting and prayer; and come together again, that Satan tempt you not for your incontinency."

1 Thessalonians 4:3-6 "3For this is the will of God, even your sanctification, that ye should abstain from fornication: 4That every one of you should know how to possess his vessel in sanctification and honour; 5Not in the lust of concupiscence, even as the Gentiles which know not God: 6That no man go beyond and defraud his brother in any matter:

because that the Lord is the avenger of all such, as we also have forewarned you and testified."

DELIGHT

Delighting Yourself In The Lord
Psalm 37:4 "Delight thyself also in the LORD; and he shall give thee the desires of thine heart."

Psalm 40:8 "I delight to do thy will, O my God: yea, thy law is within my heart."

God Delighting In His Servant
Isaiah 42:1-7 "¹Behold my servant, whom I uphold; mine elect, in whom my soul delighteth; I have put my spirit upon him: he shall bring forth judgment to the Gentiles. ²He shall not cry, nor lift up, nor cause his voice to be heard in the street. ³A bruised reed shall he not break, and the smoking flax shall he not quench: he shall bring forth judgment unto truth. ⁴He shall not fail nor be discouraged, till he have set judgment in the earth: and the isles shall wait for his law. ⁵Thus saith God the LORD, he that created the heavens, and stretched them out; he that spread forth the earth, and that which cometh out of it; he that giveth breath unto the people upon it, and spirit to them that walk therein: ⁶I the LORD have called thee in righteousness, and will hold thine hand, and will keep thee, and give thee for a covenant of the people, for a light of the Gentiles; ⁷To open the blind eyes, to bring out the prisoners from the prison, and them that sit in darkness out of the prison house."

Malachi 3:1 "Behold, I will send my messenger, and he shall prepare the way before me: and the Lord, whom ye seek, shall suddenly come to his temple, even the messenger of the covenant, whom ye delight in: behold, he shall come, saith the LORD of hosts."

The Reward For Delighting Yourself In The Lord
Psalm 37:4 "Delight thyself also in the LORD; and he shall give thee the desires of thine heart."

Those That Delight In The Commandments Of The Lord
Psalm 112:1-3 "¹Praise ye the LORD. Blessed is the man that feareth the LORD, that delighteth greatly in his commandments. ²His seed shall be mighty upon earth: the generation of the upright shall be blessed. ³Wealth and riches shall be in his house: and his righteousness endureth for ever."

What The Lord Delights In
1 Samuel 15:22 "And Samuel said, Hath the LORD as great delight in burnt offerings and sacrifices, as in obeying the voice of the LORD? Behold, to obey is better than sacrifice, and to hearken than the fat of rams."

Psalm 37:23 "The steps of a good man are ordered by the LORD: and he delighteth in his way."

Proverbs 11:1 "A false balance is abomination to the LORD: but a just weight is his delight."

Proverbs 15:8 "The sacrifice of the wicked is an abomination to the LORD: but the prayer of the upright is his delight."

Jeremiah 9:23-24 "²³Thus saith the LORD, Let not the wise man glory in his wisdom, neither let the mighty man glory in his might, let not the rich man glory in his riches: ²⁴But let him that glorieth glory in this, that he understandeth and knoweth me, that I am the LORD which exercise lovingkindness, judgment, and righteousness, in the earth: for in these things I delight, saith the LORD."

Micah 7:18 "Who is a God like unto thee, that pardoneth iniquity, and passeth by the transgression of the remnant of his heritage? he retaineth not his anger for ever, because he delighteth in mercy."

What The Lord Does Not Delight In
1 Samuel 15:22 "And Samuel said, Hath the LORD as great delight in burnt offerings and sacrifices, as in obeying the voice of the LORD? Behold, to obey is better than sacrifice, and to hearken than the fat of rams."

Isaiah 1:10-14 "¹⁰Hear the word of the LORD, ye rulers of Sodom; give ear unto the law of our God, ye people of Gomorrah. ¹¹To what purpose is the multitude of your sacrifices unto me? saith the LORD: I am full of the burnt offerings of rams, and the fat of fed beasts; and I delight not in the blood of bullocks, or of lambs, or of he goats. ¹²When ye come to appear before me, who hath required this at your hand, to tread my courts? ¹³Bring no more vain oblations; incense is an abomination unto me; the new moons and sabbaths, the calling of assemblies,

I cannot away with; it is iniquity, even the solemn meeting. ¹⁴Your new moons and your appointed feasts my soul hateth: they are a trouble unto me; I am weary to bear them."

Who Delight Is Not Seemly For
Proverbs 19:10 "Delight is not seemly for a fool; much less for a servant to have rule over princes."

Who Delights In Frowardness
Proverbs 2:11-14 "¹¹Discretion shall preserve thee, understanding shall keep thee: ¹²To deliver thee from the way of the evil man, from the man that speaketh froward things; ¹³Who leave the paths of uprightness, to walk in the ways of darkness; ¹⁴Who rejoice to do evil, and delight in the frowardness of the wicked."

Who Shall Delight Themselves In The Abundance Of Peace
Psalm 37:11 "But the meek shall inherit the earth; and shall delight themselves in the abundance of peace."

Who The Lord Delights In
Psalm 37:23 "The steps of a good man are ordered by the LORD: and he delighteth in his way."

Proverbs 11:20 "They that are of a froward heart are abomination to the LORD: but such as are upright in their way are his delight."

Proverbs 12:22 "Lying lips are abomination to the LORD: but they that deal truly are his delight."

Whose Delight Is In The Law Of The Lord
Psalm 1:1-2 "¹Blessed is the man that walketh not in the counsel of the ungodly, nor standeth in the way of sinners, nor sitteth in the seat of the scornful. ²But his delight is in the law of the LORD; and in his law doth he meditate day and night."

DELIVERANCE

Nobody Being Able To Deliver Out Of The Hand Of The Lord
Deuteronomy 32:36-39 "³⁶For the LORD shall judge his people, and repent himself for his servants, when he seeth that their power is gone, and there is none shut up, or left. ³⁷And he shall say, Where are their gods, their rock in whom they trusted, ³⁸Which did eat the fat of their sacrifices,

and drank the wine of their drink offerings? let them rise up and help you, and be your protection. ³⁹See now that I, even I, am he, and there is no god with me: I kill, and I make alive; I wound, and I heal: neither is there any that can deliver out of my hand."

Isaiah 43:12-13 "¹²I have declared, and have saved, and I have shewed, when there was no strange god among you: therefore ye are my witnesses, saith the LORD, that I am God. ¹³Yea, before the day was I am he; and there is none that can deliver out of my hand: I will work, and who shall let it?"

The Lord Being Your Deliverer
2 Samuel 22:2 "And he said, The LORD is my rock, and my fortress, and my deliverer."

Psalm 18:2 "The LORD is my rock, and my fortress, and my deliverer; my God, my strength, in whom I will trust; my buckler, and the horn of my salvation, and my high tower."

Psalm 40:17 "But I am poor and needy; yet the Lord thinketh upon me: thou art my help and my deliverer; make no tarrying, O my God."

Psalm 144:1-2 "¹Blessed be the LORD my strength, which teacheth my hands to war, and my fingers to fight: ²My goodness, and my fortress; my high tower, and my deliverer; my shield, and he in whom I trust; who subdueth my people under me."

Jeremiah 1:19 "And they shall fight against thee; but they shall not prevail against thee; for I am with thee, saith the LORD, to deliver thee."

Daniel 3:29 "Therefore I make a decree, That every people, nation, and language, which speak any thing amiss against the God of Shadrach, Meshach, and Abed-nego, shall be cut in pieces, and their houses shall be made a dunghill: because there is no other God that can deliver after this sort."

What Cannot Deliver
Ecclesiastes 8:8 "There is no man that hath power over the spirit to retain the spirit; neither hath he power in the day of death: and there is no

discharge in that war; neither shall wickedness deliver those that are given to it."

What Delivers

Proverbs 2:10-12 "¹⁰When wisdom entereth into thine heart, and knowledge is pleasant unto thy soul; ¹¹Discretion shall preserve thee, understanding shall keep thee: ¹²To deliver thee from the way of the evil man, from the man that speaketh froward things."

Proverbs 10:2 "Treasures of wickedness profit nothing: but righteousness delivereth from death."

Proverbs 11:4 "Riches profit not in the day of wrath: but righteousness delivereth from death."

Proverbs 11:6 "The righteousness of the upright shall deliver them: but transgressors shall be taken in their own naughtiness."

Proverbs 11:8-9 "⁸The righteous is delivered out of trouble, and the wicked cometh in his stead. ⁹An hypocrite with his mouth destroyeth his neighbour: but through knowledge shall the just be delivered."

Proverbs 23:13-14 "¹³Withhold not correction from the child: for if thou beatest him with the rod, he shall not die. ¹⁴Thou shalt beat him with the rod, and shalt deliver his soul from hell."

What The Lord Delivers You From

Exodus 18:8-10 "⁸And Moses told his father in law all that the LORD had done unto Pharaoh and to the Egyptians for Israel's sake, and all the travail that had come upon them by the way, and how the LORD delivered them. ⁹And Jethro rejoiced for all the goodness which the LORD had done to Israel, whom he had delivered out of the hand of the Egyptians. ¹⁰And Jethro said, Blessed be the LORD, who hath delivered you out of the hand of the Egyptians, and out of the hand of Pharaoh, who hath delivered the people from under the hand of the Egyptians."

Judges 10:11-12 "¹¹And the LORD said unto the children of Israel, Did not I deliver you from the Egyptians, and from the Amorites, from the children of Ammon, and from the Philistines? ¹²The Zidonians also, and the Amalekites, and the Maonites, did oppress you; and ye cried to me, and I delivered you out of their hand."

1 Samuel 17:37 "David said moreover, The LORD that delivered me out of the paw of the lion, and out of the paw of the bear, he will deliver me out of the hand of this Philistine. And Saul said unto David, Go, and the LORD be with thee."

2 Samuel 22:18-20 "¹⁸He delivered me from my strong enemy, and from them that hated me: for they were too strong for me. ¹⁹They prevented me in the day of my calamity: but the LORD was my stay. ²⁰He brought me forth also into a large place: he delivered me, because he delighted in me."

2 Kings 17:39 "But the LORD your God ye shall fear; and he shall deliver you out of the hand of all your enemies."

Job 33:19-30 "¹⁹He is chastened also with pain upon his bed, and the multitude of his bones with strong pain: ²⁰So that his life abhorreth bread, and his soul dainty meat. ²¹His flesh is consumed away, that it cannot be seen; and his bones that were not seen stick out. ²²Yea, his soul draweth near unto the grave, and his life to the destroyers. ²³If there be a messenger with him, an interpreter, one among a thousand, to shew unto man his uprightness: ²⁴Then he is gracious unto him, and saith, Deliver him from going down to the pit: I have found a ransom. ²⁵His flesh shall be fresher than a child's: he shall return to the days of his youth: ²⁶He shall pray unto God, and he will be favourable unto him: and he shall see his face with joy: for he will render unto man his righteousness. ²⁷He looketh upon men, and if any say, I have sinned, and perverted that which was right, and it profited me not; ²⁸He will deliver his soul from going into the pit, and his life shall see the light. ²⁹Lo, all these things worketh God oftentimes with man, ³⁰To bring back his soul from the pit, to be enlightened with the light of the living."

Psalm 18:46-48 "⁴⁶The LORD liveth; and blessed be my rock; and let the God of my salvation be exalted. ⁴⁷It is God that avengeth me, and subdueth the people under me. ⁴⁸He delivereth me from mine enemies: yea, thou liftest me up above those that rise up against me: thou hast delivered me from the violent man."

Psalm 30:3 "O LORD, thou hast brought up my soul from the grave: thou hast kept me alive, that I should not go down to the pit."

Psalm 32:5-7 "⁵I acknowledged my sin unto thee, and mine iniquity have I not hid. I said, I will confess my transgressions unto the LORD; and thou forgavest the iniquity of my sin. Selah. ⁶For this shall every one that is godly pray unto thee in a time when thou mayest be found: surely in the floods of great waters they shall not come nigh unto him. ⁷Thou art my hiding place; thou shalt preserve me from trouble; thou shalt compass me about with songs of deliverance. Selah."

Psalm 34:4 "I sought the LORD, and he heard me, and delivered me from all my fears."

Psalm 34:19 "Many are the afflictions of the righteous: but the LORD delivereth him out of them all."

Psalm 37:40 "And the LORD shall help them and deliver them: he shall deliver them from the wicked, and save them, because they trust in him."

Psalm 49:15 "But God will redeem my soul from the power of the grave: for he shall receive me. Selah."

Psalm 55:16-18 "¹⁶As for me, I will call upon God; and the LORD shall save me. ¹⁷Evening, and morning, and at noon, will I pray, and cry aloud: and he shall hear my voice. ¹⁸He hath delivered my soul in peace from the battle that was against me: for there were many with me."

Psalm 56:13 "For thou hast delivered my soul from death: wilt not thou deliver my feet from falling, that I may walk before God in the light of the living?"

Psalm 91:2-3 "²I will say of the LORD, He is my refuge and my fortress: my God; in him will I trust. ³Surely he shall deliver thee from the snare of the fowler, and from the noisome pestilence."

Psalm 97:10 "Ye that love the LORD, hate evil: he preserveth the souls of his saints; he delivereth them out of the hand of the wicked."

Psalm 107:17-20 "¹⁷Fools because of their transgression, and because of their iniquities, are afflicted. ¹⁸Their soul abhorreth all manner of meat; and they draw near unto the gates of death. ¹⁹Then they cry unto the LORD in their trouble, and he saveth them out of their distresses. ²⁰He sent his word, and healed them, and delivered them from their destructions."

Psalm 116:7-8 "⁷Return unto thy rest, O my soul; for the LORD hath dealt bountifully with thee. ⁸For thou hast delivered my soul from death, mine eyes from tears, and my feet from falling."

Psalm 144:9-11 "⁹I will sing a new song unto thee, O God: upon a psaltery and an instrument of ten strings will I sing praises unto thee. ¹⁰It is he that giveth salvation unto kings: who delivereth David his servant from the hurtful sword. ¹¹Rid me, and deliver me from the hand of strange children, whose mouth speaketh vanity, and their right hand is a right hand of falsehood."

Isaiah 38:16-17 "¹⁶O Lord, by these things men live, and in all these things is the life of my spirit: so wilt thou recover me, and make me to live. ¹⁷Behold, for peace I had great bitterness: but thou hast in love to my soul delivered it from the pit of corruption: for thou hast cast all my sins behind thy back."

Ezekiel 13:21-23 "²¹Your kerchiefs also will I tear, and deliver my people out of your hand, and they shall be no more in your hand to be hunted; and ye shall know that I am the LORD. ²²Because with lies ye have made the heart of the righteous sad, whom I have not made sad; and strengthened the hands of the wicked, that he should not return from his wicked way, by promising him life: ²³Therefore ye shall see no more vanity, nor divine divinations: for I will deliver my people out of your hand: and ye shall know that I am the LORD."

Luke 1:68-74 "⁶⁸Blessed be the Lord God of Israel; for he hath visited and redeemed his people, ⁶⁹And hath raised up an horn of salvation for us in the house of his servant David; ⁷⁰As he spake by the mouth of his holy prophets, which have been since the world began: ⁷¹That we should be saved from our enemies, and from the hand of all that hate us; ⁷²To perform the mercy promised to our fathers, and to remember his holy covenant; ⁷³The oath which he sware to our father Abraham, ⁷⁴That he would grant unto us, that we being delivered out of the hand of our enemies might serve him without fear."

Romans 7:6 "But now we are delivered from the law, that being dead wherein we were held; that we should serve in newness of spirit, and not in the oldness of the letter."

Romans 8:20-21 "20For the creature was made subject to vanity, not willingly, but by reason of him who hath subjected the same in hope, 21Because the creature itself also shall be delivered from the bondage of corruption into the glorious liberty of the children of God."

Galatians 1:3-4 "3Grace be to you and peace from God the Father, and from our Lord Jesus Christ, 4Who gave himself for our sins, that he might deliver us from this present evil world, according to the will of God and our Father."

Colossians 1:12-13 "12Giving thanks unto the Father, which hath made us meet to be partakers of the inheritance of the saints in light: 13Who hath delivered us from the power of darkness, and hath translated us into the kingdom of his dear Son."

1 Thessalonians 1:9-10 "9For they themselves shew of us what manner of entering in we had unto you, and how ye turned to God from idols to serve the living and true God; 10And to wait for his Son from heaven, whom he raised from the dead, even Jesus, which delivered us from the wrath to come."

Who Delivers Souls
Proverbs 14:25 "A true witness delivereth souls: but a deceitful witness speaketh lies."

Who Shall Be Delivered
Proverbs 11:8-9 "8The righteous is delivered out of trouble, and the wicked cometh in his stead. 9An hypocrite with his mouth destroyeth his neighbour: but through knowledge shall the just be delivered."

Proverbs 11:21 "Though hand join in hand, the wicked shall not be unpunished: but the seed of the righteous shall be delivered."

Proverbs 28:26 "He that trusteth in his own heart is a fool: but whoso walketh wisely, he shall be delivered."

Joel 2:32 "And it shall come to pass, that whosoever shall call on the name of the LORD shall be delivered: for in mount Zion and in Jerusalem shall be deliverance, as the LORD hath said, and in the remnant whom the LORD shall call."

Who The Lord Delivers
1 Samuel 7:3 "And Samuel spake unto all the house of Israel, saying, If ye do return unto the LORD with all your hearts, then put away the strange gods and Ashtaroth from among you, and prepare your hearts unto the LORD, and serve him only: and he will deliver you out of the hand of the Philistines."

Job 36:5-15 "5Behold, God is mighty, and despiseth not any: he is mighty in strength and wisdom. 6He preserveth not the life of the wicked: but giveth right to the poor. 7He withdraweth not his eyes from the righteous: but with kings are they on the throne; yea, he doth establish them for ever, and they are exalted. 8And if they be bound in fetters, and be holden in cords of affliction; 9Then he sheweth them their work, and their transgressions that they have exceeded. 10He openeth also their ear to discipline, and commandeth that they return from iniquity. 11If they obey and serve him, they shall spend their days in prosperity, and their years in pleasures. 12But if they obey not, they shall perish by the sword, and they shall die without knowledge. 13But the hypocrites in heart heap up wrath: they cry not when he bindeth them. 14They die in youth, and their life is among the unclean. 15He delivereth the poor in his affliction, and openeth their ears in oppression."

Psalm 22:1-5 "1My God, my God, why hast thou forsaken me? why art thou so far from helping me, and from the words of my roaring? 2O my God, I cry in the daytime, but thou hearest not; and in the night season, and am not silent. 3But thou art holy, O thou that inhabitest the praises of Israel. 4Our fathers trusted in thee: they trusted, and thou didst deliver them. 5They cried unto thee, and were delivered: they trusted in thee, and were not confounded."

Psalm 34:6-7 "6This poor man cried, and the LORD heard him, and saved him out of all his troubles. 7The angel of the LORD encampeth round about them that fear him, and delivereth them."

Psalm 34:17 "The righteous cry, and the LORD heareth, and delivereth them out of all their troubles."

Psalm 37:40 "And the Lord shall help them and deliver them: he shall deliver them from the wicked, and save them, because they trust in him."

Psalm 41:1 "Blessed is he that considereth the poor: the Lord will deliver him in time of trouble."

Psalm 50:14-15 "14Offer unto God thanksgiving; and pay thy vows unto the most High: 15And call upon me in the day of trouble: I will deliver thee, and thou shalt glorify me."

Psalm 55:16-18 "16As for me, I will call upon God; and the Lord shall save me. 17Evening, and morning, and at noon, will I pray, and cry aloud: and he shall hear my voice. 18He hath delivered my soul in peace from the battle that was against me: for there were many with me."

Psalm 91:9-15 "9Because thou hast made the Lord, which is my refuge, even the most High, thy habitation; 10There shall no evil befall thee, neither shall any plague come nigh thy dwelling. 11For he shall give his angels charge over thee, to keep thee in all thy ways. 12They shall bear thee up in their hands, lest thou dash thy foot against a stone. 13Thou shalt tread upon the lion and adder: the young lion and the dragon shalt thou trample under feet. 14Because he hath set his love upon me, therefore will I deliver him: I will set him on high, because he hath known my name. 15He shall call upon me, and I will answer him: I will be with him in trouble; I will deliver him, and honour him."

Psalm 97:10 "Ye that love the Lord, hate evil: he preserveth the souls of his saints; he delivereth them out of the hand of the wicked."

Psalm 107:17-29 "17Fools because of their transgression, and because of their iniquities, are afflicted. 18Their soul abhorreth all manner of meat; and they draw near unto the gates of death. 19Then they cry unto the Lord in their trouble, and he saveth them out of their distresses. 20He sent his word, and healed them, and delivered them from their destructions. 21Oh that men would praise the Lord for his goodness, and for his wonderful works to the children of men! 22And let them sacrifice the sacrifices of thanksgiving, and declare his works with rejoicing. 23They that go down to the sea in ships, that do business in great waters; 24These see the works of the Lord, and his wonders in the deep. 25For he commandeth, and raiseth the stormy wind, which lifteth up the waves thereof. 26They mount up to the heaven, they go down again to the depths: their soul is melted because of trouble. 27They reel to and fro, and stagger like a drunken man, and are at their wits' end. 28Then they cry unto the Lord in their trouble, and he bringeth them out of their distresses. 29He maketh the storm a calm, so that the waves thereof are still."

Jeremiah 1:19 "And they shall fight against thee; but they shall not prevail against thee; for I am with thee, saith the Lord, to deliver thee."

Ezekiel 13:17-23 "17Likewise, thou son of man, set thy face against the daughters of thy people, which prophesy out of their own heart; and prophesy thou against them, 18And say, Thus saith the Lord God; Woe to the women that sew pillows to all armholes, and make kerchiefs upon the head of every stature to hunt souls! Will ye hunt the souls of my people, and will ye save the souls alive that come unto you? 19And will ye pollute me among my people for handfuls of barley and for pieces of bread, to slay the souls that should not die, and to save the souls alive that should not live, by your lying to my people that hear your lies? 20Wherefore thus saith the Lord God; Behold, I am against your pillows, wherewith ye there hunt the souls to make them fly, and I will tear them from your arms, and will let the souls go, even the souls that ye hunt to make them fly. 21Your kerchiefs also will I tear, and deliver my people out of your hand, and they shall be no more in your hand to be hunted; and ye shall know that I am the Lord. 22Because with lies ye have made the heart of the righteous sad, whom I have not made sad; and strengthened the hands of the wicked, that he should not return from his wicked way, by promising him life: 23Therefore ye shall see no more vanity, nor divine divinations: for I will deliver my people out of your hand: and ye shall know that I am the Lord."

Ezekiel 34:11-12 "11For thus saith the Lord God; Behold, I, even I, will both search my sheep, and seek them out. 12As a shepherd seeketh out his flock in the day that he is among his sheep that are scattered; so will I seek out my sheep, and will deliver them out of all places where they have been scattered in the cloudy and dark day."

Daniel 3:28 "Then Nebuchadnezzar spake, and said, Blessed be the God of Shadrach, Meshach, and Abed-nego, who hath sent his angel, and delivered his servants that trusted in him, and have changed the king's word, and yielded their bodies, that they might not serve nor worship any god, except their own God."

Daniel 6:26-27 "²⁶I make a decree, That in every dominion of my kingdom men tremble and fear before the God of Daniel: for he is the living God, and stedfast for ever, and his kingdom that which shall not be destroyed, and his dominion shall be even unto the end. ²⁷He delivereth and rescueth, and he worketh signs and wonders in heaven and in earth, who hath delivered Daniel from the power of the lions."

Daniel 12:1 "And at that time shall Michael stand up, the great prince which standeth for the children of thy people: and there shall be a time of trouble, such as never was since there was a nation even to that same time: and at that time thy people shall be delivered, every one that shall be found written in the book."

Joel 2:32 "And it shall come to pass, that whosoever shall call on the name of the LORD shall be delivered: for in mount Zion and in Jerusalem shall be deliverance, as the LORD hath said, and in the remnant whom the LORD shall call."

Hebrews 2:9-15 "⁹But we see Jesus, who was made a little lower than the angels for the suffering of death, crowned with glory and honour; that he by the grace of God should taste death for every man. ¹⁰For it became him, for whom are all things, and by whom are all things, in bringing many sons unto glory, to make the captain of their salvation perfect through sufferings. ¹¹For both he that sanctifieth and they who are sanctified are all of one: for which cause he is not ashamed to call them brethren, ¹²Saying, I will declare thy name unto my brethren, in the midst of the church will I sing praise unto thee. ¹³And again, I will put my trust in him. And again, Behold I and the children which God hath given me. ¹⁴Forasmuch then as the children are partakers of flesh and blood, he also himself likewise

took part of the same; that through death he might destroy him that had the power of death, that is, the devil; ¹⁵And deliver them who through fear of death were all their lifetime subject to bondage."

2 Peter 2:9 "The Lord knoweth how to deliver the godly out of temptations, and to reserve the unjust unto the day of judgment to be punished."

Who The Lord Does Not Deliver
Judges 10:11-14 "¹¹And the LORD said unto the children of Israel, Did not I deliver you from the Egyptians, and from the Amorites, from the children of Ammon, and from the Philistines? ¹²The Zidonians also, and the Amalekites, and the Maonites, did oppress you; and ye cried to me, and I delivered you out of their hand. ¹³Yet ye have forsaken me, and served other gods: wherefore I will deliver you no more. ¹⁴Go and cry unto the gods which ye have chosen; let them deliver you in the time of your tribulation."

DENIAL

Denying Yourself For Jesus Christ
Matthew 16:24-25 "²⁴Then said Jesus unto his disciples, If any man will come after me, let him deny himself, and take up his cross, and follow me. ²⁵For whosoever will save his life shall lose it: and whosoever will lose his life for my sake shall find it."

Mark 8:31-35 "³¹And he began to teach them, that the Son of man must suffer many things, and be rejected of the elders, and of the chief priests, and scribes, and be killed, and after three days rise again. ³²And he spake that saying openly. And Peter took him, and began to rebuke him. ³³But when he had turned about and looked on his disciples, he rebuked Peter, saying, Get thee behind me, Satan: for thou savourest not the things that be of God, but the things that be of men. ³⁴And when he had called the people unto him with his disciples also, he said unto them, Whosoever will come after me, let him deny himself, and take up his cross, and follow me. ³⁵For whosoever will save his life shall lose it; but whosoever shall lose his life for my sake and the gospel's, the same shall save it."

Luke 9:22-25 "²²Saying, The Son of man must suffer many things, and be rejected of the elders and chief priests and scribes, and be slain, and be raised the third day. ²³And he said to them all, If any man will come after me, let him deny himself, and take up his cross daily, and follow me. ²⁴For whosoever will save his life shall lose it: but whosoever will lose his life for my sake, the same shall save it. ²⁵For what is a man advantaged, if he gain the whole world, and lose himself, or be cast away?"

Those That Deny The Lord
Matthew 10:33 "But whosoever shall deny me before men, him will I also deny before my Father which is in heaven."

Luke 12:8-9 "⁸Also I say unto you, Whosoever shall confess me before men, him shall the Son of man also confess before the angels of God: ⁹But he that denieth me before men shall be denied before the angels of God."

2 Timothy 2:10-12 "¹⁰Therefore I endure all things for the elect's sakes, that they may also obtain the salvation which is in Christ Jesus with eternal glory. ¹¹It is a faithful saying: For if we be dead with him, we shall also live with him: ¹²If we suffer, we shall also reign with him: if we deny him, he also will deny us."

2 Peter 2:1 "But there were false prophets also among the people, even as there shall be false teachers among you, who privily shall bring in damnable heresies, even denying the Lord that bought them, and bring upon themselves swift destruction."

1 John 2:22-23 "²²Who is a liar but he that denieth that Jesus is the Christ? He is antichrist, that denieth the Father and the Son. ²³Whosoever denieth the Son, the same hath not the Father: (but) he that acknowledgeth the Son hath the Father also."

Who Denies The Lord
Titus 1:10-16 "¹⁰For there are many unruly and vain talkers and deceivers, specially they of the circumcision: ¹¹Whose mouths must be stopped, who subvert whole houses, teaching things which they ought not, for filthy lucre's sake. ¹²One of themselves, even a prophet of their own, said, The Cretians are alway liars, evil beasts, slow bellies. ¹³This witness is true. Wherefore rebuke them sharply, that they may be sound in the faith; ¹⁴Not giving heed to Jewish fables, and commandments of men, that turn from the truth. ¹⁵Unto the pure all things are pure: but unto them that are defiled and unbelieving is nothing pure; but even their mind and conscience is defiled. ¹⁶They profess that they know God; but in works they deny him, being abominable, and disobedient, and unto every good work reprobate."

2 Peter 2:1 "But there were false prophets also among the people, even as there shall be false teachers among you, who privily shall bring in damnable heresies, even denying the Lord that bought them, and bring upon themselves swift destruction."

Jude 4 "For there are certain men crept in unawares, who were before of old ordained to this condemnation, ungodly men, turning the grace of our God into lasciviousness, and denying the only Lord God, and our Lord Jesus Christ."

**Who Jesus Christ Will Deny
Before God And The Angels**
Matthew 10:33 "But whosoever shall deny me before men, him will I also deny before my Father which is in heaven."

Luke 12:8-9 "⁸Also I say unto you, Whosoever shall confess me before men, him shall the Son of man also confess before the angels of God: ⁹But he that denieth me before men shall be denied before the angels of God."

DESIRE

Desiring The Lord
Psalm 73:25-26 "²⁵Whom have I in heaven but thee? and there is none upon earth that I desire beside thee. ²⁶My flesh and my heart faileth: but God is the strength of my heart, and my portion for ever."

Isaiah 26:8-9 "⁸Yea, in the way of thy judgments, O LORD, have we waited for thee; the desire of our soul is to thy name, and to the remembrance of thee. ⁹With my soul have I desired thee in the night; yea, with my spirit within me will I seek thee early: for when thy judgments are in the earth, the inhabitants of the world will learn righteousness."

Evil Concupiscence
Colossians 3:5-6 "⁵Mortify therefore your members which are upon the earth; fornication, uncleanness, inordinate affection, evil concupiscence, and covetousness, which is idolatry: ⁶For which things' sake the wrath of God cometh on the children of disobedience."

The Desire Accomplished
Proverbs 13:19 "The desire accomplished is sweet to the soul: but it is abomination to fools to depart from evil."

The Desire Of A Man
Proverbs 19:22 "The desire of a man is his kindness: and a poor man is better than a liar."

The Desire Of The Righteous
Proverbs 10:24 "The fear of the wicked, it shall come upon him: but the desire of the righteous shall be granted."

Proverbs 11:23 "The desire of the righteous is only good: but the expectation of the wicked is wrath."

The Desire Of The Slothful
Proverbs 21:25 "The desire of the slothful killeth him; for his hands refuse to labour."

The Desire Of The Wicked
Psalm 112:10 "The wicked shall see it, and be grieved; he shall gnash with his teeth, and melt away: the desire of the wicked shall perish."

The Time When The Desire Comes
Proverbs 13:12 "Hope deferred maketh the heart sick: but when the desire cometh, it is a tree of life."

The Wandering Of The Desire
Ecclesiastes 6:9 "Better is the sight of the eyes than the wandering of the desire: this is also vanity and vexation of spirit."

What Not To Desire
Proverbs 23:1-8 "¹When thou sittest to eat with a ruler, consider diligently what is before thee: ²And put a knife to thy throat, if thou be a man given to appetite. ³Be not desirous of his dainties: for they are deceitful meat. ⁴Labour not to be rich: cease from thine own wisdom. ⁵Wilt thou set thine eyes upon that which is not? for riches certainly make themselves wings; they fly away as an eagle toward heaven. ⁶Eat thou not the bread of him that hath an evil eye, neither desire thou his dainty meats: ⁷For as he thinketh in his heart, so is he: Eat and drink, saith he to thee; but his heart is not with thee. ⁸The morsel which thou hast eaten shalt thou vomit up, and lose thy sweet words."

Proverbs 24:1-2 "¹Be not thou envious against evil men, neither desire to be with them. ²For their heart studieth destruction, and their lips talk of mischief."

Galatians 5:26 "Let us not be desirous of vain glory, provoking one another, envying one another."

What The Lord Desires
1 Samuel 15:22 "And Samuel said, Hath the LORD as great delight in burnt offerings and sacrifices, as in obeying the voice of the LORD? Behold, to obey is better than sacrifice, and to hearken than the fat of rams."

Job 33:29-32 "²⁹Lo, all these things worketh God oftentimes with man, ³⁰To bring back his soul from the pit, to be enlightened with the light of the living. ³¹Mark well, O Job, hearken unto me: hold thy peace, and I will speak. ³²If thou hast any thing to say, answer me: speak, for I desire to justify thee."

Psalm 132:13-14 "¹³For the LORD hath chosen Zion; he hath desired it for his habitation. ¹⁴This is my rest for ever: here will I dwell; for I have desired it."

Hosea 6:6 "For I desired mercy, and not sacrifice; and the knowledge of God more than burnt offerings."

Matthew 9:12-13 "¹²But when Jesus heard that, he said unto them, They that be whole need not a physician, but they that are sick. ¹³But go ye and learn what that meaneth, I will have mercy, and not sacrifice: for I am not come to call the righteous, but sinners to repentance."

1 Timothy 2:3-4 "³For this is good and acceptable in the sight of God our Saviour; ⁴Who will have all men to be saved, and to come unto the knowledge of the truth."

What The Lord Does Not Desire

1 Samuel 15:22 "And Samuel said, Hath the LORD as great delight in burnt offerings and sacrifices, as in obeying the voice of the LORD? Behold, to obey is better than sacrifice, and to hearken than the fat of rams."

Psalm 40:5-6 "5Many, O LORD my God, are thy wonderful works which thou hast done, and thy thoughts which are to us-ward: they cannot be reckoned up in order unto thee: if I would declare and speak of them, they are more than can be numbered. 6Sacrifice and offering thou didst not desire; mine ears hast thou opened: burnt offering and sin offering hast thou not required."

Hosea 6:6 "For I desired mercy, and not sacrifice; and the knowledge of God more than burnt offerings."

Matthew 9:12-13 "12But when Jesus heard that, he said unto them, They that be whole need not a physician, but they that are sick. 13But go ye and learn what that meaneth, I will have mercy, and not sacrifice: for I am not come to call the righteous, but sinners to repentance."

Hebrews 10:1-9 "1For the law having a shadow of good things to come, and not the very image of the things, can never with those sacrifices which they offered year by year continually make the comers thereunto perfect. 2For then would they not have ceased to be offered? because that the worshippers once purged should have had no more conscience of sins. 3But in those sacrifices there is a remembrance again made of sins every year. 4For it is not possible that the blood of bulls and of goats should take away sins. 5Wherefore when he cometh into the world, he saith, Sacrifice and offering thou wouldest not, but a body hast thou prepared me: 6In burnt offerings and sacrifices for sin thou hast had no pleasure. 7Then said I, Lo, I come (in the volume of the book it is written of me,) to do thy will, O God. 8Above when he said, Sacrifice and offering and burnt offerings and offering for sin thou wouldest not, neither hadst pleasure therein; which are offered by the law; 9Then said he, Lo, I come to do thy will, O God. He taketh away the first, that he may establish the second."

What To Desire

1 Corinthians 12:27-31 "27Now ye are the body of Christ, and members in particular. 28And God hath set some in the church, first apostles, secondarily prophets, thirdly teachers, after that miracles, then gifts of healings, helps, governments, diversities of tongues. 29Are all apostles? are all prophets? are all teachers? are all workers of miracles? 30Have all the gifts of healing? do all speak with tongues? do all interpret? 31But covet earnestly the best gifts: and yet shew I unto you a more excellent way."

1 Corinthians 14:1 "Follow after charity, and desire spiritual gifts, but rather that ye may prophesy."

1 Peter 2:2-3 "2As newborn babes, desire the sincere milk of the word, that ye may grow thereby: 3If so be ye have tasted that the Lord is gracious."

Who Desires

Proverbs 13:4 "The soul of the sluggard desireth, and hath nothing: but the soul of the diligent shall be made fat."

Proverbs 13:25 "The righteous eateth to the satisfying of his soul: but the belly of the wicked shall want."

Proverbs 19:15 "Slothfulness casteth into a deep sleep; and an idle soul shall suffer hunger."

Proverbs 20:4 "The sluggard will not plow by reason of the cold; therefore shall he beg in harvest, and have nothing."

Who Desires Evil

Proverbs 12:12 "The wicked desireth the net of evil men: but the root of the righteous yieldeth fruit."

Proverbs 21:10 "The soul of the wicked desireth evil: his neighbour findeth no favour in his eyes."

Who Does Not Desire God

Job 21:7-15 "7Wherefore do the wicked live, become old, yea, are mighty in power? 8Their seed is established in their sight with them, and their offspring before their eyes. 9Their houses are safe from fear, neither is the rod of God upon them. 10Their bull gendereth, and faileth not; their cow calveth, and casteth not her calf. 11They send forth their little ones like a flock, and their children dance. [12]They take the timbrel and harp, and rejoice at the sound of the organ. [13]They spend their days in wealth, and in a moment go down to the grave. [14]Therefore they say unto God, Depart from us; for we desire not the knowledge of thy ways. [15]What is the Almighty, that we should serve him? and what profit should we have, if we pray unto him?"

Who Shall Have Their Desires Fulfilled By The Lord
Psalm 37:4 "Delight thyself also in the LORD; and he shall give thee the desires of thine heart."

Psalm 145:18-19 "[18]The LORD is nigh unto all them that call upon him, to all that call upon him in truth. [19]He will fulfil the desire of them that fear him: he also will hear their cry, and will save them."

DESOLATION

What Shall Be Desolate
Job 15:34 "For the congregation of hypocrites shall be desolate, and fire shall consume the tabernacles of bribery."

Isaiah 5:8-10 "[8]Woe unto them that join house to house, that lay field to field, till there be no place, that they may be placed alone in the midst of the earth! [9]In mine ears said the LORD of hosts, Of a truth many houses shall be desolate, even great and fair, without inhabitant. [10]Yea, ten acres of vineyard shall yield one bath, and the seed of an homer shall yield an ephah."

Matthew 12:25 "And Jesus knew their thoughts, and said unto them, Every kingdom divided against itself is brought to desolation; and every city or house divided against itself shall not stand."

Luke 11:17 "But he, knowing their thoughts, said unto them, Every kingdom divided against itself is brought to desolation; and a house divided against a house falleth."

Who Shall Be Desolate
Psalm 34:21 "Evil shall slay the wicked: and they that hate the righteous shall be desolate."

Ezekiel 35:1-15 "[1]Moreover the word of the LORD came unto me, saying, [2]Son of man, set thy face against mount Seir, and prophesy against it, [3]And say unto it, Thus saith the Lord GOD; Behold, O mount Seir, I am against thee, and I will stretch out mine hand against thee, and I will make thee most desolate. [4]I will lay thy cities waste, and thou shalt be desolate, and thou shalt know that I am the LORD. [5]Because thou hast had a perpetual hatred, and hast shed the blood of the children of Israel by the force of the sword in the time of their calamity, in the time that their iniquity had an end: [6]Therefore, as I live, saith the Lord GOD, I will prepare thee unto blood, and blood shall pursue thee: sith thou hast not hated blood, even blood shall pursue thee. [7]Thus will I make mount Seir most desolate, and cut off from it him that passeth out and him that returneth. [8]And I will fill his mountains with his slain men: in thy hills, and in thy valleys, and in all thy rivers, shall they fall that are slain with the sword. [9]I will make thee perpetual desolations, and thy cities shall not return: and ye shall know that I am the LORD. [10]Because thou hast said, These two nations and these two countries shall be mine, and we will possess it; whereas the LORD was there: [11]Therefore, as I live, saith the Lord GOD, I will even do according to thine anger, and according to thine envy which thou hast used out of thy hatred against them; and I will make myself known among them, when I have judged thee. [12]And thou shalt know that I am the LORD, and that I have heard all thy blasphemies which thou hast spoken against the mountains of Israel, saying, They are laid desolate, they are given us to consume. [13]Thus with your mouth ye have boasted against me, and have multiplied your words against me: I have heard them. [14]Thus saith the Lord GOD; When the whole earth rejoiceth, I will make thee desolate. [15]As thou didst rejoice at the inheritance of the house of Israel, because it was desolate, so will I do unto thee: thou shalt be desolate, O mount Seir, and all Idumea, even all of it: and they shall know that I am the LORD."

Who Shall Not Be Desolate
Psalm 34:22 "The LORD redeemeth the soul of his servants: and none of them that trust in him shall be desolate."

Why Desolation Comes

Leviticus 26:13-32 "¹³I am the LORD your God, which brought you forth out of the land of Egypt, that ye should not be their bondmen; and I have broken the bands of your yoke, and made you go upright. ¹⁴But if ye will not hearken unto me, and will not do all these commandments; ¹⁵And if ye shall despise my statutes, or if your soul abhor my judgments, so that ye will not do all my commandments, but that ye break my covenant: ¹⁶I also will do this unto you; I will even appoint over you terror, consumption, and the burning ague, that shall consume the eyes, and cause sorrow of heart: and ye shall sow your seed in vain, for your enemies shall eat it. ¹⁷And I will set my face against you, and ye shall be slain before your enemies: they that hate you shall reign over you; and ye shall flee when none pursueth you. ¹⁸And if ye will not yet for all this hearken unto me, then I will punish you seven times more for your sins. ¹⁹And I will break the pride of your power; and I will make your heaven as iron, and your earth as brass: ²⁰And your strength shall be spent in vain: for your land shall not yield her increase, neither shall the trees of the land yield their fruits. ²¹And if ye walk contrary unto me, and will not hearken unto me; I will bring seven times more plagues upon you according to your sins. ²²I will also send wild beasts among you, which shall rob you of your children, and destroy your cattle, and make you few in number; and your highways shall be desolate. ²³And if ye will not be reformed by me by these things, but will walk contrary unto me; ²⁴Then will I also walk contrary unto you, and will punish you yet seven times for your sins. ²⁵And I will bring a sword upon you, that shall avenge the quarrel of my covenant: and when ye are gathered together within your cities, I will send the pestilence among you; and ye shall be delivered into the hand of the enemy. ²⁶And when I have broken the staff of your bread, ten women shall bake your bread in one oven, and they shall deliver you your bread again by weight: and ye shall eat, and not be satisfied. ²⁷And if ye will not for all this hearken unto me, but walk contrary unto me; ²⁸Then I will walk contrary unto you also in fury; and I, even I, will chastise you seven times for your sins. ²⁹And ye shall eat the flesh of your sons, and the flesh of your daughters shall ye eat.

³⁰And I will destroy your high places, and cut down your images, and cast your carcases upon the carcases of your idols, and my soul shall abhor you. ³¹And I will make your cities waste, and bring your sanctuaries unto desolation, and I will not smell the savour of your sweet odours. ³²And I will bring the land into desolation: and your enemies which dwell therein shall be astonished at it."

2 Chronicles 30:7 "And be not ye like your fathers, and like your brethren, which trespassed against the LORD God of their fathers, who therefore gave them up to desolation, as ye see."

Isaiah 47:10-11 "¹⁰For thou hast trusted in thy wickedness: thou hast said, None seeth me. Thy wisdom and thy knowledge, it hath perverted thee; and thou hast said in thine heart, I am, and none else beside me. ¹¹Therefore shall evil come upon thee; thou shalt not know from whence it riseth: and mischief shall fall upon thee; thou shalt not be able to put it off: and desolation shall come upon thee suddenly, which thou shalt not know."

Jeremiah 12:10-13 "¹⁰Many pastors have destroyed my vineyard, they have trodden my portion under foot, they have made my pleasant portion a desolate wilderness. ¹¹They have made it desolate, and being desolate it mourneth unto me; the whole land is made desolate, because no man layeth it to heart. ¹²The spoilers are come upon all high places through the wilderness: for the sword of the LORD shall devour from the one end of the land even to the other end of the land: no flesh shall have peace. ¹³They have sown wheat, but shall reap thorns: they have put themselves to pain, but shall not profit: and they shall be ashamed of your revenues because of the fierce anger of the LORD."

Jeremiah 25:4-12 "⁴And the LORD hath sent unto you all his servants the prophets, rising early and sending them; but ye have not hearkened, nor inclined your ear to hear. ⁵They said, Turn ye again now every one from his evil way, and from the evil of your doings, and dwell in the land that the LORD hath given unto you and to your fathers for ever and ever: ⁶And go not after other gods to serve them, and to worship them, and provoke me not to anger with the works of your hands;

and I will do you no hurt. [7]Yet ye have not hearkened unto me, saith the LORD; that ye might provoke me to anger with the works of your hands to your own hurt. [8]Therefore thus saith the LORD of hosts; Because ye have not heard my words, [9]Behold, I will send and take all the families of the north, saith the LORD, and Nebuchadrezzar the king of Babylon, my servant, and will bring them against this land, and against the inhabitants thereof, and against all these nations round about, and will utterly destroy them, and make them an astonishment, and an hissing, and perpetual desolations. [10]Moreover I will take from them the voice of mirth, and the voice of gladness, the voice of the bridegroom, and the voice of the bride, the sound of the millstones, and the light of the candle. [11]And this whole land shall be a desolation, and an astonishment; and these nations shall serve the king of Babylon seventy years. [12]And it shall come to pass, when seventy years are accomplished, that I will punish the king of Babylon, and that nation, saith the LORD, for their iniquity, and the land of the Chaldeans, and will make it perpetual desolations."

Zephaniah 2:4-15 "[4]For Gaza shall be forsaken, and Ashkelon a desolation: they shall drive out Ashdod at the noon day, and Ekron shall be rooted up. [5]Woe unto the inhabitants of the sea coast, the nation of the Cherethites! the word of the LORD is against you; O Canaan, the land of the Philistines, I will even destroy thee, that there shall be no inhabitant. [6]And the sea coast shall be dwellings and cottages for shepherds, and folds for flocks. [7]And the coast shall be for the remnant of the house of Judah; they shall feed thereupon: in the houses of Ashkelon shall they lie down in the evening: for the LORD their God shall visit them, and turn away their captivity. [8]I have heard the reproach of Moab, and the revilings of the children of Ammon, whereby they have reproached my people, and magnified themselves against their border. [9]Therefore as I live, saith the LORD of hosts, the God of Israel, Surely Moab shall be as Sodom, and the children of Ammon as Gomorrah, even the breeding of nettles, and saltpits, and a perpetual desolation: the residue of my people shall spoil them, and the remnant of my people shall possess them. [10]This

shall they have for their pride, because they have reproached and magnified themselves against the people of the LORD of hosts. [11]The LORD will be terrible unto them: for he will famish all the gods of the earth; and men shall worship him, every one from his place, even all the isles of the heathen. [12]Ye Ethiopians also, ye shall be slain by my sword. [13]And he will stretch out his hand against the north, and destroy Assyria; and will make Nineveh a desolation, and dry like a wilderness. [14]And flocks shall lie down in the midst of her, all the beasts of the nations: both the cormorant and the bittern shall lodge in the upper lintels of it; their voice shall sing in the windows; desolation shall be in the thresholds: for he shall uncover the cedar work. [15]This is the rejoicing city that dwelt carelessly, that said in her heart, I am, and there is none beside me: how is she become a desolation, a place for beasts to lie down in! every one that passeth by her shall hiss, and wag his hand."

Zechariah 7:11-14 "[11]But they refused to hearken, and pulled away the shoulder, and stopped their ears, that they should not hear. [12]Yea, they made their hearts as an adamant stone, lest they should hear the law, and the words which the LORD of hosts hath sent in his spirit by the former prophets: therefore came a great wrath from the LORD of hosts. [13]Therefore it is come to pass, that as he cried, and they would not hear; so they cried, and I would not hear, saith the LORD of hosts: [14]But I scattered them with a whirlwind among all the nations whom they knew not. Thus the land was desolate after them, that no man passed through nor returned: for they laid the pleasant land desolate."

DESPISEMENT

God Not Despising Anyone

Job 36:5 "Behold, God is mighty, and despiseth not any: he is mighty in strength and wisdom."

The Reward For Despising The Word Of God

Numbers 15:30-31 "[30]But the soul that doeth ought presumptuously, whether he be born in the land, or a stranger, the same reproacheth the LORD; and that soul shall be cut off from among his people. [31]Because he hath despised the word of the LORD, and hath broken his commandment, that soul shall utterly be cut off; his iniquity shall be upon him."

2 Chronicles 36:16 "But they mocked the messengers of God, and despised his words, and misused his prophets, until the wrath of the LORD arose against his people, till there was no remedy."

Isaiah 5:24 "Therefore as the fire devoureth the stubble, and the flame consumeth the chaff, so their root shall be as rottenness, and their blossom shall go up as dust: because they have cast away the law of the LORD of hosts, and despised the word of the Holy One of Israel."

Isaiah 30:8-17 "8Now go, write it before them in a table, and note it in a book, that it may be for the time to come for ever and ever: 9That this is a rebellious people, lying children, children that will not hear the law of the LORD: 10Which say to the seers, See not; and to the prophets, Prophesy not unto us right things, speak unto us smooth things, prophesy deceits: 11Get you out of the way, turn aside out of the path, cause the Holy One of Israel to cease from before us. 12Wherefore thus saith the Holy One of Israel, Because ye despise this word, and trust in oppression and perverseness, and stay thereon: 13Therefore this iniquity shall be to you as a breach ready to fall, swelling out in a high wall, whose breaking cometh suddenly at an instant. 14And he shall break it as the breaking of the potters' vessel that is broken in pieces; he shall not spare: so that there shall not be found in the bursting of it a sherd to take fire from the hearth, or to take water withal out of the pit. 15For thus saith the Lord GOD, the Holy One of Israel; In returning and rest shall ye be saved; in quietness and in confidence shall be your strength: and ye would not. 16But ye said, No; for we will flee upon horses; therefore shall ye flee: and, We will ride upon the swift; therefore shall they that pursue you be swift. 17One thousand shall flee at the rebuke of one; at the rebuke of five shall ye flee: till ye be left as a beacon upon the top of a mountain, and as an ensign on an hill."

Amos 2:4-5 "4Thus saith the LORD; For three transgressions of Judah, and for four, I will not turn away the punishment thereof; because they have despised the law of the LORD, and have not kept his commandments, and their lies caused them to err, after the which their fathers have walked: 5But I will send a fire upon Judah, and it shall devour the palaces of Jerusalem."

The Reward For Despising Wisdom

Proverbs 1:20-32 "20Wisdom crieth without; she uttereth her voice in the streets: 21She crieth in the chief place of concourse, in the openings of the gates: in the city she uttereth her words, saying, 22How long, ye simple ones, will ye love simplicity? and the scorners delight in their scorning, and fools hate knowledge? 23Turn you at my reproof: behold, I will pour out my spirit unto you, I will make known my words unto you. 24Because I have called, and ye refused; I have stretched out my hand, and no man regarded; 25But ye have set at nought all my counsel, and would none of my reproof: 26I also will laugh at your calamity; I will mock when your fear cometh; 27When your fear cometh as desolation, and your destruction cometh as a whirlwind; when distress and anguish cometh upon you. 28Then shall they call upon me, but I will not answer; they shall seek me early, but they shall not find me: 29For that they hated knowledge, and did not choose the fear of the LORD: 30They would none of my counsel: they despised all my reproof. 31Therefore shall they eat of the fruit of their own way, and be filled with their own devices. 32For the turning away of the simple shall slay them, and the prosperity of fools shall destroy them."

Those That Despise A Disciple Of Christ

Luke 10:1-16 "1After these things the Lord appointed other seventy also, and sent them two and two before his face into every city and place, whither he himself would come. 2Therefore said he unto them, The harvest truly is great, but the labourers are few: pray ye therefore the Lord of the harvest, that he would send forth labourers into his harvest. 3Go your ways: behold, I send you forth as lambs among wolves. 4Carry neither purse, nor scrip, nor shoes: and salute no man by the way. 5And into whatsoever house ye enter, first say, Peace be to this house. 6And if the son of peace be there, your peace shall rest upon it: if not, it shall turn to you again. 7And in the same house remain, eating and drinking such things as they give: for the labourer is worthy of his hire. Go not from house to house. [8]And into whatsoever city ye enter, and they receive you, eat such things as are set before you: [9]And heal the sick that are therein, and say unto them, The kingdom of God is come nigh unto you. [10]But into whatsoever city ye enter, and they receive you not, go your ways out into the streets of the same, and say, [11]Even the very dust of your city, which cleaveth on us, we do wipe off against you: notwithstanding be ye sure of this, that the kingdom of God is come nigh unto you. [12]But I say unto you, that it shall be more tolerable in that day for Sodom, than for that city. [13]Woe unto thee, Chorazin! woe unto thee, Bethsaida! for if the mighty works had been done in Tyre and Sidon, which have been done in you, they had a great while ago repented, sitting in sackcloth and ashes. [14]But it shall be more tolerable for Tyre and Sidon at the judgment, than for you. [15]And thou, Capernaum, which art exalted to heaven, shalt be thrust down to hell. [16]He that heareth you heareth me; and he that despiseth you despiseth me; and he that despiseth me despiseth him that sent me."

Those That Despise Israel
Ezekiel 28:24-26 "[24]And there shall be no more a pricking brier unto the house of Israel, nor any grieving thorn of all that are round about them, that despised them; and they shall know that I am the Lord GOD. [25]Thus saith the Lord GOD; When I shall have gathered the house of Israel from the people among whom they are scattered, and shall be sanctified in them in the sight of the heathen, then shall they dwell in their land that I have given to my servant Jacob. [26]And they shall dwell safely therein, and shall build houses, and plant vineyards; yea, they shall dwell with confidence, when I have executed judgments upon all those that despise them round about them; and they shall know that I am the LORD their God."

Those That Despise The Commandments Of The Lord
Proverbs 19:16 "He that keepeth the commandment keepeth his own soul; but he that despiseth his ways shall die."

1 Thessalonians 4:2-8 "[2]For ye know what commandments we gave you by the Lord Jesus. [3]For this is the will of God, even your sanctification, that ye should abstain from fornication: [4]That every one of you should know how to possess his vessel in sanctification and honour; [5]Not in the lust of concupiscence, even as the Gentiles which know not God: [6]That no man go beyond and defraud his brother in any matter: because that the Lord is the avenger of all such, as we also have forewarned you and testified. [7]For God hath not called us unto uncleanness, but unto holiness. [8]He therefore that despiseth, despiseth not man, but God, who hath also given unto us his holy Spirit."

Those That Despise The Lord
1 Samuel 2:30 "Wherefore the LORD God of Israel saith, I said indeed that thy house, and the house of thy father, should walk before me for ever: but now the LORD saith, Be it far from me; for them that honour me I will honour, and they that despise me shall be lightly esteemed."

Malachi 1:6 "A son honoureth his father, and a servant his master: if then I be a father, where is mine honour? and if I be a master, where is my fear? saith the LORD of hosts unto you, O priests, that despise my name. And ye say, Wherein have we despised thy name?"

Luke 10:1-16 "[1]After these things the Lord appointed other seventy also, and sent them two and two before his face into every city and place, whither he himself would come. [2]Therefore said he unto them, The harvest truly is great, but the labourers are few: pray ye therefore the Lord of the harvest, that he would send forth labourers into his harvest. [3]Go your ways: behold, I send you forth as lambs among wolves. [4]Carry neither purse, nor scrip, nor shoes: and salute no man by the way. [5]And into whatsoever house ye enter, first say, Peace be to this house. [6]And if the son of peace be there, your peace shall rest upon it: if not, it shall turn to you again. [7]And in the same house remain, eating and drinking such things as they give: for the labourer is worthy of his hire. Go not from house to house. [8]And into whatsoever city ye enter, and they receive you, eat such things as are set before you: [9]And heal the sick that are therein, and say unto them, The kingdom of God is come nigh unto you. [10]But into whatsoever city ye enter, and they receive you not, go your ways out into the streets of the same, and say, [11]Even the very dust of your city, which cleaveth on us, we do wipe off against you: notwithstanding be ye sure of this, that the kingdom of God is come nigh unto you. [12]But I say unto you, that it shall be more tolerable in that day for Sodom, than for that city. [13]Woe unto thee, Chorazin! woe unto thee, Bethsaida! for if the mighty works had been done in Tyre and Sidon, which have been done in you, they had a great while ago repented, sitting in sackcloth and ashes. [14]But it shall be more tolerable for Tyre and Sidon at the judgment, than for you. [15]And thou, Capernaum, which art exalted to heaven, shalt be thrust down to hell. [16]He that heareth you heareth me; and he that despiseth you despiseth me; and he that despiseth me despiseth him that sent me."

Those That Despise
The Word Of God
Proverbs 13:13 "Whoso despiseth the word shall be destroyed: but he that feareth the commandment shall be rewarded."

Those That Despise Their Neighbor
Proverbs 14:21 "He that despiseth his neighbour sinneth: but he that hath mercy on the poor, happy is he."

What Fools Despise
Proverbs 1:7 "The fear of the LORD is the beginning of knowledge: but fools despise wisdom and instruction."

Proverbs 1:22 "How long, ye simple ones, will ye love simplicity? and the scorners delight in their scorning, and fools hate knowledge?"

Proverbs 15:5 "A fool despiseth his father's instruction: but he that regardeth reproof is prudent."

Proverbs 23:9 "Speak not in the ears of a fool: for he will despise the wisdom of thy words."

What Not To Despise
Job 5:17 "Behold, happy is the man whom God correcteth: therefore despise not thou the chastening of the Almighty."

Proverbs 3:11-12 "[11]My son, despise not the chastening of the LORD; neither be weary of his correction: [12]For whom the LORD loveth he correcteth; even as a father the son in whom he delighteth."

Hebrews 12:5-6 "[5]And ye have forgotten the exhortation which speaketh unto you as unto children, My son, despise not thou the chastening of the Lord, nor faint when thou art rebuked of him: [6]For whom the Lord loveth he chasteneth, and scourgeth every son whom he receiveth."

1 Thessalonians 5:20 "Despise not prophesyings."

Who Despises Dominion
Jude 7-8 "[7]Even as Sodom and Gomorrha, and the cities about them in like manner, giving themselves over to fornication, and going after strange flesh, are set forth for an example, suffering the vengeance of eternal fire. [8]Likewise also these filthy dreamers defile the flesh, despise dominion, and speak evil of dignities."

Who Despises The Lord
Proverbs 14:2 "He that walketh in his uprightness feareth the LORD: but he that is perverse in his ways despiseth him."

Luke 10:1-16 "[1]After these things the Lord appointed other seventy also, and sent them two and two before his face into every city and place, whither he himself would come. [2]Therefore said he unto them, The harvest truly is great, but the labourers are few: pray ye therefore the Lord of the harvest, that he would send forth labourers into his harvest. [3]Go your ways: behold, I send you forth as lambs among wolves. [4]Carry neither purse, nor scrip, nor shoes: and salute no man by the way. [5]And into whatsoever house ye enter, first say, Peace be to this house. [6]And if the son of peace be there, your peace shall rest upon it: if not, it shall turn to you again. [7]And in the same house remain, eating and drinking such things as they give: for the labourer is worthy of his hire. Go not from house to house. [8]And into whatsoever city ye enter, and they receive you, eat such things as are set before you: [9]And heal the sick that are therein, and say unto them, The kingdom of God is come nigh unto you. [10]But into whatsoever city ye enter, and they receive you not, go your ways out into the streets of the same, and say, [11]Even the very dust of your city, which cleaveth on us, we do wipe off against you: notwithstanding be ye sure of this, that the kingdom of God is come nigh unto you. [12]But I say unto you, that it shall be more tolerable in that day for Sodom, than for that city. [13]Woe unto thee,

Chorazin! woe unto thee, Bethsaida! for if the mighty works had been done in Tyre and Sidon, which have been done in you, they had a great while ago repented, sitting in sackcloth and ashes. [14]But it shall be more tolerable for Tyre and Sidon at the judgment, than for you. [15]And thou, Capernaum, which art exalted to heaven, shalt be thrust down to hell. [16]He that heareth you heareth me; and he that despiseth you despiseth me; and he that despiseth me despiseth him that sent me."

1 Thessalonians 4:2-8 "[2]For ye know what commandments we gave you by the Lord Jesus. [3]For this is the will of God, even your sanctification, that ye should abstain from fornication: [4]That every one of you should know how to possess his vessel in sanctification and honour; [5]Not in the lust of concupiscence, even as the Gentiles which know not God: [6]That no man go beyond and defraud his brother in any matter: because that the Lord is the avenger of all such, as we also have forewarned you and testified. [7]For God hath not called us unto uncleanness, but unto holiness. [8]He therefore that despiseth, despiseth not man, but God, who hath also given unto us his holy Spirit."

Who Despises Their Mother
Proverbs 15:20 "A wise son maketh a glad father: but a foolish man despiseth his mother."

Who Despises Their Neighbor
Proverbs 11:12 "He that is void of wisdom despiseth his neighbour: but a man of understanding holdeth his peace."

Who Despises Their Own Soul
Proverbs 15:32 "He that refuseth instruction despiseth his own soul: but he that heareth reproof getteth understanding."

Who Is Despised
Proverbs 12:8 "A man shall be commended according to his wisdom: but he that is of a perverse heart shall be despised."

Ecclesiastes 9:16 "Then said I, Wisdom is better than strength: nevertheless the poor man's wisdom is despised, and his words are not heard."

1 Corinthians 4:9-10 "[9]For I think that God hath set forth us the apostles last, as it were appointed to death: for we are made a spectacle unto the world, and to angels, and to men. [10]We are fools for Christ's sake, but ye are wise in Christ; we are weak, but ye are strong; ye are honourable, but we are despised."

Who Not To Despise
Proverbs 23:22 "Hearken unto thy father that begat thee, and despise not thy mother when she is old."

Matthew 18:2-10 "[2]And Jesus called a little child unto him, and set him in the midst of them, [3]And said, Verily I say unto you, Except ye be converted, and become as little children, ye shall not enter into the kingdom of heaven. [4]Whosoever therefore shall humble himself as this little child, the same is greatest in the kingdom of heaven. [5]And whoso shall receive one such little child in my name receiveth me. [6]But whoso shall offend one of these little ones which believe in me, it were better for him that a millstone were hanged about his neck, and that he were drowned in the depth of the sea. [7]Woe unto the world because of offences! for it must needs be that offences come; but woe to that man by whom the offence cometh! [8]Wherefore if thy hand or thy foot offend thee, cut them off, and cast them from thee: it is better for thee to enter into life halt or maimed, rather than having two hands or two feet to be cast into everlasting fire. [9]And if thine eye offend thee, pluck it out, and cast it from thee: it is better for thee to enter into life with one eye, rather than having two eyes to be cast into hell fire. [10]Take heed that ye despise not one of these little ones; for I say unto you, That in heaven their angels do always behold the face of my Father which is in heaven."

DESTRUCTION

The Way That Leads To Destruction
Matthew 7:13 "Enter ye in at the strait gate: for wide is the gate, and broad is the way, that leadeth to destruction, and many there be which go in thereat."

What Destroys People
Proverbs 11:3 "The integrity of the upright shall guide them: but the perverseness of transgressors shall destroy them."

Proverbs 18:7 "A fool's mouth is his destruction, and his lips are the snare of his soul."

Proverbs 21:7 "The robbery of the wicked shall destroy them; because they refuse to do judgment."

1 Timothy 6:7-9 "[7]For we brought nothing into this world, and it is certain we can carry nothing out. [8]And having food and raiment let us be therewith content. [9]But they that will be rich fall into temptation and a snare, and into many foolish and hurtful lusts, which drown men in destruction and perdition."

What Precedes Destruction
Proverbs 16:18 "Pride goeth before destruction, and an haughty spirit before a fall."

Proverbs 18:12 "Before destruction the heart of man is haughty, and before honour is humility."

When Sudden Destruction Shall Come
1 Thessalonians 5:1-3 "[1]But of the times and the seasons, brethren, ye have no need that I write unto you. [2]For yourselves know perfectly that the day of the Lord so cometh as a thief in the night. [3]For when they shall say, Peace and safety; then sudden destruction cometh upon them, as travail upon a woman with child; and they shall not escape."

Who Destroys Much Good
Ecclesiastes 9:18 "Wisdom is better than weapons of war: but one sinner destroyeth much good."

Who Destroys Their Own Soul
Proverbs 6:32 "But whoso committeth adultery with a woman lacketh understanding: he that doeth it destroyeth his own soul."

Who Seeks Destruction
Proverbs 17:19 "He loveth transgression that loveth strife: and he that exalteth his gate seeketh destruction."

Who Shall Be Destroyed
Genesis 6:12-13 "[12]And God looked upon the earth, and, behold, it was corrupt; for all flesh had corrupted his way upon the earth. [13]And God said unto Noah, The end of all flesh is come before me; for the earth is filled with violence through them; and, behold, I will destroy them with the earth."

Exodus 15:6-9 "[6]Thy right hand, O LORD, is become glorious in power: thy right hand, O LORD, hath dashed in pieces the enemy. [7]And in the greatness of thine excellency thou hast overthrown them that rose up against thee: thou sentest forth thy wrath, which consumed them as stubble. [8]And with the blast of thy nostrils the waters were gathered together, the floods stood upright as an heap, and the depths were congealed in the heart of the sea. [9]The enemy said, I will pursue, I will overtake, I will divide the spoil; my lust shall be satisfied upon them; I will draw my sword, my hand shall destroy them."

Exodus 22:20 "He that sacrificeth unto any god, save unto the LORD only, he shall be utterly destroyed."

Deuteronomy 4:3 "Your eyes have seen what the LORD did because of Baal-peor: for all the men that followed Baal-peor, the LORD thy God hath destroyed them from among you."

Deuteronomy 6:14-15 "[14]Ye shall not go after other gods, of the gods of the people which are round about you; [15](For the LORD thy God is a jealous God among you) lest the anger of the LORD thy God be kindled against thee, and destroy thee from off the face of the earth."

Deuteronomy 7:9-10 "[9]Know therefore that the LORD thy God, he is God, the faithful God, which keepeth covenant and mercy with them that love him and keep his commandments to a thousand generations; [10]And repayeth them that hate him to their face, to destroy them: he will not be slack to him that hateth him, he will repay him to his face."

Deuteronomy 28:15-20 "[15]But it shall come to pass, if thou wilt not hearken unto the voice of the LORD thy God, to observe to do all his commandments and his statutes which I command thee this day; that all these curses shall come upon thee, and overtake thee: [16]Cursed shalt thou be in the city, and cursed shalt thou be in the field. [17]Cursed shall be thy basket and thy store. [18]Cursed shall be the fruit of thy body, and the fruit of thy land, the increase of thy kine, and the flocks of thy sheep. [19]Cursed shalt thou be when thou comest in, and cursed shalt thou be when thou goest out. [20]The LORD shall send upon thee cursing, vexation, and rebuke, in all that thou settest thine hand unto for to do, until thou be destroyed, and until thou perish quickly; because of the wickedness of thy doings, whereby thou hast forsaken me."

Deuteronomy 28:45-47 "⁴⁵Moreover all these curses shall come upon thee, and shall pursue thee, and overtake thee, till thou be destroyed; because thou hearkenedst not unto the voice of the LORD thy God, to keep his commandments and his statutes which he commanded thee: ⁴⁶And they shall be upon thee for a sign and for a wonder, and upon thy seed for ever. ⁴⁷Because thou servedst not the LORD thy God with joyfulness, and with gladness of heart, for the abundance of all things."

Deuteronomy 32:17-24 "¹⁷They sacrificed unto devils, not to God; to gods whom they knew not, to new gods that came newly up, whom your fathers feared not. ¹⁸Of the Rock that begat thee thou art unmindful, and hast forgotten God that formed thee. ¹⁹And when the LORD saw it, he abhorred them, because of the provoking of his sons, and of his daughters. ²⁰And he said, I will hide my face from them, I will see what their end shall be: for they are a very froward generation, children in whom is no faith. ²¹They have moved me to jealousy with that which is not God; they have provoked me to anger with their vanities: and I will move them to jealousy with those which are not a people; I will provoke them to anger with a foolish nation. ²²For a fire is kindled in mine anger, and shall burn unto the lowest hell, and shall consume the earth with her increase, and set on fire the foundations of the mountains. ²³I will heap mischiefs upon them; I will spend mine arrows upon them. ²⁴They shall be burnt with hunger, and devoured with burning heat, and with bitter destruction: I will also send the teeth of beasts upon them, with the poison of serpents of the dust."

Job 15:20-30 "²⁰The wicked man travaileth with pain all his days, and the number of years is hidden to the oppressor. ²¹A dreadful sound is in his ears: in prosperity the destroyer shall come upon him. ²²He believeth not that he shall return out of darkness, and he is waited for of the sword. ²³He wandereth abroad for bread, saying, Where is it? he knoweth that the day of darkness is ready at his hand. ²⁴Trouble and anguish shall make him

afraid; they shall prevail against him, as a king ready to the battle. ²⁵For he stretcheth out his hand against God, and strengtheneth himself against the Almighty. ²⁶He runneth upon him, even on his neck, upon the thick bosses of his bucklers: ²⁷Because he covereth his face with his fatness, and maketh collops of fat on his flanks. ²⁸And he dwelleth in desolate cities, and in houses which no man inhabiteth, which are ready to become heaps. ²⁹He shall not be rich, neither shall his substance continue, neither shall he prolong the perfection thereof upon the earth. ³⁰He shall not depart out of darkness; the flame shall dry up his branches, and by the breath of his mouth shall he go away."

Psalm 28:3-5 "³Draw me not away with the wicked, and with the workers of iniquity, which speak peace to their neighbours, but mischief is in their hearts. ⁴Give them according to their deeds, and according to the wickedness of their endeavours: give them after the work of their hands; render to them their desert. ⁵Because they regard not the works of the LORD, nor the operation of his hands, he shall destroy them, and not build them up."

Psalm 37:38 "But the transgressors shall be destroyed together: the end of the wicked shall be cut off."

Psalm 52:1-5 "¹Why boastest thou thyself in mischief, O mighty man? the goodness of God endureth continually. ²Thy tongue deviseth mischiefs; like a sharp rasor, working deceitfully. ³Thou lovest evil more than good; and lying rather than to speak righteousness. Selah. ⁴Thou lovest all devouring words, O thou deceitful tongue. ⁵God shall likewise destroy thee for ever, he shall take thee away, and pluck thee out of thy dwelling place, and root thee out of the land of the living. Selah."

Psalm 55:16-23 "¹⁶As for me, I will call upon God; and the LORD shall save me. ¹⁷Evening, and morning, and at noon, will I pray, and cry aloud: and he shall hear my voice. ¹⁸He hath delivered my soul in peace from the battle that was against me: for there were many with me. ¹⁹God shall hear, and afflict them, even he that abideth of old. Selah. Because they have no changes, therefore they fear not God. ²⁰He hath put forth his hands against such as be at peace with him: he hath broken his covenant. [21]The words of his mouth were smoother than butter, but war was in his heart: his words were softer than oil, yet were they drawn swords. [22]Cast thy burden upon the LORD, and he shall sustain thee: he shall never suffer the righteous to be moved. [23]But thou, O God, shalt bring them down into the pit of destruction: bloody and deceitful men shall not live out half their days; but I will trust in thee."

Psalm 73:26-27 "[26]My flesh and my heart faileth: but God is the strength of my heart, and my portion for ever. [27]For, lo, they that are far from thee shall perish: thou hast destroyed all them that go a whoring from thee."

Psalm 145:20 "The LORD preserveth all them that love him: but all the wicked will he destroy."

Proverbs 10:29 "The way of the LORD is strength to the upright: but destruction shall be to the workers of iniquity."

Proverbs 13:3 "He that keepeth his mouth keepeth his life: but he that openeth wide his lips shall have destruction."

Proverbs 13:13 "Whoso despiseth the word shall be destroyed: but he that feareth the commandment shall be rewarded."

Proverbs 13:20 "He that walketh with wise men shall be wise: but a companion of fools shall be destroyed."

Proverbs 15:25 "The LORD will destroy the house of the proud: but he will establish the border of the widow."

Proverbs 21:15 "It is joy to the just to do judgment: but destruction shall be to the workers of iniquity."

Proverbs 29:1 "He, that being often reproved hardeneth his neck, shall suddenly be destroyed, and that without remedy."

Jeremiah 12:17 "But if they will not obey, I will utterly pluck up and destroy that nation, saith the LORD."

Jeremiah 15:6-7 "[6]Thou hast forsaken me, saith the LORD, thou art gone backward: therefore will I stretch out my hand against thee, and destroy thee; I am weary with repenting. [7]And I will fan them with a fan in the gates of the land; I will bereave them of children, I will destroy my people, since they return not from their ways."

Jeremiah 30:10-11 "[10]Therefore fear thou not, O my servant Jacob, saith the LORD; neither be dismayed, O Israel: for, lo, I will save thee from afar, and thy seed from the land of their captivity; and Jacob shall return, and shall be in rest, and be quiet, and none shall make him afraid. [11]For I am with thee, saith the LORD, to save thee: though I make a full end of all nations whither I have scattered thee, yet will I not make a full end of thee: but I will correct thee in measure, and will not leave thee altogether unpunished."

Jeremiah 46:28 "Fear thou not, O Jacob my servant, saith the LORD: for I am with thee; for I will make a full end of all the nations whither I have driven thee: but I will not make a full end of thee, but correct thee in measure; yet will I not leave thee wholly unpunished."

Jeremiah 48:42 "And Moab shall be destroyed from being a people, because he hath magnified himself against the LORD."

Ezekiel 34:11-16 "[11]For thus saith the Lord GOD; Behold, I, even I, will both search my sheep, and seek them out. [12]As a shepherd seeketh out his flock in the day that he is among his sheep that are scattered; so will I seek out my sheep, and will deliver them out of all places where they have been scattered in the cloudy and dark day. [13]And I will bring them out from the people, and gather them from the countries, and will bring them to their own land, and feed them upon the mountains of Israel by the rivers, and in all the inhabited places of the country. [14]I will feed them in a good pasture, and upon the high mountains of Israel shall their fold be: there shall they lie in a good fold, and in a fat pasture shall they feed upon the mountains of Israel. [15]I will feed my flock, and I will cause them to lie down, saith the Lord GOD. [16]I will seek that which was lost, and bring again that which was driven away, and will bind up that which was broken, and will strengthen that which was sick: but I will destroy the fat and the strong; I will feed them with judgment."

Amos 9:7-8 "⁷Are ye not as children of the Ethiopians unto me, O children of Israel? saith the LORD. Have not I brought up Israel out of the land of Egypt? and the Philistines from Caphtor, and the Syrians from Kir? ⁸Behold, the eyes of the Lord GOD are upon the sinful kingdom, and I will destroy it from off the face of the earth; saving that I will not utterly destroy the house of Jacob, saith the LORD."

Zechariah 12:9 "And it shall come to pass in that day, that I will seek to destroy all the nations that come against Jerusalem."

Acts 3:22-23 "²²For Moses truly said unto the fathers, A prophet shall the Lord your God raise up unto you of your brethren, like unto me; him shall ye hear in all things whatsoever he shall say unto you. ²³And it shall come to pass, that every soul, which will not hear that prophet, shall be destroyed from among the people."

1 Corinthians 3:16-17 "¹⁶Know ye not that ye are the temple of God, and that the Spirit of God dwelleth in you? ¹⁷If any man defile the temple of God, him shall God destroy; for the temple of God is holy, which temple ye are."

Philippians 3:18-19 "¹⁸(For many walk, of whom I have told you often, and now tell you even weeping, that they are the enemies of the cross of Christ: ¹⁹Whose end is destruction, whose God is their belly, and whose glory is in their shame, who mind earthly things.)"

2 Thessalonians 1:7-9 "⁷And to you who are troubled rest with us, when the Lord Jesus shall be revealed from heaven with his mighty angels, ⁸In flaming fire taking vengeance on them that know not God, and that obey not the gospel of our Lord Jesus Christ: ⁹Who shall be punished with everlasting destruction from the presence of the Lord, and from the glory of his power."

2 Peter 2:1 "But there were false prophets also among the people, even as there shall be false teachers among you, who privily shall bring in damnable heresies, even denying the Lord that bought them, and bring upon themselves swift destruction."

Revelation 11:18 "And the nations were angry, and thy wrath is come, and the time of the dead, that they should be judged, and that thou shouldest give reward unto thy servants the prophets, and to the saints, and them that fear thy name, small and great; and shouldest destroy them which destroy the earth."

Who Shall Not Be Destroyed

Genesis 18:23-32 "²³And Abraham drew near, and said, Wilt thou also destroy the righteous with the wicked? ²⁴Peradventure there be fifty righteous within the city: wilt thou also destroy and not spare the place for the fifty righteous that are therein? ²⁵That be far from thee to do after this manner, to slay the righteous with the wicked: and that the righteous should be as the wicked, that be far from thee: Shall not the Judge of all the earth do right? ²⁶And the LORD said, If I find in Sodom fifty righteous within the city, then I will spare all the place for their sakes. ²⁷And Abraham answered and said, Behold now, I have taken upon me to speak unto the Lord, which am but dust and ashes: ²⁸Peradventure there shall lack five of the fifty righteous: wilt thou destroy all the city for lack of five? And he said, If I find there forty and five, I will not destroy it. ²⁹And he spake unto him yet again, and said, Peradventure there shall be forty found there. And he said, I will not do it for forty's sake. ³⁰And he said unto him, Oh let not the Lord be angry, and I will speak: Peradventure there shall thirty be found there. And he said, I will not do it, if I find thirty there. ³¹And he said, Behold now, I have taken upon me to speak unto the Lord: Peradventure there shall be twenty found there. And he said, I will not destroy it for twenty's sake. ³²And he said, Oh let not the Lord be angry, and I will speak yet but this once: Peradventure ten shall be found there. And he said, I will not destroy it for ten's sake."

Deuteronomy 4:30-31 "³⁰When thou art in tribulation, and all these things are come upon thee, even in the latter days, if thou turn to the LORD thy God, and shalt be obedient unto his voice; ³¹(For the LORD thy God is a merciful God;) he will not forsake thee, neither destroy thee, nor forget the covenant of thy fathers which he sware unto them."

Isaiah 65:8-10 "⁸Thus saith the LORD, As the new wine is found in the cluster, and one saith, Destroy it not; for a blessing is in it: so will I do for my servants' sakes, that I may not destroy them all. ⁹And I will bring forth a seed out of Jacob, and out of Judah an inheritor of my mountains: and mine elect shall inherit it, and my servants shall dwell there. ¹⁰And Sharon shall be a fold of flocks, and the valley of Achor a place for the herds to lie down in, for my people that have sought me."

Jeremiah 30:10-11 "¹⁰Therefore fear thou not, O my servant Jacob, saith the LORD; neither be dismayed, O Israel: for, lo, I will save thee from afar, and thy seed from the land of their captivity; and Jacob shall return, and shall be in rest, and be quiet, and none shall make him afraid. ¹¹For I am with thee, saith the LORD, to save thee: though I make a full end of all nations whither I have scattered thee, yet will I not make a full end of thee: but I will correct thee in measure, and will not leave thee altogether unpunished."

Jeremiah 46:28 "Fear thou not, O Jacob my servant, saith the LORD: for I am with thee; for I will make a full end of all the nations whither I have driven thee: but I will not make a full end of thee, but correct thee in measure; yet will I not leave thee wholly unpunished."

Amos 9:7-8 "⁷Are ye not as children of the Ethiopians unto me, O children of Israel? saith the LORD. Have not I brought up Israel out of the land of Egypt? and the Philistines from Caphtor, and the Syrians from Kir? ⁸Behold, the eyes of the Lord GOD are upon the sinful kingdom, and I will destroy it from off the face of the earth; saving that I will not utterly destroy the house of Jacob, saith the LORD."

Who Shall Destroy Many
Daniel 8:23-25 "²³And in the latter time of their kingdom, when the transgressors are come to the full, a king of fierce countenance, and understanding dark sentences, shall stand up. ²⁴And his power shall be mighty, but not by his own power: and he shall destroy wonderfully, and shall prosper, and practise, and shall destroy the mighty and the holy people. ²⁵And through his policy also he shall cause craft to prosper in his hand; and he shall magnify himself in his heart, and by peace shall destroy many: he shall also stand up against the Prince of princes; but he shall be broken without hand."

Who Studies Destruction
Proverbs 24:1-2 "¹Be not thou envious against evil men, neither desire to be with them. ²For their heart studieth destruction, and their lips talk of mischief."

Why People Are Destroyed
Genesis 6:5-7 "⁵And GOD saw that the wickedness of man was great in the earth, and that every imagination of the thoughts of his heart was only evil continually. ⁶And it repented the LORD that he had made man on the earth, and it grieved him at his heart. ⁷And the LORD said, I will destroy man whom I have created from the face of the earth; both man, and beast, and the creeping thing, and the fowls of the air; for it repenteth me that I have made them."

Isaiah 5:13 "Therefore my people are gone into captivity, because they have no knowledge: and their honourable men are famished, and their multitude dried up with thirst."

Jeremiah 48:42 "And Moab shall be destroyed from being a people, because he hath magnified himself against the LORD."

Hosea 4:6 "My people are destroyed for lack of knowledge: because thou hast rejected knowledge, I will also reject thee, that thou shalt be no priest to me: seeing thou hast forgotten the law of thy God, I will also forget thy children."

DEVIL/DEVILS

Devils Believing In God
James 2:19 "Thou believest that there is one God; thou doest well: the devils also believe, and tremble."

Resisting The Devil
Ephesians 4:27 "Neither give place to the devil."

James 4:7 "Submit yourselves therefore to God. Resist the devil, and he will flee from you."

1 Peter 5:8-9 "⁸Be sober, be vigilant; because your adversary the devil, as a roaring lion, walketh about, seeking whom he may devour: ⁹Whom resist stedfast in the faith, knowing that the same afflictions are accomplished in your brethren that are in the world."

The Binding And Loosening Of Satan
Revelation 20:1-3 "¹And I saw an angel come down from heaven, having the key of the bottomless pit

and a great chain in his hand. ²And he laid hold on the dragon, that old serpent, which is the Devil, and Satan, and bound him a thousand years, ³And cast him into the bottomless pit, and shut him up, and set a seal upon him, that he should deceive the nations no more, till the thousand years should be fulfilled: and after that he must be loosed a little season."

Revelation 20:7-9 "⁷And when the thousand years are expired, Satan shall be loosed out of his prison, ⁸And shall go out to deceive the nations which are in the four quarters of the earth, Gog and Magog, to gather them together to battle: the number of whom is as the sand of the sea. ⁹And they went up on the breadth of the earth, and compassed the camp of the saints about, and the beloved city: and fire came down from God out of heaven, and devoured them."

The Character Of Satan
Genesis 3:1 "Now the serpent was more subtil than any beast of the field which the LORD God had made. And he said unto the woman, Yea, hath God said, Ye shall not eat of every tree of the garden?"

Isaiah 14:12-14 "¹²How art thou fallen from heaven, O Lucifer, son of the morning! how art thou cut down to the ground, which didst weaken the nations! ¹³For thou hast said in thine heart, I will ascend into heaven, I will exalt my throne above the stars of God: I will sit also upon the mount of the congregation, in the sides of the north: ¹⁴I will ascend above the heights of the clouds; I will be like the most High."

John 8:44 "Ye are of your father the devil, and the lusts of your father ye will do. He was a murderer from the beginning, and abode not in the truth, because there is no truth in him. When he speaketh a lie, he speaketh of his own: for he is a liar, and the father of it."

1 John 3:8 "He that committeth sin is of the devil; for the devil sinneth from the beginning. For this purpose the Son of God was manifested, that he might destroy the works of the devil."

The Devil Being Cast Down From Heaven
Isaiah 14:12-15 "¹²How art thou fallen from heaven, O Lucifer, son of the morning! how art thou cut

down to the ground, which didst weaken the nations! ¹³For thou hast said in thine heart, I will ascend into heaven, I will exalt my throne above the stars of God: I will sit also upon the mount of the congregation, in the sides of the north: ¹⁴I will ascend above the heights of the clouds; I will be like the most High. ¹⁵Yet thou shalt be brought down to hell, to the sides of the pit."

Luke 10:18 "And he said unto them, I beheld Satan as lightning fall from heaven."

John 12:30-31 "³⁰Jesus answered and said, This voice came not because of me, but for your sakes. ³¹Now is the judgment of this world: now shall the prince of this world be cast out."

Revelation 12:7-13 "⁷And there was war in heaven: Michael and his angels fought against the dragon; and the dragon fought and his angels, ⁸And prevailed not; neither was their place found any more in heaven. ⁹And the great dragon was cast out, that old serpent, called the Devil, and Satan, which deceiveth the whole world: he was cast out into the earth, and his angels were cast out with him. ¹⁰And I heard a loud voice saying in heaven, Now is come salvation, and strength, and the kingdom of our God, and the power of his Christ: for the accuser of our brethren is cast down, which accused them before our God day and night. ¹¹And they overcame him by the blood of the Lamb, and by the word of their testimony; and they loved not their lives unto the death. ¹²Therefore rejoice, ye heavens, and ye that dwell in them. Woe to the inhabiters of the earth and of the sea! for the devil is come down unto you, having great wrath, because he knoweth that he hath but a short time. ¹³And when the dragon saw that he was cast unto the earth, he persecuted the woman which brought forth the man child."

The Devil Being Cast Down To The Pit Of Hell
Isaiah 14:12-15 "¹²How art thou fallen from heaven, O Lucifer, son of the morning! how art thou cut down to the ground, which didst weaken the nations! ¹³For thou hast said in thine heart, I will ascend into heaven, I will exalt my throne above the stars of God: I will sit also upon the mount of the congregation, in the sides of the north: ¹⁴I will ascend above the heights of the clouds; I will be like

the most High. [15]Yet thou shalt be brought down to hell, to the sides of the pit."

Matthew 25:41 "Then shall he say also unto them on the left hand, Depart from me, ye cursed, into everlasting fire, prepared for the devil and his angels."

Revelation 20:1-3 "[1]And I saw an angel come down from heaven, having the key of the bottomless pit and a great chain in his hand. [2]And he laid hold on the dragon, that old serpent, which is the Devil, and Satan, and bound him a thousand years, [3]And cast him into the bottomless pit, and shut him up, and set a seal upon him, that he should deceive the nations no more, till the thousand years should be fulfilled: and after that he must be loosed a little season."

Revelation 20:7-10 "[7]And when the thousand years are expired, Satan shall be loosed out of his prison, [8]And shall go out to deceive the nations which are in the four quarters of the earth, Gog and Magog, to gather them together to battle: the number of whom is as the sand of the sea. [9]And they went up on the breadth of the earth, and compassed the camp of the saints about, and the beloved city: and fire came down from God out of heaven, and devoured them. [10]And the devil that deceived them was cast into the lake of fire and brimstone, where the beast and the false prophet are, and shall be tormented day and night for ever and ever."

The Lord Destroying The Devil
Genesis 3:14-15 "[14]And the LORD God said unto the serpent, Because thou hast done this, thou art cursed above all cattle, and above every beast of the field; upon thy belly shalt thou go, and dust shalt thou eat all the days of thy life: [15]And I will put enmity between thee and the woman, and between thy seed and her seed; it shall bruise thy head, and thou shalt bruise his heel."

Hebrews 2:9-15 "[9]But we see Jesus, who was made a little lower than the angels for the suffering of death, crowned with glory and honour; that he by the grace of God should taste death for every man. [10]For it became him, for whom are all things, and by whom are all things, in bringing many sons unto glory, to make the captain of their salvation perfect through sufferings. [11]For both he that

sanctifieth and they who are sanctified are all of one: for which cause he is not ashamed to call them brethren, [12]Saying, I will declare thy name unto my brethren, in the midst of the church will I sing praise unto thee. [13]And again, I will put my trust in him. And again, Behold I and the children which God hath given me. [14]Forasmuch then as the children are partakers of flesh and blood, he also himself likewise took part of the same; that through death he might destroy him that had the power of death, that is, the devil; [15]And deliver them who through fear of death were all their lifetime subject to bondage."

1 John 3:8 "He that committeth sin is of the devil; for the devil sinneth from the beginning. For this purpose the Son of God was manifested, that he might destroy the works of the devil."

What Satan Does
Genesis 3:13 "And the LORD God said unto the woman, What is this that thou hast done? And the woman said, The serpent beguiled me, and I did eat."

Job 1:6-7 "[6]Now there was a day when the sons of God came to present themselves before the LORD, and Satan came also among them. [7]And the LORD said unto Satan, Whence comest thou? Then Satan answered the LORD, and said, From going to and fro in the earth, and from walking up and down in it."

Matthew 13:18-19 "[18]Hear ye therefore the parable of the sower. [19]When any one heareth the word of the kingdom, and understandeth it not, then cometh the wicked one, and catcheth away that which was sown in his heart. This is he which received seed by the way side."

Mark 4:13-15 "[13]And he said unto them, Know ye not this parable? and how then will ye know all parables? [14]The sower soweth the word. [15]And these are they by the way side, where the word is sown; but when they have heard, Satan cometh immediately, and taketh away the word that was sown in their hearts."

Luke 8:11-12 "[11]Now the parable is this: The seed is the word of God. [12]Those by the way side are they that hear; then cometh the devil, and taketh away the word out of their hearts, lest they should believe and be saved."

2 Corinthians 11:3 "But I fear, lest by any means, as the serpent beguiled Eve through his subtilty, so your minds should be corrupted from the simplicity that is in Christ."

2 Corinthians 11:13-15 "¹³For such are false apostles, deceitful workers, transforming themselves into the apostles of Christ. ¹⁴And no marvel; for Satan himself is transformed into an angel of light. ¹⁵Therefore it is no great thing if his ministers also be transformed as the ministers of righteousness; whose end shall be according to their works."

1 Peter 5:8 "Be sober, be vigilant; because your adversary the devil, as a roaring lion, walketh about, seeking whom he may devour."

Revelation 2:10 "Fear none of those things which thou shalt suffer: behold, the devil shall cast some of you into prison, that ye may be tried; and ye shall have tribulation ten days: be thou faithful unto death, and I will give thee a crown of life."

Revelation 12:1-17 "¹And there appeared a great wonder in heaven; a woman clothed with the sun, and the moon under her feet, and upon her head a crown of twelve stars: ²And she being with child cried, travailing in birth, and pained to be delivered. ³And there appeared another wonder in heaven; and behold a great red dragon, having seven heads and ten horns, and seven crowns upon his heads. ⁴And his tail drew the third part of the stars of heaven, and did cast them to the earth: and the dragon stood before the woman which was ready to be delivered, for to devour her child as soon as it was born. ⁵And she brought forth a man child, who was to rule all nations with a rod of iron: and her child was caught up unto God, and to his throne. ⁶And the woman fled into the wilderness, where she hath a place prepared of God, that they should feed her there a thousand two hundred and threescore days. ⁷And there was war in heaven: Michael and his angels fought against the dragon; and the dragon fought and his angels, ⁸And prevailed not; neither was their place found any more in heaven. ⁹And the great dragon was cast out, that old serpent, called the Devil, and Satan, which deceiveth the whole

world: he was cast out into the earth, and his angels were cast out with him. ¹⁰And I heard a loud voice saying in heaven, Now is come salvation, and strength, and the kingdom of our God, and the power of his Christ: for the accuser of our brethren is cast down, which accused them before our God day and night. ¹¹And they overcame him by the blood of the Lamb, and by the word of their testimony; and they loved not their lives unto the death. ¹²Therefore rejoice, ye heavens, and ye that dwell in them. Woe to the inhabiters of the earth and of the sea! for the devil is come down unto you, having great wrath, because he knoweth that he hath but a short time. ¹³And when the dragon saw that he was cast unto the earth, he persecuted the woman which brought forth the man child. ¹⁴And to the woman were given two wings of a great eagle, that she might fly into the wilderness, into her place, where she is nourished for a time, and times, and half a time, from the face of the serpent. ¹⁵And the serpent cast out of his mouth water as a flood after the woman, that he might cause her to be carried away of the flood. ¹⁶And the earth helped the woman, and the earth opened her mouth, and swallowed up the flood which the dragon cast out of his mouth. ¹⁷And the dragon was wroth with the woman, and went to make war with the remnant of her seed, which keep the commandments of God, and have the testimony of Jesus Christ."

Revelation 20:1-3 "¹And I saw an angel come down from heaven, having the key of the bottomless pit and a great chain in his hand. ²And he laid hold on the dragon, that old serpent, which is the Devil, and Satan, and bound him a thousand years, ³And cast him into the bottomless pit, and shut him up, and set a seal upon him, that he should deceive the nations no more, till the thousand years should be fulfilled: and after that he must be loosed a little season."

Revelation 20:7-10 "⁷And when the thousand years are expired, Satan shall be loosed out of his prison, ⁸And shall go out to deceive the nations which are in the four quarters of the earth, Gog and Magog, to gather them together to battle: the number of whom is as the sand of the sea. ⁹And they went up on the breadth of the earth, and compassed the camp of the saints about, and the beloved city: and fire came down from God out of heaven, and devoured them. ¹⁰And the devil that deceived them was cast into the lake of fire and brimstone, where the beast and the false prophet are, and shall be tormented day and night for ever and ever."

What The Devil Is
Matthew 13:36-39 "³⁶Then Jesus sent the multitude away, and went into the house: and his disciples came unto him, saying, Declare unto us the parable of the tares of the field. ³⁷He answered and said unto them, He that soweth the good seed is the Son of man; ³⁸The field is the world; the good seed are the children of the kingdom; but the tares are the children of the wicked one; ³⁹The enemy that sowed them is the devil; the harvest is the end of the world; and the reapers are the angels."

John 8:44 "Ye are of your father the devil, and the lusts of your father ye will do. He was a murderer from the beginning, and abode not in the truth, because there is no truth in him. When he speaketh a lie, he speaketh of his own: for he is a liar, and the father of it."

Who Has Authority Over Devils
Mark 16:14-19 "¹⁴Afterward he appeared unto the eleven as they sat at meat, and upbraided them with their unbelief and hardness of heart, because they believed not them which had seen him after he was risen. ¹⁵And he said unto them, Go ye into all the world, and preach the gospel to every creature. ¹⁶He that believeth and is baptized shall be saved; but he that believeth not shall be damned. ¹⁷And these signs shall follow them that believe; In my name shall they cast out devils; they shall speak with new tongues; ¹⁸They shall take up serpents; and if they drink any deadly thing, it shall not hurt them; they shall lay hands on the sick, and they shall recover. ¹⁹So then after the Lord had spoken unto them, he was received up into heaven, and sat on the right hand of God."

Luke 10:17 "And the seventy returned again with joy, saying, Lord, even the devils are subject unto us through thy name."

Who Is Of The Devil
John 8:42-44 "⁴²Jesus said unto them, If God were your Father, ye would love me: for I proceeded forth and came from God; neither came I of myself, but he sent me. ⁴³Why do ye not understand my speech? even because ye cannot hear my word. ⁴⁴Ye are of your father the devil, and the lusts of your father ye will do. He was a murderer from the beginning, and abode not in the truth, because there is no truth in him. When he speaketh a lie, he speaketh of his own: for he is a liar, and the father of it."

1 John 3:8 "He that committeth sin is of the devil; for the devil sinneth from the beginning. For this purpose the Son of God was manifested, that he might destroy the works of the devil."

Who The Devil Flees From
James 4:7 "Submit yourselves therefore to God. Resist the devil, and he will flee from you."

Who The Wicked One Cannot Touch
1 John 5:18 "We know that whosoever is born of God sinneth not; but he that is begotten of God keepeth himself, and that wicked one toucheth him not."

DILIGENCE

Being Diligent
Proverbs 27:23-24 "²³Be thou diligent to know the state of thy flocks, and look well to thy herds. ²⁴For riches are not for ever: and doth the crown endure to every generation?"

Hebrews 6:11-12 "¹¹And we desire that every one of you do shew the same diligence to the full assurance of hope unto the end: ¹²That ye be not slothful, but followers of them who through faith and patience inherit the promises."

2 Peter 3:14 "Wherefore, beloved, seeing that ye look for such things, be diligent that ye may be found of him in peace, without spot, and blameless."

The Diligent
Proverbs 10:4 "He becometh poor that dealeth with a slack hand: but the hand of the diligent maketh rich."

Proverbs 12:24 "The hand of the diligent shall bear rule: but the slothful shall be under tribute."

Proverbs 12:27 "The slothful man roasteth not that which he took in hunting: but the substance of a diligent man is precious."

Proverbs 13:4 "The soul of the sluggard desireth, and hath nothing: but the soul of the diligent shall be made fat."

Proverbs 21:5 "The thoughts of the diligent tend only to plenteousness; but of every one that is hasty only to want."

Proverbs 22:29 "Seest thou a man diligent in his business? he shall stand before kings; he shall not stand before mean men."

DIRECTION

What Gate To Enter Into
Matthew 7:13 "Enter ye in at the strait gate: for wide is the gate, and broad is the way, that leadeth to destruction, and many there be which go in thereat."

Luke 13:23-24 "²³Then said one unto him, Lord, are there few that be saved? And he said unto them, ²⁴Strive to enter in at the strait gate: for many, I say unto you, will seek to enter in, and shall not be able."

DISCERNING

Discerning The Times
Matthew 24:32-34 "³²Now learn a parable of the fig tree; When his branch is yet tender, and putteth forth leaves, ye know that summer is nigh: ³³So likewise ye, when ye shall see all these things, know that it is near, even at the doors. ³⁴Verily I say unto you, This generation shall not pass, till all these things be fulfilled."

Mark 13:28-30 "²⁸Now learn a parable of the fig tree; When her branch is yet tender, and putteth forth leaves, ye know that summer is near: ²⁹So ye in like manner, when ye shall see these things come to pass, know that it is nigh, even at the doors. ³⁰Verily I say unto you, that this generation shall not pass, till all these things be done."

Luke 12:54-56 "⁵⁴And he said also to the people, When ye see a cloud rise out of the west, straightway ye say, There cometh a shower; and so it is. ⁵⁵And when ye see the south wind blow, ye say, There will be heat; and it cometh to pass. ⁵⁶Ye

hypocrites, ye can discern the face of the sky and of the earth; but how is it that ye do not discern this time?"

Luke 21:29-32 "²⁹And he spake to them a parable; Behold the fig tree, and all the trees; ³⁰When they now shoot forth, ye see and know of your own selves that summer is now nigh at hand. ³¹So likewise ye, when ye see these things come to pass, know ye that the kingdom of God is nigh at hand. ³²Verily I say unto you, This generation shall not pass away, till all be fulfilled."

What Is A Discerner Of The Thoughts And Intents Of The Heart
Hebrews 4:12 "For the word of God is quick, and powerful, and sharper than any twoedged sword, piercing even to the dividing asunder of soul and spirit, and of the joints and marrow, and is a discerner of the thoughts and intents of the heart."

What Is Spiritually Discerned
1 Corinthians 2:14 "But the natural man receiveth not the things of the Spirit of God: for they are foolishness unto him: neither can he know them, because they are spiritually discerned."

Who Discerns
Ecclesiastes 8:2-5 "²I counsel thee to keep the king's commandment, and that in regard of the oath of God. ³Be not hasty to go out of his sight: stand not in an evil thing; for he doeth whatsoever pleaseth him. ⁴Where the word of a king is, there is power: and who may say unto him, What doest thou? ⁵Whoso keepeth the commandment shall feel no evil thing: and a wise man's heart discerneth both time and judgment."

Malachi 3:16-18 "¹⁶Then they that feared the LORD spake often one to another: and the LORD hearkened, and heard it, and a book of remembrance was written before him for them that feared the LORD, and that thought upon his name. ¹⁷And they shall be mine, saith the LORD of hosts, in that day when I make up my jewels; and I will spare them, as a man spareth his own son that serveth him. ¹⁸Then shall ye return, and discern between the righteous and the wicked, between him that serveth God and him that serveth him not."

Hebrews 5:14 "But strong meat belongeth to them that are of full age, even those who by reason of use have their senses exercised to discern both good and evil."

DISCIPLES/APOSTLES

What Apostles Are For
Ephesians 4:11-14 "[11]And he gave some, apostles; and some, prophets; and some, evangelists; and some, pastors and teachers; [12]For the perfecting of the saints, for the work of the ministry, for the edifying of the body of Christ: [13]Till we all come in the unity of the faith, and of the knowledge of the Son of God, unto a perfect man, unto the measure of the stature of the fulness of Christ: [14]That we henceforth be no more children, tossed to and fro, and carried about with every wind of doctrine, by the sleight of men, and cunning craftiness, whereby they lie in wait to deceive."

What Disciples Should Be Aware Of
Matthew 10:16-23 "[16]Behold, I send you forth as sheep in the midst of wolves: be ye therefore wise as serpents, and harmless as doves. [17]But beware of men: for they will deliver you up to the councils, and they will scourge you in their synagogues; [18]And ye shall be brought before governors and kings for my sake, for a testimony against them and the Gentiles. [19]But when they deliver you up, take no thought how or what ye shall speak: for it shall be given you in that same hour what ye shall speak. [20]For it is not ye that speak, but the Spirit of your Father which speaketh in you. [21]And the brother shall deliver up the brother to death, and the father the child: and the children shall rise up against their parents, and cause them to be put to death. [22]And ye shall be hated of all men for my name's sake: but he that endureth to the end shall be saved. [23]But when they persecute you in this city, flee ye into another: for verily I say unto you, Ye shall not have gone over the cities of Israel, till the Son of man be come."

What Jesus Christ Gave
His Disciples Authority Over
Matthew 10:1 "And when he had called unto him his twelve disciples, he gave them power against unclean spirits, to cast them out, and to heal all manner of sickness and all manner of disease."

Mark 6:7 "And he called unto him the twelve, and began to send them forth by two and two; and gave them power over unclean spirits."

Luke 9:1 "Then he called his twelve disciples together, and gave them power and authority over all devils, and to cure diseases."

What Jesus Christ Sent His Disciples To Do
Matthew 10:5-8 "[5]These twelve Jesus sent forth, and commanded them, saying, Go not into the way of the Gentiles, and into any city of the Samaritans enter ye not: [6]But go rather to the lost sheep of the house of Israel. [7]And as ye go, preach, saying, The kingdom of heaven is at hand. [8]Heal the sick, cleanse the lepers, raise the dead, cast out devils: freely ye have received, freely give."

Matthew 28:16-20 "[16]Then the eleven disciples went away into Galilee, into a mountain where Jesus had appointed them. [17]And when they saw him, they worshipped him: but some doubted. [18]And Jesus came and spake unto them, saying, All power is given unto me in heaven and in earth. [19]Go ye therefore, and teach all nations, baptizing them in the name of the Father, and of the Son, and of the Holy Ghost: [20]Teaching them to observe all things whatsoever I have commanded you: and, lo, I am with you alway, even unto the end of the world. Amen."

Mark 6:7-13 "[7]And he called unto him the twelve, and began to send them forth by two and two; and gave them power over unclean spirits; [8]And commanded them that they should take nothing for their journey, save a staff only; no scrip, no bread, no money in their purse: [9]But be shod with sandals; and not put on two coats. [10]And he said unto them, In what place soever ye enter into an house, there abide till ye depart from that place. [11]And whosoever shall not receive you, nor hear you, when ye depart thence, shake off the dust under your feet for a testimony against them. Verily I say unto you, It shall be more tolerable for Sodom and Gomorrha in the day of judgment, than for that city. [12]And they went out, and preached that men should repent. [13]And they cast out many devils, and anointed with oil many that were sick, and healed them."

Mark 16:14-20 "[14]Afterward he appeared unto the eleven as they sat at meat, and upbraided them with their unbelief and hardness of heart, because they believed not them which had seen him after he was risen. [15]And he said unto them, Go ye into all the world, and preach the gospel to every creature. [16]He that believeth and is baptized shall be saved; but he that believeth not shall be damned. [17]And these signs shall follow them that believe; In my name shall they cast out devils; they shall speak with new tongues; [18]They shall take up serpents; and if they drink any deadly thing, it shall not hurt them; they shall lay hands on the sick, and they shall recover. [19]So then after the Lord had spoken unto them, he was received up into heaven, and sat on the right hand of God. [20]And they went forth, and preached everywhere, the Lord working with them, and confirming the word with signs following. Amen."

Luke 9:1-6 "[1]Then he called his twelve disciples together, and gave them power and authority over all devils, and to cure diseases. [2]And he sent them to preach the kingdom of God, and to heal the sick. [3]And he said unto them, Take nothing for your journey, neither staves, nor scrip, neither bread, neither money; neither have two coats apiece. [4]And whatsoever house ye enter into, there abide, and thence depart. [5]And whosoever will not receive you, when ye go out of that city, shake off the very dust from your feet for a testimony against them. [6]And they departed, and went through the towns, preaching the gospel, and healing every where."

Luke 10:1-12 "[1]After these things the Lord appointed other seventy also, and sent them two and two before his face into every city and place, whither he himself would come. [2]Therefore said he unto them, The harvest truly is great, but the labourers are few: pray ye therefore the Lord of the harvest, that he would send forth labourers into his harvest. [3]Go your ways: behold, I send you forth as lambs among wolves. [4]Carry neither purse, nor scrip, nor shoes: and salute no man by the way. [5]And into whatsoever house ye enter, first say, Peace be to this house. [6]And if the son of peace be there, your peace shall rest upon it: if not, it shall turn to you again. [7]And in the same house remain, eating and drinking such things as they give: for the labourer is worthy of his hire. Go not from house to house. [8]And into whatsoever city ye enter,

and they receive you, eat such things as are set before you: [9]And heal the sick that are therein, and say unto them, The kingdom of God is come nigh unto you. [10]But into whatsoever city ye enter, and they receive you not, go your ways out into the streets of the same, and say, [11]Even the very dust of your city, which cleaveth on us, we do wipe off against you: notwithstanding be ye sure of this, that the kingdom of God is come nigh unto you. [12]But I say unto you, that it shall be more tolerable in that day for Sodom, than for that city."

Luke 24:44-49 "[44]And he said unto them, These are the words which I spake unto you, while I was yet with you, that all things must be fulfilled, which were written in the law of Moses, and in the prophets, and in the psalms, concerning me. [45]Then opened he their understanding, that they might understand the scriptures, [46]And said unto them, Thus it is written, and thus it behoved Christ to suffer, and to rise from the dead the third day: [47]And that repentance and remission of sins should be preached in his name among all nations, beginning at Jerusalem. [48]And ye are witnesses of these things. [49]And, behold, I send the promise of my Father upon you: but tarry ye in the city of Jerusalem, until ye be endued with power from on high."

1 Corinthians 1:12-17 "[12]Now this I say, that every one of you saith, I am of Paul; and I of Apollos; and I of Cephas; and I of Christ. [13]Is Christ divided? was Paul crucified for you? or were ye baptized in the name of Paul? [14]I thank God that I baptized none of you, but Crispus and Gaius; [15]Lest any should say that I had baptized in mine own name. [16]And I baptized also the household of Stephanas: besides, I know not whether I baptized any other. [17]For Christ sent me not to baptize, but to preach the gospel: not with wisdom of words, lest the cross of Christ should be made of none effect."

What The Disciples Are

Matthew 5:1-16 "[1]And seeing the multitudes, he went up into a mountain: and when he was set, his disciples came unto him: [2]And he opened his mouth, and taught them, saying, [3]Blessed are the poor in spirit: for theirs is the kingdom of heaven. [4]Blessed are they that mourn: for they shall be comforted. [5]Blessed are the meek: for they shall inherit the earth. 6Blessed are they which do hunger and thirst after righteousness: for they shall be filled. 7Blessed are the merciful: for they shall obtain mercy. 8Blessed are the pure in heart: for they shall see God. 9Blessed are the peacemakers: for they shall be called the children of God. 10Blessed are they which are persecuted for righteousness' sake: for theirs is the kingdom of heaven. 11Blessed are ye, when men shall revile you, and persecute you, and shall say all manner of evil against you falsely, for my sake. 12Rejoice, and be exceeding glad: for great is your reward in heaven: for so persecuted they the prophets which were before you. 13Ye are the salt of the earth: but if the salt have lost his savour, wherewith shall it be salted? it is thenceforth good for nothing, but to be cast out, and to be trodden under foot of men. 14Ye are the light of the world. A city that is set on an hill cannot be hid. 15Neither do men light a candle, and put it under a bushel, but on a candlestick; and it giveth light unto all that are in the house. 16Let your light so shine before men, that they may see your good works, and glorify your Father which is in heaven."

Matthew 12:46-50 "46While he yet talked to the people, behold, his mother and his brethren stood without, desiring to speak with him. 47Then one said unto him, Behold, thy mother and thy brethren stand without, desiring to speak with thee. 48But he answered and said unto him that told him, Who is my mother? and who are my brethren? 49And he stretched forth his hand toward his disciples, and said, Behold my mother and my brethren! 50For whosoever shall do the will of my Father which is in heaven, the same is my brother, and sister, and mother."

Matthew 16:17-18 "17And Jesus answered and said unto him, Blessed art thou, Simon Barjona: for flesh and blood hath not revealed it unto thee, but my Father which is in heaven. 18And I say also unto thee, That thou art Peter, and upon this rock I will build my church; and the gates of hell shall not prevail against it."

Mark 3:31-35 "31There came then his brethren and his mother, and, standing without, sent unto him, calling him. 32And the multitude sat about him, and they said unto him, Behold, thy mother and thy brethren without seek for thee. 33And he answered them, saying, Who is my mother, or my brethren? 34And he looked round about on them which sat about him, and said, Behold my mother and my brethren! 35For whosoever shall do the will of God, the same is my brother, and my sister, and mother."

1 Corinthians 4:9-13 "9For I think that God hath set forth us the apostles last, as it were appointed to death: for we are made a spectacle unto the world, and to angels, and to men. 10We are fools for Christ's sake, but ye are wise in Christ; we are weak, but ye are strong; ye are honourable, but we are despised. 11Even unto this present hour we both hunger, and thirst, and are naked, and are buffeted, and have no certain dwellingplace; 12And labour, working with our own hands: being reviled, we bless; being persecuted, we suffer it: 13Being defamed, we intreat: we are made as the filth of the world, and are the offscouring of all things unto this day."

Ephesians 2:19-20 "19Now therefore ye are no more strangers and foreigners, but fellowcitizens with the saints, and of the household of God; 20And are built upon the foundation of the apostles and prophets, Jesus Christ himself being the chief corner stone."

Revelation 21:14 "And the wall of the city had twelve foundations, and in them the names of the twelve apostles of the Lamb."

What The Disciples Know

Matthew 13:10-11 "10And the disciples came, and said unto him, Why speakest thou unto them in parables? 11He answered and said unto them, Because it is given unto you to know the mysteries of the kingdom of heaven, but to them it is not given."

Mark 4:10-11 "10And when he was alone, they that were about him with the twelve asked of him the parable. 11And he said unto them, Unto you it is given to know the mystery of the kingdom of God: but unto them that are without, all these things are done in parables."

Luke 8:9-10 "9And his disciples asked him, saying, What might this parable be? 10And he said, Unto you it is given to know the mysteries of the kingdom of God: but to others in parables; that seeing they might not see, and hearing they might not understand."

John 13:5-9 "⁵After that he poureth water into a bason, and began to wash the disciples' feet, and to wipe them with the towel wherewith he was girded. ⁶Then cometh he to Simon Peter: and Peter saith unto him, Lord, dost thou wash my feet? ⁷Jesus answered and said unto him, What I do thou knowest not now; but thou shalt know hereafter. ⁸Peter saith unto him, Thou shalt never wash my feet. Jesus answered him, If I wash thee not, thou hast no part with me. ⁹Simon Peter saith unto him, Lord, not my feet only, but also my hands and my head."

Ephesians 3:1-6 "¹For this cause I Paul, the prisoner of Jesus Christ for you Gentiles, ²If ye have heard of the dispensation of the grace of God which is given me to youward: ³How that by revelation he made known unto me the mystery; (as I wrote afore in few words, ⁴Whereby, when ye read, ye may understand my knowledge in the mystery of Christ) ⁵Which in other ages was not made known unto the sons of men, as it is now revealed unto his holy apostles and prophets by the Spirit; ⁶That the Gentiles should be fellowheirs, and of the same body, and partakers of his promise in Christ by the gospel."

What Was Done By The Apostles
Acts 2:43 "And fear came upon every soul: and many wonders and signs were done by the apostles."

Who Cannot Be A Disciple Of Christ
Matthew 10:32-37 "³²Whosoever therefore shall confess me before men, him will I confess also before my Father which is in heaven. ³³But whosoever shall deny me before men, him will I also deny before my Father which is in heaven. ³⁴Think not that I am come to send peace on earth: I came not to send peace, but a sword. ³⁵For I am come to set a man at variance against his father, and the daughter against her mother, and the daughter in law against her mother in law. ³⁶And a man's foes shall be they of his own household. ³⁷He that loveth father or mother more than me is not worthy of me: and he that loveth son or daughter more than me is not worthy of me."

Luke 14:25-33 "²⁵And there went great multitudes with him: and he turned, and said unto them, ²⁶If any man come to me, and hate not his father, and mother, and wife, and children, and brethren, and sisters, yea, and his own life also, he cannot be my disciple. ²⁷And whosoever doth not bear his cross, and come after me, cannot be my disciple. ²⁸For which of you, intending to build a tower, sitteth not down first, and counteth the cost, whether he have sufficient to finish it? ²⁹Lest haply, after he hath laid the foundation, and is not able to finish it, all that behold it begin to mock him, ³⁰Saying, This man began to build, and was not able to finish. ³¹Or what king, going to make war against another king, sitteth not down first, and consulteth whether he be able with ten thousand to meet him that cometh against him with twenty thousand? ³²Or else, while the other is yet a great way off, he sendeth an ambassage, and desireth conditions of peace. ³³So likewise, whosoever he be of you that forsaketh not all that he hath, he cannot be my disciple."

Who Is A Disciple Of Christ
John 8:31 "Then said Jesus to those Jews which believed on him, If ye continue in my word, then are ye my disciples indeed."

John 13:31-35 "³¹Therefore, when he was gone out, Jesus said, Now is the Son of man glorified, and God is glorified in him. ³²If God be glorified in him, God shall also glorify him in himself, and shall straightway glorify him. ³³Little children, yet a little while I am with you. Ye shall seek me: and as I said unto the Jews, Whither I go, ye cannot come; so now I say to you. ³⁴A new commandment I give unto you, That ye love one another; as I have loved you, that ye also love one another. ³⁵By this shall all men know that ye are my disciples, if ye have love one to another."

John 15:1-8 "¹I am the true vine, and my Father is the husbandman. ²Every branch in me that beareth not fruit he taketh away: and every branch that beareth fruit, he purgeth it, that it may bring forth more fruit. ³Now ye are clean through the word which I have spoken unto you. ⁴Abide in me, and I in you. As the branch cannot bear fruit of itself, except it abide in the vine; no more can ye, except ye abide in me. ⁵I am the vine, ye are the branches: He that abideth in me, and I in him, the same bringeth forth much fruit: for without me ye can do nothing. ⁶If a man abide not in me, he is cast forth as a branch, and is withered; and men gather them, and cast them into the fire, and they are burned. ⁷If ye abide in me, and my words abide in you, ye shall ask what ye will, and it shall be done unto you. [8]Herein is my Father glorified, that ye bear much fruit; so shall ye be my disciples."

Who Is A False Apostle

2 Corinthians 11:3-15 "[3]But I fear, lest by any means, as the serpent beguiled Eve through his subtilty, so your minds should be corrupted from the simplicity that is in Christ. [4]For if he that cometh preacheth another Jesus, whom we have not preached, or if ye receive another spirit, which ye have not received, or another gospel, which ye have not accepted, ye might well bear with him. [5]For I suppose I was not a whit behind the very chiefest apostles. [6]But though I be rude in speech, yet not in knowledge; but we have been throughly made manifest among you in all things. [7]Have I committed an offence in abasing myself that ye might be exalted, because I have preached to you the gospel of God freely? [8]I robbed other churches, taking wages of them, to do you service. [9]And when I was present with you, and wanted, I was chargeable to no man: for that which was lacking to me the brethren which came from Macedonia supplied: and in all things I have kept myself from being burdensome unto you, and so will I keep myself. [10]As the truth of Christ is in me, no man shall stop me of this boasting in the regions of Achaia. [11]Wherefore? because I love you not? God knoweth. [12]But what I do, that I will do, that I may cut off occasion from them which desire occasion; that wherein they glory, they may be found even as we. [13]For such are false apostles, deceitful workers, transforming themselves into the apostles of Christ. [14]And no marvel; for Satan himself is transformed into an angel of light. [15]Therefore it is no great thing if his ministers also be transformed as the ministers of righteousness; whose end shall be according to their works."

Who The Disciple Is Not Greater Than

Matthew 10:24-25 "[24]The disciple is not above his master, nor the servant above his lord. [25]It is enough for the disciple that he be as his master, and the servant as his lord. If they have called the master of the house Beelzebub, how much more shall they call them of his household?"

Luke 6:40 "The disciple is not above his master: but every one that is perfect shall be as his master."

Why The World Hates Christ's Disciples

John 17:1-16 "[1]These words spake Jesus, and lifted up his eyes to heaven, and said, Father, the hour is come; glorify thy Son, that thy Son also may glorify thee: [2]As thou hast given him power over all flesh, that he should give eternal life to as many as thou hast given him. [3]And this is life eternal, that they might know thee the only true God, and Jesus Christ, whom thou hast sent. [4]I have glorified thee on the earth: I have finished the work which thou gavest me to do. [5]And now, O Father, glorify thou me with thine own self with the glory which I had with thee before the world was. [6]I have manifested thy name unto the men which thou gavest me out of the world: thine they were, and thou gavest them me; and they have kept thy word. [7]Now they have known that all things whatsoever thou hast given me are of thee. [8]For I have given unto them the words which thou gavest me; and they have received them, and have known surely that I came out from thee, and they have believed that thou didst send me. [9]I pray for them: I pray not for the world, but for them which thou hast given me; for they are thine. [10]And all mine are thine, and thine are mine; and I am glorified in them. [11]And now I am no more in the world, but these are in the world, and I come to thee. Holy Father, keep through thine own name those whom thou hast given me, that they may be one, as we are. [12]While I was with them in the world, I kept them in thy name: those that thou gavest me I have kept, and none of them is lost, but the son of perdition; that the scripture might be fulfilled. [13]And now come I to thee; and these things I speak in the world, that they might have my joy fulfilled in themselves. [14]I have given them thy word; and the world hath hated them, because they are not of the world, even as I am not of the world. [15]I pray not that thou shouldest take them out of the world, but that thou shouldest keep them from the evil. [16]They are not of the world, even as I am not of the world."

DISCORD

The Sowing Of Discord Among Brethren

Proverbs 6:16-19 "[16]These six things doth the LORD hate: yea, seven are an abomination unto him: [17]A proud look, a lying tongue, and hands that shed innocent blood, [18]An heart that deviseth wicked imaginations, feet that be swift in running to mischief, [19]A false witness that speaketh lies, and he that soweth discord among brethren."

DISHONESTY

Who Renounces The
Hidden Things Of Dishonesty

2 Corinthians 4:1-2 "[1]Therefore seeing we have this ministry, as we have received mercy, we faint not; [2]But have renounced the hidden things of dishonesty, not walking in craftiness, nor handling the word of God deceitfully; but by manifestation of the truth commending ourselves to every man's conscience in the sight of God."

DISHONOR

Who Dishonors God

Romans 2:21-24 "[21]Thou therefore which teachest another, teachest thou not thyself? thou that preachest a man should not steal, dost thou steal? [22]Thou that sayest a man should not commit adultery, dost thou commit adultery? thou that abhorrest idols, dost thou commit sacrilege? [23]Thou that makest thy boast of the law, through breaking the law dishonourest thou God? [24]For the name of God is blasphemed among the Gentiles through you, as it is written."

DISOBEDIENCE

The Reward For Being Disobedient To God

Genesis 3:1-24 "[1]Now the serpent was more subtil than any beast of the field which the LORD God had made. And he said unto the woman, Yea, hath God said, Ye shall not eat of every tree of the garden? [2]And the woman said unto the serpent, We may eat of the fruit of the trees of the garden: [3]But of the fruit of the tree which is in the midst of the garden, God hath said, Ye shall not eat of it, neither shall ye touch it, lest ye die. [4]And the serpent said unto the woman, Ye shall not surely die: [5]For God doth know that in the day ye eat thereof, then your eyes shall be opened, and ye shall be as gods, knowing good and evil. [6]And when the woman saw that the tree was good for food, and that it was pleasant to the eyes, and a tree to be desired to make one wise, she took of the fruit thereof, and did eat, and gave also unto her husband with her; and he did eat. [7]And the eyes of them both were opened, and they knew that they were naked; and they sewed fig leaves together, and made themselves aprons. [8]And they heard the voice of the LORD God walking in the garden in the cool of the day: and Adam and his wife hid themselves from the presence of the LORD God amongst the trees of the garden. [9]And the LORD God called unto Adam, and said unto him, Where art thou? [10]And he said, I heard thy voice in the garden, and I was afraid, because I was naked; and I hid myself. [11]And he said, Who told thee that thou wast naked? Hast thou eaten of the tree, whereof I commanded thee that thou shouldest not eat? [12]And the man said, The woman whom thou gavest to be with me, she gave me of the tree, and I did eat. [13]And the LORD God said unto the woman, What is this that thou hast done? And the woman said, The serpent beguiled me, and I did eat. [14]And the LORD God said unto the serpent, Because thou hast done this, thou art cursed above all cattle, and above every beast of the field; upon thy belly shalt thou go, and dust shalt thou eat all the days of thy life: [15]And I will put enmity between thee and the woman, and between thy seed and her seed; it shall bruise thy head, and thou shalt bruise his heel. [16]Unto the woman he said, I will greatly multiply thy sorrow and thy conception; in sorrow thou shalt bring forth children; and thy desire shall be to thy husband, and he shall rule over thee. [17]And unto Adam he said, Because thou hast hearkened unto the voice of thy wife, and hast eaten of the tree, of which I commanded thee, saying, Thou shalt not eat of it: cursed is the ground for thy sake; in sorrow shalt thou eat of it all the days of thy life; [18]Thorns also and thistles shall it bring forth to thee; and thou shalt eat the herb of the field; [19]In the sweat of thy face shalt thou eat bread, till thou return unto the ground; for out of it wast thou taken: for dust thou art, and unto dust shalt thou return. [20]And Adam called his wife's name Eve; because she was the mother of all living. [21]Unto Adam also and to his wife did the LORD God make coats of skins, and clothed them. [22]And the LORD God said, Behold, the man is become as one of us, to know good and evil: and now, lest he put forth his hand, and take also of the tree of life, and eat, and live for ever:

²³Therefore the LORD God sent him forth from the garden of Eden, to till the ground from whence he was taken. ²⁴So he drove out the man; and he placed at the east of the garden of Eden Cherubims, and a flaming sword which turned every way, to keep the way of the tree of life."

Leviticus 20:22-24 "²²Ye shall therefore keep all my statutes, and all my judgments, and do them: that the land, whither I bring you to dwell therein, spue you not out. ²³And ye shall not walk in the manners of the nation, which I cast out before you: for they committed all these things, and therefore I abhorred them. ²⁴But I have said unto you, Ye shall inherit their land, and I will give it unto you to possess it, a land that floweth with milk and honey: I am the LORD your God, which have separated you from other people."

Leviticus 26:13-39 "¹³I am the LORD your God, which brought you forth out of the land of Egypt, that ye should not be their bondmen; and I have broken the bands of your yoke, and made you go upright. ¹⁴But if ye will not hearken unto me, and will not do all these commandments; ¹⁵And if ye shall despise my statutes, or if your soul abhor my judgments, so that ye will not do all my commandments, but that ye break my covenant: ¹⁶I also will do this unto you; I will even appoint over you terror, consumption, and the burning ague, that shall consume the eyes, and cause sorrow of heart: and ye shall sow your seed in vain, for your enemies shall eat it. ¹⁷And I will set my face against you, and ye shall be slain before your enemies: they that hate you shall reign over you; and ye shall flee when none pursueth you. ¹⁸And if ye will not yet for all this hearken unto me, then I will punish you seven times more for your sins. ¹⁹And I will break the pride of your power; and I will make your heaven as iron, and your earth as brass: ²⁰And your strength shall be spent in vain: for your land shall not yield her increase, neither shall the trees of the land yield their fruits. ²¹And if ye walk contrary unto me, and will not hearken unto me; I will bring seven times more plagues upon you according to your sins. ²²I will also send wild beasts among you, which shall rob you of your children, and destroy your cattle, and make you few in number; and

your highways shall be desolate. ²³And if ye will not be reformed by me by these things, but will walk contrary unto me; ²⁴Then will I also walk contrary unto you, and will punish you yet seven times for your sins. ²⁵And I will bring a sword upon you, that shall avenge the quarrel of my covenant: and when ye are gathered together within your cities, I will send the pestilence among you; and ye shall be delivered into the hand of the enemy. ²⁶And when I have broken the staff of your bread, ten women shall bake your bread in one oven, and they shall deliver you your bread again by weight: and ye shall eat, and not be satisfied. ²⁷And if ye will not for all this hearken unto me, but walk contrary unto me; ²⁸Then I will walk contrary unto you also in fury; and I, even I, will chastise you seven times for your sins. ²⁹And ye shall eat the flesh of your sons, and the flesh of your daughters shall ye eat. ³⁰And I will destroy your high places, and cut down your images, and cast your carcases upon the carcases of your idols, and my soul shall abhor you. ³¹And I will make your cities waste, and bring your sanctuaries unto desolation, and I will not smell the savour of your sweet odours. ³²And I will bring the land into desolation: and your enemies which dwell therein shall be astonished at it. ³³And I will scatter you among the heathen, and will draw out a sword after you: and your land shall be desolate, and your cities waste. ³⁴Then shall the land enjoy her sabbaths, as long as it lieth desolate, and ye be in your enemies' land; even then shall the land rest, and enjoy her sabbaths. ³⁵As long as it lieth desolate it shall rest; because it did not rest in your sabbaths, when ye dwelt upon it. ³⁶And upon them that are left alive of you I will send a faintness into their hearts in the lands of their enemies; and the sound of a shaken leaf shall chase them; and they shall flee, as fleeing from a sword; and they shall fall when none pursueth. ³⁷And they shall fall one upon another, as it were before a sword, when none pursueth: and ye shall have no power to stand before your enemies. ³⁸And ye shall perish among the heathen, and the land of your enemies shall eat you up. ³⁹And they that are left of you shall pine away in their iniquity in your enemies' lands; and also in the iniquities of their fathers shall they pine away with them."

Numbers 15:30-31 "³⁰But the soul that doeth ought presumptuously, whether he be born in the land, or a stranger, the same reproacheth the LORD; and that soul shall be cut off from among his people. ³¹Because he hath despised the word of the LORD, and hath broken his commandment, that soul shall utterly be cut off; his iniquity shall be upon him."

Deuteronomy 4:3 "Your eyes have seen what the LORD did because of Baal-peor: for all the men that followed Baal-peor, the LORD thy God hath destroyed them from among you."

Deuteronomy 8:19-20 "¹⁹And it shall be, if thou do at all forget the LORD thy God, and walk after other gods, and serve them, and worship them, I testify against you this day that ye shall surely perish. ²⁰As the nations which the LORD destroyeth before your face, so shall ye perish; because ye would not be obedient unto the voice of the LORD your God."

Deuteronomy 11:26-28 "²⁶Behold, I set before you this day a blessing and a curse; ²⁷A blessing, if ye obey the commandments of the LORD your God, which I command you this day: ²⁸And a curse, if ye will not obey the commandments of the LORD your God, but turn aside out of the way which I command you this day, to go after other gods, which ye have not known."

Deuteronomy 28:15-62 "¹⁵But it shall come to pass, if thou wilt not hearken unto the voice of the LORD thy God, to observe to do all his commandments and his statutes which I command thee this day; that all these curses shall come upon thee, and overtake thee: ¹⁶Cursed shalt thou be in the city, and cursed shalt thou be in the field. ¹⁷Cursed shall be thy basket and thy store. ¹⁸Cursed shall be the fruit of thy body, and the fruit of thy land, the increase of thy kine, and the flocks of thy sheep. ¹⁹Cursed shalt thou be when thou comest in, and cursed shalt thou be when thou goest out. ²⁰The LORD shall send upon thee cursing, vexation, and rebuke, in all that thou settest thine hand unto for to do, until thou be destroyed, and until thou perish quickly; because of the wickedness of thy doings, whereby thou hast forsaken me. ²¹The LORD shall make the pestilence cleave unto thee, until he have consumed thee from off the land, whither thou goest to possess it. ²²The LORD shall smite thee with a consumption, and with a fever, and with an inflammation, and with an extreme burning, and with the sword, and with blasting, and with mildew; and they shall pursue thee until thou perish. ²³And thy heaven that is over thy head shall be brass, and the earth that is under thee shall be iron. ²⁴The LORD shall make the rain of thy land powder and dust: from heaven shall it come down upon thee, until thou be destroyed. ²⁵The LORD shall cause thee to be smitten before thine enemies: thou shalt go out one way against them, and flee seven ways before them: and shalt be removed into all the kingdoms of the earth. ²⁶And thy carcase shall be meat unto all fowls of the air, and unto the beasts of the earth, and no man shall fray them away. ²⁷The LORD will smite thee with the botch of Egypt, and with the emerods, and with the scab, and with the itch, whereof thou canst not be healed. ²⁸The LORD shall smite thee with madness, and blindness, and astonishment of heart: ²⁹And thou shalt grope at noonday, as the blind gropeth in darkness, and thou shalt not prosper in thy ways: and thou shalt be only oppressed and spoiled evermore, and no man shall save thee. ³⁰Thou shalt betroth a wife, and another man shall lie with her: thou shalt build an house, and thou shalt not dwell therein: thou shalt plant a vineyard, and shalt not gather the grapes thereof. ³¹Thine ox shall be slain before thine eyes, and thou shalt not eat thereof: thine ass shall be violently taken away from before thy face, and shall not be restored to thee: thy sheep shall be given unto thine enemies, and thou shalt have none to rescue them. ³²Thy sons and thy daughters shall be given unto another people, and thine eyes shall look, and fail with longing for them all the day long: and there shall be no might in thine hand. ³³The fruit of thy land, and all thy labours, shall a nation which thou knowest not eat up; and thou shalt be only oppressed and crushed alway: ³⁴So that thou shalt be mad for the sight of thine eyes which thou shalt see. ³⁵The LORD shall smite thee in the knees, and in the legs, with a sore botch that cannot be healed, from the sole of thy foot unto the top of thy head. ³⁶The LORD shall bring thee, and thy king which thou shalt set over thee, unto a nation which neither thou nor thy fathers have known;

and there shalt thou serve other gods, wood and stone. ³⁷And thou shalt become an astonishment, a proverb, and a byword, among all nations whither the LORD shall lead thee. ³⁸Thou shalt carry much seed out into the field, and shalt gather but little in; for the locust shall consume it. ³⁹Thou shalt plant vineyards, and dress them, but shalt neither drink of the wine, nor gather the grapes; for the worms shall eat them. ⁴⁰Thou shalt have olive trees throughout all thy coasts, but thou shalt not anoint thyself with the oil; for thine olive shall cast his fruit. ⁴¹Thou shalt beget sons and daughters, but thou shalt not enjoy them; for they shall go into captivity. ⁴²All thy trees and fruit of thy land shall the locust consume. ⁴³The stranger that is within thee shall get up above thee very high; and thou shalt come down very low. ⁴⁴He shall lend to thee, and thou shalt not lend to him: he shall be the head, and thou shalt be the tail. ⁴⁵Moreover all these curses shall come upon thee, and shall pursue thee, and overtake thee, till thou be destroyed; because thou hearkenedst not unto the voice of the LORD thy God, to keep his commandments and his statutes which he commanded thee: ⁴⁶And they shall be upon thee for a sign and for a wonder, and upon thy seed for ever. ⁴⁷Because thou servedst not the LORD thy God with joyfulness, and with gladness of heart, for the abundance of all things; ⁴⁸Therefore shalt thou serve thine enemies which the LORD shall send against thee, in hunger, and in thirst, and in nakedness, and in want of all things: and he shall put a yoke of iron upon thy neck, until he have destroyed thee. ⁴⁹The LORD shall bring a nation against thee from far, from the end of the earth, as swift as the eagle flieth; a nation whose tongue thou shalt not understand; ⁵⁰A nation of fierce countenance, which shall not regard the person of the old, nor shew favour to the young: ⁵¹And he shall eat the fruit of thy cattle, and the fruit of thy land, until thou be destroyed: which also shall not leave thee either corn, wine, or oil, or the increase of thy kine, or flocks of thy sheep, until he have destroyed thee. ⁵²And he shall besiege thee in all thy gates, until thy high and fenced walls come down, wherein thou trustedst, throughout all thy land: and he shall besiege thee in all thy gates throughout all thy land, which the LORD thy God hath given thee. ⁵³And thou shalt eat the fruit of thine own body, the flesh of thy sons and of thy daughters, which the LORD thy God hath given thee, in the siege, and in the straitness, wherewith thine enemies shall distress thee: ⁵⁴So that the man that is tender among you, and very delicate, his eye shall be evil toward his brother, and toward the wife of his bosom, and toward the remnant of his children which he shall leave: ⁵⁵So that he will not give to any of them of the flesh of his children whom he shall eat: because he hath nothing left him in the siege, and in the straitness, wherewith thine enemies shall distress thee in all thy gates. ⁵⁶The tender and delicate woman among you, which would not adventure to set the sole of her foot upon the ground for delicateness and tenderness, her eye shall be evil toward the husband of her bosom, and toward her son, and toward her daughter, ⁵⁷And toward her young one that cometh out from between her feet, and toward her children which she shall bear: for she shall eat them for want of all things secretly in the siege and straitness, wherewith thine enemy shall distress thee in thy gates. ⁵⁸If thou wilt not observe to do all the words of this law that are written in this book, that thou mayest fear this glorious and fearful name, THE LORD THY GOD; ⁵⁹Then the LORD will make thy plagues wonderful, and the plagues of thy seed, even great plagues, and of long continuance, and sore sicknesses, and of long continuance. ⁶⁰Moreover he will bring upon thee all the diseases of Egypt, which thou wast afraid of; and they shall cleave unto thee. ⁶¹Also every sickness, and every plague, which is not written in the book of this law, them will the LORD bring upon thee, until thou be destroyed. ⁶²And ye shall be left few in number, whereas ye were as the stars of heaven for multitude; because thou wouldest not obey the voice of the LORD thy God."

Deuteronomy 30:15-20 "¹⁵See, I have set before thee this day life and good, and death and evil; ¹⁶In that I command thee this day to love the LORD thy God, to walk in his ways, and to keep his commandments and his statutes and his judgments, that thou mayest live and multiply: and the LORD thy God shall bless thee in the land whither thou goest to possess it. ¹⁷But if thine heart turn away, so that thou wilt not hear, but shalt be drawn away, and worship other gods, and serve them; ¹⁸I denounce unto you this day, that ye shall surely perish, and that ye shall not prolong your days upon the land, whither thou passest over Jordan to go to possess it. [19]I call heaven and earth to record this day against you, that I have set before you life and death, blessing and cursing: therefore choose life, that both thou and thy seed may live: [20]That thou mayest love the LORD thy God, and that thou mayest obey his voice, and that thou mayest cleave unto him: for he is thy life, and the length of thy days: that thou mayest dwell in the land which the LORD sware unto thy fathers, to Abraham, to Isaac, and to Jacob, to give them."

Judges 2:1-3 "[1]And an angel of the LORD came up from Gilgal to Bochim, and said, I made you to go up out of Egypt, and have brought you unto the land which I sware unto your fathers; and I said, I will never break my covenant with you. [2]And ye shall make no league with the inhabitants of this land; ye shall throw down their altars: but ye have not obeyed my voice: why have ye done this? [3]Wherefore I also said, I will not drive them out from before you; but they shall be as thorns in your sides, and their gods shall be a snare unto you."

Judges 2:20-23 "[20]And the anger of the LORD was hot against Israel; and he said, Because that this people hath transgressed my covenant which I commanded their fathers, and have not hearkened unto my voice; [21]I also will not henceforth drive out any from before them of the nations which Joshua left when he died: [22]That through them I may prove Israel, whether they will keep the way of the LORD to walk therein, as their fathers did keep it, or not. [23]Therefore the LORD left those nations, without driving them out hastily; neither delivered he them into the hand of Joshua."

1 Samuel 12:15 "But if ye will not obey the voice of the LORD, but rebel against the commandment of the LORD, then shall the hand of the LORD be against you, as it was against your fathers."

1 Samuel 13:13-14 "[13]And Samuel said to Saul, Thou hast done foolishly: thou hast not kept the commandment of the LORD thy God, which he commanded thee: for now would the LORD have established thy kingdom upon Israel for ever. [14]But now thy kingdom shall not continue: the LORD hath sought him a man after his own heart, and the LORD hath commanded him to be captain over his people, because thou hast not kept that which the LORD commanded thee."

1 Samuel 15:23 "For rebellion is as the sin of witchcraft, and stubbornness is as iniquity and idolatry. Because thou hast rejected the word of the LORD, he hath also rejected thee from being king."

1 Samuel 28:17-18 "[17]And the LORD hath done to him, as he spake by me: for the LORD hath rent the kingdom out of thine hand, and given it to thy neighbour, even to David: [18]Because thou obeyedst not the voice of the LORD, nor executedst his fierce wrath upon Amalek, therefore hath the LORD done this thing unto thee this day."

1 Kings 9:6-9 "[6]But if ye shall at all turn from following me, ye or your children, and will not keep my commandments and my statutes which I have set before you, but go and serve other gods, and worship them: [7]Then will I cut off Israel out of the land which I have given them; and this house, which I have hallowed for my name, will I cast out of my sight; and Israel shall be a proverb and a byword among all people: [8]And at this house, which is high, every one that passeth by it shall be astonished, and shall hiss; and they shall say, Why hath the LORD done thus unto this land, and to this house? [9]And they shall answer, Because they forsook the LORD their God, who brought forth their fathers out of the land of Egypt, and have taken hold upon other gods, and have worshipped them, and served them: therefore hath the LORD brought upon them all this evil."

1 Kings 11:31-37 "[31]And he said to Jeroboam, Take thee ten pieces: for thus saith the LORD, the God of Israel, Behold, I will rend the kingdom out of the hand of Solomon, and will give ten tribes to thee: [32](But he shall have one tribe for my servant David's sake, and for Jerusalem's sake, the city which I have chosen out of all the tribes of Israel:) [33]Because that they have forsaken me, and have worshipped Ashtoreth the goddess of the Zidonians, Chemosh the god of the Moabites, and Milcom the god of the children of Ammon, and have not walked in my ways, to do that which is right in mine eyes, and to keep my statutes and my judgments, as did David his father. [34]Howbeit I will not take the whole kingdom out of his hand: but I will make him prince all the days of his life for David my servant's sake, whom I chose, because he kept my commandments and my statutes: ³⁵But I will take the kingdom out of his son's hand, and will give it unto thee, even ten tribes. ³⁶And unto his son will I give one tribe, that David my servant may have a light alway before me in Jerusalem, the city which I have chosen me to put my name there. ³⁷And I will take thee, and thou shalt reign according to all that thy soul desireth, and shalt be king over Israel."

2 Kings 17:7-23 "⁷For so it was, that the children of Israel had sinned against the LORD their God, which had brought them up out of the land of Egypt, from under the hand of Pharoah king of Egypt, and had feared other gods, ⁸And walked in the statutes of the heathen, whom the LORD cast out from before the children of Israel, and of the kings of Israel, which they had made. ⁹And the children of Israel did secretly those things that were not right against the LORD their God, and they built them high places in all their cities, from the tower of the watchmen to the fenced city. ¹⁰And they set them up images and groves in every high hill, and under every green tree: ¹¹And there they burnt incense in all the high places, as did the heathen whom the LORD carried away before them; and wrought wicked things to provoke the LORD to anger: ¹²For they served idols, whereof the LORD had said unto them, Ye shall not do this thing. ¹³Yet the LORD testified against Israel, and against Judah, by all the prophets, and by all the seers, saying, Turn ye from your evil ways, and keep my commandments and my statutes, according to all the law which I commanded your fathers, and which I sent to you by my servants the prophets. ¹⁴Notwithstanding they would not hear, but hardened their necks, like to the neck of their fathers, that did not believe in the LORD their God. ¹⁵And they rejected his statutes, and his covenant that he made with their fathers, and his testimonies which he testified against them; and they followed vanity, and became vain, and went after the heathen that were round about them, concerning whom the LORD had charged them, that they should not do like them. ¹⁶And they left all the commandments of the LORD their God, and made them molten images, even two calves, and made a grove, and

worshipped all the host of heaven, and served Baal. ¹⁷And they caused their sons and their daughters to pass through the fire, and used divination and enchantments, and sold themselves to do evil in the sight of the LORD, to provoke him to anger. ¹⁸Therefore the LORD was very angry with Israel, and removed them out of his sight: there was none left but the tribe of Judah only. ¹⁹Also Judah kept not the commandments of the LORD their God, but walked in the statutes of Israel which they made. ²⁰And the LORD rejected all the seed of Israel, and afflicted them, and delivered them into the hand of spoilers, until he had cast them out of his sight. ²¹For he rent Israel from the house of David; and they made Jeroboam the son of Nebat king: and Jeroboam drave Israel from following the LORD, and made them sin a great sin. ²²For the children of Israel walked in all the sins of Jeroboam which he did; they departed not from them; ²³Until the LORD removed Israel out of his sight, as he had said by all his servants the prophets. So was Israel carried away out of their own land to Assyria unto this day."

2 Kings 18:11-12 "¹¹And the king of Assyria did carry away Israel unto Assyria, and put them in Halah and in Habor by the river of Gozan, and in the cities of the Medes: ¹²Because they obeyed not the voice of the LORD their God, but transgressed his covenant, and all that Moses the servant of the LORD commanded, and would not hear them, nor do them."

2 Kings 22:13 "Go ye, inquire of the LORD for me, and for the people, and for all Judah, concerning the words of this book that is found: for great is the wrath of the LORD that is kindled against us, because our fathers have not hearkened unto the words of this book, to do according unto all that which is written concerning us."

1 Chronicles 10:13-14 "¹³So Saul died for his transgression which he committed against the LORD, even against the word of the LORD, which he kept not, and also for asking counsel of one that had a familiar spirit, to inquire of it; ¹⁴And inquired not of the LORD: therefore he slew him, and turned the kingdom unto David the son of Jesse."

2 Chronicles 24:20 "And the Spirit of God came upon Zechariah the son of Jehoiada the priest, which stood above the people, and said unto them, Thus saith God, Why transgress ye the commandments of the LORD, that ye cannot prosper? because ye have forsaken the LORD, he hath also forsaken you."

2 Chronicles 30:7 "And be not ye like your fathers, and like your brethren, which trespassed against the LORD God of their fathers, who therefore gave them up to desolation, as ye see."

2 Chronicles 33:10-11 "10And the LORD spake to Manasseh, and to his people: but they would not hearken. 11Wherefore the LORD brought upon them the captains of the host of the king of Assyria, which took Manasseh among the thorns, and bound him with fetters, and carried him to Babylon."

2 Chronicles 34:21 "Go, inquire of the LORD for me, and for them that are left in Israel and in Judah, concerning the words of the book that is found: for great is the wrath of the LORD that is poured out upon us, because our fathers have not kept the word of the LORD, to do after all that is written in this book."

Nehemiah 1:5-8 "5And said, I beseech thee, O LORD God of heaven, the great and terrible God, that keepeth covenant and mercy for them that love him and observe his commandments: 6Let thine ear now be attentive, and thine eyes open, that thou mayest hear the prayer of thy servant, which I pray before thee now, day and night, for the children of Israel thy servants, and confess the sins of the children of Israel, which we have sinned against thee: both I and my father's house have sinned. 7We have dealt very corruptly against thee, and have not kept the commandments, nor the statutes, nor the judgments, which thou commandedst thy servant Moses. 8Remember, I beseech thee, the word that thou commandedst thy servant Moses, saying, If ye transgress, I will scatter you abroad among the nations."

Nehemiah 9:26-31 "26Nevertheless they were disobedient, and rebelled against thee, and cast thy law behind their backs, and slew thy prophets which testified against them to turn them to thee, and they wrought great provocations. 27Therefore thou deliveredst them into the hand of their enemies, who vexed them: and in the time of their trouble, when they cried unto thee, thou heardest them from heaven; and according to thy manifold mercies thou gavest them saviours, who saved them out of the hand of their enemies. 28But after they had rest, they did evil again before thee: therefore leftest thou them in the hand of their enemies, so that they had the dominion over them: yet when they returned, and cried unto thee, thou heardest them from heaven; and many times didst thou deliver them according to thy mercies; 29And testifiedst against them, that thou mightest bring them again unto thy law: yet they dealt proudly, and hearkened not unto thy commandments, but sinned against thy judgments, (which if a man do, he shall live in them;) and withdrew the shoulder, and hardened their neck, and would not hear. 30Yet many years didst thou forbear them, and testifiedst against them by thy spirit in thy prophets: yet would they not give ear: therefore gavest thou them into the hand of the people of the lands. 31Nevertheless for thy great mercies' sake thou didst not utterly consume them, nor forsake them; for thou art a gracious and merciful God."

Job 36:5-12 "5Behold, God is mighty, and despiseth not any: he is mighty in strength and wisdom. 6He preserveth not the life of the wicked: but giveth right to the poor. 7He withdraweth not his eyes from the righteous: but with kings are they on the throne; yea, he doth establish them for ever, and they are exalted. 8And if they be bound in fetters, and be holden in cords of affliction; 9Then he sheweth them their work, and their transgressions that they have exceeded. 10He openeth also their ear to discipline, and commandeth that they return from iniquity. 11If they obey and serve him, they shall spend their days in prosperity, and their years in pleasures. 12But if they obey not, they shall perish by the sword, and they shall die without knowledge."

Psalm 81:10-12 "10I am the LORD thy God, which brought thee out of the land of Egypt: open thy mouth wide, and I will fill it. 11But my people would not hearken to my voice; and Israel would none of me. 12So I gave them up unto their own hearts' lust: and they walked in their own counsels."

Psalm 89:26-32 "26He shall cry unto me, Thou art my father, my God, and the rock of my salvation.

27Also I will make him my firstborn, higher than the kings of the earth. 28My mercy will I keep for him for evermore, and my covenant shall stand fast with him. 29His seed also will I make to endure for ever, and his throne as the days of heaven. 30If his children forsake my law, and walk not in my judgments; 31If they break my statutes, and keep not my commandments; 32Then will I visit their transgression with the rod, and their iniquity with stripes."

Psalm 106:24-27 "24Yea, they despised the pleasant land, they believed not his word: 25But murmured in their tents, and hearkened not unto the voice of the LORD. 26Therefore he lifted up his hand against them, to overthrow them in the wilderness: 27To overthrow their seed also among the nations, and to scatter them in the lands."

Isaiah 1:20 "But if ye refuse and rebel, ye shall be devoured with the sword: for the mouth of the LORD hath spoken it."

Isaiah 5:24 "Therefore as the fire devoureth the stubble, and the flame consumeth the chaff, so their root shall be as rottenness, and their blossom shall go up as dust: because they have cast away the law of the LORD of hosts, and despised the word of the Holy One of Israel."

Isaiah 24:5 "The earth also is defiled under the inhabitants thereof; because they have transgressed the laws, changed the ordinance, broken the everlasting covenant."

Isaiah 30:8-17 "8Now go, write it before them in a table, and note it in a book, that it may be for the time to come for ever and ever: 9That this is a rebellious people, lying children, children that will not hear the law of the LORD: 10Which say to the seers, See not; and to the prophets, Prophesy not unto us right things, speak unto us smooth things, prophesy deceits: 11Get you out of the way, turn aside out of the path, cause the Holy One of Israel to cease from before us. 12Wherefore thus saith the Holy One of Israel, Because ye despise this word, and trust in oppression and perverseness, and stay thereon: 13Therefore this iniquity shall be to you as a breach ready to fall, swelling out in a high wall, whose breaking cometh suddenly at an instant. 14And he shall break it as the breaking of the potters' vessel that is broken in pieces; he shall not spare: so that there shall not be found in

the bursting of it a sherd to take fire from the hearth, or to take water withal out of the pit. 15For thus saith the Lord GOD, the Holy One of Israel; In returning and rest shall ye be saved; in quietness and in confidence shall be your strength: and ye would not. 16But ye said, No; for we will flee upon horses; therefore shall ye flee: and, We will ride upon the swift; therefore shall they that pursue you be swift. 17One thousand shall flee at the rebuke of one; at the rebuke of five shall ye flee: till ye be left as a beacon upon the top of a mountain, and as an ensign on an hill."

Isaiah 43:22-28 "22But thou hast not called upon me, O Jacob; but thou hast been weary of me, O Israel. 23Thou hast not brought me the small cattle of thy burnt offerings; neither hast thou honoured me with thy sacrifices. I have not caused thee to serve with an offering, nor wearied thee with incense. 24Thou hast bought me no sweet cane with money, neither hast thou filled me with the fat of thy sacrifices: but thou hast made me to serve with thy sins, thou hast wearied me with thine iniquities. 25I, even I, am he that blotteth out thy transgressions for mine own sake, and will not remember thy sins. 26Put me in remembrance: let us plead together: declare thou, that thou mayest be justified. 27Thy first father hath sinned, and thy teachers have transgressed against me. 28Therefore I have profaned the princes of the sanctuary, and have given Jacob to the curse, and Israel to reproaches."

Isaiah 65:11-15 "11But ye are they that forsake the LORD, that forget my holy mountain, that prepare a table for that troop, and that furnish the drink offering unto that number. 12Therefore will I number you to the sword, and ye shall all bow down to the slaughter: because when I called, ye did not answer; when I spake, ye did not hear; but did evil before mine eyes, and did choose that wherein I delighted not. 13Therefore thus saith the Lord GOD, Behold, my servants shall eat, but ye shall be hungry: behold, my servants shall drink, but ye shall be thirsty: behold, my servants shall rejoice, but ye shall be ashamed: 14Behold, my servants shall sing for joy of heart, but ye shall cry for sorrow of heart, and shall howl for vexation of spirit. 15And ye shall leave your name for a curse unto my chosen: for the Lord GOD shall slay thee, and call his servants by another name."

Isaiah 66:1-4 "¹Thus saith the LORD, The heaven is my throne, and the earth is my footstool: where is the house that ye build unto me? and where is the place of my rest? ²For all those things hath mine hand made, and those things have been, saith the LORD: but to this man will I look, even to him that is poor and of a contrite spirit, and trembleth at my word. ³He that killeth an ox is as if he slew a man; he that sacrificeth a lamb, as if he cut off a dog's neck; he that offereth an oblation, as if he offered swine's blood; he that burneth incense, as if he blessed an idol. Yea, they have chosen their own ways, and their soul delighteth in their abominations. ⁴I also will choose their delusions, and will bring their fears upon them; because when I called, none did answer; when I spake, they did not hear: but they did evil before mine eyes, and chose that in which I delighted not."

Jeremiah 6:10-19 "¹⁰To whom shall I speak, and give warning, that they may hear? behold, their ear is uncircumcised, and they cannot hearken: behold, the word of the LORD is unto them a reproach; they have no delight in it. ¹¹Therefore I am full of the fury of the LORD; I am weary with holding in: I will pour it out upon the children abroad, and upon the assembly of young men together: for even the husband with the wife shall be taken, the aged with him that is full of days. ¹²And their houses shall be turned unto others, with their fields and wives together: for I will stretch out my hand upon the inhabitants of the land, saith the LORD. ¹³For from the least of them even unto the greatest of them every one is given to covetousness; and from the prophet even unto the priest every one dealeth falsely. ¹⁴They have healed also the hurt of the daughter of my people slightly, saying, Peace, peace; when there is no peace. ¹⁵Were they ashamed when they had committed abomination? nay, they were not at all ashamed, neither could they blush: therefore they shall fall among them that fall: at the time that I visit them they shall be cast down, saith the LORD. ¹⁶Thus saith the LORD, Stand ye in the ways, and see, and ask for the old paths, where is the good way, and walk therein, and ye shall find rest for your souls. But they said, We will not walk therein. ¹⁷Also I set watchmen over you, saying, Hearken to the sound of the trumpet. But they said, We will not hearken. ¹⁸Therefore hear, ye nations, and know, O congregation, what is among them. ¹⁹Hear, O earth: behold, I will bring evil upon this people, even the fruit of their thoughts, because they have not hearkened unto my words, nor to my law, but rejected it."

Jeremiah 9:13-16 "¹³And the LORD saith, Because they have forsaken my law which I set before them, and have not obeyed my voice, neither walked therein; ¹⁴But have walked after the imagination of their own heart, and after Baalim, which their fathers taught them: ¹⁵Therefore thus saith the LORD of hosts, the God of Israel; Behold, I will feed them, even this people, with wormwood, and give them water of gall to drink. ¹⁶I will scatter them also among the heathen, whom neither they nor their fathers have known: and I will send a sword after them, till I have consumed them."

Jeremiah 12:17 "But if they will not obey, I will utterly pluck up and destroy that nation, saith the LORD."

Jeremiah 14:10 "Thus saith the LORD unto this people, Thus have they loved to wander, they have not refrained their feet, therefore the LORD doth not accept them; he will now remember their iniquity, and visit their sins."

Jeremiah 15:6-7 "⁶Thou hast forsaken me, saith the LORD, thou art gone backward: therefore will I stretch out my hand against thee, and destroy thee; I am weary with repenting. ⁷And I will fan them with a fan in the gates of the land; I will bereave them of children, I will destroy my people, since they return not from their ways."

Jeremiah 16:11-13 "¹¹Then shalt thou say unto them, Because your fathers have forsaken me, saith the LORD, and have walked after other gods, and have served them, and have worshipped them, and have forsaken me, and have not kept my law; ¹²And ye have done worse than your fathers; for, behold, ye walk every one after the imagination of his evil heart, that they may not hearken unto me: ¹³Therefore will I cast you out of this land into a land that ye know not, neither ye nor your fathers; and there shall ye serve other gods day and night; where I will not shew you favour."

Jeremiah 17:24-27 "24And it shall come to pass, if ye diligently hearken unto me, saith the LORD, to bring in no burden through the gates of this city on the sabbath day, but hallow the sabbath day, to do no work therein; 25Then shall there enter into the gates of this city kings and princes sitting upon the throne of David, riding in chariots and on horses, they, and their princes, the men of Judah, and the inhabitants of Jerusalem: and this city shall remain for ever. 26And they shall come from the cities of Judah, and from the places about Jerusalem, and from the land of Benjamin, and from the plain, and from the mountains, and from the south, bringing burnt offerings, and sacrifices, and meat offerings, and incense, and bringing sacrifices of praise, unto the house of the LORD. 27But if ye will not hearken unto me to hallow the sabbath day, and not to bear a burden, even entering in at the gates of Jerusalem on the sabbath day; then will I kindle a fire in the gates thereof, and it shall devour the palaces of Jerusalem, and it shall not be quenched."

Jeremiah 18:5-10 "5Then the word of the LORD came to me, saying, 6O house of Israel, cannot I do with you as this potter? saith the LORD. Behold, as the clay is in the potter's hand, so are ye in mine hand, O house of Israel. 7At what instant I shall speak concerning a nation, and concerning a kingdom, to pluck up, and to pull down, and to destroy it; 8If that nation, against whom I have pronounced, turn from their evil, I will repent of the evil that I thought to do unto them. 9And at what instant I shall speak concerning a nation, and concerning a kingdom, to build and to plant it; 10If it do evil in my sight, that it obey not my voice, then I will repent of the good, wherewith I said I would benefit them."

Jeremiah 19:15 "Thus saith the LORD of hosts, the God of Israel; Behold, I will bring upon this city and upon all her towns all the evil that I have pronounced against it, because they have hardened their necks, that they might not hear my words."

Jeremiah 25:4-14 "4And the LORD hath sent unto you all his servants the prophets, rising early and sending them; but ye have not hearkened, nor inclined your ear to hear. 5They said, Turn ye again now every one from his evil way, and from the evil of your doings, and dwell in the land that the LORD hath given unto you and to your fathers for ever and ever: 6And go not after other gods to serve them, and to worship them, and provoke me not to anger with the works of your hands; and I will do you no hurt. 7Yet ye have not hearkened unto me, saith the LORD; that ye might provoke me to anger with the works of your hands to your own hurt. 8Therefore thus saith the LORD of hosts; Because ye have not heard my words, 9Behold, I will send and take all the families of the north, saith the LORD, and Nebuchadrezzar the king of Babylon, my servant, and will bring them against this land, and against the inhabitants thereof, and against all these nations round about, and will utterly destroy them, and make them an astonishment, and an hissing, and perpetual desolations. 10Moreover I will take from them the voice of mirth, and the voice of gladness, the voice of the bridegroom, and the voice of the bride, the sound of the millstones, and the light of the candle. 11And this whole land shall be a desolation, and an astonishment; and these nations shall serve the king of Babylon seventy years. 12And it shall come to pass, when seventy years are accomplished, that I will punish the king of Babylon, and that nation, saith the LORD, for their iniquity, and the land of the Chaldeans, and will make it perpetual desolations. 13And I will bring upon that land all my words which I have pronounced against it, even all that is written in this book, which Jeremiah hath prophesied against all the nations. 14For many nations and great kings shall serve themselves of them also: and I will recompense them according to their deeds, and according to the works of their own hands."

Jeremiah 32:32-36 "32Because of all the evil of the children of Israel and of the children of Judah, which they have done to provoke me to anger, they, their kings, their princes, their priests, and their prophets, and the men of Judah, and the inhabitants of Jerusalem. 33And they have turned unto me the back, and not the face: though I taught them, rising up early and teaching them, yet they have not hearkened to receive instruction. 34But they set their abominations in the house, which is called by my name, to defile it. 35And they built the high places of Baal, which are in the valley of the son of Hinnom, to cause their sons and their daughters to pass through the fire unto Molech; which I commanded them not, neither came it into my mind, that they should do this abomination, to cause Judah to sin. 36And now therefore thus saith the LORD, the God of Israel, concerning this city, whereof ye say, It shall be delivered into the hand of the king of Babylon by the sword, and by the famine, and by the pestilence."

Jeremiah 35:17 "Therefore thus saith the LORD God of hosts, the God of Israel; Behold, I will bring upon Judah and upon all the inhabitants of Jerusalem all the evil that I have pronounced against them: because I have spoken unto them, but they have not heard; and I have called unto them, but they have not answered."

Jeremiah 44:23 "Because ye have burned incense, and because ye have sinned against the LORD, and have not obeyed the voice of the LORD, nor walked in his law, nor in his statutes, nor in his testimonies; therefore this evil is happened unto you, as at this day."

Ezekiel 39:22-24 "22So the house of Israel shall know that I am the LORD their God from that day and forward. 23And the heathen shall know that the house of Israel went into captivity for their iniquity: because they trespassed against me, therefore hid I my face from them, and gave them into the hand of their enemies: so fell they all by the sword. 24According to their uncleanness and according to their transgressions have I done unto them, and hid my face from them."

Daniel 9:5-14 "5We have sinned, and have committed iniquity, and have done wickedly, and have rebelled, even by departing from thy precepts and from thy judgments: 6Neither have we hearkened unto thy servants the prophets, which spake in thy name to our kings, our princes, and our fathers, and to all the people of the land. 7O Lord, righteousness belongeth unto thee, but unto us confusion of faces, as at this day; to the men of Judah, and to the inhabitants of Jerusalem, and unto all Israel, that are near, and that are far off, through all the countries whither thou hast driven them, because of their trespass that they have trespassed against thee. 8O Lord, to us belongeth confusion of face, to our kings, to our princes, and to our fathers, because we have sinned against thee. 9To the Lord our God belong mercies and forgivenesses, though we have rebelled against him; 10Neither have we obeyed the voice of the LORD our God, to walk in his laws, which he set before us by his servants the prophets. 11Yea, all Israel have transgressed thy law, even by departing, that they might not obey thy voice; therefore the curse is poured upon us, and the oath that is written in the law of Moses the servant of God, because we have sinned against him. 12And he hath confirmed his words, which he spake against us, and against our judges that judged us, by bringing upon us a great evil: for under the whole heaven hath not been done as hath been done upon Jerusalem. 13As it is written in the law of Moses, all this evil is come upon us: yet made we not our prayer before the LORD our God, that we might turn from our iniquities, and understand thy truth. 14Therefore hath the LORD watched upon the evil, and brought it upon us: for the LORD our God is righteous in all his works which he doeth: for we obeyed not his voice."

Hosea 4:10 "For they shall eat, and not have enough: they shall commit whoredom, and shall not increase: because they have left off to take heed to the LORD."

Amos 2:4-5 "4Thus saith the LORD; For three transgressions of Judah, and for four, I will not turn away the punishment thereof; because they have despised the law of the LORD, and have not kept his commandments, and their lies caused them to err, after the which their fathers have walked: 5But I will send a fire upon Judah, and it shall devour the palaces of Jerusalem."

Zephaniah 3:1-2 "1Woe to her that is filthy and polluted, to the oppressing city! 2She obeyed not the voice; she received not correction; she trusted not in the LORD; she drew not near to her God."

Zechariah 1:4-6 "4Be ye not as your fathers, unto whom the former prophets have cried, saying, Thus saith the LORD of hosts; Turn ye now from your evil ways, and from your evil doings: but they did not hear, nor hearken unto me, saith the LORD. 5Your fathers, where are they? and the prophets, do they live for ever? 6But my words and my statutes, which I commanded my servants the prophets, did they not take hold of your fathers? and they returned and said, Like as the LORD of hosts thought to do unto us, according to our ways, and according to our doings, so hath he dealt with us."

Zechariah 7:11-14 "11But they refused to hearken, and pulled away the shoulder, and stopped their ears, that they should not hear. 12Yea, they made their hearts as an adamant stone, lest they should hear the law, and the words which the LORD of hosts hath sent in his spirit by the former prophets: therefore came a great wrath from the LORD of hosts. 13Therefore it is come to pass, that as he cried, and they would not hear; so they cried, and I would not hear, saith the LORD of hosts: 14But I scattered them with a whirlwind among all the nations whom they knew not. Thus the land was desolate after them, that no man passed through nor returned: for they laid the pleasant land desolate."

Malachi 2:1-9 "1And now, O ye priests, this commandment is for you. 2If ye will not hear, and if ye will not lay it to heart, to give glory unto my name, saith the LORD of hosts, I will even send a curse upon you, and I will curse your blessings: yea, I have cursed them already, because ye do not lay it to heart. 3Behold, I will corrupt your seed, and spread dung upon your faces, even the dung of your solemn feasts; and one shall take you away with it. 4And ye shall know that I have sent this commandment unto you, that my covenant might be with Levi, saith the LORD of hosts. 5My covenant was with him of life and peace; and I gave them to him for the fear wherewith he feared me, and was afraid before my name. 6The law of truth was in his mouth, and iniquity was not found in his lips: he walked with me in peace and equity, and did turn many away from iniquity. 7For the priest's lips should keep knowledge, and they should seek the law at his mouth: for he is the messenger of the LORD of hosts. 8But ye are departed out of the way; ye have caused many to stumble at the law; ye have corrupted the covenant of Levi, saith the LORD of hosts. 9Therefore have I also made you contemptible and base before all the people, according as ye have not kept my ways, but have been partial in the law."

Romans 5:18-19 "18Therefore as by the offence of one judgment came upon all men to condemnation; even so by the righteousness of one the free gift came upon all men unto justification of life. 19For as by one man's disobedience many were made sinners, so by the obedience of one shall many be made righteous."

Ephesians 5:5-7 "5For this ye know, that no whoremonger, nor unclean person, nor covetous man, who is an idolater, hath any inheritance in the kingdom of Christ and of God. 6Let no man deceive you with vain words: for because of these things cometh the wrath of God upon the children of disobedience. 7Be not ye therefore partakers with them."

Colossians 3:5-6 "5Mortify therefore your members which are upon the earth; fornication, uncleanness, inordinate affection, evil concupiscence, and covetousness, which is idolatry: 6For which things' sake the wrath of God cometh on the children of disobedience."

The Reward For Being Disobedient To Your Instructors

Proverbs 5:1-14 "1My son, attend unto my wisdom, and bow thine ear to my understanding: 2That thou mayest regard discretion, and that thy lips may keep knowledge. 3For the lips of a strange woman drop as an honeycomb, and her mouth is smoother than oil: 4But her end is bitter as wormwood, sharp as a twoedged sword. 5Her feet go down to death; her steps take hold on hell. 6Lest thou shouldest ponder the path of life, her ways are moveable, that thou canst not know them. 7Hear me now therefore, O ye children, and depart not from the words of my mouth. 8Remove thy way far from her, and come not nigh the door of her house: 9Lest thou give thine honour unto others, and thy years unto the cruel: 10Lest strangers be filled with thy wealth; and thy labours be in the house of a stranger; 11And thou mourn at the last, when thy flesh and thy body are consumed, 12And say, How have I hated instruction, and my heart despised reproof; 13And have not obeyed the voice of my teachers, nor inclined mine ear to them that instructed me! 14I was almost in all evil in the midst of the congregation and assembly."

Those That Are Disobedient To God

Deuteronomy 18:18-19 "[18]I will raise them up a Prophet from among their brethren, like unto thee, and will put my words in his mouth; and he shall speak unto them all that I shall command him. [19]And it shall come to pass, that whosoever will not hearken unto my words which he shall speak in my name, I will require it of him."

Deuteronomy 27:26 "Cursed be he that confirmeth not all the words of this law to do them. And all the people shall say, Amen."

Job 36:5-12 "[5]Behold, God is mighty, and despiseth not any: he is mighty in strength and wisdom. [6]He preserveth not the life of the wicked: but giveth right to the poor. [7]He withdraweth not his eyes from the righteous: but with kings are they on the throne; yea, he doth establish them for ever, and they are exalted. [8]And if they be bound in fetters, and be holden in cords of affliction; [9]Then he sheweth them their work, and their transgressions that they have exceeded. [10]He openeth also their ear to discipline, and commandeth that they return from iniquity. [11]If they obey and serve him, they shall spend their days in prosperity, and their years in pleasures. [12]But if they obey not, they shall perish by the sword, and they shall die without knowledge."

Psalm 119:113-118 "[113]I hate vain thoughts: but thy law do I love. [114]Thou art my hiding place and my shield: I hope in thy word. [115]Depart from me, ye evildoers: for I will keep the commandments of my God. [116]Uphold me according unto thy word, that I may live: and let me not be ashamed of my hope. [117]Hold thou me up, and I shall be safe: and I will have respect unto thy statutes continually. [118]Thou hast trodden down all them that err from thy statutes: for their deceit is falsehood."

Proverbs 28:9 "He that turneth away his ear from hearing the law, even his prayer shall be abomination."

Jeremiah 3:24-25 "[24]For shame hath devoured the labour of our fathers from our youth; their flocks and their herds, their sons and their daughters. [25]We lie down in our shame, and our confusion covereth us: for we have sinned against the LORD our God, we and our fathers, from our youth even unto this day, and have not obeyed the voice of the LORD our God."

Jeremiah 11:3 "And say thou unto them, Thus saith the LORD God of Israel; Cursed be the man that obeyeth not the words of this covenant."

Jeremiah 13:9-10 "[9]Thus saith the LORD, After this manner will I mar the pride of Judah, and the great pride of Jerusalem. [10]This evil people, which refuse to hear my words, which walk in the imagination of their heart, and walk after other gods, to serve them, and to worship them, shall even be as this girdle, which is good for nothing."

Matthew 5:19 "Whosoever therefore shall break one of these least commandments, and shall teach men so, he shall be called the least in the kingdom of heaven: but whosoever shall do and teach them, the same shall be called great in the kingdom of heaven."

Matthew 7:26-28 "[26]And every one that heareth these sayings of mine, and doeth them not, shall be likened unto a foolish man, which built his house upon the sand: [27]And the rain descended, and the floods came, and the winds blew, and beat upon that house; and it fell: and great was the fall of it. [28]And it came to pass, when Jesus had ended these sayings, the people were astonished at his doctrine."

Matthew 13:19-22 "[19]When any one heareth the word of the kingdom, and understandeth it not, then cometh the wicked one, and catcheth away that which was sown in his heart. This is he which received seed by the way side. [20]But he that received the seed into stony places, the same is he that heareth the word, and anon with joy receiveth it; [21]Yet hath he not root in himself, but dureth for a while: for when tribulation or persecution ariseth because of the word, by and by he is offended. [22]He also that received seed among the thorns is he that heareth the word; and the care of this world, and the deceitfulness of riches, choke the word, and he becometh unfruitful."

Mark 4:15-19 "[15]And these are they by the way side, where the word is sown; but when they have heard, Satan cometh immediately, and taketh away the word that was sown in their hearts. [16]And these are they likewise which are sown on stony ground; who, when they have heard the word, immediately receive it with gladness; ¹⁷And have no root in themselves, and so endure but for a time: afterward, when affliction or persecution ariseth for the word's sake, immediately they are offended. ¹⁸And these are they which are sown among thorns; such as hear the word, ¹⁹And the cares of this world, and the deceitfulness of riches, and the lusts of other things entering in, choke the word, and it becometh unfruitful."

Luke 6:46-49 "⁴⁶And why call ye me, Lord, Lord, and do not the things which I say? ⁴⁷Whosoever cometh to me, and heareth my sayings, and doeth them, I will shew you to whom he is like: ⁴⁸He is like a man which built an house, and digged deep, and laid the foundation on a rock: and when the flood arose, the stream beat vehemently upon that house, and could not shake it: for it was founded upon a rock. ⁴⁹But he that heareth, and doeth not, is like a man that without a foundation built an house upon the earth; against which the stream did beat vehemently, and immediately it fell; and the ruin of that house was great."

Luke 8:12-14 "¹²Those by the way side are they that hear; then cometh the devil, and taketh away the word out of their hearts, lest they should believe and be saved. ¹³They on the rock are they, which, when they hear, receive the word with joy; and these have no root, which for a while believe, and in time of temptation fall away. ¹⁴And that which fell among thorns are they, which, when they have heard, go forth, and are choked with cares and riches and pleasures of this life, and bring no fruit to perfection."

John 12:44-48 "⁴⁴Jesus cried and said, He that believeth on me, believeth not on me, but on him that sent me. ⁴⁵And he that seeth me seeth him that sent me. ⁴⁶I am come a light into the world, that whosoever believeth on me should not abide in darkness. ⁴⁷And if any man hear my words, and believe not, I judge him not: for I came not to judge the world, but to save the world. ⁴⁸He that rejecteth me, and receiveth not my words, hath one that judgeth him: the word that I have spoken, the same shall judge him in the last day."

Acts 3:22-23 "²²For Moses truly said unto the fathers, A prophet shall the Lord your God raise up unto you of your brethren, like unto me; him

shall ye hear in all things whatsoever he shall say unto you. ²³And it shall come to pass, that every soul, which will not hear that prophet, shall be destroyed from among the people."

Romans 2:8 "But unto them that are contentious, and do not obey the truth, but obey unrighteousness, indignation and wrath."

Romans 2:13 "(For not the hearers of the law are just before God, but the doers of the law shall be justified."

Romans 2:25 "For circumcision verily profiteth, if thou keep the law: but if thou be a breaker of the law, thy circumcision is made uncircumcision."

Romans 13:1-2 "¹Let every soul be subject unto the higher powers. For there is no power but of God: the powers that be are ordained of God. ²Whosoever therefore resisteth the power, resisteth the ordinance of God: and they that resist shall receive to themselves damnation."

Galatians 3:10 "For as many as are of the works of the law are under the curse: for it is written, Cursed is every one that continueth not in all things which are written in the book of the law to do them."

Ephesians 5:5-6 "⁵For this ye know, that no whoremonger, nor unclean person, nor covetous man, who is an idolater, hath any inheritance in the kingdom of Christ and of God. ⁶Let no man deceive you with vain words: for because of these things cometh the wrath of God upon the children of disobedience."

Colossians 3:5-6 "⁵Mortify therefore your members which are upon the earth; fornication, uncleanness, inordinate affection, evil concupiscence, and covetousness, which is idolatry: ⁶For which things' sake the wrath of God cometh on the children of disobedience."

2 Thessalonians 1:7-10 "⁷And to you who are troubled rest with us, when the Lord Jesus shall be revealed from heaven with his mighty angels, ⁸In flaming fire taking vengeance on them that know not God, and that obey not the gospel of our Lord Jesus Christ: ⁹Who shall be punished with everlasting destruction from the presence of the Lord, and from the glory of his power; ¹⁰When he shall come to be glorified in his saints, and to be admired in all them that believe (because our testimony among you was believed) in that day."

2 Thessalonians 3:14-15 "¹⁴And if any man obey not our word by this epistle, note that man, and have no company with him, that he may be ashamed. ¹⁵Yet count him not as an enemy, but admonish him as a brother."

1 Timothy 1:8-10 "⁸But we know that the law is good, if a man use it lawfully; ⁹Knowing this, that the law is not made for a righteous man, but for the lawless and disobedient, for the ungodly and for sinners, for unholy and profane, for murderers of fathers and murderers of mothers, for manslayers, ¹⁰For whoremongers, for them that defile themselves with mankind, for menstealers, for liars, for perjured persons, and if there be any other thing that is contrary to sound doctrine."

James 1:22-24 "²²But be ye doers of the word, and not hearers only, deceiving your own selves. ²³For if any be a hearer of the word, and not a doer, he is like unto a man beholding his natural face in a glass: ²⁴For he beholdeth himself, and goeth his way, and straightway forgetteth what manner of man he was."

James 2:10 "For whosoever shall keep the whole law, and yet offend in one point, he is guilty of all."

1 Peter 2:6-7 "⁶Wherefore also it is contained in the scripture, Behold, I lay in Sion a chief corner stone, elect, precious: and he that believeth on him shall not be confounded. ⁷Unto you therefore which believe he is precious: but unto them which be disobedient, the stone which the builders disallowed, the same is made the head of the corner."

1 John 1:5-6 "⁵This then is the message which we have heard of him, and declare unto you, that God is light, and in him is no darkness at all. ⁶If we say that we have fellowship with him, and walk in darkness, we lie, and do not the truth."

1 John 2:1-4 "¹My little children, these things write I unto you, that ye sin not. And if any man sin, we have an advocate with the Father, Jesus Christ the righteous: ²And he is the propitiation for our sins: and not for ours only, but also for the sins of the whole world. ³And hereby we do know that we know him, if we keep his commandments. ⁴He that saith, I know him, and keepeth not his commandments, is a liar, and the truth is not in him."

2 John 9 "Whosoever transgresseth, and abideth not in the doctrine of Christ, hath not God. He that abideth in the doctrine of Christ, he hath both the Father and the Son."

Who Is Disobedient To God

Isaiah 29:13 "Wherefore the Lord said, Forasmuch as this people draw near me with their mouth, and with their lips do honour me, but have removed their heart far from me, and their fear toward me is taught by the precept of men."

Ezekiel 33:30-32 "³⁰Also, thou son of man, the children of thy people still are talking against thee by the walls and in the doors of the houses, and speak one to another, every one to his brother, saying, Come, I pray you, and hear what is the word that cometh forth from the LORD. ³¹And they come unto thee as the people cometh, and they sit before thee as my people, and they hear thy words, but they will not do them: for with their mouth they shew much love, but their heart goeth after their covetousness. ³²And, lo, thou art unto them as a very lovely song of one that hath a pleasant voice, and can play well on an instrument: for they hear thy words, but they do them not."

Matthew 13:19-22 "¹⁹When any one heareth the word of the kingdom, and understandeth it not, then cometh the wicked one, and catcheth away that which was sown in his heart. This is he which received seed by the way side. ²⁰But he that received the seed into stony places, the same is he that heareth the word, and anon with joy receiveth it; ²¹Yet hath he not root in himself, but dureth for a while: for when tribulation or persecution ariseth because of the word, by and by he is offended. ²²He also that received seed among the thorns is he that heareth the word; and the care of this world, and the deceitfulness of riches, choke the word, and he becometh unfruitful."

Mark 4:15-19 "¹⁵And these are they by the way side, where the word is sown; but when they have heard, Satan cometh immediately, and taketh away the word that was sown in their hearts. ¹⁶And these are they likewise which are sown on stony ground; who, when they have heard the word, immediately receive it with gladness; [17]And have no root in themselves, and so endure but for a time: afterward, when affliction or persecution ariseth for the word's sake, immediately they are offended. [18]And these are they which are sown among thorns; such as hear the word, [19]And the cares of this world, and the deceitfulness of riches, and the lusts of other things entering in, choke the word, and it becometh unfruitful."

Mark 7:6-9 "[6]He answered and said unto them, Well hath Esaias prophesied of you hypocrites, as it is written, This people honoureth me with their lips, but their heart is far from me. [7]Howbeit in vain do they worship me, teaching for doctrines the commandments of men. [8]For laying aside the commandment of God, ye hold the tradition of men, as the washing of pots and cups: and many other such like things ye do. [9]And he said unto them, Full well ye reject the commandment of God, that ye may keep your own tradition."

Luke 8:12-14 "[12]Those by the way side are they that hear; then cometh the devil, and taketh away the word out of their hearts, lest they should believe and be saved. [13]They on the rock are they, which, when they hear, receive the word with joy; and these have no root, which for a while believe, and in time of temptation fall away. [14]And that which fell among thorns are they, which, when they have heard, go forth, and are choked with cares and riches and pleasures of this life, and bring no fruit to perfection."

John 14:23-24 "[23]Jesus answered and said unto him, If a man love me, he will keep my words: and my Father will love him, and we will come unto him, and make our abode with him. [24]He that loveth me not keepeth not my sayings: and the word which ye hear is not mine, but the Father's which sent me."

Titus 1:10-16 "[10]For there are many unruly and vain talkers and deceivers, specially they of the circumcision: [11]Whose mouths must be stopped, who subvert whole houses, teaching things which they ought not, for filthy lucre's sake. [12]One of themselves, even a prophet of their own, said, The Cretians are alway liars, evil beasts, slow bellies. [13]This witness is true. Wherefore rebuke them sharply, that they may be sound in the faith;

[14]Not giving heed to Jewish fables, and commandments of men, that turn from the truth. [15]Unto the pure all things are pure: but unto them that are defiled and unbelieving is nothing pure; but even their mind and conscience is defiled. [16]They profess that they know God; but in works they deny him, being abominable, and disobedient, and unto every good work reprobate."

DIVISION

Every Kingdom That Is Divided Against Itself
Matthew 12:25-28 "[25]And Jesus knew their thoughts, and said unto them, Every kingdom divided against itself is brought to desolation; and every city or house divided against itself shall not stand: [26]And if Satan cast out Satan, he is divided against himself; how shall then his kingdom stand? [27]And if I by Beelzebub cast out devils, by whom do your children cast them out? therefore they shall be your judges. [28]But if I cast out devils by the Spirit of God, then the kingdom of God is come unto you."

Luke 11:17-20 "[17]But he, knowing their thoughts, said unto them, Every kingdom divided against itself is brought to desolation; and a house divided against a house falleth. [18]If Satan also be divided against himself, how shall his kingdom stand? because ye say that I cast out devils through Beelzebub. [19]And if I by Beelzebub cast out devils, by whom do your sons cast them out? therefore shall they be your judges. [20]But if I with the finger of God cast out devils, no doubt the kingdom of God is come upon you."

Jesus Christ Coming
For The Purpose Of Dividing
Matthew 10:33-36 "[33]But whosoever shall deny me before men, him will I also deny before my Father which is in heaven. [34]Think not that I am come to send peace on earth: I came not to send peace, but a sword. [35]For I am come to set a man at variance against his father, and the daughter against her mother, and the daughter in law against her mother in law. [36]And a man's foes shall be they of his own household."

Matthew 25:31-33 "[31]When the Son of man shall come in his glory, and all the holy angels with him, then shall he sit upon the throne of his glory:

[32]And before him shall be gathered all nations: and he shall separate them one from another, as a shepherd divideth his sheep from the goats: [33]And he shall set the sheep on his right hand, but the goats on the left."

Luke 12:49-53 "[49]I am come to send fire on the earth; and what will I if it be already kindled? [50]But I have a baptism to be baptized with; and how am I straitened till it be accomplished! [51]Suppose ye that I am come to give peace on earth? I tell you, Nay; but rather division: [52]For from henceforth there shall be five in one house divided, three against two, and two against three. [53]The father shall be divided against the son, and the son against the father; the mother against the daughter, and the daughter against the mother; the mother in law against her daughter in law, and the daughter in law against her mother in law."

Not Being Divided
1 Corinthians 1:10-17 "[10]Now I beseech you, brethren, by the name of our Lord Jesus Christ, that ye all speak the same thing, and that there be no divisions among you; but that ye be perfectly joined together in the same mind and in the same judgment. [11]For it hath been declared unto me of you, my brethren, by them which are of the house of Chloe, that there are contentions among you. [12]Now this I say, that every one of you saith, I am of Paul; and I of Apollos; and I of Cephas; and I of Christ. [13]Is Christ divided? was Paul crucified for you? or were ye baptized in the name of Paul? [14]I thank God that I baptized none of you, but Crispus and Gaius; [15]Lest any should say that I had baptized in mine own name. [16]And I baptized also the household of Stephanas: besides, I know not whether I baptized any other. [17]For Christ sent me not to baptize, but to preach the gospel: not with wisdom of words, lest the cross of Christ should be made of none effect."

Who Is Divided
1 Corinthians 3:3-9 "[3]For ye are yet carnal: for whereas there is among you envying, and strife, and divisions, are ye not carnal, and walk as men? [4]For while one saith, I am of Paul; and another, I am of Apollos; are ye not carnal? [5]Who then is Paul, and who is Apollos, but ministers by whom ye believed, even as the Lord gave to every

man? [6]I have planted, Apollos watered; but God gave the increase. [7]So then neither is he that planteth any thing, neither he that watereth; but God that giveth the increase. [8]Now he that planteth and he that watereth are one: and every man shall receive his own reward according to his own labour. [9]For we are labourers together with God: ye are God's husbandry, ye are God's building."

1 Corinthians 11:17-21 "[17]Now in this that I declare unto you I praise you not, that ye come together not for the better, but for the worse. [18]For first of all, when ye come together in the church, I hear that there be divisions among you; and I partly believe it. [19]For there must be also heresies among you, that they which are approved may be made manifest among you. [20]When ye come together therefore into one place, this is not to eat the Lord's supper. [21]For in eating every one taketh before other his own supper: and one is hungry, and another is drunken."

DIVORCE

Not Getting Divorced
1 Corinthians 7:10-11 "[10]And unto the married I command, yet not I, but the Lord, Let not the wife depart from her husband: [11]But and if she depart, let her remain unmarried, or be reconciled to her husband: and let not the husband put away his wife."

The Requirements Of Divorcement
Deuteronomy 24:1-4 "[1]When a man hath taken a wife, and married her, and it come to pass that she find no favour in his eyes, because he hath found some uncleanness in her: then let him write her a bill of divorcement, and give it in her hand, and send her out of his house. [2]And when she is departed out of his house, she may go and be another man's wife. [3]And if the latter husband hate her, and write her a bill of divorcement, and giveth it in her hand, and sendeth her out of his house; or if the latter husband die, which took her to be his wife; [4]Her former husband, which sent her away, may not take her again to be his wife, after that she is defiled; for that is abomination before the LORD: and thou shalt not cause the land to sin, which the LORD thy God giveth thee for an inheritance."

Those Who Get Divorced And Remarry Again
Matthew 5:31-32 "[31]It hath been said, Whosoever shall put away his wife, let him give her a writing of divorcement: [32]But I say unto you, That whosoever shall put away his wife, saving for the cause of fornication, causeth her to commit adultery: and whosoever shall marry her that is divorced committeth adultery."

Matthew 19:9 "And I say unto you, Whosoever shall put away his wife, except it be for fornication, and shall marry another, committeth adultery: and whoso marrieth her which is put away doth commit adultery."

Mark 10:11-12 "[11]And he saith unto them, Whosoever shall put away his wife, and marry another, committeth adultery against her. [12]And if a woman shall put away her husband, and be married to another, she committeth adultery."

Why Moses Allowed Divorce
Matthew 19:7-8 "[7]They say unto him, Why did Moses then command to give a writing of divorcement, and to put her away? [8]He saith unto them, Moses because of the hardness of your hearts suffered you to put away your wives: but from the beginning it was not so."

Mark 10:2-6 "[2]And the Pharisees came to him, and asked him, Is it lawful for a man to put away his wife? tempting him. [3]And he answered and said unto them, What did Moses command you? [4]And they said, Moses suffered to write a bill of divorcement, and to put her away. [5]And Jesus answered and said unto them, For the hardness of your heart he wrote you this precept. [6]But from the beginning of the creation God made them male and female."

DOCTRINE

Not Being Attracted To Strange Doctrines
1 Timothy 1:3-4 "[3]As I besought thee to abide still at Ephesus, when I went into Macedonia, that thou mightest charge some that they teach no other doctrine, [4]Neither give heed to fables and endless genealogies, which minister questions, rather than godly edifying which is in faith: so do."

Hebrews 13:9 "Be not carried about with divers and strange doctrines. For it is a good thing that the heart be established with grace; not with meats, which have not profited them that have been occupied therein."

Some Not Enduring Sound Doctrine
2 Timothy 4:2-4 "[2]Preach the word; be instant in season, out of season; reprove, rebuke, exhort with all longsuffering and doctrine. [3]For the time will come when they will not endure sound doctrine; but after their own lusts shall they heap to themselves teachers, having itching ears; [4]And they shall turn away their ears from the truth, and shall be turned unto fables."

The Doctrine Of Jesus Christ
John 7:16-18 "[16]Jesus answered them, and said, My doctrine is not mine, but his that sent me. [17]If any man will do his will, he shall know of the doctrine, whether it be of God, or whether I speak of myself. [18]He that speaketh of himself seeketh his own glory: but he that seeketh his glory that sent him, the same is true, and no unrighteousness is in him."

Those That Abide In The Doctrine Of Christ
2 John 9 "Whosoever transgresseth, and abideth not in the doctrine of Christ, hath not God. He that abideth in the doctrine of Christ, he hath both the Father and the Son."

Those That Do Not Abide In The Doctrine Of Christ
2 John 9 "Whosoever transgresseth, and abideth not in the doctrine of Christ, hath not God. He that abideth in the doctrine of Christ, he hath both the Father and the Son."

What Is Profitable For Doctrine
2 Timothy 3:16-17 "[16]All scripture is given by inspiration of God, and is profitable for doctrine, for reproof, for correction, for instruction in righteousness: [17]That the man of God may be perfect, throughly furnished unto all good works."

Who Teaches The Doctrine Of Men
Isaiah 29:13-14 "[13]Wherefore the Lord said, Forasmuch as this people draw near me with their mouth, and with their lips do honour me, but have removed their heart far from me, and their fear toward me is taught by the precept of men: [14]Therefore, behold, I will proceed to do a marvellous work among this people, even a marvellous work and a wonder: for the wisdom of their

wise men shall perish, and the understanding of their prudent men shall be hid."

Mark 7:6-13 "⁶He answered and said unto them, Well hath Esaias prophesied of you hypocrites, as it is written, This people honoureth me with their lips, but their heart is far from me. ⁷Howbeit in vain do they worship me, teaching for doctrines the commandments of men. ⁸For laying aside the commandment of God, ye hold the tradition of men, as the washing of pots and cups: and many other such like things ye do. ⁹And he said unto them, Full well ye reject the commandment of God, that ye may keep your own tradition. ¹⁰For Moses said, Honour thy father and thy mother; and, Whoso curseth father or mother, let him die the death: ¹¹But ye say, If a man shall say to his father or mother, It is Corban, that is to say, a gift, by whatsoever thou mightest be profited by me; he shall be free. ¹²And ye suffer him no more to do ought for his father or his mother; ¹³Making the word of God of none effect through your tradition, which ye have delivered: and many such like things do ye."

DOUBT

Not Being Doubtfully Minded
Luke 12:22-29 "²²And he said unto his disciples, Therefore I say unto you, Take no thought for your life, what ye shall eat; neither for the body, what ye shall put on. ²³The life is more than meat, and the body is more than raiment. ²⁴Consider the ravens: for they neither sow nor reap; which neither have storehouse nor barn; and God feedeth them: how much more are ye better than the fowls? ²⁵And which of you with taking thought can add to his stature one cubit? ²⁶If ye then be not able to do that thing which is least, why take ye thought for the rest? ²⁷Consider the lilies how they grow: they toil not, they spin not; and yet I say unto you, that Solomon in all his glory was not arrayed like one of these. ²⁸If then God so clothe the grass, which is to day in the field, and to morrow is cast into the oven; how much more will he clothe you, O ye of little faith? ²⁹And seek not ye what ye shall eat, or what ye shall drink, neither be ye of doubtful mind."

Those That Do Not Doubt
Matthew 21:21-22 "²¹Jesus answered and said unto them, Verily I say unto you, If ye have faith, and doubt not, ye shall not only do this which is done to the fig tree, but also if ye shall say unto this mountain, Be thou removed, and be thou cast into the sea; it shall be done. ²²And all things, whatsoever ye shall ask in prayer, believing, ye shall receive."

Mark 11:23 "For verily I say unto you, That whosoever shall say unto this mountain, Be thou removed, and be thou cast into the sea; and shall not doubt in his heart, but shall believe that those things which he saith shall come to pass; he shall have whatsoever he saith."

Those That Doubt
Romans 14:22-23 "²²Hast thou faith? have it to thyself before God. Happy is he that condemneth not himself in that thing which he alloweth. ²³And he that doubteth is damned if he eat, because he eateth not of faith: for whatsoever is not of faith is sin."

DRUNKENNESS

Drunks
Proverbs 20:1 "Wine is a mocker, strong drink is raging: and whosoever is deceived thereby is not wise."

Proverbs 23:20-21 "²⁰Be not among winebibbers; among riotous eaters of flesh: ²¹For the drunkard and the glutton shall come to poverty: and drowsiness shall clothe a man with rags."

Proverbs 23:29-35 "²⁹Who hath woe? who hath sorrow? who hath contentions? who hath babbling? who hath wounds without cause? who hath redness of eyes? ³⁰They that tarry long at the wine; they that go to seek mixed wine. ³¹Look not thou upon the wine when it is red, when it giveth his colour in the cup, when it moveth itself aright. ³²At the last it biteth like a serpent, and stingeth like an adder. ³³Thine eyes shall behold strange women, and thine heart shall utter perverse things. ³⁴Yea, thou shalt be as he that lieth down in the midst of the sea, or as he that lieth upon the top of a mast. ³⁵They have stricken me, shalt thou say, and I was not sick; they have beaten me, and I felt it not: when shall I awake? I will seek it yet again."

Proverbs 26:9 "As a thorn goeth up into the hand of a drunkard, so is a parable in the mouth of fools."

Isaiah 5:11-12 "¹¹Woe unto them that rise up early in the morning, that they may follow strong drink; that continue until night, till wine inflame them! ¹²And the harp, and the viol, the tabret, and pipe, and wine, are in their feasts: but they regard not the work of the LORD, neither consider the operation of his hands."

Isaiah 5:22 "Woe unto them that are mighty to drink wine, and men of strength to mingle strong drink."

Isaiah 28:7 "But they also have erred through wine, and through strong drink are out of the way; the priest and the prophet have erred through strong drink, they are swallowed up of wine, they are out of the way through strong drink; they err in vision, they stumble in judgment."

1 Thessalonians 5:7 "For they that sleep sleep in the night; and they that be drunken are drunken in the night."

Not Being Drunk
Proverbs 23:31 "Look not thou upon the wine when it is red, when it giveth his colour in the cup, when it moveth itself aright."

Romans 13:13 "Let us walk honestly, as in the day; not in rioting and drunkenness, not in chambering and wantonness, not in strife and envying."

Ephesians 5:18 "And be not drunk with wine, wherein is excess; but be filled with the Spirit."

What Alcohol Does
Proverbs 23:31-32 "³¹Look not thou upon the wine when it is red, when it giveth his colour in the cup, when it moveth itself aright. ³²At the last it biteth like a serpent, and stingeth like an adder."

Isaiah 28:7 "But they also have erred through wine, and through strong drink are out of the way; the priest and the prophet have erred through strong drink, they are swallowed up of wine, they are out of the way through strong drink; they err in vision, they stumble in judgment."

Hosea 4:11 "Whoredom and wine and new wine take away the heart."

Who Should Not Drink
Proverbs 31:4-7 "⁴It is not for kings, O Lemuel, it is not for kings to drink wine; nor for princes strong drink: ⁵Lest they drink, and forget the law, and pervert the judgment of any of the afflicted. ⁶Give strong drink unto him that is ready to perish, and wine unto those that be of heavy hearts. ⁷Let him drink, and forget his poverty, and remember his misery no more."

1 Timothy 3:1-11 "¹This is a true saying, If a man desire the office of a bishop, he desireth a good work. ²A bishop then must be blameless, the husband of one wife, vigilant, sober, of good behaviour, given to hospitality, apt to teach; ³Not given to wine, no striker, not greedy of filthy lucre; but patient, not a brawler, not covetous; ⁴One that ruleth well his own house, having his children in subjection with all gravity; ⁵(For if a man know not how to rule his own house, how shall he take care of the church of God?) ⁶Not a novice, lest being lifted up with pride he fall into the condemnation of the devil. ⁷Moreover he must have a good report of them which are without; lest he fall into reproach and the snare of the devil. ⁸Likewise must the deacons be grave, not double-tongued, not given to much wine, not greedy of filthy lucre; ⁹Holding the mystery of the faith in a pure conscience. ¹⁰And let these also first be proved; then let them use the office of a deacon, being found blameless. ¹¹Even so must their wives be grave, not slanderers, sober, faithful in all things."

E*e*

EARTH

Earth Belonging To The Lord

Genesis 14:19 "And he blessed him, and said, Blessed be Abram of the most high God, possessor of heaven and earth."

Exodus 19:3-5 "³And Moses went up unto God, and the LORD called unto him out of the mountain, saying, Thus shalt thou say to the house of Jacob, and tell the children of Israel; ⁴Ye have seen what I did unto the Egyptians, and how I bare you on eagles' wings, and brought you unto myself. ⁵Now therefore, if ye will obey my voice indeed, and keep my covenant, then ye shall be a peculiar treasure unto me above all people: for all the earth is mine."

Deuteronomy 10:14 "Behold, the heaven and the heaven of heavens is the LORD's thy God, the earth also, with all that therein is."

1 Samuel 2:8 "He raiseth up the poor out of the dust, and lifteth up the beggar from the dunghill, to set them among princes, and to make them inherit the throne of glory: for the pillars of the earth are the LORD's, and he hath set the world upon them."

1 Chronicles 29:11 "Thine, O LORD, is the greatness, and the power, and the glory, and the victory, and the majesty: for all that is in the heaven and in the earth is thine; thine is the kingdom, O LORD, and thou art exalted as head above all."

Psalm 24:1 "The earth is the LORD's, and the fulness thereof; the world, and they that dwell therein."

Psalm 47:7-9 "⁷For God is the King of all the earth: sing ye praises with understanding. ⁸God reigneth over the heathen: God sitteth upon the throne of his holiness. ⁹The princes of the people are gathered together, even the people of the God of Abraham: for the shields of the earth belong unto God: he is greatly exalted."

Psalm 50:7-12 "⁷Hear, O my people, and I will speak; O Israel, and I will testify against thee: I am God, even thy God. ⁸I will not reprove thee for thy sacrifices or thy burnt offerings, to have been continually before me. ⁹I will take no bullock out of thy house, nor he goats out of thy folds. ¹⁰For every beast of the forest is mine, and the cattle upon a thousand hills. ¹¹I know all the fowls of the mountains: and the wild beasts of the field are mine. ¹²If I were hungry, I would not tell thee: for the world is mine, and the fulness thereof."

Psalm 89:8-11 "⁸O LORD God of hosts, who is a strong LORD like unto thee? or to thy faithfulness round about thee? ⁹Thou rulest the raging of the sea: when the waves thereof arise, thou stillest them. ¹⁰Thou hast broken Rahab in pieces, as one that is slain; thou hast scattered thine enemies with thy strong arm. ¹¹The heavens are thine, the earth also is thine: as for the world and the fulness thereof, thou hast founded them."

1 Corinthians 10:26-28 "²⁶For the earth is the Lord's, and the fulness thereof. ²⁷If any of them that believe not bid you to a feast, and ye be disposed to go; whatsoever is set before you, eat, asking no question for conscience sake. ²⁸But if any man say unto you, This is offered in sacrifice unto idols, eat not for his sake that shewed it, and for conscience sake: for the earth is the Lord's, and the fulness thereof."

Earth Passing Away

Psalm 102:24-27 "²⁴I said, O my God, take me not away in the midst of my days: thy years are throughout all generations. ²⁵Of old hast thou laid the foundation of the earth: and the heavens are the work of thy hands. ²⁶They shall perish, but thou shalt endure: yea, all of them shall wax old like a garment; as a vesture shalt thou change them, and they shall be changed: ²⁷But thou art the same, and thy years shall have no end."

Isaiah 51:6 "Lift up your eyes to the heavens, and look upon the earth beneath: for the heavens shall vanish away like smoke, and the earth shall wax old like a garment, and they that dwell therein shall die in like manner: but my salvation shall be for ever, and my righteousness shall not be abolished."

Matthew 24:35 "Heaven and earth shall pass away, but my words shall not pass away."

Mark 13:31 "Heaven and earth shall pass away: but my words shall not pass away."

Luke 21:33 "Heaven and earth shall pass away: but my words shall not pass away."

Hebrews 1:10-12 "[10]And, Thou, Lord, in the beginning hast laid the foundation of the earth; and the heavens are the works of thine hands: [11]They shall perish; but thou remainest; and they all shall wax old as doth a garment; [12]And as a vesture shalt thou fold them up, and they shall be changed: but thou art the same, and thy years shall not fail."

2 Peter 3:10-12 "[10]But the day of the Lord will come as a thief in the night; in the which the heavens shall pass away with a great noise, and the elements shall melt with fervent heat, the earth also and the works that are therein shall be burned up. [11]Seeing then that all these things shall be dissolved, what manner of persons ought ye to be in all holy conversation and godliness, [12]Looking for and hasting unto the coming of the day of God, wherein the heavens being on fire shall be dissolved, and the elements shall melt with fervent heat?"

Revelation 21:1-4 "[1]And I saw a new heaven and a new earth: for the first heaven and the first earth were passed away; and there was no more sea. [2]And 1 John saw the holy city, new Jerusalem, coming down from God out of heaven, prepared as a bride adorned for her husband. [3]And I heard a great voice out of heaven saying, Behold, the tabernacle of God is with men, and he will dwell with them, and they shall be his people, and God himself shall be with them, and be their God. [4]And God shall wipe away all tears from their eyes; and there shall be no more death, neither sorrow, nor crying, neither shall there be any more pain: for the former things are passed away."

The Earth Which Exists Now

2 Peter 3:3-8 "[3]Knowing this first, that there shall come in the last days scoffers, walking after their own lusts, [4]And saying, Where is the promise of his coming? for since the fathers fell asleep, all things continue as they were from the beginning of the creation. [5]For this they willingly are ignorant of, that by the word of God the heavens were of old, and the earth standing out of the water and in the water: [6]Whereby the world that then was, being overflowed with water, perished: [7]But the heavens and the earth, which are now, by the same word are kept in store, reserved unto fire against the day of judgment and perdition of ungodly men. [8]But, beloved, be not ignorant of this one thing, that one day is with the Lord as a thousand years, and a thousand years as one day."

The Lord Creating A New Earth

Psalm 102:24-27 "[24]I said, O my God, take me not away in the midst of my days: thy years are throughout all generations. [25]Of old hast thou laid the foundation of the earth: and the heavens are the work of thy hands. [26]They shall perish, but thou shalt endure: yea, all of them shall wax old like a garment; as a vesture shalt thou change them, and they shall be changed: [27]But thou art the same, and thy years shall have no end."

Isaiah 65:14-18 "[14]Behold, my servants shall sing for joy of heart, but ye shall cry for sorrow of heart, and shall howl for vexation of spirit. [15]And ye shall leave your name for a curse unto my chosen: for the Lord GOD shall slay thee, and call his servants by another name: [16]That he who blesseth himself in the earth shall bless himself in the God of truth; and he that sweareth in the earth shall swear by the God of truth; because the former troubles are forgotten, and because they are hid from mine eyes. [17]For, behold, I create new heavens and a new earth: and the former shall not be remembered, nor come into mind. [18]But be ye glad and rejoice for ever in that which I create: for, behold, I create Jerusalem a rejoicing, and her people a joy."

Isaiah 66:22 "For as the new heavens and the new earth, which I will make, shall remain before me, saith the LORD, so shall your seed and your name remain."

Hebrews 1:10-12 "[10]And, Thou, Lord, in the beginning hast laid the foundation of the earth; and the heavens are the works of thine hands: [11]They shall perish; but thou remainest; and they all shall wax old as doth a garment; [12]And as a vesture shalt thou fold them up, and they shall be changed: but thou art the same, and thy years shall not fail."

Revelation 21:1-5 "[1]And I saw a new heaven and a new earth: for the first heaven and the first earth were passed away; and there was no more sea. [2]And I John saw the holy city, new Jerusalem, coming down from God out of heaven, prepared as a bride adorned for her husband. ³And I heard a great voice out of heaven saying, Behold, the tabernacle of God is with men, and he will dwell with them, and they shall be his people, and God himself shall be with them, and be their God. ⁴And God shall wipe away all tears from their eyes; and there shall be no more death, neither sorrow, nor crying, neither shall there be any more pain: for the former things are passed away. ⁵And he that sat upon the throne said, Behold, I make all things new. And he said unto me, Write: for these words are true and faithful."

The Lord Creating The Earth

Genesis 1:1-31 "¹In the beginning God created the Heaven and the earth. ²And the earth was without form, and void; and darkness was upon the face of the deep. And the Spirit of God moved upon the face of the waters. ³And God said, Let there be light: and there was light. ⁴And God saw the light, that it was good: and God divided the light from the darkness. ⁵And God called the light Day, and the darkness he called Night. And the evening and the morning were the first day. ⁶And God said, Let there be a firmament in the midst of the waters, and let it divide the waters from the waters. ⁷And God made the firmament, and divided the waters which were under the firmament from the waters which were above the firmament: and it was so. ⁸And God called the firmament Heaven. And the evening and the morning were the second day. ⁹And God said, Let the waters under the heaven be gathered together unto one place, and let the dry land appear: and it was so. ¹⁰And God called the dry land Earth; and the gathering together of the waters called he Seas: and God saw that it was good. ¹¹And God said, Let the earth bring forth grass, the herb yielding seed, and the fruit tree yielding fruit after his kind, whose seed is in itself, upon the earth: and it was so. ¹²And the earth brought forth grass, and herb yielding seed after his kind, and the tree yielding fruit, whose seed was in itself, after his kind: and God saw that it was good. ¹³And the evening and the morning were the third day. ¹⁴And God said, Let there be lights in the firmament of the heaven to divide the day from the night; and let them be for signs, and for seasons, and for days, and years: ¹⁵And let them be for lights in the firmament of the heaven to give light upon the earth: and it was so. ¹⁶And God made two great lights; the greater light to rule the day, and the lesser light to rule the night: he made the stars also. ¹⁷And God set them in the firmament of the heaven to give light upon the earth, ¹⁸And to rule over the day and over the night, and to divide the light from the darkness: and God saw that it was good. ¹⁹And the evening and the morning were the fourth day. ²⁰And God said, Let the waters bring forth abundantly the moving creature that hath life, and fowl that may fly above the earth in the open firmament of heaven. ²¹And God created great whales, and every living creature that moveth, which the waters brought forth abundantly, after their kind, and every winged fowl after his kind: and God saw that it was good. ²²And God blessed them, saying, Be fruitful, and multiply, and fill the waters in the seas, and let fowl multiply in the earth. ²³And the evening and the morning were the fifth day. ²⁴And God said, Let the earth bring forth the living creature after his kind, cattle, and creeping thing, and beast of the earth after his kind: and it was so. ²⁵And God made the beast of the earth after his kind, and cattle after their kind, and every thing that creepeth upon the earth after his kind: and God saw that it was good. ²⁶And God said, Let us make man in our image, after our likeness: and let them have dominion over the fish of the sea, and over the fowl of the air, and over the cattle, and over all the earth, and over every creeping thing that creepeth upon the earth. ²⁷So God created man in his own image, in the image of God created he him; male and female created he them. ²⁸And God blessed them, and God said unto them, Be fruitful, and multiply, and replenish the earth, and subdue it: and have dominion over the fish of the sea, and over the fowl of the air, and over every living thing that moveth upon the earth. ²⁹And God said, Behold, I have given you every herb bearing seed, which is upon the face of all the earth, and every tree, in the which is the fruit of a tree yielding seed; to you it shall be for meat. ³⁰And to every beast of the earth, and to every fowl of the air, and to every thing that creepeth upon the earth, wherein there is life, I have given every green herb for meat: and it was so. ³¹And God saw every thing that he had made, and, behold, it was very good. And the evening and the morning were the sixth day."

Genesis 2:4 "These are the generations of the heavens and of the earth when they were created, in the day that the LORD God made the earth and the heavens."

Exodus 20:11 "For in six days the LORD made heaven and earth, the sea, and all that in them is, and rested the seventh day: wherefore the LORD blessed the sabbath day, and hallowed it."

Exodus 31:17 "It is a sign between me and the children of Israel for ever: for in six days the LORD made heaven and earth, and on the seventh day he rested, and was refreshed."

2 Kings 19:15 "And Hezekiah prayed before the LORD, and said, O LORD God of Israel, which dwellest between the cherubims, thou art the God, even thou alone, of all the kingdoms of the earth: thou hast made heaven and earth."

Nehemiah 9:6 "Thou, even thou, art LORD alone; thou hast made heaven, the heaven of heavens, with all their host, the earth, and all things that are therein, the seas, and all that is therein, and thou preservest them all; and the host of heaven worshippeth thee."

Psalm 89:8-11 "8O LORD God of hosts, who is a strong LORD like unto thee? or to thy faithfulness round about thee? 9Thou rulest the raging of the sea: when the waves thereof arise, thou stillest them. 10Thou hast broken Rahab in pieces, as one that is slain; thou hast scattered thine enemies with thy strong arm. 11The heavens are thine, the earth also is thine: as for the world and the fulness thereof, thou hast founded them."

Psalm 90:2 "Before the mountains were brought forth, or ever thou hadst formed the earth and the world, even from everlasting to everlasting, thou art God."

Psalm 95:3-5 "3For the LORD is a great God, and a great King above all gods. 4In his hand are the deep places of the earth: the strength of the hills is his also. 5The sea is his, and he made it: and his hands formed the dry land."

Psalm 102:24-25 "24I said, O my God, take me not away in the midst of my days: thy years are throughout all generations. 25Of old hast thou laid the foundation of the earth: and the heavens are the work of thy hands."

Psalm 104:1-13 "1Bless the LORD, O my soul. O LORD my God, thou art very great; thou art clothed with honour and majesty. 2Who coverest thyself with light as with a garment: who stretchest out the heavens like a curtain: 3Who layeth the beams of his chambers in the waters: who maketh the clouds his chariot: who walketh upon the wings of the wind: 4Who maketh his angels spirits; his ministers a flaming fire: 5Who laid the foundations of the earth, that it should not be removed for ever. 6Thou coveredst it with the deep as with a garment: the waters stood above the mountains. 7At thy rebuke they fled; at the voice of thy thunder they hasted away. 8They go up by the mountains; they go down by the valleys unto the place which thou hast founded for them. 9Thou hast set a bound that they may not pass over; that they turn not again to cover the earth. 10He sendeth the springs into the valleys, which run among the hills. 11They give drink to every beast of the field: the wild asses quench their thirst. 12By them shall the fowls of the heaven have their habitation, which sing among the branches. 13He watereth the hills from his chambers: the earth is satisfied with the fruit of thy works."

Psalm 115:13-15 "13He will bless them that fear the LORD, both small and great. 14The LORD shall increase you more and more, you and your children. 15Ye are blessed of the LORD which made heaven and earth."

Psalm 119:89-90 "89For ever, O LORD, thy word is settled in heaven. 90Thy faithfulness is unto all generations: thou hast established the earth, and it abideth."

Psalm 121:2 "My help cometh from the LORD, which made heaven and earth."

Psalm 124:8 "Our help is in the name of the LORD, who made heaven and earth."

Psalm 136:1-6 "1O give thanks unto the LORD; for he is good: for his mercy endureth for ever. 2O give thanks unto the God of gods: for his mercy endureth for ever. 3O give thanks to the Lord of lords: for his mercy endureth for ever. 4To him who alone doeth great wonders: for his mercy endureth for ever. 5To him that by wisdom made the heavens: for his mercy endureth for ever. 6To him that stretched out the earth above the waters: for his mercy endureth for ever."

Psalm 146:5-6 "⁵Happy is he that hath the God of Jacob for his help, whose hope is in the LORD his God: ⁶Which made heaven, and earth, the sea, and all that therein is: which keepeth truth for ever."

Proverbs 3:19 "The LORD by wisdom hath founded the earth; by understanding hath he established the heavens."

Proverbs 8:22-31 "²²The LORD possessed me in the beginning of his way, before his works of old. ²³I was set up from everlasting, from the beginning, or ever the earth was. ²⁴When there were no depths, I was brought forth; when there were no fountains abounding with water. ²⁵Before the mountains were settled, before the hills was I brought forth: ²⁶While as yet he had not made the earth, nor the fields, nor the highest part of the dust of the world. ²⁷When he prepared the heavens, I was there: when he set a compass upon the face of the depth: ²⁸When he established the clouds above: when he strengthened the fountains of the deep: ²⁹When he gave to the sea his decree, that the waters should not pass his commandment: when he appointed the foundations of the earth: ³⁰Then I was by him, as one brought up with him: and I was daily his delight, rejoicing always before him; ³¹Rejoicing in the habitable part of his earth; and my delights were with the sons of men."

Isaiah 37:16 "O LORD of hosts, God of Israel, that dwellest between the cherubims, thou art the God, even thou alone, of all the kingdoms of the earth: thou hast made heaven and earth."

Isaiah 40:28 "Hast thou not known? hast thou not heard, that the everlasting God, the LORD, the Creator of the ends of the earth, fainteth not, neither is weary? there is no searching of his understanding."

Isaiah 42:5 "Thus saith God the LORD, he that created the heavens, and stretched them out; he that spread forth the earth, and that which cometh out of it; he that giveth breath unto the people upon it, and spirit to them that walk therein."

Isaiah 44:24 "Thus saith the LORD, thy redeemer, and he that formed thee from the womb, I am the LORD that maketh all things; that stretcheth forth

the heavens alone; that spreadeth abroad the earth by myself."

Isaiah 45:11-12 "¹¹Thus saith the LORD, the Holy One of Israel, and his Maker, Ask me of things to come concerning my sons, and concerning the work of my hands command ye me. ¹²I have made the earth, and created man upon it: I, even my hands, have stretched out the heavens, and all their host have I commanded."

Isaiah 45:18 "For thus saith the LORD that created the heavens; God himself that formed the earth and made it; he hath established it, he created it not in vain, he formed it to be inhabited: I am the LORD; and there is none else."

Isaiah 48:12-13 "¹²Hearken unto me, O Jacob and Israel, my called; I am he; I am the first, I also am the last. ¹³Mine hand also hath laid the foundation of the earth, and my right hand hath spanned the heavens: when I call unto them, they stand up together."

Isaiah 51:13-16 "¹³And forgettest the LORD thy maker, that hath stretched forth the heavens, and laid the foundations of the earth; and hast feared continually every day because of the fury of the oppressor, as if he were ready to destroy? and where is the fury of the oppressor? ¹⁴The captive exile hasteneth that he may be loosed, and that he should not die in the pit, nor that his bread should fail. ¹⁵But I am the LORD thy God, that divided the sea, whose waves roared: The LORD of hosts is his name. ¹⁶And I have put my words in thy mouth, and I have covered thee in the shadow of mine hand, that I may plant the heavens, and lay the foundations of the earth, and say unto Zion, Thou art my people."

Isaiah 66:1-2 "¹Thus saith the LORD, The heaven is my throne, and the earth is my footstool: where is the house that ye build unto me? and where is the place of my rest? ²For all those things hath mine hand made, and those things have been, saith the LORD: but to this man will I look, even to him that is poor and of a contrite spirit, and trembleth at my word."

Jeremiah 10:10-12 "¹⁰But the LORD is the true God, he is the living God, and an everlasting king: at his wrath the earth shall tremble, and the nations shall not be able to abide his indignation.

11Thus shall ye say unto them, The gods that have not made the heavens and the earth, even they shall perish from the earth, and from under these heavens. 12He hath made the earth by his power, he hath established the world by his wisdom, and hath stretched out the heavens by his discretion."

Jeremiah 27:4-5 "4And command them to say unto their masters, Thus saith the LORD of hosts, the God of Israel; Thus shall ye say unto your masters; 5I have made the earth, the man and the beast that are upon the ground, by my great power and by my outstretched arm, and have given it unto whom it seemed meet unto me."

Jeremiah 32:17 "Ah Lord GOD! behold, thou hast made the heaven and the earth by thy great power and stretched out arm, and there is nothing too hard for thee."

Jonah 1:9 "And he said unto them, I am an Hebrew; and I fear the LORD, the God of heaven, which hath made the sea and the dry land."

Zechariah 12:1 "The burden of the word of the LORD for Israel, saith the LORD, which stretcheth forth the heavens, and layeth the foundation of the earth, and formeth the spirit of man within him."

Acts 4:24 "And when they heard that, they lifted up their voice to God with one accord, and said, Lord, thou art God, which hast made heaven, and earth, and the sea, and all that in them is."

Acts 14:15 "And saying, Sirs, why do ye these things? We also are men of like passions with you, and preach unto you that ye should turn from these vanities unto the living God, which made heaven, and earth, and the sea, and all things that are therein."

Hebrews 1:10-12 "10And, Thou, Lord, in the beginning hast laid the foundation of the earth; and the heavens are the works of thine hands: 11They shall perish; but thou remainest; and they all shall wax old as doth a garment; 12And as a vesture shalt thou fold them up, and they shall be changed: but thou art the same, and thy years shall not fail."

Revelation 10:5-6 "5And the angel which I saw stand upon the sea and upon the earth lifted up his hand to heaven, 6And sware by him that

liveth for ever and ever, who created heaven, and the things that therein are, and the earth, and the things that therein are, and the sea, and the things which are therein, that there should be time no longer."

Revelation 14:7 "Saying with a loud voice, Fear God, and give glory to him; for the hour of his judgment is come: and worship him that made heaven, and earth, and the sea, and the fountains of waters."

The New Earth
Isaiah 66:22 "For as the new heavens and the new earth, which I will make, shall remain before me, saith the LORD, so shall your seed and your name remain."

2 Peter 3:13 "Nevertheless we, according to his promise, look for new heavens and a new earth, wherein dwelleth righteousness."

Revelation 21:1-4 "1And I saw a new heaven and a new earth: for the first heaven and the first earth were passed away; and there was no more sea. 2And I John saw the holy city, new Jerusalem, coming down from God out of heaven, prepared as a bride adorned for her husband. 3And I heard a great voice out of heaven saying, Behold, the tabernacle of God is with men, and he will dwell with them, and they shall be his people, and God himself shall be with them, and be their God. 4And God shall wipe away all tears from their eyes; and there shall be no more death, neither sorrow, nor crying, neither shall there be any more pain: for the former things are passed away."

Those That Are Of The Earth
John 3:31 "He that cometh from above is above all: he that is of the earth is earthly, and speaketh of the earth: he that cometh from heaven is above all."

What Defiles The Earth
Genesis 6:11-13 "11The earth also was corrupt before God, and the earth was filled with violence. 12And God looked upon the earth, and, behold, it was corrupt; for all flesh had corrupted his way upon the earth. 13And God said unto Noah, The end of all flesh is come before me; for the earth is filled with violence through them; and, behold, I will destroy them with the earth."

Numbers 35:33 "So ye shall not pollute the land wherein ye are: for blood it defileth the land: and the land cannot be cleansed of the blood that is shed therein, but by the blood of him that shed it."

Isaiah 24:5 "The earth also is defiled under the inhabitants thereof; because they have transgressed the laws, changed the ordinance, broken the everlasting covenant."

What Is In The Earth

1 Chronicles 16:14 "He is the LORD our God; his judgments are in all the earth."

Psalm 33:5 "He loveth righteousness and judgment: the earth is full of the goodness of the LORD."

Psalm 72:18-19 "¹⁸Blessed be the LORD God, the God of Israel, who only doeth wondrous things. ¹⁹And blessed be his glorious name for ever: and let the whole earth be filled with his glory; Amen, and Amen."

Psalm 104:24 "O LORD, how manifold are thy works! in wisdom hast thou made them all: the earth is full of thy riches."

Psalm 105:7 "He is the LORD our God: his judgments are in all the earth."

Isaiah 6:1-3 "¹In the year that king Uzziah died I saw also the Lord sitting upon a throne, high and lifted up, and his train filled the temple. ²Above it stood the seraphims: each one had six wings; with twain he covered his face, and with twain he covered his feet, and with twain he did fly. ³And one cried unto another, and said, Holy, holy, holy, is the LORD of hosts: the whole earth is full of his glory."

Habakkuk 2:14 "For the earth shall be filled with the knowledge of the glory of the LORD, as the waters cover the sea."

What The Earth Is

Isaiah 66:1 "Thus saith the LORD, The heaven is my throne, and the earth is my footstool: where is the house that ye build unto me? and where is the place of my rest?"

Matthew 5:34-35 "³⁴But I say unto you, Swear not at all; neither by heaven; for it is God's throne: ³⁵Nor by the earth; for it is his footstool: neither by Jerusalem; for it is the city of the great King."

Who Is Earthly

John 3:31 "He that cometh from above is above all: he that is of the earth is earthly, and speaketh of the earth: he that cometh from heaven is above all."

Who Was Given Dominion Over The Earth

Genesis 1:26-28 "²⁶And God said, Let us make man in our image, after our likeness: and let them have dominion over the fish of the sea, and over the fowl of the air, and over the cattle, and over all the earth, and over every creeping thing that creepeth upon the earth. ²⁷So God created man in his own image, in the image of God created he him; male and female created he them. ²⁸And God blessed them, and God said unto them, Be fruitful, and multiply, and replenish the earth, and subdue it: and have dominion over the fish of the sea, and over the fowl of the air, and over every living thing that moveth upon the earth."

Psalm 8:4-9 "⁴What is man, that thou art mindful of him? and the son of man, that thou visitest him? ⁵For thou hast made him a little lower than the angels, and hast crowned him with glory and honour. ⁶Thou madest him to have dominion over the works of thy hands; thou hast put all things under his feet: ⁷All sheep and oxen, yea, and the beasts of the field; ⁸The fowl of the air, and the fish of the sea, and whatsoever passeth through the paths of the seas. ⁹O LORD our Lord, how excellent is thy name in all the earth!"

Psalm 115:16 "The heaven, even the heavens, are the LORD's: but the earth hath he given to the children of men."

EARTHQUAKES

The Earth Being Shaken

Psalm 60:1-2 "¹O God, thou hast cast us off, thou hast scattered us, thou hast been displeased; O turn thyself to us again. ²Thou hast made the earth to tremble; thou hast broken it: heal the breaches thereof; for it shaketh."

Psalm 114:7 "Tremble, thou earth, at the presence of the Lord, at the presence of the God of Jacob."

Isaiah 2:11-21 "¹¹The lofty looks of man shall be humbled, and the haughtiness of men shall be bowed down, and the LORD alone shall be exalted in that day. [12]For the day of the L ORD of hosts shall be upon every one that is proud and lofty, and upon every one that is lifted up; and he shall be brought low: [13]And upon all the cedars of Lebanon, that are high and lifted up, and upon all the oaks of Bashan, [14]And upon all the high mountains, and upon all the hills that are lifted up, [15]And upon every high tower, and upon every fenced wall, [16]And upon all the ships of Tarshish, and upon all pleasant pictures. [17]And the loftiness of man shall be bowed down, and the haughtiness of men shall be made low: and the L ORD alone shall be exalted in that day. [18]And the idols he shall utterly abolish. [19]And they shall go into the holes of the rocks, and into the caves of the earth, for fear of the L ORD, and for the glory of his majesty, when he ariseth to shake terribly the earth. [20]In that day a man shall cast his idols of silver, and his idols of gold, which they made each one for himself to worship, to the moles and to the bats; [21]To go into the clefts of the rocks, and into the tops of the ragged rocks, for fear of the L ORD, and for the glory of his majesty, when he ariseth to shake terribly the earth."

Isaiah 13:9-13 "[9]Behold, the day of the L ORD cometh, cruel both with wrath and fierce anger, to lay the land desolate: and he shall destroy the sinners thereof out of it. [10]For the stars of heaven and the constellations thereof shall not give their light: the sun shall be darkened in his going forth, and the moon shall not cause her light to shine. [11]And I will punish the world for their evil, and the wicked for their iniquity; and I will cause the arrogancy of the proud to cease, and will lay low the haughtiness of the terrible. [12]I will make a man more precious than fine gold; even a man than the golden wedge of Ophir. [13]Therefore I will shake the heavens, and the earth shall remove out of her place, in the wrath of the L ORD of hosts, and in the day of his fierce anger."

Jeremiah 10:10 "But the L ORD is the true God, he is the living God, and an everlasting king: at his wrath the earth shall tremble, and the nations shall not be able to abide his indignation."

Ezekiel 38:18-20 "[18]And it shall come to pass at the same time when Gog shall come against the land of Israel, saith the Lord G OD, that my fury shall come up in my face. [19]For in my jealousy and in the fire of my wrath have I spoken, Surely in that day there shall be a great shaking in the land of Israel; [20]So that the fishes of the sea, and the fowls of the heaven, and the beasts of the field, and all creeping things that creep upon the earth, and all the men that are upon the face of the earth, shall shake at my presence, and the mountains shall be thrown down, and the steep places shall fall, and every wall shall fall to the ground."

Joel 3:16 "The L ORD also shall roar out of Zion, and utter his voice from Jerusalem; and the heavens and the earth shall shake: but the L ORD will be the hope of his people, and the strength of the children of Israel."

Zechariah 14:1-5 "[1]Behold, the day of the L ORD cometh, and thy spoil shall be divided in the midst of thee. [2]For I will gather all nations against Jerusalem to battle; and the city shall be taken, and the houses rifled, and the women ravished; and half of the city shall go forth into captivity, and the residue of the people shall not be cut off from the city. [3]Then shall the L ORD go forth, and fight against those nations, as when he fought in the day of battle. [4]And his feet shall stand in that day upon the mount of Olives, which is before Jerusalem on the east, and the mount of Olives shall cleave in the midst thereof toward the east and toward the west, and there shall be a very great valley; and half of the mountain shall remove toward the north, and half of it toward the south. [5]And ye shall flee to the valley of the mountains; for the valley of the mountains shall reach unto Azal: yea, ye shall flee, like as ye fled from before the earthquake in the days of Uzziah king of Judah: and the L ORD my God shall come, and all the saints with thee."

Hebrews 12:22-27 "[22]But ye are come unto mount Sion, and unto the city of the living God, the heavenly Jerusalem, and to an innumerable company of angels, [23]To the general assembly and church of the firstborn, which are written in heaven, and to God the Judge of all, and to the spirits of just men made perfect, [24]And to Jesus the mediator of the new covenant, and to the blood of sprinkling, that speaketh better things than that of Abel. [25]See that ye refuse not him that speaketh. For if they escaped not who refused him that spake on earth, much more shall not we escape, if we turn away from him that speaketh from heaven: ²⁶Whose voice then shook the earth: but now he hath promised, saying, Yet once more I shake not the earth only, but also heaven. ²⁷And this word, Yet once more, signifieth the removing of those things that are shaken, as of things that are made, that those things which cannot be shaken may remain."

Revelation 6:12-17 "¹²And I beheld when he had opened the sixth seal, and, lo, there was a great earthquake; and the sun became black as sackcloth of hair, and the moon became as blood; ¹³And the stars of heaven fell unto the earth, even as a fig tree casteth her untimely figs, when she is shaken of a mighty wind. ¹⁴And the heaven departed as a scroll when it is rolled together; and every mountain and island were moved out of their places. ¹⁵And the kings of the earth, and the great men, and the rich men, and the chief captains, and the mighty men, and every bondman, and every free man, hid themselves in the dens and in the rocks of the mountains; ¹⁶And said to the mountains and rocks, Fall on us, and hide us from the face of him that sitteth on the throne, and from the wrath of the Lamb: ¹⁷For the great day of his wrath is come; and who shall be able to stand?"

Revelation 11:10-14 "¹⁰And they that dwell upon the earth shall rejoice over them, and make merry, and shall send gifts one to another; because these two prophets tormented them that dwelt on the earth. ¹¹And after three days and an half the Spirit of life from God entered into them, and they stood upon their feet; and great fear fell upon them which saw them. ¹²And they heard a great voice from heaven saying unto them, Come up hither. And they ascended up to heaven in a cloud; and their enemies beheld them. ¹³And the same hour was there a great earthquake, and the tenth part of the city fell, and in the earthquake were slain of men seven thousand: and the remnant were affrighted, and gave glory to the God of heaven. ¹⁴The second woe is past; and, behold, the third woe cometh quickly."

Revelation 16:17-21 "¹⁷And the seventh angel poured out his vial into the air; and there came a great voice out of the temple of heaven, from the throne, saying, It is done. ¹⁸And there were voices, and thunders, and lightnings; and there was a great earthquake, such as was not since men

were upon the earth, so mighty an earthquake, and so great. ¹⁹And the great city was divided into three parts, and the cities of the nations fell: and great Babylon came in remembrance before God, to give unto her the cup of the wine of the fierceness of his wrath. ²⁰And every island fled away, and the mountains were not found. ²¹And there fell upon men a great hail out of heaven, every stone about the weight of a talent: and men blasphemed God because of the plague of the hail; for the plague thereof was exceeding great."

There Being Earthquakes In Diverse Places Prior To The Coming Of The Lord

Matthew 24:1-7 "¹And Jesus went out, and departed from the temple: and his disciples came to him for to shew him the buildings of the temple. ²And Jesus said unto them, See ye not all these things? verily I say unto you, There shall not be left here one stone upon another, that shall not be thrown down. ³And as he sat upon the mount of Olives, the disciples came unto him privately, saying, Tell us, when shall these things be? and what shall be the sign of thy coming, and of the end of the world? ⁴And Jesus answered and said unto them, Take heed that no man deceive you. ⁵For many shall come in my name, saying, I am Christ; and shall deceive many. ⁶And ye shall hear of wars and rumours of wars: see that ye be not troubled: for all these things must come to pass, but the end is not yet. ⁷For nation shall rise against nation, and kingdom against kingdom: and there shall be famines, and pestilences, and earthquakes, in divers places."

Mark 13:1-8 "¹And as he went out of the temple, one of his disciples saith unto him, Master, see what manner of stones and what buildings are here! ²And Jesus answering said unto him, Seest thou these great buildings? there shall not be left one stone upon another, that shall not be thrown down. ³And as he sat upon the mount of Olives over against the temple, Peter and James and John and Andrew asked him privately, ⁴Tell us, when shall these things be? and what shall be the sign when all these things shall be fulfilled? ⁵And Jesus answering them began to say, Take heed lest any man deceive you: ⁶For many shall come in my name, saying, I am Christ; and shall deceive many. ⁷And when ye shall hear of wars and rumours of wars, be ye not troubled: for such things must needs be; but the end shall not be yet. [8]For nation shall rise against nation, and kingdom against kingdom: and there shall be earthquakes in divers places, and there shall be famines and troubles: these are the beginnings of sorrows."

Luke 21:5-11 "[5]And as some spake of the temple, how it was adorned with goodly stones and gifts, he said, [6]As for these things which ye behold, the days will come, in the which there shall not be left one stone upon another, that shall not be thrown down. [7]And they asked him, saying, Master, but when shall these things be? and what sign will there be when these things shall come to pass? [8]And he said, Take heed that ye be not deceived: for many shall come in my name, saying, I am Christ; and the time draweth near: go ye not therefore after them. [9]But when ye shall hear of wars and commotions, be not terrified: for these things must first come to pass; but the end is not by and by. [10]Then said he unto them, Nation shall rise against nation, and kingdom against kingdom: [11]And great earthquakes shall be in divers places, and famines, and pestilences; and fearful sights and great signs shall there be from heaven."

EDIFICATION

All Things Not Edifying
1 Corinthians 6:12 "All things are lawful unto me, but all things are not expedient: all things are lawful for me, but I will not be brought under the power of any."

1 Corinthians 10:23 "All things are lawful for me, but all things are not expedient: all things are lawful for me, but all things edify not."

Edifying One Another
Romans 15:2-3 "[2]Let every one of us please his neighbour for his good to edification. [3]For even Christ pleased not himself; but, as it is written, The reproaches of them that reproached thee fell on me."

1 Thessalonians 5:11 "Wherefore comfort yourselves together, and edify one another, even as also ye do."

Godly Edifying
1 Timothy 1:4 "Neither give heed to fables and endless genealogies, which minister questions, rather than godly edifying which is in faith: so do."

What Christ Provided For The Purpose Of Edification
Ephesians 4:7-12 "[7]But unto every one of us is given grace according to the measure of the gift of Christ. [8]Wherefore he saith, When he ascended up on high, he led captivity captive, and gave gifts unto men. [9](Now that he ascended, what is it but that he also descended first into the lower parts of the earth? [10]He that descended is the same also that ascended up far above all heavens, that he might fill all things.) [11]And he gave some, apostles; and some, prophets; and some, evangelists; and some, pastors and teachers; [12]For the perfecting of the saints, for the work of the ministry, for the edifying of the body of Christ."

What Edifies
1 Corinthians 8:1 "Now as touching things offered unto idols, we know that we all have knowledge. Knowledge puffeth up, but charity edifieth."

ELECTION

The Elect Of God
Isaiah 45:3-5 "[3]And I will give thee the treasures of darkness, and hidden riches of secret places, that thou mayest know that I, the LORD, which call thee by thy name, am the God of Israel. [4]For Jacob my servant's sake, and Israel mine elect, I have even called thee by thy name: I have surnamed thee, though thou hast not known me. [5]I am the LORD, and there is none else, there is no God beside me: I girded thee, though thou hast not known me."

Isaiah 65:8-10 "[8]Thus saith the LORD, As the new wine is found in the cluster, and one saith, Destroy it not; for a blessing is in it: so will I do for my servants' sakes, that I may not destroy them all. [9]And I will bring forth a seed out of Jacob, and out of Judah an inheritor of my mountains: and mine elect shall inherit it, and my servants shall dwell there. [10]And Sharon shall be a fold of flocks, and the valley of Achor a place for the herds to lie down in, for my people that have sought me."

Isaiah 65:21-24 "²¹And they shall build houses, and inhabit them; and they shall plant vineyards, and eat the fruit of them. ²²They shall not build, and another inhabit; they shall not plant, and another eat: for as the days of a tree are the days of my people, and mine elect shall long enjoy the work of their hands. ²³They shall not labour in vain, nor bring forth for trouble; for they are the seed of the blessed of the LORD, and their off-spring with them. ²⁴And it shall come to pass, that before they call, I will answer; and while they are yet speaking, I will hear."

Matthew 24:29-31 "²⁹Immediately after the tribulation of those days shall the sun be darkened, and the moon shall not give her light, and the stars shall fall from heaven, and the powers of the heavens shall be shaken: ³⁰And then shall appear the sign of the Son of man in heaven: and then shall all the tribes of the earth mourn, and they shall see the Son of man coming in the clouds of heaven with power and great glory. ³¹And he shall send his angels with a great sound of a trumpet, and they shall gather together his elect from the four winds, from one end of heaven to the other."

Mark 13:24-27 "²⁴But in those days, after that tribulation, the sun shall be darkened, and the moon shall not give her light, ²⁵And the stars of heaven shall fall, and the powers that are in heaven shall be shaken. ²⁶And then shall they see the Son of man coming in the clouds with great power and glory. ²⁷And then shall he send his angels, and shall gather together his elect from the four winds, from the uttermost part of the earth to the uttermost part of heaven."

Luke 18:7-8 "⁷And shall not God avenge his own elect, which cry day and night unto him, though he bear long with them? ⁸I tell you that he will avenge them speedily. Nevertheless when the Son of man cometh, shall he find faith on the earth?"

Romans 8:33 "Who shall lay any thing to the charge of God's elect? It is God that justifieth."

The Elected One
Isaiah 42:1-7 "¹Behold my servant, whom I uphold; mine elect, in whom my soul delighteth; I have put my spirit upon him: he shall bring forth judgment to the Gentiles. ²He shall not cry, nor lift up, nor cause his voice to be heard in the

street. ³A bruised reed shall he not break, and the smoking flax shall he not quench: he shall bring forth judgment unto truth. ⁴He shall not fail nor be discouraged, till he have set judgment in the earth: and the isles shall wait for his law. ⁵Thus saith God the LORD, he that created the heavens, and stretched them out; he that spread forth the earth, and that which cometh out of it; he that giveth breath unto the people upon it, and spirit to them that walk therein: ⁶I the LORD have called thee in righteousness, and will hold thine hand, and will keep thee, and give thee for a covenant of the people, for a light of the Gentiles; ⁷To open the blind eyes, to bring out the prisoners from the prison, and them that sit in darkness out of the prison house."

Malachi 3:1-5 "¹Behold, I will send my messenger, and he shall prepare the way before me: and the Lord, whom ye seek, shall suddenly come to his temple, even the messenger of the covenant, whom ye delight in: behold, he shall come, saith the LORD of hosts. ²But who may abide the day of his coming? and who shall stand when he appeareth? for he is like a refiner's fire, and like fullers' soap: ³And he shall sit as a refiner and purifer of silver: and he shall purify the sons of Levi, and purge them as gold and silver, that they may offer unto the LORD an offering in righteousness. ⁴Then shall the offering of Judah and Jerusalem be pleasant unto the LORD, as in the days of old, and as in former years. ⁵And I will come near to you to judgment; and I will be a swift witness against the sorcerers, and against the adulterers, and against false swearers, and against those that oppress the hireling in his wages, the widow, and the fatherless, and that turn aside the stranger from his right, and fear not me, saith the LORD of hosts."

EMPIRES/WORLD POWERS

Mystery Babylon
Revelation 17:1-18 "¹And there came one of the seven angels which had the seven vials, and talked with me, saying unto me, Come hither; I will shew unto thee the judgment of the great whore that sitteth upon many waters: ²With whom the kings of the earth have committed fornication, and the inhabitants of the earth have

been made drunk with the wine of her fornication. ³So he carried me away in the spirit into the wilderness: and I saw a woman sit upon a scarlet coloured beast, full of names of blasphemy, having seven heads and ten horns. ⁴And the woman was arrayed in purple and scarlet colour, and decked with gold and precious stones and pearls, having a golden cup in her hand full of abominations and filthiness of her fornication: ⁵And upon her forehead was a name written, MYSTERY, BABYLON THE GREAT, THE MOTHER OF HARLOTS AND ABOMINATIONS OF THE EARTH. ⁶And I saw the woman drunken with the blood of the saints, and with the blood of the martyrs of Jesus: and when I saw her, I wondered with great admiration. ⁷And the angel said unto me, Wherefore didst thou marvel? I will tell thee the mystery of the woman, and of the beast that carrieth her, which hath the seven heads and ten horns. ⁸The beast that thou sawest was, and is not; and shall ascend out of the bottomless pit, and go into perdition: and they that dwell on the earth shall wonder, whose names were not written in the book of life from the foundation of the world, when they behold the beast that was, and is not, and yet is. ⁹And here is the mind which hath wisdom. The seven heads are seven mountains, on which the woman sitteth. ¹⁰And there are seven kings: five are fallen, and one is, and the other is not yet come; and when he cometh, he must continue a short space. ¹¹And the beast that was, and is not, even he is the eighth, and is of the seven, and goeth into perdition. ¹²And the ten horns which thou sawest are ten kings, which have received no kingdom as yet; but receive power as kings one hour with the beast. ¹³These have one mind, and shall give their power and strength unto the beast. ¹⁴These shall make war with the Lamb, and the Lamb shall overcome them: for he is Lord of lords, and King of kings: and they that are with him are called, and chosen, and faithful. ¹⁵And he saith unto me, The waters which thou sawest, where the whore sitteth, are peoples, and multitudes, and nations, and tongues. ¹⁶And the ten horns which thou sawest upon the beast, these shall hate the whore, and shall make her desolate and naked, and shall eat her flesh, and burn her with fire. ¹⁷For God hath put in their hearts to fulfil his will, and to agree, and give their kingdom unto the beast, until the words of God shall be fulfilled. ¹⁸And the woman which thou sawest is that great city, which reigneth over the kings of the earth."

The Beast From The Sea
And The Beast From The Earth

Daniel 7:1-28 "¹In the first year of Belshazzar king of Babylon Daniel had a dream and visions of his head upon his bed: then he wrote the dream, and told the sum of the matters. ²Daniel spake and said, I saw in my vision by night, and, behold, the four winds of the heaven strove upon the great sea. ³And four great beasts came up from the sea, diverse one from another. ⁴The first was like a lion, and had eagle's wings: I beheld till the wings thereof were plucked, and it was lifted up from the earth, and made stand upon the feet as a man, and a man's heart was given to it. ⁵And behold another beast, a second, like to a bear, and it raised up itself on one side, and it had three ribs in the mouth of it between the teeth of it: and they said thus unto it, Arise, devour much flesh. ⁶After this I beheld, and lo another, like a leopard, which had upon the back of it four wings of a fowl; the beast had also four heads; and dominion was given to it. ⁷After this I saw in the night visions, and behold a fourth beast, dreadful and terrible, and strong exceedingly; and it had great iron teeth: it devoured and brake in pieces, and stamped the residue with the feet of it: and it was diverse from all the beasts that were before it; and it had ten horns. ⁸I considered the horns, and, behold, there came up among them another little horn, before whom there were three of the first horns plucked up by the roots: and, behold, in this horn were eyes like the eyes of man, and a mouth speaking great things. ⁹I beheld till the thrones were cast down, and the Ancient of days did sit, whose garment was white as snow, and the hair of his head like the pure wool: his throne was like the fiery flame, and his wheels as burning fire. ¹⁰A fiery stream issued and came forth from before him: thousand thousands ministered unto him, and ten thousand times ten thousand stood before him: the judgment was set, and the books were opened. ¹¹I beheld then because of the voice of the great words which the horn spake: I beheld even till the beast was slain, and his body destroyed, and given to the burning flame. ¹²As concerning the rest of the beasts, they had their dominion taken away: yet their lives were prolonged for a season and time. [13]I saw in the night visions, and, behold, one like the Son of man came with the clouds of heaven, and came to the Ancient of days, and they brought him near before him. [14]And there was given him dominion, and glory, and a kingdom, that all people, nations, and languages, should serve him: his dominion is an everlasting dominion, which shall not pass away, and his kingdom that which shall not be destroyed. [15]I Daniel was grieved in my spirit in the midst of my body, and the visions of my head troubled me. [16]I came near unto one of them that stood by, and asked him the truth of all this. So he told me, and made me know the interpretation of the things. [17]These great beasts, which are four, are four kings, which shall arise out of the earth. [18]But the saints of the most High shall take the kingdom, and possess the kingdom for ever, even for ever and ever. [19]Then I would know the truth of the fourth beast, which was diverse from all the others, exceeding dreadful, whose teeth were of iron, and his nails of brass; which devoured, brake in pieces, and stamped the residue with his feet; [20]And of the ten horns that were in his head, and of the other which came up, and before whom three fell; even of that horn that had eyes, and a mouth that spake very great things, whose look was more stout than his fellows. [21]I beheld, and the same horn made war with the saints, and prevailed against them; [22]Until the Ancient of days came, and judgment was given to the saints of the most High; and the time came that the saints possessed the kingdom. [23]Thus he said, The fourth beast shall be the fourth kingdom upon earth, which shall be diverse from all kingdoms, and shall devour the whole earth, and shall tread it down, and break it in pieces. [24]And the ten horns out of this kingdom are ten kings that shall arise: and another shall rise after them; and he shall be diverse from the first, and he shall subdue three kings. [25]And he shall speak great words against the most High, and shall wear out the saints of the most High, and think to change times and laws: and they shall be given into his hand until a time and times and the dividing of time. [26]But the judgment shall sit, and they shall take away his dominion, to consume and to destroy it unto the end. [27]And the kingdom and dominion, and the greatness of the kingdom under the whole heaven, shall be given to the people of the saints of the most High, whose kingdom is an everlasting kingdom, and all dominions shall serve and obey him. [28]Hitherto is the end of the matter. As for me Daniel, my cogitations much troubled me, and my countenance changed in me: but I kept the matter in my heart."

Revelation 13:1-18 "[1]And I stood upon the sand of the sea, and saw a beast rise up out of the sea, having seven heads and ten horns, and upon his horns ten crowns, and upon his heads the name of blasphemy. [2]And the beast which I saw was like unto a leopard, and his feet were as the feet of a bear, and his mouth as the mouth of a lion: and the dragon gave him his power, and his seat, and great authority. [3]And I saw one of his heads as it were wounded to death; and his deadly wound was healed: and all the world wondered after the beast. [4]And they worshipped the dragon which gave power unto the beast: and they worshipped the beast, saying, Who is like unto the beast? who is able to make war with him? [5]And there was given unto him a mouth speaking great things and blasphemies; and power was given unto him to continue forty and two months. [6]And he opened his mouth in blasphemy against God, to blaspheme his name, and his tabernacle, and them that dwell in heaven. [7]And it was given unto him to make war with the saints, and to overcome them: and power was given him over all kindreds, and tongues, and nations. [8]And all that dwell upon the earth shall worship him, whose names are not written in the book of life of the Lamb slain from the foundation of the world. [9]If any man have an ear, let him hear. [10]He that leadeth into captivity shall go into captivity: he that killeth with the sword must be killed with the sword. Here is the patience and the faith of the saints. [11]And I beheld another beast coming up out of the earth; and he had two horns like a lamb, and he spake as a dragon. [12]And he exerciseth all the power of the first beast before him, and causeth the earth and them which dwell therein to worship the first beast, whose deadly wound was healed. [13]And he doeth great wonders, so that he maketh fire come down from heaven on the earth in the sight of men, [14]And deceiveth them that dwell on the earth by the means of those miracles which he had power to do in the sight of the beast; saying to them that dwell on the earth, that they should make an image to the beast, which had the wound by a sword, and did live. [15]And he had power to give life unto the image of the beast, that the image of the beast should both speak, and cause that as many as would not worship the image of the beast should be killed. [16]And he causeth all, both small and great, rich and poor, free and bond, to receive a mark in their right hand, or in their foreheads: [17]And that no man might buy or sell, save he that had the mark, or the name of the beast, or the number of his name. [18]Here is wisdom. Let him that hath understanding count the number of the beast: for it is the number of a man; and his number is Six hundred threescore and six."

The Great Image

Daniel 2:31-45 "[31]Thou, O king, sawest, and behold a great image. This great image, whose brightness was excellent, stood before thee; and the form thereof was terrible. [32]This image's head was of fine gold, his breast and his arms of silver, his belly and his thighs of brass, [33]His legs of iron, his feet part of iron and part of clay. [34]Thou sawest till that a stone was cut out without hands, which smote the image upon his feet that were of iron and clay, and brake them to pieces. [35]Then was the iron, the clay, the brass, the silver, and the gold, broken to pieces together, and became like the chaff of the summer threshingfloors; and the wind carried them away, that no place was found for them: and the stone that smote the image became a great mountain, and filled the whole earth. [36]This is the dream; and we will tell the interpretation thereof before the king. [37]Thou, O king, art a king of kings: for the God of heaven hath given thee a kingdom, power, and strength, and glory. [38]And wheresoever the children of men dwell, the beasts of the field and the fowls of the heaven hath he given into thine hand, and hath made thee ruler over them all. Thou art this head of gold. [39]And after thee shall arise another kingdom inferior to thee, and another third kingdom of brass, which shall bear rule over all the earth. [40]And the fourth kingdom shall be strong as iron: forasmuch as iron breaketh in pieces and subdueth all things: and as iron that breaketh all these, shall it break in pieces and bruise. [41]And whereas thou sawest the feet and toes, part of potters' clay, and part of iron, the kingdom shall be divided; but there shall be in it of the strength of the iron, forasmuch as thou sawest the iron mixed with miry clay. [42]And as the toes of the feet were part of iron, and part of clay, so the kingdom shall be partly strong, and partly broken. [43]And whereas thou sawest iron mixed with miry clay, they shall mingle themselves with the seed of men: but they shall not cleave one to another, even as iron is not mixed with clay. [44]And in the days of these kings shall the God of heaven set up a kingdom, which shall never be destroyed: and the kingdom shall not be left to other people, but it shall break in pieces and consume all these kingdoms, and it shall stand for ever. [45]Forasmuch as thou sawest that the stone was cut out of the mountain without hands, and that it brake in pieces the iron, the brass, the clay, the silver, and the gold; the great God hath made known to the king what shall come to pass hereafter: and the dream is certain, and the interpretation thereof sure."

The King Of The North
And The King Of The South

Daniel 11:5-45 "[5]And the king of the south shall be strong, and one of his princes; and he shall be strong above him, and have dominion; his dominion shall be a great dominion. [6]And in the end of years they shall join themselves together; for the king's daughter of the south shall come to the king of the north to make an agreement: but she shall not retain the power of the arm; neither shall he stand, nor his arm: but she shall be given up, and they that brought her, and he that begat her, and he that strengthened her in these times. [7]But out of a branch of her roots shall one stand up in his estate, which shall come with an army, and shall enter into the fortress of the king of the north, and shall deal against them, and shall prevail: [8]And shall also carry captives into Egypt their gods, with their princes, and with their precious vessels of silver and of gold; and he shall continue more years than the king of the north. [9]So the king of the south shall come into his kingdom, and shall return into his own land. [10]But his sons shall be stirred up, and shall assemble a multitude of great forces: and one shall certainly come, and overflow, and pass through: then shall he return, and be stirred up, even to his fortress. [11]And the king of the south shall be moved with choler, and shall come forth and fight with him, even with the king of the north: and he shall set forth a great multitude; but the multitude shall be given into his hand. 12And when he hath taken away the multitude, his heart shall be lifted up; and he shall cast down many ten thousands: but he shall not be strengthened by it. 13For the king of the north shall return, and shall set forth a multitude greater than the former, and shall certainly come after certain years with a great army and with much riches. 14And in those times there shall many stand up against the king of the south: also the robbers of thy people shall exalt themselves to establish the vision; but they shall fall. 15So the king of the north shall come, and cast up a mount, and take the most fenced cities: and the arms of the south shall not withstand, neither his chosen people, neither shall there be any strength to withstand. 16But he that cometh against him shall do according to his own will, and none shall stand before him: and he shall stand in the glorious land, which by his hand shall be consumed. 17He shall also set his face to enter with the strength of his whole kingdom, and upright ones with him; thus shall he do: and he shall give him the daughter of women, corrupting her: but she shall not stand on his side, neither be for him. 18After this shall he turn his face unto the isles, and shall take many: but a prince for his own behalf shall cause the reproach offered by him to cease; without his own reproach he shall cause it to turn upon him. 19Then he shall turn his face toward the fort of his own land: but he shall stumble and fall, and not be found. 20Then shall stand up in his estate a raiser of taxes in the glory of the kingdom: but within few days he shall be destroyed, neither in anger, nor in battle. 21And in his estate shall stand up a vile person, to whom they shall not give the honour of the kingdom: but he shall come in peaceably, and obtain the kingdom by flatteries. 22And with the arms of a flood shall they be overflown from before him, and shall be broken; yea, also the prince of the covenant. 23And after the league made with him he shall work deceitfully: for he shall come up, and shall become strong with a small people. 24He shall enter peaceably even upon the fattest places of the province; and he shall do that which his fathers have not done, nor his fathers' fathers; he shall scatter among them the prey, and spoil, and riches: yea, and he shall forecast his devices against the strong holds, even for a time. 25And he shall stir up his power and his courage against the king of the south with a great army; and the king of the south shall be stirred up to battle with a very great and mighty army; but he shall not stand: for they shall forecast devices against him. 26Yea, they that feed of the portion of his meat shall destroy him, and his army shall overflow: and many shall fall down slain. 27And both these kings' hearts shall be to do mischief, and they shall speak lies at one table; but it shall not prosper: for yet the end shall be at the time appointed. 28Then shall he return into his land with great riches; and his heart shall be against the holy covenant; and he shall do exploits, and return to his own land. 29At the time appointed he shall return, and come toward the south; but it shall not be as the former, or as the latter. 30For the ships of Chittim shall come against him: therefore he shall be grieved, and return, and have indignation against the holy covenant: so shall he do; he shall even return, and have intelligence with them that forsake the holy covenant. 31And arms shall stand on his part, and they shall pollute the sanctuary of strength, and shall take away the daily sacrifice, and they shall place the abomination that maketh desolate. 32And such as do wickedly against the covenant shall he corrupt by flatteries: but the people that do know their God shall be strong, and do exploits. 33And they that understand among the people shall instruct many: yet they shall fall by the sword, and by flame, by captivity, and by spoil, many days. 34Now when they shall fall, they shall be holpen with a little help: but many shall cleave to them with flatteries. 35And some of them of understanding shall fall, to try them, and to purge, and to make them white, even to the time of the end: because it is yet for a time appointed. 36And the king shall do according to his will; and he shall exalt himself, and magnify himself above every god, and shall speak marvellous things against the God of gods, and shall prosper till the indignation be accomplished: for that that is determined shall be done. 37Neither shall he regard the God of his fathers, nor the desire of women, nor regard any god: for he shall magnify himself above all. 38But in his estate shall he honour the God of forces: and a god whom his fathers knew not shall he honour with gold, and silver, and with precious stones, and pleasant things. [39]Thus shall he do in the most strong holds with a strange god, whom he shall acknowledge and increase with glory: and he shall cause them to rule over many, and shall divide the land for gain. [40]And at the time of the end shall the king of the south push at him: and the king of the north shall come against him like a whirlwind, with chariots, and with horsemen, and with many ships; and he shall enter into the countries, and shall overflow and pass over. [41]He shall enter also into the glorious land, and many countries shall be overthrown: but these shall escape out of his hand, even Edom, and Moab, and the chief of the children of Ammon. [42]He shall stretch forth his hand also upon the countries: and the land of Egypt shall not escape. [43]But he shall have power over the treasures of gold and of silver, and over all the precious things of Egypt: and the Libyans and the Ethiopians shall be at his steps. [44]But tidings out of the east and out of the north shall trouble him: therefore he shall go forth with great fury to destroy, and utterly to make away many. [45]And he shall plant the tabernacles of his palace between the seas in the glorious holy mountain; yet he shall come to his end, and none shall help him."

The Ram And The He Goat

Daniel 8:1-26 "[1]In the third year of the reign of king Belshazzar a vision appeared unto me, even unto me Daniel, after that which appeared unto me at the first. [2]And I saw in a vision; and it came to pass, when I saw, that I was at Shushan in the palace, which is in the province of Elam; and I saw in a vision, and I was by the river of Ulai. [3]Then I lifted up mine eyes, and saw, and, behold, there stood before the river a ram which had two horns: and the two horns were high; but one was higher than the other, and the higher came up last. [4]I saw the ram pushing westward, and northward, and southward; so that no beasts might stand before him, neither was there any that could deliver out of his hand; but he did according to his will, and became great. [5]And as I was considering, behold, an he goat came from the west on the face of the whole earth, and touched not the ground: and the goat had a notable horn between his eyes. [6]And he came to the ram that had two horns, which I had there seen standing before the river, and ran unto him

in the fury of his power. [7]And I saw him come close unto the ram, and he was moved with choler against him, and smote the ram, and brake his two horns: and there was no power in the ram to stand before him, but he cast him down to the ground, and stamped upon him: and there was none that could deliver the ram out of his hand. [8]Therefore the he goat waxed very great: and when he was strong, the great horn was broken; and for it came up four notable ones toward the four winds of heaven. [9]And out of one of them came forth a little horn, which waxed exceeding great, toward the south, and toward the east, and toward the pleasant land. [10]And it waxed great, even to the host of heaven; and it cast down some of the host and of the stars to the ground, and stamped upon them. [11]Yea, he magnified himself even to the prince of the host, and by him the daily sacrifice was taken away, and the place of his sanctuary was cast down. [12]And an host was given him against the daily sacrifice by reason of transgression, and it cast down the truth to the ground; and it practised, and prospered. [13]Then I heard one saint speaking, and another saint said unto that certain saint which spake, How long shall be the vision concerning the daily sacrifice, and the transgression of desolation, to give both the sanctuary and the host to be trodden under foot? [14]And he said unto me, Unto two thousand and three hundred days; then shall the sanctuary be cleansed. [15]And it came to pass, when I, even I Daniel, had seen the vision, and sought for the meaning, then, behold, there stood before me as the appearance of a man. [16]And I heard a man's voice between the banks of Ulai, which called, and said, Gabriel, make this man to understand the vision. [17]So he came near where I stood: and when he came, I was afraid, and fell upon my face: but he said unto me, Understand, O son of man: for at the time of the end shall be the vision. [18]Now as he was speaking with me, I was in a deep sleep on my face toward the ground: but he touched me, and set me upright. [19]And he said, Behold, I will make thee know what shall be in the last end of the indignation: for at the time appointed the end shall be. [20]The ram which thou sawest having two horns are the kings of Media and Persia. [21]And the rough goat is the king of Grecia: and the great horn that is between his eyes is the first king. [22]Now that being broken, whereas four stood up for it, four kingdoms shall stand up out of the nation, but not in his power. 23And in the latter time of their kingdom, when the transgressors are come to the full, a king of fierce countenance, and understanding dark sentences, shall stand up. 24And his power shall be mighty, but not by his own power: and he shall destroy wonderfully, and shall prosper, and practise, and shall destroy the mighty and the holy people. 25And through his policy also he shall cause craft to prosper in his hand; and he shall magnify himself in his heart, and by peace shall destroy many: he shall also stand up against the Prince of princes; but he shall be broken without hand. 26And the vision of the evening and the morning which was told is true: wherefore shut thou up the vision; for it shall be for many days."

Daniel 10:20-21 "20Then said he, Knowest thou wherefore I come unto thee? and now will I return to fight with the prince of Persia: and when I am gone forth, lo, the prince of Grecia shall come. 21But I will shew thee that which is noted in the scripture of truth: and there is none that holdeth with me in these things, but Michael your prince."

Daniel 11:1-4 "1Also I in the first year of Darius the Mede, even I, stood to confirm and to strengthen him. 2And now will I shew thee the truth. Behold, there shall stand up yet three kings in Persia; and the fourth shall be far richer than they all: and by his strength through his riches he shall stir up all against the realm of Grecia. 3And a mighty king shall stand up, that shall rule with great dominion, and do according to his will. 4And when he shall stand up, his kingdom shall be broken, and shall be divided toward the four winds of heaven; and not to his posterity, nor according to his dominion which he ruled: for his kingdom shall be plucked up, even for others beside those."

END OF THE WORLD

The End Of All Things Being At Hand

1 Peter 4:7 "But the end of all things is at hand: be ye therefore sober, and watch unto prayer."

What Events Signal The End Of The World

Matthew 24:1-44 "1And Jesus went out, and departed from the temple: and his disciples came to him for to shew him the buildings of the temple. 2And Jesus said unto them, See ye not all these things? verily I say unto you, There shall not be left here one stone upon another, that shall not be thrown down. 3And as he sat upon the mount of Olives, the disciples came unto him privately, saying, Tell us, when shall these things be? and what shall be the sign of thy coming, and of the end of the world? 4And Jesus answered and said unto them, Take heed that no man deceive you. 5For many shall come in my name, saying, I am Christ; and shall deceive many. 6And ye shall hear of wars and rumours of wars: see that ye be not troubled: for all these things must come to pass, but the end is not yet. 7For nation shall rise against nation, and kingdom against kingdom: and there shall be famines, and pestilences, and earthquakes, in divers places. 8All these are the beginning of sorrows. 9Then shall they deliver you up to be afflicted, and shall kill you: and ye shall be hated of all nations for my name's sake. 10And then shall many be offended, and shall betray one another, and shall hate one another. 11And many false prophets shall rise, and shall deceive many. 12And because iniquity shall abound, the love of many shall wax cold. 13But he that shall endure unto the end, the same shall be saved. 14And this gospel of the kingdom shall be preached in all the world for a witness unto all nations; and then shall the end come. 15When ye therefore shall see the abomination of desolation, spoken of by Daniel the prophet, stand in the holy place, (whoso readeth, let him understand:) 16Then let them which be in Judaea flee into the mountains: 17Let him which is on the housetop not come down to take any thing out of his house: 18Neither let him which is in the field return back to take his clothes. 19And woe unto them that are with child, and to them that give suck in those days! 20But pray ye that your flight be not in the winter, neither on the sabbath day: 21For then shall be great tribulation, such as was not since the beginning of the world to this time, no, nor ever shall be. 22And except those days should be shortened, there should no flesh be saved: but for the elect's sake those days shall be shortened. 23Then if any man shall say unto you, Lo, here is Christ, or there; believe it not. 24For there shall arise false Christs, and false prophets, and shall shew great signs and wonders; insomuch that, if it were possible, they shall deceive the very elect. [25]Behold, I have told you before. [26]Wherefore if they shall say unto you, Behold, he is in the desert; go not forth: behold, he is in the secret chambers; believe it not. [27]For as the lightning cometh   out of the east, and shineth even unto the west; so shall also the coming of the Son of man be. [28]For wheresoever the carcase is, there will the eagles be gathered together. [29]Immediately after the tribulation of those days shall the sun be darkened, and the moon shall not give her light, and the stars shall fall from heaven, and the powers of the heavens shall be shaken: [30]And then shall appear the sign of the Son of man in heaven: and then shall all the tribes of the earth mourn, and they shall see the Son of man coming in the clouds of heaven with power and great glory. [31]And he shall send his angels with a great sound of a trumpet, and they shall gather together his elect from the four winds, from one end of heaven to the other. [32]Now learn a parable of the fig tree; When his branch is yet tender, and putteth forth leaves, ye know that summer is nigh: [33]So likewise ye, when ye shall see all these things, know that it is near, even at the doors. [34]Verily I say unto you, This generation shall not pass, till all these things be fulfilled. [35]Heaven and earth shall pass away, but my words shall not pass away. [36]But of that day and hour knoweth no man, no, not the angels of heaven, but my Father only. [37]But as the days of Noe were, so shall also the coming of the Son of man be. [38]For as in the days that were before the flood they were eating and drinking, marrying and giving in marriage, until the day that Noe entered into the ark, [39]And knew not until the flood came, and took them all away; so shall also the coming of the Son of man be. [40]Then shall two be in the field; the one shall be taken, and the other left. [41]Two women shall be grinding at the mill; the one shall be taken, and the other left. [42]Watch therefore: for ye know not what hour your Lord doth come. [43]But know this, that if the goodman of the house had known in what watch the thief would come, he would have watched, and would not have suffered his house to be broken up. [44]Therefore be ye also ready: for in such an hour as ye think not the Son of man cometh."

Mark 13:1-30 "[1]And as he went out of the temple, one of his disciples saith unto him, Master, see what manner of stones and what buildings are here! [2]And Jesus answering said unto him, Seest thou these great buildings? there shall not be left one stone upon another, that shall not be thrown down. [3]And as he sat upon the mount of Olives over against the temple, Peter and James and John and Andrew asked him privately, [4]Tell us, when shall these things be? and what shall be the sign when all these things shall be fulfilled? [5]And Jesus answering them began to say, Take heed lest any man deceive you: [6]For many shall come in my name, saying, I am Christ; and shall deceive many. [7] And when ye shall hear of wars and rumours of wars, be ye not troubled: for such things must needs be; but the end shall not be yet. [8]For nation shall rise against nation, and kingdom against kingdom: and there shall be earthquakes in divers places, and there shall be famines and troubles: these are the beginnings of sorrows. [9]But take heed to yourselves: for they shall deliver you up to councils; and in the synagogues ye shall be beaten: and ye shall be brought before rulers and kings for my sake, for a testimony against them. [10]And the gospel must first be published among all nations. [11]But when they shall lead you, and deliver you up, take no thought beforehand what ye shall speak, neither do ye premeditate: but whatsoever shall be given you in that hour, that speak ye: for it is not ye that speak, but the Holy Ghost. [12]Now the brother shall betray the brother to death, and the father the son; and children shall rise up against their parents, and shall cause them to be put to death. [13]And ye shall be hated of all men for my name's sake: but he that shall endure unto the end, the same shall be saved. [14]But when ye shall see the abomination of desolation, spoken of by Daniel the prophet, standing where it ought not, (let him that readeth understand,) then let them that be in Judaea flee to the mountains: [15]And let him that is on the housetop not go down into the house, neither enter therein, to take any thing out of his house: [16]And let him that is in the field not turn back again for to take up his garment. [17]But woe to them that are with child, and to them that give suck in those days! [18]And pray ye that your flight be not in the winter. [19]For in those days shall be affliction, such as was not from the beginning of the creation which God created unto this time, neither shall be. [20]And except that the Lord had shortened those days, no flesh should be saved: but for the elect's sake, whom he hath chosen, he hath shortened the days. [21]And then if any man shall say to you, Lo, here is Christ; or, lo, he is there; believe him not: [22]For false Christs and false prophets shall rise, and shall shew signs and wonders, to seduce, if it were possible, even the elect. [23]But take ye heed: behold, I have foretold you all things. [24]But in those days, after that tribulation, the sun shall be darkened, and the moon shall not give her light, [25]And the stars of heaven shall fall, and the powers that are in heaven shall be shaken. [26]And then shall they see the Son of man coming in the clouds with great power and glory. [27]And then shall he send his angels, and shall gather together his elect from the four winds, from the uttermost part of the earth to the uttermost part of heaven. [28]Now learn a parable of the fig tree; When her branch is yet tender, and putteth forth leaves, ye know that summer is near: [29]So ye in like manner, when ye shall see these things come to pass, know that it is nigh, even at the doors. [30]Verily I say unto you, that this generation shall not pass, till all these things be done."

Luke 21:5-36 "[5]And as some spake of the temple, how it was adorned with goodly stones and gifts, he said, [6]As for these things which ye behold, the days will come, in the which there shall not be left one stone upon another, that shall not be thrown down. [7]And they asked him, saying, Master, but when shall these things be? and what sign will there be when these things shall come to pass? [8]And he said, Take heed that ye be not deceived: for many shall come in my name, saying, I am Christ; and the time draweth near: go ye not therefore after them. [9]But when ye shall hear of wars and commotions, be not terrified: for these things must first come to pass; but the end is not by and by. [10]Then said he unto them, Nation shall rise against nation, and kingdom against kingdom: [11]And great earthquakes shall be in divers places, and famines, and pestilences; and fearful sights and great signs shall there be from heaven. [12]But before all these, they shall lay their hands on you, and persecute you, delivering you up to the synagogues, and into prisons, being brought before kings and rulers for my name's sake. [13]And it shall turn to you for a testimony. [14]Settle it therefore in your hearts, not to meditate before what ye shall answer: [15]For I will give you a mouth and wisdom, which all your adversaries shall not be able to gainsay nor resist. [16]And ye shall be betrayed both by parents, and brethren, and kinsfolks, and friends; and some of you shall they cause to be put to death. [17]And ye shall be hated of all men for my name's sake. [18]But there shall not an hair of your head perish. [19]In your patience possess ye your souls. [20]And when ye shall see Jerusalem compassed with armies, then know that the desolation thereof is nigh. [21]Then let them which are in Judaea flee to the mountains; and let them which are in the midst of it depart out; and let not them that are in the countries enter thereinto. [22]For these be the days of vengeance, that all things which are written may be fulfilled. [23]But woe unto them that are with child, and to them that give suck, in those days! for there shall be great distress in the land, and wrath upon this people. [24]And they shall fall by the edge of the sword, and shall be led away captive into all nations: and Jerusalem shall be trodden down of the Gentiles, until the times of the Gentiles be fulfilled. [25]And there shall be signs in the sun, and in the moon, and in the stars; and upon the earth distress of nations, with perplexity; the sea and the waves roaring; [26]Men's hearts failing them for fear, and for looking after those things which are coming on the earth: for the powers of heaven shall be shaken. [27]And then shall they see the Son of man coming in a cloud with power and great glory. [28]And when these things begin to come to pass, then look up, and lift up your heads; for your redemption draweth nigh. [29]And he spake to them a parable; Behold the fig tree, and all the trees; [30]When they now shoot forth, ye see and know of your own selves that summer is now nigh at hand. [31]So likewise ye, when ye see these things come to pass, know ye that the kingdom of God is nigh at hand. [32]Verily I say unto you, This generation shall not pass away, till all be fulfilled. [33]Heaven and earth shall pass away: but my words shall not pass away. [34]And take heed to yourselves, lest at any time your hearts be overcharged with surfeiting, and drunkenness, and cares of this life, and so that day come upon you unawares. [35]For as a snare shall it come on all them that dwell on the face of the whole earth. [36]Watch ye therefore, and pray always, that ye may be accounted worthy to escape all these things that shall come to pass, and to stand before the Son of man."

What The End Of The World Is Likened To

Matthew 13:24-52 "²⁴Another parable put he forth unto them, saying, The kingdom of heaven is likened unto a man which sowed good seed in his field: ²⁵But while men slept, his enemy came and sowed tares among the wheat, and went his way. ²⁶But when the blade was sprung up, and brought forth fruit, then appeared the tares also. ²⁷So the servants of the householder came and said unto him, Sir, didst not thou sow good seed in thy field? from whence then hath it tares? ²⁸He said unto them, An enemy hath done this. The servants said unto him, Wilt thou then that we go and gather them up? ²⁹But he said, Nay; lest while ye gather up the tares, ye root up also the wheat with them. ³⁰Let both grow together until the harvest: and in the time of harvest I will say to the reapers, Gather ye together first the tares, and bind them in bundles to burn them: but gather the wheat into my barn. ³¹Another parable put he forth unto them, saying, The kingdom of heaven is like to a grain of mustard seed, which a man took, and sowed in his field: ³²Which indeed is the least of all seeds: but when it is grown, it is the greatest among herbs, and becometh a tree, so that the birds of the air come and lodge in the branches thereof. ³³Another parable spake he unto them; The kingdom of heaven is like unto leaven, which a woman took, and hid in three measures of meal, till the whole was leavened. ³⁴All these things spake Jesus unto the multitude in parables; and without a parable spake he not unto them: ³⁵That it might be fulfilled which was spoken by the prophet, saying, I will open my mouth in parables; I will utter things which have been kept secret from the foundation of the world. ³⁶Then Jesus sent the multitude away, and went into the house: and his disciples came unto him, saying, Declare unto us the parable of the tares of the field. ³⁷He answered and said unto them, He that soweth the good seed is the Son of man; ³⁸The field is the world; the good seed are the children of the kingdom; but the tares are the children of the wicked one; ³⁹The enemy that sowed them is the devil; the harvest is the end of the world; and the reapers are the angels. ⁴⁰As therefore the tares are gathered and burned in the fire; so shall it be in the end of this world. ⁴¹The Son of man shall send forth his angels, and they shall gather out of his kingdom all things that offend, and them which do iniquity; ⁴²And shall cast them into a furnace of fire: there shall be wailing and gnashing of teeth. ⁴³Then shall the righteous shine forth as the sun in the kingdom of their Father. Who hath ears to hear, let him hear. ⁴⁴Again, the kingdom of heaven is like unto treasure hid in a field; the which when a man hath found, he hideth, and for joy thereof goeth and selleth all that he hath, and buyeth that field. ⁴⁵Again, the kingdom of heaven is like unto a merchant man, seeking goodly pearls: ⁴⁶Who, when he had found one pearl of great price, went and sold all that he had, and bought it. ⁴⁷Again, the kingdom of heaven is like unto a net, that was cast into the sea, and gathered of every kind: ⁴⁸Which, when it was full, they drew to shore, and sat down, and gathered the good into vessels, but cast the bad away. ⁴⁹So shall it be at the end of the world: the angels shall come forth, and sever the wicked from among the just, ⁵⁰And shall cast them into the furnace of fire: there shall be wailing and gnashing of teeth. ⁵¹Jesus saith unto them, Have ye understood all these things? They say unto him, Yea, Lord. ⁵²Then said he unto them, Therefore every scribe which is instructed unto the kingdom of heaven is like unto a man that is an householder, which bringeth forth out of his treasure things new and old."

When The End Of The World Will Come

Matthew 24:1-14 "¹And Jesus went out, and departed from the temple: and his disciples came to him for to shew him the buildings of the temple. ²And Jesus said unto them, See ye not all these things? verily I say unto you, There shall not be left here one stone upon another, that shall not be thrown down. ³And as he sat upon the mount of Olives, the disciples came unto him privately, saying, Tell us, when shall these things be? and what shall be the sign of thy coming, and of the end of the world? ⁴And Jesus answered and said unto them, Take heed that no man deceive you. ⁵For many shall come in my name, saying, I am Christ; and shall deceive many. ⁶And ye shall hear of wars and rumours of wars: see that ye be not troubled: for all these things must come to pass, but the end is not yet. ⁷For nation shall rise against nation, and kingdom against kingdom:

and there shall be famines, and pestilences, and earthquakes, in divers places. ⁸All these are the beginning of sorrows. ⁹Then shall they deliver you up to be afflicted, and shall kill you: and ye shall be hated of all nations for my name's sake. ¹⁰And then shall many be offended, and shall betray one another, and shall hate one another. ¹¹And many false prophets shall rise, and shall deceive many. ¹²And because iniquity shall abound, the love of many shall wax cold. ¹³But he that shall endure unto the end, the same shall be saved. ¹⁴And this gospel of the kingdom shall be preached in all the world for a witness unto all nations; and then shall the end come."

Mark 13:1-10 "¹And as he went out of the temple, one of his disciples saith unto him, Master, see what manner of stones and what buildings are here! ²And Jesus answering said unto him, Seest thou these great buildings? there shall not be left one stone upon another, that shall not be thrown down. ³And as he sat upon the mount of Olives over against the temple, Peter and James and John and Andrew asked him privately, ⁴Tell us, when shall these things be? and what shall be the sign when all these things shall be fulfilled? ⁵And Jesus answering them began to say, Take heed lest any man deceive you: ⁶For many shall come in my name, saying, I am Christ; and shall deceive many. ⁷And when ye shall hear of wars and rumours of wars, be ye not troubled: for such things must needs be; but the end shall not be yet. ⁸For nation shall rise against nation, and kingdom against kingdom: and there shall be earthquakes in divers places, and there shall be famines and troubles: these are the beginnings of sorrows. ⁹But take heed to yourselves: for they shall deliver you up to councils; and in the synagogues ye shall be beaten: and ye shall be brought before rulers and kings for my sake, for a testimony against them. ¹⁰And the gospel must first be published among all nations."

1 Corinthians 15:20-24 "²⁰But now is Christ risen from the dead, and become the firstfruits of them that slept. ²¹For since by man came death, by man came also the resurrection of the dead. ²²For as in Adam all die, even so in Christ shall all be made alive. ²³But every man in his own order: Christ the firstfruits; afterward they that are Christ's at his coming. ²⁴Then cometh the end, when he shall have delivered up the kingdom to God, even the Father; when he shall have put down all rule and all authority and power."

ENDURANCE

Finishing The Course
Acts 20:24 "But none of these things move me, neither count I my life dear unto myself, so that I might finish my course with joy, and the ministry, which I have received of the Lord Jesus, to testify the gospel of the grace of God."

2 Timothy 4:7-8 "⁷I have fought a good fight, I have finished my course, I have kept the faith: ⁸Henceforth there is laid up for me a crown of righteousness, which the Lord, the righteous judge, shall give me at that day: and not to me only, but unto all them also that love his appearing."

Hebrews 12:1-3 "¹Wherefore seeing we also are compassed about with so great a cloud of witnesses, let us lay aside every weight, and the sin which doth so easily beset us, and let us run with patience the race that is set before us, ²Looking unto Jesus the author and finisher of our faith; who for the joy that was set before him endured the cross, despising the shame, and is set down at the right hand of the throne of God. ³For consider him that endured such contradiction of sinners against himself, lest ye be wearied and faint in your minds."

Jesus Christ Enduring The Cross
Hebrews 12:1-2 "¹Wherefore seeing we also are compassed about with so great a cloud of witnesses, let us lay aside every weight, and the sin which doth so easily beset us, and let us run with patience the race that is set before us, ²Looking unto Jesus the author and finisher of our faith; who for the joy that was set before him endured the cross, despising the shame, and is set down at the right hand of the throne of God."

The Lord Enduring Forever
Psalm 9:7 "But the LORD shall endure for ever: he hath prepared his throne for judgment."

Psalm 10:16 "The LORD is King for ever and ever: the heathen are perished out of his land."

Psalm 45:6 "Thy throne, O God, is for ever and ever: the sceptre of thy kingdom is a right sceptre."

Psalm 93:1-2 "¹The LORD reigneth, he is clothed with majesty; the LORD is clothed with strength, wherewith he hath girded himself: the world also is stablished, that it cannot be moved. ²Thy throne is established of old: thou art from everlasting."

Psalm 102:24-27 "²⁴I said, O my God, take me not away in the midst of my days: thy years are throughout all generations. ²⁵Of old hast thou laid the foundation of the earth: and the heavens are the work of thy hands. ²⁶They shall perish, but thou shalt endure: yea, all of them shall wax old like a garment; as a vesture shalt thou change them, and they shall be changed: ²⁷But thou art the same, and thy years shall have no end."

Isaiah 40:28 "Hast thou not known? hast thou not heard, that the everlasting God, the LORD, the Creator of the ends of the earth, fainteth not, neither is weary? there is no searching of his understanding."

Lamentations 5:19 "Thou, O LORD, remainest for ever; thy throne from generation to generation."

Daniel 4:34 "And at the end of the days I Nebuchadnezzar lifted up mine eyes unto heaven, and mine understanding returned unto me, and I blessed the most High, and I praised and honoured him that liveth for ever, whose dominion is an everlasting dominion, and his kingdom is from generation to generation."

Daniel 6:26 "I make a decree, That in every dominion of my kingdom men tremble and fear before the God of Daniel: for he is the living God, and stedfast for ever, and his kingdom that which shall not be destroyed, and his dominion shall be even unto the end."

Hebrews 1:8-12 "⁸But unto the Son he saith, Thy throne, O God, is for ever and ever: a sceptre of righteousness is the sceptre of thy kingdom. ⁹Thou hast loved righteousness, and hated iniquity; therefore God, even thy God, hath anointed thee with the oil of gladness above thy fellows. ¹⁰And, Thou, Lord, in the beginning hast laid the foundation of the earth; and the heavens are the works of thine hands: ¹¹They shall perish; but thou remainest; and they all shall wax old as doth a garment; ¹²And as a vesture shalt thou fold them up, and they shall be changed: but thou art the same, and thy years shall not fail."

1 Peter 4:11 "If any man speak, let him speak as the oracles of God; if any man minister, let him do it as of the ability which God giveth: that God in all things may be glorified through Jesus Christ, to whom be praise and dominion for ever and ever. Amen."

The Reward For Enduring

Galatians 6:9 "And let us not be weary in well doing: for in due season we shall reap, if we faint not."

2 Timothy 4:7-8 "⁷I have fought a good fight, I have finished my course, I have kept the faith: ⁸Henceforth there is laid up for me a crown of righteousness, which the Lord, the righteous judge, shall give me at that day: and not to me only, but unto all them also that love his appearing."

Hebrews 12:7-10 "⁷If ye endure chastening, God dealeth with you as with sons; for what son is he whom the father chasteneth not? ⁸But if ye be without chastisement, whereof all are partakers, then are ye bastards, and not sons. ⁹Furthermore we have had fathers of our flesh which corrected us, and we gave them reverence: shall we not much rather be in subjection unto the Father of spirits, and live? ¹⁰For they verily for a few days chastened us after their own pleasure; but he for our profit, that we might be partakers of his holiness."

Revelation 2:8-10 "⁸And unto the angel of the church in Smyrna write; These things saith the first and the last, which was dead, and is alive; ⁹I know thy works, and tribulation, and poverty, (but thou art rich) and I know the blasphemy of them which say they are Jews, and are not, but are the synagogue of Satan. ¹⁰Fear none of those things which thou shalt suffer: behold, the devil shall cast some of you into prison, that ye may be tried; and ye shall have tribulation ten days: be thou faithful unto death, and I will give thee a crown of life."

Those That Endure

Matthew 10:16-22 "¹⁶Behold, I send you forth as sheep in the midst of wolves: be ye therefore wise as serpents, and harmless as doves. ¹⁷But beware of men: for they will deliver you up to the councils, and they will scourge you in their synagogues; ¹⁸And ye shall be brought before governors and kings for my sake, for a testimony against them and the Gentiles. ¹⁹But when they deliver you up, take no thought how or what ye shall speak: for it shall be given you in that same hour what ye shall speak. [20]For it is not ye that speak, but the Spirit of your Father which speaketh in you. [21]And the brother shall deliver up the brother to death, and the father the child: and the children shall rise up against their parents, and cause them to be put to death. [22]And ye shall be hated of all men for my name's sake: but he that endureth to the end shall be saved."

Matthew 24:8-13 "[8]All these are the beginning of sorrows. [9]Then shall they deliver you up to be afflicted, and shall kill you: and ye shall be hated of all nations for my name's sake. [10]And then shall many be offended, and shall betray one another, and shall hate one another. [11]And many false prophets shall rise, and shall deceive many. [12]And because iniquity shall abound, the love of many shall wax cold. [13]But he that shall endure unto the end, the same shall be saved."

Mark 13:12-13 "[12]Now the brother shall betray the brother to death, and the father the son; and children shall rise up against their parents, and shall cause them to be put to death. [13]And ye shall be hated of all men for my name's sake: but he that shall endure unto the end, the same shall be saved."

Luke 22:28-30 "[28]Ye are they which have continued with me in my temptations. [29]And I appoint unto you a kingdom, as my Father hath appointed unto me; [30]That ye may eat and drink at my table in my kingdom, and sit on thrones judging the twelve tribes of Israel."

What Endures Forever

2 Samuel 7:8-16 "[8]Now therefore so shalt thou say unto my servant David, Thus saith the LORD of hosts, I took thee from the sheepcote, from following the sheep, to be ruler over my people, over Israel: [9]And I was with thee whithersoever thou wentest, and have cut off all thine enemies out of thy sight, and have made thee a great name, like unto the name of the great men that are in the earth. [10]Moreover I will appoint a place for my people Israel, and will plant them, that they may dwell in a place of their own, and move no more; neither shall the children of wickedness afflict them any more, as beforetime, [11]And as since the time that I commanded judges to be over my people Israel,

and have caused thee to rest from all thine enemies. Also the LORD telleth thee that he will make thee an house. [12]And when thy days be fulfilled, and thou shalt sleep with thy fathers, I will set up thy seed after thee, which shall proceed out of thy bowels, and I will establish his kingdom. [13]He shall build an house for my name, and I will stablish the throne of his kingdom for ever. [14]I will be his father, and he shall be my son. If he commit iniquity, I will chasten him with the rod of men, and with the stripes of the children of men: [15]But my mercy shall not depart away from him, as I took it from Saul, whom I put away before thee. [16]And thine house and thy kingdom shall be established for ever before thee: thy throne shall be established for ever."

1 Chronicles 16:34 "O give thanks unto the LORD; for he is good; for his mercy endureth for ever."

1 Chronicles 17:7-14 "[7]Now therefore thus shalt thou say unto my servant David, Thus saith the LORD of hosts, I took thee from the sheepcote, even from following the sheep, that thou shouldest be ruler over my people Israel: [8]And I have been with thee whithersoever thou hast walked, and have cut off all thine enemies from before thee, and have made thee a name like the name of the great men that are in the earth. [9]Also I will ordain a place for my people Israel, and will plant them, and they shall dwell in their place, and shall be moved no more; neither shall the children of wickedness waste them any more, as at the beginning, [10]And since the time that I commanded judges to be over my people Israel. Moreover I will subdue all thine enemies. Furthermore I tell thee that the LORD will build thee an house. [11]And it shall come to pass, when thy days be expired that thou must go to be with thy fathers, that I will raise up thy seed after thee, which shall be of thy sons; and I will establish his kingdom. [12]He shall build me an house, and I will stablish his throne for ever. [13]I will be his father, and he shall be my son: and I will not take my mercy away from him, as I took it from him that was before thee: [14]But I will settle him in mine house and in my kingdom for ever: and his throne shall be established for evermore."

1 Chronicles 28:2-7 "[2]Then David the king stood up upon his feet, and said, Hear me, my brethren, and my people: As for me, I had in mine heart to build an house of rest for the ark of the covenant of the LORD, and for the footstool of our God, and had made ready for the building: ³But God said unto me, Thou shalt not build an house for my name, because thou hast been a man of war, and hast shed blood. ⁴Howbeit the LORD God of Israel chose me before all the house of my father to be king over Israel for ever: for he hath chosen Judah to be the ruler; and of the house of Judah, the house of my father; and among the sons of my father he liked me to make me king over all Israel: ⁵And of all my sons, (for the LORD hath given me many sons,) he hath chosen Solomon my son to sit upon the throne of the kingdom of the LORD over Israel. ⁶And he said unto me, Solomon thy son, he shall build my house and my courts: for I have chosen him to be my son, and I will be his father. ⁷Moreover I will establish his kingdom for ever, if he be constant to do my commandments and my judgments, as at this day."

Psalm 33:11 "The counsel of the LORD standeth for ever, the thoughts of his heart to all generations."

Psalm 37:18 "The LORD knoweth the days of the upright: and their inheritance shall be for ever."

Psalm 52:1 "Why boastest thou thyself in mischief, O mighty man? the goodness of God endureth continually."

Psalm 100:5 "For the LORD is good; his mercy is everlasting; and his truth endureth to all generations."

Psalm 103:17 "But the mercy of the LORD is from everlasting to everlasting upon them that fear him, and his righteousness unto children's children."

Psalm 104:31 "The glory of the LORD shall endure for ever: the LORD shall rejoice in his works."

Psalm 107:1 "O give thanks unto the LORD, for he is good: for his mercy endureth for ever."

Psalm 111:2-3 "²The works of the LORD are great, sought out of all them that have pleasure therein. ³His work is honourable and glorious: and his righteousness endureth for ever."

Psalm 111:10 "The fear of the LORD is the beginning of wisdom: a good understanding have all they that do his commandments: his praise endureth for ever."

Psalm 112:1-3 "¹Praise ye the LORD. Blessed is the man that feareth the LORD, that delighteth greatly in his commandments. ²His seed shall be mighty upon earth: the generation of the upright shall be blessed. ³Wealth and riches shall be in his house: and his righteousness endureth for ever."

Psalm 117:2 "For his merciful kindness is great toward us: and the truth of the LORD endureth for ever. Praise ye the LORD."

Psalm 118:1-4 "¹O give thanks unto the LORD; for he is good: because his mercy endureth for ever. ²Let Israel now say, that his mercy endureth for ever. ³Let the house of Aaron now say, that his mercy endureth for ever. ⁴Let them now that fear the LORD say, that his mercy endureth for ever."

Psalm 118:29 "O give thanks unto the LORD; for he is good: for his mercy endureth for ever."

Psalm 119:89-90 "⁸⁹For ever, O LORD, thy word is settled in heaven. ⁹⁰Thy faithfulness is unto all generations: thou hast established the earth, and it abideth."

Psalm 119:159-160 "¹⁵⁹Consider how I love thy precepts: quicken me, O LORD, according to thy lovingkindness. ¹⁶⁰Thy word is true from the beginning: and every one of thy righteous judgments endureth for ever."

Psalm 136:1-26 "¹O give thanks unto the LORD; for he is good: for his mercy endureth for ever. ²O give thanks unto the God of gods: for his mercy endureth for ever. ³O give thanks to the Lord of lords: for his mercy endureth for ever. ⁴To him who alone doeth great wonders: for his mercy endureth for ever. ⁵To him that by wisdom made the heavens: for his mercy endureth for ever. ⁶To him that stretched out the earth above the waters: for his mercy endureth for ever. ⁷To him that made great lights: for his mercy endureth for ever: ⁸The sun to rule by day: for his mercy endureth for ever: ⁹The moon and stars to rule by night: for his mercy endureth for ever. ¹⁰To him that smote Egypt in their firstborn: for his mercy endureth for ever: [11]And brought out Israel from among them: for his mercy endureth for ever: [12]With a strong hand, and with a stretched out arm: for his mercy endureth for ever. [13]To him which divided the Red sea into parts: for his mercy endureth for ever: [14]And made Israel to pass through the midst of it: for his mercy endureth for ever: [15]But overthrew Pharaoh and his host in the Red sea: for his mercy endureth for ever. [16]To him which led his people through the wilderness: for his mercy endureth for ever. [17]To him which smote great kings: for his mercy endureth for ever: [18]And slew famous kings: for his mercy endureth for ever: [19]Sihon king of the Amorites: for his mercy endureth for ever: [20]And Og the king of Bashan: for his mercy endureth for ever: [21]And gave their land for an heritage: for his mercy endureth for ever: [22]Even an heritage unto Israel his servant: for his mercy endureth for ever. [23]Who remembered us in our low estate: for his mercy endureth for ever: [24]And hath redeemed us from our enemies: for his mercy endureth for ever. [25]Who giveth food to all flesh: for his mercy endureth for ever. [26]O give thanks unto the God of heaven: for his mercy endureth for ever."

Psalm 138:8 "The LORD will perfect that which concerneth me: thy mercy, O LORD, endureth for ever: forsake not the works of thine own hands."

Psalm 145:10-13 "[10]All thy works shall praise thee, O LORD; and thy saints shall bless thee. [11]They shall speak of the glory of thy kingdom, and talk of thy power; [12]To make known to the sons of men his mighty acts, and the glorious majesty of his kingdom. [13]Thy kingdom is an everlasting kingdom, and thy dominion endureth throughout all generations."

Proverbs 12:19 "The lip of truth shall be established for ever: but a lying tongue is but for a moment."

Isaiah 40:8 "The grass withereth, the flower fadeth: but the word of our God shall stand for ever."

Isaiah 51:6-8 "[6]Lift up your eyes to the heavens, and look upon the earth beneath: for the heavens shall vanish away like smoke, and the earth shall wax old like a garment, and they that dwell therein shall die in like manner: but my salvation shall be for ever, and my righteousness shall not be abolished. [7]Hearken unto me, ye that know righteousness, the people in whose heart is my law; fear ye not the reproach of men, neither be ye afraid of their revilings. [8]For the moth shall eat them up like a garment, and the worm shall eat them like wool: but my righteousness shall be for ever, and my salvation from generation to generation."

Jeremiah 33:11 "The voice of joy, and the voice of gladness, the voice of the bridegroom, and the voice of the bride, the voice of them that shall say, Praise the LORD of hosts: for the LORD is good; for his mercy endureth for ever: and of them that shall bring the sacrifice of praise into the house of the LORD. For I will cause to return the captivity of the land, as at the first, saith the LORD."

Daniel 2:44 "And in the days of these kings shall the God of heaven set up a kingdom, which shall never be destroyed: and the kingdom shall not be left to other people, but it shall break in pieces and consume all these kingdoms, and it shall stand for ever."

Daniel 4:2-3 "[2]I thought it good to shew the signs and wonders that the high God hath wrought toward me. [3]How great are his signs! and how mighty are his wonders! his kingdom is an everlasting kingdom, and his dominion is from generation to generation."

Daniel 4:34 "And at the end of the days I Nebuchadnezzar lifted up mine eyes unto heaven, and mine understanding returned unto me, and I blessed the most High, and I praised and honoured him that liveth for ever, whose dominion is an everlasting dominion, and his kingdom is from generation to generation."

Daniel 6:26 "I make a decree, That in every dominion of my kingdom men tremble and fear before the God of Daniel: for he is the living God, and stedfast for ever, and his kingdom that which shall not be destroyed, and his dominion shall be even unto the end."

Matthew 24:35 "Heaven and earth shall pass away, but my words shall not pass away."

Mark 13:31 "Heaven and earth shall pass away: but my words shall not pass away."

Luke 1:31-33 "31And, behold, thou shalt conceive in thy womb, and bring forth a son, and shalt call his name JESUS. 32He shall be great, and shall be called the Son of the Highest: and the Lord God shall give unto him the throne of his father David: 33And he shall reign over the house of Jacob for ever; and of his kingdom there shall be no end."

Luke 21:33 "Heaven and earth shall pass away: but my words shall not pass away."

1 Peter 1:3-4 "3Blessed be the God and Father of our Lord Jesus Christ, which according to his abundant mercy hath begotten us again unto a lively hope by the resurrection of Jesus Christ from the dead, 4To an inheritance incorruptible, and undefiled, and that fadeth not away, reserved in heaven for you."

1 Peter 1:22-23 "22Seeing ye have purified your souls in obeying the truth through the Spirit unto unfeigned love of the brethren, see that ye love one another with a pure heart fervently: 23Being born again, not of corruptible seed, but of incorruptible, by the word of God, which liveth and abideth for ever."

1 Peter 1:25 "But the word of the Lord endureth for ever. And this is the word which by the gospel is preached unto you."

What Does Not Endure
Job 8:11-15 "11Can the rush grow up without mire? can the flag grow without water? 12Whilst it is yet in his greenness, and not cut down, it withereth before any other herb. 13So are the paths of all that forget God; and the hypocrite's hope shall perish: 14Whose hope shall be cut off, and whose trust shall be a spider's web. 15He shall lean upon his house, but it shall not stand: he shall hold it fast, but it shall not endure."

Psalm 103:15-16 "15As for man, his days are as grass: as a flower of the field, so he flourisheth. 16For the wind passeth over it, and it is gone; and the place thereof shall know it no more."

Proverbs 12:19 "The lip of truth shall be established for ever: but a lying tongue is but for a moment."

Proverbs 27:23-24 "23Be thou diligent to know the state of thy flocks, and look well to thy herds. 24For riches are not for ever: and doth the crown endure to every generation?"

Isaiah 40:6-8 "6The voice said, Cry. And he said, What shall I cry? All flesh is grass, and all the goodliness thereof is as the flower of the field: 7The grass withereth, the flower fadeth: because the spirit of the LORD bloweth upon it: surely the people is grass. 8The grass withereth, the flower fadeth: but the word of our God shall stand for ever."

James 4:14 "Whereas ye know not what shall be on the morrow. For what is your life? It is even a vapour, that appeareth for a little time, and then vanisheth away."

1 Peter 1:24 "For all flesh is as grass, and all the glory of man as the flower of grass. The grass withereth, and the flower thereof falleth away."

What To Endure
2 Timothy 2:3 "Thou therefore endure hardness, as a good soldier of Jesus Christ."

2 Timothy 4:5 "But watch thou in all things, endure afflictions, do the work of an evangelist, make full proof of thy ministry."

ENEMIES

How To Treat Your Enemies
Exodus 23:4-5 "4If thou meet thine enemy's ox or his ass going astray, thou shalt surely bring it back to him again. 5If thou see the ass of him that hateth thee lying under his burden, and wouldest forbear to help him, thou shalt surely help with him."

Proverbs 25:21-22 "21If thine enemy be hungry, give him bread to eat; and if he be thirsty, give him water to drink: 22For thou shalt heap coals of fire upon his head, and the LORD shall reward thee."

Matthew 5:43-44 "43Ye have heard that it hath been said, Thou shalt love thy neighbour, and hate thine enemy. 44But I say unto you, Love your enemies, bless them that curse you, do good to them that hate you, and pray for them which despitefully use you, and persecute you."

Luke 6:27-28 "27But I say unto you which hear, Love your enemies, do good to them which hate you, 28Bless them that curse you, and pray for them which despitefully use you."

Romans 12:14 "Bless them which persecute you: bless, and curse not."

Romans 12:17-21 "17Recompense to no man evil for evil. Provide things honest in the sight of all men. 18If it be possible, as much as lieth in you, live peaceably with all men. 19Dearly beloved, avenge not yourselves, but rather give place unto wrath: for it is written, Vengeance is mine; I will repay, saith the Lord. 20Therefore if thine enemy hunger, feed him; if he thirst, give him drink: for in so doing thou shalt heap coals of fire on his head. 21Be not overcome of evil, but overcome evil with good."

Loving Your Enemies
Proverbs 24:17 "Rejoice not when thine enemy falleth, and let not thine heart be glad when he stumbleth."

Matthew 5:43-48 "43Ye have heard that it hath been said, Thou shalt love thy neighbour, and hate thine enemy. 44But I say unto you, Love your enemies, bless them that curse you, do good to them that hate you, and pray for them which despitefully use you, and persecute you; 45That ye may be the children of your Father which is in heaven: for he maketh his sun to rise on the evil and on the good, and sendeth rain on the just and on the unjust. 46For if ye love them which love you, what reward have ye? do not even the publicans the same? 47And if ye salute your brethren only, what do ye more than others? do not even the publicans so? 48Be ye therefore perfect, even as your Father which is in heaven is perfect."

Luke 6:27-35 "27But I say unto you which hear, Love your enemies, do good to them which hate you, 28Bless them that curse you, and pray for them which despitefully use you. 29And unto him that smiteth thee on the one cheek offer also the other; and him that taketh away thy cloke forbid not to take thy coat also. 30Give to every man that asketh of thee; and of him that taketh away thy goods ask them not again. 31And as ye would that men should do to you, do ye also to them likewise. 32For if ye love them which love you, what

thank have ye? for sinners also love those that love them. 33And if ye do good to them which do good to you, what thank have ye? for sinners also do even the same. 34And if ye lend to them of whom ye hope to receive, what thank have ye? for sinners also lend to sinners, to receive as much again. 35But love ye your enemies, and do good, and lend, hoping for nothing again; and your reward shall be great, and ye shall be the children of the Highest: for he is kind unto the unthankful and to the evil."

The Enemies Of Israel
Exodus 23:15-27 "15Thou shalt keep the feast of unleavened bread: (thou shalt eat unleavened bread seven days, as I commanded thee, in the time appointed of the month Abib; for in it thou camest out from Egypt: and none shall appear before me empty:) 16And the feast of harvest, the firstfruits of thy labours, which thou hast sown in the field: and the feast of ingathering, which is in the end of the year, when thou hast gathered in thy labours out of the field. 17Three times in the year all thy males shall appear before the Lord GOD. 18Thou shalt not offer the blood of my sacrifice with leavened bread; neither shall the fat of my sacrifice remain until the morning. 19The first of the firstfruits of thy land thou shalt bring into the house of the LORD thy God. Thou shalt not seethe a kid in his mother's milk. 20Behold, I send an Angel before thee, to keep thee in the way, and to bring thee into the place which I have prepared. 21Beware of him, and obey his voice, provoke him not; for he will not pardon your transgressions: for my name is in him. 22But if thou shalt indeed obey his voice, and do all that I speak; then I will be an enemy unto thine enemies, and an adversary unto thine adversaries. 23For mine Angel shall go before thee, and bring thee in unto the Amorites, and the Hittites, and the Perizzites, and the Canaanites, and the Hivites, and the Jebusites: and I will cut them off. 24Thou shalt not bow down to their gods, nor serve them, nor do after their works: but thou shalt utterly overthrow them, and quite break down their images. 25And ye shall serve the LORD your God, and he shall bless thy bread, and thy water; and I will take sickness away from the midst of thee. 26There shall nothing cast their young, nor be barren, in thy land: the number of

thy days I will fulfil. ²⁷I will send my fear before thee, and will destroy all the people to whom thou shalt come, and I will make all thine enemies turn their backs unto thee."

Numbers 24:8 "God brought him forth out of Egypt; he hath as it were the strength of an unicorn: he shall eat up the nations his enemies, and shall break their bones, and pierce them through with his arrows."

Numbers 33:50-55 "⁵⁰And the LORD spake unto Moses in the plains of Moab by Jordan near Jericho, saying, ⁵¹Speak unto the children of Israel, and say unto them, When ye are passed over Jordan into the land of Canaan; ⁵²Then ye shall drive out all the inhabitants of the land from before you, and destroy all their pictures, and destroy all their molten images, and quite pluck down all their high places: ⁵³And ye shall dispossess the inhabitants of the land, and dwell therein: for I have given you the land to possess it. ⁵⁴And ye shall divide the land by lot for an inheritance among your families: and to the more ye shall give the more inheritance, and to the fewer ye shall give the less inheritance: every man's inheritance shall be in the place where his lot falleth; according to the tribes of your fathers ye shall inherit. ⁵⁵But if ye will not drive out the inhabitants of the land from before you; then it shall come to pass, that those which ye let remain of them shall be pricks in your eyes, and thorns in your sides, and shall vex you in the land wherein ye dwell."

Deuteronomy 7:6-15 "⁶For thou art an holy people unto the LORD thy God: the LORD thy God hath chosen thee to be a special people unto himself, above all people that are upon the face of the earth. ⁷The LORD did not set his love upon you, nor choose you, because ye were more in number than any people; for ye were the fewest of all people: ⁸But because the LORD loved you, and because he would keep the oath which he had sworn unto your fathers, hath the LORD brought you out with a mighty hand, and redeemed you out of the house of bondmen, from the hand of Pharaoh king of Egypt. ⁹Know therefore that the LORD thy God, he is God, the faithful God, which keepeth covenant and mercy with them that love him and keep his commandments to a

thousand generations; ¹⁰And repayeth them that hate him to their face, to destroy them: he will not be slack to him that hateth him, he will repay him to his face. ¹¹Thou shalt therefore keep the commandments, and the statutes, and the judgments, which I command thee this day, to do them. ¹²Wherefore it shall come to pass, if ye hearken to these judgments, and keep, and do them, that the LORD thy God shall keep unto thee the covenant and the mercy which he sware unto thy fathers: ¹³And he will love thee, and bless thee, and multiply thee: he will also bless the fruit of thy womb, and the fruit of thy land, thy corn, and thy wine, and thine oil, the increase of thy kine, and the flocks of thy sheep, in the land which he sware unto thy fathers to give thee. ¹⁴Thou shalt be blessed above all people: there shall not be male or female barren among you, or among your cattle. ¹⁵And the LORD will take away from thee all sickness, and will put none of the evil diseases of Egypt, which thou knowest, upon thee; but will lay them upon all them that hate thee."

Deuteronomy 30:1-7 "¹And it shall come to pass, when all these things are come upon thee, the blessing and the curse, which I have set before thee, and thou shalt call them to mind among all the nations, whither the LORD thy God hath driven thee, ²And shalt return unto the LORD thy God, and shalt obey his voice according to all that I command thee this day, thou and thy children, with all thine heart, and with all thy soul; ³That then the LORD thy God will turn thy captivity, and have compassion upon thee, and will return and gather thee from all the nations, whither the LORD thy God hath scattered thee. ⁴If any of thine be driven out unto the outmost parts of heaven, from thence will the LORD thy God gather thee, and from thence will he fetch thee: ⁵And the LORD thy God will bring thee into the land which thy fathers possessed, and thou shalt possess it; and he will do thee good, and multiply thee above thy fathers. ⁶And the LORD thy God will circumcise thine heart, and the heart of thy seed, to love the LORD thy God with all thine heart, and with all thy soul, that thou mayest live. ⁷And the LORD thy God will put all these curses upon thine enemies, and on them that hate thee, which persecuted thee."

Joshua 23:11-13 "¹¹Take good heed therefore unto yourselves, that ye love the LORD your God. ¹²Else if ye do in any wise go back, and cleave unto the remnant of these nations, even these that remain among you, and shall make marriages with them, and go in unto them, and they to you: ¹³Know for a certainty that the LORD your God will no more drive out any of these nations from before you; but they shall be snares and traps unto you, and scourges in your sides, and thorns in your eyes, until ye perish from off this good land which the LORD your God hath given you."

Judges 2:1-3 "¹And an angel of the LORD came up from Gilgal to Bochim, and said, I made you to go up out of Egypt, and have brought you unto the land which I sware unto your fathers; and I said, I will never break my covenant with you. ²And ye shall make no league with the inhabitants of this land; ye shall throw down their altars: but ye have not obeyed my voice: why have ye done this? ³Wherefore I also said, I will not drive them out from before you; but they shall be as thorns in your sides, and their gods shall be a snare unto you."

Esther 9:25 "But when Esther came before the king, he commanded by letters that his wicked device, which he devised against the Jews, should return upon his own head, and that he and his sons should be hanged on the gallows."

Psalm 60:3-12 "³Thou hast shewed thy people hard things: thou hast made us to drink the wine of astonishment. ⁴Thou hast given a banner to them that fear thee, that it may be displayed because of the truth. Selah. ⁵That thy beloved may be delivered; save with thy right hand, and hear me. ⁶God hath spoken in his holiness; I will rejoice, I will divide Shechem, and mete out the valley of Succoth. ⁷Gilead is mine, and Manasseh is mine; Ephraim also is the strength of mine head; Judah is my lawgiver; ⁸Moab is my washpot; over Edom will I cast out my shoe: Philistia, triumph thou because of me. ⁹Who will bring me into the strong city? who will lead me into Edom? ¹⁰Wilt not thou, O God, which hadst cast us off? and thou, O God, which didst not go out with our armies? ¹¹Give us help from trouble: for vain is the help of man. ¹²Through God we shall do valiantly: for he it is that shall tread down our enemies."

Psalm 108:7-13 "⁷God hath spoken in his holiness; I will rejoice, I will divide Shechem, and mete out the valley of Succoth. ⁸Gilead is mine; Manasseh is mine; Ephraim also is the strength of mine head; Judah is my lawgiver; ⁹Moab is my washpot; over Edom will I cast out my shoe; over Philistia will I triumph. ¹⁰Who will bring me into the strong city? who will lead me into Edom? ¹¹Wilt not thou, O God, who hast cast us off? and wilt not thou, O God, go forth with our hosts? ¹²Give us help from trouble: for vain is the help of man. ¹³Through God we shall do valiantly: for he it is that shall tread down our enemies."

Isaiah 49:14-26 "¹⁴But Zion said, The LORD hath forsaken me, and my Lord hath forgotten me. ¹⁵Can a woman forget her sucking child, that she should not have compassion on the son of her womb? yea, they may forget, yet will I not forget thee. ¹⁶Behold, I have graven thee upon the palms of my hands; thy walls are continually before me. ¹⁷Thy children shall make haste; thy destroyers and they that made thee waste shall go forth of thee. ¹⁸Lift up thine eyes round about, and behold: all these gather themselves together, and come to thee. As I live, saith the LORD, thou shalt surely clothe thee with them all, as with an ornament, and bind them on thee, as a bride doeth. ¹⁹For thy waste and thy desolate places, and the land of thy destruction, shall even now be too narrow by reason of the inhabitants, and they that swallowed thee up shall be far away. ²⁰The children which thou shalt have, after thou hast lost the other, shall say again in thine ears, The place is too strait for me: give place to me that I may dwell. ²¹Then shalt thou say in thine heart, Who hath begotten me these, seeing I have lost my children, and am desolate, a captive, and removing to and fro? and who hath brought up these? Behold, I was left alone; these, where had they been? ²²Thus saith the Lord GOD, Behold, I will lift up mine hand to the Gentiles, and set up my standard to the people: and they shall bring thy sons in their arms, and thy daughters shall be carried upon their shoulders. ²³And kings shall be thy nursing fathers, and their queens thy nursing mothers: they shall bow down to thee with their face toward the earth, and lick up the dust of thy feet; and thou shalt know that I am the LORD: for they shall not be ashamed that wait for me.

[24]Shall the prey be taken from the mighty, or the lawful captive delivered? [25]But thus saith the LORD, Even the captives of the mighty shall be taken away, and the prey of the terrible shall be delivered: for I will contend with him that contendeth with thee, and I will save thy children. [26]And I will feed them that oppress thee with their own flesh; and they shall be drunken with their own blood, as with sweet wine: and all flesh shall know that I the LORD am thy Saviour and thy Redeemer, the mighty One of Jacob."

Isaiah 54:5-17 "[5]For thy Maker is thine husband; the LORD of hosts is his name; and thy Redeemer the Holy One of Israel; The God of the whole earth shall he be called. [6]For the LORD hath called thee as a woman forsaken and grieved in spirit, and a wife of youth, when thou wast refused, saith thy God. [7]For a small moment have I forsaken thee; but with great mercies will I gather thee. [8]In a little wrath I hid my face from thee for a moment; but with everlasting kindness will I have mercy on thee, saith the LORD thy Redeemer. [9]For this is as the waters of Noah unto me: for as I have sworn that the waters of Noah should no more go over the earth; so have I sworn that I would not be wroth with thee, nor rebuke thee. [10]For the mountains shall depart, and the hills be removed; but my kindness shall not depart from thee, neither shall the covenant of my peace be removed, saith the LORD that hath mercy on thee. [11]O thou afflicted, tossed with tempest, and not comforted, behold, I will lay thy stones with fair colours, and lay thy foundations with sapphires. [12]And I will make thy windows of agates, and thy gates of carbuncles, and all thy borders of pleasant stones. [13]And all thy children shall be taught of the LORD; and great shall be the peace of thy children. [14]In righteousness shalt thou be established: thou shalt be far from oppression; for thou shalt not fear: and from terror; for it shall not come near thee. [15]Behold, they shall surely gather together, but not by me: whosoever shall gather together against thee shall fall for thy sake. [16]Behold, I have created the smith that bloweth the coals in the fire, and that bringeth forth an instrument for his work; and I have created the waster to destroy. [17]No weapon that is formed against thee shall prosper; and every tongue that shall rise against thee in judgment thou shalt condemn. This is the heritage of the servants of the LORD, and their righteousness is of me, saith the LORD."

Isaiah 59:15-20 "[15]Yea, truth faileth; and he that departeth from evil maketh himself a prey: and the LORD saw it, and it displeased him that there was no judgment. [16]And he saw that there was no man, and wondered that there was no intercessor: therefore his arm brought salvation unto him; and his righteousness, it sustained him. [17]For he put on righteousness as a breastplate, and an helmet of salvation upon his head; and he put on the garments of vengeance for clothing, and was clad with zeal as a cloke. [18]According to their deeds, accordingly he will repay, fury to his adversaries, recompence to his enemies; to the islands he will repay recompence. [19]So shall they fear the name of the LORD from the west, and his glory from the rising of the sun. When the enemy shall come in like a flood, the Spirit of the LORD shall lift up a standard against him. [20]And the Redeemer shall come to Zion, and unto them that turn from transgression in Jacob, saith the LORD."

Jeremiah 30:16-20 "[16]Therefore all they that devour thee shall be devoured; and all thine adversaries, every one of them, shall go into captivity; and they that spoil thee shall be a spoil, and all that prey upon thee will I give for a prey. [17]For I will restore health unto thee, and I will heal thee of thy wounds, saith the LORD; because they called thee an Outcast, saying, This is Zion, whom no man seeketh after. [18]Thus saith the LORD; Behold, I will bring again the captivity of Jacob's tents, and have mercy on his dwellingplaces; and the city shall be builded upon her own heap, and the palace shall remain after the manner thereof. [19]And out of them shall proceed thanksgiving and the voice of them that make merry: and I will multiply them, and they shall not be few; I will also glorify them, and they shall not be small. [20]Their children also shall be as aforetime, and their congregation shall be established before me, and I will punish all that oppress them."

Lamentations 2:14-17 "[14]Thy prophets have seen vain and foolish things for thee: and they have not discovered thine iniquity, to turn away thy captivity; but have seen for thee false burdens and causes of banishment. [15]All that pass by clap their hands at thee; they hiss and wag their head at the daughter of Jerusalem, saying, Is this the city that men call The perfection of beauty, The joy of the whole earth? [16]All thine enemies have opened their mouth against thee: they hiss and gnash the teeth: they say, We have swallowed her up: certainly this is the day that we looked for; we have found, we have seen it. [17]The LORD hath done that which he had devised; he hath fulfilled his word that he had commanded in the days of old: he hath thrown down, and hath not pitied: and he hath caused thine enemy to rejoice over thee, he hath set up the horn of thine adversaries."

Ezekiel 28:24-26 "[24]And there shall be no more a pricking brier unto the house of Israel, nor any grieving thorn of all that are round about them, that despised them; and they shall know that I am the Lord GOD. [25]Thus saith the Lord GOD; When I shall have gathered the house of Israel from the people among whom they are scattered, and shall be sanctified in them in the sight of the heathen, then shall they dwell in their land that I have given to my servant Jacob. [26]And they shall dwell safely therein, and shall build houses, and plant vineyards; yea, they shall dwell with confidence, when I have executed judgments upon all those that despise them round about them; and they shall know that I am the LORD their God."

Ezekiel 35:1-15 "[1]Moreover the word of the LORD came unto me, saying, [2]Son of man, set thy face against mount Seir, and prophesy against it, [3]And say unto it, Thus saith the Lord GOD; Behold, O mount Seir, I am against thee, and I will stretch out mine hand against thee, and I will make thee most desolate. [4]I will lay thy cities waste, and thou shalt be desolate, and thou shalt know that I am the LORD. [5]Because thou hast had a perpetual hatred, and hast shed the blood of the children of Israel by the force of the sword in the time of their calamity, in the time that their iniquity had an end: [6]Therefore, as I live, saith the Lord GOD, I will prepare thee unto blood, and blood shall pursue thee: sith thou hast not hated blood, even blood shall pursue thee. [7]Thus will I make mount Seir most desolate, and cut off from it him that passeth out and him that returneth. [8]And I will fill his mountains with his slain men: in thy hills, and in thy valleys, and in all thy rivers, shall they fall that are slain with the sword. [9]I will make thee perpetual desolations, and thy cities shall not

return: and ye shall know that I am the LORD. [10]Because thou hast said, These two nations and these two countries shall be mine, and we will possess it; whereas the LORD was there: [11]Therefore, as I live, saith the Lord GOD, I will even do according to thine anger, and according to thine envy which thou hast used out of thy hatred against them; and I will make myself known among them, when I have judged thee. [12]And thou shalt know that I am the LORD, and that I have heard all thy blasphemies which thou hast spoken against the mountains of Israel, saying, They are laid desolate, they are given us to consume. [13]Thus with your mouth ye have boasted against me, and have multiplied your words against me: I have heard them. [14]Thus saith the Lord GOD; When the whole earth rejoiceth, I will make thee desolate. [15]As thou didst rejoice at the inheritance of the house of Israel, because it was desolate, so will I do unto thee: thou shalt be desolate, O mount Seir, and all Idumea, even all of it: and they shall know that I am the LORD."

Ezekiel 36:1-7 "[1]Also, thou son of man, prophesy unto the mountains of Israel, and say, Ye mountains of Israel, hear the word of the LORD: [2]Thus saith the Lord GOD; Because the enemy hath said against you, Aha, even the ancient high places are ours in possession: [3]Therefore prophesy and say, Thus saith the Lord GOD; Because they have made you desolate, and swallowed you up on every side, that ye might be a possession unto the residue of the heathen, and ye are taken up in the lips of talkers, and are an infamy of the people: [4]Therefore, ye mountains of Israel, hear the word of the Lord GOD; Thus saith the Lord GOD to the mountains, and to the hills, to the rivers, and to the valleys, to the desolate wastes, and to the cities that are forsaken, which became a prey and derision to the residue of the heathen that are round about; [5]Therefore thus saith the Lord GOD; Surely in the fire of my jealousy have I spoken against the residue of the heathen, and against all Idumea, which have appointed my land into their possession with the joy of all their heart, with despiteful minds, to cast it out for a prey. [6]Prophesy therefore concerning the land of Israel, and say unto the mountains, and to the hills, to the rivers, and to the valleys, Thus saith the Lord GOD; Behold, I have spoken in my jealousy and in my fury, because ye have borne the shame of the heathen: ⁷Therefore thus saith the Lord GOD; I have lifted up mine hand, Surely the heathen that are about you, they shall bear their shame."

Joel 3:1-21 "¹For, behold, in those days, and in that time, when I shall bring again the captivity of Judah and Jerusalem, ²I will also gather all nations, and will bring them down into the valley of Jehoshaphat, and will plead with them there for my people and for my heritage Israel, whom they have scattered among the nations, and parted my land. ³And they have cast lots for my people; and have given a boy for an harlot, and sold a girl for wine, that they might drink. ⁴Yea, and what have ye to do with me, O Tyre, and Zidon, and all the coasts of Palestine? will ye render me a recompence? and if ye recompence me, swiftly and speedily will I return your recompence upon your own head; ⁵Because ye have taken my silver and my gold, and have carried into your temples my goodly pleasant things: ⁶The children also of Judah and the children of Jerusalem have ye sold unto the Grecians, that ye might remove them far from their border. ⁷Behold, I will raise them out of the place whither ye have sold them, and will return your recompence upon your own head: ⁸And I will sell your sons and your daughters into the hand of the children of Judah, and they shall sell them to the Sabeans, to a people far off: for the LORD hath spoken it. ⁹Proclaim ye this among the Gentiles; Prepare war, wake up the mighty men, let all the men of war draw near; let them come up: ¹⁰Beat your plowshares into swords, and your pruning-hooks into spears: let the weak say, I am strong. ¹¹Assemble yourselves, and come, all ye heathen, and gather yourselves together round about: thither cause thy mighty ones to come down, O LORD. ¹²Let the heathen be wakened, and come up to the valley of Jehoshaphat: for there will I sit to judge all the heathen round about. ¹³Put ye in the sickle, for the harvest is ripe: come, get you down; for the press is full, the fats overflow; for their wickedness is great. ¹⁴Multitudes, multitudes in the valley of decision: for the day of the LORD is near in the valley of decision. ¹⁵The sun and the moon shall be darkened, and the stars shall withdraw their shining. ¹⁶The LORD also shall roar out of Zion, and utter his voice from Jerusalem; and the heavens and the earth shall shake: but the LORD will be the hope of his people, and the strength of the children of Israel. ¹⁷So shall ye know that I am the LORD your God dwelling in Zion, my holy mountain: then shall Jerusalem be holy, and there shall no strangers pass through her any more. ¹⁸And it shall come to pass in that day, that the mountains shall drop down new wine, and the hills shall flow with milk, and all the rivers of Judah shall flow with waters, and a fountain shall come forth of the house of the LORD, and shall water the valley of Shittim. ¹⁹Egypt shall be a desolation, and Edom shall be a desolate wilderness, for the violence against the children of Judah, because they have shed innocent blood in their land. ²⁰But Judah shall dwell for ever, and Jerusalem from generation to generation. ²¹For I will cleanse their blood that I have not cleansed: for the LORD dwelleth in Zion."

Obadiah 1-21 "¹The vision of Obadiah. Thus saith the Lord GOD concerning Edom; We have heard a rumour from the LORD, and an ambassador is sent among the heathen, Arise ye, and let us rise up against her in battle. ²Behold, I have made thee small among the heathen: thou art greatly despised. ³The pride of thine heart hath deceived thee, thou that dwellest in the clefts of the rock, whose habitation is high; that saith in his heart, Who shall bring me down to the ground? ⁴Though thou exalt thyself as the eagle, and though thou set thy nest among the stars, thence will I bring thee down, saith the LORD. ⁵If thieves came to thee, if robbers by night, (how art thou cut off!) would they not have stolen till they had enough? if the grapegatherers came to thee, would they not leave some grapes? ⁶How are the things of Esau searched out! how are his hidden things sought up! ⁷All the men of thy confederacy have brought thee even to the border: the men that were at peace with thee have deceived thee, and prevailed against thee; they that eat thy bread have laid a wound under thee: there is none understanding in him. ⁸Shall I not in that day, saith the LORD, even destroy the wise men out of Edom, and understanding out of the mount of Esau? ⁹And thy mighty men, O Teman, shall be dismayed, to the end that every one of the mount of Esau may be cut off by slaughter. ¹⁰For thy violence against thy brother Jacob shame shall cover thee, and thou shalt be cut off for ever. [11]In the day that thou stoodest on the other side, in the day that the strangers carried away captive his forces, and foreigners entered into his gates, and cast lots upon Jerusalem, even thou wast as one of them. [12]But thou shouldest not have looked on the day of thy brother in the day that he became a stranger; neither shouldest thou have rejoiced over the children of Judah in the day of their destruction; neither shouldest thou have spoken proudly in the day of distress. [13]Thou shouldest not have entered into the gate of my people in the day of their calamity; yea, thou shouldest not have looked on their affliction in the day of their calamity, nor have laid hands on their substance in the day of their calamity; [14]Neither shouldest thou have stood in the crossway, to cut off those of his that did escape; neither shouldest thou have delivered up those of his that did remain in the day of distress. [15]For the day of the LORD is near upon all the heathen: as thou hast done, it shall be done unto thee: thy reward shall return upon thine own head. [16]For as ye have drunk upon my holy mountain, so shall all the heathen drink continually, yea, they shall drink, and they shall swallow down, and they shall be as though they had not been. [17]But upon mount Zion shall be deliverance, and there shall be holiness; and the house of Jacob shall possess their possessions. [18]And the house of Jacob shall be a fire, and the house of Joseph a flame, and the house of Esau for stubble, and they shall kindle in them, and devour them; and there shall not be any remaining of the house of Esau; for the LORD hath spoken it. [19]And they of the south shall possess the mount of Esau; and they of the plain the Philistines: and they shall possess the fields of Ephraim, and the fields of Samaria: and Benjamin shall possess Gilead. [20]And the captivity of this host of the children of Israel shall possess that of the Canaanites, even unto Zarephath; and the captivity of Jerusalem, which is in Sepharad, shall possess the cities of the south. [21]And saviours shall come up on mount Zion to judge the mount of Esau; and the kingdom shall be the LORD's."

Micah 5:7-9 "[7]And the remnant of Jacob shall be in the midst of many people as a dew from the LORD, as the showers upon the grass, that tarrieth not for man, nor waiteth for the sons of men. [8]And the remnant of Jacob shall be among the Gentiles in the midst of many people as a lion among the beasts of the forest, as a young lion among the flocks of sheep: who, if he go through, both treadeth down, and teareth in pieces, and none can deliver. [9]Thine hand shall be lifted up upon thine adversaries, and all thine enemies shall be cut off."

Zephaniah 2:4-15 "[4]For Gaza shall be forsaken, and Ashkelon a desolation: they shall drive out Ashdod at the noon day, and Ekron shall be rooted up. [5]Woe unto the inhabitants of the sea coast, the nation of the Cherethites! the word of the LORD is against you; O Canaan, the land of the Philistines, I will even destroy thee, that there shall be no inhabitant. [6]And the sea coast shall be dwellings and cottages for shepherds, and folds for flocks. [7]And the coast shall be for the remnant of the house of Judah; they shall feed thereupon: in the houses of Ashkelon shall they lie down in the evening: for the LORD their God shall visit them, and turn away their captivity. [8]I have heard the reproach of Moab, and the revilings of the children of Ammon, whereby they have reproached my people, and magnified themselves against their border. [9]Therefore as I live, saith the LORD of hosts, the God of Israel, Surely Moab shall be as Sodom, and the children of Ammon as Gomorrah, even the breeding of nettles, and saltpits, and a perpetual desolation: the residue of my people shall spoil them, and the remnant of my people shall possess them. [10]This shall they have for their pride, because they have reproached and magnified themselves against the people of the LORD of hosts. [11]The LORD will be terrible unto them: for he will famish all the gods of the earth; and men shall worship him, every one from his place, even all the isles of the heathen. [12]Ye Ethiopians also, ye shall be slain by my sword. [13]And he will stretch out his hand against the north, and destroy Assyria; and will make Nineveh a desolation, and dry like a wilderness. [14]And flocks shall lie down in the midst of her, all the beasts of the nations: both the cormorant and the bittern shall lodge in the upper lintels of it; their voice shall sing in the windows; desolation shall be in the thresholds: for he shall uncover the cedar work. [15]This is the rejoicing city that dwelt carelessly, that said in her heart, I am, and there is none beside me: how is she become a desolation, a place for beasts to lie down in! every one that passeth by her shall hiss, and wag his hand."

Zechariah 12:9 "And it shall come to pass in that day, that I will seek to destroy all the nations that come against Jerusalem."

Zechariah 14:9-16 "⁹And the LORD shall be king over all the earth: in that day shall there be one LORD, and his name one. ¹⁰All the land shall be turned as a plain from Geba to Rimmon south of Jerusalem: and it shall be lifted up, and inhabited in her place, from Benjamin's gate unto the place of the first gate, unto the corner gate, and from the tower of Hananeel unto the king's winepresses. ¹¹And men shall dwell in it, and there shall be no more utter destruction; but Jerusalem shall be safely inhabited. ¹²And this shall be the plague wherewith the LORD will smite all the people that have fought against Jerusalem; Their flesh shall consume away while they stand upon their feet, and their eyes shall consume away in their holes, and their tongue shall consume away in their mouth. ¹³And it shall come to pass in that day, that a great tumult from the LORD shall be among them; and they shall lay hold every one on the hand of his neighbour, and his hand shall rise up against the hand of his neighbour. ¹⁴And Judah also shall fight at Jerusalem; and the wealth of all the heathen round about shall be gathered together, gold, and silver, and apparel, in great abundance. ¹⁵And so shall be the plague of the horse, of the mule, of the camel, and of the ass, and of all the beasts that shall be in these tents, as this plague. ¹⁶And it shall come to pass, that every one that is left of all the nations which came against Jerusalem shall even go up from year to year to worship the King, the LORD of hosts, and to keep the feast of tabernacles."

The Enemies Of The Lord

Deuteronomy 32:36-43 "³⁶For the LORD shall judge his people, and repent himself for his servants, when he seeth that their power is gone, and there is none shut up, or left. ³⁷And he shall say, Where are their gods, their rock in whom they trusted, ³⁸Which did eat the fat of their sacrifices, and drank the wine of their drink offerings? let

them rise up and help you, and be your protection. ³⁹See now that I, even I, am he, and there is no god with me: I kill, and I make alive; I wound, and I heal: neither is there any that can deliver out of my hand. ⁴⁰For I lift up my hand to heaven, and say, I live for ever. ⁴¹If I whet my glittering sword, and mine hand take hold on judgment; I will render vengeance to mine enemies, and will reward them that hate me. ⁴²I will make mine arrows drunk with blood, and my sword shall devour flesh; and that with the blood of the slain and of the captives, from the beginning of revenges upon the enemy. ⁴³Rejoice, O ye nations, with his people: for he will avenge the blood of his servants, and will render vengeance to his adversaries, and will be merciful unto his land, and to his people."

1 Samuel 2:10 "The adversaries of the LORD shall be broken to pieces; out of heaven shall he thunder upon them: the LORD shall judge the ends of the earth; and he shall give strength unto his king, and exalt the horn of his anointed."

Psalm 21:7-12 "⁷For the king trusteth in the LORD, and through the mercy of the most High he shall not be moved. ⁸Thine hand shall find out all thine enemies: thy right hand shall find out those that hate thee. ⁹Thou shalt make them as a fiery oven in the time of thine anger: the LORD shall swallow them up in his wrath, and the fire shall devour them. ¹⁰Their fruit shalt thou destroy from the earth, and their seed from among the children of men. ¹¹For they intended evil against thee: they imagined a mischievous device, which they are not able to perform. ¹²Therefore shalt thou make them turn their back, when thou shalt make ready thine arrows upon thy strings against the face of them."

Psalm 35:17-19 "¹⁷Lord, how long wilt thou look on? rescue my soul from their destructions, my darling from the lions. ¹⁸I will give thee thanks in the great congregation: I will praise thee among much people. ¹⁹Let not them that are mine enemies wrongfully rejoice over me: neither let them wink with the eye that hate me without a cause."

Psalm 37:20 "But the wicked shall perish, and the enemies of the LORD shall be as the fat of lambs: they shall consume; into smoke shall they consume away."

Psalm 66:3 "Say unto God, How terrible art thou in thy works! through the greatness of thy power shall thine enemies submit themselves unto thee."

Psalm 69:1-4 "¹Save me, O God; for the waters are come in unto my soul. ²I sink in deep mire, where there is no standing: I am come into deep waters, where the floods overflow me. ³I am weary of my crying: my throat is dried: mine eyes fail while I wait for my God. ⁴They that hate me without a cause are more than the hairs of mine head: they that would destroy me, being mine enemies wrongfully, are mighty: then I restored that which I took not away."

Psalm 74:18 "Remember this, that the enemy hath reproached, O LORD, and that the foolish people have blasphemed thy name."

Psalm 83:1-17 "¹Keep not thou silence, O God: hold not thy peace, and be not still, O God. ²For, lo, thine enemies make a tumult: and they that hate thee have lifted up the head. ³They have taken crafty counsel against thy people, and consulted against thy hidden ones. ⁴They have said, Come, and let us cut them off from being a nation; that the name of Israel may be no more in remembrance. ⁵For they have consulted together with one consent: they are confederate against thee: ⁶The tabernacles of Edom, and the Ishmaelites; of Moab, and the Hagarenes; ⁷Gebal, and Ammon, and Amalek; the Philistines with the inhabitants of Tyre; ⁸Assur also is joined with them: they have holpen the children of Lot. Selah. ⁹Do unto them as unto the Midianites; as to Sisera, as to Jabin, at the brook of Kison: ¹⁰Which perished at Endor: they became as dung for the earth. ¹¹Make their nobles like Oreb, and like Zeeb: yea, all their princes as Zebah, and as Zalmunna: ¹²Who said, Let us take to ourselves the houses of God in possession. ¹³O my God, make them like a wheel; as the stubble before the wind. ¹⁴As the fire burneth a wood, and as the flame setteth the mountains on fire; ¹⁵So persecute them with thy tempest, and make them afraid with thy storm. ¹⁶Fill their faces with shame; that they may seek thy name, O LORD. ¹⁷Let them be confounded and troubled for ever; yea, let them be put to shame, and perish."

Psalm 89:8-10 "⁸O LORD God of hosts, who is a strong LORD like unto thee? or to thy faithfulness round about thee? ⁹Thou rulest the raging of the sea: when the waves thereof arise, thou stillest them. ¹⁰Thou hast broken Rahab in pieces, as one that is slain; thou hast scattered thine enemies with thy strong arm."

Psalm 92:9 "For, lo, thine enemies, O LORD, for, lo, thine enemies shall perish; all the workers of iniquity shall be scattered."

Psalm 110:1-7 "¹The LORD said unto my Lord, Sit thou at my right hand, until I make thine enemies thy footstool. ²The LORD shall send the rod of thy strength out of Zion: rule thou in the midst of thine enemies. ³Thy people shall be willing in the day of thy power, in the beauties of holiness from the womb of the morning: thou hast the dew of thy youth. ⁴The LORD hath sworn, and will not repent, Thou art a priest for ever after the order of Melchizedek. ⁵The Lord at thy right hand shall strike through kings in the day of his wrath. ⁶He shall judge among the heathen, he shall fill the places with the dead bodies; he shall wound the heads over many countries. ⁷He shall drink of the brook in the way: therefore shall he lift up the head."

Psalm 139:19-20 "¹⁹Surely thou wilt slay the wicked, O God: depart from me therefore, ye bloody men. ²⁰For they speak against thee wickedly, and thine enemies take thy name in vain."

Isaiah 42:13 "The LORD shall go forth as a mighty man, he shall stir up jealousy like a man of war: he shall cry, yea, roar; he shall prevail against his enemies."

Isaiah 66:6 "A voice of noise from the city, a voice from the temple, a voice of the LORD that rendereth recompence to his enemies."

Isaiah 66:14 "And when ye see this, your heart shall rejoice, and your bones shall flourish like an herb: and the hand of the LORD shall be known toward his servants, and his indignation toward his enemies."

Nahum 1:2 "God is jealous, and the LORD revengeth; the LORD revengeth, and is furious; the LORD will take vengeance on his adversaries, and he reserveth wrath for his enemies."

Matthew 22:42-44 "⁴²Saying, What think ye of Christ? whose son is he? They say unto him, The Son of David. ⁴³He saith unto them, How then doth David in spirit call him Lord, saying, ⁴⁴The LORD said unto my Lord, Sit thou on my right hand, till I make thine enemies thy footstool?"

Mark 12:35-36 "³⁵And Jesus answered and said, while he taught in the temple, How say the scribes that Christ is the Son of David? ³⁶For David himself said by the Holy Ghost, The Lord said to my Lord, Sit thou on my right hand, till I make thine enemies thy footstool."

Luke 20:41-43 "⁴¹And he said unto them, How say they that Christ is David's son? ⁴²And David himself saith in the book of Psalm, The LORD said unto my Lord, Sit thou on my right hand, ⁴³Till I make thine enemies thy footstool."

John 15:1-25 "¹I am the true vine, and my Father is the husbandman. ²Every branch in me that beareth not fruit he taketh away: and every branch that beareth fruit, he purgeth it, that it may bring forth more fruit. ³Now ye are clean through the word which I have spoken unto you. ⁴Abide in me, and I in you. As the branch cannot bear fruit of itself, except it abide in the vine; no more can ye, except ye abide in me. ⁵I am the vine, ye are the branches: He that abideth in me, and I in him, the same bringeth forth much fruit: for without me ye can do nothing. ⁶If a man abide not in me, he is cast forth as a branch, and is withered; and men gather them, and cast them into the fire, and they are burned. ⁷If ye abide in me, and my words abide in you, ye shall ask what ye will, and it shall be done unto you. ⁸Herein is my Father glorified, that ye bear much fruit; so shall ye be my disciples. ⁹As the Father hath loved me, so have I loved you: continue ye in my love. ¹⁰If ye keep my commandments, ye shall abide in my love; even as I have kept my Father's commandments, and abide in his love. ¹¹These things have I spoken unto you, that my joy might remain in you, and that your joy might be full. ¹²This is my commandment, That ye love one another, as I have loved you. ¹³Greater love hath no man than this, that a man lay down his life for his friends. ¹⁴Ye are my friends, if ye do whatsoever I command you. ¹⁵Henceforth I call you not servants; for the servant knoweth not what his lord doeth: but I have called you friends; for all things that I have heard of my Father I have made known unto you. ¹⁶Ye have not chosen me, but I have chosen you, and ordained you, that ye should go and bring forth fruit, and that your fruit should remain: that whatsoever ye shall ask of the Father in my name, he may give it you. ¹⁷These things I command you, that ye love one another. ¹⁸If the world hate you, ye know that it hated me before it hated you. ¹⁹If ye were of the world, the world would love his own: but because ye are not of the world, but I have chosen you out of the world, therefore the world hateth you. ²⁰Remember the word that I said unto you, The servant is not greater than his lord. If they have persecuted me, they will also persecute you; if they have kept my saying, they will keep yours also. ²¹But all these things will they do unto you for my name's sake, because they know not him that sent me. ²²If I had not come and spoken unto them, they had not had sin: but now they have no cloke for their sin. ²³He that hateth me hateth my Father also. ²⁴If I had not done among them the works which none other man did, they had not had sin: but now have they both seen and hated both me and my Father. ²⁵But this cometh to pass, that the word might be fulfilled that is written in their law, They hated me without a cause."

Acts 2:32-35 "³²This Jesus hath God raised up, whereof we all are witnesses. ³³Therefore being by the right hand of God exalted, and having received of the Father the promise of the Holy Ghost, he hath shed forth this, which ye now see and hear. ³⁴For David is not ascended into the heavens: but he saith himself, The LORD said unto my Lord, Sit thou on my right hand, ³⁵Until I make thy foes thy footstool."

1 Corinthians 15:25-28 "²⁵For he must reign, till he hath put all enemies under his feet. ²⁶The last enemy that shall be destroyed is death. ²⁷For he hath put all things under his feet. But when he saith, all things are put under him, it is manifest that he is excepted, which did put all things under him. ²⁸And when all things shall be subdued unto him, then shall the Son also himself be subject unto him that put all things under him, that God may be all in all."

Philippians 3:18-19 "¹⁸(For many walk, of whom I have told you often, and now tell you even weeping, that they are the enemies of the cross of Christ: [19]Whose end is destruction, whose God is their belly, and whose glory is in their shame, who mind earthly things.)"

The Kisses Of An Enemy
Proverbs 27:6 "Faithful are the wounds of a friend; but the kisses of an enemy are deceitful."

The Last Enemy That Shall Be Destroyed
1 Corinthians 15:25-28 "[25]For he must reign, till he hath put all enemies under his feet. [26]The last enemy that shall be destroyed is death. [27]For he hath put all things under his feet. But when he saith, all things are put under him, it is manifest that he is excepted, which did put all things under him. [28]And when all things shall be subdued unto him, then shall the Son also himself be subject unto him that put all things under him, that God may be all in all."

Hebrews 2:14-15 "[14]Forasmuch then as the children are partakers of flesh and blood, he also himself likewise took part of the same; that through death he might destroy him that had the power of death, that is, the devil; [15]And deliver them who through fear of death were all their lifetime subject to bondage."

Who Is The Enemy Of God
James 4:4 "Ye adulterers and adulteresses, know ye not that the friendship of the world is enmity with God? whosoever therefore will be a friend of the world is the enemy of God."

Who Not To Consider An Enemy
2 Thessalonians 3:14-15 "[14]And if any man obey not our word by this epistle, note that man, and have no company with him, that he may be ashamed. [15]Yet count him not as an enemy, but admonish him as a brother."

Whose Enemies Are At Peace With Him
Proverbs 16:7 "When a man's ways please the LORD, he maketh even his enemies to be at peace with him."

ENJOYMENT

Enjoying The Fruits Of Your Labor
Ecclesiastes 3:12-13 "[12]I know that there is no good in them, but for a man to rejoice, and to do good in his life. [13]And also that every man should eat and drink, and enjoy the good of all his labour, it is the gift of God."

Ecclesiastes 3:22 "Wherefore I perceive that there is nothing better, than that a man should rejoice in his own works; for that is his portion: for who shall bring him to see what shall be after him?"

Ecclesiastes 5:18-20 "[18]Behold that which I have seen: it is good and comely for one to eat and to drink, and to enjoy the good of all his labour that he taketh under the sun all the days of his life, which God giveth him: for it is his portion. [19]Every man also to whom God hath given riches and wealth, and hath given him power to eat thereof, and to take his portion, and to rejoice in his labour; this is the gift of God. [20]For he shall not much remember the days of his life; because God answereth him in the joy of his heart."

ENLIGHTENMENT

The Lord Enlightening
Ezra 9:7-8 "[7]Since the days of our fathers have we been in a great trespass unto this day; and for our iniquities have we, our kings, and our priests, been delivered into the hand of the kings of the lands, to the sword, to captivity, and to a spoil, and to confusion of face, as it is this day. [8]And now for a little space grace hath been shewed from the LORD our God, to leave us a remnant to escape, and to give us a nail in his holy place, that our God may lighten our eyes, and give us a little reviving in our bondage."

Job 33:27-30 "[27]He looketh upon men, and if any say, I have sinned, and perverted that which was right, and it profited me not; [28]He will deliver his soul from going into the pit, and his life shall see the light. [29]Lo, all these things worketh God oftentimes with man, [30]To bring back his soul from the pit, to be enlightened with the light of the living."

Psalm 18:28 "For thou wilt light my candle: the LORD my God will enlighten my darkness."

What Enlightens The Eyes
Psalm 19:8 "The statutes of the LORD are right, rejoicing the heart: the commandment of the LORD is pure, enlightening the eyes."

ENMITY

What Is Enmity Against God

Romans 8:6-7 "⁶For to be carnally minded is death; but to be spiritually minded is life and peace. ⁷Because the carnal mind is enmity against God: for it is not subject to the law of God, neither indeed can be."

James 4:4 "Ye adulterers and adulteresses, know ye not that the friendship of the world is enmity with God? whosoever therefore will be a friend of the world is the enemy of God."

ENVY

Not Envying

Romans 13:13 "Let us walk honestly, as in the day; not in rioting and drunkenness, not in chambering and wantonness, not in strife and envying."

Galatians 5:26 "Let us not be desirous of vain glory, provoking one another, envying one another."

1 Peter 2:1 "Wherefore laying aside all malice, and all guile, and hypocrisies, and envies, and all evil speakings."

The Place Where Envy Exists

James 3:13-16 "¹³Who is a wise man and endued with knowledge among you? let him shew out of a good conversation his works with meekness of wisdom. ¹⁴But if ye have bitter envying and strife in your hearts, glory not, and lie not against the truth. ¹⁵This wisdom descendeth not from above, but is earthly, sensual, devilish. ¹⁶For where envying and strife is, there is confusion and every evil work."

What Envy Does

Job 5:1-2 "¹Call now, if there be any that will answer thee; and to which of the saints wilt thou turn? ²For wrath killeth the foolish man, and envy slayeth the silly one."

Proverbs 14:30 "A sound heart is the life of the flesh: but envy the rottenness of the bones."

What Lusts To Envy

James 4:5 "Do ye think that the scripture saith in vain, The spirit that dwelleth in us lusteth to envy?"

Who Has Envy Among Them

1 Corinthians 3:3 "For ye are yet carnal: for whereas there is among you envying, and strife, and divisions, are ye not carnal, and walk as men?"

Who Not To Envy

Psalm 37:1-2 "¹Fret not thyself because of evildoers, neither be thou envious against the workers of iniquity. ²For they shall soon be cut down like the grass, and wither as the green herb."

Proverbs 3:31 "Envy thou not the oppressor, and choose none of his ways."

Proverbs 23:17 "Let not thine heart envy sinners: but be thou in the fear of the LORD all the day long."

Proverbs 24:1-2 "¹Be not thou envious against evil men, neither desire to be with them. ²For their heart studieth destruction, and their lips talk of mischief."

Proverbs 24:19 "Fret not thyself because of evil men, neither be thou envious at the wicked."

EPISTLE

The Epistle Of Christ

2 Corinthians 3:2-3 "²Ye are our epistle written in our hearts, known and read of all men: ³Forasmuch as ye are manifestly declared to be the epistle of Christ ministered by us, written not with ink, but with the Spirit of the living God; not in tables of stone, but in fleshy tables of the heart."

ETERNAL LIFE

God Promising Eternal Life

Titus 1:2 "In hope of eternal life, which God, that cannot lie, promised before the world began."

1 John 2:24-25 "²⁴Let that therefore abide in you, which ye have heard from the beginning. If that which ye have heard from the beginning shall remain in you, ye also shall continue in the Son, and in the Father. ²⁵And this is the promise that he hath promised us, even eternal life."

1 John 5:11 "And this is the record, that God hath given to us eternal life, and this life is in his Son."

Laying Hold On Eternal Life

1 Timothy 6:12 "Fight the good fight of faith, lay hold on eternal life, whereunto thou art also called, and hast professed a good profession before many witnesses."

Some Awaking To Everlasting Life

Daniel 12:1-2 "[1]And at that time shall Michael stand up, the great prince which standeth for the children of thy people: and there shall be a time of trouble, such as never was since there was a nation even to that same time: and at that time thy people shall be delivered, every one that shall be found written in the book. [2]And many of them that sleep in the dust of the earth shall awake, some to everlasting life, and some to shame and everlasting contempt."

John 5:26-29 "[26]For as the Father hath life in himself; so hath he given to the Son to have life in himself; [27]And hath given him authority to execute judgment also, because he is the Son of man. [28]Marvel not at this: for the hour is coming, in the which all that are in the graves shall hear his voice, [29]And shall come forth; they that have done good, unto the resurrection of life; and they that have done evil, unto the resurrection of damnation."

What Is Eternal Life

John 12:49-50 "[49]For I have not spoken of myself; but the Father which sent me, he gave me a commandment, what I should say, and what I should speak. [50]And I know that his commandment is life everlasting: whatsoever I speak therefore, even as the Father said unto me, so I speak."

John 17:3 "And this is life eternal, that they might know thee the only true God, and Jesus Christ, whom thou hast sent."

Romans 6:23 "For the wages of sin is death; but the gift of God is eternal life through Jesus Christ our Lord."

1 John 5:20 "And we know that the Son of God is come, and hath given us an understanding, that we may know him that is true, and we are in him that is true, even in his Son Jesus Christ. This is the true God, and eternal life."

Who Shall Not Receive Eternal Life

John 3:36 "He that believeth on the Son hath everlasting life: and he that believeth not the Son shall not see life; but the wrath of God abideth on him."

1 John 3:15 "Whosoever hateth his brother is a murderer: and ye know that no murderer hath eternal life abiding in him."

1 John 5:12 "He that hath the Son hath life; and he that hath not the Son of God hath not life."

Who Shall Receive Eternal Life

Psalm 22:26 "The meek shall eat and be satisfied: they shall praise the LORD that seek him: your heart shall live for ever."

Matthew 19:16-21 "[16]And, behold, one came and said unto him, Good Master, what good thing shall I do, that I may have eternal life? [17]And he said unto him, Why callest thou me good? there is none good but one, that is, God: but if thou wilt enter into life, keep the commandments. [18]He saith unto him, Which? Jesus said, Thou shalt do no murder, Thou shalt not commit adultery, Thou shalt not steal, Thou shalt not bear false witness, [19]Honour thy father and thy mother: and, Thou shalt love thy neighbour as thyself. [20]The young man saith unto him, All these things have I kept from my youth up: what lack I yet? [21]Jesus said unto him, If thou wilt be perfect, go and sell that thou hast, and give to the poor, and thou shalt have treasure in heaven: and come and follow me."

Matthew 19:28-30 "[28]And Jesus said unto them, Verily I say unto you, That ye which have followed me, in the regeneration when the Son of man shall sit in the throne of his glory, ye also shall sit upon twelve thrones, judging the twelve tribes of Israel. [29]And every one that hath forsaken houses, or brethren, or sisters, or father, or mother, or wife, or children, or lands, for my name's sake, shall receive an hundredfold, and shall inherit everlasting life. [30]But many that are first shall be last; and the last shall be first."

Matthew 25:31-46 "[31]When the Son of man shall come in his glory, and all the holy angels with him, then shall he sit upon the throne of his glory: [32]And before him shall be gathered all nations: and he shall separate them one from another, as a shepherd divideth his sheep from the goats: [33]And he shall set the sheep on his right hand, but the goats on the left. [34]Then shall the King say unto them on his right hand, Come, ye blessed of my Father, inherit the kingdom prepared for you from the foundation of the world: ³⁵For I was an hungred, and ye gave me meat: I was thirsty, and ye gave me drink: I was a stranger, and ye took me in: ³⁶Naked, and ye clothed me: I was sick, and ye visited me: I was in prison, and ye came unto me. ³⁷Then shall the righteous answer him, saying, Lord, when saw we thee an hungred, and fed thee? or thirsty, and gave thee drink? ³⁸When saw we thee a stranger, and took thee in? or naked, and clothed thee? ³⁹Or when saw we thee sick, or in prison, and came unto thee? ⁴⁰And the King shall answer and say unto them, Verily I say unto you, Inasmuch as ye have done it unto one of the least of these my brethren, ye have done it unto me. ⁴¹Then shall he say also unto them on the left hand, Depart from me, ye cursed, into everlasting fire, prepared for the devil and his angels: ⁴²For I was an hungred, and ye gave me no meat: I was thirsty, and ye gave me no drink: ⁴³I was a stranger, and ye took me not in: naked, and ye clothed me not: sick, and in prison, and ye visited me not. ⁴⁴Then shall they also answer him, saying, Lord, when saw we thee an hungred, or athirst, or a stranger, or naked, or sick, or in prison, and did not minister unto thee? ⁴⁵Then shall he answer them, saying, Verily I say unto you, Inasmuch as ye did it not to one of the least of these, ye did it not to me. ⁴⁶And these shall go away into everlasting punishment: but the righteous into life eternal."

Luke 10:25-28 "²⁵And, behold, a certain lawyer stood up, and tempted him, saying, Master, what shall I do to inherit eternal life? ²⁶He said unto him, What is written in the law? how readest thou? ²⁷And he answering said, Thou shalt love the Lord thy God with all thy heart, and with all thy soul, and with all thy strength, and with all thy mind; and thy neighbour as thyself. ²⁸And he said unto him, Thou hast answered right: this do, and thou shalt live."

Luke 18:24-30 "²⁴And when Jesus saw that he was very sorrowful, he said, How hardly shall they that have riches enter into the kingdom of God! ²⁵For it is easier for a camel to go through a needle's eye, than for a rich man to enter into the kingdom of God. ²⁶And they that heard it said, Who then can be saved? ²⁷And he said, The things which are impossible with men are possible with God. ²⁸Then Peter said, Lo, we have left

all, and followed thee. ²⁹And he said unto them, Verily I say unto you, There is no man that hath left house, or parents, or brethren, or wife, or children, for the kingdom of God's sake, ³⁰Who shall not receive manifold more in this present time, and in the world to come life everlasting."

John 3:14-16 "¹⁴And as Moses lifted up the serpent in the wilderness, even so must the Son of man be lifted up: ¹⁵That whosoever believeth in him should not perish, but have eternal life. ¹⁶For God so loved the world, that he gave his only begotten Son, that whosoever believeth in him should not perish, but have everlasting life."

John 3:36 "He that believeth on the Son hath everlasting life: and he that believeth not the Son shall not see life; but the wrath of God abideth on him."

John 4:13-14 "¹³Jesus answered and said unto her, Whosoever drinketh of this water shall thirst again: ¹⁴But whosoever drinketh of the water that I shall give him shall never thirst; but the water that I shall give him shall be in him a well of water springing up into everlasting life."

John 5:24-29 "²⁴Verily, verily, I say unto you, He that heareth my word, and believeth on him that sent me, hath everlasting life, and shall not come into condemnation; but is passed from death unto life. ²⁵Verily, verily, I say unto you, The hour is coming, and now is, when the dead shall hear the voice of the Son of God: and they that hear shall live. ²⁶For as the Father hath life in himself; so hath he given to the Son to have life in himself; ²⁷And hath given him authority to execute judgment also, because he is the Son of man. ²⁸Marvel not at this: for the hour is coming, in the which all that are in the graves shall hear his voice, ²⁹And shall come forth; they that have done good, unto the resurrection of life; and they that have done evil, unto the resurrection of damnation."

John 6:38-40 "³⁸For I came down from heaven, not to do mine own will, but the will of him that sent me. ³⁹And this is the Father's will which hath sent me, that of all which he hath given me I should lose nothing, but should raise it up again at the last day. ⁴⁰And this is the will of him that sent me, that every one which seeth the Son, and believeth on him, may have everlasting life: and I will raise him up at the last day."

John 6:43-47 "⁴³Jesus therefore answered and said unto them, Murmur not among yourselves. ⁴⁴No man can come to me, except the Father which hath sent me draw him: and I will raise him up at the last day. ⁴⁵It is written in the prophets, And they shall be all taught of God. Every man therefore that hath heard, and hath learned of the Father, cometh unto me. ⁴⁶Not that any man hath seen the Father, save he which is of God, he hath seen the Father. ⁴⁷Verily, verily, I say unto you, He that believeth on me hath everlasting life."

John 6:53-58 "⁵³Then Jesus said unto them, Verily, verily, I say unto you, Except ye eat the flesh of the Son of man, and drink his blood, ye have no life in you. ⁵⁴Whoso eateth my flesh, and drinketh my blood, hath eternal life; and I will raise him up at the last day. ⁵⁵For my flesh is meat indeed, and my blood is drink indeed. ⁵⁶He that eateth my flesh, and drinketh my blood, dwelleth in me, and I in him. ⁵⁷As the living Father hath sent me, and I live by the Father: so he that eateth me, even he shall live by me. ⁵⁸This is that bread which came down from heaven: not as your fathers did eat manna, and are dead: he that eateth of this bread shall live for ever."

John 10:25-28 "²⁵Jesus answered them, I told you, and ye believed not: the works that I do in my Father's name, they bear witness of me. ²⁶But ye believe not, because ye are not of my sheep, as I said unto you. ²⁷My sheep hear my voice, and I know them, and they follow me: ²⁸And I give unto them eternal life; and they shall never perish, neither shall any man pluck them out of my hand."

John 11:25-26 "²⁵Jesus said unto her, I am the resurrection, and the life: he that believeth in me, though he were dead, yet shall he live: ²⁶And whosoever liveth and believeth in me shall never die. Believest thou this?"

John 12:25 "He that loveth his life shall lose it; and he that hateth his life in this world shall keep it unto life eternal."

John 17:1-3 "¹These words spake Jesus, and lifted up his eyes to heaven, and said, Father, the hour is come; glorify thy Son, that thy Son also may glorify thee: ²As thou hast given him power over all flesh, that he should give eternal life to as many as thou hast given him. ³And this is life eternal, that they might know thee the only true God, and Jesus Christ, whom thou hast sent."

Romans 6:22-23 "²²But now being made free from sin, and become servants to God, ye have your fruit unto holiness, and the end everlasting life. ²³For the wages of sin is death; but the gift of God is eternal life through Jesus Christ our Lord."

Galatians 6:8 "For he that soweth to his flesh shall of the flesh reap corruption; but he that soweth to the Spirit shall of the Spirit reap life everlasting."

2 Timothy 2:10-11 "¹⁰Therefore I endure all things for the elect's sakes, that they may also obtain the salvation which is in Christ Jesus with eternal glory. ¹¹It is a faithful saying: For if we be dead with him, we shall also live with him."

1 John 5:12-13 "¹²He that hath the Son hath life; and he that hath not the Son of God hath not life. ¹³These things have I written unto you that believe on the name of the Son of God; that ye may know that ye have eternal life, and that ye may believe on the name of the Son of God."

EUNUCHS

What Type Of Eunuchs There Are

Matthew 19:10-12 "¹⁰His disciples say unto him, If the case of the man be so with his wife, it is not good to marry. ¹¹But he said unto them, All men cannot receive this saying, save they to whom it is given. ¹²For there are some eunuchs, which were so born from their mother's womb: and there are some eunuchs, which were made eunuchs of men: and there be eunuchs, which have made themselves eunuchs for the kingdom of heaven's sake. He that is able to receive it, let him receive it."

EVANGELISM

Doing The Work Of An Evangelist

2 Timothy 4:5 "But watch thou in all things, endure afflictions, do the work of an evangelist, make full proof of thy ministry."

How You Should Preach

1 Peter 4:11 "If any man speak, let him speak as the oracles of God; if any man minister, let him do it as of the ability which God giveth: that God in all things may be glorified through Jesus Christ, to whom be praise and dominion for ever and ever. Amen."

Jesus Christ Sending Forth Disciples To Preach

Matthew 10:5-16 "⁵These twelve Jesus sent forth, and commanded them, saying, Go not into the way of the Gentiles, and into any city of the Samaritans enter ye not: ⁶But go rather to the lost sheep of the house of Israel. ⁷And as ye go, preach, saying, The kingdom of heaven is at hand. ⁸Heal the sick, cleanse the lepers, raise the dead, cast out devils: freely ye have received, freely give. ⁹Provide neither gold, nor silver, nor brass in your purses, ¹⁰Nor scrip for your journey, neither two coats, neither shoes, nor yet staves: for the workman is worthy of his meat. ¹¹And into whatsoever city or town ye shall enter, inquire who in it is worthy; and there abide till ye go thence. ¹²And when ye come into an house, salute it. ¹³And if the house be worthy, let your peace come upon it: but if it be not worthy, let your peace return to you. ¹⁴And whosoever shall not receive you, nor hear your words, when ye depart out of that house or city, shake off the dust of your feet. ¹⁵Verily I say unto you, It shall be more tolerable for the land of Sodom and Gomorrha in the day of judgment, than for that city. ¹⁶Behold, I send you forth as sheep in the midst of wolves: be ye therefore wise as serpents, and harmless as doves."

Matthew 28:16-20 "¹⁶Then the eleven disciples went away into Galilee, into a mountain where Jesus had appointed them. ¹⁷And when they saw him, they worshipped him: but some doubted. ¹⁸And Jesus came and spake unto them, saying, All power is given unto me in heaven and in earth. ¹⁹Go ye therefore, and teach all nations, baptizing them in the name of the Father, and of the Son, and of the Holy Ghost: ²⁰Teaching them to observe all things whatsoever I have commanded you: and, lo, I am with you alway, even unto the end of the world. Amen."

Mark 6:4-12 "⁴But Jesus said unto them, A prophet is not without honour, but in his own country, and among his own kin, and in his own house. ⁵And he could there do no mighty work, save that he laid his hands upon a few sick folk, and healed them. ⁶And he marvelled because of

their unbelief. And he went round about the villages, teaching. ⁷And he called unto him the twelve, and began to send them forth by two and two; and gave them power over unclean spirits; ⁸And commanded them that they should take nothing for their journey, save a staff only; no scrip, no bread, no money in their purse: ⁹But be shod with sandals; and not put on two coats. ¹⁰And he said unto them, In what place soever ye enter into an house, there abide till ye depart from that place. ¹¹And whosoever shall not receive you, nor hear you, when ye depart thence, shake off the dust under your feet for a testimony against them. Verily I say unto you, It shall be more tolerable for Sodom and Gomorrha in the day of judgment, than for that city. ¹²And they went out, and preached that men should repent."

Mark 16:14-20 "¹⁴Afterward he appeared unto the eleven as they sat at meat, and upbraided them with their unbelief and hardness of heart, because they believed not them which had seen him after he was risen. ¹⁵And he said unto them, Go ye into all the world, and preach the gospel to every creature. ¹⁶He that believeth and is baptized shall be saved; but he that believeth not shall be damned. ¹⁷And these signs shall follow them that believe; In my name shall they cast out devils; they shall speak with new tongues; ¹⁸They shall take up serpents; and if they drink any deadly thing, it shall not hurt them; they shall lay hands on the sick, and they shall recover. ¹⁹So then after the Lord had spoken unto them, he was received up into heaven, and sat on the right hand of God. ²⁰And they went forth, and preached everywhere, the Lord working with them, and confirming the word with signs following. Amen."

Luke 9:1-2 "¹Then he called his twelve disciples together, and gave them power and authority over all devils, and to cure diseases. ²And he sent them to preach the kingdom of God, and to heal the sick."

Luke 10:1-12 "¹After these things the Lord appointed other seventy also, and sent them two and two before his face into every city and place, whither he himself would come. ²Therefore said he unto them, The harvest truly is great, but the labourers are few: pray ye therefore the Lord of the harvest, that he would send forth labourers into his harvest. ³Go your ways: behold, I send you forth as lambs among wolves. ⁴Carry neither purse, nor scrip, nor shoes: and salute no man by the way. ⁵And into whatsoever house ye enter, first say, Peace be to this house. ⁶And if the son of peace be there, your peace shall rest upon it: if not, it shall turn to you again. ⁷And in the same house remain, eating and drinking such things as they give: for the labourer is worthy of his hire. Go not from house to house. ⁸And into whatsoever city ye enter, and they receive you, eat such things as are set before you: ⁹And heal the sick that are therein, and say unto them, The kingdom of God is come nigh unto you. ¹⁰But into whatsoever city ye enter, and they receive you not, go your ways out into the streets of the same, and say, ¹¹Even the very dust of your city, which cleaveth on us, we do wipe off against you: notwithstanding be ye sure of this, that the kingdom of God is come nigh unto you. ¹²But I say unto you, that it shall be more tolerable in that day for Sodom, than for that city."

Luke 24:44-49 "⁴⁴And he said unto them, These are the words which I spake unto you, while I was yet with you, that all things must be fulfilled, which were written in the law of Moses, and in the prophets, and in the psalms, concerning me. ⁴⁵Then opened he their understanding, that they might understand the scriptures, ⁴⁶And said unto them, Thus it is written, and thus it behoved Christ to suffer, and to rise from the dead the third day: ⁴⁷And that repentance and remission of sins should be preached in his name among all nations, beginning at Jerusalem. ⁴⁸And ye are witnesses of these things. ⁴⁹And, behold, I send the promise of my Father upon you: but tarry ye in the city of Jerusalem, until ye be endued with power from on high."

1 Corinthians 1:12-17 "¹²Now this I say, that every one of you saith, I am of Paul; and I of Apollos; and I of Cephas; and I of Christ. ¹³Is Christ divided? was Paul crucified for you? or were ye baptized in the name of Paul? ¹⁴I thank God that I baptized none of you, but Crispus and Gaius; ¹⁵Lest any should say that I had baptized in mine own name. ¹⁶And I baptized also the household of Stephanas: besides, I know not whether I baptized any other. ¹⁷For Christ sent me not to baptize, but to preach the gospel: not with wisdom of

words, lest the cross of Christ should be made of none effect."

The Preaching Of The Cross

1 Corinthians 1:18-25 "¹⁸For the preaching of the cross is to them that perish foolishness; but unto us which are saved it is the power of God. ¹⁹For it is written, I will destroy the wisdom of the wise, and will bring to nothing the understanding of the prudent. ²⁰Where is the wise? where is the scribe? where is the disputer of this world? hath not God made foolish the wisdom of this world? ²¹For after that in the wisdom of God the world by wisdom knew not God, it pleased God by the foolishness of preaching to save them that believe. ²²For the Jews require a sign, and the Greeks seek after wisdom: ²³But we preach Christ crucified, unto the Jews a stumblingblock, and unto the Greeks foolishness; ²⁴But unto them which are called, both Jews and Greeks, Christ the power of God, and the wisdom of God. ²⁵Because the foolishness of God is wiser than men; and the weakness of God is stronger than men."

Those That Preach Other Gospels

Galatians 1:6-10 "⁶I marvel that ye are so soon removed from him that called you into the grace of Christ unto another gospel: ⁷Which is not another; but there be some that trouble you, and would pervert the gospel of Christ. ⁸But though we, or an angel from heaven, preach any other gospel unto you than that which we have preached unto you, let him be accursed. ⁹As we said before, so say I now again, If any man preach any other gospel unto you than that ye have received, let him be accursed. ¹⁰For do I now persuade men, or God? or do I seek to please men? for if I yet pleased men, I should not be the servant of Christ."

Those That Preach The Gospel

Isaiah 52:7 "How beautiful upon the mountains are the feet of him that bringeth good tidings, that publisheth peace; that bringeth good tidings of good, that publisheth salvation; that saith unto Zion, Thy God reigneth!"

Romans 10:14-15 "¹⁴How then shall they call on him in whom they have not believed? and how shall they believe in him of whom they have not heard? and how shall they hear without a preacher? ¹⁵And how shall they preach, except they be sent? as it is written, How beautiful are the feet of them that preach the gospel of peace, and bring glad tidings of good things!"

What Evangelists Are

2 Corinthians 2:12-17 "[12]Furthermore, when I came to Troas to preach Christ's gospel, and a door was opened unto me of the Lord, [13]I had no rest in my spirit, because I found not Titus my brother: but taking my leave of them, I went from thence into Macedonia. [14]Now thanks be unto God, which always causeth us to triumph in Christ, and maketh manifest the savour of his knowledge by us in every place. [15]For we are unto God a sweet savour of Christ, in them that are saved, and in them that perish: [16]To the one we are the savour of death unto death; and to the other the savour of life unto life. And who is sufficient for these things? [17]For we are not as many, which corrupt the word of God: but as of sincerity, but as of God, in the sight of God speak we in Christ."

What Evangelists Are For

Ephesians 4:11-14 "[11]And he gave some, apostles; and some, prophets; and some, evangelists; and some, pastors and teachers; [12]For the perfecting of the saints, for the work of the ministry, for the edifying of the body of Christ: [13]Till we all come in the unity of the faith, and of the knowledge of the Son of God, unto a perfect man, unto the measure of the stature of the fulness of Christ: [14]That we henceforth be no more children, tossed to and fro, and carried about with every wind of doctrine, by the sleight of men, and cunning craftiness, whereby they lie in wait to deceive."

What Preachers Should Do

1 Corinthians 9:13-14 "[13]Do ye not know that they which minister about holy things live of the things of the temple? and they which wait at the altar are partakers with the altar? [14]Even so hath the Lord ordained that they which preach the gospel should live of the gospel."

1 John 2:1-6 "[1]My little children, these things write I unto you, that ye sin not. And if any man sin, we have an advocate with the Father, Jesus Christ the righteous: [2]And he is the propitiation for our sins: and not for ours only, but also for the sins of the whole world. [3]And hereby we do know that we know him, if we keep his commandments. [4]He that saith, I know him, and keepeth not his commandments, is a liar, and the truth is not in him. [5]But whoso keepeth his word, in him verily is the love of God perfected: hereby know we that we are in him. [6]He that saith he abideth in him ought himself also so to walk, even as he walked."

What Preachers Should Not Do

Romans 2:21-24 "[21]Thou therefore which teachest another, teachest thou not thyself? thou that preachest a man should not steal, dost thou steal? [22]Thou that sayest a man should not commit adultery, dost thou commit adultery? thou that abhorrest idols, dost thou commit sacrilege? [23]Thou that makest thy boast of the law, through breaking the law dishonourest thou God? [24]For the name of God is blasphemed among the Gentiles through you, as it is written."

What Shall Be Preached To All Nations

Matthew 24:1-14 "[1]And Jesus went out, and departed from the temple: and his disciples came to him for to shew him the buildings of the temple. [2]And Jesus said unto them, See ye not all these things? verily I say unto you, There shall not be left here one stone upon another, that shall not be thrown down. [3]And as he sat upon the mount of Olives, the disciples came unto him privately, saying, Tell us, when shall these things be? and what shall be the sign of thy coming, and of the end of the world? [4]And Jesus answered and said unto them, Take heed that no man deceive you. [5]For many shall come in my name, saying, I am Christ; and shall deceive many. [6]And ye shall hear of wars and rumours of wars: see that ye be not troubled: for all these things must come to pass, but the end is not yet. [7]For nation shall rise against nation, and kingdom against kingdom: and there shall be famines, and pestilences, and earthquakes, in divers places. [8]All these are the beginning of sorrows. [9]Then shall they deliver you up to be afflicted, and shall kill you: and ye shall be hated of all nations for my name's sake. [10]And then shall many be offended, and shall betray one another, and shall hate one another. [11]And many false prophets shall rise, and shall deceive many. [12]And because iniquity shall abound, the love of many shall wax cold. [13]But he that shall endure unto the end, the same shall be saved. [14]And this gospel of the kingdom shall be preached in all the world for a witness unto all nations; and then shall the end come."

Mark 13:7-10 "7And when ye shall hear of wars and rumours of wars, be ye not troubled: for such things must needs be; but the end shall not be yet. 8For nation shall rise against nation, and kingdom against kingdom: and there shall be earthquakes in divers places, and there shall be famines and troubles: these are the beginnings of sorrows. 9But take heed to yourselves: for they shall deliver you up to councils; and in the synagogues ye shall be beaten: and ye shall be brought before rulers and kings for my sake, for a testimony against them. 10And the gospel must first be published among all nations."

Luke 24:44-47 "44And he said unto them, These are the words which I spake unto you, while I was yet with you, that all things must be fulfilled, which were written in the law of Moses, and in the prophets, and in the psalms, concerning me. 45Then opened he their understanding, that they might understand the scriptures, 46And said unto them, Thus it is written, and thus it behoved Christ to suffer, and to rise from the dead the third day: 47And that repentance and remission of sins should be preached in his name among all nations, beginning at Jerusalem."

What To Preach

Matthew 10:5-7 "5These twelve Jesus sent forth, and commanded them, saying, Go not into the way of the Gentiles, and into any city of the Samaritans enter ye not: 6But go rather to the lost sheep of the house of Israel. 7And as ye go, preach, saying, The kingdom of heaven is at hand."

Mark 6:7-12 "7And he called unto him the twelve, and began to send them forth by two and two; and gave them power over unclean spirits; 8And commanded them that they should take nothing for their journey, save a staff only; no scrip, no bread, no money in their purse: 9But be shod with sandals; and not put on two coats. 10And he said unto them, In what place soever ye enter into an house, there abide till ye depart from that place. 11And whosoever shall not receive you, nor hear you, when ye depart thence, shake off the dust under your feet for a testimony against them. Verily I say unto you, It shall be more tolerable for Sodom and Gomorrha in the day of judgment,

than for that city. 12And they went out, and preached that men should repent."

Mark 16:9-15 "9Now when Jesus was risen early the first day of the week, he appeared first to Mary Magdalene, out of whom he had cast seven devils. 10And she went and told them that had been with him, as they mourned and wept. 11And they, when they had heard that he was alive, and had been seen of her, believed not. 12After that he appeared in another form unto two of them, as they walked, and went into the country. 13And they went and told it unto the residue: neither believed they them. 14Afterward he appeared unto the eleven as they sat at meat, and upbraided them with their unbelief and hardness of heart, because they believed not them which had seen him after he was risen. 15And he said unto them, Go ye into all the world, and preach the gospel to every creature."

Luke 9:60 "Jesus said unto him, Let the dead bury their dead: but go thou and preach the kingdom of God."

Luke 24:44-47 "44And he said unto them, These are the words which I spake unto you, while I was yet with you, that all things must be fulfilled, which were written in the law of Moses, and in the prophets, and in the psalms, concerning me. 45Then opened he their understanding, that they might understand the scriptures, 46And said unto them, Thus it is written, and thus it behoved Christ to suffer, and to rise from the dead the third day: 47And that repentance and remission of sins should be preached in his name among all nations, beginning at Jerusalem."

2 Corinthians 4:5 "For we preach not ourselves, but Christ Jesus the Lord; and ourselves your servants for Jesus' sake."

Colossians 1:26-28 "26Even the mystery which hath been hid from ages and from generations, but now is made manifest to his saints: 27To whom God would make known what is the riches of the glory of this mystery among the Gentiles; which is Christ in you, the hope of glory: 28Whom we preach, warning every man, and teaching every man in all wisdom; that we may present every man perfect in Christ Jesus."

2 Timothy 4:2-3 "2Preach the word; be instant in season, out of season; reprove, rebuke, exhort with all longsuffering and doctrine. ³For the time will come when they will not endure sound doctrine; but after their own lusts shall they heap to themselves teachers, having itching ears."

When The Kingdom Of God
Began To Be Preached
Luke 16:16-17 "¹⁶The law and the prophets were until John: since that time the kingdom of God is preached, and every man presseth into it. ¹⁷And it is easier for heaven and earth to pass, than one tittle of the law to fail."

Who To Preach To
Mark 16:9-15 "⁹Now when Jesus was risen early the first day of the week, he appeared first to Mary Magdalene, out of whom he had cast seven devils. ¹⁰And she went and told them that had been with him, as they mourned and wept. ¹¹And they, when they had heard that he was alive, and had been seen of her, believed not. ¹²After that he appeared in another form unto two of them, as they walked, and went into the country. ¹³And they went and told it unto the residue: neither believed they them. ¹⁴Afterward he appeared unto the eleven as they sat at meat, and upbraided them with their unbelief and hardness of heart, because they believed not them which had seen him after he was risen. ¹⁵And he said unto them, Go ye into all the world, and preach the gospel to every creature."

Acts 10:42-43 "⁴²And he commanded us to preach unto the people, and to testify that it is he which was ordained of God to be the Judge of quick and dead. ⁴³To him give all the prophets witness, that through his name whosoever believeth in him shall receive remission of sins."

EVIL

Departing From Evil
Job 28:28 "And unto man he said, Behold, the fear of the Lord, that is wisdom; and to depart from evil is understanding."

Psalm 34:14 "Depart from evil, and do good; seek peace, and pursue it."

Psalm 37:27 "Depart from evil, and do good; and dwell for evermore."

Proverbs 3:7 "Be not wise in thine own eyes: fear the LORD, and depart from evil."

Proverbs 4:14-15 "¹⁴Enter not into the path of the wicked, and go not in the way of evil men. ¹⁵Avoid it, pass not by it, turn from it, and pass away."

Proverbs 16:17 "The highway of the upright is to depart from evil: he that keepeth his way preserveth his soul."

Isaiah 1:16 "Wash you, make you clean; put away the evil of your doings from before mine eyes; cease to do evil."

1 Thessalonians 5:22 "Abstain from all appearance of evil."

1 Peter 3:11 "Let him eschew evil, and do good; let him seek peace, and ensue it."

Evil Communications
1 Corinthians 15:33 "Be not deceived: evil communications corrupt good manners."

Evil Concupiscence
Colossians 3:5-6 "⁵Mortify therefore your members which are upon the earth; fornication, uncleanness, inordinate affection, evil concupiscence, and covetousness, which is idolatry: ⁶For which things' sake the wrath of God cometh on the children of disobedience."

Evil Not Dwelling With God
Psalm 5:4 "For thou art not a God that hath pleasure in wickedness: neither shall evil dwell with thee."

Evil People
Job 8:20 "Behold, God will not cast away a perfect man, neither will he help the evil doers."

Psalm 34:16 "The face of the LORD is against them that do evil, to cut off the remembrance of them from the earth."

Psalm 37:9 "For evildoers shall be cut off: but those that wait upon the LORD, they shall inherit the earth."

Proverbs 2:11-15 "¹¹Discretion shall preserve thee, understanding shall keep thee: ¹²To deliver thee from the way of the evil man, from the man that speaketh froward things; ¹³Who leave the paths of uprightness, to walk in the ways of darkness; ¹⁴Who rejoice to do evil, and delight in the frowardness of the wicked; ¹⁵Whose ways are crooked, and they froward in their paths."

Proverbs 4:14-17 "¹⁴Enter not into the path of the wicked, and go not in the way of evil men. ¹⁵Avoid it, pass not by it, turn from it, and pass away. ¹⁶For they sleep not, except they have done mischief; and their sleep is taken away, unless they cause some to fall. ¹⁷For they eat the bread of wickedness, and drink the wine of violence."

Proverbs 12:20 "Deceit is in the heart of them that imagine evil: but to the counsellers of peace is joy."

Proverbs 14:19 "The evil bow before the good; and the wicked at the gates of the righteous."

Proverbs 14:22 "Do they not err that devise evil? but mercy and truth shall be to them that devise good."

Proverbs 17:11 "An evil man seeketh only rebellion: therefore a cruel messenger shall be sent against him."

Proverbs 24:8 "He that deviseth to do evil shall be called a mischievous person."

Proverbs 24:20 "For there shall be no reward to the evil man; the candle of the wicked shall be put out."

Proverbs 28:5 "Evil men understand not judgment: but they that seek the LORD understand all things."

Proverbs 29:5-6 "⁵A man that flattereth his neighbour spreadeth a net for his feet. ⁶In the transgression of an evil man there is a snare: but the righteous doth sing and rejoice."

Matthew 12:35 "A good man out of the good treasure of the heart bringeth forth good things: and an evil man out of the evil treasure bringeth forth evil things."

Luke 6:43-45 "⁴³For a good tree bringeth not forth corrupt fruit; neither doth a corrupt tree bring forth good fruit. ⁴⁴For every tree is known by his own fruit. For of thorns men do not gather figs, nor of a bramble bush gather they grapes. ⁴⁵A good man out of the good treasure of his heart bringeth forth that which is good; and an evil man out of the evil treasure of his heart bringeth forth that which is evil: for of the abundance of the heart his mouth speaketh."

John 3:19-20 "¹⁹And this is the condemnation, that light is come into the world, and men loved darkness rather than light, because their deeds were evil. ²⁰For every one that doeth evil hateth the light, neither cometh to the light, lest his deeds should be reproved."

John 5:26-29 "²⁶For as the Father hath life in himself; so hath he given to the Son to have life in himself; ²⁷And hath given him authority to execute judgment also, because he is the Son of man. ²⁸Marvel not at this: for the hour is coming, in the which all that are in the graves shall hear his voice, ²⁹And shall come forth; they that have done good, unto the resurrection of life; and they that have done evil, unto the resurrection of damnation."

Romans 2:9 "Tribulation and anguish, upon every soul of man that doeth evil, of the Jew first, and also of the Gentile."

2 Timothy 3:13 "But evil men and seducers shall wax worse and worse, deceiving, and being deceived."

1 Peter 3:12 "For the eyes of the Lord are over the righteous, and his ears are open unto their prayers: but the face of the Lord is against them that do evil."

3 John 11 "Beloved, follow not that which is evil, but that which is good. He that doeth good is of God: but he that doeth evil hath not seen God."

Hating Evil
Amos 5:15 "Hate the evil, and love the good, and establish judgment in the gate: it may be that the LORD God of hosts will be gracious unto the remnant of Joseph."

Romans 12:9 "Let love be without dissimulation. Abhor that which is evil; cleave to that which is good."

How People Depart From Evil
Proverbs 16:6 "By mercy and truth iniquity is purged: and by the fear of the LORD men depart from evil."

Not Plotting Evil
Proverbs 3:29 "Devise not evil against thy neighbour, seeing he dwelleth securely by thee."

Not Seeking Evil
Amos 5:14 "Seek good, and not evil, that ye may live: and so the LORD, the God of hosts, shall be with you, as ye have spoken."

Not Speaking Evil
Psalm 34:13 "Keep thy tongue from evil, and thy lips from speaking guile."

Ephesians 4:31 "Let all bitterness, and wrath, and anger, and clamour, and evil speaking, be put away from you, with all malice."

Titus 3:1-2 "¹Put them in mind to be subject to principalities and powers, to obey magistrates, to be ready to every good work, ²To speak evil of no man, to be no brawlers, but gentle, shewing all meekness unto all men."

The Lord Creating Evil
Proverbs 16:4 "The LORD hath made all things for himself: yea, even the wicked for the day of evil."

Isaiah 45:7 "I form the light, and create darkness: I make peace, and create evil: I the LORD do all these things."

The Reward For Doing Evil
Deuteronomy 31:29 "For I know that after my death ye will utterly corrupt yourselves, and turn aside from the way which I have commanded you; and evil will befall you in the latter days; because ye will do evil in the sight of the LORD, to provoke him to anger through the work of your hands."

2 Kings 21:10-16 "¹⁰And the LORD spake by his servants the prophets, saying, ¹¹Because Manasseh king of Judah hath done these abominations, and hath done wickedly above all that the Amorites did, which were before him, and hath made Judah also to sin with his idols: ¹²Therefore thus saith the LORD God of Israel, Behold, I am bringing such evil upon Jerusalem and Judah, that whosoever heareth of it, both his ears shall tingle. ¹³And I will stretch over Jerusalem the line of Samaria, and the plummet of the house of Ahab: and I will wipe Jerusalem as a man wipeth a dish, wiping it, and turning it upside down. ¹⁴And I will forsake the remnant of mine inheritance, and deliver them into the hand of their enemies; and they shall become a prey and a spoil to all their enemies; ¹⁵Because they have done that which was evil in my sight, and have provoked me to anger, since the day their fathers came forth out of Egypt, even unto this day. ¹⁶Moreover Manasseh shed innocent blood very much, till he had filled

Jerusalem from one end to another; beside his sin wherewith he made Judah to sin, in doing that which was evil in the sight of the LORD."

2 Chronicles 29:6-9 "⁶For our fathers have trespassed, and done that which was evil in the eyes of the LORD our God, and have forsaken him, and have turned away their faces from the habitation of the LORD, and turned their backs. ⁷Also they have shut up the doors of the porch, and put out the lamps, and have not burned incense nor offered burnt offerings in the holy place unto the God of Israel. ⁸Wherefore the wrath of the LORD was upon Judah and Jerusalem, and he hath delivered them to trouble, to astonishment, and to hissing, as ye see with your eyes. ⁹For, lo, our fathers have fallen by the sword, and our sons and our daughters and our wives are in captivity for this."

Nehemiah 9:28-31 "²⁸But after they had rest, they did evil again before thee: therefore leftest thou them in the hand of their enemies, so that they had the dominion over them: yet when they returned, and cried unto thee, thou heardest them from heaven; and many times didst thou deliver them according to thy mercies; ²⁹And testifiedst against them, that thou mightest bring them again unto thy law: yet they dealt proudly, and hearkened not unto thy commandments, but sinned against thy judgments, (which if a man do, he shall live in them;) and withdrew the shoulder, and hardened their neck, and would not hear. ³⁰Yet many years didst thou forbear them, and testifiedst against them by thy spirit in thy prophets: yet would they not give ear: therefore gavest thou them into the hand of the people of the lands. ³¹Nevertheless for thy great mercies' sake thou didst not utterly consume them, nor forsake them; for thou art a gracious and merciful God."

Isaiah 65:11-15 "¹¹But ye are they that forsake the LORD, that forget my holy mountain, that prepare a table for that troop, and that furnish the drink offering unto that number. ¹²Therefore will I number you to the sword, and ye shall all bow down to the slaughter: because when I called, ye did not answer; when I spake, ye did not hear; but did evil before mine eyes, and did choose that wherein I delighted not. ¹³Therefore thus saith the Lord GOD, Behold, my servants shall eat, but ye shall be hungry: behold, my servants shall drink, but ye shall be thirsty: behold, my servants shall rejoice, but ye shall be ashamed: [14]Behold, my servants shall sing for joy of heart, but ye shall cry for sorrow of heart, and shall howl for vexation of spirit. [15]And ye shall leave your name for a curse unto my chosen: for the Lord GOD shall slay thee, and call his servants by another name."

Isaiah 66:1-4 "[1]Thus saith the LORD, The heaven is my throne, and the earth is my footstool: where is the house that ye build unto me? and where is the place of my rest? [2]For all those things hath mine hand made, and those things have been, saith the LORD: but to this man will I look, even to him that is poor and of a contrite spirit, and trembleth at my word. [3]He that killeth an ox is as if he slew a man; he that sacrificeth a lamb, as if he cut off a dog's neck; he that offereth an oblation, as if he offered swine's blood; he that burneth incense, as if he blessed an idol. Yea, they have chosen their own ways, and their soul delighteth in their abominations. [4]I also will choose their delusions, and will bring their fears upon them; because when I called, none did answer; when I spake, they did not hear: but they did evil before mine eyes, and chose that in which I delighted not."

Jeremiah 4:3-4 "[3]For thus saith the LORD to the men of Judah and Jerusalem, Break up your fallow ground, and sow not among thorns. [4]Circumcise yourselves to the LORD, and take away the foreskins of your heart, ye men of Judah and inhabitants of Jerusalem: lest my fury come forth like fire, and burn that none can quench it, because of the evil of your doings."

Jeremiah 18:5-10 "[5]Then the word of the LORD came to me, saying, [6]O house of Israel, cannot I do with you as this potter? saith the LORD. Behold, as the clay is in the potter's hand, so are ye in mine hand, O house of Israel. [7]At what instant I shall speak concerning a nation, and concerning a kingdom, to pluck up, and to pull down, and to destroy it; [8]If that nation, against whom I have pronounced, turn from their evil, I will repent of the evil that I thought to do unto them. [9]And at what instant I shall speak concerning a nation, and concerning a kingdom, to build and to plant it; [10]If it do evil in my sight, that it obey not my voice, then I will repent of the good, wherewith I said I would benefit them."

Jeremiah 32:32-36 "[32]Because of all the evil of the children of Israel and of the children of Judah, which they have done to provoke me to anger, they, their kings, their princes, their priests, and their prophets, and the men of Judah, and the inhabitants of Jerusalem. [33]And they have turned unto me the back, and not the face: though I taught them, rising up early and teaching them, yet they have not hearkened to receive instruction. [34]But they set their abominations in the house, which is called by my name, to defile it. [35]And they built the high places of Baal, which are in the valley of the son of Hinnom, to cause their sons and their daughters to pass through the fire unto Molech; which I commanded them not, neither came it into my mind, that they should do this abomination, to cause Judah to sin. [36]And now therefore thus saith the LORD, the God of Israel, concerning this city, whereof ye say, It shall be delivered into the hand of the king of Babylon by the sword, and by the famine, and by the pestilence."

Romans 13:1-4 "[1]Let every soul be subject unto the higher powers. For there is no power but of God: the powers that be are ordained of God. [2]Whosoever therefore resisteth the power, resisteth the ordinance of God: and they that resist shall receive to themselves damnation. [3]For rulers are not a terror to good works, but to the evil. Wilt thou then not be afraid of the power? do that which is good, and thou shalt have praise of the same: [4]For he is the minister of God to thee for good. But if thou do that which is evil, be afraid; for he beareth not the sword in vain: for he is the minister of God, a revenger to execute wrath upon him that doeth evil."

The Root Of All Evil
1 Timothy 6:10 "For the love of money is the root of all evil: which while some coveted after, they have erred from the faith, and pierced themselves through with many sorrows."

The Time When Your Eye Is Evil
Luke 11:34 "The light of the body is the eye: therefore when thine eye is single, thy whole body also is full of light; but when thine eye is evil, thy body also is full of darkness."

Those That Call Evil Good
Proverbs 24:24-25 "[24]He that saith unto the wicked, Thou are righteous; him shall the people curse,

nations shall abhor him: ²⁵But to them that rebuke him shall be delight, and a good blessing shall come upon them."

Isaiah 5:20 "Woe unto them that call evil good, and good evil; that put darkness for light, and light for darkness; that put bitter for sweet, and sweet for bitter!"

Malachi 2:17 "Ye have wearied the LORD with your words. Yet ye say, Wherein have we wearied him? When ye say, Every one that doeth evil is good in the sight of the LORD, and he delighteth in them; or, Where is the God of judgment?"

Those That Eschew Evil

Job 1:6-10 "⁶Now there was a day when the sons of God came to present themselves before the LORD, and Satan came also among them. ⁷And the LORD said unto Satan, Whence comest thou? Then Satan answered the LORD, and said, From going to and fro in the earth, and from walking up and down in it. ⁸And the LORD said unto Satan, Hast thou considered my servant Job, that there is none like him in the earth, a perfect and an upright man, one that feareth God, and escheweth evil? ⁹Then Satan answered the LORD, and said, Doth Job fear God for nought? ¹⁰Hast not thou made an hedge about him, and about his house, and about all that he hath on every side? thou hast blessed the work of his hands, and his substance is increased in the land."

Isaiah 56:1-2 "¹Thus saith the LORD, Keep ye judgment, and do justice: for my salvation is near to come, and my righteousness to be revealed. ²Blessed is the man that doeth this, and the son of man that layeth hold on it; that keepeth the sabbath from polluting it, and keepeth his hand from doing any evil."

Those That Pursue Evil

Proverbs 11:19 "As righteousness tendeth to life: so he that pursueth evil pursueth it to his own death."

Isaiah 59:7-8 "⁷Their feet run to evil, and they make haste to shed innocent blood: their thoughts are thoughts of iniquity; wasting and destruction are in their paths. ⁸The way of peace they know not; and there is no judgment in their goings: they have made them crooked paths: whosoever goeth therein shall not know peace."

Those That Reward Evil For Good

Proverbs 17:13 "Whoso rewardeth evil for good, evil shall not depart from his house."

What Brings Forth Evil Fruit

Matthew 7:17-20 "¹⁷Even so every good tree bringeth forth good fruit; but a corrupt tree bringeth forth evil fruit. ¹⁸A good tree cannot bring forth evil fruit, neither can a corrupt tree bring forth good fruit. ¹⁹Every tree that bringeth not forth good fruit is hewn down, and cast into the fire. ²⁰Wherefore by their fruits ye shall know them."

Matthew 12:35 "A good man out of the good treasure of the heart bringeth forth good things: and an evil man out of the evil treasure bringeth forth evil things."

Luke 6:43-45 "⁴³For a good tree bringeth not forth corrupt fruit; neither doth a corrupt tree bring forth good fruit. ⁴⁴For every tree is known by his own fruit. For of thorns men do not gather figs, nor of a bramble bush gather they grapes. ⁴⁵A good man out of the good treasure of his heart bringeth forth that which is good; and an evil man out of the evil treasure of his heart bringeth forth that which is evil: for of the abundance of the heart his mouth speaketh."

What Cleanses Away Evil

Proverbs 20:30 "The blueness of a wound cleanseth away evil: so do stripes the inward parts of the belly."

What Is Evil

Genesis 6:5 "And GOD saw that the wickedness of man was great in the earth, and that every imagination of the thoughts of his heart was only evil continually."

Genesis 8:21 "And the LORD smelled a sweet savour; and the LORD said in his heart, I will not again curse the ground any more for man's sake; for the imagination of man's heart is evil from his youth; neither will I again smite any more every thing living, as I have done."

Ecclesiastes 9:3 "This is an evil among all things that are done under the sun, that there is one event unto all: yea, also the heart of the sons of men is full of evil, and madness is in their heart while they live, and after that they go to the dead."

Ecclesiastes 10:5-7 "⁵There is an evil which I have seen under the sun, as an error which proceedeth from the ruler: ⁶Folly is set in great dignity, and the rich sit in low place. ⁷I have seen servants upon horses, and princes walking as servants upon the earth."

Isaiah 32:7 "The instruments also of the churl are evil: he deviseth wicked devices to destroy the poor with lying words, even when the needy speaketh right."

Jeremiah 2:13 "For my people have committed two evils; they have forsaken me the fountain of living waters, and hewed them out cisterns, broken cisterns, that can hold no water."

Jeremiah 2:19 "Thine own wickedness shall correct thee, and thy backslidings shall reprove thee: know therefore and see that it is an evil thing and bitter, that thou hast forsaken the LORD thy God, and that my fear is not in thee, saith the Lord GOD of hosts."

Jeremiah 17:9-10 "⁹The heart is deceitful above all things, and desperately wicked: who can know it? ¹⁰I the LORD search the heart, I try the reins, even to give every man according to his ways, and according to the fruit of his doings."

James 4:13-16 "¹³Go to now, ye that say, To day or to morrow we will go into such a city, and continue there a year, and buy and sell, and get gain: ¹⁴Whereas ye know not what shall be on the morrow. For what is your life? It is even a vapour, that appeareth for a little time, and then vanisheth away. ¹⁵For that ye ought to say, If the Lord will, we shall live, and do this, or that. ¹⁶But now ye rejoice in your boastings: all such rejoicing is evil."

What Is To Hate Evil
Proverbs 8:13 "The fear of the LORD is to hate evil: pride, and arrogancy, and the evil way, and the froward mouth, do I hate."

Where Evil Comes From
Matthew 15:15-20 "¹⁵Then answered Peter and said unto him, Declare unto us this parable. ¹⁶And Jesus said, Are ye also yet without understanding? ¹⁷Do not ye yet understand, that whatsoever entereth in at the mouth goeth into the belly, and is cast out into the draught? ¹⁸But those things which proceed out of the mouth come forth from the heart; and they defile the man. ¹⁹For out of the heart proceed evil thoughts, murders, adulteries, fornications, thefts, false witness, blasphemies: ²⁰These are the things which defile a man: but to eat with unwashen hands defileth not a man."

Mark 7:17-23 "¹⁷And when he was entered into the house from the people, his disciples asked him concerning the parable. ¹⁸And he saith unto them, Are ye so without understanding also? Do ye not perceive, that whatsoever thing from without entereth into the man, it cannot defile him; ¹⁹Because it entereth not into his heart, but into the belly, and goeth out into the draught, purging all meats? ²⁰And he said, That which cometh out of the man, that defileth the man. ²¹For from within, out of the heart of men, proceed evil thoughts, adulteries, fornications, murders, ²²Thefts, covetousness, wickedness, deceit, lasciviousness, an evil eye, blasphemy, pride, foolishness: ²³All these evil things come from within, and defile the man."

Romans 7:14-23 "¹⁴For we know that the law is spiritual: but I am carnal, sold under sin. ¹⁵For that which I do I allow not: for what I would, that do I not; but what I hate, that do I. ¹⁶If then I do that which I would not, I consent unto the law that it is good. ¹⁷Now then it is no more I that do it, but sin that dwelleth in me. ¹⁸For I know that in me (that is, in my flesh,) dwelleth no good thing: for to will is present with me; but how to perform that which is good I find not. ¹⁹For the good that I would I do not: but the evil which I would not, that I do. ²⁰Now if I do that I would not, it is no more I that do it, but sin that dwelleth in me. ²¹I find then a law, that, when I would do good, evil is present with me. ²²For I delight in the law of God after the inward man: ²³But I see another law in my members, warring against the law of my mind, and bringing me into captivity to the law of sin which is in my members."

Where Evil Is
James 3:13-16 "¹³Who is a wise man and endued with knowledge among you? let him shew out of a good conversation his works with meekness of wisdom. ¹⁴But if ye have bitter envying and strife in your hearts, glory not, and lie not against the truth. ¹⁵This wisdom descendeth not from above, but is earthly, sensual, devilish. ¹⁶For where envying

and strife is, there is confusion and every evil work."

Who Brings Evil To Pass
Proverbs 16:29-30 "29A violent man enticeth his neighbour, and leadeth him into the way that is not good. 30He shutteth his eyes to devise froward things: moving his lips he bringeth evil to pass."

Who Departs From Evil
Proverbs 14:16 "A wise man feareth, and departeth from evil: but the fool rageth, and is confident."

Who Desires Evil
Proverbs 12:12 "The wicked desireth the net of evil men: but the root of the righteous yieldeth fruit."

Proverbs 21:10 "The soul of the wicked desireth evil: his neighbour findeth no favour in his eyes."

Who Digs Up Evil
Proverbs 16:27 "An ungodly man diggeth up evil: and in his lips there is as a burning fire."

Who Evil Pursues
Proverbs 13:21 "Evil pursueth sinners: but to the righteous good shall be repayed."

Who Evil Shall Not Depart From
Proverbs 17:13 "Whoso rewardeth evil for good, evil shall not depart from his house."

Who Evil Shall Slay
Psalm 34:21 "Evil shall slay the wicked: and they that hate the righteous shall be desolate."

Who Has An Evil Eye
Proverbs 28:22 "He that hasteth to be rich hath an evil eye, and considereth not that poverty shall come upon him."

Who Hates Evil
Psalm 97:10 "Ye that love the LORD, hate evil: he preserveth the souls of his saints; he delivereth them out of the hand of the wicked."

Who Hates To Depart From Evil
Proverbs 13:19 "The desire accomplished is sweet to the soul: but it is abomination to fools to depart from evil."

Who Loves Evil More Than Good
Psalm 52:1-7 "1Why boastest thou thyself in mischief, O mighty man? the goodness of God endureth continually. 2Thy tongue deviseth mischiefs; like a sharp rasor, working deceitfully. 3Thou lovest evil more than good; and lying rather than to speak righteousness. Selah. 4Thou lovest all devouring words, O thou deceitful tongue. 5God shall likewise destroy thee for ever, he shall take thee away, and pluck thee out of thy dwelling place, and root thee out of the land of the living. Selah. 6The righteous also shall see, and fear, and shall laugh at him: 7Lo, this is the man that made not God his strength; but trusted in the abundance of his riches, and strengthened himself in his wickedness."

Who Rewards Evil Unto Themselves
Isaiah 3:9 "The shew of their countenance doth witness against them; and they declare their sin as Sodom, they hide it not. Woe unto their soul! for they have rewarded evil unto themselves."

Who Shall Have Evil Upon Them
Deuteronomy 31:29 "For I know that after my death ye will utterly corrupt yourselves, and turn aside from the way which I have commanded you; and evil will befall you in the latter days; because ye will do evil in the sight of the LORD, to provoke him to anger through the work of your hands."

2 Kings 21:10-16 "10And the LORD spake by his servants the prophets, saying, 11Because Manasseh king of Judah hath done these abominations, and hath done wickedly above all that the Amorites did, which were before him, and hath made Judah also to sin with his idols: 12Therefore thus saith the LORD God of Israel, Behold, I am bringing such evil upon Jerusalem and Judah, that whosoever heareth of it, both his ears shall tingle. 13And I will stretch over Jerusalem the line of Samaria, and the plummet of the house of Ahab: and I will wipe Jerusalem as a man wipeth a dish, wiping it, and turning it upside down. 14And I will forsake the remnant of mine inheritance, and deliver them into the hand of their enemies; and they shall become a prey and a spoil to all their enemies; 15Because they have done that which was evil in my sight, and have provoked me to anger, since the day their fathers came forth out of Egypt, even unto this day. 16Moreover Manasseh shed innocent blood very much, till he had filled Jerusalem from one end to another; beside his sin wherewith he made Judah to sin, in doing that which was evil in the sight of the LORD."

2 Kings 22:16-17 "16Thus saith the LORD, Behold, I will bring evil upon this place, and upon the inhabitants thereof, even all the words of the book which the king of Judah hath read: 17Because they have forsaken me, and have burned incense unto other gods, that they might provoke me to anger with all the works of their hands; therefore my wrath shall be kindled against this place, and shall not be quenched."

2 Chronicles 34:24-25 "24Thus saith the LORD, Behold, I will bring evil upon this place, and upon the inhabitants thereof, even all the curses that are written in the book which they have read before the king of Judah: 25Because they have forsaken me, and have burned incense unto other gods, that they might provoke me to anger with all the works of their hands; therefore my wrath shall be poured out upon this place, and shall not be quenched."

Isaiah 47:10-11 "10For thou hast trusted in thy wickedness: thou hast said, None seeth me. Thy wisdom and thy knowledge, it hath perverted thee; and thou hast said in thine heart, I am, and none else beside me. 11Therefore shall evil come upon thee; thou shalt not know from whence it riseth: and mischief shall fall upon thee; thou shalt not be able to put it off: and desolation shall come upon thee suddenly, which thou shalt not know."

Jeremiah 23:9-12 "9Mine heart within me is broken because of the prophets; all my bones shake; I am like a drunken man, and like a man whom wine hath overcome, because of the LORD, and because of the words of his holiness. 10For the land is full of adulterers; for because of swearing the land mourneth; the pleasant places of the wilderness are dried up, and their course is evil, and their force is not right. 11For both prophet and priest are profane; yea, in my house have I found their wickedness, saith the LORD. 12Wherefore their way shall be unto them as slippery ways in the darkness: they shall be driven on, and fall therein: for I will bring evil upon them, even the year of their visitation, saith the LORD."

Who Shall Not Have Evil Upon Them

Proverbs 1:20-33 "20Wisdom crieth without; she uttereth her voice in the streets: 21She crieth in the chief place of concourse, in the openings of the gates: in the city she uttereth her words, saying, 22How long, ye simple ones, will ye love simplicity? and the scorners delight in their scorning, and fools hate knowledge? 23Turn you at my reproof: behold, I will pour out my spirit unto you, I will make known my words unto you. 24Because I have called, and ye refused; I have stretched out my hand, and no man regarded; 25But ye have set at nought all my counsel, and would none of my reproof: 26I also will laugh at your calamity; I will mock when your fear cometh; 27When your fear cometh as desolation, and your destruction cometh as a whirlwind; when distress and anguish cometh upon you. 28Then shall they call upon me, but I will not answer; they shall seek me early, but they shall not find me: 29For that they hated knowledge, and did not choose the fear of the LORD: 30They would none of my counsel: they despised all my reproof. 31Therefore shall they eat of the fruit of their own way, and be filled with their own devices. 32For the turning away of the simple shall slay them, and the prosperity of fools shall destroy them. 33But whoso hearkeneth unto me shall dwell safely, and shall be quiet from fear of evil."

Proverbs 12:21 "There shall no evil happen to the just: but the wicked shall be filled with mischief."

Proverbs 19:23 "The fear of the LORD tendeth to life: and he that hath it shall abide satisfied; he shall not be visited with evil."

Who Strengthens The Hands Of Evildoers

Jeremiah 23:13-14 "13And I have seen folly in the prophets of Samaria; they prophesied in Baal, and caused my people Israel to err. 14I have seen also in the prophets of Jerusalem an horrible thing: they commit adultery, and walk in lies: they strengthen also the hands of evildoers, that none doth return from his wickedness: they are all of them unto me as Sodom, and the inhabitants thereof as Gomorrah."

Ezekiel 13:17-22 "17Likewise, thou son of man, set thy face against the daughters of thy people, which prophesy out of their own heart; and prophesy thou against them, [18]And say, Thus saith the Lord GOD; Woe to the women that sew pillows to all armholes, and make kerchiefs upon the head of every stature to hunt souls! Will ye hunt the souls of my people, and will ye save the souls alive that come unto you? [19]And will ye pollute me among my people for handfuls of barley and for pieces of bread, to slay the souls that should not die, and to save the souls alive that should not live, by your lying to my people that hear your lies? [20]Wherefore thus saith the Lord GOD; Behold, I am against your pillows, wherewith ye there hunt the souls to make them fly, and I will tear them from your arms, and will let the souls go, even the souls that ye hunt to make them fly. [21]Your kerchiefs also will I tear, and deliver my people out of your hand, and they shall be no more in your hand to be hunted; and ye shall know that I am the LORD. [22]Because with lies ye have made the heart of the righteous sad, whom I have not made sad; and strengthened the hands of the wicked, that he should not return from his wicked way, by promising him life."

Who The Lord Created For The Day Of Evil
Proverbs 16:4 "The LORD hath made all things for himself: yea, even the wicked for the day of evil."

EXALTATION

Exalting The Lord
Exodus 15:2 "The LORD is my strength and song, and he is become my salvation: he is my God, and I will prepare him an habitation; my father's God, and I will exalt him."

Psalm 99:5 "Exalt ye the LORD our God, and worship at his footstool; for he is holy."

Psalm 99:9 "Exalt the LORD our God, and worship at his holy hill; for the LORD our God is holy."

Psalm 107:31-32 "[31]Oh that men would praise the LORD for his goodness, and for his wonderful works to the children of men! [32]Let them exalt him also in the congregation of the people, and praise him in the assembly of the elders."

Psalm 118:28 "Thou art my God, and I will praise thee: thou art my God, I will exalt thee."

Isaiah 25:1 "O LORD, thou art my God; I will exalt thee, I will praise thy name; for thou hast done wonderful things; thy counsels of old are faithfulness and truth."

God The Father Exalting Jesus Christ
Acts 5:30-31 "[30]The God of our fathers raised up Jesus, whom ye slew and hanged on a tree. [31]Him hath God exalted with his right hand to be a Prince and a Saviour, for to give repentance to Israel, and forgiveness of sins."

Philippians 2:5-11 "[5]Let this mind be in you, which was also in Christ Jesus: [6]Who, being in the form of God, thought it not robbery to be equal with God: [7]But made himself of no reputation, and took upon him the form of a servant, and was made in the likeness of men: [8]And being found in fashion as a man, he humbled himself, and became obedient unto death, even the death of the cross. [9]Wherefore God also hath highly exalted him, and given him a name which is above every name: [10]That at the name of Jesus every knee should bow, of things in heaven, and things in earth, and things under the earth; [11]And that every tongue should confess that Jesus Christ is Lord, to the glory of God the Father."

The Lord Being Exalted
2 Samuel 22:47 "The LORD liveth; and blessed be my rock; and exalted be the God of the rock of my salvation."

1 Chronicles 29:11 "Thine, O LORD, is the greatness, and the power, and the glory, and the victory, and the majesty: for all that is in the heaven and in the earth is thine; thine is the kingdom, O LORD, and thou art exalted as head above all."

Psalm 18:46 "The LORD liveth; and blessed be my rock; and let the God of my salvation be exalted."

Psalm 46:10 "Be still, and know that I am God: I will be exalted among the heathen, I will be exalted in the earth."

Psalm 47:7-9 "[7]For God is the King of all the earth: sing ye praises with understanding. [8]God reigneth over the heathen: God sitteth upon the throne of his holiness. [9]The princes of the people are gathered together, even the people of the God of Abraham: for the shields of the earth belong unto God: he is greatly exalted."

Psalm 97:9 "For thou, LORD, art high above all the earth: thou art exalted far above all gods."

Psalm 118:16 "The right hand of the LORD is exalted: the right hand of the LORD doeth valiantly."

Isaiah 2:11 "The lofty looks of man shall be humbled, and the haughtiness of men shall be bowed down, and the LORD alone shall be exalted in that day."

Isaiah 2:17 "And the loftiness of man shall be bowed down, and the haughtiness of men shall be made low: and the LORD alone shall be exalted in that day."

Isaiah 5:16 "But the LORD of hosts shall be exalted in judgment, and God that is holy shall be sanctified in righteousness."

Isaiah 30:18 "And therefore will the LORD wait, that he may be gracious unto you, and therefore will he be exalted, that he may have mercy upon you: for the LORD is a God of judgment: blessed are all they that wait for him."

Isaiah 33:5 "The LORD is exalted; for he dwelleth on high: he hath filled Zion with judgment and righteousness."

Isaiah 33:10 "Now will I rise, saith the LORD; now will I be exalted; now will I lift up myself."

Those That Exalt Themselves
Proverbs 17:19 "He loveth transgression that loveth strife: and he that exalteth his gate seeketh destruction."

Isaiah 2:12 "For the day of the LORD of hosts shall be upon every one that is proud and lofty, and upon every one that is lifted up; and he shall be brought low."

Isaiah 14:12-15 "12How art thou fallen from heaven, O Lucifer, son of the morning! how art thou cut down to the ground, which didst weaken the nations! 13For thou hast said in thine heart, I will ascend into heaven, I will exalt my throne above the stars of God: I will sit also upon the mount of the congregation, in the sides of the north: 14I will ascend above the heights of the clouds; I will be like the most High. 15Yet thou shalt be brought down to hell, to the sides of the pit."

Jeremiah 48:42-43 "42And Moab shall be destroyed from being a people, because he hath magnified himself against the LORD. 43Fear, and the pit, and the snare, shall be upon thee, O inhabitant of Moab, saith the LORD."

Daniel 4:37 "Now I Nebuchadnezzar praise and extol and honour the King of heaven, all whose works are truth, and his ways judgment: and those that walk in pride he is able to abase."

Matthew 23:12 "And whosoever shall exalt himself shall be abased; and he that shall humble himself shall be exalted."

Luke 14:11 "For whosoever exalteth himself shall be abased; and he that humbleth himself shall be exalted."

Luke 18:9-14 "9And he spake this parable unto certain which trusted in themselves that they were righteous, and despised others: 10Two men went up into the temple to pray; the one a Pharisee, and the other a publican. 11The Pharisee stood and prayed thus with himself, God, I thank thee, that I am not as other men are, extortioners, unjust, adulterers, or even as this publican. 12I fast twice in the week, I give tithes of all that I possess. 13And the publican, standing afar off, would not lift up so much as his eyes unto heaven, but smote upon his breast, saying, God be merciful to me a sinner. 14I tell you, this man went down to his house justified rather than the other: for every one that exalteth himself shall be abased; and he that humbleth himself shall be exalted."

What Exalts A Nation
Proverbs 14:34 "Righteousness exalteth a nation: but sin is a reproach to any people."

Who Is Exalted For A Little While
Job 24:13-24 "13They are of those that rebel against the light; they know not the ways thereof, nor abide in the paths thereof. 14The murderer rising with the light killeth the poor and needy, and in the night is as a thief. 15The eye also of the adulterer waiteth for the twilight, saying, No eye shall see me: and disguiseth his face. 16In the dark they dig through houses, which they had marked for themselves in the daytime: they know not the light. 17For the morning is to them even as the shadow of death: if one know them, they are in the terrors of the shadow of death. 18He is swift as the waters; their portion is cursed in the earth: he

beholdeth not the way of the vineyards. [19]Drought and heat consume the snow waters: so doth the grave those which have sinned. [20]The womb shall forget him; the worm shall feed sweetly on him; he shall be no more remembered; and wickedness shall be broken as a tree. [21]He evil entreateth the barren that beareth not: and doeth not good to the widow. [22]He draweth also the mighty with his power: he riseth up, and no man is sure of life. [23]Though it be given him to be in safety, whereon he resteth; yet his eyes are upon their ways. [24]They are exalted for a little while, but are gone and brought low; they are taken out of the way as all other, and cut off as the tops of the ears of corn."

Who Shall Be Exalted

Numbers 24:5-7 "[5]How goodly are thy tents, O Jacob, and thy tabernacles, O Israel! [6]As the valleys are they spread forth, as gardens by the river's side, as the trees of lign aloes which the LORD hath planted, and as cedar trees beside the waters. [7]He shall pour the water out of his buckets, and his seed shall be in many waters, and his king shall be higher than Agag, and his kingdom shall be exalted."

1 Samuel 2:10 "The adversaries of the LORD shall be broken to pieces; out of heaven shall he thunder upon them: the LORD shall judge the ends of the earth; and he shall give strength unto his king, and exalt the horn of his anointed."

Job 5:8-11 "[8]I would seek unto God, and unto God would I commit my cause: [9]Which doeth great things and unsearchable; marvellous things without number: [10]Who giveth rain upon the earth, and sendeth waters upon the fields: [11]To set up on high those that be low; that those which mourn may be exalted to safety."

Job 36:5-7 "[5]Behold, God is mighty, and despiseth not any: he is mighty in strength and wisdom. [6]He preserveth not the life of the wicked: but giveth right to the poor. [7]He withdraweth not his eyes from the righteous: but with kings are they on the throne; yea, he doth establish them for ever, and they are exalted."

Psalm 37:34 "Wait on the LORD, and keep his way, and he shall exalt thee to inherit the land: when the wicked are cut off, thou shalt see it."

Psalm 75:10 "All the horns of the wicked also will I cut off; but the horns of the righteous shall be exalted."

Psalm 89:15-16 "[15]Blessed is the people that know the joyful sound: they shall walk, O LORD, in the light of thy countenance. [16]In thy name shall they rejoice all the day: and in thy righteousness shall they be exalted."

Psalm 112:6-9 "[6]Surely he shall not be moved for ever: the righteous shall be in everlasting remembrance. [7]He shall not be afraid of evil tidings: his heart is fixed, trusting in the LORD. [8]His heart is established, he shall not be afraid, until he see his desire upon his enemies. [9]He hath dispersed, he hath given to the poor; his righteousness endureth for ever; his horn shall be exalted with honour."

Psalm 148:13-14 "[13]Let them praise the name of the LORD: for his name alone is excellent; his glory is above the earth and heaven. [14]He also exalteth the horn of his people, the praise of all his saints; even of the children of Israel, a people near unto him. Praise ye the LORD."

Matthew 23:12 "And whosoever shall exalt himself shall be abased; and he that shall humble himself shall be exalted."

Luke 14:11 "For whosoever exalteth himself shall be abased; and he that humbleth himself shall be exalted."

Luke 18:9-14 "[9]And he spake this parable unto certain which trusted in themselves that they were righteous, and despised others: [10]Two men went up into the temple to pray; the one a Pharisee, and the other a publican. [11]The Pharisee stood and prayed thus with himself, God, I thank thee, that I am not as other men are, extortioners, unjust, adulterers, or even as this publican. [12]I fast twice in the week, I give tithes of all that I possess. [13]And the publican, standing afar off, would not lift up so much as his eyes unto heaven, but smote upon his breast, saying, God be merciful to me a sinner. [14]I tell you, this man went down to his house justified rather than the other: for every one that exalteth himself shall be abased; and he that humbleth himself shall be exalted."

1 Peter 5:5-6 "[5]Likewise, ye younger, submit yourselves unto the elder. Yea, all of you be subject one to another, and be clothed with humility: for God resisteth the proud, and giveth grace to the humble. ⁶Humble yourselves therefore under the mighty hand of God, that he may exalt you in due time."

EXAMPLES

Jesus Christ Being An Example

John 13:10-15 "¹⁰Jesus saith to him, He that is washed needeth not save to wash his feet, but is clean every whit: and ye are clean, but not all. ¹¹For he knew who should betray him; therefore said he, Ye are not all clean. ¹²So after he had washed their feet, and had taken his garments, and was set down again, he said unto them, Know ye what I have done to you? ¹³Ye call me Master and Lord: and ye say well; for so I am. ¹⁴If I then, your Lord and Master, have washed your feet; ye also ought to wash one another's feet. ¹⁵For I have given you an example, that ye should do as I have done to you."

John 13:31-35 "³¹Therefore, when he was gone out, Jesus said, Now is the Son of man glorified, and God is glorified in him. ³²If God be glorified in him, God shall also glorify him in himself, and shall straightway glorify him. ³³Little children, yet a little while I am with you. Ye shall seek me: and as I said unto the Jews, Whither I go, ye cannot come; so now I say to you. ³⁴A new commandment I give unto you, That ye love one another; as I have loved you, that ye also love one another. ³⁵By this shall all men know that ye are my disciples, if ye have love one to another."

1 Peter 2:21-23 "²¹For even hereunto were ye called: because Christ also suffered for us, leaving us an example, that ye should follow his steps: ²²Who did no sin, neither was guile found in his mouth: ²³Who, when he was reviled, reviled not again; when he suffered, he threatened not; but committed himself to him that judgeth righteously."

What And Who Are Examples

1 Corinthians 10:1-12 "¹Moreover, brethren, I would not that ye should be ignorant, how that all our fathers were under the cloud, and all passed through the sea; ²And were all baptized unto Moses in the cloud and in the sea; ³And did all eat the same spiritual meat; ⁴And did all drink the same spiritual drink: for they drank of that spiritual Rock that followed them: and that Rock was Christ. ⁵But with many of them God was not well pleased: for they were overthrown in the wilderness. ⁶Now these things were our examples, to the intent we should not lust after evil things, as they also lusted. ⁷Neither be ye idolaters, as were some of them; as it is written, The people sat down to eat and drink, and rose up to play. ⁸Neither let us commit fornication, as some of them committed, and fell in one day three and twenty thousand. ⁹Neither let us tempt Christ, as some of them also tempted, and were destroyed of serpents. ¹⁰Neither murmur ye, as some of them also murmured, and were destroyed of the destroyer. ¹¹Now all these things happened unto them for ensamples: and they are written for our admonition, upon whom the ends of the world are come. ¹²Wherefore let him that thinketh he standeth take heed lest he fall."

2 Peter 2:1-6 "¹But there were false prophets also among the people, even as there shall be false teachers among you, who privily shall bring in damnable heresies, even denying the Lord that bought them, and bring upon themselves swift destruction. ²And many shall follow their pernicious ways; by reason of whom the way of truth shall be evil spoken of. ³And through covetousness shall they with feigned words make merchandise of you: whose judgment now of a long time lingereth not, and their damnation slumbereth not. ⁴For if God spared not the angels that sinned, but cast them down to hell, and delivered them into chains of darkness, to be reserved unto judgment; ⁵And spared not the old world, but saved Noah the eighth person, a preacher of righteousness, bringing in the flood upon the world of the ungodly; ⁶And turning the cities of Sodom and Gomorrha into ashes condemned them with an overthrow, making them an ensample unto those that after should live ungodly."

Jude 7 "Even as Sodom and Gomorrha, and the cities about them in like manner, giving themselves over to fornication, and going after strange flesh, are set forth for an example, suffering the vengeance of eternal fire."

EXECUTION

Those That Have Been Executed

Deuteronomy 21:22-23 "²²And if a man have committed a sin worthy of death, and he be to be put to death, and thou hang him on a tree: ²³His body shall not remain all night upon the tree, but thou shalt in any wise bury him that day; (for he that is hanged is accursed of God;) that thy land be not defiled, which the LORD thy God giveth thee for an inheritance."

Galatians 3:13 "Christ hath redeemed us from the curse of the law, being made a curse for us: for it is written, Cursed is every one that hangeth on a tree."

Who Should Be Executed
According To The Law

Genesis 9:5-6 "⁵And surely your blood of your lives will I require; at the hand of every beast will I require it, and at the hand of man; at the hand of every man's brother will I require the life of man. ⁶Whoso sheddeth man's blood, by man shall his blood be shed: for in the image of God made he man."

Exodus 21:12-17 "¹²He that smiteth a man, so that he die, shall be surely put to death. ¹³And if a man lie not in wait, but God deliver him into his hand; then I will appoint thee a place whither he shall flee. ¹⁴But if a man come presumptuously upon his neighbour, to slay him with guile; thou shalt take him from mine altar, that he may die. ¹⁵And he that smiteth his father, or his mother, shall be surely put to death. ¹⁶And he that stealeth a man, and selleth him, or if he be found in his hand, he shall be surely put to death. ¹⁷And he that curseth his father, or his mother, shall surely be put to death."

Exodus 21:29 "But if the ox were wont to push with his horn in time past, and it hath been testified to his owner, and he hath not kept him in, but that he hath killed a man or a woman; the ox shall be stoned, and his owner also shall be put to death."

Exodus 22:18-19 "¹⁸Thou shalt not suffer a witch to live. ¹⁹Whosoever lieth with a beast shall surely be put to death."

Exodus 31:14-15 "¹⁴Ye shall keep the sabbath therefore; for it is holy unto you: every one that defileth it shall surely be put to death: for whosoever doeth any work therein, that soul shall be cut off from among his people. ¹⁵Six days may work be done; but in the seventh is the sabbath of rest, holy to the LORD: whosoever doeth any work in the sabbath day, he shall surely be put to death."

Leviticus 20:2 "Again, thou shalt say to the children of Israel, Whosoever he be of the children of Israel, or of the strangers that sojourn in Israel, that giveth any of his seed unto Molech; he shall surely be put to death: the people of the land shall stone him with stones."

Leviticus 20:9-16 "⁹For every one that curseth his father or his mother shall be surely put to death: he hath cursed his father or his mother; his blood shall be upon him. ¹⁰And the man that committeth adultery with another man's wife, even he that committeth adultery with his neighbour's wife, the adulterer and the adulteress shall surely be put to death. ¹¹And the man that lieth with his father's wife hath uncovered his father's nakedness: both of them shall surely be put to death; their blood shall be upon them. ¹²And if a man lie with his daughter in law, both of them shall surely be put to death: they have wrought confusion; their blood shall be upon them. ¹³If a man also lie with mankind, as he lieth with a woman, both of them have committed an abomination: they shall surely be put to death; their blood shall be upon them. ¹⁴And if a man take a wife and her mother, it is wickedness: they shall be burnt with fire, both he and they; that there be no wickedness among you. ¹⁵And if a man lie with a beast, he shall surely be put to death: and ye shall slay the beast. ¹⁶And if a woman approach unto any beast, and lie down thereto, thou shalt kill the woman, and the beast: they shall surely be put to death; their blood shall be upon them."

Leviticus 20:27 "A man also or woman that hath a familiar spirit, or that is a wizard, shall surely be put to death: they shall stone them with stones: their blood shall be upon them."

Leviticus 24:16-17 "¹⁶And he that blasphemeth the name of the LORD, he shall be surely put to death, and all the congregation shall certainly stone him: as well the stranger, as he that is born in the land, when he blasphemeth the name of the LORD, shall be put to death. ¹⁷And he that killeth any man shall surely be put to death."

Leviticus 24:21 "And he that killeth a beast, he shall restore it: and he that killeth a man, he shall be put to death."

Numbers 35:30-33 "[30]Whoso killeth any person, the murderer shall be put to death by the mouth of witnesses: but one witness shall not testify against any person to cause him to die. [31]Moreover ye shall take no satisfaction for the life of a murderer, which is guilty of death: but he shall be surely put to death. [32]And ye shall take no satisfaction for him that is fled to the city of his refuge, that he should come again to dwell in the land, until the death of the priest. [33]So ye shall not pollute the land wherein ye are: for blood it defileth the land: and the land cannot be cleansed of the blood that is shed therein, but by the blood of him that shed it."

Deuteronomy 13:1-10 "[1]If there arise among you a prophet, or a dreamer of dreams, and giveth thee a sign or a wonder, [2]And the sign or the wonder come to pass, whereof he spake unto thee, saying, Let us go after other gods, which thou hast not known, and let us serve them; [3]Thou shalt not hearken unto the words of that prophet, or that dreamer of dreams: for the LORD your God proveth you, to know whether ye love the LORD your God with all your heart and with all your soul. [4]Ye shall walk after the LORD your God, and fear him, and keep his commandments, and obey his voice, and ye shall serve him, and cleave unto him. [5]And that prophet, or that dreamer of dreams, shall be put to death; because he hath spoken to turn you away from the LORD your God, which brought you out of the land of Egypt, and redeemed you out of the house of bondage, to thrust thee out of the way which the LORD thy God commanded thee to walk in. So shalt thou put the evil away from the midst of thee. [6]If thy brother, the son of thy mother, or thy son, or thy daughter, or the wife of thy bosom, or thy friend, which is as thine own soul, entice thee secretly, saying, Let us go and serve other gods, which thou hast not known, thou, nor thy fathers; [7]Namely, of the gods of the people which are round about you, nigh unto thee, or far off from thee, from the one end of the earth even unto the other end of the earth; [8]Thou shalt not consent unto him, nor hearken unto him; neither shall thine eye pity him, neither shalt thou spare, neither shalt thou conceal him: [9]But thou shalt surely kill him; thine hand shall be first upon him to put him to death, and afterwards the hand of all the people. [10]And thou shalt stone him with stones, that he die; because he hath sought to thrust thee away from the LORD thy God, which brought thee out of the land of Egypt, from the house of bondage."

Deuteronomy 17:2-7 "[2]If there be found among you, within any of thy gates which the LORD thy God giveth thee, man or woman, that hath wrought wickedness in the sight of the LORD thy God, in transgressing his covenant, [3]And hath gone and served other gods, and worshipped them, either the sun, or moon, or any of the host of heaven, which I have not commanded; [4]And it be told thee, and thou hast heard of it, and inquired diligently, and, behold, it be true, and the thing certain, that such abomination is wrought in Israel: [5]Then shalt thou bring forth that man or that woman, which have committed that wicked thing, unto thy gates, even that man or that woman, and shalt stone them with stones, till they die. [6]At the mouth of two witnesses, or three witnesses, shall he that is worthy of death be put to death; but at the mouth of one witness he shall not be put to death. [7]The hands of the witnesses shall be first upon him to put him to death, and afterward the hands of all the people. So thou shalt put the evil away from among you."

Deuteronomy 22:13-25 "[13]If any man take a wife, and go in unto her, and hate her, [14]And give occasions of speech against her, and bring up an evil name upon her, and say, I took this woman, and when I came to her, I found her not a maid: [15]Then shall the father of the damsel, and her mother, take and bring forth the tokens of the damsel's virginity unto the elders of the city in the gate: [16]And the damsel's father shall say unto the elders, I gave my daughter unto this man to wife, and he hateth her; [17]And, lo, he hath given occasions of speech against her, saying, I found not thy daughter a maid; and yet these are the tokens of my daughter's virginity. And they shall spread the cloth before the elders of the city. [18]And the elders of that city shall take that man and chastise him; [19]And they shall amerce him in an hundred shekels of silver, and give them unto the father of the damsel, because he hath brought up an evil name upon a virgin of Israel: and she shall be his wife; he may not put her away all his days. [20]But if this thing be true, and the tokens of virginity be not found for the damsel: ²¹Then they shall bring out the damsel to the door of her father's house, and the men of her city shall stone her with stones that she die: because she hath wrought folly in Israel, to play the whore in her father's house: so shalt thou put evil away from among you. ²²If a man be found lying with a woman married to an husband, then they shall both of them die, both the man that lay with the woman, and the woman: so shalt thou put away evil from Israel. ²³If a damsel that is a virgin be betrothed unto an husband, and a man find her in the city, and lie with her; ²⁴Then ye shall bring them both out unto the gate of that city, and ye shall stone them with stones that they die; the damsel, because she cried not, being in the city; and the man, because he hath humbled his neighbour's wife: so thou shalt put away evil from among you. ²⁵But if a man find a betrothed damsel in the field, and the man force her, and lie with her: then the man only that lay with her shall die."

Ezekiel 18:1-13 "¹The word of the LORD came unto me again, saying, ²What mean ye, that ye use this proverb concerning the land of Israel, saying, The fathers have eaten sour grapes, and the children's teeth are set on edge? ³As I live, saith the Lord GOD, ye shall not have occasion any more to use this proverb in Israel. ⁴Behold, all souls are mine; as the soul of the father, so also the soul of the son is mine: the soul that sinneth, it shall die. ⁵But if a man be just, and do that which is lawful and right, ⁶And hath not eaten upon the mountains, neither hath lifted up his eyes to the idols of the house of Israel, neither hath defiled his neighbour's wife, neither hath come near to a menstruous woman, ⁷And hath not oppressed any, but hath restored to the debtor his pledge, hath spoiled none by violence, hath given his bread to the hungry, and hath covered the naked with a garment; ⁸He that hath not given forth upon usury, neither hath taken any increase, that hath withdrawn his hand from iniquity, hath executed true judgment between man and man, ⁹Hath walked in my statutes, and hath kept my judgments, to deal truly; he is just, he shall surely live, saith the Lord GOD. ¹⁰If he beget a son that is a robber, a shedder of blood, and that doeth the like to any one of these things, ¹¹And that doeth not any of those duties, but even hath eaten upon the mountains, and defiled his neighbour's wife,

¹²Hath oppressed the poor and needy, hath spoiled by violence, hath not restored the pledge, and hath lifted up his eyes to the idols, hath committed abomination, ¹³Hath given forth upon usury, and hath taken increase: shall he then live? he shall not live: he hath done all these abominations; he shall surely die; his blood shall be upon him."

Mark 7:10 "For Moses said, Honour thy father and thy mother; and, Whoso curseth father or mother, let him die the death."

John 8:3-5 "³And the scribes and Pharisees brought unto him a woman taken in adultery; and when they had set her in the midst, ⁴They say unto him, Master, this woman was taken in adultery, in the very act. ⁵Now Moses in the law commanded us, that such should be stoned: but what sayest thou?"

Romans 1:28-32 "²⁸And even as they did not like to retain God in their knowledge, God gave them over to a reprobate mind, to do those things which are not convenient; ²⁹Being filled with all unrighteousness, fornication, wickedness, covetousness, maliciousness; full of envy, murder, debate, deceit, malignity; whisperers, ³⁰Backbiters, haters of God, despiteful, proud, boasters, inventors of evil things, disobedient to parents, ³¹Without understanding, covenantbreakers, without natural affection, implacable, unmerciful: ³²Who knowing the judgment of God, that they which commit such things are worthy of death, not only do the same, but have pleasure in them that do them."

Who Should Not Be Executed According To The Law

Exodus 23:7 "Keep thee far from a false matter; and the innocent and righteous slay thou not: for I will not justify the wicked."

Leviticus 19:20 "And whosoever lieth carnally with a woman, that is a bondmaid, betrothed to an husband, and not at all redeemed, nor freedom given her; she shall be scourged; they shall not be put to death, because she was not free."

Deuteronomy 22:25-27 "²⁵But if a man find a betrothed damsel in the field, and the man force her, and lie with her: then the man only that lay with her shall die: ²⁶But unto the damsel thou shalt do nothing; there is in the damsel no sin worthy of death: for as when a man riseth against his neighbour, and slayeth him, even so is this matter: ²⁷For he found her in the field, and the betrothed damsel cried, and there was none to save her."

Deuteronomy 24:16 "The fathers shall not be put to death for the children, neither shall the children be put to death for the fathers: every man shall be put to death for his own sin."

2 Kings 14:6 "But the children of the murderers he slew not: according unto that which is written in the book of the law of Moses, wherein the LORD commanded, saying, The fathers shall not be put to death for the children, nor the children be put to death for the fathers; but every man shall be put to death for his own sin."

2 Chronicles 25:4 "But he slew not their children, but did as it is written in the law in the book of Moses, where the LORD commanded, saying, The fathers shall not die for the children, neither shall the children die for the fathers, but every man shall die for his own sin."

Ezekiel 18:1-20 "¹The word of the LORD came unto me again, saying, ²What mean ye, that ye use this proverb concerning the land of Israel, saying, The fathers have eaten sour grapes, and the children's teeth are set on edge? ³As I live, saith the Lord GOD, ye shall not have occasion any more to use this proverb in Israel. ⁴Behold, all souls are mine; as the soul of the father, so also the soul of the son is mine: the soul that sinneth, it shall die. ⁵But if a man be just, and do that which is lawful and right, ⁶And hath not eaten upon the mountains, neither hath lifted up his eyes to the idols of the house of Israel, neither hath defiled his neighbour's wife, neither hath come near to a menstruous woman, ⁷And hath not oppressed any, but hath restored to the debtor his pledge, hath spoiled none by violence, hath given his bread to the hungry, and hath covered the naked with a garment; ⁸He that hath not given forth upon usury, neither hath taken any increase, that hath withdrawn his hand from iniquity, hath executed true judgment between man and man, ⁹Hath walked in my statutes, and hath kept my judgments, to deal truly; he is just, he shall surely live, saith the Lord GOD. ¹⁰If he beget a son that is a robber, a shedder of blood, and that doeth the like to any one of these things, ¹¹And that doeth

not any of those duties, but even hath eaten upon the mountains, and defiled his neighbour's wife, ¹²Hath oppressed the poor and needy, hath spoiled by violence, hath not restored the pledge, and hath lifted up his eyes to the idols, hath committed abomination, ¹³Hath given forth upon usury, and hath taken increase: shall he then live? he shall not live: he hath done all these abominations; he shall surely die; his blood shall be upon him. ¹⁴Now, lo, if he beget a son, that seeth all his father's sins which he hath done, and considereth, and doeth not such like, ¹⁵That hath not eaten upon the mountains, neither hath lifted up his eyes to the idols of the house of Israel, hath not defiled his neighbour's wife, ¹⁶Neither hath oppressed any, hath not withholden the pledge, neither hath spoiled by violence, but hath given his bread to the hungry, and hath covered the naked with a garment, ¹⁷That hath taken off his hand from the poor, that hath not received usury nor increase, hath executed my judgments, hath walked in my statutes; he shall not die for the iniquity of his father, he shall surely live. ¹⁸As for his father, because he cruelly oppressed, spoiled his brother by violence, and did that which is not good among his people, lo, even he shall die in his iniquity. ¹⁹Yet say ye, Why? doth not the son bear the iniquity of the father? When the son hath done that which is lawful and right, and hath kept all my statutes, and hath done them, he shall surely live. ²⁰The soul that sinneth, it shall die. The son shall not bear the iniquity of the father, neither shall the father bear the iniquity of the son: the righteousness of the righteous shall be upon him, and the wickedness of the wicked shall be upon him."

EXERCISE

Bodily Exercise

1 Timothy 4:8 "For bodily exercise profiteth little: but godliness is profitable unto all things, having promise of the life that now is, and of that which is to come."

EXHORTATION

Exhorting Others

2 Timothy 4:2-3 "²Preach the word; be instant in season, out of season; reprove, rebuke, exhort with all longsuffering and doctrine. ³For the time will come when they will not endure sound doctrine; but after their own lusts shall they heap to themselves teachers, having itching ears."

Hebrews 10:23-25 "²³Let us hold fast the profession of our faith without wavering; (for he is faithful that promised;) ²⁴And let us consider one another to provoke unto love and to good works: ²⁵Not forsaking the assembling of ourselves together, as the manner of some is; but exhorting one another: and so much the more, as ye see the day approaching."

EXPEDIENCY

All Things Not Being Expedient
1 Corinthians 6:12 "All things are lawful unto me, but all things are not expedient: all things are lawful for me, but I will not be brought under the power of any."

1 Corinthians 10:23 "All things are lawful for me, but all things are not expedient: all things are lawful for me, but all things edify not."

EXPERIENCE

What Develops Experience
Romans 5:3-4 "³And not only so, but we glory in tribulations also: knowing that tribulation worketh patience; ⁴And patience, experience; and experience, hope."

What Experience Develops
Romans 5:3-4 "³And not only so, but we glory in tribulations also: knowing that tribulation worketh patience; ⁴And patience, experience; and experience, hope."

FABLES

Not Giving Heed To Fables
1 Timothy 1:3-4 "3As I besought thee to abide still at Ephesus, when I went into Macedonia, that thou mightest charge some that they teach no other doctrine, 4Neither give heed to fables and endless genealogies, which minister questions, rather than godly edifying which is in faith: so do."

Titus 1:10-14 "10For there are many unruly and vain talkers and deceivers, specially they of the circumcision: 11Whose mouths must be stopped, who subvert whole houses, teaching things which they ought not, for filthy lucre's sake. 12One of themselves, even a prophet of their own, said, The Cretians are alway liars, evil beasts, slow bellies. 13This witness is true. Wherefore rebuke them sharply, that they may be sound in the faith; 14Not giving heed to Jewish fables, and commandments of men, that turn from the truth."

Some Being Turned To Fables
2 Timothy 4:2-4 "2Preach the word; be instant in season, out of season; reprove, rebuke, exhort with all longsuffering and doctrine. 3For the time will come when they will not endure sound doctrine; but after their own lusts shall they heap to themselves teachers, having itching ears; 4And they shall turn away their ears from the truth, and shall be turned unto fables."

FAILURE

The Lord Not Failing
Deuteronomy 31:6-8 "6Be strong and of a good courage, fear not, nor be afraid of them: for the LORD thy God, he it is that doth go with thee; he will not fail thee, nor forsake thee. 7And Moses called unto Joshua, and said unto him in the sight of all Israel, Be strong and of a good courage: for thou must go with this people unto the land which the LORD hath sworn unto their fathers to give them; and thou shalt cause them to inherit it. 8And the LORD, he it is that doth go before thee; he will be with thee, he will not fail thee, neither forsake thee: fear not, neither be dismayed."

Psalm 89:26-33 "26He shall cry unto me, Thou art my father, my God, and the rock of my salvation. 27Also I will make him my firstborn, higher than the kings of the earth. 28My mercy will I keep for him for evermore, and my covenant shall stand fast with him. 29His seed also will I make to endure for ever, and his throne as the days of heaven. 30If his children forsake my law, and walk not in my judgments; 31If they break my statutes, and keep not my commandments; 32Then will I visit their transgression with the rod, and their iniquity with stripes. 33Nevertheless my lovingkindness will I not utterly take from him, nor suffer my faithfulness to fail."

Isaiah 42:1-4 "1Behold my servant, whom I uphold; mine elect, in whom my soul delighteth; I have put my spirit upon him: he shall bring forth judgment to the Gentiles. 2He shall not cry, nor lift up, nor cause his voice to be heard in the street. 3A bruised reed shall he not break, and the smoking flax shall he not quench: he shall bring forth judgment unto truth. 4He shall not fail nor be discouraged, till he have set judgment in the earth: and the isles shall wait for his law."

Lamentations 3:22 "It is of the LORD's mercies that we are not consumed, because his compassions fail not."

Zephaniah 3:5 "The just LORD is in the midst thereof; he will not do iniquity: every morning doth he bring his judgment to light, he faileth not; but the unjust knoweth no shame."

Hebrews 1:10-12 "10And, Thou, Lord, in the beginning hast laid the foundation of the earth; and the heavens are the works of thine hands: 11They shall perish; but thou remainest; and they all shall wax old as doth a garment; 12And as a vesture shalt thou fold them up, and they shall be changed: but thou art the same, and thy years shall not fail."

What Does Not Fail
Luke 12:31-34 "31But rather seek ye the kingdom of God; and all these things shall be added unto you. 32Fear not, little flock; for it is your Father's good pleasure to give you the kingdom. 33Sell that ye have, and give alms; provide yourselves bags which wax not old, a treasure in the heavens that faileth not, where no thief approacheth, neither moth corrupteth. 34For where your treasure is, there will your heart be also."

Luke 16:16-17 "[16]The law and the prophets were until John: since that time the kingdom of God is preached, and every man presseth into it. [17]And it is easier for heaven and earth to pass, than one tittle of the law to fail."

1 Corinthians 13:8 "Charity never faileth: but whether there be prophecies, they shall fail; whether there be tongues, they shall cease; whether there be knowledge, it shall vanish away."

What Fails
Psalm 73:26 "My flesh and my heart faileth: but God is the strength of my heart, and my portion for ever."

Psalm 143:7 "Hear me speedily, O LORD: my spirit faileth: hide not thy face from me, lest I be like unto them that go down into the pit."

1 Corinthians 13:8 "Charity never faileth: but whether there be prophecies, they shall fail; whether there be tongues, they shall cease; whether there be knowledge, it shall vanish away."

FAINTING

If You Faint
Proverbs 24:10 "If thou faint in the day of adversity, thy strength is small."

Not Fainting
Luke 18:1 "And he spake a parable unto them to this end, that men ought always to pray, and not to faint;"

Ephesians 3:13 "Wherefore I desire that ye faint not at my tribulations for you, which is your glory."

The Faint
Isaiah 40:28-29 "[28]Hast thou not known? hast thou not heard, that the everlasting God, the LORD, the Creator of the ends of the earth, fainteth not, neither is weary? there is no searching of his understanding. [29]He giveth power to the faint; and to them that have no might he increaseth strength."

The Lord Not Fainting
Isaiah 40:28 "Hast thou not known? hast thou not heard, that the everlasting God, the LORD, the Creator of the ends of the earth, fainteth not, neither is weary? there is no searching of his understanding."

Who Does Not Faint
Isaiah 40:30-31 "[30]Even the youths shall faint and be weary, and the young men shall utterly fall: [31]But they that wait upon the LORD shall renew their strength; they shall mount up with wings as eagles; they shall run, and not be weary; and they shall walk, and not faint."

2 Corinthians 4:1 "Therefore seeing we have this ministry, as we have received mercy, we faint not;"

Why Christians Do Not Faint
2 Corinthians 4:14-16 "[14]Knowing that he which raised up the Lord Jesus shall raise up us also by Jesus, and shall present us with you. [15]For all things are for your sakes, that the abundant grace might through the thanksgiving of many redound to the glory of God. [16]For which cause we faint not; but though our outward man perish, yet the inward man is renewed day by day."

FAITH/FAITHFULNESS

Faith Availing
Galatians 5:6 "For in Jesus Christ neither circumcision availeth anything, nor uncircumcision; but faith which worketh by love."

Faith Without Works
James 2:17-26 "[17]Even so faith, if it hath not works, is dead, being alone. [18]Yea, a man may say, Thou hast faith, and I have works: shew me thy faith without thy works, and I will shew thee my faith by my works. [19]Thou believest that there is one God; thou doest well: the devils also believe, and tremble. [20]But wilt thou know, O vain man, that faith without works is dead? [21]Was not Abraham our father justified by works, when he had offered Isaac his son upon the altar? [22]Seest thou how faith wrought with his works, and by works was faith made perfect? [23]And the scripture was fulfilled which saith, Abraham believed God, and it was imputed unto him for righteousness: and he was called the Friend of God. [24]Ye see then how that by works a man is justified, and not by faith only. [25]Likewise also was not Rahab the harlot justified by works, when she had received the messengers, and had sent them out another way? [26]For as the body without the spirit is dead, so faith without works is dead also."

Living By Faith

2 Corinthians 5:6-8 "⁶Therefore we are always confident, knowing that, whilst we are at home in the body, we are absent from the Lord: ⁷(For we walk by faith, not by sight:) ⁸We are confident, I say, and willing rather to be absent from the body, and to be present with the Lord."

Galatians 2:20 "I am crucified with Christ: nevertheless I live; yet not I, but Christ liveth in me: and the life which I now live in the flesh I live by the faith of the Son of God, who loved me, and gave himself for me."

Standing Fast In The Faith

1 Corinthians 16:13 "Watch ye, stand fast in the faith, quit you like men, be strong."

Hebrews 10:23 "Let us hold fast the profession of our faith without wavering; (for he is faithful that promised;)"

The Faithful

Psalm 31:23 "O love the LORD, all ye his saints: for the LORD preserveth the faithful, and plentifully rewardeth the proud doer."

Proverbs 11:13 "A talebearer revealeth secrets: but he that is of a faithful spirit concealeth the matter."

Proverbs 13:17 "A wicked messenger falleth into mischief: but a faithful ambassador is health."

Proverbs 25:13 "As the cold of snow in the time of harvest, so is a faithful messenger to them that send him: for he refresheth the soul of his masters."

Proverbs 28:20 "A faithful man shall abound with blessings: but he that maketh haste to be rich shall not be innocent."

Mark 11:23 "For verily I say unto you, That whosoever shall say unto this mountain, Be thou removed, and be thou cast into the sea; and shall not doubt in his heart, but shall believe that those things which he saith shall come to pass; he shall have whatsoever he saith."

Luke 16:10-12 "¹⁰He that is faithful in that which is least is faithful also in much: and he that is unjust in the least is unjust also in much. ¹¹If therefore ye have not been faithful in the unrighteous mammon, who will commit to your trust the true riches? ¹²And if ye have not been faithful in that which is another man's, who shall give you that which is your own?"

Galatians 3:6-7 "⁶Even as Abraham believed God, and it was accounted to him for righteousness. ⁷Know ye therefore that they which are of faith, the same are the children of Abraham."

The Faithfulness Of The Lord

Psalm 89:26-33 "²⁶He shall cry unto me, Thou art my father, my God, and the rock of my salvation. ²⁷Also I will make him my firstborn, higher than the kings of the earth. ²⁸My mercy will I keep for him for evermore, and my covenant shall stand fast with him. ²⁹His seed also will I make to endure for ever, and his throne as the days of heaven. ³⁰If his children forsake my law, and walk not in my judgments; ³¹If they break my statutes, and keep not my commandments; ³²Then will I visit their transgression with the rod, and their iniquity with stripes. ³³Nevertheless my lovingkindness will I not utterly take from him, nor suffer my faithfulness to fail."

Psalm 119:89-90 "⁸⁹For ever, O LORD, thy word is settled in heaven. ⁹⁰Thy faithfulness is unto all generations: thou hast established the earth, and it abideth."

Lamentations 3:22-23 "²²It is of the LORD's mercies that we are not consumed, because his compassions fail not. ²³They are new every morning: great is thy faithfulness."

The Lord Being Faithful

Deuteronomy 7:9 "Know therefore that the LORD thy God, he is God, the faithful God, which keepeth covenant and mercy with them that love him and keep his commandments to a thousand generations;"

Isaiah 49:7 "Thus saith the LORD, the Redeemer of Israel, and his Holy One, to him whom man despiseth, to him whom the nation abhorreth, to a servant of rulers, Kings shall see and arise, princes also shall worship, because of the LORD that is faithful, and the Holy One of Israel, and he shall choose thee."

1 Corinthians 1:9 "God is faithful, by whom ye were called unto the fellowship of his Son Jesus Christ our Lord."

1 Corinthians 10:13 "There hath no temptation taken you but such as is common to man: but God is faithful, who will not suffer you to be tempted above that ye are able; but will with the temptation also make a way to escape, that ye may be able to bear it."

1 Thessalonians 5:23-24 "²³And the very God of peace sanctify you wholly; and I pray God your whole spirit and soul and body be preserved blameless unto the coming of our Lord Jesus Christ. ²⁴Faithful is he that calleth you, who also will do it."

2 Thessalonians 3:3 "But the Lord is faithful, who shall stablish you, and keep you from evil."

Hebrews 10:23 "Let us hold fast the profession of our faith without wavering; (for he is faithful that promised;)"

Revelation 3:14 "And unto the angel of the church of the Laodiceans write; These things saith the Amen, the faithful and true witness, the beginning of the creation of God;"

The Reward For Having Faith
Matthew 17:20 "And Jesus said unto them, Because of your unbelief: for verily I say unto you, If ye have faith as a grain of mustard seed, ye shall say unto this mountain, Remove hence to yonder place; and it shall remove; and nothing shall be impossible unto you."

Matthew 21:21-22 "²¹Jesus answered and said unto them, Verily I say unto you, If ye have faith, and doubt not, ye shall not only do this which is done to the fig tree, but also if ye shall say unto this mountain, Be thou removed, and be thou cast into the sea; it shall be done. ²²And all things, whatsoever ye shall ask in prayer, believing, ye shall receive."

Luke 17:6 "And the Lord said, If ye had faith as a grain of mustard seed, ye might say unto this sycamine tree, Be thou plucked up by the root, and be thou planted in the sea; and it should obey you."

The Reward For Keeping The Faith
2 Timothy 4:7-8 "⁷I have fought a good fight, I have finished my course, I have kept the faith: ⁸Henceforth there is laid up for me a crown of righteousness, which the Lord, the righteous judge, shall give me at that day: and not to me only, but unto all them also that love his appearing."

Revelation 2:8-10 "⁸And unto the angel of the church in Smyrna write; These things saith the first and the last, which was dead, and is alive; ⁹I know thy works, and tribulation, and poverty, (but thou art rich) and I know the blasphemy of them which say they are Jews, and are not, but are the synagogue of Satan. ¹⁰Fear none of those things which thou shalt suffer: behold, the devil shall cast some of you into prison, that ye may be tried; and ye shall have tribulation ten days: be thou faithful unto death, and I will give thee a crown of life."

The Time Following The Coming Of Faith
Galatians 3:25-29 "²⁵But after that faith is come, we are no longer under a schoolmaster. ²⁶For ye are all the children of God by faith in Christ Jesus. ²⁷For as many of you as have been baptized into Christ have put on Christ. ²⁸There is neither Jew nor Greek, there is neither bond nor free, there is neither male nor female: for ye are all one in Christ Jesus. ²⁹And if ye be Christ's, then are ye Abraham's seed, and heirs according to the promise."

The Time Prior To The Coming Of Faith
Galatians 3:23-24 "²³But before faith came, we were kept under the law, shut up unto the faith which should afterwards be revealed. ²⁴Wherefore the law was our schoolmaster to bring us unto Christ, that we might be justified by faith."

The Trying Of Your Faith
James 1:2-3 "²My brethren, count it all joy when ye fall into divers temptations; ³Knowing this, that the trying of your faith worketh patience."

1 Peter 1:6-9 "⁶Wherein ye greatly rejoice, though now for a season, if need be, ye are in heaviness through manifold temptations: ⁷That the trial of your faith, being much more precious than of gold that perisheth, though it be tried with fire, might be found unto praise and honour and glory at the appearing of Jesus Christ: ⁸Whom having not seen, ye love; in whom, though now ye see him not, yet believing, ye rejoice with joy unspeakable and full of glory: ⁹Receiving the end of your faith, even the salvation of your souls."

There Being One Faith
Ephesians 4:4-6 "⁴There is one body, and one Spirit, even as ye are called in one hope of your calling; ⁵One Lord, one faith, one baptism, ⁶One

God and Father of all, who is above all, and through all, and in you all."

What Faith Comes By

Romans 10:17 "So then faith cometh by hearing, and hearing by the word of God."

What Faith Does

Matthew 9:22 "But Jesus turned him about, and when he saw her, he said, Daughter, be of good comfort; thy faith hath made thee whole. And the woman was made whole from that hour."

Mark 5:34 "And he said unto her, Daughter, thy faith hath made thee whole; go in peace, and be whole of thy plague."

Mark 10:52 "And Jesus said unto him, Go thy way; thy faith hath made thee whole. And immediately he received his sight, and followed Jesus in the way."

Luke 7:50 "And he said to the woman, Thy faith hath saved thee; go in peace."

Luke 8:48 "And he said unto her, Daughter, be of good comfort: thy faith hath made thee whole; go in peace."

Luke 17:19 "And he said unto him, Arise, go thy way: thy faith hath made thee whole."

Luke 18:42 "And Jesus said unto him, Receive thy sight: thy faith hath saved thee."

Acts 14:8-10 "8And there sat a certain man at Lystra, impotent in his feet, being a cripple from his mother's womb, who never had walked: 9The same heard Paul speak: who stedfastly beholding him, and perceiving that he had faith to be healed, 10Said with a loud voice, Stand upright on thy feet. And he leaped and walked."

What Faith Is

Hebrews 11:1-3 "1Now faith is the substance of things hoped for, the evidence of things not seen. 2For by it the elders obtained a good report. 3Through faith we understand that the worlds were framed by the word of God, so that things which are seen were not made of things which do appear."

What Is Achieved Through And By Faith

Acts 3:11-16 "11And as the lame man which was healed held Peter and John, all the people ran together unto them in the porch that is called Solomon's, greatly wondering. 12And when Peter saw it, he answered unto the people, Ye men of Israel, why marvel ye at this? or why look ye so earnestly on us, as though by our own power or holiness we had made this man to walk? 13The God of Abraham, and of Isaac, and of Jacob, the God of our fathers, hath glorified his Son Jesus; whom ye delivered up, and denied him in the presence of Pilate, when he was determined to let him go. 14But ye denied the Holy One and the Just, and desired a murderer to be granted unto you; 15And killed the Prince of life, whom God hath raised from the dead; whereof we are witnesses. 16And his name through faith in his name hath made this man strong, whom ye see and know: yea, the faith which is by him hath given him this perfect soundness in the presence of you all."

Romans 3:28-31 "28Therefore we conclude that a man is justified by faith without the deeds of the law. 29Is he the God of the Jews only? is he not also of the Gentiles? Yes, of the Gentiles also: 30Seeing it is one God, which shall justify the circumcision by faith, and uncircumcision through faith. 31Do we then make void the law through faith? God forbid: yea, we establish the law."

Romans 9:30 "What shall we say then? That the Gentiles, which followed not after righteousness, have attained to righteousness, even the righteousness which is of faith."

Galatians 3:8-14 "8And the scripture, foreseeing that God would justify the heathen through faith, preached before the gospel unto Abraham, saying, In thee shall all nations be blessed. 9So then they which be of faith are blessed with faithful Abraham. 10For as many as are of the works of the law are under the curse: for it is written, Cursed is every one that continueth not in all things which are written in the book of the law to do them. 11But that no man is justified by the law in the sight of God, it is evident: for, The just shall live by faith. 12And the law is not of faith: but, The man that doeth them shall live in them. 13Christ hath redeemed us from the curse of the law, being made a curse for us: for it is written, Cursed is every one that hangeth on a tree: 14That the blessing of Abraham might come on the Gentiles through Jesus Christ; that we might receive the promise of the Spirit through faith."

Galatians 3:23-29 "[23]But before faith came, we were kept under the law, shut up unto the faith which should afterwards be revealed. [24]Wherefore the law was our schoolmaster to bring us unto Christ, that we might be justified by faith. [25]But after that faith is come, we are no longer under a schoolmaster. [26]For ye are all the children of God by faith in Christ Jesus. [27]For as many of you as have been baptized into Christ have put on Christ. [28]There is neither Jew nor Greek, there is neither bond nor free, there is neither male nor female: for ye are all one in Christ Jesus. [29]And if ye be Christ's, then are ye Abraham's seed, and heirs according to the promise."

Ephesians 2:8-10 "[8]For by grace are ye saved through faith; and that not of yourselves: it is the gift of God: [9]Not of works, lest any man should boast. [10]For we are his workmanship, created in Christ Jesus unto good works, which God hath before ordained that we should walk in them."

Hebrews 11:1-11 "[1]Now faith is the substance of things hoped for, the evidence of things not seen. [2]For by it the elders obtained a good report. [3]Through faith we understand that the worlds were framed by the word of God, so that things which are seen were not made of things which do appear. [4]By faith Abel offered unto God a more excellent sacrifice than Cain, by which he obtained witness that he was righteous, God testifying of his gifts: and by it he being dead yet speaketh. [5]By faith Enoch was translated that he should not see death; and was not found, because God had translated him: for before his translation he had this testimony, that he pleased God. [6]But without faith it is impossible to please him: for he that cometh to God must believe that he is, and that he is a rewarder of them that diligently seek him. [7]By faith Noah, being warned of God of things not seen as yet, moved with fear, prepared an ark to the saving of his house; by the which he condemned the world, and became heir of the righteousness which is by faith. [8]By faith Abraham, when he was called to go out into a place which he should after receive for an inheritance, obeyed; and he went out, not knowing whither he went. [9]By faith he sojourned in the land of promise, as in a strange country, dwelling in tabernacles with Isaac and Jacob, the heirs with him of the same promise: [10]For he looked for a city which hath foundations, whose builder and maker is God. [11]Through faith also Sara herself received strength to conceive seed, and was delivered of a child when she was past age, because she judged him faithful who had promised."

Hebrews 11:17 "By faith Abraham, when he was tried, offered up Isaac: and he that had received the promises offered up his only begotten son,"

Hebrews 11:20-40 "[20]By faith Isaac blessed Jacob and Esau concerning things to come. [21]By faith Jacob, when he was a dying, blessed both the sons of Joseph; and worshipped, leaning upon the top of his staff. [22]By faith Joseph, when he died, made mention of the departing of the children of Israel; and gave commandment concerning his bones. [23]By faith Moses, when he was born, was hid three months of his parents, because they saw he was a proper child; and they were not afraid of the king's commandment. [24]By faith Moses, when he was come to years, refused to be called the son of Pharaoh's daughter; [25]Choosing rather to suffer affliction with the people of God, than to enjoy the pleasures of sin for a season; [26]Esteeming the reproach of Christ greater riches than the treasures in Egypt: for he had respect unto the recompence of the reward. [27]By faith he forsook Egypt, not fearing the wrath of the king: for he endured, as seeing him who is invisible. [28]Through faith he kept the passover, and the sprinkling of blood, lest he that destroyed the firstborn should touch them. [29]By faith they passed through the Red sea as by dry land: which the Egyptians assaying to do were drowned. [30]By faith the walls of Jericho fell down, after they were compassed about seven days. [31]By faith the harlot Rahab perished not with them that believed not, when she had received the spies with peace. [32]And what shall I more say? for the time would fail me to tell of Gedeon, and of Barak, and of Samson, and of Jephthae; of David also, and Samuel, and of the prophets: [33]Who through faith subdued kingdoms, wrought righteousness, obtained promises, stopped the mouths of lions, [34]Quenched the violence of fire, escaped the edge of the sword, out of weakness were made strong, waxed valiant in fight, turned to flight the armies of the aliens. [35]Women received their dead raised to life again: and others were tortured, not accepting deliverance; that they might obtain a better resurrection: ³⁶And others had trial of cruel mockings and scourgings, yea, moreover of bonds and imprisonment: ³⁷They were stoned, they were sawn asunder, were tempted, were slain with the sword: they wandered about in sheepskins and goatskins; being destitute, afflicted, tormented; ³⁸(Of whom the world was not worthy:) they wandered in deserts, and in mountains, and in dens and caves of the earth. ³⁹And these all, having obtained a good report through faith, received not the promise: ⁴⁰God having provided some better thing for us, that they without us should not be made perfect."

What Is Achieved Through And By The Faith Of Jesus Christ
Romans 3:21-22 "²¹But now the righteousness of God without the law is manifested, being witnessed by the law and the prophets; ²²Even the righteousness of God which is by faith of Jesus Christ unto all and upon all them that believe: for there is no difference:"

Ephesians 3:10-12 "¹⁰To the intent that now unto the principalities and powers in heavenly places might be known by the church the manifold wisdom of God, ¹¹According to the eternal purpose which he purposed in Christ Jesus our Lord: ¹²In whom we have boldness and access with confidence by the faith of him."

Philippians 3:9 "And be found in him, not having mine own righteousness, which is of the law, but that which is through the faith of Christ, the righteousness which is of God by faith:"

What Is Faithful
Psalm 119:137-138 "¹³⁷Righteous art thou, O LORD, and upright are thy judgments. ¹³⁸Thy testimonies that thou hast commanded are righteous and very faithful."

Proverbs 27:6 "Faithful are the wounds of a friend; but the kisses of an enemy are deceitful."

Isaiah 25:1 "O LORD, thou art my God; I will exalt thee, I will praise thy name; for thou hast done wonderful things; thy counsels of old are faithfulness and truth."

What Is Impossible Without Faith
Hebrews 11:6 "But without faith it is impossible to please him: for he that cometh to God must believe that he is, and that he is a rewarder of them that diligently seek him."

What Is In Faith
1 Timothy 1:4 "Neither give heed to fables and endless genealogies, which minister questions, rather than godly edifying which is in faith: so do."

What Your Faith Should Not Stand In
1 Corinthians 2:4-5 "⁴And my speech and my preaching was not with enticing words of man's wisdom, but in demonstration of the Spirit and of power: ⁵That your faith should not stand in the wisdom of men, but in the power of God."

What Your Faith Should Stand In
1 Corinthians 2:4-5 "⁴And my speech and my preaching was not with enticing words of man's wisdom, but in demonstration of the Spirit and of power: ⁵That your faith should not stand in the wisdom of men, but in the power of God."

Whatsoever Is Not Of Faith
Romans 14:22-23 "²²Hast thou faith? have it to thyself before God. Happy is he that condemneth not himself in that thing which he alloweth. ²³And he that doubteth is damned if he eat, because he eateth not of faith: for whatsoever is not of faith is sin."

Who Is Faithful
Luke 16:10-12 "¹⁰He that is faithful in that which is least is faithful also in much: and he that is unjust in the least is unjust also in much. ¹¹If therefore ye have not been faithful in the unrighteous mammon, who will commit to your trust the true riches? ¹²And if ye have not been faithful in that which is another man's, who shall give you that which is your own?"

Revelation 17:14 "These shall make war with the Lamb, and the Lamb shall overcome them: for he is Lord of lords, and King of kings: and they that are with him are called, and chosen, and faithful."

Who Shall Live By Faith
Habakkuk 2:4 "Behold, his soul which is lifted up is not upright in him: but the just shall live by his faith."

Romans 1:16-17 "¹⁶For I am not ashamed of the gospel of Christ: for it is the power of God unto salvation to every one that believeth; to the Jew first, and also to the Greek. ¹⁷For therein is the righteousness of God revealed from faith to faith: as it is written, The just shall live by faith."

Galatians 3:11 "But that no man is justified by the law in the sight of God, it is evident: for, The just shall live by faith."

Hebrews 10:38 "Now the just shall live by faith: but if any man draw back, my soul shall have no pleasure in him."

FAMILY

Brothers
Proverbs 17:17 "A friend loveth at all times, and a brother is born for adversity."

Who Are Members Of The Lord's Family
Matthew 12:46-50 "⁴⁶While he yet talked to the people, behold, his mother and his brethren stood without, desiring to speak with him. ⁴⁷Then one said unto him, Behold, thy mother and thy brethren stand without, desiring to speak with thee. ⁴⁸But he answered and said unto him that told him, Who is my mother? and who are my brethren? ⁴⁹And he stretched forth his hand toward his disciples, and said, Behold my mother and my brethren! ⁵⁰For whosoever shall do the will of my Father which is in heaven, the same is my brother, and sister, and mother."

Mark 3:31-35 "³¹There came then his brethren and his mother, and, standing without, sent unto him, calling him. ³²And the multitude sat about him, and they said unto him, Behold, thy mother and thy brethren without seek for thee. ³³And he answered them, saying, Who is my mother, or my brethren? ³⁴And he looked round about on them which sat about him, and said, Behold my mother and my brethren! ³⁵For whosoever shall do the will of God, the same is my brother, and my sister, and mother."

Luke 8:19-21 "¹⁹Then came to him his mother and his brethren, and could not come at him for the press. ²⁰And it was told him by certain which said, Thy mother and thy brethren stand without, desiring to see thee. ²¹And he answered and said unto them, My mother and my brethren are these which hear the word of God, and do it."

Romans 8:14-17 "¹⁴For as many as are led by the Spirit of God, they are the sons of God. ¹⁵For ye have not received the spirit of bondage again to fear; but ye have received the Spirit of adoption, whereby we cry, Abba, Father. ¹⁶The Spirit itself beareth witness with our spirit, that we are the children of God: ¹⁷And if children, then heirs; heirs of God, and joint-heirs with Christ; if so be that we suffer with him, that we may be also glorified together."

2 Corinthians 6:14-18 "¹⁴Be ye not unequally yoked together with unbelievers: for what fellowship hath righteousness with unrighteousness? and what communion hath light with darkness? ¹⁵And what concord hath Christ with Belial? or what part hath he that believeth with an infidel? ¹⁶And what agreement hath the temple of God with idols? for ye are the temple of the living God; as God hath said, I will dwell in them, and walk in them; and I will be their God, and they shall be my people. ¹⁷Wherefore come out from among them, and be ye separate, saith the Lord, and touch not the unclean thing; and I will receive you, ¹⁸And will be a Father unto you, and ye shall be my sons and daughters, saith the Lord Almighty."

Hebrews 2:9-11 "⁹But we see Jesus, who was made a little lower than the angels for the suffering of death, crowned with glory and honour; that he by the grace of God should taste death for every man. ¹⁰For it became him, for whom are all things, and by whom are all things, in bringing many sons unto glory, to make the captain of their salvation perfect through sufferings. ¹¹For both he that sanctifieth and they who are sanctified are all of one: for which cause he is not ashamed to call them brethren,"

FASTING

How Not To Fast
Matthew 6:16-18 "¹⁶Moreover when ye fast, be not, as the hypocrites, of a sad countenance: for they disfigure their faces, that they may appear unto men to fast. Verily I say unto you, They have their reward. ¹⁷But thou, when thou fastest, anoint thine head, and wash thy face; ¹⁸That thou appear not unto men to fast, but unto thy Father which is in secret: and thy Father, which seeth in secret, shall reward thee openly."

How To Fast
Matthew 6:16-18 "¹⁶Moreover when ye fast, be not, as the hypocrites, of a sad countenance: for they disfigure their faces, that they may appear

unto men to fast. Verily I say unto you, They have their reward. [17]But thou, when thou fastest, anoint thine head, and wash thy face; [18]That thou appear not unto men to fast, but unto thy Father which is in secret: and thy Father, which seeth in secret, shall reward thee openly."

FAVORITISM

Not Respecting Persons
(Not Showing Favoritism)

Deuteronomy 1:17 "Ye shall not respect persons in judgment; but ye shall hear the small as well as the great; ye shall not be afraid of the face of man; for the judgment is God's: and the cause that is too hard for you, bring it unto me, and I will hear it."

2 Chronicles 19:7 "Wherefore now let the fear of the LORD be upon you; take heed and do it: for there is no iniquity with the LORD our God, nor respect of persons, nor taking of gifts."

The Lord Not Respecting Persons
(Not Showing Favoritism)

Deuteronomy 10:17 "For the LORD your God is God of gods, and Lord of lords, a great God, a mighty, and a terrible, which regardeth not persons, nor taketh reward:"

Job 34:12-20 "[12]Yea, surely God will not do wickedly, neither will the Almighty pervert judgment. [13]Who hath given him a charge over the earth? or who hath disposed the whole world? [14]If he set his heart upon man, if he gather unto himself his spirit and his breath; [15]All flesh shall perish together, and man shall turn again unto dust. [16]If now thou hast understanding, hear this: hearken to the voice of my words. [17]Shall even he that hateth right govern? and wilt thou condemn him that is most just? [18]Is it fit to say to a king, Thou art wicked? and to princes, Ye are ungodly? [19]How much less to him that accepteth not the persons of princes, nor regardeth the rich more than the poor? for they all are the work of his hands. [20]In a moment shall they die, and the people shall be troubled at midnight, and pass away: and the mighty shall be taken away without hand."

Matthew 22:16 "And they sent out unto him their disciples with the Herodians, saying, Master, we know that thou art true, and teachest the way of

God in truth, neither carest thou for any man: for thou regardest not the person of men.'"

Mark 12:14 "And when they were come, they say unto him, Master, we know that thou art true, and carest for no man: for thou regardest not the person of men, but teachest the way of God in truth: Is it lawful to give tribute to Caesar, or not?"

Luke 20:21 "And they asked him, saying, Master, we know that thou sayest and teachest rightly, neither acceptest thou the person of any, but teachest the way of God truly:"

Acts 10:34 "Then Peter opened his mouth, and said, Of a truth I perceive that God is no respecter of persons:"

Romans 2:11 "For there is no respect of persons with God."

Ephesians 6:9 "And, ye masters, do the same things unto them, forbearing threatening: knowing that your Master also is in heaven; neither is there respect of persons with him."

Colossians 3:24-25 "[24]Knowing that of the Lord ye shall receive the reward of the inheritance: for ye serve the Lord Christ. [25]But he that doeth wrong shall receive for the wrong which he hath done: and there is no respect of persons."

1 Peter 1:15-17 "[15]But as he which hath called you is holy, so be ye holy in all manner of conversation; [16]Because it is written, Be ye holy; for I am holy. [17]And if ye call on the Father, who without respect of persons judgeth according to every man's work, pass the time of your sojourning here in fear:"

The Respecting Of Persons (Favoritism)

Proverbs 28:21 "To have respect of persons is not good: for for a piece of bread that man will transgress."

Those That Have Respect Of Persons
(Show Favoritism)

James 2:1-4 "[1]My brethren, have not the faith of our Lord Jesus Christ, the Lord of glory, with respect of persons. [2]For if there come unto your assembly a man with a gold ring, in goodly apparel, and there come in also a poor man in vile raiment; [3]And ye have respect to him that weareth the gay clothing, and say unto him, Sit thou here in a good place; and say to the poor,

Stand thou there, or sit here under my footstool: ⁴Are ye not then partial in yourselves, and are become judges of evil thoughts?"

James 2:9 "But if ye have respect to persons, ye commit sin, and are convinced of the law as transgressors."

FEAR

Fearing The Lord

Leviticus 19:14 "Thou shalt not curse the deaf, nor put a stumblingblock before the blind, but shalt fear thy God: I am the LORD."

Leviticus 25:17 "Ye shall not therefore oppress one another; but thou shalt fear thy God: for I am the LORD your God."

Deuteronomy 6:1-2 "¹Now these are the commandments, the statutes, and the judgments, which the LORD your God commanded to teach you, that ye might do them in the land whither ye go to possess it: ²That thou mightest fear the LORD thy God, to keep all his statutes and his commandments, which I command thee, thou, and thy son, and thy son's son, all the days of thy life; and that thy days may be prolonged."

Deuteronomy 6:13 "Thou shalt fear the LORD thy God, and serve him, and shalt swear by his name."

Deuteronomy 8:6 "Therefore thou shalt keep the commandments of the LORD thy God, to walk in his ways, and to fear him."

Deuteronomy 10:12 "And now, Israel, what doth the LORD thy God require of thee, but to fear the LORD thy God, to walk in all his ways, and to love him, and to serve the LORD thy God with all thy heart and with all thy soul,"

Deuteronomy 10:20 "Thou shalt fear the LORD thy God; him shalt thou serve, and to him shalt thou cleave, and swear by his name."

Deuteronomy 13:4 "Ye shall walk after the LORD your God, and fear him, and keep his commandments, and obey his voice, and ye shall serve him, and cleave unto him."

Joshua 4:24 "That all the people of the earth might know the hand of the LORD, that it is mighty: that ye might fear the LORD your God for ever."

Joshua 24:14 "Now therefore fear the LORD, and serve him in sincerity and in truth: and put away the gods which your fathers served on the other side of the flood, and in Egypt; and serve ye the LORD."

1 Samuel 12:24 "Only fear the LORD, and serve him in truth with all your heart: for consider how great things he hath done for you."

2 Kings 17:36-39 "³⁶But the LORD, who brought you up out of the land of Egypt with great power and a stretched out arm, him shall ye fear, and him shall ye worship, and to him shall ye do sacrifice. ³⁷And the statutes, and the ordinances, and the law, and the commandment, which he wrote for you, ye shall observe to do for evermore; and ye shall not fear other gods. ³⁸And the covenant that I have made with you ye shall not forget; neither shall ye fear other gods. ³⁹But the LORD your God ye shall fear; and he shall deliver you out of the hand of all your enemies."

1 Chronicles 16:25 "For great is the LORD, and greatly to be praised: he also is to be feared above all gods."

1 Chronicles 16:29-30 "²⁹Give unto the LORD the glory due unto his name: bring an offering, and come before him: worship the LORD in the beauty of holiness. ³⁰Fear before him, all the earth: the world also shall be stable, that it be not moved."

2 Chronicles 19:7 "Wherefore now let the fear of the LORD be upon you; take heed and do it: for there is no iniquity with the LORD our God, nor respect of persons, nor taking of gifts."

Psalm 9:20 "Put them in fear, O LORD: that the nations may know themselves to be but men. Selah."

Psalm 22:23 "Ye that fear the LORD, praise him; all ye the seed of Jacob, glorify him; and fear him, all ye the seed of Israel."

Psalm 33:8 "Let all the earth fear the LORD: let all the inhabitants of the world stand in awe of him."

Psalm 34:9 "O fear the LORD, ye his saints: for there is no want to them that fear him."

Psalm 89:7 "God is greatly to be feared in the assembly of the saints, and to be had in reverence of all them that are about him."

Psalm 96:4 "For the LORD is great, and greatly to be praised: he is to be feared above all gods."

Psalm 119:120 "My flesh trembleth for fear of thee; and I am afraid of thy judgments."

Psalm 130:3-4 "³If thou, LORD, shouldest mark iniquities, O Lord, who shall stand? ⁴But there is forgiveness with thee, that thou mayest be feared."

Proverbs 3:7 "Be not wise in thine own eyes: fear the LORD, and depart from evil."

Proverbs 23:17 "Let not thine heart envy sinners: but be thou in the fear of the LORD all the day long."

Proverbs 24:21-22 "²¹My son, fear thou the LORD and the king: and meddle not with them that are given to change: ²²For their calamity shall rise suddenly; and who knoweth the ruin of them both?"

Ecclesiastes 5:7 "For in the multitude of dreams and many words there are also divers vanities: but fear thou God."

Ecclesiastes 12:13 "Let us hear the conclusion of the whole matter: Fear God, and keep his commandments: for this is the whole duty of man."

Isaiah 8:12-13 "¹²Say ye not, A confederacy, to all them to whom this people shall say, A confederacy; neither fear ye their fear, nor be afraid. ¹³Sanctify the LORD of hosts himself; and let him be your fear, and let him be your dread."

Daniel 6:26 "I make a decree, That in every dominion of my kingdom men tremble and fear before the God of Daniel: for he is the living God, and stedfast for ever, and his kingdom that which shall not be destroyed, and his dominion shall be even unto the end."

Matthew 10:28 "And fear not them which kill the body, but are not able to kill the soul: but rather fear him which is able to destroy both soul and body in hell."

Luke 12:4-5 "⁴And I say unto you my friends, Be not afraid of them that kill the body, and after that have no more that they can do. ⁵But I will forewarn you whom ye shall fear: Fear him, which after he hath killed hath power to cast into hell; yea, I say unto you, Fear him."

Romans 11:20-21 "²⁰Well; because of unbelief they were broken off, and thou standest by faith. Be not highminded, but fear: ²¹For if God spared not the natural branches, take heed lest he also spare not thee."

2 Corinthians 7:1 "Having therefore these promises, dearly beloved, let us cleanse ourselves from all filthiness of the flesh and spirit, perfecting holiness in the fear of God."

1 Peter 2:17 "Honour all men. Love the brotherhood. Fear God. Honour the king."

Revelation 14:7 "Saying with a loud voice, Fear God, and give glory to him; for the hour of his judgment is come: and worship him that made heaven, and earth, and the sea, and the fountains of waters."

Not Being Afraid

Genesis 21:17 "And God heard the voice of the lad; and the angel of God called Hagar out of heaven, and said unto her, What aileth thee, Hagar? fear not; for God hath heard the voice of the lad where he is."

Exodus 20:18-20 "¹⁸And all the people saw the thunderings, and the lightnings, and the noise of the trumpet, and the mountain smoking: and when the people saw it, they removed, and stood afar off. ¹⁹And they said unto Moses, Speak thou with us, and we will hear: but let not God speak with us, lest we die. ²⁰And Moses said unto the people, Fear not: for God is come to prove you, and that his fear may be before your faces, that ye sin not."

Numbers 14:9 "Only rebel not ye against the LORD, neither fear ye the people of the land; for they are bread for us: their defence is departed from them, and the LORD is with us: fear them not."

Deuteronomy 31:6-8 "⁶Be strong and of a good courage, fear not, nor be afraid of them: for the LORD thy God, he it is that doth go with thee; he will not fail thee, nor forsake thee. ⁷And Moses called unto Joshua, and said unto him in the sight of all Israel, Be strong and of a good courage: for thou must go with this people unto the land which the LORD hath sworn unto their fathers to give them; and thou shalt cause them to inherit it. [8]And the LORD, he it is that doth go before thee; he will be with thee, he will not fail thee, neither forsake thee: fear not, neither be dismayed."

Joshua 1:9 "Have not I commanded thee? Be strong and of a good courage; be not afraid, neither be thou dismayed: for the LORD thy God is with thee whithersoever thou goest."

1 Chronicles 22:13 "Then shalt thou prosper, if thou takest heed to fulfil the statutes and judgments which the LORD charged Moses with concerning Israel: be strong, and of good courage; dread not, nor be dismayed."

2 Chronicles 32:7-8 "[7]Be strong and courageous, be not afraid nor dismayed for the king of Assyria, nor for all the multitude that is with him: for there be more with us than with him: [8]With him is an arm of flesh; but with us is the LORD our God to help us, and to fight our battles. And the people rested themselves upon the words of Hezekiah king of Judah."

Proverbs 3:25 "Be not afraid of sudden fear, neither of the desolation of the wicked, when it cometh."

Isaiah 8:12-13 "[12]Say ye not, A confederacy, to all them to whom this people shall say, A confederacy; neither fear ye their fear, nor be afraid. [13]Sanctify the LORD of hosts himself; and let him be your fear, and let him be your dread."

Isaiah 41:10 "Fear thou not; for I am with thee: be not dismayed; for I am thy God: I will strengthen thee; yea, I will help thee; yea, I will uphold thee with the right hand of my righteousness."

Isaiah 43:5 "Fear not: for I am with thee: I will bring thy seed from the east, and gather thee from the west;"

Isaiah 44:2 "Thus saith the LORD that made thee, and formed thee from the womb, which will help thee; Fear not, O Jacob, my servant; and thou, Jesurun, whom I have chosen."

Isaiah 44:8 "Fear ye not, neither be afraid: have not I told thee from that time, and have declared it? ye are even my witnesses. Is there a God beside me? yea, there is no God; I know not any."

Jeremiah 30:10 "Therefore fear thou not, O my servant Jacob, saith the LORD; neither be dismayed, O Israel: for, lo, I will save thee from afar, and thy seed from the land of their captivity; and Jacob shall return, and shall be in rest, and be quiet, and none shall make him afraid."

Jeremiah 46:28 "Fear thou not, O Jacob my servant, saith the LORD: for I am with thee; for I will make a full end of all the nations whither I have driven thee: but I will not make a full end of thee, but correct thee in measure; yet will I not leave thee wholly unpunished."

Daniel 10:18-19 "[18]Then there came again and touched me one like the appearance of a man, and he strengthened me, [19]And said, O man greatly beloved, fear not: peace be unto thee, be strong, yea, be strong. And when he had spoken unto me, I was strengthened, and said, Let my lord speak; for thou hast strengthened me."

Joel 2:21-22 "[21]Fear not, O land; be glad and rejoice: for the LORD will do great things. [22]Be not afraid, ye beasts of the field: for the pastures of the wilderness do spring, for the tree beareth her fruit, the fig tree and the vine do yield their strength."

Matthew 10:26-31 "[26]Fear them not therefore: for there is nothing covered, that shall not be revealed; and hid, that shall not be known. [27]What I tell you in darkness, that speak ye in light: and what ye hear in the ear, that preach ye upon the housetops. [28]And fear not them which kill the body, but are not able to kill the soul: but rather fear him which is able to destroy both soul and body in hell. [29]Are not two sparrows sold for a farthing? and one of them shall not fall on the ground without your Father. [30]But the very hairs of your head are all numbered. [31]Fear ye not therefore, ye are of more value than many sparrows."

Luke 8:50 "But when Jesus heard it, he answered him, saying, Fear not: believe only, and she shall be made whole."

John 14:27 "Peace I leave with you, my peace I give unto you: not as the world giveth, give I unto you. Let not your heart be troubled, neither let it be afraid."

1 Peter 3:14 "But and if ye suffer for righteousness' sake, happy are ye: and be not afraid of their terror, neither be troubled;"

Revelation 1:17 "And when I saw him, I fell at his feet as dead. And he laid his right hand upon me, saying unto me, Fear not; I am the first and the last:"

Revelation 2:10 "Fear none of those things which thou shalt suffer: behold, the devil shall cast some of you into prison, that ye may be tried; and ye shall have tribulation ten days: be thou faithful unto death, and I will give thee a crown of life."

The Fear Of Man
Proverbs 29:25 "The fear of man bringeth a snare: but whoso putteth his trust in the LORD shall be safe."

The Fear Of The Lord
Job 28:28 "And unto man he said, Behold, the fear of the Lord, that is wisdom; and to depart from evil is understanding."

Psalm 19:9 "The fear of the LORD is clean, enduring for ever: the judgments of the LORD are true and righteous altogether."

Psalm 111:10 "The fear of the LORD is the beginning of wisdom: a good understanding have all they that do his commandments: his praise endureth for ever."

Proverbs 1:7 "The fear of the LORD is the beginning of knowledge: but fools despise wisdom and instruction."

Proverbs 8:13 "The fear of the LORD is to hate evil: pride, and arrogancy, and the evil way, and the froward mouth, do I hate."

Proverbs 9:10 "The fear of the LORD is the beginning of wisdom: and the knowledge of the holy is understanding."

Proverbs 10:27 "The fear of the LORD prolongeth days: but the years of the wicked shall be shortened."

Proverbs 14:26-27 "26In the fear of the LORD is strong confidence: and his children shall have a place of refuge. 27The fear of the LORD is a fountain of life, to depart from the snares of death."

Proverbs 15:16 "Better is little with the fear of the LORD than great treasure and trouble therewith."

Proverbs 15:33 "The fear of the LORD is the instruction of wisdom; and before honour is humility."

Proverbs 16:6 "By mercy and truth iniquity is purged: and by the fear of the LORD men depart from evil."

Proverbs 19:23 "The fear of the LORD tendeth to life: and he that hath it shall abide satisfied; he shall not be visited with evil."

Proverbs 22:4 "By humility and the fear of the LORD are riches, and honour, and life."

Isaiah 33:5-6 "5The LORD is exalted; for he dwelleth on high: he hath filled Zion with judgment and righteousness. 6And wisdom and knowledge shall be the stability of thy times, and strength of salvation: the fear of the LORD is his treasure."

The Fear Of The Wicked
Proverbs 10:24 "The fear of the wicked, it shall come upon him: but the desire of the righteous shall be granted."

The Fearful
1 John 4:18 "There is no fear in love; but perfect love casteth out fear: because fear hath torment. He that feareth is not made perfect in love."

Revelation 21:8 "But the fearful, and unbelieving, and the abominable, and murderers, and whoremongers, and sorcerers, and idolaters, and all liars, shall have their part in the lake which burneth with fire and brimstone: which is the second death."

The Lord Delivering You From Your Fears
Psalm 34:4 "I sought the LORD, and he heard me, and delivered me from all my fears."

The Reward For Fearing Other gods
2 Kings 17:7-23 "7For so it was, that the children of Israel had sinned against the LORD their God, which had brought them up out of the land of Egypt, from under the hand of Pharoah king of Egypt, and had feared other gods, 8And walked in the statutes of the heathen, whom the LORD cast out from before the children of Israel, and of the kings of Israel, which they had made. 9And the children of Israel did secretly those things that were not right against the LORD their God, and they built them high places in all their

cities, from the tower of the watchmen to the fenced city. [10]And they set them up images and groves in every high hill, and under every green tree: [11]And there they burnt incense in all the high places, as did the heathen whom the LORD carried away before them; and wrought wicked things to provoke the LORD to anger: [12]For they served idols, whereof the LORD had said unto them, Ye shall not do this thing. [13]Yet the LORD testified against Israel, and against Judah, by all the prophets, and by all the seers, saying, Turn ye from your evil ways, and keep my commandments and my statutes, according to all the law which I commanded your fathers, and which I sent to you by my servants the prophets. [14]Notwithstanding they would not hear, but hardened their necks, like to the neck of their fathers, that did not believe in the LORD their God. [15]And they rejected his statutes, and his covenant that he made with their fathers, and his testimonies which he testified against them; and they followed vanity, and became vain, and went after the heathen that were round about them, concerning whom the LORD had charged them, that they should not do like them. [16]And they left all the commandments of the LORD their God, and made them molten images, even two calves, and made a grove, and worshipped all the host of heaven, and served Baal. [17]And they caused their sons and their daughters to pass through the fire, and used divination and enchantments, and sold themselves to do evil in the sight of the LORD, to provoke him to anger. [18]Therefore the LORD was very angry with Israel, and removed them out of his sight: there was none left but the tribe of Judah only. [19]Also Judah kept not the commandments of the LORD their God, but walked in the statutes of Israel which they made. [20]And the LORD rejected all the seed of Israel, and afflicted them, and delivered them into the hand of spoilers, until he had cast them out of his sight. [21]For he rent Israel from the house of David; and they made Jeroboam the son of Nebat king: and Jeroboam drave Israel from following the LORD, and made them sin a great sin. [22]For the children of Israel walked in all the sins of Jeroboam which he did; they departed not from them; [23]Until the LORD removed Israel out of his sight, as he had said by all his servants the prophets. So was Israel carried away out of their own land to Assyria unto this day."

The Reward For Fearing The Lord
Exodus 1:21 "And it came to pass, because the midwives feared God, that he made them houses."

1 Samuel 12:14 "If ye will fear the LORD, and serve him, and obey his voice, and not rebel against the commandment of the LORD, then shall both ye and also the king that reigneth over you continue following the LORD your God:"

Isaiah 8:13-14 "[13]Sanctify the LORD of hosts himself; and let him be your fear, and let him be your dread. [14]And he shall be for a sanctuary; but for a stone of stumbling and for a rock of offence to both the houses of Israel, for a gin and for a snare to the inhabitants of Jerusalem."

Those That Do Not Fear The Lord
Proverbs 1:20-29 "[20]Wisdom crieth without; she uttereth her voice in the streets: [21]She crieth in the chief place of concourse, in the openings of the gates: in the city she uttereth her words, saying, [22]How long, ye simple ones, will ye love simplicity? and the scorners delight in their scorning, and fools hate knowledge? [23]Turn you at my reproof: behold, I will pour out my spirit unto you, I will make known my words unto you. [24]Because I have called, and ye refused; I have stretched out my hand, and no man regarded; [25]But ye have set at nought all my counsel, and would none of my reproof: [26]I also will laugh at your calamity; I will mock when your fear cometh; [27]When your fear cometh as desolation, and your destruction cometh as a whirlwind; when distress and anguish cometh upon you. [28]Then shall they call upon me, but I will not answer; they shall seek me early, but they shall not find me: [29]For that they hated knowledge, and did not choose the fear of the LORD:"

Those That Fear The Commandment
Proverbs 13:13 "Whoso despiseth the word shall be destroyed: but he that feareth the commandment shall be rewarded."

Those That Fear The Lord
Job 1:6-10 "[6]Now there was a day when the sons of God came to present themselves before the LORD, and Satan came also among them. [7]And the LORD said unto Satan, Whence comest thou? Then Satan

answered the LORD, and said, From going to and fro in the earth, and from walking up and down in it. [8]And the LORD said unto Satan, Hast thou considered my servant Job, that there is none like him in the earth, a perfect and an upright man, one that feareth God, and escheweth evil? [9]Then Satan answered the LORD, and said, Doth Job fear God for nought? [10]Hast not thou made an hedge about him, and about his house, and about all that he hath on every side? thou hast blessed the work of his hands, and his substance is increased in the land."

Psalm 22:23 "Ye that fear the LORD, praise him; all ye the seed of Jacob, glorify him; and fear him, all ye the seed of Israel."

Psalm 25:14 "The secret of the LORD is with them that fear him; and he will shew them his covenant."

Psalm 33:18 "Behold, the eye of the LORD is upon them that fear him, upon them that hope in his mercy;"

Psalm 34:7 "The angel of the LORD encampeth round about them that fear him, and delivereth them."

Psalm 34:9 "O fear the LORD, ye his saints: for there is no want to them that fear him."

Psalm 103:8-11 "[8]The LORD is merciful and gracious, slow to anger, and plenteous in mercy. [9]He will not always chide: neither will he keep his anger for ever. [10]He hath not dealt with us after our sins; nor rewarded us according to our iniquities. [11]For as the heaven is high above the earth, so great is his mercy toward them that fear him."

Psalm 103:13 "Like as a father pitieth his children, so the LORD pitieth them that fear him."

Psalm 103:17 "But the mercy of the LORD is from everlasting to everlasting upon them that fear him, and his righteousness unto children's children;"

Psalm 111:4-5 "[4]He hath made his wonderful works to be remembered: the LORD is gracious and full of compassion. [5]He hath given meat unto them that fear him: he will ever be mindful of his covenant."

Psalm 112:1-3 "[1]Praise ye the LORD. Blessed is the man that feareth the LORD, that delighteth greatly in his commandments. [2]His seed shall be mighty upon earth: the generation of the upright shall be blessed. [3]Wealth and riches shall be in his house: and his righteousness endureth for ever."

Psalm 115:11-15 "[11]Ye that fear the LORD, trust in the LORD: he is their help and their shield. [12]The LORD hath been mindful of us: he will bless us; he will bless the house of Israel; he will bless the house of Aaron. [13]He will bless them that fear the LORD, both small and great. [14]The LORD shall increase you more and more, you and your children. [15]Ye are blessed of the LORD which made heaven and earth."

Psalm 119:73-75 "[73]Thy hands have made me and fashioned me: give me understanding, that I may learn thy commandments. [74]They that fear thee will be glad when they see me; because I have hoped in thy word. [75]I know, O LORD, that thy judgments are right, and that thou in faithfulness hast afflicted me."

Psalm 128:1-6 "[1]Blessed is every one that feareth the LORD; that walketh in his ways. [2]For thou shalt eat the labour of thine hands: happy shalt thou be, and it shall be well with thee. [3]Thy wife shall be as a fruitful vine by the sides of thine house: thy children like olive plants round about thy table. [4]Behold, that thus shall the man be blessed that feareth the LORD. [5]The LORD shall bless thee out of Zion: and thou shalt see the good of Jerusalem all the days of thy life. [6]Yea, thou shalt see thy children's children, and peace upon Israel."

Psalm 145:18-19 "[18]The LORD is nigh unto all them that call upon him, to all that call upon him in truth. [19]He will fulfil the desire of them that fear him: he also will hear their cry, and will save them."

Psalm 147:11 "The LORD taketh pleasure in them that fear him, in those that hope in his mercy."

Proverbs 19:23 "The fear of the LORD tendeth to life: and he that hath it shall abide satisfied; he shall not be visited with evil."

Proverbs 28:14 "Happy is the man that feareth alway: but he that hardeneth his heart shall fall into mischief."

Proverbs 31:30 "Favour is deceitful, and beauty is vain: but a woman that feareth the LORD, she shall be praised."

Ecclesiastes 7:16-18 "¹⁶Be not righteous over much; neither make thyself over wise: why shouldest thou destroy thyself? ¹⁷Be not over much wicked, neither be thou foolish: why shouldest thou die before thy time? ¹⁸It is good that thou shouldest take hold of this; yea, also from this withdraw not thine hand: for he that feareth God shall come forth of them all."

Isaiah 66:1-2 "¹Thus saith the LORD, The heaven is my throne, and the earth is my footstool: where is the house that ye build unto me? and where is the place of my rest? ²For all those things hath mine hand made, and those things have been, saith the LORD: but to this man will I look, even to him that is poor and of a contrite spirit, and trembleth at my word."

Malachi 3:16-18 "¹⁶Then they that feared the LORD spake often one to another: and the LORD hearkened, and heard it, and a book of remembrance was written before him for them that feared the LORD, and that thought upon his name. ¹⁷And they shall be mine, saith the LORD of hosts, in that day when I make up my jewels; and I will spare them, as a man spareth his own son that serveth him. ¹⁸Then shall ye return, and discern between the righteous and the wicked, between him that serveth God and him that serveth him not."

Malachi 4:1-3 "¹For, behold, the day cometh, that shall burn as an oven; and all the proud, yea, and all that do wickedly, shall be stubble: and the day that cometh shall burn them up, saith the LORD of hosts, that it shall leave them neither root nor branch. ²But unto you that fear my name shall the Sun of righteousness arise with healing in his wings; and ye shall go forth, and grow up as calves of the stall. ³And ye shall tread down the wicked; for they shall be ashes under the soles of your feet in the day that I shall do this, saith the LORD of hosts."

Acts 10:34-35 "³⁴Then Peter opened his mouth, and said, Of a truth I perceive that God is no respecter of persons: ³⁵But in every nation he that feareth him, and worketh righteousness, is accepted with him."

Revelation 19:5 "And a voice came out of the throne, saying, Praise our God, all ye his servants, and ye that fear him, both small and great."

What Casts Out Fear

1 John 4:18 "There is no fear in love; but perfect love casteth out fear: because fear hath torment. He that feareth is not made perfect in love."

What Is Fearful

Hebrews 10:31 "It is a fearful thing to fall into the hands of the living God."

What Not To Fear

Deuteronomy 1:17 "Ye shall not respect persons in judgment; but ye shall hear the small as well as the great; ye shall not be afraid of the face of man; for the judgment is God's: and the cause that is too hard for you, bring it unto me, and I will hear it."

2 Kings 17:35-38 "³⁵With whom the LORD had made a covenant, and charged them saying, Ye shall not fear other gods, nor bow yourselves to them, nor serve them, nor sacrifice to them: ³⁶But the LORD, who brought you up out of the land of Egypt with great power and a stretched out arm, him shall ye fear, and him shall ye worship, and to him shall ye do sacrifice. ³⁷And the statutes, and the ordinances, and the law, and the commandment, which he wrote for you, ye shall observe to do for evermore; and ye shall not fear other gods. ³⁸And the covenant that I have made with you ye shall not forget; neither shall ye fear other gods."

Psalm 56:4 "In God I will praise his word, in God I have put my trust; I will not fear what flesh can do unto me."

Psalm 56:11 "In God have I put my trust: I will not be afraid what man can do unto me."

Psalm 118:6 "The LORD is on my side; I will not fear: what can man do unto me?"

Proverbs 3:25 "Be not afraid of sudden fear, neither of the desolation of the wicked, when it cometh."

Isaiah 8:12-13 "¹²Say ye not, A confederacy, to all them to whom this people shall say, A confederacy; neither fear ye their fear, nor be afraid. ¹³Sanctify the LORD of hosts himself; and let him be your fear, and let him be your dread."

Isaiah 51:7-8 "⁷Hearken unto me, ye that know righteousness, the people in whose heart is my law;

fear ye not the reproach of men, neither be ye afraid of their revilings. [8]For the moth shall eat them up like a garment, and the worm shall eat them like wool: but my righteousness shall be for ever, and my salvation from generation to generation."

Hebrews 13:6 "So that we may boldly say, The Lord is my helper, and I will not fear what man shall do unto me."

1 Peter 3:14 "But and if ye suffer for righteousness' sake, happy are ye: and be not afraid of their terror, neither be troubled;"

Revelation 2:10 "Fear none of those things which thou shalt suffer: behold, the devil shall cast some of you into prison, that ye may be tried; and ye shall have tribulation ten days: be thou faithful unto death, and I will give thee a crown of life."

What Should Be Done With Fear
Psalm 2:11 "Serve the LORD with fear, and rejoice with trembling."

Where There Is No Fear
1 John 4:18 "There is no fear in love; but perfect love casteth out fear: because fear hath torment. He that feareth is not made perfect in love."

Who Fears The Lord
Proverbs 14:2 "He that walketh in his uprightness feareth the LORD: but he that is perverse in his ways despiseth him."

Jonah 1:7-9 "[7]And they said every one to his fellow, Come, and let us cast lots, that we may know for whose cause this evil is upon us. So they cast lots, and the lot fell upon Jonah. [8]Then said they unto him, Tell us, we pray thee, for whose cause this evil is upon us; What is thine occupation? and whence comest thou? what is thy country? and of what people art thou? [9]And he said unto them, I am an Hebrew; and I fear the LORD, the God of heaven, which hath made the sea and the dry land."

Who Not To Fear
Numbers 14:9 "Only rebel not ye against the LORD, neither fear ye the people of the land; for they are bread for us: their defence is departed from them, and the LORD is with us: fear them not."

Matthew 10:28 "And fear not them which kill the body, but are not able to kill the soul: but rather fear him which is able to destroy both soul and body in hell."

Luke 12:4-5 "[4]And I say unto you my friends, Be not afraid of them that kill the body, and after that have no more that they can do. [5]But I will forewarn you whom ye shall fear: Fear him, which after he hath killed hath power to cast into hell; yea, I say unto you, Fear him."

Who Shall Fear The Lord
Psalm 64:9 "And all men shall fear, and shall declare the work of God; for they shall wisely consider of his doing."

Psalm 67:7 "God shall bless us; and all the ends of the earth shall fear him."

Isaiah 25:1-3 "[1]O LORD, thou art my God; I will exalt thee, I will praise thy name; for thou hast done wonderful things; thy counsels of old are faithfulness and truth. [2]For thou hast made of a city an heap; of a defenced city a ruin: a palace of strangers to be no city; it shall never be built. [3]Therefore shall the strong people glorify thee, the city of the terrible nations shall fear thee."

Hosea 3:4-5 "[4]For the children of Israel shall abide many days without a king, and without a prince, and without a sacrifice, and without an image, and without an ephod, and without teraphim: [5]Afterward shall the children of Israel return, and seek the LORD their God, and David their king; and shall fear the LORD and his goodness in the latter days."

Who Shall Not Be Afraid
Psalm 112:5-8 "[5]A good man sheweth favour, and lendeth: he will guide his affairs with discretion. [6]Surely he shall not be moved for ever: the righteous shall be in everlasting remembrance. [7]He shall not be afraid of evil tidings: his heart is fixed, trusting in the LORD. [8]His heart is established, he shall not be afraid, until he see his desire upon his enemies."

Proverbs 1:20-33 "[20]Wisdom crieth without; she uttereth her voice in the streets: [21]She crieth in the chief place of concourse, in the openings of the gates: in the city she uttereth her words, saying,

[22]How long, ye simple ones, will ye love simplicity? and the scorners delight in their scorning, and fools hate knowledge? [23]Turn you at my reproof: behold, I will pour out my spirit unto you, I will make known my words unto you. [24]Because I have called, and ye refused; I have stretched out my hand, and no man regarded; [25]But ye have set at nought all my counsel, and would none of my reproof: [26]I also will laugh at your calamity; I will mock when your fear cometh; [27]When your fear cometh as desolation, and your destruction cometh as a whirlwind; when distress and anguish cometh upon you. [28]Then shall they call upon me, but I will not answer; they shall seek me early, but they shall not find me: [29]For that they hated knowledge, and did not choose the fear of the LORD: [30]They would none of my counsel: they despised all my reproof. [31]Therefore shall they eat of the fruit of their own way, and be filled with their own devices. [32]For the turning away of the simple shall slay them, and the prosperity of fools shall destroy them. [33]But whoso hearkeneth unto me shall dwell safely, and shall be quiet from fear of evil."

Isaiah 54:5-14 "[5]For thy Maker is thine husband; the LORD of hosts is his name; and thy Redeemer the Holy One of Israel; The God of the whole earth shall he be called. [6]For the LORD hath called thee as a woman forsaken and grieved in spirit, and a wife of youth, when thou wast refused, saith thy God. [7]For a small moment have I forsaken thee; but with great mercies will I gather thee. [8]In a little wrath I hid my face from thee for a moment; but with everlasting kindness will I have mercy on thee, saith the LORD thy Redeemer. [9]For this is as the waters of Noah unto me: for as I have sworn that the waters of Noah should no more go over the earth; so have I sworn that I would not be wroth with thee, nor rebuke thee. [10]For the mountains shall depart, and the hills be removed; but my kindness shall not depart from thee, neither shall the covenant of my peace be removed, saith the LORD that hath mercy on thee. [11]O thou afflicted, tossed with tempest, and not comforted, behold, I will lay thy stones with fair colours, and lay thy foundations with sapphires. [12]And I will make thy windows of agates, and thy gates of carbuncles, and all thy borders of pleasant stones. [13]And all thy children shall be taught of the LORD; and great shall be the peace of thy children. [14]In righteousness shalt thou be established: thou shalt be far from oppression; for thou shalt not fear: and from terror; for it shall not come near thee."

Who Shall Understand The Fear Of The Lord

Proverbs 2:1-5 "[1]My son, if thou wilt receive my words, and hide my commandments with thee; [2]So that thou incline thine ear unto wisdom, and apply thine heart to understanding; [3]Yea, if thou criest after knowledge, and liftest up thy voice for understanding; [4]If thou seekest her as silver, and searchest for her as for hid treasures; [5]Then shalt thou understand the fear of the LORD, and find the knowledge of God."

Who To Fear

Leviticus 19:3 "Ye shall fear every man his mother, and his father, and keep my sabbaths: I am the LORD your God."

Why Men Fear The Lord

Job 37:23-24 "[23]Touching the Almighty, we cannot find him out: he is excellent in power, and in judgment, and in plenty of justice: he will not afflict. [24]Men do therefore fear him: he respecteth not any that are wise of heart."

Why You Should Not Be Afraid

Genesis 21:17 "And God heard the voice of the lad; and the angel of God called Hagar out of heaven, and said unto her, What aileth thee, Hagar? fear not; for God hath heard the voice of the lad where he is."

Exodus 20:18-20 "[18]And all the people saw the thunderings, and the lightnings, and the noise of the trumpet, and the mountain smoking: and when the people saw it, they removed, and stood afar off. [19]And they said unto Moses, Speak thou with us, and we will hear: but let not God speak with us, lest we die. [20]And Moses said unto the people, Fear not: for God is come to prove you, and that his fear may be before your faces, that ye sin not."

Numbers 14:9 "Only rebel not ye against the LORD, neither fear ye the people of the land; for they are bread for us: their defence is departed from them, and the LORD is with us: fear them not."

Deuteronomy 31:6-8 "[6]Be strong and of a good courage, fear not, nor be afraid of them: for the LORD thy God, he it is that doth go with thee; he will not fail thee, nor forsake thee. [7]And Moses called unto Joshua, and said unto him in the sight of all Israel, Be strong and of a good courage: for thou must go with this people unto the land which the LORD hath sworn unto their fathers to give them; and thou shalt cause them to inherit it. ⁸And the LORD, he it is that doth go before thee; he will be with thee, he will not fail thee, neither forsake thee: fear not, neither be dismayed."

Joshua 1:9 "Have not I commanded thee? Be strong and of a good courage; be not afraid, neither be thou dismayed: for the LORD thy God is with thee whithersoever thou goest."

2 Chronicles 32:7-8 "⁷Be strong and courageous, be not afraid nor dismayed for the king of Assyria, nor for all the multitude that is with him: for there be more with us than with him: ⁸With him is an arm of flesh; but with us is the LORD our God to help us, and to fight our battles. And the people rested themselves upon the words of Hezekiah king of Judah."

Psalm 23:1-4 "¹The LORD is my shepherd; I shall not want. ²He maketh me to lie down in green pastures: he leadeth me beside the still waters. ³He restoreth my soul: he leadeth me in the paths of righteousness for his name's sake. ⁴Yea, though I walk through the valley of the shadow of death, I will fear no evil: for thou art with me; thy rod and thy staff they comfort me."

Psalm 27:1-2 "¹The LORD is my light and my salvation; whom shall I fear? the LORD is the strength of my life; of whom shall I be afraid? ²When the wicked, even mine enemies and my foes, came upon me to eat up my flesh, they stumbled and fell."

Psalm 46:1-11 "¹God is our refuge and strength, a very present help in trouble. ²Therefore will not we fear, though the earth be removed, and though the mountains be carried into the midst of the sea; ³Though the waters thereof roar and be troubled, though the mountains shake with the swelling thereof. Selah. ⁴There is a river, the streams whereof shall make glad the city of God, the holy place of the tabernacles of the most High. ⁵God is in the midst of her; she shall not be moved: God shall help her, and that right early. ⁶The heathen raged, the kingdoms were moved: he uttered his voice, the earth melted. ⁷The LORD

of hosts is with us; the God of Jacob is our refuge. Selah. ⁸Come, behold the works of the LORD, what desolations he hath made in the earth. ⁹He maketh wars to cease unto the end of the earth; he breaketh the bow, and cutteth the spear in sunder; he burneth the chariot in the fire. ¹⁰Be still, and know that I am God: I will be exalted among the heathen, I will be exalted in the earth. ¹¹The LORD of hosts is with us; the God of Jacob is our refuge. Selah."

Psalm 118:6 "The LORD is on my side; I will not fear: what can man do unto me?"

Psalm 138:6-7 "⁶Though the LORD be high, yet hath he respect unto the lowly: but the proud he knoweth afar off. ⁷Though I walk in the midst of trouble, thou wilt revive me: thou shalt stretch forth thine hand against the wrath of mine enemies, and thy right hand shall save me."

Proverbs 3:25-26 "²⁵Be not afraid of sudden fear, neither of the desolation of the wicked, when it cometh. ²⁶For the LORD shall be thy confidence, and shall keep thy foot from being taken."

Isaiah 12:2 "Behold, God is my salvation; I will trust, and not be afraid: for the LORD JEHOVAH is my strength and my song; he also is become my salvation."

Isaiah 35:3-4 "³Strengthen ye the weak hands, and confirm the feeble knees. ⁴Say to them that are of a fearful heart, Be strong, fear not: behold, your God will come with vengeance, even God with a recompence; he will come and save you."

Isaiah 41:10 "Fear thou not; for I am with thee: be not dismayed; for I am thy God: I will strengthen thee; yea, I will help thee; yea, I will uphold thee with the right hand of my righteousness."

Isaiah 43:3-5 "³For I am the LORD thy God, the Holy One of Israel, thy Saviour: I gave Egypt for thy ransom, Ethiopia and Seba for thee. ⁴Since thou wast precious in my sight, thou hast been honourable, and I have loved thee: therefore will I give men for thee, and people for thy life. ⁵Fear not: for I am with thee: I will bring thy seed from the east, and gather thee from the west;"

Isaiah 44:8 "Fear ye not, neither be afraid: have not I told thee from that time, and have declared it? ye are even my witnesses. Is there a God beside me? yea, there is no God; I know not any."

Isaiah 51:7-8 "⁷Hearken unto me, ye that know righteousness, the people in whose heart is my law; fear ye not the reproach of men, neither be ye afraid of their revilings. ⁸For the moth shall eat them up like a garment, and the worm shall eat them like wool: but my righteousness shall be for ever, and my salvation from generation to generation."

Jeremiah 30:10 "Therefore fear thou not, O my servant Jacob, saith the LORD; neither be dismayed, O Israel: for, lo, I will save thee from afar, and thy seed from the land of their captivity; and Jacob shall return, and shall be in rest, and be quiet, and none shall make him afraid."

Jeremiah 46:28 "Fear thou not, O Jacob my servant, saith the LORD: for I am with thee; for I will make a full end of all the nations whither I have driven thee: but I will not make a full end of thee, but correct thee in measure; yet will I not leave thee wholly unpunished."

Joel 2:21-22 "²¹Fear not, O land; be glad and rejoice: for the LORD will do great things. ²²Be not afraid, ye beasts of the field: for the pastures of the wilderness do spring, for the tree beareth her fruit, the fig tree and the vine do yield their strength."

Matthew 10:26-31 "²⁶Fear them not therefore: for there is nothing covered, that shall not be revealed; and hid, that shall not be known. ²⁷What I tell you in darkness, that speak ye in light: and what ye hear in the ear, that preach ye upon the housetops. ²⁸And fear not them which kill the body, but are not able to kill the soul: but rather fear him which is able to destroy both soul and body in hell. ²⁹Are not two sparrows sold for a farthing? and one of them shall not fall on the ground without your Father. ³⁰But the very hairs of your head are all numbered. ³¹Fear ye not therefore, ye are of more value than many sparrows."

Luke 12:31-32 "³¹But rather seek ye the kingdom of God; and all these things shall be added unto you. ³²Fear not, little flock; for it is your Father's good pleasure to give you the kingdom."

John 14:1-4 "¹Let not your heart be troubled: ye believe in God, believe also in me. ²In my Father's house are many mansions: if it were not so, I would have told you. I go to prepare a place for you. ³And if I go and prepare a place for you, I will come again, and receive you unto myself; that where I am, there ye may be also. ⁴And whither I go ye know, and the way ye know."

Hebrews 13:6 "So that we may boldly say, The Lord is my helper, and I will not fear what man shall do unto me."

1 Peter 3:12-14 "¹²For the eyes of the Lord are over the righteous, and his ears are open unto their prayers: but the face of the Lord is against them that do evil. ¹³And who is he that will harm you, if ye be followers of that which is good? ¹⁴But and if ye suffer for righteousness' sake, happy are ye: and be not afraid of their terror, neither be troubled;"

FELLOWSHIP

Not Forsaking Fellowship

Hebrews 10:23-25 "²³Let us hold fast the profession of our faith without wavering; (for he is faithful that promised;) ²⁴And let us consider one another to provoke unto love and to good works: ²⁵Not forsaking the assembling of ourselves together, as the manner of some is; but exhorting one another: and so much the more, as ye see the day approaching."

Those That Say They Have Fellowship With The Lord, But Are Disobedient

1 John 1:5-6 "⁵This then is the message which we have heard of him, and declare unto you, that God is light, and in him is no darkness at all. ⁶If we say that we have fellowship with him, and walk in darkness, we lie, and do not the truth:"

1 John 2:1-4 "¹My little children, these things write I unto you, that ye sin not. And if any man sin, we have an advocate with the Father, Jesus Christ the righteous: ²And he is the propitiation for our sins: and not for ours only, but also for the sins of the whole world. ³And hereby we do know that we know him, if we keep his commandments. ⁴He that saith, I know him, and keepeth not his commandments, is a liar, and the truth is not in him."

What Not To Have Fellowship With

1 Corinthians 10:20-21 "²⁰But I say, that the things which the Gentiles sacrifice, they sacrifice to devils, and not to God: and I would not that ye should have fellowship with devils. ²¹Ye cannot drink the cup of the Lord, and the cup of devils: ye cannot be partakers of the Lord's table, and of the table of devils."

Ephesians 5:11 "And have no fellowship with the unfruitful works of darkness, but rather reprove them."

Who Has Fellowship With Each Other
1 John 1:7 "But if we walk in the light, as he is in the light, we have fellowship one with another, and the blood of Jesus Christ his Son cleanseth us from all sin."

FINDING

Those That Find Wisdom
Proverbs 3:13 "Happy is the man that findeth wisdom, and the man that getteth understanding."

Proverbs 8:32-35 "32Now therefore hearken unto me, O ye children: for blessed are they that keep my ways. 33Hear instruction, and be wise, and refuse it not. 34Blessed is the man that heareth me, watching daily at my gates, waiting at the posts of my doors. 35For whoso findeth me findeth life, and shall obtain favour of the LORD."

Who Does Not Find Wisdom
Proverbs 14:6 "A scorner seeketh wisdom, and findeth it not: but knowledge is easy unto him that understandeth."

Who Finds
Matthew 7:7-8 "7Ask, and it shall be given you; seek, and ye shall find; knock, and it shall be opened unto you: 8For every one that asketh receiveth; and he that seeketh findeth; and to him that knocketh it shall be opened."

Luke 11:9-10 "9And I say unto you, Ask, and it shall be given you; seek, and ye shall find; knock, and it shall be opened unto you. 10For every one that asketh receiveth; and he that seeketh findeth; and to him that knocketh it shall be opened."

Who Shall Find Good
Proverbs 16:20 "He that handleth a matter wisely shall find good: and whoso trusteth in the LORD, happy is he."

Proverbs 19:8 "He that getteth wisdom loveth his own soul: he that keepeth understanding shall find good."

Who Shall Find Life
Proverbs 8:32-35 "32Now therefore hearken unto me, O ye children: for blessed are they that keep my ways. 33Hear instruction, and be wise, and refuse it not. 34Blessed is the man that heareth me, watching daily at my gates, waiting at the posts of my doors. 35For whoso findeth me findeth life, and shall obtain favour of the LORD."

Proverbs 21:21 "He that followeth after righteousness and mercy findeth life, righteousness, and honour."

Matthew 10:38-39 "38And he that taketh not his cross, and followeth after me, is not worthy of me. 39He that findeth his life shall lose it: and he that loseth his life for my sake shall find it."

Matthew 16:24-25 "24Then said Jesus unto his disciples, If any man will come after me, let him deny himself, and take up his cross, and follow me. 25For whosoever will save his life shall lose it: and whosoever will lose his life for my sake shall find it."

Who Shall Find The Lord
Deuteronomy 4:29 "But if from thence thou shalt seek the LORD thy God, thou shalt find him, if thou seek him with all thy heart and with all thy soul."

1 Chronicles 28:9 "And thou, Solomon my son, know thou the God of thy father, and serve him with a perfect heart and with a willing mind: for the LORD searcheth all hearts, and understandeth all the imaginations of the thoughts: if thou seek him, he will be found of thee; but if thou forsake him, he will cast thee off for ever."

2 Chronicles 15:2 "And he went out to meet Asa, and said unto him, Hear ye me, Asa, and all Judah and Benjamin; The LORD is with you, while ye be with him; and if ye seek him, he will be found of you; but if ye forsake him, he will forsake you."

2 Chronicles 15:14-15 "14And they sware unto the LORD with a loud voice, and with shouting, and with trumpets, and with cornets. 15And all Judah rejoiced at the oath: for they had sworn with all their heart, and sought him with their whole desire; and he was found of them: and the LORD gave them rest round about."

Proverbs 2:1-5 "¹My son, if thou wilt receive my words, and hide my commandments with thee; ²So that thou incline thine ear unto wisdom, and apply thine heart to understanding; ³Yea, if thou criest after knowledge, and liftest up thy voice for understanding; ⁴If thou seekest her as silver, and searchest for her as for hid treasures; ⁵Then shalt thou understand the fear of the LORD, and find the knowledge of God."

Jeremiah 29:10-14 "¹⁰For thus saith the LORD, That after seventy years be accomplished at Babylon I will visit you, and perform my good word toward you, in causing you to return to this place. ¹¹For I know the thoughts that I think toward you, saith the LORD, thoughts of peace, and not of evil, to give you an expected end. ¹²Then shall ye call upon me, and ye shall go and pray unto me, and I will hearken unto you. ¹³And ye shall seek me, and find me, when ye shall search for me with all your heart. ¹⁴And I will be found of you, saith the LORD: and I will turn away your captivity, and I will gather you from all the nations, and from all the places whither I have driven you, saith the LORD; and I will bring you again into the place whence I caused you to be carried away captive."

Luke 11:9-10 "⁹And I say unto you, Ask, and it shall be given you; seek, and ye shall find; knock, and it shall be opened unto you. ¹⁰For every one that asketh receiveth; and he that seeketh findeth; and to him that knocketh it shall be opened."

Who Shall Find Wisdom
Proverbs 8:12-17 "¹²I wisdom dwell with prudence, and find out knowledge of witty inventions. ¹³The fear of the LORD is to hate evil: pride, and arrogancy, and the evil way, and the froward mouth, do I hate. ¹⁴Counsel is mine, and sound wisdom: I am understanding; I have strength. ¹⁵By me kings reign, and princes decree justice. ¹⁶By me princes rule, and nobles, even all the judges of the earth. ¹⁷I love them that love me; and those that seek me early shall find me."

Who Shall Not Find Wisdom
Proverbs 1:20-30 "²⁰Wisdom crieth without; she uttereth her voice in the streets: ²¹She crieth in the chief place of concourse, in the openings of the gates: in the city she uttereth her words, saying,

²²How long, ye simple ones, will ye love simplicity? and the scorners delight in their scorning, and fools hate knowledge? ²³Turn you at my reproof: behold, I will pour out my spirit unto you, I will make known my words unto you. ²⁴Because I have called, and ye refused; I have stretched out my hand, and no man regarded; ²⁵But ye have set at nought all my counsel, and would none of my reproof: ²⁶I also will laugh at your calamity; I will mock when your fear cometh; ²⁷When your fear cometh as desolation, and your destruction cometh as a whirlwind; when distress and anguish cometh upon you. ²⁸Then shall they call upon me, but I will not answer; they shall seek me early, but they shall not find me: ²⁹For that they hated knowledge, and did not choose the fear of the LORD: ³⁰They would none of my counsel: they despised all my reproof."

FLATTERY

Flattering Mouths
Proverbs 26:28 "A lying tongue hateth those that are afflicted by it; and a flattering mouth worketh ruin."

Those That Flatter With The Tongue
Proverbs 20:19 "He that goeth about as a talebearer revealeth secrets: therefore meddle not with him that flattereth with his lips."

Proverbs 28:23 "He that rebuketh a man afterwards shall find more favour than he that flattereth with the tongue."

Proverbs 29:5 "A man that flattereth his neighbour spreadeth a net for his feet."

FLESH

Abstaining From The Lusts Of The Flesh
Romans 13:14 "But put ye on the Lord Jesus Christ, and make not provision for the flesh, to fulfil the lusts thereof."

1 Peter 2:11 "Dearly beloved, I beseech you as strangers and pilgrims, abstain from fleshly lusts, which war against the soul;"

All Flesh Not Being The Same
1 Corinthians 15:39-40 "³⁹All flesh is not the same flesh: but there is one kind of flesh of men,

another flesh of beasts, another of fishes, and another of birds. ⁴⁰There are also celestial bodies, and bodies terrestrial: but the glory of the celestial is one, and the glory of the terrestrial is another."

Fleshly Lusts

1 Peter 2:11 "Dearly beloved, I beseech you as strangers and pilgrims, abstain from fleshly lusts, which war against the soul;"

1 John 2:16 "For all that is in the world, the lust of the flesh, and the lust of the eyes, and the pride of life, is not of the Father, but is of the world."

That Which Is Born Of The Flesh

John 3:6 "That which is born of the flesh is flesh; and that which is born of the Spirit is spirit."

The Flesh

Job 34:15 "All flesh shall perish together, and man shall turn again unto dust."

Psalm 73:26 "My flesh and my heart faileth: but God is the strength of my heart, and my portion for ever."

Isaiah 40:6-8 "⁶The voice said, Cry. And he said, What shall I cry? All flesh is grass, and all the goodliness thereof is as the flower of the field: ⁷The grass withereth, the flower fadeth: because the spirit of the LORD bloweth upon it: surely the people is grass. ⁸The grass withereth, the flower fadeth: but the word of our God shall stand for ever."

Matthew 26:41 "Watch and pray, that ye enter not into temptation: the spirit indeed is willing, but the flesh is weak."

Mark 14:38 "Watch ye and pray, lest ye enter into temptation. The spirit truly is ready, but the flesh is weak."

John 6:63 "It is the spirit that quickeneth; the flesh profiteth nothing: the words that I speak unto you, they are spirit, and they are life."

Romans 7:25 "I thank God through Jesus Christ our Lord. So then with the mind I myself serve the law of God; but with the flesh the law of sin."

Galatians 5:16-21 "¹⁶This I say then, Walk in the Spirit, and ye shall not fulfil the lust of the flesh. ¹⁷For the flesh lusteth against the Spirit, and the Spirit against the flesh: and these are contrary the one to the other: so that ye cannot do the things

that ye would. ¹⁸But if ye be led of the Spirit, ye are not under the law. ¹⁹Now the works of the flesh are manifest, which are these; Adultery, fornication, uncleanness, lasciviousness, ²⁰Idolatry, witchcraft, hatred, variance, emulations, wrath, strife, seditions, heresies, ²¹Envyings, murders, drunkenness, revellings, and such like: of the which I tell you before, as I have also told you in time past, that they which do such things shall not inherit the kingdom of God."

1 Peter 1:24 "For all flesh is as grass, and all the glory of man as the flower of grass. The grass withereth, and the flower thereof falleth away:"

The Life Of The Flesh

Genesis 9:4 "But flesh with the life thereof, which is the blood thereof, shall ye not eat."

Leviticus 17:11 "For the life of the flesh is in the blood: and I have given it to you upon the altar to make an atonement for your souls: for it is the blood that maketh an atonement for the soul."

Proverbs 14:30 "A sound heart is the life of the flesh: but envy the rottenness of the bones."

The Reward For Living After The Flesh

Romans 8:13 "For if ye live after the flesh, ye shall die: but if ye through the Spirit do mortify the deeds of the body, ye shall live."

The Son Of God (Jesus Christ) Becoming Flesh

John 1:14 "And the Word was made flesh, and dwelt among us, (and we beheld his glory, the glory as of the only begotten of the Father,) full of grace and truth."

Galatians 4:4 "But when the fulness of the time was come, God sent forth his Son, made of a woman, made under the law,"

1 Timothy 3:16 "And without controversy great is the mystery of godliness: God was manifest in the flesh, justified in the Spirit, seen of angels, preached unto the Gentiles, believed on in the world, received up into glory."

Hebrews 2:9-14 "⁹But we see Jesus, who was made a little lower than the angels for the suffering of death, crowned with glory and honour; that he by the grace of God should taste death for every man. ¹⁰For it became him, for whom are all things, and by whom are all things, in bringing many sons unto glory, to make the captain of their salvation perfect through sufferings. [11]For both he that sanctifieth and they who are sanctified are all of one: for which cause he is not ashamed to call them brethren, [12]Saying, I will declare thy name unto my brethren, in the midst of the church will I sing praise unto thee. [13]And again, I will put my trust in him. And again, Behold I and the children which God hath given me. [14]Forasmuch then as the children are partakers of flesh and blood, he also himself likewise took part of the same; that through death he might destroy him that had the power of death, that is, the devil;"

Those That Walk After The Flesh

Romans 8:5-8 "[5]For they that are after the flesh do mind the things of the flesh; but they that are after the Spirit the things of the Spirit. [6]For to be carnally minded is death; but to be spiritually minded is life and peace. [7]Because the carnal mind is enmity against God: for it is not subject to the law of God, neither indeed can be. [8]So then they that are in the flesh cannot please God."

2 Peter 2:10-11 "[10]But chiefly them that walk after the flesh in the lust of uncleanness, and despise government. Presumptuous are they, self-willed, they are not afraid to speak evil of dignities. [11]Whereas angels, which are greater in power and might, bring not railing accusation against them before the Lord."

Those That Eat The Flesh Of Christ

John 6:53-58 "[53]Then Jesus said unto them, Verily, verily, I say unto you, Except ye eat the flesh of the Son of man, and drink his blood, ye have no life in you. [54]Whoso eateth my flesh, and drinketh my blood, hath eternal life; and I will raise him up at the last day. [55]For my flesh is meat indeed, and my blood is drink indeed. [56]He that eateth my flesh, and drinketh my blood, dwelleth in me, and I in him. [57]As the living Father hath sent me, and I live by the Father: so he that eateth me, even he shall live by me. [58]This is that bread which came down from heaven: not as your fathers did eat manna, and are dead: he that eateth of this bread shall live for ever."

Those That Sow To Their Flesh

Galatians 6:8 "For he that soweth to his flesh shall of the flesh reap corruption; but he that soweth to the Spirit shall of the Spirit reap life everlasting."

What Dwells In The Flesh

Romans 7:17-23 "[17]Now then it is no more I that do it, but sin that dwelleth in me. [18]For I know that in me (that is, in my flesh,) dwelleth no good thing: for to will is present with me; but how to perform that which is good I find not. [19]For the good that I would I do not: but the evil which I would not, that I do. [20]Now if I do that I would not, it is no more I that do it, but sin that dwelleth in me. [21]I find then a law, that, when I would do good, evil is present with me. [22]For I delight in the law of God after the inward man: [23]But I see another law in my members, warring against the law of my mind, and bringing me into captivity to the law of sin which is in my members."

What Is Flesh

John 3:6 "That which is born of the flesh is flesh; and that which is born of the Spirit is spirit."

What Should Not Be Done To Your Flesh

Leviticus 19:28 "Ye shall not make any cuttings in your flesh for the dead, nor print any marks upon you: I am the LORD."

Who Defiles The Flesh

Jude 7-8 "[7]Even as Sodom and Gomorrha, and the cities about them in like manner, giving themselves over to fornication, and going after strange flesh, are set forth for an example, suffering the vengeance of eternal fire. [8]Likewise also these filthy dreamers defile the flesh, despise dominion, and speak evil of dignities."

Who Does Not Walk After The Flesh

Romans 8:1 "There is therefore now no condemnation to them which are in Christ Jesus, who walk not after the flesh, but after the Spirit."

Romans 8:9 "But ye are not in the flesh, but in the Spirit, if so be that the Spirit of God dwell in you. Now if any man have not the Spirit of Christ, he is none of his."

Who Has No Confidence In The Flesh

Philippians 3:3-4 "[3]For we are the circumcision, which worship God in the spirit, and rejoice in Christ Jesus, and have no confidence in the flesh. [4]Though I might also have confidence in the flesh. If any other man thinketh that he hath whereof he might trust in the flesh, I more:"

Who Has Crucified The Flesh
Galatians 5:24 "And they that are Christ's have crucified the flesh with the affections and lusts."

FOLLOWING

Following The Lord
Matthew 16:24 "Then said Jesus unto his disciples, If any man will come after me, let him deny himself, and take up his cross, and follow me."

Matthew 19:21 "Jesus said unto him, If thou wilt be perfect, go and sell that thou hast, and give to the poor, and thou shalt have treasure in heaven: and come and follow me."

Mark 8:31-34 "31And he began to teach them, that the Son of man must suffer many things, and be rejected of the elders, and of the chief priests, and scribes, and be killed, and after three days rise again. 32And he spake that saying openly. And Peter took him, and began to rebuke him. 33But when he had turned about and looked on his disciples, he rebuked Peter, saying, Get thee behind me, Satan: for thou savourest not the things that be of God, but the things that be of men. 34And when he had called the people unto him with his disciples also, he said unto them, Whosoever will come after me, let him deny himself, and take up his cross, and follow me."

Luke 9:22-23 "22Saying, The Son of man must suffer many things, and be rejected of the elders and chief priests and scribes, and be slain, and be raised the third day. 23And he said to them all, If any man will come after me, let him deny himself, and take up his cross daily, and follow me."

John 12:23-26 "23And Jesus answered them, saying, The hour is come, that the Son of man should be glorified. 24Verily, verily, I say unto you, Except a corn of wheat fall into the ground and die, it abideth alone: but if it die, it bringeth forth much fruit. 25He that loveth his life shall lose it; and he that hateth his life in this world shall keep it unto life eternal. 26If any man serve me, let him follow me; and where I am, there shall also my servant be: if any man serve me, him will my Father honour."

Ephesians 5:1 "Be ye therefore followers of God, as dear children;"

The Reward For Following Jesus Christ
Matthew 4:18-19 "18And Jesus, walking by the sea of Galilee, saw two brethren, Simon called Peter, and Andrew his brother, casting a net into the sea: for they were fishers. 19And he saith unto them, Follow me, and I will make you fishers of men."

Mark 1:17 "And Jesus said unto them, Come ye after me, and I will make you to become fishers of men."

Luke 5:10-11 "10And so was also James, and John, the sons of Zebedee, which were partners with Simon. And Jesus said unto Simon, Fear not; from henceforth thou shalt catch men. 11And when they had brought their ships to land, they forsook all, and followed him."

The Reward For Following Vanity
2 Kings 17:7-23 "7For so it was, that the children of Israel had sinned against the LORD their God, which had brought them up out of the land of Egypt, from under the hand of Pharoah king of Egypt, and had feared other gods, 8And walked in the statutes of the heathen, whom the LORD cast out from before the children of Israel, and of the kings of Israel, which they had made. 9And the children of Israel did secretly those things that were not right against the LORD their God, and they built them high places in all their cities, from the tower of the watchmen to the fenced city. 10And they set them up images and groves in every high hill, and under every green tree: 11And there they burnt incense in all the high places, as did the heathen whom the LORD carried away before them; and wrought wicked things to provoke the LORD to anger: 12For they served idols, whereof the LORD had said unto them, Ye shall not do this thing. 13Yet the LORD testified against Israel, and against Judah, by all the prophets, and by all the seers, saying, Turn ye from your evil ways, and keep my commandments and my statutes, according to all the law which I commanded your fathers, and which I sent to you by my servants the prophets. 14Notwithstanding they would not hear, but hardened their necks, like to the neck of their fathers, that did not believe in the LORD their God. 15And they rejected his statutes, and his covenant that he made with their

fathers, and his testimonies which he testified against them; and they followed vanity, and became vain, and went after the heathen that were round about them, concerning whom the LORD had charged them, that they should not do like them. [16]And they left all the commandments of the LORD their God, and made them molten images, even two calves, and made a grove, and worshipped all the host of heaven, and served Baal. [17]And they caused their sons and their daughters to pass through the fire, and used divination and enchantments, and sold themselves to do evil in the sight of the LORD, to provoke him to anger. [18]Therefore the LORD was very angry with Israel, and removed them out of his sight: there was none left but the tribe of Judah only. [19]Also Judah kept not the commandments of the LORD their God, but walked in the statutes of Israel which they made. [20]And the LORD rejected all the seed of Israel, and afflicted them, and delivered them into the hand of spoilers, until he had cast them out of his sight. [21]For he rent Israel from the house of David; and they made Jeroboam the son of Nebat king: and Jeroboam drave Israel from following the LORD, and made them sin a great sin. [22]For the children of Israel walked in all the sins of Jeroboam which he did; they departed not from them; [23]Until the LORD removed Israel out of his sight, as he had said by all his servants the prophets. So was Israel carried away out of their own land to Assyria unto this day."

Job 15:31 "Let not him that is deceived trust in vanity: for vanity shall be his recompence."

Jeremiah 18:13-17 "[13]Therefore thus saith the LORD; Ask ye now among the heathen, who hath heard such things: the virgin of Israel hath done a very horrible thing. [14]Will a man leave the snow of Lebanon which cometh from the rock of the field? or shall the cold flowing waters that come from another place be forsaken? [15]Because my people hath forgotten me, they have burned incense to vanity, and they have caused them to stumble in their ways from the ancient paths, to walk in paths, in a way not cast up; [16]To make their land desolate, and a perpetual hissing; every one that passeth thereby shall be astonished, and wag his head. [17]I will scatter them as with an east wind before the enemy; I will shew them the back, and not the face, in the day of their calamity."

Those That Follow After Mercy
Proverbs 21:21 "He that followeth after righteousness and mercy findeth life, righteousness, and honour."

Those That Follow After Righteousness
Proverbs 15:9 "The way of the wicked is an abomination unto the LORD: but he loveth him that followeth after righteousness."

Proverbs 21:21 "He that followeth after righteousness and mercy findeth life, righteousness, and honour."

Those That Follow Jesus Christ
Matthew 19:27-30 "[27]Then answered Peter and said unto him, Behold, we have forsaken all, and followed thee; what shall we have therefore? [28]And Jesus said unto them, Verily I say unto you, That ye which have followed me, in the regeneration when the Son of man shall sit in the throne of his glory, ye also shall sit upon twelve thrones, judging the twelve tribes of Israel. [29]And every one that hath forsaken houses, or brethren, or sisters, or father, or mother, or wife, or children, or lands, for my name's sake, shall receive an hundredfold, and shall inherit everlasting life. [30]But many that are first shall be last; and the last shall be first."

Luke 18:24-30 "[24]And when Jesus saw that he was very sorrowful, he said, How hardly shall they that have riches enter into the kingdom of God! [25]For it is easier for a camel to go through a needle's eye, than for a rich man to enter into the kingdom of God. [26]And they that heard it said, Who then can be saved? [27]And he said, The things which are impossible with men are possible with God. [28]Then Peter said, Lo, we have left all, and followed thee. [29]And he said unto them, Verily I say unto you, There is no man that hath left house, or parents, or brethren, or wife, or children, for the kingdom of God's sake, [30]Who shall not receive manifold more in this present time, and in the world to come life everlasting."

John 8:12 "Then spake Jesus again unto them, saying, I am the light of the world: he that followeth me shall not walk in darkness, but shall have the light of life."

John 10:25-28 "[25]Jesus answered them, I told you, and ye believed not: the works that I do in my Father's name, they bear witness of me. [26]But ye believe not, because ye are not of my sheep, as I said unto you. ²⁷My sheep hear my voice, and I know them, and they follow me: ²⁸And I give unto them eternal life; and they shall never perish, neither shall any man pluck them out of my hand."

Those That Follow Vain People
Proverbs 12:11 "He that tilleth his land shall be satisfied with bread: but he that followeth vain persons is void of understanding."

Proverbs 28:19 "He that tilleth his land shall have plenty of bread: but he that followeth after vain persons shall have poverty enough."

Those That Do Not Follow Jesus Christ
Matthew 10:38-39 "³⁸And he that taketh not his cross, and followeth after me, is not worthy of me. ³⁹He that findeth his life shall lose it: and he that loseth his life for my sake shall find it."

What Not To Follow After
Exodus 23:2 "Thou shalt not follow a multitude to do evil; neither shalt thou speak in a cause to decline after many to wrest judgment:"

3 John 11 "Beloved, follow not that which is evil, but that which is good. He that doeth good is of God: but he that doeth evil hath not seen God."

What To Follow After
Deuteronomy 16:20 "That which is altogether just shalt thou follow, that thou mayest live, and inherit the land which the LORD thy God giveth thee."

Romans 14:19 "Let us therefore follow after the things which make for peace, and things wherewith one may edify another."

1 Corinthians 14:1 "Follow after charity, and desire spiritual gifts, but rather that ye may prophesy."

1 Thessalonians 5:15 "See that none render evil for evil unto any man; but ever follow that which is good, both among yourselves, and to all men."

2 Timothy 2:22 "Flee also youthful lusts: but follow righteousness, faith, charity, peace, with them that call on the Lord out of a pure heart."

Hebrews 12:14 "Follow peace with all men, and holiness, without which no man shall see the Lord:"

3 John 11 "Beloved, follow not that which is evil, but that which is good. He that doeth good is of God: but he that doeth evil hath not seen God."

Who Follows The Lord
Isaiah 40:10-11 "¹⁰Behold, the Lord GOD will come with strong hand, and his arm shall rule for him: behold, his reward is with him, and his work before him. ¹¹He shall feed his flock like a shepherd: he shall gather the lambs with his arm, and carry them in his bosom, and shall gently lead those that are with young."

Ezekiel 34:11-24 "¹¹For thus saith the Lord GOD; Behold, I, even I, will both search my sheep, and seek them out. ¹²As a shepherd seeketh out his flock in the day that he is among his sheep that are scattered; so will I seek out my sheep, and will deliver them out of all places where they have been scattered in the cloudy and dark day. ¹³And I will bring them out from the people, and gather them from the countries, and will bring them to their own land, and feed them upon the mountains of Israel by the rivers, and in all the inhabited places of the country. ¹⁴I will feed them in a good pasture, and upon the high mountains of Israel shall their fold be: there shall they lie in a good fold, and in a fat pasture shall they feed upon the mountains of Israel. ¹⁵I will feed my flock, and I will cause them to lie down, saith the Lord GOD. ¹⁶I will seek that which was lost, and bring again that which was driven away, and will bind up that which was broken, and will strengthen that which was sick: but I will destroy the fat and the strong; I will feed them with judgment. ¹⁷And as for you, O my flock, thus saith the Lord GOD; Behold, I judge between cattle and cattle, between the rams and the he goats. ¹⁸Seemeth it a small thing unto you to have eaten up the good pasture, but ye must tread down with your feet the residue of your pastures? and to have drunk of the deep waters, but ye must foul the residue with your feet? ¹⁹And as for my flock, they eat that which ye have trodden with your feet; and they drink that which ye have fouled with your feet. ²⁰Therefore thus saith the Lord GOD unto them; Behold, I, even I, will judge between the fat cattle and between the lean cattle. ²¹Because ye have thrust with side and with shoulder, and pushed all the diseased with your horns, till ye have scattered them abroad; ²²Therefore will I save my flock, and they shall no more be a prey; and I will judge between cattle and cattle. 23And I will set up one shepherd over them, and he shall feed them, even my servant David; he shall feed them, and he shall be their shepherd. 24And I the LORD will be their God, and my servant David a prince among them; I the LORD have spoken it."

John 10:1-5 "1Verily, verily, I say unto you, He that entereth not by the door into the sheepfold, but climbeth up some other way, the same is a thief and a robber. 2But he that entereth in by the door is the shepherd of the sheep. 3To him the porter openeth; and the sheep hear his voice: and he calleth his own sheep by name, and leadeth them out. 4And when he putteth forth his own sheep, he goeth before them, and the sheep follow him: for they know his voice. 5And a stranger will they not follow, but will flee from him: for they know not the voice of strangers."

John 10:25-27 "25Jesus answered them, I told you, and ye believed not: the works that I do in my Father's name, they bear witness of me. 26But ye believe not, because ye are not of my sheep, as I said unto you. 27My sheep hear my voice, and I know them, and they follow me:"

Revelation 7:9-17 "9After this I beheld, and, lo, a great multitude, which no man could number, of all nations, and kindreds, and people, and tongues, stood before the throne, and before the Lamb, clothed with white robes, and palms in their hands; 10And cried with a loud voice, saying, Salvation to our God which sitteth upon the throne, and unto the Lamb. 11And all the angels stood round about the throne, and about the elders and the four beasts, and fell before the throne on their faces, and worshipped God, 12Saying, Amen: Blessing, and glory, and wisdom, and thanksgiving, and honour, and power, and might, be unto our God for ever and ever. Amen. 13And one of the elders answered, saying unto me, What are these which are arrayed in white robes? and whence came they? 14And I said unto him, Sir, thou knowest. And he said to me, These are they which came out of great tribulation, and have washed their robes, and made them white in the blood of the Lamb. 15Therefore are they before the throne of God, and serve him day and night in his temple: and he that sitteth on the throne shall dwell among them. 16They shall hunger no more, neither thirst any more; neither shall the sun light on them, nor any heat. 17For the Lamb which is in the midst of the throne shall feed them, and shall lead them unto living fountains of waters: and God shall wipe away all tears from their eyes."

FOLLY

A Little Folly For Those Who Have A Good Reputation

Ecclesiastes 10:1 "Dead flies cause the ointment of the apothecary to send forth a stinking savour: so doth a little folly him that is in reputation for wisdom and honour."

The Folly Of Fools

Proverbs 14:8 "The wisdom of the prudent is to understand his way: but the folly of fools is deceit."

What Is Folly

Psalm 49:6-13 "6They that trust in their wealth, and boast themselves in the multitude of their riches; 7None of them can by any means redeem his brother, nor give to God a ransom for him: 8(For the redemption of their soul is precious, and it ceaseth for ever:) 9That he should still live for ever, and not see corruption. 10For he seeth that wise men die, likewise the fool and the brutish person perish, and leave their wealth to others. 11Their inward thought is, that their houses shall continue for ever, and their dwelling places to all generations; they call their lands after their own names. 12Nevertheless man being in honour abideth not: he is like the beasts that perish. 13This their way is their folly: yet their posterity approve their sayings. Selah."

Proverbs 14:24 "The crown of the wise is their riches: but the foolishness of fools is folly."

Proverbs 16:22 "Understanding is a wellspring of life unto him that hath it: but the instruction of fools is folly."

Proverbs 18:13 "He that answereth a matter before he heareth it, it is folly and shame unto him."

Who Enjoys Folly

Proverbs 15:21 "Folly is joy to him that is destitute of wisdom: but a man of understanding walketh uprightly."

Who Exalts Folly

Proverbs 14:29 "He that is slow to wrath is of great understanding: but he that is hasty of spirit exalteth folly."

Who Inherits Folly

Proverbs 14:18 "The simple inherit folly: but the prudent are crowned with knowledge."

Who Lays Open Their Folly

Proverbs 13:16 "Every prudent man dealeth with knowledge: but a fool layeth open his folly."

Who Returns To Their Folly

Proverbs 26:11 "As a dog returneth to his vomit, so a fool returneth to his folly."

2 Peter 2:1-22 "¹But there were false prophets also among the people, even as there shall be false teachers among you, who privily shall bring in damnable heresies, even denying the Lord that bought them, and bring upon themselves swift destruction. ²And many shall follow their pernicious ways; by reason of whom the way of truth shall be evil spoken of. ³And through covetousness shall they with feigned words make merchandise of you: whose judgment now of a long time lingereth not, and their damnation slumbereth not. ⁴For if God spared not the angels that sinned, but cast them down to hell, and delivered them into chains of darkness, to be reserved unto judgment; ⁵And spared not the old world, but saved Noah the eighth person, a preacher of righteousness, bringing in the flood upon the world of the ungodly; ⁶And turning the cities of Sodom and Gomorrha into ashes condemned them with an overthrow, making them an ensample unto those that after should live ungodly; ⁷And delivered just Lot, vexed with the filthy conversation of the wicked: ⁸(For that righteous man dwelling among them, in seeing and hearing, vexed his righteous soul from day to day with their unlawful deeds;) ⁹The Lord knoweth how to deliver the godly out of temptations, and to reserve the unjust unto the day of judgment to be punished: ¹⁰But chiefly them that walk after the flesh in the lust of uncleanness, and despise government. Presumptuous are they, selfwilled, they are not afraid to speak evil of dignities. ¹¹Whereas angels, which are greater in power and might, bring not railing accusation against them before the Lord. ¹²But these, as natural brute beasts, made to be taken and destroyed, speak evil of the things that they understand not; and shall utterly perish in their own corruption; ¹³And shall receive the reward of unrighteousness, as they that count it pleasure to riot in the day time. Spots they are and blemishes, sporting themselves with their own deceivings while they feast with you; ¹⁴Having eyes full of adultery, and that cannot cease from sin; beguiling unstable souls: an heart they have exercised with covetous practices; cursed children: ¹⁵Which have forsaken the right way, and are gone astray, following the way of Balaam the son of Bosor, who loved the wages of unrighteousness; ¹⁶But was rebuked for his iniquity: the dumb ass speaking with man's voice forbad the madness of the prophet. ¹⁷These are wells without water, clouds that are carried with a tempest; to whom the mist of darkness is reserved for ever. ¹⁸For when they speak great swelling words of vanity, they allure through the lusts of the flesh, through much wantonness, those that were clean escaped from them who live in error. ¹⁹While they promise them liberty, they themselves are the servants of corruption: for of whom a man is overcome, of the same is he brought in bondage. ²⁰For if after they have escaped the pollutions of the world through the knowledge of the Lord and Saviour Jesus Christ, they are again entangled therein, and overcome, the latter end is worse with them than the beginning. ²¹For it had been better for them not to have known the way of righteousness, than, after they have known it, to turn from the holy commandment delivered unto them. ²²But it is happened unto them according to the true proverb, The dog is turned to his own vomit again; and the sow that was washed to her wallowing in the mire."

Whose Folly Shall Be Made Manifest

2 Timothy 3:6-9 "⁶For of this sort are they which creep into houses, and lead captive silly women laden with sins, led away with divers lusts, ⁷Ever learning, and never able to come to the knowledge of the truth. ⁸Now as Jannes and Jambres withstood Moses, so do these also resist the truth: men of corrupt minds, reprobate concerning the faith. ⁹But they shall proceed no further: for their folly shall be manifest unto all men, as theirs also was."

FOOLISHNESS

Fools

Job 5:1-2 "¹Call now, if there be any that will answer thee; and to which of the saints wilt thou turn? ²For wrath killeth the foolish man, and envy slayeth the silly one."

Psalm 5:4-5 "⁴For thou art not a God that hath pleasure in wickedness: neither shall evil dwell with thee. ⁵The foolish shall not stand in thy sight: thou hatest all workers of iniquity."

Psalm 14:1 "The fool hath said in his heart, There is no God. They are corrupt, they have done abominable works, there is none that doeth good."

Psalm 53:1 "The fool hath said in his heart, There is no God. Corrupt are they, and have done abominable iniquity: there is none that doeth good."

Psalm 74:18 "Remember this, that the enemy hath reproached, O LORD, and that the foolish people have blasphemed thy name."

Psalm 74:22 "Arise, O God, plead thine own cause: remember how the foolish man reproacheth thee daily."

Psalm 92:5-6 "⁵O LORD, how great are thy works! and thy thoughts are very deep. ⁶A brutish man knoweth not; neither doth a fool understand this."

Psalm 107:17-20 "¹⁷Fools because of their transgression, and because of their iniquities, are afflicted. ¹⁸Their soul abhorreth all manner of meat; and they draw near unto the gates of death. ¹⁹Then they cry unto the LORD in their trouble, and he saveth them out of their distresses. ²⁰He sent his word, and healed them, and delivered them from their destructions."

Proverbs 1:7 "The fear of the LORD is the beginning of knowledge: but fools despise wisdom and instruction."

Proverbs 1:22 "How long, ye simple ones, will ye love simplicity? and the scorners delight in their scorning, and fools hate knowledge?"

Proverbs 3:35 "The wise shall inherit glory: but shame shall be the promotion of fools."

Proverbs 10:1 "The proverbs of Solomon. A wise son maketh a glad father: but a foolish son is the heaviness of his mother."

Proverbs 10:8 "The wise in heart will receive commandments: but a prating fool shall fall."

Proverbs 10:10 "He that winketh with the eye causeth sorrow: but a prating fool shall fall."

Proverbs 10:14 "Wise men lay up knowledge: but the mouth of the foolish is near destruction."

Proverbs 10:21 "The lips of the righteous feed many: but fools die for want of wisdom."

Proverbs 10:23 "It is as sport to a fool to do mischief: but a man of understanding hath wisdom."

Proverbs 11:29 "He that troubleth his own house shall inherit the wind: and the fool shall be servant to the wise of heart."

Proverbs 12:15-16 "¹⁵The way of a fool is right in his own eyes: but he that hearkeneth unto counsel is wise. ¹⁶A fool's wrath is presently known: but a prudent man covereth shame."

Proverbs 12:23 "A prudent man concealeth knowledge: but the heart of fools proclaimeth foolishness."

Proverbs 13:16 "Every prudent man dealeth with knowledge: but a fool layeth open his folly."

Proverbs 13:19 "The desire accomplished is sweet to the soul: but it is abomination to fools to depart from evil."

Proverbs 14:1 "Every wise woman buildeth her house: but the foolish plucketh it down with her hands."

Proverbs 14:3 "In the mouth of the foolish is a rod of pride: but the lips of the wise shall preserve them."

Proverbs 14:8-9 "⁸The wisdom of the prudent is to understand his way: but the folly of fools is deceit. ⁹Fools make a mock at sin: but among the righteous there is favour."

Proverbs 14:16 "A wise man feareth, and departeth from evil: but the fool rageth, and is confident."

Proverbs 14:24 "The crown of the wise is their riches: but the foolishness of fools is folly."

Proverbs 14:33 "Wisdom resteth in the heart of him that hath understanding: but that which is in the midst of fools is made known."

Proverbs 15:2 "The tongue of the wise useth knowledge aright: but the mouth of fools poureth out foolishness."

Proverbs 15:5 "A fool despiseth his father's instruction: but he that regardeth reproof is prudent."

Proverbs 15:7 "The lips of the wise disperse knowledge: but the heart of the foolish doeth not so."

Proverbs 15:14 "The heart of him that hath understanding seeketh knowledge: but the mouth of fools feedeth on foolishness."

Proverbs 15:20 "A wise son maketh a glad father: but a foolish man despiseth his mother."

Proverbs 17:7 "Excellent speech becometh not a fool: much less do lying lips a prince."

Proverbs 17:10 "A reproof entereth more into a wise man than an hundred stripes into a fool."

Proverbs 17:16 "Wherefore is there a price in the hand of a fool to get wisdom, seeing he hath no heart to it?"

Proverbs 17:24-25 "24Wisdom is before him that hath understanding; but the eyes of a fool are in the ends of the earth. 25A foolish son is a grief to his father, and bitterness to her that bare him."

Proverbs 17:28 "Even a fool, when he holdeth his peace, is counted wise: and he that shutteth his lips is esteemed a man of understanding."

Proverbs 18:2 "A fool hath no delight in understanding, but that his heart may discover itself."

Proverbs 18:6-7 "6A fool's lips enter into contention, and his mouth calleth for strokes. 7A fool's mouth is his destruction, and his lips are the snare of his soul."

Proverbs 19:1 "Better is the poor that walketh in his integrity, than he that is perverse in his lips, and is a fool."

Proverbs 19:10 "Delight is not seemly for a fool; much less for a servant to have rule over princes."

Proverbs 19:13 "A foolish son is the calamity of his father: and the contentions of a wife are a continual dropping."

Proverbs 19:29 "Judgments are prepared for scorners, and stripes for the back of fools."

Proverbs 20:3 "It is an honour for a man to cease from strife: but every fool will be meddling."

Proverbs 21:20 "There is treasure to be desired and oil in the dwelling of the wise; but a foolish man spendeth it up."

Proverbs 23:9 "Speak not in the ears of a fool: for he will despise the wisdom of thy words."

Proverbs 24:7 "Wisdom is too high for a fool: he openeth not his mouth in the gate."

Proverbs 26:1 "As snow in summer, and as rain in harvest, so honour is not seemly for a fool."

Proverbs 26:3 "A whip for the horse, a bridle for the ass, and a rod for the fool's back."

Proverbs 26:7 "The legs of the lame are not equal: so is a parable in the mouth of fools."

Proverbs 26:9-11 "9As a thorn goeth up into the hand of a drunkard, so is a parable in the mouth of fools. 10The great God that formed all things both rewardeth the fool, and rewardeth transgressors. 11As a dog returneth to his vomit, so a fool returneth to his folly."

Proverbs 27:3 "A stone is heavy, and the sand weighty; but a fool's wrath is heavier than them both."

Proverbs 29:11 "A fool uttereth all his mind: but a wise man keepeth it in till afterwards."

Ecclesiastes 2:14 "The wise man's eyes are in his head; but the fool walketh in darkness: and I myself perceived also that one event happeneth to them all."

Ecclesiastes 4:5-6 "5The fool foldeth his hands together, and eateth his own flesh. 6Better is an handful with quietness, than both the hands full with travail and vexation of spirit."

Ecclesiastes 4:13-14 "13Better is a poor and a wise child than an old and foolish king, who will no more be admonished. 14For out of prison he cometh to reign; whereas also he that is born in his kingdom becometh poor."

Ecclesiastes 5:1 "Keep thy foot when thou goest to the house of God, and be more ready to hear, than to give the sacrifice of fools: for they consider not that they do evil."

Ecclesiastes 5:3-4 "³For a dream cometh through the multitude of business; and a fool's voice is known by multitude of words. ⁴When thou vowest a vow unto God, defer not to pay it; for he hath no pleasure in fools: pay that which thou hast vowed."

Ecclesiastes 7:4-6 "⁴The heart of the wise is in the house of mourning; but the heart of fools is in the house of mirth. ⁵It is better to hear the rebuke of the wise, than for a man to hear the song of fools. ⁶For as the crackling of thorns under a pot, so is the laughter of the fool: this also is vanity."

Ecclesiastes 7:9 "Be not hasty in thy spirit to be angry: for anger resteth in the bosom of fools."

Ecclesiastes 10:2-3 "²A wise man's heart is at his right hand; but a fool's heart at his left. ³Yea also, when he that is a fool walketh by the way, his wisdom faileth him, and he saith to every one that he is a fool."

Ecclesiastes 10:12-15 "¹²The words of a wise man's mouth are gracious; but the lips of a fool will swallow up himself. ¹³The beginning of the words of his mouth is foolishness: and the end of his talk is mischievous madness. ¹⁴A fool also is full of words: a man cannot tell what shall be; and what shall be after him, who can tell him? ¹⁵The labour of the foolish wearieth every one of them, because he knoweth not how to go to the city."

Jeremiah 5:20-21 "²⁰Declare this in the house of Jacob, and publish it in Judah, saying, ²¹Hear now this, O foolish people, and without understanding; which have eyes, and see not; which have ears, and hear not:"

Not Being Foolish
Ecclesiastes 7:17 "Be not over much wicked, neither be thou foolish: why shouldest thou die before thy time?"

Ephesians 5:3-4 "³But fornication, and all uncleanness, or covetousness, let it not be once named among you, as becometh saints; ⁴Neither filthiness, nor foolish talking, nor jesting, which are not convenient: but rather giving of thanks."

Ephesians 5:15 "See then that ye walk circumspectly, not as fools, but as wise,"

The Foolishness Of Man
Proverbs 19:3 "The foolishness of man perverteth his way: and his heart fretteth against the LORD."

The Lord Making The Wisdom Of The World Foolish
Isaiah 29:13-14 "¹³Wherefore the Lord said, Forasmuch as this people draw near me with their mouth, and with their lips do honour me, but have removed their heart far from me, and their fear toward me is taught by the precept of men: ¹⁴Therefore, behold, I will proceed to do a marvellous work among this people, even a marvellous work and a wonder: for the wisdom of their wise men shall perish, and the understanding of their prudent men shall be hid."

Isaiah 44:24-25 "²⁴Thus saith the LORD, thy redeemer, and he that formed thee from the womb, I am the LORD that maketh all things; that stretcheth forth the heavens alone; that spreadeth abroad the earth by myself; ²⁵That frustrateth the tokens of the liars, and maketh diviners mad; that turneth wise men backward, and maketh their knowledge foolish;"

1 Corinthians 1:20-25 "²⁰Where is the wise? where is the scribe? where is the disputer of this world? hath not God made foolish the wisdom of this world? ²¹For after that in the wisdom of God the world by wisdom knew not God, it pleased God by the foolishness of preaching to save them that believe. ²²For the Jews require a sign, and the Greeks seek after wisdom: ²³But we preach Christ crucified, unto the Jews a stumblingblock, and unto the Greeks foolishness; ²⁴But unto them which are called, both Jews and Greeks, Christ the power of God, and the wisdom of God. ²⁵Because the foolishness of God is wiser than men; and the weakness of God is stronger than men."

The Reward For Foolishness
2 Chronicles 16:9 "For the eyes of the LORD run to and fro throughout the whole earth, to shew himself strong in the behalf of them whose heart is perfect toward him. Herein thou hast done foolishly: therefore from henceforth thou shalt have wars."

The Thought Of Foolishness
Proverbs 24:9 "The thought of foolishness is sin: and the scorner is an abomination to men."

What Is Foolishness To The Natural Man
1 Corinthians 1:18 "For the preaching of the cross is to them that perish foolishness; but unto us which are saved it is the power of God."

1 Corinthians 1:22-23 "22For the Jews require a sign, and the Greeks seek after wisdom: 23But we preach Christ crucified, unto the Jews a stumblingblock, and unto the Greeks foolishness;"

1 Corinthians 2:14 "But the natural man receiveth not the things of the Spirit of God: for they are foolishness unto him: neither can he know them, because they are spiritually discerned."

What Is Foolishness With God
1 Corinthians 3:18-19 "18Let no man deceive himself. If any man among you seemeth to be wise in this world, let him become a fool, that he may be wise. 19For the wisdom of this world is foolishness with God. For it is written, He taketh the wise in their own craftiness."

Where Foolishness Is Bound
Proverbs 22:15 "Foolishness is bound in the heart of a child; but the rod of correction shall drive it far from him."

Who Are Fools For Christ's Sake
1 Corinthians 4:9-10 "9For I think that God hath set forth us the apostles last, as it were appointed to death: for we are made a spectacle unto the world, and to angels, and to men. 10We are fools for Christ's sake, but ye are wise in Christ; we are weak, but ye are strong; ye are honourable, but we are despised."

Who Is A Fool
Proverbs 10:18 "He that hideth hatred with lying lips, and he that uttereth a slander, is a fool."

Proverbs 14:17 "He that is soon angry dealeth foolishly: and a man of wicked devices is hated."

Proverbs 28:26 "He that trusteth in his own heart is a fool: but whoso walketh wisely, he shall be delivered."

Matthew 7:26-28 "26And every one that heareth these sayings of mine, and doeth them not, shall be likened unto a foolish man, which built his house upon the sand: 27And the rain descended, and the floods came, and the winds blew, and beat upon that house; and it fell: and great was the fall of it. 28And it came to pass, when Jesus had ended these sayings, the people were astonished at his doctrine:"

Luke 6:46-49 "46And why call ye me, Lord, Lord, and do not the things which I say? 47Whosoever cometh to me, and heareth my sayings, and doeth them, I will shew you to whom he is like: 48He is like a man which built an house, and digged deep, and laid the foundation on a rock: and when the flood arose, the stream beat vehemently upon that house, and could not shake it: for it was founded upon a rock. 49But he that heareth, and doeth not, is like a man that without a foundation built an house upon the earth; against which the stream did beat vehemently, and immediately it fell; and the ruin of that house was great."

Romans 1:21-22 "21Because that, when they knew God, they glorified him not as God, neither were thankful; but became vain in their imaginations, and their foolish heart was darkened. 22Professing themselves to be wise, they became fools,"

FORGETTING

The Nations That Forget God
Psalm 9:17 "The wicked shall be turned into hell, and all the nations that forget God."

The Reward For Forgetting The Lord
Deuteronomy 8:19-20 "19And it shall be, if thou do at all forget the LORD thy God, and walk after other gods, and serve them, and worship them, I testify against you this day that ye shall surely perish. 20As the nations which the LORD destroyeth before your face, so shall ye perish; because ye would not be obedient unto the voice of the LORD your God."

Deuteronomy 32:17-24 "17They sacrificed unto devils, not to God; to gods whom they knew not, to new gods that came newly up, whom your fathers feared not. 18Of the Rock that begat thee thou art unmindful, and hast forgotten God that formed thee. 19And when the LORD saw it, he abhorred them, because of the provoking of his sons, and of his daughters. [20]And he said, I will hide my face from them, I will see what their end shall be: for they are a very froward generation, children in whom is no faith. [21]They have moved me to jealousy with that which is not God; they have provoked me to anger with their vanities: and I will move them to jealousy with those which are not a people; I will provoke them to anger with a foolish nation. [22]For a fire is kindled in mine anger, and shall burn unto the lowest hell, and shall consume the earth with her increase, and set on fire the foundations of the mountains. [23]I will heap mischiefs upon them; I will spend mine arrows upon them. [24]They shall be burnt with hunger, and devoured with burning heat, and with bitter destruction: I will also send the teeth of beasts upon them, with the poison of serpents of the dust."

Psalm 106:19-23 "[19]They made a calf in Horeb, and worshipped the molten image. [20]Thus they changed their glory into the similitude of an ox that eateth grass. [21]They forgat God their saviour, which had done great things in Egypt; [22]Wondrous works in the land of Ham, and terrible things by the Red sea. [23]Therefore he said that he would destroy them, had not Moses his chosen stood before him in the breach, to turn away his wrath, lest he should destroy them."

Isaiah 65:11-15 "[11]But ye are they that forsake the LORD, that forget my holy mountain, that prepare a table for that troop, and that furnish the drink offering unto that number. [12]Therefore will I number you to the sword, and ye shall all bow down to the slaughter: because when I called, ye did not answer; when I spake, ye did not hear; but did evil before mine eyes, and did choose that wherein I delighted not. [13]Therefore thus saith the Lord GOD, Behold, my servants shall eat, but ye shall be hungry: behold, my servants shall drink, but ye shall be thirsty: behold, my servants shall rejoice, but ye shall be ashamed: [14]Behold, my servants shall sing for joy of heart, but ye shall cry for sorrow of heart, and shall howl for vexation of spirit. [15]And ye shall leave your name for a curse unto my chosen: for the Lord GOD shall slay thee, and call his servants by another name:"

Jeremiah 18:13-17 "[13]Therefore thus saith the LORD; Ask ye now among the heathen, who hath heard such things: the virgin of Israel hath done a very horrible thing. [14]Will a man leave the snow of Lebanon which cometh from the rock of the field? or shall the cold flowing waters that come from another place be forsaken? [15]Because my people hath forgotten me, they have burned incense to vanity, and they have caused them to stumble in their ways from the ancient paths, to walk in paths, in a way not cast up; [16]To make their land desolate, and a perpetual hissing; every one that passeth thereby shall be astonished, and wag his head. [17]I will scatter them as with an east wind before the enemy; I will shew them the back, and not the face, in the day of their calamity."

Hosea 4:6 "My people are destroyed for lack of knowledge: because thou hast rejected knowledge, I will also reject thee, that thou shalt be no priest to me: seeing thou hast forgotten the law of thy God, I will also forget thy children."

Hosea 8:14 "For Israel hath forgotten his Maker, and buildeth temples; and Judah hath multiplied fenced cities: but I will send a fire upon his cities, and it shall devour the palaces thereof."

Hosea 13:4-8 "[4]Yet I am the LORD thy God from the land of Egypt, and thou shalt know no god but me: for there is no saviour beside me. [5]I did know thee in the wilderness, in the land of great drought. [6]According to their pasture, so were they filled; they were filled, and their heart was exalted; therefore have they forgotten me. [7]Therefore I will be unto them as a lion: as a leopard by the way will I observe them: [8]I will meet them as a bear that is bereaved of her whelps, and will rend the caul of their heart, and there will I devour them like a lion: the wild beast shall tear them."

Those That Forget The Lord

Job 8:11-18 "[11]Can the rush grow up without mire? can the flag grow without water? [12]Whilst it is yet in his greenness, and not cut down, it withereth before any other herb. [13]So are the paths of all that forget God; and the hypocrite's hope shall perish: [14]Whose hope shall be cut off, and whose trust shall be a spider's web. [15]He shall lean upon his house, but it shall not stand: he shall hold it fast, but it shall not endure. [16]He is green before the sun, and his branch shooteth forth in his garden. [17]His roots are wrapped about the heap, and seeth the place of stones. [18]If he destroy him from his place, then it shall deny him, saying, I have not seen thee."

Psalm 50:16-22 "16But unto the wicked God saith, What hast thou to do to declare my statutes, or that thou shouldest take my covenant in thy mouth? 17Seeing thou hatest instruction, and castest my words behind thee. 18When thou sawest a thief, then thou consentedst with him, and hast been partaker with adulterers. 19Thou givest thy mouth to evil, and thy tongue frameth deceit. 20Thou sittest and speakest against thy brother; thou slanderest thine own mother's son. 21These things hast thou done, and I kept silence; thou thoughtest that I was altogether such an one as thyself: but I will reprove thee, and set them in order before thine eyes. 22Now consider this, ye that forget God, lest I tear you in pieces, and there be none to deliver."

Isaiah 65:11-15 "11But ye are they that forsake the LORD, that forget my holy mountain, that prepare a table for that troop, and that furnish the drink offering unto that number. 12Therefore will I number you to the sword, and ye shall all bow down to the slaughter: because when I called, ye did not answer; when I spake, ye did not hear; but did evil before mine eyes, and did choose that wherein I delighted not. 13Therefore thus saith the Lord GOD, Behold, my servants shall eat, but ye shall be hungry: behold, my servants shall drink, but ye shall be thirsty: behold, my servants shall rejoice, but ye shall be ashamed: 14Behold, my servants shall sing for joy of heart, but ye shall cry for sorrow of heart, and shall howl for vexation of spirit. 15And ye shall leave your name for a curse unto my chosen: for the Lord GOD shall slay thee, and call his servants by another name:"

Jeremiah 50:5-6 "5They shall ask the way to Zion with their faces thitherward, saying, Come, and let us join ourselves to the LORD in a perpetual covenant that shall not be forgotten. 6My people hath been lost sheep: their shepherds have caused them to go astray, they have turned them away on the mountains: they have gone from mountain to hill, they have forgotten their restingplace."

What Shall Be Forgotten

Isaiah 65:11-17 "11But ye are they that forsake the LORD, that forget my holy mountain, that prepare a table for that troop, and that furnish the drink

offering unto that number. 12Therefore will I number you to the sword, and ye shall all bow down to the slaughter: because when I called, ye did not answer; when I spake, ye did not hear; but did evil before mine eyes, and did choose that wherein I delighted not. 13Therefore thus saith the Lord GOD, Behold, my servants shall eat, but ye shall be hungry: behold, my servants shall drink, but ye shall be thirsty: behold, my servants shall rejoice, but ye shall be ashamed: 14Behold, my servants shall sing for joy of heart, but ye shall cry for sorrow of heart, and shall howl for vexation of spirit. 15And ye shall leave your name for a curse unto my chosen: for the Lord GOD shall slay thee, and call his servants by another name: 16That he who blesseth himself in the earth shall bless himself in the God of truth; and he that sweareth in the earth shall swear by the God of truth; because the former troubles are forgotten, and because they are hid from mine eyes. 17For, behold, I create new heavens and a new earth: and the former shall not be remembered, nor come into mind."

What The Lord Will Forget

Isaiah 38:16-17 "16O Lord, by these things men live, and in all these things is the life of my spirit: so wilt thou recover me, and make me to live. 17Behold, for peace I had great bitterness: but thou hast in love to my soul delivered it from the pit of corruption: for thou hast cast all my sins behind thy back."

Isaiah 43:16-25 "16Thus saith the LORD, which maketh a way in the sea, and a path in the mighty waters; 17Which bringeth forth the chariot and horse, the army and the power; they shall lie down together, they shall not rise: they are extinct, they are quenched as tow. 18Remember ye not the former things, neither consider the things of old. 19Behold, I will do a new thing; now it shall spring forth; shall ye not know it? I will even make a way in the wilderness, and rivers in the desert. 20The beast of the field shall honour me, the dragons and the owls: because I give waters in the wilderness, and rivers in the desert, to give drink to my people, my chosen. 21This people have I formed for myself; they shall shew forth my praise. 22But thou hast not called upon me, O Jacob; but thou hast been weary of me, O Israel. 23Thou hast not brought me the small cattle of thy burnt offerings; neither hast thou honoured me with thy sacrifices. I have not caused thee to serve with an offering, nor wearied thee with incense. 24Thou hast bought me no sweet cane with money, neither hast thou filled me with the fat of thy sacrifices: but thou hast made me to serve with thy sins, thou hast wearied me with thine iniquities. 25I, even I, am he that blotteth out thy transgressions for mine own sake, and will not remember thy sins."

Jeremiah 31:33-34 "33But this shall be the covenant that I will make with the house of Israel; After those days, saith the LORD, I will put my law in their inward parts, and write it in their hearts; and will be their God, and they shall be my people. 34And they shall teach no more every man his neighbour, and every man his brother, saying, Know the LORD: for they shall all know me, from the least of them unto the greatest of them, saith the LORD; for I will forgive their iniquity, and I will remember their sin no more."

Micah 7:18-20 "18Who is a God like unto thee, that pardoneth iniquity, and passeth by the transgression of the remnant of his heritage? he retaineth not his anger for ever, because he delighteth in mercy. 19He will turn again, he will have compassion upon us; he will subdue our iniquities; and thou wilt cast all their sins into the depths of the sea. 20Thou wilt perform the truth to Jacob, and the mercy to Abraham, which thou hast sworn unto our fathers from the days of old."

Hebrews 8:10-12 "10For this is the covenant that I will make with the house of Israel after those days, saith the Lord; I will put my laws into their mind, and write them in their hearts: and I will be to them a God, and they shall be to me a people: 11And they shall not teach every man his neighbour, and every man his brother, saying, Know the Lord: for all shall know me, from the least to the greatest. 12For I will be merciful to their unrighteousness, and their sins and their iniquities will I remember no more."

Hebrews 10:16-18 "16This is the covenant that I will make with them after those days, saith the Lord, I will put my laws into their hearts, and in their minds will I write them; 17And their sins and iniquities will I remember no more. 18Now where remission of these is, there is no more offering for sin."

Who Shall Be Forgotten

Job 24:13-20 "13They are of those that rebel against the light; they know not the ways thereof, nor abide in the paths thereof. 14The murderer rising with the light killeth the poor and needy, and in the night is as a thief. 15The eye also of the adulterer waiteth for the twilight, saying, No eye shall see me: and disguiseth his face. 16In the dark they dig through houses, which they had marked for themselves in the daytime: they know not the light. 17For the morning is to them even as the shadow of death: if one know them, they are in the terrors of the shadow of death. 18He is swift as the waters; their portion is cursed in the earth: he beholdeth not the way of the vineyards. 19Drought and heat consume the snow waters: so doth the grave those which have sinned. 20The womb shall forget him; the worm shall feed sweetly on him; he shall be no more remembered; and wickedness shall be broken as a tree."

FORGIVENESS

Forgiveness Belonging To The Lord

Daniel 9:9 "To the Lord our God belong mercies and forgivenesses, though we have rebelled against him;"

Forgiving Others

Luke 17:3-4 "3Take heed to yourselves: If thy brother trespass against thee, rebuke him; and if he repent, forgive him. 4And if he trespass against thee seven times in a day, and seven times in a day turn again to thee, saying, I repent; thou shalt forgive him."

Ephesians 4:32 "And be ye kind one to another, tenderhearted, forgiving one another, even as God for Christ's sake hath forgiven you."

Colossians 3:12-13 "12Put on therefore, as the elect of God, holy and beloved, bowels of mercies, kindness, humbleness of mind, meekness, longsuffering; 13Forbearing one another, and forgiving one another, if any man have a quarrel against any: even as Christ forgave you, so also do ye."

How Many Times You Should Forgive Someone

Matthew 18:21-22 "²¹Then came Peter to him, and said, Lord, how oft shall my brother sin against me, and I forgive him? till seven times? ²²Jesus saith unto him, I say not unto thee, Until seven times: but, Until seventy times seven."

Luke 17:3-4 "³Take heed to yourselves: If thy brother trespass against thee, rebuke him; and if he repent, forgive him. ⁴And if he trespass against thee seven times in a day, and seven times in a day turn again to thee, saying, I repent; thou shalt forgive him."

The Forgiveness Of Sins Coming Through The Blood Of Jesus Christ

Acts 5:30-31 "³⁰The God of our fathers raised up Jesus, whom ye slew and hanged on a tree. ³¹Him hath God exalted with his right hand to be a Prince and a Saviour, for to give repentance to Israel, and forgiveness of sins."

Acts 10:37-43 "³⁷That word, I say, ye know, which was published throughout all Judaea, and began from Galilee, after the baptism which John preached; ³⁸How God anointed Jesus of Nazareth with the Holy Ghost and with power: who went about doing good, and healing all that were oppressed of the devil; for God was with him. ³⁹And we are witnesses of all things which he did both in the land of the Jews, and in Jerusalem; whom they slew and hanged on a tree: ⁴⁰Him God raised up the third day, and shewed him openly; ⁴¹Not to all the people, but unto witnesses chosen before of God, even to us, who did eat and drink with him after he rose from the dead. ⁴²And he commanded us to preach unto the people, and to testify that it is he which was ordained of God to be the Judge of quick and dead. ⁴³To him give all the prophets witness, that through his name whosoever believeth in him shall receive remission of sins."

Ephesians 1:3-7 "³Blessed be the God and Father of our Lord Jesus Christ, who hath blessed us with all spiritual blessings in heavenly places in Christ: ⁴According as he hath chosen us in him before the foundation of the world, that we should be holy and without blame before him in love: ⁵Having predestinated us unto the adoption of children by Jesus Christ to himself, according to the good pleasure of his will, ⁶To the praise of the glory of his grace, wherein he hath made us accepted in the beloved. ⁷In whom we have redemption through his blood, the forgiveness of sins, according to the riches of his grace;"

Colossians 1:12-14 "¹²Giving thanks unto the Father, which hath made us meet to be partakers of the inheritance of the saints in light: ¹³Who hath delivered us from the power of darkness, and hath translated us into the kingdom of his dear Son: ¹⁴In whom we have redemption through his blood, even the forgiveness of sins:"

The Lord Forgiving

Exodus 34:6-7 "⁶And the LORD passed by before him, and proclaimed, The LORD, The LORD God, merciful and gracious, longsuffering, and abundant in goodness and truth, ⁷Keeping mercy for thousands, forgiving iniquity and transgression and sin, and that will by no means clear the guilty; visiting the iniquity of the fathers upon the children, and upon the children's children, unto the third and to the fourth generation."

Numbers 14:18-19 "¹⁸The LORD is longsuffering, and of great mercy, forgiving iniquity and transgression, and by no means clearing the guilty, visiting the iniquity of the fathers upon the children unto the third and fourth generation. ¹⁹Pardon, I beseech thee, the iniquity of this people according unto the greatness of thy mercy, and as thou hast forgiven this people, from Egypt even until now."

Psalm 78:32-38 "³²For all this they sinned still, and believed not for his wondrous works. ³³Therefore their days did he consume in vanity, and their years in trouble. ³⁴When he slew them, then they sought him: and they returned and inquired early after God. ³⁵And they remembered that God was their rock, and the high God their redeemer. ³⁶Nevertheless they did flatter him with their mouth, and they lied unto him with their tongues. ³⁷For their heart was not right with him, neither were they stedfast in his covenant. ³⁸But he, being full of compassion, forgave their iniquity, and destroyed them not: yea, many a time turned he his anger away, and did not stir up all his wrath."

Psalm 86:5 "For thou, Lord, art good, and ready to forgive; and plenteous in mercy unto all them that call upon thee."

Psalm 99:8 "Thou answeredst them, O LORD our God: thou wast a God that forgavest them, though thou tookest vengeance of their inventions."

Psalm 103:1-3 "¹Bless the LORD, O my soul: and all that is within me, bless his holy name. ²Bless the LORD, O my soul, and forget not all his benefits: ³Who forgiveth all thine iniquities; who healeth all thy diseases;"

Psalm 130:3-4 "³If thou, LORD, shouldest mark iniquities, O Lord, who shall stand? ⁴But there is forgiveness with thee, that thou mayest be feared."

Jeremiah 31:33-34 "³³But this shall be the covenant that I will make with the house of Israel; After those days, saith the LORD, I will put my law in their inward parts, and write it in their hearts; and will be their God, and they shall be my people. ³⁴And they shall teach no more every man his neighbour, and every man his brother, saying, Know the LORD: for they shall all know me, from the least of them unto the greatest of them, saith the LORD; for I will forgive their iniquity, and I will remember their sin no more."

Ephesians 4:32 "And be ye kind one to another, tenderhearted, forgiving one another, even as God for Christ's sake hath forgiven you."

Colossians 2:8-13 "⁸Beware lest any man spoil you through philosophy and vain deceit, after the tradition of men, after the rudiments of the world, and not after Christ. ⁹For in him dwelleth all the fulness of the Godhead bodily. ¹⁰And ye are complete in him, which is the head of all principality and power: ¹¹In whom also ye are circumcised with the circumcision made without hands, in putting off the body of the sins of the flesh by the circumcision of Christ: ¹²Buried with him in baptism, wherein also ye are risen with him through the faith of the operation of God, who hath raised him from the dead. ¹³And you, being dead in your sins and the uncircumcision of your flesh, hath he quickened together with him, having forgiven you all trespasses;"

Colossians 3:12-13 "¹²Put on therefore, as the elect of God, holy and beloved, bowels of mercies, kindness, humbleness of mind, meekness, longsuffering; ¹³Forbearing one another, and forgiving one another, if any man have a quarrel against any: even as Christ forgave you, so also do ye."

The Reward For Forgiving Others

Matthew 6:14 "For if ye forgive men their trespasses, your heavenly Father will also forgive you:"

Mark 11:25 "And when ye stand praying, forgive, if ye have ought against any: that your Father also which is in heaven may forgive you your trespasses."

Luke 6:37 "Judge not, and ye shall not be judged: condemn not, and ye shall not be condemned: forgive, and ye shall be forgiven:"

The Reward For Not Forgiving Others

Matthew 6:15 "But if ye forgive not men their trespasses, neither will your Father forgive your trespasses."

Matthew 18:23-35 "²³Therefore is the kingdom of heaven likened unto a certain king, which would take account of his servants. ²⁴And when he had begun to reckon, one was brought unto him, which owed him ten thousand talents. ²⁵But forasmuch as he had not to pay, his lord commanded him to be sold, and his wife, and children, and all that he had, and payment to be made. ²⁶The servant therefore fell down, and worshipped him, saying, Lord, have patience with me, and I will pay thee all. ²⁷Then the lord of that servant was moved with compassion, and loosed him, and forgave him the debt. ²⁸But the same servant went out, and found one of his fellowservants, which owed him an hundred pence: and he laid hands on him, and took him by the throat, saying, Pay me that thou owest. ²⁹And his fellowservant fell down at his feet, and besought him, saying, Have patience with me, and I will pay thee all. ³⁰And he would not: but went and cast him into prison, till he should pay the debt. ³¹So when his fellowservants saw what was done, they were very sorry, and came and told unto their lord all that was done. ³²Then his lord, after that he had called him, said unto him, O thou wicked servant, I forgave thee all that debt, because thou desiredst me: ³³Shouldest not thou also have had compassion on thy fellowservant, even as I had pity on thee? ³⁴And his lord was wroth, and delivered him to the tormentors, till he should pay all that was due unto him. ³⁵So likewise shall my heavenly Father do also unto you, if ye from your hearts forgive not every one his brother their trespasses."

Mark 11:26 "But if ye do not forgive, neither will your Father which is in heaven forgive your trespasses."

Those Whose Iniquities Are Forgiven

Psalm 32:1-2 "¹Blessed is he whose transgression is forgiven, whose sin is covered. ²Blessed is the man unto whom the LORD imputeth not iniquity, and in whose spirit there is no guile."

Romans 4:6-7 "⁶Even as David also describeth the blessedness of the man, unto whom God imputeth righteousness without works, ⁷Saying, Blessed are they whose iniquities are forgiven, and whose sins are covered."

Who Shall Be Forgiven

2 Chronicles 7:12-14 "¹²And the LORD appeared to Solomon by night, and said unto him, I have heard thy prayer, and have chosen this place to myself for an house of sacrifice. ¹³If I shut up heaven that there be no rain, or if I command the locusts to devour the land, or if I send pestilence among my people; ¹⁴If my people, which are called by my name, shall humble themselves, and pray, and seek my face, and turn from their wicked ways; then will I hear from heaven, and will forgive their sin, and will heal their land."

Psalm 32:5 "I acknowledged my sin unto thee, and mine iniquity have I not hid. I said, I will confess my transgressions unto the LORD; and thou forgavest the iniquity of my sin. Selah."

Matthew 12:31-32 "³¹Wherefore I say unto you, All manner of sin and blasphemy shall be forgiven unto men: but the blasphemy against the Holy Ghost shall not be forgiven unto men. ³²And whosoever speaketh a word against the Son of man, it shall be forgiven him: but whosoever speaketh against the Holy Ghost, it shall not be forgiven him, neither in this world, neither in the world to come."

Mark 3:28 "Verily I say unto you, All sins shall be forgiven unto the sons of men, and blasphemies wherewith soever they shall blaspheme:"

Luke 7:40-48 "⁴⁰And Jesus answering said unto him, Simon, I have somewhat to say unto thee. And he saith, Master, say on. ⁴¹There was a certain creditor which had two debtors: the one owed five hundred pence, and the other fifty. ⁴²And when they had nothing to pay, he frankly forgave them both. Tell me therefore, which of them will love him most? ⁴³Simon answered and said, I suppose that he, to whom he forgave most. And he said unto him, Thou hast rightly judged. ⁴⁴And he turned to the woman, and said unto Simon, Seest thou this woman? I entered into thine house, thou gavest me no water for my feet: but she hath washed my feet with tears, and wiped them with the hairs of her head. ⁴⁵Thou gavest me no kiss: but this woman since the time I came in hath not ceased to kiss my feet. ⁴⁶My head with oil thou didst not anoint: but this woman hath anointed my feet with ointment. ⁴⁷Wherefore I say unto thee, Her sins, which are many, are forgiven; for she loved much: but to whom little is forgiven, the same loveth little. ⁴⁸And he said unto her, Thy sins are forgiven."

Luke 12:10 "And whosoever shall speak a word against the Son of man, it shall be forgiven him: but unto him that blasphemeth against the Holy Ghost it shall not be forgiven."

Acts 10:37-43 "³⁷That word, I say, ye know, which was published throughout all Judaea, and began from Galilee, after the baptism which John preached; ³⁸How God anointed Jesus of Nazareth with the Holy Ghost and with power: who went about doing good, and healing all that were oppressed of the devil; for God was with him. ³⁹And we are witnesses of all things which he did both in the land of the Jews, and in Jerusalem; whom they slew and hanged on a tree: ⁴⁰Him God raised up the third day, and shewed him openly; ⁴¹Not to all the people, but unto witnesses chosen before of God, even to us, who did eat and drink with him after he rose from the dead. ⁴²And he commanded us to preach unto the people, and to testify that it is he which was ordained of God to be the Judge of quick and dead. ⁴³To him give all the prophets witness, that through his name whosoever believeth in him shall receive remission of sins."

James 5:14-15 "¹⁴Is any sick among you? let him call for the elders of the church; and let them pray over him, anointing him with oil in the name of the Lord: ¹⁵And the prayer of faith shall save the sick, and the Lord shall raise him up; and if he have committed sins, they shall be forgiven him."

1 John 1:9 "If we confess our sins, he is faithful and just to forgive us our sins, and to cleanse us from all unrighteousness."

Who Shall Not Be Forgiven

Matthew 12:31-32 "[31]Wherefore I say unto you, All manner of sin and blasphemy shall be forgiven unto men: but the blasphemy against the Holy Ghost shall not be forgiven unto men. [32]And whosoever speaketh a word against the Son of man, it shall be forgiven him: but whosoever speaketh against the Holy Ghost, it shall not be forgiven him, neither in this world, neither in the world to come."

Mark 3:28-29 "[28]Verily I say unto you, All sins shall be forgiven unto the sons of men, and blasphemies wherewith soever they shall blaspheme: [29]But he that shall blaspheme against the Holy Ghost hath never forgiveness, but is in danger of eternal damnation:"

Luke 12:10 "And whosoever shall speak a word against the Son of man, it shall be forgiven him: but unto him that blasphemeth against the Holy Ghost it shall not be forgiven."

Hebrews 6:4-8 "[4]For it is impossible for those who were once enlightened, and have tasted of the heavenly gift, and were made partakers of the Holy Ghost, [5]And have tasted the good word of God, and the powers of the world to come, [6]If they shall fall away, to renew them again unto repentance; seeing they crucify to themselves the Son of God afresh, and put him to an open shame. [7]For the earth which drinketh in the rain that cometh oft upon it, and bringeth forth herbs meet for them by whom it is dressed, receiveth blessing from God: [8]But that which beareth thorns and briers is rejected, and is nigh unto cursing; whose end is to be burned."

Hebrews 10:26-29 "[26]For if we sin wilfully after that we have received the knowledge of the truth, there remaineth no more sacrifice for sins, [27]But a certain fearful looking for of judgment and fiery indignation, which shall devour the adversaries. [28]He that despised Moses' law died without mercy under two or three witnesses: [29]Of how much sorer punishment, suppose ye, shall he be thought worthy, who hath trodden under foot the Son of God, and hath counted the blood of the covenant, wherewith he was sanctified, an unholy thing, and hath done despite unto the Spirit of grace?"

1 John 5:16-17 "[16]If any man see his brother sin a sin which is not unto death, he shall ask, and he shall give him life for them that sin not unto death. There is a sin unto death: I do not say that he shall pray for it. [17]All unrighteousness is sin: and there is a sin not unto death."

Whose Sins Are Forgiven

1 John 2:10-12 "[10]He that loveth his brother abideth in the light, and there is none occasion of stumbling in him. [11]But he that hateth his brother is in darkness, and walketh in darkness, and knoweth not whither he goeth, because that darkness hath blinded his eyes. [12]I write unto you, little children, because your sins are forgiven you for his name's sake."

Why Jesus Christ Asked God The Father To Forgive Man

Luke 23:34 "Then said Jesus, Father, forgive them; for they know not what they do. And they parted his raiment, and cast lots."

FORSAKING

Forsaking The Lord

Jeremiah 2:13 "For my people have committed two evils; they have forsaken me the fountain of living waters, and hewed them out cisterns, broken cisterns, that can hold no water."

Jeremiah 2:19 "Thine own wickedness shall correct thee, and thy backslidings shall reprove thee: know therefore and see that it is an evil thing and bitter, that thou hast forsaken the LORD thy God, and that my fear is not in thee, saith the Lord GOD of hosts."

Not Forsaking Your Friends

Proverbs 27:10 "Thine own friend, and thy father's friend, forsake not; neither go into thy brother's house in the day of thy calamity: for better is a neighbour that is near than a brother far off."

The Reward For Forsaking The Lord

Deuteronomy 28:15-20 "[15]But it shall come to pass, if thou wilt not hearken unto the voice of the LORD thy God, to observe to do all his commandments and his statutes which I command thee this day; that all these curses shall come upon thee, and overtake thee: [16]Cursed shalt thou be in the city, and cursed shalt thou be in the field. [17]Cursed shall be thy basket and thy store. [18]Cursed shall be the fruit of thy body, and the fruit of thy land, the increase of thy kine, and the flocks of thy sheep. [19]Cursed shalt thou be when thou comest in, and cursed shalt thou be when thou goest out. [20]The LORD shall send upon thee cursing, vexation, and rebuke, in all that thou settest thine hand unto for to do, until thou be destroyed, and until thou perish quickly; because of the wickedness of thy doings, whereby thou hast forsaken me."

Deuteronomy 29:19-25 "[19]And it come to pass, when he heareth the words of this curse, that he bless himself in his heart, saying, I shall have peace, though I walk in the imagination of mine heart, to add drunkenness to thirst: [20]The LORD will not spare him, but then the anger of the LORD and his jealousy shall smoke against that man, and all the curses that are written in this book shall lie upon him, and the LORD shall blot out his name from under heaven. [21]And the LORD shall separate him unto evil out of all the tribes of Israel, according to all the curses of the covenant that are written in this book of the law: [22]So that the generation to come of your children that shall rise up after you, and the stranger that shall come from a far land, shall say, when they see the plagues of that land, and the sicknesses which the LORD hath laid upon it; [23]And that the whole land thereof is brimstone, and salt, and burning, that it is not sown, nor beareth, nor any grass groweth therein, like the overthrow of Sodom, and Gomorrah, Admah, and Zeboim, which the LORD overthrew in his anger, and in his wrath: [24]Even all nations shall say, Wherefore hath the LORD done thus unto this land? what meaneth the heat of this great anger? [25]Then men shall say, Because they have forsaken the covenant of the LORD God of their fathers, which he made with them when he brought them forth out of the land of Egypt:"

Deuteronomy 31:16-18 "[16]And the LORD said unto Moses, Behold, thou shalt sleep with thy fathers; and this people will rise up, and go a whoring after the gods of the strangers of the land, whither they go to be among them, and will forsake me, and break my covenant which I have made with them. [17]Then my anger shall be kindled against them in that day, and I will forsake them, and I will hide my face from them, and they shall be devoured, and many evils and troubles shall befall them; so that they will say in that

day. Are not these evils come upon us, because our God is not among us? [18]And I will surely hide my face in that day for all the evils which they shall have wrought, in that they are turned unto other gods."

Joshua 24:20 "If ye forsake the LORD, and serve strange gods, then he will turn and do you hurt, and consume you, after that he hath done you good."

Judges 10:11-14 "[11]And the LORD said unto the children of Israel, Did not I deliver you from the Egyptians, and from the Amorites, from the children of Ammon, and from the Philistines? [12]The Zidonians also, and the Amalekites, and the Maonites, did oppress you; and ye cried to me, and I delivered you out of their hand. [13]Yet ye have forsaken me, and served other gods: wherefore I will deliver you no more. [14]Go and cry unto the gods which ye have chosen; let them deliver you in the time of your tribulation."

1 Samuel 8:4-18 "[4]Then all the elders of Israel gathered themselves together, and came to Samuel unto Ramah, [5]And said unto him, Behold, thou art old, and thy sons walk not in thy ways: now make us a king to judge us like all the nations. [6]But the thing displeased Samuel, when they said, Give us a king to judge us. And Samuel prayed unto the LORD. [7]And the LORD said unto Samuel, Hearken unto the voice of the people in all that they say unto thee: for they have not rejected thee, but they have rejected me, that I should not reign over them. [8]According to all the works which they have done since the day that I brought them up out of Egypt even unto this day, wherewith they have forsaken me, and served other gods, so do they also unto thee. [9]Now therefore hearken unto their voice: howbeit yet protest solemnly unto them, and shew them the manner of the king that shall reign over them. [10]And Samuel told all the words of the LORD unto the people that asked of him a king. [11]And he said, This will be the manner of the king that shall reign over you: He will take your sons, and appoint them for himself, for his chariots, and to be his horsemen; and some shall run before his chariots. [12]And he will appoint him captains over thousands, and captains over fifties; and will set them to ear his ground, and to reap his harvest, and to make his instruments of war, and instruments of his chariots. ¹³And he will take your daughters to be confectionaries, and to be cooks, and to be bakers. ¹⁴And he will take your fields, and your vineyards, and your oliveyards, even the best of them, and give them to his servants. ¹⁵And he will take the tenth of your seed, and of your vineyards, and give to his officers, and to his servants. ¹⁶And he will take your menservants, and your maidservants, and your goodliest young men, and your asses, and put them to his work. ¹⁷He will take the tenth of your sheep: and ye shall be his servants. ¹⁸And ye shall cry out in that day because of your king which ye shall have chosen you; and the LORD will not hear you in that day."

1 Kings 9:6-9 "⁶But if ye shall at all turn from following me, ye or your children, and will not keep my commandments and my statutes which I have set before you, but go and serve other gods, and worship them: ⁷Then will I cut off Israel out of the land which I have given them; and this house, which I have hallowed for my name, will I cast out of my sight; and Israel shall be a proverb and a byword among all people: ⁸And at this house, which is high, every one that passeth by it shall be astonished, and shall hiss; and they shall say, Why hath the LORD done thus unto this land, and to this house? ⁹And they shall answer, Because they forsook the LORD their God, who brought forth their fathers out of the land of Egypt, and have taken hold upon other gods, and have worshipped them, and served them: therefore hath the LORD brought upon them all this evil."

1 Kings 11:31-37 "³¹And he said to Jeroboam, Take thee ten pieces: for thus saith the LORD, the God of Israel, Behold, I will rend the kingdom out of the hand of Solomon, and will give ten tribes to thee: ³²(But he shall have one tribe for my servant David's sake, and for Jerusalem's sake, the city which I have chosen out of all the tribes of Israel:) ³³Because that they have forsaken me, and have worshipped Ashtoreth the goddess of the Zidonians, Chemosh the god of the Moabites, and Milcom the god of the children of Ammon, and have not walked in my ways, to do that which is right in mine eyes, and to keep my statutes and my judgments, as did David his father. ³⁴Howbeit I will not take the whole kingdom out of his hand: but I will make him prince all the days of his life

for David my servant's sake, whom I chose, because he kept my commandments and my statutes: ³⁵But I will take the kingdom out of his son's hand, and will give it unto thee, even ten tribes. ³⁶And unto his son will I give one tribe, that David my servant may have a light alway before me in Jerusalem, the city which I have chosen me to put my name there. ³⁷And I will take thee, and thou shalt reign according to all that thy soul desireth, and shalt be king over Israel."

2 Kings 22:16-17 "¹⁶Thus saith the LORD, Behold, I will bring evil upon this place, and upon the inhabitants thereof, even all the words of the book which the king of Judah hath read: ¹⁷Because they have forsaken me, and have burned incense unto other gods, that they might provoke me to anger with all the works of their hands; therefore my wrath shall be kindled against this place, and shall not be quenched."

1 Chronicles 28:9 "And thou, Solomon my son, know thou the God of thy father, and serve him with a perfect heart and with a willing mind: for the LORD searcheth all hearts, and understandeth all the imaginations of the thoughts: if thou seek him, he will be found of thee; but if thou forsake him, he will cast thee off for ever."

2 Chronicles 15:2 "And he went out to meet Asa, and said unto him, Hear ye me, Asa, and all Judah and Benjamin; The LORD is with you, while ye be with him; and if ye seek him, he will be found of you; but if ye forsake him, he will forsake you."

2 Chronicles 24:20 "And the Spirit of God came upon Zechariah the son of Jehoiada the priest, which stood above the people, and said unto them, Thus saith God, Why transgress ye the commandments of the LORD, that ye cannot prosper? because ye have forsaken the LORD, he hath also forsaken you."

2 Chronicles 29:6-9 "⁶For our fathers have trespassed, and done that which was evil in the eyes of the LORD our God, and have forsaken him, and have turned away their faces from the habitation of the LORD, and turned their backs. ⁷Also they have shut up the doors of the porch, and put out the lamps, and have not burned incense nor offered burnt offerings in the holy place unto the God of Israel. ⁸Wherefore the wrath of the LORD was upon Judah and Jerusalem, and he hath delivered them to trouble, to astonishment, and to hissing, as ye see with your eyes. [9]For, lo, our fathers have fallen by the sword, and our sons and our daughters and our wives are in captivity for this."

2 Chronicles 34:24-25 "[24]Thus saith the LORD, Behold, I will bring evil upon this place, and upon the inhabitants thereof, even all the curses that are written in the book which they have read before the king of Judah: [25]Because they have forsaken me, and have burned incense unto other gods, that they might provoke me to anger with all the works of their hands; therefore my wrath shall be poured out upon this place, and shall not be quenched."

Jeremiah 5:18-19 "[18]Nevertheless in those days, saith the LORD, I will not make a full end with you. [19]And it shall come to pass, when ye shall say, Wherefore doeth the LORD our God all these things unto us? then shalt thou answer them, Like as ye have forsaken me, and served strange gods in your land, so shall ye serve strangers in a land that is not yours."

Jeremiah 15:6-7 "[6]Thou hast forsaken me, saith the LORD, thou art gone backward: therefore will I stretch out my hand against thee, and destroy thee; I am weary with repenting. [7]And I will fan them with a fan in the gates of the land; I will bereave them of children, I will destroy my people, since they return not from their ways."

Jeremiah 16:11-13 "[11]Then shalt thou say unto them, Because your fathers have forsaken me, saith the LORD, and have walked after other gods, and have served them, and have worshipped them, and have forsaken me, and have not kept my law; [12]And ye have done worse than your fathers; for, behold, ye walk every one after the imagination of his evil heart, that they may not hearken unto me: [13]Therefore will I cast you out of this land into a land that ye know not, neither ye nor your fathers; and there shall ye serve other gods day and night; where I will not shew you favour."

Jeremiah 17:13 "O LORD, the hope of Israel, all that forsake thee shall be ashamed, and they that depart from me shall be written in the earth, because they have forsaken the LORD, the fountain of living waters."

Jeremiah 19:3-15 "[3]And say, Hear ye the word of the LORD, O kings of Judah, and inhabitants of Jerusalem; Thus saith the LORD of hosts, the God of Israel; Behold, I will bring evil upon this place, the which whosoever heareth, his ears shall tingle. [4]Because they have forsaken me, and have estranged this place, and have burned incense in it unto other gods, whom neither they nor their fathers have known, nor the kings of Judah, and have filled this place with the blood of innocents; [5]They have built also the high places of Baal, to burn their sons with fire for burnt offerings unto Baal, which I commanded not, nor spake it, neither came it into my mind: [6]Therefore, behold, the days come, saith the LORD, that this place shall no more be called Tophet, nor The valley of the son of Hinnom, but The valley of slaughter. [7]And I will make void the counsel of Judah and Jerusalem in this place; and I will cause them to fall by the sword before their enemies, and by the hands of them that seek their lives: and their carcases will I give to be meat for the fowls of the heaven, and for the beasts of the earth. [8]And I will make this city desolate, and an hissing; every one that passeth thereby shall be astonished and hiss because of all the plagues thereof. [9]And I will cause them to eat the flesh of their sons and the flesh of their daughters, and they shall eat every one the flesh of his friend in the siege and straitness, wherewith their enemies, and they that seek their lives, shall straiten them. [10]Then shalt thou break the bottle in the sight of the men that go with thee, [11]And shalt say unto them, Thus saith the LORD of hosts; Even so will I break this people and this city, as one breaketh a potter's vessel, that cannot be made whole again: and they shall bury them in Tophet, till there be no place to bury. [12]Thus will I do unto this place, saith the LORD, and to the inhabitants thereof, and even make this city as Tophet: [13]And the houses of Jerusalem, and the houses of the kings of Judah, shall be defiled as the place of Tophet, because of all the houses upon whose roofs they have burned incense unto all the host of heaven, and have poured out drink offerings unto other gods. [14]Then came Jeremiah from Tophet, whither the LORD had sent him to prophesy; and he stood in the court of the LORD's house; and said to all the people, [15]Thus saith the LORD of hosts, the God of Israel; Behold, I will bring upon this city and upon all her towns all the evil that I have pronounced against it, because they have hardened their necks, that they might not hear my words."

Jeremiah 22:8-9 "⁸And many nations shall pass by this city, and they shall say every man to his neighbour, Wherefore hath the LORD done thus unto this great city? ⁹Then they shall answer, Because they have forsaken the covenant of the LORD their God, and worshipped other gods, and served them."

The Reward For Forsaking The Law
Psalm 89:26-32 "²⁶He shall cry unto me, Thou art my father, my God, and the rock of my salvation. ²⁷Also I will make him my firstborn, higher than the kings of the earth. ²⁸My mercy will I keep for him for evermore, and my covenant shall stand fast with him. ²⁹His seed also will I make to endure for ever, and his throne as the days of heaven. ³⁰If his children forsake my law, and walk not in my judgments; ³¹If they break my statutes, and keep not my commandments; ³²Then will I visit their transgression with the rod, and their iniquity with stripes."

Jeremiah 9:13-16 "¹³And the LORD saith, Because they have forsaken my law which I set before them, and have not obeyed my voice, neither walked therein; ¹⁴But have walked after the imagination of their own heart, and after Baalim, which their fathers taught them: ¹⁵Therefore thus saith the LORD of hosts, the God of Israel; Behold, I will feed them, even this people, with wormwood, and give them water of gall to drink. ¹⁶I will scatter them also among the heathen, whom neither they nor their fathers have known: and I will send a sword after them, till I have consumed them."

The Time When Parents
Forsake Their Children
Psalm 27:10 "When my father and my mother forsake me, then the LORD will take me up."

Those That Forsake Sin
Proverbs 28:13 "He that covereth his sins shall not prosper: but whoso confesseth and forsaketh them shall have mercy."

Those That Forsake The Law
Proverbs 28:4 "They that forsake the law praise the wicked: but such as keep the law contend with them."

Proverbs 28:9 "He that turneth away his ear from hearing the law, even his prayer shall be abomination."

Those That Forsake The Lord
Joshua 24:20 "If ye forsake the LORD, and serve strange gods, then he will turn and do you hurt, and consume you, after that he hath done you good."

Judges 10:11-14 "¹¹And the LORD said unto the children of Israel, Did not I deliver you from the Egyptians, and from the Amorites, from the children of Ammon, and from the Philistines? ¹²The Zidonians also, and the Amalekites, and the Maonites, did oppress you; and ye cried to me, and I delivered you out of their hand. ¹³Yet ye have forsaken me, and served other gods: wherefore I will deliver you no more. ¹⁴Go and cry unto the gods which ye have chosen; let them deliver you in the time of your tribulation."

1 Chronicles 28:9 "And thou, Solomon my son, know thou the God of thy father, and serve him with a perfect heart and with a willing mind: for the LORD searcheth all hearts, and understandeth all the imaginations of the thoughts: if thou seek him, he will be found of thee; but if thou forsake him, he will cast thee off for ever."

2 Chronicles 15:2 "And he went out to meet Asa, and said unto him, Hear ye me, Asa, and all Judah and Benjamin; The LORD is with you, while ye be with him; and if ye seek him, he will be found of you; but if ye forsake him, he will forsake you."

2 Chronicles 24:20 "And the Spirit of God came upon Zechariah the son of Jehoiada the priest, which stood above the people, and said unto them, Thus saith God, Why transgress ye the commandments of the LORD, that ye cannot prosper? because ye have forsaken the LORD, he hath also forsaken you."

Ezra 8:22 "For I was ashamed to require of the king a band of soldiers and horsemen to help us against the enemy in the way: because we had spoken unto the king, saying, The hand of our God is upon all them for good that seek him; but his power and his wrath is against all them that forsake him."

Isaiah 65:11-15 "¹¹But ye are they that forsake the LORD, that forget my holy mountain, that prepare a table for that troop, and that furnish the drink offering unto that number. [12]Therefore will I number you to the sword, and ye shall all bow down to the slaughter: because when I called, ye did not answer; when I spake, ye did not hear; but did evil before mine eyes, and did choose that wherein I delighted not. [13]Therefore thus saith the Lord GOD, Behold, my servants shall eat, but ye shall be hungry: behold, my servants shall drink, but ye shall be thirsty: behold, my servants shall rejoice, but ye shall be ashamed: [14]Behold, my servants shall sing for joy of heart, but ye shall cry for sorrow of heart, and shall howl for vexation of spirit. [15]And ye shall leave your name for a curse unto my chosen: for the Lord GOD shall slay thee, and call his servants by another name:"

Jeremiah 15:6-7 "[6]Thou hast forsaken me, saith the LORD, thou art gone backward: therefore will I stretch out my hand against thee, and destroy thee; I am weary with repenting. [7]And I will fan them with a fan in the gates of the land; I will bereave them of children, I will destroy my people, since they return not from their ways."

Jeremiah 17:13 "O LORD, the hope of Israel, all that forsake thee shall be ashamed, and they that depart from me shall be written in the earth, because they have forsaken the LORD, the fountain of living waters."

Those That Forsake The Way
Proverbs 15:10 "Correction is grievous unto him that forsaketh the way: and he that hateth reproof shall die."

Those That Forsake Themselves For Christ
Matthew 19:27-29 "[27]Then answered Peter and said unto him, Behold, we have forsaken all, and followed thee; what shall we have therefore? [28]And Jesus said unto them, Verily I say unto you, That ye which have followed me, in the regeneration when the Son of man shall sit in the throne of his glory, ye also shall sit upon twelve thrones, judging the twelve tribes of Israel. [29]And every one that hath forsaken houses, or brethren, or sisters, or father, or mother, or wife, or children, or lands, for my name's sake, shall receive an hundredfold, and shall inherit everlasting life."

Luke 18:24-30 "[24]And when Jesus saw that he was very sorrowful, he said, How hardly shall they that have riches enter into the kingdom of God! [25]For it is easier for a camel to go through a needle's eye, than for a rich man to enter into the kingdom of God. [26]And they that heard it said, Who then can be saved? [27]And he said, The things which are impossible with men are possible with God. [28]Then Peter said, Lo, we have left all, and followed thee. [29]And he said unto them, Verily I say unto you, There is no man that hath left house, or parents, or brethren, or wife, or children, for the kingdom of God's sake, [30]Who shall not receive manifold more in this present time, and in the world to come life everlasting."

What Not To Forsake
Hebrews 10:23-25 "[23]Let us hold fast the profession of our faith without wavering; (for he is faithful that promised;) [24]And let us consider one another to provoke unto love and to good works: [25]Not forsaking the assembling of ourselves together, as the manner of some is; but exhorting one another: and so much the more, as ye see the day approaching."

What To Forsake
Psalm 37:8 "Cease from anger, and forsake wrath: fret not thyself in any wise to do evil."

Ephesians 4:31 "Let all bitterness, and wrath, and anger, and clamour, and evil speaking, be put away from you, with all malice:"

Who Has Forsaken The Right Way
2 Peter 2:1-15 "[1]But there were false prophets also among the people, even as there shall be false teachers among you, who privily shall bring in damnable heresies, even denying the Lord that bought them, and bring upon themselves swift destruction. [2]And many shall follow their pernicious ways; by reason of whom the way of truth shall be evil spoken of. [3]And through covetousness shall they with feigned words make merchandise of you: whose judgment now of a long time lingereth not, and their damnation slumbereth not. [4]For if God spared not the angels that sinned, but cast them down to hell, and delivered them into chains of darkness, to be reserved unto judgment; [5]And spared not the old world, but saved Noah the eighth person, a preacher of righteousness, bringing in the flood upon the world of the ungodly; [6]And turning the cities of Sodom and Gomorrha into ashes condemned them with an overthrow, making them an ensample unto

those that after should live ungodly; [7]And delivered just Lot, vexed with the filthy conversation of the wicked: [8](For that righteous man dwelling among them, in seeing and hearing, vexed his righteous soul from day to day with their unlawful deeds;) [9]The Lord knoweth how to deliver the godly out of temptations, and to reserve the unjust unto the day of judgment to be punished: [10]But chiefly them that walk after the flesh in the lust of uncleanness, and despise government. Presumptuous are they, selfwilled, they are not afraid to speak evil of dignities. [11]Whereas angels, which are greater in power and might, bring not railing accusation against them before the Lord. [12]But these, as natural brute beasts, made to be taken and destroyed, speak evil of the things that they understand not; and shall utterly perish in their own corruption; [13]And shall receive the reward of unrighteousness, as they that count it pleasure to riot in the day time. Spots they are and blemishes, sporting themselves with their own deceivings while they feast with you; [14]Having eyes full of adultery, and that cannot cease from sin; beguiling unstable souls: an heart they have exercised with covetous practices; cursed children: [15]Which have forsaken the right way, and are gone astray, following the way of Balaam the son of Bosor, who loved the wages of unrighteousness;"

Who Should Forsake Their Way
Isaiah 55:7 "Let the wicked forsake his way, and the unrighteous man his thoughts: and let him return unto the LORD, and he will have mercy upon him; and to our God, for he will abundantly pardon."

Who The Lord Will Forsake
Deuteronomy 31:16-17 "[16]And the LORD said unto Moses, Behold, thou shalt sleep with thy fathers; and this people will rise up, and go a whoring after the gods of the strangers of the land, whither they go to be among them, and will forsake me, and break my covenant which I have made with them. [17]Then my anger shall be kindled against them in that day, and I will forsake them, and I will hide my face from them, and they shall be devoured, and many evils and troubles shall befall them; so that they will say in that day, Are not these evils come upon us, because our God is not among us?"

2 Chronicles 15:2 "And he went out to meet Asa, and said unto him, Hear ye me, Asa, and all Judah and Benjamin; The LORD is with you, while ye be with him; and if ye seek him, he will be found of you; but if ye forsake him, he will forsake you."

2 Chronicles 24:20 "And the Spirit of God came upon Zechariah the son of Jehoiada the priest, which stood above the people, and said unto them, Thus saith God, Why transgress ye the commandments of the LORD, that ye cannot prosper? because ye have forsaken the LORD, he hath also forsaken you."

Who The Lord Will Not Forsake
Deuteronomy 4:29-31 "[29]But if from thence thou shalt seek the LORD thy God, thou shalt find him, if thou seek him with all thy heart and with all thy soul. [30]When thou art in tribulation, and all these things are come upon thee, even in the latter days, if thou turn to the LORD thy God, and shalt be obedient unto his voice; [31](For the LORD thy God is a merciful God;) he will not forsake thee, neither destroy thee, nor forget the covenant of thy fathers which he sware unto them."

Deuteronomy 31:1-8 "[1]And Moses went and spake these words unto all Israel. [2]And he said unto them, I am an hundred and twenty years old this day; I can no more go out and come in: also the LORD hath said unto me, Thou shalt not go over this Jordan. [3]The LORD thy God, he will go over before thee, and he will destroy these nations from before thee, and thou shalt possess them: and Joshua, he shall go over before thee, as the LORD hath said. [4]And the LORD shall do unto them as he did to Sihon and to Og, kings of the Amorites, and unto the land of them, whom he destroyed. [5]And the LORD shall give them up before your face, that ye may do unto them according unto all the commandments which I have commanded you. [6]Be strong and of a good courage, fear not, nor be afraid of them: for the LORD thy God, he it is that doth go with thee; he will not fail thee, nor forsake thee. [7]And Moses called unto Joshua, and said unto him in the sight of all Israel, Be strong and of a good courage: for thou must go with this people unto the land which the LORD hath sworn unto their fathers to give them; and thou shalt cause them to inherit it. [8]And the LORD, he it is that doth go before thee;

he will be with thee, he will not fail thee, neither forsake thee: fear not, neither be dismayed."

Joshua 1:1-5 "¹Now after the death of Moses the servant of the LORD it came to pass, that the LORD spake unto Joshua the son of Nun, Moses' minister, saying, ²Moses my servant is dead; now therefore arise, go over this Jordan, thou, and all this people, unto the land which I do give to them, even to the children of Israel. ³Every place that the sole of your foot shall tread upon, that have I given unto you, as I said unto Moses. ⁴From the wilderness and this Lebanon even unto the great river, the river Euphrates, all the land of the Hittites, and unto the great sea toward the going down of the sun, shall be your coast. ⁵There shall not any man be able to stand before thee all the days of thy life: as I was with Moses, so I will be with thee: I will not fail thee, nor forsake thee."

1 Samuel 12:22 "For the LORD will not forsake his people for his great name's sake: because it hath pleased the LORD to make you his people."

Ezra 9:7-9 "⁷Since the days of our fathers have we been in a great trespass unto this day; and for our iniquities have we, our kings, and our priests, been delivered into the hand of the kings of the lands, to the sword, to captivity, and to a spoil, and to confusion of face, as it is this day. ⁸And now for a little space grace hath been shewed from the LORD our God, to leave us a remnant to escape, and to give us a nail in his holy place, that our God may lighten our eyes, and give us a little reviving in our bondage. ⁹For we were bondmen; yet our God hath not forsaken us in our bondage, but hath extended mercy unto us in the sight of the kings of Persia, to give us a reviving, to set up the house of our God, and to repair the desolations thereof, and to give us a wall in Judah and in Jerusalem."

Nehemiah 9:16-19 "¹⁶But they and our fathers dealt proudly, and hardened their necks, and hearkened not to thy commandments, ¹⁷And refused to obey, neither were mindful of thy wonders that thou didst among them; but hardened their necks, and in their rebellion appointed a captain to return to their bondage: but thou art a God ready to pardon, gracious and merciful, slow to anger, and of great kindness, and forsookest them not. ¹⁸Yea, when they had made them a

molten calf, and said, This is thy God that brought thee up out of Egypt, and had wrought great provocations; ¹⁹Yet thou in thy manifold mercies forsookest them not in the wilderness: the pillar of the cloud departed not from them by day, to lead them in the way; neither the pillar of fire by night, to shew them light, and the way wherein they should go."

Nehemiah 9:31-33 "³¹Nevertheless for thy great mercies' sake thou didst not utterly consume them, nor forsake them; for thou art a gracious and merciful God. ³²Now therefore, our God, the great, the mighty, and the terrible God, who keepest covenant and mercy, let not all the trouble seem little before thee, that hath come upon us, on our kings, on our princes, and on our priests, and on our prophets, and on our fathers, and on all thy people, since the time of the kings of Assyria unto this day. ³³Howbeit thou art just in all that is brought upon us; for thou hast done right, but we have done wickedly:"

Job 8:20 "Behold, God will not cast away a perfect man, neither will he help the evil doers:"

Psalm 9:10 "And they that know thy name will put their trust in thee: for thou, LORD, hast not forsaken them that seek thee."

Psalm 37:25 "I have been young, and now am old; yet have I not seen the righteous forsaken, nor his seed begging bread."

Psalm 37:28 "For the LORD loveth judgment, and forsaketh not his saints; they are preserved for ever: but the seed of the wicked shall be cut off."

Psalm 94:14 "For the LORD will not cast off his people, neither will he forsake his inheritance."

Isaiah 49:14-16 "¹⁴But Zion said, The LORD hath forsaken me, and my Lord hath forgotten me. ¹⁵Can a woman forget her sucking child, that she should not have compassion on the son of her womb? yea, they may forget, yet will I not forget thee. ¹⁶Behold, I have graven thee upon the palms of my hands; thy walls are continually before me."

Romans 11:1-4 "¹I say then, Hath God cast away his people? God forbid. For I also am an Israelite, of the seed of Abraham, of the tribe of Benjamin. ²God hath not cast away his people which he foreknew. Wot ye not what the scripture saith of Elias? how he maketh intercession to God against Israel, saying, ³Lord, they have killed thy prophets, and digged down thine altars; and I am left alone, and they seek my life. ⁴But what saith the answer of God unto him? I have reserved to myself seven thousand men, who have not bowed the knee to the image of Baal."

Hebrews 13:5-6 "⁵Let your conversation be without covetousness; and be content with such things as ye have: for he hath said, I will never leave thee, nor forsake thee. ⁶So that we may boldly say, The Lord is my helper, and I will not fear what man shall do unto me."

FOUNDATION

The Apostles Being A Foundation
Matthew 16:17-18 "¹⁷And Jesus answered and said unto him, Blessed art thou, Simon Barjona: for flesh and blood hath not revealed it unto thee, but my Father which is in heaven. ¹⁸And I say also unto thee, That thou art Peter, and upon this rock I will build my church; and the gates of hell shall not prevail against it."

Ephesians 2:19-20 "¹⁹Now therefore ye are no more strangers and foreigners, but fellowcitizens with the saints, and of the household of God; ²⁰And are built upon the foundation of the apostles and prophets, Jesus Christ himself being the chief corner stone;"

Revelation 21:14 "And the wall of the city had twelve foundations, and in them the names of the twelve apostles of the Lamb."

The Cornerstone (Jesus Christ)
Genesis 49:24 "But his bow abode in strength, and the arms of his hands were made strong by the hands of the mighty God of Jacob; (from thence is the shepherd, the stone of Israel:)"

Psalm 118:19-22 "¹⁹Open to me the gates of righteousness: I will go into them, and I will praise the LORD: ²⁰This gate of the LORD, into which the righteous shall enter. ²¹I will praise thee: for thou hast heard me, and art become my salvation. ²²The stone which the builders refused is become the head stone of the corner."

Isaiah 28:14-16 "¹⁴Wherefore hear the word of the LORD, ye scornful men, that rule this people which is in Jerusalem. ¹⁵Because ye have said, We have made a covenant with death, and with hell are we at agreement; when the overflowing scourge shall pass through, it shall not come unto us: for we have made lies our refuge, and under falsehood have we hid ourselves: ¹⁶Therefore thus saith the Lord GOD, Behold, I lay in Zion for a foundation a stone, a tried stone, a precious corner stone, a sure foundation: he that believeth shall not make haste."

Zechariah 6:12 "And speak unto him, saying, Thus speaketh the LORD of hosts, saying, Behold the man whose name is The BRANCH; and he shall grow up out of his place, and he shall build the temple of the LORD:"

Matthew 21:42 "Jesus saith unto them, Did ye never read in the scriptures, The stone which the builders rejected, the same is become the head of the corner: this is the Lord's doing, and it is marvellous in our eyes?"

Luke 20:9-18 "⁹Then began he to speak to the people this parable; A certain man planted a vineyard, and let it forth to husbandmen, and went into a far country for a long time. ¹⁰And at the season he sent a servant to the husbandmen, that they should give him of the fruit of the vineyard: but the husbandmen beat him, and sent him away empty. ¹¹And again he sent another servant: and they beat him also, and entreated him shamefully, and sent him away empty. ¹²And again he sent a third: and they wounded him also, and cast him out. ¹³Then said the lord of the vineyard, What shall I do? I will send my beloved son: it may be they will reverence him when they see him. ¹⁴But when the husbandmen saw him, they reasoned among themselves, saying, This is the heir: come, let us kill him, that the inheritance may be ours. ¹⁵So they cast him out of the vineyard, and killed him. What therefore shall the lord of the vineyard do unto them? ¹⁶He shall come and destroy these husbandmen, and shall give the vineyard to others. And when they heard it, they said, God forbid. ¹⁷And he beheld them, and said, What is this then that is written, The stone which the builders rejected, the same is become the head of the corner? ¹⁸Whosoever shall fall upon that stone shall be broken; but on whomsoever it shall fall, it will grind him to powder."

Acts 4:9-11 "⁹If we this day be examined of the good deed done to the impotent man, by what means he is made whole; ¹⁰Be it known unto you all, and to all the people of Israel, that by the name of Jesus Christ of Nazareth, whom ye crucified, whom God raised from the dead, even by him doth this man stand here before you whole. ¹¹This is the stone which was set at nought of you builders, which is become the head of the corner."

Romans 9:30-33 "³⁰What shall we say then? That the Gentiles, which followed not after righteousness, have attained to righteousness, even the righteousness which is of faith. ³¹But Israel, which followed after the law of righteousness, hath not attained to the law of righteousness. ³²Wherefore? Because they sought it not by faith, but as it were by the works of the law. For they stumbled at that stumblingstone; ³³As it is written, Behold, I lay in Sion a stumblingstone and rock of offence: and whosoever believeth on him shall not be ashamed."

Ephesians 2:19-22 "¹⁹Now therefore ye are no more strangers and foreigners, but fellowcitizens with the saints, and of the household of God; ²⁰And are built upon the foundation of the apostles and prophets, Jesus Christ himself being the chief corner stone; ²¹In whom all the building fitly framed together groweth unto an holy temple in the Lord: ²²In whom ye also are builded together for an habitation of God through the Spirit."

1 Peter 2:4-8 "⁴To whom coming, as unto a living stone, disallowed indeed of men, but chosen of God, and precious, ⁵Ye also, as lively stones, are built up a spiritual house, an holy priesthood, to offer up spiritual sacrifices, acceptable to God by Jesus Christ. ⁶Wherefore also it is contained in the scripture, Behold, I lay in Sion a chief corner stone, elect, precious: and he that believeth on him shall not be confounded. ⁷Unto you therefore which believe he is precious: but unto them which be disobedient, the stone which the builders disallowed, the same is made the head of the corner, ⁸And a stone of stumbling, and a rock of offence, even to them which stumble at the

word, being disobedient: whereunto also they were appointed."

The Foundation Of God

2 Timothy 2:19 "Nevertheless the foundation of God standeth sure, having this seal, The Lord knoweth them that are his. And, Let every one that nameth the name of Christ depart from iniquity."

The Lord Being A Rock

Genesis 49:24 "But his bow abode in strength, and the arms of his hands were made strong by the hands of the mighty God of Jacob; (from thence is the shepherd, the stone of Israel:)"

Exodus 17:6 "Behold, I will stand before thee there upon the rock in Horeb; and thou shalt smite the rock, and there shall come water out of it, that the people may drink. And Moses did so in the sight of the elders of Israel."

Numbers 20:10-11 "¹⁰And Moses and Aaron gathered the congregation together before the rock, and he said unto them, Hear now, ye rebels; must we fetch you water out of this rock? ¹¹And Moses lifted up his hand, and with his rod he smote the rock twice: and the water came out abundantly, and the congregation drank, and their beasts also."

Deuteronomy 32:4 "He is the Rock, his work is perfect: for all his ways are judgment: a God of truth and without iniquity, just and right is he."

Deuteronomy 32:17-18 "¹⁷They sacrificed unto devils, not to God; to gods whom they knew not, to new gods that came newly up, whom your fathers feared not. ¹⁸Of the Rock that begat thee thou art unmindful, and hast forgotten God that formed thee."

Deuteronomy 32:31 "For their rock is not as our Rock, even our enemies themselves being judges."

1 Samuel 2:2 "There is none holy as the LORD: for there is none beside thee: neither is there any rock like our God."

2 Samuel 22:2-3 "²And he said, The LORD is my rock, and my fortress, and my deliverer; ³The God of my rock; in him will I trust: he is my shield, and the horn of my salvation, my high tower, and my refuge, my saviour; thou savest me from violence."

2 Samuel 22:32 "For who is God, save the LORD? and who is a rock, save our God?"

2 Samuel 22:47 "The LORD liveth; and blessed be my rock; and exalted be the God of the rock of my salvation."

2 Samuel 23:3 "The God of Israel said, the Rock of Israel spake to me, He that ruleth over men must be just, ruling in the fear of God."

Psalm 18:2 "The LORD is my rock, and my fortress, and my deliverer; my God, my strength, in whom I will trust; my buckler, and the horn of my salvation, and my high tower."

Psalm 18:31 "For who is God save the LORD? or who is a rock save our God?"

Psalm 18:46 "The LORD liveth; and blessed be my rock; and let the God of my salvation be exalted."

Psalm 28:1 "Unto thee will I cry, O LORD my rock; be not silent to me: lest, if thou be silent to me, I become like them that go down into the pit."

Psalm 31:1-3 "1In thee, O LORD, do I put my trust; let me never be ashamed: deliver me in thy righteousness. 2Bow down thine ear to me; deliver me speedily: be thou my strong rock, for an house of defence to save me. 3For thou art my rock and my fortress; therefore for thy name's sake lead me, and guide me."

Psalm 62:1-2 "1Truly my soul waiteth upon God: from him cometh my salvation. 2He only is my rock and my salvation; he is my defence; I shall not be greatly moved."

Psalm 62:6-7 "6He only is my rock and my salvation: he is my defence; I shall not be moved. 7In God is my salvation and my glory: the rock of my strength, and my refuge, is in God."

Psalm 71:1-3 "1In thee, O LORD, do I put my trust: let me never be put to confusion. 2Deliver me in thy righteousness, and cause me to escape: incline thine ear unto me, and save me. 3Be thou my strong habitation, whereunto I may continually resort: thou hast given commandment to save me; for thou art my rock and my fortress."

Psalm 78:15 "He clave the rocks in the wilderness, and gave them drink as out of the great depths."

Psalm 78:19-20 "19Yea, they spake against God; they said, Can God furnish a table in the wilderness? 20Behold, he smote the rock, that the waters gushed out, and the streams overflowed; can he give bread also? can he provide flesh for his people?"

Psalm 78:34-35 "34When he slew them, then they sought him: and they returned and inquired early after God. 35And they remembered that God was their rock, and the high God their redeemer."

Psalm 89:26 "He shall cry unto me, Thou art my father, my God, and the rock of my salvation."

Psalm 92:15 "To shew that the LORD is upright: he is my rock, and there is no unrighteousness in him."

Psalm 95:1 "O come, let us sing unto the LORD: let us make a joyful noise to the rock of our salvation."

1 Corinthians 10:1-4 "1Moreover, brethren, I would not that ye should be ignorant, how that all our fathers were under the cloud, and all passed through the sea; 2And were all baptized unto Moses in the cloud and in the sea; 3And did all eat the same spiritual meat; 4And did all drink the same spiritual drink: for they drank of that spiritual Rock that followed them: and that Rock was Christ."

There Being No Real Foundation
Other Than Jesus Christ

Acts 4:9-12 "9If we this day be examined of the good deed done to the impotent man, by what means he is made whole; 10Be it known unto you all, and to all the people of Israel, that by the name of Jesus Christ of Nazareth, whom ye crucified, whom God raised from the dead, even by him doth this man stand here before you whole. 11This is the stone which was set at nought of you builders, which is become the head of the corner. 12Neither is there salvation in any other: for there is none other name under heaven given among men, whereby we must be saved."

1 Corinthians 3:10-11 "10According to the grace of God which is given unto me, as a wise masterbuilder, I have laid the foundation, and another buildeth thereon. But let every man take heed how he buildeth thereupon. 11For other foundation can no man lay than that is laid, which is Jesus Christ."

Who Is Likened To A Man
That Built His House Upon A Rock

Matthew 7:24-28 "24Therefore whosoever heareth these sayings of mine, and doeth them, I will liken him unto a wise man, which built his house upon a rock: 25And the rain descended, and the floods came, and the winds blew, and beat upon that house; and it fell not: for it was founded upon a rock. 26And every one that heareth these sayings of mine, and doeth them not, shall be likened unto a foolish man, which built his house upon the sand: 27And the rain descended, and the floods came, and the winds blew, and beat upon that house; and it fell: and great was the fall of it. 28And it came to pass, when Jesus had ended these sayings, the people were astonished at his doctrine:"

Luke 6:46-48 "46And why call ye me, Lord, Lord, and do not the things which I say? 47Whosoever cometh to me, and heareth my sayings, and doeth them, I will shew you to whom he is like: 48He is like a man which built an house, and digged deep, and laid the foundation on a rock: and when the flood arose, the stream beat vehemently upon that house, and could not shake it: for it was founded upon a rock."

Who Is Likened To A Man
That Built His House Upon Sand

Matthew 7:26-28 "26And every one that heareth these sayings of mine, and doeth them not, shall be likened unto a foolish man, which built his house upon the sand: 27And the rain descended, and the floods came, and the winds blew, and beat upon that house; and it fell: and great was the fall of it. 28And it came to pass, when Jesus had ended these sayings, the people were astonished at his doctrine:"

Luke 6:46-49 "46And why call ye me, Lord, Lord, and do not the things which I say? 47Whosoever cometh to me, and heareth my sayings, and doeth them, I will shew you to whom he is like: 48He is like a man which built an house, and digged deep, and laid the foundation on a rock: and when the flood arose, the stream beat vehemently upon that house, and could not shake it: for it was founded upon a rock. 49But he that heareth, and doeth not, is like a man that without a foundation built an house upon the earth; against which the stream did beat vehemently, and immediately it fell; and the ruin of that house was great."

FREEDOM/LIBERTY

Jesus Christ Making You Free

John 8:36 "If the Son therefore shall make you free, ye shall be free indeed."

Galatians 5:1 "Stand fast therefore in the liberty wherewith Christ hath made us free, and be not entangled again with the yoke of bondage."

What Frees You

John 8:32 "And ye shall know the truth, and the truth shall make you free."

Romans 8:1-2 "1There is therefore now no condemnation to them which are in Christ Jesus, who walk not after the flesh, but after the Spirit. 2For the law of the Spirit of life in Christ Jesus hath made me free from the law of sin and death."

What Not To Use Liberty For

Galatians 5:13 "For, brethren, ye have been called unto liberty; only use not liberty for an occasion to the flesh, but by love serve one another."

1 Peter 2:16 "As free, and not using your liberty for a cloke of maliciousness, but as the servants of God."

What Shall Be Liberated From
The Bondage Of Corruption

Romans 8:20-21 "20For the creature was made subject to vanity, not willingly, but by reason of him who hath subjected the same in hope, 21Because the creature itself also shall be delivered from the bondage of corruption into the glorious liberty of the children of God."

Where Liberty Is

2 Corinthians 3:17 "Now the Lord is that Spirit: and where the Spirit of the Lord is, there is liberty."

Who Is Free

Psalm 119:41-45 "41Let thy mercies come also unto me, O LORD, even thy salvation, according to thy word. 42So shall I have wherewith to answer him that reproacheth me: for I trust in thy word. 43And take not the word of truth utterly out of my mouth; for I have hoped in thy judgments. 44So shall I keep thy law continually for ever and ever. 45And I will walk at liberty: for I seek thy precepts."

John 8:36 "If the Son therefore shall make you free, ye shall be free indeed."

Romans 6:1-7 "¹What shall we say then? Shall we continue in sin, that grace may abound? ²God forbid. How shall we, that are dead to sin, live any longer therein? ³Know ye not, that so many of us as were baptized into Jesus Christ were baptized into his death? ⁴Therefore we are buried with him by baptism into death: that like as Christ was raised up from the dead by the glory of the Father, even so we also should walk in newness of life. ⁵For if we have been planted together in the likeness of his death, we shall be also in the likeness of his resurrection: ⁶Knowing this, that our old man is crucified with him, that the body of sin might be destroyed, that henceforth we should not serve sin. ⁷For he that is dead is freed from sin."

Romans 8:1-2 "¹There is therefore now no condemnation to them which are in Christ Jesus, who walk not after the flesh, but after the Spirit. ²For the law of the Spirit of life in Christ Jesus hath made me free from the law of sin and death."

1 Corinthians 7:22-23 "²²For he that is called in the Lord, being a servant, is the Lord's freeman: likewise also he that is called, being free, is Christ's servant. ²³Ye are bought with a price; be not ye the servants of men."

Who The Lord Liberates

Psalm 146:5-7 "⁵Happy is he that hath the God of Jacob for his help, whose hope is in the LORD his God: ⁶Which made heaven, and earth, the sea, and all that therein is: which keepeth truth for ever: ⁷Which executeth judgment for the oppressed: which giveth food to the hungry. The LORD looseth the prisoners:"

Isaiah 42:1-7 "¹Behold my servant, whom I uphold; mine elect, in whom my soul delighteth; I have put my spirit upon him: he shall bring forth judgment to the Gentiles. ²He shall not cry, nor lift up, nor cause his voice to be heard in the street. ³A bruised reed shall he not break, and the smoking flax shall he not quench: he shall bring forth judgment unto truth. ⁴He shall not fail nor be discouraged, till he have set judgment in the earth: and the isles shall wait for his law. ⁵Thus saith God the LORD, he that created the heavens, and stretched them out; he that spread forth the earth, and that which cometh out of it; he that giveth breath unto the people upon it, and spirit

to them that walk therein: ⁶I the LORD have called thee in righteousness, and will hold thine hand, and will keep thee, and give thee for a covenant of the people, for a light of the Gentiles; ⁷To open the blind eyes, to bring out the prisoners from the prison, and them that sit in darkness out of the prison house."

Isaiah 61:1 "The Spirit of the Lord GOD is upon me; because the LORD hath anointed me to preach good tidings unto the meek; he hath sent me to bind up the brokenhearted, to proclaim liberty to the captives, and the opening of the prison to them that are bound;"

Luke 4:14-18 "¹⁴And Jesus returned in the power of the Spirit into Galilee: and there went out a fame of him through all the region round about. ¹⁵And he taught in their synagogues, being glorified of all. ¹⁶And he came to Nazareth, where he had been brought up: and, as his custom was, he went into the synagogue on the sabbath day, and stood up for to read. ¹⁷And there was delivered unto him the book of the prophet Esaias. And when he had opened the book, he found the place where it was written, ¹⁸The Spirit of the Lord is upon me, because he hath anointed me to preach the gospel to the poor; he hath sent me to heal the brokenhearted, to preach deliverance to the captives, and recovering of sight to the blind, to set at liberty them that are bruised,"

FRIENDSHIP

Friends

Proverbs 17:17 "A friend loveth at all times, and a brother is born for adversity."

The Friendship Of The World

James 4:4 "Ye adulterers and adulteresses, know ye not that the friendship of the world is enmity with God? whosoever therefore will be a friend of the world is the enemy of God."

The Wounds Of A Friend

Proverbs 27:6 "Faithful are the wounds of a friend; but the kisses of an enemy are deceitful."

There Being A Friend
That Sticks Closer Than A Brother

Proverbs 18:24 "A man that hath friends must shew himself friendly: and there is a friend that sticketh closer than a brother."

Those That Are A Friend Of The World
James 4:4 "Ye adulterers and adulteresses, know ye not that the friendship of the world is enmity with God? whosoever therefore will be a friend of the world is the enemy of God."

Those That Have Friends
Proverbs 18:24 "A man that hath friends must shew himself friendly: and there is a friend that sticketh closer than a brother."

Who Is Everyone's Friend
Proverbs 19:6 "Many will intreat the favour of the prince: and every man is a friend to him that giveth gifts."

Who Is The Lord's Friend
Isaiah 41:8-10 "8But thou, Israel, art my servant, Jacob whom I have chosen, the seed of Abraham my friend. 9Thou whom I have taken from the ends of the earth, and called thee from the chief men thereof, and said unto thee, Thou art my servant; I have chosen thee, and not cast thee away. 10Fear thou not; for I am with thee: be not dismayed; for I am thy God: I will strengthen thee; yea, I will help thee; yea, I will uphold thee with the right hand of my righteousness."

John 15:1-16 "1I am the true vine, and my Father is the husbandman. 2Every branch in me that beareth not fruit he taketh away: and every branch that beareth fruit, he purgeth it, that it may bring forth more fruit. 3Now ye are clean through the word which I have spoken unto you. 4Abide in me, and I in you. As the branch cannot bear fruit of itself, except it abide in the vine; no more can ye, except ye abide in me. 5I am the vine, ye are the branches: He that abideth in me, and I in him, the same bringeth forth much fruit: for without me ye can do nothing. 6If a man abide not in me, he is cast forth as a branch, and is withered; and men gather them, and cast them into the fire, and they are burned. 7If ye abide in me, and my words abide in you, ye shall ask what ye will, and it shall be done unto you. 8Herein is my Father glorified, that ye bear much fruit; so shall ye be my disciples. 9As the Father hath loved me, so have I loved you: continue ye in my love. 10If ye keep my commandments, ye shall abide in my love; even as I have kept my Father's commandments, and abide in his love. 11These things have I spoken unto you, that my joy might remain in you, and that your joy might be full. 12This is my commandment, That ye love one another, as I have loved you. 13Greater love hath no man than this, that a man lay down his life for his friends. 14Ye are my friends, if ye do whatsoever I command you. 15Henceforth I call you not servants; for the servant knoweth not what his lord doeth: but I have called you friends; for all things that I have heard of my Father I have made known unto you. 16Ye have not chosen me, but I have chosen you, and ordained you, that ye should go and bring forth fruit, and that your fruit should remain: that whatsoever ye shall ask of the Father in my name, he may give it you."

James 2:23 "And the scripture was fulfilled which saith, Abraham believed God, and it was imputed unto him for righteousness: and he was called the Friend of God."

Who Separates Friends
Proverbs 17:9 "He that covereth a transgression seeketh love; but he that repeateth a matter separateth very friends."

FROWARDNESS

Putting Away A Froward Mouth
Proverbs 4:24 "Put away from thee a froward mouth, and perverse lips put far from thee."

The Froward
2 Samuel 22:21-27 "21The LORD rewarded me according to my righteousness: according to the cleanness of my hands hath he recompensed me. 22For I have kept the ways of the LORD, and have not wickedly departed from my God. 23For all his judgments were before me: and as for his statutes, I did not depart from them. 24I was also upright before him, and have kept myself from mine iniquity. 25Therefore the LORD hath recompensed me according to my righteousness; according to my cleanness in his eye sight. 26With the merciful thou wilt shew thyself merciful, and with the upright man thou wilt shew thyself upright. 27With the pure thou wilt shew thyself pure; and with the froward thou wilt shew thyself unsavoury."

Job 5:12-14 "12He disappointeth the devices of the crafty, so that their hands cannot perform their enterprise. 13He taketh the wise in their own craftiness: and the counsel of the froward is carried headlong. [14]They meet with darkness in the day-time, and grope in the noonday as in the night."

Psalm 18:24-26 "[24]Therefore hath the LORD recompensed me according to my righteousness, according to the cleanness of my hands in his eyesight. [25]With the merciful thou wilt shew thyself merciful; with an upright man thou wilt shew thyself upright; [26]With the pure thou wilt shew thyself pure; and with the froward thou wilt shew thyself froward."

Proverbs 3:32 "For the froward is abomination to the LORD: but his secret is with the righteous."

Proverbs 16:28 "A froward man soweth strife: and a whisperer separateth chief friends."

Proverbs 22:5 "Thorns and snares are in the way of the froward: he that doth keep his soul shall be far from them."

The Froward Mouth
Proverbs 8:12-13 "[12]I wisdom dwell with prudence, and find out knowledge of witty inventions. [13]The fear of the LORD is to hate evil: pride, and arrogancy, and the evil way, and the froward mouth, do I hate."

Proverbs 10:31 "The mouth of the just bringeth forth wisdom: but the froward tongue shall be cut out."

Those That Have A Froward Heart
Proverbs 11:20 "They that are of a froward heart are abomination to the LORD: but such as are upright in their way are his delight."

Proverbs 17:20 "He that hath a froward heart findeth no good: and he that hath a perverse tongue falleth into mischief."

What Has Nothing Froward In It
Proverbs 8:1-8 "[1]Doth not wisdom cry? and understanding put forth her voice? [2]She standeth in the top of high places, by the way in the places of the paths. [3]She crieth at the gates, at the entry of the city, at the coming in at the doors. [4]Unto you, O men, I call; and my voice is to the sons of man. [5]O ye simple, understand wisdom: and, ye fools, be ye of an understanding heart. [6]Hear; for I will speak of excellent things; and the opening of my lips shall be right things. [7]For my mouth shall speak truth;

and wickedness is an abomination to my lips. [8]All the words of my mouth are in righteousness; there is nothing froward or perverse in them."

What Is Froward
Proverbs 21:8 "The way of man is froward and strange: but as for the pure, his work is right."

Who Speaks Frowardness
Proverbs 2:11-14 "[11]Discretion shall preserve thee, understanding shall keep thee: [12]To deliver thee from the way of the evil man, from the man that speaketh froward things; [13]Who leave the paths of uprightness, to walk in the ways of darkness; [14]Who rejoice to do evil, and delight in the frowardness of the wicked;"

Proverbs 10:32 "The lips of the righteous know what is acceptable: but the mouth of the wicked speaketh frowardness."

Proverbs 16:29-30 "[29]A violent man enticeth his neighbour, and leadeth him into the way that is not good. [30]He shutteth his eyes to devise froward things: moving his lips he bringeth evil to pass."

Who The Lord Shows Himself Froward Toward
2 Samuel 22:21-27 "[21]The LORD rewarded me according to my righteousness: according to the cleanness of my hands hath he recompensed me. [22]For I have kept the ways of the LORD, and have not wickedly departed from my God. [23]For all his judgments were before me: and as for his statutes, I did not depart from them. [24]I was also upright before him, and have kept myself from mine iniquity. [25]Therefore the LORD hath recompensed me according to my righteousness; according to my cleanness in his eye sight. [26]With the merciful thou wilt shew thyself merciful, and with the upright man thou wilt shew thyself upright. [27]With the pure thou wilt shew thyself pure; and with the froward thou wilt shew thyself unsavoury."

Psalm 18:24-26 "[24]Therefore hath the LORD recompensed me according to my righteousness, according to the cleanness of my hands in his eyesight. [25]With the merciful thou wilt shew thyself merciful; with an upright man thou wilt shew thyself upright; [26]With the pure thou wilt shew thyself pure; and with the froward thou wilt shew thyself froward."

G g

GATHERING

Gathering People Together
To Learn Of The Lord

Deuteronomy 31:12-13 "[12]Gather the people to-gether, men, and women, and children, and thy stranger that is within thy gates, that they may hear, and that they may learn, and fear the LORD your God, and observe to do all the words of this law: [13]And that their children, which have not known any thing, may hear, and learn to fear the LORD your God, as long as ye live in the land whither ye go over Jordan to possess it."

The Lord Gathering His Saints

Psalm 50:1-6 "[1]The mighty God, even the LORD, hath spoken, and called the earth from the rising of the sun unto the going down thereof. [2]Out of Zion, the perfection of beauty, God hath shined. [3]Our God shall come, and shall not keep silence: a fire shall devour before him, and it shall be very tempestuous round about him. [4]He shall call to the heavens from above, and to the earth, that he may judge his people. [5]Gather my saints together unto me; those that have made a covenant with me by sacrifice. [6]And the heavens shall declare his righteousness: for God is judge himself. Selah."

Matthew 24:29-31 "[29]Immediately after the tribulation of those days shall the sun be darkened, and the moon shall not give her light, and the stars shall fall from heaven, and the powers of the heavens shall be shaken: [30]And then shall appear the sign of the Son of man in heaven: and then shall all the tribes of the earth mourn, and they shall see the Son of man coming in the clouds of heaven with power and great glory. [31]And he shall send his angels with a great sound of a trumpet, and they shall gather together his elect from the four winds, from one end of heaven to the other."

Mark 13:24-27 "[24]But in those days, after that tribulation, the sun shall be darkened, and the moon shall not give her light, [25]And the stars of heaven shall fall, and the powers that are in heaven shall be shaken. [26]And then shall they see the Son of man coming in the clouds with great power and glory. [27]And then shall he send his angels, and shall gather together his elect from the four winds, from the uttermost part of the earth to the uttermost part of heaven."

Ephesians 1:3-10 "[3]Blessed be the God and Father of our Lord Jesus Christ, who hath blessed us with all spiritual blessings in heavenly places in Christ: [4]According as he hath chosen us in him before the foundation of the world, that we should be holy and without blame before him in love: [5]Having predestinated us unto the adoption of children by Jesus Christ to himself, according to the good pleasure of his will, [6]To the praise of the glory of his grace, wherein he hath made us accepted in the beloved. [7]In whom we have redemption through his blood, the forgiveness of sins, according to the riches of his grace; [8]Wherein he hath abounded toward us in all wisdom and prudence; [9]Having made known unto us the mystery of his will, according to his good pleasure which he hath purposed in himself: [10]That in the dispensation of the fulness of times he might gather together in one all things in Christ, both which are in heaven, and which are on earth; even in him:"

The Lord Gathering The Nations Together

Isaiah 66:17-18 "[17]They that sanctify themselves, and purify themselves in the gardens behind one tree in the midst, eating swine's flesh, and the abomination, and the mouse, shall be consumed together, saith the LORD. [18]For I know their works and their thoughts: it shall come, that I will gather all nations and tongues; and they shall come, and see my glory."

Joel 3:1-14 "[1]For, behold, in those days, and in that time, when I shall bring again the captivity of Judah and Jerusalem, [2]I will also gather all nations, and will bring them down into the valley of Jehoshaphat, and will plead with them there for my people and for my heritage Israel, whom they have scattered among the nations, and parted my land. [3]And they have cast lots for my people; and have given a boy for an harlot, and sold a girl for wine, that they might drink. [4]Yea, and what have ye to do with me, O Tyre, and Zidon, and all the coasts of Palestine? will ye render me a recompence? and if ye recompence me, swiftly and speedily will I return your recompence upon your own head; [5]Because ye have taken my silver and my gold, and have carried into your temples my goodly pleasant things: ⁶The children also of Judah and the children of Jerusalem have ye sold unto the Grecians, that ye might remove them far from their border. ⁷Behold, I will raise them out of the place whither ye have sold them, and will return your recompence upon your own head: ⁸And I will sell your sons and your daughters into the hand of the children of Judah, and they shall sell them to the Sabeans, to a people far off: for the LORD hath spoken it. ⁹Proclaim ye this among the Gentiles; Prepare war, wake up the mighty men, let all the men of war draw near; let them come up: ¹⁰Beat your plowshares into swords, and your pruninghooks into spears: let the weak say, I am strong. ¹¹Assemble yourselves, and come, all ye heathen, and gather yourselves together round about: thither cause thy mighty ones to come down, O LORD. ¹²Let the heathen be wakened, and come up to the valley of Jehoshaphat: for there will I sit to judge all the heathen round about. ¹³Put ye in the sickle, for the harvest is ripe: come, get you down; for the press is full, the fats overflow; for their wickedness is great. ¹⁴Multitudes, multitudes in the valley of decision: for the day of the LORD is near in the valley of decision."

Zephaniah 3:8 "Therefore wait ye upon me, saith the LORD, until the day that I rise up to the prey: for my determination is to gather the nations, that I may assemble the kingdoms, to pour upon them mine indignation, even all my fierce anger: for all the earth shall be devoured with the fire of my jealousy."

Zechariah 12:1-3 "¹The burden of the word of the LORD for Israel, saith the LORD, which stretcheth forth the heavens, and layeth the foundation of the earth, and formeth the spirit of man within him. ²Behold, I will make Jerusalem a cup of trembling unto all the people round about, when they shall be in the siege both against Judah and against Jerusalem. ³And in that day will I make Jerusalem a burdensome stone for all people: all that burden themselves with it shall be cut in pieces, though all the people of the earth be gathered together against it."

Zechariah 14:1-2 "¹Behold, the day of the LORD cometh, and thy spoil shall be divided in the midst of thee. ²For I will gather all nations against Jerusalem to battle; and the city shall be taken, and the houses rifled, and the women ravished; and half of the city shall go forth into captivity, and the residue of the people shall not be cut off from the city."

Matthew 25:31-33 "³¹When the Son of man shall come in his glory, and all the holy angels with him, then shall he sit upon the throne of his glory: ³²And before him shall be gathered all nations: and he shall separate them one from another, as a shepherd divideth his sheep from the goats: ³³And he shall set the sheep on his right hand, but the goats on the left."

Revelation 16:13-16 "¹³And I saw three unclean spirits like frogs come out of the mouth of the dragon, and out of the mouth of the beast, and out of the mouth of the false prophet. ¹⁴For they are the spirits of devils, working miracles, which go forth unto the kings of the earth and of the whole world, to gather them to the battle of that great day of God Almighty. ¹⁵Behold, I come as a thief. Blessed is he that watcheth, and keepeth his garments, lest he walk naked, and they see his shame. ¹⁶And he gathered them together into a place called in the Hebrew tongue Armageddon."

The Place Where People Are Gathered In Christ's Name

Matthew 18:19-22 "¹⁹Again I say unto you, That if two of you shall agree on earth as touching any thing that they shall ask, it shall be done for them of my Father which is in heaven. ²⁰For where two or three are gathered together in my name, there am I in the midst of them. ²¹Then came Peter to him, and said, Lord, how oft shall my brother sin against me, and I forgive him? till seven times? ²²Jesus saith unto him, I say not unto thee, Until seven times: but, Until seventy times seven."

GENTILES/HEATHEN

Gentiles And Jews Being Equal In Christ

Acts 15:6-9 "⁶And the apostles and elders came together for to consider of this matter. ⁷And when there had been much disputing, Peter rose up, and said unto them, Men and brethren, ye know how that a good while ago God made choice among us, that the Gentiles by my mouth should hear the word of the gospel, and believe. [8]And God, which knoweth the hearts, bare them witness, giving them the Holy Ghost, even as he did unto us; [9]And put no difference between us and them, purifying their hearts by faith."

Romans 3:21-22 "[21]But now the righteousness of God without the law is manifested, being witnessed by the law and the prophets; [22]Even the righteousness of God which is by faith of Jesus Christ unto all and upon all them that believe: for there is no difference:"

Romans 10:12-13 "[12]For there is no difference between the Jew and the Greek: for the same Lord over all is rich unto all that call upon him. [13]For whosoever shall call upon the name of the Lord shall be saved."

1 Corinthians 12:12-13 "[12]For as the body is one, and hath many members, and all the members of that one body, being many, are one body: so also is Christ. [13]For by one Spirit are we all baptized into one body, whether we be Jews or Gentiles, whether we be bond or free; and have been all made to drink into one Spirit."

Galatians 3:27-29 "[27]For as many of you as have been baptized into Christ have put on Christ. [28]There is neither Jew nor Greek, there is neither bond nor free, there is neither male nor female: for ye are all one in Christ Jesus. [29]And if ye be Christ's, then are ye Abraham's seed, and heirs according to the promise."

Colossians 3:8-11 "[8]But now ye also put off all these; anger, wrath, malice, blasphemy, filthy communication out of your mouth. [9]Lie not one to another, seeing that ye have put off the old man with his deeds; [10]And have put on the new man, which is renewed in knowledge after the image of him that created him: [11]Where there is neither Greek nor Jew, circumcision nor uncircumcision, Barbarian, Scythian, bond nor free: but Christ is all, and in all."

Gentiles Being Under Sin
Romans 3:9-12 "[9]What then? are we better than they? No, in no wise: for we have before proved both Jews and Gentiles, that they are all under sin; [10]As it is written, There is none righteous, no, not one: [11]There is none that understandeth, there is none that seeketh after God. [12]They are

all gone out of the way, they are together become unprofitable; there is none that doeth good, no, not one."

Salvation Coming To The Gentiles
Acts 15:6-11 "[6]And the apostles and elders came together for to consider of this matter. [7]And when there had been much disputing, Peter rose up, and said unto them, Men and brethren, ye know how that a good while ago God made choice among us, that the Gentiles by my mouth should hear the word of the gospel, and believe. [8]And God, which knoweth the hearts, bare them witness, giving them the Holy Ghost, even as he did unto us; [9]And put no difference between us and them, purifying their hearts by faith. [10]Now therefore why tempt ye God, to put a yoke upon the neck of the disciples, which neither our fathers nor we were able to bear? [11]But we believe that through the grace of the Lord Jesus Christ we shall be saved, even as they."

Acts 28:25-28 "[25]And when they agreed not among themselves, they departed, after that Paul had spoken one word, Well spake the Holy Ghost by Esaias the prophet unto our fathers, [26]Saying, Go unto this people, and say, Hearing ye shall hear, and shall not understand; and seeing ye shall see, and not perceive: [27]For the heart of this people is waxed gross, and their ears are dull of hearing, and their eyes have they closed; lest they should see with their eyes, and hear with their ears, and understand with their heart, and should be converted, and I should heal them. [28]Be it known therefore unto you, that the salvation of God is sent unto the Gentiles, and that they will hear it."

Romans 9:30-33 "[30]What shall we say then? That the Gentiles, which followed not after righteousness, have attained to righteousness, even the righteousness which is of faith. [31]But Israel, which followed after the law of righteousness, hath not attained to the law of righteousness. [32]Wherefore? Because they sought it not by faith, but as it were by the works of the law. For they stumbled at that stumblingstone; [33]As it is written, Behold, I lay in Sion a stumblingstone and rock of offence: and whosoever believeth on him shall not be ashamed."

Romans 11:1-32 "[1]I say then, Hath God cast away his people? God forbid. For I also am an Israelite, of the seed of Abraham, of the tribe of Benjamin. [2]God hath not cast away his people which he foreknew. Wot ye not what the scripture saith of Elias? how he maketh intercession to God against Israel, saying, [3]Lord, they have killed thy prophets, and digged down thine altars; and I am left alone, and they seek my life. [4]But what saith the answer of God unto him? I have reserved to myself seven thousand men, who have not bowed the knee to the image of Baal. [5]Even so then at this present time also there is a remnant according to the election of grace. [6]And if by grace, then is it no more of works: otherwise grace is no more grace. But if it be of works, then is it no more grace: otherwise work is no more work. [7]What then? Israel hath not obtained that which he seeketh for; but the election hath obtained it, and the rest were blinded [8](According as it is written, God hath given them the spirit of slumber, eyes that they should not see, and ears that they should not hear;) unto this day. [9]And David saith, Let their table be made a snare, and a trap, and a stumbling block, and a recompence unto them: [10]Let their eyes be darkened, that they may not see, and bow down their back alway. [11]I say then, Have they stumbled that they should fall? God forbid: but rather through their fall salvation is come unto the Gentiles, for to provoke them to jealousy. [12]Now if the fall of them be the riches of the world, and the diminishing of them the riches of the Gentiles; how much more their fulness? [13]For I speak to you Gentiles, inasmuch as I am the apostle of the Gentiles, I magnify mine office: [14]If by any means I may provoke to emulation them which are my flesh, and might save some of them. [15]For if the casting away of them be the reconciling of the world, what shall the receiving of them be, but life from the dead? [16]For if the firstfruit be holy, the lump is also holy: and if the root be holy, so are the branches. [17]And if some of the branches be broken off, and thou, being a wild olive tree, wert graffed in among them, and with them partakest of the root and fatness of the olive tree; [18]Boast not against the branches. But if thou boast, thou bearest not the root, but the root thee. [19]Thou wilt say then, The branches were broken off, that I might be graffed in. [20]Well; because of unbelief they were broken off, and thou standest by faith. Be not highminded, but fear: [21]For if God spared not the natural branches, take heed

lest he also spare not thee. [22]Behold therefore the goodness and severity of God: on them which fell, severity; but toward thee, goodness, if thou continue in his goodness: otherwise thou also shalt be cut off. [23]And they also, if they abide not still in unbelief, shall be graffed in: for God is able to graff them in again. [24]For if thou wert cut out of the olive tree which is wild by nature, and wert graffed contrary to nature into a good olive tree: how much more shall these, which be the natural branches, be graffed into their own olive tree? [25]For I would not, brethren, that ye should be ignorant of this mystery, lest ye should be wise in your own conceits; that blindness in part is happened to Israel, until the fulness of the Gentiles be come in. [26]And so all Israel shall be saved: as it is written, There shall come out of Sion the Deliverer, and shall turn away ungodliness from Jacob: [27]For this is my covenant unto them, when I shall take away their sins. [28]As concerning the gospel, they are enemies for your sakes: but as touching the election, they are beloved for the fathers' sakes. [29]For the gifts and calling of God are without repentance. [30]For as ye in times past have not believed God, yet have now obtained mercy through their unbelief: [31]Even so have these also now not believed, that through your mercy they also may obtain mercy. [32]For God hath concluded them all in unbelief, that he might have mercy upon all."

Galatians 3:6-14 "[6]Even as Abraham believed God, and it was accounted to him for righteousness. [7]Know ye therefore that they which are of faith, the same are the children of Abraham. [8]And the scripture, foreseeing that God would justify the heathen through faith, preached before the gospel unto Abraham, saying, In thee shall all nations be blessed. [9]So then they which be of faith are blessed with faithful Abraham. [10]For as many as are of the works of the law are under the curse: for it is written, Cursed is every one that continueth not in all things which are written in the book of the law to do them. [11]But that no man is justified by the law in the sight of God, it is evident: for, The just shall live by faith. [12]And the law is not of faith: but, The man that doeth them shall live in them. [13]Christ hath redeemed us from the curse of the law, being made a curse for us: for it is written, Cursed is every one that hangeth on a tree: [14]That the blessing of Abraham might come on the Gentiles through Jesus Christ; that we might receive the promise of the Spirit through faith."

The Apostle Of The Gentiles/Heathen

Acts 9:11-15 "[11]And the Lord said unto him, Arise, and go into the street which is called Straight, and inquire in the house of Judas for one called Saul, of Tarsus: for, behold, he prayeth, [12]And hath seen in a vision a man named Ananias coming in, and putting his hand on him, that he might receive his sight. [13]Then Ananias answered, Lord, I have heard by many of this man, how much evil he hath done to thy saints at Jerusalem: [14]And here he hath authority from the chief priests to bind all that call on thy name. [15]But the Lord said unto him, Go thy way: for he is a chosen vessel unto me, to bear my name before the Gentiles, and kings, and the children of Israel:"

Acts 26:12-18 "[12]Whereupon as I went to Damascus with authority and commission from the chief priests, [13]At midday, O king, I saw in the way a light from heaven, above the brightness of the sun, shining round about me and them which journeyed with me. [14]And when we were all fallen to the earth, I heard a voice speaking unto me, and saying in the Hebrew tongue, Saul, Saul, why persecutest thou me? it is hard for thee to kick against the pricks. [15]And I said, Who art thou, Lord? And he said, I am Jesus whom thou persecutest. [16]But rise, and stand upon thy feet: for I have appeared unto thee for this purpose, to make thee a minister and a witness both of these things which thou hast seen, and of those things in the which I will appear unto thee; [17]Delivering thee from the people, and from the Gentiles, unto whom now I send thee, [18]To open their eyes, and to turn them from darkness to light, and from the power of Satan unto God, that they may receive forgiveness of sins, and inheritance among them which are sanctified by faith that is in me."

Romans 11:13 "For I speak to you Gentiles, inasmuch as I am the apostle of the Gentiles, I magnify mine office:"

Galatians 1:13-16 "[13]For ye have heard of my conversation in time past in the Jews' religion, how that beyond measure I persecuted the church of God, and wasted it: [14]And profited in the Jews'

religion above many my equals in mine own nation, being more exceedingly zealous of the traditions of my fathers. [15]But when it pleased God, who separated me from my mother's womb, and called me by his grace, [16]To reveal his Son in me, that I might preach him among the heathen; immediately I conferred not with flesh and blood:"

Ephesians 3:1-8 "[1]For this cause I Paul, the prisoner of Jesus Christ for you Gentiles, [2]If ye have heard of the dispensation of the grace of God which is given me to youward: [3]How that by revelation he made known unto me the mystery; (as I wrote afore in few words, [4]Whereby, when ye read, ye may understand my knowledge in the mystery of Christ) [5]Which in other ages was not made known unto the sons of men, as it is now revealed unto his holy apostles and prophets by the Spirit; [6]That the Gentiles should be fellowheirs, and of the same body, and partakers of his promise in Christ by the gospel: [7]Whereof I was made a minister, according to the gift of the grace of God given unto me by the effectual working of his power. [8]Unto me, who am less than the least of all saints, is this grace given, that I should preach among the Gentiles the unsearchable riches of Christ;"

1 Timothy 2:7 "Whereunto I am ordained a preacher, and an apostle, (I speak the truth in Christ, and lie not;) a teacher of the Gentiles in faith and verity."

The Counsel Of The Heathen

Psalm 33:10 "The LORD bringeth the counsel of the heathen to nought: he maketh the devices of the people of none effect."

The Gentiles Being Fellowheirs With The Jews

Ephesians 3:6 "That the Gentiles should be fellowheirs, and of the same body, and partakers of his promise in Christ by the gospel:"

The Gentiles Nursing Israel

Isaiah 49:14-23 "[14]But Zion said, The LORD hath forsaken me, and my Lord hath forgotten me. [15]Can a woman forget her sucking child, that she should not have compassion on the son of her womb? yea, they may forget, yet will I not forget thee. [16]Behold, I have graven thee upon the palms of my hands; thy walls are continually before me. [17]Thy children shall make haste; thy destroyers and they that made thee waste shall go forth of thee. [18]Lift up thine eyes round about, and behold: all these gather themselves together, and come to thee. As I live, saith the LORD, thou shalt surely clothe thee with them all, as with an ornament, and bind them on thee, as a bride doeth. [19]For thy waste and thy desolate places, and the land of thy destruction, shall even now be too narrow by reason of the inhabitants, and they that swallowed thee up shall be far away. [20]The children which thou shalt have, after thou hast lost the other, shall say again in thine ears, The place is too strait for me: give place to me that I may dwell. [21]Then shalt thou say in thine heart, Who hath begotten me these, seeing I have lost my children, and am desolate, a captive, and removing to and fro? and who hath brought up these? Behold, I was left alone; these, where had they been? [22]Thus saith the Lord GOD, Behold, I will lift up mine hand to the Gentiles, and set up my standard to the people: and they shall bring thy sons in their arms, and thy daughters shall be carried upon their shoulders. [23]And kings shall be thy nursing fathers, and their queens thy nursing mothers: they shall bow down to thee with their face toward the earth, and lick up the dust of thy feet; and thou shalt know that I am the LORD: for they shall not be ashamed that wait for me."

Isaiah 60:15-16 "[15]Whereas thou hast been forsaken and hated, so that no man went through thee, I will make thee an eternal excellency, a joy of many generations. [16]Thou shalt also suck the milk of the Gentiles, and shalt suck the breast of kings: and thou shalt know that I the LORD am thy Saviour and thy Redeemer, the mighty One of Jacob."

The Gentiles/Heathen Treading Jerusalem Under Their Feet
Psalm 79:1 "O God, the heathen are come into thine inheritance; thy holy temple have they defiled; they have laid Jerusalem on heaps."

Luke 21:24 "And they shall fall by the edge of the sword, and shall be led away captive into all nations: and Jerusalem shall be trodden down of the Gentiles, until the times of the Gentiles be fulfilled."

Revelation 11:1-2 "[1]And there was given me a reed like unto a rod: and the angel stood, saying,

Rise, and measure the temple of God, and the altar, and them that worship therein. [2]But the court which is without the temple leave out, and measure it not; for it is given unto the Gentiles: and the holy city shall they tread under foot forty and two months."

The Gentiles Trusting In The Branch Of Jesse
Isaiah 11:1 "And there shall come forth a rod out of the stem of Jesse, and a Branch shall grow out of his roots:"

Isaiah 11:10 "And in that day there shall be a root of Jesse, which shall stand for an ensign of the people; to it shall the Gentiles seek: and his rest shall be glorious."

Zechariah 6:12 "And speak unto him, saying, Thus speaketh the LORD of hosts, saying, Behold the man whose name is The BRANCH; and he shall grow up out of his place, and he shall build the temple of the LORD:"

Romans 15:8-12 "[8]Now I say that Jesus Christ was a minister of the circumcision for the truth of God, to confirm the promises made unto the fathers: [9]And that the Gentiles might glorify God for his mercy; as it is written, For this cause I will confess to thee among the Gentiles, and sing unto thy name. [10]And again he saith, Rejoice, ye Gentiles, with his people. [11]And again, Praise the Lord, all ye Gentiles; and laud him, all ye people. [12]And again, Esaias saith, There shall be a root of Jesse, and he that shall rise to reign over the Gentiles; in him shall the Gentiles trust."

The Heathen Perishing Out Of The Lord's Land
Psalm 10:16 "The LORD is King for ever and ever: the heathen are perished out of his land."

The King Of Israel Speaking Peace To The Heathen
Zechariah 9:9-10 "[9]Rejoice greatly, O daughter of Zion; shout, O daughter of Jerusalem: behold, thy King cometh unto thee: he is just, and having salvation; lowly, and riding upon an ass, and upon a colt the foal of an ass. [10]And I will cut off the chariot from Ephraim, and the horse from Jerusalem, and the battle bow shall be cut off: and he shall speak peace unto the heathen: and his dominion shall be from sea even to sea, and from river even to the ends of the earth."

The Lord Being The God
Of The Gentiles/Heathen

Psalm 47:7-9 "⁷For God is the King of all the earth: sing ye praises with understanding. ⁸God reigneth over the heathen: God sitteth upon the throne of his holiness. ⁹The princes of the people are gathered together, even the people of the God of Abraham: for the shields of the earth belong unto God: he is greatly exalted."

Isaiah 54:5 "For thy Maker is thine husband; the LORD of hosts is his name; and thy Redeemer the Holy One of Israel; The God of the whole earth shall he be called."

Romans 3:29-30 "²⁹Is he the God of the Jews only? is he not also of the Gentiles? Yes, of the Gentiles also: ³⁰Seeing it is one God, which shall justify the circumcision by faith, and uncircumcision through faith."

Romans 10:12-13 "¹²For there is no difference between the Jew and the Greek: for the same Lord over all is rich unto all that call upon him. ¹³For whosoever shall call upon the name of the Lord shall be saved."

The Lord Judging The Heathen

Psalm 110:5-7 "⁵The Lord at thy right hand shall strike through kings in the day of his wrath. ⁶He shall judge among the heathen, he shall fill the places with the dead bodies; he shall wound the heads over many countries. ⁷He shall drink of the brook in the way: therefore shall he lift up the head."

Ezekiel 28:24-26 "²⁴And there shall be no more a pricking brier unto the house of Israel, nor any grieving thorn of all that are round about them, that despised them; and they shall know that I am the Lord GOD. ²⁵Thus saith the Lord GOD; When I shall have gathered the house of Israel from the people among whom they are scattered, and shall be sanctified in them in the sight of the heathen, then shall they dwell in their land that I have given to my servant Jacob. ²⁶And they shall dwell safely therein, and shall build houses, and plant vineyards; yea, they shall dwell with confidence, when I have executed judgments upon all those that despise them round about them; and they shall know that I am the LORD their God."

Ezekiel 36:1-7 "¹Also, thou son of man, prophesy unto the mountains of Israel, and say, Ye mountains of Israel, hear the word of the LORD: ²Thus saith the Lord GOD; Because the enemy hath said against you, Aha, even the ancient high places are ours in possession: ³Therefore prophesy and say, Thus saith the Lord GOD; Because they have made you desolate, and swallowed you up on every side, that ye might be a possession unto the residue of the heathen, and ye are taken up in the lips of talkers, and are an infamy of the people: ⁴Therefore, ye mountains of Israel, hear the word of the Lord GOD; Thus saith the Lord GOD to the mountains, and to the hills, to the rivers, and to the valleys, to the desolate wastes, and to the cities that are forsaken, which became a prey and derision to the residue of the heathen that are round about; ⁵Therefore thus saith the Lord GOD; Surely in the fire of my jealousy have I spoken against the residue of the heathen, and against all Idumea, which have appointed my land into their possession with the joy of all their heart, with despiteful minds, to cast it out for a prey. ⁶Prophesy therefore concerning the land of Israel, and say unto the mountains, and to the hills, to the rivers, and to the valleys, Thus saith the Lord GOD; Behold, I have spoken in my jealousy and in my fury, because ye have borne the shame of the heathen: ⁷Therefore thus saith the Lord GOD; I have lifted up mine hand, Surely the heathen that are about you, they shall bear their shame."

Joel 3:9-16 "⁹Proclaim ye this among the Gentiles; Prepare war, wake up the mighty men, let all the men of war draw near; let them come up: ¹⁰Beat your plowshares into swords, and your pruning-hooks into spears: let the weak say, I am strong. ¹¹Assemble yourselves, and come, all ye heathen, and gather yourselves together round about: thither cause thy mighty ones to come down, O LORD. ¹²Let the heathen be wakened, and come up to the valley of Jehoshaphat: for there will I sit to judge all the heathen round about. ¹³Put ye in the sickle, for the harvest is ripe: come, get you down; for the press is full, the fats overflow; for their wickedness is great. ¹⁴Multitudes, multitudes in the valley of decision: for the day of the LORD is near in the valley of decision. ¹⁵The sun and the moon shall be darkened, and the stars shall withdraw their shining. ¹⁶The LORD also shall roar out of Zion, and utter his voice from Jerusalem; and the heavens and the earth shall shake: but the LORD will be the hope of his people, and the strength of the children of Israel."

Obadiah 15-16 "[15]For the day of the LORD is near upon all the heathen: as thou hast done, it shall be done unto thee: thy reward shall return upon thine own head. [16]For as ye have drunk upon my holy mountain, so shall all the heathen drink continually, yea, they shall drink, and they shall swallow down, and they shall be as though they had not been."

The Lord Laughing At The Heathen
Psalm 59:8 "But thou, O LORD, shalt laugh at them; thou shalt have all the heathen in derision."

The Lord Showing Light To The Gentiles
Isaiah 49:5-6 "[5]And now, saith the LORD that formed me from the womb to be his servant, to bring Jacob again to him, Though Israel be not gathered, yet shall I be glorious in the eyes of the LORD, and my God shall be my strength. [6]And he said, It is a light thing that thou shouldest be my servant to raise up the tribes of Jacob, and to restore the preserved of Israel: I will also give thee for a light to the Gentiles, that thou mayest be my salvation unto the end of the earth."

Isaiah 60:1-3 "[1]Arise, shine; for thy light is come, and the glory of the LORD is risen upon thee. [2]For, behold, the darkness shall cover the earth, and gross darkness the people: but the LORD shall arise upon thee, and his glory shall be seen upon thee. [3]And the Gentiles shall come to thy light, and kings to the brightness of thy rising."

Acts 26:23 "That Christ should suffer, and that he should be the first that should rise from the dead, and should shew light unto the people, and to the Gentiles."

The Servant Of The Lord
Bringing Forth Judgment To The Gentiles
Isaiah 42:1 "Behold my servant, whom I uphold; mine elect, in whom my soul delighteth; I have put my spirit upon him: he shall bring forth judgment to the Gentiles."

What Is Dreadful Among The Heathen
Malachi 1:14 "But cursed be the deceiver, which hath in his flock a male, and voweth, and sacrificeth unto the LORD a corrupt thing: for I am a great King, saith the LORD of hosts, and my name is dreadful among the heathen."

What The Gentiles/Heathen Shall Know
Exodus 7:5 "And the Egyptians shall know that I am the LORD, when I stretch forth mine hand upon Egypt, and bring out the children of Israel from among them."

Psalm 98:2 "The LORD hath made known his salvation: his righteousness hath he openly shewed in the sight of the heathen."

Ezekiel 36:22-24 "[22]Therefore say unto the house of Israel, Thus saith the Lord GOD; I do not this for your sakes, O house of Israel, but for mine holy name's sake, which ye have profaned among the heathen, whither ye went. [23]And I will sanctify my great name, which was profaned among the heathen, which ye have profaned in the midst of them; and the heathen shall know that I am the LORD, saith the Lord GOD, when I shall be sanctified in you before their eyes. [24]For I will take you from among the heathen, and gather you out of all countries, and will bring you into your own land."

Ezekiel 36:33-38 "[33]Thus saith the Lord GOD; In the day that I shall have cleansed you from all your iniquities I will also cause you to dwell in the cities, and the wastes shall be builded. [34]And the desolate land shall be tilled, whereas it lay desolate in the sight of all that passed by. [35]And they shall say, This land that was desolate is become like the garden of Eden; and the waste and desolate and ruined cities are become fenced, and are inhabited. [36]Then the heathen that are left round about you shall know that I the LORD build the ruined places, and plant that that was desolate: I the LORD have spoken it, and I will do it. [37]Thus saith the Lord GOD; I will yet for this be inquired of by the house of Israel, to do it for them; I will increase them with men like a flock. [38]As the holy flock, as the flock of Jerusalem in her solemn feasts; so shall the waste cities be filled with flocks of men: and they shall know that I am the LORD."

Ezekiel 39:6-8 "[6]And I will send a fire on Magog, and among them that dwell carelessly in the isles: and they shall know that I am the LORD. [7]So will I make my holy name known in the midst of my people Israel; and I will not let them pollute my holy name any more: and the heathen shall know that I am the LORD, the Holy One in Israel.

⁸Behold, it is come, and it is done, saith the Lord GOD; this is the day whereof I have spoken."

Ezekiel 39:22-24 "²²So the house of Israel shall know that I am the LORD their God from that day and forward. ²³And the heathen shall know that the house of Israel went into captivity for their iniquity: because they trespassed against me, therefore hid I my face from them, and gave them into the hand of their enemies: so fell they all by the sword. ²⁴According to their uncleanness and according to their transgressions have I done unto them, and hid my face from them."

Colossians 1:26-27 "²⁶Even the mystery which hath been hid from ages and from generations, but now is made manifest to his saints: ²⁷To whom God would make known what is the riches of the glory of this mystery among the Gentiles; which is Christ in you, the hope of glory:"

GIVING AND GIFTS

Desiring Spiritual Gifts

1 Corinthians 12:27-31 "²⁷Now ye are the body of Christ, and members in particular. ²⁸And God hath set some in the church, first apostles, secondarily prophets, thirdly teachers, after that miracles, then gifts of healings, helps, governments, diversities of tongues. ²⁹Are all apostles? are all prophets? are all teachers? are all workers of miracles? ³⁰Have all the gifts of healing? do all speak with tongues? do all interpret? ³¹But covet earnestly the best gifts: and yet shew I unto you a more excellent way."

1 Corinthians 14:1 "Follow after charity, and desire spiritual gifts, but rather that ye may prophesy."

Giving Being More Blessed Than Receiving

Acts 20:35 "I have shewed you all things, how that so labouring ye ought to support the weak, and to remember the words of the Lord Jesus, how he said, It is more blessed to give than to receive."

Good Gifts

John 3:27 "John answered and said, A man can receive nothing, except it be given him from heaven."

James 1:17 "Every good gift and every perfect gift is from above, and cometh down from the Father of lights, with whom is no variableness, neither shadow of turning."

Spiritual Gifts

Acts 19:4-6 "⁴Then said Paul, John verily baptized with the baptism of repentance, saying unto the people, that they should believe on him which should come after him, that is, on Christ Jesus. ⁵When they heard this, they were baptized in the name of the Lord Jesus. ⁶And when Paul had laid his hands upon them, the Holy Ghost came on them; and they spake with tongues, and prophesied."

Romans 12:4-8 "⁴For as we have many members in one body, and all members have not the same office: ⁵So we, being many, are one body in Christ, and every one members one of another. ⁶Having then gifts differing according to the grace that is given to us, whether prophecy, let us prophesy according to the proportion of faith; ⁷Or ministry, let us wait on our ministering: or he that teacheth, on teaching; ⁸Or he that exhorteth, on exhortation: he that giveth, let him do it with simplicity; he that ruleth, with diligence; he that sheweth mercy, with cheerfulness."

1 Corinthians 12:1-11 "¹Now concerning spiritual gifts, brethren, I would not have you ignorant. ²Ye know that ye were Gentiles, carried away unto these dumb idols, even as ye were led. ³Wherefore I give you to understand, that no man speaking by the Spirit of God calleth Jesus accursed: and that no man can say that Jesus is the Lord, but by the Holy Ghost. ⁴Now there are diversities of gifts, but the same Spirit. ⁵And there are differences of administrations, but the same Lord. ⁶And there are diversities of operations, but it is the same God which worketh all in all. ⁷But the manifestation of the Spirit is given to every man to profit withal. ⁸For to one is given by the Spirit the word of wisdom; to another the word of knowledge by the same Spirit; ⁹To another faith by the same Spirit; to another the gifts of healing by the same Spirit; ¹⁰To another the working of miracles; to another prophecy; to another discerning of spirits; to another divers kinds of tongues; to another the interpretation of tongues: ¹¹But all these worketh that one and the selfsame Spirit, dividing to every man severally as he will."

1 Corinthians 12:27-31 "²⁷Now ye are the body of Christ, and members in particular. ²⁸And God hath set some in the church, first apostles, secondarily prophets, thirdly teachers, after that miracles, then gifts of healings, helps, governments, diversities of tongues. [29]Are all apostles? are all prophets? are all teachers? are all workers of miracles? [30]Have all the gifts of healing? do all speak with tongues? do all interpret? [31]But covet earnestly the best gifts: and yet shew I unto you a more excellent way."

The Gift Of God
Ecclesiastes 3:13 "And also that every man should eat and drink, and enjoy the good of all his labour, it is the gift of God."

Ecclesiastes 5:18-20 "[18]Behold that which I have seen: it is good and comely for one to eat and to drink, and to enjoy the good of all his labour that he taketh under the sun all the days of his life, which God giveth him: for it is his portion. [19]Every man also to whom God hath given riches and wealth, and hath given him power to eat thereof, and to take his portion, and to rejoice in his labour; this is the gift of God. [20]For he shall not much remember the days of his life; because God answereth him in the joy of his heart."

Acts 8:20 "But Peter said unto him, Thy money perish with thee, because thou hast thought that the gift of God may be purchased with money."

Romans 5:14-18 "[14]Nevertheless death reigned from Adam to Moses, even over them that had not sinned after the similitude of Adam's transgression, who is the figure of him that was to come. [15]But not as the offence, so also is the free gift. For if through the offence of one many be dead, much more the grace of God, and the gift by grace, which is by one man, Jesus Christ, hath abounded unto many. [16]And not as it was by one that sinned, so is the gift: for the judgment was by one to condemnation, but the free gift is of many offences unto justification. [17]For if by one man's offence death reigned by one; much more they which receive abundance of grace and of the gift of righteousness shall reign in life by one, Jesus Christ.) [18]Therefore as by the offence of one judgment came upon all men to condemnation; even so by the righteousness of one the free gift came upon all men unto justification of life."

Romans 6:23 "For the wages of sin is death; but the gift of God is eternal life through Jesus Christ our Lord."

Romans 11:29 "For the gifts and calling of God are without repentance."

Ephesians 2:8-10 "[8]For by grace are ye saved through faith; and that not of yourselves: it is the gift of God: [9]Not of works, lest any man should boast. [10]For we are his workmanship, created in Christ Jesus unto good works, which God hath before ordained that we should walk in them."

Ephesians 4:7 "But unto every one of us is given grace according to the measure of the gift of Christ."

2 Timothy 1:6 "Wherefore I put thee in remembrance that thou stir up the gift of God, which is in thee by the putting on of my hands."

The Lord Giving
Job 1:20-21 "[20]Then Job arose, and rent his mantle, and shaved his head, and fell down upon the ground, and worshipped, [21]And said, Naked came I out of my mother's womb, and naked shall I return thither: the LORD gave, and the LORD hath taken away; blessed be the name of the LORD."

Psalm 68:19 "Blessed be the Lord, who daily loadeth us with benefits, even the God of our salvation. Selah."

1 Timothy 6:17 "Charge them that are rich in this world, that they be not highminded, nor trust in uncertain riches, but in the living God, who giveth us richly all things to enjoy;"

The Reward For Giving
Ecclesiastes 11:1-2 "[1]Cast thy bread upon the waters: for thou shalt find it after many days. [2]Give a portion to seven, and also to eight; for thou knowest not what evil shall be upon the earth."

Luke 6:38 "Give, and it shall be given unto you; good measure, pressed down, and shaken together, and running over, shall men give into your bosom. For with the same measure that ye mete withal it shall be measured to you again."

Those That Are Given Much
Luke 12:48 "But he that knew not, and did commit things worthy of stripes, shall be beaten with few stripes. For unto whomsoever much is given, of him shall be much required: and to whom men have committed much, of him they will ask the more."

Those That Give Gifts

Proverbs 19:6 "Many will intreat the favour of the prince: and every man is a friend to him that giveth gifts."

Those That Give To The Rich

Proverbs 22:16 "He that oppresseth the poor to increase his riches, and he that giveth to the rich, shall surely come to want."

Those That God The Father Gave To Jesus Christ

Isaiah 8:16-18 "16Bind up the testimony, seal the law among my disciples. 17And I will wait upon the LORD, that hideth his face from the house of Jacob, and I will look for him. 18Behold, I and the children whom the LORD hath given me are for signs and for wonders in Israel from the LORD of hosts, which dwelleth in mount Zion."

John 6:35-39 "35And Jesus said unto them, I am the bread of life: he that cometh to me shall never hunger; and he that believeth on me shall never thirst. 36But I said unto you, That ye also have seen me, and believe not. 37All that the Father giveth me shall come to me; and him that cometh to me I will in no wise cast out. 38For I came down from heaven, not to do mine own will, but the will of him that sent me. 39And this is the Father's will which hath sent me, that of all which he hath given me I should lose nothing, but should raise it up again at the last day."

John 10:25-29 "25Jesus answered them, I told you, and ye believed not: the works that I do in my Father's name, they bear witness of me. 26But ye believe not, because ye are not of my sheep, as I said unto you. 27My sheep hear my voice, and I know them, and they follow me: 28And I give unto them eternal life; and they shall never perish, neither shall any man pluck them out of my hand. 29My Father, which gave them me, is greater than all; and no man is able to pluck them out of my Father's hand."

John 17:1-26 "1These words spake Jesus, and lifted up his eyes to heaven, and said, Father, the hour is come; glorify thy Son, that thy Son also may glorify thee: 2As thou hast given him power over all flesh, that he should give eternal life to as many as thou hast given him. 3And this is life eternal, that they might know thee the only true God, and Jesus Christ, whom thou hast sent. 4I have glorified thee on the earth: I have finished the work which thou gavest me to do. 5And now, O Father, glorify thou me with thine own self with the glory which I had with thee before the world was. 6I have manifested thy name unto the men which thou gavest me out of the world: thine they were, and thou gavest them me; and they have kept thy word. 7Now they have known that all things whatsoever thou hast given me are of thee. 8For I have given unto them the words which thou gavest me; and they have received them, and have known surely that I came out from thee, and they have believed that thou didst send me. 9I pray for them: I pray not for the world, but for them which thou hast given me; for they are thine. 10And all mine are thine, and thine are mine; and I am glorified in them. 11And now I am no more in the world, but these are in the world, and I come to thee. Holy Father, keep through thine own name those whom thou hast given me, that they may be one, as we are. 12While I was with them in the world, I kept them in thy name: those that thou gavest me I have kept, and none of them is lost, but the son of perdition; that the scripture might be fulfilled. 13And now come I to thee; and these things I speak in the world, that they might have my joy fulfilled in themselves. 14I have given them thy word; and the world hath hated them, because they are not of the world, even as I am not of the world. 15I pray not that thou shouldest take them out of the world, but that thou shouldest keep them from the evil. 16They are not of the world, even as I am not of the world. 17Sanctify them through thy truth: thy word is truth. 18As thou hast sent me into the world, even so have I also sent them into the world. 19And for their sakes I sanctify myself, that they also might be sanctified through the truth. 20Neither pray I for these alone, but for them also which shall believe on me through their word; 21That they all may be one; as thou, Father, art in me, and I in thee, that they also may be one in us: that the world may believe that thou hast sent me. 22And the glory which thou gavest me I have given them; that they may be one, even as we are one: 23I in them, and thou in me, that they may be made perfect in one; and that the world may know that thou hast sent me, and hast loved them, as thou hast loved me. 24Father, I will that they also, whom thou hast given me, be with me where I am; that they may behold my glory, which thou hast given me: for thou lovedst me before the foundation of the world. ²⁵O righteous Father, the world hath not known thee: but I have known thee, and these have known that thou hast sent me. ²⁶And I have declared unto them thy name, and will declare it: that the love wherewith thou hast loved me may be in them, and I in them."

What Is Given To Believers By The Lord

Genesis 9:1-3 "¹And God blessed Noah and his sons, and said unto them, Be fruitful, and multiply, and replenish the earth. ²And the fear of you and the dread of you shall be upon every beast of the earth, and upon every fowl of the air, upon all that moveth upon the earth, and upon all the fishes of the sea; into your hand are they delivered. ³Every moving thing that liveth shall be meat for you; even as the green herb have I given you all things."

2 Samuel 22:33-36 "³³God is my strength and power: and he maketh my way perfect. ³⁴He maketh my feet like hinds' feet: and setteth me upon my high places. ³⁵He teacheth my hands to war; so that a bow of steel is broken by mine arms. ³⁶Thou hast also given me the shield of thy salvation: and thy gentleness hath made me great."

1 Chronicles 22:12 "Only the LORD give thee wisdom and understanding, and give thee charge concerning Israel, that thou mayest keep the law of the LORD thy God."

Nehemiah 9:7-20 "⁷Thou art the LORD the God, who didst choose Abram, and broughtest him forth out of Ur of the Chaldees, and gavest him the name of Abraham; ⁸And foundest his heart faithful before thee, and madest a covenant with him to give the land of the Canaanites, the Hittites, the Amorites, and the Perizzites, and the Jebusites, and the Girgashites, to give it, I say, to his seed, and hast performed thy words; for thou art righteous: ⁹And didst see the affliction of our fathers in Egypt, and heardest their cry by the Red sea; ¹⁰And shewedst signs and wonders upon Pharoah, and on all his servants, and on all the people of his land: for thou knewest that they dealt proudly against them. So didst thou get thee a name, as it is this day. ¹¹And thou didst divide the sea before them, so that they went through the midst of the sea on the dry land; and their persecutors thou threwest into the deeps, as a stone into the mighty waters. ¹²Moreover thou leddest them in the day by a cloudy pillar; and in the night by a pillar of fire, to give them light in the way wherein they should go. ¹³Thou camest down also upon mount Sinai, and spakest with them from heaven, and gavest them right judgments, and true laws, good statutes and commandments: ¹⁴And madest known unto them thy holy sabbath, and commandedst them precepts, statutes, and laws, by the hand of Moses thy servant: ¹⁵And gavest them bread from heaven for their hunger, and broughtest forth water for them out of the rock for their thirst, and promisedst them that they should go in to possess the land which thou hadst sworn to give them. ¹⁶But they and our fathers dealt proudly, and hardened their necks, and hearkened not to thy commandments, ¹⁷And refused to obey, neither were mindful of thy wonders that thou didst among them; but hardened their necks, and in their rebellion appointed a captain to return to their bondage: but thou art a God ready to pardon, gracious and merciful, slow to anger, and of great kindness, and forsookest them not. ¹⁸Yea, when they had made them a molten calf, and said, This is thy God that brought thee up out of Egypt, and had wrought great provocations; ¹⁹Yet thou in thy manifold mercies forsookest them not in the wilderness: the pillar of the cloud departed not from them by day, to lead them in the way; neither the pillar of fire by night, to shew them light, and the way wherein they should go. ²⁰Thou gavest also thy good spirit to instruct them, and withheldest not thy manna from their mouth, and gavest them water for their thirst."

Psalm 18:31-35 "³¹For who is God save the LORD? or who is a rock save our God? ³²It is God that girdeth me with strength, and maketh my way perfect. ³³He maketh my feet like hinds' feet, and setteth me upon my high places. ³⁴He teacheth my hands to war, so that a bow of steel is broken by mine arms. ³⁵Thou hast also given me the shield of thy salvation: and thy right hand hath holden me up, and thy gentleness hath made me great."

Psalm 61:5 "For thou, O God, hast heard my vows: thou hast given me the heritage of those that fear thy name."

Psalm 68:18 "Thou hast ascended on high, thou hast led captivity captive: thou hast received gifts for men; yea, for the rebellious also, that the LORD God might dwell among them."

Psalm 68:35 "O God, thou art terrible out of thy holy places: the God of Israel is he that giveth strength and power unto his people. Blessed be God."

Psalm 84:11 "For the LORD God is a sun and shield: the LORD will give grace and glory: no good thing will he withhold from them that walk uprightly."

Psalm 119:73-75 "[73]Thy hands have made me and fashioned me: give me understanding, that I may learn thy commandments. [74]They that fear thee will be glad when they see me; because I have hoped in thy word. [75]I know, O LORD, that thy judgments are right, and that thou in faithfulness hast afflicted me."

Proverbs 2:6 "For the LORD giveth wisdom: out of his mouth cometh knowledge and understanding."

Proverbs 3:33-34 "[33]The curse of the LORD is in the house of the wicked: but he blesseth the habitation of the just. [34]Surely he scorneth the scorners: but he giveth grace unto the lowly."

Ecclesiastes 2:24-26 "[24]There is nothing better for a man, than that he should eat and drink, and that he should make his soul enjoy good in his labour. This also I saw, that it was from the hand of God. [25]For who can eat, or who else can hasten hereunto, more than I? [26]For God giveth to a man that is good in his sight wisdom, and knowledge, and joy: but to the sinner he giveth travail, to gather and to heap up, that he may give to him that is good before God. This also is vanity and vexation of spirit."

Isaiah 50:4 "The Lord GOD hath given me the tongue of the learned, that I should know how to speak a word in season to him that is weary: he wakeneth morning by morning, he wakeneth mine ear to hear as the learned."

Isaiah 56:4-5 "[4]For thus saith the LORD unto the eunuchs that keep my sabbaths, and choose the things that please me, and take hold of my covenant; [5]Even unto them will I give in mine house and within my walls a place and a name

better than of sons and of daughters: I will give them an everlasting name, that shall not be cut off."

Daniel 1:17 "As for these four children, God gave them knowledge and skill in all learning and wisdom: and Daniel had understanding in all visions and dreams."

Daniel 2:20-21 "[20]Daniel answered and said, Blessed be the name of God for ever and ever: for wisdom and might are his: [21]And he changeth the times and the seasons: he removeth kings, and setteth up kings: he giveth wisdom unto the wise, and knowledge to them that know understanding:"

John 1:1-12 "[1]In the beginning was the Word, and the Word was with God, and the Word was God. [2]The same was in the beginning with God. [3]All things were made by him; and without him was not any thing made that was made. [4]In him was life; and the life was the light of men. [5]And the light shineth in darkness; and the darkness comprehended it not. [6]There was a man sent from God, whose name was John. [7]The same came for a witness, to bear witness of the Light, that all men through him might believe. [8]He was not that Light, but was sent to bear witness of that Light. [9]That was the true Light, which lighteth every man that cometh into the world. [10]He was in the world, and the world was made by him, and the world knew him not. [11]He came unto his own, and his own received him not. [12]But as many as received him, to them gave he power to become the sons of God, even to them that believe on his name:"

John 6:26-27 "[26]Jesus answered them and said, Verily, verily, I say unto you, Ye seek me, not because ye saw the miracles, but because ye did eat of the loaves, and were filled. [27]Labour not for the meat which perisheth, but for that meat which endureth unto everlasting life, which the Son of man shall give unto you: for him hath God the Father sealed."

John 10:25-29 "[25]Jesus answered them, I told you, and ye believed not: the works that I do in my Father's name, they bear witness of me. [26]But ye believe not, because ye are not of my sheep, as I said unto you. [27]My sheep hear my voice, and I know them, and they follow me: [28]And I give unto them eternal life; and they shall never perish, neither shall any man pluck them out of my hand. [29]My Father, which gave them me, is greater than all; and no man is able to pluck them out of my Father's hand."

John 14:9-18 "[9]Jesus saith unto him, Have I been so long time with you, and yet hast thou not known me, Philip? he that hath seen me hath seen the Father; and how sayest thou then, Shew us the Father? [10]Believest thou not that I am in the Father, and the Father in me? the words that I speak unto you I speak not of myself: but the Father that dwelleth in me, he doeth the works. [11]Believe me that I am in the Father, and the Father in me: or else believe me for the very works' sake. [12]Verily, verily, I say unto you, He that believeth on me, the works that I do shall he do also; and greater works than these shall he do; because I go unto my Father. [13]And whatsoever ye shall ask in my name, that will I do, that the Father may be glorified in the Son. [14]If ye shall ask any thing in my name, I will do it. [15]If ye love me, keep my commandments. [16]And I will pray the Father, and he shall give you another Comforter, that he may abide with you for ever; [17]Even the Spirit of truth; whom the world cannot receive, because it seeth him not, neither knoweth him: but ye know him; for he dwelleth with you, and shall be in you. [18]I will not leave you comfortless: I will come to you."

John 17:1-22 "[1]These words spake Jesus, and lifted up his eyes to heaven, and said, Father, the hour is come; glorify thy Son, that thy Son also may glorify thee: [2]As thou hast given him power over all flesh, that he should give eternal life to as many as thou hast given him. [3]And this is life eternal, that they might know thee the only true God, and Jesus Christ, whom thou hast sent. [4]I have glorified thee on the earth: I have finished the work which thou gavest me to do. [5]And now, O Father, glorify thou me with thine own self with the glory which I had with thee before the world was. [6]I have manifested thy name unto the men which thou gavest me out of the world: thine they were, and thou gavest them me; and they have kept thy word. [7]Now they have known that all things whatsoever thou hast given me are of thee. [8]For I have given unto them the words which thou gavest me; and they have received them, and have known surely that I came out from thee, and they have believed that thou didst send me. [9]I pray for them: I pray not for the world, but for them which thou hast given me; for they are thine. [10]And all mine are thine, and thine are mine; and I am glorified in them. [11]And now I am no more in the world, but these are in the world, and I come to thee. Holy Father, keep through thine own name those whom thou hast given me, that they may be one, as we are. [12]While I was with them in the world, I kept them in thy name: those that thou gavest me I have kept, and none of them is lost, but the son of perdition; that the scripture might be fulfilled. [13]And now come I to thee; and these things I speak in the world, that they might have my joy fulfilled in themselves. [14]I have given them thy word; and the world hath hated them, because they are not of the world, even as I am not of the world. [15]I pray not that thou shouldest take them out of the world, but that thou shouldest keep them from the evil. [16]They are not of the world, even as I am not of the world. [17]Sanctify them through thy truth: thy word is truth. [18]As thou hast sent me into the world, even so have I also sent them into the world. [19]And for their sakes I sanctify myself, that they also might be sanctified through the truth. [20]Neither pray I for these alone, but for them also which shall believe on me through their word; [21]That they all may be one; as thou, Father, art in me, and I in thee, that they also may be one in us: that the world may believe that thou hast sent me. [22]And the glory which thou gavest me I have given them; that they may be one, even as we are one:"

Acts 2:38 "Then Peter said unto them, Repent, and be baptized every one of you in the name of Jesus Christ for the remission of sins, and ye shall receive the gift of the Holy Ghost."

Acts 5:30-32 "[30]The God of our fathers raised up Jesus, whom ye slew and hanged on a tree. [31]Him hath God exalted with his right hand to be a Prince and a Saviour, for to give repentance to Israel, and forgiveness of sins. [32]And we are his witnesses of these things; and so is also the Holy Ghost, whom God hath given to them that obey him."

Acts 10:44-48 "[44]While Peter yet spake these words, the Holy Ghost fell on all them which heard the word. [45]And they of the circumcision which believed were astonished, as many as came with Peter, because that on the Gentiles also was poured out the gift of the Holy Ghost. ⁴⁶For they heard them speak with tongues, and magnify God. Then answered Peter, ⁴⁷Can any man forbid water, that these should not be baptized, which have received the Holy Ghost as well as we? ⁴⁸And he commanded them to be baptized in the name of the Lord. Then prayed they him to tarry certain days."

Acts 15:8 "And God, which knoweth the hearts, bare them witness, giving them the Holy Ghost, even as he did unto us;"

Romans 5:5 "And hope maketh not ashamed; because the love of God is shed abroad in our hearts by the Holy Ghost which is given unto us."

Romans 8:31-32 "³¹What shall we then say to these things? If God be for us, who can be against us? ³²He that spared not his own Son, but delivered him up for us all, how shall he not with him also freely give us all things?"

Romans 12:1-3 "¹I beseech you therefore, brethren, by the mercies of God, that ye present your bodies a living sacrifice, holy, acceptable unto God, which is your reasonable service. ²And be not conformed to this world: but be ye transformed by the renewing of your mind, that ye may prove what is that good, and acceptable, and perfect, will of God. ³For I say, through the grace given unto me, to every man that is among you, not to think of himself more highly than he ought to think; but to think soberly, according as God hath dealt to every man the measure of faith."

1 Corinthians 1:4 "I thank my God always on your behalf, for the grace of God which is given you by Jesus Christ;"

1 Corinthians 2:12-14 "¹²Now we have received, not the spirit of the world, but the spirit which is of God; that we might know the things that are freely given to us of God. ¹³Which things also we speak, not in the words which man's wisdom teacheth, but which the Holy Ghost teacheth; comparing spiritual things with spiritual. ¹⁴But the natural man receiveth not the things of the Spirit of God: for they are foolishness unto him: neither can he know them, because they are spiritually discerned."

1 Corinthians 3:10 "According to the grace of God which is given unto me, as a wise masterbuilder, I have laid the foundation, and another buildeth thereon. But let every man take heed how he buildeth thereupon."

1 Corinthians 6:19-20 "¹⁹What? know ye not that your body is the temple of the Holy Ghost which is in you, which ye have of God, and ye are not your own? ²⁰For ye are bought with a price: therefore glorify God in your body, and in your spirit, which are God's."

1 Corinthians 12:3-7 "³Wherefore I give you to understand, that no man speaking by the Spirit of God calleth Jesus accursed: and that no man can say that Jesus is the Lord, but by the Holy Ghost. ⁴Now there are diversities of gifts, but the same Spirit. ⁵And there are differences of administrations, but the same Lord. ⁶And there are diversities of operations, but it is the same God which worketh all in all. ⁷But the manifestation of the Spirit is given to every man to profit withal."

1 Corinthians 15:9-10 "⁹For I am the least of the apostles, that am not meet to be called an apostle, because I persecuted the church of God. ¹⁰But by the grace of God I am what I am: and his grace which was bestowed upon me was not in vain; but I laboured more abundantly than they all: yet not I, but the grace of God which was with me."

2 Corinthians 4:6 "For God, who commanded the light to shine out of darkness, hath shined in our hearts, to give the light of the knowledge of the glory of God in the face of Jesus Christ."

2 Corinthians 5:5 "Now he that hath wrought us for the selfsame thing is God, who also hath given unto us the earnest of the Spirit."

Ephesians 3:7-8 "⁷Whereof I was made a minister, according to the gift of the grace of God given unto me by the effectual working of his power. ⁸Unto me, who am less than the least of all saints, is this grace given, that I should preach among the Gentiles the unsearchable riches of Christ;"

Ephesians 4:7-14 "⁷But unto every one of us is given grace according to the measure of the gift of Christ. ⁸Wherefore he saith, When he ascended up on high, he led captivity captive, and gave gifts unto men. ⁹(Now that he ascended, what is it but that he also descended first into the lower parts of the earth? ¹⁰He that descended is the same also that ascended up far above all heavens, that he might fill all things.) ¹¹And he gave some, apostles; and some, prophets; and some, evangelists; and some, pastors and teachers; ¹²For the perfecting of the saints, for the work of the ministry, for the edifying of the body of Christ: ¹³Till we all come in the unity of the faith, and of the knowledge of the Son of God, unto a perfect man, unto the measure of the stature of the fulness of Christ: ¹⁴That we henceforth be no more children, tossed to and fro, and carried about with every wind of doctrine, by the sleight of men, and cunning craftiness, whereby they lie in wait to deceive;"

Ephesians 5:14 "Wherefore he saith, Awake thou that sleepest, and arise from the dead, and Christ shall give thee light."

1 Thessalonians 4:8 "He therefore that despiseth, despiseth not man, but God, who hath also given unto us his holy Spirit."

2 Timothy 1:7 "For God hath not given us the spirit of fear; but of power, and of love, and of a sound mind."

2 Timothy 4:7-8 "⁷I have fought a good fight, I have finished my course, I have kept the faith: ⁸Henceforth there is laid up for me a crown of righteousness, which the Lord, the righteous judge, shall give me at that day: and not to me only, but unto all them also that love his appearing."

James 1:5 "If any of you lack wisdom, let him ask of God, that giveth to all men liberally, and upbraideth not; and it shall be given him."

James 4:6 "But he giveth more grace. Wherefore he saith, God resisteth the proud, but giveth grace unto the humble."

1 Peter 5:5 "Likewise, ye younger, submit yourselves unto the elder. Yea, all of you be subject one to another, and be clothed with humility: for God resisteth the proud, and giveth grace to the humble."

2 Peter 1:1-4 "¹Simon Peter, a servant and an apostle of Jesus Christ, to them that have obtained like precious faith with us through the righteousness of God and our Saviour Jesus Christ: ²Grace and peace be multiplied unto you

through the knowledge of God, and of Jesus our Lord, ³According as his divine power hath given unto us all things that pertain unto life and godliness, through the knowledge of him that hath called us to glory and virtue: ⁴Whereby are given unto us exceeding great and precious promises: that by these ye might be partakers of the divine nature, having escaped the corruption that is in the world through lust."

1 John 3:21-24 "²¹Beloved, if our heart condemn us not, then have we confidence toward God. ²²And whatsoever we ask, we receive of him, because we keep his commandments, and do those things that are pleasing in his sight. ²³And this is his commandment, That we should believe on the name of his Son Jesus Christ, and love one another, as he gave us commandment. ²⁴And he that keepeth his commandments dwelleth in him, and he in him. And hereby we know that he abideth in us, by the Spirit which he hath given us."

1 John 4:12-13 "¹²No man hath seen God at any time. If we love one another, God dwelleth in us, and his love is perfected in us. ¹³Hereby know we that we dwell in him, and he in us, because he hath given us of his Spirit."

1 John 5:11 "And this is the record, that God hath given to us eternal life, and this life is in his Son."

1 John 5:20 "And we know that the Son of God is come, and hath given us an understanding, that we may know him that is true, and we are in him that is true, even in his Son Jesus Christ. This is the true God, and eternal life."

Revelation 2:8-10 "⁸And unto the angel of the church in Smyrna write; These things saith the first and the last, which was dead, and is alive; ⁹I know thy works, and tribulation, and poverty, (but thou art rich) and I know the blasphemy of them which say they are Jews, and are not, but are the synagogue of Satan. ¹⁰Fear none of those things which thou shalt suffer: behold, the devil shall cast some of you into prison, that ye may be tried; and ye shall have tribulation ten days: be thou faithful unto death, and I will give thee a crown of life."

Revelation 21:6 "And he said unto me, It is done. I am Alpha and Omega, the beginning and the end. I will give unto him that is athirst of the fountain of the water of life freely."

Revelation 22:3-5 "³And there shall be no more curse: but the throne of God and of the Lamb shall be in it; and his servants shall serve him: ⁴And they shall see his face; and his name shall be in their foreheads. ⁵And there shall be no night there; and they need no candle, neither light of the sun; for the Lord God giveth them light: and they shall reign for ever and ever."

What Should Be Given To The Lord
1 Chronicles 16:28-29 "²⁸Give unto the LORD, ye kindreds of the people, give unto the LORD glory and strength. ²⁹Give unto the LORD the glory due unto his name: bring an offering, and come before him: worship the LORD in the beauty of holiness."

Psalm 29:2 "Give unto the LORD the glory due unto his name; worship the LORD in the beauty of holiness."

Psalm 96:8 "Give unto the LORD the glory due unto his name: bring an offering, and come into his courts."

Romans 12:1-2 "¹I beseech you therefore, brethren, by the mercies of God, that ye present your bodies a living sacrifice, holy, acceptable unto God, which is your reasonable service. ²And be not conformed to this world: but be ye transformed by the renewing of your mind, that ye may prove what is that good, and acceptable, and perfect, will of God."

Revelation 14:7 "Saying with a loud voice, Fear God, and give glory to him; for the hour of his judgment is come: and worship him that made heaven, and earth, and the sea, and the fountains of waters."

Who Gives
Psalm 37:21 "The wicked borroweth, and payeth not again: but the righteous sheweth mercy, and giveth."

GLORY

All Coming Short Of The Glory Of God
Romans 3:23 "For all have sinned, and come short of the glory of God;"

Giving Glory To The Lord
1 Chronicles 16:28-29 "²⁸Give unto the LORD, ye kindreds of the people, give unto the LORD glory and strength. ²⁹Give unto the LORD the glory due unto his name: bring an offering, and come before him: worship the LORD in the beauty of holiness."

Psalm 29:2 "Give unto the LORD the glory due unto his name; worship the LORD in the beauty of holiness."

Psalm 96:8 "Give unto the LORD the glory due unto his name: bring an offering, and come into his courts."

Revelation 14:7 "Saying with a loud voice, Fear God, and give glory to him; for the hour of his judgment is come: and worship him that made heaven, and earth, and the sea, and the fountains of waters."

Glorifying The Lord
Psalm 22:23 "Ye that fear the LORD, praise him; all ye the seed of Jacob, glorify him; and fear him, all ye the seed of Israel."

Isaiah 24:15 "Wherefore glorify ye the LORD in the fires, even the name of the LORD God of Israel in the isles of the sea."

1 Corinthians 6:19-20 "¹⁹What? know ye not that your body is the temple of the Holy Ghost which is in you, which ye have of God, and ye are not your own? ²⁰For ye are bought with a price: therefore glorify God in your body, and in your spirit, which are God's."

1 Corinthians 10:31 "Whether therefore ye eat, or drink, or whatsoever ye do, do all to the glory of God."

Glory Belonging To The Lord
1 Chronicles 29:11 "Thine, O LORD, is the greatness, and the power, and the glory, and the victory, and the majesty: for all that is in the heaven and in the earth is thine; thine is the kingdom, O LORD, and thou art exalted as head above all."

Glorying In The Lord
Psalm 105:1-3 "¹O give thanks unto the LORD; call upon his name: make known his deeds among the people. ²Sing unto him, sing psalms unto him: talk ye of all his wondrous works. ³Glory ye in his holy

name: let the heart of them rejoice that seek the LORD."

Jeremiah 9:23-24 "23Thus saith the LORD, Let not the wise man glory in his wisdom, neither let the mighty man glory in his might, let not the rich man glory in his riches: 24But let him that glorieth glory in this, that he understandeth and knoweth me, that I am the LORD which exercise lovingkindness, judgment, and righteousness, in the earth: for in these things I delight, saith the LORD."

1 Corinthians 1:31 "That, according as it is written, He that glorieth, let him glory in the Lord."

2 Corinthians 10:17 "But he that glorieth, let him glory in the Lord."

Galatians 6:14 "But God forbid that I should glory, save in the cross of our Lord Jesus Christ, by whom the world is crucified unto me, and I unto the world."

God The Father Being Glorified
In God The Son (Jesus Christ)
John 12:23-28 "23And Jesus answered them, saying, The hour is come, that the Son of man should be glorified. 24Verily, verily, I say unto you, Except a corn of wheat fall into the ground and die, it abideth alone: but if it die, it bringeth forth much fruit. 25He that loveth his life shall lose it; and he that hateth his life in this world shall keep it unto life eternal. 26If any man serve me, let him follow me; and where I am, there shall also my servant be: if any man serve me, him will my Father honour. 27Now is my soul troubled; and what shall I say? Father, save me from this hour: but for this cause came I unto this hour. 28Father, glorify thy name. Then came there a voice from heaven, saying, I have both glorified it, and will glorify it again."

John 13:31-32 "31Therefore, when he was gone out, Jesus said, Now is the Son of man glorified, and God is glorified in him. 32If God be glorified in him, God shall also glorify him in himself, and shall straightway glorify him."

John 14:13 "And whatsoever ye shall ask in my name, that will I do, that the Father may be glorified in the Son."

John 17:1-5 "1These words spake Jesus, and lifted up his eyes to heaven, and said, Father, the hour is come; glorify thy Son, that thy Son also may glorify thee: 2As thou hast given him power over all flesh, that he should give eternal life to as many as thou hast given him. 3And this is life eternal, that they might know thee the only true God, and Jesus Christ, whom thou hast sent. 4I have glorified thee on the earth: I have finished the work which thou gavest me to do. 5And now, O Father, glorify thou me with thine own self with the glory which I had with thee before the world was."

1 Peter 4:11 "If any man speak, let him speak as the oracles of God; if any man minister, let him do it as of the ability which God giveth: that God in all things may be glorified through Jesus Christ, to whom be praise and dominion for ever and ever. Amen."

God The Father Giving Jesus Christ Glory
John 13:31-32 "31Therefore, when he was gone out, Jesus said, Now is the Son of man glorified, and God is glorified in him. 32If God be glorified in him, God shall also glorify him in himself, and shall straightway glorify him."

John 17:1-24 "1These words spake Jesus, and lifted up his eyes to heaven, and said, Father, the hour is come; glorify thy Son, that thy Son also may glorify thee: 2As thou hast given him power over all flesh, that he should give eternal life to as many as thou hast given him. 3And this is life eternal, that they might know thee the only true God, and Jesus Christ, whom thou hast sent. 4I have glorified thee on the earth: I have finished the work which thou gavest me to do. 5And now, O Father, glorify thou me with thine own self with the glory which I had with thee before the world was. 6I have manifested thy name unto the men which thou gavest me out of the world: thine they were, and thou gavest them me; and they have kept thy word. 7Now they have known that all things whatsoever thou hast given me are of thee. 8For I have given unto them the words which thou gavest me; and they have received them, and have known surely that I came out from thee, and they have believed that thou didst send me. 9I pray for them: I pray not for the world, but for them which thou hast given me; for they are thine. 10And all mine are thine, and thine are mine; and I am glorified in them. 11And now I am no more in the world, but these are in the world, and I come to thee. Holy Father, keep through thine own name those whom thou hast given me, that they may be one, as we are. [12]While I was with them in the world, I kept them in thy name: those that thou gavest me I have kept, and none of them is lost, but the son of perdition; that the scripture might be fulfilled. [13]And now come I to thee; and these things I speak in the world, that they might have my joy fulfilled in themselves. [14]I have given them thy word; and the world hath hated them, because they are not of the world, even as I am not of the world. [15]I pray not that thou shouldest take them out of the world, but that thou shouldest keep them from the evil. [16]They are not of the world, even as I am not of the world. [17]Sanctify them through thy truth: thy word is truth. [18]As thou hast sent me into the world, even so have I also sent them into the world. [19]And for their sakes I sanctify myself, that they also might be sanctified through the truth. [20]Neither pray I for these alone, but for them also which shall believe on me through their word; [21]That they all may be one; as thou, Father, art in me, and I in thee, that they also may be one in us: that the world may believe that thou hast sent me. [22]And the glory which thou gavest me I have given them; that they may be one, even as we are one: [23]I in them, and thou in me, that they may be made perfect in one; and that the world may know that thou hast sent me, and hast loved them, as thou hast loved me. [24]Father, I will that they also, whom thou hast given me, be with me where I am; that they may behold my glory, which thou hast given me: for thou lovedst me before the foundation of the world."

Acts 3:13 "The God of Abraham, and of Isaac, and of Jacob, the God of our fathers, hath glorified his Son Jesus; whom ye delivered up, and denied him in the presence of Pilate, when he was determined to let him go."

Hebrews 2:9 "But we see Jesus, who was made a little lower than the angels for the suffering of death, crowned with glory and honour; that he by the grace of God should taste death for every man."

1 Peter 1:18-21 "[18]Forasmuch as ye know that ye were not redeemed with corruptible things, as silver and gold, from your vain conversation received by tradition from your fathers; [19]But with the precious blood of Christ, as of a lamb without blemish and without spot: [20]Who verily was fore-ordained before the foundation of the world, but was manifest in these last times for you, [21]Who by him do believe in God, that raised him up from the dead, and gave him glory; that your faith and hope might be in God."

2 Peter 1:16-18 "[16]For we have not followed cunningly devised fables, when we made known unto you the power and coming of our Lord Jesus Christ, but were eyewitnesses of his majesty. [17]For he received from God the Father honour and glory, when there came such a voice to him from the excellent glory, This is my beloved Son, in whom I am well pleased. [18]And this voice which came from heaven we heard, when we were with him in the holy mount."

Jesus Christ Being Glorified In His Saints
2 Thessalonians 1:7-10 "[7]And to you who are troubled rest with us, when the Lord Jesus shall be revealed from heaven with his mighty angels, [8]In flaming fire taking vengeance on them that know not God, and that obey not the gospel of our Lord Jesus Christ: [9]Who shall be punished with everlasting destruction from the presence of the Lord, and from the glory of his power; [10]When he shall come to be glorified in his saints, and to be admired in all them that believe (because our testimony among you was believed) in that day."

Jesus Christ Not Seeking His Own Glory
John 8:49-50 "[49]Jesus answered, I have not a devil; but I honour my Father, and ye do dishonour me. [50]And I seek not mine own glory: there is one that seeketh and judgeth."

The Glory Of Man
1 Peter 1:24 "For all flesh is as grass, and all the glory of man as the flower of grass. The grass withereth, and the flower thereof falleth away:"

The Glory Of The Lord
Psalm 72:18-19 "[18]Blessed be the LORD God, the God of Israel, who only doeth wondrous things. [19]And blessed be his glorious name for ever: and let the whole earth be filled with his glory; Amen, and Amen."

Psalm 104:31 "The glory of the LORD shall endure for ever: the LORD shall rejoice in his works."

Psalm 108:3-5 "3I will praise thee, O LORD, among the people: and I will sing praises unto thee among the nations. 4For thy mercy is great above the heavens: and thy truth reacheth unto the clouds. 5Be thou exalted, O God, above the heavens: and thy glory above all the earth;"

Psalm 113:4 "The LORD is high above all nations, and his glory above the heavens."

Psalm 138:5 "Yea, they shall sing in the ways of the LORD: for great is the glory of the LORD."

Psalm 148:13 "Let them praise the name of the LORD: for his name alone is excellent; his glory is above the earth and heaven."

Isaiah 6:1-3 "1In the year that king Uzziah died I saw also the Lord sitting upon a throne, high and lifted up, and his train filled the temple. 2Above it stood the seraphims: each one had six wings; with twain he covered his face, and with twain he covered his feet, and with twain he did fly. 3And one cried unto another, and said, Holy, holy, holy, is the LORD of hosts: the whole earth is full of his glory."

Isaiah 40:5 "And the glory of the LORD shall be revealed, and all flesh shall see it together: for the mouth of the LORD hath spoken it."

Isaiah 42:8 "I am the LORD: that is my name: and my glory will I not give to another, neither my praise to graven images."

Isaiah 60:1-2 "1Arise, shine; for thy light is come, and the glory of the LORD is risen upon thee. 2For, behold, the darkness shall cover the earth, and gross darkness the people: but the LORD shall arise upon thee, and his glory shall be seen upon thee."

Habakkuk 2:14 "For the earth shall be filled with the knowledge of the glory of the LORD, as the waters cover the sea."

Romans 8:18 "For I reckon that the sufferings of this present time are not worthy to be compared with the glory which shall be revealed in us."

1 Peter 4:13 "But rejoice, inasmuch as ye are partakers of Christ's sufferings; that, when his glory shall be revealed, ye may be glad also with exceeding joy."

Revelation 21:21-23 "21And the twelve gates were twelve pearls; every several gate was of one pearl: and the street of the city was pure gold, as it were transparent glass. 22And I saw no temple therein: for the Lord God Almighty and the Lamb are the temple of it. 23And the city had no need of the sun, neither of the moon, to shine in it: for the glory of God did lighten it, and the Lamb is the light thereof."

The Holy Spirit Glorifying Jesus Christ

John 16:5-15 "5But now I go my way to him that sent me; and none of you asketh me, Whither goest thou? 6But because I have said these things unto you, sorrow hath filled your heart. 7Nevertheless I tell you the truth; It is expedient for you that I go away: for if I go not away, the Comforter will not come unto you; but if I depart, I will send him unto you. 8And when he is come, he will reprove the world of sin, and of righteousness, and of judgment: 9Of sin, because they believe not on me; 10Of righteousness, because I go to my Father, and ye see me no more; 11Of judgment, because the prince of this world is judged. 12I have yet many things to say unto you, but ye cannot bear them now. 13Howbeit when he, the Spirit of truth, is come, he will guide you into all truth: for he shall not speak of himself; but whatsoever he shall hear, that shall he speak: and he will shew you things to come. 14He shall glorify me: for he shall receive of mine, and shall shew it unto you. 15All things that the Father hath are mine: therefore said I, that he shall take of mine, and shall shew it unto you."

The Lord Being Glorious

Exodus 15:11 "Who is like unto thee, O LORD, among the gods? who is like thee, glorious in holiness, fearful in praises, doing wonders?"

The Lord Being Glory

Psalm 3:3 "But thou, O LORD, art a shield for me; my glory, and the lifter up of mine head."

Psalm 24:10 "Who is this King of glory? The LORD of hosts, he is the King of glory. Selah."

Isaiah 60:19 "The sun shall be no more thy light by day; neither for brightness shall the moon give light unto thee: but the LORD shall be unto thee an everlasting light, and thy God thy glory."

Zechariah 2:4-5 "⁴And said unto him, Run, speak to this young man, saying, Jerusalem shall be inhabited as towns without walls for the multitude of men and cattle therein: ⁵For I, saith the LORD, will be unto her a wall of fire round about, and will be the glory in the midst of her."

James 2:1 "My brethren, have not the faith of our Lord Jesus Christ, the Lord of glory, with respect of persons."

The Lord Giving Glory
Psalm 62:6-7 "⁶He only is my rock and my salvation: he is my defence; I shall not be moved. ⁷In God is my salvation and my glory: the rock of my strength, and my refuge, is in God."

Psalm 84:11 "For the LORD God is a sun and shield: the LORD will give grace and glory: no good thing will he withhold from them that walk uprightly."

The Reward For Not Glorifying God
Daniel 5:23-31 "²³But hast lifted up thyself against the LORD of heaven; and they have brought the vessels of his house before thee, and thou, and thy lords, thy wives, and thy concubines, have drunk wine in them; and thou hast praised the gods of silver, and gold, of brass, iron, wood, and stone, which see not, nor hear, nor know: and the God in whose hand thy breath is, and whose are all thy ways, hast thou not glorified: ²⁴Then was the part of the hand sent from him; and this writing was written. ²⁵And this is the writing that was written, MENE, MENE, TEKEL, UPHARSIN. ²⁶This is the interpretation of the thing: MENE; God hath numbered thy kingdom, and finished it. ²⁷TEKEL; Thou art weighed in the balances, and art found wanting. ²⁸PERES; Thy kingdom is divided, and given to the Medes and Persians. ²⁹Then commanded Belshazzar, and they clothed Daniel with scarlet, and put a chain of gold about his neck, and made a proclamation concerning him, that he should be the third ruler in the kingdom. ³⁰In that night was Belshazzar the king of the Chaldeans slain. ³¹And Darius the Median took the kingdom, being about threescore and two years old."

Romans 1:18-22 "¹⁸For the wrath of God is revealed from heaven against all ungodliness and unrighteousness of men, who hold the truth in unrighteousness; ¹⁹Because that which may be known of God is manifest in them; for God hath shewed it unto them. ²⁰For the invisible things of him from the creation of the world are clearly seen, being understood by the things that are made, even his eternal power and Godhead; so that they are without excuse: ²¹Because that, when they knew God, they glorified him not as God, neither were thankful; but became vain in their imaginations, and their foolish heart was darkened. ²²Professing themselves to be wise, they became fools,"

What Is Not Glory
Proverbs 25:27 "It is not good to eat much honey: so for men to search their own glory is not glory."

What Not To Glory In
Jeremiah 9:23-24 "²³Thus saith the LORD, Let not the wise man glory in his wisdom, neither let the mighty man glory in his might, let not the rich man glory in his riches: ²⁴But let him that glorieth glory in this, that he understandeth and knoweth me, that I am the LORD which exercise lovingkindness, judgment, and righteousness, in the earth: for in these things I delight, saith the LORD."

1 Corinthians 3:20-21 "²⁰And again, The Lord knoweth the thoughts of the wise, that they are vain. ²¹Therefore let no man glory in men. For all things are yours;"

When There Is Great Glory
Proverbs 28:12 "When righteous men do rejoice, there is great glory: but when the wicked rise, a man is hidden."

Where Glory Is
1 Chronicles 16:26-27 "²⁶For all the gods of the people are idols: but the LORD made the heavens. ²⁷Glory and honour are in his presence; strength and gladness are in his place."

Who Can Reflect The Glory Of The Lord
2 Corinthians 3:17-18 "¹⁷Now the Lord is that Spirit: and where the Spirit of the Lord is, there is liberty. ¹⁸But we all, with open face beholding as in a glass the glory of the Lord, are changed into the same image from glory to glory, even as by the Spirit of the Lord."

Who Glorifies The Lord
Psalm 50:16-23 "¹⁶But unto the wicked God saith, What hast thou to do to declare my statutes, or that thou shouldest take my covenant in thy

mouth? [17]Seeing thou hatest instruction, and castest my words behind thee. [18]When thou sawest a thief, then thou consentedst with him, and hast been partaker with adulterers. [19]Thou givest thy mouth to evil, and thy tongue frameth deceit. [20]Thou sittest and speakest against thy brother; thou slanderest thine own mother's son. [21]These things hast thou done, and I kept silence; thou thoughtest that I was altogether such an one as thyself: but I will reprove thee, and set them in order before thine eyes. [22]Now consider this, ye that forget God, lest I tear you in pieces, and there be none to deliver. [23]Whoso offereth praise glorifieth me: and to him that ordereth his conversation aright will I shew the salvation of God."

Matthew 5:11-16 "[11]Blessed are ye, when men shall revile you, and persecute you, and shall say all manner of evil against you falsely, for my sake. [12]Rejoice, and be exceeding glad: for great is your reward in heaven: for so persecuted they the prophets which were before you. [13]Ye are the salt of the earth: but if the salt have lost his savour, wherewith shall it be salted? it is thenceforth good for nothing, but to be cast out, and to be trodden under foot of men. [14]Ye are the light of the world. A city that is set on an hill cannot be hid. [15]Neither do men light a candle, and put it under a bushel, but on a candlestick; and it giveth light unto all that are in the house. [16]Let your light so shine before men, that they may see your good works, and glorify your Father which is in heaven."

Luke 13:10-13 "[10]And he was teaching in one of the synagogues on the sabbath. [11]And, behold, there was a woman which had a spirit of infirmity eighteen years, and was bowed together, and could in no wise lift up herself. [12]And when Jesus saw her, he called her to him, and said unto her, Woman, thou art loosed from thine infirmity. [13]And he laid his hands on her: and immediately she was made straight, and glorified God."

Who Shall Glorify The Lord
Isaiah 25:1-3 "[1]O LORD, thou art my God; I will exalt thee, I will praise thy name; for thou hast done wonderful things; thy counsels of old are faithfulness and truth. [2]For thou hast made of a city an heap; of a defenced city a ruin: a palace of strangers to be no city; it shall never be built. [3]Therefore shall the strong people glorify thee, the city of the terrible nations shall fear thee."

Who Shall Glory
Psalm 63:11 "But the king shall rejoice in God; every one that sweareth by him shall glory: but the mouth of them that speak lies shall be stopped."

Psalm 64:9-10 "[9]And all men shall fear, and shall declare the work of God; for they shall wisely consider of his doing. [10]The righteous shall be glad in the LORD, and shall trust in him; and all the upright in heart shall glory."

Isaiah 45:25 "In the LORD shall all the seed of Israel be justified, and shall glory."

Who Shall Receive Glory
1 Samuel 2:7-8 "[7]The LORD maketh poor, and maketh rich: he bringeth low, and lifteth up. [8]He raiseth up the poor out of the dust, and lifteth up the beggar from the dunghill, to set them among princes, and to make them inherit the throne of glory: for the pillars of the earth are the LORD's, and he hath set the world upon them."

Proverbs 3:35 "The wise shall inherit glory: but shame shall be the promotion of fools."

Romans 2:10 "But glory, honour, and peace, to every man that worketh good, to the Jew first, and also to the Gentile:"

Romans 8:16-17 "[16]The Spirit itself beareth witness with our spirit, that we are the children of God: [17]And if children, then heirs; heirs of God, and joint-heirs with Christ; if so be that we suffer with him, that we may be also glorified together."

Who Shall See The Glory Of God
Psalm 97:5-6 "[5]The hills melted like wax at the presence of the LORD, at the presence of the Lord of the whole earth. [6]The heavens declare his righteousness, and all the people see his glory."

Isaiah 40:5 "And the glory of the LORD shall be revealed, and all flesh shall see it together: for the mouth of the LORD hath spoken it."

Isaiah 66:17-18 "[17]They that sanctify themselves, and purify themselves in the gardens behind one tree in the midst, eating swine's flesh, and the abomination, and the mouse, shall be consumed together, saith the LORD. [18]For I know their works and their thoughts: it shall come, that I will gather all nations and tongues; and they shall come, and see my glory."

John 11:40 "Jesus saith unto her, Said I not unto thee, that, if thou wouldest believe, thou shouldest see the glory of God?"

Who The Lord Glorifies

Psalm 8:1-5 "¹O LORD our Lord, how excellent is thy name in all the earth! who hast set thy glory above the heavens. ²Out of the mouth of babes and sucklings hast thou ordained strength because of thine enemies, that thou mightest still the enemy and the avenger. ³When I consider thy heavens, the work of thy fingers, the moon and the stars, which thou hast ordained; ⁴What is man, that thou art mindful of him? and the son of man, that thou visitest him? ⁵For thou hast made him a little lower than the angels, and hast crowned him with glory and honour."

Isaiah 55:1-5 "¹Ho, every one that thirsteth, come ye to the waters, and he that hath no money; come ye, buy, and eat; yea, come, buy wine and milk without money and without price. ²Wherefore do ye spend money for that which is not bread? and your labour for that which satisfieth not? hearken diligently unto me, and eat ye that which is good, and let your soul delight itself in fatness. ³Incline your ear, and come unto me: hear, and your soul shall live; and I will make an everlasting covenant with you, even the sure mercies of David. ⁴Behold, I have given him for a witness to the people, a leader and commander to the people. ⁵Behold, thou shalt call a nation that thou knowest not, and nations that knew not thee shall run unto thee because of the LORD thy God, and for the Holy One of Israel; for he hath glorified thee."

John 17:1-22 "¹These words spake Jesus, and lifted up his eyes to heaven, and said, Father, the hour is come; glorify thy Son, that thy Son also may glorify thee: ²As thou hast given him power over all flesh, that he should give eternal life to as many as thou hast given him. ³And this is life eternal, that they might know thee the only true God, and Jesus Christ, whom thou hast sent. ⁴I have glorified thee on the earth: I have finished the work which thou gavest me to do. ⁵And now, O Father, glorify thou me with thine own self with the glory which I had with thee before the world was. ⁶I have manifested thy name unto the men which thou gavest me out of the world: thine they were, and thou gavest them me; and they have kept thy word. ⁷Now they have known that all things whatsoever thou hast given me are of thee. ⁸For I have given unto them the words which thou gavest me; and they have received them, and have known surely that I came out from thee, and they have believed that thou didst send me. ⁹I pray for them: I pray not for the world, but for them which thou hast given me; for they are thine. ¹⁰And all mine are thine, and thine are mine; and I am glorified in them. ¹¹And now I am no more in the world, but these are in the world, and I come to thee. Holy Father, keep through thine own name those whom thou hast given me, that they may be one, as we are. ¹²While I was with them in the world, I kept them in thy name: those that thou gavest me I have kept, and none of them is lost, but the son of perdition; that the scripture might be fulfilled. ¹³And now come I to thee; and these things I speak in the world, that they might have my joy fulfilled in themselves. ¹⁴I have given them thy word; and the world hath hated them, because they are not of the world, even as I am not of the world. ¹⁵I pray not that thou shouldest take them out of the world, but that thou shouldest keep them from the evil. ¹⁶They are not of the world, even as I am not of the world. ¹⁷Sanctify them through thy truth: thy word is truth. ¹⁸As thou hast sent me into the world, even so have I also sent them into the world. ¹⁹And for their sakes I sanctify myself, that they also might be sanctified through the truth. ²⁰Neither pray I for these alone, but for them also which shall believe on me through their word; ²¹That they all may be one; as thou, Father, art in me, and I in thee, that they also may be one in us: that the world may believe that thou hast sent me. ²²And the glory which thou gavest me I have given them; that they may be one, even as we are one:"

Romans 8:28-30 "²⁸And we know that all things work together for good to them that love God, to them who are the called according to his purpose. ²⁹For whom he did foreknow, he also did predestinate to be conformed to the image of his Son, that he might be the firstborn among many brethren. ³⁰Moreover whom he did predestinate, them he also called: and whom he called, them he also justified: and whom he justified, them he also glorified."

Whose Glory Becomes Shame

Hosea 4:6-7 "⁶My people are destroyed for lack of knowledge: because thou hast rejected knowledge, I will also reject thee, that thou shalt be no priest to me: seeing thou hast forgotten the law of thy God, I will also forget thy children. 7As they were increased, so they sinned against me: therefore will I change their glory into shame."

Habakkuk 2:6-16 "6Shall not all these take up a parable against him, and a taunting proverb against him, and say, Woe to him that increaseth that which is not his! how long? and to him that ladeth himself with thick clay! 7Shall they not rise up suddenly that shall bite thee, and awake that shall vex thee, and thou shalt be for booties unto them? 8Because thou hast spoiled many nations, all the remnant of the people shall spoil thee; because of men's blood, and for the violence of the land, of the city, and of all that dwell therein. 9Woe to him that coveteth an evil covetousness to his house, that he may set his nest on high, that he may be delivered from the power of evil! 10Thou hast consulted shame to thy house by cutting off many people, and hast sinned against thy soul. 11For the stone shall cry out of the wall, and the beam out of the timber shall answer it. 12Woe to him that buildeth a town with blood, and stablisheth a city by iniquity! 13Behold, is it not of the LORD of hosts that the people shall labour in the very fire, and the people shall weary themselves for very vanity? 14For the earth shall be filled with the knowledge of the glory of the LORD, as the waters cover the sea. 15Woe unto him that giveth his neighbour drink, that puttest thy bottle to him, and makest him drunken also, that thou mayest look on their nakedness! 16Thou art filled with shame for glory: drink thou also, and let thy foreskin be uncovered: the cup of the LORD's right hand shall be turned unto thee, and shameful spewing shall be on thy glory."

Whose Glory Is In Their Shame
Philippians 3:18-19 "18(For many walk, of whom I have told you often, and now tell you even weeping, that they are the enemies of the cross of Christ: 19Whose end is destruction, whose God is their belly, and whose glory is in their shame, who mind earthly things.)"

GOD

God The Father, God The Son, And God The Holy Spirit Being One
1 John 5:7 "For there are three that bear record in heaven, the Father, the Word, and the Holy Ghost: and these three are one."

Nothing Being Too Difficult For The Lord God
Genesis 18:14 "Is any thing too hard for the LORD? At the time appointed I will return unto thee, according to the time of life, and Sarah shall have a son."

Jeremiah 32:17 "Ah Lord GOD! behold, thou hast made the heaven and the earth by thy great power and stretched out arm, and there is nothing too hard for thee:"

The Character Of The Lord God
Genesis 18:22-26 "22And the men turned their faces from thence, and went toward Sodom: but Abraham stood yet before the LORD. 23And Abraham drew near, and said, Wilt thou also destroy the righteous with the wicked? 24Peradventure there be fifty righteous within the city: wilt thou also destroy and not spare the place for the fifty righteous that are therein? 25That be far from thee to do after this manner, to slay the righteous with the wicked: and that the righteous should be as the wicked, that be far from thee: Shall not the Judge of all the earth do right? 26And the LORD said, If I find in Sodom fifty righteous within the city, then I will spare all the place for their sakes."

Exodus 20:3-6 "3Thou shalt have no other gods before me. 4Thou shalt not make unto thee any graven image, or any likeness of any thing that is in heaven above, or that is in the earth beneath, or that is in the water under the earth: 5Thou shalt not bow down thyself to them, nor serve them: for I the LORD thy God am a jealous God, visiting the iniquity of the fathers upon the children unto the third and fourth generation of them that hate me; 6And shewing mercy unto thousands of them that love me, and keep my commandments."

Exodus 22:20-27 "20He that sacrificeth unto any god, save unto the LORD only, he shall be utterly destroyed. 21Thou shalt neither vex a stranger, nor oppress him: for ye were strangers in the land of Egypt. 22Ye shall not afflict any widow, or fatherless child. 23If thou afflict them in any wise, and they cry at all unto me, I will surely hear their cry; 24And my wrath shall wax hot, and I will kill you with the sword; and your wives shall be widows, and your children fatherless. 25If thou lend money to any of my people that is poor by thee, thou shalt not be to him as an usurer, neither shalt thou lay upon him usury. 26If thou at all take thy neighbour's raiment to pledge, thou shalt deliver it unto him by that the sun goeth down: 27For that is his covering only, it is his raiment for his skin: wherein shall he sleep? and it shall come to pass, when he crieth unto me, that I will hear; for I am gracious."

Exodus 33:17-19 "17And the LORD said unto Moses, I will do this thing also that thou hast spoken: for thou hast found grace in my sight, and I know thee by name. 18And he said, I beseech thee, shew me thy glory. 19And he said, I will make all my goodness pass before thee, and I will proclaim the name of the LORD before thee; and will be gracious to whom I will be gracious, and will shew mercy on whom I will shew mercy."

Exodus 34:6-7 "6And the LORD passed by before him, and proclaimed, The LORD, The LORD God, merciful and gracious, longsuffering, and abundant in goodness and truth, 7Keeping mercy for thousands, forgiving iniquity and transgression and sin, and that will by no means clear the guilty; visiting the iniquity of the fathers upon the children, and upon the children's children, unto the third and to the fourth generation."

Exodus 34:14 "For thou shalt worship no other god: for the LORD, whose name is Jealous, is a jealous God:"

Leviticus 11:44-45 "44For I am the LORD your God: ye shall therefore sanctify yourselves, and ye shall be holy; for I am holy: neither shall ye defile yourselves with any manner of creeping thing that creepeth upon the earth. 45For I am the LORD that bringeth you up out of the land of Egypt, to be your God: ye shall therefore be holy, for I am holy."

Leviticus 19:2 "Speak unto all the congregation of the children of Israel, and say unto them, Ye shall be holy: for I the LORD your God am holy."

Leviticus 20:26 "And ye shall be holy unto me: for I the LORD am holy, and have severed you from other people, that ye should be mine."

Leviticus 21:8 "Thou shalt sanctify him therefore; for he offereth the bread of thy God: he shall be holy unto thee: for I the LORD, which sanctify you, am holy."

Numbers 14:18-19 "18The LORD is longsuffering, and of great mercy, forgiving iniquity and transgression, and by no means clearing the guilty, visiting the iniquity of the fathers upon the children unto the third and fourth generation. 19Pardon, I beseech thee, the iniquity of this people according unto the greatness of thy mercy, and as thou hast forgiven this people, from Egypt even until now."

Numbers 23:19 "God is not a man, that he should lie; neither the son of man, that he should repent: hath he said, and shall he not do it? or hath he spoken, and shall he not make it good?"

Deuteronomy 4:24 "For the LORD thy God is a consuming fire, even a jealous God."

Deuteronomy 4:31 "(For the LORD thy God is a merciful God;) he will not forsake thee, neither destroy thee, nor forget the covenant of thy fathers which he sware unto them."

Deuteronomy 5:7-10 "7Thou shalt have none other gods before me. 8Thou shalt not make thee any graven image, or any likeness of any thing that is in heaven above, or that is in the earth beneath, or that is in the waters beneath the earth: 9Thou shalt not bow down thyself unto them, nor serve them: for I the LORD thy God am a jealous God, visiting the iniquity of the fathers upon the children unto the third and fourth generation of them that hate me, 10And shewing mercy unto thousands of them that love me and keep my commandments."

Deuteronomy 6:15 "(For the LORD thy God is a jealous God among you) lest the anger of the LORD thy God be kindled against thee, and destroy thee from off the face of the earth."

Deuteronomy 7:9 "Know therefore that the LORD thy God, he is God, the faithful God, which keepeth covenant and mercy with them that love him and keep his commandments to a thousand generations;"

Deuteronomy 10:17 "For the LORD your God is God of gods, and Lord of lords, a great God, a mighty, and a terrible, which regardeth not persons, nor taketh reward:"

Deuteronomy 32:4 "He is the Rock, his work is perfect: for all his ways are judgment: a God of truth and without iniquity, just and right is he."

1 Samuel 15:29 "And also the Strength of Israel will not lie nor repent: for he is not a man, that he should repent."

1 Samuel 16:7 "But the LORD said unto Samuel, Look not on his countenance, or on the height of his stature; because I have refused him: for the LORD seeth not as man seeth; for man looketh on the outward appearance, but the LORD looketh on the heart."

1 Chronicles 16:34 "O give thanks unto the LORD; for he is good; for his mercy endureth for ever."

2 Chronicles 19:7 "Wherefore now let the fear of the LORD be upon you; take heed and do it: for there is no iniquity with the LORD our God, nor respect of persons, nor taking of gifts."

2 Chronicles 30:9 "For if ye turn again unto the LORD, your brethren and your children shall find compassion before them that lead them captive, so that they shall come again into this land: for the LORD your God is gracious and merciful, and will not turn away his face from you, if ye return unto him."

Ezra 9:9 "For we were bondmen; yet our God hath not forsaken us in our bondage, but hath extended mercy unto us in the sight of the kings of Persia, to give us a reviving, to set up the house of our God, and to repair the desolations thereof, and to give us a wall in Judah and in Jerusalem."

Ezra 9:15 "O LORD God of Israel, thou art righteous: for we remain yet escaped, as it is this day: behold, we are before thee in our trespasses: for we cannot stand before thee because of this."

Nehemiah 1:5 "And said, I beseech thee, O LORD God of heaven, the great and terrible God, that keepeth covenant and mercy for them that love him and observe his commandments:"

Nehemiah 9:7-8 "⁷Thou art the LORD the God, who didst choose Abram, and broughtest him forth out of Ur of the Chaldees, and gavest him the name of Abraham; ⁸And foundest his heart faithful before thee, and madest a covenant with him to give the land of the Canaanites, the Hittites, the Amorites, and the Perizzites, and the Jebusites, and the Girgashites, to give it, I say, to his seed, and hast performed thy words; for thou art righteous:"

Nehemiah 9:16-19 "¹⁶But they and our fathers dealt proudly, and hardened their necks, and hearkened not to thy commandments, ¹⁷And refused to obey, neither were mindful of thy wonders that thou didst among them; but hardened their necks, and in their rebellion appointed a captain to return to their bondage: but thou art a God ready to pardon, gracious and merciful, slow to anger, and of great kindness, and forsookest them not. ¹⁸Yea, when they had made them a molten calf, and said, This is thy God that brought thee up out of Egypt, and had wrought great provocations; ¹⁹Yet thou in thy manifold mercies forsookest them not in the wilderness: the pillar of the cloud departed not from them by day, to lead them in the way; neither the pillar of fire by night, to shew them light, and the way wherein they should go."

Nehemiah 9:31-33 "³¹Nevertheless for thy great mercies' sake thou didst not utterly consume them, nor forsake them; for thou art a gracious and merciful God. ³²Now therefore, our God, the great, the mighty, and the terrible God, who keepest covenant and mercy, let not all the trouble seem little before thee, that hath come upon us, on our kings, on our princes, and on our priests, and on our prophets, and on our fathers, and on all thy people, since the time of the kings of Assyria unto this day. ³³Howbeit thou art just in all that is brought upon us; for thou hast done right, but we have done wickedly:"

Job 8:20 "Behold, God will not cast away a perfect man, neither will he help the evil doers:"

Job 34:10-19 "¹⁰Therefore hearken unto me, ye men of understanding: far be it from God, that he should do wickedness; and from the Almighty, that he should commit iniquity. ¹¹For the work of a man shall he render unto him, and cause every man to find according to his ways. ¹²Yea, surely God will not do wickedly, neither will the Almighty pervert judgment. ¹³Who hath given him a charge over the earth? or who hath disposed the whole world? ¹⁴If he set his heart upon man, if he gather unto himself his spirit and his breath; ¹⁵All flesh shall perish together, and man shall turn again unto dust. ¹⁶If now thou hast understanding, hear this: hearken to the voice of my words. ¹⁷Shall even he that hateth right govern? and wilt thou condemn him that is most just? ¹⁸Is it fit to say to a king, Thou art wicked? and to princes, Ye are ungodly? [19]How much less to him that accepteth not the persons of princes, nor regardeth the rich more than the poor? for they all are the work of his hands."

Job 35:13 "Surely God will not hear vanity, neither will the Almighty regard it."

Job 36:5-7 "[5]Behold, God is mighty, and despiseth not any: he is mighty in strength and wisdom. [6]He preserveth not the life of the wicked: but giveth right to the poor. [7]He withdraweth not his eyes from the righteous: but with kings are they on the throne; yea, he doth establish them for ever, and they are exalted."

Job 37:23-24 "[23]Touching the Almighty, we cannot find him out: he is excellent in power, and in judgment, and in plenty of justice: he will not afflict. [24]Men do therefore fear him: he respecteth not any that are wise of heart."

Psalm 5:4 "For thou art not a God that hath pleasure in wickedness: neither shall evil dwell with thee."

Psalm 7:9 "Oh let the wickedness of the wicked come to an end; but establish the just: for the righteous God trieth the hearts and reins."

Psalm 11:7 "For the righteous LORD loveth righteousness; his countenance doth behold the upright."

Psalm 25:8 "Good and upright is the LORD: therefore will he teach sinners in the way."

Psalm 34:8 "O taste and see that the LORD is good: blessed is the man that trusteth in him."

Psalm 78:32-38 "[32]For all this they sinned still, and believed not for his wondrous works. [33]Therefore their days did he consume in vanity, and their years in trouble. [34]When he slew them, then they sought him: and they returned and inquired early after God. [35]And they remembered that God was their rock, and the high God their redeemer. [36]Nevertheless they did flatter him with their mouth, and they lied unto him with their tongues. [37]For their heart was not right with him, neither were they stedfast in his covenant. [38]But he, being full of compassion, forgave their iniquity, and destroyed them not: yea, many a

time turned he his anger away, and did not stir up all his wrath."

Psalm 86:5 "For thou, Lord, art good, and ready to forgive; and plenteous in mercy unto all them that call upon thee."

Psalm 86:15 "But thou, O Lord, art a God full of compassion, and gracious, longsuffering, and plenteous in mercy and truth."

Psalm 92:15 "To shew that the LORD is upright: he is my rock, and there is no unrighteousness in him."

Psalm 94:14 "For the LORD will not cast off his people, neither will he forsake his inheritance."

Psalm 99:5 "Exalt ye the LORD our God, and worship at his footstool; for he is holy."

Psalm 99:9 "Exalt the LORD our God, and worship at his holy hill; for the LORD our God is holy."

Psalm 100:5 "For the LORD is good; his mercy is everlasting; and his truth endureth to all generations."

Psalm 102:24-27 "[24]I said, O my God, take me not away in the midst of my days: thy years are throughout all generations. [25]Of old hast thou laid the foundation of the earth: and the heavens are the work of thy hands. [26]They shall perish, but thou shalt endure: yea, all of them shall wax old like a garment; as a vesture shalt thou change them, and they shall be changed: [27]But thou art the same, and thy years shall have no end."

Psalm 103:8-10 "[8]The LORD is merciful and gracious, slow to anger, and plenteous in mercy. [9]He will not always chide: neither will he keep his anger for ever. [10]He hath not dealt with us after our sins; nor rewarded us according to our iniquities."

Psalm 107:1 "O give thanks unto the LORD, for he is good: for his mercy endureth for ever."

Psalm 111:4-5 "[4]He hath made his wonderful works to be remembered: the LORD is gracious and full of compassion. [5]He hath given meat unto them that fear him: he will ever be mindful of his covenant."

Psalm 116:5 "Gracious is the LORD, and righteous; yea, our God is merciful."

Psalm 117:2 "For his merciful kindness is great toward us: and the truth of the LORD endureth for ever. Praise ye the LORD."

Psalm 118:1 "O give thanks unto the LORD; for he is good: because his mercy endureth for ever."

Psalm 118:29 "O give thanks unto the LORD; for he is good: for his mercy endureth for ever."

Psalm 119:65-68 "65Thou hast dealt well with thy servant, O LORD, according unto thy word. 66Teach me good judgment and knowledge: for I have believed thy commandments. 67Before I was afflicted I went astray: but now have I kept thy word. 68Thou art good, and doest good; teach me thy statutes."

Psalm 119:137 "Righteous art thou, O LORD, and upright are thy judgments."

Psalm 130:7-8 "7Let Israel hope in the LORD: for with the LORD there is mercy, and with him is plenteous redemption. 8And he shall redeem Israel from all his iniquities."

Psalm 136:1 "O give thanks unto the LORD; for he is good: for his mercy endureth for ever."

Psalm 143:10 "Teach me to do thy will; for thou art my God: thy spirit is good; lead me into the land of uprightness."

Psalm 145:8-9 "8The LORD is gracious, and full of compassion; slow to anger, and of great mercy. 9The LORD is good to all: and his tender mercies are over all his works."

Psalm 145:17 "The LORD is righteous in all his ways, and holy in all his works."

Psalm 146:5-6 "5Happy is he that hath the God of Jacob for his help, whose hope is in the LORD his God: 6Which made heaven, and earth, the sea, and all that therein is: which keepeth truth for ever:"

Isaiah 5:16 "But the LORD of hosts shall be exalted in judgment, and God that is holy shall be sanctified in righteousness."

Isaiah 6:1-3 "1In the year that king Uzziah died I saw also the Lord sitting upon a throne, high and lifted up, and his train filled the temple. 2Above it stood the seraphims: each one had six wings; with twain he covered his face, and with twain he covered his feet, and with twain he did fly. 3And one cried unto another, and said, Holy, holy, holy, is the LORD of hosts: the whole earth is full of his glory."

Isaiah 26:4-7 "4Trust ye in the LORD for ever: for in the LORD JEHOVAH is everlasting strength: 5For he bringeth down them that dwell on high; the lofty city, he layeth it low; he layeth it low, even to the ground; he bringeth it even to the dust. 6The foot shall tread it down, even the feet of the poor, and the steps of the needy. 7The way of the just is uprightness: thou, most upright, dost weigh the path of the just."

Isaiah 30:18 "And therefore will the LORD wait, that he may be gracious unto you, and therefore will he be exalted, that he may have mercy upon you: for the LORD is a God of judgment: blessed are all they that wait for him."

Isaiah 40:28 "Hast thou not known? hast thou not heard, that the everlasting God, the LORD, the Creator of the ends of the earth, fainteth not, neither is weary? there is no searching of his understanding."

Isaiah 49:7 "Thus saith the LORD, the Redeemer of Israel, and his Holy One, to him whom man despiseth, to him whom the nation abhorreth, to a servant of rulers, Kings shall see and arise, princes also shall worship, because of the LORD that is faithful, and the Holy One of Israel, and he shall choose thee."

Isaiah 54:5-10 "5For thy Maker is thine husband; the LORD of hosts is his name; and thy Redeemer the Holy One of Israel; The God of the whole earth shall he be called. 6For the LORD hath called thee as a woman forsaken and grieved in spirit, and a wife of youth, when thou wast refused, saith thy God. 7For a small moment have I forsaken thee; but with great mercies will I gather thee. 8In a little wrath I hid my face from thee for a moment; but with everlasting kindness will I have mercy on thee, saith the LORD thy Redeemer. 9For this is as the waters of Noah unto me: for as I have sworn that the waters of Noah should no more go over the earth; so have I sworn that I would not be wroth with thee, nor rebuke thee. 10For the mountains shall depart, and the hills be removed; but my kindness shall not depart from thee, neither shall the covenant of my peace be removed, saith the LORD that hath mercy on thee."

Jeremiah 3:11-12 "11And the LORD said unto me, The backsliding Israel hath justified herself more than treacherous Judah. 12Go and proclaim these words toward the north, and say, Return, thou backsliding Israel, saith the LORD; and I will not cause mine anger to fall upon you: for I am merciful, saith the LORD, and I will not keep anger for ever."

Jeremiah 9:23-24 "23Thus saith the LORD, Let not the wise man glory in his wisdom, neither let the mighty man glory in his might, let not the rich man glory in his riches: 24But let him that glorieth glory in this, that he understandeth and knoweth me, that I am the LORD which exercise lovingkindness, judgment, and righteousness, in the earth: for in these things I delight, saith the LORD."

Jeremiah 32:17-19 "17Ah Lord GOD! behold, thou hast made the heaven and the earth by thy great power and stretched out arm, and there is nothing too hard for thee: 18Thou shewest lovingkindness unto thousands, and recompensest the iniquity of the fathers into the bosom of their children after them: the Great, the Mighty God, the LORD of hosts, is his name, 19Great in counsel, and mighty in work: for thine eyes are open upon all the ways of the sons of men: to give every one according to his ways, and according to the fruit of his doings:"

Jeremiah 33:11 "The voice of joy, and the voice of gladness, the voice of the bridegroom, and the voice of the bride, the voice of them that shall say, Praise the LORD of hosts: for the LORD is good; for his mercy endureth for ever: and of them that shall bring the sacrifice of praise into the house of the LORD. For I will cause to return the captivity of the land, as at the first, saith the LORD."

Lamentations 3:31-36 "31For the Lord will not cast off for ever: 32But though he cause grief, yet will he have compassion according to the multitude of his mercies. 33For he doth not afflict willingly nor grieve the children of men. 34To crush under his feet all the prisoners of the earth, 35To turn aside the right of a man before the face of the most High, 36To subvert a man in his cause, the Lord approveth not."

Daniel 6:26 "I make a decree, That in every dominion of my kingdom men tremble and fear before the God of Daniel: for he is the living God, and stedfast for ever, and his kingdom that which shall not be destroyed, and his dominion shall be even unto the end."

Daniel 9:4 "And I prayed unto the LORD my God, and made my confession, and said, O Lord, the great and dreadful God, keeping the covenant and mercy to them that love him, and to them that keep his commandments;"

Daniel 9:14 "Therefore hath the LORD watched upon the evil, and brought it upon us: for the LORD our God is righteous in all his works which he doeth: for we obeyed not his voice."

Joel 2:12-13 "12Therefore also now, saith the LORD, turn ye even to me with all your heart, and with fasting, and with weeping, and with mourning: 13And rend your heart, and not your garments, and turn unto the LORD your God: for he is gracious and merciful, slow to anger, and of great kindness, and repenteth him of the evil."

Amos 5:15 "Hate the evil, and love the good, and establish judgment in the gate: it may be that the LORD God of hosts will be gracious unto the remnant of Joseph."

Micah 7:18-20 "18Who is a God like unto thee, that pardoneth iniquity, and passeth by the transgression of the remnant of his heritage? he retaineth not his anger for ever, because he delighteth in mercy. 19He will turn again, he will have compassion upon us; he will subdue our iniquities; and thou wilt cast all their sins into the depths of the sea. 20Thou wilt perform the truth to Jacob, and the mercy to Abraham, which thou hast sworn unto our fathers from the days of old."

Nahum 1:2-3 "2God is jealous, and the LORD revengeth; the LORD revengeth, and is furious; the LORD will take vengeance on his adversaries, and he reserveth wrath for his enemies. 3The LORD is slow to anger, and great in power, and will not at all acquit the wicked: the LORD hath his way in the whirlwind and in the storm, and the clouds are the dust of his feet."

Nahum 1:7 "The LORD is good, a strong hold in the day of trouble; and he knoweth them that trust in him."

Zephaniah 3:5 "The just LORD is in the midst thereof; he will not do iniquity: every morning doth he bring his judgment to light, he faileth not; but the unjust knoweth no shame."

Zechariah 9:9 "Rejoice greatly, O daughter of Zion; shout, O daughter of Jerusalem: behold, thy King cometh unto thee: he is just, and having salvation; lowly, and riding upon an ass, and upon a colt the foal of an ass."

Malachi 3:6 "For I am the LORD, I change not; therefore ye sons of Jacob are not consumed."

Matthew 5:48 "Be ye therefore perfect, even as your Father which is in heaven is perfect."

Luke 6:35-36 "35But love ye your enemies, and do good, and lend, hoping for nothing again; and your reward shall be great, and ye shall be the children of the Highest: for he is kind unto the unthankful and to the evil. 36Be ye therefore merciful, as your Father also is merciful."

John 17:25 "O righteous Father, the world hath not known thee: but I have known thee, and these have known that thou hast sent me."

Acts 10:34 "Then Peter opened his mouth, and said, Of a truth I perceive that God is no respecter of persons:"

Romans 2:11 "For there is no respect of persons with God."

1 Corinthians 1:9 "God is faithful, by whom ye were called unto the fellowship of his Son Jesus Christ our Lord."

1 Corinthians 10:13 "There hath no temptation taken you but such as is common to man: but God is faithful, who will not suffer you to be tempted above that ye are able; but will with the temptation also make a way to escape, that ye may be able to bear it."

Ephesians 2:4-5 "4But God, who is rich in mercy, for his great love wherewith he loved us, 5Even when we were dead in sins, hath quickened us together with Christ, (by grace ye are saved;)"

Ephesians 6:9 "And, ye masters, do the same things unto them, forbearing threatening: knowing that your Master also is in heaven; neither is there respect of persons with him."

Philippians 2:5-8 "5Let this mind be in you, which was also in Christ Jesus: 6Who, being in the form of God, thought it not robbery to be equal with God: 7But made himself of no reputation, and took upon him the form of a servant, and was made in the likeness of men: 8And being found in fashion as a man, he humbled himself, and became obedient unto death, even the death of the cross."

1 Thessalonians 5:23-24 "23And the very God of peace sanctify you wholly; and I pray God your whole spirit and soul and body be preserved blameless unto the coming of our Lord Jesus Christ. 24Faithful is he that calleth you, who also will do it."

2 Thessalonians 3:3 "But the Lord is faithful, who shall stablish you, and keep you from evil."

Titus 1:2 "In hope of eternal life, which God, that cannot lie, promised before the world began;"

Hebrews 1:10-12 "10And, Thou, Lord, in the beginning hast laid the foundation of the earth; and the heavens are the works of thine hands: 11They shall perish; but thou remainest; and they all shall wax old as doth a garment; 12And as a vesture shalt thou fold them up, and they shall be changed: but thou art the same, and thy years shall not fail."

Hebrews 6:10 "For God is not unrighteous to forget your work and labour of love, which ye have shewed toward his name, in that ye have ministered to the saints, and do minister."

Hebrews 8:10-12 "10For this is the covenant that I will make with the house of Israel after those days, saith the Lord; I will put my laws into their mind, and write them in their hearts: and I will be to them a God, and they shall be to me a people: 11And they shall not teach every man his neighbour, and every man his brother, saying, Know the Lord: for all shall know me, from the least to the greatest. 12For I will be merciful to their unrighteousness, and their sins and their iniquities will I remember no more."

Hebrews 10:23 "Let us hold fast the profession of our faith without wavering; (for he is faithful that promised;)"

James 1:13 "Let no man say when he is tempted, I am tempted of God: for God cannot be tempted with evil, neither tempteth he any man:"

James 1:17 "Every good gift and every perfect gift is from above, and cometh down from the Father of lights, with whom is no variableness, neither shadow of turning."

1 Peter 1:15-17 "15But as he which hath called you is holy, so be ye holy in all manner of conversation; 16Because it is written, Be ye holy; for I am holy. 17And if ye call on the Father, who without respect of persons judgeth according to every man's work, pass the time of your sojourning here in fear:"

1 Peter 2:2-3 "2As newborn babes, desire the sincere milk of the word, that ye may grow thereby: 3If so be ye have tasted that the Lord is gracious."

2 Peter 3:9 "The Lord is not slack concerning his promise, as some men count slackness; but is longsuffering to us-ward, not willing that any should perish, but that all should come to repentance."

1 John 1:5 "This then is the message which we have heard of him, and declare unto you, that God is light, and in him is no darkness at all."

Revelation 3:14 "And unto the angel of the church of the Laodiceans write; These things saith the Amen, the faithful and true witness, the beginning of the creation of God;"

Revelation 15:3-4 "3And they sing the song of Moses the servant of God, and the song of the Lamb, saying, Great and marvellous are thy works, Lord God Almighty; just and true are thy ways, thou King of saints. 4Who shall not fear thee, O Lord, and glorify thy name? for thou only art holy: for all nations shall come and worship before thee; for thy judgments are made manifest."

Revelation 16:5 "And I heard the angel of the waters say, Thou art righteous, O Lord, which art, and wast, and shalt be, because thou hast judged thus."

The Lord God Being The Living God

2 Samuel 22:47 "The LORD liveth; and blessed be my rock; and exalted be the God of the rock of my salvation."

Job 19:25-26 "25For I know that my redeemer liveth, and that he shall stand at the latter day upon the earth: 26And though after my skin worms destroy this body, yet in my flesh shall I see God:"

Psalm 18:46 "The LORD liveth; and blessed be my rock; and let the God of my salvation be exalted."

Jeremiah 10:10 "But the LORD is the true God, he is the living God, and an everlasting king: at his wrath the earth shall tremble, and the nations shall not be able to abide his indignation."

Ezekiel 18:3 "As I live, saith the Lord GOD, ye shall not have occasion any more to use this proverb in Israel."

Daniel 6:26 "I make a decree, That in every dominion of my kingdom men tremble and fear before the God of Daniel: for he is the living God, and stedfast for ever, and his kingdom that which shall not be destroyed, and his dominion shall be even unto the end."

John 6:57 "As the living Father hath sent me, and I live by the Father: so he that eateth me, even he shall live by me."

Acts 14:11-15 "11And when the people saw what Paul had done, they lifted up their voices, saying in the speech of Lycaonia, The gods are come down to us in the likeness of men. 12And they called Barnabas, Jupiter; and Paul, Mercurius, because he was the chief speaker. 13Then the priest of Jupiter, which was before their city, brought oxen and garlands unto the gates, and would have done sacrifice with the people. 14Which when the apostles, Barnabas and Paul, heard of, they rent their clothes, and ran in among the people, crying out, 15And saying, Sirs, why do ye these things? We also are men of like passions with you, and preach unto you that ye should turn from these vanities unto the living God, which made heaven, and earth, and the sea, and all things that are therein:"

2 Corinthians 3:3 "Forasmuch as ye are manifestly declared to be the epistle of Christ ministered by us, written not with ink, but with the Spirit of the living God; not in tables of stone, but in fleshy tables of the heart."

2 *Corinthians 6:16* "And what agreement hath the temple of God with idols? for ye are the temple of the living God; as God hath said, I will dwell in them, and walk in them; and I will be their God, and they shall be my people."

1 *Thessalonians 1:9* "For they themselves shew of us what manner of entering in we had unto you, and how ye turned to God from idols to serve the living and true God;"

Revelation 10:5-6 "⁵And the angel which I saw stand upon the sea and upon the earth lifted up his hand to heaven, ⁶And sware by him that liveth for ever and ever, who created heaven, and the things that therein are, and the earth, and the things that therein are, and the sea, and the things which are therein, that there should be time no longer:"

The Lord God Being The Only God

Deuteronomy 4:35 "Unto thee it was shewed, that thou mightest know that the LORD he is God; there is none else beside him."

Deuteronomy 4:39 "Know therefore this day, and consider it in thine heart, that the LORD he is God in heaven above, and upon the earth beneath: there is none else."

Deuteronomy 6:4 "Hear, O Israel: The LORD our God is one LORD:"

Deuteronomy 32:36-39 "³⁶For the LORD shall judge his people, and repent himself for his servants, when he seeth that their power is gone, and there is none shut up, or left. ³⁷And he shall say, Where are their gods, their rock in whom they trusted, ³⁸Which did eat the fat of their sacrifices, and drank the wine of their drink offerings? let them rise up and help you, and be your protection. ³⁹See now that I, even I, am he, and there is no god with me: I kill, and I make alive; I wound, and I heal: neither is there any that can deliver out of my hand."

1 *Samuel 2:2* "There is none holy as the LORD: for there is none beside thee: neither is there any rock like our God."

2 *Samuel 7:22* "Wherefore thou art great, O LORD God: for there is none like thee, neither is there any God beside thee, according to all that we have heard with our ears."

1 *Kings 8:23* "And he said, LORD God of Israel, there is no God like thee, in heaven above, or on earth beneath, who keepest covenant and mercy with thy servants that walk before thee with all their heart:"

1 *Kings 8:60* "That all the people of the earth may know that the LORD is God, and that there is none else."

2 *Kings 5:15* "And he returned to the man of God, he and all his company, and came, and stood before him: and he said, Behold, now I know that there is no God in all earth, but in Israel: now therefore, I pray thee, take a blessing of thy servant."

2 *Kings 19:15* "And Hezekiah prayed before the LORD, and said, O LORD God of Israel, which dwellest between the cherubims, thou art the God, even thou alone, of all the kingdoms of the earth: thou hast made heaven and earth."

2 *Kings 19:19* "Now therefore, O LORD our God, I beseech thee, save thou us out of his hand, that all the kingdoms of the earth may know that thou art the LORD God, even thou only."

1 *Chronicles 17:20* "O LORD, there is none like thee, neither is there any God beside thee, according to all that we have heard with our ears."

2 *Chronicles 6:14* "And said, O LORD God of Israel, there is no God like thee in the heaven, nor in the earth; which keepest covenant, and shewest mercy unto thy servants, that walk before thee with all their hearts:"

Nehemiah 9:6 "Thou, even thou, art LORD alone; thou hast made heaven, the heaven of heavens, with all their host, the earth, and all things that are therein, the seas, and all that is therein, and thou preservest them all; and the host of heaven worshippeth thee."

Psalm 62:6-7 "⁶He only is my rock and my salvation: he is my defence; I shall not be moved. ⁷In God is my salvation and my glory: the rock of my strength, and my refuge, is in God."

Psalm 73:25-26 "²⁵Whom have I in heaven but thee? and there is none upon earth that I desire beside thee. ²⁶My flesh and my heart faileth: but God is the strength of my heart, and my portion for ever."

Psalm 83:18 "That men may know that thou, whose name alone is JEHOVAH, art the most high over all the earth."

Psalm 86:8 "Among the gods there is none like unto thee, O Lord; neither are there any works like unto thy works."

Psalm 86:10 "For thou art great, and doest wondrous things: thou art God alone."

Psalm 89:8 "O LORD God of hosts, who is a strong LORD like unto thee? or to thy faithfulness round about thee?"

Psalm 148:13 "Let them praise the name of the LORD: for his name alone is excellent; his glory is above the earth and heaven."

Proverbs 30:4-5 "4Who hath ascended up into heaven, or descended? who hath gathered the wind in his fists? who hath bound the waters in a garment? who hath established all the ends of the earth? what is his name, and what is his son's name, if thou canst tell? 5Every word of God is pure: he is a shield unto them that put their trust in him."

Isaiah 37:16 "O LORD of hosts, God of Israel, that dwellest between the cherubims, thou art the God, even thou alone, of all the kingdoms of the earth: thou hast made heaven and earth."

Isaiah 37:18-20 "18Of a truth, LORD, the kings of Assyria have laid waste all the nations, and their countries, 19And have cast their gods into the fire: for they were no gods, but the work of men's hands, wood and stone: therefore they have destroyed them. 20Now therefore, O LORD our God, save us from his hand, that all the kingdoms of the earth may know that thou art the LORD, even thou only."

Isaiah 43:10-12 "10Ye are my witnesses, saith the LORD, and my servant whom I have chosen: that ye may know and believe me, and understand that I am he: before me there was no God formed, neither shall there be after me. 11I, even I, am the LORD; and beside me there is no saviour. 12I have declared, and have saved, and I have shewed, when there was no strange god among you: therefore ye are my witnesses, saith the LORD, that I am God."

Isaiah 44:6-8 "6Thus saith the LORD the King of Israel, and his redeemer the LORD of hosts; I am the first, and I am the last; and beside me there is no

God. 7And who, as I, shall call, and shall declare it, and set it in order for me, since I appointed the ancient people? and the things that are coming, and shall come, let them shew unto them. 8Fear ye not, neither be afraid: have not I told thee from that time, and have declared it? ye are even my witnesses. Is there a God beside me? yea, there is no God; I know not any."

Isaiah 44:24 "Thus saith the LORD, thy redeemer, and he that formed thee from the womb, I am the LORD that maketh all things; that stretcheth forth the heavens alone; that spreadeth abroad the earth by myself;"

Isaiah 45:5-6 "5I am the LORD, and there is none else, there is no God beside me: I girded thee, though thou hast not known me: 6That they may know from the rising of the sun, and from the west, that there is none beside me. I am the LORD, and there is none else."

Isaiah 45:18 "For thus saith the LORD that created the heavens; God himself that formed the earth and made it; he hath established it, he created it not in vain, he formed it to be inhabited: I am the LORD; and there is none else."

Isaiah 45:22-23 "22Look unto me, and be ye saved, all the ends of the earth: for I am God, and there is none else. 23I have sworn by myself, the word is gone out of my mouth in righteousness, and shall not return, That unto me every knee shall bow, every tongue shall swear."

Isaiah 46:9 "Remember the former things of old: for I am God, and there is none else; I am God, and there is none like me,"

Jeremiah 10:6 "Forasmuch as there is none like unto thee, O LORD; thou art great, and thy name is great in might."

Daniel 3:29 "Therefore I make a decree, That every people, nation, and language, which speak any thing amiss against the God of Shadrach, Meshach, and Abed-nego, shall be cut in pieces, and their houses shall be made a dunghill: because there is no other God that can deliver after this sort."

Hosea 13:4 "Yet I am the LORD thy God from the land of Egypt, and thou shalt know no god but me: for there is no saviour beside me."

Joel 2:27 "And ye shall know that I am in the midst of Israel, and that I am the LORD your God, and none else: and my people shall never be ashamed."

Zechariah 14:9 "And the LORD shall be king over all the earth: in that day shall there be one LORD, and his name one."

Malachi 2:10 "Have we not all one father? hath not one God created us? why do we deal treacherously every man against his brother, by profaning the covenant of our fathers?"

Matthew 23:8-10 "8But be not ye called Rabbi: for one is your Master, even Christ; and all ye are brethren. 9And call no man your father upon the earth: for one is your Father, which is in heaven. 10Neither be ye called masters: for one is your Master, even Christ."

Mark 12:29 "And Jesus answered him, The first of all the commandments is, Hear, O Israel; The Lord our God is one Lord:"

Mark 12:32 "And the scribe said unto him, Well, Master, thou hast said the truth: for there is one God; and there is none other but he:"

John 17:1-3 "1These words spake Jesus, and lifted up his eyes to heaven, and said, Father, the hour is come; glorify thy Son, that thy Son also may glorify thee: 2As thou hast given him power over all flesh, that he should give eternal life to as many as thou hast given him. 3And this is life eternal, that they might know thee the only true God, and Jesus Christ, whom thou hast sent."

Romans 3:29-30 "29Is he the God of the Jews only? is he not also of the Gentiles? Yes, of the Gentiles also: 30Seeing it is one God, which shall justify the circumcision by faith, and uncircumcision through faith."

1 Corinthians 8:4-6 "4As concerning therefore the eating of those things that are offered in sacrifice unto idols, we know that an idol is nothing in the world, and that there is none other God but one. 5For though there be that are called gods, whether in heaven or in earth, (as there be gods many, and lords many,) 6But to us there is but one God, the Father, of whom are all things, and we in him; and one Lord Jesus Christ, by whom are all things, and we by him."

1 Corinthians 12:3-6 "3Wherefore I give you to understand, that no man speaking by the Spirit of God calleth Jesus accursed: and that no man can say that Jesus is the Lord, but by the Holy Ghost. 4Now there are diversities of gifts, but the same Spirit. 5And there are differences of administrations, but the same Lord. 6And there are diversities of operations, but it is the same God which worketh all in all."

Galatians 3:19-20 "19Wherefore then serveth the law? It was added because of transgressions, till the seed should come to whom the promise was made; and it was ordained by angels in the hand of a mediator. 20Now a mediator is not a mediator of one, but God is one."

Ephesians 4:4-6 "4There is one body, and one Spirit, even as ye are called in one hope of your calling; 5One Lord, one faith, one baptism, 6One God and Father of all, who is above all, and through all, and in you all."

1 Timothy 1:17 "Now unto the King eternal, immortal, invisible, the only wise God, be honour and glory for ever and ever. Amen."

1 Timothy 2:5 "For there is one God, and one mediator between God and men, the man Christ Jesus;"

James 4:10-12 "10Humble yourselves in the sight of the Lord, and he shall lift you up. 11Speak not evil one of another, brethren. He that speaketh evil of his brother, and judgeth his brother, speaketh evil of the law, and judgeth the law: but if thou judge the law, thou art not a doer of the law, but a judge. 12There is one lawgiver, who is able to save and to destroy: who art thou that judgest another?"

Jude 4 "For there are certain men crept in unawares, who were before of old ordained to this condemnation, ungodly men, turning the grace of our God into lasciviousness, and denying the only Lord God, and our Lord Jesus Christ."

Revelation 15:4 "Who shall not fear thee, O Lord, and glorify thy name? for thou only art holy: for all nations shall come and worship before thee; for thy judgments are made manifest."

The Ways Of The Lord God

Deuteronomy 32:4 "He is the Rock, his work is perfect: for all his ways are judgment: a God of truth and without iniquity, just and right is he."

2 Samuel 22:31 "As for God, his way is perfect; the word of the LORD is tried: he is a buckler to all them that trust in him."

Psalm 18:30 "As for God, his way is perfect: the word of the LORD is tried: he is a buckler to all those that trust in him."

Psalm 103:6-7 "⁶The LORD executeth righteousness and judgment for all that are oppressed. ⁷He made known his ways unto Moses, his acts unto the children of Israel."

Proverbs 10:29 "The way of the LORD is strength to the upright: but destruction shall be to the workers of iniquity."

Isaiah 55:7-9 "⁷Let the wicked forsake his way, and the unrighteous man his thoughts: and let him return unto the LORD, and he will have mercy upon him; and to our God, for he will abundantly pardon. ⁸For my thoughts are not your thoughts, neither are your ways my ways, saith the LORD. ⁹For as the heavens are higher than the earth, so are my ways higher than your ways, and my thoughts than your thoughts."

Ezekiel 18:25-30 "²⁵Yet ye say, The way of the Lord is not equal. Hear now, O house of Israel; Is not my way equal? are not your ways unequal? ²⁶When a righteous man turneth away from his righteousness, and committeth iniquity, and dieth in them; for his iniquity that he hath done shall he die. ²⁷Again, when the wicked man turneth away from his wickedness that he hath committed, and doeth that which is lawful and right, he shall save his soul alive. ²⁸Because he considereth, and turneth away from all his transgressions that he hath committed, he shall surely live, he shall not die. ²⁹Yet saith the house of Israel, The way of the Lord is not equal. O house of Israel, are not my ways equal? are not your ways unequal? ³⁰Therefore I will judge you, O house of Israel, every one according to his ways, saith the Lord GOD. Repent, and turn yourselves from all your transgressions; so iniquity shall not be your ruin."

Ezekiel 33:17-20 "¹⁷Yet the children of thy people say, The way of the Lord is not equal: but as for them, their way is not equal. ¹⁸When the righteous turneth from his righteousness, and committeth iniquity, he shall even die thereby. ¹⁹But if the wicked turn from his wickedness, and do that which is lawful and right, he shall live thereby. ²⁰Yet ye say, The way of the Lord is not equal. O ye house of Israel, I will judge you every one after his ways."

Daniel 4:37 "Now I Nebuchadnezzar praise and extol and honour the King of heaven, all whose works are truth, and his ways judgment: and those that walk in pride he is able to abase."

Hosea 14:9 "Who is wise, and he shall understand these things? prudent, and he shall know them? for the ways of the LORD are right, and the just shall walk in them: but the transgressors shall fall therein."

Romans 11:33-36 "³³O the depth of the riches both of the wisdom and knowledge of God! how unsearchable are his judgments, and his ways past finding out! ³⁴For who hath known the mind of the Lord? or who hath been his counseller? ³⁵Or who hath first given to him, and it shall be recompensed unto him again? ³⁶For of him, and through him, and to him, are all things: to whom be glory for ever. Amen."

Revelation 15:3 "And they sing the song of Moses the servant of God, and the song of the Lamb, saying, Great and marvellous are thy works, Lord God Almighty; just and true are thy ways, thou King of saints."

The Works Of The Lord God

Deuteronomy 32:4 "He is the Rock, his work is perfect: for all his ways are judgment: a God of truth and without iniquity, just and right is he."

Psalm 33:4 "For the word of the LORD is right; and all his works are done in truth."

Psalm 40:5 "Many, O LORD my God, are thy wonderful works which thou hast done, and thy thoughts which are to us-ward: they cannot be reckoned up in order unto thee: if I would declare and speak of them, they are more than can be numbered."

Psalm 66:3-5 "³Say unto God, How terrible art thou in thy works! through the greatness of thy power shall thine enemies submit themselves unto thee. ⁴All the earth shall worship thee, and shall sing unto thee; they shall sing to thy name. Selah. ⁵Come and see the works of God: he is terrible in his doing toward the children of men."

Psalm 86:8 "Among the gods there is none like unto thee, O Lord; neither are there any works like unto thy works."

Psalm 92:5-6 "⁵O LORD, how great are thy works! and thy thoughts are very deep. ⁶A brutish man knoweth not; neither doth a fool understand this."

Psalm 104:1-13 "¹Bless the LORD, O my soul. O LORD my God, thou art very great; thou art clothed with honour and majesty. ²Who coverest thyself with light as with a garment: who stretchest out the heavens like a curtain: ³Who layeth the beams of his chambers in the waters: who maketh the clouds his chariot: who walketh upon the wings of the wind: ⁴Who maketh his angels spirits; his ministers a flaming fire: ⁵Who laid the foundations of the earth, that it should not be removed for ever. ⁶Thou coveredst it with the deep as with a garment: the waters stood above the mountains. ⁷At thy rebuke they fled; at the voice of thy thunder they hasted away. ⁸They go up by the mountains; they go down by the valleys unto the place which thou hast founded for them. ⁹Thou hast set a bound that they may not pass over; that they turn not again to cover the earth. ¹⁰He sendeth the springs into the valleys, which run among the hills. ¹¹They give drink to every beast of the field: the wild asses quench their thirst. ¹²By them shall the fowls of the heaven have their habitation, which sing among the branches. ¹³He watereth the hills from his chambers: the earth is satisfied with the fruit of thy works."

Psalm 104:24-31 "²⁴O LORD, how manifold are thy works! in wisdom hast thou made them all: the earth is full of thy riches. ²⁵So is this great and wide sea, wherein are things creeping innumerable, both small and great beasts. ²⁶There go the ships: there is that leviathan, whom thou hast made to play therein. ²⁷These wait all upon thee; that thou mayest give them their meat in due season. ²⁸That

thou givest them they gather: thou openest thine hand, they are filled with good. ²⁹Thou hidest thy face, they are troubled: thou takest away their breath, they die, and return to their dust. ³⁰Thou sendest forth thy spirit, they are created: and thou renewest the face of the earth. ³¹The glory of the LORD shall endure for ever: the LORD shall rejoice in his works."

Psalm 111:2-8 "²The works of the LORD are great, sought out of all them that have pleasure therein. ³His work is honourable and glorious: and his righteousness endureth for ever. ⁴He hath made his wonderful works to be remembered: the LORD is gracious and full of compassion. ⁵He hath given meat unto them that fear him: he will ever be mindful of his covenant. ⁶He hath shewed his people the power of his works, that he may give them the heritage of the heathen. ⁷The works of his hands are verity and judgment; all his commandments are sure. ⁸They stand fast for ever and ever, and are done in truth and uprightness."

Psalm 139:14-17 "¹⁴I will praise thee; for I am fearfully and wonderfully made: marvellous are thy works; and that my soul knoweth right well. ¹⁵My substance was not hid from thee, when I was made in secret, and curiously wrought in the lowest parts of the earth. ¹⁶Thine eyes did see my substance, yet being unperfect; and in thy book all my members were written, which in continuance were fashioned, when as yet there was none of them. ¹⁷How precious also are thy thoughts unto me, O God! how great is the sum of them!"

Psalm 145:9-10 "⁹The LORD is good to all: and his tender mercies are over all his works. ¹⁰All thy works shall praise thee, O LORD; and thy saints shall bless thee."

Proverbs 16:11 "A just weight and balance are the LORD's: all the weights of the bag are his work."

Ecclesiastes 3:10-15 "¹⁰I have seen the travail, which God hath given to the sons of men to be exercised in it. ¹¹He hath made every thing beautiful in his time: also he hath set the world in their heart, so that no man can find out the work that God maketh from the beginning to the end. ¹²I know that there is no good in them, but for a man to rejoice, and to do good in his life. ¹³And also that every man should eat and drink, and enjoy the good of all his labour, it is the gift of

God. [14]I know that, whatsoever God doeth, it shall be for ever: nothing can be put to it, nor any thing taken from it: and God doeth it, that men should fear before him. [15]That which hath been is now; and that which is to be hath already been; and God requireth that which is past."

Ecclesiastes 8:17 "Then I beheld all the work of God, that a man cannot find out the work that is done under the sun: because though a man labour to seek it out, yet he shall not find it; yea further; though a wise man think to know it, yet shall he not be able to find it."

Ecclesiastes 11:5 "As thou knowest not what is the way of the spirit, nor how the bones do grow in the womb of her that is with child: even so thou knowest not the works of God who maketh all."

Daniel 4:37 "Now I Nebuchadnezzar praise and extol and honour the King of heaven, all whose works are truth, and his ways judgment: and those that walk in pride he is able to abase."

Acts 15:18 "Known unto God are all his works from the beginning of the world."

Revelation 15:3 "And they sing the song of Moses the servant of God, and the song of the Lamb, saying, Great and marvellous are thy works, Lord God Almighty; just and true are thy ways, thou King of saints."

What Is From The Lord God

Psalm 62:1-2 "[1]Truly my soul waiteth upon God: from him cometh my salvation. [2]He only is my rock and my salvation; he is my defence; I shall not be greatly moved."

Proverbs 16:1 "The preparations of the heart in man, and the answer of the tongue, is from the LORD."

What Is In The Hand Of The Lord God

1 Chronicles 29:11-12 "[11]Thine, O LORD, is the greatness, and the power, and the glory, and the victory, and the majesty: for all that is in the heaven and in the earth is thine; thine is the kingdom, O LORD, and thou art exalted as head above all. [12]Both riches and honour come of thee, and thou reignest over all; and in thine hand is power and might; and in thine hand it is to make great, and to give strength unto all."

Job 12:9-10 "[9]Who knoweth not in all these that the hand of the LORD hath wrought this? [10]In whose hand is the soul of every living thing, and the breath of all mankind."

Psalm 66:8-9 "[8]O bless our God, ye people, and make the voice of his praise to be heard: [9]Which holdeth our soul in life, and suffereth not our feet to be moved."

Psalm 75:7-8 "[7]But God is the judge: he putteth down one, and setteth up another. [8]For in the hand of the LORD there is a cup, and the wine is red; it is full of mixture; and he poureth out of the same: but the dregs thereof, all the wicked of the earth shall wring them out, and drink them."

Psalm 95:3-5 "[3]For the LORD is a great God, and a great King above all gods. [4]In his hand are the deep places of the earth: the strength of the hills is his also. [5]The sea is his, and he made it: and his hands formed the dry land."

Proverbs 21:1 "The king's heart is in the hand of the LORD, as the rivers of water: he turneth it whithersoever he will."

Ecclesiastes 9:1 "For all this I considered in my heart even to declare all this, that the righteous, and the wise, and their works, are in the hand of God: no man knoweth either love or hatred by all that is before them."

Jeremiah 18:5-6 "[5]Then the word of the LORD came to me, saying, [6]O house of Israel, cannot I do with you as this potter? saith the LORD. Behold, as the clay is in the potter's hand, so are ye in mine hand, O house of Israel."

Daniel 5:23 "But hast lifted up thyself against the LORD of heaven; and they have brought the vessels of his house before thee, and thou, and thy lords, thy wives, and thy concubines, have drunk wine in them; and thou hast praised the gods of silver, and gold, of brass, iron, wood, and stone, which see not, nor hear, nor know: and the God in whose hand thy breath is, and whose are all thy ways, hast thou not glorified:"

What Is Of The Lord God

Psalm 37:39 "But the salvation of the righteous is of the LORD: he is their strength in the time of trouble."

Proverbs 16:33 "The lot is cast into the lap; but the whole disposing thereof is of the LORD."

Proverbs 20:24 "Man's goings are of the LORD; how can a man then understand his own way?"

Proverbs 21:31 "The horse is prepared against the day of battle: but safety is of the LORD."

Romans 11:34-36 "34For who hath known the mind of the Lord? or who hath been his counseller? 35Or who hath first given to him, and it shall be recompensed unto him again? 36For of him, and through him, and to him, are all things: to whom be glory for ever. Amen."

1 Corinthians 8:6 "But to us there is but one God, the Father, of whom are all things, and we in him; and one Lord Jesus Christ, by whom are all things, and we by him."

What The Lord God Does

Exodus 15:11 "Who is like unto thee, O LORD, among the gods? who is like thee, glorious in holiness, fearful in praises, doing wonders?"

Deuteronomy 10:17-18 "17For the LORD your God is God of gods, and Lord of lords, a great God, a mighty, and a terrible, which regardeth not persons, nor taketh reward: 18He doth execute the judgment of the fatherless and widow, and loveth the stranger, in giving him food and raiment."

Deuteronomy 32:36-39 "36For the LORD shall judge his people, and repent himself for his servants, when he seeth that their power is gone, and there is none shut up, or left. 37And he shall say, Where are their gods, their rock in whom they trusted, 38Which did eat the fat of their sacrifices, and drank the wine of their drink offerings? let them rise up and help you, and be your protection. 39See now that I, even I, am he, and there is no god with me: I kill, and I make alive; I wound, and I heal: neither is there any that can deliver out of my hand."

1 Samuel 2:6-9 "6The LORD killeth, and maketh alive: he bringeth down to the grave, and bringeth up. 7The LORD maketh poor, and maketh rich: he bringeth low, and lifteth up. 8He raiseth up the poor out of the dust, and lifteth up the beggar from the dunghill, to set them among princes, and to make them inherit the throne of glory: for the pillars of the earth are the LORD's,

and he hath set the world upon them. 9He will keep the feet of his saints, and the wicked shall be silent in darkness; for by strength shall no man prevail."

1 Samuel 12:24 "Only fear the LORD, and serve him in truth with all your heart: for consider how great things he hath done for you."

2 Samuel 22:33-40 "33God is my strength and power: and he maketh my way perfect. 34He maketh my feet like hinds' feet: and setteth me upon my high places. 35He teacheth my hands to war; so that a bow of steel is broken by mine arms. 36Thou hast also given me the shield of thy salvation: and thy gentleness hath made me great. 37Thou hast enlarged my steps under me; so that my feet did not slip. 38I have pursued mine enemies, and destroyed them; and turned not again until I had consumed them. 39And I have consumed them, and wounded them, that they could not arise: yea, they are fallen under my feet. 40For thou hast girded me with strength to battle: them that rose up against me hast thou subdued under me."

Job 1:20-21 "20Then Job arose, and rent his mantle, and shaved his head, and fell down upon the ground, and worshipped, 21And said, Naked came I out of my mother's womb, and naked shall I return thither: the LORD gave, and the LORD hath taken away; blessed be the name of the LORD."

Job 5:8-16 "8I would seek unto God, and unto God would I commit my cause: 9Which doeth great things and unsearchable; marvellous things without number: 10Who giveth rain upon the earth, and sendeth waters upon the fields: 11To set up on high those that be low; that those which mourn may be exalted to safety. 12He disappointeth the devices of the crafty, so that their hands cannot perform their enterprise. 13He taketh the wise in their own craftiness: and the counsel of the froward is carried headlong. 14They meet with darkness in the daytime, and grope in the noonday as in the night. 15But he saveth the poor from the sword, from their mouth, and from the hand of the mighty. 16So the poor hath hope, and iniquity stoppeth her mouth."

Job 12:9-25 "9Who knoweth not in all these that the hand of the LORD hath wrought this? 10In whose hand is the soul of every living thing, and the breath of all mankind. [11]Doth not the ear try words? and the mouth taste his meat? [12]With the ancient is wisdom; and in length of days understanding. [13]With him is wisdom and strength, he hath counsel and understanding. [14]Behold, he breaketh down, and it cannot be built again: he shutteth up a man, and there can be no opening. [15]Behold, he withholdeth the waters, and they dry up: also he sendeth them out, and they overturn the earth. [16]With him is strength and wisdom: the deceived and the deceiver are his. [17]He leadeth counsellers away spoiled, and maketh the judges fools. [18]He looseth the bond of kings, and girdeth their loins with a girdle. [19]He leadeth princes away spoiled, and overthroweth the mighty. [20]He removeth away the speech of the trusty, and taketh away the understanding of the aged. [21]He poureth contempt upon princes, and weakeneth the strength of the mighty. [22]He discovereth deep things out of darkness, and bringeth out to light the shadow of death. [23]He increaseth the nations, and destroyeth them: he enlargeth the nations, and straiteneth them again. [24]He taketh away the heart of the chief of the people of the earth, and causeth them to wander in a wilderness where there is no way. [25]They grope in the dark without light, and he maketh them to stagger like a drunken man."

Job 26:7-14 "[7]He stretcheth out the north over the empty place, and hangeth the earth upon nothing. [8]He bindeth up the waters in his thick clouds; and the cloud is not rent under them. [9]He holdeth back the face of his throne, and spreadeth his cloud upon it. [10]He hath compassed the waters with bounds, until the day and night come to an end. [11]The pillars of heaven tremble and are astonished at his reproof. [12]He divideth the sea with his power, and by his understanding he smiteth through the proud. [13]By his spirit he hath garnished the heavens; his hand hath formed the crooked serpent. [14]Lo, these are parts of his ways: but how little a portion is heard of him? but the thunder of his power who can understand?"

Job 35:10-11 "[10]But none saith, Where is God my maker, who giveth songs in the night; [11]Who teacheth us more than the beasts of the earth, and maketh us wiser than the fowls of heaven?"

Job 36:5-15 "[5]Behold, God is mighty, and despiseth not any: he is mighty in strength and wisdom. [6]He

preserveth not the life of the wicked: but giveth right to the poor. [7]He withdraweth not his eyes from the righteous: but with kings are they on the throne; yea, he doth establish them for ever, and they are exalted. [8]And if they be bound in fetters, and be holden in cords of affliction; [9]Then he sheweth them their work, and their transgressions that they have exceeded. [10]He openeth also their ear to discipline, and commandeth that they return from iniquity. [11]If they obey and serve him, they shall spend their days in prosperity, and their years in pleasures. [12]But if they obey not, they shall perish by the sword, and they shall die without knowledge. [13]But the hypocrites in heart heap up wrath: they cry not when he bindeth them. [14]They die in youth, and their life is among the unclean. [15]He delivereth the poor in his affliction, and openeth their ears in oppression."

Job 36:26-33 "[26]Behold, God is great, and we know him not, neither can the number of his years be searched out. [27]For he maketh small the drops of water: they pour down rain according to the vapour thereof: [28]Which the clouds do drop and distil upon man abundantly. [29]Also can any understand the spreadings of the clouds, or the noise of his tabernacle? [30]Behold, he spreadeth his light upon it, and covereth the bottom of the sea. [31]For by them judgeth he the people; he giveth meat in abundance. [32]With clouds he covereth the light; and commandeth it not to shine by the cloud that cometh betwixt. [33]The noise thereof sheweth concerning it, the cattle also concerning the vapour."

Job 37:5 "God thundereth marvellously with his voice; great things doeth he, which we cannot comprehend."

Job 42:1-2 "[1]Then Job answered the LORD, and said, [2]I know that thou canst do every thing, and that no thought can be withholden from thee."

Psalm 18:31-36 "[31]For who is God save the LORD? or who is a rock save our God? [32]It is God that girdeth me with strength, and maketh my way perfect. [33]He maketh my feet like hinds' feet, and setteth me upon my high places. [34]He teacheth my hands to war, so that a bow of steel is broken by mine arms. [35]Thou hast also given me the shield of thy salvation: and thy right hand hath holden me up, and thy gentleness hath made me great. [36]Thou hast enlarged my steps under me, that my feet did not slip."

Psalm 33:10 "The LORD bringeth the counsel of the heathen to nought: he maketh the devices of the people of none effect."

Psalm 46:1-9 "[1]God is our refuge and strength, a very present help in trouble. [2]Therefore will not we fear, though the earth be removed, and though the mountains be carried into the midst of the sea; [3]Though the waters thereof roar and be troubled, though the mountains shake with the swelling thereof. Selah. [4]There is a river, the streams whereof shall make glad the city of God, the holy place of the tabernacles of the most High. [5]God is in the midst of her; she shall not be moved: God shall help her, and that right early. [6]The heathen raged, the kingdoms were moved: he uttered his voice, the earth melted. [7]The LORD of hosts is with us; the God of Jacob is our refuge. Selah. [8]Come, behold the works of the LORD, what desolations he hath made in the earth. [9]He maketh wars to cease unto the end of the earth; he breaketh the bow, and cutteth the spear in sunder; he burneth the chariot in the fire."

Psalm 66:3-7 "[3]Say unto God, How terrible art thou in thy works! through the greatness of thy power shall thine enemies submit themselves unto thee. [4]All the earth shall worship thee, and shall sing unto thee; they shall sing to thy name. Selah. [5]Come and see the works of God: he is terrible in his doing toward the children of men. [6]He turned the sea into dry land: they went through the flood on foot: there did we rejoice in him. [7]He ruleth by his power for ever; his eyes behold the nations: let not the rebellious exalt themselves. Selah."

Psalm 72:18 "Blessed be the LORD God, the God of Israel, who only doeth wondrous things."

Psalm 86:10 "For thou art great, and doest wondrous things: thou art God alone."

Psalm 89:8-10 "[8]O LORD God of hosts, who is a strong LORD like unto thee? or to thy faithfulness round about thee? [9]Thou rulest the raging of the sea: when the waves thereof arise, thou stillest them. [10]Thou hast broken Rahab in pieces, as one that is slain; thou hast scattered thine enemies with thy strong arm."

Psalm 90:1-3 "[1]LORD, thou hast been our dwelling place in all generations. [2]Before the mountains were brought forth, or ever thou hadst formed the earth and the world, even from everlasting to everlasting, thou art God. [3]Thou turnest man to destruction; and sayest, Return, ye children of men."

Psalm 98:1 "O sing unto the LORD a new song; for he hath done marvellous things: his right hand, and his holy arm, hath gotten him the victory."

Psalm 100:2-5 "[2]Serve the LORD with gladness: come before his presence with singing. [3]Know ye that the LORD he is God: it is he that hath made us, and not we ourselves; we are his people, and the sheep of his pasture. [4]Enter into his gates with thanksgiving, and into his courts with praise: be thankful unto him, and bless his name. [5]For the LORD is good; his mercy is everlasting; and his truth endureth to all generations."

Psalm 104:1-20 "[1]Bless the LORD, O my soul. O LORD my God, thou art very great; thou art clothed with honour and majesty. [2]Who coverest thyself with light as with a garment: who stretchest out the heavens like a curtain: [3]Who layeth the beams of his chambers in the waters: who maketh the clouds his chariot: who walketh upon the wings of the wind: [4]Who maketh his angels spirits; his ministers a flaming fire: [5]Who laid the foundations of the earth, that it should not be removed for ever. [6]Thou coveredst it with the deep as with a garment: the waters stood above the mountains. [7]At thy rebuke they fled; at the voice of thy thunder they hasted away. [8]They go up by the mountains; they go down by the valleys unto the place which thou hast founded for them. [9]Thou hast set a bound that they may not pass over; that they turn not again to cover the earth. [10]He sendeth the springs into the valleys, which run among the hills. [11]They give drink to every beast of the field: the wild asses quench their thirst. [12]By them shall the fowls of the heaven have their habitation, which sing among the branches. [13]He watereth the hills from his chambers: the earth is satisfied with the fruit of thy works. [14]He causeth the grass to grow for the cattle, and herb for the service of man: that he may bring forth food out of the earth; [15]And wine that maketh glad the heart of man, and oil to make his face to shine, and bread which strengtheneth man's heart. [16]The trees of the LORD are full of sap; the cedars of Lebanon, which he hath planted; [17]Where the birds make their nests: as for the stork, the fir trees are her house. [18]The high hills are a refuge for the wild goats; and the rocks for the conies. [19]He appointed the moon for seasons: the sun knoweth his going down. [20]Thou makest darkness, and it is night: wherein all the beasts of the forest do creep forth."

Psalm 104:24-30 "[24]O LORD, how manifold are thy works! in wisdom hast thou made them all: the earth is full of thy riches. [25]So is this great and wide sea, wherein are things creeping innumerable, both small and great beasts [26]There go the ships: there is that leviathan, whom thou hast made to play therein. [27]These wait all upon thee; that thou mayest give them their meat in due season. [28]That thou givest them they gather: thou openest thine hand, they are filled with good. [29]Thou hidest thy face, they are troubled: thou takest away their breath, they die, and return to their dust. [30]Thou sendest forth thy spirit, they are created: and thou renewest the face of the earth."

Psalm 106:21-22 "[21]They forgat God their saviour, which had done great things in Egypt; [22]Wondrous works in the land of Ham, and terrible things by the Red sea."

Psalm 107:8-9 "[8]Oh that men would praise the LORD for his goodness, and for his wonderful works to the children of men! [9]For he satisfieth the longing soul, and filleth the hungry soul with goodness."

Psalm 107:23-41 "[23]They that go down to the sea in ships, that do business in great waters; [24]These see the works of the LORD, and his wonders in the deep. [25]For he commandeth, and raiseth the stormy wind, which lifteth up the waves thereof. [26]They mount up to the heaven, they go down again to the depths: their soul is melted because of trouble. [27]They reel to and fro, and stagger like a drunken man, and are at their wits' end. [28]Then they cry unto the LORD in their trouble, and he bringeth them out of their distresses. [29]He maketh the storm a calm, so that the waves thereof are still. [30]Then are they glad because they be quiet; so he bringeth them unto their desired haven. [31]Oh that men would praise the LORD for his goodness, and for his wonderful works to the children of

men! [32]Let them exalt him also in the congregation of the people, and praise him in the assembly of the elders. [33]He turneth rivers into a wilderness, and the watersprings into dry ground; [34]A fruitful land into barrenness, for the wickedness of them that dwell therein. [35]He turneth the wilderness into a standing water, and dry ground into watersprings. [36]And there he maketh the hungry to dwell, that they may prepare a city for habitation; [37]And sow the fields, and plant vineyards, which may yield fruits of increase. [38]He blesseth them also, so that they are multiplied greatly; and suffereth not their cattle to decrease. [39]Again, they are minished and brought low through oppression, affliction, and sorrow. [40]He poureth contempt upon princes, and causeth them to wander in the wilderness, where there is no way. [41]Yet setteth he the poor on high from affliction, and maketh him families like a flock."

Psalm 113:5-9 "[5]Who is like unto the LORD our God, who dwelleth on high, [6]Who humbleth himself to behold the things that are in heaven, and in the earth! [7]He raiseth up the poor out of the dust, and lifteth the needy out of the dunghill; [8]That he may set him with princes, even with the princes of his people. [9]He maketh the barren woman to keep house, and to be a joyful mother of children. Praise ye the LORD."

Psalm 115:3 "But our God is in the heavens: he hath done whatsoever he hath pleased."

Psalm 118:15-16 "[15]The voice of rejoicing and salvation is in the tabernacles of the righteous: the right hand of the LORD doeth valiantly. [16]The right hand of the LORD is exalted: the right hand of the LORD doeth valiantly."

Psalm 119:65-68 "[65]Thou hast dealt well with thy servant, O LORD, according unto thy word. [66]Teach me good judgment and knowledge: for I have believed thy commandments. [67]Before I was afflicted I went astray: but now have I kept thy word. [68]Thou art good, and doest good; teach me thy statutes."

Psalm 135:6 "Whatsoever the LORD pleased, that did he in heaven, and in earth, in the seas, and all deep places."

Psalm 136:1-25 "[1]O give thanks unto the LORD; for he is good: for his mercy endureth for ever. [2]O give thanks unto the God of gods: for his mercy endureth for ever. ³O give thanks to the Lord of lords: for his mercy endureth for ever. ⁴To him who alone doeth great wonders: for his mercy endureth for ever. ⁵To him that by wisdom made the heavens: for his mercy endureth for ever. ⁶To him that stretched out the earth above the waters: for his mercy endureth for ever. ⁷To him that made great lights: for his mercy endureth for ever: ⁸The sun to rule by day: for his mercy endureth for ever: ⁹The moon and stars to rule by night: for his mercy endureth for ever. ¹⁰To him that smote Egypt in their firstborn: for his mercy endureth for ever: ¹¹And brought out Israel from among them: for his mercy endureth for ever: ¹²With a strong hand, and with a stretched out arm: for his mercy endureth for ever. ¹³To him which divided the Red sea into parts: for his mercy endureth for ever: ¹⁴And made Israel to pass through the midst of it: for his mercy endureth for ever: ¹⁵But overthrew Pharaoh and his host in the Red sea: for his mercy endureth for ever. ¹⁶To him which led his people through the wilderness: for his mercy endureth for ever. ¹⁷To him which smote great kings: for his mercy endureth for ever: ¹⁸And slew famous kings: for his mercy endureth for ever: ¹⁹Sihon king of the Amorites: for his mercy endureth for ever: ²⁰And Og the king of Bashan: for his mercy endureth for ever: ²¹And gave their land for an heritage: for his mercy endureth for ever: ²²Even an heritage unto Israel his servant: for his mercy endureth for ever. ²³Who remembered us in our low estate: for his mercy endureth for ever: ²⁴And hath redeemed us from our enemies: for his mercy endureth for ever. ²⁵Who giveth food to all flesh: for his mercy endureth for ever."

Psalm 144:1 "Blessed be the LORD my strength, which teacheth my hands to war, and my fingers to fight:"

Psalm 146:5-8 "⁵Happy is he that hath the God of Jacob for his help, whose hope is in the LORD his God: ⁶Which made heaven, and earth, the sea, and all that therein is: which keepeth truth for ever: ⁷Which executeth judgment for the oppressed: which giveth food to the hungry. The LORD looseth the prisoners: ⁸The LORD openeth the eyes of the blind: the LORD raiseth them that are bowed down: the LORD loveth the righteous:"

Isaiah 12:5 "Sing unto the LORD; for he hath done excellent things: this is known in all the earth."

Isaiah 25:1-2 "¹O LORD, thou art my God; I will exalt thee, I will praise thy name; for thou hast done wonderful things; thy counsels of old are faithfulness and truth. ²For thou hast made of a city an heap; of a defenced city a ruin: a palace of strangers to be no city; it shall never be built."

Isaiah 40:22-23 "²²It is he that sitteth upon the circle of the earth, and the inhabitants thereof are as grasshoppers; that stretcheth out the heavens as a curtain, and spreadeth them out as a tent to dwell in: ²³That bringeth the princes to nothing; he maketh the judges of the earth as vanity."

Isaiah 43:16-20 "¹⁶Thus saith the LORD, which maketh a way in the sea, and a path in the mighty waters; ¹⁷Which bringeth forth the chariot and horse, the army and the power; they shall lie down together, they shall not rise: they are extinct, they are quenched as tow. ¹⁸Remember ye not the former things, neither consider the things of old. ¹⁹Behold, I will do a new thing; now it shall spring forth; shall ye not know it? I will even make a way in the wilderness, and rivers in the desert. ²⁰The beast of the field shall honour me, the dragons and the owls: because I give waters in the wilderness, and rivers in the desert, to give drink to my people, my chosen."

Isaiah 44:1-3 "¹Yet now hear, O Jacob my servant; and Israel, whom I have chosen: ²Thus saith the LORD that made thee, and formed thee from the womb, which will help thee; Fear not, O Jacob, my servant; and thou, Jesurun, whom I have chosen. ³For I will pour water upon him that is thirsty, and floods upon the dry ground: I will pour my spirit upon thy seed, and my blessing upon thine offspring:"

Isaiah 44:24-28 "²⁴Thus saith the LORD, thy redeemer, and he that formed thee from the womb, I am the LORD that maketh all things; that stretcheth forth the heavens alone; that spreadeth abroad the earth by myself; ²⁵That frustrateth the tokens of the liars, and maketh diviners mad; that turneth wise men backward, and maketh their knowledge foolish; ²⁶That confirmeth the word of his servant, and performeth the counsel of his messengers; that saith to Jerusalem, Thou shalt be inhabited; and to the cities of Judah, Ye shall be built, and I will raise up the decayed places thereof: [27]That saith to the deep, Be dry, and I will dry up thy rivers: [28]That saith of Cyrus, He is my shepherd, and shall perform all my pleasure: even saying to Jerusalem, Thou shalt be built; and to the temple, Thy foundation shall be laid."

Isaiah 45:7 "I form the light, and create darkness: I make peace, and create evil: I the LORD do all these things."

Isaiah 51:15-16 "[15]But I am the LORD thy God, that divided the sea, whose waves roared: The LORD of hosts is his name. [16]And I have put my words in thy mouth, and I have covered thee in the shadow of mine hand, that I may plant the heavens, and lay the foundations of the earth, and say unto Zion, Thou art my people."

Jeremiah 9:23-24 "[23]Thus saith the LORD, Let not the wise man glory in his wisdom, neither let the mighty man glory in his might, let not the rich man glory in his riches: [24]But let him that glorieth glory in this, that he understandeth and knoweth me, that I am the LORD which exercise lovingkindness, judgment, and righteousness, in the earth: for in these things I delight, saith the LORD."

Jeremiah 10:10-13 "[10]But the LORD is the true God, he is the living God, and an everlasting king: at his wrath the earth shall tremble, and the nations shall not be able to abide his indignation. [11]Thus shall ye say unto them, The gods that have not made the heavens and the earth, even they shall perish from the earth, and from under these heavens. [12]He hath made the earth by his power, he hath established the world by his wisdom, and hath stretched out the heavens by his discretion. [13]When he uttereth his voice, there is a multitude of waters in the heavens, and he causeth the vapours to ascend from the ends of the earth; he maketh lightnings with rain, and bringeth forth the wind out of his treasures."

Jeremiah 17:10 "I the LORD search the heart, I try the reins, even to give every man according to his ways, and according to the fruit of his doings."

Jeremiah 31:35 "Thus saith the LORD, which giveth the sun for a light by day, and the ordinances of the moon and of the stars for a light by night, which divideth the sea when the waves thereof roar; The LORD of hosts is his name:"

Daniel 2:20-22 "[20]Daniel answered and said, Blessed be the name of God for ever and ever: for wisdom and might are his: [21]And he changeth the times and the seasons: he removeth kings, and setteth up kings: he giveth wisdom unto the wise, and knowledge to them that know understanding: [22]He revealeth the deep and secret things: he knoweth what is in the darkness, and the light dwelleth with him."

Daniel 4:34-35 "[34]And at the end of the days I Nebuchadnezzar lifted up mine eyes unto heaven, and mine understanding returned unto me, and I blessed the most High, and I praised and honoured him that liveth for ever, whose dominion is an everlasting dominion, and his kingdom is from generation to generation: [35]And all the inhabitants of the earth are reputed as nothing: and he doeth according to his will in the army of heaven, and among the inhabitants of the earth: and none can stay his hand, or say unto him, What doest thou?"

Daniel 6:26-27 "[26]I make a decree, That in every dominion of my kingdom men tremble and fear before the God of Daniel: for he is the living God, and stedfast for ever, and his kingdom that which shall not be destroyed, and his dominion shall be even unto the end. [27]He delivereth and rescueth, and he worketh signs and wonders in heaven and in earth, who hath delivered Daniel from the power of the lions."

Joel 2:21 "Fear not, O land; be glad and rejoice: for the LORD will do great things."

Amos 4:13 "For, lo, he that formeth the mountains, and createth the wind, and declareth unto man what is his thought, that maketh the morning darkness, and treadeth upon the high places of the earth, The LORD, The God of hosts, is his name."

Amos 5:8-9 "[8]Seek him that maketh the seven stars and Orion, and turneth the shadow of death into the morning, and maketh the day dark with night: that calleth for the waters of the sea, and poureth them out upon the face of the earth: The LORD is his name: [9]That strengtheneth the spoiled against the strong, so that the spoiled shall come against the fortress."

Amos 9:6 "It is he that buildeth his stories in the heaven, and hath founded his troop in the earth; he that calleth for the waters of the sea, and poureth them out upon the face of the earth: The LORD is his name."

Habakkuk 3:19 "The LORD God is my strength, and he will make my feet like hinds' feet, and he will make me to walk upon mine high places. To the chief singer on my stringed instruments."

Matthew 21:42 "Jesus saith unto them, Did ye never read in the scriptures, The stone which the builders rejected, the same is become the head of the corner: this is the Lord's doing, and it is marvellous in our eyes?"

Acts 17:23-25 "²³For as I passed by, and beheld your devotions, I found an altar with this inscription, TO THE UNKNOWN GOD. Whom therefore ye ignorantly worship, him declare I unto you. ²⁴God that made the world and all things therein, seeing that he is Lord of heaven and earth, dwelleth not in temples made with hands; ²⁵Neither is worshipped with men's hands, as though he needed any thing, seeing he giveth to all life, and breath, and all things;"

Philippians 2:13 "For it is God which worketh in you both to will and to do of his good pleasure."

2 Thessalonians 3:3 "But the Lord is faithful, who shall stablish you, and keep you from evil."

What The Lord God Is
Genesis 14:19-20 "¹⁹And he blessed him, and said, Blessed be Abram of the most high God, possessor of heaven and earth: ²⁰And blessed be the most high God, which hath delivered thine enemies into thy hand. And he gave him tithes of all."

Genesis 17:1 "And when Abram was ninety years old and nine, the LORD appeared to Abram, and said unto him, I am the Almighty God; walk before me, and be thou perfect."

Exodus 3:14 "And God said unto Moses, I AM THAT I AM: and he said, Thus shalt thou say unto the children of Israel, I AM hath sent me unto you."

Exodus 15:2-3 "²The LORD is my strength and song, and he is become my salvation: he is my God, and I will prepare him an habitation; my father's God, and I will exalt him. ³The LORD is a man of war: the LORD is his name."

Exodus 15:11 "Who is like unto thee, O LORD, among the gods? who is like thee, glorious in holiness, fearful in praises, doing wonders?"

Exodus 18:11 "Now I know that the LORD is greater than all gods: for in the thing wherein they dealt proudly he was above them."

Leviticus 20:7 "Sanctify yourselves therefore, and be ye holy: for I am the LORD your God."

Deuteronomy 4:24 "For the LORD thy God is a consuming fire, even a jealous God."

Deuteronomy 10:17 "For the LORD your God is God of gods, and Lord of lords, a great God, a mighty, and a terrible, which regardeth not persons, nor taketh reward:"

Deuteronomy 30:20 "That thou mayest love the LORD thy God, and that thou mayest obey his voice, and that thou mayest cleave unto him: for he is thy life, and the length of thy days: that thou mayest dwell in the land which the LORD sware unto thy fathers, to Abraham, to Isaac, and to Jacob, to give them."

Deuteronomy 32:4 "He is the Rock, his work is perfect: for all his ways are judgment: a God of truth and without iniquity, just and right is he."

Joshua 4:24 "That all the people of the earth might know the hand of the LORD, that it is mighty: that ye might fear the LORD your God for ever."

1 Samuel 2:3 "Talk no more so exceeding proudly; let not arrogancy come out of your mouth: for the LORD is a God of knowledge, and by him actions are weighed."

1 Samuel 15:29 "And also the Strength of Israel will not lie nor repent: for he is not a man, that he should repent."

2 Samuel 7:22 "Wherefore thou art great, O LORD God: for there is none like thee, neither is there any God beside thee, according to all that we have heard with our ears."

2 Samuel 22:2-3 "²And he said, The LORD is my rock, and my fortress, and my deliverer; ³The God of my rock; in him will I trust: he is my shield, and the horn of my salvation, my high tower, and my refuge, my saviour; thou savest me from violence."

2 Samuel 22:29 "For thou art my lamp, O LORD: and the LORD will lighten my darkness."

2 Samuel 22:31-33 "³¹As for God, his way is perfect; the word of the LORD is tried: he is a buckler to all them that trust in him. ³²For who is God, save the LORD? and who is a rock, save our God? ³³God is my strength and power: and he maketh my way perfect."

2 Samuel 22:47 "The LORD liveth; and blessed be my rock; and exalted be the God of the rock of my salvation."

2 Samuel 22:50-51 "⁵⁰Therefore I will give thanks unto thee, O LORD, among the heathen, and I will sing praises unto thy name. ⁵¹He is the tower of salvation for his king: and sheweth mercy to his anointed, unto David, and to his seed for evermore."

1 Chronicles 16:11-14 "¹¹Seek the LORD and his strength, seek his face continually. ¹²Remember his marvellous works that he hath done, his wonders, and the judgments of his mouth; ¹³O ye seed of Israel his servant, ye children of Jacob, his chosen ones. ¹⁴He is the LORD our God; his judgments are in all the earth."

1 Chronicles 16:25 "For great is the LORD, and greatly to be praised: he also is to be feared above all gods."

2 Chronicles 2:5 "And the house which I build is great: for great is our God above all gods."

Nehemiah 8:6 "And Ezra blessed the LORD, the great God. And all the people answered, Amen, Amen, with lifting up their hands: and they bowed their heads, and worshipped the LORD with their faces to the ground."

Nehemiah 9:32 "Now therefore, our God, the great, the mighty, and the terrible God, who keepest covenant and mercy, let not all the trouble seem little before thee, that hath come upon us, on our kings, on our princes, and on our priests, and on our prophets, and on our fathers, and on all thy people, since the time of the kings of Assyria unto this day."

Job 13:16 "He also shall be my salvation: for an hypocrite shall not come before him."

Job 22:25 "Yea, the Almighty shall be thy defence, and thou shalt have plenty of silver."

Job 33:12 "Behold, in this thou art not just: I will answer thee, that God is greater than man."

Job 36:5 "Behold, God is mighty, and despiseth not any: he is mighty in strength and wisdom."

Job 36:26 "Behold, God is great, and we know him not, neither can the number of his years be searched out."

Job 37:23 "Touching the Almighty, we cannot find him out: he is excellent in power, and in judgment, and in plenty of justice: he will not afflict."

Psalm 3:3 "But thou, O LORD, art a shield for me; my glory, and the lifter up of mine head."

Psalm 7:10 "My defence is of God, which saveth the upright in heart."

Psalm 9:9 "The LORD also will be a refuge for the oppressed, a refuge in times of trouble."

Psalm 10:16 "The LORD is King for ever and ever: the heathen are perished out of his land."

Psalm 18:2-3 "²The LORD is my rock, and my fortress, and my deliverer; my God, my strength, in whom I will trust; my buckler, and the horn of my salvation, and my high tower. ³I will call upon the LORD, who is worthy to be praised: so shall I be saved from mine enemies."

Psalm 18:30-31 "³⁰As for God, his way is perfect: the word of the LORD is tried: he is a buckler to all those that trust in him. ³¹For who is God save the LORD? or who is a rock save our God?"

Psalm 18:46 "The LORD liveth; and blessed be my rock; and let the God of my salvation be exalted."

Psalm 22:28 "For the kingdom is the LORD's: and he is the governor among the nations."

Psalm 23:1-4 "¹The LORD is my shepherd; I shall not want. ²He maketh me to lie down in green pastures: he leadeth me beside the still waters. [3]He restoreth my soul: he leadeth me in the paths of righteousness for his name's sake. [4]Yea, though I walk through the valley of the shadow of death, I will fear no evil: for thou art with me; thy rod and thy staff they comfort me."

Psalm 24:10 "Who is this King of glory? The LORD of hosts, he is the King of glory. Selah."

Psalm 25:5 "Lead me in thy truth, and teach me: for thou art the God of my salvation; on thee do I wait all the day."

Psalm 27:1 "The LORD is my light and my salvation; whom shall I fear? the LORD is the strength of my life; of whom shall I be afraid?"

Psalm 28:1 "Unto thee will I cry, O LORD my rock; be not silent to me: lest, if thou be silent to me, I become like them that go down into the pit."

Psalm 28:6-8 "[6]Blessed be the LORD, because he hath heard the voice of my supplications. [7]The LORD is my strength and my shield; my heart trusted in him, and I am helped: therefore my heart greatly rejoiceth; and with my song will I praise him. [8]The LORD is their strength, and he is the saving strength of his anointed."

Psalm 30:10 "Hear, O LORD, and have mercy upon me: LORD, be thou my helper."

Psalm 31:1-5 "[1]In thee, O LORD, do I put my trust; let me never be ashamed: deliver me in thy righteousness. [2]Bow down thine ear to me; deliver me speedily: be thou my strong rock, for an house of defence to save me. [3]For thou art my rock and my fortress; therefore for thy name's sake lead me, and guide me. [4]Pull me out of the net that they have laid privily for me: for thou art my strength. [5]Into thine hand I commit my spirit: thou hast redeemed me, O LORD God of truth."

Psalm 31:14 "But I trusted in thee, O LORD: I said, Thou art my God."

Psalm 32:5-7 "[5]I acknowledged my sin unto thee, and mine iniquity have I not hid. I said, I will confess my transgressions unto the LORD; and thou forgavest the iniquity of my sin. Selah. [6]For this shall every one that is godly pray unto thee in a time when thou mayest be found: surely in the floods of great waters they shall not come nigh unto him. [7]Thou art my hiding place; thou shalt

preserve me from trouble; thou shalt compass me about with songs of deliverance. Selah."

Psalm 33:20 "Our soul waiteth for the LORD: he is our help and our shield."

Psalm 37:39 "But the salvation of the righteous is of the LORD: he is their strength in the time of trouble."

Psalm 40:17 "But I am poor and needy; yet the Lord thinketh upon me: thou art my help and my deliverer; make no tarrying, O my God."

Psalm 42:11 "Why art thou cast down, O my soul? and why art thou disquieted within me? hope thou in God: for I shall yet praise him, who is the health of my countenance, and my God."

Psalm 43:5 "Why art thou cast down, O my soul? and why art thou disquieted within me? hope in God: for I shall yet praise him, who is the health of my countenance, and my God."

Psalm 46:1-11 "[1]God is our refuge and strength, a very present help in trouble. [2]Therefore will not we fear, though the earth be removed, and though the mountains be carried into the midst of the sea; [3]Though the waters thereof roar and be troubled, though the mountains shake with the swelling thereof. Selah. [4]There is a river, the streams whereof shall make glad the city of God, the holy place of the tabernacles of the most High. [5]God is in the midst of her; she shall not be moved: God shall help her, and that right early. [6]The heathen raged, the kingdoms were moved: he uttered his voice, the earth melted. [7]The LORD of hosts is with us; the God of Jacob is our refuge. Selah. [8]Come, behold the works of the LORD, what desolations he hath made in the earth. [9]He maketh wars to cease unto the end of the earth; he breaketh the bow, and cutteth the spear in sunder; he burneth the chariot in the fire. [10]Be still, and know that I am God: I will be exalted among the heathen, I will be exalted in the earth. [11]The LORD of hosts is with us; the God of Jacob is our refuge. Selah."

Psalm 47:2 "For the LORD most high is terrible; he is a great King over all the earth."

Psalm 47:7-9 "[7]For God is the King of all the earth: sing ye praises with understanding. [8]God reigneth over the heathen: God sitteth upon the throne of his holiness. ⁹The princes of the people are gathered together, even the people of the God of Abraham: for the shields of the earth belong unto God: he is greatly exalted."

Psalm 48:14 "For this God is our God for ever and ever: he will be our guide even unto death."

Psalm 50:6 "And the heavens shall declare his righteousness: for God is judge himself. Selah."

Psalm 54:4 "Behold, God is mine helper: the Lord is with them that uphold my soul."

Psalm 59:9 "Because of his strength will I wait upon thee: for God is my defence."

Psalm 59:16-17 "¹⁶But I will sing of thy power; yea, I will sing aloud of thy mercy in the morning: for thou hast been my defence and refuge in the day of my trouble. ¹⁷Unto thee, O my strength, will I sing: for God is my defence, and the God of my mercy."

Psalm 61:1-3 "¹Hear my cry, O God; attend unto my prayer. ²From the end of the earth will I cry unto thee, when my heart is overwhelmed: lead me to the rock that is higher than I. ³For thou hast been a shelter for me, and a strong tower from the enemy."

Psalm 62:1-2 "¹Truly my soul waiteth upon God: from him cometh my salvation. ²He only is my rock and my salvation; he is my defence; I shall not be greatly moved."

Psalm 62:6-8 "⁶He only is my rock and my salvation: he is my defence; I shall not be moved. ⁷In God is my salvation and my glory: the rock of my strength, and my refuge, is in God. ⁸Trust in him at all times; ye people, pour out your heart before him: God is a refuge for us. Selah."

Psalm 63:1-7 "¹O God, thou art my God; early will I seek thee: my soul thirsteth for thee, my flesh longeth for thee in a dry and thirsty land, where no water is; ²To see thy power and thy glory, so as I have seen thee in the sanctuary. ³Because thy lovingkindness is better than life, my lips shall praise thee. ⁴Thus will I bless thee while I live: I will lift up my hands in thy name. ⁵My soul shall be satisfied as with marrow and fatness; and my mouth shall praise thee with joyful lips: ⁶When I remember thee upon my bed, and meditate on thee in the night watches. ⁷Because

thou hast been my help, therefore in the shadow of thy wings will I rejoice."

Psalm 68:4-5 "⁴Sing unto God, sing praises to his name: extol him that rideth upon the heavens by his name JAH, and rejoice before him. ⁵A father of the fatherless, and a judge of the widows, is God in his holy habitation."

Psalm 68:35 "O God, thou art terrible out of thy holy places: the God of Israel is he that giveth strength and power unto his people. Blessed be God."

Psalm 71:1-7 "¹In thee, O LORD, do I put my trust: let me never be put to confusion. ²Deliver me in thy righteousness, and cause me to escape: incline thine ear unto me, and save me. ³Be thou my strong habitation, whereunto I may continually resort: thou hast given commandment to save me; for thou art my rock and my fortress. ⁴Deliver me, O my God, out of the hand of the wicked, out of the hand of the unrighteous and cruel man. ⁵For thou art my hope, O Lord GOD: thou art my trust from my youth. ⁶By thee have I been holden up from the womb: thou art he that took me out of my mother's bowels: my praise shall be continually of thee. ⁷I am as a wonder unto many; but thou art my strong refuge."

Psalm 72:18-19 "¹⁸Blessed be the LORD God, the God of Israel, who only doeth wondrous things. ¹⁹And blessed be his glorious name for ever: and let the whole earth be filled with his glory; Amen, and Amen."

Psalm 73:26 "My flesh and my heart faileth: but God is the strength of my heart, and my portion for ever."

Psalm 74:12 "For God is my King of old, working salvation in the midst of the earth."

Psalm 75:7 "But God is the judge: he putteth down one, and setteth up another."

Psalm 78:34-35 "³⁴When he slew them, then they sought him: and they returned and inquired early after God. ³⁵And they remembered that God was their rock, and the high God their redeemer."

Psalm 83:18 "That men may know that thou, whose name alone is JEHOVAH, art the most high over all the earth."

Psalm 84:11 "For the LORD God is a sun and shield: the LORD will give grace and glory: no good thing will he withhold from them that walk uprightly."

Psalm 86:10 "For thou art great, and doest wondrous things: thou art God alone."

Psalm 89:18 "For the LORD is our defence; and the Holy One of Israel is our king."

Psalm 89:26 "He shall cry unto me, Thou art my father, my God, and the rock of my salvation."

Psalm 90:1-2 "¹LORD, thou hast been our dwelling place in all generations. ²Before the mountains were brought forth, or ever thou hadst formed the earth and the world, even from everlasting to everlasting, thou art God."

Psalm 91:2 "I will say of the LORD, He is my refuge and my fortress: my God; in him will I trust."

Psalm 91:9 "Because thou hast made the LORD, which is my refuge, even the most High, thy habitation;"

Psalm 92:8 "But thou, LORD, art most high for evermore."

Psalm 92:15 "To shew that the LORD is upright: he is my rock, and there is no unrighteousness in him."

Psalm 94:1-2 "¹O LORD God, to whom vengeance belongeth; O God, to whom vengeance belongeth, shew thyself. ²Lift up thyself, thou judge of the earth: render a reward to the proud."

Psalm 94:22 "But the LORD is my defence; and my God is the rock of my refuge."

Psalm 95:1-3 "¹O come, let us sing unto the LORD: let us make a joyful noise to the rock of our salvation. ²Let us come before his presence with thanksgiving, and make a joyful noise unto him with psalms. ³For the LORD is a great God, and a great King above all gods."

Psalm 95:7 "For he is our God; and we are the people of his pasture, and the sheep of his hand. To day if ye will hear his voice,"

Psalm 96:4 "For the LORD is great, and greatly to be praised: he is to be feared above all gods."

Psalm 97:9 "For thou, LORD, art high above all the earth: thou art exalted far above all gods."

Psalm 99:2 "The LORD is great in Zion; and he is high above all the people."

Psalm 104:1 "Bless the LORD, O my soul. O LORD my God, thou art very great; thou art clothed with honour and majesty."

Psalm 115:9-11 "⁹O Israel, trust thou in the LORD: he is their help and their shield. ¹⁰O house of Aaron, trust in the LORD: he is their help and their shield. ¹¹Ye that fear the LORD, trust in the LORD: he is their help and their shield."

Psalm 118:14 "The LORD is my strength and song, and is become my salvation."

Psalm 118:19-21 "¹⁹Open to me the gates of righteousness: I will go into them, and I will praise the LORD: ²⁰This gate of the LORD, into which the righteous shall enter. ²¹I will praise thee: for thou hast heard me, and art become my salvation."

Psalm 118:26-27 "²⁶Blessed be he that cometh in the name of the LORD: we have blessed you out of the house of the LORD. ²⁷God is the LORD, which hath shewed us light: bind the sacrifice with cords, even unto the horns of the altar."

Psalm 119:113-115 "¹¹³I hate vain thoughts: but thy law do I love. ¹¹⁴Thou art my hiding place and my shield: I hope in thy word. ¹¹⁵Depart from me, ye evildoers: for I will keep the commandments of my God."

Psalm 135:5 "For I know that the LORD is great, and that our Lord is above all gods."

Psalm 138:6 "Though the LORD be high, yet hath he respect unto the lowly: but the proud he knoweth afar off."

Psalm 143:10 "Teach me to do thy will; for thou art my God: thy spirit is good; lead me into the land of uprightness."

Psalm 144:1-2 "¹Blessed be the LORD my strength, which teacheth my hands to war, and my fingers to fight: ²My goodness, and my fortress; my high tower, and my deliverer; my shield, and he in whom I trust; who subdueth my people under me."

Psalm 145:3 "Great is the LORD, and greatly to be praised; and his greatness is unsearchable."

Psalm 147:5 "Great is our Lord, and of great power: his understanding is infinite."

Proverbs 2:6-7 "⁶For the LORD giveth wisdom: out of his mouth cometh knowledge and understanding. ⁷He layeth up sound wisdom for the righteous: he is a buckler to them that walk uprightly."

Proverbs 3:25-26 "²⁵Be not afraid of sudden fear, neither of the desolation of the wicked, when it cometh. ²⁶For the LORD shall be thy confidence, and shall keep thy foot from being taken."

Proverbs 22:2 "The rich and poor meet together: the LORD is the maker of them all."

Proverbs 30:5 "Every word of God is pure: he is a shield unto them that put their trust in him."

Isaiah 12:2 "Behold, God is my salvation; I will trust, and not be afraid: for the LORD JEHOVAH is my strength and my song; he also is become my salvation."

Isaiah 12:6 "Cry out and shout, thou inhabitant of Zion: for great is the Holy One of Israel in the midst of thee."

Isaiah 25:1-4 "¹O LORD, thou art my God; I will exalt thee, I will praise thy name; for thou hast done wonderful things; thy counsels of old are faithfulness and truth. ²For thou hast made of a city an heap; of a defenced city a ruin: a palace of strangers to be no city; it shall never be built. ³Therefore shall the strong people glorify thee, the city of the terrible nations shall fear thee. ⁴For thou hast been a strength to the poor, a strength to the needy in his distress, a refuge from the storm, a shadow from the heat, when the blast of the terrible ones is as a storm against the wall."

Isaiah 26:4 "Trust ye in the LORD for ever: for in the LORD JEHOVAH is everlasting strength:"

Isaiah 30:18 "And therefore will the LORD wait, that he may be gracious unto you, and therefore will he be exalted, that he may have mercy upon you: for the LORD is a God of judgment: blessed are all they that wait for him."

Isaiah 33:2 "O LORD, be gracious unto us; we have waited for thee: be thou their arm every morning, our salvation also in the time of trouble."

Isaiah 33:22 "For the LORD is our judge, the LORD is our lawgiver, the LORD is our king; he will save us."

Isaiah 43:3 "For I am the LORD thy God, the Holy One of Israel, thy Saviour: I gave Egypt for thy ransom, Ethiopia and Seba for thee."

Isaiah 43:11 "I, even I, am the LORD; and beside me there is no saviour."

Isaiah 43:14-15 "¹⁴Thus saith the LORD, your redeemer, the Holy One of Israel; For your sake I have sent to Babylon, and have brought down all their nobles, and the Chaldeans, whose cry is in the ships. ¹⁵I am the LORD, your Holy One, the creator of Israel, your King."

Isaiah 44:6 "Thus saith the LORD the King of Israel, and his redeemer the LORD of hosts; I am the first, and I am the last; and beside me there is no God."

Isaiah 44:24 "Thus saith the LORD, thy redeemer, and he that formed thee from the womb, I am the LORD that maketh all things; that stretcheth forth the heavens alone; that spreadeth abroad the earth by myself;"

Isaiah 45:3 "And I will give thee the treasures of darkness, and hidden riches of secret places, that thou mayest know that I, the LORD, which call thee by thy name, am the God of Israel."

Isaiah 45:11 "Thus saith the LORD, the Holy One of Israel, and his Maker, Ask me of things to come concerning my sons, and concerning the work of my hands command ye me."

Isaiah 47:4 "As for our redeemer, the LORD of hosts is his name, the Holy One of Israel."

Isaiah 48:12-14 "¹²Hearken unto me, O Jacob and Israel, my called; I am he; I am the first, I also am the last. ¹³Mine hand also hath laid the foundation of the earth, and my right hand hath spanned the heavens: when I call unto them, they stand up together. ¹⁴All ye, assemble yourselves, and hear; which among them hath declared these things? The LORD hath loved him: he will do his pleasure on Babylon, and his arm shall be on the Chaldeans."

Isaiah 48:17 "Thus saith the LORD, thy Redeemer, the Holy One of Israel; I am the LORD thy God which teacheth thee to profit, which leadeth thee by the way that thou shouldest go."

Isaiah 49:5 "And now, saith the LORD that formed me from the womb to be his servant, to bring Jacob again to him, Though Israel be not gathered, yet shall I be glorious in the eyes of the LORD, and my God shall be my strength."

Isaiah 49:7 "Thus saith the LORD, the Redeemer of Israel, and his Holy One, to him whom man despiseth, to him whom the nation abhorreth, to a servant of rulers, Kings shall see and arise, princes also shall worship, because of the LORD that is faithful, and the Holy One of Israel, and he shall choose thee."

Isaiah 49:26 "And I will feed them that oppress thee with their own flesh; and they shall be drunken with their own blood, as with sweet wine: and all flesh shall know that I the LORD am thy Saviour and thy Redeemer, the mighty One of Jacob."

Isaiah 52:12 "For ye shall not go out with haste, nor go by flight: for the LORD will go before you; and the God of Israel will be your rereward."

Isaiah 54:5-8 "⁵For thy Maker is thine husband; the LORD of hosts is his name; and thy Redeemer the Holy One of Israel; The God of the whole earth shall he be called. ⁶For the LORD hath called thee as a woman forsaken and grieved in spirit, and a wife of youth, when thou wast refused, saith thy God. ⁷For a small moment have I forsaken thee; but with great mercies will I gather thee. ⁸In a little wrath I hid my face from thee for a moment; but with everlasting kindness will I have mercy on thee, saith the LORD thy Redeemer."

Isaiah 60:15-16 "¹⁵Whereas thou hast been forsaken and hated, so that no man went through thee, I will make thee an eternal excellency, a joy of many generations. ¹⁶Thou shalt also suck the milk of the Gentiles, and shalt suck the breast of kings: and thou shalt know that I the LORD am thy Saviour and thy Redeemer, the mighty One of Jacob."

Isaiah 60:19-20 "¹⁹The sun shall be no more thy light by day; neither for brightness shall the moon give light unto thee: but the LORD shall be unto thee an everlasting light, and thy God thy glory. ²⁰Thy sun shall no more go down; neither shall thy moon withdraw itself: for the LORD shall be thine everlasting light, and the days of thy mourning shall be ended."

Isaiah 63:7-8 "⁷I will mention the lovingkindnesses of the LORD, and the praises of the LORD, according to all that the LORD hath bestowed on us, and the great goodness toward the house of Israel, which he hath bestowed on them according to his mercies, and according to the multitude of his lovingkindnesses. ⁸For he said, Surely they are my people, children that will not lie: so he was their Saviour."

Isaiah 64:8 "But now, O LORD, thou art our father; we are the clay, and thou our potter; and we all are the work of thy hand."

Jeremiah 2:12-13 "¹²Be astonished, O ye heavens, at this, and be horribly afraid, be ye very desolate, saith the LORD. ¹³For my people have committed two evils; they have forsaken me the fountain of living waters, and hewed them out cisterns, broken cisterns, that can hold no water."

Jeremiah 10:6 "Forasmuch as there is none like unto thee, O LORD; thou art great, and thy name is great in might."

Jeremiah 10:10 "But the LORD is the true God, he is the living God, and an everlasting king: at his wrath the earth shall tremble, and the nations shall not be able to abide his indignation."

Jeremiah 16:19 "O LORD, my strength, and my fortress, and my refuge in the day of affliction, the Gentiles shall come unto thee from the ends of the earth, and shall say, Surely our fathers have inherited lies, vanity, and things wherein there is no profit."

Jeremiah 17:13-14 "¹³O LORD, the hope of Israel, all that forsake thee shall be ashamed, and they that depart from me shall be written in the earth, because they have forsaken the LORD, the fountain of living waters. ¹⁴Heal me, O LORD, and I shall be healed; save me, and I shall be saved: for thou art my praise."

Jeremiah 31:7-9 "⁷For thus saith the LORD; Sing with gladness for Jacob, and shout among the chief of the nations: publish ye, praise ye, and say, O LORD, save thy people, the remnant of Israel. [8]Behold, I will bring them from the north country, and gather them from the coasts of the earth, and with them the blind and the lame, the woman with child and her that travaileth with child together: a great company shall return thither. [9]They shall come with weeping, and with supplications will I lead them: I will cause them to walk by the rivers of waters in a straight way, wherein they shall not stumble: for I am a father to Israel, and Ephraim is my firstborn."

Jeremiah 32:18-19 "[18]Thou shewest lovingkindness unto thousands, and recompensest the iniquity of the fathers into the bosom of their children after them: the Great, the Mighty God, the LORD of hosts, is his name, [19]Great in counsel, and mighty in work: for thine eyes are open upon all the ways of the sons of men: to give every one according to his ways, and according to the fruit of his doings:"

Jeremiah 32:36 "And now therefore thus saith the LORD, the God of Israel, concerning this city, whereof ye say, It shall be delivered into the hand of the king of Babylon by the sword, and by the famine, and by the pestilence;"

Jeremiah 50:34 "Their Redeemer is strong; the LORD of hosts is his name: he shall throughly plead their cause, that he may give rest to the land, and disquiet the inhabitants of Babylon."

Lamentations 3:24 "The LORD is my portion, saith my soul; therefore will I hope in him."

Ezekiel 11:16 "Therefore say, Thus saith the Lord GOD; Although I have cast them far off among the heathen, and although I have scattered them among the countries, yet will I be to them as a little sanctuary in the countries where they shall come."

Ezekiel 34:11-24 "[11]For thus saith the Lord GOD; Behold, I, even I, will both search my sheep, and seek them out. [12]As a shepherd seeketh out his flock in the day that he is among his sheep that are scattered; so will I seek out my sheep, and will deliver them out of all places where they have been scattered in the cloudy and dark day. [13]And I will bring them out from the people, and gather them from the countries, and will bring them to their own land, and feed them upon the mountains of Israel by the rivers, and in all the inhabited places of the country. [14]I will feed them in a good pasture, and upon the high mountains of Israel shall their fold be: there shall they lie in a good fold, and in a fat pasture shall they feed upon the mountains of Israel. [15]I will feed my flock, and I will cause them to lie down, saith the Lord GOD. [16]I will seek that which was lost, and bring again that which was driven away, and will bind up that which was broken, and will strengthen that which was sick: but I will destroy the fat and the strong; I will feed them with judgment. [17]And as for you, O my flock, thus saith the Lord GOD; Behold, I judge between cattle and cattle, between the rams and the he goats. [18]Seemeth it a small thing unto you to have eaten up the good pasture, but ye must tread down with your feet the residue of your pastures? and to have drunk of the deep waters, but ye must foul the residue with your feet? [19]And as for my flock, they eat that which ye have trodden with your feet; and they drink that which ye have fouled with your feet. [20]Therefore thus saith the Lord GOD unto them; Behold, I, even I, will judge between the fat cattle and between the lean cattle. [21]Because ye have thrust with side and with shoulder, and pushed all the diseased with your horns, till ye have scattered them abroad; [22]Therefore will I save my flock, and they shall no more be a prey; and I will judge between cattle and cattle. [23]And I will set up one shepherd over them, and he shall feed them, even my servant David; he shall feed them, and he shall be their shepherd. [24]And I the LORD will be their God, and my servant David a prince among them; I the LORD have spoken it."

Daniel 2:47 "The king answered unto Daniel, and said, Of a truth it is, that your God is a God of gods, and a Lord of kings, and a revealer of secrets, seeing thou couldest reveal this secret."

Daniel 6:26 "I make a decree, That in every dominion of my kingdom men tremble and fear before the God of Daniel: for he is the living God, and stedfast for ever, and his kingdom that which shall not be destroyed, and his dominion shall be even unto the end."

Hosea 13:4 "Yet I am the LORD thy God from the land of Egypt, and thou shalt know no god but me: for there is no saviour beside me."

Joel 3:16 "The LORD also shall roar out of Zion, and utter his voice from Jerusalem; and the heavens and the earth shall shake: but the LORD will be the hope of his people, and the strength of the children of Israel."

Micah 7:8 "Rejoice not against me, O mine enemy: when I fall, I shall arise; when I sit in darkness, the LORD shall be a light unto me."

Nahum 1:3 "The LORD is slow to anger, and great in power, and will not at all acquit the wicked: the LORD hath his way in the whirlwind and in the storm, and the clouds are the dust of his feet."

Nahum 1:7 "The LORD is good, a strong hold in the day of trouble; and he knoweth them that trust in him."

Habakkuk 3:19 "The LORD God is my strength, and he will make my feet like hinds' feet, and he will make me to walk upon mine high places. To the chief singer on my stringed instruments."

Zechariah 2:4-5 "⁴And said unto him, Run, speak to this young man, saying, Jerusalem shall be inhabited as towns without walls for the multitude of men and cattle therein: ⁵For I, saith the LORD, will be unto her a wall of fire round about, and will be the glory in the midst of her."

Zechariah 14:9 "And the LORD shall be king over all the earth: in that day shall there be one LORD, and his name one."

Malachi 1:14 "But cursed be the deceiver, which hath in his flock a male, and voweth, and sacrificeth unto the LORD a corrupt thing: for I am a great King, saith the LORD of hosts, and my name is dreadful among the heathen."

Malachi 3:1-2 "¹Behold, I will send my messenger, and he shall prepare the way before me: and the Lord, whom ye seek, shall suddenly come to his temple, even the messenger of the covenant, whom ye delight in: behold, he shall come, saith the LORD of hosts. ²But who may abide the day of his coming? and who shall stand when he appeareth? for he is like a refiner's fire, and like fullers' soap:"

Matthew 11:25 "At that time Jesus answered and said, I thank thee, O Father, Lord of heaven and earth, because thou hast hid these things from the wise and prudent, and hast revealed them unto babes."

Matthew 22:31-32 "³¹But as touching the resurrection of the dead, have ye not read that which was spoken unto you by God, saying, ³²I am the God of Abraham, and the God of Isaac, and the God of Jacob? God is not the God of the dead, but of the living."

Mark 12:26-27 "²⁶And as touching the dead, that they rise: have ye not read in the book of Moses, how in the bush God spake unto him, saying, I am the God of Abraham, and the God of Isaac, and the God of Jaco ²⁷He is not the God of the dead, but the God of the living: ye therefore do greatly err."

Luke 1:68 "Blessed be the Lord God of Israel; for he hath visited and redeemed his people,"

Luke 20:37-38 "³⁷Now that the dead are raised, even Moses shewed at the bush, when he calleth the Lord the God of Abraham, and the God of Isaac, and the God of Jacob. ³⁸For he is not a God of the dead, but of the living: for all live unto him."

John 3:31-33 "³¹He that cometh from above is above all: he that is of the earth is earthly, and speaketh of the earth: he that cometh from heaven is above all. ³²And what he hath seen and heard, that he testifieth; and no man receiveth his testimony. ³³He that hath received his testimony hath set to his seal that God is true."

John 4:24 "God is a Spirit: and they that worship him must worship him in spirit and in truth."

John 7:28 "Then cried Jesus in the temple as he taught, saying, Ye both know me, and ye know whence I am: and I am not come of myself, but he that sent me is true, whom ye know not."

John 8:25-26 "²⁵Then said they unto him, Who art thou? And Jesus saith unto them, Even the same that I said unto you from the beginning. ²⁶I have many things to say and to judge of you: but he that sent me is true; and I speak to the world those things which I have heard of him."

John 10:25-29 "²⁵Jesus answered them, I told you, and ye believed not: the works that I do in my

Father's name, they bear witness of me. ²⁶But ye believe not, because ye are not of my sheep, as I said unto you. ²⁷My sheep hear my voice, and I know them, and they follow me: ²⁸And I give unto them eternal life; and they shall never perish, neither shall any man pluck them out of my hand. ²⁹My Father, which gave them me, is greater than all; and no man is able to pluck them out of my Father's hand."

Romans 3:29 "Is he the God of the Jews only? is he not also of the Gentiles? Yes, of the Gentiles also:"

1 Corinthians 1:25 "Because the foolishness of God is wiser than men; and the weakness of God is stronger than men."

1 Corinthians 11:2-3 "²Now I praise you, brethren, that ye remember me in all things, and keep the ordinances, as I delivered them to you. ³But I would have you know, that the head of every man is Christ; and the head of the woman is the man; and the head of Christ is God."

1 Corinthians 14:33 "For God is not the author of confusion, but of peace, as in all churches of the saints."

2 Corinthians 1:3 "Blessed be God, even the Father of our Lord Jesus Christ, the Father of mercies, and the God of all comfort;"

2 Corinthians 3:14-17 "¹⁴But their minds were blinded: for until this day remaineth the same vail untaken away in the reading of the old testament; which vail is done away in Christ. ¹⁵But even unto this day, when Moses is read, the vail is upon their heart. ¹⁶Nevertheless when it shall turn to the Lord, the vail shall be taken away. ¹⁷Now the Lord is that Spirit: and where the Spirit of the Lord is, there is liberty."

Ephesians 3:14-15 "¹⁴For this cause I bow my knees unto the Father of our Lord Jesus Christ, ¹⁵Of whom the whole family in heaven and earth is named,"

1 Timothy 1:1-2 "¹Paul, an apostle of Jesus Christ by the commandment of God our Saviour, and Lord Jesus Christ, which is our hope; ²Unto Timothy, my own son in the faith: Grace, mercy, and peace, from God our Father and Jesus Christ our Lord."

1 Timothy 1:17 "Now unto the King eternal, immortal, invisible, the only wise God, be honour and glory for ever and ever. Amen."

1 Timothy 2:3 "For this is good and acceptable in the sight of God our Saviour;"

Titus 2:13 "Looking for that blessed hope, and the glorious appearing of the great God and our Saviour Jesus Christ;"

Hebrews 3:4 "For every house is builded by some man; but he that built all things is God."

Hebrews 12:23 "To the general assembly and church of the firstborn, which are written in heaven, and to God the Judge of all, and to the spirits of just men made perfect,"

Hebrews 12:29 "For our God is a consuming fire."

Hebrews 13:6 "So that we may boldly say, The Lord is my helper, and I will not fear what man shall do unto me."

1 John 1:5 "This then is the message which we have heard of him, and declare unto you, that God is light, and in him is no darkness at all."

1 John 3:20 "For if our heart condemn us, God is greater than our heart, and knoweth all things."

1 John 4:4 "Ye are of God, little children, and have overcome them: because greater is he that is in you, than he that is in the world."

1 John 4:8 "He that loveth not knoweth not God; for God is love."

1 John 4:16 "And we have known and believed the love that God hath to us. God is love; and he that dwelleth in love dwelleth in God, and God in him."

1 John 5:20 "And we know that the Son of God is come, and hath given us an understanding, that we may know him that is true, and we are in him that is true, even in his Son Jesus Christ. This is the true God, and eternal life."

Jude 25 "To the only wise God our Saviour, be glory and majesty, dominion and power, both now and ever. Amen."

Revelation 4:8 "And the four beasts had each of them six wings about him; and they were full of eyes within: and they rest not day and night, saying,

Holy, holy, holy, Lord God Almighty, which was, and is, and is to come."

Revelation 4:11 "Thou art worthy, O Lord, to receive glory and honour and power: for thou hast created all things, and for thy pleasure they are and were created."

Revelation 15:3-4 "³And they sing the song of Moses the servant of God, and the song of the Lamb, saying, Great and marvellous are thy works, Lord God Almighty; just and true are thy ways, thou King of saints. ⁴Who shall not fear thee, O Lord, and glorify thy name? for thou only art holy: for all nations shall come and worship before thee; for thy judgments are made manifest."

Revelation 16:5 "And I heard the angel of the waters say, Thou art righteous, O Lord, which art, and wast, and shalt be, because thou hast judged thus."

Revelation 18:8 "Therefore shall her plagues come in one day, death, and mourning, and famine; and she shall be utterly burned with fire: for strong is the Lord God who judgeth her."

Revelation 21:21-23 "²¹And the twelve gates were twelve pearls; every several gate was of one pearl: and the street of the city was pure gold, as it were transparent glass. ²²And I saw no temple therein: for the Lord God Almighty and the Lamb are the temple of it. ²³And the city had no need of the sun, neither of the moon, to shine in it: for the glory of God did lighten it, and the Lamb is the light thereof."

What The Lord God Is Not

Numbers 23:19 "God is not a man, that he should lie; neither the son of man, that he should repent: hath he said, and shall he not do it? or hath he spoken, and shall he not make it good?"

1 Samuel 15:29 "And also the Strength of Israel will not lie nor repent: for he is not a man, that he should repent."

Matthew 22:31-32 "³¹But as touching the resurrection of the dead, have ye not read that which was spoken unto you by God, saying, ³²I am the God of Abraham, and the God of Isaac, and the God of Jacob? God is not the God of the dead, but of the living."

Mark 12:26-27 "²⁶And as touching the dead, that they rise: have ye not read in the book of Moses, how in the bush God spake unto him, saying, I am the God of Abraham, and the God of Isaac, and the God of Jacob? ²⁷He is not the God of the dead, but the God of the living: ye therefore do greatly err."

Luke 20:37-38 "³⁷Now that the dead are raised, even Moses shewed at the bush, when he calleth the Lord the God of Abraham, and the God of Isaac, and the God of Jacob. ³⁸For he is not a God of the dead, but of the living: for all live unto him."

Acts 17:29 "Forasmuch then as we are the offspring of God, we ought not to think that the Godhead is like unto gold, or silver, or stone, graven by art and man's device."

1 Corinthians 14:33 "For God is not the author of confusion, but of peace, as in all churches of the saints."

Where The Lord God Is

Numbers 35:34 "Defile not therefore the land which ye shall inhabit, wherein I dwell: for I the LORD dwell among the children of Israel."

Deuteronomy 4:39 "Know therefore this day, and consider it in thine heart, that the LORD he is God in heaven above, and upon the earth beneath: there is none else."

Joshua 2:11 "And as soon as we had heard these things, our hearts did melt, neither did there remain any more courage in any man, because of you: for the LORD your God, he is God in heaven above, and in earth beneath."

1 Kings 8:28-43 "²⁸Yet have thou respect unto the prayer of thy servant, and to his supplication, O LORD my God, to hearken unto the cry and to the prayer, which thy servant prayeth before thee to day: ²⁹That thine eyes may be open toward this house night and day, even toward the place of which thou hast said, My name shall be there: that thou mayest hearken unto the prayer which thy servant shall make toward this place. ³⁰And hearken thou to the supplication of thy servant, and of thy people Israel, when they shall pray toward this place: and hear thou in heaven thy dwelling place: and when thou hearest, forgive.

31If any man trespass against his neighbour, and an oath be laid upon him to cause him to swear, and the oath come before thine altar in this house: 32Then hear thou in heaven, and do, and judge thy servants, condemning the wicked, to bring his way upon his head; and justifying the righteous, to give him according to his righteousness. 33When thy people Israel be smitten down before the enemy, because they have sinned against thee, and shall turn again to thee, and confess thy name, and pray, and make supplication unto thee in this house: 34Then hear thou in heaven, and forgive the sin of thy people Israel, and bring them again unto the land which thou gavest unto their fathers. 35When heaven is shut up, and there is no rain, because they have sinned against thee; if they pray toward this place, and confess thy name, and turn from their sin, when thou afflictest them: 36Then hear thou in heaven, and forgive the sin of thy servants, and of thy people Israel, that thou teach them the good way wherein they should walk, and give rain upon thy land, which thou hast given to thy people for an inheritance. 37If there be in the land famine, if there be pestilence, blasting, mildew, locust, or if there be caterpiller; if their enemy besiege them in the land of their cities; whatsoever plague, whatsoever sickness there be; 38What prayer and supplication soever be made by any man, or by all thy people Israel, which shall know every man the plague of his own heart, and spread forth his hands toward this house: 39Then hear thou in heaven thy dwelling place, and forgive, and do, and give to every man according to his ways, whose heart thou knowest; (for thou, even thou only, knowest the hearts of all the children of men;) 40That they may fear thee all the days that they live in the land which thou gavest unto our fathers. 41Moreover concerning a stranger, that is not of thy people Israel, but cometh out of a far country for thy name's sake; 42(For they shall hear of thy great name, and of thy strong hand, and of thy stretched out arm;) when he shall come and pray toward this house; 43Hear thou in heaven thy dwelling place, and do according to all that the stranger calleth to thee for: that all people of the earth may know thy name, to fear thee, as do thy people Israel; and that they may know that this house, which I have builded, is called by thy name."

1 Kings 9:3 "And the LORD said unto him, I have heard thy prayer and thy supplication, that thou hast made before me: I have hallowed this house, which thou hast built, to put my name there for ever; and mine eyes and mine heart shall be there perpetually."

2 Kings 19:15 "And Hezekiah prayed before the LORD, and said, O LORD God of Israel, which dwellest between the cherubims, thou art the God, even thou alone, of all the kingdoms of the earth: thou hast made heaven and earth."

2 Chronicles 6:19-33 "19Have respect therefore to the prayer of thy servant, and to his supplication, O LORD my God, to hearken unto the cry and the prayer which thy servant prayeth before thee: 20That thine eyes may be open upon this house day and night, upon the place whereof thou hast said that thou wouldest put thy name there; to hearken unto the prayer which thy servant prayeth toward this place. 21Hearken therefore unto the supplications of thy servant, and of thy people Israel, which they shall make toward this place: hear thou from thy dwelling place, even from heaven; and when thou hearest, forgive. 22If a man sin against his neighbour, and an oath be laid upon him to make him swear, and the oath come before thine altar in this house; 23Then hear thou from heaven, and do, and judge thy servants, by requiting the wicked, by recompensing his way upon his own head; and by justifying the righteous, by giving him according to his righteousness. 24And if thy people Israel be put to the worse before the enemy, because they have sinned against thee; and shall return and confess thy name, and pray and make supplication before thee in this house; 25Then hear thou from the heavens, and forgive the sin of thy people Israel, and bring them again unto the land which thou gavest to them and to their fathers. 26When the heaven is shut up, and there is no rain, because they have sinned against thee; yet if they pray toward this place, and confess thy name, and turn from their sin, when thou dost afflict them; 27Then hear thou from heaven, and forgive the sin of thy servants, and of thy people Israel, when thou hast taught them the good way, wherein they should walk; and send rain upon thy land, which thou hast given unto thy people for an inheritance. 28If there be dearth in the land, if there be pestilence, if there be blasting, or mildew, locusts, or caterpillers; if their enemies besiege them in the cities of their land; whatsoever sore or whatsoever sickness there be: 29Then what prayer or what supplication soever shall be made of any man, or of all thy people Israel, when every one shall know his own sore and his own grief, and shall spread forth his hands in this house: 30Then hear thou from heaven thy dwelling place, and forgive, and render unto every man according unto all his ways, whose heart thou knowest; (for thou only knowest the hearts of the children of men:) 31That they may fear thee, to walk in thy ways, so long as they live in the land which thou gavest unto our fathers. 32Moreover concerning the stranger, which is not of thy people Israel, but is come from a far country for thy great name's sake, and thy mighty hand, and thy stretched out arm; if they come and pray in this house; 33Then hear thou from the heavens, even from thy dwelling place, and do according to all that the stranger calleth to thee for; that all people of the earth may know thy name, and fear thee, as doth thy people Israel, and may know that this house which I have built is called by thy name."

Psalm 11:4 "The LORD is in his holy temple, the LORD's throne is in heaven: his eyes behold, his eyelids try, the children of men."

Psalm 16:8 "I have set the LORD always before me: because he is at my right hand, I shall not be moved."

Psalm 47:7-8 "7For God is the King of all the earth: sing ye praises with understanding. 8God reigneth over the heathen: God sitteth upon the throne of his holiness."

Psalm 68:15-18 "15The hill of God is as the hill of Bashan; an high hill as the hill of Bashan. 16Why leap ye, ye high hills? this is the hill which God desireth to dwell in; yea, the LORD will dwell in it for ever. 17The chariots of God are twenty thousand, even thousands of angels: the Lord is among them, as in Sinai, in the holy place. 18Thou hast ascended on high, thou hast led captivity captive: thou hast received gifts for men; yea, for the rebellious also, that the LORD God might dwell among them."

Psalm 99:1-2 "1The LORD reigneth; let the people tremble: he sitteth between the cherubims; let the

earth be moved. 2The LORD is great in Zion; and he is high above all the people."

Psalm 113:4-5 "4The LORD is high above all nations, and his glory above the heavens. 5Who is like unto the LORD our God, who dwelleth on high,"

Psalm 115:3 "But our God is in the heavens: he hath done whatsoever he hath pleased."

Psalm 132:13-14 "13For the LORD hath chosen Zion; he hath desired it for his habitation. 14This is my rest for ever: here will I dwell; for I have desired it."

Psalm 139:4-8 "4For there is not a word in my tongue, but, lo, O LORD, thou knowest it altogether. 5Thou hast beset me behind and before, and laid thine hand upon me. 6Such knowledge is too wonderful for me; it is high, I cannot attain unto it. 7Whither shall I go from thy spirit? or whither shall I flee from thy presence? 8If I ascend up into heaven, thou art there: if I make my bed in hell, behold, thou art there."

Ecclesiastes 5:2 "Be not rash with thy mouth, and let not thine heart be hasty to utter any thing before God: for God is in heaven, and thou upon earth: therefore let thy words be few."

Isaiah 8:16-18 "16Bind up the testimony, seal the law among my disciples. 17And I will wait upon the LORD, that hideth his face from the house of Jacob, and I will look for him. 18Behold, I and the children whom the LORD hath given me are for signs and for wonders in Israel from the LORD of hosts, which dwelleth in mount Zion."

Isaiah 33:5 "The LORD is exalted; for he dwelleth on high: he hath filled Zion with judgment and righteousness."

Isaiah 37:16 "O LORD of hosts, God of Israel, that dwellest between the cherubims, thou art the God, even thou alone, of all the kingdoms of the earth: thou hast made heaven and earth."

Isaiah 40:22 "It is he that sitteth upon the circle of the earth, and the inhabitants thereof are as grasshoppers; that stretcheth out the heavens as a curtain, and spreadeth them out as a tent to dwell in:"

Isaiah 57:15 "For thus saith the high and lofty One that inhabiteth eternity, whose name is Holy; I dwell in the high and holy place, with him also that is of a contrite and humble spirit, to revive the spirit of the humble, and to revive the heart of the contrite ones."

Jeremiah 23:24 "Can any hide himself in secret places that I shall not see him? saith the LORD. Do not I fill heaven and earth? saith the LORD."

Joel 3:17-21 "¹⁷So shall ye know that I am the LORD your God dwelling in Zion, my holy mountain: then shall Jerusalem be holy, and there shall no strangers pass through her any more. ¹⁸And it shall come to pass in that day, that the mountains shall drop down new wine, and the hills shall flow with milk, and all the rivers of Judah shall flow with waters, and a fountain shall come forth of the house of the LORD, and shall water the valley of Shittim. ¹⁹Egypt shall be a desolation, and Edom shall be a desolate wilderness, for the violence against the children of Judah, because they have shed innocent blood in their land. ²⁰But Judah shall dwell for ever, and Jerusalem from generation to generation. ²¹For I will cleanse their blood that I have not cleansed: for the LORD dwelleth in Zion."

Amos 9:6 "It is he that buildeth his stories in the heaven, and hath founded his troop in the earth; he that calleth for the waters of the sea, and poureth them out upon the face of the earth: The LORD is his name."

Habakkuk 2:20 "But the LORD is in his holy temple: let all the earth keep silence before him."

Zechariah 8:3 "Thus saith the LORD; I am returned unto Zion, and will dwell in the midst of Jerusalem: and Jerusalem shall be called a city of truth; and the mountain of the LORD of hosts the holy mountain."

Matthew 6:9 "After this manner therefore pray ye: Our Father which art in heaven, Hallowed be thy name."

Matthew 10:32-33 "³²Whosoever therefore shall confess me before men, him will I confess also before my Father which is in heaven. ³³But whosoever shall deny me before men, him will I also deny before my Father which is in heaven."

Matthew 18:10 "Take heed that ye despise not one of these little ones; for I say unto you, That in heaven their angels do always behold the face of my Father which is in heaven."

Matthew 18:19-22 "¹⁹Again I say unto you, That if two of you shall agree on earth as touching any thing that they shall ask, it shall be done for them of my Father which is in heaven. ²⁰For where two or three are gathered together in my name, there am I in the midst of them. ²¹Then came Peter to him, and said, Lord, how oft shall my brother sin against me, and I forgive him? till seven times? ²²Jesus saith unto him, I say not unto thee, Until seven times: but, Until seventy times seven."

Matthew 23:9 "And call no man your father upon the earth: for one is your Father, which is in heaven."

Ephesians 6:9 "And, ye masters, do the same things unto them, forbearing threatening: knowing that your Master also is in heaven; neither is there respect of persons with him."

Where The Lord God Is Not
1 Kings 19:11-12 "¹¹And he said, Go forth, and stand upon the mount before the LORD. And, behold, the LORD passed by, and a great and strong wind rent the mountains, and brake in pieces the rocks before the LORD; but the LORD was not in the wind: and after the wind an earthquake; but the LORD was not in the earthquake: ¹²And after the earthquake a fire; but the LORD was not in the fire: and after the fire a still small voice."

Acts 17:22-24 "²²Then Paul stood in the midst of Mars' hill, and said, Ye men of Athens, I perceive that in all things ye are too superstitious. ²³For as I passed by, and beheld your devotions, I found an altar with this inscription, TO THE UNKNOWN GOD. Whom therefore ye ignorantly worship, him declare I unto you. ²⁴God that made the world and all things therein, seeing that he is Lord of heaven and earth, dwelleth not in temples made with hands;"

Who The Lord God Dwells In
1 John 4:16 "And we have known and believed the love that God hath to us. God is love; and he that dwelleth in love dwelleth in God, and God in him."

GODLINESS

Godliness With Contentment
1 Timothy 6:6 "But godliness with contentment is great gain."

The Godly
Psalm 4:3 "But know that the LORD hath set apart him that is godly for himself: the LORD will hear when I call unto him."

2 Timothy 3:12 "Yea, and all that will live godly in Christ Jesus shall suffer persecution."

2 Peter 1:1-11 "¹Simon Peter, a servant and an apostle of Jesus Christ, to them that have obtained like precious faith with us through the righteousness of God and our Saviour Jesus Christ: ²Grace and peace be multiplied unto you through the knowledge of God, and of Jesus our Lord, ³According as his divine power hath given unto us all things that pertain unto life and godliness, through the knowledge of him that hath called us to glory and virtue: ⁴Whereby are given unto us exceeding great and precious promises: that by these ye might be partakers of the divine nature, having escaped the corruption that is in the world through lust. ⁵And beside this, giving all diligence, add to your faith virtue; and to virtue knowledge; ⁶And to knowledge temperance; and to temperance patience; and to patience godliness; ⁷And to godliness brotherly kindness; and to brotherly kindness charity. ⁸For if these things be in you, and abound, they make you that ye shall neither be barren nor unfruitful in the knowledge of our Lord Jesus Christ. ⁹But he that lacketh these things is blind, and cannot see afar off, and hath forgotten that he was purged from his old sins. ¹⁰Wherefore the rather, brethren, give diligence to make your calling and election sure: for if ye do these things, ye shall never fall: ¹¹For so an entrance shall be ministered unto you abundantly into the everlasting kingdom of our Lord and Saviour Jesus Christ."

2 Peter 2:9 "The Lord knoweth how to deliver the godly out of temptations, and to reserve the unjust unto the day of judgment to be punished:"

What Godliness Is Profitable Unto
1 Timothy 4:8 "For bodily exercise profiteth little: but godliness is profitable unto all things, having promise of the life that now is, and of that which is to come."

GOODNESS

Doing Good
Deuteronomy 6:18 "And thou shalt do that which is right and good in the sight of the LORD: that it may be well with thee, and that thou mayest go in and possess the good land which the LORD sware unto thy fathers,"

Psalm 34:14 "Depart from evil, and do good; seek peace, and pursue it."

Psalm 37:3 "Trust in the LORD, and do good; so shalt thou dwell in the land, and verily thou shalt be fed."

Psalm 37:27 "Depart from evil, and do good; and dwell for evermore."

Matthew 5:43-44 "⁴³Ye have heard that it hath been said, Thou shalt love thy neighbour, and hate thine enemy. ⁴⁴But I say unto you, Love your enemies, bless them that curse you, do good to them that hate you, and pray for them which despitefully use you, and persecute you;"

Luke 6:27-28 "²⁷But I say unto you which hear, Love your enemies, do good to them which hate you, ²⁸Bless them that curse you, and pray for them which despitefully use you."

Luke 6:35 "But love ye your enemies, and do good, and lend, hoping for nothing again; and your reward shall be great, and ye shall be the children of the Highest: for he is kind unto the unthankful and to the evil."

Galatians 6:10 "As we have therefore opportunity, let us do good unto all men, especially unto them who are of the household of faith."

1 Thessalonians 5:15 "See that none render evil for evil unto any man; but ever follow that which is good, both among yourselves, and to all men."

1 Peter 3:11 "Let him eschew evil, and do good; let him seek peace, and ensue it."

Good People
Psalm 37:23 "The steps of a good man are ordered by the LORD: and he delighteth in his way."

Psalm 112:5-9 "⁵A good man sheweth favour, and lendeth: he will guide his affairs with discretion. ⁶Surely he shall not be moved for ever: the righteous shall be in everlasting remembrance. ⁷He shall not be afraid of evil tidings: his heart is fixed, trusting in the LORD. ⁸His heart is established, he shall not be afraid, until he see his desire upon his enemies. ⁹He hath dispersed, he hath given to the poor; his righteousness endureth for ever; his horn shall be exalted with honour."

Proverbs 12:2 "A good man obtaineth favour of the LORD: but a man of wicked devices will he condemn."

Proverbs 13:22 "A good man leaveth an inheritance to his children's children: and the wealth of the sinner is laid up for the just."

Proverbs 14:14 "The backslider in heart shall be filled with his own ways: and a good man shall be satisfied from himself."

Proverbs 14:19 "The evil bow before the good; and the wicked at the gates of the righteous."

Proverbs 14:22 "Do they not err that devise evil? but mercy and truth shall be to them that devise good."

Ecclesiastes 2:24-26 "²⁴There is nothing better for a man, than that he should eat and drink, and that he should make his soul enjoy good in his labour. This also I saw, that it was from the hand of God. ²⁵For who can eat, or who else can hasten hereunto, more than I? ²⁶For God giveth to a man that is good in his sight wisdom, and knowledge, and joy: but to the sinner he giveth travail, to gather and to heap up, that he may give to him that is good before God. This also is vanity and vexation of spirit."

Matthew 12:35 "A good man out of the good treasure of the heart bringeth forth good things: and an evil man out of the evil treasure bringeth forth evil things."

Luke 6:43-45 "⁴³For a good tree bringeth not forth corrupt fruit; neither doth a corrupt tree bring forth good fruit. ⁴⁴For every tree is known by his own fruit. For of thorns men do not gather figs, nor of a bramble bush gather they grapes. ⁴⁵A good man out of the good treasure of his heart bringeth forth that which is good; and an evil man out of the evil treasure of his heart bringeth forth that which is evil: for of the abundance of the heart his mouth speaketh."

John 5:26-29 "²⁶For as the Father hath life in himself; so hath he given to the Son to have life in himself; ²⁷And hath given him authority to execute judgment also, because he is the Son of man. ²⁸Marvel not at this: for the hour is coming, in the which all that are in the graves shall hear his voice, ²⁹And shall come forth; they that have done good, unto the resurrection of life; and they that have done evil, unto the resurrection of damnation."

Romans 2:10 "But glory, honour, and peace, to every man that worketh good, to the Jew first, and also to the Gentile:"

3 John 11 "Beloved, follow not that which is evil, but that which is good. He that doeth good is of God: but he that doeth evil hath not seen God."

Overcoming Evil With Good

Romans 12:17-21 "¹⁷Recompense to no man evil for evil. Provide things honest in the sight of all men. ¹⁸If it be possible, as much as lieth in you, live peaceably with all men. ¹⁹Dearly beloved, avenge not yourselves, but rather give place unto wrath: for it is written, Vengeance is mine; I will repay, saith the Lord. ²⁰Therefore if thine enemy hunger, feed him; if he thirst, give him drink: for in so doing thou shalt heap coals of fire on his head. ²¹Be not overcome of evil, but overcome evil with good."

Seeking Good

Amos 5:14 "Seek good, and not evil, that ye may live: and so the LORD, the God of hosts, shall be with you, as ye have spoken."

1 Thessalonians 5:15 "See that none render evil for evil unto any man; but ever follow that which is good, both among yourselves, and to all men."

3 John 11 "Beloved, follow not that which is evil, but that which is good. He that doeth good is of God: but he that doeth evil hath not seen God."

The Goodness Of The Lord

Psalm 33:5 "He loveth righteousness and judgment: the earth is full of the goodness of the LORD."

Psalm 52:1 "Why boastest thou thyself in mischief, O mighty man? the goodness of God endureth continually."

Jeremiah 31:14 "And I will satiate the soul of the priests with fatness, and my people shall be satisfied with my goodness, saith the LORD."

Romans 2:4 "Or despisest thou the riches of his goodness and forbearance and longsuffering; not knowing that the goodness of God leadeth thee to repentance?"

The Lord Being Good

Exodus 34:6 "And the LORD passed by before him, and proclaimed, The LORD, The LORD God, merciful and gracious, longsuffering, and abundant in goodness and truth,"

1 Chronicles 16:34 "O give thanks unto the LORD; for he is good; for his mercy endureth for ever."

Psalm 25:8 "Good and upright is the LORD: therefore will he teach sinners in the way."

Psalm 34:8 "O taste and see that the LORD is good: blessed is the man that trusteth in him."

Psalm 86:5 "For thou, Lord, art good, and ready to forgive; and plenteous in mercy unto all them that call upon thee."

Psalm 100:5 "For the LORD is good; his mercy is everlasting; and his truth endureth to all generations."

Psalm 107:1 "O give thanks unto the LORD, for he is good: for his mercy endureth for ever."

Psalm 118:1 "O give thanks unto the LORD; for he is good: because his mercy endureth for ever."

Psalm 118:29 "O give thanks unto the LORD; for he is good: for his mercy endureth for ever."

Psalm 119:65-68 "65Thou hast dealt well with thy servant, O LORD, according unto thy word. 66Teach me good judgment and knowledge: for I have believed thy commandments. 67Before I was afflicted I went astray: but now have I kept thy word. 68Thou art good, and doest good; teach me thy statutes."

Psalm 136:1 "O give thanks unto the LORD; for he is good: for his mercy endureth for ever."

Psalm 143:10 "Teach me to do thy will; for thou art my God: thy spirit is good; lead me into the land of uprightness."

Psalm 145:9 "The LORD is good to all: and his tender mercies are over all his works."

Jeremiah 33:11 "The voice of joy, and the voice of gladness, the voice of the bridegroom, and the voice of the bride, the voice of them that shall say, Praise the LORD of hosts: for the LORD is good; for his mercy endureth for ever: and of them that shall bring the sacrifice of praise into the house of the LORD. For I will cause to return the captivity of the land, as at the first, saith the LORD."

Nahum 1:7 "The LORD is good, a strong hold in the day of trouble; and he knoweth them that trust in him."

The Reward For Doing Good

Deuteronomy 6:18 "And thou shalt do that which is right and good in the sight of the LORD: that it may be well with thee, and that thou mayest go in and possess the good land which the LORD sware unto thy fathers,"

Psalm 37:3 "Trust in the LORD, and do good; so shalt thou dwell in the land, and verily thou shalt be fed."

Jeremiah 6:16 "Thus saith the LORD, Stand ye in the ways, and see, and ask for the old paths, where is the good way, and walk therein, and ye shall find rest for your souls. But they said, We will not walk therein."

Matthew 5:43-45 "43Ye have heard that it hath been said, Thou shalt love thy neighbour, and hate thine enemy. 44But I say unto you, Love your enemies, bless them that curse you, do good to them that hate you, and pray for them which despitefully use you, and persecute you; 45That ye may be the children of your Father which is in heaven: for he maketh his sun to rise on the evil and on the good, and sendeth rain on the just and on the unjust."

Luke 6:33-35 "33And if ye do good to them which do good to you, what thank have ye? for sinners also do even the same. 34And if ye lend to them of whom ye hope to receive, what thank have ye? for sinners also lend to sinners, to receive as much again. 35But love ye your enemies, and do good, and lend, hoping for nothing again; and your reward shall be great, and ye shall be the children of the Highest: for he is kind unto the unthankful and to the evil."

Romans 13:1-3 "¹Let every soul be subject unto the higher powers. For there is no power but of God: the powers that be are ordained of God. ²Whosoever therefore resisteth the power, resisteth the ordinance of God: and they that resist shall receive to themselves damnation. ³For rulers are not a terror to good works, but to the evil. Wilt thou then not be afraid of the power? do that which is good, and thou shalt have praise of the same:"

Ephesians 6:5-8 "⁵Servants, be obedient to them that are your masters according to the flesh, with fear and trembling, in singleness of your heart, as unto Christ; ⁶Not with eyeservice, as menpleasers; but as the servants of Christ, doing the will of God from the heart; ⁷With good will doing service, as to the Lord, and not to men: ⁸Knowing that whatsoever good thing any man doeth, the same shall he receive of the Lord, whether he be bond or free."

There Being None That Do Good

Psalm 14:1-4 "¹The fool hath said in his heart, There is no God. They are corrupt, they have done abominable works, there is none that doeth good. ²The LORD looked down from heaven upon the children of men, to see if there were any that did understand, and seek God. ³They are all gone aside, they are all together become filthy: there is none that doeth good, no, not one. ⁴Have all the workers of iniquity no knowledge? who eat up my people as they eat bread, and call not upon the LORD."

Psalm 53:1 "The fool hath said in his heart, There is no God. Corrupt are they, and have done abominable iniquity: there is none that doeth good."

Ecclesiastes 7:20 "For there is not a just man upon earth, that doeth good, and sinneth not."

Matthew 19:16-17 "¹⁶And, behold, one came and said unto him, Good Master, what good thing shall I do, that I may have eternal life? ¹⁷And he said unto him, Why callest thou me good? there is none good but one, that is, God: but if thou wilt enter into life, keep the commandments."

Romans 3:9-12 "⁹What then? are we better than they? No, in no wise: for we have before proved both Jews and Gentiles, that they are all under sin; ¹⁰As it is written, There is none righteous, no, not one: ¹¹There is none that understandeth, there is none that seeketh after God. ¹²They are all gone out of the way, they are together become unprofitable; there is none that doeth good, no, not one."

Those That Seek Good

Proverbs 11:27 "He that diligently seeketh good procureth favour: but he that seeketh mischief, it shall come unto him."

Those That Call Good Evil

Isaiah 5:20 "Woe unto them that call evil good, and good evil; that put darkness for light, and light for darkness; that put bitter for sweet, and sweet for bitter!"

What Brings Forth Good Fruit

Matthew 7:17-20 "¹⁷Even so every good tree bringeth forth good fruit; but a corrupt tree bringeth forth evil fruit. ¹⁸A good tree cannot bring forth evil fruit, neither can a corrupt tree bring forth good fruit. ¹⁹Every tree that bringeth not forth good fruit is hewn down, and cast into the fire. ²⁰Wherefore by their fruits ye shall know them."

Matthew 12:35 "A good man out of the good treasure of the heart bringeth forth good things: and an evil man out of the evil treasure bringeth forth evil things."

Luke 6:43-45 "⁴³For a good tree bringeth not forth corrupt fruit; neither doth a corrupt tree bring forth good fruit. ⁴⁴For every tree is known by his own fruit. For of thorns men do not gather figs, nor of a bramble bush gather they grapes. ⁴⁵A good man out of the good treasure of his heart bringeth forth that which is good; and an evil man out of the evil treasure of his heart bringeth forth that which is evil: for of the abundance of the heart his mouth speaketh."

Colossians 1:5-6 "⁵For the hope which is laid up for you in heaven, whereof ye heard before in the word of the truth of the gospel; ⁶Which is come unto you, as it is in all the world; and bringeth forth fruit, as it doth also in you, since the day ye heard of it, and knew the grace of God in truth:"

What Is Good

Genesis 1:4 "And God saw the light, that it was good: and God divided the light from the darkness."

Genesis 1:10 "And God called the dry land Earth; and the gathering together of the waters called he Seas: and God saw that it was good."

Genesis 1:12 "And the earth brought forth grass, and herb yielding seed after his kind, and the tree yielding fruit, whose seed was in itself, after his kind: and God saw that it was good."

Genesis 1:16-18 "[16]And God made two great lights; the greater light to rule the day, and the lesser light to rule the night: he made the stars also. [17]And God set them in the firmament of the heaven to give light upon the earth, [18]And to rule over the day and over the night, and to divide the light from the darkness: and God saw that it was good."

Genesis 1:21 "And God created great whales, and every living creature that moveth, which the waters brought forth abundantly, after their kind, and every winged fowl after his kind: and God saw that it was good."

Genesis 1:25 "And God made the beast of the earth after his kind, and cattle after their kind, and every thing that creepeth upon the earth after his kind: and God saw that it was good."

Genesis 1:31 "And God saw every thing that he had made, and, behold, it was very good. And the evening and the morning were the sixth day."

Psalm 92:1 "It is a good thing to give thanks unto the LORD, and to sing praises unto thy name, O most High:"

Psalm 119:65-71 "[65]Thou hast dealt well with thy servant, O LORD, according unto thy word. [66]Teach me good judgment and knowledge: for I have believed thy commandments. [67]Before I was afflicted I went astray: but now have I kept thy word. [68]Thou art good, and doest good; teach me thy statutes. [69]The proud have forged a lie against me: but I will keep thy precepts with my whole heart. [70]Their heart is as fat as grease; but I delight in thy law. [71]It is good for me that I have been afflicted; that I might learn thy statutes."

Psalm 133:1 "Behold, how good and how pleasant it is for brethren to dwell together in unity!"

Proverbs 11:23 "The desire of the righteous is only good: but the expectation of the wicked is wrath."

Proverbs 15:23 "A man hath joy by the answer of his mouth: and a word spoken in due season, how good is it!"

Ecclesiastes 7:11 "Wisdom is good with an inheritance: and by it there is profit to them that see the sun."

Isaiah 39:8 "Then said Hezekiah to Isaiah, Good is the word of the LORD which thou hast spoken. He said moreover, For there shall be peace and truth in my days."

Lamentations 3:26-27 "[26]It is good that a man should both hope and quietly wait for the salvation of the LORD. [27]It is good for a man that he bear the yoke in his youth."

Romans 7:12 "Wherefore the law is holy, and the commandment holy, and just, and good."

1 Timothy 1:8 "But we know that the law is good, if a man use it lawfully;"

1 Timothy 2:1-4 "[1]I exhort therefore, that, first of all, supplications, prayers, intercessions, and giving of thanks, be made for all men; [2]For kings, and for all that are in authority; that we may lead a quiet and peaceable life in all godliness and honesty. [3]For this is good and acceptable in the sight of God our Saviour; [4]Who will have all men to be saved, and to come unto the knowledge of the truth."

1 Timothy 4:1-5 "[1]Now the Spirit speaketh expressly, that in the latter times some shall depart from the faith, giving heed to seducing spirits, and doctrines of devils; [2]Speaking lies in hypocrisy; having their conscience seared with a hot iron; [3]Forbidding to marry, and commanding to abstain from meats, which God hath created to be received with thanksgiving of them which believe and know the truth. [4]For every creature of God is good, and nothing to be refused, if it be received with thanksgiving: [5]For it is sanctified by the word of God and prayer."

Titus 3:1-8 "[1]Put them in mind to be subject to principalities and powers, to obey magistrates, to be ready to every good work, [2]To speak evil of no man, to be no brawlers, but gentle, shewing all meekness unto all men. [3]For we ourselves also were sometimes foolish, disobedient, deceived, serving divers lusts and pleasures, living in malice and envy, hateful, and hating one another. [4]But after that the kindness and love of God our Saviour toward man appeared, [5]Not by works of righteousness which we have done, but according to his mercy he saved us, by the washing of regeneration, and renewing of the Holy Ghost; [6]Which he shed on us abundantly through Jesus Christ our Saviour; [7]That being justified by his grace, we should be made heirs according to the hope of eternal life. [8]This is a faithful saying, and these things I will that thou affirm constantly, that they which have believed in God might be careful to maintain good works. These things are good and profitable unto men."

Hebrews 13:9 "Be not carried about with divers and strange doctrines. For it is a good thing that the heart be established with grace; not with meats, which have not profited them that have been occupied therein."

Who Does Not Find Any Good
Proverbs 17:20 "He that hath a froward heart findeth no good: and he that hath a perverse tongue falleth into mischief."

Who Shall Find Good
Proverbs 16:20 "He that handleth a matter wisely shall find good: and whoso trusteth in the LORD, happy is he."

Proverbs 19:8 "He that getteth wisdom loveth his own soul: he that keepeth understanding shall find good."

Who To Do Good To
Matthew 5:43-45 "[43]Ye have heard that it hath been said, Thou shalt love thy neighbour, and hate thine enemy. [44]But I say unto you, Love your enemies, bless them that curse you, do good to them that hate you, and pray for them which despitefully use you, and persecute you; [45]That ye may be the children of your Father which is in heaven: for he maketh his sun to rise on the evil and on the good, and sendeth rain on the just and on the unjust."

Luke 6:27-28 "[27]But I say unto you which hear, Love your enemies, do good to them which hate you, [28]Bless them that curse you, and pray for them which despitefully use you."

Luke 6:33-35 "[33]And if ye do good to them which do good to you, what thank have ye? for sinners also do even the same. [34]And if ye lend to them of whom ye hope to receive, what thank have ye? for sinners also lend to sinners, to receive as much again. [35]But love ye your enemies, and do good, and lend, hoping for nothing again; and your reward shall be great, and ye shall be the children of the Highest: for he is kind unto the unthankful and to the evil."

Galatians 6:10 "As we have therefore opportunity, let us do good unto all men, especially unto them who are of the household of faith."

GOSPEL

The Gospel Being Preached To All Nations
Matthew 24:14 "And this gospel of the kingdom shall be preached in all the world for a witness unto all nations; and then shall the end come."

Matthew 28:18-20 "[18]And Jesus came and spake unto them, saying, All power is given unto me in heaven and in earth. [19]Go ye therefore, and teach all nations, baptizing them in the name of the Father, and of the Son, and of the Holy Ghost: [20]Teaching them to observe all things whatsoever I have commanded you: and, lo, I am with you alway, even unto the end of the world. Amen."

Mark 13:10 "And the gospel must first be published among all nations."

Luke 24:44-47 "[44]And he said unto them, These are the words which I spake unto you, while I was yet with you, that all things must be fulfilled, which were written in the law of Moses, and in the prophets, and in the psalms, concerning me. [45]Then opened he their understanding, that they might understand the scriptures, [46]And said unto them, Thus it is written, and thus it behoved Christ to suffer, and to rise from the dead the third day: [47]And that repentance and remission of sins should be preached in his name among all nations, beginning at Jerusalem."

Colossians 1:5-6 "[5]For the hope which is laid up for you in heaven, whereof ye heard before in the word of the truth of the gospel; [6]Which is come unto you, as it is in all the world; and bringeth forth fruit, as it doth also in you, since the day ye heard of it, and knew the grace of God in truth:"

The Poor Receiving The Gospel
Matthew 11:4-5 "⁴Jesus answered and said unto them, Go and shew John again those things which ye do hear and see: ⁵The blind receive their sight, and the lame walk, the lepers are cleansed, and the deaf hear, the dead are raised up, and the poor have the gospel preached to them."

Luke 7:22 "Then Jesus answering said unto them, Go your way, and tell John what things ye have seen and heard; how that the blind see, the lame walk, the lepers are cleansed, the deaf hear, the dead are raised, to the poor the gospel is preached."

What The Gospel Does
1 Corinthians 15:1-2 "¹Moreover, brethren, I declare unto you the gospel which I preached unto you, which also ye have received, and wherein ye stand; ²By which also ye are saved, if ye keep in memory what I preached unto you, unless ye have believed in vain."

Colossians 1:5-6 "⁵For the hope which is laid up for you in heaven, whereof ye heard before in the word of the truth of the gospel; ⁶Which is come unto you, as it is in all the world; and bringeth forth fruit, as it doth also in you, since the day ye heard of it, and knew the grace of God in truth:"

What The Gospel Is
Romans 1:16-17 "¹⁶For I am not ashamed of the gospel of Christ: for it is the power of God unto salvation to every one that believeth; to the Jew first, and also to the Greek. ¹⁷For therein is the righteousness of God revealed from faith to faith: as it is written, The just shall live by faith."

Where The Gospel Comes From
Galatians 1:11-12 "¹¹But I certify you, brethren, that the gospel which was preached of me is not after man. ¹²For I neither received it of man, neither was I taught it, but by the revelation of Jesus Christ."

Who Should Live Of The Gospel
1 Corinthians 9:13-14 "¹³Do ye not know that they which minister about holy things live of the things of the temple? and they which wait at the altar are partakers with the altar? ¹⁴Even so hath the Lord ordained that they which preach the gospel should live of the gospel."

Who The Gospel Is Hid From
2 Corinthians 4:3-4 "³But if our gospel be hid, it is hid to them that are lost: ⁴In whom the god of this world hath blinded the minds of them which believe not, lest the light of the glorious gospel of Christ, who is the image of God, should shine unto them."

Why The Gospel Did Not Profit Those In The Time Of Moses
Hebrews 4:1-2 "¹Let us therefore fear, lest, a promise being left us of entering into his rest, any of you should seem to come short of it. ²For unto us was the gospel preached, as well as unto them: but the word preached did not profit them, not being mixed with faith in them that heard it."

Why The Gospel Was Preached
1 Peter 4:1-6 "¹Forasmuch then as Christ hath suffered for us in the flesh, arm yourselves likewise with the same mind: for he that hath suffered in the flesh hath ceased from sin; ²That he no longer should live the rest of his time in the flesh to the lusts of men, but to the will of God. ³For the time past of our life may suffice us to have wrought the will of the Gentiles, when we walked in lasciviousness, lusts, excess of wine, revellings, banquetings, and abominable idolatries: ⁴Wherein they think it strange that ye run not with them to the same excess of riot, speaking evil of you: ⁵Who shall give account to him that is ready to judge the quick and the dead. ⁶For for this cause was the gospel preached also to them that are dead, that they might be judged according to men in the flesh, but live according to God in the spirit."

GOVERNMENT

Fearing The King
Proverbs 24:21-22 "²¹My son, fear thou the LORD and the king: and meddle not with them that are given to change: ²²For their calamity shall rise suddenly; and who knoweth the ruin of them both?"

Foolish Kings
Ecclesiastes 4:13-14 "¹³Better is a poor and a wise child than an old and foolish king, who will no more be admonished. ¹⁴For out of prison he cometh to reign; whereas also he that is born in his kingdom becometh poor."

God Setting Up And Removing Kings

Job 12:9-23 "⁹Who knoweth not in all these that the hand of the LORD hath wrought this? ¹⁰In whose hand is the soul of every living thing, and the breath of all mankind. ¹¹Doth not the ear try words? and the mouth taste his meat? ¹²With the ancient is wisdom; and in length of days understanding. ¹³With him is wisdom and strength, he hath counsel and understanding. ¹⁴Behold, he breaketh down, and it cannot be built again: he shutteth up a man, and there can be no opening. ¹⁵Behold, he withholdeth the waters, and they dry up: also he sendeth them out, and they overturn the earth. ¹⁶With him is strength and wisdom: the deceived and the deceiver are his. ¹⁷He leadeth counsellers away spoiled, and maketh the judges fools. ¹⁸He looseth the bond of kings, and girdeth their loins with a girdle. ¹⁹He leadeth princes away spoiled, and overthroweth the mighty. ²⁰He removeth away the speech of the trusty, and taketh away the understanding of the aged. ²¹He poureth contempt upon princes, and weakeneth the strength of the mighty. ²²He discovereth deep things out of darkness, and bringeth out to light the shadow of death. ²³He increaseth the nations, and destroyeth them: he enlargeth the nations, and straiteneth them again."

Isaiah 40:22-23 "²²It is he that sitteth upon the circle of the earth, and the inhabitants thereof are as grasshoppers; that stretcheth out the heavens as a curtain, and spreadeth them out as a tent to dwell in: ²³That bringeth the princes to nothing; he maketh the judges of the earth as vanity."

Jeremiah 18:5-10 "⁵Then the word of the LORD came to me, saying, ⁶O house of Israel, cannot I do with you as this potter? saith the LORD. Behold, as the clay is in the potter's hand, so are ye in mine hand, O house of Israel. ⁷At what instant I shall speak concerning a nation, and concerning a kingdom, to pluck up, and to pull down, and to destroy it; ⁸If that nation, against whom I have pronounced, turn from their evil, I will repent of the evil that I thought to do unto them. ⁹And at what instant I shall speak concerning a nation, and concerning a kingdom, to build and to plant it; ¹⁰If it do evil in my sight, that it obey not my voice, then I will repent of the good, wherewith I said I would benefit them."

Jeremiah 27:4-8 "⁴And command them to say unto their masters, Thus saith the LORD of hosts, the God of Israel; Thus shall ye say unto your masters; ⁵I have made the earth, the man and the beast that are upon the ground, by my great power and by my outstretched arm, and have given it unto whom it seemed meet unto me. ⁶And now have I given all these lands unto the hand of Nebuchadnezzar the king of Babylon, my servant; and the beasts of the field have I given him also to serve him. ⁷And all nations shall serve him, and his son, and his son's son, until the very time of his land come: and then many nations and great kings shall serve themselves of him. ⁸And it shall come to pass, that the nation and kingdom which will not serve the same Nebuchadnezzar the king of Babylon, and that will not put their neck under the yoke of the king of Babylon, that nation will I punish, saith the LORD, with the sword, and with the famine, and with the pestilence, until I have consumed them by his hand."

Daniel 2:20-21 "²⁰Daniel answered and said, Blessed be the name of God for ever and ever: for wisdom and might are his: ²¹And he changeth the times and the seasons: he removeth kings, and setteth up kings: he giveth wisdom unto the wise, and knowledge to them that know understanding:"

Daniel 2:31-45 "³¹Thou, O king, sawest, and behold a great image. This great image, whose brightness was excellent, stood before thee; and the form thereof was terrible. ³²This image's head was of fine gold, his breast and his arms of silver, his belly and his thighs of brass, ³³His legs of iron, his feet part of iron and part of clay. ³⁴Thou sawest till that a stone was cut out without hands, which smote the image upon his feet that were of iron and clay, and brake them to pieces. ³⁵Then was the iron, the clay, the brass, the silver, and the gold, broken to pieces together, and became like the chaff of the summer threshingfloors; and the wind carried them away, that no place was found for them: and the stone that smote the image became a great mountain, and filled the whole earth. ³⁶This is the dream; and we will tell the interpretation thereof before the king. ³⁷Thou, O king, art a king of kings: for the God of heaven hath given thee a kingdom, power, and strength, and glory. [38]And wheresoever the children of men dwell, the beasts of the field and the fowls of the heaven hath he given into thine hand, and hath made thee ruler over them all. Thou art this head of gold. [39]And after thee shall arise another kingdom inferior to thee, and another third kingdom of brass, which shall bear rule over all the earth. [40]And the fourth kingdom shall be strong as iron: forasmuch as iron breaketh in pieces and subdueth all things: and as iron that breaketh all these, shall it break in pieces and bruise. [41]And whereas thou sawest the feet and toes, part of potters' clay, and part of iron, the kingdom shall be divided; but there shall be in it of the strength of the iron, forasmuch as thou sawest the iron mixed with miry clay. [42]And as the toes of the feet were part of iron, and part of clay, so the kingdom shall be partly strong, and partly broken. [43]And whereas thou sawest iron mixed with miry clay, they shall mingle themselves with the seed of men: but they shall not cleave one to another, even as iron is not mixed with clay. [44]And in the days of these kings shall the God of heaven set up a kingdom, which shall never be destroyed: and the kingdom shall not be left to other people, but it shall break in pieces and consume all these kingdoms, and it shall stand for ever. [45]Forasmuch as thou sawest that the stone was cut out of the mountain without hands, and that it brake in pieces the iron, the brass, the clay, the silver, and the gold; the great God hath made known to the king what shall come to pass hereafter: and the dream is certain, and the interpretation thereof sure."

Daniel 4:17 "This matter is by the decree of the watchers, and the demand by the word of the holy ones: to the intent that the living may know that the most High ruleth in the kingdom of men, and giveth it to whomsoever he will, and setteth up over it the basest of men."

Daniel 4:32 "And they shall drive thee from men, and thy dwelling shall be with the beasts of the field: they shall make thee to eat grass as oxen, and seven times shall pass over thee, until thou know that the most High ruleth in the kingdom of men, and giveth it to whomsoever he will."

Daniel 5:18-31 "[18]O thou king, the most high God gave Nebuchadnezzar thy father a kingdom, and majesty, and glory, and honour: [19]And for the majesty that he gave him, all people, nations, and languages, trembled and feared before him: whom he would he slew; and whom he would he kept alive; and whom he would he set up; and whom he would he put down. [20]But when his heart was lifted up, and his mind hardened in pride, he was deposed from his kingly throne, and they took his glory from him: [21]And he was driven from the sons of men; and his heart was made like the beasts, and his dwelling was with the wild asses: they fed him with grass like oxen, and his body was wet with the dew of heaven; till he knew that the most high God ruled in the kingdom of men, and that he appointeth over it whomsoever he will. [22]And thou his son, O Belshazzar, hast not humbled thine heart, though thou knewest all this; [23]But hast lifted up thyself against the LORD of heaven; and they have brought the vessels of his house before thee, and thou, and thy lords, thy wives, and thy concubines, have drunk wine in them; and thou hast praised the gods of silver, and gold, of brass, iron, wood, and stone, which see not, nor hear, nor know: and the God in whose hand thy breath is, and whose are all thy ways, hast thou not glorified: [24]Then was the part of the hand sent from him; and this writing was written. [25]And this is the writing that was written, MENE, MENE, TEKEL, UPHARSIN. [26]This is the interpretation of the thing: MENE; God hath numbered thy kingdom, and finished it. [27]TEKEL; Thou art weighed in the balances, and art found wanting. [28]PERES; Thy kingdom is divided, and given to the Medes and Persians. [29]Then commanded Belshazzar, and they clothed Daniel with scarlet, and put a chain of gold about his neck, and made a proclamation concerning him, that he should be the third ruler in the kingdom. [30]In that night was Belshazzar the king of the Chaldeans slain. [31]And Darius the Median took the kingdom, being about threescore and two years old."

Honoring The King
1 Peter 2:17 "Honour all men. Love the brotherhood. Fear God. Honour the king."

How Long The Lord Will Reign
Exodus 15:18 "The LORD shall reign for ever and ever."

Psalm 66:3-7 "³Say unto God, How terrible art thou in thy works! through the greatness of thy power shall thine enemies submit themselves unto thee. ⁴All the earth shall worship thee, and shall sing unto thee; they shall sing to thy name. Selah. ⁵Come and see the works of God: he is terrible in his doing toward the children of men. ⁶He turned the sea into dry land: they went through the flood on foot: there did we rejoice in him. ⁷He ruleth by his power for ever; his eyes behold the nations: let not the rebellious exalt themselves. Selah."

Psalm 146:10 "The LORD shall reign for ever, even thy God, O Zion, unto all generations. Praise ye the LORD."

Isaiah 9:6-7 "⁶For unto us a child is born, unto us a son is given: and the government shall be upon his shoulder: and his name shall be called Wonderful, Counseller, The mighty God, The everlasting Father, The Prince of Peace. ⁷Of the increase of his government and peace there shall be no end, upon the throne of David, and upon his kingdom, to order it, and to establish it with judgment and with justice from henceforth even for ever. The zeal of the LORD of hosts will perform this."

Revelation 11:15-17 "¹⁵And the seventh angel sounded; and there were great voices in heaven, saying, The kingdoms of this world are become the kingdoms of our Lord, and of his Christ; and he shall reign for ever and ever. ¹⁶And the four and twenty elders, which sat before God on their seats, fell upon their faces, and worshipped God, ¹⁷Saying, We give thee thanks, O Lord God Almighty, which art, and wast, and art to come; because thou hast taken to thee thy great power, and hast reigned."

How States Fall And How States Are Prolonged
Proverbs 28:1-2 "¹The wicked flee when no man pursueth: but the righteous are bold as a lion. ²For the transgression of a land many are the princes thereof: but by a man of understanding and knowledge the state thereof shall be prolonged."

If Rulers Listen To Lies
Proverbs 29:12 "If a ruler hearken to lies, all his servants are wicked."

Not Cursing Rulers
Exodus 22:28 "Thou shalt not revile the gods, nor curse the ruler of thy people."

Ecclesiastes 10:20 "Curse not the king, no not in thy thought; and curse not the rich in thy bedchamber: for a bird of the air shall carry the voice, and that which hath wings shall tell the matter."

The King That Faithfully Judges The Poor
Proverbs 29:14 "The king that faithfully judgeth the poor, his throne shall be established for ever."

The Kings Of The Earth
2 Samuel 23:3 "The God of Israel said, the Rock of Israel spake to me, He that ruleth over men must be just, ruling in the fear of God."

Psalm 61:5-7 "⁵For thou, O God, hast heard my vows: thou hast given me the heritage of those that fear thy name. ⁶Thou wilt prolong the king's life: and his years as many generations. ⁷He shall abide before God for ever: O prepare mercy and truth, which may preserve him."

Psalm 76:11-12 "¹¹Vow, and pay unto the LORD your God: let all that be round about him bring presents unto him that ought to be feared. ¹²He shall cut off the spirit of princes: he is terrible to the kings of the earth."

Psalm 138:4-5 "⁴All the kings of the earth shall praise thee, O LORD, when they hear the words of thy mouth. ⁵Yea, they shall sing in the ways of the LORD: for great is the glory of the LORD."

Proverbs 14:28 "In the multitude of people is the king's honour: but in the want of people is the destruction of the prince."

Proverbs 16:12-15 "¹²It is an abomination to kings to commit wickedness: for the throne is established by righteousness. ¹³Righteous lips are the delight of kings; and they love him that speaketh right. ¹⁴The wrath of a king is as messengers of death: but a wise man will pacify it. ¹⁵In the light of the king's countenance is life; and his favour is as a cloud of the latter rain."

Proverbs 17:7 "Excellent speech becometh not a fool: much less do lying lips a prince."

Proverbs 20:8 "A king that sitteth in the throne of judgment scattereth away all evil with his eyes."

Proverbs 20:28 "Mercy and truth preserve the king: and his throne is upholden by mercy."

Proverbs 25:2-5 "²It is the glory of God to conceal a thing: but the honour of kings is to search out a matter. ³The heaven for height, and the earth for depth, and the heart of kings is unsearchable. ⁴Take away the dross from the silver, and there shall come forth a vessel for the finer. ⁵Take away the wicked from before the king, and his throne shall be established in righteousness."

Proverbs 29:4 "The king by judgment establisheth the land: but he that receiveth gifts overthroweth it."

Proverbs 31:4-7 "⁴It is not for kings, O Lemuel, it is not for kings to drink wine; nor for princes strong drink: ⁵Lest they drink, and forget the law, and pervert the judgment of any of the afflicted. ⁶Give strong drink unto him that is ready to perish, and wine unto those that be of heavy hearts. ⁷Let him drink, and forget his poverty, and remember his misery no more."

Ecclesiastes 8:4 "Where the word of a king is, there is power: and who may say unto him, What doest thou?"

The Lord Being King

Psalm 10:16 "The LORD is King for ever and ever: the heathen are perished out of his land."

Psalm 22:28-29 "²⁸For the kingdom is the LORD's: and he is the governor among the nations. ²⁹All they that be fat upon earth shall eat and worship: all they that go down to the dust shall bow before him: and none can keep alive his own soul."

Psalm 24:10 "Who is this King of glory? The LORD of hosts, he is the King of glory. Selah."

Psalm 47:2 "For the LORD most high is terrible; he is a great King over all the earth."

Psalm 47:7-9 "⁷For God is the King of all the earth: sing ye praises with understanding. ⁸God reigneth over the heathen: God sitteth upon the throne of his holiness. ⁹The princes of the people are gathered together, even the people of the God of Abraham: for the shields of the earth belong unto God: he is greatly exalted."

Psalm 74:12 "For God is my King of old, working salvation in the midst of the earth."

Psalm 89:18 "For the LORD is our defence; and the Holy One of Israel is our king."

Psalm 95:3 "For the LORD is a great God, and a great King above all gods."

Isaiah 33:22 "For the LORD is our judge, the LORD is our lawgiver, the LORD is our king; he will save us."

Isaiah 43:14-15 "¹⁴Thus saith the LORD, your redeemer, the Holy One of Israel; For your sake I have sent to Babylon, and have brought down all their nobles, and the Chaldeans, whose cry is in the ships. ¹⁵I am the LORD, your Holy One, the creator of Israel, your King."

Isaiah 44:6 "Thus saith the LORD the King of Israel, and his redeemer the LORD of hosts; I am the first, and I am the last; and beside me there is no God."

Jeremiah 10:10 "But the LORD is the true God, he is the living God, and an everlasting king: at his wrath the earth shall tremble, and the nations shall not be able to abide his indignation."

Daniel 4:37 "Now I Nebuchadnezzar praise and extol and honour the King of heaven, all whose works are truth, and his ways judgment: and those that walk in pride he is able to abase."

Zechariah 14:9 "And the LORD shall be king over all the earth: in that day shall there be one LORD, and his name one."

Malachi 1:14 "But cursed be the deceiver, which hath in his flock a male, and voweth, and sacrificeth unto the LORD a corrupt thing: for I am a great King, saith the LORD of hosts, and my name is dreadful among the heathen."

Matthew 2:1-2 "¹Now when Jesus was born in Bethlehem of Judaea in the days of Herod the king, behold, there came wise men from the east to Jerusalem, ²Saying, Where is he that is born King of the Jews? for we have seen his star in the east, and are come to worship him."

Matthew 11:25 "At that time Jesus answered and said, I thank thee, O Father, Lord of heaven and earth, because thou hast hid these things from the wise and prudent, and hast revealed them unto babes."

1 Timothy 1:17 "Now unto the King eternal, immortal, invisible, the only wise God, be honour and glory for ever and ever. Amen."

Revelation 15:3 "And they sing the song of Moses the servant of God, and the song of the Lamb, saying, Great and marvellous are thy works, Lord God Almighty; just and true are thy ways, thou King of saints."

The Lord Governing

Exodus 15:18 "The LORD shall reign for ever and ever."

Judges 8:23 "And Gideon said unto them, I will not rule over you, neither shall my son rule over you: the LORD shall rule over you."

1 Chronicles 16:31 "Let the heavens be glad, and let the earth rejoice: and let men say among the nations, The LORD reigneth."

1 Chronicles 29:11-12 "11Thine, O LORD, is the greatness, and the power, and the glory, and the victory, and the majesty: for all that is in the heaven and in the earth is thine; thine is the kingdom, O LORD, and thou art exalted as head above all. 12Both riches and honour come of thee, and thou reignest over all; and in thine hand is power and might; and in thine hand it is to make great, and to give strength unto all."

Psalm 66:3-7 "3Say unto God, How terrible art thou in thy works! through the greatness of thy power shall thine enemies submit themselves unto thee. 4All the earth shall worship thee, and shall sing unto thee; they shall sing to thy name. Selah. 5Come and see the works of God: he is terrible in his doing toward the children of men. 6He turned the sea into dry land: they went through the flood on foot: there did we rejoice in him. 7He ruleth by his power for ever; his eyes behold the nations: let not the rebellious exalt themselves. Selah."

Psalm 67:3-4 "3Let the people praise thee, O God; let all the people praise thee. 4O let the nations be glad and sing for joy: for thou shalt judge the people righteously, and govern the nations upon earth. Selah."

Psalm 93:1-5 "1The LORD reigneth, he is clothed with majesty; the LORD is clothed with strength, wherewith he hath girded himself: the world also is stablished, that it cannot be moved. 2Thy throne is established of old: thou art from everlasting. 3The floods have lifted up, O LORD, the floods have lifted up their voice; the floods lift up their waves. 4The LORD on high is mightier than the noise of many waters, yea, than the mighty waves of the sea. 5Thy testimonies are very sure: holiness becometh thine house, O LORD, for ever."

Psalm 99:1 "The LORD reigneth; let the people tremble: he sitteth between the cherubims; let the earth be moved."

Psalm 103:19 "The LORD hath prepared his throne in the heavens; and his kingdom ruleth over all."

Psalm 146:10 "The LORD shall reign for ever, even thy God, O Zion, unto all generations. Praise ye the LORD."

Isaiah 40:10 "Behold, the Lord GOD will come with strong hand, and his arm shall rule for him: behold, his reward is with him, and his work before him."

Daniel 4:17 "This matter is by the decree of the watchers, and the demand by the word of the holy ones: to the intent that the living may know that the most High ruleth in the kingdom of men, and giveth it to whomsoever he will, and setteth up over it the basest of men."

Daniel 4:32 "And they shall drive thee from men, and thy dwelling shall be with the beasts of the field: they shall make thee to eat grass as oxen, and seven times shall pass over thee, until thou know that the most High ruleth in the kingdom of men, and giveth it to whomsoever he will."

Daniel 5:21 "And he was driven from the sons of men; and his heart was made like the beasts, and his dwelling was with the wild asses: they fed him with grass like oxen, and his body was wet with the dew of heaven; till he knew that the most high God ruled in the kingdom of men, and that he appointeth over it whomsoever he will."

Revelation 11:15-17 "15And the seventh angel sounded; and there were great voices in heaven, saying, The kingdoms of this world are become the kingdoms of our Lord, and of his Christ; and he shall reign for ever and ever. 16And the four and twenty elders, which sat before God on their seats, fell upon their faces, and worshipped God,

[17]Saying, We give thee thanks, O Lord God Almighty, which art, and wast, and art to come; because thou hast taken to thee thy great power, and hast reigned."

The Messianic King

2 Samuel 7:8-17 "[8]Now therefore so shalt thou say unto my servant David, Thus saith the LORD of hosts, I took thee from the sheepcote, from following the sheep, to be ruler over my people, over Israel: [9]And I was with thee whithersoever thou wentest, and have cut off all thine enemies out of thy sight, and have made thee a great name, like unto the name of the great men that are in the earth. [10]Moreover I will appoint a place for my people Israel, and will plant them, that they may dwell in a place of their own, and move no more; neither shall the children of wickedness afflict them any more, as beforetime, [11]And as since the time that I commanded judges to be over my people Israel, and have caused thee to rest from all thine enemies. Also the LORD telleth thee that he will make thee an house. [12]And when thy days be fulfilled, and thou shalt sleep with thy fathers, I will set up thy seed after thee, which shall proceed out of thy bowels, and I will establish his kingdom. [13]He shall build an house for my name, and I will stablish the throne of his kingdom for ever. [14]I will be his father, and he shall be my son. If he commit iniquity, I will chasten him with the rod of men, and with the stripes of the children of men: [15]But my mercy shall not depart away from him, as I took it from Saul, whom I put away before thee. [16]And thine house and thy kingdom shall be established for ever before thee: thy throne shall be established for ever. [17]According to all these words, and according to all this vision, so did Nathan speak unto David."

1 Chronicles 17:7-15 "[7]Now therefore thus shalt thou say unto my servant David, Thus saith the LORD of hosts, I took thee from the sheepcote, even from following the sheep, that thou shouldest be ruler over my people Israel: [8]And I have been with thee whithersoever thou hast walked, and have cut off all thine enemies from before thee, and have made thee a name like the name of the great men that are in the earth. [9]Also I will ordain a place for my people Israel, and will plant them, and they shall dwell in their place, and shall be moved no more; neither shall the children of wickedness waste them any more, as at the beginning, [10]And since the time that I commanded judges to be over my people Israel. Moreover I will subdue all thine enemies. Furthermore I tell thee that the LORD will build thee an house. [11]And it shall come to pass, when thy days be expired that thou must go to be with thy fathers, that I will raise up thy seed after thee, which shall be of thy sons; and I will establish his kingdom. [12]He shall build me an house, and I will stablish his throne for ever. [13]I will be his father, and he shall be my son: and I will not take my mercy away from him, as I took it from him that was before thee: [14]But I will settle him in mine house and in my kingdom for ever: and his throne shall be established for evermore. [15]According to all these words, and according to all this vision, so did Nathan speak unto David."

Psalm 2:1-12 "[1]Why do the heathen rage, and the people imagine a vain thing? [2]The kings of the earth set themselves, and the rulers take counsel together, against the LORD, and against his anointed, saying, [3]Let us break their bands asunder, and cast away their cords from us. [4]He that sitteth in the heavens shall laugh: the Lord shall have them in derision. [5]Then shall he speak unto them in his wrath, and vex them in his sore displeasure. [6]Yet have I set my king upon my holy hill of Zion. [7]I will declare the decree: the LORD hath said unto me, Thou art my Son; this day have I begotten thee. [8]Ask of me, and I shall give thee the heathen for thine inheritance, and the uttermost parts of the earth for thy possession. [9]Thou shalt break them with a rod of iron; thou shalt dash them in pieces like a potter's vessel. [10]Be wise now therefore, O ye kings: be instructed, ye judges of the earth. [11]Serve the LORD with fear, and rejoice with trembling. [12]Kiss the Son, lest he be angry, and ye perish from the way, when his wrath is kindled but a little. Blessed are all they that put their trust in him."

Isaiah 9:6-7 "[6]For unto us a child is born, unto us a son is given: and the government shall be upon his shoulder: and his name shall be called Wonderful, Counseller, The mighty God, The everlasting Father, The Prince of Peace. [7]Of the increase of his government and peace there shall be no end, upon the throne of David, and upon his kingdom, to order it, and to establish it with judgment and with justice from henceforth even for ever. The zeal of the LORD of hosts will perform this."

Isaiah 32:1-8 "¹Behold, a king shall reign in righteousness, and princes shall rule in judgment. ²And a man shall be as an hiding place from the wind, and a covert from the tempest; as rivers of water in a dry place, as the shadow of a great rock in a weary land. ³And the eyes of them that see shall not be dim, and the ears of them that hear shall hearken. ⁴The heart also of the rash shall understand knowledge, and the tongue of the stammerers shall be ready to speak plainly. ⁵The vile person shall be no more called liberal, nor the churl said to be bountiful. ⁶For the vile person will speak villany, and his heart will work iniquity, to practise hypocrisy, and to utter error against the LORD, to make empty the soul of the hungry, and he will cause the drink of the thirsty to fail. ⁷The instruments also of the churl are evil: he deviseth wicked devices to destroy the poor with lying words, even when the needy speaketh right. ⁸But the liberal deviseth liberal things; and by liberal things shall he stand."

Jeremiah 23:5-8 "⁵Behold, the days come, saith the LORD, that I will raise unto David a righteous Branch, and a King shall reign and prosper, and shall execute judgment and justice in the earth. ⁶In his days Judah shall be saved, and Israel shall dwell safely: and this is his name whereby he shall be called, THE LORD OUR RIGHTEOUSNESS. ⁷Therefore, behold, the days come, saith the LORD, that they shall no more say, The LORD liveth, which brought up the children of Israel out of the land of Egypt; ⁸But, The LORD liveth, which brought up and which led the seed of the house of Israel out of the north country, and from all countries whither I had driven them; and they shall dwell in their own land."

Daniel 7:13-14 "¹³I saw in the night visions, and, behold, one like the Son of man came with the clouds of heaven, and came to the Ancient of days, and they brought him near before him. ¹⁴And there was given him dominion, and glory, and a kingdom, that all people, nations, and languages, should serve him: his dominion is an everlasting dominion, which shall not pass away, and his kingdom that which shall not be destroyed."

Micah 5:2-6 "²But thou, Bethlehem Ephratah, though thou be little among the thousands of Judah, yet out of thee shall he come forth unto me that is to be ruler in Israel; whose goings forth have been from of old, from everlasting. ³Therefore will he give them up, until the time that she which travaileth hath brought forth: then the remnant of his brethren shall return unto the children of Israel. ⁴And he shall stand and feed in the strength of the LORD, in the majesty of the name of the LORD his God; and they shall abide: for now shall he be great unto the ends of the earth. ⁵And this man shall be the peace, when the Assyrian shall come into our land: and when he shall tread in our palaces, then shall we raise against him seven shepherds, and eight principal men. ⁶And they shall waste the land of Assyria with the sword, and the land of Nimrod in the entrances thereof: thus shall he deliver us from the Assyrian, when he cometh into our land, and when he treadeth within our borders."

Zechariah 9:9-10 "⁹Rejoice greatly, O daughter of Zion; shout, O daughter of Jerusalem: behold, thy King cometh unto thee: he is just, and having salvation; lowly, and riding upon an ass, and upon a colt the foal of an ass. ¹⁰And I will cut off the chariot from Ephraim, and the horse from Jerusalem, and the battle bow shall be cut off: and he shall speak peace unto the heathen: and his dominion shall be from sea even to sea, and from river even to the ends of the earth."

Matthew 2:1-6 "¹Now when Jesus was born in Bethlehem of Judaea in the days of Herod the king, behold, there came wise men from the east to Jerusalem, ²Saying, Where is he that is born King of the Jews? for we have seen his star in the east, and are come to worship him. ³When Herod the king had heard these things, he was troubled, and all Jerusalem with him. ⁴And when he had gathered all the chief priests and scribes of the people together, he demanded of them where Christ should be born. ⁵And they said unto him, In Bethlehem of Judaea: for thus it is written by the prophet, ⁶And thou Bethlehem, in the land of Juda, art not the least among the princes of Juda: for out of thee shall come a Governor, that shall rule my people Israel."

Matthew 21:9-11 "⁹And the multitudes that went before, and that followed, cried, saying, Hosanna to the Son of David: Blessed is he that cometh in the name of the Lord; Hosanna in the highest. [10]And when he was come into Jerusalem, all the city was moved, saying, Who is this? [11]And the multitude said, This is Jesus the prophet of Nazareth of Galilee."

Mark 11:9-11 "[9]And they that went before, and they that followed, cried, saying, Hosanna; Blessed is he that cometh in the name of the Lord: [10]Blessed be the kingdom of our father David, that cometh in the name of the Lord: Hosanna in the highest. [11]And Jesus entered into Jerusalem, and into the temple: and when he had looked round about upon all things, and now the eventide was come, he went out unto Bethany with the twelve."

Luke 1:31-33 "[31]And, behold, thou shalt conceive in thy womb, and bring forth a son, and shalt call his name JESUS. [32]He shall be great, and shall be called the Son of the Highest: and the Lord God shall give unto him the throne of his father David: [33]And he shall reign over the house of Jacob for ever; and of his kingdom there shall be no end."

Luke 19:35-38 "[35]And they brought him to Jesus: and they cast their garments upon the colt, and they set Jesus thereon. [36]And as he went, they spread their clothes in the way. [37]And when he was come nigh, even now at the descent of the mount of Olives, the whole multitude of the disciples began to rejoice and praise God with a loud voice for all the mighty works that they had seen; [38]Saying, Blessed be the King that cometh in the name of the Lord: peace in heaven, and glory in the highest."

John 12:12-13 "[12]On the next day much people that were come to the feast, when they heard that Jesus was coming to Jerusalem, [13]Took branches of palm trees, and went forth to meet him, and cried, Hosanna: Blessed is the King of Israel that cometh in the name of the Lord."

Revelation 12:1-5 "[1]And there appeared a great wonder in heaven; a woman clothed with the sun, and the moon under her feet, and upon her head a crown of twelve stars: [2]And she being with child cried, travailing in birth, and pained to be delivered. [3]And there appeared another wonder in heaven; and behold a great red dragon, having seven heads and ten horns, and seven crowns upon his heads. [4]And his tail drew the third part of the stars of heaven, and did cast them to the earth: and the dragon stood before the woman which was ready to be delivered, for to devour her child as soon as it was born. [5]And she brought forth a man child, who was to rule all nations with a rod of iron: and her child was caught up unto God, and to his throne."

Revelation 19:11-15 "[11]And I saw heaven opened, and behold a white horse; and he that sat upon him was called Faithful and True, and in righteousness he doth judge and make war. [12]His eyes were as a flame of fire, and on his head were many crowns; and he had a name written, that no man knew, but he himself. [13]And he was clothed with a vesture dipped in blood: and his name is called The Word of God. [14]And the armies which were in heaven followed him upon white horses, clothed in fine linen, white and clean. [15]And out of his mouth goeth a sharp sword, that with it he should smite the nations: and he shall rule them with a rod of iron: and he treadeth the winepress of the fierceness and wrath of Almighty God."

The Prince That Wants Understanding
Proverbs 28:16 "The prince that wanteth understanding is also a great oppressor: but he that hateth covetousness shall prolong his days."

The Prince(s) Of This World
Psalm 107:31-40 "[31]Oh that men would praise the LORD for his goodness, and for his wonderful works to the children of men! [32]Let them exalt him also in the congregation of the people, and praise him in the assembly of the elders. [33]He turneth rivers into a wilderness, and the watersprings into dry ground; [34]A fruitful land into barrenness, for the wickedness of them that dwell therein. [35]He turneth the wilderness into a standing water, and dry ground into watersprings. [36]And there he maketh the hungry to dwell, that they may prepare a city for habitation; [37]And sow the fields, and plant vineyards, which may yield fruits of increase. [38]He blesseth them also, so that they are multiplied greatly; and suffereth not their cattle to decrease. [39]Again, they are minished and brought low through oppression, affliction, and sorrow. [40]He poureth contempt upon

princes, and causeth them to wander in the wilderness, where there is no way."

John 12:30-32 "30Jesus answered and said, This voice came not because of me, but for your sakes. 31Now is the judgment of this world: now shall the prince of this world be cast out. 32And I, if I be lifted up from the earth, will draw all men unto me."

John 14:23-30 "23Jesus answered and said unto him, If a man love me, he will keep my words: and my Father will love him, and we will come unto him, and make our abode with him. 24He that loveth me not keepeth not my sayings: and the word which ye hear is not mine, but the Father's which sent me. 25These things have I spoken unto you, being yet present with you. 26But the Comforter, which is the Holy Ghost, whom the Father will send in my name, he shall teach you all things, and bring all things to your remembrance, whatsoever I have said unto you. 27Peace I leave with you, my peace I give unto you: not as the world giveth, give I unto you. Let not your heart be troubled, neither let it be afraid. 28Ye have heard how I said unto you, I go away, and come again unto you. If ye loved me, ye would rejoice, because I said, I go unto the Father: for my Father is greater than I. 29And now I have told you before it come to pass, that, when it is come to pass, ye might believe. 30Hereafter I will not talk much with you: for the prince of this world cometh, and hath nothing in me."

John 16:7-11 "7Nevertheless I tell you the truth; It is expedient for you that I go away: for if I go not away, the Comforter will not come unto you; but if I depart, I will send him unto you. 8And when he is come, he will reprove the world of sin, and of righteousness, and of judgment: 9Of sin, because they believe not on me; 10Of righteousness, because I go to my Father, and ye see me no more; 11Of judgment, because the prince of this world is judged."

1 Corinthians 2:6-8 "6Howbeit we speak wisdom among them that are perfect: yet not the wisdom of this world, nor of the princes of this world, that come to nought: 7But we speak the wisdom of God in a mystery, even the hidden wisdom, which God ordained before the world unto our glory: 8Which none of the princes of this world knew: for had they known it, they would not have crucified the Lord of glory."

2 Corinthians 4:3-4 "3But if our gospel be hid, it is hid to them that are lost: 4In whom the god of this world hath blinded the minds of them which believe not, lest the light of the glorious gospel of Christ, who is the image of God, should shine unto them."

The Purpose Of Government
Romans 13:1-7 "1Let every soul be subject unto the higher powers. For there is no power but of God: the powers that be are ordained of God. 2Whosoever therefore resisteth the power, resisteth the ordinance of God: and they that resist shall receive to themselves damnation. 3For rulers are not a terror to good works, but to the evil. Wilt thou then not be afraid of the power? do that which is good, and thou shalt have praise of the same: 4For he is the minister of God to thee for good. But if thou do that which is evil, be afraid; for he beareth not the sword in vain: for he is the minister of God, a revenger to execute wrath upon him that doeth evil. 5Wherefore ye must needs be subject, not only for wrath, but also for conscience sake. 6For for this cause pay ye tribute also: for they are God's ministers, attending continually upon this very thing. 7Render therefore to all their dues: tribute to whom tribute is due; custom to whom custom; fear to whom fear; honour to whom honour."

1 Peter 2:13-14 "13Submit yourselves to every ordinance of man for the Lord's sake: whether it be to the king, as supreme; 14Or unto governors, as unto them that are sent by him for the punishment of evildoers, and for the praise of them that do well."

The Time When Children Rule
Ecclesiastes 10:16 "Woe to thee, O land, when thy king is a child, and thy princes eat in the morning!"

The Time When Nobles Rule
Ecclesiastes 10:17 "Blessed art thou, O land, when thy king is the son of nobles, and thy princes eat in due season, for strength, and not for drunkenness!"

The Time When The Righteous Rule
Proverbs 29:2 "When the righteous are in authority, the people rejoice: but when the wicked beareth rule, the people mourn."

The Time When The Wicked Rule
Proverbs 29:2 "When the righteous are in authority, the people rejoice: but when the wicked beareth rule, the people mourn."

Proverbs 29:16 "When the wicked are multiplied, transgression increaseth: but the righteous shall see their fall."

Those That Rule Among Fools
Ecclesiastes 9:17 "The words of wise men are heard in quiet more than the cry of him that ruleth among fools."

Who Shall Bear Rule
Proverbs 12:24 "The hand of the diligent shall bear rule: but the slothful shall be under tribute."

Who Shall Not Rule The Righteous
Psalm 125:3 "For the rod of the wicked shall not rest upon the lot of the righteous; lest the righteous put forth their hands unto iniquity."

Who Shall Reign With The Lord
Daniel 7:15-27 "[15]I Daniel was grieved in my spirit in the midst of my body, and the visions of my head troubled me. [16]I came near unto one of them that stood by, and asked him the truth of all this. So he told me, and made me know the interpretation of the things. [17]These great beasts, which are four, are four kings, which shall arise out of the earth. [18]But the saints of the most High shall take the kingdom, and possess the kingdom for ever, even for ever and ever. [19]Then I would know the truth of the fourth beast, which was diverse from all the others, exceeding dreadful, whose teeth were of iron, and his nails of brass; which devoured, brake in pieces, and stamped the residue with his feet; [20]And of the ten horns that were in his head, and of the other which came up, and before whom three fell; even of that horn that had eyes, and a mouth that spake very great things, whose look was more stout than his fellows. [21]I beheld, and the same horn made war with the saints, and prevailed against them; [22]Until the Ancient of days came, and judgment was given to the saints of the most High; and the time came that the saints possessed the kingdom. [23]Thus he said, The fourth beast shall be the fourth kingdom upon earth, which shall be diverse from all kingdoms, and shall devour the whole earth, and shall tread it down, and break it in pieces. [24]And the ten horns out of this kingdom are ten kings that shall arise: and another shall rise after them; and he shall be diverse from the first, and he shall subdue three kings. [25]And he shall speak great words against the most High, and shall wear out the saints of the most High, and think to change times and laws: and they shall be given into his hand until a time and times and the dividing of time. [26]But the judgment shall sit, and they shall take away his dominion, to consume and to destroy it unto the end. [27]And the kingdom and dominion, and the greatness of the kingdom under the whole heaven, shall be given to the people of the saints of the most High, whose kingdom is an everlasting kingdom, and all dominions shall serve and obey him."

Luke 22:22-30 "[22]And truly the Son of man goeth, as it was determined: but woe unto that man by whom he is betrayed! [23]And they began to inquire among themselves, which of them it was that should do this thing. [24]And there was also a strife among them, which of them should be accounted the greatest. [25]And he said unto them, The kings of the Gentiles exercise lordship over them; and they that exercise authority upon them are called benefactors. [26]But ye shall not be so: but he that is greatest among you, let him be as the younger; and he that is chief, as he that doth serve. [27]For whether is greater, he that sitteth at meat, or he that serveth? is not he that sitteth at meat? but I am among you as he that serveth. [28]Ye are they which have continued with me in my temptations. [29]And I appoint unto you a kingdom, as my Father hath appointed unto me; [30]That ye may eat and drink at my table in my kingdom, and sit on thrones judging the twelve tribes of Israel."

2 Timothy 2:10-12 "[10]Therefore I endure all things for the elect's sakes, that they may also obtain the salvation which is in Christ Jesus with eternal glory. [11]It is a faithful saying: For if we be dead with him, we shall also live with him: [12]If we suffer, we shall also reign with him: if we deny him, he also will deny us:"

Revelation 2:18-28 "[18]And unto the angel of the church in Thyatira write; These things saith the Son of God, who hath his eyes like unto a flame of fire, and his feet are like fine brass; [19]I know thy works, and charity, and service, and faith, and thy patience, and thy works; and the last to be more than the first. [20]Notwithstanding I have a few things against thee, because thou sufferest that woman Jezebel, which calleth herself a prophetess, to teach and to seduce my servants to commit fornication, and to eat things sacrificed unto idols. [21]And I gave her space to repent of her fornication; and she repented not. [22]Behold, I will cast her into a bed, and them that commit adultery with her into great tribulation, except they repent of their deeds. [23]And I will kill her children with death; and all the churches shall know that I am he which searcheth the reins and hearts: and I will give unto every one of you according to your works. [24]But unto you I say, and unto the rest in Thyatira, as many as have not this doctrine, and which have not known the depths of Satan, as they speak; I will put upon you none other burden. [25]But that which ye have already hold fast till I come. [26]And he that overcometh, and keepeth my works unto the end, to him will I give power over the nations: [27]And he shall rule them with a rod of iron; as the vessels of a potter shall they be broken to shivers: even as I received of my Father. [28]And I will give him the morning star."

Revelation 3:14-21 "[14]And unto the angel of the church of the Laodiceans write; These things saith the Amen, the faithful and true witness, the beginning of the creation of God; [15]I know thy works, that thou art neither cold nor hot: I would thou wert cold or hot. [16]So then because thou art lukewarm, and neither cold nor hot, I will spue thee out of my mouth. [17]Because thou sayest, I am rich, and increased with goods, and have need of nothing; and knowest not that thou art wretched, and miserable, and poor, and blind, and naked: [18]I counsel thee to buy of me gold tried in the fire, that thou mayest be rich; and white raiment, that thou mayest be clothed, and that the shame of thy nakedness do not appear; and anoint thine eyes with eyesalve, that thou mayest see. [19]As many as I love, I rebuke and chasten: be zealous therefore, and repent. [20]Behold, I stand at the door, and knock: if any man hear my voice, and open the door, I will come in to him, and will sup with him, and he with me. [21]To him that overcometh will I grant to sit with me in my throne, even as I also overcame, and am set down with my Father in his throne."

Revelation 5:8-10 "[8]And when he had taken the book, the four beasts and four and twenty elders fell down before the Lamb, having every one of them harps, and golden vials full of odours, which are the prayers of saints. [9]And they sung a new song, saying, Thou art worthy to take the book, and to open the seals thereof: for thou wast slain, and hast redeemed us to God by thy blood out of every kindred, and tongue, and people, and nation; [10]And hast made us unto our God kings and priests: and we shall reign on the earth."

Revelation 20:4-6 "[4]And I saw thrones, and they sat upon them, and judgment was given unto them: and I saw the souls of them that were beheaded for the witness of Jesus, and for the word of God, and which had not worshipped the beast, neither his image, neither had received his mark upon their foreheads, or in their hands; and they lived and reigned with Christ a thousand years. [5]But the rest of the dead lived not again until the thousand years were finished. This is the first resurrection. [6]Blessed and holy is he that hath part in the first resurrection: on such the second death hath no power, but they shall be priests of God and of Christ, and shall reign with him a thousand years."

Revelation 22:3-5 "[3]And there shall be no more curse: but the throne of God and of the Lamb shall be in it; and his servants shall serve him: [4]And they shall see his face; and his name shall be in their foreheads. [5]And there shall be no night there; and they need no candle, neither light of the sun; for the Lord God giveth them light: and they shall reign for ever and ever."

Who Should Be Chosen To Govern Israel
Deuteronomy 17:14-20 "[14]When thou art come unto the land which the LORD thy God giveth thee, and shalt possess it, and shalt dwell therein, and shalt say, I will set a king over me, like as all the nations that are about me; [15]Thou shalt in any wise set him king over thee, whom the LORD thy God shall choose: one from among thy brethren shalt thou set king over thee: thou mayest not set a stranger over thee, which is not thy brother. [16]But he shall not multiply horses to himself, nor cause the people to return to Egypt, to the end that he should multiply horses: forasmuch as the LORD hath said unto you, Ye shall henceforth return no more that way. [17]Neither shall he multiply wives

to himself, that his heart turn not away: neither shall he greatly multiply to himself silver and gold. [18]And it shall be, when he sitteth upon the throne of his kingdom, that he shall write him a copy of this law in a book out of that which is before the priests the Levites: [19]And it shall be with him, and he shall read therein all the days of his life: that he may learn to fear the LORD his God, to keep all the words of this law and these statutes, to do them: [20]That his heart be not lifted up above his brethren, and that he turn not aside from the commandment, to the right hand, or to the left: to the end that he may prolong his days in his kingdom, he, and his children, in the midst of Israel."

Whose Throne Shall Be Established

2 Samuel 7:8-16 "[8]Now therefore so shalt thou say unto my servant David, Thus saith the LORD of hosts, I took thee from the sheepcote, from following the sheep, to be ruler over my people, over Israel: [9]And I was with thee whithersoever thou wentest, and have cut off all thine enemies out of thy sight, and have made thee a great name, like unto the name of the great men that are in the earth. [10]Moreover I will appoint a place for my people Israel, and will plant them, that they may dwell in a place of their own, and move no more; neither shall the children of wickedness afflict them any more, as beforetime, [11]And as since the time that I commanded judges to be over my people Israel, and have caused thee to rest from all thine enemies. Also the LORD telleth thee that he will make thee an house. [12]And when thy days be fulfilled, and thou shalt sleep with thy fathers, I will set up thy seed after thee, which shall proceed out of thy bowels, and I will establish his kingdom. [13]He shall build an house for my name, and I will stablish the throne of his kingdom for ever. [14]I will be his father, and he shall be my son. If he commit iniquity, I will chasten him with the rod of men, and with the stripes of the children of men: [15]But my mercy shall not depart away from him, as I took it from Saul, whom I put away before thee. [16]And thine house and thy kingdom shall be established for ever before thee: thy throne shall be established for ever."

1 Chronicles 28:2-7 "[2]Then David the king stood up upon his feet, and said, Hear me, my brethren, and my people: As for me, I had in mine heart to build an house of rest for the ark of the covenant of the LORD, and for the footstool of our God, and had made ready for the building: [3]But God said unto me, Thou shalt not build an house for my name, because thou hast been a man of war, and hast shed blood. [4]Howbeit the LORD God of Israel chose me before all the house of my father to be king over Israel for ever: for he hath chosen Judah to be the ruler; and of the house of Judah, the house of my father; and among the sons of my father he liked me to make me king over all Israel: [5]And of all my sons, (for the LORD hath given me many sons,) he hath chosen Solomon my son to sit upon the throne of the kingdom of the LORD over Israel. [6]And he said unto me, Solomon thy son, he shall build my house and my courts: for I have chosen him to be my son, and I will be his father. [7]Moreover I will establish his kingdom for ever, if he be constant to do my commandments and my judgments, as at this day."

Job 36:5-7 "[5]Behold, God is mighty, and despiseth not any: he is mighty in strength and wisdom. [6]He preserveth not the life of the wicked: but giveth right to the poor. [7]He withdraweth not his eyes from the righteous: but with kings are they on the throne; yea, he doth establish them for ever, and they are exalted."

Psalm 89:19-37 "[19]Then thou spakest in vision to thy holy one, and saidst, I have laid help upon one that is mighty; I have exalted one chosen out of the people. [20]I have found David my servant; with my holy oil have I anointed him: [21]With whom my hand shall be established: mine arm also shall strengthen him. [22]The enemy shall not exact upon him; nor the son of wickedness afflict him. [23]And I will beat down his foes before his face, and plague them that hate him. [24]But my faithfulness and my mercy shall be with him: and in my name shall his horn be exalted. [25]I will set his hand also in the sea, and his right hand in the rivers. [26]He shall cry unto me, Thou art my father, my God, and the rock of my salvation. [27]Also I will make him my firstborn, higher than the kings of the earth. [28]My mercy will I keep for him for evermore, and my covenant shall stand fast with him. [29]His seed also will I make to endure for ever, and his throne as the days of heaven. [30]If his children forsake my law, and walk not in my judgments; [31]If they break my statutes, and keep not my commandments; 32Then will I visit their transgression with the rod, and their iniquity with stripes. 33Nevertheless my lovingkindness will I not utterly take from him, nor suffer my faithfulness to fail. 34My covenant will I not break, nor alter the thing that is gone out of my lips. 35Once have I sworn by my holiness that I will not lie unto David. 36His seed shall endure forever, and his throne as the sun before me. 37It shall be established for ever as the moon, and as a faithful witness in heaven. Selah."

Proverbs 25:4-5 "4Take away the dross from the silver, and there shall come forth a vessel for the finer. 5Take away the wicked from before the king, and his throne shall be established in righteousness."

Proverbs 29:14 "The king that faithfully judgeth the poor, his throne shall be established for ever."

Wicked Rulers
Proverbs 28:15 "As a roaring lion, and a ranging bear; so is a wicked ruler over the poor people."

Micah 3:9-12 "9Hear this, I pray you, ye heads of the house of Jacob, and princes of the house of Israel, that abhor judgment, and pervert all equity. 10They build up Zion with blood, and Jerusalem with iniquity. 11The heads thereof judge for reward, and the priests thereof teach for hire, and the prophets thereof divine for money: yet will they lean upon the LORD, and say, Is not the LORD among us? none evil can come upon us. 12Therefore shall Zion for your sake be plowed as a field, and Jerusalem shall become heaps, and the mountain of the house as the high places of the forest."

Wise Kings
Psalm 72:1-17 "1Give the king thy judgments, O God, and thy righteousness unto the king's son. 2He shall judge thy people with righteousness, and thy poor with judgment. 3The mountains shall bring peace to the people, and the little hills, by righteousness. 4He shall judge the poor of the people, he shall save the children of the needy, and shall break in pieces the oppressor. 5They shall fear thee as long as the sun and moon endure, throughout all generations. 6He shall come down like rain upon the mown grass: as showers that water the earth. 7In his days shall the righteous flourish; and abundance of peace so long as the moon endureth. 8He shall have dominion also

from sea to sea, and from the river unto the ends of the earth. 9They that dwell in the wilderness shall bow before him; and his enemies shall lick the dust. 10The kings of Tarshish and of the isles shall bring presents: the kings of Sheba and Seba shall offer gifts. 11Yea, all kings shall fall down before him: all nations shall serve him. 12For he shall deliver the needy when he crieth; the poor also, and him that hath no helper. 13He shall spare the poor and needy, and shall save the souls of the needy. 14He shall redeem their soul from deceit and violence: and precious shall their blood be in his sight. 15And he shall live, and to him shall be given of the gold of Sheba: prayer also shall be made for him continually; and daily shall he be praised. 16There shall be an handful of corn in the earth upon the top of the mountains; the fruit thereof shall shake like Lebanon: and they of the city shall flourish like grass of the earth. 17His name shall endure for ever: his name shall be continued as long as the sun: and men shall be blessed in him: all nations shall call him blessed."

Proverbs 20:26 "A wise king scattereth the wicked, and bringeth the wheel over them."

GRACE

Gracious Women
Proverbs 11:16 "A gracious woman retaineth honour: and strong men retain riches."

The Grace Of God
John 1:17 "For the law was given by Moses, but grace and truth came by Jesus Christ."

Acts 15:10-11 "10Now therefore why tempt ye God, to put a yoke upon the neck of the disciples, which neither our fathers nor we were able to bear? 11But we believe that through the grace of the Lord Jesus Christ we shall be saved, even as they."

Romans 5:12-21 "12Wherefore, as by one man sin entered into the world, and death by sin; and so death passed upon all men, for that all have sinned: 13(For until the law sin was in the world: but sin is not imputed when there is no law. 14Nevertheless death reigned from Adam to Moses, even over them that had not sinned after the similitude of Adam's transgression, who is the figure of him that was to come. 15But not as the offence, so also is the free gift. For if through the offence of one many be dead, much more the grace of God, and the gift by grace, which is by one man, Jesus Christ, hath abounded unto many. 16And not as it was by one that sinned, so is the gift: for the judgment was by one to condemnation, but the free gift is of many offences unto justification. 17For if by one man's offence death reigned by one; much more they which receive abundance of grace and of the gift of righteousness shall reign in life by one, Jesus Christ.) 18Therefore as by the offence of one judgment came upon all men to condemnation; even so by the righteousness of one the free gift came upon all men unto justification of life. 19For as by one man's disobedience many were made sinners, so by the obedience of one shall many be made righteous. 20Moreover the law entered, that the offence might abound. But where sin abounded, grace did much more abound: 21That as sin hath reigned unto death, even so might grace reign through righteousness unto eternal life by Jesus Christ our Lord."

1 Corinthians 1:4 "I thank my God always on your behalf, for the grace of God which is given you by Jesus Christ;"

1 Corinthians 3:10 "According to the grace of God which is given unto me, as a wise masterbuilder, I have laid the foundation, and another buildeth thereon. But let every man take heed how he buildeth thereupon."

1 Corinthians 15:9-10 "9For I am the least of the apostles, that am not meet to be called an apostle, because I persecuted the church of God. 10But by the grace of God I am what I am: and his grace which was bestowed upon me was not in vain; but I laboured more abundantly than they all: yet not I, but the grace of God which was with me."

2 Corinthians 8:9 "For ye know the grace of our Lord Jesus Christ, that, though he was rich, yet for your sakes he became poor, that ye through his poverty might be rich."

2 Corinthians 12:8-9 "8For this thing I besought the Lord thrice, that it might depart from me. 9And he said unto me, My grace is sufficient for thee: for my strength is made perfect in weakness. Most gladly therefore will I rather glory in my infirmities, that the power of Christ may rest upon me."

Ephesians 1:3-7 "3Blessed be the God and Father of our Lord Jesus Christ, who hath blessed us with all spiritual blessings in heavenly places in Christ: 4According as he hath chosen us in him before the foundation of the world, that we should be holy and without blame before him in love: 5Having predestinated us unto the adoption of children by Jesus Christ to himself, according to the good pleasure of his will, 6To the praise of the glory of his grace, wherein he hath made us accepted in the beloved. 7In whom we have redemption through his blood, the forgiveness of sins, according to the riches of his grace;"

Ephesians 2:4-9 "4But God, who is rich in mercy, for his great love wherewith he loved us, 5Even when we were dead in sins, hath quickened us together with Christ, (by grace ye are saved;) 6And hath raised us up together, and made us sit together in heavenly places in Christ Jesus: 7That in the ages to come he might shew the exceeding riches of his grace in his kindness toward us through Christ Jesus. 8For by grace are ye saved through faith; and that not of yourselves: it is the gift of God: 9Not of works, lest any man should boast."

Ephesians 3:7-8 "7Whereof I was made a minister, according to the gift of the grace of God given unto me by the effectual working of his power. 8Unto me, who am less than the least of all saints, is this grace given, that I should preach among the Gentiles the unsearchable riches of Christ;"

1 Timothy 1:14 "And the grace of our Lord was exceeding abundant with faith and love which is in Christ Jesus."

Titus 2:11-12 "11For the grace of God that bringeth salvation hath appeared to all men, 12Teaching us that, denying ungodliness and worldly lusts, we should live soberly, righteously, and godly, in this present world;"

Titus 3:3-7 "3For we ourselves also were sometimes foolish, disobedient, deceived, serving divers lusts and pleasures, living in malice and envy, hateful, and hating one another. 4But after that the kindness and love of God our Saviour toward man appeared, [5]Not by works of righteousness which we have done, but according to his mercy he saved us, by the washing of regeneration, and renewing of the Holy Ghost; [6]Which he shed on us abundantly through Jesus Christ our Saviour; [7]That being justified by his grace, we should be made heirs according to the hope of eternal life."

Hebrews 2:9 "But we see Jesus, who was made a little lower than the angels for the suffering of death, crowned with glory and honour; that he by the grace of God should taste death for every man."

The Heart Being Established With Grace
Hebrews 13:9 "Be not carried about with divers and strange doctrines. For it is a good thing that the heart be established with grace; not with meats, which have not profited them that have been occupied therein."

The Lord Being Gracious
Exodus 22:20-27 "[20]He that sacrificeth unto any god, save unto the LORD only, he shall be utterly destroyed. [21]Thou shalt neither vex a stranger, nor oppress him: for ye were strangers in the land of Egypt. [22]Ye shall not afflict any widow, or fatherless child. [23]If thou afflict them in any wise, and they cry at all unto me, I will surely hear their cry; [24]And my wrath shall wax hot, and I will kill you with the sword; and your wives shall be widows, and your children fatherless. [25]If thou lend money to any of my people that is poor by thee, thou shalt not be to him as an usurer, neither shalt thou lay upon him usury. [26]If thou at all take thy neighbour's raiment to pledge, thou shalt deliver it unto him by that the sun goeth down: [27]For that is his covering only, it is his raiment for his skin: wherein shall he sleep? and it shall come to pass, when he crieth unto me, that I will hear; for I am gracious."

Exodus 33:17-19 "[17]And the LORD said unto Moses, I will do this thing also that thou hast spoken: for thou hast found grace in my sight, and I know thee by name. [18]And he said, I beseech thee, shew me thy glory. [19]And he said, I will make all my goodness pass before thee, and I will proclaim the name of the LORD before thee; and will be gracious to whom I will be gracious, and will shew mercy on whom I will shew mercy."

Exodus 34:6 "And the LORD passed by before him, and proclaimed, The LORD, The LORD God, merciful and gracious, longsuffering, and abundant in goodness and truth,"

2 Chronicles 30:9 "For if ye turn again unto the LORD, your brethren and your children shall find compassion before them that lead them captive, so that they shall come again into this land: for the LORD your God is gracious and merciful, and will not turn away his face from you, if ye return unto him."

Nehemiah 9:16-17 "[16]But they and our fathers dealt proudly, and hardened their necks, and hearkened not to thy commandments, [17]And refused to obey, neither were mindful of thy wonders that thou didst among them; but hardened their necks, and in their rebellion appointed a captain to return to their bondage: but thou art a God ready to pardon, gracious and merciful, slow to anger, and of great kindness, and forsookest them not."

Nehemiah 9:31 "Nevertheless for thy great mercies' sake thou didst not utterly consume them, nor forsake them; for thou art a gracious and merciful God."

Job 33:19-33 "[19]He is chastened also with pain upon his bed, and the multitude of his bones with strong pain: [20]So that his life abhorreth bread, and his soul dainty meat. [21]His flesh is consumed away, that it cannot be seen; and his bones that were not seen stick out. [22]Yea, his soul draweth near unto the grave, and his life to the destroyers. [23]If there be a messenger with him, an interpreter, one among a thousand, to shew unto man his uprightness: [24]Then he is gracious unto him, and saith, Deliver him from going down to the pit: I have found a ransom. [25]His flesh shall be fresher than a child's: he shall return to the days of his youth: [26]He shall pray unto God, and he will be favourable unto him: and he shall see his face with joy: for he will render unto man his righteousness. [27]He looketh upon men, and if any say, I have sinned, and perverted that which was right, and it profited me not; [28]He will deliver his soul from going into the pit, and his life shall see the light. [29]Lo, all these things worketh God oftentimes with man, [30]To bring back his soul from the pit, to be enlightened with the light of the living. [31]Mark well, O Job, hearken unto me: hold thy peace, and I will speak. [32]If thou hast any thing to say, answer me: speak, for I desire to justify thee. [33]If not, hearken unto me: hold thy peace, and I shall teach thee wisdom."

Psalm 86:15 "But thou, O Lord, art a God full of compassion, and gracious, longsuffering, and plenteous in mercy and truth."

Psalm 103:8 "The LORD is merciful and gracious, slow to anger, and plenteous in mercy."

Psalm 111:4 "He hath made his wonderful works to be remembered: the LORD is gracious and full of compassion."

Psalm 116:5 "Gracious is the LORD, and righteous; yea, our God is merciful."

Psalm 145:8 "The LORD is gracious, and full of compassion; slow to anger, and of great mercy."

Isaiah 30:18 "And therefore will the LORD wait, that he may be gracious unto you, and therefore will he be exalted, that he may have mercy upon you: for the LORD is a God of judgment: blessed are all they that wait for him."

Joel 2:12-13 "[12]Therefore also now, saith the LORD, turn ye even to me with all your heart, and with fasting, and with weeping, and with mourning: [13]And rend your heart, and not your garments, and turn unto the LORD your God: for he is gracious and merciful, slow to anger, and of great kindness, and repenteth him of the evil."

Amos 5:15 "Hate the evil, and love the good, and establish judgment in the gate: it may be that the LORD God of hosts will be gracious unto the remnant of Joseph."

1 Peter 2:2-3 "[2]As newborn babes, desire the sincere milk of the word, that ye may grow thereby: [3]If so be ye have tasted that the Lord is gracious."

1 Peter 5:10 "But the God of all grace, who hath called us unto his eternal glory by Christ Jesus, after that ye have suffered a while, make you perfect, stablish, strengthen, settle you."

The Reward For Being Under Grace
Romans 6:1-14 "[1]What shall we say then? Shall we continue in sin, that grace may abound? [2]God forbid. How shall we, that are dead to sin, live any longer therein? [3]Know ye not, that so many of us as were baptized into Jesus Christ were baptized into his death? [4]Therefore we are buried with him by baptism into death: that like as Christ was raised up from the dead by the glory of the Father, even so we also should walk in newness of life. [5]For if we have been planted together in the likeness of his death, we shall be also in the likeness of his resurrection: [6]Knowing this, that our old man is crucified with him, that the body of sin might be destroyed, that henceforth we should not serve sin. [7]For he that is dead is freed from sin. [8]Now if we be dead with Christ, we believe that we shall also live with him: [9]Knowing that Christ being raised from the dead dieth no more; death hath no more dominion over him. [10]For in that he died, he died unto sin once: but in that he liveth, he liveth unto God. [11]Likewise reckon ye also yourselves to be dead indeed unto sin, but alive unto God through Jesus Christ our Lord. [12]Let not sin therefore reign in your mortal body, that ye should obey it in the lusts thereof. [13]Neither yield ye your members as instruments of unrighteousness unto sin: but yield yourselves unto God, as those that are alive from the dead, and your members as instruments of righteousness unto God. [14]For sin shall not have dominion over you: for ye are not under the law, but under grace."

What Is Gracious
Ecclesiastes 10:12 "The words of a wise man's mouth are gracious; but the lips of a fool will swallow up himself."

Who Is Fallen From Grace
Galatians 5:4-6 "[4]Christ is become of no effect unto you, whosoever of you are justified by the law; ye are fallen from grace. [5]For we through the Spirit wait for the hope of righteousness by faith. [6]For in Jesus Christ neither circumcision availeth anything, nor uncircumcision; but faith which worketh by love."

Who The Lord Gives Grace To
Psalm 84:11 "For the LORD God is a sun and shield: the LORD will give grace and glory: no good thing will he withhold from them that walk uprightly."

Proverbs 3:33-34 "[33]The curse of the LORD is in the house of the wicked: but he blesseth the habitation of the just. [34]Surely he scorneth the scorners: but he giveth grace unto the lowly."

1 Corinthians 15:9-10 "⁹For I am the least of the apostles, that am not meet to be called an apostle, because I persecuted the church of God. ¹⁰But by the grace of God I am what I am: and his grace which was bestowed upon me was not in vain; but I laboured more abundantly than they all: yet not I, but the grace of God which was with me."

Ephesians 3:7-8 "⁷Whereof I was made a minister, according to the gift of the grace of God given unto me by the effectual working of his power. ⁸Unto me, who am less than the least of all saints, is this grace given, that I should preach among the Gentiles the unsearchable riches of Christ;"

Ephesians 4:1-7 "¹I therefore, the prisoner of the Lord, beseech you that ye walk worthy of the vocation wherewith ye are called, ²With all lowliness and meekness, with longsuffering, forbearing one another in love; ³Endeavouring to keep the unity of the Spirit in the bond of peace. ⁴There is one body, and one Spirit, even as ye are called in one hope of your calling; ⁵One Lord, one faith, one baptism, ⁶One God and Father of all, who is above all, and through all, and in you all. ⁷But unto every one of us is given grace according to the measure of the gift of Christ."

James 4:6 "But he giveth more grace. Wherefore he saith, God resisteth the proud, but giveth grace unto the humble."

1 Peter 5:5 "Likewise, ye younger, submit yourselves unto the elder. Yea, all of you be subject one to another, and be clothed with humility: for God resisteth the proud, and giveth grace to the humble."

GREATNESS

Great Men
Job 32:9 "Great men are not always wise: neither do the aged understand judgment."

Greatness Belonging To The Lord
1 Chronicles 29:11 "Thine, O LORD, is the greatness, and the power, and the glory, and the victory, and the majesty: for all that is in the heaven and in the earth is thine; thine is the kingdom, O LORD, and thou art exalted as head above all."

The Greatest Of Men
Matthew 20:25-27 "²⁵But Jesus called them unto him, and said, Ye know that the princes of the Gentiles exercise dominion over them, and they that are great exercise authority upon them. ²⁶But it shall not be so among you: but whosoever will be great among you, let him be your minister; ²⁷And whosoever will be chief among you, let him be your servant:"

Matthew 23:8-11 "⁸But be not ye called Rabbi: for one is your Master, even Christ; and all ye are brethren. ⁹And call no man your father upon the earth: for one is your Father, which is in heaven. ¹⁰Neither be ye called masters: for one is your Master, even Christ. ¹¹But he that is greatest among you shall be your servant."

Mark 10:42-44 "⁴²But Jesus called them to him, and saith unto them, Ye know that they which are accounted to rule over the Gentiles exercise lordship over them; and their great ones exercise authority upon them. ⁴³But so shall it not be among you: but whosoever will be great among you, shall be your minister: ⁴⁴And whosoever of you will be the chiefest, shall be servant of all."

Luke 22:22-27 "²²And truly the Son of man goeth, as it was determined: but woe unto that man by whom he is betrayed! ²³And they began to inquire among themselves, which of them it was that should do this thing. ²⁴And there was also a strife among them, which of them should be accounted the greatest. ²⁵And he said unto them, The kings of the Gentiles exercise lordship over them; and they that exercise authority upon them are called benefactors. ²⁶But ye shall not be so: but he that is greatest among you, let him be as the younger; and he that is chief, as he that doth serve. ²⁷For whether is greater, he that sitteth at meat, or he that serveth? is not he that sitteth at meat? but I am among you as he that serveth."

The Greatness Of The Lord
Psalm 145:3 "Great is the LORD, and greatly to be praised; and his greatness is unsearchable."

The Lord Being Great
Deuteronomy 10:17 "For the LORD your God is God of gods, and Lord of lords, a great God, a mighty, and a terrible, which regardeth not persons, nor taketh reward:"

Deuteronomy 32:2-3 "²My doctrine shall drop as the rain, my speech shall distil as the dew, as the small rain upon the tender herb, and as the showers upon the grass: ³Because I will publish the name of the LORD: ascribe ye greatness unto our God."

2 Samuel 7:22 "Wherefore thou art great, O LORD God: for there is none like thee, neither is there any God beside thee, according to all that we have heard with our ears."

1 Chronicles 16:25 "For great is the LORD, and greatly to be praised: he also is to be feared above all gods."

2 Chronicles 2:5 "And the house which I build is great: for great is our God above all gods."

Nehemiah 8:6 "And Ezra blessed the LORD, the great God. And all the people answered, Amen, Amen, with lifting up their hands: and they bowed their heads, and worshipped the LORD with their faces to the ground."

Nehemiah 9:32 "Now therefore, our God, the great, the mighty, and the terrible God, who keepest covenant and mercy, let not all the trouble seem little before thee, that hath come upon us, on our kings, on our princes, and on our priests, and on our prophets, and on our fathers, and on all thy people, since the time of the kings of Assyria unto this day."

Job 36:26 "Behold, God is great, and we know him not, neither can the number of his years be searched out."

Psalm 86:10 "For thou art great, and doest wondrous things: thou art God alone."

Psalm 95:3 "For the LORD is a great God, and a great King above all gods."

Psalm 96:4 "For the LORD is great, and greatly to be praised: he is to be feared above all gods."

Psalm 99:2 "The LORD is great in Zion; and he is high above all the people."

Psalm 104:1 "Bless the LORD, O my soul. O LORD my God, thou art very great; thou art clothed with honour and majesty."

Psalm 135:5 "For I know that the LORD is great, and that our Lord is above all gods."

Psalm 145:3 "Great is the LORD, and greatly to be praised; and his greatness is unsearchable."

Psalm 147:5 "Great is our Lord, and of great power: his understanding is infinite."

Proverbs 26:10 "The great God that formed all things both rewardeth the fool, and rewardeth transgressors."

Isaiah 12:6 "Cry out and shout, thou inhabitant of Zion: for great is the Holy One of Israel in the midst of thee."

Jeremiah 10:6 "Forasmuch as there is none like unto thee, O LORD; thou art great, and thy name is great in might."

Jeremiah 32:18-19 "¹⁸Thou shewest lovingkindness unto thousands, and recompensest the iniquity of the fathers into the bosom of their children after them: the Great, the Mighty God, the LORD of hosts, is his name, ¹⁹Great in counsel, and mighty in work: for thine eyes are open upon all the ways of the sons of men: to give every one according to his ways, and according to the fruit of his doings:"

Daniel 9:4 "And I prayed unto the LORD my God, and made my confession, and said, O Lord, the great and dreadful God, keeping the covenant and mercy to them that love him, and to them that keep his commandments;"

Nahum 1:3 "The LORD is slow to anger, and great in power, and will not at all acquit the wicked: the LORD hath his way in the whirlwind and in the storm, and the clouds are the dust of his feet."

Luke 1:31-32 "³¹And, behold, thou shalt conceive in thy womb, and bring forth a son, and shalt call his name JESUS. ³²He shall be great, and shall be called the Son of the Highest: and the Lord God shall give unto him the throne of his father David:"

Titus 2:13 "Looking for that blessed hope, and the glorious appearing of the great God and our Saviour Jesus Christ;"

1 John 3:20 "For if our heart condemn us, God is greater than our heart, and knoweth all things."

The Lord Being Greater Than All Gods

Exodus 18:11 "Now I know that the LORD is greater than all gods: for in the thing wherein they dealt proudly he was above them."

Deuteronomy 10:17 "For the LORD your God is God of gods, and Lord of lords, a great God, a mighty, and a terrible, which regardeth not persons, nor taketh reward:"

1 Chronicles 16:25 "For great is the LORD, and greatly to be praised: he also is to be feared above all gods."

2 Chronicles 2:5 "And the house which I build is great: for great is our God above all gods."

Psalm 95:3 "For the LORD is a great God, and a great King above all gods."

Psalm 96:4 "For the LORD is great, and greatly to be praised: he is to be feared above all gods."

Psalm 135:5 "For I know that the LORD is great, and that our Lord is above all gods."

The Lord Doing Great Things

Joel 2:21 "Fear not, O land; be glad and rejoice: for the LORD will do great things."

What Is Great

2 Chronicles 2:4-5 "⁴Behold, I build an house to the name of the LORD my God, to dedicate it to him, and to burn before him sweet incense, and for the continual shewbread, and for the burnt offerings morning and evening, on the sabbaths, and on the new moons, and on the solemn feasts of the LORD our God. This is an ordinance for ever to Israel. ⁵And the house which I build is great: for great is our God above all gods."

Psalm 92:5-6 "⁵O LORD, how great are thy works! and thy thoughts are very deep. ⁶A brutish man knoweth not; neither doth a fool understand this."

Psalm 103:8-11 "⁸The LORD is merciful and gracious, slow to anger, and plenteous in mercy. ⁹He will not always chide: neither will he keep his anger for ever. ¹⁰He hath not dealt with us after our sins; nor rewarded us according to our iniquities. ¹¹For as the heaven is high above the earth, so great is his mercy toward them that fear him."

Psalm 108:3-4 "³I will praise thee, O LORD, among the people: and I will sing praises unto thee among the nations. ⁴For thy mercy is great above the heavens: and thy truth reacheth unto the clouds."

Psalm 111:2 "The works of the LORD are great, sought out of all them that have pleasure therein."

Psalm 117:2 "For his merciful kindness is great toward us: and the truth of the LORD endureth for ever. Praise ye the LORD."

Psalm 138:5 "Yea, they shall sing in the ways of the LORD: for great is the glory of the LORD."

Psalm 139:17 "How precious also are thy thoughts unto me, O God! how great is the sum of them!"

Lamentations 3:22-23 "²²It is of the LORD's mercies that we are not consumed, because his compassions fail not. ²³They are new every morning: great is thy faithfulness."

Revelation 15:3 "And they sing the song of Moses the servant of God, and the song of the Lamb, saying, Great and marvellous are thy works, Lord God Almighty; just and true are thy ways, thou King of saints."

What Makes You Great

2 Samuel 22:33-36 "³³God is my strength and power: and he maketh my way perfect. ³⁴He maketh my feet like hinds' feet: and setteth me upon my high places. ³⁵He teacheth my hands to war; so that a bow of steel is broken by mine arms. ³⁶Thou hast also given me the shield of thy salvation: and thy gentleness hath made me great."

Psalm 18:31-35 "³¹For who is God save the LORD? or who is a rock save our God? ³²It is God that girdeth me with strength, and maketh my way perfect. ³³He maketh my feet like hinds' feet, and setteth me upon my high places. ³⁴He teacheth my hands to war, so that a bow of steel is broken by mine arms. ³⁵Thou hast also given me the shield of thy salvation: and thy right hand hath holden me up, and thy gentleness hath made me great."

Who Shall Be Great

Luke 9:46-48 "⁴⁶Then there arose a reasoning among them, which of them should be greatest. ⁴⁷And Jesus, perceiving the thought of their heart, took a child, and set him by him, ⁴⁸And said unto them, Whosoever shall receive this child in my name receiveth me: and whosoever shall receive me receiveth him that sent me: for he that is least among you all, the same shall be great."

GREED/GLUTTONY

Gluttons

Proverbs 23:20-21 "[20]Be not among winebibbers; among riotous eaters of flesh: [21]For the drunkard and the glutton shall come to poverty: and drowsiness shall clothe a man with rags."

Greedy Gain With Trouble

Proverbs 15:16 "Better is little with the fear of the LORD than great treasure and trouble therewith."

Proverbs 16:8 "Better is a little with righteousness than great revenues without right."

Not Gleaning

Leviticus 19:9-10 "[9]And when ye reap the harvest of your land, thou shalt not wholly reap the corners of thy field, neither shalt thou gather the gleanings of thy harvest. [10]And thou shalt not glean thy vineyard, neither shalt thou gather every grape of thy vineyard; thou shalt leave them for the poor and stranger: I am the LORD your God."

Deuteronomy 24:19-22 "[19]When thou cuttest down thine harvest in thy field, and hast forgot a sheaf in the field, thou shalt not go again to fetch it: it shall be for the stranger, for the fatherless, and for the widow: that the LORD thy God may bless thee in all the work of thine hands. [20]When thou beatest thine olive tree, thou shalt not go over the boughs again: it shall be for the stranger, for the fatherless, and for the widow. [21]When thou gatherest the grapes of thy vineyard, thou shalt not glean it afterward: it shall be for the stranger, for the fatherless, and for the widow. [22]And thou shalt remember that thou wast a bondman in the land of Egypt: therefore I command thee to do this thing."

The Greedy

Proverbs 1:10-19 "[10]My son, if sinners entice thee, consent thou not. [11]If they say, Come with us, let us lay wait for blood, let us lurk privily for the innocent without cause: [12]Let us swallow them up alive as the grave; and whole, as those that go down into the pit: [13]We shall find all precious substance, we shall fill our houses with spoil: [14]Cast in thy lot among us; let us all have one purse: [15]My son, walk not thou in the way with them; refrain thy foot from their path: [16]For their feet run to evil, and make haste to shed blood. [17]Surely in vain the net is spread in the sight of any bird. [18]And they lay wait for their own blood; they lurk privily for their own lives. [19]So are the ways of every one that is greedy of gain; which taketh away the life of the owners thereof."

Proverbs 15:27 "He that is greedy of gain troubleth his own house; but he that hateth gifts shall live."

Ecclesiastes 5:10 "He that loveth silver shall not be satisfied with silver; nor he that loveth abundance with increase: this is also vanity."

Isaiah 5:8-10 "[8]Woe unto them that join house to house, that lay field to field, till there be no place, that they may be placed alone in the midst of the earth! [9]In mine ears said the LORD of hosts, Of a truth many houses shall be desolate, even great and fair, without inhabitant. [10]Yea, ten acres of vineyard shall yield one bath, and the seed of an homer shall yield an ephah."

Isaiah 56:9-12 "[9]All ye beasts of the field, come to devour, yea, all ye beasts in the forest. [10]His watchmen are blind: they are all ignorant, they are all dumb dogs, they cannot bark; sleeping, lying down, loving to slumber. [11]Yea, they are greedy dogs which can never have enough, and they are shepherds that cannot understand: they all look to their own way, every one for his gain, from his quarter. [12]Come ye, say they, I will fetch wine, and we will fill ourselves with strong drink; and to morrow shall be as this day, and much more abundant."

Luke 12:13-21 "[13]And one of the company said unto him, Master, speak to my brother, that he divide the inheritance with me. [14]And he said unto him, Man, who made me a judge or a divider over you? [15]And he said unto them, Take heed, and beware of covetousness: for a man's life consisteth not in the abundance of the things which he possesseth. [16]And he spake a parable unto them, saying, The ground of a certain rich man brought forth plentifully: [17]And he thought within himself, saying, What shall I do, because I have no room where to bestow my fruits? [18]And he said, This will I do: I will pull down my barns, and build greater; and there will I bestow all my fruits and my goods. ¹⁹And I will say to my soul, Soul, thou hast much goods laid up for many years; take thine ease, eat, drink, and be merry. ²⁰But God said unto him, Thou fool, this night thy soul shall be required of thee: then whose shall those things be, which thou hast provided? ²¹So is he that layeth up treasure for himself, and is not rich toward God."

GRUDGE

Not Holding A Grudge Against Others
Leviticus 19:18 "Thou shalt not avenge, nor bear any grudge against the children of thy people, but thou shalt love thy neighbour as thyself: I am the LORD."

James 5:9 "Grudge not one against another, brethren, lest ye be condemned: behold, the judge standeth before the door."

GUIDANCE

Blind Guides
Isaiah 56:9-12 "⁹All ye beasts of the field, come to devour, yea, all ye beasts in the forest. ¹⁰His watchmen are blind: they are all ignorant, they are all dumb dogs, they cannot bark; sleeping, lying down, loving to slumber. ¹¹Yea, they are greedy dogs which can never have enough, and they are shepherds that cannot understand: they all look to their own way, every one for his gain, from his quarter. ¹²Come ye, say they, I will fetch wine, and we will fill ourselves with strong drink; and to morrow shall be as this day, and much more abundant."

Matthew 15:12-14 "¹²Then came his disciples, and said unto him, Knowest thou that the Pharisees were offended, after they heard this saying? ¹³But he answered and said, Every plant, which my heavenly Father hath not planted, shall be rooted up. ¹⁴Let them alone: they be blind leaders of the blind. And if the blind lead the blind, both shall fall into the ditch."

Matthew 23:16-26 "¹⁶Woe unto you, ye blind guides, which say, Whosoever shall swear by the temple, it is nothing; but whosoever shall swear by the gold of the temple, he is a debtor! ¹⁷Ye fools and blind: for whether is greater, the gold, or the temple that sanctifieth the gold? ¹⁸And, Whosoever shall swear by the altar, it is nothing; but whosoever sweareth by the gift that is upon it, he is guilty. ¹⁹Ye fools and blind: for whether is greater, the gift, or the altar that sanctifieth the gift? ²⁰Whoso therefore shall swear by the altar, sweareth by it, and by all things thereon. ²¹And whoso shall swear by the temple, sweareth by it, and by him that dwelleth therein. ²²And he that shall swear by heaven, sweareth by the throne of God, and by him that sitteth thereon. ²³Woe unto you, scribes and Pharisees, hypocrites! for ye pay tithe of mint and anise and cummin, and have omitted the weightier matters of the law, judgment, mercy, and faith: these ought ye to have done, and not to leave the other undone. ²⁴Ye blind guides, which strain at a gnat, and swallow a camel. ²⁵Woe unto you, scribes and Pharisees, hypocrites! for ye make clean the outside of the cup and of the platter, but within they are full of extortion and excess. ²⁶Thou blind Pharisee, cleanse first that which is within the cup and platter, that the outside of them may be clean also."

Luke 6:39 "And he spake a parable unto them, Can the blind lead the blind? shall they not both fall into the ditch?"

The Lord Guiding
Nehemiah 9:7-19 "⁷Thou art the LORD the God, who didst choose Abram, and broughtest him forth out of Ur of the Chaldees, and gavest him the name of Abraham; ⁸And foundest his heart faithful before thee, and madest a covenant with him to give the land of the Canaanites, the Hittites, the Amorites, and the Perizzites, and the Jebusites, and the Girgashites, to give it, I say, to his seed, and hast performed thy words; for thou art righteous: ⁹And didst see the affliction of our fathers in Egypt, and heardest their cry by the Red sea; ¹⁰And shewedst signs and wonders upon Pharoah, and on all his servants, and on all the people of his land: for thou knewest that they dealt proudly against them. So didst thou get thee a name, as it is this day. ¹¹And thou didst divide the sea before them, so that they went through the midst of the sea on the dry land; and their persecutors thou threwest into the deeps, as a stone into the mighty waters. ¹²Moreover thou leddest them in the day by a cloudy pillar; and in the night by a pillar of fire, to give them light in

the way wherein they should go. [13]Thou camest down also upon mount Sinai, and spakest with them from heaven, and gavest them right judgments, and true laws, good statutes and commandments: [14]And madest known unto them thy holy sabbath, and commandedst them precepts, statutes, and laws, by the hand of Moses thy servant: [15]And gavest them bread from heaven for their hunger, and broughtest forth water for them out of the rock for their thirst, and promisedst them that they should go in to possess the land which thou hadst sworn to give them. [16]But they and our fathers dealt proudly, and hardened their necks, and hearkened not to thy commandments, [17]And refused to obey, neither were mindful of thy wonders that thou didst among them; but hardened their necks, and in their rebellion appointed a captain to return to their bondage: but thou art a God ready to pardon, gracious and merciful, slow to anger, and of great kindness, and forsookest them not. [18]Yea, when they had made them a molten calf, and said, This is thy God that brought thee up out of Egypt, and had wrought great provocations; [19]Yet thou in thy manifold mercies forsookest them not in the wilderness: the pillar of the cloud departed not from them by day, to lead them in the way; neither the pillar of fire by night, to shew them light, and the way wherein they should go."

Psalm 16:8-11 "[8]I have set the LORD always before me: because he is at my right hand, I shall not be moved. [9]Therefore my heart is glad, and my glory rejoiceth: my flesh also shall rest in hope. [10]For thou wilt not leave my soul in hell; neither wilt thou suffer thine Holy One to see corruption. [11]Thou wilt shew me the path of life: in thy presence is fulness of joy; at thy right hand there are pleasures for evermore."

Psalm 23:1-4 "[1]The LORD is my shepherd; I shall not want. [2]He maketh me to lie down in green pastures: he leadeth me beside the still waters. [3]He restoreth my soul: he leadeth me in the paths of righteousness for his name's sake. [4]Yea, though I walk through the valley of the shadow of death, I will fear no evil: for thou art with me; thy rod and thy staff they comfort me."

Psalm 25:5 "Lead me in thy truth, and teach me: for thou art the God of my salvation; on thee do I wait all the day."

Psalm 31:1-3 "[1]In thee, O LORD, do I put my trust; let me never be ashamed: deliver me in thy righteousness. [2]Bow down thine ear to me; deliver me speedily: be thou my strong rock, for an house of defence to save me. [3]For thou art my rock and my fortress; therefore for thy name's sake lead me, and guide me."

Psalm 40:1-2 "[1]I waited patiently for the LORD; and he inclined unto me, and heard my cry. [2]He brought me up also out of an horrible pit, out of the miry clay, and set my feet upon a rock, and established my goings."

Psalm 48:14 "For this God is our God for ever and ever: he will be our guide even unto death."

Psalm 61:1-2 "[1]Hear my cry, O God; attend unto my prayer. [2]From the end of the earth will I cry unto thee, when my heart is overwhelmed: lead me to the rock that is higher than I."

Psalm 73:24-26 "[24]Thou shalt guide me with thy counsel, and afterward receive me to glory. [25]Whom have I in heaven but thee? and there is none upon earth that I desire beside thee. [26]My flesh and my heart faileth: but God is the strength of my heart, and my portion for ever."

Psalm 138:6-7 "[6]Though the LORD be high, yet hath he respect unto the lowly: but the proud he knoweth afar off. [7]Though I walk in the midst of trouble, thou wilt revive me: thou shalt stretch forth thine hand against the wrath of mine enemies, and thy right hand shall save me."

Psalm 139:4-10 "[4]For there is not a word in my tongue, but, lo, O LORD, thou knowest it altogether. [5]Thou hast beset me behind and before, and laid thine hand upon me. [6]Such knowledge is too wonderful for me; it is high, I cannot attain unto it. [7]Whither shall I go from thy spirit? or whither shall I flee from thy presence? [8]If I ascend up into heaven, thou art there: if I make my bed in hell, behold, thou art there. [9]If I take the wings of the morning, and dwell in the uttermost parts of the sea; [10]Even there shall thy hand lead me, and thy right hand shall hold me."

Psalm 143:7-10 "⁷Hear me speedily, O LORD: my spirit faileth: hide not thy face from me, lest I be like unto them that go down into the pit. ⁸Cause me to hear thy lovingkindness in the morning; for in thee do I trust: cause me to know the way wherein I should walk; for I lift up my soul unto thee. ⁹Deliver me, O LORD, from mine enemies: I flee unto thee to hide me. ¹⁰Teach me to do thy will; for thou art my God: thy spirit is good; lead me into the land of uprightness."

Proverbs 16:9 "A man's heart deviseth his way: but the LORD directeth his steps."

Isaiah 48:17 "Thus saith the LORD, thy Redeemer, the Holy One of Israel; I am the LORD thy God which teacheth thee to profit, which leadeth thee by the way that thou shouldest go."

Isaiah 58:11 "And the LORD shall guide thee continually, and satisfy thy soul in drought, and make fat thy bones: and thou shalt be like a watered garden, and like a spring of water, whose waters fail not."

What Guides The Upright
Proverbs 11:3 "The integrity of the upright shall guide them: but the perverseness of transgressors shall destroy them."

Proverbs 11:5 "The righteousness of the perfect shall direct his way: but the wicked shall fall by his own wickedness."

Who The Lord Shall Guide
Exodus 15:11-13 "¹¹Who is like unto thee, O LORD, among the gods? who is like thee, glorious in holiness, fearful in praises, doing wonders? ¹²Thou stretchedst out thy right hand, the earth swallowed them. ¹³Thou in thy mercy hast led forth the people which thou hast redeemed: thou

hast guided them in thy strength unto thy holy habitation."

Psalm 25:8-9 "⁸Good and upright is the LORD: therefore will he teach sinners in the way. ⁹The meek will he guide in judgment: and the meek will he teach his way."

Proverbs 3:5-6 "⁵Trust in the LORD with all thine heart; and lean not unto thine own understanding. ⁶In all thy ways acknowledge him, and he shall direct thy paths."

GUILE

Abstaining From Guile
Psalm 34:13 "Keep thy tongue from evil, and thy lips from speaking guile."

1 Peter 2:1 "Wherefore laying aside all malice, and all guile, and hypocrisies, and envies, and all evil speakings,"

Those That Have No Guile
Psalm 32:1-2 "¹Blessed is he whose transgression is forgiven, whose sin is covered. ²Blessed is the man unto whom the LORD imputeth not iniquity, and in whose spirit there is no guile."

GULLIBLENESS

Some Being Gullible
2 Corinthians 11:3-4 "³But I fear, lest by any means, as the serpent beguiled Eve through his subtilty, so your minds should be corrupted from the simplicity that is in Christ. ⁴For if he that cometh preacheth another Jesus, whom we have not preached, or if ye receive another spirit, which ye have not received, or another gospel, which ye have not accepted, ye might well bear with him."

H*h*

HAPPINESS/JOY

Being Glad In The Lord
Psalm 32:11 "Be glad in the LORD, and rejoice, ye righteous: and shout for joy, all ye that are upright in heart."

The Joy Of The Hypocrite
Job 20:1-5 "¹Then answered Zophar the Naamathite, and said, ²Therefore do my thoughts cause me to answer, and for this I make haste. ³I have heard the check of my reproach, and the spirit of my understanding causeth me to answer. ⁴Knowest thou not this of old, since man was placed upon earth, ⁵That the triumphing of the wicked is short, and the joy of the hypocrite but for a moment?"

The Joy Of The Lord
Nehemiah 8:10 "Then he said unto them, Go your way, eat the fat, and drink the sweet, and send portions unto them for whom nothing is prepared: for this day is holy unto our Lord: neither be ye sorry; for the joy of the LORD is your strength."

The Lord Bringing Joy
Psalm 30:10-11 "¹⁰Hear, O LORD, and have mercy upon me: LORD, be thou my helper. ¹¹Thou hast turned for me my mourning into dancing: thou hast put off my sackcloth, and girded me with gladness;"

Jeremiah 31:13-14 "¹³Then shall the virgin rejoice in the dance, both young men and old together: for I will turn their mourning into joy, and will comfort them, and make them rejoice from their sorrow. ¹⁴And I will satiate the soul of the priests with fatness, and my people shall be satisfied with my goodness, saith the LORD."

Isaiah 35:10 "And the ransomed of the LORD shall return, and come to Zion with songs and everlasting joy upon their heads: they shall obtain joy and gladness, and sorrow and sighing shall flee away."

Isaiah 51:11 "Therefore the redeemed of the LORD shall return, and come with singing unto Zion; and everlasting joy shall be upon their head: they shall obtain gladness and joy; and sorrow and mourning shall flee away."

Romans 15:13 "Now the God of hope fill you with all joy and peace in believing, that ye may abound in hope, through the power of the Holy Ghost."

Those That Are Of A Merry Heart
Proverbs 15:15 "All the days of the afflicted are evil: but he that is of a merry heart hath a continual feast."

Where Joy Is
1 Chronicles 16:26-27 "²⁶For all the gods of the people are idols: but the LORD made the heavens. ²⁷Glory and honour are in his presence; strength and gladness are in his place."

Psalm 16:8-11 "⁸I have set the LORD always before me: because he is at my right hand, I shall not be moved. ⁹Therefore my heart is glad, and my glory rejoiceth: my flesh also shall rest in hope. ¹⁰For thou wilt not leave my soul in hell; neither wilt thou suffer thine Holy One to see corruption. ¹¹Thou wilt shew me the path of life: in thy presence is fulness of joy; at thy right hand there are pleasures for evermore."

Who God Gives Joy To
Ecclesiastes 2:24-26 "²⁴There is nothing better for a man, than that he should eat and drink, and that he should make his soul enjoy good in his labour. This also I saw, that it was from the hand of God. ²⁵For who can eat, or who else can hasten hereunto, more than I? ²⁶For God giveth to a man that is good in his sight wisdom, and knowledge, and joy: but to the sinner he giveth travail, to gather and to heap up, that he may give to him that is good before God. This also is vanity and vexation of spirit."

Who Is Happy
Job 5:17 "Behold, happy is the man whom God correcteth: therefore despise not thou the chastening of the Almighty:"

Psalm 127:3-5 "³Lo, children are an heritage of the LORD: and the fruit of the womb is his reward. ⁴As arrows are in the hand of a mighty man; so are children of the youth. ⁵Happy is the man that hath his quiver full of them: they shall not be ashamed, but they shall speak with the enemies in the gate."

Psalm 128:1-2 "¹Blessed is every one that feareth the LORD; that walketh in his ways. ²For thou shalt eat the labour of thine hands: happy shalt thou be, and it shall be well with thee."

Psalm 144:9-15 "⁹I will sing a new song unto thee, O God: upon a psaltery and an instrument of ten strings will I sing praises unto thee. ¹⁰It is he that giveth salvation unto kings: who delivereth David his servant from the hurtful sword. ¹¹Rid me, and deliver me from the hand of strange children, whose mouth speaketh vanity, and their right hand is a right hand of falsehood: ¹²That our sons may be as plants grown up in their youth; that our daughters may be as corner stones, polished after the similitude of a palace: ¹³That our garners may be full, affording all manner of store: that our sheep may bring forth thousands and ten thousands in our streets: ¹⁴That our oxen may be strong to labour; that there be no breaking in, nor going out; that there be no complaining in our streets. ¹⁵Happy is that people, that is in such a case: yea, happy is that people, whose God is the LORD."

Psalm 146:5 "Happy is he that hath the God of Jacob for his help, whose hope is in the LORD his God:"

Proverbs 3:13 "Happy is the man that findeth wisdom, and the man that getteth understanding."

Proverbs 12:20 "Deceit is in the heart of them that imagine evil: but to the counsellers of peace is joy."

Proverbs 14:21 "He that despiseth his neighbour sinneth: but he that hath mercy on the poor, happy is he."

Proverbs 16:20 "He that handleth a matter wisely shall find good: and whoso trusteth in the LORD, happy is he."

Proverbs 23:24 "The father of the righteous shall greatly rejoice: and he that begetteth a wise child shall have joy of him."

Proverbs 28:14 "Happy is the man that feareth alway: but he that hardeneth his heart shall fall into mischief."

Proverbs 29:18 "Where there is no vision, the people perish: but he that keepeth the law, happy is he."

Isaiah 65:13-14 "¹³Therefore thus saith the Lord GOD, Behold, my servants shall eat, but ye shall be hungry: behold, my servants shall drink, but ye shall be thirsty: behold, my servants shall rejoice, but ye shall be ashamed: ¹⁴Behold, my servants shall sing for joy of heart, but ye shall cry for sorrow of heart, and shall howl for vexation of spirit."

John 13:13-17 "¹³Ye call me Master and Lord: and ye say well; for so I am. ¹⁴If I then, your Lord and Master, have washed your feet; ye also ought to wash one another's feet. ¹⁵For I have given you an example, that ye should do as I have done to you. ¹⁶Verily, verily, I say unto you, The servant is not greater than his lord; neither he that is sent greater than he that sent him. ¹⁷If ye know these things, happy are ye if ye do them."

Romans 14:22 "Hast thou faith? have it to thyself before God. Happy is he that condemneth not himself in that thing which he alloweth."

1 Peter 3:14 "But and if ye suffer for righteousness' sake, happy are ye: and be not afraid of their terror, neither be troubled;"

1 Peter 4:12-14 "¹²Beloved, think it not strange concerning the fiery trial which is to try you, as though some strange thing happened unto you: ¹³But rejoice, inasmuch as ye are partakers of Christ's sufferings; that, when his glory shall be revealed, ye may be glad also with exceeding joy. ¹⁴If ye be reproached for the name of Christ, happy are ye; for the spirit of glory and of God resteth upon you: on their part he is evil spoken of, but on your part he is glorified."

Why You Should Be Of Good Cheer
John 15:1-11 "¹I am the true vine, and my Father is the husbandman. ²Every branch in me that beareth not fruit he taketh away: and every branch that beareth fruit, he purgeth it, that it may bring forth more fruit. ³Now ye are clean through the word which I have spoken unto you. ⁴Abide in me, and I in you. As the branch cannot bear fruit of itself, except it abide in the vine; no more can ye, except ye abide in me. ⁵I am the vine, ye are the branches: He that abideth in me, and I in him, the same bringeth forth much fruit: for without me ye can do nothing. ⁶If a man abide not in me, he is cast forth as a branch, and is

withered; and men gather them, and cast them into the fire, and they are burned. [7]If ye abide in me, and my words abide in you, ye shall ask what ye will, and it shall be done unto you. [8]Herein is my Father glorified, that ye bear much fruit; so shall ye be my disciples. [9]As the Father hath loved me, so have I loved you: continue ye in my love. [10]If ye keep my commandments, ye shall abide in my love; even as I have kept my Father's commandments, and abide in his love. [11]These things have I spoken unto you, that my joy might remain in you, and that your joy might be full."

John 16:31-33 "[31]Jesus answered them, Do ye now believe? [32]Behold, the hour cometh, yea, is now come, that ye shall be scattered, every man to his own, and shall leave me alone: and yet I am not alone, because the Father is with me. [33]These things I have spoken unto you, that in me ye might have peace. In the world ye shall have tribulation: but be of good cheer; I have overcome the world."

HARVEST

The Day Of The Lord's Harvest

Joel 3:9-16 "[9]Proclaim ye this among the Gentiles; Prepare war, wake up the mighty men, let all the men of war draw near; let them come up: [10]Beat your plowshares into swords, and your pruning-hooks into spears: let the weak say, I am strong. [11]Assemble yourselves, and come, all ye heathen, and gather yourselves together round about: thither cause thy mighty ones to come down, O LORD. [12]Let the heathen be wakened, and come up to the valley of Jehoshaphat: for there will I sit to judge all the heathen round about. [13]Put ye in the sickle, for the harvest is ripe: come, get you down; for the press is full, the fats overflow; for their wickedness is great. [14]Multitudes, multitudes in the valley of decision: for the day of the LORD is near in the valley of decision. [15]The sun and the moon shall be darkened, and the stars shall withdraw their shining. [16]The LORD also shall roar out of Zion, and utter his voice from Jerusalem; and the heavens and the earth shall shake: but the LORD will be the hope of his people, and the strength of the children of Israel."

Matthew 3:10-12 "[10]And now also the axe is laid unto the root of the trees: therefore every tree which bringeth not forth good fruit is hewn down, and cast into the fire. [11]I indeed baptize you with water unto repentance: but he that cometh after me is mightier than I, whose shoes I am not worthy to bear: he shall baptize you with the Holy Ghost, and with fire: [12]Whose fan is in his hand, and he will throughly purge his floor, and gather his wheat into the garner; but he will burn up the chaff with unquenchable fire."

Matthew 13:24-43 "[24]Another parable put he forth unto them, saying, The kingdom of heaven is likened unto a man which sowed good seed in his field: [25]But while men slept, his enemy came and sowed tares among the wheat, and went his way. [26]But when the blade was sprung up, and brought forth fruit, then appeared the tares also. [27]So the servants of the householder came and said unto him, Sir, didst not thou sow good seed in thy field? from whence then hath it tares? [28]He said unto them, An enemy hath done this. The servants said unto him, Wilt thou then that we go and gather them up? [29]But he said, Nay; lest while ye gather up the tares, ye root up also the wheat with them. [30]Let both grow together until the harvest: and in the time of harvest I will say to the reapers, Gather ye together first the tares, and bind them in bundles to burn them: but gather the wheat into my barn. [31]Another parable put he forth unto them, saying, The kingdom of heaven is like to a grain of mustard seed, which a man took, and sowed in his field: [32]Which indeed is the least of all seeds: but when it is grown, it is the greatest among herbs, and becometh a tree, so that the birds of the air come and lodge in the branches thereof. [33]Another parable spake he unto them; The kingdom of heaven is like unto leaven, which a woman took, and hid in three measures of meal, till the whole was leavened. [34]All these things spake Jesus unto the multitude in parables; and without a parable spake he not unto them: [35]That it might be fulfilled which was spoken by the prophet, saying, I will open my mouth in parables; I will utter things which have been kept secret from the foundation of the world. [36]Then Jesus sent the multitude away, and went into the house: and his disciples came unto him, saying, Declare unto us the parable of the tares of the field. [37]He answered and said unto them, He that soweth the good seed is the Son of man; [38]The field is the world; the good seed are the children of the kingdom; but the tares are the children of the wicked one; ³⁹The enemy that sowed them is the devil; the harvest is the end of the world; and the reapers are the angels. ⁴⁰As therefore the tares are gathered and burned in the fire; so shall it be in the end of this world. ⁴¹The Son of man shall send forth his angels, and they shall gather out of his kingdom all things that offend, and them which do iniquity; ⁴²And shall cast them into a furnace of fire: there shall be wailing and gnashing of teeth. ⁴³Then shall the righteous shine forth as the sun in the kingdom of their Father. Who hath ears to hear, let him hear."

Matthew 13:47-50 "⁴⁷Again, the kingdom of heaven is like unto a net, that was cast into the sea, and gathered of every kind: ⁴⁸Which, when it was full, they drew to shore, and sat down, and gathered the good into vessels, but cast the bad away. ⁴⁹So shall it be at the end of the world: the angels shall come forth, and sever the wicked from among the just, ⁵⁰And shall cast them into the furnace of fire: there shall be wailing and gnashing of teeth."

Luke 3:15-17 "¹⁵And as the people were in expectation, and all men mused in their hearts of John, whether he were the Christ, or not; ¹⁶John answered, saying unto them all, I indeed baptize you with water; but one mightier than I cometh, the latchet of whose shoes I am not worthy to unloose: he shall baptize you with the Holy Ghost and with fire: ¹⁷Whose fan is in his hand, and he will throughly purge his floor, and will gather the wheat into his garner; but the chaff he will burn with fire unquenchable."

Revelation 14:15-20 "¹⁵And another angel came out of the temple, crying with a loud voice to him that sat on the cloud, Thrust in thy sickle, and reap: for the time is come for thee to reap; for the harvest of the earth is ripe. ¹⁶And he that sat on the cloud thrust in his sickle on the earth; and the earth was reaped. ¹⁷And another angel came out of the temple which is in heaven, he also having a sharp sickle. ¹⁸And another angel came out from the altar, which had power over fire; and cried with a loud cry to him that had the sharp sickle, saying, Thrust in thy sharp sickle, and gather the clusters of the vine of the earth; for her grapes are fully ripe. ¹⁹And the angel thrust in his sickle into the earth, and gathered the vine of the

earth, and cast it into the great winepress of the wrath of God. ²⁰And the winepress was trodden without the city, and blood came out of the winepress, even unto the horse bridles, by the space of a thousand and six hundred furlongs."

The Laborers Of The Harvest

Matthew 9:35-38 "³⁵And Jesus went about all the cities and villages, teaching in their synagogues, and preaching the gospel of the kingdom, and healing every sickness and every disease among the people. ³⁶But when he saw the multitudes, he was moved with compassion on them, because they fainted, and were scattered abroad, as sheep having no shepherd. ³⁷Then saith he unto his disciples, The harvest truly is plenteous, but the labourers are few; ³⁸Pray ye therefore the Lord of the harvest, that he will send forth labourers into his harvest."

Luke 10:1-12 "¹After these things the Lord appointed other seventy also, and sent them two and two before his face into every city and place, whither he himself would come. ²Therefore said he unto them, The harvest truly is great, but the labourers are few: pray ye therefore the Lord of the harvest, that he would send forth labourers into his harvest. ³Go your ways: behold, I send you forth as lambs among wolves. ⁴Carry neither purse, nor scrip, nor shoes: and salute no man by the way. ⁵And into whatsoever house ye enter, first say, Peace be to this house. ⁶And if the son of peace be there, your peace shall rest upon it: if not, it shall turn to you again. ⁷And in the same house remain, eating and drinking such things as they give: for the labourer is worthy of his hire. Go not from house to house. ⁸And into whatsoever city ye enter, and they receive you, eat such things as are set before you: ⁹And heal the sick that are therein, and say unto them, The kingdom of God is come nigh unto you. ¹⁰But into whatsoever city ye enter, and they receive you not, go your ways out into the streets of the same, and say, ¹¹Even the very dust of your city, which cleaveth on us, we do wipe off against you: notwithstanding be ye sure of this, that the kingdom of God is come nigh unto you. ¹²But I say unto you, that it shall be more tolerable in that day for Sodom, than for that city."

Those That Sleep In Harvest

Proverbs 10:5 "He that gathereth in summer is a wise son: but he that sleepeth in harvest is a son that causeth shame."

When The Earth Will Yield Her Increase
Psalm 67:5-7 "⁵Let the people praise thee, O God; let all the people praise thee. ⁶Then shall the earth yield her increase; and God, even our own God, shall bless us. ⁷God shall bless us; and all the ends of the earth shall fear him."

Who Shall Beg In Harvest
Proverbs 20:4 "The sluggard will not plow by reason of the cold; therefore shall he beg in harvest, and have nothing."

HASTE

Not Being Hasty
Proverbs 25:8-10 "⁸Go not forth hastily to strive, lest thou know not what to do in the end thereof, when thy neighbour hath put thee to shame. ⁹Debate thy cause with thy neighbour himself; and discover not a secret to another: ¹⁰Lest he that heareth it put thee to shame, and thine infamy turn not away."

Ecclesiastes 5:2 "Be not rash with thy mouth, and let not thine heart be hasty to utter any thing before God: for God is in heaven, and thou upon earth: therefore let thy words be few."

Ecclesiastes 7:9 "Be not hasty in thy spirit to be angry: for anger resteth in the bosom of fools."

1 Timothy 5:22 "Lay hands suddenly on no man, neither be partaker of other men's sins: keep thyself pure."

Those That Are Hasty
Proverbs 14:29 "He that is slow to wrath is of great understanding: but he that is hasty of spirit exalteth folly."

Proverbs 18:13 "He that answereth a matter before he heareth it, it is folly and shame unto him."

Proverbs 19:2 "Also, that the soul be without knowledge, it is not good; and he that hasteth with his feet sinneth."

Proverbs 21:5 "The thoughts of the diligent tend only to plenteousness; but of every one that is hasty only to want."

Proverbs 28:20 "A faithful man shall abound with blessings: but he that maketh haste to be rich shall not be innocent."

Proverbs 28:22 "He that hasteth to be rich hath an evil eye, and considereth not that poverty shall come upon him."

Proverbs 29:20 "Seest thou a man that is hasty in his words? there is more hope of a fool than of him."

HATE

The Place Where There Is Hatred
Proverbs 15:17 "Better is a dinner of herbs where love is, than a stalled ox and hatred therewith."

The Reward For Hating Knowledge
Proverbs 1:20-32 "²⁰Wisdom crieth without; she uttereth her voice in the streets: ²¹She crieth in the chief place of concourse, in the openings of the gates: in the city she uttereth her words, saying, ²²How long, ye simple ones, will ye love simplicity? and the scorners delight in their scorning, and fools hate knowledge? ²³Turn you at my reproof: behold, I will pour out my spirit unto you, I will make known my words unto you. ²⁴Because I have called, and ye refused; I have stretched out my hand, and no man regarded; ²⁵But ye have set at nought all my counsel, and would none of my reproof: ²⁶I also will laugh at your calamity; I will mock when your fear cometh; ²⁷When your fear cometh as desolation, and your destruction cometh as a whirlwind; when distress and anguish cometh upon you. ²⁸Then shall they call upon me, but I will not answer; they shall seek me early, but they shall not find me: ²⁹For that they hated knowledge, and did not choose the fear of the LORD: ³⁰They would none of my counsel: they despised all my reproof. ³¹Therefore shall they eat of the fruit of their own way, and be filled with their own devices. ³²For the turning away of the simple shall slay them, and the prosperity of fools shall destroy them."

The World Hating Jesus Christ
John 7:6-8 "⁶Then Jesus said unto them, My time is not yet come: but your time is alway ready. ⁷The world cannot hate you; but me it hateth, because I testify of it, that the works thereof are evil. ⁸Go ye up unto this feast: I go not up yet unto this feast; for my time is not yet full come."

John 15:1-25 "¹I am the true vine, and my Father is the husbandman. ²Every branch in me that beareth not fruit he taketh away: and every branch that beareth fruit, he purgeth it, that it may bring forth more fruit. ³Now ye are clean through the word which I have spoken unto you. ⁴Abide in me, and I in you. As the branch cannot bear fruit of itself, except it abide in the vine; no more can ye, except ye abide in me. ⁵I am the vine, ye are the branches: He that abideth in me, and I in him, the same bringeth forth much fruit: for without me ye can do nothing. ⁶If a man abide not in me, he is cast forth as a branch, and is withered; and men gather them, and cast them into the fire, and they are burned. ⁷If ye abide in me, and my words abide in you, ye shall ask what ye will, and it shall be done unto you. ⁸Herein is my Father glorified, that ye bear much fruit; so shall ye be my disciples. ⁹As the Father hath loved me, so have I loved you: continue ye in my love. ¹⁰If ye keep my commandments, ye shall abide in my love; even as I have kept my Father's commandments, and abide in his love. ¹¹These things have I spoken unto you, that my joy might remain in you, and that your joy might be full. ¹²This is my commandment, That ye love one another, as I have loved you. ¹³Greater love hath no man than this, that a man lay down his life for his friends. ¹⁴Ye are my friends, if ye do whatsoever I command you. ¹⁵Henceforth I call you not servants; for the servant knoweth not what his lord doeth: but I have called you friends; for all things that I have heard of my Father I have made known unto you. ¹⁶Ye have not chosen me, but I have chosen you, and ordained you, that ye should go and bring forth fruit, and that your fruit should remain: that whatsoever ye shall ask of the Father in my name, he may give it you. ¹⁷These things I command you, that ye love one another. ¹⁸If the world hate you, ye know that it hated me before it hated you. ¹⁹If ye were of the world, the world would love his own: but because ye are not of the world, but I have chosen you out of the world, therefore the world hateth you. ²⁰Remember the word that I said unto you, The servant is not greater than his lord. If they have persecuted me, they will also persecute you; if they have kept my saying, they will keep yours also. ²¹But all these things will they do unto you for my name's sake, because they know not him that sent me. ²²If I had not come and spoken unto them, they had not had sin: but now they have no cloke for their sin. ²³He that hateth me hateth my Father also. ²⁴If I had not done among them the works which none other man did, they had not had sin: but now have they both seen and hated both me and my Father. ²⁵But this cometh to pass, that the word might be fulfilled that is written in their law, They hated me without a cause."

Those That Do Not Hate Their Life In This World

Matthew 10:32-37 "³²Whosoever therefore shall confess me before men, him will I confess also before my Father which is in heaven. ³³But whosoever shall deny me before men, him will I also deny before my Father which is in heaven. ³⁴Think not that I am come to send peace on earth: I came not to send peace, but a sword. ³⁵For I am come to set a man at variance against his father, and the daughter against her mother, and the daughter in law against her mother in law. ³⁶And a man's foes shall be they of his own household. ³⁷He that loveth father or mother more than me is not worthy of me: and he that loveth son or daughter more than me is not worthy of me."

Luke 14:25-33 "²⁵And there went great multitudes with him: and he turned, and said unto them, ²⁶If any man come to me, and hate not his father, and mother, and wife, and children, and brethren, and sisters, yea, and his own life also, he cannot be my disciple. ²⁷And whosoever doth not bear his cross, and come after me, cannot be my disciple. ²⁸For which of you, intending to build a tower, sitteth not down first, and counteth the cost, whether he have sufficient to finish it? ²⁹Lest haply, after he hath laid the foundation, and is not able to finish it, all that behold it begin to mock him, ³⁰Saying, This man began to build, and was not able to finish. ³¹Or what king, going to make war against another king, sitteth not down first, and consulteth whether he be able with ten thousand to meet him that cometh against him with twenty thousand? ³²Or else, while the other is yet a great way off, he sendeth an ambassage, and desireth conditions of peace. ³³So likewise, whosoever he be of you that forsaketh not all that he hath, he cannot be my disciple."

Those That Hate

Proverbs 26:24 "He that hateth dissembleth with his lips, and layeth up deceit within him;"

Those That Hate Israel

Deuteronomy 7:6-15 "⁶For thou art an holy people unto the LORD thy God: the LORD thy God hath chosen thee to be a special people unto himself, above all people that are upon the face of the earth. ⁷The LORD did not set his love upon you, nor choose you, because ye were more in number than any people; for ye were the fewest of all people: ⁸But because the LORD loved you, and because he would keep the oath which he had sworn unto your fathers, hath the LORD brought you out with a mighty hand, and redeemed you out of the house of bondmen, from the hand of Pharaoh king of Egypt. ⁹Know therefore that the LORD thy God, he is God, the faithful God, which keepeth covenant and mercy with them that love him and keep his commandments to a thousand generations; ¹⁰And repayeth them that hate him to their face, to destroy them: he will not be slack to him that hateth him, he will repay him to his face. ¹¹Thou shalt therefore keep the commandments, and the statutes, and the judgments, which I command thee this day, to do them. ¹²Wherefore it shall come to pass, if ye hearken to these judgments, and keep, and do them, that the LORD thy God shall keep unto thee the covenant and the mercy which he sware unto thy fathers: ¹³And he will love thee, and bless thee, and multiply thee: he will also bless the fruit of thy womb, and the fruit of thy land, thy corn, and thy wine, and thine oil, the increase of thy kine, and the flocks of thy sheep, in the land which he sware unto thy fathers to give thee. ¹⁴Thou shalt be blessed above all people: there shall not be male or female barren among you, or among your cattle. ¹⁵And the LORD will take away from thee all sickness, and will put none of the evil diseases of Egypt, which thou knowest, upon thee; but will lay them upon all them that hate thee."

Deuteronomy 30:1-7 "¹And it shall come to pass, when all these things are come upon thee, the blessing and the curse, which I have set before thee, and thou shalt call them to mind among all the nations, whither the LORD thy God hath driven thee, ²And shalt return unto the LORD thy God, and shalt obey his voice according to all that I command thee this day, thou and thy children, with all thine heart, and with all thy soul; ³That then the LORD thy God will turn thy captivity, and have compassion upon thee, and will return and gather thee from all the nations, whither the LORD thy God hath scattered thee. ⁴If any of thine be driven out unto the outmost parts of heaven, from thence will the LORD thy God gather thee, and from thence will he fetch thee: ⁵And the LORD thy God will bring thee into the land which thy fathers possessed, and thou shalt possess it; and he will do thee good, and multiply thee above thy fathers. ⁶And the LORD thy God will circumcise thine heart, and the heart of thy seed, to love the LORD thy God with all thine heart, and with all thy soul, that thou mayest live. ⁷And the LORD thy God will put all these curses upon thine enemies, and on them that hate thee, which persecuted thee."

Ezekiel 35:1-15 "¹Moreover the word of the LORD came unto me, saying, ²Son of man, set thy face against mount Seir, and prophesy against it, ³And say unto it, Thus saith the Lord GOD; Behold, O mount Seir, I am against thee, and I will stretch out mine hand against thee, and I will make thee most desolate. ⁴I will lay thy cities waste, and thou shalt be desolate, and thou shalt know that I am the LORD. ⁵Because thou hast had a perpetual hatred, and hast shed the blood of the children of Israel by the force of the sword in the time of their calamity, in the time that their iniquity had an end: ⁶Therefore, as I live, saith the Lord GOD, I will prepare thee unto blood, and blood shall pursue thee: sith thou hast not hated blood, even blood shall pursue thee. ⁷Thus will I make mount Seir most desolate, and cut off from it him that passeth out and him that returneth. ⁸And I will fill his mountains with his slain men: in thy hills, and in thy valleys, and in all thy rivers, shall they fall that are slain with the sword. ⁹I will make thee perpetual desolations, and thy cities shall not return: and ye shall know that I am the LORD. ¹⁰Because thou hast said, These two nations and these two countries shall be mine, and we will possess it; whereas the LORD was there: ¹¹Therefore, as I live, saith the Lord GOD, I will even do according to thine anger, and according to thine envy which thou hast used out of thy hatred against them; and I will make myself known among them, when I have judged thee. ¹²And thou shalt know that I am the LORD, and that I have heard all thy blasphemies which thou hast spoken against the mountains of Israel, saying, They are laid desolate, they are given us to consume. ¹³Thus with your mouth ye have boasted against me, and have multiplied your words against me: I have heard them. ¹⁴Thus saith the Lord GOD; When the whole earth rejoiceth, I will make thee desolate. ¹⁵As thou didst rejoice at the inheritance of the house of Israel, because it was desolate, so will I do unto thee: thou shalt be desolate, O mount Seir, and all Idumea, even all of it: and they shall know that I am the LORD."

Those That Hate Reproof

Proverbs 12:1 "Whoso loveth instruction loveth knowledge: but he that hateth reproof is brutish."

Proverbs 15:10 "Correction is grievous unto him that forsaketh the way: and he that hateth reproof shall die."

Those That Hate The Lord

Exodus 20:2-5 "²I am the LORD thy God, which have brought thee out of the land of Egypt, out of the house of bondage. ³Thou shalt have no other gods before me. ⁴Thou shalt not make unto thee any graven image, or any likeness of any thing that is in heaven above, or that is in the earth beneath, or that is in the water under the earth: ⁵Thou shalt not bow down thyself to them, nor serve them: for I the LORD thy God am a jealous God, visiting the iniquity of the fathers upon the children unto the third and fourth generation of them that hate me;"

Deuteronomy 5:6-9 "⁶I am the LORD thy God, which brought thee out of the land of Egypt, from the house of bondage. ⁷Thou shalt have none other gods before me. ⁸Thou shalt not make thee any graven image, or any likeness of any thing that is in heaven above, or that is in the earth beneath, or that is in the waters beneath the earth: ⁹Thou shalt not bow down thyself unto them, nor serve them: for I the LORD thy God am a jealous God, visiting the iniquity of the fathers upon the children unto the third and fourth generation of them that hate me,"

Deuteronomy 7:9-10 "⁹Know therefore that the LORD thy God, he is God, the faithful God, which keepeth covenant and mercy with them that love him and keep his commandments to a thousand generations; ¹⁰And repayeth them that hate him to their face, to destroy them: he will not be slack to him that hateth him, he will repay him to his face."

Deuteronomy 32:36-41 "³⁶For the LORD shall judge his people, and repent himself for his servants, when he seeth that their power is gone, and there is none shut up, or left. ³⁷And he shall say, Where are their gods, their rock in whom they trusted, ³⁸Which did eat the fat of their sacrifices, and drank the wine of their drink offerings? let them rise up and help you, and be your protection. ³⁹See now that I, even I, am he, and there is no god with me: I kill, and I make alive; I wound, and I heal: neither is there any that can deliver out of my hand. ⁴⁰For I lift up my hand to heaven, and say, I live for ever. ⁴¹If I whet my glittering sword, and mine hand take hold on judgment; I will render vengeance to mine enemies, and will reward them that hate me."

Job 8:20-22 "²⁰Behold, God will not cast away a perfect man, neither will he help the evil doers: ²¹Till he fill thy mouth with laughing, and thy lips with rejoicing. ²²They that hate thee shall be clothed with shame; and the dwelling place of the wicked shall come to nought."

Psalm 21:7-12 "⁷For the king trusteth in the LORD, and through the mercy of the most High he shall not be moved. ⁸Thine hand shall find out all thine enemies: thy right hand shall find out those that hate thee. ⁹Thou shalt make them as a fiery oven in the time of thine anger: the LORD shall swallow them up in his wrath, and the fire shall devour them. ¹⁰Their fruit shalt thou destroy from the earth, and their seed from among the children of men. ¹¹For they intended evil against thee: they imagined a mischievous device, which they are not able to perform. ¹²Therefore shalt thou make them turn their back, when thou shalt make ready thine arrows upon thy strings against the face of them."

Psalm 83:1-17 "¹Keep not thou silence, O God: hold not thy peace, and be not still, O God. ²For, lo, thine enemies make a tumult: and they that hate thee have lifted up the head. ³They have taken crafty counsel against thy people, and consulted against thy hidden ones. ⁴They have said,

Come, and let us cut them off from being a nation; that the name of Israel may be no more in remembrance. ⁵For they have consulted together with one consent: they are confederate against thee: ⁶The tabernacles of Edom, and the Ishmaelites; of Moab, and the Hagarenes; ⁷Gebal, and Ammon, and Amalek; the Philistines with the inhabitants of Tyre; ⁸Assur also is joined with them: they have holpen the children of Lot. Selah. ⁹Do unto them as unto the Midianites; as to Sisera, as to Jabin, at the brook of Kison: ¹⁰Which perished at Endor: they became as dung for the earth. ¹¹Make their nobles like Oreb, and like Zeeb: yea, all their princes as Zebah, and as Zalmunna: ¹²Who said, Let us take to ourselves the houses of God in possession. ¹³O my God, make them like a wheel; as the stubble before the wind. ¹⁴As the fire burneth a wood, and as the flame setteth the mountains on fire; ¹⁵So persecute them with thy tempest, and make them afraid with thy storm. ¹⁶Fill their faces with shame; that they may seek thy name, O LORD. ¹⁷Let them be confounded and troubled for ever; yea, let them be put to shame, and perish:"

Luke 10:1-16 "¹After these things the Lord appointed other seventy also, and sent them two and two before his face into every city and place, whither he himself would come. ²Therefore said he unto them, The harvest truly is great, but the labourers are few: pray ye therefore the Lord of the harvest, that he would send forth labourers into his harvest. ³Go your ways: behold, I send you forth as lambs among wolves. ⁴Carry neither purse, nor scrip, nor shoes: and salute no man by the way. ⁵And into whatsoever house ye enter, first say, Peace be to this house. ⁶And if the son of peace be there, your peace shall rest upon it: if not, it shall turn to you again. ⁷And in the same house remain, eating and drinking such things as they give: for the labourer is worthy of his hire. Go not from house to house. ⁸And into whatsoever city ye enter, and they receive you, eat such things as are set before you: ⁹And heal the sick that are therein, and say unto them, The kingdom of God is come nigh unto you. ¹⁰But into whatsoever city ye enter, and they receive you not, go your ways out into the streets of the same, and say, ¹¹Even the very dust of your city, which cleaveth on us, we do wipe off against you: notwithstanding be ye sure of this, that the kingdom of God is come nigh unto

you. ¹²But I say unto you, that it shall be more tolerable in that day for Sodom, than for that city. ¹³Woe unto thee, Chorazin! woe unto thee, Bethsaida! for if the mighty works had been done in Tyre and Sidon, which have been done in you, they had a great while ago repented, sitting in sackcloth and ashes. ¹⁴But it shall be more tolerable for Tyre and Sidon at the judgment, than for you. ¹⁵And thou, Capernaum, which art exalted to heaven, shalt be thrust down to hell. ¹⁶He that heareth you heareth me; and he that despiseth you despiseth me; and he that despiseth me despiseth him that sent me."

John 15:1-25 "¹I am the true vine, and my Father is the husbandman. ²Every branch in me that beareth not fruit he taketh away: and every branch that beareth fruit, he purgeth it, that it may bring forth more fruit. ³Now ye are clean through the word which I have spoken unto you. ⁴Abide in me, and I in you. As the branch cannot bear fruit of itself, except it abide in the vine; no more can ye, except ye abide in me. ⁵I am the vine, ye are the branches: He that abideth in me, and I in him, the same bringeth forth much fruit: for without me ye can do nothing. ⁶If a man abide not in me, he is cast forth as a branch, and is withered; and men gather them, and cast them into the fire, and they are burned. ⁷If ye abide in me, and my words abide in you, ye shall ask what ye will, and it shall be done unto you. ⁸Herein is my Father glorified, that ye bear much fruit; so shall ye be my disciples. ⁹As the Father hath loved me, so have I loved you: continue ye in my love. ¹⁰If ye keep my commandments, ye shall abide in my love; even as I have kept my Father's commandments, and abide in his love. ¹¹These things have I spoken unto you, that my joy might remain in you, and that your joy might be full. ¹²This is my commandment, That ye love one another, as I have loved you. ¹³Greater love hath no man than this, that a man lay down his life for his friends. ¹⁴Ye are my friends, if ye do whatsoever I command you. ¹⁵Henceforth I call you not servants; for the servant knoweth not what his lord doeth: but I have called you friends; for all things that I have heard of my Father I have made known unto you. ¹⁶Ye have not chosen me, but I have chosen you, and ordained you, that ye should go and bring forth fruit, and that your fruit should remain: that whatsoever ye shall ask of the Father in my name, he may give it you. [17]These things I command you, that ye love one another. [18]If the world hate you, ye know that it hated me before it hated you. [19]If ye were of the world, the world would love his own: but because ye are not of the world, but I have chosen you out of the world, therefore the world hateth you. [20]Remember the word that I said unto you, The servant is not greater than his lord. If they have persecuted me, they will also persecute you; if they have kept my saying, they will keep yours also. [21]But all these things will they do unto you for my name's sake, because they know not him that sent me. [22]If I had not come and spoken unto them, they had not had sin: but now they have no cloke for their sin. [23]He that hateth me hateth my Father also. [24]If I had not done among them the works which none other man did, they had not had sin: but now have they both seen and hated both me and my Father. [25]But this cometh to pass, that the word might be fulfilled that is written in their law, They hated me without a cause."

Those That Hate The Righteous
Psalm 34:21 "Evil shall slay the wicked: and they that hate the righteous shall be desolate."

Those That Hate Their Brother
1 John 2:9-11 "[9]He that saith he is in the light, and hateth his brother, is in darkness even until now. [10]He that loveth his brother abideth in the light, and there is none occasion of stumbling in him. [11]But he that hateth his brother is in darkness, and walketh in darkness, and knoweth not whither he goeth, because that darkness hath blinded his eyes."

1 John 3:14-15 "[14]We know that we have passed from death unto life, because we love the brethren. He that loveth not his brother abideth in death. [15]Whosoever hateth his brother is a murderer: and ye know that no murderer hath eternal life abiding in him."

1 John 4:20 "If a man say, I love God, and hateth his brother, he is a liar: for he that loveth not his brother whom he hath seen, how can he love God whom he hath not seen?"

Those That Hate Their Life In This World
John 12:25 "He that loveth his life shall lose it; and he that hateth his life in this world shall keep it unto life eternal."

Those That Hate Wisdom
Proverbs 8:32-36 "[32]Now therefore hearken unto me, O ye children: for blessed are they that keep my ways. [33]Hear instruction, and be wise, and refuse it not. [34]Blessed is the man that heareth me, watching daily at my gates, waiting at the posts of my doors. [35]For whoso findeth me findeth life, and shall obtain favour of the LORD. [36]But he that sinneth against me wrongeth his own soul: all they that hate me love death."

What Fools Hate
Proverbs 1:7 "The fear of the LORD is the beginning of knowledge: but fools despise wisdom and instruction."

Proverbs 1:22 "How long, ye simple ones, will ye love simplicity? and the scorners delight in their scorning, and fools hate knowledge?"

Proverbs 13:19 "The desire accomplished is sweet to the soul: but it is abomination to fools to depart from evil."

What Hatred Does
Proverbs 10:12 "Hatred stirreth up strifes: but love covereth all sins."

What Is To Hate Evil
Proverbs 8:13 "The fear of the LORD is to hate evil: pride, and arrogancy, and the evil way, and the froward mouth, do I hate."

What The Lord Hates
Deuteronomy 7:25 "The graven images of their gods shall ye burn with fire: thou shalt not desire the silver or gold that is on them, nor take it unto thee, lest thou be snared therein: for it is an abomination to the LORD thy God."

Deuteronomy 12:31 "Thou shalt not do so unto the LORD thy God: for every abomination to the LORD, which he hateth, have they done unto their gods; for even their sons and their daughters they have burnt in the fire to their gods."

Deuteronomy 16:22 "Neither shalt thou set thee up any image; which the LORD thy God hateth."

Deuteronomy 18:9-12 "[9]When thou art come into the land which the LORD thy God giveth thee, thou shalt not learn to do after the abominations of those nations. [10]There shall not be found among you any one that maketh his son or his daughter to pass through the fire, or that useth divination, or an observer of times, or an enchanter, or a witch, [11]Or a charmer, or a consulter with familiar spirits, or a wizard, or a necromancer. [12]For all that do these things are an abomination unto the LORD: and because of these abominations the LORD thy God doth drive them out from before thee."

Deuteronomy 22:5 "The woman shall not wear that which pertaineth unto a man, neither shall a man put on a woman's garment: for all that do so are abomination unto the LORD thy God."

Deuteronomy 23:17-18 "[17]There shall be no whore of the daughters of Israel, nor a sodomite of the sons of Israel. [18]Thou shalt not bring the hire of a whore, or the price of a dog, into the house of the LORD thy God for any vow: for even both these are abomination unto the LORD thy God."

Deuteronomy 24:1-4 "[1]When a man hath taken a wife, and married her, and it come to pass that she find no favour in his eyes, because he hath found some uncleanness in her: then let him write her a bill of divorcement, and give it in her hand, and send her out of his house. [2]And when she is departed out of his house, she may go and be another man's wife. [3]And if the latter husband hate her, and write her a bill of divorcement, and giveth it in her hand, and sendeth her out of his house; or if the latter husband die, which took her to be his wife; [4]Her former husband, which sent her away, may not take her again to be his wife, after that she is defiled; for that is abomination before the LORD: and thou shalt not cause the land to sin, which the LORD thy God giveth thee for an inheritance."

Deuteronomy 27:15 "Cursed be the man that maketh any graven or molten image, an abomination unto the LORD, the work of the hands of the craftsman, and putteth it in a secret place. And all the people shall answer and say, Amen."

Psalm 5:4-5 "[4]For thou art not a God that hath pleasure in wickedness: neither shall evil dwell with thee. [5]The foolish shall not stand in thy sight: thou hatest all workers of iniquity."

Psalm 11:5 "The LORD trieth the righteous: but the wicked and him that loveth violence his soul hateth."

Proverbs 3:32 "For the froward is abomination to the LORD: but his secret is with the righteous."

Proverbs 6:16-19 "[16]These six things doth the LORD hate: yea, seven are an abomination unto him: [17]A proud look, a lying tongue, and hands that shed innocent blood, [18]An heart that deviseth wicked imaginations, feet that be swift in running to mischief, [19]A false witness that speaketh lies, and he that soweth discord among brethren."

Proverbs 11:1 "A false balance is abomination to the LORD: but a just weight is his delight."

Proverbs 11:20 "They that are of a froward heart are abomination to the LORD: but such as are upright in their way are his delight."

Proverbs 12:22 "Lying lips are abomination to the LORD: but they that deal truly are his delight."

Proverbs 15:8-9 "[8]The sacrifice of the wicked is an abomination to the LORD: but the prayer of the upright is his delight. [9]The way of the wicked is an abomination unto the LORD: but he loveth him that followeth after righteousness."

Proverbs 15:26 "The thoughts of the wicked are an abomination to the LORD: but the words of the pure are pleasant words."

Proverbs 16:5 "Every one that is proud in heart is an abomination to the LORD: though hand join in hand, he shall not be unpunished."

Proverbs 17:15 "He that justifieth the wicked, and he that condemneth the just, even they both are abomination to the LORD."

Proverbs 20:10 "Divers weights, and divers measures, both of them are alike abomination to the LORD."

Proverbs 20:23 "Divers weights are an abomination unto the LORD; and a false balance is not good."

Isaiah 1:10-14 "[10]Hear the word of the LORD, ye rulers of Sodom; give ear unto the law of our God, ye people of Gomorrah. [11]To what purpose is the multitude of your sacrifices unto me? saith the LORD: I am full of the burnt offerings of rams, and the fat of fed beasts; and I delight not in the blood of bullocks, or of lambs, or of he goats. [12]When ye come to appear before me, who hath required this at your hand, to tread my courts? [13]Bring no more vain oblations; incense is an abomination unto me; the new moons and sabbaths, the calling of assemblies, I cannot away with; it is iniquity, even the solemn meeting. [14]Your new moons and your appointed feasts my soul hateth: they are a trouble unto me; I am weary to bear them."

Isaiah 61:8 "For I the LORD love judgment, I hate robbery for burnt offering; and I will direct their work in truth, and I will make an everlasting covenant with them."

Zechariah 8:17 "And let none of you imagine evil in your hearts against his neighbour; and love no false oath: for all these are things that I hate, saith the LORD."

Luke 16:15 "And he said unto them, Ye are they which justify yourselves before men; but God knoweth your hearts: for that which is highly esteemed among men is abomination in the sight of God."

Revelation 2:1-6 "[1]Unto the angel of the church of Ephesus write; These things saith he that holdeth the seven stars in his right hand, who walketh in the midst of the seven golden candlesticks; [2]I know thy works, and thy labour, and thy patience, and how thou canst not bear them which are evil: and thou hast tried them which say they are apostles, and are not, and hast found them liars: [3]And hast borne, and hast patience, and for my name's sake hast laboured, and hast not fainted. [4]Nevertheless I have somewhat against thee, because thou hast left thy first love. [5]Remember therefore from whence thou art fallen, and repent, and do the first works; or else I will come unto thee quickly, and will remove thy candlestick out of his place, except thou repent. [6]But this thou hast, that thou hatest the deeds of the Nicolaitans, which I also hate."

Revelation 2:12-15 "[12]And to the angel of the church in Pergamos write; These things saith he which hath the sharp sword with two edges; [13]I know thy works, and where thou dwellest, even where Satan's seat is: and thou holdest fast my name, and hast not denied my faith, even in those days wherein Antipas was my faithful martyr, who was slain among you, where Satan dwelleth. [14]But I have a few things against thee, because thou hast there them that hold the doctrine of Balaam, who taught Balac to cast a stumblingblock before the children of Israel, to eat things sacrificed unto idols, and to commit fornication. [15]So hast thou also them that hold the doctrine of the Nicolaitans, which thing I hate."

What To Hate
Amos 5:15 "Hate the evil, and love the good, and establish judgment in the gate: it may be that the LORD God of hosts will be gracious unto the remnant of Joseph."

Romans 12:9 "Let love be without dissimulation. Abhor that which is evil; cleave to that which is good."

Who Hates Evil
Psalm 97:10 "Ye that love the LORD, hate evil: he preserveth the souls of his saints; he delivereth them out of the hand of the wicked."

Who Hates The Light
John 3:20 "For every one that doeth evil hateth the light, neither cometh to the light, lest his deeds should be reproved."

Who Hates The Upright
Proverbs 29:10 "The bloodthirsty hate the upright: but the just seek his soul."

Who Not To Hate
Leviticus 19:17 "Thou shalt not hate thy brother in thine heart: thou shalt in any wise rebuke thy neighbour, and not suffer sin upon him."

Who The World Hates
Matthew 10:16-22 "[16]Behold, I send you forth as sheep in the midst of wolves: be ye therefore wise as serpents, and harmless as doves. [17]But beware of men: for they will deliver you up to the councils, and they will scourge you in their synagogues; [18]And ye shall be brought before governors and kings for my sake, for a testimony against them and the Gentiles. [19]But when they deliver you up, take no thought how or what ye shall speak: for it shall be given you in that same hour what ye shall speak. [20]For it is not ye that speak, but the Spirit of your Father which speaketh in you. [21]And the brother shall deliver up the brother to death, and the father the child: and the children shall rise up against their parents, and cause them to be put to death. [22]And ye shall be hated of all men for my name's sake: but he that endureth to the end shall be saved."

Matthew 24:1-9 "[1]And Jesus went out, and departed from the temple: and his disciples came to him for to shew him the buildings of the temple. [2]And Jesus said unto them, See ye not all these things? verily I say unto you, There shall not be left here one stone upon another, that shall not be thrown down. ³And as he sat upon the mount of Olives, the disciples came unto him privately, saying, Tell us, when shall these things be? and what shall be the sign of thy coming, and of the end of the world? ⁴And Jesus answered and said unto them, Take heed that no man deceive you. ⁵For many shall come in my name, saying, I am Christ; and shall deceive many. ⁶And ye shall hear of wars and rumours of wars: see that ye be not troubled: for all these things must come to pass, but the end is not yet. ⁷For nation shall rise against nation, and kingdom against kingdom: and there shall be famines, and pestilences, and earthquakes, in divers places. ⁸All these are the beginning of sorrows. ⁹Then shall they deliver you up to be afflicted, and shall kill you: and ye shall be hated of all nations for my name's sake."

Mark 13:1-13 "¹And as he went out of the temple, one of his disciples saith unto him, Master, see what manner of stones and what buildings are here! ²And Jesus answering said unto him, Seest thou these great buildings? there shall not be left one stone upon another, that shall not be thrown down. ³And as he sat upon the mount of Olives over against the temple, Peter and James and John and Andrew asked him privately, ⁴Tell us, when shall these things be? and what shall be the sign when all these things shall be fulfilled? ⁵And Jesus answering them began to say, Take heed lest any man deceive you: ⁶For many shall come in my name, saying, I am Christ; and shall deceive many. ⁷And when ye shall hear of wars and rumours of wars, be ye not troubled: for such things must needs be; but the end shall not be yet. ⁸For nation shall rise against nation, and kingdom against kingdom: and there shall be earthquakes in divers places, and there shall be famines and troubles: these are the beginnings of sorrows. ⁹But take heed to yourselves: for they shall deliver you up to councils; and in the synagogues ye shall be beaten: and ye shall be brought before rulers and kings for my sake, for a testimony against them. ¹⁰And the gospel must first be published among all nations. ¹¹But when they shall lead you, and deliver you up, take no thought beforehand what ye shall speak, neither do ye premeditate: but whatsoever shall be given you in that hour, that speak ye: for it is not ye that speak, but the Holy Ghost. ¹²Now the brother shall betray the brother to death, and the father the son; and children shall rise up against their parents, and shall cause them to be put to death. ¹³And ye shall be hated of all men for my name's sake: but he that shall endure unto the end, the same shall be saved."

Luke 21:5-17 "⁵And as some spake of the temple, how it was adorned with goodly stones and gifts, he said, ⁶As for these things which ye behold, the days will come, in the which there shall not be left one stone upon another, that shall not be thrown down. ⁷And they asked him, saying, Master, but when shall these things be? and what sign will there be when these things shall come to pass? ⁸And he said, Take heed that ye be not deceived: for many shall come in my name, saying, I am Christ; and the time draweth near: go ye not therefore after them. ⁹But when ye shall hear of wars and commotions, be not terrified: for these things must first come to pass; but the end is not by and by. ¹⁰Then said he unto them, Nation shall rise against nation, and kingdom against kingdom: ¹¹And great earthquakes shall be in divers places, and famines, and pestilences; and fearful sights and great signs shall there be from heaven. ¹²But before all these, they shall lay their hands on you, and persecute you, delivering you up to the synagogues, and into prisons, being brought before kings and rulers for my name's sake. ¹³And it shall turn to you for a testimony. ¹⁴Settle it therefore in your hearts, not to meditate before what ye shall answer: ¹⁵For I will give you a mouth and wisdom, which all your adversaries shall not be able to gainsay nor resist. ¹⁶And ye shall be betrayed both by parents, and brethren, and kinsfolks, and friends; and some of you shall they cause to be put to death. ¹⁷And ye shall be hated of all men for my name's sake."

John 15:1-19 "¹I am the true vine, and my Father is the husbandman. ²Every branch in me that beareth not fruit he taketh away: and every branch that beareth fruit, he purgeth it, that it may bring forth more fruit. ³Now ye are clean through the word which I have spoken unto you. ⁴Abide in me, and I in you. As the branch cannot bear fruit of itself, except it abide in the vine; no more can ye, except ye abide in me. ⁵I am the vine, ye are the branches: He that abideth in me, and I in him, the same bringeth forth much fruit:

for without me ye can do nothing. ⁶If a man abide not in me, he is cast forth as a branch, and is withered; and men gather them, and cast them into the fire, and they are burned. ⁷If ye abide in me, and my words abide in you, ye shall ask what ye will, and it shall be done unto you. ⁸Herein is my Father glorified, that ye bear much fruit; so shall ye be my disciples. ⁹As the Father hath loved me, so have I loved you: continue ye in my love. ¹⁰If ye keep my commandments, ye shall abide in my love; even as I have kept my Father's commandments, and abide in his love. ¹¹These things have I spoken unto you, that my joy might remain in you, and that your joy might be full. ¹²This is my commandment, That ye love one another, as I have loved you. ¹³Greater love hath no man than this, that a man lay down his life for his friends. ¹⁴Ye are my friends, if ye do whatsoever I command you. ¹⁵Henceforth I call you not servants; for the servant knoweth not what his lord doeth: but I have called you friends; for all things that I have heard of my Father I have made known unto you. ¹⁶Ye have not chosen me, but I have chosen you, and ordained you, that ye should go and bring forth fruit, and that your fruit should remain: that whatsoever ye shall ask of the Father in my name, he may give it you. ¹⁷These things I command you, that ye love one another. ¹⁸If the world hate you, ye know that it hated me before it hated you. ¹⁹If ye were of the world, the world would love his own: but because ye are not of the world, but I have chosen you out of the world, therefore the world hateth you."

John 17:1-14 "¹These words spake Jesus, and lifted up his eyes to heaven, and said, Father, the hour is come; glorify thy Son, that thy Son also may glorify thee: ²As thou hast given him power over all flesh, that he should give eternal life to as many as thou hast given him. ³And this is life eternal, that they might know thee the only true God, and Jesus Christ, whom thou hast sent. ⁴I have glorified thee on the earth: I have finished the work which thou gavest me to do. ⁵And now, O Father, glorify thou me with thine own self with the glory which I had with thee before the world was. ⁶I have manifested thy name unto the men which thou gavest me out of the world: thine they were, and thou gavest them me; and they have kept thy word. ⁷Now they have known that all things whatsoever thou hast given me are of

thee. ⁸For I have given unto them the words which thou gavest me; and they have received them, and have known surely that I came out from thee, and they have believed that thou didst send me. ⁹I pray for them: I pray not for the world, but for them which thou hast given me; for they are thine. ¹⁰And all mine are thine, and thine are mine; and I am glorified in them. ¹¹And now I am no more in the world, but these are in the world, and I come to thee. Holy Father, keep through thine own name those whom thou hast given me, that they may be one, as we are. ¹²While I was with them in the world, I kept them in thy name: those that thou gavest me I have kept, and none of them is lost, but the son of perdition; that the scripture might be fulfilled. ¹³And now come I to thee; and these things I speak in the world, that they might have my joy fulfilled in themselves. ¹⁴I have given them thy word; and the world hath hated them, because they are not of the world, even as I am not of the world."

1 John 3:11-13 "¹¹For this is the message that ye heard from the beginning, that we should love one another. ¹²Not as Cain, who was of that wicked one, and slew his brother. And wherefore slew he him? Because his own works were evil, and his brother's righteous. ¹³Marvel not, my brethren, if the world hate you."

Why The World Hates Jesus Christ And Those That Believe In Him

John 7:6-7 "⁶Then Jesus said unto them, My time is not yet come: but your time is alway ready. ⁷The world cannot hate you; but me it hateth, because I testify of it, that the works thereof are evil."

John 15:1-19 "¹I am the true vine, and my Father is the husbandman. ²Every branch in me that beareth not fruit he taketh away: and every branch that beareth fruit, he purgeth it, that it may bring forth more fruit. ³Now ye are clean through the word which I have spoken unto you. ⁴Abide in me, and I in you. As the branch cannot bear fruit of itself, except it abide in the vine; no more can ye, except ye abide in me. ⁵I am the vine, ye are the branches: He that abideth in me, and I in him, the same bringeth forth much fruit: for without me ye can do nothing. ⁶If a man abide not in me, he is cast forth as a branch, and is withered; and men gather them, and cast them into the fire, and they are burned. ⁷If ye abide in me, and my words abide in you, ye shall ask what ye will, and it shall be done unto you. ⁸Herein is my Father glorified, that ye bear much fruit; so shall ye be my disciples. ⁹As the Father hath loved me, so have I loved you: continue ye in my love. ¹⁰If ye keep my commandments, ye shall abide in my love; even as I have kept my Father's commandments, and abide in his love. ¹¹These things have I spoken unto you, that my joy might remain in you, and that your joy might be full. ¹²This is my commandment, That ye love one another, as I have loved you. ¹³Greater love hath no man than this, that a man lay down his life for his friends. ¹⁴Ye are my friends, if ye do whatsoever I command you. ¹⁵Henceforth I call you not servants; for the servant knoweth not what his lord doeth: but I have called you friends; for all things that I have heard of my Father I have made known unto you. ¹⁶Ye have not chosen me, but I have chosen you, and ordained you, that ye should go and bring forth fruit, and that your fruit should remain: that whatsoever ye shall ask of the Father in my name, he may give it you. ¹⁷These things I command you, that ye love one another. ¹⁸If the world hate you, ye know that it hated me before it hated you. ¹⁹If ye were of the world, the world would love his own: but because ye are not of the world, but I have chosen you out of the world, therefore the world hateth you."

John 17:1-16 "¹These words spake Jesus, and lifted up his eyes to heaven, and said, Father, the hour is come; glorify thy Son, that thy Son also may glorify thee: ²As thou hast given him power over all flesh, that he should give eternal life to as many as thou hast given him. ³And this is life eternal, that they might know thee the only true God, and Jesus Christ, whom thou hast sent. ⁴I have glorified thee on the earth: I have finished the work which thou gavest me to do. ⁵And now, O Father, glorify thou me with thine own self with the glory which I had with thee before the world was. ⁶I have manifested thy name unto the men which thou gavest me out of the world: thine they were, and thou gavest them me; and they have kept thy word. ⁷Now they have known that all things whatsoever thou hast given me are of thee. ⁸For I have given unto them the words which thou gavest me; and they have received them, and have known surely that I came out

from thee, and they have believed that thou didst send me. ⁹I pray for them: I pray not for the world, but for them which thou hast given me; for they are thine. ¹⁰And all mine are thine, and thine are mine; and I am glorified in them. ¹¹And now I am no more in the world, but these are in the world, and I come to thee. Holy Father, keep through thine own name those whom thou hast given me, that they may be one, as we are. ¹²While I was with them in the world, I kept them in thy name: those that thou gavest me I have kept, and none of them is lost, but the son of perdition; that the scripture might be fulfilled. ¹³And now come I to thee; and these things I speak in the world, that they might have my joy fulfilled in themselves. ¹⁴I have given them thy word; and the world hath hated them, because they are not of the world, even as I am not of the world. ¹⁵I pray not that thou shouldest take them out of the world, but that thou shouldest keep them from the evil. ¹⁶They are not of the world, even as I am not of the world."

HEALING

The Lord Healing

Exodus 15:26 "And said, If thou wilt diligently hearken to the voice of the LORD thy God, and wilt do that which is right in his sight, and wilt give ear to his commandments, and keep all his statutes, I will put none of these diseases upon thee, which I have brought upon the Egyptians: for I am the LORD that healeth thee."

2 Kings 20:5 "Turn again, and tell Hezekiah the captain of my people, Thus saith the LORD, the God of David thy father, I have heard thy prayer, I have seen thy tears: behold, I will heal thee: on the third day thou shalt go up unto the house of the LORD."

Psalm 30:2 "O LORD my God, I cried unto thee, and thou hast healed me."

Psalm 103:1-3 "¹Bless the LORD, O my soul: and all that is within me, bless his holy name. ²Bless the LORD, O my soul, and forget not all his benefits: ³Who forgiveth all thine iniquities; who healeth all thy diseases;"

Isaiah 53:1-5 "¹Who hath believed our report? and to whom is the arm of the LORD revealed?

²For he shall grow up before him as a tender plant, and as a root out of a dry ground: he hath no form nor comeliness; and when we shall see him, there is no beauty that we should desire him. ³He is despised and rejected of men; a man of sorrows, and acquainted with grief: and we hid as it were our faces from him; he was despised, and we esteemed him not. ⁴Surely he hath borne our griefs, and carried our sorrows: yet we did esteem him stricken, smitten of God, and afflicted. ⁵But he was wounded for our transgressions, he was bruised for our iniquities: the chastisement of our peace was upon him; and with his stripes we are healed."

Isaiah 57:15-19 "¹⁵For thus saith the high and lofty One that inhabiteth eternity, whose name is Holy; I dwell in the high and holy place, with him also that is of a contrite and humble spirit, to revive the spirit of the humble, and to revive the heart of the contrite ones. ¹⁶For I will not contend for ever, neither will I be always wroth: for the spirit should fail before me, and the souls which I have made. ¹⁷For the iniquity of his covetousness was I wroth, and smote him: I hid me, and was wroth, and he went on frowardly in the way of his heart. ¹⁸I have seen his ways, and will heal him: I will lead him also, and restore comforts unto him and to his mourners. ¹⁹I create the fruit of the lips; Peace, peace to him that is far off, and to him that is near, saith the LORD; and I will heal him."

Jeremiah 3:21-22 "²¹A voice was heard upon the high places, weeping and supplications of the children of Israel: for they have perverted their way, and they have forgotten the LORD their God. ²²Return, ye backsliding children, and I will heal your backslidings. Behold, we come unto thee; for thou art the LORD our God."

Jeremiah 17:14 "Heal me, O LORD, and I shall be healed; save me, and I shall be saved: for thou art my praise."

Jeremiah 30:16-17 "¹⁶Therefore all they that devour thee shall be devoured; and all thine adversaries, every one of them, shall go into captivity; and they that spoil thee shall be a spoil, and all that prey upon thee will I give for a prey. ¹⁷For I will restore health unto thee, and I will heal thee of thy wounds, saith the LORD; because they called thee

an Outcast, saying, This is Zion, whom no man seeketh after."

Jeremiah 33:4-6 "⁴For thus saith the LORD, the God of Israel, concerning the houses of this city, and concerning the houses of the kings of Judah, which are thrown down by the mounts, and by the sword; ⁵They come to fight with the Chaldeans, but it is to fill them with the dead bodies of men, whom I have slain in mine anger and in my fury, and for all whose wickedness I have hid my face from this city. ⁶Behold, I will bring it health and cure, and I will cure them, and will reveal unto them the abundance of peace and truth."

Hosea 6:1 "Come, and let us return unto the LORD: for he hath torn, and he will heal us; he hath smitten, and he will bind us up."

Matthew 11:4-5 "⁴Jesus answered and said unto them, Go and shew John again those things which ye do hear and see: ⁵The blind receive their sight, and the lame walk, the lepers are cleansed, and the deaf hear, the dead are raised up, and the poor have the gospel preached to them."

Matthew 13:10-15 "¹⁰And the disciples came, and said unto him, Why speakest thou unto them in parables? ¹¹He answered and said unto them, Because it is given unto you to know the mysteries of the kingdom of heaven, but to them it is not given. ¹²For whosoever hath, to him shall be given, and he shall have more abundance: but whosoever hath not, from him shall be taken away even that he hath. ¹³Therefore speak I to them in parables: because they seeing see not; and hearing they hear not, neither do they understand. ¹⁴And in them is fulfilled the prophecy of Esaias, which saith, By hearing ye shall hear, and shall not understand; and seeing ye shall see, and shall not perceive: ¹⁵For this people's heart is waxed gross, and their ears are dull of hearing, and their eyes they have closed; lest at any time they should see with their eyes, and hear with their ears, and should understand with their heart, and should be converted, and I should heal them."

Mark 3:7-10 "⁷But Jesus withdrew himself with his disciples to the sea: and a great multitude from Galilee followed him, and from Judaea, ⁸And from Jerusalem, and from Idumaea, and from beyond Jordan; and they about Tyre and Sidon, a great multitude, when they had heard what great things he did, came unto him. ⁹And he spake to his disciples, that a small ship should wait on him because of the multitude, lest they should throng him. ¹⁰For he had healed many; insomuch that they pressed upon him for to touch him, as many as had plagues."

Mark 6:4-5 "⁴But Jesus said unto them, A prophet is not without honour, but in his own country, and among his own kin, and in his own house. ⁵And he could there do no mighty work, save that he laid his hands upon a few sick folk, and healed them."

Luke 4:40-41 "⁴⁰Now when the sun was setting, all they that had any sick with divers diseases brought them unto him; and he laid his hands on every one of them, and healed them. ⁴¹And devils also came out of many, crying out, and saying, Thou art Christ the Son of God. And he rebuking them suffered them not to speak: for they knew that he was Christ."

Luke 5:12-15 "¹²And it came to pass, when he was in a certain city, behold a man full of leprosy: who seeing Jesus fell on his face, and besought him, saying, Lord, if thou wilt, thou canst make me clean. ¹³And he put forth his hand, and touched him, saying, I will: be thou clean. And immediately the leprosy departed from him. ¹⁴And he charged him to tell no man: but go, and shew thyself to the priest, and offer for thy cleansing, according as Moses commanded, for a testimony unto them. ¹⁵But so much the more went there a fame abroad of him: and great multitudes came together to hear, and to be healed by him of their infirmities."

Luke 7:22 "Then Jesus answering said unto them, Go your way, and tell John what things ye have seen and heard; how that the blind see, the lame walk, the lepers are cleansed, the deaf hear, the dead are raised, to the poor the gospel is preached."

Acts 4:9-10 "⁹If we this day be examined of the good deed done to the impotent man, by what means he is made whole; ¹⁰Be it known unto you all, and to all the people of Israel, that by the name of Jesus Christ of Nazareth, whom ye crucified, whom God raised from the dead, even by him doth this man stand here before you whole."

1 Peter 2:21-24 "²¹For even hereunto were ye called: because Christ also suffered for us, leaving us an example, that ye should follow his steps: ²²Who did no sin, neither was guile found in his mouth: ²³Who, when he was reviled, reviled not again; when he suffered, he threatened not; but committed himself to him that judgeth righteously: ²⁴Who his own self bare our sins in his own body on the tree, that we, being dead to sins, should live unto righteousness: by whose stripes ye were healed."

Who Is Given Power To Heal

Matthew 10:1 "And when he had called unto him his twelve disciples, he gave them power against unclean spirits, to cast them out, and to heal all manner of sickness and all manner of disease."

Matthew 10:5-8 "⁵These twelve Jesus sent forth, and commanded them, saying, Go not into the way of the Gentiles, and into any city of the Samaritans enter ye not: ⁶But go rather to the lost sheep of the house of Israel. ⁷And as ye go, preach, saying, The kingdom of heaven is at hand. ⁸Heal the sick, cleanse the lepers, raise the dead, cast out devils: freely ye have received, freely give."

Mark 6:7-13 "⁷And he called unto him the twelve, and began to send them forth by two and two; and gave them power over unclean spirits; ⁸And commanded them that they should take nothing for their journey, save a staff only; no scrip, no bread, no money in their purse: ⁹But be shod with sandals; and not put on two coats. ¹⁰And he said unto them, In what place soever ye enter into an house, there abide till ye depart from that place. ¹¹And whosoever shall not receive you, nor hear you, when ye depart thence, shake off the dust under your feet for a testimony against them. Verily I say unto you, It shall be more tolerable for Sodom and Gomorrha in the day of judgment, than for that city. ¹²And they went out, and preached that men should repent. ¹³And they cast out many devils, and anointed with oil many that were sick, and healed them."

Mark 16:14-20 "¹⁴Afterward he appeared unto the eleven as they sat at meat, and upbraided them with their unbelief and hardness of heart, because they believed not them which had seen him after he was risen. ¹⁵And he said unto them, Go ye into all the world, and preach the gospel to every creature. [16]He that believeth and is baptized shall be saved; but he that believeth not shall be damned. [17]And these signs shall follow them that believe; In my name shall they cast out devils; they shall speak with new tongues; [18]They shall take up serpents; and if they drink any deadly thing, it shall not hurt them; they shall lay hands on the sick, and they shall recover. [19]So then after the Lord had spoken unto them, he was received up into heaven, and sat on the right hand of God. [20]And they went forth, and preached everywhere, the Lord working with them, and confirming the word with signs following. Amen."

Luke 9:1-6 "[1]Then he called his twelve disciples together, and gave them power and authority over all devils, and to cure diseases. [2]And he sent them to preach the kingdom of God, and to heal the sick. [3]And he said unto them, Take nothing for your journey, neither staves, nor scrip, neither bread, neither money; neither have two coats apiece. [4]And whatsoever house ye enter into, there abide, and thence depart. [5]And whosoever will not receive you, when ye go out of that city, shake off the very dust from your feet for a testimony against them. [6]And they departed, and went through the towns, preaching the gospel, and healing every where."

Luke 10:1-9 "[1]After these things the Lord appointed other seventy also, and sent them two and two before his face into every city and place, whither he himself would come. [2]Therefore said he unto them, The harvest truly is great, but the labourers are few: pray ye therefore the Lord of the harvest, that he would send forth labourers into his harvest. [3]Go your ways: behold, I send you forth as lambs among wolves. [4]Carry neither purse, nor scrip, nor shoes: and salute no man by the way. [5]And into whatsoever house ye enter, first say, Peace be to this house. [6]And if the son of peace be there, your peace shall rest upon it: if not, it shall turn to you again. [7]And in the same house remain, eating and drinking such things as they give: for the labourer is worthy of his hire. Go not from house to house. [8]And into whatsoever city ye enter, and they receive you, eat such things as are set before you: [9]And heal the sick that are therein, and say unto them, The kingdom of God is come nigh unto you."

Acts 3:1-12 "[1]Now Peter and John went together into the temple at the hour of prayer, being the ninth hour. [2]And a certain man lame from his mother's womb was carried, whom they laid daily at the gate of the temple which is called Beautiful, to ask alms of them that entered into the temple; [3]Who seeing Peter and John about to go into the temple asked an alms. [4]And Peter, fastening his eyes upon him with John, said, Look on us. [5]And he gave heed unto them, expecting to receive something of them. [6]Then Peter said, Silver and gold have I none; but such as I have give I thee: In the name of Jesus Christ of Nazareth rise up and walk. [7]And he took him by the right hand, and lifted him up: and immediately his feet and ancle bones received strength. [8]And he leaping up stood, and walked, and entered with them into the temple, walking, and leaping, and praising God. [9]And all the people saw him walking and praising God: [10]And they knew that it was he which sat for alms at the Beautiful gate of the temple: and they were filled with wonder and amazement at that which had happened unto him. [11]And as the lame man which was healed held Peter and John, all the people ran together unto them in the porch that is called Solomon's, greatly wondering. [12]And when Peter saw it, he answered unto the people, Ye men of Israel, why marvel ye at this? or why look ye so earnestly on us, as though by our own power or holiness we had made this man to walk?"

Acts 5:15-16 "[15]Insomuch that they brought forth the sick into the streets, and laid them on beds and couches, that at the least the shadow of Peter passing by might overshadow some of them. [16]There came also a multitude out of the cities round about unto Jerusalem, bringing sick folks, and them which were vexed with unclean spirits: and they were healed every one."

Acts 14:8-10 "[8]And there sat a certain man at Lystra, impotent in his feet, being a cripple from his mother's womb, who never had walked: [9]The same heard Paul speak: who stedfastly beholding him, and perceiving that he had faith to be healed, [10]Said with a loud voice, Stand upright on thy feet. And he leaped and walked."

Who The Lord Heals

2 Chronicles 7:12-14 "[12]And the LORD appeared to Solomon by night, and said unto him, I have heard thy prayer, and have chosen this place to myself for an house of sacrifice. ¹³If I shut up heaven that there be no rain, or if I command the locusts to devour the land, or if I send pestilence among my people; ¹⁴If my people, which are called by my name, shall humble themselves, and pray, and seek my face, and turn from their wicked ways; then will I hear from heaven, and will forgive their sin, and will heal their land."

Psalm 107:17-20 "¹⁷Fools because of their transgression, and because of their iniquities, are afflicted. ¹⁸Their soul abhorreth all manner of meat; and they draw near unto the gates of death. ¹⁹Then they cry unto the LORD in their trouble, and he saveth them out of their distresses. ²⁰He sent his word, and healed them, and delivered them from their destructions."

Isaiah 61:1 "The Spirit of the Lord GOD is upon me; because the LORD hath anointed me to preach good tidings unto the meek; he hath sent me to bind up the brokenhearted, to proclaim liberty to the captives, and the opening of the prison to them that are bound;"

Matthew 9:11-13 "¹¹And when the Pharisees saw it, they said unto his disciples, Why eateth your Master with publicans and sinners? ¹²But when Jesus heard that, he said unto them, They that be whole need not a physician, but they that are sick. ¹³But go ye and learn what that meaneth, I will have mercy, and not sacrifice: for I am not come to call the righteous, but sinners to repentance."

Mark 2:16-17 "¹⁶And when the scribes and Pharisees saw him eat with publicans and sinners, they said unto his disciples, How is it that he eateth and drinketh with publicans and sinners? ¹⁷When Jesus heard it, he saith unto them, They that are whole have no need of the physician, but they that are sick: I came not to call the righteous, but sinners to repentance."

Luke 4:14-18 "¹⁴And Jesus returned in the power of the Spirit into Galilee: and there went out a fame of him through all the region round about. ¹⁵And he taught in their synagogues, being glorified of all. ¹⁶And he came to Nazareth, where he had been brought up: and, as his custom was, he went into the synagogue on the sabbath day, and stood up for to read. ¹⁷And there was delivered unto him the book of the prophet Esaias. And when he had opened the book, he found the place where it was written, ¹⁸The Spirit of the Lord is upon me, because he hath anointed me to preach the gospel to the poor; he hath sent me to heal the brokenhearted, to preach deliverance to the captives, and recovering of sight to the blind, to set at liberty them that are bruised,"

Luke 5:30-32 "³⁰But their scribes and Pharisees murmured against his disciples, saying, Why do ye eat and drink with publicans and sinners? ³¹And Jesus answering said unto them, They that are whole need not a physician; but they that are sick. ³²I came not to call the righteous, but sinners to repentance."

James 5:14-16 "¹⁴Is any sick among you? let him call for the elders of the church; and let them pray over him, anointing him with oil in the name of the Lord: ¹⁵And the prayer of faith shall save the sick, and the Lord shall raise him up; and if he have committed sins, they shall be forgiven him. ¹⁶Confess your faults one to another, and pray one for another, that ye may be healed. The effectual fervent prayer of a righteous man availeth much."

HEALTH

What Is Health
Proverbs 12:18 "There is that speaketh like the piercings of a sword: but the tongue of the wise is health."

Proverbs 13:17 "A wicked messenger falleth into mischief: but a faithful ambassador is health."

HEARING

Being Swift To Hear
James 1:19 "Wherefore, my beloved brethren, let every man be swift to hear, slow to speak, slow to wrath:"

Hearing The Lord
Deuteronomy 4:1 "Now therefore hearken, O Israel, unto the statutes and unto the judgments, which I teach you, for to do them, that ye may live, and go in and possess the land which the LORD God of your fathers giveth you."

Deuteronomy 18:15 "The LORD thy God will raise up unto thee a Prophet from the midst of thee, of thy brethren, like unto me; unto him ye shall hearken;"

Isaiah 1:10 "Hear the word of the LORD, ye rulers of Sodom; give ear unto the law of our God, ye people of Gomorrah."

Isaiah 46:9-12 "9Remember the former things of old: for I am God, and there is none else; I am God, and there is none like me, 10Declaring the end from the beginning, and from ancient times the things that are not yet done, saying, My counsel shall stand, and I will do all my pleasure: 11Calling a ravenous bird from the east, the man that executeth my counsel from a far country: yea, I have spoken it, I will also bring it to pass; I have purposed it, I will also do it. 12Hearken unto me, ye stouthearted, that are far from righteousness:"

Isaiah 48:12 "Hearken unto me, O Jacob and Israel, my called; I am he; I am the first, I also am the last."

Isaiah 51:1-7 "1Hearken to me, ye that follow after righteousness, ye that seek the LORD: look unto the rock whence ye are hewn, and to the hole of the pit whence ye are digged. 2Look unto Abraham your father, and unto Sarah that bare you: for I called him alone, and blessed him, and increased him. 3For the LORD shall comfort Zion: he will comfort all her waste places; and he will make her wilderness like Eden, and her desert like the garden of the LORD; joy and gladness shall be found therein, thanksgiving, and the voice of melody. 4Hearken unto me, my people; and give ear unto me, O my nation: for a law shall proceed from me, and I will make my judgment to rest for a light of the people. 5My righteousness is near; my salvation is gone forth, and mine arms shall judge the people; the isles shall wait upon me, and on mine arm shall they trust. 6Lift up your eyes to the heavens, and look upon the earth beneath: for the heavens shall vanish away like smoke, and the earth shall wax old like a garment, and they that dwell therein shall die in like manner: but my salvation shall be for ever, and my righteousness shall not be abolished. 7Hearken unto me, ye that know righteousness, the people in whose heart is my law; fear ye not the reproach of men, neither be ye afraid of their revilings."

Isaiah 55:1-3 "1Ho, every one that thirsteth, come ye to the waters, and he that hath no money; come ye, buy, and eat; yea, come, buy wine and milk without money and without price. 2Wherefore do ye spend money for that which is not bread? and your labour for that which satisfieth not? hearken diligently unto me, and eat ye that which is good, and let your soul delight itself in fatness. 3Incline your ear, and come unto me: hear, and your soul shall live; and I will make an everlasting covenant with you, even the sure mercies of David."

Matthew 17:4-5 "4Then answered Peter, and said unto Jesus, Lord, it is good for us to be here: if thou wilt, let us make here three tabernacles; one for thee, and one for Moses, and one for Elias. 5While he yet spake, behold, a bright cloud overshadowed them: and behold a voice out of the cloud, which said, This is my beloved Son, in whom I am well pleased; hear ye him."

Mark 9:5-7 "5And Peter answered and said to Jesus, Master, it is good for us to be here: and let us make three tabernacles; one for thee, and one for Moses, and one for Elias. 6For he wist not what to say; for they were sore afraid. 7And there was a cloud that overshadowed them: and a voice came out of the cloud, saying, This is my beloved Son: hear him."

Luke 9:33-35 "33And it came to pass, as they departed from him, Peter said unto Jesus, Master, it is good for us to be here: and let us make three tabernacles; one for thee, and one for Moses, and one for Elias: not knowing what he said. 34While he thus spake, there came a cloud, and overshadowed them: and they feared as they entered into the cloud. 35And there came a voice out of the cloud, saying, This is my beloved Son: hear him."

Acts 3:22 "For Moses truly said unto the fathers, A prophet shall the Lord your God raise up unto you of your brethren, like unto me; him shall ye hear in all things whatsoever he shall say unto you."

Acts 7:37 "This is that Moses, which said unto the children of Israel, A prophet shall the Lord your God raise up unto you of your brethren, like unto me; him shall ye hear."

The Ear

Job 34:2-3 "2Hear my words, O ye wise men; and give ear unto me, ye that have knowledge. 3For the ear trieth words, as the mouth tasteth meat."

The Ear Of The Wise
Proverbs 18:15 "The heart of the prudent getteth knowledge; and the ear of the wise seeketh knowledge."

The Hearing Ear
Proverbs 15:31 "The ear that heareth the reproof of life abideth among the wise."

Proverbs 20:12 "The hearing ear, and the seeing eye, the LORD hath made even both of them."

The Lord Hearing
Genesis 21:17 "And God heard the voice of the lad; and the angel of God called Hagar out of heaven, and said unto her, What aileth thee, Hagar? fear not; for God hath heard the voice of the lad where he is."

Exodus 22:20-27 "20He that sacrificeth unto any god, save unto the LORD only, he shall be utterly destroyed. 21Thou shalt neither vex a stranger, nor oppress him: for ye were strangers in the land of Egypt. 22Ye shall not afflict any widow, or fatherless child. 23If thou afflict them in any wise, and they cry at all unto me, I will surely hear their cry; 24And my wrath shall wax hot, and I will kill you with the sword; and your wives shall be widows, and your children fatherless. 25If thou lend money to any of my people that is poor by thee, thou shalt not be to him as an usurer, neither shalt thou lay upon him usury. 26If thou at all take thy neighbour's raiment to pledge, thou shalt deliver it unto him by that the sun goeth down: 27For that is his covering only, it is his raiment for his skin: wherein shall he sleep? and it shall come to pass, when he crieth unto me, that I will hear; for I am gracious."

2 Samuel 22:4-7 "4I will call on the LORD, who is worthy to be praised: so shall I be saved from mine enemies. 5When the waves of death compassed me, the floods of ungodly men made me afraid; 6The sorrows of hell compassed me about; the snares of death prevented me; 7In my distress I called upon the LORD, and cried to my God: and he did hear my voice out of his temple, and my cry did enter into his ears."

1 Kings 8:28 "Yet have thou respect unto the prayer of thy servant, and to his supplication, O LORD my God, to hearken unto the cry and to the prayer, which thy servant prayeth before thee to day:"

1 Kings 9:3 "And the LORD said unto him, I have heard thy prayer and thy supplication, that thou hast made before me: I have hallowed this house, which thou hast built, to put my name there for ever; and mine eyes and mine heart shall be there perpetually."

2 Kings 20:5 "Turn again, and tell Hezekiah the captain of my people, Thus saith the LORD, the God of David thy father, I have heard thy prayer, I have seen thy tears: behold, I will heal thee: on the third day thou shalt go up unto the house of the LORD."

2 Chronicles 7:12 "And the LORD appeared to Solomon by night, and said unto him, I have heard thy prayer, and have chosen this place to myself for an house of sacrifice."

Nehemiah 9:7-9 "7Thou art the LORD the God, who didst choose Abram, and broughtest him forth out of Ur of the Chaldees, and gavest him the name of Abraham; 8And foundest his heart faithful before thee, and madest a covenant with him to give the land of the Canaanites, the Hittites, the Amorites, and the Perizzites, and the Jebusites, and the Girgashites, to give it, I say, to his seed, and hast performed thy words; for thou art righteous: 9And didst see the affliction of our fathers in Egypt, and heardest their cry by the Red sea;"

Nehemiah 9:26-31 "26Nevertheless they were disobedient, and rebelled against thee, and cast thy law behind their backs, and slew thy prophets which testified against them to turn them to thee, and they wrought great provocations. 27Therefore thou deliveredst them into the hand of their enemies, who vexed them: and in the time of their trouble, when they cried unto thee, thou heardest them from heaven; and according to thy manifold mercies thou gavest them saviours, who saved them out of the hand of their enemies. 28But after they had rest, they did evil again before thee: therefore leftest thou them in the hand of their enemies, so that they had the dominion over them: yet when they returned, and cried unto thee, thou heardest them from heaven; and many times didst thou deliver them according to thy mercies; 29And testifiedst against them, that thou mightest bring them again unto thy law: yet they dealt proudly, and hearkened not unto thy commandments, but sinned against thy judgments, (which if a man do, he shall live in them;) and withdrew the shoulder, and hardened their neck, and would not hear. ³⁰Yet many years didst thou forbear them, and testifiedst against them by thy spirit in thy prophets: yet would they not give ear: therefore gavest thou them into the hand of the people of the lands. ³¹Nevertheless for thy great mercies' sake thou didst not utterly consume them, nor forsake them; for thou art a gracious and merciful God."

Job 34:23-28 "²³For he will not lay upon man more than right; that he should enter into judgment with God. ²⁴He shall break in pieces mighty men without number, and set others in their stead. ²⁵Therefore he knoweth their works, and he overturneth them in the night, so that they are destroyed. ²⁶He striketh them as wicked men in the open sight of others; ²⁷Because they turned back from him, and would not consider any of his ways: ²⁸So that they cause the cry of the poor to come unto him, and he heareth the cry of the afflicted."

Psalm 3:4 "I cried unto the LORD with my voice, and he heard me out of his holy hill. Selah."

Psalm 4:3 "But know that the LORD hath set apart him that is godly for himself: the LORD will hear when I call unto him."

Psalm 6:9 "The LORD hath heard my supplication; the LORD will receive my prayer."

Psalm 17:6 "I have called upon thee, for thou wilt hear me, O God: incline thine ear unto me, and hear my speech."

Psalm 18:6 "In my distress I called upon the LORD, and cried unto my God: he heard my voice out of his temple, and my cry came before him, even into his ears."

Psalm 28:6 "Blessed be the LORD, because he hath heard the voice of my supplications."

Psalm 34:4 "I sought the LORD, and he heard me, and delivered me from all my fears."

Psalm 34:6 "This poor man cried, and the LORD heard him, and saved him out of all his troubles."

Psalm 34:17 "The righteous cry, and the LORD heareth, and delivereth them out of all their troubles."

Psalm 40:1 "I waited patiently for the LORD; and he inclined unto me, and heard my cry."

Psalm 55:16-19 "¹⁶As for me, I will call upon God; and the LORD shall save me. ¹⁷Evening, and morning, and at noon, will I pray, and cry aloud: and he shall hear my voice. ¹⁸He hath delivered my soul in peace from the battle that was against me: for there were many with me. ¹⁹God shall hear, and afflict them, even he that abideth of old. Selah. Because they have no changes, therefore they fear not God."

Psalm 61:1-5 "¹Hear my cry, O God; attend unto my prayer. ²From the end of the earth will I cry unto thee, when my heart is overwhelmed: lead me to the rock that is higher than I. ³For thou hast been a shelter for me, and a strong tower from the enemy. ⁴I will abide in thy tabernacle for ever: I will trust in the covert of thy wings. Selah. ⁵For thou, O God, hast heard my vows: thou hast given me the heritage of those that fear thy name."

Psalm 65:1-2 "¹Praise waiteth for thee, O God, in Sion: and unto thee shall the vow be performed. ²O thou that hearest prayer, unto thee shall all flesh come."

Psalm 86:6-7 "⁶Give ear, O LORD, unto my prayer; and attend to the voice of my supplications. ⁷In the day of my trouble I will call upon thee: for thou wilt answer me."

Psalm 99:6 "Moses and Aaron among his priests, and Samuel among them that call upon his name; they called upon the LORD, and he answered them."

Psalm 106:40-47 "⁴⁰Therefore was the wrath of the LORD kindled against his people, insomuch that he abhorred his own inheritance. ⁴¹And he gave them into the hand of the heathen; and they that hated them ruled over them. ⁴²Their enemies also oppressed them, and they were brought into subjection under their hand. ⁴³Many times did he deliver them; but they provoked him with their counsel, and were brought low for their iniquity. ⁴⁴Nevertheless he regarded their affliction, when he heard their cry: ⁴⁵And he remembered for them his covenant, and repented according to the multitude of his mercies. ⁴⁶He made them also to be pitied of all those that carried them captives. ⁴⁷Save us, O LORD our God, and gather us from among the heathen, to give thanks unto thy holy name, and to triumph in thy praise."

Psalm 116:1 "I love the LORD, because he hath heard my voice and my supplications."

Psalm 118:5 "I called upon the LORD in distress: the LORD answered me, and set me in a large place."

Psalm 118:19-21 "19Open to me the gates of righteousness: I will go into them, and I will praise the LORD: 20This gate of the LORD, into which the righteous shall enter. 21I will praise thee: for thou hast heard me, and art become my salvation."

Psalm 130:1-2 "1Out of the depths have I cried unto thee, O LORD. 2Lord, hear my voice: let thine ears be attentive to the voice of my supplications."

Psalm 138:3-4 "3In the day when I cried thou answeredst me, and strengthenedst me with strength in my soul. 4All the kings of the earth shall praise thee, O LORD, when they hear the words of thy mouth."

Proverbs 15:29 "The LORD is far from the wicked: but he heareth the prayer of the righteous."

Isaiah 59:1 "Behold, the LORD's hand is not shortened, that it cannot save; neither his ear heavy, that it cannot hear:"

Isaiah 65:23-24 "23They shall not labour in vain, nor bring forth for trouble; for they are the seed of the blessed of the LORD, and their offspring with them. 24And it shall come to pass, that before they call, I will answer; and while they are yet speaking, I will hear."

Jeremiah 29:11-12 "11For I know the thoughts that I think toward you, saith the LORD, thoughts of peace, and not of evil, to give you an expected end. 12Then shall ye call upon me, and ye shall go and pray unto me, and I will hearken unto you."

Micah 7:7 "Therefore I will look unto the LORD; I will wait for the God of my salvation: my God will hear me."

Zechariah 13:9 "And I will bring the third part through the fire, and will refine them as silver is refined, and will try them as gold is tried: they shall call on my name, and I will hear them: I will say, It is my people: and they shall say, The LORD is my God."

1 John 5:13-15 "13These things have I written unto you that believe on the name of the Son of God; that ye may know that ye have eternal life, and that ye may believe on the name of the Son of God. 14And this is the confidence that we have in him, that, if we ask any thing according to his will, he heareth us: 15And if we know that he hear us, whatsoever we ask, we know that we have the petitions that we desired of him."

The Lord Opening Ears

Job 33:14-19 "14For God speaketh once, yea twice, yet man perceiveth it not. 15In a dream, in a vision of the night, when deep sleep falleth upon men, in slumberings upon the bed; 16Then he openeth the ears of men, and sealeth their instruction, 17That he may withdraw man from his purpose, and hide pride from man. 18He keepeth back his soul from the pit, and his life from perishing by the sword. 19He is chastened also with pain upon his bed, and the multitude of his bones with strong pain:"

Job 36:5-15 "5Behold, God is mighty, and despiseth not any: he is mighty in strength and wisdom. 6He preserveth not the life of the wicked: but giveth right to the poor. 7He withdraweth not his eyes from the righteous: but with kings are they on the throne; yea, he doth establish them for ever, and they are exalted. 8And if they be bound in fetters, and be holden in cords of affliction; 9Then he sheweth them their work, and their transgressions that they have exceeded. 10He openeth also their ear to discipline, and commandeth that they return from iniquity. 11If they obey and serve him, they shall spend their days in prosperity, and their years in pleasures. 12But if they obey not, they shall perish by the sword, and they shall die without knowledge. 13But the hypocrites in heart heap up wrath: they cry not when he bindeth them. 14They die in youth, and their life is among the unclean. 15He delivereth the poor in his affliction, and openeth their ears in oppression."

Psalm 40:5-6 "5Many, O LORD my God, are thy wonderful works which thou hast done, and thy thoughts which are to us-ward: they cannot be reckoned up in order unto thee: if I would declare and speak of them, they are more than can be numbered. 6Sacrifice and offering thou didst not desire; mine ears hast thou opened: burnt offering and sin offering hast thou not required."

Isaiah 50:4-5 "4The Lord GOD hath given me the tongue of the learned, that I should know how to speak a word in season to him that is weary: he wakeneth morning by morning, he wakeneth mine ear to hear as the learned. 5The Lord GOD hath opened mine ear, and I was not rebellious, neither turned away back."

Matthew 11:4-5 "4Jesus answered and said unto them, Go and shew John again those things which ye do hear and see: 5The blind receive their sight, and the lame walk, the lepers are cleansed, and the deaf hear, the dead are raised up, and the poor have the gospel preached to them."

Luke 7:22 "Then Jesus answering said unto them, Go your way, and tell John what things ye have seen and heard; how that the blind see, the lame walk, the lepers are cleansed, the deaf hear, the dead are raised, to the poor the gospel is preached."

Luke 24:44-47 "44And he said unto them, These are the words which I spake unto you, while I was yet with you, that all things must be fulfilled, which were written in the law of Moses, and in the prophets, and in the psalms, concerning me. 45Then opened he their understanding, that they might understand the scriptures, 46And said unto them, Thus it is written, and thus it behoved Christ to suffer, and to rise from the dead the third day: 47And that repentance and remission of sins should be preached in his name among all nations, beginning at Jerusalem."

The Reward For Not Hearing The Lord
Isaiah 65:11-15 "11But ye are they that forsake the LORD, that forget my holy mountain, that prepare a table for that troop, and that furnish the drink offering unto that number. 12Therefore will I number you to the sword, and ye shall all bow down to the slaughter: because when I called, ye did not answer; when I spake, ye did not hear; but did evil before mine eyes, and did choose that wherein I delighted not. 13Therefore thus saith the Lord GOD, Behold, my servants shall eat, but ye shall be hungry: behold, my servants shall drink, but ye shall be thirsty: behold, my servants shall rejoice, but ye shall be ashamed: 14Behold, my servants shall sing for joy of heart, but ye shall cry for sorrow of heart, and shall howl for vexation of spirit. 15And ye shall leave your name for a curse unto my chosen: for

the Lord GOD shall slay thee, and call his servants by another name:"

Isaiah 66:1-4 "1Thus saith the LORD, The heaven is my throne, and the earth is my footstool: where is the house that ye build unto me? and where is the place of my rest? 2For all those things hath mine hand made, and those things have been, saith the LORD: but to this man will I look, even to him that is poor and of a contrite spirit, and trembleth at my word. 3He that killeth an ox is as if he slew a man; he that sacrificeth a lamb, as if he cut off a dog's neck; he that offereth an oblation, as if he offered swine's blood; he that burneth incense, as if he blessed an idol. Yea, they have chosen their own ways, and their soul delighteth in their abominations. 4I also will choose their delusions, and will bring their fears upon them; because when I called, none did answer; when I spake, they did not hear: but they did evil before mine eyes, and chose that in which I delighted not."

Zechariah 1:4-6 "4Be ye not as your fathers, unto whom the former prophets have cried, saying, Thus saith the LORD of hosts; Turn ye now from your evil ways, and from your evil doings: but they did not hear, nor hearken unto me, saith the LORD. 5Your fathers, where are they? and the prophets, do they live for ever? 6But my words and my statutes, which I commanded my servants the prophets, did they not take hold of your fathers? and they returned and said, Like as the LORD of hosts thought to do unto us, according to our ways, and according to our doings, so hath he dealt with us."

Those That Do Not Hear The Lord's Disciples
Matthew 10:5-15 "5These twelve Jesus sent forth, and commanded them, saying, Go not into the way of the Gentiles, and into any city of the Samaritans enter ye not: 6But go rather to the lost sheep of the house of Israel. 7And as ye go, preach, saying, The kingdom of heaven is at hand. 8Heal the sick, cleanse the lepers, raise the dead, cast out devils: freely ye have received, freely give. 9Provide neither gold, nor silver, nor brass in your purses, 10Nor scrip for your journey, neither two coats, neither shoes, nor yet staves: for the workman is worthy of his meat. 11And into whatsoever city or town ye shall enter, inquire who in it is worthy; and there abide till ye go thence. 12And when ye come into an house,

salute it. [13]And if the house be worthy, let your peace come upon it: but if it be not worthy, let your peace return to you. [14]And whosoever shall not receive you, nor hear your words, when ye depart out of that house or city, shake off the dust of your feet. [15]Verily I say unto you, It shall be more tolerable for the land of Sodom and Gomorrha in the day of judgment, than for that city."

Mark 6:7-11 "[7]And he called unto him the twelve, and began to send them forth by two and two; and gave them power over unclean spirits; [8]And commanded them that they should take nothing for their journey, save a staff only; no scrip, no bread, no money in their purse: [9]But be shod with sandals; and not put on two coats. [10]And he said unto them, In what place soever ye enter into an house, there abide till ye depart from that place. [11]And whosoever shall not receive you, nor hear you, when ye depart thence, shake off the dust under your feet for a testimony against them. Verily I say unto you, It shall be more tolerable for Sodom and Gomorrha in the day of judgment, than for that city."

Luke 9:1-6 "[1]Then he called his twelve disciples together, and gave them power and authority over all devils, and to cure diseases. [2]And he sent them to preach the kingdom of God, and to heal the sick. [3]And he said unto them, Take nothing for your journey, neither staves, nor scrip, neither bread, neither money; neither have two coats apiece. [4]And whatsoever house ye enter into, there abide, and thence depart. [5]And whosoever will not receive you, when ye go out of that city, shake off the very dust from your feet for a testimony against them. [6]And they departed, and went through the towns, preaching the gospel, and healing every where."

Luke 10:1-12 "[1]After these things the Lord appointed other seventy also, and sent them two and two before his face into every city and place, whither he himself would come. [2]Therefore said he unto them, The harvest truly is great, but the labourers are few: pray ye therefore the Lord of the harvest, that he would send forth labourers into his harvest. [3]Go your ways: behold, I send you forth as lambs among wolves. [4]Carry neither purse, nor scrip, nor shoes: and salute no man by the way. [5]And into whatsoever house ye enter, first say, Peace be to this house. [6]And if the son of peace be there,

your peace shall rest upon it: if not, it shall turn to you again. [7]And in the same house remain, eating and drinking such things as they give: for the labourer is worthy of his hire. Go not from house to house. [8]And into whatsoever city ye enter, and they receive you, eat such things as are set before you: [9]And heal the sick that are therein, and say unto them, The kingdom of God is come nigh unto you. [10]But into whatsoever city ye enter, and they receive you not, go your ways out into the streets of the same, and say, [11]Even the very dust of your city, which cleaveth on us, we do wipe off against you: notwithstanding be ye sure of this, that the kingdom of God is come nigh unto you. [12]But I say unto you, that it shall be more tolerable in that day for Sodom, than for that city."

Those That Do Not Hear The Law
Proverbs 28:9 "He that turneth away his ear from hearing the law, even his prayer shall be abomination."

Those That Hear Instruction
Proverbs 8:32-34 "[32]Now therefore hearken unto me, O ye children: for blessed are they that keep my ways. [33]Hear instruction, and be wise, and refuse it not. [34]Blessed is the man that heareth me, watching daily at my gates, waiting at the posts of my doors."

Those That Hear Reproof
Proverbs 15:31-32 "[31]The ear that heareth the reproof of life abideth among the wise. [32]He that refuseth instruction despiseth his own soul: but he that heareth reproof getteth understanding."

Those That Hear The Lord
Matthew 7:24-28 "[24]Therefore whosoever heareth these sayings of mine, and doeth them, I will liken him unto a wise man, which built his house upon a rock: [25]And the rain descended, and the floods came, and the winds blew, and beat upon that house; and it fell not: for it was founded upon a rock. [26]And every one that heareth these sayings of mine, and doeth them not, shall be likened unto a foolish man, which built his house upon the sand: [27]And the rain descended, and the floods came, and the winds blew, and beat upon that house; and it fell: and great was the fall of it. [28]And it came to pass, when Jesus had ended these sayings, the people were astonished at his doctrine:"

Matthew 13:23 "But he that received seed into the good ground is he that heareth the word, and understandeth it; which also beareth fruit, and bringeth forth, some an hundredfold, some sixty, some thirty."

Mark 4:20 "And these are they which are sown on good ground; such as hear the word, and receive it, and bring forth fruit, some thirtyfold, some sixty, and some an hundred."

Luke 6:46-48 "⁴⁶And why call ye me, Lord, Lord, and do not the things which I say? ⁴⁷Whosoever cometh to me, and heareth my sayings, and doeth them, I will shew you to whom he is like: ⁴⁸He is like a man which built an house, and digged deep, and laid the foundation on a rock: and when the flood arose, the stream beat vehemently upon that house, and could not shake it: for it was founded upon a rock."

Luke 8:15 "But that on the good ground are they, which in an honest and good heart, having heard the word, keep it, and bring forth fruit with patience."

Luke 8:19-21 "¹⁹Then came to him his mother and his brethren, and could not come at him for the press. ²⁰And it was told him by certain which said, Thy mother and thy brethren stand without, desiring to see thee. ²¹And he answered and said unto them, My mother and my brethren are these which hear the word of God, and do it."

Luke 11:27-28 "²⁷And it came to pass, as he spake these things, a certain woman of the company lifted up her voice, and said unto him, Blessed is the womb that bare thee, and the paps which thou hast sucked. ²⁸But he said, Yea rather, blessed are they that hear the word of God, and keep it."

John 5:23-25 "²³That all men should honour the Son, even as they honour the Father. He that honoureth not the Son honoureth not the Father which hath sent him. ²⁴Verily, verily, I say unto you, He that heareth my word, and believeth on him that sent me, hath everlasting life, and shall not come into condemnation; but is passed from death unto life. ²⁵Verily, verily, I say unto you, The hour is coming, and now is, when the dead shall hear the voice of the Son of God: and they that hear shall live."

Revelation 1:1-3 "¹The Revelation of Jesus Christ, which God gave unto him, to shew unto his servants things which must shortly come to pass; and he sent and signified it by his angel unto his servant John: ²Who bare record of the word of God, and of the testimony of Jesus Christ, and of all things that he saw. ³Blessed is he that readeth, and they that hear the words of this prophecy, and keep those things which are written therein: for the time is at hand."

Revelation 3:14-20 "¹⁴And unto the angel of the church of the Laodiceans write; These things saith the Amen, the faithful and true witness, the beginning of the creation of God; ¹⁵I know thy works, that thou art neither cold nor hot: I would thou wert cold or hot. ¹⁶So then because thou art lukewarm, and neither cold nor hot, I will spue thee out of my mouth. ¹⁷Because thou sayest, I am rich, and increased with goods, and have need of nothing; and knowest not that thou art wretched, and miserable, and poor, and blind, and naked: ¹⁸I counsel thee to buy of me gold tried in the fire, that thou mayest be rich; and white raiment, that thou mayest be clothed, and that the shame of thy nakedness do not appear; and anoint thine eyes with eyesalve, that thou mayest see. ¹⁹As many as I love, I rebuke and chasten: be zealous therefore, and repent. ²⁰Behold, I stand at the door, and knock: if any man hear my voice, and open the door, I will come in to him, and will sup with him, and he with me."

Those That Hear The Lord's Disciples
Luke 10:1-16 "¹After these things the Lord appointed other seventy also, and sent them two and two before his face into every city and place, whither he himself would come. ²Therefore said he unto them, The harvest truly is great, but the labourers are few: pray ye therefore the Lord of the harvest, that he would send forth labourers into his harvest. ³Go your ways: behold, I send you forth as lambs among wolves. ⁴Carry neither purse, nor scrip, nor shoes: and salute no man by the way. ⁵And into whatsoever house ye enter, first say, Peace be to this house. ⁶And if the son of peace be there, your peace shall rest upon it: if not, it shall turn to you again. ⁷And in the same house remain, eating and drinking such things as they give: for the labourer is worthy of his hire. Go not from house to house. ⁸And into whatsoever city ye enter,

and they receive you, eat such things as are set before you: [9]And heal the sick that are therein, and say unto them, The kingdom of God is come nigh unto you. [10]But into whatsoever city ye enter, and they receive you not, go your ways out into the streets of the same, and say, [11]Even the very dust of your city, which cleaveth on us, we do wipe off against you: notwithstanding be ye sure of this, that the kingdom of God is come nigh unto you. [12]But I say unto you, that it shall be more tolerable in that day for Sodom, than for that city. [13]Woe unto thee, Chorazin! woe unto thee, Bethsaida! for if the mighty works had been done in Tyre and Sidon, which have been done in you, they had a great while ago repented, sitting in sackcloth and ashes. [14]But it shall be more tolerable for Tyre and Sidon at the judgment, than for you. [15]And thou, Capernaum, which art exalted to heaven, shalt be thrust down to hell. [16]He that heareth you heareth me; and he that despiseth you despiseth me; and he that despiseth me despiseth him that sent me."

Those That Hear Wisdom
Proverbs 1:20-33 "[20]Wisdom crieth without; she uttereth her voice in the streets: [21]She crieth in the chief place of concourse, in the openings of the gates: in the city she uttereth her words, saying, [22]How long, ye simple ones, will ye love simplicity? and the scorners delight in their scorning, and fools hate knowledge? [23]Turn you at my reproof: behold, I will pour out my spirit unto you, I will make known my words unto you. [24]Because I have called, and ye refused; I have stretched out my hand, and no man regarded; [25]But ye have set at nought all my counsel, and would none of my reproof: [26]I also will laugh at your calamity; I will mock when your fear cometh; [27]When your fear cometh as desolation, and your destruction cometh as a whirlwind; when distress and anguish cometh upon you. [28]Then shall they call upon me, but I will not answer; they shall seek me early, but they shall not find me: [29]For that they hated knowledge, and did not choose the fear of the LORD: [30]They would none of my counsel: they despised all my reproof. [31]Therefore shall they eat of the fruit of their own way, and be filled with their own devices. [32]For the turning away of the simple shall slay them, and the prosperity of fools shall

destroy them. [33]But whoso hearkeneth unto me shall dwell safely, and shall be quiet from fear of evil."

Proverbs 8:32-34 "[32]Now therefore hearken unto me, O ye children: for blessed are they that keep my ways. [33]Hear instruction, and be wise, and refuse it not. [34]Blessed is the man that heareth me, watching daily at my gates, waiting at the posts of my doors."

Those That Listen To Counsel
Proverbs 12:15 "The way of a fool is right in his own eyes: but he that hearkeneth unto counsel is wise."

What Comes By Hearing
Romans 10:17 "So then faith cometh by hearing, and hearing by the word of God."

What God Will Not Hear
Job 35:13 "Surely God will not hear vanity, neither will the Almighty regard it."

What Not To Hear
1 Timothy 1:3-4 "[3]As I besought thee to abide still at Ephesus, when I went into Macedonia, that thou mightest charge some that they teach no other doctrine, [4]Neither give heed to fables and endless genealogies, which minister questions, rather than godly edifying which is in faith: so do."

Titus 1:10-14 "[10]For there are many unruly and vain talkers and deceivers, specially they of the circumcision: [11]Whose mouths must be stopped, who subvert whole houses, teaching things which they ought not, for filthy lucre's sake. [12]One of themselves, even a prophet of their own, said, The Cretians are alway liars, evil beasts, slow bellies. [13]This witness is true. Wherefore rebuke them sharply, that they may be sound in the faith; [14]Not giving heed to Jewish fables, and commandments of men, that turn from the truth."

What The Ear Has Not Heard
Isaiah 64:4 "For since the beginning of the world men have not heard, nor perceived by the ear, neither hath the eye seen, O God, beside thee, what he hath prepared for him that waiteth for him."

1 Corinthians 2:9 "But as it is written, Eye hath not seen, nor ear heard, neither have entered into the heart of man, the things which God hath prepared for them that love him."

What To Hear
Proverbs 5:1 "My son, attend unto my wisdom, and bow thine ear to my understanding:"

Proverbs 8:32-33 "32Now therefore hearken unto me, O ye children: for blessed are they that keep my ways. 33Hear instruction, and be wise, and refuse it not."

Proverbs 19:20 "Hear counsel, and receive instruction, that thou mayest be wise in thy latter end."

Proverbs 22:17 "Bow down thine ear, and hear the words of the wise, and apply thine heart unto my knowledge."

Proverbs 23:12 "Apply thine heart unto instruction, and thine ears to the words of knowledge."

Isaiah 28:14 "Wherefore hear the word of the LORD, ye scornful men, that rule this people which is in Jerusalem."

Jeremiah 10:1 "Hear ye the word which the LORD speaketh unto you, O house of Israel:"

1 Timothy 1:3-4 "3As I besought thee to abide still at Ephesus, when I went into Macedonia, that thou mightest charge some that they teach no other doctrine, 4Neither give heed to fables and endless genealogies, which minister questions, rather than godly edifying which is in faith: so do."

Hebrews 2:1 "Therefore we ought to give the more earnest heed to the things which we have heard, lest at any time we should let them slip."

Who Does Not Hear God
Jeremiah 5:19-21 "19And it shall come to pass, when ye shall say, Wherefore doeth the LORD our God all these things unto us? then shalt thou answer them, Like as ye have forsaken me, and served strange gods in your land, so shall ye serve strangers in a land that is not yours. 20Declare this in the house of Jacob, and publish it in Judah, saying, 21Hear now this, O foolish people, and without understanding; which have eyes, and see not; which have ears, and hear not:"

John 8:47 "He that is of God heareth God's words: ye therefore hear them not, because ye are not of God."

Who Does Not Hear Rebuke
Proverbs 13:1 "A wise son heareth his father's instruction: but a scorner heareth not rebuke."

Who Does Not Hear The Lord's Disciples
1 John 4:1-6 "1Beloved, believe not every spirit, but try the spirits whether they are of God: because many false prophets are gone out into the world. 2Hereby know ye the Spirit of God: Every spirit that confesseth that Jesus Christ is come in the flesh is of God: 3And every spirit that confesseth not that Jesus Christ is come in the flesh is not of God: and this is that spirit of antichrist, whereof ye have heard that it should come; and even now already is it in the world. 4Ye are of God, little children, and have overcome them: because greater is he that is in you, than he that is in the world. 5They are of the world: therefore speak they of the world, and the world heareth them. 6We are of God: he that knoweth God heareth us; he that is not of God heareth not us. Hereby know we the spirit of truth, and the spirit of error."

Who Hears His Father's Instruction
Proverbs 13:1 "A wise son heareth his father's instruction: but a scorner heareth not rebuke."

Who Hears The Lord
Matthew 13:23 "But he that received seed into the good ground is he that heareth the word, and understandeth it; which also beareth fruit, and bringeth forth, some an hundredfold, some sixty, some thirty."

Mark 4:20 "And these are they which are sown on good ground; such as hear the word, and receive it, and bring forth fruit, some thirtyfold, some sixty, and some an hundred."

Luke 8:15 "But that on the good ground are they, which in an honest and good heart, having heard the word, keep it, and bring forth fruit with patience."

Luke 10:1-16 "1After these things the Lord appointed other seventy also, and sent them two and two before his face into every city and place, whither he himself would come. ²Therefore said he unto them, The harvest truly is great, but the labourers are few: pray ye therefore the Lord of the harvest, that he would send forth labourers into his harvest. ³Go your ways: behold, I send you forth as lambs among wolves. ⁴Carry neither purse, nor scrip, nor shoes: and salute no man by the way. ⁵And into whatsoever house ye enter, first say, Peace be to this house. ⁶And if the son of peace be there, your peace shall rest upon it: if not, it shall turn to you again. ⁷And in the same house remain, eating and drinking such things as they give: for the labourer is worthy of his hire. Go not from house to house. ⁸And into whatsoever city ye enter, and they receive you, eat such things as are set before you: ⁹And heal the sick that are therein, and say unto them, The kingdom of God is come nigh unto you. ¹⁰But into whatsoever city ye enter, and they receive you not, go your ways out into the streets of the same, and say, ¹¹Even the very dust of your city, which cleaveth on us, we do wipe off against you: notwithstanding be ye sure of this, that the kingdom of God is come nigh unto you. ¹²But I say unto you, that it shall be more tolerable in that day for Sodom, than for that city. ¹³Woe unto thee, Chorazin! woe unto thee, Bethsaida! for if the mighty works had been done in Tyre and Sidon, which have been done in you, they had a great while ago repented, sitting in sackcloth and ashes. ¹⁴But it shall be more tolerable for Tyre and Sidon at the judgment, than for you. ¹⁵And thou, Capernaum, which art exalted to heaven, shalt be thrust down to hell. ¹⁶He that heareth you heareth me; and he that despiseth you despiseth me; and he that despiseth me despiseth him that sent me."

John 8:47 "He that is of God heareth God's words: ye therefore hear them not, because ye are not of God."

John 10:1-5 "¹Verily, verily, I say unto you, He that entereth not by the door into the sheepfold, but climbeth up some other way, the same is a thief and a robber. ²But he that entereth in by the door is the shepherd of the sheep. ³To him the porter openeth; and the sheep hear his voice: and he calleth his own sheep by name, and leadeth them out. ⁴And when he putteth forth his own sheep, he goeth before them, and the sheep follow him: for they know his voice. ⁵And a stranger will they not follow, but will flee from him: for they know not the voice of strangers."

John 10:14-16 "¹⁴I am the good shepherd, and know my sheep, and am known of mine. ¹⁵As the Father knoweth me, even so know I the Father: and I lay down my life for the sheep. ¹⁶And other sheep I have, which are not of this fold: them also I must bring, and they shall hear my voice; and there shall be one fold, and one shepherd."

John 10:25-27 "²⁵Jesus answered them, I told you, and ye believed not: the works that I do in my Father's name, they bear witness of me. ²⁶But ye believe not, because ye are not of my sheep, as I said unto you. ²⁷My sheep hear my voice, and I know them, and they follow me."

John 18:37 "Pilate therefore said unto him, Art thou a king then? Jesus answered, Thou sayest that I am a king. To this end was I born, and for this cause came I into the world, that I should bear witness unto the truth. Every one that is of the truth heareth my voice."

Who Hears The Lord's Disciples
1 John 4:1-6 "¹Beloved, believe not every spirit, but try the spirits whether they are of God: because many false prophets are gone out into the world. ²Hereby know ye the Spirit of God: Every spirit that confesseth that Jesus Christ is come in the flesh is of God: ³And every spirit that confesseth not that Jesus Christ is come in the flesh is not of God: and this is that spirit of antichrist, whereof ye have heard that it should come; and even now already is it in the world. ⁴Ye are of God, little children, and have overcome them: because greater is he that is in you, than he that is in the world. ⁵They are of the world: therefore speak they of the world, and the world heareth them. ⁶We are of God: he that knoweth God heareth us; he that is not of God heareth not us. Hereby know we the spirit of truth, and the spirit of error."

Who Not To Listen To
Deuteronomy 13:1-3 "¹If there arise among you a prophet, or a dreamer of dreams, and giveth thee a sign or a wonder, ²And the sign or the wonder come to pass, whereof he spake unto thee, saying, Let us go after other gods, which thou hast not

known, and let us serve them; ³Thou shalt not hearken unto the words of that prophet, or that dreamer of dreams: for the LORD your God proveth you, to know whether ye love the LORD your God with all your heart and with all your soul."

Deuteronomy 13:6-8 "⁶If thy brother, the son of thy mother, or thy son, or thy daughter, or the wife of thy bosom, or thy friend, which is as thine own soul, entice thee secretly, saying, Let us go and serve other gods, which thou hast not known, thou, nor thy fathers; ⁷Namely, of the gods of the people which are round about you, nigh unto thee, or far off from thee, from the one end of the earth even unto the other end of the earth; ⁸Thou shalt not consent unto him, nor hearken unto him; neither shall thine eye pity him, neither shalt thou spare, neither shalt thou conceal him:"

Proverbs 14:7 "Go from the presence of a foolish man, when thou perceivest not in him the lips of knowledge."

Jeremiah 29:8-9 "⁸For thus saith the LORD of hosts, the God of Israel; Let not your prophets and your diviners, that be in the midst of you, deceive you, neither hearken to your dreams which ye cause to be dreamed. ⁹For they prophesy falsely unto you in my name: I have not sent them, saith the LORD."

Who Shall Not Be Heard
Proverbs 21:13 "Whoso stoppeth his ears at the cry of the poor, he also shall cry himself, but shall not be heard."

Who The Lord Hears
Exodus 22:20-23 "²⁰He that sacrificeth unto any god, save unto the LORD only, he shall be utterly destroyed. ²¹Thou shalt neither vex a stranger, nor oppress him: for ye were strangers in the land of Egypt. ²²Ye shall not afflict any widow, or fatherless child. ²³If thou afflict them in any wise, and they cry at all unto me, I will surely hear their cry;"

2 Chronicles 7:12-14 "¹²And the LORD appeared to Solomon by night, and said unto him, I have heard thy prayer, and have chosen this place to myself for an house of sacrifice. ¹³If I shut up heaven that there be no rain, or if I command the locusts to devour the land, or if I send pestilence among my people;¹⁴ If my people, which are called by my name, shall humble themselves, and pray, and seek my face, and turn from their wicked ways; then will I hear from heaven, and will forgive their sin, and will heal their land."

Job 34:23-28 "²³For he will not lay upon man more than right; that he should enter into judgment with God. ²⁴He shall break in pieces mighty men without number, and set others in their stead. ²⁵Therefore he knoweth their works, and he overturneth them in the night, so that they are destroyed. ²⁶He striketh them as wicked men in the open sight of others; ²⁷Because they turned back from him, and would not consider any of his ways: ²⁸So that they cause the cry of the poor to come unto him, and he heareth the cry of the afflicted."

Psalm 4:3 "But know that the LORD hath set apart him that is godly for himself: the LORD will hear when I call unto him."

Psalm 20:6 "Now know I that the LORD saveth his anointed; he will hear him from his holy heaven with the saving strength of his right hand."

Psalm 34:6 "This poor man cried, and the LORD heard him, and saved him out of all his troubles."

Psalm 34:15 "The eyes of the LORD are upon the righteous, and his ears are open unto their cry."

Psalm 34:17 "The righteous cry, and the LORD heareth, and delivereth them out of all their troubles."

Psalm 40:1 "I waited patiently for the LORD; and he inclined unto me, and heard my cry."

Psalm 91:9-15 "⁹Because thou hast made the LORD, which is my refuge, even the most High, thy habitation; ¹⁰There shall no evil befall thee, neither shall any plague come nigh thy dwelling. ¹¹For he shall give his angels charge over thee, to keep thee in all thy ways. ¹²They shall bear thee up in their hands, lest thou dash thy foot against a stone. ¹³Thou shalt tread upon the lion and adder: the young lion and the dragon shalt thou trample under feet. ¹⁴Because he hath set his love upon me, therefore will I deliver him: I will set him on high, because he hath known my name. ¹⁵He shall call upon me, and I will answer him: I will be with him in trouble; I will deliver him, and honour him."

Psalm 145:18-19 "[18]The LORD is nigh unto all them that call upon him, to all that call upon him in truth. [19]He will fulfil the desire of them that fear him: he also will hear their cry, and will save them."

Proverbs 15:29 "The LORD is far from the wicked: but he heareth the prayer of the righteous."

Isaiah 65:22-24 "[22]They shall not build, and another inhabit; they shall not plant, and another eat: for as the days of a tree are the days of my people, and mine elect shall long enjoy the work of their hands. [23]They shall not labour in vain, nor bring forth for trouble; for they are the seed of the blessed of the LORD, and their offspring with them. [24]And it shall come to pass, that before they call, I will answer; and while they are yet speaking, I will hear."

Daniel 10:12 "Then said he unto me, Fear not, Daniel: for from the first day that thou didst set thine heart to understand, and to chasten thyself before thy God, thy words were heard, and I am come for thy words."

1 Peter 3:12 "For the eyes of the Lord are over the righteous, and his ears are open unto their prayers: but the face of the Lord is against them that do evil."

Who The Lord Will Not Hear

1 Samuel 8:4-18 "[4]Then all the elders of Israel gathered themselves together, and came to Samuel unto Ramah, [5]And said unto him, Behold, thou art old, and thy sons walk not in thy ways: now make us a king to judge us like all the nations. [6]But the thing displeased Samuel, when they said, Give us a king to judge us. And Samuel prayed unto the LORD. [7]And the LORD said unto Samuel, Hearken unto the voice of the people in all that they say unto thee: for they have not rejected thee, but they have rejected me, that I should not reign over them. [8]According to all the works which they have done since the day that I brought them up out of Egypt even unto this day, wherewith they have forsaken me, and served other gods, so do they also unto thee. [9]Now therefore hearken unto their voice: howbeit yet protest solemnly unto them, and shew them the manner of the king that shall reign over them. [10]And Samuel told all the words of the LORD unto the people that asked of him a king. [11]And he said,

This will be the manner of the king that shall reign over you: He will take your sons, and appoint them for himself, for his chariots, and to be his horsemen; and some shall run before his chariots. [12]And he will appoint him captains over thousands, and captains over fifties; and will set them to ear his ground, and to reap his harvest, and to make his instruments of war, and instruments of his chariots. [13]And he will take your daughters to be confectionaries, and to be cooks, and to be bakers. [14]And he will take your fields, and your vineyards, and your oliveyards, even the best of them, and give them to his servants. [15]And he will take the tenth of your seed, and of your vineyards, and give to his officers, and to his servants. [16]And he will take your menservants, and your maidservants, and your goodliest young men, and your asses, and put them to his work. [17]He will take the tenth of your sheep: and ye shall be his servants. [18]And ye shall cry out in that day because of your king which ye shall have chosen you; and the LORD will not hear you in that day."

Job 27:8-10 "[8]For what is the hope of the hypocrite, though he hath gained, when God taketh away his soul? [9]Will God hear his cry when trouble cometh upon him? [10]Will he delight himself in the Almighty? will he always call upon God?"

Psalm 66:18 "If I regard iniquity in my heart, the Lord will not hear me."

Isaiah 1:10-15 "[10]Hear the word of the LORD, ye rulers of Sodom; give ear unto the law of our God, ye people of Gomorrah. [11]To what purpose is the multitude of your sacrifices unto me? saith the LORD: I am full of the burnt offerings of rams, and the fat of fed beasts; and I delight not in the blood of bullocks, or of lambs, or of he goats. [12]When ye come to appear before me, who hath required this at your hand, to tread my courts? [13]Bring no more vain oblations; incense is an abomination unto me; the new moons and sabbaths, the calling of assemblies, I cannot away with; it is iniquity, even the solemn meeting. [14]Your new moons and your appointed feasts my soul hateth: they are a trouble unto me; I am weary to bear them. [15]And when ye spread forth your hands, I will hide mine eyes from you: yea, when ye make many prayers, I will not hear: your hands are full of blood."

Isaiah 59:1-2 "¹Behold, the LORD's hand is not shortened, that it cannot save; neither his ear heavy, that it cannot hear: ²But your iniquities have separated between you and your God, and your sins have hid his face from you, that he will not hear."

Zechariah 7:11-13 "¹¹But they refused to hearken, and pulled away the shoulder, and stopped their ears, that they should not hear. ¹²Yea, they made their hearts as an adamant stone, lest they should hear the law, and the words which the LORD of hosts hath sent in his spirit by the former prophets: therefore came a great wrath from the LORD of hosts. ¹³Therefore it is come to pass, that as he cried, and they would not hear; so they cried, and I would not hear, saith the LORD of hosts:"

Who The World Hears

1 John 4:1-5 "¹Beloved, believe not every spirit, but try the spirits whether they are of God: because many false prophets are gone out into the world. ²Hereby know ye the Spirit of God: Every spirit that confesseth that Jesus Christ is come in the flesh is of God: ³And every spirit that confesseth not that Jesus Christ is come in the flesh is not of God: and this is that spirit of antichrist, whereof ye have heard that it should come; and even now already is it in the world. ⁴Ye are of God, little children, and have overcome them: because greater is he that is in you, than he that is in the world. ⁵They are of the world: therefore speak they of the world, and the world heareth them."

Who To Listen To

Proverbs 23:22 "Hearken unto thy father that begat thee, and despise not thy mother when she is old."

Who Will Not Hear The Law Of The Lord

Isaiah 30:1-9 "¹Woe to the rebellious children, saith the LORD, that take counsel, but not of me; and that cover with a covering, but not of my spirit, that they may add sin to sin: ²That walk to go down into Egypt, and have not asked at my mouth; to strengthen themselves in the strength of Pharaoh, and to trust in the shadow of Egypt! ³Therefore shall the strength of Pharaoh be your shame, and the trust in the shadow of Egypt your confusion. ⁴For his princes were at Zoan, and his ambassadors came to Hanes. ⁵They were all ashamed of a people that could not profit them, nor be an help nor profit, but a shame, and also a reproach. ⁶The burden of the beasts of the south: into the land of trouble and anguish, from whence come the young and old lion, the viper and fiery flying serpent, they will carry their riches upon the shoulders of young asses, and their treasures upon the bunches of camels, to a people that shall not profit them. ⁷For the Egyptians shall help in vain, and to no purpose: therefore have I cried concerning this, Their strength is to sit still. ⁸Now go, write it before them in a table, and note it in a book, that it may be for the time to come for ever and ever: ⁹That this is a rebellious people, lying children, children that will not hear the law of the LORD:"

Why Some Do Not Hear The Word Of God

John 8:47 "He that is of God heareth God's words: ye therefore hear them not, because ye are not of God."

1 John 4:1-6 "¹Beloved, believe not every spirit, but try the spirits whether they are of God: because many false prophets are gone out into the world. ²Hereby know ye the Spirit of God: Every spirit that confesseth that Jesus Christ is come in the flesh is of God: ³And every spirit that confesseth not that Jesus Christ is come in the flesh is not of God: and this is that spirit of antichrist, whereof ye have heard that it should come; and even now already is it in the world. ⁴Ye are of God, little children, and have overcome them: because greater is he that is in you, than he that is in the world. ⁵They are of the world: therefore speak they of the world, and the world heareth them. ⁶We are of God: he that knoweth God heareth us; he that is not of God heareth not us. Hereby know we the spirit of truth, and the spirit of error."

HEART

God Being The Strength Of Your Heart

Psalm 73:26 "My flesh and my heart faileth: but God is the strength of my heart, and my portion for ever."

Hearts That Devise Wicked Imaginations

Proverbs 6:16-18 "[16]These six things doth the LORD hate: yea, seven are an abomination unto him: [17]A proud look, a lying tongue, and hands that shed innocent blood, [18]An heart that deviseth wicked imaginations, feet that be swift in running to mischief,"

Heaviness In The Heart

Proverbs 12:25 "Heaviness in the heart of man maketh it stoop: but a good word maketh it glad."

Inclining Your Heart To The Lord

Joshua 24:23 "Now therefore put away, said he, the strange gods which are among you, and incline your heart unto the LORD God of Israel."

Letting Your Heart Be Perfect With The Lord

1 Kings 8:61 "Let your heart therefore be perfect with the LORD our God, to walk in his statutes, and to keep his commandments, as at this day."

Merry Hearts

Proverbs 15:13 "A merry heart maketh a cheerful countenance: but by sorrow of the heart the spirit is broken."

Proverbs 17:22 "A merry heart doeth good like a medicine: but a broken spirit drieth the bones."

Not Imagining Evil In Your Heart

Zechariah 7:9-10 "[9]Thus speaketh the LORD of hosts, saying, Execute true judgment, and shew mercy and compassions every man to his brother: [10]And oppress not the widow, nor the fatherless, the stranger, nor the poor; and let none of you imagine evil against his brother in your heart."

Zechariah 8:17 "And let none of you imagine evil in your hearts against his neighbour; and love no false oath: for all these are things that I hate, saith the LORD."

Not Letting Your Heart Be Troubled

John 14:27 "Peace I leave with you, my peace I give unto you: not as the world giveth, give I unto you. Let not your heart be troubled, neither let it be afraid."

Pouring Out Your Heart Before God

Psalm 62:7-8 "[7]In God is my salvation and my glory: the rock of my strength, and my refuge, is in God. [8]Trust in him at all times; ye people, pour out your heart before him: God is a refuge for us. Selah."

Proud Hearts

Psalm 119:69-70 "[69]The proud have forged a lie against me: but I will keep thy precepts with my whole heart. [70]Their heart is as fat as grease; but I delight in thy law."

Proverbs 21:4 "An high look, and a proud heart, and the plowing of the wicked, is sin."

Obadiah 1-3 "[1]The vision of Obadiah. Thus saith the Lord GOD concerning Edom; We have heard a rumour from the LORD, and an ambassador is sent among the heathen, Arise ye, and let us rise up against her in battle. [2]Behold, I have made thee small among the heathen: thou art greatly despised. [3]The pride of thine heart hath deceived thee, thou that dwellest in the clefts of the rock, whose habitation is high; that saith in his heart, Who shall bring me down to the ground?"

Purifying Your Heart

James 4:8 "Draw nigh to God, and he will draw nigh to you. Cleanse your hands, ye sinners; and purify your hearts, ye double minded."

Sorrow Of The Heart

Proverbs 15:13 "A merry heart maketh a cheerful countenance: but by sorrow of the heart the spirit is broken."

Sound Hearts

Proverbs 14:30 "A sound heart is the life of the flesh: but envy the rottenness of the bones."

The Heart Being Established With Grace

Hebrews 13:9 "Be not carried about with divers and strange doctrines. For it is a good thing that the heart be established with grace; not with meats, which have not profited them that have been occupied therein."

The Heart Of Fools

Psalm 14:1 "The fool hath said in his heart, There is no God. They are corrupt, they have done abominable works, there is none that doeth good."

Psalm 53:1 "The fool hath said in his heart, There is no God. Corrupt are they, and have done abominable iniquity: there is none that doeth good."

Proverbs 12:23 "A prudent man concealeth knowledge: but the heart of fools proclaimeth foolishness."

Proverbs 15:7 "The lips of the wise disperse knowledge: but the heart of the foolish doeth not so."

Proverbs 18:2 "A fool hath no delight in understanding, but that his heart may discover itself."

Ecclesiastes 7:4 "The heart of the wise is in the house of mourning; but the heart of fools is in the house of mirth."

Ecclesiastes 10:2 "A wise man's heart is at his right hand; but a fool's heart at his left."

The Heart Of Man
Genesis 6:5 "And GOD saw that the wickedness of man was great in the earth, and that every imagination of the thoughts of his heart was only evil continually."

Genesis 8:21 "And the LORD smelled a sweet savour; and the LORD said in his heart, I will not again curse the ground any more for man's sake; for the imagination of man's heart is evil from his youth; neither will I again smite any more every thing living, as I have done."

Psalm 73:26 "My flesh and my heart faileth: but God is the strength of my heart, and my portion for ever."

Proverbs 16:9 "A man's heart deviseth his way: but the LORD directeth his steps."

Proverbs 18:12 "Before destruction the heart of man is haughty, and before honour is humility."

Proverbs 19:3 "The foolishness of man perverteth his way: and his heart fretteth against the LORD."

Proverbs 19:21 "There are many devices in a man's heart; nevertheless the counsel of the LORD, that shall stand."

Ecclesiastes 9:3 "This is an evil among all things that are done under the sun, that there is one event unto all: yea, also the heart of the sons of men is full of evil, and madness is in their heart while they live, and after that they go to the dead."

Jeremiah 17:9-10 "⁹The heart is deceitful above all things, and desperately wicked: who can know it? ¹⁰I the LORD search the heart, I try the reins, even to give every man according to his ways, and according to the fruit of his doings."

Romans 1:21-22 "²¹Because that, when they knew God, they glorified him not as God, neither were thankful; but became vain in their imaginations, and their foolish heart was darkened. ²²Professing themselves to be wise, they became fools,"

1 John 3:20 "For if our heart condemn us, God is greater than our heart, and knoweth all things."

The Heart Of The Prudent
Proverbs 18:15 "The heart of the prudent getteth knowledge; and the ear of the wise seeketh knowledge."

The Heart Of The Righteous
Psalm 112:6-8 "⁶Surely he shall not be moved for ever: the righteous shall be in everlasting remembrance. ⁷He shall not be afraid of evil tidings: his heart is fixed, trusting in the LORD. ⁸His heart is established, he shall not be afraid, until he see his desire upon his enemies."

Proverbs 15:28 "The heart of the righteous studieth to answer: but the mouth of the wicked poureth out evil things."

The Heart Of The Wicked
Proverbs 10:20 "The tongue of the just is as choice silver: the heart of the wicked is little worth."

Proverbs 26:23 "Burning lips and a wicked heart are like a potsherd covered with silver dross."

The Heart Of The Wise
Proverbs 16:23 "The heart of the wise teacheth his mouth, and addeth learning to his lips."

Ecclesiastes 7:4 "The heart of the wise is in the house of mourning; but the heart of fools is in the house of mirth."

Ecclesiastes 8:2-5 "²I counsel thee to keep the king's commandment, and that in regard of the oath of God. ³Be not hasty to go out of his sight: stand not in an evil thing; for he doeth whatsoever pleaseth him. ⁴Where the word of a king is, there is power: and who may say unto him, What doest thou? ⁵Whoso keepeth the commandment shall feel no evil thing: and a wise man's heart discerneth both time and judgment."

Ecclesiastes 10:2 "A wise man's heart is at his right hand; but a fool's heart at his left."

The Heart Of Those That Have Understanding
Proverbs 14:33 "Wisdom resteth in the heart of him that hath understanding: but that which is in the midst of fools is made known."

Proverbs 15:14 "The heart of him that hath understanding seeketh knowledge: but the mouth of fools feedeth on foolishness."

The Hypocrites In Heart

Job 36:13-14 "13But the hypocrites in heart heap up wrath: they cry not when he bindeth them. 14They die in youth, and their life is among the unclean."

Isaiah 29:13 "Wherefore the Lord said, Forasmuch as this people draw near me with their mouth, and with their lips do honour me, but have removed their heart far from me, and their fear toward me is taught by the precept of men:"

Ezekiel 33:30-32 "30Also, thou son of man, the children of thy people still are talking against thee by the walls and in the doors of the houses, and speak one to another, every one to his brother, saying, Come, I pray you, and hear what is the word that cometh forth from the LORD. 31And they come unto thee as the people cometh, and they sit before thee as my people, and they hear thy words, but they will not do them: for with their mouth they shew much love, but their heart goeth after their covetousness. 32And, lo, thou art unto them as a very lovely song of one that hath a pleasant voice, and can play well on an instrument: for they hear thy words, but they do them not."

Mark 7:6-13 "6He answered and said unto them, Well hath Esaias prophesied of you hypocrites, as it is written, This people honoureth me with their lips, but their heart is far from me. 7Howbeit in vain do they worship me, teaching for doctrines the commandments of men. 8For laying aside the commandment of God, ye hold the tradition of men, as the washing of pots and cups: and many other such like things ye do. 9And he said unto them, Full well ye reject the commandment of God, that ye may keep your own tradition. 10For Moses said, Honour thy father and thy mother; and, Whoso curseth father or mother, let him die the death: 11But ye say, If a man shall say to his father or mother, It is Corban, that is to say, a gift, by whatsoever thou mightest be profited by me; he shall be free. 12And ye suffer him no more to do ought for his father or his mother; 13Making the word of God of none effect through your tradition, which ye have delivered: and many such like things do ye."

The Lord Knowing The Heart

1 Kings 8:28-39 "28Yet have thou respect unto the prayer of thy servant, and to his supplication, O LORD my God, to hearken unto the cry and to the prayer, which thy servant prayeth before thee to day: 29That thine eyes may be open toward this house night and day, even toward the place of which thou hast said, My name shall be there: that thou mayest hearken unto the prayer which thy servant shall make toward this place. 30And hearken thou to the supplication of thy servant, and of thy people Israel, when they shall pray toward this place: and hear thou in heaven thy dwelling place: and when thou hearest, forgive. 31If any man trespass against his neighbour, and an oath be laid upon him to cause him to swear, and the oath come before thine altar in this house: 32Then hear thou in heaven, and do, and judge thy servants, condemning the wicked, to bring his way upon his head; and justifying the righteous, to give him according to his righteousness. 33When thy people Israel be smitten down before the enemy, because they have sinned against thee, and shall turn again to thee, and confess thy name, and pray, and make supplication unto thee in this house: 34Then hear thou in heaven, and forgive the sin of thy people Israel, and bring them again unto the land which thou gavest unto their fathers. 35When heaven is shut up, and there is no rain, because they have sinned against thee; if they pray toward this place, and confess thy name, and turn from their sin, when thou afflictest them: 36Then hear thou in heaven, and forgive the sin of thy servants, and of thy people Israel, that thou teach them the good way wherein they should walk, and give rain upon thy land, which thou hast given to thy people for an inheritance. 37If there be in the land famine, if there be pestilence, blasting, mildew, locust, or if there be caterpiller; if their enemy besiege them in the land of their cities; whatsoever plague, whatsoever sickness there be; 38What prayer and supplication soever be made by any man, or by all thy people Israel, which shall know every man the plague of his own heart, and spread forth his hands toward this house: 39Then hear thou in heaven thy dwelling place, and forgive, and do, and give to every man according to his ways, whose heart thou knowest; (for thou, even thou only, knowest the hearts of all the children of men;)"

1 Chronicles 28:9 "And thou, Solomon my son, know thou the God of thy father, and serve him with a perfect heart and with a willing mind: for the LORD searcheth all hearts, and understandeth all the imaginations of the thoughts: if thou seek him, he will be found of thee; but if thou forsake him, he will cast thee off for ever."

2 Chronicles 6:19-30 "19Have respect therefore to the prayer of thy servant, and to his supplication, O LORD my God, to hearken unto the cry and the prayer which thy servant prayeth before thee: 20That thine eyes may be open upon this house day and night, upon the place whereof thou hast said that thou wouldest put thy name there; to hearken unto the prayer which thy servant prayeth toward this place. 21Hearken therefore unto the supplications of thy servant, and of thy people Israel, which they shall make toward this place: hear thou from thy dwelling place, even from heaven; and when thou hearest, forgive. 22If a man sin against his neighbour, and an oath be laid upon him to make him swear, and the oath come before thine altar in this house; 23Then hear thou from heaven, and do, and judge thy servants, by requiting the wicked, by recompensing his way upon his own head; and by justifying the righteous, by giving him according to his righteousness. 24And if thy people Israel be put to the worse before the enemy, because they have sinned against thee; and shall return and confess thy name, and pray and make supplication before thee in this house; 25Then hear thou from the heavens, and forgive the sin of thy people Israel, and bring them again unto the land which thou gavest to them and to their fathers. 26When the heaven is shut up, and there is no rain, because they have sinned against thee; yet if they pray toward this place, and confess thy name, and turn from their sin, when thou dost afflict them; 27Then hear thou from heaven, and forgive the sin of thy servants, and of thy people Israel, when thou hast taught them the good way, wherein they should walk; and send rain upon thy land, which thou hast given unto thy people for an inheritance. 28If there be dearth in the land, if there be pestilence, if there be blasting, or mildew, locusts, or caterpillers; if their enemies besiege them in the cities of their land; whatsoever sore or whatsoever sickness there be: 29Then what prayer or what supplication soever shall be made of any man, or of all thy people Israel, when every one shall know his own sore and his own grief, and shall spread forth his hands in this house: 30Then hear thou from heaven thy dwelling place, and forgive, and render unto every man according unto all his ways, whose heart thou knowest; (for thou only knowest the hearts of the children of men:)"

Luke 16:15 "And he said unto them, Ye are they which justify yourselves before men; but God knoweth your hearts: for that which is highly esteemed among men is abomination in the sight of God."

Acts 15:8 "And God, which knoweth the hearts, bare them witness, giving them the Holy Ghost, even as he did unto us;"

The Lord Looking Upon The Heart
1 Samuel 16:7 "But the LORD said unto Samuel, Look not on his countenance, or on the height of his stature; because I have refused him: for the LORD seeth not as man seeth; for man looketh on the outward appearance, but the LORD looketh on the heart."

1 Chronicles 28:9 "And thou, Solomon my son, know thou the God of thy father, and serve him with a perfect heart and with a willing mind: for the LORD searcheth all hearts, and understandeth all the imaginations of the thoughts: if thou seek him, he will be found of thee; but if thou forsake him, he will cast thee off for ever."

Proverbs 5:21 "For the ways of man are before the eyes of the LORD, and he pondereth all his goings."

Proverbs 21:2 "Every way of a man is right in his own eyes: but the LORD pondereth the hearts."

Proverbs 24:11-12 "11If thou forbear to deliver them that are drawn unto death, and those that are ready to be slain; 12If thou sayest, Behold, we knew it not; doth not he that pondereth the heart consider it? and he that keepeth thy soul, doth not he know it? and shall not he render to every man according to his works?"

Jeremiah 17:9-10 "9The heart is deceitful above all things, and desperately wicked: who can know it? 10I the LORD search the heart, I try the reins, even to give every man according to his ways, and according to the fruit of his doings."

Revelation 2:18-23 "¹⁸And unto the angel of the church in Thyatira write; These things saith the Son of God, who hath his eyes like unto a flame of fire, and his feet are like fine brass; ¹⁹I know thy works, and charity, and service, and faith, and thy patience, and thy works; and the last to be more than the first. ²⁰Notwithstanding I have a few things against thee, because thou sufferest that woman Jezebel, which calleth herself a prophetess, to teach and to seduce my servants to commit fornication, and to eat things sacrificed unto idols. ²¹And I gave her space to repent of her fornication; and she repented not. ²²Behold, I will cast her into a bed, and them that commit adultery with her into great tribulation, except they repent of their deeds. ²³And I will kill her children with death; and all the churches shall know that I am he which searcheth the reins and hearts: and I will give unto every one of you according to your works."

The Lord Shining In Your Heart
2 Corinthians 4:6 "For God, who commanded the light to shine out of darkness, hath shined in our hearts, to give the light of the knowledge of the glory of God in the face of Jesus Christ."

The Pure In Heart
Matthew 5:8 "Blessed are the pure in heart: for they shall see God."

The Reward For Walking After The Imagination Of Your Own Heart
Deuteronomy 29:17-29 "¹⁷And ye have seen their abominations, and their idols, wood and stone, silver and gold, which were among them:) ¹⁸Lest there should be among you man, or woman, or family, or tribe, whose heart turneth away this day from the LORD our God, to go and serve the gods of these nations; lest there should be among you a root that beareth gall and wormwood; ¹⁹And it come to pass, when he heareth the words of this curse, that he bless himself in his heart, saying, I shall have peace, though I walk in the imagination of mine heart, to add drunkenness to thirst: ²⁰The LORD will not spare him, but then the anger of the LORD and his jealousy shall smoke against that man, and all the curses that are written in this book shall lie upon him, and the LORD shall blot out his name from under heaven. ²¹And the LORD shall separate him unto evil out of all the tribes of Israel, according to all the curses of the covenant that are written in this book of the law: ²²So that the generation to come of your children that shall rise up after you, and the stranger that shall come from a far land, shall say, when they see the plagues of that land, and the sicknesses which the LORD hath laid upon it; ²³And that the whole land thereof is brimstone, and salt, and burning, that it is not sown, nor beareth, nor any grass groweth therein, like the overthrow of Sodom, and Gomorrah, Admah, and Zeboim, which the LORD overthrew in his anger, and in his wrath: ²⁴Even all nations shall say, Wherefore hath the LORD done thus unto this land? what meaneth the heat of this great anger? ²⁵Then men shall say, Because they have forsaken the covenant of the LORD God of their fathers, which he made with them when he brought them forth out of the land of Egypt: ²⁶For they went and served other gods, and worshipped them, gods whom they knew not, and whom he had not given unto them: ²⁷And the anger of the LORD was kindled against this land, to bring upon it all the curses that are written in this book: ²⁸And the LORD rooted them out of their land in anger, and in wrath, and in great indignation, and cast them into another land, as it is this day. ²⁹The secret things belong unto the LORD our God: but those things which are revealed belong unto us and to our children for ever, that we may do all the words of this law."

Jeremiah 9:13-16 "¹³And the LORD saith, Because they have forsaken my law which I set before them, and have not obeyed my voice, neither walked therein; ¹⁴But have walked after the imagination of their own heart, and after Baalim, which their fathers taught them: ¹⁵Therefore thus saith the LORD of hosts, the God of Israel; Behold, I will feed them, even this people, with wormwood, and give them water of gall to drink. ¹⁶I will scatter them also among the heathen, whom neither they nor their fathers have known: and I will send a sword after them, till I have consumed them."

Jeremiah 16:11-13 "¹¹Then shalt thou say unto them, Because your fathers have forsaken me, saith the LORD, and have walked after other gods, and have served them, and have worshipped them, and have forsaken me, and have not kept my law; ¹²And ye have done worse than your fathers; for, behold, ye walk every one after the imagination of his evil heart, that they may not hearken unto me: [13]Therefore will I cast you out of this land into a land that ye know not, neither ye nor your fathers; and there shall ye serve other gods day and night; where I will not shew you favour."

The Wise In Heart
Proverbs 10:8 "The wise in heart will receive commandments: but a prating fool shall fall."

Proverbs 16:21 "The wise in heart shall be called prudent: and the sweetness of the lips increaseth learning."

The Wise Of Heart
Job 37:23-24 "[23]Touching the Almighty, we cannot find him out: he is excellent in power, and in judgment, and in plenty of justice: he will not afflict. [24]Men do therefore fear him: he respecteth not any that are wise of heart."

Those That Are Of A Proud Heart
Proverbs 28:25 "He that is of a proud heart stirreth up strife: but he that putteth his trust in the LORD shall be made fat."

Those That Are Upright In Heart
Psalm 32:11 "Be glad in the LORD, and rejoice, ye righteous: and shout for joy, all ye that are upright in heart."

Those That Harden Their Heart
Proverbs 28:14 "Happy is the man that feareth alway: but he that hardeneth his heart shall fall into mischief."

Those That Have A Froward Heart
Proverbs 11:20 "They that are of a froward heart are abomination to the LORD: but such as are upright in their way are his delight."

Proverbs 17:20 "He that hath a froward heart findeth no good: and he that hath a perverse tongue falleth into mischief."

Those That Have A Perverse Heart
Proverbs 12:8 "A man shall be commended according to his wisdom: but he that is of a perverse heart shall be despised."

Those That Trust In Their Own Heart
Proverbs 28:26 "He that trusteth in his own heart is a fool: but whoso walketh wisely, he shall be delivered."

Those That Walk In The Imagination Of Their Heart
Jeremiah 13:9-10 "[9]Thus saith the LORD, After this manner will I mar the pride of Judah, and the great pride of Jerusalem. [10]This evil people, which refuse to hear my words, which walk in the imagination of their heart, and walk after other gods, to serve them, and to worship them, shall even be as this girdle, which is good for nothing."

Jeremiah 23:16-17 "[16]Thus saith the LORD of hosts, Hearken not unto the words of the prophets that prophesy unto you: they make you vain: they speak a vision of their own heart, and not out of the mouth of the LORD. [17]They say still unto them that despise me, The LORD hath said, Ye shall have peace; and they say unto every one that walketh after the imagination of his own heart, No evil shall come upon you."

Those Whose Hearts Are Perfect Toward The Lord
2 Chronicles 16:9 "For the eyes of the LORD run to and fro throughout the whole earth, to shew himself strong in the behalf of them whose heart is perfect toward him. Herein thou hast done foolishly: therefore from henceforth thou shalt have wars."

Those Whose Hearts Depart From The Lord
Jeremiah 17:5-6 "[5]Thus saith the LORD; Cursed be the man that trusteth in man, and maketh flesh his arm, and whose heart departeth from the LORD. [6]For he shall be like the heath in the desert, and shall not see when good cometh; but shall inhabit the parched places in the wilderness, in a salt land and not inhabited."

Those Whose Hearts Walk After Detestable Things
Ezekiel 11:21 "But as for them whose heart walketh after the heart of their detestable things and their abominations, I will recompense their way upon their own heads, saith the Lord GOD."

What Destroys The Heart
Ecclesiastes 7:7 "Surely oppression maketh a wise man mad; and a gift destroyeth the heart."

What Not To Set Your Heart Upon
Psalm 62:10 "Trust not in oppression, and become not vain in robbery: if riches increase, set not your heart upon them."

What Proceeds From The Heart

Matthew 15:10-11 "[10]And he called the multitude, and said unto them, Hear, and understand: [11]Not that which goeth into the mouth defileth a man; but that which cometh out of the mouth, this defileth a man."

Matthew 15:15-20 "[15]Then answered Peter and said unto him, Declare unto us this parable. [16]And Jesus said, Are ye also yet without understanding? [17]Do not ye yet understand, that whatsoever entereth in at the mouth goeth into the belly, and is cast out into the draught? [18]But those things which proceed out of the mouth come forth from the heart; and they defile the man. [19]For out of the heart proceed evil thoughts, murders, adulteries, fornications, thefts, false witness, blasphemies: [20]These are the things which defile a man: but to eat with unwashen hands defileth not a man."

Mark 7:14-23 "[14]And when he had called all the people unto him, he said unto them, Hearken unto me every one of you, and understand: [15]There is nothing from without a man, that entering into him can defile him: but the things which come out of him, those are they that defile the man. [16]If any man have ears to hear, let him hear. [17]And when he was entered into the house from the people, his disciples asked him concerning the parable. [18]And he saith unto them, Are ye so without understanding also? Do ye not perceive, that whatsoever thing from without entereth into the man, it cannot defile him; [19]Because it entereth not into his heart, but into the belly, and goeth out into the draught, purging all meats? [20]And he said, That which cometh out of the man, that defileth the man. [21]For from within, out of the heart of men, proceed evil thoughts, adulteries, fornications, murders, [22]Thefts, covetousness, wickedness, deceit, lasciviousness, an evil eye, blasphemy, pride, foolishness: [23]All these evil things come from within, and defile the man."

What Rejoices The Heart

Psalm 19:8 "The statutes of the LORD are right, rejoicing the heart: the commandment of the LORD is pure, enlightening the eyes."

Proverbs 15:30 "The light of the eyes rejoiceth the heart: and a good report maketh the bones fat."

Proverbs 27:9 "Ointment and perfume rejoice the heart: so doth the sweetness of a man's friend by hearty counsel."

What Shall Keep Your Heart

Philippians 4:7 "And the peace of God, which passeth all understanding, shall keep your hearts and minds through Christ Jesus."

What Takes Away The Heart

Hosea 4:11-12 "[11]Whoredom and wine and new wine take away the heart. [12]My people ask counsel at their stocks, and their staff declareth unto them: for the spirit of whoredoms hath caused them to err, and they have gone a whoring from under their God."

Where Your Heart Will Be

Matthew 6:19-21 "[19]Lay not up for yourselves treasures upon earth, where moth and rust doth corrupt, and where thieves break through and steal: [20]But lay up for yourselves treasures in heaven, where neither moth nor rust doth corrupt, and where thieves do not break through nor steal: [21]For where your treasure is, there will your heart be also."

Luke 12:33-34 "[33]Sell that ye have, and give alms; provide yourselves bags which wax not old, a treasure in the heavens that faileth not, where no thief approacheth, neither moth corrupteth. [34]For where your treasure is, there will your heart be also."

Whose Heart Becomes Darkened

Romans 1:21-22 "[21]Because that, when they knew God, they glorified him not as God, neither were thankful; but became vain in their imaginations, and their foolish heart was darkened. [22]Professing themselves to be wise, they became fools,"

Ephesians 4:17-18 "[17]This I say therefore, and testify in the Lord, that ye henceforth walk not as other Gentiles walk, in the vanity of their mind, [18]Having the understanding darkened, being alienated from the life of God through the ignorance that is in them, because of the blindness of their heart:"

Whose Heart Is Right With God

Romans 2:29 "But he is a Jew, which is one inwardly; and circumcision is that of the heart, in the spirit, and not in the letter; whose praise is not of men, but of God."

Whose Heart Shall Be Strengthened

Psalm 27:14 "Wait on the LORD: be of good courage, and he shall strengthen thine heart: wait, I say, on the LORD."

Psalm 31:24 "Be of good courage, and he shall strengthen your heart, all ye that hope in the LORD."

HEAVEN/THE HEAVENS

Paul's Vision Of Paradise
2 Corinthians 12:1-4 "[1]It is not expedient for me doubtless to glory. I will come to visions and revelations of the Lord. [2]I knew a man in Christ above fourteen years ago, (whether in the body, I cannot tell; or whether out of the body, I cannot tell: God knoweth;) such an one caught up to the third heaven. [3]And I knew such a man, (whether in the body, or out of the body, I cannot tell: God knoweth;) [4]How that he was caught up into paradise, and heard unspeakable words, which it is not lawful for a man to utter."

The Heavens Being Shaken
Isaiah 13:9-13 "[9]Behold, the day of the LORD cometh, cruel both with wrath and fierce anger, to lay the land desolate: and he shall destroy the sinners thereof out of it. [10]For the stars of heaven and the constellations thereof shall not give their light: the sun shall be darkened in his going forth, and the moon shall not cause her light to shine. [11]And I will punish the world for their evil, and the wicked for their iniquity; and I will cause the arrogancy of the proud to cease, and will lay low the haughtiness of the terrible. [12]I will make a man more precious than fine gold; even a man than the golden wedge of Ophir. [13]Therefore I will shake the heavens, and the earth shall remove out of her place, in the wrath of the LORD of hosts, and in the day of his fierce anger."

Joel 3:16 "The LORD also shall roar out of Zion, and utter his voice from Jerusalem; and the heavens and the earth shall shake: but the LORD will be the hope of his people, and the strength of the children of Israel."

Matthew 24:29 "Immediately after the tribulation of those days shall the sun be darkened, and the moon shall not give her light, and the stars shall fall from heaven, and the powers of the heavens shall be shaken:"

Mark 13:24-25 "[24]But in those days, after that tribulation, the sun shall be darkened, and the moon shall not give her light, [25]And the stars of heaven shall fall, and the powers that are in heaven shall be shaken."

Luke 21:25-26 "[25]And there shall be signs in the sun, and in the moon, and in the stars; and upon the earth distress of nations, with perplexity; the sea and the waves roaring; [26]Men's hearts failing them for fear, and for looking after those things which are coming on the earth: for the powers of heaven shall be shaken."

Hebrews 12:22-27 "[22]But ye are come unto mount Sion, and unto the city of the living God, the heavenly Jerusalem, and to an innumerable company of angels, [23]To the general assembly and church of the firstborn, which are written in heaven, and to God the Judge of all, and to the spirits of just men made perfect, [24]And to Jesus the mediator of the new covenant, and to the blood of sprinkling, that speaketh better things than that of Abel. [25]See that ye refuse not him that speaketh. For if they escaped not who refused him that spake on earth, much more shall not we escape, if we turn away from him that speaketh from heaven: [26]Whose voice then shook the earth: but now he hath promised, saying, Yet once more I shake not the earth only, but also heaven. [27]And this word, Yet once more, signifieth the removing of those things that are shaken, as of things that are made, that those things which cannot be shaken may remain."

The Heavens Belonging To The Lord
Genesis 14:19 "And he blessed him, and said, Blessed be Abram of the most high God, possessor of heaven and earth:"

Deuteronomy 10:14 "Behold, the heaven and the heaven of heavens is the LORD's thy God, the earth also, with all that therein is."

1 Chronicles 29:11 "Thine, O LORD, is the greatness, and the power, and the glory, and the victory, and the majesty: for all that is in the heaven and in the earth is thine; thine is the kingdom, O LORD, and thou art exalted as head above all."

Psalm 89:8-11 "[8]O LORD God of hosts, who is a strong LORD like unto thee? or to thy faithfulness round about thee? [9]Thou rulest the raging of the sea: when the waves thereof arise, thou stillest them. [10]Thou hast broken Rahab in pieces, as one that is slain; thou hast scattered thine enemies with thy strong arm. [11]The heavens are thine, the earth also is thine: as for the world and the fulness thereof, thou hast founded them."

Psalm 115:16 "The heaven, even the heavens, are the Lord's: but the earth hath he given to the children of men."

The Heavens Passing Away
Psalm 102:24-27 "[24]I said, O my God, take me not away in the midst of my days: thy years are throughout all generations. [25]Of old hast thou laid the foundation of the earth: and the heavens are the work of thy hands. [26]They shall perish, but thou shalt endure: yea, all of them shall wax old like a garment; as a vesture shalt thou change them, and they shall be changed: [27]But thou art the same, and thy years shall have no end."

Isaiah 51:6 "Lift up your eyes to the heavens, and look upon the earth beneath: for the heavens shall vanish away like smoke, and the earth shall wax old like a garment, and they that dwell therein shall die in like manner: but my salvation shall be for ever, and my righteousness shall not be abolished."

Matthew 24:35 "Heaven and earth shall pass away, but my words shall not pass away."

Mark 13:31 "Heaven and earth shall pass away: but my words shall not pass away."

Luke 21:33 "Heaven and earth shall pass away: but my words shall not pass away."

Hebrews 1:10-12 "[10]And, Thou, Lord, in the beginning hast laid the foundation of the earth; and the heavens are the works of thine hands: [11]They shall perish; but thou remainest; and they all shall wax old as doth a garment; [12]And as a vesture shalt thou fold them up, and they shall be changed: but thou art the same, and thy years shall not fail."

2 Peter 3:10-12 "[10]But the day of the Lord will come as a thief in the night; in the which the heavens shall pass away with a great noise, and the elements shall melt with fervent heat, the earth also and the works that are therein shall be burned up. [11]Seeing then that all these things shall be dissolved, what manner of persons ought ye to be in all holy conversation and godliness, [12]Looking for and hasting unto the coming of the day of God, wherein the heavens being on fire shall be dissolved, and the elements shall melt with fervent heat?"

Revelation 21:1-4 "[1]And I saw a new heaven and a new earth: for the first heaven and the first earth were passed away; and there was no more sea. [2]And I John saw the holy city, new Jerusalem, coming down from God out of heaven, prepared as a bride adorned for her husband. [3]And I heard a great voice out of heaven saying, Behold, the tabernacle of God is with men, and he will dwell with them, and they shall be his people, and God himself shall be with them, and be their God. [4]And God shall wipe away all tears from their eyes; and there shall be no more death, neither sorrow, nor crying, neither shall there be any more pain: for the former things are passed away."

The Heavens Which Exist Now
2 Peter 3:3-8 "[3]Knowing this first, that there shall come in the last days scoffers, walking after their own lusts, [4]And saying, Where is the promise of his coming? for since the fathers fell asleep, all things continue as they were from the beginning of the creation. [5]For this they willingly are ignorant of, that by the word of God the heavens were of old, and the earth standing out of the water and in the water: [6]Whereby the world that then was, being overflowed with water, perished: [7]But the heavens and the earth, which are now, by the same word are kept in store, reserved unto fire against the day of judgment and perdition of ungodly men. [8]But, beloved, be not ignorant of this one thing, that one day is with the Lord as a thousand years, and a thousand years as one day."

The Lord Being King Of Heaven
Daniel 4:37 "Now I Nebuchadnezzar praise and extol and honour the King of heaven, all whose works are truth, and his ways judgment: and those that walk in pride he is able to abase."

Matthew 11:25 "At that time Jesus answered and said, I thank thee, O Father, Lord of heaven and earth, because thou hast hid these things from the wise and prudent, and hast revealed them unto babes."

The Lord Creating New Heavens
Isaiah 65:14-18 "[14]Behold, my servants shall sing for joy of heart, but ye shall cry for sorrow of heart, and shall howl for vexation of spirit. [15]And ye shall leave your name for a curse unto my chosen: for the Lord God shall slay thee, and call his servants by another name: [16]That he who blesseth

himself in the earth shall bless himself in the God of truth; and he that sweareth in the earth shall swear by the God of truth; because the former troubles are forgotten, and because they are hid from mine eyes. [17]For, behold, I create new heavens and a new earth: and the former shall not be remembered, nor come into mind. [18]But be ye glad and rejoice for ever in that which I create: for, behold, I create Jerusalem a rejoicing, and her people a joy."

Isaiah 66:22 "For as the new heavens and the new earth, which I will make, shall remain before me, saith the LORD, so shall your seed and your name remain."

Hebrews 1:10-12 "[10]And, Thou, Lord, in the beginning hast laid the foundation of the earth; and the heavens are the works of thine hands: [11]They shall perish; but thou remainest; and they all shall wax old as doth a garment; [12]And as a vesture shalt thou fold them up, and they shall be changed: but thou art the same, and thy years shall not fail."

Revelation 21:1-5 "[1]And I saw a new heaven and a new earth: for the first heaven and the first earth were passed away; and there was no more sea. [2]And I John saw the holy city, new Jerusalem, coming down from God out of heaven, prepared as a bride adorned for her husband. [3]And I heard a great voice out of heaven saying, Behold, the tabernacle of God is with men, and he will dwell with them, and they shall be his people, and God himself shall be with them, and be their God. [4]And God shall wipe away all tears from their eyes; and there shall be no more death, neither sorrow, nor crying, neither shall there be any more pain: for the former things are passed away. [5]And he that sat upon the throne said, Behold, I make all things new. And he said unto me, Write: for these words are true and faithful."

The Lord Creating The Heavens
Genesis 1:1-19 "[1]In the beginning God created the Heaven and the earth. [2]And the earth was without form, and void; and darkness was upon the face of the deep. And the Spirit of God moved upon the face of the waters. [3]And God said, Let there be light: and there was light. [4]And God saw the light, that it was good: and God divided the light from the darkness. [5]And God called the light Day, and the darkness he called Night. And the evening and the morning were the first day. [6]And God said, Let there be a firmament in the midst of the waters, and let it divide the waters from the waters. [7]And God made the firmament, and divided the waters which were under the firmament from the waters which were above the firmament: and it was so. [8]And God called the firmament Heaven. And the evening and the morning were the second day. [9]And God said, Let the waters under the heaven be gathered together unto one place, and let the dry land appear: and it was so. [10]And God called the dry land Earth; and the gathering together of the waters called he Seas: and God saw that it was good. [11]And God said, Let the earth bring forth grass, the herb yielding seed, and the fruit tree yielding fruit after his kind, whose seed is in itself, upon the earth: and it was so. [12]And the earth brought forth grass, and herb yielding seed after his kind, and the tree yielding fruit, whose seed was in itself, after his kind: and God saw that it was good. [13]And the evening and the morning were the third day. [14]And God said, Let there be lights in the firmament of the heaven to divide the day from the night; and let them be for signs, and for seasons, and for days, and years: [15]And let them be for lights in the firmament of the heaven to give light upon the earth: and it was so. [16]And God made two great lights; the greater light to rule the day, and the lesser light to rule the night: he made the stars also. [17]And God set them in the firmament of the heaven to give light upon the earth, [18]And to rule over the day and over the night, and to divide the light from the darkness: and God saw that it was good. [19]And the evening and the morning were the fourth day."

Genesis 2:4 "These are the generations of the heavens and of the earth when they were created, in the day that the LORD God made the earth and the heavens,"

Exodus 20:11 "For in six days the LORD made heaven and earth, the sea, and all that in them is, and rested the seventh day: wherefore the LORD blessed the sabbath day, and hallowed it."

Exodus 31:17 "It is a sign between me and the children of Israel for ever: for in six days the LORD made heaven and earth, and on the seventh day he rested, and was refreshed."

2 Kings 19:15 "And Hezekiah prayed before the LORD, and said, O LORD God of Israel, which dwellest between the cherubims, thou art the God, even thou alone, of all the kingdoms of the earth: thou hast made heaven and earth."

1 Chronicles 16:26 "For all the gods of the people are idols: but the LORD made the heavens."

Nehemiah 9:6 "Thou, even thou, art LORD alone; thou hast made heaven, the heaven of heavens, with all their host, the earth, and all things that are therein, the seas, and all that is therein, and thou preservest them all; and the host of heaven worshippeth thee."

Psalm 8:1-3 "¹O LORD our Lord, how excellent is thy name in all the earth! who hast set thy glory above the heavens. ²Out of the mouth of babes and sucklings hast thou ordained strength because of thine enemies, that thou mightest still the enemy and the avenger. ³When I consider thy heavens, the work of thy fingers, the moon and the stars, which thou hast ordained;"

Psalm 33:6 "By the word of the LORD were the heavens made; and all the host of them by the breath of his mouth."

Psalm 89:8-11 "⁸O LORD God of hosts, who is a strong LORD like unto thee? or to thy faithfulness round about thee? ⁹Thou rulest the raging of the sea: when the waves thereof arise, thou stillest them. ¹⁰Thou hast broken Rahab in pieces, as one that is slain; thou hast scattered thine enemies with thy strong arm. ¹¹The heavens are thine, the earth also is thine: as for the world and the fulness thereof, thou hast founded them."

Psalm 96:5 "For all the gods of the nations are idols: but the LORD made the heavens."

Psalm 102:24-25 "²⁴I said, O my God, take me not away in the midst of my days: thy years are throughout all generations. ²⁵Of old hast thou laid the foundation of the earth: and the heavens are the work of thy hands."

Psalm 104:1-2 "¹Bless the LORD, O my soul. O LORD my God, thou art very great; thou art clothed with honour and majesty. ²Who coverest thyself with light as with a garment: who stretchest out the heavens like a curtain:"

Psalm 115:15 "Ye are blessed of the LORD which made heaven and earth."

Psalm 121:2 "My help cometh from the LORD, which made heaven and earth."

Psalm 124:8 "Our help is in the name of the LORD, who made heaven and earth."

Psalm 136:3-5 "³O give thanks to the Lord of lords: for his mercy endureth for ever. ⁴To him who alone doeth great wonders: for his mercy endureth for ever. ⁵To him that by wisdom made the heavens: for his mercy endureth for ever."

Psalm 146:5-6 "⁵Happy is he that hath the God of Jacob for his help, whose hope is in the LORD his God: ⁶Which made heaven, and earth, the sea, and all that therein is: which keepeth truth for ever:"

Proverbs 3:19 "The LORD by wisdom hath founded the earth; by understanding hath he established the heavens."

Proverbs 8:22-27 "²²The LORD possessed me in the beginning of his way, before his works of old. ²³I was set up from everlasting, from the beginning, or ever the earth was. ²⁴When there were no depths, I was brought forth; when there were no fountains abounding with water. ²⁵Before the mountains were settled, before the hills was I brought forth: ²⁶While as yet he had not made the earth, nor the fields, nor the highest part of the dust of the world. ²⁷When he prepared the heavens, I was there: when he set a compass upon the face of the depth:"

Isaiah 37:16 "O LORD of hosts, God of Israel, that dwellest between the cherubims, thou art the God, even thou alone, of all the kingdoms of the earth: thou hast made heaven and earth."

Isaiah 40:22 "It is he that sitteth upon the circle of the earth, and the inhabitants thereof are as grasshoppers; that stretcheth out the heavens as a curtain, and spreadeth them out as a tent to dwell in:"

Isaiah 42:5 "Thus saith God the LORD, he that created the heavens, and stretched them out; he that spread forth the earth, and that which cometh out of it; he that giveth breath unto the people upon it, and spirit to them that walk therein:"

Isaiah 44:24 "Thus saith the LORD, thy redeemer, and he that formed thee from the womb, I am the LORD that maketh all things; that stretcheth forth the heavens alone; that spreadeth abroad the earth by myself;"

Isaiah 45:11-12 "11Thus saith the LORD, the Holy One of Israel, and his Maker, Ask me of things to come concerning my sons, and concerning the work of my hands command ye me. 12I have made the earth, and created man upon it: I, even my hands, have stretched out the heavens, and all their host have I commanded."

Isaiah 45:18 "For thus saith the LORD that created the heavens; God himself that formed the earth and made it; he hath established it, he created it not in vain, he formed it to be inhabited: I am the LORD; and there is none else."

Isaiah 48:12-13 "12Hearken unto me, O Jacob and Israel, my called; I am he; I am the first, I also am the last. 13Mine hand also hath laid the foundation of the earth, and my right hand hath spanned the heavens: when I call unto them, they stand up together."

Isaiah 51:13-16 "13And forgettest the LORD thy maker, that hath stretched forth the heavens, and laid the foundations of the earth; and hast feared continually every day because of the fury of the oppressor, as if he were ready to destroy? and where is the fury of the oppressor? 14The captive exile hasteneth that he may be loosed, and that he should not die in the pit, nor that his bread should fail. 15But I am the LORD thy God, that divided the sea, whose waves roared: The LORD of hosts is his name. 16And I have put my words in thy mouth, and I have covered thee in the shadow of mine hand, that I may plant the heavens, and lay the foundations of the earth, and say unto Zion, Thou art my people."

Isaiah 66:1-2 "1Thus saith the LORD, The heaven is my throne, and the earth is my footstool: where is the house that ye build unto me? and where is the place of my rest? 2For all those things hath mine hand made, and those things have been, saith the LORD: but to this man will I look, even to him that is poor and of a contrite spirit, and trembleth at my word."

Jeremiah 10:10-12 "10But the LORD is the true God, he is the living God, and an everlasting king: at his wrath the earth shall tremble, and the nations shall not be able to abide his indignation. 11Thus shall ye say unto them, The gods that have not made the heavens and the earth, even they shall perish from the earth, and from under these heavens. 12He hath made the earth by his power, he hath established the world by his wisdom, and hath stretched out the heavens by his discretion."

Jeremiah 32:17 "Ah Lord GOD! behold, thou hast made the heaven and the earth by thy great power and stretched out arm, and there is nothing too hard for thee:"

Amos 5:8 "Seek him that maketh the seven stars and Orion, and turneth the shadow of death into the morning, and maketh the day dark with night: that calleth for the waters of the sea, and poureth them out upon the face of the earth: The LORD is his name:"

Zechariah 12:1 "The burden of the word of the LORD for Israel, saith the LORD, which stretcheth forth the heavens, and layeth the foundation of the earth, and formeth the spirit of man within him."

Acts 4:24 "And when they heard that, they lifted up their voice to God with one accord, and said, Lord, thou art God, which hast made heaven, and earth, and the sea, and all that in them is:"

Acts 14:15 "And saying, Sirs, why do ye these things? We also are men of like passions with you, and preach unto you that ye should turn from these vanities unto the living God, which made heaven, and earth, and the sea, and all things that are therein:"

Hebrews 1:10-12 "10And, Thou, Lord, in the beginning hast laid the foundation of the earth; and the heavens are the works of thine hands: 11They shall perish; but thou remainest; and they all shall wax old as doth a garment; 12And as a vesture shalt thou fold them up, and they shall be changed: but thou art the same, and thy years shall not fail."

Revelation 10:5-6 "5And the angel which I saw stand upon the sea and upon the earth lifted up his hand to heaven, 6And sware by him that liveth for ever and ever, who created heaven, and the things that therein are, and the earth, and the things that therein are, and the sea, and the things which are therein, that there should be time no longer:"

Revelation 14:7 "Saying with a loud voice, Fear God, and give glory to him; for the hour of his judgment is come: and worship him that made heaven, and earth, and the sea, and the fountains of waters."

The Lord Stretching Out The Heavens

Psalm 104:1-2 "¹Bless the LORD, O my soul. O LORD my God, thou art very great; thou art clothed with honour and majesty. ²Who coverest thyself with light as with a garment: who stretchest out the heavens like a curtain:"

Isaiah 40:22 "It is he that sitteth upon the circle of the earth, and the inhabitants thereof are as grasshoppers; that stretcheth out the heavens as a curtain, and spreadeth them out as a tent to dwell in:"

Isaiah 42:5 "Thus saith God the LORD, he that created the heavens, and stretched them out; he that spread forth the earth, and that which cometh out of it; he that giveth breath unto the people upon it, and spirit to them that walk therein:"

Isaiah 44:24 "Thus saith the LORD, thy redeemer, and he that formed thee from the womb, I am the LORD that maketh all things; that stretcheth forth the heavens alone; that spreadeth abroad the earth by myself;"

Isaiah 45:11-12 "¹¹Thus saith the LORD, the Holy One of Israel, and his Maker, Ask me of things to come concerning my sons, and concerning the work of my hands command ye me. ¹²I have made the earth, and created man upon it: I, even my hands, have stretched out the heavens, and all their host have I commanded."

Isaiah 48:12-13 "¹²Hearken unto me, O Jacob and Israel, my called; I am he; I am the first, I also am the last. ¹³Mine hand also hath laid the foundation of the earth, and my right hand hath spanned the heavens: when I call unto them, they stand up together."

Isaiah 51:13 "And forgettest the LORD thy maker, that hath stretched forth the heavens, and laid the foundations of the earth; and hast feared continually every day because of the fury of the oppressor, as if he were ready to destroy? and where is the fury of the oppressor?"

Jeremiah 10:10-12 "¹⁰But the LORD is the true God, he is the living God, and an everlasting king: at his wrath the earth shall tremble, and the nations shall not be able to abide his indignation. ¹¹Thus shall ye say unto them, The gods that have not made the heavens and the earth, even they shall perish from the earth, and from under these heavens. ¹²He hath made the earth by his power, he hath established the world by his wisdom, and hath stretched out the heavens by his discretion."

Zechariah 12:1 "The burden of the word of the LORD for Israel, saith the LORD, which stretcheth forth the heavens, and layeth the foundation of the earth, and formeth the spirit of man within him."

The New Heavens

Isaiah 66:22 "For as the new heavens and the new earth, which I will make, shall remain before me, saith the LORD, so shall your seed and your name remain."

2 Peter 3:13 "Nevertheless we, according to his promise, look for new heavens and a new earth, wherein dwelleth righteousness."

Revelation 21:1-4 "¹And I saw a new heaven and a new earth: for the first heaven and the first earth were passed away; and there was no more sea. ²And I John saw the holy city, new Jerusalem, coming down from God out of heaven, prepared as a bride adorned for her husband. ³And I heard a great voice out of heaven saying, Behold, the tabernacle of God is with men, and he will dwell with them, and they shall be his people, and God himself shall be with them, and be their God. ⁴And God shall wipe away all tears from their eyes; and there shall be no more death, neither sorrow, nor crying, neither shall there be any more pain: for the former things are passed away."

What Heaven Is

Psalm 103:11 "For as the heaven is high above the earth, so great is his mercy toward them that fear him."

Isaiah 66:1 "Thus saith the LORD, The heaven is my throne, and the earth is my footstool: where is the house that ye build unto me? and where is the place of my rest?"

Matthew 5:34-35 "³⁴But I say unto you, Swear not at all; neither by heaven; for it is God's throne: ³⁵Nor by the earth; for it is his footstool: neither by Jerusalem; for it is the city of the great King."

What Shall Be Bound In Heaven

Matthew 18:18 "Verily I say unto you, Whatsoever ye shall bind on earth shall be bound in heaven: and whatsoever ye shall loose on earth shall be loosed in heaven."

What Shall Be Loosed In Heaven
Matthew 18:18 "Verily I say unto you, Whatsoever ye shall bind on earth shall be bound in heaven: and whatsoever ye shall loose on earth shall be loosed in heaven."

Who Shall Be Great
In The Kingdom Of Heaven
Matthew 5:19 "Whosoever therefore shall break one of these least commandments, and shall teach men so, he shall be called the least in the kingdom of heaven: but whosoever shall do and teach them, the same shall be called great in the kingdom of heaven."

Matthew 18:1-4 "¹At the same time came the disciples unto Jesus, saying, Who is the greatest in the kingdom of heaven? ²And Jesus called a little child unto him, and set him in the midst of them, ³And said, Verily I say unto you, Except ye be converted, and become as little children, ye shall not enter into the kingdom of heaven. ⁴Whosoever therefore shall humble himself as this little child, the same is greatest in the kingdom of heaven."

Luke 9:46-48 "⁴⁶Then there arose a reasoning among them, which of them should be greatest. ⁴⁷And Jesus, perceiving the thought of their heart, took a child, and set him by him, ⁴⁸And said unto them, Whosoever shall receive this child in my name receiveth me: and whosoever shall receive me receiveth him that sent me: for he that is least among you all, the same shall be great."

Luke 22:22-27 "²²And truly the Son of man goeth, as it was determined: but woe unto that man by whom he is betrayed! ²³And they began to inquire among themselves, which of them it was that should do this thing. ²⁴And there was also a strife among them, which of them should be accounted the greatest. ²⁵And he said unto them, The kings of the Gentiles exercise lordship over them; and they that exercise authority upon them are called benefactors. ²⁶But ye shall not be so: but he that is greatest among you, let him be as the younger; and he that is chief, as he that doth serve. ²⁷For whether is greater, he that sitteth at

meat, or he that serveth? is not he that sitteth at meat? but I am among you as he that serveth."

Who Shall Be Least
In The Kingdom Of Heaven
Matthew 5:19 "Whosoever therefore shall break one of these least commandments, and shall teach men so, he shall be called the least in the kingdom of heaven: but whosoever shall do and teach them, the same shall be called great in the kingdom of heaven."

Mark 9:33-35 "³³And he came to Capernaum: and being in the house he asked them, What was it that ye disputed among yourselves by the way? ³⁴But they held their peace: for by the way they had disputed among themselves, who should be the greatest. ³⁵And he sat down, and called the twelve, and saith unto them, If any man desire to be first, the same shall be last of all, and servant of all."

Luke 22:22-27 "²²And truly the Son of man goeth, as it was determined: but woe unto that man by whom he is betrayed! ²³And they began to inquire among themselves, which of them it was that should do this thing. ²⁴And there was also a strife among them, which of them should be accounted the greatest. ²⁵And he said unto them, The kings of the Gentiles exercise lordship over them; and they that exercise authority upon them are called benefactors. ²⁶But ye shall not be so: but he that is greatest among you, let him be as the younger; and he that is chief, as he that doth serve. ²⁷For whether is greater, he that sitteth at meat, or he that serveth? is not he that sitteth at meat? but I am among you as he that serveth."

Who Shall Have Treasure In Heaven
Matthew 19:21 "Jesus said unto him, If thou wilt be perfect, go and sell that thou hast, and give to the poor, and thou shalt have treasure in heaven: and come and follow me."

Luke 12:31-34 "³¹But rather seek ye the kingdom of God; and all these things shall be added unto you. ³²Fear not, little flock; for it is your Father's good pleasure to give you the kingdom. ³³Sell that ye have, and give alms; provide yourselves bags which wax not old, a treasure in the heavens that faileth not, where no thief approacheth, neither moth corrupteth. ³⁴For where your treasure is, there will your heart be also."

HELL

Avoiding Hell

Matthew 5:29-30 "29And if thy right eye offend thee, pluck it out, and cast it from thee: for it is profitable for thee that one of thy members should perish, and not that thy whole body should be cast into hell. 30And if thy right hand offend thee, cut if off, and cast it from thee: for it is profitable for thee that one of thy members should perish, and not that thy whole body should be cast into hell."

Matthew 18:7-9 "7Woe unto the world because of offences! for it must needs be that offences come; but woe to that man by whom the offence cometh! 8Wherefore if thy hand or thy foot offend thee, cut them off, and cast them from thee: it is better for thee to enter into life halt or maimed, rather than having two hands or two feet to be cast into everlasting fire. 9And if thine eye offend thee, pluck it out, and cast it from thee: it is better for thee to enter into life with one eye, rather than having two eyes to be cast into hell fire."

Mark 9:43-48 "43And if thy hand offend thee, cut it off: it is better for thee to enter into life maimed, than having two hands to go into hell, into the fire that never shall be quenched: 44Where their worm dieth not, and the fire is not quenched. 45And if thy foot offend thee, cut it off: it is better for thee to enter halt into life, than having two feet to be cast into hell, into the fire that never shall be quenched: 46Where their worm dieth not, and the fire is not quenched. 47And if thine eye offend thee, pluck it out: it is better for thee to enter into the kingdom of God with one eye, than having two eyes to be cast into hell fire: 48Where their worm dieth not, and the fire is not quenched."

Jesus Christ Having The Keys Of Hell

Revelation 1:18 "I am he that liveth, and was dead; and, behold, I am alive for evermore, Amen; and have the keys of hell and of death."

What Shall Be Turned Into Hell

Psalm 9:17 "The wicked shall be turned into hell, and all the nations that forget God."

Who Shall Be Cast Into The Everlasting Fire

Isaiah 14:12-15 "12How art thou fallen from heaven, O Lucifer, son of the morning! how art thou cut down to the ground, which didst weaken the nations! 13For thou hast said in thine heart, I will ascend into heaven, I will exalt my throne above the stars of God: I will sit also upon the mount of the congregation, in the sides of the north: 14I will ascend above the heights of the clouds; I will be like the most High. 15Yet thou shalt be brought down to hell, to the sides of the pit."

Isaiah 33:10-14 "10Now will I rise, saith the LORD; now will I be exalted; now will I lift up myself. 11Ye shall conceive chaff, ye shall bring forth stubble: your breath, as fire, shall devour you. 12And the people shall be as the burnings of lime: as thorns cut up shall they be burned in the fire. 13Hear, ye that are far off, what I have done; and, ye that are near, acknowledge my might. 14The sinners in Zion are afraid; fearfulness hath surprised the hypocrites. Who among us shall dwell with the devouring fire? who among us shall dwell with everlasting burnings?"

Daniel 7:11 "I beheld then because of the voice of the great words which the horn spake: I beheld even till the beast was slain, and his body destroyed, and given to the burning flame."

Matthew 3:10-12 "10And now also the axe is laid unto the root of the trees: therefore every tree which bringeth not forth good fruit is hewn down, and cast into the fire. 11I indeed baptize you with water unto repentance: but he that cometh after me is mightier than I, whose shoes I am not worthy to bear: he shall baptize you with the Holy Ghost, and with fire: 12Whose fan is in his hand, and he will throughly purge his floor, and gather his wheat into the garner; but he will burn up the chaff with unquenchable fire."

Matthew 7:15-19 "15Beware of false prophets, which come to you in sheep's clothing, but inwardly they are ravening wolves. 16Ye shall know them by their fruits. Do men gather grapes of thorns, or figs of thistles? 17Even so every good tree bringeth forth good fruit; but a corrupt tree bringeth forth evil fruit. 18A good tree cannot bring forth evil fruit, neither can a corrupt tree bring forth good fruit. 19Every tree that bringeth not forth good fruit is hewn down, and cast into the fire."

Matthew 13:24-30 "24Another parable put he forth unto them, saying, The kingdom of heaven is likened unto a man which sowed good seed in his field: [25]But while men slept, his enemy came and sowed tares among the wheat, and went his way. [26]But when the blade was sprung up, and brought forth fruit, then appeared the tares also. [27]So the servants of the householder came and said unto him, Sir, didst not thou sow good seed in thy field? from whence then hath it tares? [28]He said unto them, An enemy hath done this. The servants said unto him, Wilt thou then that we go and gather them up? [29]But he said, Nay; lest while ye gather up the tares, ye root up also the wheat with them. [30]Let both grow together until the harvest: and in the time of harvest I will say to the reapers, Gather ye together first the tares, and bind them in bundles to burn them: but gather the wheat into my barn."

Matthew 13:36-40 "[36]Then Jesus sent the multitude away, and went into the house: and his disciples came unto him, saying, Declare unto us the parable of the tares of the field. [37]He answered and said unto them, He that soweth the good seed is the Son of man; [38]The field is the world; the good seed are the children of the kingdom; but the tares are the children of the wicked one; [39]The enemy that sowed them is the devil; the harvest is the end of the world; and the reapers are the angels. [40]As therefore the tares are gathered and burned in the fire; so shall it be in the end of this world."

Matthew 13:47-50 "[47]Again, the kingdom of heaven is like unto a net, that was cast into the sea, and gathered of every kind: [48]Which, when it was full, they drew to shore, and sat down, and gathered the good into vessels, but cast the bad away. [49]So shall it be at the end of the world: the angels shall come forth, and sever the wicked from among the just, [50]And shall cast them into the furnace of fire: there shall be wailing and gnashing of teeth."

Matthew 25:31-46 "[31]When the Son of man shall come in his glory, and all the holy angels with him, then shall he sit upon the throne of his glory: [32]And before him shall be gathered all nations: and he shall separate them one from another, as a shepherd divideth his sheep from the goats: [33]And he shall set the sheep on his right hand, but the goats on the left. [34]Then shall the King say unto them on his right hand, Come, ye blessed of my Father, inherit the kingdom prepared for you from the foundation of the world: [35]For I was an hungred, and ye gave me meat: I was thirsty, and ye gave me drink: I was a stranger, and ye took me in: [36]Naked, and ye clothed me: I was sick, and ye visited me: I was in prison, and ye came unto me. [37]Then shall the righteous answer him, saying, Lord, when saw we thee an hungred, and fed thee? or thirsty, and gave thee drink? [38]When saw we thee a stranger, and took thee in? or naked, and clothed thee? [39]Or when saw we thee sick, or in prison, and came unto thee? [40]And the King shall answer and say unto them, Verily I say unto you, Inasmuch as ye have done it unto one of the least of these my brethren, ye have done it unto me. [41]Then shall he say also unto them on the left hand, Depart from me, ye cursed, into everlasting fire, prepared for the devil and his angels: [42]For I was an hungred, and ye gave me no meat: I was thirsty, and ye gave me no drink: [43]I was a stranger, and ye took me not in: naked, and ye clothed me not: sick, and in prison, and ye visited me not. [44]Then shall they also answer him, saying, Lord, when saw we thee an hungred, or athirst, or a stranger, or naked, or sick, or in prison, and did not minister unto thee? [45]Then shall he answer them, saying, Verily I say unto you, Inasmuch as ye did it not to one of the least of these, ye did it not to me. [46]And these shall go away into everlasting punishment: but the righteous into life eternal."

Luke 3:8-9 "[8]Bring forth therefore fruits worthy of repentance, and begin not to say within yourselves, We have Abraham to our father: for I say unto you, That God is able of these stones to raise up children unto Abraham. [9]And now also the axe is laid unto the root of the trees: every tree therefore which bringeth not forth good fruit is hewn down, and cast into the fire."

Luke 3:15-17 "[15]And as the people were in expectation, and all men mused in their hearts of John, whether he were the Christ, or not; [16]John answered, saying unto them all, I indeed baptize you with water; but one mightier than I cometh, the latchet of whose shoes I am not worthy to unloose: he shall baptize you with the Holy Ghost and with fire: [17]Whose fan is in his hand, and he will throughly purge his floor, and will gather the wheat into his garner; but the chaff he will burn with fire unquenchable."

John 15:1-6 "[1]I am the true vine, and my Father is the husbandman. [2]Every branch in me that beareth not fruit he taketh away: and every branch that beareth fruit, he purgeth it, that it may bring forth more fruit. [3]Now ye are clean through the word which I have spoken unto you. [4]Abide in me, and I in you. As the branch cannot bear fruit of itself, except it abide in the vine; no more can ye, except ye abide in me. [5]I am the vine, ye are the branches: He that abideth in me, and I in him, the same bringeth forth much fruit: for without me ye can do nothing. [6]If a man abide not in me, he is cast forth as a branch, and is withered; and men gather them, and cast them into the fire, and they are burned."

2 Thessalonians 1:7-9 "[7]And to you who are troubled rest with us, when the Lord Jesus shall be revealed from heaven with his mighty angels, [8]In flaming fire taking vengeance on them that know not God, and that obey not the gospel of our Lord Jesus Christ: [9]Who shall be punished with everlasting destruction from the presence of the Lord, and from the glory of his power;"

2 Peter 2:4 "For if God spared not the angels that sinned, but cast them down to hell, and delivered them into chains of darkness, to be reserved unto judgment;"

Jude 7 "Even as Sodom and Gomorrha, and the cities about them in like manner, giving themselves over to fornication, and going after strange flesh, are set forth for an example, suffering the vengeance of eternal fire."

Revelation 19:19-20 "[19]And I saw the beast, and the kings of the earth, and their armies, gathered together to make war against him that sat on the horse, and against his army. [20]And the beast was taken, and with him the false prophet that wrought miracles before him, with which he deceived them that had received the mark of the beast, and them that worshipped his image. These both were cast alive into a lake of fire burning with brimstone."

Revelation 20:7-15 "[7]And when the thousand years are expired, Satan shall be loosed out of his prison, [8]And shall go out to deceive the nations which are in the four quarters of the earth, Gog and Magog, to gather them together to battle: the number of whom is as the sand of the sea. [9]And they went up on the breadth of the earth, and compassed the camp of the saints about, and the beloved city: and fire came down from God out of heaven, and devoured them. [10]And the devil that deceived them was cast into the lake of fire and brimstone, where the beast and the false prophet are, and shall be tormented day and night for ever and ever. [11]And I saw a great white throne, and him that sat on it, from whose face the earth and the heaven fled away; and there was found no place for them. [12]And I saw the dead, small and great, stand before God; and the books were opened: and another book was opened, which is the book of life: and the dead were judged out of those things which were written in the books, according to their works. [13]And the sea gave up the dead which were in it; and death and hell delivered up the dead which were in them: and they were judged every man according to their works. [14]And death and hell were cast into the lake of fire. This is the second death. [15]And whosoever was not found written in the book of life was cast into the lake of fire."

Revelation 21:8 "But the fearful, and unbelieving, and the abominable, and murderers, and whoremongers, and sorcerers, and idolaters, and all liars, shall have their part in the lake which burneth with fire and brimstone: which is the second death."

HELP

Helping Others

Exodus 23:4-5 "[4]If thou meet thine enemy's ox or his ass going astray, thou shalt surely bring it back to him again. [5]If thou see the ass of him that hateth thee lying under his burden, and wouldest forbear to help him, thou shalt surely help with him."

Deuteronomy 22:1-4 "[1]Thou shalt not see the brother's ox or his sheep go astray, and hide thyself from them: thou shalt in any case bring them again unto thy brother. [2]And if thy brother be not nigh unto thee, or if thou know him not, then thou shalt bring it unto thine own house, and it shall be with thee until thy brother seek after it, and thou shalt restore it to him again. ³In like manner shalt thou do with his ass; and so shalt thou do with his raiment; and with all lost thing of thy brother's, which he hath lost, and thou hast found, shalt thou do likewise: thou mayest not hide thyself. ⁴Thou shalt not see thy brother's ass or his ox fall down by the way, and hide thyself from them: thou shalt surely help him to lift them up again."

Proverbs 31:8-9 "⁸Open thy mouth for the dumb in the cause of all such as are appointed to destruction. ⁹Open thy mouth, judge righteously, and plead the cause of the poor and needy."

Isaiah 1:17 "Learn to do well; seek judgment, relieve the oppressed, judge the fatherless, plead for the widow."

Acts 20:35 "I have shewed you all things, how that so labouring ye ought to support the weak, and to remember the words of the Lord Jesus, how he said, It is more blessed to give than to receive."

Romans 15:1-3 "¹We then that are strong ought to bear the infirmities of the weak, and not to please ourselves. ²Let every one of us please his neighbour for his good to edification. ³For even Christ pleased not himself; but, as it is written, The reproaches of them that reproached thee fell on me."

Galatians 6:1-2 "¹Brethren, if a man be overtaken in a fault, ye which are spiritual, restore such an one in the spirit of meekness; considering thyself, lest thou also be tempted. ²Bear ye one another's burdens, and so fulfil the law of Christ."

Philippians 4:3 "And I intreat thee also, true yokefellow, help those women which laboured with me in the gospel, with Clement also, and with other my fellowlabourers, whose names are in the book of life."

1 Thessalonians 5:14 "Now we exhort you, brethren, warn them that are unruly, comfort the feebleminded, support the weak, be patient toward all men."

The Help Of Man
Psalm 60:11-12 "¹¹Give us help from trouble: for vain is the help of man. ¹²Through God we shall

do valiantly: for he it is that shall tread down our enemies."

Psalm 108:12-13 "¹²Give us help from trouble: for vain is the help of man. ¹³Through God we shall do valiantly: for he it is that shall tread down our enemies."

Psalm 146:3 "Put not your trust in princes, nor in the son of man, in whom there is no help."

The Lord Being Your Help
Psalm 30:10 "Hear, O LORD, and have mercy upon me: LORD, be thou my helper."

Psalm 33:20 "Our soul waiteth for the LORD: he is our help and our shield."

Psalm 40:17 "But I am poor and needy; yet the Lord thinketh upon me: thou art my help and my deliverer; make no tarrying, O my God."

Psalm 46:1 "God is our refuge and strength, a very present help in trouble."

Psalm 54:4 "Behold, God is mine helper: the Lord is with them that uphold my soul."

Psalm 63:1-7 "¹O God, thou art my God; early will I seek thee: my soul thirsteth for thee, my flesh longeth for thee in a dry and thirsty land, where no water is; ²To see thy power and thy glory, so as I have seen thee in the sanctuary. ³Because thy lovingkindness is better than life, my lips shall praise thee. ⁴Thus will I bless thee while I live: I will lift up my hands in thy name. ⁵My soul shall be satisfied as with marrow and fatness; and my mouth shall praise thee with joyful lips: ⁶When I remember thee upon my bed, and meditate on thee in the night watches. ⁷Because thou hast been my help, therefore in the shadow of thy wings will I rejoice."

Psalm 94:17 "Unless the LORD had been my help, my soul had almost dwelt in silence."

Psalm 115:9-11 "⁹O Israel, trust thou in the LORD: he is their help and their shield. ¹⁰O house of Aaron, trust in the LORD: he is their help and their shield. ¹¹Ye that fear the LORD, trust in the LORD: he is their help and their shield."

Hosea 13:4-9 "⁴Yet I am the LORD thy God from the land of Egypt, and thou shalt know no god but me: for there is no saviour beside me. ⁵I did know thee in the wilderness, in the land of great drought. ⁶According to their pasture, so were they filled; they were filled, and their heart was exalted; therefore have they forgotten me. ⁷Therefore I will be unto them as a lion: as a leopard by the way will I observe them: ⁸I will meet them as a bear that is bereaved of her whelps, and will rend the caul of their heart, and there will I devour them like a lion: the wild beast shall tear them. ⁹O Israel, thou hast destroyed thyself; but in me is thine help."

Hebrews 13:6 "So that we may boldly say, The Lord is my helper, and I will not fear what man shall do unto me."

The Lord Helping
2 Chronicles 25:8 "But if thou wilt go, do it, be strong for the battle: God shall make thee fall before the enemy: for God hath power to help, and to cast down."

2 Chronicles 32:7-8 "⁷Be strong and courageous, be not afraid nor dismayed for the king of Assyria, nor for all the multitude that is with him: for there be more with us than with him: ⁸With him is an arm of flesh; but with us is the LORD our God to help us, and to fight our battles. And the people rested themselves upon the words of Hezekiah king of Judah."

Psalm 25:15 "Mine eyes are ever toward the LORD; for he shall pluck my feet out of the net."

Psalm 28:7-8 "⁷The LORD is my strength and my shield; my heart trusted in him, and I am helped: therefore my heart greatly rejoiceth; and with my song will I praise him. ⁸The LORD is their strength, and he is the saving strength of his anointed."

Psalm 37:40 "And the LORD shall help them and deliver them: he shall deliver them from the wicked, and save them, because they trust in him."

Psalm 46:5 "God is in the midst of her; she shall not be moved: God shall help her, and that right early."

Psalm 55:22 "Cast thy burden upon the LORD, and he shall sustain thee: he shall never suffer the righteous to be moved."

Psalm 116:6 "The LORD preserveth the simple: I was brought low, and he helped me."

Psalm 118:13 "Thou hast thrust sore at me that I might fall: but the LORD helped me."

Psalm 121:2 "My help cometh from the LORD, which made heaven and earth."

Psalm 124:8 "Our help is in the name of the LORD, who made heaven and earth."

Isaiah 41:10 "Fear thou not; for I am with thee: be not dismayed; for I am thy God: I will strengthen thee; yea, I will help thee; yea, I will uphold thee with the right hand of my righteousness."

Isaiah 44:2 "Thus saith the LORD that made thee, and formed thee from the womb, which will help thee; Fear not, O Jacob, my servant; and thou, Jesurun, whom I have chosen."

Isaiah 50:7 "For the Lord GOD will help me; therefore shall I not be confounded: therefore have I set my face like a flint, and I know that I shall not be ashamed."

Isaiah 50:9 "Behold, the Lord GOD will help me; who is he that shall condemn me? lo, they all shall wax old as a garment; the moth shall eat them up."

Philippians 4:19 "But my God shall supply all your need according to his riches in glory by Christ Jesus."

Those That Have God For Their Help
Psalm 146:5 "Happy is he that hath the God of Jacob for his help, whose hope is in the LORD his God:"

Those That Help Christ's People
Matthew 25:31-40 "³¹When the Son of man shall come in his glory, and all the holy angels with him, then shall he sit upon the throne of his glory: ³²And before him shall be gathered all nations: and he shall separate them one from another, as a shepherd divideth his sheep from the goats: ³³And he shall set the sheep on his right hand, but the goats on the left. ³⁴Then shall the King say unto them on his right hand, Come, ye blessed of my Father, inherit the kingdom prepared for you from the foundation of the world: ³⁵For I was an hungred, and ye gave me meat: I was thirsty, and ye gave me drink: I was a stranger, and ye took me in: ³⁶Naked, and ye clothed me: I was sick, and ye visited me: I was in prison, and ye came unto me.

[37]Then shall the righteous answer him, saying, Lord, when saw we thee an hungred, and fed thee? or thirsty, and gave thee drink? [38]When saw we thee a stranger, and took thee in? or naked, and clothed thee? [39]Or when saw we thee sick, or in prison, and came unto thee? [40]And the King shall answer and say unto them, Verily I say unto you, Inasmuch as ye have done it unto one of the least of these my brethren, ye have done it unto me."

Mark 9:41 "For whosoever shall give you a cup of water to drink in my name, because ye belong to Christ, verily I say unto you, he shall not lose his reward."

Those That Seek The Help Of Evildoers
Isaiah 31:1-3 "[1]Woe to them that go down to Egypt for help; and stay on horses, and trust in chariots, because they are many; and in horsemen, because they are very strong; but they look not unto the Holy One of Israel, neither seek the LORD! [2]Yet he also is wise, and will bring evil, and will not call back his words: but will arise against the house of the evildoers, and against the help of them that work iniquity. [3]Now the Egyptians are men, and not God; and their horses flesh, and not spirit. When the LORD shall stretch out his hand, both he that helpeth shall fall, and he that is holpen shall fall down, and they all shall fail together."

What Helps
Romans 8:26-28 "[26]Likewise the Spirit also helpeth our infirmities: for we know not what we should pray for as we ought: but the Spirit itself maketh intercession for us with groanings which cannot be uttered. [27]And he that searcheth the hearts knoweth what is the mind of the Spirit, because he maketh intercession for the saints according to the will of God. [28]And we know that all things work together for good to them that love God, to them who are the called according to his purpose."

Who God Will Not Help
Job 8:20 "Behold, God will not cast away a perfect man, neither will he help the evil doers:"

Who The Lord Helps
Psalm 37:40 "And the LORD shall help them and deliver them: he shall deliver them from the wicked, and save them, because they trust in him."

Psalm 46:1-5 "[1]God is our refuge and strength, a very present help in trouble. [2]Therefore will not we fear, though the earth be removed, and though the mountains be carried into the midst of the sea; [3]Though the waters thereof roar and be troubled, though the mountains shake with the swelling thereof. Selah. [4]There is a river, the streams whereof shall make glad the city of God, the holy place of the tabernacles of the most High. [5]God is in the midst of her; she shall not be moved: God shall help her, and that right early."

HIDING

It Being The Glory Of God To Conceal
Proverbs 25:2-3 "[2]It is the glory of God to conceal a thing: but the honour of kings is to search out a matter. [3]The heaven for height, and the earth for depth, and the heart of kings is unsearchable."

Nobody Being Able To Hide From The Lord
Jeremiah 23:24 "Can any hide himself in secret places that I shall not see him? saith the LORD. Do not I fill heaven and earth? saith the LORD."

That Which Has Been Hidden
Matthew 10:26 "Fear them not therefore: for there is nothing covered, that shall not be revealed; and hid, that shall not be known."

Mark 4:21-22 "[21]And he said unto them, Is a candle brought to be put under a bushel, or under a bed? and not to be set on a candlestick? [22]For there is nothing hid, which shall not be manifested; neither was any thing kept secret, but that it should come abroad."

Luke 8:16-17 "[16]No man, when he hath lighted a candle, covereth it with a vessel, or putteth it under a bed; but setteth it on a candlestick, that they which enter in may see the light. [17]For nothing is secret, that shall not be made manifest; neither any thing hid, that shall not be known and come abroad."

Luke 12:2 "For there is nothing covered, that shall not be revealed; neither hid, that shall not be known."

1 Corinthians 4:5 "Therefore judge nothing before the time, until the Lord come, who both will bring to light the hidden things of darkness, and will make manifest the counsels of the hearts: and then shall every man have praise of God."

The Lord Being A Hiding Place

Psalm 32:5-7 "⁵I acknowledged my sin unto thee, and mine iniquity have I not hid. I said, I will confess my transgressions unto the Lord; and thou forgavest the iniquity of my sin. Selah. ⁶For this shall every one that is godly pray unto thee in a time when thou mayest be found: surely in the floods of great waters they shall not come nigh unto him. ⁷Thou art my hiding place; thou shalt preserve me from trouble; thou shalt compass me about with songs of deliverance. Selah."

Those That Seek Deep To
Hide Their Counsel From The Lord

Isaiah 29:15-16 "¹⁵Woe unto them that seek deep to hide their counsel from the Lord, and their works are in the dark, and they say, Who seeth us? and who knoweth us? ¹⁶Surely your turning of things upside down shall be esteemed as the potter's clay: for shall the work say of him that made it, He made me not? or shall the thing framed say of him that framed it, He had no understanding?"

What Is Hidden From Mankind

Job 28:20-24 "²⁰Whence then cometh wisdom? and where is the place of understanding? ²¹Seeing it is hid from the eyes of all living, and kept close from the fowls of the air. ²²Destruction and death say, We have heard the fame thereof with our ears. ²³God understandeth the way thereof, and he knoweth the place thereof. ²⁴For he looketh to the ends of the earth, and seeth under the whole heaven;"

When People Hide Themselves

Proverbs 28:12 "When righteous men do rejoice, there is great glory: but when the wicked rise, a man is hidden."

Proverbs 28:28 "When the wicked rise, men hide themselves: but when they perish, the righteous increase."

Who Hides When They See Evil Coming

Proverbs 22:3 "A prudent man foreseeth the evil, and hideth himself: but the simple pass on, and are punished."

Proverbs 27:12 "A prudent man foreseeth the evil, and hideth himself; but the simple pass on, and are punished."

Who Knowledge Is Hid From

Matthew 11:25-27 "²⁵At that time Jesus answered and said, I thank thee, O Father, Lord of heaven and earth, because thou hast hid these things from the wise and prudent, and hast revealed them unto babes. ²⁶Even so, Father: for so it seemed good in thy sight. ²⁷All things are delivered unto me of my Father: and no man knoweth the Son, but the Father; neither knoweth any man the Father, save the Son, and he to whomsoever the Son will reveal him."

Luke 10:21-22 "²¹In that hour Jesus rejoiced in spirit, and said, I thank thee, O Father, Lord of heaven and earth, that thou hast hid these things from the wise and prudent, and hast revealed them unto babes: even so, Father; for so it seemed good in thy sight. ²²All things are delivered to me of my Father: and no man knoweth who the Son is, but the Father; and who the Father is, but the Son, and he to whom the Son will reveal him."

Who The Lord Hides Himself From

Deuteronomy 31:16-18 "¹⁶And the Lord said unto Moses, Behold, thou shalt sleep with thy fathers; and this people will rise up, and go a whoring after the gods of the strangers of the land, whither they go to be among them, and will forsake me, and break my covenant which I have made with them. ¹⁷Then my anger shall be kindled against them in that day, and I will forsake them, and I will hide my face from them, and they shall be devoured, and many evils and troubles shall befall them; so that they will say in that day. Are not these evils come upon us, because our God is not among us? ¹⁸And I will surely hide my face in that day for all the evils which they shall have wrought, in that they are turned unto other gods."

Deuteronomy 32:17-20 "¹⁷They sacrificed unto devils, not to God; to gods whom they knew not, to new gods that came newly up, whom your fathers feared not. ¹⁸Of the Rock that begat thee thou art unmindful, and hast forgotten God that formed thee. ¹⁹And when the Lord saw it, he abhorred them, because of the provoking of his sons, and of his daughters. ²⁰And he said, I will hide my face from them, I will see what their end shall be: for they are a very froward generation, children in whom is no faith."

Isaiah 1:10-15 "[10]Hear the word of the LORD, ye rulers of Sodom; give ear unto the law of our God, ye people of Gomorrah. [11]To what purpose is the multitude of your sacrifices unto me? saith the LORD: I am full of the burnt offerings of rams, and the fat of fed beasts; and I delight not in the blood of bullocks, or of lambs, or of he goats. [12]When ye come to appear before me, who hath required this at your hand, to tread my courts? [13]Bring no more vain oblations; incense is an abomination unto me; the new moons and sabbaths, the calling of assemblies, I cannot away with; it is iniquity, even the solemn meeting. [14]Your new moons and your appointed feasts my soul hateth: they are a trouble unto me; I am weary to bear them. [15]And when ye spread forth your hands, I will hide mine eyes from you: yea, when ye make many prayers, I will not hear: your hands are full of blood."

Isaiah 59:1-2 "[1]Behold, the LORD's hand is not shortened, that it cannot save; neither his ear heavy, that it cannot hear: [2]But your iniquities have separated between you and your God, and your sins have hid his face from you, that he will not hear."

Isaiah 64:4-7 "[4]For since the beginning of the world men have not heard, nor perceived by the ear, neither hath the eye seen, O God, beside thee, what he hath prepared for him that waiteth for him. [5]Thou meetest him that rejoiceth and worketh righteousness, those that remember thee in thy ways: behold, thou art wroth; for we have sinned: in those is continuance, and we shall be saved. [6]But we are all as an unclean thing, and all our righteousnesses are as filthy rags; and we all do fade as a leaf; and our iniquities, like the wind, have taken us away. [7]And there is none that calleth upon thy name, that stirreth up himself to take hold of thee: for thou hast hid thy face from us, and hast consumed us, because of our iniquities."

Jeremiah 33:1-5 "[1]Moreover the word of the LORD came unto Jeremiah the second time, while he was yet shut up in the court of the prison, saying, [2]Thus saith the LORD the maker thereof, the LORD that formed it, to establish it; the LORD is his name; [3]Call unto me, and I will answer thee, and shew thee great and mighty things, which thou knowest not. [4]For thus saith the LORD, the God of Israel, concerning the houses of this city, and concerning the houses of the kings of Judah, which are thrown down by the mounts, and by the sword; [5]They come to fight with the Chaldeans, but it is to fill them with the dead bodies of men, whom I have slain in mine anger and in my fury, and for all whose wickedness I have hid my face from this city."

Ezekiel 39:22-24 "[22]So the house of Israel shall know that I am the LORD their God from that day and forward. [23]And the heathen shall know that the house of Israel went into captivity for their iniquity: because they trespassed against me, therefore hid I my face from them, and gave them into the hand of their enemies: so fell they all by the sword. [24]According to their uncleanness and according to their transgressions have I done unto them, and hid my face from them."

HOLINESS

Being Holy

Exodus 22:31 "And ye shall be holy men unto me: neither shall ye eat any flesh that is torn of beasts in the field; ye shall cast it to the dogs."

Leviticus 11:44-45 "[44]For I am the LORD your God: ye shall therefore sanctify yourselves, and ye shall be holy; for I am holy: neither shall ye defile yourselves with any manner of creeping thing that creepeth upon the earth. [45]For I am the LORD that bringeth you up out of the land of Egypt, to be your God: ye shall therefore be holy, for I am holy."

Leviticus 19:2 "Speak unto all the congregation of the children of Israel, and say unto them, Ye shall be holy: for I the LORD your God am holy."

Leviticus 20:7 "Sanctify yourselves therefore, and be ye holy: for I am the LORD your God."

Leviticus 20:26 "And ye shall be holy unto me: for I the LORD am holy, and have severed you from other people, that ye should be mine."

1 Peter 1:15-16 "[15]But as he which hath called you is holy, so be ye holy in all manner of conversation; [16]Because it is written, Be ye holy; for I am holy."

God Calling Us To Holiness

1 Thessalonians 4:7 "For God hath not called us unto uncleanness, but unto holiness."

Not Giving That Which Is Holy Unto Dogs

Matthew 7:6 "Give not that which is holy unto the dogs, neither cast ye your pearls before swine, lest they trample them under their feet, and turn again and rend you."

The Lord Being Holy

Leviticus 11:44-45 "[44]For I am the LORD your God: ye shall therefore sanctify yourselves, and ye shall be holy; for I am holy: neither shall ye defile yourselves with any manner of creeping thing that creepeth upon the earth. [45]For I am the LORD that bringeth you up out of the land of Egypt, to be your God: ye shall therefore be holy, for I am holy."

Leviticus 19:2 "Speak unto all the congregation of the children of Israel, and say unto them, Ye shall be holy: for I the LORD your God am holy."

Leviticus 20:26 "And ye shall be holy unto me: for I the LORD am holy, and have severed you from other people, that ye should be mine."

Leviticus 21:8 "Thou shalt sanctify him therefore; for he offereth the bread of thy God: he shall be holy unto thee: for I the LORD, which sanctify you, am holy."

Psalm 99:5 "Exalt ye the LORD our God, and worship at his footstool; for he is holy."

Psalm 99:9 "Exalt the LORD our God, and worship at his holy hill; for the LORD our God is holy."

Psalm 145:17 "The LORD is righteous in all his ways, and holy in all his works."

Isaiah 5:16 "But the LORD of hosts shall be exalted in judgment, and God that is holy shall be sanctified in righteousness."

Isaiah 6:1-3 "[1]In the year that king Uzziah died I saw also the Lord sitting upon a throne, high and lifted up, and his train filled the temple. [2]Above it stood the seraphims: each one had six wings; with twain he covered his face, and with twain he covered his feet, and with twain he did fly. [3]And one cried unto another, and said, Holy, holy, holy, is the LORD of hosts: the whole earth is full of his glory."

Isaiah 43:3 "For I am the LORD thy God, the Holy One of Israel, thy Saviour: I gave Egypt for thy ransom, Ethiopia and Seba for thee."

Isaiah 43:14-15 "[14]Thus saith the LORD, your redeemer, the Holy One of Israel; For your sake I have sent to Babylon, and have brought down all their nobles, and the Chaldeans, whose cry is in the ships. [15]I am the LORD, your Holy One, the creator of Israel, your King."

Isaiah 57:15 "For thus saith the high and lofty One that inhabiteth eternity, whose name is Holy; I dwell in the high and holy place, with him also that is of a contrite and humble spirit, to revive the spirit of the humble, and to revive the heart of the contrite ones."

Acts 3:13-14 "[13]The God of Abraham, and of Isaac, and of Jacob, the God of our fathers, hath glorified his Son Jesus; whom ye delivered up, and denied him in the presence of Pilate, when he was determined to let him go. [14]But ye denied the Holy One and the Just, and desired a murderer to be granted unto you;"

Hebrews 7:22-26 "[22]By so much was Jesus made a surety of a better testament. [23]And they truly were many priests, because they were not suffered to continue by reason of death: [24]But this man, because he continueth ever, hath an unchangeable priesthood. [25]Wherefore he is able also to save them to the uttermost that come unto God by him, seeing he ever liveth to make intercession for them. [26]For such an high priest became us, who is holy, harmless, undefiled, separate from sinners, and made higher than the heavens;"

1 Peter 1:15-17 "[15]But as he which hath called you is holy, so be ye holy in all manner of conversation; [16]Because it is written, Be ye holy; for I am holy. [17]And if ye call on the Father, who without respect of persons judgeth according to every man's work, pass the time of your sojourning here in fear:"

Revelation 3:7 "And to the angel of the church in Philadelphia write; These things saith he that is holy, he that is true, he that hath the key of David, he that openeth, and no man shutteth; and shutteth, and no man openeth;"

Revelation 4:8 "And the four beasts had each of them six wings about him; and they were full of eyes within: and they rest not day and night, saying, Holy, holy, holy, Lord God Almighty, which was, and is, and is to come."

Revelation 15:4 "Who shall not fear thee, O Lord, and glorify thy name? for thou only art holy: for all nations shall come and worship before thee; for thy judgments are made manifest."

What Is Holy

Exodus 31:14-15 "¹⁴Ye shall keep the sabbath therefore; for it is holy unto you: every one that defileth it shall surely be put to death: for whosoever doeth any work therein, that soul shall be cut off from among his people. ¹⁵Six days may work be done; but in the seventh is the sabbath of rest, holy to the LORD: whosoever doeth any work in the sabbath day, he shall surely be put to death."

Leviticus 27:30 "And all the tithe of the land, whether of the seed of the land, or of the fruit of the tree, is the LORD's: it is holy unto the LORD."

Romans 7:12 "Wherefore the law is holy, and the commandment holy, and just, and good."

Who Is Holy

Revelation 20:6 "Blessed and holy is he that hath part in the first resurrection: on such the second death hath no power, but they shall be priests of God and of Christ, and shall reign with him a thousand years."

HOLY SPIRIT

Being Filled With The Spirit

Ephesians 5:18 "And be not drunk with wine, wherein is excess; but be filled with the Spirit;"

God Giving Us The Holy Spirit

Nehemiah 9:16-20 "¹⁶But they and our fathers dealt proudly, and hardened their necks, and hearkened not to thy commandments, ¹⁷And refused to obey, neither were mindful of thy wonders that thou didst among them; but hardened their necks, and in their rebellion appointed a captain to return to their bondage: but thou art a God ready to pardon, gracious and merciful, slow to anger, and of great kindness, and forsookest them not. ¹⁸Yea, when they had made them a molten calf, and said, This is thy God that brought thee up out of Egypt, and had wrought great provocations; ¹⁹Yet thou in thy manifold mercies forsookest them not in the wilderness: the pillar of the cloud departed not from them by day, to lead them in the way; neither the pillar of fire by night,

to shew them light, and the way wherein they should go. ²⁰Thou gavest also thy good spirit to instruct them, and withheldest not thy manna from their mouth, and gavest them water for their thirst."

John 14:9-18 "⁹Jesus saith unto him, Have I been so long time with you, and yet hast thou not known me, Philip? he that hath seen me hath seen the Father; and how sayest thou then, Shew us the Father? ¹⁰Believest thou not that I am in the Father, and the Father in me? the words that I speak unto you I speak not of myself: but the Father that dwelleth in me, he doeth the works. ¹¹Believe me that I am in the Father, and the Father in me: or else believe me for the very works' sake. ¹² Verily, verily, I say unto you, He that believeth on me, the works that I do shall he do also; and greater works than these shall he do; because I go unto my Father. ¹³And whatsoever ye shall ask in my name, that will I do, that the Father may be glorified in the Son. ¹⁴If ye shall ask any thing in my name, I will do it. ¹⁵If ye love me, keep my commandments. ¹⁶And I will pray the Father, and he shall give you another Comforter, that he may abide with you for ever; ¹⁷Even the Spirit of truth; whom the world cannot receive, because it seeth him not, neither knoweth him: but ye know him; for he dwelleth with you, and shall be in you. ¹⁸I will not leave you comfortless: I will come to you."

Romans 5:5 "And hope maketh not ashamed; because the love of God is shed abroad in our hearts by the Holy Ghost which is given unto us."

1 Corinthians 12:3-7 "³Wherefore I give you to understand, that no man speaking by the Spirit of God calleth Jesus accursed: and that no man can say that Jesus is the Lord, but by the Holy Ghost. ⁴Now there are diversities of gifts, but the same Spirit. ⁵And there are differences of administrations, but the same Lord. ⁶And there are diversities of operations, but it is the same God which worketh all in all. ⁷But the manifestation of the Spirit is given to every man to profit withal."

2 Corinthians 5:5 "Now he that hath wrought us for the selfsame thing is God, who also hath given unto us the earnest of the Spirit."

Ephesians 3:14-16 "¹⁴For this cause I bow my knees unto the Father of our Lord Jesus Christ,

15Of whom the whole family in heaven and earth is named, 16That he would grant you, according to the riches of his glory, to be strengthened with might by his Spirit in the inner man;"

1 Thessalonians 4:8 "He therefore that despiseth, despiseth not man, but God, who hath also given unto us his holy Spirit."

2 Timothy 1:7 "For God hath not given us the spirit of fear; but of power, and of love, and of a sound mind."

1 John 3:21-24 "21Beloved, if our heart condemn us not, then have we confidence toward God. 22And whatsoever we ask, we receive of him, because we keep his commandments, and do those things that are pleasing in his sight. 23And this is his commandment, That we should believe on the name of his Son Jesus Christ, and love one another, as he gave us commandment. 24And he that keepeth his commandments dwelleth in him, and he in him. And hereby we know that he abideth in us, by the Spirit which he hath given us."

1 John 4:12-13 "12No man hath seen God at any time. If we love one another, God dwelleth in us, and his love is perfected in us. 13Hereby know we that we dwell in him, and he in us, because he hath given us of his Spirit."

God The Father Anointing Jesus Christ With The Holy Spirit

Isaiah 11:1-2 "1And there shall come forth a rod out of the stem of Jesse, and a Branch shall grow out of his roots: 2And the spirit of the LORD shall rest upon him, the spirit of wisdom and understanding, the spirit of counsel and might, the spirit of knowledge and of the fear of the LORD;"

Isaiah 42:1 "Behold my servant, whom I uphold; mine elect, in whom my soul delighteth; I have put my spirit upon him: he shall bring forth judgment to the Gentiles."

Isaiah 61:1-3 "1The Spirit of the Lord GOD is upon me; because the LORD hath anointed me to preach good tidings unto the meek; he hath sent me to bind up the brokenhearted, to proclaim liberty to the captives, and the opening of the prison to them that are bound; 2To proclaim the acceptable year of the LORD, and the day of vengeance of our God; to comfort all that mourn; 3To appoint unto them that mourn in Zion, to give unto them beauty for ashes, the oil of joy for mourning, the garment of praise for the spirit of heaviness; that they might be called trees of righteousness, the planting of the LORD, that he might be glorified."

Luke 4:14-19 "14And Jesus returned in the power of the Spirit into Galilee: and there went out a fame of him through all the region round about. 15And he taught in their synagogues, being glorified of all. 16And he came to Nazareth, where he had been brought up: and, as his custom was, he went into the synagogue on the sabbath day, and stood up for to read. 17And there was delivered unto him the book of the prophet Esaias. And when he had opened the book, he found the place where it was written, 18The Spirit of the Lord is upon me, because he hath anointed me to preach the gospel to the poor; he hath sent me to heal the brokenhearted, to preach deliverance to the captives, and recovering of sight to the blind, to set at liberty them that are bruised, 19To preach the acceptable year of the Lord."

Acts 10:37-38 "37That word, I say, ye know, which was published throughout all Judaea, and began from Galilee, after the baptism which John preached; 38How God anointed Jesus of Nazareth with the Holy Ghost and with power: who went about doing good, and healing all that were oppressed of the devil; for God was with him."

Not Quenching The Spirit

1 Thessalonians 5:19 "Quench not the Spirit."

Jesus Christ Baptizing With The Holy Spirit

Matthew 3:11-14 "11I indeed baptize you with water unto repentance: but he that cometh after me is mightier than I, whose shoes I am not worthy to bear: he shall baptize you with the Holy Ghost, and with fire: 12Whose fan is in his hand, and he will throughly purge his floor, and gather his wheat into the garner; but he will burn up the chaff with unquenchable fire. 13Then cometh Jesus from Galilee to Jordan unto John, to be baptized of him. 14But John forbad him, saying, I have need to be baptized of thee, and comest thou to me?"

Mark 1:7-9 "7And preached, saying, There cometh one mightier than I after me, the latchet of whose shoes I am not worthy to stoop down and unloose. [8]I indeed have baptized you with water: but he shall baptize you with the Holy Ghost. [9]And it came to pass in those days, that Jesus came from Nazareth of Galilee, and was baptized of John in Jordan."

Luke 3:15-21 "[15]And as the people were in expectation, and all men mused in their hearts of John, whether he were the Christ, or not; [16]John answered, saying unto them all, I indeed baptize you with water; but one mightier than I cometh, the latchet of whose shoes I am not worthy to unloose: he shall baptize you with the Holy Ghost and with fire: [17]Whose fan is in his hand, and he will throughly purge his floor, and will gather the wheat into his garner; but the chaff he will burn with fire unquenchable. [18]And many other things in his exhortation preached he unto the people. [19]But Herod the tetrarch, being reproved by him for Herodias his brother Philip's wife, and for all the evils which Herod had done, [20]Added yet this above all, that he shut up John in prison. [21]Now when all the people were baptized, it came to pass, that Jesus also being baptized, and praying, the heaven was opened,"

John 1:29-34 "[29]The next day John seeth Jesus coming unto him, and saith, Behold the Lamb of God, which taketh away the sin of the world. [30]This is he of whom I said, After me cometh a man which is preferred before me: for he was before me. [31]And I knew him not: but that he should be made manifest to Israel, therefore am I come baptizing with water. [32]And John bare record, saying, I saw the Spirit descending from heaven like a dove, and it abode upon him. [33]And I knew him not: but he that sent me to baptize with water, the same said unto me, Upon whom thou shalt see the Spirit descending, and remaining on him, the same is he which baptizeth with the Holy Ghost. [34]And I saw, and bare record that this is the Son of God."

Acts 1:5 "For John truly baptized with water; but ye shall be baptized with the Holy Ghost not many days hence."

Acts 11:16 "Then remembered I the word of the Lord, how that he said, John indeed baptized with water; but ye shall be baptized with the Holy Ghost."

Acts 19:4-6 "[4]Then said Paul, John verily baptized with the baptism of repentance, saying unto the people, that they should believe on him which should come after him, that is, on Christ Jesus. [5]When they heard this, they were baptized in the name of the Lord Jesus. [6]And when Paul had laid his hands upon them, the Holy Ghost came on them; and they spake with tongues, and prophesied."

The Descention Of The Holy Spirit
Matthew 3:16-17 "[16]And Jesus, when he was baptized, went up straightway out of the water: and, lo, the heavens were opened unto him, and he saw the Spirit of God descending like a dove, and lighting upon him: [17]And lo a voice from heaven, saying, This is my beloved Son, in whom I am well pleased."

Mark 1:9-11 "[9]And it came to pass in those days, that Jesus came from Nazareth of Galilee, and was baptized of John in Jordan. [10]And straightway coming up out of the water, he saw the heavens opened, and the Spirit like a dove descending upon him: [11]And there came a voice from heaven, saying, Thou art my beloved Son, in whom I am well pleased."

Luke 3:21-22 "[21]Now when all the people were baptized, it came to pass, that Jesus also being baptized, and praying, the heaven was opened, [22]And the Holy Ghost descended in a bodily shape like a dove upon him, and a voice came from heaven, which said, Thou art my beloved Son; in thee I am well pleased."

John 1:32-34 "[32]And John bare record, saying, I saw the Spirit descending from heaven like a dove, and it abode upon him. [33]And I knew him not: but he that sent me to baptize with water, the same said unto me, Upon whom thou shalt see the Spirit descending, and remaining on him, the same is he which baptizeth with the Holy Ghost. [34]And I saw, and bare record that this is the Son of God."

The Fruit Of The Spirit
Galatians 5:22-24 "[22]But the fruit of the Spirit is love, joy, peace, longsuffering, gentleness, goodness, faith, [23]Meekness, temperance: against such there is no law. [24]And they that are Christ's have crucified the flesh with the affections and lusts."

Ephesians 5:9-10 "⁹(For the fruit of the Spirit is in all goodness and righteousness and truth;) ¹⁰Proving what is acceptable unto the Lord."

The Holy Spirit Being Sent By God

Psalm 104:24-30 "²⁴O LORD, how manifold are thy works! in wisdom hast thou made them all: the earth is full of thy riches. ²⁵So is this great and wide sea, wherein are things creeping innumerable, both small and great beasts. ²⁶There go the ships: there is that leviathan, whom thou hast made to play therein. ²⁷These wait all upon thee; that thou mayest give them their meat in due season. ²⁸That thou givest them they gather: thou openest thine hand, they are filled with good. ²⁹Thou hidest thy face, they are troubled: thou takest away their breath, they die, and return to their dust. ³⁰Thou sendest forth thy spirit, they are created: and thou renewest the face of the earth."

Luke 24:44-49 "⁴⁴And he said unto them, These are the words which I spake unto you, while I was yet with you, that all things must be fulfilled, which were written in the law of Moses, and in the prophets, and in the psalms, concerning me. ⁴⁵Then opened he their understanding, that they might understand the scriptures, ⁴⁶And said unto them, Thus it is written, and thus it behoved Christ to suffer, and to rise from the dead the third day: ⁴⁷And that repentance and remission of sins should be preached in his name among all nations, beginning at Jerusalem. ⁴⁸And ye are witnesses of these things. ⁴⁹And, behold, I send the promise of my Father upon you: but tarry ye in the city of Jerusalem, until ye be endued with power from on high."

John 14:23-26 "²³Jesus answered and said unto him, If a man love me, he will keep my words: and my Father will love him, and we will come unto him, and make our abode with him. ²⁴He that loveth me not keepeth not my sayings: and the word which ye hear is not mine, but the Father's which sent me. ²⁵These things have I spoken unto you, being yet present with you. ²⁶But the Comforter, which is the Holy Ghost, whom the Father will send in my name, he shall teach you all things, and bring all things to your remembrance, whatsoever I have said unto you."

John 15:26-27 "²⁶But when the Comforter is come, whom I will send unto you from the Father, even the Spirit of truth, which proceedeth from the Father, he shall testify of me: ²⁷And ye also shall bear witness, because ye have been with me from the beginning."

John 16:1-7 "¹These things have I spoken unto you, that ye should not be offended. ²They shall put you out of the synagogues: yea, the time cometh, that whosoever killeth you will think that he doeth God service. ³And these things will they do unto you, because they have not known the Father, nor me. ⁴But these things have I told you, that when the time shall come, ye may remember that I told you of them. And these things I said not unto you at the beginning, because I was with you. ⁵But now I go my way to him that sent me; and none of you asketh me, Whither goest thou? ⁶But because I have said these things unto you, sorrow hath filled your heart. ⁷Nevertheless I tell you the truth; It is expedient for you that I go away: for if I go not away, the Comforter will not come unto you; but if I depart, I will send him unto you."

Galatians 4:6-7 "⁶And because ye are sons, God hath sent forth the Spirit of his Son into your hearts, crying, Abba, Father. ⁷Wherefore thou art no more a servant, but a son; and if a son, then an heir of God through Christ."

1 Peter 1:12 "Unto whom it was revealed, that not unto themselves, but unto us they did minister the things, which are now reported unto you by them that have preached the gospel unto you with the Holy Ghost sent down from heaven; which things the angels desire to look into."

The Holy Spirit Speaking Through People

Isaiah 50:4-5 "⁴The Lord GOD hath given me the tongue of the learned, that I should know how to speak a word in season to him that is weary: he wakeneth morning by morning, he wakeneth mine ear to hear as the learned. ⁵The Lord GOD hath opened mine ear, and I was not rebellious, neither turned away back."

Isaiah 51:15-16 "¹⁵But I am the LORD thy God, that divided the sea, whose waves roared: The LORD of hosts is his name. ¹⁶And I have put my words in thy mouth, and I have covered thee in the shadow of mine hand, that I may plant the heavens, and lay the foundations of the earth, and say unto Zion, Thou art my people."

Isaiah 59:21 "As for me, this is my covenant with them, saith the LORD; My spirit that is upon thee, and my words which I have put in thy mouth, shall not depart out of thy mouth, nor out of the mouth of thy seed, nor out of the mouth of thy seed's seed, saith the LORD, from henceforth and for ever."

Matthew 10:19-20 "19But when they deliver you up, take no thought how or what ye shall speak: for it shall be given you in that same hour what ye shall speak. 20For it is not ye that speak, but the Spirit of your Father which speaketh in you."

Mark 13:11 "But when they shall lead you, and deliver you up, take no thought beforehand what ye shall speak, neither do ye premeditate: but whatsoever shall be given you in that hour, that speak ye: for it is not ye that speak, but the Holy Ghost."

Luke 12:11-12 "11And when they bring you unto the synagogues, and unto magistrates, and powers, take ye no thought how or what thing ye shall answer, or what ye shall say: 12For the Holy Ghost shall teach you in the same hour what ye ought to say."

Luke 21:12-15 "12But before all these, they shall lay their hands on you, and persecute you, delivering you up to the synagogues, and into prisons, being brought before kings and rulers for my name's sake. 13And it shall turn to you for a testimony. 14Settle it therefore in your hearts, not to meditate before what ye shall answer: 15For I will give you a mouth and wisdom, which all your adversaries shall not be able to gainsay nor resist."

Acts 2:4 "And they were all filled with the Holy Ghost, and began to speak with other tongues, as the Spirit gave them utterance."

1 Corinthians 12:3 "Wherefore I give you to understand, that no man speaking by the Spirit of God calleth Jesus accursed: and that no man can say that Jesus is the Lord, but by the Holy Ghost."

2 Peter 1:19-21 "19We have also a more sure word of prophecy; whereunto ye do well that ye take heed, as unto a light that shineth in a dark place, until the day dawn, and the day star arise in your hearts: 20Knowing this first, that no prophecy of the scripture is of any private interpretation. 21For the prophecy came not in old time by the will of man: but holy men of God spake as they were moved by the Holy Ghost."

The Holy Spirit Teaching

Nehemiah 9:16-20 "16But they and our fathers dealt proudly, and hardened their necks, and hearkened not to thy commandments, 17And refused to obey, neither were mindful of thy wonders that thou didst among them; but hardened their necks, and in their rebellion appointed a captain to return to their bondage: but thou art a God ready to pardon, gracious and merciful, slow to anger, and of great kindness, and forsookest them not. 18Yea, when they had made them a molten calf, and said, This is thy God that brought thee up out of Egypt, and had wrought great provocations; 19Yet thou in thy manifold mercies forsookest them not in the wilderness: the pillar of the cloud departed not from them by day, to lead them in the way; neither the pillar of fire by night, to shew them light, and the way wherein they should go. 20Thou gavest also thy good spirit to instruct them, and withheldest not thy manna from their mouth, and gavest them water for their thirst."

Luke 12:11-12 "11And when they bring you unto the synagogues, and unto magistrates, and powers, take ye no thought how or what thing ye shall answer, or what ye shall say: 12For the Holy Ghost shall teach you in the same hour what ye ought to say."

John 14:23-26 "23Jesus answered and said unto him, If a man love me, he will keep my words: and my Father will love him, and we will come unto him, and make our abode with him. 24He that loveth me not keepeth not my sayings: and the word which ye hear is not mine, but the Father's which sent me. 25These things have I spoken unto you, being yet present with you. 26But the Comforter, which is the Holy Ghost, whom the Father will send in my name, he shall teach you all things, and bring all things to your remembrance, whatsoever I have said unto you."

John 16:13-14 "13Howbeit when he, the Spirit of truth, is come, he will guide you into all truth: for he shall not speak of himself; but whatsoever he shall hear, that shall he speak: and he will shew you things to come. 14He shall glorify me: for he shall receive of mine, and shall shew it unto you."

1 Corinthians 2:12-14 "¹²Now we have received, not the spirit of the world, but the spirit which is of God; that we might know the things that are freely given to us of God. ¹³Which things also we speak, not in the words which man's wisdom teacheth, but which the Holy Ghost teacheth; comparing spiritual things with spiritual. ¹⁴But the natural man receiveth not the things of the Spirit of God: for they are foolishness unto him: neither can he know them, because they are spiritually discerned."

The Holy Spirit Witnessing

John 15:1-27 "¹I am the true vine, and my Father is the husbandman. ²Every branch in me that beareth not fruit he taketh away: and every branch that beareth fruit, he purgeth it, that it may bring forth more fruit. ³Now ye are clean through the word which I have spoken unto you. ⁴Abide in me, and I in you. As the branch cannot bear fruit of itself, except it abide in the vine; no more can ye, except ye abide in me. ⁵I am the vine, ye are the branches: He that abideth in me, and I in him, the same bringeth forth much fruit: for without me ye can do nothing. ⁶If a man abide not in me, he is cast forth as a branch, and is withered; and men gather them, and cast them into the fire, and they are burned. ⁷If ye abide in me, and my words abide in you, ye shall ask what ye will, and it shall be done unto you. ⁸Herein is my Father glorified, that ye bear much fruit; so shall ye be my disciples. ⁹As the Father hath loved me, so have I loved you: continue ye in my love. ¹⁰If ye keep my commandments, ye shall abide in my love; even as I have kept my Father's commandments, and abide in his love. ¹¹These things have I spoken unto you, that my joy might remain in you, and that your joy might be full. ¹²This is my commandment, That ye love one another, as I have loved you. ¹³Greater love hath no man than this, that a man lay down his life for his friends. ¹⁴Ye are my friends, if ye do whatsoever I command you. ¹⁵Henceforth I call you not servants; for the servant knoweth not what his lord doeth: but I have called you friends; for all things that I have heard of my Father I have made known unto you. ¹⁶Ye have not chosen me, but I have chosen you, and ordained you, that ye should go and bring forth fruit, and that your fruit should remain: that whatsoever ye shall ask of the Father in my name, he may give it you. ¹⁷These things I command you, that ye love one another. ¹⁸If the world hate you, ye know that it hated me before it hated you. ¹⁹If ye were of the world, the world would love his own: but because ye are not of the world, but I have chosen you out of the world, therefore the world hateth you. ²⁰Remember the word that I said unto you, The servant is not greater than his lord. If they have persecuted me, they will also persecute you; if they have kept my saying, they will keep yours also. ²¹But all these things will they do unto you for my name's sake, because they know not him that sent me. ²²If I had not come and spoken unto them, they had not had sin: but now they have no cloke for their sin. ²³He that hateth me hateth my Father also. ²⁴If I had not done among them the works which none other man did, they had not had sin: but now have they both seen and hated both me and my Father. ²⁵But this cometh to pass, that the word might be fulfilled that is written in their law, They hated me without a cause. ²⁶But when the Comforter is come, whom I will send unto you from the Father, even the Spirit of truth, which proceedeth from the Father, he shall testify of me: ²⁷And ye also shall bear witness, because ye have been with me from the beginning."

Acts 5:30-32 "³⁰The God of our fathers raised up Jesus, whom ye slew and hanged on a tree. ³¹Him hath God exalted with his right hand to be a Prince and a Saviour, for to give repentance to Israel, and forgiveness of sins. ³²And we are his witnesses of these things; and so is also the Holy Ghost, whom God hath given to them that obey him."

Acts 20:22-23 "²²And now, behold, I go bound in the spirit unto Jerusalem, not knowing the things that shall befall me there: ²³Save that the Holy Ghost witnesseth in every city, saying that bonds and afflictions abide me."

Romans 8:16 "The Spirit itself beareth witness with our spirit, that we are the children of God:"

Ephesians 3:1-5 "¹For this cause I Paul, the prisoner of Jesus Christ for you Gentiles, ²If ye have heard of the dispensation of the grace of God which is given me to youward: ³How that by revelation he made known unto me the mystery; (as

I wrote afore in few words, ⁴Whereby, when ye read, ye may understand my knowledge in the mystery of Christ) ⁵Which in other ages was not made known unto the sons of men, as it is now revealed unto his holy apostles and prophets by the Spirit;"

Hebrews 10:15 "Whereof the Holy Ghost also is a witness to us: for after that he had said before,"

1 John 5:5-7 "⁵Who is he that overcometh the world, but he that believeth that Jesus is the Son of God? ⁶This is he that came by water and blood, even Jesus Christ; not by water only, but by water and blood. And it is the Spirit that beareth witness, because the Spirit is truth. ⁷For there are three that bear record in heaven, the Father, the Word, and the Holy Ghost: and these three are one."

The Lord Pouring Out His Spirit

Isaiah 44:1-3 "¹Yet now hear, O Jacob my servant; and Israel, whom I have chosen: ²Thus saith the LORD that made thee, and formed thee from the womb, which will help thee; Fear not, O Jacob, my servant; and thou, Jesurun, whom I have chosen. ³For I will pour water upon him that is thirsty, and floods upon the dry ground: I will pour my spirit upon thy seed, and my blessing upon thine offspring:"

Joel 2:27-29 "²⁷And ye shall know that I am in the midst of Israel, and that I am the LORD your God, and none else: and my people shall never be ashamed. ²⁸And it shall come to pass afterward, that I will pour out my spirit upon all flesh; and your sons and your daughters shall prophesy, your old men shall dream dreams, your young men shall see visions: ²⁹And also upon the servants and upon the handmaids in those days will I pour out my spirit."

Zechariah 12:8-10 "⁸In that day shall the LORD defend the inhabitants of Jerusalem; and he that is feeble among them at that day shall be as David; and the house of David shall be as God, as the angel of the LORD before them. ⁹And it shall come to pass in that day, that I will seek to destroy all the nations that come against Jerusalem. ¹⁰And I will pour upon the house of David, and upon the inhabitants of Jerusalem, the spirit of grace and of supplications: and they shall look upon me whom they have pierced, and they shall mourn for him,

as one mourneth for his only son, and shall be in bitterness for him, as one that is in bitterness for his firstborn."

Acts 2:17-18 "¹⁷And it shall come to pass in the last days, saith God, I will pour out of my Spirit upon all flesh: and your sons and your daughters shall prophesy, and your young men shall see visions, and your old men shall dream dreams: ¹⁸And on my servants and on my handmaidens I will pour out in those days of my Spirit; and they shall prophesy:"

Acts 10:44-48 "⁴⁴While Peter yet spake these words, the Holy Ghost fell on all them which heard the word. ⁴⁵And they of the circumcision which believed were astonished, as many as came with Peter, because that on the Gentiles also was poured out the gift of the Holy Ghost. ⁴⁶For they heard them speak with tongues, and magnify God. Then answered Peter, ⁴⁷Can any man forbid water, that these should not be baptized, which have received the Holy Ghost as well as we? ⁴⁸And he commanded them to be baptized in the name of the Lord. Then prayed they him to tarry certain days."

The Place Where The Spirit Of The Lord Is

2 Corinthians 3:14-17 "¹⁴But their minds were blinded: for until this day remaineth the same vail untaken away in the reading of the old testament; which vail is done away in Christ. ¹⁵But even unto this day, when Moses is read, the vail is upon their heart. ¹⁶Nevertheless when it shall turn to the Lord, the vail shall be taken away. ¹⁷Now the Lord is that Spirit: and where the Spirit of the Lord is, there is liberty."

There Being One Spirit

1 Corinthians 12:3-7 "³Wherefore I give you to understand, that no man speaking by the Spirit of God calleth Jesus accursed: and that no man can say that Jesus is the Lord, but by the Holy Ghost. ⁴Now there are diversities of gifts, but the same Spirit. ⁵And there are differences of administrations, but the same Lord. ⁶And there are diversities of operations, but it is the same God which worketh all in all. ⁷But the manifestation of the Spirit is given to every man to profit withal."

Ephesians 4:4-6 "⁴There is one body, and one Spirit, even as ye are called in one hope of your calling; 5One Lord, one faith, one baptism, 6One God and Father of all, who is above all, and through all, and in you all."

Those That Are Born Of The Spirit
John 3:3-8 "3Jesus answered and said unto him, Verily, verily, I say unto thee, Except a man be born again, he cannot see the kingdom of God. 4Nicodemus saith unto him, How can a man be born when he is old? can he enter the second time into his mother's womb, and be born? 5Jesus answered, Verily, verily, I say unto thee, Except a man be born of water and of the Spirit, he cannot enter into the kingdom of God. 6That which is born of the flesh is flesh; and that which is born of the Spirit is spirit. 7Marvel not that I said unto thee, Ye must be born again. 8The wind bloweth where it listeth, and thou hearest the sound thereof, but canst not tell whence it cometh, and whither it goeth: so is every one that is born of the Spirit."

Those That Do Not Have The Spirit Of Christ
Romans 8:9 "But ye are not in the flesh, but in the Spirit, if so be that the Spirit of God dwell in you. Now if any man have not the Spirit of Christ, he is none of his."

Those That Follow After The Spirit
Romans 8:1-5 "1There is therefore now no condemnation to them which are in Christ Jesus, who walk not after the flesh, but after the Spirit. 2For the law of the Spirit of life in Christ Jesus hath made me free from the law of sin and death. 3For what the law could not do, in that it was weak through the flesh, God sending his own Son in the likeness of sinful flesh, and for sin, condemned sin in the flesh: 4That the righteousness of the law might be fulfilled in us, who walk not after the flesh, but after the Spirit. 5For they that are after the flesh do mind the things of the flesh; but they that are after the Spirit the things of the Spirit."

Romans 8:14 "For as many as are led by the Spirit of God, they are the sons of God."

Galatians 5:16-18 "16This I say then, Walk in the Spirit, and ye shall not fulfil the lust of the flesh. 17For the flesh lusteth against the Spirit, and the Spirit against the flesh: and these are contrary the one to the other: so that ye cannot do the things that ye would. 18But if ye be led of the Spirit, ye are not under the law."

Those That Have The Spirit Of God Dwelling In Them
Romans 8:9-11 "9But ye are not in the flesh, but in the Spirit, if so be that the Spirit of God dwell in you. Now if any man have not the Spirit of Christ, he is none of his. 10And if Christ be in you, the body is dead because of sin; but the Spirit is life because of righteousness. 11But if the Spirit of him that raised up Jesus from the dead dwell in you, he that raised up Christ from the dead shall also quicken your mortal bodies by his Spirit that dwelleth in you."

Those That Sin Against The Holy Spirit
Matthew 12:31-32 "31Wherefore I say unto you, All manner of sin and blasphemy shall be forgiven unto men: but the blasphemy against the Holy Ghost shall not be forgiven unto men. 32And whosoever speaketh a word against the Son of man, it shall be forgiven him: but whosoever speaketh against the Holy Ghost, it shall not be forgiven him, neither in this world, neither in the world to come."

Mark 3:28-29 "28Verily I say unto you, All sins shall be forgiven unto the sons of men, and blasphemies wherewith soever they shall blaspheme: 29But he that shall blaspheme against the Holy Ghost hath never forgiveness, but is in danger of eternal damnation:"

Luke 12:10 "And whosoever shall speak a word against the Son of man, it shall be forgiven him: but unto him that blasphemeth against the Holy Ghost it shall not be forgiven."

Hebrews 6:4-8 "4For it is impossible for those who were once enlightened, and have tasted of the heavenly gift, and were made partakers of the Holy Ghost, 5And have tasted the good word of God, and the powers of the world to come, 6If they shall fall away, to renew them again unto repentance; seeing they crucify to themselves the Son of God afresh, and put him to an open shame. 7For the earth which drinketh in the rain that cometh oft upon it, and bringeth forth herbs meet for them by whom it is dressed, receiveth blessing from God: 8But that which beareth thorns and briers is rejected, and is nigh unto cursing; whose end is to be burned."

Hebrews 10:26-29 "26For if we sin wilfully after that we have received the knowledge of the truth, there remaineth no more sacrifice for sins, ²⁷But a certain fearful looking for of judgment and fiery indignation, which shall devour the adversaries. ²⁸He that despised Moses' law died without mercy under two or three witnesses: ²⁹Of how much sorer punishment, suppose ye, shall he be thought worthy, who hath trodden under foot the Son of God, and hath counted the blood of the covenant, wherewith he was sanctified, an unholy thing, and hath done despite unto the Spirit of grace?"

1 John 5:16-17 "¹⁶If any man see his brother sin a sin which is not unto death, he shall ask, and he shall give him life for them that sin not unto death. There is a sin unto death: I do not say that he shall pray for it. ¹⁷All unrighteousness is sin: and there is a sin not unto death."

Those That Sow To The Spirit
Galatians 6:8 "For he that soweth to his flesh shall of the flesh reap corruption; but he that soweth to the Spirit shall of the Spirit reap life everlasting."

Walking In The Spirit
Galatians 5:25 "If we live in the Spirit, let us also walk in the Spirit."

What Can Be Accomplished Through The Power Of The Holy Spirit
Acts 1:6-8 "⁶When they therefore were come together, they asked of him, saying, Lord, wilt thou at this time restore again the kingdom to Israel? ⁷And he said unto them, It is not for you to know the times or the seasons, which the Father hath put in his own power. ⁸But ye shall receive power, after that the Holy Ghost is come upon you: and ye shall be witnesses unto me both in Jerusalem, and in all Judaea, and in Samaria, and unto the uttermost part of the earth."

Romans 15:13 "Now the God of hope fill you with all joy and peace in believing, that ye may abound in hope, through the power of the Holy Ghost."

1 Corinthians 6:9-11 "⁹Know ye not that the unrighteous shall not inherit the kingdom of God? Be not deceived: neither fornicators, nor idolaters, nor adulterers, nor effeminate, nor abusers of themselves with mankind, ¹⁰Nor thieves, nor covetous, nor drunkards, nor revilers, nor extortioners, shall inherit the kingdom of God. ¹¹And such were some of you: but ye are washed, but ye are

sanctified, but ye are justified in the name of the Lord Jesus, and by the Spirit of our God."

2 Corinthians 3:14-18 "¹⁴But their minds were blinded: for until this day remaineth the same vail untaken away in the reading of the old testament; which vail is done away in Christ. ¹⁵But even unto this day, when Moses is read, the vail is upon their heart. ¹⁶Nevertheless when it shall turn to the Lord, the vail shall be taken away. ¹⁷Now the Lord is that Spirit: and where the Spirit of the Lord is, there is liberty. ¹⁸But we all, with open face beholding as in a glass the glory of the Lord, are changed into the same image from glory to glory, even as by the Spirit of the Lord."

What Is Contrary To The Spirit
Galatians 5:16-17 "¹⁶This I say then, Walk in the Spirit, and ye shall not fulfil the lust of the flesh. ¹⁷For the flesh lusteth against the Spirit, and the Spirit against the flesh: and these are contrary the one to the other: so that ye cannot do the things that ye would."

What Occurs When The Holy Spirit Comes Upon You
1 Samuel 10:6 "And the Spirit of the LORD will come upon thee, and thou shalt prophesy with them, and shalt be turned into another man."

What The Holy Spirit Does
John 15:1-26 "¹I am the true vine, and my Father is the husbandman. ²Every branch in me that beareth not fruit he taketh away: and every branch that beareth fruit, he purgeth it, that it may bring forth more fruit. ³Now ye are clean through the word which I have spoken unto you. ⁴Abide in me, and I in you. As the branch cannot bear fruit of itself, except it abide in the vine; no more can ye, except ye abide in me. ⁵I am the vine, ye are the branches: He that abideth in me, and I in him, the same bringeth forth much fruit: for without me ye can do nothing. ⁶If a man abide not in me, he is cast forth as a branch, and is withered; and men gather them, and cast them into the fire, and they are burned. ⁷If ye abide in me, and my words abide in you, ye shall ask what ye will, and it shall be done unto you. ⁸Herein is my Father glorified, that ye bear much fruit; so shall ye be my disciples. ⁹As the Father hath loved me, so have I loved you: continue ye in my love. ¹⁰If ye

keep my commandments, ye shall abide in my love; even as I have kept my Father's commandments, and abide in his love. ¹¹These things have I spoken unto you, that my joy might remain in you, and that your joy might be full. ¹²This is my commandment, That ye love one another, as I have loved you. ¹³Greater love hath no man than this, that a man lay down his life for his friends. ¹⁴Ye are my friends, if ye do whatsoever I command you. ¹⁵Henceforth I call you not servants; for the servant knoweth not what his lord doeth: but I have called you friends; for all things that I have heard of my Father I have made known unto you. ¹⁶Ye have not chosen me, but I have chosen you, and ordained you, that ye should go and bring forth fruit, and that your fruit should remain: that whatsoever ye shall ask of the Father in my name, he may give it you. ¹⁷These things I command you, that ye love one another. ¹⁸If the world hate you, ye know that it hated me before it hated you. ¹⁹If ye were of the world, the world would love his own: but because ye are not of the world, but I have chosen you out of the world, therefore the world hateth you. ²⁰Remember the word that I said unto you, The servant is not greater than his lord. If they have persecuted me, they will also persecute you; if they have kept my saying, they will keep yours also. ²¹But all these things will they do unto you for my name's sake, because they know not him that sent me. ²²If I had not come and spoken unto them, they had not had sin: but now they have no cloke for their sin. ²³He that hateth me hateth my Father also. ²⁴If I had not done among them the works which none other man did, they had not had sin: but now have they both seen and hated both me and my Father. ²⁵But this cometh to pass, that the word might be fulfilled that is written in their law, They hated me without a cause. ²⁶But when the Comforter is come, whom I will send unto you from the Father, even the Spirit of truth, which proceedeth from the Father, he shall testify of me:"

John 16:1-14 "¹These things have I spoken unto you, that ye should not be offended. ²They shall put you out of the synagogues: yea, the time cometh, that whosoever killeth you will think that he doeth God service. ³And these things will they do unto you, because they have not known the Father, nor me. ⁴But these things have I told you,

that when the time shall come, ye may remember that I told you of them. And these things I said not unto you at the beginning, because I was with you. ⁵But now I go my way to him that sent me; and none of you asketh me, Whither goest thou? ⁶But because I have said these things unto you, sorrow hath filled your heart. ⁷Nevertheless I tell you the truth; It is expedient for you that I go away: for if I go not away, the Comforter will not come unto you; but if I depart, I will send him unto you. ⁸And when he is come, he will reprove the world of sin, and of righteousness, and of judgment: ⁹Of sin, because they believe not on me; ¹⁰Of righteousness, because I go to my Father, and ye see me no more; ¹¹Of judgment, because the prince of this world is judged. ¹²I have yet many things to say unto you, but ye cannot bear them now. ¹³Howbeit when he, the Spirit of truth, is come, he will guide you into all truth: for he shall not speak of himself; but whatsoever he shall hear, that shall he speak: and he will shew you things to come. ¹⁴He shall glorify me: for he shall receive of mine, and shall shew it unto you."

Romans 8:26-28 "²⁶Likewise the Spirit also helpeth our infirmities: for we know not what we should pray for as we ought: but the Spirit itself maketh intercession for us with groanings which cannot be uttered. ²⁷And he that searcheth the hearts knoweth what is the mind of the Spirit, because he maketh intercession for the saints according to the will of God. ²⁸And we know that all things work together for good to them that love God, to them who are the called according to his purpose."

1 Corinthians 2:9-10 "⁹But as it is written, Eye hath not seen, nor ear heard, neither have entered into the heart of man, the things which God hath prepared for them that love him. ¹⁰But God hath revealed them unto us by his Spirit: for the Spirit searcheth all things, yea, the deep things of God."

2 Corinthians 3:4-6 "⁴And such trust have we through Christ to God-ward: ⁵Not that we are sufficient of ourselves to think any thing as of ourselves; but our sufficiency is of God; ⁶Who also hath made us able ministers of the new testament; not of the letter, but of the spirit: for the letter killeth, but the spirit giveth life."

Ephesians 4:30 "And grieve not the holy Spirit of God, whereby ye are sealed unto the day of redemption."

1 John 5:6 "This is he that came by water and blood, even Jesus Christ; not by water only, but by water and blood. And it is the Spirit that beareth witness, because the Spirit is truth."

What The Holy Spirit Is

John 14:23-26 "²³Jesus answered and said unto him, If a man love me, he will keep my words: and my Father will love him, and we will come unto him, and make our abode with him. ²⁴He that loveth me not keepeth not my sayings: and the word which ye hear is not mine, but the Father's which sent me. ²⁵These things have I spoken unto you, being yet present with you. ²⁶But the Comforter, which is the Holy Ghost, whom the Father will send in my name, he shall teach you all things, and bring all things to your remembrance, whatsoever I have said unto you."

John 15:26-27 "²⁶But when the Comforter is come, whom I will send unto you from the Father, even the Spirit of truth, which proceedeth from the Father, he shall testify of me: ²⁷And ye also shall bear witness, because ye have been with me from the beginning."

Acts 5:30-32 "³⁰The God of our fathers raised up Jesus, whom ye slew and hanged on a tree. ³¹Him hath God exalted with his right hand to be a Prince and a Saviour, for to give repentance to Israel, and forgiveness of sins. ³²And we are his witnesses of these things; and so is also the Holy Ghost, whom God hath given to them that obey him."

Hebrews 10:15 "Whereof the Holy Ghost also is a witness to us: for after that he had said before,"

1 John 5:6 "This is he that came by water and blood, even Jesus Christ; not by water only, but by water and blood. And it is the Spirit that beareth witness, because the Spirit is truth."

Where The Holy Spirit Dwells

Ezekiel 11:19 "And I will give them one heart, and I will put a new spirit within you; and I will take the stony heart out of their flesh, and will give them an heart of flesh:"

Ezekiel 36:22-27 "²²Therefore say unto the house of Israel, Thus saith the Lord GOD; I do not this for your sakes, O house of Israel, but for mine holy name's sake, which ye have profaned among the heathen, whither ye went. ²³And I will sanctify my great name, which was profaned among the heathen, which ye have profaned in the midst of them; and the heathen shall know that I am the LORD, saith the Lord GOD, when I shall be sanctified in you before their eyes. ²⁴For I will take you from among the heathen, and gather you out of all countries, and will bring you into your own land. ²⁵Then will I sprinkle clean water upon you, and ye shall be clean: from all your filthiness, and from all your idols, will I cleanse you. ²⁶A new heart also will I give you, and a new spirit will I put within you: and I will take away the stony heart out of your flesh, and I will give you an heart of flesh. ²⁷And I will put my spirit within you, and cause you to walk in my statutes, and ye shall keep my judgments, and do them."

Ezekiel 37:12-14 "¹²Therefore prophesy and say unto them, Thus saith the Lord GOD; Behold, O my people, I will open your graves, and cause you to come up out of your graves, and bring you into the land of Israel. ¹³And ye shall know that I am the LORD, when I have opened your graves, O my people, and brought you up out of your graves, ¹⁴And shall put my spirit in you, and ye shall live, and I shall place you in your own land: then shall ye know that I the LORD have spoken it, and performed it, saith the LORD."

John 14:9-18 "⁹Jesus saith unto him, Have I been so long time with you, and yet hast thou not known me, Philip? he that hath seen me hath seen the Father; and how sayest thou then, Shew us the Father? ¹⁰Believest thou not that I am in the Father, and the Father in me? the words that I speak unto you I speak not of myself: but the Father that dwelleth in me, he doeth the works. ¹¹Believe me that I am in the Father, and the Father in me: or else believe me for the very works' sake. ¹²Verily, verily, I say unto you, He that believeth on me, the works that I do shall he do also; and greater works than these shall he do; because I go unto my Father. ¹³And whatsoever ye shall ask in my name, that will I do, that the Father may be glorified in the Son. ¹⁴If ye shall ask any thing in my name, I will do it. ¹⁵If ye love me, keep my commandments. ¹⁶And I will pray the Father, and he shall give you another Comforter, that he may abide with you for ever; ¹⁷Even the Spirit of truth; whom the world cannot receive, because it seeth him not, neither knoweth him: but ye know him; for he dwelleth with you, and shall be in you. [18]I will not leave you comfortless: I will come to you."

1 Corinthians 3:16-17 "[16]Know ye not that ye are the temple of God, and that the Spirit of God dwelleth in you? [17]If any man defile the temple of God, him shall God destroy; for the temple of God is holy, which temple ye are."

1 Corinthians 6:19-20 "[19]What? know ye not that your body is the temple of the Holy Ghost which is in you, which ye have of God, and ye are not your own? [20]For ye are bought with a price: therefore glorify God in your body, and in your spirit, which are God's."

2 Corinthians 6:16 "And what agreement hath the temple of God with idols? for ye are the temple of the living God; as God hath said, I will dwell in them, and walk in them; and I will be their God, and they shall be my people."

1 Peter 1:10-11 "[10]Of which salvation the prophets have inquired and searched diligently, who prophesied of the grace that should come unto you: [11]Searching what, or what manner of time the Spirit of Christ which was in them did signify, when it testified beforehand the sufferings of Christ, and the glory that should follow."

Who Does Not Have The Holy Spirit
Jude 17-19 "[17]But, beloved, remember ye the words which were spoken before of the apostles of our Lord Jesus Christ; [18]How that they told you there should be mockers in the last time, who should walk after their own ungodly lusts. [19]These be they who separate themselves, sensual, having not the Spirit."

Who The Holy Spirit Is Given To
Luke 11:9-13 "[9]And I say unto you, Ask, and it shall be given you; seek, and ye shall find; knock, and it shall be opened unto you. [10]For every one that asketh receiveth; and he that seeketh findeth; and to him that knocketh it shall be opened. [11]If a son shall ask bread of any of you that is a father, will he give him a stone? or if he ask a fish, will he for a fish give him a serpent? [12]Or if he shall ask an egg, will he offer him a scorpion? [13]If ye then, being evil, know how to give good gifts unto your children: how much more shall your heavenly Father give the Holy Spirit to them that ask him?"

John 7:37-39 "[37]In the last day, that great day of the feast, Jesus stood and cried, saying, If any man thirst, let him come unto me, and drink. [38]He that believeth on me, as the scripture hath said, out of his belly shall flow rivers of living water. [39](But this spake he of the Spirit, which they that believe on him should receive: for the Holy Ghost was not yet given; because that Jesus was not yet glorified.)"

Acts 2:38 "Then Peter said unto them, Repent, and be baptized every one of you in the name of Jesus Christ for the remission of sins, and ye shall receive the gift of the Holy Ghost."

Acts 5:30-32 "[30]The God of our fathers raised up Jesus, whom ye slew and hanged on a tree. [31]Him hath God exalted with his right hand to be a Prince and a Saviour, for to give repentance to Israel, and forgiveness of sins. [32]And we are his witnesses of these things; and so is also the Holy Ghost, whom God hath given to them that obey him."

Acts 15:6-8 "[6]And the apostles and elders came together for to consider of this matter. [7]And when there had been much disputing, Peter rose up, and said unto them, Men and brethren, ye know how that a good while ago God made choice among us, that the Gentiles by my mouth should hear the word of the gospel, and believe. [8]And God, which knoweth the hearts, bare them witness, giving them the Holy Ghost, even as he did unto us;"

Why The World Cannot Receive Nor Know The Spirit Of God
John 14:9-19 "[9]Jesus saith unto him, Have I been so long time with you, and yet hast thou not known me, Philip? he that hath seen me hath seen the Father; and how sayest thou then, Shew us the Father? [10]Believest thou not that I am in the Father, and the Father in me? the words that I speak unto you I speak not of myself: but the Father that dwelleth in me, he doeth the works. [11]Believe me that I am in the Father, and the Father in me: or else believe me for the very works' sake. [12]Verily, verily, I say unto you, He that believeth on me, the works that I do shall he do also; and greater works than these shall he do; because I go unto my Father. [13]And whatsoever ye shall ask in my name, that will I do, that the Father may be glorified in the Son. [14]If ye shall ask any thing in my name, I will do it. [15]If ye love me, keep my commandments.

[16]And I will pray the Father, and he shall give you another Comforter, that he may abide with you for ever; [17]Even the Spirit of truth; whom the world cannot receive, because it seeth him not, neither knoweth him: but ye know him; for he dwelleth with you, and shall be in you. [18]I will not leave you comfortless: I will come to you. [19]Yet a little while, and the world seeth me no more; but ye see me: because I live, ye shall live also."

1 Corinthians 2:14-16 "[14]But the natural man receiveth not the things of the Spirit of God: for they are foolishness unto him: neither can he know them, because they are spiritually discerned. [15]But he that is spiritual judgeth all things, yet he himself is judged of no man. [16]For who hath known the mind of the Lord, that he may instruct him? But we have the mind of Christ."

HONESTY

Being Honest
Romans 12:17 "Recompense to no man evil for evil. Provide things honest in the sight of all men."

Romans 13:13 "Let us walk honestly, as in the day; not in rioting and drunkenness, not in chambering and wantonness, not in strife and envying."

HONOR

God The Father And
Jesus Christ Honoring Each Other
John 8:49 "Jesus answered, I have not a devil; but I honour my Father, and ye do dishonour me."

John 8:54-55 "[54]Jesus answered, If I honour myself, my honour is nothing: it is my Father that honoureth me; of whom ye say, that he is your God: [55]Yet ye have not known him; but I know him: and if I should say, I know him not, I shall be a liar like unto you: but I know him, and keep his saying."

Jesus Christ Being Crowned With Honor
Hebrews 2:9 "But we see Jesus, who was made a little lower than the angels for the suffering of death, crowned with glory and honour; that he by the grace of God should taste death for every man."

2 Peter 1:16-18 "[16]For we have not followed cunningly devised fables, when we made known unto you the power and coming of our Lord Jesus Christ, but were eyewitnesses of his majesty. [17]For he received from God the Father honour and glory, when there came such a voice to him from the excellent glory, This is my beloved Son, in whom I am well pleased. [18]And this voice which came from heaven we heard, when we were with him in the holy mount."

Honor Coming From The Lord
1 Chronicles 29:11-12 "[11]Thine, O LORD, is the greatness, and the power, and the glory, and the victory, and the majesty: for all that is in the heaven and in the earth is thine; thine is the kingdom, O LORD, and thou art exalted as head above all. [12]Both riches and honour come of thee, and thou reignest over all; and in thine hand is power and might; and in thine hand it is to make great, and to give strength unto all."

Those That Do Not Honor Jesus Christ
John 5:22-23 "[22]For the Father judgeth no man, but hath committed all judgment unto the Son: [23]That all men should honour the Son, even as they honour the Father. He that honoureth not the Son honoureth not the Father which hath sent him."

Those That Give Honor To A Fool
Proverbs 26:8 "As he that bindeth a stone in a sling, so is he that giveth honour to a fool."

Those That Honor The Lord
1 Samuel 2:30 "Wherefore the LORD God of Israel saith, I said indeed that thy house, and the house of thy father, should walk before me for ever: but now the LORD saith, Be it far from me; for them that honour me I will honour, and they that despise me shall be lightly esteemed."

Proverbs 14:31 "He that oppresseth the poor reproacheth his Maker: but he that honoureth him hath mercy on the poor."

What Brings Honor
Proverbs 22:4 "By humility and the fear of the LORD are riches, and honour, and life."

What Is Before Honor
Proverbs 15:33 "The fear of the LORD is the instruction of wisdom; and before honour is humility."

Proverbs 18:12 "Before destruction the heart of man is haughty, and before honour is humility."

What Is Honorable In All
Hebrews 13:4 "Marriage is honourable in all, and the bed undefiled: but whoremongers and adulterers God will judge."

Where A Prophet Does Not Have Honor
Matthew 13:57 "And they were offended in him. But Jesus said unto them, A prophet is not without honour, save in his own country, and in his own house."

Mark 6:4 "But Jesus said unto them, A prophet is not without honour, but in his own country, and among his own kin, and in his own house."

Luke 4:24 "And he said, Verily I say unto you, No prophet is accepted in his own country."

John 4:44 "For Jesus himself testified, that a prophet hath no honour in his own country."

Where Honor Is
1 Chronicles 16:26-27 "²⁶For all the gods of the people are idols: but the LORD made the heavens. ²⁷Glory and honour are in his presence; strength and gladness are in his place."

Proverbs 8:12-18 "¹²I wisdom dwell with prudence, and find out knowledge of witty inventions. ¹³The fear of the LORD is to hate evil: pride, and arrogancy, and the evil way, and the froward mouth, do I hate. ¹⁴Counsel is mine, and sound wisdom: I am understanding; I have strength. ¹⁵By me kings reign, and princes decree justice. ¹⁶By me princes rule, and nobles, even all the judges of the earth. ¹⁷I love them that love me; and those that seek me early shall find me. ¹⁸Riches and honour are with me; yea, durable riches and righteousness."

Who Does Not Honor God The Father
John 5:22-23 "²²For the Father judgeth no man, but hath committed all judgment unto the Son: ²³That all men should honour the Son, even as they honour the Father. He that honoureth not the Son honoureth not the Father which hath sent him."

Who Has Honor
Psalm 8:1-5 "¹O LORD our Lord, how excellent is thy name in all the earth! who hast set thy glory above the heavens. ²Out of the mouth of babes and sucklings hast thou ordained strength because of thine enemies, that thou mightest still the enemy and the avenger. ³When I consider thy heavens, the work of thy fingers, the moon and the stars, which thou hast ordained; ⁴What is man, that thou art mindful of him? and the son of man, that thou visitest him? ⁵For thou hast made him a little lower than the angels, and hast crowned him with glory and honour."

Psalm 112:6-9 "⁶Surely he shall not be moved for ever: the righteous shall be in everlasting remembrance. ⁷He shall not be afraid of evil tidings: his heart is fixed, trusting in the LORD. ⁸His heart is established, he shall not be afraid, until he see his desire upon his enemies. ⁹He hath dispersed, he hath given to the poor; his righteousness endureth for ever; his horn shall be exalted with honour."

Proverbs 13:18 "Poverty and shame shall be to him that refuseth instruction: but he that regardeth reproof shall be honoured."

Proverbs 21:21 "He that followeth after righteousness and mercy findeth life, righteousness, and honour."

Proverbs 27:18 "Whoso keepeth the fig tree shall eat the fruit thereof: so he that waiteth on his master shall be honoured."

Romans 2:10 "But glory, honour, and peace, to every man that worketh good, to the Jew first, and also to the Gentile:"

1 Corinthians 4:8-10 "⁸Now ye are full, now ye are rich, ye have reigned as kings without us: and I would to God ye did reign, that we also might reign with you. ⁹For I think that God hath set forth us the apostles last, as it were appointed to death: for we are made a spectacle unto the world, and to angels, and to men. ¹⁰We are fools for Christ's sake, but ye are wise in Christ; we are weak, but ye are strong; ye are honourable, but we are despised."

Who Honor Is Not Seemly For
Proverbs 26:1 "As snow in summer, and as rain in harvest, so honour is not seemly for a fool."

Who Honor Upholds
Proverbs 29:23 "A man's pride shall bring him low: but honour shall uphold the humble in spirit."

Who Honors The Lord With Their Lips, But Not With Their Heart

Isaiah 29:13 "Wherefore the Lord said, Forasmuch as this people draw near me with their mouth, and with their lips do honour me, but have removed their heart far from me, and their fear toward me is taught by the precept of men:"

Mark 7:6-13 "⁶He answered and said unto them, Well hath Esaias prophesied of you hypocrites, as it is written, This people honoureth me with their lips, but their heart is far from me. ⁷Howbeit in vain do they worship me, teaching for doctrines the commandments of men. ⁸For laying aside the commandment of God, ye hold the tradition of men, as the washing of pots and cups: and many other such like things ye do. ⁹And he said unto them, Full well ye reject the commandment of God, that ye may keep your own tradition. ¹⁰For Moses said, Honour thy father and thy mother; and, Whoso curseth father or mother, let him die the death: ¹¹But ye say, If a man shall say to his father or mother, It is Corban, that is to say, a gift, by whatsoever thou mightest be profited by me; he shall be free. ¹²And ye suffer him no more to do ought for his father or his mother; ¹³Making the word of God of none effect through your tradition, which ye have delivered: and many such like things do ye."

Who Retains Honor

Proverbs 11:16 "A gracious woman retaineth honour: and strong men retain riches."

Who The Lord Honors

1 Samuel 2:30 "Wherefore the Lord God of Israel saith, I said indeed that thy house, and the house of thy father, should walk before me for ever: but now the Lord saith, Be it far from me; for them that honour me I will honour, and they that despise me shall be lightly esteemed."

Psalm 91:9-15 "⁹Because thou hast made the Lord, which is my refuge, even the most High, thy habitation; ¹⁰There shall no evil befall thee, neither shall any plague come nigh thy dwelling. ¹¹For he shall give his angels charge over thee, to keep thee in all thy ways. ¹²They shall bear thee up in their hands, lest thou dash thy foot against a stone. ¹³Thou shalt tread upon the lion and adder: the young lion and the dragon shalt thou trample under feet. ¹⁴Because he hath set his love upon me, therefore will I deliver him: I will set him on high, because he hath known my name. ¹⁵He shall call upon me, and I will answer him: I will be with him in trouble; I will deliver him, and honour him."

John 12:23-26 "²³And Jesus answered them, saying, The hour is come, that the Son of man should be glorified. ²⁴Verily, verily, I say unto you, Except a corn of wheat fall into the ground and die, it abideth alone: but if it die, it bringeth forth much fruit. ²⁵He that loveth his life shall lose it; and he that hateth his life in this world shall keep it unto life eternal. ²⁶If any man serve me, let him follow me; and where I am, there shall also my servant be: if any man serve me, him will my Father honour."

Who To Honor

Exodus 20:12 "Honour thy father and thy mother: that thy days may be long upon the land which the Lord thy God giveth thee."

Deuteronomy 5:16 "Honour thy father and thy mother, as the Lord thy God hath commanded thee; that thy days may be prolonged, and that it may go well with thee, in the land which the Lord thy God giveth thee."

Matthew 19:19 "Honour thy father and thy mother: and, Thou shalt love thy neighbour as thyself."

Mark 7:10 "For Moses said, Honour thy father and thy mother; and, Whoso curseth father or mother, let him die the death:"

Romans 12:10 "Be kindly affectioned one to another with brotherly love; in honour preferring one another;"

Ephesians 6:2-3 "²Honour thy father and mother; (which is the first commandment with promise;) ³That it may be well with thee, and thou mayest live long on the earth."

1 Peter 2:17 "Honour all men. Love the brotherhood. Fear God. Honour the king."

1 Peter 3:7 "Likewise, ye husbands, dwell with them according to knowledge, giving honour unto the wife, as unto the weaker vessel, and as being heirs together of the grace of life; that your prayers be not hindered."

HOPE

Hope Deferred
Proverbs 13:12 "Hope deferred maketh the heart sick: but when the desire cometh, it is a tree of life."

Hope That Is Seen
Romans 8:24-25 "24For we are saved by hope: but hope that is seen is not hope: for what a man seeth, why doth he yet hope for? 25But if we hope for that we see not, then do we with patience wait for it."

Hoping In The Lord
Psalm 42:11 "Why art thou cast down, O my soul? and why art thou disquieted within me? hope thou in God: for I shall yet praise him, who is the health of my countenance, and my God."

Psalm 43:5 "Why art thou cast down, O my soul? and why art thou disquieted within me? hope in God: for I shall yet praise him, who is the health of my countenance, and my God."

Lamentations 3:24 "The LORD is my portion, saith my soul; therefore will I hope in him."

The Hope Of The Hypocrite
Job 8:11-13 "11Can the rush grow up without mire? can the flag grow without water? 12Whilst it is yet in his greenness, and not cut down, it withereth before any other herb. 13So are the paths of all that forget God; and the hypocrite's hope shall perish:"

Job 27:8-10 "8For what is the hope of the hypocrite, though he hath gained, when God taketh away his soul? 9Will God hear his cry when trouble cometh upon him? 10Will he delight himself in the Almighty? will he always call upon God?"

The Hope Of The Righteous
Proverbs 10:28 "The hope of the righteous shall be gladness: but the expectation of the wicked shall perish."

The Hope Of The Unjust
Proverbs 11:7 "When a wicked man dieth, his expectation shall perish: and the hope of unjust men perisheth."

The Lord Being Hope
Psalm 71:4-5 "4Deliver me, O my God, out of the hand of the wicked, out of the hand of the unrighteous and cruel man. 5For thou art my hope, O Lord GOD: thou art my trust from my youth."

Romans 15:13 "Now the God of hope fill you with all joy and peace in believing, that ye may abound in hope, through the power of the Holy Ghost."

1 Timothy 1:1 "Paul, an apostle of Jesus Christ by the commandment of God our Saviour, and Lord Jesus Christ, which is our hope;"

The Substance Of Things Hoped For
Hebrews 11:1-3 "1Now faith is the substance of things hoped for, the evidence of things not seen. 2For by it the elders obtained a good report. 3Through faith we understand that the worlds were framed by the word of God, so that things which are seen were not made of things which do appear."

Those That Hope In The Lord
Psalm 31:24 "Be of good courage, and he shall strengthen your heart, all ye that hope in the LORD."

Psalm 33:18 "Behold, the eye of the LORD is upon them that fear him, upon them that hope in his mercy;"

Psalm 146:5 "Happy is he that hath the God of Jacob for his help, whose hope is in the LORD his God:"

Psalm 147:11 "The LORD taketh pleasure in them that fear him, in those that hope in his mercy."

Jeremiah 17:7-8 "7Blessed is the man that trusteth in the LORD, and whose hope the LORD is. 8For he shall be as a tree planted by the waters, and that spreadeth out her roots by the river, and shall not see when heat cometh, but her leaf shall be green; and shall not be careful in the year of drought, neither shall cease from yielding fruit."

What Gives Hope
Romans 15:1-4 "1We then that are strong ought to bear the infirmities of the weak, and not to please ourselves. 2Let every one of us please his neighbour for his good to edification. 3For even Christ pleased not himself; but, as it is written, The reproaches of them that reproached thee fell on me. 4For whatsoever things were written aforetime were written

for our learning, that we through patience and comfort of the scriptures might have hope."

What Is Not Hope
Romans 8:24-25 "[24]For we are saved by hope: but hope that is seen is not hope: for what a man seeth, why doth he yet hope for? [25]But if we hope for that we see not, then do we with patience wait for it."

What To Hope In
Psalm 130:5 "I wait for the LORD, my soul doth wait, and in his word do I hope."

What Works Hope
Romans 5:3-5 "[3]And not only so, but we glory in tribulations also: knowing that tribulation worketh patience; [4]And patience, experience; and experience, hope: [5]And hope maketh not ashamed; because the love of God is shed abroad in our hearts by the Holy Ghost which is given unto us."

Who Cannot Hope For The Truth Of The Lord
Isaiah 38:16-18 "[16]O Lord, by these things men live, and in all these things is the life of my spirit: so wilt thou recover me, and make me to live. [17]Behold, for peace I had great bitterness: but thou hast in love to my soul delivered it from the pit of corruption: for thou hast cast all my sins behind thy back. [18]For the grave cannot praise thee, death can not celebrate thee: they that go down into the pit cannot hope for thy truth."

Who Has Hope
Ecclesiastes 9:4 "For to him that is joined to all the living there is hope: for a living dog is better than a dead lion."

HUMBLENESS

Being Of A Humble Spirit
Proverbs 16:19 "Better it is to be of an humble spirit with the lowly, than to divide the spoil with the proud."

Humbling Yourself Before The Lord
James 4:10 "Humble yourselves in the sight of the Lord, and he shall lift you up."

1 Peter 5:6 "Humble yourselves therefore under the mighty hand of God, that he may exalt you in due time:"

Jesus Christ Humbling Himself
Philippians 2:5-8 "[5]Let this mind be in you, which was also in Christ Jesus: [6]Who, being in the form of God, thought it not robbery to be equal with God: [7]But made himself of no reputation, and took upon him the form of a servant, and was made in the likeness of men: [8]And being found in fashion as a man, he humbled himself, and became obedient unto death, even the death of the cross."

The Reward For Humbling Yourself
Leviticus 26:40-45 "[40]If they shall confess their iniquity, and the iniquity of their fathers, with their trespass which they trespassed against me, and that also they have walked contrary unto me; [41]And that I also have walked contrary unto them, and have brought them into the land of their enemies; if then their uncircumcised hearts be humbled, and they then accept of the punishment of their iniquity: [42]Then will I remember my covenant with Jacob, and also my covenant with Isaac, and also my covenant with Abraham will I remember; and I will remember the land. [43]The land also shall be left of them, and shall enjoy her sabbaths, while she lieth desolate without them: and they shall accept of the punishment of their iniquity: because, even because they despised my judgments, and because their soul abhorred my statutes. [44]And yet for all that, when they be in the land of their enemies, I will not cast them away, neither will I abhor them, to destroy them utterly, and to break my covenant with them: for I am the LORD their God. [45]But I will for their sakes remember the covenant of their ancestors, whom I brought forth out of the land of Egypt in the sight of the heathen, that I might be their God: I am the LORD."

2 Chronicles 7:12-14 "[12]And the LORD appeared to Solomon by night, and said unto him, I have heard thy prayer, and have chosen this place to myself for an house of sacrifice. [13]If I shut up heaven that there be no rain, or if I command the locusts to devour the land, or if I send pestilence among my people; [14]If my people, which are called by my name, shall humble themselves, and pray, and seek my face, and turn from their wicked ways; then will I hear from heaven, and will forgive their sin, and will heal their land."

James 4:10 "Humble yourselves in the sight of the Lord, and he shall lift you up."

1 Peter 5:6 "Humble yourselves therefore under the mighty hand of God, that he may exalt you in due time:"

The Humble
Proverbs 29:23 "A man's pride shall bring him low: but honour shall uphold the humble in spirit."

Isaiah 57:15 "For thus saith the high and lofty One that inhabiteth eternity, whose name is Holy; I dwell in the high and holy place, with him also that is of a contrite and humble spirit, to revive the spirit of the humble, and to revive the heart of the contrite ones."

Matthew 18:1-4 "¹At the same time came the disciples unto Jesus, saying, Who is the greatest in the kingdom of heaven? ²And Jesus called a little child unto him, and set him in the midst of them, ³And said, Verily I say unto you, Except ye be converted, and become as little children, ye shall not enter into the kingdom of heaven. ⁴Whosoever therefore shall humble himself as this little child, the same is greatest in the kingdom of heaven."

Matthew 23:12 "And whosoever shall exalt himself shall be abased; and he that shall humble himself shall be exalted."

Luke 14:11 "For whosoever exalteth himself shall be abased; and he that humbleth himself shall be exalted."

Luke 18:9-14 "⁹And he spake this parable unto certain which trusted in themselves that they were righteous, and despised others: ¹⁰Two men went up into the temple to pray; the one a Pharisee, and the other a publican. ¹¹The Pharisee stood and prayed thus with himself, God, I thank thee, that I am not as other men are, extortioners, unjust, adulterers, or even as this publican. ¹²I fast twice in the week, I give tithes of all that I possess. ¹³And the publican, standing afar off, would not lift up so much as his eyes unto heaven, but smote upon his breast, saying, God be merciful to me a sinner. ¹⁴I tell you, this man went down to his house justified rather than the other: for every one that exalteth himself shall be abased; and he that humbleth himself shall be exalted."

James 4:6 "But he giveth more grace. Wherefore he saith, God resisteth the proud, but giveth grace unto the humble."

1 Peter 5:5-6 "⁵Likewise, ye younger, submit yourselves unto the elder. Yea, all of you be subject one to another, and be clothed with humility: for God resisteth the proud, and giveth grace to the humble. ⁶Humble yourselves therefore under the mighty hand of God, that he may exalt you in due time:"

What Shall Be Humbled
Isaiah 2:11-12 "¹¹The lofty looks of man shall be humbled, and the haughtiness of men shall be bowed down, and the LORD alone shall be exalted in that day. ¹²For the day of the LORD of hosts shall be upon every one that is proud and lofty, and upon every one that is lifted up; and he shall be brought low:"

Isaiah 2:17 "And the loftiness of man shall be bowed down, and the haughtiness of men shall be made low: and the LORD alone shall be exalted in that day."

Isaiah 13:9-11 "⁹Behold, the day of the LORD cometh, cruel both with wrath and fierce anger, to lay the land desolate: and he shall destroy the sinners thereof out of it. ¹⁰For the stars of heaven and the constellations thereof shall not give their light: the sun shall be darkened in his going forth, and the moon shall not cause her light to shine. ¹¹And I will punish the world for their evil, and the wicked for their iniquity; and I will cause the arrogancy of the proud to cease, and will lay low the haughtiness of the terrible."

HUMILITY

What Humility Precedes
Proverbs 15:33 "The fear of the LORD is the instruction of wisdom; and before honour is humility."

Proverbs 18:12 "Before destruction the heart of man is haughty, and before honour is humility."

What Humility Brings
Proverbs 22:4 "By humility and the fear of the LORD are riches, and honour, and life."

HUNGER

Hungry Souls
Psalm 107:8-9 "⁸Oh that men would praise the LORD for his goodness, and for his wonderful

works to the children of men! [9]For he satisfieth the longing soul, and filleth the hungry soul with goodness."

Proverbs 27:7 "The full soul loatheth an honeycomb; but to the hungry soul every bitter thing is sweet."

Those That Hunger After Righteousness
Matthew 5:6 "Blessed are they which do hunger and thirst after righteousness: for they shall be filled."

Luke 6:21 "Blessed are ye that hunger now: for ye shall be filled. Blessed are ye that weep now: for ye shall laugh."

Who Shall Hunger
Deuteronomy 32:17-24 "[17]They sacrificed unto devils, not to God; to gods whom they knew not, to new gods that came newly up, whom your fathers feared not. [18]Of the Rock that begat thee thou art unmindful, and hast forgotten God that formed thee. [19]And when the LORD saw it, he abhorred them, because of the provoking of his sons, and of his daughters. [20]And he said, I will hide my face from them, I will see what their end shall be: for they are a very froward generation, children in whom is no faith. [21]They have moved me to jealousy with that which is not God; they have provoked me to anger with their vanities: and I will move them to jealousy with those which are not a people; I will provoke them to anger with a foolish nation. [22]For a fire is kindled in mine anger, and shall burn unto the lowest hell, and shall consume the earth with her increase, and set on fire the foundations of the mountains. [23]I will heap mischiefs upon them; I will spend mine arrows upon them. [24]They shall be burnt with hunger, and devoured with burning heat, and with bitter destruction: I will also send the teeth of beasts upon them, with the poison of serpents of the dust."

Proverbs 19:15 "Slothfulness casteth into a deep sleep; and an idle soul shall suffer hunger."

Isaiah 65:11-13 "[11]But ye are they that forsake the LORD, that forget my holy mountain, that prepare a table for that troop, and that furnish the drink offering unto that number. [12]Therefore will I number you to the sword, and ye shall all bow down to the slaughter: because when I called, ye did not answer; when I spake, ye did not hear; but did evil before mine eyes, and did choose that wherein I delighted not. [13]Therefore thus saith the Lord GOD, Behold, my servants shall eat, but ye shall be hungry: behold, my servants shall drink, but ye shall be thirsty: behold, my servants shall rejoice, but ye shall be ashamed:"

Luke 6:24-25 "[24]But woe unto you that are rich! for ye have received your consolation. [25]Woe unto you that are full! for ye shall hunger. Woe unto you that laugh now! for ye shall mourn and weep."

Who Shall Not Hunger
Deuteronomy 11:13-15 "[13]And it shall come to pass, if ye shall hearken diligently unto my commandments which I command you this day, to love the LORD your God, and to serve him with all your heart and with all your soul, [14]That I will give you the rain of your land in his due season, the first rain and the latter rain, that thou mayest gather in thy corn, and thy wine, and thine oil. [15]And I will send grass in thy fields for thy cattle, that thou mayest eat and be full."

Psalm 34:10 "The young lions do lack, and suffer hunger: but they that seek the LORD shall not want any good thing."

Proverbs 10:3 "The LORD will not suffer the soul of the righteous to famish: but he casteth away the substance of the wicked."

Isaiah 65:13 "Therefore thus saith the Lord GOD, Behold, my servants shall eat, but ye shall be hungry: behold, my servants shall drink, but ye shall be thirsty: behold, my servants shall rejoice, but ye shall be ashamed:"

Matthew 5:6 "Blessed are they which do hunger and thirst after righteousness: for they shall be filled."

Luke 6:21 "Blessed are ye that hunger now: for ye shall be filled. Blessed are ye that weep now: for ye shall laugh."

John 6:35 "And Jesus said unto them, I am the bread of life: he that cometh to me shall never hunger; and he that believeth on me shall never thirst."

Revelation 7:9-17 "[9]After this I beheld, and, lo, a great multitude, which no man could number, of all nations, and kindreds, and people, and tongues, stood before the throne, and before the Lamb, clothed with white robes, and palms in their hands; 10And cried with a loud voice, saying, Salvation to our God which sitteth upon the throne, and unto the Lamb. 11And all the angels stood round about the throne, and about the elders and the four beasts, and fell before the throne on their faces, and worshipped God, 12Saying, Amen: Blessing, and glory, and wisdom, and thanksgiving, and honour, and power, and might, be unto our God for ever and ever. Amen. 13And one of the elders answered, saying unto me, What are these which are arrayed in white robes? and whence came they? 14And I said unto him, Sir, thou knowest. And he said to me, These are they which came out of great tribulation, and have washed their robes, and made them white in the blood of the Lamb. 15Therefore are they before the throne of God, and serve him day and night in his temple: and he that sitteth on the throne shall dwell among them. 16They shall hunger no more, neither thirst any more; neither shall the sun light on them, nor any heat. 17For the Lamb which is in the midst of the throne shall feed them, and shall lead them unto living fountains of waters: and God shall wipe away all tears from their eyes."

HYPOCRISY

Abstaining From Hypocrisy
1 Peter 2:1 "Wherefore laying aside all malice, and all guile, and hypocrisies, and envies, and all evil speakings,"

Hypocrites
Job 8:11-18 "11Can the rush grow up without mire? can the flag grow without water? 12Whilst it is yet in his greenness, and not cut down, it withereth before any other herb. 13So are the paths of all that forget God; and the hypocrite's hope shall perish: 14Whose hope shall be cut off, and whose trust shall be a spider's web. 15He shall lean upon his house, but it shall not stand: he shall hold it fast, but it shall not endure. 16He is green before the sun, and his branch shooteth forth in his garden. 17His roots are wrapped about the heap, and seeth the place of stones. 18If he destroy him from his place, then it shall deny him, saying, I have not seen thee."

Job 13:16 "He also shall be my salvation: for an hypocrite shall not come before him."

Job 15:34-35 "34For the congregation of hypocrites shall be desolate, and fire shall consume the tabernacles of bribery. 35They conceive mischief, and bring forth vanity, and their belly prepareth deceit."

Job 20:1-5 "1Then answered Zophar the Naamathite, and said, 2Therefore do my thoughts cause me to answer, and for this I make haste. 3I have heard the check of my reproach, and the spirit of my understanding causeth me to answer. 4Knowest thou not this of old, since man was placed upon earth, 5That the triumphing of the wicked is short, and the joy of the hypocrite but for a moment?"

Job 27:8-10 "8For what is the hope of the hypocrite, though he hath gained, when God taketh away his soul? 9Will God hear his cry when trouble cometh upon him? 10Will he delight himself in the Almighty? will he always call upon God?"

Job 36:13-14 "13But the hypocrites in heart heap up wrath: they cry not when he bindeth them. 14They die in youth, and their life is among the unclean."

Proverbs 11:9 "An hypocrite with his mouth destroyeth his neighbour: but through knowledge shall the just be delivered."

Isaiah 29:13 "Wherefore the Lord said, Forasmuch as this people draw near me with their mouth, and with their lips do honour me, but have removed their heart far from me, and their fear toward me is taught by the precept of men:"

Isaiah 33:14 "The sinners in Zion are afraid; fearfulness hath surprised the hypocrites. Who among us shall dwell with the devouring fire? who among us shall dwell with everlasting burnings?"

Matthew 6:16 "Moreover when ye fast, be not, as the hypocrites, of a sad countenance: for they disfigure their faces, that they may appear unto men to fast. Verily I say unto you, They have their reward."

Matthew 23:2-7 "2Saying, The scribes and the Pharisees sit in Moses' seat: 3All therefore whatsoever they bid you observe, that observe and do; but do not ye after their works: for they say, and do not. [4]For they bind heavy burdens and grievous to be borne, and lay them on men's shoulders; but they themselves will not move them with one of their fingers. [5]But all their works they do for to be seen of men: they make broad their phylacteries, and enlarge the borders of their garments, [6]And love the uppermost rooms at feasts, and the chief seats in the synagogues, [7]And greetings in the markets, and to be called of men, Rabbi, Rabbi."

Matthew 23:13-36 "[13]But woe unto you, scribes and Pharisees, hypocrites! for ye shut up the kingdom of heaven against men: for ye neither go in yourselves, neither suffer ye them that are entering to go in. [14]Woe unto you, scribes and Pharisees, hypocrites! for ye devour widows' houses, and for a pretence make long prayer: therefore ye shall receive the greater damnation. [15]Woe unto you, scribes and Pharisees, hypocrites! for ye compass sea and land to make one proselyte, and when he is made, ye make him twofold more the child of hell than yourselves. [16]Woe unto you, ye blind guides, which say, Whosoever shall swear by the temple, it is nothing; but whosoever shall swear by the gold of the temple, he is a debtor! [17]Ye fools and blind: for whether is greater, the gold, or the temple that sanctifieth the gold? [18]And, Whosoever shall swear by the altar, it is nothing; but whosoever sweareth by the gift that is upon it, he is guilty. [19]Ye fools and blind: for whether is greater, the gift, or the altar that sanctifieth the gift? [20]Whoso therefore shall swear by the altar, sweareth by it, and by all things thereon. [21]And whoso shall swear by the temple, sweareth by it, and by him that dwelleth therein. [22]And he that shall swear by heaven, sweareth by the throne of God, and by him that sitteth thereon. [23]Woe unto you, scribes and Pharisees, hypocrites! for ye pay tithe of mint and anise and cummin, and have omitted the weightier matters of the law, judgment, mercy, and faith: these ought ye to have done, and not to leave the other undone. [24]Ye blind guides, which strain at a gnat, and swallow a camel. [25]Woe unto you, scribes and Pharisees, hypocrites! for ye make clean the outside of the cup and of the platter, but within they are full of extortion and excess. [26]Thou blind Pharisee, cleanse first that which is within the cup and platter, that the outside of them may be clean also. [27]Woe unto you, scribes and Pharisees, hypocrites! for ye are like unto whited sepulchres, which indeed appear beautiful outward, but are within full of dead men's bones, and of all uncleanness. [28]Even so ye also outwardly appear righteous unto men, but within ye are full of hypocrisy and iniquity. [29]Woe unto you, scribes and Pharisees, hypocrites! because ye build the tombs of the prophets, and garnish the sepulchres of the righteous, [30]And say, If we had been in the days of our fathers, we would not have been partakers with them in the blood of the prophets. [31]Wherefore ye be witnesses unto yourselves, that ye are the children of them which killed the prophets. [32]Fill ye up then the measure of your fathers. [33]Ye serpents, ye generation of vipers, how can ye escape the damnation of hell? [34]Wherefore, behold, I send unto you prophets, and wise men, and scribes: and some of them ye shall kill and crucify; and some of them shall ye scourge in your synagogues, and persecute them from city to city: [35]That upon you may come all the righteous blood shed upon the earth, from the blood of righteous Abel unto the blood of Zacharias son of Barachias, whom ye slew between the temple and the altar. [36]Verily I say unto you, All these things shall come upon this generation."

Mark 7:6-13 "[6]He answered and said unto them, Well hath Esaias prophesied of you hypocrites, as it is written, This people honoureth me with their lips, but their heart is far from me. [7]Howbeit in vain do they worship me, teaching for doctrines the commandments of men. [8]For laying aside the commandment of God, ye hold the tradition of men, as the washing of pots and cups: and many other such like things ye do. [9]And he said unto them, Full well ye reject the commandment of God, that ye may keep your own tradition. [10]For Moses said, Honour thy father and thy mother; and, Whoso curseth father or mother, let him die the death: [11]But ye say, If a man shall say to his father or mother, It is Corban, that is to say, a gift, by whatsoever thou mightest be profited by me; he shall be free. [12]And ye suffer him no more to do ought for his father or his mother; [13]Making the word of God of none effect through your tradition, which ye have delivered: and many such like things do ye."

Luke 11:39-52 "[39]And the Lord said unto him, Now do ye Pharisees make clean the outside of the cup and the platter; but your inward part is full of ravening and wickedness. [40]Ye fools, did not he that made that which is without make that which is within also? [41]But rather give alms of such things as ye have; and, behold, all things are clean unto you. [42]But woe unto you, Pharisees! for ye tithe mint and rue and all manner of herbs, and pass over judgment and the love of God: these ought ye to have done, and not to leave the other undone. [43]Woe unto you, Pharisees! for ye love the uppermost seats in the synagogues, and greetings in the markets. [44]Woe unto you, scribes and Pharisees, hypocrites! for ye are as graves which appear not, and the men that walk over them are not aware of them. [45]Then answered one of the lawyers, and said unto him, Master, thus saying thou reproachest us also. [46]And he said, Woe unto you also, ye lawyers! for ye lade men with burdens grievous to be borne, and ye yourselves touch not the burdens with one of your fingers. [47]Woe unto you! for ye build the sepulchres of the prophets, and your fathers killed them. [48]Truly ye bear witness that ye allow the deeds of your fathers: for they indeed killed them, and ye build their sepulchres. [49]Therefore also said the wisdom of God, I will send them prophets and apostles, and some of them they shall slay and persecute: [50]That the blood of all the prophets, which was shed from the foundation of the world, may be required of this generation; [51]From the blood of Abel unto the blood of Zacharias, which perished between the altar and the temple: verily I say unto you, It shall be required of this generation. [52]Woe unto you, lawyers! for ye have taken away the key of knowledge: ye entered not in yourselves, and them that were entering in ye hindered.”

Luke 18:9-14 “[9]And he spake this parable unto certain which trusted in themselves that they were righteous, and despised others: [10]Two men went up into the temple to pray; the one a Pharisee, and the other a publican. [11]The Pharisee stood and prayed thus with himself, God, I thank thee, that I am not as other men are, extortioners, unjust, adulterers, or even as this publican. [12]I fast twice in the week, I give tithes of all that I possess. [13]And the publican, standing afar off, would not lift up so much as his eyes unto heaven, but smote upon his breast, saying, God be merciful to me a sinner. [14]I tell you, this man went down to his house justified rather than the other: for every one that exalteth himself shall be abased; and he that humbleth himself shall be exalted.”

Luke 20:46-47 “[46]Beware of the scribes, which desire to walk in long robes, and love greetings in the markets, and the highest seats in the synagogues, and the chief rooms at feasts; [47]Which devour widows’ houses, and for a shew make long prayers: the same shall receive greater damnation.”

Romans 2:1-3 “[1]Therefore thou art inexcusable, O man, whosoever thou art that judgest: for wherein thou judgest another, thou condemnest thyself; for thou that judgest doest the same things. [2]But we are sure that the judgment of God is according to truth against them which commit such things. [3]And thinkest thou this, O man, that judgest them which do such things, and doest the same, that thou shalt escape the judgment of God?”

What Is Hypocrisy
Luke 12:1 “In the mean time, when there were gathered together an innumerable multitude of people, insomuch that they trode one upon another, he began to say unto his disciples first of all, Beware ye of the leaven of the Pharisees, which is hypocrisy.”

What Lacks Hypocrisy
James 3:17 “But the wisdom that is from above is first pure, then peaceable, gentle, and easy to be intreated, full of mercy and good fruits, without partiality, and without hypocrisy.”

I*i*

IDOLATRY

Idolaters

Exodus 22:20 "He that sacrificeth unto any god, save unto the LORD only, he shall be utterly destroyed."

Leviticus 20:1-5 "¹And the LORD spake unto Moses, saying, ²Again, thou shalt say to the children of Israel, Whosoever he be of the children of Israel, or of the strangers that sojourn in Israel, that giveth any of his seed unto Molech; he shall surely be put to death: the people of the land shall stone him with stones. ³And I will set my face against that man, and will cut him off from among his people; because he hath given of his seed unto Molech, to defile my sanctuary, and to profane my holy name. ⁴And if the people of the land do any ways hide their eyes from the man, when he giveth of his seed unto Molech, and kill him not: ⁵Then I will set my face against that man, and against his family, and will cut him off, and all that go a whoring after him, to commit whoredom with Molech, from among their people."

Deuteronomy 27:15 "Cursed be the man that maketh any graven or molten image, an abomination unto the LORD, the work of the hands of the craftsman, and putteth it in a secret place. And all the people shall answer and say, Amen."

Psalm 73:26-27 "²⁶My flesh and my heart faileth: but God is the strength of my heart, and my portion for ever. ²⁷For, lo, they that are far from thee shall perish: thou hast destroyed all them that go a whoring from thee."

Psalm 97:7 "Confounded be all they that serve graven images, that boast themselves of idols: worship him, all ye gods."

Psalm 115:4-8 "⁴Their idols are silver and gold, the work of men's hands. ⁵They have mouths, but they speak not: eyes have they, but they see not: ⁶They have ears, but they hear not: noses have they, but they smell not: ⁷They have hands, but they handle not: feet have they, but they walk not: neither speak they through their throat. ⁸They that make them are like unto them; so is every one that trusteth in them."

Psalm 135:15-18 "¹⁵The idols of the heathen are silver and gold, the work of men's hands. ¹⁶They have mouths, but they speak not; eyes have they, but they see not; ¹⁷They have ears, but they hear not; neither is there any breath in their mouths. ¹⁸They that make them are like unto them: so is every one that trusteth in them."

Isaiah 42:17 "They shall be turned back, they shall be greatly ashamed, that trust in graven images, that say to the molten images, Ye are our gods."

Isaiah 44:9-19 "⁹They that make a graven image are all of them vanity; and their delectable things shall not profit; and they are their own witnesses; they see not, nor know; that they may be ashamed. ¹⁰Who hath formed a god, or molten a graven image that is profitable for nothing? ¹¹Behold, all his fellows shall be ashamed: and the workmen, they are of men: let them all be gathered together, let them stand up; yet they shall fear, and they shall be ashamed together. ¹²The smith with the tongs both worketh in the coals, and fashioneth it with hammers, and worketh it with the strength of his arms: yea, he is hungry, and his strength faileth: he drinketh no water, and is faint. ¹³The carpenter stretcheth out his rule; he marketh it out with a line; he fitteth it with planes, and he marketh it out with the compass, and maketh it after the figure of a man, according to the beauty of a man; that it may remain in the house. ¹⁴He heweth him down cedars, and taketh the cypress and the oak, which he strengtheneth for himself among the trees of the forest: he planteth an ash, and the rain doth nourish it. ¹⁵Then shall it be for a man to burn: for he will take thereof, and warm himself; yea, he kindleth it, and baketh bread; yea, he maketh a god, and worshippeth it; he maketh it a graven image, and falleth down thereto. ¹⁶He burneth part thereof in the fire; with part thereof he eateth flesh; he roasteth roast, and is satisfied: yea, he warmeth himself, and saith, Aha, I am warm, I have seen the fire: ¹⁷And the residue thereof he maketh a god, even his graven image: he falleth down unto it, and worshippeth it, and prayeth unto it, and saith, Deliver me; for thou art my god. ¹⁸They have not known nor understood: for he hath shut their eyes, that they cannot see; and their hearts, that they cannot understand. [19]And none considereth in his heart, neither is there knowledge nor understanding to say, I have burned part of it in the fire; yea, also I have baked bread upon the coals thereof; I have roasted flesh, and eaten it: and shall I make the residue thereof an abomination? shall I fall down to the stock of a tree?"

Isaiah 45:20 "Assemble yourselves and come; draw near together, ye that are escaped of the nations: they have no knowledge that set up the wood of their graven image, and pray unto a god that cannot save."

Isaiah 57:3-13 "[3]But draw near hither, ye sons of the sorceress, the seed of the adulterer and the whore. [4]Against whom do ye sport yourselves? against whom make ye a wide mouth, and draw out the tongue? are ye not children of transgression, a seed of falsehood, [5]Enflaming yourselves with idols under every green tree, slaying the children in the valleys under the clifts of the rocks? [6]Among the smooth stones of the stream is thy portion; they, they are thy lot: even to them hast thou poured a drink offering, thou hast offered a meat offering. Should I receive comfort in these? [7]Upon a lofty and high mountain hast thou set thy bed: even thither wentest thou up to offer sacrifice. [8]Behind the doors also and the posts hast thou set up thy remembrance: for thou hast discovered thyself to another than me, and art gone up; thou hast enlarged thy bed, and made thee a covenant with them; thou lovedst their bed where thou sawest it. [9]And thou wentest to the king with ointment, and didst increase thy perfumes, and didst send thy messengers far off, and didst debase thyself even unto hell. [10]Thou art wearied in the greatness of thy way; yet saidst thou not, There is no hope: thou hast found the life of thine hand; therefore thou wast not grieved. [11]And of whom hast thou been afraid or feared, that thou hast lied, and hast not remembered me, nor laid it to thy heart? have not I held my peace even of old, and thou fearest me not? [12]I will declare thy righteousness, and thy works; for they shall not profit thee. [13]When thou criest, let thy companies deliver thee; but the wind shall carry them all away; vanity shall take them: but he that putteth his trust in me shall possess the land, and shall inherit my holy mountain;"

Jeremiah 13:9-10 "[9]Thus saith the LORD, After this manner will I mar the pride of Judah, and the great pride of Jerusalem. [10]This evil people, which refuse to hear my words, which walk in the imagination of their heart, and walk after other gods, to serve them, and to worship them, shall even be as this girdle, which is good for nothing."

Ezekiel 14:6-10 "[6]Therefore say unto the house of Israel, Thus saith the Lord GOD; Repent, and turn yourselves from your idols; and turn away your faces from all your abominations. [7]For every one of the house of Israel, or of the stranger that sojourneth in Israel, which separateth himself from me, and setteth up his idols in his heart, and putteth the stumblingblock of his iniquity before his face, and cometh to a prophet to inquire of him concerning me; I the LORD will answer him by myself: [8]And I will set my face against that man, and will make him a sign and a proverb, and I will cut him off from the midst of my people; and ye shall know that I am the LORD. [9]And if the prophet be deceived when he hath spoken a thing, I the LORD have deceived that prophet, and I will stretch out my hand upon him, and will destroy him from the midst of my people Israel. [10]And they shall bear the punishment of their iniquity: the punishment of the prophet shall be even as the punishment of him that seeketh unto him;"

Amos 8:14 "They that swear by the sin of Samaria, and say, Thy god, O Dan, liveth; and, The manner of Beer-sheba liveth; even they shall fall, and never rise up again."

Habakkuk 2:18-19 "[18]What profiteth the graven image that the maker thereof hath graven it; the molten image, and a teacher of lies, that the maker of his work trusteth therein, to make dumb idols? [19]Woe unto him that saith to the wood, Awake; to the dumb stone, Arise, it shall teach! Behold, it is laid over with gold and silver, and there is no breath at all in the midst of it."

Revelation 21:8 "But the fearful, and unbelieving, and the abominable, and murderers, and whoremongers, and sorcerers, and idolaters, and all liars, shall have their part in the lake which burneth with fire and brimstone: which is the second death."

Revelation 22:13-15 "[13]I am Alpha and Omega, the beginning and the end, the first and the last. [14]Blessed are they that do his commandments, that they may have right to the tree of life, and may enter in through the gates into the city. [15]For without are dogs, and sorcerers, and whoremongers, and murderers, and idolaters, and whosoever loveth and maketh a lie."

Idols

Exodus 32:1-6 "[1]And when the people saw that Moses delayed to come down out of the mount, the people gathered themselves together unto Aaron, and said unto him, Up, make us gods, which shall go before us; for as for this Moses, the man that brought us up out of the land of Egypt, we wot not what is become of him. [2]And Aaron said unto them, Break off the golden earrings, which are in the ears of your wives, of your sons, and of your daughters, and bring them unto me. [3]And all the people brake off the golden earrings which were in their ears, and brought them unto Aaron. [4]And he received them at their hand, and fashioned it with a graving tool, after he had made it a molten calf: and they said, These be thy gods, O Israel, which brought thee up out of the land of Egypt. [5]And when Aaron saw it, he built an altar before it; and Aaron made proclamation, and said, To morrow is a feast to the LORD. [6]And they rose up early on the morrow, and offered burnt offerings, and brought peace offerings; and the people sat down to eat and to drink, and rose up to play."

Deuteronomy 4:27-28 "[27]And the LORD shall scatter you among the nations, and ye shall be left few in number among the heathen, whither the LORD shall lead you. [28]And there ye shall serve gods, the work of men's hands, wood and stone, which neither see, nor hear, nor eat, nor smell."

Deuteronomy 7:25 "The graven images of their gods shall ye burn with fire: thou shalt not desire the silver or gold that is on them, nor take it unto thee, lest thou be snared therein: for it is an abomination to the LORD thy God."

Deuteronomy 16:22 "Neither shalt thou set thee up any image; which the LORD thy God hateth."

Deuteronomy 27:15 "Cursed be the man that maketh any graven or molten image, an abomination unto the LORD, the work of the hands of the craftsman, and putteth it in a secret place. And all the people shall answer and say, Amen."

2 Kings 19:17-18 "[17]Of a truth, LORD, the kings of Assyria have destroyed the nations and their lands, [18]And have cast their gods into the fire: for they were no gods, but the work of men's hands, wood and stone: therefore they have destroyed them."

Psalm 106:35-36 "[35]But were mingled among the heathen, and learned their works. [36]And they served their idols: which were a snare unto them."

Psalm 115:4-7 "[4]Their idols are silver and gold, the work of men's hands. [5]They have mouths, but they speak not: eyes have they, but they see not: [6]They have ears, but they hear not: noses have they, but they smell not: [7]They have hands, but they handle not: feet have they, but they walk not: neither speak they through their throat."

Psalm 135:15-17 "[15]The idols of the heathen are silver and gold, the work of men's hands. [16]They have mouths, but they speak not; eyes have they, but they see not; [17]They have ears, but they hear not; neither is there any breath in their mouths."

Isaiah 2:12-20 "[12]For the day of the LORD of hosts shall be upon every one that is proud and lofty, and upon every one that is lifted up; and he shall be brought low: [13]And upon all the cedars of Lebanon, that are high and lifted up, and upon all the oaks of Bashan, [14]And upon all the high mountains, and upon all the hills that are lifted up, [15]And upon every high tower, and upon every fenced wall, [16]And upon all the ships of Tarshish, and upon all pleasant pictures. [17]And the loftiness of man shall be bowed down, and the haughtiness of men shall be made low: and the LORD alone shall be exalted in that day. [18]And the idols he shall utterly abolish. [19]And they shall go into the holes of the rocks, and into the caves of the earth, for fear of the LORD, and for the glory of his majesty, when he ariseth to shake terribly the earth. [20]In that day a man shall cast his idols of silver, and his idols of gold, which they made each one for himself to worship, to the moles and to the bats;"

Isaiah 37:18-19 "[18]Of a truth, LORD, the kings of Assyria have laid waste all the nations, and their countries, [19]And have cast their gods into the fire:

for they were no gods, but the work of men's hands, wood and stone: therefore they have destroyed them."

Isaiah 41:29 "Behold, they are all vanity; their works are nothing: their molten images are wind and confusion."

Isaiah 44:9-10 "⁹They that make a graven image are all of them vanity; and their delectable things shall not profit; and they are their own witnesses; they see not, nor know; that they may be ashamed. ¹⁰Who hath formed a god, or molten a graven image that is profitable for nothing?"

Isaiah 46:6-7 "⁶They lavish gold out of the bag, and weigh silver in the balance, and hire a goldsmith; and he maketh it a god: they fall down, yea, they worship. ⁷They bear him upon the shoulder, they carry him, and set him in his place, and he standeth; from his place shall he not remove: yea, one shall cry unto him, yet can he not answer, nor save him out of his trouble."

Jeremiah 2:11 "Hath a nation changed their gods, which are yet no gods? but my people have changed their glory for that which doth not profit."

Jeremiah 2:28 "But where are thy gods that thou hast made thee? let them arise, if they can save thee in the time of thy trouble: for according to the number of thy cities are thy gods, O Judah."

Jeremiah 10:2-5 "²Thus saith the LORD, Learn not the way of the heathen, and be not dismayed at the signs of heaven; for the heathen are dismayed at them. ³For the customs of the people are vain: for one cutteth a tree out of the forest, the work of the hands of the workman, with the axe. ⁴They deck it with silver and with gold; they fasten it with nails and with hammers, that it move not. ⁵They are upright as the palm tree, but speak not: they must needs be borne, because they cannot go. Be not afraid of them; for they cannot do evil, neither also is it in them to do good."

Jeremiah 10:11 "Thus shall ye say unto them, The gods that have not made the heavens and the earth, even they shall perish from the earth, and from under these heavens."

Jeremiah 10:14-15 "¹⁴Every man is brutish in his knowledge: every founder is confounded by the graven image: for his molten image is falsehood, and there is no breath in them. ¹⁵They are vanity, and the work of errors: in the time of their visitation they shall perish."

Jeremiah 11:12 "Then shall the cities of Judah and inhabitants of Jerusalem go, and cry unto the gods unto whom they offer incense: but they shall not save them at all in the time of their trouble."

Jeremiah 16:19-20 "¹⁹O LORD, my strength, and my fortress, and my refuge in the day of affliction, the Gentiles shall come unto thee from the ends of the earth, and shall say, Surely our fathers have inherited lies, vanity, and things wherein there is no profit. ²⁰Shall a man make gods unto himself, and they are no gods?"

Jeremiah 18:13-15 "¹³Therefore thus saith the LORD; Ask ye now among the heathen, who hath heard such things: the virgin of Israel hath done a very horrible thing. ¹⁴Will a man leave the snow of Lebanon which cometh from the rock of the field? or shall the cold flowing waters that come from another place be forsaken? ¹⁵Because my people hath forgotten me, they have burned incense to vanity, and they have caused them to stumble in their ways from the ancient paths, to walk in paths, in a way not cast up;"

Jeremiah 51:17-18 "¹⁷Every man is brutish by his knowledge; every founder is confounded by the graven image: for his molten image is falsehood, and there is no breath in them. ¹⁸They are vanity, the work of errors: in the time of their visitation they shall perish."

Daniel 5:23 "But hast lifted up thyself against the LORD of heaven; and they have brought the vessels of his house before thee, and thou, and thy lords, thy wives, and thy concubines, have drunk wine in them; and thou hast praised the gods of silver, and gold, of brass, iron, wood, and stone, which see not, nor hear, nor know: and the God in whose hand thy breath is, and whose are all thy ways, hast thou not glorified:"

Micah 5:10-15 "¹⁰And it shall come to pass in that day, saith the LORD, that I will cut off thy horses out of the midst of thee, and I will destroy thy chariots: ¹¹And I will cut off the cities of thy land, and throw down all thy strong holds: ¹²And I will cut off witchcrafts out of thine hand; and thou shalt have no more soothsayers: ¹³Thy graven images also will I cut off, and thy standing images out of the midst of thee; and thou shalt no more worship the work of thine hands. ¹⁴And I will pluck up thy groves out of the midst of thee: so will I destroy thy cities. ¹⁵And I will execute vengeance in anger and fury upon the heathen, such as they have not heard."

Habakkuk 2:18-19 "¹⁸What profiteth the graven image that the maker thereof hath graven it; the molten image, and a teacher of lies, that the maker of his work trusteth therein, to make dumb idols? ¹⁹Woe unto him that saith to the wood, Awake; to the dumb stone, Arise, it shall teach! Behold, it is laid over with gold and silver, and there is no breath at all in the midst of it."

Acts 14:11-15 "¹¹And when the people saw what Paul had done, they lifted up their voices, saying in the speech of Lycaonia, The gods are come down to us in the likeness of men. ¹²And they called Barnabas, Jupiter; and Paul, Mercurius, because he was the chief speaker. ¹³Then the priest of Jupiter, which was before their city, brought oxen and garlands unto the gates, and would have done sacrifice with the people. ¹⁴Which when the apostles, Barnabas and Paul, heard of, they rent their clothes, and ran in among the people, crying out, ¹⁵And saying, Sirs, why do ye these things? We also are men of like passions with you, and preach unto you that ye should turn from these vanities unto the living God, which made heaven, and earth, and the sea, and all things that are therein:"

Revelation 9:20 "And the rest of the men which were not killed by these plagues yet repented not of the works of their hands, that they should not worship devils, and idols of gold, and silver, and brass, and stone, and of wood: which neither can see, nor hear, nor walk:"

Not Being An Idolater

Exodus 20:2-5 "²I am the LORD thy God, which have brought thee out of the land of Egypt, out of the house of bondage. ³Thou shalt have no other gods before me. ⁴Thou shalt not make unto thee any graven image, or any likeness of any thing that is in heaven above, or that is in the earth beneath, or that is in the water under the earth: ⁵Thou shalt not bow down thyself to them, nor serve them: for I the LORD thy God am a jealous

God, visiting the iniquity of the fathers upon the children unto the third and fourth generation of them that hate me;"

Exodus 20:23 "Ye shall not make with me gods of silver, neither shall ye make unto you gods of gold."

Exodus 23:13 "And in all things that I have said unto you be circumspect: and make no mention of the name of other gods, neither let it be heard out of thy mouth."

Exodus 23:24 "Thou shalt not bow down to their gods, nor serve them, nor do after their works: but thou shalt utterly overthrow them, and quite break down their images."

Exodus 34:11-17 "¹¹Observe thou that which I command thee this day: behold, I drive out before thee the Amorite, and the Canaanite, and the Hittite, and the Perizzite, and the Hivite, and the Jebusite. ¹²Take heed to thyself, lest thou make a covenant with the inhabitants of the land whither thou goest, lest it be for a snare in the midst of thee: ¹³But ye shall destroy their altars, break their images, and cut down their groves: ¹⁴For thou shalt worship no other god: for the LORD, whose name is Jealous, is a jealous God: ¹⁵Lest thou make a covenant with the inhabitants of the land, and they go a whoring after their gods, and do sacrifice unto their gods, and one call thee, and thou eat of his sacrifice; ¹⁶And thou take of their daughters unto thy sons, and their daughters go a whoring after their gods, and make thy sons go a whoring after their gods. ¹⁷Thou shalt make thee no molten gods."

Leviticus 19:4 "Turn ye not unto idols, nor make to yourselves molten gods: I am the LORD your God."

Leviticus 26:1 "Ye shall make you no idols nor graven image, neither rear you up a standing image, neither shall ye set up any image of stone in your land, to bow down unto it: for I am the LORD your God."

Deuteronomy 4:15-18 "¹⁵Take ye therefore good heed unto yourselves; for ye saw no manner of similitude on the day that the LORD spake unto you in Horeb out of the midst of the fire: ¹⁶Lest ye corrupt yourselves, and make you a graven image, the similitude of any figure, the likeness of male or female, ¹⁷The likeness of any beast that is on the earth, the likeness of any winged fowl that flieth in the air, [18]The likeness of any thing that creepeth on the ground, the likeness of any fish that is in the waters beneath the earth:"

Deuteronomy 5:6-9 "[6]I am the LORD thy God, which brought thee out of the land of Egypt, from the house of bondage. [7]Thou shalt have none other gods before me. [8]Thou shalt not make thee any graven image, or any likeness of any thing that is in heaven above, or that is in the earth beneath, or that is in the waters beneath the earth: [9]Thou shalt not bow down thyself unto them, nor serve them: for I the LORD thy God am a jealous God, visiting the iniquity of the fathers upon the children unto the third and fourth generation of them that hate me,"

Deuteronomy 6:14 "Ye shall not go after other gods, of the gods of the people which are round about you;"

Deuteronomy 7:16 "And thou shalt consume all the people which the LORD thy God shall deliver thee; thine eye shall have no pity upon them: neither shalt thou serve their gods; for that will be a snare unto thee."

Deuteronomy 12:29-31 "[29]When the LORD thy God shall cut off the nations from before thee, whither thou goest to possess them, and thou succeedest them, and dwellest in their land; [30]Take heed to thyself that thou be not snared by following them, after that they be destroyed from before thee; and that thou inquire not after their gods, saying, How did these nations serve their gods? even so will I do likewise. [31]Thou shalt not do so unto the LORD thy God: for every abomination to the LORD, which he hateth, have they done unto their gods; for even their sons and their daughters they have burnt in the fire to their gods."

Deuteronomy 16:22 "Neither shalt thou set thee up any image; which the LORD thy God hateth."

Deuteronomy 28:14 "And thou shalt not go aside from any of the words which I command thee this day, to the right hand, or to the left, to go after other gods to serve them."

Joshua 23:6-7 "[6]Be ye therefore very courageous to keep and to do all that is written in the book of the law of Moses, that ye turn not aside therefrom to the right hand or to the left; [7]That ye come not

among these nations, these that remain among you; neither make mention of the name of their gods, nor cause to swear by them, neither serve them, nor bow yourselves unto them:"

Joshua 24:14-15 "[14]Now therefore fear the LORD, and serve him in sincerity and in truth: and put away the gods which your fathers served on the other side of the flood, and in Egypt; and serve ye the LORD. [15]And if it seem evil unto you to serve the LORD, choose you this day whom ye will serve; whether the gods which your fathers served that were on the other side of the flood, or the gods of the Amorites, in whose land ye dwell: but as for me and my house, we will serve the LORD."

2 Kings 17:12 "For they served idols, whereof the LORD had said unto them, Ye shall not do this thing."

2 Kings 17:35-38 "[35]With whom the LORD had made a covenant, and charged them saying, Ye shall not fear other gods, nor bow yourselves to them, nor serve them, nor sacrifice to them: [36]But the LORD, who brought you up out of the land of Egypt with great power and a stretched out arm, him shall ye fear, and him shall ye worship, and to him shall ye do sacrifice. [37]And the statutes, and the ordinances, and the law, and the commandment, which he wrote for you, ye shall observe to do for evermore; and ye shall not fear other gods. [38]And the covenant that I have made with you ye shall not forget; neither shall ye fear other gods."

Psalm 81:9-10 "[9]There shall no strange god be in thee; neither shalt thou worship any strange god. [10]I am the LORD thy God, which brought thee out of the land of Egypt: open thy mouth wide, and I will fill it."

Jeremiah 25:4-6 "[4]And the LORD hath sent unto you all his servants the prophets, rising early and sending them; but ye have not hearkened, nor inclined your ear to hear. [5]They said, Turn ye again now every one from his evil way, and from the evil of your doings, and dwell in the land that the LORD hath given unto you and to your fathers for ever and ever: [6]And go not after other gods to serve them, and to worship them, and provoke me not to anger with the works of your hands; and I will do you no hurt."

Hosea 13:4 "Yet I am the LORD thy God from the land of Egypt, and thou shalt know no god but me: for there is no saviour beside me."

1 Corinthians 10:7 "Neither be ye idolaters, as were some of them; as it is written, The people sat down to eat and drink, and rose up to play."

1 Corinthians 10:14 "Wherefore, my dearly beloved, flee from idolatry."

1 John 5:21 "Little children, keep yourselves from idols. Amen."

The Reward For Idolatry

Exodus 23:31-33 "³¹And I will set thy bounds from the Red sea even unto the sea of the Philistines, and from the desert unto the river: for I will deliver the inhabitants of the land into your hand; and thou shalt drive them out before thee. ³²Thou shalt make no covenant with them, nor with their gods. ³³They shall not dwell in thy land, lest they make thee sin against me: for if thou serve their gods, it will surely be a snare unto thee."

Exodus 32:7-8 "⁷And the LORD said unto Moses, Go, get thee down; for thy people, which thou broughtest out of the land of Egypt, have corrupted themselves: ⁸They have turned aside quickly out of the way which I commanded them: they have made them a molten calf, and have worshipped it, and have sacrificed thereunto, and said, These be thy gods, O Israel, which have brought thee up out of the land of Egypt."

Deuteronomy 4:23-28 "²³Take heed unto yourselves, lest ye forget the covenant of the LORD your God, which he made with you, and make you a graven image, or the likeness of any thing, which the LORD thy God hath forbidden thee. ²⁴For the LORD thy God is a consuming fire, even a jealous God. ²⁵When thou shalt beget children, and children's children, and ye shall have remained long in the land, and shall corrupt yourselves, and make a graven image, or the likeness of any thing, and shall do evil in the sight of the LORD thy God, to provoke him to anger: ²⁶I call heaven and earth to witness against you this day, that ye shall soon utterly perish from off the land whereunto ye go over Jordan to possess it; ye shall not prolong your days upon it, but shall utterly be destroyed. ²⁷And the LORD shall scatter you among the nations, and ye shall be left few in number among the heathen, whither the LORD shall lead you. ²⁸And there ye shall serve gods, the work of men's hands, wood and stone, which neither see, nor hear, nor eat, nor smell."

Deuteronomy 8:19-20 "¹⁹And it shall be, if thou do at all forget the LORD thy God, and walk after other gods, and serve them, and worship them, I testify against you this day that ye shall surely perish. ²⁰As the nations which the LORD destroyeth before your face, so shall ye perish; because ye would not be obedient unto the voice of the LORD your God."

Deuteronomy 11:16-18 "¹⁶Take heed to yourselves, that your heart be not deceived, and ye turn aside, and serve other gods, and worship them; ¹⁷And then the LORD's wrath be kindled against you, and he shut up the heaven, that there be no rain, and that the land yield not her fruit; and lest ye perish quickly from off the good land which the LORD giveth you. ¹⁸Therefore shall ye lay up these my words in your heart and in your soul, and bind them for a sign upon your hand, that they may be as frontlets between your eyes."

Deuteronomy 11:26-28 "²⁶Behold, I set before you this day a blessing and a curse; ²⁷A blessing, if ye obey the commandments of the LORD your God, which I command you this day: ²⁸And a curse, if ye will not obey the commandments of the LORD your God, but turn aside out of the way which I command you this day, to go after other gods, which ye have not known."

Deuteronomy 29:17-29 "¹⁷And ye have seen their abominations, and their idols, wood and stone, silver and gold, which were among them:) ¹⁸Lest there should be among you man, or woman, or family, or tribe, whose heart turneth away this day from the LORD our God, to go and serve the gods of these nations; lest there should be among you a root that beareth gall and wormwood; ¹⁹And it come to pass, when he heareth the words of this curse, that he bless himself in his heart, saying, I shall have peace, though I walk in the imagination of mine heart, to add drunkenness to thirst: ²⁰The LORD will not spare him, but then the anger of the LORD and his jealousy shall smoke against that man, and all the curses that are written in this book shall lie upon him, and the LORD shall blot out his name from under heaven. [21]And the LORD shall separate him unto evil out of all the tribes of Israel, according to all the curses of the covenant that are written in this book of the law: [22]So that the generation to come of your children that shall rise up after you, and the stranger that shall come from a far land, shall say, when they see the plagues of that land, and the sicknesses which the LORD hath laid upon it; [23]And that the whole land thereof is brimstone, and salt, and burning, that it is not sown, nor beareth, nor any grass groweth therein, like the overthrow of Sodom, and Gomorrah, Admah, and Zeboim, which the LORD overthrew in his anger, and in his wrath: [24]Even all nations shall say, Wherefore hath the LORD done thus unto this land? what meaneth the heat of this great anger? [25]Then men shall say, Because they have forsaken the covenant of the LORD God of their fathers, which he made with them when he brought them forth out of the land of Egypt: [26]For they went and served other gods, and worshipped them, gods whom they knew not, and whom he had not given unto them: [27]And the anger of the LORD was kindled against this land, to bring upon it all the curses that are written in this book: [28]And the LORD rooted them out of their land in anger, and in wrath, and in great indignation, and cast them into another land, as it is this day. [29]The secret things belong unto the LORD our God: but those things which are revealed belong unto us and to our children for ever, that we may do all the words of this law."

Deuteronomy 30:15-18 "[15]See, I have set before thee this day life and good, and death and evil; [16]In that I command thee this day to love the LORD thy God, to walk in his ways, and to keep his commandments and his statutes and his judgments, that thou mayest live and multiply: and the LORD thy God shall bless thee in the land whither thou goest to possess it. [17]But if thine heart turn away, so that thou wilt not hear, but shalt be drawn away, and worship other gods, and serve them; [18]I denounce unto you this day, that ye shall surely perish, and that ye shall not prolong your days upon the land, whither thou passest over Jordan to go to possess it."

Deuteronomy 31:16-18 "[16]And the LORD said unto Moses, Behold, thou shalt sleep with thy fathers;

and this people will rise up, and go a whoring after the gods of the strangers of the land, whither they go to be among them, and will forsake me, and break my covenant which I have made with them. [17]Then my anger shall be kindled against them in that day, and I will forsake them, and I will hide my face from them, and they shall be devoured, and many evils and troubles shall befall them; so that they will say in that day, Are not these evils come upon us, because our God is not among us? [18]And I will surely hide my face in that day for all the evils which they shall have wrought, in that they are turned unto other gods."

Deuteronomy 32:17-24 "[17]They sacrificed unto devils, not to God; to gods whom they knew not, to new gods that came newly up, whom your fathers feared not. [18]Of the Rock that begat thee thou art unmindful, and hast forgotten God that formed thee. [19]And when the LORD saw it, he abhorred them, because of the provoking of his sons, and of his daughters. [20]And he said, I will hide my face from them, I will see what their end shall be: for they are a very froward generation, children in whom is no faith. [21]They have moved me to jealousy with that which is not God; they have provoked me to anger with their vanities: and I will move them to jealousy with those which are not a people; I will provoke them to anger with a foolish nation. [22]For a fire is kindled in mine anger, and shall burn unto the lowest hell, and shall consume the earth with her increase, and set on fire the foundations of the mountains. [23]I will heap mischiefs upon them; I will spend mine arrows upon them. [24]They shall be burnt with hunger, and devoured with burning heat, and with bitter destruction: I will also send the teeth of beasts upon them, with the poison of serpents of the dust."

Joshua 23:15-16 "[15]Therefore it shall come to pass, that as all good things are come upon you, which the LORD your God promised you; so shall the LORD bring upon you all evil things, until he have destroyed you from off this good land which the LORD your God hath given you. [16]When ye have transgressed the covenant of the LORD your God, which he commanded you, and have gone and served other gods, and bowed yourselves to them; then shall the anger of the LORD be kindled against you, and ye shall perish quickly from off the good land which he hath given unto you."

Joshua 24:20 "If ye forsake the LORD, and serve strange gods, then he will turn and do you hurt, and consume you, after that he hath done you good."

Judges 2:19 "And it came to pass, when the judge was dead, that they returned, and corrupted themselves more than their fathers, in following other gods to serve them, and to bow down unto them; they ceased not from their own doings, nor from their stubborn way."

Judges 10:11-14 "11And the LORD said unto the children of Israel, Did not I deliver you from the Egyptians, and from the Amorites, from the children of Ammon, and from the Philistines? 12The Zidonians also, and the Amalekites, and the Maonites, did oppress you; and ye cried to me, and I delivered you out of their hand. 13Yet ye have forsaken me, and served other gods: wherefore I will deliver you no more. 14Go and cry unto the gods which ye have chosen; let them deliver you in the time of your tribulation."

1 Samuel 8:4-18 "4Then all the elders of Israel gathered themselves together, and came to Samuel unto Ramah, 5And said unto him, Behold, thou art old, and thy sons walk not in thy ways: now make us a king to judge us like all the nations. 6But the thing displeased Samuel, when they said, Give us a king to judge us. And Samuel prayed unto the LORD. 7And the LORD said unto Samuel, Hearken unto the voice of the people in all that they say unto thee: for they have not rejected thee, but they have rejected me, that I should not reign over them. 8According to all the works which they have done since the day that I brought them up out of Egypt even unto this day, wherewith they have forsaken me, and served other gods, so do they also unto thee. 9Now therefore hearken unto their voice: howbeit yet protest solemnly unto them, and shew them the manner of the king that shall reign over them. 10And Samuel told all the words of the LORD unto the people that asked of him a king. 11And he said, This will be the manner of the king that shall reign over you: He will take your sons, and appoint them for himself, for his chariots, and to be his horsemen; and some shall run before his chariots. 12And he will appoint him captains over thousands, and captains over fifties; and will set them to ear his ground, and to reap his harvest, and to make his instruments of war, and instruments of his chariots. 13And he will take your daughters to be confectionaries, and to be cooks, and to be bakers. 14And he will take your fields, and your vineyards, and your oliveyards, even the best of them, and give them to his servants. 15And he will take the tenth of your seed, and of your vineyards, and give to his officers, and to his servants. 16And he will take your menservants, and your maidservants, and your goodliest young men, and your asses, and put them to his work. 17He will take the tenth of your sheep: and ye shall be his servants. 18And ye shall cry out in that day because of your king which ye shall have chosen you; and the LORD will not hear you in that day."

1 Kings 9:6-9 "6But if ye shall at all turn from following me, ye or your children, and will not keep my commandments and my statutes which I have set before you, but go and serve other gods, and worship them: 7Then will I cut off Israel out of the land which I have given them; and this house, which I have hallowed for my name, will I cast out of my sight; and Israel shall be a proverb and a byword among all people: 8And at this house, which is high, every one that passeth by it shall be astonished, and shall hiss; and they shall say, Why hath the LORD done thus unto this land, and to this house? 9And they shall answer, Because they forsook the LORD their God, who brought forth their fathers out of the land of Egypt, and have taken hold upon other gods, and have worshipped them, and served them: therefore hath the LORD brought upon them all this evil."

1 Kings 11:31-37 "31And he said to Jeroboam, Take thee ten pieces: for thus saith the LORD, the God of Israel, Behold, I will rend the kingdom out of the hand of Solomon, and will give ten tribes to thee: 32(But he shall have one tribe for my servant David's sake, and for Jerusalem's sake, the city which I have chosen out of all the tribes of Israel:) 33Because that they have forsaken me, and have worshipped Ashtoreth the goddess of the Zidonians, Chemosh the god of the Moabites, and Milcom the god of the children of Ammon, and have not walked in my ways, to do that which is right in mine eyes, and to keep my statutes and my judgments, as did David his father. 34Howbeit

I will not take the whole kingdom out of his hand: but I will make him prince all the days of his life for David my servant's sake, whom I chose, because he kept my commandments and my statutes: [35]But I will take the kingdom out of his son's hand, and will give it unto thee, even ten tribes. [36]And unto his son will I give one tribe, that David my servant may have a light alway before me in Jerusalem, the city which I have chosen me to put my name there. [37]And I will take thee, and thou shalt reign according to all that thy soul desireth, and shalt be king over Israel."

1 Kings 14:15-16 "[15]For the LORD shall smite Israel, as a reed is shaken in the water, and he shall root up Israel out of this good land, which he gave to their fathers, and shall scatter them beyond the river, because they have made their groves, provoking the LORD to anger. [16]And he shall give Israel up because of the sins of Jeroboam, who did sin, and who made Israel to sin."

2 Kings 17:7-23 "[7]For so it was, that the children of Israel had sinned against the LORD their God, which had brought them up out of the land of Egypt, from under the hand of Pharoah king of Egypt, and had feared other gods, [8]And walked in the statutes of the heathen, whom the LORD cast out from before the children of Israel, and of the kings of Israel, which they had made. [9]And the children of Israel did secretly those things that were not right against the LORD their God, and they built them high places in all their cities, from the tower of the watchmen to the fenced city. [10]And they set them up images and groves in every high hill, and under every green tree: [11]And there they burnt incense in all the high places, as did the heathen whom the LORD carried away before them; and wrought wicked things to provoke the LORD to anger: [12]For they served idols, whereof the LORD had said unto them, Ye shall not do this thing. [13]Yet the LORD testified against Israel, and against Judah, by all the prophets, and by all the seers, saying, Turn ye from your evil ways, and keep my commandments and my statutes, according to all the law which I commanded your fathers, and which I sent to you by my servants the prophets. [14]Notwithstanding they would not hear, but hardened their necks, like to the neck of their fathers, that did not believe in the LORD their God. [15]And they rejected his statutes, and his covenant that he made with their fathers, and his testimonies which he testified against them; and they followed vanity, and became vain, and went after the heathen that were round about them, concerning whom the LORD had charged them, that they should not do like them. [16]And they left all the commandments of the LORD their God, and made them molten images, even two calves, and made a grove, and worshipped all the host of heaven, and served Baal. [17]And they caused their sons and their daughters to pass through the fire, and used divination and enchantments, and sold themselves to do evil in the sight of the LORD, to provoke him to anger. [18]Therefore the LORD was very angry with Israel, and removed them out of his sight: there was none left but the tribe of Judah only. [19]Also Judah kept not the commandments of the LORD their God, but walked in the statutes of Israel which they made. [20]And the LORD rejected all the seed of Israel, and afflicted them, and delivered them into the hand of spoilers, until he had cast them out of his sight. [21]For he rent Israel from the house of David; and they made Jeroboam the son of Nebat king: and Jeroboam drave Israel from following the LORD, and made them sin a great sin. [22]For the children of Israel walked in all the sins of Jeroboam which he did; they departed not from them; [23]Until the LORD removed Israel out of his sight, as he had said by all his servants the prophets. So was Israel carried away out of their own land to Assyria unto this day."

2 Kings 21:10-16 "[10]And the LORD spake by his servants the prophets, saying, [11]Because Manasseh king of Judah hath done these abominations, and hath done wickedly above all that the Amorites did, which were before him, and hath made Judah also to sin with his idols: [12]Therefore thus saith the LORD God of Israel, Behold, I am bringing such evil upon Jerusalem and Judah, that whosoever heareth of it, both his ears shall tingle. [13]And I will stretch over Jerusalem the line of Samaria, and the plummet of the house of Ahab: and I will wipe Jerusalem as a man wipeth a dish, wiping it, and turning it upside down. [14]And I will forsake the remnant of mine inheritance, and deliver them into the hand of their enemies; and they shall become a prey and a spoil to all their enemies; [15]Because they have done that which was evil in my sight, and have provoked me to anger, since the day their fathers came forth out of Egypt, even unto this day. ¹⁶Moreover Manasseh shed innocent blood very much, till he had filled Jerusalem from one end to another; beside his sin where-with he made Judah to sin, in doing that which was evil in the sight of the LORD."

2 Kings 22:16-17 "¹⁶Thus saith the LORD, Behold, I will bring evil upon this place, and upon the inhabitants thereof, even all the words of the book which the king of Judah hath read: ¹⁷Because they have forsaken me, and have burned incense unto other gods, that they might provoke me to anger with all the works of their hands; therefore my wrath shall be kindled against this place, and shall not be quenched."

2 Chronicles 28:23 "For he sacrificed unto the gods of Damascus, which smote him: and he said, Because the gods of the kings of Syria help them, therefore will I sacrifice to them, that they may help me. But they were the ruin of him, and of all Israel."

2 Chronicles 34:24-25 "²⁴Thus saith the LORD, Behold, I will bring evil upon this place, and upon the inhabitants thereof, even all the curses that are written in the book which they have read before the king of Judah: ²⁵Because they have forsaken me, and have burned incense unto other gods, that they might provoke me to anger with all the works of their hands; therefore my wrath shall be poured out upon this place, and shall not be quenched."

Psalm 106:19-23 "¹⁹They made a calf in Horeb, and worshipped the molten image. ²⁰Thus they changed their glory into the similitude of an ox that eateth grass. ²¹They forgat God their saviour, which had done great things in Egypt; ²²Wondrous works in the land of Ham, and terrible things by the Red sea. ²³Therefore he said that he would destroy them, had not Moses his chosen stood before him in the breach, to turn away his wrath, lest he should destroy them."

Psalm 106:35-36 "³⁵But were mingled among the heathen, and learned their works. ³⁶And they served their idols: which were a snare unto them."

Jeremiah 5:18-19 "¹⁸Nevertheless in those days, saith the LORD, I will not make a full end with

you. ¹⁹And it shall come to pass, when ye shall say, Wherefore doeth the LORD our God all these things unto us? then shalt thou answer them, Like as ye have forsaken me, and served strange gods in your land, so shall ye serve strangers in a land that is not yours."

Jeremiah 11:17 "For the LORD of hosts, that planted thee, hath pronounced evil against thee, for the evil of the house of Israel and of the house of Judah, which they have done against them-selves to provoke me to anger in offering incense unto Baal."

Jeremiah 16:11-13 "¹¹Then shalt thou say unto them, Because your fathers have forsaken me, saith the LORD, and have walked after other gods, and have served them, and have worshipped them, and have forsaken me, and have not kept my law; ¹²And ye have done worse than your fathers; for, behold, ye walk every one after the imagination of his evil heart, that they may not hearken unto me: ¹³Therefore will I cast you out of this land into a land that ye know not, neither ye nor your fathers; and there shall ye serve other gods day and night; where I will not shew you favour."

Jeremiah 18:13-17 "¹³Therefore thus saith the LORD; Ask ye now among the heathen, who hath heard such things: the virgin of Israel hath done a very horrible thing. ¹⁴Will a man leave the snow of Lebanon which cometh from the rock of the field? or shall the cold flowing waters that come from another place be forsaken? ¹⁵Because my people hath forgotten me, they have burned incense to vanity, and they have caused them to stumble in their ways from the ancient paths, to walk in paths, in a way not cast up; ¹⁶To make their land desolate, and a perpetual hissing; every one that passeth thereby shall be astonished, and wag his head. ¹⁷I will scatter them as with an east wind before the enemy; I will shew them the back, and not the face, in the day of their calamity."

Jeremiah 19:3-15 "³And say, Hear ye the word of the LORD, O kings of Judah, and inhabitants of Jerusalem; Thus saith the LORD of hosts, the God of Israel; Behold, I will bring evil upon this place, the which whosoever heareth, his ears shall tingle. ⁴Because they have forsaken me, and have estranged this place, and have burned incense in it unto other gods, whom neither they nor their fathers have known, nor the kings of Judah, and have filled this place with the blood of innocents; [5]They have built also the high places of Baal, to burn their sons with fire for burnt offerings unto Baal, which I commanded not, nor spake it, neither came it into my mind: [6]Therefore, behold, the days come, saith the LORD, that this place shall no more be called Tophet, nor The valley of the son of Hinnom, but The valley of slaughter. [7]And I will make void the counsel of Judah and Jerusalem in this place; and I will cause them to fall by the sword before their enemies, and by the hands of them that seek their lives: and their carcases will I give to be meat for the fowls of the heaven, and for the beasts of the earth. [8]And I will make this city desolate, and an hissing; every one that passeth thereby shall be astonished and hiss because of all the plagues thereof. [9]And I will cause them to eat the flesh of their sons and the flesh of their daughters, and they shall eat every one the flesh of his friend in the siege and straitness, wherewith their enemies, and they that seek their lives, shall straiten them. [10]Then shalt thou break the bottle in the sight of the men that go with thee, [11]And shalt say unto them, Thus saith the LORD of hosts; Even so will I break this people and this city, as one breaketh a potter's vessel, that cannot be made whole again: and they shall bury them in Tophet, till there be no place to bury. [12]Thus will I do unto this place, saith the LORD, and to the inhabitants thereof, and even make this city as Tophet: [13]And the houses of Jerusalem, and the houses of the kings of Judah, shall be defiled as the place of Tophet, because of all the houses upon whose roofs they have burned incense unto all the host of heaven, and have poured out drink offerings unto other gods. [14]Then came Jeremiah from Tophet, whither the LORD had sent him to prophesy; and he stood in the court of the LORD's house; and said to all the people, [15]Thus saith the LORD of hosts, the God of Israel; Behold, I will bring upon this city and upon all her towns all the evil that I have pronounced against it, because they have hardened their necks, that they might not hear my words."

Jeremiah 22:8-9 "[8]And many nations shall pass by this city, and they shall say every man to his neighbour, Wherefore hath the LORD done thus unto this great city? [9]Then they shall answer, Because they have forsaken the covenant of the LORD their God, and worshipped other gods, and served them."

Jeremiah 25:4-14 "[4]And the LORD hath sent unto you all his servants the prophets, rising early and sending them; but ye have not hearkened, nor inclined your ear to hear. [5]They said, Turn ye again now every one from his evil way, and from the evil of your doings, and dwell in the land that the LORD hath given unto you and to your fathers for ever and ever: [6]And go not after other gods to serve them, and to worship them, and provoke me not to anger with the works of your hands; and I will do you no hurt. [7]Yet ye have not hearkened unto me, saith the LORD; that ye might provoke me to anger with the works of your hands to your own hurt. [8]Therefore thus saith the LORD of hosts; Because ye have not heard my words, [9]Behold, I will send and take all the families of the north, saith the LORD, and Nebuchadrezzar the king of Babylon, my servant, and will bring them against this land, and against the inhabitants thereof, and against all these nations round about, and will utterly destroy them, and make them an astonishment, and an hissing, and perpetual desolations. [10]Moreover I will take from them the voice of mirth, and the voice of gladness, the voice of the bridegroom, and the voice of the bride, the sound of the millstones, and the light of the candle. [11]And this whole land shall be a desolation, and an astonishment; and these nations shall serve the king of Babylon seventy years. [12]And it shall come to pass, when seventy years are accomplished, that I will punish the king of Babylon, and that nation, saith the LORD, for their iniquity, and the land of the Chaldeans, and will make it perpetual desolations. [13]And I will bring upon that land all my words which I have pronounced against it, even all that is written in this book, which Jeremiah hath prophesied against all the nations. [14]For many nations and great kings shall serve themselves of them also: and I will recompense them according to their deeds, and according to the works of their own hands."

Jeremiah 32:34-36 "[34]But they set their abominations in the house, which is called by my name, to defile it. [35]And they built the high places of Baal, which are in the valley of the son of Hinnom, to cause their sons and their daughters to pass through the fire unto Molech; which I commanded them not, neither came it into my mind, that they should do this abomination, to cause Judah to sin. [36]And now therefore thus saith the LORD, the God of Israel, concerning this city, whereof ye say, It shall be delivered into the hand of the king of Babylon by the sword, and by the famine, and by the pestilence;"

Ezekiel 36:16-19 "[16]Moreover the word of the LORD came unto me, saying, [17]Son of man, when the house of Israel dwelt in their own land, they defiled it by their own way and by their doings: their way was before me as the uncleanness of a removed woman. [18]Wherefore I poured my fury upon them for the blood that they had shed upon the land, and for their idols wherewith they had polluted it: [19]And I scattered them among the heathen, and they were dispersed through the countries: according to their way and according to their doings I judged them."

Hosea 9:1-9 "[1]Rejoice not, O Israel, for joy, as other people: for thou hast gone a whoring from thy God, thou hast loved a reward upon every cornfloor. [2]The floor and the winepress shall not feed them, and the new wine shall fail in her. [3]They shall not dwell in the LORD's land; but Ephraim shall return to Egypt, and they shall eat unclean things in Assyria. [4]They shall not offer wine offerings to the LORD, neither shall they be pleasing unto him: their sacrifices shall be unto them as the bread of mourners; all that eat thereof shall be polluted: for their bread for their soul shall not come into the house of the LORD. [5]What will ye do in the solemn day, and in the day of the feast of the LORD? [6]For, lo, they are gone because of destruction: Egypt shall gather them up, Memphis shall bury them: the pleasant places for their silver, nettles shall possess them: thorns shall be in their tabernacles. [7]The days of visitation are come, the days of recompence are come; Israel shall know it: the prophet is a fool, the spiritual man is mad, for the multitude of thine iniquity, and the great hatred. [8]The watchman of Ephraim was with my God: but the prophet is a snare of a fowler in all his ways, and hatred in the house of his God. [9]They have deeply corrupted themselves, as in the days of Gibeah: therefore he will remember their iniquity, he will visit their sins."

Zechariah 10:2 "For the idols have spoken vanity, and the diviners have seen a lie, and have told false dreams; they comfort in vain: therefore they went their way as a flock, they were troubled, because there was no shepherd."

Acts 7:42-43 "[42]Then God turned, and gave them up to worship the host of heaven; as it is written in the book of the prophets, O ye house of Israel, have ye offered to me slain beasts and sacrifices by the space of forty years in the wilderness? [43]Yea, ye took up the tabernacle of Moloch, and the star of your god Remphan, figures which ye made to worship them: and I will carry you away beyond Babylon."

Colossians 3:5-6 "[5]Mortify therefore your members which are upon the earth; fornication, uncleanness, inordinate affection, evil concupiscence, and covetousness, which is idolatry: [6]For which things' sake the wrath of God cometh on the children of disobedience:"

Those That Are Not Idolaters
Ezekiel 18:5-9 "[5]But if a man be just, and do that which is lawful and right, [6]And hath not eaten upon the mountains, neither hath lifted up his eyes to the idols of the house of Israel, neither hath defiled his neighbour's wife, neither hath come near to a menstruous woman, [7]And hath not oppressed any, but hath restored to the debtor his pledge, hath spoiled none by violence, hath given his bread to the hungry, and hath covered the naked with a garment; [8]He that hath not given forth upon usury, neither hath taken any increase, that hath withdrawn his hand from iniquity, hath executed true judgment between man and man, [9]Hath walked in my statutes, and hath kept my judgments, to deal truly; he is just, he shall surely live, saith the Lord GOD."

What Is Idolatry
1 Samuel 15:23 "For rebellion is as the sin of witchcraft, and stubbornness is as iniquity and idolatry. Because thou hast rejected the word of the LORD, he hath also rejected thee from being king."

1 Chronicles 16:26 "For all the gods of the people are idols: but the LORD made the heavens."

Psalm 96:5 "For all the gods of the nations are idols: but the LORD made the heavens."

Colossians 3:5 "Mortify therefore your members which are upon the earth; fornication, uncleanness, inordinate affection, evil concupiscence, and covetousness, which is idolatry:"

What Should Be Done To Idols
Exodus 23:24 "Thou shalt not bow down to their gods, nor serve them, nor do after their works: but thou shalt utterly overthrow them, and quite break down their images."

Exodus 34:11-13 "[11]Observe thou that which I command thee this day: behold, I drive out before thee the Amorite, and the Canaanite, and the Hittite, and the Perizzite, and the Hivite, and the Jebusite. [12]Take heed to thyself, lest thou make a covenant with the inhabitants of the land whither thou goest, lest it be for a snare in the midst of thee: [13]But ye shall destroy their altars, break their images, and cut down their groves:"

Numbers 33:50-52 "[50]And the Lord spake unto Moses in the plains of Moab by Jordan near Jericho, saying, [51]Speak unto the children of Israel, and say unto them, When ye are passed over Jordan into the land of Canaan; [52]Then ye shall drive out all the inhabitants of the land from before you, and destroy all their pictures, and destroy all their molten images, and quite pluck down all their high places:"

Deuteronomy 7:5 "But thus shall ye deal with them; ye shall destroy their altars, and break down their images, and cut down their groves, and burn their graven images with fire."

Deuteronomy 7:25 "The graven images of their gods shall ye burn with fire: thou shalt not desire the silver or gold that is on them, nor take it unto thee, lest thou be snared therein: for it is an abomination to the Lord thy God."

Deuteronomy 12:2-3 "[2]Ye shall utterly destroy all the places, wherein the nations which ye shall possess served their gods, upon the high mountains, and upon the hills, and under every green tree: [3]And ye shall overthrow their altars, and break their pillars, and burn their groves with fire; and ye shall hew down the graven images of their gods, and destroy the names of them out of that place."

Joshua 24:23 "Now therefore put away, said he, the strange gods which are among you, and incline your heart unto the Lord God of Israel."

Judges 2:1-2 "[1]And an angel of the Lord came up from Gilgal to Bochim, and said, I made you to go up out of Egypt, and have brought you unto the land which I sware unto your fathers; and I said, I will never break my covenant with you. [2]And ye shall make no league with the inhabitants of this land; ye shall throw down their altars: but ye have not obeyed my voice: why have ye done this?"

Who Is An Idolater
Ephesians 5:5 "For this ye know, that no whoremonger, nor unclean person, nor covetous man, who is an idolater, hath any inheritance in the kingdom of Christ and of God."

IMMATURITY

The Time When You Are Immature
1 Corinthians 13:11-12 "[11]When I was a child, I spake as a child, I understood as a child, I thought as a child: but when I became a man, I put away childish things. [12]For now we see through a glass, darkly; but then face to face: now I know in part; but then shall I know even as also I am known."

Who Is Immature
1 Corinthians 3:1-3 "[1]And I, brethren, could not speak unto you as unto spiritual, but as unto carnal, even as unto babes in Christ. [2]I have fed you with milk, and not with meat: for hitherto ye were not able to bear it, neither yet now are ye able. [3]For ye are yet carnal: for whereas there is among you envying, and strife, and divisions, are ye not carnal, and walk as men?"

Hebrews 5:11-13 "[11]Of whom we have many things to say, and hard to be uttered, seeing ye are dull of hearing. [12]For when for the time ye ought to be teachers, ye have need that one teach you again which be the first principles of the oracles of God; and are become such as have need of milk, and not of strong meat. [13]For every one that useth milk is unskilful in the word of righteousness: for he is a babe."

INCREASE

God Giving The Increase
1 Corinthians 3:6-9 "[6]I have planted, Apollos watered; but God gave the increase. [7]So then neither is he that planteth any thing, neither he that

watereth; but God that giveth the increase. [8]Now he that planteth and he that watereth are one: and every man shall receive his own reward according to his own labour. [9]For we are labourers together with God: ye are God's husbandry, ye are God's building."

When The Righteous Increase
Proverbs 28:28 "When the wicked rise, men hide themselves: but when they perish, the righteous increase."

Who Shall Increase
Proverbs 13:11 "Wealth gotten by vanity shall be diminished: but he that gathereth by labour shall increase."

INDIFFERENCE

The Reward For Being Lukewarm
Revelation 3:14-16 "[14]And unto the angel of the church of the Laodiceans write; These things saith the Amen, the faithful and true witness, the beginning of the creation of God; [15]I know thy works, that thou art neither cold nor hot: I would thou wert cold or hot. [16]So then because thou art lukewarm, and neither cold nor hot, I will spue thee out of my mouth."

INDIGNATION

The Indignation Of The Lord
Jeremiah 10:10 "But the LORD is the true God, he is the living God, and an everlasting king: at his wrath the earth shall tremble, and the nations shall not be able to abide his indignation."

Zephaniah 3:8 "Therefore wait ye upon me, saith the LORD, until the day that I rise up to the prey: for my determination is to gather the nations, that I may assemble the kingdoms, to pour upon them mine indignation, even all my fierce anger: for all the earth shall be devoured with the fire of my jealousy."

Who Shall Bear The Indignation Of The Lord
Psalm 69:22-26 "[22]Let their table become a snare before them: and that which should have been for their welfare, let it become a trap. [23]Let their eyes be darkened, that they see not; and make their loins continually to shake. [24]Pour out thine indignation upon them, and let thy wrathful anger take hold of them. [25]Let their habitation be desolate; and let none dwell in their tents. [26]For they persecute him whom thou hast smitten; and they talk to the grief of those whom thou hast wounded."

Isaiah 66:14 "And when ye see this, your heart shall rejoice, and your bones shall flourish like an herb: and the hand of the LORD shall be known toward his servants, and his indignation toward his enemies."

Micah 7:9 "I will bear the indignation of the LORD, because I have sinned against him, until he plead my cause, and execute judgment for me: he will bring me forth to the light, and I shall behold his righteousness."

Romans 2:8 "But unto them that are contentious, and do not obey the truth, but obey unrighteousness, indignation and wrath,"

Revelation 14:9-11 "[9]And the third angel followed them, saying with a loud voice, If any man worship the beast and his image, and receive his mark in his forehead, or in his hand, [10]The same shall drink of the wine of the wrath of God, which is poured out without mixture into the cup of his indignation; and he shall be tormented with fire and brimstone in the presence of the holy angels, and in the presence of the Lamb: [11]And the smoke of their torment ascendeth up for ever and ever: and they have no rest day nor night, who worship the beast and his image, and whosoever receiveth the mark of his name."

INHERITANCE

The Inheritance Of The Lord
Psalm 94:14 "For the LORD will not cast off his people, neither will he forsake his inheritance."

The Inheritance Of The Upright
Psalm 37:18 "The LORD knoweth the days of the upright: and their inheritance shall be for ever."

1 Peter 1:3-5 "[3]Blessed be the God and Father of our Lord Jesus Christ, which according to his abundant mercy hath begotten us again unto a lively hope by the resurrection of Jesus Christ from the dead, [4]To an inheritance incorruptible, and undefiled, and that fadeth not away, reserved in heaven for you, [5]Who are kept by the power of God through faith unto salvation ready to be revealed in the last time."

What Cannot Inherit The Kingdom Of God
1 Corinthians 15:50 "Now this I say, brethren, that flesh and blood cannot inherit the kingdom of God; neither doth corruption inherit incorruption."

What Is Able To Give You An Inheritance
Acts 20:32 "And now, brethren, I commend you to God, and to the word of his grace, which is able to build you up, and to give you an inheritance among all them which are sanctified."

Who Inherits Folly
Proverbs 14:18 "The simple inherit folly: but the prudent are crowned with knowledge."

Who Inherits Substance
Proverbs 8:12-21 "12I wisdom dwell with prudence, and find out knowledge of witty inventions. 13The fear of the LORD is to hate evil: pride, and arrogancy, and the evil way, and the froward mouth, do I hate. 14Counsel is mine, and sound wisdom: I am understanding; I have strength. 15By me kings reign, and princes decree justice. 16By me princes rule, and nobles, even all the judges of the earth. 17I love them that love me; and those that seek me early shall find me. 18Riches and honour are with me; yea, durable riches and righteousness. 19My fruit is better than gold, yea, than fine gold; and my revenue than choice silver. 20I lead in the way of righteousness, in the midst of the paths of judgment: 21That I may cause those that love me to inherit substance; and I will fill their treasures."

Who Is An Heir Of God Through Christ
Romans 8:16-17 "16The Spirit itself beareth witness with our spirit, that we are the children of God: 17And if children, then heirs; heirs of God, and joint-heirs with Christ; if so be that we suffer with him, that we may be also glorified together."

Galatians 3:27-29 "27For as many of you as have been baptized into Christ have put on Christ. 28There is neither Jew nor Greek, there is neither bond nor free, there is neither male nor female: for ye are all one in Christ Jesus. 29And if ye be Christ's, then are ye Abraham's seed, and heirs according to the promise."

Galatians 4:3-7 "3Even so we, when we were children, were in bondage under the elements of the world: 4But when the fulness of the time was come, God sent forth his Son, made of a woman, made under the law, 5To redeem them that were under the law, that we might receive the adoption of sons. 6And because ye are sons, God hath sent forth the Spirit of his Son into your hearts, crying, Abba, Father. 7Wherefore thou art no more a servant, but a son; and if a son, then an heir of God through Christ."

Ephesians 1:10-11 "10That in the dispensation of the fulness of times he might gather together in one all things in Christ, both which are in heaven, and which are on earth; even in him: 11In whom also we have obtained an inheritance, being predestinated according to the purpose of him who worketh all things after the counsel of his own will."

Ephesians 3:6 "That the Gentiles should be fellowheirs, and of the same body, and partakers of his promise in Christ by the gospel."

Colossians 1:9-12 "9For this cause we also, since the day we heard it, do not cease to pray for you, and to desire that ye might be filled with the knowledge of his will in all wisdom and spiritual understanding; 10That ye might walk worthy of the Lord unto all pleasing, being fruitful in every good work, and increasing in the knowledge of God; 11Strengthened with all might, according to his glorious power, unto all patience and longsuffering with joyfulness; 12Giving thanks unto the Father, which hath made us meet to be partakers of the inheritance of the saints in light."

Titus 3:3-7 "3For we ourselves also were sometimes foolish, disobedient, deceived, serving divers lusts and pleasures, living in malice and envy, hateful, and hating one another. 4But after that the kindness and love of God our Saviour toward man appeared, 5Not by works of righteousness which we have done, but according to his mercy he saved us, by the washing of regeneration, and renewing of the Holy Ghost; 6Which he shed on us abundantly through Jesus Christ our Saviour; 7That being justified by his grace, we should be made heirs according to the hope of eternal life."

Who Shall Inherit All Things
Revelation 21:7 "He that overcometh shall inherit all things; and I will be his God, and he shall be my son."

Who Shall Inherit Eternal Life
Matthew 19:16-21 "16And, behold, one came and said unto him, Good Master, what good thing

shall I do, that I may have eternal life? [17]And he said unto him, Why callest thou me good? there is none good but one, that is, God: but if thou wilt enter into life, keep the commandments. [18]He saith unto him, Which? Jesus said, Thou shalt do no murder, Thou shalt not commit adultery, Thou shalt not steal, Thou shalt not bear false witness, [19]Honour thy father and thy mother: and, Thou shalt love thy neighbour as thyself. [20]The young man saith unto him, All these things have I kept from my youth up: what lack I yet? [21]Jesus said unto him, If thou wilt be perfect, go and sell that thou hast, and give to the poor, and thou shalt have treasure in heaven: and come and follow me."

Matthew 19:28-30 "[28]And Jesus said unto them, Verily I say unto you, That ye which have followed me, in the regeneration when the Son of man shall sit in the throne of his glory, ye also shall sit upon twelve thrones, judging the twelve tribes of Israel. [29]And every one that hath forsaken houses, or brethren, or sisters, or father, or mother, or wife, or children, or lands, for my name's sake, shall receive an hundredfold, and shall inherit everlasting life. [30]But many that are first shall be last; and the last shall be first."

Matthew 25:31-46 "[31]When the Son of man shall come in his glory, and all the holy angels with him, then shall he sit upon the throne of his glory: [32]And before him shall be gathered all nations: and he shall separate them one from another, as a shepherd divideth his sheep from the goats: [33]And he shall set the sheep on his right hand, but the goats on the left. [34]Then shall the King say unto them on his right hand, Come, ye blessed of my Father, inherit the kingdom prepared for you from the foundation of the world: [35]For I was an hungred, and ye gave me meat: I was thirsty, and ye gave me drink: I was a stranger, and ye took me in: [36]Naked, and ye clothed me: I was sick, and ye visited me: I was in prison, and ye came unto me. [37]Then shall the righteous answer him, saying, Lord, when saw we thee an hungred, and fed thee? or thirsty, and gave thee drink? [38]When saw we thee a stranger, and took thee in? or naked, and clothed thee? [39]Or when saw we thee sick, or in prison, and came unto thee? [40]And the King shall answer and say unto them, Verily I say unto you, Inasmuch as ye have done it unto one

of the least of these my brethren, ye have done it unto me. [41]Then shall he say also unto them on the left hand, Depart from me, ye cursed, into everlasting fire, prepared for the devil and his angels: [42]For I was an hungred, and ye gave me no meat: I was thirsty, and ye gave me no drink: [43]I was a stranger, and ye took me not in: naked, and ye clothed me not: sick, and in prison, and ye visited me not. [44]Then shall they also answer him, saying, Lord, when saw we thee an hungred, or athirst, or a stranger, or naked, or sick, or in prison, and did not minister unto thee? [45]Then shall he answer them, saying, Verily I say unto you, Inasmuch as ye did it not to one of the least of these, ye did it not to me. [46]And these shall go away into everlasting punishment: but the righteous into life eternal."

Luke 10:25-28 "[25]And, behold, a certain lawyer stood up, and tempted him, saying, Master, what shall I do to inherit eternal life? [26]He said unto him, What is written in the law? how readest thou? [27]And he answering said, Thou shalt love the Lord thy God with all thy heart, and with all thy soul, and with all thy strength, and with all thy mind; and thy neighbour as thyself. [28]And he said unto him, Thou hast answered right: this do, and thou shalt live."

Who Shall Inherit Glory
1 Samuel 2:8 "He raiseth up the poor out of the dust, and lifteth up the beggar from the dunghill, to set them among princes, and to make them inherit the throne of glory: for the pillars of the earth are the LORD's, and he hath set the world upon them."

Proverbs 3:35 "The wise shall inherit glory: but shame shall be the promotion of fools."

Who Shall Inherit The Earth
Psalm 37:9 "For evildoers shall be cut off: but those that wait upon the LORD, they shall inherit the earth."

Psalm 37:11 "But the meek shall inherit the earth; and shall delight themselves in the abundance of peace."

Psalm 37:18-22 "[18]The LORD knoweth the days of the upright: and their inheritance shall be for ever. [19]They shall not be ashamed in the evil time: and in the days of famine they shall be satisfied.

[20]But the wicked shall perish, and the enemies of the LORD shall be as the fat of lambs: they shall consume; into smoke shall they consume away. [21]The wicked borroweth, and payeth not again: but the righteous sheweth mercy, and giveth. [22]For such as be blessed of him shall inherit the earth; and they that be cursed of him shall be cut off."

Isaiah 57:13-15 "[13]When thou criest, let thy companies deliver thee; but the wind shall carry them all away; vanity shall take them: but he that putteth his trust in me shall possess the land, and shall inherit my holy mountain; [14]And shall say, Cast ye up, cast ye up, prepare the way, take up the stumblingblock out of the way of my people. [15]For thus saith the high and lofty One that inhabiteth eternity, whose name is Holy; I dwell in the high and holy place, with him also that is of a contrite and humble spirit, to revive the spirit of the humble, and to revive the heart of the contrite ones."

Matthew 5:5 "Blessed are the meek: for they shall inherit the earth."

Who Shall Inherit The Kingdom Of God

Matthew 25:31-46 "[31]When the Son of man shall come in his glory, and all the holy angels with him, then shall he sit upon the throne of his glory: [32]And before him shall be gathered all nations: and he shall separate them one from another, as a shepherd divideth his sheep from the goats: [33]And he shall set the sheep on his right hand, but the goats on the left. [34]Then shall the King say unto them on his right hand, Come, ye blessed of my Father, inherit the kingdom prepared for you from the foundation of the world: [35]For I was an hungred, and ye gave me meat: I was thirsty, and ye gave me drink: I was a stranger, and ye took me in: [36]Naked, and ye clothed me: I was sick, and ye visited me: I was in prison, and ye came unto me. [37]Then shall the righteous answer him, saying, Lord, when saw we thee an hungred, and fed thee? or thirsty, and gave thee drink? [38]When saw we thee a stranger, and took thee in? or naked, and clothed thee? [39]Or when saw we thee sick, or in prison, and came unto thee? [40]And the King shall answer and say unto them, Verily I say unto you, Inasmuch as ye have done it unto one of the least of these my brethren, ye have done it unto me. [41]Then shall he say also unto them on the left hand, Depart from me, ye cursed, into everlasting fire, prepared for the devil and his angels: [42]For I was an hungred, and ye gave me no meat: I was thirsty, and ye gave me no drink: [43]I was a stranger, and ye took me not in: naked, and ye clothed me not: sick, and in prison, and ye visited me not. [44]Then shall they also answer him, saying, Lord, when saw we thee an hungred, or athirst, or a stranger, or naked, or sick, or in prison, and did not minister unto thee? [45]Then shall he answer them, saying, Verily I say unto you, Inasmuch as ye did it not to one of the least of these, ye did it not to me. [46]And these shall go away into everlasting punishment: but the righteous into life eternal."

Who Shall Inherit The Wind

Proverbs 11:29 "He that troubleth his own house shall inherit the wind: and the fool shall be servant to the wise of heart."

Who Shall Not Inherit The Kingdom Of God

Matthew 25:31-46 "[31]When the Son of man shall come in his glory, and all the holy angels with him, then shall he sit upon the throne of his glory: [32]And before him shall be gathered all nations: and he shall separate them one from another, as a shepherd divideth his sheep from the goats: [33]And he shall set the sheep on his right hand, but the goats on the left. [34]Then shall the King say unto them on his right hand, Come, ye blessed of my Father, inherit the kingdom prepared for you from the foundation of the world: [35]For I was an hungred, and ye gave me meat: I was thirsty, and ye gave me drink: I was a stranger, and ye took me in: [36]Naked, and ye clothed me: I was sick, and ye visited me: I was in prison, and ye came unto me. [37]Then shall the righteous answer him, saying, Lord, when saw we thee an hungred, and fed thee? or thirsty, and gave thee drink? [38]When saw we thee a stranger, and took thee in? or naked, and clothed thee? [39]Or when saw we thee sick, or in prison, and came unto thee? [40]And the King shall answer and say unto them, Verily I say unto you, Inasmuch as ye have done it unto one of the least of these my brethren, ye have done it unto me. [41]Then shall he say also unto them on the left hand, Depart from me, ye cursed, into everlasting fire, prepared for the devil and his angels: [42]For I was an hungred, and ye gave me no meat: I was thirsty, and ye gave me no drink: [43]I was a stranger, and ye took me not in: naked, and ye clothed me not: sick, and in prison, and ye visited me not. [44]Then shall they also answer him, saying, Lord, when saw we thee an hungred, or athirst, or a stranger, or naked, or sick, or in prison, and did not minister unto thee? [45]Then shall he answer them, saying, Verily I say unto you, Inasmuch as ye did it not to one of the least of these, ye did it not to me. [46]And these shall go away into everlasting punishment: but the righteous into life eternal."

1 Corinthians 6:9-11 "[9]Know ye not that the unrighteous shall not inherit the kingdom of God? Be not deceived: neither fornicators, nor idolaters, nor adulterers, nor effeminate, nor abusers of themselves with mankind, [10]Nor thieves, nor covetous, nor drunkards, nor revilers, nor extortioners, shall inherit the kingdom of God. [11]And such were some of you: but ye are washed, but ye are sanctified, but ye are justified in the name of the Lord Jesus, and by the Spirit of our God."

Galatians 5:16-21 "[16]This I say then, Walk in the Spirit, and ye shall not fulfil the lust of the flesh. [17]For the flesh lusteth against the Spirit, and the Spirit against the flesh: and these are contrary the one to the other: so that ye cannot do the things that ye would. [18]But if ye be led of the Spirit, ye are not under the law. [19]Now the works of the flesh are manifest, which are these; Adultery, fornication, uncleanness, lasciviousness, [20]Idolatry, witchcraft, hatred, variance, emulations, wrath, strife, seditions, heresies, [21]Envyings, murders, drunkenness, revellings, and such like: of the which I tell you before, as I have also told you in time past, that they which do such things shall not inherit the kingdom of God."

Ephesians 5:5-7 "[5]For this ye know, that no whoremonger, nor unclean person, nor covetous man, who is an idolater, hath any inheritance in the kingdom of Christ and of God. [6]Let no man deceive you with vain words: for because of these things cometh the wrath of God upon the children of disobedience. [7]Be not ye therefore partakers with them."

INIQUITY

Departing From Iniquity
2 Timothy 2:19 "Nevertheless the foundation of God standeth sure, having this seal, The Lord knoweth them that are his. And, Let every one that nameth the name of Christ depart from iniquity."

God Hating Iniquity
Psalm 5:4-5 "[4]For thou art not a God that hath pleasure in wickedness: neither shall evil dwell with thee. [5]The foolish shall not stand in thy sight: thou hatest all workers of iniquity."

The Lord Being Without Iniquity
Deuteronomy 32:4 "He is the Rock, his work is perfect: for all his ways are judgment: a God of truth and without iniquity, just and right is he."

2 Chronicles 19:7 "Wherefore now let the fear of the LORD be upon you; take heed and do it: for there is no iniquity with the LORD our God, nor respect of persons, nor taking of gifts."

Zephaniah 3:5 "The just LORD is in the midst thereof; he will not do iniquity: every morning doth he bring his judgment to light, he faileth not; but the unjust knoweth no shame."

The Reward For Abstaining From Iniquity
2 Samuel 22:21-25 "[21]The LORD rewarded me according to my righteousness: according to the cleanness of my hands hath he recompensed me. [22]For I have kept the ways of the LORD, and have not wickedly departed from my God. [23]For all his judgments were before me: and as for his statutes, I did not depart from them. [24]I was also upright before him, and have kept myself from mine iniquity. [25]Therefore the LORD hath recompensed me according to my righteousness; according to my cleanness in his eye sight."

The Reward For Iniquity
Psalm 66:18 "If I regard iniquity in my heart, the Lord will not hear me:"

Psalm 107:17 "Fools because of their transgression, and because of their iniquities, are afflicted."

Isaiah 13:9-11 "[9]Behold, the day of the LORD cometh, cruel both with wrath and fierce anger, to lay the land desolate: and he shall destroy the sinners thereof out of it. [10]For the stars of heaven and the constellations thereof shall not give their light: the sun shall be darkened in his going forth, and the moon shall not cause her light to shine. [11]And I will punish the world for their evil, and the wicked for their iniquity; and I will cause the arrogancy of the proud to cease, and will lay low the haughtiness of the terrible."

Isaiah 59:1-2 "[1]Behold, the LORD's hand is not shortened, that it cannot save; neither his ear heavy, that it cannot hear: ²But your iniquities have separated between you and your God, and your sins have hid his face from you, that he will not hear."

Isaiah 64:4-7 "⁴For since the beginning of the world men have not heard, nor perceived by the ear, neither hath the eye seen, O God, beside thee, what he hath prepared for him that waiteth for him. ⁵Thou meetest him that rejoiceth and worketh righteousness, those that remember thee in thy ways: behold, thou art wroth; for we have sinned: in those is continuance, and we shall be saved. ⁶But we are all as an unclean thing, and all our righteousnesses are as filthy rags; and we all do fade as a leaf; and our iniquities, like the wind, have taken us away. ⁷And there is none that calleth upon thy name, that stirreth up himself to take hold of thee: for thou hast hid thy face from us, and hast consumed us, because of our iniquities."

Jeremiah 16:16-18 "¹⁶Behold, I will send for many fishers, saith the LORD, and they shall fish them; and after will I send for many hunters, and they shall hunt them from every mountain, and from every hill, and out of the holes of the rocks. ¹⁷For mine eyes are upon all their ways: they are not hid from my face, neither is their iniquity hid from mine eyes. ¹⁸And first I will recompense their iniquity and their sin double; because they have defiled my land, they have filled mine inheritance with the carcases of their detestable and abominable things."

Jeremiah 30:12-15 "¹²For thus saith the LORD, Thy bruise is incurable, and thy wound is grievous. ¹³There is none to plead thy cause, that thou mayest be bound up: thou hast no healing medicines. ¹⁴All thy lovers have forgotten thee; they seek thee not; for I have wounded thee with the wound of an enemy, with the chastisement of a cruel one, for the multitude of thine iniquity; because thy sins were increased. ¹⁵Why criest thou for thine affliction? thy sorrow is incurable for the multitude of thine iniquity: because thy sins were increased, I have done these things unto thee."

Daniel 9:4-14 "⁴And I prayed unto the LORD my God, and made my confession, and said, O Lord, the great and dreadful God, keeping the covenant and mercy to them that love him, and to them that keep his commandments; ⁵We have sinned, and have committed iniquity, and have done wickedly, and have rebelled, even by departing from thy precepts and from thy judgments: ⁶Neither have we hearkened unto thy servants the prophets, which spake in thy name to our kings, our princes, and our fathers, and to all the people of the land. ⁷O Lord, righteousness belongeth unto thee, but unto us confusion of faces, as at this day; to the men of Judah, and to the inhabitants of Jerusalem, and unto all Israel, that are near, and that are far off, through all the countries whither thou hast driven them, because of their trespass that they have trespassed against thee. ⁸O Lord, to us belongeth confusion of face, to our kings, to our princes, and to our fathers, because we have sinned against thee. ⁹To the Lord our God belong mercies and forgivenesses, though we have rebelled against him; ¹⁰Neither have we obeyed the voice of the LORD our God, to walk in his laws, which he set before us by his servants the prophets. ¹¹Yea, all Israel have transgressed thy law, even by departing, that they might not obey thy voice; therefore the curse is poured upon us, and the oath that is written in the law of Moses the servant of God, because we have sinned against him. ¹²And he hath confirmed his words, which he spake against us, and against our judges that judged us, by bringing upon us a great evil: for under the whole heaven hath not been done as hath been done upon Jerusalem. ¹³As it is written in the law of Moses, all this evil is come upon us: yet made we not our prayer before the LORD our God, that we might turn from our iniquities, and understand thy truth. ¹⁴Therefore hath the LORD watched upon the evil, and brought it upon us: for the LORD our God is righteous in all his works which he doeth: for we obeyed not his voice."

Matthew 24:12 "And because iniquity shall abound, the love of many shall wax cold."

The Workers Of Iniquity
Psalm 14:2-4 "²The LORD looked down from heaven upon the children of men, to see if there were any that did understand, and seek God. ³They are all gone aside, they are all together become filthy: there is none that doeth good, no, not one. ⁴Have all the workers of iniquity no knowledge? who eat up my people as they eat bread, and call not upon the LORD."

Psalm 28:3-5 "³Draw me not away with the wicked, and with the workers of iniquity, which speak peace to their neighbours, but mischief is in their hearts. ⁴Give them according to their deeds, and according to the wickedness of their endeavours: give them after the work of their hands; render to them their desert. ⁵Because they regard not the works of the LORD, nor the operation of his hands, he shall destroy them, and not build them up."

Psalm 92:9 "For, lo, thine enemies, O LORD, for, lo, thine enemies shall perish; all the workers of iniquity shall be scattered."

Psalm 94:3-7 "³LORD, how long shall the wicked, how long shall the wicked triumph? ⁴How long shall they utter and speak hard things? and all the workers of iniquity boast themselves? ⁵They break in pieces thy people, O LORD, and afflict thine heritage. ⁶They slay the widow and the stranger, and murder the fatherless. ⁷Yet they say, The LORD shall not see, neither shall the God of Jacob regard it."

Proverbs 10:29 "The way of the LORD is strength to the upright: but destruction shall be to the workers of iniquity."

Proverbs 21:15 "It is joy to the just to do judgment: but destruction shall be to the workers of iniquity."

Those That Abstain From Iniquity
Ezekiel 18:5-9 "⁵But if a man be just, and do that which is lawful and right, ⁶And hath not eaten upon the mountains, neither hath lifted up his eyes to the idols of the house of Israel, neither hath defiled his neighbour's wife, neither hath come near to a menstruous woman, ⁷And hath not oppressed any, but hath restored to the debtor his pledge, hath spoiled none by violence, hath given his bread to the hungry, and hath covered the naked with a garment; ⁸He that hath not given forth upon usury, neither hath taken any increase, that hath withdrawn his hand from iniquity, hath executed true judgment between man and man, ⁹Hath walked in my statutes, and hath kept my judgments, to deal truly; he is just, he shall surely live, saith the Lord GOD."

Those That Build A City With Iniquity
Habakkuk 2:6-17 "⁶Shall not all these take up a parable against him, and a taunting proverb against him, and say, Woe to him that increaseth that which is not his! how long? and to him that ladeth himself with thick clay! ⁷Shall they not rise up suddenly that shall bite thee, and awake that shall vex thee, and thou shalt be for booties unto them? ⁸Because thou hast spoiled many nations, all the remnant of the people shall spoil thee; because of men's blood, and for the violence of the land, of the city, and of all that dwell therein. ⁹Woe to him that coveteth an evil covetousness to his house, that he may set his nest on high, that he may be delivered from the power of evil! ¹⁰Thou hast consulted shame to thy house by cutting off many people, and hast sinned against thy soul. ¹¹For the stone shall cry out of the wall, and the beam out of the timber shall answer it. ¹²Woe to him that buildeth a town with blood, and stablisheth a city by iniquity! ¹³Behold, is it not of the LORD of hosts that the people shall labour in the very fire, and the people shall weary themselves for very vanity? ¹⁴For the earth shall be filled with the knowledge of the glory of the LORD, as the waters cover the sea. ¹⁵Woe unto him that giveth his neighbour drink, that puttest thy bottle to him, and makest him drunken also, that thou mayest look on their nakedness! ¹⁶Thou art filled with shame for glory: drink thou also, and let thy foreskin be uncovered: the cup of the LORD's right hand shall be turned unto thee, and shameful spewing shall be on thy glory. ¹⁷For the violence of Lebanon shall cover thee, and the spoil of beasts, which made them afraid, because of men's blood, and for the violence of the land, of the city, and of all that dwell therein."

Those That Sow Iniquity
Job 4:8 "Even as I have seen, they that plow iniquity, and sow wickedness, reap the same."

Proverbs 22:8 "He that soweth iniquity shall reap vanity: and the rod of his anger shall fail."

Colossians 3:25 "But he that doeth wrong shall receive for the wrong which he hath done: and there is no respect of persons."

What Iniquity Is Purged By
Proverbs 16:6 "By mercy and truth iniquity is purged: and by the fear of the LORD men depart from evil."

What Is As Iniquity
1 Samuel 15:23 "For rebellion is as the sin of witchcraft, and stubbornness is as iniquity and idolatry. Because thou hast rejected the word of

the LORD, he hath also rejected thee from being king."

Who Does No Iniquity
Psalm 119:1-3 "¹Blessed are the undefiled in the way, who walk in the law of the LORD. ²Blessed are they that keep his testimonies, and that seek him with the whole heart. ³They also do no iniquity: they walk in his ways."

Zephaniah 3:13 "The remnant of Israel shall not do iniquity, nor speak lies; neither shall a deceitful tongue be found in their mouth: for they shall feed and lie down, and none shall make them afraid."

Who Reaps Iniquity
Hosea 10:13 "Ye have plowed wickedness, ye have reaped iniquity; ye have eaten the fruit of lies: because thou didst trust in thy way, in the multitude of thy mighty men."

Who Works Iniquity
Isaiah 59:1-6 "¹Behold, the LORD's hand is not shortened, that it cannot save; neither his ear heavy, that it cannot hear: ²But your iniquities have separated between you and your God, and your sins have hid his face from you, that he will not hear. ³For your hands are defiled with blood, and your fingers with iniquity; your lips have spoken lies, your tongue hath muttered perverseness. ⁴None calleth for justice, nor any pleadeth for truth: they trust in vanity, and speak lies; they conceive mischief, and bring forth iniquity. ⁵They hatch cockatrice' eggs, and weave the spider's web: he that eateth of their eggs dieth, and that which is crushed breaketh out into a viper. ⁶Their webs shall not become garments, neither shall they cover themselves with their works: their works are works of iniquity, and the act of violence is in their hands."

INSTRUCTION

Hearing Instruction
Proverbs 8:32-33 "³²Now therefore hearken unto me, O ye children: for blessed are they that keep my ways. ³³Hear instruction, and be wise, and refuse it not."

Proverbs 19:20 "Hear counsel, and receive instruction, that thou mayest be wise in thy latter end."

Proverbs 23:12 "Apply thine heart unto instruction, and thine ears to the words of knowledge."

The Instruction Of Fools
Proverbs 16:22 "Understanding is a wellspring of life unto him that hath it: but the instruction of fools is folly."

The Time When The Wise Are Instructed
Proverbs 9:7-10 "⁷He that reproveth a scorner getteth to himself shame: and he that rebuketh a wicked man getteth himself a blot. ⁸Reprove not a scorner, lest he hate thee: rebuke a wise man, and he will love thee. ⁹Give instruction to a wise man, and he will be yet wiser: teach a just man, and he will increase in learning. ¹⁰The fear of the LORD is the beginning of wisdom: and the knowledge of the holy is understanding."

Proverbs 21:11 "When the scorner is punished, the simple is made wise: and when the wise is instructed, he receiveth knowledge."

Those That Keep Instruction
Proverbs 10:17 "He is in the way of life that keepeth instruction: but he that refuseth reproof erreth."

Those That Love Instruction
Proverbs 12:1 "Whoso loveth instruction loveth knowledge: but he that hateth reproof is brutish."

Those That Refuse Instruction
Proverbs 13:18 "Poverty and shame shall be to him that refuseth instruction: but he that regardeth reproof shall be honoured."

Proverbs 15:32 "He that refuseth instruction despiseth his own soul: but he that heareth reproof getteth understanding."

What Instruction Not To Hear
Proverbs 19:27 "Cease, my son, to hear the instruction that causeth to err from the words of knowledge."

What Instruction Is
Proverbs 4:13 "Take fast hold of instruction; let her not go: keep her; for she is thy life."

Proverbs 6:23 "For the commandment is a lamp; and the law is light; and reproofs of instruction are the way of life:"

What Is Profitable For Instruction
2 Timothy 3:16-17 "¹⁶All scripture is given by inspiration of God, and is profitable for doctrine, for reproof, for correction, for instruction in

righteousness: [17]That the man of God may be perfect, throughly furnished unto all good works."

Who Despises Instruction
Psalm 50:16-17 "[16]But unto the wicked God saith, What hast thou to do to declare my statutes, or that thou shouldest take my covenant in thy mouth? [17]Seeing thou hatest instruction, and castest my words behind thee."

Proverbs 1:7 "The fear of the LORD is the beginning of knowledge: but fools despise wisdom and instruction."

Proverbs 15:5 "A fool despiseth his father's instruction: but he that regardeth reproof is prudent."

Proverbs 23:9 "Speak not in the ears of a fool: for he will despise the wisdom of thy words."

Who Hears Their Father's Instruction
Proverbs 13:1 "A wise son heareth his father's instruction: but a scorner heareth not rebuke."

ISRAEL/JEWS

Israel Becoming Lost
Jeremiah 23:1-4 "[1]Woe be unto the pastors that destroy and scatter the sheep of my pasture! saith the LORD. [2]Therefore thus saith the LORD God of Israel against the pastors that feed my people; Ye have scattered my flock, and driven them away, and have not visited them: behold, I will visit upon you the evil of your doings, saith the LORD. [3]And I will gather the remnant of my flock out of all countries whither I have driven them, and will bring them again to their folds; and they shall be fruitful and increase. [4]And I will set up shepherds over them which shall feed them: and they shall fear no more, nor be dismayed, neither shall they be lacking, saith the LORD."

Jeremiah 50:4-6 "[4]In those days, and in that time, saith the LORD, the children of Israel shall come, they and the children of Judah together, going and weeping: they shall go, and seek the LORD their God. [5]They shall ask the way to Zion with their faces thitherward, saying, Come, and let us join ourselves to the LORD in a perpetual covenant that shall not be forgotten. [6]My people hath been lost sheep: their shepherds have caused them to go astray, they have turned them away on the mountains: they have gone from mountain to hill, they have forgotten their restingplace."

Ezekiel 34:1-10 "[1]And the word of the LORD came unto me, saying, [2]Son of man, prophesy against the shepherds of Israel, prophesy, and say unto them, Thus saith the Lord GOD unto the shepherds; Woe be to the shepherds of Israel that do feed themselves! should not the shepherds feed the flocks? [3]Ye eat the fat, and ye clothe you with the wool, ye kill them that are fed: but ye feed not the flock. [4]The diseased have ye not strengthened, neither have ye healed that which was sick, neither have ye bound up that which was broken, neither have ye brought again that which was driven away, neither have ye sought that which was lost; but with force and with cruelty have ye ruled them. [5]And they were scattered, because there is no shepherd: and they became meat to all the beasts of the field, when they were scattered. [6]My sheep wandered through all the mountains, and upon every high hill: yea, my flock was scattered upon all the face of the earth, and none did search or seek after them. [7]Therefore, ye shepherds, hear the word of the LORD; [8]As I live, saith the Lord GOD, surely because my flock became a prey, and my flock became meat to every beast of the field, because there was no shepherd, neither did my shepherds search for my flock, but the shepherds fed themselves, and fed not my flock; [9]Therefore, O ye shepherds, hear the word of the LORD; [10]Thus saith the Lord GOD; Behold, I am against the shepherds; and I will require my flock at their hand, and cause them to cease from feeding the flock; neither shall the shepherds feed themselves any more; for I will deliver my flock from their mouth, that they may not be meat for them."

Zechariah 13:7-9 "[7]Awake, O sword, against my shepherd, and against the man that is my fellow, saith the LORD of hosts: smite the shepherd, and the sheep shall be scattered: and I will turn mine hand upon the little ones. [8]And it shall come to pass, that in all the land, saith the LORD, two parts therein shall be cut off and die; but the third shall be left therein. [9]And I will bring the third part through the fire, and will refine them as silver is refined, and will try them as gold is tried: they shall call on my name, and I will hear them: I will say, It is my people: and they shall say, The LORD is my God."

Matthew 10:5-7 "⁵These twelve Jesus sent forth, and commanded them, saying, Go not into the way of the Gentiles, and into any city of the Samaritans enter ye not: ⁶But go rather to the lost sheep of the house of Israel. ⁷And as ye go, preach, saying, The kingdom of heaven is at hand."

Israel Being Attacked

Ezekiel 38:1-23 "¹And the word of the LORD came unto me, saying, ²Son of man, set thy face against Gog, the land of Magog, the chief prince of Meshech and Tubal, and prophesy against him, ³And say, Thus saith the Lord GOD; Behold I am against thee, O Gog, the chief prince of Meshech and Tubal: ⁴And I will turn thee back, and put hooks into thy jaws, and I will bring thee forth, and all thine army, horses and horsemen, all of them clothed with all sorts of armour, even a great company with bucklers and shields, all of them handling swords: ⁵Persia, Ethiopia, and Libya with them; all of them with shield and helmet: ⁶Gomer, and all his bands; the house of Togarmah of the north quarters, and all his bands: and many people with thee. ⁷Be thou prepared, and prepare for thyself, thou, and all thy company that are assembled unto thee, and be thou a guard unto them. ⁸After many days thou shalt be visited: in the latter years thou shalt come into the land that is brought back from the sword, and is gathered out of many people, against the mountains of Israel, which have been always waste: but it is brought forth out of the nations, and they shall dwell safely all of them. ⁹Thou shalt ascend and come like a storm, thou shalt be like a cloud to cover the land, thou, and all thy bands, and many people with thee. ¹⁰Thus saith the Lord GOD; It shall also come to pass, that at the same time shall things come into thy mind, and thou shalt think an evil thought: ¹¹And thou shalt say, I will go up to the land of unwalled villages; I will go to them that are at rest, that dwell safely, all of them dwelling without walls, and having neither bars nor gates, ¹²To take a spoil, and to take a prey; to turn thine hand upon the desolate places that are now inhabited, and upon the people that are gathered out of the nations, which have gotten cattle and goods, that dwell in the midst of the land. ¹³Sheba, and Dedan, and the merchants of Tarshish, with all the young lions thereof, shall say unto thee, Art thou come to take

a spoil? hast thou gathered thy company to take a prey? to carry away silver and gold, to take away cattle and goods, to take a great spoil? ¹⁴Therefore, son of man, prophesy and say unto Gog, Thus saith the Lord GOD; In that day when my people of Israel dwelleth safely, shalt thou not know it? ¹⁵And thou shalt come from thy place out of the north parts, thou, and many people with thee, all of them riding upon horses, a great company, and a mighty army: ¹⁶And thou shalt come up against my people of Israel, as a cloud to cover the land; it shall be in the latter days, and I will bring thee against my land, that the heathen may know me, when I shall be sanctified in thee, O Gog, before their eyes. ¹⁷Thus saith the Lord GOD; Art thou he of whom I have spoken in old time by my servants the prophets of Israel, which prophesied in those days many years that I would bring thee against them? ¹⁸And it shall come to pass at the same time when Gog shall come against the land of Israel, saith the Lord GOD, that my fury shall come up in my face. ¹⁹For in my jealousy and in the fire of my wrath have I spoken, Surely in that day there shall be a great shaking in the land of Israel; ²⁰So that the fishes of the sea, and the fowls of the heaven, and the beasts of the field, and all creeping things that creep upon the earth, and all the men that are upon the face of the earth, shall shake at my presence, and the mountains shall be thrown down, and the steep places shall fall, and every wall shall fall to the ground. ²¹And I will call for a sword against him throughout all my mountains, saith the Lord GOD: every man's sword shall be against his brother. ²²And I will plead against him with pestilence and with blood; and I will rain upon him, and upon his bands, and upon the many people that are with him, an overflowing rain, and great hailstones, fire, and brimstone. ²³Thus will I magnify myself, and sanctify myself; and I will be known in the eyes of many nations, and they shall know that I am the LORD."

Ezekiel 39:1-24 "¹Therefore, thou son of man, prophesy against Gog, and say, Thus saith the Lord GOD; Behold, I am against thee, O Gog, the chief prince of Meshech and Tubal: ²And I will turn thee back, and leave but the sixth part of thee, and will cause thee to come up from the north parts, and will bring thee upon the mountains of

Israel: ³And I will smite thy bow out of thy left hand, and will cause thine arrows to fall out of thy right hand. ⁴Thou shalt fall upon the mountains of Israel, thou, and all thy bands, and the people that is with thee: I will give thee unto the ravenous birds of every sort, and to the beasts of the field to be devoured. ⁵Thou shalt fall upon the open field: for I have spoken it, saith the Lord GOD. ⁶And I will send a fire on Magog, and among them that dwell carelessly in the isles: and they shall know that I am the LORD. ⁷So will I make my holy name known in the midst of my people Israel; and I will not let them pollute my holy name any more: and the heathen shall know that I am the LORD, the Holy One in Israel. ⁸Behold, it is come, and it is done, saith the Lord GOD; this is the day whereof I have spoken. ⁹And they that dwell in the cities of Israel shall go forth, and shall set on fire and burn the weapons, both the shields and the bucklers, the bows and the arrows, and the handstaves, and the spears, and they shall burn them with fire seven years: ¹⁰So that they shall take no wood out of the field, neither cut down any out of the forests; for they shall burn the weapons with fire: and they shall spoil those that spoiled them, and rob those that robbed them, saith the Lord GOD. ¹¹And it shall come to pass in that day, that I will give unto Gog a place there of graves in Israel, the valley of the passengers on the east of the sea: and it shall stop the noses of the passengers: and there shall they bury Gog and all his multitude: and they shall call it The valley of Hamon-gog. ¹²And seven months shall the house of Israel be burying of them, that they may cleanse the land. ¹³Yea, all the people of the land shall bury them; and it shall be to them a renown the day that I shall be glorified, saith the Lord GOD. ¹⁴And they shall sever out men of continual employment, passing through the land to bury with the passengers those that remain upon the face of the earth, to cleanse it: after the end of seven months shall they search. ¹⁵And the passengers that pass through the land, when any seeth a man's bone, then shall he set up a sign by it, till the buriers have buried it in the valley of Hamon-gog. ¹⁶And also the name of the city shall be Hamonah. Thus shall they cleanse the land. ¹⁷And, thou son of man, thus saith the Lord GOD; Speak unto every feathered fowl, and to every beast of the field, Assemble yourselves, and come; gather yourselves on every side to my sacrifice that I do sacrifice for you, even a great sacrifice upon the mountains of Israel, that ye may eat flesh, and drink blood. ¹⁸Ye shall eat the flesh of the mighty, and drink the blood of the princes of the earth, of rams, of lambs, and of goats, of bullocks, all of them fatlings of Bashan. ¹⁹And ye shall eat fat till ye be full, and drink blood till ye be drunken, of my sacrifice which I have sacrificed for you. ²⁰Thus ye shall be filled at my table with horses and chariots, with mighty men, and with all men of war, saith the Lord GOD. ²¹And I will set my glory among the heathen, and all the heathen shall see my judgment that I have executed, and my hand that I have laid upon them. ²²So the house of Israel shall know that I am the LORD their God from that day and forward. ²³And the heathen shall know that the house of Israel went into captivity for their iniquity: because they trespassed against me, therefore hid I my face from them, and gave them into the hand of their enemies: so fell they all by the sword. ²⁴According to their uncleanness and according to their transgressions have I done unto them, and hid my face from them."

Joel 3:1-16 "¹For, behold, in those days, and in that time, when I shall bring again the captivity of Judah and Jerusalem, ²I will also gather all nations, and will bring them down into the valley of Jehoshaphat, and will plead with them there for my people and for my heritage Israel, whom they have scattered among the nations, and parted my land. ³And they have cast lots for my people; and have given a boy for an harlot, and sold a girl for wine, that they might drink. ⁴Yea, and what have ye to do with me, O Tyre, and Zidon, and all the coasts of Palestine? will ye render me a recompence? and if ye recompence me, swiftly and speedily will I return your recompence upon your own head; ⁵Because ye have taken my silver and my gold, and have carried into your temples my goodly pleasant things: ⁶The children also of Judah and the children of Jerusalem have ye sold unto the Grecians, that ye might remove them far from their border. ⁷Behold, I will raise them out of the place whither ye have sold them, and will return your recompence upon your own head: ⁸And I will sell your sons and your daughters into the hand of the children of Judah, and they shall sell them to the Sabeans, to a people far off: for the LORD hath spoken it. [9]Proclaim ye this among the Gentiles; Prepare war, wake up the mighty men, let all the men of war draw near; let them come up: [10]Beat your plowshares into swords, and your pruninghooks into spears: let the weak say, I am strong. [11]Assemble yourselves, and come, all ye heathen, and gather yourselves together round about: thither cause thy mighty ones to come down, O LORD. [12]Let the heathen be wakened, and come up to the valley of Jehoshaphat: for there will I sit to judge all the heathen round about. [13]Put ye in the sickle, for the harvest is ripe: come, get you down; for the press is full, the fats overflow; for their wickedness is great. [14]Multitudes, multitudes in the valley of decision: for the day of the LORD is near in the valley of decision. [15]The sun and the moon shall be darkened, and the stars shall withdraw their shining. [16]The LORD also shall roar out of Zion, and utter his voice from Jerusalem; and the heavens and the earth shall shake: but the LORD will be the hope of his people, and the strength of the children of Israel."

Zechariah 12:1-10 "[1]The burden of the word of the LORD for Israel, saith the LORD, which stretcheth forth the heavens, and layeth the foundation of the earth, and formeth the spirit of man within him. [2]Behold, I will make Jerusalem a cup of trembling unto all the people round about, when they shall be in the siege both against Judah and against Jerusalem. [3]And in that day will I make Jerusalem a burdensome stone for all people: all that burden themselves with it shall be cut in pieces, though all the people of the earth be gathered together against it. [4]In that day, saith the LORD, I will smite every horse with astonishment, and his rider with madness: and I will open mine eyes upon the house of Judah, and will smite every horse of the people with blindness. [5]And the governors of Judah shall say in their heart, The inhabitants of Jerusalem shall be my strength in the LORD of hosts their God. [6]In that day will I make the governors of Judah like an hearth of fire among the wood, and like a torch of fire in a sheaf; and they shall devour all the people round about, on the right hand and on the left: and Jerusalem shall be inhabited again in her own place, even in Jerusalem. [7]The LORD also shall

save the tents of Judah first, that the glory of the house of David and the glory of the inhabitants of Jerusalem do not magnify themselves against Judah. [8]In that day shall the LORD defend the inhabitants of Jerusalem; and he that is feeble among them at that day shall be as David; and the house of David shall be as God, as the angel of the LORD before them. [9]And it shall come to pass in that day, that I will seek to destroy all the nations that come against Jerusalem. [10]And I will pour upon the house of David, and upon the inhabitants of Jerusalem, the spirit of grace and of supplications: and they shall look upon me whom they have pierced, and they shall mourn for him, as one mourneth for his only son, and shall be in bitterness for him, as one that is in bitterness for his firstborn."

Zechariah 14:1-13 "[1]Behold, the day of the LORD cometh, and thy spoil shall be divided in the midst of thee. [2]For I will gather all nations against Jerusalem to battle; and the city shall be taken, and the houses rifled, and the women ravished; and half of the city shall go forth into captivity, and the residue of the people shall not be cut off from the city. [3]Then shall the LORD go forth, and fight against those nations, as when he fought in the day of battle. [4]And his feet shall stand in that day upon the mount of Olives, which is before Jerusalem on the east, and the mount of Olives shall cleave in the midst thereof toward the east and toward the west, and there shall be a very great valley; and half of the mountain shall remove toward the north, and half of it toward the south. [5]And ye shall flee to the valley of the mountains; for the valley of the mountains shall reach unto Azal: yea, ye shall flee, like as ye fled from before the earthquake in the days of Uzziah king of Judah: and the LORD my God shall come, and all the saints with thee. [6]And it shall come to pass in that day, that the light shall not be clear, nor dark: [7]But it shall be one day which shall be known to the LORD, not day, nor night: but it shall come to pass, that at evening time it shall be light. [8]And it shall be in that day, that living waters shall go out from Jerusalem; half of them toward the former sea, and half of them toward the hinder sea: in summer and in winter shall it be. [9]And the LORD shall be king over all the earth: in that day shall there be one LORD, and his name one. [10]All the land shall be turned as a plain from Geba to Rimmon south of Jerusalem: and it shall be lifted up, and inhabited in her place, from Benjamin's gate unto the place of the first gate, unto the corner gate, and from the tower of Hananeel unto the king's winepresses. [11]And men shall dwell in it, and there shall be no more utter destruction; but Jerusalem shall be safely inhabited. [12]And this shall be the plague wherewith the LORD will smite all the people that have fought against Jerusalem; Their flesh shall consume away while they stand upon their feet, and their eyes shall consume away in their holes, and their tongue shall consume away in their mouth. [13]And it shall come to pass in that day, that a great tumult from the LORD shall be among them; and they shall lay hold every one on the hand of his neighbour, and his hand shall rise up against the hand of his neighbour."

Luke 19:41-44 "[41]And when he was come near, he beheld the city, and wept over it, [42]Saying, If thou hadst known, even thou, at least in this thy day, the things which belong unto thy peace! but now they are hid from thine eyes. [43]For the days shall come upon thee, that thine enemies shall cast a trench about thee, and compass thee round, and keep thee in on every side, [44]And shall lay thee even with the ground, and thy children within thee; and they shall not leave in thee one stone upon another; because thou knewest not the time of thy visitation."

Luke 21:20-24 "[20]And when ye shall see Jerusalem compassed with armies, then know that the desolation thereof is nigh. [21]Then let them which are in Judaea flee to the mountains; and let them which are in the midst of it depart out; and let not them that are in the countries enter thereinto. [22]For these be the days of vengeance, that all things which are written may be fulfilled. [23]But woe unto them that are with child, and to them that give suck, in those days! for there shall be great distress in the land, and wrath upon this people. [24]And they shall fall by the edge of the sword, and shall be led away captive into all nations: and Jerusalem shall be trodden down of the Gentiles, until the times of the Gentiles be fulfilled."

Revelation 16:12-21 "[12]And the sixth angel poured out his vial upon the great river Euphrates; and the water thereof was dried up, that the way of the kings of the east might be prepared. [13]And I saw three unclean spirits like frogs come out of the mouth of the dragon, and out of the mouth of the beast, and out of the mouth of the false prophet. [14]For they are the spirits of devils, working miracles, which go forth unto the kings of the earth and of the whole world, to gather them to the battle of that great day of God Almighty. [15]Behold, I come as a thief. Blessed is he that watcheth, and keepeth his garments, lest he walk naked, and they see his shame. [16]And he gathered them together into a place called in the Hebrew tongue Armageddon. [17]And the seventh angel poured out his vial into the air; and there came a great voice out of the temple of heaven, from the throne, saying, It is done. [18]And there were voices, and thunders, and lightnings; and there was a great earthquake, such as was not since men were upon the earth, so mighty an earthquake, and so great. [19]And the great city was divided into three parts, and the cities of the nations fell: and great Babylon came in remembrance before God, to give unto her the cup of the wine of the fierceness of his wrath. [20]And every island fled away, and the mountains were not found. [21]And there fell upon men a great hail out of heaven, every stone about the weight of a talent: and men blasphemed God because of the plague of the hail; for the plague thereof was exceeding great."

Revelation 20:7-10 "[7]And when the thousand years are expired, Satan shall be loosed out of his prison, [8]And shall go out to deceive the nations which are in the four quarters of the earth, Gog and Magog, to gather them together to battle: the number of whom is as the sand of the sea. [9]And they went up on the breadth of the earth, and compassed the camp of the saints about, and the beloved city: and fire came down from God out of heaven, and devoured them. [10]And the devil that deceived them was cast into the lake of fire and brimstone, where the beast and the false prophet are, and shall be tormented day and night for ever and ever."

Israel Being Returned To The Promised Land

Deuteronomy 30:1-5 "[1]And it shall come to pass, when all these things are come upon thee, the blessing and the curse, which I have set before thee, and thou shalt call them to mind among all the nations, whither the LORD thy God hath driven thee, [2]And shalt return unto the LORD thy God, and shalt obey his voice according to all that

I command thee this day, thou and thy children, with all thine heart, and with all thy soul; ³That then the LORD thy God will turn thy captivity, and have compassion upon thee, and will return and gather thee from all the nations, whither the LORD thy God hath scattered thee. ⁴If any of thine be driven out unto the outmost parts of heaven, from thence will the LORD thy God gather thee, and from thence will he fetch thee: ⁵And the LORD thy God will bring thee into the land which thy fathers possessed, and thou shalt possess it; and he will do thee good, and multiply thee above thy fathers."

1 Kings 8:33-34 "³³When thy people Israel be smitten down before the enemy, because they have sinned against thee, and shall turn again to thee, and confess thy name, and pray, and make supplication unto thee in this house: ³⁴Then hear thou in heaven, and forgive the sin of thy people Israel, and bring them again unto the land which thou gavest unto their fathers."

Nehemiah 1:2-9 "²That Hanani, one of my brethren, came, he and certain men of Judah; and I asked them concerning the Jews that had escaped, which were left of the captivity, and concerning Jerusalem. ³And they said unto me, The remnant that are left of the captivity there in the province are in great affliction and reproach: the wall of Jerusalem also is broken down, and the gates thereof are burned with fire. ⁴And it came to pass, when I heard these words, that I sat down and wept, and mourned certain days, and fasted, and prayed before the God of heaven, ⁵And said, I beseech thee, O LORD God of heaven, the great and terrible God, that keepeth covenant and mercy for them that love him and observe his commandments: ⁶Let thine ear now be attentive, and thine eyes open, that thou mayest hear the prayer of thy servant, which I pray before thee now, day and night, for the children of Israel thy servants, and confess the sins of the children of Israel, which we have sinned against thee: both I and my father's house have sinned. ⁷We have dealt very corruptly against thee, and have not kept the commandments, nor the statutes, nor the judgments, which thou commandedst thy servant Moses. ⁸Remember, I beseech thee, the word that thou commandedst thy servant Moses, saying, If ye transgress, I will scatter you abroad among the nations: ⁹But if ye turn unto me, and keep my commandments, and do them; though there were of you cast out unto the uttermost part of the heaven, yet will I gather them from thence, and will bring them unto the place that I have chosen to set my name there."

Isaiah 11:11-16 "¹¹And it shall come to pass in that day, that the Lord shall set his hand again the second time to recover the remnant of his people, which shall be left, from Assyria, and from Egypt, and from Pathros, and from Cush, and from Elam, and from Shinar, and from Hamath, and from the islands of the sea. ¹²And he shall set up an ensign for the nations, and shall assemble the outcasts of Israel, and gather together the dispersed of Judah from the four corners of the earth. ¹³The envy also of Ephraim shall depart, and the adversaries of Judah shall be cut off: Ephraim shall not envy Judah, and Judah shall not vex Ephraim. ¹⁴But they shall fly upon the shoulders of the Philistines toward the west; they shall spoil them of the east together: they shall lay their hand upon Edom and Moab; and the children of Ammon shall obey them. ¹⁵And the LORD shall utterly destroy the tongue of the Egyptian sea; and with his mighty wind shall he shake his hand over the river, and shall smite it in the seven streams, and make men go over dryshod. ¹⁶And there shall be an highway for the remnant of his people, which shall be left, from Assyria; like as it was to Israel in the day that he came up out of the land of Egypt."

Isaiah 14:1 "For the LORD will have mercy on Jacob, and will yet choose Israel, and set them in their own land: and the strangers shall be joined with them, and they shall cleave to the house of Jacob."

Isaiah 35:1-10 "¹The wilderness and the solitary place shall be glad for them; and the desert shall rejoice, and blossom as the rose. ²It shall blossom abundantly, and rejoice even with joy and singing: the glory of Lebanon shall be given unto it, the excellency of Carmel and Sharon, they shall see the glory of the LORD, and the excellency of our God. ³Strengthen ye the weak hands, and confirm the feeble knees. ⁴Say to them that are of a fearful heart, Be strong, fear not: behold, your God will come with vengeance, even God with a recompence; he will come and save you. ⁵Then the eyes of the blind shall be opened, and the ears of the deaf shall be unstopped. ⁶Then shall the lame man leap as an hart, and the tongue of the dumb sing: for in the wilderness shall waters break out, and streams in the desert. ⁷And the parched ground shall become a pool, and the thirsty land springs of water: in the habitation of dragons, where each lay, shall be grass with reeds and rushes. ⁸And an highway shall be there, and a way, and it shall be called The way of holiness; the unclean shall not pass over it; but it shall be for those: the wayfaring men, though fools, shall not err therein. ⁹No lion shall be there, nor any ravenous beast shall go up thereon, it shall not be found there; but the redeemed shall walk there: ¹⁰And the ransomed of the LORD shall return, and come to Zion with songs and everlasting joy upon their heads: they shall obtain joy and gladness, and sorrow and sighing shall flee away."

Isaiah 43:3-6 "³For I am the LORD thy God, the Holy One of Israel, thy Saviour: I gave Egypt for thy ransom, Ethiopia and Seba for thee. ⁴Since thou wast precious in my sight, thou hast been honourable, and I have loved thee: therefore will I give men for thee, and people for thy life. ⁵Fear not: for I am with thee: I will bring thy seed from the east, and gather thee from the west; ⁶I will say to the north, Give up; and to the south, Keep not back: bring my sons from far, and my daughters from the ends of the earth;"

Isaiah 43:15-21 "¹⁵I am the LORD, your Holy One, the creator of Israel, your King. ¹⁶Thus saith the LORD, which maketh a way in the sea, and a path in the mighty waters; ¹⁷Which bringeth forth the chariot and horse, the army and the power; they shall lie down together, they shall not rise: they are extinct, they are quenched as tow. ¹⁸Remember ye not the former things, neither consider the things of old. ¹⁹Behold, I will do a new thing; now it shall spring forth; shall ye not know it? I will even make a way in the wilderness, and rivers in the desert. ²⁰The beast of the field shall honour me, the dragons and the owls: because I give waters in the wilderness, and rivers in the desert, to give drink to my people, my chosen. ²¹This people have I formed for myself; they shall shew forth my praise."

Isaiah 49:14-23 "¹⁴But Zion said, The LORD hath forsaken me, and my Lord hath forgotten me. ¹⁵Can a woman forget her sucking child, that she should not have compassion on the son of her womb? yea, they may forget, yet will I not forget

thee. ¹⁶Behold, I have graven thee upon the palms of my hands; thy walls are continually before me. ¹⁷Thy children shall make haste; thy destroyers and they that made thee waste shall go forth of thee. ¹⁸Lift up thine eyes round about, and behold: all these gather themselves together, and come to thee. As I live, saith the LORD, thou shalt surely clothe thee with them all, as with an ornament, and bind them on thee, as a bride doeth. ¹⁹For thy waste and thy desolate places, and the land of thy destruction, shall even now be too narrow by reason of the inhabitants, and they that swallowed thee up shall be far away. ²⁰The children which thou shalt have, after thou hast lost the other, shall say again in thine ears, The place is too strait for me: give place to me that I may dwell. ²¹Then shalt thou say in thine heart, Who hath begotten me these, seeing I have lost my children, and am desolate, a captive, and removing to and fro? and who hath brought up these? Behold, I was left alone; these, where had they been? ²²Thus saith the Lord GOD, Behold, I will lift up mine hand to the Gentiles, and set up my standard to the people: and they shall bring thy sons in their arms, and thy daughters shall be carried upon their shoulders. ²³And kings shall be thy nursing fathers, and their queens thy nursing mothers: they shall bow down to thee with their face toward the earth, and lick up the dust of thy feet; and thou shalt know that I am the LORD: for they shall not be ashamed that wait for me."

Isaiah 66:18-20 "¹⁸For I know their works and their thoughts: it shall come, that I will gather all nations and tongues; and they shall come, and see my glory. ¹⁹And I will set a sign among them, and I will send those that escape of them unto the nations, to Tarshish, Pul, and Lud, that draw the bow, to Tubal, and Javan, to the isles afar off, that have not heard my fame, neither have seen my glory; and they shall declare my glory among the Gentiles. ²⁰And they shall bring all your brethren for an offering unto the LORD out of all nations upon horses, and in chariots, and in litters, and upon mules, and upon swift beasts, to my holy mountain Jerusalem, saith the LORD, as the children of Israel bring an offering in a clean vessel into the house of the LORD."

Jeremiah 3:14-18 "¹⁴Turn, O backsliding children, saith the LORD; for I am married unto you: and I will take you one of a city, and two of a family, and I will bring you to Zion: 15And I will give you pastors according to mine heart, which shall feed you with knowledge and understanding. 16And it shall come to pass, when ye be multiplied and increased in the land, in those days, saith the LORD, they shall say no more, The ark of the covenant of the LORD: neither shall it come to mind: neither shall they remember it; neither shall they visit it; neither shall that be done any more. 17At that time they shall call Jerusalem the throne of the LORD; and all the nations shall be gathered unto it, to the name of the LORD, to Jerusalem: neither shall they walk any more after the imagination of their evil heart. 18In those days the house of Judah shall walk with the house of Israel, and they shall come together out of the land of the north to the land that I have given for an inheritance unto your fathers."

Jeremiah 12:14-15 "14Thus saith the LORD against all mine evil neighbours, that touch the inheritance which I have caused my people Israel to inherit; Behold, I will pluck them out of their land, and pluck out the house of Judah from among them. 15And it shall come to pass, after that I have plucked them out I will return, and have compassion on them, and will bring them again, every man to his heritage, and every man to his land."

Jeremiah 16:14-16 "14Therefore, behold, the days come, saith the LORD, that it shall no more be said, The LORD liveth, that brought up the children of Israel out of the land of Egypt; 15But, The LORD liveth, that brought up the children of Israel from the land of the north, and from all the lands whither he had driven them: and I will bring them again into their land that I gave unto their fathers. 16Behold, I will send for many fishers, saith the LORD, and they shall fish them; and after will I send for many hunters, and they shall hunt them from every mountain, and from every hill, and out of the holes of the rocks."

Jeremiah 23:1-8 "1Woe be unto the pastors that destroy and scatter the sheep of my pasture! saith the LORD. 2Therefore thus saith the LORD God of Israel against the pastors that feed my people; Ye have scattered my flock, and driven them away, and have not visited them: behold, I will visit upon you the evil of your doings, saith the LORD. 3And I will gather the remnant of my flock out of

all countries whither I have driven them, and will bring them again to their folds; and they shall be fruitful and increase. 4And I will set up shepherds over them which shall feed them: and they shall fear no more, nor be dismayed, neither shall they be lacking, saith the LORD. 5Behold, the days come, saith the LORD, that I will raise unto David a righteous Branch, and a King shall reign and prosper, and shall execute judgment and justice in the earth. 6In his days Judah shall be saved, and Israel shall dwell safely: and this is his name whereby he shall be called, THE LORD OUR RIGHTEOUSNESS. 7Therefore, behold, the days come, saith the LORD, that they shall no more say, The LORD liveth, which brought up the children of Israel out of the land of Egypt; 8But, The LORD liveth, which brought up and which led the seed of the house of Israel out of the north country, and from all countries whither I had driven them; and they shall dwell in their own land."

Jeremiah 24:1-10 "1The LORD shewed me, and, behold, two baskets of figs were set before the temple of the LORD, after that Nebuchadrezzar king of Babylon had carried away captive Jeconiah the son of Jehoiakim king of Judah, and the princes of Judah, with the carpenters and smiths, from Jerusalem, and had brought them to Babylon. 2One basket had very good figs, even like the figs that are first ripe: and the other basket had very naughty figs, which could not be eaten, they were so bad. 3Then said the LORD unto me, What seest thou, Jeremiah? And I said, Figs; the good figs, very good; and the evil, very evil, that cannot be eaten, they are so evil. 4Again the word of the LORD came unto me, saying, 5Thus saith the LORD, the God of Israel; Like these good figs, so will I acknowledge them that are carried away captive of Judah, whom I have sent out of this place into the land of the Chaldeans for their good. 6For I will set mine eyes upon them for good, and I will bring them again to this land: and I will build them, and not pull them down; and I will plant them, and not pluck them up. 7And I will give them an heart to know me, that I am the LORD: and they shall be my people, and I will be their God: for they shall return unto me with their whole heart. 8And as the evil figs, which cannot be eaten, they are so evil; surely thus saith the LORD, So will I give Zedekiah the king of Judah, and his princes, and the residue of Jerusalem, that remain in this land, and them that dwell in the land of Egypt: ⁹And I will deliver them to be removed into all the kingdoms of the earth for their hurt, to be a reproach and a proverb, a taunt and a curse, in all places whither I shall drive them. ¹⁰And I will send the sword, the famine, and the pestilence, among them, till they be consumed from off the land that I gave unto them and to their fathers."

Jeremiah 29:8-14 "⁸For thus saith the LORD of hosts, the God of Israel; Let not your prophets and your diviners, that be in the midst of you, deceive you, neither hearken to your dreams which ye cause to be dreamed. ⁹For they prophesy falsely unto you in my name: I have not sent them, saith the LORD. ¹⁰For thus saith the LORD, That after seventy years be accomplished at Babylon I will visit you, and perform my good word toward you, in causing you to return to this place. ¹¹For I know the thoughts that I think toward you, saith the LORD, thoughts of peace, and not of evil, to give you an expected end. ¹²Then shall ye call upon me, and ye shall go and pray unto me, and I will hearken unto you. ¹³And ye shall seek me, and find me, when ye shall search for me with all your heart. ¹⁴And I will be found of you, saith the LORD: and I will turn away your captivity, and I will gather you from all the nations, and from all the places whither I have driven you, saith the LORD; and I will bring you again into the place whence I caused you to be carried away captive."

Jeremiah 30:1-24 "¹The word that came to Jeremiah from the LORD, saying, ²Thus speaketh the LORD God of Israel, saying, Write thee all the words that I have spoken unto thee in a book. ³For, lo, the days come, saith the LORD, that I will bring again the captivity of my people Israel and Judah, saith the LORD: and I will cause them to return to the land that I gave to their fathers, and they shall possess it. ⁴And these are the words that the LORD spake concerning Israel and concerning Judah. ⁵For thus saith the LORD; We have heard a voice of trembling, of fear, and not of peace. ⁶Ask ye now, and see whether a man doth travail with child? wherefore do I see every man with his hands on his loins, as a woman in travail,

and all faces are turned into paleness? ⁷Alas! for that day is great, so that none is like it: it is even the time of Jacob's trouble; but he shall be saved out of it. ⁸For it shall come to pass in that day, saith the LORD of hosts, that I will break his yoke from off thy neck, and will burst thy bonds, and strangers shall no more serve themselves of him: ⁹But they shall serve the LORD their God, and David their king, whom I will raise up unto them. ¹⁰Therefore fear thou not, O my servant Jacob, saith the LORD; neither be dismayed, O Israel: for, lo, I will save thee from afar, and thy seed from the land of their captivity; and Jacob shall return, and shall be in rest, and be quiet, and none shall make him afraid. ¹¹For I am with thee, saith the LORD, to save thee: though I make a full end of all nations whither I have scattered thee, yet will I not make a full end of thee: but I will correct thee in measure, and will not leave thee altogether unpunished. ¹²For thus saith the LORD, Thy bruise is incurable, and thy wound is grievous. ¹³There is none to plead thy cause, that thou mayest be bound up: thou hast no healing medicines. ¹⁴All thy lovers have forgotten thee; they seek thee not; for I have wounded thee with the wound of an enemy, with the chastisement of a cruel one, for the multitude of thine iniquity; because thy sins were increased. ¹⁵Why criest thou for thine affliction? thy sorrow is incurable for the multitude of thine iniquity: because thy sins were increased, I have done these things unto thee. ¹⁶Therefore all they that devour thee shall be devoured; and all thine adversaries, every one of them, shall go into captivity; and they that spoil thee shall be a spoil, and all that prey upon thee will I give for a prey. ¹⁷For I will restore health unto thee, and I will heal thee of thy wounds, saith the LORD; because they called thee an Outcast, saying, This is Zion, whom no man seeketh after. ¹⁸Thus saith the LORD; Behold, I will bring again the captivity of Jacob's tents, and have mercy on his dwellingplaces; and the city shall be builded upon her own heap, and the palace shall remain after the manner thereof. ¹⁹And out of them shall proceed thanksgiving and the voice of them that make merry: and I will multiply them, and they shall not be few; I will also glorify them, and they shall not be small. ²⁰Their children also shall be as aforetime, and their congregation shall be established before me, and I will punish all that oppress them. ²¹And their nobles shall be of themselves, and their governor shall proceed from the midst of them; and I will cause him to draw near, and he shall approach unto me: for who is this that engaged his heart to approach unto me? saith the LORD. ²²And ye shall be my people, and I will be your God. ²³Behold, the whirlwind of the LORD goeth forth with fury, a continuing whirlwind: it shall fall with pain upon the head of the wicked. ²⁴The fierce anger of the LORD shall not return, until he have done it, and until he have performed the intents of his heart: in the latter days ye shall consider it."

Jeremiah 31:7-14 "⁷For thus saith the LORD; Sing with gladness for Jacob, and shout among the chief of the nations: publish ye, praise ye, and say, O LORD, save thy people, the remnant of Israel. ⁸Behold, I will bring them from the north country, and gather them from the coasts of the earth, and with them the blind and the lame, the woman with child and her that travaileth with child together: a great company shall return thither. ⁹They shall come with weeping, and with supplications will I lead them: I will cause them to walk by the rivers of waters in a straight way, wherein they shall not stumble: for I am a father to Israel, and Ephraim is my firstborn. ¹⁰Hear the word of the LORD, O ye nations, and declare it in the isles afar off, and say, He that scattered Israel will gather him, and keep him, as a shepherd doth his flock. ¹¹For the LORD hath redeemed Jacob, and ransomed him from the hand of him that was stronger than he. ¹²Therefore they shall come and sing in the height of Zion, and shall flow together to the goodness of the LORD, for wheat, and for wine, and for oil, and for the young of the flock and of the herd: and their soul shall be as a watered garden; and they shall not sorrow any more at all. ¹³Then shall the virgin rejoice in the dance, both young men and old together: for I will turn their mourning into joy, and will comfort them, and make them rejoice from their sorrow. ¹⁴And I will satiate the soul of the priests with fatness, and my people shall be satisfied with my goodness, saith the LORD."

Jeremiah 32:32-37 "³²Because of all the evil of the children of Israel and of the children of Judah, which they have done to provoke me to anger,

they, their kings, their princes, their priests, and their prophets, and the men of Judah, and the inhabitants of Jerusalem. ³³And they have turned unto me the back, and not the face: though I taught them, rising up early and teaching them, yet they have not hearkened to receive instruction. ³⁴But they set their abominations in the house, which is called by my name, to defile it. ³⁵And they built the high places of Baal, which are in the valley of the son of Hinnom, to cause their sons and their daughters to pass through the fire unto Molech; which I commanded them not, neither came it into my mind, that they should do this abomination, to cause Judah to sin. ³⁶And now therefore thus saith the LORD, the God of Israel, concerning this city, whereof ye say, It shall be delivered into the hand of the king of Babylon by the sword, and by the famine, and by the pestilence; ³⁷Behold, I will gather them out of all countries, whither I have driven them in mine anger, and in my fury, and in great wrath; and I will bring them again unto this place, and I will cause them to dwell safely."

Jeremiah 33:1-13 "¹Moreover the word of the LORD came unto Jeremiah the second time, while he was yet shut up in the court of the prison, saying, ²Thus saith the LORD the maker thereof, the LORD that formed it, to establish it; the LORD is his name; ³Call unto me, and I will answer thee, and shew thee great and mighty things, which thou knowest not. ⁴For thus saith the LORD, the God of Israel, concerning the houses of this city, and concerning the houses of the kings of Judah, which are thrown down by the mounts, and by the sword; ⁵They come to fight with the Chaldeans, but it is to fill them with the dead bodies of men, whom I have slain in mine anger and in my fury, and for all whose wickedness I have hid my face from this city. ⁶Behold, I will bring it health and cure, and I will cure them, and will reveal unto them the abundance of peace and truth. ⁷And I will cause the captivity of Judah and the captivity of Israel to return, and will build them, as at the first. ⁸And I will cleanse them from all their iniquity, whereby they have sinned against me; and I will pardon all their iniquities, whereby they have sinned, and whereby they have transgressed against me. ⁹And it shall be to me a name of joy, a praise and an honour before all the nations of the earth, which shall hear all the good that I do unto them: and they shall fear and tremble for all the goodness and for all the prosperity that I procure unto it. [10]Thus saith the LORD; Again there shall be heard in this place, which ye say shall be desolate without man and without beast, even in the cities of Judah, and in the streets of Jerusalem, that are desolate, without man, and without inhabitant, and without beast, [11]The voice of joy, and the voice of gladness, the voice of the bridegroom, and the voice of the bride, the voice of them that shall say, Praise the LORD of hosts: for the LORD is good; for his mercy endureth for ever: and of them that shall bring the sacrifice of praise into the house of the LORD. For I will cause to return the captivity of the land, as at the first, saith the LORD. [12]Thus saith the LORD of hosts; Again in this place, which is desolate without man and without beast, and in all the cities thereof, shall be an habitation of shepherds causing their flocks to lie down. [13]In the cities of the mountains, in the cities of the vale, and in the cities of the south, and in the land of Benjamin, and in the places about Jerusalem, and in the cities of Judah, shall the flocks pass again under the hands of him that telleth them, saith the LORD."

Ezekiel 11:16-18 "[16]Therefore say, Thus saith the Lord GOD; Although I have cast them far off among the heathen, and although I have scattered them among the countries, yet will I be to them as a little sanctuary in the countries where they shall come. [17]Therefore say, Thus saith the Lord GOD; I will even gather you from the people, and assemble you out of the countries where ye have been scattered, and I will give you the land of Israel. [18]And they shall come thither, and they shall take away all the detestable things thereof and all the abominations thereof from thence."

Ezekiel 20:32-38 "[32]And that which cometh into your mind shall not be at all, that ye say, We will be as the heathen, as the families of the countries, to serve wood and stone. [33]As I live, saith the Lord GOD, surely with a mighty hand, and with a stretched out arm, and with fury poured out, will I rule over you: [34]And I will bring you out from the people, and will gather you out of the countries wherein ye are scattered, with a mighty hand, and with a stretched out arm, and with fury poured out. [35]And I will bring you into the wilderness of the people, and there will I plead with you face to face. [36]Like as I pleaded with your fathers in the wilderness of the land of Egypt, so will I plead with you, saith the Lord GOD. [37]And I will cause you to pass under the rod, and I will bring you into the bond of the covenant: [38]And I will purge out from among you the rebels, and them that transgress against me: I will bring them forth out of the country where they sojourn, and they shall not enter into the land of Israel: and ye shall know that I am the LORD."

Ezekiel 28:24-26 "[24]And there shall be no more a pricking brier unto the house of Israel, nor any grieving thorn of all that are round about them, that despised them; and they shall know that I am the Lord GOD. [25]Thus saith the Lord GOD; When I shall have gathered the house of Israel from the people among whom they are scattered, and shall be sanctified in them in the sight of the heathen, then shall they dwell in their land that I have given to my servant Jacob. [26]And they shall dwell safely therein, and shall build houses, and plant vineyards; yea, they shall dwell with confidence, when I have executed judgments upon all those that despise them round about them; and they shall know that I am the LORD their God."

Ezekiel 34:11-13 "[11]For thus saith the Lord GOD; Behold, I, even I, will both search my sheep, and seek them out. [12]As a shepherd seeketh out his flock in the day that he is among his sheep that are scattered; so will I seek out my sheep, and will deliver them out of all places where they have been scattered in the cloudy and dark day. [13]And I will bring them out from the people, and gather them from the countries, and will bring them to their own land, and feed them upon the mountains of Israel by the rivers, and in all the inhabited places of the country."

Ezekiel 36:8-15 "[8]But ye, O mountains of Israel, ye shall shoot forth your branches, and yield your fruit to my people of Israel; for they are at hand to come. [9]For, behold, I am for you, and I will turn unto you, and ye shall be tilled and sown: [10]And I will multiply men upon you, all the house of Israel, even all of it: and the cities shall be inhabited, and the wastes shall be builded: [11]And I will multiply upon you man and beast; and they shall increase and bring fruit: and I will settle you after your old estates, and will do better unto you than at your beginnings: and ye shall know that I am the LORD. [12]Yea, I will cause men to walk upon you, even my people Israel; and they shall possess thee, and thou shalt be their inheritance, and thou shalt no more henceforth bereave them of men. [13]Thus saith the Lord GOD; Because they say unto you, Thou land devourest up men, and hast bereaved thy nations; [14]Therefore thou shalt devour men no more, neither bereave thy nations any more, saith the Lord GOD. [15]Neither will I cause men to hear in thee the shame of the heathen any more, neither shalt thou bear the reproach of the people any more, neither shalt thou cause thy nations to fall any more, saith the Lord GOD."

Ezekiel 36:22-38 "[22]Therefore say unto the house of Israel, Thus saith the Lord GOD; I do not this for your sakes, O house of Israel, but for mine holy name's sake, which ye have profaned among the heathen, whither ye went. [23]And I will sanctify my great name, which was profaned among the heathen, which ye have profaned in the midst of them; and the heathen shall know that I am the LORD, saith the Lord GOD, when I shall be sanctified in you before their eyes. [24]For I will take you from among the heathen, and gather you out of all countries, and will bring you into your own land. [25]Then will I sprinkle clean water upon you, and ye shall be clean: from all your filthiness, and from all your idols, will I cleanse you. [26]A new heart also will I give you, and a new spirit will I put within you: and I will take away the stony heart out of your flesh, and I will give you an heart of flesh. [27]And I will put my spirit within you, and cause you to walk in my statutes, and ye shall keep my judgments, and do them. [28]And ye shall dwell in the land that I gave to your fathers; and ye shall be my people, and I will be your God. [29]I will also save you from all your uncleannesses: and I will call for the corn, and will increase it, and lay no famine upon you. [30]And I will multiply the fruit of the tree, and the increase of the field, that ye shall receive no more reproach of famine among the heathen. [31]Then shall ye remember your own evil ways, and your doings that were not good, and shall lothe yourselves in your own sight for your iniquities and for your abominations. [32]Not for your sakes do I this, saith the Lord GOD, be it known unto you: be ashamed and confounded for your own ways,

O house of Israel. [33]Thus saith the Lord GOD; In the day that I shall have cleansed you from all your iniquities I will also cause you to dwell in the cities, and the wastes shall be builded. [34]And the desolate land shall be tilled, whereas it lay desolate in the sight of all that passed by. [35]And they shall say, This land that was desolate is become like the garden of Eden; and the waste and desolate and ruined cities are become fenced, and are inhabited. [36]Then the heathen that are left round about you shall know that I the LORD build the ruined places, and plant that that was desolate: I the LORD have spoken it, and I will do it. [37]Thus saith the Lord GOD; I will yet for this be inquired of by the house of Israel, to do it for them; I will increase them with men like a flock. [38]As the holy flock, as the flock of Jerusalem in her solemn feasts; so shall the waste cities be filled with flocks of men: and they shall know that I am the LORD."

Ezekiel 37:1-14 "[1]The hand of the LORD was upon me, and carried me out in the spirit of the LORD, and set me down in the midst of the valley which was full of bones, [2]And caused me to pass by them round about: and, behold, there were very many in the open valley; and, lo, they were very dry. [3]And he said unto me, Son of man, can these bones live? And I answered, O Lord GOD, thou knowest. [4]Again he said unto me, Prophesy upon these bones, and say unto them, O ye dry bones, hear the word of the LORD. [5]Thus saith the Lord GOD unto these bones; Behold, I will cause breath to enter into you, and ye shall live: [6]And I will lay sinews upon you, and will bring up flesh upon you, and cover you with skin, and put breath in you, and ye shall live; and ye shall know that I am the LORD. [7]So I prophesied as I was commanded: and as I prophesied, there was a noise, and behold a shaking, and the bones came together, bone to his bone. [8]And when I beheld, lo, the sinews and the flesh came up upon them, and the skin covered them above: but there was no breath in them. [9]Then said he unto me, Prophesy unto the wind, prophesy, son of man, and say to the wind, Thus saith the Lord GOD; Come from the four winds, O breath, and breathe upon these slain, that they may live. [10]So I prophesied as he commanded me, and the breath came into them, and they lived, and stood up upon their feet, an exceeding great army. [11]Then he said unto me, Son of man, these bones are the whole house of Israel: behold, they say, Our bones are dried, and our hope is lost: we are cut off for our parts. [12]Therefore prophesy and say unto them, Thus saith the Lord GOD; Behold, O my people, I will open your graves, and cause you to come up out of your graves, and bring you into the land of Israel. [13]And ye shall know that I am the LORD, when I have opened your graves, O my people, and brought you up out of your graves, [14]And shall put my spirit in you, and ye shall live, and I shall place you in your own land: then shall ye know that I the LORD have spoken it, and performed it, saith the LORD."

Ezekiel 39:25-29 "[25]Therefore thus saith the Lord GOD; Now will I bring again the captivity of Jacob, and have mercy upon the whole house of Israel, and will be jealous for my holy name; [26]After that they have borne their shame, and all their trespasses whereby they have trespassed against me, when they dwelt safely in their land, and none made them afraid. [27]When I have brought them again from the people, and gathered them out of their enemies' lands, and am sanctified in them in the sight of many nations; [28]Then shall they know that I am the LORD their God, which cause them to be led into captivity among the heathen: but I have gathered them unto their own land, and have left none of them any more there. [29]Neither will I hide my face any more from them: for I have poured out my spirit upon the house of Israel, saith the Lord GOD."

Amos 9:11-15 "[11]In that day will I raise up the tabernacle of David that is fallen, and close up the breaches thereof; and I will raise up his ruins, and I will build it as in the days of old: [12]That they may possess the remnant of Edom, and of all the heathen, which are called by my name, saith the LORD that doeth this. [13]Behold, the days come, saith the LORD, that the plowman shall overtake the reaper, and the treader of grapes him that soweth seed; and the mountains shall drop sweet wine, and all the hills shall melt. [14]And I will bring again the captivity of my people of Israel, and they shall build the waste cities, and inhabit them; and they shall plant vineyards, and drink the wine thereof; they shall also make gardens, and eat the fruit of them. [15]And I will plant them

upon their land, and they shall no more be pulled up out of their land which I have given them, saith the LORD thy God."

Obadiah 17-21 "[17]But upon mount Zion shall be deliverance, and there shall be holiness; and the house of Jacob shall possess their possessions. [18]And the house of Jacob shall be a fire, and the house of Joseph a flame, and the house of Esau for stubble, and they shall kindle in them, and devour them; and there shall not be any remaining of the house of Esau; for the LORD hath spoken it. [19]And they of the south shall possess the mount of Esau; and they of the plain the Philistines: and they shall possess the fields of Ephraim, and the fields of Samaria: and Benjamin shall possess Gilead. [20]And the captivity of this host of the children of Israel shall possess that of the Canaanites, even unto Zarephath; and the captivity of Jerusalem, which is in Sepharad, shall possess the cities of the south. [21]And saviours shall come up on mount Zion to judge the mount of Esau; and the kingdom shall be the LORD's."

Micah 5:2-3 "[2]But thou, Bethlehem Ephratah, though thou be little among the thousands of Judah, yet out of thee shall he come forth unto me that is to be ruler in Israel; whose goings forth have been from of old, from everlasting. [3]Therefore will he give them up, until the time that she which travaileth hath brought forth: then the remnant of his brethren shall return unto the children of Israel."

Zechariah 2:4-7 "[4]And said unto him, Run, speak to this young man, saying, Jerusalem shall be inhabited as towns without walls for the multitude of men and cattle therein: [5]For I, saith the LORD, will be unto her a wall of fire round about, and will be the glory in the midst of her. [6]Ho, ho, come forth, and flee from the land of the north, saith the LORD: for I have spread you abroad as the four winds of the heaven, saith the LORD. [7]Deliver thyself, O Zion, that dwellest with the daughter of Babylon."

Zechariah 8:3-8 "[3]Thus saith the LORD; I am returned unto Zion, and will dwell in the midst of Jerusalem: and Jerusalem shall be called a city of truth; and the mountain of the LORD of hosts the holy mountain. [4]Thus saith the LORD of hosts; There shall yet old men and old women dwell in the streets of Jerusalem, and every man with his staff in his hand for very age. [5]And the streets of the city shall be full of boys and girls playing in the streets thereof. [6]Thus saith the LORD of hosts; If it be marvellous in the eyes of the remnant of this people in these days, should it also be marvellous in mine eyes? saith the LORD of hosts. [7]Thus saith the LORD of hosts; Behold, I will save my people from the east country, and from the west country; [8]And I will bring them, and they shall dwell in the midst of Jerusalem: and they shall be my people, and I will be their God, in truth and in righteousness."

Israel Being Revived

Ezekiel 37:1-14 "[1]The hand of the LORD was upon me, and carried me out in the spirit of the LORD, and set me down in the midst of the valley which was full of bones, [2]And caused me to pass by them round about: and, behold, there were very many in the open valley; and, lo, they were very dry. [3]And he said unto me, Son of man, can these bones live? And I answered, O Lord GOD, thou knowest. [4]Again he said unto me, Prophesy upon these bones, and say unto them, O ye dry bones, hear the word of the LORD. [5]Thus saith the Lord GOD unto these bones; Behold, I will cause breath to enter into you, and ye shall live: [6]And I will lay sinews upon you, and will bring up flesh upon you, and cover you with skin, and put breath in you, and ye shall live; and ye shall know that I am the LORD. [7]So I prophesied as I was commanded: and as I prophesied, there was a noise, and behold a shaking, and the bones came together, bone to his bone. [8]And when I beheld, lo, the sinews and the flesh came up upon them, and the skin covered them above: but there was no breath in them. [9]Then said he unto me, Prophesy unto the wind, prophesy, son of man, and say to the wind, Thus saith the Lord GOD; Come from the four winds, O breath, and breathe upon these slain, that they may live. [10]So I prophesied as he commanded me, and the breath came into them, and they lived, and stood up upon their feet, an exceeding great army. [11]Then he said unto me, Son of man, these bones are the whole house of Israel: behold, they say, Our bones are dried, and our hope is lost: we are cut off for our parts. [12]Therefore prophesy and say unto them, Thus saith the Lord GOD; Behold, O my people, I will open your graves, and cause you to come up out of your graves, and bring you into the land of Israel. [13]And ye shall know that I am the LORD, when I have opened your graves, O my people, and brought you up out of your graves, [14]And shall put my spirit in you, and ye shall live, and I shall place you in your own land: then shall ye know that I the LORD have spoken it, and performed it, saith the LORD."

Israel Being Scattered Across The Globe

Deuteronomy 4:26-28 "[26]I call heaven and earth to witness against you this day, that ye shall soon utterly perish from off the land whereunto ye go over Jordan to possess it; ye shall not prolong your days upon it, but shall utterly be destroyed. [27]And the LORD shall scatter you among the nations, and ye shall be left few in number among the heathen, whither the LORD shall lead you. [28]And there ye shall serve gods, the work of men's hands, wood and stone, which neither see, nor hear, nor eat, nor smell."

Deuteronomy 28:36-37 "[36]The LORD shall bring thee, and thy king which thou shalt set over thee, unto a nation which neither thou nor thy fathers have known; and there shalt thou serve other gods, wood and stone. [37]And thou shalt become an astonishment, a proverb, and a byword, among all nations whither the LORD shall lead thee."

Deuteronomy 28:63-68 "[63]And it shall come to pass, that as the LORD rejoiced over you to do you good, and to multiply you; so the LORD will rejoice over you to destroy you, and to bring you to nought; and ye shall be plucked from off the land whither thou goest to possess it. [64]And the LORD shall scatter thee among all people, from the one end of the earth even unto the other; and there thou shalt serve other gods, which neither thou nor thy fathers have known, even wood and stone. [65]And among these nations shalt thou find no ease, neither shall the sole of thy foot have rest: but the LORD shall give thee there a trembling heart, and failing of eyes, and sorrow of mind: [66]And thy life shall hang in doubt before thee; and thou shalt fear day and night, and shalt have none assurance of thy life: [67]In the morning thou shalt say, Would God it were even! and at even thou shalt say, Would God it were morning! for the fear of thine heart wherewith thou shalt fear, and for the sight of thine eyes which thou shalt see. ⁶⁸And the LORD shall bring thee into Egypt again with ships, by the way whereof I spake unto thee, Thou shalt see it no more again: and there ye shall be sold unto your enemies for bondmen and bondwomen, and no man shall buy you."

Deuteronomy 30:1-4 "¹And it shall come to pass, when all these things are come upon thee, the blessing and the curse, which I have set before thee, and thou shalt call them to mind among all the nations, whither the LORD thy God hath driven thee, ²And shalt return unto the LORD thy God, and shalt obey his voice according to all that I command thee this day, thou and thy children, with all thine heart, and with all thy soul; ³That then the LORD thy God will turn thy captivity, and have compassion upon thee, and will return and gather thee from all the nations, whither the LORD thy God hath scattered thee. ⁴If any of thine be driven out unto the outmost parts of heaven, from thence will the LORD thy God gather thee, and from thence will he fetch thee:"

1 Kings 14:15 "For the LORD shall smite Israel, as a reed is shaken in the water, and he shall root up Israel out of this good land, which he gave to their fathers, and shall scatter them beyond the river, because they have made their groves, provoking the LORD to anger."

Nehemiah 1:2-8 "²That Hanani, one of my brethren, came, he and certain men of Judah; and I asked them concerning the Jews that had escaped, which were left of the captivity, and concerning Jerusalem. ³And they said unto me, The remnant that are left of the captivity there in the province are in great affliction and reproach: the wall of Jerusalem also is broken down, and the gates thereof are burned with fire. ⁴And it came to pass, when I heard these words, that I sat down and wept, and mourned certain days, and fasted, and prayed before the God of heaven, ⁵And said, I beseech thee, O LORD God of heaven, the great and terrible God, that keepeth covenant and mercy for them that love him and observe his commandments: ⁶Let thine ear now be attentive, and thine eyes open, that thou mayest hear the prayer of thy servant, which I pray before thee now, day and night, for the children of Israel thy servants, and confess the sins of the children of Israel, which we have sinned against thee: both I and my father's house have sinned. ⁷We have dealt very corruptly against thee, and have not kept the commandments, nor the statutes, nor the judgments, which thou commandedst thy servant Moses. ⁸Remember, I beseech thee, the word that thou commandedst thy servant Moses, saying, If ye transgress, I will scatter you abroad among the nations:"

Jeremiah 9:13-16 "¹³And the LORD saith, Because they have forsaken my law which I set before them, and have not obeyed my voice, neither walked therein; ¹⁴But have walked after the imagination of their own heart, and after Baalim, which their fathers taught them: ¹⁵Therefore thus saith the LORD of hosts, the God of Israel; Behold, I will feed them, even this people, with wormwood, and give them water of gall to drink. ¹⁶I will scatter them also among the heathen, whom neither they nor their fathers have known: and I will send a sword after them, till I have consumed them."

Jeremiah 12:14-15 "¹⁴Thus saith the LORD against all mine evil neighbours, that touch the inheritance which I have caused my people Israel to inherit; Behold, I will pluck them out of their land, and pluck out the house of Judah from among them. ¹⁵And it shall come to pass, after that I have plucked them out I will return, and have compassion on them, and will bring them again, every man to his heritage, and every man to his land."

Jeremiah 18:13-17 "¹³Therefore thus saith the LORD; Ask ye now among the heathen, who hath heard such things: the virgin of Israel hath done a very horrible thing. ¹⁴Will a man leave the snow of Lebanon which cometh from the rock of the field? or shall the cold flowing waters that come from another place be forsaken? ¹⁵Because my people hath forgotten me, they have burned incense to vanity, and they have caused them to stumble in their ways from the ancient paths, to walk in paths, in a way not cast up; ¹⁶To make their land desolate, and a perpetual hissing; every one that passeth thereby shall be astonished, and wag his head. ¹⁷I will scatter them as with an east wind before the enemy; I will shew them the back, and not the face, in the day of their calamity."

Jeremiah 23:1-8 "¹Woe be unto the pastors that destroy and scatter the sheep of my pasture! saith the LORD. ²Therefore thus saith the LORD God of Israel against the pastors that feed my people; Ye have scattered my flock, and driven them away, and have not visited them: behold, I will visit upon you the evil of your doings, saith the LORD. ³And I will gather the remnant of my flock out of all countries whither I have driven them, and will bring them again to their folds; and they shall be fruitful and increase. ⁴And I will set up shepherds over them which shall feed them: and they shall fear no more, nor be dismayed, neither shall they be lacking, saith the LORD. ⁵Behold, the days come, saith the LORD, that I will raise unto David a righteous Branch, and a King shall reign and prosper, and shall execute judgment and justice in the earth. ⁶In his days Judah shall be saved, and Israel shall dwell safely: and this is his name whereby he shall be called, THE LORD OUR RIGHTEOUSNESS. ⁷Therefore, behold, the days come, saith the LORD, that they shall no more say, The LORD liveth, which brought up the children of Israel out of the land of Egypt; ⁸But, The LORD liveth, which brought up and which led the seed of the house of Israel out of the north country, and from all countries whither I had driven them; and they shall dwell in their own land."

Jeremiah 24:1-10 "¹The LORD shewed me, and, behold, two baskets of figs were set before the temple of the LORD, after that Nebuchadrezzar king of Babylon had carried away captive Jeconiah the son of Jehoiakim king of Judah, and the princes of Judah, with the carpenters and smiths, from Jerusalem, and had brought them to Babylon. ²One basket had very good figs, even like the figs that are first ripe: and the other basket had very naughty figs, which could not be eaten, they were so bad. ³Then said the LORD unto me, What seest thou, Jeremiah? And I said, Figs; the good figs, very good; and the evil, very evil, that cannot be eaten, they are so evil. ⁴Again the word of the LORD came unto me, saying, ⁵Thus saith the LORD, the God of Israel; Like these good figs, so will I acknowledge them that are carried away captive of Judah, whom I have sent out of this place into the land of the Chaldeans for their good. ⁶For I will set mine eyes upon them for

good, and I will bring them again to this land: and I will build them, and not pull them down; and I will plant them, and not pluck them up. ⁷And I will give them an heart to know me, that I am the LORD: and they shall be my people, and I will be their God: for they shall return unto me with their whole heart. ⁸And as the evil figs, which cannot be eaten, they are so evil; surely thus saith the LORD, So will I give Zedekiah the king of Judah, and his princes, and the residue of Jerusalem, that remain in this land, and them that dwell in the land of Egypt: ⁹And I will deliver them to be removed into all the kingdoms of the earth for their hurt, to be a reproach and a proverb, a taunt and a curse, in all places whither I shall drive them. ¹⁰And I will send the sword, the famine, and the pestilence, among them, till they be consumed from off the land that I gave unto them and to their fathers."

Jeremiah 30:10-11 "¹⁰Therefore fear thou not, O my servant Jacob, saith the LORD; neither be dismayed, O Israel: for, lo, I will save thee from afar, and thy seed from the land of their captivity; and Jacob shall return, and shall be in rest, and be quiet, and none shall make him afraid. ¹¹For I am with thee, saith the LORD, to save thee: though I make a full end of all nations whither I have scattered thee, yet will I not make a full end of thee: but I will correct thee in measure, and will not leave thee altogether unpunished."

Jeremiah 31:10 "Hear the word of the LORD, O ye nations, and declare it in the isles afar off, and say, He that scattered Israel will gather him, and keep him, as a shepherd doth his flock."

Jeremiah 32:32-37 "³²Because of all the evil of the children of Israel and of the children of Judah, which they have done to provoke me to anger, they, their kings, their princes, their priests, and their prophets, and the men of Judah, and the inhabitants of Jerusalem. ³³And they have turned unto me the back, and not the face: though I taught them, rising up early and teaching them, yet they have not hearkened to receive instruction. ³⁴But they set their abominations in the house, which is called by my name, to defile it. ³⁵And they built the high places of Baal, which are in the valley of the son of Hinnom, to cause their sons and their daughters to pass through the fire unto Molech; which I commanded them not, neither came it into my mind, that they should do this abomination, to cause Judah to sin. ³⁶And now therefore thus saith the LORD, the God of Israel, concerning this city, whereof ye say, It shall be delivered into the hand of the king of Babylon by the sword, and by the famine, and by the pestilence; ³⁷Behold, I will gather them out of all countries, whither I have driven them in mine anger, and in my fury, and in great wrath; and I will bring them again unto this place, and I will cause them to dwell safely:"

Jeremiah 46:28 "Fear thou not, O Jacob my servant, saith the LORD: for I am with thee; for I will make a full end of all the nations whither I have driven thee: but I will not make a full end of thee, but correct thee in measure; yet will I not leave thee wholly unpunished."

Ezekiel 11:16-17 "¹⁶Therefore say, Thus saith the Lord GOD; Although I have cast them far off among the heathen, and although I have scattered them among the countries, yet will I be to them as a little sanctuary in the countries where they shall come. ¹⁷Therefore say, Thus saith the Lord GOD; I will even gather you from the people, and assemble you out of the countries where ye have been scattered, and I will give you the land of Israel."

Ezekiel 28:25 "Thus saith the Lord GOD; When I shall have gathered the house of Israel from the people among whom they are scattered, and shall be sanctified in them in the sight of the heathen, then shall they dwell in their land that I have given to my servant Jacob."

Ezekiel 34:1-6 "¹And the word of the LORD came unto me, saying, ²Son of man, prophesy against the shepherds of Israel, prophesy, and say unto them, Thus saith the Lord GOD unto the shepherds; Woe be to the shepherds of Israel that do feed themselves! should not the shepherds feed the flocks? ³Ye eat the fat, and ye clothe you with the wool, ye kill them that are fed: but ye feed not the flock. ⁴The diseased have ye not strengthened, neither have ye healed that which was sick, neither have ye bound up that which was broken, neither have ye brought again that which was driven away, neither have ye sought that which was lost; but with force and with cruelty have ye ruled them. ⁵And they were scattered, because there is no shepherd: and they became meat to all the beasts of the field, when they were scattered. ⁶My sheep wandered through all the mountains, and upon every high hill: yea, my flock was scattered upon all the face of the earth, and none did search or seek after them."

Ezekiel 34:11-12 "¹¹For thus saith the Lord GOD; Behold, I, even I, will both search my sheep, and seek them out. ¹²As a shepherd seeketh out his flock in the day that he is among his sheep that are scattered; so will I seek out my sheep, and will deliver them out of all places where they have been scattered in the cloudy and dark day."

Ezekiel 36:16-19 "¹⁶Moreover the word of the LORD came unto me, saying, ¹⁷Son of man, when the house of Israel dwelt in their own land, they defiled it by their own way and by their doings: their way was before me as the uncleanness of a removed woman. ¹⁸Wherefore I poured my fury upon them for the blood that they had shed upon the land, and for their idols wherewith they had polluted it: ¹⁹And I scattered them among the heathen, and they were dispersed through the countries: according to their way and according to their doings I judged them."

Daniel 9:7 "O Lord, righteousness belongeth unto thee, but unto us confusion of faces, as at this day; to the men of Judah, and to the inhabitants of Jerusalem, and unto all Israel, that are near, and that are far off, through all the countries whither thou hast driven them, because of their trespass that they have trespassed against thee."

Amos 9:7-9 "⁷Are ye not as children of the Ethiopians unto me, O children of Israel? saith the LORD. Have not I brought up Israel out of the land of Egypt? and the Philistines from Caphtor, and the Syrians from Kir? ⁸Behold, the eyes of the Lord GOD are upon the sinful kingdom, and I will destroy it from off the face of the earth; saving that I will not utterly destroy the house of Jacob, saith the LORD. ⁹For, lo, I will command, and I will sift the house of Israel among all nations, like as corn is sifted in a sieve, yet shall not the least grain fall upon the earth."

Zechariah 2:4-7 "⁴And said unto him, Run, speak to this young man, saying, Jerusalem shall be inhabited as towns without walls for the multitude of men and cattle therein: ⁵For I, saith the LORD, will be unto her a wall of fire round about, and will be the glory in the midst of her. [6]Ho, ho, come forth, and flee from the land of the north, saith the Lord: for I have spread you abroad as the four winds of the heaven, saith the Lord. [7]Deliver thyself, O Zion, that dwellest with the daughter of Babylon."

Zechariah 7:11-14 "[11]But they refused to hearken, and pulled away the shoulder, and stopped their ears, that they should not hear. [12]Yea, they made their hearts as an adamant stone, lest they should hear the law, and the words which the Lord of hosts hath sent in his spirit by the former prophets: therefore came a great wrath from the Lord of hosts. [13]Therefore it is come to pass, that as he cried, and they would not hear; so they cried, and I would not hear, saith the Lord of hosts: [14]But I scattered them with a whirlwind among all the nations whom they knew not. Thus the land was desolate after them, that no man passed through nor returned: for they laid the pleasant land desolate."

Jews And Gentiles Being Equal In Christ

Acts 15:6-9 "[6]And the apostles and elders came together for to consider of this matter. [7]And when there had been much disputing, Peter rose up, and said unto them, Men and brethren, ye know how that a good while ago God made choice among us, that the Gentiles by my mouth should hear the word of the gospel, and believe. [8]And God, which knoweth the hearts, bare them witness, giving them the Holy Ghost, even as he did unto us; [9]And put no difference between us and them, purifying their hearts by faith."

Romans 3:21-22 "[21]But now the righteousness of God without the law is manifested, being witnessed by the law and the prophets; [22]Even the righteousness of God which is by faith of Jesus Christ unto all and upon all them that believe: for there is no difference:"

Romans 10:12-13 "[12]For there is no difference between the Jew and the Greek: for the same Lord over all is rich unto all that call upon him. [13]For whosoever shall call upon the name of the Lord shall be saved."

1 Corinthians 12:12-13 "[12]For as the body is one, and hath many members, and all the members of that one body, being many, are one body: so also is Christ. [13]For by one Spirit are we all baptized into one body, whether we be Jews or Gentiles, whether we be bond or free; and have been all made to drink into one Spirit."

Galatians 3:27-29 "[27]For as many of you as have been baptized into Christ have put on Christ. [28]There is neither Jew nor Greek, there is neither bond nor free, there is neither male nor female: for ye are all one in Christ Jesus. [29]And if ye be Christ's, then are ye Abraham's seed, and heirs according to the promise."

Colossians 3:8-11 "[8]But now ye also put off all these; anger, wrath, malice, blasphemy, filthy communication out of your mouth. [9]Lie not one to another, seeing that ye have put off the old man with his deeds; [10]And have put on the new man, which is renewed in knowledge after the image of him that created him: [11]Where there is neither Greek nor Jew, circumcision nor uncircumcision, Barbarian, Scythian, bond nor free: but Christ is all, and in all."

Jews Being Under Sin

Romans 3:9-12 "[9]What then? are we better than they? No, in no wise: for we have before proved both Jews and Gentiles, that they are all under sin; [10]As it is written, There is none righteous, no, not one: [11]There is none that understandeth, there is none that seeketh after God. [12]They are all gone out of the way, they are together become unprofitable; there is none that doeth good, no, not one."

The Fate Of Israel

Zechariah 12:1-14 "[1]The burden of the word of the Lord for Israel, saith the Lord, which stretcheth forth the heavens, and layeth the foundation of the earth, and formeth the spirit of man within him. [2]Behold, I will make Jerusalem a cup of trembling unto all the people round about, when they shall be in the siege both against Judah and against Jerusalem. [3]And in that day will I make Jerusalem a burdensome stone for all people: all that burden themselves with it shall be cut in pieces, though all the people of the earth be gathered together against it. [4]In that day, saith the Lord, I will smite every horse with astonishment, and his rider with madness: and I will open mine eyes upon the house of Judah, and will smite every horse of the people with blindness. [5]And the governors of Judah shall say in their heart, The inhabitants of

Jerusalem shall be my strength in the LORD of hosts their God. [6]In that day will I make the governors of Judah like an hearth of fire among the wood, and like a torch of fire in a sheaf; and they shall devour all the people round about, on the right hand and on the left: and Jerusalem shall be inhabited again in her own place, even in Jerusalem. [7]The LORD also shall save the tents of Judah first, that the glory of the house of David and the glory of the inhabitants of Jerusalem do not magnify themselves against Judah. [8]In that day shall the LORD defend the inhabitants of Jerusalem; and he that is feeble among them at that day shall be as David; and the house of David shall be as God, as the angel of the LORD before them. [9]And it shall come to pass in that day, that I will seek to destroy all the nations that come against Jerusalem. [10]And I will pour upon the house of David, and upon the inhabitants of Jerusalem, the spirit of grace and of supplications: and they shall look upon me whom they have pierced, and they shall mourn for him, as one mourneth for his only son, and shall be in bitterness for him, as one that is in bitterness for his firstborn. [11]In that day shall there be a great mourning in Jerusalem, as the mourning of Hadadrimmon in the valley of Megiddon. [12]And the land shall mourn, every family apart; the family of the house of David apart, and their wives apart; the family of the house of Nathan apart, and their wives apart; [13]The family of the house of Levi apart, and their wives apart; the family of Shimei apart, and their wives apart; [14]All the families that remain, every family apart, and their wives apart."

The Lord Being A Father To Israel
Jeremiah 31:7-9 "[7]For thus saith the LORD; Sing with gladness for Jacob, and shout among the chief of the nations: publish ye, praise ye, and say, O LORD, save thy people, the remnant of Israel. [8]Behold, I will bring them from the north country, and gather them from the coasts of the earth, and with them the blind and the lame, the woman with child and her that travaileth with child together: a great company shall return thither. [9]They shall come with weeping, and with supplications will I lead them: I will cause them to walk by the rivers of waters in a straight way, wherein they shall not stumble: for I am a father to Israel, and Ephraim is my firstborn."

The Lord Being The Creator Of Israel
Isaiah 43:1 "But now thus saith the LORD that created thee, O Jacob, and he that formed thee, O Israel, Fear not: for I have redeemed thee, I have called thee by thy name; thou art mine."

Isaiah 43:14-15 "[14]Thus saith the LORD, your redeemer, the Holy One of Israel; For your sake I have sent to Babylon, and have brought down all their nobles, and the Chaldeans, whose cry is in the ships. [15]I am the LORD, your Holy One, the creator of Israel, your King."

Isaiah 45:11 "Thus saith the LORD, the Holy One of Israel, and his Maker, Ask me of things to come concerning my sons, and concerning the work of my hands command ye me."

Isaiah 54:5 "For thy Maker is thine husband; the LORD of hosts is his name; and thy Redeemer the Holy One of Israel; The God of the whole earth shall he be called."

The Lord Being The Hope Of Israel
Psalm 130:7-8 "[7]Let Israel hope in the LORD: for with the LORD there is mercy, and with him is plenteous redemption. [8]And he shall redeem Israel from all his iniquities."

Jeremiah 17:13 "O LORD, the hope of Israel, all that forsake thee shall be ashamed, and they that depart from me shall be written in the earth, because they have forsaken the LORD, the fountain of living waters."

Joel 3:16 "The LORD also shall roar out of Zion, and utter his voice from Jerusalem; and the heavens and the earth shall shake: but the LORD will be the hope of his people, and the strength of the children of Israel."

The Lord Breaking Israel's Yoke
Leviticus 26:11-13 "[11]And I will set my tabernacle among you: and my soul shall not abhor you. [12]And I will walk among you, and will be your God, and ye shall be my people. [13]I am the LORD your God, which brought you forth out of the land of Egypt, that ye should not be their bondmen; and I have broken the bands of your yoke, and made you go upright."

Ezekiel 34:27-29 "[27]And the tree of the field shall yield her fruit, and the earth shall yield her increase, and they shall be safe in their land, and shall know that I am the LORD, when I have broken the bands of their yoke, and delivered them out of the hand of those that served themselves of them. ²⁸And they shall no more be a prey to the heathen, neither shall the beast of the land devour them; but they shall dwell safely, and none shall make them afraid. ²⁹And I will raise up for them a plant of renown, and they shall be no more consumed with hunger in the land, neither bear the shame of the heathen any more."

The Lord Choosing Israel

Deuteronomy 4:35-38 "³⁵Unto thee it was shewed, that thou mightest know that the LORD he is God; there is none else beside him. ³⁶Out of heaven he made thee to hear his voice, that he might instruct thee: and upon earth he shewed thee his great fire; and thou heardest his words out of the midst of the fire. ³⁷And because he loved thy fathers, therefore he chose their seed after them, and brought thee out in his sight with his mighty power out of Egypt; ³⁸To drive out nations from before thee greater and mightier than thou art, to bring thee in, to give thee their land for an inheritance, as it is this day."

Deuteronomy 7:6-8 "⁶For thou art an holy people unto the LORD thy God: the LORD thy God hath chosen thee to be a special people unto himself, above all people that are upon the face of the earth. ⁷The LORD did not set his love upon you, nor choose you, because ye were more in number than any people; for ye were the fewest of all people: ⁸But because the LORD loved you, and because he would keep the oath which he had sworn unto your fathers, hath the LORD brought you out with a mighty hand, and redeemed you out of the house of bondmen, from the hand of Pharaoh king of Egypt."

1 Chronicles 28:2-7 "²Then David the king stood up upon his feet, and said, Hear me, my brethren, and my people: As for me, I had in mine heart to build an house of rest for the ark of the covenant of the LORD, and for the footstool of our God, and had made ready for the building: ³But God said unto me, Thou shalt not build an house for my name, because thou hast been a man of war, and hast shed blood. ⁴Howbeit the LORD God of Israel chose me before all the house of my father to be king over Israel for ever: for he hath chosen Judah to be the ruler; and of the house of Judah, the house of my father; and among the sons of my father he liked me to make me king over all Israel: ⁵And of all my sons, (for the LORD hath given me many sons,) he hath chosen Solomon my son to sit upon the throne of the kingdom of the LORD over Israel. ⁶And he said unto me, Solomon thy son, he shall build my house and my courts: for I have chosen him to be my son, and I will be his father. ⁷Moreover I will establish his kingdom for ever, if he be constant to do my commandments and my judgments, as at this day."

Psalm 105:4-6 "⁴Seek the LORD, and his strength: seek his face evermore. ⁵Remember his marvellous works that he hath done; his wonders, and the judgments of his mouth; ⁶O ye seed of Abraham his servant, ye children of Jacob his chosen."

Psalm 132:13-15 "¹³For the LORD hath chosen Zion; he hath desired it for his habitation. ¹⁴This is my rest for ever: here will I dwell; for I have desired it. ¹⁵I will abundantly bless her provision: I will satisfy her poor with bread."

Isaiah 41:8-10 "⁸But thou, Israel, art my servant, Jacob whom I have chosen, the seed of Abraham my friend. ⁹Thou whom I have taken from the ends of the earth, and called thee from the chief men thereof, and said unto thee, Thou art my servant; I have chosen thee, and not cast thee away. ¹⁰Fear thou not; for I am with thee: be not dismayed; for I am thy God: I will strengthen thee; yea, I will help thee; yea, I will uphold thee with the right hand of my righteousness."

Isaiah 43:16-21 "¹⁶Thus saith the LORD, which maketh a way in the sea, and a path in the mighty waters; ¹⁷Which bringeth forth the chariot and horse, the army and the power; they shall lie down together, they shall not rise: they are extinct, they are quenched as tow. ¹⁸Remember ye not the former things, neither consider the things of old. ¹⁹Behold, I will do a new thing; now it shall spring forth; shall ye not know it? I will even make a way in the wilderness, and rivers in the desert. ²⁰The beast of the field shall honour me, the dragons and the owls: because I give waters in the wilderness, and rivers in the desert, to give drink to my people, my chosen. ²¹This people have I formed for myself; they shall shew forth my praise."

Isaiah 44:1-2 "¹Yet now hear, O Jacob my servant; and Israel, whom I have chosen: ²Thus saith the LORD that made thee, and formed thee from the womb, which will help thee; Fear not, O Jacob, my servant; and thou, Jesurun, whom I have chosen."

Isaiah 49:7 "Thus saith the LORD, the Redeemer of Israel, and his Holy One, to him whom man despiseth, to him whom the nation abhorreth, to a servant of rulers, Kings shall see and arise, princes also shall worship, because of the LORD that is faithful, and the Holy One of Israel, and he shall choose thee."

The Lord Not Destroying Israel

Isaiah 54:5-10 "⁵For thy Maker is thine husband; the LORD of hosts is his name; and thy Redeemer the Holy One of Israel; The God of the whole earth shall he be called. ⁶For the LORD hath called thee as a woman forsaken and grieved in spirit, and a wife of youth, when thou wast refused, saith thy God. ⁷For a small moment have I forsaken thee; but with great mercies will I gather thee. ⁸In a little wrath I hid my face from thee for a moment; but with everlasting kindness will I have mercy on thee, saith the LORD thy Redeemer. ⁹For this is as the waters of Noah unto me: for as I have sworn that the waters of Noah should no more go over the earth; so have I sworn that I would not be wroth with thee, nor rebuke thee. ¹⁰For the mountains shall depart, and the hills be removed; but my kindness shall not depart from thee, neither shall the covenant of my peace be removed, saith the LORD that hath mercy on thee."

Jeremiah 5:15-18 "¹⁵Lo, I will bring a nation upon you from far, O house of Israel, saith the LORD: it is a mighty nation, it is an ancient nation, a nation whose language thou knowest not, neither understandest what they say. ¹⁶Their quiver is as an open sepulchre, they are all mighty men. ¹⁷And they shall eat up thine harvest, and thy bread, which thy sons and thy daughters should eat: they shall eat up thy flocks and thine herds: they shall eat up thy vines and thy fig trees: they shall impoverish thy fenced cities, wherein thou trustedst, with the sword. ¹⁸Nevertheless in those days, saith the LORD, I will not make a full end with you."

Jeremiah 30:10-11 "¹⁰Therefore fear thou not, O my servant Jacob, saith the LORD; neither be dismayed, O Israel: for, lo, I will save thee from afar, and thy seed from the land of their captivity; and Jacob shall return, and shall be in rest, and be quiet, and none shall make him afraid. ¹¹For I am with thee, saith the LORD, to save thee: though I make a full end of all nations whither I have scattered thee, yet will I not make a full end of thee: but I will correct thee in measure, and will not leave thee altogether unpunished."

Jeremiah 46:28 "Fear thou not, O Jacob my servant, saith the LORD: for I am with thee; for I will make a full end of all the nations whither I have driven thee: but I will not make a full end of thee, but correct thee in measure; yet will I not leave thee wholly unpunished."

Amos 9:7-8 "⁷Are ye not as children of the Ethiopians unto me, O children of Israel? saith the LORD. Have not I brought up Israel out of the land of Egypt? and the Philistines from Caphtor, and the Syrians from Kir? ⁸Behold, the eyes of the Lord GOD are upon the sinful kingdom, and I will destroy it from off the face of the earth; saving that I will not utterly destroy the house of Jacob, saith the LORD."

The Lord Redeeming Israel

Deuteronomy 7:6-8 "⁶For thou art an holy people unto the LORD thy God: the LORD thy God hath chosen thee to be a special people unto himself, above all people that are upon the face of the earth. ⁷The LORD did not set his love upon you, nor choose you, because ye were more in number than any people; for ye were the fewest of all people: ⁸But because the LORD loved you, and because he would keep the oath which he had sworn unto your fathers, hath the LORD brought you out with a mighty hand, and redeemed you out of the house of bondmen, from the hand of Pharaoh king of Egypt."

Deuteronomy 9:26 "I prayed therefore unto the LORD, and said, O Lord GOD, destroy not thy people and thine inheritance, which thou hast redeemed through thy greatness, which thou hast brought forth out of Egypt with a mighty hand."

Deuteronomy 13:5 "And that prophet, or that dreamer of dreams, shall be put to death; because he hath spoken to turn you away from the LORD your God, which brought you out of the land of Egypt, and redeemed you out of the house of bondage, to thrust thee out of the way which the LORD thy God commanded thee to walk in. So shalt thou put the evil away from the midst of thee."

Deuteronomy 24:17-18 "¹⁷Thou shalt not pervert the judgment of the stranger, nor of the fatherless; nor take a widow's raiment to pledge: ¹⁸But thou shalt remember that thou wast a bondman in Egypt, and the LORD thy God redeemed thee thence: therefore I command thee to do this thing."

Psalm 111:4-9 "⁴He hath made his wonderful works to be remembered: the LORD is gracious and full of compassion. ⁵He hath given meat unto them that fear him: he will ever be mindful of his covenant. ⁶He hath shewed his people the power of his works, that he may give them the heritage of the heathen. ⁷The works of his hands are verity and judgment; all his commandments are sure. ⁸They stand fast for ever and ever, and are done in truth and uprightness. ⁹He sent redemption unto his people: he hath commanded his covenant for ever: holy and reverend is his name."

Psalm 130:7-8 "⁷Let Israel hope in the LORD: for with the LORD there is mercy, and with him is plenteous redemption. ⁸And he shall redeem Israel from all his iniquities."

Psalm 136:1-24 "¹O give thanks unto the LORD; for he is good: for his mercy endureth for ever. ²O give thanks unto the God of gods: for his mercy endureth for ever. ³O give thanks to the Lord of lords: for his mercy endureth for ever. ⁴To him who alone doeth great wonders: for his mercy endureth for ever. ⁵To him that by wisdom made the heavens: for his mercy endureth for ever. ⁶To him that stretched out the earth above the waters: for his mercy endureth for ever. ⁷To him that made great lights: for his mercy endureth for ever: ⁸The sun to rule by day: for his mercy endureth for ever: ⁹The moon and stars to rule by night: for his mercy endureth for ever. ¹⁰To him that smote Egypt in their firstborn: for his mercy endureth for ever: ¹¹And brought out Israel from among them: for his mercy endureth for ever: ¹²With a strong hand, and with a stretched out arm: for his mercy endureth for ever. ¹³To him which divided the Red sea into parts: for his mercy endureth for ever: ¹⁴And made Israel to pass through the midst of it: for his mercy endureth for ever: ¹⁵But overthrew Pharaoh and his host in the Red sea: for his mercy endureth for ever. ¹⁶To him which led his people through the wilderness: for his mercy endureth for ever. ¹⁷To him which smote great kings: for his mercy endureth for ever: ¹⁸And slew famous kings: for his mercy endureth for ever: ¹⁹Sihon king of the Amorites: for his mercy endureth for ever: ²⁰And Og the king of Bashan: for his mercy endureth for ever: ²¹And gave their land for an heritage: for his mercy endureth for ever: ²²Even an heritage unto Israel his servant: for his mercy endureth for ever. ²³Who remembered us in our low estate: for his mercy endureth for ever: ²⁴And hath redeemed us from our enemies: for his mercy endureth for ever."

Isaiah 43:1 "But now thus saith the LORD that created thee, O Jacob, and he that formed thee, O Israel, Fear not: for I have redeemed thee, I have called thee by thy name; thou art mine."

Isaiah 48:20 "Go ye forth of Babylon, flee ye from the Chaldeans, with a voice of singing declare ye, tell this, utter it even to the end of the earth; say ye, The LORD hath redeemed his servant Jacob."

Isaiah 59:15-20 "¹⁵Yea, truth faileth; and he that departeth from evil maketh himself a prey: and the LORD saw it, and it displeased him that there was no judgment. ¹⁶And he saw that there was no man, and wondered that there was no intercessor: therefore his arm brought salvation unto him; and his righteousness, it sustained him. ¹⁷For he put on righteousness as a breastplate, and an helmet of salvation upon his head; and he put on the garments of vengeance for clothing, and was clad with zeal as a cloke. ¹⁸According to their deeds, accordingly he will repay, fury to his adversaries, recompence to his enemies; to the islands he will repay recompence. ¹⁹So shall they fear the name of the LORD from the west, and his glory from the rising of the sun. When the enemy shall come in like a flood, the Spirit of the LORD shall lift up a standard against him. ²⁰And the Redeemer shall come to Zion, and unto them that turn from transgression in Jacob, saith the LORD."

Isaiah 63:7-9 "⁷I will mention the lovingkindnesses of the LORD, and the praises of the LORD, according to all that the LORD hath bestowed on us, and the great goodness toward the house of Israel, which he hath bestowed on them according to his mercies, and according to the multitude of his lovingkindnesses. 8For he said, Surely they are my people, children that will not lie: so he was their Saviour. 9In all their affliction he was afflicted, and the angel of his presence saved them: in his love and in his pity he redeemed them; and he bare them, and carried them all the days of old."

Jeremiah 31:10-11 "10Hear the word of the LORD, O ye nations, and declare it in the isles afar off, and say, He that scattered Israel will gather him, and keep him, as a shepherd doth his flock. 11For the LORD hath redeemed Jacob, and ransomed him from the hand of him that was stronger than he."

Luke 1:68 "Blessed be the Lord God of Israel; for he hath visited and redeemed his people,"

The Lord Saving Israel

Psalm 14:7 "Oh that the salvation of Israel were come out of Zion! when the LORD bringeth back the captivity of his people, Jacob shall rejoice, and Israel shall be glad."

Psalm 53:6 "Oh that the salvation of Israel were come out of Zion! When God bringeth back the captivity of his people, Jacob shall rejoice, and Israel shall be glad."

Jeremiah 23:5-6 "5Behold, the days come, saith the LORD, that I will raise unto David a righteous Branch, and a King shall reign and prosper, and shall execute judgment and justice in the earth. 6In his days Judah shall be saved, and Israel shall dwell safely: and this is his name whereby he shall be called, THE LORD OUR RIGHTEOUSNESS."

Jeremiah 30:1-11 "1The word that came to Jeremiah from the LORD, saying, 2Thus speaketh the LORD God of Israel, saying, Write thee all the words that I have spoken unto thee in a book. 3For, lo, the days come, saith the LORD, that I will bring again the captivity of my people Israel and Judah, saith the LORD: and I will cause them to return to the land that I gave to their fathers, and they shall possess it. 4And these are the words that the LORD spake concerning Israel and concerning Judah. 5For thus saith the LORD; We have heard a voice of trembling, of fear, and not of peace. 6Ask ye now, and see whether a man doth travail with child? wherefore do I see every man with his hands on his loins, as a woman in travail, and all faces are turned into paleness? 7Alas! for that day is great, so that none is like it: it is even the time of Jacob's trouble; but he shall be saved out of it. 8For it shall come to pass in that day, saith the LORD of hosts, that I will break his yoke from off thy neck, and will burst thy bonds, and strangers shall no more serve themselves of him: 9But they shall serve the LORD their God, and David their king, whom I will raise up unto them. 10Therefore fear thou not, O my servant Jacob, saith the LORD; neither be dismayed, O Israel: for, lo, I will save thee from afar, and thy seed from the land of their captivity; and Jacob shall return, and shall be in rest, and be quiet, and none shall make him afraid. 11For I am with thee, saith the LORD, to save thee: though I make a full end of all nations whither I have scattered thee, yet will I not make a full end of thee: but I will correct thee in measure, and will not leave thee altogether unpunished."

Jeremiah 33:14-16 "14Behold, the days come, saith the LORD, that I will perform that good thing which I have promised unto the house of Israel and to the house of Judah. 15In those days, and at that time, will I cause the Branch of righteousness to grow up unto David; and he shall execute judgment and righteousness in the land. 16In those days shall Judah be saved, and Jerusalem shall dwell safely: and this is the name wherewith she shall be called, The LORD our righteousness."

Zechariah 12:1-10 "1The burden of the word of the LORD for Israel, saith the LORD, which stretcheth forth the heavens, and layeth the foundation of the earth, and formeth the spirit of man within him. 2Behold, I will make Jerusalem a cup of trembling unto all the people round about, when they shall be in the siege both against Judah and against Jerusalem. 3And in that day will I make Jerusalem a burdensome stone for all people: all that burden themselves with it shall be cut in pieces, though all the people of the earth be gathered together against it. 4In that day, saith the LORD, I will smite every horse with astonishment, and his rider with madness: and I will open mine eyes upon the house of Judah, and will smite every horse of the people with blindness. 5And the governors of Judah shall say in their heart, The inhabitants of Jerusalem shall be my strength in the LORD of hosts their God. [6]In that day will I make the governors of Judah like an hearth of fire among the wood, and like a torch of fire in a sheaf; and they shall devour all the people round about, on the right hand and on the left: and Jerusalem shall be inhabited again in her own place, even in Jerusalem. [7]The LORD also shall save the tents of Judah first, that the glory of the house of David and the glory of the inhabitants of Jerusalem do not magnify themselves against Judah. [8]In that day shall the LORD defend the inhabitants of Jerusalem; and he that is feeble among them at that day shall be as David; and the house of David shall be as God, as the angel of the LORD before them. [9]And it shall come to pass in that day, that I will seek to destroy all the nations that come against Jerusalem. [10]And I will pour upon the house of David, and upon the inhabitants of Jerusalem, the spirit of grace and of supplications: and they shall look upon me whom they have pierced, and they shall mourn for him, as one mourneth for his only son, and shall be in bitterness for him, as one that is in bitterness for his firstborn."

Luke 1:68-71 "[68]Blessed be the Lord God of Israel; for he hath visited and redeemed his people, [69]And hath raised up an horn of salvation for us in the house of his servant David; [70]As he spake by the mouth of his holy prophets, which have been since the world began: [71]That we should be saved from our enemies, and from the hand of all that hate us;"

Romans 11:26 "And so all Israel shall be saved: as it is written, There shall come out of Sion the Deliverer, and shall turn away ungodliness from Jacob:"

The Lord Separating Israel
From All Other People

Leviticus 20:22-26 "[22]Ye shall therefore keep all my statutes, and all my judgments, and do them: that the land, whither I bring you to dwell therein, spue you not out. [23]And ye shall not walk in the manners of the nation, which I cast out before you: for they committed all these things, and therefore I abhorred them. [24]But I have said unto you, Ye shall inherit their land, and I will give it unto you to possess it, a land that floweth with milk and honey: I am the LORD your God, which have separated you from other people. [25]Ye

shall therefore put difference between clean beasts and unclean, and between unclean fowls and clean: and ye shall not make your souls abominable by beast, or by fowl, or by any manner of living thing that creepeth on the ground, which I have separated from you as unclean. [26]And ye shall be holy unto me: for I the LORD am holy, and have severed you from other people, that ye should be mine."

1 Kings 8:51-53 "[51]For they be thy people, and thine inheritance, which thou broughtest forth out of Egypt, from the midst of the furnace of iron: [52]That thine eyes may be open unto the supplication of thy servant, and unto the supplication of thy people Israel, to hearken unto them in all that they call for unto thee. [53]For thou didst separate them from among all the people of the earth, to be thine inheritance, as thou spakest by the hand of Moses thy servant, when thou broughtest our fathers out of Egypt, O Lord GOD."

The Remnant Of Israel

1 Kings 19:18 "Yet I have left me seven thousand in Israel, all the knees which have not bowed unto Baal, and every mouth which hath not kissed him."

Ezra 9:7-9 "[7]Since the days of our fathers have we been in a great trespass unto this day; and for our iniquities have we, our kings, and our priests, been delivered into the hand of the kings of the lands, to the sword, to captivity, and to a spoil, and to confusion of face, as it is this day. [8]And now for a little space grace hath been shewed from the LORD our God, to leave us a remnant to escape, and to give us a nail in his holy place, that our God may lighten our eyes, and give us a little reviving in our bondage. [9]For we were bondmen; yet our God hath not forsaken us in our bondage, but hath extended mercy unto us in the sight of the kings of Persia, to give us a reviving, to set up the house of our God, and to repair the desolations thereof, and to give us a wall in Judah and in Jerusalem."

Nehemiah 1:2-3 "[2]That Hanani, one of my brethren, came, he and certain men of Judah; and I asked them concerning the Jews that had escaped, which were left of the captivity, and concerning Jerusalem. [3]And they said unto me, The remnant that are left of the captivity there in the province are in great affliction and reproach: the wall of Jerusalem also is broken down, and the gates thereof are burned with fire."

Isaiah 10:20-23 "²⁰And it shall come to pass in that day, that the remnant of Israel, and such as are escaped of the house of Jacob, shall no more again stay upon him that smote them; but shall stay upon the LORD, the Holy One of Israel, in truth. ²¹The remnant shall return, even the remnant of Jacob, unto the mighty God. ²²For though thy people Israel be as the sand of the sea, yet a remnant of them shall return: the consumption decreed shall overflow with righteousness. ²³For the Lord GOD of hosts shall make a consumption, even determined, in the midst of all the land."

Jeremiah 23:1-4 "¹Woe be unto the pastors that destroy and scatter the sheep of my pasture! saith the LORD. ²Therefore thus saith the LORD God of Israel against the pastors that feed my people; Ye have scattered my flock, and driven them away, and have not visited them: behold, I will visit upon you the evil of your doings, saith the LORD. ³And I will gather the remnant of my flock out of all countries whither I have driven them, and will bring them again to their folds; and they shall be fruitful and increase. ⁴And I will set up shepherds over them which shall feed them: and they shall fear no more, nor be dismayed, neither shall they be lacking, saith the LORD."

Jeremiah 31:7-9 "⁷For thus saith the LORD; Sing with gladness for Jacob, and shout among the chief of the nations: publish ye, praise ye, and say, O LORD, save thy people, the remnant of Israel. ⁸Behold, I will bring them from the north country, and gather them from the coasts of the earth, and with them the blind and the lame, the woman with child and her that travaileth with child together: a great company shall return thither. ⁹They shall come with weeping, and with supplications will I lead them: I will cause them to walk by the rivers of waters in a straight way, wherein they shall not stumble: for I am a father to Israel, and Ephraim is my firstborn."

Joel 2:32 "And it shall come to pass, that whosoever shall call on the name of the LORD shall be delivered: for in mount Zion and in Jerusalem shall be deliverance, as the LORD hath said, and in the remnant whom the LORD shall call."

Micah 5:7-9 "⁷And the remnant of Jacob shall be in the midst of many people as a dew from the LORD, as the showers upon the grass, that tarrieth not for man, nor waiteth for the sons of men. ⁸And the remnant of Jacob shall be among the Gentiles in the midst of many people as a lion among the beasts of the forest, as a young lion among the flocks of sheep: who, if he go through, both treadeth down, and teareth in pieces, and none can deliver. ⁹Thine hand shall be lifted up upon thine adversaries, and all thine enemies shall be cut off."

Zephaniah 3:13 "The remnant of Israel shall not do iniquity, nor speak lies; neither shall a deceitful tongue be found in their mouth: for they shall feed and lie down, and none shall make them afraid."

Romans 9:27 "Esaias also crieth concerning Israel, Though the number of the children of Israel be as the sand of the sea, a remnant shall be saved:"

Romans 11:1-5 "¹I say then, Hath God cast away his people? God forbid. For I also am an Israelite, of the seed of Abraham, of the tribe of Benjamin. ²God hath not cast away his people which he foreknew. Wot ye not what the scripture saith of Elias? how he maketh intercession to God against Israel, saying, ³Lord, they have killed thy prophets, and digged down thine altars; and I am left alone, and they seek my life. ⁴But what saith the answer of God unto him? I have reserved to myself seven thousand men, who have not bowed the knee to the image of Baal. ⁵Even so then at this present time also there is a remnant according to the election of grace."

The Salvation Of Israel
Psalm 14:7 "Oh that the salvation of Israel were come out of Zion! when the LORD bringeth back the captivity of his people, Jacob shall rejoice, and Israel shall be glad."

Psalm 53:6 "Oh that the salvation of Israel were come out of Zion! When God bringeth back the captivity of his people, Jacob shall rejoice, and Israel shall be glad."

Jeremiah 3:23 "Truly in vain is salvation hoped for from the hills, and from the multitude of mountains: truly in the LORD our God is the salvation of Israel."

Romans 11:1-32 "[1]I say then, Hath God cast away his people? God forbid. For I also am an Israelite, of the seed of Abraham, of the tribe of Benjamin. [2]God hath not cast away his people which he foreknew. Wot ye not what the scripture saith of Elias? how he maketh intercession to God against Israel, saying, [3]Lord, they have killed thy prophets, and digged down thine altars; and I am left alone, and they seek my life. [4]But what saith the answer of God unto him? I have reserved to myself seven thousand men, who have not bowed the knee to the image of Baal. [5]Even so then at this present time also there is a remnant according to the election of grace. [6]And if by grace, then is it no more of works: otherwise grace is no more grace. But if it be of works, then is it no more grace: otherwise work is no more work. [7]What then? Israel hath not obtained that which he seeketh for; but the election hath obtained it, and the rest were blinded [8](According as it is written, God hath given them the spirit of slumber, eyes that they should not see, and ears that they should not hear;) unto this day. [9]And David saith, Let their table be made a snare, and a trap, and a stumbling block, and a recompence unto them: [10]Let their eyes be darkened, that they may not see, and bow down their back alway. [11]I say then, Have they stumbled that they should fall? God forbid: but rather through their fall salvation is come unto the Gentiles, for to provoke them to jealousy. [12]Now if the fall of them be the riches of the world, and the diminishing of them the riches of the Gentiles; how much more their fulness? [13]For I speak to you Gentiles, inasmuch as I am the apostle of the Gentiles, I magnify mine office: [14]If by any means I may provoke to emulation them which are my flesh, and might save some of them. [15]For if the casting away of them be the reconciling of the world, what shall the receiving of them be, but life from the dead? [16]For if the firstfruit be holy, the lump is also holy: and if the root be holy, so are the branches. [17]And if some of the branches be broken off, and thou, being a wild olive tree, wert graffed in among them, and with them partakest of the root and fatness of the olive tree; [18]Boast not against the branches. But if thou boast, thou bearest not the root, but the root thee. [19]Thou wilt say then, The branches were broken off, that I might be graffed in. [20]Well; because of unbelief they were broken off, and thou standest by faith. Be not highminded, but fear: [21]For if God spared not the natural branches, take heed lest he also spare not thee. [22]Behold therefore the goodness and severity of God: on them which fell, severity; but toward thee, goodness, if thou continue in his goodness: otherwise thou also shalt be cut off. [23]And they also, if they abide not still in unbelief, shall be graffed in: for God is able to graff them in again. [24]For if thou wert cut out of the olive tree which is wild by nature, and wert graffed contrary to nature into a good olive tree: how much more shall these, which be the natural branches, be graffed into their own olive tree? [25]For I would not, brethren, that ye should be ignorant of this mystery, lest ye should be wise in your own conceits; that blindness in part is happened to Israel, until the fulness of the Gentiles be come in. [26]And so all Israel shall be saved: as it is written, There shall come out of Sion the Deliverer, and shall turn away ungodliness from Jacob: [27]For this is my covenant unto them, when I shall take away their sins. [28]As concerning the gospel, they are enemies for your sakes: but as touching the election, they are beloved for the fathers' sakes. [29]For the gifts and calling of God are without repentance. [30]For as ye in times past have not believed God, yet have now obtained mercy through their unbelief: [31]Even so have these also now not believed, that through your mercy they also may obtain mercy. [32]For God hath concluded them all in unbelief, that he might have mercy upon all."

What Israel Shall Know

Isaiah 49:22-26 "[22]Thus saith the Lord GOD, Behold, I will lift up mine hand to the Gentiles, and set up my standard to the people: and they shall bring thy sons in their arms, and thy daughters shall be carried upon their shoulders. [23]And kings shall be thy nursing fathers, and their queens thy nursing mothers: they shall bow down to thee with their face toward the earth, and lick up the dust of thy feet; and thou shalt know that I am the LORD: for they shall not be ashamed that wait for me. [24]Shall the prey be taken from the mighty, or the lawful captive delivered? [25]But thus saith the LORD, Even the captives of the mighty shall be taken away, and the prey of the terrible shall be delivered: for I will contend with him that contendeth with thee, and I will save thy children. 26And I will feed them that oppress thee with their own flesh; and they shall be drunken with their own blood, as with sweet wine: and all flesh shall know that I the LORD am thy Saviour and thy Redeemer, the mighty One of Jacob."

Ezekiel 28:24-26 "24And there shall be no more a pricking brier unto the house of Israel, nor any grieving thorn of all that are round about them, that despised them; and they shall know that I am the Lord GOD. 25Thus saith the Lord GOD; When I shall have gathered the house of Israel from the people among whom they are scattered, and shall be sanctified in them in the sight of the heathen, then shall they dwell in their land that I have given to my servant Jacob. 26And they shall dwell safely therein, and shall build houses, and plant vineyards; yea, they shall dwell with confidence, when I have executed judgments upon all those that despise them round about them; and they shall know that I am the LORD their God."

Ezekiel 34:27-31 "27And the tree of the field shall yield her fruit, and the earth shall yield her increase, and they shall be safe in their land, and shall know that I am the LORD, when I have broken the bands of their yoke, and delivered them out of the hand of those that served themselves of them. 28And they shall no more be a prey to the heathen, neither shall the beast of the land devour them; but they shall dwell safely, and none shall make them afraid. 29And I will raise up for them a plant of renown, and they shall be no more consumed with hunger in the land, neither bear the shame of the heathen any more. 30Thus shall they know that I the LORD their God am with them, and that they, even the house of Israel, are my people, saith the Lord GOD. 31And ye my flock, the flock of my pasture, are men, and I am your God, saith the Lord GOD."

Ezekiel 36:8-11 "8But ye, O mountains of Israel, ye shall shoot forth your branches, and yield your fruit to my people of Israel; for they are at hand to come. 9For, behold, I am for you, and I will turn unto you, and ye shall be tilled and sown: 10And I will multiply men upon you, all the house of Israel, even all of it: and the cities shall be inhabited, and the wastes shall be builded: 11And I will multiply upon you man and beast; and they shall increase and bring fruit: and I will settle you

after your old estates, and will do better unto you than at your beginnings: and ye shall know that I am the LORD."

Ezekiel 37:11-14 "11Then he said unto me, Son of man, these bones are the whole house of Israel: behold, they say, Our bones are dried, and our hope is lost: we are cut off for our parts. 12Therefore prophesy and say unto them, Thus saith the Lord GOD; Behold, O my people, I will open your graves, and cause you to come up out of your graves, and bring you into the land of Israel. 13And ye shall know that I am the LORD, when I have opened your graves, O my people, and brought you up out of your graves, 14And shall put my spirit in you, and ye shall live, and I shall place you in your own land: then shall ye know that I the LORD have spoken it, and performed it, saith the LORD."

Ezekiel 39:17-22 "17And, thou son of man, thus saith the Lord GOD; Speak unto every feathered fowl, and to every beast of the field, Assemble yourselves, and come; gather yourselves on every side to my sacrifice that I do sacrifice for you, even a great sacrifice upon the mountains of Israel, that ye may eat flesh, and drink blood. 18Ye shall eat the flesh of the mighty, and drink the blood of the princes of the earth, of rams, of lambs, and of goats, of bullocks, all of them fatlings of Bashan. 19And ye shall eat fat till ye be full, and drink blood till ye be drunken, of my sacrifice which I have sacrificed for you. 20Thus ye shall be filled at my table with horses and chariots, with mighty men, and with all men of war, saith the Lord GOD. 21And I will set my glory among the heathen, and all the heathen shall see my judgment that I have executed, and my hand that I have laid upon them. 22So the house of Israel shall know that I am the LORD their God from that day and forward."

Ezekiel 39:25-28 "25Therefore thus saith the Lord GOD; Now will I bring again the captivity of Jacob, and have mercy upon the whole house of Israel, and will be jealous for my holy name; 26After that they have borne their shame, and all their trespasses whereby they have trespassed against me, when they dwelt safely in their land, and none made them afraid. 27When I have brought them again from the people, and gathered them out of their enemies' lands, and am sanctified in them in the sight of many nations; [28]Then shall they know that I am the LORD their God, which cause them to be led into captivity among the heathen: but I have gathered them unto their own land, and have left none of them any more there."

Joel 2:23-27 "[23]Be glad then, ye children of Zion, and rejoice in the LORD your God: for he hath given you the former rain moderately, and he will cause to come down for you the rain, the former rain, and the latter rain in the first month. [24]And the floors shall be full of wheat, and the fats shall overflow with wine and oil. [25]And I will restore to you the years that the locust hath eaten, the cankerworm, and the caterpiller, and the palmerworm, my great army which I sent among you. [26]And ye shall eat in plenty, and be satisfied, and praise the name of the LORD your God, that hath dealt wondrously with you: and my people shall never be ashamed. [27]And ye shall know that I am in the midst of Israel, and that I am the LORD your God, and none else: and my people shall never be ashamed."

Joel 3:16-17 "[16]The LORD also shall roar out of Zion, and utter his voice from Jerusalem; and the heavens and the earth shall shake: but the LORD will be the hope of his people, and the strength of the children of Israel. [17]So shall ye know that I am the LORD your God dwelling in Zion, my holy mountain: then shall Jerusalem be holy, and there shall no strangers pass through her any more."

What Israelites Are

Exodus 19:3-5 "[3]And Moses went up unto God, and the LORD called unto him out of the mountain, saying, Thus shalt thou say to the house of Jacob, and tell the children of Israel; [4]Ye have seen what I did unto the Egyptians, and how I bare you on eagles' wings, and brought you unto myself. [5]Now therefore, if ye will obey my voice indeed, and keep my covenant, then ye shall be a peculiar treasure unto me above all people: for all the earth is mine:"

Leviticus 25:55 "For unto me the children of Israel are servants; they are my servants whom I brought forth out of the land of Egypt: I am the LORD your God."

Deuteronomy 4:20 "But the LORD hath taken you, and brought you forth out of the iron furnace, even out of Egypt, to be unto him a people of inheritance, as ye are this day."

Deuteronomy 7:6-8 "[6]For thou art an holy people unto the LORD thy God: the LORD thy God hath chosen thee to be a special people unto himself, above all people that are upon the face of the earth. [7]The LORD did not set his love upon you, nor choose you, because ye were more in number than any people; for ye were the fewest of all people: [8]But because the LORD loved you, and because he would keep the oath which he had sworn unto your fathers, hath the LORD brought you out with a mighty hand, and redeemed you out of the house of bondmen, from the hand of Pharaoh king of Egypt."

Deuteronomy 9:26-29 "[26]I prayed therefore unto the LORD, and said, O Lord GOD, destroy not thy people and thine inheritance, which thou hast redeemed through thy greatness, which thou hast brought forth out of Egypt with a mighty hand. [27]Remember thy servants, Abraham, Isaac, and Jacob; look not unto the stubbornness of this people, nor to their wickedness, nor to their sin: [28]Lest the land whence thou broughtest us out say, Because the LORD was not able to bring them into the land which he promised them, and because he hated them, he hath brought them out to slay them in the wilderness. [29]Yet they are thy people and thine inheritance, which thou broughtest out by thy mighty power and by thy stretched out arm."

Deuteronomy 14:21 "Ye shall not eat of any thing that dieth of itself: thou shalt give it unto the stranger that is in thy gates, that he may eat it; or thou mayest sell it unto an alien: for thou art an holy people unto the LORD thy God. Thou shalt not seethe a kid in his mother's milk."

Deuteronomy 27:9 "And Moses and the priests the Levites spake unto all Israel, saying, Take heed, and hearken, O Israel; this day thou art become the people of the LORD thy God."

Deuteronomy 28:1-10 "[1]And it shall come to pass, if thou shalt hearken diligently unto the voice of the LORD thy God, to observe and to do all his commandments which I command thee this day, that the LORD thy God will set thee on high above all nations of the earth: [2]And all these blessings shall come on thee, and overtake thee, if thou shalt hearken unto the voice of the LORD thy

God. ³Blessed shalt thou be in the city, and blessed shalt thou be in the field. ⁴Blessed shall be the fruit of thy body, and the fruit of thy ground, and the fruit of thy cattle, the increase of thy kine, and the flocks of thy sheep. ⁵Blessed shall be thy basket and thy store. ⁶Blessed shalt thou be when thou comest in, and blessed shalt thou be when thou goest out. ⁷The LORD shall cause thine enemies that rise up against thee to be smitten before thy face: they shall come out against thee one way, and flee before thee seven ways. ⁸The LORD shall command the blessing upon thee in thy storehouses, and in all that thou settest thine hand unto; and he shall bless thee in the land which the LORD thy God giveth thee. ⁹The LORD shall establish thee an holy people unto himself, as he hath sworn unto thee, if thou shalt keep the commandments of the LORD thy God, and walk in his ways. ¹⁰And all people of the earth shall see that thou art called by the name of the LORD; and they shall be afraid of thee."

1 Kings 8:51-53 "⁵¹For they be thy people, and thine inheritance, which thou broughtest forth out of Egypt, from the midst of the furnace of iron: ⁵²That thine eyes may be open unto the supplication of thy servant, and unto the supplication of thy people Israel, to hearken unto them in all that they call for unto thee. ⁵³For thou didst separate them from among all the people of the earth, to be thine inheritance, as thou spakest by the hand of Moses thy servant, when thou broughtest our fathers out of Egypt, O Lord GOD."

1 Chronicles 16:11-13 "¹¹Seek the LORD and his strength, seek his face continually. ¹²Remember his marvellous works that he hath done, his wonders, and the judgments of his mouth; ¹³O ye seed of Israel his servant, ye children of Jacob, his chosen ones."

Nehemiah 1:5-6 "⁵And said, I beseech thee, O LORD God of heaven, the great and terrible God, that keepeth covenant and mercy for them that love him and observe his commandments: ⁶Let thine ear now be attentive, and thine eyes open, that thou mayest hear the prayer of thy servant, which I pray before thee now, day and night, for the children of Israel thy servants, and confess the sins of the children of Israel, which we have sinned against thee: both I and my father's house have sinned."

Psalm 105:4-6 "⁴Seek the LORD, and his strength: seek his face evermore. ⁵Remember his marvellous works that he hath done; his wonders, and the judgments of his mouth; ⁶O ye seed of Abraham his servant, ye children of Jacob his chosen."

Psalm 136:3-22 "³O give thanks to the Lord of lords: for his mercy endureth for ever. ⁴To him who alone doeth great wonders: for his mercy endureth for ever. ⁵To him that by wisdom made the heavens: for his mercy endureth for ever. ⁶To him that stretched out the earth above the waters: for his mercy endureth for ever. ⁷To him that made great lights: for his mercy endureth for ever: ⁸The sun to rule by day: for his mercy endureth for ever: ⁹The moon and stars to rule by night: for his mercy endureth for ever. ¹⁰To him that smote Egypt in their firstborn: for his mercy endureth for ever: ¹¹And brought out Israel from among them: for his mercy endureth for ever: ¹²With a strong hand, and with a stretched out arm: for his mercy endureth for ever. ¹³To him which divided the Red sea into parts: for his mercy endureth for ever: ¹⁴And made Israel to pass through the midst of it: for his mercy endureth for ever: ¹⁵But overthrew Pharaoh and his host in the Red sea: for his mercy endureth for ever. ¹⁶To him which led his people through the wilderness: for his mercy endureth for ever. ¹⁷To him which smote great kings: for his mercy endureth for ever: ¹⁸And slew famous kings: for his mercy endureth for ever: ¹⁹Sihon king of the Amorites: for his mercy endureth for ever: ²⁰And Og the king of Bashan: for his mercy endureth for ever: ²¹And gave their land for an heritage: for his mercy endureth for ever: ²²Even an heritage unto Israel his servant: for his mercy endureth for ever."

Psalm 148:13-14 "¹³Let them praise the name of the LORD: for his name alone is excellent; his glory is above the earth and heaven. ¹⁴He also exalteth the horn of his people, the praise of all his saints; even of the children of Israel, a people near unto him. Praise ye the LORD."

Isaiah 5:7 "For the vineyard of the LORD of hosts is the house of Israel, and the men of Judah his pleasant plant: and he looked for judgment, but behold oppression; for righteousness, but behold a cry."

Isaiah 41:8-10 "8But thou, Israel, art my servant, Jacob whom I have chosen, the seed of Abraham my friend. 9Thou whom I have taken from the ends of the earth, and called thee from the chief men thereof, and said unto thee, Thou art my servant; I have chosen thee, and not cast thee away. 10Fear thou not; for I am with thee: be not dismayed; for I am thy God: I will strengthen thee; yea, I will help thee; yea, I will uphold thee with the right hand of my righteousness."

Isaiah 43:3-10 "3For I am the LORD thy God, the Holy One of Israel, thy Saviour: I gave Egypt for thy ransom, Ethiopia and Seba for thee. 4Since thou wast precious in my sight, thou hast been honourable, and I have loved thee: therefore will I give men for thee, and people for thy life. 5Fear not: for I am with thee: I will bring thy seed from the east, and gather thee from the west; 6I will say to the north, Give up; and to the south, Keep not back: bring my sons from far, and my daughters from the ends of the earth; 7Even every one that is called by my name: for I have created him for my glory, I have formed him; yea, I have made him. 8Bring forth the blind people that have eyes, and the deaf that have ears. 9Let all the nations be gathered together, and let the people be assembled: who among them can declare this, and shew us former things? let them bring forth their witnesses, that they may be justified: or let them hear, and say, It is truth. 10Ye are my witnesses, saith the LORD, and my servant whom I have chosen: that ye may know and believe me, and understand that I am he: before me there was no God formed, neither shall there be after me."

Isaiah 44:1-8 "1Yet now hear, O Jacob my servant; and Israel, whom I have chosen: 2Thus saith the LORD that made thee, and formed thee from the womb, which will help thee; Fear not, O Jacob, my servant; and thou, Jesurun, whom I have chosen. 3For I will pour water upon him that is thirsty, and floods upon the dry ground: I will pour my spirit upon thy seed, and my blessing upon thine offspring: 4And they shall spring up as among the grass, as willows by the water courses. 5One shall say, I am the LORD's; and another shall call himself by the name of Jacob; and another shall subscribe with his hand unto the LORD, and surname himself by the name of Israel. 6Thus saith the LORD the King of Israel, and his redeemer the LORD of hosts; I am the first, and I am the last; and beside me there is no God. 7And who, as I, shall call, and shall declare it, and set it in order for me, since I appointed the ancient people? and the things that are coming, and shall come, let them shew unto them. 8Fear ye not, neither be afraid: have not I told thee from that time, and have declared it? ye are even my witnesses. Is there a God beside me? yea, there is no God; I know not any."

Isaiah 45:3-5 "3And I will give thee the treasures of darkness, and hidden riches of secret places, that thou mayest know that I, the LORD, which call thee by thy name, am the God of Israel. 4For Jacob my servant's sake, and Israel mine elect, I have even called thee by thy name: I have surnamed thee, though thou hast not known me. 5I am the LORD, and there is none else, there is no God beside me: I girded thee, though thou hast not known me:"

Isaiah 48:12 "Hearken unto me, O Jacob and Israel, my called; I am he; I am the first, I also am the last."

Isaiah 48:20 "Go ye forth of Babylon, flee ye from the Chaldeans, with a voice of singing declare ye, tell this, utter it even to the end of the earth; say ye, The LORD hath redeemed his servant Jacob."

Isaiah 49:1-5 "1Listen, O isles, unto me; and hearken, ye people, from far; The LORD hath called me from the womb; from the bowels of my mother hath he made mention of my name. 2And he hath made my mouth like a sharp sword; in the shadow of his hand hath he hid me, and made me a polished shaft; in his quiver hath he hid me; 3And said unto me, Thou art my servant, O Israel, in whom I will be glorified. 4Then I said, I have laboured in vain, I have spent my strength for nought, and in vain: yet surely my judgment is with the LORD, and my work with my God. 5And now, saith the LORD that formed me from the womb to be his servant, to bring Jacob again to him, Though Israel be not gathered, yet shall I be glorious in the eyes of the LORD, and my God shall be my strength."

Isaiah 51:15-16 "15But I am the LORD thy God, that divided the sea, whose waves roared: The LORD of hosts is his name. 16And I have put my words in thy mouth, and I have covered thee in the shadow of mine hand, that I may plant the heavens, and lay the foundations of the earth, and say unto Zion, Thou art my people."

Isaiah 61:1-9 "¹The Spirit of the Lord GOD is upon me; because the LORD hath anointed me to preach good tidings unto the meek; he hath sent me to bind up the brokenhearted, to proclaim liberty to the captives, and the opening of the prison to them that are bound; ²To proclaim the acceptable year of the LORD, and the day of vengeance of our God; to comfort all that mourn; ³To appoint unto them that mourn in Zion, to give unto them beauty for ashes, the oil of joy for mourning, the garment of praise for the spirit of heaviness; that they might be called trees of righteousness, the planting of the LORD, that he might be glorified. ⁴And they shall build the old wastes, they shall raise up the former desolations, and they shall repair the waste cities, the desolations of many generations. ⁵And strangers shall stand and feed your flocks, and the sons of the alien shall be your plowmen and your vinedressers. ⁶But ye shall be named the Priests of the LORD: men shall call you the Ministers of our God: ye shall eat the riches of the Gentiles, and in their glory shall ye boast yourselves. ⁷For your shame ye shall have double; and for confusion they shall rejoice in their portion: therefore in their land they shall possess the double: everlasting joy shall be unto them. ⁸For I the LORD love judgment, I hate robbery for burnt offering; and I will direct their work in truth, and I will make an everlasting covenant with them. ⁹And their seed shall be known among the Gentiles, and their offspring among the people: all that see them shall acknowledge them, that they are the seed which the LORD hath blessed."

Isaiah 63:7-8 "⁷I will mention the lovingkindnesses of the LORD, and the praises of the LORD, according to all that the LORD hath bestowed on us, and the great goodness toward the house of Israel, which he hath bestowed on them according to his mercies, and according to the multitude of his lovingkindnesses. ⁸For he said, Surely they are my people, children that will not lie: so he was their Saviour."

Jeremiah 10:16 "The portion of Jacob is not like them: for he is the former of all things; and Israel is the rod of his inheritance: The LORD of hosts is his name."

Jeremiah 30:10 "Therefore fear thou not, O my servant Jacob, saith the LORD; neither be dismayed, O Israel: for, lo, I will save thee from afar, and thy seed from the land of their captivity; and Jacob shall return, and shall be in rest, and be quiet, and none shall make him afraid."

Jeremiah 46:28 "Fear thou not, O Jacob my servant, saith the LORD: for I am with thee; for I will make a full end of all the nations whither I have driven thee: but I will not make a full end of thee, but correct thee in measure; yet will I not leave thee wholly unpunished."

Ezekiel 28:25 "Thus saith the Lord GOD; When I shall have gathered the house of Israel from the people among whom they are scattered, and shall be sanctified in them in the sight of the heathen, then shall they dwell in their land that I have given to my servant Jacob."

Ezekiel 34:30-31 "³⁰Thus shall they know that I the LORD their God am with them, and that they, even the house of Israel, are my people, saith the Lord GOD. ³¹And ye my flock, the flock of my pasture, are men, and I am your God, saith the Lord GOD."

Zechariah 13:7-9 "⁷Awake, O sword, against my shepherd, and against the man that is my fellow, saith the LORD of hosts: smite the shepherd, and the sheep shall be scattered: and I will turn mine hand upon the little ones. ⁸And it shall come to pass, that in all the land, saith the LORD, two parts therein shall be cut off and die; but the third shall be left therein. ⁹And I will bring the third part through the fire, and will refine them as silver is refined, and will try them as gold is tried: they shall call on my name, and I will hear them: I will say, It is my people: and they shall say, The LORD is my God."

When Israel Will Dwell Safely

Jeremiah 23:5-8 "⁵Behold, the days come, saith the LORD, that I will raise unto David a righteous Branch, and a King shall reign and prosper, and shall execute judgment and justice in the earth. ⁶In his days Judah shall be saved, and Israel shall dwell safely: and this is his name whereby he shall be called, THE LORD OUR RIGHTEOUSNESS. ⁷Therefore, behold, the days come, saith the LORD, that they shall no more say, The LORD liveth, which brought up the children of

Israel out of the land of Egypt; ⁸But, The LORD liveth, which brought up and which led the seed of the house of Israel out of the north country, and from all countries whither I had driven them; and they shall dwell in their own land."

Jeremiah 33:14-17 "¹⁴Behold, the days come, saith the LORD, that I will perform that good thing which I have promised unto the house of Israel and to the house of Judah. ¹⁵In those days, and at that time, will I cause the Branch of righteousness to grow up unto David; and he shall execute judgment and righteousness in the land. ¹⁶In those days shall Judah be saved, and Jerusalem shall dwell safely: and this is the name wherewith she shall be called, The LORD our righteousness. ¹⁷For thus saith the LORD; David shall never want a man to sit upon the throne of the house of Israel;"

Ezekiel 28:25-26 "²⁵Thus saith the Lord GOD; When I shall have gathered the house of Israel from the people among whom they are scattered, and shall be sanctified in them in the sight of the heathen, then shall they dwell in their land that I have given to my servant Jacob. ²⁶And they shall dwell safely therein, and shall build houses, and plant vineyards; yea, they shall dwell with confidence, when I have executed judgments upon all those that despise them round about them; and they shall know that I am the LORD their God."

Ezekiel 34:25-31 "²⁵And I will make with them a covenant of peace, and will cause the evil beasts to cease out of the land: and they shall dwell safely in the wilderness, and sleep in the woods. ²⁶And I will make them and the places round about my hill a blessing; and I will cause the shower to come down in his season; there shall be showers of blessing. ²⁷And the tree of the field shall yield her fruit, and the earth shall yield her increase, and they shall be safe in their land, and shall know that I am the LORD, when I have broken the bands of their yoke, and delivered them out of the hand of those that served themselves of them. ²⁸And they shall no more be a prey to the heathen, neither shall the beast of the land devour them; but they shall dwell safely, and none shall make them afraid. ²⁹And I will raise up for them a plant of renown, and they shall be no more consumed with hunger in the land, neither bear the shame of the heathen any more. ³⁰Thus shall they

know that I the LORD their God am with them, and that they, even the house of Israel, are my people, saith the Lord GOD. ³¹And ye my flock, the flock of my pasture, are men, and I am your God, saith the Lord GOD."

Zechariah 14:9-21 "⁹And the LORD shall be king over all the earth: in that day shall there be one LORD, and his name one. ¹⁰All the land shall be turned as a plain from Geba to Rimmon south of Jerusalem: and it shall be lifted up, and inhabited in her place, from Benjamin's gate unto the place of the first gate, unto the corner gate, and from the tower of Hananeel unto the king's winepresses. ¹¹And men shall dwell in it, and there shall be no more utter destruction; but Jerusalem shall be safely inhabited. ¹²And this shall be the plague wherewith the LORD will smite all the people that have fought against Jerusalem; Their flesh shall consume away while they stand upon their feet, and their eyes shall consume away in their holes, and their tongue shall consume away in their mouth. ¹³And it shall come to pass in that day, that a great tumult from the LORD shall be among them; and they shall lay hold every one on the hand of his neighbour, and his hand shall rise up against the hand of his neighbour. ¹⁴And Judah also shall fight at Jerusalem; and the wealth of all the heathen round about shall be gathered together, gold, and silver, and apparel, in great abundance. ¹⁵And so shall be the plague of the horse, of the mule, of the camel, and of the ass, and of all the beasts that shall be in these tents, as this plague. ¹⁶And it shall come to pass, that every one that is left of all the nations which came against Jerusalem shall even go up from year to year to worship the King, the LORD of hosts, and to keep the feast of tabernacles. ¹⁷And it shall be, that whoso will not come up of all the families of the earth unto Jerusalem to worship the King, the LORD of hosts, even upon them shall be no rain. ¹⁸And if the family of Egypt go not up, and come not, that have no rain; there shall be the plague, wherewith the LORD will smite the heathen that come not up to keep the feast of tabernacles. ¹⁹This shall be the punishment of Egypt, and the punishment of all nations that come not up to keep the feast of tabernacles. ²⁰In that day shall there be upon the bells of the horses, HOLINESS UNTO THE LORD; and the pots in the LORD's house shall be like the bowl's before the altar. [21]Yea, every pot in Jerusalem and in Judah shall be holiness unto the LORD of hosts: and all they that sacrifice shall come and take of them, and seethe therein: and in that day there shall be no more the Canaanite in the house of the LORD of hosts."

Who Destroyed Israel
Hosea 13:9 "O Israel, thou hast destroyed thyself; but in me is thine help."

Who Is A Jew
Romans 2:29 "But he is a Jew, which is one inwardly; and circumcision is that of the heart, in the spirit, and not in the letter; whose praise is not of men, but of God."

Who Is Not A Jew
Romans 2:28 "For he is not a Jew, which is one outwardly; neither is that circumcision, which is outward in the flesh:"

Why Israel Fell
1 Kings 14:15-16 "[15]For the LORD shall smite Israel, as a reed is shaken in the water, and he shall root up Israel out of this good land, which he gave to their fathers, and shall scatter them beyond the river, because they have made their groves, provoking the LORD to anger. [16]And he shall give Israel up because of the sins of Jeroboam, who did sin, and who made Israel to sin."

2 Chronicles 28:23 "For he sacrificed unto the gods of Damascus, which smote him: and he said, Because the gods of the kings of Syria help them, therefore will I sacrifice to them, that they may help me. But they were the ruin of him, and of all Israel."

2 Chronicles 29:6-9 "[6]For our fathers have trespassed, and done that which was evil in the eyes of the LORD our God, and have forsaken him, and have turned away their faces from the habitation of the LORD, and turned their backs. [7]Also they have shut up the doors of the porch, and put out the lamps, and have not burned incense nor offered burnt offerings in the holy place unto the God of Israel. [8]Wherefore the wrath of the LORD was upon Judah and Jerusalem, and he hath delivered them to trouble, to astonishment, and to hissing, as ye see with your eyes. [9]For, lo, our fathers have fallen by the sword, and our sons and our daughters and our wives are in captivity for this."

Isaiah 3:8 "For Jerusalem is ruined, and Judah is fallen: because their tongue and their doings are against the LORD, to provoke the eyes of his glory."

Isaiah 5:11-13 "[11]Woe unto them that rise up early in the morning, that they may follow strong drink; that continue until night, till wine inflame them! [12]And the harp, and the viol, the tabret, and pipe, and wine, are in their feasts: but they regard not the work of the LORD, neither consider the operation of his hands. [13]Therefore my people are gone into captivity, because they have no knowledge: and their honourable men are famished, and their multitude dried up with thirst."

Jeremiah 9:13-16 "[13]And the LORD saith, Because they have forsaken my law which I set before them, and have not obeyed my voice, neither walked therein; [14]But have walked after the imagination of their own heart, and after Baalim, which their fathers taught them: [15]Therefore thus saith the LORD of hosts, the God of Israel; Behold, I will feed them, even this people, with wormwood, and give them water of gall to drink. [16]I will scatter them also among the heathen, whom neither they nor their fathers have known: and I will send a sword after them, till I have consumed them."

Jeremiah 11:17 "For the LORD of hosts, that planted thee, hath pronounced evil against thee, for the evil of the house of Israel and of the house of Judah, which they have done against themselves to provoke me to anger in offering incense unto Baal."

Jeremiah 18:13-17 "[13]Therefore thus saith the LORD; Ask ye now among the heathen, who hath heard such things: the virgin of Israel hath done a very horrible thing. [14]Will a man leave the snow of Lebanon which cometh from the rock of the field? or shall the cold flowing waters that come from another place be forsaken? [15]Because my people hath forgotten me, they have burned incense to vanity, and they have caused them to stumble in their ways from the ancient paths, to walk in paths, in a way not cast up; [16]To make their land desolate, and a perpetual hissing; every one that passeth thereby shall be astonished, and wag his head. ¹⁷I will scatter them as with an east wind before the enemy; I will shew them the back, and not the face, in the day of their calamity."

Ezekiel 36:16-19 "¹⁶Moreover the word of the LORD came unto me, saying, ¹⁷Son of man, when the house of Israel dwelt in their own land, they defiled it by their own way and by their doings: their way was before me as the uncleanness of a removed woman. ¹⁸Wherefore I poured my fury upon them for the blood that they had shed upon the land, and for their idols wherewith they had polluted it: ¹⁹And I scattered them among the heathen, and they were dispersed through the countries: according to their way and according to their doings I judged them."

Ezekiel 39:22-24 "²²So the house of Israel shall know that I am the LORD their God from that day and forward. ²³And the heathen shall know that the house of Israel went into captivity for their iniquity: because they trespassed against me, therefore hid I my face from them, and gave them into the hand of their enemies: so fell they all by the sword. ²⁴According to their uncleanness and according to their transgressions have I done unto them, and hid my face from them."

Daniel 9:4-14 "⁴And I prayed unto the LORD my God, and made my confession, and said, O Lord, the great and dreadful God, keeping the covenant and mercy to them that love him, and to them that keep his commandments; ⁵We have sinned, and have committed iniquity, and have done wickedly, and have rebelled, even by departing from thy precepts and from thy judgments: ⁶Neither have we hearkened unto thy servants the prophets, which spake in thy name to our kings, our princes, and our fathers, and to all the people of the land. ⁷O Lord, righteousness belongeth unto thee, but unto us confusion of faces, as at this day; to the men of Judah, and to the inhabitants of Jerusalem, and unto all Israel, that are near, and that are far off, through all the countries whither thou hast driven them, because of their trespass that they have trespassed against thee. ⁸O Lord, to us belongeth confusion of face, to our kings, to our princes, and to our fathers, because we have sinned against thee. ⁹To the Lord our God belong mercies and forgivenesses, though we have rebelled against him; ¹⁰Neither

have we obeyed the voice of the LORD our God, to walk in his laws, which he set before us by his servants the prophets. ¹¹Yea, all Israel have transgressed thy law, even by departing, that they might not obey thy voice; therefore the curse is poured upon us, and the oath that is written in the law of Moses the servant of God, because we have sinned against him. ¹²And he hath confirmed his words, which he spake against us, and against our judges that judged us, by bringing upon us a great evil: for under the whole heaven hath not been done as hath been done upon Jerusalem. ¹³As it is written in the law of Moses, all this evil is come upon us: yet made we not our prayer before the LORD our God, that we might turn from our iniquities, and understand thy truth. ¹⁴Therefore hath the LORD watched upon the evil, and brought it upon us: for the LORD our God is righteous in all his works which he doeth: for we obeyed not his voice."

Hosea 4:1 "Hear the word of the LORD, ye children of Israel: for the LORD hath a controversy with the inhabitants of the land, because there is no truth, nor mercy, nor knowledge of God in the land."

Hosea 4:6 "My people are destroyed for lack of knowledge: because thou hast rejected knowledge, I will also reject thee, that thou shalt be no priest to me: seeing thou hast forgotten the law of thy God, I will also forget thy children."

Amos 2:4-5 "⁴Thus saith the LORD; For three transgressions of Judah, and for four, I will not turn away the punishment thereof; because they have despised the law of the LORD, and have not kept his commandments, and their lies caused them to err, after the which their fathers have walked: ⁵But I will send a fire upon Judah, and it shall devour the palaces of Jerusalem."

Zechariah 7:7-14 "⁷Should ye not hear the words which the LORD hath cried by the former prophets, when Jerusalem was inhabited and in prosperity, and the cities thereof round about her, when men inhabited the south and the plain? ⁸And the word of the LORD came unto Zechariah, saying, ⁹Thus speaketh the LORD of hosts, saying, Execute true judgment, and shew mercy and compassions every man to his brother: ¹⁰And oppress not the widow, nor the fatherless, the stranger, nor the poor; and let none of you imagine evil against his brother in your heart. [11]But they refused to hearken, and pulled away the shoulder, and stopped their ears, that they should not hear. [12]Yea, they made their hearts as an adamant stone, lest they should hear the law, and the words which the LORD of hosts hath sent in his spirit by the former prophets: therefore came a great wrath from the LORD of hosts. [13]Therefore it is come to pass, that as he cried, and they would not hear; so they cried, and I would not hear, saith the LORD of hosts: [14]But I scattered them with a whirlwind among all the nations whom they knew not. Thus the land was desolate after them, that no man passed through nor returned: for they laid the pleasant land desolate."

Why Jews Stumbled

Isaiah 8:13-15 "[13]Sanctify the LORD of hosts himself; and let him be your fear, and let him be your dread. [14]And he shall be for a sanctuary; but for a stone of stumbling and for a rock of offence to both the houses of Israel, for a gin and for a snare to the inhabitants of Jerusalem. [15]And many among them shall stumble, and fall, and be broken, and be snared, and be taken."

Romans 9:30-33 "[30]What shall we say then? That the Gentiles, which followed not after righteousness, have attained to righteousness, even the righteousness which is of faith. [31]But Israel, which followed after the law of righteousness, hath not attained to the law of righteousness. [32]Wherefore? Because they sought it not by faith, but as it were by the works of the law. For they stumbled at that stumblingstone; [33]As it is written, Behold, I lay in Sion a stumblingstone and rock of offence: and whosoever believeth on him shall not be ashamed."

Romans 11:1-11 "[1]I say then, Hath God cast away his people? God forbid. For I also am an Israelite, of the seed of Abraham, of the tribe of Benjamin. [2]God hath not cast away his people which he foreknew. Wot ye not what the scripture saith of Elias? how he maketh intercession to God against Israel, saying, [3]Lord, they have killed thy prophets, and digged down thine altars; and I am left alone, and they seek my life. [4]But what saith the answer of God unto him? I have reserved to myself seven thousand men, who have not bowed the knee to the image of Baal. [5]Even so then at this present time also there is a remnant according to the election of grace. [6]And if by grace, then is it no more of works: otherwise grace is no more grace. But if it be of works, then is it no more grace: otherwise work is no more work. [7]What then? Israel hath not obtained that which he seeketh for; but the election hath obtained it, and the rest were blinded [8](According as it is written, God hath given them the spirit of slumber, eyes that they should not see, and ears that they should not hear;) unto this day. [9]And David saith, Let their table be made a snare, and a trap, and a stumbling block, and a recompence unto them: [10]Let their eyes be darkened, that they may not see, and bow down their back alway. [11]I say then, Have they stumbled that they should fall? God forbid: but rather through their fall salvation is come unto the Gentiles, for to provoke them to jealousy."

1 Corinthians 1:22-23 "[22]For the Jews require a sign, and the Greeks seek after wisdom: [23]But we preach Christ crucified, unto the Jews a stumblingblock, and unto the Greeks foolishness;"

Jj

JERUSALEM

The Gentiles Treading
Jerusalem Under Their Feet

Psalm 79:1 "O God, the heathen are come into thine inheritance; thy holy temple have they defiled; they have laid Jerusalem on heaps."

Luke 21:24 "And they shall fall by the edge of the sword, and shall be led away captive into all nations: and Jerusalem shall be trodden down of the Gentiles, until the times of the Gentiles be fulfilled."

Revelation 11:1-2 "¹And there was given me a reed like unto a rod: and the angel stood, saying, Rise, and measure the temple of God, and the altar, and them that worship therein. ²But the court which is without the temple leave out, and measure it not; for it is given unto the Gentiles: and the holy city shall they tread under foot forty and two months."

The Lord Choosing Jerusalem

Deuteronomy 12:11 "Then there shall be a place which the LORD your God shall choose to cause his name to dwell there; thither shall ye bring all that I command you; your burnt offerings, and your sacrifices, your tithes, and the heave offering of your hand, and all your choice vows which ye vow unto the LORD:"

1 Kings 8:38-48 "³⁸What prayer and supplication soever be made by any man, or by all thy people Israel, which shall know every man the plague of his own heart, and spread forth his hands toward this house: ³⁹Then hear thou in heaven thy dwelling place, and forgive, and do, and give to every man according to his ways, whose heart thou knowest; (for thou, even thou only, knowest the hearts of all the children of men;) ⁴⁰That they may fear thee all the days that they live in the land which thou gavest unto our fathers. ⁴¹Moreover concerning a stranger, that is not of thy people Israel, but cometh out of a far country for thy name's sake; ⁴²(For they shall hear of thy great name, and of thy strong hand, and of thy stretched out arm;) when he shall come and pray toward

this house; ⁴³Hear thou in heaven thy dwelling place, and do according to all that the stranger calleth to thee for: that all people of the earth may know thy name, to fear thee, as do thy people Israel; and that they may know that this house, which I have builded, is called by thy name. ⁴⁴If thy people go out to battle against their enemy, whithersoever thou shalt send them, and shall pray unto the LORD toward the city which thou hast chosen, and toward the house that I have built for thy name: ⁴⁵Then hear thou in heaven their prayer and their supplication, and maintain their cause. ⁴⁶If they sin against thee, (for there is no man that sinneth not,) and thou be angry with them, and deliver them to the enemy, so that they carry them away captives unto the land of the enemy, far or near; ⁴⁷Yet if they shall bethink themselves in the land whither they were carried captives, and repent, and make supplication unto thee in the land of them that carried them captives, saying, We have sinned, and have done perversely, we have committed wickedness; ⁴⁸And so return unto thee with all their heart, and with all their soul, in the land of their enemies, which led them away captive, and pray unto thee toward their land, which thou gavest unto their fathers, the city which thou hast chosen, and the house which I have built for thy name:"

1 Kings 11:31-36 "³¹And he said to Jeroboam, Take thee ten pieces: for thus saith the LORD, the God of Israel, Behold, I will rend the kingdom out of the hand of Solomon, and will give ten tribes to thee: ³²(But he shall have one tribe for my servant David's sake, and for Jerusalem's sake, the city which I have chosen out of all the tribes of Israel:) ³³Because that they have forsaken me, and have worshipped Ashtoreth the goddess of the Zidonians, Chemosh the god of the Moabites, and Milcom the god of the children of Ammon, and have not walked in my ways, to do that which is right in mine eyes, and to keep my statutes and my judgments, as did David his father. ³⁴Howbeit I will not take the whole kingdom out of his hand: but I will make him prince all the days of his life for David my servant's sake, whom I chose, because he kept my commandments and my statutes: ³⁵But I will take the kingdom out of his son's hand, and will give it unto thee, even ten tribes. ³⁶And unto his son will I give one tribe, that David my servant may have a light alway before me in Jerusalem, the city which I have chosen me to put my name there."

2 Kings 21:7 "And he set a graven image of the grove that he had made in the house, of which the LORD said to David, and to Solomon his son, In this house, and in Jerusalem, which I have chosen out of all tribes of Israel, will I put my name for ever:"

2 Chronicles 6:19-40 "¹⁹Have respect therefore to the prayer of thy servant, and to his supplication, O LORD my God, to hearken unto the cry and the prayer which thy servant prayeth before thee: ²⁰That thine eyes may be open upon this house day and night, upon the place whereof thou hast said that thou wouldest put thy name there; to hearken unto the prayer which thy servant prayeth toward this place. ²¹Hearken therefore unto the supplications of thy servant, and of thy people Israel, which they shall make toward this place: hear thou from thy dwelling place, even from heaven; and when thou hearest, forgive. ²²If a man sin against his neighbour, and an oath be laid upon him to make him swear, and the oath come before thine altar in this house; ²³Then hear thou from heaven, and do, and judge thy servants, by requiting the wicked, by recompensing his way upon his own head; and by justifying the righteous, by giving him according to his righteousness. ²⁴And if thy people Israel be put to the worse before the enemy, because they have sinned against thee; and shall return and confess thy name, and pray and make supplication before thee in this house; ²⁵Then hear thou from the heavens, and forgive the sin of thy people Israel, and bring them again unto the land which thou gavest to them and to their fathers. ²⁶When the heaven is shut up, and there is no rain, because they have sinned against thee; yet if they pray toward this place, and confess thy name, and turn from their sin, when thou dost afflict them; ²⁷Then hear thou from heaven, and forgive the sin of thy servants, and of thy people Israel, when thou hast taught them the good way, wherein they should walk; and send rain upon thy land, which thou hast given unto thy people for an inheritance. ²⁸If there be dearth in the land, if there be pestilence, if there be blasting, or mildew, locusts, or caterpillers; if their enemies besiege

them in the cities of their land; whatsoever sore or whatsoever sickness there be: ²⁹Then what prayer or what supplication soever shall be made of any man, or of all thy people Israel, when every one shall know his own sore and his own grief, and shall spread forth his hands in this house: ³⁰Then hear thou from heaven thy dwelling place, and forgive, and render unto every man according unto all his ways, whose heart thou knowest; (for thou only knowest the hearts of the children of men:) ³¹That they may fear thee, to walk in thy ways, so long as they live in the land which thou gavest unto our fathers. ³²Moreover concerning the stranger, which is not of thy people Israel, but is come from a far country for thy great name's sake, and thy mighty hand, and thy stretched out arm; if they come and pray in this house; ³³Then hear thou from the heavens, even from thy dwelling place, and do according to all that the stranger calleth to thee for; that all people of the earth may know thy name, and fear thee, as doth thy people Israel, and may know that this house which I have built is called by thy name. ³⁴If thy people go out to war against their enemies by the way that thou shalt send them, and they pray unto thee toward this city which thou hast chosen, and the house which I have built for thy name; ³⁵Then hear thou from the heavens their prayer and their supplication, and maintain their cause. ³⁶If they sin against thee, (for there is no man which sinneth not,) and thou be angry with them, and deliver them over before their enemies, and they carry them away captives unto a land far off or near; ³⁷Yet if they bethink themselves in the land whither they are carried captive, and turn and pray unto thee in the land of their captivity, saying, We have sinned, we have done amiss, and have dealt wickedly; ³⁸If they return to thee with all their heart and with all their soul in the land of their captivity, whither they have carried them captives, and pray toward their land, which thou gavest unto their fathers, and toward the city which thou hast chosen, and toward the house which I have built for thy name: ³⁹Then hear thou from the heavens, even from thy dwelling place, their prayer and their supplications, and maintain their cause, and forgive thy people which have sinned against thee. ⁴⁰Now, my God, let, I beseech thee, thine eyes be open, and let thine ears be attent unto the prayer that is made in this place."

2 Chronicles 33:7 "And he set a carved image, the idol which he had made, in the house of God, of which God had said to David and to Solomon his son, In this house, and in Jerusalem, which I have chosen before all the tribes of Israel, will I put my name for ever:"

Nehemiah 1:2-9 "²That Hanani, one of my brethren, came, he and certain men of Judah; and I asked them concerning the Jews that had escaped, which were left of the captivity, and concerning Jerusalem. ³And they said unto me, The remnant that are left of the captivity there in the province are in great affliction and reproach: the wall of Jerusalem also is broken down, and the gates thereof are burned with fire. ⁴And it came to pass, when I heard these words, that I sat down and wept, and mourned certain days, and fasted, and prayed before the God of heaven, ⁵And said, I beseech thee, O LORD God of heaven, the great and terrible God, that keepeth covenant and mercy for them that love him and observe his commandments: ⁶Let thine ear now be attentive, and thine eyes open, that thou mayest hear the prayer of thy servant, which I pray before thee now, day and night, for the children of Israel thy servants, and confess the sins of the children of Israel, which we have sinned against thee: both I and my father's house have sinned. ⁷We have dealt very corruptly against thee, and have not kept the commandments, nor the statutes, nor the judgments, which thou commandedst thy servant Moses. ⁸Remember, I beseech thee, the word that thou commandedst thy servant Moses, saying, If ye transgress, I will scatter you abroad among the nations: ⁹But if ye turn unto me, and keep my commandments, and do them; though there were of you cast out unto the uttermost part of the heaven, yet will I gather them from thence, and will bring them unto the place that I have chosen to set my name there."

Psalm 132:13-15 "¹³For the LORD hath chosen Zion; he hath desired it for his habitation. ¹⁴This is my rest for ever: here will I dwell; for I have desired it. ¹⁵I will abundantly bless her provision: I will satisfy her poor with bread."

Zechariah 2:10-13 "¹⁰Sing and rejoice, O daughter of Zion: for, lo, I come, and I will dwell in the midst of thee, saith the LORD. ¹¹And many nations shall be joined to the LORD in that day, and shall be my people: and I will dwell in the midst of thee, and thou shalt know that the LORD of hosts hath sent me unto thee. ¹²And the LORD shall inherit Judah his portion in the holy land, and shall choose Jerusalem again. ¹³Be silent, O all flesh, before the LORD: for he is raised up out of his holy habitation."

The Lord Making Jerusalem
A Cup Of Trembling
Zechariah 12:1-3 "¹The burden of the word of the LORD for Israel, saith the LORD, which stretcheth forth the heavens, and layeth the foundation of the earth, and formeth the spirit of man within him. ²Behold, I will make Jerusalem a cup of trembling unto all the people round about, when they shall be in the siege both against Judah and against Jerusalem. ³And in that day will I make Jerusalem a burdensome stone for all people: all that burden themselves with it shall be cut in pieces, though all the people of the earth be gathered together against it."

The New Jerusalem
Isaiah 65:14-25 "¹⁴Behold, my servants shall sing for joy of heart, but ye shall cry for sorrow of heart, and shall howl for vexation of spirit. ¹⁵And ye shall leave your name for a curse unto my chosen: for the Lord GOD shall slay thee, and call his servants by another name: ¹⁶That he who blesseth himself in the earth shall bless himself in the God of truth; and he that sweareth in the earth shall swear by the God of truth; because the former troubles are forgotten, and because they are hid from mine eyes. ¹⁷For, behold, I create new heavens and a new earth: and the former shall not be remembered, nor come into mind. ¹⁸But be ye glad and rejoice for ever in that which I create: for, behold, I create Jerusalem a rejoicing, and her people a joy. ¹⁹And I will rejoice in Jerusalem, and joy in my people: and the voice of weeping shall be no more heard in her, nor the voice of crying. ²⁰There shall be no more thence an infant of days, nor an old man that hath not filled his days: for the child shall die an hundred years old; but the sinner being an hundred years old shall be accursed. ²¹And they shall build houses, and inhabit them; and they shall plant vineyards, and eat the fruit of them. ²²They shall not build, and another inhabit; they shall not plant, and another eat: for as the days of a tree are the days of my people, and mine elect shall long enjoy the work

of their hands. ²³They shall not labour in vain, nor bring forth for trouble; for they are the seed of the blessed of the LORD, and their offspring with them. ²⁴And it shall come to pass, that before they call, I will answer; and while they are yet speaking, I will hear. ²⁵The wolf and the lamb shall feed together, and the lion shall eat straw like the bullock: and dust shall be the serpent's meat. They shall not hurt nor destroy in all my holy mountain, saith the LORD."

Ezekiel 48:30-35 "³⁰And these are the goings out of the city on the north side, four thousand and five hundred measures. ³¹And the gates of the city shall be after the names of the tribes of Israel: three gates northward; one gate of Reuben, one gate of Judah, one gate of Levi. ³²And at the east side four thousand and five hundred: and three gates; and one gate of Joseph, one gate of Benjamin, one gate of Dan. ³³And at the south side four thousand and five hundred measures: and three gates; one gate of Simeon, one gate of Issachar, one gate of Zebulun. ³⁴At the west side four thousand and five hundred, with their three gates; one gate of Gad, one gate of Asher, one gate of Naphtali. ³⁵It was round about eighteen thousand measures: and the name of the city from that day shall be, The LORD is there."

Galatians 4:21-26 "²¹Tell me, ye that desire to be under the law, do ye not hear the law? ²²For it is written, that Abraham had two sons, the one by a bondmaid, the other by a freewoman. ²³But he who was of the bondwoman was born after the flesh; but he of the freewoman was by promise. ²⁴Which things are an allegory: for these are the two covenants; the one from the mount Sinai, which gendereth to bondage, which is Agar. ²⁵For this Agar is mount Sinai in Arabia, and answereth to Jerusalem which now is, and is in bondage with her children. ²⁶But Jerusalem which is above is free, which is the mother of us all."

Hebrews 12:22-28 "²²But ye are come unto mount Sion, and unto the city of the living God, the heavenly Jerusalem, and to an innumerable company of angels, ²³To the general assembly and church of the firstborn, which are written in heaven, and to God the Judge of all, and to the spirits of just men made perfect, ²⁴And to Jesus the mediator of the new covenant, and to the blood of sprinkling, that speaketh better things

than that of Abel. ²⁵See that ye refuse not him that speaketh. For if they escaped not who refused him that spake on earth, much more shall not we escape, if we turn away from him that speaketh from heaven: ²⁶Whose voice then shook the earth: but now he hath promised, saying, Yet once more I shake not the earth only, but also heaven. ²⁷And this word, Yet once more, signifieth the removing of those things that are shaken, as of things that are made, that those things which cannot be shaken may remain. ²⁸Wherefore we receiving a kingdom which cannot be moved, let us have grace, whereby we may serve God acceptably with reverence and godly fear:"

Revelation 3:12 "Him that overcometh will I make a pillar in the temple of my God, and he shall go no more out: and I will write upon him the name of my God, and the name of the city of my God, which is new Jerusalem, which cometh down out of heaven from my God: and I will write upon him my new name."

Revelation 21:1-5 "¹And I saw a new heaven and a new earth: for the first heaven and the first earth were passed away; and there was no more sea. ²And I John saw the holy city, new Jerusalem, coming down from God out of heaven, prepared as a bride adorned for her husband. ³And I heard a great voice out of heaven saying, Behold, the tabernacle of God is with men, and he will dwell with them, and they shall be his people, and God himself shall be with them, and be their God. ⁴And God shall wipe away all tears from their eyes; and there shall be no more death, neither sorrow, nor crying, neither shall there be any more pain: for the former things are passed away. ⁵And he that sat upon the throne said, Behold, I make all things new. And he said unto me, Write: for these words are true and faithful."

Revelation 21:9-27 "⁹And there came unto me one of the seven angels which had the seven vials full of the seven last plagues, and talked with me, saying, Come hither, I will shew thee the bride, the Lamb's wife. ¹⁰And he carried me away in the spirit to a great and high mountain, and shewed me that great city, the holy Jerusalem, descending out of heaven from God, ¹¹Having the glory of God: and her light was like unto a stone most precious, even like a jasper stone, clear as crystal; ¹²And had a wall great and high, and had twelve gates, and at the gates twelve angels, and names written thereon, which are the names of the twelve tribes of the children of Israel: ¹³On the east three gates; on the north three gates; on the south three gates; and on the west three gates. ¹⁴And the wall of the city had twelve foundations, and in them the names of the twelve apostles of the Lamb. ¹⁵And he that talked with me had a golden reed to measure the city, and the gates thereof, and the wall thereof. ¹⁶And the city lieth foursquare, and the length is as large as the breadth: and he measured the city with the reed, twelve thousand furlongs. The length and the breadth and the height of it are equal. ¹⁷And he measured the wall thereof, an hundred and forty and four cubits, according to the measure of a man, that is, of the angel. ¹⁸And the building of the wall of it was of jasper: and the city was pure gold, like unto clear glass. ¹⁹And the foundations of the wall of the city were garnished with all manner of precious stones. The first foundation was jasper; the second, sapphire; the third, a chalcedony; the fourth, an emerald; ²⁰The fifth, sardonyx; the sixth, sardius; the seventh, chrysolite; the eighth, beryl; the ninth, a topaz; the tenth, a chrysoprasus; the eleventh, a jacinth; the twelfth, an amethyst. ²¹And the twelve gates were twelve pearls; every several gate was of one pearl: and the street of the city was pure gold, as it were transparent glass. ²²And I saw no temple therein: for the Lord God Almighty and the Lamb are the temple of it. ²³And the city had no need of the sun, neither of the moon, to shine in it: for the glory of God did lighten it, and the Lamb is the light thereof. ²⁴And the nations of them which are saved shall walk in the light of it: and the kings of the earth do bring their glory and honour into it. ²⁵And the gates of it shall not be shut at all by day: for there shall be no night there. ²⁶And they shall bring the glory and honour of the nations into it. ²⁷And there shall in no wise enter into it any thing that defileth, neither whatsoever worketh abomination, or maketh a lie: but they which are written in the Lamb's book of life."

Those That Love Jerusalem
Psalm 122:1-7 "¹I was glad when they said unto me, Let us go into the house of the LORD. ²Our feet shall stand within thy gates, O Jerusalem. ³Jerusalem is builded as a city that is compact together: ⁴Whither the tribes go up, the tribes of the LORD, unto the testimony of Israel, to give thanks unto the name of the LORD. ⁵For there are set thrones of judgment, the thrones of the house of David. ⁶Pray for the peace of Jerusalem: they shall prosper that love thee. ⁷Peace be within thy walls, and prosperity within thy palaces."

What Jerusalem Is
1 Kings 11:31-36 "³¹And he said to Jeroboam, Take thee ten pieces: for thus saith the LORD, the God of Israel, Behold, I will rend the kingdom out of the hand of Solomon, and will give ten tribes to thee: ³²(But he shall have one tribe for my servant David's sake, and for Jerusalem's sake, the city which I have chosen out of all the tribes of Israel:) ³³Because that they have forsaken me, and have worshipped Ashtoreth the goddess of the Zidonians, Chemosh the god of the Moabites, and Milcom the god of the children of Ammon, and have not walked in my ways, to do that which is right in mine eyes, and to keep my statutes and my judgments, as did David his father. ³⁴Howbeit I will not take the whole kingdom out of his hand: but I will make him prince all the days of his life for David my servant's sake, whom I chose, because he kept my commandments and my statutes: ³⁵But I will take the kingdom out of his son's hand, and will give it unto thee, even ten tribes. ³⁶And unto his son will I give one tribe, that David my servant may have a light alway before me in Jerusalem, the city which I have chosen me to put my name there."

Psalm 132:13-15 "¹³For the LORD hath chosen Zion; he hath desired it for his habitation. ¹⁴This is my rest for ever: here will I dwell; for I have desired it. ¹⁵I will abundantly bless her provision: I will satisfy her poor with bread."

Jeremiah 3:14-17 "¹⁴Turn, O backsliding children, saith the LORD; for I am married unto you: and I will take you one of a city, and two of a family, and I will bring you to Zion: ¹⁵And I will give you pastors according to mine heart, which shall feed you with knowledge and understanding. ¹⁶And it shall come to pass, when ye be multiplied and increased in the land, in those days, saith the LORD, they shall say no more, The ark of the covenant of the LORD: neither shall it come to mind: neither shall they remember it; neither shall they visit it; neither shall that be done any more. ¹⁷At that time they shall call Jerusalem the throne of the LORD; and all the nations shall be gathered unto it, to the name of the LORD, to Jerusalem: neither shall they walk any more after the imagination of their evil heart."

Zechariah 8:3 "Thus saith the LORD; I am returned unto Zion, and will dwell in the midst of Jerusalem: and Jerusalem shall be called a city of truth; and the mountain of the LORD of hosts the holy mountain."

Matthew 5:34-35 "³⁴But I say unto you, Swear not at all; neither by heaven; for it is God's throne: ³⁵Nor by the earth; for it is his footstool: neither by Jerusalem; for it is the city of the great King."

What Shall Be Put In Jerusalem
Deuteronomy 12:11 "Then there shall be a place which the LORD your God shall choose to cause his name to dwell there; thither shall ye bring all that I command you; your burnt offerings, and your sacrifices, your tithes, and the heave offering of your hand, and all your choice vows which ye vow unto the LORD:"

1 Kings 8:28-43 "²⁸Yet have thou respect unto the prayer of thy servant, and to his supplication, O LORD my God, to hearken unto the cry and to the prayer, which thy servant prayeth before thee to day: ²⁹That thine eyes may be open toward this house night and day, even toward the place of which thou hast said, My name shall be there: that thou mayest hearken unto the prayer which thy servant shall make toward this place. ³⁰And hearken thou to the supplication of thy servant, and of thy people Israel, when they shall pray toward this place: and hear thou in heaven thy dwelling place: and when thou hearest, forgive. ³¹If any man trespass against his neighbour, and an oath be laid upon him to cause him to swear, and the oath come before thine altar in this house: ³²Then hear thou in heaven, and do, and judge thy servants, condemning the wicked, to bring his way upon his head; and justifying the righteous, to give him according to his righteousness. ³³When thy people Israel be smitten down before the enemy, because they have sinned against thee, and shall turn again to thee, and confess thy name, and pray, and make supplication unto thee in this house: ³⁴Then hear thou in heaven, and forgive the sin of thy people Israel, and bring them again unto the land which thou gavest unto their fathers. ³⁵When heaven is shut up, and there is no rain, because they have sinned against thee; if they pray toward this place, and confess thy name, and turn from their sin, when thou afflictest them: ³⁶Then hear thou in heaven, and forgive the sin of thy servants, and of thy people Israel, that thou teach them the good way wherein they should walk, and give rain upon thy land, which thou hast given to thy people for an inheritance. ³⁷If there be in the land famine, if there be pestilence, blasting, mildew, locust, or if there be caterpiller; if their enemy besiege them in the land of their cities; whatsoever plague, whatsoever sickness there be; ³⁸What prayer and supplication soever be made by any man, or by all thy people Israel, which shall know every man the plague of his own heart, and spread forth his hands toward this house: ³⁹Then hear thou in heaven thy dwelling place, and forgive, and do, and give to every man according to his ways, whose heart thou knowest; (for thou, even thou only, knowest the hearts of all the children of men;) ⁴⁰That they may fear thee all the days that they live in the land which thou gavest unto our fathers. ⁴¹Moreover concerning a stranger, that is not of thy people Israel, but cometh out of a far country for thy name's sake; ⁴²(For they shall hear of thy great name, and of thy strong hand, and of thy stretched out arm;) when he shall come and pray toward this house; ⁴³Hear thou in heaven thy dwelling place, and do according to all that the stranger calleth to thee for: that all people of the earth may know thy name, to fear thee, as do thy people Israel; and that they may know that this house, which I have builded, is called by thy name."

1 Kings 9:1-3 "¹And it came to pass, when Solomon had finished the building of the house of the LORD, and the king's house, and all Solomon's desire which he was pleased to do, ²That the LORD appeared to Solomon the second time, as he had appeared unto him at Gibeon. ³And the LORD said unto him, I have heard thy prayer and thy supplication, that thou hast made before me: I have hallowed this house, which thou hast built, to put my name there for ever; and mine eyes and mine heart shall be there perpetually."

1 Kings 11:31-36 "³¹And he said to Jeroboam, Take thee ten pieces: for thus saith the LORD, the

God of Israel, Behold, I will rend the kingdom out of the hand of Solomon, and will give ten tribes to thee: ³²(But he shall have one tribe for my servant David's sake, and for Jerusalem's sake, the city which I have chosen out of all the tribes of Israel:) ³³Because that they have forsaken me, and have worshipped Ashtoreth the goddess of the Zidonians, Chemosh the god of the Moabites, and Milcom the god of the children of Ammon, and have not walked in my ways, to do that which is right in mine eyes, and to keep my statutes and my judgments, as did David his father. ³⁴Howbeit I will not take the whole kingdom out of his hand: but I will make him prince all the days of his life for David my servant's sake, whom I chose, because he kept my commandments and my statutes: ³⁵But I will take the kingdom out of his son's hand, and will give it unto thee, even ten tribes. ³⁶And unto his son will I give one tribe, that David my servant may have a light alway before me in Jerusalem, the city which I have chosen me to put my name there."

2 Kings 21:4 "And he built altars in the house of the LORD, of which the LORD said, In Jerusalem will I put my name."

2 Kings 21:7 "And he set a graven image of the grove that he had made in the house, of which the LORD said to David, and to Solomon his son, In this house, and in Jerusalem, which I have chosen out of all tribes of Israel, will I put my name for ever."

2 Chronicles 6:19-38 "¹⁹Have respect therefore to the prayer of thy servant, and to his supplication, O LORD my God, to hearken unto the cry and the prayer which thy servant prayeth before thee: ²⁰That thine eyes may be open upon this house day and night, upon the place whereof thou hast said that thou wouldest put thy name there; to hearken unto the prayer which thy servant prayeth toward this place. ²¹Hearken therefore unto the supplications of thy servant, and of thy people Israel, which they shall make toward this place: hear thou from thy dwelling place, even from heaven; and when thou hearest, forgive. ²²If a man sin against his neighbour, and an oath be laid upon him to make him swear, and the oath come before thine altar in this house; ²³Then hear thou from heaven, and do, and judge thy servants, by requiting the wicked, by recompensing his way upon his own head; and by justifying the righteous, by giving him according to his righteousness. ²⁴And if thy people Israel be put to the worse before the enemy, because they have sinned against thee; and shall return and confess thy name, and pray and make supplication before thee in this house; ²⁵Then hear thou from the heavens, and forgive the sin of thy people Israel, and bring them again unto the land which thou gavest to them and to their fathers. ²⁶When the heaven is shut up, and there is no rain, because they have sinned against thee; yet if they pray toward this place, and confess thy name, and turn from their sin, when thou dost afflict them; ²⁷Then hear thou from heaven, and forgive the sin of thy servants, and of thy people Israel, when thou hast taught them the good way, wherein they should walk; and send rain upon thy land, which thou hast given unto thy people for an inheritance. ²⁸If there be dearth in the land, if there be pestilence, if there be blasting, or mildew, locusts, or caterpillers; if their enemies besiege them in the cities of their land; whatsoever sore or whatsoever sickness there be: ²⁹Then what prayer or what supplication soever shall be made of any man, or of all thy people Israel, when every one shall know his own sore and his own grief, and shall spread forth his hands in this house: ³⁰Then hear thou from heaven thy dwelling place, and forgive, and render unto every man according unto all his ways, whose heart thou knowest; (for thou only knowest the hearts of the children of men:) ³¹That they may fear thee, to walk in thy ways, so long as they live in the land which thou gavest unto our fathers. ³²Moreover concerning the stranger, which is not of thy people Israel, but is come from a far country for thy great name's sake, and thy mighty hand, and thy stretched out arm; if they come and pray in this house; ³³Then hear thou from the heavens, even from thy dwelling place, and do according to all that the stranger calleth to thee for; that all people of the earth may know thy name, and fear thee, as doth thy people Israel, and may know that this house which I have built is called by thy name. ³⁴If thy people go out to war against their enemies by the way that thou shalt send them, and they pray unto thee toward this city which thou hast chosen, and the house which I have built for thy name; ³⁵Then hear thou from the heavens their prayer and their supplication, and maintain their cause. [36]If they sin against thee, (for there is no man which sinneth not,) and thou be angry with them, and deliver them over before their enemies, and they carry them away captives unto a land far off or near; [37]Yet if they bethink themselves in the land whither they are carried captive, and turn and pray unto thee in the land of their captivity, saying, We have sinned, we have done amiss, and have dealt wickedly; [38]If they return to thee with all their heart and with all their soul in the land of their captivity, whither they have carried them captives, and pray toward their land, which thou gavest unto their fathers, and toward the city which thou hast chosen, and toward the house which I have built for thy name:"

2 Chronicles 33:4 "Also he built altars in the house of the LORD, whereof the LORD had said, In Jerusalem shall my name be for ever."

2 Chronicles 33:7 "And he set a carved image, the idol which he had made, in the house of God, of which God had said to David and to Solomon his son, In this house, and in Jerusalem, which I have chosen before all the tribes of Israel, will I put my name for ever:"

Nehemiah 1:2-9 "[2]That Hanani, one of my brethren, came, he and certain men of Judah; and I asked them concerning the Jews that had escaped, which were left of the captivity, and concerning Jerusalem. [3]And they said unto me, The remnant that are left of the captivity there in the province are in great affliction and reproach: the wall of Jerusalem also is broken down, and the gates thereof are burned with fire. [4]And it came to pass, when I heard these words, that I sat down and wept, and mourned certain days, and fasted, and prayed before the God of heaven, [5]And said, I beseech thee, O LORD God of heaven, the great and terrible God, that keepeth covenant and mercy for them that love him and observe his commandments: [6]Let thine ear now be attentive, and thine eyes open, that thou mayest hear the prayer of thy servant, which I pray before thee now, day and night, for the children of Israel thy servants, and confess the sins of the children of Israel, which we have sinned against thee: both I and my father's house have sinned. [7]We have dealt very corruptly against thee, and have not kept the commandments, nor the statutes, nor the

judgments, which thou commandedst thy servant Moses. [8]Remember, I beseech thee, the word that thou commandedst thy servant Moses, saying, If ye transgress, I will scatter you abroad among the nations: [9]But if ye turn unto me, and keep my commandments, and do them; though there were of you cast out unto the uttermost part of the heaven, yet will I gather them from thence, and will bring them unto the place that I have chosen to set my name there."

What Shall Go Forth From Jerusalem

Isaiah 2:1-3 "[1]the word that Isaiah the son of Amoz saw concerning Judah and Jerusalem. [2]And it shall come to pass in the last days, that the mountain of the LORD's house shall be established in the top of the mountains, and shall be exalted above the hills; and all nations shall flow unto it. [3]And many people shall go and say, Come ye, and let us go up to the mountain of the LORD, to the house of the God of Jacob; and he will teach us of his ways, and we will walk in his paths: for out of Zion shall go forth the law, and the word of the LORD from Jerusalem."

Micah 4:1-2 "[1]But in the last days it shall come to pass, that the mountain of the house of the LORD shall be established in the top of the mountains, and it shall be exalted above the hills; and people shall flow unto it. [2]And many nations shall come, and say, Come, and let us go up to the mountain of the LORD, and to the house of the God of Jacob; and he will teach us of his ways, and we will walk in his paths: for the law shall go forth of Zion, and the word of the LORD from Jerusalem."

Zechariah 14:8 "And it shall be in that day, that living waters shall go out from Jerusalem; half of them toward the former sea, and half of them toward the hinder sea: in summer and in winter shall it be."

When Jerusalem Will Be Desolated

Luke 21:20-24 "[20]And when ye shall see Jerusalem compassed with armies, then know that the desolation thereof is nigh. [21]Then let them which are in Judaea flee to the mountains; and let them which are in the midst of it depart out; and let not them that are in the countries enter thereinto. [22]For these be the days of vengeance, that all things which are written may be fulfilled. [23]But woe unto them that are with child, and to them that give suck, in those days! for there shall be great distress in the land, and wrath upon this people. ²⁴And they shall fall by the edge of the sword, and shall be led away captive into all nations: and Jerusalem shall be trodden down of the Gentiles, until the times of the Gentiles be fulfilled."

JESTING

Not Jesting
Ephesians 5:3-4 "³But fornication, and all uncleanness, or covetousness, let it not be once named among you, as becometh saints; ⁴Neither filthiness, nor foolish talking, nor jesting, which are not convenient: but rather giving of thanks."

JESUS CHRIST

God The Father Being
The Head Of Jesus Christ
John 10:25-29 "²⁵Jesus answered them, I told you, and ye believed not: the works that I do in my Father's name, they bear witness of me. ²⁶But ye believe not, because ye are not of my sheep, as I said unto you. ²⁷My sheep hear my voice, and I know them, and they follow me: ²⁸And I give unto them eternal life; and they shall never perish, neither shall any man pluck them out of my hand. ²⁹My Father, which gave them me, is greater than all; and no man is able to pluck them out of my Father's hand."

John 14:23-28 "²³Jesus answered and said unto him, If a man love me, he will keep my words: and my Father will love him, and we will come unto him, and make our abode with him. ²⁴He that loveth me not keepeth not my sayings: and the word which ye hear is not mine, but the Father's which sent me. ²⁵These things have I spoken unto you, being yet present with you. ²⁶But the Comforter, which is the Holy Ghost, whom the Father will send in my name, he shall teach you all things, and bring all things to your remembrance, whatsoever I have said unto you. ²⁷Peace I leave with you, my peace I give unto you: not as the world giveth, give I unto you. Let not your heart be troubled, neither let it be afraid. ²⁸Ye have heard how I said unto you, I go away, and come again unto you. If ye loved me, ye

would rejoice, because I said, I go unto the Father: for my Father is greater than I."

1 Corinthians 3:23 "And ye are Christ's; and Christ is God's."

1 Corinthians 11:2-3 "²Now I praise you, brethren, that ye remember me in all things, and keep the ordinances, as I delivered them to you. ³But I would have you know, that the head of every man is Christ; and the head of the woman is the man; and the head of Christ is God."

1 Corinthians 15:28 "And when all things shall be subdued unto him, then shall the Son also himself be subject unto him that put all things under him, that God may be all in all."

Ephesians 4:4-6 "⁴There is one body, and one Spirit, even as ye are called in one hope of your calling; ⁵One Lord, one faith, one baptism, ⁶One God and Father of all, who is above all, and through all, and in you all."

God The Father Being With Jesus Christ
John 16:31-32 "³¹Jesus answered them, Do ye now believe? ³²Behold, the hour cometh, yea, is now come, that ye shall be scattered, every man to his own, and shall leave me alone: and yet I am not alone, because the Father is with me."

Acts 10:37-38 "³⁷That word, I say, ye know, which was published throughout all Judaea, and began from Galilee, after the baptism which John preached; ³⁸How God anointed Jesus of Nazareth with the Holy Ghost and with power: who went about doing good, and healing all that were oppressed of the devil; for God was with him."

Jesus Christ And God The Father
Being In Each Other
John 10:34-38 "³⁴Jesus answered them, Is it not written in your law, I said, Ye are gods? ³⁵If he called them gods, unto whom the word of God came, and the scripture cannot be broken; ³⁶Say ye of him, whom the Father hath sanctified, and sent into the world, Thou blasphemest; because I said, I am the Son of God? ³⁷If I do not the works of my Father, believe me not. ³⁸But if I do, though ye believe not me, believe the works: that ye may know, and believe, that the Father is in me, and I in him."

John 14:6-11 "⁶Jesus saith unto him, I am the way, the truth, and the life: no man cometh unto the Father, but by me. ⁷If ye had known me, ye should have known my Father also: and from henceforth ye know him, and have seen him. ⁸Philip saith unto him, Lord, shew us the Father, and it sufficeth us. ⁹Jesus saith unto him, Have I been so long time with you, and yet hast thou not known me, Philip? he that hath seen me hath seen the Father; and how sayest thou then, Shew us the Father? ¹⁰Believest thou not that I am in the Father, and the Father in me? the words that I speak unto you I speak not of myself: but the Father that dwelleth in me, he doeth the works. ¹¹Believe me that I am in the Father, and the Father in me: or else believe me for the very works' sake."

John 14:20 "At that day ye shall know that I am in my Father, and ye in me, and I in you."

John 17:1-23 "¹These words spake Jesus, and lifted up his eyes to heaven, and said, Father, the hour is come; glorify thy Son, that thy Son also may glorify thee: ²As thou hast given him power over all flesh, that he should give eternal life to as many as thou hast given him. ³And this is life eternal, that they might know thee the only true God, and Jesus Christ, whom thou hast sent. ⁴I have glorified thee on the earth: I have finished the work which thou gavest me to do. ⁵And now, O Father, glorify thou me with thine own self with the glory which I had with thee before the world was. ⁶I have manifested thy name unto the men which thou gavest me out of the world: thine they were, and thou gavest them me; and they have kept thy word. ⁷Now they have known that all things whatsoever thou hast given me are of thee. ⁸For I have given unto them the words which thou gavest me; and they have received them, and have known surely that I came out from thee, and they have believed that thou didst send me. ⁹I pray for them: I pray not for the world, but for them which thou hast given me; for they are thine. ¹⁰And all mine are thine, and thine are mine; and I am glorified in them. ¹¹And now I am no more in the world, but these are in the world, and I come to thee. Holy Father, keep through thine own name those whom thou hast given me, that they may be one, as we are. ¹²While I was with them in the world, I kept them in thy name: those that thou gavest me I have kept, and none of them is lost, but the son of perdition; that the scripture might be fulfilled. ¹³And now come I to thee; and these things I speak in the world, that they might have my joy fulfilled in themselves. ¹⁴I have given them thy word; and the world hath hated them, because they are not of the world, even as I am not of the world. ¹⁵I pray not that thou shouldest take them out of the world, but that thou shouldest keep them from the evil. ¹⁶They are not of the world, even as I am not of the world. ¹⁷Sanctify them through thy truth: thy word is truth. ¹⁸As thou hast sent me into the world, even so have I also sent them into the world. ¹⁹And for their sakes I sanctify myself, that they also might be sanctified through the truth. ²⁰Neither pray I for these alone, but for them also which shall believe on me through their word; ²¹That they all may be one; as thou, Father, art in me, and I in thee, that they also may be one in us: that the world may believe that thou hast sent me. ²²And the glory which thou gavest me I have given them; that they may be one, even as we are one: ²³I in them, and thou in me, that they may be made perfect in one; and that the world may know that thou hast sent me, and hast loved them, as thou hast loved me."

Jesus Christ Being The Only Christ

Matthew 23:8-10 "⁸But be not ye called Rabbi: for one is your Master, even Christ; and all ye are brethren. ⁹And call no man your father upon the earth: for one is your Father, which is in heaven. ¹⁰Neither be ye called masters: for one is your Master, even Christ."

Acts 4:9-12 "⁹If we this day be examined of the good deed done to the impotent man, by what means he is made whole; ¹⁰Be it known unto you all, and to all the people of Israel, that by the name of Jesus Christ of Nazareth, whom ye crucified, whom God raised from the dead, even by him doth this man stand here before you whole. ¹¹This is the stone which was set at nought of you builders, which is become the head of the corner. ¹²Neither is there salvation in any other: for there is none other name under heaven given among men, whereby we must be saved."

1 Corinthians 8:4-6 "⁴As concerning therefore the eating of those things that are offered in sacrifice unto idols, we know that an idol is nothing in the world, and that there is none other God but one. [5]For though there be that are called gods, whether in heaven or in earth, (as there be gods many, and lords many,) [6]But to us there is but one God, the Father, of whom are all things, and we in him; and one Lord Jesus Christ, by whom are all things, and we by him."

1 Timothy 2:5 "For there is one God, and one mediator between God and men, the man Christ Jesus;"

Jesus Christ Doing The Will Of God The Father

Psalm 40:7-9 "[7]Then said I, Lo, I come: in the volume of the book it is written of me, [8]I delight to do thy will, O my God: yea, thy law is within my heart. [9]I have preached righteousness in the great congregation: lo, I have not refrained my lips, O LORD, thou knowest."

John 4:34 "Jesus saith unto them, My meat is to do the will of him that sent me, and to finish his work."

John 5:17-20 "[17]But Jesus answered them, My Father worketh hitherto, and I work. [18]Therefore the Jews sought the more to kill him, because he not only had broken the sabbath, but said also that God was his Father, making himself equal with God. [19]Then answered Jesus and said unto them, Verily, verily, I say unto you, The Son can do nothing of himself, but what he seeth the Father do: for what things soever he doeth, these also doeth the Son likewise. [20]For the Father loveth the Son, and sheweth him all things that himself doeth: and he will shew him greater works than these, that ye may marvel."

John 5:23-30 "[23]That all men should honour the Son, even as they honour the Father. He that honoureth not the Son honoureth not the Father which hath sent him. [24]Verily, verily, I say unto you, He that heareth my word, and believeth on him that sent me, hath everlasting life, and shall not come into condemnation; but is passed from death unto life. [25]Verily, verily, I say unto you, The hour is coming, and now is, when the dead shall hear the voice of the Son of God: and they that hear shall live. [26]For as the Father hath life in himself; so hath he given to the Son to have life in himself; [27]And hath given him authority to execute judgment also, because he is the Son of man.

[28]Marvel not at this: for the hour is coming, in the which all that are in the graves shall hear his voice, [29]And shall come forth; they that have done good, unto the resurrection of life; and they that have done evil, unto the resurrection of damnation. [30]I can of mine own self do nothing: as I hear, I judge: and my judgment is just; because I seek not mine own will, but the will of the Father which hath sent me."

John 6:35-38 "[35]And Jesus said unto them, I am the bread of life: he that cometh to me shall never hunger; and he that believeth on me shall never thirst. [36]But I said unto you, That ye also have seen me, and believe not. [37]All that the Father giveth me shall come to me; and him that cometh to me I will in no wise cast out. [38]For I came down from heaven, not to do mine own will, but the will of him that sent me."

John 8:25-29 "[25]Then said they unto him, Who art thou? And Jesus saith unto them, Even the same that I said unto you from the beginning. [26]I have many things to say and to judge of you: but he that sent me is true; and I speak to the world those things which I have heard of him. [27]They understood not that he spake to them of the Father. [28]Then said Jesus unto them, When ye have lifted up the Son of man, then shall ye know that I am he, and that I do nothing of myself; but as my Father hath taught me, I speak these things. [29]And he that sent me is with me: the Father hath not left me alone; for I do always those things that please him."

John 9:3-4 "[3]Jesus answered, Neither hath this man sinned, nor his parents: but that the works of God should be made manifest in him. [4]I must work the works of him that sent me, while it is day: the night cometh, when no man can work."

John 14:23-31 "[23]Jesus answered and said unto him, If a man love me, he will keep my words: and my Father will love him, and we will come unto him, and make our abode with him. [24]He that loveth me not keepeth not my sayings: and the word which ye hear is not mine, but the Father's which sent me. [25]These things have I spoken unto you, being yet present with you. [26]But the Comforter, which is the Holy Ghost, whom the Father will send in my name, he shall teach you all things, and bring all things to your remembrance, whatsoever I have said unto you. [27]Peace I leave with you, my peace I give unto you: not as the world giveth, give I unto you. Let not your heart be troubled, neither let it be afraid. [28]Ye have heard how I said unto you, I go away, and come again unto you. If ye loved me, ye would rejoice, because I said, I go unto the Father: for my Father is greater than I. [29]And now I have told you before it come to pass, that, when it is come to pass, ye might believe. [30]Hereafter I will not talk much with you: for the prince of this world cometh, and hath nothing in me. [31]But that the world may know that I love the Father; and as the Father gave me commandment, even so I do. Arise, let us go hence."

John 17:1-4 "[1]These words spake Jesus, and lifted up his eyes to heaven, and said, Father, the hour is come; glorify thy Son, that thy Son also may glorify thee: [2]As thou hast given him power over all flesh, that he should give eternal life to as many as thou hast given him. [3]And this is life eternal, that they might know thee the only true God, and Jesus Christ, whom thou hast sent. [4]I have glorified thee on the earth: I have finished the work which thou gavest me to do."

Hebrews 10:4-10 "[4]For it is not possible that the blood of bulls and of goats should take away sins. [5]Wherefore when he cometh into the world, he saith, Sacrifice and offering thou wouldest not, but a body hast thou prepared me: [6]In burnt offerings and sacrifices for sin thou hast had no pleasure. [7]Then said I, Lo, I come (in the volume of the book it is written of me,) to do thy will, O God. [8]Above when he said, Sacrifice and offering and burnt offerings and offering for sin thou wouldest not, neither hadst pleasure therein; which are offered by the law; [9]Then said he, Lo, I come to do thy will, O God. He taketh away the first, that he may establish the second. [10]By the which will we are sanctified through the offering of the body of Jesus Christ once for all."

Jesus Christ Existing Before All Things
Psalm 90:2 "Before the mountains were brought forth, or ever thou hadst formed the earth and the world, even from everlasting to everlasting, thou art God."

John 1:1-4 "[1]In the beginning was the Word, and the Word was with God, and the Word was God. [2]The same was in the beginning with God. [3]All things were made by him; and without him was not any thing made that was made. [4]In him was life; and the life was the light of men."

John 8:58 "Jesus said unto them, Verily, verily, I say unto you, Before Abraham was, I am."

John 17:1-5 "[1]These words spake Jesus, and lifted up his eyes to heaven, and said, Father, the hour is come; glorify thy Son, that thy Son also may glorify thee: [2]As thou hast given him power over all flesh, that he should give eternal life to as many as thou hast given him. [3]And this is life eternal, that they might know thee the only true God, and Jesus Christ, whom thou hast sent. [4]I have glorified thee on the earth: I have finished the work which thou gavest me to do. [5]And now, O Father, glorify thou me with thine own self with the glory which I had with thee before the world was."

Colossians 1:12-17 "[12]Giving thanks unto the Father, which hath made us meet to be partakers of the inheritance of the saints in light: [13]Who hath delivered us from the power of darkness, and hath translated us into the kingdom of his dear Son: [14]In whom we have redemption through his blood, even the forgiveness of sins: [15]Who is the image of the invisible God, the firstborn of every creature: [16]For by him were all things created, that are in heaven, and that are in earth, visible and invisible, whether they be thrones, or dominions, or principalities, or powers: all things were created by him, and for him: [17]And he is before all things, and by him all things consist."

1 John 1:1-3 "[1]That which was from the beginning, which we have heard, which we have seen with our eyes, which we have looked upon, and our hands have handled, of the Word of life; [2](For the life was manifested, and we have seen it, and bear witness, and shew unto you that eternal life, which was with the Father, and was manifested unto us;) [3]That which we have seen and heard declare we unto you, that ye also may have fellowship with us: and truly our fellowship is with the Father, and with his Son Jesus Christ."

Jesus Christ, God The Father, And The Holy Spirit Being One
John 10:25-30 "[25]Jesus answered them, I told you, and ye believed not: the works that I do in my

Father's name, they bear witness of me. [26]But ye believe not, because ye are not of my sheep, as I said unto you. [27]My sheep hear my voice, and I know them, and they follow me: [28]And I give unto them eternal life; and they shall never perish, neither shall any man pluck them out of my hand. [29]My Father, which gave them me, is greater than all; and no man is able to pluck them out of my Father's hand. [30]I and my Father are one."

John 17:1-22 "[1]These words spake Jesus, and lifted up his eyes to heaven, and said, Father, the hour is come; glorify thy Son, that thy Son also may glorify thee: [2]As thou hast given him power over all flesh, that he should give eternal life to as many as thou hast given him. [3]And this is life eternal, that they might know thee the only true God, and Jesus Christ, whom thou hast sent. [4]I have glorified thee on the earth: I have finished the work which thou gavest me to do. [5]And now, O Father, glorify thou me with thine own self with the glory which I had with thee before the world was. [6]I have manifested thy name unto the men which thou gavest me out of the world: thine they were, and thou gavest them me; and they have kept thy word. [7]Now they have known that all things whatsoever thou hast given me are of thee. [8]For I have given unto them the words which thou gavest me; and they have received them, and have known surely that I came out from thee, and they have believed that thou didst send me. [9]I pray for them: I pray not for the world, but for them which thou hast given me; for they are thine. [10]And all mine are thine, and thine are mine; and I am glorified in them. [11]And now I am no more in the world, but these are in the world, and I come to thee. Holy Father, keep through thine own name those whom thou hast given me, that they may be one, as we are. [12]While I was with them in the world, I kept them in thy name: those that thou gavest me I have kept, and none of them is lost, but the son of perdition; that the scripture might be fulfilled. [13]And now come I to thee; and these things I speak in the world, that they might have my joy fulfilled in themselves. [14]I have given them thy word; and the world hath hated them, because they are not of the world, even as I am not of the world. [15]I pray not that thou shouldest take them out of the world, but that thou shouldest keep them from the evil. [16]They are not of the world, even as I am not of the world. [17]Sanctify them through thy truth: thy word is truth. [18]As thou hast sent me into the world, even so have I also sent them into the world. [19]And for their sakes I sanctify myself, that they also might be sanctified through the truth. [20]Neither pray I for these alone, but for them also which shall believe on me through their word; [21]That they all may be one; as thou, Father, art in me, and I in thee, that they also may be one in us: that the world may believe that thou hast sent me. [22]And the glory which thou gavest me I have given them; that they may be one, even as we are one:"

1 John 5:7 "For there are three that bear record in heaven, the Father, the Word, and the Holy Ghost: and these three are one."

Jesus Christ Having Life In Himself
John 5:26 "For as the Father hath life in himself; so hath he given to the Son to have life in himself;"

Jesus Christ Living By God The Father
John 6:53-57 "[53]Then Jesus said unto them, Verily, verily, I say unto you, Except ye eat the flesh of the Son of man, and drink his blood, ye have no life in you. [54]Whoso eateth my flesh, and drinketh my blood, hath eternal life; and I will raise him up at the last day. [55]For my flesh is meat indeed, and my blood is drink indeed. [56]He that eateth my flesh, and drinketh my blood, dwelleth in me, and I in him. [57]As the living Father hath sent me, and I live by the Father: so he that eateth me, even he shall live by me."

2 Corinthians 13:3-5 "[3]Since ye seek a proof of Christ speaking in me, which to you-ward is not weak, but is mighty in you. [4]For though he was crucified through weakness, yet he liveth by the power of God. For we also are weak in him, but we shall live with him by the power of God toward you. [5]Examine yourselves, whether ye be in the faith; prove your own selves. Know ye not your own selves, how that Jesus Christ is in you, except ye be reprobates?"

The Character Of Jesus Christ
Isaiah 53:1-9 "[1]Who hath believed our report? and to whom is the arm of the Lord revealed? [2]For he shall grow up before him as a tender plant, and as a root out of a dry ground: he hath no form nor

comeliness; and when we shall see him, there is no beauty that we should desire him. ³He is despised and rejected of men; a man of sorrows, and acquainted with grief: and we hid as it were our faces from him; he was despised, and we esteemed him not. ⁴Surely he hath borne our griefs, and carried our sorrows: yet we did esteem him stricken, smitten of God, and afflicted. ⁵But he was wounded for our transgressions, he was bruised for our iniquities: the chastisement of our peace was upon him; and with his stripes we are healed. ⁶All we like sheep have gone astray; we have turned every one to his own way; and the LORD hath laid on him the iniquity of us all. ⁷He was oppressed, and he was afflicted, yet he opened not his mouth: he is brought as a lamb to the slaughter, and as a sheep before her shearers is dumb, so he openeth not his mouth. ⁸He was taken from prison and from judgment: and who shall declare his generation? for he was cut off out of the land of the living: for the transgression of my people was he stricken. ⁹And he made his grave with the wicked, and with the rich in his death; because he had done no violence, neither was any deceit in his mouth."

Zechariah 9:9 "Rejoice greatly, O daughter of Zion; shout, O daughter of Jerusalem: behold, thy King cometh unto thee: he is just, and having salvation; lowly, and riding upon an ass, and upon a colt the foal of an ass."

Matthew 11:25-30 "²⁵At that time Jesus answered and said, I thank thee, O Father, Lord of heaven and earth, because thou hast hid these things from the wise and prudent, and hast revealed them unto babes. ²⁶Even so, Father: for so it seemed good in thy sight. ²⁷All things are delivered unto me of my Father: and no man knoweth the Son, but the Father; neither knoweth any man the Father, save the Son, and he to whomsoever the Son will reveal him. ²⁸Come unto me, all ye that labour and are heavy laden, and I will give you rest. ²⁹Take my yoke upon you, and learn of me; for I am meek and lowly in heart: and ye shall find rest unto your souls. ³⁰For my yoke is easy, and my burden is light."

Matthew 22:16 "And they sent out unto him their disciples with the Herodians, saying, Master, we know that thou art true, and teachest the way of God in truth, neither carest thou for any man: for thou regardest not the person of men."

Mark 12:14 "And when they were come, they say unto him, Master, we know that thou art true, and carest for no man: for thou regardest not the person of men, but teachest the way of God in truth: Is it lawful to give tribute to Caesar, or not?"

Luke 20:21 "And they asked him, saying, Master, we know that thou sayest and teachest rightly, neither acceptest thou the person of any, but teachest the way of God truly:"

Philippians 2:5-8 "⁵Let this mind be in you, which was also in Christ Jesus: ⁶Who, being in the form of God, thought it not robbery to be equal with God: ⁷But made himself of no reputation, and took upon him the form of a servant, and was made in the likeness of men: ⁸And being found in fashion as a man, he humbled himself, and became obedient unto death, even the death of the cross."

Hebrews 4:14-15 "¹⁴Seeing then that we have a great high priest, that is passed into the heavens, Jesus the Son of God, let us hold fast our profession. ¹⁵For we have not an high priest which cannot be touched with the feeling of our infirmities; but was in all points tempted like as we are, yet without sin."

Hebrews 7:22-26 "²²By so much was Jesus made a surety of a better testament. ²³And they truly were many priests, because they were not suffered to continue by reason of death: ²⁴But this man, because he continueth ever, hath an unchangeable priesthood. ²⁵Wherefore he is able also to save them to the uttermost that come unto God by him, seeing he ever liveth to make intercession for them. ²⁶For such an high priest became us, who is holy, harmless, undefiled, separate from sinners, and made higher than the heavens;"

Hebrews 13:8 "Jesus Christ the same yesterday, and today, and for ever."

1 Peter 2:21-23 "²¹For even hereunto were ye called: because Christ also suffered for us, leaving us an example, that ye should follow his steps: ²²Who did no sin, neither was guile found in his mouth: ²³Who, when he was reviled, reviled not again; when he suffered, he threatened not; but committed himself to him that judgeth righteously:"

1 John 2:1 "My little children, these things write I unto you, that ye sin not. And if any man sin, we have an advocate with the Father, Jesus Christ the righteous:"

1 John 3:1-7 "[1]Behold, what manner of love the Father hath bestowed upon us, that we should be called the sons of God: therefore the world knoweth us not, because it knew him not. [2]Beloved, now are we the sons of God, and it doth not yet appear what we shall be: but we know that, when he shall appear, we shall be like him; for we shall see him as he is. [3]And every man that hath this hope in him purifieth himself, even as he is pure. [4]Whosoever committeth sin transgresseth also the law: for sin is the transgression of the law. [5]And ye know that he was manifested to take away our sins; and in him is no sin. [6]Whosoever abideth in him sinneth not: whosoever sinneth hath not seen him, neither known him. [7]Little children, let no man deceive you: he that doeth righteousness is righteous, even as he is righteous."

The Doctrine Of Jesus Christ

John 7:16-18 "[16]Jesus answered them, and said, My doctrine is not mine, but his that sent me. [17]If any man will do his will, he shall know of the doctrine, whether it be of God, or whether I speak of myself. [18]He that speaketh of himself seeketh his own glory: but he that seeketh his glory that sent him, the same is true, and no unrighteousness is in him."

The Lineage Of Jesus Christ

2 Samuel 7:8-17 "[8]Now therefore so shalt thou say unto my servant David, Thus saith the LORD of hosts, I took thee from the sheepcote, from following the sheep, to be ruler over my people, over Israel: [9]And I was with thee whithersoever thou wentest, and have cut off all thine enemies out of thy sight, and have made thee a great name, like unto the name of the great men that are in the earth. [10]Moreover I will appoint a place for my people Israel, and will plant them, that they may dwell in a place of their own, and move no more; neither shall the children of wickedness afflict them any more, as beforetime, [11]And as since the time that I commanded judges to be over my people Israel, and have caused thee to rest from all thine enemies. Also the LORD telleth thee that he will make thee an house. [12]And when thy days be

fulfilled, and thou shalt sleep with thy fathers, I will set up thy seed after thee, which shall proceed out of thy bowels, and I will establish his kingdom. [13]He shall build an house for my name, and I will stablish the throne of his kingdom for ever. [14]I will be his father, and he shall be my son. If he commit iniquity, I will chasten him with the rod of men, and with the stripes of the children of men: [15]But my mercy shall not depart away from him, as I took it from Saul, whom I put away before thee. [16]And thine house and thy kingdom shall be established for ever before thee: thy throne shall be established for ever. [17]According to all these words, and according to all this vision, so did Nathan speak unto David."

1 Chronicles 17:7-15 "[7]Now therefore thus shalt thou say unto my servant David, Thus saith the LORD of hosts, I took thee from the sheepcote, even from following the sheep, that thou shouldest be ruler over my people Israel: [8]And I have been with thee whithersoever thou hast walked, and have cut off all thine enemies from before thee, and have made thee a name like the name of the great men that are in the earth. [9]Also I will ordain a place for my people Israel, and will plant them, and they shall dwell in their place, and shall be moved no more; neither shall the children of wickedness waste them any more, as at the beginning, [10]And since the time that I commanded judges to be over my people Israel. Moreover I will subdue all thine enemies. Furthermore I tell thee that the LORD will build thee an house. [11]And it shall come to pass, when thy days be expired that thou must go to be with thy fathers, that I will raise up thy seed after thee, which shall be of thy sons; and I will establish his kingdom. [12]He shall build me an house, and I will stablish his throne for ever. [13]I will be his father, and he shall be my son: and I will not take my mercy away from him, as I took it from him that was before thee: [14]But I will settle him in mine house and in my kingdom for ever: and his throne shall be established for evermore. [15]According to all these words, and according to all this vision, so did Nathan speak unto David."

1 Chronicles 28:2-7 "[2]Then David the king stood up upon his feet, and said, Hear me, my brethren, and my people: As for me, I had in mine heart to build an house of rest for the ark of the covenant of the LORD, and for the footstool of our God, and had made ready for the building: ³But God said unto me, Thou shalt not build an house for my name, because thou hast been a man of war, and hast shed blood. ⁴Howbeit the LORD God of Israel chose me before all the house of my father to be king over Israel for ever: for he hath chosen Judah to be the ruler; and of the house of Judah, the house of my father; and among the sons of my father he liked me to make me king over all Israel: ⁵And of all my sons, (for the LORD hath given me many sons,) he hath chosen Solomon my son to sit upon the throne of the kingdom of the LORD over Israel. ⁶And he said unto me, Solomon thy son, he shall build my house and my courts: for I have chosen him to be my son, and I will be his father. ⁷Moreover I will establish his kingdom for ever, if he be constant to do my commandments and my judgments, as at this day."

Psalm 132:11 "The LORD hath sworn in truth unto David; he will not turn from it; Of the fruit of thy body will I set upon thy throne."

Jeremiah 23:5 "Behold, the days come, saith the LORD, that I will raise unto David a righteous Branch, and a King shall reign and prosper, and shall execute judgment and justice in the earth."

Matthew 1:1-17 "¹The book of the generation of Jesus Christ, the son of David, the son of Abraham. ²Abraham begat Isaac; and Isaac begat Jacob; and Jacob begat Judas and his brethren; ³And Judas begat Phares and Zara of Thamar; and Phares begat Esrom; and Esrom begat Aram; ⁴And Aram begat Aminadab; and Aminadab begat Naasson; and Naasson begat Salmon; ⁵And Salmon begat Booz of Rachab; and Booz begat Obed of Ruth; and Obed begat Jesse; ⁶And Jesse begat David the king; and David the king begat Solomon of her that had been the wife of Urias; ⁷And Solomon begat Roboam; and Roboam begat Abia; and Abia begat Asa; ⁸And Asa begat Josaphat; and Josaphat begat Joram; and Joram begat Ozias; ⁹And Ozias begat Joatham; and Joatham begat Achaz; and Achaz begat Ezekias; ¹⁰And Ezekias begat Manasses; and Manasses begat Amon; and Amon begat Josias; ¹¹And Josias begat Jechonias and his brethren, about the time they were carried away to Babylon: ¹²And after they were brought to Babylon, Jechonias begat Salathiel; and Salathiel begat Zorobabel; ¹³And

Zorobabel begat Abiud; and Abiud begat Eliakim; and Eliakim begat Azor; ¹⁴And Azor begat Sadoc; and Sadoc begat Achim; and Achim begat Eliud; ¹⁵And Eliud begat Eleazar; and Eleazar begat Matthan; and Matthan begat Jacob; ¹⁶And Jacob begat Joseph the husband of Mary, of whom was born Jesus, who is called Christ. ¹⁷So all the generations from Abraham to David are fourteen generations; and from David until the carrying away into Babylon are fourteen generations; and from the carrying away into Babylon unto Christ are fourteen generations."

Matthew 1:20 "But while he thought on these things, behold, the angel of the Lord appeared unto him in a dream, saying, Joseph, thou son of David, fear not to take unto thee Mary thy wife: for that which is conceived in her is of the Holy Ghost."

Matthew 21:9-11 "⁹And the multitudes that went before, and that followed, cried, saying, Hosanna to the Son of David: Blessed is he that cometh in the name of the Lord; Hosanna in the highest. ¹⁰And when he was come into Jerusalem, all the city was moved, saying, Who is this? ¹¹And the multitude said, This is Jesus the prophet of Nazareth of Galilee."

Matthew 22:42-45 "⁴²Saying, What think ye of Christ? whose son is he? They say unto him, The Son of David. ⁴³He saith unto them, How then doth David in spirit call him Lord, saying, ⁴⁴The LORD said unto my Lord, Sit thou on my right hand, till I make thine enemies thy footstool? ⁴⁵If David then call him Lord, how is he his son?"

Mark 11:9-11 "⁹And they that went before, and they that followed, cried, saying, Hosanna; Blessed is he that cometh in the name of the Lord: ¹⁰Blessed be the kingdom of our father David, that cometh in the name of the Lord: Hosanna in the highest. ¹¹And Jesus entered into Jerusalem, and into the temple: and when he had looked round about upon all things, and now the eventide was come, he went out unto Bethany with the twelve."

Mark 12:35-37 "³⁵And Jesus answered and said, while he taught in the temple, How say the scribes that Christ is the Son of David? ³⁶For David himself said by the Holy Ghost, The Lord said to my Lord, Sit thou on my right hand, till I make thine enemies thy footstool. [37]David therefore himself calleth him Lord; and whence is he then his son? And the common people heard him gladly."

Luke 1:31-32 "[31]And, behold, thou shalt conceive in thy womb, and bring forth a son, and shalt call his name JESUS. [32]He shall be great, and shall be called the Son of the Highest: and the Lord God shall give unto him the throne of his father David:"

Luke 2:1-5 "[1]And it came to pass in those days, that there went out a decree from Caesar Augustus, that all the world should be taxed. [2](And this taxing was first made when Cyrenius was governor of Syria.) [3]And all went to be taxed, every one into his own city. [4]And Joseph also went up from Galilee, out of the city of Nazareth, into Judaea, unto the city of David, which is called Bethlehem; (because he was of the house and lineage of David:) [5]To be taxed with Mary his espoused wife, being great with child."

Luke 3:23-38 "[23]And Jesus himself began to be about thirty years of age, being (as was supposed) the son of Joseph, which was the son of Heli, [24]Which was the son of Matthat, which was the son of Levi, which was the son of Melchi, which was the son of Janna, which was the son of Joseph, [25]Which was the son of Mattathias, which was the son of Amos, which was the son of Naum, which was the son of Esli, which was the son of Nagge, [26]Which was the son of Maath, which was the son of Mattathias, which was the son of Semei, which was the son of Joseph, which was the son of Juda, [27]Which was the son of Joanna, which was the son of Rhesa, which was the son of Zorobabel, which was the son of Salathiel, which was the son of Neri, [28]Which was the son of Melchi, which was the son of Addi, which was the son of Cosam, which was the son of Elmodam, which was the son of Er, [29]Which was the son of Jose, which was the son of Eliezer, which was the son of Jorim, which was the son of Matthat, which was the son of Levi, [30]Which was the son of Simeon, which was the son of Juda, which was the son of Joseph, which was the son of Jonan, which was the son of Eliakim, [31]Which was the son of Melea, which was the son of Menan, which was the son of Mattatha, which was the son of Nathan, which was the son of David, [32]Which

was the son of Jesse, which was the son of Obed, which was the son of Booz, which was the son of Salmon, which was the son of Naasson, [33]Which was the son of Aminadab, which was the son of Aram, which was the son of Esrom, which was the son of Phares, which was the son of Juda, [34]Which was the son of Jacob, which was the son of Isaac, which was the son of Abraham, which was the son of Thara, which was the son of Nachor, [35]Which was the son of Saruch, which was the son of Ragau, which was the son of Phalec, which was the son of Heber, which was the son of Sala, [36]Which was the son of Cainan, which was the son of Arphaxad, which was the son of Sem, which was the son of Noe, which was the son of Lamech, [37]Which was the son of Mathusala, which was the son of Enoch, which was the son of Jared, which was the son of Maleleel, which was the son of Cainan, [38]Which was the son of Enos, which was the son of Seth, which was the son of Adam, which was the son of God."

Luke 20:41-44 "[41]And he said unto them, How say they that Christ is David's son? [42]And David himself saith in the book of Psalm, The LORD said unto my Lord, Sit thou on my right hand, [43]Till I make thine enemies thy footstool. [44]David therefore calleth him Lord, how is he then his son?"

John 7:42 "Hath not the scripture said, That Christ cometh of the seed of David, and out of the town of Bethlehem, where David was?"

Acts 2:29-30 "[29]Men and brethren, let me freely speak unto you of the patriarch David, that he is both dead and buried, and his sepulchre is with us unto this day. [30]Therefore being a prophet, and knowing that God had sworn with an oath to him, that of the fruit of his loins, according to the flesh, he would raise up Christ to sit on his throne;"

Acts 13:22-23 "[22]And when he had removed him, he raised up unto them David to be their king; to whom also he gave testimony, and said, I have found David the son of Jesse, a man after mine own heart, which shall fulfil all my will. [23]Of this man's seed hath God according to his promise raised unto Israel a Saviour, Jesus:"

Romans 1:3 "Concerning his Son Jesus Christ our Lord, which was made of the seed of David according to the flesh;"

2 Timothy 2:8 "Remember that Jesus Christ of the seed of David was raised from the dead according to my gospel:"

Revelation 5:5 "And one of the elders saith unto me, Weep not: behold, the Lion of the tribe of Juda, the Root of David, hath prevailed to open the book, and to loose the seven seals thereof."

Revelation 22:16 "I Jesus have sent mine angel to testify unto you these things in the churches. I am the root and the offspring of David, and the bright and morning star."

The Testimony Of Jesus Christ
Revelation 19:10 "And I fell at his feet to worship him. And he said unto me, See thou do it not: I am thy fellowservant, and of thy brethren that have the testimony of Jesus: worship God: for the testimony of Jesus is the spirit of prophecy."

The Words That Jesus Christ Spoke
John 6:63-64 "⁶³It is the spirit that quickeneth; the flesh profiteth nothing: the words that I speak unto you, they are spirit, and they are life. ⁶⁴But there are some of you that believe not. For Jesus knew from the beginning who they were that believed not, and who should betray him."

John 8:37-47 "³⁷I know that ye are Abraham's seed; but ye seek to kill me, because my word hath no place in you. ³⁸I speak that which I have seen with my Father: and ye do that which ye have seen with your father. ³⁹They answered and said unto him, Abraham is our father. Jesus saith unto them, If ye were Abraham's children, ye would do the works of Abraham. ⁴⁰But now ye seek to kill me, a man that hath told you the truth, which I have heard of God: this did not Abraham. ⁴¹Ye do the deeds of your father. Then said they to him, We be not born of fornication; we have one Father, even God. ⁴²Jesus said unto them, If God were your Father, ye would love me: for I proceeded forth and came from God; neither came I of myself, but he sent me. ⁴³Why do ye not understand my speech? even because ye cannot hear my word. ⁴⁴Ye are of your father the devil, and the lusts of your father ye will do. He was a murderer from the beginning, and abode not in the truth, because there is no truth in him. When he speaketh a lie, he speaketh of his own: for he is a liar, and the father of it. ⁴⁵And because I tell you the truth, ye believe me not. ⁴⁶Which of

you convinceth me of sin? And if I say the truth, why do ye not believe me? ⁴⁷He that is of God heareth God's words: ye therefore hear them not, because ye are not of God."

John 12:44-48 "⁴⁴Jesus cried and said, He that believeth on me, believeth not on me, but on him that sent me. ⁴⁵And he that seeth me seeth him that sent me. ⁴⁶I am come a light into the world, that whosoever believeth on me should not abide in darkness. ⁴⁷And if any man hear my words, and believe not, I judge him not: for I came not to judge the world, but to save the world. ⁴⁸He that rejecteth me, and receiveth not my words, hath one that judgeth him: the word that I have spoken, the same shall judge him in the last day."

John 14:6-11 "⁶Jesus saith unto him, I am the way, the truth, and the life: no man cometh unto the Father, but by me. ⁷If ye had known me, ye should have known my Father also: and from henceforth ye know him, and have seen him. ⁸Philip saith unto him, Lord, shew us the Father, and it sufficeth us. ⁹Jesus saith unto him, Have I been so long time with you, and yet hast thou not known me, Philip? he that hath seen me hath seen the Father; and how sayest thou then, Shew us the Father? ¹⁰Believest thou not that I am in the Father, and the Father in me? the words that I speak unto you I speak not of myself: but the Father that dwelleth in me, he doeth the works. ¹¹Believe me that I am in the Father, and the Father in me: or else believe me for the very works' sake."

John 14:23-24 "²³Jesus answered and said unto him, If a man love me, he will keep my words: and my Father will love him, and we will come unto him, and make our abode with him. ²⁴He that loveth me not keepeth not my sayings: and the word which ye hear is not mine, but the Father's which sent me."

John 15:1-3 "¹I am the true vine, and my Father is the husbandman. ²Every branch in me that beareth not fruit he taketh away: and every branch that beareth fruit, he purgeth it, that it may bring forth more fruit. ³Now ye are clean through the word which I have spoken unto you."

What Is In Jesus Christ
Romans 8:39 "Nor height, nor depth, nor any other creature, shall be able to separate us from

the love of God, which is in Christ Jesus our Lord."

Colossians 2:8-15 "⁸Beware lest any man spoil you through philosophy and vain deceit, after the tradition of men, after the rudiments of the world, and not after Christ. ⁹For in him dwelleth all the fulness of the Godhead bodily. ¹⁰And ye are complete in him, which is the head of all principality and power: ¹¹In whom also ye are circumcised with the circumcision made without hands, in putting off the body of the sins of the flesh by the circumcision of Christ: ¹²Buried with him in baptism, wherein also ye are risen with him through the faith of the operation of God, who hath raised him from the dead. ¹³And you, being dead in your sins and the uncircumcision of your flesh, hath he quickened together with him, having forgiven you all trespasses; ¹⁴Blotting out the handwriting of ordinances that was against us, which was contrary to us, and took it out of the way, nailing it to his cross; ¹⁵And having spoiled principalities and powers, he made a shew of them openly, triumphing over them in it."

1 Timothy 1:14 "And the grace of our Lord was exceeding abundant with faith and love which is in Christ Jesus."

2 Timothy 2:10 "Therefore I endure all things for the elect's sakes, that they may also obtain the salvation which is in Christ Jesus with eternal glory."

What Jesus Christ Came To Do
1 Chronicles 16:33 "Then shall the trees of the wood sing out at the presence of the LORD, because he cometh to judge the earth."

Psalm 40:7-10 "⁷Then said I, Lo, I come: in the volume of the book it is written of me, ⁸I delight to do thy will, O my God: yea, thy law is within my heart. ⁹I have preached righteousness in the great congregation: lo, I have not refrained my lips, O LORD, thou knowest. ¹⁰I have not hid thy righteousness within my heart; I have declared thy faithfulness and thy salvation: I have not concealed thy lovingkindness and thy truth from the great congregation."

Psalm 96:13 "Before the LORD: for he cometh, for he cometh to judge the earth: he shall judge the world with righteousness, and the people with his truth."

Isaiah 42:5-7 "⁵Thus saith God the LORD, he that created the heavens, and stretched them out; he that spread forth the earth, and that which cometh out of it; he that giveth breath unto the people upon it, and spirit to them that walk therein: ⁶I the LORD have called thee in righteousness, and will hold thine hand, and will keep thee, and give thee for a covenant of the people, for a light of the Gentiles; ⁷To open the blind eyes, to bring out the prisoners from the prison, and them that sit in darkness out of the prison house."

Isaiah 61:1-3 "¹The Spirit of the Lord GOD is upon me; because the LORD hath anointed me to preach good tidings unto the meek; he hath sent me to bind up the brokenhearted, to proclaim liberty to the captives, and the opening of the prison to them that are bound; ²To proclaim the acceptable year of the LORD, and the day of vengeance of our God; to comfort all that mourn; ³To appoint unto them that mourn in Zion, to give unto them beauty for ashes, the oil of joy for mourning, the garment of praise for the spirit of heaviness; that they might be called trees of righteousness, the planting of the LORD, that he might be glorified."

Matthew 1:20-21 "²⁰But while he thought on these things, behold, the angel of the Lord appeared unto him in a dream, saying, Joseph, thou son of David, fear not to take unto thee Mary thy wife: for that which is conceived in her is of the Holy Ghost. ²¹And she shall bring forth a son, and thou shalt call his name JESUS: for he shall save his people from their sins."

Matthew 3:11-14 "¹¹I indeed baptize you with water unto repentance: but he that cometh after me is mightier than I, whose shoes I am not worthy to bear: he shall baptize you with the Holy Ghost, and with fire: ¹²Whose fan is in his hand, and he will throughly purge his floor, and gather his wheat into the garner; but he will burn up the chaff with unquenchable fire. ¹³Then cometh Jesus from Galilee to Jordan unto John, to be baptized of him. ¹⁴But John forbad him, saying, I have need to be baptized of thee, and comest thou to me?"

Matthew 5:17-18 "¹⁷Think not that I am come to destroy the law, or the prophets: I am not come to destroy, but to fulfil. ¹⁸For verily I say unto you,

Till heaven and earth pass, one jot or one tittle shall in no wise pass from the law, till all be fulfilled."

Matthew 9:11-13 "¹¹And when the Pharisees saw it, they said unto his disciples, Why eateth your Master with publicans and sinners? ¹²But when Jesus heard that, he said unto them, They that be whole need not a physician, but they that are sick. ¹³But go ye and learn what that meaneth, I will have mercy, and not sacrifice: for I am not come to call the righteous, but sinners to repentance."

Matthew 10:33-36 "³³But whosoever shall deny me before men, him will I also deny before my Father which is in heaven. ³⁴Think not that I am come to send peace on earth: I came not to send peace, but a sword. ³⁵For I am come to set a man at variance against his father, and the daughter against her mother, and the daughter in law against her mother in law. ³⁶And a man's foes shall be they of his own household."

Matthew 18:11 "For the Son of man is come to save that which was lost."

Matthew 20:28 "Even as the Son of man came not to be ministered unto, but to minister, and to give his life a ransom for many."

Mark 2:16-17 "¹⁶And when the scribes and Pharisees saw him eat with publicans and sinners, they said unto his disciples, How is it that he eateth and drinketh with publicans and sinners? ¹⁷When Jesus heard it, he saith unto them, They that are whole have no need of the physician, but they that are sick: I came not to call the righteous, but sinners to repentance."

Mark 10:45 "For even the Son of man came not to be ministered unto, but to minister, and to give his life a ransom for many."

Luke 4:14-19 "¹⁴And Jesus returned in the power of the Spirit into Galilee: and there went out a fame of him through all the region round about. ¹⁵And he taught in their synagogues, being glorified of all. ¹⁶And he came to Nazareth, where he had been brought up: and, as his custom was, he went into the synagogue on the sabbath day, and stood up for to read. ¹⁷And there was delivered unto him the book of the prophet Esaias. And when he had opened the book, he found the place where it was written, ¹⁸The Spirit of the Lord is upon me, because he hath anointed me to preach the gospel to the poor; he hath sent me to heal the brokenhearted, to preach deliverance to the captives, and recovering of sight to the blind, to set at liberty them that are bruised, ¹⁹To preach the acceptable year of the Lord."

Luke 5:30-32 "³⁰But their scribes and Pharisees murmured against his disciples, saying, Why do ye eat and drink with publicans and sinners? ³¹And Jesus answering said unto them, They that are whole need not a physician; but they that are sick. ³²I came not to call the righteous, but sinners to repentance."

Luke 9:54-56 "⁵⁴And when his disciples James and John saw this, they said, Lord, wilt thou that we command fire to come down from heaven, and consume them, even as Elias did? ⁵⁵But he turned, and rebuked them, and said, Ye know not what manner of spirit ye are of. ⁵⁶For the Son of man is not come to destroy men's lives, but to save them. And they went to another village."

Luke 12:49-53 "⁴⁹I am come to send fire on the earth; and what will I if it be already kindled? ⁵⁰But I have a baptism to be baptized with; and how am I straitened till it be accomplished! ⁵¹Suppose ye that I am come to give peace on earth? I tell you, Nay; but rather division: ⁵²For from henceforth there shall be five in one house divided, three against two, and two against three. ⁵³The father shall be divided against the son, and the son against the father; the mother against the daughter, and the daughter against the mother; the mother in law against her daughter in law, and the daughter in law against her mother in law."

Luke 19:9-10 "⁹And Jesus said unto him, This day is salvation come to this house, forsomuch as he also is a son of Abraham. ¹⁰For the Son of man is come to seek and to save that which was lost."

John 1:29 "The next day John seeth Jesus coming unto him, and saith, Behold the Lamb of God, which taketh away the sin of the world."

John 3:16-17 "¹⁶For God so loved the world, that he gave his only begotten Son, that whosoever believeth in him should not perish, but have everlasting life. ¹⁷For God sent not his Son into the world to condemn the world; but that the world through him might be saved."

John 4:25-26 "²⁵The woman saith unto him, I know that Messias cometh, which is called Christ: when he is come, he will tell us all things. ²⁶Jesus saith unto her, I that speak unto thee am he."

John 4:34 "Jesus saith unto them, My meat is to do the will of him that sent me, and to finish his work."

John 6:35-38 "³⁵And Jesus said unto them, I am the bread of life: he that cometh to me shall never hunger; and he that believeth on me shall never thirst. ³⁶But I said unto you, That ye also have seen me, and believe not. ³⁷All that the Father giveth me shall come to me; and him that cometh to me I will in no wise cast out. ³⁸For I came down from heaven, not to do mine own will, but the will of him that sent me."

John 9:39 "And Jesus said, For judgment I am come into this world, that they which see not might see; and that they which see might be made blind."

John 10:7-10 "⁷Then said Jesus unto them again, Verily, verily, I say unto you, I am the door of the sheep. ⁸All that ever came before me are thieves and robbers: but the sheep did not hear them. ⁹I am the door: by me if any man enter in, he shall be saved, and shall go in and out, and find pasture. ¹⁰The thief cometh not, but for to steal, and to kill, and to destroy: I am come that they might have life, and that they might have it more abundantly."

John 12:23-27 "²³And Jesus answered them, saying, The hour is come, that the Son of man should be glorified. ²⁴Verily, verily, I say unto you, Except a corn of wheat fall into the ground and die, it abideth alone: but if it die, it bringeth forth much fruit. ²⁵He that loveth his life shall lose it; and he that hateth his life in this world shall keep it unto life eternal. ²⁶If any man serve me, let him follow me; and where I am, there shall also my servant be: if any man serve me, him will my Father honour. ²⁷Now is my soul troubled; and what shall I say? Father, save me from this hour: but for this cause came I unto this hour."

John 12:44-47 "⁴⁴Jesus cried and said, He that believeth on me, believeth not on me, but on him that sent me. ⁴⁵And he that seeth me seeth him that sent me. ⁴⁶I am come a light into the world, that whosoever believeth on me should not abide in darkness. ⁴⁷And if any man hear my words, and believe not, I judge him not: for I came not to judge the world, but to save the world."

John 18:37 "Pilate therefore said unto him, Art thou a king then? Jesus answered, Thou sayest that I am a king. To this end was I born, and for this cause came I into the world, that I should bear witness unto the truth. Every one that is of the truth heareth my voice."

Acts 3:26 "Unto you first God, having raised up his Son Jesus, sent him to bless you, in turning away every one of you from his iniquities."

Acts 5:30-31 "³⁰The God of our fathers raised up Jesus, whom ye slew and hanged on a tree. ³¹Him hath God exalted with his right hand to be a Prince and a Saviour, for to give repentance to Israel, and forgiveness of sins."

Romans 14:9 "For to this end Christ both died, and rose, and revived, that he might be Lord both of the dead and living."

Romans 15:5-9 "⁵Now the God of patience and consolation grant you to be likeminded one toward another according to Christ Jesus: ⁶That ye may with one mind and one mouth glorify God, even the Father of our Lord Jesus Christ. ⁷Wherefore receive ye one another, as Christ also received us to the glory of God. ⁸Now I say that Jesus Christ was a minister of the circumcision for the truth of God, to confirm the promises made unto the fathers: ⁹And that the Gentiles might glorify God for his mercy; as it is written, For this cause I will confess to thee among the Gentiles, and sing unto thy name."

1 Corinthians 1:30 "But of him are ye in Christ Jesus, who of God is made unto us wisdom, and righteousness, and sanctification, and redemption:"

Galatians 4:3-5 "³Even so we, when we were children, were in bondage under the elements of the world: ⁴But when the fulness of the time was come, God sent forth his Son, made of a woman, made under the law, ⁵To redeem them that were under the law, that we might receive the adoption of sons."

Ephesians 2:13-18 "¹³But now in Christ Jesus ye who sometimes were far off are made nigh by the blood of Christ. ¹⁴For he is our peace, who hath made both one, and hath broken down the middle wall of partition between us; ¹⁵Having abolished in his flesh the enmity, even the law of commandments contained in ordinances; for to make in himself of twain one new man, so making peace; ¹⁶And that he might reconcile both unto God in one body by the cross, having slain the enmity thereby: ¹⁷And came and preached peace to you which were afar off, and to them that were nigh. ¹⁸For through him we both have access by one Spirit unto the Father."

1 Timothy 1:15 "This is a faithful saying, and worthy of all acceptation, that Christ Jesus came into the world to save sinners; of whom I am chief."

Hebrews 1:1-3 "¹God, who at sundry times and in divers manners spake in time past unto the fathers by the prophets, ²Hath in these last days spoken unto us by his Son, whom he hath appointed heir of all things, by whom also he made the worlds; ³Who being the brightness of his glory, and the express image of his person, and upholding all things by the word of his power, when he had by himself purged our sins, sat down on the right hand of the Majesty on high;"

Hebrews 10:7-10 "⁷Then said I, Lo, I come (in the volume of the book it is written of me,) to do thy will, O God. ⁸Above when he said, Sacrifice and offering and burnt offerings and offering for sin thou wouldest not, neither hadst pleasure therein; which are offered by the law; ⁹Then said he, Lo, I come to do thy will, O God. He taketh away the first, that he may establish the second. ¹⁰By the which will we are sanctified through the offering of the body of Jesus Christ once for all."

1 John 3:1-5 "¹Behold, what manner of love the Father hath bestowed upon us, that we should be called the sons of God: therefore the world knoweth us not, because it knew him not. ²Beloved, now are we the sons of God, and it doth not yet appear what we shall be: but we know that, when he shall appear, we shall be like him; for we shall see him as he is. ³And every man that hath this hope in him purifieth himself, even as he is pure. ⁴Whosoever committeth sin transgresseth also the law: for sin is the transgression of the law. ⁵And ye know that he was manifested to take away our sins; and in him is no sin."

1 John 3:8 "He that committeth sin is of the devil; for the devil sinneth from the beginning. For this purpose the Son of God was manifested, that he might destroy the works of the devil."

1 John 4:9-10 "⁹In this was manifested the love of God toward us, because that God sent his only begotten Son into the world, that we might live through him. ¹⁰Herein is love, not that we loved God, but that he loved us, and sent his Son to be the propitiation for our sins."

1 John 4:14 "And we have seen and do testify that the Father sent the Son to be the Saviour of the world."

1 John 5:20 "And we know that the Son of God is come, and hath given us an understanding, that we may know him that is true, and we are in him that is true, even in his Son Jesus Christ. This is the true God, and eternal life."

Jude 14-15 "¹⁴And Enoch also, the seventh from Adam, prophesied of these, saying, Behold, the Lord cometh with ten thousands of his saints, ¹⁵To execute judgment upon all, and to convince all that are ungodly among them of all their ungodly deeds which they have ungodly committed, and of all their hard speeches which ungodly sinners have spoken against him."

Revelation 1:4-6 "⁴John to the seven churches which are in Asia: Grace be unto you, and peace, from him which is, and which was, and which is to come; and from the seven Spirits which are before his throne; ⁵And from Jesus Christ, who is the faithful witness, and the first begotten of the dead, and the prince of the kings of the earth. Unto him that loved us, and washed us from our sins in his own blood, ⁶And hath made us kings and priests unto God and his Father; to him be glory and dominion for ever and ever. Amen."

Revelation 5:8-10 "⁸And when he had taken the book, the four beasts and four and twenty elders fell down before the Lamb, having every one of them harps, and golden vials full of odours, which are the prayers of saints. ⁹And they sung a new song, saying, Thou art worthy to take the book, and to open the seals thereof: for thou wast slain, and hast redeemed us to God by thy blood out of every kindred, and tongue, and people, and nation; ¹⁰And hast made us unto our God kings and priests: and we shall reign on the earth."

What Jesus Christ Is

Psalm 110:1-4 "[1]The LORD said unto my Lord, Sit thou at my right hand, until I make thine enemies thy footstool. [2]The LORD shall send the rod of thy strength out of Zion: rule thou in the midst of thine enemies. [3]Thy people shall be willing in the day of thy power, in the beauties of holiness from the womb of the morning: thou hast the dew of thy youth. [4]The LORD hath sworn, and will not repent, Thou art a priest for ever after the order of Melchizedek."

Isaiah 9:6 "For unto us a child is born, unto us a son is given: and the government shall be upon his shoulder: and his name shall be called Wonderful, Counseller, The mighty God, The everlasting Father, The Prince of Peace."

Isaiah 44:6 "Thus saith the LORD the King of Israel, and his redeemer the LORD of hosts; I am the first, and I am the last; and beside me there is no God."

Isaiah 48:12-14 "[12]Hearken unto me, O Jacob and Israel, my called; I am he; I am the first, I also am the last. [13]Mine hand also hath laid the foundation of the earth, and my right hand hath spanned the heavens: when I call unto them, they stand up together. [14]All ye, assemble yourselves, and hear; which among them hath declared these things? The LORD hath loved him: he will do his pleasure on Babylon, and his arm shall be on the Chaldeans."

Micah 5:2-5 "[2]But thou, Bethlehem Ephratah, though thou be little among the thousands of Judah, yet out of thee shall he come forth unto me that is to be ruler in Israel; whose goings forth have been from of old, from everlasting. [3]Therefore will he give them up, until the time that she which travaileth hath brought forth: then the remnant of his brethren shall return unto the children of Israel. [4]And he shall stand and feed in the strength of the LORD, in the majesty of the name of the LORD his God; and they shall abide: for now shall he be great unto the ends of the earth. [5]And this man shall be the peace, when the Assyrian shall come into our land: and when he shall tread in our palaces, then shall we raise against him seven shepherds, and eight principal men."

Matthew 1:20-21 "[20]But while he thought on these things, behold, the angel of the Lord appeared unto him in a dream, saying, Joseph, thou son of David, fear not to take unto thee Mary thy wife: for that which is conceived in her is of the Holy Ghost. [21]And she shall bring forth a son, and thou shalt call his name JESUS: for he shall save his people from their sins."

Matthew 2:1-2 "[1]Now when Jesus was born in Bethlehem of Judaea in the days of Herod the king, behold, there came wise men from the east to Jerusalem, [2]Saying, Where is he that is born King of the Jews? for we have seen his star in the east, and are come to worship him."

Matthew 3:16-17 "[16]And Jesus, when he was baptized, went up straightway out of the water: and, lo, the heavens were opened unto him, and he saw the Spirit of God descending like a dove, and lighting upon him: [17]And lo a voice from heaven, saying, This is my beloved Son, in whom I am well pleased."

Matthew 13:36-39 "[36]Then Jesus sent the multitude away, and went into the house: and his disciples came unto him, saying, Declare unto us the parable of the tares of the field. [37]He answered and said unto them, He that soweth the good seed is the Son of man; [38]The field is the world; the good seed are the children of the kingdom; but the tares are the children of the wicked one; [39]The enemy that sowed them is the devil; the harvest is the end of the world; and the reapers are the angels."

Matthew 16:13-16 "[13]When Jesus came into the coasts of Caesarea Philippi, he asked his disciples, saying, Whom do men say that I the Son of man am? [14]And they said, Some say that thou art John the Baptist: some, Elias; and others, Jeremias, or one of the prophets. [15]He saith unto them, But whom say ye that I am? [16]And Simon Peter answered and said, Thou art the Christ, the Son of the living God."

Matthew 17:4-5 "[4]Then answered Peter, and said unto Jesus, Lord, it is good for us to be here: if thou wilt, let us make here three tabernacles; one for thee, and one for Moses, and one for Elias. [5]While he yet spake, behold, a bright cloud overshadowed them: and behold a voice out of the cloud, which said, This is my beloved Son, in whom I am well pleased; hear ye him."

Matthew 21:9-11 "⁹And the multitudes that went before, and that followed, cried, saying, Hosanna to the Son of David: Blessed is he that cometh in the name of the Lord; Hosanna in the highest. ¹⁰And when he was come into Jerusalem, all the city was moved, saying, Who is this? ¹¹And the multitude said, This is Jesus the prophet of Nazareth of Galilee."

Matthew 23:8-10 "⁸But be not ye called Rabbi: for one is your Master, even Christ; and all ye are brethren. ⁹And call no man your father upon the earth: for one is your Father, which is in heaven. ¹⁰Neither be ye called masters: for one is your Master, even Christ."

Matthew 27:54 "Now when the centurion, and they that were with him, watching Jesus, saw the earthquake, and those things that were done, they feared greatly, saying, Truly this was the Son of God."

Mark 1:1 "The beginning of the gospel of Jesus Christ, the Son of God;"

Mark 1:9-11 "⁹And it came to pass in those days, that Jesus came from Nazareth of Galilee, and was baptized of John in Jordan. ¹⁰And straightway coming up out of the water, he saw the heavens opened, and the Spirit like a dove descending upon him: ¹¹And there came a voice from heaven, saying, Thou art my beloved Son, in whom I am well pleased."

Mark 2:27-28 "²⁷And he said unto them, The sabbath was made for man, and not man for the sabbath: ²⁸Therefore the Son of man is Lord also of the sabbath."

Mark 3:7-11 "⁷But Jesus withdrew himself with his disciples to the sea: and a great multitude from Galilee followed him, and from Judaea, ⁸And from Jerusalem, and from Idumaea, and from beyond Jordan; and they about Tyre and Sidon, a great multitude, when they had heard what great things he did, came unto him. ⁹And he spake to his disciples, that a small ship should wait on him because of the multitude, lest they should throng him. ¹⁰For he had healed many; insomuch that they pressed upon him for to touch him, as many as had plagues. ¹¹And unclean spirits, when they saw him, fell down before him, and cried, saying, Thou art the Son of God."

Mark 9:5-7 "⁵And Peter answered and said to Jesus, Master, it is good for us to be here: and let us make three tabernacles; one for thee, and one for Moses, and one for Elias. ⁶For he wist not what to say; for they were sore afraid. ⁷And there was a cloud that overshadowed them: and a voice came out of the cloud, saying, This is my beloved Son: hear him."

Mark 14:61-62 "⁶¹But he held his peace, and answered nothing. Again the high priest asked him, and said unto him, Art thou the Christ, the Son of the Blessed? ⁶²And Jesus said, I am: and ye shall see the Son of man sitting on the right hand of power, and coming in the clouds of heaven."

Mark 15:37-39 "³⁷And Jesus cried with a loud voice, and gave up the ghost. ³⁸And the veil of the temple was rent in twain from the top to the bottom. ³⁹And when the centurion, which stood over against him, saw that he so cried out, and gave up the ghost, he said, Truly this man was the Son of God."

Luke 1:31-32 "³¹And, behold, thou shalt conceive in thy womb, and bring forth a son, and shalt call his name JESUS. ³²He shall be great, and shall be called the Son of the Highest: and the Lord God shall give unto him the throne of his father David:"

Luke 2:11 "For unto you is born this day in the city of David a Saviour, which is Christ the Lord."

Luke 3:21-22 "²¹Now when all the people were baptized, it came to pass, that Jesus also being baptized, and praying, the heaven was opened, ²²And the Holy Ghost descended in a bodily shape like a dove upon him, and a voice came from heaven, which said, Thou art my beloved Son; in thee I am well pleased."

Luke 4:33-34 "³³And in the synagogue there was a man, which had a spirit of an unclean devil, and cried out with a loud voice, ³⁴Saying, Let us alone; what have we to do with thee, thou Jesus of Nazareth? art thou come to destroy us? I know thee who thou art; the Holy One of God."

Luke 4:40-41 "⁴⁰Now when the sun was setting, all they that had any sick with divers diseases brought them unto him; and he laid his hands on every one of them, and healed them. [41]And devils also came out of many, crying out, and saying, Thou art Christ the Son of God. And he rebuking them suffered them not to speak: for they knew that he was Christ."

Luke 8:28 "When he saw Jesus, he cried out, and fell down before him, and with a loud voice said, What have I to do with thee, Jesus, thou Son of God most high? I beseech thee, torment me not."

Luke 9:33-35 "[33]And it came to pass, as they departed from him, Peter said unto Jesus, Master, it is good for us to be here: and let us make three tabernacles; one for thee, and one for Moses, and one for Elias: not knowing what he said. [34]While he thus spake, there came a cloud, and overshadowed them: and they feared as they entered into the cloud. [35]And there came a voice out of the cloud, saying, This is my beloved Son: hear him."

Luke 19:35-38 "[35]And they brought him to Jesus: and they cast their garments upon the colt, and they set Jesus thereon. [36]And as he went, they spread their clothes in the way. [37]And when he was come nigh, even now at the descent of the mount of Olives, the whole multitude of the disciples began to rejoice and praise God with a loud voice for all the mighty works that they had seen; [38]Saying, Blessed be the King that cometh in the name of the Lord: peace in heaven, and glory in the highest."

John 1:1-9 "[1]In the beginning was the Word, and the Word was with God, and the Word was God. [2]The same was in the beginning with God. [3]All things were made by him; and without him was not any thing made that was made. [4]In him was life; and the life was the light of men. [5]And the light shineth in darkness; and the darkness comprehended it not [6]There was a man sent from God, whose name was John. [7]The same came for a witness, to bear witness of the Light, that all men through him might believe. [8]He was not that Light, but was sent to bear witness of that Light. [9]That was the true Light, which lighteth every man that cometh into the world."

John 1:18 "No man hath seen God at any time; the only begotten Son, which is in the bosom of the Father, he hath declared him."

John 1:29-34 "[29]The next day John seeth Jesus coming unto him, and saith, Behold the Lamb of God, which taketh away the sin of the world. [30]This is he of whom I said, After me cometh a man which is preferred before me: for he was before me. [31]And I knew him not: but that he should be made manifest to Israel, therefore am I come baptizing with water. [32]And John bare record, saying, I saw the Spirit descending from heaven like a dove, and it abode upon him. [33]And I knew him not: but he that sent me to baptize with water, the same said unto me, Upon whom thou shalt see the Spirit descending, and remaining on him, the same is he which baptizeth with the Holy Ghost. [34]And I saw, and bare record that this is the Son of God."

John 3:1-2 "[1]There was a man of the Pharisees, named Nicodemus, a ruler of the Jews: [2]The same came to Jesus by night, and said unto him, Rabbi, we know that thou art a teacher come from God: for no man can do these miracles that thou doest, except God be with him."

John 3:17-19 "[17]For God sent not his Son into the world to condemn the world; but that the world through him might be saved. [18]He that believeth on him is not condemned: but he that believeth not is condemned already, because he hath not believed in the name of the only begotten Son of God. [19]And this is the condemnation, that light is come into the world, and men loved darkness rather than light, because their deeds were evil."

John 3:27-35 "[27]John answered and said, A man can receive nothing, except it be given him from heaven. [28]Ye yourselves bear me witness, that I said, I am not the Christ, but that I am sent before him. [29]He that hath the bride is the bridegroom: but the friend of the bridegroom, which standeth and heareth him, rejoiceth greatly because of the bridegroom's voice: this my joy therefore is fulfilled. [30]He must increase, but I must decrease. [31]He that cometh from above is above all: he that is of the earth is earthly, and speaketh of the earth: he that cometh from heaven is above all. [32]And what he hath seen and heard, that he testifieth; and no man receiveth his testimony. [33]He that hath received his testimony hath set to his seal that God is true. [34]For he whom God hath sent speaketh the words of God: for God giveth not the Spirit by measure unto him. [35]The Father loveth the Son, and hath given all things into his hand."

John 4:25-26 "²⁵The woman saith unto him, I know that Messias cometh, which is called Christ: when he is come, he will tell us all things. ²⁶Jesus saith unto her, I that speak unto thee am he."

John 5:26-27 "²⁶For as the Father hath life in himself; so hath he given to the Son to have life in himself; ²⁷And hath given him authority to execute judgment also, because he is the Son of man."

John 6:31-35 "³¹Our fathers did eat manna in the desert; as it is written, He gave them bread from heaven to eat. ³²Then Jesus said unto them, Verily, verily, I say unto you, Moses gave you not that bread from heaven; but my Father giveth you the true bread from heaven. ³³For the bread of God is he which cometh down from heaven, and giveth life unto the world. ³⁴Then said they unto him, Lord, evermore give us this bread. ³⁵And Jesus said unto them, I am the bread of life: he that cometh to me shall never hunger; and he that believeth on me shall never thirst."

John 6:41-42 "⁴¹The Jews then murmured at him, because he said, I am the bread which came down from heaven. ⁴²And they said, Is not this Jesus, the son of Joseph, whose father and mother we know? how is it then that he saith, I came down from heaven?"

John 6:48-58 "⁴⁸I am that bread of life. ⁴⁹Your fathers did eat manna in the wilderness, and are dead. ⁵⁰This is the bread which cometh down from heaven, that a man may eat thereof, and not die. ⁵¹I am the living bread which came down from heaven: if any man eat of this bread, he shall live for ever: and the bread that I will give is my flesh, which I will give for the life of the world. ⁵²The Jews therefore strove among themselves, saying, How can this man give us his flesh to eat? ⁵³Then Jesus said unto them, Verily, verily, I say unto you, Except ye eat the flesh of the Son of man, and drink his blood, ye have no life in you. ⁵⁴Whoso eateth my flesh, and drinketh my blood, hath eternal life; and I will raise him up at the last day. ⁵⁵For my flesh is meat indeed, and my blood is drink indeed. ⁵⁶He that eateth my flesh, and drinketh my blood, dwelleth in me, and I in him. ⁵⁷As the living Father hath sent me, and I live by the Father: so he that eateth me, even he shall live by me. ⁵⁸This is that bread which came down from heaven: not as your fathers did eat manna,

and are dead: he that eateth of this bread shall live for ever."

John 6:67-69 "⁶⁷Then said Jesus unto the twelve, Will ye also go away? ⁶⁸Then Simon Peter answered him, Lord, to whom shall we go? thou hast the words of eternal life. ⁶⁹And we believe and are sure that thou art that Christ, the Son of the living God."

John 8:12 "Then spake Jesus again unto them, saying, I am the light of the world: he that followeth me shall not walk in darkness, but shall have the light of life."

John 8:25-29 "²⁵Then said they unto him, Who art thou? And Jesus saith unto them, Even the same that I said unto you from the beginning. ²⁶I have many things to say and to judge of you: but he that sent me is true; and I speak to the world those things which I have heard of him. ²⁷They understood not that he spake to them of the Father. ²⁸Then said Jesus unto them, When ye have lifted up the Son of man, then shall ye know that I am he, and that I do nothing of myself; but as my Father hath taught me, I speak these things. ²⁹And he that sent me is with me: the Father hath not left me alone; for I do always those things that please him."

John 9:3-5 "³Jesus answered, Neither hath this man sinned, nor his parents: but that the works of God should be made manifest in him. ⁴I must work the works of him that sent me, while it is day: the night cometh, when no man can work. ⁵As long as I am in the world, I am the light of the world."

John 10:1-18 "¹Verily, verily, I say unto you, He that entereth not by the door into the sheepfold, but climbeth up some other way, the same is a thief and a robber. ²But he that entereth in by the door is the shepherd of the sheep. ³To him the porter openeth; and the sheep hear his voice: and he calleth his own sheep by name, and leadeth them out. ⁴And when he putteth forth his own sheep, he goeth before them, and the sheep follow him: for they know his voice. ⁵And a stranger will they not follow, but will flee from him: for they know not the voice of strangers. ⁶This parable spake Jesus unto them: but they understood not what things they were which he spake unto them. ⁷Then said Jesus unto them again, Verily, verily, I say unto you, I am the door of the sheep.

[8]All that ever came before me are thieves and robbers: but the sheep did not hear them. [9]I am the door: by me if any man enter in, he shall be saved, and shall go in and out, and find pasture. [10]The thief cometh not, but for to steal, and to kill, and to destroy: I am come that they might have life, and that they might have it more abundantly. [11]I am the good shepherd: the good shepherd giveth his life for the sheep. [12]But he that is an hireling, and not the shepherd, whose own the sheep are not, seeth the wolf coming, and leaveth the sheep, and fleeth: and the wolf catcheth them, and scattereth the sheep. [13]The hireling fleeth, because he is an hireling, and careth not for the sheep. [14]I am the good shepherd, and know my sheep, and am known of mine. [15]As the Father knoweth me, even so know I the Father: and I lay down my life for the sheep. [16]And other sheep I have, which are not of this fold: them also I must bring, and they shall hear my voice; and there shall be one fold, and one shepherd. [17]Therefore doth my Father love me, because I lay down my life, that I might take it again. [18]No man taketh it from me, but I lay it down of myself. I have power to lay it down, and I have power to take it again. This commandment have I received of my Father."

John 10:34-38 "[34]Jesus answered them, Is it not written in your law, I said, Ye are gods? [35]If he called them gods, unto whom the word of God came, and the scripture cannot be broken; [36]Say ye of him, whom the Father hath sanctified, and sent into the world, Thou blasphemest; because I said, I am the Son of God? [37]If I do not the works of my Father, believe me not. [38]But if I do, though ye believe not me, believe the works: that ye may know, and believe, that the Father is in me, and I in him."

John 11:25 "Jesus said unto her, I am the resurrection, and the life: he that believeth in me, though he were dead, yet shall he live:"

John 12:12-13 "[12]On the next day much people that were come to the feast, when they heard that Jesus was coming to Jerusalem, [13]Took branches of palm trees, and went forth to meet him, and cried, Hosanna: Blessed is the King of Israel that cometh in the name of the Lord."

John 12:35-36 "[35]Then Jesus said unto them, Yet a little while is the light with you. Walk while ye have the light, lest darkness come upon you: for he that walketh in darkness knoweth not whither he goeth. [36]While ye have light, believe in the light, that ye may be the children of light. These things spake Jesus, and departed, and did hide himself from them."

John 12:44-46 "[44]Jesus cried and said, He that believeth on me, believeth not on me, but on him that sent me. [45]And he that seeth me seeth him that sent me. [46]I am come a light into the world, that whosoever believeth on me should not abide in darkness."

John 13:10-19 "[10]Jesus saith to him, He that is washed needeth not save to wash his feet, but is clean every whit: and ye are clean, but not all. [11]For he knew who should betray him; therefore said he, Ye are not all clean. [12]So after he had washed their feet, and had taken his garments, and was set down again, he said unto them, Know ye what I have done to you? [13]Ye call me Master and Lord: and ye say well; for so I am. [14]If I then, your Lord and Master, have washed your feet; ye also ought to wash one another's feet. [15]For I have given you an example, that ye should do as I have done to you. [16]Verily, verily, I say unto you, The servant is not greater than his lord; neither he that is sent greater than he that sent him. [17]If ye know these things, happy are ye if ye do them. [18]I speak not of you all: I know whom I have chosen: but that the scripture may be fulfilled, He that eateth bread with me hath lifted up his heel against me. [19]Now I tell you before it come, that, when it is come to pass, ye may believe that I am he."

John 14:6 "Jesus saith unto him, I am the way, the truth, and the life: no man cometh unto the Father, but by me."

John 15:1-8 "[1]I am the true vine, and my Father is the husbandman. [2]Every branch in me that beareth not fruit he taketh away: and every branch that beareth fruit, he purgeth it, that it may bring forth more fruit. [3]Now ye are clean through the word which I have spoken unto you. [4]Abide in me, and I in you. As the branch cannot bear fruit of itself, except it abide in the vine; no more can ye, except ye abide in me. [5]I am the vine, ye are the branches: He that abideth in me, and I in him, the same bringeth forth much fruit: for without me ye can do nothing. [6]If a man abide not in me, he is cast forth as a branch, and is withered; and men gather them, and cast them into the fire, and they are burned. [7]If ye abide in me, and my words abide in you, ye shall ask what ye will, and it shall be done unto you. [8]Herein is my Father glorified, that ye bear much fruit; so shall ye be my disciples."

John 18:37 "Pilate therefore said unto him, Art thou a king then? Jesus answered, Thou sayest that I am a king. To this end was I born, and for this cause came I into the world, that I should bear witness unto the truth. Every one that is of the truth heareth my voice."

John 20:31 "But these are written, that ye might believe that Jesus is the Christ, the Son of God; and that believing ye might have life through his name."

Acts 2:22 "Ye men of Israel, hear these words; Jesus of Nazareth, a man approved of God among you by miracles and wonders and signs, which God did by him in the midst of you, as ye yourselves also know:"

Acts 2:36 "Therefore let all the house of Israel know assuredly, that God hath made that same Jesus, whom ye have crucified, both Lord and Christ."

Acts 3:13-15 "[13]The God of Abraham, and of Isaac, and of Jacob, the God of our fathers, hath glorified his Son Jesus; whom ye delivered up, and denied him in the presence of Pilate, when he was determined to let him go. [14]But ye denied the Holy One and the Just, and desired a murderer to be granted unto you; [15]And killed the Prince of life, whom God hath raised from the dead; whereof we are witnesses."

Acts 3:26 "Unto you first God, having raised up his Son Jesus, sent him to bless you, in turning away every one of you from his iniquities."

Acts 4:9-11 "[9]If we this day be examined of the good deed done to the impotent man, by what means he is made whole; [10]Be it known unto you all, and to all the people of Israel, that by the name of Jesus Christ of Nazareth, whom ye crucified, whom God raised from the dead, even by him doth this man stand here before you whole. [11]This is the stone which was set at nought of you builders, which is become the head of the corner."

Acts 5:30-31 "[30]The God of our fathers raised up Jesus, whom ye slew and hanged on a tree. [31]Him hath God exalted with his right hand to be a Prince and a Saviour, for to give repentance to Israel, and forgiveness of sins."

Acts 10:36-42 "[36]The word which God sent unto the children of Israel, preaching peace by Jesus Christ: (he is Lord of all:) [37]That word, I say, ye know, which was published throughout all Judaea, and began from Galilee, after the baptism which John preached; [38]How God anointed Jesus of Nazareth with the Holy Ghost and with power: who went about doing good, and healing all that were oppressed of the devil; for God was with him. [39]And we are witnesses of all things which he did both in the land of the Jews, and in Jerusalem; whom they slew and hanged on a tree: [40]Him God raised up the third day, and shewed him openly; [41]Not to all the people, but unto witnesses chosen before of God, even to us, who did eat and drink with him after he rose from the dead. [42]And he commanded us to preach unto the people, and to testify that it is he which was ordained of God to be the Judge of quick and dead."

Acts 13:22-23 "[22]And when he had removed him, he raised up unto them David to be their king; to whom also he gave testimony, and said, I have found David the son of Jesse, a man after mine own heart, which shall fulfil all my will. [23]Of this man's seed hath God according to his promise raised unto Israel a Saviour, Jesus:"

Acts 17:3 "Opening and alleging, that Christ must needs have suffered, and risen again from the dead; and that this Jesus, whom I preach unto you, is Christ."

Romans 10:4 "For Christ is the end of the law for righteousness to every one that believeth."

Romans 14:9 "For to this end Christ both died, and rose, and revived, that he might be Lord both of the dead and living."

Romans 15:8 "Now I say that Jesus Christ was a minister of the circumcision for the truth of God, to confirm the promises made unto the fathers:"

1 Corinthians 10:1-4 "[1]Moreover, brethren, I would not that ye should be ignorant, how that all our fathers were under the cloud, and all passed through the sea; ²And were all baptized unto Moses in the cloud and in the sea; ³And did all eat the same spiritual meat; ⁴And did all drink the same spiritual drink: for they drank of that spiritual Rock that followed them: and that Rock was Christ."

1 Corinthians 11:2-3 "²Now I praise you, brethren, that ye remember me in all things, and keep the ordinances, as I delivered them to you. ³But I would have you know, that the head of every man is Christ; and the head of the woman is the man; and the head of Christ is God."

1 Corinthians 15:20-23 "²⁰But now is Christ risen from the dead, and become the firstfruits of them that slept. ²¹For since by man came death, by man came also the resurrection of the dead. ²²For as in Adam all die, even so in Christ shall all be made alive. ²³But every man in his own order: Christ the firstfruits; afterward they that are Christ's at his coming."

1 Corinthians 15:45 "And so it is written, The first man Adam was made a living soul; the last Adam was made a quickening spirit."

2 Corinthians 4:3-4 "³But if our gospel be hid, it is hid to them that are lost: ⁴In whom the god of this world hath blinded the minds of them which believe not, lest the light of the glorious gospel of Christ, who is the image of God, should shine unto them."

Ephesians 1:19-23 "¹⁹And what is the exceeding greatness of his power to usward who believe, according to the working of his mighty power, ²⁰Which he wrought in Christ, when he raised him from the dead, and set him at his own right hand in the heavenly places, ²¹Far above all principality, and power, and might, and dominion, and every name that is named, not only in this world, but also in that which is to come: ²²And hath put all things under his feet, and gave him to be the head over all things to the church, ²³Which is his body, the fulness of him that filleth all in all."

Ephesians 2:13-14 "¹³But now in Christ Jesus ye who sometimes were far off are made nigh by the blood of Christ. ¹⁴For he is our peace, who hath made both one, and hath broken down the middle wall of partition between us;"

Ephesians 2:19-20 "¹⁹Now therefore ye are no more strangers and foreigners, but fellowcitizens with the saints, and of the household of God; ²⁰And are built upon the foundation of the apostles and prophets, Jesus Christ himself being the chief corner stone;"

Ephesians 5:22-23 "²²Wives, submit yourselves unto your own husbands, as unto the Lord. ²³For the husband is the head of the wife, even as Christ is the head of the church: and he is the saviour of the body."

Philippians 2:5-6 "⁵Let this mind be in you, which was also in Christ Jesus: ⁶Who, being in the form of God, thought it not robbery to be equal with God:"

Philippians 3:20-21 "²⁰For our conversation is in heaven; from whence also we look for the Saviour, the Lord Jesus Christ: ²¹Who shall change our vile body, that it may be fashioned like unto his glorious body, according to the working whereby he is able even to subdue all things unto himself."

Colossians 1:12-20 "¹²Giving thanks unto the Father, which hath made us meet to be partakers of the inheritance of the saints in light: ¹³Who hath delivered us from the power of darkness, and hath translated us into the kingdom of his dear Son: ¹⁴In whom we have redemption through his blood, even the forgiveness of sins: ¹⁵Who is the image of the invisible God, the firstborn of every creature: ¹⁶For by him were all things created, that are in heaven, and that are in earth, visible and invisible, whether they be thrones, or dominions, or principalities, or powers: all things were created by him, and for him: ¹⁷And he is before all things, and by him all things consist. ¹⁸And he is the head of the body, the church: who is the beginning, the firstborn from the dead; that in all things he might have the preeminence. ¹⁹For it pleased the Father that in him should all fulness dwell; ²⁰And, having made peace through the blood of his cross, by him to reconcile all things unto himself; by him, I say, whether they be things in earth, or things in heaven."

Colossians 2:8-10 "⁸Beware lest any man spoil you through philosophy and vain deceit, after the tradition of men, after the rudiments of the world, and not after Christ. ⁹For in him dwelleth all the fulness of the Godhead bodily. ¹⁰And ye are complete in him, which is the head of all principality and power:"

Colossians 3:4 "When Christ, who is our life, shall appear, then shall ye also appear with him in glory."

Colossians 3:11 "Where there is neither Greek nor Jew, circumcision nor uncircumcision, Barbarian, Scythian, bond nor free: but Christ is all, and in all."

1 Thessalonians 1:9-10 "⁹For they themselves shew of us what manner of entering in we had unto you, and how ye turned to God from idols to serve the living and true God; ¹⁰And to wait for his Son from heaven, whom he raised from the dead, even Jesus, which delivered us from the wrath to come."

1 Timothy 1:1-2 "¹Paul, an apostle of Jesus Christ by the commandment of God our Saviour, and Lord Jesus Christ, which is our hope; ²Unto Timothy, my own son in the faith: Grace, mercy, and peace, from God our Father and Jesus Christ our Lord."

1 Timothy 2:5 "For there is one God, and one mediator between God and men, the man Christ Jesus;"

Titus 2:13 "Looking for that blessed hope, and the glorious appearing of the great God and our Saviour Jesus Christ;"

Titus 3:6 "Which he shed on us abundantly through Jesus Christ our Saviour;"

Hebrews 1:1-7 "¹God, who at sundry times and in divers manners spake in time past unto the fathers by the prophets, ²Hath in these last days spoken unto us by his Son, whom he hath appointed heir of all things, by whom also he made the worlds; ³Who being the brightness of his glory, and the express image of his person, and upholding all things by the word of his power, when he had by himself purged our sins, sat down on the right hand of the Majesty on high; ⁴Being made so much better than the angels, as he hath by inheritance obtained a more excellent name than they. ⁵For unto which of the angels said he at any time, Thou art my Son, this day have I begotten thee? And again, I will be to him a Father, and he shall be to me a Son? ⁶And again, when he bringeth in the firstbegotten into the world, he saith, And let

all the angels of God worship him. ⁷And of the angels he saith, Who maketh his angels spirits, and his ministers a flame of fire."

Hebrews 2:9-17 "⁹But we see Jesus, who was made a little lower than the angels for the suffering of death, crowned with glory and honour; that he by the grace of God should taste death for every man. ¹⁰For it became him, for whom are all things, and by whom are all things, in bringing many sons unto glory, to make the captain of their salvation perfect through sufferings. ¹¹For both he that sanctifieth and they who are sanctified are all of one: for which cause he is not ashamed to call them brethren, ¹²Saying, I will declare thy name unto my brethren, in the midst of the church will I sing praise unto thee. ¹³And again, I will put my trust in him. And again, Behold I and the children which God hath given me. ¹⁴Forasmuch then as the children are partakers of flesh and blood, he also himself likewise took part of the same; that through death he might destroy him that had the power of death, that is, the devil; ¹⁵And deliver them who through fear of death were all their lifetime subject to bondage. ¹⁶For verily he took not on him the nature of angels; but he took on him the seed of Abraham. ¹⁷Wherefore in all things it behoved him to be made like unto his brethren, that he might be a merciful and faithful high priest in things pertaining to God, to make reconciliation for the sins of the people."

Hebrews 4:14-15 "¹⁴Seeing then that we have a great high priest, that is passed into the heavens, Jesus the Son of God, let us hold fast our profession. ¹⁵For we have not an high priest which cannot be touched with the feeling of our infirmities; but was in all points tempted like as we are, yet without sin."

Hebrews 5:5-10 "⁵So also Christ glorified not himself to be made an high priest; but he that said unto him, Thou art my Son, to day have I begotten thee. ⁶As he saith also in another place, Thou art a priest for ever after the order of Melchisedec. ⁷Who in the days of his flesh, when he had offered up prayers and supplications with strong crying and tears unto him that was able to save him from death, and was heard in that he feared; ⁸Though he were a Son, yet learned he obedience by the things which he suffered; ⁹And being made perfect, he became the author of eternal salvation unto all them that obey him; ¹⁰Called of God an high priest after the order of Melchisedec."

Hebrews 6:20 "Whither the forerunner is for us entered, even Jesus, made an high priest for ever after the order of Melchisedec."

Hebrews 7:15-28 "¹⁵And it is yet far more evident: for that after the similitude of Melchisedec there ariseth another priest, ¹⁶Who is made, not after the law of a carnal commandment, but after the power of an endless life. ¹⁷For he testifieth, Thou art a priest for ever after the order of Melchisedec. ¹⁸For there is verily a disannulling of the commandment going before for the weakness and unprofitableness thereof. ¹⁹For the law made nothing perfect, but the bringing in of a better hope did; by the which we draw nigh unto God. ²⁰And inasmuch as not without an oath he was made priest: ²¹(For those priests were made without an oath; but this with an oath by him that said unto him, The Lord sware and will not repent, Thou art a priest for ever after the order of Melchisedec:) ²²By so much was Jesus made a surety of a better testament. ²³And they truly were many priests, because they were not suffered to continue by reason of death: ²⁴But this man, because he continueth ever, hath an unchangeable priesthood. ²⁵Wherefore he is able also to save them to the uttermost that come unto God by him, seeing he ever liveth to make intercession for them. ²⁶For such an high priest became us, who is holy, harmless, undefiled, separate from sinners, and made higher than the heavens; ²⁷Who needeth not daily, as those high priests, to offer up sacrifice, first for his own sins, and then for the people's: for this he did once, when he offered up himself. ²⁸For the law maketh men high priests which have infirmity; but the word of the oath, which was since the law, maketh the Son, who is consecrated for evermore."

Hebrews 9:11-14 "¹¹But Christ being come an high priest of good things to come, by a greater and more perfect tabernacle, not made with hands, that is to say, not of this building; ¹²Neither by the blood of goats and calves, but by his own blood he entered in once into the holy place, having obtained eternal redemption for us. ¹³For if the blood of bulls and of goats, and the ashes of an heifer sprinkling the unclean, sanctifieth to the purifying of the flesh: ¹⁴How much more shall the blood of Christ, who through the eternal Spirit offered himself without spot to God, purge your conscience from dead works to serve the living God?"

Hebrews 12:1-2 "¹Wherefore seeing we also are compassed about with so great a cloud of witnesses, let us lay aside every weight, and the sin which doth so easily beset us, and let us run with patience the race that is set before us, ²Looking unto Jesus the author and finisher of our faith; who for the joy that was set before him endured the cross, despising the shame, and is set down at the right hand of the throne of God."

Hebrews 12:24 "And to Jesus the mediator of the new covenant, and to the blood of sprinkling, that speaketh better things than that of Abel."

James 2:1 "My brethren, have not the faith of our Lord Jesus Christ, the Lord of glory, with respect of persons."

1 Peter 2:21-25 "²¹For even hereunto were ye called: because Christ also suffered for us, leaving us an example, that ye should follow his steps: ²²Who did no sin, neither was guile found in his mouth: ²³Who, when he was reviled, reviled not again; when he suffered, he threatened not; but committed himself to him that judgeth righteously: ²⁴Who his own self bare our sins in his own body on the tree, that we, being dead to sins, should live unto righteousness: by whose stripes ye were healed. ²⁵For ye were as sheep going astray; but are now returned unto the Shepherd and Bishop of your souls."

2 Peter 1:1 "Simon Peter, a servant and an apostle of Jesus Christ, to them that have obtained like precious faith with us through the righteousness of God and our Saviour Jesus Christ:"

2 Peter 1:11 "For so an entrance shall be ministered unto you abundantly into the everlasting kingdom of our Lord and Saviour Jesus Christ."

2 Peter 1:16-17 "¹⁶For we have not followed cunningly devised fables, when we made known unto you the power and coming of our Lord Jesus Christ, but were eyewitnesses of his majesty. ¹⁷For he received from God the Father honour and glory, when there came such a voice to him from the excellent glory, This is my beloved Son, in whom I am well pleased."

2 Peter 3:18 "But grow in grace, and in the knowledge of our Lord and Saviour Jesus Christ. To him be glory both now and for ever. Amen."

1 John 1:1-3 "¹That which was from the beginning, which we have heard, which we have seen with our eyes, which we have looked upon, and our hands have handled, of the Word of life; ²(For the life was manifested, and we have seen it, and bear witness, and shew unto you that eternal life, which was with the Father, and was manifested unto us;) ³That which we have seen and heard declare we unto you, that ye also may have fellowship with us: and truly our fellowship is with the Father, and with his Son Jesus Christ."

1 John 2:1-2 "¹My little children, these things write I unto you, that ye sin not. And if any man sin, we have an advocate with the Father, Jesus Christ the righteous: ²And he is the propitiation for our sins: and not for ours only, but also for the sins of the whole world."

1 John 4:9-10 "⁹In this was manifested the love of God toward us, because that God sent his only begotten Son into the world, that we might live through him. ¹⁰Herein is love, not that we loved God, but that he loved us, and sent his Son to be the propitiation for our sins."

1 John 4:14 "And we have seen and do testify that the Father sent the Son to be the Saviour of the world."

1 John 5:20 "And we know that the Son of God is come, and hath given us an understanding, that we may know him that is true, and we are in him that is true, even in his Son Jesus Christ. This is the true God, and eternal life."

2 John 3 "Grace be with you, mercy, and peace, from God the Father, and from the Lord Jesus Christ, the Son of the Father, in truth and love."

Revelation 1:4-5 "⁴John to the seven churches which are in Asia: Grace be unto you, and peace, from him which is, and which was, and which is to come; and from the seven Spirits which are before his throne; ⁵And from Jesus Christ, who is the faithful witness, and the first begotten of the dead, and the prince of the kings of the earth. Unto him that loved us, and washed us from our sins in his own blood,"

Revelation 1:8 "I am Alpha and Omega, the beginning and the ending, saith the Lord, which is, and which was, and which is to come, the Almighty."

Revelation 1:11 "Saying, I am Alpha and Omega, the first and the last: and, What thou seest, write in a book, and send it unto the seven churches which are in Asia; unto Ephesus, and unto Smyrna, and unto Pergamos, and unto Thyatira, and unto Sardis, and unto Philadelphia, and unto Laodicea."

Revelation 1:17-18 "¹⁷And when I saw him, I fell at his feet as dead. And he laid his right hand upon me, saying unto me, Fear not; I am the first and the last: ¹⁸I am he that liveth, and was dead; and, behold, I am alive for evermore, Amen; and have the keys of hell and of death."

Revelation 2:8 "And unto the angel of the church in Smyrna write; These things saith the first and the last, which was dead, and is alive;"

Revelation 3:1 "And unto the angel of the church in Sardis write; These things saith he that hath the seven Spirits of God, and the seven stars; I know thy works, that thou hast a name that thou livest, and art dead."

Revelation 3:7 "And to the angel of the church in Philadelphia write; These things saith he that is holy, he that is true, he that hath the key of David, he that openeth, and no man shutteth; and shutteth, and no man openeth;"

Revelation 3:14 "And unto the angel of the church of the Laodiceans write; These things saith the Amen, the faithful and true witness, the beginning of the creation of God;"

Revelation 5:5 "And one of the elders saith unto me, Weep not: behold, the Lion of the tribe of Juda, the Root of David, hath prevailed to open the book, and to loose the seven seals thereof."

Revelation 17:14 "These shall make war with the Lamb, and the Lamb shall overcome them: for he is Lord of lords, and King of kings: and they that are with him are called, and chosen, and faithful."

Revelation 19:11-16 "¹¹And I saw heaven opened, and behold a white horse; and he that sat upon him was called Faithful and True, and in righteousness he doth judge and make war. ¹²His eyes were as a flame of fire, and on his head were many crowns;

and he had a name written, that no man knew, but he himself. [13]And he was clothed with a vesture dipped in blood: and his name is called The Word of God. [14]And the armies which were in heaven followed him upon white horses, clothed in fine linen, white and clean. [15]And out of his mouth goeth a sharp sword, that with it he should smite the nations: and he shall rule them with a rod of iron: and he treadeth the winepress of the fierceness and wrath of Almighty God. [16]And he hath on his vesture and on his thigh a name written, KING OF KINGS, AND LORD OF LORDS."

Revelation 21:6 "And he said unto me, It is done. I am Alpha and Omega, the beginning and the end. I will give unto him that is athirst of the fountain of the water of life freely."

Revelation 21:21-23 "[21]And the twelve gates were twelve pearls; every several gate was of one pearl: and the street of the city was pure gold, as it were transparent glass. [22]And I saw no temple therein: for the Lord God Almighty and the Lamb are the temple of it. [23]And the city had no need of the sun, neither of the moon, to shine in it: for the glory of God did lighten it, and the Lamb is the light thereof."

Revelation 22:13 "I am Alpha and Omega, the beginning and the end, the first and the last."

Revelation 22:16 "I Jesus have sent mine angel to testify unto you these things in the churches. I am the root and the offspring of David, and the bright and morning star."

What Jesus Christ Is In

Colossians 3:11 "Where there is neither Greek nor Jew, circumcision nor uncircumcision, Barbarian, Scythian, bond nor free: but Christ is all, and in all."

What Jesus Christ Is Over

John 17:1-2 "[1]These words spake Jesus, and lifted up his eyes to heaven, and said, Father, the hour is come; glorify thy Son, that thy Son also may glorify thee: [2]As thou hast given him power over all flesh, that he should give eternal life to as many as thou hast given him."

Romans 9:5 "Whose are the fathers, and of whom as concerning the flesh Christ came, who is over all, God blessed for ever. Amen."

What Jesus Christ Left To Do

John 14:1-6 "[1]Let not your heart be troubled: ye believe in God, believe also in me. [2]In my Father's house are many mansions: if it were not so, I would have told you. I go to prepare a place for you. [3]And if I go and prepare a place for you, I will come again, and receive you unto myself; that where I am, there ye may be also. [4]And whither I go ye know, and the way ye know. [5]Thomas saith unto him, Lord, we know not whither thou goest; and how can we know the way? [6]Jesus saith unto him, I am the way, the truth, and the life: no man cometh unto the Father, but by me."

What Jesus Christ Speaks

Deuteronomy 18:17-19 "[17]And the LORD said unto me, They have well spoken that which they have spoken. [18]I will raise them up a Prophet from among their brethren, like unto thee, and will put my words in his mouth; and he shall speak unto them all that I shall command him. [19]And it shall come to pass, that whosoever will not hearken unto my words which he shall speak in my name, I will require it of him."

John 3:34-35 "[34]For he whom God hath sent speaketh the words of God: for God giveth not the Spirit by measure unto him. [35]The Father loveth the Son, and hath given all things into his hand."

John 8:25-29 "[25]Then said they unto him, Who art thou? And Jesus saith unto them, Even the same that I said unto you from the beginning. [26]I have many things to say and to judge of you: but he that sent me is true; and I speak to the world those things which I have heard of him. [27]They understood not that he spake to them of the Father. [28]Then said Jesus unto them, When ye have lifted up the Son of man, then shall ye know that I am he, and that I do nothing of myself; but as my Father hath taught me, I speak these things. [29]And he that sent me is with me: the Father hath not left me alone; for I do always those things that please him."

John 8:36-38 "[36]If the Son therefore shall make you free, ye shall be free indeed. [37]I know that ye are Abraham's seed; but ye seek to kill me, because my word hath no place in you. [38]I speak that which I have seen with my Father: and ye do that which ye have seen with your father."

John 12:44-50 "[44]Jesus cried and said, He that believeth on me, believeth not on me, but on him that sent me. [45]And he that seeth me seeth him that sent me. [46]I am come a light into the world, that whosoever believeth on me should not abide in darkness. [47]And if any man hear my words, and believe not, I judge him not: for I came not to judge the world, but to save the world. [48]He that rejecteth me, and receiveth not my words, hath one that judgeth him: the word that I have spoken, the same shall judge him in the last day. [49]For I have not spoken of myself; but the Father which sent me, he gave me a commandment, what I should say, and what I should speak. [50]And I know that his commandment is life everlasting: whatsoever I speak therefore, even as the Father said unto me, so I speak."

John 15:1-15 "[1]I am the true vine, and my Father is the husbandman. [2]Every branch in me that beareth not fruit he taketh away: and every branch that beareth fruit, he purgeth it, that it may bring forth more fruit. [3]Now ye are clean through the word which I have spoken unto you. [4]Abide in me, and I in you. As the branch cannot bear fruit of itself, except it abide in the vine; no more can ye, except ye abide in me. [5]I am the vine, ye are the branches: He that abideth in me, and I in him, the same bringeth forth much fruit: for without me ye can do nothing. [6]If a man abide not in me, he is cast forth as a branch, and is withered; and men gather them, and cast them into the fire, and they are burned. [7]If ye abide in me, and my words abide in you, ye shall ask what ye will, and it shall be done unto you. [8]Herein is my Father glorified, that ye bear much fruit; so shall ye be my disciples. [9]As the Father hath loved me, so have I loved you: continue ye in my love. [10]If ye keep my commandments, ye shall abide in my love; even as I have kept my Father's commandments, and abide in his love. [11]These things have I spoken unto you, that my joy might remain in you, and that your joy might be full. [12]This is my commandment, That ye love one another, as I have loved you. [13]Greater love hath no man than this, that a man lay down his life for his friends. [14]Ye are my friends, if ye do whatsoever I command you. [15]Henceforth I call you not servants; for the servant knoweth not what his lord doeth: but I have called you friends; for all things that I have heard of my Father I have made known unto you."

John 16:29-33 "[29]His disciples said unto him, Lo, now speakest thou plainly, and speakest no proverb. [30]Now are we sure that thou knowest all things, and needest not that any man should ask thee: by this we believe that thou camest forth from God. [31]Jesus answered them, Do ye now believe? [32]Behold, the hour cometh, yea, is now come, that ye shall be scattered, every man to his own, and shall leave me alone: and yet I am not alone, because the Father is with me. [33]These things I have spoken unto you, that in me ye might have peace. In the world ye shall have tribulation: but be of good cheer; I have overcome the world."

John 17:1-14 "[1]These words spake Jesus, and lifted up his eyes to heaven, and said, Father, the hour is come; glorify thy Son, that thy Son also may glorify thee: [2]As thou hast given him power over all flesh, that he should give eternal life to as many as thou hast given him. [3]And this is life eternal, that they might know thee the only true God, and Jesus Christ, whom thou hast sent. [4]I have glorified thee on the earth: I have finished the work which thou gavest me to do. [5]And now, O Father, glorify thou me with thine own self with the glory which I had with thee before the world was. [6]I have manifested thy name unto the men which thou gavest me out of the world: thine they were, and thou gavest them me; and they have kept thy word. [7]Now they have known that all things whatsoever thou hast given me are of thee. [8]For I have given unto them the words which thou gavest me; and they have received them, and have known surely that I came out from thee, and they have believed that thou didst send me. [9]I pray for them: I pray not for the world, but for them which thou hast given me; for they are thine. [10]And all mine are thine, and thine are mine; and I am glorified in them. [11]And now I am no more in the world, but these are in the world, and I come to thee. Holy Father, keep through thine own name those whom thou hast given me, that they may be one, as we are. [12]While I was with them in the world, I kept them in thy name: those that thou gavest me I have kept, and none of them is lost, but the son of perdition; that the scripture might be fulfilled. [13]And now come I to thee; and these things I speak in the world, that they might have my joy fulfilled in themselves. [14]I have given them thy word; and the world hath hated them, because they are not of the world, even as I am not of the world."

John 18:22-23 "²²And when he had thus spoken, one of the officers which stood by struck Jesus with the palm of his hand, saying, Answerest thou the high priest so? ²³Jesus answered him, If I have spoken evil, bear witness of the evil: but if well, why smitest thou me?"

Acts 1:1-3 "¹The former treatise have I made, O Theophilus, of all that Jesus began both to do and teach, ²Until the day in which he was taken up, after that he through the Holy Ghost had given commandments unto the apostles whom he had chosen: ³To whom also he shewed himself alive after his passion by many infallible proofs, being seen of them forty days, and speaking of the things pertaining to the kingdom of God:"

What Was Foretold About Jesus Christ

Genesis 3:14-15 "¹⁴And the LORD God said unto the serpent, Because thou hast done this, thou art cursed above all cattle, and above every beast of the field; upon thy belly shalt thou go, and dust shalt thou eat all the days of thy life: ¹⁵And I will put enmity between thee and the woman, and between thy seed and her seed; it shall bruise thy head, and thou shalt bruise his heel."

Genesis 49:24 "But his bow abode in strength, and the arms of his hands were made strong by the hands of the mighty God of Jacob; (from thence is the shepherd, the stone of Israel:)"

Exodus 12:46 "In one house shall it be eaten; thou shalt not carry forth ought of the flesh abroad out of the house; neither shall ye break a bone thereof."

Exodus 17:6 "Behold, I will stand before thee there upon the rock in Horeb; and thou shalt smite the rock, and there shall come water out of it, that the people may drink. And Moses did so in the sight of the elders of Israel."

Numbers 9:12 "They shall leave none of it unto the morning, nor break any bone of it: according to all the ordinances of the passover they shall keep it."

Numbers 20:10-11 "¹⁰And Moses and Aaron gathered the congregation together before the rock, and he said unto them, Hear now, ye rebels; must we fetch you water out of this rock? ¹¹And Moses lifted up his hand, and with his rod he smote the rock twice: and the water came out abundantly, and the congregation drank, and their beasts also."

Deuteronomy 18:15-19 "¹⁵The LORD thy God will raise up unto thee a Prophet from the midst of thee, of thy brethren, like unto me; unto him ye shall hearken; ¹⁶According to all that thou desiredst of the LORD thy God in Horeb in the day of the assembly, saying, Let me not hear again the voice of the LORD my God, neither let me see this great fire any more, that I die not. ¹⁷And the LORD said unto me, They have well spoken that which they have spoken. ¹⁸I will raise them up a Prophet from among their brethren, like unto thee, and will put my words in his mouth; and he shall speak unto them all that I shall command him. ¹⁹And it shall come to pass, that whosoever will not hearken unto my words which he shall speak in my name, I will require it of him."

2 Samuel 7:8-17 "⁸Now therefore so shalt thou say unto my servant David, Thus saith the LORD of hosts, I took thee from the sheepcote, from following the sheep, to be ruler over my people, over Israel: ⁹And I was with thee whithersoever thou wentest, and have cut off all thine enemies out of thy sight, and have made thee a great name, like unto the name of the great men that are in the earth. ¹⁰Moreover I will appoint a place for my people Israel, and will plant them, that they may dwell in a place of their own, and move no more; neither shall the children of wickedness afflict them any more, as beforetime, ¹¹And as since the time that I commanded judges to be over my people Israel, and have caused thee to rest from all thine enemies. Also the LORD telleth thee that he will make thee an house. ¹²And when thy days be fulfilled, and thou shalt sleep with thy fathers, I will set up thy seed after thee, which shall proceed out of thy bowels, and I will establish his kingdom. ¹³He shall build an house for my name, and I will stablish the throne of his kingdom for ever. ¹⁴I will be his father, and he shall be my son. If he commit iniquity, I will chasten him with the rod of men, and with the stripes of the children of men: ¹⁵But my mercy shall not depart away from him, as I took it from Saul, whom I put away before thee. ¹⁶And thine house and thy kingdom shall be established for ever before thee: thy throne shall be established for ever. ¹⁷According to all these words, and according to all this vision, so did Nathan speak unto David."

1 Kings 8:25 "Therefore now, LORD God of Israel, keep with thy servant David my father that thou promisedst him, saying, There shall not fail thee a man in my sight to sit on the throne of Israel; so that thy children take heed to their way, that they walk before me as thou hast walked before me."

1 Chronicles 17:7-15 "7Now therefore thus shalt thou say unto my servant David, Thus saith the LORD of hosts, I took thee from the sheepcote, even from following the sheep, that thou shouldest be ruler over my people Israel: 8And I have been with thee whithersoever thou hast walked, and have cut off all thine enemies from before thee, and have made thee a name like the name of the great men that are in the earth. 9Also I will ordain a place for my people Israel, and will plant them, and they shall dwell in their place, and shall be moved no more; neither shall the children of wickedness waste them any more, as at the beginning, 10And since the time that I commanded judges to be over my people Israel. Moreover I will subdue all thine enemies. Furthermore I tell thee that the LORD will build thee an house. 11And it shall come to pass, when thy days be expired that thou must go to be with thy fathers, that I will raise up thy seed after thee, which shall be of thy sons; and I will establish his kingdom. 12He shall build me an house, and I will stablish his throne for ever. 13I will be his father, and he shall be my son: and I will not take my mercy away from him, as I took it from him that was before thee: 14But I will settle him in mine house and in my kingdom for ever: and his throne shall be established for evermore. 15According to all these words, and according to all this vision, so did Nathan speak unto David."

1 Chronicles 28:2-7 "2Then David the king stood up upon his feet, and said, Hear me, my brethren, and my people: As for me, I had in mine heart to build an house of rest for the ark of the covenant of the LORD, and for the footstool of our God, and had made ready for the building: 3But God said unto me, Thou shalt not build an house for my name, because thou hast been a man of war, and hast shed blood. 4Howbeit the LORD God of Israel chose me before all the house of my father to be king over Israel for ever: for he hath chosen Judah to be the ruler; and of the house of Judah, the house of my father; and among the sons of my father he liked me to make me king over all Israel: 5And of all my sons, (for the LORD hath given me many sons,) he hath chosen Solomon my son to sit upon the throne of the kingdom of the LORD over Israel. 6And he said unto me, Solomon thy son, he shall build my house and my courts: for I have chosen him to be my son, and I will be his father. 7Moreover I will establish his kingdom for ever, if he be constant to do my commandments and my judgments, as at this day."

Psalm 2:1-12 "1Why do the heathen rage, and the people imagine a vain thing? 2The kings of the earth set themselves, and the rulers take counsel together, against the LORD, and against his anointed, saying, 3Let us break their bands asunder, and cast away their cords from us. 4He that sitteth in the heavens shall laugh: the Lord shall have them in derision. 5Then shall he speak unto them in his wrath, and vex them in his sore displeasure. 6Yet have I set my king upon my holy hill of Zion. 7I will declare the decree: the LORD hath said unto me, Thou art my Son; this day have I begotten thee. 8Ask of me, and I shall give thee the heathen for thine inheritance, and the uttermost parts of the earth for thy possession. 9Thou shalt break them with a rod of iron; thou shalt dash them in pieces like a potter's vessel. 10Be wise now therefore, O ye kings: be instructed, ye judges of the earth. 11Serve the LORD with fear, and rejoice with trembling. 12Kiss the Son, lest he be angry, and ye perish from the way, when his wrath is kindled but a little. Blessed are all they that put their trust in him."

Psalm 16:8-10 "8I have set the LORD always before me: because he is at my right hand, I shall not be moved. 9Therefore my heart is glad, and my glory rejoiceth: my flesh also shall rest in hope. 10For thou wilt not leave my soul in hell; neither wilt thou suffer thine Holy One to see corruption."

Psalm 22:1-21 "1My God, my God, why hast thou forsaken me? why art thou so far from helping me, and from the words of my roaring? 2O my God, I cry in the daytime, but thou hearest not; and in the night season, and am not silent. 3But thou art holy, O thou that inhabitest the praises of Israel. 4Our fathers trusted in thee: they trusted, and thou didst deliver them. 5They cried unto thee, and were delivered: they trusted in thee, and were not confounded. ⁶But I am a worm, and no man; a reproach of men, and despised of the people. ⁷All they that see me laugh me to scorn: they shoot out the lip, they shake the head saying, ⁸He trusted on the LORD that he would deliver him: let him deliver him, seeing he delighted in him. ⁹But thou art he that took me out of the womb: thou didst make me hope when I was upon my mother's breasts. ¹⁰I was cast upon thee from the womb: thou art my God from my mother's belly. ¹¹Be not far from me; for trouble is near; for there is none to help. ¹²Many bulls have compassed me: strong bulls of Bashan have beset me round. ¹³They gaped upon me with their mouths, as a ravening and a roaring lion. ¹⁴I am poured out like water, and all my bones are out of joint: my heart is like wax; it is melted in the midst of my bowels. ¹⁵My strength is dried up like a potsherd; and my tongue cleaveth to my jaws; and thou hast brought me into the dust of death. ¹⁶For dogs have compassed me: the assembly of the wicked have inclosed me: they pierced my hands and my feet. ¹⁷I may tell all my bones: they look and stare upon me. ¹⁸They part my garments among them, and cast lots upon my vesture. ¹⁹But be not thou far from me, O LORD: O my strength, haste thee to help me. ²⁰Deliver my soul from the sword; my darling from the power of the dog. ²¹Save me from the lion's mouth: for thou hast heard me from the horns of the unicorns."

Psalm 34:19-20 "¹⁹Many are the afflictions of the righteous: but the LORD delivereth him out of them all. ²⁰He keepeth all his bones: not one of them is broken."

Psalm 35:17-19 "¹⁷Lord, how long wilt thou look on? rescue my soul from their destructions, my darling from the lions. ¹⁸I will give thee thanks in the great congregation: I will praise thee among much people. ¹⁹Let not them that are mine enemies wrongfully rejoice over me: neither let them wink with the eye that hate me without a cause."

Psalm 40:6-10 "⁶Sacrifice and offering thou didst not desire; mine ears hast thou opened: burnt offering and sin offering hast thou not required. ⁷Then said I, Lo, I come: in the volume of the book it is written of me, ⁸I delight to do thy will, O my God: yea, thy law is within my heart. ⁹I have preached righteousness in the great congregation: lo, I have not refrained my lips, O LORD,

thou knowest. ¹⁰I have not hid thy righteousness within my heart; I have declared thy faithfulness and thy salvation: I have not concealed thy lovingkindness and thy truth from the great congregation."

Psalm 41:9 "Yea, mine own familiar friend, in whom I trusted, which did eat of my bread, hath lifted up his heel against me."

Psalm 69:1-12 "¹Save me, O God; for the waters are come in unto my soul. ²I sink in deep mire, where there is no standing: I am come into deep waters, where the floods overflow me. ³I am weary of my crying: my throat is dried: mine eyes fail while I wait for my God. ⁴They that hate me without a cause are more than the hairs of mine head: they that would destroy me, being mine enemies wrongfully, are mighty: then I restored that which I took not away. ⁵O God, thou knowest my foolishness; and my sins are not hid from thee. ⁶Let not them that wait on thee, O Lord GOD of hosts, be ashamed for my sake: let not those that seek thee be confounded for my sake, O God of Israel. ⁷Because for thy sake I have borne reproach; shame hath covered my face. ⁸I am become a stranger unto my brethren, and an alien unto my mother's children. ⁹For the zeal of thine house hath eaten me up; and the reproaches of them that reproached thee are fallen upon me. ¹⁰When I wept, and chastened my soul with fasting, that was to my reproach. ¹¹I made sackcloth also my garment; and I became a proverb to them. ¹²They that sit in the gate speak against me; and I was the song of the drunkards."

Psalm 110:1-7 "¹The LORD said unto my Lord, Sit thou at my right hand, until I make thine enemies thy footstool. ²The LORD shall send the rod of thy strength out of Zion: rule thou in the midst of thine enemies. ³Thy people shall be willing in the day of thy power, in the beauties of holiness from the womb of the morning: thou hast the dew of thy youth. ⁴The LORD hath sworn, and will not repent, Thou art a priest for ever after the order of Melchizedek. ⁵The Lord at thy right hand shall strike through kings in the day of his wrath. ⁶He shall judge among the heathen, he shall fill the places with the dead bodies; he shall wound the heads over many countries. ⁷He shall drink of the brook in the way: therefore shall he lift up the head."

Psalm 118:19-22 "¹⁹Open to me the gates of right-eousness: I will go into them, and I will praise the LORD: ²⁰This gate of the LORD, into which the righteous shall enter. ²¹I will praise thee: for thou hast heard me, and art become my salvation. ²²The stone which the builders refused is become the head stone of the corner."

Psalm 132:11 "The LORD hath sworn in truth unto David; he will not turn from it; Of the fruit of thy body will I set upon thy throne."

Proverbs 30:4 "Who hath ascended up into heaven, or descended? who hath gathered the wind in his fists? who hath bound the waters in a garment? who hath established all the ends of the earth? what is his name, and what is his son's name, if thou canst tell?"

Isaiah 4:2-6 "²In that day shall the branch of the LORD be beautiful and glorious, and the fruit of the earth shall be excellent and comely for them that are escaped of Israel. ³And it shall come to pass, that he that is left in Zion, and he that remaineth in Jerusalem, shall be called holy, even every one that is written among the living in Jerusalem: ⁴When the Lord shall have washed away the filth of the daughters of Zion, and shall have purged the blood of Jerusalem from the midst thereof by the spirit of judgment, and by the spirit of burning. ⁵And the LORD will create upon every dwelling place of mount Zion, and upon her assemblies, a cloud and smoke by day, and the shining of a flaming fire by night: for upon all the glory shall be a defence. ⁶And there shall be a tabernacle for a shadow in the daytime from the heat, and for a place of refuge, and for a covert from storm and from rain."

Isaiah 7:14-16 "¹⁴Therefore the Lord himself shall give you a sign; Behold, a virgin shall conceive, and bear a son, and shall call his name Immanuel. ¹⁵Butter and honey shall he eat, that he may know to refuse the evil, and choose the good. ¹⁶For before the child shall know to refuse the evil, and choose the good, the land that thou abhorrest shall be forsaken of both her kings."

Isaiah 9:6-7 "⁶For unto us a child is born, unto us a son is given: and the government shall be upon his shoulder: and his name shall be called Wonderful, Counseller, The mighty God, The everlasting Father, The Prince of Peace. ⁷Of the increase of his government and peace there shall be no end, upon the throne of David, and upon his kingdom, to order it, and to establish it with judgment and with justice from henceforth even for ever. The zeal of the LORD of hosts will perform this."

Isaiah 11:1-16 "¹And there shall come forth a rod out of the stem of Jesse, and a Branch shall grow out of his roots: ²And the spirit of the LORD shall rest upon him, the spirit of wisdom and under-standing, the spirit of counsel and might, the spirit of knowledge and of the fear of the LORD; ³And shall make him of quick understanding in the fear of the LORD: and he shall not judge after the sight of his eyes, neither reprove after the hearing of his ears: ⁴But with righteousness shall he judge the poor, and reprove with equity for the meek of the earth: and he shall smite the earth with the rod of his mouth, and with the breath of his lips shall he slay the wicked. ⁵And righteousness shall be the girdle of his loins, and faithfulness the girdle of his reins. ⁶The wolf also shall dwell with the lamb, and the leopard shall lie down with the kid; and the calf and the young lion and the fatling together; and a little child shall lead them. ⁷And the cow and the bear shall feed; their young ones shall lie down together: and the lion shall eat straw like the ox. ⁸And the sucking child shall play on the hole of the asp, and the weaned child shall put his hand on the cockatrice' den. ⁹They shall not hurt nor destroy in all my holy mountain: for the earth shall be full of the knowledge of the LORD, as the waters cover the sea. ¹⁰And in that day there shall be a root of Jesse, which shall stand for an ensign of the people; to it shall the Gentiles seek: and his rest shall be glorious. ¹¹And it shall come to pass in that day, that the Lord shall set his hand again the second time to recover the remnant of his peo-ple, which shall be left, from Assyria, and from Egypt, and from Pathros, and from Cush, and from Elam, and from Shinar, and from Hamath, and from the islands of the sea. ¹²And he shall set up an ensign for the nations, and shall assemble the outcasts of Israel, and gather together the dis-persed of Judah from the four corners of the earth. ¹³The envy also of Ephraim shall depart, and the adversaries of Judah shall be cut off: Ephraim shall not envy Judah, and Judah shall not vex Ephraim. ¹⁴But they shall fly upon the shoulders of the Philistines toward the west; they shall spoil them of the east together: they shall lay their hand upon Edom and Moab; and the children of Ammon shall obey them. ¹⁵And the LORD shall utterly destroy the tongue of the Egyptian sea; and with his mighty wind shall he shake his hand over the river, and shall smite it in the seven streams, and make men go over dryshod. ¹⁶And there shall be an highway for the remnant of his people, which shall be left, from Assyria; like as it was to Israel in the day that he came up out of the land of Egypt."

Isaiah 28:14-16 "¹⁴Wherefore hear the word of the LORD, ye scornful men, that rule this people which is in Jerusalem. ¹⁵Because ye have said, We have made a covenant with death, and with hell are we at agreement; when the overflowing scourge shall pass through, it shall not come unto us: for we have made lies our refuge, and under falsehood have we hid ourselves: ¹⁶Therefore thus saith the Lord GOD, Behold, I lay in Zion for a foundation a stone, a tried stone, a precious corner stone, a sure foundation: he that believeth shall not make haste."

Isaiah 32:1-8 "¹Behold, a king shall reign in righteousness, and princes shall rule in judgment. ²And a man shall be as an hiding place from the wind, and a covert from the tempest; as rivers of water in a dry place, as the shadow of a great rock in a weary land. ³And the eyes of them that see shall not be dim, and the ears of them that hear shall hearken. ⁴The heart also of the rash shall understand knowledge, and the tongue of the stammerers shall be ready to speak plainly. ⁵The vile person shall be no more called liberal, nor the churl said to be bountiful. ⁶For the vile person will speak villany, and his heart will work iniquity, to practise hypocrisy, and to utter error against the LORD, to make empty the soul of the hungry, and he will cause the drink of the thirsty to fail. ⁷The instruments also of the churl are evil: he deviseth wicked devices to destroy the poor with lying words, even when the needy speaketh right. ⁸But the liberal deviseth liberal things; and by liberal things shall he stand."

Isaiah 40:1-11 "¹Comfort ye, comfort ye my people, saith your God. ²Speak ye comfortably to Jerusalem, and cry unto her, that her warfare is accomplished, that her iniquity is pardoned: for she hath received of the LORD's hand double for all her sins. ³The voice of him that crieth in the wilderness, Prepare ye the way of the LORD, make straight in the desert a highway for our God. ⁴Every valley shall be exalted, and every mountain and hill shall be made low: and the crooked shall be made straight, and the rough places plain: ⁵And the glory of the LORD shall be revealed, and all flesh shall see it together: for the mouth of the LORD hath spoken it. ⁶The voice said, Cry. And he said, What shall I cry? All flesh is grass, and all the goodliness thereof is as the flower of the field: ⁷The grass withereth, the flower fadeth: because the spirit of the LORD bloweth upon it: surely the people is grass. ⁸The grass withereth, the flower fadeth: but the word of our God shall stand for ever. ⁹O Zion, that bringest good tidings, get thee up into the high mountain; O Jerusalem, that bringest good tidings, lift up thy voice with strength; lift it up, be not afraid; say unto the cities of Judah, Behold your God! ¹⁰Behold, the Lord GOD will come with strong hand, and his arm shall rule for him: behold, his reward is with him, and his work before him. ¹¹He shall feed his flock like a shepherd: he shall gather the lambs with his arm, and carry them in his bosom, and shall gently lead those that are with young."

Isaiah 42:1-9 "¹Behold my servant, whom I uphold; mine elect, in whom my soul delighteth; I have put my spirit upon him: he shall bring forth judgment to the Gentiles. ²He shall not cry, nor lift up, nor cause his voice to be heard in the street. ³A bruised reed shall he not break, and the smoking flax shall he not quench: he shall bring forth judgment unto truth. ⁴He shall not fail nor be discouraged, till he have set judgment in the earth: and the isles shall wait for his law. ⁵Thus saith God the LORD, he that created the heavens, and stretched them out; he that spread forth the earth, and that which cometh out of it; he that giveth breath unto the people upon it, and spirit to them that walk therein: ⁶I the LORD have called thee in righteousness, and will hold thine hand, and will keep thee, and give thee for a covenant of the people, for a light of the Gentiles; ⁷To open the blind eyes, to bring out the prisoners from the prison, and them that sit in darkness out of the prison house. ⁸I am the LORD: that is my name: and my glory will I not give to another, neither my praise to graven images. ⁹Behold, the former things are come to pass, and new things do I declare: before they spring forth I tell you of them."

Isaiah 44:1-3 "¹Yet now hear, O Jacob my servant; and Israel, whom I have chosen: ²Thus saith the LORD that made thee, and formed thee from the womb, which will help thee; Fear not, O Jacob, my servant; and thou, Jesurun, whom I have chosen. ³For I will pour water upon him that is thirsty, and floods upon the dry ground: I will pour my spirit upon thy seed, and my blessing upon thine offspring:"

Isaiah 50:4-10 "⁴The Lord GOD hath given me the tongue of the learned, that I should know how to speak a word in season to him that is weary: he wakeneth morning by morning, he wakeneth mine ear to hear as the learned. ⁵The Lord GOD hath opened mine ear, and I was not rebellious, neither turned away back. ⁶I gave my back to the smiters, and my cheeks to them that plucked off the hair: I hid not my face from shame and spitting. ⁷For the Lord GOD will help me; therefore shall I not be confounded: therefore have I set my face like a flint, and I know that I shall not be ashamed. ⁸He is near that justifieth me; who will contend with me? let us stand together: who is mine adversary? let him come near to me. ⁹Behold, the Lord GOD will help me; who is he that shall condemn me? lo, they all shall wax old as a garment; the moth shall eat them up. ¹⁰Who is among you that feareth the LORD, that obeyeth the voice of his servant, that walketh in darkness, and hath no light? let him trust in the name of the LORD, and stay upon his God."

Isaiah 52:12-15 "¹²For ye shall not go out with haste, nor go by flight: for the LORD will go before you; and the God of Israel will be your rereward. ¹³Behold, my servant shall deal prudently, he shall be exalted and extolled, and be very high. ¹⁴As many were astonied at thee; his visage was so marred more than any man, and his form more than the sons of men: ¹⁵So shall he sprinkle many nations; the kings shall shut their mouths at him: for that which had not been told them shall they see; and that which they had not heard shall they consider."

Isaiah 53:1-12 "¹Who hath believed our report? and to whom is the arm of the LORD revealed?

²For he shall grow up before him as a tender plant, and as a root out of a dry ground: he hath no form nor comeliness; and when we shall see him, there is no beauty that we should desire him. ³He is despised and rejected of men; a man of sorrows, and acquainted with grief: and we hid as it were our faces from him; he was despised, and we esteemed him not. ⁴Surely he hath borne our griefs, and carried our sorrows: yet we did esteem him stricken, smitten of God, and afflicted. ⁵But he was wounded for our transgressions, he was bruised for our iniquities: the chastisement of our peace was upon him; and with his stripes we are healed. ⁶All we like sheep have gone astray; we have turned every one to his own way; and the LORD hath laid on him the iniquity of us all. ⁷He was oppressed, and he was afflicted, yet he opened not his mouth: he is brought as a lamb to the slaughter, and as a sheep before her shearers is dumb, so he openeth not his mouth. ⁸He was taken from prison and from judgment: and who shall declare his generation? for he was cut off out of the land of the living: for the transgression of my people was he stricken. ⁹And he made his grave with the wicked, and with the rich in his death; because he had done no violence, neither was any deceit in his mouth. ¹⁰Yet it pleased the LORD to bruise him; he hath put him to grief: when thou shalt make his soul an offering for sin, he shall see his seed, he shall prolong his days, and the pleasure of the LORD shall prosper in his hand. ¹¹He shall see of the travail of his soul, and shall be satisfied: by his knowledge shall my righteous servant justify many; for he shall bear their iniquities. ¹²Therefore will I divide him a portion with the great, and he shall divide the spoil with the strong; because he hath poured out his soul unto death: and he was numbered with the transgressors; and he bare the sin of many, and made intercession for the transgressors."

Isaiah 55:1-3 "¹Ho, every one that thirsteth, come ye to the waters, and he that hath no money; come ye, buy, and eat; yea, come, buy wine and milk without money and without price. ²Wherefore do ye spend money for that which is not bread? and your labour for that which satisfieth not? hearken diligently unto me, and eat ye that which is good, and let your soul delight itself in fatness. ³Incline your ear, and come unto me: hear, and your soul shall live; and I will make an everlasting covenant with you, even the sure mercies of David."

Isaiah 59:20 "And the Redeemer shall come to Zion, and unto them that turn from transgression in Jacob, saith the LORD."

Isaiah 61:1-3 "¹The Spirit of the Lord GOD is upon me; because the LORD hath anointed me to preach good tidings unto the meek; he hath sent me to bind up the brokenhearted, to proclaim liberty to the captives, and the opening of the prison to them that are bound; ²To proclaim the acceptable year of the LORD, and the day of vengeance of our God; to comfort all that mourn; ³To appoint unto them that mourn in Zion, to give unto them beauty for ashes, the oil of joy for mourning, the garment of praise for the spirit of heaviness; that they might be called trees of righteousness, the planting of the LORD, that he might be glorified."

Jeremiah 23:5-8 "⁵Behold, the days come, saith the LORD, that I will raise unto David a righteous Branch, and a King shall reign and prosper, and shall execute judgment and justice in the earth. ⁶In his days Judah shall be saved, and Israel shall dwell safely: and this is his name whereby he shall be called, THE LORD OUR RIGHTEOUSNESS. ⁷Therefore, behold, the days come, saith the LORD, that they shall no more say, The LORD liveth, which brought up the children of Israel out of the land of Egypt; ⁸But, The LORD liveth, which brought up and which led the seed of the house of Israel out of the north country, and from all countries whither I had driven them; and they shall dwell in their own land."

Jeremiah 33:14-17 "¹⁴Behold, the days come, saith the LORD, that I will perform that good thing which I have promised unto the house of Israel and to the house of Judah. ¹⁵In those days, and at that time, will I cause the Branch of righteousness to grow up unto David; and he shall execute judgment and righteousness in the land. ¹⁶In those days shall Judah be saved, and Jerusalem shall dwell safely: and this is the name wherewith she shall be called, The LORD our righteousness. ¹⁷For thus saith the LORD; David shall never want a man to sit upon the throne of the house of Israel;"

Ezekiel 34:11-24 "¹¹For thus saith the Lord GOD; Behold, I, even I, will both search my sheep, and seek them out. ¹²As a shepherd seeketh out his flock in the day that he is among his sheep that are scattered; so will I seek out my sheep, and will deliver them out of all places where they have been scattered in the cloudy and dark day. ¹³And I will bring them out from the people, and gather them from the countries, and will bring them to their own land, and feed them upon the mountains of Israel by the rivers, and in all the inhabited places of the country. ¹⁴I will feed them in a good pasture, and upon the high mountains of Israel shall their fold be: there shall they lie in a good fold, and in a fat pasture shall they feed upon the mountains of Israel. ¹⁵I will feed my flock, and I will cause them to lie down, saith the Lord GOD. ¹⁶I will seek that which was lost, and bring again that which was driven away, and will bind up that which was broken, and will strengthen that which was sick: but I will destroy the fat and the strong; I will feed them with judgment. ¹⁷And as for you, O my flock, thus saith the Lord GOD; Behold, I judge between cattle and cattle, between the rams and the he goats. ¹⁸Seemeth it a small thing unto you to have eaten up the good pasture, but ye must tread down with your feet the residue of your pastures? and to have drunk of the deep waters, but ye must foul the residue with your feet? ¹⁹And as for my flock, they eat that which ye have trodden with your feet; and they drink that which ye have fouled with your feet. ²⁰Therefore thus saith the Lord GOD unto them; Behold, I, even I, will judge between the fat cattle and between the lean cattle. ²¹Because ye have thrust with side and with shoulder, and pushed all the diseased with your horns, till ye have scattered them abroad; ²²Therefore will I save my flock, and they shall no more be a prey; and I will judge between cattle and cattle. ²³And I will set up one shepherd over them, and he shall feed them, even my servant David; he shall feed them, and he shall be their shepherd. ²⁴And I the LORD will be their God, and my servant David a prince among them; I the LORD have spoken it."

Daniel 3:23-25 "²³And these three men, Shadrach, Meshach, and Abed-nego, fell down bound into the midst of the burning fiery furnace. ²⁴Then Nebuchadnezzar the king was astonied, and rose up in haste, and spake, and said unto his coun-sellers, Did not we cast three men bound into the midst of the fire? They answered and said unto the king, True, O king. 25He answered and said, Lo, I see four men loose, walking in the midst of the fire, and they have no hurt; and the form of the fourth is like the Son of God."

Daniel 7:9-14 "9I beheld till the thrones were cast down, and the Ancient of days did sit, whose gar-ment was white as snow, and the hair of his head like the pure wool: his throne was like the fiery flame, and his wheels as burning fire. 10A fiery stream issued and came forth from before him: thousand thousands ministered unto him, and ten thousand times ten thousand stood before him: the judgment was set, and the books were opened. 11I beheld then because of the voice of the great words which the horn spake: I beheld even till the beast was slain, and his body destroyed, and given to the burning flame. 12As concerning the rest of the beasts, they had their dominion taken away: yet their lives were prolonged for a season and time. 13I saw in the night visions, and, behold, one like the Son of man came with the clouds of heaven, and came to the Ancient of days, and they brought him near before him. 14And there was given him dominion, and glory, and a kingdom, that all people, nations, and languages, should serve him: his dominion is an everlasting domin-ion, which shall not pass away, and his kingdom that which shall not be destroyed."

Daniel 9:24-27 "24Seventy weeks are determined upon thy people and upon thy holy city, to finish the transgression, and to make an end of sins, and to make reconciliation for iniquity, and to bring in everlasting righteousness, and to seal up the vision and prophecy, and to anoint the most Holy. 25Know therefore and understand, that from the going forth of the commandment to restore and to build Jerusalem unto the Messiah the Prince shall be seven weeks, and threescore and two weeks: the street shall be built again, and the wall, even in troublous times. 26And after threescore and two weeks shall Messiah be cut off, but not for himself: and the people of the prince that shall come shall destroy the city and the sanctuary; and the end thereof shall be with a flood, and unto the end of the war desolations are determined. 27And

he shall confirm the covenant with many for one week: and in the midst of the week he shall cause the sacrifice and the oblation to cease, and for the overspreading of abominations he shall make it desolate, even until the consummation, and that determined shall be poured upon the desolate."

Hosea 6:1-3 "1Come, and let us return unto the LORD: for he hath torn, and he will heal us; he hath smitten, and he will bind us up. 2After two days will he revive us: in the third day he will raise us up, and we shall live in his sight. 3Then shall we know, if we follow on to know the LORD: his going forth is prepared as the morning; and he shall come unto us as the rain, as the lat-ter and former rain unto the earth."

Micah 5:2-9 "2But thou, Bethlehem Ephratah, though thou be little among the thousands of Judah, yet out of thee shall he come forth unto me that is to be ruler in Israel; whose goings forth have been from of old, from everlasting. 3There-fore will he give them up, until the time that she which travaileth hath brought forth: then the remnant of his brethren shall return unto the children of Israel. 4And he shall stand and feed in the strength of the LORD, in the majesty of the name of the LORD his God; and they shall abide: for now shall he be great unto the ends of the earth. 5And this man shall be the peace, when the Assyrian shall come into our land: and when he shall tread in our palaces, then shall we raise against him seven shepherds, and eight principal men. 6And they shall waste the land of Assyria with the sword, and the land of Nimrod in the entrances thereof: thus shall he deliver us from the Assyrian, when he cometh into our land, and when he treadeth within our borders. 7And the remnant of Jacob shall be in the midst of many people as a dew from the LORD, as the showers upon the grass, that tarrieth not for man, nor waiteth for the sons of men. 8And the remnant of Jacob shall be among the Gentiles in the midst of many people as a lion among the beasts of the for-est, as a young lion among the flocks of sheep: who, if he go through, both treadeth down, and teareth in pieces, and none can deliver. 9Thine hand shall be lifted up upon thine adversaries, and all thine enemies shall be cut off."

Zechariah 2:4-13 "⁴And said unto him, Run, speak to this young man, saying, Jerusalem shall be inhabited as towns without walls for the multitude of men and cattle therein: ⁵For I, saith the LORD, will be unto her a wall of fire round about, and will be the glory in the midst of her. ⁶Ho, ho, come forth, and flee from the land of the north, saith the LORD: for I have spread you abroad as the four winds of the heaven, saith the LORD. ⁷Deliver thyself, O Zion, that dwellest with the daughter of Babylon. ⁸For thus saith the LORD of hosts; After the glory hath he sent me unto the nations which spoiled you: for he that toucheth you toucheth the apple of his eye. ⁹For, behold, I will shake mine hand upon them, and they shall be a spoil to their servants: and ye shall know that the LORD of hosts hath sent me. ¹⁰Sing and rejoice, O daughter of Zion: for, lo, I come, and I will dwell in the midst of thee, saith the LORD. ¹¹And many nations shall be joined to the LORD in that day, and shall be my people: and I will dwell in the midst of thee, and thou shalt know that the LORD of hosts hath sent me unto thee. ¹²And the LORD shall inherit Judah his portion in the holy land, and shall choose Jerusalem again. ¹³Be silent, O all flesh, before the LORD: for he is raised up out of his holy habitation."

Zechariah 6:12 "And speak unto him, saying, Thus speaketh the LORD of hosts, saying, Behold the man whose name is The BRANCH; and he shall grow up out of his place, and he shall build the temple of the LORD:"

Zechariah 9:9-10 "⁹Rejoice greatly, O daughter of Zion; shout, O daughter of Jerusalem: behold, thy King cometh unto thee: he is just, and having salvation; lowly, and riding upon an ass, and upon a colt the foal of an ass. ¹⁰And I will cut off the chariot from Ephraim, and the horse from Jerusalem, and the battle bow shall be cut off: and he shall speak peace unto the heathen: and his dominion shall be from sea even to sea, and from river even to the ends of the earth."

Zechariah 12:10-14 "¹⁰And I will pour upon the house of David, and upon the inhabitants of Jerusalem, the spirit of grace and of supplications: and they shall look upon me whom they have pierced, and they shall mourn for him, as one mourneth for his only son, and shall be in bitterness for him,

as one that is in bitterness for his firstborn. ¹¹In that day shall there be a great mourning in Jerusalem, as the mourning of Hadadrimmon in the valley of Megiddon. ¹²And the land shall mourn, every family apart; the family of the house of David apart, and their wives apart; the family of the house of Nathan apart, and their wives apart; ¹³The family of the house of Levi apart, and their wives apart; the family of Shimei apart, and their wives apart; ¹⁴All the families that remain, every family apart, and their wives apart."

Zechariah 13:7 "Awake, O sword, against my shepherd, and against the man that is my fellow, saith the LORD of hosts: smite the shepherd, and the sheep shall be scattered: and I will turn mine hand upon the little ones."

Zechariah 14:1-21 "¹Behold, the day of the LORD cometh, and thy spoil shall be divided in the midst of thee. ²For I will gather all nations against Jerusalem to battle; and the city shall be taken, and the houses rifled, and the women ravished; and half of the city shall go forth into captivity, and the residue of the people shall not be cut off from the city. ³Then shall the LORD go forth, and fight against those nations, as when he fought in the day of battle. ⁴And his feet shall stand in that day upon the mount of Olives, which is before Jerusalem on the east, and the mount of Olives shall cleave in the midst thereof toward the east and toward the west, and there shall be a very great valley; and half of the mountain shall remove toward the north, and half of it toward the south. ⁵And ye shall flee to the valley of the mountains; for the valley of the mountains shall reach unto Azal: yea, ye shall flee, like as ye fled from before the earthquake in the days of Uzziah king of Judah: and the LORD my God shall come, and all the saints with thee. ⁶And it shall come to pass in that day, that the light shall not be clear, nor dark: ⁷But it shall be one day which shall be known to the LORD, not day, nor night: but it shall come to pass, that at evening time it shall be light. ⁸And it shall be in that day, that living waters shall go out from Jerusalem; half of them toward the former sea, and half of them toward the hinder sea: in summer and in winter shall it be. ⁹And the LORD shall be king over all the earth: in that day shall there be one LORD, and his name one. ¹⁰All the land shall be turned as a plain from Geba to Rimmon south of Jerusalem: and it shall be lifted up, and inhabited in her place, from Benjamin's gate unto the place of the first gate, unto the corner gate, and from the tower of Hananeel unto the king's winepresses. ¹¹And men shall dwell in it, and there shall be no more utter destruction; but Jerusalem shall be safely inhabited. ¹²And this shall be the plague wherewith the LORD will smite all the people that have fought against Jerusalem; Their flesh shall consume away while they stand upon their feet, and their eyes shall consume away in their holes, and their tongue shall consume away in their mouth. ¹³And it shall come to pass in that day, that a great tumult from the LORD shall be among them; and they shall lay hold every one on the hand of his neighbour, and his hand shall rise up against the hand of his neighbour. ¹⁴And Judah also shall fight at Jerusalem; and the wealth of all the heathen round about shall be gathered together, gold, and silver, and apparel, in great abundance. ¹⁵And so shall be the plague of the horse, of the mule, of the camel, and of the ass, and of all the beasts that shall be in these tents, as this plague. ¹⁶And it shall come to pass, that every one that is left of all the nations which came against Jerusalem shall even go up from year to year to worship the King, the LORD of hosts, and to keep the feast of tabernacles. ¹⁷And it shall be, that whoso will not come up of all the families of the earth unto Jerusalem to worship the King, the LORD of hosts, even upon them shall be no rain. ¹⁸And if the family of Egypt go not up, and come not, that have no rain; there shall be the plague, wherewith the LORD will smite the heathen that come not up to keep the feast of tabernacles. ¹⁹This shall be the punishment of Egypt, and the punishment of all nations that come not up to keep the feast of tabernacles. ²⁰In that day shall there be upon the bells of the horses, HOLINESS UNTO THE LORD; and the pots in the LORD's house shall be like the bowl's before the altar. ²¹Yea, every pot in Jerusalem and in Judah shall be holiness unto the LORD of hosts: and all they that sacrifice shall come and take of them, and seethe therein: and in that day there shall be no more the Canaanite in the house of the LORD of hosts."

Malachi 3:1-5 "¹Behold, I will send my messenger, and he shall prepare the way before me: and the Lord, whom ye seek, shall suddenly come to his temple, even the messenger of the covenant, whom ye delight in: behold, he shall come, saith the LORD of hosts. ²But who may abide the day of his coming? and who shall stand when he appeareth? for he is like a refiner's fire, and like fullers' soap: ³And he shall sit as a refiner and purifer of silver: and he shall purify the sons of Levi, and purge them as gold and silver, that they may offer unto the LORD an offering in righteousness. ⁴Then shall the offering of Judah and Jerusalem be pleasant unto the LORD, as in the days of old, and as in former years. ⁵And I will come near to you to judgment; and I will be a swift witness against the sorcerers, and against the adulterers, and against false swearers, and against those that oppress the hireling in his wages, the widow, and the fatherless, and that turn aside the stranger from his right, and fear not me, saith the LORD of hosts."

Matthew 1:20-23 "²⁰But while he thought on these things, behold, the angel of the Lord appeared unto him in a dream, saying, Joseph, thou son of David, fear not to take unto thee Mary thy wife: for that which is conceived in her is of the Holy Ghost. ²¹And she shall bring forth a son, and thou shalt call his name JESUS: for he shall save his people from their sins. ²²Now all this was done, that it might be fulfilled which was spoken of the Lord by the prophet, saying, ²³Behold, a virgin shall be with child, and shall bring forth a son, and they shall call his name Emmanuel, which being interpreted is, God with us."

Matthew 2:1-6 "¹Now when Jesus was born in Bethlehem of Judaea in the days of Herod the king, behold, there came wise men from the east to Jerusalem, ²Saying, Where is he that is born King of the Jews? for we have seen his star in the east, and are come to worship him. ³When Herod the king had heard these things, he was troubled, and all Jerusalem with him. ⁴And when he had gathered all the chief priests and scribes of the people together, he demanded of them where Christ should be born. ⁵And they said unto him, In Bethlehem of Judaea: for thus it is written by the prophet, ⁶And thou Bethlehem, in the land of Juda, art not the least among the princes of Juda: for out of thee shall come a Governor, that shall rule my people Israel."

Matthew 3:11-14 "[11]I indeed baptize you with water unto repentance: but he that cometh after me is mightier than I, whose shoes I am not worthy to bear: he shall baptize you with the Holy Ghost, and with fire: [12]Whose fan is in his hand, and he will throughly purge his floor, and gather his wheat into the garner; but he will burn up the chaff with unquenchable fire. [13]Then cometh Jesus from Galilee to Jordan unto John, to be baptized of him. [14]But John forbad him, saying, I have need to be baptized of thee, and comest thou to me?"

Matthew 21:42 "Jesus saith unto them, Did ye never read in the scriptures, The stone which the builders rejected, the same is become the head of the corner: this is the Lord's doing, and it is marvellous in our eyes?"

Matthew 26:24 "The Son of man goeth as it is written of him: but woe unto that man by whom the Son of man is betrayed! it had been good for that man if he had not been born."

Mark 1:7-9 "[7]And preached, saying, There cometh one mightier than I after me, the latchet of whose shoes I am not worthy to stoop down and unloose. [8]I indeed have baptized you with water: but he shall baptize you with the Holy Ghost. [9]And it came to pass in those days, that Jesus came from Nazareth of Galilee, and was baptized of John in Jordan."

Mark 9:12 "And he answered and told them, Elias verily cometh first, and restoreth all things; and how it is written of the Son of man, that he must suffer many things, and be set at nought."

Mark 12:35-37 "[35]And Jesus answered and said, while he taught in the temple, How say the scribes that Christ is the Son of David? [36]For David himself said by the Holy Ghost, The Lord said to my Lord, Sit thou on my right hand, till I make thine enemies thy footstool. [37]David therefore himself calleth him Lord; and whence is he then his son? And the common people heard him gladly."

Mark 14:21 "The Son of man indeed goeth, as it is written of him: but woe to that man by whom the Son of man is betrayed! good were it for that man if he had never been born."

Mark 15:24-28 "[24]And when they had crucified him, they parted his garments, casting lots upon them, what every man should take. [25]And it was the third hour, and they crucified him. [26]And the superscription of his accusation was written over, THE KING OF THE JEWS. [27]And with him they crucify two thieves; the one on his right hand, and the other on his left. [28]And the scripture was fulfilled, which saith, And he was numbered with the transgressors."

Luke 3:15-21 "[15]And as the people were in expectation, and all men mused in their hearts of John, whether he were the Christ, or not; [16]John answered, saying unto them all, I indeed baptize you with water; but one mightier than I cometh, the latchet of whose shoes I am not worthy to unloose: he shall baptize you with the Holy Ghost and with fire: [17]Whose fan is in his hand, and he will throughly purge his floor, and will gather the wheat into his garner; but the chaff he will burn with fire unquenchable. [18]And many other things in his exhortation preached he unto the people. [19]But Herod the tetrarch, being reproved by him for Herodias his brother Philip's wife, and for all the evils which Herod had done, [20]Added yet this above all, that he shut up John in prison. [21]Now when all the people were baptized, it came to pass, that Jesus also being baptized, and praying, the heaven was opened,"

Luke 22:22 "And truly the Son of man goeth, as it was determined: but woe unto that man by whom he is betrayed!"

Luke 22:37-38 "[37]For I say unto you, that this that is written must yet be accomplished in me, And he was reckoned among the transgressors: for the things concerning me have an end. [38]And they said, Lord, behold, here are two swords. And he said unto them, It is enough."

Luke 24:25-26 "[25]Then he said unto them, O fools, and slow of heart to believe all that the prophets have spoken: [26]Ought not Christ to have suffered these things, and to enter into his glory?"

Luke 24:44-47 "[44]And he said unto them, These are the words which I spake unto you, while I was yet with you, that all things must be fulfilled, which were written in the law of Moses, and in the prophets, and in the psalms, concerning me. [45]Then opened he their understanding, that they might understand the scriptures, [46]And said unto them, Thus it is written, and thus it behoved Christ to suffer, and to rise from the dead the third day: [47]And that repentance and remission of sins should be preached in his name among all nations, beginning at Jerusalem."

John 1:1-15 "[1]In the beginning was the Word, and the Word was with God, and the Word was God. [2]The same was in the beginning with God. [3]All things were made by him; and without him was not any thing made that was made. [4]In him was life; and the life was the light of men. [5]And the light shineth in darkness; and the darkness comprehended it not. [6]There was a man sent from God, whose name was John. [7]The same came for a witness, to bear witness of the Light, that all men through him might believe. [8]He was not that Light, but was sent to bear witness of that Light. [9]That was the true Light, which lighteth every man that cometh into the world. [10]He was in the world, and the world was made by him, and the world knew him not. [11]He came unto his own, and his own received him not. [12]But as many as received him, to them gave he power to become the sons of God, even to them that believe on his name: [13]Which were born, not of blood, nor of the will of the flesh, nor of the will of man, but of God. [14]And the Word was made flesh, and dwelt among us, (and we beheld his glory, the glory as of the only begotten of the Father,) full of grace and truth. [15]John bare witness of him, and cried, saying, This was he of whom I spake, He that cometh after me is preferred before me: for he was before me."

John 1:29-34 "[29]The next day John seeth Jesus coming unto him, and saith, Behold the Lamb of God, which taketh away the sin of the world. [30]This is he of whom I said, After me cometh a man which is preferred before me: for he was before me. [31]And I knew him not: but that he should be made manifest to Israel, therefore am I come baptizing with water. [32]And John bare record, saying, I saw the Spirit descending from heaven like a dove, and it abode upon him. [33]And I knew him not: but he that sent me to baptize with water, the same said unto me, Upon whom thou shalt see the Spirit descending, and remaining on him, the same is he which baptizeth with the Holy Ghost. [34]And I saw, and bare record that this is the Son of God."

John 5:23-47 "[23]That all men should honour the Son, even as they honour the Father. He that honoureth not the Son honoureth not the Father which hath sent him. [24]Verily, verily, I say unto you, He that heareth my word, and believeth on him that sent me, hath everlasting life, and shall not come into condemnation; but is passed from death unto life. [25]Verily, verily, I say unto you, The hour is coming, and now is, when the dead shall hear the voice of the Son of God: and they that hear shall live. [26]For as the Father hath life in himself; so hath he given to the Son to have life in himself; [27]And hath given him authority to execute judgment also, because he is the Son of man. [28]Marvel not at this: for the hour is coming, in the which all that are in the graves shall hear his voice, [29]And shall come forth; they that have done good, unto the resurrection of life; and they that have done evil, unto the resurrection of damnation. [30]I can of mine own self do nothing: as I hear, I judge: and my judgment is just; because I seek not mine own will, but the will of the Father which hath sent me. [31]If I bear witness of myself, my witness is not true. [32]There is another that beareth witness of me; and I know that the witness which he witnesseth of me is true. [33]Ye sent unto John, and he bare witness unto the truth. [34]But I receive not testimony from man: but these things I say, that ye might be saved. [35]He was a burning and a shining light: and ye were willing for a season to rejoice in his light. [36]But I have greater witness than that of John: for the works which the Father hath given me to finish, the same works that I do, bear witness of me, that the Father hath sent me. [37]And the Father himself, which hath sent me, hath borne witness of me. Ye have neither heard his voice at any time, nor seen his shape. [38]And ye have not his word abiding in you: for whom he hath sent, him ye believe not. [39]Search the scriptures; for in them ye think ye have eternal life: and they are they which testify of me. [40]And ye will not come to me, that ye might have life. [41]I receive not honour from men. [42]But I know you, that ye have not the love of God in you. [43]I am come in my Father's name, and ye receive me not: if another shall come in his own name, him ye will receive. ⁴⁴How can ye believe, which receive honour one of another, and seek not the honour that cometh from God only? ⁴⁵Do not think that I will accuse you to the Father: there is one that accuseth you, even Moses, in whom ye trust. ⁴⁶For had ye believed Moses, ye would have believed me: for he wrote of me. ⁴⁷But if ye believe not his writings, how shall ye believe my words?"

John 7:37-38 "³⁷In the last day, that great day of the feast, Jesus stood and cried, saying, If any man thirst, let him come unto me, and drink. ³⁸He that believeth on me, as the scripture hath said, out of his belly shall flow rivers of living water."

John 7:42 "Hath not the scripture said, That Christ cometh of the seed of David, and out of the town of Bethlehem, where David was?"

John 15:1-25 "¹I am the true vine, and my Father is the husbandman. ²Every branch in me that beareth not fruit he taketh away: and every branch that beareth fruit, he purgeth it, that it may bring forth more fruit. ³Now ye are clean through the word which I have spoken unto you. ⁴Abide in me, and I in you. As the branch cannot bear fruit of itself, except it abide in the vine; no more can ye, except ye abide in me. ⁵I am the vine, ye are the branches: He that abideth in me, and I in him, the same bringeth forth much fruit: for without me ye can do nothing. ⁶If a man abide not in me, he is cast forth as a branch, and is withered; and men gather them, and cast them into the fire, and they are burned. ⁷If ye abide in me, and my words abide in you, ye shall ask what ye will, and it shall be done unto you. ⁸Herein is my Father glorified, that ye bear much fruit; so shall ye be my disciples. ⁹As the Father hath loved me, so have I loved you: continue ye in my love. ¹⁰If ye keep my commandments, ye shall abide in my love; even as I have kept my Father's commandments, and abide in his love. ¹¹These things have I spoken unto you, that my joy might remain in you, and that your joy might be full. ¹²This is my commandment, That ye love one another, as I have loved you. ¹³Greater love hath no man than this, that a man lay down his life for his friends. ¹⁴Ye are my friends, if ye do whatsoever I command you. ¹⁵Henceforth I call you not servants; for the servant knoweth not what his lord doeth: but I have called you friends; for all things that I have heard of my Father I have made known unto you. ¹⁶Ye have not chosen me, but I have chosen you, and ordained you, that ye should go and bring forth fruit, and that your fruit should remain: that whatsoever ye shall ask of the Father in my name, he may give it you. ¹⁷These things I command you, that ye love one another. ¹⁸If the world hate you, ye know that it hated me before it hated you. ¹⁹If ye were of the world, the world would love his own: but because ye are not of the world, but I have chosen you out of the world, therefore the world hateth you. ²⁰Remember the word that I said unto you, The servant is not greater than his lord. If they have persecuted me, they will also persecute you; if they have kept my saying, they will keep yours also. ²¹But all these things will they do unto you for my name's sake, because they know not him that sent me. ²²If I had not come and spoken unto them, they had not had sin: but now they have no cloke for their sin. ²³He that hateth me hateth my Father also. ²⁴If I had not done among them the works which none other man did, they had not had sin: but now have they both seen and hated both me and my Father. ²⁵But this cometh to pass, that the word might be fulfilled that is written in their law, They hated me without a cause."

John 19:31-37 "³¹The Jews therefore, because it was the preparation, that the bodies should not remain upon the cross on the sabbath day, (for that sabbath day was an high day,) besought Pilate that their legs might be broken, and that they might be taken away. ³²Then came the soldiers, and brake the legs of the first, and of the other which was crucified with him. ³³But when they came to Jesus, and saw that he was dead already, they brake not his legs: ³⁴But one of the soldiers with a spear pierced his side, and forthwith came there out blood and water. ³⁵And he that saw it bare record, and his record is true: and he knoweth that he saith true, that ye might believe. ³⁶For these things were done, that the scripture should be fulfilled, A bone of him shall not be broken. ³⁷And again another scripture saith, They shall look on him whom they pierced."

Acts 2:22-35 "²²Ye men of Israel, hear these words; Jesus of Nazareth, a man approved of God among you by miracles and wonders and signs, which God did by him in the midst of you, as ye yourselves also know: [23]Him, being delivered by the determinate counsel and foreknowledge of God, ye have taken, and by wicked hands have crucified and slain: [24]Whom God hath raised up, having loosed the pains of death: because it was not possible that he should be holden of it. [25]For David speaketh concerning him, I foresaw the Lord always before my face, for he is on my right hand, that I should not be moved: [26]Therefore did my heart rejoice, and my tongue was glad; moreover also my flesh shall rest in hope: [27]Because thou wilt not leave my soul in hell, neither wilt thou suffer thine Holy One to see corruption. [28]Thou hast made known to me the ways of life; thou shalt make me full of joy with thy countenance. [29]Men and brethren, let me freely speak unto you of the patriarch David, that he is both dead and buried, and his sepulchre is with us unto this day. [30]Therefore being a prophet, and knowing that God had sworn with an oath to him, that of the fruit of his loins, according to the flesh, he would raise up Christ to sit on his throne; [31]He seeing this before spake of the resurrection of Christ, that his soul was not left in hell, neither his flesh did see corruption. [32]This Jesus hath God raised up, whereof we all are witnesses. [33]Therefore being by the right hand of God exalted, and having received of the Father the promise of the Holy Ghost, he hath shed forth this, which ye now see and hear. [34]For David is not ascended into the heavens: but he saith himself, The LORD said unto my Lord, Sit thou on my right hand, [35]Until I make thy foes thy footstool.”

Acts 3:13-24 “[13]The God of Abraham, and of Isaac, and of Jacob, the God of our fathers, hath glorified his Son Jesus; whom ye delivered up, and denied him in the presence of Pilate, when he was determined to let him go. [14]But ye denied the Holy One and the Just, and desired a murderer to be granted unto you; [15]And killed the Prince of life, whom God hath raised from the dead; whereof we are witnesses. [16]And his name through faith in his name hath made this man strong, whom ye see and know: yea, the faith which is by him hath given him this perfect soundness in the presence of you all. [17]And now, brethren, I wot that through ignorance ye did it, as did also your rulers. [18]But

those things, which God before had shewed by the mouth of all his prophets, that Christ should suffer, he hath so fulfilled. [19]Repent ye therefore, and be converted, that your sins may be blotted out, when the times of refreshing shall come from the presence of the Lord; [20]And he shall send Jesus Christ, which before was preached unto you: [21]Whom the heaven must receive until the times of restitution of all things, which God hath spoken by the mouth of all his holy prophets since the world began. [22]For Moses truly said unto the fathers, A prophet shall the Lord your God raise up unto you of your brethren, like unto me; him shall ye hear in all things whatsoever he shall say unto you. [23]And it shall come to pass, that every soul, which will not hear that prophet, shall be destroyed from among the people. [24]Yea, and all the prophets from Samuel and those that follow after, as many as have spoken, have likewise foretold of these days.”

Acts 4:25-28 “[25]Who by the mouth of thy servant David hast said, Why did the heathen rage, and the people imagine vain things? [26]The kings of the earth stood up, and the rulers were gathered together against the Lord, and against his Christ. [27]For of a truth against thy holy child Jesus, whom thou hast anointed, both Herod, and Pontius Pilate, with the Gentiles, and the people of Israel, were gathered together, [28]For to do whatsoever thy hand and thy counsel determined before to be done.”

Acts 7:37 “This is that Moses, which said unto the children of Israel, A prophet shall the Lord your God raise up unto you of your brethren, like unto me; him shall ye hear.”

Acts 7:52 “Which of the prophets have not your fathers persecuted? and they have slain them which shewed before of the coming of the Just One; of whom ye have been now the betrayers and murderers:”

Acts 13:32-39 “[32]And we declare unto you glad tidings, how that the promise which was made unto the fathers, [33]God hath fulfilled the same unto us their children, in that he hath raised up Jesus again; as it is also written in the second psalm, Thou art my Son, this day have I begotten thee. [34]And as concerning that he raised him up from the dead, now no more to return to corruption, he said on this wise, I will give you the sure mercies of David. [35]Wherefore he saith also in another psalm, Thou shalt not suffer thine Holy One to see corruption. [36]For David, after he had served his own generation by the will of God, fell on sleep, and was laid unto his fathers, and saw corruption: [37]But he, whom God raised again, saw no corruption. [38]Be it known unto you therefore, men and brethren, that through this man is preached unto you the forgiveness of sins: [39]And by him all that believe are justified from all things, from which ye could not be justified by the law of Moses."

Acts 17:2-3 "[2]And Paul, as his manner was, went in unto them, and three sabbath days reasoned with them out of the scriptures, [3]Opening and alleging, that Christ must needs have suffered, and risen again from the dead; and that this Jesus, whom I preach unto you, is Christ."

Acts 26:22-23 "[22]Having therefore obtained help of God, I continue unto this day, witnessing both to small and great, saying none other things than those which the prophets and Moses did say should come: [23]That Christ should suffer, and that he should be the first that should rise from the dead, and should shew light unto the people, and to the Gentiles."

Romans 10:9-11 "[9]That if thou shalt confess with thy mouth the Lord Jesus, and shalt believe in thine heart that God hath raised him from the dead, thou shalt be saved. [10]For with the heart man believeth unto righteousness; and with the mouth confession is made unto salvation. [11]For the scripture saith, Whosoever believeth on him shall not be ashamed."

Romans 11:26-27 "[26]And so all Israel shall be saved: as it is written, There shall come out of Sion the Deliverer, and shall turn away ungodliness from Jacob: [27]For this is my covenant unto them, when I shall take away their sins."

Romans 15:2-3 "[2]Let every one of us please his neighbour for his good to edification. [3]For even Christ pleased not himself; but, as it is written, The reproaches of them that reproached thee fell on me."

Romans 15:8-12 "[8]Now I say that Jesus Christ was a minister of the circumcision for the truth of God, to confirm the promises made unto the fathers: [9]And that the Gentiles might glorify God for his mercy; as it is written, For this cause I will confess to thee among the Gentiles, and sing unto thy name. [10]And again he saith, Rejoice, ye Gentiles, with his people. [11]And again, Praise the Lord, all ye Gentiles; and laud him, all ye people. [12]And again, Esaias saith, There shall be a root of Jesse, and he that shall rise to reign over the Gentiles; in him shall the Gentiles trust."

1 Corinthians 15:3-4 "[3]For I delivered unto you first of all that which I also received, how that Christ died for our sins according to the scriptures; [4]And that he was buried, and that he rose again the third day according to the scriptures:"

2 Thessalonians 2:8 "And then shall that Wicked be revealed, whom the Lord shall consume with the spirit of his mouth, and shall destroy with the brightness of his coming:"

Hebrews 10:1-15 "[1]For the law having a shadow of good things to come, and not the very image of the things, can never with those sacrifices which they offered year by year continually make the comers thereunto perfect. [2]For then would they not have ceased to be offered? because that the worshippers once purged should have had no more conscience of sins. [3]But in those sacrifices there is a remembrance again made of sins every year. [4]For it is not possible that the blood of bulls and of goats should take away sins. [5]Wherefore when he cometh into the world, he saith, Sacrifice and offering thou wouldest not, but a body hast thou prepared me: [6]In burnt offerings and sacrifices for sin thou hast had no pleasure. [7]Then said I, Lo, I come (in the volume of the book it is written of me,) to do thy will, O God. [8]Above when he said, Sacrifice and offering and burnt offerings and offering for sin thou wouldest not, neither hadst pleasure therein; which are offered by the law; [9]Then said he, Lo, I come to do thy will, O God. He taketh away the first, that he may establish the second. [10]By the which will we are sanctified through the offering of the body of Jesus Christ once for all. [11]And every priest standeth daily ministering and offering oftentimes the same sacrifices, which can never take away sins: [12]But this man, after he had offered one sacrifice for sins for ever, sat down on the right hand of God; [13]From henceforth expecting till his enemies be made his footstool. [14]For by one offering he hath perfected for ever them that are sanctified. [15]Whereof the Holy Ghost also is a witness to us: for after that he had said before,"

1 Peter 1:10-12 "[10]Of which salvation the prophets have inquired and searched diligently, who prophesied of the grace that should come unto you: [11]Searching what, or what manner of time the Spirit of Christ which was in them did signify, when it testified beforehand the sufferings of Christ, and the glory that should follow. [12]Unto whom it was revealed, that not unto themselves, but unto us they did minister the things, which are now reported unto you by them that have preached the gospel unto you with the Holy Ghost sent down from heaven; which things the angels desire to look into."

Revelation 1:7-8 "[7]Behold, he cometh with clouds; and every eye shall see him, and they also which pierced him: and all kindreds of the earth shall wail because of him. Even so, Amen. [8]I am Alpha and Omega, the beginning and the ending, saith the Lord, which is, and which was, and which is to come, the Almighty."

Revelation 1:14-17 "[14]His head and his hairs were white like wool, as white as snow; and his eyes were as a flame of fire; [15]And his feet like unto fine brass, as if they burned in a furnace; and his voice as the sound of many waters. [16]And he had in his right hand seven stars: and out of his mouth went a sharp twoedged sword: and his countenance was as the sun shineth in his strength. [17]And when I saw him, I fell at his feet as dead. And he laid his right hand upon me, saying unto me, Fear not; I am the first and the last:"

Revelation 19:11-16 "[11]And I saw heaven opened, and behold a white horse; and he that sat upon him was called Faithful and True, and in righteousness he doth judge and make war. [12]His eyes were as a flame of fire, and on his head were many crowns; and he had a name written, that no man knew, but he himself. [13]And he was clothed with a vesture dipped in blood: and his name is called The Word of God. [14]And the armies which were in heaven followed him upon white horses, clothed in fine linen, white and clean. [15]And out of his mouth goeth a sharp sword, that with it he should smite the nations: and he shall rule them with a rod of iron: and he treadeth the winepress of the fierceness and wrath of Almighty God. [16]And he hath on his vesture and on his thigh a name written, KING OF KINGS, AND LORD OF LORDS."

Where Jesus Christ Ascended To

Mark 16:19 "So then after the Lord had spoken unto them, he was received up into heaven, and sat on the right hand of God."

Luke 24:45-51 "[45]Then opened he their understanding, that they might understand the scriptures, [46]And said unto them, Thus it is written, and thus it behoved Christ to suffer, and to rise from the dead the third day: [47]And that repentance and remission of sins should be preached in his name among all nations, beginning at Jerusalem. [48]And ye are witnesses of these things. [49]And, behold, I send the promise of my Father upon you: but tarry ye in the city of Jerusalem, until ye be endued with power from on high. [50]And he led them out as far as to Bethany, and he lifted up his hands, and blessed them. [51]And it came to pass, while he blessed them, he was parted from them, and carried up into heaven."

John 3:13-14 "[13]And no man hath ascended up to heaven, but he that came down from heaven, even the Son of man which is in heaven. [14]And as Moses lifted up the serpent in the wilderness, even so must the Son of man be lifted up:"

John 13:1-3 "[1]Now before the feast of the passover, when Jesus knew that his hour was come that he should depart out of this world unto the Father, having loved his own which were in the world, he loved them unto the end. [2]And supper being ended, the devil having now put into the heart of Judas Iscariot, Simon's son, to betray him; [3]Jesus knowing that the Father had given all things into his hands, and that he was come from God, and went to God;"

John 20:17 "Jesus saith unto her, Touch me not; for I am not yet ascended to my Father: but go to my brethren, and say unto them, I ascend unto my Father, and your Father; and to my God, and your God."

Ephesians 4:7-10 "[7]But unto every one of us is given grace according to the measure of the gift of

Christ. ⁸Wherefore he saith, When he ascended up on high, he led captivity captive, and gave gifts unto men. ⁹(Now that he ascended, what is it but that he also descended first into the lower parts of the earth? ¹⁰He that descended is the same also that ascended up far above all heavens, that he might fill all things.)"

1 Peter 3:21-22 "²¹The like figure whereunto even baptism doth also now save us (not the putting away of the filth of the flesh, but the answer of a good conscience toward God,) by the resurrection of Jesus Christ: ²²Who is gone into heaven, and is on the right hand of God; angels and authorities and powers being made subject unto him."

Where Jesus Christ Descended From

John 3:13-14 "¹³And no man hath ascended up to heaven, but he that came down from heaven, even the Son of man which is in heaven. ¹⁴And as Moses lifted up the serpent in the wilderness, even so must the Son of man be lifted up:"

John 3:31-35 "³¹He that cometh from above is above all: he that is of the earth is earthly, and speaketh of the earth: he that cometh from heaven is above all. ³²And what he hath seen and heard, that he testifieth; and no man receiveth his testimony. ³³He that hath received his testimony hath set to his seal that God is true. ³⁴For he whom God hath sent speaketh the words of God: for God giveth not the Spirit by measure unto him. ³⁵The Father loveth the Son, and hath given all things into his hand."

John 6:35-38 "³⁵And Jesus said unto them, I am the bread of life: he that cometh to me shall never hunger; and he that believeth on me shall never thirst. ³⁶But I said unto you, That ye also have seen me, and believe not. ³⁷All that the Father giveth me shall come to me; and him that cometh to me I will in no wise cast out. ³⁸For I came down from heaven, not to do mine own will, but the will of him that sent me."

John 6:41-42 "⁴¹The Jews then murmured at him, because he said, I am the bread which came down from heaven. ⁴²And they said, Is not this Jesus, the son of Joseph, whose father and mother we know? how is it then that he saith, I came down from heaven?"

John 8:21-23 "²¹Then said Jesus again unto them, I go my way, and ye shall seek me, and shall die in your sins: whither I go, ye cannot come. ²²Then said the Jews, Will he kill himself? because he saith, Whither I go, ye cannot come. ²³And he said unto them, Ye are from beneath; I am from above: ye are of this world; I am not of this world."

John 13:3 "Jesus knowing that the Father had given all things into his hands, and that he was come from God, and went to God;"

Ephesians 4:7-10 "⁷But unto every one of us is given grace according to the measure of the gift of Christ. ⁸Wherefore he saith, When he ascended up on high, he led captivity captive, and gave gifts unto men. ⁹(Now that he ascended, what is it but that he also descended first into the lower parts of the earth? ¹⁰He that descended is the same also that ascended up far above all heavens, that he might fill all things.)"

Where Jesus Christ Sits

Psalm 110:1-5 "¹The LORD said unto my Lord, Sit thou at my right hand, until I make thine enemies thy footstool. ²The LORD shall send the rod of thy strength out of Zion: rule thou in the midst of thine enemies. ³Thy people shall be willing in the day of thy power, in the beauties of holiness from the womb of the morning: thou hast the dew of thy youth. ⁴The LORD hath sworn, and will not repent, Thou art a priest for ever after the order of Melchizedek. ⁵The Lord at thy right hand shall strike through kings in the day of his wrath."

Matthew 22:42-44 "⁴²Saying, What think ye of Christ? whose son is he? They say unto him, The Son of David. ⁴³He saith unto them, How then doth David in spirit call him Lord, saying, ⁴⁴The LORD said unto my Lord, Sit thou on my right hand, till I make thine enemies thy footstool?"

Mark 12:35-36 "³⁵And Jesus answered and said, while he taught in the temple, How say the scribes that Christ is the Son of David? ³⁶For David himself said by the Holy Ghost, The Lord said to my Lord, Sit thou on my right hand, till I make thine enemies thy footstool."

Mark 14:60-62 "⁶⁰And the high priest stood up in the midst, and asked Jesus, saying, Answerest thou nothing? what is it which these witness against thee? ⁶¹But he held his peace, and answered nothing.

Again the high priest asked him, and said unto him, Art thou the Christ, the Son of the Blessed? [62]And Jesus said, I am: and ye shall see the Son of man sitting on the right hand of power, and coming in the clouds of heaven."

Mark 16:19 "So then after the Lord had spoken unto them, he was received up into heaven, and sat on the right hand of God."

Luke 20:41-43 "[41]And he said unto them, How say they that Christ is David's son? [42]And David himself saith in the book of Psalm, The LORD said unto my Lord, Sit thou on my right hand, [43]Till I make thine enemies thy footstool."

Acts 2:32-35 "[32]This Jesus hath God raised up, whereof we all are witnesses. [33]Therefore being by the right hand of God exalted, and having received of the Father the promise of the Holy Ghost, he hath shed forth this, which ye now see and hear. [34]For David is not ascended into the heavens: but he saith himself, The LORD said unto my Lord, Sit thou on my right hand, [35]Until I make thy foes thy footstool."

Romans 8:34 "Who is he that condemneth? It is Christ that died, yea rather, that is risen again, who is even at the right hand of God, who also maketh intercession for us."

Ephesians 1:19-22 "[19]And what is the exceeding greatness of his power to usward who believe, according to the working of his mighty power, [20]Which he wrought in Christ, when he raised him from the dead, and set him at his own right hand in the heavenly places, [21]Far above all principality, and power, and might, and dominion, and every name that is named, not only in this world, but also in that which is to come: [22]And hath put all things under his feet, and gave him to be the head over all things to the church,"

Colossians 3:1 "If ye then be risen with Christ, seek those things which are above, where Christ sitteth on the right hand of God."

Hebrews 1:1-3 "[1]God, who at sundry times and in divers manners spake in time past unto the fathers by the prophets, [2]Hath in these last days spoken unto us by his Son, whom he hath appointed heir of all things, by whom also he made the worlds; [3]Who being the brightness of his glory, and the express image of his person, and upholding all things by the word of his power, when he had by himself purged our sins, sat down on the right hand of the Majesty on high;"

Hebrews 1:8-13 "[8]But unto the Son he saith, Thy throne, O God, is for ever and ever: a sceptre of righteousness is the sceptre of thy kingdom. [9]Thou hast loved righteousness, and hated iniquity; therefore God, even thy God, hath anointed thee with the oil of gladness above thy fellows. [10]And, Thou, Lord, in the beginning hast laid the foundation of the earth; and the heavens are the works of thine hands: [11]They shall perish; but thou remainest; and they all shall wax old as doth a garment; [12]And as a vesture shalt thou fold them up, and they shall be changed: but thou art the same, and thy years shall not fail. [13]But to which of the angels said he at any time, Sit on my right hand, until I make thine enemies thy footstool?"

Hebrews 10:10-13 "[10]By the which will we are sanctified through the offering of the body of Jesus Christ once for all. [11]And every priest standeth daily ministering and offering oftentimes the same sacrifices, which can never take away sins: [12]But this man, after he had offered one sacrifice for sins for ever, sat down on the right hand of God; [13]From henceforth expecting till his enemies be made his footstool."

Hebrews 12:1-2 "[1]Wherefore seeing we also are compassed about with so great a cloud of witnesses, let us lay aside every weight, and the sin which doth so easily beset us, and let us run with patience the race that is set before us, [2]Looking unto Jesus the author and finisher of our faith; who for the joy that was set before him endured the cross, despising the shame, and is set down at the right hand of the throne of God."

1 Peter 3:21-22 "[21]The like figure whereunto even baptism doth also now save us (not the putting away of the filth of the flesh, but the answer of a good conscience toward God,) by the resurrection of Jesus Christ: [22]Who is gone into heaven, and is on the right hand of God; angels and authorities and powers being made subject unto him."

Revelation 3:14-21 "[14]And unto the angel of the church of the Laodiceans write; These things saith the Amen, the faithful and true witness, the beginning of the creation of God; [15]I know thy works, that thou art neither cold nor hot: I would thou wert cold or hot. [16]So then because thou art lukewarm, and neither cold nor hot, I will spue thee out of my mouth. [17]Because thou sayest, I am rich, and increased with goods, and have need of nothing; and knowest not that thou art wretched, and miserable, and poor, and blind, and naked: [18]I counsel thee to buy of me gold tried in the fire, that thou mayest be rich; and white raiment, that thou mayest be clothed, and that the shame of thy nakedness do not appear; and anoint thine eyes with eyesalve, that thou mayest see. [19]As many as I love, I rebuke and chasten: be zealous therefore, and repent. [20]Behold, I stand at the door, and knock: if any man hear my voice, and open the door, I will come in to him, and will sup with him, and he with me. [21]To him that overcometh will I grant to sit with me in my throne, even as I also overcame, and am set down with my Father in his throne."

Revelation 12:5 "And she brought forth a man child, who was to rule all nations with a rod of iron: and her child was caught up unto God, and to his throne."

Who Is In Jesus Christ

John 6:53-56 "[53]Then Jesus said unto them, Verily, verily, I say unto you, Except ye eat the flesh of the Son of man, and drink his blood, ye have no life in you. [54]Whoso eateth my flesh, and drinketh my blood, hath eternal life; and I will raise him up at the last day. [55]For my flesh is meat indeed, and my blood is drink indeed. [56]He that eateth my flesh, and drinketh my blood, dwelleth in me, and I in him."

John 14:8-20 "[8]Philip saith unto him, Lord, shew us the Father, and it sufficeth us. [9]Jesus saith unto him, Have I been so long time with you, and yet hast thou not known me, Philip? he that hath seen me hath seen the Father; and how sayest thou then, Shew us the Father? [10]Believest thou not that I am in the Father, and the Father in me? the words that I speak unto you I speak not of myself: but the Father that dwelleth in me, he doeth the works. [11]Believe me that I am in the Father, and the Father in me: or else believe me for the very works' sake. [12]Verily, verily, I say unto you, He that believeth on me, the works that I do shall he do also; and greater works than these

shall he do; because I go unto my Father. [13]And whatsoever ye shall ask in my name, that will I do, that the Father may be glorified in the Son. [14]If ye shall ask any thing in my name, I will do it. [15]If ye love me, keep my commandments. [16]And I will pray the Father, and he shall give you another Comforter, that he may abide with you for ever; [17]Even the Spirit of truth; whom the world cannot receive, because it seeth him not, neither knoweth him: but ye know him; for he dwelleth with you, and shall be in you. [18]I will not leave you comfortless: I will come to you. [19]Yet a little while, and the world seeth me no more; but ye see me: because I live, ye shall live also. [20]At that day ye shall know that I am in my Father, and ye in me, and I in you."

1 Corinthians 1:26-30 "[26]For ye see your calling, brethren, how that not many wise men after the flesh, not many mighty, not many noble, are called: [27]But God hath chosen the foolish things of the world to confound the wise; and God hath chosen the weak things of the world to confound the things which are mighty; [28]And base things of the world, and things which are despised, hath God chosen, yea, and things which are not, to bring to nought things that are: [29]That no flesh should glory in his presence. [30]But of him are ye in Christ Jesus, who of God is made unto us wisdom, and righteousness, and sanctification, and redemption:"

Colossians 2:8-12 "[8]Beware lest any man spoil you through philosophy and vain deceit, after the tradition of men, after the rudiments of the world, and not after Christ. [9]For in him dwelleth all the fulness of the Godhead bodily. [10]And ye are complete in him, which is the head of all principality and power: [11]In whom also ye are circumcised with the circumcision made without hands, in putting off the body of the sins of the flesh by the circumcision of Christ: [12]Buried with him in baptism, wherein also ye are risen with him through the faith of the operation of God, who hath raised him from the dead."

1 John 2:1-6 "[1]My little children, these things write I unto you, that ye sin not. And if any man sin, we have an advocate with the Father, Jesus Christ the righteous: [2]And he is the propitiation for our sins: and not for ours only, but also for the sins of the whole world. [3]And hereby we do know that we know him, if we keep his commandments. [4]He that saith, I know him, and keepeth not his commandments, is a liar, and the truth is not in him. [5]But whoso keepeth his word, in him verily is the love of God perfected: hereby know we that we are in him. [6]He that saith he abideth in him ought himself also so to walk, even as he walked."

1 John 3:21-24 "[21]Beloved, if our heart condemn us not, then have we confidence toward God. [22]And whatsoever we ask, we receive of him, because we keep his commandments, and do those things that are pleasing in his sight. [23]And this is his commandment, That we should believe on the name of his Son Jesus Christ, and love one another, as he gave us commandment. [24]And he that keepeth his commandments dwelleth in him, and he in him. And hereby we know that he abideth in us, by the Spirit which he hath given us."

1 John 5:19-20 "[19]And we know that we are of God, and the whole world lieth in wickedness. [20]And we know that the Son of God is come, and hath given us an understanding, that we may know him that is true, and we are in him that is true, even in his Son Jesus Christ. This is the true God, and eternal life."

Who Is Subject To Jesus Christ

1 Peter 3:21-22 "[21]The like figure whereunto even baptism doth also now save us (not the putting away of the filth of the flesh, but the answer of a good conscience toward God,) by the resurrection of Jesus Christ: [22]Who is gone into heaven, and is on the right hand of God; angels and authorities and powers being made subject unto him."

Who Jesus Christ Is In

John 6:53-56 "[53]Then Jesus said unto them, Verily, verily, I say unto you, Except ye eat the flesh of the Son of man, and drink his blood, ye have no life in you. [54]Whoso eateth my flesh, and drinketh my blood, hath eternal life; and I will raise him up at the last day. [55]For my flesh is meat indeed, and my blood is drink indeed. [56]He that eateth my flesh, and drinketh my blood, dwelleth in me, and I in him."

John 14:8-20 "[8]Philip saith unto him, Lord, shew us the Father, and it sufficeth us. [9]Jesus saith unto him, Have I been so long time with you, and yet hast thou not known me, Philip? he that hath seen me hath seen the Father; and how sayest thou then, Shew us the Father? [10]Believest thou not that I am in the Father, and the Father in me? the words that I speak unto you I speak not of myself: but the Father that dwelleth in me, he doeth the works. [11]Believe me that I am in the Father, and the Father in me: or else believe me for the very works' sake. [12]Verily, verily, I say unto you, He that believeth on me, the works that I do shall he do also; and greater works than these shall he do; because I go unto my Father. [13]And whatsoever ye shall ask in my name, that will I do, that the Father may be glorified in the Son. [14]If ye shall ask any thing in my name, I will do it. [15]If ye love me, keep my commandments. [16]And I will pray the Father, and he shall give you another Comforter, that he may abide with you for ever; [17]Even the Spirit of truth; whom the world cannot receive, because it seeth him not, neither knoweth him: but ye know him; for he dwelleth with you, and shall be in you. [18]I will not leave you comfortless: I will come to you. [19]Yet a little while, and the world seeth me no more; but ye see me: because I live, ye shall live also. [20]At that day ye shall know that I am in my Father, and ye in me, and I in you."

John 17:1-26 "[1]These words spake Jesus, and lifted up his eyes to heaven, and said, Father, the hour is come; glorify thy Son, that thy Son also may glorify thee: [2]As thou hast given him power over all flesh, that he should give eternal life to as many as thou hast given him. [3]And this is life eternal, that they might know thee the only true God, and Jesus Christ, whom thou hast sent. [4]I have glorified thee on the earth: I have finished the work which thou gavest me to do. [5]And now, O Father, glorify thou me with thine own self with the glory which I had with thee before the world was. [6]I have manifested thy name unto the men which thou gavest me out of the world: thine they were, and thou gavest them me; and they have kept thy word. [7]Now they have known that all things whatsoever thou hast given me are of thee. [8]For I have given unto them the words which thou gavest me; and they have received them, and have known surely that I came out from thee, and they have believed that thou didst send me. [9]I pray for them: I pray not for the world, but for them which thou hast given me; for they are thine. [10]And all mine are thine, and thine are mine; and I am glorified in them. [11]And now I am no more in the world, but these are in the world, and I come to thee. Holy Father, keep through thine own name those whom thou hast given me, that they may be one, as we are. [12]While I was with them in the world, I kept them in thy name: those that thou gavest me I have kept, and none of them is lost, but the son of perdition; that the scripture might be fulfilled. [13]And now come I to thee; and these things I speak in the world, that they might have my joy fulfilled in themselves. [14]I have given them thy word; and the world hath hated them, because they are not of the world, even as I am not of the world. [15]I pray not that thou shouldest take them out of the world, but that thou shouldest keep them from the evil. [16]They are not of the world, even as I am not of the world. [17]Sanctify them through thy truth: thy word is truth. [18]As thou hast sent me into the world, even so have I also sent them into the world. [19]And for their sakes I sanctify myself, that they also might be sanctified through the truth. [20]Neither pray I for these alone, but for them also which shall believe on me through their word; [21]That they all may be one; as thou, Father, art in me, and I in thee, that they also may be one in us: that the world may believe that thou hast sent me. [22]And the glory which thou gavest me I have given them; that they may be one, even as we are one: [23]I in them, and thou in me, that they may be made perfect in one; and that the world may know that thou hast sent me, and hast loved them, as thou hast loved me. [24]Father, I will that they also, whom thou hast given me, be with me where I am; that they may behold my glory, which thou hast given me: for thou lovedst me before the foundation of the world. [25]O righteous Father, the world hath not known thee: but I have known thee, and these have known that thou hast sent me. [26]And I have declared unto them thy name, and will declare it: that the love wherewith thou hast loved me may be in them, and I in them."

2 Corinthians 13:4-5 "[4]For though he was crucified through weakness, yet he liveth by the power of God. For we also are weak in him, but we shall live with him by the power of God toward you.

[5]Examine yourselves, whether ye be in the faith; prove your own selves. Know ye not your own selves, how that Jesus Christ is in you, except ye be reprobates?"

1 John 3:21-24 "[21]Beloved, if our heart condemn us not, then have we confidence toward God. [22]And whatsoever we ask, we receive of him, because we keep his commandments, and do those things that are pleasing in his sight. [23]And this is his commandment, That we should believe on the name of his Son Jesus Christ, and love one another, as he gave us commandment. [24]And he that keepeth his commandments dwelleth in him, and he in him. And hereby we know that he abideth in us, by the Spirit which he hath given us."

Who Lives By Jesus Christ
John 6:53-57 "[53]Then Jesus said unto them, Verily, verily, I say unto you, Except ye eat the flesh of the Son of man, and drink his blood, ye have no life in you. [54]Whoso eateth my flesh, and drinketh my blood, hath eternal life; and I will raise him up at the last day. [55]For my flesh is meat indeed, and my blood is drink indeed. [56]He that eateth my flesh, and drinketh my blood, dwelleth in me, and I in him. [57]As the living Father hath sent me, and I live by the Father: so he that eateth me, even he shall live by me."

Galatians 2:20 "I am crucified with Christ: nevertheless I live; yet not I, but Christ liveth in me: and the life which I now live in the flesh I live by the faith of the Son of God, who loved me, and gave himself for me."

JOHN THE BAPTIST

John The Baptist Being Sent To Prepare The Way For Jesus Christ
Luke 1:63-76 "[63]And he asked for a writing table, and wrote, saying, His name is John. And they marvelled all. [64]And his mouth was opened immediately, and his tongue loosed, and he spake, and praised God. [65]And fear came on all that dwelt round about them: and all these sayings were noised abroad throughout all the hill country of Judaea. [66]And all they that heard them laid them up in their hearts, saying, What manner of child shall this be! And the hand of the Lord was with him. [67]And his father Zacharias was filled

with the Holy Ghost, and prophesied, saying, 68Blessed be the Lord God of Israel; for he hath visited and redeemed his people, 69And hath raised up an horn of salvation for us in the house of his servant David; 70As he spake by the mouth of his holy prophets, which have been since the world began: 71That we should be saved from our enemies, and from the hand of all that hate us; 72To perform the mercy promised to our fathers, and to remember his holy covenant; 73The oath which he sware to our father Abraham, 74That he would grant unto us, that we being delivered out of the hand of our enemies might serve him without fear, 75In holiness and righteousness before him, all the days of our life. 76And thou, child, shalt be called the prophet of the Highest: for thou shalt go before the face of the Lord to prepare his ways;"

John 1:6-15 "6There was a man sent from God, whose name was John. 7The same came for a witness, to bear witness of the Light, that all men through him might believe. 8He was not that Light, but was sent to bear witness of that Light. 9That was the true Light, which lighteth every man that cometh into the world. 10He was in the world, and the world was made by him, and the world knew him not. 11He came unto his own, and his own received him not. 12But as many as received him, to them gave he power to become the sons of God, even to them that believe on his name: 13Which were born, not of blood, nor of the will of the flesh, nor of the will of man, but of God. 14And the Word was made flesh, and dwelt among us, (and we beheld his glory, the glory as of the only begotten of the Father,) full of grace and truth. 15John bare witness of him, and cried, saying, This was he of whom I spake, He that cometh after me is preferred before me: for he was before me."

John 3:27-28 "27John answered and said, A man can receive nothing, except it be given him from heaven. 28Ye yourselves bear me witness, that I said, I am not the Christ, but that I am sent before him."

John 5:33-35 "33Ye sent unto John, and he bare witness unto the truth. 34But I receive not testimony from man: but these things I say, that ye might be saved. 35He was a burning and a shining light: and ye were willing for a season to rejoice in his light."

John The Baptist Being The Greatest Prophet

Matthew 11:11 "Verily I say unto you, Among them that are born of women there hath not risen a greater than John the Baptist: notwithstanding he that is least in the kingdom of heaven is greater than he."

Luke 7:28 "For I say unto you, Among those that are born of women there is not a greater prophet than John the Baptist: but he that is least in the kingdom of God is greater than he."

What John The Baptist Baptized With

Matthew 3:1-11 "1In those days came John the Baptist, preaching in the wilderness of Judaea, 2And saying, Repent ye: for the kingdom of heaven is at hand. 3For this is he that was spoken of by the prophet Esaias, saying, The voice of one crying in the wilderness, Prepare ye the way of the Lord, make his paths straight. 4And the same John had his raiment of camel's hair, and a leathern girdle about his loins; and his meat was locusts and wild honey. 5Then went out to him Jerusalem, and all Judaea, and all the region round about Jordan, 6And were baptized of him in Jordan, confessing their sins. 7But when he saw many of the Pharisees and Sadducees come to his baptism, he said unto them, O generation of vipers, who hath warned you to flee from the wrath to come? 8Bring forth therefore fruits meet for repentance: 9And think not to say within yourselves, We have Abraham to our father: for I say unto you, that God is able of these stones to raise up children unto Abraham. 10And now also the axe is laid unto the root of the trees: therefore every tree which bringeth not forth good fruit is hewn down, and cast into the fire. 11I indeed baptize you with water unto repentance: but he that cometh after me is mightier than I, whose shoes I am not worthy to bear: he shall baptize you with the Holy Ghost, and with fire:"

Mark 1:7-8 "7And preached, saying, There cometh one mightier than I after me, the latchet of whose shoes I am not worthy to stoop down and unloose. 8I indeed have baptized you with water: but he shall baptize you with the Holy Ghost."

Luke 3:16 "John answered, saying unto them all, I indeed baptize you with water; but one mightier than I cometh, the latchet of whose shoes I am not worthy to unloose: he shall baptize you with the Holy Ghost and with fire:"

John 1:26-34 "²⁶John answered them, saying, I baptize with water: but there standeth one among you, whom ye know not; ²⁷He it is, who coming after me is preferred before me, whose shoe's latchet I am not worthy to unloose. ²⁸These things were done in Bethabara beyond Jordan, where John was baptizing. ²⁹The next day John seeth Jesus coming unto him, and saith, Behold the Lamb of God, which taketh away the sin of the world. ³⁰This is he of whom I said, After me cometh a man which is preferred before me: for he was before me. ³¹And I knew him not: but that he should be made manifest to Israel, therefore am I come baptizing with water. ³²And John bare record, saying, I saw the Spirit descending from heaven like a dove, and it abode upon him. ³³And I knew him not: but he that sent me to baptize with water, the same said unto me, Upon whom thou shalt see the Spirit descending, and remaining on him, the same is he which baptizeth with the Holy Ghost. ³⁴And I saw, and bare record that this is the Son of God."

Acts 1:5 "For John truly baptized with water; but ye shall be baptized with the Holy Ghost not many days hence."

Acts 11:16 "Then remembered I the word of the Lord, how that he said, John indeed baptized with water; but ye shall be baptized with the Holy Ghost."

Acts 19:4 "Then said Paul, John verily baptized with the baptism of repentance, saying unto the people, that they should believe on him which should come after him, that is, on Christ Jesus."

What Was Foretold About John The Baptist

Isaiah 40:1-4 "¹Comfort ye, comfort ye my people, saith your God. ²Speak ye comfortably to Jerusalem, and cry unto her, that her warfare is accomplished, that her iniquity is pardoned: for she hath received of the Lord's hand double for all her sins. ³The voice of him that crieth in the wilderness, Prepare ye the way of the Lord, make straight in the desert a highway for our God. ⁴Every valley shall be exalted, and every mountain and hill shall be made low: and the crooked shall be made straight, and the rough places plain:"

Malachi 3:1 "Behold, I will send my messenger, and he shall prepare the way before me: and the Lord, whom ye seek, shall suddenly come to his temple, even the messenger of the covenant, whom ye delight in: behold, he shall come, saith the Lord of hosts."

Matthew 3:1-3 "¹In those days came John the Baptist, preaching in the wilderness of Judaea, ²And saying, Repent ye: for the kingdom of heaven is at hand. ³For this is he that was spoken of by the prophet Esaias, saying, The voice of one crying in the wilderness, Prepare ye the way of the Lord, make his paths straight."

Matthew 11:7-11 "⁷And as they departed, Jesus began to say unto the multitudes concerning John, What went ye out into the wilderness to see? A reed shaken with the wind? ⁸But what went ye out for to see? A man clothed in soft raiment? behold, they that wear soft clothing are in kings' houses. ⁹But what went ye out for to see? A prophet? yea, I say unto you, and more than a prophet. ¹⁰For this is he, of whom it is written, Behold, I send my messenger before thy face, which shall prepare thy way before thee. ¹¹Verily I say unto you, Among them that are born of women there hath not risen a greater than John the Baptist: notwithstanding he that is least in the kingdom of heaven is greater than he."

Mark 1:1-3 "¹The beginning of the gospel of Jesus Christ, the Son of God; ²As it is written in the prophets, Behold, I send my messenger before thy face, which shall prepare thy way before thee. ³The voice of one crying in the wilderness, Prepare ye the way of the Lord, make his paths straight."

Luke 3:2-6 "²Annas and Caiaphas being the high priests, the word of God came unto John the son of Zacharias in the wilderness. ³And he came into all the country about Jordan, preaching the baptism of repentance for the remission of sins; ⁴As it is written in the book of the words of Esaias the prophet, saying, The voice of one crying in the wilderness, Prepare ye the way of the Lord, make his paths straight. ⁵Every valley shall be filled, and every mountain and hill shall be brought low; and the crooked shall be made straight, and the rough ways shall be made smooth; ⁶And all flesh shall see the salvation of God."

Luke 7:22-28 "²²Then Jesus answering said unto them, Go your way, and tell John what things ye have seen and heard; how that the blind see, the lame walk, the lepers are cleansed, the deaf hear, the dead are raised, to the poor the gospel is preached. 23And blessed is he, whosoever shall not be offended in me. 24And when the messengers of John were departed, he began to speak unto the people concerning John, What went ye out into the wilderness for to see? A reed shaken with the wind? 25But what went ye out for to see? A man clothed in soft raiment? Behold, they which are gorgeously apparelled, and live delicately, are in kings' courts. 26But what went ye out for to see? A prophet? Yea, I say unto you, and much more than a prophet. 27This is he, of whom it is written, Behold, I send my messenger before thy face, which shall prepare thy way before thee. 28For I say unto you, Among those that are born of women there is not a greater prophet than John the Baptist: but he that is least in the kingdom of God is greater than he."

John 1:19-23 "19And this is the record of John, when the Jews sent priests and Levites from Jerusalem to ask him, Who art thou? 20And he confessed, and denied not; but confessed, I am not the Christ. 21And they asked him, What then? Art thou Elias? And he saith, I am not.Art thou that prophet? And he answered, No. 22Then said they unto him, Who art thou? that we may give an answer to them that sent us. What sayest thou of thyself? 23He said, I am the voice of one crying in the wilderness, Make straight the way of the Lord, as said the prophet Esaias."

JUDAS ISCARIOT

Judas Iscariot Betraying Jesus Christ

Matthew 26:14-16 "14Then one of the twelve, called Judas Iscariot, went unto the chief priests, 15And said unto them, What will ye give me, and I will deliver him unto you? And they covenanted with him for thirty pieces of silver. 16And from that time he sought opportunity to betray him."

Matthew 26:19-25 "19And the disciples did as Jesus had appointed them; and they made ready the passover. 20Now when the even was come, he sat down with the twelve. 21And as they did eat, he said, Verily I say unto you, that one of you shall betray me. 22And they were exceeding sorrowful, and began every one of them to say unto him, Lord, is it I? 23And he answered and said, He that dippeth his hand with me in the dish, the same shall betray me. 24The Son of man goeth as it is written of him: but woe unto that man by whom the Son of man is betrayed! it had been good for that man if he had not been born. 25Then Judas, which betrayed him, answered and said, Master, is it I? He said unto him, Thou hast said."

Matthew 27:3-5 "3Then Judas, which had betrayed him, when he saw that he was condemned, repented himself, and brought again the thirty pieces of silver to the chief priests and elders, 4Saying, I have sinned in that I have betrayed the innocent blood. And they said, What is that to us? see thou to that. 5And he cast down the pieces of silver in the temple, and departed, and went and hanged himself."

Mark 14:10-11 "10And Judas Iscariot, one of the twelve, went unto the chief priests, to betray him unto them. 11And when they heard it, they were glad, and promised to give him money. And he sought how he might conveniently betray him."

Mark 14:18-20 "18And as they sat and did eat, Jesus said, Verily I say unto you, One of you which eateth with me shall betray me. 19And they began to be sorrowful, and to say unto him one by one, Is it I? and another said, Is it I? 20And he answered and said unto them, It is one of the twelve, that dippeth with me in the dish."

Luke 22:1-6 "1Now the feast of unleavened bread drew nigh, which is called the Passover. 2And the chief priests and scribes sought how they might kill him; for they feared the people. 3Then entered Satan into Judas surnamed Iscariot, being of the number of the twelve. 4And he went his way, and communed with the chief priests and captains, how he might betray him unto them. 5And they were glad, and covenanted to give him money. 6And he promised, and sought opportunity to betray him unto them in the absence of the multitude."

Luke 22:21-22 "21But, behold, the hand of him that betrayeth me is with me on the table. 22And truly the Son of man goeth, as it was determined: but woe unto that man by whom he is betrayed!"

Luke 22:47-48 "47And while he yet spake, behold a multitude, and he that was called Judas, one of the twelve, went before them, and drew near unto Jesus to kiss him. 48But Jesus said unto him, Judas, betrayest thou the Son of man with a kiss?"

John 6:70-71 "⁷⁰Jesus answered them, Have not I chosen you twelve, and one of you is a devil? ⁷¹He spake of Judas Iscariot the son of Simon: for he it was that should betray him, being one of the twelve."

John 13:1-2 "¹Now before the feast of the passover, when Jesus knew that his hour was come that he should depart out of this world unto the Father, having loved his own which were in the world, he loved them unto the end. ²And supper being ended, the devil having now put into the heart of Judas Iscariot, Simon's son, to betray him;"

John 18:1-5 "¹When Jesus had spoken these words, he went forth with his disciples over the brook Cedron, where was a garden, into the which he entered, and his disciples. ²And Judas also, which betrayed him, knew the place: for Jesus ofttimes resorted thither with his disciples. ³Judas then, having received a band of men and officers from the chief priests and Pharisees, cometh thither with lanterns and torches and weapons. ⁴Jesus therefore, knowing all things that should come upon him, went forth, and said unto them, Whom seek ye? ⁵They answered him, Jesus of Nazareth. Jesus saith unto them, I am he. And Judas also, which betrayed him, stood with them."

What Was Foretold About Judas Iscariot

Psalm 41:9 "Yea, mine own familiar friend, in whom I trusted, which did eat of my bread, hath lifted up his heel against me."

Psalm 69:22-26 "²²Let their table become a snare before them: and that which should have been for their welfare, let it become a trap. ²³Let their eyes be darkened, that they see not; and make their loins continually to shake. ²⁴Pour out thine indignation upon them, and let thy wrathful anger take hold of them. ²⁵Let their habitation be desolate; and let none dwell in their tents. ²⁶For they persecute him whom thou hast smitten; and they talk to the grief of those whom thou hast wounded."

Psalm 109:6-10 "⁶Set thou a wicked man over him: and let Satan stand at his right hand. ⁷When he shall be judged, let him be condemned: and let his prayer become sin. ⁸Let his days be few; and let another take his office. ⁹Let his children be fatherless, and his wife a widow. ¹⁰Let his children be continually vagabonds, and beg: let them seek their bread also out of their desolate places."

Zechariah 11:12-13 "¹²And I said unto them, If ye think good, give me my price; and if not, forbear. So they weighed for my price thirty pieces of silver. ¹³And the LORD said unto me, Cast it unto the potter: a goodly price that I was prised at of them. And I took the thirty pieces of silver, and cast them to the potter in the house of the LORD."

Matthew 27:3-10 "³Then Judas, which had betrayed him, when he saw that he was condemned, repented himself, and brought again the thirty pieces of silver to the chief priests and elders, ⁴Saying, I have sinned in that I have betrayed the innocent blood. And they said, What is that to us? see thou to that. ⁵And he cast down the pieces of silver in the temple, and departed, and went and hanged himself. ⁶And the chief priests took the silver pieces, and said, It is not lawful for to put them into the treasury, because it is the price of blood. ⁷And they took counsel, and bought with them the potter's field, to bury strangers in. ⁸Wherefore that field was called, The field of blood, unto this day. ⁹Then was fulfilled that which was spoken by Jeremy the prophet, saying, And they took the thirty pieces of silver, the price of him that was valued, whom they of the children of Israel did value; ¹⁰And gave them for the potter's field, as the Lord appointed me."

John 13:10-18 "¹⁰Jesus saith to him, He that is washed needeth not save to wash his feet, but is clean every whit: and ye are clean, but not all. ¹¹For he knew who should betray him; therefore said he, Ye are not all clean. ¹²So after he had washed their feet, and had taken his garments, and was set down again, he said unto them, Know ye what I have done to you? ¹³Ye call me Master and Lord: and ye say well; for so I am. ¹⁴If I then, your Lord and Master, have washed your feet; ye also ought to wash one another's feet. ¹⁵For I have given you an example, that ye should do as I have done to you. ¹⁶Verily, verily, I say unto you, The servant is not greater than his lord; neither he that is sent greater than he that sent him. ¹⁷If ye know these things, happy are ye if ye do them. ¹⁸I speak not of you all: I know whom I have chosen: but that the scripture may be fulfilled, He that eateth bread with me hath lifted up his heel against me."

John 17:1-12 "¹These words spake Jesus, and lifted up his eyes to heaven, and said, Father, the hour is come; glorify thy Son, that thy Son also may glorify thee: ²As thou hast given him power over all flesh, that he should give eternal life to as many as thou hast given him. ³And this is life eternal, that they might know thee the only true God, and Jesus Christ, whom thou hast sent. ⁴I have glorified thee on the earth: I have finished the work which thou gavest me to do. ⁵And now, O Father, glorify thou me with thine own self with the glory which I had with thee before the world was. ⁶I have manifested thy name unto the men which thou gavest me out of the world: thine they were, and thou gavest them me; and they have kept thy word. ⁷Now they have known that all things whatsoever thou hast given me are of thee. ⁸For I have given unto them the words which thou gavest me; and they have received them, and have known surely that I came out from thee, and they have believed that thou didst send me. ⁹I pray for them: I pray not for the world, but for them which thou hast given me; for they are thine. ¹⁰And all mine are thine, and thine are mine; and I am glorified in them. ¹¹And now I am no more in the world, but these are in the world, and I come to thee. Holy Father, keep through thine own name those whom thou hast given me, that they may be one, as we are. ¹²While I was with them in the world, I kept them in thy name: those that thou gavest me I have kept, and none of them is lost, but the son of perdition; that the scripture might be fulfilled."

Acts 1:16-20 "¹⁶Men and brethren, this scripture must needs have been fulfilled, which the Holy Ghost by the mouth of David spake before concerning Judas, which was guide to them that took Jesus. ¹⁷For he was numbered with us, and had obtained part of this ministry. ¹⁸Now this man purchased a field with the reward of iniquity; and falling headlong, he burst asunder in the midst, and all his bowels gushed out. ¹⁹And it was known unto all the dwellers at Jerusalem; insomuch as that field is called in their proper tongue, Aceldama, that is to say, The field of blood. ²⁰For it is written in the book of Psalm, Let his habitation be desolate, and let no man dwell therein: and his bishoprick let another take."

JUDGMENT

Doing Judgment

Proverbs 21:3 "To do justice and judgment is more acceptable to the LORD than sacrifice."

Everyone Appearing Before
The Judgment Seat Of Christ

Daniel 7:9-14 "⁹I beheld till the thrones were cast down, and the Ancient of days did sit, whose garment was white as snow, and the hair of his head like the pure wool: his throne was like the fiery flame, and his wheels as burning fire. ¹⁰A fiery stream issued and came forth from before him: thousand thousands ministered unto him, and ten thousand times ten thousand stood before him: the judgment was set, and the books were opened. ¹¹I beheld then because of the voice of the great words which the horn spake: I beheld even till the beast was slain, and his body destroyed, and given to the burning flame. ¹²As concerning the rest of the beasts, they had their dominion taken away: yet their lives were prolonged for a season and time. ¹³I saw in the night visions, and, behold, one like the Son of man came with the clouds of heaven, and came to the Ancient of days, and they brought him near before him. ¹⁴And there was given him dominion, and glory, and a kingdom, that all people, nations, and languages, should serve him: his dominion is an everlasting dominion, which shall not pass away, and his kingdom that which shall not be destroyed."

Matthew 25:31-46 "³¹When the Son of man shall come in his glory, and all the holy angels with him, then shall he sit upon the throne of his glory: ³²And before him shall be gathered all nations: and he shall separate them one from another, as a shepherd divideth his sheep from the goats: ³³And he shall set the sheep on his right hand, but the goats on the left. ³⁴Then shall the King say unto them on his right hand, Come, ye blessed of my Father, inherit the kingdom prepared for you from the foundation of the world: ³⁵For I was an hungred, and ye gave me meat: I was thirsty, and ye gave me drink: I was a stranger, and ye took me in: ³⁶Naked, and ye clothed me: I was sick, and ye visited me: I was in prison, and ye came unto me. ³⁷Then shall the righteous answer him, saying, Lord, when saw we thee an hungred, and fed thee? or thirsty, and gave thee drink? ³⁸When saw we thee a stranger, and took thee in? or naked, and clothed thee? [39]Or when saw we thee sick, or in prison, and came unto thee? [40]And the King shall answer and say unto them, Verily I say unto you, Inasmuch as ye have done it unto one of the least of these my brethren, ye have done it unto me. [41]Then shall he say also unto them on the left hand, Depart from me, ye cursed, into everlasting fire, prepared for the devil and his angels: [42]For I was an hungred, and ye gave me no meat: I was thirsty, and ye gave me no drink: [43]I was a stranger, and ye took me not in: naked, and ye clothed me not: sick, and in prison, and ye visited me not. [44]Then shall they also answer him, saying, Lord, when saw we thee an hungred, or athirst, or a stranger, or naked, or sick, or in prison, and did not minister unto thee? [45]Then shall he answer them, saying, Verily I say unto you, Inasmuch as ye did it not to one of the least of these, ye did it not to me. [46]And these shall go away into everlasting punishment: but the righteous into life eternal."

John 5:22 "For the Father judgeth no man, but hath committed all judgment unto the Son:"

John 5:26-27 "[26]For as the Father hath life in himself; so hath he given to the Son to have life in himself; [27]And hath given him authority to execute judgment also, because he is the Son of man."

Romans 14:10-12 "[10]But why dost thou judge thy brother? or why dost thou set at nought thy brother? for we shall all stand before the judgment seat of Christ. [11]For it is written, As I live, saith the Lord, every knee shall bow to me, and every tongue shall confess to God. [12]So then every one of us shall give account of himself to God."

2 Corinthians 5:10 "For we must all appear before the judgment seat of Christ; that every one may receive the things done in his body, according to that he hath done, whether it be good or bad."

Revelation 20:11-15 "[11]And I saw a great white throne, and him that sat on it, from whose face the earth and the heaven fled away; and there was found no place for them. [12]And I saw the dead, small and great, stand before God; and the books were opened: and another book was opened,

which is the book of life: and the dead were judged out of those things which were written in the books, according to their works. [13]And the sea gave up the dead which were in it; and death and hell delivered up the dead which were in them: and they were judged every man according to their works. [14]And death and hell were cast into the lake of fire. This is the second death. [15]And whosoever was not found written in the book of life was cast into the lake of fire."

Executing Judgment
Zechariah 7:9 "Thus speaketh the LORD of hosts, saying, Execute true judgment, and shew mercy and compassions every man to his brother:"

Zechariah 8:16 "These are the things that ye shall do; Speak ye every man the truth to his neighbour; execute the judgment of truth and peace in your gates:"

God Not Perverting Judgment
Job 34:12 "Yea, surely God will not do wickedly, neither will the Almighty pervert judgment."

How Judgment Came Upon All Men
Romans 5:12-19 "[12]Wherefore, as by one man sin entered into the world, and death by sin; and so death passed upon all men, for that all have sinned: [13](For until the law sin was in the world: but sin is not imputed when there is no law. [14]Nevertheless death reigned from Adam to Moses, even over them that had not sinned after the similitude of Adam's transgression, who is the figure of him that was to come. [15]But not as the offence, so also is the free gift. For if through the offence of one many be dead, much more the grace of God, and the gift by grace, which is by one man, Jesus Christ, hath abounded unto many. [16]And not as it was by one that sinned, so is the gift: for the judgment was by one to condemnation, but the free gift is of many offences unto justification. [17]For if by one man's offence death reigned by one; much more they which receive abundance of grace and of the gift of righteousness shall reign in life by one, Jesus Christ.) [18]Therefore as by the offence of one judgment came upon all men to condemnation; even so by the righteousness of one the free gift came upon all men unto justification of life. [19]For as by one man's disobedience many were made sinners, so by the obedience of one shall many be made righteous."

How Man Judges

1 Samuel 16:7 "But the LORD said unto Samuel, Look not on his countenance, or on the height of his stature; because I have refused him: for the LORD seeth not as man seeth; for man looketh on the outward appearance, but the LORD looketh on the heart."

How Not To Judge

Exodus 23:2-3 "²Thou shalt not follow a multitude to do evil; neither shalt thou speak in a cause to decline after many to wrest judgment: ³Neither shalt thou countenance a poor man in his cause."

Exodus 23:6-7 "⁶Thou shalt not wrest the judgment of thy poor in his cause. ⁷Keep thee far from a false matter; and the innocent and righteous slay thou not: for I will not justify the wicked."

Leviticus 19:15 "Ye shall do no unrighteousness in judgment: thou shalt not respect the person of the poor, nor honour the person of the mighty: but in righteousness shalt thou judge thy neighbour."

Leviticus 19:35 "Ye shall do no unrighteousness in judgment, in meteyard, in weight, or in measure."

Deuteronomy 1:17 "Ye shall not respect persons in judgment; but ye shall hear the small as well as the great; ye shall not be afraid of the face of man; for the judgment is God's: and the cause that is too hard for you, bring it unto me, and I will hear it."

Deuteronomy 16:19 "Thou shalt not wrest judgment; thou shalt not respect persons, neither take a gift: for a gift doth blind the eyes of the wise, and pervert the words of the righteous."

1 Samuel 16:7 "But the LORD said unto Samuel, Look not on his countenance, or on the height of his stature; because I have refused him: for the LORD seeth not as man seeth; for man looketh on the outward appearance, but the LORD looketh on the heart."

Proverbs 18:5 "It is not good to accept the person of the wicked, to overthrow the righteous in judgment."

Proverbs 24:23 "These things also belong to the wise. It is not good to have respect of persons in judgment."

John 7:24 "Judge not according to the appearance, but judge righteous judgment."

How The Lord Judges

1 Samuel 16:7 "But the LORD said unto Samuel, Look not on his countenance, or on the height of his stature; because I have refused him: for the LORD seeth not as man seeth; for man looketh on the outward appearance, but the LORD looketh on the heart."

Psalm 67:3-4 "³Let the people praise thee, O God; let all the people praise thee. ⁴O let the nations be glad and sing for joy: for thou shalt judge the people righteously, and govern the nations upon earth. Selah."

How To Judge

Leviticus 19:15 "Ye shall do no unrighteousness in judgment: thou shalt not respect the person of the poor, nor honour the person of the mighty: but in righteousness shalt thou judge thy neighbour."

Leviticus 19:35-36 "³⁵Ye shall do no unrighteousness in judgment, in meteyard, in weight, or in measure. ³⁶Just balances, just weights, a just ephah, and a just hin, shall ye have: I am the LORD your God, which brought you out of the land of Egypt."

Deuteronomy 1:16-17 "¹⁶And I charged your judges at that time, saying, Hear the causes between your brethren, and judge righteously between every man and his brother, and the stranger that is with him. ¹⁷Ye shall not respect persons in judgment; but ye shall hear the small as well as the great; ye shall not be afraid of the face of man; for the judgment is God's: and the cause that is too hard for you, bring it unto me, and I will hear it."

2 Chronicles 19:5-7 "⁵And he set judges in the land throughout all the fenced cities of Judah, city by city, ⁶And said to the judges, Take heed what ye do: for ye judge not for man, but for the LORD, who is with you in the judgment. ⁷Wherefore now let the fear of the LORD be upon you; take heed and do it: for there is no iniquity with the LORD our God, nor respect of persons, nor taking of gifts."

John 7:24 "Judge not according to the appearance, but judge righteous judgment."

Judges Judging For The Lord

2 Chronicles 19:5-7 "⁵And he set judges in the land throughout all the fenced cities of Judah, city by city, ⁶And said to the judges, Take heed what ye do: for ye judge not for man, but for the LORD, who is with you in the judgment. ⁷Wherefore now let the fear of the LORD be upon you; take heed and do it: for there is no iniquity with the LORD our God, nor respect of persons, nor taking of gifts."

Judgment Belonging To God
Deuteronomy 1:17 "Ye shall not respect persons in judgment; but ye shall hear the small as well as the great; ye shall not be afraid of the face of man; for the judgment is God's: and the cause that is too hard for you, bring it unto me, and I will hear it."

Keeping Judgment
Isaiah 56:1 "Thus saith the LORD, Keep ye judgment, and do justice: for my salvation is near to come, and my righteousness to be revealed."

Hosea 12:6 "Therefore turn thou to thy God: keep mercy and judgment, and wait on thy God continually."

Kings That Sit In The Throne Of Judgment
Proverbs 20:8 "A king that sitteth in the throne of judgment scattereth away all evil with his eyes."

Not Judging Others
Matthew 7:1-5 "¹Judge not, that ye be not judged. ²For with what judgment ye judge, ye shall be judged: and with what measure ye mete, it shall be measured to you again. ³And why beholdest thou the mote that is in thy brother's eye, but considerest not the beam that is in thine own eye? ⁴Or how wilt thou say to thy brother, Let me pull out the mote out of thine eye; and, behold, a beam is in thine own eye? ⁵Thou hypocrite, first cast out the beam out of thine own eye; and then shalt thou see clearly to cast out the mote out of thy brother's eye."

Luke 6:37-42 "³⁷Judge not, and ye shall not be judged: condemn not, and ye shall not be condemned: forgive, and ye shall be forgiven: ³⁸Give, and it shall be given unto you; good measure, pressed down, and shaken together, and running over, shall men give into your bosom. For with the same measure that ye mete withal it shall be measured to you again. ³⁹And he spake a parable unto them, Can the blind lead the blind? shall they not both fall into the ditch? ⁴⁰The disciple is not above his master: but every one that is perfect shall be as his master. ⁴¹And why beholdest thou the mote that is in thy brother's eye, but perceivest not the beam that is in thine own eye? ⁴²Either how canst

thou say to thy brother, Brother, let me pull out the mote that is in thine eye, when thou thyself beholdest not the beam that is in thine own eye? Thou hypocrite, cast out first the beam out of thine own eye, and then shalt thou see clearly to pull out the mote that is in thy brother's eye."

John 8:3-7 "³And the scribes and Pharisees brought unto him a woman taken in adultery; and when they had set her in the midst, ⁴They say unto him, Master, this woman was taken in adultery, in the very act. ⁵Now Moses in the law commanded us, that such should be stoned: but what sayest thou? ⁶This they said, tempting him, that they might have to accuse him. But Jesus stooped down, and with his finger wrote on the ground, as though he heard them not. ⁷So when they continued asking him, he lifted up himself, and said unto them, He that is without sin among you, let him first cast a stone at her."

Romans 14:10-13 "¹⁰But why dost thou judge thy brother? or why dost thou set at nought thy brother? for we shall all stand before the judgment seat of Christ. ¹¹For it is written, As I live, saith the Lord, every knee shall bow to me, and every tongue shall confess to God. ¹²So then every one of us shall give account of himself to God. ¹³Let us not therefore judge one another any more: but judge this rather, that no man put a stumblingblock or an occasion to fall in his brother's way."

Not Perverting Judgment
Deuteronomy 24:17 "Thou shalt not pervert the judgment of the stranger, nor of the fatherless; nor take a widow's raiment to pledge:"

Seeking Judgment
Isaiah 1:17 "Learn to do well; seek judgment, relieve the oppressed, judge the fatherless, plead for the widow."

The Judgment Of Babylon
Isaiah 13:17-22 "¹⁷Behold, I will stir up the Medes against them, which shall not regard silver; and as for gold, they shall not delight in it. ¹⁸Their bows also shall dash the young men to pieces; and they shall have no pity on the fruit of the womb; their eye shall not spare children. ¹⁹And Babylon, the glory of kingdoms, the beauty of the Chaldees' excellency, shall be as when God overthrew

Sodom and Gomorrah. 20It shall never be inhabited, neither shall it be dwelt in from generation to generation: neither shall the Arabian pitch tent there; neither shall the shepherds make their fold there. 21But wild beasts of the desert shall lie there; and their houses shall be full of doleful creatures; and owls shall dwell there, and satyrs shall dance there. 22And the wild beasts of the islands shall cry in their desolate houses, and dragons in their pleasant palaces: and her time is near to come, and her days shall not be prolonged."

Isaiah 14:21-23 "21Prepare slaughter for his children for the iniquity of their fathers; that they do not rise, nor possess the land, nor fill the face of the world with cities. 22For I will rise up against them, saith the LORD of hosts, and cut off from Babylon the name, and remnant, and son, and nephew, saith the LORD. 23I will also make it a possession for the bittern, and pools of water: and I will sweep it with the besom of destruction, saith the LORD of hosts."

Isaiah 48:12-14 "12Hearken unto me, O Jacob and Israel, my called; I am he; I am the first, I also am the last. 13Mine hand also hath laid the foundation of the earth, and my right hand hath spanned the heavens: when I call unto them, they stand up together. 14All ye, assemble yourselves, and hear; which among them hath declared these things? The LORD hath loved him: he will do his pleasure on Babylon, and his arm shall be on the Chaldeans."

Jeremiah 25:1-14 "1The word that came to Jeremiah concerning all the people of Judah in the fourth year of Jehoiakim the son of Josiah king of Judah, that was the first year of Nebuchadrezzar king of Babylon; 2The which Jeremiah the prophet spake unto all the people of Judah, and to all the inhabitants of Jerusalem, saying, 3From the thirteenth year of Josiah the son of Amon king of Judah, even unto this day, that is the three and twentieth year, the word of the LORD hath come unto me, and I have spoken unto you, rising early and speaking; but ye have not hearkened. 4And the LORD hath sent unto you all his servants the prophets, rising early and sending them; but ye have not hearkened, nor inclined your ear to hear. 5They said, Turn ye again now every one

from his evil way, and from the evil of your doings, and dwell in the land that the LORD hath given unto you and to your fathers for ever and ever: 6And go not after other gods to serve them, and to worship them, and provoke me not to anger with the works of your hands; and I will do you no hurt. 7Yet ye have not hearkened unto me, saith the LORD; that ye might provoke me to anger with the works of your hands to your own hurt. 8Therefore thus saith the LORD of hosts; Because ye have not heard my words, 9Behold, I will send and take all the families of the north, saith the LORD, and Nebuchadrezzar the king of Babylon, my servant, and will bring them against this land, and against the inhabitants thereof, and against all these nations round about, and will utterly destroy them, and make them an astonishment, and an hissing, and perpetual desolations. 10Moreover I will take from them the voice of mirth, and the voice of gladness, the voice of the bridegroom, and the voice of the bride, the sound of the millstones, and the light of the candle. 11And this whole land shall be a desolation, and an astonishment; and these nations shall serve the king of Babylon seventy years. 12And it shall come to pass, when seventy years are accomplished, that I will punish the king of Babylon, and that nation, saith the LORD, for their iniquity, and the land of the Chaldeans, and will make it perpetual desolations. 13And I will bring upon that land all my words which I have pronounced against it, even all that is written in this book, which Jeremiah hath prophesied against all the nations. 14For many nations and great kings shall serve themselves of them also: and I will recompense them according to their deeds, and according to the works of their own hands."

Jeremiah 51:1-12 "1Thus saith the LORD; Behold, I will raise up against Babylon, and against them that dwell in the midst of them that rise up against me, a destroying wind; 2And will send unto Babylon fanners, that shall fan her, and shall empty her land: for in the day of trouble they shall be against her round about. 3Against him that bendeth let the archer bend his bow, and against him that lifteth himself up in his brigandine: and spare ye not her young men; destroy ye utterly all her host. 4Thus the slain shall fall in the land of the Chaldeans, and they that are thrust through in her streets. 5For Israel hath not been forsaken, nor Judah of his God, of the LORD of hosts; though their land was filled with sin against the Holy One of Israel. ⁶Flee out of the midst of Babylon, and deliver every man his soul: be not cut off in her iniquity; for this is the time of the LORD's vengeance; he will render unto her a recompence. ⁷Babylon hath been a golden cup in the LORD's hand, that made all the earth drunken: the nations have drunken of her wine; therefore the nations are mad. ⁸Babylon is suddenly fallen and destroyed: howl for her; take balm for her pain, if so she may be healed. ⁹We would have healed Babylon, but she is not healed: forsake her, and let us go every one into his own country: for her judgment reacheth unto heaven, and is lifted up even to the skies. ¹⁰The LORD hath brought forth our righteousness: come, and let us declare in Zion the work of the LORD our God. ¹¹Make bright the arrows; gather the shields: the LORD hath raised up the spirit of the kings of the Medes: for his device is against Babylon, to destroy it; because it is the vengeance of the LORD, the vengeance of his temple. ¹²Set up the standard upon the walls of Babylon, make the watch strong, set up the watchmen, prepare the ambushes: for the LORD hath both devised and done that which he spake against the inhabitants of Babylon."

Revelation 17:1-18 "¹And there came one of the seven angels which had the seven vials, and talked with me, saying unto me, Come hither; I will shew unto thee the judgment of the great whore that sitteth upon many waters: ²With whom the kings of the earth have committed fornication, and the inhabitants of the earth have been made drunk with the wine of her fornication. ³So he carried me away in the spirit into the wilderness: and I saw a woman sit upon a scarlet coloured beast, full of names of blasphemy, having seven heads and ten horns. ⁴And the woman was arrayed in purple and scarlet colour, and decked with gold and precious stones and pearls, having a golden cup in her hand full of abominations and filthiness of her fornication: ⁵And upon her forehead was a name written, MYSTERY, BABYLON THE GREAT, THE MOTHER OF HARLOTS AND ABOMINATIONS OF THE EARTH. ⁶And I saw the woman drunken with the blood of the saints, and with the blood

of the martyrs of Jesus: and when I saw her, I wondered with great admiration. ⁷And the angel said unto me, Wherefore didst thou marvel? I will tell thee the mystery of the woman, and of the beast that carrieth her, which hath the seven heads and ten horns. ⁸The beast that thou sawest was, and is not; and shall ascend out of the bottomless pit, and go into perdition: and they that dwell on the earth shall wonder, whose names were not written in the book of life from the foundation of the world, when they behold the beast that was, and is not, and yet is. ⁹And here is the mind which hath wisdom. The seven heads are seven mountains, on which the woman sitteth. ¹⁰And there are seven kings: five are fallen, and one is, and the other is not yet come; and when he cometh, he must continue a short space. ¹¹And the beast that was, and is not, even he is the eighth, and is of the seven, and goeth into perdition. ¹²And the ten horns which thou sawest are ten kings, which have received no kingdom as yet; but receive power as kings one hour with the beast. ¹³These have one mind, and shall give their power and strength unto the beast. ¹⁴These shall make war with the Lamb, and the Lamb shall overcome them: for he is Lord of lords, and King of kings: and they that are with him are called, and chosen, and faithful. ¹⁵And he saith unto me, The waters which thou sawest, where the whore sitteth, are peoples, and multitudes, and nations, and tongues. ¹⁶And the ten horns which thou sawest upon the beast, these shall hate the whore, and shall make her desolate and naked, and shall eat her flesh, and burn her with fire. ¹⁷For God hath put in their hearts to fulfil his will, and to agree, and give their kingdom unto the beast, until the words of God shall be fulfilled. ¹⁸And the woman which thou sawest is that great city, which reigneth over the kings of the earth."

Revelation 18:1-24 "¹And after these things I saw another angel come down from heaven, having great power; and the earth was lightened with his glory. ²And he cried mightily with a strong voice, saying, Babylon the great is fallen, is fallen, and is become the habitation of devils, and the hold of every foul spirit, and a cage of every unclean and hateful bird. ³For all nations have drunk of the wine of the wrath of her fornication, and the kings of the earth have committed fornication with her, and the merchants of the earth are waxed rich through the abundance of her delicacies. ⁴And I heard another voice from heaven, saying, Come out of her, my people, that ye be not partakers of her sins, and that ye receive not of her plagues. ⁵For her sins have reached unto heaven, and God hath remembered her iniquities. ⁶Reward her even as she rewarded you, and double unto her double according to her works: in the cup which she hath filled fill to her double. ⁷How much she hath glorified herself, and lived deliciously, so much torment and sorrow give her: for she saith in her heart, I sit a queen, and am no widow, and shall see no sorrow. ⁸Therefore shall her plagues come in one day, death, and mourning, and famine; and she shall be utterly burned with fire: for strong is the Lord God who judgeth her. ⁹And the kings of the earth, who have committed fornication and lived deliciously with her, shall bewail her, and lament for her, when they shall see the smoke of her burning, ¹⁰Standing afar off for the fear of her torment, saying, Alas, alas, that great city Babylon, that mighty city! for in one hour is thy judgment come. ¹¹And the merchants of the earth shall weep and mourn over her; for no man buyeth their merchandise any more: ¹²The merchandise of gold, and silver, and precious stones, and of pearls, and fine linen, and purple, and silk, and scarlet, and all thyine wood, and all manner vessels of ivory, and all manner vessels of most precious wood, and of brass, and iron, and marble, ¹³And cinnamon, and odours, and ointments, and frankincense, and wine, and oil, and fine flour, and wheat, and beasts, and sheep, and horses, and chariots, and slaves, and souls of men. ¹⁴And the fruits that thy soul lusted after are departed from thee, and all things which were dainty and goodly are departed from thee, and thou shalt find them no more at all. ¹⁵The merchants of these things, which were made rich by her, shall stand afar off for the fear of her torment, weeping and wailing, ¹⁶And saying, Alas, alas, that great city, that was clothed in fine linen, and purple, and scarlet, and decked with gold, and precious stones, and pearls! ¹⁷For in one hour so great riches is come to nought. And every shipmaster, and all the company in ships, and sailors, and as many as trade by sea, stood afar off, ¹⁸And cried when they saw the smoke of her burning, saying, What city is like unto this great city! ¹⁹And they cast dust on their heads, and cried, weeping and wailing, saying, Alas, alas, that great city, wherein were made rich all that had ships in the sea by reason of her costliness! for in one hour is she made desolate. ²⁰Rejoice over her, thou heaven, and ye holy apostles and prophets; for God hath avenged you on her. ²¹And a mighty angel took up a stone like a great millstone, and cast it into the sea, saying, Thus with violence shall that great city Babylon be thrown down, and shall be found no more at all. ²²And the voice of harpers, and musicians, and of pipers, and trumpeters, shall be heard no more at all in thee; and no craftsman, of whatsoever craft he be, shall be found any more in thee; and the sound of a millstone shall be heard no more at all in thee; ²³And the light of a candle shall shine no more at all in thee; and the voice of the bridegroom and of the bride shall be heard no more at all in thee: for thy merchants were the great men of the earth; for by thy sorceries were all nations deceived. ²⁴And in her was found the blood of prophets, and of saints, and of all that were slain upon the earth."

Revelation 19:1-2 "¹And after these things I heard a great voice of much people in heaven, saying, Alleluia; Salvation, and glory, and honour, and power, unto the Lord our God: ²For true and righteous are his judgments: for he hath judged the great whore, which did corrupt the earth with her fornication, and hath avenged the blood of his servants at her hand."

The Judgment(s) Of The Lord
1 Chronicles 16:14 "He is the Lord our God; his judgments are in all the earth."

Psalm 19:9-11 "⁹The fear of the Lord is clean, enduring for ever: the judgments of the Lord are true and righteous altogether. ¹⁰More to be desired are they than gold, yea, than much fine gold: sweeter also than honey and the honeycomb. ¹¹Moreover by them is thy servant warned: and in keeping of them there is great reward."

Psalm 36:6 "Thy righteousness is like the great mountains; thy judgments are a great deep: O Lord, thou preservest man and beast."

Psalm 105:7 "He is the Lord our God: his judgments are in all the earth."

Psalm 119:75 "I know, O Lord, that thy judgments are right, and that thou in faithfulness hast afflicted me."

Psalm 119:137 "Righteous art thou, O Lord, and upright are thy judgments."

Psalm 119:159-160 "159Consider how I love thy precepts: quicken me, O Lord, according to thy lovingkindness. 160Thy word is true from the beginning: and every one of thy righteous judgments endureth for ever."

Isaiah 26:4-9 "4Trust ye in the Lord for ever: for in the Lord JEHOVAH is everlasting strength: 5For he bringeth down them that dwell on high; the lofty city, he layeth it low; he layeth it low, even to the ground; he bringeth it even to the dust. 6The foot shall tread it down, even the feet of the poor, and the steps of the needy. 7The way of the just is uprightness: thou, most upright, dost weigh the path of the just. 8Yea, in the way of thy judgments, O Lord, have we waited for thee; the desire of our soul is to thy name, and to the remembrance of thee. 9With my soul have I desired thee in the night; yea, with my spirit within me will I seek thee early: for when thy judgments are in the earth, the inhabitants of the world will learn righteousness."

Isaiah 51:3-4 "3For the Lord shall comfort Zion: he will comfort all her waste places; and he will make her wilderness like Eden, and her desert like the garden of the Lord; joy and gladness shall be found therein, thanksgiving, and the voice of melody. 4Hearken unto me, my people; and give ear unto me, O my nation: for a law shall proceed from me, and I will make my judgment to rest for a light of the people."

Zephaniah 3:5 "The just Lord is in the midst thereof; he will not do iniquity: every morning doth he bring his judgment to light, he faileth not; but the unjust knoweth no shame."

Romans 2:1-16 "1Therefore thou art inexcusable, O man, whosoever thou art that judgest: for wherein thou judgest another, thou condemnest thyself; for thou that judgest doest the same things. 2But we are sure that the judgment of God is according to truth against them which commit such things. 3And thinkest thou this, O man, that judgest them which do such things, and doest the same, that thou shalt escape the judgment of God? 4Or despisest thou the riches of his goodness and forbearance and longsuffering; not knowing that the goodness of God leadeth thee to repentance? 5But after thy hardness and impenitent heart treasurest up unto thyself wrath against the day of wrath and revelation of the righteous judgment of God; 6Who will render to every man according to his deeds: 7To them who by patient continuance in well doing seek for glory and honour and immortality, eternal life: 8But unto them that are contentious, and do not obey the truth, but obey unrighteousness, indignation and wrath, 9Tribulation and anguish, upon every soul of man that doeth evil, of the Jew first, and also of the Gentile; 10But glory, honour, and peace, to every man that worketh good, to the Jew first, and also to the Gentile: 11For there is no respect of persons with God. 12For as many as have sinned without law shall also perish without law: and as many as have sinned in the law shall be judged by the law; 13(For not the hearers of the law are just before God, but the doers of the law shall be justified. 14For when the Gentiles, which have not the law, do by nature the things contained in the law, these, having not the law, are a law unto themselves: 15Which shew the work of the law written in their hearts, their conscience also bearing witness, and their thoughts the mean while accusing or else excusing one another;) 16In the day when God shall judge the secrets of men by Jesus Christ according to my gospel."

Romans 11:33-36 "33O the depth of the riches both of the wisdom and knowledge of God! how unsearchable are his judgments, and his ways past finding out! 34For who hath known the mind of the Lord? or who hath been his counsellor? 35Or who hath first given to him, and it shall be recompensed unto him again? 36For of him, and through him, and to him, are all things: to whom be glory for ever. Amen."

Revelation 15:4 "Who shall not fear thee, O Lord, and glorify thy name? for thou only art holy: for all nations shall come and worship before thee; for thy judgments are made manifest."

Revelation 16:7 "And I heard another out of the altar say, Even so, Lord God Almighty, true and righteous are thy judgments."

Revelation 19:1-2 "¹And after these things I heard a great voice of much people in heaven, saying, Alleluia; Salvation, and glory, and honour, and power, unto the Lord our God: ²For true and righteous are his judgments: for he hath judged the great whore, which did corrupt the earth with her fornication, and hath avenged the blood of his servants at her hand."

The Lord Being A God Of Judgment

Isaiah 30:18 "And therefore will the LORD wait, that he may be gracious unto you, and therefore will he be exalted, that he may have mercy upon you: for the LORD is a God of judgment: blessed are all they that wait for him."

Jeremiah 9:23-24 "²³Thus saith the LORD, Let not the wise man glory in his wisdom, neither let the mighty man glory in his might, let not the rich man glory in his riches: ²⁴But let him that glorieth glory in this, that he understandeth and knoweth me, that I am the LORD which exercise lovingkindness, judgment, and righteousness, in the earth: for in these things I delight, saith the LORD."

The Lord Being Judge

Psalm 50:6 "And the heavens shall declare his righteousness: for God is judge himself. Selah."

Psalm 68:4-5 "⁴Sing unto God, sing praises to his name: extol him that rideth upon the heavens by his name JAH, and rejoice before him. ⁵A father of the fatherless, and a judge of the widows, is God in his holy habitation."

Psalm 75:7 "But God is the judge: he putteth down one, and setteth up another."

Psalm 94:1-2 "¹O LORD God, to whom vengeance belongeth; O God, to whom vengeance belongeth, shew thyself. ²Lift up thyself, thou judge of the earth: render a reward to the proud."

Isaiah 33:22 "For the LORD is our judge, the LORD is our lawgiver, the LORD is our king; he will save us."

Acts 10:37-42 "³⁷That word, I say, ye know, which was published throughout all Judaea, and began from Galilee, after the baptism which John preached; ³⁸How God anointed Jesus of Nazareth with the Holy Ghost and with power: who went about doing good, and healing all that were oppressed of the devil; for God was with him. ³⁹And we are witnesses of all things which he did both in the land of the Jews, and in Jerusalem; whom they slew and hanged on a tree: ⁴⁰Him God raised up the third day, and shewed him openly; ⁴¹Not to all the people, but unto witnesses chosen before of God, even to us, who did eat and drink with him after he rose from the dead. ⁴²And he commanded us to preach unto the people, and to testify that it is he which was ordained of God to be the Judge of quick and dead."

2 Timothy 4:7-8 "⁷I have fought a good fight, I have finished my course, I have kept the faith: ⁸Henceforth there is laid up for me a crown of righteousness, which the Lord, the righteous judge, shall give me at that day: and not to me only, but unto all them also that love his appearing."

Hebrews 12:23 "To the general assembly and church of the firstborn, which are written in heaven, and to God the Judge of all, and to the spirits of just men made perfect,"

The Lord Judging

Deuteronomy 32:36 "For the LORD shall judge his people, and repent himself for his servants, when he seeth that their power is gone, and there is none shut up, or left."

1 Samuel 2:10 "The adversaries of the LORD shall be broken to pieces; out of heaven shall he thunder upon them: the LORD shall judge the ends of the earth; and he shall give strength unto his king, and exalt the horn of his anointed."

1 Chronicles 16:33 "Then shall the trees of the wood sing out at the presence of the LORD, because he cometh to judge the earth."

Job 36:26-31 "²⁶Behold, God is great, and we know him not, neither can the number of his years be searched out. ²⁷For he maketh small the drops of water: they pour down rain according to the vapour thereof: ²⁸Which the clouds do drop and distil upon man abundantly. ²⁹Also can any understand the spreadings of the clouds, or the noise of his tabernacle? ³⁰Behold, he spreadeth his light upon it, and covereth the bottom of the sea. ³¹For by them judgeth he the people; he giveth meat in abundance."

Psalm 7:8 "The LORD shall judge the people: judge me, O LORD, according to my righteousness, and according to mine integrity that is in me."

Psalm 7:11 "God judgeth the righteous, and God is angry with the wicked every day."

Psalm 9:7-8 "⁷But the LORD shall endure for ever: he hath prepared his throne for judgment. ⁸And he shall judge the world in righteousness, he shall minister judgment to the people in uprightness."

Psalm 9:16 "The LORD is known by the judgment which he executeth: the wicked is snared in the work of his own hands. Higgaion. Selah."

Psalm 50:1-5 "¹The mighty God, even the LORD, hath spoken, and called the earth from the rising of the sun unto the going down thereof. ²Out of Zion, the perfection of beauty, God hath shined. ³Our God shall come, and shall not keep silence: a fire shall devour before him, and it shall be very tempestuous round about him. ⁴He shall call to the heavens from above, and to the earth, that he may judge his people. ⁵Gather my saints together unto me; those that have made a covenant with me by sacrifice."

Psalm 58:10-11 "¹⁰The righteous shall rejoice when he seeth the vengeance: he shall wash his feet in the blood of the wicked. ¹¹So that a man shall say, Verily there is a reward for the righteous: verily he is a God that judgeth in the earth."

Psalm 67:3-4 "³Let the people praise thee, O God; let all the people praise thee. ⁴O let the nations be glad and sing for joy: for thou shalt judge the people righteously, and govern the nations upon earth. Selah."

Psalm 96:13 "Before the LORD: for he cometh, for he cometh to judge the earth: he shall judge the world with righteousness, and the people with his truth."

Ecclesiastes 12:14 "For God shall bring every work into judgment, with every secret thing, whether it be good, or whether it be evil."

Isaiah 2:3-4 "³And many people shall go and say, Come ye, and let us go up to the mountain of the LORD, to the house of the God of Jacob; and he will teach us of his ways, and we will walk in his paths: for out of Zion shall go forth the law, and the word of the LORD from Jerusalem. ⁴And he shall judge among the nations, and shall rebuke many people: and they shall beat their swords into plowshares, and their spears into pruning-

hooks: nation shall not lift up sword against nation, neither shall they learn war any more."

Isaiah 51:3-5 "³For the LORD shall comfort Zion: he will comfort all her waste places; and he will make her wilderness like Eden, and her desert like the garden of the LORD; joy and gladness shall be found therein, thanksgiving, and the voice of melody. ⁴Hearken unto me, my people; and give ear unto me, O my nation: for a law shall proceed from me, and I will make my judgment to rest for a light of the people. ⁵My righteousness is near; my salvation is gone forth, and mine arms shall judge the people; the isles shall wait upon me, and on mine arm shall they trust."

Jeremiah 23:5 "Behold, the days come, saith the LORD, that I will raise unto David a righteous Branch, and a King shall reign and prosper, and shall execute judgment and justice in the earth."

Jeremiah 33:14-15 "¹⁴Behold, the days come, saith the LORD, that I will perform that good thing which I have promised unto the house of Israel and to the house of Judah. ¹⁵In those days, and at that time, will I cause the Branch of righteousness to grow up unto David; and he shall execute judgment and righteousness in the land."

Ezekiel 18:29-30 "²⁹Yet saith the house of Israel, The way of the Lord is not equal. O house of Israel, are not my ways equal? are not your ways unequal? ³⁰Therefore I will judge you, O house of Israel, every one according to his ways, saith the Lord GOD. Repent, and turn yourselves from all your transgressions; so iniquity shall not be your ruin."

Ezekiel 33:17-20 "¹⁷Yet the children of thy people say, The way of the Lord is not equal: but as for them, their way is not equal. ¹⁸When the righteous turneth from his righteousness, and committeth iniquity, he shall even die thereby. ¹⁹But if the wicked turn from his wickedness, and do that which is lawful and right, he shall live thereby. ²⁰Yet ye say, The way of the Lord is not equal. O ye house of Israel, I will judge you every one after his ways."

Ezekiel 36:16-19 "¹⁶Moreover the word of the LORD came unto me, saying, ¹⁷Son of man, when the house of Israel dwelt in their own land, they defiled it by their own way and by their doings:

their way was before me as the uncleanness of a removed woman. [18]Wherefore I poured my fury upon them for the blood that they had shed upon the land, and for their idols wherewith they had polluted it: [19]And I scattered them among the heathen, and they were dispersed through the countries: according to their way and according to their doings I judged them."

Micah 4:1-3 "[1]But in the last days it shall come to pass, that the mountain of the house of the LORD shall be established in the top of the mountains, and it shall be exalted above the hills; and people shall flow unto it. [2]And many nations shall come, and say, Come, and let us go up to the mountain of the LORD, and to the house of the God of Jacob; and he will teach us of his ways, and we will walk in his paths: for the law shall go forth of Zion, and the word of the LORD from Jerusalem. [3]And he shall judge among many people, and rebuke strong nations afar off; and they shall beat their swords into plowshares, and their spears into pruninghooks: nation shall not lift up a sword against nation, neither shall they learn war any more."

John 5:22 "For the Father judgeth no man, but hath committed all judgment unto the Son:"

John 5:26-27 "[26]For as the Father hath life in himself; so hath he given to the Son to have life in himself; [27]And hath given him authority to execute judgment also, because he is the Son of man."

John 9:39 "And Jesus said, For judgment I am come into this world, that they which see not might see; and that they which see might be made blind."

Acts 17:30-31 "[30]And the times of this ignorance God winked at; but now commandeth all men every where to repent: [31]Because he hath appointed a day, in the which he will judge the world in righteousness by that man whom he hath ordained; whereof he hath given assurance unto all men, in that he hath raised him from the dead."

1 Corinthians 4:3-5 "[3]But with me it is a very small thing that I should be judged of you, or of man's judgment: yea, I judge not mine own self. [4]For I know nothing by myself; yet am I not hereby justified: but he that judgeth me is the Lord. [5]Therefore judge nothing before the time,

until the Lord come, who both will bring to light the hidden things of darkness, and will make manifest the counsels of the hearts: and then shall every man have praise of God."

Hebrews 10:30 "For we know him that hath said, Vengeance belongeth unto me, I will recompense, saith the Lord. And again, The Lord shall judge his people."

Jude 14-15 "[14]And Enoch also, the seventh from Adam, prophesied of these, saying, Behold, the Lord cometh with ten thousands of his saints, [15]To execute judgment upon all, and to convince all that are ungodly among them of all their ungodly deeds which they have ungodly committed, and of all their hard speeches which ungodly sinners have spoken against him."

Revelation 16:5 "And I heard the angel of the waters say, Thou art righteous, O Lord, which art, and wast, and shalt be, because thou hast judged thus."

Revelation 18:8 "Therefore shall her plagues come in one day, death, and mourning, and famine; and she shall be utterly burned with fire: for strong is the Lord God who judgeth her."

Revelation 19:11 "And I saw heaven opened, and behold a white horse; and he that sat upon him was called Faithful and True, and in righteousness he doth judge and make war."

The Lord Loving Judgment
Psalm 33:5 "He loveth righteousness and judgment: the earth is full of the goodness of the LORD."

Psalm 37:28 "For the LORD loveth judgment, and forsaketh not his saints; they are preserved for ever: but the seed of the wicked shall be cut off."

Isaiah 61:8 "For I the LORD love judgment, I hate robbery for burnt offering; and I will direct their work in truth, and I will make an everlasting covenant with them."

The Reward For Refusing To Do Judgment
Proverbs 21:7 "The robbery of the wicked shall destroy them; because they refuse to do judgment."

Those That Execute True Judgment
Ezekiel 18:5-9 "[5]But if a man be just, and do that which is lawful and right, [6]And hath not eaten upon the mountains, neither hath lifted up his

eyes to the idols of the house of Israel, neither hath defiled his neighbour's wife, neither hath come near to a menstruous woman, [7]And hath not oppressed any, but hath restored to the debtor his pledge, hath spoiled none by violence, hath given his bread to the hungry, and hath covered the naked with a garment; [8]He that hath not given forth upon usury, neither hath taken any increase, that hath withdrawn his hand from iniquity, hath executed true judgment between man and man, [9]Hath walked in my statutes, and hath kept my judgments, to deal truly; he is just, he shall surely live, saith the Lord GOD."

Those That Judge Others
Romans 2:1-3 "[1]Therefore thou art inexcusable, O man, whosoever thou art that judgest: for wherein thou judgest another, thou condemnest thyself; for thou that judgest doest the same things. [2]But we are sure that the judgment of God is according to truth against them which commit such things. [3]And thinkest thou this, O man, that judgest them which do such things, and doest the same, that thou shalt escape the judgment of God?"

James 4:11-12 "[11]Speak not evil one of another, brethren. He that speaketh evil of his brother, and judgeth his brother, speaketh evil of the law, and judgeth the law: but if thou judge the law, thou art not a doer of the law, but a judge. [12]There is one lawgiver, who is able to save and to destroy: who art thou that judgest another?"

Those That Judge Themselves
1 Corinthians 11:31-32 "[31]For if we would judge ourselves, we should not be judged. [32]But when we are judged, we are chastened of the Lord, that we should not be condemned with the world."

Those That Keep Judgment
Psalm 106:3 "Blessed are they that keep judgment, and he that doeth righteousness at all times."

Those That Pervert Judgment
Deuteronomy 27:19 "Cursed be he that perverteth the judgment of the stranger, fatherless, and widow. And all the people shall say, Amen."

What Is Judgment
Deuteronomy 32:3-4 "[3]Because I will publish the name of the LORD: ascribe ye greatness unto our God. [4]He is the Rock, his work is perfect: for all his ways are judgment: a God of truth and without iniquity, just and right is he."

Psalm 111:4-7 "[4]He hath made his wonderful works to be remembered: the LORD is gracious and full of compassion. [5]He hath given meat unto them that fear him: he will ever be mindful of his covenant. [6]He hath shewed his people the power of his works, that he may give them the heritage of the heathen. [7]The works of his hands are verity and judgment; all his commandments are sure."

Daniel 4:37 "Now I Nebuchadnezzar praise and extol and honour the King of heaven, all whose works are truth, and his ways judgment: and those that walk in pride he is able to abase."

What The Saints Shall Judge
1 Corinthians 6:1-8 "[1]Dare any of you, having a matter against another, go to law before the unjust, and not before the saints? [2]Do ye not know that the saints shall judge the world? and if the world shall be judged by you, are ye unworthy to judge the smallest matters? [3]Know ye not that we shall judge angels? how much more things that pertain to this life? [4]If then ye have judgments of things pertaining to this life, set them to judge who are least esteemed in the church. [5]I speak to your shame. Is it so, that there is not a wise man among you? no, not one that shall be able to judge between his brethren? [6]But brother goeth to law with brother, and that before the unbelievers. [7]Now therefore there is utterly a fault among you, because ye go to law one with another. Why do ye not rather take wrong? why do ye not rather suffer yourselves to be defrauded? [8]Nay, ye do wrong, and defraud, and that your brethren."

Where Judgment Comes From
Proverbs 29:26 "Many seek the ruler's favour; but every man's judgment cometh from the LORD."

Where Judgment Will Begin
1 Peter 4:17-18 "[17]For the time is come that judgment must begin at the house of God: and if it first begin at us, what shall the end be of them that obey not the gospel of God? [18]And if the righteous scarcely be saved, where shall the ungodly and the sinner appear?"

Who Does Not Understand Judgment
Proverbs 28:5 "Evil men understand not judgment: but they that seek the LORD understand all things."

Who Enjoys Doing Judgment
Proverbs 21:15 "It is joy to the just to do judgment: but destruction shall be to the workers of iniquity."

Who Is Reserved Unto Judgment
2 Peter 2:4 "For if God spared not the angels that sinned, but cast them down to hell, and delivered them into chains of darkness, to be reserved unto judgment;"

Who Judges All Things
1 Corinthians 2:15 "But he that is spiritual judgeth all things, yet he himself is judged of no man."

Who Judgments Are Prepared For
Proverbs 19:29 "Judgments are prepared for scorners, and stripes for the back of fools."

Who Perverts The Ways Of Judgment
Proverbs 17:23 "A wicked man taketh a gift out of the bosom to pervert the ways of judgment."

Who Refuses To Do Judgment
Proverbs 21:7 "The robbery of the wicked shall destroy them; because they refuse to do judgment."

Who Scorns Judgment
Proverbs 19:28 "An ungodly witness scorneth judgment: and the mouth of the wicked devoureth iniquity."

Who Shall Be Judged
Psalm 110:5-7 "5The Lord at thy right hand shall strike through kings in the day of his wrath. 6He shall judge among the heathen, he shall fill the places with the dead bodies; he shall wound the heads over many countries. 7He shall drink of the brook in the way: therefore shall he lift up the head."

Ecclesiastes 3:16-17 "16And moreover I saw under the sun the place of judgment, that wickedness was there; and the place of righteousness, that iniquity was there. 17I said in mine heart, God shall judge the righteous and the wicked: for there is a time there for every purpose and for every work."

Ecclesiastes 11:9 "Rejoice, O young man, in thy youth; and let thy heart cheer thee in the days of thy youth, and walk in the ways of thine heart, and in the sight of thine eyes: but know thou, that for all these things God will bring thee into judgment."

Ezekiel 16:23-38 "23And it came to pass after all thy wickedness, (woe, woe unto thee! saith the Lord GOD;) 24That thou hast also built unto thee an eminent place, and hast made thee an high place in every street. 25Thou hast built thy high place at every head of the way, and hast made thy beauty to be abhorred, and hast opened thy feet to every one that passed by, and multiplied thy whoredoms. 26Thou hast also committed fornication with the Egyptians thy neighbours, great of flesh; and hast increased thy whoredoms, to provoke me to anger. 27Behold, therefore I have stretched out my hand over thee, and have diminished thine ordinary food, and delivered thee unto the will of them that hate thee, the daughters of the Philistines, which are ashamed of thy lewd way. 28Thou hast played the whore also with the Assyrians, because thou wast unsatiable; yea, thou hast played the harlot with them, and yet couldest not be satisfied. 29 Thou hast moreover multiplied thy fornication in the land of Canaan unto Chaldea; and yet thou wast not satisfied herewith. 30How weak is thine heart, saith the Lord GOD, seeing thou doest all these things, the work of an imperious whorish woman; 31In that thou buildest thine eminent place in the head of every way, and makest thine high place in every street; and hast not been as an harlot, in that thou scornest hire; 32But as a wife that committeth adultery, which taketh strangers instead of her husband! 33They give gifts to all whores: but thou givest thy gifts to all thy lovers, and hirest them, that they may come unto thee on every side for thy whoredom. 34And the contrary is in thee from other women in thy whoredoms, whereas none followeth thee to commit whoredoms: and in that thou givest a reward, and no reward is given unto thee, therefore thou art contrary. 35Wherefore, O harlot, hear the word of the LORD: 36Thus saith the Lord GOD; Because thy filthiness was poured out, and thy nakedness discovered through thy whoredoms with thy lovers, and with all the idols of thy abominations, and by the blood of thy children, which thou didst give unto them; 37Behold, therefore I will gather all thy lovers, with whom thou hast taken pleasure, and all them that thou hast loved, with all them that thou hast hated; I will even gather them round about against thee, and will discover thy nakedness unto them, that they may see all thy nakedness. 38And I will judge thee, as women that break wedlock and shed blood are judged; and I will give thee blood in fury and jealousy."

Ezekiel 28:24-26 "24And there shall be no more a pricking brier unto the house of Israel, nor any grieving thorn of all that are round about them, that despised them; and they shall know that I am the Lord GOD. 25Thus saith the Lord GOD; When I shall have gathered the house of Israel from the people among whom they are scattered, and shall be sanctified in them in the sight of the heathen, then shall they dwell in their land that I have given to my servant Jacob. 26And they shall dwell safely therein, and shall build houses, and plant vineyards; yea, they shall dwell with confidence, when I have executed judgments upon all those that despise them round about them; and they shall know that I am the LORD their God."

Joel 3:9-12 "9Proclaim ye this among the Gentiles; Prepare war, wake up the mighty men, let all the men of war draw near; let them come up: 10Beat your plowshares into swords, and your pruning-hooks into spears: let the weak say, I am strong. 11Assemble yourselves, and come, all ye heathen, and gather yourselves together round about: thither cause thy mighty ones to come down, O LORD. 12Let the heathen be wakened, and come up to the valley of Jehoshaphat: for there will I sit to judge all the heathen round about."

John 12:44-48 "44Jesus cried and said, He that believeth on me, believeth not on me, but on him that sent me. 45And he that seeth me seeth him that sent me. 46I am come a light into the world, that whosoever believeth on me should not abide in darkness. 47And if any man hear my words, and believe not, I judge him not: for I came not to judge the world, but to save the world. 48He that rejecteth me, and receiveth not my words, hath one that judgeth him: the word that I have spoken, the same shall judge him in the last day."

2 Timothy 4:1 "I charge thee therefore before God, and the Lord Jesus Christ, who shall judge the quick and the dead at his appearing and his kingdom;"

Hebrews 10:26-30 "26For if we sin wilfully after that we have received the knowledge of the truth, there remaineth no more sacrifice for sins, 27But a certain fearful looking for of judgment and fiery

indignation, which shall devour the adversaries. 28He that despised Moses' law died without mercy under two or three witnesses: 29Of how much sorer punishment, suppose ye, shall he be thought worthy, who hath trodden under foot the Son of God, and hath counted the blood of the covenant, wherewith he was sanctified, an unholy thing, and hath done despite unto the Spirit of grace? 30For we know him that hath said, Vengeance belongeth unto me, I will recompense, saith the Lord. And again, The Lord shall judge his people."

Hebrews 13:4 "Marriage is honourable in all, and the bed undefiled: but whoremongers and adulterers God will judge."

2 Peter 2:9 "The Lord knoweth how to deliver the godly out of temptations, and to reserve the unjust unto the day of judgment to be punished:"

Revelation 19:1-2 "1And after these things I heard a great voice of much people in heaven, saying, Alleluia; Salvation, and glory, and honour, and power, unto the Lord our God: 2For true and righteous are his judgments: for he hath judged the great whore, which did corrupt the earth with her fornication, and hath avenged the blood of his servants at her hand."

Who Shall Not Be Judged
Matthew 7:1 "Judge not, that ye be not judged."

Luke 6:37 "Judge not, and ye shall not be judged: condemn not, and ye shall not be condemned: forgive, and ye shall be forgiven:"

1 Corinthians 11:31 "For if we would judge ourselves, we should not be judged."

Who The Lord Executes Judgment For
Deuteronomy 10:17-18 "17For the LORD your God is God of gods, and Lord of lords, a great God, a mighty, and a terrible, which regardeth not persons, nor taketh reward: 18He doth execute the judgment of the fatherless and widow, and loveth the stranger, in giving him food and raiment."

Psalm 103:6 "The LORD executeth righteousness and judgment for all that are oppressed."

Psalm 146:5-7 "5Happy is he that hath the God of Jacob for his help, whose hope is in the LORD his God: 6Which made heaven, and earth, the sea, and all that therein is: which keepeth truth for ever: [7]Which executeth judgment for the oppressed: which giveth food to the hungry. The LORD looseth the prisoners:"

JUSTICE

Doing Justice
Proverbs 21:3 "To do justice and judgment is more acceptable to the LORD than sacrifice."

Isaiah 56:1 "Thus saith the LORD, Keep ye judgment, and do justice: for my salvation is near to come, and my righteousness to be revealed."

False Balances/Divers Weights
Proverbs 11:1 "A false balance is abomination to the LORD: but a just weight is his delight."

Proverbs 20:10 "Divers weights, and divers measures, both of them are alike abomination to the LORD."

Proverbs 20:23 "Divers weights are an abomination unto the LORD; and a false balance is not good."

Just Weights
Proverbs 11:1 "A false balance is abomination to the LORD: but a just weight is his delight."

Proverbs 16:11 "A just weight and balance are the LORD's: all the weights of the bag are his work."

The Just
Proverbs 3:33 "The curse of the LORD is in the house of the wicked: but he blesseth the habitation of the just."

Proverbs 4:18 "But the path of the just is as the shining light, that shineth more and more unto the perfect day."

Proverbs 9:9 "Give instruction to a wise man, and he will be yet wiser: teach a just man, and he will increase in learning."

Proverbs 10:6-7 "[6]Blessings are upon the head of the just: but violence covereth the mouth of the wicked. [7]The memory of the just is blessed: but the name of the wicked shall rot."

Proverbs 10:20 "The tongue of the just is as choice silver: the heart of the wicked is little worth."

Proverbs 10:31 "The mouth of the just bringeth forth wisdom: but the froward tongue shall be cut out."

Proverbs 11:9 "An hypocrite with his mouth destroyeth his neighbour: but through knowledge shall the just be delivered."

Proverbs 12:13 "The wicked is snared by the transgression of his lips: but the just shall come out of trouble."

Proverbs 12:21 "There shall no evil happen to the just: but the wicked shall be filled with mischief."

Proverbs 13:22 "A good man leaveth an inheritance to his children's children: and the wealth of the sinner is laid up for the just."

Proverbs 20:7 "The just man walketh in his integrity: his children are blessed after him."

Proverbs 21:15 "It is joy to the just to do judgment: but destruction shall be to the workers of iniquity."

Proverbs 24:16 "For a just man falleth seven times, and riseth up again: but the wicked shall fall into mischief."

Proverbs 29:10 "The bloodthirsty hate the upright: but the just seek his soul."

Proverbs 29:27 "An unjust man is an abomination to the just: and he that is upright in the way is abomination to the wicked."

Isaiah 26:7 "The way of the just is uprightness: thou, most upright, dost weigh the path of the just."

Ezekiel 18:5-9 "[5]But if a man be just, and do that which is lawful and right, [6]And hath not eaten upon the mountains, neither hath lifted up his eyes to the idols of the house of Israel, neither hath defiled his neighbour's wife, neither hath come near to a menstruous woman, [7]And hath not oppressed any, but hath restored to the debtor his pledge, hath spoiled none by violence, hath given his bread to the hungry, and hath covered the naked with a garment; [8]He that hath not given forth upon usury, neither hath taken any increase, that hath withdrawn his hand from iniquity, hath executed true judgment between man and man, [9]Hath walked in my statutes, and hath kept my judgments, to deal truly; he is just, he shall surely live, saith the Lord GOD."

Hosea 14:9 "Who is wise, and he shall understand these things? prudent, and he shall know them? for the ways of the LORD are right, and the just shall walk in them: but the transgressors shall fall therein."

Habakkuk 2:4 "Behold, his soul which is lifted up is not upright in him: but the just shall live by his faith."

Matthew 5:45 "That ye may be the children of your Father which is in heaven: for he maketh his sun to rise on the evil and on the good, and sendeth rain on the just and on the unjust."

Romans 1:16-17 "[16]For I am not ashamed of the gospel of Christ: for it is the power of God unto salvation to every one that believeth; to the Jew first, and also to the Greek. [17]For therein is the righteousness of God revealed from faith to faith: as it is written, The just shall live by faith."

Galatians 3:11 "But that no man is justified by the law in the sight of God, it is evident: for, The just shall live by faith."

Hebrews 10:38 "Now the just shall live by faith: but if any man draw back, my soul shall have no pleasure in him."

The Lord Being Just
Deuteronomy 32:4 "He is the Rock, his work is perfect: for all his ways are judgment: a God of truth and without iniquity, just and right is he."

Nehemiah 9:32-33 "[32]Now therefore, our God, the great, the mighty, and the terrible God, who keepest covenant and mercy, let not all the trouble seem little before thee, that hath come upon us, on our kings, on our princes, and on our priests, and on our prophets, and on our fathers, and on all thy people, since the time of the kings of Assyria unto this day. [33]Howbeit thou art just in all that is brought upon us; for thou hast done right, but we have done wickedly:"

Job 37:23 "Touching the Almighty, we cannot find him out: he is excellent in power, and in judgment, and in plenty of justice: he will not afflict."

Zephaniah 3:5 "The just LORD is in the midst thereof; he will not do iniquity: every morning doth he bring his judgment to light, he faileth not; but the unjust knoweth no shame."

Zechariah 9:9 "Rejoice greatly, O daughter of Zion; shout, O daughter of Jerusalem: behold, thy King cometh unto thee: he is just, and having salvation; lowly, and riding upon an ass, and upon a colt the foal of an ass."

Acts 3:13-14 "[13]The God of Abraham, and of Isaac, and of Jacob, the God of our fathers, hath glorified his Son Jesus; whom ye delivered up, and denied him in the presence of Pilate, when he was determined to let him go. [14]But ye denied the Holy One and the Just, and desired a murderer to be granted unto you;"

What Is Just
John 5:26-30 "[26]For as the Father hath life in himself; so hath he given to the Son to have life in himself; [27]And hath given him authority to execute judgment also, because he is the Son of man. [28]Marvel not at this: for the hour is coming, in the which all that are in the graves shall hear his voice, [29]And shall come forth; they that have done good, unto the resurrection of life; and they that have done evil, unto the resurrection of damnation. [30]I can of mine own self do nothing: as I hear, I judge: and my judgment is just; because I seek not mine own will, but the will of the Father which hath sent me."

Romans 7:12 "Wherefore the law is holy, and the commandment holy, and just, and good."

Revelation 15:3 "And they sing the song of Moses the servant of God, and the song of the Lamb, saying, Great and marvellous are thy works, Lord God Almighty; just and true are thy ways, thou King of saints."

Who Is Just
Ezekiel 18:5-9 "[5]But if a man be just, and do that which is lawful and right, [6]And hath not eaten upon the mountains, neither hath lifted up his eyes to the idols of the house of Israel, neither hath defiled his neighbour's wife, neither hath come near to a menstruous woman, [7]And hath not oppressed any, but hath restored to the debtor his pledge, hath spoiled none by violence, hath given his bread to the hungry, and hath covered the naked with a garment; [8]He that hath not given forth upon usury, neither hath taken any increase, that hath withdrawn his hand from iniquity, hath executed true judgment between man and man, [9]Hath walked in my statutes, and hath kept my judgments, to deal truly; he is just, he shall surely live, saith the Lord GOD."

Who Must Be Just

2 Samuel 23:3 "The God of Israel said, the Rock of Israel spake to me, He that ruleth over men must be just, ruling in the fear of God."

JUSTIFICATION

Justification Coming By Jesus Christ

Isaiah 53:1-11 "¹Who hath believed our report? and to whom is the arm of the LORD revealed? ²For he shall grow up before him as a tender plant, and as a root out of a dry ground: he hath no form nor comeliness; and when we shall see him, there is no beauty that we should desire him. ³He is despised and rejected of men; a man of sorrows, and acquainted with grief: and we hid as it were our faces from him; he was despised, and we esteemed him not. ⁴Surely he hath borne our griefs, and carried our sorrows: yet we did esteem him stricken, smitten of God, and afflicted. ⁵But he was wounded for our transgressions, he was bruised for our iniquities: the chastisement of our peace was upon him; and with his stripes we are healed. ⁶All we like sheep have gone astray; we have turned every one to his own way; and the LORD hath laid on him the iniquity of us all. ⁷He was oppressed, and he was afflicted, yet he opened not his mouth: he is brought as a lamb to the slaughter, and as a sheep before her shearers is dumb, so he openeth not his mouth. ⁸He was taken from prison and from judgment: and who shall declare his generation? for he was cut off out of the land of the living: for the transgression of my people was he stricken. ⁹And he made his grave with the wicked, and with the rich in his death; because he had done no violence, neither was any deceit in his mouth. ¹⁰Yet it pleased the LORD to bruise him; he hath put him to grief: when thou shalt make his soul an offering for sin, he shall see his seed, he shall prolong his days, and the pleasure of the LORD shall prosper in his hand. ¹¹He shall see of the travail of his soul, and shall be satisfied: by his knowledge shall my righteous servant justify many; for he shall bear their iniquities."

Acts 13:33-39 "³³God hath fulfilled the same unto us their children, in that he hath raised up Jesus again; as it is also written in the second psalm, Thou art my Son, this day have I begotten thee. ³⁴And as concerning that he raised him up from the dead, now no more to return to corruption, he said on this wise, I will give you the sure mercies of David. ³⁵Wherefore he saith also in another psalm, Thou shalt not suffer thine Holy One to see corruption. ³⁶For David, after he had served his own generation by the will of God, fell on sleep, and was laid unto his fathers, and saw corruption: ³⁷But he, whom God raised again, saw no corruption. ³⁸Be it known unto you therefore, men and brethren, that through this man is preached unto you the forgiveness of sins: ³⁹And by him all that believe are justified from all things, from which ye could not be justified by the law of Moses."

Romans 3:23-24 "²³For all have sinned, and come short of the glory of God; ²⁴Being justified freely by his grace through the redemption that is in Christ Jesus:"

Romans 5:6-19 "⁶For when we were yet without strength, in due time Christ died for the ungodly. ⁷For scarcely for a righteous man will one die: yet peradventure for a good man some would even dare to die. ⁸But God commendeth his love toward us, in that, while we were yet sinners, Christ died for us. ⁹Much more then, being now justified by his blood, we shall be saved from wrath through him. ¹⁰For if, when we were enemies, we were reconciled to God by the death of his Son, much more, being reconciled, we shall be saved by his life. ¹¹And not only so, but we also joy in God through our Lord Jesus Christ, by whom we have now received the atonement. ¹²Wherefore, as by one man sin entered into the world, and death by sin; and so death passed upon all men, for that all have sinned: ¹³(For until the law sin was in the world: but sin is not imputed when there is no law. ¹⁴Nevertheless death reigned from Adam to Moses, even over them that had not sinned after the similitude of Adam's transgression, who is the figure of him that was to come. ¹⁵But not as the offence, so also is the free gift. For if through the offence of one many be dead, much more the grace of God, and the gift by grace, which is by one man, Jesus Christ, hath abounded unto many. ¹⁶And not as it was by one that sinned, so is the gift: for the judgment was by one to condemnation, but the free gift is of many offences unto justification. ¹⁷For if by one man's offence death reigned by one; much more they which receive abundance of grace and of the gift of righteousness shall reign in life by one, Jesus Christ.) [18]Therefore as by the offence of one judgment came upon all men to condemnation; even so by the righteousness of one the free gift came upon all men unto justification of life. [19]For as by one man's disobedience many were made sinners, so by the obedience of one shall many be made righteous."

1 Corinthians 6:9-11 "[9]Know ye not that the unrighteous shall not inherit the kingdom of God? Be not deceived: neither fornicators, nor idolaters, nor adulterers, nor effeminate, nor abusers of themselves with mankind, [10]Nor thieves, nor covetous, nor drunkards, nor revilers, nor extortioners, shall inherit the kingdom of God. [11]And such were some of you: but ye are washed, but ye are sanctified, but ye are justified in the name of the Lord Jesus, and by the Spirit of our God."

Galatians 2:16-20 "[16]Knowing that a man is not justified by the works of the law, but by the faith of Jesus Christ, even we have believed in Jesus Christ, that we might be justified by the faith of Christ, and not by the works of the law: for by the works of the law shall no flesh be justified. [17]But if, while we seek to be justified by Christ, we ourselves also are found sinners, is therefore Christ the minister of sin? God forbid. [18]For if I build again the things which I destroyed, I make myself a transgressor. [19]For I through the law am dead to the law, that I might live unto God. [20]I am crucified with Christ: nevertheless I live; yet not I, but Christ liveth in me: and the life which I now live in the flesh I live by the faith of the Son of God, who loved me, and gave himself for me."

Titus 3:3-7 "[3]For we ourselves also were sometimes foolish, disobedient, deceived, serving divers lusts and pleasures, living in malice and envy, hateful, and hating one another. [4]But after that the kindness and love of God our Saviour toward man appeared, [5]Not by works of righteousness which we have done, but according to his mercy he saved us, by the washing of regeneration, and renewing of the Holy Ghost; [6]Which he shed on us abundantly through Jesus Christ our Saviour; [7]That being justified by his grace, we should be made heirs according to the hope of eternal life."

Hebrews 10:9-14 "[9]Then said he, Lo, I come to do thy will, O God. He taketh away the first, that he may establish the second. [10]By the which will we are sanctified through the offering of the body of Jesus Christ once for all. [11]And every priest standeth daily ministering and offering oftentimes the same sacrifices, which can never take away sins: [12]But this man, after he had offered one sacrifice for sins for ever, sat down on the right hand of God; [13]From henceforth expecting till his enemies be made his footstool. [14]For by one offering he hath perfected for ever them that are sanctified."

The Lord Justifying
Job 33:29-32 "[29]Lo, all these things worketh God oftentimes with man, [30]To bring back his soul from the pit, to be enlightened with the light of the living. [31]Mark well, O Job, hearken unto me: hold thy peace, and I will speak. [32]If thou hast any thing to say, answer me: speak, for I desire to justify thee."

Isaiah 50:7-8 "[7]For the Lord GOD will help me; therefore shall I not be confounded: therefore have I set my face like a flint, and I know that I shall not be ashamed. [8]He is near that justifieth me; who will contend with me? let us stand together: who is mine adversary? let him come near to me."

Romans 8:33 "Who shall lay any thing to the charge of God's elect? It is God that justifieth."

Those That Are Justified
Romans 8:28-30 "[28]And we know that all things work together for good to them that love God, to them who are the called according to his purpose. [29]For whom he did foreknow, he also did predestinate to be conformed to the image of his Son, that he might be the firstborn among many brethren. [30]Moreover whom he did predestinate, them he also called: and whom he called, them he also justified: and whom he justified, them he also glorified."

Those That Are Justified By The Law
Galatians 5:4-6 "[4]Christ is become of no effect unto you, whosoever of you are justified by the law; ye are fallen from grace. [5]For we through the Spirit wait for the hope of righteousness by faith. [6]For in Jesus Christ neither circumcision availeth anything, nor uncircumcision; but faith which worketh by love."

Those That Justify The Wicked
Proverbs 17:15 "He that justifieth the wicked, and he that condemneth the just, even they both are abomination to the LORD."

Proverbs 24:24 "He that saith unto the wicked, Thou are righteous; him shall the people curse, nations shall abhor him:"

Isaiah 5:22-23 "22Woe unto them that are mighty to drink wine, and men of strength to mingle strong drink: 23Which justify the wicked for reward, and take away the righteousness of the righteous from him!"

Those That Justify Themselves
Luke 16:14-15 "14And the Pharisees also, who were covetous, heard all these things: and they derided him. 15And he said unto them, Ye are they which justify yourselves before men; but God knoweth your hearts: for that which is highly esteemed among men is abomination in the sight of God."

What You Are Justified By
Matthew 12:36-37 "3But I say unto you, That every idle word that men shall speak, they shall give account thereof in the day of judgment. 37For by thy words thou shalt be justified, and by thy words thou shalt be condemned."

Romans 3:28-30 "28Therefore we conclude that a man is justified by faith without the deeds of the law. 29Is he the God of the Jews only? is he not also of the Gentiles? Yes, of the Gentiles also: 30Seeing it is one God, which shall justify the circumcision by faith, and uncircumcision through faith."

Galatians 3:6-14 "6Even as Abraham believed God, and it was accounted to him for righteousness. 7Know ye therefore that they which are of faith, the same are the children of Abraham. 8And the scripture, foreseeing that God would justify the heathen through faith, preached before the gospel unto Abraham, saying, In thee shall all nations be blessed. 9So then they which be of faith are blessed with faithful Abraham. 10For as many as are of the works of the law are under the curse: for it is written, Cursed is every one that continueth not in all things which are written in the book of the law to do them. 11But that no man is justified by the law in the sight of God, it is evident: for,

The just shall live by faith. 12And the law is not of faith: but, The man that doeth them shall live in them. 13Christ hath redeemed us from the curse of the law, being made a curse for us: for it is written, Cursed is every one that hangeth on a tree: 14That the blessing of Abraham might come on the Gentiles through Jesus Christ; that we might receive the promise of the Spirit through faith."

James 2:20-25 "20But wilt thou know, O vain man, that faith without works is dead? 21Was not Abraham our father justified by works, when he had offered Isaac his son upon the altar? 22Seest thou how faith wrought with his works, and by works was faith made perfect? 23And the scripture was fulfilled which saith, Abraham believed God, and it was imputed unto him for righteousness: and he was called the Friend of God. 24Ye see then how that by works a man is justified, and not by faith only. 25Likewise also was not Rahab the harlot justified by works, when she had received the messengers, and had sent them out another way?"

What You Are Not Justified By
Acts 13:33-39 "33God hath fulfilled the same unto us their children, in that he hath raised up Jesus again; as it is also written in the second psalm, Thou art my Son, this day have I begotten thee. 34And as concerning that he raised him up from the dead, now no more to return to corruption, he said on this wise, I will give you the sure mercies of David. 35Wherefore he saith also in another psalm, Thou shalt not suffer thine Holy One to see corruption. 36For David, after he had served his own generation by the will of God, fell on sleep, and was laid unto his fathers, and saw corruption: 37But he, whom God raised again, saw no corruption. 38Be it known unto you therefore, men and brethren, that through this man is preached unto you the forgiveness of sins: 39And by him all that believe are justified from all things, from which ye could not be justified by the law of Moses."

Romans 3:20 "Therefore by the deeds of the law there shall no flesh be justified in his sight: for by the law is the knowledge of sin."

Galatians 2:16 "Knowing that a man is not justified by the works of the law, but by the faith of

Jesus Christ, even we have believed in Jesus Christ, that we might be justified by the faith of Christ, and not by the works of the law: for by the works of the law shall no flesh be justified."

Galatians 3:10-11 "¹⁰For as many as are of the works of the law are under the curse: for it is written, Cursed is every one that continueth not in all things which are written in the book of the law to do them. ¹¹But that no man is justified by the law in the sight of God, it is evident: for, The just shall live by faith."

James 2:20-24 "²⁰But wilt thou know, O vain man, that faith without works is dead? ²¹Was not Abraham our father justified by works, when he had offered Isaac his son upon the altar? ²²Seest thou how faith wrought with his works, and by works was faith made perfect? ²³And the scripture was fulfilled which saith, Abraham believed God, and it was imputed unto him for righteousness: and he was called the Friend of God. ²⁴Ye see then how that by works a man is justified, and not by faith only."

Who Shall Be Justified
Isaiah 45:25 "In the LORD shall all the seed of Israel be justified, and shall glory."

Acts 13:33-39 "³³God hath fulfilled the same unto us their children, in that he hath raised up Jesus again; as it is also written in the second psalm, Thou art my Son, this day have I begotten thee. ³⁴And as concerning that he raised him up from the dead, now no more to return to corruption, he said on this wise, I will give you the sure mercies of David. ³⁵Wherefore he saith also in another psalm, Thou shalt not suffer thine Holy One to see corruption. ³⁶For David, after he had served his own generation by the will of God, fell on sleep, and was laid unto his fathers, and saw corruption: ³⁷But he, whom God raised again, saw no corruption. ³⁸Be it known unto you therefore, men and brethren, that through this man is preached unto you the forgiveness of sins: ³⁹And by him all that believe are justified from all things, from which ye could not be justified by the law of Moses."

Romans 2:13 "(For not the hearers of the law are just before God, but the doers of the law shall be justified."

Romans 8:28-30 "²⁸And we know that all things work together for good to them that love God, to them who are the called according to his purpose. ²⁹For whom he did foreknow, he also did predestinate to be conformed to the image of his Son, that he might be the firstborn among many brethren. ³⁰Moreover whom he did predestinate, them he also called: and whom he called, them he also justified: and whom he justified, them he also glorified."

Who Shall Not Be Justified
Exodus 23:7 "Keep thee far from a false matter; and the innocent and righteous slay thou not: for I will not justify the wicked."

Romans 2:13 "(For not the hearers of the law are just before God, but the doers of the law shall be justified."

KINDNESS

Being Kind

Romans 12:10 "Be kindly affectioned one to another with brotherly love; in honour preferring one another."

Ephesians 4:32 "And be ye kind one to another, tenderhearted, forgiving one another, even as God for Christ's sake hath forgiven you."

Colossians 3:12 "Put on therefore, as the elect of God, holy and beloved, bowels of mercies, kindness, humbleness of mind, meekness, longsuffering."

The Kindness Of The Lord

Psalm 63:1-3 "¹O God, thou art my God; early will I seek thee: my soul thirsteth for thee, my flesh longeth for thee in a dry and thirsty land, where no water is; ²To see thy power and thy glory, so as I have seen thee in the sanctuary. ³Because thy lovingkindness is better than life, my lips shall praise thee."

Psalm 89:26-33 "²⁶He shall cry unto me, Thou art my father, my God, and the rock of my salvation. ²⁷Also I will make him my firstborn, higher than the kings of the earth. ²⁸My mercy will I keep for him for evermore, and my covenant shall stand fast with him. ²⁹His seed also will I make to endure for ever, and his throne as the days of heaven. ³⁰If his children forsake my law, and walk not in my judgments; ³¹If they break my statutes, and keep not my commandments; ³²Then will I visit their transgression with the rod, and their iniquity with stripes. ³³Nevertheless my lovingkindness will I not utterly take from him, nor suffer my faithfulness to fail."

Psalm 117:2 "For his merciful kindness is great toward us: and the truth of the LORD endureth for ever. Praise ye the LORD."

Isaiah 54:10 "For the mountains shall depart, and the hills be removed; but my kindness shall not depart from thee, neither shall the covenant of my peace be removed, saith the LORD that hath mercy on thee."

Isaiah 63:7 "I will mention the lovingkindnesses of the LORD, and the praises of the LORD, according to all that the LORD hath bestowed on us, and the great goodness toward the house of Israel, which he hath bestowed on them according to his mercies, and according to the multitude of his lovingkindnesses."

Titus 3:3-5 "³For we ourselves also were sometimes foolish, disobedient, deceived, serving divers lusts and pleasures, living in malice and envy, hateful, and hating one another. ⁴But after that the kindness and love of God our Saviour toward man appeared, ⁵Not by works of righteousness which we have done, but according to his mercy he saved us, by the washing of regeneration, and renewing of the Holy Ghost."

The Lord Being Kind

Nehemiah 9:16-17 "¹⁶But they and our fathers dealt proudly, and hardened their necks, and hearkened not to thy commandments, ¹⁷And refused to obey, neither were mindful of thy wonders that thou didst among them; but hardened their necks, and in their rebellion appointed a captain to return to their bondage: but thou art a God ready to pardon, gracious and merciful, slow to anger, and of great kindness, and forsookest them not."

Joel 2:12-13 "¹²Therefore also now, saith the LORD, turn ye even to me with all your heart, and with fasting, and with weeping, and with mourning: ¹³And rend your heart, and not your garments, and turn unto the LORD your God: for he is gracious and merciful, slow to anger, and of great kindness, and repenteth him of the evil."

Luke 6:35 "But love ye your enemies, and do good, and lend, hoping for nothing again; and your reward shall be great, and ye shall be the children of the Highest: for he is kind unto the unthankful and to the evil."

Those That Are Kind

2 Peter 1:1-11 "¹Simon Peter, a servant and an apostle of Jesus Christ, to them that have obtained like precious faith with us through the righteousness of God and our Saviour Jesus Christ: ²Grace and peace be multiplied unto you through the knowledge of God, and of Jesus our Lord, ³According as his divine power hath given unto us all things that pertain unto life and godliness, through the knowledge of him that hath called us to glory and virtue: ⁴Whereby are given unto us exceeding great and precious promises: that by these ye might be partakers of the divine nature, having escaped the corruption that is in the world through lust. [5]And beside this, giving all diligence, add to your faith virtue; and to virtue knowledge; [6]And to knowledge temperance; and to temperance patience; and to patience godliness; [7]And to godliness brotherly kindness; and to brotherly kindness charity. [8]For if these things be in you, and abound, they make you that ye shall neither be barren nor unfruitful in the knowledge of our Lord Jesus Christ. [9]But he that lacketh these things is blind, and cannot see afar off, and hath forgotten that he was purged from his old sins. [10]Wherefore the rather, brethren, give diligence to make your calling and election sure: for if ye do these things, ye shall never fall: [11]For so an entrance shall be ministered unto you abundantly into the everlasting kingdom of our Lord and Saviour Jesus Christ."

Those That Are Not Kind

2 Peter 1:1-9 "[1]Simon Peter, a servant and an apostle of Jesus Christ, to them that have obtained like precious faith with us through the righteousness of God and our Saviour Jesus Christ: [2]Grace and peace be multiplied unto you through the knowledge of God, and of Jesus our Lord, [3]According as his divine power hath given unto us all things that pertain unto life and godliness, through the knowledge of him that hath called us to glory and virtue: [4]Whereby are given unto us exceeding great and precious promises: that by these ye might be partakers of the divine nature, having escaped the corruption that is in the world through lust. [5]And beside this, giving all diligence, add to your faith virtue; and to virtue knowledge; [6]And to knowledge temperance; and to temperance patience; and to patience godliness; [7]And to godliness brotherly kindness; and to brotherly kindness charity. [8]For if these things be in you, and abound, they make you that ye shall neither be barren nor unfruitful in the knowledge of our Lord Jesus Christ. [9]But he that lacketh these things is blind, and cannot see afar off, and hath forgotten that he was purged from his old sins."

KINGDOM OF GOD

The Kingdom Of God Having No End

Psalm 145:10-13 "[10]All thy works shall praise thee, O LORD; and thy saints shall bless thee. [11] They shall speak of the glory of thy kingdom, and talk of thy power; [12] To make known to the sons of men his mighty acts, and the glorious majesty of his kingdom. [13] Thy kingdom is an everlasting kingdom, and thy dominion endureth throughout all generations."

Daniel 2:44 "And in the days of these kings shall the God of heaven set up a kingdom, which shall never be destroyed: and the kingdom shall not be left to other people, but it shall break in pieces and consume all these kingdoms, and it shall stand for ever."

Daniel 4:2-3 "[2]I thought it good to shew the signs and wonders that the high God hath wrought toward me. [3] How great are his signs! and how mighty are his wonders! his kingdom is an everlasting kingdom, and his dominion is from generation to generation."

Daniel 4:34 "And at the end of the days I Nebuchadnezzar lifted up mine eyes unto heaven, and mine understanding returned unto me, and I blessed the most High, and I praised and honoured him that liveth for ever, whose dominion is an everlasting dominion, and his kingdom is from generation to generation."

Daniel 6:26 "I make a decree, That in every dominion of my kingdom men tremble and fear before the God of Daniel: for he is the living God, and stedfast for ever, and his kingdom that which shall not be destroyed, and his dominion shall be even unto the end."

Daniel 7:13-14 "[13]I saw in the night visions, and, behold, one like the Son of man came with the clouds of heaven, and came to the Ancient of days, and they brought him near before him. [14] And there was given him dominion, and glory, and a kingdom, that all people, nations, and languages, should serve him: his dominion is an everlasting dominion, which shall not pass away, and his kingdom that which shall not be destroyed."

Daniel 7:27 "And the kingdom and dominion, and the greatness of the kingdom under the whole heaven, shall be given to the people of the saints of the most High, whose kingdom is an everlasting kingdom, and all dominions shall serve and obey him."

Luke 1:31-33 "³¹And, behold, thou shalt conceive in thy womb, and bring forth a son, and shalt call his name JESUS. ³² He shall be great, and shall be called the Son of the Highest: and the Lord God shall give unto him the throne of his father David: ³³ And he shall reign over the house of Jacob for ever; and of his kingdom there shall be no end."

Hebrews 1:8 "But unto the Son he saith, Thy throne, O God, is for ever and ever: a sceptre of righteousness is the sceptre of thy kingdom."

Those That Are Least In The Kingdom Of God

Matthew 11:11 "Verily I say unto you, Among them that are born of women there hath not risen a greater than John the Baptist: notwithstanding he that is least in the kingdom of heaven is greater than he."

Luke 7:28 "For I say unto you, Among those that are born of women there is not a greater prophet than John the Baptist: but he that is least in the kingdom of God is greater than he."

What Cannot Inherit The Kingdom Of God

1 Corinthians 15:50 "Now this I say, brethren, that flesh and blood cannot inherit the kingdom of God; neither doth corruption inherit incorruption."

What The Kingdom Of God Is

Matthew 3:1-2 "¹In those days came John the Baptist, preaching in the wilderness of Judaea, ²And saying, Repent ye: for the kingdom of heaven is at hand."

Matthew 10:5-7 "⁵These twelve Jesus sent forth, and commanded them, saying, Go not into the way of the Gentiles, and into any city of the Samaritans enter ye not: ⁶But go rather to the lost sheep of the house of Israel. ⁷And as ye go, preach, saying, The kingdom of heaven is at hand."

Mark 1:15 "And saying, The time is fulfilled, and the kingdom of God is at hand: repent ye, and believe the gospel."

Luke 10:1-11 "¹After these things the Lord appointed other seventy also, and sent them two and two before his face into every city and place, whither he himself would come. ²Therefore said he unto them, The harvest truly is great, but the labourers are few: pray ye therefore the Lord of the harvest, that he would send forth labourers into his harvest. ³Go your ways: behold, I send you forth as lambs among wolves. ⁴Carry neither purse, nor scrip, nor shoes: and salute no man by the way. ⁵And into whatsoever house ye enter, first say, Peace be to this house. ⁶And if the son of peace be there, your peace shall rest upon it: if not, it shall turn to you again. ⁷And in the same house remain, eating and drinking such things as they give: for the labourer is worthy of his hire. Go not from house to house. ⁸And into whatsoever city ye enter, and they receive you, eat such things as are set before you: ⁹And heal the sick that are therein, and say unto them, The kingdom of God is come nigh unto you. ¹⁰But into whatsoever city ye enter, and they receive you not, go your ways out into the streets of the same, and say, ¹¹Even the very dust of your city, which cleaveth on us, we do wipe off against you: notwithstanding be ye sure of this, that the kingdom of God is come nigh unto you."

Romans 14:17 "For the kingdom of God is not meat and drink; but righteousness, and peace, and joy in the Holy Ghost."

1 Corinthians 4:20 "For the kingdom of God is not in word, but in power."

What The Kingdom Of God Is Likened To

Matthew 13:24-52 "²⁴Another parable put he forth unto them, saying, The kingdom of heaven is likened unto a man which sowed good seed in his field: ²⁵But while men slept, his enemy came and sowed tares among the wheat, and went his way. ²⁶But when the blade was sprung up, and brought forth fruit, then appeared the tares also. ²⁷So the servants of the householder came and said unto him, Sir, didst not thou sow good seed in thy field? from whence then hath it tares? ²⁸He said unto them, An enemy hath done this. The servants said unto him, Wilt thou then that we go and gather them up? ²⁹But he said, Nay; lest while ye gather up the tares, ye root up also the wheat with them. ³⁰Let both grow together until the harvest: and in the time of harvest I will say to the reapers, Gather ye together first the tares, and bind them in bundles to burn them: but gather the wheat into my barn. ³¹Another parable put he forth unto them, saying, The kingdom of heaven is like to a grain of mustard seed, which a man took, and sowed in his field: ³²Which indeed is the least of all seeds: but when it is grown, it is the greatest among herbs, and becometh a tree, so that the birds of the air come and lodge in the branches thereof. [33]Another parable spake he unto them; The kingdom of heaven is like unto leaven, which a woman took, and hid in three measures of meal, till the whole was leavened. [34]All these things spake Jesus unto the multitude in parables; and without a parable spake he not unto them: [35]That it might be fulfilled which was spoken by the prophet, saying, I will open my mouth in parables; I will utter things which have been kept secret from the foundation of the world. [36]Then Jesus sent the multitude away, and went into the house: and his disciples came unto him, saying, Declare unto us the parable of the tares of the field. [37]He answered and said unto them, He that soweth the good seed is the Son of man; [38]The field is the world; the good seed are the children of the kingdom; but the tares are the children of the wicked one; [39]The enemy that sowed them is the devil; the harvest is the end of the world; and the reapers are the angels. [40]As therefore the tares are gathered and burned in the fire; so shall it be in the end of this world. [41]The Son of man shall send forth his angels, and they shall gather out of his kingdom all things that offend, and them which do iniquity; [42]And shall cast them into a furnace of fire: there shall be wailing and gnashing of teeth. [43]Then shall the righteous shine forth as the sun in the kingdom of their Father. Who hath ears to hear, let him hear. [44]Again, the kingdom of heaven is like unto treasure hid in a field; the which when a man hath found, he hideth, and for joy thereof goeth and selleth all that he hath, and buyeth that field. [45]Again, the kingdom of heaven is like unto a merchant man, seeking goodly pearls: [46]Who, when he had found one pearl of great price, went and sold all that he had, and bought it. [47]Again, the kingdom of heaven is like unto a net, that was cast into the sea, and gathered of every kind: [48]Which, when it was full, they drew to shore, and sat down, and gathered the good into vessels, but cast the bad away. [49]So shall it be at the end of the world: the angels shall come forth, and sever the wicked from among the just, [50]And shall cast them into the furnace of fire: there shall be wailing and gnashing of teeth. [51]Jesus saith unto them, Have ye understood all these things? They say unto him, Yea, Lord. [52]Then said he unto them, Therefore every scribe which is instructed unto the kingdom of heaven is like unto a man that is an householder, which

bringeth forth out of his treasure things new and old."

Matthew 18:23-35 "[23]Therefore is the kingdom of heaven likened unto a certain king, which would take account of his servants. [24]And when he had begun to reckon, one was brought unto him, which owed him ten thousand talents. [25]But forasmuch as he had not to pay, his lord commanded him to be sold, and his wife, and children, and all that he had, and payment to be made. [26]The servant therefore fell down, and worshipped him, saying, Lord, have patience with me, and I will pay thee all. [27]Then the lord of that servant was moved with compassion, and loosed him, and forgave him the debt. [28]But the same servant went out, and found one of his fellowservants, which owed him an hundred pence: and he laid hands on him, and took him by the throat, saying, Pay me that thou owest. [29]And his fellowservant fell down at his feet, and besought him, saying, Have patience with me, and I will pay thee all. [30]And he would not: but went and cast him into prison, till he should pay the debt. [31]So when his fellowservants saw what was done, they were very sorry, and came and told unto their lord all that was done. [32]Then his lord, after that he had called him, said unto him, O thou wicked servant, I forgave thee all that debt, because thou desiredst me: [33]Shouldest not thou also have had compassion on thy fellowservant, even as I had pity on thee? [34]And his lord was wroth, and delivered him to the tormentors, till he should pay all that was due unto him. [35]So likewise shall my heavenly Father do also unto you, if ye from your hearts forgive not every one his brother their trespasses."

Matthew 20:1-16 "[1]For the kingdom of heaven is like unto a man that is an householder, which went out early in the morning to hire labourers into his vineyard. [2]And when he had agreed with the labourers for a penny a day, he sent them into his vineyard. [3]And he went out about the third hour, and saw others standing idle in the marketplace, [4]And said unto them; Go ye also into the vineyard, and whatsoever is right I will give you. And they went their way. [5]Again he went out about the sixth and ninth hour, and did likewise. [6]And about the eleventh hour he went out, and found others standing idle, and saith unto them, Why stand ye here all the day idle? [7]They say unto him, Because no man hath hired us. He saith unto them, Go ye also into the vineyard; and whatsoever is right, that shall ye receive. ⁸So when even was come, the lord of the vineyard saith unto his steward, Call the labourers, and give them their hire, beginning from the last unto the first. ⁹And when they came that were hired about the eleventh hour, they received every man a penny. ¹⁰But when the first came, they supposed that they should have received more; and they likewise received every man a penny. ¹¹And when they had received it, they murmured against the goodman of the house, ¹²Saying, These last have wrought but one hour, and thou hast made them equal unto us, which have borne the burden and heat of the day. ¹³But he answered one of them, and said, Friend, I do thee no wrong: didst not thou agree with me for a penny? ¹⁴Take that thine is, and go thy way: I will give unto this last, even as unto thee. ¹⁵Is it not lawful for me to do what I will with mine own? Is thine eye evil, because I am good? ¹⁶So the last shall be first, and the first last: for many be called, but few chosen."

Matthew 22:2-14 "²The kingdom of heaven is like unto a certain king, which made a marriage for his son, ³And sent forth his servants to call them that were bidden to the wedding: and they would not come. ⁴Again, he sent forth other servants, saying, Tell them which are bidden, Behold, I have prepared my dinner: my oxen and my fatlings are killed, and all things are ready: come unto the marriage. ⁵But they made light of it, and went their ways, one to his farm, another to his merchandise: ⁶And the remnant took his servants, and entreated them spitefully, and slew them. ⁷But when the king heard thereof, he was wroth: and he sent forth his armies, and destroyed those murderers, and burned up their city. ⁸Then saith he to his servants, The wedding is ready, but they which were bidden were not worthy. ⁹Go ye therefore into the highways, and as many as ye shall find, bid to the marriage. ¹⁰So those servants went out into the highways, and gathered together all as many as they found, both bad and good: and the wedding was furnished with guests. ¹¹And when the king came in to see the guests, he saw there a man which had not on a wedding garment: ¹²And he saith unto him, Friend, how camest thou in hither not having a wedding garment? And he was speechless. ¹³Then said the king to the servants, Bind him hand and foot, and take him away, and cast him into outer darkness;

there shall be weeping and gnashing of teeth. ¹⁴For many are called, but few are chosen."

Matthew 25:1-30 "¹Then shall the kingdom of heaven be likened unto ten virgins, which took their lamps, and went forth to meet the bridegroom. ²And five of them were wise, and five were foolish. ³They that were foolish took their lamps, and took no oil with them: ⁴But the wise took oil in their vessels with their lamps. ⁵While the bridegroom tarried, they all slumbered and slept. ⁶And at midnight there was a cry made, Behold, the bridegroom cometh; go ye out to meet him. ⁷Then all those virgins arose, and trimmed their lamps. ⁸And the foolish said unto the wise, Give us of your oil; for our lamps are gone out. ⁹But the wise answered, saying, Not so; lest there be not enough for us and you: but go ye rather to them that sell, and buy for yourselves. ¹⁰And while they went to buy, the bridegroom came; and they that were ready went in with him to the marriage: and the door was shut. ¹¹Afterward came also the other virgins, saying, Lord, Lord, open to us. ¹²But he answered and said, Verily I say unto you, I know you not. ¹³Watch therefore, for ye know neither the day nor the hour wherein the Son of man cometh. ¹⁴For the kingdom of heaven is as a man travelling into a far country, who called his own servants, and delivered unto them his goods. ¹⁵And unto one he gave five talents, to another two, and to another one; to every man according to his several ability; and straightway took his journey. ¹⁶Then he that had received the five talents went and traded with the same, and made them other five talents. ¹⁷And likewise he that had received two, he also gained other two. ¹⁸But he that had received one went and digged in the earth, and hid his lord's money. ¹⁹After a long time the lord of those servants cometh, and reckoneth with them. ²⁰And so he that had received five talents came and brought other five talents, saying, Lord, thou deliveredst unto me five talents: behold, I have gained beside them five talents more. ²¹His lord said unto him, Well done, thou good and faithful servant: thou hast been faithful over a few things, I will make thee ruler over many things: enter thou into the joy of thy lord. ²²He also that had received two talents came and said, Lord, thou deliveredst unto me two talents: behold, I have gained two other talents beside them. ²³His lord said unto him, Well done, good and faithful servant; thou hast been faithful over a few things, I will make thee ruler over many things: enter thou into the joy of thy lord. ²⁴Then he which had received the one talent came and said, Lord, I knew thee that thou art an hard man, reaping where thou hast not sown, and gathering where thou hast not strawed: ²⁵And I was afraid, and went and hid thy talent in the earth: lo, there thou hast that is thine. ²⁶His lord answered and said unto him, Thou wicked and slothful servant, thou knewest that I reap where I sowed not, and gather where I have not strawed: ²⁷Thou oughtest therefore to have put my money to the exchangers, and then at my coming I should have received mine own with usury. ²⁸Take therefore the talent from him, and give it unto him which hath ten talents. ²⁹For unto every one that hath shall be given, and he shall have abundance: but from him that hath not shall be taken away even that which he hath. ³⁰And cast ye the unprofitable servant into outer darkness: there shall be weeping and gnashing of teeth."

Mark 4:21-34 "²¹And he said unto them, Is a candle brought to be put under a bushel, or under a bed? and not to be set on a candlestick? ²²For there is nothing hid, which shall not be manifested; neither was there any thing kept secret, but that it should come abroad. ²³If any man have ears to hear, let him hear. ²⁴And he said unto them, Take heed what ye hear: with what measure ye mete, it shall be measured to you: and unto you that hear shall more be given. ²⁵For he that hath, to him shall be given: and he that hath not, from him shall be taken even that which he hath. ²⁶And he said, So is the kingdom of God, as if a man should cast seed into the ground; ²⁷And should sleep, and rise night and day, and the seed should spring and grow up, he knoweth not how. ²⁸For the earth bringeth forth fruit of herself; first the blade, then the ear, after that the full corn in the ear. ²⁹But when the fruit is brought forth, immediately he putteth in the sickle, because the harvest is come. ³⁰And he said, Whereunto shall we liken the kingdom of God? or with what comparison shall we compare it? ³¹It is like a grain of mustard seed, which, when it is sown in the earth, is less than all the seeds that be in the earth: ³²But when it is sown, it groweth up, and becometh greater than all herbs, and shooteth out great branches; so that the fowls of the air may lodge under the shadow of it. ³³And with many such parables spake he the word unto them, as they were able to hear it. ³⁴But without a parable spake he not unto them: and when they were alone, he expounded all things to his disciples."

Luke 13:18-21 "¹⁸Then said he, Unto what is the kingdom of God like? and whereunto shall I resemble it? ¹⁹It is like a grain of mustard seed, which a man took, and cast into his garden; and it grew, and waxed a great tree; and the fowls of the air lodged in the branches of it. ²⁰And again he said, Whereunto shall I liken the kingdom of God? ²¹It is like leaven, which a woman took and hid in three measures of meal, till the whole was leavened."

Luke 14:15-24 "¹⁵And when one of them that sat at meat with him heard these things, he said unto him, Blessed is he that shall eat bread in the kingdom of God. ¹⁶Then said he unto him, A certain man made a great supper, and bade many: ¹⁷And sent his servant at supper time to say to them that were bidden, Come; for all things are now ready. ¹⁸And they all with one consent began to make excuse. The first said unto him, I have bought a piece of ground, and I must needs go and see it: I pray thee have me excused. ¹⁹And another said, I have bought five yoke of oxen, and I go to prove them: I pray thee have me excused. ²⁰And another said, I have married a wife, and therefore I cannot come. ²¹So that servant came, and shewed his lord these things. Then the master of the house being angry said to his servant, Go out quickly into the streets and lanes of the city, and bring in hither the poor, and the maimed, and the halt, and the blind. ²²And the servant said, Lord, it is done as thou hast commanded, and yet there is room. ²³And the lord said unto the servant, Go out into the highways and hedges, and compel them to come in, that my house may be filled. ²⁴For I say unto you, That none of those men which were bidden shall taste of my supper."

Luke 19:11-27 "¹¹And as they heard these things, he added and spake a parable, because he was nigh to Jerusalem, and because they thought that the kingdom of God should immediately appear. ¹²He said therefore, A certain nobleman went into a far country to receive for himself a kingdom, and to return. ¹³And he called his ten servants, and delivered them ten pounds, and said unto them, Occupy till I come. ¹⁴But his citizens hated him, and sent a message after him, saying, We will not have this man to reign over us. [15]And it came to pass, that when he was returned, having received the kingdom, then he commanded these servants to be called unto him, to whom he had given the money, that he might know how much every man had gained by trading. [16]Then came the first, saying, Lord, thy pound hath gained ten pounds. [17]And he said unto him, Well, thou good servant: because thou hast been faithful in a very little, have thou authority over ten cities. [18]And the second came, saying, Lord, thy pound hath gained five pounds. [19]And he said likewise to him, Be thou also over five cities. [20]And another came, saying, Lord, behold, here is thy pound, which I have kept laid up in a napkin: [21]For I feared thee, because thou art an austere man: thou takest up that thou layedst not down, and reapest that thou didst not sow. [22]And he saith unto him, Out of thine own mouth will I judge thee, thou wicked servant. Thou knewest that I was an austere man, taking up that I laid not down, and reaping that I did not sow: [23]Wherefore then gavest not thou my money into the bank, that at my coming I might have required mine own with usury? [24]And he said unto them that stood by, Take from him the pound, and give it to him that hath ten pounds. [25](And they said unto him, Lord, he hath ten pounds.) [26]For I say unto you, That unto every one which hath shall be given; and from him that hath not, even that he hath shall be taken away from him. [27]But those mine enemies, which would not that I should reign over them, bring hither, and slay them before me."

What The Kingdom Of God Is Not
John 18:35-36 "[35]Pilate answered, Am I a Jew? Thine own nation and the chief priests have delivered thee unto me: what hast thou done? [36]Jesus answered, My kingdom is not of this world: if my kingdom were of this world, then would my servants fight, that I should not be delivered to the Jews: but now is my kingdom not from hence."

Romans 14:17 "For the kingdom of God is not meat and drink; but righteousness, and peace, and joy in the Holy Ghost."

1 Corinthians 4:20 "For the kingdom of God is not in word, but in power."

When The Kingdom Of God Was Introduced
Luke 16:16-17 "[16]The law and the prophets were until John: since that time the kingdom of God is preached, and every man presseth into it. [17]And it is easier for heaven and earth to pass, than one tittle of the law to fail."

When The Kingdom Of God Will Be Near
Luke 21:5-32 "[5]And as some spake of the temple, how it was adorned with goodly stones and gifts, he said, [6]As for these things which ye behold, the days will come, in the which there shall not be left one stone upon another, that shall not be thrown down. [7]And they asked him, saying, Master, but when shall these things be? and what sign will there be when these things shall come to pass? [8]And he said, Take heed that ye be not deceived: for many shall come in my name, saying, I am Christ; and the time draweth near: go ye not therefore after them. [9]But when ye shall hear of wars and commotions, be not terrified: for these things must first come to pass; but the end is not by and by. [10]Then said he unto them, Nation shall rise against nation, and kingdom against kingdom: [11]And great earthquakes shall be in divers places, and famines, and pestilences; and fearful sights and great signs shall there be from heaven. [12]But before all these, they shall lay their hands on you, and persecute you, delivering you up to the synagogues, and into prisons, being brought before kings and rulers for my name's sake. [13]And it shall turn to you for a testimony. [14]Settle it therefore in your hearts, not to meditate before what ye shall answer: [15]For I will give you a mouth and wisdom, which all your adversaries shall not be able to gainsay nor resist. [16]And ye shall be betrayed both by parents, and brethren, and kinsfolks, and friends; and some of you shall they cause to be put to death. [17]And ye shall be hated of all men for my name's sake. [18]But there shall not an hair of your head perish. [19]In your patience possess ye your souls. [20]And when ye shall see Jerusalem compassed with armies, then know that the desolation thereof is nigh. [21]Then let them which are in Judaea flee to the mountains; and let them which are in the midst of it depart out; and let not them that are in the countries enter thereinto. [22]For these be the days of vengeance, that all things which are written may be fulfilled. [23]But woe unto them that are with child, and to them that give suck, in those days! for there shall be great distress in the land, and wrath upon this people. [24]And they shall fall by the edge of the sword, and shall be led away captive into all nations: and Jerusalem shall be trodden

down of the Gentiles, until the times of the Gentiles be fulfilled. [25]And there shall be signs in the sun, and in the moon, and in the stars; and upon the earth distress of nations, with perplexity; the sea and the waves roaring; [26]Men's hearts failing them for fear, and for looking after those things which are coming on the earth: for the powers of heaven shall be shaken. [27]And then shall they see the Son of man coming in a cloud with power and great glory. [28]And when these things begin to come to pass, then look up, and lift up your heads; for your redemption draweth nigh. [29]And he spake to them a parable; Behold the fig tree, and all the trees; [30]When they now shoot forth, ye see and know of your own selves that summer is now nigh at hand. [31]So likewise ye, when ye see these things come to pass, know ye that the kingdom of God is nigh at hand. [32]Verily I say unto you, This generation shall not pass away, till all be fulfilled."

Where The Kingdom Of God Is
Luke 17:20-21 "[20]And when he was demanded of the Pharisees, when the kingdom of God should come, he answered them and said, The kingdom of God cometh not with observation: [21]Neither shall they say, Lo here! or, lo there! for, behold, the kingdom of God is within you."

Who Can Enter Into The Kingdom Of God
Daniel 7:18 "But the saints of the most High shall take the kingdom, and possess the kingdom for ever, even for ever and ever."

Daniel 7:27 "And the kingdom and dominion, and the greatness of the kingdom under the whole heaven, shall be given to the people of the saints of the most High, whose kingdom is an everlasting kingdom, and all dominions shall serve and obey him."

Matthew 5:3 "Blessed are the poor in spirit: for theirs is the kingdom of heaven."

Matthew 5:10 "Blessed are they which are persecuted for righteousness' sake: for theirs is the kingdom of heaven."

Matthew 7:21 "Not every one that saith unto me, Lord, Lord, shall enter into the kingdom of heaven; but he that doeth the will of my Father which is in heaven."

Matthew 25:31-46 "[31]When the Son of man shall come in his glory, and all the holy angels with him,

then shall he sit upon the throne of his glory: [32]And before him shall be gathered all nations: and he shall separate them one from another, as a shepherd divideth his sheep from the goats: [33]And he shall set the sheep on his right hand, but the goats on the left. [34]Then shall the King say unto them on his right hand, Come, ye blessed of my Father, inherit the kingdom prepared for you from the foundation of the world: [35]For I was an hungred, and ye gave me meat: I was thirsty, and ye gave me drink: I was a stranger, and ye took me in: [36]Naked, and ye clothed me: I was sick, and ye visited me: I was in prison, and ye came unto me. [37]Then shall the righteous answer him, saying, Lord, when saw we thee an hungred, and fed thee? or thirsty, and gave thee drink? [38]When saw we thee a stranger, and took thee in? or naked, and clothed thee? [39]Or when saw we thee sick, or in prison, and came unto thee? [40]And the King shall answer and say unto them, Verily I say unto you, Inasmuch as ye have done it unto one of the least of these my brethren, ye have done it unto me. [41]Then shall he say also unto them on the left hand, Depart from me, ye cursed, into everlasting fire, prepared for the devil and his angels: [42]For I was an hungred, and ye gave me no meat: I was thirsty, and ye gave me no drink: [43]I was a stranger, and ye took me not in: naked, and ye clothed me not: sick, and in prison, and ye visited me not. [44]Then shall they also answer him, saying, Lord, when saw we thee an hungred, or athirst, or a stranger, or naked, or sick, or in prison, and did not minister unto thee? [45]Then shall he answer them, saying, Verily I say unto you, Inasmuch as ye did it not to one of the least of these, ye did it not to me. [46]And these shall go away into everlasting punishment: but the righteous into life eternal."

Luke 6:20 "And he lifted up his eyes on his disciples, and said, Blessed be ye poor: for yours is the kingdom of God."

2 Peter 1:1-11 "[1]Simon Peter, a servant and an apostle of Jesus Christ, to them that have obtained like precious faith with us through the righteousness of God and our Saviour Jesus Christ: [2]Grace and peace be multiplied unto you through the knowledge of God, and of Jesus our Lord, [3]According as his divine power hath given unto us all things that pertain unto life and godliness, through the knowledge of him that hath called us to glory and virtue:

⁴Whereby are given unto us exceeding great and precious promises: that by these ye might be partakers of the divine nature, having escaped the corruption that is in the world through lust. ⁵And beside this, giving all diligence, add to your faith virtue; and to virtue knowledge; ⁶And to knowledge temperance; and to temperance patience; and to patience godliness; ⁷And to godliness brotherly kindness; and to brotherly kindness charity. ⁸For if these things be in you, and abound, they make you that ye shall neither be barren nor unfruitful in the knowledge of our Lord Jesus Christ. ⁹But he that lacketh these things is blind, and cannot see afar off, and hath forgotten that he was purged from his old sins. ¹⁰Wherefore the rather, brethren, give diligence to make your calling and election sure: for if ye do these things, ye shall never fall: ¹¹For so an entrance shall be ministered unto you abundantly into the everlasting kingdom of our Lord and Saviour Jesus Christ."

Revelation 22:13-14 "¹³I am Alpha and Omega, the beginning and the end, the first and the last. ¹⁴Blessed are they that do his commandments, that they may have right to the tree of life, and may enter in through the gates into the city."

Who Cannot Enter Into The Kingdom Of God

Matthew 5:20 "For I say unto you, That except your righteousness shall exceed the righteousness of the scribes and Pharisees, ye shall in no case enter into the kingdom of heaven."

Matthew 7:21-23 "²¹Not every one that saith unto me, Lord, Lord, shall enter into the kingdom of heaven; but he that doeth the will of my Father which is in heaven. ²²Many will say to me in that day, Lord, Lord, have we not prophesied in thy name? and in thy name have cast out devils? and in thy name done many wonderful works? ²³And then will I profess unto them, I never knew you: depart from me, ye that work iniquity."

Matthew 18:1-3 "¹At the same time came the disciples unto Jesus, saying, Who is the greatest in the kingdom of heaven? ²And Jesus called a little child unto him, and set him in the midst of them, ³And said, Verily I say unto you, Except ye be converted, and become as little children, ye shall not enter into the kingdom of heaven."

Matthew 25:31-46 "³¹When the Son of man shall come in his glory, and all the holy angels with him, then shall he sit upon the throne of his glory: ³²And before him shall be gathered all nations: and he shall separate them one from another, as a shepherd divideth his sheep from the goats: ³³And he shall set the sheep on his right hand, but the goats on the left. ³⁴Then shall the King say unto them on his right hand, Come, ye blessed of my Father, inherit the kingdom prepared for you from the foundation of the world: ³⁵For I was an hungred, and ye gave me meat: I was thirsty, and ye gave me drink: I was a stranger, and ye took me in: ³⁶Naked, and ye clothed me: I was sick, and ye visited me: I was in prison, and ye came unto me. ³⁷Then shall the righteous answer him, saying, Lord, when saw we thee an hungred, and fed thee? or thirsty, and gave thee drink? ³⁸When saw we thee a stranger, and took thee in? or naked, and clothed thee? ³⁹Or when saw we thee sick, or in prison, and came unto thee? ⁴⁰And the King shall answer and say unto them, Verily I say unto you, Inasmuch as ye have done it unto one of the least of these my brethren, ye have done it unto me. ⁴¹Then shall he say also unto them on the left hand, Depart from me, ye cursed, into everlasting fire, prepared for the devil and his angels: ⁴²For I was an hungred, and ye gave me no meat: I was thirsty, and ye gave me no drink: ⁴³I was a stranger, and ye took me not in: naked, and ye clothed me not: sick, and in prison, and ye visited me not. ⁴⁴Then shall they also answer him, saying, Lord, when saw we thee an hungred, or athirst, or a stranger, or naked, or sick, or in prison, and did not minister unto thee? ⁴⁵Then shall he answer them, saying, Verily I say unto you, Inasmuch as ye did it not to one of the least of these, ye did it not to me. ⁴⁶And these shall go away into everlasting punishment: but the righteous into life eternal."

Luke 13:24-29 "²⁴Strive to enter in at the strait gate: for many, I say unto you, will seek to enter in, and shall not be able. ²⁵When once the master of the house is risen up, and hath shut to the door, and ye begin to stand without, and to knock at the door, saying, Lord, Lord, open unto us; and he shall answer and say unto you, I know you not whence ye are: ²⁶Then shall ye begin to say, We have eaten and drunk in thy presence, and thou hast taught in our streets. ²⁷But he shall say, I tell you, I know you not whence ye are; depart from me, all ye workers of iniquity. [28]There shall be weeping and gnashing of teeth, when ye shall see Abraham, and Isaac, and Jacob, and all the prophets, in the kingdom of God, and you yourselves thrust out. [29]And they shall come from the east, and from the west, and from the north, and from the south, and shall sit down in the kingdom of God."

Luke 18:16-17 "[16]But Jesus called them unto him, and said, Suffer little children to come unto me, and forbid them not: for of such is the kingdom of God. [17]Verily I say unto you, Whosoever shall not receive the kingdom of God as a little child shall in no wise enter therein."

John 3:3-8 "[3]Jesus answered and said unto him, Verily, verily, I say unto thee, Except a man be born again, he cannot see the kingdom of God. [4]Nicodemus saith unto him, How can a man be born when he is old? can he enter the second time into his mother's womb, and be born? [5]Jesus answered, Verily, verily, I say unto thee, Except a man be born of water and of the Spirit, he cannot enter into the kingdom of God. [6]That which is born of the flesh is flesh; and that which is born of the Spirit is spirit. [7]Marvel not that I said unto thee, Ye must be born again. [8]The wind bloweth where it listeth, and thou hearest the sound thereof, but canst not tell whence it cometh, and whither it goeth: so is every one that is born of the Spirit."

1 Corinthians 6:9-11 "[9]Know ye not that the unrighteous shall not inherit the kingdom of God? Be not deceived: neither fornicators, nor idolaters, nor adulterers, nor effeminate, nor abusers of themselves with mankind, [10]Nor thieves, nor covetous, nor drunkards, nor revilers, nor extortioners, shall inherit the kingdom of God. [11]And such were some of you: but ye are washed, but ye are sanctified, but ye are justified in the name of the Lord Jesus, and by the Spirit of our God."

Galatians 5:16-21 "[16]This I say then, Walk in the Spirit, and ye shall not fulfil the lust of the flesh. [17]For the flesh lusteth against the Spirit, and the Spirit against the flesh: and these are contrary the one to the other: so that ye cannot do the things that ye would. [18]But if ye be led of the Spirit, ye are not under the law. [19]Now the works of the flesh are manifest, which are these; Adultery, fornication, uncleanness, lasciviousness, [20]Idolatry, witchcraft, hatred, variance, emulations, wrath, strife, seditions, heresies, [21]Envyings, murders, drunkenness, revellings, and such like: of the which I tell you before, as I have also told you in time past, that they which do such things shall not inherit the kingdom of God."

Ephesians 5:5-7 "[5]For this ye know, that no whoremonger, nor unclean person, nor covetous man, who is an idolater, hath any inheritance in the kingdom of Christ and of God. [6]Let no man deceive you with vain words: for because of these things cometh the wrath of God upon the children of disobedience. [7]Be not ye therefore partakers with them."

Revelation 22:13-19 "[13]I am Alpha and Omega, the beginning and the end, the first and the last. [14]Blessed are they that do his commandments, that they may have right to the tree of life, and may enter in through the gates into the city. [15]For without are dogs, and sorcerers, and whoremongers, and murderers, and idolaters, and whosoever loveth and maketh a lie. [16]I Jesus have sent mine angel to testify unto you these things in the churches. I am the root and the offspring of David, and the bright and morning star. [17]And the Spirit and the bride say, Come. And let him that heareth say, Come. And let him that is athirst come. And whosoever will, let him take the water of life freely. [18]For I testify unto every man that heareth the words of the prophecy of this book, If any man shall add unto these things, God shall add unto him the plagues that are written in this book: [19]And if any man shall take away from the words of the book of this prophecy, God shall take away his part out of the book of life, and out of the holy city, and from the things which are written in this book."

Who Shall Be Great In The Kingdom Of God

Matthew 5:19 "Whosoever therefore shall break one of these least commandments, and shall teach men so, he shall be called the least in the kingdom of heaven: but whosoever shall do and teach them, the same shall be called great in the kingdom of heaven."

Matthew 18:1-4 "[1]At the same time came the disciples unto Jesus, saying, Who is the greatest in the kingdom of heaven? [2]And Jesus called a little child unto him, and set him in the midst of them, [3]And said, Verily I say unto you, Except ye be converted, and become as little children, ye shall not enter into the kingdom of heaven. [4]Whosoever therefore shall humble himself as this little child, the same is greatest in the kingdom of heaven."

Luke 9:46-48 "⁴⁶Then there arose a reasoning among them, which of them should be greatest. ⁴⁷And Jesus, perceiving the thought of their heart, took a child, and set him by him, ⁴⁸And said unto them, Whosoever shall receive this child in my name receiveth me: and whosoever shall receive me receiveth him that sent me: for he that is least among you all, the same shall be great."

Luke 22:22-27 "²²And truly the Son of man goeth, as it was determined: but woe unto that man by whom he is betrayed! ²³And they began to inquire among themselves, which of them it was that should do this thing. ²⁴And there was also a strife among them, which of them should be accounted the greatest. ²⁵And he said unto them, The kings of the Gentiles exercise lordship over them; and they that exercise authority upon them are called benefactors. ²⁶But ye shall not be so: but he that is greatest among you, let him be as the younger; and he that is chief, as he that doth serve. ²⁷For whether is greater, he that sitteth at meat, or he that serveth? is not he that sitteth at meat? but I am among you as he that serveth."

Who Shall Be Least In The Kingdom Of God
Matthew 5:19 "Whosoever therefore shall break one of these least commandments, and shall teach men so, he shall be called the least in the kingdom of heaven: but whosoever shall do and teach them, the same shall be called great in the kingdom of heaven."

Mark 9:33-35 "³³And he came to Capernaum: and being in the house he asked them, What was it that ye disputed among yourselves by the way? ³⁴But they held their peace: for by the way they had disputed among themselves, who should be the greatest. ³⁵And he sat down, and called the twelve, and saith unto them, If any man desire to be first, the same shall be last of all, and servant of all."

Luke 22:22-27 "²²And truly the Son of man goeth, as it was determined: but woe unto that man by whom he is betrayed! ²³And they began to inquire among themselves, which of them it was that should do this thing. ²⁴And there was also a strife among them, which of them should be accounted the greatest. ²⁵And he said unto them, The kings of

the Gentiles exercise lordship over them; and they that exercise authority upon them are called benefactors. ²⁶But ye shall not be so: but he that is greatest among you, let him be as the younger; and he that is chief, as he that doth serve. ²⁷For whether is greater, he that sitteth at meat, or he that serveth? is not he that sitteth at meat? but I am among you as he that serveth."

Who Shall Have A Hard Time Entering Into The Kingdom Of God
Matthew 19:23-26 "²³Then said Jesus unto his disciples, Verily I say unto you, That a rich man shall hardly enter into the kingdom of heaven. ²⁴And again I say unto you, It is easier for a camel to go through the eye of a needle, than for a rich man to enter into the kingdom of God. ²⁵When his disciples heard it, they were exceedingly amazed, saying, Who then can be saved? ²⁶But Jesus beheld them, and said unto them, With men this is impossible; but with God all things are possible."

Mark 10:23-27 "²³And Jesus looked round about, and saith unto his disciples, How hardly shall they that have riches enter into the kingdom of God! ²⁴And the disciples were astonished at his words. But Jesus answereth again, and saith unto them, Children, how hard is it for them that trust in riches to enter into the kingdom of God! ²⁵It is easier for a camel to go through the eye of a needle, than for a rich man to enter into the kingdom of God. ²⁶And they were astonished out of measure, saying among themselves, Who then can be saved? ²⁷And Jesus looking upon them saith, With men it is impossible, but not with God: for with God all things are possible."

Luke 18:24-27 "²⁴And when Jesus saw that he was very sorrowful, he said, How hardly shall they that have riches enter into the kingdom of God! ²⁵For it is easier for a camel to go through a needle's eye, than for a rich man to enter into the kingdom of God. ²⁶And they that heard it said, Who then can be saved? ²⁷And he said, The things which are impossible with men are possible with God."

KNOWLEDGE

God Being A God Of Knowledge
1 Samuel 2:3 "Talk no more so exceeding proudly; let not arrogancy come out of your mouth: for the

LORD is a God of knowledge, and by him actions are weighed."

God The Father And
Jesus Christ Knowing Each Other

Matthew 11:25-27 "²⁵At that time Jesus answered and said, I thank thee, O Father, Lord of heaven and earth, because thou hast hid these things from the wise and prudent, and hast revealed them unto babes. ²⁶Even so, Father: for so it seemed good in thy sight. ²⁷All things are delivered unto me of my Father: and no man knoweth the Son, but the Father; neither knoweth any man the Father, save the Son, and he to whomsoever the Son will reveal him."

Luke 10:22 "All things are delivered to me of my Father: and no man knoweth who the Son is, but the Father; and who the Father is, but the Son, and he to whom the Son will reveal him."

John 7:28-29 "²⁸Then cried Jesus in the temple as he taught, saying, Ye both know me, and ye know whence I am: and I am not come of myself, but he that sent me is true, whom ye know not. ²⁹But I know him: for I am from him, and he hath sent me."

John 8:53-58 "⁵³Art thou greater than our father Abraham, which is dead? and the prophets are dead: whom makest thou thyself? ⁵⁴Jesus answered, If I honour myself, my honour is nothing: it is my Father that honoureth me; of whom ye say, that he is your God: ⁵⁵Yet ye have not known him; but I know him: and if I should say, I know him not, I shall be a liar like unto you: but I know him, and keep his saying. ⁵⁶Your father Abraham rejoiced to see my day: and he saw it, and was glad. ⁵⁷Then said the Jews unto him, Thou art not yet fifty years old, and hast thou seen Abraham? ⁵⁸Jesus said unto them, Verily, verily, I say unto you, Before Abraham was, I am."

John 10:14-15 "¹⁴I am the good shepherd, and know my sheep, and am known of mine. ¹⁵As the Father knoweth me, even so know I the Father: and I lay down my life for the sheep."

John 17:1-25 "¹These words spake Jesus, and lifted up his eyes to heaven, and said, Father, the hour is come; glorify thy Son, that thy Son also may glorify thee: ²As thou hast given him power over all flesh, that he should give eternal life to as many as thou hast given him. ³And this is life eternal, that they might know thee the only true God, and Jesus

Christ, whom thou hast sent. ⁴I have glorified thee on the earth: I have finished the work which thou gavest me to do. ⁵And now, O Father, glorify thou me with thine own self with the glory which I had with thee before the world was. ⁶I have manifested thy name unto the men which thou gavest me out of the world: thine they were, and thou gavest them me; and they have kept thy word. ⁷Now they have known that all things whatsoever thou hast given me are of thee. ⁸For I have given unto them the words which thou gavest me; and they have received them, and have known surely that I came out from thee, and they have believed that thou didst send me. ⁹I pray for them: I pray not for the world, but for them which thou hast given me; for they are thine. ¹⁰And all mine are thine, and thine are mine; and I am glorified in them. ¹¹And now I am no more in the world, but these are in the world, and I come to thee. Holy Father, keep through thine own name those whom thou hast given me, that they may be one, as we are. ¹²While I was with them in the world, I kept them in thy name: those that thou gavest me I have kept, and none of them is lost, but the son of perdition; that the scripture might be fulfilled. ¹³And now come I to thee; and these things I speak in the world, that they might have my joy fulfilled in themselves. ¹⁴I have given them thy word; and the world hath hated them, because they are not of the world, even as I am not of the world. ¹⁵I pray not that thou shouldest take them out of the world, but that thou shouldest keep them from the evil. ¹⁶They are not of the world, even as I am not of the world. ¹⁷Sanctify them through thy truth: thy word is truth. ¹⁸As thou hast sent me into the world, even so have I also sent them into the world. ¹⁹And for their sakes I sanctify myself, that they also might be sanctified through the truth. ²⁰Neither pray I for these alone, but for them also which shall believe on me through their word; ²¹That they all may be one; as thou, Father, art in me, and I in thee, that they also may be one in us: that the world may believe that thou hast sent me. ²²And the glory which thou gavest me I have given them; that they may be one, even as we are one: ²³I in them, and thou in me, that they may be made perfect in one; and that the world may know that thou hast sent me, and hast loved them, as thou hast loved me. ²⁴Father, I will that they also, whom thou hast given me, be with me where I am; that they may behold my glory, which thou hast given me: for thou lovedst me before the foundation of the world. [25]O righteous Father, the world hath not known thee: but I have known thee, and these have known that thou hast sent me."

Hearing Knowledge
Proverbs 22:17 "Bow down thine ear, and hear the words of the wise, and apply thine heart unto my knowledge."

Proverbs 23:12 "Apply thine heart unto instruction, and thine ears to the words of knowledge."

If Any Man Thinks That He Knows Anything
1 Corinthians 8:1-2 "[1]Now as touching things offered unto idols, we know that we all have knowledge. Knowledge puffeth up, but charity edifieth. [2]And if any man think that he knoweth anything, he knoweth nothing yet as he ought to know."

If You Know Jesus Christ
John 8:17-19 "[17]It is also written in your law, that the testimony of two men is true. [18]I am one that bear witness of myself, and the Father that sent me beareth witness of me. [19]Then said they unto him, Where is thy Father? Jesus answered, Ye neither know me, nor my Father: if ye had known me, ye should have known my Father also."

John 14:6-7 "[6]Jesus saith unto him, I am the way, the truth, and the life: no man cometh unto the Father, but by me. [7]If ye had known me, ye should have known my Father also: and from henceforth ye know him, and have seen him."

Men Of Knowledge
Proverbs 24:5 "A wise man is strong; yea, a man of knowledge increaseth strength."

The Lack Of Knowledge
Proverbs 19:2 "Also, that the soul be without knowledge, it is not good; and he that hasteth with his feet sinneth."

The Lips Of Knowledge
Proverbs 20:15 "There is gold, and a multitude of rubies: but the lips of knowledge are a precious jewel."

The Reward For Hating Knowledge
Proverbs 1:20-32 "[20]Wisdom crieth without; she uttereth her voice in the streets: [21]She crieth in the chief place of concourse, in the openings of the gates: in the city she uttereth her words, saying, [22]How long, ye simple ones, will ye love simplicity? and the scorners delight in their scorning, and fools hate knowledge? [23]Turn you at my reproof: behold, I will pour out my spirit unto you, I will make known my words unto you. [24]Because I have called, and ye refused; I have stretched out my hand, and no man regarded; [25]But ye have set at nought all my counsel, and would none of my reproof: [26]I also will laugh at your calamity; I will mock when your fear cometh; [27]When your fear cometh as desolation, and your destruction cometh as a whirlwind; when distress and anguish cometh upon you. [28]Then shall they call upon me, but I will not answer; they shall seek me early, but they shall not find me: [29]For that they hated knowledge, and did not choose the fear of the LORD: [30]They would none of my counsel: they despised all my reproof. [31]Therefore shall they eat of the fruit of their own way, and be filled with their own devices. [32]For the turning away of the simple shall slay them, and the prosperity of fools shall destroy them."

The Reward For Lacking Knowledge
Isaiah 5:13 "Therefore my people are gone into captivity, because they have no knowledge: and their honourable men are famished, and their multitude dried up with thirst."

Hosea 4:1-6 "[1]Hear the word of the LORD, ye children of Israel: for the LORD hath a controversy with the inhabitants of the land, because there is no truth, nor mercy, nor knowledge of God in the land. [2]By swearing, and lying, and killing, and stealing, and committing adultery, they break out, and blood toucheth blood. [3]Therefore shall the land mourn, and every one that dwelleth therein shall languish, with the beasts of the field, and with the fowls of heaven; yea, the fishes of the sea also shall be taken away. [4]Yet let no man strive, nor reprove another: for thy people are as they that strive with the priest. [5]Therefore shalt thou fall in the day, and the prophet also shall fall with thee in the night, and I will destroy thy mother. [6]My people are destroyed for lack of knowledge: because thou hast rejected knowledge, I will also reject thee, that thou shalt be no priest to me: seeing thou hast forgotten the law of thy God, I will also forget thy children."

Those That Do Not Know The Lord
Job 18:5-21 "[5]Yea, the light of the wicked shall be put out, and the spark of his fire shall not shine.

⁶The light shall be dark in his tabernacle, and his candle shall be put out with him. ⁷The steps of his strength shall be straitened, and his own counsel shall cast him down. ⁸For he is cast into a net by his own feet, and he walketh upon a snare. ⁹The gin shall take him by the heel, and the robber shall prevail against him. ¹⁰The snare is laid for him in the ground, and a trap for him in the way. ¹¹Terrors shall make him afraid on every side, and shall drive him to his feet. ¹²His strength shall be hungerbitten, and destruction shall be ready at his side. ¹³It shall devour the strength of his skin: even the firstborn of death shall devour his strength. ¹⁴His confidence shall be rooted out of his tabernacle, and it shall bring him to the king of terrors. ¹⁵It shall dwell in his tabernacle, because it is none of his: brimstone shall be scattered upon his habitation. ¹⁶His roots shall be dried up beneath, and above shall his branch be cut off. ¹⁷His remembrance shall perish from the earth, and he shall have no name in the street. ¹⁸He shall be driven from light into darkness, and chased out of the world. ¹⁹He shall neither have son nor nephew among his people, nor any remaining in his dwellings. ²⁰They that come after him shall be astonied at his day, as they that went before were affrighted. ²¹Surely such are the dwellings of the wicked, and this is the place of him that knoweth not God."

Jeremiah 10:24-25 "²⁴O LORD, correct me, but with judgment; not in thine anger, lest thou bring me to nothing. ²⁵Pour out thy fury upon the heathen that know thee not, and upon the families that call not on thy name: for they have eaten up Jacob, and devoured him, and consumed him, and have made his habitation desolate."

John 16:2-3 "²They shall put you out of the synagogues: yea, the time cometh, that whosoever killeth you will think that he doeth God service. ³And these things will they do unto you, because they have not known the Father, nor me."

2 Thessalonians 1:7-9 "⁷And to you who are troubled rest with us, when the Lord Jesus shall be revealed from heaven with his mighty angels, ⁸In flaming fire taking vengeance on them that know not God, and that obey not the gospel of our Lord Jesus Christ: ⁹Who shall be punished with everlasting destruction from the presence of the Lord, and from the glory of his power."

1 John 3:1 "Behold, what manner of love the Father hath bestowed upon us, that we should be called the sons of God: therefore the world knoweth us not, because it knew him not."

Those That Do Not Like To Retain God In Their Knowledge

Romans 1:28-31 "²⁸And even as they did not like to retain God in their knowledge, God gave them over to a reprobate mind, to do those things which are not convenient; ²⁹Being filled with all unrighteousness, fornication, wickedness, covetousness, maliciousness; full of envy, murder, debate, deceit, malignity; whisperers, ³⁰Backbiters, haters of God, despiteful, proud, boasters, inventors of evil things, disobedient to parents, ³¹Without understanding, covenantbreakers, without natural affection, implacable, unmerciful."

Those That Find Knowledge

Proverbs 8:1-9 "¹Doth not wisdom cry? and understanding put forth her voice? ²She standeth in the top of high places, by the way in the places of the paths. ³She crieth at the gates, at the entry of the city, at the coming in at the doors. ⁴Unto you, O men, I call; and my voice is to the sons of man. ⁵O ye simple, understand wisdom: and, ye fools, be ye of an understanding heart. ⁶Hear; for I will speak of excellent things; and the opening of my lips shall be right things. ⁷For my mouth shall speak truth; and wickedness is an abomination to my lips. ⁸All the words of my mouth are in righteousness; there is nothing froward or perverse in them. ⁹They are all plain to him that understandeth, and right to them that find knowledge."

Those That Have Knowledge

Proverbs 17:27 "He that hath knowledge spareth his words: and a man of understanding is of an excellent spirit."

Proverbs 28:2 "For the transgression of a land many are the princes thereof: but by a man of understanding and knowledge the state thereof shall be prolonged."

2 Peter 1:1-11 "¹Simon Peter, a servant and an apostle of Jesus Christ, to them that have obtained like precious faith with us through the righteousness of God and our Saviour Jesus Christ: ²Grace and peace be multiplied unto you through the knowledge of God, and of Jesus our Lord, ³According as his divine power hath given unto us all things that pertain unto life and godliness, through the knowledge of him that hath called us to glory and virtue: [4]Whereby are given unto us exceeding great and precious promises: that by these ye might be partakers of the divine nature, having escaped the corruption that is in the world through lust. [5]And beside this, giving all diligence, add to your faith virtue; and to virtue knowledge; [6]And to knowledge temperance; and to temperance patience; and to patience godliness; [7]And to godliness brotherly kindness; and to brotherly kindness charity. [8]For if these things be in you, and abound, they make you that ye shall neither be barren nor unfruitful in the knowledge of our Lord Jesus Christ. [9]But he that lacketh these things is blind, and cannot see afar off, and hath forgotten that he was purged from his old sins. [10]Wherefore the rather, brethren, give diligence to make your calling and election sure: for if ye do these things, ye shall never fall: [11]For so an entrance shall be ministered unto you abundantly into the everlasting kingdom of our Lord and Saviour Jesus Christ."

Those That Increase Knowledge
Ecclesiastes 1:18 "For in much wisdom is much grief: and he that increaseth knowledge increaseth sorrow."

Those That Know The Joyful Sound
Psalm 89:15-16 "[15]Blessed is the people that know the joyful sound: they shall walk, O LORD, in the light of thy countenance. [16]In thy name shall they rejoice all the day: and in thy righteousness shall they be exalted."

Those That Know The Lord
Psalm 9:10 "And they that know thy name will put their trust in thee: for thou, LORD, hast not forsaken them that seek thee."

Psalm 91:9-14 "[9]Because thou hast made the LORD, which is my refuge, even the most High, thy habitation; [10]There shall no evil befall thee, neither shall any plague come nigh thy dwelling. [11]For he shall give his angels charge over thee, to keep thee in all thy ways. [12]They shall bear thee up in their hands, lest thou dash thy foot against a stone. [13]Thou shalt tread upon the lion and adder: the young lion and the dragon shalt thou trample under feet. [14]Because he hath set his love upon me, therefore will I deliver him: I will set him on high, because he hath known my name."

1 John 2:13-14 "[13]I write unto you, fathers, because ye have known him that is from the beginning. I write unto you, young men, because ye have overcome the wicked one. I write unto you, little children, because ye have known the Father. [14]I have written unto you, fathers, because ye have known him that is from the beginning. I have written unto you, young men, because ye are strong, and the word of God abideth in you, and ye have overcome the wicked one."

1 John 4:6 "We are of God: he that knoweth God heareth us; he that is not of God heareth not us. Hereby know we the spirit of truth, and the spirit of error."

Those That Lack Knowledge
2 Peter 1:1-9 "[1]Simon Peter, a servant and an apostle of Jesus Christ, to them that have obtained like precious faith with us through the righteousness of God and our Saviour Jesus Christ: [2]Grace and peace be multiplied unto you through the knowledge of God, and of Jesus our Lord, [3]According as his divine power hath given unto us all things that pertain unto life and godliness, through the knowledge of him that hath called us to glory and virtue: [4]Whereby are given unto us exceeding great and precious promises: that by these ye might be partakers of the divine nature, having escaped the corruption that is in the world through lust. [5]And beside this, giving all diligence, add to your faith virtue; and to virtue knowledge; [6]And to knowledge temperance; and to temperance patience; and to patience godliness; [7]And to godliness brotherly kindness; and to brotherly kindness charity. [8]For if these things be in you, and abound, they make you that ye shall neither be barren nor unfruitful in the knowledge of our Lord Jesus Christ. [9]But he that lacketh these things is blind, and cannot see afar off, and hath forgotten that he was purged from his old sins."

What Is Renewed In Knowledge
Colossians 3:9-10 "[9]Lie not one to another, seeing that ye have put off the old man with his deeds; [10]And have put on the new man, which is renewed in knowledge after the image of him that created him."

What Is The Beginning Of Knowledge
Proverbs 1:7 "The fear of the LORD is the beginning of knowledge: but fools despise wisdom and instruction."

Proverbs 9:10 "The fear of the LORD is the beginning of wisdom: and the knowledge of the holy is understanding."

What Israel Shall Know

Isaiah 49:22-26 "²²Thus saith the Lord GOD, Behold, I will lift up mine hand to the Gentiles, and set up my standard to the people: and they shall bring thy sons in their arms, and thy daughters shall be carried upon their shoulders. ²³And kings shall be thy nursing fathers, and their queens thy nursing mothers: they shall bow down to thee with their face toward the earth, and lick up the dust of thy feet; and thou shalt know that I am the LORD: for they shall not be ashamed that wait for me. ²⁴Shall the prey be taken from the mighty, or the lawful captive delivered? ²⁵But thus saith the LORD, Even the captives of the mighty shall be taken away, and the prey of the terrible shall be delivered: for I will contend with him that contendeth with thee, and I will save thy children. ²⁶And I will feed them that oppress thee with their own flesh; and they shall be drunken with their own blood, as with sweet wine: and all flesh shall know that I the LORD am thy Saviour and thy Redeemer, the mighty One of Jacob."

Ezekiel 28:24-26 "²⁴And there shall be no more a pricking brier unto the house of Israel, nor any grieving thorn of all that are round about them, that despised them; and they shall know that I am the Lord GOD. ²⁵Thus saith the Lord GOD; When I shall have gathered the house of Israel from the people among whom they are scattered, and shall be sanctified in them in the sight of the heathen, then shall they dwell in their land that I have given to my servant Jacob. ²⁶And they shall dwell safely therein, and shall build houses, and plant vineyards; yea, they shall dwell with confidence, when I have executed judgments upon all those that despise them round about them; and they shall know that I am the LORD their God."

Ezekiel 34:27-31 "²⁷And the tree of the field shall yield her fruit, and the earth shall yield her increase, and they shall be safe in their land, and shall know that I am the LORD, when I have broken the bands of their yoke, and delivered them out of the hand of those that served themselves of them. ²⁸And they shall no more be a prey to the heathen, neither shall the beast of the land devour them; but they shall dwell safely, and none shall make them afraid. ²⁹And I will raise up for them a plant of renown, and they shall be no more consumed with hunger in the land, neither bear the shame of the heathen any more. ³⁰Thus shall they know that I the LORD their God am with them, and that they, even the house of Israel, are my people, saith the Lord GOD. ³¹And ye my flock, the flock of my pasture, are men, and I am your God, saith the Lord GOD."

Ezekiel 36:8-11 "⁸But ye, O mountains of Israel, ye shall shoot forth your branches, and yield your fruit to my people of Israel; for they are at hand to come. ⁹For, behold, I am for you, and I will turn unto you, and ye shall be tilled and sown: ¹⁰And I will multiply men upon you, all the house of Israel, even all of it: and the cities shall be inhabited, and the wastes shall be builded: ¹¹And I will multiply upon you man and beast; and they shall increase and bring fruit: and I will settle you after your old estates, and will do better unto you than at your beginnings: and ye shall know that I am the LORD."

Ezekiel 37:11-14 "¹¹Then he said unto me, Son of man, these bones are the whole house of Israel: behold, they say, Our bones are dried, and our hope is lost: we are cut off for our parts. ¹²Therefore prophesy and say unto them, Thus saith the Lord GOD; Behold, O my people, I will open your graves, and cause you to come up out of your graves, and bring you into the land of Israel. ¹³And ye shall know that I am the LORD, when I have opened your graves, O my people, and brought you up out of your graves, ¹⁴And shall put my spirit in you, and ye shall live, and I shall place you in your own land: then shall ye know that I the LORD have spoken it, and performed it, saith the LORD."

Ezekiel 39:17-22 "¹⁷And, thou son of man, thus saith the Lord GOD; Speak unto every feathered fowl, and to every beast of the field, Assemble yourselves, and come; gather yourselves on every side to my sacrifice that I do sacrifice for you, even a great sacrifice upon the mountains of Israel, that ye may eat flesh, and drink blood. ¹⁸Ye shall eat the flesh of the mighty, and drink the blood of the princes of the earth, of rams, of lambs, and of goats, of bullocks, all of them fatlings of Bashan.

¹⁹And ye shall eat fat till ye be full, and drink blood till ye be drunken, of my sacrifice which I have sacrificed for you. ²⁰Thus ye shall be filled at my table with horses and chariots, with mighty men, and with all men of war, saith the Lord GOD. ²¹And I will set my glory among the heathen, and all the heathen shall see my judgment that I have executed, and my hand that I have laid upon them. ²²So the house of Israel shall know that I am the LORD their God from that day and forward."

Ezekiel 39:25-28 "²⁵Therefore thus saith the Lord GOD; Now will I bring again the captivity of Jacob, and have mercy upon the whole house of Israel, and will be jealous for my holy name; ²⁶After that they have borne their shame, and all their trespasses whereby they have trespassed against me, when they dwelt safely in their land, and none made them afraid. ²⁷When I have brought them again from the people, and gathered them out of their enemies' lands, and am sanctified in them in the sight of many nations; ²⁸Then shall they know that I am the LORD their God, which cause them to be led into captivity among the heathen: but I have gathered them unto their own land, and have left none of them any more there."

Joel 2:23-27 "²³Be glad then, ye children of Zion, and rejoice in the LORD your God: for he hath given you the former rain moderately, and he will cause to come down for you the rain, the former rain, and the latter rain in the first month. ²⁴And the floors shall be full of wheat, and the fats shall overflow with wine and oil. ²⁵And I will restore to you the years that the locust hath eaten, the cankerworm, and the caterpiller, and the palmerworm, my great army which I sent among you. ²⁶And ye shall eat in plenty, and be satisfied, and praise the name of the LORD your God, that hath dealt wondrously with you: and my people shall never be ashamed. ²⁷And ye shall know that I am in the midst of Israel, and that I am the LORD your God, and none else: and my people shall never be ashamed."

Joel 3:16-17 "¹⁶The LORD also shall roar out of Zion, and utter his voice from Jerusalem; and the heavens and the earth shall shake: but the LORD will be the hope of his people, and the strength of the children of Israel. ¹⁷So shall ye know that I am the LORD your God dwelling in Zion, my holy mountain: then shall Jerusalem be holy, and there shall no strangers pass through her any more."

What Knowledge Does
Proverbs 11:9 "An hypocrite with his mouth destroyeth his neighbour: but through knowledge shall the just be delivered."

Proverbs 24:3-4 "³Through wisdom is an house builded; and by understanding it is established: ⁴And by knowledge shall the chambers be filled with all precious and pleasant riches."

What Knowledge Is
Isaiah 33:5-6 "⁵The LORD is exalted; for he dwelleth on high: he hath filled Zion with judgment and righteousness. ⁶And wisdom and knowledge shall be the stability of thy times, and strength of salvation: the fear of the LORD is his treasure."

What Man Does Not Know
Proverbs 27:1 "Boast not thyself of to morrow; for thou knowest not what a day may bring forth."

Ecclesiastes 11:1-5 "¹Cast thy bread upon the waters: for thou shalt find it after many days. ²Give a portion to seven, and also to eight; for thou knowest not what evil shall be upon the earth. ³If the clouds be full of rain, they empty themselves upon the earth: and if the tree fall toward the south, or toward the north, in the place where the tree falleth, there it shall be. ⁴He that observeth the wind shall not sow; and he that regardeth the clouds shall not reap. ⁵As thou knowest not what is the way of the spirit, nor how the bones do grow in the womb of her that is with child: even so thou knowest not the works of God who maketh all."

Jeremiah 33:2-3 "²Thus saith the LORD the maker thereof, the LORD that formed it, to establish it; the LORD is his name; ³Call unto me, and I will answer thee, and shew thee great and mighty things, which thou knowest not."

Matthew 24:29-36 "²⁹Immediately after the tribulation of those days shall the sun be darkened, and the moon shall not give her light, and the stars shall fall from heaven, and the powers of the heavens shall be shaken: ³⁰And then shall appear the sign of the Son of man in heaven: and then shall all the tribes of the earth mourn, and they shall see the Son of man coming in the clouds of heaven with power and great glory. [31]And he shall send his angels with a great sound of a trumpet, and they shall gather together his elect from the four winds, from one end of heaven to the other. [32]Now learn a parable of the fig tree; When his branch is yet tender, and putteth forth leaves, ye know that summer is nigh: [33]So likewise ye, when ye shall see all these things, know that it is near, even at the doors. [34]Verily I say unto you, This generation shall not pass, till all these things be fulfilled. [35]Heaven and earth shall pass away, but my words shall not pass away. [36]But of that day and hour knoweth no man, no, not the angels of heaven, but my Father only."

Matthew 25:13 "Watch therefore, for ye know neither the day nor the hour wherein the Son of man cometh."

Mark 13:28-33 "[28]Now learn a parable of the fig tree; When her branch is yet tender, and putteth forth leaves, ye know that summer is near: [29]So ye in like manner, when ye shall see these things come to pass, know that it is nigh, even at the doors. [30]Verily I say unto you, that this generation shall not pass, till all these things be done. [31]Heaven and earth shall pass away: but my words shall not pass away. [32]But of that day and that hour knoweth no man, no, not the angels which are in heaven, neither the Son, but the Father. [33]Take ye heed, watch and pray: for ye know not when the time is."

Luke 23:34 "Then said Jesus, Father, forgive them; for they know not what they do. And they parted his raiment, and cast lots."

Acts 1:6-7 "[6]When they therefore were come together, they asked of him, saying, Lord, wilt thou at this time restore again the kingdom to Israel? [7]And he said unto them, It is not for you to know the times or the seasons, which the Father hath put in his own power."

Romans 11:34-36 "[34]For who hath known the mind of the Lord? or who hath been his counseller? [35]Or who hath first given to him, and it shall be recompensed unto him again? [36]For of him, and through him, and to him, are all things: to whom be glory for ever. Amen."

1 Corinthians 2:6-8 "[6]Howbeit we speak wisdom among them that are perfect: yet not the wisdom

of this world, nor of the princes of this world, that come to nought: [7]But we speak the wisdom of God in a mystery, even the hidden wisdom, which God ordained before the world unto our glory: [8]Which none of the princes of this world knew: for had they known it, they would not have crucified the Lord of glory."

1 Corinthians 2:12-16 "[12]Now we have received, not the spirit of the world, but the spirit which is of God; that we might know the things that are freely given to us of God. [13]Which things also we speak, not in the words which man's wisdom teacheth, but which the Holy Ghost teacheth; comparing spiritual things with spiritual. [14]But the natural man receiveth not the things of the Spirit of God: for they are foolishness unto him: neither can he know them, because they are spiritually discerned. [15]But he that is spiritual judgeth all things, yet he himself is judged of no man. [16]For who hath known the mind of the Lord, that he may instruct him? But we have the mind of Christ."

James 4:13-14 "[13]Go to now, ye that say, To day or to morrow we will go into such a city, and continue there a year, and buy and sell, and get gain: [14]Whereas ye know not what shall be on the morrow. For what is your life? It is even a vapour, that appeareth for a little time, and then vanisheth away."

Revelation 3:1-3 "[1]And unto the angel of the church in Sardis write; These things saith he that hath the seven Spirits of God, and the seven stars; I know thy works, that thou hast a name that thou livest, and art dead. [2]Be watchful, and strengthen the things which remain, that are ready to die: for I have not found thy works perfect before God. [3]Remember therefore how thou hast received and heard, and hold fast, and repent. If therefore thou shalt not watch, I will come on thee as a thief, and thou shalt not know what hour I will come upon thee."

What Preserves Knowledge
Proverbs 22:12 "The eyes of the LORD preserve knowledge, and he overthroweth the words of the transgressor."

What The Disciples Know
Matthew 13:10-11 "[10]And the disciples came, and said unto him, Why speakest thou unto them in parables? [11]He answered and said unto them, Because it is given unto you to know the mysteries

of the kingdom of heaven, but to them it is not given."

Mark 4:10-11 "¹⁰And when he was alone, they that were about him with the twelve asked of him the parable. ¹¹And he said unto them, Unto you it is given to know the mystery of the kingdom of God: but unto them that are without, all these things are done in parables."

Luke 8:9-10 "⁹And his disciples asked him, saying, What might this parable be? ¹⁰And he said, Unto you it is given to know the mysteries of the kingdom of God: but to others in parables; that seeing they might not see, and hearing they might not understand."

John 13:5-9 "⁵After that he poureth water into a bason, and began to wash the disciples' feet, and to wipe them with the towel wherewith he was girded. ⁶Then cometh he to Simon Peter: and Peter saith unto him, Lord, dost thou wash my feet? ⁷Jesus answered and said unto him, What I do thou knowest not now; but thou shalt know hereafter. ⁸Peter saith unto him, Thou shalt never wash my feet. Jesus answered him, If I wash thee not, thou hast no part with me. ⁹Simon Peter saith unto him, Lord, not my feet only, but also my hands and my head."

Ephesians 3:1-6 "¹For this cause I Paul, the prisoner of Jesus Christ for you Gentiles, ²If ye have heard of the dispensation of the grace of God which is given me to youward: ³How that by revelation he made known unto me the mystery; (as I wrote afore in few words, ⁴Whereby, when ye read, ye may understand my knowledge in the mystery of Christ) ⁵Which in other ages was not made known unto the sons of men, as it is now revealed unto his holy apostles and prophets by the Spirit; ⁶That the Gentiles should be fellowheirs, and of the same body, and partakers of his promise in Christ by the gospel."

What The Gentiles/Heathen Shall Know

Exodus 7:5 "And the Egyptians shall know that I am the LORD, when I stretch forth mine hand upon Egypt, and bring out the children of Israel from among them."

Psalm 98:2 "The LORD hath made known his salvation: his righteousness hath he openly shewed in the sight of the heathen."

Ezekiel 36:22-24 "²²Therefore say unto the house of Israel, Thus saith the Lord GOD; I do not this for your sakes, O house of Israel, but for mine holy name's sake, which ye have profaned among the heathen, whither ye went. ²³And I will sanctify my great name, which was profaned among the heathen, which ye have profaned in the midst of them; and the heathen shall know that I am the LORD, saith the Lord GOD, when I shall be sanctified in you before their eyes. ²⁴For I will take you from among the heathen, and gather you out of all countries, and will bring you into your own land."

Ezekiel 36:33-38 "³³Thus saith the Lord GOD; In the day that I shall have cleansed you from all your iniquities I will also cause you to dwell in the cities, and the wastes shall be builded. ³⁴And the desolate land shall be tilled, whereas it lay desolate in the sight of all that passed by. ³⁵And they shall say, This land that was desolate is become like the garden of Eden; and the waste and desolate and ruined cities are become fenced, and are inhabited. ³⁶Then the heathen that are left round about you shall know that I the LORD build the ruined places, and plant that that was desolate: I the LORD have spoken it, and I will do it. ³⁷Thus saith the Lord GOD; I will yet for this be inquired of by the house of Israel, to do it for them; I will increase them with men like a flock. ³⁸As the holy flock, as the flock of Jerusalem in her solemn feasts; so shall the waste cities be filled with flocks of men: and they shall know that I am the LORD."

Ezekiel 39:6-8 "⁶And I will send a fire on Magog, and among them that dwell carelessly in the isles: and they shall know that I am the LORD. ⁷So will I make my holy name known in the midst of my people Israel; and I will not let them pollute my holy name any more: and the heathen shall know that I am the LORD, the Holy One in Israel. ⁸Behold, it is come, and it is done, saith the Lord GOD; this is the day whereof I have spoken."

Ezekiel 39:22-24 "²²So the house of Israel shall know that I am the LORD their God from that day and forward. ²³And the heathen shall know that the house of Israel went into captivity for their iniquity: because they trespassed against me, therefore hid I my face from them, and gave them into the hand of their enemies: so fell they all by the sword. ²⁴According to their uncleanness and according to their transgressions have I done unto them, and hid my face from them."

Colossians 1:26-27 "²⁶Even the mystery which hath been hid from ages and from generations, but now is made manifest to his saints: ²⁷To whom God would make known what is the riches of the glory of this mystery among the Gentiles; which is Christ in you, the hope of glory."

What The Lord Knows
Genesis 3:4-5 "⁴And the serpent said unto the woman, Ye shall not surely die: ⁵For God doth know that in the day ye eat thereof, then your eyes shall be opened, and ye shall be as gods, knowing good and evil."

1 Kings 8:28-39 "²⁸Yet have thou respect unto the prayer of thy servant, and to his supplication, O LORD my God, to hearken unto the cry and to the prayer, which thy servant prayeth before thee to day: ²⁹That thine eyes may be open toward this house night and day, even toward the place of which thou hast said, My name shall be there: that thou mayest hearken unto the prayer which thy servant shall make toward this place. ³⁰And hearken thou to the supplication of thy servant, and of thy people Israel, when they shall pray toward this place: and hear thou in heaven thy dwelling place: and when thou hearest, forgive. ³¹If any man trespass against his neighbour, and an oath be laid upon him to cause him to swear, and the oath come before thine altar in this house: ³²Then hear thou in heaven, and do, and judge thy servants, condemning the wicked, to bring his way upon his head; and justifying the righteous, to give him according to his righteousness. ³³When thy people Israel be smitten down before the enemy, because they have sinned against thee, and shall turn again to thee, and confess thy name, and pray, and make supplication unto thee in this house: ³⁴Then hear thou in heaven, and forgive the sin of thy people Israel, and bring them again unto the land which thou gavest unto their fathers. ³⁵When heaven is shut up, and there is no rain, because they have sinned against thee; if they pray toward this place, and confess thy name, and turn from their sin, when thou afflictest them: ³⁶Then hear thou in heaven, and forgive the sin of thy servants, and of thy people Israel, that thou teach them the good way wherein they should walk, and give rain upon thy land,

which thou hast given to thy people for an inheritance. ³⁷If there be in the land famine, if there be pestilence, blasting, mildew, locust, or if there be caterpiller; if their enemy besiege them in the land of their cities; whatsoever plague, whatsoever sickness there be; ³⁸What prayer and supplication soever be made by any man, or by all thy people Israel, which shall know every man the plague of his own heart, and spread forth his hands toward this house: ³⁹Then hear thou in heaven thy dwelling place, and forgive, and do, and give to every man according to his ways, whose heart thou knowest; (for thou, even thou only, knowest the hearts of all the children of men;)"

1 Chronicles 28:9 "And thou, Solomon my son, know thou the God of thy father, and serve him with a perfect heart and with a willing mind: for the LORD searcheth all hearts, and understandeth all the imaginations of the thoughts: if thou seek him, he will be found of thee; but if thou forsake him, he will cast thee off for ever."

2 Chronicles 6:19-30 "¹⁹Have respect therefore to the prayer of thy servant, and to his supplication, O LORD my God, to hearken unto the cry and the prayer which thy servant prayeth before thee: ²⁰That thine eyes may be open upon this house day and night, upon the place whereof thou hast said that thou wouldest put thy name there; to hearken unto the prayer which thy servant prayeth toward this place. ²¹Hearken therefore unto the supplications of thy servant, and of thy people Israel, which they shall make toward this place: hear thou from thy dwelling place, even from heaven; and when thou hearest, forgive. ²²If a man sin against his neighbour, and an oath be laid upon him to make him swear, and the oath come before thine altar in this house; ²³Then hear thou from heaven, and do, and judge thy servants, by requiting the wicked, by recompensing his way upon his own head; and by justifying the righteous, by giving him according to his righteousness. ²⁴And if thy people Israel be put to the worse before the enemy, because they have sinned against thee; and shall return and confess thy name, and pray and make supplication before thee in this house; ²⁵Then hear thou from the heavens, and forgive the sin of thy people Israel, and bring them again unto the land which thou gavest to them and to their fathers. ²⁶When the heaven is shut up, and there is no rain, because they have sinned against thee; yet if they pray toward this place, and confess thy name, and turn from their sin, when thou dost afflict them; 27Then hear thou from heaven, and forgive the sin of thy servants, and of thy people Israel, when thou hast taught them the good way, wherein they should walk; and send rain upon thy land, which thou hast given unto thy people for an inheritance. 28If there be dearth in the land, if there be pestilence, if there be blasting, or mildew, locusts, or caterpillers; if their enemies besiege them in the cities of their land; whatsoever sore or whatsoever sickness there be: 29Then what prayer or what supplication soever shall be made of any man, or of all thy people Israel, when every one shall know his own sore and his own grief, and shall spread forth his hands in this house: 30Then hear thou from heaven thy dwelling place, and forgive, and render unto every man according unto all his ways, whose heart thou knowest; (for thou only knowest the hearts of the children of men:)"

Job 11:7-11 "7Canst thou by searching find out God? canst thou find out the Almighty unto perfection? 8It is as high as heaven; what canst thou do? deeper than hell; what canst thou know? 9The measure thereof is longer than the earth, and broader than the sea. 10If he cut off, and shut up, or gather together, then who can hinder him? 11For he knoweth vain men: he seeth wickedness also; will he not then consider it?"

Job 28:20-23 "20Whence then cometh wisdom? and where is the place of understanding? 21Seeing it is hid from the eyes of all living, and kept close from the fowls of the air. 22Destruction and death say, We have heard the fame thereof with our ears. 23God understandeth the way thereof, and he knoweth the place thereof."

Job 34:21-25 "21For his eyes are upon the ways of man, and he seeth all his goings. 22There is no darkness, nor shadow of death, where the workers of iniquity may hide themselves. 23For he will not lay upon man more than right; that he should enter into judgment with God. 24He shall break in pieces mighty men without number, and set others in their stead. 25Therefore he knoweth their works, and he overturneth them in the night, so that they are destroyed."

Psalm 1:6 "For the LORD knoweth the way of the righteous: but the way of the ungodly shall perish."

Psalm 37:18 "The LORD knoweth the days of the upright: and their inheritance shall be for ever."

Psalm 69:5 "O God, thou knowest my foolishness; and my sins are not hid from thee."

Psalm 94:3-11 "3LORD, how long shall the wicked, how long shall the wicked triumph? 4How long shall they utter and speak hard things? and all the workers of iniquity boast themselves? 5They break in pieces thy people, O LORD, and afflict thine heritage. 6They slay the widow and the stranger, and murder the fatherless. 7Yet they say, The LORD shall not see, neither shall the God of Jacob regard it. 8Understand, ye brutish among the people: and ye fools, when will ye be wise? 9He that planted the ear, shall he not hear? he that formed the eye, shall he not see? 10He that chastiseth the heathen, shall not he correct? he that teacheth man knowledge, shall not he know? 11The LORD knoweth the thoughts of man, that they are vanity."

Psalm 103:13-14 "13Like as a father pitieth his children, so the LORD pitieth them that fear him. 14For he knoweth our frame; he remembereth that we are dust."

Psalm 139:1-4 "1O LORD, thou hast searched me, and known me. 2Thou knowest my downsitting and mine uprising, thou understandest my thought afar off. 3Thou compassest my path and my lying down, and art acquainted with all my ways. 4For there is not a word in my tongue, but, lo, O LORD, thou knowest it altogether."

Proverbs 24:11-12 "11If thou forbear to deliver them that are drawn unto death, and those that are ready to be slain; 12If thou sayest, Behold, we knew it not; doth not he that pondereth the heart consider it? and he that keepeth thy soul, doth not he know it? and shall not he render to every man according to his works?"

Isaiah 66:17-18 "17They that sanctify themselves, and purify themselves in the gardens behind one tree in the midst, eating swine's flesh, and the abomination, and the mouse, shall be consumed together, saith the LORD. 18For I know their works and their thoughts: it shall come, that I will gather all nations and tongues; and they shall come, and see my glory."

Jeremiah 29:8-11 "⁸For thus saith the LORD of hosts, the God of Israel; Let not your prophets and your diviners, that be in the midst of you, deceive you, neither hearken to your dreams which ye cause to be dreamed. ⁹For they prophesy falsely unto you in my name: I have not sent them, saith the LORD. ¹⁰For thus saith the LORD, That after seventy years be accomplished at Babylon I will visit you, and perform my good word toward you, in causing you to return to this place. ¹¹For I know the thoughts that I think toward you, saith the LORD, thoughts of peace, and not of evil, to give you an expected end."

Daniel 2:20-22 "²⁰Daniel answered and said, Blessed be the name of God for ever and ever: for wisdom and might are his: ²¹And he changeth the times and the seasons: he removeth kings, and setteth up kings: he giveth wisdom unto the wise, and knowledge to them that know understanding: ²²He revealeth the deep and secret things: he knoweth what is in the darkness, and the light dwelleth with him."

Amos 4:13 "For, lo, he that formeth the mountains, and createth the wind, and declareth unto man what is his thought, that maketh the morning darkness, and treadeth upon the high places of the earth, The LORD, The God of hosts, is his name."

Matthew 12:25 "And Jesus knew their thoughts, and said unto them, Every kingdom divided against itself is brought to desolation; and every city or house divided against itself shall not stand."

Matthew 24:29-36 "²⁹Immediately after the tribulation of those days shall the sun be darkened, and the moon shall not give her light, and the stars shall fall from heaven, and the powers of the heavens shall be shaken: ³⁰And then shall appear the sign of the Son of man in heaven: and then shall all the tribes of the earth mourn, and they shall see the Son of man coming in the clouds of heaven with power and great glory. ³¹And he shall send his angels with a great sound of a trumpet, and they shall gather together his elect from the four winds, from one end of heaven to the other. ³²Now learn a parable of the fig tree; When his branch is yet tender, and putteth forth leaves, ye

know that summer is nigh: ³³So likewise ye, when ye shall see all these things, know that it is near, even at the doors. ³⁴Verily I say unto you, This generation shall not pass, till all these things be fulfilled. ³⁵Heaven and earth shall pass away, but my words shall not pass away. ³⁶But of that day and hour knoweth no man, no, not the angels of heaven, but my Father only."

Mark 13:28-33 "²⁸Now learn a parable of the fig tree; When her branch is yet tender, and putteth forth leaves, ye know that summer is near: ²⁹So ye in like manner, when ye shall see these things come to pass, know that it is nigh, even at the doors. ³⁰Verily I say unto you, that this generation shall not pass, till all these things be done. ³¹Heaven and earth shall pass away: but my words shall not pass away. ³²But of that day and that hour knoweth no man, no, not the angels which are in heaven, neither the Son, but the Father. ³³Take ye heed, watch and pray: for ye know not when the time is."

Luke 11:17 "But he, knowing their thoughts, said unto them, Every kingdom divided against itself is brought to desolation; and a house divided against a house falleth."

Luke 16:15 "And he said unto them, Ye are they which justify yourselves before men; but God knoweth your hearts: for that which is highly esteemed among men is abomination in the sight of God."

John 2:24-25 "²⁴But Jesus did not commit himself unto them, because he knew all men, ²⁵And needed not that any should testify of man: for he knew what was in man."

John 6:64 "But there are some of you that believe not. For Jesus knew from the beginning who they were that believed not, and who should betray him."

John 13:1-3 "¹Now before the feast of the passover, when Jesus knew that his hour was come that he should depart out of this world unto the Father, having loved his own which were in the world, he loved them unto the end. ²And supper being ended, the devil having now put into the heart of Judas Iscariot, Simon's son, to betray him; ³Jesus knowing that the Father had given all things into his hands, and that he was come from God, and went to God."

John 13:10-11 "¹⁰Jesus saith to him, He that is washed needeth not save to wash his feet, but is clean every whit: and ye are clean, but not all. ¹¹For he knew who should betray him; therefore said he, Ye are not all clean."

John 16:28-31 "²⁸I came forth from the Father, and am come into the world: again, I leave the world, and go to the Father. ²⁹His disciples said unto him, Lo, now speakest thou plainly, and speakest no proverb. ³⁰Now are we sure that thou knowest all things, and needest not that any man should ask thee: by this we believe that thou camest forth from God. ³¹Jesus answered them, Do ye now believe?"

John 18:4 "Jesus therefore, knowing all things that should come upon him, went forth, and said unto them, Whom seek ye?"

Acts 15:8 "And God, which knoweth the hearts, bare them witness, giving them the Holy Ghost, even as he did unto us."

1 Corinthians 3:20-21 "²⁰And again, The Lord knoweth the thoughts of the wise, that they are vain. ²¹Therefore let no man glory in men. For all things are yours."

1 John 3:20 "For if our heart condemn us, God is greater than our heart, and knoweth all things."

Revelation 2:1-2 "¹Unto the angel of the church of Ephesus write; These things saith he that holdeth the seven stars in his right hand, who walketh in the midst of the seven golden candlesticks; ²I know thy works, and thy labour, and thy patience, and how thou canst not bear them which are evil: and thou hast tried them which say they are apostles, and are not, and hast found them liars."

Revelation 2:8-9 "⁸And unto the angel of the church in Smyrna write; These things saith the first and the last, which was dead, and is alive; ⁹I know thy works, and tribulation, and poverty, (but thou art rich) and I know the blasphemy of them which say they are Jews, and are not, but are the synagogue of Satan."

Revelation 2:12-13 "¹²And to the angel of the church in Pergamos write; These things saith he which hath the sharp sword with two edges; ¹³I know thy works, and where thou dwellest, even where Satan's seat is: and thou holdest fast my name, and hast not denied my faith, even in those days wherein Antipas was my faithful martyr, who was slain among you, where Satan dwelleth."

Revelation 2:18-19 "¹⁸And unto the angel of the church in Thyatira write; These things saith the Son of God, who hath his eyes like unto a flame of fire, and his feet are like fine brass; ¹⁹I know thy works, and charity, and service, and faith, and thy patience, and thy works; and the last to be more than the first."

Revelation 3:1 "And unto the angel of the church in Sardis write; These things saith he that hath the seven Spirits of God, and the seven stars; I know thy works, that thou hast a name that thou livest, and art dead."

Revelation 3:7-8 "⁷And to the angel of the church in Philadelphia write; These things saith he that is holy, he that is true, he that hath the key of David, he that openeth, and no man shutteth; and shutteth, and no man openeth; ⁸I know thy works: behold, I have set before thee an open door, and no man can shut it: for thou hast a little strength, and hast kept my word, and hast not denied my name."

Revelation 3:14-15 "¹⁴And unto the angel of the church of the Laodiceans write; These things saith the Amen, the faithful and true witness, the beginning of the creation of God; ¹⁵I know thy works, that thou art neither cold nor hot: I would thou wert cold or hot."

What The Nations Shall Know

1 Kings 8:60 "That all the people of the earth may know that the LORD is God, and that there is none else."

Psalm 9:20 "Put them in fear, O LORD: that the nations may know themselves to be but men. Selah."

Isaiah 49:26 "And I will feed them that oppress thee with their own flesh; and they shall be drunken with their own blood, as with sweet wine: and all flesh shall know that I the LORD am thy Saviour and thy Redeemer, the mighty One of Jacob."

Ezekiel 38:23 "Thus will I magnify myself, and sanctify myself; and I will be known in the eyes of many nations, and they shall know that I am the LORD."

Romans 16:25-26 "²⁵Now to him that is of power to stablish you according to my gospel, and the preaching of Jesus Christ, according to the revelation of the mystery, which was kept secret since the world began, ²⁶But now is made manifest, and by the scriptures of the prophets, according to the commandment of the everlasting God, made known to all nations for the obedience of faith."

When Knowledge Shall Be Increased
Daniel 12:4 "But thou, O Daniel, shut up the words, and seal the book, even to the time of the end: many shall run to and fro, and knowledge shall be increased."

Where Knowledge Comes From
Proverbs 2:6 "For the LORD giveth wisdom: out of his mouth cometh knowledge and understanding."

Who Conceals Knowledge
Proverbs 10:14 "Wise men lay up knowledge: but the mouth of the foolish is near destruction."

Proverbs 12:23 "A prudent man concealeth knowledge: but the heart of fools proclaimeth foolishness."

Who Deals With Knowledge
Proverbs 13:16 "Every prudent man dealeth with knowledge: but a fool layeth open his folly."

Who Disperses Knowledge
Proverbs 15:7 "The lips of the wise disperse knowledge: but the heart of the foolish doeth not so."

Who Does Not Know God
1 John 3:1-6 "¹Behold, what manner of love the Father hath bestowed upon us, that we should be called the sons of God: therefore the world knoweth us not, because it knew him not. ²Beloved, now are we the sons of God, and it doth not yet appear what we shall be: but we know that, when he shall appear, we shall be like him; for we shall see him as he is. ³And every man that hath this hope in him purifieth himself, even as he is pure. ⁴Whosoever committeth sin transgresseth also the law: for sin is the transgression of the law. ⁵And ye know that he was manifested to take away our sins; and in him is no sin. ⁶Whosoever abideth in him sinneth not: whosoever sinneth hath not seen him, neither known him."

1 John 4:8 "He that loveth not knoweth not God; for God is love."

Who Gets Knowledge
Proverbs 18:15 "The heart of the prudent getteth knowledge; and the ear of the wise seeketh knowledge."

Proverbs 21:11 "When the scorner is punished, the simple is made wise: and when the wise is instructed, he receiveth knowledge."

Who God Gives Knowledge To
Ecclesiastes 2:24-26 "²⁴There is nothing better for a man, than that he should eat and drink, and that he should make his soul enjoy good in his labour. This also I saw, that it was from the hand of God. ²⁵For who can eat, or who else can hasten hereunto, more than I? ²⁶For God giveth to a man that is good in his sight wisdom, and knowledge, and joy: but to the sinner he giveth travail, to gather and to heap up, that he may give to him that is good before God. This also is vanity and vexation of spirit."

Daniel 1:8-17 "⁸But Daniel purposed in his heart that he would not defile himself with the portion of the king's meat, nor with the wine which he drank: therefore he requested of the prince of the eunuchs that he might not defile himself. ⁹Now God had brought Daniel into favour and tender love with the prince of the eunuchs. ¹⁰And the prince of the eunuchs said unto Daniel, I fear my lord the king, who hath appointed your meat and your drink: for why should he see your faces worse liking than the children which are of your sort? then shall ye make me endanger my head to the king. ¹¹Then said Daniel to Melzar, whom the prince of the eunuchs had set over Daniel, Hananiah, Mishael, and Azariah, ¹²Prove thy servants, I beseech thee, ten days; and let them give us pulse to eat, and water to drink. ¹³Then let our countenances be looked upon before thee, and the countenance of the children that eat of the portion of the king's meat: and as thou seest, deal with thy servants. ¹⁴So he consented to them in this matter, and proved them ten days. ¹⁵And at the end of ten days their countenances appeared fairer and fatter in flesh than all the children which did eat the portion of the king's meat. ¹⁶Thus Melzar took away the portion of their meat, and the wine that they should drink; and gave them pulse. ¹⁷As for these four children, God gave them knowledge and skill in all learning and wisdom: and Daniel had understanding in all visions and dreams."

Daniel 2:20-21 "20Daniel answered and said, Blessed be the name of God for ever and ever: for wisdom and might are his: 21And he changeth the times and the seasons: he removeth kings, and setteth up kings: he giveth wisdom unto the wise, and knowledge to them that know understanding."

Who Has Knowledge
Proverbs 14:18 "The simple inherit folly: but the prudent are crowned with knowledge."

2 Peter 1:1-8 "1Simon Peter, a servant and an apostle of Jesus Christ, to them that have obtained like precious faith with us through the righteousness of God and our Saviour Jesus Christ: 2Grace and peace be multiplied unto you through the knowledge of God, and of Jesus our Lord, 3According as his divine power hath given unto us all things that pertain unto life and godliness, through the knowledge of him that hath called us to glory and virtue: 4Whereby are given unto us exceeding great and precious promises: that by these ye might be partakers of the divine nature, having escaped the corruption that is in the world through lust. 5And beside this, giving all diligence, add to your faith virtue; and to virtue knowledge; 6And to knowledge temperance; and to temperance patience; and to patience godliness; 7And to godliness brotherly kindness; and to brotherly kindness charity. 8For if these things be in you, and abound, they make you that ye shall neither be barren nor unfruitful in the knowledge of our Lord Jesus Christ."

Who Has No Knowledge
Isaiah 44:9-19 "9They that make a graven image are all of them vanity; and their delectable things shall not profit; and they are their own witnesses; they see not, nor know; that they may be ashamed. 10 Who hath formed a god, or molten a graven image that is profitable for nothing? 11Behold, all his fellows shall be ashamed: and the workmen, they are of men: let them all be gathered together, let them stand up; yet they shall fear, and they shall be ashamed together. 12The smith with the tongs both worketh in the coals, and fashioneth it with hammers, and worketh it with the strength of his arms: yea, he is hungry, and his strength faileth: he drinketh no water, and is faint. 13The carpenter stretcheth out his rule; he marketh it out with a line; he fitteth it with planes, and he marketh it out with the compass, and maketh it after the figure of a man, according to the beauty of a man; that it may remain in the house. 14He heweth him down cedars, and taketh the cypress and the oak, which he strengtheneth for himself among the trees of the forest: he planteth an ash, and the rain doth nourish it. 15Then shall it be for a man to burn: for he will take thereof, and warm himself; yea, he kindleth it, and baketh bread; yea, he maketh a god, and worshippeth it; he maketh it a graven image, and falleth down thereto. 16He burneth part thereof in the fire; with part thereof he eateth flesh; he roasteth roast, and is satisfied: yea, he warmeth himself, and saith, Aha, I am warm, I have seen the fire: 17And the residue thereof he maketh a god, even his graven image: he falleth down unto it, and worshippeth it, and prayeth unto it, and saith, Deliver me; for thou art my god. 18They have not known nor understood: for he hath shut their eyes, that they cannot see; and their hearts, that they cannot understand. 19And none considereth in his heart, neither is there knowledge nor understanding to say, I have burned part of it in the fire; yea, also I have baked bread upon the coals thereof; I have roasted flesh, and eaten it: and shall I make the residue thereof an abomination? shall I fall down to the stock of a tree?"

Isaiah 45:20 "Assemble yourselves and come; draw near together, ye that are escaped of the nations: they have no knowledge that set up the wood of their graven image, and pray unto a god that cannot save."

1 Timothy 6:3-5 "3If any man teach otherwise, and consent not to wholesome words, even the words of our Lord Jesus Christ, and to the doctrine which is according to godliness; 4He is proud, knowing nothing, but doting about questions and strifes of words, whereof cometh envy, strife, railings, evil surmisings, 5Perverse disputings of men of corrupt minds, and destitute of the truth, supposing that gain is godliness: from such withdraw thyself."

2 Timothy 3:1-7 "1This know also, that in the last days perilous times shall come. 2For men shall be lovers of their own selves, covetous, boasters, proud, blasphemers, disobedient to parents, unthankful, unholy, 3Without natural affection, trucebreakers, false accusers, incontinent, fierce, despisers of those that are good, 4Traitors, heady, highminded, lovers of pleasures more than lovers of God; [5]Having a form of godliness, but denying the power thereof: from such turn away. [6]For of this sort are they which creep into houses, and lead captive silly women laden with sins, led away with divers lusts, Justification [7]Ever learning, and never able to come to the knowledge of the truth."

Who Hates Knowledge
Proverbs 1:22 "How long, ye simple ones, will ye love simplicity? and the scorners delight in their scorning, and fools hate knowledge?"

Who Knowledge Is Easy To
Proverbs 14:6 "A scorner seeketh wisdom, and findeth it not: but knowledge is easy unto him that understandeth."

Who Knows All Things
1 John 2:20-21 "[20]But ye have an unction from the Holy One, and ye know all things. [21]I have not written unto you because ye know not the truth, but because ye know it, and that no lie is of the truth."

Who Knows The Lord
Matthew 11:25-27 "[25]At that time Jesus answered and said, I thank thee, O Father, Lord of heaven and earth, because thou hast hid these things from the wise and prudent, and hast revealed them unto babes. [26]Even so, Father: for so it seemed good in thy sight. [27]All things are delivered unto me of my Father: and no man knoweth the Son, but the Father; neither knoweth any man the Father, save the Son, and he to whomsoever the Son will reveal him."

Luke 10:22 "All things are delivered to me of my Father: and no man knoweth who the Son is, but the Father; and who the Father is, but the Son, and he to whom the Son will reveal him."

John 10:14-16 "[14]I am the good shepherd, and know my sheep, and am known of mine. [15]As the Father knoweth me, even so know I the Father: and I lay down my life for the sheep. [16]And other sheep I have, which are not of this fold: them also I must bring, and they shall hear my voice; and there shall be one fold, and one shepherd."

1 John 2:1-3 "[1]My little children, these things write I unto you, that ye sin not. And if any man sin, we have an advocate with the Father, Jesus Christ the

righteous: [2]And he is the propitiation for our sins: and not for ours only, but also for the sins of the whole world. [3]And hereby we do know that we know him, if we keep his commandments."

1 John 4:7 "Beloved, let us love one another: for love is of God; and every one that loveth is born of God, and knoweth God."

Who Loves Knowledge
Proverbs 12:1 "Whoso loveth instruction loveth knowledge: but he that hateth reproof is brutish."

Who Seeks Knowledge
Proverbs 15:14 "The heart of him that hath understanding seeketh knowledge: but the mouth of fools feedeth on foolishness."

Proverbs 18:15 "The heart of the prudent getteth knowledge; and the ear of the wise seeketh knowledge."

Who Shall Find The Knowledge Of God
Proverbs 2:1-5 "[1]My son, if thou wilt receive my words, and hide my commandments with thee; [2]So that thou incline thine ear unto wisdom, and apply thine heart to understanding; [3]Yea, if thou criest after knowledge, and liftest up thy voice for understanding; [4]If thou seekest her as silver, and searchest for her as for hid treasures; [5]Then shalt thou understand the fear of the LORD, and find the knowledge of God."

Who Shall Know Of Jesus Christ's Doctrine
John 7:16-18 "[16]Jesus answered them, and said, My doctrine is not mine, but his that sent me. [17]If any man will do his will, he shall know of the doctrine, whether it be of God, or whether I speak of myself. [18]He that speaketh of himself seeketh his own glory: but he that seeketh his glory that sent him, the same is true, and no unrighteousness is in him."

Who The Lord Knows
Nahum 1:7 "The LORD is good, a strong hold in the day of trouble; and he knoweth them that trust in him."

John 10:14-16 "[14]I am the good shepherd, and know my sheep, and am known of mine. [15]As the Father knoweth me, even so know I the Father: and I lay down my life for the sheep. [16]And other sheep I have, which are not of this fold: them also

I must bring, and they shall hear my voice; and there shall be one fold, and one shepherd."

John 10:25-27 "²⁵Jesus answered them, I told you, and ye believed not: the works that I do in my Father's name, they bear witness of me. ²⁶But ye believe not, because ye are not of my sheep, as I said unto you. ²⁷My sheep hear my voice, and I know them, and they follow me."

1 Corinthians 8:3 "But if any man love God, the same is known of him."

2 Timothy 2:19 "Nevertheless the foundation of God standeth sure, having this seal, The Lord knoweth them that are his. And, Let every one that nameth the name of Christ depart from iniquity."

Who Uses Knowledge Aright
Proverbs 15:2 "The tongue of the wise useth knowledge aright: but the mouth of fools poureth out foolishness."

Who Will Understand Knowledge
Proverbs 19:25 "Smite a scorner, and the simple will beware: and reprove one that hath understanding, and he will understand knowledge."

Whose Knowledge The Lord Makes Foolish
Isaiah 29:13-14 "¹³Wherefore the Lord said, Forasmuch as this people draw near me with their mouth, and with their lips do honour me, but have removed their heart far from me, and their fear toward me is taught by the precept of men: ¹⁴Therefore, behold, I will proceed to do a marvellous work among this people, even a marvellous work and a wonder: for the wisdom of their wise men shall perish, and the understanding of their prudent men shall be hid."

Isaiah 44:24-25 "²⁴Thus saith the LORD, thy redeemer, and he that formed thee from the womb, I am the LORD that maketh all things; that stretcheth forth the heavens alone; that spreadeth abroad the earth by myself; ²⁵That frustrateth the tokens of the liars, and maketh diviners mad; that turneth wise men backward, and maketh their knowledge foolish."

1 Corinthians 1:20 "Where is the wise? where is the scribe? where is the disputer of this world? hath not God made foolish the wisdom of this world?"

L l

LABOR

God Working In You
Philippians 2:13 "For it is God which worketh in you both to will and to do of his good pleasure."

Labor Profiting
Proverbs 14:23 "In all labour there is profit: but the talk of the lips tendeth only to penury."

Laboring
Ephesians 4:28 "Let him that stole steal no more: but rather let him labour, working with his hands the thing which is good, that he may have to give to him that needeth."

1 Thessalonians 4:11-12 "11And that ye study to be quiet, and to do your own business, and to work with your own hands, as we commanded you; 12That ye may walk honestly toward them that are without, and that ye may have lack of nothing."

Man's Work
1 Corinthians 3:10-15 "10According to the grace of God which is given unto me, as a wise master-builder, I have laid the foundation, and another buildeth thereon. But let every man take heed how he buildeth thereupon. 11For other foundation can no man lay than that is laid, which is Jesus Christ. 12Now if any man build upon this foundation gold, silver, precious stones, wood, hay, stubble; 13Every man's work shall be made manifest: for the day shall declare it, because it shall be revealed by fire; and the fire shall try every man's work of what sort it is. 14If any man's work abide which he hath built thereupon, he shall receive a reward. 15If any man's work shall be burned, he shall suffer loss: but he himself shall be saved; yet so as by fire."

The Labor Of The Righteous
Proverbs 10:16 "The labour of the righteous tendeth to life: the fruit of the wicked to sin."

The Laborers Of The Harvest
Matthew 9:35-38 "35And Jesus went about all the cities and villages, teaching in their synagogues, and preaching the gospel of the kingdom, and healing every sickness and every disease among the people. 36But when he saw the multitudes, he was moved with compassion on them, because they fainted, and were scattered abroad, as sheep having no shepherd. 37Then saith he unto his disciples, The harvest truly is plenteous, but the labourers are few; 38Pray ye therefore the Lord of the harvest, that he will send forth labourers into his harvest."

Luke 10:1-12 "1After these things the Lord appointed other seventy also, and sent them two and two before his face into every city and place, whither he himself would come. 2Therefore said he unto them, The harvest truly is great, but the labourers are few: pray ye therefore the Lord of the harvest, that he would send forth labourers into his harvest. 3Go your ways: behold, I send you forth as lambs among wolves. 4Carry neither purse, nor scrip, nor shoes: and salute no man by the way. 5And into whatsoever house ye enter, first say, Peace be to this house. 6And if the son of peace be there, your peace shall rest upon it: if not, it shall turn to you again. 7And in the same house remain, eating and drinking such things as they give: for the labourer is worthy of his hire. Go not from house to house. 8And into whatsoever city ye enter, and they receive you, eat such things as are set before you: 9And heal the sick that are therein, and say unto them, The kingdom of God is come nigh unto you. 10But into whatsoever city ye enter, and they receive you not, go your ways out into the streets of the same, and say, 11Even the very dust of your city, which cleaveth on us, we do wipe off against you: notwithstanding be ye sure of this, that the kingdom of God is come nigh unto you. 12But I say unto you, that it shall be more tolerable in that day for Sodom, than for that city."

The Recompense Of A Man's Hands
Proverbs 12:14 "A man shall be satisfied with good by the fruit of his mouth: and the recompence of a man's hands shall be rendered unto him."

The Work Of The Lord
John 6:29 "Jesus answered and said unto them, This is the work of God, that ye believe on him whom he hath sent."

Those That Do The Work Of The Lord Deceitfully
Jeremiah 48:10 "Cursed be he that doeth the work of the LORD deceitfully, and cursed be he that keepeth back his sword from blood."

Those That Labor

Proverbs 12:11 "He that tilleth his land shall be satisfied with bread: but he that followeth vain persons is void of understanding."

Proverbs 13:11 "Wealth gotten by vanity shall be diminished: but he that gathereth by labour shall increase."

Proverbs 16:26 "He that laboureth laboureth for himself; for his mouth craveth it of him."

Proverbs 28:19 "He that tilleth his land shall have plenty of bread: but he that followeth after vain persons shall have poverty enough."

Ecclesiastes 5:12 "The sleep of a labouring man is sweet, whether he eat little or much: but the abundance of the rich will not suffer him to sleep."

What Not To Labor For

Proverbs 23:4 "Labour not to be rich: cease from thine own wisdom."

John 6:26-27 "26Jesus answered them and said, Verily, verily, I say unto you, Ye seek me, not because ye saw the miracles, but because ye did eat of the loaves, and were filled. 27Labour not for the meat which perisheth, but for that meat which endureth unto everlasting life, which the Son of man shall give unto you: for him hath God the Father sealed."

What To Labor For

John 6:26-27 "26Jesus answered them and said, Verily, verily, I say unto you, Ye seek me, not because ye saw the miracles, but because ye did eat of the loaves, and were filled. 27Labour not for the meat which perisheth, but for that meat which endureth unto everlasting life, which the Son of man shall give unto you: for him hath God the Father sealed."

Who Labors In Vain

Psalm 127:1 "Except the LORD build the house, they labour in vain that build it: except the LORD keep the city, the watchman waketh but in vain."

Who Refuses To Labor

Proverbs 21:25 "The desire of the slothful killeth him; for his hands refuse to labour."

Who Shall Eat The Fruits Of Their Labor

Psalm 128:1-2 "1Blessed is every one that feareth the LORD; that walketh in his ways. 2For thou shalt eat the labour of thine hands: happy shalt thou be, and it shall be well with thee."

Isaiah 65:22-23 "22They shall not build, and another inhabit; they shall not plant, and another eat: for as the days of a tree are the days of my people, and mine elect shall long enjoy the work of their hands. 23They shall not labour in vain, nor bring forth for trouble; for they are the seed of the blessed of the LORD, and their offspring with them."

1 Corinthians 3:3-9 "3For ye are yet carnal: for whereas there is among you envying, and strife, and divisions, are ye not carnal, and walk as men? 4For while one saith, I am of Paul; and another, I am of Apollos; are ye not carnal? 5Who then is Paul, and who is Apollos, but ministers by whom ye believed, even as the Lord gave to every man? 6I have planted, Apollos watered; but God gave the increase. 7So then neither is he that planteth any thing, neither he that watereth; but God that giveth the increase. 8Now he that planteth and he that watereth are one: and every man shall receive his own reward according to his own labour. 9For we are labourers together with God: ye are God's husbandry, ye are God's building."

Who Shall Not Labor In Vain

Isaiah 65:22-23 "22They shall not build, and another inhabit; they shall not plant, and another eat: for as the days of a tree are the days of my people, and mine elect shall long enjoy the work of their hands. 23They shall not labour in vain, nor bring forth for trouble; for they are the seed of the blessed of the LORD, and their offspring with them."

1 Corinthians 15:58 "Therefore, my beloved brethren, be ye stedfast, unmoveable, always abounding in the work of the Lord, forasmuch as ye know that your labour is not in vain in the Lord."

Who Shall Rest From Their Labors

Isaiah 55:1-2 "1Ho, every one that thirsteth, come ye to the waters, and he that hath no money; come ye, buy, and eat; yea, come, buy wine and milk without money and without price. 2Wherefore do ye spend money for that which is not bread? and your labour for that which satisfieth not? hearken diligently unto me, and eat ye that which is good, and let your soul delight itself in fatness."

Matthew 11:25-30 "²⁵At that time Jesus answered and said, I thank thee, O Father, Lord of heaven and earth, because thou hast hid these things from the wise and prudent, and hast revealed them unto babes. ²⁶Even so, Father: for so it seemed good in thy sight. ²⁷All things are delivered unto me of my Father: and no man knoweth the Son, but the Father; neither knoweth any man the Father, save the Son, and he to whomsoever the Son will reveal him. ²⁸Come unto me, all ye that labour and are heavy laden, and I will give you rest. ²⁹Take my yoke upon you, and learn of me; for I am meek and lowly in heart: and ye shall find rest unto your souls. ³⁰For my yoke is easy, and my burden is light."

Revelation 14:13 "And I heard a voice from heaven saying unto me, Write, Blessed are the dead which die in the Lord from henceforth: Yea, saith the Spirit, that they may rest from their labours; and their works do follow them."

Why You Should Labor

2 Thessalonians 3:8 "Neither did we eat any man's bread for nought; but wrought with labour and travail night and day, that we might not be chargeable to any of you."

LAST DAYS

The Last Days Being Here

Hebrews 1:1-2 "¹God, who at sundry times and in divers manners spake in time past unto the fathers by the prophets, ² Hath in these last days spoken unto us by his Son, whom he hath appointed heir of all things, by whom also he made the worlds."

1 Peter 1:18-20 "¹⁸Forasmuch as ye know that ye were not redeemed with corruptible things, as silver and gold, from your vain conversation received by tradition from your fathers; ¹⁹ But with the precious blood of Christ, as of a lamb without blemish and without spot: ²⁰ Who verily was foreordained before the foundation of the world, but was manifest in these last times for you,"

1 John 2:18-19 "¹⁸Little children, it is the last time: and as ye have heard that antichrist shall come, even now are there many antichrists; whereby we know that it is the last time. ¹⁹ They went out from us, but they were not of us; for if they had been of us, they would no doubt have continued with us: but they went out, that they might be made manifest that they were not all of us."

What Shall Come To Pass In The Last Days

Deuteronomy 4:20-31 "²⁰But the LORD hath taken you, and brought you forth out of the iron furnace, even out of Egypt, to be unto him a people of inheritance, as ye are this day. ²¹Furthermore the LORD was angry with me for your sakes, and sware that I should not go over Jordan, and that I should not go in unto that good land, which the LORD thy God giveth thee for an inheritance: ²²But I must die in this land, I must not go over Jordan: but ye shall go over, and possess that good land. ²³Take heed unto yourselves, lest ye forget the covenant of the LORD your God, which he made with you, and make you a graven image, or the likeness of any thing, which the LORD thy God hath forbidden thee. ²⁴For the LORD thy God is a consuming fire, even a jealous God. ²⁵When thou shalt beget children, and children's children, and ye shall have remained long in the land, and shall corrupt yourselves, and make a graven image, or the likeness of any thing, and shall do evil in the sight of the LORD thy God, to provoke him to anger: ²⁶I call heaven and earth to witness against you this day, that ye shall soon utterly perish from off the land whereunto ye go over Jordan to possess it; ye shall not prolong your days upon it, but shall utterly be destroyed. ²⁷And the LORD shall scatter you among the nations, and ye shall be left few in number among the heathen, whither the LORD shall lead you. ²⁸And there ye shall serve gods, the work of men's hands, wood and stone, which neither see, nor hear, nor eat, nor smell. ²⁹But if from thence thou shalt seek the LORD thy God, thou shalt find him, if thou seek him with all thy heart and with all thy soul. ³⁰When thou art in tribulation, and all these things are come upon thee, even in the latter days, if thou turn to the LORD thy God, and shalt be obedient unto his voice; ³¹(For the LORD thy God is a merciful God;) he will not forsake thee, neither destroy thee, nor forget the covenant of thy fathers which he sware unto them."

Job 19:25-27 "²⁵For I know that my redeemer liveth, and that he shall stand at the latter day upon the earth: ²⁶And though after my skin worms destroy this body, yet in my flesh shall I see God: ²⁷Whom I shall see for myself, and mine eyes shall behold, and not another; though my reins be consumed within me."

Isaiah 2:1-4 "¹the word that Isaiah the son of Amoz saw concerning Judah and Jerusalem. ²And it shall come to pass in the last days, that the mountain of the LORD's house shall be established in the top of the mountains, and shall be exalted above the hills; and all nations shall flow unto it. ³And many people shall go and say, Come ye, and let us go up to the mountain of the LORD, to the house of the God of Jacob; and he will teach us of his ways, and we will walk in his paths: for out of Zion shall go forth the law, and the word of the LORD from Jerusalem. ⁴And he shall judge among the nations, and shall rebuke many people: and they shall beat their swords into plowshares, and their spears into pruninghooks: nation shall not lift up sword against nation, neither shall they learn war any more."

Jeremiah 23:18-20 "¹⁸For who hath stood in the counsel of the LORD, and hath perceived and heard his word? who hath marked his word, and heard it? ¹⁹Behold, a whirlwind of the LORD is gone forth in fury, even a grievous whirlwind: it shall fall grievously upon the head of the wicked. ²⁰The anger of the LORD shall not return, until he have executed, and till he have performed the thoughts of his heart: in the latter days ye shall consider it perfectly."

Jeremiah 30:23-24 "²³Behold, the whirlwind of the LORD goeth forth with fury, a continuing whirlwind: it shall fall with pain upon the head of the wicked. ²⁴The fierce anger of the LORD shall not return, until he have done it, and until he have performed the intents of his heart: in the latter days ye shall consider it."

Ezekiel 38:1-23 "¹And the word of the LORD came unto me, saying, ²Son of man, set thy face against Gog, the land of Magog, the chief prince of Meshech and Tubal, and prophesy against him, ³And say, Thus saith the Lord GOD; Behold I am against thee, O Gog, the chief prince of Meshech and Tubal: ⁴And I will turn thee back, and put hooks into thy jaws, and I will bring thee forth, and all thine army, horses and horsemen, all of them clothed with all sorts of armour, even a great company with bucklers and shields, all of them handling swords: ⁵Persia, Ethiopia, and Libya with them; all of them with shield and helmet: ⁶Gomer, and all his bands; the house of Togarmah of the north quarters, and all his bands: and many people

with thee. ⁷Be thou prepared, and prepare for thyself, thou, and all thy company that are assembled unto thee, and be thou a guard unto them. ⁸After many days thou shalt be visited: in the latter years thou shalt come into the land that is brought back from the sword, and is gathered out of many people, against the mountains of Israel, which have been always waste: but it is brought forth out of the nations, and they shall dwell safely all of them. ⁹Thou shalt ascend and come like a storm, thou shalt be like a cloud to cover the land, thou, and all thy bands, and many people with thee. ¹⁰Thus saith the Lord GOD; It shall also come to pass, that at the same time shall things come into thy mind, and thou shalt think an evil thought: ¹¹And thou shalt say, I will go up to the land of unwalled villages; I will go to them that are at rest, that dwell safely, all of them dwelling without walls, and having neither bars nor gates, ¹²To take a spoil, and to take a prey; to turn thine hand upon the desolate places that are now inhabited, and upon the people that are gathered out of the nations, which have gotten cattle and goods, that dwell in the midst of the land. ¹³Sheba, and Dedan, and the merchants of Tarshish, with all the young lions thereof, shall say unto thee, Art thou come to take a spoil? hast thou gathered thy company to take a prey? to carry away silver and gold, to take away cattle and goods, to take a great spoil? ¹⁴Therefore, son of man, prophesy and say unto Gog, Thus saith the Lord GOD; In that day when my people of Israel dwelleth safely, shalt thou not know it? ¹⁵And thou shalt come from thy place out of the north parts, thou, and many people with thee, all of them riding upon horses, a great company, and a mighty army: ¹⁶And thou shalt come up against my people of Israel, as a cloud to cover the land; it shall be in the latter days, and I will bring thee against my land, that the heathen may know me, when I shall be sanctified in thee, O Gog, before their eyes. ¹⁷Thus saith the Lord GOD; Art thou he of whom I have spoken in old time by my servants the prophets of Israel, which prophesied in those days many years that I would bring thee against them? ¹⁸And it shall come to pass at the same time when Gog shall come against the land of Israel, saith the Lord GOD, that my fury shall come up in my face. ¹⁹For in my jealousy and in the fire of my wrath have I spoken, Surely in that day there shall be a great shaking in the land of Israel; ²⁰So that the fishes of the sea, and the fowls of the heaven, and the beasts of the field, and all creeping things that creep upon the earth, and all the men that are upon the face of the earth, shall shake at my presence, and the mountains shall be thrown down, and the steep places shall fall, and every wall shall fall to the ground. ²¹And I will call for a sword against him throughout all my mountains, saith the Lord GOD: every man's sword shall be against his brother. ²²And I will plead against him with pestilence and with blood; and I will rain upon him, and upon his bands, and upon the many people that are with him, an overflowing rain, and great hailstones, fire, and brimstone. ²³Thus will I magnify myself, and sanctify myself; and I will be known in the eyes of many nations, and they shall know that I am the LORD."

Ezekiel 39:1-24 "¹Therefore, thou son of man, prophesy against Gog, and say, Thus saith the Lord GOD; Behold, I am against thee, O Gog, the chief prince of Meshech and Tubal: ²And I will turn thee back, and leave but the sixth part of thee, and will cause thee to come up from the north parts, and will bring thee upon the mountains of Israel: ³And I will smite thy bow out of thy left hand, and will cause thine arrows to fall out of thy right hand. ⁴Thou shalt fall upon the mountains of Israel, thou, and all thy bands, and the people that is with thee: I will give thee unto the ravenous birds of every sort, and to the beasts of the field to be devoured. ⁵Thou shalt fall upon the open field: for I have spoken it, saith the Lord GOD. ⁶And I will send a fire on Magog, and among them that dwell carelessly in the isles: and they shall know that I am the LORD. ⁷So will I make my holy name known in the midst of my people Israel; and I will not let them pollute my holy name any more: and the heathen shall know that I am the LORD, the Holy One in Israel. ⁸Behold, it is come, and it is done, saith the Lord GOD; this is the day whereof I have spoken. ⁹And they that dwell in the cities of Israel shall go forth, and shall set on fire and burn the weapons, both the shields and the bucklers, the bows and the arrows, and the handstaves, and the spears, and they shall burn them with fire seven years: ¹⁰So that they shall take no wood out of the field, neither cut down any out of the forests; for they shall burn the weapons with fire: and they shall spoil those that spoiled them, and rob those that robbed them, saith the Lord GOD. ¹¹And it shall come to pass in that day,

that I will give unto Gog a place there of graves in Israel, the valley of the passengers on the east of the sea: and it shall stop the noses of the passengers: and there shall they bury Gog and all his multitude: and they shall call it The valley of Hamon-gog. ¹²And seven months shall the house of Israel be burying of them, that they may cleanse the land. ¹³Yea, all the people of the land shall bury them; and it shall be to them a renown the day that I shall be glorified, saith the Lord GOD. ¹⁴And they shall sever out men of continual employment, passing through the land to bury with the passengers those that remain upon the face of the earth, to cleanse it: after the end of seven months shall they search. ¹⁵And the passengers that pass through the land, when any seeth a man's bone, then shall he set up a sign by it, till the buriers have buried it in the valley of Hamon-gog. ¹⁶And also the name of the city shall be Hamonah. Thus shall they cleanse the land. ¹⁷And, thou son of man, thus saith the Lord GOD; Speak unto every feathered fowl, and to every beast of the field, Assemble yourselves, and come; gather yourselves on every side to my sacrifice that I do sacrifice for you, even a great sacrifice upon the mountains of Israel, that ye may eat flesh, and drink blood. ¹⁸Ye shall eat the flesh of the mighty, and drink the blood of the princes of the earth, of rams, of lambs, and of goats, of bullocks, all of them fatlings of Bashan. ¹⁹And ye shall eat fat till ye be full, and drink blood till ye be drunken, of my sacrifice which I have sacrificed for you. ²⁰Thus ye shall be filled at my table with horses and chariots, with mighty men, and with all men of war, saith the Lord GOD. ²¹And I will set my glory among the heathen, and all the heathen shall see my judgment that I have executed, and my hand that I have laid upon them. ²²So the house of Israel shall know that I am the LORD their God from that day and forward. ²³And the heathen shall know that the house of Israel went into captivity for their iniquity: because they trespassed against me, therefore hid I my face from them, and gave them into the hand of their enemies: so fell they all by the sword. ²⁴According to their uncleanness and according to their transgressions have I done unto them, and hid my face from them."

Daniel 8:1-26 "¹In the third year of the reign of king Belshazzar a vision appeared unto me, even unto me Daniel, after that which appeared unto me at the first. ²And I saw in a vision; and it came to pass, when I saw, that I was at Shushan in the palace, which is in the province of Elam; and I saw in a vision, and I was by the river of Ulai. ³Then I lifted up mine eyes, and saw, and, behold, there stood before the river a ram which had two horns: and the two horns were high; but one was higher than the other, and the higher came up last. ⁴I saw the ram pushing westward, and northward, and southward; so that no beasts might stand before him, neither was there any that could deliver out of his hand; but he did according to his will, and became great. ⁵And as I was considering, behold, an he goat came from the west on the face of the whole earth, and touched not the ground: and the goat had a notable horn between his eyes. ⁶And he came to the ram that had two horns, which I had there seen standing before the river, and ran unto him in the fury of his power. ⁷And I saw him come close unto the ram, and he was moved with choler against him, and smote the ram, and brake his two horns: and there was no power in the ram to stand before him, but he cast him down to the ground, and stamped upon him: and there was none that could deliver the ram out of his hand. ⁸Therefore the he goat waxed very great: and when he was strong, the great horn was broken; and for it came up four notable ones toward the four winds of heaven. ⁹And out of one of them came forth a little horn, which waxed exceeding great, toward the south, and toward the east, and toward the pleasant land. ¹⁰And it waxed great, even to the host of heaven; and it cast down some of the host and of the stars to the ground, and stamped upon them. ¹¹Yea, he magnified himself even to the prince of the host, and by him the daily sacrifice was taken away, and the place of his sanctuary was cast down. ¹²And an host was given him against the daily sacrifice by reason of transgression, and it cast down the truth to the ground; and it practised, and prospered. ¹³Then I heard one saint speaking, and another saint said unto that certain saint which spake, How long shall be the vision concerning the daily sacrifice, and the transgression of desolation, to give both the sanctuary and the host to be trodden under foot? ¹⁴And he said unto me, Unto two thousand and three hundred days; then shall the sanctuary be cleansed. ¹⁵And it came to pass, when I, even I Daniel, had seen the vision, and sought for the meaning, then, behold, there stood before me as the appearance of a man. ¹⁶And I heard a man's voice between the banks of Ulai, which called, and said, Gabriel, make this man to understand the vision. ¹⁷So he came near where I stood: and when he came, I was afraid, and fell upon my face: but he said unto me, Understand, O son of man: for at the time of the end shall be the vision. ¹⁸Now as he was speaking with me, I was in a deep sleep on my face toward the ground: but he touched me, and set me upright. ¹⁹And he said, Behold, I will make thee know what shall be in the last end of the indignation: for at the time appointed the end shall be. ²⁰The ram which thou sawest having two horns are the kings of Media and Persia. ²¹And the rough goat is the king of Grecia: and the great horn that is between his eyes is the first king. ²²Now that being broken, whereas four stood up for it, four kingdoms shall stand up out of the nation, but not in his power. ²³And in the latter time of their kingdom, when the transgressors are come to the full, a king of fierce countenance, and understanding dark sentences, shall stand up. ²⁴And his power shall be mighty, but not by his own power: and he shall destroy wonderfully, and shall prosper, and practise, and shall destroy the mighty and the holy people. ²⁵And through his policy also he shall cause craft to prosper in his hand; and he shall magnify himself in his heart, and by peace shall destroy many: he shall also stand up against the Prince of princes; but he shall be broken without hand. ²⁶And the vision of the evening and the morning which was told is true: wherefore shut thou up the vision; for it shall be for many days."

Daniel 12:1-13 "¹And at that time shall Michael stand up, the great prince which standeth for the children of thy people: and there shall be a time of trouble, such as never was since there was a nation even to that same time: and at that time thy people shall be delivered, every one that shall be found written in the book. ²And many of them that sleep in the dust of the earth shall awake, some to everlasting life, and some to shame and everlasting contempt. ³And they that be wise shall shine as the brightness of the firmament; and they that turn many to righteousness as the stars for ever and ever. ⁴But thou, O Daniel, shut up the words, and seal the book, even to the time of the end: many shall run to and fro, and knowledge shall be increased. ⁵Then I Daniel looked, and, behold, there stood other two, the one on this side of the bank of the river, and the other on that side of the bank of the river. ⁶And one said to the man clothed in linen, which was upon the waters of the river, How long shall it be to the end of these wonders? ⁷And I heard the man clothed in linen, which was upon the waters of the river, when he held up his right hand and his left hand unto heaven, and sware by him that liveth for ever that it shall be for a time, times, and an half; and when he shall have accomplished to scatter the power of the holy people, all these things shall be finished. ⁸And I heard, but I understood not: then said I, O my Lord, what shall be the end of these things? ⁹And he said, Go thy way, Daniel: for the words are closed up and sealed till the time of the end. ¹⁰Many shall be purified, and made white, and tried; but the wicked shall do wickedly: and none of the wicked shall understand; but the wise shall understand. ¹¹And from the time that the daily sacrifice shall be taken away, and the abomination that maketh desolate set up, there shall be a thousand two hundred and ninety days. ¹²Blessed is he that waiteth, and cometh to the thousand three hundred and five and thirty days. ¹³But go thou thy way till the end be: for thou shalt rest, and stand in thy lot at the end of the days."

Hosea 3:4-5 "⁴For the children of Israel shall abide many days without a king, and without a prince, and without a sacrifice, and without an image, and without an ephod, and without teraphim: ⁵Afterward shall the children of Israel return, and seek the LORD their God, and David their king; and shall fear the LORD and his goodness in the latter days."

Joel 2:27-32 "²⁷And ye shall know that I am in the midst of Israel, and that I am the LORD your God, and none else: and my people shall never be ashamed. ²⁸And it shall come to pass afterward, that I will pour out my spirit upon all flesh; and your sons and your daughters shall prophesy, your old men shall dream dreams, your young men shall see visions: ²⁹And also upon the servants and upon the handmaids in those days will I pour out my spirit. ³⁰And I will shew wonders in the heavens and in the earth, blood, and fire, and pillars of smoke. ³¹The sun shall be turned into darkness, and the moon into blood, before the great and the terrible day of the LORD come. ³²And it shall come to pass, that whosoever shall call on the name of the

LORD shall be delivered: for in mount Zion and in Jerusalem shall be deliverance, as the LORD hath said, and in the remnant whom the LORD shall call."

Micah 4:1-5 "¹But in the last days it shall come to pass, that the mountain of the house of the LORD shall be established in the top of the mountains, and it shall be exalted above the hills; and people shall flow unto it. ²And many nations shall come, and say, Come, and let us go up to the mountain of the LORD, and to the house of the God of Jacob; and he will teach us of his ways, and we will walk in his paths: for the law shall go forth of Zion, and the word of the LORD from Jerusalem. ³And he shall judge among many people, and rebuke strong nations afar off; and they shall beat their swords into plowshares, and their spears into pruninghooks: nation shall not lift up a sword against nation, neither shall they learn war any more. ⁴But they shall sit every man under his vine and under his fig tree; and none shall make them afraid: for the mouth of the LORD of hosts hath spoken it. ⁵For all people will walk every one in the name of his god, and we will walk in the name of the LORD our God for ever and ever."

Acts 2:17-22 "¹⁷And it shall come to pass in the last days, saith God, I will pour out of my Spirit upon all flesh: and your sons and your daughters shall prophesy, and your young men shall see visions, and your old men shall dream dreams: ¹⁸And on my servants and on my handmaidens I will pour out in those days of my Spirit; and they shall prophesy: ¹⁹And I will shew wonders in heaven above, and signs in the earth beneath; blood, and fire, and vapour of smoke: ²⁰The sun shall be turned into darkness, and the moon into blood, before that great and notable day of the Lord come: ²¹And it shall come to pass, that whosoever shall call on the name of the Lord shall be saved. ²²Ye men of Israel, hear these words; Jesus of Nazareth, a man approved of God among you by miracles and wonders and signs, which God did by him in the midst of you, as ye yourselves also know."

1 Timothy 4:1-5 "¹Now the Spirit speaketh expressly, that in the latter times some shall depart from the faith, giving heed to seducing spirits, and doctrines of devils; ²Speaking lies in hypocrisy; having their conscience seared with a hot iron; ³Forbidding to marry, and commanding to abstain from meats, which God hath created to be received with thanksgiving of them which believe and know the truth. [4]For every creature of God is good, and nothing to be refused, if it be received with thanksgiving: [5]For it is sanctified by the word of God and prayer."

2 Timothy 3:1-9 "[1]This know also, that in the last days perilous times shall come. [2]For men shall be lovers of their own selves, covetous, boasters, proud, blasphemers, disobedient to parents, unthankful, unholy, [3]Without natural affection, trucebreakers, false accusers, incontinent, fierce, despisers of those that are good, [4]Traitors, heady, highminded, lovers of pleasures more than lovers of God; [5]Having a form of godliness, but denying the power thereof: from such turn away. [6]For of this sort are they which creep into houses, and lead captive silly women laden with sins, led away with divers lusts, [7]Ever learning, and never able to come to the knowledge of the truth. [8]Now as Jannes and Jambres withstood Moses, so do these also resist the truth: men of corrupt minds, reprobate concerning the faith. [9]But they shall proceed no further: for their folly shall be manifest unto all men, as theirs also was."

2 Timothy 4:1-4 "[1]I charge thee therefore before God, and the Lord Jesus Christ, who shall judge the quick and the dead at his appearing and his kingdom; [2]Preach the word; be instant in season, out of season; reprove, rebuke, exhort with all longsuffering and doctrine. [3]For the time will come when they will not endure sound doctrine; but after their own lusts shall they heap to themselves teachers, having itching ears; [4]And they shall turn away their ears from the truth, and shall be turned unto fables."

2 Peter 3:1-4 "[1]This second epistle, beloved, I now write unto you; in both which I stir up your pure minds by way of remembrance: [2]That ye may be mindful of the words which were spoken before by the holy prophets, and of the commandment of us the apostles of the Lord and Saviour: [3]Knowing this first, that there shall come in the last days scoffers, walking after their own lusts, [4]And saying, Where is the promise of his coming? for since the fathers fell asleep, all things continue as they were from the beginning of the creation."

1 John 2:18-19 "[18]Little children, it is the last time: and as ye have heard that antichrist shall come, even now are there many antichrists; whereby we know that it is the last time. [19]They went out from us, but they were not of us; for if they had been of us, they would no doubt have continued with us: but they went out, that they might be made manifest that they were not all of us."

Jude 17-19 "[17]But, beloved, remember ye the words which were spoken before of the apostles of our Lord Jesus Christ; [18]How that they told you there should be mockers in the last time, who should walk after their own ungodly lusts. [19]These be they who separate themselves, sensual, having not the Spirit."

Who Will Be Raised Up At The Last Day

John 6:35-40 "[35]And Jesus said unto them, I am the bread of life: he that cometh to me shall never hunger; and he that believeth on me shall never thirst. [36]But I said unto you, That ye also have seen me, and believe not. [37]All that the Father giveth me shall come to me; and him that cometh to me I will in no wise cast out. [38]For I came down from heaven, not to do mine own will, but the will of him that sent me. [39]And this is the Father's will which hath sent me, that of all which he hath given me I should lose nothing, but should raise it up again at the last day. [40]And this is the will of him that sent me, that every one which seeth the Son, and believeth on him, may have everlasting life: and I will raise him up at the last day."

John 6:43-44 "[43]Jesus therefore answered and said unto them, Murmur not among yourselves. [44]No man can come to me, except the Father which hath sent me draw him: and I will raise him up at the last day."

John 6:53-54 "[53]Then Jesus said unto them, Verily, verily, I say unto you, Except ye eat the flesh of the Son of man, and drink his blood, ye have no life in you. [54]Whoso eateth my flesh, and drinketh my blood, hath eternal life; and I will raise him up at the last day."

LAW

Christ Being The End Of The Law

Romans 7:1-25 "[1]Know ye not, brethren, (for I speak to them that know the law,) how that the law hath dominion over a man as long as he liveth? 2 For the woman which hath an husband is bound by the law to her husband so long as he liveth; but if the husband be dead, she is loosed from the law of her husband. 3 So then if, while her husband liveth, she be married to another man, she shall be called an adulteress: but if her husband be dead, she is free from that law; so that she is no adulteress, though she be married to another man. 4 Wherefore, my brethren, ye also are become dead to the law by the body of Christ; that ye should be married to another, even to him who is raised from the dead, that we should bring forth fruit unto God. 5 For when we were in the flesh, the motions of sins, which were by the law, did work in our members to bring forth fruit unto death. 6 But now we are delivered from the law, that being dead wherein we were held; that we should serve in newness of spirit, and not in the oldness of the letter. 7 What shall we say then? Is the law sin? God forbid. Nay, I had not known sin, but by the law: for I had not known lust, except the law had said, Thou shalt not covet. 8 But sin, taking occasion by the commandment, wrought in me all manner of concupiscence. For without the law sin was dead. 9 For I was alive without the law once: but when the commandment came, sin revived, and I died. 10 And the commandment, which was ordained to life, I found to be unto death. 11 For sin, taking occasion by the commandment, deceived me, and by it slew me. 12 Wherefore the law is holy, and the commandment holy, and just, and good. 13 Was then that which is good made death unto me? God forbid. But sin, that it might appear sin, working death in me by that which is good; that sin by the commandment might become exceeding sinful. 14 For we know that the law is spiritual: but I am carnal, sold under sin. 15 For that which I do I allow not: for what I would, that do I not; but what I hate, that do I. 16 If then I do that which I would not, I consent unto the law that it is good. 17 Now then it is no more I that do it, but sin that dwelleth in me. 18 For I know that in me (that is, in my flesh,) dwelleth no good thing: for to will is present with me; but how to perform that which is good I find not. 19 For the good that I would I do not: but the evil which I would not, that I do. 20 Now if I do that I would not, it is no more I that do it, but sin that dwelleth in me. 21 I find then a law, that, when I would do good, evil is present with me. 22 For I delight in the law of God after the inward man: 23 But I see another law in my members, warring against the law of my mind, and bringing me into captivity to the law of sin which is in my members. 24 O wretched man that I am! who shall deliver me from the body of this death? 25 I thank God through Jesus Christ our Lord. So then with the mind I myself serve the law of God; but with the flesh the law of sin."

Romans 8:1-4 "1There is therefore now no condemnation to them which are in Christ Jesus, who walk not after the flesh, but after the Spirit. 2 For the law of the Spirit of life in Christ Jesus hath made me free from the law of sin and death. 3 For what the law could not do, in that it was weak through the flesh, God sending his own Son in the likeness of sinful flesh, and for sin, condemned sin in the flesh: 4 That the righteousness of the law might be fulfilled in us, who walk not after the flesh, but after the Spirit."

Romans 10:4 "For Christ is the end of the law for righteousness to every one that believeth."

2 Corinthians 3:14-16 "14But their minds were blinded: for until this day remaineth the same vail untaken away in the reading of the old testament; which vail is done away in Christ. 15 But even unto this day, when Moses is read, the vail is upon their heart. 16 Nevertheless when it shall turn to the Lord, the vail shall be taken away."

Galatians 2:16-21 "16Knowing that a man is not justified by the works of the law, but by the faith of Jesus Christ, even we have believed in Jesus Christ, that we might be justified by the faith of Christ, and not by the works of the law: for by the works of the law shall no flesh be justified. 17 But if, while we seek to be justified by Christ, we ourselves also are found sinners, is therefore Christ the minister of sin? God forbid. 18 For if I build again the things which I destroyed, I make myself a transgressor. 19 For I through the law am dead to the law, that I might live unto God. 20 I am crucified with Christ: nevertheless I live; yet not I, but Christ liveth in me: and the life which I now live in the flesh I live by the faith of the Son of God, who loved me, and gave himself for me. 21 I do not frustrate the grace of God: for if righteousness come by the law, then Christ is dead in vain."

Galatians 3:10-14 "10For as many as are of the works of the law are under the curse: for it is written,

Cursed is every one that continueth not in all things which are written in the book of the law to do them. [11] But that no man is justified by the law in the sight of God, it is evident: for, The just shall live by faith. [12] And the law is not of faith: but, The man that doeth them shall live in them. [13] Christ hath redeemed us from the curse of the law, being made a curse for us: for it is written, Cursed is every one that hangeth on a tree: [14] That the blessing of Abraham might come on the Gentiles through Jesus Christ; that we might receive the promise of the Spirit through faith."

Galatians 3:19-29 "[19]Wherefore then serveth the law? It was added because of transgressions, till the seed should come to whom the promise was made; and it was ordained by angels in the hand of a mediator. [20] Now a mediator is not a mediator of one, but God is one. [21] Is the law then against the promises of God? God forbid: for if there had been a law given which could have given life, verily righteousness should have been by the law. [22] But the scripture hath concluded all under sin, that the promise by faith of Jesus Christ might be given to them that believe. [23] But before faith came, we were kept under the law, shut up unto the faith which should afterwards be revealed. [24] Wherefore the law was our schoolmaster to bring us unto Christ, that we might be justified by faith. [25] But after that faith is come, we are no longer under a schoolmaster. [26] For ye are all the children of God by faith in Christ Jesus. [27] For as many of you as have been baptized into Christ have put on Christ. [28] There is neither Jew nor Greek, there is neither bond nor free, there is neither male nor female: for ye are all one in Christ Jesus. [29] And if ye be Christ's, then are ye Abraham's seed, and heirs according to the promise."

Galatians 4:3-11 "[3]Even so we, when we were children, were in bondage under the elements of the world: [4] But when the fulness of the time was come, God sent forth his Son, made of a woman, made under the law, [5] To redeem them that were under the law, that we might receive the adoption of sons. [6] And because ye are sons, God hath sent forth the Spirit of his Son into your hearts, crying, Abba, Father. [7] Wherefore thou art no more a servant, but a son; and if a son, then an heir of God through Christ. [8] Howbeit then, when ye knew not God, ye did service unto them which by nature are no gods. [9] But now, after that ye have known God, or rather are known of God, how turn ye again to the weak and beggarly elements, whereunto ye desire again to be in bondage? [10] Ye observe days, and months, and times, and years. [11] I am afraid of you, lest I have bestowed upon you labour in vain."

Ephesians 2:13-15 "[13]But now in Christ Jesus ye who sometimes were far off are made nigh by the blood of Christ. [14] For he is our peace, who hath made both one, and hath broken down the middle wall of partition between us; [15] Having abolished in his flesh the enmity, even the law of commandments contained in ordinances; for to make in himself of twain one new man, so making peace."

Having One Manner Of Law
Leviticus 24:22 "Ye shall have one manner of law, as well for the stranger, as for one of your own country: for I am the LORD your God."

Numbers 15:15-16 "[15]One ordinance shall be both for you of the congregation, and also for the stranger that sojourneth with you, an ordinance for ever in your generations: as ye are, so shall the stranger be before the LORD. [16]One law and one manner shall be for you, and for the stranger that sojourneth with you."

Numbers 15:29 "Ye shall have one law for him that sinneth through ignorance, both for him that is born among the children of Israel, and for the stranger that sojourneth among them."

Jesus Christ Coming To Fulfill The Law
Matthew 5:17-18 "[17]Think not that I am come to destroy the law, or the prophets: I am not come to destroy, but to fulfil. [18]For verily I say unto you, Till heaven and earth pass, one jot or one tittle shall in no wise pass from the law, till all be fulfilled."

The Law Of The Wise
Proverbs 13:14 "The law of the wise is a fountain of life, to depart from the snares of death."

The Lord Being The Lawgiver
Isaiah 33:22 "For the LORD is our judge, the LORD is our lawgiver, the LORD is our king; he will save us."

Isaiah 51:3-7 "[3]For the LORD shall comfort Zion: he will comfort all her waste places; and he will make her wilderness like Eden, and her desert like the garden of the LORD; joy and gladness shall be found therein, thanksgiving, and the voice of melody. [4]Hearken unto me, my people; and give ear unto me, O my nation: for a law shall proceed from me, and I will make my judgment to rest for a light of the people. ⁵My righteousness is near; my salvation is gone forth, and mine arms shall judge the people; the isles shall wait upon me, and on mine arm shall they trust. ⁶Lift up your eyes to the heavens, and look upon the earth beneath: for the heavens shall vanish away like smoke, and the earth shall wax old like a garment, and they that dwell therein shall die in like manner: but my salvation shall be for ever, and my righteousness shall not be abolished. ⁷Hearken unto me, ye that know righteousness, the people in whose heart is my law; fear ye not the reproach of men, neither be ye afraid of their revilings."

James 4:10-12 "¹⁰Humble yourselves in the sight of the Lord, and he shall lift you up. ¹¹Speak not evil one of another, brethren. He that speaketh evil of his brother, and judgeth his brother, speaketh evil of the law, and judgeth the law: but if thou judge the law, thou art not a doer of the law, but a judge. ¹²There is one lawgiver, who is able to save and to destroy: who art thou that judgest another?"

The Reward For Ignoring The Law
Isaiah 5:24 "Therefore as the fire devoureth the stubble, and the flame consumeth the chaff, so their root shall be as rottenness, and their blossom shall go up as dust: because they have cast away the law of the LORD of hosts, and despised the word of the Holy One of Israel."

Hosea 4:6-7 "⁶My people are destroyed for lack of knowledge: because thou hast rejected knowledge, I will also reject thee, that thou shalt be no priest to me: seeing thou hast forgotten the law of thy God, I will also forget thy children. ⁷As they were increased, so they sinned against me: therefore will I change their glory into shame."

Those That Are Justified By The Law
Galatians 5:4-6 "⁴Christ is become of no effect unto you, whosoever of you are justified by the law; ye are fallen from grace. ⁵For we through the Spirit wait for the hope of righteousness by faith. ⁶For in Jesus Christ neither circumcision availeth anything, nor uncircumcision; but faith which worketh by love."

Those That Do By Nature
The Things Contained In The Law
Romans 2:14-15 "¹⁴For when the Gentiles, which have not the law, do by nature the things contained in the law, these, having not the law, are a law unto themselves: ¹⁵Which shew the work of the law written in their hearts, their conscience also bearing witness, and their thoughts the mean while accusing or else excusing one another;)"

Those That Love The Law
Psalm 119:165 "Great peace have they which love thy law: and nothing shall offend them."

Those That Follow The Law
Without Any Faith
Romans 9:30-33 "³⁰What shall we say then? That the Gentiles, which followed not after righteousness, have attained to righteousness, even the righteousness which is of faith. ³¹But Israel, which followed after the law of righteousness, hath not attained to the law of righteousness. ³²Wherefore? Because they sought it not by faith, but as it were by the works of the law. For they stumbled at that stumblingstone; ³³As it is written, Behold, I lay in Sion a stumblingstone and rock of offence: and whosoever believeth on him shall not be ashamed."

Those That Forsake The Law
Proverbs 28:4 "They that forsake the law praise the wicked: but such as keep the law contend with them."

Proverbs 28:9 "He that turneth away his ear from hearing the law, even his prayer shall be abomination."

Those That Keep The Law
Proverbs 28:4 "They that forsake the law praise the wicked: but such as keep the law contend with them."

Proverbs 28:7 "Whoso keepeth the law is a wise son: but he that is a companion of riotous men shameth his father."

Proverbs 29:18 "Where there is no vision, the people perish: but he that keepeth the law, happy is he."

What Is Lawful For Believers
1 Corinthians 6:12 "All things are lawful unto me, but all things are not expedient: all things are lawful for me, but I will not be brought under the power of any."

1 Corinthians 10:23 "All things are lawful for me, but all things are not expedient: all things are lawful for me, but all things edify not."

What Is The Fulfilling Of The Law

Matthew 7:12 "Therefore all things whatsoever ye would that men should do to you, do ye even so to them: for this is the law and the prophets."

Matthew 22:36-40 "³⁶Master, which is the great commandment in the law? ³⁷Jesus said unto him, Thou shalt love the Lord thy God with all thy heart, and with all thy soul, and with all thy mind. ³⁸This is the first and great commandment. ³⁹And the second is like unto it, Thou shalt love thy neighbour as thyself. ⁴⁰On these two commandments hang all the law and the prophets."

Mark 12:28-33 "²⁸And one of the scribes came, and having heard them reasoning together, and perceiving that he had answered them well, asked him, Which is the first commandment of all? ²⁹And Jesus answered him, The first of all the commandments is, Hear, O Israel; The Lord our God is one Lord: ³⁰And thou shalt love the Lord thy God with all thy heart, and with all thy soul, and with all thy mind, and with all thy strength: this is the first commandment. ³¹And the second is like, namely this, Thou shalt love thy neighbour as thyself. There is none other commandment greater than these. ³²And the scribe said unto him, Well, Master, thou hast said the truth: for there is one God; and there is none other but he: ³³And to love him with all the heart, and with all the understanding, and with all the soul, and with all the strength, and to love his neighbour as himself, is more than all whole burnt offerings and sacrifices."

Luke 10:25-28 "²⁵And, behold, a certain lawyer stood up, and tempted him, saying, Master, what shall I do to inherit eternal life? ²⁶He said unto him, What is written in the law? how readest thou? ²⁷And he answering said, Thou shalt love the Lord thy God with all thy heart, and with all thy soul, and with all thy strength, and with all thy mind; and thy neighbour as thyself. ²⁸And he said unto him, Thou hast answered right: this do, and thou shalt live."

Romans 13:8-10 "⁸Owe no man any thing, but to love one another: for he that loveth another hath fulfilled the law. ⁹For this, Thou shalt not commit adultery, Thou shalt not kill, Thou shalt not steal, Thou shalt not bear false witness, Thou shalt not covet; and if there be any other commandment, it is briefly comprehended in this saying, namely, Thou shalt love thy neighbour as thyself. ¹⁰Love worketh

no ill to his neighbour: therefore love is the fulfilling of the law."

Galatians 5:14 "For all the law is fulfilled in one word, even in this; Thou shalt love thy neighbour as thyself."

James 2:8 "If ye fulfil the royal law according to the scripture, Thou shalt love thy neighbour as thyself, ye do well."

What Occurs When There Is No Law

Romans 5:12-13 "¹²Wherefore, as by one man sin entered into the world, and death by sin; and so death passed upon all men, for that all have sinned: ¹³(For until the law sin was in the world: but sin is not imputed when there is no law."

Romans 7:1-8 "¹Know ye not, brethren, (for I speak to them that know the law,) how that the law hath dominion over a man as long as he liveth? ²For the woman which hath an husband is bound by the law to her husband so long as he liveth; but if the husband be dead, she is loosed from the law of her husband. ³So then if, while her husband liveth, she be married to another man, she shall be called an adulteress: but if her husband be dead, she is free from that law; so that she is no adulteress, though she be married to another man. ⁴Wherefore, my brethren, ye also are become dead to the law by the body of Christ; that ye should be married to another, even to him who is raised from the dead, that we should bring forth fruit unto God. ⁵For when we were in the flesh, the motions of sins, which were by the law, did work in our members to bring forth fruit unto death. ⁶But now we are delivered from the law, that being dead wherein we were held; that we should serve in newness of spirit, and not in the oldness of the letter. ⁷What shall we say then? Is the law sin? God forbid. Nay, I had not known sin, but by the law: for I had not known lust, except the law had said, Thou shalt not covet. ⁸But sin, taking occasion by the commandment, wrought in me all manner of concupiscence. For without the law sin was dead."

What The Law Cannot Do

Acts 13:33-39 "³³God hath fulfilled the same unto us their children, in that he hath raised up Jesus again; as it is also written in the second psalm, Thou art my Son, this day have I begotten thee. ³⁴And as concerning that he raised him up from the dead, now no more to return to corruption, he said on this wise, I will give you the sure mercies of David. 35Wherefore he saith also in another psalm, Thou shalt not suffer thine Holy One to see corruption. 36For David, after he had served his own generation by the will of God, fell on sleep, and was laid unto his fathers, and saw corruption: 37But he, whom God raised again, saw no corruption. 38Be it known unto you therefore, men and brethren, that through this man is preached unto you the forgiveness of sins: 39And by him all that believe are justified from all things, from which ye could not be justified by the law of Moses."

Romans 3:20 "Therefore by the deeds of the law there shall no flesh be justified in his sight: for by the law is the knowledge of sin."

Romans 8:1-4 "1There is therefore now no condemnation to them which are in Christ Jesus, who walk not after the flesh, but after the Spirit. 2For the law of the Spirit of life in Christ Jesus hath made me free from the law of sin and death. 3For what the law could not do, in that it was weak through the flesh, God sending his own Son in the likeness of sinful flesh, and for sin, condemned sin in the flesh: 4That the righteousness of the law might be fulfilled in us, who walk not after the flesh, but after the Spirit."

Galatians 2:16 "Knowing that a man is not justified by the works of the law, but by the faith of Jesus Christ, even we have believed in Jesus Christ, that we might be justified by the faith of Christ, and not by the works of the law: for by the works of the law shall no flesh be justified."

Galatians 3:6-11 "6Even as Abraham believed God, and it was accounted to him for righteousness. 7Know ye therefore that they which are of faith, the same are the children of Abraham. 8And the scripture, foreseeing that God would justify the heathen through faith, preached before the gospel unto Abraham, saying, In thee shall all nations be blessed. 9So then they which be of faith are blessed with faithful Abraham. 10For as many as are of the works of the law are under the curse: for it is written, Cursed is every one that continueth not in all things which are written in the book of the law to do them. 11But that no man is justified by the law in the sight of God, it is evident: for, The just shall live by faith."

Hebrews 7:19 "For the law made nothing perfect, but the bringing in of a better hope did; by the which we draw nigh unto God."

Hebrews 10:1-15 "1For the law having a shadow of good things to come, and not the very image of the things, can never with those sacrifices which they offered year by year continually make the comers thereunto perfect. 2For then would they not have ceased to be offered? because that the worshippers once purged should have had no more conscience of sins. 3But in those sacrifices there is a remembrance again made of sins every year. 4For it is not possible that the blood of bulls and of goats should take away sins. 5Wherefore when he cometh into the world, he saith, Sacrifice and offering thou wouldest not, but a body hast thou prepared me: 6In burnt offerings and sacrifices for sin thou hast had no pleasure. 7Then said I, Lo, I come (in the volume of the book it is written of me,) to do thy will, O God. 8Above when he said, Sacrifice and offering and burnt offerings and offering for sin thou wouldest not, neither hadst pleasure therein; which are offered by the law; 9Then said he, Lo, I come to do thy will, O God. He taketh away the first, that he may establish the second. 10By the which will we are sanctified through the offering of the body of Jesus Christ once for all. 11And every priest standeth daily ministering and offering oftentimes the same sacrifices, which can never take away sins: 12But this man, after he had offered one sacrifice for sins for ever, sat down on the right hand of God; 13From henceforth expecting till his enemies be made his footstool. 14For by one offering he hath perfected for ever them that are sanctified. 15Whereof the Holy Ghost also is a witness to us: for after that he had said before,"

What The Law Is

Psalm 19:7 "The law of the LORD is perfect, converting the soul: the testimony of the LORD is sure, making wise the simple."

Psalm 119:72-75 "72The law of thy mouth is better unto me than thousands of gold and silver. 73Thy hands have made me and fashioned me: give me understanding, that I may learn thy commandments. 74They that fear thee will be glad when they see me; because I have hoped in thy word. 75I know, O LORD, that thy judgments are right, and that thou in faithfulness hast afflicted me."

Psalm 119:137-142 "137Righteous art thou, O LORD, and upright are thy judgments. 138Thy testimonies that thou hast commanded are righteous and very faithful. 139My zeal hath consumed me, because mine enemies have forgotten thy words. [140]Thy word is very pure: therefore thy servant loveth it. [141]I am small and despised: yet do not I forget thy precepts. [142]Thy righteousness is an everlasting righteousness, and thy law is the truth."

Proverbs 6:23 "For the commandment is a lamp; and the law is light; and reproofs of instruction are the way of life."

Romans 3:20 "Therefore by the deeds of the law there shall no flesh be justified in his sight: for by the law is the knowledge of sin."

Romans 7:7-16 "[7]What shall we say then? Is the law sin? God forbid. Nay, I had not known sin, but by the law: for I had not known lust, except the law had said, Thou shalt not covet. [8]But sin, taking occasion by the commandment, wrought in me all manner of concupiscence. For without the law sin was dead. [9]For I was alive without the law once: but when the commandment came, sin revived, and I died. [10]And the commandment, which was ordained to life, I found to be unto death. [11]For sin, taking occasion by the commandment, deceived me, and by it slew me. [12]Wherefore the law is holy, and the commandment holy, and just, and good. [13]Was then that which is good made death unto me? God forbid. But sin, that it might appear sin, working death in me by that which is good; that sin by the commandment might become exceeding sinful. [14]For we know that the law is spiritual: but I am carnal, sold under sin. [15]For that which I do I allow not: for what I would, that do I not; but what I hate, that do I. [16]If then I do that which I would not, I consent unto the law that it is good."

1 Corinthians 15:56 "The sting of death is sin; and the strength of sin is the law."

Galatians 3:19-29 "[19]Wherefore then serveth the law? It was added because of transgressions, till the seed should come to whom the promise was made; and it was ordained by angels in the hand of a mediator. [20]Now a mediator is not a mediator of one, but God is one. [21]Is the law then against the promises of God? God forbid: for if there had been a law given which could have given life, verily righteousness should have been by the law. [22]But the scripture hath concluded all under sin, that the promise by faith of Jesus Christ might be given to them that believe. [23]But before faith came, we were kept under the law, shut up unto the faith which should afterwards be revealed. [24]Wherefore the law was our schoolmaster to bring us unto Christ, that we might be justified by faith. [25]But after that faith is come, we are no longer under a schoolmaster. [26]For ye are all the children of God by faith in Christ Jesus. [27]For as many of you as have been baptized into Christ have put on Christ. [28]There is neither Jew nor Greek, there is neither bond nor free, there is neither male nor female: for ye are all one in Christ Jesus. [29]And if ye be Christ's, then are ye Abraham's seed, and heirs according to the promise."

1 Timothy 1:8 "But we know that the law is good, if a man use it lawfully."

What The Law Is Not
Galatians 3:10-12 "[10]For as many as are of the works of the law are under the curse: for it is written, Cursed is every one that continueth not in all things which are written in the book of the law to do them. [11]But that no man is justified by the law in the sight of God, it is evident: for, The just shall live by faith. [12]And the law is not of faith: but, The man that doeth them shall live in them."

When The Law Was A Guide
Luke 16:16-17 "[16]The law and the prophets were until John: since that time the kingdom of God is preached, and every man presseth into it. [17]And it is easier for heaven and earth to pass, than one tittle of the law to fail."

Where The Law Shall Go Forth From
Isaiah 2:1-3 "[1]the word that Isaiah the son of Amoz saw concerning Judah and Jerusalem. [2]And it shall come to pass in the last days, that the mountain of the LORD's house shall be established in the top of the mountains, and shall be exalted above the hills; and all nations shall flow unto it. [3]And many people shall go and say, Come ye, and let us go up to the mountain of the LORD, to the house of the God of Jacob; and he will teach us of his ways, and we will walk in his paths: for out of Zion shall go forth the law, and the word of the LORD from Jerusalem."

Micah 4:1-2 "[1]But in the last days it shall come to pass, that the mountain of the house of the LORD shall be established in the top of the mountains, and it shall be exalted above the hills; and people shall flow unto it. [2]And many nations shall come, and say, Come, and let us go up to the mountain of the LORD, and to the house of the God of Jacob; and he will teach us of his ways, and we will walk in his paths: for the law shall go forth of Zion, and the word of the LORD from Jerusalem."

Who Delights In The Law
Psalm 1:1-2 "[1]Blessed is the man that walketh not in the counsel of the ungodly, nor standeth in the way of sinners, nor sitteth in the seat of the scornful. [2]But his delight is in the law of the LORD; and in his law doth he meditate day and night."

Who Establishes The Law
Romans 3:28-31 "[28]Therefore we conclude that a man is justified by faith without the deeds of the law. [29]Is he the God of the Jews only? is he not also of the Gentiles? Yes, of the Gentiles also: [30]Seeing it is one God, which shall justify the circumcision by faith, and uncircumcision through faith. [31]Do we then make void the law through faith? God forbid: yea, we establish the law."

Who Gave The Law
Deuteronomy 4:44-45 "[44]And this is the law which Moses set before the children of Israel: [45]These are the testimonies, and the statutes, and the judgments, which Moses spake unto the children of Israel, after they came forth out of Egypt,"

John 1:17 "For the law was given by Moses, but grace and truth came by Jesus Christ."

Who Has Fulfilled The Law
Romans 8:1-4 "[1]There is therefore now no condemnation to them which are in Christ Jesus, who walk not after the flesh, but after the Spirit. [2]For the law of the Spirit of life in Christ Jesus hath made me free from the law of sin and death. [3]For what the law could not do, in that it was weak through the flesh, God sending his own Son in the likeness of sinful flesh, and for sin, condemned sin in the flesh: [4]That the righteousness of the law might be fulfilled in us, who walk not after the flesh, but after the Spirit."

Romans 13:8-9 "[8]Owe no man any thing, but to love one another: for he that loveth another hath fulfilled the law. [9]For this, Thou shalt not commit adultery, Thou shalt not kill, Thou shalt not steal, Thou shalt not bear false witness, Thou shalt not covet; and if there be any other commandment, it is briefly comprehended in this saying, namely, Thou shalt love thy neighbour as thyself."

James 2:8 "If ye fulfil the royal law according to the scripture, Thou shalt love thy neighbour as thyself, ye do well."

Who Is Not Under The Law
Galatians 5:16-18 "[16]This I say then, Walk in the Spirit, and ye shall not fulfil the lust of the flesh. [17]For the flesh lusteth against the Spirit, and the Spirit against the flesh: and these are contrary the one to the other: so that ye cannot do the things that ye would. [18]But if ye be led of the Spirit, ye are not under the law."

Who The Law Is Made For
1 Timothy 1:8-10 "[8]But we know that the law is good, if a man use it lawfully; [9]Knowing this, that the law is not made for a righteous man, but for the lawless and disobedient, for the ungodly and for sinners, for unholy and profane, for murderers of fathers and murderers of mothers, for manslayers, [10]For whoremongers, for them that defile themselves with mankind, for menstealers, for liars, for perjured persons, and if there be any other thing that is contrary to sound doctrine."

Why The Law Was Given
Romans 5:18-21 "[18]Therefore as by the offence of one judgment came upon all men to condemnation; even so by the righteousness of one the free gift came upon all men unto justification of life. [19]For as by one man's disobedience many were made sinners, so by the obedience of one shall many be made righteous. [20]Moreover the law entered, that the offence might abound. But where sin abounded, grace did much more abound: [21]That as sin hath reigned unto death, even so might grace reign through righteousness unto eternal life by Jesus Christ our Lord."

LAZINESS

Lazy People
Proverbs 10:4-5 "[4]He becometh poor that dealeth with a slack hand: but the hand of the diligent maketh rich. [5] He that gathereth in summer is a wise son: but he that sleepeth in harvest is a son that causeth shame."

Proverbs 10:26 "As vinegar to the teeth, and as smoke to the eyes, so is the sluggard to them that send him."

Proverbs 12:24 "The hand of the diligent shall bear rule: but the slothful shall be under tribute."

Proverbs 12:27 "The slothful man roasteth not that which he took in hunting: but the substance of a diligent man is precious."

Proverbs 13:4 "The soul of the sluggard desireth, and hath nothing: but the soul of the diligent shall be made fat."

Proverbs 15:19 "The way of the slothful man is as an hedge of thorns: but the way of the righteous is made plain."

Proverbs 18:9 "He also that is slothful in his work is brother to him that is a great waster."

Proverbs 19:15 "Slothfulness casteth into a deep sleep; and an idle soul shall suffer hunger."

Proverbs 19:24 "A slothful man hideth his hand in his bosom, and will not so much as bring it to his mouth again."

Proverbs 20:4 "The sluggard will not plow by reason of the cold; therefore shall he beg in harvest, and have nothing."

Proverbs 21:25-26 "25The desire of the slothful killeth him; for his hands refuse to labour. 26 He coveteth greedily all the day long: but the righteous giveth and spareth not."

Proverbs 22:13 "The slothful man saith, There is a lion without, I shall be slain in the streets."

Proverbs 24:30-34 "30I went by the field of the slothful, and by the vineyard of the man void of understanding; 31 And, lo, it was all grown over with thorns, and nettles had covered the face thereof, and the stone wall thereof was broken down. 32 Then I saw, and considered it well: I looked upon it, and received instruction. 33 Yet a little sleep, a little slumber, a little folding of the hands to sleep: 34 So shall thy poverty come as one that travelleth; and thy want as an armed man."

Proverbs 26:13-16 "13The slothful man saith, There is a lion in the way; a lion is in the streets. 14 As the door turneth upon his hinges, so doth the slothful upon his bed. 15 The slothful hideth his hand in his bosom; it grieveth him to bring it again to his mouth. 16 The sluggard is wiser in his own conceit than seven men that can render a reason."

Not Being Lazy

Proverbs 20:13 "Love not sleep, lest thou come to poverty; open thine eyes, and thou shalt be satisfied with bread."

Romans 12:10-11 "10Be kindly affectioned one to another with brotherly love; in honour preferring one another; 11Not slothful in business; fervent in spirit; serving the Lord."

Hebrews 6:11-12 "11And we desire that every one of you do shew the same diligence to the full assurance of hope unto the end: 12That ye be not slothful, but followers of them who through faith and patience inherit the promises."

What Laziness Does

Proverbs 19:15 "Slothfulness casteth into a deep sleep; and an idle soul shall suffer hunger."

Proverbs 23:20-21 "20Be not among winebibbers; among riotous eaters of flesh: 21For the drunkard and the glutton shall come to poverty: and drowsiness shall clothe a man with rags."

Ecclesiastes 10:18 "By much slothfulness the building decayeth; and through idleness of the hands the house droppeth through."

LEARNING

The Reward For Learning Of The Lord

Isaiah 54:13-14 "13And all thy children shall be taught of the LORD; and great shall be the peace of thy children. 14 In righteousness shalt thou be established: thou shalt be far from oppression; for thou shalt not fear: and from terror; for it shall not come near thee."

Jeremiah 12:16 "And it shall come to pass, if they will diligently learn the ways of my people, to swear by my name, The LORD liveth; as they taught my people to swear by Baal; then shall they be built in the midst of my people."

Matthew 11:25-30 "25At that time Jesus answered and said, I thank thee, O Father, Lord of heaven and earth, because thou hast hid these things from the wise and prudent, and hast revealed them unto babes. 26 Even so, Father: for so it seemed good in thy sight. 27 All things are delivered unto me of my Father: and no man knoweth the Son, but the Father; neither knoweth any man the

Father, save the Son, and he to whomsoever the Son will reveal him. ²⁸ Come unto me, all ye that labour and are heavy laden, and I will give you rest. ²⁹ Take my yoke upon you, and learn of me; for I am meek and lowly in heart: and ye shall find rest unto your souls. ³⁰ For my yoke is easy, and my burden is light."

The Reward For Learning
The Works Of The Heathen
Psalm 106:35-36 "³⁵But were mingled among the heathen, and learned their works. ³⁶And they served their idols: which were a snare unto them."

Those That Learn Of The Lord
John 6:43-45 "⁴³Jesus therefore answered and said unto them, Murmur not among yourselves. ⁴⁴No man can come to me, except the Father which hath sent me draw him: and I will raise him up at the last day. ⁴⁵It is written in the prophets, And they shall be all taught of God. Every man therefore that hath heard, and hath learned of the Father, cometh unto me."

What Increases Learning
Proverbs 16:21 "The wise in heart shall be called prudent: and the sweetness of the lips increaseth learning."

What To Learn
Deuteronomy 5:1 "And Moses called all Israel, and said unto them, Hear, O Israel, the statutes and judgments which I speak in your ears this day, that ye may learn them, and keep, and do them."

Deuteronomy 31:12-13 "¹²Gather the people together, men, and women, and children, and thy stranger that is within thy gates, that they may hear, and that they may learn, and fear the LORD your God, and observe to do all the words of this law: ¹³And that their children, which have not known any thing, may hear, and learn to fear the LORD your God, as long as ye live in the land whither ye go over Jordan to possess it."

Isaiah 1:17 "Learn to do well; seek judgment, relieve the oppressed, judge the fatherless, plead for the widow."

When The World Will Learn Righteousness
Isaiah 26:4-9 "⁴Trust ye in the LORD for ever: for in the LORD JEHOVAH is everlasting strength: ⁵For he bringeth down them that dwell on high;

the lofty city, he layeth it low; he layeth it low, even to the ground; he bringeth it even to the dust. ⁶The foot shall tread it down, even the feet of the poor, and the steps of the needy. ⁷The way of the just is uprightness: thou, most upright, dost weigh the path of the just. ⁸Yea, in the way of thy judgments, O LORD, have we waited for thee; the desire of our soul is to thy name, and to the remembrance of thee. ⁹With my soul have I desired thee in the night; yea, with my spirit within me will I seek thee early: for when thy judgments are in the earth, the inhabitants of the world will learn righteousness."

Whose Ways You Should
Not Learn
Deuteronomy 18:9-14 "⁹When thou art come into the land which the LORD thy God giveth thee, thou shalt not learn to do after the abominations of those nations. ¹⁰There shall not be found among you any one that maketh his son or his daughter to pass through the fire, or that useth divination, or an observer of times, or an enchanter, or a witch, ¹¹Or a charmer, or a consulter with familiar spirits, or a wizard, or a necromancer. ¹²For all that do these things are an abomination unto the LORD: and because of these abominations the LORD thy God doth drive them out from before thee. ¹³Thou shalt be perfect with the LORD thy God. ¹⁴For these nations, which thou shalt possess, hearkened unto observers of times, and unto diviners: but as for thee, the LORD thy God hath not suffered thee so to do."

Proverbs 22:24-25 "²⁴Make no friendship with an angry man; and with a furious man thou shalt not go: ²⁵Lest thou learn his ways, and get a snare to thy soul."

Jeremiah 10:2-5 "²Thus saith the LORD, Learn not the way of the heathen, and be not dismayed at the signs of heaven; for the heathen are dismayed at them. ³For the customs of the people are vain: for one cutteth a tree out of the forest, the work of the hands of the workman, with the axe. ⁴They deck it with silver and with gold; they fasten it with nails and with hammers, that it move not. ⁵They are upright as the palm tree, but speak not: they must needs be borne, because they cannot go. Be not afraid of them; for they cannot do evil, neither also is it in them to do good."

LEGALISM

Liberty Being Threatened By Legalism
Galatians 5:1-13 "¹Stand fast therefore in the liberty wherewith Christ hath made us free, and be not entangled again with the yoke of bondage. ² Behold, I Paul say unto you, that if ye be circumcised, Christ shall profit you nothing. ³ For I testify again to every man that is circumcised, that he is a debtor to do the whole law. ⁴ Christ is become of no effect unto you, whosoever of you are justified by the law; ye are fallen from grace. ⁵ For we through the Spirit wait for the hope of righteousness by faith. ⁶ For in Jesus Christ neither circumcision availeth anything, nor uncircumcision; but faith which worketh by love. ⁷ Ye did run well; who did hinder you that ye should not obey the truth? ⁸ This persuasion cometh not of him that calleth you. ⁹ A little leaven leaveneth the whole lump. ¹⁰ I have confidence in you through the Lord, that ye will be none otherwise minded: but he that troubleth you shall bear his judgment, whosoever he be. ¹¹ And I, brethren, if I yet preach circumcision, why do I yet suffer persecution? then is the offence of the cross ceased. ¹² I would they were even cut off which trouble you. ¹³ For, brethren, ye have been called unto liberty; only use not liberty for an occasion to the flesh, but by love serve one another."

What Legalism Does
2 Corinthians 3:6 "Who also hath made us able ministers of the new testament; not of the letter, but of the spirit: for the letter killeth, but the spirit giveth life."

LENDING

Those That Lend Without Hoping For Anything In Return
Luke 6:33-35 "³³And if ye do good to them which do good to you, what thank have ye? for sinners also do even the same. ³⁴ And if ye lend to them of whom ye hope to receive, what thank have ye? for sinners also lend to sinners, to receive as much again. ³⁵ But love ye your enemies, and do good, and lend, hoping for nothing again; and your reward shall be great, and ye shall be the children of the Highest: for he is kind unto the unthankful and to the evil."

Who Is A Servant To The Lender
Proverbs 22:7 "The rich ruleth over the poor, and the borrower is servant to the lender."

Who Lends
Psalm 37:21 "The wicked borroweth, and payeth not again: but the righteous sheweth mercy, and giveth."

Psalm 112:5 "A good man sheweth favour, and lendeth: he will guide his affairs with discretion."

Who Lends To The Lord
Proverbs 19:17 "He that hath pity upon the poor lendeth unto the LORD; and that which he hath given will he pay him again."

LEVIATHAN

The Lord Destroying The Leviathan
Psalm 74:12-14 "¹²For God is my King of old, working salvation in the midst of the earth. ¹³ Thou didst divide the sea by thy strength: thou brakest the heads of the dragons in the waters. ¹⁴ Thou brakest the heads of leviathan in pieces, and gavest him to be meat to the people inhabiting the wilderness."

Isaiah 27:1 "In that day the LORD with his sore and great and strong sword shall punish leviathan the piercing serpent, even leviathan that crooked serpent; and he shall slay the dragon that is in the sea."

LIFE

How You Should Live Your Life
2 Corinthians 5:14-15 "¹⁴For the love of Christ constraineth us; because we thus judge, that if one died for all, then were all dead: ¹⁵ And that he died for all, that they which live should not henceforth live unto themselves, but unto him which died for them, and rose again."

Galatians 2:20 "I am crucified with Christ: nevertheless I live; yet not I, but Christ liveth in me: and the life which I now live in the flesh I live by the faith of the Son of God, who loved me, and gave himself for me."

Jesus Christ Giving Life
John 6:31-33 "³¹Our fathers did eat manna in the desert; as it is written, He gave them bread from

heaven to eat. [32] Then Jesus said unto them, Verily, verily, I say unto you, Moses gave you not that bread from heaven; but my Father giveth you the true bread from heaven. [33] For the bread of God is he which cometh down from heaven, and giveth life unto the world."

John 6:48-58 "[48]I am that bread of life. [49] Your fathers did eat manna in the wilderness, and are dead. [50] This is the bread which cometh down from heaven, that a man may eat thereof, and not die. [51] I am the living bread which came down from heaven: if any man eat of this bread, he shall live for ever: and the bread that I will give is my flesh, which I will give for the life of the world. [52] The Jews therefore strove among themselves, saying, How can this man give us his flesh to eat? [53] Then Jesus said unto them, Verily, verily, I say unto you, Except ye eat the flesh of the Son of man, and drink his blood, ye have no life in you. [54] Whoso eateth my flesh, and drinketh my blood, hath eternal life; and I will raise him up at the last day. [55] For my flesh is meat indeed, and my blood is drink indeed. [56] He that eateth my flesh, and drinketh my blood, dwelleth in me, and I in him. [57] As the living Father hath sent me, and I live by the Father: so he that eateth me, even he shall live by me. [58] This is that bread which came down from heaven: not as your fathers did eat manna, and are dead: he that eateth of this bread shall live for ever."

John 10:7-10 "[7]Then said Jesus unto them again, Verily, verily, I say unto you, I am the door of the sheep. [8] All that ever came before me are thieves and robbers: but the sheep did not hear them. [9] I am the door: by me if any man enter in, he shall be saved, and shall go in and out, and find pasture. [10] The thief cometh not, but for to steal, and to kill, and to destroy: I am come that they might have life, and that they might have it more abundantly."

Acts 17:23-25 "[23]For as I passed by, and beheld your devotions, I found an altar with this inscription, TO THE UNKNOWN GOD. Whom therefore ye ignorantly worship, him declare I unto you. [24] God that made the world and all things therein, seeing that he is Lord of heaven and earth, dwelleth not in temples made with hands; [25] Neither is worshipped with men's hands,

as though he needed any thing, seeing he giveth to all life, and breath, and all things."

1 John 5:11 "And this is the record, that God hath given to us eternal life, and this life is in his Son."

Revelation 2:8-10 "[8]And unto the angel of the church in Smyrna write; These things saith the first and the last, which was dead, and is alive; [9] I know thy works, and tribulation, and poverty, (but thou art rich) and I know the blasphemy of them which say they are Jews, and are not, but are the synagogue of Satan. [10] Fear none of those things which thou shalt suffer: behold, the devil shall cast some of you into prison, that ye may be tried; and ye shall have tribulation ten days: be thou faithful unto death, and I will give thee a crown of life."

Nobody Living To Himself

Romans 14:7-8 "[7]For none of us liveth to himself, and no man dieth to himself. [8]For whether we live, we live unto the Lord; and whether we die, we die unto the Lord: whether we live therefore, or die, we are the Lord's."

The Gate And Way Which Leads To Life

Proverbs 15:24 "The way of life is above to the wise, that he may depart from hell beneath."

Matthew 7:13-14 "[13]Enter ye in at the strait gate: for wide is the gate, and broad is the way, that leadeth to destruction, and many there be which go in thereat: [14]Because strait is the gate, and narrow is the way, which leadeth unto life, and few there be that find it."

Luke 13:22-24 "[22]And he went through the cities and villages, teaching, and journeying toward Jerusalem. [23]Then said one unto him, Lord, are there few that be saved? And he said unto them, [24]Strive to enter in at the strait gate: for many, I say unto you, will seek to enter in, and shall not be able."

The Lord Being Life

Deuteronomy 30:20 "That thou mayest love the LORD thy God, and that thou mayest obey his voice, and that thou mayest cleave unto him: for he is thy life, and the length of thy days: that thou mayest dwell in the land which the LORD sware unto thy fathers, to Abraham, to Isaac, and to Jacob, to give them."

John 6:31-35 "[31]Our fathers did eat manna in the desert; as it is written, He gave them bread from heaven to eat. ³²Then Jesus said unto them, Verily, verily, I say unto you, Moses gave you not that bread from heaven; but my Father giveth you the true bread from heaven. ³³For the bread of God is he which cometh down from heaven, and giveth life unto the world. ³⁴Then said they unto him, Lord, evermore give us this bread. ³⁵And Jesus said unto them, I am the bread of life: he that cometh to me shall never hunger; and he that believeth on me shall never thirst."

John 6:48-58 "⁴⁸I am that bread of life. ⁴⁹Your fathers did eat manna in the wilderness, and are dead. ⁵⁰This is the bread which cometh down from heaven, that a man may eat thereof, and not die. ⁵¹I am the living bread which came down from heaven: if any man eat of this bread, he shall live for ever: and the bread that I will give is my flesh, which I will give for the life of the world. ⁵²The Jews therefore strove among themselves, saying, How can this man give us his flesh to eat? ⁵³Then Jesus said unto them, Verily, verily, I say unto you, Except ye eat the flesh of the Son of man, and drink his blood, ye have no life in you. ⁵⁴Whoso eateth my flesh, and drinketh my blood, hath eternal life; and I will raise him up at the last day. ⁵⁵For my flesh is meat indeed, and my blood is drink indeed. ⁵⁶He that eateth my flesh, and drinketh my blood, dwelleth in me, and I in him. ⁵⁷As the living Father hath sent me, and I live by the Father: so he that eateth me, even he shall live by me. ⁵⁸This is that bread which came down from heaven: not as your fathers did eat manna, and are dead: he that eateth of this bread shall live for ever."

John 11:25 "Jesus said unto her, I am the resurrection, and the life: he that believeth in me, though he were dead, yet shall he live."

John 14:6 "Jesus saith unto him, I am the way, the truth, and the life: no man cometh unto the Father, but by me."

Acts 3:13-15 "¹³The God of Abraham, and of Isaac, and of Jacob, the God of our fathers, hath glorified his Son Jesus; whom ye delivered up, and denied him in the presence of Pilate, when he was determined to let him go. ¹⁴But ye denied the Holy One and the Just, and desired a murderer to be granted unto you; ¹⁵And killed the Prince of life, whom God hath raised from the dead; whereof we are witnesses."

Colossians 3:4 "When Christ, who is our life, shall appear, then shall ye also appear with him in glory."

1 John 1:1-3 "¹That which was from the beginning, which we have heard, which we have seen with our eyes, which we have looked upon, and our hands have handled, of the Word of life; ²(For the life was manifested, and we have seen it, and bear witness, and shew unto you that eternal life, which was with the Father, and was manifested unto us;) ³That which we have seen and heard declare we unto you, that ye also may have fellowship with us: and truly our fellowship is with the Father, and with his Son Jesus Christ."

The Lord Being The Creator Of All Life

Genesis 2:7 "And the LORD God formed man of the dust of the ground, and breathed into his nostrils the breath of life; and man became a living soul."

Job 33:4-6 "⁴The Spirit of God hath made me, and the breath of the Almighty hath given me life. ⁵If thou canst answer me, set thy words in order before me, stand up. ⁶Behold, I am according to thy wish in God's stead: I also am formed out of the clay."

Isaiah 42:5 "Thus saith God the LORD, he that created the heavens, and stretched them out; he that spread forth the earth, and that which cometh out of it; he that giveth breath unto the people upon it, and spirit to them that walk therein."

John 1:1-4 "¹In the beginning was the Word, and the Word was with God, and the Word was God. ²The same was in the beginning with God. ³All things were made by him; and without him was not any thing made that was made. ⁴In him was life; and the life was the light of men."

Acts 17:23-25 "²³For as I passed by, and beheld your devotions, I found an altar with this inscription, TO THE UNKNOWN GOD. Whom therefore ye ignorantly worship, him declare I unto you. ²⁴God that made the world and all things therein, seeing that he is Lord of heaven and earth, dwelleth not in temples made with hands; ²⁵Neither is worshipped with men's hands, as though he needed any thing, seeing he giveth to all life, and breath, and all things."

The Lord Holding Your Life In His Hands

Psalm 66:8-9 "⁸O bless our God, ye people, and make the voice of his praise to be heard: ⁹Which holdeth our soul in life, and suffereth not our feet to be moved."

What Brings Life

Proverbs 22:4 "By humility and the fear of the LORD are riches, and honour, and life."

What Gives Life

Proverbs 6:20-23 "²⁰My son, keep thy father's commandment, and forsake not the law of thy mother: ²¹Bind them continually upon thine heart, and tie them about thy neck. ²²When thou goest, it shall lead thee; when thou sleepest, it shall keep thee; and when thou awakest, it shall talk with thee. ²³For the commandment is a lamp; and the law is light; and reproofs of instruction are the way of life."

Ecclesiastes 7:12 "For wisdom is a defence, and money is a defence: but the excellency of knowledge is, that wisdom giveth life to them that have it."

2 Corinthians 3:4-6 "⁴And such trust have we through Christ to God-ward: ⁵Not that we are sufficient of ourselves to think any thing as of ourselves; but our sufficiency is of God; ⁶Who also hath made us able ministers of the new testament; not of the letter, but of the spirit: for the letter killeth, but the spirit giveth life."

What Is Life

Deuteronomy 32:45-47 "⁴⁵And Moses made an end of speaking all these words to all Israel: ⁴⁶And he said unto them, Set your hearts unto all the words which I testify among you this day, which ye shall command your children to observe to do, all the words of this law. ⁴⁷For it is not a vain thing for you; because it is your life: and through this thing ye shall prolong your days in the land, whither ye go over Jordan to possess it."

Proverbs 4:13 "Take fast hold of instruction; let her not go: keep her; for she is thy life."

Proverbs 6:23 "For the commandment is a lamp; and the law is light; and reproofs of instruction are the way of life."

Proverbs 10:11 "The mouth of a righteous man is a well of life: but violence covereth the mouth of the wicked."

Proverbs 11:30 "The fruit of the righteous is a tree of life; and he that winneth souls is wise."

Proverbs 13:12 "Hope deferred maketh the heart sick: but when the desire cometh, it is a tree of life."

Proverbs 13:14 "The law of the wise is a fountain of life, to depart from the snares of death."

Proverbs 14:27 "The fear of the LORD is a fountain of life, to depart from the snares of death."

Proverbs 15:4 "A wholesome tongue is a tree of life: but perverseness therein is a breach in the spirit."

Proverbs 16:22 "Understanding is a wellspring of life unto him that hath it: but the instruction of fools is folly."

John 6:63-64 "⁶³It is the spirit that quickeneth; the flesh profiteth nothing: the words that I speak unto you, they are spirit, and they are life. ⁶⁴But there are some of you that believe not. For Jesus knew from the beginning who they were that believed not, and who should betray him."

Romans 8:6 "For to be carnally minded is death; but to be spiritually minded is life and peace."

What Life Is

James 4:14 "Whereas ye know not what shall be on the morrow. For what is your life? It is even a vapour, that appeareth for a little time, and then vanisheth away."

What Man Lives By

Deuteronomy 8:3 "And he humbled thee, and suffered thee to hunger, and fed thee with manna, which thou knewest not, neither did thy fathers know; that he might make thee know that man doth not live by bread only, but by every word that proceedeth out of the mouth of the LORD doth man live."

Isaiah 38:13-16 "¹³I reckoned till morning, that, as a lion, so will he break all my bones: from day even to night wilt thou make an end of me. ¹⁴Like a crane or a swallow, so did I chatter: I did mourn as a dove: mine eyes fail with looking upward: O LORD, I am oppressed; undertake for me. ¹⁵What shall I say? he hath both spoken unto me, and himself hath done it: I shall go softly all my years in the bitterness of my soul. ¹⁶O Lord, by these things men live, and in all these things is the life of my spirit: so wilt thou recover me, and make me to live."

Matthew 4:4 "But he answered and said, It is written, Man shall not live by bread alone, but by every word that proceedeth out of the mouth of God."

Luke 4:4 "And Jesus answered him, saying, It is written, That man shall not live by bread alone, but by every word of God."

What Tends To Life
Proverbs 11:19 "As righteousness tendeth to life: so he that pursueth evil pursueth it to his own death."

Proverbs 19:23 "The fear of the LORD tendeth to life: and he that hath it shall abide satisfied; he shall not be visited with evil."

Where Life Is
Psalm 30:4-5 "⁴Sing unto the LORD, O ye saints of his, and give thanks at the remembrance of his holiness. ⁵For his anger endureth but a moment; in his favour is life: weeping may endure for a night, but joy cometh in the morning."

Proverbs 12:28 "In the way of righteousness is life; and in the pathway thereof there is no death."

Who Is In The Way Of Life
Proverbs 10:17 "He is in the way of life that keepeth instruction: but he that refuseth reproof erreth."

Who Keeps Their Life
Proverbs 13:3 "He that keepeth his mouth keepeth his life: but he that openeth wide his lips shall have destruction."

Who Lives By Jesus Christ
John 6:53-57 "⁵³Then Jesus said unto them, Verily, verily, I say unto you, Except ye eat the flesh of the Son of man, and drink his blood, ye have no life in you. ⁵⁴Whoso eateth my flesh, and drinketh my blood, hath eternal life; and I will raise him up at the last day. ⁵⁵For my flesh is meat indeed, and my blood is drink indeed. ⁵⁶He that eateth my flesh, and drinketh my blood, dwelleth in me, and I in him. ⁵⁷As the living Father hath sent me, and I live by the Father: so he that eateth me, even he shall live by me."

Galatians 2:20 "I am crucified with Christ: nevertheless I live; yet not I, but Christ liveth in me: and the life which I now live in the flesh I live by the faith of the Son of God, who loved me, and gave himself for me."

Who Shall Find Life
Proverbs 8:32-35 "³²Now therefore hearken unto me, O ye children: for blessed are they that keep my ways. ³³Hear instruction, and be wise, and refuse it not. ³⁴Blessed is the man that heareth me, watching daily at my gates, waiting at the posts of my doors. ³⁵For whoso findeth me findeth life, and shall obtain favour of the LORD."

Proverbs 21:21 "He that followeth after righteousness and mercy findeth life, righteousness, and honour."

Matthew 10:38-39 "³⁸And he that taketh not his cross, and followeth after me, is not worthy of me. ³⁹He that findeth his life shall lose it: and he that loseth his life for my sake shall find it."

Matthew 16:24-25 "²⁴Then said Jesus unto his disciples, If any man will come after me, let him deny himself, and take up his cross, and follow me. ²⁵For whosoever will save his life shall lose it: and whosoever will lose his life for my sake shall find it."

Who Shall Live
Leviticus 18:4-5 "⁴Ye shall do my judgments, and keep mine ordinances, to walk therein: I am the LORD your God. ⁵Ye shall therefore keep my statutes, and my judgments: which if a man do, he shall live in them: I am the LORD."

Deuteronomy 4:1 "Now therefore hearken, O Israel, unto the statutes and unto the judgments, which I teach you, for to do them, that ye may live, and go in and possess the land which the LORD God of your fathers giveth you."

Deuteronomy 5:32-33 "³²Ye shall observe to do therefore as the LORD your God hath commanded you: ye shall not turn aside to the right hand or to the left. ³³Ye shall walk in all the ways which the LORD your God hath commanded you, that ye may live, and that it may be well with you, and that ye may prolong your days in the land which ye shall possess."

Deuteronomy 8:1 "All the commandments which I command thee this day shall ye observe to do, that ye may live, and multiply, and go in and possess the land which the LORD sware unto your fathers."

Deuteronomy 16:20 "That which is altogether just shalt thou follow, that thou mayest live, and inherit the land which the LORD thy God giveth thee."

Deuteronomy 30:15-16 "15See, I have set before thee this day life and good, and death and evil; 16In that I command thee this day to love the LORD thy God, to walk in his ways, and to keep his commandments and his statutes and his judgments, that thou mayest live and multiply: and the LORD thy God shall bless thee in the land whither thou goest to possess it."

Nehemiah 9:29-31 "29And testifiedst against them, that thou mightest bring them again unto thy law: yet they dealt proudly, and hearkened not unto thy commandments, but sinned against thy judgments, (which if a man do, he shall live in them;) and withdrew the shoulder, and hardened their neck, and would not hear. 30Yet many years didst thou forbear them, and testifiedst against them by thy spirit in thy prophets: yet would they not give ear: therefore gavest thou them into the hand of the people of the lands. 31Nevertheless for thy great mercies' sake thou didst not utterly consume them, nor forsake them; for thou art a gracious and merciful God."

Proverbs 7:1-3 "1My son, keep my words, and lay up my commandments with thee. 2Keep my commandments, and live; and my law as the apple of thine eye. 3Bind them upon thy fingers, write them upon the table of thine heart."

Proverbs 15:27 "He that is greedy of gain troubleth his own house; but he that hateth gifts shall live."

Isaiah 55:1-3 "1Ho, every one that thirsteth, come ye to the waters, and he that hath no money; come ye, buy, and eat; yea, come, buy wine and milk without money and without price. 2Wherefore do ye spend money for that which is not bread? and your labour for that which satisfieth not? hearken diligently unto me, and eat ye that which is good, and let your soul delight itself in fatness. 3Incline your ear, and come unto me: hear, and your soul shall live; and I will make an everlasting covenant with you, even the sure mercies of David."

Ezekiel 3:21 "Nevertheless if thou warn the righteous man, that the righteous sin not, and he doth not sin, he shall surely live, because he is warned; also thou hast delivered thy soul."

Ezekiel 18:5-9 "5But if a man be just, and do that which is lawful and right, 6And hath not eaten upon the mountains, neither hath lifted up his eyes to the idols of the house of Israel, neither hath defiled his neighbour's wife, neither hath come near to a menstruous woman, 7And hath not oppressed any, but hath restored to the debtor his pledge, hath spoiled none by violence, hath given his bread to the hungry, and hath covered the naked with a garment; 8He that hath not given forth upon usury, neither hath taken any increase, that hath withdrawn his hand from iniquity, hath executed true judgment between man and man, 9Hath walked in my statutes, and hath kept my judgments, to deal truly; he is just, he shall surely live, saith the Lord GOD."

Ezekiel 18:14-19 "14Now, lo, if he beget a son, that seeth all his father's sins which he hath done, and considereth, and doeth not such like, 15That hath not eaten upon the mountains, neither hath lifted up his eyes to the idols of the house of Israel, hath not defiled his neighbour's wife, 16Neither hath oppressed any, hath not withholden the pledge, neither hath spoiled by violence, but hath given his bread to the hungry, and hath covered the naked with a garment, 17That hath taken off his hand from the poor, that hath not received usury nor increase, hath executed my judgments, hath walked in my statutes; he shall not die for the iniquity of his father, he shall surely live. 18As for his father, because he cruelly oppressed, spoiled his brother by violence, and did that which is not good among his people, lo, even he shall die in his iniquity. 19Yet say ye, Why? doth not the son bear the iniquity of the father? When the son hath done that which is lawful and right, and hath kept all my statutes, and hath done them, he shall surely live."

Ezekiel 18:21-23 "21But if the wicked will turn from all his sins that he hath committed, and keep all my statutes, and do that which is lawful and right, he shall surely live, he shall not die. 22All his transgressions that he hath committed, they shall not be mentioned unto him: in his righteousness that he hath done he shall live. 23Have I any pleasure at all that the wicked should die? saith the Lord GOD: and not that he should return from his ways, and live?"

Ezekiel 18:27-32 "27Again, when the wicked man turneth away from his wickedness that he hath committed, and doeth that which is lawful and right, he shall save his soul alive. ²⁸Because he considereth, and turneth away from all his transgressions that he hath committed, he shall surely live, he shall not die. ²⁹Yet saith the house of Israel, The way of the Lord is not equal. O house of Israel, are not my ways equal? are not your ways unequal? ³⁰Therefore I will judge you, O house of Israel, every one according to his ways, saith the Lord GOD. Repent, and turn yourselves from all your transgressions; so iniquity shall not be your ruin. ³¹Cast away from you all your transgressions, whereby ye have transgressed; and make you a new heart and a new spirit: for why will ye die, O house of Israel? ³²For I have no pleasure in the death of him that dieth, saith the Lord GOD: wherefore turn yourselves, and live ye."

Ezekiel 33:14-16 "¹⁴Again, when I say unto the wicked, Thou shalt surely die; if he turn from his sin, and do that which is lawful and right; ¹⁵If the wicked restore the pledge, give again that he had robbed, walk in the statutes of life, without committing iniquity; he shall surely live, he shall not die. ¹⁶None of his sins that he hath committed shall be mentioned unto him: he hath done that which is lawful and right; he shall surely live."

Ezekiel 33:19 "But if the wicked turn from his wickedness, and do that which is lawful and right, he shall live thereby."

Amos 5:4 "For thus saith the LORD unto the house of Israel, Seek ye me, and ye shall live."

Luke 10:25-28 "²⁵And, behold, a certain lawyer stood up, and tempted him, saying, Master, what shall I do to inherit eternal life? ²⁶He said unto him, What is written in the law? how readest thou? ²⁷And he answering said, Thou shalt love the Lord thy God with all thy heart, and with all thy soul, and with all thy strength, and with all thy mind; and thy neighbour as thyself. ²⁸And he said unto him, Thou hast answered right: this do, and thou shalt live."

John 5:24-25 "²⁴Verily, verily, I say unto you, He that heareth my word, and believeth on him that sent me, hath everlasting life, and shall not come into condemnation; but is passed from death unto life. ²⁵Verily, verily, I say unto you, The hour is coming, and now is, when the dead shall hear the voice of the Son of God: and they that hear shall live."

John 6:53-58 "⁵³Then Jesus said unto them, Verily, verily, I say unto you, Except ye eat the flesh of the Son of man, and drink his blood, ye have no life in you. ⁵⁴Whoso eateth my flesh, and drinketh my blood, hath eternal life; and I will raise him up at the last day. ⁵⁵For my flesh is meat indeed, and my blood is drink indeed. ⁵⁶He that eateth my flesh, and drinketh my blood, dwelleth in me, and I in him. ⁵⁷As the living Father hath sent me, and I live by the Father: so he that eateth me, even he shall live by me. ⁵⁸This is that bread which came down from heaven: not as your fathers did eat manna, and are dead: he that eateth of this bread shall live for ever."

John 11:25-26 "²⁵Jesus said unto her, I am the resurrection, and the life: he that believeth in me, though he were dead, yet shall he live: ²⁶And whosoever liveth and believeth in me shall never die. Believest thou this?"

John 14:16-19 "¹⁶And I will pray the Father, and he shall give you another Comforter, that he may abide with you for ever; ¹⁷Even the Spirit of truth; whom the world cannot receive, because it seeth him not, neither knoweth him: but ye know him; for he dwelleth with you, and shall be in you. ¹⁸I will not leave you comfortless: I will come to you. ¹⁹Yet a little while, and the world seeth me no more; but ye see me: because I live, ye shall live also."

John 20:31 "But these are written, that ye might believe that Jesus is the Christ, the Son of God; and that believing ye might have life through his name."

Romans 8:13 "For if ye live after the flesh, ye shall die: but if ye through the Spirit do mortify the deeds of the body, ye shall live."

2 Timothy 2:10-11 "¹⁰Therefore I endure all things for the elect's sakes, that they may also obtain the salvation which is in Christ Jesus with eternal glory. ¹¹It is a faithful saying: For if we be dead with him, we shall also live with him."

Revelation 2:8-10 "⁸And unto the angel of the church in Smyrna write; These things saith the first and the last, which was dead, and is alive; ⁹I know thy works, and tribulation, and poverty, (but thou art rich) and I know the blasphemy of them which say they are Jews, and are not, but are the synagogue of Satan. [10]Fear none of those things which thou shalt suffer: behold, the devil shall cast some of you into prison, that ye may be tried; and ye shall have tribulation ten days: be thou faithful unto death, and I will give thee a crown of life."

Who Shall Lose Their Life
Matthew 10:38-39 "[38]And he that taketh not his cross, and followeth after me, is not worthy of me. [39]He that findeth his life shall lose it: and he that loseth his life for my sake shall find it."

Matthew 16:24-25 "[24]Then said Jesus unto his disciples, If any man will come after me, let him deny himself, and take up his cross, and follow me. [25]For whosoever will save his life shall lose it: and whosoever will lose his life for my sake shall find it."

Mark 8:31-36 "[31]And he began to teach them, that the Son of man must suffer many things, and be rejected of the elders, and of the chief priests, and scribes, and be killed, and after three days rise again. [32]And he spake that saying openly. And Peter took him, and began to rebuke him. [33]But when he had turned about and looked on his disciples, he rebuked Peter, saying, Get thee behind me, Satan: for thou savourest not the things that be of God, but the things that be of men. [34]And when he had called the people unto him with his disciples also, he said unto them, Whosoever will come after me, let him deny himself, and take up his cross, and follow me. [35]For whosoever will save his life shall lose it; but whosoever shall lose his life for my sake and the gospel's, the same shall save it. [36]For what shall it profit a man, if he shall gain the whole world, and lose his own soul?"

Luke 9:22-25 "[22]Saying, The Son of man must suffer many things, and be rejected of the elders and chief priests and scribes, and be slain, and be raised the third day. [23]And he said to them all, If any man will come after me, let him deny himself, and take up his cross daily, and follow me. [24]For whosoever will save his life shall lose it: but whosoever will lose his life for my sake, the same shall save it. [25]For what is a man advantaged, if he gain the whole world, and lose himself, or be cast away?"

Luke 17:33 "Whosoever shall seek to save his life shall lose it; and whosoever shall lose his life shall preserve it."

John 12:25 "He that loveth his life shall lose it; and he that hateth his life in this world shall keep it unto life eternal."

Who Shall Not Live Out Half Their Days
Psalm 55:23 "But thou, O God, shalt bring them down into the pit of destruction: bloody and deceitful men shall not live out half their days; but I will trust in thee."

Who Shall Not See Life
John 3:36 "He that believeth on the Son hath everlasting life: and he that believeth not the Son shall not see life; but the wrath of God abideth on him."

Who Shall Save Their Life
Mark 8:31-35 "[31]And he began to teach them, that the Son of man must suffer many things, and be rejected of the elders, and of the chief priests, and scribes, and be killed, and after three days rise again. [32]And he spake that saying openly. And Peter took him, and began to rebuke him. [33]But when he had turned about and looked on his disciples, he rebuked Peter, saying, Get thee behind me, Satan: for thou savourest not the things that be of God, but the things that be of men. [34]And when he had called the people unto him with his disciples also, he said unto them, Whosoever will come after me, let him deny himself, and take up his cross, and follow me. [35]For whosoever will save his life shall lose it; but whosoever shall lose his life for my sake and the gospel's, the same shall save it."

Luke 9:22-25 "[22]Saying, The Son of man must suffer many things, and be rejected of the elders and chief priests and scribes, and be slain, and be raised the third day. [23]And he said to them all, If any man will come after me, let him deny himself, and take up his cross daily, and follow me. [24]For whosoever will save his life shall lose it: but whosoever will lose his life for my sake, the same shall save it. [25]For what is a man advantaged, if he gain the whole world, and lose himself, or be cast away?"

Luke 17:33 "Whosoever shall seek to save his life shall lose it; and whosoever shall lose his life shall preserve it."

John 12:25 "He that loveth his life shall lose it; and he that hateth his life in this world shall keep it unto life eternal."

Whose Life Will Not Be Preserved
Job 36:5-6 "⁵Behold, God is mighty, and despiseth not any: he is mighty in strength and wisdom. ⁶He preserveth not the life of the wicked: but giveth right to the poor."

LIGHT

The Lamp Of The Wicked
Proverbs 13:9 "The light of the righteous rejoiceth: but the lamp of the wicked shall be put out."

The Light Of The Body
Luke 11:33-36 "³³No man, when he hath lighted a candle, putteth it in a secret place, neither under a bushel, but on a candlestick, that they which come in may see the light. ³⁴The light of the body is the eye: therefore when thine eye is single, thy whole body also is full of light; but when thine eye is evil, thy body also is full of darkness. ³⁵Take heed therefore that the light which is in thee be not darkness. ³⁶If thy whole body therefore be full of light, having no part dark, the whole shall be full of light, as when the bright shining of a candle doth give thee light."

The Light Of The Eyes
Proverbs 15:30 "The light of the eyes rejoiceth the heart: and a good report maketh the bones fat."

The Light Of The Righteous
Proverbs 13:9 "The light of the righteous rejoiceth: but the lamp of the wicked shall be put out."

The Lord Being Light
2 Samuel 22:29 "For thou art my lamp, O LORD: and the LORD will lighten my darkness."

Psalm 27:1 "The LORD is my light and my salvation; whom shall I fear? the LORD is the strength of my life; of whom shall I be afraid?"

Psalm 104:1-2 "¹Bless the LORD, O my soul. O LORD my God, thou art very great; thou art clothed with honour and majesty. ²Who coverest thyself with light as with a garment: who stretchest out the heavens like a curtain."

Isaiah 42:1-7 "¹Behold my servant, whom I uphold; mine elect, in whom my soul delighteth; I have put my spirit upon him: he shall bring forth judgment to the Gentiles. ²He shall not cry, nor lift up, nor cause his voice to be heard in the street. ³A bruised reed shall he not break, and the smoking flax shall he not quench: he shall bring forth judgment unto truth. ⁴He shall not fail nor be discouraged, till he have set judgment in the earth: and the isles shall wait for his law. ⁵Thus saith God the LORD, he that created the heavens, and stretched them out; he that spread forth the earth, and that which cometh out of it; he that giveth breath unto the people upon it, and spirit to them that walk therein: ⁶I the LORD have called thee in righteousness, and will hold thine hand, and will keep thee, and give thee for a covenant of the people, for a light of the Gentiles; ⁷To open the blind eyes, to bring out the prisoners from the prison, and them that sit in darkness out of the prison house."

Isaiah 60:19-20 "¹⁹The sun shall be no more thy light by day; neither for brightness shall the moon give light unto thee: but the LORD shall be unto thee an everlasting light, and thy God thy glory. ²⁰Thy sun shall no more go down; neither shall thy moon withdraw itself: for the LORD shall be thine everlasting light, and the days of thy mourning shall be ended."

Daniel 2:20-22 "²⁰Daniel answered and said, Blessed be the name of God for ever and ever: for wisdom and might are his: ²¹And he changeth the times and the seasons: he removeth kings, and setteth up kings: he giveth wisdom unto the wise, and knowledge to them that know understanding: ²²He revealeth the deep and secret things: he knoweth what is in the darkness, and the light dwelleth with him."

Micah 7:8 "Rejoice not against me, O mine enemy: when I fall, I shall arise; when I sit in darkness, the LORD shall be a light unto me."

John 1:1-9 "¹In the beginning was the Word, and the Word was with God, and the Word was God. ²The same was in the beginning with God. ³All things were made by him; and without him was not any thing made that was made. ⁴In him was life; and the life was the light of men. ⁵And the light shineth in darkness; and the darkness comprehended it not. ⁶There was a man sent from God, whose name was John. ⁷The same came for a witness, to bear witness of the Light, that all men through him might believe. [8]He was not that Light, but was sent to bear witness of that Light. [9]That was the true Light, which lighteth every man that cometh into the world."

John 3:17-19 "[17]For God sent not his Son into the world to condemn the world; but that the world through him might be saved. [18]He that believeth on him is not condemned: but he that believeth not is condemned already, because he hath not believed in the name of the only begotten Son of God. [19]And this is the condemnation, that light is come into the world, and men loved darkness rather than light, because their deeds were evil."

John 8:12 "Then spake Jesus again unto them, saying, I am the light of the world: he that followeth me shall not walk in darkness, but shall have the light of life."

John 9:3-5 "[3]Jesus answered, Neither hath this man sinned, nor his parents: but that the works of God should be made manifest in him. [4]I must work the works of him that sent me, while it is day: the night cometh, when no man can work. [5]As long as I am in the world, I am the light of the world."

John 12:35-36 "[35]Then Jesus said unto them, Yet a little while is the light with you. Walk while ye have the light, lest darkness come upon you: for he that walketh in darkness knoweth not whither he goeth. [36]While ye have light, believe in the light, that ye may be the children of light. These things spake Jesus, and departed, and did hide himself from them."

John 12:44-46 "[44]Jesus cried and said, He that believeth on me, believeth not on me, but on him that sent me. [45]And he that seeth me seeth him that sent me. [46]I am come a light into the world, that whosoever believeth on me should not abide in darkness."

1 John 1:5 "This then is the message which we have heard of him, and declare unto you, that God is light, and in him is no darkness at all."

Revelation 21:21-23 "[21]And the twelve gates were twelve pearls; every several gate was of one pearl: and the street of the city was pure gold, as it were transparent glass. [22]And I saw no temple therein: for the Lord God Almighty and the Lamb are the temple of it. [23]And the city had no need of the sun, neither of the moon, to shine in it: for the glory of God did lighten it, and the Lamb is the light thereof."

Revelation 22:16 "I Jesus have sent mine angel to testify unto you these things in the churches. I am the root and the offspring of David, and the bright and morning star."

The Lord Being The Creator Of Light
Genesis 1:1-5 "[1]In the beginning God created the Heaven and the earth. [2]And the earth was without form, and void; and darkness was upon the face of the deep. And the Spirit of God moved upon the face of the waters. [3]And God said, Let there be light: and there was light. [4]And God saw the light, that it was good: and God divided the light from the darkness. [5]And God called the light Day, and the darkness he called Night. And the evening and the morning were the first day."

Isaiah 45:7 "I form the light, and create darkness: I make peace, and create evil: I the LORD do all these things."

2 Corinthians 4:6 "For God, who commanded the light to shine out of darkness, hath shined in our hearts, to give the light of the knowledge of the glory of God in the face of Jesus Christ."

The Lord Lighting Darkness
2 Samuel 22:29 "For thou art my lamp, O LORD: and the LORD will lighten my darkness."

Psalm 18:28 "For thou wilt light my candle: the LORD my God will enlighten my darkness."

Proverbs 29:13 "The poor and the deceitful man meet together: the LORD lighteneth both their eyes."

1 Corinthians 4:5 "Therefore judge nothing before the time, until the Lord come, who both will bring to light the hidden things of darkness, and will make manifest the counsels of the hearts: and then shall every man have praise of God."

The Lord Showing Light
Psalm 118:27 "God is the LORD, which hath shewed us light: bind the sacrifice with cords, even unto the horns of the altar."

Acts 26:23 "That Christ should suffer, and that he should be the first that should rise from the dead, and should shew light unto the people, and to the Gentiles."

Those That Put Darkness For Light, And Light For Darkness

Isaiah 5:20 "Woe unto them that call evil good, and good evil; that put darkness for light, and light for darkness; that put bitter for sweet, and sweet for bitter!"

Those That Walk In The Light

John 11:9-10 "⁹Jesus answered, Are there not twelve hours in the day? If any man walk in the day, he stumbleth not, because he seeth the light of this world. ¹⁰But if a man walk in the night, he stumbleth, because there is no light in him."

John 12:35-36 "³⁵Then Jesus said unto them, Yet a little while is the light with you. Walk while ye have the light, lest darkness come upon you: for he that walketh in darkness knoweth not whither he goeth. ³⁶While ye have light, believe in the light, that ye may be the children of light. These things spake Jesus, and departed, and did hide himself from them."

1 John 1:7 "But if we walk in the light, as he is in the light, we have fellowship one with another, and the blood of Jesus Christ his Son cleanseth us from all sin."

What Gives Light

Psalm 119:126-130 "¹²⁶It is time for thee, LORD, to work: for they have made void thy law. ¹²⁷Therefore I love thy commandments above gold; yea, above fine gold. ¹²⁸Therefore I esteem all thy precepts concerning all things to be right; and I hate every false way. ¹²⁹Thy testimonies are wonderful: therefore doth my soul keep them. ¹³⁰The entrance of thy words giveth light; it giveth understanding unto the simple."

What Is Light

Proverbs 6:23 "For the commandment is a lamp; and the law is light; and reproofs of instruction are the way of life."

Proverbs 20:27 "The spirit of man is the candle of the LORD, searching all the inward parts of the belly."

Ephesians 5:13 "But all things that are reproved are made manifest by the light: for whatsoever doth make manifest is light."

Who Abides In The Light

1 John 2:7-10 "⁷Brethren, I write no new commandment unto you, but an old commandment which ye had from the beginning. The old commandment is the word which ye have heard from the beginning. ⁸Again, a new commandment I write unto you, which thing is true in him and in you: because the darkness is past, and the true light now shineth. ⁹He that saith he is in the light, and hateth his brother, is in darkness even until now. ¹⁰He that loveth his brother abideth in the light, and there is none occasion of stumbling in him."

Who Comes To The Light

John 3:21 "But he that doeth truth cometh to the light, that his deeds may be made manifest, that they are wrought in God."

Who Does Not Come To The Light

John 3:20 "For every one that doeth evil hateth the light, neither cometh to the light, lest his deeds should be reproved."

Who Hates The Light

John 3:20 "For every one that doeth evil hateth the light, neither cometh to the light, lest his deeds should be reproved."

Who Is A Light

Matthew 5:1-16 "¹And seeing the multitudes, he went up into a mountain: and when he was set, his disciples came unto him: ²And he opened his mouth, and taught them, saying, ³Blessed are the poor in spirit: for theirs is the kingdom of heaven. ⁴Blessed are they that mourn: for they shall be comforted. ⁵Blessed are the meek: for they shall inherit the earth. ⁶Blessed are they which do hunger and thirst after righteousness: for they shall be filled. ⁷Blessed are the merciful: for they shall obtain mercy. ⁸Blessed are the pure in heart: for they shall see God. ⁹Blessed are the peacemakers: for they shall be called the children of God. ¹⁰Blessed are they which are persecuted for righteousness' sake: for theirs is the kingdom of heaven. ¹¹Blessed are ye, when men shall revile you, and persecute you, and shall say all manner of evil against you falsely, for my sake. ¹²Rejoice, and be exceeding glad: for great is your reward in heaven: for so persecuted they the prophets which were before you. ¹³Ye are the salt of the earth: but if the salt have lost his savour, wherewith shall it be salted? it is thenceforth good for nothing, but to be cast out, and to be trodden under foot of men. ¹⁴Ye are the light of the world. A city that is set on an hill cannot be hid. ¹⁵Neither do men light a candle, and put it under a bushel, but on a candlestick; and it giveth light unto all that are in the house. [16]Let your light so shine before men, that they may see your good works, and glorify your Father which is in heaven."

John 12:35-36 "[35]Then Jesus said unto them, Yet a little while is the light with you. Walk while ye have the light, lest darkness come upon you: for he that walketh in darkness knoweth not whither he goeth. [36]While ye have light, believe in the light, that ye may be the children of light. These things spake Jesus, and departed, and did hide himself from them."

Ephesians 5:1-8 "[1]Be ye therefore followers of God, as dear children; [2]And walk in love, as Christ also hath loved us, and hath given himself for us an offering and a sacrifice to God for a sweetsmelling savour. [3]But fornication, and all uncleanness, or covetousness, let it not be once named among you, as becometh saints; [4]Neither filthiness, nor foolish talking, nor jesting, which are not convenient: but rather giving of thanks. [5]For this ye know, that no whoremonger, nor unclean person, nor covetous man, who is an idolater, hath any inheritance in the kingdom of Christ and of God. [6]Let no man deceive you with vain words: for because of these things cometh the wrath of God upon the children of disobedience. [7]Be not ye therefore partakers with them. [8]For ye were sometimes darkness, but now are ye light in the Lord: walk as children of light."

Philippians 2:14-15 "[14]Do all things without murmurings and disputings: [15]That ye may be blameless and harmless, the sons of God, without rebuke, in the midst of a crooked and perverse nation, among whom ye shine as lights in the world."

1 Thessalonians 5:1-5 "[1]But of the times and the seasons, brethren, ye have no need that I write unto you. [2]For yourselves know perfectly that the day of the Lord so cometh as a thief in the night. [3]For when they shall say, Peace and safety; then sudden destruction cometh upon them, as travail upon a woman with child; and they shall not escape. [4]But ye, brethren, are not in darkness, that that day should overtake you as a thief. [5]Ye are all the children of light, and the children of the day: we are not of the night, nor of darkness."

Who Shall See The Light
Job 33:27-30 "[27]He looketh upon men, and if any say, I have sinned, and perverted that which was right, and it profited me not; [28]He will deliver his soul from going into the pit, and his life shall see the light. [29]Lo, all these things worketh God oftentimes with man, [30]To bring back his soul from the pit, to be enlightened with the light of the living."

Psalm 36:7-9 "[7]How excellent is thy lovingkindness, O God! therefore the children of men put their trust under the shadow of thy wings. [8]They shall be abundantly satisfied with the fatness of thy house; and thou shalt make them drink of the river of thy pleasures. [9]For with thee is the fountain of life: in thy light shall we see light."

Who Shall Walk In The Light
John 8:12 "Then spake Jesus again unto them, saying, I am the light of the world: he that followeth me shall not walk in darkness, but shall have the light of life."

John 12:44-46 "[44]Jesus cried and said, He that believeth on me, believeth not on me, but on him that sent me. [45]And he that seeth me seeth him that sent me. [46]I am come a light into the world, that whosoever believeth on me should not abide in darkness."

Who The Lord Gives Light To
Ephesians 5:14 "Wherefore he saith, Awake thou that sleepest, and arise from the dead, and Christ shall give thee light."

Revelation 22:3-5 "[3]And there shall be no more curse: but the throne of God and of the Lamb shall be in it; and his servants shall serve him: [4]And they shall see his face; and his name shall be in their foreheads. [5]And there shall be no night there; and they need no candle, neither light of the sun; for the Lord God giveth them light: and they shall reign for ever and ever."

LIKEMINDEDNESS

Being Likeminded
Romans 12:16 "Be of the same mind one toward another. Mind not high things, but condescend to men of low estate. Be not wise in your own conceits."

Romans 15:5-6 "⁵Now the God of patience and consolation grant you to be likeminded one toward another according to Christ Jesus: ⁶ That ye may with one mind and one mouth glorify God, even the Father of our Lord Jesus Christ."

1 Corinthians 1:10 "Now I beseech you, brethren, by the name of our Lord Jesus Christ, that ye all speak the same thing, and that there be no divisions among you; but that ye be perfectly joined together in the same mind and in the same judgment."

2 Corinthians 13:11 "Finally, brethren, farewell. Be perfect, be of good comfort, be of one mind, live in peace; and the God of love and peace shall be with you."

Philippians 1:27 "Only let your conversation be as it becometh the gospel of Christ: that whether I come and see you, or else be absent, I may hear of your affairs, that ye stand fast in one spirit, with one mind striving together for the faith of the gospel."

Philippians 2:2 "Fulfil ye my joy, that ye be likeminded, having the same love, being of one accord, of one mind."

Philippians 3:14-16 "¹⁴I press toward the mark for the prize of the high calling of God in Christ Jesus. ¹⁵ Let us therefore, as many as be perfect, be thus minded: and if in any thing ye be otherwise minded, God shall reveal even this unto you. ¹⁶ Nevertheless, whereto we have already attained, let us walk by the same rule, let us mind the same thing."

Philippians 4:2 "I beseech Euodias, and beseech Syntyche, that they be of the same mind in the Lord."

1 Peter 3:8 "Finally, be ye all of one mind, having compassion one of another, love as brethren, be pitiful, be courteous."

LIVESTOCK

Laws Concerning Livestock
Exodus 21:28-36 "²⁸If an ox gore a man or a woman, that they die: then the ox shall be surely stoned, and his flesh shall not be eaten; but the owner of the ox shall be quit. ²⁹ But if the ox were wont to push with his horn in time past, and it hath been testified to his owner, and he hath not kept him in, but that he hath killed a man or a woman; the ox shall be stoned, and his owner also

shall be put to death. ³⁰ If there be laid on him a sum of money, then he shall give for the ransom of his life whatsoever is laid upon him. ³¹ Whether he have gored a son, or have gored a daughter, according to this judgment shall it be done unto him. ³² If the ox shall push a manservant or a maidservant; he shall give unto their master thirty shekels of silver, and the ox shall be stoned. ³³ And if a man shall open a pit, or if a man shall dig a pit, and not cover it, and an ox or an ass fall therein; ³⁴ The owner of the pit shall make it good, and give money unto the owner of them; and the dead beast shall be his. ³⁵ And if one man's ox hurt another's, that he die; then they shall sell the live ox, and divide the money of it; and the dead ox also they shall divide. ³⁶ Or if it be known that the ox hath used to push in time past, and his owner hath not kept him in; he shall surely pay ox for ox; and the dead shall be his own."

Leviticus 19:19 "Ye shall keep my statutes. Thou shalt not let thy cattle gender with a diverse kind: thou shalt not sow thy field with mingled seed: neither shall a garment mingled of linen and woollen come upon thee."

LIVING WATERS

Jesus Christ Leading People
To Living Fountains Of Water
Isaiah 55:1-3 "¹Ho, every one that thirsteth, come ye to the waters, and he that hath no money; come ye, buy, and eat; yea, come, buy wine and milk without money and without price. ² Wherefore do ye spend money for that which is not bread? and your labour for that which satisfieth not? hearken diligently unto me, and eat ye that which is good, and let your soul delight itself in fatness. ³ Incline your ear, and come unto me: hear, and your soul shall live; and I will make an everlasting covenant with you, even the sure mercies of David."

Revelation 7:17 "For the Lamb which is in the midst of the throne shall feed them, and shall lead them unto living fountains of waters: and God shall wipe away all tears from their eyes."

The Lord Being The
Fountain Of Living Waters
Jeremiah 2:12-13 "¹²Be astonished, O ye heavens, at this, and be horribly afraid, be ye very desolate,

saith the LORD. [13]For my people have committed two evils; they have forsaken me the fountain of living waters, and hewed them out cisterns, broken cisterns, that can hold no water."

Jeremiah 17:13 "O LORD, the hope of Israel, all that forsake thee shall be ashamed, and they that depart from me shall be written in the earth, because they have forsaken the LORD, the fountain of living waters."

Psalm 36:7-9 "[7]How excellent is thy lovingkindness, O God! therefore the children of men put their trust under the shadow of thy wings. [8]They shall be abundantly satisfied with the fatness of thy house; and thou shalt make them drink of the river of thy pleasures. [9]For with thee is the fountain of life: in thy light shall we see light."

John 19:33-34 "[33]But when they came to Jesus, and saw that he was dead already, they brake not his legs: [34]But one of the soldiers with a spear pierced his side, and forthwith came there out blood and water."

1 Corinthians 10:1-4 "[1]Moreover, brethren, I would not that ye should be ignorant, how that all our fathers were under the cloud, and all passed through the sea; [2]And were all baptized unto Moses in the cloud and in the sea; [3]And did all eat the same spiritual meat; [4]And did all drink the same spiritual drink: for they drank of that spiritual Rock that followed them: and that Rock was Christ."

The Water That Jesus Christ Gives
John 4:13-14 "[13]Jesus answered and said unto her, Whosoever drinketh of this water shall thirst again: [14]But whosoever drinketh of the water that I shall give him shall never thirst; but the water that I shall give him shall be in him a well of water springing up into everlasting life."

Those That Drink Of The Water
That Jesus Christ Gives
John 4:13-14 "[13]Jesus answered and said unto her, Whosoever drinketh of this water shall thirst again: [14]But whosoever drinketh of the water that I shall give him shall never thirst; but the water that I shall give him shall be in him a well of water springing up into everlasting life."

Waters Coming Forth From The Rock
Exodus 17:6 "Behold, I will stand before thee there upon the rock in Horeb; and thou shalt smite the rock, and there shall come water out of it, that the people may drink. And Moses did so in the sight of the elders of Israel."

Numbers 20:10-11 "[10]And Moses and Aaron gathered the congregation together before the rock, and he said unto them, Hear now, ye rebels; must we fetch you water out of this rock? [11]And Moses lifted up his hand, and with his rod he smote the rock twice: and the water came out abundantly, and the congregation drank, and their beasts also."

Nehemiah 9:7-15 "[7]Thou art the LORD the God, who didst choose Abram, and broughtest him forth out of Ur of the Chaldees, and gavest him the name of Abraham; [8]And foundest his heart faithful before thee, and madest a covenant with him to give the land of the Canaanites, the Hittites, the Amorites, and the Perizzites, and the Jebusites, and the Girgashites, to give it, I say, to his seed, and hast performed thy words; for thou art righteous: [9]And didst see the affliction of our fathers in Egypt, and heardest their cry by the Red sea; [10]And shewedst signs and wonders upon Pharoah, and on all his servants, and on all the people of his land: for thou knewest that they dealt proudly against them. So didst thou get thee a name, as it is this day. [11]And thou didst divide the sea before them, so that they went through the midst of the sea on the dry land; and their persecutors thou threwest into the deeps, as a stone into the mighty waters. [12]Moreover thou leddest them in the day by a cloudy pillar; and in the night by a pillar of fire, to give them light in the way wherein they should go. [13]Thou camest down also upon mount Sinai, and spakest with them from heaven, and gavest them right judgments, and true laws, good statutes and commandments: [14]And madest known unto them thy holy sabbath, and commandedst them precepts, statutes, and laws, by the hand of Moses thy servant: [15]And gavest them bread from heaven for their hunger, and broughtest forth water for them out of the rock for their thirst, and promisedst them that they should go in to possess the land which thou hadst sworn to give them."

Psalm 78:15 "He clave the rocks in the wilderness, and gave them drink as out of the great depths."

Psalm 78:19-20 "¹⁹Yea, they spake against God; they said, Can God furnish a table in the wilderness? ²⁰Behold, he smote the rock, that the waters gushed out, and the streams overflowed; can he give bread also? can he provide flesh for his people?"

John 19:33-34 "³³But when they came to Jesus, and saw that he was dead already, they brake not his legs: ³⁴But one of the soldiers with a spear pierced his side, and forthwith came there out blood and water."

1 Corinthians 10:1-4 "¹Moreover, brethren, I would not that ye should be ignorant, how that all our fathers were under the cloud, and all passed through the sea; ²And were all baptized unto Moses in the cloud and in the sea; ³And did all eat the same spiritual meat; ⁴And did all drink the same spiritual drink: for they drank of that spiritual Rock that followed them: and that Rock was Christ."

What Is A Fountain Of Life
Proverbs 10:11 "The mouth of a righteous man is a well of life: but violence covereth the mouth of the wicked."

Proverbs 13:14 "The law of the wise is a fountain of life, to depart from the snares of death."

Proverbs 14:27 "The fear of the LORD is a fountain of life, to depart from the snares of death."

Proverbs 16:22 "Understanding is a wellspring of life unto him that hath it: but the instruction of fools is folly."

Where The Fountain Of Water Shall Go Out From

Ezekiel 47:1-12 "¹Afterward he brought me again unto the door of the house; and, behold, waters issued out from under the threshold of the house eastward: for the forefront of the house stood toward the east, and the waters came down from under from the right side of the house, at the south side of the altar. ²Then brought he me out of the way of the gate northward, and led me about the way without unto the utter gate by the way that looketh eastward; and, behold, there ran out waters on the right side. ³And when the man that had the line in his hand went forth eastward, he measured a thousand cubits, and he brought me through the waters; the waters were to the ancles. ⁴Again he measured a thousand, and brought me through the waters; the waters were to the knees. Again he measured a thousand, and brought me through; the waters were to the loins. ⁵Afterward he measured a thousand; and it was a river that I could not pass over: for the waters were risen, waters to swim in, a river that could not be passed over. ⁶And he said unto me, Son of man, hast thou seen this? Then he brought me, and caused me to return to the brink of the river. ⁷Now when I had returned, behold, at the bank of the river were very many trees on the one side and on the other. ⁸Then said he unto me, These waters issue out toward the east country, and go down into the desert, and go into the sea: which being brought forth into the sea, the waters shall be healed. ⁹And it shall come to pass, that every thing that liveth, which moveth, whithersoever the rivers shall come, shall live: and there shall be a very great multitude of fish, because these waters shall come thither: for they shall be healed; and every thing shall live whither the river cometh. ¹⁰And it shall come to pass, that the fishers shall stand upon it from En-gedi even unto En-eglaim; they shall be a place to spread forth nets; their fish shall be according to their kinds, as the fish of the great sea, exceeding many. ¹¹But the miry places thereof and the marishes thereof shall not be healed; they shall be given to salt. ¹²And by the river upon the bank thereof, on this side and on that side, shall grow all trees for meat, whose leaf shall not fade, neither shall the fruit thereof be consumed: it shall bring forth new fruit according to his months, because their waters they issued out of the sanctuary: and the fruit thereof shall be for meat, and the leaf thereof for medicine."

Joel 3:18 "And it shall come to pass in that day, that the mountains shall drop down new wine, and the hills shall flow with milk, and all the rivers of Judah shall flow with waters, and a fountain shall come forth of the house of the LORD, and shall water the valley of Shittim."

Zechariah 13:1 "In that day there shall be a fountain opened to the house of David and to the inhabitants of Jerusalem for sin and for uncleanness."

Zechariah 14:8 "And it shall be in that day, that living waters shall go out from Jerusalem; half of them toward the former sea, and half of them toward the hinder sea: in summer and in winter shall it be."

Revelation 22:1 "And he shewed me a pure river of water of life, clear as crystal, proceeding out of the throne of God and of the Lamb."

Who Shall Have Rivers Of
Living Water Flowing Out Of Them

John 7:37-38 "37In the last day, that great day of the feast, Jesus stood and cried, saying, If any man thirst, let him come unto me, and drink. 38He that believeth on me, as the scripture hath said, out of his belly shall flow rivers of living water."

Who Shall Receive The Water Of Life

Isaiah 12:1-3 "1And in that day thou shalt say, O LORD, I will praise thee: though thou wast angry with me, thine anger is turned away, and thou comfortedst me. 2Behold, God is my salvation; I will trust, and not be afraid: for the LORD JEHOVAH is my strength and my song; he also is become my salvation. 3Therefore with joy shall ye draw water out of the wells of salvation."

Isaiah 44:1-3 "1Yet now hear, O Jacob my servant; and Israel, whom I have chosen: 2Thus saith the LORD that made thee, and formed thee from the womb, which will help thee; Fear not, O Jacob, my servant; and thou, Jesurun, whom I have chosen. 3For I will pour water upon him that is thirsty, and floods upon the dry ground: I will pour my spirit upon thy seed, and my blessing upon thine offspring."

Revelation 21:6 "And he said unto me, It is done. I am Alpha and Omega, the beginning and the end. I will give unto him that is athirst of the fountain of the water of life freely."

Revelation 22:17 "And the Spirit and the bride say, Come. And let him that heareth say, Come. And let him that is athirst come. And whosoever will, let him take the water of life freely."

Who Will Be Like A Watered Garden

Isaiah 58:10-11 "10And if thou draw out thy soul to the hungry, and satisfy the afflicted soul; then shall thy light rise in obscurity, and thy darkness be as the noonday: 11And the LORD shall guide thee continually, and satisfy thy soul in drought, and make fat thy bones: and thou shalt be like a watered garden, and like a spring of water, whose waters fail not."

LOSING AND THINGS LOST

The Lord Seeking And Saving
That Which Was Lost

Jeremiah 31:10 "Hear the word of the LORD, O ye nations, and declare it in the isles afar off, and say, He that scattered Israel will gather him, and keep him, as a shepherd doth his flock."

Ezekiel 34:11-16 "11For thus saith the Lord GOD; Behold, I, even I, will both search my sheep, and seek them out. 12 As a shepherd seeketh out his flock in the day that he is among his sheep that are scattered; so will I seek out my sheep, and will deliver them out of all places where they have been scattered in the cloudy and dark day. 13 And I will bring them out from the people, and gather them from the countries, and will bring them to their own land, and feed them upon the mountains of Israel by the rivers, and in all the inhabited places of the country. 14 I will feed them in a good pasture, and upon the high mountains of Israel shall their fold be: there shall they lie in a good fold, and in a fat pasture shall they feed upon the mountains of Israel. 15 I will feed my flock, and I will cause them to lie down, saith the Lord GOD. 16 I will seek that which was lost, and bring again that which was driven away, and will bind up that which was broken, and will strengthen that which was sick: but I will destroy the fat and the strong; I will feed them with judgment."

Matthew 18:11-14 "11For the Son of man is come to save that which was lost. 12 How think ye? if a man have an hundred sheep, and one of them be gone astray, doth he not leave the ninety and nine, and goeth into the mountains, and seeketh that which is gone astray? 13 And if so be that he find it, verily I say unto you, he rejoiceth more of that sheep, than of the ninety and nine which went not astray. 14 Even so it is not the will of your Father which is in heaven, that one of these little ones should perish."

Luke 15:3-32 "3And he spake this parable unto them, saying, 4 What man of you, having an hundred sheep, if he lose one of them, doth not leave the ninety and nine in the wilderness, and go after that which is lost, until he find it? 5 And when he hath found it, he layeth it on his shoulders, rejoicing. 6 And when he cometh home, he calleth together his friends and neighbours, saying unto them, Rejoice with me; for I have found my sheep which was lost. 7 I say unto you, that likewise joy shall be in heaven over one sinner that repenteth, more than over ninety and nine just persons, which need no repentance. 8 Either what woman having ten pieces of silver, if she lose one piece, doth not light a candle, and sweep the house, and seek diligently till she find it? 9 And when she hath found it, she calleth her friends and her neighbours together, saying, Rejoice with me; for I have found the piece which I had lost. 10 Likewise, I say unto you, there is joy in the presence of the angels of God over one sinner that repenteth. 11 And he said, A certain man had two sons: 12 And the younger of them said to his father, Father, give me the portion of goods that falleth to me. And he divided unto them his living. 13 And not many days after the younger son gathered all together, and took his journey into a far country, and there wasted his substance with riotous living. 14 And when he had spent all, there arose a mighty famine in that land; and he began to be in want. 15 And he went and joined himself to a citizen of that country; and he sent him into his fields to feed swine. 16 And he would fain have filled his belly with the husks that the swine did eat: and no man gave unto him. 17 And when he came to himself, he said, How many hired servants of my father's have bread enough and to spare, and I perish with hunger! 18 I will arise and go to my father, and will say unto him, Father, I have sinned against heaven, and before thee, 19 And am no more worthy to be called thy son: make me as one of thy hired servants. 20 And he arose, and came to his father. But when he was yet a great way off, his father saw him, and had compassion, and ran, and fell on his neck, and kissed him. 21 And the son said unto him, Father, I have sinned against heaven, and in thy sight, and am no more worthy to be called thy son. 22 But the father said to his servants, Bring forth the best robe, and put it on him; and put a ring on his hand, and shoes on his feet: 23 And bring hither the fatted calf, and kill it; and let us eat, and be merry: 24 For this my son was dead, and is alive again; he was lost, and is found. And they began to be merry. 25 Now his elder son was in the field: and as he came and drew nigh to the house, he heard musick and dancing. 26 And he called one of the servants, and asked what these things meant. 27 And he said unto him, Thy brother is come; and thy father hath killed the fatted calf, because he hath received him safe and sound. 28 And he was angry, and would not go in: therefore came his father out, and intreated him. 29 And he answering said to his father, Lo, these many years do I serve thee, neither transgressed I at any time thy commandment: and yet thou never gavest me a kid, that I might make merry with my friends: 30 But as soon as this thy son was come, which hath devoured thy living with harlots, thou hast killed for him the fatted calf. 31 And he said unto him, Son, thou art ever with me, and all that I have is thine. 32 It was meet that we should make merry, and be glad: for this thy brother was dead, and is alive again; and was lost, and is found."

Luke 19:9-10 "9And Jesus said unto him, This day is salvation come to this house, forsomuch as he also is a son of Abraham. 10 For the Son of man is come to seek and to save that which was lost."

Those That Are Lost
2 Corinthians 4:3-4 "3But if our gospel be hid, it is hid to them that are lost: 4In whom the god of this world hath blinded the minds of them which believe not, lest the light of the glorious gospel of Christ, who is the image of God, should shine unto them."

Who Is Not Lost
John 17:1-12 "1These words spake Jesus, and lifted up his eyes to heaven, and said, Father, the hour is come; glorify thy Son, that thy Son also may glorify thee: 2As thou hast given him power over all flesh, that he should give eternal life to as many as thou hast given him. 3And this is life eternal, that they might know thee the only true God, and Jesus Christ, whom thou hast sent. 4I have glorified thee on the earth: I have finished the work which thou gavest me to do. 5And now, O Father, glorify thou me with thine own self with the glory which I had with thee before the world was. 6I have manifested thy name unto the men which thou gavest me out of the world: thine they were, and thou gavest them me; and they have kept thy word. 7Now they have known that all things whatsoever thou hast given me are of thee. 8For I

have given unto them the words which thou gavest me; and they have received them, and have known surely that I came out from thee, and they have believed that thou didst send me. 9I pray for them: I pray not for the world, but for them which thou hast given me; for they are thine. 10And all mine are thine, and thine are mine; and I am glorified in them. 11And now I am no more in the world, but these are in the world, and I come to thee. Holy Father, keep through thine own name those whom thou hast given me, that they may be one, as we are. 12While I was with them in the world, I kept them in thy name: those that thou gavest me I have kept, and none of them is lost, but the son of perdition; that the scripture might be fulfilled."

Who Shall Lose Their Life
Matthew 10:38-39 "38And he that taketh not his cross, and followeth after me, is not worthy of me. 39He that findeth his life shall lose it: and he that loseth his life for my sake shall find it."

Matthew 16:24-25 "24Then said Jesus unto his disciples, If any man will come after me, let him deny himself, and take up his cross, and follow me. 25For whosoever will save his life shall lose it: and whosoever will lose his life for my sake shall find it."

Mark 8:31-36 "31And he began to teach them, that the Son of man must suffer many things, and be rejected of the elders, and of the chief priests, and scribes, and be killed, and after three days rise again. 32And he spake that saying openly. And Peter took him, and began to rebuke him. 33But when he had turned about and looked on his disciples, he rebuked Peter, saying, Get thee behind me, Satan: for thou savourest not the things that be of God, but the things that be of men. 34And when he had called the people unto him with his disciples also, he said unto them, Whosoever will come after me, let him deny himself, and take up his cross, and follow me. 35For whosoever will save his life shall lose it; but whosoever shall lose his life for my sake and the gospel's, the same shall save it. 36For what shall it profit a man, if he shall gain the whole world, and lose his own soul?"

Luke 9:22-25 "22Saying, The Son of man must suffer many things, and be rejected of the elders and chief priests and scribes, and be slain, and be raised the third day. 23And he said to them all, If any man

will come after me, let him deny himself, and take up his cross daily, and follow me. 24For whosoever will save his life shall lose it: but whosoever will lose his life for my sake, the same shall save it. 25For what is a man advantaged, if he gain the whole world, and lose himself, or be cast away?"

Luke 17:33 "Whosoever shall seek to save his life shall lose it; and whosoever shall lose his life shall preserve it."

John 12:25 "He that loveth his life shall lose it; and he that hateth his life in this world shall keep it unto life eternal."

LOVE

God Being Love
1 John 4:7-8 "7Beloved, let us love one another: for love is of God; and every one that loveth is born of God, and knoweth God. 8 He that loveth not knoweth not God; for God is love."

1 John 4:16 "And we have known and believed the love that God hath to us. God is love; and he that dwelleth in love dwelleth in God, and God in him."

God The Father And
Jesus Christ Loving Each Other
John 3:35 "The Father loveth the Son, and hath given all things into his hand."

John 5:20 "For the Father loveth the Son, and sheweth him all things that himself doeth: and he will shew him greater works than these, that ye may marvel."

John 10:7-17 "7Then said Jesus unto them again, Verily, verily, I say unto you, I am the door of the sheep. 8All that ever came before me are thieves and robbers: but the sheep did not hear them. 9I am the door: by me if any man enter in, he shall be saved, and shall go in and out, and find pasture. 10The thief cometh not, but for to steal, and to kill, and to destroy: I am come that they might have life, and that they might have it more abundantly. 11I am the good shepherd: the good shepherd giveth his life for the sheep. 12But he that is an hireling, and not the shepherd, whose own the sheep are not, seeth the wolf coming, and leaveth the sheep, and fleeth: and the wolf catcheth them, and scattereth the sheep. 13The hireling fleeth, because he is an hireling, and careth not for the sheep. [14]I am the good shepherd, and know my sheep, and am known of mine. [15]As the Father knoweth me, even so know I the Father: and I lay down my life for the sheep. [16]And other sheep I have, which are not of this fold: them also I must bring, and they shall hear my voice; and there shall be one fold, and one shepherd. [17]Therefore doth my Father love me, because I lay down my life, that I might take it again."

John 14:23-31 "[23]Jesus answered and said unto him, If a man love me, he will keep my words: and my Father will love him, and we will come unto him, and make our abode with him. [24]He that loveth me not keepeth not my sayings: and the word which ye hear is not mine, but the Father's which sent me. [25]These things have I spoken unto you, being yet present with you. [26]But the Comforter, which is the Holy Ghost, whom the Father will send in my name, he shall teach you all things, and bring all things to your remembrance, whatsoever I have said unto you. [27]Peace I leave with you, my peace I give unto you: not as the world giveth, give I unto you. Let not your heart be troubled, neither let it be afraid. [28]Ye have heard how I said unto you, I go away, and come again unto you. If ye loved me, ye would rejoice, because I said, I go unto the Father: for my Father is greater than I. [29]And now I have told you before it come to pass, that, when it is come to pass, ye might believe. [30]Hereafter I will not talk much with you: for the prince of this world cometh, and hath nothing in me. [31]But that the world may know that I love the Father; and as the Father gave me commandment, even so I do. Arise, let us go hence."

John 15:1-9 "[1]I am the true vine, and my Father is the husbandman. [2]Every branch in me that beareth not fruit he taketh away: and every branch that beareth fruit, he purgeth it, that it may bring forth more fruit. [3]Now ye are clean through the word which I have spoken unto you. [4]Abide in me, and I in you. As the branch cannot bear fruit of itself, except it abide in the vine; no more can ye, except ye abide in me. [5]I am the vine, ye are the branches: He that abideth in me, and I in him, the same bringeth forth much fruit: for without me ye can do nothing. [6]If a man abide not in me, he is cast forth as a branch, and is withered; and men gather them, and cast them into the fire, and they are burned. [7]If ye abide in me, and my words abide in you, ye shall ask what ye will, and it shall be done unto you. [8]Herein is my Father glorified, that ye bear much fruit; so shall ye be my disciples. [9]As the Father hath loved me, so have I loved you: continue ye in my love."

John 17:1-26 "[1]These words spake Jesus, and lifted up his eyes to heaven, and said, Father, the hour is come; glorify thy Son, that thy Son also may glorify thee: [2]As thou hast given him power over all flesh, that he should give eternal life to as many as thou hast given him. [3]And this is life eternal, that they might know thee the only true God, and Jesus Christ, whom thou hast sent. [4]I have glorified thee on the earth: I have finished the work which thou gavest me to do. [5]And now, O Father, glorify thou me with thine own self with the glory which I had with thee before the world was. [6]I have manifested thy name unto the men which thou gavest me out of the world: thine they were, and thou gavest them me; and they have kept thy word. [7]Now they have known that all things whatsoever thou hast given me are of thee. [8]For I have given unto them the words which thou gavest me; and they have received them, and have known surely that I came out from thee, and they have believed that thou didst send me. [9]I pray for them: I pray not for the world, but for them which thou hast given me; for they are thine. [10]And all mine are thine, and thine are mine; and I am glorified in them. [11]And now I am no more in the world, but these are in the world, and I come to thee. Holy Father, keep through thine own name those whom thou hast given me, that they may be one, as we are. [12]While I was with them in the world, I kept them in thy name: those that thou gavest me I have kept, and none of them is lost, but the son of perdition; that the scripture might be fulfilled. [13]And now come I to thee; and these things I speak in the world, that they might have my joy fulfilled in themselves. [14]I have given them thy word; and the world hath hated them, because they are not of the world, even as I am not of the world. [15]I pray not that thou shouldest take them out of the world, but that thou shouldest keep them from the evil. [16]They are not of the world, even as I am not of the world. [17]Sanctify them through thy truth: thy word is truth. [18]As thou hast sent me into the world, even so have I also sent them into the world. [19]And for their sakes I sanctify myself, that they also might be sanctified through the truth. [20]Neither pray I for these alone, but for them also which shall believe on me through their word; [21]That they all may be one; as thou, Father, art in me, and I in thee, that they also may be one in us: that the world may believe that thou hast sent me. [22]And the glory which thou gavest me I have given them; that they may be one, even as we are one: [23]I in them, and thou in me, that they may be made perfect in one; and that the world may know that thou hast sent me, and hast loved them, as thou hast loved me. [24]Father, I will that they also, whom thou hast given me, be with me where I am; that they may behold my glory, which thou hast given me: for thou lovedst me before the foundation of the world. [25]O righteous Father, the world hath not known thee: but I have known thee, and these have known that thou hast sent me. [26]And I have declared unto them thy name, and will declare it: that the love wherewith thou hast loved me may be in them, and I in them."

God The Father And
Jesus Christ Loving People

Deuteronomy 7:8 "But because the LORD loved you, and because he would keep the oath which he had sworn unto your fathers, hath the LORD brought you out with a mighty hand, and redeemed you out of the house of bondmen, from the hand of Pharaoh king of Egypt."

John 3:16 "For God so loved the world, that he gave his only begotten Son, that whosoever believeth in him should not perish, but have everlasting life."

John 13:1 "Now before the feast of the passover, when Jesus knew that his hour was come that he should depart out of this world unto the Father, having loved his own which were in the world, he loved them unto the end."

John 13:31-34 "[31]Therefore, when he was gone out, Jesus said, Now is the Son of man glorified, and God is glorified in him. [32]If God be glorified in him, God shall also glorify him in himself, and shall straightway glorify him. [33]Little children, yet a little while I am with you. Ye shall seek me: and as I said unto the Jews, Whither I go, ye cannot come; so now I say to you. [34]A new commandment I give unto you, That ye love one another; as I have loved you, that ye also love one another."

John 15:1-13 "[1]I am the true vine, and my Father is the husbandman. [2]Every branch in me that beareth not fruit he taketh away: and every branch that beareth fruit, he purgeth it, that it may bring forth more fruit. [3]Now ye are clean through the word which I have spoken unto you. [4]Abide in me, and I in you. As the branch cannot bear fruit of itself, except it abide in the vine; no more can ye, except ye abide in me. [5]I am the vine, ye are the branches: He that abideth in me, and I in him, the same bringeth forth much fruit: for without me ye can do nothing. [6]If a man abide not in me, he is cast forth as a branch, and is withered; and men gather them, and cast them into the fire, and they are burned. [7]If ye abide in me, and my words abide in you, ye shall ask what ye will, and it shall be done unto you. [8]Herein is my Father glorified, that ye bear much fruit; so shall ye be my disciples. [9]As the Father hath loved me, so have I loved you: continue ye in my love. [10]If ye keep my commandments, ye shall abide in my love; even as I have kept my Father's commandments, and abide in his love. [11]These things have I spoken unto you, that my joy might remain in you, and that your joy might be full. [12]This is my commandment, That ye love one another, as I have loved you. [13]Greater love hath no man than this, that a man lay down his life for his friends."

John 16:27 "For the Father himself loveth you, because ye have loved me, and have believed that I came out from God."

John 17:1-23 "[1]These words spake Jesus, and lifted up his eyes to heaven, and said, Father, the hour is come; glorify thy Son, that thy Son also may glorify thee: [2]As thou hast given him power over all flesh, that he should give eternal life to as many as thou hast given him. [3]And this is life eternal, that they might know thee the only true God, and Jesus Christ, whom thou hast sent. [4]I have glorified thee on the earth: I have finished the work which thou gavest me to do. [5]And now, O Father, glorify thou me with thine own self with the glory which I had with thee before the world was. [6]I have manifested thy name unto the men which thou gavest me out of the world: thine they were, and thou gavest them me; and they have kept thy word. [7]Now they have known that all things whatsoever thou hast given me are of thee. [8]For I have given unto them the words which thou gavest me; and they have received them, and have known surely that I came out from thee, and they have believed that thou didst send me. [9]I pray for them: I pray not for the world, but for them which thou hast given me; for they are thine. [10]And all mine are thine, and thine are mine; and I am glorified in them. [11]And now I am no more in the world, but these are in the world, and I come to thee. Holy Father, keep through thine own name those whom thou hast given me, that they may be one, as we are. [12]While I was with them in the world, I kept them in thy name: those that thou gavest me I have kept, and none of them is lost, but the son of perdition; that the scripture might be fulfilled. [13]And now come I to thee; and these things I speak in the world, that they might have my joy fulfilled in themselves. [14]I have given them thy word; and the world hath hated them, because they are not of the world, even as I am not of the world. [15]I pray not that thou shouldest take them out of the world, but that thou shouldest keep them from the evil. [16]They are not of the world, even as I am not of the world. [17]Sanctify them through thy truth: thy word is truth. [18]As thou hast sent me into the world, even so have I also sent them into the world. [19]And for their sakes I sanctify myself, that they also might be sanctified through the truth. [20]Neither pray I for these alone, but for them also which shall believe on me through their word; [21]That they all may be one; as thou, Father, art in me, and I in thee, that they also may be one in us: that the world may believe that thou hast sent me. [22]And the glory which thou gavest me I have given them; that they may be one, even as we are one: [23]I in them, and thou in me, that they may be made perfect in one; and that the world may know that thou hast sent me, and hast loved them, as thou hast loved me."

Galatians 2:20 "I am crucified with Christ: nevertheless I live; yet not I, but Christ liveth in me: and the life which I now live in the flesh I live by the faith of the Son of God, who loved me, and gave himself for me."

Ephesians 2:4-5 "[4]But God, who is rich in mercy, for his great love wherewith he loved us, [5]Even when we were dead in sins, hath quickened us together with Christ, (by grace ye are saved;)"

Ephesians 5:2 "And walk in love, as Christ also hath loved us, and hath given himself for us an offering and a sacrifice to God for a sweetsmelling savour."

1 Peter 5:6-7 "[6]Humble yourselves therefore under the mighty hand of God, that he may exalt you in due time: [7]Casting all your care upon him; for he careth for you."

1 John 3:1 "Behold, what manner of love the Father hath bestowed upon us, that we should be called the sons of God: therefore the world knoweth us not, because it knew him not."

1 John 4:9-11 "[9]In this was manifested the love of God toward us, because that God sent his only begotten Son into the world, that we might live through him. [10]Herein is love, not that we loved God, but that he loved us, and sent his Son to be the propitiation for our sins. [11]Beloved, if God so loved us, we ought also to love one another."

1 John 4:16-19 "[16]And we have known and believed the love that God hath to us. God is love; and he that dwelleth in love dwelleth in God, and God in him. [17]Herein is our love made perfect, that we may have boldness in the day of judgment: because as he is, so are we in this world. [18]There is no fear in love; but perfect love casteth out fear: because fear hath torment. He that feareth is not made perfect in love. [19]We love him, because he first loved us."

Revelation 1:4-5 "[4]John to the seven churches which are in Asia: Grace be unto you, and peace, from him which is, and which was, and which is to come; and from the seven Spirits which are before his throne; [5]And from Jesus Christ, who is the faithful witness, and the first begotten of the dead, and the prince of the kings of the earth. Unto him that loved us, and washed us from our sins in his own blood,"

How To Love
1 John 3:18 "My little children, let us not love in word, neither in tongue; but in deed and in truth."

Keeping Yourself In The Love Of God
Jude 20-21 "[20]But ye, beloved, building up yourselves on your most holy faith, praying in the Holy Ghost, [21]Keep yourselves in the love of God, looking for the mercy of our Lord Jesus Christ unto eternal life."

Loving Others

Leviticus 19:18 "Thou shalt not avenge, nor bear any grudge against the children of thy people, but thou shalt love thy neighbour as thyself: I am the LORD."

Matthew 19:19 "Honour thy father and thy mother: and, Thou shalt love thy neighbour as thyself."

Matthew 22:36-40 "[36]Master, which is the great commandment in the law? [37]Jesus said unto him, Thou shalt love the Lord thy God with all thy heart, and with all thy soul, and with all thy mind. [38]This is the first and great commandment. [39]And the second is like unto it, Thou shalt love thy neighbour as thyself. [40]On these two commandments hang all the law and the prophets."

Mark 12:28-33 "[28]And one of the scribes came, and having heard them reasoning together, and perceiving that he had answered them well, asked him, Which is the first commandment of all? [29]And Jesus answered him, The first of all the commandments is, Hear, O Israel; The Lord our God is one Lord: [30]And thou shalt love the Lord thy God with all thy heart, and with all thy soul, and with all thy mind, and with all thy strength: this is the first commandment. [31]And the second is like, namely this, Thou shalt love thy neighbour as thyself. There is none other commandment greater than these. [32]And the scribe said unto him, Well, Master, thou hast said the truth: for there is one God; and there is none other but he: [33]And to love him with all the heart, and with all the understanding, and with all the soul, and with all the strength, and to love his neighbour as himself, is more than all whole burnt offerings and sacrifices."

Luke 10:25-28 "[25]And, behold, a certain lawyer stood up, and tempted him, saying, Master, what shall I do to inherit eternal life? [26]He said unto him, What is written in the law? how readest thou? [27]And he answering said, Thou shalt love the Lord thy God with all thy heart, and with all thy soul, and with all thy strength, and with all thy mind; and thy neighbour as thyself. [28]And he said unto him, Thou hast answered right: this do, and thou shalt live."

John 13:34-35 "[34]A new commandment I give unto you, That ye love one another; as I have loved you, that ye also love one another. [35]By this shall all men know that ye are my disciples, if ye have love one to another."

John 15:12-13 "[12]This is my commandment, That ye love one another, as I have loved you. [13]Greater love hath no man than this, that a man lay down his life for his friends."

John 15:17 "These things I command you, that ye love one another."

Romans 12:10 "Be kindly affectioned one to another with brotherly love; in honour preferring one another."

Romans 13:8-10 "[8]Owe no man any thing, but to love one another: for he that loveth another hath fulfilled the law. [9]For this, Thou shalt not commit adultery, Thou shalt not kill, Thou shalt not steal, Thou shalt not bear false witness, Thou shalt not covet; and if there be any other commandment, it is briefly comprehended in this saying, namely, Thou shalt love thy neighbour as thyself. [10]Love worketh no ill to his neighbour: therefore love is the fulfilling of the law."

Galatians 5:13-14 "[13]For, brethren, ye have been called unto liberty; only use not liberty for an occasion to the flesh, but by love serve one another. [14]For all the law is fulfilled in one word, even in this; Thou shalt love thy neighbour as thyself."

Ephesians 4:1-2 "I therefore, the prisoner of the Lord, beseech you that ye walk worthy of the vocation wherewith ye are called, [2]With all lowliness and meekness, with longsuffering, forbearing one another in love."

Ephesians 5:25 "Husbands, love your wives, even as Christ also loved the church, and gave himself for it."

Ephesians 5:28 "So ought men to love their wives as their own bodies. He that loveth his wife loveth himself."

Ephesians 5:33 "Nevertheless let every one of you in particular so love his wife even as himself; and the wife see that she reverence her husband."

Colossians 3:19 "Husbands, love your wives, and be not bitter against them."

1 Thessalonians 4:9-10 "[9]But as touching brotherly love ye need not that I write unto you: for ye yourselves are taught of God to love one another. [10]And indeed ye do it toward all the brethren which are in all Macedonia: but we beseech you, brethren, that ye increase more and more."

Hebrews 13:1 "Let brotherly love continue."

James 2:8 "If ye fulfil the royal law according to the scripture, Thou shalt love thy neighbour as thyself, ye do well."

1 Peter 1:22-23 "22Seeing ye have purified your souls in obeying the truth through the Spirit unto unfeigned love of the brethren, see that ye love one another with a pure heart fervently: 23Being born again, not of corruptible seed, but of incorruptible, by the word of God, which liveth and abideth for ever."

1 Peter 2:17 "Honour all men. Love the brotherhood. Fear God. Honour the king."

1 John 3:11-12 "11For this is the message that ye heard from the beginning, that we should love one another. 12Not as Cain, who was of that wicked one, and slew his brother. And wherefore slew he him? Because his own works were evil, and his brother's righteous."

1 John 3:23 "And this is his commandment, That we should believe on the name of his Son Jesus Christ, and love one another, as he gave us commandment."

1 John 4:7 "Beloved, let us love one another: for love is of God; and every one that loveth is born of God, and knoweth God."

1 John 4:11 "Beloved, if God so loved us, we ought also to love one another."

1 John 4:21 "And this commandment have we from him, That he who loveth God love his brother also."

2 John 4-6 "4I rejoiced greatly that I found of thy children walking in truth, as we have received a commandment from the Father. 5And now I beseech thee, lady, not as though I wrote a new commandment unto thee, but that which we had from the beginning, that we love one another. 6And this is love, that we walk after his commandments. This is the commandment, That, as ye have heard from the beginning, ye should walk in it."

Loving The Lord

Deuteronomy 6:5 "And thou shalt love the LORD thy God with all thine heart, and with all thy soul, and with all thy might."

Deuteronomy 10:12 "And now, Israel, what doth the LORD thy God require of thee, but to fear the LORD thy God, to walk in all his ways, and to love him, and to serve the LORD thy God with all thy heart and with all thy soul,"

Deuteronomy 11:1 "Therefore thou shalt love the LORD thy God, and keep his charge, and his statutes, and his judgments, and his commandments, always."

Deuteronomy 30:15-16 "15See, I have set before thee this day life and good, and death and evil; 16In that I command thee this day to love the LORD thy God, to walk in his ways, and to keep his commandments and his statutes and his judgments, that thou mayest live and multiply: and the LORD thy God shall bless thee in the land whither thou goest to possess it."

Deuteronomy 30:19-20 "19I call heaven and earth to record this day against you, that I have set before you life and death, blessing and cursing: therefore choose life, that both thou and thy seed may live: 20That thou mayest love the LORD thy God, and that thou mayest obey his voice, and that thou mayest cleave unto him: for he is thy life, and the length of thy days: that thou mayest dwell in the land which the LORD sware unto thy fathers, to Abraham, to Isaac, and to Jacob, to give them."

Joshua 22:5 "But take diligent heed to do the commandment and the law, which Moses the servant of the LORD charged you, to love the LORD your God, and to walk in all his ways, and to keep his commandments, and to cleave unto him, and to serve him with all your heart and with all your soul."

Joshua 23:11 "Take good heed therefore unto yourselves, that ye love the LORD your God."

Psalm 31:23 "O love the LORD, all ye his saints: for the LORD preserveth the faithful, and plentifully rewardeth the proud doer."

Matthew 22:36-40 "36Master, which is the great commandment in the law? 37Jesus said unto him, Thou shalt love the Lord thy God with all thy heart, and with all thy soul, and with all thy mind. 38This is the first and great commandment. 39And the second is like unto it, Thou shalt love thy neighbour as thyself. 40On these two commandments hang all the law and the prophets."

Mark 12:28-33 "[28]And one of the scribes came, and having heard them reasoning together, and perceiving that he had answered them well, asked him, Which is the first commandment of all? [29]And Jesus answered him, The first of all the commandments is, Hear, O Israel; The Lord our God is one Lord: [30]And thou shalt love the Lord thy God with all thy heart, and with all thy soul, and with all thy mind, and with all thy strength: this is the first commandment. [31]And the second is like, namely this, Thou shalt love thy neighbour as thyself. There is none other commandment greater than these. [32]And the scribe said unto him, Well, Master, thou hast said the truth: for there is one God; and there is none other but he: [33]And to love him with all the heart, and with all the understanding, and with all the soul, and with all the strength, and to love his neighbour as himself, is more than all whole burnt offerings and sacrifices."

Luke 10:25-28 "[25]And, behold, a certain lawyer stood up, and tempted him, saying, Master, what shall I do to inherit eternal life? [26]He said unto him, What is written in the law? how readest thou? [27]And he answering said, Thou shalt love the Lord thy God with all thy heart, and with all thy soul, and with all thy strength, and with all thy mind; and thy neighbour as thyself. [28]And he said unto him, Thou hast answered right: this do, and thou shalt live."

Not Faking Love

Romans 12:9 "Let love be without dissimulation. Abhor that which is evil; cleave to that which is good."

1 John 3:18 "My little children, let us not love in word, neither in tongue; but in deed and in truth."

Perfect Love

1 John 4:18 "There is no fear in love; but perfect love casteth out fear: because fear hath torment. He that feareth is not made perfect in love."

Secret Love

Proverbs 27:5 "Open rebuke is better than secret love."

The Lord Exercising Lovingkindness

Jeremiah 9:23-24 "[23]Thus saith the LORD, Let not the wise man glory in his wisdom, neither let the mighty man glory in his might, let not the rich man glory in his riches: [24]But let him that glorieth glory

in this, that he understandeth and knoweth me, that I am the LORD which exercise lovingkindness, judgment, and righteousness, in the earth: for in these things I delight, saith the LORD."

The Love Of God

Psalm 36:7 "How excellent is thy lovingkindness, O God! therefore the children of men put their trust under the shadow of thy wings."

Psalm 63:1-3 "[1]O God, thou art my God; early will I seek thee: my soul thirsteth for thee, my flesh longeth for thee in a dry and thirsty land, where no water is; [2]To see thy power and thy glory, so as I have seen thee in the sanctuary. [3]Because thy lovingkindness is better than life, my lips shall praise thee."

Romans 5:5 "And hope maketh not ashamed; because the love of God is shed abroad in our hearts by the Holy Ghost which is given unto us."

Romans 8:39 "Nor height, nor depth, nor any other creature, shall be able to separate us from the love of God, which is in Christ Jesus our Lord."

Ephesians 3:19 "And to know the love of Christ, which passeth knowledge, that ye might be filled with all the fulness of God."

Titus 3:3-5 "[3]For we ourselves also were sometimes foolish, disobedient, deceived, serving divers lusts and pleasures, living in malice and envy, hateful, and hating one another. [4]But after that the kindness and love of God our Saviour toward man appeared, [5]Not by works of righteousness which we have done, but according to his mercy he saved us, by the washing of regeneration, and renewing of the Holy Ghost."

1 John 5:3 "For this is the love of God, that we keep his commandments: and his commandments are not grievous."

The Place Where There Is Love

Proverbs 15:17 "Better is a dinner of herbs where love is, than a stalled ox and hatred therewith."

The Reward For Loving The Lord

Deuteronomy 11:13-15 "[13]And it shall come to pass, if ye shall hearken diligently unto my commandments which I command you this day, to love the LORD your God, and to serve him with all your heart and with all your soul, [14]That I will give you the rain of your land in his due season, the first rain and the latter rain, that thou mayest gather in thy corn, and thy wine, and thine oil. ¹⁵And I will send grass in thy fields for thy cattle, that thou mayest eat and be full."

Deuteronomy 11:22-23 "²²For if ye shall diligently keep all these commandments which I command you, to do them, to love the LORD your God, to walk in all his ways, and to cleave unto him; ²³Then will the LORD drive out all these nations from before you, and ye shall possess greater nations and mightier than yourselves."

Deuteronomy 30:15-16 "¹⁵See, I have set before thee this day life and good, and death and evil; ¹⁶In that I command thee this day to love the LORD thy God, to walk in his ways, and to keep his commandments and his statutes and his judgments, that thou mayest live and multiply: and the LORD thy God shall bless thee in the land whither thou goest to possess it."

Psalm 91:9-16 "⁹Because thou hast made the LORD, which is my refuge, even the most High, thy habitation; ¹⁰There shall no evil befall thee, neither shall any plague come nigh thy dwelling. ¹¹For he shall give his angels charge over thee, to keep thee in all thy ways. ¹²They shall bear thee up in their hands, lest thou dash thy foot against a stone. ¹³Thou shalt tread upon the lion and adder: the young lion and the dragon shalt thou trample under feet. ¹⁴Because he hath set his love upon me, therefore will I deliver him: I will set him on high, because he hath known my name. ¹⁵He shall call upon me, and I will answer him: I will be with him in trouble; I will deliver him, and honour him. ¹⁶With long life will I satisfy him, and shew him my salvation."

Luke 7:40-48 "⁴⁰And Jesus answering said unto him, Simon, I have somewhat to say unto thee. And he saith, Master, say on. ⁴¹There was a certain creditor which had two debtors: the one owed five hundred pence, and the other fifty. ⁴²And when they had nothing to pay, he frankly forgave them both. Tell me therefore, which of them will love him most? ⁴³Simon answered and said, I suppose that he, to whom he forgave most. And he said unto him, Thou hast rightly judged. ⁴⁴And he turned to the woman, and said unto Simon, Seest thou this woman? I entered into thine house, thou gavest me no water for my feet: but she hath washed my feet with tears, and wiped them with the hairs of her head. ⁴⁵Thou gavest me no kiss: but this woman since the time I came in hath not ceased to kiss my feet. ⁴⁶My head with oil thou didst not anoint: but this woman hath anointed my feet with ointment. ⁴⁷Wherefore I say unto thee, Her sins, which are many, are forgiven; for she loved much: but to whom little is forgiven, the same loveth little. ⁴⁸And he said unto her, Thy sins are forgiven."

John 16:19-27 "¹⁹Now Jesus knew that they were desirous to ask him, and said unto them, Do ye inquire among yourselves of that I said, A little while, and ye shall not see me: and again, a little while, and ye shall see me? ²⁰Verily, verily, I say unto you, That ye shall weep and lament, but the world shall rejoice: and ye shall be sorrowful, but your sorrow shall be turned into joy. ²¹A woman when she is in travail hath sorrow, because her hour is come: but as soon as she is delivered of the child, she remembereth no more the anguish, for joy that a man is born into the world. ²²And ye now therefore have sorrow: but I will see you again, and your heart shall rejoice, and your joy no man taketh from you. ²³And in that day ye shall ask me nothing. Verily, verily, I say unto you, Whatsoever ye shall ask the Father in my name, he will give it you. ²⁴Hitherto have ye asked nothing in my name: ask, and ye shall receive, that your joy may be full. ²⁵These things have I spoken unto you in proverbs: but the time cometh, when I shall no more speak unto you in proverbs, but I shall shew you plainly of the Father. ²⁶At that day ye shall ask in my name: and I say not unto you, that I will pray the Father for you: ²⁷For the Father himself loveth you, because ye have loved me, and have believed that I came out from God."

The Source Of Love

1 John 4:7-21 "⁷Beloved, let us love one another: for love is of God; and every one that loveth is born of God, and knoweth God. ⁸He that loveth not knoweth not God; for God is love. ⁹In this was manifested the love of God toward us, because that God sent his only begotten Son into the world, that we might live through him. ¹⁰Herein is love, not that we loved God, but that he loved us, and sent his Son to be the propitiation for our sins. ¹¹Beloved, if God so loved us, we ought also to love one another. ¹²No man hath seen God at any time. If we love one another, God dwelleth in us, and his love is perfected in us. [13]Hereby know we that we dwell in him, and he in us, because he hath given us of his Spirit. [14]And we have seen and do testify that the Father sent the Son to be the Saviour of the world. [15]Whosoever shall confess that Jesus is the Son of God, God dwelleth in him, and he in God. [16]And we have known and believed the love that God hath to us. God is love; and he that dwelleth in love dwelleth in God, and God in him. [17]Herein is our love made perfect, that we may have boldness in the day of judgment: because as he is, so are we in this world. [18]There is no fear in love; but perfect love casteth out fear: because fear hath torment. He that feareth is not made perfect in love. [19]We love him, because he first loved us. [20]If a man say, I love God, and hateth his brother, he is a liar: for he that loveth not his brother whom he hath seen, how can he love God whom he hath not seen? [21]And this commandment have we from him, That he who loveth God love his brother also."

Those That Do Not Love Jesus Christ
John 14:23-24 "[23]Jesus answered and said unto him, If a man love me, he will keep my words: and my Father will love him, and we will come unto him, and make our abode with him. [24]He that loveth me not keepeth not my sayings: and the word which ye hear is not mine, but the Father's which sent me."

Those That Do Not Love Others
1 John 3:10 "In this the children of God are manifest, and the children of the devil: whosoever doeth not righteousness is not of God, neither he that loveth not his brother."

1 John 3:14 "We know that we have passed from death unto life, because we love the brethren. He that loveth not his brother abideth in death."

1 John 4:8 "He that loveth not knoweth not God; for God is love."

1 John 4:20 "If a man say, I love God, and hateth his brother, he is a liar: for he that loveth not his brother whom he hath seen, how can he love God whom he hath not seen?"

Those That Dwell In Love
1 John 4:16 "And we have known and believed the love that God hath to us. God is love; and he that

dwelleth in love dwelleth in God, and God in him."

Those That Love Others
Romans 13:8 "Owe no man any thing, but to love one another: for he that loveth another hath fulfilled the law."

Ephesians 5:28 "So ought men to love their wives as their own bodies. He that loveth his wife loveth himself."

James 2:8 "If ye fulfil the royal law according to the scripture, Thou shalt love thy neighbour as thyself, ye do well."

1 John 2:10 "He that loveth his brother abideth in the light, and there is none occasion of stumbling in him."

1 John 3:14 "We know that we have passed from death unto life, because we love the brethren. He that loveth not his brother abideth in death."

1 John 4:7 "Beloved, let us love one another: for love is of God; and every one that loveth is born of God, and knoweth God."

1 John 4:12 "No man hath seen God at any time. If we love one another, God dwelleth in us, and his love is perfected in us."

Those That Love Others
More Than Jesus Christ
Matthew 10:33-37 "[33]But whosoever shall deny me before men, him will I also deny before my Father which is in heaven. [34]Think not that I am come to send peace on earth: I came not to send peace, but a sword. [35]For I am come to set a man at variance against his father, and the daughter against her mother, and the daughter in law against her mother in law. [36]And a man's foes shall be they of his own household. [37]He that loveth father or mother more than me is not worthy of me: and he that loveth son or daughter more than me is not worthy of me."

Luke 14:26 "If any man come to me, and hate not his father, and mother, and wife, and children, and brethren, and sisters, yea, and his own life also, he cannot be my disciple."

Those That Love The Lord
Exodus 20:2-6 "[2]I am the LORD thy God, which have brought thee out of the land of Egypt, out of the house of bondage. [3]Thou shalt have no other

gods before me. ⁴Thou shalt not make unto thee any graven image, or any likeness of any thing that is in heaven above, or that is in the earth beneath, or that is in the water under the earth: ⁵Thou shalt not bow down thyself to them, nor serve them: for I the LORD thy God am a jealous God, visiting the iniquity of the fathers upon the children unto the third and fourth generation of them that hate me; ⁶And shewing mercy unto thousands of them that love me, and keep my commandments."

Deuteronomy 5:6-10 "⁶I am the LORD thy God, which brought thee out of the land of Egypt, from the house of bondage. ⁷Thou shalt have none other gods before me. ⁸Thou shalt not make thee any graven image, or any likeness of any thing that is in heaven above, or that is in the earth beneath, or that is in the waters beneath the earth: ⁹Thou shalt not bow down thyself unto them, nor serve them: for I the LORD thy God am a jealous God, visiting the iniquity of the fathers upon the children unto the third and fourth generation of them that hate me, ¹⁰And shewing mercy unto thousands of them that love me and keep my commandments."

Deuteronomy 7:9 "Know therefore that the LORD thy God, he is God, the faithful God, which keepeth covenant and mercy with them that love him and keep his commandments to a thousand generations."

Nehemiah 1:5 "And said, I beseech thee, O LORD God of heaven, the great and terrible God, that keepeth covenant and mercy for them that love him and observe his commandments."

Psalm 97:10 "Ye that love the LORD, hate evil: he preserveth the souls of his saints; he delivereth them out of the hand of the wicked."

Psalm 145:20 "The LORD preserveth all them that love him: but all the wicked will he destroy."

Isaiah 56:6-7 "⁶Also the sons of the stranger, that join themselves to the LORD, to serve him, and to love the name of the LORD, to be his servants, every one that keepeth the sabbath from polluting it, and taketh hold of my covenant; ⁷Even them will I bring to my holy mountain, and make them joyful in my house of prayer: their burnt offerings and their sacrifices shall be accepted upon mine altar; for mine house shall be called an house of prayer for all people."

Isaiah 64:4 "For since the beginning of the world men have not heard, nor perceived by the ear, neither hath the eye seen, O God, beside thee, what he hath prepared for him that waiteth for him."

Daniel 9:4 "And I prayed unto the LORD my God, and made my confession, and said, O Lord, the great and dreadful God, keeping the covenant and mercy to them that love him, and to them that keep his commandments."

John 14:21-28 "²¹He that hath my commandments, and keepeth them, he it is that loveth me: and he that loveth me shall be loved of my Father, and I will love him, and will manifest myself to him. ²²Judas saith unto him, not Iscariot, Lord, how is it that thou wilt manifest thyself unto us, and not unto the world? ²³Jesus answered and said unto him, If a man love me, he will keep my words: and my Father will love him, and we will come unto him, and make our abode with him. ²⁴He that loveth me not keepeth not my sayings: and the word which ye hear is not mine, but the Father's which sent me. ²⁵These things have I spoken unto you, being yet present with you. ²⁶But the Comforter, which is the Holy Ghost, whom the Father will send in my name, he shall teach you all things, and bring all things to your remembrance, whatsoever I have said unto you. ²⁷Peace I leave with you, my peace I give unto you: not as the world giveth, give I unto you. Let not your heart be troubled, neither let it be afraid. ²⁸Ye have heard how I said unto you, I go away, and come again unto you. If ye loved me, ye would rejoice, because I said, I go unto the Father: for my Father is greater than I."

Romans 8:28 "And we know that all things work together for good to them that love God, to them who are the called according to his purpose."

1 Corinthians 2:9 "But as it is written, Eye hath not seen, nor ear heard, neither have entered into the heart of man, the things which God hath prepared for them that love him."

1 Corinthians 8:3 "But if any man love God, the same is known of him."

James 2:5 "Hearken, my beloved brethren, Hath not God chosen the poor of this world rich in faith, and heirs of the kingdom which he hath promised to them that love him?"

1 John 4:21 "And this commandment have we from him, That he who loveth God love his brother also."

1 John 5:1-2 "¹Whosoever believeth that Jesus is the Christ is born of God: and every one that loveth him that begat loveth him also that is begotten of him. ²By this we know that we love the children of God, when we love God, and keep his commandments."

Those That Love The World
1 John 2:15 "Love not the world, neither the things that are in the world. If any man love the world, the love of the Father is not in him."

Those That Love Wisdom
Proverbs 8:12-21 "¹²I wisdom dwell with prudence, and find out knowledge of witty inventions. ¹³The fear of the LORD is to hate evil: pride, and arrogancy, and the evil way, and the froward mouth, do I hate. ¹⁴Counsel is mine, and sound wisdom: I am understanding; I have strength. ¹⁵By me kings reign, and princes decree justice. ¹⁶By me princes rule, and nobles, even all the judges of the earth. ¹⁷I love them that love me; and those that seek me early shall find me. ¹⁸Riches and honour are with me; yea, durable riches and righteousness. ¹⁹My fruit is better than gold, yea, than fine gold; and my revenue than choice silver. ²⁰I lead in the way of righteousness, in the midst of the paths of judgment: ²¹That I may cause those that love me to inherit substance; and I will fill their treasures."

Proverbs 29:3 "Whoso loveth wisdom rejoiceth his father: but he that keepeth company with harlots spendeth his substance."

Those Whom The Lord Loves
Proverbs 3:11-12 "¹¹My son, despise not the chastening of the LORD; neither be weary of his correction: ¹²For whom the LORD loveth he correcteth; even as a father the son in whom he delighteth."

Revelation 3:14-19 "¹⁴And unto the angel of the church of the Laodiceans write; These things saith the Amen, the faithful and true witness, the beginning of the creation of God; ¹⁵I know thy works, that thou art neither cold nor hot: I would thou wert cold or hot. ¹⁶So then because thou art lukewarm, and neither cold nor hot, I will spue thee out of my mouth. ¹⁷Because thou sayest, I am rich, and increased with goods, and have need of nothing; and knowest not that thou art wretched, and miserable, and poor, and blind, and naked: ¹⁸I counsel thee to buy of me gold tried in the fire, that thou mayest be rich; and white raiment, that thou mayest be clothed, and that the shame of thy nakedness do not appear; and anoint thine eyes with eyesalve, that thou mayest see. ¹⁹As many as I love, I rebuke and chasten: be zealous therefore, and repent."

Walking In Love
Ephesians 5:2 "And walk in love, as Christ also hath loved us, and hath given himself for us an offering and a sacrifice to God for a sweetsmelling savour."

What Love Does
Proverbs 10:12 "Hatred stirreth up strifes: but love covereth all sins."

What Love Is
Romans 13:8-10 "⁸Owe no man any thing, but to love one another: for he that loveth another hath fulfilled the law. ⁹For this, Thou shalt not commit adultery, Thou shalt not kill, Thou shalt not steal, Thou shalt not bear false witness, Thou shalt not covet; and if there be any other commandment, it is briefly comprehended in this saying, namely, Thou shalt love thy neighbour as thyself. ¹⁰Love worketh no ill to his neighbour: therefore love is the fulfilling of the law."

2 John 3-6 "³Grace be with you, mercy, and peace, from God the Father, and from the Lord Jesus Christ, the Son of the Father, in truth and love. ⁴I rejoiced greatly that I found of thy children walking in truth, as we have received a commandment from the Father. ⁵And now I beseech thee, lady, not as though I wrote a new commandment unto thee, but that which we had from the beginning, that we love one another. ⁶And this is love, that we walk after his commandments. This is the commandment, That, as ye have heard from the beginning, ye should walk in it."

What Not To Love
Zechariah 8:17 "And let none of you imagine evil in your hearts against his neighbour; and love no false oath: for all these are things that I hate, saith the LORD."

1 John 2:15 "Love not the world, neither the things that are in the world. If any man love the world, the love of the Father is not in him."

What The Lord Loves
Psalm 11:7 "For the righteous LORD loveth righteousness; his countenance doth behold the upright."

Psalm 33:4-5 "⁴For the word of the LORD is right; and all his works are done in truth. ⁵He loveth righteousness and judgment: the earth is full of the goodness of the LORD."

Psalm 37:28 "For the LORD loveth judgment, and forsaketh not his saints; they are preserved for ever: but the seed of the wicked shall be cut off."

Isaiah 61:8 "For I the LORD love judgment, I hate robbery for burnt offering; and I will direct their work in truth, and I will make an everlasting covenant with them."

What To Love
Amos 5:15 "Hate the evil, and love the good, and establish judgment in the gate: it may be that the LORD God of hosts will be gracious unto the remnant of Joseph."

Who Loves Jesus Christ
John 8:42 "Jesus said unto them, If God were your Father, ye would love me: for I proceeded forth and came from God; neither came I of myself, but he sent me."

John 14:9-15 "⁹Jesus saith unto him, Have I been so long time with you, and yet hast thou not known me, Philip? he that hath seen me hath seen the Father; and how sayest thou then, Shew us the Father? ¹⁰Believest thou not that I am in the Father, and the Father in me? the words that I speak unto you I speak not of myself: but the Father that dwelleth in me, he doeth the works. ¹¹Believe me that I am in the Father, and the Father in me: or else believe me for the very works' sake. ¹²Verily, verily, I say unto you, He that believeth on me, the works that I do shall he do also; and greater works than these shall he do; because I go unto my Father. ¹³And whatsoever ye shall ask in my name, that will I do, that the Father may be glorified in the Son. ¹⁴If ye shall ask any thing in my name, I will do it. ¹⁵If ye love me, keep my commandments."

John 14:21-23 "²¹He that hath my commandments, and keepeth them, he it is that loveth me: and he that loveth me shall be loved of my Father, and I will love him, and will manifest myself to him. ²²Judas saith unto him, not Iscariot, Lord, how is it that thou wilt manifest thyself unto us, and not unto the world? ²³Jesus answered and said unto him, If a man love me, he will keep my words: and my Father will love him, and we will come unto him, and make our abode with him."

Who Loves God's Children
1 John 5:1-2 "¹Whosoever believeth that Jesus is the Christ is born of God: and every one that loveth him that begat loveth him also that is begotten of him. ²By this we know that we love the children of God, when we love God, and keep his commandments."

Who Seeks Love
Proverbs 17:9 "He that covereth a transgression seeketh love; but he that repeateth a matter separateth very friends."

Who Shall Abide In Christ's Love
John 15:1-10 "¹I am the true vine, and my Father is the husbandman. ²Every branch in me that beareth not fruit he taketh away: and every branch that beareth fruit, he purgeth it, that it may bring forth more fruit. ³Now ye are clean through the word which I have spoken unto you. ⁴Abide in me, and I in you. As the branch cannot bear fruit of itself, except it abide in the vine; no more can ye, except ye abide in me. ⁵I am the vine, ye are the branches: He that abideth in me, and I in him, the same bringeth forth much fruit: for without me ye can do nothing. ⁶If a man abide not in me, he is cast forth as a branch, and is withered; and men gather them, and cast them into the fire, and they are burned. ⁷If ye abide in me, and my words abide in you, ye shall ask what ye will, and it shall be done unto you. ⁸Herein is my Father glorified, that ye bear much fruit; so shall ye be my disciples. ⁹As the Father hath loved me, so have I loved you: continue ye in my love. ¹⁰If ye keep my commandments, ye shall abide in my love; even as I have kept my Father's commandments, and abide in his love."

Who The Lord Loves
Deuteronomy 7:6-8 "⁶For thou art an holy people unto the LORD thy God: the LORD thy God hath chosen thee to be a special people unto himself, above all people that are upon the face of the

earth. [7]The LORD did not set his love upon you, nor choose you, because ye were more in number than any people; for ye were the fewest of all people: [8]But because the LORD loved you, and because he would keep the oath which he had sworn unto your fathers, hath the LORD brought you out with a mighty hand, and redeemed you out of the house of bondmen, from the hand of Pharaoh king of Egypt."

Deuteronomy 7:11-13 "[11]Thou shalt therefore keep the commandments, and the statutes, and the judgments, which I command thee this day, to do them. [12]Wherefore it shall come to pass, if ye hearken to these judgments, and keep, and do them, that the LORD thy God shall keep unto thee the covenant and the mercy which he sware unto thy fathers: [13]And he will love thee, and bless thee, and multiply thee: he will also bless the fruit of thy womb, and the fruit of thy land, thy corn, and thy wine, and thine oil, the increase of thy kine, and the flocks of thy sheep, in the land which he sware unto thy fathers to give thee."

Deuteronomy 10:17-18 "[17]For the LORD your God is God of gods, and Lord of lords, a great God, a mighty, and a terrible, which regardeth not persons, nor taketh reward: [18]He doth execute the judgment of the fatherless and widow, and loveth the stranger, in giving him food and raiment."

Psalm 146:8 "The LORD openeth the eyes of the blind: the LORD raiseth them that are bowed down: the LORD loveth the righteous."

Proverbs 15:9 "The way of the wicked is an abomination unto the LORD: but he loveth him that followeth after righteousness."

Isaiah 43:3-4 "[3]For I am the LORD thy God, the Holy One of Israel, thy Saviour: I gave Egypt for thy ransom, Ethiopia and Seba for thee. [4]Since thou wast precious in my sight, thou hast been honourable, and I have loved thee: therefore will I give men for thee, and people for thy life."

John 14:21-23 "[21]He that hath my commandments, and keepeth them, he it is that loveth me: and he that loveth me shall be loved of my Father, and I will love him, and will manifest myself to him. [22]Judas saith unto him, not Iscariot, Lord, how is it that thou wilt manifest thyself unto us, and not unto the world? [23]Jesus answered and said unto

him, If a man love me, he will keep my words: and my Father will love him, and we will come unto him, and make our abode with him."

2 Corinthians 9:6-7 "[6]But this I say, He which soweth sparingly shall reap also sparingly; and he which soweth bountifully shall reap also bountifully. [7]Every man according as he purposeth in his heart, so let him give; not grudgingly, or of necessity: for God loveth a cheerful giver."

Revelation 3:7-9 "[7]And to the angel of the church in Philadelphia write; These things saith he that is holy, he that is true, he that hath the key of David, he that openeth, and no man shutteth; and shutteth, and no man openeth; [8]I know thy works: behold, I have set before thee an open door, and no man can shut it: for thou hast a little strength, and hast kept my word, and hast not denied my name. [9]Behold, I will make them of the synagogue of Satan, which say they are Jews, and are not, but do lie; behold, I will make them to come and worship before thy feet, and to know that I have loved thee."

Who The Love Of God Is Perfected In

1 John 2:1-5 "[1]My little children, these things write I unto you, that ye sin not. And if any man sin, we have an advocate with the Father, Jesus Christ the righteous: [2]And he is the propitiation for our sins: and not for ours only, but also for the sins of the whole world. [3]And hereby we do know that we know him, if we keep his commandments. [4]He that saith, I know him, and keepeth not his commandments, is a liar, and the truth is not in him. [5]But whoso keepeth his word, in him verily is the love of God perfected: hereby know we that we are in him."

Who The Love Of The Father Is Not In

1 John 2:15 "Love not the world, neither the things that are in the world. If any man love the world, the love of the Father is not in him."

Who To Love

Deuteronomy 10:17-19 "[17]For the LORD your God is God of gods, and Lord of lords, a great God, a mighty, and a terrible, which regardeth not persons, nor taketh reward: [18]He doth execute the judgment of the fatherless and widow, and loveth the stranger, in giving him food and raiment. [19]Love ye therefore the stranger: for ye were strangers in the land of Egypt."

Matthew 5:43-48 "⁴³Ye have heard that it hath been said, Thou shalt love thy neighbour, and hate thine enemy. ⁴⁴But I say unto you, Love your enemies, bless them that curse you, do good to them that hate you, and pray for them which despitefully use you, and persecute you; ⁴⁵That ye may be the children of your Father which is in heaven: for he maketh his sun to rise on the evil and on the good, and sendeth rain on the just and on the unjust. ⁴⁶For if ye love them which love you, what reward have ye? do not even the publicans the same? ⁴⁷And if ye salute your brethren only, what do ye more than others? do not even the publicans so? ⁴⁸Be ye therefore perfect, even as your Father which is in heaven is perfect."

Luke 6:27-35 "²⁷But I say unto you which hear, Love your enemies, do good to them which hate you, ²⁸Bless them that curse you, and pray for them which despitefully use you. ²⁹And unto him that smiteth thee on the one cheek offer also the other; and him that taketh away thy cloke forbid not to take thy coat also. ³⁰Give to every man that asketh of thee; and of him that taketh away thy goods ask them not again. ³¹And as ye would that men should do to you, do ye also to them likewise. ³²For if ye love them which love you, what thank have ye? for sinners also love those that love them. ³³And if ye do good to them which do good to you, what thank have ye? for sinners also do even the same. ³⁴And if ye lend to them of whom ye hope to receive, what thank have ye? for sinners also lend to sinners, to receive as much again. ³⁵But love ye your enemies, and do good, and lend, hoping for nothing again; and your reward shall be great, and ye shall be the children of the Highest: for he is kind unto the unthankful and to the evil."

Why Love Waxes Cold
Matthew 24:12 "And because iniquity shall abound, the love of many shall wax cold."

LOWLINESS

Jesus Christ Being Lowly In Heart
Zechariah 9:9 "Rejoice greatly, O daughter of Zion; shout, O daughter of Jerusalem: behold, thy King cometh unto thee: he is just, and having salvation; lowly, and riding upon an ass, and upon a colt the foal of an ass."

Matthew 11:25-30 "²⁵At that time Jesus answered and said, I thank thee, O Father, Lord of heaven and earth, because thou hast hid these things from the wise and prudent, and hast revealed them unto babes. ²⁶ Even so, Father: for so it seemed good in thy sight. ²⁷ All things are delivered unto me of my Father: and no man knoweth the Son, but the Father; neither knoweth any man the Father, save the Son, and he to whomsoever the Son will reveal him. ²⁸ Come unto me, all ye that labour and are heavy laden, and I will give you rest. ²⁹ Take my yoke upon you, and learn of me; for I am meek and lowly in heart: and ye shall find rest unto your souls. ³⁰ For my yoke is easy, and my burden is light."

The Lowly
Psalm 138:6 "Though the LORD be high, yet hath he respect unto the lowly: but the proud he knoweth afar off."

Proverbs 3:33-34 "³³The curse of the LORD is in the house of the wicked: but he blesseth the habitation of the just. ³⁴Surely he scorneth the scorners: but he giveth grace unto the lowly."

Proverbs 11:2 "When pride cometh, then cometh shame: but with the lowly is wisdom."

Walking With Lowliness
Ephesians 4:1-2 "¹I therefore, the prisoner of the Lord, beseech you that ye walk worthy of the vocation wherewith ye are called, ²With all lowliness and meekness, with longsuffering, forbearing one another in love."

LUST

Abstaining From Lusts
Romans 13:14 "But put ye on the Lord Jesus Christ, and make not provision for the flesh, to fulfil the lusts thereof."

1 Peter 2:11 "Dearly beloved, I beseech you as strangers and pilgrims, abstain from fleshly lusts, which war against the soul."

Fleeing From Youthful Lusts
2 Timothy 2:22 "Flee also youthful lusts: but follow righteousness, faith, charity, peace, with them that call on the Lord out of a pure heart."

The Lust Of The Flesh And Eyes

1 John 2:16 "For all that is in the world, the lust of the flesh, and the lust of the eyes, and the pride of life, is not of the Father, but is of the world."

Those That Lust After A Woman

Matthew 5:28 "But I say unto you, That whosoever looketh on a woman to lust after her hath committed adultery with her already in his heart."

What Comes Out Of Lust

James 4:1-3 "¹From whence come wars and fightings among you? come they not hence, even of your lusts that war in your members? ²Ye lust, and have not: ye kill, and desire to have, and cannot obtain: ye fight and war, yet ye have not, because ye ask not. ³Ye ask, and receive not, because ye ask amiss, that ye may consume it upon your lusts."

What Lust Does

1 Timothy 6:9 "But they that will be rich fall into temptation and a snare, and into many foolish and hurtful lusts, which drown men in destruction and perdition."

James 1:15 "Then when lust hath conceived, it bringeth forth sin: and sin, when it is finished, bringeth forth death."

1 Peter 2:11 "Dearly beloved, I beseech you as strangers and pilgrims, abstain from fleshly lusts, which war against the soul."

What Lusts Against The Spirit

Galatians 5:16-17 "¹⁶This I say then, Walk in the Spirit, and ye shall not fulfil the lust of the flesh. ¹⁷For the flesh lusteth against the Spirit, and the Spirit against the flesh: and these are contrary the one to the other: so that ye cannot do the things that ye would."

Who Falls Into Many Lusts

1 Timothy 6:9 "But they that will be rich fall into temptation and a snare, and into many foolish and hurtful lusts, which drown men in destruction and perdition."

Who Has Crucified Their Lusts

Galatians 5:24 "And they that are Christ's have crucified the flesh with the affections and lusts."

Who Shall Not Fulfill The Lust Of The Flesh

Galatians 5:16-21 "¹⁶This I say then, Walk in the Spirit, and ye shall not fulfil the lust of the flesh. ¹⁷For the flesh lusteth against the Spirit, and the Spirit against the flesh: and these are contrary the one to the other: so that ye cannot do the things that ye would. ¹⁸But if ye be led of the Spirit, ye are not under the law. ¹⁹Now the works of the flesh are manifest, which are these; Adultery, fornication, uncleanness, lasciviousness, ²⁰Idolatry, witchcraft, hatred, variance, emulations, wrath, strife, seditions, heresies, ²¹Envyings, murders, drunkenness, revellings, and such like: of the which I tell you before, as I have also told you in time past, that they which do such things shall not inherit the kingdom of God."

Who Walks After Their Own Lusts

Jude 7-16 "⁷Even as Sodom and Gomorrha, and the cities about them in like manner, giving themselves over to fornication, and going after strange flesh, are set forth for an example, suffering the vengeance of eternal fire. ⁸Likewise also these filthy dreamers defile the flesh, despise dominion, and speak evil of dignities. ⁹Yet Michael the archangel, when contending with the devil he disputed about the body of Moses, durst not bring against him a railing accusation, but said, The Lord rebuke thee. ¹⁰But these speak evil of those things which they know not: but what they know naturally, as brute beasts, in those things they corrupt themselves. ¹¹Woe unto them! for they have gone in the way of Cain, and ran greedily after the error of Balaam for reward, and perished in the gainsaying of Core. ¹²These are spots in your feasts of charity, when they feast with you, feeding themselves without fear: clouds they are without water, carried about of winds; trees whose fruit withereth, without fruit, twice dead, plucked up by the roots; ¹³Raging waves of the sea, foaming out their own shame; wandering stars, to whom is reserved the blackness of darkness for ever. ¹⁴And Enoch also, the seventh from Adam, prophesied of these, saying, Behold, the Lord cometh with ten thousands of his saints, ¹⁵To execute judgment upon all, and to convince all that are ungodly among them of all their ungodly deeds which they have ungodly committed, and of all their hard speeches which ungodly sinners have spoken against him. ¹⁶These are murmurers, complainers, walking after their own lusts; and their mouth speaketh great swelling words, having men's persons in admiration because of advantage."

LYING/LIES

God Not Being Able To Lie
Titus 1:2 "In hope of eternal life, which God, that cannot lie, promised before the world began."

If Rulers Listen To Lies
Proverbs 29:12 "If a ruler hearken to lies, all his servants are wicked."

Liars
Psalm 63:11 "But the king shall rejoice in God; every one that sweareth by him shall glory: but the mouth of them that speak lies shall be stopped."

Proverbs 10:18 "He that hideth hatred with lying lips, and he that uttereth a slander, is a fool."

Proverbs 17:4 "A wicked doer giveth heed to false lips; and a liar giveth ear to a naughty tongue."

Proverbs 19:5 "A false witness shall not be unpunished, and he that speaketh lies shall not escape."

Proverbs 19:9 "A false witness shall not be unpunished, and he that speaketh lies shall perish."

Proverbs 19:22 "The desire of a man is his kindness: and a poor man is better than a liar."

Proverbs 25:18 "A man that beareth false witness against his neighbour is a maul, and a sword, and a sharp arrow."

1 Timothy 1:8-10 "[8]But we know that the law is good, if a man use it lawfully; [9]Knowing this, that the law is not made for a righteous man, but for the lawless and disobedient, for the ungodly and for sinners, for unholy and profane, for murderers of fathers and murderers of mothers, for manslayers, [10]For whoremongers, for them that defile themselves with mankind, for menstealers, for liars, for perjured persons, and if there be any other thing that is contrary to sound doctrine."

Revelation 21:8 "But the fearful, and unbelieving, and the abominable, and murderers, and whoremongers, and sorcerers, and idolaters, and all liars, shall have their part in the lake which burneth with fire and brimstone: which is the second death."

Revelation 22:13-15 "[13]I am Alpha and Omega, the beginning and the end, the first and the last. [14]Blessed are they that do his commandments, that they may have right to the tree of life, and may enter in through the gates into the city. [15]For without are dogs, and sorcerers, and whoremongers, and murderers, and idolaters, and whosoever loveth and maketh a lie."

Lying Lips
Psalm 31:18 "Let the lying lips be put to silence; which speak grievous things proudly and contemptuously against the righteous."

Proverbs 6:16-19 "[16]These six things doth the LORD hate: yea, seven are an abomination unto him: [17]A proud look, a lying tongue, and hands that shed innocent blood, [18]An heart that deviseth wicked imaginations, feet that be swift in running to mischief, [19]A false witness that speaketh lies, and he that soweth discord among brethren."

Proverbs 12:19 "The lip of truth shall be established for ever: but a lying tongue is but for a moment."

Proverbs 12:22 "Lying lips are abomination to the LORD: but they that deal truly are his delight."

Proverbs 17:7 "Excellent speech becometh not a fool: much less do lying lips a prince."

Proverbs 26:28 "A lying tongue hateth those that are afflicted by it; and a flattering mouth worketh ruin."

Not Lying
Exodus 20:16 "Thou shalt not bear false witness against thy neighbour."

Exodus 23:1 "Thou shalt not raise a false report: put not thine hand with the wicked to be an unrighteous witness."

Exodus 23:7 "Keep thee far from a false matter; and the innocent and righteous slay thou not: for I will not justify the wicked."

Leviticus 19:11 "Ye shall not steal, neither deal falsely, neither lie one to another."

Deuteronomy 5:20 "Neither shalt thou bear false witness against thy neighbour."

Psalm 31:18 "Let the lying lips be put to silence; which speak grievous things proudly and contemptuously against the righteous."

Proverbs 24:28 "Be not a witness against thy neighbour without cause; and deceive not with thy lips."

Matthew 19:18 "He saith unto him, Which? Jesus said, Thou shalt do no murder, Thou shalt not commit adultery, Thou shalt not steal, Thou shalt not bear false witness,"

Luke 3:14 "And the soldiers likewise demanded of him, saying, And what shall we do? And he said unto them, Do violence to no man, neither accuse any falsely; and be content with your wages."

Romans 13:8-9 "⁸Owe no man any thing, but to love one another: for he that loveth another hath fulfilled the law. ⁹For this, Thou shalt not commit adultery, Thou shalt not kill, Thou shalt not steal, Thou shalt not bear false witness, Thou shalt not covet; and if there be any other commandment, it is briefly comprehended in this saying, namely, Thou shalt love thy neighbour as thyself."

Ephesians 4:25 "Wherefore putting away lying, speak every man truth with his neighbour: for we are members one of another."

Colossians 3:9 "Lie not one to another, seeing that ye have put off the old man with his deeds."

The Acquiring Of Wealth By Lying

Proverbs 21:6 "The getting of treasures by a lying tongue is a vanity tossed to and fro of them that seek death."

The Reward For Lying

Hosea 4:1-3 "¹Hear the word of the LORD, ye children of Israel: for the LORD hath a controversy with the inhabitants of the land, because there is no truth, nor mercy, nor knowledge of God in the land. ²By swearing, and lying, and killing, and stealing, and committing adultery, they break out, and blood toucheth blood. ³Therefore shall the land mourn, and every one that dwelleth therein shall languish, with the beasts of the field, and with the fowls of heaven; yea, the fishes of the sea also shall be taken away."

Amos 2:4 "Thus saith the LORD; For three transgressions of Judah, and for four, I will not turn away the punishment thereof; because they have despised the law of the LORD, and have not kept his commandments, and their lies caused them to err, after the which their fathers have walked."

Who Hates Lying

Proverbs 13:5 "A righteous man hateth lying: but a wicked man is loathsome, and cometh to shame."

Who Is A Liar

Proverbs 14:5 "A faithful witness will not lie: but a false witness will utter lies."

Proverbs 14:25 "A true witness delivereth souls: but a deceitful witness speaketh lies."

Proverbs 30:5-6 "⁵Every word of God is pure: he is a shield unto them that put their trust in him. ⁶Add thou not unto his words, lest he reprove thee, and thou be found a liar."

Isaiah 59:1-4 "¹Behold, the LORD's hand is not shortened, that it cannot save; neither his ear heavy, that it cannot hear: ²But your iniquities have separated between you and your God, and your sins have hid his face from you, that he will not hear. ³For your hands are defiled with blood, and your fingers with iniquity; your lips have spoken lies, your tongue hath muttered perverseness. ⁴None calleth for justice, nor any pleadeth for truth: they trust in vanity, and speak lies; they conceive mischief, and bring forth iniquity."

Micah 6:10-12 "¹⁰Are there yet the treasures of wickedness in the house of the wicked, and the scant measure that is abominable? ¹¹Shall I count them pure with the wicked balances, and with the bag of deceitful weights? ¹²For the rich men thereof are full of violence, and the inhabitants thereof have spoken lies, and their tongue is deceitful in their mouth."

John 8:42-44 "⁴²Jesus said unto them, If God were your Father, ye would love me: for I proceeded forth and came from God; neither came I of myself, but he sent me. ⁴³Why do ye not understand my speech? even because ye cannot hear my word. ⁴⁴Ye are of your father the devil, and the lusts of your father ye will do. He was a murderer from the beginning, and abode not in the truth, because there is no truth in him. When he speaketh a lie, he speaketh of his own: for he is a liar, and the father of it."

1 John 1:5-6 "⁵This then is the message which we have heard of him, and declare unto you, that God is light, and in him is no darkness at all. ⁶If we say that we have fellowship with him, and walk in darkness, we lie, and do not the truth."

1 John 2:1-4 "¹My little children, these things write I unto you, that ye sin not. And if any man sin, we have an advocate with the Father, Jesus Christ the righteous: ²And he is the propitiation for our sins: and not for ours only, but also for the sins of the whole world. ³And hereby we do know that we know him, if we keep his commandments. ⁴He that saith, I know him, and keepeth not his commandments, is a liar, and the truth is not in him."

1 John 2:22 "Who is a liar but he that denieth that Jesus is the Christ? He is antichrist, that denieth the Father and the Son."

1 John 4:20 "If a man say, I love God, and hateth his brother, he is a liar: for he that loveth not his brother whom he hath seen, how can he love God whom he hath not seen?"

Who Will Believe Lies

2 Thessalonians 2:8-12 "⁸And then shall that Wicked be revealed, whom the Lord shall consume with the spirit of his mouth, and shall destroy with the brightness of his coming: ⁹Even him, whose coming is after the working of Satan with all power and signs and lying wonders, ¹⁰And with all deceivableness of unrighteousness in them that perish; because they received not the love of the truth, that they might be saved. ¹¹And for this cause God shall send them strong delusion, that they should believe a lie: ¹²That they all might be damned who believed not the truth, but had pleasure in unrighteousness."

Who Will Not Lie

Proverbs 14:5 "A faithful witness will not lie: but a false witness will utter lies."

Zephaniah 3:13 "The remnant of Israel shall not do iniquity, nor speak lies; neither shall a deceitful tongue be found in their mouth: for they shall feed and lie down, and none shall make them afraid."

Mm

MALICE

Not Being Malicious

Ephesians 4:31 "Let all bitterness, and wrath, and anger, and clamour, and evil speaking, be put away from you, with all malice."

1 Peter 2:1 "Wherefore laying aside all malice, and all guile, and hypocrisies, and envies, and all evil speakings,"

MAN

Jesus Christ Being The Head Of Man

1 Corinthians 3:23 "And ye are Christ's; and Christ is God's."

1 Corinthians 11:2-3 "²Now I praise you, brethren, that ye remember me in all things, and keep the ordinances, as I delivered them to you. ³ But I would have you know, that the head of every man is Christ; and the head of the woman is the man; and the head of Christ is God."

Ephesians 5:22-23 "²²Wives, submit yourselves unto your own husbands, as unto the Lord. ²³ For the husband is the head of the wife, even as Christ is the head of the church: and he is the saviour of the body."

Man Being Born Into Trouble

Job 5:7 "Yet man is born unto trouble, as the sparks fly upward."

Job 14:1-2 "¹Man that is born of a woman is of few days, and full of trouble. ²He cometh forth like a flower, and is cut down: he fleeth also as a shadow, and continueth not."

Man Entering And Leaving The World With Nothing

Job 1:20-21 "²⁰Then Job arose, and rent his mantle, and shaved his head, and fell down upon the ground, and worshipped, ²¹And said, Naked came I out of my mother's womb, and naked shall I return thither: the LORD gave, and the LORD hath taken away; blessed be the name of the LORD."

1 Timothy 6:6-8 "⁶But godliness with contentment is great gain. ⁷For we brought nothing into this world, and it is certain we can carry nothing out. ⁸And having food and raiment let us be therewith content."

Man Having Authority Over God's Creation

Genesis 1:26-28 "²⁶And God said, Let us make man in our image, after our likeness: and let them have dominion over the fish of the sea, and over the fowl of the air, and over the cattle, and over all the earth, and over every creeping thing that creepeth upon the earth. ²⁷So God created man in his own image, in the image of God created he him; male and female created he them. ²⁸And God blessed them, and God said unto them, Be fruitful, and multiply, and replenish the earth, and subdue it: and have dominion over the fish of the sea, and over the fowl of the air, and over every living thing that moveth upon the earth."

Genesis 9:1-2 "¹And God blessed Noah and his sons, and said unto them, Be fruitful, and multiply, and replenish the earth. ²And the fear of you and the dread of you shall be upon every beast of the earth, and upon every fowl of the air, upon all that moveth upon the earth, and upon all the fishes of the sea; into your hand are they delivered."

Psalm 8:4-8 "⁴What is man, that thou art mindful of him? and the son of man, that thou visitest him? ⁵For thou hast made him a little lower than the angels, and hast crowned him with glory and honour. ⁶Thou madest him to have dominion over the works of thy hands; thou hast put all things under his feet: ⁷All sheep and oxen, yea, and the beasts of the field; ⁸The fowl of the air, and the fish of the sea, and whatsoever passeth through the paths of the seas."

Hebrews 2:6-8 "⁶But one in a certain place testified, saying, What is man, that thou art mindful of him? or the son of man, that thou visitest him? ⁷Thou madest him a little lower than the angels; thou crownedst him with glory and honour, and didst set him over the works of thy hands: ⁸Thou hast put all things in subjection under his feet. For in that he put all in subjection under him, he left nothing that is not put under him. But now we see not yet all things put under him."

Man Living By The Word Of God

Deuteronomy 8:3 "And he humbled thee, and suffered thee to hunger, and fed thee with manna, which thou knewest not, neither did thy fathers know; that he might make thee know that man doth not live by bread only, but by every word that proceedeth out of the mouth of the LORD doth man live."

Matthew 4:4 "But he answered and said, It is written, Man shall not live by bread alone, but by every word that proceedeth out of the mouth of God."

Luke 4:4 "And Jesus answered him, saying, It is written, That man shall not live by bread alone, but by every word of God."

Man's Goings
Proverbs 20:24 "Man's goings are of the LORD; how can a man then understand his own way?"

That Which Is Highly Esteemed Among Men
Luke 16:15 "And he said unto them, Ye are they which justify yourselves before men; but God knoweth your hearts: for that which is highly esteemed among men is abomination in the sight of God."

The Days Of Man
Job 14:1-5 "[1]Man that is born of a woman is of few days, and full of trouble. [2]He cometh forth like a flower, and is cut down: he fleeth also as a shadow, and continueth not. [3]And dost thou open thine eyes upon such an one, and bringest me into judgment with thee? [4]Who can bring a clean thing out of an unclean? not one. [5]Seeing his days are determined, the number of his months are with thee, thou hast appointed his bounds that he cannot pass."

Psalm 103:15-16 "[15]As for man, his days are as grass: as a flower of the field, so he flourisheth. [16]For the wind passeth over it, and it is gone; and the place thereof shall know it no more."

The Duty Of Man
Ecclesiastes 12:13 "Let us hear the conclusion of the whole matter: Fear God, and keep his commandments: for this is the whole duty of man."

The First Man
Genesis 2:7 "And the LORD God formed man of the dust of the ground, and breathed into his nostrils the breath of life; and man became a living soul."

1 Corinthians 15:45 "And so it is written, The first man Adam was made a living soul; the last Adam was made a quickening spirit."

The Glory Of Man
1 Peter 1:24 "For all flesh is as grass, and all the glory of man as the flower of grass. The grass withereth, and the flower thereof falleth away."

The Heart Of Man
Genesis 6:5 "And GOD saw that the wickedness of man was great in the earth, and that every imagination of the thoughts of his heart was only evil continually."

Genesis 8:21 "And the LORD smelled a sweet savour; and the LORD said in his heart, I will not again curse the ground any more for man's sake; for the imagination of man's heart is evil from his youth; neither will I again smite any more every thing living, as I have done."

Psalm 73:26 "My flesh and my heart faileth: but God is the strength of my heart, and my portion for ever."

Proverbs 16:9 "A man's heart deviseth his way: but the LORD directeth his steps."

Proverbs 18:12 "Before destruction the heart of man is haughty, and before honour is humility."

Proverbs 19:3 "The foolishness of man perverteth his way: and his heart fretteth against the LORD."

Proverbs 19:21 "There are many devices in a man's heart; nevertheless the counsel of the LORD, that shall stand."

Jeremiah 17:9-10 "[9]The heart is deceitful above all things, and desperately wicked: who can know it? [10]I the LORD search the heart, I try the reins, even to give every man according to his ways, and according to the fruit of his doings."

Romans 1:21-22 "[21]Because that, when they knew God, they glorified him not as God, neither were thankful; but became vain in their imaginations, and their foolish heart was darkened. [22]Professing themselves to be wise, they became fools,"

1 John 3:20 "For if our heart condemn us, God is greater than our heart, and knoweth all things."

The Lord Being Greater Than Man
Job 33:12 "Behold, in this thou art not just: I will answer thee, that God is greater than man."

Isaiah 55:7-9 "[7]Let the wicked forsake his way, and the unrighteous man his thoughts: and let him return unto the LORD, and he will have mercy upon him; and to our God, for he will abundantly pardon. [8]For my thoughts are not your thoughts, neither are your ways my ways, saith the LORD. [9]For as the heavens are higher than the earth, so are my ways higher than your ways, and my thoughts than your thoughts."

1 Corinthians 1:25 "Because the foolishness of God is wiser than men; and the weakness of God is stronger than men."

1 John 4:4 "Ye are of God, little children, and have overcome them: because greater is he that is in you, than he that is in the world."

The Lord Creating Man

Genesis 1:26-31 "[26]And God said, Let us make man in our image, after our likeness: and let them have dominion over the fish of the sea, and over the fowl of the air, and over the cattle, and over all the earth, and over every creeping thing that creepeth upon the earth. [27]So God created man in his own image, in the image of God created he him; male and female created he them. [28]And God blessed them, and God said unto them, Be fruitful, and multiply, and replenish the earth, and subdue it: and have dominion over the fish of the sea, and over the fowl of the air, and over every living thing that moveth upon the earth. [29]And God said, Behold, I have given you every herb bearing seed, which is upon the face of all the earth, and every tree, in the which is the fruit of a tree yielding seed; to you it shall be for meat. [30]And to every beast of the earth, and to every fowl of the air, and to every thing that creepeth upon the earth, wherein there is life, I have given every green herb for meat: and it was so. [31]And God saw every thing that he had made, and, behold, it was very good. And the evening and the morning were the sixth day."

Genesis 2:7 "And the LORD God formed man of the dust of the ground, and breathed into his nostrils the breath of life; and man became a living soul."

Genesis 5:1-2 "[1]This is the book of the generations of Adam. In the day that God created man, in the likeness of God made he him; [2]Male and female created he them; and blessed them, and called their name Adam, in the day when they were created."

Deuteronomy 32:18 "Of the Rock that begat thee thou art unmindful, and hast forgotten God that formed thee."

Job 33:4-6 "[4]The Spirit of God hath made me, and the breath of the Almighty hath given me life. [5]If thou canst answer me, set thy words in order before me, stand up. [6]Behold, I am according to thy wish in God's stead: I also am formed out of the clay."

Job 35:10 "But none saith, Where is God my maker, who giveth songs in the night."

Psalm 100:3 "Know ye that the LORD he is God: it is he that hath made us, and not we ourselves; we are his people, and the sheep of his pasture."

Psalm 119:73-75 "[73]Thy hands have made me and fashioned me: give me understanding, that I may learn thy commandments. [74]They that fear thee will be glad when they see me; because I have hoped in thy word. [75]I know, O LORD, that thy judgments are right, and that thou in faithfulness hast afflicted me."

Psalm 139:13-17 "[13]For thou hast possessed my reins: thou hast covered me in my mother's womb. [14]I will praise thee; for I am fearfully and wonderfully made: marvellous are thy works; and that my soul knoweth right well. [15]My substance was not hid from thee, when I was made in secret, and curiously wrought in the lowest parts of the earth. [16]Thine eyes did see my substance, yet being unperfect; and in thy book all my members were written, which in continuance were fashioned, when as yet there was none of them. [17]How precious also are thy thoughts unto me, O God! how great is the sum of them!"

Isaiah 42:5 "Thus saith God the LORD, he that created the heavens, and stretched them out; he that spread forth the earth, and that which cometh out of it; he that giveth breath unto the people upon it, and spirit to them that walk therein."

Isaiah 44:2 "Thus saith the LORD that made thee, and formed thee from the womb, which will help thee; Fear not, O Jacob, my servant; and thou, Jesurun, whom I have chosen."

Isaiah 44:24 "Thus saith the LORD, thy redeemer, and he that formed thee from the womb, I am the

LORD that maketh all things; that stretcheth forth the heavens alone; that spreadeth abroad the earth by myself."

Isaiah 45:11-12 "[11]Thus saith the LORD, the Holy One of Israel, and his Maker, Ask me of things to come concerning my sons, and concerning the work of my hands command ye me. [12]I have made the earth, and created man upon it: I, even my hands, have stretched out the heavens, and all their host have I commanded."

Isaiah 51:13 "And forgettest the LORD thy maker, that hath stretched forth the heavens, and laid the foundations of the earth; and hast feared continually every day because of the fury of the oppressor, as if he were ready to destroy? and where is the fury of the oppressor?"

Isaiah 54:5 "For thy Maker is thine husband; the LORD of hosts is his name; and thy Redeemer the Holy One of Israel; The God of the whole earth shall he be called."

Isaiah 57:15-16 "[15]For thus saith the high and lofty One that inhabiteth eternity, whose name is Holy; I dwell in the high and holy place, with him also that is of a contrite and humble spirit, to revive the spirit of the humble, and to revive the heart of the contrite ones. [16]For I will not contend for ever, neither will I be always wroth: for the spirit should fail before me, and the souls which I have made."

Isaiah 64:8 "But now, O LORD, thou art our father; we are the clay, and thou our potter; and we all are the work of thy hand."

Jeremiah 1:4-5 "[4]Then the word of the LORD came unto me, saying, [5]Before I formed thee in the belly I knew thee; and before thou camest forth out of the womb I sanctified thee, and I ordained thee a prophet unto the nations."

Jeremiah 27:4-5 "[4]And command them to say unto their masters, Thus saith the LORD of hosts, the God of Israel; Thus shall ye say unto your masters; [5]I have made the earth, the man and the beast that are upon the ground, by my great power and by my outstretched arm, and have given it unto whom it seemed meet unto me."

Zechariah 12:1 "The burden of the word of the LORD for Israel, saith the LORD, which stretcheth forth the heavens, and layeth the foundation of the earth, and formeth the spirit of man within him."

Malachi 2:10 "Have we not all one father? hath not one God created us? why do we deal treacherously every man against his brother, by profaning the covenant of our fathers?"

Matthew 19:4-6 "[4]And he answered and said unto them, Have ye not read, that he which made them at the beginning made them male and female, [5]And said, For this cause shall a man leave father and mother, and shall cleave to his wife: and they twain shall be one flesh? [6]Wherefore they are no more twain, but one flesh. What therefore God hath joined together, let not man put asunder."

Mark 10:6 "But from the beginning of the creation God made them male and female."

Acts 17:23-26 "[23]For as I passed by, and beheld your devotions, I found an altar with this inscription, TO THE UNKNOWN GOD. Whom therefore ye ignorantly worship, him declare I unto you. [24]God that made the world and all things therein, seeing that he is Lord of heaven and earth, dwelleth not in temples made with hands; [25]Neither is worshipped with men's hands, as though he needed any thing, seeing he giveth to all life, and breath, and all things; [26]And hath made of one blood all nations of men for to dwell on all the face of the earth, and hath determined the times before appointed, and the bounds of their habitation."

James 3:9 "Therewith bless we God, even the Father; and therewith curse we men, which are made after the similitude of God."

The Misery Of Man
Ecclesiastes 8:6 "Because to every purpose there is time and judgment, therefore the misery of man is great upon him."

The New Man
Ephesians 4:22-24 "[22]That ye put off concerning the former conversation the old man, which is corrupt according to the deceitful lusts; [23]And be renewed in the spirit of your mind; [24]And that ye put on the new man, which after God is created in righteousness and true holiness."

Colossians 3:1-10 "[1]If ye then be risen with Christ, seek those things which are above, where Christ sitteth on the right hand of God. ²Set your affection on things above, not on things on the earth. ³For ye are dead, and your life is hid with Christ in God. ⁴When Christ, who is our life, shall appear, then shall ye also appear with him in glory. ⁵Mortify therefore your members which are upon the earth; fornication, uncleanness, inordinate affection, evil concupiscence, and covetousness, which is idolatry: ⁶For which things' sake the wrath of God cometh on the children of disobedience: ⁷In the which ye also walked some time, when ye lived in them. ⁸But now ye also put off all these; anger, wrath, malice, blasphemy, filthy communication out of your mouth. ⁹Lie not one to another, seeing that ye have put off the old man with his deeds; ¹⁰And have put on the new man, which is renewed in knowledge after the image of him that created him."

The Old Man
Romans 6:3-6 "³Know ye not, that so many of us as were baptized into Jesus Christ were baptized into his death? ⁴Therefore we are buried with him by baptism into death: that like as Christ was raised up from the dead by the glory of the Father, even so we also should walk in newness of life. ⁵For if we have been planted together in the likeness of his death, we shall be also in the likeness of his resurrection: ⁶Knowing this, that our old man is crucified with him, that the body of sin might be destroyed, that henceforth we should not serve sin."

Ephesians 4:22 "That ye put off concerning the former conversation the old man, which is corrupt according to the deceitful lusts."

The Spirit Of Man
Proverbs 18:14 "The spirit of a man will sustain his infirmity; but a wounded spirit who can bear?"

Proverbs 20:27 "The spirit of man is the candle of the LORD, searching all the inward parts of the belly."

Ecclesiastes 12:7 "Then shall the dust return to the earth as it was: and the spirit shall return unto God who gave it."

1 Corinthians 6:19-20 "¹⁹What? know ye not that your body is the temple of the Holy Ghost which is in you, which ye have of God, and ye are not your own? ²⁰For ye are bought with a price: therefore glorify God in your body, and in your spirit, which are God's."

The Ways Of Man
Proverbs 5:21 "For the ways of man are before the eyes of the LORD, and he pondereth all his goings."

Proverbs 16:2 "All the ways of a man are clean in his own eyes; but the LORD weigheth the spirits."

Proverbs 21:2 "Every way of a man is right in his own eyes: but the LORD pondereth the hearts."

Proverbs 21:8 "The way of man is froward and strange: but as for the pure, his work is right."

Isaiah 55:7-9 "⁷Let the wicked forsake his way, and the unrighteous man his thoughts: and let him return unto the LORD, and he will have mercy upon him; and to our God, for he will abundantly pardon. ⁸For my thoughts are not your thoughts, neither are your ways my ways, saith the LORD. ⁹For as the heavens are higher than the earth, so are my ways higher than your ways, and my thoughts than your thoughts."

Jeremiah 10:23 "O LORD, I know that the way of man is not in himself: it is not in man that walketh to direct his steps."

Ezekiel 18:25-30 "²⁵Yet ye say, The way of the Lord is not equal. Hear now, O house of Israel; Is not my way equal? are not your ways unequal? ²⁶When a righteous man turneth away from his righteousness, and committeth iniquity, and dieth in them; for his iniquity that he hath done shall he die. ²⁷Again, when the wicked man turneth away from his wickedness that he hath committed, and doeth that which is lawful and right, he shall save his soul alive. ²⁸Because he considereth, and turneth away from all his transgressions that he hath committed, he shall surely live, he shall not die. ²⁹Yet saith the house of Israel, The way of the Lord is not equal. O house of Israel, are not my ways equal? are not your ways unequal? ³⁰Therefore I will judge you, O house of Israel, every one according to his ways, saith the Lord GOD. Repent, and turn yourselves from all your transgressions; so iniquity shall not be your ruin."

Ezekiel 33:17-20 "¹⁷Yet the children of thy people say, The way of the Lord is not equal: but as for them, their way is not equal. ¹⁸When the righteous turneth from his righteousness, and committeth iniquity, he shall even die thereby. [19]But if the wicked turn from his wickedness, and do that which is lawful and right, he shall live thereby. [20]Yet ye say, The way of the Lord is not equal. O ye house of Israel, I will judge you every one after his ways."

What Man Is

Genesis 2:7 "And the LORD God formed man of the dust of the ground, and breathed into his nostrils the breath of life; and man became a living soul."

Genesis 3:17-19 "[17]And unto Adam he said, Because thou hast hearkened unto the voice of thy wife, and hast eaten of the tree, of which I commanded thee, saying, Thou shalt not eat of it: cursed is the ground for thy sake; in sorrow shalt thou eat of it all the days of thy life; [18]Thorns also and thistles shall it bring forth to thee; and thou shalt eat the herb of the field; [19]In the sweat of thy face shalt thou eat bread, till thou return unto the ground; for out of it wast thou taken: for dust thou art, and unto dust shalt thou return."

Genesis 6:3 "And the LORD said, My spirit shall not always strive with man, for that he also is flesh: yet his days shall be an hundred and twenty years."

Genesis 18:27 "And Abraham answered and said, Behold now, I have taken upon me to speak unto the Lord, which am but dust and ashes."

Job 4:17-21 "[17]Shall mortal man be more just than God? shall a man be more pure than his maker? [18]Behold, he put no trust in his servants; and his angels he charged with folly: [19]How much less in them that dwell in houses of clay, whose foundation is in the dust, which are crushed before the moth? [20]They are destroyed from morning to evening: they perish for ever without any regarding it. [21]Doth not their excellency which is in them go away? they die, even without wisdom."

Job 14:1-2 "[1]Man that is born of a woman is of few days, and full of trouble. [2]He cometh forth like a flower, and is cut down: he fleeth also as a shadow, and continueth not."

Job 33:4-6 "[4]The Spirit of God hath made me, and the breath of the Almighty hath given me life. [5]If thou canst answer me, set thy words in order before me, stand up. [6]Behold, I am according to thy wish in God's stead: I also am formed out of the clay."

Job 34:15 "All flesh shall perish together, and man shall turn again unto dust."

Psalm 8:4-8 "[4]What is man, that thou art mindful of him? and the son of man, that thou visitest him? [5]For thou hast made him a little lower than the angels, and hast crowned him with glory and honour. [6]Thou madest him to have dominion over the works of thy hands; thou hast put all things under his feet: [7]All sheep and oxen, yea, and the beasts of the field; [8]The fowl of the air, and the fish of the sea, and whatsoever passeth through the paths of the seas."

Psalm 39:5 "Behold, thou hast made my days as an handbreadth; and mine age is as nothing before thee: verily every man at his best state is altogether vanity. Selah."

Psalm 49:12 "Nevertheless man being in honour abideth not: he is like the beasts that perish."

Psalm 49:20 "Man that is in honour, and understandeth not, is like the beasts that perish."

Psalm 78:32-39 "[32]For all this they sinned still, and believed not for his wondrous works. [33]Therefore their days did he consume in vanity, and their years in trouble. [34]When he slew them, then they sought him: and they returned and inquired early after God. [35]And they remembered that God was their rock, and the high God their redeemer. [36]Nevertheless they did flatter him with their mouth, and they lied unto him with their tongues. [37]For their heart was not right with him, neither were they stedfast in his covenant. [38]But he, being full of compassion, forgave their iniquity, and destroyed them not: yea, many a time turned he his anger away, and did not stir up all his wrath. [39]For he remembered that they were but flesh; a wind that passeth away, and cometh not again."

Psalm 103:13-14 "[13]Like as a father pitieth his children, so the LORD pitieth them that fear him. [14]For he knoweth our frame; he remembereth that we are dust."

Psalm 144:3-4 "[3]LORD, what is man, that thou takest knowledge of him! or the son of man, that thou makest account of him! [4]Man is like to vanity: his days are as a shadow that passeth away."

Ecclesiastes 3:18-21 "¹⁸I said in mine heart concerning the estate of the sons of men, that God might manifest them, and that they might see that they themselves are beasts. ¹⁹For that which befalleth the sons of men befalleth beasts; even one thing befalleth them: as the one dieth, so dieth the other; yea, they have all one breath; so that a man hath no preeminence above a beast: for all is vanity. ²⁰All go unto one place; all are of the dust, and all turn to dust again. ²¹Who knoweth the spirit of man that goeth upward, and the spirit of the beast that goeth downward to the earth?"

Ecclesiastes 12:7-8 "⁷Then shall the dust return to the earth as it was: and the spirit shall return unto God who gave it. ⁸Vanity of vanities, saith the preacher; all is vanity."

Isaiah 64:8 "But now, O LORD, thou art our father; we are the clay, and thou our potter; and we all are the work of thy hand."

Daniel 4:34-35 "³⁴And at the end of the days I Nebuchadnezzar lifted up mine eyes unto heaven, and mine understanding returned unto me, and I blessed the most High, and I praised and honoured him that liveth for ever, whose dominion is an everlasting dominion, and his kingdom is from generation to generation: ³⁵And all the inhabitants of the earth are reputed as nothing: and he doeth according to his will in the army of heaven, and among the inhabitants of the earth: and none can stay his hand, or say unto him, What doest thou?"

1 Corinthians 15:45 "And so it is written, The first man Adam was made a living soul; the last Adam was made a quickening spirit."

Hebrews 2:6-8 "⁶But one in a certain place testified, saying, What is man, that thou art mindful of him? or the son of man, that thou visitest him? ⁷Thou madest him a little lower than the angels; thou crownedst him with glory and honour, and didst set him over the works of thy hands: ⁸Thou hast put all things in subjection under his feet. For in that he put all in subjection under him, he left nothing that is not put under him. But now we see not yet all things put under him."

What Not To Call A Man
Matthew 23:9 "And call no man your father upon the earth: for one is your Father, which is in heaven."

Acts 10:28 "And he said unto them, Ye know how that it is an unlawful thing for a man that is a Jew to keep company, or come unto one of another nation; but God hath shewed me that I should not call any man common or unclean."

What Was Given To Man
Genesis 9:1-3 "¹And God blessed Noah and his sons, and said unto them, Be fruitful, and multiply, and replenish the earth. ²And the fear of you and the dread of you shall be upon every beast of the earth, and upon every fowl of the air, upon all that moveth upon the earth, and upon all the fishes of the sea; into your hand are they delivered. ³Every moving thing that liveth shall be meat for you; even as the green herb have I given you all things."

Psalm 115:16 "The heaven, even the heavens, are the LORD's: but the earth hath he given to the children of men."

MANIFESTATION

Jesus Christ Being Manifested In The Last Times
1 Peter 1:18-20 "¹⁸Forasmuch as ye know that ye were not redeemed with corruptible things, as silver and gold, from your vain conversation received by tradition from your fathers; ¹⁹ But with the precious blood of Christ, as of a lamb without blemish and without spot: ²⁰ Who verily was foreordained before the foundation of the world, but was manifest in these last times for you,"

1 John 1:1-3 "¹That which was from the beginning, which we have heard, which we have seen with our eyes, which we have looked upon, and our hands have handled, of the Word of life; ² (For the life was manifested, and we have seen it, and bear witness, and shew unto you that eternal life, which was with the Father, and was manifested unto us;) ³ That which we have seen and heard declare we unto you, that ye also may have fellowship with us: and truly our fellowship is with the Father, and with his Son Jesus Christ."

The Manifestation Of The Spirit
1 Corinthians 12:4-7 "⁴Now there are diversities of gifts, but the same Spirit. ⁵And there are differences of administrations, but the same Lord. ⁶And there are diversities of operations, but it is the same God which worketh all in all. ⁷But the

manifestation of the Spirit is given to every man to profit withal."

What Is Made Manifest

Romans 16:25-26 "²⁵Now to him that is of power to stablish you according to my gospel, and the preaching of Jesus Christ, according to the revelation of the mystery, which was kept secret since the world began, ²⁶But now is made manifest, and by the scriptures of the prophets, according to the commandment of the everlasting God, made known to all nations for the obedience of faith."

2 Corinthians 2:14 "Now thanks be unto God, which always causeth us to triumph in Christ, and maketh manifest the savour of his knowledge by us in every place."

Colossians 1:26-27 "²⁶Even the mystery which hath been hid from ages and from generations, but now is made manifest to his saints: ²⁷To whom God would make known what is the riches of the glory of this mystery among the Gentiles; which is Christ in you, the hope of glory."

Revelation 15:4 "Who shall not fear thee, O Lord, and glorify thy name? for thou only art holy: for all nations shall come and worship before thee; for thy judgments are made manifest."

What Manifests Things

John 3:19-21 "¹⁹And this is the condemnation, that light is come into the world, and men loved darkness rather than light, because their deeds were evil. ²⁰For every one that doeth evil hateth the light, neither cometh to the light, lest his deeds should be reproved. ²¹But he that doeth truth cometh to the light, that his deeds may be made manifest, that they are wrought in God."

Ephesians 5:13-14 "¹³But all things that are reproved are made manifest by the light: for whatsoever doth make manifest is light. ¹⁴Wherefore he saith, Awake thou that sleepest, and arise from the dead, and Christ shall give thee light."

What Shall Be Manifested

Matthew 10:26-27 "²⁶Fear them not therefore: for there is nothing covered, that shall not be revealed; and hid, that shall not be known. ²⁷What I tell you in darkness, that speak ye in light: and what ye hear in the ear, that preach ye upon the housetops."

Mark 4:21-22 "²¹And he said unto them, Is a candle brought to be put under a bushel, or under a bed? and not to be set on a candlestick? ²²For there is nothing hid, which shall not be manifested; neither was any thing kept secret, but that it should come abroad."

Luke 8:16-18 "¹⁶No man, when he hath lighted a candle, covereth it with a vessel, or putteth it under a bed; but setteth it on a candlestick, that they which enter in may see the light. ¹⁷For nothing is secret, that shall not be made manifest; neither any thing hid, that shall not be known and come abroad. ¹⁸Take heed therefore how ye hear: for whosoever hath, to him shall be given; and whosoever hath not, from him shall be taken even that which he seemeth to have."

Luke 12:2-3 "²For there is nothing covered, that shall not be revealed; neither hid, that shall not be known. ³Therefore whatsoever ye have spoken in darkness shall be heard in the light; and that which ye have spoken in the ear in closets shall be proclaimed upon the housetops."

1 Corinthians 3:10-13 "¹⁰According to the grace of God which is given unto me, as a wise masterbuilder, I have laid the foundation, and another buildeth thereon. But let every man take heed how he buildeth thereupon. ¹¹For other foundation can no man lay than that is laid, which is Jesus Christ. ¹²Now if any man build upon this foundation gold, silver, precious stones, wood, hay, stubble; ¹³Every man's work shall be made manifest: for the day shall declare it, because it shall be revealed by fire; and the fire shall try every man's work of what sort it is."

1 Corinthians 4:5 "Therefore judge nothing before the time, until the Lord come, who both will bring to light the hidden things of darkness, and will make manifest the counsels of the hearts: and then shall every man have praise of God."

2 Timothy 3:6-9 "⁶For of this sort are they which creep into houses, and lead captive silly women laden with sins, led away with divers lusts, ⁷Ever learning, and never able to come to the knowledge of the truth. ⁸Now as Jannes and Jambres withstood Moses, so do these also resist the truth: men of corrupt minds, reprobate concerning the faith. ⁹But they shall proceed no further: for their folly shall be manifest unto all men, as theirs also was."

1 Peter 4:13 "But rejoice, inasmuch as ye are partakers of Christ's sufferings; that, when his glory shall be revealed, ye may be glad also with exceeding joy."

Who Jesus Christ Manifested God's Name To
John 17:1-26 "[1]These words spake Jesus, and lifted up his eyes to heaven, and said, Father, the hour is come; glorify thy Son, that thy Son also may glorify thee: [2]As thou hast given him power over all flesh, that he should give eternal life to as many as thou hast given him. [3]And this is life eternal, that they might know thee the only true God, and Jesus Christ, whom thou hast sent. [4]I have glorified thee on the earth: I have finished the work which thou gavest me to do. [5]And now, O Father, glorify thou me with thine own self with the glory which I had with thee before the world was. [6]I have manifested thy name unto the men which thou gavest me out of the world: thine they were, and thou gavest them me; and they have kept thy word. [7]Now they have known that all things whatsoever thou hast given me are of thee. [8]For I have given unto them the words which thou gavest me; and they have received them, and have known surely that I came out from thee, and they have believed that thou didst send me. [9]I pray for them: I pray not for the world, but for them which thou hast given me; for they are thine. [10]And all mine are thine, and thine are mine; and I am glorified in them. [11]And now I am no more in the world, but these are in the world, and I come to thee. Holy Father, keep through thine own name those whom thou hast given me, that they may be one, as we are. [12]While I was with them in the world, I kept them in thy name: those that thou gavest me I have kept, and none of them is lost, but the son of perdition; that the scripture might be fulfilled. [13]And now come I to thee; and these things I speak in the world, that they might have my joy fulfilled in themselves. [14]I have given them thy word; and the world hath hated them, because they are not of the world, even as I am not of the world. [15]I pray not that thou shouldest take them out of the world, but that thou shouldest keep them from the evil. [16]They are not of the world, even as I am not of the world. [17]Sanctify them through thy truth: thy word is truth. [18]As thou hast sent me into the world, even so have I also sent them into the world. [19]And for their sakes I sanctify myself, that they also might be sanctified through the truth. [20]Neither pray I for these alone, but for them also which shall believe on me through their word; [21]That they all may be one; as thou, Father, art in me, and I in thee, that they also may be one in us: that the world may believe that thou hast sent me. [22]And the glory which thou gavest me I have given them; that they may be one, even as we are one: [23]I in them, and thou in me, that they may be made perfect in one; and that the world may know that thou hast sent me, and hast loved them, as thou hast loved me. [24]Father, I will that they also, whom thou hast given me, be with me where I am; that they may behold my glory, which thou hast given me: for thou lovedst me before the foundation of the world. [25]O righteous Father, the world hath not known thee: but I have known thee, and these have known that thou hast sent me. [26]And I have declared unto them thy name, and will declare it: that the love wherewith thou hast loved me may be in them, and I in them."

Who Jesus Christ Manifests Himself To
John 14:21-23 "[21]He that hath my commandments, and keepeth them, he it is that loveth me: and he that loveth me shall be loved of my Father, and I will love him, and will manifest myself to him. [22]Judas saith unto him, not Iscariot, Lord, how is it that thou wilt manifest thyself unto us, and not unto the world? [23]Jesus answered and said unto him, If a man love me, he will keep my words: and my Father will love him, and we will come unto him, and make our abode with him."

MARRIAGE

How Long Wives Are Bound To Their Husbands
Romans 7:1-3 "[1]Know ye not, brethren, (for I speak to them that know the law,) how that the law hath dominion over a man as long as he liveth? [2]For the woman which hath an husband is bound by the law to her husband so long as he liveth; but if the husband be dead, she is loosed from the law of her husband. [3]So then if, while her husband liveth, she be married to another man, she shall be called an adulteress: but if her husband be dead, she is free from that law; so that she is no adulteress, though she be married to another man."

1 Corinthians 7:39-40 "[39]The wife is bound by the law as long as her husband liveth; but if her

Marriage 727

husband be dead, she is at liberty to be married to whom she will; only in the Lord. 40 But she is happier if she so abide, after my judgment: and I think also that I have the Spirit of God."

Husbands And Wives Becoming One
Genesis 2:24 "Therefore shall a man leave his father and his mother, and shall cleave unto his wife: and they shall be one flesh."

Matthew 19:4-6 "4And he answered and said unto them, Have ye not read, that he which made them at the beginning made them male and female, 5And said, For this cause shall a man leave father and mother, and shall cleave to his wife: and they twain shall be one flesh? 6Wherefore they are no more twain, but one flesh. What therefore God hath joined together, let not man put asunder."

Mark 10:6-9 "6But from the beginning of the creation God made them male and female. 7For this cause shall a man leave his father and mother, and cleave to his wife; 8And they twain shall be one flesh: so then they are no more twain, but one flesh. 9What therefore God hath joined together, let not man put asunder."

1 Corinthians 6:15-16 "15Know ye not that your bodies are the members of Christ? shall I then take the members of Christ, and make them the members of an harlot? God forbid. 16What? know ye not that he which is joined to an harlot is one body? for two, saith he, shall be one flesh."

Ephesians 5:28-31 "28So ought men to love their wives as their own bodies. He that loveth his wife loveth himself. 29For no man ever yet hated his own flesh; but nourisheth and cherisheth it, even as the Lord the church: 30For we are members of his body, of his flesh, and of his bones. 31For this cause shall a man leave his father and mother, and shall be joined unto his wife, and they two shall be one flesh."

Prudent Wives
Proverbs 19:14 "House and riches are the inheritance of fathers and a prudent wife is from the LORD."

The Contentions Of A Wife
Proverbs 19:13 "A foolish son is the calamity of his father: and the contentions of a wife are a continual dropping."

The Duties Of A Husband
Deuteronomy 24:5 "When a man hath taken a new wife, he shall not go out to war, neither shall he be charged with any business: but he shall be free at home one year, and shall cheer up his wife which he hath taken."

Proverbs 5:15-20 "15Drink waters out of thine own cistern, and running waters out of thine own well. 16Let thy fountains be dispersed abroad, and rivers of waters in the streets. 17Let them be only thine own, and not strangers' with thee. 18Let thy fountain be blessed: and rejoice with the wife of thy youth. 19Let her be as the loving hind and pleasant roe; let her breasts satisfy thee at all times; and be thou ravished always with her love. 20And why wilt thou, my son, be ravished with a strange woman, and embrace the bosom of a stranger?"

1 Corinthians 7:1-3 "1Now concerning the things whereof ye wrote unto me: It is good for a man not to touch a woman. 2Nevertheless, to avoid fornication, let every man have his own wife, and let every woman have her own husband. 3Let the husband render unto the wife due benevolence: and likewise also the wife unto the husband."

Ephesians 5:25 "Husbands, love your wives, even as Christ also loved the church, and gave himself for it."

Ephesians 5:28 "So ought men to love their wives as their own bodies. He that loveth his wife loveth himself."

Ephesians 5:33 "Nevertheless let every one of you in particular so love his wife even as himself; and the wife see that she reverence her husband."

Colossians 3:19 "Husbands, love your wives, and be not bitter against them."

1 Peter 3:7 "Likewise, ye husbands, dwell with them according to knowledge, giving honour unto the wife, as unto the weaker vessel, and as being heirs together of the grace of life; that your prayers be not hindered."

The Duties Of A Wife
1 Corinthians 7:1-3 "1Now concerning the things whereof ye wrote unto me: It is good for a man not to touch a woman. 2Nevertheless, to avoid fornication, let every man have his own wife, and let

every woman have her own husband. ³Let the husband render unto the wife due benevolence: and likewise also the wife unto the husband."

Ephesians 5:22 "Wives, submit yourselves unto your own husbands, as unto the Lord."

Ephesians 5:33 "Nevertheless let every one of you in particular so love his wife even as himself; and the wife see that she reverence her husband."

Colossians 3:18 "Wives, submit yourselves unto your own husbands, as it is fit in the Lord."

1 Peter 3:1-6 "¹Likewise, ye wives, be in subjection to your own husbands; that, if any obey not the word, they also may without the word be won by the conversation of the wives; ²While they behold your chaste conversation coupled with fear. ³Whose adorning let it not be that outward adorning of plaiting the hair, and of wearing of gold, or of putting on of apparel; ⁴But let it be the hidden man of the heart, in that which is not corruptible, even the ornament of a meek and quiet spirit, which is in the sight of God of great price. ⁵For after this manner in the old time the holy women also, who trusted in God, adorned themselves, being in subjection unto their own husbands: ⁶Even as Sara obeyed Abraham, calling him lord: whose daughters ye are, as long as ye do well, and are not afraid with any amazement."

The Reward For Marrying Idolaters

Exodus 34:11-16 "¹¹Observe thou that which I command thee this day: behold, I drive out before thee the Amorite, and the Canaanite, and the Hittite, and the Perizzite, and the Hivite, and the Jebusite. ¹²Take heed to thyself, lest thou make a covenant with the inhabitants of the land whither thou goest, lest it be for a snare in the midst of thee: ¹³But ye shall destroy their altars, break their images, and cut down their groves: ¹⁴For thou shalt worship no other god: for the LORD, whose name is Jealous, is a jealous God: ¹⁵Lest thou make a covenant with the inhabitants of the land, and they go a whoring after their gods, and do sacrifice unto their gods, and one call thee, and thou eat of his sacrifice; ¹⁶And thou take of their daughters unto thy sons, and their daughters go a whoring after their gods, and make thy sons go a whoring after their gods."

Deuteronomy 7:1-4 "¹When the LORD thy God shall bring thee into the land whither thou goest

to possess it, and hath cast out many nations before thee, the Hittites, and the Girgashites, and the Amorites, and the Canaanites, and the Perizzites, and the Hivites, and the Jebusites, seven nations greater and mightier than thou; ²And when the LORD thy God shall deliver them before thee; thou shalt smite them, and utterly destroy them; thou shalt make no covenant with them, nor shew mercy unto them: ³Neither shalt thou make marriages with them; thy daughter thou shalt not give unto his son, nor his daughter shalt thou take unto thy son. ⁴For they will turn away thy son from following me, that they may serve other gods: so will the anger of the LORD be kindled against you, and destroy thee suddenly."

1 Kings 11:1-8 "¹But king Solomon loved many strange women, together with the daughter of Pharaoh, women of the Moabites, Ammonites, Edomites, Zidonians, and Hittites; ²Of the nations concerning which the LORD said unto the children of Israel, Ye shall not go in to them, neither shall they come in unto you: for surely they will turn away your heart after their gods: Solomon clave unto these in love. ³And he had seven hundred wives, princesses, and three hundred concubines: and his wives turned away his heart. ⁴For it came to pass, when Solomon was old, that his wives turned away his heart after other gods: and his heart was not perfect with the LORD his God, as was the heart of David his father. ⁵For Solomon went after Ashtoreth the goddess of the Zidonians, and after Milcom the abomination of the Ammonites. ⁶And Solomon did evil in the sight of the LORD, and went not fully after the LORD, as did David his father. ⁷Then did Solomon build an high place for Chemosh, the abomination of Moab, in the hill that is before Jerusalem, and for Molech, the abomination of the children of Ammon. ⁸And likewise did he for all his strange wives, which burnt incense and sacrificed unto their gods."

Nehemiah 13:23-27 "²³In those days also saw I Jews that had married wives of Ashdod, of Ammon, and of Moab: ²⁴And their children spake half in the speech of Ashdod, and could not speak in the Jews' language, but according to the language of each people. ²⁵And I contended with them, and cursed them, and smote certain of them, and plucked off their hair, and made them swear by

God, saying, Ye shall not give your daughters unto their sons, nor take their daughters unto your sons, or for yourselves. ²⁶Did not Solomon king of Israel sin by these things? yet among many nations was there no king like him, who was beloved of his God, and God made him king over all Israel: nevertheless even him did outlandish women cause to sin. ²⁷Shall we then hearken unto you to do all this great evil, to transgress against our God in marrying strange wives?"

Malachi 2:11-13 "¹¹Judah hath dealt treacherously, and an abomination is committed in Israel and in Jerusalem; for Judah hath profaned the holiness of the LORD which he loved, and hath married the daughter of a strange god. ¹²The LORD will cut off the man that doeth this, the master and the scholar, out of the tabernacles of Jacob, and him that offereth an offering unto the LORD of hosts. ¹³And this have ye done again, covering the altar of the LORD with tears, with weeping, and with crying out, insomuch that he regardeth not the offering any more, or receiveth it with good will at your hand."

The Rights Of Marriage
1 Corinthians 7:3-5 "³Let the husband render unto the wife due benevolence: and likewise also the wife unto the husband. ⁴The wife hath not power of her own body, but the husband: and likewise also the husband hath not power of his own body, but the wife. ⁵Defraud ye not one the other, except it be with consent for a time, that ye may give yourselves to fasting and prayer; and come together again, that Satan tempt you not for your incontinency."

Those That Do Not Marry
1 Corinthians 7:25-38 "²⁵Now concerning virgins I have no commandment of the Lord: yet I give my judgment, as one that hath obtained mercy of the Lord to be faithful. ²⁶I suppose therefore that this is good for the present distress, I say, that it is good for a man so to be. ²⁷Art thou bound unto a wife? seek not to be loosed. Art thou loosed from a wife? seek not a wife. ²⁸But and if thou marry, thou hast not sinned; and if a virgin marry, she hath not sinned. Nevertheless such shall have trouble in the flesh: but I spare you. ²⁹But this I say, brethren, the time is short: it remaineth, that both they that have wives be as though they had

none; ³⁰And they that weep, as though they wept not; and they that rejoice, as though they rejoiced not; and they that buy, as though they possessed not; ³¹And they that use this world, as not abusing it: for the fashion of this world passeth away. ³²But I would have you without carefulness. He that is unmarried careth for the things that belong to the Lord, how he may please the Lord: ³³But he that is married careth for the things that are of the world, how he may please his wife. ³⁴There is difference also between a wife and a virgin. The unmarried woman careth for the things of the Lord, that she may be holy both in body and in spirit: but she that is married careth for the things of the world, how she may please her husband. ³⁵And this I speak for your own profit; not that I may cast a snare upon you, but for that which is comely, and that ye may attend upon the Lord without distraction. ³⁶But if any man think that he behaveth himself uncomely toward his virgin, if she pass the flower of her age, and need so require, let him do what he will, he sinneth not: let them marry. ³⁷Nevertheless he that standeth stedfast in his heart, having no necessity, but hath power over his own will, and hath so decreed in his heart that he will keep his virgin, doeth well. ³⁸So then he that giveth her in marriage doeth well; but he that giveth her not in marriage doeth better."

Those That Love Their Wife
Ephesians 5:28-29 "²⁸So ought men to love their wives as their own bodies. He that loveth his wife loveth himself. ²⁹For no man ever yet hated his own flesh; but nourisheth and cherisheth it, even as the Lord the church."

Those That Marry
Proverbs 18:22 "Whoso findeth a wife findeth a good thing, and obtaineth favour of the LORD."

1 Corinthians 7:25-38 "²⁵Now concerning virgins I have no commandment of the Lord: yet I give my judgment, as one that hath obtained mercy of the Lord to be faithful. ²⁶I suppose therefore that this is good for the present distress, I say, that it is good for a man so to be. ²⁷Art thou bound unto a wife? seek not to be loosed. Art thou loosed from a wife? seek not a wife. ²⁸But and if thou marry, thou hast not sinned; and if a virgin marry, she hath not sinned. Nevertheless such shall have trouble in the flesh: but I spare you. ²⁹But this I say, brethren, the time is short: it remaineth, that both they that have wives be as though they had none; [30]And they that weep, as though they wept not; and they that rejoice, as though they rejoiced not; and they that buy, as though they possessed not; [31]And they that use this world, as not abusing it: for the fashion of this world passeth away. [32]But I would have you without carefulness. He that is unmarried careth for the things that belong to the Lord, how he may please the Lord: [33]But he that is married careth for the things that are of the world, how he may please his wife. [34]There is difference also between a wife and a virgin. The unmarried woman careth for the things of the Lord, that she may be holy both in body and in spirit: but she that is married careth for the things of the world, how she may please her husband. [35]And this I speak for your own profit; not that I may cast a snare upon you, but for that which is comely, and that ye may attend upon the Lord without distraction. [36]But if any man think that he behaveth himself uncomely toward his virgin, if she pass the flower of her age, and need so require, let him do what he will, he sinneth not: let them marry. [37]Nevertheless he that standeth stedfast in his heart, having no necessity, but hath power over his own will, and hath so decreed in his heart that he will keep his virgin, doeth well. [38]So then he that giveth her in marriage doeth well; but he that giveth her not in marriage doeth better."

Those That Remarry Or
Marry Those Who Have Been Divorced
Matthew 5:31-32 "[31]It hath been said, Whosoever shall put away his wife, let him give her a writing of divorcement: [32]But I say unto you, That whosoever shall put away his wife, saving for the cause of fornication, causeth her to commit adultery: and whosoever shall marry her that is divorced committeth adultery."

Matthew 19:9 "And I say unto you, Whosoever shall put away his wife, except it be for fornication, and shall marry another, committeth adultery: and whoso marrieth her which is put away doth commit adultery."

Mark 10:11-12 "[11]And he saith unto them, Whosoever shall put away his wife, and marry another, committeth adultery against her. [12]And if a woman shall put away her husband, and be married to another, she committeth adultery."

Luke 16:18 "Whosoever putteth away his wife, and marrieth another, committeth adultery: and whosoever marrieth her that is put away from her husband committeth adultery."

Romans 7:1-3 "[1]Know ye not, brethren, (for I speak to them that know the law,) how that the law hath dominion over a man as long as he liveth? [2]For the woman which hath an husband is bound by the law to her husband so long as he liveth; but if the husband be dead, she is loosed from the law of her husband. [3]So then if, while her husband liveth, she be married to another man, she shall be called an adulteress: but if her husband be dead, she is free from that law; so that she is no adulteress, though she be married to another man."

Unbelieving Spouses
1 Corinthians 7:10-16 "[10]And unto the married I command, yet not I, but the Lord, Let not the wife depart from her husband: [11]But and if she depart, let her remain unmarried, or be reconciled to her husband: and let not the husband put away his wife. [12]But to the rest speak I, not the Lord: If any brother hath a wife that believeth not, and she be pleased to dwell with him, let him not put her away. [13]And the woman which hath an husband that believeth not, and if he be pleased to dwell with her, let her not leave him. [14]For the unbelieving husband is sanctified by the wife, and the unbelieving wife is sanctified by the husband: else were your children unclean; but now are they holy. [15]But if the unbelieving depart, let him depart. A brother or a sister is not under bondage in such cases: but God hath called us to peace. [16]For what knowest thou, O wife, whether thou shalt save thy husband? or how knowest thou, O man, whether thou shalt save thy wife?"

What Marriage Is
Hebrews 13:4 "Marriage is honourable in all, and the bed undefiled: but whoremongers and adulterers God will judge."

What Marriage Is Analogous To
Ephesians 5:22-33 "[22]Wives, submit yourselves unto your own husbands, as unto the Lord. [23]For the husband is the head of the wife, even as Christ is the head of the church: and he is the saviour of the body. [24]Therefore as the church is subject unto Christ, so let the wives be to their own husbands in every thing. [25]Husbands, love your wives, even

as Christ also loved the church, and gave himself for it; [26]That he might sanctify and cleanse it with the washing of water by the word, [27]That he might present it to himself a glorious church, not having spot, or wrinkle, or any such thing; but that it should be holy and without blemish. [28]So ought men to love their wives as their own bodies. He that loveth his wife loveth himself. [29]For no man ever yet hated his own flesh; but nourisheth and cherisheth it, even as the Lord the church: [30]For we are members of his body, of his flesh, and of his bones. [31]For this cause shall a man leave his father and mother, and shall be joined unto his wife, and they two shall be one flesh. [32]This is a great mystery: but I speak concerning Christ and the church. [33]Nevertheless let every one of you in particular so love his wife even as himself; and the wife see that she reverence her husband."

Who Does Not Marry

Matthew 22:23-32 "[23]The same day came to him the Sadducees, which say that there is no resurrection, and asked him, [24]Saying, Master, Moses said, If a man die, having no children, his brother shall marry his wife, and raise up seed unto his brother. [25]Now there were with us seven brethren: and the first, when he had married a wife, deceased, and, having no issue, left his wife unto his brother: [26]Likewise the second also, and the third, unto the seventh. [27]And last of all the woman died also. [28]Therefore in the resurrection whose wife shall she be of the seven? for they all had her. [29]Jesus answered and said unto them, Ye do err, not knowing the scriptures, nor the power of God. [30]For in the resurrection they neither marry, nor are given in marriage, but are as the angels of God in heaven. [31]But as touching the resurrection of the dead, have ye not read that which was spoken unto you by God, saying, [32]I am the God of Abraham, and the God of Isaac, and the God of Jacob? God is not the God of the dead, but of the living."

Mark 12:18-27 "[18]Then come unto him the Sadducees, which say there is no resurrection; and they asked him, saying, [19]Master, Moses wrote unto us, If a man's brother die, and leave his wife behind him, and leave no children, that his brother should take his wife, and raise up seed unto his brother. [20]Now there were seven brethren: and the first took a wife, and dying left no seed. [21]And the second took her, and died, neither left he any seed:

and the third likewise. [22]And the seven had her, and left no seed: last of all the woman died also. [23]In the resurrection therefore, when they shall rise, whose wife shall she be of them? for the seven had her to wife. [24]And Jesus answering said unto them, Do ye not therefore err, because ye know not the scriptures, neither the power of God? [25]For when they shall rise from the dead, they neither marry, nor are given in marriage; but are as the angels which are in heaven. [26]And as touching the dead, that they rise: have ye not read in the book of Moses, how in the bush God spake unto him, saying, I am the God of Abraham, and the God of Isaac, and the God of Jacob? [27]He is not the God of the dead, but the God of the living: ye therefore do greatly err."

Luke 20:27-38 "[27]Then came to him certain of the Sadducees, which deny that there is any resurrection; and they asked him, [28]Saying, Master, Moses wrote unto us, If any man's brother die, having a wife, and he die without children, that his brother should take his wife, and raise up seed unto his brother. [29]There were therefore seven brethren: and the first took a wife, and died without children. [30]And the second took her to wife, and he died childless. [31]And the third took her; and in like manner the seven also: and they left no children, and died. [32]Last of all the woman died also. [33]Therefore in the resurrection whose wife of them is she? for seven had her to wife. [34]And Jesus answering said unto them, The children of this world marry, and are given in marriage: [35]But they which shall be accounted worthy to obtain that world, and the resurrection from the dead, neither marry, nor are given in marriage: [36]Neither can they die any more: for they are equal unto the angels; and are the children of God, being the children of the resurrection. [37]Now that the dead are raised, even Moses shewed at the bush, when he calleth the Lord the God of Abraham, and the God of Isaac, and the God of Jacob. [38]For he is not a God of the dead, but of the living: for all live unto him."

Who Not To Marry

Deuteronomy 7:1-4 "[1]When the LORD thy God shall bring thee into the land whither thou goest to possess it, and hath cast out many nations before thee, the Hittites, and the Girgashites, and the Amorites, and the Canaanites, and the Perizzites, and the Hivites, and the Jebusites, seven nations greater and mightier than thou; [2]And when the LORD thy God shall deliver them before thee; thou shalt smite them, and utterly destroy them; thou shalt make no covenant with them, nor shew mercy unto them: [3]Neither shalt thou make marriages with them; thy daughter thou shalt not give unto his son, nor his daughter shalt thou take unto thy son. [4]For they will turn away thy son from following me, that they may serve other gods: so will the anger of the LORD be kindled against you, and destroy thee suddenly."

Joshua 23:1-12 "[1]And it came to pass a long time after that the LORD had given rest unto Israel from all their enemies round about, that Joshua waxed old and stricken in age. [2]And Joshua called for all Israel, and for their elders, and for their heads, and for their judges, and for their officers, and said unto them, I am old and stricken in age: [3]And ye have seen all that the LORD your God hath done unto all these nations because of you; for the LORD your God is he that hath fought for you. [4]Behold, I have divided unto you by lot these nations that remain, to be an inheritance for your tribes, from Jordan, with all the nations that I have cut off, even unto the great sea westward. [5]And the LORD your God, he shall expel them from before you, and drive them from out of your sight; and ye shall possess their land, as the LORD your God hath promised unto you. [6]Be ye therefore very courageous to keep and to do all that is written in the book of the law of Moses, that ye turn not aside therefrom to the right hand or to the left; [7]That ye come not among these nations, these that remain among you; neither make mention of the name of their gods, nor cause to swear by them, neither serve them, nor bow yourselves unto them: [8]But cleave unto the LORD your God, as ye have done unto this day. [9]For the LORD hath driven out from before you great nations and strong: but as for you, no man hath been able to stand before you unto this day. [10]One man of you shall chase a thousand: for the LORD your God, he it is that fighteth for you, as he hath promised you. [11]Take good heed therefore unto yourselves, that ye love the LORD your God. [12]Else if ye do in any wise go back, and cleave unto the remnant of these nations, even these that remain among you, and shall make marriages with them, and go in unto them, and they to you."

Ezra 9:1-2 "[1]Now when these things were done, the princes came to me, saying, The people of Israel, and the priests, and the Levites, have not separated themselves from the people of the lands, doing according to their abominations, even of the Canaanites, the Hittites, the Perizzites, the Jebusites, the Ammonites, the Moabites, the Egyptians, and the Amorites. [2]For they have taken of their daughters for themselves, and for their sons: so that the holy seed have mingled themselves with the people of those lands: yea, the hand of the princes and rulers hath been chief in this trespass."

Ezra 9:10-12 "[10]And now, O our God, what shall we say after this? for we have forsaken thy commandments, [11]Which thou hast commanded by thy servants the prophets, saying, The land, unto which ye go to possess it, is an unclean land with the filthiness of the people of the lands, with their abominations, which have filled it from one end to another with their uncleanness. [12]Now therefore give not your daughters unto their sons, neither take their daughters unto your sons, nor seek their peace or their wealth for ever: that ye may be strong, and eat the good of the land, and leave it for an inheritance to your children for ever."

Ezra 10:2-3 "[2]And Shechaniah the son of Jehiel, one of the sons of Elam, answered and said unto Ezra, We have trespassed against our God, and have taken strange wives of the people of the land: yet now there is hope in Israel concerning this thing. [3]Now therefore let us make a covenant with our God to put away all the wives, and such as are born of them, according to the counsel of my lord, and of those that tremble at the commandment of our God; and let it be done according to the law."

Nehemiah 10:29-30 "[29]They clave to their brethren, their nobles, and entered into a curse, and into an oath, to walk in God's law, which was given by Moses the servant of God, and to observe and do all the commandments of the LORD our Lord, and his judgments and his statutes; [30]And that we would not give our daughters unto the people of the land, nor take their daughters for our sons."

Nehemiah 13:23-27 "[23]In those days also saw I Jews that had married wives of Ashdod, of Ammon, and of Moab: [24]And their children spake half in the speech of Ashdod, and could not speak in the Jews' language, but according to the language of each people. [25]And I contended with them, and cursed them, and smote certain of them, and plucked off their hair, and made them swear by God, saying, Ye shall not give your daughters unto their sons, nor take their daughters unto your sons, or for yourselves. [26]Did not Solomon king of Israel sin by these things? yet among many nations was there no king like him, who was beloved of his God, and God made him king over all Israel: nevertheless even him did outlandish women cause to sin. [27]Shall we then hearken unto you to do all this great evil, to transgress against our God in marrying strange wives?"

Who Should Get Married
Exodus 22:16-17 "[16]And if a man entice a maid that is not betrothed, and lie with her, he shall surely endow her to be his wife. [17]If her father utterly refuse to give her unto him, he shall pay money according to the dowry of virgins."

1 Corinthians 7:6-9 "[6]But I speak this by permission, and not of commandment. [7]For I would that all men were even as I myself. But every man hath his proper gift of God, one after this manner, and another after that. [8]I say therefore to the unmarried and widows, It is good for them if they abide even as I. [9]But if they cannot contain, let them marry: for it is better to marry than to burn."

Why You Should Get Married
1 Corinthians 7:1-2 "[1]Now concerning the things whereof ye wrote unto me: It is good for a man not to touch a woman. [2]Nevertheless, to avoid fornication, let every man have his own wife, and let every woman have her own husband."

1 Corinthians 7:6-9 "[6]But I speak this by permission, and not of commandment. [7]For I would that all men were even as I myself. But every man hath his proper gift of God, one after this manner, and another after that. [8]I say therefore to the unmarried and widows, It is good for them if they abide even as I. [9]But if they cannot contain, let them marry: for it is better to marry than to burn."

MASTERS

Masters That Delicately Bring Up Their Servants From A Child
Proverbs 29:21 "He that delicately bringeth up his servant from a child shall have him become his son at the length."

What Masters Should Do
Ephesians 6:5-9 "[5]Servants, be obedient to them that are your masters according to the flesh, with fear and trembling, in singleness of your heart, as unto Christ; [6]Not with eyeservice, as menpleasers; but as the servants of Christ, doing the will of God from the heart; [7]With good will doing service, as to the Lord, and not to men: [8]Knowing that whatsoever good thing any man doeth, the same shall he receive of the Lord, whether he be bond or free. [9]And, ye masters, do the same things unto them, forbearing threatening: knowing that your Master also is in heaven; neither is there respect of persons with him."

Colossians 4:1 "Masters, give unto your servants that which is just and equal; knowing that ye also have a Master in heaven."

What Masters Should Not Do
Deuteronomy 24:14 "Thou shalt not oppress an hired servant that is poor and needy, whether he be of thy brethren, or of thy strangers that are in thy land within thy gates."

MATURITY

The Time When You Are Mature
1 Corinthians 13:11-12 "[11]When I was a child, I spake as a child, I understood as a child, I thought as a child: but when I became a man, I put away childish things. [12]For now we see through a glass, darkly; but then face to face: now I know in part; but then shall I know even as also I am known."

Those That Are Full Of Age
Hebrews 5:11-14 "[11]Of whom we have many things to say, and hard to be uttered, seeing ye are dull of hearing. [12]For when for the time ye ought to be teachers, ye have need that one teach you again which be the first principles of the oracles of God; and are become such as have need of milk, and not of strong meat. [13]For every one that useth milk is unskilful in the word of righteousness: for he is a babe. [14]But strong meat belongeth to them that are of full age, even those who by reason of use have their senses exercised to discern both good and evil."

MEAT

Animals Being Meat For Humans
Genesis 9:1-4 "[1]And God blessed Noah and his sons, and said unto them, Be fruitful, and multiply,

and replenish the earth. 2 And the fear of you and the dread of you shall be upon every beast of the earth, and upon every fowl of the air, upon all that moveth upon the earth, and upon all the fishes of the sea; into your hand are they delivered. 3 Every moving thing that liveth shall be meat for you; even as the green herb have I given you all things. 4 But flesh with the life thereof, which is the blood thereof, shall ye not eat."

Separating The Clean Animals
From The Unclean Animals

Exodus 22:31 "And ye shall be holy men unto me: neither shall ye eat any flesh that is torn of beasts in the field; ye shall cast it to the dogs."

Leviticus 11:2-47 "2Speak unto the children of Israel, saying, These are the beasts which ye shall eat among all the beasts that are on the earth. 3Whatsoever parteth the hoof, and is clovenfooted, and cheweth the cud, among the beasts, that shall ye eat. 4Nevertheless these shall ye not eat of them that chew the cud, or of them that divide the hoof: as the camel, because he cheweth the cud, but divideth not the hoof; he is unclean unto you. 5And the coney, because he cheweth the cud, but divideth not the hoof; he is unclean unto you. 6And the hare, because he cheweth the cud, but divideth not the hoof; he is unclean unto you. 7And the swine, though he divide the hoof, and be clovenfooted, yet he cheweth not the cud; he is unclean to you. 8Of their flesh shall ye not eat, and their carcase shall ye not touch; they are unclean to you. 9These shall ye eat of all that are in the waters: whatsoever hath fins and scales in the waters, in the seas, and in the rivers, them shall ye eat. 10And all that have not fins and scales in the seas, and in the rivers, of all that move in the waters, and of any living thing which is in the waters, they shall be an abomination unto you: 11They shall be even an abomination unto you; ye shall not eat of their flesh, but ye shall have their carcases in abomination. 12Whatsoever hath no fins nor scales in the waters, that shall be an abomination unto you. 13And these are they which ye shall have in abomination among the fowls; they shall not be eaten, they are an abomination: the eagle, and the ossifrage, and the ospray, 14And the vulture, and the kite after his kind; 15Every raven after his kind; 16And the owl, and the night hawk, and the cuckow, and the hawk after his

kind, 17And the little owl, and the cormorant, and the great owl, 18And the swan, and the pelican, and the gier eagle, 19And the stork, the heron after her kind, and the lapwing, and the bat. 20All fowls that creep, going upon all four, shall be an abomination unto you. 21Yet these may ye eat of every flying creeping thing that goeth upon all four, which have legs above their feet, to leap withal upon the earth; 22Even these of them ye may eat; the locust after his kind, and the bald locust after his kind, and the beetle after his kind, and the grasshopper after his kind. 23But all other flying creeping things, which have four feet, shall be an abomination unto you. 24And for these ye shall be unclean: whosoever toucheth the carcase of them shall be unclean until the even. 25And whosoever beareth ought of the carcase of them shall wash his clothes, and be unclean until the even. 26The carcases of every beast which divideth the hoof, and is not clovenfooted, nor cheweth the cud, are unclean unto you: every one that toucheth them shall be unclean. 27And whatsoever goeth upon his paws, among all manner of beasts that go on all four, those are unclean unto you: whoso toucheth their carcase shall be unclean until the even. 28And he that beareth the carcase of them shall wash his clothes, and be unclean until the even: they are unclean unto you. 29These also shall be unclean unto you among the creeping things that creep upon the earth; the weasel, and the mouse, and the tortoise after his kind, 30And the ferret, and the chameleon, and the lizard, and the snail, and the mole. 31These are unclean to you among all that creep: whosoever doth touch them, when they be dead, shall be unclean until the even. 32And upon whatsoever any of them, when they are dead, doth fall, it shall be unclean; whether it be any vessel of wood, or raiment, or skin, or sack, whatsoever vessel it be, wherein any work is done, it must be put into water, and it shall be unclean until the even; so it shall be cleansed. 33And every earthen vessel, whereinto any of them falleth, whatsoever is in it shall be unclean; and ye shall break it. 34Of all meat which may be eaten, that on which such water cometh shall be unclean: and all drink that may be drunk in every such vessel shall be unclean. 35And every thing whereupon any part of their carcase falleth shall be unclean; whether it be oven, or ranges for pots, they shall be broken down: for they are unclean, and shall be unclean unto you. 36Nevertheless a fountain or pit, wherein there is plenty of water, shall be clean: but that which toucheth their carcase shall be unclean. 37And if any part of their carcase fall upon any sowing seed which is to be sown, it shall be clean. 38But if any water be put upon the seed, and any part of their carcase fall thereon, it shall be unclean unto you. 39And if any beast, of which ye may eat, die; he that toucheth the carcase thereof shall be unclean until the even. 40And he that eateth of the carcase of it shall wash his clothes, and be unclean until the even: he also that beareth the carcase of it shall wash his clothes, and be unclean until the even. 41And every creeping thing that creepeth upon the earth shall be an abomination; it shall not be eaten. 42Whatsoever goeth upon the belly, and whatsoever goeth upon all four, or whatsoever hath more feet among all creeping things that creep upon the earth, them ye shall not eat; for they are an abomination. 43Ye shall not make yourselves abominable with any creeping thing that creepeth, neither shall ye make yourselves unclean with them, that ye should be defiled thereby. 44For I am the LORD your God: ye shall therefore sanctify yourselves, and ye shall be holy; for I am holy: neither shall ye defile yourselves with any manner of creeping thing that creepeth upon the earth. 45For I am the LORD that bringeth you up out of the land of Egypt, to be your God: ye shall therefore be holy, for I am holy. 46This is the law of the beasts, and of the fowl, and of every living creature that moveth in the waters, and of every creature that creepeth upon the earth: 47To make a difference between the unclean and the clean, and between the beast that may be eaten and the beast that may not be eaten."

Leviticus 20:25 "Ye shall therefore put difference between clean beasts and unclean, and between unclean fowls and clean: and ye shall not make your souls abominable by beast, or by fowl, or by any manner of living thing that creepeth on the ground, which I have separated from you as unclean."

Deuteronomy 14:3-21 "3Thou shalt not eat any abominable thing. 4These are the beasts which ye shall eat: the ox, the sheep, and the goat, 5The hart, and the roebuck, and the fallow deer, and the wild goat, and the pygarg, and the wild ox, and the chamois. 6And every beast that parteth the hoof, and cleaveth the cleft into two claws, and cheweth the cud among the beasts, that ye shall eat. 7Nevertheless these ye shall not eat of them that chew the cud, or of them that divide the cloven hoof; as the camel, and the hare, and the coney: for they chew the cud, but divide not the hoof; therefore they are unclean unto you. 8And the swine, because it divideth the hoof, yet cheweth not the cud, it is unclean unto you: ye shall not eat of their flesh, nor touch their dead carcase. 9These ye shall eat of all that are in the waters: all that have fins and scales shall ye eat: 10And whatsoever hath not fins and scales ye may not eat; it is unclean unto you. 11Of all clean birds ye shall eat. 12But these are they of which ye shall not eat: the eagle, and ossifrage, and the ospray, 13And the glede, and the kite, and the vulture after his kind, 14And every raven after his kind, 15And the owl, and the night hawk, and the cuckow, and the hawk after his kind, 16The little owl, and the great owl, and the swan, 17And the pelican, and the gier eagle, and the cormorant, 18And the stork, and the heron after her kind, and the lapwing, and the bat. 19And every creeping thing that flieth is unclean unto you: they shall not be eaten. 20But of all clean fowls ye may eat. 21Ye shall not eat of any thing that dieth of itself: thou shalt give it unto the stranger that is in thy gates, that he may eat it; or thou mayest sell it unto an alien: for thou art an holy people unto the LORD thy God. Thou shalt not seethe a kid in his mother's milk."

The Meat Sacrificed To Idols

Romans 14:14-23 "14I know, and am persuaded by the Lord Jesus, that there is nothing unclean of itself: but to him that esteemeth any thing to be unclean, to him it is unclean. 15But if thy brother be grieved with thy meat, now walkest thou not charitably. Destroy not him with thy meat, for whom Christ died. 16Let not then your good be evil spoken of: 17For the kingdom of God is not meat and drink; but righteousness, and peace, and joy in the Holy Ghost. 18For he that in these things serveth Christ is acceptable to God, and approved of men. 19Let us therefore follow after the things which make for peace, and things wherewith one may edify another. 20For meat destroy not the work of God. All things indeed are pure; but it is evil for that man who eateth with offence. 21It is good neither to eat flesh, nor to drink wine, nor any thing whereby thy brother stumbleth, or is offended, or is made weak. ²²Hast thou faith? have it to thyself before God. Happy is he that condemneth not himself in that thing which he alloweth. ²³And he that doubteth is damned if he eat, because he eateth not of faith: for whatsoever is not of faith is sin."

1 Corinthians 8:1-13 "¹Now as touching things offered unto idols, we know that we all have knowledge. Knowledge puffeth up, but charity edifieth. ²And if any man think that he knoweth anything, he knoweth nothing yet as he ought to know. ³But if any man love God, the same is known of him. ⁴As concerning therefore the eating of those things that are offered in sacrifice unto idols, we know that an idol is nothing in the world, and that there is none other God but one. ⁵For though there be that are called gods, whether in heaven or in earth, (as there be gods many, and lords many,) ⁶But to us there is but one God, the Father, of whom are all things, and we in him; and one Lord Jesus Christ, by whom are all things, and we by him. ⁷Howbeit there is not in every man that knowledge: for some with conscience of the idol unto this hour eat it as a thing offered unto an idol; and their conscience being weak is defiled. ⁸But meat commendeth us not to God: for neither, if we eat, are we the better; neither, if we eat not, are we the worse. ⁹But take heed lest by any means this liberty of yours become a stumblingblock to them that are weak. ¹⁰For if any man see thee which hast knowledge sit at meat in the idol's temple, shall not the conscience of him which is weak be emboldened to eat those things which are offered to idols; ¹¹And through thy knowledge shall the weak brother perish, for whom Christ died? ¹²But when ye sin so against the brethren, and wound their weak conscience, ye sin against Christ. ¹³Wherefore, if meat make my brother to offend, I will eat no flesh while the world standeth, lest I make my brother to offend."

1 Corinthians 10:14-33 "¹⁴Wherefore, my dearly beloved, flee from idolatry. ¹⁵I speak as to wise men; judge ye what I say. ¹⁶The cup of blessing which we bless, is it not the communion of the blood of Christ? The bread which we break, is it not the communion of the body of Christ? ¹⁷For we being many are one bread, and one body: for we are all partakers of that one bread. ¹⁸Behold Israel after the flesh: are not they which eat of the sacrifices partakers of the altar? ¹⁹What say I then? that the idol is any thing, or that which is offered in sacrifice to idols is any thing? ²⁰But I say, that the things which the Gentiles sacrifice, they sacrifice to devils, and not to God: and I would not that ye should have fellowship with devils. ²¹Ye cannot drink the cup of the Lord, and the cup of devils: ye cannot be partakers of the Lord's table, and of the table of devils. ²²Do we provoke the Lord to jealousy? are we stronger than he? ²³All things are lawful for me, but all things are not expedient: all things are lawful for me, but all things edify not. ²⁴Let no man seek his own, but every man another's wealth. ²⁵Whatsoever is sold in the shambles, that eat, asking no question for conscience sake: ²⁶For the earth is the Lord's, and the fulness thereof. ²⁷If any of them that believe not bid you to a feast, and ye be disposed to go; whatsoever is set before you, eat, asking no question for conscience sake. ²⁸But if any man say unto you, This is offered in sacrifice unto idols, eat not for his sake that shewed it, and for conscience sake: for the earth is the Lord's, and the fulness thereof: ²⁹Conscience, I say, not thine own, but of the other: for why is my liberty judged of another man's conscience? ³⁰For if I by grace be a partaker, why am I evil spoken of for that for which I give thanks? ³¹Whether therefore ye eat, or drink, or whatsoever ye do, do all to the glory of God. ³²Give none offence, neither to the Jews, nor to the Gentiles, nor to the church of God: ³³Even as I please all men in all things, not seeking mine own profit, but the profit of many, that they may be saved."

MEEKNESS

Being Meek

Ephesians 4:1-2 "¹I therefore, the prisoner of the Lord, beseech you that ye walk worthy of the vocation wherewith ye are called, ² With all lowliness and meekness, with longsuffering, forbearing one another in love."

Titus 3:1-2 "¹Put them in mind to be subject to principalities and powers, to obey magistrates, to be ready to every good work, ² To speak evil of no man, to be no brawlers, but gentle, shewing all meekness unto all men."

Jesus Christ Being Meek

Matthew 11:25-30 "²⁵At that time Jesus answered and said, I thank thee, O Father, Lord of heaven and earth, because thou hast hid these things from the wise and prudent, and hast revealed them unto babes. ²⁶Even so, Father: for so it seemed good in thy sight. ²⁷All things are delivered unto me of my Father: and no man knoweth the Son, but the Father; neither knoweth any man the Father, save the Son, and he to whomsoever the Son will reveal him. ²⁸Come unto me, all ye that labour and are heavy laden, and I will give you rest. ²⁹Take my yoke upon you, and learn of me; for I am meek and lowly in heart: and ye shall find rest unto your souls. ³⁰For my yoke is easy, and my burden is light."

Philippians 2:5-8 "⁵Let this mind be in you, which was also in Christ Jesus: ⁶Who, being in the form of God, thought it not robbery to be equal with God: ⁷But made himself of no reputation, and took upon him the form of a servant, and was made in the likeness of men: ⁸And being found in fashion as a man, he humbled himself, and became obedient unto death, even the death of the cross."

Seeking Meekness

Zephaniah 2:3 "Seek ye the LORD, all ye meek of the earth, which have wrought his judgment; seek righteousness, seek meekness: it may be ye shall be hid in the day of the LORD's anger."

The Meek

Psalm 22:26 "The meek shall eat and be satisfied: they shall praise the LORD that seek him: your heart shall live for ever."

Psalm 25:8-9 "⁸Good and upright is the LORD: therefore will he teach sinners in the way. ⁹The meek will he guide in judgment: and the meek will he teach his way."

Psalm 37:11 "But the meek shall inherit the earth; and shall delight themselves in the abundance of peace."

Psalm 147:6 "The LORD lifteth up the meek: he casteth the wicked down to the ground."

Psalm 149:4 "For the LORD taketh pleasure in his people: he will beautify the meek with salvation."

Matthew 5:5 "Blessed are the meek: for they shall inherit the earth."

MEN

Men Being Equal To Women In Christ

Galatians 3:27-29 "²⁷For as many of you as have been baptized into Christ have put on Christ. ²⁸ There is neither Jew nor Greek, there is neither bond nor free, there is neither male nor female: for ye are all one in Christ Jesus. ²⁹ And if ye be Christ's, then are ye Abraham's seed, and heirs according to the promise."

Men Being The Head Of Women

Genesis 3:16 "Unto the woman he said, I will greatly multiply thy sorrow and thy conception; in sorrow thou shalt bring forth children; and thy desire shall be to thy husband, and he shall rule over thee."

1 Corinthians 11:2-16 "²Now I praise you, brethren, that ye remember me in all things, and keep the ordinances, as I delivered them to you. ³But I would have you know, that the head of every man is Christ; and the head of the woman is the man; and the head of Christ is God. ⁴Every man praying or prophesying, having his head covered, dishonoureth his head. ⁵But every woman that prayeth or prophesieth with her head uncovered dishonoureth her head: for that is even all one as if she were shaven. ⁶For if the woman be not covered, let her also be shorn: but if it be a shame for a woman to be shorn or shaven, let her be covered. ⁷For a man indeed ought not to cover his head, forasmuch as he is the image and glory of God: but the woman is the glory of the man. ⁸For the man is not of the woman; but the woman of the man. ⁹Neither was the man created for the woman; but the woman for the man. ¹⁰For this cause ought the woman to have power on her head because of the angels. ¹¹Nevertheless neither is the man without the woman, neither the woman without the man, in the Lord. ¹²For as the woman is of the man, even so is the man also by the woman; but all things of God. ¹³Judge in yourselves: is it comely that a woman pray unto God uncovered? ¹⁴Doth not even nature itself teach you, that, if a man have long hair, it is a shame unto him? ¹⁵But if a woman have long hair, it is a glory to her: for her hair is given her for a covering. ¹⁶But if any man seem to be contentious, we have no such custom, neither the churches of God."

Ephesians 5:22-23 "²²Wives, submit yourselves unto your own husbands, as unto the Lord. ²³For the husband is the head of the wife, even as Christ is the head of the church: and he is the saviour of the body."

1 Timothy 2:11-14 "¹¹Let the woman learn in silence with all subjection. ¹²But I suffer not a woman to teach, nor to usurp authority over the man, but to be in silence. ¹³For Adam was first formed, then Eve. ¹⁴And Adam was not deceived, but the woman being deceived was in the transgression."

Men Needing Women
1 Corinthians 11:11-12 "¹¹Nevertheless neither is the man without the woman, neither the woman without the man, in the Lord. ¹²For as the woman is of the man, even so is the man also by the woman; but all things of God."

Strong Men
Proverbs 11:16 "A gracious woman retaineth honour: and strong men retain riches."

The Curse On Men
Genesis 3:17-19 "¹⁷And unto Adam he said, Because thou hast hearkened unto the voice of thy wife, and hast eaten of the tree, of which I commanded thee, saying, Thou shalt not eat of it: cursed is the ground for thy sake; in sorrow shalt thou eat of it all the days of thy life; ¹⁸Thorns also and thistles shall it bring forth to thee; and thou shalt eat the herb of the field; ¹⁹In the sweat of thy face shalt thou eat bread, till thou return unto the ground; for out of it wast thou taken: for dust thou art, and unto dust shalt thou return."

What Men Should Not Do
Deuteronomy 22:5 "The woman shall not wear that which pertaineth unto a man, neither shall a man put on a woman's garment: for all that do so are abomination unto the LORD thy God."

1 Corinthians 11:2-16 "²Now I praise you, brethren, that ye remember me in all things, and keep the ordinances, as I delivered them to you. ³But I would have you know, that the head of every man is Christ; and the head of the woman is the man; and the head of Christ is God. ⁴Every man praying or prophesying, having his head covered, dishonoureth his head. ⁵But every woman that prayeth or prophesieth with her head uncovered dishonoureth her head: for that is even all one as if she were shaven. ⁶For if the woman be not covered, let her also be shorn: but if it be a shame for a woman to be shorn or shaven, let her be covered. ⁷For a man indeed ought not to cover his head, forasmuch as he is the image and glory of God: but the woman is the glory of the man. ⁸For the man is not of the woman; but the woman of the man. ⁹Neither was the man created for the woman; but the woman for the man. ¹⁰For this cause ought the woman to have power on her head because of the angels. ¹¹Nevertheless neither is the man without the woman, neither the woman without the man, in the Lord. ¹²For as the woman is of the man, even so is the man also by the woman; but all things of God. ¹³Judge in yourselves: is it comely that a woman pray unto God uncovered? ¹⁴Doth not even nature itself teach you, that, if a man have long hair, it is a shame unto him? ¹⁵But if a woman have long hair, it is a glory to her: for her hair is given her for a covering. ¹⁶But if any man seem to be contentious, we have no such custom, neither the churches of God."

Where Men Come From
1 Corinthians 11:11-12 "¹¹Nevertheless neither is the man without the woman, neither the woman without the man, in the Lord. ¹²For as the woman is of the man, even so is the man also by the woman; but all things of God."

MERCY

Being Merciful
Zechariah 7:9 "Thus speaketh the LORD of hosts, saying, Execute true judgment, and shew mercy and compassions every man to his brother."

Luke 6:36 "Be ye therefore merciful, as your Father also is merciful."

Colossians 3:12 "Put on therefore, as the elect of God, holy and beloved, bowels of mercies, kindness, humbleness of mind, meekness, longsuffering."

Keeping Mercy
Hosea 12:6 "Therefore turn thou to thy God: keep mercy and judgment, and wait on thy God continually."

Mercy Belonging To The Lord

Psalm 62:12 "Also unto thee, O Lord, belongeth mercy: for thou renderest to every man according to his work."

Daniel 9:9 "To the Lord our God belong mercies and forgivenesses, though we have rebelled against him."

The Lord Being Merciful

Exodus 33:17-19 "[17]And the LORD said unto Moses, I will do this thing also that thou hast spoken: for thou hast found grace in my sight, and I know thee by name. [18]And he said, I beseech thee, shew me thy glory. [19]And he said, I will make all my goodness pass before thee, and I will proclaim the name of the LORD before thee; and will be gracious to whom I will be gracious, and will shew mercy on whom I will shew mercy."

Exodus 34:6-7 "[6]And the LORD passed by before him, and proclaimed, The LORD, The LORD God, merciful and gracious, longsuffering, and abundant in goodness and truth, [7]Keeping mercy for thousands, forgiving iniquity and transgression and sin, and that will by no means clear the guilty; visiting the iniquity of the fathers upon the children, and upon the children's children, unto the third and to the fourth generation."

Numbers 14:18 "The LORD is longsuffering, and of great mercy, forgiving iniquity and transgression, and by no means clearing the guilty, visiting the iniquity of the fathers upon the children unto the third and fourth generation."

Deuteronomy 4:31 "(For the LORD thy God is a merciful God;) he will not forsake thee, neither destroy thee, nor forget the covenant of thy fathers which he sware unto them."

2 Chronicles 30:9 "For if ye turn again unto the LORD, your brethren and your children shall find compassion before them that lead them captive, so that they shall come again into this land: for the LORD your God is gracious and merciful, and will not turn away his face from you, if ye return unto him."

Ezra 9:9 "For we were bondmen; yet our God hath not forsaken us in our bondage, but hath extended mercy unto us in the sight of the kings of Persia, to give us a reviving, to set up the house of our God, and to repair the desolations thereof, and to give us a wall in Judah and in Jerusalem."

Nehemiah 9:16-19 "[16]But they and our fathers dealt proudly, and hardened their necks, and hearkened not to thy commandments, [17]And refused to obey, neither were mindful of thy wonders that thou didst among them; but hardened their necks, and in their rebellion appointed a captain to return to their bondage: but thou art a God ready to pardon, gracious and merciful, slow to anger, and of great kindness, and forsookest them not. [18]Yea, when they had made them a molten calf, and said, This is thy God that brought thee up out of Egypt, and had wrought great provocations; [19]Yet thou in thy manifold mercies forsookest them not in the wilderness: the pillar of the cloud departed not from them by day, to lead them in the way; neither the pillar of fire by night, to shew them light, and the way wherein they should go."

Nehemiah 9:31 "Nevertheless for thy great mercies' sake thou didst not utterly consume them, nor forsake them; for thou art a gracious and merciful God."

Psalm 59:16-17 "[16]But I will sing of thy power; yea, I will sing aloud of thy mercy in the morning: for thou hast been my defence and refuge in the day of my trouble. [17]Unto thee, O my strength, will I sing: for God is my defence, and the God of my mercy."

Psalm 86:5 "For thou, Lord, art good, and ready to forgive; and plenteous in mercy unto all them that call upon thee."

Psalm 86:15 "But thou, O Lord, art a God full of compassion, and gracious, longsuffering, and plenteous in mercy and truth."

Psalm 103:8 "The LORD is merciful and gracious, slow to anger, and plenteous in mercy."

Psalm 116:5 "Gracious is the LORD, and righteous; yea, our God is merciful."

Psalm 130:7 "Let Israel hope in the LORD: for with the LORD there is mercy, and with him is plenteous redemption."

Psalm 145:8 "The LORD is gracious, and full of compassion; slow to anger, and of great mercy."

Isaiah 30:18 "And therefore will the LORD wait, that he may be gracious unto you, and therefore will he be exalted, that he may have mercy upon you: for the LORD is a God of judgment: blessed are all they that wait for him."

Isaiah 54:5-10 "⁵For thy Maker is thine husband; the LORD of hosts is his name; and thy Redeemer the Holy One of Israel; The God of the whole earth shall he be called. ⁶For the LORD hath called thee as a woman forsaken and grieved in spirit, and a wife of youth, when thou wast refused, saith thy God. ⁷For a small moment have I forsaken thee; but with great mercies will I gather thee. ⁸In a little wrath I hid my face from thee for a moment; but with everlasting kindness will I have mercy on thee, saith the LORD thy Redeemer. ⁹For this is as the waters of Noah unto me: for as I have sworn that the waters of Noah should no more go over the earth; so have I sworn that I would not be wroth with thee, nor rebuke thee. ¹⁰For the mountains shall depart, and the hills be removed; but my kindness shall not depart from thee, neither shall the covenant of my peace be removed, saith the LORD that hath mercy on thee."

Jeremiah 3:11-12 "¹¹And the LORD said unto me, The backsliding Israel hath justified herself more than treacherous Judah. ¹²Go and proclaim these words toward the north, and say, Return, thou backsliding Israel, saith the LORD; and I will not cause mine anger to fall upon you: for I am merciful, saith the LORD, and I will not keep anger for ever."

Joel 2:12-13 "¹²Therefore also now, saith the LORD, turn ye even to me with all your heart, and with fasting, and with weeping, and with mourning: ¹³And rend your heart, and not your garments, and turn unto the LORD your God: for he is gracious and merciful, slow to anger, and of great kindness, and repenteth him of the evil."

Luke 6:36 "Be ye therefore merciful, as your Father also is merciful."

Ephesians 2:4-5 "⁴But God, who is rich in mercy, for his great love wherewith he loved us, ⁵Even when we were dead in sins, hath quickened us together with Christ, (by grace ye are saved;)"

Hebrews 8:10-12 "¹⁰For this is the covenant that I will make with the house of Israel after those days, saith the Lord; I will put my laws into their mind, and write them in their hearts: and I will be to them a God, and they shall be to me a people:

¹¹And they shall not teach every man his neighbour, and every man his brother, saying, Know the Lord: for all shall know me, from the least to the greatest. ¹²For I will be merciful to their unrighteousness, and their sins and their iniquities will I remember no more."

The Mercies Of The Lord

1 Chronicles 16:34 "O give thanks unto the LORD; for he is good; for his mercy endureth for ever."

Psalm 21:7 "For the king trusteth in the LORD, and through the mercy of the most High he shall not be moved."

Psalm 66:20 "Blessed be God, which hath not turned away my prayer, nor his mercy from me."

Psalm 94:18 "When I said, My foot slippeth; thy mercy, O LORD, held me up."

Psalm 100:5 "For the LORD is good; his mercy is everlasting; and his truth endureth to all generations."

Psalm 103:8-11 "⁸The LORD is merciful and gracious, slow to anger, and plenteous in mercy. ⁹He will not always chide: neither will he keep his anger for ever. ¹⁰He hath not dealt with us after our sins; nor rewarded us according to our iniquities. ¹¹For as the heaven is high above the earth, so great is his mercy toward them that fear him."

Psalm 103:17 "But the mercy of the LORD is from everlasting to everlasting upon them that fear him, and his righteousness unto children's children."

Psalm 107:1 "O give thanks unto the LORD, for he is good: for his mercy endureth for ever."

Psalm 108:3-4 "³I will praise thee, O LORD, among the people: and I will sing praises unto thee among the nations. ⁴For thy mercy is great above the heavens: and thy truth reacheth unto the clouds."

Psalm 117:2 "For his merciful kindness is great toward us: and the truth of the LORD endureth for ever. Praise ye the LORD."

Psalm 118:1-4 "¹O give thanks unto the LORD; for he is good: because his mercy endureth for ever. ²Let Israel now say, that his mercy endureth for ever. ³Let the house of Aaron now say, that his mercy endureth for ever. ⁴Let them now that fear the LORD say, that his mercy endureth for ever."

Psalm 136:1-26 "[1]O give thanks unto the LORD; for he is good: for his mercy endureth for ever. [2]O give thanks unto the God of gods: for his mercy endureth for ever. [3]O give thanks to the Lord of lords: for his mercy endureth for ever. [4]To him who alone doeth great wonders: for his mercy endureth for ever. [5]To him that by wisdom made the heavens: for his mercy endureth for ever. [6]To him that stretched out the earth above the waters: for his mercy endureth for ever. [7]To him that made great lights: for his mercy endureth for ever: [8]The sun to rule by day: for his mercy endureth for ever: [9]The moon and stars to rule by night: for his mercy endureth for ever. [10]To him that smote Egypt in their firstborn: for his mercy endureth for ever: [11]And brought out Israel from among them: for his mercy endureth for ever: [12]With a strong hand, and with a stretched out arm: for his mercy endureth for ever. [13]To him which divided the Red sea into parts: for his mercy endureth for ever: [14]And made Israel to pass through the midst of it: for his mercy endureth for ever: [15]But overthrew Pharaoh and his host in the Red sea: for his mercy endureth for ever. [16]To him which led his people through the wilderness: for his mercy endureth for ever. [17]To him which smote great kings: for his mercy endureth for ever: [18]And slew famous kings: for his mercy endureth for ever: [19]Sihon king of the Amorites: for his mercy endureth for ever: [20]And Og the king of Bashan: for his mercy endureth for ever: [21]And gave their land for an heritage: for his mercy endureth for ever: [22]Even an heritage unto Israel his servant: for his mercy endureth for ever. [23]Who remembered us in our low estate: for his mercy endureth for ever: [24]And hath redeemed us from our enemies: for his mercy endureth for ever. [25]Who giveth food to all flesh: for his mercy endureth for ever. [26]O give thanks unto the God of heaven: for his mercy endureth for ever."

Psalm 138:8 "The LORD will perfect that which concerneth me: thy mercy, O LORD, endureth for ever: forsake not the works of thine own hands."

Psalm 145:9 "The LORD is good to all: and his tender mercies are over all his works."

Jeremiah 33:11 "The voice of joy, and the voice of gladness, the voice of the bridegroom, and the voice of the bride, the voice of them that shall say, Praise the LORD of hosts: for the LORD is good; for his mercy endureth for ever: and of them that shall bring the sacrifice of praise into the house of the LORD. For I will cause to return the captivity of the land, as at the first, saith the LORD."

Lamentations 3:22 "It is of the LORD's mercies that we are not consumed, because his compassions fail not."

Lamentations 3:31-32 "[31]For the Lord will not cast off for ever: [32]But though he cause grief, yet will he have compassion according to the multitude of his mercies."

The Merciful

2 Samuel 22:21-26 "[21]The LORD rewarded me according to my righteousness: according to the cleanness of my hands hath he recompensed me. [22]For I have kept the ways of the LORD, and have not wickedly departed from my God. [23]For all his judgments were before me: and as for his statutes, I did not depart from them. [24]I was also upright before him, and have kept myself from mine iniquity. [25]Therefore the LORD hath recompensed me according to my righteousness; according to my cleanness in his eye sight. [26]With the merciful thou wilt shew thyself merciful, and with the upright man thou wilt shew thyself upright."

Psalm 18:24-25 "[24]Therefore hath the LORD recompensed me according to my righteousness, according to the cleanness of my hands in his eyesight. [25]With the merciful thou wilt shew thyself merciful; with an upright man thou wilt shew thyself upright."

Proverbs 14:21 "He that despiseth his neighbour sinneth: but he that hath mercy on the poor, happy is he."

Isaiah 57:1-2 "[1]The righteous perisheth, and no man layeth it to heart: and merciful men are taken away, none considering that the righteous is taken away from the evil to come. [2]He shall enter into peace: they shall rest in their beds, each one walking in his uprightness."

Matthew 5:7 "Blessed are the merciful: for they shall obtain mercy."

Those That Follow After Mercy

Proverbs 21:21 "He that followeth after righteousness and mercy findeth life, righteousness, and honour."

What Is Full Of Mercy
Psalm 25:10 "All the paths of the LORD are mercy and truth unto such as keep his covenant and his testimonies."

James 3:17 "But the wisdom that is from above is first pure, then peaceable, gentle, and easy to be intreated, full of mercy and good fruits, without partiality, and without hypocrisy."

What Mercy Does
Psalm 61:5-7 "[5]For thou, O God, hast heard my vows: thou hast given me the heritage of those that fear thy name. [6]Thou wilt prolong the king's life: and his years as many generations. [7]He shall abide before God for ever: O prepare mercy and truth, which may preserve him."

Proverbs 16:6 "By mercy and truth iniquity is purged: and by the fear of the LORD men depart from evil."

Proverbs 20:28 "Mercy and truth preserve the king: and his throne is upholden by mercy."

Who Shall Have Mercy
Psalm 25:10 "All the paths of the LORD are mercy and truth unto such as keep his covenant and his testimonies."

Psalm 32:10 "Many sorrows shall be to the wicked: but he that trusteth in the LORD, mercy shall compass him about."

Proverbs 14:22 "Do they not err that devise evil? but mercy and truth shall be to them that devise good."

Proverbs 28:13 "He that covereth his sins shall not prosper: but whoso confesseth and forsaketh them shall have mercy."

Hosea 10:12 "Sow to yourselves in righteousness, reap in mercy; break up your fallow ground: for it is time to seek the LORD, till he come and rain righteousness upon you."

Matthew 5:7 "Blessed are the merciful: for they shall obtain mercy."

Who Shows Mercy
Psalm 37:21 "The wicked borroweth, and payeth not again: but the righteous sheweth mercy, and giveth."

Proverbs 14:31 "He that oppresseth the poor reproacheth his Maker: but he that honoureth him hath mercy on the poor."

Who The Lord Is Merciful With
Exodus 20:2-6 "[2]I am the LORD thy God, which have brought thee out of the land of Egypt, out of the house of bondage. [3]Thou shalt have no other gods before me. [4]Thou shalt not make unto thee any graven image, or any likeness of any thing that is in heaven above, or that is in the earth beneath, or that is in the water under the earth: [5]Thou shalt not bow down thyself to them, nor serve them: for I the LORD thy God am a jealous God, visiting the iniquity of the fathers upon the children unto the third and fourth generation of them that hate me; [6]And shewing mercy unto thousands of them that love me, and keep my commandments."

Deuteronomy 5:6-10 "[6]I am the LORD thy God, which brought thee out of the land of Egypt, from the house of bondage. [7]Thou shalt have none other gods before me. [8]Thou shalt not make thee any graven image, or any likeness of any thing that is in heaven above, or that is in the earth beneath, or that is in the waters beneath the earth: [9]Thou shalt not bow down thyself unto them, nor serve them: for I the LORD thy God am a jealous God, visiting the iniquity of the fathers upon the children unto the third and fourth generation of them that hate me, [10]And shewing mercy unto thousands of them that love me and keep my commandments."

Deuteronomy 7:9 "Know therefore that the LORD thy God, he is God, the faithful God, which keepeth covenant and mercy with them that love him and keep his commandments to a thousand generations."

Deuteronomy 32:36-43 "[36]For the LORD shall judge his people, and repent himself for his servants, when he seeth that their power is gone, and there is none shut up, or left. [37]And he shall say, Where are their gods, their rock in whom they trusted, [38]Which did eat the fat of their sacrifices, and drank the wine of their drink offerings? let them rise up and help you, and be your protection. [39]See now that I, even I, am he, and there is no god with me: I kill, and I make alive; I wound, and I heal: neither is there any that can deliver out of my hand. [40]For I lift up my hand to heaven, and say, I live for ever. [41]If I whet my glittering sword, and mine hand take hold on judgment; I will render vengeance to mine enemies, and will reward them that hate me. ⁴²I will make mine arrows drunk with blood, and my sword shall devour flesh; and that with the blood of the slain and of the captives, from the beginning of revenges upon the enemy. ⁴³Rejoice, O ye nations, with his people: for he will avenge the blood of his servants, and will render vengeance to his adversaries, and will be merciful unto his land, and to his people."

2 Samuel 22:21-26 "²¹The LORD rewarded me according to my righteousness: according to the cleanness of my hands hath he recompensed me. ²²For I have kept the ways of the LORD, and have not wickedly departed from my God. ²³For all his judgments were before me: and as for his statutes, I did not depart from them. ²⁴I was also upright before him, and have kept myself from mine iniquity. ²⁵Therefore the LORD hath recompensed me according to my righteousness; according to my cleanness in his eye sight. ²⁶With the merciful thou wilt shew thyself merciful, and with the upright man thou wilt shew thyself upright."

2 Samuel 22:50-51 "⁵⁰Therefore I will give thanks unto thee, O LORD, among the heathen, and I will sing praises unto thy name. ⁵¹He is the tower of salvation for his king: and sheweth mercy to his anointed, unto David, and to his seed for evermore."

1 Kings 8:23 "And he said, LORD God of Israel, there is no God like thee, in heaven above, or on earth beneath, who keepest covenant and mercy with thy servants that walk before thee with all their heart."

2 Chronicles 6:14 "And said, O LORD God of Israel, there is no God like thee in the heaven, nor in the earth; which keepest covenant, and shewest mercy unto thy servants, that walk before thee with all their hearts."

Nehemiah 1:5 "And said, I beseech thee, O LORD God of heaven, the great and terrible God, that keepeth covenant and mercy for them that love him and observe his commandments."

Psalm 18:24-25 "²⁴Therefore hath the LORD recompensed me according to my righteousness, according to the cleanness of my hands in his eyesight. ²⁵With the merciful thou wilt shew thyself merciful;

with an upright man thou wilt shew thyself upright."

Psalm 86:5 "For thou, Lord, art good, and ready to forgive; and plenteous in mercy unto all them that call upon thee."

Psalm 103:8-11 "⁸The LORD is merciful and gracious, slow to anger, and plenteous in mercy. ⁹He will not always chide: neither will he keep his anger for ever. ¹⁰He hath not dealt with us after our sins; nor rewarded us according to our iniquities. ¹¹For as the heaven is high above the earth, so great is his mercy toward them that fear him."

Isaiah 14:1 "For the LORD will have mercy on Jacob, and will yet choose Israel, and set them in their own land: and the strangers shall be joined with them, and they shall cleave to the house of Jacob."

Isaiah 55:7 "Let the wicked forsake his way, and the unrighteous man his thoughts: and let him return unto the LORD, and he will have mercy upon him; and to our God, for he will abundantly pardon."

Hosea 2:21-23 "²¹And it shall come to pass in that day, I will hear, saith the LORD, I will hear the heavens, and they shall hear the earth; ²²And the earth shall hear the corn, and the wine, and the oil; and they shall hear Jezreel. ²³And I will sow her unto me in the earth; and I will have mercy upon her that had not obtained mercy; and I will say to them which were not my people, Thou art my people; and they shall say, Thou art my God."

Micah 7:18-20 "¹⁸Who is a God like unto thee, that pardoneth iniquity, and passeth by the transgression of the remnant of his heritage? he retaineth not his anger for ever, because he delighteth in mercy. ¹⁹He will turn again, he will have compassion upon us; he will subdue our iniquities; and thou wilt cast all their sins into the depths of the sea. ²⁰Thou wilt perform the truth to Jacob, and the mercy to Abraham, which thou hast sworn unto our fathers from the days of old."

MIND

Having Christ's Mind

Philippians 2:5-8 "⁵Let this mind be in you, which was also in Christ Jesus: ⁶ Who, being in the form of God, thought it not robbery to be equal with God: 7 But made himself of no reputation, and took upon him the form of a servant, and was made in the likeness of men: 8 And being found in fashion as a man, he humbled himself, and became obedient unto death, even the death of the cross."

1 Peter 4:1 "Forasmuch then as Christ hath suffered for us in the flesh, arm yourselves likewise with the same mind: for he that hath suffered in the flesh hath ceased from sin."

The Carnal Mind
Romans 8:6-7 "⁶For to be carnally minded is death; but to be spiritually minded is life and peace. ⁷Because the carnal mind is enmity against God: for it is not subject to the law of God, neither indeed can be."

What Shall Keep Your Mind
Philippians 4:7 "And the peace of God, which passeth all understanding, shall keep your hearts and minds through Christ Jesus."

What Wars Against The Mind
Romans 7:21-25 "²¹I find then a law, that, when I would do good, evil is present with me. ²²For I delight in the law of God after the inward man: ²³But I see another law in my members, warring against the law of my mind, and bringing me into captivity to the law of sin which is in my members. ²⁴O wretched man that I am! who shall deliver me from the body of this death? ²⁵I thank God through Jesus Christ our Lord. So then with the mind I myself serve the law of God; but with the flesh the law of sin."

Who Has The Mind Of Christ
1 Corinthians 2:12-16 "¹²Now we have received, not the spirit of the world, but the spirit which is of God; that we might know the things that are freely given to us of God. ¹³Which things also we speak, not in the words which man's wisdom teacheth, but which the Holy Ghost teacheth; comparing spiritual things with spiritual. ¹⁴But the natural man receiveth not the things of the Spirit of God: for they are foolishness unto him: neither can he know them, because they are spiritually discerned. ¹⁵But he that is spiritual judgeth all things, yet he himself is judged of no man. ¹⁶For who hath known the mind of the Lord, that he may instruct him? But we have the mind of Christ."

MINISTRY

How To Minister
1 Peter 4:11 "If any man speak, let him speak as the oracles of God; if any man minister, let him do it as of the ability which God giveth: that God in all things may be glorified through Jesus Christ, to whom be praise and dominion for ever and ever. Amen."

Who Is A Minister Of God
Romans 13:1-6 "¹Let every soul be subject unto the higher powers. For there is no power but of God: the powers that be are ordained of God. ²Whosoever therefore resisteth the power, resisteth the ordinance of God: and they that resist shall receive to themselves damnation. ³For rulers are not a terror to good works, but to the evil. Wilt thou then not be afraid of the power? do that which is good, and thou shalt have praise of the same: ⁴For he is the minister of God to thee for good. But if thou do that which is evil, be afraid; for he beareth not the sword in vain: for he is the minister of God, a revenger to execute wrath upon him that doeth evil. ⁵Wherefore ye must needs be subject, not only for wrath, but also for conscience sake. ⁶For for this cause pay ye tribute also: for they are God's ministers, attending continually upon this very thing."

2 Corinthians 3:1-6 "¹Do we begin again to commend ourselves? or need we, as some others, epistles of commendation to you, or letters of commendation from you? ²Ye are our epistle written in our hearts, known and read of all men: ³Forasmuch as ye are manifestly declared to be the epistle of Christ ministered by us, written not with ink, but with the Spirit of the living God; not in tables of stone, but in fleshy tables of the heart. ⁴And such trust have we through Christ to God-ward: ⁵Not that we are sufficient of ourselves to think any thing as of ourselves; but our sufficiency is of God; ⁶Who also hath made us able ministers of the new testament; not of the letter, but of the spirit: for the letter killeth, but the spirit giveth life."

MISCHIEF

Feet That Run To Mischief
Proverbs 6:16-18 "¹⁶These six things doth the LORD hate: yea, seven are an abomination unto him: ¹⁷ A

proud look, a lying tongue, and hands that shed innocent blood, 18 An heart that deviseth wicked imaginations, feet that be swift in running to mischief,"

Those That Seek Mischief
Proverbs 11:27 "He that diligently seeketh good procureth favour: but he that seeketh mischief, it shall come unto him."

Who Falls Into Mischief
Proverbs 11:27 "He that diligently seeketh good procureth favour: but he that seeketh mischief, it shall come unto him."

Proverbs 13:17 "A wicked messenger falleth into mischief: but a faithful ambassador is health."

Proverbs 17:20 "He that hath a froward heart findeth no good: and he that hath a perverse tongue falleth into mischief."

Proverbs 24:16 "For a just man falleth seven times, and riseth up again: but the wicked shall fall into mischief."

Proverbs 28:14 "Happy is the man that feareth alway: but he that hardeneth his heart shall fall into mischief."

Isaiah 47:10-11 "10For thou hast trusted in thy wickedness: thou hast said, None seeth me. Thy wisdom and thy knowledge, it hath perverted thee; and thou hast said in thine heart, I am, and none else beside me. 11Therefore shall evil come upon thee; thou shalt not know from whence it riseth: and mischief shall fall upon thee; thou shalt not be able to put it off: and desolation shall come upon thee suddenly, which thou shalt not know."

Who Is Mischievous
Psalm 28:3 "Draw me not away with the wicked, and with the workers of iniquity, which speak peace to their neighbours, but mischief is in their hearts."

Proverbs 24:8 "He that deviseth to do evil shall be called a mischievous person."

Isaiah 59:1-4 "1Behold, the LORD's hand is not shortened, that it cannot save; neither his ear heavy, that it cannot hear: 2But your iniquities have separated between you and your God, and your sins have hid his face from you, that he will not hear. 3For your hands are defiled with blood, and your fingers with iniquity; your lips have spoken lies,

your tongue hath muttered perverseness. 4None calleth for justice, nor any pleadeth for truth: they trust in vanity, and speak lies; they conceive mischief, and bring forth iniquity."

Who Shall Be Filled With Mischief
Proverbs 12:21 "There shall no evil happen to the just: but the wicked shall be filled with mischief."

Who Speaks Of Mischief
Psalm 52:1-7 "1Why boastest thou thyself in mischief, O mighty man? the goodness of God endureth continually. 2Thy tongue deviseth mischiefs; like a sharp rasor, working deceitfully. 3Thou lovest evil more than good; and lying rather than to speak righteousness. Selah. 4Thou lovest all devouring words, O thou deceitful tongue. 5God shall likewise destroy thee for ever, he shall take thee away, and pluck thee out of thy dwelling place, and root thee out of the land of the living. Selah. 6The righteous also shall see, and fear, and shall laugh at him: 7Lo, this is the man that made not God his strength; but trusted in the abundance of his riches, and strengthened himself in his wickedness."

Proverbs 24:1-2 "1Be not thou envious against evil men, neither desire to be with them. 2For their heart studieth destruction, and their lips talk of mischief."

Who Thinks Mischief Is Fun
Proverbs 10:23 "It is as sport to a fool to do mischief: but a man of understanding hath wisdom."

MOCKERY

God Not Being Mocked
Galatians 6:7 "Be not deceived; God is not mocked: for whatsoever a man soweth, that shall he also reap."

Those That Mock The Poor
Proverbs 17:5 "Whoso mocketh the poor reproacheth his Maker: and he that is glad at calamities shall not be unpunished."

What Is A Mocker
Proverbs 20:1 "Wine is a mocker, strong drink is raging: and whosoever is deceived thereby is not wise."

Who Makes A Mock At Sin
Proverbs 14:9 "Fools make a mock at sin: but among the righteous there is favour."

MOURNING

Those That Mourn

Job 5:8-11 "⁸I would seek unto God, and unto God would I commit my cause: ⁹ Which doeth great things and unsearchable; marvellous things without number: ¹⁰ Who giveth rain upon the earth, and sendeth waters upon the fields: ¹¹ To set up on high those that be low; that those which mourn may be exalted to safety."

Matthew 5:4 "Blessed are they that mourn: for they shall be comforted."

Luke 6:21 "Blessed are ye that hunger now: for ye shall be filled. Blessed are ye that weep now: for ye shall laugh."

When People Mourn

Proverbs 29:2 "When the righteous are in authority, the people rejoice: but when the wicked beareth rule, the people mourn."

Who Shall Mourn

Luke 6:24-25 "²⁴But woe unto you that are rich! for ye have received your consolation. ²⁵Woe unto you that are full! for ye shall hunger. Woe unto you that laugh now! for ye shall mourn and weep."

Who To Mourn With

Romans 12:15 "Rejoice with them that do rejoice, and weep with them that weep."

MURMURING

Not Murmuring

John 6:41-43 "⁴¹The Jews then murmured at him, because he said, I am the bread which came down from heaven. ⁴² And they said, Is not this Jesus, the son of Joseph, whose father and mother we know? how is it then that he saith, I came down from heaven? ⁴³ Jesus therefore answered and said unto them, Murmur not among yourselves."

1 Corinthians 10:10 "Neither murmur ye, as some of them also murmured, and were destroyed of the destroyer."

Philippians 2:14-15 "¹⁴Do all things without murmurings and disputings: ¹⁵ That ye may be blameless and harmless, the sons of God, without rebuke, in the midst of a crooked and perverse nation, among whom ye shine as lights in the world."

The Reward For Murmuring Against God

Numbers 14:36-37 "³⁶And the men, which Moses sent to search the land, who returned, and made all the congregation to murmur against him, by bringing up a slander upon the land, ³⁷Even those men that did bring up the evil report upon the land, died by the plague before the LORD."

Psalm 106:24-27 "²⁴Yea, they despised the pleasant land, they believed not his word: ²⁵But murmured in their tents, and hearkened not unto the voice of the LORD. ²⁶Therefore he lifted up his hand against them, to overthrow them in the wilderness: ²⁷To overthrow their seed also among the nations, and to scatter them in the lands."

1 Corinthians 10:10 "Neither murmur ye, as some of them also murmured, and were destroyed of the destroyer."

Who Are Murmurers

Jude 7-16 "⁷Even as Sodom and Gomorrha, and the cities about them in like manner, giving themselves over to fornication, and going after strange flesh, are set forth for an example, suffering the vengeance of eternal fire. ⁸Likewise also these filthy dreamers defile the flesh, despise dominion, and speak evil of dignities. ⁹Yet Michael the archangel, when contending with the devil he disputed about the body of Moses, durst not bring against him a railing accusation, but said, The Lord rebuke thee. ¹⁰But these speak evil of those things which they know not: but what they know naturally, as brute beasts, in those things they corrupt themselves. ¹¹Woe unto them! for they have gone in the way of Cain, and ran greedily after the error of Balaam for reward, and perished in the gainsaying of Core. ¹²These are spots in your feasts of charity, when they feast with you, feeding themselves without fear: clouds they are without water, carried about of winds; trees whose fruit withereth, without fruit, twice dead, plucked up by the roots; ¹³Raging waves of the sea, foaming out their own shame; wandering stars, to whom is reserved the blackness of darkness for ever. ¹⁴And Enoch also, the seventh from Adam, prophesied of these, saying, Behold, the Lord cometh with ten thousands of his saints, ¹⁵To execute judgment upon all, and to convince all that are ungodly among them of all their ungodly deeds which they have ungodly committed, and of all their hard speeches which ungodly sinners have spoken against him. [16]These are murmurers, complainers, walking after their own lusts; and their mouth speaketh great swelling words, having men's persons in admiration because of advantage."

MYSTERY

The Mystery Of God
Psalm 25:14 "The secret of the LORD is with them that fear him; and he will shew them his covenant."

Romans 16:25-26 "[25]Now to him that is of power to stablish you according to my gospel, and the preaching of Jesus Christ, according to the revelation of the mystery, which was kept secret since the world began, [26] But now is made manifest, and by the scriptures of the prophets, according to the commandment of the everlasting God, made known to all nations for the obedience of faith."

1 Corinthians 2:6-8 "[6]Howbeit we speak wisdom among them that are perfect: yet not the wisdom of this world, nor of the princes of this world, that come to nought: [7] But we speak the wisdom of God in a mystery, even the hidden wisdom, which God ordained before the world unto our glory: [8] Which none of the princes of this world knew: for had they known it, they would not have crucified the Lord of glory."

1 Corinthians 15:50-57 "[50]Now this I say, brethren, that flesh and blood cannot inherit the kingdom of God; neither doth corruption inherit incorruption. [51] Behold, I shew you a mystery; We shall not all sleep, but we shall all be changed, [52] In a moment, in the twinkling of an eye, at the last trump: for the trumpet shall sound, and the dead shall be raised incorruptible, and we shall be changed. [53] For this corruptible must put on incorruption, and this mortal must put on immortality. [54] So when this corruptible shall have put on incorruption, and this mortal shall have put on immortality, then shall be brought to pass the saying that is written, Death is swallowed up in victory. [55] O death, where is thy sting? O grave, where is thy victory? [56] The sting of death is sin; and the strength of sin is the law.

[57] But thanks be to God, which giveth us the victory through our Lord Jesus Christ."

Ephesians 3:1-9 "[1]For this cause I Paul, the prisoner of Jesus Christ for you Gentiles, [2] If ye have heard of the dispensation of the grace of God which is given me to youward: [3] How that by revelation he made known unto me the mystery; (as I wrote afore in few words, [4] Whereby, when ye read, ye may understand my knowledge in the mystery of Christ) [5] Which in other ages was not made known unto the sons of men, as it is now revealed unto his holy apostles and prophets by the Spirit; [6] That the Gentiles should be fellowheirs, and of the same body, and partakers of his promise in Christ by the gospel: [7] Whereof I was made a minister, according to the gift of the grace of God given unto me by the effectual working of his power. [8] Unto me, who am less than the least of all saints, is this grace given, that I should preach among the Gentiles the unsearchable riches of Christ; [9] And to make all men see what is the fellowship of the mystery, which from the beginning of the world hath been hid in God, who created all things by Jesus Christ."

Colossians 1:26-27 "[26]Even the mystery which hath been hid from ages and from generations, but now is made manifest to his saints: [27] To whom God would make known what is the riches of the glory of this mystery among the Gentiles; which is Christ in you, the hope of glory."

Revelation 10:7 "But in the days of the voice of the seventh angel, when he shall begin to sound, the mystery of God should be finished, as he hath declared to his servants the prophets."

The Secret Things
Deuteronomy 29:29 "The secret things belong unto the LORD our God: but those things which are revealed belong unto us and to our children for ever, that we may do all the words of this law."

Who Speaks Mysteries
1 Corinthians 14:2 "For he that speaketh in an unknown tongue speaketh not unto men, but unto God: for no man understandeth him; howbeit in the spirit he speaketh mysteries."

N*n*

NAME

A Place Being Established
For The Name Of The Lord

Deuteronomy 12:11 "Then there shall be a place which the LORD your God shall choose to cause his name to dwell there; thither shall ye bring all that I command you; your burnt offerings, and your sacrifices, your tithes, and the heave offering of your hand, and all your choice vows which ye vow unto the LORD."

2 Samuel 7:8-13 "⁸Now therefore so shalt thou say unto my servant David, Thus saith the LORD of hosts, I took thee from the sheepcote, from following the sheep, to be ruler over my people, over Israel: ⁹ And I was with thee whithersoever thou wentest, and have cut off all thine enemies out of thy sight, and have made thee a great name, like unto the name of the great men that are in the earth. ¹⁰ Moreover I will appoint a place for my people Israel, and will plant them, that they may dwell in a place of their own, and move no more; neither shall the children of wickedness afflict them any more, as beforetime, ¹¹ And as since the time that I commanded judges to be over my people Israel, and have caused thee to rest from all thine enemies. Also the LORD telleth thee that he will make thee an house. ¹² And when thy days be fulfilled, and thou shalt sleep with thy fathers, I will set up thy seed after thee, which shall proceed out of thy bowels, and I will establish his kingdom. ¹³ He shall build an house for my name, and I will stablish the throne of his kingdom for ever."

1 Kings 8:28-48 "²⁸Yet have thou respect unto the prayer of thy servant, and to his supplication, O LORD my God, to hearken unto the cry and to the prayer, which thy servant prayeth before thee to day: ²⁹ That thine eyes may be open toward this house night and day, even toward the place of which thou hast said, My name shall be there: that thou mayest hearken unto the prayer which thy servant shall make toward this place. ³⁰ And hearken thou to the supplication of thy servant, and of thy people Israel, when they shall pray toward this place: and hear thou in heaven thy dwelling place: and when thou hearest, forgive. ³¹

If any man trespass against his neighbour, and an oath be laid upon him to cause him to swear, and the oath come before thine altar in this house: ³² Then hear thou in heaven, and do, and judge thy servants, condemning the wicked, to bring his way upon his head; and justifying the righteous, to give him according to his righteousness. ³³ When thy people Israel be smitten down before the enemy, because they have sinned against thee, and shall turn again to thee, and confess thy name, and pray, and make supplication unto thee in this house: ³⁴ Then hear thou in heaven, and forgive the sin of thy people Israel, and bring them again unto the land which thou gavest unto their fathers. ³⁵ When heaven is shut up, and there is no rain, because they have sinned against thee; if they pray toward this place, and confess thy name, and turn from their sin, when thou afflictest them: ³⁶ Then hear thou in heaven, and forgive the sin of thy servants, and of thy people Israel, that thou teach them the good way wherein they should walk, and give rain upon thy land, which thou hast given to thy people for an inheritance. ³⁷ If there be in the land famine, if there be pestilence, blasting, mildew, locust, or if there be caterpiller; if their enemy besiege them in the land of their cities; whatsoever plague, whatsoever sickness there be; ³⁸ What prayer and supplication soever be made by any man, or by all thy people Israel, which shall know every man the plague of his own heart, and spread forth his hands toward this house: ³⁹ Then hear thou in heaven thy dwelling place, and forgive, and do, and give to every man according to his ways, whose heart thou knowest; (for thou, even thou only, knowest the hearts of all the children of men;) ⁴⁰ That they may fear thee all the days that they live in the land which thou gavest unto our fathers. ⁴¹ Moreover concerning a stranger, that is not of thy people Israel, but cometh out of a far country for thy name's sake; ⁴² (For they shall hear of thy great name, and of thy strong hand, and of thy stretched out arm;) when he shall come and pray toward this house; ⁴³ Hear thou in heaven thy dwelling place, and do according to all that the stranger calleth to thee for: that all people of the earth may know thy name, to fear thee, as do thy people Israel; and that they may know that this house, which I have builded, is called by thy name. ⁴⁴ If thy people go out to battle against their enemy, whithersoever thou shalt send them, and shall pray unto the LORD toward the city which thou hast chosen, and toward the house that I have built for thy name: [45] Then hear thou in heaven their prayer and their supplication, and maintain their cause. [46] If they sin against thee, (for there is no man that sinneth not,) and thou be angry with them, and deliver them to the enemy, so that they carry them away captives unto the land of the enemy, far or near; [47] Yet if they shall bethink themselves in the land whither they were carried captives, and repent, and make supplication unto thee in the land of them that carried them captives, saying, We have sinned, and have done perversely, we have committed wickedness; [48] And so return unto thee with all their heart, and with all their soul, in the land of their enemies, which led them away captive, and pray unto thee toward their land, which thou gavest unto their fathers, the city which thou hast chosen, and the house which I have built for thy name."

1 Kings 9:1-3 "[1]And it came to pass, when Solomon had finished the building of the house of the LORD, and the king's house, and all Solomon's desire which he was pleased to do, [2] That the LORD appeared to Solomon the second time, as he had appeared unto him at Gibeon. [3] And the LORD said unto him, I have heard thy prayer and thy supplication, that thou hast made before me: I have hallowed this house, which thou hast built, to put my name there for ever; and mine eyes and mine heart shall be there perpetually."

1 Kings 11:31-36 "[31]And he said to Jeroboam, Take thee ten pieces: for thus saith the LORD, the God of Israel, Behold, I will rend the kingdom out of the hand of Solomon, and will give ten tribes to thee: [32] (But he shall have one tribe for my servant David's sake, and for Jerusalem's sake, the city which I have chosen out of all the tribes of Israel:) [33] Because that they have forsaken me, and have worshipped Ashtoreth the goddess of the Zidonians, Chemosh the god of the Moabites, and Milcom the god of the children of Ammon, and have not walked in my ways, to do that which is right in mine eyes, and to keep my statutes and my judgments, as did David his father. [34] Howbeit I will not take the whole kingdom out of his hand: but I will make him prince all the days of his life for David my servant's sake, whom I chose, because he kept my commandments and my statutes: [35] But I

will take the kingdom out of his son's hand, and will give it unto thee, even ten tribes. [36] And unto his son will I give one tribe, that David my servant may have a light alway before me in Jerusalem, the city which I have chosen me to put my name there."

2 Kings 21:4 "And he built altars in the house of the LORD, of which the LORD said, In Jerusalem will I put my name."

2 Kings 21:7 "And he set a graven image of the grove that he had made in the house, of which the LORD said to David, and to Solomon his son, In this house, and in Jerusalem, which I have chosen out of all tribes of Israel, will I put my name for ever."

2 Chronicles 6:19-38 "[19]Have respect therefore to the prayer of thy servant, and to his supplication, O LORD my God, to hearken unto the cry and the prayer which thy servant prayeth before thee: [20] That thine eyes may be open upon this house day and night, upon the place whereof thou hast said that thou wouldest put thy name there; to hearken unto the prayer which thy servant prayeth toward this place. [21] Hearken therefore unto the supplications of thy servant, and of thy people Israel, which they shall make toward this place: hear thou from thy dwelling place, even from heaven; and when thou hearest, forgive. [22] If a man sin against his neighbour, and an oath be laid upon him to make him swear, and the oath come before thine altar in this house; [23] Then hear thou from heaven, and do, and judge thy servants, by requiting the wicked, by recompensing his way upon his own head; and by justifying the righteous, by giving him according to his righteousness. [24] And if thy people Israel be put to the worse before the enemy, because they have sinned against thee; and shall return and confess thy name, and pray and make supplication before thee in this house; [25] Then hear thou from the heavens, and forgive the sin of thy people Israel, and bring them again unto the land which thou gavest to them and to their fathers. [26] When the heaven is shut up, and there is no rain, because they have sinned against thee; yet if they pray toward this place, and confess thy name, and turn from their sin, when thou dost afflict them; [27] Then hear thou from heaven, and forgive the sin of thy servants, and of thy people Israel, when thou hast taught them the good way, wherein they should walk; and send rain upon thy land, which thou hast given unto thy people for an inheritance. [28] If there be dearth in the land, if there be pestilence, if there be blasting, or mildew, locusts, or caterpillers; if their enemies besiege them in the cities of their land; whatsoever sore or whatsoever sickness there be: [29] Then what prayer or what supplication soever shall be made of any man, or of all thy people Israel, when every one shall know his own sore and his own grief, and shall spread forth his hands in this house: [30] Then hear thou from heaven thy dwelling place, and forgive, and render unto every man according unto all his ways, whose heart thou knowest; (for thou only knowest the hearts of the children of men:) [31] That they may fear thee, to walk in thy ways, so long as they live in the land which thou gavest unto our fathers. [32] Moreover concerning the stranger, which is not of thy people Israel, but is come from a far country for thy great name's sake, and thy mighty hand, and thy stretched out arm; if they come and pray in this house; [33] Then hear thou from the heavens, even from thy dwelling place, and do according to all that the stranger calleth to thee for; that all people of the earth may know thy name, and fear thee, as doth thy people Israel, and may know that this house which I have built is called by thy name. [34] If thy people go out to war against their enemies by the way that thou shalt send them, and they pray unto thee toward this city which thou hast chosen, and the house which I have built for thy name; [35] Then hear thou from the heavens their prayer and their supplication, and maintain their cause. [36] If they sin against thee, (for there is no man which sinneth not,) and thou be angry with them, and deliver them over before their enemies, and they carry them away captives unto a land far off or near; [37] Yet if they bethink themselves in the land whither they are carried captive, and turn and pray unto thee in the land of their captivity, saying, We have sinned, we have done amiss, and have dealt wickedly; [38] If they return to thee with all their heart and with all their soul in the land of their captivity, whither they have carried them captives, and pray toward their land, which thou gavest unto their fathers, and toward the city which thou hast chosen, and toward the house which I have built for thy name."

2 Chronicles 33:4 "Also he built altars in the house of the LORD, whereof the LORD had said, In Jerusalem shall my name be for ever."

2 Chronicles 33:7 "And he set a carved image, the idol which he had made, in the house of God, of which God had said to David and to Solomon his son, In this house, and in Jerusalem, which I have chosen before all the tribes of Israel, will I put my name for ever."

Nehemiah 1:2-9 "[2]That Hanani, one of my brethren, came, he and certain men of Judah; and I asked them concerning the Jews that had escaped, which were left of the captivity, and concerning Jerusalem. [3] And they said unto me, The remnant that are left of the captivity there in the province are in great affliction and reproach: the wall of Jerusalem also is broken down, and the gates thereof are burned with fire. [4] And it came to pass, when I heard these words, that I sat down and wept, and mourned certain days, and fasted, and prayed before the God of heaven, [5] And said, I beseech thee, O LORD God of heaven, the great and terrible God, that keepeth covenant and mercy for them that love him and observe his commandments: [6] Let thine ear now be attentive, and thine eyes open, that thou mayest hear the prayer of thy servant, which I pray before thee now, day and night, for the children of Israel thy servants, and confess the sins of the children of Israel, which we have sinned against thee: both I and my father's house have sinned. [7] We have dealt very corruptly against thee, and have not kept the commandments, nor the statutes, nor the judgments, which thou commandedst thy servant Moses. [8] Remember, I beseech thee, the word that thou commandedst thy servant Moses, saying, If ye transgress, I will scatter you abroad among the nations: [9] But if ye turn unto me, and keep my commandments, and do them; though there were of you cast out unto the uttermost part of the heaven, yet will I gather them from thence, and will bring them unto the place that I have chosen to set my name there."

God's Name
Exodus 3:13-14 "[13]And Moses said unto God, Behold, when I come unto the children of Israel, and shall say unto them, The God of your fathers hath sent me unto you; and they shall say to me, What is his name? what shall I say unto them? [14]And God said unto Moses, I AM THAT I AM: and he said, Thus shalt thou say unto the children of Israel, I AM hath sent me unto you."

Exodus 6:3 "And I appeared unto Abraham, unto Isaac, and unto Jacob, by the name of God Almighty, but by my name JEHOVAH was I not known to them."

Exodus 15:3 "The LORD is a man of war: the LORD is his name."

Exodus 34:14 "For thou shalt worship no other god: for the LORD, whose name is Jealous, is a jealous God."

Deuteronomy 28:58 "If thou wilt not observe to do all the words of this law that are written in this book, that thou mayest fear this glorious and fearful name, THE LORD THY GOD."

Psalm 68:4 "Sing unto God, sing praises to his name: extol him that rideth upon the heavens by his name JAH, and rejoice before him."

Psalm 83:18 "That men may know that thou, whose name alone is JEHOVAH, art the most high over all the earth."

Isaiah 7:14 "Therefore the Lord himself shall give you a sign; Behold, a virgin shall conceive, and bear a son, and shall call his name Immanuel."

Isaiah 9:6 "For unto us a child is born, unto us a son is given: and the government shall be upon his shoulder: and his name shall be called Wonderful, Counseller, The mighty God, The everlasting Father, The Prince of Peace."

Isaiah 42:8 "I am the LORD: that is my name: and my glory will I not give to another, neither my praise to graven images."

Isaiah 47:4 "As for our redeemer, the LORD of hosts is his name, the Holy One of Israel."

Isaiah 48:2 "For they call themselves of the holy city, and stay themselves upon the God of Israel; The LORD of hosts is his name."

Isaiah 51:15 "But I am the LORD thy God, that divided the sea, whose waves roared: The LORD of hosts is his name."

Isaiah 54:5 "For thy Maker is thine husband; the LORD of hosts is his name; and thy Redeemer the Holy One of Israel; The God of the whole earth shall he be called."

Isaiah 57:15 "For thus saith the high and lofty One that inhabiteth eternity, whose name is Holy; I dwell in the high and holy place, with him also that is of a contrite and humble spirit, to revive the spirit of the humble, and to revive the heart of the contrite ones."

Jeremiah 10:16 "The portion of Jacob is not like them: for he is the former of all things; and Israel is the rod of his inheritance: The LORD of hosts is his name."

Jeremiah 16:21 "Therefore, behold, I will this once cause them to know, I will cause them to know mine hand and my might; and they shall know that my name is The LORD."

Jeremiah 23:5-6 "⁵Behold, the days come, saith the LORD, that I will raise unto David a righteous Branch, and a King shall reign and prosper, and shall execute judgment and justice in the earth. ⁶In his days Judah shall be saved, and Israel shall dwell safely: and this is his name whereby he shall be called, THE LORD OUR RIGHTEOUSNESS."

Jeremiah 31:35 "Thus saith the LORD, which giveth the sun for a light by day, and the ordinances of the moon and of the stars for a light by night, which divideth the sea when the waves thereof roar; The LORD of hosts is his name."

Jeremiah 32:17-18 "¹⁷Ah Lord GOD! behold, thou hast made the heaven and the earth by thy great power and stretched out arm, and there is nothing too hard for thee: ¹⁸Thou shewest lovingkindness unto thousands, and recompensest the iniquity of the fathers into the bosom of their children after them: the Great, the Mighty God, the LORD of hosts, is his name,"

Jeremiah 33:2 "Thus saith the LORD the maker thereof, the LORD that formed it, to establish it; the LORD is his name."

Jeremiah 50:34 "Their Redeemer is strong; the LORD of hosts is his name: he shall throughly plead their cause, that he may give rest to the land, and disquiet the inhabitants of Babylon."

Amos 4:13 "For, lo, he that formeth the mountains, and createth the wind, and declareth unto man what is his thought, that maketh the morning darkness, and treadeth upon the high places of the earth, The LORD, The God of hosts, is his name."

Amos 5:8 "Seek him that maketh the seven stars and Orion, and turneth the shadow of death into the morning, and maketh the day dark with night: that calleth for the waters of the sea, and poureth them out upon the face of the earth: The LORD is his name."

Amos 9:6 "It is he that buildeth his stories in the heaven, and hath founded his troop in the earth; he that calleth for the waters of the sea, and poureth them out upon the face of the earth: The LORD is his name."

Matthew 1:20-25 "20But while he thought on these things, behold, the angel of the Lord appeared unto him in a dream, saying, Joseph, thou son of David, fear not to take unto thee Mary thy wife: for that which is conceived in her is of the Holy Ghost. 21And she shall bring forth a son, and thou shalt call his name JESUS: for he shall save his people from their sins. 22Now all this was done, that it might be fulfilled which was spoken of the Lord by the prophet, saying, 23Behold, a virgin shall be with child, and shall bring forth a son, and they shall call his name Emmanuel, which being interpreted is, God with us. 24Then Joseph being raised from sleep did as the angel of the Lord had bidden him, and took unto him his wife: 25And knew her not till she had brought forth her first-born son: and he called his name JESUS."

Luke 1:31-32 "31And, behold, thou shalt conceive in thy womb, and bring forth a son, and shalt call his name JESUS. 32He shall be great, and shall be called the Son of the Highest: and the Lord God shall give unto him the throne of his father David."

Luke 2:21 "And when eight days were accomplished for the circumcising of the child, his name was called JESUS, which was so named of the angel before he was conceived in the womb."

John 8:58 "Jesus said unto them, Verily, verily, I say unto you, Before Abraham was, I am."

Revelation 19:11-13 "11And I saw heaven opened, and behold a white horse; and he that sat upon him was called Faithful and True, and in righteousness he doth judge and make war. 12His eyes were as a flame of fire, and on his head were many crowns; and he had a name written, that no man knew, but he himself. 13And he was clothed with a vesture dipped in blood: and his name is called The Word of God."

Revelation 19:11-16 "11And I saw heaven opened, and behold a white horse; and he that sat upon him was called Faithful and True, and in righteousness he doth judge and make war. 12His eyes were as a flame of fire, and on his head were many crowns; and he had a name written, that no man knew, but he himself. 13And he was clothed with a vesture dipped in blood: and his name is called The Word of God. 14And the armies which were in heaven followed him upon white horses, clothed in fine linen, white and clean. 15And out of his mouth goeth a sharp sword, that with it he should smite the nations: and he shall rule them with a rod of iron: and he treadeth the winepress of the fierceness and wrath of Almighty God. 16And he hath on his vesture and on his thigh a name written, KING OF KINGS, AND LORD OF LORDS."

Good Names
Proverbs 22:1 "A good name is rather to be chosen than great riches, and loving favour rather than silver and gold."

Ecclesiastes 7:1 "A good name is better than precious ointment; and the day of death than the day of one's birth."

Not Misusing The Name Of The Lord
Exodus 20:7 "Thou shalt not take the name of the LORD thy God in vain; for the LORD will not hold him guiltless that taketh his name in vain."

Leviticus 18:21 "And thou shalt not let any of thy seed pass through the fire to Molech, neither shalt thou profane the name of thy God: I am the LORD."

Leviticus 19:12 "And ye shall not swear by my name falsely, neither shalt thou profane the name of thy God: I am the LORD."

Deuteronomy 5:11 "Thou shalt not take the name of the LORD thy God in vain: for the LORD will not hold him guiltless that taketh his name in vain."

The Name Of The Lord
Job 1:20-21 "20Then Job arose, and rent his mantle, and shaved his head, and fell down upon the ground, and worshipped, 21And said, Naked came I out of my mother's womb, and naked shall I return thither: the LORD gave, and the LORD hath taken away; blessed be the name of the LORD."

Psalm 8:1 "O LORD our Lord, how excellent is thy name in all the earth! who hast set thy glory above the heavens."

Psalm 8:9 "O LORD our Lord, how excellent is thy name in all the earth!"

Psalm 72:18-19 "18Blessed be the LORD God, the God of Israel, who only doeth wondrous things. 19And blessed be his glorious name for ever: and let the whole earth be filled with his glory; Amen, and Amen."

Psalm 111:4-9 "4He hath made his wonderful works to be remembered: the LORD is gracious and full of compassion. 5He hath given meat unto them that fear him: he will ever be mindful of his covenant. 6He hath shewed his people the power of his works, that he may give them the heritage of the heathen. 7The works of his hands are verity and judgment; all his commandments are sure. 8They stand fast for ever and ever, and are done in truth and uprightness. 9He sent redemption unto his people: he hath commanded his covenant for ever: holy and reverend is his name."

Psalm 124:8 "Our help is in the name of the LORD, who made heaven and earth."

Psalm 148:13 "Let them praise the name of the LORD: for his name alone is excellent; his glory is above the earth and heaven."

Proverbs 18:10 "The name of the LORD is a strong tower: the righteous runneth into it, and is safe."

Jeremiah 10:6 "Forasmuch as there is none like unto thee, O LORD; thou art great, and thy name is great in might."

Daniel 2:20 "Daniel answered and said, Blessed be the name of God for ever and ever: for wisdom and might are his."

Malachi 1:14 "But cursed be the deceiver, which hath in his flock a male, and voweth, and sacrificeth unto the LORD a corrupt thing: for I am a great King, saith the LORD of hosts, and my name is dreadful among the heathen."

John 20:31 "But these are written, that ye might believe that Jesus is the Christ, the Son of God; and that believing ye might have life through his name."

Acts 4:9-10 "9If we this day be examined of the good deed done to the impotent man, by what means he is made whole; 10Be it known unto you all, and to all the people of Israel, that by the name of Jesus Christ of Nazareth, whom ye crucified, whom God raised from the dead, even by him doth this man stand here before you whole."

Acts 10:37-43 "37That word, I say, ye know, which was published throughout all Judaea, and began from Galilee, after the baptism which John preached; 38How God anointed Jesus of Nazareth with the Holy Ghost and with power: who went about doing good, and healing all that were oppressed of the devil; for God was with him. 39And we are witnesses of all things which he did both in the land of the Jews, and in Jerusalem; whom they slew and hanged on a tree: 40Him God raised up the third day, and shewed him openly; 41Not to all the people, but unto witnesses chosen before of God, even to us, who did eat and drink with him after he rose from the dead. 42And he commanded us to preach unto the people, and to testify that it is he which was ordained of God to be the Judge of quick and dead. 43To him give all the prophets witness, that through his name whosoever believeth in him shall receive remission of sins."

1 Corinthians 6:9-11 "9Know ye not that the unrighteous shall not inherit the kingdom of God? Be not deceived: neither fornicators, nor idolaters, nor adulterers, nor effeminate, nor abusers of themselves with mankind, 10Nor thieves, nor covetous, nor drunkards, nor revilers, nor extortioners, shall inherit the kingdom of God. 11And such were some of you: but ye are washed, but ye are sanctified, but ye are justified in the name of the Lord Jesus, and by the Spirit of our God."

Philippians 2:5-11 "5Let this mind be in you, which was also in Christ Jesus: 6Who, being in the form of God, thought it not robbery to be equal with God: 7But made himself of no reputation, and took upon him the form of a servant, and was made in the likeness of men: 8And being found in fashion as a man, he humbled himself, and became obedient unto death, even the death of the cross. 9Wherefore God also hath highly exalted him, and given him a name which is above every name: 10That at the name of Jesus every knee should bow, of things in heaven, and things in earth, and things under the earth; [11]And that every tongue should confess that Jesus Christ is Lord, to the glory of God the Father."

The Name Of The Wicked
Proverbs 10:7 "The memory of the just is blessed: but the name of the wicked shall rot."

Those Whose Names Are Not Written In The Book Of Life
Revelation 13:1-8 "[1]And I stood upon the sand of the sea, and saw a beast rise up out of the sea, having seven heads and ten horns, and upon his horns ten crowns, and upon his heads the name of blasphemy. [2]And the beast which I saw was like unto a leopard, and his feet were as the feet of a bear, and his mouth as the mouth of a lion: and the dragon gave him his power, and his seat, and great authority. [3]And I saw one of his heads as it were wounded to death; and his deadly wound was healed: and all the world wondered after the beast. [4]And they worshipped the dragon which gave power unto the beast: and they worshipped the beast, saying, Who is like unto the beast? who is able to make war with him? [5]And there was given unto him a mouth speaking great things and blasphemies; and power was given unto him to continue forty and two months. [6]And he opened his mouth in blasphemy against God, to blaspheme his name, and his tabernacle, and them that dwell in heaven. [7]And it was given unto him to make war with the saints, and to overcome them: and power was given him over all kindreds, and tongues, and nations. [8]And all that dwell upon the earth shall worship him, whose names are not written in the book of life of the Lamb slain from the foundation of the world."

Revelation 20:15 "And whosoever was not found written in the book of life was cast into the lake of fire."

Those Whose Names Are Written In The Book Of Life
Psalm 139:13-17 "[13]For thou hast possessed my reins: thou hast covered me in my mother's womb. [14]I will praise thee; for I am fearfully and wonderfully made: marvellous are thy works; and that my soul knoweth right well. [15]My substance was not hid from thee, when I was made in secret, and curiously wrought in the lowest parts of the earth. [16]Thine eyes did see my substance, yet being unperfect; and in thy book all my members were written, which in continuance were fashioned, when as yet there was none of them. [17]How precious also are thy thoughts unto me, O God! how great is the sum of them!"

Daniel 12:1 "And at that time shall Michael stand up, the great prince which standeth for the children of thy people: and there shall be a time of trouble, such as never was since there was a nation even to that same time: and at that time thy people shall be delivered, every one that shall be found written in the book."

Revelation 21:22-27 "[22]And I saw no temple therein: for the Lord God Almighty and the Lamb are the temple of it. [23]And the city had no need of the sun, neither of the moon, to shine in it: for the glory of God did lighten it, and the Lamb is the light thereof. [24]And the nations of them which are saved shall walk in the light of it: and the kings of the earth do bring their glory and honour into it. [25]And the gates of it shall not be shut at all by day: for there shall be no night there. [26]And they shall bring the glory and honour of the nations into it. [27]And there shall in no wise enter into it any thing that defileth, neither whatsoever worketh abomination, or maketh a lie: but they which are written in the Lamb's book of life."

What Can Be Accomplished In The Name Of The Lord
Mark 9:38 "And John answered him, saying, Master, we saw one casting out devils in thy name, and he followeth not us: and we forbad him, because he followeth not us."

Mark 16:17-19 "[17]And these signs shall follow them that believe; In my name shall they cast out devils; they shall speak with new tongues; [18]They shall take up serpents; and if they drink any deadly thing, it shall not hurt them; they shall lay hands on the sick, and they shall recover. [19]So then after the Lord had spoken unto them, he was received up into heaven, and sat on the right hand of God."

Luke 9:49 "And John answered and said, Master, we saw one casting out devils in thy name; and we forbad him, because he followeth not with us."

Luke 10:17 "And the seventy returned again with joy, saying, Lord, even the devils are subject unto us through thy name."

Who Shall Have God's Name In Their Foreheads

Revelation 22:3-4 "³And there shall be no more curse: but the throne of God and of the Lamb shall be in it; and his servants shall serve him: ⁴And they shall see his face; and his name shall be in their foreheads."

Who Shall Receive A New Name

Isaiah 56:4-5 "⁴For thus saith the LORD unto the eunuchs that keep my sabbaths, and choose the things that please me, and take hold of my covenant; ⁵Even unto them will I give in mine house and within my walls a place and a name better than of sons and of daughters: I will give them an everlasting name, that shall not be cut off."

Revelation 2:17 "He that hath an ear, let him hear what the Spirit saith unto the churches; To him that overcometh will I give to eat of the hidden manna, and will give him a white stone, and in the stone a new name written, which no man knoweth saving he that receiveth it."

Revelation 3:12 "Him that overcometh will I make a pillar in the temple of my God, and he shall go no more out: and I will write upon him the name of my God, and the name of the city of my God, which is new Jerusalem, which cometh down out of heaven from my God: and I will write upon him my new name."

Who Takes The Name Of The Lord In Vain

Psalm 139:19-20 "¹⁹Surely thou wilt slay the wicked, O God: depart from me therefore, ye bloody men. ²⁰For they speak against thee wickedly, and thine enemies take thy name in vain."

Whose Name Shall Remain

Isaiah 66:20-22 "²⁰And they shall bring all your brethren for an offering unto the LORD out of all nations upon horses, and in chariots, and in litters, and upon mules, and upon swift beasts, to my holy mountain Jerusalem, saith the LORD, as the children of Israel bring an offering in a clean vessel into the house of the LORD. ²¹And I will also take of them for priests and for Levites, saith the LORD. ²²For as the new heavens and the new earth, which I will make, shall remain before me, saith the LORD, so shall your seed and your name remain."

Whose Names Are Written In Heaven

Luke 10:17-20 "¹⁷And the seventy returned again with joy, saying, Lord, even the devils are subject unto us through thy name. ¹⁸And he said unto them, I beheld Satan as lightning fall from heaven. ¹⁹Behold, I give unto you power to tread on serpents and scorpions, and over all the power of the enemy: and nothing shall by any means hurt you. ²⁰Notwithstanding in this rejoice not, that the spirits are subject unto you; but rather rejoice, because your names are written in heaven."

Hebrews 12:22-23 "²²But ye are come unto mount Sion, and unto the city of the living God, the heavenly Jerusalem, and to an innumerable company of angels, ²³To the general assembly and church of the firstborn, which are written in heaven, and to God the Judge of all, and to the spirits of just men made perfect,"

Whose Name Shall Be Blotted Out Of The Book Of Life

Revelation 22:18-19 "¹⁸For I testify unto every man that heareth the words of the prophecy of this book, If any man shall add unto these things, God shall add unto him the plagues that are written in this book: ¹⁹And if any man shall take away from the words of the book of this prophecy, God shall take away his part out of the book of life, and out of the holy city, and from the things which are written in this book."

Whose Name Shall Not Be Blotted Out Of The Book Of Life

Revelation 3:5 "He that overcometh, the same shall be clothed in white raiment; and I will not blot out his name out of the book of life, but I will confess his name before my Father, and before his angels."

NATIONS

All Nations Serving The Lord

Psalm 22:27 "All the ends of the world shall remember and turn unto the LORD: and all the kindreds of the nations shall worship before thee."

Daniel 7:13-14 "¹³I saw in the night visions, and, behold, one like the Son of man came with the clouds of heaven, and came to the Ancient of days, and they brought him near before him. ¹⁴And there was given him dominion, and glory, and a kingdom, that all people, nations, and languages, should serve him: his dominion is an everlasting dominion, which shall not pass away, and his kingdom that which shall not be destroyed."

Daniel 7:27 "And the kingdom and dominion, and the greatness of the kingdom under the whole heaven, shall be given to the people of the saints of the most High, whose kingdom is an everlasting kingdom, and all dominions shall serve and obey him."

God Beholding The Nations
Psalm 66:3-7 "³Say unto God, How terrible art thou in thy works! through the greatness of thy power shall thine enemies submit themselves unto thee. ⁴All the earth shall worship thee, and shall sing unto thee; they shall sing to thy name. Selah. ⁵Come and see the works of God: he is terrible in his doing toward the children of men. ⁶He turned the sea into dry land: they went through the flood on foot: there did we rejoice in him. ⁷He ruleth by his power for ever; his eyes behold the nations: let not the rebellious exalt themselves. Selah."

God Making All Nations Out Of One Blood
Acts 17:23-26 "²³For as I passed by, and beheld your devotions, I found an altar with this inscription, TO THE UNKNOWN GOD. Whom therefore ye ignorantly worship, him declare I unto you. ²⁴God that made the world and all things therein, seeing that he is Lord of heaven and earth, dwelleth not in temples made with hands; ²⁵Neither is worshipped with men's hands, as though he needed any thing, seeing he giveth to all life, and breath, and all things; ²⁶And hath made of one blood all nations of men for to dwell on all the face of the earth, and hath determined the times before appointed, and the bounds of their habitation."

How States Fall And How States Are Prolonged
Proverbs 28:1-2 "¹The wicked flee when no man pursueth: but the righteous are bold as a lion. ²For the transgression of a land many are the princes thereof: but by a man of understanding and knowledge the state thereof shall be prolonged."

The Lord Destroying Nations
Job 12:9-23 "⁹Who knoweth not in all these that the hand of the LORD hath wrought this? ¹⁰In whose hand is the soul of every living thing, and the breath of all mankind. ¹¹Doth not the ear try words? and the mouth taste his meat? ¹²With the ancient is wisdom; and in length of days understanding. ¹³With him is wisdom and strength, he hath counsel and understanding. ¹⁴Behold, he breaketh down, and it cannot be built again: he shutteth up a man, and there can be no opening. ¹⁵Behold, he withholdeth the waters, and they dry up: also he sendeth them out, and they overturn the earth. ¹⁶With him is strength and wisdom: the deceived and the deceiver are his. ¹⁷He leadeth counsellers away spoiled, and maketh the judges fools. ¹⁸He looseth the bond of kings, and girdeth their loins with a girdle. ¹⁹He leadeth princes away spoiled, and overthroweth the mighty. ²⁰He removeth away the speech of the trusty, and taketh away the understanding of the aged. ²¹He poureth contempt upon princes, and weakeneth the strength of the mighty. ²²He discovereth deep things out of darkness, and bringeth out to light the shadow of death. ²³He increaseth the nations, and destroyeth them: he enlargeth the nations, and straiteneth them again."

Psalm 110:5-6 "⁵The Lord at thy right hand shall strike through kings in the day of his wrath. ⁶He shall judge among the heathen, he shall fill the places with the dead bodies; he shall wound the heads over many countries."

The Lord Gathering The Nations Together
Isaiah 66:17-18 "¹⁷They that sanctify themselves, and purify themselves in the gardens behind one tree in the midst, eating swine's flesh, and the abomination, and the mouse, shall be consumed together, saith the LORD. ¹⁸For I know their works and their thoughts: it shall come, that I will gather all nations and tongues; and they shall come, and see my glory."

Joel 3:1-14 "¹For, behold, in those days, and in that time, when I shall bring again the captivity of Judah and Jerusalem, ²I will also gather all nations, and will bring them down into the valley of Jehoshaphat, and will plead with them there for my people and for my heritage Israel, whom they have scattered among the nations, and parted my land. ³And they have cast lots for my people; and have given a boy for an harlot, and sold a girl for wine, that they might drink. ⁴Yea, and what have ye to do with me, O Tyre, and Zidon, and all the coasts of Palestine? will ye render me a recompence? and if ye recompence me, swiftly and speedily will I return your recompence upon your own head; [5]Because ye have taken my silver and my gold, and have carried into your temples my goodly pleasant things: [6]The children also of Judah and the children of Jerusalem have ye sold unto the Grecians, that ye might remove them far from their border. [7]Behold, I will raise them out of the place whither ye have sold them, and will return your recompence upon your own head: [8]And I will sell your sons and your daughters into the hand of the children of Judah, and they shall sell them to the Sabeans, to a people far off: for the LORD hath spoken it. [9]Proclaim ye this among the Gentiles; Prepare war, wake up the mighty men, let all the men of war draw near; let them come up: [10]Beat your plowshares into swords, and your pruninghooks into spears: let the weak say, I am strong. [11]Assemble yourselves, and come, all ye heathen, and gather yourselves together round about: thither cause thy mighty ones to come down, O LORD. [12]Let the heathen be wakened, and come up to the valley of Jehoshaphat: for there will I sit to judge all the heathen round about. [13]Put ye in the sickle, for the harvest is ripe: come, get you down; for the press is full, the fats overflow; for their wickedness is great. [14]Multitudes, multitudes in the valley of decision: for the day of the LORD is near in the valley of decision."

Zephaniah 3:8 "Therefore wait ye upon me, saith the LORD, until the day that I rise up to the prey: for my determination is to gather the nations, that I may assemble the kingdoms, to pour upon them mine indignation, even all my fierce anger: for all the earth shall be devoured with the fire of my jealousy."

Zechariah 12:1-3 "[1]The burden of the word of the LORD for Israel, saith the LORD, which stretcheth forth the heavens, and layeth the foundation of the earth, and formeth the spirit of man within him. [2]Behold, I will make Jerusalem a cup of trembling unto all the people round about, when they shall be in the siege both against Judah and against Jerusalem. [3]And in that day will I make Jerusalem a burdensome stone for all people: all that burden themselves with it shall be cut in pieces, though all the people of the earth be gathered together against it."

Zechariah 14:1-2 "[1]Behold, the day of the LORD cometh, and thy spoil shall be divided in the midst

of thee. [2]For I will gather all nations against Jerusalem to battle; and the city shall be taken, and the houses rifled, and the women ravished; and half of the city shall go forth into captivity, and the residue of the people shall not be cut off from the city."

Matthew 25:31-33 "[31]When the Son of man shall come in his glory, and all the holy angels with him, then shall he sit upon the throne of his glory: [32]And before him shall be gathered all nations: and he shall separate them one from another, as a shepherd divideth his sheep from the goats: [33]And he shall set the sheep on his right hand, but the goats on the left."

Revelation 16:13-16 "[13]And I saw three unclean spirits like frogs come out of the mouth of the dragon, and out of the mouth of the beast, and out of the mouth of the false prophet. [14]For they are the spirits of devils, working miracles, which go forth unto the kings of the earth and of the whole world, to gather them to the battle of that great day of God Almighty. [15]Behold, I come as a thief. Blessed is he that watcheth, and keepeth his garments, lest he walk naked, and they see his shame. [16]And he gathered them together into a place called in the Hebrew tongue Armageddon."

The Lord Judging Among The Nations

Isaiah 2:3-4 "[3]And many people shall go and say, Come ye, and let us go up to the mountain of the LORD, to the house of the God of Jacob; and he will teach us of his ways, and we will walk in his paths: for out of Zion shall go forth the law, and the word of the LORD from Jerusalem. [4]And he shall judge among the nations, and shall rebuke many people: and they shall beat their swords into plowshares, and their spears into pruninghooks: nation shall not lift up sword against nation, neither shall they learn war any more."

Micah 4:1-3 "[1]But in the last days it shall come to pass, that the mountain of the house of the LORD shall be established in the top of the mountains, and it shall be exalted above the hills; and people shall flow unto it. [2]And many nations shall come, and say, Come, and let us go up to the mountain of the LORD, and to the house of the God of Jacob; and he will teach us of his ways, and we will walk in his paths: for the law shall go forth of Zion, and the word of the LORD from Jerusalem. [3]And he shall judge among many people, and rebuke strong nations afar off; and they shall beat their swords into plowshares, and their spears into pruning-hooks: nation shall not lift up a sword against nation, neither shall they learn war any more.”

The Nation Whose God Is The Lord
Psalm 33:12 “Blessed is the nation whose God is the LORD: and the people whom he hath chosen for his own inheritance.”

The Nations That Oppose The Lord
Psalm 2:1-6 “¹Why do the heathen rage, and the people imagine a vain thing? ²The kings of the earth set themselves, and the rulers take counsel together, against the LORD, and against his anointed, saying, ³Let us break their bands asunder, and cast away their cords from us. ⁴He that sitteth in the heavens shall laugh: the Lord shall have them in derision. ⁵Then shall he speak unto them in his wrath, and vex them in his sore displeasure. ⁶Yet have I set my king upon my holy hill of Zion.”

The Nations That Forget God
Psalm 9:17 “The wicked shall be turned into hell, and all the nations that forget God.”

The Origin Of The Post-Flood Nations
Genesis 9:18-19 “¹⁸And the sons of Noah, that went forth of the ark, were Shem, and Ham, and Japheth: and Ham is the father of Canaan. ¹⁹These are the three sons of Noah: and of them was the whole earth overspread.”

Genesis 10:1-32 “¹Now these are the generations of the sons of Noah, Shem, Ham, and Japheth: and unto them were sons born after the flood. ²The sons of Japheth; Gomer, and Magog, and Madai, and Javan, and Tubal, and Meshech, and Tiras. ³And the sons of Gomer; Ashkenaz, and Riphath, and Togarmah. ⁴And the sons of Javan; Elishah, and Tarshish, Kittim, and Dodanim. ⁵By these were the isles of the Gentiles divided in their lands; every one after his tongue, after their families, in their nations. ⁶And the sons of Ham; Cush, and Mizraim, and Phut, and Canaan. ⁷And the sons of Cush; Seba, and Havilah, and Sabtah, and Raamah, and Sabtecha: and the sons of Raamah; Sheba, and Dedan. ⁸And Cush begat Nimrod: he began to be a mighty one in the earth. ⁹He was a mighty hunter before the LORD: wherefore it is said, Even as Nimrod the mighty hunter before the LORD. ¹⁰And the beginning of his kingdom was Babel, and Erech, and Accad, and Calneh, in the land of Shinar. ¹¹Out of that land went forth Asshur, and builded Nineveh, and the city Rehoboth, and Calah, ¹²And Resen between Nineveh and Calah: the same is a great city. ¹³And Mizraim begat Ludim, and Anamim, and Lehabim, and Naphtuhim, ¹⁴And Pathrusim, and Casluhim, (out of whom came Philistim,) and Caphtorim. ¹⁵And Canaan begat Sidon his firstborn, and Heth, ¹⁶And the Jebusite, and the Amorite, and the Girgasite, ¹⁷And the Hivite, and the Arkite, and the Sinite, ¹⁸And the Arvadite, and the Zemarite, and the Hamathite: and afterward were the families of the Canaanites spread abroad. ¹⁹And the border of the Canaanites was from Sidon, as thou comest to Gerar, unto Gaza; as thou goest, unto Sodom, and Gomorrah, and Admah, and Zeboim, even unto Lasha. ²⁰These are the sons of Ham, after their families, after their tongues, in their countries, and in their nations. ²¹Unto Shem also, the father of all the children of Eber, the brother of Japheth the elder, even to him were children born. ²²The children of Shem; Elam, and Asshur, and Arphaxad, and Lud, and Aram. ²³And the children of Aram; Uz, and Hul, and Gether, and Mash. ²⁴And Arphaxad begat Salah; and Salah begat Eber. ²⁵And unto Eber were born two sons: the name of one was Peleg; for in his days was the earth divided; and his brother’s name was Joktan. ²⁶And Joktan begat Almodad, and Sheleph, and Hazar-maveth, and Jerah, ²⁷And Hadoram, and Uzal, and Diklah, ²⁸And Obal, and Abimael, and Sheba, ²⁹And Ophir, and Havilah, and Jobab: all these were the sons of Joktan. ³⁰And their dwelling was from Mesha, as thou goest unto Sephar a mount of the east. ³¹These are the sons of Shem, after their families, after their tongues, in their lands, after their nations. ³²These are the families of the sons of Noah, after their generations, in their nations: and by these were the nations divided in the earth after the flood.”

What Exalts A Nation
Proverbs 14:34 “Righteousness exalteth a nation: but sin is a reproach to any people.”

What Nations The Lord Shall Destroy

Jeremiah 30:10-11 "¹⁰Therefore fear thou not, O my servant Jacob, saith the LORD; neither be dismayed, O Israel: for, lo, I will save thee from afar, and thy seed from the land of their captivity; and Jacob shall return, and shall be in rest, and be quiet, and none shall make him afraid. ¹¹For I am with thee, saith the LORD, to save thee: though I make a full end of all nations whither I have scattered thee, yet will I not make a full end of thee: but I will correct thee in measure, and will not leave thee altogether unpunished."

Jeremiah 46:28 "Fear thou not, O Jacob my servant, saith the LORD: for I am with thee; for I will make a full end of all the nations whither I have driven thee: but I will not make a full end of thee, but correct thee in measure; yet will I not leave thee wholly unpunished."

Daniel 2:31-44 "³¹Thou, O king, sawest, and behold a great image. This great image, whose brightness was excellent, stood before thee; and the form thereof was terrible. ³²This image's head was of fine gold, his breast and his arms of silver, his belly and his thighs of brass, ³³His legs of iron, his feet part of iron and part of clay. ³⁴Thou sawest till that a stone was cut out without hands, which smote the image upon his feet that were of iron and clay, and brake them to pieces. ³⁵Then was the iron, the clay, the brass, the silver, and the gold, broken to pieces together, and became like the chaff of the summer threshingfloors; and the wind carried them away, that no place was found for them: and the stone that smote the image became a great mountain, and filled the whole earth. ³⁶This is the dream; and we will tell the interpretation thereof before the king. ³⁷Thou, O king, art a king of kings: for the God of heaven hath given thee a kingdom, power, and strength, and glory. ³⁸And wheresoever the children of men dwell, the beasts of the field and the fowls of the heaven hath he given into thine hand, and hath made thee ruler over them all. Thou art this head of gold. ³⁹And after thee shall arise another kingdom inferior to thee, and another third kingdom of brass, which shall bear rule over all the earth. ⁴⁰And the fourth kingdom shall be strong as iron: forasmuch as iron breaketh in pieces and subdueth all things: and as iron that breaketh all these, shall it break in pieces

and bruise. ⁴¹And whereas thou sawest the feet and toes, part of potters' clay, and part of iron, the kingdom shall be divided; but there shall be in it of the strength of the iron, forasmuch as thou sawest the iron mixed with miry clay. ⁴²And as the toes of the feet were part of iron, and part of clay, so the kingdom shall be partly strong, and partly broken. ⁴³And whereas thou sawest iron mixed with miry clay, they shall mingle themselves with the seed of men: but they shall not cleave one to another, even as iron is not mixed with clay. ⁴⁴And in the days of these kings shall the God of heaven set up a kingdom, which shall never be destroyed: and the kingdom shall not be left to other people, but it shall break in pieces and consume all these kingdoms, and it shall stand for ever."

Amos 9:7-8 "⁷Are ye not as children of the Ethiopians unto me, O children of Israel? saith the LORD. Have not I brought up Israel out of the land of Egypt? and the Philistines from Caphtor, and the Syrians from Kir? ⁸Behold, the eyes of the Lord GOD are upon the sinful kingdom, and I will destroy it from off the face of the earth; saving that I will not utterly destroy the house of Jacob, saith the LORD."

Zechariah 12:8-9 "⁸In that day shall the LORD defend the inhabitants of Jerusalem; and he that is feeble among them at that day shall be as David; and the house of David shall be as God, as the angel of the LORD before them. ⁹And it shall come to pass in that day, that I will seek to destroy all the nations that come against Jerusalem."

What The Nations Shall Know

1 Kings 8:60 "That all the people of the earth may know that the LORD is God, and that there is none else."

Psalm 9:20 "Put them in fear, O LORD: that the nations may know themselves to be but men. Selah."

Isaiah 49:26 "And I will feed them that oppress thee with their own flesh; and they shall be drunken with their own blood, as with sweet wine: and all flesh shall know that I the LORD am thy Saviour and thy Redeemer, the mighty One of Jacob."

Ezekiel 38:23 "Thus will I magnify myself, and sanctify myself; and I will be known in the eyes of many nations, and they shall know that I am the LORD."

Romans 16:25-26 "25Now to him that is of power to stablish you according to my gospel, and the preaching of Jesus Christ, according to the revelation of the mystery, which was kept secret since the world began, 26But now is made manifest, and by the scriptures of the prophets, according to the commandment of the everlasting God, made known to all nations for the obedience of faith."

Who All Nations Are Blessed In

Genesis 12:1-3 "1Now the LORD had said unto Abram, Get thee out of thy country, and from thy kindred, and from thy father's house, unto a land that I will shew thee: 2And I will make of thee a great nation, and I will bless thee, and make thy name great; and thou shalt be a blessing: 3And I will bless them that bless thee, and curse him that curseth thee: and in thee shall all families of the earth be blessed."

Genesis 18:18 "Seeing that Abraham shall surely become a great and mighty nation, and all the nations of the earth shall be blessed in him?"

Genesis 22:15-18 "15And the angel of the LORD called unto Abraham out of heaven the second time, 16And said, By myself have I sworn, saith the LORD, for because thou hast done this thing, and hast not withheld thy son, thine only son: 17That in blessing I will bless thee, and in multiplying I will multiply thy seed as the stars of the heaven, and as the sand which is upon the sea shore; and thy seed shall possess the gate of his enemies; 18And in thy seed shall all the nations of the earth be blessed; because thou hast obeyed my voice."

Genesis 26:3-4 "3Sojourn in this land, and I will be with thee, and will bless thee; for unto thee, and unto thy seed, I will give all these countries, and I will perform the oath which I sware unto Abraham thy father; 4And I will make thy seed to multiply as the stars of heaven, and will give unto thy seed all these countries; and in thy seed shall all the nations of the earth be blessed."

Acts 3:25 "Ye are the children of the prophets, and of the covenant which God made with our fathers, saying unto Abraham, And in thy seed shall all the kindreds of the earth be blessed."

Galatians 3:6-8 "6Even as Abraham believed God, and it was accounted to him for righteousness. 7Know ye therefore that they which are of faith, the same are the children of Abraham. 8And the scripture, foreseeing that God would justify the heathen through faith, preached before the gospel unto Abraham, saying, In thee shall all nations be blessed."

Who Are The Parents Of Many Nations

Genesis 17:4-6 "4As for me, behold, my covenant is with thee, and thou shalt be a father of many nations. 5Neither shall thy name any more be called Abram, but thy name shall be Abraham; for a father of many nations have I made thee. 6And I will make thee exceeding fruitful, and I will make nations of thee, and kings shall come out of thee."

Genesis 17:15-16 "15And God said unto Abraham, As for Sarai thy wife, thou shalt not call her name Sarai, but Sarah shall her name be. 16And I will bless her, and give thee a son also of her: yea, I will bless her, and she shall be a mother of nations; kings of people shall be of her."

Who Became A Great Nation

Genesis 17:20 "And as for Ishmael, I have heard thee: Behold, I have blessed him, and will make him fruitful, and will multiply him exceedingly; twelve princes shall he beget, and I will make him a great nation."

Genesis 21:8-13 "8And the child grew, and was weaned: and Abraham made a great feast the same day that Isaac was weaned. 9And Sarah saw the son of Hagar the Egyptian, which she had born unto Abraham, mocking. 10Wherefore she said unto Abraham, Cast out this bondwoman and her son: for the son of this bondwoman shall not be heir with my son, even with Isaac. 11And the thing was very grievous in Abraham's sight because of his son. 12And God said unto Abraham, Let it not be grievous in thy sight because of the lad, and because of thy bondwoman; in all that Sarah hath said unto thee, hearken unto her voice; for in Isaac shall thy seed be called. 13And also of the son of the bondwoman will I make a nation, because he is thy seed."

Genesis 21:17-18 "17And God heard the voice of the lad; and the angel of God called Hagar out of lad, and because of thy bondwoman; in all that Sarah hath said unto thee, hearken unto her voice; for in Isaac shall thy seed be called. [13]And also of the son of the bondwoman will I make a nation, because he is thy seed."

NEWNESS

Newness Availing
Galatians 6:15 "For in Christ Jesus neither circumcision availeth anything, nor uncircumcision, but a new creature."

Renewing Yourself
Ezekiel 18:31 "Cast away from you all your transgressions, whereby ye have transgressed; and make you a new heart and a new spirit: for why will ye die, O house of Israel?"

Ezekiel 33:11 "Say unto them, As I live, saith the Lord GOD, I have no pleasure in the death of the wicked; but that the wicked turn from his way and live: turn ye, turn ye from your evil ways; for why will ye die, O house of Israel?"

Romans 12:1-2 "[1]I beseech you therefore, brethren, by the mercies of God, that ye present your bodies a living sacrifice, holy, acceptable unto God, which is your reasonable service. [2]And be not conformed to this world: but be ye transformed by the renewing of your mind, that ye may prove what is that good, and acceptable, and perfect, will of God."

Ephesians 4:22-24 "[22]That ye put off concerning the former conversation the old man, which is corrupt according to the deceitful lusts; [23]And be renewed in the spirit of your mind; [24]And that ye put on the new man, which after God is created in righteousness and true holiness."

The Lord Creating News Heavens And A New Earth
Psalm 102:24-27 "[24]I said, O my God, take me not away in the midst of my days: thy years are throughout all generations. [25]Of old hast thou laid the foundation of the earth: and the heavens are the work of thy hands. [26]They shall perish, but thou shalt endure: yea, all of them shall wax old like a garment; as a vesture shalt thou change them, and they shall be changed: [27]But thou art the same, and thy years shall have no end."

Isaiah 65:14-18 "[14]Behold, my servants shall sing for joy of heart, but ye shall cry for sorrow of heart, and shall howl for vexation of spirit. [15]And ye shall leave your name for a curse unto my chosen: for the Lord GOD shall slay thee, and call his servants by another name: [16]That he who blesseth himself in the earth shall bless himself in the God of truth; and he that sweareth in the earth shall swear by the God of truth; because the former troubles are forgotten, and because they are hid from mine eyes. [17]For, behold, I create new heavens and a new earth: and the former shall not be remembered, nor come into mind. [18]But be ye glad and rejoice for ever in that which I create: for, behold, I create Jerusalem a rejoicing, and her people a joy."

Isaiah 66:22 "For as the new heavens and the new earth, which I will make, shall remain before me, saith the LORD, so shall your seed and your name remain."

Hebrews 1:10-12 "[10]And, Thou, Lord, in the beginning hast laid the foundation of the earth; and the heavens are the works of thine hands: [11]They shall perish; but thou remainest; and they all shall wax old as doth a garment; [12]And as a vesture shalt thou fold them up, and they shall be changed: but thou art the same, and thy years shall not fail."

Revelation 21:1-5 "[1]And I saw a new heaven and a new earth: for the first heaven and the first earth were passed away; and there was no more sea. [2]And I John saw the holy city, new Jerusalem, coming down from God out of heaven, prepared as a bride adorned for her husband. [3]And I heard a great voice out of heaven saying, Behold, the tabernacle of God is with men, and he will dwell with them, and they shall be his people, and God himself shall be with them, and be their God. [4]And God shall wipe away all tears from their eyes; and there shall be no more death, neither sorrow, nor crying, neither shall there be any more pain: for the former things are passed away. [5]And he that sat upon the throne said, Behold, I make all things new. And he said unto me, Write: for these words are true and faithful."

The Lord Putting A New Spirit Within You
1 Samuel 10:6 "And the Spirit of the LORD will come upon thee, and thou shalt prophesy with them, and shalt be turned into another man."

Psalm 51:10 "Create in me a clean heart, O God; and renew a right spirit within me."

Ezekiel 11:16-19 "[16]Therefore say, Thus saith the Lord GOD; Although I have cast them far off among the heathen, and although I have scattered them among the countries, yet will I be to them as a little sanctuary in the countries where they shall come. [17]Therefore say, Thus saith the Lord GOD; I will even gather you from the people, and assemble you out of the countries where ye have been scattered, and I will give you the land of Israel. [18]And they shall come thither, and they shall take away all the detestable things thereof and all the abominations thereof from thence. [19]And I will give them one heart, and I will put a new spirit within you; and I will take the stony heart out of their flesh, and will give them an heart of flesh."

Ezekiel 36:22-27 "[22]Therefore say unto the house of Israel, Thus saith the Lord GOD; I do not this for your sakes, O house of Israel, but for mine holy name's sake, which ye have profaned among the heathen, whither ye went. [23]And I will sanctify my great name, which was profaned among the heathen, which ye have profaned in the midst of them; and the heathen shall know that I am the LORD, saith the Lord GOD, when I shall be sanctified in you before their eyes. [24]For I will take you from among the heathen, and gather you out of all countries, and will bring you into your own land. [25]Then will I sprinkle clean water upon you, and ye shall be clean: from all your filthiness, and from all your idols, will I cleanse you. [26]A new heart also will I give you, and a new spirit will I put within you: and I will take away the stony heart out of your flesh, and I will give you an heart of flesh. [27]And I will put my spirit within you, and cause you to walk in my statutes, and ye shall keep my judgments, and do them."

Ezekiel 37:12-14 "[12]Therefore prophesy and say unto them, Thus saith the Lord GOD; Behold, O my people, I will open your graves, and cause you to come up out of your graves, and bring you into the land of Israel. [13]And ye shall know that I am the LORD, when I have opened your graves, O my people, and brought you up out of your graves, [14]And shall put my spirit in you, and ye shall live, and I shall place you in your own land: then shall

ye know that I the LORD have spoken it, and performed it, saith the LORD."

The New Heavens And Earth

Isaiah 66:22 "For as the new heavens and the new earth, which I will make, shall remain before me, saith the LORD, so shall your seed and your name remain."

2 Peter 3:13 "Nevertheless we, according to his promise, look for new heavens and a new earth, wherein dwelleth righteousness."

Revelation 21:1-4 "[1]And I saw a new heaven and a new earth: for the first heaven and the first earth were passed away; and there was no more sea. [2]And I John saw the holy city, new Jerusalem, coming down from God out of heaven, prepared as a bride adorned for her husband. [3]And I heard a great voice out of heaven saying, Behold, the tabernacle of God is with men, and he will dwell with them, and they shall be his people, and God himself shall be with them, and be their God. [4]And God shall wipe away all tears from their eyes; and there shall be no more death, neither sorrow, nor crying, neither shall there be any more pain: for the former things are passed away."

The New Jerusalem

Isaiah 65:14-25 "[14]Behold, my servants shall sing for joy of heart, but ye shall cry for sorrow of heart, and shall howl for vexation of spirit. [15]And ye shall leave your name for a curse unto my chosen: for the Lord GOD shall slay thee, and call his servants by another name: [16]That he who blesseth himself in the earth shall bless himself in the God of truth; and he that sweareth in the earth shall swear by the God of truth; because the former troubles are forgotten, and because they are hid from mine eyes. [17]For, behold, I create new heavens and a new earth: and the former shall not be remembered, nor come into mind. [18]But be ye glad and rejoice for ever in that which I create: for, behold, I create Jerusalem a rejoicing, and her people a joy. [19]And I will rejoice in Jerusalem, and joy in my people: and the voice of weeping shall be no more heard in her, nor the voice of crying. [20]There shall be no more thence an infant of days, nor an old man that hath not filled his days: for the child shall die an hundred years old; but the sinner being an hundred years old shall be accursed. [21]And they shall build houses, and inhabit them; and they shall plant vineyards, and eat the fruit of them. ²²They shall not build, and another inhabit; they shall not plant, and another eat: for as the days of a tree are the days of my people, and mine elect shall long enjoy the work of their hands. ²³They shall not labour in vain, nor bring forth for trouble; for they are the seed of the blessed of the LORD, and their offspring with them. ²⁴And it shall come to pass, that before they call, I will answer; and while they are yet speaking, I will hear. ²⁵The wolf and the lamb shall feed together, and the lion shall eat straw like the bullock: and dust shall be the serpent's meat. They shall not hurt nor destroy in all my holy mountain, saith the LORD."

Ezekiel 48:30-35 "³⁰And these are the goings out of the city on the north side, four thousand and five hundred measures. ³¹And the gates of the city shall be after the names of the tribes of Israel: three gates northward; one gate of Reuben, one gate of Judah, one gate of Levi. ³²And at the east side four thousand and five hundred: and three gates; and one gate of Joseph, one gate of Benjamin, one gate of Dan. ³³And at the south side four thousand and five hundred measures: and three gates; one gate of Simeon, one gate of Issachar, one gate of Zebulun. ³⁴At the west side four thousand and five hundred, with their three gates; one gate of Gad, one gate of Asher, one gate of Naphtali. ³⁵It was round about eighteen thousand measures: and the name of the city from that day shall be, The LORD is there."

Galatians 4:21-26 "²¹Tell me, ye that desire to be under the law, do ye not hear the law? ²²For it is written, that Abraham had two sons, the one by a bondmaid, the other by a freewoman. ²³But he who was of the bondwoman was born after the flesh; but he of the freewoman was by promise. ²⁴Which things are an allegory: for these are the two covenants; the one from the mount Sinai, which gendereth to bondage, which is Agar. ²⁵For this Agar is mount Sinai in Arabia, and answereth to Jerusalem which now is, and is in bondage with her children. ²⁶But Jerusalem which is above is free, which is the mother of us all."

Hebrews 12:22-28 "²²But ye are come unto mount Sion, and unto the city of the living God, the heavenly Jerusalem, and to an innumerable company of angels, ²³To the general assembly and church of the firstborn, which are written in heaven, and to God the Judge of all, and to the spirits of just men made perfect, ²⁴And to Jesus the mediator of the new covenant, and to the blood of sprinkling, that speaketh better things than that of Abel. ²⁵See that ye refuse not him that speaketh. For if they escaped not who refused him that spake on earth, much more shall not we escape, if we turn away from him that speaketh from heaven: ²⁶Whose voice then shook the earth: but now he hath promised, saying, Yet once more I shake not the earth only, but also heaven. ²⁷And this word, Yet once more, signifieth the removing of those things that are shaken, as of things that are made, that those things which cannot be shaken may remain. ²⁸Wherefore we receiving a kingdom which cannot be moved, let us have grace, whereby we may serve God acceptably with reverence and godly fear."

Revelation 3:12 "Him that overcometh will I make a pillar in the temple of my God, and he shall go no more out: and I will write upon him the name of my God, and the name of the city of my God, which is new Jerusalem, which cometh down out of heaven from my God: and I will write upon him my new name."

Revelation 21:1-5 "¹And I saw a new heaven and a new earth: for the first heaven and the first earth were passed away; and there was no more sea. ²And I John saw the holy city, new Jerusalem, coming down from God out of heaven, prepared as a bride adorned for her husband. ³And I heard a great voice out of heaven saying, Behold, the tabernacle of God is with men, and he will dwell with them, and they shall be his people, and God himself shall be with them, and be their God. ⁴And God shall wipe away all tears from their eyes; and there shall be no more death, neither sorrow, nor crying, neither shall there be any more pain: for the former things are passed away. ⁵And he that sat upon the throne said, Behold, I make all things new. And he said unto me, Write: for these words are true and faithful."

Revelation 21:9-27 "⁹And there came unto me one of the seven angels which had the seven vials full of the seven last plagues, and talked with me, saying, Come hither, I will shew thee the bride, the

Lamb's wife. ¹⁰And he carried me away in the spirit to a great and high mountain, and shewed me that great city, the holy Jerusalem, descending out of heaven from God, ¹¹Having the glory of God: and her light was like unto a stone most precious, even like a jasper stone, clear as crystal; ¹²And had a wall great and high, and had twelve gates, and at the gates twelve angels, and names written thereon, which are the names of the twelve tribes of the children of Israel: ¹³On the east three gates; on the north three gates; on the south three gates; and on the west three gates. ¹⁴And the wall of the city had twelve foundations, and in them the names of the twelve apostles of the Lamb. ¹⁵And he that talked with me had a golden reed to measure the city, and the gates thereof, and the wall thereof. ¹⁶And the city lieth foursquare, and the length is as large as the breadth: and he measured the city with the reed, twelve thousand furlongs. The length and the breadth and the height of it are equal. ¹⁷And he measured the wall thereof, an hundred and forty and four cubits, according to the measure of a man, that is, of the angel. ¹⁸And the building of the wall of it was of jasper: and the city was pure gold, like unto clear glass. ¹⁹And the foundations of the wall of the city were garnished with all manner of precious stones. The first foundation was jasper; the second, sapphire; the third, a chalcedony; the fourth, an emerald; ²⁰The fifth, sardonyx; the sixth, sardius; the seventh, chrysolite; the eighth, beryl; the ninth, a topaz; the tenth, a chrysoprasus; the eleventh, a jacinth; the twelfth, an amethyst. ²¹And the twelve gates were twelve pearls; every several gate was of one pearl: and the street of the city was pure gold, as it were transparent glass. ²²And I saw no temple therein: for the Lord God Almighty and the Lamb are the temple of it. ²³And the city had no need of the sun, neither of the moon, to shine in it: for the glory of God did lighten it, and the Lamb is the light thereof. ²⁴And the nations of them which are saved shall walk in the light of it: and the kings of the earth do bring their glory and honour into it. ²⁵And the gates of it shall not be shut at all by day: for there shall be no night there. ²⁶And they shall bring the glory and honour of the nations into it. ²⁷And there shall in no wise enter into it any thing that defileth, neither whatsoever worketh abomination, or maketh a lie: but they which are written in the Lamb's book of life."

The New Man
Ephesians 4:22-24 "²²That ye put off concerning the former conversation the old man, which is corrupt according to the deceitful lusts; ²³And be renewed in the spirit of your mind; ²⁴And that ye put on the new man, which after God is created in righteousness and true holiness."

Colossians 3:1-10 "¹If ye then be risen with Christ, seek those things which are above, where Christ sitteth on the right hand of God. ²Set your affection on things above, not on things on the earth. ³For ye are dead, and your life is hid with Christ in God. ⁴When Christ, who is our life, shall appear, then shall ye also appear with him in glory. ⁵Mortify therefore your members which are upon the earth; fornication, uncleanness, inordinate affection, evil concupiscence, and covetousness, which is idolatry: ⁶For which things' sake the wrath of God cometh on the children of disobedience: ⁷In the which ye also walked some time, when ye lived in them. ⁸But now ye also put off all these; anger, wrath, malice, blasphemy, filthy communication out of your mouth. ⁹Lie not one to another, seeing that ye have put off the old man with his deeds; ¹⁰And have put on the new man, which is renewed in knowledge after the image of him that created him."

What Is Renewed
2 Corinthians 4:16 "For which cause we faint not; but though our outward man perish, yet the inward man is renewed day by day."

Colossians 3:9-10 "⁹Lie not one to another, seeing that ye have put off the old man with his deeds; ¹⁰And have put on the new man, which is renewed in knowledge after the image of him that created him."

Who Is A New Creature
Romans 6:3-7 "³Know ye not, that so many of us as were baptized into Jesus Christ were baptized into his death? ⁴Therefore we are buried with him by baptism into death: that like as Christ was raised up from the dead by the glory of the Father, even so we also should walk in newness of life. ⁵For if we have been planted together in the likeness of his death, we shall be also in the likeness of his resurrection: ⁶Knowing this, that our old man is crucified with him, that the body of sin might be destroyed, that henceforth we should not serve sin. ⁷For he that is dead is freed from sin."

2 Corinthians 5:17 "Therefore if any man be in Christ, he is a new creature: old things are passed away; behold, all things are become new."

Ephesians 2:5-10 "⁵Even when we were dead in sins, hath quickened us together with Christ, (by grace ye are saved;) ⁶And hath raised us up together, and made us sit together in heavenly places in Christ Jesus: ⁷That in the ages to come he might shew the exceeding riches of his grace in his kindness toward us through Christ Jesus. ⁸For by grace are ye saved through faith; and that not of yourselves: it is the gift of God: ⁹Not of works, lest any man should boast. ¹⁰For we are his workmanship, created in Christ Jesus unto good works, which God hath before ordained that we should walk in them."

OBEDIENCE

Jesus Christ Being Obedient

Romans 5:17-19 "¹⁷For if by one man's offence death reigned by one; much more they which receive abundance of grace and of the gift of righteousness shall reign in life by one, Jesus Christ.) ¹⁸ Therefore as by the offence of one judgment came upon all men to condemnation; even so by the righteousness of one the free gift came upon all men unto justification of life. ¹⁹ For as by one man's disobedience many were made sinners, so by the obedience of one shall many be made righteous."

Philippians 2:5-8 "⁵Let this mind be in you, which was also in Christ Jesus: ⁶ Who, being in the form of God, thought it not robbery to be equal with God: ⁷ But made himself of no reputation, and took upon him the form of a servant, and was made in the likeness of men: ⁸ And being found in fashion as a man, he humbled himself, and became obedient unto death, even the death of the cross."

Hebrews 5:5-8 "⁵So also Christ glorified not himself to be made an high priest; but he that said unto him, Thou art my Son, to day have I begotten thee. ⁶ As he saith also in another place, Thou art a priest for ever after the order of Melchisedec. ⁷ Who in the days of his flesh, when he had offered up prayers and supplications with strong crying and tears unto him that was able to save him from death, and was heard in that he feared; ⁸ Though he were a Son, yet learned he obedience by the things which he suffered."

Hebrews 10:9-14 "⁹Then said he, Lo, I come to do thy will, O God. He taketh away the first, that he may establish the second. ¹⁰ By the which will we are sanctified through the offering of the body of Jesus Christ once for all. ¹¹ And every priest standeth daily ministering and offering oftentimes the same sacrifices, which can never take away sins: ¹² But this man, after he had offered one sacrifice for sins for ever, sat down on the right hand of God; ¹³ From henceforth expecting till his enemies be made his footstool. ¹⁴ For by one offering he hath perfected for ever them that are sanctified."

Keeping The Commandments Of The Lord (Obeying The Lord)

Exodus 34:11-14 "¹¹Observe thou that which I command thee this day: behold, I drive out before thee the Amorite, and the Canaanite, and the Hittite, and the Perizzite, and the Hivite, and the Jebusite. ¹²Take heed to thyself, lest thou make a covenant with the inhabitants of the land whither thou goest, lest it be for a snare in the midst of thee: ¹³But ye shall destroy their altars, break their images, and cut down their groves: ¹⁴For thou shalt worship no other god: for the LORD, whose name is Jealous, is a jealous God."

Leviticus 18:4-5 "⁴Ye shall do my judgments, and keep mine ordinances, to walk therein: I am the LORD your God. ⁵Ye shall therefore keep my statutes, and my judgments: which if a man do, he shall live in them: I am the LORD."

Leviticus 18:26-30 "²⁶Ye shall therefore keep my statutes and my judgments, and shall not commit any of these abominations; neither any of your own nation, nor any stranger that sojourneth among you: ²⁷(For all these abominations have the men of the land done, which were before you, and the land is defiled;) ²⁸That the land spue not you out also, when ye defile it, as it spued out the nations that were before you. ²⁹For whosoever shall commit any of these abominations, even the souls that commit them shall be cut off from among their people. ³⁰Therefore shall ye keep mine ordinance, that ye commit not any one of these abominable customs, which were committed before you, and that ye defile not yourselves therein: I am the LORD your God."

Leviticus 19:18-19 "¹⁸Thou shalt not avenge, nor bear any grudge against the children of thy people, but thou shalt love thy neighbour as thyself: I am the LORD. ¹⁹Ye shall keep my statutes. Thou shalt not let thy cattle gender with a diverse kind: thou shalt not sow thy field with mingled seed: neither shall a garment mingled of linen and woollen come upon thee."

Leviticus 19:37 "Therefore shall ye observe all my statutes, and all my judgments, and do them: I am the LORD."

Leviticus 20:8 "And ye shall keep my statutes, and do them: I am the LORD which sanctify you."

Leviticus 20:22-24 "²²Ye shall therefore keep all my statutes, and all my judgments, and do them: that the land, whither I bring you to dwell therein, spue you not out. ²³And ye shall not walk in the manners of the nation, which I cast out before you: for they committed all these things, and therefore I abhorred them. ²⁴But I have said unto you, Ye shall inherit their land, and I will give it unto you to possess it, a land that floweth with milk and honey: I am the LORD your God, which have separated you from other people."

Leviticus 25:17-18 "¹⁷Ye shall not therefore oppress one another; but thou shalt fear thy God: for I am the LORD your God. ¹⁸Wherefore ye shall do my statutes, and keep my judgments, and do them; and ye shall dwell in the land in safety."

Deuteronomy 4:1-2 "¹Now therefore hearken, O Israel, unto the statutes and unto the judgments, which I teach you, for to do them, that ye may live, and go in and possess the land which the LORD God of your fathers giveth you. ²Ye shall not add unto the word which I command you, neither shall ye diminish ought from it, that ye may keep the commandments of the LORD your God which I command you."

Deuteronomy 4:5-6 "⁵Behold, I have taught you statutes and judgments, even as the LORD my God commanded me, that ye should do so in the land whither ye go to possess it. ⁶Keep therefore and do them; for this is your wisdom and your understanding in the sight of the nations, which shall hear all these statutes, and say, Surely this great nation is a wise and understanding people."

Deuteronomy 4:40 "Thou shalt keep therefore his statutes, and his commandments, which I command thee this day, that it may go well with thee, and with thy children after thee, and that thou mayest prolong thy days upon the earth, which the LORD thy God giveth thee, for ever."

Deuteronomy 5:1 "And Moses called all Israel, and said unto them, Hear, O Israel, the statutes and judgments which I speak in your ears this day, that ye may learn them, and keep, and do them."

Deuteronomy 5:32-33 "³²Ye shall observe to do therefore as the LORD your God hath commanded you: ye shall not turn aside to the right hand or to the left. ³³Ye shall walk in all the ways which the LORD your God hath commanded you, that ye may live, and that it may be well with you, and that ye may prolong your days in the land which ye shall possess."

Deuteronomy 6:1-3 "¹Now these are the commandments, the statutes, and the judgments, which the LORD your God commanded to teach you, that ye might do them in the land whither ye go to possess it: ²That thou mightest fear the LORD thy God, to keep all his statutes and his commandments, which I command thee, thou, and thy son, and thy son's son, all the days of thy life; and that thy days may be prolonged. ³Hear therefore, O Israel, and observe to do it; that it may be well with thee, and that ye may increase mightily, as the LORD God of thy fathers hath promised thee, in the land that floweth with milk and honey."

Deuteronomy 6:17 "Ye shall diligently keep the commandments of the LORD your God, and his testimonies, and his statutes, which he hath commanded thee."

Deuteronomy 7:9-11 "⁹Know therefore that the LORD thy God, he is God, the faithful God, which keepeth covenant and mercy with them that love him and keep his commandments to a thousand generations; ¹⁰And repayeth them that hate him to their face, to destroy them: he will not be slack to him that hateth him, he will repay him to his face. ¹¹Thou shalt therefore keep the commandments, and the statutes, and the judgments, which I command thee this day, to do them."

Deuteronomy 8:1 "All the commandments which I command thee this day shall ye observe to do, that ye may live, and multiply, and go in and possess the land which the LORD sware unto your fathers."

Deuteronomy 8:6 "Therefore thou shalt keep the commandments of the LORD thy God, to walk in his ways, and to fear him."

Deuteronomy 10:12-13 "¹²And now, Israel, what doth the LORD thy God require of thee, but to fear the LORD thy God, to walk in all his ways, and to love him, and to serve the LORD thy God with all thy heart and with all thy soul, ¹³To keep the commandments of the LORD, and his statutes, which I command thee this day for thy good?"

Deuteronomy 11:1 "Therefore thou shalt love the LORD thy God, and keep his charge, and his statutes, and his judgments, and his commandments, always."

Deuteronomy 11:31-32 "³¹For ye shall pass over Jordan to go in to possess the land which the LORD your God giveth you, and ye shall possess it, and dwell therein. ³²And ye shall observe to do all the statutes and judgments which I set before you this day."

Deuteronomy 12:31-32 "³¹Thou shalt not do so unto the LORD thy God: for every abomination to the LORD, which he hateth, have they done unto their gods; for even their sons and their daughters they have burnt in the fire to their gods. ³²What thing soever I command you, observe to do it: thou shalt not add thereto, nor diminish from it."

Deuteronomy 13:4 "Ye shall walk after the LORD your God, and fear him, and keep his commandments, and obey his voice, and ye shall serve him, and cleave unto him."

Deuteronomy 26:16 "This day the LORD thy God hath commanded thee to do these statutes and judgments: thou shalt therefore keep and do them with all thine heart, and with all thy soul."

Deuteronomy 27:9-10 "⁹And Moses and the priests the Levites spake unto all Israel, saying, Take heed, and hearken, O Israel; this day thou art become the people of the LORD thy God. ¹⁰Thou shalt therefore obey the voice of the LORD thy God, and do his commandments and his statutes, which I command thee this day."

Deuteronomy 30:15-16 "¹⁵See, I have set before thee this day life and good, and death and evil; ¹⁶In that I command thee this day to love the LORD thy God, to walk in his ways, and to keep his commandments and his statutes and his judgments, that thou mayest live and multiply: and the LORD thy God shall bless thee in the land whither thou goest to possess it."

Deuteronomy 30:19-20 "¹⁹I call heaven and earth to record this day against you, that I have set before you life and death, blessing and cursing: therefore choose life, that both thou and thy seed may live: ²⁰That thou mayest love the LORD thy God, and that thou mayest obey his voice, and that thou

mayest cleave unto him: for he is thy life, and the length of thy days: that thou mayest dwell in the land which the LORD sware unto thy fathers, to Abraham, to Isaac, and to Jacob, to give them."

Deuteronomy 32:45-46 "⁴⁵And Moses made an end of speaking all these words to all Israel: ⁴⁶And he said unto them, Set your hearts unto all the words which I testify among you this day, which ye shall command your children to observe to do, all the words of this law."

Joshua 1:7-8 "⁷Only be thou strong and very courageous, that thou mayest observe to do according to all the law, which Moses my servant commanded thee: turn not from it to the right hand or to the left, that thou mayest prosper whithersoever thou goest. ⁸This book of the law shall not depart out of thy mouth; but thou shalt meditate therein day and night, that thou mayest observe to do according to all that is written therein: for then thou shalt make thy way prosperous, and then thou shalt have good success."

Joshua 22:5 "But take diligent heed to do the commandment and the law, which Moses the servant of the LORD charged you, to love the LORD your God, and to walk in all his ways, and to keep his commandments, and to cleave unto him, and to serve him with all your heart and with all your soul."

Joshua 23:6 "Be ye therefore very courageous to keep and to do all that is written in the book of the law of Moses, that ye turn not aside therefrom to the right hand or to the left."

1 Kings 2:3 "And keep the charge of the LORD thy God, to walk in his ways, to keep his statutes, and his commandments, and his judgments, and his testimonies, as it is written in the law of Moses, that thou mayest prosper in all that thou doest, and whithersoever thou turnest thyself."

1 Kings 8:61 "Let your heart therefore be perfect with the LORD our God, to walk in his statutes, and to keep his commandments, as at this day."

2 Kings 17:13 "Yet the LORD testified against Israel, and against Judah, by all the prophets, and by all the seers, saying, Turn ye from your evil ways, and keep my commandments and my statutes, according to all the law which I commanded your fathers, and which I sent to you by my servants the prophets."

1 Chronicles 16:14-15 "¹⁴He is the LORD our God; his judgments are in all the earth. ¹⁵Be ye mindful always of his covenant; the word which he commanded to a thousand generations."

Psalm 37:34 "Wait on the LORD, and keep his way, and he shall exalt thee to inherit the land: when the wicked are cut off, thou shalt see it."

Psalm 119:1-8 "¹Blessed are the undefiled in the way, who walk in the law of the LORD. ²Blessed are they that keep his testimonies, and that seek him with the whole heart. ³They also do no iniquity: they walk in his ways. ⁴Thou hast commanded us to keep thy precepts diligently. ⁵O that my ways were directed to keep thy statutes! ⁶Then shall I not be ashamed, when I have respect unto all thy commandments. ⁷I will praise thee with uprightness of heart, when I shall have learned thy righteous judgments. ⁸I will keep thy statutes: O forsake me not utterly."

Ecclesiastes 12:13 "Let us hear the conclusion of the whole matter: Fear God, and keep his commandments: for this is the whole duty of man."

Jeremiah 7:23 "But this thing commanded I them, saying, Obey my voice, and I will be your God, and ye shall be my people: and walk ye in all the ways that I have commanded you, that it may be well unto you."

Jeremiah 26:12-13 "¹²Then spake Jeremiah unto all the princes and to all the people, saying, The LORD sent me to prophesy against this house and against this city all the words that ye have heard. ¹³Therefore now amend your ways and your doings, and obey the voice of the LORD your God; and the LORD will repent him of the evil that he hath pronounced against you."

Matthew 19:16-17 "¹⁶And, behold, one came and said unto him, Good Master, what good thing shall I do, that I may have eternal life? ¹⁷And he said unto him, Why callest thou me good? there is none good but one, that is, God: but if thou wilt enter into life, keep the commandments."

Acts 5:28-29 "²⁸Saying, Did not we straitly command you that ye should not teach in this name? and, behold, ye have filled Jerusalem with your doctrine, and intend to bring this man's blood upon us. ²⁹Then Peter and the other apostles answered and said, We ought to obey God rather than men."

John 14:9-15 "⁹Jesus saith unto him, Have I been so long time with you, and yet hast thou not known me, Philip? he that hath seen me hath seen the Father; and how sayest thou then, Shew us the Father? ¹⁰Believest thou not that I am in the Father, and the Father in me? the words that I speak unto you I speak not of myself: but the Father that dwelleth in me, he doeth the works. ¹¹Believe me that I am in the Father, and the Father in me: or else believe me for the very works' sake. ¹² Verily, verily, I say unto you, He that believeth on me, the works that I do shall he do also; and greater works than these shall he do; because I go unto my Father. ¹³And whatsoever ye shall ask in my name, that will I do, that the Father may be glorified in the Son. ¹⁴If ye shall ask any thing in my name, I will do it. ¹⁵If ye love me, keep my commandments."

1 Peter 1:13-14 "¹³Wherefore gird up the loins of your mind, be sober, and hope to the end for the grace that is to be brought unto you at the revelation of Jesus Christ; ¹⁴As obedient children, not fashioning yourselves according to the former lusts in your ignorance."

1 John 5:3 "For this is the love of God, that we keep his commandments: and his commandments are not grievous."

2 John 4-6 "⁴I rejoiced greatly that I found of thy children walking in truth, as we have received a commandment from the Father. ⁵And now I beseech thee, lady, not as though I wrote a new commandment unto thee, but that which we had from the beginning, that we love one another. ⁶And this is love, that we walk after his commandments. This is the commandment, That, as ye have heard from the beginning, ye should walk in it."

The Obeying Of The Lord

1 Samuel 15:22 "And Samuel said, Hath the LORD as great delight in burnt offerings and sacrifices, as in obeying the voice of the LORD? Behold, to obey is better than sacrifice, and to hearken than the fat of rams."

1 Corinthians 7:19 "Circumcision is nothing, and uncircumcision is nothing, but the keeping of the commandments of God."

The Reward For Being Obedient To God

Genesis 22:15-18 "¹⁵And the angel of the LORD called unto Abraham out of heaven the second time, ¹⁶And said, By myself have I sworn, saith the LORD, for because thou hast done this thing, and hast not withheld thy son, thine only son: ¹⁷That in blessing I will bless thee, and in multiplying I will multiply thy seed as the stars of the heaven, and as the sand which is upon the sea shore; and thy seed shall possess the gate of his enemies; ¹⁸And in thy seed shall all the nations of the earth be blessed; because thou hast obeyed my voice."

Genesis 26:2-5 "²And the LORD appeared unto him, and said, Go not down into Egypt; dwell in the land which I shall tell thee of: ³Sojourn in this land, and I will be with thee, and will bless thee; for unto thee, and unto thy seed, I will give all these countries, and I will perform the oath which I sware unto Abraham thy father; ⁴And I will make thy seed to multiply as the stars of heaven, and will give unto thy seed all these countries; and in thy seed shall all the nations of the earth be blessed; ⁵Because that Abraham obeyed my voice, and kept my charge, my commandments, my statutes, and my laws."

Exodus 15:26 "And said, If thou wilt diligently hearken to the voice of the LORD thy God, and wilt do that which is right in his sight, and wilt give ear to his commandments, and keep all his statutes, I will put none of these diseases upon thee, which I have brought upon the Egyptians: for I am the LORD that healeth thee."

Exodus 19:3-5 "³And Moses went up unto God, and the LORD called unto him out of the mountain, saying, Thus shalt thou say to the house of Jacob, and tell the children of Israel; ⁴Ye have seen what I did unto the Egyptians, and how I bare you on eagles' wings, and brought you unto myself. ⁵Now therefore, if ye will obey my voice indeed, and keep my covenant, then ye shall be a peculiar treasure unto me above all people: for all the earth is mine."

Exodus 23:20-25 "²⁰Behold, I send an Angel before thee, to keep thee in the way, and to bring thee into the place which I have prepared. ²¹Beware of him, and obey his voice, provoke him not; for he will not pardon your transgressions: for my name is in him. ²²But if thou shalt indeed obey his voice, and do all that I speak; then I will be an enemy unto thine enemies, and an adversary unto thine adversaries. ²³For mine Angel shall go before thee, and bring thee in unto the Amorites, and the Hittites, and the Perizzites, and the Canaanites, and the Hivites, and the Jebusites: and I will cut them off. ²⁴Thou shalt not bow down to their gods, nor serve them, nor do after their works: but thou shalt utterly overthrow them, and quite break down their images. ²⁵And ye shall serve the LORD your God, and he shall bless thy bread, and thy water; and I will take sickness away from the midst of thee."

Leviticus 18:4-5 "⁴Ye shall do my judgments, and keep mine ordinances, to walk therein: I am the LORD your God. ⁵Ye shall therefore keep my statutes, and my judgments: which if a man do, he shall live in them: I am the LORD."

Leviticus 20:22-24 "²²Ye shall therefore keep all my statutes, and all my judgments, and do them: that the land, whither I bring you to dwell therein, spue you not out. ²³And ye shall not walk in the manners of the nation, which I cast out before you: for they committed all these things, and therefore I abhorred them. ²⁴But I have said unto you, Ye shall inherit their land, and I will give it unto you to possess it, a land that floweth with milk and honey: I am the LORD your God, which have separated you from other people."

Leviticus 25:17-18 "¹⁷Ye shall not therefore oppress one another; but thou shalt fear thy God: for I am the LORD your God. ¹⁸Wherefore ye shall do my statutes, and keep my judgments, and do them; and ye shall dwell in the land in safety."

Leviticus 26:1-13 "¹Ye shall make you no idols nor graven image, neither rear you up a standing image, neither shall ye set up any image of stone in your land, to bow down unto it: for I am the LORD your God. ²Ye shall keep my sabbaths, and reverence my sanctuary: I am the LORD. ³If ye walk in my statutes, and keep my commandments, and do them; ⁴Then I will give you rain in due season, and the land shall yield her increase, and the trees of the field shall yield their fruit.

⁵And your threshing shall reach unto the vintage, and the vintage shall reach unto the sowing time: and ye shall eat your bread to the full, and dwell in your land safely. ⁶And I will give peace in the land, and ye shall lie down, and none shall make you afraid: and I will rid evil beasts out of the land, neither shall the sword go through your land. ⁷And ye shall chase your enemies, and they shall fall before you by the sword. ⁸And five of you shall chase an hundred, and an hundred of you shall put ten thousand to flight: and your enemies shall fall before you by the sword. ⁹For I will have respect unto you, and make you fruitful, and multiply you, and establish my covenant with you. ¹⁰And ye shall eat old store, and bring forth the old because of the new. ¹¹And I will set my tabernacle among you: and my soul shall not abhor you. ¹²And I will walk among you, and will be your God, and ye shall be my people. ¹³I am the Lord your God, which brought you forth out of the land of Egypt, that ye should not be their bondmen; and I have broken the bands of your yoke, and made you go upright."

Deuteronomy 4:29-31 "²⁹But if from thence thou shalt seek the Lord thy God, thou shalt find him, if thou seek him with all thy heart and with all thy soul. ³⁰When thou art in tribulation, and all these things are come upon thee, even in the latter days, if thou turn to the Lord thy God, and shalt be obedient unto his voice; ³¹(For the Lord thy God is a merciful God;) he will not forsake thee, neither destroy thee, nor forget the covenant of thy fathers which he sware unto them."

Deuteronomy 4:40 "Thou shalt keep therefore his statutes, and his commandments, which I command thee this day, that it may go well with thee, and with thy children after thee, and that thou mayest prolong thy days upon the earth, which the Lord thy God giveth thee, for ever."

Deuteronomy 5:32-33 "³²Ye shall observe to do therefore as the Lord your God hath commanded you: ye shall not turn aside to the right hand or to the left. ³³Ye shall walk in all the ways which the Lord your God hath commanded you, that ye may live, and that it may be well with you, and that ye may prolong your days in the land which ye shall possess."

Deuteronomy 6:1-3 "¹Now these are the commandments, the statutes, and the judgments, which the Lord your God commanded to teach you, that ye might do them in the land whither ye go to possess it: ²That thou mightest fear the Lord thy God, to keep all his statutes and his commandments, which I command thee, thou, and thy son, and thy son's son, all the days of thy life; and that thy days may be prolonged. ³Hear therefore, O Israel, and observe to do it; that it may be well with thee, and that ye may increase mightily, as the Lord God of thy fathers hath promised thee, in the land that floweth with milk and honey."

Deuteronomy 6:25 "And it shall be our righteousness, if we observe to do all these commandments before the Lord our God, as he hath commanded us."

Deuteronomy 7:11-15 "¹¹Thou shalt therefore keep the commandments, and the statutes, and the judgments, which I command thee this day, to do them. ¹²Wherefore it shall come to pass, if ye hearken to these judgments, and keep, and do them, that the Lord thy God shall keep unto thee the covenant and the mercy which he sware unto thy fathers: ¹³And he will love thee, and bless thee, and multiply thee: he will also bless the fruit of thy womb, and the fruit of thy land, thy corn, and thy wine, and thine oil, the increase of thy kine, and the flocks of thy sheep, in the land which he sware unto thy fathers to give thee. ¹⁴Thou shalt be blessed above all people: there shall not be male or female barren among you, or among your cattle. ¹⁵And the Lord will take away from thee all sickness, and will put none of the evil diseases of Egypt, which thou knowest, upon thee; but will lay them upon all them that hate thee."

Deuteronomy 8:1 "All the commandments which I command thee this day shall ye observe to do, that ye may live, and multiply, and go in and possess the land which the Lord sware unto your fathers."

Deuteronomy 11:13-15 "¹³And it shall come to pass, if ye shall hearken diligently unto my commandments which I command you this day, to love the Lord your God, and to serve him with all your heart and with all your soul, ¹⁴That I will give you the rain of your land in his due season, the first rain and the latter rain, that thou mayest gather in thy corn, and thy wine, and thine oil. ¹⁵And I will send grass in thy fields for thy cattle, that thou mayest eat and be full."

Deuteronomy 11:22-23 "²²For if ye shall diligently keep all these commandments which I command you, to do them, to love the Lord your God, to walk in all his ways, and to cleave unto him; ²³Then will the Lord drive out all these nations from before you, and ye shall possess greater nations and mightier than yourselves."

Deuteronomy 11:26-28 "²⁶Behold, I set before you this day a blessing and a curse; ²⁷A blessing, if ye obey the commandments of the Lord your God, which I command you this day: ²⁸And a curse, if ye will not obey the commandments of the Lord your God, but turn aside out of the way which I command you this day, to go after other gods, which ye have not known."

Deuteronomy 15:4-6 "⁴Save when there shall be no poor among you; for the Lord shall greatly bless thee in the land which the Lord thy God giveth thee for an inheritance to possess it: ⁵Only if thou carefully hearken unto the voice of the Lord thy God, to observe to do all these commandments which I command thee this day. ⁶For the Lord thy God blesseth thee, as he promised thee: and thou shalt lend unto many nations, but thou shalt not borrow; and thou shalt reign over many nations, but they shall not reign over thee."

Deuteronomy 28:1-14 "¹And it shall come to pass, if thou shalt hearken diligently unto the voice of the Lord thy God, to observe and to do all his commandments which I command thee this day, that the Lord thy God will set thee on high above all nations of the earth: ²And all these blessings shall come on thee, and overtake thee, if thou shalt hearken unto the voice of the Lord thy God. ³Blessed shalt thou be in the city, and blessed shalt thou be in the field. ⁴Blessed shall be the fruit of thy body, and the fruit of thy ground, and the fruit of thy cattle, the increase of thy kine, and the flocks of thy sheep. ⁵Blessed shall be thy basket and thy store. ⁶Blessed shalt thou be when thou comest in, and blessed shalt thou be when thou goest out. ⁷The Lord shall cause thine enemies that rise up against thee to be smitten before thy face: they shall come out against thee one way, and flee before thee seven ways. ⁸The Lord shall command the blessing upon thee in thy storehouses, and in all that thou settest thine hand unto; and he shall bless thee in the land which the Lord thy God giveth thee. ⁹The Lord shall establish thee an holy people unto himself, as he hath sworn unto thee, if thou shalt keep the commandments of the Lord thy God, and walk in his ways. ¹⁰And all people of the earth shall see that thou art called by the name of the Lord; and they shall be afraid of thee. ¹¹And the Lord shall make thee plenteous in goods, in the fruit of thy body, and in the fruit of thy cattle, and in the fruit of thy ground, in the land which the Lord sware unto thy fathers to give thee. ¹²The Lord shall open unto thee his good treasure, the heaven to give the rain unto thy land in his season, and to bless all the work of thine hand: and thou shalt lend unto many nations, and thou shalt not borrow. ¹³And the Lord shall make thee the head, and not the tail; and thou shalt be above only, and thou shalt not be beneath; if that thou hearken unto the commandments of the Lord thy God, which I command thee this day, to observe and to do them: ¹⁴And thou shalt not go aside from any of the words which I command thee this day, to the right hand, or to the left, to go after other gods to serve them."

Deuteronomy 30:8-10 "⁸And thou shalt return and obey the voice of the Lord, and do all his commandments which I command thee this day. ⁹And the Lord thy God will make thee plenteous in every work of thine hand, in the fruit of thy body, and in the fruit of thy cattle, and in the fruit of thy land, for good: for the Lord will again rejoice over thee for good, as he rejoiced over thy fathers: ¹⁰ If thou shalt hearken unto the voice of the Lord thy God, to keep his commandments and his statutes which are written in this book of the law, and if thou turn unto the Lord thy God with all thine heart, and with all thy soul."

Deuteronomy 30:15-20 "¹⁵See, I have set before thee this day life and good, and death and evil; ¹⁶In that I command thee this day to love the Lord thy God, to walk in his ways, and to keep his commandments and his statutes and his judgments, that thou mayest live and multiply: and the Lord thy God shall bless thee in the land whither thou goest to possess it. ¹⁷But if thine heart turn away, so that thou wilt not hear, but shalt be drawn away, and worship other gods, and serve them; ¹⁸I denounce unto you this day, that ye shall surely perish, and that ye shall not prolong your days upon the land, whither thou passest over Jordan to go to possess it. ¹⁹I call heaven and earth to record this day against you, that I have set before you life and death, blessing and cursing: therefore choose life, that both thou and thy seed may live: ²⁰That thou mayest love the LORD thy God, and that thou mayest obey his voice, and that thou mayest cleave unto him: for he is thy life, and the length of thy days: that thou mayest dwell in the land which the LORD sware unto thy fathers, to Abraham, to Isaac, and to Jacob, to give them.”

Deuteronomy 32:45-47 “⁴⁵And Moses made an end of speaking all these words to all Israel: ⁴⁶And he said unto them, Set your hearts unto all the words which I testify among you this day, which ye shall command your children to observe to do, all the words of this law. ⁴⁷For it is not a vain thing for you; because it is your life: and through this thing ye shall prolong your days in the land, whither ye go over Jordan to possess it.”

Joshua 1:7-8 “⁷Only be thou strong and very courageous, that thou mayest observe to do according to all the law, which Moses my servant commanded thee: turn not from it to the right hand or to the left, that thou mayest prosper whithersoever thou goest. ⁸This book of the law shall not depart out of thy mouth; but thou shalt meditate therein day and night, that thou mayest observe to do according to all that is written therein: for then thou shalt make thy way prosperous, and then thou shalt have good success.”

1 Samuel 12:14 “If ye will fear the LORD, and serve him, and obey his voice, and not rebel against the commandment of the LORD, then shall both ye and also the king that reigneth over you continue following the LORD your God.”

2 Samuel 22:21-25 “²¹The LORD rewarded me according to my righteousness: according to the cleanness of my hands hath he recompensed me. ²²For I have kept the ways of the LORD, and have not wickedly departed from my God. ²³For all his judgments were before me: and as for his statutes, I did not depart from them. ²⁴I was also upright before him, and have kept myself from mine iniquity. ²⁵Therefore the LORD hath recompensed me according to my righteousness; according to my cleanness in his eye sight.”

1 Kings 2:3-4 “³And keep the charge of the LORD thy God, to walk in his ways, to keep his statutes, and his commandments, and his judgments, and his testimonies, as it is written in the law of Moses, that thou mayest prosper in all that thou doest, and whithersoever thou turnest thyself: ⁴That the LORD may continue his word which he spake concerning me, saying, If thy children take heed to their way, to walk before me in truth with all their heart and with all their soul, there shall not fail thee (said he) a man on the throne of Israel.”

1 Kings 3:11-14 “¹¹And God said unto him, Because thou hast asked this thing, and hast not asked for thyself long life; neither hast asked riches for thyself, nor hast asked the life of thine enemies; but hast asked for thyself understanding to discern judgment; ¹²Behold, I have done according to thy words: lo, I have given thee a wise and an understanding heart; so that there was none like thee before thee, neither after thee shall any arise like unto thee. ¹³And I have also given thee that which thou hast not asked, both riches, and honour: so that there shall not be any among the kings like unto thee all thy days. ¹⁴And if thou wilt walk in my ways, to keep my statutes and my commandments, as thy father David did walk, then I will lengthen thy days.”

1 Kings 9:3-5 “³And the LORD said unto him, I have heard thy prayer and thy supplication, that thou hast made before me: I have hallowed this house, which thou hast built, to put my name there for ever; and mine eyes and mine heart shall be there perpetually. ⁴And if thou wilt walk before me, as David thy father walked, in integrity of heart, and in uprightness, to do according to all that I have commanded thee, and wilt keep my statutes and my judgments: ⁵Then I will establish the throne of thy kingdom upon Israel for ever, as I promised to David thy father, saying, There shall not fail thee a man upon the throne of Israel.”

1 Kings 11:31-38 “³¹And he said to Jeroboam, Take thee ten pieces: for thus saith the LORD, the God of Israel, Behold, I will rend the kingdom out of the hand of Solomon, and will give ten tribes to thee: ³²(But he shall have one tribe for my servant David’s sake, and for Jerusalem’s sake, the city which I have chosen out of all the tribes of Israel:) ³³Because that they have forsaken me, and have worshipped Ashtoreth the goddess of the Zidonians, Chemosh the god of the Moabites, and Milcom the god of the children of Ammon, and have not walked in my ways, to do that which is right in mine eyes, and to keep my statutes and my judgments, as did David his father. 34Howbeit I will not take the whole kingdom out of his hand: but I will make him prince all the days of his life for David my servant's sake, whom I chose, because he kept my commandments and my statutes: 35But I will take the kingdom out of his son's hand, and will give it unto thee, even ten tribes. 36And unto his son will I give one tribe, that David my servant may have a light alway before me in Jerusalem, the city which I have chosen me to put my name there. 37And I will take thee, and thou shalt reign according to all that thy soul desireth, and shalt be king over Israel. 38And it shall be, if thou wilt hearken unto all that I command thee, and wilt walk in my ways, and do that is right in my sight, to keep my statutes and my commandments, as David my servant did; that I will be with thee, and build thee a sure house, as I built for David, and will give Israel unto thee."

2 Kings 18:5-8 "5He trusted in the LORD God of Israel; so that after him was none like him among all the kings of Judah, nor any that were before him. 6For he clave to the LORD, and departed not from following him, but kept his commandments, which the LORD commanded Moses. 7And the LORD was with him; and he prospered whithersoever he went forth: and he rebelled against the king of Assyria, and served him not. 8He smote the Philistines, even unto Gaza, and the borders thereof, from the tower of the watchmen to the fenced city."

2 Kings 21:7-8 "7And he set a graven image of the grove that he had made in the house, of which the LORD said to David, and to Solomon his son, In this house, and in Jerusalem, which I have chosen out of all tribes of Israel, will I put my name for ever: 8Neither will I make the feet of Israel move any more out of the land which I gave their fathers; only if they will observe to do according to all that I have commanded them, and according to all the law that my servant Moses commanded them."

1 Chronicles 22:13 "Then shalt thou prosper, if thou takest heed to fulfil the statutes and judgments

which the LORD charged Moses with concerning Israel: be strong, and of good courage; dread not, nor be dismayed."

Nehemiah 1:5-9 "5And said, I beseech thee, O LORD God of heaven, the great and terrible God, that keepeth covenant and mercy for them that love him and observe his commandments: 6Let thine ear now be attentive, and thine eyes open, that thou mayest hear the prayer of thy servant, which I pray before thee now, day and night, for the children of Israel thy servants, and confess the sins of the children of Israel, which we have sinned against thee: both I and my father's house have sinned. 7We have dealt very corruptly against thee, and have not kept the commandments, nor the statutes, nor the judgments, which thou commandedst thy servant Moses. 8Remember, I beseech thee, the word that thou commandedst thy servant Moses, saying, If ye transgress, I will scatter you abroad among the nations: 9But if ye turn unto me, and keep my commandments, and do them; though there were of you cast out unto the uttermost part of the heaven, yet will I gather them from thence, and will bring them unto the place that I have chosen to set my name there."

Nehemiah 9:29-31 "29And testifiedst against them, that thou mightest bring them again unto thy law: yet they dealt proudly, and hearkened not unto thy commandments, but sinned against thy judgments, (which if a man do, he shall live in them;) and withdrew the shoulder, and hardened their neck, and would not hear. 30Yet many years didst thou forbear them, and testifiedst against them by thy spirit in thy prophets: yet would they not give ear: therefore gavest thou them into the hand of the people of the lands. 31Nevertheless for thy great mercies' sake thou didst not utterly consume them, nor forsake them; for thou art a gracious and merciful God."

Job 36:5-11 "5Behold, God is mighty, and despiseth not any: he is mighty in strength and wisdom. 6He preserveth not the life of the wicked: but giveth right to the poor. 7He withdraweth not his eyes from the righteous: but with kings are they on the throne; yea, he doth establish them for ever, and they are exalted. 8And if they be bound in fetters, and be holden in cords of affliction; 9Then he sheweth them their work, and their transgressions that they have exceeded. [10]He openeth also their ear to discipline, and commandeth that they return from iniquity. [11]If they obey and serve him, they shall spend their days in prosperity, and their years in pleasures."

Psalm 18:20-24 "[20]The LORD rewarded me according to my righteousness; according to the cleanness of my hands hath he recompensed me. [21]For I have kept the ways of the LORD, and have not wickedly departed from my God. [22]For all his judgments were before me, and I did not put away his statutes from me. [23]I was also upright before him, and I kept myself from mine iniquity. [24]Therefore hath the LORD recompensed me according to my righteousness, according to the cleanness of my hands in his eyesight."

Psalm 19:9-11 "[9]The fear of the LORD is clean, enduring for ever: the judgments of the LORD are true and righteous altogether. [10]More to be desired are they than gold, yea, than much fine gold: sweeter also than honey and the honeycomb. [11]Moreover by them is thy servant warned: and in keeping of them there is great reward."

Psalm 37:34 "Wait on the LORD, and keep his way, and he shall exalt thee to inherit the land: when the wicked are cut off, thou shalt see it."

Psalm 119:1-8 "[1]Blessed are the undefiled in the way, who walk in the law of the LORD. [2]Blessed are they that keep his testimonies, and that seek him with the whole heart. [3]They also do no iniquity: they walk in his ways. [4]Thou hast commanded us to keep thy precepts diligently. [5]O that my ways were directed to keep thy statutes! [6]Then shall I not be ashamed, when I have respect unto all thy commandments. [7]I will praise thee with uprightness of heart, when I shall have learned thy righteous judgments. [8]I will keep thy statutes: O forsake me not utterly."

Psalm 119:41-45 "[41]Let thy mercies come also unto me, O LORD, even thy salvation, according to thy word. [42]So shall I have wherewith to answer him that reproacheth me: for I trust in thy word. [43]And take not the word of truth utterly out of my mouth; for I have hoped in thy judgments. [44]So shall I keep thy law continually for ever and ever. [45]And I will walk at liberty: for I seek thy precepts."

Psalm 119:89-100 "[89]For ever, O LORD, thy word is settled in heaven. [90]Thy faithfulness is unto all generations: thou hast established the earth, and it abideth. [91]They continue this day according to thine ordinances: for all are thy servants. [92]Unless thy law had been my delights, I should then have perished in mine affliction. [93]I will never forget thy precepts: for with them thou hast quickened me. [94]I am thine, save me; for I have sought thy precepts. [95]The wicked have waited for me to destroy me: but I will consider thy testimonies. [96]I have seen an end of all perfection: but thy commandment is exceeding broad. [97]O how love I thy law! it is my meditation all the day. [98]Thou through thy commandments hast made me wiser than mine enemies: for they are ever with me. [99]I have more understanding than all my teachers: for thy testimonies are my meditation. [100]I understand more than the ancients, because I keep thy precepts."

Proverbs 2:1-5 "[1]My son, if thou wilt receive my words, and hide my commandments with thee; [2]So that thou incline thine ear unto wisdom, and apply thine heart to understanding; [3]Yea, if thou criest after knowledge, and liftest up thy voice for understanding; [4]If thou seekest her as silver, and searchest for her as for hid treasures; [5]Then shalt thou understand the fear of the LORD, and find the knowledge of God."

Isaiah 1:19-20 "[19]If ye be willing and obedient, ye shall eat the good of the land: [20]But if ye refuse and rebel, ye shall be devoured with the sword: for the mouth of the LORD hath spoken it."

Isaiah 48:17-19 "[17]Thus saith the LORD, thy Redeemer, the Holy One of Israel; I am the LORD thy God which teacheth thee to profit, which leadeth thee by the way that thou shouldest go. [18]O that thou hadst hearkened to my commandments! then had thy peace been as a river, and thy righteousness as the waves of the sea: [19]Thy seed also had been as the sand, and the offspring of thy bowels like the gravel thereof; his name should not have been cut off nor destroyed from before me."

Jeremiah 7:23 "But this thing commanded I them, saying, Obey my voice, and I will be your God, and ye shall be my people: and walk ye in all the ways that I have commanded you, that it may be well unto you."

Jeremiah 17:24-26 "²⁴And it shall come to pass, if ye diligently hearken unto me, saith the LORD, to bring in no burden through the gates of this city on the sabbath day, but hallow the sabbath day, to do no work therein; ²⁵Then shall there enter into the gates of this city kings and princes sitting upon the throne of David, riding in chariots and on horses, they, and their princes, the men of Judah, and the inhabitants of Jerusalem: and this city shall remain for ever. ²⁶And they shall come from the cities of Judah, and from the places about Jerusalem, and from the land of Benjamin, and from the plain, and from the mountains, and from the south, bringing burnt offerings, and sacrifices, and meat offerings, and incense, and bringing sacrifices of praise, unto the house of the LORD."

Jeremiah 26:12-13 "¹²Then spake Jeremiah unto all the princes and to all the people, saying, The LORD sent me to prophesy against this house and against this city all the words that ye have heard. ¹³Therefore now amend your ways and your doings, and obey the voice of the LORD your God; and the LORD will repent him of the evil that he hath pronounced against you."

John 8:49-51 "⁴⁹Jesus answered, I have not a devil; but I honour my Father, and ye do dishonour me. ⁵⁰And I seek not mine own glory: there is one that seeketh and judgeth. ⁵¹Verily, verily, I say unto you, If a man keep my saying, he shall never see death."

1 John 3:21-22 "²¹Beloved, if our heart condemn us not, then have we confidence toward God. ²²And whatsoever we ask, we receive of him, because we keep his commandments, and do those things that are pleasing in his sight."

Those That Are Obedient To God

Exodus 20:2-6 "²I am the LORD thy God, which have brought thee out of the land of Egypt, out of the house of bondage. ³Thou shalt have no other gods before me. ⁴Thou shalt not make unto thee any graven image, or any likeness of any thing that is in heaven above, or that is in the earth beneath, or that is in the water under the earth: ⁵Thou shalt not bow down thyself to them, nor serve them: for I the LORD thy God am a jealous God, visiting the iniquity of the fathers upon the children unto the third and fourth generation of them that hate me; ⁶And shewing mercy unto thousands of them that love me, and keep my commandments."

Deuteronomy 5:6-10 "⁶I am the LORD thy God, which brought thee out of the land of Egypt, from the house of bondage. ⁷Thou shalt have none other gods before me. ⁸Thou shalt not make thee any graven image, or any likeness of any thing that is in heaven above, or that is in the earth beneath, or that is in the waters beneath the earth: ⁹Thou shalt not bow down thyself unto them, nor serve them: for I the LORD thy God am a jealous God, visiting the iniquity of the fathers upon the children unto the third and fourth generation of them that hate me, ¹⁰And shewing mercy unto thousands of them that love me and keep my commandments."

Deuteronomy 7:9 "Know therefore that the LORD thy God, he is God, the faithful God, which keepeth covenant and mercy with them that love him and keep his commandments to a thousand generations."

Nehemiah 1:5 "And said, I beseech thee, O LORD God of heaven, the great and terrible God, that keepeth covenant and mercy for them that love him and observe his commandments."

Psalm 25:10 "All the paths of the LORD are mercy and truth unto such as keep his covenant and his testimonies."

Psalm 103:17-18 "¹⁷But the mercy of the LORD is from everlasting to everlasting upon them that fear him, and his righteousness unto children's children; ¹⁸To such as keep his covenant, and to those that remember his commandments to do them."

Psalm 111:10 "The fear of the LORD is the beginning of wisdom: a good understanding have all they that do his commandments: his praise endureth for ever."

Psalm 119:1-3 "¹Blessed are the undefiled in the way, who walk in the law of the LORD. ²Blessed are they that keep his testimonies, and that seek him with the whole heart. ³They also do no iniquity: they walk in his ways."

Proverbs 19:16 "He that keepeth the commandment keepeth his own soul; but he that despiseth his ways shall die."

Proverbs 28:4 "They that forsake the law praise the wicked: but such as keep the law contend with them."

Proverbs 28:7 "Whoso keepeth the law is a wise son: but he that is a companion of riotous men shameth his father."

Proverbs 29:18 "Where there is no vision, the people perish: but he that keepeth the law, happy is he."

Ezekiel 18:5-9 "⁵But if a man be just, and do that which is lawful and right, ⁶And hath not eaten upon the mountains, neither hath lifted up his eyes to the idols of the house of Israel, neither hath defiled his neighbour's wife, neither hath come near to a menstruous woman, ⁷And hath not oppressed any, but hath restored to the debtor his pledge, hath spoiled none by violence, hath given his bread to the hungry, and hath covered the naked with a garment; ⁸He that hath not given forth upon usury, neither hath taken any increase, that hath withdrawn his hand from iniquity, hath executed true judgment between man and man, ⁹Hath walked in my statutes, and hath kept my judgments, to deal truly; he is just, he shall surely live, saith the Lord GOD."

Daniel 9:4 "And I prayed unto the LORD my God, and made my confession, and said, O Lord, the great and dreadful God, keeping the covenant and mercy to them that love him, and to them that keep his commandments."

Matthew 5:19 "Whosoever therefore shall break one of these least commandments, and shall teach men so, he shall be called the least in the kingdom of heaven: but whosoever shall do and teach them, the same shall be called great in the kingdom of heaven."

Matthew 7:21-25 "²¹Not every one that saith unto me, Lord, Lord, shall enter into the kingdom of heaven; but he that doeth the will of my Father which is in heaven. ²²Many will say to me in that day, Lord, Lord, have we not prophesied in thy name? and in thy name have cast out devils? and in thy name done many wonderful works? ²³And then will I profess unto them, I never knew you: depart from me, ye that work iniquity. ²⁴Therefore whosoever heareth these sayings of mine, and doeth them, I will liken him unto a wise man, which built his house upon a rock: ²⁵And the rain descended, and the floods came, and the winds blew, and beat upon that house; and it fell not: for it was founded upon a rock."

Luke 6:46-48 "⁴⁶And why call ye me, Lord, Lord, and do not the things which I say? ⁴⁷Whosoever cometh to me, and heareth my sayings, and doeth them, I will shew you to whom he is like: ⁴⁸He is like a man which built an house, and digged deep, and laid the foundation on a rock: and when the flood arose, the stream beat vehemently upon that house, and could not shake it: for it was founded upon a rock."

Luke 8:19-21 "¹⁹Then came to him his mother and his brethren, and could not come at him for the press. ²⁰And it was told him by certain which said, Thy mother and thy brethren stand without, desiring to see thee. ²¹And he answered and said unto them, My mother and my brethren are these which hear the word of God, and do it."

Luke 11:27-28 "²⁷And it came to pass, as he spake these things, a certain woman of the company lifted up her voice, and said unto him, Blessed is the womb that bare thee, and the paps which thou hast sucked. ²⁸But he said, Yea rather, blessed are they that hear the word of God, and keep it."

John 5:24-25 "²⁴Verily, verily, I say unto you, He that heareth my word, and believeth on him that sent me, hath everlasting life, and shall not come into condemnation; but is passed from death unto life. ²⁵Verily, verily, I say unto you, The hour is coming, and now is, when the dead shall hear the voice of the Son of God: and they that hear shall live."

John 14:21 "He that hath my commandments, and keepeth them, he it is that loveth me: and he that loveth me shall be loved of my Father, and I will love him, and will manifest myself to him."

John 15:1-14 "¹I am the true vine, and my Father is the husbandman. ²Every branch in me that beareth not fruit he taketh away: and every branch that beareth fruit, he purgeth it, that it may bring forth more fruit. ³Now ye are clean through the word which I have spoken unto you. ⁴Abide in me, and I in you. As the branch cannot bear fruit of itself, except it abide in the vine; no more can ye, except ye abide in me. ⁵I am the vine, ye are the branches: He that abideth in me, and I in him, the same bringeth forth much fruit: for without me ye can do nothing. [6]If a man abide not in me, he is cast forth as a branch, and is withered; and men gather them, and cast them into the fire, and they are burned. [7]If ye abide in me, and my words abide in you, ye shall ask what ye will, and it shall be done unto you. [8]Herein is my Father glorified, that ye bear much fruit; so shall ye be my disciples. [9]As the Father hath loved me, so have I loved you: continue ye in my love. [10]If ye keep my commandments, ye shall abide in my love; even as I have kept my Father's commandments, and abide in his love. [11]These things have I spoken unto you, that my joy might remain in you, and that your joy might be full. [12]This is my commandment, That ye love one another, as I have loved you. [13]Greater love hath no man than this, that a man lay down his life for his friends. [14]Ye are my friends, if ye do whatsoever I command you."

Acts 5:32 "And we are his witnesses of these things; and so is also the Holy Ghost, whom God hath given to them that obey him."

Romans 2:13 "(For not the hearers of the law are just before God, but the doers of the law shall be justified."

Galatians 3:10-12 "[10]For as many as are of the works of the law are under the curse: for it is written, Cursed is every one that continueth not in all things which are written in the book of the law to do them. [11]But that no man is justified by the law in the sight of God, it is evident: for, The just shall live by faith. [12]And the law is not of faith: but, The man that doeth them shall live in them."

Hebrews 5:8-9 "[8]Though he were a Son, yet learned he obedience by the things which he suffered; [9]And being made perfect, he became the author of eternal salvation unto all them that obey him."

James 1:25 "But whoso looketh into the perfect law of liberty, and continueth therein, he being not a forgetful hearer, but a doer of the work, this man shall be blessed in his deed."

1 John 2:1-5 "[1]My little children, these things write I unto you, that ye sin not. And if any man sin, we have an advocate with the Father, Jesus Christ the righteous: [2]And he is the propitiation for our sins: and not for ours only, but also for the sins of the whole world. [3]And hereby we do know that we know him, if we keep his commandments. [4]He that saith, I know him, and keepeth not his commandments, is a liar, and the truth is not in him. [5]But whoso keepeth his word, in him verily is the love of God perfected: hereby know we that we are in him."

1 John 3:21-24 "[21]Beloved, if our heart condemn us not, then have we confidence toward God. [22]And whatsoever we ask, we receive of him, because we keep his commandments, and do those things that are pleasing in his sight. [23]And this is his commandment, That we should believe on the name of his Son Jesus Christ, and love one another, as he gave us commandment. [24]And he that keepeth his commandments dwelleth in him, and he in him. And hereby we know that he abideth in us, by the Spirit which he hath given us."

2 John 9 "Whosoever transgresseth, and abideth not in the doctrine of Christ, hath not God. He that abideth in the doctrine of Christ, he hath both the Father and the Son."

Revelation 1:3 "Blessed is he that readeth, and they that hear the words of this prophecy, and keep those things which are written therein: for the time is at hand."

Revelation 2:18-28 "[18]And unto the angel of the church in Thyatira write; These things saith the Son of God, who hath his eyes like unto a flame of fire, and his feet are like fine brass; [19]I know thy works, and charity, and service, and faith, and thy patience, and thy works; and the last to be more than the first. [20]Notwithstanding I have a few things against thee, because thou sufferest that woman Jezebel, which calleth herself a prophetess, to teach and to seduce my servants to commit fornication, and to eat things sacrificed unto idols. [21]And I gave her space to repent of her fornication; and she repented not. [22]Behold, I will cast her into a bed, and them that commit adultery with her into great tribulation, except they repent of their deeds. [23]And I will kill her children with death; and all the churches shall know that I am he which searcheth the reins and hearts: and I will give unto every one of you according to your works. [24]But unto you I say, and unto the rest in Thyatira, as many as have not this doctrine, and which have not known the depths of Satan, as they speak; I will put upon you none other burden. 25But that which ye have already hold fast till I come. 26And he that overcometh, and keepeth my works unto the end, to him will I give power over the nations: 27And he shall rule them with a rod of iron; as the vessels of a potter shall they be broken to shivers: even as I received of my Father. 28And I will give him the morning star."

Revelation 3:7-10 "7And to the angel of the church in Philadelphia write; These things saith he that is holy, he that is true, he that hath the key of David, he that openeth, and no man shutteth; and shutteth, and no man openeth; 8I know thy works: behold, I have set before thee an open door, and no man can shut it: for thou hast a little strength, and hast kept my word, and hast not denied my name. 9Behold, I will make them of the synagogue of Satan, which say they are Jews, and are not, but do lie; behold, I will make them to come and worship before thy feet, and to know that I have loved thee. 10Because thou hast kept the word of my patience, I also will keep thee from the hour of temptation, which shall come upon all the world, to try them that dwell upon the earth."

Revelation 22:7 "Behold, I come quickly: blessed is he that keepeth the sayings of the prophecy of this book."

Revelation 22:13-14 "13I am Alpha and Omega, the beginning and the end, the first and the last. 14Blessed are they that do his commandments, that they may have right to the tree of life, and may enter in through the gates into the city."

Those That Obey The King

Ecclesiastes 8:2-5 "2I counsel thee to keep the king's commandment, and that in regard of the oath of God. 3Be not hasty to go out of his sight: stand not in an evil thing; for he doeth whatsoever pleaseth him. 4Where the word of a king is, there is power: and who may say unto him, What doest thou? 5Whoso keepeth the commandment shall feel no evil thing: and a wise man's heart discerneth both time and judgment."

Who To Obey

Proverbs 6:20-21 "20My son, keep thy father's commandment, and forsake not the law of thy mother: 21Bind them continually upon thine heart, and tie them about thy neck."

Ecclesiastes 8:2-4 "2I counsel thee to keep the king's commandment, and that in regard of the oath of God. 3Be not hasty to go out of his sight: stand not in an evil thing; for he doeth whatsoever pleaseth him. 4Where the word of a king is, there is power: and who may say unto him, What doest thou?"

Romans 13:1 "Let every soul be subject unto the higher powers. For there is no power but of God: the powers that be are ordained of God."

Ephesians 6:1 "Children, obey your parents in the Lord: for this is right."

Ephesians 6:5-8 "5Servants, be obedient to them that are your masters according to the flesh, with fear and trembling, in singleness of your heart, as unto Christ; 6Not with eyeservice, as menpleasers; but as the servants of Christ, doing the will of God from the heart; 7With good will doing service, as to the Lord, and not to men: 8Knowing that whatsoever good thing any man doeth, the same shall he receive of the Lord, whether he be bond or free."

Colossians 3:20 "Children, obey your parents in all things: for this is well pleasing unto the Lord."

Colossians 3:22-23 "22Servants, obey in all things your masters according to the flesh; not with eyeservice, as menpleasers; but in singleness of heart, fearing God: 23And whatsoever ye do, do it heartily, as to the Lord, and not unto men."

Titus 2:9 "Exhort servants to be obedient unto their own masters, and to please them well in all things; not answering again."

Titus 3:1 "Put them in mind to be subject to principalities and powers, to obey magistrates, to be ready to every good work,"

Hebrews 13:17 "Obey them that have the rule over you, and submit yourselves: for they watch for your souls, as they that must give account, that they may do it with joy, and not with grief: for that is unprofitable for you."

Who Will Keep The Commandments Of The Lord

Proverbs 10:8 "The wise in heart will receive commandments: but a prating fool shall fall."

John 14:9-15 "9Jesus saith unto him, Have I been so long time with you, and yet hast thou not known me, Philip? he that hath seen me hath seen the Father; and how sayest thou then, Shew us the Father? [10]Believest thou not that I am in the Father, and the Father in me? the words that I speak unto you I speak not of myself: but the Father that dwelleth in me, he doeth the works. [11]Believe me that I am in the Father, and the Father in me: or else believe me for the very works' sake. [12]Verily, verily, I say unto you, He that believeth on me, the works that I do shall he do also; and greater works than these shall he do; because I go unto my Father. [13]And whatsoever ye shall ask in my name, that will I do, that the Father may be glorified in the Son. [14]If ye shall ask any thing in my name, I will do it. [15]If ye love me, keep my commandments."

John 14:22-23 "[22]Judas saith unto him, not Iscariot, Lord, how is it that thou wilt manifest thyself unto us, and not unto the world? [23]Jesus answered and said unto him, If a man love me, he will keep my words: and my Father will love him, and we will come unto him, and make our abode with him."

OFFENSE

A Brother Offended
Proverbs 18:19 "A brother offended is harder to be won than a strong city: and their contentions are like the bars of a castle."

The Reward For Offences
Matthew 18:7 "Woe unto the world because of offences! for it must needs be that offences come; but woe to that man by whom the offence cometh!"

Those That Are Not Offended In Christ
Matthew 11:4-6 "[4]Jesus answered and said unto them, Go and shew John again those things which ye do hear and see: [5]The blind receive their sight, and the lame walk, the lepers are cleansed, and the deaf hear, the dead are raised up, and the poor have the gospel preached to them. [6]And blessed is he, whosoever shall not be offended in me."

Luke 7:22-23 "[22]Then Jesus answering said unto them, Go your way, and tell John what things ye have seen and heard; how that the blind see, the lame walk, the lepers are cleansed, the deaf hear, the dead are raised, to the poor the gospel is preached. [23]And blessed is he, whosoever shall not be offended in me."

Those That Offend People
Who Believe In Christ
Matthew 18:1-6 "[1]At the same time came the disciples unto Jesus, saying, Who is the greatest in the kingdom of heaven? [2]And Jesus called a little child unto him, and set him in the midst of them, [3]And said, Verily I say unto you, Except ye be converted, and become as little children, ye shall not enter into the kingdom of heaven. [4]Whosoever therefore shall humble himself as this little child, the same is greatest in the kingdom of heaven. [5]And whoso shall receive one such little child in my name receiveth me. [6]But whoso shall offend one of these little ones which believe in me, it were better for him that a millstone were hanged about his neck, and that he were drowned in the depth of the sea."

Mark 9:38-42 "[38]And John answered him, saying, Master, we saw one casting out devils in thy name, and he followeth not us: and we forbad him, because he followeth not us. [39]But Jesus said, Forbid him not: for there is no man which shall do a miracle in my name, that can lightly speak evil of me. [40]For he that is not against us is on our part. [41]For whosoever shall give you a cup of water to drink in my name, because ye belong to Christ, verily I say unto you, he shall not lose his reward. [42]And whosoever shall offend one of these little ones that believe in me, it is better for him that a millstone were hanged about his neck, and he were cast into the sea."

Luke 17:1-2 "[1]Then said he unto the disciples, It is impossible but that offences will come: but woe unto him, through whom they come! [2]It were better for him that a millstone were hanged about his neck, and he cast into the sea, than that he should offend one of these little ones."

Who Shall Not Be Offended By Anything
Psalm 119:165 "Great peace have they which love thy law: and nothing shall offend them."

OFFERINGS

Whose Offering The Lord Will Not Accept
Genesis 4:1-7 "[1]And Adam knew Eve his wife; and she conceived, and bare Cain, and said, I have gotten a man from the LORD. [2] And she again bare his brother Abel. And Abel was a keeper of sheep,

but Cain was a tiller of the ground. ³ And in process of time it came to pass, that Cain brought of the fruit of the ground an offering unto the LORD. ⁴ And Abel, he also brought of the firstlings of his flock and of the fat thereof. And the LORD had respect unto Abel and to his offering: ⁵ But unto Cain and to his offering he had not respect. And Cain was very wroth, and his countenance fell. ⁶ And the LORD said unto Cain, Why art thou wroth? and why is thy countenance fallen? ⁷ If thou doest well, shalt thou not be accepted? and if thou doest not well, sin lieth at the door. And unto thee shall be his desire, and thou shalt rule over him."

Malachi 1:6-10 "⁶A son honoureth his father, and a servant his master: if then I be a father, where is mine honour? and if I be a master, where is my fear? saith the LORD of hosts unto you, O priests, that despise my name. And ye say, Wherein have we despised thy name? ⁷ Ye offer polluted bread upon mine altar; and ye say, Wherein have we polluted thee? In that ye say, The table of the LORD is contemptible. ⁸ And if ye offer the blind for sacrifice, is it not evil? and if ye offer the lame and sick, is it not evil? offer it now unto thy governor; will he be pleased with thee, or accept thy person? saith the LORD of hosts. ⁹ And now, I pray you, beseech God that he will be gracious unto us: this hath been by your means: will he regard your persons? saith the LORD of hosts. ¹⁰ Who is there even among you that would shut the doors for nought? neither do ye kindle fire on mine altar for nought. I have no pleasure in you, saith the LORD of hosts, neither will I accept an offering at your hand."

OMNIPRESENCE

The Lord Filling Heaven And Earth
Jeremiah 23:24 "Can any hide himself in secret places that I shall not see him? saith the LORD. Do not I fill heaven and earth? saith the LORD."

OPPOSITION

The Reward For Opposing The Lord
Isaiah 3:8 "For Jerusalem is ruined, and Judah is fallen: because their tongue and their doings are against the LORD, to provoke the eyes of his glory."

There Being No Opposition To The Lord
Job 11:7-10 "⁷Canst thou by searching find out God? canst thou find out the Almighty unto perfection? ⁸It is as high as heaven; what canst thou do? deeper than hell; what canst thou know? ⁹The measure thereof is longer than the earth, and broader than the sea. ¹⁰If he cut off, and shut up, or gather together, then who can hinder him?"

Job 42:1-2 "¹Then Job answered the LORD, and said, ²I know that thou canst do every thing, and that no thought can be withholden from thee."

Proverbs 21:30 "There is no wisdom nor understanding nor counsel against the LORD."

Isaiah 43:12-13 "¹²I have declared, and have saved, and I have shewed, when there was no strange god among you: therefore ye are my witnesses, saith the LORD, that I am God. ¹³Yea, before the day was I am he; and there is none that can deliver out of my hand: I will work, and who shall let it?"

Isaiah 50:7-9 "⁷For the Lord GOD will help me; therefore shall I not be confounded: therefore have I set my face like a flint, and I know that I shall not be ashamed. ⁸He is near that justifieth me; who will contend with me? let us stand together: who is mine adversary? let him come near to me. ⁹Behold, the Lord GOD will help me; who is he that shall condemn me? lo, they all shall wax old as a garment; the moth shall eat them up."

Daniel 4:34-35 "³⁴And at the end of the days I Nebuchadnezzar lifted up mine eyes unto heaven, and mine understanding returned unto me, and I blessed the most High, and I praised and honoured him that liveth for ever, whose dominion is an everlasting dominion, and his kingdom is from generation to generation: ³⁵And all the inhabitants of the earth are reputed as nothing: and he doeth according to his will in the army of heaven, and among the inhabitants of the earth: and none can stay his hand, or say unto him, What doest thou?"

Those That Oppose The Lord
Exodus 15:6-12 "⁶Thy right hand, O LORD, is become glorious in power: thy right hand, O LORD, hath dashed in pieces the enemy. ⁷And in the greatness of thine excellency thou hast overthrown them that rose up against thee: thou sentest forth

thy wrath, which consumed them as stubble. ⁸And with the blast of thy nostrils the waters were gathered together, the floods stood upright as an heap, and the depths were congealed in the heart of the sea. ⁹The enemy said, I will pursue, I will overtake, I will divide the spoil; my lust shall be satisfied upon them; I will draw my sword, my hand shall destroy them. ¹⁰Thou didst blow with thy wind, the sea covered them: they sank as lead in the mighty waters. ¹¹Who is like unto thee, O LORD, among the gods? who is like thee, glorious in holiness, fearful in praises, doing wonders? ¹²Thou stretchedst out thy right hand, the earth swallowed them."

Deuteronomy 32:36-43 "³⁶For the LORD shall judge his people, and repent himself for his servants, when he seeth that their power is gone, and there is none shut up, or left. ³⁷And he shall say, Where are their gods, their rock in whom they trusted, ³⁸Which did eat the fat of their sacrifices, and drank the wine of their drink offerings? let them rise up and help you, and be your protection. ³⁹See now that I, even I, am he, and there is no god with me: I kill, and I make alive; I wound, and I heal: neither is there any that can deliver out of my hand. ⁴⁰For I lift up my hand to heaven, and say, I live for ever. ⁴¹If I whet my glittering sword, and mine hand take hold on judgment; I will render vengeance to mine enemies, and will reward them that hate me. ⁴²I will make mine arrows drunk with blood, and my sword shall devour flesh; and that with the blood of the slain and of the captives, from the beginning of revenges upon the enemy. ⁴³Rejoice, O ye nations, with his people: for he will avenge the blood of his servants, and will render vengeance to his adversaries, and will be merciful unto his land, and to his people."

1 Samuel 2:10 "The adversaries of the LORD shall be broken to pieces; out of heaven shall he thunder upon them: the LORD shall judge the ends of the earth; and he shall give strength unto his king, and exalt the horn of his anointed."

Psalm 2:1-6 "¹Why do the heathen rage, and the people imagine a vain thing? ²The kings of the earth set themselves, and the rulers take counsel together, against the LORD, and against his anointed, saying, ³Let us break their bands asunder, and cast away their cords from us. ⁴He that sitteth in the heavens shall laugh: the Lord shall have them in derision. ⁵Then shall he speak unto them in his wrath, and vex them in his sore displeasure. ⁶Yet have I set my king upon my holy hill of Zion."

Isaiah 59:15-18 "¹⁵Yea, truth faileth; and he that departeth from evil maketh himself a prey: and the LORD saw it, and it displeased him that there was no judgment. ¹⁶And he saw that there was no man, and wondered that there was no intercessor: therefore his arm brought salvation unto him; and his righteousness, it sustained him. ¹⁷For he put on righteousness as a breastplate, and an helmet of salvation upon his head; and he put on the garments of vengeance for clothing, and was clad with zeal as a cloke. ¹⁸According to their deeds, accordingly he will repay, fury to his adversaries, recompence to his enemies; to the islands he will repay recompence."

Micah 5:7-9 "⁷And the remnant of Jacob shall be in the midst of many people as a dew from the LORD, as the showers upon the grass, that tarrieth not for man, nor waiteth for the sons of men. ⁸And the remnant of Jacob shall be among the Gentiles in the midst of many people as a lion among the beasts of the forest, as a young lion among the flocks of sheep: who, if he go through, both treadeth down, and teareth in pieces, and none can deliver. ⁹Thine hand shall be lifted up upon thine adversaries, and all thine enemies shall be cut off."

Nahum 1:2 "God is jealous, and the LORD revengeth; the LORD revengeth, and is furious; the LORD will take vengeance on his adversaries, and he reserveth wrath for his enemies."

1 John 2:18-19 "¹⁸Little children, it is the last time: and as ye have heard that antichrist shall come, even now are there many antichrists; whereby we know that it is the last time. ¹⁹They went out from us, but they were not of us; for if they had been of us, they would no doubt have continued with us: but they went out, that they might be made manifest that they were not all of us."

What Cannot Be Opposed
Acts 5:39 "But if it be of God, ye cannot overthrow it; lest haply ye be found even to fight against God."

Who Opposes The Lord

Job 15:20-26 "²⁰The wicked man travaileth with pain all his days, and the number of years is hidden to the oppressor. ²¹A dreadful sound is in his ears: in prosperity the destroyer shall come upon him. ²²He believeth not that he shall return out of darkness, and he is waited for of the sword. ²³He wandereth abroad for bread, saying, Where is it? he knoweth that the day of darkness is ready at his hand. ²⁴Trouble and anguish shall make him afraid; they shall prevail against him, as a king ready to the battle. ²⁵For he stretcheth out his hand against God, and strengtheneth himself against the Almighty. ²⁶He runneth upon him, even on his neck, upon the thick bosses of his bucklers."

Matthew 12:25-30 "²⁵And Jesus knew their thoughts, and said unto them, Every kingdom divided against itself is brought to desolation; and every city or house divided against itself shall not stand: ²⁶And if Satan cast out Satan, he is divided against himself; how shall then his kingdom stand? ²⁷And if I by Beelzebub cast out devils, by whom do your children cast them out? therefore they shall be your judges. ²⁸But if I cast out devils by the Spirit of God, then the kingdom of God is come unto you. ²⁹Or else how can one enter into a strong man's house, and spoil his goods, except he first bind the strong man? and then he will spoil his house. ³⁰He that is not with me is against me; and he that gathereth not with me scattereth abroad."

Luke 11:17-23 "¹⁷But he, knowing their thoughts, said unto them, Every kingdom divided against itself is brought to desolation; and a house divided against a house falleth. ¹⁸If Satan also be divided against himself, how shall his kingdom stand? because ye say that I cast out devils through Beelzebub. ¹⁹And if I by Beelzebub cast out devils, by whom do your sons cast them out? therefore shall they be your judges. ²⁰But if I with the finger of God cast out devils, no doubt the kingdom of God is come upon you. ²¹When a strong man armed keepeth his palace, his goods are in peace: ²²But when a stronger than he shall come upon him, and overcome him, he taketh from him all his armour wherein he trusted, and divideth his spoils. ²³He that is not with me is against me: and he that gathereth not with me scattereth."

Who Cannot Be Opposed

Jeremiah 1:19 "And they shall fight against thee; but they shall not prevail against thee; for I am with thee, saith the Lᴏʀᴅ, to deliver thee."

Romans 8:31 "What shall we then say to these things? If God be for us, who can be against us?"

1 Peter 3:12-14 "¹²For the eyes of the Lord are over the righteous, and his ears are open unto their prayers: but the face of the Lord is against them that do evil. ¹³And who is he that will harm you, if ye be followers of that which is good? ¹⁴But and if ye suffer for righteousness' sake, happy are ye: and be not afraid of their terror, neither be troubled."

Who Does Not Oppose To The Lord

Mark 9:38-41 "³⁸And John answered him, saying, Master, we saw one casting out devils in thy name, and he followeth not us: and we forbad him, because he followeth not us. ³⁹But Jesus said, Forbid him not: for there is no man which shall do a miracle in my name, that can lightly speak evil of me. ⁴⁰For he that is not against us is on our part. ⁴¹For whosoever shall give you a cup of water to drink in my name, because ye belong to Christ, verily I say unto you, he shall not lose his reward."

Luke 9:49-50 "⁴⁹And John answered and said, Master, we saw one casting out devils in thy name; and we forbad him, because he followeth not with us. ⁵⁰And Jesus said unto him, Forbid him not: for he that is not against us is for us."

Who The Lord Opposes

Psalm 34:16 "The face of the Lᴏʀᴅ is against them that do evil, to cut off the remembrance of them from the earth."

Isaiah 49:14-25 "¹⁴But Zion said, The Lᴏʀᴅ hath forsaken me, and my Lord hath forgotten me. ¹⁵Can a woman forget her sucking child, that she should not have compassion on the son of her womb? yea, they may forget, yet will I not forget thee. ¹⁶Behold, I have graven thee upon the palms of my hands; thy walls are continually before me. ¹⁷Thy children shall make haste; thy destroyers and they that made thee waste shall go forth of thee. ¹⁸Lift up thine eyes round about, and behold: all these gather themselves together, and come to thee. As I live, saith the Lᴏʀᴅ, thou shalt surely clothe thee with them all, as with an ornament, and bind them on thee, as a bride doeth. ¹⁹For thy waste and thy desolate places, and the land of thy destruction, shall even now be too narrow by reason of the inhabitants, and they that swallowed thee up shall be far away. ²⁰The children which thou shalt have, after thou hast lost the other, shall say again in thine ears, The place is too strait for me: give place to me that I may dwell. ²¹Then shalt thou say in thine heart, Who hath begotten me these, seeing I have lost my children, and am desolate, a captive, and removing to and fro? and who hath brought up these? Behold, I was left alone; these, where had they been? ²²Thus saith the Lord GOD, Behold, I will lift up mine hand to the Gentiles, and set up my standard to the people: and they shall bring thy sons in their arms, and thy daughters shall be carried upon their shoulders. ²³And kings shall be thy nursing fathers, and their queens thy nursing mothers: they shall bow down to thee with their face toward the earth, and lick up the dust of thy feet; and thou shalt know that I am the LORD: for they shall not be ashamed that wait for me. ²⁴Shall the prey be taken from the mighty, or the lawful captive delivered? ²⁵But thus saith the LORD, Even the captives of the mighty shall be taken away, and the prey of the terrible shall be delivered: for I will contend with him that contendeth with thee, and I will save thy children."

Jeremiah 23:30-32 "³⁰Therefore, behold, I am against the prophets, saith the LORD, that steal my words every one from his neighbour. ³¹Behold, I am against the prophets, saith the LORD, that use their tongues, and say, He saith. ³²Behold, I am against them that prophesy false dreams, saith the LORD, and do tell them, and cause my people to err by their lies, and by their lightness; yet I sent them not, nor commanded them: therefore they shall not profit this people at all, saith the LORD."

Ezekiel 13:3-8 "³Thus saith the Lord GOD; Woe unto the foolish prophets, that follow their own spirit, and have seen nothing! ⁴O Israel, thy prophets are like the foxes in the deserts. ⁵Ye have not gone up into the gaps, neither made up the hedge for the house of Israel to stand in the battle in the day of the LORD. ⁶They have seen vanity and lying divination, saying, The LORD saith: and the LORD hath not sent them: and they have made others to hope that they would confirm the word. ⁷Have ye not seen a vain vision, and have ye not spoken a lying divination, whereas ye say, The LORD saith it; albeit I have not spoken? ⁸Therefore thus saith the Lord GOD; Because ye have spoken vanity, and seen lies, therefore, behold, I am against you, saith the Lord GOD."

Ezekiel 13:17-20 "¹⁷Likewise, thou son of man, set thy face against the daughters of thy people, which prophesy out of their own heart; and prophesy thou against them, ¹⁸And say, Thus saith the Lord GOD; Woe to the women that sew pillows to all armholes, and make kerchiefs upon the head of every stature to hunt souls! Will ye hunt the souls of my people, and will ye save the souls alive that come unto you? ¹⁹And will ye pollute me among my people for handfuls of barley and for pieces of bread, to slay the souls that should not die, and to save the souls alive that should not live, by your lying to my people that hear your lies? ²⁰Wherefore thus saith the Lord GOD; Behold, I am against your pillows, wherewith ye there hunt the souls to make them fly, and I will tear them from your arms, and will let the souls go, even the souls that ye hunt to make them fly."

1 Peter 3:12 "For the eyes of the Lord are over the righteous, and his ears are open unto their prayers: but the face of the Lord is against them that do evil."

OPPRESSION

Not Oppressing Others

Exodus 22:21 "Thou shalt neither vex a stranger, nor oppress him: for ye were strangers in the land of Egypt."

Exodus 23:9 "Also thou shalt not oppress a stranger: for ye know the heart of a stranger, seeing ye were strangers in the land of Egypt."

Leviticus 25:17 "Ye shall not therefore oppress one another; but thou shalt fear thy God: for I am the LORD your God."

Deuteronomy 24:14 "Thou shalt not oppress an hired servant that is poor and needy, whether he be of thy brethren, or of thy strangers that are in thy land within thy gates."

Proverbs 22:22 "Rob not the poor, because he is poor: neither oppress the afflicted in the gate."

Zechariah 7:9-10 "⁹Thus speaketh the LORD of hosts, saying, Execute true judgment, and shew mercy and compassions every man to his brother: ¹⁰ And oppress not the widow, nor the fatherless, the stranger, nor the poor; and let none of you imagine evil against his brother in your heart."

The Oppressed
Psalm 9:9 "The LORD also will be a refuge for the oppressed, a refuge in times of trouble."

Psalm 103:6 "The LORD executeth righteousness and judgment for all that are oppressed."

Psalm 146:5-7 "⁵Happy is he that hath the God of Jacob for his help, whose hope is in the LORD his God: ⁶Which made heaven, and earth, the sea, and all that therein is: which keepeth truth for ever: ⁷Which executeth judgment for the oppressed: which giveth food to the hungry. The LORD looseth the prisoners."

The Servant Of The Lord Being Oppressed
Isaiah 53:1-11 "¹Who hath believed our report? and to whom is the arm of the LORD revealed? ²For he shall grow up before him as a tender plant, and as a root out of a dry ground: he hath no form nor comeliness; and when we shall see him, there is no beauty that we should desire him. ³He is despised and rejected of men; a man of sorrows, and acquainted with grief: and we hid as it were our faces from him; he was despised, and we esteemed him not. ⁴Surely he hath borne our griefs, and carried our sorrows: yet we did esteem him stricken, smitten of God, and afflicted. ⁵But he was wounded for our transgressions, he was bruised for our iniquities: the chastisement of our peace was upon him; and with his stripes we are healed. ⁶All we like sheep have gone astray; we have turned every one to his own way; and the LORD hath laid on him the iniquity of us all. ⁷He was oppressed, and he was afflicted, yet he opened not his mouth: he is brought as a lamb to the slaughter, and as a sheep before her shearers is dumb, so he openeth not his mouth. ⁸He was taken from prison and from judgment: and who shall declare his generation? for he was cut off out of the land of the living: for the transgression of my people was he stricken. ⁹And he made his grave with the wicked, and with the rich in his death; because he had done no violence, neither was any deceit in his mouth. ¹⁰Yet it pleased the LORD to bruise him; he hath put him to grief: when thou shalt make his soul an offering for sin, he shall see his seed, he shall prolong his days, and the pleasure of the LORD shall prosper in his hand. ¹¹He shall see of the travail of his soul, and shall be satisfied: by his knowledge shall my righteous servant justify many; for he shall bear their iniquities."

Those That Have Not Oppressed Others
Isaiah 33:15-16 "¹⁵He that walketh righteously, and speaketh uprightly; he that despiseth the gain of oppressions, that shaketh his hands from holding of bribes, that stoppeth his ears from hearing of blood, and shutteth his eyes from seeing evil; ¹⁶He shall dwell on high: his place of defence shall be the munitions of rocks: bread shall be given him; his waters shall be sure."

Ezekiel 18:5-9 "⁵But if a man be just, and do that which is lawful and right, ⁶And hath not eaten upon the mountains, neither hath lifted up his eyes to the idols of the house of Israel, neither hath defiled his neighbour's wife, neither hath come near to a menstruous woman, ⁷And hath not oppressed any, but hath restored to the debtor his pledge, hath spoiled none by violence, hath given his bread to the hungry, and hath covered the naked with a garment; ⁸He that hath not given forth upon usury, neither hath taken any increase, that hath withdrawn his hand from iniquity, hath executed true judgment between man and man, ⁹Hath walked in my statutes, and hath kept my judgments, to deal truly; he is just, he shall surely live, saith the Lord GOD."

Those That Oppress Israel
Isaiah 49:14-26 "¹⁴But Zion said, The LORD hath forsaken me, and my Lord hath forgotten me. ¹⁵Can a woman forget her sucking child, that she should not have compassion on the son of her womb? yea, they may forget, yet will I not forget thee. ¹⁶Behold, I have graven thee upon the palms of my hands; thy walls are continually before me. ¹⁷Thy children shall make haste; thy destroyers and they that made thee waste shall go forth of thee. ¹⁸Lift up thine eyes round about, and behold: all these gather themselves together, and come to thee. As I live, saith the LORD, thou shalt surely clothe thee with them all, as with an ornament, and bind them on thee, as a bride doeth. ¹⁹For thy waste and thy desolate

places, and the land of thy destruction, shall even now be too narrow by reason of the inhabitants, and they that swallowed thee up shall be far away. ²⁰The children which thou shalt have, after thou hast lost the other, shall say again in thine ears, The place is too strait for me: give place to me that I may dwell. ²¹Then shalt thou say in thine heart, Who hath begotten me these, seeing I have lost my children, and am desolate, a captive, and removing to and fro? and who hath brought up these? Behold, I was left alone; these, where had they been? ²²Thus saith the Lord GOD, Behold, I will lift up mine hand to the Gentiles, and set up my standard to the people: and they shall bring thy sons in their arms, and thy daughters shall be carried upon their shoulders. ²³And kings shall be thy nursing fathers, and their queens thy nursing mothers: they shall bow down to thee with their face toward the earth, and lick up the dust of thy feet; and thou shalt know that I am the LORD: for they shall not be ashamed that wait for me. ²⁴Shall the prey be taken from the mighty, or the lawful captive delivered? ²⁵But thus saith the LORD, Even the captives of the mighty shall be taken away, and the prey of the terrible shall be delivered: for I will contend with him that contendeth with thee, and I will save thy children. ²⁶And I will feed them that oppress thee with their own flesh; and they shall be drunken with their own blood, as with sweet wine: and all flesh shall know that I the LORD am thy Saviour and thy Redeemer, the mighty One of Jacob."

Jeremiah 30:16-20 "¹⁶Therefore all they that devour thee shall be devoured; and all thine adversaries, every one of them, shall go into captivity; and they that spoil thee shall be a spoil, and all that prey upon thee will I give for a prey. ¹⁷For I will restore health unto thee, and I will heal thee of thy wounds, saith the LORD; because they called thee an Outcast, saying, This is Zion, whom no man seeketh after. ¹⁸Thus saith the LORD; Behold, I will bring again the captivity of Jacob's tents, and have mercy on his dwelling-places; and the city shall be builded upon her own heap, and the palace shall remain after the manner thereof. ¹⁹And out of them shall proceed thanksgiving and the voice of them that make merry: and I will multiply them, and they shall

not be few; I will also glorify them, and they shall not be small. ²⁰Their children also shall be as aforetime, and their congregation shall be established before me, and I will punish all that oppress them."

Those That Oppress The Poor

Job 20:1-19 "¹Then answered Zophar the Naamathite, and said, ²Therefore do my thoughts cause me to answer, and for this I make haste. ³I have heard the check of my reproach, and the spirit of my understanding causeth me to answer. ⁴Knowest thou not this of old, since man was placed upon earth, ⁵That the triumphing of the wicked is short, and the joy of the hypocrite but for a moment? ⁶Though his excellency mount up to the heavens, and his head reach unto the clouds; ⁷Yet he shall perish for ever like his own dung: they which have seen him shall say, Where is he? ⁸He shall fly away as a dream, and shall not be found: yea, he shall be chased away as a vision of the night. ⁹The eye also which saw him shall see him no more; neither shall his place any more behold him. ¹⁰His children shall seek to please the poor, and his hands shall restore their goods. ¹¹His bones are full of the sin of his youth, which shall lie down with him in the dust. ¹²Though wickedness be sweet in his mouth, though he hide it under his tongue; ¹³Though he spare it, and forsake it not; but keep it still within his mouth: ¹⁴Yet his meat in his bowels is turned, it is the gall of asps within him. ¹⁵He hath swallowed down riches, and he shall vomit them up again: God shall cast them out of his belly. ¹⁶He shall suck the poison of asps: the viper's tongue shall slay him. ¹⁷He shall not see the rivers, the floods, the brooks of honey and butter. ¹⁸That which he laboured for shall he restore, and shall not swallow it down: according to his substance shall the restitution be, and he shall not rejoice therein. ¹⁹Because he hath oppressed and hath forsaken the poor; because he hath violently taken away an house which he builded not."

Proverbs 14:31 "He that oppresseth the poor reproacheth his Maker: but he that honoureth him hath mercy on the poor."

Proverbs 22:16 "He that oppresseth the poor to increase his riches, and he that giveth to the rich, shall surely come to want."

Proverbs 22:22-23 "²²Rob not the poor, because he is poor: neither oppress the afflicted in the gate: ²³For the LORD will plead their cause, and spoil the soul of those that spoiled them."

Proverbs 28:3 "A poor man that oppresseth the poor is like a sweeping rain which leaveth no food."

Who Is An Oppressor
Proverbs 28:16 "The prince that wanteth understanding is also a great oppressor: but he that hateth covetousness shall prolong his days."

Who Shall Be Far From Oppression
Isaiah 54:5-14 "⁵For thy Maker is thine husband; the LORD of hosts is his name; and thy Redeemer the Holy One of Israel; The God of the whole earth shall he be called. ⁶For the LORD hath called thee as a woman forsaken and grieved in spirit, and a wife of youth, when thou wast refused, saith thy God. ⁷For a small moment have I forsaken thee; but with great mercies will I gather thee. ⁸In a little wrath I hid my face from thee for a moment; but with everlasting kindness will I have mercy on thee, saith the LORD thy Redeemer. ⁹For this is as the waters of Noah unto me: for as I have sworn that the waters of Noah should no more go over the earth; so have I sworn that I would not be wroth with thee, nor rebuke thee. ¹⁰For the mountains shall depart, and the hills be removed; but my kindness shall not depart from thee, neither shall the covenant of my peace be removed, saith the LORD that hath mercy on thee. ¹¹O thou afflicted, tossed with tempest, and not comforted, behold, I will lay thy stones with fair colours, and lay thy foundations with sapphires. ¹²And I will make thy windows of agates, and thy gates of carbuncles, and all thy borders of pleasant stones. ¹³And all thy children shall be taught of the LORD; and great shall be the peace of thy children. ¹⁴In righteousness shalt thou be established: thou shalt be far from oppression; for thou shalt not fear: and from terror; for it shall not come near thee."

ORDINATION

Jesus Christ Being Ordained
Acts 10:37-43 "³⁷That word, I say, ye know, which was published throughout all Judaea, and began from Galilee, after the baptism which John preached; ³⁸ How God anointed Jesus of Nazareth with the Holy Ghost and with power: who went about doing good, and healing all that were oppressed of the devil; for God was with him. ³⁹ And we are witnesses of all things which he did both in the land of the Jews, and in Jerusalem; whom they slew and hanged on a tree: ⁴⁰ Him God raised up the third day, and shewed him openly; ⁴¹ Not to all the people, but unto witnesses chosen before of God, even to us, who did eat and drink with him after he rose from the dead. ⁴² And he commanded us to preach unto the people, and to testify that it is he which was ordained of God to be the Judge of quick and dead. ⁴³ To him give all the prophets witness, that through his name whosoever believeth in him shall receive remission of sins."

Acts 17:30-31 "³⁰And the times of this ignorance God winked at; but now commandeth all men every where to repent: ³¹ Because he hath appointed a day, in the which he will judge the world in righteousness by that man whom he hath ordained; whereof he hath given assurance unto all men, in that he hath raised him from the dead."

1 Peter 1:18-20 "¹⁸Forasmuch as ye know that ye were not redeemed with corruptible things, as silver and gold, from your vain conversation received by tradition from your fathers; ¹⁹ But with the precious blood of Christ, as of a lamb without blemish and without spot: ²⁰ Who verily was foreordained before the foundation of the world, but was manifest in these last times for you."

What Has Been Ordained
Romans 7:10 "And the commandment, which was ordained to life, I found to be unto death."

Romans 13:1-2 "¹Let every soul be subject unto the higher powers. For there is no power but of God: the powers that be are ordained of God. ²Whosoever therefore resisteth the power, resisteth the ordinance of God: and they that resist shall receive to themselves damnation."

1 Corinthians 2:7 "But we speak the wisdom of God in a mystery, even the hidden wisdom, which God ordained before the world unto our glory."

1 Corinthians 9:13-14 "¹³Do ye not know that they which minister about holy things live of the things of the temple? and they which wait at the altar are partakers with the altar? ¹⁴Even so hath the Lord ordained that they which preach the gospel should live of the gospel."

Galatians 3:19-20 "¹⁹Wherefore then serveth the law? It was added because of transgressions, till the seed should come to whom the promise was made; and it was ordained by angels in the hand of a mediator. ²⁰Now a mediator is not a mediator of one, but God is one."

Ephesians 2:8-10 "⁸For by grace are ye saved through faith; and that not of yourselves: it is the gift of God: ⁹Not of works, lest any man should boast. ¹⁰For we are his workmanship, created in Christ Jesus unto good works, which God hath before ordained that we should walk in them."

Who Is Ordained

Jeremiah 1:5 "Before I formed thee in the belly I knew thee; and before thou camest forth out of the womb I sanctified thee, and I ordained thee a prophet unto the nations."

John 15:1-16 "¹I am the true vine, and my Father is the husbandman. ²Every branch in me that beareth not fruit he taketh away: and every branch that beareth fruit, he purgeth it, that it may bring forth more fruit. ³Now ye are clean through the word which I have spoken unto you. ⁴Abide in me, and I in you. As the branch cannot bear fruit of itself, except it abide in the vine; no more can ye, except ye abide in me. ⁵I am the vine, ye are the branches: He that abideth in me, and I in him, the same bringeth forth much fruit: for without me ye can do nothing. ⁶If a man abide not in me, he is cast forth as a branch, and is withered; and men gather them, and cast them into the fire, and they are burned. ⁷If ye abide in me, and my words abide in you, ye shall ask what ye will, and it shall be done unto you. ⁸Herein is my Father glorified, that ye bear much fruit; so shall ye be my disciples. ⁹As the Father hath loved me, so have I loved you: continue ye in my love. ¹⁰If ye keep my commandments, ye shall abide in my love; even as I have kept my Father's commandments, and abide in his love. ¹¹These things have I spoken unto you, that my joy might remain in you, and that your joy might be full. ¹²This is my commandment, That ye love one another, as I have loved you. ¹³Greater love hath no man than this, that a man lay down his life for his friends. ¹⁴Ye are my friends, if ye do whatsoever I command you. ¹⁵Henceforth I call you not servants; for the servant knoweth not what his lord doeth: but I have called you friends; for all things that I have heard of my Father I have made known unto you. ¹⁶Ye have not chosen me, but I have chosen you, and ordained you, that ye should go and bring forth fruit, and that your fruit should remain: that whatsoever ye shall ask of the Father in my name, he may give it you."

1 Timothy 2:7 "Whereunto I am ordained a preacher, and an apostle, (I speak the truth in Christ, and lie not;) a teacher of the Gentiles in faith and verity."

PAGANISM

Diviners

Zechariah 10:1-2 "¹Ask ye of the LORD rain in the time of the latter rain; so the LORD shall make bright clouds, and give them showers of rain, to every one grass in the field. ²For the idols have spoken vanity, and the diviners have seen a lie, and have told false dreams; they comfort in vain: therefore they went their way as a flock, they were troubled, because there was no shepherd."

Not Practicing Paganism

Leviticus 19:26 "Ye shall not eat any thing with the blood: neither shall ye use enchantment, nor observe times."

Leviticus 19:31 "Regard not them that have familiar spirits, neither seek after wizards, to be defiled by them: I am the LORD your God."

Deuteronomy 18:9-14 "⁹When thou art come into the land which the LORD thy God giveth thee, thou shalt not learn to do after the abominations of those nations. ¹⁰There shall not be found among you any one that maketh his son or his daughter to pass through the fire, or that useth divination, or an observer of times, or an enchanter, or a witch, ¹¹Or a charmer, or a consulter with familiar spirits, or a wizard, or a necromancer. ¹²For all that do these things are an abomination unto the LORD: and because of these abominations the LORD thy God doth drive them out from before thee. ¹³Thou shalt be perfect with the LORD thy God. ¹⁴For these nations, which thou shalt possess, hearkened unto observers of times, and unto diviners: but as for thee, the LORD thy God hath not suffered thee so to do."

Sorcerers

Revelation 21:8 "But the fearful, and unbelieving, and the abominable, and murderers, and whoremongers, and sorcerers, and idolaters, and all liars, shall have their part in the lake which burneth with fire and brimstone: which is the second death."

Revelation 22:13-15 "¹³I am Alpha and Omega, the beginning and the end, the first and the last.

¹⁴Blessed are they that do his commandments, that they may have right to the tree of life, and may enter in through the gates into the city. ¹⁵For without are dogs, and sorcerers, and whoremongers, and murderers, and idolaters, and whosoever loveth and maketh a lie."

The Reward For Practicing Paganism

2 Kings 21:6 "And he made his son pass through the fire, and observed times, and used enchantments, and dealt with familiar spirits and wizards: he wrought much wickedness in the sight of the LORD, to provoke him to anger."

1 Chronicles 10:13-14 "¹³So Saul died for his transgression which he committed against the LORD, even against the word of the LORD, which he kept not, and also for asking counsel of one that had a familiar spirit, to inquire of it; ¹⁴And inquired not of the LORD: therefore he slew him, and turned the kingdom unto David the son of Jesse."

2 Chronicles 33:6 "And he caused his children to pass through the fire in the valley of the son of Hinnom: also he observed times, and used enchantments, and used witchcraft, and dealt with a familiar spirit, and with wizards: he wrought much evil in the sight of the LORD, to provoke him to anger."

Psalm 106:37-43 "³⁷Yea, they sacrificed their sons and their daughters unto devils, ³⁸And shed innocent blood, even the blood of their sons and of their daughters, whom they sacrificed unto the idols of Canaan: and the land was polluted with blood. ³⁹Thus were they defiled with their own works, and went a whoring with their own inventions. ⁴⁰Therefore was the wrath of the LORD kindled against his people, insomuch that he abhorred his own inheritance. ⁴¹And he gave them into the hand of the heathen; and they that hated them ruled over them. ⁴²Their enemies also oppressed them, and they were brought into subjection under their hand. ⁴³Many times did he deliver them; but they provoked him with their counsel, and were brought low for their iniquity."

Jeremiah 19:3-15 "³And say, Hear ye the word of the LORD, O kings of Judah, and inhabitants of Jerusalem; Thus saith the LORD of hosts, the God of Israel; Behold, I will bring evil upon this place, the which whosoever heareth, his ears shall tingle.

[4]Because they have forsaken me, and have estranged this place, and have burned incense in it unto other gods, whom neither they nor their fathers have known, nor the kings of Judah, and have filled this place with the blood of innocents; [5]They have built also the high places of Baal, to burn their sons with fire for burnt offerings unto Baal, which I commanded not, nor spake it, neither came it into my mind: [6]Therefore, behold, the days come, saith the LORD, that this place shall no more be called Tophet, nor The valley of the son of Hinnom, but The valley of slaughter. [7]And I will make void the counsel of Judah and Jerusalem in this place; and I will cause them to fall by the sword before their enemies, and by the hands of them that seek their lives: and their carcases will I give to be meat for the fowls of the heaven, and for the beasts of the earth. [8]And I will make this city desolate, and an hissing; every one that passeth thereby shall be astonished and hiss because of all the plagues thereof. [9]And I will cause them to eat the flesh of their sons and the flesh of their daughters, and they shall eat every one the flesh of his friend in the siege and straitness, wherewith their enemies, and they that seek their lives, shall straiten them. [10]Then shalt thou break the bottle in the sight of the men that go with thee, [11]And shalt say unto them, Thus saith the LORD of hosts; Even so will I break this people and this city, as one breaketh a potter's vessel, that cannot be made whole again: and they shall bury them in Tophet, till there be no place to bury. [12]Thus will I do unto this place, saith the LORD, and to the inhabitants thereof, and even make this city as Tophet: [13]And the houses of Jerusalem, and the houses of the kings of Judah, shall be defiled as the place of Tophet, because of all the houses upon whose roofs they have burned incense unto all the host of heaven, and have poured out drink offerings unto other gods. [14]Then came Jeremiah from Tophet, whither the LORD had sent him to prophesy; and he stood in the court of the LORD's house; and said to all the people, [15]Thus saith the LORD of hosts, the God of Israel; Behold, I will bring upon this city and upon all her towns all the evil that I have pronounced against it, because they have hardened their necks, that they might not hear my words."

Jeremiah 32:35-36 "[35]And they built the high places of Baal, which are in the valley of the son of Hinnom, to cause their sons and their daughters to pass through the fire unto Molech; which I commanded them not, neither came it into my mind, that they should do this abomination, to cause Judah to sin. [36]And now therefore thus saith the LORD, the God of Israel, concerning this city, whereof ye say, It shall be delivered into the hand of the king of Babylon by the sword, and by the famine, and by the pestilence."

Micah 5:10-15 "[10]And it shall come to pass in that day, saith the LORD, that I will cut off thy horses out of the midst of thee, and I will destroy thy chariots: [11]And I will cut off the cities of thy land, and throw down all thy strong holds: [12]And I will cut off witchcrafts out of thine hand; and thou shalt have no more soothsayers: [13]Thy graven images also will I cut off, and thy standing images out of the midst of thee; and thou shalt no more worship the work of thine hands. [14]And I will pluck up thy groves out of the midst of thee: so will I destroy thy cities. [15]And I will execute vengeance in anger and fury upon the heathen, such as they have not heard."

Nahum 3:4-7 "[4]Because of the multitude of the whoredoms of the wellfavoured harlot, the mistress of witchcrafts, that selleth nations through her whoredoms, and families through her witchcrafts. [5]Behold, I am against thee, saith the LORD of hosts; and I will discover thy skirts upon thy face, and I will shew the nations thy nakedness, and the kingdoms thy shame. [6]And I will cast abominable filth upon thee, and make thee vile, and will set thee as a gazingstock. [7]And it shall come to pass, that all they that look upon thee shall flee from thee, and say, Nineveh is laid waste: who will bemoan her? whence shall I seek comforters for thee?"

Those That Practice Paganism

Deuteronomy 18:9-12 "[9]When thou art come into the land which the LORD thy God giveth thee, thou shalt not learn to do after the abominations of those nations. [10]There shall not be found among you any one that maketh his son or his daughter to pass through the fire, or that useth divination, or an observer of times, or an enchanter, or a witch, [11]Or a charmer, or a consulter with familiar spirits, or a wizard, or a necromancer. ¹²For all that do these things are an abomination unto the LORD: and because of these abominations the LORD thy God doth drive them out from before thee."

What Should Be Done To Pagans According To The Law

Exodus 22:18 "Thou shalt not suffer a witch to live."

Leviticus 20:27 "A man also or woman that hath a familiar spirit, or that is a wizard, shall surely be put to death: they shall stone them with stones: their blood shall be upon them."

2 Kings 23:24 "Moreover the workers with familiar spirits, and the wizards, and the images, and the idols, and all the abominations that were spied in the land of Judah and in Jerusalem, did Josiah put away, that he might perform the words of the law which were written in the book that Hilkiah the priest found in the house of the LORD."

PARABLES

Jesus Christ Speaking In Parables

Psalm 78:1-2 "¹Give ear, O my people, to my law: incline your ears to the words of my mouth. ²I will open my mouth in a parable: I will utter dark sayings of old."

Matthew 13:34-35 "³⁴All these things spake Jesus unto the multitude in parables; and without a parable spake he not unto them: ³⁵That it might be fulfilled which was spoken by the prophet, saying, I will open my mouth in parables; I will utter things which have been kept secret from the foundation of the world."

Mark 4:33-34 "³³And with many such parables spake he the word unto them, as they were able to hear it. ³⁴But without a parable spake he not unto them: and when they were alone, he expounded all things to his disciples."

Parables In The Mouths Of Fools

Proverbs 26:7 "The legs of the lame are not equal: so is a parable in the mouth of fools."

Proverbs 26:9 "As a thorn goeth up into the hand of a drunkard, so is a parable in the mouth of fools."

Why Jesus Christ Spoke In Parables

Matthew 13:10-17 "¹⁰And the disciples came, and said unto him, Why speakest thou unto them in parables? ¹¹He answered and said unto them, Because it is given unto you to know the mysteries of the kingdom of heaven, but to them it is not given. ¹²For whosoever hath, to him shall be given, and he shall have more abundance: but whosoever hath not, from him shall be taken away even that he hath. ¹³Therefore speak I to them in parables: because they seeing see not; and hearing they hear not, neither do they understand. ¹⁴And in them is fulfilled the prophecy of Esaias, which saith, By hearing ye shall hear, and shall not understand; and seeing ye shall see, and shall not perceive: ¹⁵For this people's heart is waxed gross, and their ears are dull of hearing, and their eyes they have closed; lest at any time they should see with their eyes, and hear with their ears, and should understand with their heart, and should be converted, and I should heal them. ¹⁶But blessed are your eyes, for they see: and your ears, for they hear. ¹⁷For verily I say unto you, That many prophets and righteous men have desired to see those things which ye see, and have not seen them; and to hear those things which ye hear, and have not heard them."

Matthew 13:34-35 "³⁴All these things spake Jesus unto the multitude in parables; and without a parable spake he not unto them: ³⁵That it might be fulfilled which was spoken by the prophet, saying, I will open my mouth in parables; I will utter things which have been kept secret from the foundation of the world."

Mark 4:10-12 "¹⁰And when he was alone, they that were about him with the twelve asked of him the parable. ¹¹And he said unto them, Unto you it is given to know the mystery of the kingdom of God: but unto them that are without, all these things are done in parables: ¹²That seeing they may see, and not perceive; and hearing they may hear, and not understand; lest at any time they should be converted, and their sins should be forgiven them."

Luke 8:9-10 "⁹And his disciples asked him, saying, What might this parable be? ¹⁰And he said, Unto you it is given to know the mysteries of the kingdom of God: but to others in parables; that seeing they might not see, and hearing they might not understand."

PARENTS

Fathers
Proverbs 17:6 "Children's children are the crown of old men; and the glory of children are their fathers."

Honoring Your Parents
Exodus 20:12 "Honour thy father and thy mother: that thy days may be long upon the land which the LORD thy God giveth thee."

Leviticus 19:3 "Ye shall fear every man his mother, and his father, and keep my sabbaths: I am the LORD your God."

Deuteronomy 5:16 "Honour thy father and thy mother, as the LORD thy God hath commanded thee; that thy days may be prolonged, and that it may go well with thee, in the land which the LORD thy God giveth thee."

Proverbs 23:22 "Hearken unto thy father that begat thee, and despise not thy mother when she is old."

Matthew 19:19 "Honour thy father and thy mother: and, Thou shalt love thy neighbour as thyself."

Mark 7:10 "For Moses said, Honour thy father and thy mother; and, Whoso curseth father or mother, let him die the death."

Ephesians 6:2-3 "²Honour thy father and mother; (which is the first commandment with promise;) ³That it may be well with thee, and thou mayest live long on the earth."

The Father Of The Righteous
Proverbs 23:24 "The father of the righteous shall greatly rejoice: and he that begetteth a wise child shall have joy of him."

The Reward For Parenting Strange Children
Hosea 5:7 "They have dealt treacherously against the LORD: for they have begotten strange children: now shall a month devour them with their portions."

The Time When Parents Forsake Their Children
Psalm 27:10 "When my father and my mother forsake me, then the LORD will take me up."

Those That Curse Their Parents
Exodus 21:17 "And he that curseth his father, or his mother, shall surely be put to death."

Leviticus 20:9 "For every one that curseth his father or his mother shall be surely put to death: he hath cursed his father or his mother; his blood shall be upon him."

Proverbs 20:20 "Whoso curseth his father or his mother, his lamp shall be put out in obscure darkness."

Mark 7:10 "For Moses said, Honour thy father and thy mother; and, Whoso curseth father or mother, let him die the death."

Those That Parent Fools
Proverbs 17:21 "He that begetteth a fool doeth it to his sorrow: and the father of a fool hath no joy."

Proverbs 17:25 "A foolish son is a grief to his father, and bitterness to her that bare him."

Proverbs 19:13 "A foolish son is the calamity of his father: and the contentions of a wife are a continual dropping."

Those That Rob Their Parents
Proverbs 28:24 "Whoso robbeth his father or his mother, and saith, It is no transgression; the same is the companion of a destroyer."

Those That Set Light By Their Parents
Deuteronomy 27:16 "Cursed be he that setteth light by his father or his mother. And all the people shall say, Amen."

Those That Smite Their Parents
Exodus 21:15 "And he that smiteth his father, or his mother, shall be surely put to death."

What Fathers Should Do
Ephesians 6:4 "And, ye fathers, provoke not your children to wrath: but bring them up in the nurture and admonition of the Lord."

What Fathers Should Not Do
Ephesians 6:4 "And, ye fathers, provoke not your children to wrath: but bring them up in the nurture and admonition of the Lord."

Colossians 3:21 "Fathers, provoke not your children to anger, lest they be discouraged."

Who Despises Their Mother
Proverbs 15:20 "A wise son maketh a glad father: but a foolish man despiseth his mother."

Who Is The Heaviness Of Their Mother

Proverbs 10:1 "The proverbs of Solomon. A wise son maketh a glad father: but a foolish son is the heaviness of his mother."

Who Makes A Glad Father

Proverbs 10:1 "The proverbs of Solomon. A wise son maketh a glad father: but a foolish son is the heaviness of his mother."

Proverbs 15:20 "A wise son maketh a glad father: but a foolish man despiseth his mother."

PARTAKING

What Cannot Be Partaken Together

1 Corinthians 10:19-21 "19What say I then? that the idol is any thing, or that which is offered in sacrifice to idols is any thing? 20But I say, that the things which the Gentiles sacrifice, they sacrifice to devils, and not to God: and I would not that ye should have fellowship with devils. 21Ye cannot drink the cup of the Lord, and the cup of devils: ye cannot be partakers of the Lord's table, and of the table of devils."

What Not To Partake In

1 Timothy 5:22 "Lay hands suddenly on no man, neither be partaker of other men's sins: keep thyself pure."

Who Not To Partake With

Ephesians 5:5-7 "5For this ye know, that no whoremonger, nor unclean person, nor covetous man, who is an idolater, hath any inheritance in the kingdom of Christ and of God. 6Let no man deceive you with vain words: for because of these things cometh the wrath of God upon the children of disobedience. 7Be not ye therefore partakers with them."

Revelation 18:1-5 "1And after these things I saw another angel come down from heaven, having great power; and the earth was lightened with his glory. 2And he cried mightily with a strong voice, saying, Babylon the great is fallen, is fallen, and is become the habitation of devils, and the hold of every foul spirit, and a cage of every unclean and hateful bird. 3For all nations have drunk of the wine of the wrath of her fornication, and the kings of the earth have committed fornication with her, and the merchants of the earth are waxed rich through the abundance of her delicacies. 4And I heard another voice from heaven, saying, Come out of her, my people, that ye be not partakers of her sins, and that ye receive not of her plagues. 5For her sins have reached unto heaven, and God hath remembered her iniquities."

Who Partakes With Evil

Psalm 50:16-18 "16But unto the wicked God saith, What hast thou to do to declare my statutes, or that thou shouldest take my covenant in thy mouth? 17Seeing thou hatest instruction, and castest my words behind thee. 18When thou sawest a thief, then thou consentedst with him, and hast been partaker with adulterers."

2 John 9-11 "9Whosoever transgresseth, and abideth not in the doctrine of Christ, hath not God. He that abideth in the doctrine of Christ, he hath both the Father and the Son. 10If there come any unto you, and bring not this doctrine, receive him not into your house, neither bid him God speed: 11For he that biddeth him God speed is partaker of his evil deeds."

Who Partakes With The Lord

Romans 11:1-17 "1I say then, Hath God cast away his people? God forbid. For I also am an Israelite, of the seed of Abraham, of the tribe of Benjamin. 2God hath not cast away his people which he foreknew. Wot ye not what the scripture saith of Elias? how he maketh intercession to God against Israel, saying, 3Lord, they have killed thy prophets, and digged down thine altars; and I am left alone, and they seek my life. 4But what saith the answer of God unto him? I have reserved to myself seven thousand men, who have not bowed the knee to the image of Baal. 5Even so then at this present time also there is a remnant according to the election of grace. 6And if by grace, then is it no more of works: otherwise grace is no more grace. But if it be of works, then is it no more grace: otherwise work is no more work. 7What then? Israel hath not obtained that which he seeketh for; but the election hath obtained it, and the rest were blinded 8(According as it is written, God hath given them the spirit of slumber, eyes that they should not see, and ears that they should not hear;) unto this day. 9And David saith, Let their table be made a snare, and a trap, and a stumbling block, and a recompence unto them: 10Let their eyes be darkened, that they may not see, and bow down their back alway. [11]I say then, Have they stumbled that they should fall? God forbid: but rather through their fall salvation is come unto the Gentiles, for to provoke them to jealousy. [12]Now if the fall of them be the riches of the world, and the diminishing of them the riches of the Gentiles; how much more their fulness? [13]For I speak to you Gentiles, inasmuch as I am the apostle of the Gentiles, I magnify mine office: [14]If by any means I may provoke to emulation them which are my flesh, and might save some of them. [15]For if the casting away of them be the reconciling of the world, what shall the receiving of them be, but life from the dead? [16]For if the firstfruit be holy, the lump is also holy: and if the root be holy, so are the branches. [17]And if some of the branches be broken off, and thou, being a wild olive tree, wert graffed in among them, and with them partakest of the root and fatness of the olive tree."

1 Corinthians 10:14-18 "[14]Wherefore, my dearly beloved, flee from idolatry. [15]I speak as to wise men; judge ye what I say. [16]The cup of blessing which we bless, is it not the communion of the blood of Christ? The bread which we break, is it not the communion of the body of Christ? [17]For we being many are one bread, and one body: for we are all partakers of that one bread. [18]Behold Israel after the flesh: are not they which eat of the sacrifices partakers of the altar?"

Ephesians 3:1-6 "[1]For this cause I Paul, the prisoner of Jesus Christ for you Gentiles, [2]If ye have heard of the dispensation of the grace of God which is given me to youward: [3]How that by revelation he made known unto me the mystery; (as I wrote afore in few words, [4]Whereby, when ye read, ye may understand my knowledge in the mystery of Christ) [5]Which in other ages was not made known unto the sons of men, as it is now revealed unto his holy apostles and prophets by the Spirit; [6]That the Gentiles should be fellowheirs, and of the same body, and partakers of his promise in Christ by the gospel."

Colossians 1:9-14 "[9]For this cause we also, since the day we heard it, do not cease to pray for you, and to desire that ye might be filled with the knowledge of his will in all wisdom and spiritual understanding; [10]That ye might walk worthy of the Lord unto all pleasing, being fruitful in every

good work, and increasing in the knowledge of God; [11]Strengthened with all might, according to his glorious power, unto all patience and longsuffering with joyfulness; [12]Giving thanks unto the Father, which hath made us meet to be partakers of the inheritance of the saints in light: [13]Who hath delivered us from the power of darkness, and hath translated us into the kingdom of his dear Son: [14]In whom we have redemption through his blood, even the forgiveness of sins."

1 Timothy 6:1-2 "[1]Let as many servants as are under the yoke count their own masters worthy of all honour, that the name of God and his doctrine be not blasphemed. [2]And they that have believing masters, let them not despise them, because they are brethren; but rather do them service, because they are faithful and beloved, partakers of the benefit. These things teach and exhort."

Hebrews 12:7-10 "[7]If ye endure chastening, God dealeth with you as with sons; for what son is he whom the father chasteneth not? [8]But if ye be without chastisement, whereof all are partakers, then are ye bastards, and not sons. [9]Furthermore we have had fathers of our flesh which corrected us, and we gave them reverence: shall we not much rather be in subjection unto the Father of spirits, and live? [10]For they verily for a few days chastened us after their own pleasure; but he for our profit, that we might be partakers of his holiness."

1 Peter 4:12-14 "[12]Beloved, think it not strange concerning the fiery trial which is to try you, as though some strange thing happened unto you: [13]But rejoice, inasmuch as ye are partakers of Christ's sufferings; that, when his glory shall be revealed, ye may be glad also with exceeding joy. [14]If ye be reproached for the name of Christ, happy are ye; for the spirit of glory and of God resteth upon you: on their part he is evil spoken of, but on your part he is glorified."

2 Peter 1:1-4 "[1]Simon Peter, a servant and an apostle of Jesus Christ, to them that have obtained like precious faith with us through the righteousness of God and our Saviour Jesus Christ: [2]Grace and peace be multiplied unto you through the knowledge of God, and of Jesus our Lord, [3]According as his divine power hath given unto us all things that pertain unto life and godliness, through the knowledge of him that hath called us to glory and virtue: [4]Whereby are given unto us exceeding great and precious promises: that by these ye might be partakers of the divine nature, having escaped the corruption that is in the world through lust."

PATIENCE

Being Patient

Romans 12:10-12 "[10]Be kindly affectioned one to another with brotherly love; in honour preferring one another; [11]Not slothful in business; fervent in spirit; serving the Lord; [12]Rejoicing in hope; patient in tribulation; continuing instant in prayer."

1 Thessalonians 5:14 "Now we exhort you, brethren, warn them that are unruly, comfort the feebleminded, support the weak, be patient toward all men."

Hebrews 10:36-37 "[36]For ye have need of patience, that, after ye have done the will of God, ye might receive the promise. [37]For yet a little while, and he that shall come will come, and will not tarry."

Hebrews 12:1-3 "[1]Wherefore seeing we also are compassed about with so great a cloud of witnesses, let us lay aside every weight, and the sin which doth so easily beset us, and let us run with patience the race that is set before us, [2]Looking unto Jesus the author and finisher of our faith; who for the joy that was set before him endured the cross, despising the shame, and is set down at the right hand of the throne of God. [3]For consider him that endured such contradiction of sinners against himself, lest ye be wearied and faint in your minds."

James 5:7-8 "[7]Be patient therefore, brethren, unto the coming of the Lord. Behold, the husbandman waiteth for the precious fruit of the earth, and hath long patience for it, until he receive the early and latter rain. [8]Be ye also patient; stablish your hearts: for the coming of the Lord draweth nigh."

The Patient In Spirit

Ecclesiastes 7:8 "Better is the end of a thing than the beginning thereof: and the patient in spirit is better than the proud in spirit."

The Reward For Patience

Luke 21:19 "In your patience possess ye your souls."

Those That Are Not Patient

2 Peter 1:1-9 "[1]Simon Peter, a servant and an apostle of Jesus Christ, to them that have obtained like precious faith with us through the righteousness of God and our Saviour Jesus Christ: [2]Grace and peace be multiplied unto you through the knowledge of God, and of Jesus our Lord, [3]According as his divine power hath given unto us all things that pertain unto life and godliness, through the knowledge of him that hath called us to glory and virtue: [4]Whereby are given unto us exceeding great and precious promises: that by these ye might be partakers of the divine nature, having escaped the corruption that is in the world through lust. [5]And beside this, giving all diligence, add to your faith virtue; and to virtue knowledge; [6]And to knowledge temperance; and to temperance patience; and to patience godliness; [7]And to godliness brotherly kindness; and to brotherly kindness charity. [8]For if these things be in you, and abound, they make you that ye shall neither be barren nor unfruitful in the knowledge of our Lord Jesus Christ. [9]But he that lacketh these things is blind, and cannot see afar off, and hath forgotten that he was purged from his old sins."

Those That Are Patient

2 Peter 1:1-11 "[1]Simon Peter, a servant and an apostle of Jesus Christ, to them that have obtained like precious faith with us through the righteousness of God and our Saviour Jesus Christ: [2]Grace and peace be multiplied unto you through the knowledge of God, and of Jesus our Lord, [3]According as his divine power hath given unto us all things that pertain unto life and godliness, through the knowledge of him that hath called us to glory and virtue: [4]Whereby are given unto us exceeding great and precious promises: that by these ye might be partakers of the divine nature, having escaped the corruption that is in the world through lust. [5]And beside this, giving all diligence, add to your faith virtue; and to virtue knowledge; [6]And to knowledge temperance; and to temperance patience; and to patience godliness; [7]And to godliness brotherly kindness; and to brotherly kindness charity. [8]For if these things be in you, and abound, they make you that ye shall neither be barren nor unfruitful in the knowledge of our Lord Jesus Christ. [9]But he that lacketh these things is blind, and cannot see afar off, and hath forgotten that he was purged from his old sins. [10]Wherefore the rather, brethren, give diligence to make your calling and election sure: for if ye do these things, ye shall never fall: [11]For so an entrance shall be ministered unto you abundantly into the everlasting kingdom of our Lord and Saviour Jesus Christ."

What Teaches Patience
Romans 15:1-4 "[1]We then that are strong ought to bear the infirmities of the weak, and not to please ourselves. [2]Let every one of us please his neighbour for his good to edification. [3]For even Christ pleased not himself; but, as it is written, The reproaches of them that reproached thee fell on me. [4]For whatsoever things were written aforetime were written for our learning, that we through patience and comfort of the scriptures might have hope."

What Works Patience
Romans 5:3-4 "[3]And not only so, but we glory in tribulations also: knowing that tribulation worketh patience; [4]And patience, experience; and experience, hope."

James 1:2-3 "[2]My brethren, count it all joy when ye fall into divers temptations; [3]Knowing this, that the trying of your faith worketh patience."

PEACE

A Dry Morsel With Quietness
Proverbs 17:1 "Better is a dry morsel, and quietness therewith, than an house full of sacrifices with strife."

Jesus Christ Giving Peace
John 14:23-27 "[23]Jesus answered and said unto him, If a man love me, he will keep my words: and my Father will love him, and we will come unto him, and make our abode with him. [24]He that loveth me not keepeth not my sayings: and the word which ye hear is not mine, but the Father's which sent me. [25]These things have I spoken unto you, being yet present with you. [26]But the Comforter, which is the Holy Ghost, whom the Father will send in my name, he shall teach you all things, and bring all things to your remembrance, whatsoever I have said unto you. [27]Peace I leave with you, my peace I give unto you: not as the world giveth, give I unto you. Let not your heart be troubled, neither let it be afraid."

John 16:31-33 "[31]Jesus answered them, Do ye now believe? [32]Behold, the hour cometh, yea, is now come, that ye shall be scattered, every man to his own, and shall leave me alone: and yet I am not alone, because the Father is with me. [33]These things I have spoken unto you, that in me ye might have peace. In the world ye shall have tribulation: but be of good cheer; I have overcome the world."

Letting The Peace Of God Rule In Your Heart
Colossians 3:15 "And let the peace of God rule in your hearts, to the which also ye are called in one body; and be ye thankful."

Living Peaceably
Mark 9:50 "Salt is good: but if the salt have lost his saltness, wherewith will ye season it? Have salt in yourselves, and have peace one with another."

Romans 12:17-18 "[17]Recompense to no man evil for evil. Provide things honest in the sight of all men. [18]If it be possible, as much as lieth in you, live peaceably with all men."

2 Corinthians 13:11 "Finally, brethren, farewell. Be perfect, be of good comfort, be of one mind, live in peace; and the God of love and peace shall be with you."

Peacemakers
Matthew 5:9 "Blessed are the peacemakers: for they shall be called the children of God."

James 3:18 "And the fruit of righteousness is sown in peace of them that make peace."

Seeking Peace
Psalm 34:14 "Depart from evil, and do good; seek peace, and pursue it."

Romans 14:19 "Let us therefore follow after the things which make for peace, and things wherewith one may edify another."

2 Timothy 2:22 "Flee also youthful lusts: but follow righteousness, faith, charity, peace, with them that call on the Lord out of a pure heart."

Hebrews 12:14 "Follow peace with all men, and holiness, without which no man shall see the Lord."

1 Peter 3:11 "Let him eschew evil, and do good; let him seek peace, and ensue it."

The Counselors Of Peace
Proverbs 12:20 "Deceit is in the heart of them that imagine evil: but to the counsellers of peace is joy."

The Lord Being Peace
Isaiah 9:6 "For unto us a child is born, unto us a son is given: and the government shall be upon his shoulder: and his name shall be called Wonderful, Counseller, The mighty God, The everlasting Father, The Prince of Peace."

Micah 5:2-5 "²But thou, Bethlehem Ephratah, though thou be little among the thousands of Judah, yet out of thee shall he come forth unto me that is to be ruler in Israel; whose goings forth have been from of old, from everlasting. ³Therefore will he give them up, until the time that she which travaileth hath brought forth: then the remnant of his brethren shall return unto the children of Israel. ⁴And he shall stand and feed in the strength of the LORD, in the majesty of the name of the LORD his God; and they shall abide: for now shall he be great unto the ends of the earth. ⁵And this man shall be the peace, when the Assyrian shall come into our land: and when he shall tread in our palaces, then shall we raise against him seven shepherds, and eight principal men."

2 Corinthians 13:11 "Finally, brethren, farewell. Be perfect, be of good comfort, be of one mind, live in peace; and the God of love and peace shall be with you."

Ephesians 2:13-14 "¹³But now in Christ Jesus ye who sometimes were far off are made nigh by the blood of Christ. ¹⁴For he is our peace, who hath made both one, and hath broken down the middle wall of partition between us."

The Lord Making Peace
Isaiah 45:7 "I form the light, and create darkness: I make peace, and create evil: I the LORD do all these things."

The Peace Of God
Philippians 4:7 "And the peace of God, which passeth all understanding, shall keep your hearts and minds through Christ Jesus."

The Time When People Shall Say Peace And Safety
1 Thessalonians 5:3 "For when they shall say, Peace and safety; then sudden destruction cometh upon them, as travail upon a woman with child; and they shall not escape."

What Is Peace
Romans 8:6 "For to be carnally minded is death; but to be spiritually minded is life and peace."

James 3:17 "But the wisdom that is from above is first pure, then peaceable, gentle, and easy to be intreated, full of mercy and good fruits, without partiality, and without hypocrisy."

Who Shall Have Peace
Psalm 29:11 "The LORD will give strength unto his people; the LORD will bless his people with peace."

Psalm 37:11 "But the meek shall inherit the earth; and shall delight themselves in the abundance of peace."

Psalm 37:37 "Mark the perfect man, and behold the upright: for the end of that man is peace."

Psalm 119:165 "Great peace have they which love thy law: and nothing shall offend them."

Proverbs 16:7 "When a man's ways please the LORD, he maketh even his enemies to be at peace with him."

Isaiah 48:17-18 "¹⁷Thus saith the LORD, thy Redeemer, the Holy One of Israel; I am the LORD thy God which teacheth thee to profit, which leadeth thee by the way that thou shouldest go. ¹⁸O that thou hadst hearkened to my commandments! then had thy peace been as a river, and thy righteousness as the waves of the sea."

Isaiah 54:5-13 "⁵For thy Maker is thine husband; the LORD of hosts is his name; and thy Redeemer the Holy One of Israel; The God of the whole earth shall he be called. ⁶For the LORD hath called thee as a woman forsaken and grieved in spirit, and a wife of youth, when thou wast refused, saith thy God. ⁷For a small moment have I forsaken thee; but with great mercies will I gather thee. ⁸In a little wrath I hid my face from thee for a moment; but with everlasting kindness will I have mercy on thee, saith the LORD thy Redeemer. ⁹For this is as the waters of Noah unto me: for as I have sworn that the waters of Noah should no more go over the earth; so have I sworn that I would not be wroth with thee, nor rebuke thee. ¹⁰For the mountains shall depart, and the hills be removed; but my kindness shall not depart from thee, neither shall the covenant of my peace be removed, saith the LORD that hath mercy on thee. ¹¹O thou afflicted, tossed with tempest, and not comforted, behold, I will lay thy stones with fair colours, and lay thy foundations with sapphires. ¹²And I will make thy windows of agates, and thy gates of carbuncles, and all thy borders of pleasant stones. ¹³And all thy children shall be taught of the LORD; and great shall be the peace of thy children."

Isaiah 57:1-2 "¹The righteous perisheth, and no man layeth it to heart: and merciful men are taken away, none considering that the righteous is taken away from the evil to come. ²He shall enter into peace: they shall rest in their beds, each one walking in his uprightness."

Romans 2:10 "But glory, honour, and peace, to every man that worketh good, to the Jew first, and also to the Gentile."

Who Shall Not Have Peace

Isaiah 48:22 "There is no peace, saith the LORD, unto the wicked."

Isaiah 57:20-21 "²⁰But the wicked are like the troubled sea, when it cannot rest, whose waters cast up mire and dirt. ²¹There is no peace, saith my God, to the wicked."

Isaiah 59:1-8 "¹Behold, the LORD's hand is not shortened, that it cannot save; neither his ear heavy, that it cannot hear: ²But your iniquities have separated between you and your God, and your sins have hid his face from you, that he will not hear. ³For your hands are defiled with blood, and your fingers with iniquity; your lips have spoken lies, your tongue hath muttered perverseness. ⁴None calleth for justice, nor any pleadeth for truth: they trust in vanity, and speak lies; they conceive mischief, and bring forth iniquity. ⁵They hatch cockatrice' eggs, and weave the spider's web: he that eateth of their eggs dieth, and that which is crushed breaketh out into a viper. ⁶Their webs shall not become garments, neither shall they cover themselves with their works: their works are works of iniquity, and the act of violence is in their hands. ⁷Their feet run to evil, and they make hast to shed innocent blood: their thoughts are thoughts of iniquity; wasting and destruction are in their

paths. ⁸The way of peace they know not; and there is no judgment in their goings: they have made them crooked paths: whosoever goeth therein shall not know peace."

PERISHING

How The Old World Perished

Genesis 6:17 "And, behold, I, even I, do bring a flood of waters upon the earth, to destroy all flesh, wherein is the breath of life, from under heaven; and every thing that is in the earth shall die."

Genesis 7:4 "For yet seven days, and I will cause it to rain upon the earth forty days and forty nights; and every living substance that I have made will I destroy from off the face of the earth."

Genesis 7:10-12 "¹⁰And it came to pass after seven days, that the waters of the flood were upon the earth. ¹¹In the six hundredth year of Noah's life, in the second month, the seventeenth day of the month, the same day were all the fountains of the great deep broken up, and the windows of heaven were opened. ¹²And the rain was upon the earth forty days and forty nights."

Genesis 7:21-24 "²¹And all flesh died that moved upon the earth, both of fowl, and of cattle, and of beast, and of every creeping thing that creepeth upon the earth, and every man: ²²All in whose nostrils was the breath of life, of all that was in the dry land, died. ²³And every living substance was destroyed which was upon the face of the ground, both man, and cattle, and the creeping things, and the fowl of the heaven; and they were destroyed from the earth: and Noah only remained alive, and they that were with him in the ark. ²⁴And the waters prevailed upon the earth an hundred and fifty days."

2 Peter 2:4-5 "⁴For if God spared not the angels that sinned, but cast them down to hell, and delivered them into chains of darkness, to be reserved unto judgment; ⁵And spared not the old world, but saved Noah the eighth person, a preacher of righteousness, bringing in the flood upon the world of the ungodly."

2 Peter 3:3-6 "³Knowing this first, that there shall come in the last days scoffers, walking after their own lusts, ⁴And saying, Where is the promise of his coming? for since the fathers fell asleep, all things continue as they were from the beginning of the creation. ⁵For this they willingly are ignorant of, that by the word of God the heavens were of old, and the earth standing out of the water and in the water: ⁶Whereby the world that then was, being overflowed with water, perished."

The Time When The Wicked Perish

Proverbs 28:28 "When the wicked rise, men hide themselves: but when they perish, the righteous increase."

Those That Perish

1 Corinthians 1:18-25 "¹⁸For the preaching of the cross is to them that perish foolishness; but unto us which are saved it is the power of God. ¹⁹For it is written, I will destroy the wisdom of the wise, and will bring to nothing the understanding of the prudent. ²⁰Where is the wise? where is the scribe? where is the disputer of this world? hath not God made foolish the wisdom of this world? ²¹For after that in the wisdom of God the world by wisdom knew not God, it pleased God by the foolishness of preaching to save them that believe. ²²For the Jews require a sign, and the Greeks seek after wisdom: ²³But we preach Christ crucified, unto the Jews a stumblingblock, and unto the Greeks foolishness; ²⁴But unto them which are called, both Jews and Greeks, Christ the power of God, and the wisdom of God. ²⁵Because the foolishness of God is wiser than men; and the weakness of God is stronger than men."

What Shall Perish

Job 8:11-13 "¹¹Can the rush grow up without mire? can the flag grow without water? ¹²Whilst it is yet in his greenness, and not cut down, it withereth before any other herb. ¹³So are the paths of all that forget God; and the hypocrite's hope shall perish."

Job 18:5-17 "⁵Yea, the light of the wicked shall be put out, and the spark of his fire shall not shine. ⁶The light shall be dark in his tabernacle, and his candle shall be put out with him. ⁷The steps of his strength shall be straitened, and his own counsel shall cast him down. ⁸For he is cast into a net by his own feet, and he walketh upon a snare. ⁹The gin shall take him by the heel, and the robber shall prevail against him. ¹⁰The snare is laid for him in the ground, and a trap for him in the way. ¹¹Terrors shall make him afraid on every side, and shall drive him to his feet. ¹²His strength shall be hungerbitten, and destruction shall be ready at his side. ¹³It shall devour the strength of his skin: even the firstborn of death shall devour his strength. ¹⁴His confidence shall be rooted out of his tabernacle, and it shall bring him to the king of terrors. ¹⁵It shall dwell in his tabernacle, because it is none of his: brimstone shall be scattered upon his habitation. ¹⁶His roots shall be dried up beneath, and above shall his branch be cut off. ¹⁷His remembrance shall perish from the earth, and he shall have no name in the street."

Job 34:15 "All flesh shall perish together, and man shall turn again unto dust."

Psalm 1:6 "For the LORD knoweth the way of the righteous: but the way of the ungodly shall perish."

Psalm 112:10 "The wicked shall see it, and be grieved; he shall gnash with his teeth, and melt away: the desire of the wicked shall perish."

Proverbs 10:28 "The hope of the righteous shall be gladness: but the expectation of the wicked shall perish."

Proverbs 11:7 "When a wicked man dieth, his expectation shall perish: and the hope of unjust men perisheth."

Ecclesiastes 9:5-6 "⁵For the living know that they shall die: but the dead know not any thing, neither have they any more a reward; for the memory of them is forgotten. ⁶Also their love, and their hatred, and their envy, is now perished; neither have they any more a portion for ever in any thing that is done under the sun."

Isaiah 29:13-14 "¹³Wherefore the Lord said, Forasmuch as this people draw near me with their mouth, and with their lips do honour me, but have removed their heart far from me, and their fear toward me is taught by the precept of men: ¹⁴Therefore, behold, I will proceed to do a marvellous work among this people, even a marvellous work and a wonder: for the wisdom of their wise men shall perish, and the understanding of their prudent men shall be hid."

Jeremiah 10:11 "Thus shall ye say unto them, The gods that have not made the heavens and the earth, even they shall perish from the earth, and from under these heavens."

Jeremiah 10:14-15 "¹⁴Every man is brutish in his knowledge: every founder is confounded by the graven image: for his molten image is falsehood, and there is no breath in them. ¹⁵They are vanity, and the work of errors: in the time of their visitation they shall perish."

Jeremiah 51:17-18 "¹⁷Every man is brutish by his knowledge; every founder is confounded by the graven image: for his molten image is falsehood, and there is no breath in them. ¹⁸They are vanity, the work of errors: in the time of their visitation they shall perish."

Acts 8:20 "But Peter said unto him, Thy money perish with thee, because thou hast thought that the gift of God may be purchased with money."

2 Corinthians 4:16 "For which cause we faint not; but though our outward man perish, yet the inward man is renewed day by day."

Where People Perish
Proverbs 29:18 "Where there is no vision, the people perish: but he that keepeth the law, happy is he."

Who Shall Not Perish
Proverbs 12:7 "The wicked are overthrown, and are not: but the house of the righteous shall stand."

Luke 21:5-18 "⁵And as some spake of the temple, how it was adorned with goodly stones and gifts, he said, ⁶As for these things which ye behold, the days will come, in the which there shall not be left one stone upon another, that shall not be thrown down. ⁷And they asked him, saying, Master, but when shall these things be? and what sign will there be when these things shall come to pass? ⁸And he said, Take heed that ye be not deceived: for many shall come in my name, saying, I am Christ; and the time draweth near: go ye not therefore after them. ⁹But when ye shall hear of wars and commotions, be not terrified: for these things must first come to pass; but the end is not by and by. ¹⁰Then said he unto them, Nation shall rise against nation, and kingdom against kingdom: ¹¹And great earthquakes shall be in divers places, and famines, and pestilences; and fearful sights and great signs shall there be from heaven. ¹²But

before all these, they shall lay their hands on you, and persecute you, delivering you up to the synagogues, and into prisons, being brought before kings and rulers for my name's sake. ¹³And it shall turn to you for a testimony. ¹⁴Settle it therefore in your hearts, not to meditate before what ye shall answer: ¹⁵For I will give you a mouth and wisdom, which all your adversaries shall not be able to gainsay nor resist. ¹⁶And ye shall be betrayed both by parents, and brethren, and kinsfolks, and friends; and some of you shall they cause to be put to death. ¹⁷And ye shall be hated of all men for my name's sake. ¹⁸But there shall not an hair of your head perish."

John 3:14-16 "¹⁴And as Moses lifted up the serpent in the wilderness, even so must the Son of man be lifted up: ¹⁵That whosoever believeth in him should not perish, but have eternal life. ¹⁶For God so loved the world, that he gave his only begotten Son, that whosoever believeth in him should not perish, but have everlasting life."

John 10:25-28 "²⁵Jesus answered them, I told you, and ye believed not: the works that I do in my Father's name, they bear witness of me. ²⁶But ye believe not, because ye are not of my sheep, as I said unto you. ²⁷My sheep hear my voice, and I know them, and they follow me: ²⁸And I give unto them eternal life; and they shall never perish, neither shall any man pluck them out of my hand."

Who Shall Perish
Leviticus 26:13-39 "¹³I am the LORD your God, which brought you forth out of the land of Egypt, that ye should not be their bondmen; and I have broken the bands of your yoke, and made you go upright. ¹⁴But if ye will not hearken unto me, and will not do all these commandments; ¹⁵And if ye shall despise my statutes, or if your soul abhor my judgments, so that ye will not do all my commandments, but that ye break my covenant: ¹⁶I also will do this unto you; I will even appoint over you terror, consumption, and the burning ague, that shall consume the eyes, and cause sorrow of heart: and ye shall sow your seed in vain, for your enemies shall eat it. ¹⁷And I will set my face against you, and ye shall be slain before your enemies: they that hate you shall reign over you; and ye shall flee when none pursueth you. ¹⁸And if ye

will not yet for all this hearken unto me, then I will punish you seven times more for your sins. [19]And I will break the pride of your power; and I will make your heaven as iron, and your earth as brass: [20]And your strength shall be spent in vain: for your land shall not yield her increase, neither shall the trees of the land yield their fruits. [21]And if ye walk contrary unto me, and will not hearken unto me; I will bring seven times more plagues upon you according to your sins. [22]I will also send wild beasts among you, which shall rob you of your children, and destroy your cattle, and make you few in number; and your highways shall be desolate. [23]And if ye will not be reformed by me by these things, but will walk contrary unto me; [24]Then will I also walk contrary unto you, and will punish you yet seven times for your sins. [25]And I will bring a sword upon you, that shall avenge the quarrel of my covenant: and when ye are gathered together within your cities, I will send the pestilence among you; and ye shall be delivered into the hand of the enemy. [26]And when I have broken the staff of your bread, ten women shall bake your bread in one oven, and they shall deliver you your bread again by weight: and ye shall eat, and not be satisfied. [27]And if ye will not for all this hearken unto me, but walk contrary unto me; [28]Then I will walk contrary unto you also in fury; and I, even I, will chastise you seven times for your sins. [29]And ye shall eat the flesh of your sons, and the flesh of your daughters shall ye eat. [30]And I will destroy your high places, and cut down your images, and cast your carcases upon the carcases of your idols, and my soul shall abhor you. [31]And I will make your cities waste, and bring your sanctuaries unto desolation, and I will not smell the savour of your sweet odours. [32]And I will bring the land into desolation: and your enemies which dwell therein shall be astonished at it. [33]And I will scatter you among the heathen, and will draw out a sword after you: and your land shall be desolate, and your cities waste. [34]Then shall the land enjoy her sabbaths, as long as it lieth desolate, and ye be in your enemies' land; even then shall the land rest, and enjoy her sabbaths. [35]As long as it lieth desolate it shall rest; because it did not rest in your sabbaths, when ye dwelt upon it. [36]And upon them that are left alive of you I will send a faintness into their hearts in the lands of their enemies; and the sound of a shaken leaf shall

chase them; and they shall flee, as fleeing from a sword; and they shall fall when none pursueth. [37]And they shall fall one upon another, as it were before a sword, when none pursueth: and ye shall have no power to stand before your enemies. [38]And ye shall perish among the heathen, and the land of your enemies shall eat you up. [39]And they that are left of you shall pine away in their iniquity in your enemies' lands; and also in the iniquities of their fathers shall they pine away with them."

Deuteronomy 4:23-26 "[23]Take heed unto yourselves, lest ye forget the covenant of the LORD your God, which he made with you, and make you a graven image, or the likeness of any thing, which the LORD thy God hath forbidden thee. [24]For the LORD thy God is a consuming fire, even a jealous God. [25]When thou shalt beget children, and children's children, and ye shall have remained long in the land, and shall corrupt yourselves, and make a graven image, or the likeness of any thing, and shall do evil in the sight of the LORD thy God, to provoke him to anger: [26]I call heaven and earth to witness against you this day, that ye shall soon utterly perish from off the land whereunto ye go over Jordan to possess it; ye shall not prolong your days upon it, but shall utterly be destroyed."

Deuteronomy 8:19-20 "[19]And it shall be, if thou do at all forget the LORD thy God, and walk after other gods, and serve them, and worship them, I testify against you this day that ye shall surely perish. [20]As the nations which the LORD destroyeth before your face, so shall ye perish; because ye would not be obedient unto the voice of the LORD your God."

Deuteronomy 11:16-18 "[16]Take heed to yourselves, that your heart be not deceived, and ye turn aside, and serve other gods, and worship them; [17]And then the LORD's wrath be kindled against you, and he shut up the heaven, that there be no rain, and that the land yield not her fruit; and lest ye perish quickly from off the good land which the LORD giveth you. [18]Therefore shall ye lay up these my words in your heart and in your soul, and bind them for a sign upon your hand, that they may be as frontlets between your eyes."

Deuteronomy 28:15-20 "[15]But it shall come to pass, if thou wilt not hearken unto the voice of the LORD thy God, to observe to do all his commandments and his statutes which I command thee this day; that all these curses shall come upon thee, and overtake thee: ¹⁶Cursed shalt thou be in the city, and cursed shalt thou be in the field. ¹⁷Cursed shall be thy basket and thy store. ¹⁸Cursed shall be the fruit of thy body, and the fruit of thy land, the increase of thy kine, and the flocks of thy sheep. ¹⁹Cursed shalt thou be when thou comest in, and cursed shalt thou be when thou goest out. ²⁰The LORD shall send upon thee cursing, vexation, and rebuke, in all that thou settest thine hand unto for to do, until thou be destroyed, and until thou perish quickly; because of the wickedness of thy doings, whereby thou hast forsaken me."

Deuteronomy 30:15-18 "¹⁵See, I have set before thee this day life and good, and death and evil; ¹⁶In that I command thee this day to love the LORD thy God, to walk in his ways, and to keep his commandments and his statutes and his judgments, that thou mayest live and multiply: and the LORD thy God shall bless thee in the land whither thou goest to possess it. ¹⁷But if thine heart turn away, so that thou wilt not hear, but shalt be drawn away, and worship other gods, and serve them; ¹⁸I denounce unto you this day, that ye shall surely perish, and that ye shall not prolong your days upon the land, whither thou passest over Jordan to go to possess it."

Joshua 23:15-16 "¹⁵Therefore it shall come to pass, that as all good things are come upon you, which the LORD your God promised you; so shall the LORD bring upon you all evil things, until he have destroyed you from off this good land which the LORD your God hath given you. ¹⁶When ye have transgressed the covenant of the LORD your God, which he commanded you, and have gone and served other gods, and bowed yourselves to them; then shall the anger of the LORD be kindled against you, and ye shall perish quickly from off the good land which he hath given unto you."

Job 4:17-21 "¹⁷Shall mortal man be more just than God? shall a man be more pure than his maker? ¹⁸Behold, he put no trust in his servants; and his angels he charged with folly: ¹⁹How much less in them that dwell in houses of clay, whose foundation is in the dust, which are crushed before the moth? ²⁰They are destroyed from morning to evening: they perish for ever without any regarding it. ²¹Doth not their excellency which is in them go away? they die, even without wisdom."

Job 20:1-7 "¹Then answered Zophar the Naamathite, and said, ²Therefore do my thoughts cause me to answer, and for this I make haste. ³I have heard the check of my reproach, and the spirit of my understanding causeth me to answer. ⁴Knowest thou not this of old, since man was placed upon earth, ⁵That the triumphing of the wicked is short, and the joy of the hypocrite but for a moment? ⁶Though his excellency mount up to the heavens, and his head reach unto the clouds; ⁷Yet he shall perish for ever like his own dung: they which have seen him shall say, Where is he?"

Job 36:5-12 "⁵Behold, God is mighty, and despiseth not any: he is mighty in strength and wisdom. ⁶He preserveth not the life of the wicked: but giveth right to the poor. ⁷He withdraweth not his eyes from the righteous: but with kings are they on the throne; yea, he doth establish them for ever, and they are exalted. ⁸And if they be bound in fetters, and be holden in cords of affliction; ⁹Then he sheweth them their work, and their transgressions that they have exceeded. ¹⁰He openeth also their ear to discipline, and commandeth that they return from iniquity. ¹¹If they obey and serve him, they shall spend their days in prosperity, and their years in pleasures. ¹²But if they obey not, they shall perish by the sword, and they shall die without knowledge."

Psalm 10:16 "The LORD is King for ever and ever: the heathen are perished out of his land."

Psalm 37:1-2 "¹Fret not thyself because of evildoers, neither be thou envious against the workers of iniquity. ²For they shall soon be cut down like the grass, and wither as the green herb."

Psalm 37:20 "But the wicked shall perish, and the enemies of the LORD shall be as the fat of lambs: they shall consume; into smoke shall they consume away."

Psalm 49:12 "Nevertheless man being in honour abideth not: he is like the beasts that perish."

Psalm 49:20 "Man that is in honour, and understandeth not, is like the beasts that perish."

Psalm 73:26-27 "²⁶My flesh and my heart faileth: but God is the strength of my heart, and my portion for ever. ²⁷For, lo, they that are far from thee shall perish: thou hast destroyed all them that go a whoring from thee."

Psalm 92:9 "For, lo, thine enemies, O LORD, for, lo, thine enemies shall perish; all the workers of iniquity shall be scattered."

Proverbs 12:7 "The wicked are overthrown, and are not: but the house of the righteous shall stand."

Proverbs 14:11 "The house of the wicked shall be overthrown: but the tabernacle of the upright shall flourish."

Proverbs 19:5 "A false witness shall not be unpunished, and he that speaketh lies shall not escape."

Proverbs 19:9 "A false witness shall not be unpunished, and he that speaketh lies shall perish."

Proverbs 21:28 "A false witness shall perish: but the man that heareth speaketh constantly."

Amos 8:14 "They that swear by the sin of Samaria, and say, Thy god, O Dan, liveth; and, The manner of Beer-sheba liveth; even they shall fall, and never rise up again."

Matthew 26:52 "Then said Jesus unto him, Put up again thy sword into his place: for all they that take the sword shall perish with the sword."

Luke 13:1-5 "[1]There were present at that season some that told him of the Galilaeans, whose blood Pilate had mingled with their sacrifices. [2]And Jesus answering said unto them, Suppose ye that these Galilaeans were sinners above all the Galilaeans, because they suffered such things? [3]I tell you, Nay: but, except ye repent, ye shall all likewise perish. [4]Or those eighteen, upon whom the tower in Siloam fell, and slew them, think ye that they were sinners above all men that dwelt in Jerusalem? [5]I tell you, Nay: but, except ye repent, ye shall all likewise perish."

Romans 2:12-13 "[12]For as many as have sinned without law shall also perish without law: and as many as have sinned in the law shall be judged by the law; [13](For not the hearers of the law are just before God, but the doers of the law shall be justified."

2 Peter 2:1-12 "[1]But there were false prophets also among the people, even as there shall be false teachers among you, who privily shall bring in damnable heresies, even denying the Lord that bought them, and bring upon themselves swift destruction. [2]And many shall follow their pernicious ways; by reason of whom the way of truth shall be evil spoken of. [3]And through covetousness shall they with feigned words make merchandise of you: whose judgment now of a long time lingereth not, and their damnation slumbereth not. [4]For if God spared not the angels that sinned, but cast them down to hell, and delivered them into chains of darkness, to be reserved unto judgment; [5]And spared not the old world, but saved Noah the eighth person, a preacher of righteousness, bringing in the flood upon the world of the ungodly; [6]And turning the cities of Sodom and Gomorrha into ashes condemned them with an overthrow, making them an ensample unto those that after should live ungodly; [7]And delivered just Lot, vexed with the filthy conversation of the wicked: [8](For that righteous man dwelling among them, in seeing and hearing, vexed his righteous soul from day to day with their unlawful deeds;) [9]The Lord knoweth how to deliver the godly out of temptations, and to reserve the unjust unto the day of judgment to be punished: [10]But chiefly them that walk after the flesh in the lust of uncleanness, and despise government. Presumptuous are they, selfwilled, they are not afraid to speak evil of dignities. [11]Whereas angels, which are greater in power and might, bring not railing accusation against them before the Lord. [12]But these, as natural brute beasts, made to be taken and destroyed, speak evil of the things that they understand not; and shall utterly perish in their own corruption."

PERSECUTION

The World Persecuting Jesus Christ

John 5:15-18 "[15]The man departed, and told the Jews that it was Jesus, which had made him whole. [16]And therefore did the Jews persecute Jesus, and sought to slay him, because he had done these things on the sabbath day. [17]But Jesus answered them, My Father worketh hitherto, and I work. [18]Therefore the Jews sought the more to kill him, because he not only had broken the sabbath, but said also that God was his Father, making himself equal with God."

John 15:1-25 "[1]I am the true vine, and my Father is the husbandman. [2]Every branch in me that beareth not fruit he taketh away: and every branch that beareth fruit, he purgeth it, that it may bring forth more fruit. [3]Now ye are clean through the word which I have spoken unto you. [4]Abide in me, and I in you. As the branch cannot bear fruit of itself, except it abide in the vine; no more can ye, except ye abide in me. [5]I am the vine, ye are the branches: He that abideth in me, and I in him, the same bringeth forth much fruit: for without me ye can do nothing. [6]If a man abide not in me, he is cast forth as a branch, and is withered; and men gather them, and cast them into the fire, and they are burned. [7]If ye abide in me, and my words abide in you, ye shall ask what ye will, and it shall be done unto you. [8]Herein is my Father glorified, that ye bear much fruit; so shall ye be my disciples. [9]As the Father hath loved me, so have I loved you: continue ye in my love. [10]If ye keep my commandments, ye shall abide in my love; even as I have kept my Father's commandments, and abide in his love. [11]These things have I spoken unto you, that my joy might remain in you, and that your joy might be full. [12]This is my commandment, That ye love one another, as I have loved you. [13]Greater love hath no man than this, that a man lay down his life for his friends. [14]Ye are my friends, if ye do whatsoever I command you. [15]Henceforth I call you not servants; for the servant knoweth not what his lord doeth: but I have called you friends; for all things that I have heard of my Father I have made known unto you. [16]Ye have not chosen me, but I have chosen you, and ordained you, that ye should go and bring forth fruit, and that your fruit should remain: that whatsoever ye shall ask of the Father in my name, he may give it you. [17]These things I command you, that ye love one another. [18]If the world hate you, ye know that it hated me before it hated you. [19]If ye were of the world, the world would love his own: but because ye are not of the world, but I have chosen you out of the world, therefore the world hateth you. [20]Remember the word that I said unto you, The servant is not greater than his lord. If they have persecuted me, they will also persecute you; if they have kept my saying, they will keep yours also. [21]But all these things will they do unto you for my name's sake, because they know not him that sent me. [22]If I had not come and spoken unto them, they had not had sin: but now they have no cloke for their sin. [23]He that hateth me hateth my Father also. [24]If I had not done among them the works which none

other man did, they had not had sin: but now have they both seen and hated both me and my Father. [25]But this cometh to pass, that the word might be fulfilled that is written in their law, They hated me without a cause."

Acts 4:24-27 "[24]And when they heard that, they lifted up their voice to God with one accord, and said, Lord, thou art God, which hast made heaven, and earth, and the sea, and all that in them is: [25]Who by the mouth of thy servant David hast said, Why did the heathen rage, and the people imagine vain things? [26]The kings of the earth stood up, and the rulers were gathered together against the Lord, and against his Christ. [27]For of a truth against thy holy child Jesus, whom thou hast anointed, both Herod, and Pontius Pilate, with the Gentiles, and the people of Israel, were gathered together."

Acts 9:1-5 "[1]And Saul, yet breathing out threatenings and slaughter against the disciples of the Lord, went unto the high priest, [2]And desired of him letters to Damascus to the synagogues, that if he found any of this way, whether they were men or women, he might bring them bound unto Jerusalem. [3]And as he journeyed, he came near Damascus: and suddenly there shined round about him a light from heaven: [4]And he fell to the earth, and heard a voice saying unto him, Saul, Saul, why persecutest thou me? [5]And he said, Who art thou, Lord? And the Lord said, I am Jesus whom thou persecutest: it is hard for thee to kick against the pricks."

Acts 22:6-8 "[6]And it came to pass, that, as I made my journey, and was come nigh unto Damascus about noon, suddenly there shone from heaven a great light round about me. [7]And I fell unto the ground, and heard a voice saying unto me, Saul, Saul, why persecutest thou me? [8]And I answered, Who art thou, Lord? And he said unto me, I am Jesus of Nazareth, whom thou persecutest."

Those That Are Persecuted For The Sake Of Christ

Matthew 5:10-12 "[10]Blessed are they which are persecuted for righteousness' sake: for theirs is the kingdom of heaven. [11]Blessed are ye, when men shall revile you, and persecute you, and shall say all manner of evil against you falsely, for my sake. [12]Rejoice, and be exceeding glad: for great is your reward in heaven: for so persecuted they the prophets which were before you."

Luke 6:22-23 "²²Blessed are ye, when men shall hate you, and when they shall separate you from their company, and shall reproach you, and cast out your name as evil, for the Son of man's sake. ²³Rejoice ye in that day, and leap for joy: for, behold, your reward is great in heaven: for in the like manner did their fathers unto the prophets."

Those That Persecute Israel

Deuteronomy 30:1-7 "¹And it shall come to pass, when all these things are come upon thee, the blessing and the curse, which I have set before thee, and thou shalt call them to mind among all the nations, whither the LORD thy God hath driven thee, ²And shalt return unto the LORD thy God, and shalt obey his voice according to all that I command thee this day, thou and thy children, with all thine heart, and with all thy soul; ³That then the LORD thy God will turn thy captivity, and have compassion upon thee, and will return and gather thee from all the nations, whither the LORD thy God hath scattered thee. ⁴If any of thine be driven out unto the outmost parts of heaven, from thence will the LORD thy God gather thee, and from thence will he fetch thee: ⁵And the LORD thy God will bring thee into the land which thy fathers possessed, and thou shalt possess it; and he will do thee good, and multiply thee above thy fathers. ⁶And the LORD thy God will circumcise thine heart, and the heart of thy seed, to love the LORD thy God with all thine heart, and with all thy soul, that thou mayest live. ⁷And the LORD thy God will put all these curses upon thine enemies, and on them that hate thee, which persecuted thee."

Who Persecutes The Poor

Psalm 10:2 "The wicked in his pride doth persecute the poor: let them be taken in the devices that they have imagined."

Who Shall Face Persecution

Matthew 10:16-25 "¹⁶Behold, I send you forth as sheep in the midst of wolves: be ye therefore wise as serpents, and harmless as doves. ¹⁷But beware of men: for they will deliver you up to the councils, and they will scourge you in their synagogues; ¹⁸And ye shall be brought before governors and kings for my sake, for a testimony against them and the Gentiles. ¹⁹But when they deliver you up,

take no thought how or what ye shall speak: for it shall be given you in that same hour what ye shall speak. ²⁰For it is not ye that speak, but the Spirit of your Father which speaketh in you. ²¹And the brother shall deliver up the brother to death, and the father the child: and the children shall rise up against their parents, and cause them to be put to death. ²²And ye shall be hated of all men for my name's sake: but he that endureth to the end shall be saved. ²³But when they persecute you in this city, flee ye into another: for verily I say unto you, Ye shall not have gone over the cities of Israel, till the Son of man be come. ²⁴The disciple is not above his master, nor the servant above his lord. ²⁵It is enough for the disciple that he be as his master, and the servant as his lord. If they have called the master of the house Beelzebub, how much more shall they call them of his household?"

Matthew 24:1-10 "¹And Jesus went out, and departed from the temple: and his disciples came to him for to shew him the buildings of the temple. ²And Jesus said unto them, See ye not all these things? verily I say unto you, There shall not be left here one stone upon another, that shall not be thrown down. ³And as he sat upon the mount of Olives, the disciples came unto him privately, saying, Tell us, when shall these things be? and what shall be the sign of thy coming, and of the end of the world? ⁴And Jesus answered and said unto them, Take heed that no man deceive you. ⁵For many shall come in my name, saying, I am Christ; and shall deceive many. ⁶And ye shall hear of wars and rumours of wars: see that ye be not troubled: for all these things must come to pass, but the end is not yet. ⁷For nation shall rise against nation, and kingdom against kingdom: and there shall be famines, and pestilences, and earthquakes, in divers places. ⁸All these are the beginning of sorrows. ⁹Then shall they deliver you up to be afflicted, and shall kill you: and ye shall be hated of all nations for my name's sake. ¹⁰And then shall many be offended, and shall betray one another, and shall hate one another."

Mark 13:1-13 "¹And as he went out of the temple, one of his disciples saith unto him, Master, see what manner of stones and what buildings are here! ²And Jesus answering said unto him, Seest thou these great buildings? there shall not be left one stone upon another, that shall not be thrown down. ³And as he sat upon the mount of Olives over against the temple, Peter and James and John and Andrew asked him privately, ⁴Tell us, when shall these things be? and what shall be the sign when all these things shall be fulfilled? ⁵And Jesus answering them began to say, Take heed lest any man deceive you: ⁶For many shall come in my name, saying, I am Christ; and shall deceive many. ⁷And when ye shall hear of wars and rumours of wars, be ye not troubled: for such things must needs be; but the end shall not be yet. ⁸For nation shall rise against nation, and kingdom against kingdom: and there shall be earthquakes in divers places, and there shall be famines and troubles: these are the beginnings of sorrows. ⁹But take heed to yourselves: for they shall deliver you up to councils; and in the synagogues ye shall be beaten: and ye shall be brought before rulers and kings for my sake, for a testimony against them. ¹⁰And the gospel must first be published among all nations. ¹¹But when they shall lead you, and deliver you up, take no thought beforehand what ye shall speak, neither do ye premeditate: but whatsoever shall be given you in that hour, that speak ye: for it is not ye that speak, but the Holy Ghost. ¹²Now the brother shall betray the brother to death, and the father the son; and children shall rise up against their parents, and shall cause them to be put to death. ¹³And ye shall be hated of all men for my name's sake: but he that shall endure unto the end, the same shall be saved."

Luke 21:5-19 "⁵And as some spake of the temple, how it was adorned with goodly stones and gifts, he said, ⁶As for these things which ye behold, the days will come, in the which there shall not be left one stone upon another, that shall not be thrown down. ⁷And they asked him, saying, Master, but when shall these things be? and what sign will there be when these things shall come to pass? ⁸And he said, Take heed that ye be not deceived: for many shall come in my name, saying, I am Christ; and the time draweth near: go ye not therefore after them. ⁹But when ye shall hear of wars and commotions, be not terrified: for these things must first come to pass; but the end is not by and by. ¹⁰Then said he unto them, Nation shall rise against nation, and kingdom against king- dom: ¹¹And great earthquakes shall be in divers

places, and famines, and pestilences; and fearful sights and great signs shall there be from heaven. ¹²But before all these, they shall lay their hands on you, and persecute you, delivering you up to the synagogues, and into prisons, being brought before kings and rulers for my name's sake. ¹³And it shall turn to you for a testimony. ¹⁴Settle it therefore in your hearts, not to meditate before what ye shall answer: ¹⁵For I will give you a mouth and wisdom, which all your adversaries shall not be able to gainsay nor resist. ¹⁶And ye shall be betrayed both by parents, and brethren, and kinsfolks, and friends; and some of you shall they cause to be put to death. ¹⁷And ye shall be hated of all men for my name's sake. ¹⁸But there shall not an hair of your head perish. ¹⁹In your patience possess ye your souls."

John 15:1-20 "¹I am the true vine, and my Father is the husbandman. ²Every branch in me that beareth not fruit he taketh away: and every branch that beareth fruit, he purgeth it, that it may bring forth more fruit. ³Now ye are clean through the word which I have spoken unto you. ⁴Abide in me, and I in you. As the branch cannot bear fruit of itself, except it abide in the vine; no more can ye, except ye abide in me. ⁵I am the vine, ye are the branches: He that abideth in me, and I in him, the same bringeth forth much fruit: for without me ye can do nothing. ⁶If a man abide not in me, he is cast forth as a branch, and is withered; and men gather them, and cast them into the fire, and they are burned. ⁷If ye abide in me, and my words abide in you, ye shall ask what ye will, and it shall be done unto you. ⁸Herein is my Father glorified, that ye bear much fruit; so shall ye be my disciples. ⁹As the Father hath loved me, so have I loved you: continue ye in my love. ¹⁰If ye keep my commandments, ye shall abide in my love; even as I have kept my Father's command- ments, and abide in his love. ¹¹These things have I spoken unto you, that my joy might remain in you, and that your joy might be full. ¹²This is my commandment, That ye love one another, as I have loved you. ¹³Greater love hath no man than this, that a man lay down his life for his friends. ¹⁴Ye are my friends, if ye do whatsoever I com- mand you. ¹⁵Henceforth I call you not servants; for the servant knoweth not what his lord doeth: but I have called you friends; for all things that I have heard of my Father I have made known unto you. [16]Ye have not chosen me, but I have chosen you, and ordained you, that ye should go and bring forth fruit, and that your fruit should remain: that whatsoever ye shall ask of the Father in my name, he may give it you. [17]These things I command you, that ye love one another. [18]If the world hate you, ye know that it hated me before it hated you. [19]If ye were of the world, the world would love his own: but because ye are not of the world, but I have chosen you out of the world, therefore the world hateth you. [20]Remember the word that I said unto you, The servant is not greater than his lord. If they have persecuted me, they will also persecute you; if they have kept my saying, they will keep yours also."

John 16:1-4 "[1]These things have I spoken unto you, that ye should not be offended. [2]They shall put you out of the synagogues: yea, the time cometh, that whosoever killeth you will think that he doeth God service. [3]And these things will they do unto you, because they have not known the Father, nor me. [4]But these things have I told you, that when the time shall come, ye may remember that I told you of them. And these things I said not unto you at the beginning, because I was with you."

1 Corinthians 4:9-13 "[9]For I think that God hath set forth us the apostles last, as it were appointed to death: for we are made a spectacle unto the world, and to angels, and to men. [10]We are fools for Christ's sake, but ye are wise in Christ; we are weak, but ye are strong; ye are honourable, but we are despised. [11]Even unto this present hour we both hunger, and thirst, and are naked, and are buffeted, and have no certain dwellingplace; [12]And labour, working with our own hands: being reviled, we bless; being persecuted, we suffer it: [13]Being defamed, we intreat: we are made as the filth of the world, and are the offscouring of all things unto this day."

2 Timothy 3:12 "Yea, and all that will live godly in Christ Jesus shall suffer persecution."

PERVERSION

Perverseness Within The Tongue
Proverbs 15:4 "A wholesome tongue is a tree of life: but perverseness therein is a breach in the spirit."

The Perverse
Proverbs 10:9 "He that walketh uprightly walketh surely: but he that perverteth his ways shall be known."

Proverbs 12:8 "A man shall be commended according to his wisdom: but he that is of a perverse heart shall be despised."

Proverbs 14:2 "He that walketh in his uprightness feareth the LORD: but he that is perverse in his ways despiseth him."

Proverbs 17:20 "He that hath a froward heart findeth no good: and he that hath a perverse tongue falleth into mischief."

Proverbs 19:1 "Better is the poor that walketh in his integrity, than he that is perverse in his lips, and is a fool."

Proverbs 28:6 "Better is the poor that walketh in his uprightness, than he that is perverse in his ways, though he be rich."

Proverbs 28:18 "Whoso walketh uprightly shall be saved: but he that is perverse in his ways shall fall at once."

The Perverseness Of Transgressors
Proverbs 11:3 "The integrity of the upright shall guide them: but the perverseness of transgressors shall destroy them."

What Has Nothing Perverse In It
Proverbs 8:1-8 "[1]Doth not wisdom cry? and understanding put forth her voice? [2]She standeth in the top of high places, by the way in the places of the paths. [3]She crieth at the gates, at the entry of the city, at the coming in at the doors. [4]Unto you, O men, I call; and my voice is to the sons of man. [5]O ye simple, understand wisdom: and, ye fools, be ye of an understanding heart. [6]Hear; for I will speak of excellent things; and the opening of my lips shall be right things. [7]For my mouth shall speak truth; and wickedness is an abomination to my lips. [8]All the words of my mouth are in righteousness; there is nothing froward or perverse in them."

What Perverts
Exodus 23:8 "And thou shalt take no gift: for the gift blindeth the wise, and perverteth the words of the righteous."

Deuteronomy 16:19 "Thou shalt not wrest judgment; thou shalt not respect persons, neither take a gift: for a gift doth blind the eyes of the wise, and pervert the words of the righteous."

Proverbs 19:3 "The foolishness of man perverteth his way: and his heart fretteth against the LORD."

Isaiah 47:10 "For thou hast trusted in thy wickedness: thou hast said, None seeth me. Thy wisdom and thy knowledge, it hath perverted thee; and thou hast said in thine heart, I am, and none else beside me."

PESTILENCE

There Being Pestilences
Prior To The Coming Of The Lord
Matthew 24:1-7 "1And Jesus went out, and departed from the temple: and his disciples came to him for to shew him the buildings of the temple. 2And Jesus said unto them, See ye not all these things? verily I say unto you, There shall not be left here one stone upon another, that shall not be thrown down. 3And as he sat upon the mount of Olives, the disciples came unto him privately, saying, Tell us, when shall these things be? and what shall be the sign of thy coming, and of the end of the world? 4And Jesus answered and said unto them, Take heed that no man deceive you. 5For many shall come in my name, saying, I am Christ; and shall deceive many. 6And ye shall hear of wars and rumours of wars: see that ye be not troubled: for all these things must come to pass, but the end is not yet. 7For nation shall rise against nation, and kingdom against kingdom: and there shall be famines, and pestilences, and earthquakes, in divers places."

Mark 13:1-8 "1And as he went out of the temple, one of his disciples saith unto him, Master, see what manner of stones and what buildings are here! 2And Jesus answering said unto him, Seest thou these great buildings? there shall not be left one stone upon another, that shall not be thrown down. 3And as he sat upon the mount of Olives over against the temple, Peter and James and John and Andrew asked him privately, 4Tell us, when shall these things be? and what shall be the sign when all these things shall be fulfilled? 5And Jesus answering them began to say, Take heed lest any man deceive you: 6For many shall come in my name, saying, I am Christ; and shall deceive many. 7And when ye shall hear of wars and rumours of wars, be ye not troubled: for such things must needs be; but the end shall not be yet. 8For nation shall rise against nation, and kingdom against kingdom: and there shall be earthquakes in divers places, and there shall be famines and troubles: these are the beginnings of sorrows."

Luke 21:5-11 "5And as some spake of the temple, how it was adorned with goodly stones and gifts, he said, 6As for these things which ye behold, the days will come, in the which there shall not be left one stone upon another, that shall not be thrown down. 7And they asked him, saying, Master, but when shall these things be? and what sign will there be when these things shall come to pass? 8And he said, Take heed that ye be not deceived: for many shall come in my name, saying, I am Christ; and the time draweth near: go ye not therefore after them. 9But when ye shall hear of wars and commotions, be not terrified: for these things must first come to pass; but the end is not by and by. 10Then said he unto them, Nation shall rise against nation, and kingdom against kingdom: 11And great earthquakes shall be in divers places, and famines, and pestilences; and fearful sights and great signs shall there be from heaven."

Who The Lord Sends Pestilence Upon
Leviticus 26:13-25 "13I am the LORD your God, which brought you forth out of the land of Egypt, that ye should not be their bondmen; and I have broken the bands of your yoke, and made you go upright. 14But if ye will not hearken unto me, and will not do all these commandments; 15And if ye shall despise my statutes, or if your soul abhor my judgments, so that ye will not do all my commandments, but that ye break my covenant: 16I also will do this unto you; I will even appoint over you terror, consumption, and the burning ague, that shall consume the eyes, and cause sorrow of heart: and ye shall sow your seed in vain, for your enemies shall eat it. 17And I will set my face against you, and ye shall be slain before your enemies: they that hate you shall reign over you; and ye shall flee when none pursueth you. 18And if ye will not yet for all this hearken unto me, then I will punish you seven times more for your sins. 19And I will break the pride of your power; and I will make your heaven as iron, and your earth as

brass: [20]And your strength shall be spent in vain: for your land shall not yield her increase, neither shall the trees of the land yield their fruits. [21]And if ye walk contrary unto me, and will not hearken unto me; I will bring seven times more plagues upon you according to your sins. [22]I will also send wild beasts among you, which shall rob you of your children, and destroy your cattle, and make you few in number; and your highways shall be desolate. [23]And if ye will not be reformed by me by these things, but will walk contrary unto me; [24]Then will I also walk contrary unto you, and will punish you yet seven times for your sins. [25]And I will bring a sword upon you, that shall avenge the quarrel of my covenant: and when ye are gathered together within your cities, I will send the pestilence among you; and ye shall be delivered into the hand of the enemy."

Deuteronomy 28:15-21 "[15]But it shall come to pass, if thou wilt not hearken unto the voice of the LORD thy God, to observe to do all his commandments and his statutes which I command thee this day; that all these curses shall come upon thee, and overtake thee: [16]Cursed shalt thou be in the city, and cursed shalt thou be in the field. [17]Cursed shall be thy basket and thy store. [18]Cursed shall be the fruit of thy body, and the fruit of thy land, the increase of thy kine, and the flocks of thy sheep. [19]Cursed shalt thou be when thou comest in, and cursed shalt thou be when thou goest out. [20]The LORD shall send upon thee cursing, vexation, and rebuke, in all that thou settest thine hand unto for to do, until thou be destroyed, and until thou perish quickly; because of the wickedness of thy doings, whereby thou hast forsaken me. [21]The LORD shall make the pestilence cleave unto thee, until he have consumed thee from off the land, whither thou goest to possess it."

Jeremiah 24:1-10 "[1]The LORD shewed me, and, behold, two baskets of figs were set before the temple of the LORD, after that Nebuchadrezzar king of Babylon had carried away captive Jeconiah the son of Jehoiakim king of Judah, and the princes of Judah, with the carpenters and smiths, from Jerusalem, and had brought them to Babylon. [2]One basket had very good figs, even like the figs that are first ripe: and the other basket had very naughty figs, which could not be eaten, they were so bad. [3]Then said the LORD unto me, What

seest thou, Jeremiah? And I said, Figs; the good figs, very good; and the evil, very evil, that cannot be eaten, they are so evil. [4]Again the word of the LORD came unto me, saying, [5]Thus saith the LORD, the God of Israel; Like these good figs, so will I acknowledge them that are carried away captive of Judah, whom I have sent out of this place into the land of the Chaldeans for their good. [6]For I will set mine eyes upon them for good, and I will bring them again to this land: and I will build them, and not pull them down; and I will plant them, and not pluck them up. [7]And I will give them an heart to know me, that I am the LORD: and they shall be my people, and I will be their God: for they shall return unto me with their whole heart. [8]And as the evil figs, which cannot be eaten, they are so evil; surely thus saith the LORD, So will I give Zedekiah the king of Judah, and his princes, and the residue of Jerusalem, that remain in this land, and them that dwell in the land of Egypt: [9]And I will deliver them to be removed into all the kingdoms of the earth for their hurt, to be a reproach and a proverb, a taunt and a curse, in all places whither I shall drive them. [10]And I will send the sword, the famine, and the pestilence, among them, till they be consumed from off the land that I gave unto them and to their fathers."

Amos 4:9-10 "[9]I have smitten you with blasting and mildew: when your gardens and your vineyards and your fig trees and your olive trees increased, the palmerworm devoured them: yet have ye not returned unto me, saith the LORD. [10]I have sent among you the pestilence after the manner of Egypt: your young men have I slain with the sword, and have taken away your horses; and I have made the stink of your camps to come up unto your nostrils: yet have ye not returned unto me, saith the LORD."

PLAGUE

Who Will Be Plagued

Leviticus 26:13-22 "[13]I am the LORD your God, which brought you forth out of the land of Egypt, that ye should not be their bondmen; and I have broken the bands of your yoke, and made you go upright. [14]But if ye will not hearken unto me, and will not do all these commandments; [15]And if ye shall despise my statutes, or if your soul abhor my judgments, so that ye will not do all my commandments, but that ye break my covenant: [16]I also will do this unto you; I will even appoint over you terror, consumption, and the burning ague, that shall consume the eyes, and cause sorrow of heart: and ye shall sow your seed in vain, for your enemies shall eat it. [17]And I will set my face against you, and ye shall be slain before your enemies: they that hate you shall reign over you; and ye shall flee when none pursueth you. [18]And if ye will not yet for all this hearken unto me, then I will punish you seven times more for your sins. [19]And I will break the pride of your power; and I will make your heaven as iron, and your earth as brass: [20]And your strength shall be spent in vain: for your land shall not yield her increase, neither shall the trees of the land yield their fruits. [21]And if ye walk contrary unto me, and will not hearken unto me; I will bring seven times more plagues upon you according to your sins. [22]I will also send wild beasts among you, which shall rob you of your children, and destroy your cattle, and make you few in number; and your highways shall be desolate."

Numbers 14:36-37 "[36]And the men, which Moses sent to search the land, who returned, and made all the congregation to murmur against him, by bringing up a slander upon the land, [37]Even those men that did bring up the evil report upon the land, died by the plague before the LORD."

Deuteronomy 28:58-62 "[58]If thou wilt not observe to do all the words of this law that are written in this book, that thou mayest fear this glorious and fearful name, THE LORD THY GOD; [59]Then the LORD will make thy plagues wonderful, and the plagues of thy seed, even great plagues, and of long continuance, and sore sicknesses, and of long continuance. [60]Moreover he will bring upon thee all the diseases of Egypt, which thou wast afraid of; and they shall cleave unto thee. [61]Also every sickness, and every plague, which is not written in the book of this law, them will the LORD bring upon thee, until thou be destroyed. [62]And ye shall be left few in number, whereas ye were as the stars of heaven for multitude; because thou wouldest not obey the voice of the LORD thy God."

Psalm 106:19-29 "[19]They made a calf in Horeb, and worshipped the molten image. [20]Thus they changed their glory into the similitude of an ox that eateth grass. [21]They forgat God their saviour, which had done great things in Egypt; [22]Wondrous works in the land of Ham, and terrible things by the Red sea. [23]Therefore he said that he would destroy them, had not Moses his chosen stood before him in the breach, to turn away his wrath, lest he should destroy them. [24]Yea, they despised the pleasant land, they believed not his word: [25]But murmured in their tents, and hearkened not unto the voice of the LORD. [26]Therefore he lifted up his hand against them, to overthrow them in the wilderness: [27]To overthrow their seed also among the nations, and to scatter them in the lands. [28]They joined themselves also unto Baalpeor, and ate the sacrifices of the dead. [29]Thus they provoked him to anger with their inventions: and the plague brake in upon them."

Revelation 18:1-8 "[1]And after these things I saw another angel come down from heaven, having great power; and the earth was lightened with his glory. [2]And he cried mightily with a strong voice, saying, Babylon the great is fallen, is fallen, and is become the habitation of devils, and the hold of every foul spirit, and a cage of every unclean and hateful bird. [3]For all nations have drunk of the wine of the wrath of her fornication, and the kings of the earth have committed fornication with her, and the merchants of the earth are waxed rich through the abundance of her delicacies. [4]And I heard another voice from heaven, saying, Come out of her, my people, that ye be not partakers of her sins, and that ye receive not of her plagues. [5]For her sins have reached unto heaven, and God hath remembered her iniquities. [6]Reward her even as she rewarded you, and double unto her double according to her works: in the cup which she hath filled fill to her double. [7]How much she hath glorified herself, and lived deliciously, so much torment and sorrow give her: for she saith in her heart, I sit a queen, and am no widow, and shall see no sorrow. [8]Therefore shall her plagues come in one day, death, and mourning, and famine; and she shall be utterly burned with fire: for strong is the Lord God who judgeth her."

Revelation 22:18 "For I testify unto every man that heareth the words of the prophecy of this book, If any man shall add unto these things, God shall add unto him the plagues that are written in this book."

PLEASURE

Those That Love Pleasure
Proverbs 21:17 "He that loveth pleasure shall be a poor man: he that loveth wine and oil shall not be rich."

Those That Please The Lord
Proverbs 16:7 "When a man's ways please the LORD, he maketh even his enemies to be at peace with him."

Ecclesiastes 7:26 "And I find more bitter than death the woman, whose heart is snares and nets, and her hands as bands: whoso pleaseth God shall escape from her; but the sinner shall be taken by her."

Isaiah 56:4-5 "⁴For thus saith the LORD unto the eunuchs that keep my sabbaths, and choose the things that please me, and take hold of my covenant; ⁵Even unto them will I give in mine house and within my walls a place and a name better than of sons and of daughters: I will give them an everlasting name, that shall not be cut off."

What Is Pleasing To The Lord
Numbers 24:1 "And when Balaam saw that it pleased the LORD to bless Israel, he went not, as at other times, to seek for enchantments, but he set his face toward the wilderness."

1 Chronicles 29:17 "I know also, my God, that thou triest the heart, and hast pleasure in uprightness. As for me, in the uprightness of mine heart I have willingly offered all these things: and now have I seen with joy thy people, which are present here, to offer willingly unto thee."

Colossians 1:12-19 "¹²Giving thanks unto the Father, which hath made us meet to be partakers of the inheritance of the saints in light: ¹³Who hath delivered us from the power of darkness, and hath translated us into the kingdom of his dear Son: ¹⁴In whom we have redemption through his blood, even the forgiveness of sins: ¹⁵Who is the image of the invisible God, the firstborn of every creature: ¹⁶For by him were all things created, that are in heaven, and that are in earth, visible and invisible, whether they be thrones, or dominions, or principalities, or powers: all things were created by him, and for him: ¹⁷And he is before all things, and by him all things consist. ¹⁸And he is the head of the body, the church: who is the beginning, the firstborn from the dead; that in all things he might have the preeminence. ¹⁹For it pleased the Father that in him should all fulness dwell."

Colossians 3:20 "Children, obey your parents in all things: for this is well pleasing unto the Lord."

Hebrews 13:12-16 "¹²Wherefore Jesus also, that he might sanctify the people with his own blood, suffered without the gate. ¹³Let us go forth therefore unto him without the camp, bearing his reproach. ¹⁴For here have we no continuing city, but we seek one to come. ¹⁵By him therefore let us offer the sacrifice of praise to God continually, that is, the fruit of our lips giving thanks to his name. ¹⁶But to do good and to communicate forget not: for with such sacrifices God is well pleased."

What The Lord Has No Pleasure In
Ezekiel 18:21-23 "²¹But if the wicked will turn from all his sins that he hath committed, and keep all my statutes, and do that which is lawful and right, he shall surely live, he shall not die. ²²All his transgressions that he hath committed, they shall not be mentioned unto him: in his righteousness that he hath done he shall live. ²³Have I any pleasure at all that the wicked should die? saith the Lord GOD: and not that he should return from his ways, and live?"

Ezekiel 18:31-32 "³¹Cast away from you all your transgressions, whereby ye have transgressed; and make you a new heart and a new spirit: for why will ye die, O house of Israel? ³²For I have no pleasure in the death of him that dieth, saith the Lord GOD: wherefore turn yourselves, and live ye."

Ezekiel 33:11 "Say unto them, As I live, saith the Lord GOD, I have no pleasure in the death of the wicked; but that the wicked turn from his way and live: turn ye, turn ye from your evil ways; for why will ye die, O house of Israel?"

Hebrews 10:1-9 "¹For the law having a shadow of good things to come, and not the very image of the things, can never with those sacrifices which they offered year by year continually make the comers thereunto perfect. ²For then would they not have ceased to be offered? because that the worshippers once purged should have had no more conscience of sins. ³But in those sacrifices there is a remembrance again made of sins every year. ⁴For it is not possible that the blood of bulls and of goats should take away sins. ⁵Wherefore when he cometh into the world, he saith, Sacrifice and offering thou wouldest not, but a body hast thou prepared me: ⁶In burnt offerings and sacrifices for sin thou hast had no pleasure. ⁷Then said I, Lo, I come (in the volume of the book it is written of me,) to do thy will, O God. ⁸Above when he said, Sacrifice and offering and burnt offerings and offering for sin thou wouldest not, neither hadst pleasure therein; which are offered by the law; ⁹Then said he, Lo, I come to do thy will, O God. He taketh away the first, that he may establish the second."

Who Cannot Please God
Romans 8:8 "So then they that are in the flesh cannot please God."

Hebrews 10:36-38 "³⁶For ye have need of patience, that, after ye have done the will of God, ye might receive the promise. ³⁷For yet a little while, and he that shall come will come, and will not tarry. ³⁸Now the just shall live by faith: but if any man draw back, my soul shall have no pleasure in him."

Hebrews 11:6 "But without faith it is impossible to please him: for he that cometh to God must believe that he is, and that he is a rewarder of them that diligently seek him."

Who The Lord Takes Pleasure In
Psalm 147:11 "The Lord taketh pleasure in them that fear him, in those that hope in his mercy."

Psalm 149:4 "For the Lord taketh pleasure in his people: he will beautify the meek with salvation."

POSITION

Who Shall Be First
Matthew 19:30 "But many that are first shall be last; and the last shall be first."

Matthew 20:16 "So the last shall be first, and the first last: for many be called, but few chosen."

Mark 10:31 "But many that are first shall be last; and the last first."

Luke 13:30 "And, behold, there are last which shall be first, and there are first which shall be last."

Who Shall Be Last
Matthew 19:30 "But many that are first shall be last; and the last shall be first."

Matthew 20:16 "So the last shall be first, and the first last: for many be called, but few chosen."

Mark 9:35 "And he sat down, and called the twelve, and saith unto them, If any man desire to be first, the same shall be last of all, and servant of all."

Mark 10:31 "But many that are first shall be last; and the last first."

Luke 13:30 "And, behold, there are last which shall be first, and there are first which shall be last."

POVERTY

The Lord Being The Maker Of The Poor
1 Samuel 2:7 "The Lord maketh poor, and maketh rich: he bringeth low, and lifteth up."

Job 1:20-21 "²⁰Then Job arose, and rent his mantle, and shaved his head, and fell down upon the ground, and worshipped, ²¹And said, Naked came I out of my mother's womb, and naked shall I return thither: the Lord gave, and the Lord hath taken away; blessed be the name of the Lord."

Job 34:12-19 "¹²Yea, surely God will not do wickedly, neither will the Almighty pervert judgment. ¹³Who hath given him a charge over the earth? or who hath disposed the whole world? ¹⁴If he set his heart upon man, if he gather unto himself his spirit and his breath; ¹⁵All flesh shall perish together, and man shall turn again unto dust. ¹⁶If now thou hast understanding, hear this: hearken to the voice of my words. ¹⁷Shall even he that hateth right govern? and wilt thou condemn him that is most just? ¹⁸Is it fit to say to a king, Thou art wicked? and to princes, Ye are ungodly? ¹⁹How much less to him that accepteth not the persons of princes, nor regardeth the rich more than the poor? for they all are the work of his hands."

Proverbs 22:2 "The rich and poor meet together: the LORD is the maker of them all."

The Poor

1 Samuel 2:7-8 "⁷The LORD maketh poor, and maketh rich: he bringeth low, and lifteth up. ⁸He raiseth up the poor out of the dust, and lifteth up the beggar from the dunghill, to set them among princes, and to make them inherit the throne of glory: for the pillars of the earth are the LORD's, and he hath set the world upon them."

Job 5:8-16 "⁸I would seek unto God, and unto God would I commit my cause: ⁹Which doeth great things and unsearchable; marvellous things without number: ¹⁰Who giveth rain upon the earth, and sendeth waters upon the fields: ¹¹To set up on high those that be low; that those which mourn may be exalted to safety. ¹²He disappointeth the devices of the crafty, so that their hands cannot perform their enterprise. ¹³He taketh the wise in their own craftiness: and the counsel of the froward is carried headlong. ¹⁴They meet with darkness in the daytime, and grope in the noonday as in the night. ¹⁵But he saveth the poor from the sword, from their mouth, and from the hand of the mighty. ¹⁶So the poor hath hope, and iniquity stoppeth her mouth."

Job 36:5-15 "⁵Behold, God is mighty, and despiseth not any: he is mighty in strength and wisdom. ⁶He preserveth not the life of the wicked: but giveth right to the poor. ⁷He withdraweth not his eyes from the righteous: but with kings are they on the throne; yea, he doth establish them for ever, and they are exalted. ⁸And if they be bound in fetters, and be holden in cords of affliction; ⁹Then he sheweth them their work, and their transgressions that they have exceeded. ¹⁰He openeth also their ear to discipline, and commandeth that they return from iniquity. ¹¹If they obey and serve him, they shall spend their days in prosperity, and their years in pleasures. ¹²But if they obey not, they shall perish by the sword, and they shall die without knowledge. ¹³But the hypocrites in heart heap up wrath: they cry not when he bindeth them. ¹⁴They die in youth, and their life is among the unclean. ¹⁵He delivereth the poor in his affliction, and openeth their ears in oppression."

Psalm 34:6 "This poor man cried, and the LORD heard him, and saved him out of all his troubles."

Psalm 107:31-41 "³¹Oh that men would praise the LORD for his goodness, and for his wonderful works to the children of men! ³²Let them exalt him also in the congregation of the people, and praise him in the assembly of the elders. ³³He turneth rivers into a wilderness, and the watersprings into dry ground; ³⁴A fruitful land into barrenness, for the wickedness of them that dwell therein. ³⁵He turneth the wilderness into a standing water, and dry ground into watersprings. ³⁶And there he maketh the hungry to dwell, that they may prepare a city for habitation; ³⁷And sow the fields, and plant vineyards, which may yield fruits of increase. ³⁸He blesseth them also, so that they are multiplied greatly; and suffereth not their cattle to decrease. ³⁹Again, they are minished and brought low through oppression, affliction, and sorrow. ⁴⁰He poureth contempt upon princes, and causeth them to wander in the wilderness, where there is no way. ⁴¹Yet setteth he the poor on high from affliction, and maketh him families like a flock."

Psalm 113:5-8 "⁵Who is like unto the LORD our God, who dwelleth on high, ⁶Who humbleth himself to behold the things that are in heaven, and in the earth! ⁷He raiseth up the poor out of the dust, and lifteth the needy out of the dunghill; ⁸That he may set him with princes, even with the princes of his people."

Psalm 140:12 "I know that the LORD will maintain the cause of the afflicted, and the right of the poor."

Proverbs 10:15 "The rich man's wealth is his strong city: the destruction of the poor is their poverty."

Proverbs 13:8 "The ransom of a man's life are his riches: but the poor heareth not rebuke."

Proverbs 13:23 "Much food is in the tillage of the poor: but there is that is destroyed for want of judgment."

Proverbs 14:20 "The poor is hated even of his own neighbour: but the rich hath many friends."

Proverbs 18:23 "The poor useth intreaties; but the rich answereth roughly."

Proverbs 19:1 "Better is the poor that walketh in his integrity, than he that is perverse in his lips, and is a fool."

Proverbs 19:4 "Wealth maketh many friends; but the poor is separated from his neighbour."

Proverbs 19:7 "All the brethren of the poor do hate him: how much more do his friends go far from him? he pursueth them with words, yet they are wanting to him."

Proverbs 19:22 "The desire of a man is his kindness: and a poor man is better than a liar."

Proverbs 22:7 "The rich ruleth over the poor, and the borrower is servant to the lender."

Proverbs 22:22-23 "²²Rob not the poor, because he is poor: neither oppress the afflicted in the gate: ²³For the LORD will plead their cause, and spoil the soul of those that spoiled them."

Proverbs 28:3 "A poor man that oppresseth the poor is like a sweeping rain which leaveth no food."

Proverbs 28:6 "Better is the poor that walketh in his uprightness, than he that is perverse in his ways, though he be rich."

Proverbs 28:11 "The rich man is wise in his own conceit; but the poor that hath understanding searcheth him out."

Proverbs 29:13 "The poor and the deceitful man meet together: the LORD lighteneth both their eyes."

Ecclesiastes 4:13-14 "¹³Better is a poor and a wise child than an old and foolish king, who will no more be admonished. ¹⁴For out of prison he cometh to reign; whereas also he that is born in his kingdom becometh poor."

Ecclesiastes 9:16 "Then said I, Wisdom is better than strength: nevertheless the poor man's wisdom is despised, and his words are not heard."

The Poor In Spirit
Isaiah 66:1-2 "¹Thus saith the LORD, The heaven is my throne, and the earth is my footstool: where is the house that ye build unto me? and where is the place of my rest? ²For all those things hath mine hand made, and those things have been, saith the LORD: but to this man will I look, even to him that is poor and of a contrite spirit, and trembleth at my word."

Matthew 5:3 "Blessed are the poor in spirit: for theirs is the kingdom of heaven."

Luke 6:20 "And he lifted up his eyes on his disciples, and said, Blessed be ye poor: for yours is the kingdom of God."

What Tends To Penury
Proverbs 14:23 "In all labour there is profit: but the talk of the lips tendeth only to penury."

Who Will End Up In Poverty
Proverbs 10:4 "He becometh poor that dealeth with a slack hand: but the hand of the diligent maketh rich."

Proverbs 13:4 "The soul of the sluggard desireth, and hath nothing: but the soul of the diligent shall be made fat."

Proverbs 13:18 "Poverty and shame shall be to him that refuseth instruction: but he that regardeth reproof shall be honoured."

Proverbs 20:13 "Love not sleep, lest thou come to poverty; open thine eyes, and thou shalt be satisfied with bread."

Proverbs 21:17 "He that loveth pleasure shall be a poor man: he that loveth wine and oil shall not be rich."

Proverbs 22:16 "He that oppresseth the poor to increase his riches, and he that giveth to the rich, shall surely come to want."

Proverbs 23:20-21 "²⁰Be not among winebibbers; among riotous eaters of flesh: ²¹For the drunkard and the glutton shall come to poverty: and drowsiness shall clothe a man with rags."

Proverbs 24:30-34 "³⁰I went by the field of the slothful, and by the vineyard of the man void of understanding; ³¹And, lo, it was all grown over with thorns, and nettles had covered the face thereof, and the stone wall thereof was broken down. ³²Then I saw, and considered it well: I looked upon it, and received instruction. ³³Yet a little sleep, a little slumber, a little folding of the hands to sleep: ³⁴So shall thy poverty come as one that travelleth; and thy want as an armed man."

Proverbs 28:19 "He that tilleth his land shall have plenty of bread: but he that followeth after vain persons shall have poverty enough."

Proverbs 28:22 "He that hasteth to be rich hath an evil eye, and considereth not that poverty shall come upon him."

Why Jesus Christ Became Poor
2 Corinthians 8:9 "For ye know the grace of our Lord Jesus Christ, that, though he was rich, yet for your sakes he became poor, that ye through his poverty might be rich."

POWER

God Being Your Power
2 Samuel 22:33 "God is my strength and power: and he maketh my way perfect."

Jesus Christ Being Given Power
Matthew 28:18 "And Jesus came and spake unto them, saying, All power is given unto me in heaven and in earth."

Luke 4:31-36 "31And came down to Capernaum, a city of Galilee, and taught them on the sabbath days. 32And they were astonished at his doctrine: for his word was with power. 33And in the synagogue there was a man, which had a spirit of an unclean devil, and cried out with a loud voice, 34Saying, Let us alone; what have we to do with thee, thou Jesus of Nazareth? art thou come to destroy us? I know thee who thou art; the Holy One of God. 35And Jesus rebuked him, saying, Hold thy peace, and come out of him. And when the devil had thrown him in the midst, he came out of him, and hurt him not. 36And they were all amazed, and spake among themselves, saying, What a word is this! for with authority and power he commandeth the unclean spirits, and they come out."

John 10:14-18 "14I am the good shepherd, and know my sheep, and am known of mine. 15As the Father knoweth me, even so know I the Father: and I lay down my life for the sheep. 16And other sheep I have, which are not of this fold: them also I must bring, and they shall hear my voice; and there shall be one fold, and one shepherd. 17Therefore doth my Father love me, because I lay down my life, that I might take it again. 18No man taketh it from me, but I lay it down of myself. I have power to lay it down, and I have power to take it again. This commandment have I received of my Father."

John 17:1-3 "1These words spake Jesus, and lifted up his eyes to heaven, and said, Father, the hour is come; glorify thy Son, that thy Son also may glorify thee: 2As thou hast given him power over all flesh, that he should give eternal life to as many as thou hast given him. 3And this is life eternal, that they might know thee the only true God, and Jesus Christ, whom thou hast sent."

Acts 10:37-38 "37That word, I say, ye know, which was published throughout all Judaea, and began from Galilee, after the baptism which John preached; 38How God anointed Jesus of Nazareth with the Holy Ghost and with power: who went about doing good, and healing all that were oppressed of the devil; for God was with him."

Power Belonging To God
Psalm 62:11 "God hath spoken once; twice have I heard this; that power belongeth unto God."

The Lord Being Powerful
Joshua 4:24 "That all the people of the earth might know the hand of the LORD, that it is mighty: that ye might fear the LORD your God for ever."

2 Chronicles 25:8 "But if thou wilt go, do it, be strong for the battle: God shall make thee fall before the enemy: for God hath power to help, and to cast down."

Job 37:23 "Touching the Almighty, we cannot find him out: he is excellent in power, and in judgment, and in plenty of justice: he will not afflict."

Psalm 93:1-4 "1The LORD reigneth, he is clothed with majesty; the LORD is clothed with strength, wherewith he hath girded himself: the world also is stablished, that it cannot be moved. 2Thy throne is established of old: thou art from everlasting. 3The floods have lifted up, O LORD, the floods have lifted up their voice; the floods lift up their waves. 4The LORD on high is mightier than the noise of many waters, yea, than the mighty waves of the sea."

Psalm 147:5 "Great is our Lord, and of great power: his understanding is infinite."

Jeremiah 10:6 "Forasmuch as there is none like unto thee, O LORD; thou art great, and thy name is great in might."

Nahum 1:3 "The LORD is slow to anger, and great in power, and will not at all acquit the wicked: the LORD hath his way in the whirlwind and in the storm, and the clouds are the dust of his feet."

The Lord Giving Power

Mark 6:7 "And he called unto him the twelve, and began to send them forth by two and two; and gave them power over unclean spirits."

Luke 9:1-2 "¹Then he called his twelve disciples together, and gave them power and authority over all devils, and to cure diseases. ²And he sent them to preach the kingdom of God, and to heal the sick."

Luke 10:17-20 "¹⁷And the seventy returned again with joy, saying, Lord, even the devils are subject unto us through thy name. ¹⁸And he said unto them, I beheld Satan as lightning fall from heaven. ¹⁹Behold, I give unto you power to tread on serpents and scorpions, and over all the power of the enemy: and nothing shall by any means hurt you. ²⁰Notwithstanding in this rejoice not, that the spirits are subject unto you; but rather rejoice, because your names are written in heaven."

John 1:1-13 "¹In the beginning was the Word, and the Word was with God, and the Word was God. ²The same was in the beginning with God. ³All things were made by him; and without him was not any thing made that was made. ⁴In him was life; and the life was the light of men. ⁵And the light shineth in darkness; and the darkness comprehended it not. ⁶There was a man sent from God, whose name was John. ⁷The same came for a witness, to bear witness of the Light, that all men through him might believe. ⁸He was not that Light, but was sent to bear witness of that Light. ⁹That was the true Light, which lighteth every man that cometh into the world. ¹⁰He was in the world, and the world was made by him, and the world knew him not. ¹¹He came unto his own, and his own received him not. ¹²But as many as received him, to them gave he power to become the sons of God, even to them that believe on his name: ¹³Which were born, not of blood, nor of the will of the flesh, nor of the will of man, but of God."

Acts 1:6-8 "⁶When they therefore were come together, they asked of him, saying, Lord, wilt thou at this time restore again the kingdom to Israel? ⁷And he said unto them, It is not for you to know the times or the seasons, which the Father hath put in his own power. ⁸But ye shall receive power, after that the Holy Ghost is come upon you: and ye shall be witnesses unto me both in Jerusalem, and in all Judaea, and in Samaria, and unto the uttermost part of the earth."

The Power Of The Lord

Psalm 66:3-7 "³Say unto God, How terrible art thou in thy works! through the greatness of thy power shall thine enemies submit themselves unto thee. ⁴All the earth shall worship thee, and shall sing unto thee; they shall sing to thy name. Selah. ⁵Come and see the works of God: he is terrible in his doing toward the children of men. ⁶He turned the sea into dry land: they went through the flood on foot: there did we rejoice in him. ⁷He ruleth by his power for ever; his eyes behold the nations: let not the rebellious exalt themselves. Selah."

Jeremiah 10:10-12 "¹⁰But the LORD is the true God, he is the living God, and an everlasting king: at his wrath the earth shall tremble, and the nations shall not be able to abide his indignation. ¹¹Thus shall ye say unto them, The gods that have not made the heavens and the earth, even they shall perish from the earth, and from under these heavens. ¹²He hath made the earth by his power, he hath established the world by his wisdom, and hath stretched out the heavens by his discretion."

Jeremiah 27:4-5 "⁴And command them to say unto their masters, Thus saith the LORD of hosts, the God of Israel; Thus shall ye say unto your masters; ⁵I have made the earth, the man and the beast that are upon the ground, by my great power and by my outstretched arm, and have given it unto whom it seemed meet unto me."

Jeremiah 32:17 "Ah Lord GOD! behold, thou hast made the heaven and the earth by thy great power and stretched out arm, and there is nothing too hard for thee."

There Being No Power Other Than God

John 19:10-11 "¹⁰Then saith Pilate unto him, Speakest thou not unto me? knowest thou not that I have power to crucify thee, and have power to release thee? ¹¹Jesus answered, Thou couldest have no power at all against me, except it were given thee from above: therefore he that delivered me unto thee hath the greater sin."

Romans 13:1-2 "[1]Let every soul be subject unto the higher powers. For there is no power but of God: the powers that be are ordained of God. [2]Whosoever therefore resisteth the power, resisteth the ordinance of God: and they that resist shall receive to themselves damnation."

What Is In Power
1 Corinthians 4:20 "For the kingdom of God is not in word, but in power."

What Is Power
Romans 1:16 "For I am not ashamed of the gospel of Christ: for it is the power of God unto salvation to every one that believeth; to the Jew first, and also to the Greek."

Hebrews 4:12 "For the word of God is quick, and powerful, and sharper than any twoedged sword, piercing even to the dividing asunder of soul and spirit, and of the joints and marrow, and is a discerner of the thoughts and intents of the heart."

When You Will Receive Power
Acts 1:6-8 "[6]When they therefore were come together, they asked of him, saying, Lord, wilt thou at this time restore again the kingdom to Israel? [7]And he said unto them, It is not for you to know the times or the seasons, which the Father hath put in his own power. [8]But ye shall receive power, after that the Holy Ghost is come upon you: and ye shall be witnesses unto me both in Jerusalem, and in all Judaea, and in Samaria, and unto the uttermost part of the earth."

PRAISE

Not Praising Yourself
Proverbs 27:2 "Let another man praise thee, and not thine own mouth; a stranger, and not thine own lips."

Praising The Lord
Psalm 18:46-49 "[46]The LORD liveth; and blessed be my rock; and let the God of my salvation be exalted. [47]It is God that avengeth me, and subdueth the people under me. [48]He delivereth me from mine enemies: yea, thou liftest me up above those that rise up against me: thou hast delivered me from the violent man. [49]Therefore will I give thanks unto thee, O LORD, among the heathen, and sing praises unto thy name."

Psalm 22:22-23 "[22]I will declare thy name unto my brethren: in the midst of the congregation will I praise thee. [23]Ye that fear the LORD, praise him; all ye the seed of Jacob, glorify him; and fear him, all ye the seed of Israel."

Psalm 35:17-18 "[17]Lord, how long wilt thou look on? rescue my soul from their destructions, my darling from the lions. [18]I will give thee thanks in the great congregation: I will praise thee among much people."

Psalm 42:11 "Why art thou cast down, O my soul? and why art thou disquieted within me? hope thou in God: for I shall yet praise him, who is the health of my countenance, and my God."

Psalm 43:5 "Why art thou cast down, O my soul? and why art thou disquieted within me? hope in God: for I shall yet praise him, who is the health of my countenance, and my God."

Psalm 44:8 "In God we boast all the day long, and praise thy name for ever. Selah."

Psalm 47:1-6 "[1]O clap your hands, all ye people; shout unto God with the voice of triumph. [2]For the LORD most high is terrible; he is a great King over all the earth. [3]He shall subdue the people under us, and the nations under our feet. [4]He shall choose our inheritance for us, the excellency of Jacob whom he loved. Selah. [5]God is gone up with a shout, the LORD with the sound of a trumpet. [6]Sing praises to God, sing praises: sing praises unto our King, sing praises."

Psalm 52:8-9 "[8]But I am like a green olive tree in the house of God: I trust in the mercy of God for ever and ever. [9]I will praise thee for ever, because thou hast done it: and I will wait on thy name; for it is good before thy saints."

Psalm 57:7 "My heart is fixed, O God, my heart is fixed: I will sing and give praise."

Psalm 61:5-8 "[5]For thou, O God, hast heard my vows: thou hast given me the heritage of those that fear thy name. [6]Thou wilt prolong the king's life: and his years as many generations. [7]He shall abide before God for ever: O prepare mercy and truth, which may preserve him. [8]So will I sing praise unto thy name for ever, that I may daily perform my vows."

Psalm 63:1-5 "[1]O God, thou art my God; early will I seek thee: my soul thirsteth for thee, my flesh longeth for thee in a dry and thirsty land, where no water is; [2]To see thy power and thy glory, so as I have seen thee in the sanctuary. [3]Because thy lovingkindness is better than life, my lips shall praise thee. [4]Thus will I bless thee while I live: I will lift up my hands in thy name. [5]My soul shall be satisfied as with marrow and fatness; and my mouth shall praise thee with joyful lips."

Psalm 66:8 "O bless our God, ye people, and make the voice of his praise to be heard."

Psalm 67:5-7 "[5]Let the people praise thee, O God; let all the people praise thee. [6]Then shall the earth yield her increase; and God, even our own God, shall bless us. [7]God shall bless us; and all the ends of the earth shall fear him."

Psalm 68:4 "Sing unto God, sing praises to his name: extol him that rideth upon the heavens by his name JAH, and rejoice before him."

Psalm 75:9 "But I will declare for ever; I will sing praises to the God of Jacob."

Psalm 92:1 "It is a good thing to give thanks unto the LORD, and to sing praises unto thy name, O most High."

Psalm 104:35 "Let the sinners be consumed out of the earth, and let the wicked be no more. Bless thou the LORD, O my soul. Praise ye the LORD."

Psalm 106:48 "Blessed be the Lord God of Israel from everlasting to everlasting: and let all the people say, Amen. Praise ye the LORD."

Psalm 107:31-32 "[31]Oh that men would praise the LORD for his goodness, and for his wonderful works to the children of men! [32]Let them exalt him also in the congregation of the people, and praise him in the assembly of the elders."

Psalm 108:3 "I will praise thee, O LORD, among the people: and I will sing praises unto thee among the nations."

Psalm 111:1 "Praise ye the LORD. I will praise the LORD with my whole heart, in the assembly of the upright, and in the congregation."

Psalm 112:1 "Praise ye the LORD. Blessed is the man that feareth the LORD, that delighteth greatly in his commandments."

Psalm 113:1 "Praise ye the LORD. Praise, O ye servants of the LORD, praise the name of the LORD."

Psalm 117:1-2 "[1]O praise the LORD, all ye nations: praise him, all ye people. [2]For his merciful kindness is great toward us: and the truth of the LORD endureth for ever. Praise ye the LORD."

Psalm 118:19-21 "[19]Open to me the gates of righteousness: I will go into them, and I will praise the LORD: [20]This gate of the LORD, into which the righteous shall enter. [21]I will praise thee: for thou hast heard me, and art become my salvation."

Psalm 118:28 "Thou art my God, and I will praise thee: thou art my God, I will exalt thee."

Psalm 119:1-7 "[1]Blessed are the undefiled in the way, who walk in the law of the LORD. [2]Blessed are they that keep his testimonies, and that seek him with the whole heart. [3]They also do no iniquity: they walk in his ways. [4]Thou hast commanded us to keep thy precepts diligently. [5]O that my ways were directed to keep thy statutes! [6]Then shall I not be ashamed, when I have respect unto all thy commandments. [7]I will praise thee with uprightness of heart, when I shall have learned thy righteous judgments."

Psalm 138:1-4 "[1]I will praise thee with my whole heart: before the gods will I sing praise unto thee. [2]I will worship toward thy holy temple, and praise thy name for thy lovingkindness and for thy truth: for thou hast magnified thy word above all thy name. [3]In the day when I cried thou answeredst me, and strengthenedst me with strength in my soul. [4]All the kings of the earth shall praise thee, O LORD, when they hear the words of thy mouth."

Psalm 144:9 "I will sing a new song unto thee, O God: upon a psaltery and an instrument of ten strings will I sing praises unto thee."

Psalm 146:10 "The LORD shall reign for ever, even thy God, O Zion, unto all generations. Praise ye the LORD."

Psalm 148:1-14 "[1]Praise ye the LORD. Praise ye the LORD from the heavens: praise him in the heights. [2]Praise ye him, all his angels: praise ye him, all his hosts. [3]Praise ye him, sun and moon: praise him, all ye stars of light. [4]Praise him, ye heavens of heavens, and ye waters that be above the heavens. [5]Let them praise the name of the LORD: for he commanded, and they were created. [6]He hath also stablished them for ever and ever: he hath made a decree which shall not pass. [7]Praise the LORD from the earth, ye dragons, and all deeps: [8]Fire, and hail; snow, and vapour; stormy wind fulfilling his word: [9]Mountains, and all hills; fruitful trees, and all cedars: [10]Beasts, and all cattle; creeping things, and flying fowl: [11]Kings of the earth, and all people; princes, and all judges of the earth: [12]Both young men, and maidens; old men, and children: [13]Let them praise the name of the LORD: for his name alone is excellent; his glory is above the earth and heaven. [14]He also exalteth the horn of his people, the praise of all his saints; even of the children of Israel, a people near unto him. Praise ye the LORD."

Psalm 150:6 "Let every thing that hath breath praise the LORD. Praise ye the LORD."

Isaiah 25:1 "O LORD, thou art my God; I will exalt thee, I will praise thy name; for thou hast done wonderful things; thy counsels of old are faithfulness and truth."

Jeremiah 33:11 "The voice of joy, and the voice of gladness, the voice of the bridegroom, and the voice of the bride, the voice of them that shall say, Praise the LORD of hosts: for the LORD is good; for his mercy endureth for ever: and of them that shall bring the sacrifice of praise into the house of the LORD. For I will cause to return the captivity of the land, as at the first, saith the LORD."

Romans 15:11 "And again, Praise the Lord, all ye Gentiles; and laud him, all ye people."

Hebrews 2:9-12 "[9]But we see Jesus, who was made a little lower than the angels for the suffering of death, crowned with glory and honour; that he by the grace of God should taste death for every man. [10]For it became him, for whom are all things, and by whom are all things, in bringing many sons unto glory, to make the captain of their salvation perfect through sufferings. [11]For both he that sanctifieth and they who are sanctified are all of one: for which cause he is not ashamed to call them brethren, [12]Saying, I will declare thy name

unto my brethren, in the midst of the church will I sing praise unto thee."

Revelation 19:5 "And a voice came out of the throne, saying, Praise our God, all ye his servants, and ye that fear him, both small and great."

The Lord Being Your Praise
Jeremiah 17:14 "Heal me, O LORD, and I shall be healed; save me, and I shall be saved: for thou art my praise."

The Praise Of The Lord
Psalm 111:10 "The fear of the LORD is the beginning of wisdom: a good understanding have all they that do his commandments: his praise endureth for ever."

Isaiah 42:8 "I am the LORD: that is my name: and my glory will I not give to another, neither my praise to graven images."

Who Does Not Praise The Lord
Psalm 115:17 "The dead praise not the LORD, neither any that go down into silence."

Isaiah 38:16-18 "[16]O Lord, by these things men live, and in all these things is the life of my spirit: so wilt thou recover me, and make me to live. [17]Behold, for peace I had great bitterness: but thou hast in love to my soul delivered it from the pit of corruption: for thou hast cast all my sins behind thy back. [18]For the grave cannot praise thee, death can not celebrate thee: they that go down into the pit cannot hope for thy truth."

Who Gets Their Praise From God
Romans 2:29 "But he is a Jew, which is one inwardly; and circumcision is that of the heart, in the spirit, and not in the letter; whose praise is not of men, but of God."

Who Loves The Praise Of Men More Than The Praise Of God
John 12:37-43 "[37]But though he had done so many miracles before them, yet they believed not on him: [38]That the saying of Esaias the prophet might be fulfilled, which he spake, Lord, who hath believed our report? and to whom hath the arm of the Lord been revealed? [39]Therefore they could not believe, because that Esaias said again, [40]He hath blinded their eyes, and hardened their heart; that they should not see with their eyes, nor understand with their heart, and be converted,

and I should heal them. [41]These things said Esaias, when he saw his glory, and spake of him. [42]Nevertheless among the chief rulers also many believed on him; but because of the Pharisees they did not confess him, lest they should be put out of the synagogue: [43]For they loved the praise of men more than the praise of God."

Who Praises The Wicked
Proverbs 28:4 "They that forsake the law praise the wicked: but such as keep the law contend with them."

Who Shall Be Praised
Proverbs 31:10-30 "[10]Who can find a virtuous woman? for her price is far above rubies. [11]The heart of her husband doth safely trust in her, so that he shall have no need of spoil. [12]She will do him good and not evil all the days of her life. [13]She seeketh wool, and flax, and worketh willingly with her hands. [14]She is like the merchants' ships; she bringeth her food from afar. [15]She riseth also while it is yet night, and giveth meat to her household, and a portion to her maidens. [16]She considereth a field, and buyeth it: with the fruit of her hands she planteth a vineyard. [17]She girdeth her loins with strength, and strengtheneth her arms. [18]She perceiveth that her merchandise is good: her candle goeth not out by night. [19]She layeth her hands to the spindle, and her hands hold the distaff. [20]She stretcheth out her hand to the poor; yea, she reacheth forth her hands to the needy. [21]She is not afraid of the snow for her household: for all her household are clothed with scarlet. [22]She maketh herself coverings of tapestry; her clothing is silk and purple. [23]Her husband is known in the gates, when he sitteth among the elders of the land. [24]She maketh fine linen, and selleth it; and delivereth girdles unto the merchant. [25]Strength and honour are her clothing; and she shall rejoice in time to come. [26]She openeth her mouth with wisdom; and in her tongue is the law of kindness. [27]She looketh well to the ways of her household, and eateth not the bread of idleness. [28]Her children arise up, and call her blessed; her husband also, and he praiseth her. [29]Many daughters have done virtuously, but thou excellest them all. [30]Favour is deceitful, and beauty is vain: but a woman that feareth the LORD, she shall be praised."

Who Shall Praise The Lord
Psalm 22:26 "The meek shall eat and be satisfied: they shall praise the LORD that seek him: your heart shall live for ever."

Psalm 138:4 "All the kings of the earth shall praise thee, O LORD, when they hear the words of thy mouth."

Joel 2:23-26 "[23]Be glad then, ye children of Zion, and rejoice in the LORD your God: for he hath given you the former rain moderately, and he will cause to come down for you the rain, the former rain, and the latter rain in the first month. [24]And the floors shall be full of wheat, and the fats shall overflow with wine and oil. [25]And I will restore to you the years that the locust hath eaten, the cankerworm, and the caterpiller, and the palmerworm, my great army which I sent among you. [26]And ye shall eat in plenty, and be satisfied, and praise the name of the LORD your God, that hath dealt wondrously with you: and my people shall never be ashamed."

PRAYER

God The Father Knowing
What You Need Before You Ask
Matthew 6:5-8 "[5]And when thou prayest, thou shalt not be as the hypocrites are: for they love to pray standing in the synagogues and in the corners of the streets, that they may be seen of men. Verily I say unto you, They have their reward. [6]But thou, when thou prayest, enter into thy closet, and when thou hast shut thy door, pray to thy Father which is in secret; and thy Father which seeth in secret shall reward thee openly. [7]But when ye pray, use not vain repetitions, as the heathen do: for they think that they shall be heard for their much speaking. [8]Be not ye therefore like unto them: for your Father knoweth what things ye have need of, before ye ask him."

How Not To Pray
Matthew 6:5 "And when thou prayest, thou shalt not be as the hypocrites are: for they love to pray standing in the synagogues and in the corners of the streets, that they may be seen of men. Verily I say unto you, They have their reward."

Matthew 6:7-8 "[7]But when ye pray, use not vain repetitions, as the heathen do: for they think that they shall be heard for their much speaking. [8]Be not ye therefore like unto them: for your Father knoweth what things ye have need of, before ye ask him."

How To Pray
Matthew 6:6 "But thou, when thou prayest, enter into thy closet, and when thou hast shut thy door, pray to thy Father which is in secret; and thy Father which seeth in secret shall reward thee openly."

Matthew 6:9-13 "[9]After this manner therefore pray ye: Our Father which art in heaven, Hallowed be thy name. [10]Thy kingdom come. Thy will be done in earth, as it is in heaven. [11]Give us this day our daily bread. [12]And forgive us our debts, as we forgive our debtors. [13]And lead us not into temptation, but deliver us from evil: For thine is the kingdom, and the power, and the glory, for ever. Amen."

Mark 11:25 "And when ye stand praying, forgive, if ye have ought against any: that your Father also which is in heaven may forgive you your trespasses."

James 1:5-6 "[5]If any of you lack wisdom, let him ask of God, that giveth to all men liberally, and upbraideth not; and it shall be given him. [6]But let him ask in faith, nothing wavering. For he that wavereth is like a wave of the sea driven with the wind and tossed."

Pouring Out Your Heart Before God
Psalm 62:7-8 "[7]In God is my salvation and my glory: the rock of my strength, and my refuge, is in God. [8]Trust in him at all times; ye people, pour out your heart before him: God is a refuge for us. Selah."

Praying Continually
Matthew 26:41 "Watch and pray, that ye enter not into temptation: the spirit indeed is willing, but the flesh is weak."

Mark 14:38 "Watch ye and pray, lest ye enter into temptation. The spirit truly is ready, but the flesh is weak."

Luke 18:1 "And he spake a parable unto them to this end, that men ought always to pray, and not to faint."

Luke 21:34-36 "[34]And take heed to yourselves, lest at any time your hearts be overcharged with surfeiting, and drunkenness, and cares of this life, and so that day come upon you unawares. [35]For as a snare shall it come on all them that dwell on the face of the whole earth. [36]Watch ye therefore, and pray always, that ye may be accounted worthy to escape all these things that shall come to pass, and to stand before the Son of man."

Luke 22:40 "And when he was at the place, he said unto them, Pray that ye enter not into temptation."

Luke 22:46 "And said unto them, Why sleep ye? rise and pray, lest ye enter into temptation."

Romans 12:10-12 "[10]Be kindly affectioned one to another with brotherly love; in honour preferring one another; [11]Not slothful in business; fervent in spirit; serving the Lord; [12]Rejoicing in hope; patient in tribulation; continuing instant in prayer."

Ephesians 6:18 "Praying always with all prayer and supplication in the Spirit, and watching thereunto with all perseverance and supplication for all saints."

Philippians 4:6 "Be careful for nothing; but in every thing by prayer and supplication with thanksgiving let your requests be made known unto God."

1 Thessalonians 5:17 "Pray without ceasing."

1 Timothy 2:8 "I will therefore that men pray every where, lifting up holy hands, without wrath and doubting."

Praying For Others
Matthew 5:43-44 "[43]Ye have heard that it hath been said, Thou shalt love thy neighbour, and hate thine enemy. [44]But I say unto you, Love your enemies, bless them that curse you, do good to them that hate you, and pray for them which despitefully use you, and persecute you."

Luke 6:27-28 "[27]But I say unto you which hear, Love your enemies, do good to them which hate you, [28]Bless them that curse you, and pray for them which despitefully use you."

Ephesians 6:18 "Praying always with all prayer and supplication in the Spirit, and watching thereunto with all perseverance and supplication for all saints."

1 Timothy 2:1-3 "¹I exhort therefore, that, first of all, supplications, prayers, intercessions, and giving of thanks, be made for all men; ²For kings, and for all that are in authority; that we may lead a quiet and peaceable life in all godliness and honesty. ³For this is good and acceptable in the sight of God our Saviour."

James 5:14-16 "¹⁴Is any sick among you? let him call for the elders of the church; and let them pray over him, anointing him with oil in the name of the Lord: ¹⁵And the prayer of faith shall save the sick, and the Lord shall raise him up; and if he have committed sins, they shall be forgiven him. ¹⁶Confess your faults one to another, and pray one for another, that ye may be healed. The effectual fervent prayer of a righteous man availeth much."

1 John 5:16 "If any man see his brother sin a sin which is not unto death, he shall ask, and he shall give him life for them that sin not unto death. There is a sin unto death: I do not say that he shall pray for it."

Praying For The Peace Of Jerusalem
Psalm 122:6 "Pray for the peace of Jerusalem: they shall prosper that love thee."

Praying In The Holy Spirit
Jude 20 "But ye, beloved, building up yourselves on your most holy faith, praying in the Holy Ghost."

The Lord Hearing Prayers
2 Chronicles 7:12 "And the LORD appeared to Solomon by night, and said unto him, I have heard thy prayer, and have chosen this place to myself for an house of sacrifice."

Psalm 6:9 "The LORD hath heard my supplication; the LORD will receive my prayer."

Psalm 65:1-2 "¹Praise waiteth for thee, O God, in Sion: and unto thee shall the vow be performed. ²O thou that hearest prayer, unto thee shall all flesh come."

Psalm 66:20 "Blessed be God, which hath not turned away my prayer, nor his mercy from me."

Psalm 86:6-7 "⁶Give ear, O LORD, unto my prayer; and attend to the voice of my supplications. ⁷In the

day of my trouble I will call upon thee: for thou wilt answer me."

Psalm 99:6 "Moses and Aaron among his priests, and Samuel among them that call upon his name; they called upon the LORD, and he answered them."

The Prayer Of A Righteous Man
James 5:16 "Confess your faults one to another, and pray one for another, that ye may be healed. The effectual fervent prayer of a righteous man availeth much."

The Prayer Of Faith
James 5:15 "And the prayer of faith shall save the sick, and the Lord shall raise him up; and if he have committed sins, they shall be forgiven him."

The Prayer Of The Upright
Proverbs 15:8 "The sacrifice of the wicked is an abomination to the LORD: but the prayer of the upright is his delight."

The Reward For Praying
1 Kings 8:28-45 "²⁸Yet have thou respect unto the prayer of thy servant, and to his supplication, O LORD my God, to hearken unto the cry and to the prayer, which thy servant prayeth before thee to day: ²⁹That thine eyes may be open toward this house night and day, even toward the place of which thou hast said, My name shall be there: that thou mayest hearken unto the prayer which thy servant shall make toward this place. ³⁰And hearken thou to the supplication of thy servant, and of thy people Israel, when they shall pray toward this place: and hear thou in heaven thy dwelling place: and when thou hearest, forgive. ³¹If any man trespass against his neighbour, and an oath be laid upon him to cause him to swear, and the oath come before thine altar in this house: ³²Then hear thou in heaven, and do, and judge thy servants, condemning the wicked, to bring his way upon his head; and justifying the righteous, to give him according to his righteousness. ³³When thy people Israel be smitten down before the enemy, because they have sinned against thee, and shall turn again to thee, and confess thy name, and pray, and make supplication unto thee in this house: ³⁴Then hear thou in heaven, and forgive the sin of thy people Israel, and bring them again unto the land which thou gavest unto their fathers. ³⁵When heaven is shut up, and there is no

rain, because they have sinned against thee; if they pray toward this place, and confess thy name, and turn from their sin, when thou afflictest them: [36]Then hear thou in heaven, and forgive the sin of thy servants, and of thy people Israel, that thou teach them the good way wherein they should walk, and give rain upon thy land, which thou hast given to thy people for an inheritance. [37]If there be in the land famine, if there be pestilence, blasting, mildew, locust, or if there be caterpiller; if their enemy besiege them in the land of their cities; whatsoever plague, whatsoever sickness there be; [38]What prayer and supplication soever be made by any man, or by all thy people Israel, which shall know every man the plague of his own heart, and spread forth his hands toward this house: [39]Then hear thou in heaven thy dwelling place, and forgive, and do, and give to every man according to his ways, whose heart thou knowest; (for thou, even thou only, knowest the hearts of all the children of men;) [40]That they may fear thee all the days that they live in the land which thou gavest unto our fathers. [41]Moreover concerning a stranger, that is not of thy people Israel, but cometh out of a far country for thy name's sake; [42](For they shall hear of thy great name, and of thy strong hand, and of thy stretched out arm;) when he shall come and pray toward this house; [43]Hear thou in heaven thy dwelling place, and do according to all that the stranger calleth to thee for: that all people of the earth may know thy name, to fear thee, as do thy people Israel; and that they may know that this house, which I have builded, is called by thy name. [44]If thy people go out to battle against their enemy, whithersoever thou shalt send them, and shall pray unto the LORD toward the city which thou hast chosen, and toward the house that I have built for thy name: [45]Then hear thou in heaven their prayer and their supplication, and maintain their cause."

2 Chronicles 6:19-40 "[19]Have respect therefore to the prayer of thy servant, and to his supplication, O LORD my God, to hearken unto the cry and the prayer which thy servant prayeth before thee: [20]That thine eyes may be open upon this house day and night, upon the place whereof thou hast said that thou wouldest put thy name there; to hearken unto the prayer which thy servant prayeth toward this place. [21]Hearken therefore unto the supplications of thy servant, and of thy people Israel, which they shall make toward this place: hear thou from thy dwelling place, even from heaven; and when thou hearest, forgive. [22]If a man sin against his neighbour, and an oath be laid upon him to make him swear, and the oath come before thine altar in this house; [23]Then hear thou from heaven, and do, and judge thy servants, by requiting the wicked, by recompensing his way upon his own head; and by justifying the righteous, by giving him according to his righteousness. [24]And if thy people Israel be put to the worse before the enemy, because they have sinned against thee; and shall return and confess thy name, and pray and make supplication before thee in this house; [25]Then hear thou from the heavens, and forgive the sin of thy people Israel, and bring them again unto the land which thou gavest to them and to their fathers. [26]When the heaven is shut up, and there is no rain, because they have sinned against thee; yet if they pray toward this place, and confess thy name, and turn from their sin, when thou dost afflict them; [27]Then hear thou from heaven, and forgive the sin of thy servants, and of thy people Israel, when thou hast taught them the good way, wherein they should walk; and send rain upon thy land, which thou hast given unto thy people for an inheritance. [28]If there be dearth in the land, if there be pestilence, if there be blasting, or mildew, locusts, or caterpillers; if their enemies besiege them in the cities of their land; whatsoever sore or whatsoever sickness there be: [29]Then what prayer or what supplication soever shall be made of any man, or of all thy people Israel, when every one shall know his own sore and his own grief, and shall spread forth his hands in this house: [30]Then hear thou from heaven thy dwelling place, and forgive, and render unto every man according unto all his ways, whose heart thou knowest; (for thou only knowest the hearts of the children of men:) [31]That they may fear thee, to walk in thy ways, so long as they live in the land which thou gavest unto our fathers. [32]Moreover concerning the stranger, which is not of thy people Israel, but is come from a far country for thy great name's sake, and thy mighty hand, and thy stretched out arm; if they come and pray in this house; [33]Then hear thou from the heavens, even from thy dwelling place, and do according to all that the stranger calleth to thee for; that all people of the earth may know thy name, and fear thee, as doth thy people Israel, and may know that this house which I have built is called by thy name. 34If thy people go out to war against their enemies by the way that thou shalt send them, and they pray unto thee toward this city which thou hast chosen, and the house which I have built for thy name; 35Then hear thou from the heavens their prayer and their supplication, and maintain their cause. 36If they sin against thee, (for there is no man which sinneth not,) and thou be angry with them, and deliver them over before their enemies, and they carry them away captives unto a land far off or near; 37Yet if they bethink themselves in the land whither they are carried captive, and turn and pray unto thee in the land of their captivity, saying, We have sinned, we have done amiss, and have dealt wickedly; 38If they return to thee with all their heart and with all their soul in the land of their captivity, whither they have carried them captives, and pray toward their land, which thou gavest unto their fathers, and toward the city which thou hast chosen, and toward the house which I have built for thy name: 39Then hear thou from the heavens, even from thy dwelling place, their prayer and their supplications, and maintain their cause, and forgive thy people which have sinned against thee. 40Now, my God, let, I beseech thee, thine eyes be open, and let thine ears be attent unto the prayer that is made in this place."

2 Chronicles 7:12-14 "12And the LORD appeared to Solomon by night, and said unto him, I have heard thy prayer, and have chosen this place to myself for an house of sacrifice. 13If I shut up heaven that there be no rain, or if I command the locusts to devour the land, or if I send pestilence among my people; 14If my people, which are called by my name, shall humble themselves, and pray, and seek my face, and turn from their wicked ways; then will I hear from heaven, and will forgive their sin, and will heal their land."

Matthew 7:7-11 "7Ask, and it shall be given you; seek, and ye shall find; knock, and it shall be opened unto you: 8For every one that asketh receiveth; and he that seeketh findeth; and to him that knocketh it shall be opened. 9Or what man is there of you, whom if his son ask bread, will he give him a stone? 10Or if he ask a fish, will he give him a serpent? 11If ye then, being evil, know how to give good gifts unto your children, how much more shall your Father which is in heaven give good things to them that ask him?"

Matthew 21:21-22 "21Jesus answered and said unto them, Verily I say unto you, If ye have faith, and doubt not, ye shall not only do this which is done to the fig tree, but also if ye shall say unto this mountain, Be thou removed, and be thou cast into the sea; it shall be done. 22And all things, whatsoever ye shall ask in prayer, believing, ye shall receive."

Luke 11:8-13 "8I say unto you, Though he will not rise and give him, because he is his friend, yet because of his importunity he will rise and give him as many as he needeth. 9And I say unto you, Ask, and it shall be given you; seek, and ye shall find; knock, and it shall be opened unto you. 10For every one that asketh receiveth; and he that seeketh findeth; and to him that knocketh it shall be opened. 11If a son shall ask bread of any of you that is a father, will he give him a stone? or if he ask a fish, will he for a fish give him a serpent? 12Or if he shall ask an egg, will he offer him a scorpion? 13If ye then, being evil, know how to give good gifts unto your children: how much more shall your heavenly Father give the Holy Spirit to them that ask him?"

John 14:9-14 "9Jesus saith unto him, Have I been so long time with you, and yet hast thou not known me, Philip? he that hath seen me hath seen the Father; and how sayest thou then, Shew us the Father? 10Believest thou not that I am in the Father, and the Father in me? the words that I speak unto you I speak not of myself: but the Father that dwelleth in me, he doeth the works. 11Believe me that I am in the Father, and the Father in me: or else believe me for the very works' sake. 12Verily, verily, I say unto you, He that believeth on me, the works that I do shall he do also; and greater works than these shall he do; because I go unto my Father. 13And whatsoever ye shall ask in my name, that will I do, that the Father may be glorified in the Son. 14If ye shall ask any thing in my name, I will do it."

John 15:9-16 "9As the Father hath loved me, so have I loved you: continue ye in my love. 10If ye keep my commandments, ye shall abide in my love; even as I have kept my Father's commandments, and abide in his love. [11]These things have I spoken unto you, that my joy might remain in you, and that your joy might be full. [12]This is my commandment, That ye love one another, as I have loved you. [13]Greater love hath no man than this, that a man lay down his life for his friends. [14]Ye are my friends, if ye do whatsoever I command you. [15]Henceforth I call you not servants; for the servant knoweth not what his lord doeth: but I have called you friends; for all things that I have heard of my Father I have made known unto you. [16]Ye have not chosen me, but I have chosen you, and ordained you, that ye should go and bring forth fruit, and that your fruit should remain: that whatsoever ye shall ask of the Father in my name, he may give it you."

John 16:22-26 "[22]And ye now therefore have sorrow: but I will see you again, and your heart shall rejoice, and your joy no man taketh from you. [23]And in that day ye shall ask me nothing. Verily, verily, I say unto you, Whatsoever ye shall ask the Father in my name, he will give it you. [24]Hitherto have ye asked nothing in my name: ask, and ye shall receive, that your joy may be full. [25]These things have I spoken unto you in proverbs: but the time cometh, when I shall no more speak unto you in proverbs, but I shall shew you plainly of the Father. [26]At that day ye shall ask in my name: and I say not unto you, that I will pray the Father for you."

James 1:5 "If any of you lack wisdom, let him ask of God, that giveth to all men liberally, and upbraideth not; and it shall be given him."

James 5:14-16 "[14]Is any sick among you? let him call for the elders of the church; and let them pray over him, anointing him with oil in the name of the Lord: [15]And the prayer of faith shall save the sick, and the Lord shall raise him up; and if he have committed sins, they shall be forgiven him. [16]Confess your faults one to another, and pray one for another, that ye may be healed. The effectual fervent prayer of a righteous man availeth much."

1 John 5:13-15 "[13]These things have I written unto you that believe on the name of the Son of God; that ye may know that ye have eternal life, and that ye may believe on the name of the Son of God. [14]And this is the confidence that we have in him, that, if we ask any thing according to his will,

he heareth us: [15]And if we know that he hear us, whatsoever we ask, we know that we have the petitions that we desired of him."

Those That Pray To A God That Cannot Save
Isaiah 45:20 "Assemble yourselves and come; draw near together, ye that are escaped of the nations: they have no knowledge that set up the wood of their graven image, and pray unto a god that cannot save."

The Spirit Helps You Pray
Romans 8:26-28 "[26]Likewise the Spirit also helpeth our infirmities: for we know not what we should pray for as we ought: but the Spirit itself maketh intercession for us with groanings which cannot be uttered. [27]And he that searcheth the hearts knoweth what is the mind of the Spirit, because he maketh intercession for the saints according to the will of God. [28]And we know that all things work together for good to them that love God, to them who are the called according to his purpose."

Whose Prayer Shall Be An Abomination
Proverbs 28:9 "He that turneth away his ear from hearing the law, even his prayer shall be abomination."

Whose Prayer The Lord Does Not Hear
Isaiah 1:10-15 "[10]Hear the word of the LORD, ye rulers of Sodom; give ear unto the law of our God, ye people of Gomorrah. [11]To what purpose is the multitude of your sacrifices unto me? saith the LORD: I am full of the burnt offerings of rams, and the fat of fed beasts; and I delight not in the blood of bullocks, or of lambs, or of he goats. [12]When ye come to appear before me, who hath required this at your hand, to tread my courts? [13]Bring no more vain oblations; incense is an abomination unto me; the new moons and sabbaths, the calling of assemblies, I cannot away with; it is iniquity, even the solemn meeting. [14]Your new moons and your appointed feasts my soul hateth: they are a trouble unto me; I am weary to bear them. [15]And when ye spread forth your hands, I will hide mine eyes from you: yea, when ye make many prayers, I will not hear: your hands are full of blood."

Whose Prayer The Lord Hears
Job 33:19-26 "[19]He is chastened also with pain upon his bed, and the multitude of his bones with

strong pain: 20So that his life abhorreth bread, and his soul dainty meat. 21His flesh is consumed away, that it cannot be seen; and his bones that were not seen stick out. 22Yea, his soul draweth near unto the grave, and his life to the destroyers. 23If there be a messenger with him, an interpreter, one among a thousand, to shew unto man his uprightness: 24Then he is gracious unto him, and saith, Deliver him from going down to the pit: I have found a ransom. 25His flesh shall be fresher than a child's: he shall return to the days of his youth: 26He shall pray unto God, and he will be favourable unto him: and he shall see his face with joy: for he will render unto man his righteousness."

Psalm 91:9-15 "9Because thou hast made the LORD, which is my refuge, even the most High, thy habitation; 10There shall no evil befall thee, neither shall any plague come nigh thy dwelling. 11For he shall give his angels charge over thee, to keep thee in all thy ways. 12They shall bear thee up in their hands, lest thou dash thy foot against a stone. 13Thou shalt tread upon the lion and adder: the young lion and the dragon shalt thou trample under feet. 14Because he hath set his love upon me, therefore will I deliver him: I will set him on high, because he hath known my name. 15He shall call upon me, and I will answer him: I will be with him in trouble; I will deliver him, and honour him."

Proverbs 15:29 "The LORD is far from the wicked: but he heareth the prayer of the righteous."

1 Peter 3:12 "For the eyes of the Lord are over the righteous, and his ears are open unto their prayers: but the face of the Lord is against them that do evil."

PREDESTINATION

The Lord Predestining
Psalm 139:13-17 "13For thou hast possessed my reins: thou hast covered me in my mother's womb. 14I will praise thee; for I am fearfully and wonderfully made: marvellous are thy works; and that my soul knoweth right well. 15My substance was not hid from thee, when I was made in secret, and curiously wrought in the lowest parts of the earth. 16Thine eyes did see my substance, yet being unperfect; and in thy book all my members were written, which in continuance were fashioned,

when as yet there was none of them. 17How precious also are thy thoughts unto me, O God! how great is the sum of them!"

Habakkuk 2:1-3 "1I will stand upon my watch, and set me upon the tower, and will watch to see what he will say unto me, and what I shall answer when I am reproved. 2And the LORD answered me, and said, Write the vision, and make it plain upon tables, that he may run that readeth it. 3For the vision is yet for an appointed time, but at the end it shall speak, and not lie: though it tarry, wait for it; because it will surely come, it will not tarry."

Acts 1:6-7 "6When they therefore were come together, they asked of him, saying, Lord, wilt thou at this time restore again the kingdom to Israel? 7And he said unto them, It is not for you to know the times or the seasons, which the Father hath put in his own power."

Acts 17:23-26 "23For as I passed by, and beheld your devotions, I found an altar with this inscription, TO THE UNKNOWN GOD. Whom therefore ye ignorantly worship, him declare I unto you. 24God that made the world and all things therein, seeing that he is Lord of heaven and earth, dwelleth not in temples made with hands; 25Neither is worshipped with men's hands, as though he needed any thing, seeing he giveth to all life, and breath, and all things; 26And hath made of one blood all nations of men for to dwell on all the face of the earth, and hath determined the times before appointed, and the bounds of their habitation."

Ephesians 1:3-5 "3Blessed be the God and Father of our Lord Jesus Christ, who hath blessed us with all spiritual blessings in heavenly places in Christ: 4According as he hath chosen us in him before the foundation of the world, that we should be holy and without blame before him in love: 5Having predestinated us unto the adoption of children by Jesus Christ to himself, according to the good pleasure of his will."

Those That Are Predestined By God
Romans 8:28-30 "28And we know that all things work together for good to them that love God, to them who are the called according to his purpose. 29For whom he did foreknow, he also did predestinate to be conformed to the image of his Son, that he might be the firstborn among many

brethren. [30]Moreover whom he did predestinate, them he also called: and whom he called, them he also justified: and whom he justified, them he also glorified."

Who God Predestines
1 Kings 19:15-18 "[15]And the Lord said unto him, Go, return on thy way to the wilderness of Damascus: and when thou comest, anoint Hazael to be king over Syria: [16]And Jehu the son of Nimshi shalt thou anoint to be king over Israel: and Elisha the son of Shaphat of Abel-meholah shalt thou anoint to be prophet in thy room. [17]And it shall come to pass, that him that escapeth the sword of Hazael shall Jehu slay: and him that escapeth from the sword of Jehu shall Elisha slay. [18]Yet I have left me seven thousand in Israel, all the knees which have not bowed unto Baal, and every mouth which hath not kissed him."

Romans 8:28-29 "[28]And we know that all things work together for good to them that love God, to them who are the called according to his purpose. [29]For whom he did foreknow, he also did predestinate to be conformed to the image of his Son, that he might be the firstborn among many brethren."

Romans 11:1-4 "[1]I say then, Hath God cast away his people? God forbid. For I also am an Israelite, of the seed of Abraham, of the tribe of Benjamin. [2]God hath not cast away his people which he foreknew. Wot ye not what the scripture saith of Elias? how he maketh intercession to God against Israel, saying, [3]Lord, they have killed thy prophets, and digged down thine altars; and I am left alone, and they seek my life. [4]But what saith the answer of God unto him? I have reserved to myself seven thousand men, who have not bowed the knee to the image of Baal."

Ephesians 1:3-11 "[3]Blessed be the God and Father of our Lord Jesus Christ, who hath blessed us with all spiritual blessings in heavenly places in Christ: [4]According as he hath chosen us in him before the foundation of the world, that we should be holy and without blame before him in love: [5]Having predestinated us unto the adoption of children by Jesus Christ to himself, according to the good pleasure of his will, [6]To the praise of the glory of his grace, wherein he hath made us accepted in the beloved. [7]In whom we have redemption through his blood, the forgiveness of sins, according to the riches of his grace; [8]Wherein he hath abounded toward us in all wisdom and prudence; [9]Having made known unto us the mystery of his will, according to his good pleasure which he hath purposed in himself: [10]That in the dispensation of the fulness of times he might gather together in one all things in Christ, both which are in heaven, and which are on earth; even in him: [11]In whom also we have obtained an inheritance, being predestinated according to the purpose of him who worketh all things after the counsel of his own will."

PRESERVATION

The Lord Preserving
Psalm 32:5-7 "[5]I acknowledged my sin unto thee, and mine iniquity have I not hid. I said, I will confess my transgressions unto the Lord; and thou forgavest the iniquity of my sin. Selah. [6]For this shall every one that is godly pray unto thee in a time when thou mayest be found: surely in the floods of great waters they shall not come nigh unto him. [7]Thou art my hiding place; thou shalt preserve me from trouble; thou shalt compass me about with songs of deliverance. Selah."

Psalm 121:7 "The Lord shall preserve thee from all evil: he shall preserve thy soul."

Proverbs 22:12 "The eyes of the Lord preserve knowledge, and he overthroweth the words of the transgressor."

What Preserves
Psalm 25:21-22 "[21]Let integrity and uprightness preserve me; for I wait on thee. [22]Redeem Israel, O God, out of all his troubles."

Psalm 61:5-7 "[5]For thou, O God, hast heard my vows: thou hast given me the heritage of those that fear thy name. [6]Thou wilt prolong the king's life: and his years as many generations. [7]He shall abide before God for ever: O prepare mercy and truth, which may preserve him."

Proverbs 2:10-11 "[10]When wisdom entereth into thine heart, and knowledge is pleasant unto thy soul; [11]Discretion shall preserve thee, understanding shall keep thee."

Proverbs 20:28 "Mercy and truth preserve the king: and his throne is upholden by mercy."

Who God Does Not Preserve
Job 36:5-6 "⁵Behold, God is mighty, and despiseth not any: he is mighty in strength and wisdom. ⁶He preserveth not the life of the wicked: but giveth right to the poor."

Who Preserves Their Soul
Proverbs 16:17 "The highway of the upright is to depart from evil: he that keepeth his way preserveth his soul."

Who The Lord Preserves
Deuteronomy 6:24 "And the LORD commanded us to do all these statutes, to fear the LORD our God, for our good always, that he might preserve us alive, as it is at this day."

Psalm 31:23 "O love the LORD, all ye his saints: for the LORD preserveth the faithful, and plentifully rewardeth the proud doer."

Psalm 36:6 "Thy righteousness is like the great mountains; thy judgments are a great deep: O LORD, thou preservest man and beast."

Psalm 37:28 "For the LORD loveth judgment, and forsaketh not his saints; they are preserved for ever: but the seed of the wicked shall be cut off."

Psalm 97:10 "Ye that love the LORD, hate evil: he preserveth the souls of his saints; he delivereth them out of the hand of the wicked."

Psalm 116:6 "The LORD preserveth the simple: I was brought low, and he helped me."

Psalm 145:20 "The LORD preserveth all them that love him: but all the wicked will he destroy."

Psalm 146:9 "The LORD preserveth the strangers; he relieveth the fatherless and widow: but the way of the wicked he turneth upside down."

Proverbs 2:6-8 "⁶For the LORD giveth wisdom: out of his mouth cometh knowledge and understanding. ⁷He layeth up sound wisdom for the righteous: he is a buckler to them that walk uprightly. ⁸He keepeth the paths of judgment, and preserveth the way of his saints."

PRIDE/ARROGANCE

A Proud Look
Proverbs 6:16-19 "¹⁶These six things doth the LORD hate: yea, seven are an abomination unto him: ¹⁷A proud look, a lying tongue, and hands that shed innocent blood, ¹⁸An heart that deviseth wicked imaginations, feet that be swift in running to mischief, ¹⁹A false witness that speaketh lies, and he that soweth discord among brethren."

Proverbs 21:4 "An high look, and a proud heart, and the plowing of the wicked, is sin."

Not Being Arrogant
1 Samuel 2:3 "Talk no more so exceeding proudly; let not arrogancy come out of your mouth: for the LORD is a God of knowledge, and by him actions are weighed."

Romans 12:3 "For I say, through the grace given unto me, to every man that is among you, not to think of himself more highly than he ought to think; but to think soberly, according as God hath dealt to every man the measure of faith."

Proud Hearts
Psalm 119:69-70 "⁶⁹The proud have forged a lie against me: but I will keep thy precepts with my whole heart. ⁷⁰Their heart is as fat as grease; but I delight in thy law."

Proverbs 21:4 "An high look, and a proud heart, and the plowing of the wicked, is sin."

The Pride Of Life
1 John 2:16 "For all that is in the world, the lust of the flesh, and the lust of the eyes, and the pride of life, is not of the Father, but is of the world."

The Pride Of Man
Proverbs 29:23 "A man's pride shall bring him low: but honour shall uphold the humble in spirit."

Isaiah 2:11-12 "¹¹The lofty looks of man shall be humbled, and the haughtiness of men shall be bowed down, and the LORD alone shall be exalted in that day. ¹²For the day of the LORD of hosts shall be upon every one that is proud and lofty, and upon every one that is lifted up; and he shall be brought low."

Isaiah 2:17-19 "¹⁷And the loftiness of man shall be bowed down, and the haughtiness of men shall be made low: and the LORD alone shall be exalted in that day. ¹⁸And the idols he shall utterly abolish. ¹⁹And they shall go into the holes of the rocks, and into the caves of the earth, for fear of the LORD, and for the glory of his majesty, when he ariseth to shake terribly the earth."

Isaiah 13:9-11 "⁹Behold, the day of the LORD cometh, cruel both with wrath and fierce anger, to lay the land desolate: and he shall destroy the sinners thereof out of it. ¹⁰For the stars of heaven and the constellations thereof shall not give their light: the sun shall be darkened in his going forth, and the moon shall not cause her light to shine. ¹¹And I will punish the world for their evil, and the wicked for their iniquity; and I will cause the arrogancy of the proud to cease, and will lay low the haughtiness of the terrible."

Obadiah 1-3 "¹The vision of Obadiah. Thus saith the Lord GOD concerning Edom; We have heard a rumour from the LORD, and an ambassador is sent among the heathen, Arise ye, and let us rise up against her in battle. ²Behold, I have made thee small among the heathen: thou art greatly despised. ³The pride of thine heart hath deceived thee, thou that dwellest in the clefts of the rock, whose habitation is high; that saith in his heart, Who shall bring me down to the ground?"

The Proud And Arrogant

2 Samuel 22:21-28 "²¹The LORD rewarded me according to my righteousness: according to the cleanness of my hands hath he recompensed me. ²²For I have kept the ways of the LORD, and have not wickedly departed from my God. ²³For all his judgments were before me: and as for his statutes, I did not depart from them. ²⁴I was also upright before him, and have kept myself from mine iniquity. ²⁵Therefore the LORD hath recompensed me according to my righteousness; according to my cleanness in his eye sight. ²⁶With the merciful thou wilt shew thyself merciful, and with the upright man thou wilt shew thyself upright. ²⁷With the pure thou wilt shew thyself pure; and with the froward thou wilt shew thyself unsavoury. ²⁸And the afflicted people thou wilt save: but thine eyes are upon the haughty, that thou mayest bring them down."

Psalm 119:69-70 "⁶⁹The proud have forged a lie against me: but I will keep thy precepts with my whole heart. ⁷⁰Their heart is as fat as grease; but I delight in thy law."

Psalm 138:6 "Though the LORD be high, yet hath he respect unto the lowly: but the proud he knoweth afar off."

Proverbs 15:25 "The LORD will destroy the house of the proud: but he will establish the border of the widow."

Proverbs 16:5 "Every one that is proud in heart is an abomination to the LORD: though hand join in hand, he shall not be unpunished."

Proverbs 28:25 "He that is of a proud heart stirreth up strife: but he that putteth his trust in the LORD shall be made fat."

Isaiah 2:11-16 "¹¹The lofty looks of man shall be humbled, and the haughtiness of men shall be bowed down, and the LORD alone shall be exalted in that day. ¹²For the day of the LORD of hosts shall be upon every one that is proud and lofty, and upon every one that is lifted up; and he shall be brought low: ¹³And upon all the cedars of Lebanon, that are high and lifted up, and upon all the oaks of Bashan, ¹⁴And upon all the high mountains, and upon all the hills that are lifted up, ¹⁵And upon every high tower, and upon every fenced wall, ¹⁶And upon all the ships of Tarshish, and upon all pleasant pictures."

Isaiah 24:4 "The earth mourneth and fadeth away, the world languisheth and fadeth away, the haughty people of the earth do languish."

Isaiah 26:4-5 "⁴Trust ye in the LORD for ever: for in the LORD JEHOVAH is everlasting strength: ⁵For he bringeth down them that dwell on high; the lofty city, he layeth it low; he layeth it low, even to the ground; he bringeth it even to the dust."

Daniel 4:37 "Now I Nebuchadnezzar praise and extol and honour the King of heaven, all whose works are truth, and his ways judgment: and those that walk in pride he is able to abase."

Malachi 4:1 "For, behold, the day cometh, that shall burn as an oven; and all the proud, yea, and all that do wickedly, shall be stubble: and the day that cometh shall burn them up, saith the LORD of hosts, that it shall leave them neither root nor branch."

Galatians 6:3-4 "³For if a man think himself to be something, when he is nothing, he deceiveth himself. ⁴But let every man prove his own work, and then shall he have rejoicing in himself alone, and not in another."

James 4:6 "But he giveth more grace. Wherefore he saith, God resisteth the proud, but giveth grace unto the humble."

1 Peter 5:5 "Likewise, ye younger, submit yourselves unto the elder. Yea, all of you be subject one to another, and be clothed with humility: for God resisteth the proud, and giveth grace to the humble."

The Proud In Spirit
Ecclesiastes 7:8 "Better is the end of a thing than the beginning thereof: and the patient in spirit is better than the proud in spirit."

The Reward For Pride
Jeremiah 48:42 "And Moab shall be destroyed from being a people, because he hath magnified himself against the LORD."

Ezekiel 28:2-8 "²Son of man, say unto the prince of Tyrus, Thus saith the Lord GOD; Because thine heart is lifted up, and thou hast said, I am a God, I sit in the seat of God, in the midst of the seas; yet thou art a man, and not God, though thou set thine heart as the heart of God: ³Behold, thou art wiser than Daniel; there is no secret that they can hide from thee: ⁴With thy wisdom and with thine understanding thou hast gotten thee riches, and hast gotten gold and silver into thy treasures: ⁵By thy great wisdom and by thy traffick hast thou increased thy riches, and thine heart is lifted up because of thy riches: ⁶Therefore thus saith the Lord GOD; Because thou hast set thine heart as the heart of God; ⁷Behold, therefore I will bring strangers upon thee, the terrible of the nations: and they shall draw their swords against the beauty of thy wisdom, and they shall defile thy brightness. ⁸They shall bring thee down to the pit, and thou shalt die the deaths of them that are slain in the midst of the seas."

Ezekiel 28:12-19 "¹²Son of man, take up a lamentation upon the king of Tyrus, and say unto him, Thus saith the Lord GOD; Thou sealest up the sum, full of wisdom, and perfect in beauty. ¹³Thou hast been in Eden the garden of God; every precious stone was thy covering, the sardius, topaz, and the diamond, the beryl, the onyx, and the jasper, the sapphire, the emerald, and the carbuncle, and gold: the workmanship of thy tabrets and of thy pipes was prepared in thee in the day that thou wast created. ¹⁴Thou art the anointed cherub that covereth; and I have set thee so: thou wast upon the holy mountain of God; thou hast walked up and down in the midst of the stones of fire. ¹⁵Thou wast perfect in thy ways from the day that thou wast created, till iniquity was found in thee. ¹⁶By the multitude of thy merchandise they have filled the midst of thee with violence, and thou hast sinned: therefore I will cast thee as profane out of the mountain of God: and I will destroy thee, O covering cherub, from the midst of the stones of fire. ¹⁷Thine heart was lifted up because of thy beauty, thou hast corrupted thy wisdom by reason of thy brightness: I will cast thee to the ground, I will lay thee before kings, that they may behold thee. ¹⁸Thou hast defiled thy sanctuaries by the multitude of thine iniquities, by the iniquity of thy traffick; therefore will I bring forth a fire from the midst of thee, it shall devour thee, and I will bring thee to ashes upon the earth in the sight of all them that behold thee. ¹⁹All they that know thee among the people shall be astonished at thee: thou shalt be a terror, and never shalt thou be any more."

Daniel 5:18-31 "¹⁸O thou king, the most high God gave Nebuchadnezzar thy father a kingdom, and majesty, and glory, and honour: ¹⁹And for the majesty that he gave him, all people, nations, and languages, trembled and feared before him: whom he would he slew; and whom he would he kept alive; and whom he would he set up; and whom he would he put down. ²⁰But when his heart was lifted up, and his mind hardened in pride, he was deposed from his kingly throne, and they took his glory from him: ²¹And he was driven from the sons of men; and his heart was made like the beasts, and his dwelling was with the wild asses: they fed him with grass like oxen, and his body was wet with the dew of heaven; till he knew that the most high God ruled in the kingdom of men, and that he appointeth over it whomsoever he will. ²²And thou his son, O Belshazzar, hast not humbled thine heart, though thou knewest all this; ²³But hast lifted up thyself against the LORD of heaven; and they have brought the vessels of his house before thee, and thou, and thy lords, thy wives, and thy concubines, have drunk wine in them; and thou hast praised the gods of silver, and gold, of brass, iron, wood, and stone, which see not, nor hear, nor know: and the God in whose hand thy breath is, and whose are all thy ways, hast thou not glorified: [24]Then was the part of the hand sent from him; and this writing was written. [25]And this is the writing that was written, MENE, MENE, TEKEL, UPHARSIN. [26]This is the interpretation of the thing: MENE; God hath numbered thy kingdom, and finished it. [27]TEKEL; Thou art weighed in the balances, and art found wanting. [28]PERES; Thy kingdom is divided, and given to the Medes and Persians. [29]Then commanded Belshazzar, and they clothed Daniel with scarlet, and put a chain of gold about his neck, and made a proclamation concerning him, that he should be the third ruler in the kingdom. [30]In that night was Belshazzar the king of the Chaldeans slain. [31]And Darius the Median took the kingdom, being about threescore and two years old."

Obadiah 1-4 "[1]The vision of Obadiah. Thus saith the Lord GOD concerning Edom; We have heard a rumour from the LORD, and an ambassador is sent among the heathen, Arise ye, and let us rise up against her in battle. [2]Behold, I have made thee small among the heathen: thou art greatly despised. [3]The pride of thine heart hath deceived thee, thou that dwellest in the clefts of the rock, whose habitation is high; that saith in his heart, Who shall bring me down to the ground? [4]Though thou exalt thyself as the eagle, and though thou set thy nest among the stars, thence will I bring thee down, saith the LORD."

Zephaniah 2:9-10 "[9]Therefore as I live, saith the LORD of hosts, the God of Israel, Surely Moab shall be as Sodom, and the children of Ammon as Gomorrah, even the breeding of nettles, and saltpits, and a perpetual desolation: the residue of my people shall spoil them, and the remnant of my people shall possess them. [10]This shall they have for their pride, because they have reproached and magnified themselves against the people of the LORD of hosts."

What Accompanies Pride
Proverbs 11:2 "When pride cometh, then cometh shame: but with the lowly is wisdom."

Proverbs 13:10 "Only by pride cometh contention: but with the well advised is wisdom."

What Follows Pride
Proverbs 16:18 "Pride goeth before destruction, and an haughty spirit before a fall."

Proverbs 18:12 "Before destruction the heart of man is haughty, and before honour is humility."

Who Hates Pride And Arrogancy
Proverbs 8:13 "The fear of the LORD is to hate evil: pride, and arrogancy, and the evil way, and the froward mouth, do I hate."

Who Is Proud
Proverbs 14:3 "In the mouth of the foolish is a rod of pride: but the lips of the wise shall preserve them."

Proverbs 21:24 "Proud and haughty scorner is his name, who dealeth in proud wrath."

Habakkuk 2:4-5 "[4]Behold, his soul which is lifted up is not upright in him: but the just shall live by his faith. [5]Yea also, because he transgresseth by wine, he is a proud man, neither keepeth at home, who enlargeth his desire as hell, and is as death, and cannot be satisfied, but gathereth unto him all nations, and heapeth unto him all people."

1 Timothy 6:3-5 "[3]If any man teach otherwise, and consent not to wholesome words, even the words of our Lord Jesus Christ, and to the doctrine which is according to godliness; [4]He is proud, knowing nothing, but doting about questions and strifes of words, whereof cometh envy, strife, railings, evil surmisings, [5]Perverse disputings of men of corrupt minds, and destitute of the truth, supposing that gain is godliness: from such withdraw thyself."

PRIESTS

Disobedient Priests
Zephaniah 3:1-4 "[1]Woe to her that is filthy and polluted, to the oppressing city! [2]She obeyed not the voice; she received not correction; she trusted not in the LORD; she drew not near to her God. [3]Her princes within her are roaring lions; her judges are evening wolves; they gnaw not the bones till the morrow. [4]Her prophets are light and treacherous persons: her priests have polluted the sanctuary, they have done violence to the law."

Malachi 2:1-9 "[1]And now, O ye priests, this commandment is for you. [2]If ye will not hear, and if ye will not lay it to heart, to give glory unto my name, saith the LORD of hosts, I will even send a curse upon you, and I will curse your blessings: yea, I have cursed them already, because ye do not lay it to heart. ³Behold, I will corrupt your seed, and spread dung upon your faces, even the dung of your solemn feasts; and one shall take you away with it. ⁴And ye shall know that I have sent this commandment unto you, that my covenant might be with Levi, saith the LORD of hosts. ⁵My covenant was with him of life and peace; and I gave them to him for the fear wherewith he feared me, and was afraid before my name. ⁶The law of truth was in his mouth, and iniquity was not found in his lips: he walked with me in peace and equity, and did turn many away from iniquity. ⁷For the priest's lips should keep knowledge, and they should seek the law at his mouth: for he is the messenger of the LORD of hosts. ⁸But ye are departed out of the way; ye have caused many to stumble at the law; ye have corrupted the covenant of Levi, saith the LORD of hosts. ⁹Therefore have I also made you contemptible and base before all the people, according as ye have not kept my ways, but have been partial in the law."

Priests That Despise The Name Of The Lord

Malachi 1:6 "A son honoureth his father, and a servant his master: if then I be a father, where is mine honour? and if I be a master, where is my fear? saith the LORD of hosts unto you, O priests, that despise my name. And ye say, Wherein have we despised thy name?"

The Duties Of A Priest

Leviticus 21:1-15 "¹And the LORD said unto Moses, Speak unto the priests the sons of Aaron, and say unto them, There shall none be defiled for the dead among his people: ²But for his kin, that is near unto him, that is, for his mother, and for his father, and for his son, and for his daughter, and for his brother, ³And for his sister a virgin, that is nigh unto him, which hath had no husband; for her may he be defiled. ⁴But he shall not defile himself, being a chief man among his people, to profane himself. ⁵They shall not make baldness upon their head, neither shall they shave off the corner of their beard, nor make any cuttings in their flesh. ⁶They shall be holy unto their God, and not profane the name of their God: for the offerings of the LORD made by fire, and the bread of their God, they do offer: therefore they shall be holy. ⁷They shall not take a wife that is a whore, or profane; neither shall they take a woman put away from her husband: for he is holy unto his God. ⁸Thou shalt sanctify him therefore; for he offereth the bread of thy God: he shall be holy unto thee: for I the LORD, which sanctify you, am holy. ⁹And the daughter of any priest, if she profane herself by playing the whore, she profaneth her father: she shall be burnt with fire. ¹⁰And he that is the high priest among his brethren, upon whose head the anointing oil was poured, and that is consecrated to put on the garments, shall not uncover his head, nor rend his clothes; ¹¹Neither shall he go in to any dead body, nor defile himself for his father, or for his mother; ¹²Neither shall he go out of the sanctuary, nor profane the sanctuary of his God; for the crown of the anointing oil of his God is upon him: I am the LORD. ¹³And he shall take a wife in her virginity. ¹⁴A widow, or a divorced woman, or profane, or an harlot, these shall he not take: but he shall take a virgin of his own people to wife. ¹⁵Neither shall he profane his seed among his people: for I the LORD do sanctify him."

Malachi 2:1-7 "¹And now, O ye priests, this commandment is for you. ²If ye will not hear, and if ye will not lay it to heart, to give glory unto my name, saith the LORD of hosts, I will even send a curse upon you, and I will curse your blessings: yea, I have cursed them already, because ye do not lay it to heart. ³Behold, I will corrupt your seed, and spread dung upon your faces, even the dung of your solemn feasts; and one shall take you away with it. ⁴And ye shall know that I have sent this commandment unto you, that my covenant might be with Levi, saith the LORD of hosts. ⁵My covenant was with him of life and peace; and I gave them to him for the fear wherewith he feared me, and was afraid before my name. ⁶The law of truth was in his mouth, and iniquity was not found in his lips: he walked with me in peace and equity, and did turn many away from iniquity. ⁷For the priest's lips should keep knowledge, and they should seek the law at his mouth: for he is the messenger of the LORD of hosts."

Who Shall Be Priests Of God And Of Christ

Revelation 20:6 "Blessed and holy is he that hath part in the first resurrection: on such the second death hath no power, but they shall be priests of

God and of Christ, and shall reign with him a thousand years."

PROFIT

Those That Profit From Violence

Deuteronomy 27:24-25 "24Cursed be he that smiteth his neighbour secretly. And all the people shall say, Amen. 25Cursed be he that taketh reward to slay an innocent person. And all the people shall say, Amen."

Proverbs 1:10-19 "10My son, if sinners entice thee, consent thou not. 11If they say, Come with us, let us lay wait for blood, let us lurk privily for the innocent without cause: 12Let us swallow them up alive as the grave; and whole, as those that go down into the pit: 13We shall find all precious substance, we shall fill our houses with spoil: 14Cast in thy lot among us; let us all have one purse: 15My son, walk not thou in the way with them; refrain thy foot from their path: 16For their feet run to evil, and make haste to shed blood. 17Surely in vain the net is spread in the sight of any bird. 18And they lay wait for their own blood; they lurk privily for their own lives. 19So are the ways of every one that is greedy of gain; which taketh away the life of the owners thereof."

Ezekiel 18:1-13 "1The word of the LORD came unto me again, saying, 2What mean ye, that ye use this proverb concerning the land of Israel, saying, The fathers have eaten sour grapes, and the children's teeth are set on edge? 3As I live, saith the Lord GOD, ye shall not have occasion any more to use this proverb in Israel. 4Behold, all souls are mine; as the soul of the father, so also the soul of the son is mine: the soul that sinneth, it shall die. 5But if a man be just, and do that which is lawful and right, 6And hath not eaten upon the mountains, neither hath lifted up his eyes to the idols of the house of Israel, neither hath defiled his neighbour's wife, neither hath come near to a menstruous woman, 7And hath not oppressed any, but hath restored to the debtor his pledge, hath spoiled none by violence, hath given his bread to the hungry, and hath covered the naked with a garment; 8He that hath not given forth upon usury, neither hath taken any increase, that hath withdrawn his hand from iniquity, hath executed true judgment between man and man, 9Hath walked in my statutes, and hath kept my judgments, to deal truly; he is just, he shall surely live, saith the Lord GOD. 10If he beget a son that is a robber, a shedder of blood, and that doeth the like to any one of these things, 11And that doeth not any of those duties, but even hath eaten upon the mountains, and defiled his neighbour's wife, 12Hath oppressed the poor and needy, hath spoiled by violence, hath not restored the pledge, and hath lifted up his eyes to the idols, hath committed abomination, 13Hath given forth upon usury, and hath taken increase: shall he then live? he shall not live: he hath done all these abominations; he shall surely die; his blood shall be upon him."

Habakkuk 2:6-17 "6Shall not all these take up a parable against him, and a taunting proverb against him, and say, Woe to him that increaseth that which is not his! how long? and to him that ladeth himself with thick clay! 7Shall they not rise up suddenly that shall bite thee, and awake that shall vex thee, and thou shalt be for booties unto them? 8Because thou hast spoiled many nations, all the remnant of the people shall spoil thee; because of men's blood, and for the violence of the land, of the city, and of all that dwell therein. 9Woe to him that coveteth an evil covetousness to his house, that he may set his nest on high, that he may be delivered from the power of evil! 10Thou hast consulted shame to thy house by cutting off many people, and hast sinned against thy soul. 11For the stone shall cry out of the wall, and the beam out of the timber shall answer it. 12Woe to him that buildeth a town with blood, and stablisheth a city by iniquity! 13Behold, is it not of the LORD of hosts that the people shall labour in the very fire, and the people shall weary themselves for very vanity? 14For the earth shall be filled with the knowledge of the glory of the LORD, as the waters cover the sea. 15Woe unto him that giveth his neighbour drink, that puttest thy bottle to him, and makest him drunken also, that thou mayest look on their nakedness! 16Thou art filled with shame for glory: drink thou also, and let thy foreskin be uncovered: the cup of the LORD's right hand shall be turned unto thee, and shameful spewing shall be on thy glory. 17For the violence of Lebanon shall cover thee, and the spoil of beasts, which made them afraid, because of men's blood, and for the violence of the land, of the city, and of all that dwell therein."

What Is Not Profitable

Proverbs 10:2 "Treasures of wickedness profit nothing: but righteousness delivereth from death."

Isaiah 44:9-10 "⁹They that make a graven image are all of them vanity; and their delectable things shall not profit; and they are their own witnesses; they see not, nor know; that they may be ashamed. ¹⁰Who hath formed a god, or molten a graven image that is profitable for nothing?"

Isaiah 57:3-12 "³But draw near hither, ye sons of the sorceress, the seed of the adulterer and the whore. ⁴Against whom do ye sport yourselves? against whom make ye a wide mouth, and draw out the tongue? are ye not children of transgression, a seed of falsehood, ⁵Enflaming yourselves with idols under every green tree, slaying the children in the valleys under the clifts of the rocks? ⁶Among the smooth stones of the stream is thy portion; they, they are thy lot: even to them hast thou poured a drink offering, thou hast offered a meat offering. Should I receive comfort in these? ⁷Upon a lofty and high mountain hast thou set thy bed: even thither wentest thou up to offer sacrifice. ⁸Behind the doors also and the posts hast thou set up thy remembrance: for thou hast discovered thyself to another than me, and art gone up; thou hast enlarged thy bed, and made thee a covenant with them; thou lovedst their bed where thou sawest it. ⁹And thou wentest to the king with ointment, and didst increase thy perfumes, and didst send thy messengers far off, and didst debase thyself even unto hell. ¹⁰Thou art wearied in the greatness of thy way; yet saidst thou not, There is no hope: thou hast found the life of thine hand; therefore thou wast not grieved. ¹¹And of whom hast thou been afraid or feared, that thou hast lied, and hast not remembered me, nor laid it to thy heart? have not I held my peace even of old, and thou fearest me not? ¹²I will declare thy righteousness, and thy works; for they shall not profit thee."

Jeremiah 2:11 "Hath a nation changed their gods, which are yet no gods? but my people have changed their glory for that which doth not profit."

Jeremiah 16:19-20 "¹⁹O LORD, my strength, and my fortress, and my refuge in the day of affliction, the Gentiles shall come unto thee from the ends of the earth, and shall say, Surely our fathers have inherited lies, vanity, and things wherein there is no profit. ²⁰Shall a man make gods unto himself, and they are no gods?"

Habakkuk 2:18-19 "¹⁸What profiteth the graven image that the maker thereof hath graven it; the molten image, and a teacher of lies, that the maker of his work trusteth therein, to make dumb idols? ¹⁹Woe unto him that saith to the wood, Awake; to the dumb stone, Arise, it shall teach! Behold, it is laid over with gold and silver, and there is no breath at all in the midst of it."

Matthew 16:26 "For what is a man profited, if he shall gain the whole world, and lose his own soul? or what shall a man give in exchange for his soul?"

Mark 8:36-37 "³⁶For what shall it profit a man, if he shall gain the whole world, and lose his own soul? ³⁷Or what shall a man give in exchange for his soul?"

Luke 9:25 "For what is a man advantaged, if he gain the whole world, and lose himself, or be cast away?"

John 6:63 "It is the spirit that quickeneth; the flesh profiteth nothing: the words that I speak unto you, they are spirit, and they are life."

What Is Profitable

Job 35:8 "Thy wickedness may hurt a man as thou art; and thy righteousness may profit the son of man."

Proverbs 14:23 "In all labour there is profit: but the talk of the lips tendeth only to penury."

Ecclesiastes 7:11 "Wisdom is good with an inheritance: and by it there is profit to them that see the sun."

1 Timothy 4:8 "For bodily exercise profiteth little: but godliness is profitable unto all things, having promise of the life that now is, and of that which is to come."

Titus 3:1-8 "¹Put them in mind to be subject to principalities and powers, to obey magistrates, to be ready to every good work, ²To speak evil of no man, to be no brawlers, but gentle, shewing all meekness unto all men. ³For we ourselves also were sometimes foolish, disobedient, deceived, serving divers lusts and pleasures, living in malice and envy, hateful, and hating one another. [4]But after that the kindness and love of God our Saviour toward man appeared, [5]Not by works of righteousness which we have done, but according to his mercy he saved us, by the washing of regeneration, and renewing of the Holy Ghost; [6]Which he shed on us abundantly through Jesus Christ our Saviour; [7]That being justified by his grace, we should be made heirs according to the hope of eternal life. [8]This is a faithful saying, and these things I will that thou affirm constantly, that they which have believed in God might be careful to maintain good works. These things are good and profitable unto men."

What Will Not Profit In The Day Of Wrath

Proverbs 11:4 "Riches profit not in the day of wrath: but righteousness delivereth from death."

Zephaniah 1:18 "Neither their silver nor their gold shall be able to deliver them in the day of the LORD's wrath; but the whole land shall be devoured by the fire of his jealousy: for he shall make even a speedy riddance of all them that dwell in the land."

Who Does Not Profit Others

Jeremiah 23:30-32 "[30]Therefore, behold, I am against the prophets, saith the LORD, that steal my words every one from his neighbour. [31]Behold, I am against the prophets, saith the LORD, that use their tongues, and say, He saith. [32]Behold, I am against them that prophesy false dreams, saith the LORD, and do tell them, and cause my people to err by their lies, and by their lightness; yet I sent them not, nor commanded them: therefore they shall not profit this people at all, saith the LORD."

PROOF

The Lord Proving

Exodus 20:18-20 "[18]And all the people saw the thunderings, and the lightnings, and the noise of the trumpet, and the mountain smoking: and when the people saw it, they removed, and stood afar off. [19]And they said unto Moses, Speak thou with us, and we will hear: but let not God speak with us, lest we die. [20]And Moses said unto the people, Fear not: for God is come to prove you, and that his fear may be before your faces, that ye sin not."

Deuteronomy 13:1-3 "[1]If there arise among you a prophet, or a dreamer of dreams, and giveth thee a sign or a wonder, [2]And the sign or the wonder come to pass, whereof he spake unto thee, saying, Let us go after other gods, which thou hast not known, and let us serve them; [3]Thou shalt not hearken unto the words of that prophet, or that dreamer of dreams: for the LORD your God proveth you, to know whether ye love the LORD your God with all your heart and with all your soul."

Judges 2:20-23 "[20]And the anger of the LORD was hot against Israel; and he said, Because that this people hath transgressed my covenant which I commanded their fathers, and have not hearkened unto my voice; [21]I also will not henceforth drive out any from before them of the nations which Joshua left when he died: [22]That through them I may prove Israel, whether they will keep the way of the LORD to walk therein, as their fathers did keep it, or not. [23]Therefore the LORD left those nations, without driving them out hastily; neither delivered he them into the hand of Joshua."

Psalm 26:2 "Examine me, O LORD, and prove me; try my reins and my heart."

What To Prove

Romans 12:1-2 "[1]I beseech you therefore, brethren, by the mercies of God, that ye present your bodies a living sacrifice, holy, acceptable unto God, which is your reasonable service. [2]And be not conformed to this world: but be ye transformed by the renewing of your mind, that ye may prove what is that good, and acceptable, and perfect, will of God."

Galatians 6:3-4 "[3]For if a man think himself to be something, when he is nothing, he deceiveth himself. [4]But let every man prove his own work, and then shall he have rejoicing in himself alone, and not in another."

1 Thessalonians 5:21 "Prove all things; hold fast that which is good."

PROPHECY AND PROPHETS

False Prophets

Deuteronomy 18:17-20 "[17]And the LORD said unto me, They have well spoken that which they have spoken. ¹⁸I will raise them up a Prophet from among their brethren, like unto thee, and will put my words in his mouth; and he shall speak unto them all that I shall command him. ¹⁹And it shall come to pass, that whosoever will not hearken unto my words which he shall speak in my name, I will require it of him. ²⁰But the prophet, which shall presume to speak a word in my name, which I have not commanded him to speak, or that shall speak in the name of other gods, even that prophet shall die."

Jeremiah 14:13-15 "¹³Then said I, Ah, Lord GOD! behold, the prophets say unto them, Ye shall not see the sword, neither shall ye have famine; but I will give you assured peace in this place. ¹⁴Then the LORD said unto me, The prophets prophesy lies in my name: I sent them not, neither have I commanded them, neither spake unto them: they prophesy unto you a false vision and divination, and a thing of nought, and the deceit of their heart. ¹⁵Therefore thus saith the LORD concerning the prophets that prophesy in my name, and I sent them not, yet they say, Sword and famine shall not be in this land; By sword and famine shall those prophets be consumed."

Jeremiah 23:9-32 "⁹Mine heart within me is broken because of the prophets; all my bones shake; I am like a drunken man, and like a man whom wine hath overcome, because of the LORD, and because of the words of his holiness. ¹⁰For the land is full of adulterers; for because of swearing the land mourneth; the pleasant places of the wilderness are dried up, and their course is evil, and their force is not right. ¹¹For both prophet and priest are profane; yea, in my house have I found their wickedness, saith the LORD. ¹²Wherefore their way shall be unto them as slippery ways in the darkness: they shall be driven on, and fall therein: for I will bring evil upon them, even the year of their visitation, saith the LORD. ¹³And I have seen folly in the prophets of Samaria; they prophesied in Baal, and caused my people Israel to err. ¹⁴I have seen also in the prophets of Jerusalem an horrible thing: they commit adultery, and walk in lies: they strengthen also the hands of evildoers, that none doth return from his wickedness: they are all of them unto me as Sodom, and the inhabitants thereof as Gomorrah. ¹⁵Therefore thus saith the LORD of hosts concerning the prophets;

Behold, I will feed them with wormwood, and make them drink the water of gall: for from the prophets of Jerusalem is profaneness gone forth into all the land. ¹⁶Thus saith the LORD of hosts, Hearken not unto the words of the prophets that prophesy unto you: they make you vain: they speak a vision of their own heart, and not out of the mouth of the LORD. ¹⁷They say still unto them that despise me, The LORD hath said, Ye shall have peace; and they say unto every one that walketh after the imagination of his own heart, No evil shall come upon you. ¹⁸For who hath stood in the counsel of the LORD, and hath perceived and heard his word? who hath marked his word, and heard it? ¹⁹Behold, a whirlwind of the LORD is gone forth in fury, even a grievous whirlwind: it shall fall grievously upon the head of the wicked. ²⁰The anger of the LORD shall not return, until he have executed, and till he have performed the thoughts of his heart: in the latter days ye shall consider it perfectly. ²¹I have not sent these prophets, yet they ran: I have not spoken to them, yet they prophesied. ²²But if they had stood in my counsel, and had caused my people to hear my words, then they should have turned them from their evil way, and from the evil of their doings. ²³Am I a God at hand, saith the LORD, and not a God afar off? ²⁴Can any hide himself in secret places that I shall not see him? saith the LORD. Do not I fill heaven and earth? saith the LORD. ²⁵I have heard what the prophets said, that prophesy lies in my name, saying, I have dreamed, I have dreamed. ²⁶How long shall this be in the heart of the prophets that prophesy lies? yea, they are prophets of the deceit of their own heart; ²⁷Which think to cause my people to forget my name by their dreams which they tell every man to his neighbour, as their fathers have forgotten my name for Baal. ²⁸The prophet that hath a dream, let him tell a dream; and he that hath my word, let him speak my word faithfully. What is the chaff to the wheat? saith the LORD. ²⁹Is not my word like as a fire? saith the LORD; and like a hammer that breaketh the rock in pieces? ³⁰Therefore, behold, I am against the prophets, saith the LORD, that steal my words every one from his neighbour. ³¹Behold, I am against the prophets, saith the LORD, that use their tongues, and say, He saith. ³²Behold, I am against them that prophesy false dreams, saith the LORD, and do tell them, and cause my people to err by their lies, and by their lightness; yet I sent them not, nor commanded them: therefore they shall not profit this people at all, saith the LORD."

Jeremiah 27:9-10 "⁹Therefore hearken not ye to your prophets, nor to your diviners, nor to your dreamers, nor to your enchanters, nor to your sorcerers, which speak unto you, saying, Ye shall not serve the king of Babylon: ¹⁰For they prophesy a lie unto you, to remove you far from your land; and that I should drive you out, and ye should perish."

Jeremiah 28:1-17 "¹And it came to pass the same year, in the beginning of the reign of Zedekiah king of Judah, in the fourth year, and in the fifth month, that Hananiah the son of Azur the prophet, which was of Gibeon, spake unto me in the house of the LORD, in the presence of the priests and of all the people, saying, ²Thus speaketh the LORD of hosts, the God of Israel, saying, I have broken the yoke of the king of Babylon. ³Within two full years will I bring again into this place all the vessels of the LORD's house, that Nebuchadnezzar king of Babylon took away from this place, and carried them to Babylon: ⁴And I will bring again to this place Jeconiah the son of Jehoiakim king of Judah, with all the captives of Judah, that went into Babylon, saith the LORD: for I will break the yoke of the king of Babylon. ⁵Then the prophet Jeremiah said unto the prophet Hananiah in the presence of the priests, and in the presence of all the people that stood in the house of the LORD, ⁶Even the prophet Jeremiah said, Amen: the LORD do so: the LORD perform thy words which thou hast prophesied, to bring again the vessels of the LORD's house, and all that is carried away captive, from Babylon into this place. ⁷Nevertheless hear thou now this word that I speak in thine ears, and in the ears of all the people; ⁸The prophets that have been before me and before thee of old prophesied both against many countries, and against great kingdoms, of war, and of evil, and of pestilence. ⁹The prophet which prophesieth of peace, when the word of the prophet shall come to pass, then shall the prophet be known, that the LORD hath truly sent him. ¹⁰Then Hananiah the prophet took the yoke from off the prophet Jeremiah's neck, and brake it. ¹¹And Hananiah spake in the presence of all the

people, saying, Thus saith the LORD; Even so will I break the yoke of Nebuchadnezzar king of Babylon from the neck of all nations within the space of two full years. And the prophet Jeremiah went his way. ¹²Then the word of the LORD came unto Jeremiah the prophet, after that Hananiah the prophet had broken the yoke from off the neck of the prophet Jeremiah, saying, ¹³Go and tell Hananiah, saying, Thus saith the LORD; Thou hast broken the yokes of wood; but thou shalt make for them yokes of iron. ¹⁴For thus saith the LORD of hosts, the God of Israel; I have put a yoke of iron upon the neck of all these nations, that they may serve Nebuchadnezzar king of Babylon; and they shall serve him: and I have given him the beasts of the field also. ¹⁵Then said the prophet Jeremiah unto Hananiah the prophet, Hear now, Hananiah; The LORD hath not sent thee; but thou makest this people to trust in a lie. ¹⁶Therefore thus saith the LORD; Behold, I will cast thee from off the face of the earth: this year thou shalt die, because thou hast taught rebellion against the LORD. ¹⁷So Hananiah the prophet died the same year in the seventh month."

Jeremiah 29:8-9 "⁸For thus saith the LORD of hosts, the God of Israel; Let not your prophets and your diviners, that be in the midst of you, deceive you, neither hearken to your dreams which ye cause to be dreamed. ⁹For they prophesy falsely unto you in my name: I have not sent them, saith the LORD."

Lamentations 2:14 "Thy prophets have seen vain and foolish things for thee: and they have not discovered thine iniquity, to turn away thy captivity; but have seen for thee false burdens and causes of banishment."

Ezekiel 13:3-10 "³Thus saith the Lord GOD; Woe unto the foolish prophets, that follow their own spirit, and have seen nothing! ⁴O Israel, thy prophets are like the foxes in the deserts. ⁵Ye have not gone up into the gaps, neither made up the hedge for the house of Israel to stand in the battle in the day of the LORD. ⁶They have seen vanity and lying divination, saying, The LORD saith: and the LORD hath not sent them: and they have made others to hope that they would confirm the word. ⁷Have ye not seen a vain vision, and have ye not spoken a lying divination, whereas ye say, The

LORD saith it; albeit I have not spoken? [8]Therefore thus saith the Lord GOD; Because ye have spoken vanity, and seen lies, therefore, behold, I am against you, saith the Lord GOD. [9]And mine hand shall be upon the prophets that see vanity, and that divine lies: they shall not be in the assembly of my people, neither shall they be written in the writing of the house of Israel, neither shall they enter into the land of Israel; and ye shall know that I am the Lord GOD. [10]Because, even because they have seduced my people, saying, Peace; and there was no peace; and one built up a wall, and, lo, others daubed it with untempered morter."

Ezekiel 13:17-23 "[17]Likewise, thou son of man, set thy face against the daughters of thy people, which prophesy out of their own heart; and prophesy thou against them, [18]And say, Thus saith the Lord GOD; Woe to the women that sew pillows to all armholes, and make kerchiefs upon the head of every stature to hunt souls! Will ye hunt the souls of my people, and will ye save the souls alive that come unto you? [19]And will ye pollute me among my people for handfuls of barley and for pieces of bread, to slay the souls that should not die, and to save the souls alive that should not live, by your lying to my people that hear your lies? [20]Wherefore thus saith the Lord GOD; Behold, I am against your pillows, wherewith ye there hunt the souls to make them fly, and I will tear them from your arms, and will let the souls go, even the souls that ye hunt to make them fly. [21]Your kerchiefs also will I tear, and deliver my people out of your hand, and they shall be no more in your hand to be hunted; and ye shall know that I am the LORD. [22]Because with lies ye have made the heart of the righteous sad, whom I have not made sad; and strengthened the hands of the wicked, that he should not return from his wicked way, by promising him life: [23]Therefore ye shall see no more vanity, nor divine divinations: for I will deliver my people out of your hand: and ye shall know that I am the LORD."

Ezekiel 14:9-10 "[9]And if the prophet be deceived when he hath spoken a thing, I the LORD have deceived that prophet, and I will stretch out my hand upon him, and will destroy him from the midst of my people Israel. [10]And they shall bear the punishment of their iniquity: the punishment of the prophet shall be even as the punishment of him that seeketh unto him."

Ezekiel 22:28 "And her prophets have daubed them with untempered morter, seeing vanity, and divining lies unto them, saying, Thus saith the Lord GOD, when the LORD hath not spoken."

Zephaniah 3:1-4 "[1]Woe to her that is filthy and polluted, to the oppressing city! [2]She obeyed not the voice; she received not correction; she trusted not in the LORD; she drew not near to her God. [3]Her princes within her are roaring lions; her judges are evening wolves; they gnaw not the bones till the morrow. [4]Her prophets are light and treacherous persons: her priests have polluted the sanctuary, they have done violence to the law."

Matthew 7:15-23 "[15]Beware of false prophets, which come to you in sheep's clothing, but inwardly they are ravening wolves. [16]Ye shall know them by their fruits. Do men gather grapes of thorns, or figs of thistles? [17]Even so every good tree bringeth forth good fruit; but a corrupt tree bringeth forth evil fruit. [18]A good tree cannot bring forth evil fruit, neither can a corrupt tree bring forth good fruit. [19]Every tree that bringeth not forth good fruit is hewn down, and cast into the fire. [20]Wherefore by their fruits ye shall know them. [21]Not every one that saith unto me, Lord, Lord, shall enter into the kingdom of heaven; but he that doeth the will of my Father which is in heaven. [22]Many will say to me in that day, Lord, Lord, have we not prophesied in thy name? and in thy name have cast out devils? and in thy name done many wonderful works? [23]And then will I profess unto them, I never knew you: depart from me, ye that work iniquity."

Matthew 24:11 "And many false prophets shall rise, and shall deceive many."

Matthew 24:23-24 "[23]Then if any man shall say unto you, Lo, here is Christ, or there; believe it not. [24]For there shall arise false Christs, and false prophets, and shall shew great signs and wonders; insomuch that, if it were possible, they shall deceive the very elect."

Mark 13:21-22 "[21]And then if any man shall say to you, Lo, here is Christ; or, lo, he is there; believe him not: [22]For false Christs and false prophets shall rise, and shall shew signs and wonders, to seduce, if it were possible, even the elect."

2 Peter 2:1-22 "¹But there were false prophets also among the people, even as there shall be false teachers among you, who privily shall bring in damnable heresies, even denying the Lord that bought them, and bring upon themselves swift destruction. ²And many shall follow their pernicious ways; by reason of whom the way of truth shall be evil spoken of. ³And through covetousness shall they with feigned words make merchandise of you: whose judgment now of a long time lingereth not, and their damnation slumbereth not. ⁴For if God spared not the angels that sinned, but cast them down to hell, and delivered them into chains of darkness, to be reserved unto judgment; ⁵And spared not the old world, but saved Noah the eighth person, a preacher of righteousness, bringing in the flood upon the world of the ungodly; ⁶And turning the cities of Sodom and Gomorrha into ashes condemned them with an overthrow, making them an ensample unto those that after should live ungodly; ⁷And delivered just Lot, vexed with the filthy conversation of the wicked: ⁸(For that righteous man dwelling among them, in seeing and hearing, vexed his righteous soul from day to day with their unlawful deeds;) ⁹The Lord knoweth how to deliver the godly out of temptations, and to reserve the unjust unto the day of judgment to be punished: ¹⁰But chiefly them that walk after the flesh in the lust of uncleanness, and despise government. Presumptuous are they, selfwilled, they are not afraid to speak evil of dignities. ¹¹Whereas angels, which are greater in power and might, bring not railing accusation against them before the Lord. ¹²But these, as natural brute beasts, made to be taken and destroyed, speak evil of the things that they understand not; and shall utterly perish in their own corruption; ¹³And shall receive the reward of unrighteousness, as they that count it pleasure to riot in the day time. Spots they are and blemishes, sporting themselves with their own deceivings while they feast with you; ¹⁴Having eyes full of adultery, and that cannot cease from sin; beguiling unstable souls: an heart they have exercised with covetous practices; cursed children: ¹⁵Which have forsaken the right way, and are gone astray, following the way of Balaam the son of Bosor, who loved the wages of unrighteousness; ¹⁶But was rebuked for his iniquity: the dumb ass speaking with man's voice forbad the madness of the prophet. ¹⁷These are wells without water, clouds that are carried with a tempest; to whom the mist of darkness is reserved for ever. ¹⁸For when they speak great swelling words of vanity, they allure through the lusts of the flesh, through much wantonness, those that were clean escaped from them who live in error. ¹⁹While they promise them liberty, they themselves are the servants of corruption: for of whom a man is overcome, of the same is he brought in bondage. ²⁰For if after they have escaped the pollutions of the world through the knowledge of the Lord and Saviour Jesus Christ, they are again entangled therein, and overcome, the latter end is worse with them than the beginning. ²¹For it had been better for them not to have known the way of righteousness, than, after they have known it, to turn from the holy commandment delivered unto them. ²²But it is happened unto them according to the true proverb, The dog is turned to his own vomit again; and the sow that was washed to her wallowing in the mire."

1 John 4:1 "Beloved, believe not every spirit, but try the spirits whether they are of God: because many false prophets are gone out into the world."

Revelation 2:18-23 "¹⁸And unto the angel of the church in Thyatira write; These things saith the Son of God, who hath his eyes like unto a flame of fire, and his feet are like fine brass; ¹⁹I know thy works, and charity, and service, and faith, and thy patience, and thy works; and the last to be more than the first. ²⁰Notwithstanding I have a few things against thee, because thou sufferest that woman Jezebel, which calleth herself a prophetess, to teach and to seduce my servants to commit fornication, and to eat things sacrificed unto idols. ²¹And I gave her space to repent of her fornication; and she repented not. ²²Behold, I will cast her into a bed, and them that commit adultery with her into great tribulation, except they repent of their deeds. ²³And I will kill her children with death; and all the churches shall know that I am he which searcheth the reins and hearts: and I will give unto every one of you according to your works."

How To Prophesy

Romans 12:4-6 "⁴For as we have many members in one body, and all members have not the same office: ⁵So we, being many, are one body in Christ, and every one members one of another. [6]Having then gifts differing according to the grace that is given to us, whether prophecy, let us prophesy according to the proportion of faith."

How To Spot A True Prophet And A False Prophet

Deuteronomy 18:21-22 "[21]And if thou say in thine heart, How shall we know the word which the LORD hath not spoken? [22]When a prophet speaketh in the name of the LORD, if the thing follow not, nor come to pass, that is the thing which the LORD hath not spoken, but the prophet hath spoken it presumptuously: thou shalt not be afraid of him."

Jeremiah 28:8-9 "[8]The prophets that have been before me and before thee of old prophesied both against many countries, and against great kingdoms, of war, and of evil, and of pestilence. [9]The prophet which prophesieth of peace, when the word of the prophet shall come to pass, then shall the prophet be known, that the LORD hath truly sent him."

Ezekiel 33:27-33 "[27]Say thou thus unto them, Thus saith the Lord GOD; As I live, surely they that are in the wastes shall fall by the sword, and him that is in the open field will I give to the beasts to be devoured, and they that be in the forts and in the caves shall die of the pestilence. [28]For I will lay the land most desolate, and the pomp of her strength shall cease; and the mountains of Israel shall be desolate, that none shall pass through. [29]Then shall they know that I am the LORD, when I have laid the land most desolate because of all their abominations which they have committed. [30]Also, thou son of man, the children of thy people still are talking against thee by the walls and in the doors of the houses, and speak one to another, every one to his brother, saying, Come, I pray you, and hear what is the word that cometh forth from the LORD. [31]And they come unto thee as the people cometh, and they sit before thee as my people, and they hear thy words, but they will not do them: for with their mouth they shew much love, but their heart goeth after their covetousness. [32]And, lo, thou art unto them as a very lovely song of one that hath a pleasant voice, and can play well on an instrument: for they hear thy words, but they do them not. [33]And when this cometh to pass,

(lo, it will come,) then shall they know that a prophet hath been among them."

Prophesying Vs. Tongues

1 Corinthians 14:1-40 "[1]Follow after charity, and desire spiritual gifts, but rather that ye may prophesy. [2]For he that speaketh in an unknown tongue speaketh not unto men, but unto God: for no man understandeth him; howbeit in the spirit he speaketh mysteries. [3]But he that prophesieth speaketh unto men to edification, and exhortation, and comfort. [4]He that speaketh in an unknown tongue edifieth himself; but he that prophesieth edifieth the church. [5]I would that ye all spake with tongues, but rather that ye prophesied: for greater is he that prophesieth than he that speaketh with tongues, except he interpret, that the church may receive edifying. [6]Now, brethren, if I come unto you speaking with tongues, what shall I profit you, except I shall speak to you either by revelation, or by knowledge, or by prophesying, or by doctrine? [7]And even things without life giving sound, whether pipe or harp, except they give a distinction in the sounds, how shall it be known what is piped or harped? [8]For if the trumpet give an uncertain sound, who shall prepare himself to the battle? [9]So likewise ye, except ye utter by the tongue words easy to be understood, how shall it be known what is spoken? for ye shall speak into the air. [10]There are, it may be, so many kinds of voices in the world, and none of them is without signification. [11]Therefore if I know not the meaning of the voice, I shall be unto him that speaketh a barbarian, and he that speaketh shall be a barbarian unto me. [12]Even so ye, forasmuch as ye are zealous of spiritual gifts, seek that ye may excel to the edifying of the church. [13]Wherefore let him that speaketh in an unknown tongue pray that he may interpret. [14]For if I pray in an unknown tongue, my spirit prayeth, but my understanding is unfruitful. [15]What is it then? I will pray with the spirit, and I will pray with the understanding also: I will sing with the spirit, and I will sing with the understanding also. [16]Else when thou shalt bless with the spirit, how shall he that occupieth the room of the unlearned say Amen at thy giving of thanks, seeing he understandeth not what thou sayest? [17]For thou verily givest thanks well, but the other is not edified. [18]I thank my God, I speak with tongues more than ye all: [19]Yet in the church I had rather speak five words with my understanding, that by my voice I might teach others also, than ten thousand words in an unknown tongue. [20]Brethren, be not children in understanding: howbeit in malice be ye children, but in understanding be men. [21]In the law it is written, With men of other tongues and other lips will I speak unto this people; and yet for all that will they not hear me, saith the Lord. [22]Wherefore tongues are for a sign, not to them that believe, but to them that believe not: but prophesying serveth not for them that believe not, but for them which believe. [23]If therefore the whole church be come together into one place, and all speak with tongues, and there come in those that are unlearned, or unbelievers, will they not say that ye are mad? [24]But if all prophesy, and there come in one that believeth not, or one unlearned, he is convinced of all, he is judged of all: [25]And thus are the secrets of his heart made manifest; and so falling down on his face he will worship God, and report that God is in you of a truth. [26]How is it then, brethren? when ye come together, everyone of you hath a psalm, hath a doctrine, hath a tongue, hath a revelation, hath an interpretation. Let all things be done unto edifying. [27]If any man speak in an unknown tongue, let it be by two, or at the most by three, and that by course; and let one interpret. [28]But if there be no interpreter, let him keep silence in the church; and let him speak to himself, and to God. [29]Let the prophets speak two or three, and let the other judge. [30]If any thing be revealed to another that sitteth by, let the first hold his peace. [31]For ye may all prophesy one by one, that all may learn, and all may be comforted. [32]And the spirits of the prophets are subject to the prophets. [33]For God is not the author of confusion, but of peace, as in all churches of the saints. [34]Let your women keep silence in the churches: for it is not permitted unto them to speak; but they are commanded to be under obedience, as also saith the law. [35]And if they will learn any thing, let them ask their husbands at home: for it is a shame for women to speak in the church. [36]What? came the word of God out from you? or came it unto you only? [37]If any man think himself to be a prophet, or spiritual, let him acknowledge that the things that I write unto you are the commandments of the Lord. [38]But if any man be ignorant, let him be ignorant. [39]Wherefore, brethren,

covet to prophesy, and forbid not to speak with tongues. [40]Let all things be done decently and in order."

The Prophecy Of The Scripture

2 Peter 1:19-21 "[19]We have also a more sure word of prophecy; whereunto ye do well that ye take heed, as unto a light that shineth in a dark place, until the day dawn, and the day star arise in your hearts: [20]Knowing this first, that no prophecy of the scripture is of any private interpretation. [21]For the prophecy came not in old time by the will of man: but holy men of God spake as they were moved by the Holy Ghost."

The Reward For Prophesying

1 Corinthians 14:24-25 "[24]But if all prophesy, and there come in one that believeth not, or one unlearned, he is convinced of all, he is judged of all: [25]And thus are the secrets of his heart made manifest; and so falling down on his face he will worship God, and report that God is in you of a truth."

Those That Add To Or Remove From The Prophecies Of The Bible

Revelation 22:18-19 "[18]For I testify unto every man that heareth the words of the prophecy of this book, If any man shall add unto these things, God shall add unto him the plagues that are written in this book: [19]And if any man shall take away from the words of the book of this prophecy, God shall take away his part out of the book of life, and out of the holy city, and from the things which are written in this book."

Those That Listen To False Prophets

Jeremiah 14:15-16 "[15]Therefore thus saith the LORD concerning the prophets that prophesy in my name, and I sent them not, yet they say, Sword and famine shall not be in this land; By sword and famine shall those prophets be consumed. [16]And the people to whom they prophesy shall be cast out in the streets of Jerusalem because of the famine and the sword; and they shall have none to bury them, them, their wives, nor their sons, nor their daughters: for I will pour their wickedness upon them."

Those That Prophesy

1 Corinthians 14:1-5 "[1]Follow after charity, and desire spiritual gifts, but rather that ye may prophesy. ²For he that speaketh in an unknown tongue speaketh not unto men, but unto God: for no man understandeth him; howbeit in the spirit he speaketh mysteries. ³But he that prophesieth speaketh unto men to edification, and exhortation, and comfort. ⁴He that speaketh in an unknown tongue edifieth himself; but he that prophesieth edifieth the church. ⁵I would that ye all spake with tongues, but rather that ye prophesied: for greater is he that prophesieth than he that speaketh with tongues, except he interpret, that the church may receive edifying."

What Is The Spirit Of Prophecy
Revelation 19:10 "And I fell at his feet to worship him. And he said unto me, See thou do it not: I am thy fellowservant, and of thy brethren that have the testimony of Jesus: worship God: for the testimony of Jesus is the spirit of prophecy."

What Prophet The Lord Knew Face To Face
Deuteronomy 34:10 "And there arose not a prophet since in Israel like unto Moses, whom the LORD knew face to face."

What Prophets Are For
Ephesians 4:11-14 "¹¹And he gave some, apostles; and some, prophets; and some, evangelists; and some, pastors and teachers; ¹²For the perfecting of the saints, for the work of the ministry, for the edifying of the body of Christ: ¹³Till we all come in the unity of the faith, and of the knowledge of the Son of God, unto a perfect man, unto the measure of the stature of the fulness of Christ: ¹⁴That we henceforth be no more children, tossed to and fro, and carried about with every wind of doctrine, by the sleight of men, and cunning craftiness, whereby they lie in wait to deceive."

Where A Prophet Does Not Have Honor
Matthew 13:57 "And they were offended in him. But Jesus said unto them, A prophet is not without honour, save in his own country, and in his own house."

Mark 6:4 "But Jesus said unto them, A prophet is not without honour, but in his own country, and among his own kin, and in his own house."

Luke 4:24 "And he said, Verily I say unto you, No prophet is accepted in his own country."

John 4:44 "For Jesus himself testified, that a prophet hath no honour in his own country."

Who Prophesying Serves
1 Corinthians 14:22 "Wherefore tongues are for a sign, not to them that believe, but to them that believe not: but prophesying serveth not for them that believe not, but for them which believe."

Who Shall Prophesy
Joel 2:27-28 "²⁷And ye shall know that I am in the midst of Israel, and that I am the LORD your God, and none else: and my people shall never be ashamed. ²⁸And it shall come to pass afterward, that I will pour out my spirit upon all flesh; and your sons and your daughters shall prophesy, your old men shall dream dreams, your young men shall see visions."

Acts 2:17-18 "¹⁷And it shall come to pass in the last days, saith God, I will pour out of my Spirit upon all flesh: and your sons and your daughters shall prophesy, and your young men shall see visions, and your old men shall dream dreams: ¹⁸And on my servants and on my handmaidens I will pour out in those days of my Spirit; and they shall prophesy."

Who Shall Receive A Prophet's Reward
Matthew 10:41 "He that receiveth a prophet in the name of a prophet shall receive a prophet's reward; and he that receiveth a righteous man in the name of a righteous man shall receive a righteous man's reward."

PROSPERITY

Who Shall Not Prosper
2 Chronicles 24:20 "And the Spirit of God came upon Zechariah the son of Jehoiada the priest, which stood above the people, and said unto them, Thus saith God, Why transgress ye the commandments of the LORD, that ye cannot prosper? because ye have forsaken the LORD, he hath also forsaken you."

Proverbs 28:13 "He that covereth his sins shall not prosper: but whoso confesseth and forsaketh them shall have mercy."

Isaiah 54:5-17 "⁵For thy Maker is thine husband; the LORD of hosts is his name; and thy Redeemer the Holy One of Israel; The God of the whole earth shall he be called. ⁶For the LORD hath called thee as a woman forsaken and grieved in spirit, and a wife of youth, when thou wast refused, saith thy God. [7]For a small moment have I forsaken thee; but with great mercies will I gather thee. [8]In a little wrath I hid my face from thee for a moment; but with everlasting kindness will I have mercy on thee, saith the LORD thy Redeemer. [9]For this is as the waters of Noah unto me: for as I have sworn that the waters of Noah should no more go over the earth; so have I sworn that I would not be wroth with thee, nor rebuke thee. [10]For the mountains shall depart, and the hills be removed; but my kindness shall not depart from thee, neither shall the covenant of my peace be removed, saith the LORD that hath mercy on thee. [11]O thou afflicted, tossed with tempest, and not comforted, behold, I will lay thy stones with fair colours, and lay thy foundations with sapphires. [12]And I will make thy windows of agates, and thy gates of carbuncles, and all thy borders of pleasant stones. [13]And all thy children shall be taught of the LORD; and great shall be the peace of thy children. [14]In righteousness shalt thou be established: thou shalt be far from oppression; for thou shalt not fear: and from terror; for it shall not come near thee. [15]Behold, they shall surely gather together, but not by me: whosoever shall gather together against thee shall fall for thy sake. [16]Behold, I have created the smith that bloweth the coals in the fire, and that bringeth forth an instrument for his work; and I have created the waster to destroy. [17]No weapon that is formed against thee shall prosper; and every tongue that shall rise against thee in judgment thou shalt condemn. This is the heritage of the servants of the LORD, and their righteousness is of me, saith the LORD."

Jeremiah 10:21 "For the pastors are become brutish, and have not sought the LORD: therefore they shall not prosper, and all their flocks shall be scattered."

Who Shall Prosper

Joshua 1:7-8 "[7]Only be thou strong and very courageous, that thou mayest observe to do according to all the law, which Moses my servant commanded thee: turn not from it to the right hand or to the left, that thou mayest prosper whithersoever thou goest. [8]This book of the law shall not depart out of thy mouth; but thou shalt meditate therein day and night, that thou mayest observe to do according to all that is written therein: for then thou

shalt make thy way prosperous, and then thou shalt have good success."

1 Kings 2:3-4 "[3]And keep the charge of the LORD thy God, to walk in his ways, to keep his statutes, and his commandments, and his judgments, and his testimonies, as it is written in the law of Moses, that thou mayest prosper in all that thou doest, and whithersoever thou turnest thyself: [4]That the LORD may continue his word which he spake concerning me, saying, If thy children take heed to their way, to walk before me in truth with all their heart and with all their soul, there shall not fail thee (said he) a man on the throne of Israel."

2 Kings 18:5-8 "[5]He trusted in the LORD God of Israel; so that after him was none like him among all the kings of Judah, nor any that were before him. [6]For he clave to the LORD, and departed not from following him, but kept his commandments, which the LORD commanded Moses. [7]And the LORD was with him; and he prospered whithersoever he went forth: and he rebelled against the king of Assyria, and served him not. [8]He smote the Philistines, even unto Gaza, and the borders thereof, from the tower of the watchmen to the fenced city."

1 Chronicles 22:13 "Then shalt thou prosper, if thou takest heed to fulfil the statutes and judgments which the LORD charged Moses with concerning Israel: be strong, and of good courage; dread not, nor be dismayed."

2 Chronicles 20:20 "And they rose early in the morning, and went forth into the wilderness of Tekoa: and as they went forth, Jehoshaphat stood and said, Hear me, O Judah, and ye inhabitants of Jerusalem; Believe in the LORD your God, so shall ye be established; believe his prophets, so shall ye prosper."

2 Chronicles 26:5 "And he sought God in the days of Zechariah, who had understanding in the visions of God: and as long as he sought the LORD, God made him to prosper."

2 Chronicles 31:21 "And in every work that he began in the service of the house of God, and in the law, and in the commandments, to seek his God, he did it with all his heart, and prospered."

Job 36:5-11 "[5]Behold, God is mighty, and despiseth not any: he is mighty in strength and wisdom. [6]He preserveth not the life of the wicked: but giveth right to the poor. [7]He withdraweth not his eyes from the righteous: but with kings are they on the throne; yea, he doth establish them for ever, and they are exalted. [8]And if they be bound in fetters, and be holden in cords of affliction; [9]Then he sheweth them their work, and their transgressions that they have exceeded. [10]He openeth also their ear to discipline, and commandeth that they return from iniquity. [11]If they obey and serve him, they shall spend their days in prosperity, and their years in pleasures."

Psalm 1:1-3 "[1]Blessed is the man that walketh not in the counsel of the ungodly, nor standeth in the way of sinners, nor sitteth in the seat of the scornful. [2]But his delight is in the law of the LORD; and in his law doth he meditate day and night. [3]And he shall be like a tree planted by the rivers of water, that bringeth forth his fruit in his season; his leaf also shall not wither; and whatsoever he doeth shall prosper."

Psalm 122:6-7 "[6]Pray for the peace of Jerusalem: they shall prosper that love thee. [7]Peace be within thy walls, and prosperity within thy palaces."

Proverbs 14:11 "The house of the wicked shall be overthrown: but the tabernacle of the upright shall flourish."

PRUDENCE

The Prudent
Proverbs 12:16 "A fool's wrath is presently known: but a prudent man covereth shame."

Proverbs 12:23 "A prudent man concealeth knowledge: but the heart of fools proclaimeth foolishness."

Proverbs 13:16 "Every prudent man dealeth with knowledge: but a fool layeth open his folly."

Proverbs 14:8 "The wisdom of the prudent is to understand his way: but the folly of fools is deceit."

Proverbs 14:15 "The simple believeth every word: but the prudent man looketh well to his going."

Proverbs 14:18 "The simple inherit folly: but the prudent are crowned with knowledge."

Proverbs 18:15 "The heart of the prudent getteth knowledge; and the ear of the wise seeketh knowledge."

Proverbs 19:14 "House and riches are the inheritance of fathers and a prudent wife is from the LORD."

Proverbs 22:3 "A prudent man foreseeth the evil, and hideth himself: but the simple pass on, and are punished."

Proverbs 27:12 "A prudent man foreseeth the evil, and hideth himself; but the simple pass on, and are punished."

Those That Are Prudent In Their Own Sight
Isaiah 5:21 "Woe unto them that are wise in their own eyes, and prudent in their own sight!"

What Dwells With Prudence
Proverbs 8:12 "I wisdom dwell with prudence, and find out knowledge of witty inventions."

Who Is Prudent
Proverbs 15:5 "A fool despiseth his father's instruction: but he that regardeth reproof is prudent."

Proverbs 16:21 "The wise in heart shall be called prudent: and the sweetness of the lips increaseth learning."

PUNISHMENT

Punishing The Just
Proverbs 17:26 "Also to punish the just is not good, nor to strike princes for equity."

The Lord Punishing The World
Isaiah 13:9-16 "[9]Behold, the day of the LORD cometh, cruel both with wrath and fierce anger, to lay the land desolate: and he shall destroy the sinners thereof out of it. [10]For the stars of heaven and the constellations thereof shall not give their light: the sun shall be darkened in his going forth, and the moon shall not cause her light to shine. [11]And I will punish the world for their evil, and the wicked for their iniquity; and I will cause the arrogancy of the proud to cease, and will lay low the haughtiness of the terrible. [12]I will make a man more precious than fine gold; even a man than the golden wedge of Ophir. [13]Therefore I will shake the heavens, and the earth shall remove out of her place, in the wrath of the LORD of hosts,

and in the day of his fierce anger. ¹⁴And it shall be as the chased roe, and as a sheep that no man taketh up: they shall every man turn to his own people, and flee every one into his own land. ¹⁵Every one that is found shall be thrust through; and every one that is joined unto them shall fall by the sword. ¹⁶Their children also shall be dashed to pieces before their eyes; their houses shall be spoiled, and their wives ravished."

Isaiah 66:15-17 "¹⁵For, behold, the LORD will come with fire, and with his chariots like a whirlwind, to render his anger with fury, and his rebuke with flames of fire. ¹⁶For by fire and by his sword will the LORD plead with all flesh: and the slain of the LORD shall be many. ¹⁷They that sanctify themselves, and purify themselves in the gardens behind one tree in the midst, eating swine's flesh, and the abomination, and the mouse, shall be consumed together, saith the LORD."

The Time When A Scorner Is Punished
Proverbs 21:11 "When the scorner is punished, the simple is made wise: and when the wise is instructed, he receiveth knowledge."

Who Shall Be Punished
Leviticus 26:13-24 "¹³I am the LORD your God, which brought you forth out of the land of Egypt, that ye should not be their bondmen; and I have broken the bands of your yoke, and made you go upright. ¹⁴But if ye will not hearken unto me, and will not do all these commandments; ¹⁵And if ye shall despise my statutes, or if your soul abhor my judgments, so that ye will not do all my commandments, but that ye break my covenant: ¹⁶I also will do this unto you; I will even appoint over you terror, consumption, and the burning ague, that shall consume the eyes, and cause sorrow of heart: and ye shall sow your seed in vain, for your enemies shall eat it. ¹⁷And I will set my face against you, and ye shall be slain before your enemies: they that hate you shall reign over you; and ye shall flee when none pursueth you. ¹⁸And if ye will not yet for all this hearken unto me, then I will punish you seven times more for your sins. ¹⁹And I will break the pride of your power; and I will make your heaven as iron, and your earth as brass: ²⁰And your strength shall be spent in vain: for your land shall not yield her increase, neither shall the trees of the land yield their fruits. ²¹And if ye walk contrary unto me, and will not hearken unto me; I will bring seven times more plagues upon you according to your sins. ²²I will also send wild beasts among you, which shall rob you of your children, and destroy your cattle, and make you few in number; and your highways shall be desolate. ²³And if ye will not be reformed by me by these things, but will walk contrary unto me; ²⁴Then will I also walk contrary unto you, and will punish you yet seven times for your sins."

Proverbs 11:21 "Though hand join in hand, the wicked shall not be unpunished: but the seed of the righteous shall be delivered."

Proverbs 16:5 "Every one that is proud in heart is an abomination to the LORD: though hand join in hand, he shall not be unpunished."

Proverbs 17:5 "Whoso mocketh the poor reproacheth his Maker: and he that is glad at calamities shall not be unpunished."

Proverbs 19:5 "A false witness shall not be unpunished, and he that speaketh lies shall not escape."

Proverbs 19:9 "A false witness shall not be unpunished, and he that speaketh lies shall perish."

Proverbs 19:19 "A man of great wrath shall suffer punishment: for if thou deliver him, yet thou must do it again."

Proverbs 22:3 "A prudent man foreseeth the evil, and hideth himself: but the simple pass on, and are punished."

Proverbs 27:12 "A prudent man foreseeth the evil, and hideth himself; but the simple pass on, and are punished."

Isaiah 13:9-11 "⁹Behold, the day of the LORD cometh, cruel both with wrath and fierce anger, to lay the land desolate: and he shall destroy the sinners thereof out of it. ¹⁰For the stars of heaven and the constellations thereof shall not give their light: the sun shall be darkened in his going forth, and the moon shall not cause her light to shine. ¹¹And I will punish the world for their evil, and the wicked for their iniquity; and I will cause the arrogancy of the proud to cease, and will lay low the haughtiness of the terrible."

Isaiah 27:1 "In that day the LORD with his sore and great and strong sword shall punish leviathan the piercing serpent, even leviathan that crooked serpent; and he shall slay the dragon that is in the sea."

Jeremiah 27:4-8 "⁴And command them to say unto their masters, Thus saith the LORD of hosts, the God of Israel; Thus shall ye say unto your masters; ⁵I have made the earth, the man and the beast that are upon the ground, by my great power and by my outstretched arm, and have given it unto whom it seemed meet unto me. ⁶And now have I given all these lands unto the hand of Nebuchadnezzar the king of Babylon, my servant; and the beasts of the field have I given him also to serve him. ⁷And all nations shall serve him, and his son, and his son's son, until the very time of his land come: and then many nations and great kings shall serve themselves of him. ⁸And it shall come to pass, that the nation and kingdom which will not serve the same Nebuchadnezzar the king of Babylon, and that will not put their neck under the yoke of the king of Babylon, that nation will I punish, saith the LORD, with the sword, and with the famine, and with the pestilence, until I have consumed them by his hand."

Amos 2:4-5 "⁴Thus saith the LORD; For three transgressions of Judah, and for four, I will not turn away the punishment thereof; because they have despised the law of the LORD, and have not kept his commandments, and their lies caused them to err, after the which their fathers have walked: ⁵But I will send a fire upon Judah, and it shall devour the palaces of Jerusalem."

Matthew 25:31-46 "³¹When the Son of man shall come in his glory, and all the holy angels with him, then shall he sit upon the throne of his glory: ³²And before him shall be gathered all nations: and he shall separate them one from another, as a shepherd divideth his sheep from the goats: ³³And he shall set the sheep on his right hand, but the goats on the left. ³⁴Then shall the King say unto them on his right hand, Come, ye blessed of my Father, inherit the kingdom prepared for you from the foundation of the world: ³⁵For I was an hungred, and ye gave me meat: I was thirsty, and ye gave me drink: I was a stranger, and ye took me in: ³⁶Naked, and ye clothed me: I was sick,

and ye visited me: I was in prison, and ye came unto me. ³⁷Then shall the righteous answer him, saying, Lord, when saw we thee an hungred, and fed thee? or thirsty, and gave thee drink? ³⁸When saw we thee a stranger, and took thee in? or naked, and clothed thee? ³⁹Or when saw we thee sick, or in prison, and came unto thee? ⁴⁰And the King shall answer and say unto them, Verily I say unto you, Inasmuch as ye have done it unto one of the least of these my brethren, ye have done it unto me. ⁴¹Then shall he say also unto them on the left hand, Depart from me, ye cursed, into everlasting fire, prepared for the devil and his angels: ⁴²For I was an hungred, and ye gave me no meat: I was thirsty, and ye gave me no drink: ⁴³I was a stranger, and ye took me not in: naked, and ye clothed me not: sick, and in prison, and ye visited me not. ⁴⁴Then shall they also answer him, saying, Lord, when saw we thee an hungred, or athirst, or a stranger, or naked, or sick, or in prison, and did not minister unto thee? ⁴⁵Then shall he answer them, saying, Verily I say unto you, Inasmuch as ye did it not to one of the least of these, ye did it not to me. ⁴⁶And these shall go away into everlasting punishment: but the righteous into life eternal."

2 Thessalonians 1:7-9 "⁷And to you who are troubled rest with us, when the Lord Jesus shall be revealed from heaven with his mighty angels, ⁸In flaming fire taking vengeance on them that know not God, and that obey not the gospel of our Lord Jesus Christ: ⁹Who shall be punished with everlasting destruction from the presence of the Lord, and from the glory of his power."

Hebrews 10:26-30 "²⁶For if we sin wilfully after that we have received the knowledge of the truth, there remaineth no more sacrifice for sins, ²⁷But a certain fearful looking for of judgment and fiery indignation, which shall devour the adversaries. ²⁸He that despised Moses' law died without mercy under two or three witnesses: ²⁹Of how much sorer punishment, suppose ye, shall he be thought worthy, who hath trodden under foot the Son of God, and hath counted the blood of the covenant, wherewith he was sanctified, an unholy thing, and hath done despite unto the Spirit of grace? ³⁰For we know him that hath said, Vengeance belongeth unto me, I will recompense, saith the Lord. And again, The Lord shall judge his people."

2 Peter 2:9 "The Lord knoweth how to deliver the godly out of temptations, and to reserve the unjust unto the day of judgment to be punished."

PURITY

Keeping Yourself Pure
1 Timothy 5:22 "Lay hands suddenly on no man, neither be partaker of other men's sins: keep thyself pure."

The Pure
2 Samuel 22:21-27 "²¹The LORD rewarded me according to my righteousness: according to the cleanness of my hands hath he recompensed me. ²²For I have kept the ways of the LORD, and have not wickedly departed from my God. ²³For all his judgments were before me: and as for his statutes, I did not depart from them. ²⁴I was also upright before him, and have kept myself from mine iniquity. ²⁵Therefore the LORD hath recompensed me according to my righteousness; according to my cleanness in his eye sight. ²⁶With the merciful thou wilt shew thyself merciful, and with the upright man thou wilt shew thyself upright. ²⁷With the pure thou wilt shew thyself pure; and with the froward thou wilt shew thyself unsavoury."

Psalm 18:24-26 "²⁴Therefore hath the LORD recompensed me according to my righteousness, according to the cleanness of my hands in his eyesight. ²⁵With the merciful thou wilt shew thyself merciful; with an upright man thou wilt shew thyself upright; ²⁶With the pure thou wilt shew thyself pure; and with the froward thou wilt shew thyself froward."

Proverbs 15:26 "The thoughts of the wicked are an abomination to the LORD: but the words of the pure are pleasant words."

Proverbs 21:8 "The way of man is froward and strange: but as for the pure, his work is right."

Titus 1:15 "Unto the pure all things are pure: but unto them that are defiled and unbelieving is nothing pure; but even their mind and conscience is defiled."

What Is Pure
Psalm 12:6 "The words of the LORD are pure words: as silver tried in a furnace of earth, purified seven times."

Psalm 119:137-140 "¹³⁷Righteous art thou, O LORD, and upright are thy judgments. ¹³⁸Thy testimonies that thou hast commanded are righteous and very faithful. ¹³⁹My zeal hath consumed me, because mine enemies have forgotten thy words. ¹⁴⁰Thy word is very pure: therefore thy servant loveth it."

Proverbs 30:5-6 "⁵Every word of God is pure: he is a shield unto them that put their trust in him. ⁶Add thou not unto his words, lest he reprove thee, and thou be found a liar."

James 3:17 "But the wisdom that is from above is first pure, then peaceable, gentle, and easy to be intreated, full of mercy and good fruits, without partiality, and without hypocrisy."

Who Finds Nothing To Be Pure
Titus 1:15 "Unto the pure all things are pure: but unto them that are defiled and unbelieving is nothing pure; but even their mind and conscience is defiled."

Who Purifies Their Soul
1 Peter 1:18-23 "¹⁸Forasmuch as ye know that ye were not redeemed with corruptible things, as silver and gold, from your vain conversation received by tradition from your fathers; ¹⁹But with the precious blood of Christ, as of a lamb without blemish and without spot: ²⁰Who verily was foreordained before the foundation of the world, but was manifest in these last times for you, ²¹Who by him do believe in God, that raised him up from the dead, and gave him glory; that your faith and hope might be in God. ²²Seeing ye have purified your souls in obeying the truth through the Spirit unto unfeigned love of the brethren, see that ye love one another with a pure heart fervently: ²³Being born again, not of corruptible seed, but of incorruptible, by the word of God, which liveth and abideth for ever."

1 John 3:1-3 "¹Behold, what manner of love the Father hath bestowed upon us, that we should be called the sons of God: therefore the world knoweth us not, because it knew him not. ²Beloved, now are we the sons of God, and it doth not yet appear what we shall be: but we know that, when he shall appear, we shall be like him; for we shall see him as he is. ³And every man that hath this hope in him purifieth himself, even as he is pure."

Who The Lord Shows Himself Pure Toward

2 Samuel 22:21-27 "[21]The LORD rewarded me according to my righteousness: according to the cleanness of my hands hath he recompensed me. [22]For I have kept the ways of the LORD, and have not wickedly departed from my God. [23]For all his judgments were before me: and as for his statutes, I did not depart from them. [24]I was also upright before him, and have kept myself from mine iniquity. [25]Therefore the LORD hath recompensed me according to my righteousness; according to my cleanness in his eye sight. [26]With the merciful thou wilt shew thyself merciful, and with the upright man thou wilt shew thyself upright. [27]With the pure thou wilt shew thyself pure; and with the froward thou wilt shew thyself unsavoury."

Psalm 18:24-26 "[24]Therefore hath the LORD recompensed me according to my righteousness, according to the cleanness of my hands in his eyesight. [25]With the merciful thou wilt shew thyself merciful; with an upright man thou wilt shew thyself upright; [26]With the pure thou wilt shew thyself pure; and with the froward thou wilt shew thyself froward."

QUICKENING

What Quickens

John 6:63 "It is the spirit that quickeneth; the flesh profiteth nothing: the words that I speak unto you, they are spirit, and they are life."

Who The Lord Quickens

John 5:21 "For as the Father raiseth up the dead, and quickeneth them; even so the Son quickeneth whom he will."

Romans 8:10-14 "¹⁰And if Christ be in you, the body is dead because of sin; but the Spirit is life because of righteousness. ¹¹But if the Spirit of him that raised up Jesus from the dead dwell in you, he that raised up Christ from the dead shall also quicken your mortal bodies by his Spirit that dwelleth in you. ¹²Therefore, brethren, we are debtors, not to the flesh, to live after the flesh. ¹³For if ye live after the flesh, ye shall die: but if ye through the Spirit do mortify the deeds of the body, ye shall live. ¹⁴For as many as are led by the Spirit of God, they are the sons of God."

Ephesians 2:1-5 "¹And you hath he quickened, who were dead in trespasses and sins; ²Wherein in time past ye walked according to the course of this world, according to the prince of the power of the air, the spirit that now worketh in the children of disobedience: ³Among whom also we all had our conversation in times past in the lusts of our flesh, fulfilling the desires of the flesh and of the mind; and were by nature the children of wrath, even as others. ⁴But God, who is rich in mercy, for his great love wherewith he loved us, ⁵Even when we were dead in sins, hath quickened us together with Christ, (by grace ye are saved;)"

R*r*

REBELLION

Not Letting The Rebellious
Exalt Themselves

Psalm 66:3-7 "³Say unto God, How terrible art thou in thy works! through the greatness of thy power shall thine enemies submit themselves unto thee. ⁴All the earth shall worship thee, and shall sing unto thee; they shall sing to thy name. Selah. ⁵Come and see the works of God: he is terrible in his doing toward the children of men. ⁶He turned the sea into dry land: they went through the flood on foot: there did we rejoice in him. ⁷He ruleth by his power for ever; his eyes behold the nations: let not the rebellious exalt themselves. Selah."

Not Rebelling Against The Lord

Numbers 14:9 "Only rebel not ye against the LORD, neither fear ye the people of the land; for they are bread for us: their defence is departed from them, and the LORD is with us: fear them not."

The Rebellious

Job 24:13-24 "¹³They are of those that rebel against the light; they know not the ways thereof, nor abide in the paths thereof. ¹⁴The murderer rising with the light killeth the poor and needy, and in the night is as a thief. ¹⁵The eye also of the adulterer waiteth for the twilight, saying, No eye shall see me: and disguiseth his face. ¹⁶In the dark they dig through houses, which they had marked for themselves in the daytime: they know not the light. ¹⁷For the morning is to them even as the shadow of death: if one know them, they are in the terrors of the shadow of death. ¹⁸He is swift as the waters; their portion is cursed in the earth: he beholdeth not the way of the vineyards. ¹⁹Drought and heat consume the snow waters: so doth the grave those which have sinned. ²⁰The womb shall forget him; the worm shall feed sweetly on him; he shall be no more remembered; and wickedness shall be broken as a tree. ²¹He evil entreateth the barren that beareth not: and doeth not good to the widow. ²²He draweth also the mighty with his power: he riseth up, and no man is sure of life. ²³Though it be given him to be in safety, whereon he resteth; yet his eyes are upon their ways. ²⁴They are exalted for a little while, but are gone and brought low; they are taken out of the way as all other, and cut off as the tops of the ears of corn."

Isaiah 30:1-11 "¹Woe to the rebellious children, saith the LORD, that take counsel, but not of me; and that cover with a covering, but not of my spirit, that they may add sin to sin: ²That walk to go down into Egypt, and have not asked at my mouth; to strengthen themselves in the strength of Pharaoh, and to trust in the shadow of Egypt! ³Therefore shall the strength of Pharaoh be your shame, and the trust in the shadow of Egypt your confusion. ⁴For his princes were at Zoan, and his ambassadors came to Hanes. ⁵They were all ashamed of a people that could not profit them, nor be an help nor profit, but a shame, and also a reproach. ⁶The burden of the beasts of the south: into the land of trouble and anguish, from whence come the young and old lion, the viper and fiery flying serpent, they will carry their riches upon the shoulders of young asses, and their treasures upon the bunches of camels, to a people that shall not profit them. ⁷For the Egyptians shall help in vain, and to no purpose: therefore have I cried concerning this, Their strength is to sit still. ⁸Now go, write it before them in a table, and note it in a book, that it may be for the time to come for ever and ever: ⁹That this is a rebellious people, lying children, children that will not hear the law of the LORD: ¹⁰Which say to the seers, See not; and to the prophets, Prophesy not unto us right things, speak unto us smooth things, prophesy deceits: ¹¹Get you out of the way, turn aside out of the path, cause the Holy One of Israel to cease from before us."

Ezekiel 12:1-2 "¹The word of the LORD also came unto me, saying, ²Son of man, thou dwellest in the midst of a rebellious house, which have eyes to see, and see not; they have ears to hear, and hear not: for they are a rebellious house."

The Reward For Not Rebelling
Against The Lord

1 Samuel 12:14 "If ye will fear the LORD, and serve him, and obey his voice, and not rebel against the commandment of the LORD, then shall both ye and also the king that reigneth over you continue following the LORD your God."

The Reward For Rebelling Against The Lord

1 Samuel 12:15 "But if ye will not obey the voice of the LORD, but rebel against the commandment of the LORD, then shall the hand of the LORD be against you, as it was against your fathers."

Nehemiah 9:26-31 "²⁶Nevertheless they were disobedient, and rebelled against thee, and cast thy law behind their backs, and slew thy prophets which testified against them to turn them to thee, and they wrought great provocations. ²⁷Therefore thou deliveredst them into the hand of their enemies, who vexed them: and in the time of their trouble, when they cried unto thee, thou heardest them from heaven; and according to thy manifold mercies thou gavest them saviours, who saved them out of the hand of their enemies. ²⁸But after they had rest, they did evil again before thee: therefore leftest thou them in the hand of their enemies, so that they had the dominion over them: yet when they returned, and cried unto thee, thou heardest them from heaven; and many times didst thou deliver them according to thy mercies; ²⁹And testifiedst against them, that thou mightest bring them again unto thy law: yet they dealt proudly, and hearkened not unto thy commandments, but sinned against thy judgments, (which if a man do, he shall live in them;) and withdrew the shoulder, and hardened their neck, and would not hear. ³⁰Yet many years didst thou forbear them, and testifiedst against them by thy spirit in thy prophets: yet would they not give ear: therefore gavest thou them into the hand of the people of the lands. ³¹Nevertheless for thy great mercies' sake thou didst not utterly consume them, nor forsake them; for thou art a gracious and merciful God."

Psalm 107:8-12 "⁸Oh that men would praise the LORD for his goodness, and for his wonderful works to the children of men! ⁹For he satisfieth the longing soul, and filleth the hungry soul with goodness. ¹⁰Such as sit in darkness and in the shadow of death, being bound in affliction and iron; ¹¹Because they rebelled against the words of God, and contemned the counsel of the most High: ¹²Therefore he brought down their heart with labour; they fell down, and there was none to help."

Isaiah 1:20 "But if ye refuse and rebel, ye shall be devoured with the sword: for the mouth of the LORD hath spoken it."

Isaiah 30:8-17 "⁸Now go, write it before them in a table, and note it in a book, that it may be for the time to come for ever and ever: ⁹That this is a rebellious people, lying children, children that will not hear the law of the LORD: ¹⁰Which say to the seers, See not; and to the prophets, Prophesy not unto us right things, speak unto us smooth things, prophesy deceits: ¹¹Get you out of the way, turn aside out of the path, cause the Holy One of Israel to cease from before us. ¹²Wherefore thus saith the Holy One of Israel, Because ye despise this word, and trust in oppression and perverseness, and stay thereon: ¹³Therefore this iniquity shall be to you as a breach ready to fall, swelling out in a high wall, whose breaking cometh suddenly at an instant. ¹⁴And he shall break it as the breaking of the potters' vessel that is broken in pieces; he shall not spare: so that there shall not be found in the bursting of it a sherd to take fire from the hearth, or to take water withal out of the pit. ¹⁵For thus saith the Lord GOD, the Holy One of Israel; In returning and rest shall ye be saved; in quietness and in confidence shall be your strength: and ye would not. ¹⁶But ye said, No; for we will flee upon horses; therefore shall ye flee: and, We will ride upon the swift; therefore shall they that pursue you be swift. ¹⁷One thousand shall flee at the rebuke of one; at the rebuke of five shall ye flee: till ye be left as a beacon upon the top of a mountain, and as an ensign on an hill."

Jeremiah 28:16-17 "¹⁶Therefore thus saith the LORD; Behold, I will cast thee from off the face of the earth: this year thou shalt die, because thou hast taught rebellion against the LORD. ¹⁷So Hananiah the prophet died the same year in the seventh month."

Daniel 9:4-9 "⁴And I prayed unto the LORD my God, and made my confession, and said, O Lord, the great and dreadful God, keeping the covenant and mercy to them that love him, and to them that keep his commandments; ⁵We have sinned, and have committed iniquity, and have done wickedly, and have rebelled, even by departing from thy precepts and from thy judgments: ⁶Neither have we hearkened unto thy servants the prophets, which spake in thy name to our kings, our princes, and our fathers, and to all the people of the land. ⁷O Lord, righteousness belongeth unto thee, but unto us confusion of faces, as at this day; to the men of Judah, and to the inhabitants of Jerusalem, and unto all Israel, that are near, and that are far off, through all the countries whither thou hast driven them, because of their trespass that they have trespassed against thee. 8O Lord, to us belongeth confusion of face, to our kings, to our princes, and to our fathers, because we have sinned against thee. 9To the Lord our God belong mercies and forgivenesses, though we have rebelled against him."

What Rebellion Is
1 Samuel 15:23 "For rebellion is as the sin of witchcraft, and stubbornness is as iniquity and idolatry. Because thou hast rejected the word of the Lord, he hath also rejected thee from being king."

Who Seeks Rebellion
Proverbs 17:11 "An evil man seeketh only rebellion: therefore a cruel messenger shall be sent against him."

REBIRTH/BEING BORN AGAIN

Rebirth (Being Born Again)
Coming By The Resurrection Of Jesus Christ
1 Peter 1:3 "Blessed be the God and Father of our Lord Jesus Christ, which according to his abundant mercy hath begotten us again unto a lively hope by the resurrection of Jesus Christ from the dead."

1 Peter 1:22-23 "22Seeing ye have purified your souls in obeying the truth through the Spirit unto unfeigned love of the brethren, see that ye love one another with a pure heart fervently: 23Being born again, not of corruptible seed, but of incorruptible, by the word of God, which liveth and abideth for ever."

That Which Is Born Of The Spirit
John 3:6 "That which is born of the flesh is flesh; and that which is born of the Spirit is spirit."

Those That Are Born Of God
John 3:3-8 "3Jesus answered and said unto him, Verily, verily, I say unto thee, Except a man be born again, he cannot see the kingdom of God. 4Nicodemus saith unto him, How can a man be born when he is old? can he enter the second time into his mother's womb, and be born? 5Jesus answered, Verily, verily, I say unto thee, Except a man be born of water and of the Spirit, he cannot enter into the kingdom of God. 6That which is born of the flesh is flesh; and that which is born of

the Spirit is spirit. 7Marvel not that I said unto thee, Ye must be born again. 8The wind bloweth where it listeth, and thou hearest the sound thereof, but canst not tell whence it cometh, and whither it goeth: so is every one that is born of the Spirit."

1 John 3:9 "Whosoever is born of God doth not commit sin; for his seed remaineth in him: and he cannot sin, because he is born of God."

1 John 5:4 "For whatsoever is born of God overcometh the world: and this is the victory that overcometh the world, even our faith."

1 John 5:18 "We know that whosoever is born of God sinneth not; but he that is begotten of God keepeth himself, and that wicked one toucheth him not."

Those That Are Not Born Again
John 3:3-7 "3Jesus answered and said unto him, Verily, verily, I say unto thee, Except a man be born again, he cannot see the kingdom of God. 4Nicodemus saith unto him, How can a man be born when he is old? can he enter the second time into his mother's womb, and be born? 5Jesus answered, Verily, verily, I say unto thee, Except a man be born of water and of the Spirit, he cannot enter into the kingdom of God. 6That which is born of the flesh is flesh; and that which is born of the Spirit is spirit. 7Marvel not that I said unto thee, Ye must be born again."

Who Is Born Of God
John 1:1-13 "1In the beginning was the Word, and the Word was with God, and the Word was God. 2The same was in the beginning with God. 3All things were made by him; and without him was not any thing made that was made. 4In him was life; and the life was the light of men. 5And the light shineth in darkness; and the darkness comprehended it not. 6There was a man sent from God, whose name was John. 7The same came for a witness, to bear witness of the Light, that all men through him might believe. 8He was not that Light, but was sent to bear witness of that Light. 9That was the true Light, which lighteth every man that cometh into the world. 10He was in the world, and the world was made by him, and the world knew him not. 11He came unto his own, and his own received him not. 12But as many as received him, to them gave he power to become

the sons of God, even to them that believe on his name: [13]Which were born, not of blood, nor of the will of the flesh, nor of the will of man, but of God."

1 John 2:24-29 "[24]Let that therefore abide in you, which ye have heard from the beginning. If that which ye have heard from the beginning shall remain in you, ye also shall continue in the Son, and in the Father. [25]And this is the promise that he hath promised us, even eternal life. [26]These things have I written unto you concerning them that seduce you. [27]But the anointing which ye have received of him abideth in you, and ye need not that any man teach you: but as the same anointing teacheth you of all things, and is truth, and is no lie, and even as it hath taught you, ye shall abide in him. [28]And now, little children, abide in him; that, when he shall appear, we may have confidence, and not be ashamed before him at his coming. [29]If ye know that he is righteous, ye know that every one that doeth righteousness is born of him."

1 John 4:7 "Beloved, let us love one another: for love is of God; and every one that loveth is born of God, and knoweth God."

1 John 5:1 "Whosoever believeth that Jesus is the Christ is born of God: and every one that loveth him that begat loveth him also that is begotten of him."

REBUKE

Hearing The Rebuke Of The Wise
Ecclesiastes 7:5-6 "[5]It is better to hear the rebuke of the wise, than for a man to hear the song of fools. [6]For as the crackling of thorns under a pot, so is the laughter of the fool: this also is vanity."

Open Rebuke
Proverbs 27:5 "Open rebuke is better than secret love."

Rebuking Others
2 Timothy 4:2-3 "[2]Preach the word; be instant in season, out of season; reprove, rebuke, exhort with all longsuffering and doctrine. [3]For the time will come when they will not endure sound doctrine; but after their own lusts shall they heap to themselves teachers, having itching ears."

Titus 1:10-13 "[10]For there are many unruly and vain talkers and deceivers, specially they of the circumcision: [11]Whose mouths must be stopped, who subvert whole houses, teaching things which they ought not, for filthy lucre's sake. [12]One of themselves, even a prophet of their own, said, The Cretians are alway liars, evil beasts, slow bellies. [13]This witness is true. Wherefore rebuke them sharply, that they may be sound in the faith."

The Reward For Rebuking A Wise Man
Proverbs 9:8-9 "[8]Reprove not a scorner, lest he hate thee: rebuke a wise man, and he will love thee. [9]Give instruction to a wise man, and he will be yet wiser: teach a just man, and he will increase in learning."

Proverbs 19:25 "Smite a scorner, and the simple will beware: and reprove one that hath understanding, and he will understand knowledge."

Those That Rebuke
Proverbs 28:23 "He that rebuketh a man afterwards shall find more favour than he that flattereth with the tongue."

Those That Rebuke The Wicked
Proverbs 9:7 "He that reproveth a scorner getteth to himself shame: and he that rebuketh a wicked man getteth himself a blot."

Proverbs 24:24-25 "[24]He that saith unto the wicked, Thou are righteous; him shall the people curse, nations shall abhor him: [25]But to them that rebuke him shall be delight, and a good blessing shall come upon them."

Who Does Not Hear Rebuke
Proverbs 13:1 "A wise son heareth his father's instruction: but a scorner heareth not rebuke."

Who The Lord Rebukes
Revelation 3:14-19 "[14]And unto the angel of the church of the Laodiceans write; These things saith the Amen, the faithful and true witness, the beginning of the creation of God; [15]I know thy works, that thou art neither cold nor hot: I would thou wert cold or hot. [16]So then because thou art lukewarm, and neither cold nor hot, I will spue thee out of my mouth. [17]Because thou sayest, I am rich, and increased with goods, and have need of nothing; and knowest not that thou art wretched, and miserable, and poor, and blind, and naked: [18]I

counsel thee to buy of me gold tried in the fire, that thou mayest be rich; and white raiment, that thou mayest be clothed, and that the shame of thy nakedness do not appear; and anoint thine eyes with eyesalve, that thou mayest see. [19]As many as I love, I rebuke and chasten: be zealous therefore, and repent."

Who To Rebuke

Leviticus 19:17 "Thou shalt not hate thy brother in thine heart: thou shalt in any wise rebuke thy neighbour, and not suffer sin upon him."

Luke 17:3-4 "[3]Take heed to yourselves: If thy brother trespass against thee, rebuke him; and if he repent, forgive him. [4]And if he trespass against thee seven times in a day, and seven times in a day turn again to thee, saying, I repent; thou shalt forgive him."

RECEIVING

Receiving One Another

Romans 15:7 "Wherefore receive ye one another, as Christ also received us to the glory of God."

Those That Do Not Receive Jesus Christ

John 12:44-49 "[44]Jesus cried and said, He that believeth on me, believeth not on me, but on him that sent me. [45]And he that seeth me seeth him that sent me. [46]I am come a light into the world, that whosoever believeth on me should not abide in darkness. [47]And if any man hear my words, and believe not, I judge him not: for I came not to judge the world, but to save the world. [48]He that rejecteth me, and receiveth not my words, hath one that judgeth him: the word that I have spoken, the same shall judge him in the last day. [49]For I have not spoken of myself; but the Father which sent me, he gave me a commandment, what I should say, and what I should speak."

Those That Do Not Receive
Jesus Christ's Disciples

Matthew 10:5-15 "[5]These twelve Jesus sent forth, and commanded them, saying, Go not into the way of the Gentiles, and into any city of the Samaritans enter ye not: [6]But go rather to the lost sheep of the house of Israel. [7]And as ye go, preach, saying, The kingdom of heaven is at hand. [8]Heal the sick, cleanse the lepers, raise the dead, cast out devils: freely ye have received, freely give. [9]Provide neither gold, nor silver, nor brass in your purses, [10]Nor scrip for your journey, neither two coats, neither shoes, nor yet staves: for the workman is worthy of his meat. [11]And into whatsoever city or town ye shall enter, inquire who in it is worthy; and there abide till ye go thence. [12]And when ye come into an house, salute it. [13]And if the house be worthy, let your peace come upon it: but if it be not worthy, let your peace return to you. [14]And whosoever shall not receive you, nor hear your words, when ye depart out of that house or city, shake off the dust of your feet. [15]Verily I say unto you, It shall be more tolerable for the land of Sodom and Gomorrha in the day of judgment, than for that city."

Mark 6:7-11 "[7]And he called unto him the twelve, and began to send them forth by two and two; and gave them power over unclean spirits; [8]And commanded them that they should take nothing for their journey, save a staff only; no scrip, no bread, no money in their purse: [9]But be shod with sandals; and not put on two coats. [10]And he said unto them, In what place soever ye enter into an house, there abide till ye depart from that place. [11]And whosoever shall not receive you, nor hear you, when ye depart thence, shake off the dust under your feet for a testimony against them. Verily I say unto you, It shall be more tolerable for Sodom and Gomorrha in the day of judgment, than for that city."

Luke 9:1-5 "[1]Then he called his twelve disciples together, and gave them power and authority over all devils, and to cure diseases. [2]And he sent them to preach the kingdom of God, and to heal the sick. [3]And he said unto them, Take nothing for your journey, neither staves, nor scrip, neither bread, neither money; neither have two coats apiece. [4]And whatsoever house ye enter into, there abide, and thence depart. [5]And whosoever will not receive you, when ye go out of that city, shake off the very dust from your feet for a testimony against them."

Luke 10:1-12 "[1]After these things the Lord appointed other seventy also, and sent them two and two before his face into every city and place, whither he himself would come. [2]Therefore said he unto them, The harvest truly is great, but the labourers are few: pray ye therefore the Lord of the harvest, that he would send forth labourers into his harvest. ³Go your ways: behold, I send you forth as lambs among wolves. ⁴Carry neither purse, nor scrip, nor shoes: and salute no man by the way. ⁵And into whatsoever house ye enter, first say, Peace be to this house. ⁶And if the son of peace be there, your peace shall rest upon it: if not, it shall turn to you again. ⁷And in the same house remain, eating and drinking such things as they give: for the labourer is worthy of his hire. Go not from house to house. ⁸And into whatsoever city ye enter, and they receive you, eat such things as are set before you: ⁹And heal the sick that are therein, and say unto them, The kingdom of God is come nigh unto you. ¹⁰But into whatsoever city ye enter, and they receive you not, go your ways out into the streets of the same, and say, ¹¹Even the very dust of your city, which cleaveth on us, we do wipe off against you: notwithstanding be ye sure of this, that the kingdom of God is come nigh unto you. ¹²But I say unto you, that it shall be more tolerable in that day for Sodom, than for that city."

Those That Receive A Child
In The Name Of Jesus Christ
Matthew 18:1-5 "¹At the same time came the disciples unto Jesus, saying, Who is the greatest in the kingdom of heaven? ²And Jesus called a little child unto him, and set him in the midst of them, ³And said, Verily I say unto you, Except ye be converted, and become as little children, ye shall not enter into the kingdom of heaven. ⁴Whosoever therefore shall humble himself as this little child, the same is greatest in the kingdom of heaven. ⁵And whoso shall receive one such little child in my name receiveth me."

Mark 9:35-39 "³⁵And he sat down, and called the twelve, and saith unto them, If any man desire to be first, the same shall be last of all, and servant of all. ³⁶And he took a child, and set him in the midst of them: and when he had taken him in his arms, he said unto them, ³⁷Whosoever shall receive one of such children in my name, receiveth me: and whosoever shall receive me, receiveth not me, but him that sent me. ³⁸And John answered him, saying, Master, we saw one casting out devils in thy name, and he followeth not us: and we forbad him, because he followeth not us. ³⁹But Jesus said, Forbid him not: for there is no man which shall do a miracle in my name, that can lightly speak evil of me."

Luke 9:46-48 "⁴⁶Then there arose a reasoning among them, which of them should be greatest. ⁴⁷And Jesus, perceiving the thought of their heart, took a child, and set him by him, ⁴⁸And said unto them, Whosoever shall receive this child in my name receiveth me: and whosoever shall receive me receiveth him that sent me: for he that is least among you all, the same shall be great."

Those That Receive Jesus Christ
Matthew 10:33-41 "³³But whosoever shall deny me before men, him will I also deny before my Father which is in heaven. ³⁴Think not that I am come to send peace on earth: I came not to send peace, but a sword. ³⁵For I am come to set a man at variance against his father, and the daughter against her mother, and the daughter in law against her mother in law. ³⁶And a man's foes shall be they of his own household. ³⁷He that loveth father or mother more than me is not worthy of me: and he that loveth son or daughter more than me is not worthy of me. ³⁸And he that taketh not his cross, and followeth after me, is not worthy of me. ³⁹He that findeth his life shall lose it: and he that loseth his life for my sake shall find it. ⁴⁰He that receiveth you receiveth me, and he that receiveth me receiveth him that sent me. ⁴¹He that receiveth a prophet in the name of a prophet shall receive a prophet's reward; and he that receiveth a righteous man in the name of a righteous man shall receive a righteous man's reward."

Mark 9:37-39 "³⁷Whosoever shall receive one of such children in my name, receiveth me: and whosoever shall receive me, receiveth not me, but him that sent me. ³⁸And John answered him, saying, Master, we saw one casting out devils in thy name, and he followeth not us: and we forbad him, because he followeth not us. ³⁹But Jesus said, Forbid him not: for there is no man which shall do a miracle in my name, that can lightly speak evil of me."

Luke 9:46-48 "⁴⁶Then there arose a reasoning among them, which of them should be greatest. ⁴⁷And Jesus, perceiving the thought of their heart, took a child, and set him by him, ⁴⁸And said unto them, Whosoever shall receive this child in my name receiveth me: and whosoever shall receive me receiveth him that sent me: for he that is least among you all, the same shall be great."

John 1:1-13 "¹In the beginning was the Word, and the Word was with God, and the Word was God. ²The same was in the beginning with God. ³All things were made by him; and without him was not any thing made that was made. ⁴In him was life; and the life was the light of men. ⁵And the light shineth in darkness; and the darkness comprehended it not. ⁶There was a man sent from God, whose name was John. ⁷The same came for a witness, to bear witness of the Light, that all men through him might believe. ⁸He was not that Light, but was sent to bear witness of that Light. ⁹That was the true Light, which lighteth every man that cometh into the world. ¹⁰He was in the world, and the world was made by him, and the world knew him not. ¹¹He came unto his own, and his own received him not. ¹²But as many as received him, to them gave he power to become the sons of God, even to them that believe on his name: ¹³Which were born, not of blood, nor of the will of the flesh, nor of the will of man, but of God."

John 13:10-20 "¹⁰Jesus saith to him, He that is washed needeth not save to wash his feet, but is clean every whit: and ye are clean, but not all. ¹¹For he knew who should betray him; therefore said he, Ye are not all clean. ¹²So after he had washed their feet, and had taken his garments, and was set down again, he said unto them, Know ye what I have done to you? ¹³Ye call me Master and Lord: and ye say well; for so I am. ¹⁴If I then, your Lord and Master, have washed your feet; ye also ought to wash one another's feet. ¹⁵For I have given you an example, that ye should do as I have done to you. ¹⁶Verily, verily, I say unto you, The servant is not greater than his lord; neither he that is sent greater than he that sent him. ¹⁷If ye know these things, happy are ye if ye do them. ¹⁸I speak not of you all: I know whom I have chosen: but that the scripture may be fulfilled, He that eateth bread with me hath lifted up his heel against me. ¹⁹Now I tell you before it come, that, when it is come to pass, ye may believe that I am he. ²⁰Verily, verily, I say unto you, He that receiveth whomsoever I send receiveth me; and he that receiveth me receiveth him that sent me."

Those That Receive Jesus Christ's Disciples
Matthew 10:33-41 "³³But whosoever shall deny me before men, him will I also deny before my Father which is in heaven. ³⁴Think not that I am come to send peace on earth: I came not to send peace, but a sword. ³⁵For I am come to set a man at variance against his father, and the daughter against her mother, and the daughter in law against her mother in law. ³⁶And a man's foes shall be they of his own household. ³⁷He that loveth father or mother more than me is not worthy of me: and he that loveth son or daughter more than me is not worthy of me. ³⁸And he that taketh not his cross, and followeth after me, is not worthy of me. ³⁹He that findeth his life shall lose it: and he that loseth his life for my sake shall find it. ⁴⁰He that receiveth you receiveth me, and he that receiveth me receiveth him that sent me. ⁴¹He that receiveth a prophet in the name of a prophet shall receive a prophet's reward; and he that receiveth a righteous man in the name of a righteous man shall receive a righteous man's reward."

John 13:10-20 "¹⁰Jesus saith to him, He that is washed needeth not save to wash his feet, but is clean every whit: and ye are clean, but not all. ¹¹For he knew who should betray him; therefore said he, Ye are not all clean. ¹²So after he had washed their feet, and had taken his garments, and was set down again, he said unto them, Know ye what I have done to you? ¹³Ye call me Master and Lord: and ye say well; for so I am. ¹⁴If I then, your Lord and Master, have washed your feet; ye also ought to wash one another's feet. ¹⁵For I have given you an example, that ye should do as I have done to you. ¹⁶Verily, verily, I say unto you, The servant is not greater than his lord; neither he that is sent greater than he that sent him. ¹⁷If ye know these things, happy are ye if ye do them. ¹⁸I speak not of you all: I know whom I have chosen: but that the scripture may be fulfilled, He that eateth bread with me hath lifted up his heel against me. ¹⁹Now I tell you before it come, that, when it is come to pass, ye may believe that I am he. ²⁰Verily, verily, I say unto you, He that receiveth whomsoever I send receiveth me; and he that receiveth me receiveth him that sent me."

What Is More Blessed Than Receiving
Acts 20:35 "I have shewed you all things, how that so labouring ye ought to support the weak, and to remember the words of the Lord Jesus, how he said, It is more blessed to give than to receive."

Who Did Not Receive Jesus Christ

John 1:1-11 "¹In the beginning was the Word, and the Word was with God, and the Word was God. ²The same was in the beginning with God. ³All things were made by him; and without him was not any thing made that was made. ⁴In him was life; and the life was the light of men. ⁵And the light shineth in darkness; and the darkness comprehended it not. ⁶There was a man sent from God, whose name was John. ⁷The same came for a witness, to bear witness of the Light, that all men through him might believe. ⁸He was not that Light, but was sent to bear witness of that Light. ⁹That was the true Light, which lighteth every man that cometh into the world. ¹⁰He was in the world, and the world was made by him, and the world knew him not. ¹¹He came unto his own, and his own received him not."

John 5:23-47 "²³That all men should honour the Son, even as they honour the Father. He that honoureth not the Son honoureth not the Father which hath sent him. ²⁴Verily, verily, I say unto you, He that heareth my word, and believeth on him that sent me, hath everlasting life, and shall not come into condemnation; but is passed from death unto life. ²⁵Verily, verily, I say unto you, The hour is coming, and now is, when the dead shall hear the voice of the Son of God: and they that hear shall live. ²⁶For as the Father hath life in himself; so hath he given to the Son to have life in himself; ²⁷And hath given him authority to execute judgment also, because he is the Son of man. ²⁸Marvel not at this: for the hour is coming, in the which all that are in the graves shall hear his voice, ²⁹And shall come forth; they that have done good, unto the resurrection of life; and they that have done evil, unto the resurrection of damnation. ³⁰I can of mine own self do nothing: as I hear, I judge: and my judgment is just; because I seek not mine own will, but the will of the Father which hath sent me. ³¹If I bear witness of myself, my witness is not true. ³²There is another that beareth witness of me; and I know that the witness which he witnesseth of me is true. ³³Ye sent unto John, and he bare witness unto the truth. ³⁴But I receive not testimony from man: but these things I say, that ye might be saved. ³⁵He was a burning and a shining light: and ye were willing for a season to rejoice in his light. ³⁶But I have greater witness than that of John: for the works which the Father hath given me to finish, the same works that I do, bear witness of me, that the Father hath sent me. ³⁷And the Father himself, which hath sent me, hath borne witness of me. Ye have neither heard his voice at any time, nor seen his shape. ³⁸And ye have not his word abiding in you: for whom he hath sent, him ye believe not. ³⁹Search the scriptures; for in them ye think ye have eternal life: and they are they which testify of me. ⁴⁰And ye will not come to me, that ye might have life. ⁴¹I receive not honour from men. ⁴²But I know you, that ye have not the love of God in you. ⁴³I am come in my Father's name, and ye receive me not: if another shall come in his own name, him ye will receive. ⁴⁴How can ye believe, which receive honour one of another, and seek not the honour that cometh from God only? ⁴⁵Do not think that I will accuse you to the Father: there is one that accuseth you, even Moses, in whom ye trust. ⁴⁶For had ye believed Moses, ye would have believed me: for he wrote of me. ⁴⁷But if ye believe not his writings, how shall ye believe my words?"

Who Receives

Matthew 7:7-8 "⁷Ask, and it shall be given you; seek, and ye shall find; knock, and it shall be opened unto you: ⁸For every one that asketh receiveth; and he that seeketh findeth; and to him that knocketh it shall be opened."

Matthew 21:21-22 "²¹Jesus answered and said unto them, Verily I say unto you, If ye have faith, and doubt not, ye shall not only do this which is done to the fig tree, but also if ye shall say unto this mountain, Be thou removed, and be thou cast into the sea; it shall be done. ²²And all things, whatsoever ye shall ask in prayer, believing, ye shall receive."

Mark 11:23-24 "²³For verily I say unto you, That whosoever shall say unto this mountain, Be thou removed, and be thou cast into the sea; and shall not doubt in his heart, but shall believe that those things which he saith shall come to pass; he shall have whatsoever he saith. ²⁴Therefore I say unto you, What things soever ye desire, when ye pray, believe that ye receive them, and ye shall have them."

Luke 11:9-10 "⁹And I say unto you, Ask, and it shall be given you; seek, and ye shall find; knock, and it shall be opened unto you. ¹⁰For every one that asketh receiveth; and he that seeketh findeth; and to him that knocketh it shall be opened."

1 John 3:21-22 "²¹Beloved, if our heart condemn us not, then have we confidence toward God. ²²And whatsoever we ask, we receive of him, because we keep his commandments, and do those things that are pleasing in his sight."

1 John 5:13-15 "¹³These things have I written unto you that believe on the name of the Son of God; that ye may know that ye have eternal life, and that ye may believe on the name of the Son of God. ¹⁴And this is the confidence that we have in him, that, if we ask any thing according to his will, he heareth us: ¹⁵And if we know that he hear us, whatsoever we ask, we know that we have the petitions that we desired of him."

Who Receives Jesus Christ
And The One Who Sent Him

Matthew 10:33-41 "³³But whosoever shall deny me before men, him will I also deny before my Father which is in heaven. ³⁴Think not that I am come to send peace on earth: I came not to send peace, but a sword. ³⁵For I am come to set a man at variance against his father, and the daughter against her mother, and the daughter in law against her mother in law. ³⁶And a man's foes shall be they of his own household. ³⁷He that loveth father or mother more than me is not worthy of me: and he that loveth son or daughter more than me is not worthy of me. ³⁸And he that taketh not his cross, and followeth after me, is not worthy of me. ³⁹He that findeth his life shall lose it: and he that loseth his life for my sake shall find it. ⁴⁰He that receiveth you receiveth me, and he that receiveth me receiveth him that sent me. ⁴¹He that receiveth a prophet in the name of a prophet shall receive a prophet's reward; and he that receiveth a righteous man in the name of a righteous man shall receive a righteous man's reward."

Matthew 18:1-5 "¹At the same time came the disciples unto Jesus, saying, Who is the greatest in the kingdom of heaven? ²And Jesus called a little child unto him, and set him in the midst of them, ³And said, Verily I say unto you, Except ye be converted, and become as little children, ye shall not enter into the kingdom of heaven. ⁴Whosoever therefore shall humble himself as this little child, the same is greatest in the kingdom of heaven. ⁵And whoso shall receive one such little child in my name receiveth me."

Mark 9:35-39 "³⁵And he sat down, and called the twelve, and saith unto them, If any man desire to be first, the same shall be last of all, and servant of all. ³⁶And he took a child, and set him in the midst of them: and when he had taken him in his arms, he said unto them, ³⁷Whosoever shall receive one of such children in my name, receiveth me: and whosoever shall receive me, receiveth not me, but him that sent me. ³⁸And John answered him, saying, Master, we saw one casting out devils in thy name, and he followeth not us: and we forbad him, because he followeth not us. ³⁹But Jesus said, Forbid him not: for there is no man which shall do a miracle in my name, that can lightly speak evil of me."

Luke 9:46-48 "⁴⁶Then there arose a reasoning among them, which of them should be greatest. ⁴⁷And Jesus, perceiving the thought of their heart, took a child, and set him by him, ⁴⁸And said unto them, Whosoever shall receive this child in my name receiveth me: and whosoever shall receive me receiveth him that sent me: for he that is least among you all, the same shall be great."

John 13:10-20 "¹⁰Jesus saith to him, He that is washed needeth not save to wash his feet, but is clean every whit: and ye are clean, but not all. ¹¹For he knew who should betray him; therefore said he, Ye are not all clean. ¹²So after he had washed their feet, and had taken his garments, and was set down again, he said unto them, Know ye what I have done to you? ¹³Ye call me Master and Lord: and ye say well; for so I am. ¹⁴If I then, your Lord and Master, have washed your feet; ye also ought to wash one another's feet. ¹⁵For I have given you an example, that ye should do as I have done to you. ¹⁶Verily, verily, I say unto you, The servant is not greater than his lord; neither he that is sent greater than he that sent him. ¹⁷If ye know these things, happy are ye if ye do them. ¹⁸I speak not of you all: I know whom I have chosen: but that the scripture may be fulfilled, He that eateth bread with me hath lifted up his heel against me. ¹⁹Now I tell you before it come, that, when it is come to pass, ye may believe that I am he. ²⁰Verily,

verily, I say unto you, He that receiveth whomsoever I send receiveth me; and he that receiveth me receiveth him that sent me."

Who Receives Knowledge
Proverbs 21:11 "When the scorner is punished, the simple is made wise: and when the wise is instructed, he receiveth knowledge."

RECOMPENSE/RESTITUTION

Recompense Belonging To The Lord
Deuteronomy 32:35-36 "35To me belongeth vengeance, and recompence; their foot shall slide in due time: for the day of their calamity is at hand, and the things that shall come upon them make haste. 36For the LORD shall judge his people, and repent himself for his servants, when he seeth that their power is gone, and there is none shut up, or left."

Romans 12:17-19 "17Recompense to no man evil for evil. Provide things honest in the sight of all men. 18If it be possible, as much as lieth in you, live peaceably with all men. 19Dearly beloved, avenge not yourselves, but rather give place unto wrath: for it is written, Vengeance is mine; I will repay, saith the Lord."

Hebrews 10:30 "For we know him that hath said, Vengeance belongeth unto me, I will recompense, saith the Lord. And again, The Lord shall judge his people."

The Eye For An Eye Law
Exodus 21:18-27 "18And if men strive together, and one smite another with a stone, or with his fist, and he die not, but keepeth his bed: 19If he rise again, and walk abroad upon his staff, then shall he that smote him be quit: only he shall pay for the loss of his time, and shall cause him to be thoroughly healed. 20And if a man smite his servant, or his maid, with a rod, and he die under his hand; he shall be surely punished. 21Notwithstanding, if he continue a day or two, he shall not be punished: for he is his money. 22If men strive, and hurt a woman with child, so that her fruit depart from her, and yet no mischief follow: he shall be surely punished, according as the woman's husband will lay upon him; and he shall pay as the judges determine. 23And if any mischief follow, then thou shalt give life for life, 24Eye for eye, tooth for tooth, hand for hand, foot for foot, 25Burning for burning, wound for wound, stripe for stripe. 26And if a man smite the eye of his servant, or the eye of his maid, that it perish; he shall let him go free for his eye's sake. 27And if he smite out his manservant's tooth, or his maidservant's tooth; he shall let him go free for his tooth's sake."

Exodus 21:28-36 "28If an ox gore a man or a woman, that they die: then the ox shall be surely stoned, and his flesh shall not be eaten; but the owner of the ox shall be quit. 29But if the ox were wont to push with his horn in time past, and it hath been testified to his owner, and he hath not kept him in, but that he hath killed a man or a woman; the ox shall be stoned, and his owner also shall be put to death. 30If there be laid on him a sum of money, then he shall give for the ransom of his life whatsoever is laid upon him. 31Whether he have gored a son, or have gored a daughter, according to this judgment shall it be done unto him. 32If the ox shall push a manservant or a maidservant; he shall give unto their master thirty shekels of silver, and the ox shall be stoned. 33And if a man shall open a pit, or if a man shall dig a pit, and not cover it, and an ox or an ass fall therein; 34The owner of the pit shall make it good, and give money unto the owner of them; and the dead beast shall be his. 35And if one man's ox hurt another's, that he die; then they shall sell the live ox, and divide the money of it; and the dead ox also they shall divide. 36Or if it be known that the ox hath used to push in time past, and his owner hath not kept him in; he shall surely pay ox for ox; and the dead shall be his own."

Exodus 22:1-15 "1If a man shall steal an ox, or a sheep, and kill it, or sell it; he shall restore five oxen for an ox, and four sheep for a sheep. 2If a thief be found breaking up, and be smitten that he die, there shall no blood be shed for him. 3If the sun be risen upon him, there shall be blood shed for him; for he should make full restitution; if he have nothing, then he shall be sold for his theft. 4If the theft be certainly found in his hand alive, whether it be ox, or ass, or sheep; he shall restore double. 5If a man shall cause a field or vineyard to be eaten, and shall put in his beast, and shall feed in another man's field; of the best of his own field, and of the best of his own vineyard, shall he make restitution. 6If fire break out, and catch in thorns, so that the stacks of corn, or the standing corn, or the field, be consumed therewith; he that kindled the fire shall surely make restitution. ⁷If a man shall deliver unto his neighbour money or stuff to keep, and it be stolen out of the man's house; if the thief be found, let him pay double. ⁸If the thief be not found, then the master of the house shall be brought unto the judges, to see whether he have put his hand unto his neighbour's goods. ⁹For all manner of trespass, whether it be for ox, for ass, for sheep, for raiment, or for any manner of lost thing, which another challengeth to be his, the cause of both parties shall come before the judges; and whom the judges shall condemn, he shall pay double unto his neighbour. ¹⁰If a man deliver unto his neighbour an ass, or an ox, or a sheep, or any beast, to keep; and it die, or be hurt, or driven away, no man seeing it: ¹¹Then shall an oath of the LORD be between them both, that he hath not put his hand unto his neighbour's goods; and the owner of it shall accept thereof, and he shall not make it good. ¹²And if it be stolen from him, he shall make restitution unto the owner thereof. ¹³If it be torn in pieces, then let him bring it for witness, and he shall not make good that which was torn. ¹⁴And if a man borrow ought of his neighbour, and it be hurt, or die, the owner thereof being not with it, he shall surely make it good. ¹⁵But if the owner thereof be with it, he shall not make it good: if it be an hired thing, it came for his hire."

Leviticus 24:18-21 "¹⁸And he that killeth a beast shall make it good; beast for beast. ¹⁹And if a man cause a blemish in his neighbour; as he hath done, so shall it be done to him; ²⁰Breach for breach, eye for eye, tooth for tooth: as he hath caused a blemish in a man, so shall it be done to him again. ²¹And he that killeth a beast, he shall restore it: and he that killeth a man, he shall be put to death."

Numbers 5:5-8 "⁵And the LORD spake unto Moses, saying, ⁶Speak unto the children of Israel, When a man or woman shall commit any sin that men commit, to do a trespass against the LORD, and that person be guilty; ⁷Then they shall confess their sin which they have done: and he shall recompense his trespass with the principal thereof, and add unto it the fifth part thereof, and give it unto him against whom he hath trespassed. ⁸But if the man have no kinsman to recompense the trespass unto, let the trespass be recompensed unto

the LORD, even to the priest; beside the ram of the atonement, whereby an atonement shall be made for him."

Deuteronomy 19:15-21 "¹⁵One witness shall not rise up against a man for any iniquity, or for any sin, in any sin that he sinneth: at the mouth of two witnesses, or at the mouth of three witnesses, shall the matter be established. ¹⁶If a false witness rise up against any man to testify against him that which is wrong; ¹⁷Then both the men, between whom the controversy is, shall stand before the LORD, before the priests and the judges, which shall be in those days; ¹⁸And the judges shall make diligent inquisition: and, behold, if the witness be a false witness, and hath testified falsely against his brother; ¹⁹Then shall ye do unto him, as he had thought to have done unto his brother: so shalt thou put the evil away from among you. ²⁰And those which remain shall hear, and fear, and shall henceforth commit no more any such evil among you. ²¹And thine eye shall not pity; but life shall go for life, eye for eye, tooth for tooth, hand for hand, foot for foot."

The Eye For An Eye Law
And The New Testament

Matthew 5:38-42 "³⁸Ye have heard that it hath been said, An eye for an eye, and a tooth for a tooth: ³⁹But I say unto you, That ye resist not evil: but whosoever shall smite thee on thy right cheek, turn to him the other also. ⁴⁰And if any man will sue thee at the law, and take away thy coat, let him have thy cloke also. ⁴¹And whosoever shall compel thee to go a mile, go with him twain. ⁴²Give to him that asketh thee, and from him that would borrow of thee turn not thou away."

Luke 6:27-36 "²⁷But I say unto you which hear, Love your enemies, do good to them which hate you, ²⁸Bless them that curse you, and pray for them which despitefully use you. ²⁹And unto him that smiteth thee on the one cheek offer also the other; and him that taketh away thy cloke forbid not to take thy coat also. ³⁰Give to every man that asketh of thee; and of him that taketh away thy goods ask them not again. ³¹And as ye would that men should do to you, do ye also to them likewise. ³²For if ye love them which love you, what thank have ye? for sinners also love those that love them. ³³And if ye do good to them which do good to you, what thank have ye? for sinners also do even the same. ³⁴And if ye lend to them of whom ye hope to receive, what thank have ye? for sinners also lend to sinners, to receive as much again. ³⁵But love ye your enemies, and do good, and lend, hoping for nothing again; and your reward shall be great, and ye shall be the children of the Highest: for he is kind unto the unthankful and to the evil. ³⁶Be ye therefore merciful, as your Father also is merciful."

Romans 12:17-21 "¹⁷Recompense to no man evil for evil. Provide things honest in the sight of all men. ¹⁸If it be possible, as much as lieth in you, live peaceably with all men. ¹⁹Dearly beloved, avenge not yourselves, but rather give place unto wrath: for it is written, Vengeance is mine; I will repay, saith the Lord. ²⁰Therefore if thine enemy hunger, feed him; if he thirst, give him drink: for in so doing thou shalt heap coals of fire on his head. ²¹Be not overcome of evil, but overcome evil with good."

The Lord Recompensing

2 Samuel 22:21-25 "²¹The LORD rewarded me according to my righteousness: according to the cleanness of my hands hath he recompensed me. ²²For I have kept the ways of the LORD, and have not wickedly departed from my God. ²³For all his judgments were before me: and as for his statutes, I did not depart from them. ²⁴I was also upright before him, and have kept myself from mine iniquity. ²⁵Therefore the LORD hath recompensed me according to my righteousness; according to my cleanness in his eye sight."

Psalm 18:20-24 "²⁰The LORD rewarded me according to my righteousness; according to the cleanness of my hands hath he recompensed me. ²¹For I have kept the ways of the LORD, and have not wickedly departed from my God. ²²For all his judgments were before me, and I did not put away his statutes from me. ²³I was also upright before him, and I kept myself from mine iniquity. ²⁴Therefore hath the LORD recompensed me according to my righteousness, according to the cleanness of my hands in his eyesight."

Isaiah 59:15-18 "¹⁵Yea, truth faileth; and he that departeth from evil maketh himself a prey: and the LORD saw it, and it displeased him that there was no judgment. ¹⁶And he saw that there was no

man, and wondered that there was no intercessor: therefore his arm brought salvation unto him; and his righteousness, it sustained him. ¹⁷For he put on righteousness as a breastplate, and an helmet of salvation upon his head; and he put on the garments of vengeance for clothing, and was clad with zeal as a cloke. ¹⁸According to their deeds, accordingly he will repay, fury to his adversaries, recompence to his enemies; to the islands he will repay recompence."

Jeremiah 16:16-18 "¹⁶Behold, I will send for many fishers, saith the LORD, and they shall fish them; and after will I send for many hunters, and they shall hunt them from every mountain, and from every hill, and out of the holes of the rocks. ¹⁷For mine eyes are upon all their ways: they are not hid from my face, neither is their iniquity hid from mine eyes. ¹⁸And first I will recompense their iniquity and their sin double; because they have defiled my land, they have filled mine inheritance with the carcases of their detestable and abominable things."

Jeremiah 25:12-14 "¹²And it shall come to pass, when seventy years are accomplished, that I will punish the king of Babylon, and that nation, saith the LORD, for their iniquity, and the land of the Chaldeans, and will make it perpetual desolations. ¹³And I will bring upon that land all my words which I have pronounced against it, even all that is written in this book, which Jeremiah hath prophesied against all the nations. ¹⁴For many nations and great kings shall serve themselves of them also: and I will recompense them according to their deeds, and according to the works of their own hands."

Jeremiah 32:18-19 "¹⁸Thou shewest lovingkindness unto thousands, and recompensest the iniquity of the fathers into the bosom of their children after them: the Great, the Mighty God, the LORD of hosts, is his name, ¹⁹Great in counsel, and mighty in work: for thine eyes are open upon all the ways of the sons of men: to give every one according to his ways, and according to the fruit of his doings."

Jeremiah 51:6 "Flee out of the midst of Babylon, and deliver every man his soul: be not cut off in her iniquity; for this is the time of the LORD's vengeance; he will render unto her a recompence."

Ezekiel 11:21 "But as for them whose heart walketh after the heart of their detestable things and their abominations, I will recompense their way upon their own heads, saith the Lord GOD."

Ezekiel 16:43 "Because thou hast not remembered the days of thy youth, but hast fretted me in all these things; behold, therefore I also will recompense thy way upon thine head, saith the Lord GOD: and thou shalt not commit this lewdness above all thine abominations."

Joel 3:1-4 "¹For, behold, in those days, and in that time, when I shall bring again the captivity of Judah and Jerusalem, ²I will also gather all nations, and will bring them down into the valley of Jehoshaphat, and will plead with them there for my people and for my heritage Israel, whom they have scattered among the nations, and parted my land. ³And they have cast lots for my people; and have given a boy for an harlot, and sold a girl for wine, that they might drink. ⁴Yea, and what have ye to do with me, O Tyre, and Zidon, and all the coasts of Palestine? will ye render me a recompence? and if ye recompence me, swiftly and speedily will I return your recompence upon your own head."

Romans 12:17-19 "¹⁷Recompense to no man evil for evil. Provide things honest in the sight of all men. ¹⁸If it be possible, as much as lieth in you, live peaceably with all men. ¹⁹Dearly beloved, avenge not yourselves, but rather give place unto wrath: for it is written, Vengeance is mine; I will repay, saith the Lord."

2 Thessalonians 1:6 "Seeing it is a righteous thing with God to recompense tribulation to them that trouble you."

Hebrews 10:30 "For we know him that hath said, Vengeance belongeth unto me, I will recompense, saith the Lord. And again, The Lord shall judge his people."

The Recompense Of A Man's Hands
Proverbs 12:14 "A man shall be satisfied with good by the fruit of his mouth: and the recompence of a man's hands shall be rendered unto him."

Who Shall Be Recompensed
Proverbs 11:31 "Behold, the righteous shall be recompensed in the earth: much more the wicked and the sinner."

Luke 14:12-14 "¹²Then said he also to him that bade him, When thou makest a dinner or a supper, call not thy friends, nor thy brethren, neither thy kinsmen, nor thy rich neighbours; lest they also bid thee again, and a recompence be made thee. ¹³But when thou makest a feast, call the poor, the maimed, the lame, the blind: ¹⁴And thou shalt be blessed; for they cannot recompense thee: for thou shalt be recompensed at the resurrection of the just."

RECONCILIATION

Jesus Christ Reconciling Man To God
Romans 5:6-11 "⁶For when we were yet without strength, in due time Christ died for the ungodly. ⁷For scarcely for a righteous man will one die: yet peradventure for a good man some would even dare to die. ⁸But God commendeth his love toward us, in that, while we were yet sinners, Christ died for us. ⁹Much more then, being now justified by his blood, we shall be saved from wrath through him. ¹⁰For if, when we were enemies, we were reconciled to God by the death of his Son, much more, being reconciled, we shall be saved by his life. ¹¹And not only so, but we also joy in God through our Lord Jesus Christ, by whom we have now received the atonement."

2 Corinthians 5:18-21 "¹⁸And all things are of God, who hath reconciled us to himself by Jesus Christ, and hath given to us the ministry of reconciliation; ¹⁹To wit, that God was in Christ, reconciling the world unto himself, not imputing their trespasses unto them; and hath committed unto us the word of reconciliation. ²⁰Now then we are ambassadors for Christ, as though God did beseech you by us: we pray you in Christ's stead, be ye reconciled to God. ²¹For he hath made him to be sin for us, who knew no sin; that we might be made the righteousness of God in him."

Ephesians 2:13-16 "¹³But now in Christ Jesus ye who sometimes were far off are made nigh by the blood of Christ. ¹⁴For he is our peace, who hath made both one, and hath broken down the middle wall of partition between us; ¹⁵Having abolished in his flesh the enmity, even the law of commandments contained in ordinances; for to make in himself of twain one new man, so making peace; ¹⁶And that he might reconcile both unto God in one body by the cross, having slain the enmity thereby."

Colossians 1:12-22 "¹²Giving thanks unto the Father, which hath made us meet to be partakers of the inheritance of the saints in light: ¹³Who hath delivered us from the power of darkness, and hath translated us into the kingdom of his dear Son: ¹⁴In whom we have redemption through his blood, even the forgiveness of sins: ¹⁵Who is the image of the invisible God, the firstborn of every creature: ¹⁶For by him were all things created, that are in heaven, and that are in earth, visible and invisible, whether they be thrones, or dominions, or principalities, or powers: all things were created by him, and for him: ¹⁷And he is before all things, and by him all things consist. ¹⁸And he is the head of the body, the church: who is the beginning, the firstborn from the dead; that in all things he might have the preeminence. ¹⁹For it pleased the Father that in him should all fulness dwell; ²⁰And, having made peace through the blood of his cross, by him to reconcile all things unto himself; by him, I say, whether they be things in earth, or things in heaven. ²¹And you, that were sometime alienated and enemies in your mind by wicked works, yet now hath he reconciled ²²In the body of his flesh through death, to present you holy and unblameable and unreproveable in his sight."

Hebrews 2:9-17 "⁹But we see Jesus, who was made a little lower than the angels for the suffering of death, crowned with glory and honour; that he by the grace of God should taste death for every man. ¹⁰For it became him, for whom are all things, and by whom are all things, in bringing many sons unto glory, to make the captain of their salvation perfect through sufferings. ¹¹For both he that sanctifieth and they who are sanctified are all of one: for which cause he is not ashamed to call them brethren, ¹²Saying, I will declare thy name unto my brethren, in the midst of the church will I sing praise unto thee. ¹³And again, I will put my trust in him. And again, Behold I and the children which God hath given me. ¹⁴Forasmuch then as the children are partakers of flesh and blood, he also himself likewise took part of the same; that through death he might destroy him that had the power of death, that is, the devil; ¹⁵And deliver them who through fear of death were all their lifetime subject to bondage. ¹⁶For verily he took

not on him the nature of angels; but he took on him the seed of Abraham. ¹⁷Wherefore in all things it behoved him to be made like unto his brethren, that he might be a merciful and faithful high priest in things pertaining to God, to make reconciliation for the sins of the people."

Hebrews 10:1-14 "¹For the law having a shadow of good things to come, and not the very image of the things, can never with those sacrifices which they offered year by year continually make the comers thereunto perfect. ²For then would they not have ceased to be offered? because that the worshippers once purged should have had no more conscience of sins. ³But in those sacrifices there is a remembrance again made of sins every year. ⁴For it is not possible that the blood of bulls and of goats should take away sins. ⁵Wherefore when he cometh into the world, he saith, Sacrifice and offering thou wouldest not, but a body hast thou prepared me: ⁶In burnt offerings and sacrifices for sin thou hast had no pleasure. ⁷Then said I, Lo, I come (in the volume of the book it is written of me,) to do thy will, O God. ⁸Above when he said, Sacrifice and offering and burnt offerings and offering for sin thou wouldest not, neither hadst pleasure therein; which are offered by the law; ⁹Then said he, Lo, I come to do thy will, O God. He taketh away the first, that he may establish the second. ¹⁰By the which will we are sanctified through the offering of the body of Jesus Christ once for all. ¹¹And every priest standeth daily ministering and offering oftentimes the same sacrifices, which can never take away sins: ¹²But this man, after he had offered one sacrifice for sins for ever, sat down on the right hand of God; ¹³From henceforth expecting till his enemies be made his footstool. ¹⁴For by one offering he hath perfected for ever them that are sanctified."

1 Peter 3:18 "For Christ also hath once suffered for sins, the just for the unjust, that he might bring us to God, being put to death in the flesh, but quickened by the Spirit."

Reconciling With Others
Matthew 5:21-26 "²¹Ye have heard that it was said by them of old time, Thou shalt not kill; and whosoever shall kill shall be in danger of the judgment: ²²But I say unto you, That whosoever is angry with his brother without a cause shall be in

danger of the judgment: and whosoever shall say to his brother, Raca, shall be in danger of the council: but whosoever shall say, Thou fool, shall be in danger of hell fire. 23Therefore if thou bring thy gift to the altar, and there rememberest that thy brother hath ought against thee; 24Leave there thy gift before the altar, and go thy way; first be reconciled to thy brother, and then come and offer thy gift. 25Agree with thine adversary quickly, whiles thou art in the way with him; lest at any time the adversary deliver thee to the judge, and the judge deliver thee to the officer, and thou be cast into prison. 26Verily I say unto thee, Thou shalt by no means come out thence, till thou hast paid the uttermost farthing."

REDEMPTION

The Holy Spirit Sealing Your Redemption
Ephesians 4:30 "And grieve not the holy Spirit of God, whereby ye are sealed unto the day of redemption."

The Lord Being The Redeemer
Job 19:25-27 "25For I know that my redeemer liveth, and that he shall stand at the latter day upon the earth: 26And though after my skin worms destroy this body, yet in my flesh shall I see God: 27Whom I shall see for myself, and mine eyes shall behold, and not another; though my reins be consumed within me."

Psalm 78:34-35 "34When he slew them, then they sought him: and they returned and inquired early after God. 35And they remembered that God was their rock, and the high God their redeemer."

Isaiah 43:14-15 "14Thus saith the LORD, your redeemer, the Holy One of Israel; For your sake I have sent to Babylon, and have brought down all their nobles, and the Chaldeans, whose cry is in the ships. 15I am the LORD, your Holy One, the creator of Israel, your King."

Isaiah 44:6 "Thus saith the LORD the King of Israel, and his redeemer the LORD of hosts; I am the first, and I am the last; and beside me there is no God."

Isaiah 44:24 "Thus saith the LORD, thy redeemer, and he that formed thee from the womb, I am the LORD that maketh all things; that stretcheth forth the heavens alone; that spreadeth abroad the earth by myself."

Isaiah 47:4 "As for our redeemer, the LORD of hosts is his name, the Holy One of Israel."

Isaiah 49:7 "Thus saith the LORD, the Redeemer of Israel, and his Holy One, to him whom man despiseth, to him whom the nation abhorreth, to a servant of rulers, Kings shall see and arise, princes also shall worship, because of the LORD that is faithful, and the Holy One of Israel, and he shall choose thee."

Isaiah 49:26 "And I will feed them that oppress thee with their own flesh; and they shall be drunken with their own blood, as with sweet wine: and all flesh shall know that I the LORD am thy Saviour and thy Redeemer, the mighty One of Jacob."

Isaiah 54:5-8 "5For thy Maker is thine husband; the LORD of hosts is his name; and thy Redeemer the Holy One of Israel; The God of the whole earth shall he be called. 6For the LORD hath called thee as a woman forsaken and grieved in spirit, and a wife of youth, when thou wast refused, saith thy God. 7For a small moment have I forsaken thee; but with great mercies will I gather thee. 8In a little wrath I hid my face from thee for a moment; but with everlasting kindness will I have mercy on thee, saith the LORD thy Redeemer."

Isaiah 60:15-16 "15Whereas thou hast been forsaken and hated, so that no man went through thee, I will make thee an eternal excellency, a joy of many generations. 16Thou shalt also suck the milk of the Gentiles, and shalt suck the breast of kings: and thou shalt know that I the LORD am thy Saviour and thy Redeemer, the mighty One of Jacob."

Jeremiah 50:34 "Their Redeemer is strong; the LORD of hosts is his name: he shall throughly plead their cause, that he may give rest to the land, and disquiet the inhabitants of Babylon."

Titus 2:13-14 "13Looking for that blessed hope, and the glorious appearing of the great God and our Saviour Jesus Christ; 14Who gave himself for us, that he might redeem us from all iniquity, and purify unto himself a peculiar people, zealous of good works."

The Lord Redeeming

Deuteronomy 7:6-8 "⁶For thou art an holy people unto the Lord thy God: the Lord thy God hath chosen thee to be a special people unto himself, above all people that are upon the face of the earth. ⁷The Lord did not set his love upon you, nor choose you, because ye were more in number than any people; for ye were the fewest of all people: ⁸But because the Lord loved you, and because he would keep the oath which he had sworn unto your fathers, hath the Lord brought you out with a mighty hand, and redeemed you out of the house of bondmen, from the hand of Pharaoh king of Egypt."

Deuteronomy 13:5 "And that prophet, or that dreamer of dreams, shall be put to death; because he hath spoken to turn you away from the Lord your God, which brought you out of the land of Egypt, and redeemed you out of the house of bondage, to thrust thee out of the way which the Lord thy God commanded thee to walk in. So shalt thou put the evil away from the midst of thee."

Deuteronomy 24:17-18 "¹⁷Thou shalt not pervert the judgment of the stranger, nor of the fatherless; nor take a widow's raiment to pledge: ¹⁸But thou shalt remember that thou wast a bondman in Egypt, and the Lord thy God redeemed thee thence: therefore I command thee to do this thing."

Psalm 31:5 "Into thine hand I commit my spirit: thou hast redeemed me, O Lord God of truth."

Psalm 49:15 "But God will redeem my soul from the power of the grave: for he shall receive me. Selah."

Psalm 103:1-4 "¹Bless the Lord, O my soul: and all that is within me, bless his holy name. ²Bless the Lord, O my soul, and forget not all his benefits: ³Who forgiveth all thine iniquities; who healeth all thy diseases; ⁴Who redeemeth thy life from destruction; who crowneth thee with lovingkindness and tender mercies."

Psalm 111:2-9 "²The works of the Lord are great, sought out of all them that have pleasure therein. ³His work is honourable and glorious: and his righteousness endureth for ever. ⁴He hath made his wonderful works to be remembered: the Lord is gracious and full of compassion. ⁵He hath given meat unto them that fear him: he will ever be mindful of his covenant. ⁶He hath shewed his people the power of his works, that he may give them the heritage of the heathen. ⁷The works of his hands are verity and judgment; all his commandments are sure. ⁸They stand fast for ever and ever, and are done in truth and uprightness. ⁹He sent redemption unto his people: he hath commanded his covenant for ever: holy and reverend is his name."

Psalm 130:7-8 "⁷Let Israel hope in the Lord: for with the Lord there is mercy, and with him is plenteous redemption. ⁸And he shall redeem Israel from all his iniquities."

Psalm 136:1-24 "¹O give thanks unto the Lord; for he is good: for his mercy endureth for ever. ²O give thanks unto the God of gods: for his mercy endureth for ever. ³O give thanks to the Lord of lords: for his mercy endureth for ever. ⁴To him who alone doeth great wonders: for his mercy endureth for ever. ⁵To him that by wisdom made the heavens: for his mercy endureth for ever. ⁶To him that stretched out the earth above the waters: for his mercy endureth for ever. ⁷To him that made great lights: for his mercy endureth for ever: ⁸The sun to rule by day: for his mercy endureth for ever: ⁹The moon and stars to rule by night: for his mercy endureth for ever. ¹⁰To him that smote Egypt in their firstborn: for his mercy endureth for ever: ¹¹And brought out Israel from among them: for his mercy endureth for ever: ¹²With a strong hand, and with a stretched out arm: for his mercy endureth for ever. ¹³To him which divided the Red sea into parts: for his mercy endureth for ever: ¹⁴And made Israel to pass through the midst of it: for his mercy endureth for ever: ¹⁵But overthrew Pharaoh and his host in the Red sea: for his mercy endureth for ever. ¹⁶To him which led his people through the wilderness: for his mercy endureth for ever. ¹⁷To him which smote great kings: for his mercy endureth for ever: ¹⁸And slew famous kings: for his mercy endureth for ever: ¹⁹Sihon king of the Amorites: for his mercy endureth for ever: ²⁰And Og the king of Bashan: for his mercy endureth for ever: ²¹And gave their land for an heritage: for his mercy endureth for ever: ^{22}Even an heritage unto Israel his servant: for his mercy endureth for ever. ^{23}Who remembered us in our low estate: for his mercy endureth for ever: ^{24}And hath redeemed us from our enemies: for his mercy endureth for ever."

Isaiah 43:1 "But now thus saith the Lord that created thee, O Jacob, and he that formed thee, O Israel, Fear not: for I have redeemed thee, I have called thee by thy name; thou art mine."

Isaiah 59:19-20 "^{19}So shall they fear the name of the Lord from the west, and his glory from the rising of the sun. When the enemy shall come in like a flood, the Spirit of the Lord shall lift up a standard against him. ^{20}And the Redeemer shall come to Zion, and unto them that turn from transgression in Jacob, saith the Lord."

Isaiah 63:7-9 "^{7}I will mention the lovingkindnesses of the Lord, and the praises of the Lord, according to all that the Lord hath bestowed on us, and the great goodness toward the house of Israel, which he hath bestowed on them according to his mercies, and according to the multitude of his lovingkindnesses. ^{8}For he said, Surely they are my people, children that will not lie: so he was their Saviour. ^{9}In all their affliction he was afflicted, and the angel of his presence saved them: in his love and in his pity he redeemed them; and he bare them, and carried them all the days of old."

Jeremiah 31:10-11 "^{10}Hear the word of the Lord, O ye nations, and declare it in the isles afar off, and say, He that scattered Israel will gather him, and keep him, as a shepherd doth his flock. ^{11}For the Lord hath redeemed Jacob, and ransomed him from the hand of him that was stronger than he."

Luke 1:68 "Blessed be the Lord God of Israel; for he hath visited and redeemed his people."

Galatians 3:10-14 "^{10}For as many as are of the works of the law are under the curse: for it is written, Cursed is every one that continueth not in all things which are written in the book of the law to do them. ^{11}But that no man is justified by the law in the sight of God, it is evident: for, The just shall live by faith. ^{12}And the law is not of faith: but, The man that doeth them shall live in them. ^{13}Christ hath redeemed us from the curse of the

law, being made a curse for us: for it is written, Cursed is every one that hangeth on a tree: ^{14}That the blessing of Abraham might come on the Gentiles through Jesus Christ; that we might receive the promise of the Spirit through faith."

Hebrews 9:11-12 "^{11}But Christ being come an high priest of good things to come, by a greater and more perfect tabernacle, not made with hands, that is to say, not of this building; ^{12}Neither by the blood of goats and calves, but by his own blood he entered in once into the holy place, having obtained eternal redemption for us."

1 Peter 1:18-20 "^{18}Forasmuch as ye know that ye were not redeemed with corruptible things, as silver and gold, from your vain conversation received by tradition from your fathers; ^{19}But with the precious blood of Christ, as of a lamb without blemish and without spot: ^{20}Who verily was foreordained before the foundation of the world, but was manifest in these last times for you."

Revelation 5:8-10 "^{8}And when he had taken the book, the four beasts and four and twenty elders fell down before the Lamb, having every one of them harps, and golden vials full of odours, which are the prayers of saints. ^{9}And they sung a new song, saying, Thou art worthy to take the book, and to open the seals thereof: for thou wast slain, and hast redeemed us to God by thy blood out of every kindred, and tongue, and people, and nation; ^{10}And hast made us unto our God kings and priests: and we shall reign on the earth."

The Redeemed Of The Lord

Exodus 15:11-13 "^{11}Who is like unto thee, O Lord, among the gods? who is like thee, glorious in holiness, fearful in praises, doing wonders? ^{12}Thou stretchedst out thy right hand, the earth swallowed them. ^{13}Thou in thy mercy hast led forth the people which thou hast redeemed: thou hast guided them in thy strength unto thy holy habitation."

Psalm 107:1-3 "^{1}O give thanks unto the Lord, for he is good: for his mercy endureth for ever. ^{2}Let the redeemed of the Lord say so, whom he hath redeemed from the hand of the enemy; ^{3}And gathered them out of the lands, from the east, and from the west, from the north, and from the south."

Isaiah 35:10 "And the ransomed of the LORD shall return, and come to Zion with songs and everlasting joy upon their heads: they shall obtain joy and gladness, and sorrow and sighing shall flee away."

Isaiah 51:11 "Therefore the redeemed of the LORD shall return, and come with singing unto Zion; and everlasting joy shall be upon their head: they shall obtain gladness and joy; and sorrow and mourning shall flee away."

When Redemption Will Be Near

Matthew 24:1-34 "[1]And Jesus went out, and departed from the temple: and his disciples came to him for to shew him the buildings of the temple. [2]And Jesus said unto them, See ye not all these things? verily I say unto you, There shall not be left here one stone upon another, that shall not be thrown down. [3]And as he sat upon the mount of Olives, the disciples came unto him privately, saying, Tell us, when shall these things be? and what shall be the sign of thy coming, and of the end of the world? [4]And Jesus answered and said unto them, Take heed that no man deceive you. [5]For many shall come in my name, saying, I am Christ; and shall deceive many. [6]And ye shall hear of wars and rumours of wars: see that ye be not troubled: for all these things must come to pass, but the end is not yet. [7]For nation shall rise against nation, and kingdom against kingdom: and there shall be famines, and pestilences, and earthquakes, in divers places. [8]All these are the beginning of sorrows. [9]Then shall they deliver you up to be afflicted, and shall kill you: and ye shall be hated of all nations for my name's sake. [10]And then shall many be offended, and shall betray one another, and shall hate one another. [11]And many false prophets shall rise, and shall deceive many. [12]And because iniquity shall abound, the love of many shall wax cold. [13]But he that shall endure unto the end, the same shall be saved. [14]And this gospel of the kingdom shall be preached in all the world for a witness unto all nations; and then shall the end come. [15]When ye therefore shall see the abomination of desolation, spoken of by Daniel the prophet, stand in the holy place, (whoso readeth, let him understand:) [16]Then let them which be in Judaea flee into the mountains: [17]Let him which is on the housetop not come down to take any thing out of his house: [18]Neither let him which is in the field return back to take his clothes. [19]And woe unto them that are with child, and to them that give suck in those days! [20]But pray ye that your flight be not in the winter, neither on the sabbath day: [21]For then shall be great tribulation, such as was not since the beginning of the world to this time, no, nor ever shall be. [22]And except those days should be shortened, there should no flesh be saved: but for the elect's sake those days shall be shortened. [23]Then if any man shall say unto you, Lo, here is Christ, or there; believe it not. [24]For there shall arise false Christs, and false prophets, and shall shew great signs and wonders; insomuch that, if it were possible, they shall deceive the very elect. [25]Behold, I have told you before. [26]Wherefore if they shall say unto you, Behold, he is in the desert; go not forth: behold, he is in the secret chambers; believe it not. [27]For as the lightning cometh out of the east, and shineth even unto the west; so shall also the coming of the Son of man be. [28]For wheresoever the carcase is, there will the eagles be gathered together. [29]Immediately after the tribulation of those days shall the sun be darkened, and the moon shall not give her light, and the stars shall fall from heaven, and the powers of the heavens shall be shaken: [30]And then shall appear the sign of the Son of man in heaven: and then shall all the tribes of the earth mourn, and they shall see the Son of man coming in the clouds of heaven with power and great glory. [31]And he shall send his angels with a great sound of a trumpet, and they shall gather together his elect from the four winds, from one end of heaven to the other. [32]Now learn a parable of the fig tree; When his branch is yet tender, and putteth forth leaves, ye know that summer is nigh: [33]So likewise ye, when ye shall see all these things, know that it is near, even at the doors. [34]Verily I say unto you, This generation shall not pass, till all these things be fulfilled."

Mark 13:1-30 "[1]And as he went out of the temple, one of his disciples saith unto him, Master, see what manner of stones and what buildings are here! [2]And Jesus answering said unto him, Seest thou these great buildings? there shall not be left one stone upon another, that shall not be thrown down. [3]And as he sat upon the mount of Olives over against the temple, Peter and James and John and Andrew asked him privately, [4]Tell us, when shall these things be? and what shall be the sign when all these things shall be fulfilled? [5]And Jesus answering them began to say, Take heed lest any man deceive you: [6]For many shall come in my name, saying, I am Christ; and shall deceive many. [7]And when ye shall hear of wars and rumours of wars, be ye not troubled: for such things must needs be; but the end shall not be yet. [8]For nation shall rise against nation, and kingdom against kingdom: and there shall be earthquakes in divers places, and there shall be famines and troubles: these are the beginnings of sorrows. [9]But take heed to yourselves: for they shall deliver you up to councils; and in the synagogues ye shall be beaten: and ye shall be brought before rulers and kings for my sake, for a testimony against them. [10]And the gospel must first be published among all nations. [11]But when they shall lead you, and deliver you up, take no thought beforehand what ye shall speak, neither do ye premeditate: but whatsoever shall be given you in that hour, that speak ye: for it is not ye that speak, but the Holy Ghost. [12]Now the brother shall betray the brother to death, and the father the son; and children shall rise up against their parents, and shall cause them to be put to death. [13]And ye shall be hated of all men for my name's sake: but he that shall endure unto the end, the same shall be saved. [14]But when ye shall see the abomination of desolation, spoken of by Daniel the prophet, standing where it ought not, (let him that readeth understand,) then let them that be in Judaea flee to the mountains: [15]And let him that is on the housetop not go down into the house, neither enter therein, to take any thing out of his house: [16]And let him that is in the field not turn back again for to take up his garment. [17]But woe to them that are with child, and to them that give suck in those days! [18]And pray ye that your flight be not in the winter. [19]For in those days shall be affliction, such as was not from the beginning of the creation which God created unto this time, neither shall be. [20]And except that the Lord had shortened those days, no flesh should be saved: but for the elect's sake, whom he hath chosen, he hath shortened the days. [21]And then if any man shall say to you, Lo, here is Christ; or, lo, he is there; believe him not: [22]For false Christs and false prophets shall rise, and shall shew signs and wonders, to seduce, if it were possible, even the elect. [23]But take ye heed: behold, I have foretold you all things. [24]But in those days, after that tribulation, the sun shall be darkened, and the moon shall not give her light, [25]And the stars of heaven shall fall, and the powers that are in heaven shall be shaken. [26]And then shall they see the Son of man coming in the clouds with great power and glory. [27]And then shall he send his angels, and shall gather together his elect from the four winds, from the uttermost part of the earth to the uttermost part of heaven. [28]Now learn a parable of the fig tree; When her branch is yet tender, and putteth forth leaves, ye know that summer is near: [29]So ye in like manner, when ye shall see these things come to pass, know that it is nigh, even at the doors. [30]Verily I say unto you, that this generation shall not pass, till all these things be done."

Luke 21:5-32 "[5]And as some spake of the temple, how it was adorned with goodly stones and gifts, he said, [6]As for these things which ye behold, the days will come, in the which there shall not be left one stone upon another, that shall not be thrown down. [7]And they asked him, saying, Master, but when shall these things be? and what sign will there be when these things shall come to pass? [8]And he said, Take heed that ye be not deceived: for many shall come in my name, saying, I am Christ; and the time draweth near: go ye not therefore after them. [9]But when ye shall hear of wars and commotions, be not terrified: for these things must first come to pass; but the end is not by and by. [10]Then said he unto them, Nation shall rise against nation, and kingdom against kingdom: [11]And great earthquakes shall be in divers places, and famines, and pestilences; and fearful sights and great signs shall there be from heaven. [12]But before all these, they shall lay their hands on you, and persecute you, delivering you up to the synagogues, and into prisons, being brought before kings and rulers for my name's sake. [13]And it shall turn to you for a testimony. [14]Settle it therefore in your hearts, not to meditate before what ye shall answer: [15]For I will give you a mouth and wisdom, which all your adversaries shall not be able to gainsay nor resist. [16]And ye shall be betrayed both by parents, and brethren, and kinsfolks, and friends; and some of you shall they cause to be put to death. [17]And ye shall be hated of all men for my name's sake. [18]But there shall not an hair of your head perish. [19]In your patience possess ye your souls. [20]And when ye shall see Jerusalem compassed with armies, then know that the desolation thereof is nigh. [21]Then let them which are in Judaea flee to the mountains; and let them which are in the midst of it depart out; and let not them that are in the countries enter thereinto. [22]For these be the days of vengeance, that all things which are written may be fulfilled. [23]But woe unto them that are with child, and to them that give suck, in those days! for there shall be great distress in the land, and wrath upon this people. [24]And they shall fall by the edge of the sword, and shall be led away captive into all nations: and Jerusalem shall be trodden down of the Gentiles, until the times of the Gentiles be fulfilled. [25]And there shall be signs in the sun, and in the moon, and in the stars; and upon the earth distress of nations, with perplexity; the sea and the waves roaring; [26]Men's hearts failing them for fear, and for looking after those things which are coming on the earth: for the powers of heaven shall be shaken. [27]And then shall they see the Son of man coming in a cloud with power and great glory. [28]And when these things begin to come to pass, then look up, and lift up your heads; for your redemption draweth nigh. [29]And he spake to them a parable; Behold the fig tree, and all the trees; [30]When they now shoot forth, ye see and know of your own selves that summer is now nigh at hand. [31]So likewise ye, when ye see these things come to pass, know ye that the kingdom of God is nigh at hand. [32]Verily I say unto you, This generation shall not pass away, till all be fulfilled."

Who The Lord Redeems

Deuteronomy 7:6-8 "[6]For thou art an holy people unto the LORD thy God: the LORD thy God hath chosen thee to be a special people unto himself, above all people that are upon the face of the earth. [7]The LORD did not set his love upon you, nor choose you, because ye were more in number than any people; for ye were the fewest of all people: [8]But because the LORD loved you, and because he would keep the oath which he had sworn unto your fathers, hath the LORD brought you out with a mighty hand, and redeemed you out of the house of bondmen, from the hand of Pharaoh king of Egypt."

Deuteronomy 9:26 "I prayed therefore unto the LORD, and said, O Lord GOD, destroy not thy people and thine inheritance, which thou hast redeemed through thy greatness, which thou hast brought forth out of Egypt with a mighty hand."

Deuteronomy 13:5 "And that prophet, or that dreamer of dreams, shall be put to death; because he hath spoken to turn you away from the LORD your God, which brought you out of the land of Egypt, and redeemed you out of the house of bondage, to thrust thee out of the way which the LORD thy God commanded thee to walk in. So shalt thou put the evil away from the midst of thee."

Deuteronomy 24:17-18 "[17]Thou shalt not pervert the judgment of the stranger, nor of the fatherless; nor take a widow's raiment to pledge: [18]But thou shalt remember that thou wast a bondman in Egypt, and the LORD thy God redeemed thee thence: therefore I command thee to do this thing."

Psalm 34:22 "The LORD redeemeth the soul of his servants: and none of them that trust in him shall be desolate."

Psalm 111:4-9 "[4]He hath made his wonderful works to be remembered: the LORD is gracious and full of compassion. [5]He hath given meat unto them that fear him: he will ever be mindful of his covenant. [6]He hath shewed his people the power of his works, that he may give them the heritage of the heathen. [7]The works of his hands are verity and judgment; all his commandments are sure. [8]They stand fast for ever and ever, and are done in truth and uprightness. [9]He sent redemption unto his people: he hath commanded his covenant for ever: holy and reverend is his name."

Psalm 130:7-8 "[7]Let Israel hope in the LORD: for with the LORD there is mercy, and with him is plenteous redemption. [8]And he shall redeem Israel from all his iniquities."

Psalm 136:1-24 "[1]O give thanks unto the LORD; for he is good: for his mercy endureth for ever. [2]O give thanks unto the God of gods: for his mercy endureth for ever. [3]O give thanks to the Lord of lords: for his mercy endureth for ever. [4]To him who alone doeth great wonders: for his mercy endureth for ever. [5]To him that by wisdom made the heavens: for his mercy endureth for ever. [6]To him that stretched out the earth above the waters: for his mercy endureth for ever. [7]To him that made great lights: for his mercy endureth for ever: [8]The sun to rule by day: for his mercy endureth for ever: [9]The moon and stars to rule by night: for his mercy endureth for ever. [10]To him that smote Egypt in their firstborn: for his mercy endureth for ever: [11]And brought out Israel from among them: for his mercy endureth for ever: [12]With a strong hand, and with a stretched out arm: for his mercy endureth for ever. [13]To him which divided the Red sea into parts: for his mercy endureth for ever: [14]And made Israel to pass through the midst of it: for his mercy endureth for ever: [15]But overthrew Pharaoh and his host in the Red sea: for his mercy endureth for ever. [16]To him which led his people through the wilderness: for his mercy endureth for ever. [17]To him which smote great kings: for his mercy endureth for ever: [18]And slew famous kings: for his mercy endureth for ever: [19]Sihon king of the Amorites: for his mercy endureth for ever: [20]And Og the king of Bashan: for his mercy endureth for ever: [21]And gave their land for an heritage: for his mercy endureth for ever: [22]Even an heritage unto Israel his servant: for his mercy endureth for ever. [23]Who remembered us in our low estate: for his mercy endureth for ever: [24]And hath redeemed us from our enemies: for his mercy endureth for ever."

Isaiah 48:20 "Go ye forth of Babylon, flee ye from the Chaldeans, with a voice of singing declare ye, tell this, utter it even to the end of the earth; say ye, The LORD hath redeemed his servant Jacob."

Jeremiah 31:10-11 "[10]Hear the word of the LORD, O ye nations, and declare it in the isles afar off, and say, He that scattered Israel will gather him, and keep him, as a shepherd doth his flock. [11]For the LORD hath redeemed Jacob, and ransomed him from the hand of him that was stronger than he."

Galatians 4:3-5 "[3]Even so we, when we were children, were in bondage under the elements of the world: [4]But when the fulness of the time was come, God sent forth his Son, made of a woman, made under the law, [5]To redeem them that were under the law, that we might receive the adoption of sons."

Ephesians 1:3-7 "[3]Blessed be the God and Father of our Lord Jesus Christ, who hath blessed us with all spiritual blessings in heavenly places in Christ: [4]According as he hath chosen us in him before the foundation of the world, that we should be holy and without blame before him in love: [5]Having predestinated us unto the adoption of children by Jesus Christ to himself, according to the good pleasure of his will, [6]To the praise of the glory of his grace, wherein he hath made us accepted in the beloved. [7]In whom we have redemption through his blood, the forgiveness of sins, according to the riches of his grace."

Colossians 1:9-14 "[9]For this cause we also, since the day we heard it, do not cease to pray for you, and to desire that ye might be filled with the knowledge of his will in all wisdom and spiritual understanding; [10]That ye might walk worthy of the Lord unto all pleasing, being fruitful in every good work, and increasing in the knowledge of God; [11]Strengthened with all might, according to his glorious power, unto all patience and longsuffering with joyfulness; [12]Giving thanks unto the Father, which hath made us meet to be partakers of the inheritance of the saints in light: [13]Who hath delivered us from the power of darkness, and hath translated us into the kingdom of his dear Son: [14]In whom we have redemption through his blood, even the forgiveness of sins."

Who Waits Hopefully For Redemption

Romans 8:18-23 "[18]For I reckon that the sufferings of this present time are not worthy to be compared with the glory which shall be revealed in us. [19]For the earnest expectation of the creature waiteth for the manifestation of the sons of God. [20]For the creature was made subject to vanity, not willingly, but by reason of him who hath subjected the same in hope, [21]Because the creature itself also shall be delivered from the bondage of corruption into the glorious liberty of the children of God. [22]For we know that the whole creation groaneth and travaileth in pain together until now. [23]And not only they, but ourselves also, which have the firstfruits of the Spirit, even we ourselves groan within ourselves, waiting for the adoption, to wit, the redemption of our body."

Why The Lord Redeems

Deuteronomy 7:8 "But because the LORD loved you, and because he would keep the oath which he had sworn unto your fathers, hath the LORD brought you out with a mighty hand, and redeemed you out of the house of bondmen, from the hand of Pharaoh king of Egypt."

REFINING

The Lord Refining

Zechariah 13:7-9 "⁷Awake, O sword, against my shepherd, and against the man that is my fellow, saith the LORD of hosts: smite the shepherd, and the sheep shall be scattered: and I will turn mine hand upon the little ones. ⁸And it shall come to pass, that in all the land, saith the LORD, two parts therein shall be cut off and die; but the third shall be left therein. ⁹And I will bring the third part through the fire, and will refine them as silver is refined, and will try them as gold is tried: they shall call on my name, and I will hear them: I will say, It is my people: and they shall say, The LORD is my God."

Malachi 3:1-3 "¹Behold, I will send my messenger, and he shall prepare the way before me: and the Lord, whom ye seek, shall suddenly come to his temple, even the messenger of the covenant, whom ye delight in: behold, he shall come, saith the LORD of hosts. ²But who may abide the day of his coming? and who shall stand when he appeareth? for he is like a refiner's fire, and like fullers' soap: ³And he shall sit as a refiner and purifer of silver: and he shall purify the sons of Levi, and purge them as gold and silver, that they may offer unto the LORD an offering in righteousness."

REFUGE

The Lord Being A Refuge

2 Samuel 22:3 "The God of my rock; in him will I trust: he is my shield, and the horn of my salvation, my high tower, and my refuge, my saviour; thou savest me from violence."

Psalm 9:9 "The LORD also will be a refuge for the oppressed, a refuge in times of trouble."

Psalm 32:5-7 "⁵I acknowledged my sin unto thee, and mine iniquity have I not hid. I said, I will confess my transgressions unto the LORD; and thou forgavest the iniquity of my sin. Selah. ⁶For this shall every one that is godly pray unto thee in

a time when thou mayest be found: surely in the floods of great waters they shall not come nigh unto him. ⁷Thou art my hiding place; thou shalt preserve me from trouble; thou shalt compass me about with songs of deliverance. Selah."

Psalm 46:1-11 "¹God is our refuge and strength, a very present help in trouble. ²Therefore will not we fear, though the earth be removed, and though the mountains be carried into the midst of the sea; ³Though the waters thereof roar and be troubled, though the mountains shake with the swelling thereof. Selah. ⁴There is a river, the streams whereof shall make glad the city of God, the holy place of the tabernacles of the most High. ⁵God is in the midst of her; she shall not be moved: God shall help her, and that right early. ⁶The heathen raged, the kingdoms were moved: he uttered his voice, the earth melted. ⁷The LORD of hosts is with us; the God of Jacob is our refuge. Selah. ⁸Come, behold the works of the LORD, what desolations he hath made in the earth. ⁹He maketh wars to cease unto the end of the earth; he breaketh the bow, and cutteth the spear in sunder; he burneth the chariot in the fire. ¹⁰Be still, and know that I am God: I will be exalted among the heathen, I will be exalted in the earth. ¹¹The LORD of hosts is with us; the God of Jacob is our refuge. Selah."

Psalm 57:1 "Be merciful unto me, O God, be merciful unto me: for my soul trusteth in thee: yea, in the shadow of thy wings will I make my refuge, until these calamities be overpast."

Psalm 59:16-17 "¹⁶But I will sing of thy power; yea, I will sing aloud of thy mercy in the morning: for thou hast been my defence and refuge in the day of my trouble. ¹⁷Unto thee, O my strength, will I sing: for God is my defence, and the God of my mercy."

Psalm 61:1-3 "¹Hear my cry, O God; attend unto my prayer. ²From the end of the earth will I cry unto thee, when my heart is overwhelmed: lead me to the rock that is higher than I. ³For thou hast been a shelter for me, and a strong tower from the enemy."

Psalm 62:6-8 "⁶He only is my rock and my salvation: he is my defence; I shall not be moved. ⁷In

God is my salvation and my glory: the rock of my strength, and my refuge, is in God. [8]Trust in him at all times; ye people, pour out your heart before him: God is a refuge for us. Selah."

Psalm 71:5-7 "[5]For thou art my hope, O Lord GOD: thou art my trust from my youth. [6]By thee have I been holden up from the womb: thou art he that took me out of my mother's bowels: my praise shall be continually of thee. [7]I am as a wonder unto many; but thou art my strong refuge."

Psalm 91:2 "I will say of the LORD, He is my refuge and my fortress: my God; in him will I trust."

Psalm 91:9 "Because thou hast made the LORD, which is my refuge, even the most High, thy habitation."

Psalm 94:22 "But the LORD is my defence; and my God is the rock of my refuge."

Isaiah 8:13-14 "[13]Sanctify the LORD of hosts himself; and let him be your fear, and let him be your dread. [14]And he shall be for a sanctuary; but for a stone of stumbling and for a rock of offence to both the houses of Israel, for a gin and for a snare to the inhabitants of Jerusalem."

Isaiah 25:1-4 "[1]O LORD, thou art my God; I will exalt thee, I will praise thy name; for thou hast done wonderful things; thy counsels of old are faithfulness and truth. [2]For thou hast made of a city an heap; of a defenced city a ruin: a palace of strangers to be no city; it shall never be built. [3]Therefore shall the strong people glorify thee, the city of the terrible nations shall fear thee. [4]For thou hast been a strength to the poor, a strength to the needy in his distress, a refuge from the storm, a shadow from the heat, when the blast of the terrible ones is as a storm against the wall."

Jeremiah 16:19 "O LORD, my strength, and my fortress, and my refuge in the day of affliction, the Gentiles shall come unto thee from the ends of the earth, and shall say, Surely our fathers have inherited lies, vanity, and things wherein there is no profit."

Ezekiel 11:16 "Therefore say, Thus saith the Lord GOD; Although I have cast them far off among the heathen, and although I have scattered them among the countries, yet will I be to them as a

-little sanctuary in the countries where they shall come."

Nahum 1:7 "The LORD is good, a strong hold in the day of trouble; and he knoweth them that trust in him."

Who Shall Have A Place Of Refuge
Proverbs 14:26 "In the fear of the LORD is strong confidence: and his children shall have a place of refuge."

REJECTION

Jesus Christ Being Rejected
Isaiah 53:1-3 "[1]Who hath believed our report? and to whom is the arm of the LORD revealed? [2]For he shall grow up before him as a tender plant, and as a root out of a dry ground: he hath no form nor comeliness; and when we shall see him, there is no beauty that we should desire him. [3]He is despised and rejected of men; a man of sorrows, and acquainted with grief: and we hid as it were our faces from him; he was despised, and we esteemed him not."

Mark 8:31 "And he began to teach them, that the Son of man must suffer many things, and be rejected of the elders, and of the chief priests, and scribes, and be killed, and after three days rise again."

Luke 9:22 "Saying, The Son of man must suffer many things, and be rejected of the elders and chief priests and scribes, and be slain, and be raised the third day."

Luke 17:24-25 "[24]For as the lightning, that lighteneth out of the one part under heaven, shineth unto the other part under heaven; so shall also the Son of man be in his day. [25]But first must he suffer many things, and be rejected of this generation."

The Reward For Rejecting Knowledge
Hosea 4:1-6 "[1]Hear the word of the LORD, ye children of Israel: for the LORD hath a controversy with the inhabitants of the land, because there is no truth, nor mercy, nor knowledge of God in the land. [2]By swearing, and lying, and killing, and stealing, and committing adultery, they break out, and blood toucheth blood. [3]Therefore shall the land mourn, and every one that dwelleth therein shall languish, with the beasts of the field, and

with the fowls of heaven; yea, the fishes of the sea also shall be taken away. ⁴Yet let no man strive, nor reprove another: for thy people are as they that strive with the priest. ⁵Therefore shalt thou fall in the day, and the prophet also shall fall with thee in the night, and I will destroy thy mother. ⁶My people are destroyed for lack of knowledge: because thou hast rejected knowledge, I will also reject thee, that thou shalt be no priest to me: seeing thou hast forgotten the law of thy God, I will also forget thy children."

The Reward For Rejecting The Lord

1 Samuel 8:4-18 "⁴Then all the elders of Israel gathered themselves together, and came to Samuel unto Ramah, ⁵And said unto him, Behold, thou art old, and thy sons walk not in thy ways: now make us a king to judge us like all the nations. ⁶But the thing displeased Samuel, when they said, Give us a king to judge us. And Samuel prayed unto the LORD. ⁷And the LORD said unto Samuel, Hearken unto the voice of the people in all that they say unto thee: for they have not rejected thee, but they have rejected me, that I should not reign over them. ⁸According to all the works which they have done since the day that I brought them up out of Egypt even unto this day, wherewith they have forsaken me, and served other gods, so do they also unto thee. ⁹Now therefore hearken unto their voice: howbeit yet protest solemnly unto them, and shew them the manner of the king that shall reign over them. ¹⁰And Samuel told all the words of the LORD unto the people that asked of him a king. ¹¹And he said, This will be the manner of the king that shall reign over you: He will take your sons, and appoint them for himself, for his chariots, and to be his horsemen; and some shall run before his chariots. ¹²And he will appoint him captains over thousands, and captains over fifties; and will set them to ear his ground, and to reap his harvest, and to make his instruments of war, and instruments of his chariots. ¹³And he will take your daughters to be confectionaries, and to be cooks, and to be bakers. ¹⁴And he will take your fields, and your vineyards, and your oliveyards, even the best of them, and give them to his servants. ¹⁵And he will take the tenth of your seed, and of your vineyards, and give to his officers, and to his servants. ¹⁶And he will take your menservants, and your maidservants, and

your goodliest young men, and your asses, and put them to his work. ¹⁷He will take the tenth of your sheep: and ye shall be his servants. ¹⁸And ye shall cry out in that day because of your king which ye shall have chosen you; and the LORD will not hear you in that day."

1 Samuel 15:23 "For rebellion is as the sin of witchcraft, and stubbornness is as iniquity and idolatry. Because thou hast rejected the word of the LORD, he hath also rejected thee from being king."

2 Kings 17:15-23 "¹⁵And they rejected his statutes, and his covenant that he made with their fathers, and his testimonies which he testified against them; and they followed vanity, and became vain, and went after the heathen that were round about them, concerning whom the LORD had charged them, that they should not do like them. ¹⁶And they left all the commandments of the LORD their God, and made them molten images, even two calves, and made a grove, and worshipped all the host of heaven, and served Baal. ¹⁷And they caused their sons and their daughters to pass through the fire, and used divination and enchantments, and sold themselves to do evil in the sight of the LORD, to provoke him to anger. ¹⁸Therefore the LORD was very angry with Israel, and removed them out of his sight: there was none left but the tribe of Judah only. ¹⁹Also Judah kept not the commandments of the LORD their God, but walked in the statutes of Israel which they made. ²⁰And the LORD rejected all the seed of Israel, and afflicted them, and delivered them into the hand of spoilers, until he had cast them out of his sight. ²¹For he rent Israel from the house of David; and they made Jeroboam the son of Nebat king: and Jeroboam drave Israel from following the LORD, and made them sin a great sin. ²²For the children of Israel walked in all the sins of Jeroboam which he did; they departed not from them; ²³Until the LORD removed Israel out of his sight, as he had said by all his servants the prophets. So was Israel carried away out of their own land to Assyria unto this day."

Jeremiah 6:10-19 "¹⁰To whom shall I speak, and give warning, that they may hear? behold, their ear is uncircumcised, and they cannot hearken: behold, the word of the LORD is unto them a reproach; they have no delight in it. [11]Therefore I am full of the fury of the LORD; I am weary with holding in: I will pour it out upon the children abroad, and upon the assembly of young men together: for even the husband with the wife shall be taken, the aged with him that is full of days. [12]And their houses shall be turned unto others, with their fields and wives together: for I will stretch out my hand upon the inhabitants of the land, saith the LORD. [13]For from the least of them even unto the greatest of them every one is given to covetousness; and from the prophet even unto the priest every one dealeth falsely. [14]They have healed also the hurt of the daughter of my people slightly, saying, Peace, peace; when there is no peace. [15]Were they ashamed when they had committed abomination? nay, they were not at all ashamed, neither could they blush: therefore they shall fall among them that fall: at the time that I visit them they shall be cast down, saith the LORD. [16]Thus saith the LORD, Stand ye in the ways, and see, and ask for the old paths, where is the good way, and walk therein, and ye shall find rest for your souls. But they said, We will not walk therein. [17]Also I set watchmen over you, saying, Hearken to the sound of the trumpet. But they said, We will not hearken. [18]Therefore hear, ye nations, and know, O congregation, what is among them. [19]Hear, O earth: behold, I will bring evil upon this people, even the fruit of their thoughts, because they have not hearkened unto my words, nor to my law, but rejected it."

The Stone Which The Builders Rejected

Psalm 118:19-22 "[19]Open to me the gates of righteousness: I will go into them, and I will praise the LORD: [20]This gate of the LORD, into which the righteous shall enter. [21]I will praise thee: for thou hast heard me, and art become my salvation. [22]The stone which the builders refused is become the head stone of the corner."

Matthew 21:42 "Jesus saith unto them, Did ye never read in the scriptures, The stone which the builders rejected, the same is become the head of the corner: this is the Lord's doing, and it is marvellous in our eyes?"

Luke 20:9-18 "[9]Then began he to speak to the people this parable; A certain man planted a vineyard, and let it forth to husbandmen, and went into a far country for a long time. [10]And at the season he sent a servant to the husbandmen, that they should give him of the fruit of the vineyard: but the husbandmen beat him, and sent him away empty. [11]And again he sent another servant: and they beat him also, and entreated him shamefully, and sent him away empty. [12]And again he sent a third: and they wounded him also, and cast him out. [13]Then said the lord of the vineyard, What shall I do? I will send my beloved son: it may be they will reverence him when they see him. [14]But when the husbandmen saw him, they reasoned among themselves, saying, This is the heir: come, let us kill him, that the inheritance may be ours. [15]So they cast him out of the vineyard, and killed him. What therefore shall the lord of the vineyard do unto them? [16]He shall come and destroy these husbandmen, and shall give the vineyard to others. And when they heard it, they said, God forbid. [17]And he beheld them, and said, What is this then that is written, The stone which the builders rejected, the same is become the head of the corner? [18]Whosoever shall fall upon that stone shall be broken; but on whomsoever it shall fall, it will grind him to powder."

Acts 4:9-11 "[9]If we this day be examined of the good deed done to the impotent man, by what means he is made whole; [10]Be it known unto you all, and to all the people of Israel, that by the name of Jesus Christ of Nazareth, whom ye crucified, whom God raised from the dead, even by him doth this man stand here before you whole. [11]This is the stone which was set at nought of you builders, which is become the head of the corner."

1 Peter 2:4-8 "[4]To whom coming, as unto a living stone, disallowed indeed of men, but chosen of God, and precious, [5]Ye also, as lively stones, are built up a spiritual house, an holy priesthood, to offer up spiritual sacrifices, acceptable to God by Jesus Christ. [6]Wherefore also it is contained in the scripture, Behold, I lay in Sion a chief corner stone, elect, precious: and he that believeth on him shall not be confounded. [7]Unto you therefore which believe he is precious: but unto them which be disobedient, the stone which the builders disallowed, the same is made the head of the corner, [8]And a stone of stumbling, and a rock of offence, even to them which stumble at the word, being disobedient: whereunto also they were appointed."

Those That Reject Jesus Christ

John 12:44-49 "⁴⁴Jesus cried and said, He that believeth on me, believeth not on me, but on him that sent me. ⁴⁵And he that seeth me seeth him that sent me. ⁴⁶I am come a light into the world, that whosoever believeth on me should not abide in darkness. ⁴⁷And if any man hear my words, and believe not, I judge him not: for I came not to judge the world, but to save the world. ⁴⁸He that rejecteth me, and receiveth not my words, hath one that judgeth him: the word that I have spoken, the same shall judge him in the last day. ⁴⁹For I have not spoken of myself; but the Father which sent me, he gave me a commandment, what I should say, and what I should speak."

Who The Lord Rejects

Hosea 4:1-6 "¹Hear the word of the LORD, ye children of Israel: for the LORD hath a controversy with the inhabitants of the land, because there is no truth, nor mercy, nor knowledge of God in the land. ²By swearing, and lying, and killing, and stealing, and committing adultery, they break out, and blood toucheth blood. ³Therefore shall the land mourn, and every one that dwelleth therein shall languish, with the beasts of the field, and with the fowls of heaven; yea, the fishes of the sea also shall be taken away. ⁴Yet let no man strive, nor reprove another: for thy people are as they that strive with the priest. ⁵Therefore shalt thou fall in the day, and the prophet also shall fall with thee in the night, and I will destroy thy mother. ⁶My people are destroyed for lack of knowledge: because thou hast rejected knowledge, I will also reject thee, that thou shalt be no priest to me: seeing thou hast forgotten the law of thy God, I will also forget thy children."

REJOICE

Rejoicing In The Lord

Psalm 32:11 "Be glad in the LORD, and rejoice, ye righteous: and shout for joy, all ye that are upright in heart."

Psalm 97:12 "Rejoice in the LORD, ye righteous; and give thanks at the remembrance of his holiness."

Psalm 118:24 "This is the day which the LORD hath made; we will rejoice and be glad in it."

Joel 2:23 "Be glad then, ye children of Zion, and rejoice in the LORD your God: for he hath given you the former rain moderately, and he will cause to come down for you the rain, the former rain, and the latter rain in the first month."

Habakkuk 3:18 "Yet I will rejoice in the LORD, I will joy in the God of my salvation."

Philippians 4:4 "Rejoice in the Lord alway: and again I say, Rejoice."

The Time When Righteous Men Rejoice

Proverbs 28:12 "When righteous men do rejoice, there is great glory: but when the wicked rise, a man is hidden."

The Voice Of Rejoicing

Psalm 118:15 "The voice of rejoicing and salvation is in the tabernacles of the righteous: the right hand of the LORD doeth valiantly."

What Not To Rejoice In

Proverbs 24:17 "Rejoice not when thine enemy falleth, and let not thine heart be glad when he stumbleth."

Luke 10:19-20 "¹⁹Behold, I give unto you power to tread on serpents and scorpions, and over all the power of the enemy: and nothing shall by any means hurt you. ²⁰Notwithstanding in this rejoice not, that the spirits are subject unto you; but rather rejoice, because your names are written in heaven."

1 Corinthians 13:6 "Rejoiceth not in iniquity, but rejoiceth in the truth."

What Rejoices The Heart

Psalm 19:8 "The statutes of the LORD are right, rejoicing the heart: the commandment of the LORD is pure, enlightening the eyes."

Proverbs 15:30 "The light of the eyes rejoiceth the heart: and a good report maketh the bones fat."

Proverbs 27:9 "Ointment and perfume rejoice the heart: so doth the sweetness of a man's friend by hearty counsel."

What The Lord Shall Rejoice In

Psalm 104:31 "The glory of the LORD shall endure for ever: the LORD shall rejoice in his works."

What To Rejoice In
Ecclesiastes 3:22 "Wherefore I perceive that there is nothing better, than that a man should rejoice in his own works; for that is his portion: for who shall bring him to see what shall be after him?"

Luke 10:19-20 "19Behold, I give unto you power to tread on serpents and scorpions, and over all the power of the enemy: and nothing shall by any means hurt you. 20Notwithstanding in this rejoice not, that the spirits are subject unto you; but rather rejoice, because your names are written in heaven."

Romans 12:10-12 "10Be kindly affectioned one to another with brotherly love; in honour preferring one another; 11Not slothful in business; fervent in spirit; serving the Lord; 12Rejoicing in hope; patient in tribulation; continuing instant in prayer."

1 Corinthians 13:6 "Rejoiceth not in iniquity, but rejoiceth in the truth."

When People Rejoice
Proverbs 11:10 "When it goeth well with the righteous, the city rejoiceth: and when the wicked perish, there is shouting."

Proverbs 29:2 "When the righteous are in authority, the people rejoice: but when the wicked beareth rule, the people mourn."

Who Rejoices
1 Chronicles 16:10 "Glory ye in his holy name: let the heart of them rejoice that seek the LORD."

Psalm 13:5-6 "5But I have trusted in thy mercy; my heart shall rejoice in thy salvation. 6I will sing unto the LORD, because he hath dealt bountifully with me."

Psalm 33:20-21 "20Our soul waiteth for the LORD: he is our help and our shield. 21For our heart shall rejoice in him, because we have trusted in his holy name."

Psalm 58:10-11 "10The righteous shall rejoice when he seeth the vengeance: he shall wash his feet in the blood of the wicked. 11So that a man shall say, Verily there is a reward for the righteous: verily he is a God that judgeth in the earth."

Psalm 89:15-16 "15Blessed is the people that know the joyful sound: they shall walk, O LORD, in the light of thy countenance. 16In thy name shall they rejoice all the day: and in thy righteousness shall they be exalted."

Proverbs 23:24 "The father of the righteous shall greatly rejoice: and he that begetteth a wise child shall have joy of him."

Who To Rejoice With
Romans 12:15 "Rejoice with them that do rejoice, and weep with them that weep."

RELIANCE

The Reward For Not Relying On The Lord
2 Chronicles 16:7 "And at that time Hanani the seer came to Asa king of Judah, and said unto him, Because thou hast relied on the king of Syria, and not relied on the LORD thy God, therefore is the host of the king of Syria escaped out of thine hand."

The Reward For Relying On The Lord
2 Chronicles 13:18 "Thus the children of Israel were brought under at that time, and the children of Judah prevailed, because they relied upon the LORD God of their fathers."

2 Chronicles 16:8 "Were not the Ethiopians and the Lubims a huge host, with very many chariots and horsemen? yet, because thou didst rely on the LORD, he delivered them into thine hand."

REMEMBRANCE

Remembering The Lord
Deuteronomy 4:23 "Take heed unto yourselves, lest ye forget the covenant of the LORD your God, which he made with you, and make you a graven image, or the likeness of any thing, which LORD thy God hath forbidden thee."

Deuteronomy 6:10-12 "10And it shall be, when the LORD thy God shall have brought thee into the land which he sware unto thy fathers, to Abraham, to Isaac, and to Jacob, to give thee great and goodly cities, which thou buildedst not, 11And houses full of all good things, which thou filledst not, and wells digged, which thou diggedst not, vineyards and olive trees, which thou plantedst not; when thou shalt have eaten and be full; 12Then beware lest thou forget the LORD, which brought thee forth out of the land of Egypt, from the house of bondage."

Deuteronomy 8:11-14 "¹¹Beware that thou forget not the LORD thy God, in not keeping his commandments, and his judgments, and his statutes, which I command thee this day: ¹²Lest when thou hast eaten and art full, and hast built goodly houses, and dwelt therein; ¹³And when thy herds and thy flocks multiply, and thy silver and thy gold is multiplied, and all that thou hast is multiplied; ¹⁴Then thine heart be lifted up, and thou forget the LORD thy God, which brought thee forth out of the land of Egypt, from the house of bondage."

1 Chronicles 16:11-12 "¹¹Seek the LORD and his strength, seek his face continually. ¹²Remember his marvellous works that he hath done, his wonders, and the judgments of his mouth."

Psalm 20:7 "Some trust in chariots, and some in horses: but we will remember the name of the LORD our God."

Psalm 105:4-6 "⁴Seek the LORD, and his strength: seek his face evermore. ⁵Remember his marvellous works that he hath done; his wonders, and the judgments of his mouth; ⁶O ye seed of Abraham his servant, ye children of Jacob his chosen."

Ecclesiastes 12:1 "Remember now thy Creator in the days of thy youth, while the evil days come not, nor the years draw nigh, when thou shalt say, I have no pleasure in them."

Those That Remember God
Isaiah 64:4-5 "⁴For since the beginning of the world men have not heard, nor perceived by the ear, neither hath the eye seen, O God, beside thee, what he hath prepared for him that waiteth for him. ⁵Thou meetest him that rejoiceth and worketh righteousness, those that remember thee in thy ways: behold, thou art wroth; for we have sinned: in those is continuance, and we shall be saved."

What To Remember
2 Kings 17:35-38 "³⁵With whom the LORD had made a covenant, and charged them saying, Ye shall not fear other gods, nor bow yourselves to them, nor serve them, nor sacrifice to them: ³⁶But the LORD, who brought you up out of the land of Egypt with great power and a stretched out arm,

him shall ye fear, and him shall ye worship, and to him shall ye do sacrifice. ³⁷And the statutes, and the ordinances, and the law, and the commandment, which he wrote for you, ye shall observe to do for evermore; and ye shall not fear other gods. ³⁸And the covenant that I have made with you ye shall not forget; neither shall ye fear other gods."

Isaiah 46:8-9 "⁸Remember this, and shew yourselves men: bring it again to mind, O ye transgressors. ⁹Remember the former things of old: for I am God, and there is none else; I am God, and there is none like me."

Acts 20:35 "I have shewed you all things, how that so labouring ye ought to support the weak, and to remember the words of the Lord Jesus, how he said, It is more blessed to give than to receive."

2 Timothy 2:8 "Remember that Jesus Christ of the seed of David was raised from the dead according to my gospel."

Who The Lord Will Remember
Isaiah 49:14-16 "¹⁴But Zion said, The LORD hath forsaken me, and my Lord hath forgotten me. ¹⁵Can a woman forget her sucking child, that she should not have compassion on the son of her womb? yea, they may forget, yet will I not forget thee. ¹⁶Behold, I have graven thee upon the palms of my hands; thy walls are continually before me."

REMOVAL

The Righteous Being Removed From The Earth
Isaiah 57:1-2 "¹The righteous perisheth, and no man layeth it to heart: and merciful men are taken away, none considering that the righteous is taken away from the evil to come. ²He shall enter into peace: they shall rest in their beds, each one walking in his uprightness."

Micah 7:1-6 "¹Woe is me! for I am as when they have gathered the summer fruits, as the grapegleanings of the vintage: there is no cluster to eat: my soul desired the firstripe fruit. ²The good man is perished out of the earth: and there is none upright among men: they all lie in wait for blood; they hunt every man his brother with a net. ³That they may do evil with both hands earnestly, the prince asketh, and the judge asketh for a reward; and the great man, he uttereth his mischievous desire: so they wrap it up. ⁴The best of them is as a brier: the most upright is sharper than a thorn hedge: the day of thy watchmen and thy visitation cometh; now shall be their perplexity. ⁵Trust ye not in a friend, put ye not confidence in a guide: keep the doors of thy mouth from her that lieth in thy bosom. ⁶For the son dishonoureth the father, the daughter riseth up against her mother, the daughter in law against her mother in law; a man's enemies are the men of his own house."

RENDERING

The Lord Rendering To Every Man According To His Own Way/Works

1 Kings 8:28-39 "²⁸Yet have thou respect unto the prayer of thy servant, and to his supplication, O LORD my God, to hearken unto the cry and to the prayer, which thy servant prayeth before thee to day: ²⁹That thine eyes may be open toward this house night and day, even toward the place of which thou hast said, My name shall be there: that thou mayest hearken unto the prayer which thy servant shall make toward this place. ³⁰And hearken thou to the supplication of thy servant, and of thy people Israel, when they shall pray toward this place: and hear thou in heaven thy dwelling place: and when thou hearest, forgive. ³¹If any man trespass against his neighbour, and an oath be laid upon him to cause him to swear, and the oath come before thine altar in this house: ³²Then hear thou in heaven, and do, and judge thy servants, condemning the wicked, to bring his way upon his head; and justifying the righteous, to give him according to his righteousness. ³³When thy people Israel be smitten down before the enemy, because they have sinned against thee, and shall turn again to thee, and confess thy name, and pray, and make supplication unto thee in this house: ³⁴Then hear thou in heaven, and forgive the sin of thy people Israel, and bring them again unto the land which thou gavest unto their fathers. ³⁵When heaven is shut up, and there is no rain, because they have sinned against thee; if they pray toward this place, and confess thy name, and turn from their sin, when thou afflictest them: ³⁶Then hear thou in heaven, and forgive the sin of thy servants, and of thy people Israel, that thou teach them the good way wherein they should walk, and give rain upon thy land, which thou

hast given to thy people for an inheritance. ³⁷If there be in the land famine, if there be pestilence, blasting, mildew, locust, or if there be caterpiller; if their enemy besiege them in the land of their cities; whatsoever plague, whatsoever sickness there be; ³⁸What prayer and supplication soever be made by any man, or by all thy people Israel, which shall know every man the plague of his own heart, and spread forth his hands toward this house: ³⁹Then hear thou in heaven thy dwelling place, and forgive, and do, and give to every man according to his ways, whose heart thou knowest; (for thou, even thou only, knowest the hearts of all the children of men;)"

2 Chronicles 6:19-30 "¹⁹Have respect therefore to the prayer of thy servant, and to his supplication, O LORD my God, to hearken unto the cry and the prayer which thy servant prayeth before thee: ²⁰That thine eyes may be open upon this house day and night, upon the place whereof thou hast said that thou wouldest put thy name there; to hearken unto the prayer which thy servant prayeth toward this place. ²¹Hearken therefore unto the supplications of thy servant, and of thy people Israel, which they shall make toward this place: hear thou from thy dwelling place, even from heaven; and when thou hearest, forgive. ²²If a man sin against his neighbour, and an oath be laid upon him to make him swear, and the oath come before thine altar in this house; ²³Then hear thou from heaven, and do, and judge thy servants, by requiting the wicked, by recompensing his way upon his own head; and by justifying the righteous, by giving him according to his righteousness. ²⁴And if thy people Israel be put to the worse before the enemy, because they have sinned against thee; and shall return and confess thy name, and pray and make supplication before thee in this house; ²⁵Then hear thou from the heavens, and forgive the sin of thy people Israel, and bring them again unto the land which thou gavest to them and to their fathers. ²⁶When the heaven is shut up, and there is no rain, because they have sinned against thee; yet if they pray toward this place, and confess thy name, and turn from their sin, when thou dost afflict them; ²⁷Then hear thou from heaven, and forgive the sin of thy servants, and of thy people Israel, when thou hast taught them the good way, wherein they should walk; and send rain upon thy land, which thou hast given unto thy people for an inheritance. [28]If there be dearth in the land, if there be pestilence, if there be blasting, or mildew, locusts, or caterpillers; if their enemies besiege them in the cities of their land; whatsoever sore or whatsoever sickness there be: [29]Then what prayer or what supplication soever shall be made of any man, or of all thy people Israel, when every one shall know his own sore and his own grief, and shall spread forth his hands in this house: [30]Then hear thou from heaven thy dwelling place, and forgive, and render unto every man according unto all his ways, whose heart thou knowest; (for thou only knowest the hearts of the children of men:)"

Job 34:10-11 "[10]Therefore hearken unto me, ye men of understanding: far be it from God, that he should do wickedness; and from the Almighty, that he should commit iniquity. [11]For the work of a man shall he render unto him, and cause every man to find according to his ways."

Psalm 18:20-24 "[20]The LORD rewarded me according to my righteousness; according to the cleanness of my hands hath he recompensed me. [21]For I have kept the ways of the LORD, and have not wickedly departed from my God. [22]For all his judgments were before me, and I did not put away his statutes from me. [23]I was also upright before him, and I kept myself from mine iniquity. [24]Therefore hath the LORD recompensed me according to my righteousness, according to the cleanness of my hands in his eyesight."

Psalm 28:1-4 "[1]Unto thee will I cry, O LORD my rock; be not silent to me: lest, if thou be silent to me, I become like them that go down into the pit. [2]Hear the voice of my supplications, when I cry unto thee, when I lift up my hands toward thy holy oracle. [3]Draw me not away with the wicked, and with the workers of iniquity, which speak peace to their neighbours, but mischief is in their hearts. [4]Give them according to their deeds, and according to the wickedness of their endeavours: give them after the work of their hands; render to them their desert."

Psalm 62:12 "Also unto thee, O Lord, belongeth mercy: for thou renderest to every man according to his work."

Proverbs 24:12 "If thou sayest, Behold, we knew it not; doth not he that pondereth the heart consider it? and he that keepeth thy soul, doth not he know it? and shall not he render to every man according to his works?"

Jeremiah 17:9-10 "[9]The heart is deceitful above all things, and desperately wicked: who can know it? [10]I the LORD search the heart, I try the reins, even to give every man according to his ways, and according to the fruit of his doings."

Jeremiah 23:1-2 "[1]Woe be unto the pastors that destroy and scatter the sheep of my pasture! saith the LORD. [2]Therefore thus saith the LORD God of Israel against the pastors that feed my people; Ye have scattered my flock, and driven them away, and have not visited them: behold, I will visit upon you the evil of your doings, saith the LORD."

Zechariah 1:4-6 "[4]Be ye not as your fathers, unto whom the former prophets have cried, saying, Thus saith the LORD of hosts; Turn ye now from your evil ways, and from your evil doings: but they did not hear, nor hearken unto me, saith the LORD. [5]Your fathers, where are they? and the prophets, do they live for ever? [6]But my words and my statutes, which I commanded my servants the prophets, did they not take hold of your fathers? and they returned and said, Like as the LORD of hosts thought to do unto us, according to our ways, and according to our doings, so hath he dealt with us."

Matthew 16:27 "For the Son of man shall come in the glory of his Father with his angels; and then he shall reward every man according to his works."

Romans 2:5-6 "[5]But after thy hardness and impenitent heart treasurest up unto thyself wrath against the day of wrath and revelation of the righteous judgment of God; [6]Who will render to every man according to his deeds."

1 Corinthians 3:3-9 "[3]For ye are yet carnal: for whereas there is among you envying, and strife, and divisions, are ye not carnal, and walk as men? [4]For while one saith, I am of Paul; and another, I am of Apollos; are ye not carnal? [5]Who then is Paul, and who is Apollos, but ministers by whom ye believed, even as the Lord gave to every man? [6]I have planted, Apollos watered; but God gave the increase. [7]So then neither is he that planteth any thing, neither he that watereth; but God that giveth the increase. [8]Now he that planteth and he that watereth are one: and every man shall receive his own reward according to his own labour. [9]For we are labourers together with God: ye are God's husbandry, ye are God's building."

2 Corinthians 11:13-15 "[13]For such are false apostles, deceitful workers, transforming themselves into the apostles of Christ. [14]And no marvel; for Satan himself is transformed into an angel of light. [15]Therefore it is no great thing if his ministers also be transformed as the ministers of righteousness; whose end shall be according to their works."

Revelation 2:18-23 "[18]And unto the angel of the church in Thyatira write; These things saith the Son of God, who hath his eyes like unto a flame of fire, and his feet are like fine brass; [19]I know thy works, and charity, and service, and faith, and thy patience, and thy works; and the last to be more than the first. [20]Notwithstanding I have a few things against thee, because thou sufferest that woman Jezebel, which calleth herself a prophetess, to teach and to seduce my servants to commit fornication, and to eat things sacrificed unto idols. [21]And I gave her space to repent of her fornication; and she repented not. [22]Behold, I will cast her into a bed, and them that commit adultery with her into great tribulation, except they repent of their deeds. [23]And I will kill her children with death; and all the churches shall know that I am he which searcheth the reins and hearts: and I will give unto every one of you according to your works."

Revelation 18:4-6 "[4]And I heard another voice from heaven, saying, Come out of her, my people, that ye be not partakers of her sins, and that ye receive not of her plagues. [5]For her sins have reached unto heaven, and God hath remembered her iniquities. [6]Reward her even as she rewarded you, and double unto her double according to her works: in the cup which she hath filled fill to her double."

Revelation 22:12-13 "[12]And, behold, I come quickly; and my reward is with me, to give every man according as his work shall be. [13]I am Alpha and Omega, the beginning and the end, the first and the last."

What Shall Be Rendered To A Man

Proverbs 12:14 "A man shall be satisfied with good by the fruit of his mouth: and the recompence of a man's hands shall be rendered unto him."

What Should Be Rendered To Caesar
And What Should Be Rendered To God

Matthew 22:16-21 "[16]And they sent out unto him their disciples with the Herodians, saying, Master, we know that thou art true, and teachest the way of God in truth, neither carest thou for any man: for thou regardest not the person of men. [17]Tell us therefore, What thinkest thou? Is it lawful to give tribute unto Caesar, or not? [18]But Jesus perceived their wickedness, and said, Why tempt ye me, ye hypocrites? [19]Shew me the tribute money. And they brought unto him a penny. [20]And he saith unto them, Whose is this image and superscription? [21]They say unto him, Caesar's. Then saith he unto them, Render therefore unto Caesar the things which are Caesar's; and unto God the things that are God's."

Mark 12:14-17 "[14]And when they were come, they say unto him, Master, we know that thou art true, and carest for no man: for thou regardest not the person of men, but teachest the way of God in truth: Is it lawful to give tribute to Caesar, or not? [15]Shall we give, or shall we not give? But he, knowing their hypocrisy, said unto them, Why tempt ye me? bring me a penny, that I may see it. [16]And they brought it. And he saith unto them, Whose is this image and superscription? And they said unto him, Caesar's. [17]And Jesus answering said unto them, Render to Caesar the things that are Caesar's, and to God the things that are God's. And they marvelled at him."

Luke 20:21-25 "[21]And they asked him, saying, Master, we know that thou sayest and teachest rightly, neither acceptest thou the person of any, but teachest the way of God truly: [22]Is it lawful for us to give tribute unto Caesar, or no? [23]But he perceived their craftiness, and said unto them, Why tempt ye me? [24]Shew me a penny. Whose image and superscription hath it? They answered and said, Caesar's. [25]And he said unto them, Render therefore unto Caesar the things which be Caesar's, and unto God the things which be God's."

REPENTANCE

Jesus Christ Coming To Call
Sinners To Repentance

Matthew 9:11-13 "¹¹And when the Pharisees saw it, they said unto his disciples, Why eateth your Master with publicans and sinners? ¹²But when Jesus heard that, he said unto them, They that be whole need not a physician, but they that are sick. ¹³But go ye and learn what that meaneth, I will have mercy, and not sacrifice: for I am not come to call the righteous, but sinners to repentance."

Mark 2:16-17 "¹⁶And when the scribes and Pharisees saw him eat with publicans and sinners, they said unto his disciples, How is it that he eateth and drinketh with publicans and sinners? ¹⁷When Jesus heard it, he saith unto them, They that are whole have no need of the physician, but they that are sick: I came not to call the righteous, but sinners to repentance."

Luke 5:30-32 "³⁰But their scribes and Pharisees murmured against his disciples, saying, Why do ye eat and drink with publicans and sinners? ³¹And Jesus answering said unto them, They that are whole need not a physician; but they that are sick. ³²I came not to call the righteous, but sinners to repentance."

Acts 5:30-31 "³⁰The God of our fathers raised up Jesus, whom ye slew and hanged on a tree. ³¹Him hath God exalted with his right hand to be a Prince and a Saviour, for to give repentance to Israel, and forgiveness of sins."

Repenting

Ezekiel 14:6 "Therefore say unto the house of Israel, Thus saith the Lord GOD; Repent, and turn yourselves from your idols; and turn away your faces from all your abominations."

Ezekiel 18:29-32 "²⁹Yet saith the house of Israel, The way of the Lord is not equal. O house of Israel, are not my ways equal? are not your ways unequal? ³⁰Therefore I will judge you, O house of Israel, every one according to his ways, saith the Lord GOD. Repent, and turn yourselves from all your transgressions; so iniquity shall not be your ruin. ³¹Cast away from you all your transgressions, whereby ye have transgressed; and make you a new heart and a new spirit: for why will ye die, O house of Israel? ³²For I have no pleasure in the death of him that dieth, saith the Lord GOD: wherefore turn yourselves, and live ye."

Matthew 3:1-2 "¹In those days came John the Baptist, preaching in the wilderness of Judaea, ²And saying, Repent ye: for the kingdom of heaven is at hand."

Mark 1:15 "And saying, The time is fulfilled, and the kingdom of God is at hand: repent ye, and believe the gospel."

Acts 2:38 "Then Peter said unto them, Repent, and be baptized every one of you in the name of Jesus Christ for the remission of sins, and ye shall receive the gift of the Holy Ghost."

Acts 3:19 "Repent ye therefore, and be converted, that your sins may be blotted out, when the times of refreshing shall come from the presence of the Lord."

Acts 17:29-30 "²⁹Forasmuch then as we are the offspring of God, we ought not to think that the Godhead is like unto gold, or silver, or stone, graven by art and man's device. ³⁰And the times of this ignorance God winked at; but now commandeth all men every where to repent."

Revelation 2:5 "Remember therefore from whence thou art fallen, and repent, and do the first works; or else I will come unto thee quickly, and will remove thy candlestick out of his place, except thou repent."

Revelation 2:16 "Repent; or else I will come unto thee quickly, and will fight against them with the sword of my mouth."

Revelation 3:19 "As many as I love, I rebuke and chasten: be zealous therefore, and repent."

The Lord Giving Time
For Sinners To Repent

2 Peter 3:9 "The Lord is not slack concerning his promise, as some men count slackness; but is longsuffering to us-ward, not willing that any should perish, but that all should come to repentance."

The Reward For Not Repenting

Luke 13:1-5 "¹There were present at that season some that told him of the Galilaeans, whose blood

Pilate had mingled with their sacrifices. 2And Jesus answering said unto them, Suppose ye that these Galilaeans were sinners above all the Galilaeans, because they suffered such things? 3I tell you, Nay: but, except ye repent, ye shall all likewise perish. 4Or those eighteen, upon whom the tower in Siloam fell, and slew them, think ye that they were sinners above all men that dwelt in Jerusalem? 5I tell you, Nay: but, except ye repent, ye shall all likewise perish."

Revelation 2:1-5 "1Unto the angel of the church of Ephesus write; These things saith he that holdeth the seven stars in his right hand, who walketh in the midst of the seven golden candlesticks; 2I know thy works, and thy labour, and thy patience, and how thou canst not bear them which are evil: and thou hast tried them which say they are apostles, and are not, and hast found them liars: 3And hast borne, and hast patience, and for my name's sake hast laboured, and hast not fainted. 4Nevertheless I have somewhat against thee, because thou hast left thy first love. 5Remember therefore from whence thou art fallen, and repent, and do the first works; or else I will come unto thee quickly, and will remove thy candlestick out of his place, except thou repent."

Revelation 2:12-16 "12And to the angel of the church in Pergamos write; These things saith he which hath the sharp sword with two edges; 13I know thy works, and where thou dwellest, even where Satan's seat is: and thou holdest fast my name, and hast not denied my faith, even in those days wherein Antipas was my faithful martyr, who was slain among you, where Satan dwelleth. 14But I have a few things against thee, because thou hast there them that hold the doctrine of Balaam, who taught Balac to cast a stumblingblock before the children of Israel, to eat things sacrificed unto idols, and to commit fornication. 15So hast thou also them that hold the doctrine of the Nicolaitans, which thing I hate. 16Repent; or else I will come unto thee quickly, and will fight against them with the sword of my mouth."

Revelation 2:18-23 "18And unto the angel of the church in Thyatira write; These things saith the Son of God, who hath his eyes like unto a flame of fire, and his feet are like fine brass; 19I know thy works, and charity, and service, and faith, and thy patience, and thy works; and the last to be more than the first. 20Notwithstanding I have a few things against thee, because thou sufferest that woman Jezebel, which calleth herself a prophetess, to teach and to seduce my servants to commit fornication, and to eat things sacrificed unto idols. 21And I gave her space to repent of her fornication; and she repented not. 22Behold, I will cast her into a bed, and them that commit adultery with her into great tribulation, except they repent of their deeds. 23And I will kill her children with death; and all the churches shall know that I am he which searcheth the reins and hearts: and I will give unto every one of you according to your works."

The Reward For Repenting

1 Kings 8:43-50 "43Hear thou in heaven thy dwelling place, and do according to all that the stranger calleth to thee for: that all people of the earth may know thy name, to fear thee, as do thy people Israel; and that they may know that this house, which I have builded, is called by thy name. 44If thy people go out to battle against their enemy, whithersoever thou shalt send them, and shall pray unto the LORD toward the city which thou hast chosen, and toward the house that I have built for thy name: 45Then hear thou in heaven their prayer and their supplication, and maintain their cause. 46If they sin against thee, (for there is no man that sinneth not,) and thou be angry with them, and deliver them to the enemy, so that they carry them away captives unto the land of the enemy, far or near; 47Yet if they shall bethink themselves in the land whither they were carried captives, and repent, and make supplication unto thee in the land of them that carried them captives, saying, We have sinned, and have done perversely, we have committed wickedness; 48And so return unto thee with all their heart, and with all their soul, in the land of their enemies, which led them away captive, and pray unto thee toward their land, which thou gavest unto their fathers, the city which thou hast chosen, and the house which I have built for thy name: 49Then hear thou their prayer and their supplication in heaven thy dwelling place, and maintain their cause, 50And forgive thy people that have sinned against thee and all their transgressions wherein they have transgressed against thee, and give them compassion before them who carried them captive, that they may have compassion on them."

Ezekiel 18:27-32 "27Again, when the wicked man turneth away from his wickedness that he hath committed, and doeth that which is lawful and right, he shall save his soul alive. 28Because he considereth, and turneth away from all his transgressions that he hath committed, he shall surely live, he shall not die. 29Yet saith the house of Israel, The way of the Lord is not equal. O house of Israel, are not my ways equal? are not your ways unequal? 30Therefore I will judge you, O house of Israel, every one according to his ways, saith the Lord GOD. Repent, and turn yourselves from all your transgressions; so iniquity shall not be your ruin. 31Cast away from you all your transgressions, whereby ye have transgressed; and make you a new heart and a new spirit: for why will ye die, O house of Israel? 32For I have no pleasure in the death of him that dieth, saith the Lord GOD: wherefore turn yourselves, and live ye."

Ezekiel 33:11-20 "11Say unto them, As I live, saith the Lord GOD, I have no pleasure in the death of the wicked; but that the wicked turn from his way and live: turn ye, turn ye from your evil ways; for why will ye die, O house of Israel? 12Therefore, thou son of man, say unto the children of thy people, The righteousness of the righteous shall not deliver him in the day of his transgression: as for the wickedness of the wicked, he shall not fall thereby in the day that he turneth from his wickedness; neither shall the righteous be able to live for his righteousness in the day that he sinneth. 13When I shall say to the righteous, that he shall surely live; if he trust to his own righteousness, and commit iniquity, all his righteousnesses shall not be remembered; but for his iniquity that he hath committed, he shall die for it. 14Again, when I say unto the wicked, Thou shalt surely die; if he turn from his sin, and do that which is lawful and right; 15If the wicked restore the pledge, give again that he had robbed, walk in the statutes of life, without committing iniquity; he shall surely live, he shall not die. 16None of his sins that he hath committed shall be mentioned unto him: he hath done that which is lawful and right; he shall surely live. 17Yet the children of thy people say, The way of the Lord is not equal: but as for them, their way is not equal. 18When the righteous turneth from his righteousness, and committeth iniquity, he shall even die thereby. 19But if the wicked turn from his wickedness, and do that which is lawful and right, he shall live thereby. 20Yet ye say, The way of the Lord is not equal. O ye house of Israel, I will judge you every one after his ways."

The Sinner That Repents

Luke 15:1-10 "1Then drew near unto him all the publicans and sinners for to hear him. 2And the Pharisees and scribes murmured, saying, This man receiveth sinners, and eateth with them. 3And he spake this parable unto them, saying, 4What man of you, having an hundred sheep, if he lose one of them, doth not leave the ninety and nine in the wilderness, and go after that which is lost, until he find it? 5And when he hath found it, he layeth it on his shoulders, rejoicing. 6And when he cometh home, he calleth together his friends and neighbours, saying unto them, Rejoice with me; for I have found my sheep which was lost. 7I say unto you, that likewise joy shall be in heaven over one sinner that repenteth, more than over ninety and nine just persons, which need no repentance. 8Either what woman having ten pieces of silver, if she lose one piece, doth not light a candle, and sweep the house, and seek diligently till she find it? 9And when she hath found it, she calleth her friends and her neighbours together, saying, Rejoice with me; for I have found the piece which I had lost. 10Likewise, I say unto you, there is joy in the presence of the angels of God over one sinner that repenteth."

What Leads You To Repentance

Romans 2:4 "Or despisest thou the riches of his goodness and forbearance and longsuffering; not knowing that the goodness of God leadeth thee to repentance?"

What Works Repentance

2 Corinthians 7:10 "For godly sorrow worketh repentance to salvation not to be repented of: but the sorrow of the world worketh death."

Who Baptized With
The Baptism Of Repentance

Matthew 3:1-11 "1In those days came John the Baptist, preaching in the wilderness of Judaea, 2And saying, Repent ye: for the kingdom of heaven is at hand. ³For this is he that was spoken of by the prophet Esaias, saying, The voice of one crying in the wilderness, Prepare ye the way of the Lord, make his paths straight. ⁴And the same John had his raiment of camel's hair, and a leathern girdle about his loins; and his meat was locusts and wild honey. ⁵Then went out to him Jerusalem, and all Judaea, and all the region round about Jordan, ⁶And were baptized of him in Jordan, confessing their sins. ⁷But when he saw many of the Pharisees and Sadducees come to his baptism, he said unto them, O generation of vipers, who hath warned you to flee from the wrath to come? ⁸Bring forth therefore fruits meet for repentance: ⁹And think not to say within yourselves, We have Abraham to our father: for I say unto you, that God is able of these stones to raise up children unto Abraham. ¹⁰And now also the axe is laid unto the root of the trees: therefore every tree which bringeth not forth good fruit is hewn down, and cast into the fire. ¹¹I indeed baptize you with water unto repentance: but he that cometh after me is mightier than I, whose shoes I am not worthy to bear: he shall baptize you with the Holy Ghost, and with fire."

Luke 3:2-3 "²Annas and Caiaphas being the high priests, the word of God came unto John the son of Zacharias in the wilderness. ³And he came into all the country about Jordan, preaching the baptism of repentance for the remission of sins."

Acts 19:4 "Then said Paul, John verily baptized with the baptism of repentance, saying unto the people, that they should believe on him which should come after him, that is, on Christ Jesus."

REPROACH

How Reproach Ceases
Proverbs 22:10 "Cast out the scorner, and contention shall go out; yea, strife and reproach shall cease."

The Reproaches Of Man
Falling On Jesus Christ
Psalm 69:1-9 "¹Save me, O God; for the waters are come in unto my soul. ²I sink in deep mire, where there is no standing: I am come into deep waters, where the floods overflow me. ³I am weary of my crying: my throat is dried: mine eyes fail while I

wait for my God. ⁴They that hate me without a cause are more than the hairs of mine head: they that would destroy me, being mine enemies wrongfully, are mighty: then I restored that which I took not away. ⁵O God, thou knowest my foolishness; and my sins are not hid from thee. ⁶Let not them that wait on thee, O Lord GOD of hosts, be ashamed for my sake: let not those that seek thee be confounded for my sake, O God of Israel. ⁷Because for thy sake I have borne reproach; shame hath covered my face. ⁸I am become a stranger unto my brethren, and an alien unto my mother's children. ⁹For the zeal of thine house hath eaten me up; and the reproaches of them that reproached thee are fallen upon me."

Romans 15:3 "For even Christ pleased not himself; but, as it is written, The reproaches of them that reproached thee fell on me."

What Comes With Reproach
Proverbs 18:3 "When the wicked cometh, then cometh also contempt, and with ignominy reproach."

What Is A Reproach To Any People
Proverbs 14:34 "Righteousness exalteth a nation: but sin is a reproach to any people."

Who Is A Son That Brings Reproach
Proverbs 19:26 "He that wasteth his father, and chaseth away his mother, is a son that causeth shame, and bringeth reproach."

Who Reproaches The Lord
Psalm 74:18 "Remember this, that the enemy hath reproached, O LORD, and that the foolish people have blasphemed thy name."

Psalm 74:22 "Arise, O God, plead thine own cause: remember how the foolish man reproacheth thee daily."

Proverbs 17:5 "Whoso mocketh the poor reproacheth his Maker: and he that is glad at calamities shall not be unpunished."

REPROOF

All Things That Are Reproved
Ephesians 5:13-14 "¹³But all things that are reproved are made manifest by the light: for whatsoever doth make manifest is light. ¹⁴Wherefore he

saith, Awake thou that sleepest, and arise from the dead, and Christ shall give thee light."

God Reproving
Psalm 50:7-8 "⁷Hear, O my people, and I will speak; O Israel, and I will testify against thee: I am God, even thy God. ⁸I will not reprove thee for thy sacrifices or thy burnt offerings, to have been continually before me."

Psalm 50:16-21 "¹⁶But unto the wicked God saith, What hast thou to do to declare my statutes, or that thou shouldest take my covenant in thy mouth? ¹⁷Seeing thou hatest instruction, and castest my words behind thee. ¹⁸When thou sawest a thief, then thou consentedst with him, and hast been partaker with adulterers. ¹⁹Thou givest thy mouth to evil, and thy tongue frameth deceit. ²⁰Thou sittest and speakest against thy brother; thou slanderest thine own mother's son. ²¹These things hast thou done, and I kept silence; thou thoughtest that I was altogether such an one as thyself: but I will reprove thee, and set them in order before thine eyes."

Reproofs Of Instruction
Proverbs 6:23 "For the commandment is a lamp; and the law is light; and reproofs of instruction are the way of life."

Reproving
2 Timothy 4:2-3 "²Preach the word; be instant in season, out of season; reprove, rebuke, exhort with all longsuffering and doctrine. ³For the time will come when they will not endure sound doctrine; but after their own lusts shall they heap to themselves teachers, having itching ears."

The Comforter Reproving The World Of Sin
John 16:7-11 "⁷Nevertheless I tell you the truth; It is expedient for you that I go away: for if I go not away, the Comforter will not come unto you; but if I depart, I will send him unto you. ⁸And when he is come, he will reprove the world of sin, and of righteousness, and of judgment: ⁹Of sin, because they believe not on me; ¹⁰Of righteousness, because I go to my Father, and ye see me no more; ¹¹Of judgment, because the prince of this world is judged."

The Reward For Reproving A Wise Man
Proverbs 9:8-9 "⁸Reprove not a scorner, lest he hate thee: rebuke a wise man, and he will love thee. ⁹Give instruction to a wise man, and he will

be yet wiser: teach a just man, and he will increase in learning."

Proverbs 19:25 "Smite a scorner, and the simple will beware: and reprove one that hath understanding, and he will understand knowledge."

Those That Hate Reproof
Proverbs 12:1 "Whoso loveth instruction loveth knowledge: but he that hateth reproof is brutish."

Proverbs 15:10 "Correction is grievous unto him that forsaketh the way: and he that hateth reproof shall die."

Those That Hear Reproof
Proverbs 15:31-32 "³¹The ear that heareth the reproof of life abideth among the wise. ³²He that refuseth instruction despiseth his own soul: but he that heareth reproof getteth understanding."

Those That Refuse Reproof
Proverbs 10:17 "He is in the way of life that keepeth instruction: but he that refuseth reproof erreth."

Proverbs 29:1 "He, that being often reproved hardeneth his neck, shall suddenly be destroyed, and that without remedy."

Those That Regard Reproof
Proverbs 13:18 "Poverty and shame shall be to him that refuseth instruction: but he that regardeth reproof shall be honoured."

Proverbs 15:5 "A fool despiseth his father's instruction: but he that regardeth reproof is prudent."

Those That Reprove A Scorner
Proverbs 9:7-10 "⁷He that reproveth a scorner getteth to himself shame: and he that rebuketh a wicked man getteth himself a blot. ⁸Reprove not a scorner, lest he hate thee: rebuke a wise man, and he will love thee. ⁹Give instruction to a wise man, and he will be yet wiser: teach a just man, and he will increase in learning. ¹⁰The fear of the LORD is the beginning of wisdom: and the knowledge of the holy is understanding."

Proverbs 15:12 "A scorner loveth not one that reproveth him: neither will he go unto the wise."

What Is Profitable For Reproof
2 Timothy 3:16-17 "¹⁶All scripture is given by inspiration of God, and is profitable for doctrine,

for reproof, for correction, for instruction in righteousness: [17]That the man of God may be perfect, throughly furnished unto all good works."

What Reproof Gives
Proverbs 29:15 "The rod and reproof give wisdom: but a child left to himself bringeth his mother to shame."

What Shall Reprove You
Jeremiah 2:19 "Thine own wickedness shall correct thee, and thy backslidings shall reprove thee: know therefore and see that it is an evil thing and bitter, that thou hast forsaken the LORD thy God, and that my fear is not in thee, saith the Lord GOD of hosts."

What To Reprove
Ephesians 5:11 "And have no fellowship with the unfruitful works of darkness, but rather reprove them."

Who Despises Reproof
Proverbs 1:20-30 "[20]Wisdom crieth without; she uttereth her voice in the streets: [21]She crieth in the chief place of concourse, in the openings of the gates: in the city she uttereth her words, saying, [22]How long, ye simple ones, will ye love simplicity? and the scorners delight in their scorning, and fools hate knowledge? [23]Turn you at my reproof: behold, I will pour out my spirit unto you, I will make known my words unto you. [24]Because I have called, and ye refused; I have stretched out my hand, and no man regarded; [25]But ye have set at nought all my counsel, and would none of my reproof: [26]I also will laugh at your calamity; I will mock when your fear cometh; [27]When your fear cometh as desolation, and your destruction cometh as a whirlwind; when distress and anguish cometh upon you. [28]Then shall they call upon me, but I will not answer; they shall seek me early, but they shall not find me: [29]For that they hated knowledge, and did not choose the fear of the LORD: [30]They would none of my counsel: they despised all my reproof."

Who Reproof Enters Into
Proverbs 17:10 "A reproof entereth more into a wise man than an hundred stripes into a fool."

Wise Reprovers Upon An Obedient Ear
Proverbs 25:12 "As an earring of gold, and an ornament of fine gold, so is a wise reprover upon an obedient ear."

REQUIREMENTS
What The Lord Does Not Require
1 Samuel 15:22 "And Samuel said, Hath the LORD as great delight in burnt offerings and sacrifices, as in obeying the voice of the LORD? Behold, to obey is better than sacrifice, and to hearken than the fat of rams."

Psalm 40:5-6 "[5]Many, O LORD my God, are thy wonderful works which thou hast done, and thy thoughts which are to us-ward: they cannot be reckoned up in order unto thee: if I would declare and speak of them, they are more than can be numbered. [6]Sacrifice and offering thou didst not desire; mine ears hast thou opened: burnt offering and sin offering hast thou not required."

Isaiah 1:10-14 "[10]Hear the word of the LORD, ye rulers of Sodom; give ear unto the law of our God, ye people of Gomorrah. [11]To what purpose is the multitude of your sacrifices unto me? saith the LORD: I am full of the burnt offerings of rams, and the fat of fed beasts; and I delight not in the blood of bullocks, or of lambs, or of he goats. [12]When ye come to appear before me, who hath required this at your hand, to tread my courts? [13]Bring no more vain oblations; incense is an abomination unto me; the new moons and sabbaths, the calling of assemblies, I cannot away with; it is iniquity, even the solemn meeting. [14]Your new moons and your appointed feasts my soul hateth: they are a trouble unto me; I am weary to bear them."

What The Lord Requires
Deuteronomy 10:12-13 "[12]And now, Israel, what doth the LORD thy God require of thee, but to fear the LORD thy God, to walk in all his ways, and to love him, and to serve the LORD thy God with all thy heart and with all thy soul, [13]To keep the commandments of the LORD, and his statutes, which I command thee this day for thy good?"

Deuteronomy 23:21 "When thou shalt vow a vow unto the LORD thy God, thou shalt not slack to pay it: for the LORD thy God will surely require it of thee; and it would be sin in thee."

Ecclesiastes 12:13 "Let us hear the conclusion of the whole matter: Fear God, and keep his commandments: for this is the whole duty of man."

Micah 6:6-8 "[6]Wherewith shall I come before the LORD, and bow myself before the high God? shall I come before him with burnt offerings, with calves of a year old? [7]Will the LORD be pleased with thousands of rams, or with ten thousands of rivers of oil? shall I give my firstborn for my transgression, the fruit of my body for the sin of my soul? [8]He hath shewed thee, O man, what is good; and what doth the LORD require of thee, but to do justly, and to love mercy, and to walk humbly with thy God?"

1 Corinthians 4:1-2 "[1]Let a man so account of us, as of the ministers of Christ, and stewards of the mysteries of God. [2]Moreover it is required in stewards, that a man be found faithful."

Who Much Is Required From
Luke 12:48 "But he that knew not, and did commit things worthy of stripes, shall be beaten with few stripes. For unto whomsoever much is given, of him shall be much required: and to whom men have committed much, of him they will ask the more."

RESISTANCE

The Reward For Resisting The Devil
James 4:7 "Submit yourselves therefore to God. Resist the devil, and he will flee from you."

Those That Resist The Powers That Be
Romans 13:1-2 "[1]Let every soul be subject unto the higher powers. For there is no power but of God: the powers that be are ordained of God. [2]Whosoever therefore resisteth the power, resisteth the ordinance of God: and they that resist shall receive to themselves damnation."

What Not To Resist
Matthew 5:38-42 "[38]Ye have heard that it hath been said, An eye for an eye, and a tooth for a tooth: [39]But I say unto you, That ye resist not evil: but whosoever shall smite thee on thy right cheek, turn to him the other also. [40]And if any man will sue thee at the law, and take away thy coat, let him have thy cloke also. [41]And whosoever shall compel thee to go a mile, go with him twain. [42]Give to him that asketh thee, and from him that would borrow of thee turn not thou away."

Who God Resists
James 4:6 "But he giveth more grace. Wherefore he saith, God resisteth the proud, but giveth grace unto the humble."

1 Peter 5:5 "Likewise, ye younger, submit yourselves unto the elder. Yea, all of you be subject one to another, and be clothed with humility: for God resisteth the proud, and giveth grace to the humble."

Who Resists The Holy Spirit
Acts 7:51 "Ye stiffnecked and uncircumcised in heart and ears, ye do always resist the Holy Ghost: as your fathers did, so do ye."

Who Resists The Truth
2 Timothy 3:6-8 "[6]For of this sort are they which creep into houses, and lead captive silly women laden with sins, led away with divers lusts, [7]Ever learning, and never able to come to the knowledge of the truth. [8]Now as Jannes and Jambres withstood Moses, so do these also resist the truth: men of corrupt minds, reprobate concerning the faith."

Who To Resist
Ephesians 4:27 "Neither give place to the devil."

James 4:7 "Submit yourselves therefore to God. Resist the devil, and he will flee from you."

1 Peter 5:8-9 "[8]Be sober, be vigilant; because your adversary the devil, as a roaring lion, walketh about, seeking whom he may devour: [9]Whom resist stedfast in the faith, knowing that the same afflictions are accomplished in your brethren that are in the world."

RESPECT

Those That Do Not Respect The Proud
Psalm 40:4 "Blessed is that man that maketh the LORD his trust, and respecteth not the proud, nor such as turn aside to lies."

Who The Lord Does Not Respect
Job 37:23-24 "[23]Touching the Almighty, we cannot find him out: he is excellent in power, and in judgment, and in plenty of justice: he will not afflict. [24]Men do therefore fear him: he respecteth not any that are wise of heart."

Who The Lord Respects
Psalm 138:6 "Though the LORD be high, yet hath he respect unto the lowly: but the proud he knoweth afar off."

RESURRECTION

God Resurrecting The Dead
Job 19:25-27 "[25]For I know that my redeemer liveth, and that he shall stand at the latter day upon the earth: [26]And though after my skin

worms destroy this body, yet in my flesh shall I see God: [27]Whom I shall see for myself, and mine eyes shall behold, and not another; though my reins be consumed within me."

Daniel 12:1-2 "[1]And at that time shall Michael stand up, the great prince which standeth for the children of thy people: and there shall be a time of trouble, such as never was since there was a nation even to that same time: and at that time thy people shall be delivered, every one that shall be found written in the book. [2]And many of them that sleep in the dust of the earth shall awake, some to everlasting life, and some to shame and everlasting contempt."

Matthew 11:4-5 "[4]Jesus answered and said unto them, Go and shew John again those things which ye do hear and see: [5]The blind receive their sight, and the lame walk, the lepers are cleansed, and the deaf hear, the dead are raised up, and the poor have the gospel preached to them."

Luke 7:22 "Then Jesus answering said unto them, Go your way, and tell John what things ye have seen and heard; how that the blind see, the lame walk, the lepers are cleansed, the deaf hear, the dead are raised, to the poor the gospel is preached."

John 5:21 "For as the Father raiseth up the dead, and quickeneth them; even so the Son quickeneth whom he will."

John 5:23-29 "[23]That all men should honour the Son, even as they honour the Father. He that honoureth not the Son honoureth not the Father which hath sent him. [24]Verily, verily, I say unto you, He that heareth my word, and believeth on him that sent me, hath everlasting life, and shall not come into condemnation; but is passed from death unto life. [25]Verily, verily, I say unto you, The hour is coming, and now is, when the dead shall hear the voice of the Son of God: and they that hear shall live. [26]For as the Father hath life in himself; so hath he given to the Son to have life in himself; [27]And hath given him authority to execute judgment also, because he is the Son of man. [28]Marvel not at this: for the hour is coming, in the which all that are in the graves shall hear his voice, [29]And shall come forth; they that have done good, unto the resurrection of life; and they that have done evil, unto the resurrection of damnation."

1 Corinthians 15:50-57 "[50]Now this I say, brethren, that flesh and blood cannot inherit the kingdom of God; neither doth corruption inherit incorruption. [51]Behold, I shew you a mystery; We shall not all sleep, but we shall all be changed, [52]In a moment, in the twinkling of an eye, at the last trump: for the trumpet shall sound, and the dead shall be raised incorruptible, and we shall be changed. [53]For this corruptible must put on incorruption, and this mortal must put on immortality. [54]So when this corruptible shall have put on incorruption, and this mortal shall have put on immortality, then shall be brought to pass the saying that is written, Death is swallowed up in victory. [55]O death, where is thy sting? O grave, where is thy victory? [56]The sting of death is sin; and the strength of sin is the law. [57]But thanks be to God, which giveth us the victory through our Lord Jesus Christ."

2 Corinthians 1:9 "But we had the sentence of death in ourselves, that we should not trust in ourselves, but in God which raiseth the dead."

Ephesians 2:1-6 "[1]And you hath he quickened, who were dead in trespasses and sins; [2]Wherein in time past ye walked according to the course of this world, according to the prince of the power of the air, the spirit that now worketh in the children of disobedience: [3]Among whom also we all had our conversation in times past in the lusts of our flesh, fulfilling the desires of the flesh and of the mind; and were by nature the children of wrath, even as others. [4]But God, who is rich in mercy, for his great love wherewith he loved us, [5]Even when we were dead in sins, hath quickened us together with Christ, (by grace ye are saved;) [6]And hath raised us up together, and made us sit together in heavenly places in Christ Jesus."

Ephesians 5:13-14 "[13]But all things that are reproved are made manifest by the light: for whatsoever doth make manifest is light. [14]Wherefore he saith, Awake thou that sleepest, and arise from the dead, and Christ shall give thee light."

If There Is No Resurrection

1 Corinthians 15:12-19 "[12]Now if Christ be preached that he rose from the dead, how say some among you that there is no resurrection of the dead? [13]But if there be no resurrection of the dead, then is Christ not risen: [14]And if Christ be not risen, then is our preaching vain, and your faith is also vain. [15]Yea, and we are found false witnesses of God; because we have testified of God that he raised up Christ: whom he raised not up, if so be that the dead rise not. [16]For if the dead rise not, then is not Christ raised: [17]And if Christ be not raised, your faith is vain; ye are yet in your sins. [18]Then they also which are fallen asleep in Christ are perished. [19]If in this life only we have hope in Christ, we are of all men most miserable."

1 Corinthians 15:29-32 "[29]Else what shall they do which are baptized for the dead, if the dead rise not at all? why are they then baptized for the dead? [30]And why stand we in jeopardy every hour? [31]I protest by your rejoicing which I have in Christ Jesus our Lord, I die daily. [32]If after the manner of men I have fought with beasts at Ephesus, what advantageth it me, if the dead rise not? let us eat and drink; for to morrow we die."

Jesus Christ Being Raised From The Dead
Matthew 16:21 "From that time forth began Jesus to shew unto his disciples, how that he must go unto Jerusalem, and suffer many things of the elders and chief priests and scribes, and be killed, and be raised again the third day."

Matthew 17:22-23 "[22]And while they abode in Galilee, Jesus said unto them, The Son of man shall be betrayed into the hands of men: [23]And they shall kill him, and the third day he shall be raised again. And they were exceeding sorry."

Matthew 20:18-19 "[18]Behold, we go up to Jerusalem; and the Son of man shall be betrayed unto the chief priests and unto the scribes, and they shall condemn him to death, [19]And shall deliver him to the Gentiles to mock, and to scourge, and to crucify him: and the third day he shall rise again."

Matthew 28:5-7 "[5]And the angel answered and said unto the women, Fear not ye: for I know that ye seek Jesus, which was crucified. [6]He is not here: for he is risen, as he said. Come, see the place where the Lord lay. [7]And go quickly, and tell his disciples that he is risen from the dead; and, behold, he goeth before you into Galilee; there shall ye see him: lo, I have told you."

Mark 8:31 "And he began to teach them, that the Son of man must suffer many things, and be rejected of the elders, and of the chief priests, and scribes, and be killed, and after three days rise again."

Mark 16:6 "And he saith unto them, Be not affrighted: Ye seek Jesus of Nazareth, which was crucified: he is risen; he is not here: behold the place where they laid him."

Mark 16:9 "Now when Jesus was risen early the first day of the week, he appeared first to Mary Magdalene, out of whom he had cast seven devils."

Luke 9:22 "Saying, The Son of man must suffer many things, and be rejected of the elders and chief priests and scribes, and be slain, and be raised the third day."

Luke 18:31-33 "[31]Then he took unto him the twelve, and said unto them, Behold, we go up to Jerusalem, and all things that are written by the prophets concerning the Son of man shall be accomplished. [32]For he shall be delivered unto the Gentiles, and shall be mocked, and spitefully entreated, and spitted on: [33]And they shall scourge him, and put him to death: and the third day he shall rise again."

Luke 24:6-7 "[6]He is not here, but is risen: remember how he spake unto you when he was yet in Galilee, [7]Saying, The Son of man must be delivered into the hands of sinful men, and be crucified, and the third day rise again."

Luke 24:44-46 "[44]And he said unto them, These are the words which I spake unto you, while I was yet with you, that all things must be fulfilled, which were written in the law of Moses, and in the prophets, and in the psalms, concerning me. [45]Then opened he their understanding, that they might understand the scriptures, [46]And said unto them, Thus it is written, and thus it behoved Christ to suffer, and to rise from the dead the third day."

John 20:1-9 "[1]The first day of the week cometh Mary Magdalene early, when it was yet dark, unto the sepulchre, and seeth the stone taken away from the sepulchre. [2]Then she runneth, and cometh to Simon Peter, and to the other disciple, whom Jesus loved, and saith unto them, They have taken away the Lord out of the sepulchre, and we know not where they have laid him. [3]Peter therefore went forth, and that other disciple, and came to the sepulchre. [4]So they ran both together: and the other disciple did outrun Peter, and came first to the sepulchre. [5]And he stooping down, and looking in, saw the linen clothes lying; yet went he not in. [6]Then cometh Simon Peter following him, and went into the sepulchre, and seeth the linen clothes lie, [7]And the napkin, that was about his head, not lying with the linen clothes, but wrapped together in a place by itself. [8]Then went in also that other disciple, which came first to the sepulchre, and he saw, and believed. [9]For as yet they knew not the scripture, that he must rise again from the dead."

Acts 1:1-2 "[1]The former treatise have I made, O Theophilus, of all that Jesus began both to do and teach, [2]Until the day in which he was taken up, after that he through the Holy Ghost had given commandments unto the apostles whom he had chosen."

Acts 2:22-24 "[22]Ye men of Israel, hear these words; Jesus of Nazareth, a man approved of God among you by miracles and wonders and signs, which God did by him in the midst of you, as ye yourselves also know: [23]Him, being delivered by the determinate counsel and foreknowledge of God, ye have taken, and by wicked hands have crucified and slain: [24]Whom God hath raised up, having loosed the pains of death: because it was not possible that he should be holden of it."

Acts 2:32 "This Jesus hath God raised up, whereof we all are witnesses."

Acts 3:13-15 "[13]The God of Abraham, and of Isaac, and of Jacob, the God of our fathers, hath glorified his Son Jesus; whom ye delivered up, and denied him in the presence of Pilate, when he was determined to let him go. [14]But ye denied the Holy One and the Just, and desired a murderer to be granted unto you; [15]And killed the Prince of life, whom God hath raised from the dead; whereof we are witnesses."

Acts 3:26 "Unto you first God, having raised up his Son Jesus, sent him to bless you, in turning away every one of you from his iniquities."

Acts 4:9-10 "[9]If we this day be examined of the good deed done to the impotent man, by what means he is made whole; [10]Be it known unto you all, and to all the people of Israel, that by the name of Jesus Christ of Nazareth, whom ye crucified, whom God raised from the dead, even by him doth this man stand here before you whole."

Acts 5:30 "The God of our fathers raised up Jesus, whom ye slew and hanged on a tree."

Acts 10:37-40 "[37]That word, I say, ye know, which was published throughout all Judaea, and began from Galilee, after the baptism which John preached; [38]How God anointed Jesus of Nazareth with the Holy Ghost and with power: who went about doing good, and healing all that were oppressed of the devil; for God was with him. [39]And we are witnesses of all things which he did both in the land of the Jews, and in Jerusalem; whom they slew and hanged on a tree: [40]Him God raised up the third day, and shewed him openly."

Acts 13:33-37 "[33]God hath fulfilled the same unto us their children, in that he hath raised up Jesus again; as it is also written in the second psalm, Thou art my Son, this day have I begotten thee. [34]And as concerning that he raised him up from the dead, now no more to return to corruption, he said on this wise, I will give you the sure mercies of David. [35]Wherefore he saith also in another psalm, Thou shalt not suffer thine Holy One to see corruption. [36]For David, after he had served his own generation by the will of God, fell on sleep, and was laid unto his fathers, and saw corruption: [37]But he, whom God raised again, saw no corruption."

Acts 17:3 "Opening and alleging, that Christ must needs have suffered, and risen again from the dead; and that this Jesus, whom I preach unto you, is Christ."

Acts 17:30-31 "[30]And the times of this ignorance God winked at; but now commandeth all men every where to repent: [31]Because he hath appointed a day, in the which he will judge the world in righteousness by that man whom he hath ordained; whereof he hath given assurance unto all men, in that he hath raised him from the dead."

Acts 26:23 "That Christ should suffer, and that he should be the first that should rise from the dead, and should shew light unto the people, and to the Gentiles."

Romans 6:4-9 "⁴Therefore we are buried with him by baptism into death: that like as Christ was raised up from the dead by the glory of the Father, even so we also should walk in newness of life. ⁵For if we have been planted together in the likeness of his death, we shall be also in the likeness of his resurrection: ⁶Knowing this, that our old man is crucified with him, that the body of sin might be destroyed, that henceforth we should not serve sin. ⁷For he that is dead is freed from sin. ⁸Now if we be dead with Christ, we believe that we shall also live with him: ⁹Knowing that Christ being raised from the dead dieth no more; death hath no more dominion over him."

Romans 7:4 "Wherefore, my brethren, ye also are become dead to the law by the body of Christ; that ye should be married to another, even to him who is raised from the dead, that we should bring forth fruit unto God."

Romans 8:11 "But if the Spirit of him that raised up Jesus from the dead dwell in you, he that raised up Christ from the dead shall also quicken your mortal bodies by his Spirit that dwelleth in you."

Romans 8:34 "Who is he that condemneth? It is Christ that died, yea rather, that is risen again, who is even at the right hand of God, who also maketh intercession for us."

Romans 14:7-9 "⁷For none of us liveth to himself, and no man dieth to himself. ⁸For whether we live, we live unto the Lord; and whether we die, we die unto the Lord: whether we live therefore, or die, we are the Lord's. ⁹For to this end Christ both died, and rose, and revived, that he might be Lord both of the dead and living."

1 Corinthians 6:14 "And God hath both raised up the Lord, and will also raise up us by his own power."

1 Corinthians 15:3-4 "³For I delivered unto you first of all that which I also received, how that Christ died for our sins according to the scriptures; ⁴And that he was buried, and that he rose again the third day according to the scriptures."

1 Corinthians 15:20-23 "²⁰But now is Christ risen from the dead, and become the firstfruits of them that slept. ²¹For since by man came death, by man came also the resurrection of the dead. ²²For as in Adam all die, even so in Christ shall all be made alive. ²³But every man in his own order: Christ the firstfruits; afterward they that are Christ's at his coming."

2 Corinthians 4:14 "Knowing that he which raised up the Lord Jesus shall raise up us also by Jesus, and shall present us with you."

Ephesians 1:19-20 "¹⁹And what is the exceeding greatness of his power to usward who believe, according to the working of his mighty power, ²⁰Which he wrought in Christ, when he raised him from the dead, and set him at his own right hand in the heavenly places."

Colossians 2:8-12 "⁸Beware lest any man spoil you through philosophy and vain deceit, after the tradition of men, after the rudiments of the world, and not after Christ. ⁹For in him dwelleth all the fulness of the Godhead bodily. ¹⁰And ye are complete in him, which is the head of all principality and power: ¹¹In whom also ye are circumcised with the circumcision made without hands, in putting off the body of the sins of the flesh by the circumcision of Christ: ¹²Buried with him in baptism, wherein also ye are risen with him through the faith of the operation of God, who hath raised him from the dead."

1 Thessalonians 1:9-10 "⁹For they themselves shew of us what manner of entering in we had unto you, and how ye turned to God from idols to serve the living and true God; ¹⁰And to wait for his Son from heaven, whom he raised from the dead, even Jesus, which delivered us from the wrath to come."

2 Timothy 2:8 "Remember that Jesus Christ of the seed of David was raised from the dead according to my gospel."

1 Peter 1:18-21 "¹⁸Forasmuch as ye know that ye were not redeemed with corruptible things, as silver and gold, from your vain conversation received by tradition from your fathers; ¹⁹But with the precious blood of Christ, as of a lamb without blemish and without spot: ²⁰Who verily was foreordained before the foundation of the world, but was manifest in these last times for you, ²¹Who by him do believe in God, that raised him up from the dead, and gave him glory; that your faith and hope might be in God."

Revelation 1:17-18 "¹⁷And when I saw him, I fell at his feet as dead. And he laid his right hand upon me, saying unto me, Fear not; I am the first and the last: ¹⁸I am he that liveth, and was dead; and, behold, I am alive for evermore, Amen; and have the keys of hell and of death."

Revelation 2:8 "And unto the angel of the church in Smyrna write; These things saith the first and the last, which was dead, and is alive."

Jesus Christ Being The Resurrection
John 11:25-26 "²⁵Jesus said unto her, I am the resurrection, and the life: he that believeth in me, though he were dead, yet shall he live: ²⁶And whosoever liveth and believeth in me shall never die. Believest thou this?"

The First Resurrection
Revelation 20:4-5 "⁴And I saw thrones, and they sat upon them, and judgment was given unto them: and I saw the souls of them that were beheaded for the witness of Jesus, and for the word of God, and which had not worshipped the beast, neither his image, neither had received his mark upon their foreheads, or in their hands; and they lived and reigned with Christ a thousand years. ⁵But the rest of the dead lived not again until the thousand years were finished. This is the first resurrection."

The Resurrected
Matthew 22:23-32 "²³The same day came to him the Sadducees, which say that there is no resurrection, and asked him, ²⁴Saying, Master, Moses said, If a man die, having no children, his brother shall marry his wife, and raise up seed unto his brother. ²⁵Now there were with us seven brethren: and the first, when he had married a wife, deceased, and, having no issue, left his wife unto his brother: ²⁶Likewise the second also, and the third, unto the seventh. ²⁷And last of all the woman died also. ²⁸Therefore in the resurrection whose wife shall she be of the seven? for they all had her. ²⁹Jesus answered and said unto them, Ye do err, not knowing the scriptures, nor the power of God. ³⁰For in the resurrection they neither marry, nor are given in marriage, but are as the angels of God in heaven. ³¹But as touching the resurrection of the dead, have ye not read that which was spoken unto you by God, saying, ³²I am the God of Abraham, and the God of Isaac, and the God of

Jacob? God is not the God of the dead, but of the living."

Mark 12:18-27 "¹⁸Then come unto him the Sadducees, which say there is no resurrection; and they asked him, saying, ¹⁹Master, Moses wrote unto us, If a man's brother die, and leave his wife behind him, and leave no children, that his brother should take his wife, and raise up seed unto his brother. ²⁰Now there were seven brethren: and the first took a wife, and dying left no seed. ²¹And the second took her, and died, neither left he any seed: and the third likewise. ²²And the seven had her, and left no seed: last of all the woman died also. ²³In the resurrection therefore, when they shall rise, whose wife shall she be of them? for the seven had her to wife. ²⁴And Jesus answering said unto them, Do ye not therefore err, because ye know not the scriptures, neither the power of God? ²⁵For when they shall rise from the dead, they neither marry, nor are given in marriage; but are as the angels which are in heaven. ²⁶And as touching the dead, that they rise: have ye not read in the book of Moses, how in the bush God spake unto him, saying, I am the God of Abraham, and the God of Isaac, and the God of Jacob? ²⁷He is not the God of the dead, but the God of the living: ye therefore do greatly err."

Luke 20:27-38 "²⁷Then came to him certain of the Sadducees, which deny that there is any resurrection; and they asked him, ²⁸Saying, Master, Moses wrote unto us, If any man's brother die, having a wife, and he die without children, that his brother should take his wife, and raise up seed unto his brother. ²⁹There were therefore seven brethren: and the first took a wife, and died without children. ³⁰And the second took her to wife, and he died childless. ³¹And the third took her; and in like manner the seven also: and they left no children, and died. ³²Last of all the woman died also. ³³Therefore in the resurrection whose wife of them is she? for seven had her to wife. ³⁴And Jesus answering said unto them, The children of this world marry, and are given in marriage: ³⁵But they which shall be accounted worthy to obtain that world, and the resurrection from the dead, neither marry, nor are given in marriage: ³⁶Neither can they die any more: for they are equal unto the angels; and are the children of God, being the children of the resurrection. ³⁷Now that the dead are raised, even Moses shewed at the bush, when he calleth the Lord the God of Abraham, and the God of Isaac, and the God of Jacob. [38]For he is not a God of the dead, but of the living: for all live unto him."

Colossians 3:1-3 "[1]If ye then be risen with Christ, seek those things which are above, where Christ sitteth on the right hand of God. [2]Set your affection on things above, not on things on the earth. [3]For ye are dead, and your life is hid with Christ in God."

The Resurrection Of Jesus Christ

1 Peter 3:20-21 "[20]Which sometime were disobedient, when once the longsuffering of God waited in the days of Noah, while the ark was a preparing, wherein few, that is, eight souls were saved by water. [21]The like figure whereunto even baptism doth also now save us (not the putting away of the filth of the flesh, but the answer of a good conscience toward God,) by the resurrection of Jesus Christ."

The Resurrection Of The Dead

1 Corinthians 15:20-22 "[20]But now is Christ risen from the dead, and become the firstfruits of them that slept. [21]For since by man came death, by man came also the resurrection of the dead. [22]For as in Adam all die, even so in Christ shall all be made alive."

1 Corinthians 15:39-46 "[39]All flesh is not the same flesh: but there is one kind of flesh of men, another flesh of beasts, another of fishes, and another of birds. [40]There are also celestial bodies, and bodies terrestrial: but the glory of the celestial is one, and the glory of the terrestrial is another. [41]There is one glory of the sun, and another glory of the moon, and another glory of the stars: for one star differeth from another star in glory. [42]So also is the resurrection of the dead. It is sown in corruption; it is raised in incorruption: [43]It is sown in dishonour; it is raised in glory: it is sown in weakness; it is raised in power: [44]It is sown a natural body; it is raised a spiritual body. There is a natural body, and there is a spiritual body. [45]And so it is written, The first man Adam was made a living soul; the last Adam was made a quickening spirit. [46]Howbeit that was not first which is spiritual, but that which is natural; and afterward that which is spiritual."

Those That Have Part In The First Resurrection

Revelation 20:6 "Blessed and holy is he that hath part in the first resurrection: on such the second death hath no power, but they shall be priests of God and of Christ, and shall reign with him a thousand years."

Who Falls, And Never Rises Up Again

Amos 8:14 "They that swear by the sin of Samaria, and say, Thy god, O Dan, liveth; and, The manner of Beer-sheba liveth; even they shall fall, and never rise up again."

Who Falls, But Rises Up Again

Proverbs 24:16 "For a just man falleth seven times, and riseth up again: but the wicked shall fall into mischief."

Who Shall Be Resurrected

John 6:35-40 "[35]And Jesus said unto them, I am the bread of life: he that cometh to me shall never hunger; and he that believeth on me shall never thirst. [36]But I said unto you, That ye also have seen me, and believe not. [37]All that the Father giveth me shall come to me; and him that cometh to me I will in no wise cast out. [38]For I came down from heaven, not to do mine own will, but the will of him that sent me. [39]And this is the Father's will which hath sent me, that of all which he hath given me I should lose nothing, but should raise it up again at the last day. [40]And this is the will of him that sent me, that every one which seeth the Son, and believeth on him, may have everlasting life: and I will raise him up at the last day."

John 6:43-44 "[43]Jesus therefore answered and said unto them, Murmur not among yourselves. [44]No man can come to me, except the Father which hath sent me draw him: and I will raise him up at the last day."

John 6:53-54 "[53]Then Jesus said unto them, Verily, verily, I say unto you, Except ye eat the flesh of the Son of man, and drink his blood, ye have no life in you. [54]Whoso eateth my flesh, and drinketh my blood, hath eternal life; and I will raise him up at the last day."

Romans 6:4-9 "[4]Therefore we are buried with him by baptism into death: that like as Christ was raised up from the dead by the glory of the Father, even so we also should walk in newness of life. [5]For if we have been planted together in the likeness of his death, we shall be also in the likeness of his resurrection: [6]Knowing this, that our old man is crucified with him, that the body of sin might be destroyed, that henceforth we should not serve sin. [7]For he that is dead is freed from sin. [8]Now if we be dead with Christ, we believe that we shall also live with him: [9]Knowing that Christ being raised from the dead dieth no more; death hath no more dominion over him."

Romans 8:10-11 "[10]And if Christ be in you, the body is dead because of sin; but the Spirit is life because of righteousness. [11]But if the Spirit of him that raised up Jesus from the dead dwell in you, he that raised up Christ from the dead shall also quicken your mortal bodies by his Spirit that dwelleth in you."

1 Corinthians 6:9-14 "[9]Know ye not that the unrighteous shall not inherit the kingdom of God? Be not deceived: neither fornicators, nor idolaters, nor adulterers, nor effeminate, nor abusers of themselves with mankind, [10]Nor thieves, nor covetous, nor drunkards, nor revilers, nor extortioners, shall inherit the kingdom of God. [11]And such were some of you: but ye are washed, but ye are sanctified, but ye are justified in the name of the Lord Jesus, and by the Spirit of our God. [12]All things are lawful unto me, but all things are not expedient: all things are lawful for me, but I will not be brought under the power of any. [13]Meats for the belly, and the belly for meats: but God shall destroy both it and them. Now the body is not for fornication, but for the Lord; and the Lord for the body. [14]And God hath both raised up the Lord, and will also raise up us by his own power."

1 Corinthians 15:20-23 "[20]But now is Christ risen from the dead, and become the firstfruits of them that slept. [21]For since by man came death, by man came also the resurrection of the dead. [22]For as in Adam all die, even so in Christ shall all be made alive. [23]But every man in his own order: Christ the firstfruits; afterward they that are Christ's at his coming."

2 Corinthians 4:7-14 "[7]But we have this treasure in earthen vessels, that the excellency of the power may be of God, and not of us. [8]We are troubled on every side, yet not distressed; we are perplexed, but not in despair; [9]Persecuted, but not forsaken;

cast down, but not destroyed; [10]Always bearing about in the body the dying of the Lord Jesus, that the life also of Jesus might be made manifest in our body. [11]For we which live are alway delivered unto death for Jesus' sake, that the life also of Jesus might be made manifest in our mortal flesh. [12]So then death worketh in us, but life in you. [13]We having the same spirit of faith, according as it is written, I believed, and therefore have I spoken; we also believe, and therefore speak; [14]Knowing that he which raised up the Lord Jesus shall raise up us also by Jesus, and shall present us with you."

Colossians 2:8-15 "[8]Beware lest any man spoil you through philosophy and vain deceit, after the tradition of men, after the rudiments of the world, and not after Christ. [9]For in him dwelleth all the fulness of the Godhead bodily. [10]And ye are complete in him, which is the head of all principality and power: [11]In whom also ye are circumcised with the circumcision made without hands, in putting off the body of the sins of the flesh by the circumcision of Christ: [12]Buried with him in baptism, wherein also ye are risen with him through the faith of the operation of God, who hath raised him from the dead. [13]And you, being dead in your sins and the uncircumcision of your flesh, hath he quickened together with him, having forgiven you all trespasses; [14]Blotting out the handwriting of ordinances that was against us, which was contrary to us, and took it out of the way, nailing it to his cross; [15]And having spoiled principalities and powers, he made a shew of them openly, triumphing over them in it."

1 Thessalonians 4:13-18 "[13]But I would not have you to be ignorant, brethren, concerning them which are asleep, that ye sorrow not, even as others which have no hope. [14]For if we believe that Jesus died and rose again, even so them also which sleep in Jesus will God bring with him. [15]For this we say unto you by the word of the Lord, that we which are alive and remain unto the coming of the Lord shall not prevent them which are asleep. [16]For the Lord himself shall descend from heaven with a shout, with the voice of the archangel, and with the trump of God: and the dead in Christ shall rise first: [17]Then we which are alive and remain shall be caught up together with them in the clouds, to meet the Lord in the air: and so shall we ever be with the Lord. [18]Wherefore comfort one another with these words."

REVELATION

The Lord Revealing Secrets

Isaiah 48:2-6 "[2]For they call themselves of the holy city, and stay themselves upon the God of Israel; The LORD of hosts is his name. [3]I have declared the former things from the beginning; and they went forth out of my mouth, and I shewed them; I did them suddenly, and they came to pass. [4]Because I knew that thou art obstinate, and thy neck is an iron sinew, and thy brow brass; [5]I have even from the beginning declared it to thee; before it came to pass I shewed it thee: lest thou shouldest say, Mine idol hath done them, and my graven image, and my molten image, hath commanded them. [6]Thou hast heard, see all this; and will not ye declare it? I have shewed thee new things from this time, even hidden things, and thou didst not know them."

Daniel 2:20-22 "[20]Daniel answered and said, Blessed be the name of God for ever and ever: for wisdom and might are his: [21]And he changeth the times and the seasons: he removeth kings, and setteth up kings: he giveth wisdom unto the wise, and knowledge to them that know understanding: [22]He revealeth the deep and secret things: he knoweth what is in the darkness, and the light dwelleth with him."

Daniel 2:28 "But there is a God in heaven that revealeth secrets, and maketh known to the king Nebuchadnezzar what shall be in the latter days. Thy dream, and the visions of thy head upon thy bed, are these."

Daniel 2:47 "The king answered unto Daniel, and said, Of a truth it is, that your God is a God of gods, and a Lord of kings, and a revealer of secrets, seeing thou couldest reveal this secret."

Daniel 9:21-23 "[21]Yea, whiles I was speaking in prayer, even the man Gabriel, whom I had seen in the vision at the beginning, being caused to fly swiftly, touched me about the time of the evening oblation. [22]And he informed me, and talked with me, and said, O Daniel, I am now come forth to give thee skill and understanding. [23]At the beginning of thy supplications the commandment came

forth, and I am come to shew thee; for thou art greatly beloved: therefore understand the matter, and consider the vision."

1 Corinthians 2:9-10 "[9]But as it is written, Eye hath not seen, nor ear heard, neither have entered into the heart of man, the things which God hath prepared for them that love him. [10]But God hath revealed them unto us by his Spirit: for the Spirit searcheth all things, yea, the deep things of God."

1 Corinthians 4:5 "Therefore judge nothing before the time, until the Lord come, who both will bring to light the hidden things of darkness, and will make manifest the counsels of the hearts: and then shall every man have praise of God."

The Lord Revealing The Future

Isaiah 41:21-28 "[21]Produce your cause, saith the LORD; bring forth your strong reasons, saith the King of Jacob. [22]Let them bring them forth, and shew us what shall happen: let them shew the former things, what they be, that we may consider them, and know the latter end of them; or declare us things for to come. [23]Shew the things that are to come hereafter, that we may know that ye are gods: yea, do good, or do evil, that we may be dismayed, and behold it together. [24]Behold, ye are of nothing, and your work of nought: an abomination is he that chooseth you. [25]I have raised up one from the north, and he shall come: from the rising of the sun shall he call upon my name: and he shall come upon princes as upon morter, and as the potter treadeth clay. [26]Who hath declared from the beginning, that we may know? and beforetime, that we may say, He is righteous? yea, there is none that sheweth, yea, there is none that declareth, yea, there is none that heareth your words. [27]The first shall say to Zion, Behold, behold them: and I will give to Jerusalem one that bringeth good tidings. [28]For I beheld, and there was no man; even among them, and there was no counseller, that, when I asked of them, could answer a word."

Isaiah 42:8-9 "[8]I am the LORD: that is my name: and my glory will I not give to another, neither my praise to graven images. [9]Behold, the former things are come to pass, and new things do I declare: before they spring forth I tell you of them."

Isaiah 43:9-12 "[9]Let all the nations be gathered together, and let the people be assembled: who among them can declare this, and shew us former things? let them bring forth their witnesses, that they may be justified: or let them hear, and say, It is truth. [10]Ye are my witnesses, saith the LORD, and my servant whom I have chosen: that ye may know and believe me, and understand that I am he: before me there was no God formed, neither shall there be after me. [11]I, even I, am the LORD; and beside me there is no saviour. [12]I have declared, and have saved, and I have shewed, when there was no strange god among you: therefore ye are my witnesses, saith the LORD, that I am God."

Isaiah 44:6-8 "[6]Thus saith the LORD the King of Israel, and his redeemer the LORD of hosts; I am the first, and I am the last; and beside me there is no God. [7]And who, as I, shall call, and shall declare it, and set it in order for me, since I appointed the ancient people? and the things that are coming, and shall come, let them shew unto them. [8]Fear ye not, neither be afraid: have not I told thee from that time, and have declared it? ye are even my witnesses. Is there a God beside me? yea, there is no God; I know not any."

Isaiah 46:8-12 "[8]Remember this, and shew yourselves men: bring it again to mind, O ye transgressors. [9]Remember the former things of old: for I am God, and there is none else; I am God, and there is none like me, [10]Declaring the end from the beginning, and from ancient times the things that are not yet done, saying, My counsel shall stand, and I will do all my pleasure: [11]Calling a ravenous bird from the east, the man that executeth my counsel from a far country: yea, I have spoken it, I will also bring it to pass; I have purposed it, I will also do it. [12]Hearken unto me, ye stouthearted, that are far from righteousness."

Isaiah 48:2-8 "[2]For they call themselves of the holy city, and stay themselves upon the God of Israel; The LORD of hosts is his name. [3]I have declared the former things from the beginning; and they went forth out of my mouth, and I shewed them; I did them suddenly, and they came to pass. [4]Because I knew that thou art obstinate, and thy neck is an iron sinew, and thy brow brass; [5]I have even from the beginning declared it to thee; before it came to pass I shewed it thee: lest thou shouldest say, Mine idol hath done them, and my graven image, and my molten image, hath

commanded them. [6]Thou hast heard, see all this; and will not ye declare it? I have shewed thee new things from this time, even hidden things, and thou didst not know them. [7]They are created now, and not from the beginning; even before the day when thou heardest them not; lest thou shouldest say, Behold, I knew them. [8]Yea, thou heardest not; yea, thou knewest not; yea, from that time that thine ear was not opened: for I knew that thou wouldest deal very treacherously, and wast called a transgressor from the womb."

Ezekiel 12:25 "For I am the LORD: I will speak, and the word that I shall speak shall come to pass; it shall be no more prolonged: for in your days, O rebellious house, will I say the word, and will perform it, saith the Lord GOD."

Daniel 2:28 "But there is a God in heaven that revealeth secrets, and maketh known to the king Nebuchadnezzar what shall be in the latter days. Thy dream, and the visions of thy head upon thy bed, are these."

Daniel 2:45 "Forasmuch as thou sawest that the stone was cut out of the mountain without hands, and that it brake in pieces the iron, the brass, the clay, the silver, and the gold; the great God hath made known to the king what shall come to pass hereafter: and the dream is certain, and the interpretation thereof sure."

Daniel 10:12-14 "[12]Then said he unto me, Fear not, Daniel: for from the first day that thou didst set thine heart to understand, and to chasten thyself before thy God, thy words were heard, and I am come for thy words. [13]But the prince of the kingdom of Persia withstood me one and twenty days: but, lo, Michael, one of the chief princes, came to help me; and I remained there with the kings of Persia. [14]Now I am come to make thee understand what shall befall thy people in the latter days: for yet the vision is for many days."

Daniel 10:20-21 "[20]Then said he, Knowest thou wherefore I come unto thee? and now will I return to fight with the prince of Persia: and when I am gone forth, lo, the prince of Grecia shall come. [21]But I will shew thee that which is noted in the scripture of truth: and there is none that holdeth with me in these things, but Michael your prince."

Mark 13:1-23 "¹And as he went out of the temple, one of his disciples saith unto him, Master, see what manner of stones and what buildings are here! ²And Jesus answering said unto him, Seest thou these great buildings? there shall not be left one stone upon another, that shall not be thrown down. ³And as he sat upon the mount of Olives over against the temple, Peter and James and John and Andrew asked him privately, ⁴Tell us, when shall these things be? and what shall be the sign when all these things shall be fulfilled? ⁵And Jesus answering them began to say, Take heed lest any man deceive you: ⁶For many shall come in my name, saying, I am Christ; and shall deceive many. ⁷And when ye shall hear of wars and rumours of wars, be ye not troubled: for such things must needs be; but the end shall not be yet. ⁸For nation shall rise against nation, and kingdom against kingdom: and there shall be earthquakes in divers places, and there shall be famines and troubles: these are the beginnings of sorrows. ⁹But take heed to yourselves: for they shall deliver you up to councils; and in the synagogues ye shall be beaten: and ye shall be brought before rulers and kings for my sake, for a testimony against them. ¹⁰And the gospel must first be published among all nations. ¹¹But when they shall lead you, and deliver you up, take no thought beforehand what ye shall speak, neither do ye premeditate: but whatsoever shall be given you in that hour, that speak ye: for it is not ye that speak, but the Holy Ghost. ¹²Now the brother shall betray the brother to death, and the father the son; and children shall rise up against their parents, and shall cause them to be put to death. ¹³And ye shall be hated of all men for my name's sake: but he that shall endure unto the end, the same shall be saved. ¹⁴But when ye shall see the abomination of desolation, spoken of by Daniel the prophet, standing where it ought not, (let him that readeth understand,) then let them that be in Judaea flee to the mountains: ¹⁵And let him that is on the housetop not go down into the house, neither enter therein, to take any thing out of his house: ¹⁶And let him that is in the field not turn back again for to take up his garment. ¹⁷But woe to them that are with child, and to them that give suck in those days! ¹⁸And pray ye that your flight be not in the winter. ¹⁹For in those days shall be affliction, such as was not from the beginning of the creation which God created

unto this time, neither shall be. ²⁰And except that the Lord had shortened those days, no flesh should be saved: but for the elect's sake, whom he hath chosen, he hath shortened the days. ²¹And then if any man shall say to you, Lo, here is Christ; or, lo, he is there; believe him not: ²²For false Christs and false prophets shall rise, and shall shew signs and wonders, to seduce, if it were possible, even the elect. ²³But take ye heed: behold, I have foretold you all things."

Luke 1:68-70 "⁶⁸Blessed be the Lord God of Israel; for he hath visited and redeemed his people, ⁶⁹And hath raised up an horn of salvation for us in the house of his servant David; ⁷⁰As he spake by the mouth of his holy prophets, which have been since the world began."

John 13:10-19 "¹⁰Jesus saith to him, He that is washed needeth not save to wash his feet, but is clean every whit: and ye are clean, but not all. ¹¹For he knew who should betray him; therefore said he, Ye are not all clean. ¹²So after he had washed their feet, and had taken his garments, and was set down again, he said unto them, Know ye what I have done to you? ¹³Ye call me Master and Lord: and ye say well; for so I am. ¹⁴If I then, your Lord and Master, have washed your feet; ye also ought to wash one another's feet. ¹⁵For I have given you an example, that ye should do as I have done to you. ¹⁶Verily, verily, I say unto you, The servant is not greater than his lord; neither he that is sent greater than he that sent him. ¹⁷If ye know these things, happy are ye if ye do them. ¹⁸I speak not of you all: I know whom I have chosen: but that the scripture may be fulfilled, He that eateth bread with me hath lifted up his heel against me. ¹⁹Now I tell you before it come, that, when it is come to pass, ye may believe that I am he."

John 14:23-29 "²³Jesus answered and said unto him, If a man love me, he will keep my words: and my Father will love him, and we will come unto him, and make our abode with him. ²⁴He that loveth me not keepeth not my sayings: and the word which ye hear is not mine, but the Father's which sent me. ²⁵These things have I spoken unto you, being yet present with you. ²⁶But the Comforter, which is the Holy Ghost, whom the Father will send in my name, he shall teach you all things, and bring all things to your remembrance, whatsoever I have said unto you. ²⁷Peace I leave with you, my peace I give unto you: not as the world giveth, give I unto you. Let not your heart be troubled, neither let it be afraid. ²⁸Ye have heard how I said unto you, I go away, and come again unto you. If ye loved me, ye would rejoice, because I said, I go unto the Father: for my Father is greater than I. ²⁹And now I have told you before it come to pass, that, when it is come to pass, ye might believe."

John 16:1-4 "¹These things have I spoken unto you, that ye should not be offended. ²They shall put you out of the synagogues: yea, the time cometh, that whosoever killeth you will think that he doeth God service. ³And these things will they do unto you, because they have not known the Father, nor me. ⁴But these things have I told you, that when the time shall come, ye may remember that I told you of them. And these things I said not unto you at the beginning, because I was with you."

Revelation 1:1 "The Revelation of Jesus Christ, which God gave unto him, to shew unto his servants things which must shortly come to pass; and he sent and signified it by his angel unto his servant John."

Revelation 4:1 "After this I looked, and, behold, a door was opened in heaven: and the first voice which I heard was as it were of a trumpet talking with me; which said, Come up hither, and I will shew thee things which must be hereafter."

Revelation 22:6 "And he said unto me, These sayings are faithful and true: and the Lord God of the holy prophets sent his angel to shew unto his servants the things which must shortly be done."

The Lord Revealing Truth

Jeremiah 33:4-6 "⁴For thus saith the LORD, the God of Israel, concerning the houses of this city, and concerning the houses of the kings of Judah, which are thrown down by the mounts, and by the sword; ⁵They come to fight with the Chaldeans, but it is to fill them with the dead bodies of men, whom I have slain in mine anger and in my fury, and for all whose wickedness I have hid my face from this city. ⁶Behold, I will bring it health and cure, and I will cure them, and will reveal unto them the abundance of peace and truth."

The Things Which Are Revealed

Deuteronomy 29:29 "The secret things belong unto the LORD our God: but those things which are revealed belong unto us and to our children for ever, that we may do all the words of this law."

What Reveals

Proverbs 27:19 "As in water face answereth to face, so the heart of man to man."

James 1:22-24 "²²But be ye doers of the word, and not hearers only, deceiving your own selves. ²³For if any be a hearer of the word, and not a doer, he is like unto a man beholding his natural face in a glass: ²⁴For he beholdeth himself, and goeth his way, and straightway forgetteth what manner of man he was."

What Shall Be Revealed

Isaiah 40:5 "And the glory of the LORD shall be revealed, and all flesh shall see it together: for the mouth of the LORD hath spoken it."

Isaiah 56:1 "Thus saith the LORD, Keep ye judgment, and do justice: for my salvation is near to come, and my righteousness to be revealed."

Matthew 10:26 "Fear them not therefore: for there is nothing covered, that shall not be revealed; and hid, that shall not be known."

Luke 12:2 "For there is nothing covered, that shall not be revealed; neither hid, that shall not be known."

Romans 8:16-18 "¹⁶The Spirit itself beareth witness with our spirit, that we are the children of God: ¹⁷And if children, then heirs; heirs of God, and joint-heirs with Christ; if so be that we suffer with him, that we may be also glorified together. ¹⁸For I reckon that the sufferings of this present time are not worthy to be compared with the glory which shall be revealed in us."

1 Peter 4:13 "But rejoice, inasmuch as ye are partakers of Christ's sufferings; that, when his glory shall be revealed, ye may be glad also with exceeding joy."

What The Lord Has Revealed

Psalm 98:2 "The LORD hath made known his salvation: his righteousness hath he openly shewed in the sight of the heathen."

Romans 16:25-26 "25Now to him that is of power to stablish you according to my gospel, and the preaching of Jesus Christ, according to the revelation of the mystery, which was kept secret since the world began, 26But now is made manifest, and by the scriptures of the prophets, according to the commandment of the everlasting God, made known to all nations for the obedience of faith."

Ephesians 3:1-9 "1For this cause I Paul, the prisoner of Jesus Christ for you Gentiles, 2If ye have heard of the dispensation of the grace of God which is given me to youward: 3How that by revelation he made known unto me the mystery; (as I wrote afore in few words, 4Whereby, when ye read, ye may understand my knowledge in the mystery of Christ) 5Which in other ages was not made known unto the sons of men, as it is now revealed unto his holy apostles and prophets by the Spirit; 6That the Gentiles should be fellowheirs, and of the same body, and partakers of his promise in Christ by the gospel: 7Whereof I was made a minister, according to the gift of the grace of God given unto me by the effectual working of his power. 8Unto me, who am less than the least of all saints, is this grace given, that I should preach among the Gentiles the unsearchable riches of Christ; 9And to make all men see what is the fellowship of the mystery, which from the beginning of the world hath been hid in God, who created all things by Jesus Christ."

1 Peter 1:10-12 "10Of which salvation the prophets have inquired and searched diligently, who prophesied of the grace that should come unto you: 11Searching what, or what manner of time the Spirit of Christ which was in them did signify, when it testified beforehand the sufferings of Christ, and the glory that should follow. 12Unto whom it was revealed, that not unto themselves, but unto us they did minister the things, which are now reported unto you by them that have preached the gospel unto you with the Holy Ghost sent down from heaven; which things the angels desire to look into."

Where The Righteousness Of God Is Revealed

Romans 1:16-20 "16For I am not ashamed of the gospel of Christ: for it is the power of God unto salvation to every one that believeth; to the Jew first, and also to the Greek. 17For therein is the righteousness of God revealed from faith to faith:

as it is written, The just shall live by faith. 18For the wrath of God is revealed from heaven against all ungodliness and unrighteousness of men, who hold the truth in unrighteousness; 19Because that which may be known of God is manifest in them; for God hath shewed it unto them. 20For the invisible things of him from the creation of the world are clearly seen, being understood by the things that are made, even his eternal power and Godhead; so that they are without excuse."

Who The Lord Reveals Things To

Psalm 25:14 "The secret of the LORD is with them that fear him; and he will shew them his covenant."

Psalm 103:6-7 "6The LORD executeth righteousness and judgment for all that are oppressed. 7He made known his ways unto Moses, his acts unto the children of Israel."

Psalm 111:2-6 "2The works of the LORD are great, sought out of all them that have pleasure therein. 3His work is honourable and glorious: and his righteousness endureth for ever. 4He hath made his wonderful works to be remembered: the LORD is gracious and full of compassion. 5He hath given meat unto them that fear him: he will ever be mindful of his covenant. 6He hath shewed his people the power of his works, that he may give them the heritage of the heathen."

Matthew 11:25-26 "25At that time Jesus answered and said, I thank thee, O Father, Lord of heaven and earth, because thou hast hid these things from the wise and prudent, and hast revealed them unto babes. 26Even so, Father: for so it seemed good in thy sight."

Luke 10:21 "In that hour Jesus rejoiced in spirit, and said, I thank thee, O Father, Lord of heaven and earth, that thou hast hid these things from the wise and prudent, and hast revealed them unto babes: even so, Father; for so it seemed good in thy sight."

Ephesians 1:3-9 "3Blessed be the God and Father of our Lord Jesus Christ, who hath blessed us with all spiritual blessings in heavenly places in Christ: 4According as he hath chosen us in him before the foundation of the world, that we should be holy and without blame before him in love: 5Having predestinated us unto the adoption of children by Jesus Christ to himself, according to the good pleasure of his will, 6To the praise of the glory of his grace, wherein he hath made us accepted in the beloved. 7In whom we have redemption through his blood, the forgiveness of sins, according to the riches of his grace; 8Wherein he hath abounded toward us in all wisdom and prudence; 9Having made known unto us the mystery of his will, according to his good pleasure which he hath purposed in himself."

Who Reveals Secrets
Proverbs 11:13 "A talebearer revealeth secrets: but he that is of a faithful spirit concealeth the matter."

Proverbs 20:19 "He that goeth about as a talebearer revealeth secrets: therefore meddle not with him that flattereth with his lips."

RIGHTEOUSNESS

Awaking To Righteousness
1 Corinthians 15:34 "Awake to righteousness, and sin not; for some have not the knowledge of God: I speak this to your shame."

How Many Became Righteous
Romans 5:17-19 "17For if by one man's offence death reigned by one; much more they which receive abundance of grace and of the gift of righteousness shall reign in life by one, Jesus Christ.) 18Therefore as by the offence of one judgment came upon all men to condemnation; even so by the righteousness of one the free gift came upon all men unto justification of life. 19For as by one man's disobedience many were made sinners, so by the obedience of one shall many be made righteous."

Hebrews 10:10-14 "10By the which will we are sanctified through the offering of the body of Jesus Christ once for all. 11And every priest standeth daily ministering and offering oftentimes the same sacrifices, which can never take away sins: 12But this man, after he had offered one sacrifice for sins for ever, sat down on the right hand of God; 13From henceforth expecting till his enemies be made his footstool. 14For by one offering he hath perfected for ever them that are sanctified."

Not Letting Your Righteousness Go
Job 27:6 "My righteousness I hold fast, and will not let it go: my heart shall not reproach me so long as I live."

Righteousness Belonging To The Lord
Daniel 9:7 "O Lord, righteousness belongeth unto thee, but unto us confusion of faces, as at this day; to the men of Judah, and to the inhabitants of Jerusalem, and unto all Israel, that are near, and that are far off, through all the countries whither thou hast driven them, because of their trespass that they have trespassed against thee."

Seeking Righteousness
Zephaniah 2:3 "Seek ye the LORD, all ye meek of the earth, which have wrought his judgment; seek righteousness, seek meekness: it may be ye shall be hid in the day of the LORD's anger."

Matthew 6:33-34 "33But seek ye first the kingdom of God, and his righteousness; and all these things shall be added unto you. 34Take therefore no thought for the morrow: for the morrow shall take thought for the things of itself. Sufficient unto the day is the evil thereof."

The Fruit Of Righteousness
Proverbs 11:30 "The fruit of the righteous is a tree of life; and he that winneth souls is wise."

James 3:18 "And the fruit of righteousness is sown in peace of them that make peace."

The Lord Being Righteous
Ezra 9:15 "O LORD God of Israel, thou art righteous: for we remain yet escaped, as it is this day: behold, we are before thee in our trespasses: for we cannot stand before thee because of this."

Nehemiah 9:7-8 "7Thou art the LORD the God, who didst choose Abram, and broughtest him forth out of Ur of the Chaldees, and gavest him the name of Abraham; 8And foundest his heart faithful before thee, and madest a covenant with him to give the land of the Canaanites, the Hittites, the Amorites, and the Perizzites, and the Jebusites, and the Girgashites, to give it, I say, to his seed, and hast performed thy words; for thou art righteous."

Psalm 7:9 "Oh let the wickedness of the wicked come to an end; but establish the just: for the righteous God trieth the hearts and reins."

Psalm 11:7 "For the righteous LORD loveth righteousness; his countenance doth behold the upright."

Psalm 116:5 "Gracious is the LORD, and righteous; yea, our God is merciful."

Psalm 119:137 "Righteous art thou, O LORD, and upright are thy judgments."

Psalm 145:17 "The LORD is righteous in all his ways, and holy in all his works."

Isaiah 5:16 "But the LORD of hosts shall be exalted in judgment, and God that is holy shall be sanctified in righteousness."

Jeremiah 9:23-24 "²³Thus saith the LORD, Let not the wise man glory in his wisdom, neither let the mighty man glory in his might, let not the rich man glory in his riches: ²⁴But let him that glorieth glory in this, that he understandeth and knoweth me, that I am the LORD which exercise lovingkindness, judgment, and righteousness, in the earth: for in these things I delight, saith the LORD."

Daniel 9:14 "Therefore hath the LORD watched upon the evil, and brought it upon us: for the LORD our God is righteous in all his works which he doeth: for we obeyed not his voice."

John 17:25 "O righteous Father, the world hath not known thee: but I have known thee, and these have known that thou hast sent me."

2 Timothy 4:7-8 "⁷I have fought a good fight, I have finished my course, I have kept the faith: ⁸Henceforth there is laid up for me a crown of righteousness, which the Lord, the righteous judge, shall give me at that day: and not to me only, but unto all them also that love his appearing."

1 John 2:1 "My little children, these things write I unto you, that ye sin not. And if any man sin, we have an advocate with the Father, Jesus Christ the righteous."

1 John 3:1-7 "¹Behold, what manner of love the Father hath bestowed upon us, that we should be called the sons of God: therefore the world knoweth us not, because it knew him not. ²Beloved, now are we the sons of God, and it doth not yet appear what we shall be: but we know that, when he shall appear, we shall be like him; for we shall see him as he is. ³And every man that hath this hope in him purifieth himself, even as he is pure. ⁴Whosoever committeth sin transgresseth also the law: for sin is the transgression of the law.

⁵And ye know that he was manifested to take away our sins; and in him is no sin. ⁶Whosoever abideth in him sinneth not: whosoever sinneth hath not seen him, neither known him. ⁷Little children, let no man deceive you: he that doeth righteousness is righteous, even as he is righteous."

Revelation 16:5 "And I heard the angel of the waters say, Thou art righteous, O Lord, which art, and wast, and shalt be, because thou hast judged thus."

The Lord Bringing Forth Righteousness
Psalm 37:5-6 "⁵Commit thy way unto the LORD; trust also in him; and he shall bring it to pass. ⁶And he shall bring forth thy righteousness as the light, and thy judgment as the noonday."

Isaiah 61:10-11 "¹⁰I will greatly rejoice in the LORD, my soul shall be joyful in my God; for he hath clothed me with the garments of salvation, he hath covered me with the robe of righteousness, as a bridegroom decketh himself with ornaments, and as a bride adorneth herself with her jewels. ¹¹For as the earth bringeth forth her bud, and as the garden causeth the things that are sown in it to spring forth; so the Lord GOD will cause righteousness and praise to spring forth before all the nations."

Jeremiah 51:10 "The LORD hath brought forth our righteousness: come, and let us declare in Zion the work of the LORD our God."

The Lord Loving Righteousness
Psalm 11:7 "For the righteous LORD loveth righteousness; his countenance doth behold the upright."

Psalm 33:4-5 "⁴For the word of the LORD is right; and all his works are done in truth. ⁵He loveth righteousness and judgment: the earth is full of the goodness of the LORD."

The Reward For Sowing Righteousness
Hosea 10:12 "Sow to yourselves in righteousness, reap in mercy; break up your fallow ground: for it is time to seek the LORD, till he come and rain righteousness upon you."

The Righteous
Job 36:5-10 "⁵Behold, God is mighty, and despiseth not any: he is mighty in strength and wisdom. ⁶He

preserveth not the life of the wicked: but giveth right to the poor. [7]He withdraweth not his eyes from the righteous: but with kings are they on the throne; yea, he doth establish them for ever, and they are exalted. [8]And if they be bound in fetters, and be holden in cords of affliction; [9]Then he sheweth them their work, and their transgressions that they have exceeded. [10]He openeth also their ear to discipline, and commandeth that they return from iniquity."

Psalm 1:6 "For the LORD knoweth the way of the righteous: but the way of the ungodly shall perish."

Psalm 5:12 "For thou, LORD, wilt bless the righteous; with favour wilt thou compass him as with a shield."

Psalm 7:11 "God judgeth the righteous, and God is angry with the wicked every day."

Psalm 11:5 "The LORD trieth the righteous: but the wicked and him that loveth violence his soul hateth."

Psalm 15:1-5 "[1]LORD, who shall abide in thy tabernacle? who shall dwell in thy holy hill? [2]He that walketh uprightly, and worketh righteousness, and speaketh the truth in his heart. [3]He that backbiteth not with his tongue, nor doeth evil to his neighbour, nor taketh up a reproach against his neighbour. [4]In whose eyes a vile person is contemned; but he honoureth them that fear the LORD. He that sweareth to his own hurt, and changeth not. [5]He that putteth not out his money to usury, nor taketh reward against the innocent. He that doeth these things shall never be moved."

Psalm 32:11 "Be glad in the LORD, and rejoice, ye righteous: and shout for joy, all ye that are upright in heart."

Psalm 34:15 "The eyes of the LORD are upon the righteous, and his ears are open unto their cry."

Psalm 34:17 "The righteous cry, and the LORD heareth, and delivereth them out of all their troubles."

Psalm 34:19 "Many are the afflictions of the righteous: but the LORD delivereth him out of them all."

Psalm 37:16-17 "[16]A little that a righteous man hath is better than the riches of many wicked. [17]For the arms of the wicked shall be broken: but the LORD upholdeth the righteous."

Psalm 37:21 "The wicked borroweth, and payeth not again: but the righteous sheweth mercy, and giveth."

Psalm 37:25 "I have been young, and now am old; yet have I not seen the righteous forsaken, nor his seed begging bread."

Psalm 37:30 "The mouth of the righteous speaketh wisdom, and his tongue talketh of judgment."

Psalm 52:1-6 "[1]Why boastest thou thyself in mischief, O mighty man? the goodness of God endureth continually. [2]Thy tongue deviseth mischiefs; like a sharp rasor, working deceitfully. [3]Thou lovest evil more than good; and lying rather than to speak righteousness. Selah. [4]Thou lovest all devouring words, O thou deceitful tongue. [5]God shall likewise destroy thee for ever, he shall take thee away, and pluck thee out of thy dwelling place, and root thee out of the land of the living. Selah. [6]The righteous also shall see, and fear, and shall laugh at him."

Psalm 55:22 "Cast thy burden upon the LORD, and he shall sustain thee: he shall never suffer the righteous to be moved."

Psalm 58:10-11 "[10]The righteous shall rejoice when he seeth the vengeance: he shall wash his feet in the blood of the wicked. [11]So that a man shall say, Verily there is a reward for the righteous: verily he is a God that judgeth in the earth."

Psalm 64:10 "The righteous shall be glad in the LORD, and shall trust in him; and all the upright in heart shall glory."

Psalm 75:10 "All the horns of the wicked also will I cut off; but the horns of the righteous shall be exalted."

Psalm 92:12-13 "[12]The righteous shall flourish like the palm tree: he shall grow like a cedar in Lebanon. [13]Those that be planted in the house of the LORD shall flourish in the courts of our God."

Psalm 106:3 "Blessed are they that keep judgment, and he that doeth righteousness at all times."

Psalm 107:31-42 "³¹Oh that men would praise the LORD for his goodness, and for his wonderful works to the children of men! ³²Let them exalt him also in the congregation of the people, and praise him in the assembly of the elders. ³³He turneth rivers into a wilderness, and the watersprings into dry ground; ³⁴A fruitful land into barrenness, for the wickedness of them that dwell therein. ³⁵He turneth the wilderness into a standing water, and dry ground into watersprings. ³⁶And there he maketh the hungry to dwell, that they may prepare a city for habitation; ³⁷And sow the fields, and plant vineyards, which may yield fruits of increase. ³⁸He blesseth them also, so that they are multiplied greatly; and suffereth not their cattle to decrease. ³⁹Again, they are minished and brought low through oppression, affliction, and sorrow. ⁴⁰He poureth contempt upon princes, and causeth them to wander in the wilderness, where there is no way. ⁴¹Yet setteth he the poor on high from affliction, and maketh him families like a flock. ⁴²The righteous shall see it, and rejoice: and all iniquity shall stop her mouth."

Psalm 112:1-9 "¹Praise ye the LORD. Blessed is the man that feareth the LORD, that delighteth greatly in his commandments. ²His seed shall be mighty upon earth: the generation of the upright shall be blessed. ³Wealth and riches shall be in his house: and his righteousness endureth for ever. ⁴Unto the upright there ariseth light in the darkness: he is gracious, and full of compassion, and righteous. ⁵A good man sheweth favour, and lendeth: he will guide his affairs with discretion. ⁶Surely he shall not be moved for ever: the righteous shall be in everlasting remembrance. ⁷He shall not be afraid of evil tidings: his heart is fixed, trusting in the LORD. ⁸His heart is established, he shall not be afraid, until he see his desire upon his enemies. ⁹He hath dispersed, he hath given to the poor; his righteousness endureth for ever; his horn shall be exalted with honour."

Psalm 118:15 "The voice of rejoicing and salvation is in the tabernacles of the righteous: the right hand of the LORD doeth valiantly."

Psalm 118:19-20 "¹⁹Open to me the gates of righteousness: I will go into them, and I will praise the LORD: ²⁰This gate of the LORD, into which the righteous shall enter."

Psalm 125:3 "For the rod of the wicked shall not rest upon the lot of the righteous; lest the righteous put forth their hands unto iniquity."

Psalm 140:12-13 "¹²I know that the LORD will maintain the cause of the afflicted, and the right of the poor. ¹³Surely the righteous shall give thanks unto thy name: the upright shall dwell in thy presence."

Psalm 146:8 "The LORD openeth the eyes of the blind: the LORD raiseth them that are bowed down: the LORD loveth the righteous."

Proverbs 2:6-7 "⁶For the LORD giveth wisdom: out of his mouth cometh knowledge and understanding. ⁷He layeth up sound wisdom for the righteous: he is a buckler to them that walk uprightly."

Proverbs 3:32 "For the froward is abomination to the LORD: but his secret is with the righteous."

Proverbs 10:3 "The LORD will not suffer the soul of the righteous to famish: but he casteth away the substance of the wicked."

Proverbs 10:11 "The mouth of a righteous man is a well of life: but violence covereth the mouth of the wicked."

Proverbs 10:16 "The labour of the righteous tendeth to life: the fruit of the wicked to sin."

Proverbs 10:21 "The lips of the righteous feed many: but fools die for want of wisdom."

Proverbs 10:24-25 "²⁴The fear of the wicked, it shall come upon him: but the desire of the righteous shall be granted. ²⁵As the whirlwind passeth, so is the wicked no more: but the righteous is an everlasting foundation."

Proverbs 10:28 "The hope of the righteous shall be gladness: but the expectation of the wicked shall perish."

Proverbs 10:30 "The righteous shall never be removed: but the wicked shall not inhabit the earth."

Proverbs 10:32 "The lips of the righteous know what is acceptable: but the mouth of the wicked speaketh frowardness."

Proverbs 11:8 "The righteous is delivered out of trouble, and the wicked cometh in his stead."

Proverbs 11:10 "When it goeth well with the righteous, the city rejoiceth: and when the wicked perish, there is shouting."

Proverbs 11:18 "The wicked worketh a deceitful work: but to him that soweth righteousness shall be a sure reward."

Proverbs 11:21 "Though hand join in hand, the wicked shall not be unpunished: but the seed of the righteous shall be delivered."

Proverbs 11:23 "The desire of the righteous is only good: but the expectation of the wicked is wrath."

Proverbs 11:28 "He that trusteth in his riches shall fall: but the righteous shall flourish as a branch."

Proverbs 11:30-31 "³⁰The fruit of the righteous is a tree of life; and he that winneth souls is wise. ³¹Behold, the righteous shall be recompensed in the earth: much more the wicked and the sinner."

Proverbs 12:3 "A man shall not be established by wickedness: but the root of the righteous shall not be moved."

Proverbs 12:5 "The thoughts of the righteous are right: but the counsels of the wicked are deceit."

Proverbs 12:7 "The wicked are overthrown, and are not: but the house of the righteous shall stand."

Proverbs 12:10 "A righteous man regardeth the life of his beast: but the tender mercies of the wicked are cruel."

Proverbs 12:12 "The wicked desireth the net of evil men: but the root of the righteous yieldeth fruit."

Proverbs 12:26 "The righteous is more excellent than his neighbour: but the way of the wicked seduceth them."

Proverbs 13:5 "A righteous man hateth lying: but a wicked man is loathsome, and cometh to shame."

Proverbs 13:9 "The light of the righteous rejoiceth: but the lamp of the wicked shall be put out."

Proverbs 13:21 "Evil pursueth sinners: but to the righteous good shall be repayed."

Proverbs 13:25 "The righteous eateth to the satisfying of his soul: but the belly of the wicked shall want."

Proverbs 14:9 "Fools make a mock at sin: but among the righteous there is favour."

Proverbs 14:19 "The evil bow before the good; and the wicked at the gates of the righteous."

Proverbs 14:32 "The wicked is driven away in his wickedness: but the righteous hath hope in his death."

Proverbs 15:6 "In the house of the righteous is much treasure: but in the revenues of the wicked is trouble."

Proverbs 15:19 "The way of the slothful man is as an hedge of thorns: but the way of the righteous is made plain."

Proverbs 15:28-29 "²⁸The heart of the righteous studieth to answer: but the mouth of the wicked poureth out evil things. ²⁹The LORD is far from the wicked: but he heareth the prayer of the righteous."

Proverbs 18:10 "The name of the LORD is a strong tower: the righteous runneth into it, and is safe."

Proverbs 21:12 "The righteous man wisely considereth the house of the wicked: but God overthroweth the wicked for their wickedness."

Proverbs 21:25-26 "²⁵The desire of the slothful killeth him; for his hands refuse to labour. ²⁶He coveteth greedily all the day long: but the righteous giveth and spareth not."

Proverbs 28:1 "The wicked flee when no man pursueth: but the righteous are bold as a lion."

Proverbs 28:12 "When righteous men do rejoice, there is great glory: but when the wicked rise, a man is hidden."

Proverbs 28:28 "When the wicked rise, men hide themselves: but when they perish, the righteous increase."

Proverbs 29:2 "When the righteous are in authority, the people rejoice: but when the wicked beareth rule, the people mourn."

Proverbs 29:6-7 "⁶In the transgression of an evil man there is a snare: but the righteous doth sing and rejoice. ⁷The righteous considereth the cause of the poor: but the wicked regardeth not to know it."

Proverbs 29:16 "When the wicked are multiplied, transgression increaseth: but the righteous shall see their fall."

Ecclesiastes 3:17 "I said in mine heart, God shall judge the righteous and the wicked: for there is a time there for every purpose and for every work."

Isaiah 3:10 "Say ye to the righteous, that it shall be well with him: for they shall eat the fruit of their doings."

Isaiah 33:15-16 "15He that walketh righteously, and speaketh uprightly; he that despiseth the gain of oppressions, that shaketh his hands from holding of bribes, that stoppeth his ears from hearing of blood, and shutteth his eyes from seeing evil; 16He shall dwell on high: his place of defence shall be the munitions of rocks: bread shall be given him; his waters shall be sure."

Isaiah 57:1-2 "1The righteous perisheth, and no man layeth it to heart: and merciful men are taken away, none considering that the righteous is taken away from the evil to come. 2He shall enter into peace: they shall rest in their beds, each one walking in his uprightness."

Isaiah 64:4-5 "4For since the beginning of the world men have not heard, nor perceived by the ear, neither hath the eye seen, O God, beside thee, what he hath prepared for him that waiteth for him. 5Thou meetest him that rejoiceth and worketh righteousness, those that remember thee in thy ways: behold, thou art wroth; for we have sinned: in those is continuance, and we shall be saved."

Micah 7:1-2 "1Woe is me! for I am as when they have gathered the summer fruits, as the grapegleanings of the vintage: there is no cluster to eat: my soul desired the firstripe fruit. 2The good man is perished out of the earth: and there is none upright among men: they all lie in wait for blood; they hunt every man his brother with a net."

Matthew 13:41-43 "41The Son of man shall send forth his angels, and they shall gather out of his kingdom all things that offend, and them which do iniquity; 42And shall cast them into a furnace of fire: there shall be wailing and gnashing of teeth. 43Then shall the righteous shine forth as the sun in the kingdom of their Father. Who hath ears to hear, let him hear."

Matthew 25:46 "And these shall go away into everlasting punishment: but the righteous into life eternal."

Acts 10:34-35 "34Then Peter opened his mouth, and said, Of a truth I perceive that God is no respecter of persons: 35But in every nation he that feareth him, and worketh righteousness, is accepted with him."

1 Timothy 1:8-10 "8But we know that the law is good, if a man use it lawfully; 9Knowing this, that the law is not made for a righteous man, but for the lawless and disobedient, for the ungodly and for sinners, for unholy and profane, for murderers of fathers and murderers of mothers, for manslayers, 10For whoremongers, for them that defile themselves with mankind, for menstealers, for liars, for perjured persons, and if there be any other thing that is contrary to sound doctrine."

1 Peter 3:12 "For the eyes of the Lord are over the righteous, and his ears are open unto their prayers: but the face of the Lord is against them that do evil."

1 John 3:7 "Little children, let no man deceive you: he that doeth righteousness is righteous, even as he is righteous."

The Righteousness Of The Lord

Psalm 36:6 "Thy righteousness is like the great mountains; thy judgments are a great deep: O LORD, thou preservest man and beast."

Psalm 50:1-6 "1The mighty God, even the LORD, hath spoken, and called the earth from the rising of the sun unto the going down thereof. 2Out of Zion, the perfection of beauty, God hath shined. 3Our God shall come, and shall not keep silence: a fire shall devour before him, and it shall be very tempestuous round about him. 4He shall call to the heavens from above, and to the earth, that he may judge his people. 5Gather my saints together unto me; those that have made a covenant with me by sacrifice. 6And the heavens shall declare his righteousness: for God is judge himself. Selah."

Psalm 97:5-6 "5The hills melted like wax at the presence of the LORD, at the presence of the Lord of the whole earth. 6The heavens declare his righteousness, and all the people see his glory."

Psalm 98:2 "The LORD hath made known his salvation: his righteousness hath he openly shewed in the sight of the heathen."

Psalm 103:17 "But the mercy of the LORD is from everlasting to everlasting upon them that fear him, and his righteousness unto children's children."

Psalm 111:2-3 "²The works of the LORD are great, sought out of all them that have pleasure therein. ³His work is honourable and glorious: and his righteousness endureth for ever."

Psalm 119:137-142 "¹³⁷Righteous art thou, O LORD, and upright are thy judgments. ¹³⁸Thy testimonies that thou hast commanded are righteous and very faithful. ¹³⁹My zeal hath consumed me, because mine enemies have forgotten thy words. ¹⁴⁰Thy word is very pure: therefore thy servant loveth it. ¹⁴¹I am small and despised: yet do not I forget thy precepts. ¹⁴²Thy righteousness is an everlasting righteousness, and thy law is the truth."

Psalm 143:11 "Quicken me, O LORD, for thy name's sake: for thy righteousness' sake bring my soul out of trouble."

Isaiah 46:9-13 "⁹Remember the former things of old: for I am God, and there is none else; I am God, and there is none like me, ¹⁰Declaring the end from the beginning, and from ancient times the things that are not yet done, saying, My counsel shall stand, and I will do all my pleasure: ¹¹Calling a ravenous bird from the east, the man that executeth my counsel from a far country: yea, I have spoken it, I will also bring it to pass; I have purposed it, I will also do it. ¹²Hearken unto me, ye stouthearted, that are far from righteousness: ¹³I bring near my righteousness; it shall not be far off, and my salvation shall not tarry: and I will place salvation in Zion for Israel my glory."

Isaiah 51:3-8 "³For the LORD shall comfort Zion: he will comfort all her waste places; and he will make her wilderness like Eden, and her desert like the garden of the LORD; joy and gladness shall be found therein, thanksgiving, and the voice of melody. ⁴Hearken unto me, my people; and give ear unto me, O my nation: for a law shall proceed from me, and I will make my judgment to rest for a light of the people. ⁵My righteousness is near; my salvation is gone forth, and mine arms shall judge the people; the isles shall wait upon me, and on mine arm shall they trust. ⁶Lift up your eyes to the heavens, and look upon the earth beneath: for the heavens shall vanish away like smoke, and the earth shall wax old like a garment, and they that dwell therein shall die in like manner: but my salvation shall be for ever, and my righteousness shall not be abolished. ⁷Hearken unto me, ye that know righteousness, the people in whose heart is my law; fear ye not the reproach of men, neither be ye afraid of their revilings. ⁸For the moth shall eat them up like a garment, and the worm shall eat them like wool: but my righteousness shall be for ever, and my salvation from generation to generation."

Isaiah 56:1 "Thus saith the LORD, Keep ye judgment, and do justice: for my salvation is near to come, and my righteousness to be revealed."

Romans 3:21-22 "²¹But now the righteousness of God without the law is manifested, being witnessed by the law and the prophets; ²²Even the righteousness of God which is by faith of Jesus Christ unto all and upon all them that believe: for there is no difference."

Philippians 3:8-9 "⁸Yea doubtless, and I count all things but loss for the excellency of the knowledge of Christ Jesus my Lord: for whom I have suffered the loss of all things, and do count them but dung, that I may win Christ, ⁹And be found in him, not having mine own righteousness, which is of the law, but that which is through the faith of Christ, the righteousness which is of God by faith."

2 Peter 1:1 "Simon Peter, a servant and an apostle of Jesus Christ, to them that have obtained like precious faith with us through the righteousness of God and our Saviour Jesus Christ."

The Righteousness Of The Perfect
Proverbs 11:5 "The righteousness of the perfect shall direct his way: but the wicked shall fall by his own wickedness."

The Way Of Righteousness
Proverbs 12:28 "In the way of righteousness is life; and in the pathway thereof there is no death."

There Being None That Are Righteous
Psalm 14:1-4 "¹The fool hath said in his heart, There is no God. They are corrupt, they have

done abominable works, there is none that doeth good. ²The LORD looked down from heaven upon the children of men, to see if there were any that did understand, and seek God. ³They are all gone aside, they are all together become filthy: there is none that doeth good, no, not one. ⁴Have all the workers of iniquity no knowledge? who eat up my people as they eat bread, and call not upon the LORD."

Those That Do Not Do Righteousness
1 John 3:10 "In this the children of God are manifest, and the children of the devil: whosoever doeth not righteousness is not of God, neither he that loveth not his brother."

Psalm 53:1 "The fool hath said in his heart, There is no God. Corrupt are they, and have done abominable iniquity: there is none that doeth good."

Romans 3:9-12 "⁹What then? are we better than they? No, in no wise: for we have before proved both Jews and Gentiles, that they are all under sin; ¹⁰As it is written, There is none righteous, no, not one: ¹¹There is none that understandeth, there is none that seeketh after God. ¹²They are all gone out of the way, they are together become unprofitable; there is none that doeth good, no, not one."

Those That Follow After Righteousness
Proverbs 15:9 "The way of the wicked is an abomination unto the LORD: but he loveth him that followeth after righteousness."

Proverbs 21:21 "He that followeth after righteousness and mercy findeth life, righteousness, and honour."

Those That Hunger And Thirst
After Righteousness
Matthew 5:6 "Blessed are they which do hunger and thirst after righteousness: for they shall be filled."

Luke 6:21 "Blessed are ye that hunger now: for ye shall be filled. Blessed are ye that weep now: for ye shall laugh."

Those That Sow Righteousness
Proverbs 11:18 "The wicked worketh a deceitful work: but to him that soweth righteousness shall be a sure reward."

What Is Established By Righteousness
Proverbs 16:12 "It is an abomination to kings to commit wickedness: for the throne is established by righteousness."

What Is Righteous
Psalm 19:9-11 "⁹The fear of the LORD is clean, enduring for ever: the judgments of the LORD are true and righteous altogether. ¹⁰More to be desired are they than gold, yea, than much fine gold: sweeter also than honey and the honeycomb. ¹¹Moreover by them is thy servant warned: and in keeping of them there is great reward."

Psalm 119:137-138 "¹³⁷Righteous art thou, O LORD, and upright are thy judgments. ¹³⁸Thy testimonies that thou hast commanded are righteous and very faithful."

Proverbs 8:1-9 "¹Doth not wisdom cry? and understanding put forth her voice? ²She standeth in the top of high places, by the way in the places of the paths. ³She crieth at the gates, at the entry of the city, at the coming in at the doors. ⁴Unto you, O men, I call; and my voice is to the sons of man. ⁵O ye simple, understand wisdom: and, ye fools, be ye of an understanding heart. ⁶Hear; for I will speak of excellent things; and the opening of my lips shall be right things. ⁷For my mouth shall speak truth; and wickedness is an abomination to my lips. ⁸All the words of my mouth are in righteousness; there is nothing froward or perverse in them. ⁹They are all plain to him that understandeth, and right to them that find knowledge."

Revelation 16:7 "And I heard another out of the altar say, Even so, Lord God Almighty, true and righteous are thy judgments."

Revelation 19:1-2 "¹And after these things I heard a great voice of much people in heaven, saying, Alleluia; Salvation, and glory, and honour, and power, unto the Lord our God: ²For true and righteous are his judgments: for he hath judged the great whore, which did corrupt the earth with her fornication, and hath avenged the blood of his servants at her hand."

What Righteousness Does
Job 35:8 "Thy wickedness may hurt a man as thou art; and thy righteousness may profit the son of man."

Proverbs 10:2 "Treasures of wickedness profit nothing: but righteousness delivereth from death."

Proverbs 11:4 "Riches profit not in the day of wrath: but righteousness delivereth from death."

Proverbs 13:6 "Righteousness keepeth him that is upright in the way: but wickedness overthroweth the sinner."

Proverbs 14:34 "Righteousness exalteth a nation: but sin is a reproach to any people."

What Righteousness Tends To
Proverbs 11:19 "As righteousness tendeth to life: so he that pursueth evil pursueth it to his own death."

What Yields The Peaceable Fruit Of Righteousness
Hebrews 12:11 "Now no chastening for the present seemeth to be joyous, but grievous: nevertheless afterward it yieldeth the peaceable fruit of righteousness unto them which are exercised thereby."

When The Inhabitants Of The World Will Learn Righteousness
Isaiah 26:4-9 "⁴Trust ye in the LORD for ever: for in the LORD JEHOVAH is everlasting strength: ⁵For he bringeth down them that dwell on high; the lofty city, he layeth it low; he layeth it low, even to the ground; he bringeth it even to the dust. ⁶The foot shall tread it down, even the feet of the poor, and the steps of the needy. ⁷The way of the just is uprightness: thou, most upright, dost weigh the path of the just. ⁸Yea, in the way of thy judgments, O LORD, have we waited for thee; the desire of our soul is to thy name, and to the remembrance of thee. ⁹With my soul have I desired thee in the night; yea, with my spirit within me will I seek thee early: for when thy judgments are in the earth, the inhabitants of the world will learn righteousness."

Where Righteousness Dwells
2 Peter 3:13 "Nevertheless we, according to his promise, look for new heavens and a new earth, wherein dwelleth righteousness."

Who Attained To Righteousness
Romans 9:30 "What shall we say then? That the Gentiles, which followed not after righteousness, have attained to righteousness, even the righteousness which is of faith."

Who Did Not Attain To The Law Of Righteousness
Romans 9:31-33 "³¹But Israel, which followed after the law of righteousness, hath not attained to the law of righteousness. ³²Wherefore? Because they sought it not by faith, but as it were by the works of the law. For they stumbled at that stumblingstone; ³³As it is written, Behold, I lay in Sion a stumblingstone and rock of offence: and whosoever believeth on him shall not be ashamed."

Who Is Free From Righteousness
Romans 6:20 "For when ye were the servants of sin, ye were free from righteousness."

Who Is Righteous
Proverbs 12:17 "He that speaketh truth sheweth forth righteousness: but a false witness deceit."

1 John 3:7 "Little children, let no man deceive you: he that doeth righteousness is righteous, even as he is righteous."

Who Is The Servant Of Righteousness
Romans 6:17-18 "¹⁷But God be thanked, that ye were the servants of sin, but ye have obeyed from the heart that form of doctrine which was delivered you. ¹⁸Being then made free from sin, ye became the servants of righteousness."

Who Shall Receive A Crown Of Righteousness
2 Timothy 4:7-8 "⁷I have fought a good fight, I have finished my course, I have kept the faith: ⁸Henceforth there is laid up for me a crown of righteousness, which the Lord, the righteous judge, shall give me at that day: and not to me only, but unto all them also that love his appearing."

Revelation 2:8-10 "⁸And unto the angel of the church in Smyrna write; These things saith the first and the last, which was dead, and is alive; ⁹I know thy works, and tribulation, and poverty, (but thou art rich) and I know the blasphemy of them which say they are Jews, and are not, but are the synagogue of Satan. ¹⁰Fear none of those things which thou shalt suffer: behold, the devil shall cast some of you into prison, that ye may be tried; and ye shall have tribulation ten days: be thou faithful unto death, and I will give thee a crown of life."

Who Shall Receive A Righteous Man's Reward
Matthew 10:41 "He that receiveth a prophet in the name of a prophet shall receive a prophet's reward; and he that receiveth a righteous man in the name

of a righteous man shall receive a righteous man's reward."

Whose Righteousness Endures Forever

Psalm 112:1-3 "¹Praise ye the LORD. Blessed is the man that feareth the LORD, that delighteth greatly in his commandments. ²His seed shall be mighty upon earth: the generation of the upright shall be blessed. ³Wealth and riches shall be in his house: and his righteousness endureth for ever."

SS

SABBATH

Doing Good Works On The Sabbath

Matthew 12:10-13 "10And, behold, there was a man which had his hand withered. And they asked him, saying, Is it lawful to heal on the sabbath days? that they might accuse him. 11And he said unto them, What man shall there be among you, that shall have one sheep, and if it fall into a pit on the sabbath day, will he not lay hold on it, and lift it out? 12How much then is a man better than a sheep? Wherefore it is lawful to do well on the sabbath days. 13Then saith he to the man, Stretch forth thine hand. And he stretched it forth; and it was restored whole, like as the other."

Luke 13:10-17 "10And he was teaching in one of the synagogues on the sabbath. 11And, behold, there was a woman which had a spirit of infirmity eighteen years, and was bowed together, and could in no wise lift up herself. 12And when Jesus saw her, he called her to him, and said unto her, Woman, thou art loosed from thine infirmity. 13And he laid his hands on her: and immediately she was made straight, and glorified God. 14And the ruler of the synagogue answered with indignation, because that Jesus had healed on the sabbath day, and said unto the people, There are six days in which men ought to work: in them therefore come and be healed, and not on the sabbath day. 15The Lord then answered him, and said, Thou hypocrite, doth not each one of you on the sabbath loose his ox or his ass from the stall, and lead him away to watering? 16And ought not this woman, being a daughter of Abraham, whom Satan hath bound, lo, these eighteen years, be loosed from this bond on the sabbath day? 17And when he had said these things, all his adversaries were ashamed: and all the people rejoiced for all the glorious things that were done by him."

Luke 14:2-5 "2And, behold, there was a certain man before him which had the dropsy. 3And Jesus answering spake unto the lawyers and Pharisees, saying, Is it lawful to heal on the sabbath day? 4And they held their peace. And he took him, and healed him, and let him go; 5And answered them, saying, Which of you shall have an ass or an ox fallen into a pit, and will not straightway pull him out on the sabbath day?"

John 5:15-18 "15The man departed, and told the Jews that it was Jesus, which had made him whole. 16And therefore did the Jews persecute Jesus, and sought to slay him, because he had done these things on the sabbath day. 17But Jesus answered them, My Father worketh hitherto, and I work. 18Therefore the Jews sought the more to kill him, because he not only had broken the sabbath, but said also that God was his Father, making himself equal with God."

John 7:21-24 "21Jesus answered and said unto them, I have done one work, and ye all marvel. 22Moses therefore gave unto you circumcision; (not because it is of Moses, but of the fathers;) and ye on the sabbath day circumcise a man. 23If a man on the sabbath day receive circumcision, that the law of Moses should not be broken; are ye angry at me, because I have made a man every whit whole on the sabbath day? 24Judge not according to the appearance, but judge righteous judgment."

Jesus Christ Being Lord Of The Sabbath

Mark 2:27-28 "27And he said unto them, The sabbath was made for man, and not man for the sabbath: 28Therefore the Son of man is Lord also of the sabbath."

Keeping The Sabbath(s)

Exodus 20:8-11 "8Remember the sabbath day, to keep it holy. 9Six days shalt thou labour, and do all thy work: 10But the seventh day is the sabbath of the LORD thy God: in it thou shalt not do any work, thou, nor thy son, nor thy daughter, thy manservant, nor thy maidservant, nor thy cattle, nor thy stranger that is within thy gates: 11For in six days the LORD made heaven and earth, the sea, and all that in them is, and rested the seventh day: wherefore the LORD blessed the sabbath day, and hallowed it."

Exodus 31:12-17 "12And the LORD spake unto Moses, saying, 13Speak thou also unto the children of Israel, saying, Verily my sabbaths ye shall keep: for it is a sign between me and you throughout your generations; that ye may know that I am the LORD that doth sanctify you. 14Ye shall keep the sabbath therefore; for it is holy unto you: every one that defileth it shall surely be put to death: for whosoever doeth any work therein, that soul shall be cut off from among his people. [15]Six days may work be done; but in the seventh is the sabbath of rest, holy to the LORD: whosoever doeth any work in the sabbath day, he shall surely be put to death. [16]Wherefore the children of Israel shall keep the sabbath, to observe the sabbath throughout their generations, for a perpetual covenant. [17]It is a sign between me and the children of Israel for ever: for in six days the LORD made heaven and earth, and on the seventh day he rested, and was refreshed."

Leviticus 19:3 "Ye shall fear every man his mother, and his father, and keep my sabbaths: I am the LORD your God."

Leviticus 26:2 "Ye shall keep my sabbaths, and reverence my sanctuary: I am the LORD."

Deuteronomy 5:12-15 "[12]Keep the sabbath day to sanctify it, as the LORD thy God hath commanded thee. [13]Six days thou shalt labour, and do all thy work: [14]But the seventh day is the sabbath of the LORD thy God: in it thou shalt not do any work, thou, nor thy son, nor thy daughter, nor thy manservant, nor thy maidservant, nor thine ox, nor thine ass, nor any of thy cattle, nor thy stranger that is within thy gates; that thy manservant and thy maidservant may rest as well as thou. [15]And remember that thou wast a servant in the land of Egypt, and that the LORD thy God brought thee out thence through a mighty hand and by a stretched out arm: therefore the LORD thy God commanded thee to keep the sabbath day."

Jeremiah 17:19-22 "[19]Thus said the LORD unto me; Go and stand in the gate of the children of the people, whereby the kings of Judah come in, and by the which they go out, and in all the gates of Jerusalem; [20]And say unto them, Hear ye the word of the LORD, ye kings of Judah, and all Judah, and all the inhabitants of Jerusalem, that enter in by these gates: [21]Thus saith the LORD; Take heed to yourselves, and bear no burden on the sabbath day, nor bring it in by the gates of Jerusalem; [22]Neither carry forth a burden out of your houses on the sabbath day, neither do ye any work, but hallow ye the sabbath day, as I commanded your fathers."

The Requirements Of The Sabbath

Exodus 20:8-11 "[8]Remember the sabbath day, to keep it holy. [9]Six days shalt thou labour, and do all

thy work: [10]But the seventh day is the sabbath of the LORD thy God: in it thou shalt not do any work, thou, nor thy son, nor thy daughter, thy manservant, nor thy maidservant, nor thy cattle, nor thy stranger that is within thy gates: [11]For in six days the LORD made heaven and earth, the sea, and all that in them is, and rested the seventh day: wherefore the LORD blessed the sabbath day, and hallowed it."

Exodus 23:10-12 "[10]And six years thou shalt sow thy land, and shalt gather in the fruits thereof: [11]But the seventh year thou shalt let it rest and lie still; that the poor of thy people may eat: and what they leave the beasts of the field shall eat. In like manner thou shalt deal with thy vineyard, and with thy oliveyard. [12]Six days thou shalt do thy work, and on the seventh day thou shalt rest: that thine ox and thine ass may rest, and the son of thy handmaid, and the stranger, may be refreshed."

Leviticus 23:1-3 "[1]And the LORD spake unto Moses, saying, [2]Speak unto the children of Israel, and say unto them, Concerning the feasts of the LORD, which ye shall proclaim to be holy convocations, even these are my feasts. [3]Six days shall work be done: but the seventh day is the sabbath of rest, an holy convocation; ye shall do no work therein: it is the sabbath of the LORD in all your dwellings."

Deuteronomy 5:12-15 "[12]Keep the sabbath day to sanctify it, as the LORD thy God hath commanded thee. [13]Six days thou shalt labour, and do all thy work: [14]But the seventh day is the sabbath of the LORD thy God: in it thou shalt not do any work, thou, nor thy son, nor thy daughter, nor thy manservant, nor thy maidservant, nor thine ox, nor thine ass, nor any of thy cattle, nor thy stranger that is within thy gates; that thy manservant and thy maidservant may rest as well as thou. [15]And remember that thou wast a servant in the land of Egypt, and that the LORD thy God brought thee out thence through a mighty hand and by a stretched out arm: therefore the LORD thy God commanded thee to keep the sabbath day."

Jeremiah 17:19-22 "[19]Thus said the LORD unto me; Go and stand in the gate of the children of the people, whereby the kings of Judah come in, and by the which they go out, and in all the gates of Jerusalem; [20]And say unto them, Hear ye the word of the LORD, ye kings of Judah, and all Judah, and all the inhabitants of Jerusalem, that enter in by these gates: [21]Thus saith the LORD; Take heed to yourselves, and bear no burden on the sabbath day, nor bring it in by the gates of Jerusalem; [22]Neither carry forth a burden out of your houses on the sabbath day, neither do ye any work, but hallow ye the sabbath day, as I commanded your fathers."

The Reward For Keeping The Sabbath
Isaiah 58:13-14 "[13]If thou turn away thy foot from the sabbath, from doing thy pleasure on my holy day; and call the sabbath a delight, the holy of the LORD, honourable; and shalt honour him, not doing thine own ways, nor finding thine own pleasure, nor speaking thine own words: [14]Then shalt thou delight thyself in the LORD; and I will cause thee to ride upon the high places of the earth, and feed thee with the heritage of Jacob thy father: for the mouth of the LORD hath spoken it."

Jeremiah 17:24-26 "[24]And it shall come to pass, if ye diligently hearken unto me, saith the LORD, to bring in no burden through the gates of this city on the sabbath day, but hallow the sabbath day, to do no work therein; [25]Then shall there enter into the gates of this city kings and princes sitting upon the throne of David, riding in chariots and on horses, they, and their princes, the men of Judah, and the inhabitants of Jerusalem: and this city shall remain for ever. [26]And they shall come from the cities of Judah, and from the places about Jerusalem, and from the land of Benjamin, and from the plain, and from the mountains, and from the south, bringing burnt offerings, and sacrifices, and meat offerings, and incense, and bringing sacrifices of praise, unto the house of the LORD."

The Reward For Not Keeping The Sabbath
Jeremiah 17:24-27 "[24]And it shall come to pass, if ye diligently hearken unto me, saith the LORD, to bring in no burden through the gates of this city on the sabbath day, but hallow the sabbath day, to do no work therein; [25]Then shall there enter into the gates of this city kings and princes sitting upon the throne of David, riding in chariots and on horses, they, and their princes, the men of Judah, and the inhabitants of Jerusalem: and this city shall remain for ever. [26]And they shall come from the cities of Judah, and from the places about Jerusalem, and from the land of Benjamin, and from the plain, and from the mountains, and from the south, bringing burnt offerings, and sacrifices, and meat offerings, and incense, and bringing sacrifices of praise, unto the house of the LORD. [27]But if ye will not hearken unto me to hallow the sabbath day, and not to bear a burden, even entering in at the gates of Jerusalem on the sabbath day; then will I kindle a fire in the gates thereof, and it shall devour the palaces of Jerusalem, and it shall not be quenched."

Those That Keep The Sabbath
Isaiah 56:1-7 "[1]Thus saith the LORD, Keep ye judgment, and do justice: for my salvation is near to come, and my righteousness to be revealed. [2]Blessed is the man that doeth this, and the son of man that layeth hold on it; that keepeth the sabbath from polluting it, and keepeth his hand from doing any evil. [3]Neither let the son of the stranger, that hath joined himself to the LORD, speak, saying, The LORD hath utterly separated me from his people: neither let the eunuch say, Behold, I am a dry tree. [4]For thus saith the LORD unto the eunuchs that keep my sabbaths, and choose the things that please me, and take hold of my covenant; [5]Even unto them will I give in mine house and within my walls a place and a name better than of sons and of daughters: I will give them an everlasting name, that shall not be cut off. [6]Also the sons of the stranger, that join themselves to the LORD, to serve him, and to love the name of the LORD, to be his servants, every one that keepeth the sabbath from polluting it, and taketh hold of my covenant; [7]Even them will I bring to my holy mountain, and make them joyful in my house of prayer: their burnt offerings and their sacrifices shall be accepted upon mine altar; for mine house shall be called an house of prayer for all people."

What Day The Sabbath Falls Upon
Genesis 2:1-3 "[1]Thus the heavens and the earth were finished, and all the host of them. [2]And on the seventh day God ended his work which he had made; and he rested on the seventh day from all his work which he had made. [3]And God blessed the seventh day, and sanctified it: because that in it he had rested from all his work which God created and made."

Exodus 20:8-11 "⁸Remember the sabbath day, to keep it holy. ⁹Six days shalt thou labour, and do all thy work: ¹⁰But the seventh day is the sabbath of the LORD thy God: in it thou shalt not do any work, thou, nor thy son, nor thy daughter, thy manservant, nor thy maidservant, nor thy cattle, nor thy stranger that is within thy gates: ¹¹For in six days the LORD made heaven and earth, the sea, and all that in them is, and rested the seventh day: wherefore the LORD blessed the sabbath day, and hallowed it."

Leviticus 23:1-3 "¹And the LORD spake unto Moses, saying, ²Speak unto the children of Israel, and say unto them, Concerning the feasts of the LORD, which ye shall proclaim to be holy convocations, even these are my feasts. ³Six days shall work be done: but the seventh day is the sabbath of rest, an holy convocation; ye shall do no work therein: it is the sabbath of the LORD in all your dwellings."

Deuteronomy 5:12-15 "¹²Keep the sabbath day to sanctify it, as the LORD thy God hath commanded thee. ¹³Six days thou shalt labour, and do all thy work: ¹⁴But the seventh day is the sabbath of the LORD thy God: in it thou shalt not do any work, thou, nor thy son, nor thy daughter, nor thy manservant, nor thy maidservant, nor thine ox, nor thine ass, nor any of thy cattle, nor thy stranger that is within thy gates; that thy manservant and thy maidservant may rest as well as thou. ¹⁵And remember that thou wast a servant in the land of Egypt, and that the LORD thy God brought thee out thence through a mighty hand and by a stretched out arm: therefore the LORD thy God commanded thee to keep the sabbath day."

Who The Sabbath Was Made For
Mark 2:27-28 "²⁷And he said unto them, The sabbath was made for man, and not man for the sabbath: ²⁸Therefore the Son of man is Lord also of the sabbath."

SACRIFICE

Jesus Christ Being The Lamb Of God
John 1:29 "The next day John seeth Jesus coming unto him, and saith, Behold the Lamb of God, which taketh away the sin of the world."

Revelation 5:6-13 "⁶And I beheld, and, lo, in the midst of the throne and of the four beasts, and in the midst of the elders, stood a Lamb as it had been slain, having seven horns and seven eyes, which are the seven Spirits of God sent forth into all the earth. ⁷And he came and took the book out of the right hand of him that sat upon the throne. ⁸And when he had taken the book, the four beasts and four and twenty elders fell down before the Lamb, having every one of them harps, and golden vials full of odours, which are the prayers of saints. ⁹And they sung a new song, saying, Thou art worthy to take the book, and to open the seals thereof: for thou wast slain, and hast redeemed us to God by thy blood out of every kindred, and tongue, and people, and nation; ¹⁰And hast made us unto our God kings and priests: and we shall reign on the earth. ¹¹And I beheld, and I heard the voice of many angels round about the throne and the beasts and the elders: and the number of them was ten thousand times ten thousand, and thousands of thousands; ¹²Saying with a loud voice, Worthy is the Lamb that was slain to receive power, and riches, and wisdom, and strength, and honour, and glory, and blessing. ¹³And every creature which is in heaven, and on the earth, and under the earth, and such as are in the sea, and all that are in them, heard I saying, Blessing, and honour, and glory, and power, be unto him that sitteth upon the throne, and unto the Lamb for ever and ever."

Jesus Christ Sacrificing Himself
Psalm 69:1-9 "¹Save me, O God; for the waters are come in unto my soul. ²I sink in deep mire, where there is no standing: I am come into deep waters, where the floods overflow me. ³I am weary of my crying: my throat is dried: mine eyes fail while I wait for my God. ⁴They that hate me without a cause are more than the hairs of mine head: they that would destroy me, being mine enemies wrongfully, are mighty: then I restored that which I took not away. ⁵O God, thou knowest my foolishness; and my sins are not hid from thee. ⁶Let not them that wait on thee, O Lord GOD of hosts, be ashamed for my sake: let not those that seek thee be confounded for my sake, O God of Israel. ⁷Because for thy sake I have borne reproach; shame hath covered my face. ⁸I am become a stranger unto my brethren, and an alien unto my

mother's children. 9For the zeal of thine house hath eaten me up; and the reproaches of them that reproached thee are fallen upon me."

Isaiah 53:1-12 "1Who hath believed our report? and to whom is the arm of the LORD revealed? 2For he shall grow up before him as a tender plant, and as a root out of a dry ground: he hath no form nor comeliness; and when we shall see him, there is no beauty that we should desire him. 3He is despised and rejected of men; a man of sorrows, and acquainted with grief: and we hid as it were our faces from him; he was despised, and we esteemed him not. 4Surely he hath borne our griefs, and carried our sorrows: yet we did esteem him stricken, smitten of God, and afflicted. 5But he was wounded for our transgressions, he was bruised for our iniquities: the chastisement of our peace was upon him; and with his stripes we are healed. 6All we like sheep have gone astray; we have turned every one to his own way; and the LORD hath laid on him the iniquity of us all. 7He was oppressed, and he was afflicted, yet he opened not his mouth: he is brought as a lamb to the slaughter, and as a sheep before her shearers is dumb, so he openeth not his mouth. 8He was taken from prison and from judgment: and who shall declare his generation? for he was cut off out of the land of the living: for the transgression of my people was he stricken. 9And he made his grave with the wicked, and with the rich in his death; because he had done no violence, neither was any deceit in his mouth. 10Yet it pleased the LORD to bruise him; he hath put him to grief: when thou shalt make his soul an offering for sin, he shall see his seed, he shall prolong his days, and the pleasure of the LORD shall prosper in his hand. 11He shall see of the travail of his soul, and shall be satisfied: by his knowledge shall my righteous servant justify many; for he shall bear their iniquities. 12Therefore will I divide him a portion with the great, and he shall divide the spoil with the strong; because he hath poured out his soul unto death: and he was numbered with the transgressors; and he bare the sin of many, and made intercession for the transgressors."

Matthew 20:28 "Even as the Son of man came not to be ministered unto, but to minister, and to give his life a ransom for many."

Matthew 26:26-28 "26And as they were eating, Jesus took bread, and blessed it, and brake it, and gave it to the disciples, and said, Take, eat; this is my body. 27And he took the cup, and gave thanks, and gave it to them, saying, Drink ye all of it; 28For this is my blood of the new testament, which is shed for many for the remission of sins."

Mark 10:45 "For even the Son of man came not to be ministered unto, but to minister, and to give his life a ransom for many."

Mark 14:22-24 "22And as they did eat, Jesus took bread, and blessed, and brake it, and gave to them, and said, Take, eat: this is my body. 23And he took the cup, and when he had given thanks, he gave it to them: and they all drank of it. 24And he said unto them, This is my blood of the new testament, which is shed for many."

Luke 22:19-22 "19And he took bread, and gave thanks, and brake it, and gave unto them, saying, This is my body which is given for you: this do in remembrance of me. 20Likewise also the cup after supper, saying, This cup is the new testament in my blood, which is shed for you. 21But, behold, the hand of him that betrayeth me is with me on the table. 22And truly the Son of man goeth, as it was determined: but woe unto that man by whom he is betrayed!"

John 10:6-18 "6This parable spake Jesus unto them: but they understood not what things they were which he spake unto them. 7Then said Jesus unto them again, Verily, verily, I say unto you, I am the door of the sheep. 8All that ever came before me are thieves and robbers: but the sheep did not hear them. 9I am the door: by me if any man enter in, he shall be saved, and shall go in and out, and find pasture. 10The thief cometh not, but for to steal, and to kill, and to destroy: I am come that they might have life, and that they might have it more abundantly. 11I am the good shepherd: the good shepherd giveth his life for the sheep. 12But he that is an hireling, and not the shepherd, whose own the sheep are not, seeth the wolf coming, and leaveth the sheep, and fleeth: and the wolf catcheth them, and scattereth the sheep. 13The hireling fleeth, because he is an hireling, and careth not for the sheep. 14I am the good shepherd, and know my sheep, and am known of mine. 15As the Father knoweth me, even so know I the Father: and I lay down my life for the sheep. 16And other sheep I have, which are not of this fold: them also I must bring, and they shall hear my voice; and there shall be one fold, and one shepherd. [17]Therefore doth my Father love me, because I lay down my life, that I might take it again. [18]No man taketh it from me, but I lay it down of myself. I have power to lay it down, and I have power to take it again. This commandment have I received of my Father."

John 12:23-24 "[23]And Jesus answered them, saying, The hour is come, that the Son of man should be glorified. [24]Verily, verily, I say unto you, Except a corn of wheat fall into the ground and die, it abideth alone: but if it die, it bringeth forth much fruit."

John 12:30-34 "[30]Jesus answered and said, This voice came not because of me, but for your sakes. [31]Now is the judgment of this world: now shall the prince of this world be cast out. [32]And I, if I be lifted up from the earth, will draw all men unto me. [33]This he said, signifying what death he should die. [34]The people answered him, We have heard out of the law that Christ abideth for ever: and how sayest thou, The Son of man must be lifted up? who is this Son of man?"

John 15:1-13 "[1]I am the true vine, and my Father is the husbandman. [2]Every branch in me that beareth not fruit he taketh away: and every branch that beareth fruit, he purgeth it, that it may bring forth more fruit. [3]Now ye are clean through the word which I have spoken unto you. [4]Abide in me, and I in you. As the branch cannot bear fruit of itself, except it abide in the vine; no more can ye, except ye abide in me. [5]I am the vine, ye are the branches: He that abideth in me, and I in him, the same bringeth forth much fruit: for without me ye can do nothing. [6]If a man abide not in me, he is cast forth as a branch, and is withered; and men gather them, and cast them into the fire, and they are burned. [7]If ye abide in me, and my words abide in you, ye shall ask what ye will, and it shall be done unto you. [8]Herein is my Father glorified, that ye bear much fruit; so shall ye be my disciples. [9]As the Father hath loved me, so have I loved you: continue ye in my love. [10]If ye keep my commandments, ye shall abide in my love; even as I have kept my Father's commandments, and abide in his love. [11]These things have I spoken unto you, that my joy might remain in you, and that your joy might be full. [12]This is my commandment, That ye love one another, as I have loved you. [13]Greater love hath no man than this, that a man lay down his life for his friends."

Acts 2:22-23 "[22]Ye men of Israel, hear these words; Jesus of Nazareth, a man approved of God among you by miracles and wonders and signs, which God did by him in the midst of you, as ye yourselves also know: [23]Him, being delivered by the determinate counsel and foreknowledge of God, ye have taken, and by wicked hands have crucified and slain."

Romans 5:6-11 "[6]For when we were yet without strength, in due time Christ died for the ungodly. [7]For scarcely for a righteous man will one die: yet peradventure for a good man some would even dare to die. [8]But God commendeth his love toward us, in that, while we were yet sinners, Christ died for us. [9]Much more then, being now justified by his blood, we shall be saved from wrath through him. [10]For if, when we were enemies, we were reconciled to God by the death of his Son, much more, being reconciled, we shall be saved by his life. [11]And not only so, but we also joy in God through our Lord Jesus Christ, by whom we have now received the atonement."

Romans 8:2-3 "[2]For the law of the Spirit of life in Christ Jesus hath made me free from the law of sin and death. [3]For what the law could not do, in that it was weak through the flesh, God sending his own Son in the likeness of sinful flesh, and for sin, condemned sin in the flesh."

Romans 8:31-32 "[31]What shall we then say to these things? If God be for us, who can be against us? [32]He that spared not his own Son, but delivered him up for us all, how shall he not with him also freely give us all things?"

Romans 14:7-9 "[7]For none of us liveth to himself, and no man dieth to himself. [8]For whether we live, we live unto the Lord; and whether we die, we die unto the Lord: whether we live therefore, or die, we are the Lord's. [9]For to this end Christ both died, and rose, and revived, that he might be Lord both of the dead and living."

Romans 15:3 "For even Christ pleased not himself; but, as it is written, The reproaches of them that reproached thee fell on me."

1 Corinthians 11:23-25 "[23]For I have received of the Lord that which also I delivered unto you,

That the Lord Jesus the same night in which he was betrayed took bread: 24And when he had given thanks, he brake it, and said, Take, eat: this is my body, which is broken for you: this do in remembrance of me. 25After the same manner also he took the cup, when he had supped, saying, This cup is the new testament in my blood: this do ye, as oft as ye drink it, in remembrance of me."

1 Corinthians 15:3 "For I delivered unto you first of all that which I also received, how that Christ died for our sins according to the scriptures."

2 Corinthians 5:14 "For the love of Christ constraineth us; because we thus judge, that if one died for all, then were all dead."

2 Corinthians 5:18-21 "18And all things are of God, who hath reconciled us to himself by Jesus Christ, and hath given to us the ministry of reconciliation; 19To wit, that God was in Christ, reconciling the world unto himself, not imputing their trespasses unto them; and hath committed unto us the word of reconciliation. 20Now then we are ambassadors for Christ, as though God did beseech you by us: we pray you in Christ's stead, be ye reconciled to God. 21For he hath made him to be sin for us, who knew no sin; that we might be made the righteousness of God in him."

Galatians 1:3-5 "3Grace be to you and peace from God the Father, and from our Lord Jesus Christ, 4Who gave himself for our sins, that he might deliver us from this present evil world, according to the will of God and our Father: 5To whom be glory for ever and ever. Amen."

Galatians 2:20 "I am crucified with Christ: nevertheless I live; yet not I, but Christ liveth in me: and the life which I now live in the flesh I live by the faith of the Son of God, who loved me, and gave himself for me."

Ephesians 1:3-7 "3Blessed be the God and Father of our Lord Jesus Christ, who hath blessed us with all spiritual blessings in heavenly places in Christ: 4According as he hath chosen us in him before the foundation of the world, that we should be holy and without blame before him in love: 5Having predestinated us unto the adoption of children by Jesus Christ to himself, according to the good pleasure of his will, 6To the praise of the glory of his grace, wherein he hath made us accepted in the beloved. 7In whom we have redemption through his blood, the forgiveness of sins, according to the riches of his grace."

Ephesians 5:2 "And walk in love, as Christ also hath loved us, and hath given himself for us an offering and a sacrifice to God for a sweetsmelling savour."

Ephesians 5:25 "Husbands, love your wives, even as Christ also loved the church, and gave himself for it."

Colossians 1:12-22 "12Giving thanks unto the Father, which hath made us meet to be partakers of the inheritance of the saints in light: 13Who hath delivered us from the power of darkness, and hath translated us into the kingdom of his dear Son: 14In whom we have redemption through his blood, even the forgiveness of sins: 15Who is the image of the invisible God, the firstborn of every creature: 16For by him were all things created, that are in heaven, and that are in earth, visible and invisible, whether they be thrones, or dominions, or principalities, or powers: all things were created by him, and for him: 17And he is before all things, and by him all things consist. 18And he is the head of the body, the church: who is the beginning, the firstborn from the dead; that in all things he might have the preeminence. 19For it pleased the Father that in him should all fulness dwell; 20And, having made peace through the blood of his cross, by him to reconcile all things unto himself; by him, I say, whether they be things in earth, or things in heaven. 21And you, that were sometime alienated and enemies in your mind by wicked works, yet now hath he reconciled 22In the body of his flesh through death, to present you holy and unblameable and unreproveable in his sight."

1 Thessalonians 5:9-10 "9For God hath not appointed us to wrath, but to obtain salvation by our Lord Jesus Christ, 10Who died for us, that, whether we wake or sleep, we should live together with him."

1 Timothy 2:5-6 "5For there is one God, and one mediator between God and men, the man Christ Jesus; 6Who gave himself a ransom for all, to be testified in due time."

Titus 2:13-14 "[13]Looking for that blessed hope, and the glorious appearing of the great God and our Saviour Jesus Christ; [14]Who gave himself for us, that he might redeem us from all iniquity, and purify unto himself a peculiar people, zealous of good works."

Hebrews 2:9-15 "[9]But we see Jesus, who was made a little lower than the angels for the suffering of death, crowned with glory and honour; that he by the grace of God should taste death for every man. [10]For it became him, for whom are all things, and by whom are all things, in bringing many sons unto glory, to make the captain of their salvation perfect through sufferings. [11]For both he that sanctifieth and they who are sanctified are all of one: for which cause he is not ashamed to call them brethren, [12]Saying, I will declare thy name unto my brethren, in the midst of the church will I sing praise unto thee. [13]And again, I will put my trust in him. And again, Behold I and the children which God hath given me. [14]Forasmuch then as the children are partakers of flesh and blood, he also himself likewise took part of the same; that through death he might destroy him that had the power of death, that is, the devil; [15]And deliver them who through fear of death were all their lifetime subject to bondage."

Hebrews 7:22-27 "[22]By so much was Jesus made a surety of a better testament. [23]And they truly were many priests, because they were not suffered to continue by reason of death: [24]But this man, because he continueth ever, hath an unchangeable priesthood. [25]Wherefore he is able also to save them to the uttermost that come unto God by him, seeing he ever liveth to make intercession for them. [26]For such an high priest became us, who is holy, harmless, undefiled, separate from sinners, and made higher than the heavens; [27]Who needeth not daily, as those high priests, to offer up sacrifice, first for his own sins, and then for the people's: for this he did once, when he offered up himself."

Hebrews 9:11-28 "[11]But Christ being come an high priest of good things to come, by a greater and more perfect tabernacle, not made with hands, that is to say, not of this building; [12]Neither by the blood of goats and calves, but by his own blood he entered in once into the holy place, having obtained eternal redemption for us. [13]For if the blood of bulls and of goats, and the ashes of an heifer sprinkling the unclean, sanctifieth to the purifying of the flesh: [14]How much more shall the blood of Christ, who through the eternal Spirit offered himself without spot to God, purge your conscience from dead works to serve the living God? [15]And for this cause he is the mediator of the new testament, that by means of death, for the redemption of the transgressions that were under the first testament, they which are called might receive the promise of eternal inheritance. [16]For where a testament is, there must also of necessity be the death of the testator. [17]For a testament is of force after men are dead: otherwise it is of no strength at all while the testator liveth. [18]Whereupon neither the first testament was dedicated without blood. [19]For when Moses had spoken every precept to all the people according to the law, he took the blood of calves and of goats, with water, and scarlet wool, and hyssop, and sprinkled both the book, and all the people, [20]Saying, This is the blood of the testament which God hath enjoined unto you. [21]Moreover he sprinkled with blood both the tabernacle, and all the vessels of the ministry. [22]And almost all things are by the law purged with blood; and without shedding of blood is no remission. [23]It was therefore necessary that the patterns of things in the heavens should be purified with these; but the heavenly things themselves with better sacrifices than these. [24]For Christ is not entered into the holy places made with hands, which are the figures of the true; but into heaven itself, now to appear in the presence of God for us: [25]Nor yet that he should offer himself often, as the high priest entereth into the holy place every year with blood of others; [26]For then must he often have suffered since the foundation of the world: but now once in the end of the world hath he appeared to put away sin by the sacrifice of himself. [27]And as it is appointed unto men once to die, but after this the judgment: [28]So Christ was once offered to bear the sins of many; and unto them that look for him shall he appear the second time without sin unto salvation."

Hebrews 10:1-15 "[1]For the law having a shadow of good things to come, and not the very image of the things, can never with those sacrifices which they offered year by year continually make the comers thereunto perfect. ²For then would they not have ceased to be offered? because that the worshippers once purged should have had no more conscience of sins. ³But in those sacrifices there is a remembrance again made of sins every year. ⁴For it is not possible that the blood of bulls and of goats should take away sins. ⁵Wherefore when he cometh into the world, he saith, Sacrifice and offering thou wouldest not, but a body hast thou prepared me: ⁶In burnt offerings and sacrifices for sin thou hast had no pleasure. ⁷Then said I, Lo, I come (in the volume of the book it is written of me,) to do thy will, O God. ⁸Above when he said, Sacrifice and offering and burnt offerings and offering for sin thou wouldest not, neither hadst pleasure therein; which are offered by the law; ⁹Then said he, Lo, I come to do thy will, O God. He taketh away the first, that he may establish the second. ¹⁰By the which will we are sanctified through the offering of the body of Jesus Christ once for all. ¹¹And every priest standeth daily ministering and offering oftentimes the same sacrifices, which can never take away sins: ¹²But this man, after he had offered one sacrifice for sins for ever, sat down on the right hand of God; ¹³From henceforth expecting till his enemies be made his footstool. ¹⁴For by one offering he hath perfected for ever them that are sanctified. ¹⁵Whereof the Holy Ghost also is a witness to us: for after that he had said before."

1 Peter 2:21-24 "²¹For even hereunto were ye called: because Christ also suffered for us, leaving us an example, that ye should follow his steps: ²²Who did no sin, neither was guile found in his mouth: ²³Who, when he was reviled, reviled not again; when he suffered, he threatened not; but committed himself to him that judgeth righteously: ²⁴Who his own self bare our sins in his own body on the tree, that we, being dead to sins, should live unto righteousness: by whose stripes ye were healed."

1 Peter 3:18 "For Christ also hath once suffered for sins, the just for the unjust, that he might bring us to God, being put to death in the flesh, but quickened by the Spirit."

1 John 3:16 "Hereby perceive we the love of God, because he laid down his life for us: and we ought to lay down our lives for the brethren."

Revelation 1:4-5 "⁴John to the seven churches which are in Asia: Grace be unto you, and peace, from him which is, and which was, and which is to come; and from the seven Spirits which are before his throne; ⁵And from Jesus Christ, who is the faithful witness, and the first begotten of the dead, and the prince of the kings of the earth. Unto him that loved us, and washed us from our sins in his own blood."

Revelation 5:8-9 "⁸And when he had taken the book, the four beasts and four and twenty elders fell down before the Lamb, having every one of them harps, and golden vials full of odours, which are the prayers of saints. ⁹And they sung a new song, saying, Thou art worthy to take the book, and to open the seals thereof: for thou wast slain, and hast redeemed us to God by thy blood out of every kindred, and tongue, and people, and nation."

Revelation 5:12 "Saying with a loud voice, Worthy is the Lamb that was slain to receive power, and riches, and wisdom, and strength, and honour, and glory, and blessing."

Not Sacrificing Your Children
Leviticus 18:21 "And thou shalt not let any of thy seed pass through the fire to Molech, neither shalt thou profane the name of thy God: I am the LORD."

Sacrificing Yourself For Others
1 John 3:16 "Hereby perceive we the love of God, because he laid down his life for us: and we ought to lay down our lives for the brethren."

Sacrificing Yourself For The Lord
Romans 12:1-2 "¹I beseech you therefore, brethren, by the mercies of God, that ye present your bodies a living sacrifice, holy, acceptable unto God, which is your reasonable service. ²And be not conformed to this world: but be ye transformed by the renewing of your mind, that ye may prove what is that good, and acceptable, and perfect, will of God."

2 Corinthians 5:14-15 "¹⁴For the love of Christ constraineth us; because we thus judge, that if one died for all, then were all dead: ¹⁵And that he died for all, that they which live should not henceforth live unto themselves, but unto him which died for them, and rose again."

Galatians 2:20 "I am crucified with Christ: nevertheless I live; yet not I, but Christ liveth in me: and the life which I now live in the flesh I live by the faith of the Son of God, who loved me, and gave himself for me."

The Lord Hating Child Sacrifice
Deuteronomy 12:31 "Thou shalt not do so unto the LORD thy God: for every abomination to the LORD, which he hateth, have they done unto their gods; for even their sons and their daughters they have burnt in the fire to their gods."

The Lord Not Desiring Sacrifices
Psalm 40:5-6 "⁵Many, O LORD my God, are thy wonderful works which thou hast done, and thy thoughts which are to us-ward: they cannot be reckoned up in order unto thee: if I would declare and speak of them, they are more than can be numbered. ⁶Sacrifice and offering thou didst not desire; mine ears hast thou opened: burnt offering and sin offering hast thou not required."

Isaiah 1:10-14 "¹⁰Hear the word of the LORD, ye rulers of Sodom; give ear unto the law of our God, ye people of Gomorrah. ¹¹To what purpose is the multitude of your sacrifices unto me? saith the LORD: I am full of the burnt offerings of rams, and the fat of fed beasts; and I delight not in the blood of bullocks, or of lambs, or of he goats. ¹²When ye come to appear before me, who hath required this at your hand, to tread my courts? ¹³Bring no more vain oblations; incense is an abomination unto me; the new moons and sabbaths, the calling of assemblies, I cannot away with; it is iniquity, even the solemn meeting. ¹⁴Your new moons and your appointed feasts my soul hateth: they are a trouble unto me; I am weary to bear them."

Hosea 6:6 "For I desired mercy, and not sacrifice; and the knowledge of God more than burnt offerings."

Matthew 9:12-13 "¹²But when Jesus heard that, he said unto them, They that be whole need not a physician, but they that are sick. ¹³But go ye and learn what that meaneth, I will have mercy, and not sacrifice: for I am not come to call the righteous, but sinners to repentance."

Hebrews 10:1-9 "¹For the law having a shadow of good things to come, and not the very image of the things, can never with those sacrifices which they offered year by year continually make the comers thereunto perfect. ²For then would they not have ceased to be offered? because that the worshippers once purged should have had no more conscience of sins. ³But in those sacrifices there is a remembrance again made of sins every year. ⁴For it is not possible that the blood of bulls and of goats should take away sins. ⁵Wherefore when he cometh into the world, he saith, Sacrifice and offering thou wouldest not, but a body hast thou prepared me: ⁶In burnt offerings and sacrifices for sin thou hast had no pleasure. ⁷Then said I, Lo, I come (in the volume of the book it is written of me,) to do thy will, O God. ⁸Above when he said, Sacrifice and offering and burnt offerings and offering for sin thou wouldest not, neither hadst pleasure therein; which are offered by the law; ⁹Then said he, Lo, I come to do thy will, O God. He taketh away the first, that he may establish the second."

The Meat Sacrificed To Idols
Romans 14:14-23 "¹⁴I know, and am persuaded by the Lord Jesus, that there is nothing unclean of itself: but to him that esteemeth any thing to be unclean, to him it is unclean. ¹⁵But if thy brother be grieved with thy meat, now walkest thou not charitably. Destroy not him with thy meat, for whom Christ died. ¹⁶Let not then your good be evil spoken of: ¹⁷For the kingdom of God is not meat and drink; but righteousness, and peace, and joy in the Holy Ghost. ¹⁸For he that in these things serveth Christ is acceptable to God, and approved of men. ¹⁹Let us therefore follow after the things which make for peace, and things wherewith one may edify another. ²⁰For meat destroy not the work of God. All things indeed are pure; but it is evil for that man who eateth with offence. ²¹It is good neither to eat flesh, nor to drink wine, nor any thing whereby thy brother stumbleth, or is offended, or is made weak. ²²Hast thou faith? have it to thyself before God. Happy is he that condemneth not himself in that thing which he alloweth. ²³And he that doubteth is damned if he eat, because he eateth not of faith: for whatsoever is not of faith is sin."

1 Corinthians 8:1-13 "¹Now as touching things offered unto idols, we know that we all have knowledge. Knowledge puffeth up, but charity edifieth. ²And if any man think that he knoweth anything, he knoweth nothing yet as he ought to know. ³But if any man love God, the same is known of him. ⁴As concerning therefore the eating of those things that are offered in sacrifice unto idols, we know that an idol is nothing in the world, and that there is none other God but one. ⁵For though there be that are called gods, whether in heaven or in earth, (as there be gods many, and lords many,) ⁶But to us there is but one God, the Father, of whom are all things, and we in him; and one Lord Jesus Christ, by whom are all things, and we by him. ⁷Howbeit there is not in every man that knowledge: for some with conscience of the idol unto this hour eat it as a thing offered unto an idol; and their conscience being weak is defiled. ⁸But meat commendeth us not to God: for neither, if we eat, are we the better; neither, if we eat not, are we the worse. ⁹But take heed lest by any means this liberty of yours become a stumblingblock to them that are weak. ¹⁰For if any man see thee which hast knowledge sit at meat in the idol's temple, shall not the conscience of him which is weak be emboldened to eat those things which are offered to idols; ¹¹And through thy knowledge shall the weak brother perish, for whom Christ died? ¹²But when ye sin so against the brethren, and wound their weak conscience, ye sin against Christ. ¹³Wherefore, if meat make my brother to offend, I will eat no flesh while the world standeth, lest I make my brother to offend."

1 Corinthians 10:14-33 "¹⁴Wherefore, my dearly beloved, flee from idolatry. ¹⁵I speak as to wise men; judge ye what I say. ¹⁶The cup of blessing which we bless, is it not the communion of the blood of Christ? The bread which we break, is it not the communion of the body of Christ? ¹⁷For we being many are one bread, and one body: for we are all partakers of that one bread. ¹⁸Behold Israel after the flesh: are not they which eat of the sacrifices partakers of the altar? ¹⁹What say I then? that the idol is any thing, or that which is offered in sacrifice to idols is any thing? ²⁰But I say, that the things which the Gentiles sacrifice, they sacrifice to devils, and not to God: and I would not that ye should have fellowship with devils. ²¹Ye cannot drink the cup of the Lord, and the cup of devils: ye cannot be partakers of the Lord's table, and of the table of devils. ²²Do we provoke the Lord to jealousy? are we stronger than he? ²³All things are lawful for me, but all things are not expedient: all things are lawful for me, but all things edify not. ²⁴Let no man seek his own, but every man another's wealth. ²⁵Whatsoever is sold

in the shambles, that eat, asking no question for conscience sake: ²⁶For the earth is the Lord's, and the fulness thereof. ²⁷If any of them that believe not bid you to a feast, and ye be disposed to go; whatsoever is set before you, eat, asking no question for conscience sake. ²⁸But if any man say unto you, This is offered in sacrifice unto idols, eat not for his sake that shewed it, and for conscience sake: for the earth is the Lord's, and the fulness thereof: ²⁹Conscience, I say, not thine own, but of the other: for why is my liberty judged of another man's conscience? ³⁰For if I by grace be a partaker, why am I evil spoken of for that for which I give thanks? ³¹Whether therefore ye eat, or drink, or whatsoever ye do, do all to the glory of God. ³²Give none offence, neither to the Jews, nor to the Gentiles, nor to the church of God: ³³Even as I please all men in all things, not seeking mine own profit, but the profit of many, that they may be saved."

The Reward For Sacrificing Your Children

Psalm 106:37-43 "³⁷Yea, they sacrificed their sons and their daughters unto devils, ³⁸And shed innocent blood, even the blood of their sons and of their daughters, whom they sacrificed unto the idols of Canaan: and the land was polluted with blood. ³⁹Thus were they defiled with their own works, and went a whoring with their own inventions. ⁴⁰Therefore was the wrath of the LORD kindled against his people, insomuch that he abhorred his own inheritance. ⁴¹And he gave them into the hand of the heathen; and they that hated them ruled over them. ⁴²Their enemies also oppressed them, and they were brought into subjection under their hand. ⁴³Many times did he deliver them; but they provoked him with their counsel, and were brought low for their iniquity."

Jeremiah 19:3-15 "³And say, Hear ye the word of the LORD, O kings of Judah, and inhabitants of Jerusalem; Thus saith the LORD of hosts, the God of Israel; Behold, I will bring evil upon this place, the which whosoever heareth, his ears shall tingle. ⁴Because they have forsaken me, and have estranged this place, and have burned incense in it unto other gods, whom neither they nor their fathers have known, nor the kings of Judah, and have filled this place with the blood of innocents; ⁵They have built also the high places of Baal, to burn their sons with fire for burnt offerings unto

Baal, which I commanded not, nor spake it, neither came it into my mind: ⁶Therefore, behold, the days come, saith the LORD, that this place shall no more be called Tophet, nor The valley of the son of Hinnom, but The valley of slaughter. ⁷And I will make void the counsel of Judah and Jerusalem in this place; and I will cause them to fall by the sword before their enemies, and by the hands of them that seek their lives: and their carcases will I give to be meat for the fowls of the heaven, and for the beasts of the earth. ⁸And I will make this city desolate, and an hissing; every one that passeth thereby shall be astonished and hiss because of all the plagues thereof. ⁹And I will cause them to eat the flesh of their sons and the flesh of their daughters, and they shall eat every one the flesh of his friend in the siege and straitness, wherewith their enemies, and they that seek their lives, shall straiten them. ¹⁰Then shalt thou break the bottle in the sight of the men that go with thee, ¹¹And shalt say unto them, Thus saith the LORD of hosts; Even so will I break this people and this city, as one breaketh a potter's vessel, that cannot be made whole again: and they shall bury them in Tophet, till there be no place to bury. ¹²Thus will I do unto this place, saith the LORD, and to the inhabitants thereof, and even make this city as Tophet: ¹³And the houses of Jerusalem, and the houses of the kings of Judah, shall be defiled as the place of Tophet, because of all the houses upon whose roofs they have burned incense unto all the host of heaven, and have poured out drink offerings unto other gods. ¹⁴Then came Jeremiah from Tophet, whither the LORD had sent him to prophesy; and he stood in the court of the LORD's house; and said to all the people, ¹⁵Thus saith the LORD of hosts, the God of Israel; Behold, I will bring upon this city and upon all her towns all the evil that I have pronounced against it, because they have hardened their necks, that they might not hear my words."

Jeremiah 32:35-36 "³⁵And they built the high places of Baal, which are in the valley of the son of Hinnom, to cause their sons and their daughters to pass through the fire unto Molech; which I commanded them not, neither came it into my mind, that they should do this abomination, to cause Judah to sin. ³⁶And now therefore thus saith the LORD, the God of Israel, concerning this city,

whereof ye say, It shall be delivered into the hand of the king of Babylon by the sword, and by the famine, and by the pestilence."

The Sacrifice Of The Wicked
Proverbs 15:8 "The sacrifice of the wicked is an abomination to the LORD: but the prayer of the upright is his delight."

Proverbs 21:27 "The sacrifice of the wicked is abomination: how much more, when he bringeth it with a wicked mind?"

Those That Sacrifice Their Children
Leviticus 20:2 "Again, thou shalt say to the children of Israel, Whosoever he be of the children of Israel, or of the strangers that sojourn in Israel, that giveth any of his seed unto Molech; he shall surely be put to death: the people of the land shall stone him with stones."

2 Kings 16:2-3 "²Twenty years old was Ahaz when he began to reign, and reigned sixteen years in Jerusalem, and did not that which was right in the sight of the LORD his God, like David his father. ³But he walked in the way of the kings of Israel, yea, and made his son to pass through the fire, according to the abominations of the heathen, whom the LORD cast out from before the children of Israel."

2 Chronicles 28:1-3 "¹Ahaz was twenty years old when he began to reign, and he reigned sixteen years in Jerusalem: but he did not that which was right in the sight of the LORD, like David his father: ²For he walked in the ways of the kings of Israel, and made also molten images for Baalim. ³Moreover he burnt incense in the valley of the son of Hinnom, and burnt his children in the fire, after the abominations of the heathen whom the LORD had cast out before the children of Israel."

Isaiah 57:3-13 "³But draw near hither, ye sons of the sorceress, the seed of the adulterer and the whore. ⁴Against whom do ye sport yourselves? against whom make ye a wide mouth, and draw out the tongue? are ye not children of transgression, a seed of falsehood, ⁵Enflaming yourselves with idols under every green tree, slaying the children in the valleys under the clifts of the rocks? ⁶Among the smooth stones of the stream is thy portion; they, they are thy lot: even to them hast thou poured a drink offering, thou hast offered a meat offering. Should I receive comfort in these? [7]Upon a lofty and high mountain hast thou set thy bed: even thither wentest thou up to offer sacrifice. [8]Behind the doors also and the posts hast thou set up thy remembrance: for thou hast discovered thyself to another than me, and art gone up; thou hast enlarged thy bed, and made thee a covenant with them; thou lovedst their bed where thou sawest it. [9]And thou wentest to the king with ointment, and didst increase thy perfumes, and didst send thy messengers far off, and didst debase thyself even unto hell. [10]Thou art wearied in the greatness of thy way; yet saidst thou not, There is no hope: thou hast found the life of thine hand; therefore thou wast not grieved. [11]And of whom hast thou been afraid or feared, that thou hast lied, and hast not remembered me, nor laid it to thy heart? have not I held my peace even of old, and thou fearest me not? [12]I will declare thy righteousness, and thy works; for they shall not profit thee. [13]When thou criest, let thy companies deliver thee; but the wind shall carry them all away; vanity shall take them: but he that putteth his trust in me shall possess the land, and shall inherit my holy mountain."

Those That Sacrifice To Idols
Exodus 22:20 "He that sacrificeth unto any god, save unto the Lord only, he shall be utterly destroyed."

Isaiah 57:3-13 "[3]But draw near hither, ye sons of the sorceress, the seed of the adulterer and the whore. [4]Against whom do ye sport yourselves? against whom make ye a wide mouth, and draw out the tongue? are ye not children of transgression, a seed of falsehood, [5]Enflaming yourselves with idols under every green tree, slaying the children in the valleys under the clifts of the rocks? [6]Among the smooth stones of the stream is thy portion; they, they are thy lot: even to them hast thou poured a drink offering, thou hast offered a meat offering. Should I receive comfort in these? [7]Upon a lofty and high mountain hast thou set thy bed: even thither wentest thou up to offer sacrifice. [8]Behind the doors also and the posts hast thou set up thy remembrance: for thou hast discovered thyself to another than me, and art gone up; thou hast enlarged thy bed, and made thee a covenant with them; thou lovedst their bed where thou sawest it. [9]And thou wentest to the king with ointment, and didst increase thy perfumes, and

didst send thy messengers far off, and didst debase thyself even unto hell. [10]Thou art wearied in the greatness of thy way; yet saidst thou not, There is no hope: thou hast found the life of thine hand; therefore thou wast not grieved. [11]And of whom hast thou been afraid or feared, that thou hast lied, and hast not remembered me, nor laid it to thy heart? have not I held my peace even of old, and thou fearest me not? [12]I will declare thy righteousness, and thy works; for they shall not profit thee. [13]When thou criest, let thy companies deliver thee; but the wind shall carry them all away; vanity shall take them: but he that putteth his trust in me shall possess the land, and shall inherit my holy mountain."

What Is Better Than Sacrifice
1 Samuel 15:22 "And Samuel said, Hath the Lord as great delight in burnt offerings and sacrifices, as in obeying the voice of the Lord? Behold, to obey is better than sacrifice, and to hearken than the fat of rams."

Proverbs 21:3 "To do justice and judgment is more acceptable to the Lord than sacrifice."

Mark 12:28-33 "[28]And one of the scribes came, and having heard them reasoning together, and perceiving that he had answered them well, asked him, Which is the first commandment of all? [29]And Jesus answered him, The first of all the commandments is, Hear, O Israel; The Lord our God is one Lord: [30]And thou shalt love the Lord thy God with all thy heart, and with all thy soul, and with all thy mind, and with all thy strength: this is the first commandment. [31]And the second is like, namely this, Thou shalt love thy neighbour as thyself. There is none other commandment greater than these. [32]And the scribe said unto him, Well, Master, thou hast said the truth: for there is one God; and there is none other but he: [33]And to love him with all the heart, and with all the understanding, and with all the soul, and with all the strength, and to love his neighbour as himself, is more than all whole burnt offerings and sacrifices."

What Sacrifices To Offer
Psalm 4:5 "Offer the sacrifices of righteousness, and put your trust in the Lord."

Whose Sacrifice Is Not Pleasing To The Lord
Genesis 4:3-7 "[3]And in process of time it came to pass, that Cain brought of the fruit of the ground

an offering unto the LORD. [4]And Abel, he also brought of the firstlings of his flock and of the fat thereof. And the LORD had respect unto Abel and to his offering: [5]But unto Cain and to his offering he had not respect. And Cain was very wroth, and his countenance fell. [6]And the LORD said unto Cain, Why art thou wroth? and why is thy countenance fallen? [7]If thou doest well, shalt thou not be accepted? and if thou doest not well, sin lieth at the door. And unto thee shall be his desire, and thou shalt rule over him."

Isaiah 66:1-4 "[1]Thus saith the LORD, The heaven is my throne, and the earth is my footstool: where is the house that ye build unto me? and where is the place of my rest? [2]For all those things hath mine hand made, and those things have been, saith the LORD: but to this man will I look, even to him that is poor and of a contrite spirit, and trembleth at my word. [3]He that killeth an ox is as if he slew a man; he that sacrificeth a lamb, as if he cut off a dog's neck; he that offereth an oblation, as if he offered swine's blood; he that burneth incense, as if he blessed an idol. Yea, they have chosen their own ways, and their soul delighteth in their abominations. [4]I also will choose their delusions, and will bring their fears upon them; because when I called, none did answer; when I spake, they did not hear: but they did evil before mine eyes, and chose that in which I delighted not."

Hosea 9:1-4 "[1]Rejoice not, O Israel, for joy, as other people: for thou hast gone a whoring from thy God, thou hast loved a reward upon every cornfloor. [2]The floor and the winepress shall not feed them, and the new wine shall fail in her. [3]They shall not dwell in the LORD's land; but Ephraim shall return to Egypt, and they shall eat unclean things in Assyria. [4]They shall not offer wine offerings to the LORD, neither shall they be pleasing unto him: their sacrifices shall be unto them as the bread of mourners; all that eat thereof shall be polluted: for their bread for their soul shall not come into the house of the LORD."

Whose Sacrifice Shall Be Accepted By The Lord
Genesis 4:3-7 "[3]And in process of time it came to pass, that Cain brought of the fruit of the ground an offering unto the LORD. [4]And Abel, he also brought of the firstlings of his flock and of the fat thereof. And the LORD had respect unto Abel and

to his offering: [5]But unto Cain and to his offering he had not respect. And Cain was very wroth, and his countenance fell. [6]And the LORD said unto Cain, Why art thou wroth? and why is thy countenance fallen? [7]If thou doest well, shalt thou not be accepted? and if thou doest not well, sin lieth at the door. And unto thee shall be his desire, and thou shalt rule over him."

Isaiah 56:6-7 "[6]Also the sons of the stranger, that join themselves to the LORD, to serve him, and to love the name of the LORD, to be his servants, every one that keepeth the sabbath from polluting it, and taketh hold of my covenant; [7]Even them will I bring to my holy mountain, and make them joyful in my house of prayer: their burnt offerings and their sacrifices shall be accepted upon mine altar; for mine house shall be called an house of prayer for all people."

Hebrews 13:12-16 "[12]Wherefore Jesus also, that he might sanctify the people with his own blood, suffered without the gate. [13]Let us go forth therefore unto him without the camp, bearing his reproach. [14]For here have we no continuing city, but we seek one to come. [15]By him therefore let us offer the sacrifice of praise to God continually, that is, the fruit of our lips giving thanks to his name. [16]But to do good and to communicate forget not: for with such sacrifices God is well pleased."

SAFETY

Safety Being Of The Lord
Proverbs 21:31 "The horse is prepared against the day of battle: but safety is of the LORD."

The Time When People Shall Say Peace And Safety
1 Thessalonians 5:3 "For when they shall say, Peace and safety; then sudden destruction cometh upon them, as travail upon a woman with child; and they shall not escape."

Where Safety Is
Proverbs 11:14 "Where no counsel is, the people fall: but in the multitude of counsellers there is safety."

Proverbs 24:6 "For by wise counsel thou shalt make thy war: and in multitude of counsellers there is safety."

Who Shall Be Safe

Leviticus 25:17-18 "[17]Ye shall not therefore oppress one another; but thou shalt fear thy God: for I am the LORD your God. [18]Wherefore ye shall do my statutes, and keep my judgments, and do them; and ye shall dwell in the land in safety."

Leviticus 26:1-5 "[1]Ye shall make you no idols nor graven image, neither rear you up a standing image, neither shall ye set up any image of stone in your land, to bow down unto it: for I am the LORD your God. [2]Ye shall keep my sabbaths, and reverence my sanctuary: I am the LORD. [3]If ye walk in my statutes, and keep my commandments, and do them; [4]Then I will give you rain in due season, and the land shall yield her increase, and the trees of the field shall yield their fruit. [5]And your threshing shall reach unto the vintage, and the vintage shall reach unto the sowing time: and ye shall eat your bread to the full, and dwell in your land safely."

Job 5:8-11 "[8]I would seek unto God, and unto God would I commit my cause: [9]Which doeth great things and unsearchable; marvellous things without number: [10]Who giveth rain upon the earth, and sendeth waters upon the fields: [11]To set up on high those that be low; that those which mourn may be exalted to safety."

Psalm 91:9-13 "[9]Because thou hast made the LORD, which is my refuge, even the most High, thy habitation; [10]There shall no evil befall thee, neither shall any plague come nigh thy dwelling. [11]For he shall give his angels charge over thee, to keep thee in all thy ways. [12]They shall bear thee up in their hands, lest thou dash thy foot against a stone. [13]Thou shalt tread upon the lion and adder: the young lion and the dragon shalt thou trample under feet."

Proverbs 1:20-33 "[20]Wisdom crieth without; she uttereth her voice in the streets: [21]She crieth in the chief place of concourse, in the openings of the gates: in the city she uttereth her words, saying, [22]How long, ye simple ones, will ye love simplicity? and the scorners delight in their scorning, and fools hate knowledge? [23]Turn you at my reproof: behold, I will pour out my spirit unto you, I will make known my words unto you. [24]Because I have called, and ye refused; I have stretched out my hand, and no man regarded; [25]But ye have set at nought all my counsel, and would none of my reproof: [26]I also will laugh at your calamity; I will mock when your fear cometh; [27]When your fear cometh as desolation, and your destruction cometh as a whirlwind; when distress and anguish cometh upon you. [28]Then shall they call upon me, but I will not answer; they shall seek me early, but they shall not find me: [29]For that they hated knowledge, and did not choose the fear of the LORD: [30]They would none of my counsel: they despised all my reproof. [31]Therefore shall they eat of the fruit of their own way, and be filled with their own devices. [32]For the turning away of the simple shall slay them, and the prosperity of fools shall destroy them. [33]But whoso hearkeneth unto me shall dwell safely, and shall be quiet from fear of evil."

Proverbs 18:10 "The name of the LORD is a strong tower: the righteous runneth into it, and is safe."

Proverbs 29:25 "The fear of man bringeth a snare: but whoso putteth his trust in the LORD shall be safe."

SAINTS

Jesus Christ Being Glorified In His Saints

2 Thessalonians 1:7-10 "[7]And to you who are troubled rest with us, when the Lord Jesus shall be revealed from heaven with his mighty angels, [8]In flaming fire taking vengeance on them that know not God, and that obey not the gospel of our Lord Jesus Christ: [9]Who shall be punished with everlasting destruction from the presence of the Lord, and from the glory of his power; [10]When he shall come to be glorified in his saints, and to be admired in all them that believe (because our testimony among you was believed) in that day."

The Lord Coming With His Saints

Deuteronomy 33:1-2 "[1]And this is the blessing, wherewith Moses the man of God blessed the children of Israel before his death. [2]And he said, The LORD came from Sinai, and rose up from Seir unto them; he shined forth from mount Paran, and he came with ten thousands of saints: from his right hand went a fiery law for them."

Zechariah 14:1-5 "[1]Behold, the day of the LORD cometh, and thy spoil shall be divided in the midst of thee. ²For I will gather all nations against Jerusalem to battle; and the city shall be taken, and the houses rifled, and the women ravished; and half of the city shall go forth into captivity, and the residue of the people shall not be cut off from the city. ³Then shall the LORD go forth, and fight against those nations, as when he fought in the day of battle. ⁴And his feet shall stand in that day upon the mount of Olives, which is before Jerusalem on the east, and the mount of Olives shall cleave in the midst thereof toward the east and toward the west, and there shall be a very great valley; and half of the mountain shall remove toward the north, and half of it toward the south. ⁵And ye shall flee to the valley of the mountains; for the valley of the mountains shall reach unto Azal: yea, ye shall flee, like as ye fled from before the earthquake in the days of Uzziah king of Judah: and the LORD my God shall come, and all the saints with thee."

Jude 14 "And Enoch also, the seventh from Adam, prophesied of these, saying, Behold, the Lord cometh with ten thousands of his saints."

The Lord Gathering His Saints

Psalm 50:1-6 "¹The mighty God, even the LORD, hath spoken, and called the earth from the rising of the sun unto the going down thereof. ²Out of Zion, the perfection of beauty, God hath shined. ³Our God shall come, and shall not keep silence: a fire shall devour before him, and it shall be very tempestuous round about him. ⁴He shall call to the heavens from above, and to the earth, that he may judge his people. ⁵Gather my saints together unto me; those that have made a covenant with me by sacrifice. ⁶And the heavens shall declare his righteousness: for God is judge himself. Selah."

The Saints Of God

Deuteronomy 33:1-3 "¹And this is the blessing, wherewith Moses the man of God blessed the children of Israel before his death. ²And he said, The LORD came from Sinai, and rose up from Seir unto them; he shined forth from mount Paran, and he came with ten thousands of saints: from his right hand went a fiery law for them. ³Yea, he loved the people; all his saints are in thy hand: and they sat down at thy feet; every one shall receive of thy words."

1 Samuel 2:6-9 "⁶The LORD killeth, and maketh alive: he bringeth down to the grave, and bringeth up. ⁷The LORD maketh poor, and maketh rich: he bringeth low, and lifteth up. ⁸He raiseth up the poor out of the dust, and lifteth up the beggar from the dunghill, to set them among princes, and to make them inherit the throne of glory: for the pillars of the earth are the LORD's, and he hath set the world upon them. ⁹He will keep the feet of his saints, and the wicked shall be silent in darkness; for by strength shall no man prevail."

Psalm 37:28 "For the LORD loveth judgment, and forsaketh not his saints; they are preserved for ever: but the seed of the wicked shall be cut off."

Psalm 97:10 "Ye that love the LORD, hate evil: he preserveth the souls of his saints; he delivereth them out of the hand of the wicked."

Psalm 145:9-10 "⁹The LORD is good to all: and his tender mercies are over all his works. ¹⁰All thy works shall praise thee, O LORD; and thy saints shall bless thee."

Psalm 148:7-14 "⁷Praise the LORD from the earth, ye dragons, and all deeps: ⁸Fire, and hail; snow, and vapour; stormy wind fulfilling his word: ⁹Mountains, and all hills; fruitful trees, and all cedars: ¹⁰Beasts, and all cattle; creeping things, and flying fowl: ¹¹Kings of the earth, and all people; princes, and all judges of the earth: ¹²Both young men, and maidens; old men, and children: ¹³Let them praise the name of the LORD: for his name alone is excellent; his glory is above the earth and heaven. ¹⁴He also exalteth the horn of his people, the praise of all his saints; even of the children of Israel, a people near unto him. Praise ye the LORD."

Proverbs 2:6-8 "⁶For the LORD giveth wisdom: out of his mouth cometh knowledge and understanding. ⁷He layeth up sound wisdom for the righteous: he is a buckler to them that walk uprightly. ⁸He keepeth the paths of judgment, and preserveth the way of his saints."

Daniel 7:15-28 "¹⁵I Daniel was grieved in my spirit in the midst of my body, and the visions of my head troubled me. ¹⁶I came near unto one of them that stood by, and asked him the truth of all this. So he told me, and made me know the interpretation of the things. ¹⁷These great beasts, which are four, are four kings, which shall arise out of the earth. [18]But the saints of the most High shall take the kingdom, and possess the kingdom for ever, even for ever and ever. [19]Then I would know the truth of the fourth beast, which was diverse from all the others, exceeding dreadful, whose teeth were of iron, and his nails of brass; which devoured, brake in pieces, and stamped the residue with his feet; [20]And of the ten horns that were in his head, and of the other which came up, and before whom three fell; even of that horn that had eyes, and a mouth that spake very great things, whose look was more stout than his fellows. [21]I beheld, and the same horn made war with the saints, and prevailed against them; [22]Until the Ancient of days came, and judgment was given to the saints of the most High; and the time came that the saints possessed the kingdom. [23]Thus he said, The fourth beast shall be the fourth kingdom upon earth, which shall be diverse from all kingdoms, and shall devour the whole earth, and shall tread it down, and break it in pieces. [24]And the ten horns out of this kingdom are ten kings that shall arise: and another shall rise after them; and he shall be diverse from the first, and he shall subdue three kings. [25]And he shall speak great words against the most High, and shall wear out the saints of the most High, and think to change times and laws: and they shall be given into his hand until a time and times and the dividing of time. [26]But the judgment shall sit, and they shall take away his dominion, to consume and to destroy it unto the end. [27]And the kingdom and dominion, and the greatness of the kingdom under the whole heaven, shall be given to the people of the saints of the most High, whose kingdom is an everlasting kingdom, and all dominions shall serve and obey him. [28]Hitherto is the end of the matter. As for me Daniel, my cogitations much troubled me, and my countenance changed in me: but I kept the matter in my heart."

Romans 8:26-28 "[26]Likewise the Spirit also helpeth our infirmities: for we know not what we should pray for as we ought: but the Spirit itself maketh intercession for us with groanings which cannot be uttered. [27]And he that searcheth the hearts knoweth what is the mind of the Spirit, because he maketh intercession for the saints according to the will of God. [28]And we know that all things work together for good to them that love God,

to them who are the called according to his purpose."

1 Corinthians 6:1-3 "[1]Dare any of you, having a matter against another, go to law before the unjust, and not before the saints? [2]Do ye not know that the saints shall judge the world? and if the world shall be judged by you, are ye unworthy to judge the smallest matters? [3]Know ye not that we shall judge angels? how much more things that pertain to this life?"

Colossians 1:24-28 "[24]Who now rejoice in my sufferings for you, and fill up that which is behind of the afflictions of Christ in my flesh for his body's sake, which is the church: [25]Whereof I am made a minister, according to the dispensation of God which is given to me for you, to fulfil the word of God; [26]Even the mystery which hath been hid from ages and from generations, but now is made manifest to his saints: [27]To whom God would make known what is the riches of the glory of this mystery among the Gentiles; which is Christ in you, the hope of glory: [28]Whom we preach, warning every man, and teaching every man in all wisdom; that we may present every man perfect in Christ Jesus."

Revelation 11:15-18 "[15]And the seventh angel sounded; and there were great voices in heaven, saying, The kingdoms of this world are become the kingdoms of our Lord, and of his Christ; and he shall reign for ever and ever. [16]And the four and twenty elders, which sat before God on their seats, fell upon their faces, and worshipped God, [17]Saying, We give thee thanks, O Lord God Almighty, which art, and wast, and art to come; because thou hast taken to thee thy great power, and hast reigned. [18]And the nations were angry, and thy wrath is come, and the time of the dead, that they should be judged, and that thou shouldest give reward unto thy servants the prophets, and to the saints, and them that fear thy name, small and great; and shouldest destroy them which destroy the earth."

SALT

If Salt Loses Its Savor

Matthew 5:13 "Ye are the salt of the earth: but if the salt have lost his savour, wherewith shall it be salted? it is thenceforth good for nothing, but to be cast out, and to be trodden under foot of men."

Mark 9:49-50 "⁴⁹For every one shall be salted with fire, and every sacrifice shall be salted with salt. ⁵⁰Salt is good: but if the salt have lost his saltness, wherewith will ye season it? Have salt in yourselves, and have peace one with another."

Luke 14:34-35 "³⁴Salt is good: but if the salt have lost his savour, wherewith shall it be seasoned? ³⁵It is neither fit for the land, nor yet for the dunghill; but men cast it out. He that hath ears to hear, let him hear."

Who Is The Salt Of The Earth
Matthew 5:1-13 "¹And seeing the multitudes, he went up into a mountain: and when he was set, his disciples came unto him: ²And he opened his mouth, and taught them, saying, ³Blessed are the poor in spirit: for theirs is the kingdom of heaven. ⁴Blessed are they that mourn: for they shall be comforted. ⁵Blessed are the meek: for they shall inherit the earth. ⁶Blessed are they which do hunger and thirst after righteousness: for they shall be filled. ⁷Blessed are the merciful: for they shall obtain mercy. ⁸Blessed are the pure in heart: for they shall see God. ⁹Blessed are the peacemakers: for they shall be called the children of God. ¹⁰Blessed are they which are persecuted for righteousness' sake: for theirs is the kingdom of heaven. ¹¹Blessed are ye, when men shall revile you, and persecute you, and shall say all manner of evil against you falsely, for my sake. ¹²Rejoice, and be exceeding glad: for great is your reward in heaven: for so persecuted they the prophets which were before you. ¹³Ye are the salt of the earth: but if the salt have lost his savour, wherewith shall it be salted? it is thenceforth good for nothing, but to be cast out, and to be trodden under foot of men."

SALVATION

Jesus Christ Coming To Save
Matthew 1:20-21 "²⁰But while he thought on these things, behold, the angel of the Lord appeared unto him in a dream, saying, Joseph, thou son of David, fear not to take unto thee Mary thy wife: for that which is conceived in her is of the Holy Ghost. ²¹And she shall bring forth a son, and thou shalt call his name JESUS: for he shall save his people from their sins."

Matthew 18:11-14 "¹¹For the Son of man is come to save that which was lost. ¹²How think ye? if a man have an hundred sheep, and one of them be gone astray, doth he not leave the ninety and nine, and goeth into the mountains, and seeketh that which is gone astray? ¹³And if so be that he find it, verily I say unto you, he rejoiceth more of that sheep, than of the ninety and nine which went not astray. ¹⁴Even so it is not the will of your Father which is in heaven, that one of these little ones should perish."

Luke 9:54-56 "⁵⁴And when his disciples James and John saw this, they said, Lord, wilt thou that we command fire to come down from heaven, and consume them, even as Elias did? ⁵⁵But he turned, and rebuked them, and said, Ye know not what manner of spirit ye are of. ⁵⁶For the Son of man is not come to destroy men's lives, but to save them. And they went to another village."

Luke 15:3-32 "³And he spake this parable unto them, saying, ⁴What man of you, having an hundred sheep, if he lose one of them, doth not leave the ninety and nine in the wilderness, and go after that which is lost, until he find it? ⁵And when he hath found it, he layeth it on his shoulders, rejoicing. ⁶And when he cometh home, he calleth together his friends and neighbours, saying unto them, Rejoice with me; for I have found my sheep which was lost. ⁷I say unto you, that likewise joy shall be in heaven over one sinner that repenteth, more than over ninety and nine just persons, which need no repentance. ⁸Either what woman having ten pieces of silver, if she lose one piece, doth not light a candle, and sweep the house, and seek diligently till she find it? ⁹And when she hath found it, she calleth her friends and her neighbours together, saying, Rejoice with me; for I have found the piece which I had lost. ¹⁰Likewise, I say unto you, there is joy in the presence of the angels of God over one sinner that repenteth. ¹¹And he said, A certain man had two sons: ¹²And the younger of them said to his father, Father, give me the portion of goods that falleth to me. And he divided unto them his living. ¹³And not many days after the younger son gathered all together, and took his journey into a far country, and there wasted his substance with riotous living. [14]And when he had spent all, there arose a mighty famine in that land; and he began to be in want. [15]And he went and joined himself to a citizen of that country; and he sent him into his fields to feed swine. [16]And he would fain have filled his belly with the husks that the swine did eat: and no man gave unto him. [17]And when he came to himself, he said, How many hired servants of my father's have bread enough and to spare, and I perish with hunger! [18]I will arise and go to my father, and will say unto him, Father, I have sinned against heaven, and before thee, [19]And am no more worthy to be called thy son: make me as one of thy hired servants. [20]And he arose, and came to his father. But when he was yet a great way off, his father saw him, and had compassion, and ran, and fell on his neck, and kissed him. [21]And the son said unto him, Father, I have sinned against heaven, and in thy sight, and am no more worthy to be called thy son. [22]But the father said to his servants, Bring forth the best robe, and put it on him; and put a ring on his hand, and shoes on his feet: [23]And bring hither the fatted calf, and kill it; and let us eat, and be merry: [24]For this my son was dead, and is alive again; he was lost, and is found. And they began to be merry. [25]Now his elder son was in the field: and as he came and drew nigh to the house, he heard musick and dancing. [26]And he called one of the servants, and asked what these things meant. [27]And he said unto him, Thy brother is come; and thy father hath killed the fatted calf, because he hath received him safe and sound. [28]And he was angry, and would not go in: therefore came his father out, and intreated him. [29]And he answering said to his father, Lo, these many years do I serve thee, neither transgressed I at any time thy commandment: and yet thou never gavest me a kid, that I might make merry with my friends: [30]But as soon as this thy son was come, which hath devoured thy living with harlots, thou hast killed for him the fatted calf. [31]And he said unto him, Son, thou art ever with me, and all that I have is thine. [32]It was meet that we should make merry, and be glad: for this thy brother was dead, and is alive again; and was lost, and is found."

Luke 19:9-10 "[9]And Jesus said unto him, This day is salvation come to this house, forsomuch as he also is a son of Abraham. [10]For the Son of man is come to seek and to save that which was lost."

John 3:16-17 "[16]For God so loved the world, that he gave his only begotten Son, that whosoever believeth in him should not perish, but have everlasting life. [17]For God sent not his Son into the world to condemn the world; but that the world through him might be saved."

John 12:44-47 "[44]Jesus cried and said, He that believeth on me, believeth not on me, but on him that sent me. [45]And he that seeth me seeth him that sent me. [46]I am come a light into the world, that whosoever believeth on me should not abide in darkness. [47]And if any man hear my words, and believe not, I judge him not: for I came not to judge the world, but to save the world."

1 Timothy 1:15 "This is a faithful saying, and worthy of all acceptation, that Christ Jesus came into the world to save sinners; of whom I am chief."

Salvation Belonging To The Lord
Psalm 3:8 "Salvation belongeth unto the LORD: thy blessing is upon thy people. Selah."

Salvation Coming To The Gentiles
Acts 15:6-11 "[6]And the apostles and elders came together for to consider of this matter. [7]And when there had been much disputing, Peter rose up, and said unto them, Men and brethren, ye know how that a good while ago God made choice among us, that the Gentiles by my mouth should hear the word of the gospel, and believe. [8]And God, which knoweth the hearts, bare them witness, giving them the Holy Ghost, even as he did unto us; [9]And put no difference between us and them, purifying their hearts by faith. [10]Now therefore why tempt ye God, to put a yoke upon the neck of the disciples, which neither our fathers nor we were able to bear? [11]But we believe that through the grace of the Lord Jesus Christ we shall be saved, even as they."

Acts 28:25-28 "[25]And when they agreed not among themselves, they departed, after that Paul had spoken one word, Well spake the Holy Ghost by Esaias the prophet unto our fathers, [26]Saying, Go unto this people, and say, Hearing ye shall hear, and shall not understand; and seeing ye shall see, and not perceive: [27]For the heart of this people is waxed gross, and their ears are dull of hearing, and their eyes have they closed; lest they should see with their eyes, and hear with their ears, and understand with their heart, and should be converted, and I should heal them. ²⁸Be it known therefore unto you, that the salvation of God is sent unto the Gentiles, and that they will hear it."

Romans 9:30-33 "³⁰What shall we say then? That the Gentiles, which followed not after righteousness, have attained to righteousness, even the righteousness which is of faith. ³¹But Israel, which followed after the law of righteousness, hath not attained to the law of righteousness. ³²Wherefore? Because they sought it not by faith, but as it were by the works of the law. For they stumbled at that stumblingstone; ³³As it is written, Behold, I lay in Sion a stumblingstone and rock of offence: and whosoever believeth on him shall not be ashamed."

Romans 11:1-32 "¹I say then, Hath God cast away his people? God forbid. For I also am an Israelite, of the seed of Abraham, of the tribe of Benjamin. ²God hath not cast away his people which he foreknew. Wot ye not what the scripture saith of Elias? how he maketh intercession to God against Israel, saying, ³Lord, they have killed thy prophets, and digged down thine altars; and I am left alone, and they seek my life. ⁴But what saith the answer of God unto him? I have reserved to myself seven thousand men, who have not bowed the knee to the image of Baal. ⁵Even so then at this present time also there is a remnant according to the election of grace. ⁶And if by grace, then is it no more of works: otherwise grace is no more grace. But if it be of works, then is it no more grace: otherwise work is no more work. ⁷What then? Israel hath not obtained that which he seeketh for; but the election hath obtained it, and the rest were blinded ⁸(According as it is written, God hath given them the spirit of slumber, eyes that they should not see, and ears that they should not hear;) unto this day. ⁹And David saith, Let their table be made a snare, and a trap, and a stumbling block, and a recompence unto them: ¹⁰Let their eyes be darkened, that they may not see, and bow down their back alway. ¹¹I say then, Have they stumbled that they should fall? God forbid: but rather through their fall salvation is come unto the Gentiles, for to provoke them to jealousy. ¹²Now if the fall of them be the riches of the world, and the diminishing of them the riches

of the Gentiles; how much more their fulness? ¹³For I speak to you Gentiles, inasmuch as I am the apostle of the Gentiles, I magnify mine office: ¹⁴If by any means I may provoke to emulation them which are my flesh, and might save some of them. ¹⁵For if the casting away of them be the reconciling of the world, what shall the receiving of them be, but life from the dead? ¹⁶For if the firstfruit be holy, the lump is also holy: and if the root be holy, so are the branches. ¹⁷And if some of the branches be broken off, and thou, being a wild olive tree, wert graffed in among them, and with them partakest of the root and fatness of the olive tree; ¹⁸Boast not against the branches. But if thou boast, thou bearest not the root, but the root thee. ¹⁹Thou wilt say then, The branches were broken off, that I might be graffed in. ²⁰Well; because of unbelief they were broken off, and thou standest by faith. Be not highminded, but fear: ²¹For if God spared not the natural branches, take heed lest he also spare not thee. ²²Behold therefore the goodness and severity of God: on them which fell, severity; but toward thee, goodness, if thou continue in his goodness: otherwise thou also shalt be cut off. ²³And they also, if they abide not still in unbelief, shall be graffed in: for God is able to graff them in again. ²⁴For if thou wert cut out of the olive tree which is wild by nature, and wert graffed contrary to nature into a good olive tree: how much more shall these, which be the natural branches, be graffed into their own olive tree? ²⁵For I would not, brethren, that ye should be ignorant of this mystery, lest ye should be wise in your own conceits; that blindness in part is happened to Israel, until the fulness of the Gentiles be come in. ²⁶And so all Israel shall be saved: as it is written, There shall come out of Sion the Deliverer, and shall turn away ungodliness from Jacob: ²⁷For this is my covenant unto them, when I shall take away their sins. ²⁸As concerning the gospel, they are enemies for your sakes: but as touching the election, they are beloved for the fathers' sakes. ²⁹For the gifts and calling of God are without repentance. ³⁰For as ye in times past have not believed God, yet have now obtained mercy through their unbelief: ³¹Even so have these also now not believed, that through your mercy they also may obtain mercy. ³²For God hath concluded them all in unbelief, that he might have mercy upon all."

Galatians 3:6-14 "⁶Even as Abraham believed God, and it was accounted to him for righteousness. ⁷Know ye therefore that they which are of faith, the same are the children of Abraham. ⁸And the scripture, foreseeing that God would justify the heathen through faith, preached before the gospel unto Abraham, saying, In thee shall all nations be blessed. ⁹So then they which be of faith are blessed with faithful Abraham. ¹⁰For as many as are of the works of the law are under the curse: for it is written, Cursed is every one that continueth not in all things which are written in the book of the law to do them. ¹¹But that no man is justified by the law in the sight of God, it is evident: for, The just shall live by faith. ¹²And the law is not of faith: but, The man that doeth them shall live in them. ¹³Christ hath redeemed us from the curse of the law, being made a curse for us: for it is written, Cursed is every one that hangeth on a tree: ¹⁴That the blessing of Abraham might come on the Gentiles through Jesus Christ; that we might receive the promise of the Spirit through faith."

The Lord Being The Only Savior

Psalm 62:1-2 "¹Truly my soul waiteth upon God: from him cometh my salvation. ²He only is my rock and my salvation; he is my defence; I shall not be greatly moved."

Psalm 62:6-7 "⁶He only is my rock and my salvation: he is my defence; I shall not be moved. ⁷In God is my salvation and my glory: the rock of my strength, and my refuge, is in God."

Isaiah 43:11-12 "¹¹I, even I, am the LORD; and beside me there is no saviour. ¹²I have declared, and have saved, and I have shewed, when there was no strange god among you: therefore ye are my witnesses, saith the LORD, that I am God."

Hosea 13:4 "Yet I am the LORD thy God from the land of Egypt, and thou shalt know no god but me: for there is no saviour beside me."

Acts 4:9-12 "⁹If we this day be examined of the good deed done to the impotent man, by what means he is made whole; ¹⁰Be it known unto you all, and to all the people of Israel, that by the name of Jesus Christ of Nazareth, whom ye crucified, whom God raised from the dead, even by him doth this man stand here before you whole. ¹¹This is the stone which was set at nought of you builders, which is become the head of the corner. ¹²Neither is there salvation in any other: for there is none other name under heaven given among men, whereby we must be saved."

The Lord Being The Savior/Salvation

Exodus 15:2 "The LORD is my strength and song, and he is become my salvation: he is my God, and I will prepare him an habitation; my father's God, and I will exalt him."

2 Samuel 22:3 "The God of my rock; in him will I trust: he is my shield, and the horn of my salvation, my high tower, and my refuge, my saviour; thou savest me from violence."

2 Samuel 22:47 "The LORD liveth; and blessed be my rock; and exalted be the God of the rock of my salvation."

2 Samuel 22:50-51 "⁵⁰Therefore I will give thanks unto thee, O LORD, among the heathen, and I will sing praises unto thy name. ⁵¹He is the tower of salvation for his king: and sheweth mercy to his anointed, unto David, and to his seed for evermore."

Job 13:16 "He also shall be my salvation: for an hypocrite shall not come before him."

Psalm 18:2 "The LORD is my rock, and my fortress, and my deliverer; my God, my strength, in whom I will trust; my buckler, and the horn of my salvation, and my high tower."

Psalm 18:46 "The LORD liveth; and blessed be my rock; and let the God of my salvation be exalted."

Psalm 25:5 "Lead me in thy truth, and teach me: for thou art the God of my salvation; on thee do I wait all the day."

Psalm 27:1 "The LORD is my light and my salvation; whom shall I fear? the LORD is the strength of my life; of whom shall I be afraid?"

Psalm 28:7-8 "⁷The LORD is my strength and my shield; my heart trusted in him, and I am helped: therefore my heart greatly rejoiceth; and with my song will I praise him. ⁸The LORD is their strength, and he is the saving strength of his anointed."

Psalm 62:1-2 "¹Truly my soul waiteth upon God: from him cometh my salvation. ²He only is my rock and my salvation; he is my defence; I shall not be greatly moved."

Psalm 62:6-7 "⁶He only is my rock and my salvation: he is my defence; I shall not be moved. ⁷In God is my salvation and my glory: the rock of my strength, and my refuge, is in God."

Psalm 68:19 "Blessed be the Lord, who daily loadeth us with benefits, even the God of our salvation. Selah."

Psalm 89:26 "He shall cry unto me, Thou art my father, my God, and the rock of my salvation."

Psalm 118:14-15 "¹⁴The LORD is my strength and song, and is become my salvation. ¹⁵The voice of rejoicing and salvation is in the tabernacles of the righteous: the right hand of the LORD doeth valiantly."

Isaiah 12:2-3 "²Behold, God is my salvation; I will trust, and not be afraid: for the LORD JEHOVAH is my strength and my song; he also is become my salvation. ³Therefore with joy shall ye draw water out of the wells of salvation."

Isaiah 33:2 "O LORD, be gracious unto us; we have waited for thee: be thou their arm every morning, our salvation also in the time of trouble."

Isaiah 43:3 "For I am the LORD thy God, the Holy One of Israel, thy Saviour: I gave Egypt for thy ransom, Ethiopia and Seba for thee."

Isaiah 43:11-12 "¹¹I, even I, am the LORD; and beside me there is no saviour. ¹²I have declared, and have saved, and I have shewed, when there was no strange god among you: therefore ye are my witnesses, saith the LORD, that I am God."

Isaiah 49:26 "And I will feed them that oppress thee with their own flesh; and they shall be drunken with their own blood, as with sweet wine: and all flesh shall know that I the LORD am thy Saviour and thy Redeemer, the mighty One of Jacob."

Isaiah 60:15-16 "¹⁵Whereas thou hast been forsaken and hated, so that no man went through thee, I will make thee an eternal excellency, a joy of many generations. ¹⁶Thou shalt also suck the milk of the Gentiles, and shalt suck the breast of kings: and thou shalt know that I the LORD am thy Saviour and thy Redeemer, the mighty One of Jacob."

Isaiah 63:7-8 "⁷I will mention the lovingkindnesses of the LORD, and the praises of the LORD, according to all that the LORD hath bestowed on us, and the great goodness toward the house of Israel, which he hath bestowed on them according to his mercies, and according to the multitude of his lovingkindnesses. ⁸For he said, Surely they are my people, children that will not lie: so he was their Saviour."

Hosea 13:4 "Yet I am the LORD thy God from the land of Egypt, and thou shalt know no god but me: for there is no saviour beside me."

Habakkuk 3:18 "Yet I will rejoice in the LORD, I will joy in the God of my salvation."

Zechariah 9:9 "Rejoice greatly, O daughter of Zion; shout, O daughter of Jerusalem: behold, thy King cometh unto thee: he is just, and having salvation; lowly, and riding upon an ass, and upon a colt the foal of an ass."

Luke 2:11 "For unto you is born this day in the city of David a Saviour, which is Christ the Lord."

Acts 5:30-31 "³⁰The God of our fathers raised up Jesus, whom ye slew and hanged on a tree. ³¹Him hath God exalted with his right hand to be a Prince and a Saviour, for to give repentance to Israel, and forgiveness of sins."

Acts 13:22-23 "²²And when he had removed him, he raised up unto them David to be their king; to whom also he gave testimony, and said, I have found David the son of Jesse, a man after mine own heart, which shall fulfil all my will. ²³Of this man's seed hath God according to his promise raised unto Israel a Saviour, Jesus."

Ephesians 5:22-23 "²²Wives, submit yourselves unto your own husbands, as unto the Lord. ²³For the husband is the head of the wife, even as Christ is the head of the church: and he is the saviour of the body."

Philippians 3:20-21 "²⁰For our conversation is in heaven; from whence also we look for the Saviour, the Lord Jesus Christ: ²¹Who shall change our vile body, that it may be fashioned like unto his glorious body, according to the working whereby he is able even to subdue all things unto himself."

1 Timothy 1:1 "Paul, an apostle of Jesus Christ by the commandment of God our Saviour, and Lord Jesus Christ, which is our hope."

1 Timothy 2:3 "For this is good and acceptable in the sight of God our Saviour."

Titus 2:13 "Looking for that blessed hope, and the glorious appearing of the great God and our Saviour Jesus Christ."

Titus 3:3-6 "³For we ourselves also were sometimes foolish, disobedient, deceived, serving divers lusts and pleasures, living in malice and envy, hateful, and hating one another. ⁴But after that the kindness and love of God our Saviour toward man appeared, ⁵Not by works of righteousness which we have done, but according to his mercy he saved us, by the washing of regeneration, and renewing of the Holy Ghost; ⁶Which he shed on us abundantly through Jesus Christ our Saviour."

Hebrews 2:9-10 "⁹But we see Jesus, who was made a little lower than the angels for the suffering of death, crowned with glory and honour; that he by the grace of God should taste death for every man. ¹⁰For it became him, for whom are all things, and by whom are all things, in bringing many sons unto glory, to make the captain of their salvation perfect through sufferings."

2 Peter 1:1 "Simon Peter, a servant and an apostle of Jesus Christ, to them that have obtained like precious faith with us through the righteousness of God and our Saviour Jesus Christ."

2 Peter 1:11 "For so an entrance shall be ministered unto you abundantly into the everlasting kingdom of our Lord and Saviour Jesus Christ."

2 Peter 3:18 "But grow in grace, and in the knowledge of our Lord and Saviour Jesus Christ. To him be glory both now and for ever. Amen."

1 John 4:14 "And we have seen and do testify that the Father sent the Son to be the Saviour of the world."

Jude 25 "To the only wise God our Saviour, be glory and majesty, dominion and power, both now and ever. Amen."

The Lord Giving Salvation
2 Samuel 22:33-36 "³³God is my strength and power: and he maketh my way perfect. ³⁴He maketh my feet like hinds' feet: and setteth me upon my high places. ³⁵He teacheth my hands to war; so that a bow of steel is broken by mine arms. ³⁶Thou hast also given me the shield of thy salvation: and thy gentleness hath made me great."

Psalm 18:31-35 "³¹For who is God save the LORD? or who is a rock save our God? ³²It is God that girdeth me with strength, and maketh my way perfect. ³³He maketh my feet like hinds' feet, and setteth me upon my high places. ³⁴He teacheth my hands to war, so that a bow of steel is broken by mine arms. ³⁵Thou hast also given me the shield of thy salvation: and thy right hand hath holden me up, and thy gentleness hath made me great."

Psalm 144:9-11 "⁹I will sing a new song unto thee, O God: upon a psaltery and an instrument of ten strings will I sing praises unto thee. ¹⁰It is he that giveth salvation unto kings: who delivereth David his servant from the hurtful sword. ¹¹Rid me, and deliver me from the hand of strange children, whose mouth speaketh vanity, and their right hand is a right hand of falsehood."

Isaiah 61:10 "I will greatly rejoice in the LORD, my soul shall be joyful in my God; for he hath clothed me with the garments of salvation, he hath covered me with the robe of righteousness, as a bridegroom decketh himself with ornaments, and as a bride adorneth herself with her jewels."

The Lord Saving
2 Samuel 22:3 "The God of my rock; in him will I trust: he is my shield, and the horn of my salvation, my high tower, and my refuge, my saviour; thou savest me from violence."

Psalm 37:40 "And the LORD shall help them and deliver them: he shall deliver them from the wicked, and save them, because they trust in him."

Psalm 71:1-3 "¹In thee, O LORD, do I put my trust: let me never be put to confusion. ²Deliver me in thy righteousness, and cause me to escape: incline thine ear unto me, and save me. ³Be thou my strong habitation, whereunto I may continually resort: thou hast given commandment to save me; for thou art my rock and my fortress."

Psalm 138:6-7 "⁶Though the LORD be high, yet hath he respect unto the lowly: but the proud he knoweth afar off. ⁷Though I walk in the midst of trouble, thou wilt revive me: thou shalt stretch forth thine hand against the wrath of mine enemies, and thy right hand shall save me."

Isaiah 25:8-9 "⁸He will swallow up death in victory; and the Lord GOD will wipe away tears from off all faces; and the rebuke of his people shall he take away from off all the earth: for the LORD hath spoken it. ⁹And it shall be said in that day, Lo, this is our God; we have waited for him, and he will save us: this is the LORD; we have waited for him, we will be glad and rejoice in his salvation."

Isaiah 33:22 "For the LORD is our judge, the LORD is our lawgiver, the LORD is our king; he will save us."

Isaiah 43:12 "I have declared, and have saved, and I have shewed, when there was no strange god among you: therefore ye are my witnesses, saith the LORD, that I am God."

Isaiah 45:22 "Look unto me, and be ye saved, all the ends of the earth: for I am God, and there is none else."

Isaiah 59:1 "Behold, the LORD's hand is not shortened, that it cannot save; neither his ear heavy, that it cannot hear."

Jeremiah 17:14 "Heal me, O LORD, and I shall be healed; save me, and I shall be saved: for thou art my praise."

Jeremiah 30:1-11 "¹The word that came to Jeremiah from the LORD, saying, ²Thus speaketh the LORD God of Israel, saying, Write thee all the words that I have spoken unto thee in a book. ³For, lo, the days come, saith the LORD, that I will bring again the captivity of my people Israel and Judah, saith the LORD: and I will cause them to return to the land that I gave to their fathers, and they shall possess it. ⁴And these are the words that the LORD spake concerning Israel and concerning Judah. ⁵For thus saith the LORD; We have heard a voice of trembling, of fear, and not of peace. ⁶Ask ye now, and see whether a man doth travail with child? wherefore do I see every man with his hands on his loins, as a woman in travail, and all faces are turned into paleness? ⁷Alas! for that day is great, so that none is like it: it is even the time of Jacob's trouble; but he shall be saved out of it. ⁸For it shall come to pass in that day, saith the LORD of hosts, that I will break his yoke from off thy neck, and will burst thy bonds, and strangers shall no more serve themselves of him: ⁹But they

shall serve the LORD their God, and David their king, whom I will raise up unto them. ¹⁰Therefore fear thou not, O my servant Jacob, saith the LORD; neither be dismayed, O Israel: for, lo, I will save thee from afar, and thy seed from the land of their captivity; and Jacob shall return, and shall be in rest, and be quiet, and none shall make him afraid. ¹¹For I am with thee, saith the LORD, to save thee: though I make a full end of all nations whither I have scattered thee, yet will I not make a full end of thee: but I will correct thee in measure, and will not leave thee altogether unpunished."

Matthew 1:20-21 "²⁰But while he thought on these things, behold, the angel of the Lord appeared unto him in a dream, saying, Joseph, thou son of David, fear not to take unto thee Mary thy wife: for that which is conceived in her is of the Holy Ghost. ²¹And she shall bring forth a son, and thou shalt call his name JESUS: for he shall save his people from their sins."

Luke 1:68-71 "⁶⁸Blessed be the Lord God of Israel; for he hath visited and redeemed his people, ⁶⁹And hath raised up an horn of salvation for us in the house of his servant David; ⁷⁰As he spake by the mouth of his holy prophets, which have been since the world began: ⁷¹That we should be saved from our enemies, and from the hand of all that hate us."

1 Thessalonians 5:9-10 "⁹For God hath not appointed us to wrath, but to obtain salvation by our Lord Jesus Christ, ¹⁰Who died for us, that, whether we wake or sleep, we should live together with him."

Titus 3:3-5 "³For we ourselves also were sometimes foolish, disobedient, deceived, serving divers lusts and pleasures, living in malice and envy, hateful, and hating one another. ⁴But after that the kindness and love of God our Saviour toward man appeared, ⁵Not by works of righteousness which we have done, but according to his mercy he saved us, by the washing of regeneration, and renewing of the Holy Ghost."

James 4:10-12 "¹⁰Humble yourselves in the sight of the Lord, and he shall lift you up. ¹¹Speak not evil one of another, brethren. He that speaketh evil of his brother, and judgeth his brother, speaketh evil of the law, and judgeth the law: but if thou judge the law, thou art not a doer of the law, but a judge. ¹²There is one lawgiver, who is able to save and to destroy: who art thou that judgest another?"

The Salvation Of Israel

Psalm 14:7 "Oh that the salvation of Israel were come out of Zion! when the LORD bringeth back the captivity of his people, Jacob shall rejoice, and Israel shall be glad."

Psalm 53:6 "Oh that the salvation of Israel were come out of Zion! When God bringeth back the captivity of his people, Jacob shall rejoice, and Israel shall be glad."

Jeremiah 3:23 "Truly in vain is salvation hoped for from the hills, and from the multitude of mountains: truly in the LORD our God is the salvation of Israel."

Romans 11:1-32 "¹I say then, Hath God cast away his people? God forbid. For I also am an Israelite, of the seed of Abraham, of the tribe of Benjamin. ²God hath not cast away his people which he foreknew. Wot ye not what the scripture saith of Elias? how he maketh intercession to God against Israel, saying, ³Lord, they have killed thy prophets, and digged down thine altars; and I am left alone, and they seek my life. ⁴But what saith the answer of God unto him? I have reserved to myself seven thousand men, who have not bowed the knee to the image of Baal. ⁵Even so then at this present time also there is a remnant according to the election of grace. ⁶And if by grace, then is it no more of works: otherwise grace is no more grace. But if it be of works, then is it no more grace: otherwise work is no more work. ⁷What then? Israel hath not obtained that which he seeketh for; but the election hath obtained it, and the rest were blinded ⁸(According as it is written, God hath given them the spirit of slumber, eyes that they should not see, and ears that they should not hear;) unto this day. ⁹And David saith, Let their table be made a snare, and a trap, and a stumbling block, and a recompence unto them: ¹⁰Let their eyes be darkened, that they may not see, and bow down their back alway. ¹¹I say then, Have they stumbled that they should fall? God forbid: but rather through their fall salvation is come unto the Gentiles, for to provoke them to jealousy. ¹²Now if the fall of them be the riches of the world, and the diminishing of them the riches of the Gentiles; how much more their fulness? ¹³For I speak to you Gentiles, inasmuch as I am the apostle of the Gentiles, I magnify mine office: ¹⁴If by any means I may provoke to emulation them which are my flesh, and might save some of them. ¹⁵For if the casting away of them be the reconciling of the world, what shall the receiving of them be, but life from the dead? ¹⁶For if the firstfruit be holy, the lump is also holy: and if the root be holy, so are the branches. ¹⁷And if some of the branches be broken off, and thou, being a wild olive tree, wert graffed in among them, and with them partakest of the root and fatness of the olive tree; ¹⁸Boast not against the branches. But if thou boast, thou bearest not the root, but the root thee. ¹⁹Thou wilt say then, The branches were broken off, that I might be graffed in. ²⁰Well; because of unbelief they were broken off, and thou standest by faith. Be not highminded, but fear: ²¹For if God spared not the natural branches, take heed lest he also spare not thee. ²²Behold therefore the goodness and severity of God: on them which fell, severity; but toward thee, goodness, if thou continue in his goodness: otherwise thou also shalt be cut off. ²³And they also, if they abide not still in unbelief, shall be graffed in: for God is able to graff them in again. ²⁴For if thou wert cut out of the olive tree which is wild by nature, and wert graffed contrary to nature into a good olive tree: how much more shall these, which be the natural branches, be graffed into their own olive tree? ²⁵For I would not, brethren, that ye should be ignorant of this mystery, lest ye should be wise in your own conceits; that blindness in part is happened to Israel, until the fulness of the Gentiles be come in. ²⁶And so all Israel shall be saved: as it is written, There shall come out of Sion the Deliverer, and shall turn away ungodliness from Jacob: ²⁷For this is my covenant unto them, when I shall take away their sins. ²⁸As concerning the gospel, they are enemies for your sakes: but as touching the election, they are beloved for the fathers' sakes. ²⁹For the gifts and calling of God are without repentance. ³⁰For as ye in times past have not believed God, yet have now obtained mercy through their unbelief: ³¹Even so have these also now not believed, that through your mercy they also may obtain mercy. ³²For God hath concluded them all in unbelief, that he might have mercy upon all."

The Salvation Of The Lord

Psalm 98:2 "The LORD hath made known his salvation: his righteousness hath he openly shewed in the sight of the heathen."

Isaiah 46:9-13 "⁹Remember the former things of old: for I am God, and there is none else; I am God, and there is none like me, ¹⁰Declaring the end from the beginning, and from ancient times the things that are not yet done, saying, My counsel shall stand, and I will do all my pleasure: ¹¹Calling a ravenous bird from the east, the man that executeth my counsel from a far country: yea, I have spoken it, I will also bring it to pass; I have purposed it, I will also do it. ¹²Hearken unto me, ye stouthearted, that are far from righteousness: ¹³I bring near my righteousness; it shall not be far off, and my salvation shall not tarry: and I will place salvation in Zion for Israel my glory."

Isaiah 51:3-8 "³For the LORD shall comfort Zion: he will comfort all her waste places; and he will make her wilderness like Eden, and her desert like the garden of the LORD; joy and gladness shall be found therein, thanksgiving, and the voice of melody. ⁴Hearken unto me, my people; and give ear unto me, O my nation: for a law shall proceed from me, and I will make my judgment to rest for a light of the people. ⁵My righteousness is near; my salvation is gone forth, and mine arms shall judge the people; the isles shall wait upon me, and on mine arm shall they trust. ⁶Lift up your eyes to the heavens, and look upon the earth beneath: for the heavens shall vanish away like smoke, and the earth shall wax old like a garment, and they that dwell therein shall die in like manner: but my salvation shall be for ever, and my righteousness shall not be abolished. ⁷Hearken unto me, ye that know righteousness, the people in whose heart is my law; fear ye not the reproach of men, neither be ye afraid of their revilings. ⁸For the moth shall eat them up like a garment, and the worm shall eat them like wool: but my righteousness shall be for ever, and my salvation from generation to generation."

Isaiah 56:1 "Thus saith the LORD, Keep ye judgment, and do justice: for my salvation is near to come, and my righteousness to be revealed."

Luke 3:4-6 "⁴As it is written in the book of the words of Esaias the prophet, saying, The voice of one crying in the wilderness, Prepare ye the way of the Lord, make his paths straight. ⁵Every valley shall be filled, and every mountain and hill shall be brought low; and the crooked shall be made straight, and the rough ways shall be made smooth; ⁶And all flesh shall see the salvation of God."

Acts 28:28 "Be it known therefore unto you, that the salvation of God is sent unto the Gentiles, and that they will hear it."

The Salvation Of The Righteous

Psalm 37:39 "But the salvation of the righteous is of the LORD: he is their strength in the time of trouble."

Those That Are Saved

1 Corinthians 1:18 "For the preaching of the cross is to them that perish foolishness; but unto us which are saved it is the power of God."

What Cannot Save

Deuteronomy 32:37-38 "³⁷And he shall say, Where are their gods, their rock in whom they trusted, ³⁸Which did eat the fat of their sacrifices, and drank the wine of their drink offerings? let them rise up and help you, and be your protection."

Judges 10:11-14 "¹¹And the LORD said unto the children of Israel, Did not I deliver you from the Egyptians, and from the Amorites, from the children of Ammon, and from the Philistines? ¹²The Zidonians also, and the Amalekites, and the Maonites, did oppress you; and ye cried to me, and I delivered you out of their hand. ¹³Yet ye have forsaken me, and served other gods: wherefore I will deliver you no more. ¹⁴Go and cry unto the gods which ye have chosen; let them deliver you in the time of your tribulation."

Isaiah 45:20 "Assemble yourselves and come; draw near together, ye that are escaped of the nations: they have no knowledge that set up the wood of their graven image, and pray unto a god that cannot save."

Isaiah 46:6-7 "⁶They lavish gold out of the bag, and weigh silver in the balance, and hire a goldsmith; and he maketh it a god: they fall down, yea, they worship. ⁷They bear him upon the shoulder, they carry him, and set him in his place, and he standeth; from his place shall he not remove: yea, one shall cry unto him, yet can he not answer, nor save him out of his trouble."

Isaiah 47:13 "Thou art wearied in the multitude of thy counsels. Let now the astrologers, the stargazers, the monthly prognosticators, stand up, and save thee from these things that shall come upon thee."

Jeremiah 2:28 "But where are thy gods that thou hast made thee? let them arise, if they can save thee in the time of thy trouble: for according to the number of thy cities are thy gods, O Judah."

Jeremiah 11:12 "Then shall the cities of Judah and inhabitants of Jerusalem go, and cry unto the gods unto whom they offer incense: but they shall not save them at all in the time of their trouble."

Hosea 13:4-11 "⁴Yet I am the LORD thy God from the land of Egypt, and thou shalt know no god but me: for there is no saviour beside me. ⁵I did know thee in the wilderness, in the land of great drought. ⁶According to their pasture, so were they filled; they were filled, and their heart was exalted; therefore have they forgotten me. ⁷Therefore I will be unto them as a lion: as a leopard by the way will I observe them: ⁸I will meet them as a bear that is bereaved of her whelps, and will rend the caul of their heart, and there will I devour them like a lion: the wild beast shall tear them. ⁹O Israel, thou hast destroyed thyself; but in me is thine help. ¹⁰I will be thy king: where is any other that may save thee in all thy cities? and thy judges of whom thou saidst, Give me a king and princes? ¹¹I gave thee a king in mine anger, and took him away in my wrath."

What Saves
Luke 7:50 "And he said to the woman, Thy faith hath saved thee; go in peace."

Luke 18:42 "And Jesus said unto him, Receive thy sight: thy faith hath saved thee."

Romans 8:24-25 "²⁴For we are saved by hope: but hope that is seen is not hope: for what a man seeth, why doth he yet hope for? ²⁵But if we hope for that we see not, then do we with patience wait for it."

1 Corinthians 15:1-2 "¹Moreover, brethren, I declare unto you the gospel which I preached unto you, which also ye have received, and wherein ye stand; ²By which also ye are saved, if ye keep in memory what I preached unto you, unless ye have believed in vain."

Ephesians 2:5 "Even when we were dead in sins, hath quickened us together with Christ, (by grace ye are saved;)"

Ephesians 2:8-10 "⁸For by grace are ye saved through faith; and that not of yourselves: it is the gift of God: ⁹Not of works, lest any man should boast. ¹⁰For we are his workmanship, created in Christ Jesus unto good works, which God hath before ordained that we should walk in them."

Titus 2:11 "For the grace of God that bringeth salvation hath appeared to all men."

James 1:20-21 "²⁰For the wrath of man worketh not the righteousness of God. ²¹Wherefore lay apart all filthiness and superfluity of naughtiness, and receive with meekness the engrafted word, which is able to save your souls."

James 5:15 "And the prayer of faith shall save the sick, and the Lord shall raise him up; and if he have committed sins, they shall be forgiven him."

1 Peter 3:20-21 "²⁰Which sometime were disobedient, when once the longsuffering of God waited in the days of Noah, while the ark was a preparing, wherein few, that is, eight souls were saved by water. ²¹The like figure whereunto even baptism doth also now save us (not the putting away of the filth of the flesh, but the answer of a good conscience toward God,) by the resurrection of Jesus Christ."

Where Salvation Comes From
Psalm 62:1-2 "¹Truly my soul waiteth upon God: from him cometh my salvation. ²He only is my rock and my salvation; he is my defence; I shall not be greatly moved."

Where Salvation Is
Psalm 118:15 "The voice of rejoicing and salvation is in the tabernacles of the righteous: the right hand of the LORD doeth valiantly."

Who Salvation Is Far From
Psalm 119:155 "Salvation is far from the wicked: for they seek not thy statutes."

Who Shall Be Saved
2 Samuel 22:4-7 "⁴I will call on the LORD, who is worthy to be praised: so shall I be saved from mine enemies. ⁵When the waves of death compassed me, the floods of ungodly men made me afraid; ⁶The sorrows of hell compassed me about; the snares of death prevented me; ⁷In my distress I

called upon the LORD, and cried to my God: and he did hear my voice out of his temple, and my cry did enter into his ears."

2 Samuel 22:21-28 "²¹The LORD rewarded me according to my righteousness: according to the cleanness of my hands hath he recompensed me. ²²For I have kept the ways of the LORD, and have not wickedly departed from my God. ²³For all his judgments were before me: and as for his statutes, I did not depart from them. ²⁴I was also upright before him, and have kept myself from mine iniquity. ²⁵Therefore the LORD hath recompensed me according to my righteousness; according to my cleanness in his eye sight. ²⁶With the merciful thou wilt shew thyself merciful, and with the upright man thou wilt shew thyself upright. ²⁷With the pure thou wilt shew thyself pure; and with the froward thou wilt shew thyself unsavoury. ²⁸And the afflicted people thou wilt save: but thine eyes are upon the haughty, that thou mayest bring them down."

Job 5:8-16 "⁸I would seek unto God, and unto God would I commit my cause: ⁹Which doeth great things and unsearchable; marvellous things without number: ¹⁰Who giveth rain upon the earth, and sendeth waters upon the fields: ¹¹To set up on high those that be low; that those which mourn may be exalted to safety. ¹²He disappointeth the devices of the crafty, so that their hands cannot perform their enterprise. ¹³He taketh the wise in their own craftiness: and the counsel of the froward is carried headlong. ¹⁴They meet with darkness in the daytime, and grope in the noonday as in the night. ¹⁵But he saveth the poor from the sword, from their mouth, and from the hand of the mighty. ¹⁶So the poor hath hope, and iniquity stoppeth her mouth."

Psalm 7:10 "My defence is of God, which saveth the upright in heart."

Psalm 17:6-7 "⁶I have called upon thee, for thou wilt hear me, O God: incline thine ear unto me, and hear my speech. ⁷Shew thy marvellous lovingkindness, O thou that savest by thy right hand them which put their trust in thee from those that rise up against them."

Psalm 18:3 "I will call upon the LORD, who is worthy to be praised: so shall I be saved from mine enemies."

Psalm 20:6 "Now know I that the LORD saveth his anointed; he will hear him from his holy heaven with the saving strength of his right hand."

Psalm 34:6 "This poor man cried, and the LORD heard him, and saved him out of all his troubles."

Psalm 34:18 "The LORD is nigh unto them that are of a broken heart; and saveth such as be of a contrite spirit."

Psalm 37:40 "And the LORD shall help them and deliver them: he shall deliver them from the wicked, and save them, because they trust in him."

Psalm 55:16 "As for me, I will call upon God; and the LORD shall save me."

Psalm 107:8-13 "⁸Oh that men would praise the LORD for his goodness, and for his wonderful works to the children of men! ⁹For he satisfieth the longing soul, and filleth the hungry soul with goodness. ¹⁰Such as sit in darkness and in the shadow of death, being bound in affliction and iron; ¹¹Because they rebelled against the words of God, and contemned the counsel of the most High: ¹²Therefore he brought down their heart with labour; they fell down, and there was none to help. ¹³Then they cried unto the LORD in their trouble, and he saved them out of their distresses."

Psalm 107:17-19 "¹⁷Fools because of their transgression, and because of their iniquities, are afflicted. ¹⁸Their soul abhorreth all manner of meat; and they draw near unto the gates of death. ¹⁹Then they cry unto the LORD in their trouble, and he saveth them out of their distresses."

Psalm 145:18-19 "¹⁸The LORD is nigh unto all them that call upon him, to all that call upon him in truth. ¹⁹He will fulfil the desire of them that fear him: he also will hear their cry, and will save them."

Psalm 149:4 "For the LORD taketh pleasure in his people: he will beautify the meek with salvation."

Proverbs 20:22 "Say not thou, I will recompense evil; but wait on the LORD, and he shall save thee."

Proverbs 28:18 "Whoso walketh uprightly shall be saved: but he that is perverse in his ways shall fall at once."

Daniel 6:23 "Then was the king exceeding glad for him, and commanded that they should take Daniel up out of the den. So Daniel was taken up out of the den, and no manner of hurt was found upon him, because he believed in his God."

Matthew 10:16-22 "16Behold, I send you forth as sheep in the midst of wolves: be ye therefore wise as serpents, and harmless as doves. 17But beware of men: for they will deliver you up to the councils, and they will scourge you in their synagogues; 18And ye shall be brought before governors and kings for my sake, for a testimony against them and the Gentiles. 19But when they deliver you up, take no thought how or what ye shall speak: for it shall be given you in that same hour what ye shall speak. 20For it is not ye that speak, but the Spirit of your Father which speaketh in you. 21And the brother shall deliver up the brother to death, and the father the child: and the children shall rise up against their parents, and cause them to be put to death. 22And ye shall be hated of all men for my name's sake: but he that endureth to the end shall be saved."

Matthew 24:8-13 "8All these are the beginning of sorrows. 9Then shall they deliver you up to be afflicted, and shall kill you: and ye shall be hated of all nations for my name's sake. 10And then shall many be offended, and shall betray one another, and shall hate one another. 11And many false prophets shall rise, and shall deceive many. 12And because iniquity shall abound, the love of many shall wax cold. 13But he that shall endure unto the end, the same shall be saved."

Mark 13:12-13 "12Now the brother shall betray the brother to death, and the father the son; and children shall rise up against their parents, and shall cause them to be put to death. 13And ye shall be hated of all men for my name's sake: but he that shall endure unto the end, the same shall be saved."

Mark 16:16-19 "16He that believeth and is baptized shall be saved; but he that believeth not shall be damned. 17And these signs shall follow them that believe; In my name shall they cast out devils; they shall speak with new tongues; 18They shall take up serpents; and if they drink any deadly thing, it shall not hurt them; they shall lay hands on the sick, and they shall recover. 19So then after the Lord had spoken unto them, he was received up into heaven, and sat on the right hand of God."

Acts 2:21 "And it shall come to pass, that whosoever shall call on the name of the Lord shall be saved."

Acts 15:6-11 "6And the apostles and elders came together for to consider of this matter. 7And when there had been much disputing, Peter rose up, and said unto them, Men and brethren, ye know how that a good while ago God made choice among us, that the Gentiles by my mouth should hear the word of the gospel, and believe. 8And God, which knoweth the hearts, bare them witness, giving them the Holy Ghost, even as he did unto us; 9And put no difference between us and them, purifying their hearts by faith. 10Now therefore why tempt ye God, to put a yoke upon the neck of the disciples, which neither our fathers nor we were able to bear? 11But we believe that through the grace of the Lord Jesus Christ we shall be saved, even as they."

Acts 16:31 "And they said, Believe on the Lord Jesus Christ, and thou shalt be saved, and thy house."

Romans 5:6-11 "6For when we were yet without strength, in due time Christ died for the ungodly. 7For scarcely for a righteous man will one die: yet peradventure for a good man some would even dare to die. 8But God commendeth his love toward us, in that, while we were yet sinners, Christ died for us. 9Much more then, being now justified by his blood, we shall be saved from wrath through him. 10For if, when we were enemies, we were reconciled to God by the death of his Son, much more, being reconciled, we shall be saved by his life. 11And not only so, but we also joy in God through our Lord Jesus Christ, by whom we have now received the atonement."

Romans 9:27 "Esaias also crieth concerning Israel, Though the number of the children of Israel be as the sand of the sea, a remnant shall be saved."

Romans 10:9-10 "9That if thou shalt confess with thy mouth the Lord Jesus, and shalt believe in thine heart that God hath raised him from the dead, thou shalt be saved. [10]For with the heart man believeth unto righteousness; and with the mouth confession is made unto salvation."

Romans 10:12-13 "[12]For there is no difference between the Jew and the Greek: for the same Lord over all is rich unto all that call upon him. [13]For whosoever shall call upon the name of the Lord shall be saved."

Romans 11:26 "And so all Israel shall be saved: as it is written, There shall come out of Sion the Deliverer, and shall turn away ungodliness from Jacob."

1 Corinthians 1:21 "For after that in the wisdom of God the world by wisdom knew not God, it pleased God by the foolishness of preaching to save them that believe."

1 Corinthians 15:1-2 "[1]Moreover, brethren, I declare unto you the gospel which I preached unto you, which also ye have received, and wherein ye stand; [2]By which also ye are saved, if ye keep in memory what I preached unto you, unless ye have believed in vain."

1 Timothy 2:12-15 "[12]But I suffer not a woman to teach, nor to usurp authority over the man, but to be in silence. [13]For Adam was first formed, then Eve. [14]And Adam was not deceived, but the woman being deceived was in the transgression. [15]Notwithstanding she shall be saved in childbearing, if they continue in faith and charity and holiness with sobriety."

2 Timothy 2:10-11 "[10]Therefore I endure all things for the elect's sakes, that they may also obtain the salvation which is in Christ Jesus with eternal glory. [11]It is a faithful saying: For if we be dead with him, we shall also live with him."

Hebrews 7:22-25 "[22]By so much was Jesus made a surety of a better testament. [23]And they truly were many priests, because they were not suffered to continue by reason of death: [24]But this man, because he continueth ever, hath an unchangeable priesthood. [25]Wherefore he is able also to save them to the uttermost that come unto God by him, seeing he ever liveth to make intercession for them."

Hebrews 9:28 "So Christ was once offered to bear the sins of many; and unto them that look for him shall he appear the second time without sin unto salvation."

Who Shall Save A Soul

James 5:20 "Let him know, that he which converteth the sinner from the error of his way shall save a soul from death, and shall hide a multitude of sins."

Who Shall Save Their Life

Mark 8:31-35 "[31]And he began to teach them, that the Son of man must suffer many things, and be rejected of the elders, and of the chief priests, and scribes, and be killed, and after three days rise again. [32]And he spake that saying openly. And Peter took him, and began to rebuke him. [33]But when he had turned about and looked on his disciples, he rebuked Peter, saying, Get thee behind me, Satan: for thou savourest not the things that be of God, but the things that be of men. [34]And when he had called the people unto him with his disciples also, he said unto them, Whosoever will come after me, let him deny himself, and take up his cross, and follow me. [35]For whosoever will save his life shall lose it; but whosoever shall lose his life for my sake and the gospel's, the same shall save it."

Luke 9:22-25 "[22]Saying, The Son of man must suffer many things, and be rejected of the elders and chief priests and scribes, and be slain, and be raised the third day. [23]And he said to them all, If any man will come after me, let him deny himself, and take up his cross daily, and follow me. [24]For whosoever will save his life shall lose it: but whosoever will lose his life for my sake, the same shall save it. [25]For what is a man advantaged, if he gain the whole world, and lose himself, or be cast away?"

Luke 17:33 "Whosoever shall seek to save his life shall lose it; and whosoever shall lose his life shall preserve it."

John 12:25 "He that loveth his life shall lose it; and he that hateth his life in this world shall keep it unto life eternal."

Who Will See The Salvation Of God

Psalm 50:16-23 "[16]But unto the wicked God saith, What hast thou to do to declare my statutes, or that thou shouldest take my covenant in thy mouth? [17]Seeing thou hatest instruction, and castest my words behind thee. [18]When thou sawest a thief, then thou consentedst with him, and hast been partaker with adulterers. 19Thou givest thy mouth to evil, and thy tongue frameth deceit. 20Thou sittest and speakest against thy brother; thou slanderest thine own mother's son. 21These things hast thou done, and I kept silence; thou thoughtest that I was altogether such an one as thyself: but I will reprove thee, and set them in order before thine eyes. 22Now consider this, ye that forget God, lest I tear you in pieces, and there be none to deliver. 23Whoso offereth praise glorifieth me: and to him that ordereth his conversation aright will I shew the salvation of God."

Psalm 91:9-16 "9Because thou hast made the LORD, which is my refuge, even the most High, thy habitation; 10There shall no evil befall thee, neither shall any plague come nigh thy dwelling. 11For he shall give his angels charge over thee, to keep thee in all thy ways. 12They shall bear thee up in their hands, lest thou dash thy foot against a stone. 13Thou shalt tread upon the lion and adder: the young lion and the dragon shalt thou trample under feet. 14Because he hath set his love upon me, therefore will I deliver him: I will set him on high, because he hath known my name. 15He shall call upon me, and I will answer him: I will be with him in trouble; I will deliver him, and honour him. 16With long life will I satisfy him, and shew him my salvation."

SANCTIFICATION

Everyone Being Sanctified
Through The Blood Of Jesus Christ
1 Corinthians 6:9-11 "9Know ye not that the unrighteous shall not inherit the kingdom of God? Be not deceived: neither fornicators, nor idolaters, nor adulterers, nor effeminate, nor abusers of themselves with mankind, 10Nor thieves, nor covetous, nor drunkards, nor revilers, nor extortioners, shall inherit the kingdom of God. 11And such were some of you: but ye are washed, but ye are sanctified, but ye are justified in the name of the Lord Jesus, and by the Spirit of our God."

Hebrews 10:1-14 "1For the law having a shadow of good things to come, and not the very image of the things, can never with those sacrifices which they offered year by year continually make the comers thereunto perfect. 2For then would they not have ceased to be offered? because that the worshippers once purged should have had no more conscience of sins. 3But in those sacrifices there is a remembrance again made of sins every year. 4For it is not possible that the blood of bulls and of goats should take away sins. 5Wherefore when he cometh into the world, he saith, Sacrifice and offering thou wouldest not, but a body hast thou prepared me: 6In burnt offerings and sacrifices for sin thou hast had no pleasure. 7Then said I, Lo, I come (in the volume of the book it is written of me,) to do thy will, O God. 8Above when he said, Sacrifice and offering and burnt offerings and offering for sin thou wouldest not, neither hadst pleasure therein; which are offered by the law; 9Then said he, Lo, I come to do thy will, O God. He taketh away the first, that he may establish the second. 10By the which will we are sanctified through the offering of the body of Jesus Christ once for all. 11And every priest standeth daily ministering and offering oftentimes the same sacrifices, which can never take away sins: 12But this man, after he had offered one sacrifice for sins for ever, sat down on the right hand of God; 13From henceforth expecting till his enemies be made his footstool. 14For by one offering he hath perfected for ever them that are sanctified."

Hebrews 13:10-12 "10We have an altar, whereof they have no right to eat which serve the tabernacle. 11For the bodies of those beasts, whose blood is brought into the sanctuary by the high priest for sin, are burned without the camp. 12Wherefore Jesus also, that he might sanctify the people with his own blood, suffered without the gate."

Husbands And Wives Being Sanctified
By Their Spouses
1 Corinthians 7:10-16 "10And unto the married I command, yet not I, but the Lord, Let not the wife depart from her husband: 11But and if she depart, let her remain unmarried, or be reconciled to her husband: and let not the husband put away his wife. 12But to the rest speak I, not the Lord: If any brother hath a wife that believeth not, and she be pleased to dwell with him, let him not put her away. 13And the woman which hath an husband that believeth not, and if he be pleased to dwell with her, let her not leave him. 14For the unbelieving husband is sanctified by the wife, and the

unbelieving wife is sanctified by the husband: else were your children unclean; but now are they holy. [15]But if the unbelieving depart, let him depart. A brother or a sister is not under bondage in such cases: but God hath called us to peace. [16]For what knowest thou, O wife, whether thou shalt save thy husband? or how knowest thou, O man, whether thou shalt save thy wife?"

Jesus Christ Being Sanctified
By God The Father

John 10:34-36 "[34]Jesus answered them, Is it not written in your law, I said, Ye are gods? [35]If he called them gods, unto whom the word of God came, and the scripture cannot be broken; [36]Say ye of him, whom the Father hath sanctified, and sent into the world, Thou blasphemest; because I said, I am the Son of God?"

Sanctifying The Lord

Isaiah 8:12-13 "[12]Say ye not, A confederacy, to all them to whom this people shall say, A confederacy; neither fear ye their fear, nor be afraid. [13]Sanctify the LORD of hosts himself; and let him be your fear, and let him be your dread."

Sanctifying Yourself

Leviticus 11:44 "For I am the LORD your God: ye shall therefore sanctify yourselves, and ye shall be holy; for I am holy: neither shall ye defile yourselves with any manner of creeping thing that creepeth upon the earth."

Leviticus 20:7 "Sanctify yourselves therefore, and be ye holy: for I am the LORD your God."

Joshua 3:5 "And Joshua said unto the people, Sanctify yourselves: for to morrow the LORD will do wonders among you."

The Lord Being Sanctified

Isaiah 5:16 "But the LORD of hosts shall be exalted in judgment, and God that is holy shall be sanctified in righteousness."

Ezekiel 28:25 "Thus saith the Lord GOD; When I shall have gathered the house of Israel from the people among whom they are scattered, and shall be sanctified in them in the sight of the heathen, then shall they dwell in their land that I have given to my servant Jacob."

Ezekiel 36:22-23 "[22]Therefore say unto the house of Israel, Thus saith the Lord GOD; I do not this

for your sakes, O house of Israel, but for mine holy name's sake, which ye have profaned among the heathen, whither ye went. [23]And I will sanctify my great name, which was profaned among the heathen, which ye have profaned in the midst of them; and the heathen shall know that I am the LORD, saith the Lord GOD, when I shall be sanctified in you before their eyes."

Ezekiel 38:14-16 "[14]Therefore, son of man, prophesy and say unto Gog, Thus saith the Lord GOD; In that day when my people of Israel dwelleth safely, shalt thou not know it? [15]And thou shalt come from thy place out of the north parts, thou, and many people with thee, all of them riding upon horses, a great company, and a mighty army: [16]And thou shalt come up against my people of Israel, as a cloud to cover the land; it shall be in the latter days, and I will bring thee against my land, that the heathen may know me, when I shall be sanctified in thee, O Gog, before their eyes."

Ezekiel 39:25-27 "[25]Therefore thus saith the Lord GOD; Now will I bring again the captivity of Jacob, and have mercy upon the whole house of Israel, and will be jealous for my holy name; [26]After that they have borne their shame, and all their trespasses whereby they have trespassed against me, when they dwelt safely in their land, and none made them afraid. [27]When I have brought them again from the people, and gathered them out of their enemies' lands, and am sanctified in them in the sight of many nations."

The Lord Sanctifying

Exodus 31:12-13 "[12]And the LORD spake unto Moses, saying, [13]Speak thou also unto the children of Israel, saying, Verily my sabbaths ye shall keep: for it is a sign between me and you throughout your generations; that ye may know that I am the LORD that doth sanctify you."

Leviticus 20:8 "And ye shall keep my statutes, and do them: I am the LORD which sanctify you."

Leviticus 21:8 "Thou shalt sanctify him therefore; for he offereth the bread of thy God: he shall be holy unto thee: for I the LORD, which sanctify you, am holy."

Leviticus 21:15 "Neither shall he profane his seed among his people: for I the LORD do sanctify him."

Jeremiah 1:4-5 "⁴Then the word of the LORD came unto me, saying, ⁵Before I formed thee in the belly I knew thee; and before thou camest forth out of the womb I sanctified thee, and I ordained thee a prophet unto the nations."

Ezekiel 36:22-23 "²²Therefore say unto the house of Israel, Thus saith the Lord GOD; I do not this for your sakes, O house of Israel, but for mine holy name's sake, which ye have profaned among the heathen, whither ye went. ²³And I will sanctify my great name, which was profaned among the heathen, which ye have profaned in the midst of them; and the heathen shall know that I am the LORD, saith the Lord GOD, when I shall be sanctified in you before their eyes."

Ezekiel 38:23 "Thus will I magnify myself, and sanctify myself; and I will be known in the eyes of many nations, and they shall know that I am the LORD."

John 17:1-19 "¹These words spake Jesus, and lifted up his eyes to heaven, and said, Father, the hour is come; glorify thy Son, that thy Son also may glorify thee: ²As thou hast given him power over all flesh, that he should give eternal life to as many as thou hast given him. ³And this is life eternal, that they might know thee the only true God, and Jesus Christ, whom thou hast sent. ⁴I have glorified thee on the earth: I have finished the work which thou gavest me to do. ⁵And now, O Father, glorify thou me with thine own self with the glory which I had with thee before the world was. ⁶I have manifested thy name unto the men which thou gavest me out of the world: thine they were, and thou gavest them me; and they have kept thy word. ⁷Now they have known that all things whatsoever thou hast given me are of thee. ⁸For I have given unto them the words which thou gavest me; and they have received them, and have known surely that I came out from thee, and they have believed that thou didst send me. ⁹I pray for them: I pray not for the world, but for them which thou hast given me; for they are thine. ¹⁰And all mine are thine, and thine are mine; and I am glorified in them. ¹¹And now I am no more in the world, but these are in the world, and I come to thee. Holy Father, keep through thine own name those whom thou hast given me, that they may be one, as we are. ¹²While I was with them in the world, I kept them in thy name: those that thou gavest me I have kept, and none of them is lost, but the son of perdition; that the scripture might be fulfilled. ¹³And now come I to thee; and these things I speak in the world, that they might have my joy fulfilled in themselves. ¹⁴I have given them thy word; and the world hath hated them, because they are not of the world, even as I am not of the world. ¹⁵I pray not that thou shouldest take them out of the world, but that thou shouldest keep them from the evil. ¹⁶They are not of the world, even as I am not of the world. ¹⁷Sanctify them through thy truth: thy word is truth. ¹⁸As thou hast sent me into the world, even so have I also sent them into the world. ¹⁹And for their sakes I sanctify myself, that they also might be sanctified through the truth."

1 Thessalonians 5:23 "And the very God of peace sanctify you wholly; and I pray God your whole spirit and soul and body be preserved blameless unto the coming of our Lord Jesus Christ."

Hebrews 13:12 "Wherefore Jesus also, that he might sanctify the people with his own blood, suffered without the gate."

Those That Are Sanctified

1 Corinthians 1:2 "Unto the church of God which is at Corinth, to them that are sanctified in Christ Jesus, called to be saints, with all that in every place call upon the name of Jesus Christ our Lord, both theirs and ours."

Hebrews 2:9-11 "⁹But we see Jesus, who was made a little lower than the angels for the suffering of death, crowned with glory and honour; that he by the grace of God should taste death for every man. ¹⁰For it became him, for whom are all things, and by whom are all things, in bringing many sons unto glory, to make the captain of their salvation perfect through sufferings. ¹¹For both he that sanctifieth and they who are sanctified are all of one: for which cause he is not ashamed to call them brethren."

Hebrews 10:10-14 "¹⁰By the which will we are sanctified through the offering of the body of Jesus Christ once for all. ¹¹And every priest standeth daily ministering and offering oftentimes the same sacrifices, which can never take away sins: ¹²But this man, after he had offered one sacrifice for sins for ever, sat down on the right hand of God; ¹³From henceforth expecting till his enemies be made his footstool. ¹⁴For by one offering he hath perfected for ever them that are sanctified."

Those That Sanctify Themselves
With Abominations

Isaiah 66:15-17 "¹⁵For, behold, the LORD will come with fire, and with his chariots like a whirlwind, to render his anger with fury, and his rebuke with flames of fire. ¹⁶For by fire and by his sword will the LORD plead with all flesh: and the slain of the LORD shall be many. ¹⁷They that sanctify themselves, and purify themselves in the gardens behind one tree in the midst, eating swine's flesh, and the abomination, and the mouse, shall be consumed together, saith the LORD."

What Is Sanctified

Genesis 2:1-3 "¹Thus the heavens and the earth were finished, and all the host of them. ²And on the seventh day God ended his work which he had made; and he rested on the seventh day from all his work which he had made. ³And God blessed the seventh day, and sanctified it: because that in it he had rested from all his work which God created and made."

2 Chronicles 30:8 "Now be ye not stiffnecked, as your fathers were, but yield yourselves unto the LORD, and enter into his sanctuary, which he hath sanctified for ever: and serve the LORD your God, that the fierceness of his wrath may turn away from you."

1 Timothy 4:1-5 "¹Now the Spirit speaketh expressly, that in the latter times some shall depart from the faith, giving heed to seducing spirits, and doctrines of devils; ²Speaking lies in hypocrisy; having their conscience seared with a hot iron; ³Forbidding to marry, and commanding to abstain from meats, which God hath created to be received with thanksgiving of them which believe and know the truth. ⁴For every creature of God is good, and nothing to be refused, if it be received with thanksgiving: ⁵For it is sanctified by the word of God and prayer."

SATISFACTION

The Lord Satisfying

Psalm 91:9-16 "⁹Because thou hast made the LORD, which is my refuge, even the most High, thy habitation; ¹⁰There shall no evil befall thee,

neither shall any plague come nigh thy dwelling. ¹¹For he shall give his angels charge over thee, to keep thee in all thy ways. ¹²They shall bear thee up in their hands, lest thou dash thy foot against a stone. ¹³Thou shalt tread upon the lion and adder: the young lion and the dragon shalt thou trample under feet. ¹⁴Because he hath set his love upon me, therefore will I deliver him: I will set him on high, because he hath known my name. ¹⁵He shall call upon me, and I will answer him: I will be with him in trouble; I will deliver him, and honour him. ¹⁶With long life will I satisfy him, and shew him my salvation."

Psalm 103:1-5 "¹Bless the LORD, O my soul: and all that is within me, bless his holy name. ²Bless the LORD, O my soul, and forget not all his benefits: ³Who forgiveth all thine iniquities; who healeth all thy diseases; ⁴Who redeemeth thy life from destruction; who crowneth thee with lovingkindness and tender mercies; ⁵Who satisfieth thy mouth with good things; so that thy youth is renewed like the eagle's."

Psalm 107:8-9 "⁸Oh that men would praise the LORD for his goodness, and for his wonderful works to the children of men! ⁹For he satisfieth the longing soul, and filleth the hungry soul with goodness."

Psalm 132:13-15 "¹³For the LORD hath chosen Zion; he hath desired it for his habitation. ¹⁴This is my rest for ever: here will I dwell; for I have desired it. ¹⁵I will abundantly bless her provision: I will satisfy her poor with bread."

Isaiah 58:11 "And the LORD shall guide thee continually, and satisfy thy soul in drought, and make fat thy bones: and thou shalt be like a watered garden, and like a spring of water, whose waters fail not."

What Is Never Satisfied

Proverbs 27:20 "Hell and destruction are never full; so the eyes of man are never satisfied."

What Is Satisfied With
The Fruit Of The Lord

Psalm 104:1-13 "¹Bless the LORD, O my soul. O LORD my God, thou art very great; thou art clothed with honour and majesty. ²Who coverest thyself with light as with a garment: who stretchest out the heavens like a curtain: ³Who layeth the beams of his chambers in the waters: who maketh the clouds his chariot: who walketh upon the wings of the wind: ⁴Who maketh his angels spirits; his ministers a flaming fire: ⁵Who laid the foundations of the earth, that it should not be removed for ever. ⁶Thou coveredst it with the deep as with a garment: the waters stood above the mountains. ⁷At thy rebuke they fled; at the voice of thy thunder they hasted away. ⁸They go up by the mountains; they go down by the valleys unto the place which thou hast founded for them. ⁹Thou hast set a bound that they may not pass over; that they turn not again to cover the earth. ¹⁰He sendeth the springs into the valleys, which run among the hills. ¹¹They give drink to every beast of the field: the wild asses quench their thirst. ¹²By them shall the fowls of the heaven have their habitation, which sing among the branches. ¹³He watereth the hills from his chambers: the earth is satisfied with the fruit of thy works."

What Satisfies A Person

Proverbs 12:14 "A man shall be satisfied with good by the fruit of his mouth: and the recompence of a man's hands shall be rendered unto him."

Proverbs 18:20 "A man's belly shall be satisfied with the fruit of his mouth; and with the increase of his lips shall he be filled."

Who Eats To The Satisfying Of Their Soul

Proverbs 13:25 "The righteous eateth to the satisfying of his soul: but the belly of the wicked shall want."

Who Shall Be Satisfied

Psalm 17:13-15 "¹³Arise, O LORD, disappoint him, cast him down: deliver my soul from the wicked, which is thy sword: ¹⁴From men which are thy hand, O LORD, from men of the world, which have their portion in this life, and whose belly thou fillest with thy hid treasure: they are full of children, and leave the rest of their substance to their babes. ¹⁵As for me, I will behold thy face in righteousness: I shall be satisfied, when I awake, with thy likeness."

Psalm 22:26 "The meek shall eat and be satisfied: they shall praise the LORD that seek him: your heart shall live for ever."

Psalm 34:10 "The young lions do lack, and suffer hunger: but they that seek the LORD shall not want any good thing."

Psalm 36:7-8 "⁷How excellent is thy lovingkindness, O God! therefore the children of men put their trust under the shadow of thy wings. ⁸They shall be abundantly satisfied with the fatness of thy house; and thou shalt make them drink of the river of thy pleasures."

Psalm 37:18-19 "¹⁸The LORD knoweth the days of the upright: and their inheritance shall be for ever. ¹⁹They shall not be ashamed in the evil time: and in the days of famine they shall be satisfied."

Psalm 63:1-5 "¹O God, thou art my God; early will I seek thee: my soul thirsteth for thee, my flesh longeth for thee in a dry and thirsty land, where no water is; ²To see thy power and thy glory, so as I have seen thee in the sanctuary. ³Because thy lovingkindness is better than life, my lips shall praise thee. ⁴Thus will I bless thee while I live: I will lift up my hands in thy name. ⁵My soul shall be satisfied as with marrow and fatness; and my mouth shall praise thee with joyful lips."

Psalm 65:1-4 "¹Praise waiteth for thee, O God, in Sion: and unto thee shall the vow be performed. ²O thou that hearest prayer, unto thee shall all flesh come. ³Iniquities prevail against me: as for our transgressions, thou shalt purge them away. ⁴Blessed is the man whom thou choosest, and causest to approach unto thee, that he may dwell in thy courts: we shall be satisfied with the goodness of thy house, even of thy holy temple."

Psalm 91:9-16 "⁹Because thou hast made the LORD, which is my refuge, even the most High, thy habitation; ¹⁰There shall no evil befall thee, neither shall any plague come nigh thy dwelling. ¹¹For he shall give his angels charge over thee, to keep thee in all thy ways. ¹²They shall bear thee up in their hands, lest thou dash thy foot against a stone. ¹³Thou shalt tread upon the lion and adder: the young lion and the dragon shalt thou trample under feet. ¹⁴Because he hath set his love upon me, therefore will I deliver him: I will set him on high, because he hath known my name. ¹⁵He shall call upon me, and I will answer him: I will be with him in trouble; I will deliver him, and honour him. ¹⁶With long life will I satisfy him, and shew him my salvation."

Proverbs 12:11 "He that tilleth his land shall be satisfied with bread: but he that followeth vain persons is void of understanding."

Proverbs 13:25 "The righteous eateth to the satisfying of his soul: but the belly of the wicked shall want."

Proverbs 14:14 "The backslider in heart shall be filled with his own ways: and a good man shall be satisfied from himself."

Proverbs 19:23 "The fear of the LORD tendeth to life: and he that hath it shall abide satisfied; he shall not be visited with evil."

Proverbs 20:13 "Love not sleep, lest thou come to poverty; open thine eyes, and thou shalt be satisfied with bread."

Jeremiah 31:14 "And I will satiate the soul of the priests with fatness, and my people shall be satisfied with my goodness, saith the LORD."

Joel 2:23-26 "23Be glad then, ye children of Zion, and rejoice in the LORD your God: for he hath given you the former rain moderately, and he will cause to come down for you the rain, the former rain, and the latter rain in the first month. 24And the floors shall be full of wheat, and the fats shall overflow with wine and oil. 25And I will restore to you the years that the locust hath eaten, the cankerworm, and the caterpiller, and the palmerworm, my great army which I sent among you. 26And ye shall eat in plenty, and be satisfied, and praise the name of the LORD your God, that hath dealt wondrously with you: and my people shall never be ashamed."

Matthew 5:6 "Blessed are they which do hunger and thirst after righteousness: for they shall be filled."

Luke 6:21 "Blessed are ye that hunger now: for ye shall be filled. Blessed are ye that weep now: for ye shall laugh."

Who Shall Not Be Satisfied

Leviticus 26:13-26 "13I am the LORD your God, which brought you forth out of the land of Egypt, that ye should not be their bondmen; and I have broken the bands of your yoke, and made you go upright. 14But if ye will not hearken unto me, and will not do all these commandments; 15And if ye shall despise my statutes, or if your soul abhor my judgments, so that ye will not do all my commandments, but that ye break my covenant: 16I also will do this unto you; I will even appoint over you terror, consumption, and the burning ague, that shall consume the eyes, and cause sorrow of heart: and ye shall sow your seed in vain, for your enemies shall eat it. 17And I will set my face against you, and ye shall be slain before your enemies: they that hate you shall reign over you; and ye shall flee when none pursueth you. 18And if ye will not yet for all this hearken unto me, then I will punish you seven times more for your sins. 19And I will break the pride of your power; and I will make your heaven as iron, and your earth as brass: 20And your strength shall be spent in vain: for your land shall not yield her increase, neither shall the trees of the land yield their fruits. 21And if ye walk contrary unto me, and will not hearken unto me; I will bring seven times more plagues upon you according to your sins. 22I will also send wild beasts among you, which shall rob you of your children, and destroy your cattle, and make you few in number; and your highways shall be desolate. 23And if ye will not be reformed by me by these things, but will walk contrary unto me; 24Then will I also walk contrary unto you, and will punish you yet seven times for your sins. 25And I will bring a sword upon you, that shall avenge the quarrel of my covenant: and when ye are gathered together within your cities, I will send the pestilence among you; and ye shall be delivered into the hand of the enemy. 26And when I have broken the staff of your bread, ten women shall bake your bread in one oven, and they shall deliver you your bread again by weight: and ye shall eat, and not be satisfied."

Proverbs 13:25 "The righteous eateth to the satisfying of his soul: but the belly of the wicked shall want."

Ecclesiastes 5:10 "He that loveth silver shall not be satisfied with silver; nor he that loveth abundance with increase: this is also vanity."

Ezekiel 16:28-29 "28Thou hast played the whore also with the Assyrians, because thou wast unsatiable; yea, thou hast played the harlot with them, and yet couldest not be satisfied. 29Thou hast moreover multiplied thy fornication in the land of Canaan unto Chaldea; and yet thou wast not satisfied herewith."

Micah 6:10-14 "10Are there yet the treasures of wickedness in the house of the wicked, and the scant measure that is abominable? 11Shall I count them pure with the wicked balances, and with the bag of deceitful weights? [12]For the rich men thereof are full of violence, and the inhabitants thereof have spoken lies, and their tongue is deceitful in their mouth. [13]Therefore also will I make thee sick in smiting thee, in making thee desolate because of thy sins. [14]Thou shalt eat, but not be satisfied; and thy casting down shall be in the midst of thee; and thou shalt take hold, but shalt not deliver; and that which thou deliverest will I give up to the sword."

Habakkuk 2:4-5 "[4]Behold, his soul which is lifted up is not upright in him: but the just shall live by his faith. [5]Yea also, because he transgresseth by wine, he is a proud man, neither keepeth at home, who enlargeth his desire as hell, and is as death, and cannot be satisfied, but gathereth unto him all nations, and heapeth unto him all people."

SCORN

Scorners
Proverbs 1:22 "How long, ye simple ones, will ye love simplicity? and the scorners delight in their scorning, and fools hate knowledge?"

Proverbs 3:33-34 "[33]The curse of the LORD is in the house of the wicked: but he blesseth the habitation of the just. [34]Surely he scorneth the scorners: but he giveth grace unto the lowly."

Proverbs 13:1 "A wise son heareth his father's instruction: but a scorner heareth not rebuke."

Proverbs 14:6 "A scorner seeketh wisdom, and findeth it not: but knowledge is easy unto him that understandeth."

Proverbs 15:12 "A scorner loveth not one that reproveth him: neither will he go unto the wise."

Proverbs 19:29 "Judgments are prepared for scorners, and stripes for the back of fools."

Proverbs 24:9 "The thought of foolishness is sin: and the scorner is an abomination to men."

Proverbs 29:8 "Scornful men bring a city into a snare: but wise men turn away wrath."

Isaiah 28:14-15 "[14]Wherefore hear the word of the LORD, ye scornful men, that rule this people which is in Jerusalem. [15]Because ye have said, We

have made a covenant with death, and with hell are we at agreement; when the overflowing scourge shall pass through, it shall not come unto us: for we have made lies our refuge, and under falsehood have we hid ourselves."

The Reward For Casting Out The Scorner
Proverbs 22:10 "Cast out the scorner, and contention shall go out; yea, strife and reproach shall cease."

The Time When A Scorner Is Punished
Proverbs 19:25 "Smite a scorner, and the simple will beware: and reprove one that hath understanding, and he will understand knowledge."

Proverbs 21:11 "When the scorner is punished, the simple is made wise: and when the wise is instructed, he receiveth knowledge."

Those That Reprove A Scorner
Proverbs 9:7-10 "[7]He that reproveth a scorner getteth to himself shame: and he that rebuketh a wicked man getteth himself a blot. [8]Reprove not a scorner, lest he hate thee: rebuke a wise man, and he will love thee. [9]Give instruction to a wise man, and he will be yet wiser: teach a just man, and he will increase in learning. [10]The fear of the LORD is the beginning of wisdom: and the knowledge of the holy is understanding."

Proverbs 15:12 "A scorner loveth not one that reproveth him: neither will he go unto the wise."

Those That Do Not Sit In The Seat Of The Scornful
Psalm 1:1-2 "[1]Blessed is the man that walketh not in the counsel of the ungodly, nor standeth in the way of sinners, nor sitteth in the seat of the scornful. [2]But his delight is in the law of the LORD; and in his law doth he meditate day and night."

Who The Lord Scorns
Proverbs 3:33-34 "[33]The curse of the LORD is in the house of the wicked: but he blesseth the habitation of the just. [34]Surely he scorneth the scorners: but he giveth grace unto the lowly."

SCRIPTURE

All Scripture Being Given By Inspiration Of God
2 Timothy 3:16-17 "[16]All scripture is given by inspiration of God, and is profitable for doctrine,

for reproof, for correction, for instruction in righteousness: [17]That the man of God may be perfect, throughly furnished unto all good works."

2 Peter 1:19-21 "[19]We have also a more sure word of prophecy; whereunto ye do well that ye take heed, as unto a light that shineth in a dark place, until the day dawn, and the day star arise in your hearts: [20]Knowing this first, that no prophecy of the scripture is of any private interpretation. [21]For the prophecy came not in old time by the will of man: but holy men of God spake as they were moved by the Holy Ghost."

All Scripture Being Profitable
For Doctrine And Instruction

2 Timothy 3:16-17 "[16]All scripture is given by inspiration of God, and is profitable for doctrine, for reproof, for correction, for instruction in righteousness: [17]That the man of God may be perfect, throughly furnished unto all good works."

The Scriptures Making You Wise

2 Timothy 3:14-15 "[14]But continue thou in the things which thou hast learned and hast been assured of, knowing of whom thou hast learned them; [15]And that from a child thou hast known the holy scriptures, which are able to make thee wise unto salvation through faith which is in Christ Jesus."

The Scriptures Testifying Of Jesus Christ

Luke 24:44-46 "[44]And he said unto them, These are the words which I spake unto you, while I was yet with you, that all things must be fulfilled, which were written in the law of Moses, and in the prophets, and in the psalms, concerning me. [45]Then opened he their understanding, that they might understand the scriptures, [46]And said unto them, Thus it is written, and thus it behoved Christ to suffer, and to rise from the dead the third day."

John 5:23-47 "[23]That all men should honour the Son, even as they honour the Father. He that honoureth not the Son honoureth not the Father which hath sent him. [24]Verily, verily, I say unto you, He that heareth my word, and believeth on him that sent me, hath everlasting life, and shall not come into condemnation; but is passed from death unto life. [25]Verily, verily, I say unto you, The hour is coming, and now is, when the dead shall hear the voice of the Son of God: and they that hear shall live. [26]For as the Father hath life in himself; so hath he given to the Son to have life in himself; [27]And hath given him authority to execute judgment also, because he is the Son of man. [28]Marvel not at this: for the hour is coming, in the which all that are in the graves shall hear his voice, [29]And shall come forth; they that have done good, unto the resurrection of life; and they that have done evil, unto the resurrection of damnation. [30]I can of mine own self do nothing: as I hear, I judge: and my judgment is just; because I seek not mine own will, but the will of the Father which hath sent me. [31]If I bear witness of myself, my witness is not true. [32]There is another that beareth witness of me; and I know that the witness which he witnesseth of me is true. [33]Ye sent unto John, and he bare witness unto the truth. [34]But I receive not testimony from man: but these things I say, that ye might be saved. [35]He was a burning and a shining light: and ye were willing for a season to rejoice in his light. [36]But I have greater witness than that of John: for the works which the Father hath given me to finish, the same works that I do, bear witness of me, that the Father hath sent me. [37]And the Father himself, which hath sent me, hath borne witness of me. Ye have neither heard his voice at any time, nor seen his shape. [38]And ye have not his word abiding in you: for whom he hath sent, him ye believe not. [39]Search the scriptures; for in them ye think ye have eternal life: and they are they which testify of me. [40]And ye will not come to me, that ye might have life. [41]I receive not honour from men. [42]But I know you, that ye have not the love of God in you. [43]I am come in my Father's name, and ye receive me not: if another shall come in his own name, him ye will receive. [44]How can ye believe, which receive honour one of another, and seek not the honour that cometh from God only? [45]Do not think that I will accuse you to the Father: there is one that accuseth you, even Moses, in whom ye trust. [46]For had ye believed Moses, ye would have believed me: for he wrote of me. [47]But if ye believe not his writings, how shall ye believe my words?"

The Things Written In Scripture

Romans 15:1-4 "[1]We then that are strong ought to bear the infirmities of the weak, and not to please ourselves. ²Let every one of us please his neighbour for his good to edification. ³For even Christ pleased not himself; but, as it is written, The reproaches of them that reproached thee fell on me. ⁴For whatsoever things were written aforetime were written for our learning, that we through patience and comfort of the scriptures might have hope."

2 Corinthians 1:12-13 "¹²For our rejoicing is this, the testimony of our conscience, that in simplicity and godly sincerity, not with fleshly wisdom, but by the grace of God, we have had our conversation in the world, and more abundantly to youward. ¹³For we write none other things unto you, than what ye read or acknowledge; and I trust ye shall acknowledge even to the end."

What The Scriptures Manifest
Romans 16:25-26 "²⁵Now to him that is of power to stablish you according to my gospel, and the preaching of Jesus Christ, according to the revelation of the mystery, which was kept secret since the world began, ²⁶But now is made manifest, and by the scriptures of the prophets, according to the commandment of the everlasting God, made known to all nations for the obedience of faith."

SEALS

God The Father Sealing Jesus Christ
John 6:26-27 "²⁶Jesus answered them and said, Verily, verily, I say unto you, Ye seek me, not because ye saw the miracles, but because ye did eat of the loaves, and were filled. ²⁷Labour not for the meat which perisheth, but for that meat which endureth unto everlasting life, which the Son of man shall give unto you: for him hath God the Father sealed."

The Seven Seals
Revelation 6:1-17 "¹And I saw when the Lamb opened one of the seals, and I heard, as it were the noise of thunder, one of the four beasts saying, Come and see. ²And I saw, and behold a white horse: and he that sat on him had a bow; and a crown was given unto him: and he went forth conquering, and to conquer. ³And when he had opened the second seal, I heard the second beast say, Come and see. ⁴And there went out another horse that was red: and power was given to him that sat thereon to take peace from the earth, and

that they should kill one another: and there was given unto him a great sword. ⁵And when he had opened the third seal, I heard the third beast say, Come and see. And I beheld, and lo a black horse; and he that sat on him had a pair of balances in his hand. ⁶And I heard a voice in the midst of the four beasts say, A measure of wheat for a penny, and three measures of barley for a penny; and see thou hurt not the oil and the wine. ⁷And when he had opened the fourth seal, I heard the voice of the fourth beast say, Come and see. ⁸And I looked, and behold a pale horse: and his name that sat on him was Death, and Hell followed with him. And power was given unto them over the fourth part of the earth, to kill with sword, and with hunger, and with death, and with the beasts of the earth. ⁹And when he had opened the fifth seal, I saw under the altar the souls of them that were slain for the word of God, and for the testimony which they held: ¹⁰And they cried with a loud voice, saying, How long, O Lord, holy and true, dost thou not judge and avenge our blood on them that dwell on the earth? ¹¹And white robes were given unto every one of them; and it was said unto them, that they should rest yet for a little season, until their fellowservants also and their brethren, that should be killed as they were, should be fulfilled. ¹²And I beheld when he had opened the sixth seal, and, lo, there was a great earthquake; and the sun became black as sackcloth of hair, and the moon became as blood; ¹³And the stars of heaven fell unto the earth, even as a fig tree casteth her untimely figs, when she is shaken of a mighty wind. ¹⁴And the heaven departed as a scroll when it is rolled together; and every mountain and island were moved out of their places. ¹⁵And the kings of the earth, and the great men, and the rich men, and the chief captains, and the mighty men, and every bondman, and every free man, hid themselves in the dens and in the rocks of the mountains; ¹⁶And said to the mountains and rocks, Fall on us, and hide us from the face of him that sitteth on the throne, and from the wrath of the Lamb: ¹⁷For the great day of his wrath is come; and who shall be able to stand?"

Revelation 8:1-13 "¹And when he had opened the seventh seal, there was silence in heaven about the space of half an hour. ²And I saw the seven angels which stood before God; and to them were given seven trumpets. ³And another angel came and stood at the altar, having a golden censer; and there was given unto him much incense, that he should offer it with the prayers of all saints upon the golden altar which was before the throne. ⁴And the smoke of the incense, which came with the prayers of the saints, ascended up before God out of the angel's hand. ⁵And the angel took the censer, and filled it with fire of the altar, and cast it into the earth: and there were voices, and thunderings, and lightnings, and an earthquake. ⁶And the seven angels which had the seven trumpets prepared themselves to sound. ⁷The first angel sounded, and there followed hail and fire mingled with blood, and they were cast upon the earth: and the third part of trees was burnt up, and all green grass was burnt up. ⁸And the second angel sounded, and as it were a great mountain burning with fire was cast into the sea: and the third part of the sea became blood; ⁹And the third part of the creatures which were in the sea, and had life, died; and the third part of the ships were destroyed. ¹⁰And the third angel sounded, and there fell a great star from heaven, burning as it were a lamp, and it fell upon the third part of the rivers, and upon the fountains of waters; ¹¹And the name of the star is called Wormwood: and the third part of the waters became wormwood; and many men died of the waters, because they were made bitter. ¹²And the fourth angel sounded, and the third part of the sun was smitten, and the third part of the moon, and the third part of the stars; so as the third part of them was darkened, and the day shone not for a third part of it, and the night likewise. ¹³And I beheld, and heard an angel flying through the midst of heaven, saying with a loud voice, Woe, woe, woe, to the inhabiters of the earth by reason of the other voices of the trumpet of the three angels, which are yet to sound!"

Revelation 9:1-21 "¹And the fifth angel sounded, and I saw a star fall from heaven unto the earth: and to him was given the key of the bottomless pit. ²And he opened the bottomless pit; and there arose a smoke out of the pit, as the smoke of a great furnace; and the sun and the air were darkened by reason of the smoke of the pit. ³And there came out of the smoke locusts upon the earth: and unto them was given power, as the scorpions of the earth have power. ⁴And it was commanded

them that they should not hurt the grass of the earth, neither any green thing, neither any tree; but only those men which have not the seal of God in their foreheads. ⁵And to them it was given that they should not kill them, but that they should be tormented five months: and their torment was as the torment of a scorpion, when he striketh a man. ⁶And in those days shall men seek death, and shall not find it; and shall desire to die, and death shall flee from them. ⁷And the shapes of the locusts were like unto horses prepared unto battle; and on their heads were as it were crowns like gold, and their faces were as the faces of men. ⁸And they had hair as the hair of women, and their teeth were as the teeth of lions. ⁹And they had breastplates, as it were breastplates of iron; and the sound of their wings was as the sound of chariots of many horses running to battle. ¹⁰And they had tails like unto scorpions, and there were stings in their tails: and their power was to hurt men five months. ¹¹And they had a king over them, which is the angel of the bottomless pit, whose name in the Hebrew tongue is Abaddon, but in the Greek tongue hath his name Apollyon. ¹²One woe is past; and, behold, there come two woes more hereafter. ¹³And the sixth angel sounded, and I heard a voice from the four horns of the golden altar which is before God, ¹⁴Saying to the sixth angel which had the trumpet, Loose the four angels which are bound in the great river Euphrates. ¹⁵And the four angels were loosed, which were prepared for an hour, and a day, and a month, and a year, for to slay the third part of men. ¹⁶And the number of the army of the horsemen were two hundred thousand thousand: and I heard the number of them. ¹⁷And thus I saw the horses in the vision, and them that sat on them, having breastplates of fire, and of jacinth, and brimstone: and the heads of the horses were as the heads of lions; and out of their mouths issued fire and smoke and brimstone. ¹⁸By these three was the third part of men killed, by the fire, and by the smoke, and by the brimstone, which issued out of their mouths. ¹⁹For their power is in their mouth, and in their tails: for their tails were like unto serpents, and had heads, and with them they do hurt. ²⁰And the rest of the men which were not killed by these plagues yet repented not of the works of their hands, that they should not worship devils, and idols of gold, and silver, and brass, and stone, and of wood: which neither can see, nor hear, nor walk: ²¹Neither repented they of their murders, nor of their sorceries, nor of their fornication, nor of their thefts."

Revelation 10:1-7 "¹And I saw another mighty angel come down from heaven, clothed with a cloud: and a rainbow was upon his head, and his face was as it were the sun, and his feet as pillars of fire: ²And he had in his hand a little book open: and he set his right foot upon the sea, and his left foot on the earth, ³And cried with a loud voice, as when a lion roareth: and when he had cried, seven thunders uttered their voices. ⁴And when the seven thunders had uttered their voices, I was about to write: and I heard a voice from heaven saying unto me, Seal up those things which the seven thunders uttered, and write them not. ⁵And the angel which I saw stand upon the sea and upon the earth lifted up his hand to heaven, ⁶And sware by him that liveth for ever and ever, who created heaven, and the things that therein are, and the earth, and the things that therein are, and the sea, and the things which are therein, that there should be time no longer: ⁷But in the days of the voice of the seventh angel, when he shall begin to sound, the mystery of God should be finished, as he hath declared to his servants the prophets."

Revelation 11:15-19 "¹⁵And the seventh angel sounded; and there were great voices in heaven, saying, The kingdoms of this world are become the kingdoms of our Lord, and of his Christ; and he shall reign for ever and ever. ¹⁶And the four and twenty elders, which sat before God on their seats, fell upon their faces, and worshipped God, ¹⁷Saying, We give thee thanks, O Lord God Almighty, which art, and wast, and art to come; because thou hast taken to thee thy great power, and hast reigned. ¹⁸And the nations were angry, and thy wrath is come, and the time of the dead, that they should be judged, and that thou shouldest give reward unto thy servants the prophets, and to the saints, and them that fear thy name, small and great; and shouldest destroy them which destroy the earth. ¹⁹And the temple of God was opened in heaven, and there was seen in his temple the ark of his testament: and there were lightnings, and voices, and thunderings, and an earthquake, and great hail."

Who God Has Sealed

Revelation 7:1-4 "¹And after these things I saw four angels standing on the four corners of the earth, holding the four winds of the earth, that the wind should not blow on the earth, nor on the sea, nor on any tree. ²And I saw another angel ascending from the east, having the seal of the living God: and he cried with a loud voice to the four angels, to whom it was given to hurt the earth and the sea, ³Saying, Hurt not the earth, neither the sea, nor the trees, till we have sealed the servants of our God in their foreheads. ⁴And I heard the number of them which were sealed: and there were sealed an hundred and forty and four thousand of all the tribes of the children of Israel."

SEEING

How The Lord Sees

1 Samuel 16:7 "But the LORD said unto Samuel, Look not on his countenance, or on the height of his stature; because I have refused him: for the LORD seeth not as man seeth; for man looketh on the outward appearance, but the LORD looketh on the heart."

Jesus Christ Seeing God The Father

John 1:18 "No man hath seen God at any time; the only begotten Son, which is in the bosom of the Father, he hath declared him."

John 6:43-46 "⁴³Jesus therefore answered and said unto them, Murmur not among yourselves. ⁴⁴No man can come to me, except the Father which hath sent me draw him: and I will raise him up at the last day. ⁴⁵It is written in the prophets, And they shall be all taught of God. Every man therefore that hath heard, and hath learned of the Father, cometh unto me. ⁴⁶Not that any man hath seen the Father, save he which is of God, he hath seen the Father."

No Man Seeing God

Exodus 33:17-23 "¹⁷And the LORD said unto Moses, I will do this thing also that thou hast spoken: for thou hast found grace in my sight, and I know thee by name. ¹⁸And he said, I beseech thee, shew me thy glory. ¹⁹And he said, I will make all my goodness pass before thee, and I will proclaim the name of the LORD before thee; and will be gracious to whom I will be gracious, and will shew mercy on whom I will shew mercy. ²⁰And he said, Thou canst not see my face: for there shall no man see me, and live. ²¹And the LORD said, Behold, there is a place by me, and thou shalt stand upon a rock: ²²And it shall come to pass, while my glory passeth by, that I will put thee in a clift of the rock, and will cover thee with my hand while I pass by: ²³And I will take away mine hand, and thou shalt see my back parts: but my face shall not be seen."

John 1:18 "No man hath seen God at any time; the only begotten Son, which is in the bosom of the Father, he hath declared him."

John 5:37 "And the Father himself, which hath sent me, hath borne witness of me. Ye have neither heard his voice at any time, nor seen his shape."

John 6:43-46 "⁴³Jesus therefore answered and said unto them, Murmur not among yourselves. ⁴⁴No man can come to me, except the Father which hath sent me draw him: and I will raise him up at the last day. ⁴⁵It is written in the prophets, And they shall be all taught of God. Every man therefore that hath heard, and hath learned of the Father, cometh unto me. ⁴⁶Not that any man hath seen the Father, save he which is of God, he hath seen the Father."

1 John 4:12 "No man hath seen God at any time. If we love one another, God dwelleth in us, and his love is perfected in us."

The Eyes Of The Lord
2 Chronicles 16:9 "For the eyes of the LORD run to and fro throughout the whole earth, to shew himself strong in the behalf of them whose heart is perfect toward him. Herein thou hast done foolishly: therefore from henceforth thou shalt have wars."

Job 34:21-23 "²¹For his eyes are upon the ways of man, and he seeth all his goings. ²²There is no darkness, nor shadow of death, where the workers of iniquity may hide themselves. ²³For he will not lay upon man more than right; that he should enter into judgment with God."

Psalm 11:4 "The LORD is in his holy temple, the LORD's throne is in heaven: his eyes behold, his eyelids try, the children of men."

Psalm 33:18 "Behold, the eye of the LORD is upon them that fear him, upon them that hope in his mercy."

Psalm 34:15 "The eyes of the LORD are upon the righteous, and his ears are open unto their cry."

Psalm 66:3-7 "³Say unto God, How terrible art thou in thy works! through the greatness of thy power shall thine enemies submit themselves unto thee. ⁴All the earth shall worship thee, and shall sing unto thee; they shall sing to thy name. Selah. ⁵Come and see the works of God: he is terrible in his doing toward the children of men. ⁶He turned the sea into dry land: they went through the flood on foot: there did we rejoice in him. ⁷He ruleth by his power for ever; his eyes behold the nations: let not the rebellious exalt themselves. Selah."

Proverbs 5:21 "For the ways of man are before the eyes of the LORD, and he pondereth all his goings."

Proverbs 15:3 "The eyes of the LORD are in every place, beholding the evil and the good."

Proverbs 22:12 "The eyes of the LORD preserve knowledge, and he overthroweth the words of the transgressor."

Jeremiah 32:18-19 "¹⁸Thou shewest lovingkindness unto thousands, and recompensest the iniquity of the fathers into the bosom of their children after them: the Great, the Mighty God, the LORD of hosts, is his name, ¹⁹Great in counsel, and mighty in work: for thine eyes are open upon all the ways of the sons of men: to give every one according to his ways, and according to the fruit of his doings."

Amos 9:8 "Behold, the eyes of the Lord GOD are upon the sinful kingdom, and I will destroy it from off the face of the earth; saving that I will not utterly destroy the house of Jacob, saith the LORD."

1 Peter 3:12 "For the eyes of the Lord are over the righteous, and his ears are open unto their prayers: but the face of the Lord is against them that do evil."

The Place Where There Is No Vision
Proverbs 29:18 "Where there is no vision, the people perish: but he that keepeth the law, happy is he."

The Seeing Eye
Proverbs 20:12 "The hearing ear, and the seeing eye, the LORD hath made even both of them."

The Sight Of The Eyes
Ecclesiastes 6:9 "Better is the sight of the eyes than the wandering of the desire: this is also vanity and vexation of spirit."

The Things Which Are Not Seen
2 Corinthians 4:17-18 "17For our light affliction, which is but for a moment, worketh for us a far more exceeding and eternal weight of glory; 18While we look not at the things which are seen, but at the things which are not seen: for the things which are seen are temporal; but the things which are not seen are eternal."

The Things Which Are Seen
2 Corinthians 4:17-18 "17For our light affliction, which is but for a moment, worketh for us a far more exceeding and eternal weight of glory; 18While we look not at the things which are seen, but at the things which are not seen: for the things which are seen are temporal; but the things which are not seen are eternal."

Hebrews 11:3 "Through faith we understand that the worlds were framed by the word of God, so that things which are seen were not made of things which do appear."

The Wise Man's Eyes
Ecclesiastes 2:14 "The wise man's eyes are in his head; but the fool walketh in darkness: and I myself perceived also that one event happeneth to them all."

Those That Have Not Seen
And Yet Have Believed In Jesus Christ
John 20:29 "Jesus saith unto him, Thomas, because thou hast seen me, thou hast believed: blessed are they that have not seen, and yet have believed."

1 Peter 1:7-9 "7That the trial of your faith, being much more precious than of gold that perisheth, though it be tried with fire, might be found unto praise and honour and glory at the appearing of Jesus Christ: 8Whom having not seen, ye love; in whom, though now ye see him not, yet believing, ye rejoice with joy unspeakable and full of glory: 9Receiving the end of your faith, even the salvation of your souls."

Those That Have Seen Jesus Christ
John 14:7-9 "7If ye had known me, ye should have known my Father also: and from henceforth ye know him, and have seen him. 8Philip saith unto him, Lord, shew us the Father, and it sufficeth us. 9Jesus saith unto him, Have I been so long time with you, and yet hast thou not known me, Philip? he that hath seen me hath seen the Father; and how sayest thou then, Shew us the Father?"

What All Flesh Shall See
Isaiah 40:5 "And the glory of the LORD shall be revealed, and all flesh shall see it together: for the mouth of the LORD hath spoken it."

Isaiah 66:17-18 "17They that sanctify themselves, and purify themselves in the gardens behind one tree in the midst, eating swine's flesh, and the abomination, and the mouse, shall be consumed together, saith the LORD. 18For I know their works and their thoughts: it shall come, that I will gather all nations and tongues; and they shall come, and see my glory."

Luke 3:4-6 "4As it is written in the book of the words of Esaias the prophet, saying, The voice of one crying in the wilderness, Prepare ye the way of the Lord, make his paths straight. 5Every valley shall be filled, and every mountain and hill shall be brought low; and the crooked shall be made straight, and the rough ways shall be made smooth; 6And all flesh shall see the salvation of God."

What God Sees
Job 11:7-11 "7Canst thou by searching find out God? canst thou find out the Almighty unto perfection? 8It is as high as heaven; what canst thou do? deeper than hell; what canst thou know? 9The measure thereof is longer than the earth, and broader than the sea. 10If he cut off, and shut up, or gather together, then who can hinder him? 11For he knoweth vain men: he seeth wickedness also; will he not then consider it?"

Job 34:21-23 "21For his eyes are upon the ways of man, and he seeth all his goings. 22There is no darkness, nor shadow of death, where the workers of iniquity may hide themselves. 23For he will not lay upon man more than right; that he should enter into judgment with God."

What Is The Evidence Of Things Not Seen

Hebrews 11:1 "Now faith is the substance of things hoped for, the evidence of things not seen."

What Is The Eye

Luke 11:34-36 "34The light of the body is the eye: therefore when thine eye is single, thy whole body also is full of light; but when thine eye is evil, thy body also is full of darkness. 35Take heed therefore that the light which is in thee be not darkness. 36If thy whole body therefore be full of light, having no part dark, the whole shall be full of light, as when the bright shining of a candle doth give thee light."

What The Eye Has Not Seen

Isaiah 64:4 "For since the beginning of the world men have not heard, nor perceived by the ear, neither hath the eye seen, O God, beside thee, what he hath prepared for him that waiteth for him."

1 Corinthians 2:9 "But as it is written, Eye hath not seen, nor ear heard, neither have entered into the heart of man, the things which God hath prepared for them that love him."

Who Does Not See God

Jeremiah 5:19-21 "19And it shall come to pass, when ye shall say, Wherefore doeth the LORD our God all these things unto us? then shalt thou answer them, Like as ye have forsaken me, and served strange gods in your land, so shall ye serve strangers in a land that is not yours. 20Declare this in the house of Jacob, and publish it in Judah, saying, 21Hear now this, O foolish people, and without understanding; which have eyes, and see not; which have ears, and hear not."

Who Has Not Seen The Lord

1 John 3:1-6 "1Behold, what manner of love the Father hath bestowed upon us, that we should be called the sons of God: therefore the world knoweth us not, because it knew him not. 2Beloved, now are we the sons of God, and it doth not yet appear what we shall be: but we know that, when he shall appear, we shall be like him; for we shall see him as he is. 3And every man that hath this hope in him purifieth himself, even as he is pure. 4Whosoever committeth sin transgresseth also the law: for sin is the transgression of the law. 5And ye know that he was manifested to take away our sins; and in him is no sin. 6Whosoever abideth in him sinneth not: whosoever sinneth hath not seen him, neither known him."

3 John 11 "Beloved, follow not that which is evil, but that which is good. He that doeth good is of God: but he that doeth evil hath not seen God."

Who Has Seen God The Father

John 12:44-45 "44Jesus cried and said, He that believeth on me, believeth not on me, but on him that sent me. 45And he that seeth me seeth him that sent me."

John 14:7-9 "7If ye had known me, ye should have known my Father also: and from henceforth ye know him, and have seen him. 8Philip saith unto him, Lord, shew us the Father, and it sufficeth us. 9Jesus saith unto him, Have I been so long time with you, and yet hast thou not known me, Philip? he that hath seen me hath seen the Father; and how sayest thou then, Shew us the Father?"

Who Shall Not See The Lord

Hebrews 12:14 "Follow peace with all men, and holiness, without which no man shall see the Lord."

Who Shall See God

Job 19:25-27 "25For I know that my redeemer liveth, and that he shall stand at the latter day upon the earth: 26And though after my skin worms destroy this body, yet in my flesh shall I see God: 27Whom I shall see for myself, and mine eyes shall behold, and not another; though my reins be consumed within me."

Matthew 5:8 "Blessed are the pure in heart: for they shall see God."

1 John 3:1-2 "1Behold, what manner of love the Father hath bestowed upon us, that we should be called the sons of God: therefore the world knoweth us not, because it knew him not. 2Beloved, now are we the sons of God, and it doth not yet appear what we shall be: but we know that, when he shall appear, we shall be like him; for we shall see him as he is."

Revelation 22:3-4 "3And there shall be no more curse: but the throne of God and of the Lamb shall be in it; and his servants shall serve him: 4And they shall see his face; and his name shall be in their foreheads."

SEEKING

Seeking The Lord

1 Chronicles 16:11 "Seek the LORD and his strength, seek his face continually."

Psalm 63:1 "O God, thou art my God; early will I seek thee: my soul thirsteth for thee, my flesh longeth for thee in a dry and thirsty land, where no water is."

Psalm 105:4 "Seek the LORD, and his strength: seek his face evermore."

Isaiah 8:19 "And when they shall say unto you, Seek unto them that have familiar spirits, and unto wizards that peep, and that mutter: should not a people seek unto their God? for the living to the dead?"

Isaiah 55:6 "Seek ye the LORD while he may be found, call ye upon him while he is near."

Amos 5:8 "Seek him that maketh the seven stars and Orion, and turneth the shadow of death into the morning, and maketh the day dark with night: that calleth for the waters of the sea, and poureth them out upon the face of the earth: The LORD is his name."

Zephaniah 2:3 "Seek ye the LORD, all ye meek of the earth, which have wrought his judgment; seek righteousness, seek meekness: it may be ye shall be hid in the day of the LORD's anger."

Acts 17:23-27 "23For as I passed by, and beheld your devotions, I found an altar with this inscription, TO THE UNKNOWN GOD. Whom therefore ye ignorantly worship, him declare I unto you. 24God that made the world and all things therein, seeing that he is Lord of heaven and earth, dwelleth not in temples made with hands; 25Neither is worshipped with men's hands, as though he needed any thing, seeing he giveth to all life, and breath, and all things; 26And hath made of one blood all nations of men for to dwell on all the face of the earth, and hath determined the times before appointed, and the bounds of their habitation; 27That they should seek the Lord, if haply they might feel after him, and find him, though he be not far from every one of us."

The Lord Seeking That Which Was Lost

Jeremiah 31:10 "Hear the word of the LORD, O ye nations, and declare it in the isles afar off, and say, He that scattered Israel will gather him, and keep him, as a shepherd doth his flock."

Ezekiel 34:11-16 "11For thus saith the Lord GOD; Behold, I, even I, will both search my sheep, and seek them out. 12As a shepherd seeketh out his flock in the day that he is among his sheep that are scattered; so will I seek out my sheep, and will deliver them out of all places where they have been scattered in the cloudy and dark day. 13And I will bring them out from the people, and gather them from the countries, and will bring them to their own land, and feed them upon the mountains of Israel by the rivers, and in all the inhabited places of the country. 14I will feed them in a good pasture, and upon the high mountains of Israel shall their fold be: there shall they lie in a good fold, and in a fat pasture shall they feed upon the mountains of Israel. 15I will feed my flock, and I will cause them to lie down, saith the Lord GOD. 16I will seek that which was lost, and bring again that which was driven away, and will bind up that which was broken, and will strengthen that which was sick: but I will destroy the fat and the strong; I will feed them with judgment."

Matthew 18:11-14 "11For the Son of man is come to save that which was lost. 12How think ye? if a man have an hundred sheep, and one of them be gone astray, doth he not leave the ninety and nine, and goeth into the mountains, and seeketh that which is gone astray? 13And if so be that he find it, verily I say unto you, he rejoiceth more of that sheep, than of the ninety and nine which went not astray. 14Even so it is not the will of your Father which is in heaven, that one of these little ones should perish."

Luke 15:3-32 "3And he spake this parable unto them, saying, 4What man of you, having an hundred sheep, if he lose one of them, doth not leave the ninety and nine in the wilderness, and go after that which is lost, until he find it? 5And when he hath found it, he layeth it on his shoulders, rejoicing. 6And when he cometh home, he calleth together his friends and neighbours, saying unto them, Rejoice with me; for I have found my sheep which was lost. 7I say unto you, that likewise joy shall be in heaven over one sinner that repenteth, more than over ninety and nine just persons, which need no repentance. 8Either what woman having ten pieces of silver, if she lose one piece, doth not light a candle, and sweep the house, and seek diligently till she find it? ⁹And when she hath found it, she calleth her friends and her neighbours together, saying, Rejoice with me; for I have found the piece which I had lost. ¹⁰Likewise, I say unto you, there is joy in the presence of the angels of God over one sinner that repenteth. ¹¹And he said, A certain man had two sons: ¹²And the younger of them said to his father, Father, give me the portion of goods that falleth to me. And he divided unto them his living. ¹³And not many days after the younger son gathered all together, and took his journey into a far country, and there wasted his substance with riotous living. ¹⁴And when he had spent all, there arose a mighty famine in that land; and he began to be in want. ¹⁵And he went and joined himself to a citizen of that country; and he sent him into his fields to feed swine. ¹⁶And he would fain have filled his belly with the husks that the swine did eat: and no man gave unto him. ¹⁷And when he came to himself, he said, How many hired servants of my father's have bread enough and to spare, and I perish with hunger! ¹⁸I will arise and go to my father, and will say unto him, Father, I have sinned against heaven, and before thee, ¹⁹And am no more worthy to be called thy son: make me as one of thy hired servants. ²⁰And he arose, and came to his father. But when he was yet a great way off, his father saw him, and had compassion, and ran, and fell on his neck, and kissed him. ²¹And the son said unto him, Father, I have sinned against heaven, and in thy sight, and am no more worthy to be called thy son. ²²But the father said to his servants, Bring forth the best robe, and put it on him; and put a ring on his hand, and shoes on his feet: ²³And bring hither the fatted calf, and kill it; and let us eat, and be merry: ²⁴For this my son was dead, and is alive again; he was lost, and is found. And they began to be merry. ²⁵Now his elder son was in the field: and as he came and drew nigh to the house, he heard musick and dancing. ²⁶And he called one of the servants, and asked what these things meant. ²⁷And he said unto him, Thy brother is come; and thy father hath killed the fatted calf, because he hath received him safe and sound. ²⁸And he was angry, and would not go in: therefore came his father out, and intreated him. ²⁹And he answering said to his father, Lo, these many years do I serve thee,

neither transgressed I at any time thy commandment: and yet thou never gavest me a kid, that I might make merry with my friends: ³⁰But as soon as this thy son was come, which hath devoured thy living with harlots, thou hast killed for him the fatted calf. ³¹And he said unto him, Son, thou art ever with me, and all that I have is thine. ³²It was meet that we should make merry, and be glad: for this thy brother was dead, and is alive again; and was lost, and is found."

Luke 19:9-10 "⁹And Jesus said unto him, This day is salvation come to this house, forsomuch as he also is a son of Abraham. ¹⁰For the Son of man is come to seek and to save that which was lost."

The Reward For Not Seeking The Lord
2 Chronicles 16:12-13 "¹²And Asa in the thirty and ninth year of his reign was diseased in his feet, until his disease was exceeding great: yet in his disease he sought not to the LORD, but to the physicians. ¹³And Asa slept with his fathers, and died in the one and fortieth year of his reign."

Jeremiah 10:21 "For the pastors are become brutish, and have not sought the LORD: therefore they shall not prosper, and all their flocks shall be scattered."

The Reward For Seeking The Lord
Deuteronomy 4:29-31 "²⁹But if from thence thou shalt seek the LORD thy God, thou shalt find him, if thou seek him with all thy heart and with all thy soul. ³⁰When thou art in tribulation, and all these things are come upon thee, even in the latter days, if thou turn to the LORD thy God, and shalt be obedient unto his voice; ³¹(For the LORD thy God is a merciful God;) he will not forsake thee, neither destroy thee, nor forget the covenant of thy fathers which he sware unto them."

1 Chronicles 28:8-9 "⁸Now therefore in the sight of all Israel the congregation of the LORD, and in the audience of our God, keep and seek for all the commandments of the LORD your God: that ye may possess this good land, and leave it for an inheritance for your children after you for ever. ⁹And thou, Solomon my son, know thou the God of thy father, and serve him with a perfect heart and with a willing mind: for the LORD searcheth all hearts, and understandeth all the imaginations of the thoughts: if thou seek him, he will be found of thee; but if thou forsake him, he will cast thee off for ever."

2 Chronicles 7:12-14 "¹²And the LORD appeared to Solomon by night, and said unto him, I have heard thy prayer, and have chosen this place to myself for an house of sacrifice. ¹³If I shut up heaven that there be no rain, or if I command the locusts to devour the land, or if I send pestilence among my people; ¹⁴If my people, which are called by my name, shall humble themselves, and pray, and seek my face, and turn from their wicked ways; then will I hear from heaven, and will forgive their sin, and will heal their land."

2 Chronicles 15:2 "And he went out to meet Asa, and said unto him, Hear ye me, Asa, and all Judah and Benjamin; The LORD is with you, while ye be with him; and if ye seek him, he will be found of you; but if ye forsake him, he will forsake you."

2 Chronicles 15:14-15 "¹⁴And they sware unto the LORD with a loud voice, and with shouting, and with trumpets, and with cornets. ¹⁵And all Judah rejoiced at the oath: for they had sworn with all their heart, and sought him with their whole desire; and he was found of them: and the LORD gave them rest round about."

2 Chronicles 26:5 "And he sought God in the days of Zechariah, who had understanding in the visions of God: and as long as he sought the LORD, God made him to prosper."

Psalm 34:4 "I sought the LORD, and he heard me, and delivered me from all my fears."

Psalm 119:41-45 "⁴¹Let thy mercies come also unto me, O LORD, even thy salvation, according to thy word. ⁴²So shall I have wherewith to answer him that reproacheth me: for I trust in thy word. ⁴³And take not the word of truth utterly out of my mouth; for I have hoped in thy judgments. ⁴⁴So shall I keep thy law continually for ever and ever. ⁴⁵And I will walk at liberty: for I seek thy precepts."

Jeremiah 29:10-13 "¹⁰For thus saith the LORD, That after seventy years be accomplished at Babylon I will visit you, and perform my good word toward you, in causing you to return to this place. ¹¹For I know the thoughts that I think toward you, saith the LORD, thoughts of peace, and not of evil, to give you an expected end. ¹²Then shall ye call upon me, and ye shall go and pray unto me, and I will hearken unto you. ¹³And ye shall seek me, and find me, when ye shall search for me with all your heart."

Amos 5:4 "For thus saith the LORD unto the house of Israel, Seek ye me, and ye shall live."

Zephaniah 2:3 "Seek ye the LORD, all ye meek of the earth, which have wrought his judgment; seek righteousness, seek meekness: it may be ye shall be hid in the day of the LORD's anger."

Matthew 6:25-33 "²⁵Therefore I say unto you, Take no thought for your life, what ye shall eat, or what ye shall drink; nor yet for your body, what ye shall put on. Is not the life more than meat, and the body than raiment? ²⁶Behold the fowls of the air: for they sow not, neither do they reap, nor gather into barns; yet your heavenly Father feedeth them. Are ye not much better than they? ²⁷Which of you by taking thought can add one cubit unto his stature? ²⁸And why take ye thought for raiment? Consider the lilies of the field, how they grow; they toil not, neither do they spin: ²⁹And yet I say unto you, That even Solomon in all his glory was not arrayed like one of these. ³⁰Wherefore, if God so clothe the grass of the field, which to day is, and to morrow is cast into the oven, shall he not much more clothe you, O ye of little faith? ³¹Therefore take no thought, saying, What shall we eat? or, What shall we drink? or, Wherewithal shall we be clothed? ³²(For after all these things do the Gentiles seek:) for your heavenly Father knoweth that ye have need of all these things. ³³But seek ye first the kingdom of God, and his righteousness; and all these things shall be added unto you."

Luke 12:22-31 "²²And he said unto his disciples, Therefore I say unto you, Take no thought for your life, what ye shall eat; neither for the body, what ye shall put on. ²³The life is more than meat, and the body is more than raiment. ²⁴Consider the ravens: for they neither sow nor reap; which neither have storehouse nor barn; and God feedeth them: how much more are ye better than the fowls? ²⁵And which of you with taking thought can add to his stature one cubit? ²⁶If ye then be not able to do that thing which is least, why take ye thought for the rest? ²⁷Consider the lilies how they grow: they toil not, they spin not; and yet I say unto you, that Solomon in all his glory was not arrayed like one of these. [28]If then God so clothe the grass, which is to day in the field, and to morrow is cast into the oven; how much more will he clothe you, O ye of little faith? [29]And seek not ye what ye shall eat, or what ye shall drink, neither be ye of doubtful mind. [30]For all these things do the nations of the world seek after: and your Father knoweth that ye have need of these things. [31]But rather seek ye the kingdom of God; and all these things shall be added unto you."

The Reward For Seeking Knowledge

Proverbs 2:1-5 "[1]My son, if thou wilt receive my words, and hide my commandments with thee; [2]So that thou incline thine ear unto wisdom, and apply thine heart to understanding; [3]Yea, if thou criest after knowledge, and liftest up thy voice for understanding; [4]If thou seekest her as silver, and searchest for her as for hid treasures; [5]Then shalt thou understand the fear of the LORD, and find the knowledge of God."

Those That Do Not Seek The Lord

Isaiah 31:1-3 "[1]Woe to them that go down to Egypt for help; and stay on horses, and trust in chariots, because they are many; and in horsemen, because they are very strong; but they look not unto the Holy One of Israel, neither seek the LORD! [2]Yet he also is wise, and will bring evil, and will not call back his words: but will arise against the house of the evildoers, and against the help of them that work iniquity. [3]Now the Egyptians are men, and not God; and their horses flesh, and not spirit. When the LORD shall stretch out his hand, both he that helpeth shall fall, and he that is holpen shall fall down, and they all shall fail together."

Those That Seek Death

Proverbs 21:6 "The getting of treasures by a lying tongue is a vanity tossed to and fro of them that seek death."

Those That Seek Good

Proverbs 11:27 "He that diligently seeketh good procureth favour: but he that seeketh mischief, it shall come unto him."

Those That Seek Mischief

Proverbs 11:27 "He that diligently seeketh good procureth favour: but he that seeketh mischief, it shall come unto him."

Those That Seek The Lord

1 Chronicles 16:10 "Glory ye in his holy name: let the heart of them rejoice that seek the LORD."

2 Chronicles 30:18-19 "[18]For a multitude of the people, even many of Ephraim, and Manasseh, Issachar, and Zebulun, had not cleansed themselves, yet did they eat the passover otherwise than it was written. But Hezekiah prayed for them, saying, The good LORD pardon every one [19]That prepareth his heart to seek God, the LORD God of his fathers, though he be not cleansed according to the purification of the sanctuary."

Ezra 8:22 "For I was ashamed to require of the king a band of soldiers and horsemen to help us against the enemy in the way: because we had spoken unto the king, saying, The hand of our God is upon all them for good that seek him; but his power and his wrath is against all them that forsake him."

Psalm 9:10 "And they that know thy name will put their trust in thee: for thou, LORD, hast not forsaken them that seek thee."

Psalm 22:26 "The meek shall eat and be satisfied: they shall praise the LORD that seek him: your heart shall live for ever."

Psalm 34:10 "The young lions do lack, and suffer hunger: but they that seek the LORD shall not want any good thing."

Psalm 105:1-3 "[1]O give thanks unto the LORD; call upon his name: make known his deeds among the people. [2]Sing unto him, sing psalms unto him: talk ye of all his wondrous works. [3]Glory ye in his holy name: let the heart of them rejoice that seek the LORD."

Psalm 119:1-3 "[1]Blessed are the undefiled in the way, who walk in the law of the LORD. [2]Blessed are they that keep his testimonies, and that seek him with the whole heart. [3]They also do no iniquity: they walk in his ways."

Proverbs 28:5 "Evil men understand not judgment: but they that seek the LORD understand all things."

Lamentations 3:25 "The LORD is good unto them that wait for him, to the soul that seeketh him."

Matthew 7:7-11 "[7]Ask, and it shall be given you; seek, and ye shall find; knock, and it shall be opened unto you: [8]For every one that asketh receiveth; and he that seeketh findeth; and to him that knocketh it shall be opened. [9]Or what man is there of you, whom if his son ask bread, will he give him a stone? [10]Or if he ask a fish, will he give him a serpent? [11]If ye then, being evil, know how to give good gifts unto your children, how much more shall your Father which is in heaven give good things to them that ask him?"

Luke 11:8-13 "[8]I say unto you, Though he will not rise and give him, because he is his friend, yet because of his importunity he will rise and give him as many as he needeth. [9]And I say unto you, Ask, and it shall be given you; seek, and ye shall find; knock, and it shall be opened unto you. [10]For every one that asketh receiveth; and he that seeketh findeth; and to him that knocketh it shall be opened. [11]If a son shall ask bread of any of you that is a father, will he give him a stone? or if he ask a fish, will he for a fish give him a serpent? [12]Or if he shall ask an egg, will he offer him a scorpion? [13]If ye then, being evil, know how to give good gifts unto your children: how much more shall your heavenly Father give the Holy Spirit to them that ask him?"

Hebrews 9:28 "So Christ was once offered to bear the sins of many; and unto them that look for him shall he appear the second time without sin unto salvation."

Hebrews 11:6 "But without faith it is impossible to please him: for he that cometh to God must believe that he is, and that he is a rewarder of them that diligently seek him."

What Not To Seek

Amos 5:14 "Seek good, and not evil, that ye may live: and so the LORD, the God of hosts, shall be with you, as ye have spoken."

1 Corinthians 10:33 "Even as I please all men in all things, not seeking mine own profit, but the profit of many, that they may be saved."

Colossians 3:1-2 "[1]If ye then be risen with Christ, seek those things which are above, where Christ sitteth on the right hand of God. [2]Set your affection on things above, not on things on the earth."

What To Seek

1 Chronicles 28:8 "Now therefore in the sight of all Israel the congregation of the LORD, and in the audience of our God, keep and seek for all the commandments of the LORD your God: that ye may possess this good land, and leave it for an inheritance for your children after you for ever."

Psalm 34:14 "Depart from evil, and do good; seek peace, and pursue it."

Isaiah 1:17 "Learn to do well; seek judgment, relieve the oppressed, judge the fatherless, plead for the widow."

Amos 5:14 "Seek good, and not evil, that ye may live: and so the LORD, the God of hosts, shall be with you, as ye have spoken."

Zephaniah 2:3 "Seek ye the LORD, all ye meek of the earth, which have wrought his judgment; seek righteousness, seek meekness: it may be ye shall be hid in the day of the LORD's anger."

Matthew 6:25-33 "[25]Therefore I say unto you, Take no thought for your life, what ye shall eat, or what ye shall drink; nor yet for your body, what ye shall put on. Is not the life more than meat, and the body than raiment? [26]Behold the fowls of the air: for they sow not, neither do they reap, nor gather into barns; yet your heavenly Father feedeth them. Are ye not much better than they? [27]Which of you by taking thought can add one cubit unto his stature? [28]And why take ye thought for raiment? Consider the lilies of the field, how they grow; they toil not, neither do they spin: [29]And yet I say unto you, That even Solomon in all his glory was not arrayed like one of these. [30]Wherefore, if God so clothe the grass of the field, which to day is, and to morrow is cast into the oven, shall he not much more clothe you, O ye of little faith? [31]Therefore take no thought, saying, What shall we eat? or, What shall we drink? or, Wherewithal shall we be clothed? [32](For after all these things do the Gentiles seek:) for your heavenly Father knoweth that ye have need of all these things. [33]But seek ye first the kingdom of God, and his righteousness; and all these things shall be added unto you."

Luke 12:22-31 "[22]And he said unto his disciples, Therefore I say unto you, Take no thought for your life, what ye shall eat; neither for the body, what ye shall put on. [23]The life is more than meat, and the body is more than raiment. [24]Consider the ravens: for they neither sow nor reap; which neither have storehouse nor barn; and God feedeth them: how much more are ye better than the fowls? [25]And which of you with taking thought can add to his stature one cubit? [26]If ye then be not able to do that thing which is least, why take ye thought for the rest? [27]Consider the lilies how they grow: they toil not, they spin not; and yet I say unto you, that Solomon in all his glory was not arrayed like one of these. [28]If then God so clothe the grass, which is to day in the field, and to morrow is cast into the oven; how much more will he clothe you, O ye of little faith? [29]And seek not ye what ye shall eat, or what ye shall drink, neither be ye of doubtful mind. [30]For all these things do the nations of the world seek after: and your Father knoweth that ye have need of these things. [31]But rather seek ye the kingdom of God; and all these things shall be added unto you."

1 Corinthians 10:33 "Even as I please all men in all things, not seeking mine own profit, but the profit of many, that they may be saved."

1 Corinthians 14:12 "Even so ye, forasmuch as ye are zealous of spiritual gifts, seek that ye may excel to the edifying of the church."

Colossians 3:1-2 "[1]If ye then be risen with Christ, seek those things which are above, where Christ sitteth on the right hand of God. [2]Set your affection on things above, not on things on the earth."

1 Peter 3:11 "Let him eschew evil, and do good; let him seek peace, and ensue it."

Who Does Not Seek God
Psalm 10:4 "The wicked, through the pride of his countenance, will not seek after God: God is not in all his thoughts."

Psalm 119:155 "Salvation is far from the wicked: for they seek not thy statutes."

Who Not To Seek After
Leviticus 19:31 "Regard not them that have familiar spirits, neither seek after wizards, to be defiled by them: I am the LORD your God."

Who Seeks Destruction
Proverbs 17:19 "He loveth transgression that loveth strife: and he that exalteth his gate seeketh destruction."

Who Seeks Love
Proverbs 17:9 "He that covereth a transgression seeketh love; but he that repeateth a matter separateth very friends."

Who Seeks Rebellion
Proverbs 17:11 "An evil man seeketh only rebellion: therefore a cruel messenger shall be sent against him."

Who Shall Not Find Wisdom When They Seek It
Proverbs 1:20-29 "[20]Wisdom crieth without; she uttereth her voice in the streets: [21]She crieth in the chief place of concourse, in the openings of the gates: in the city she uttereth her words, saying, [22]How long, ye simple ones, will ye love simplicity? and the scorners delight in their scorning, and fools hate knowledge? [23]Turn you at my reproof: behold, I will pour out my spirit unto you, I will make known my words unto you. [24]Because I have called, and ye refused; I have stretched out my hand, and no man regarded; [25]But ye have set at nought all my counsel, and would none of my reproof: [26]I also will laugh at your calamity; I will mock when your fear cometh; [27]When your fear cometh as desolation, and your destruction cometh as a whirlwind; when distress and anguish cometh upon you. [28]Then shall they call upon me, but I will not answer; they shall seek me early, but they shall not find me: [29]For that they hated knowledge, and did not choose the fear of the LORD."

Proverbs 14:6 "A scorner seeketh wisdom, and findeth it not: but knowledge is easy unto him that understandeth."

Who Shall Seek The Lord
Hosea 3:4-5 "[4]For the children of Israel shall abide many days without a king, and without a prince, and without a sacrifice, and without an image, and without an ephod, and without teraphim: [5]Afterward shall the children of Israel return, and seek the LORD their God, and David their king; and shall fear the LORD and his goodness in the latter days."

Why People Seek Jesus Christ
John 6:26-27 "[26]Jesus answered them and said, Verily, verily, I say unto you, Ye seek me, not because ye saw the miracles, but because ye did eat of the loaves, and were filled. [27]Labour not for the meat which perisheth, but for that meat which endureth unto everlasting life, which the Son of man shall give unto you: for him hath God the Father sealed."

SELF-RIGHTEOUSNESS

Not Being Self-righteousness Via The Law

Philippians 3:8-11 "⁸Yea doubtless, and I count all things but loss for the excellency of the knowledge of Christ Jesus my Lord: for whom I have suffered the loss of all things, and do count them but dung, that I may win Christ, ⁹And be found in him, not having mine own righteousness, which is of the law, but that which is through the faith of Christ, the righteousness which is of God by faith: ¹⁰That I may know him, and the power of his resurrection, and the fellowship of his sufferings, being made conformable unto his death; ¹¹If by any means I might attain unto the resurrection of the dead."

The Self-righteous

Luke 18:9-14 "⁹And he spake this parable unto certain which trusted in themselves that they were righteous, and despised others: ¹⁰Two men went up into the temple to pray; the one a Pharisee, and the other a publican. ¹¹The Pharisee stood and prayed thus with himself, God, I thank thee, that I am not as other men are, extortioners, unjust, adulterers, or even as this publican. ¹²I fast twice in the week, I give tithes of all that I possess. ¹³And the publican, standing afar off, would not lift up so much as his eyes unto heaven, but smote upon his breast, saying, God be merciful to me a sinner. ¹⁴I tell you, this man went down to his house justified rather than the other: for every one that exalteth himself shall be abased; and he that humbleth himself shall be exalted."

SENDING AND THOSE SENT

God The Father Sending
Jesus Christ Into The World

Zechariah 2:4-13 "⁴And said unto him, Run, speak to this young man, saying, Jerusalem shall be inhabited as towns without walls for the multitude of men and cattle therein: ⁵For I, saith the LORD, will be unto her a wall of fire round about, and will be the glory in the midst of her. ⁶Ho, ho, come forth, and flee from the land of the north, saith the LORD: for I have spread you abroad as the four winds of the heaven, saith the LORD. ⁷Deliver thyself, O Zion, that dwellest with the daughter of Babylon. ⁸For thus saith the LORD of hosts; After the glory hath he sent me unto the nations which spoiled you: for he that toucheth you toucheth the apple of his eye. ⁹For, behold, I will shake mine hand upon them, and they shall be a spoil to their servants: and ye shall know that the LORD of hosts hath sent me. ¹⁰Sing and rejoice, O daughter of Zion: for, lo, I come, and I will dwell in the midst of thee, saith the LORD. ¹¹And many nations shall be joined to the LORD in that day, and shall be my people: and I will dwell in the midst of thee, and thou shalt know that the LORD of hosts hath sent me unto thee. ¹²And the LORD shall inherit Judah his portion in the holy land, and shall choose Jerusalem again. ¹³Be silent, O all flesh, before the LORD: for he is raised up out of his holy habitation."

Luke 20:9-18 "⁹Then began he to speak to the people this parable; A certain man planted a vineyard, and let it forth to husbandmen, and went into a far country for a long time. ¹⁰And at the season he sent a servant to the husbandmen, that they should give him of the fruit of the vineyard: but the husbandmen beat him, and sent him away empty. ¹¹And again he sent another servant: and they beat him also, and entreated him shamefully, and sent him away empty. ¹²And again he sent a third: and they wounded him also, and cast him out. ¹³Then said the lord of the vineyard, What shall I do? I will send my beloved son: it may be they will reverence him when they see him. ¹⁴But when the husbandmen saw him, they reasoned among themselves, saying, This is the heir: come, let us kill him, that the inheritance may be ours. ¹⁵So they cast him out of the vineyard, and killed him. What therefore shall the lord of the vineyard do unto them? ¹⁶He shall come and destroy these husbandmen, and shall give the vineyard to others. And when they heard it, they said, God forbid. ¹⁷And he beheld them, and said, What is this then that is written, The stone which the builders rejected, the same is become the head of the corner? ¹⁸Whosoever shall fall upon that stone shall be broken; but on whomsoever it shall fall, it will grind him to powder."

John 3:16-17 "¹⁶For God so loved the world, that he gave his only begotten Son, that whosoever believeth in him should not perish, but have everlasting life. ¹⁷For God sent not his Son into the world to condemn the world; but that the world through him might be saved."

John 5:23-38 "²³That all men should honour the Son, even as they honour the Father. He that honoureth not the Son honoureth not the Father which hath sent him. ²⁴Verily, verily, I say unto you, He that heareth my word, and believeth on him that sent me, hath everlasting life, and shall not come into condemnation; but is passed from death unto life. ²⁵Verily, verily, I say unto you, The hour is coming, and now is, when the dead shall hear the voice of the Son of God: and they that hear shall live. ²⁶For as the Father hath life in himself; so hath he given to the Son to have life in himself; ²⁷And hath given him authority to execute judgment also, because he is the Son of man. ²⁸Marvel not at this: for the hour is coming, in the which all that are in the graves shall hear his voice, ²⁹And shall come forth; they that have done good, unto the resurrection of life; and they that have done evil, unto the resurrection of damnation. ³⁰I can of mine own self do nothing: as I hear, I judge: and my judgment is just; because I seek not mine own will, but the will of the Father which hath sent me. ³¹If I bear witness of myself, my witness is not true. ³²There is another that beareth witness of me; and I know that the witness which he witnesseth of me is true. ³³Ye sent unto John, and he bare witness unto the truth. ³⁴But I receive not testimony from man: but these things I say, that ye might be saved. ³⁵He was a burning and a shining light: and ye were willing for a season to rejoice in his light. ³⁶But I have greater witness than that of John: for the works which the Father hath given me to finish, the same works that I do, bear witness of me, that the Father hath sent me. ³⁷And the Father himself, which hath sent me, hath borne witness of me. Ye have neither heard his voice at any time, nor seen his shape. ³⁸And ye have not his word abiding in you: for whom he hath sent, him ye believe not."

John 6:29 "Jesus answered and said unto them, This is the work of God, that ye believe on him whom he hath sent."

John 6:35-40 "³⁵And Jesus said unto them, I am the bread of life: he that cometh to me shall never hunger; and he that believeth on me shall never thirst. ³⁶But I said unto you, That ye also have seen me, and believe not. ³⁷All that the Father giveth me shall come to me; and him that cometh

to me I will in no wise cast out. ³⁸For I came down from heaven, not to do mine own will, but the will of him that sent me. ³⁹And this is the Father's will which hath sent me, that of all which he hath given me I should lose nothing, but should raise it up again at the last day. ⁴⁰And this is the will of him that sent me, that every one which seeth the Son, and believeth on him, may have everlasting life: and I will raise him up at the last day."

John 6:43-44 "⁴³Jesus therefore answered and said unto them, Murmur not among yourselves. ⁴⁴No man can come to me, except the Father which hath sent me draw him: and I will raise him up at the last day."

John 6:53-57 "⁵³Then Jesus said unto them, Verily, verily, I say unto you, Except ye eat the flesh of the Son of man, and drink his blood, ye have no life in you. ⁵⁴Whoso eateth my flesh, and drinketh my blood, hath eternal life; and I will raise him up at the last day. ⁵⁵For my flesh is meat indeed, and my blood is drink indeed. ⁵⁶He that eateth my flesh, and drinketh my blood, dwelleth in me, and I in him. ⁵⁷As the living Father hath sent me, and I live by the Father: so he that eateth me, even he shall live by me."

John 7:16-18 "¹⁶Jesus answered them, and said, My doctrine is not mine, but his that sent me. ¹⁷If any man will do his will, he shall know of the doctrine, whether it be of God, or whether I speak of myself. ¹⁸He that speaketh of himself seeketh his own glory: but he that seeketh his glory that sent him, the same is true, and no unrighteousness is in him."

John 7:28-29 "²⁸Then cried Jesus in the temple as he taught, saying, Ye both know me, and ye know whence I am: and I am not come of myself, but he that sent me is true, whom ye know not. ²⁹But I know him: for I am from him, and he hath sent me."

John 7:33 "Then said Jesus unto them, Yet a little while am I with you, and then I go unto him that sent me."

John 8:25-29 "²⁵Then said they unto him, Who art thou? And Jesus saith unto them, Even the same that I said unto you from the beginning. ²⁶I have many things to say and to judge of you: but he that sent me is true; and I speak to the world those things which I have heard of him. [27]They under-stood not that he spake to them of the Father. [28]Then said Jesus unto them, When ye have lifted up the Son of man, then shall ye know that I am he, and that I do nothing of myself; but as my Father hath taught me, I speak these things. [29]And he that sent me is with me: the Father hath not left me alone; for I do always those things that please him."

John 8:42 "Jesus said unto them, If God were your Father, ye would love me: for I proceeded forth and came from God; neither came I of myself, but he sent me."

John 9:3-4 "[3]Jesus answered, Neither hath this man sinned, nor his parents: but that the works of God should be made manifest in him. [4]I must work the works of him that sent me, while it is day: the night cometh, when no man can work."

John 10:34-36 "[34]Jesus answered them, Is it not written in your law, I said, Ye are gods? [35]If he called them gods, unto whom the word of God came, and the scripture cannot be broken; [36]Say ye of him, whom the Father hath sanctified, and sent into the world, Thou blasphemest; because I said, I am the Son of God?"

John 11:41-42 "[41]Then they took away the stone from the place where the dead was laid. And Jesus lifted up his eyes, and said, Father, I thank thee that thou hast heard me. [42]And I knew that thou hearest me always: but because of the people which stand by I said it, that they may believe that thou hast sent me."

John 12:44-49 "[44]Jesus cried and said, He that believeth on me, believeth not on me, but on him that sent me. [45]And he that seeth me seeth him that sent me. [46]I am come a light into the world, that whosoever believeth on me should not abide in darkness. [47]And if any man hear my words, and believe not, I judge him not: for I came not to judge the world, but to save the world. [48]He that rejecteth me, and receiveth not my words, hath one that judgeth him: the word that I have spo-ken, the same shall judge him in the last day. [49]For I have not spoken of myself; but the Father which sent me, he gave me a commandment, what I should say, and what I should speak."

John 14:23-24 "[23]Jesus answered and said unto him, If a man love me, he will keep my words: and my Father will love him, and we will come unto him, and make our abode with him. [24]He that loveth me not keepeth not my sayings: and the word which ye hear is not mine, but the Father's which sent me."

John 15:1-21 "[1]I am the true vine, and my Father is the husbandman. [2]Every branch in me that beareth not fruit he taketh away: and every branch that beareth fruit, he purgeth it, that it may bring forth more fruit. [3]Now ye are clean through the word which I have spoken unto you. [4]Abide in me, and I in you. As the branch cannot bear fruit of itself, except it abide in the vine; no more can ye, except ye abide in me. [5]I am the vine, ye are the branches: He that abideth in me, and I in him, the same bringeth forth much fruit: for without me ye can do nothing. [6]If a man abide not in me, he is cast forth as a branch, and is withered; and men gather them, and cast them into the fire, and they are burned. [7]If ye abide in me, and my words abide in you, ye shall ask what ye will, and it shall be done unto you. [8]Herein is my Father glorified, that ye bear much fruit; so shall ye be my disciples. [9]As the Father hath loved me, so have I loved you: continue ye in my love. [10]If ye keep my commandments, ye shall abide in my love; even as I have kept my Father's command-ments, and abide in his love. [11]These things have I spoken unto you, that my joy might remain in you, and that your joy might be full. [12]This is my commandment, That ye love one another, as I have loved you. [13]Greater love hath no man than this, that a man lay down his life for his friends. [14]Ye are my friends, if ye do whatsoever I com-mand you. [15]Henceforth I call you not servants; for the servant knoweth not what his lord doeth: but I have called you friends; for all things that I have heard of my Father I have made known unto you. [16]Ye have not chosen me, but I have chosen you, and ordained you, that ye should go and bring forth fruit, and that your fruit should remain: that whatsoever ye shall ask of the Father in my name, he may give it you. [17]These things I command you, that ye love one another. [18]If the world hate you, ye know that it hated me before it hated you. [19]If ye were of the world, the world would love his own: but because ye are not of the world, but I have chosen you out of the world, therefore the world hateth you. [20]Remember the word that I said unto you, The servant is not greater than his lord. If they have persecuted me, they will also persecute you; if they have kept my saying, they will keep yours also. 21But all these things will they do unto you for my name's sake, because they know not him that sent me."

John 16:3-5 "3And these things will they do unto you, because they have not known the Father, nor me. 4But these things have I told you, that when the time shall come, ye may remember that I told you of them. And these things I said not unto you at the beginning, because I was with you. 5But now I go my way to him that sent me; and none of you asketh me, Whither goest thou?"

John 16:28-31 "28I came forth from the Father, and am come into the world: again, I leave the world, and go to the Father. 29His disciples said unto him, Lo, now speakest thou plainly, and speakest no proverb. 30Now are we sure that thou knowest all things, and needest not that any man should ask thee: by this we believe that thou camest forth from God. 31Jesus answered them, Do ye now believe?"

John 17:1-25 "1These words spake Jesus, and lifted up his eyes to heaven, and said, Father, the hour is come; glorify thy Son, that thy Son also may glorify thee: 2As thou hast given him power over all flesh, that he should give eternal life to as many as thou hast given him. 3And this is life eternal, that they might know thee the only true God, and Jesus Christ, whom thou hast sent. 4I have glorified thee on the earth: I have finished the work which thou gavest me to do. 5And now, O Father, glorify thou me with thine own self with the glory which I had with thee before the world was. 6I have manifested thy name unto the men which thou gavest me out of the world: thine they were, and thou gavest them me; and they have kept thy word. 7Now they have known that all things whatsoever thou hast given me are of thee. 8For I have given unto them the words which thou gavest me; and they have received them, and have known surely that I came out from thee, and they have believed that thou didst send me. 9I pray for them: I pray not for the world, but for them which thou hast given me; for they are thine. 10And all mine are thine, and thine are mine; and I am glorified in them. 11And now I am no more in the world, but these are in the

world, and I come to thee. Holy Father, keep through thine own name those whom thou hast given me, that they may be one, as we are. 12While I was with them in the world, I kept them in thy name: those that thou gavest me I have kept, and none of them is lost, but the son of perdition; that the scripture might be fulfilled. 13And now come I to thee; and these things I speak in the world, that they might have my joy fulfilled in themselves. 14I have given them thy word; and the world hath hated them, because they are not of the world, even as I am not of the world. 15I pray not that thou shouldest take them out of the world, but that thou shouldest keep them from the evil. 16They are not of the world, even as I am not of the world. 17Sanctify them through thy truth: thy word is truth. 18As thou hast sent me into the world, even so have I also sent them into the world. 19And for their sakes I sanctify myself, that they also might be sanctified through the truth. 20Neither pray I for these alone, but for them also which shall believe on me through their word; 21That they all may be one; as thou, Father, art in me, and I in thee, that they also may be one in us: that the world may believe that thou hast sent me. 22And the glory which thou gavest me I have given them; that they may be one, even as we are one: 23I in them, and thou in me, that they may be made perfect in one; and that the world may know that thou hast sent me, and hast loved them, as thou hast loved me. 24Father, I will that they also, whom thou hast given me, be with me where I am; that they may behold my glory, which thou hast given me: for thou lovedst me before the foundation of the world. 25O righteous Father, the world hath not known thee: but I have known thee, and these have known that thou hast sent me."

John 20:21-22 "21Then said Jesus to them again, Peace be unto you: as my Father hath sent me, even so send I you. 22And when he had said this, he breathed on them, and saith unto them, Receive ye the Holy Ghost."

Acts 3:26 "Unto you first God, having raised up his Son Jesus, sent him to bless you, in turning away every one of you from his iniquities."

Romans 8:1-4 "1There is therefore now no condemnation to them which are in Christ Jesus, who walk not after the flesh, but after the Spirit. 2For the law of the Spirit of life in Christ Jesus hath made me free from the law of sin and death. ³For what the law could not do, in that it was weak through the flesh, God sending his own Son in the likeness of sinful flesh, and for sin, condemned sin in the flesh: ⁴That the righteousness of the law might be fulfilled in us, who walk not after the flesh, but after the Spirit."

Galatians 4:4 "But when the fulness of the time was come, God sent forth his Son, made of a woman, made under the law."

1 John 4:9-10 "⁹In this was manifested the love of God toward us, because that God sent his only begotten Son into the world, that we might live through him. ¹⁰Herein is love, not that we loved God, but that he loved us, and sent his Son to be the propitiation for our sins."

1 John 4:14 "And we have seen and do testify that the Father sent the Son to be the Saviour of the world."

The Holy Spirit Being Sent By God
Psalm 104:24-30 "²⁴O Lᴏʀᴅ, how manifold are thy works! in wisdom hast thou made them all: the earth is full of thy riches. ²⁵So is this great and wide sea, wherein are things creeping innumerable, both small and great beasts. ²⁶There go the ships: there is that leviathan, whom thou hast made to play therein. ²⁷These wait all upon thee; that thou mayest give them their meat in due season. ²⁸That thou givest them they gather: thou openest thine hand, they are filled with good. ²⁹Thou hidest thy face, they are troubled: thou takest away their breath, they die, and return to their dust. ³⁰Thou sendest forth thy spirit, they are created: and thou renewest the face of the earth."

Luke 24:44-49 "⁴⁴And he said unto them, These are the words which I spake unto you, while I was yet with you, that all things must be fulfilled, which were written in the law of Moses, and in the prophets, and in the psalms, concerning me. ⁴⁵Then opened he their understanding, that they might understand the scriptures, ⁴⁶And said unto them, Thus it is written, and thus it behoved Christ to suffer, and to rise from the dead the third day: ⁴⁷And that repentance and remission of sins should be preached in his name among all nations, beginning at Jerusalem. ⁴⁸And ye are witnesses of these things. ⁴⁹And, behold, I send the promise of my Father upon you: but tarry ye in

the city of Jerusalem, until ye be endued with power from on high."

John 14:23-26 "²³Jesus answered and said unto him, If a man love me, he will keep my words: and my Father will love him, and we will come unto him, and make our abode with him. ²⁴He that loveth me not keepeth not my sayings: and the word which ye hear is not mine, but the Father's which sent me. ²⁵These things have I spoken unto you, being yet present with you. ²⁶But the Comforter, which is the Holy Ghost, whom the Father will send in my name, he shall teach you all things, and bring all things to your remembrance, whatsoever I have said unto you."

John 15:26-27 "²⁶But when the Comforter is come, whom I will send unto you from the Father, even the Spirit of truth, which proceedeth from the Father, he shall testify of me: ²⁷And ye also shall bear witness, because ye have been with me from the beginning."

John 16:1-7 "¹These things have I spoken unto you, that ye should not be offended. ²They shall put you out of the synagogues: yea, the time cometh, that whosoever killeth you will think that he doeth God service. ³And these things will they do unto you, because they have not known the Father, nor me. ⁴But these things have I told you, that when the time shall come, ye may remember that I told you of them. And these things I said not unto you at the beginning, because I was with you. ⁵But now I go my way to him that sent me; and none of you asketh me, Whither goest thou? ⁶But because I have said these things unto you, sorrow hath filled your heart. ⁷Nevertheless I tell you the truth; It is expedient for you that I go away: for if I go not away, the Comforter will not come unto you; but if I depart, I will send him unto you."

Galatians 4:6-7 "⁶And because ye are sons, God hath sent forth the Spirit of his Son into your hearts, crying, Abba, Father. ⁷Wherefore thou art no more a servant, but a son; and if a son, then an heir of God through Christ."

1 Peter 1:12 "Unto whom it was revealed, that not unto themselves, but unto us they did minister the things, which are now reported unto you by them that have preached the gospel unto you with the

Holy Ghost sent down from heaven; which things the angels desire to look into."

Those That Send A Message
By The Hand Of A Fool
Proverbs 26:6 "He that sendeth a message by the hand of a fool cutteth off the feet, and drinketh damage."

Who The Lord Did Not Send
Jeremiah 14:13-15 "¹³Then said I, Ah, Lord GOD! behold, the prophets say unto them, Ye shall not see the sword, neither shall ye have famine; but I will give you assured peace in this place. ¹⁴Then the LORD said unto me, The prophets prophesy lies in my name: I sent them not, neither have I commanded them, neither spake unto them: they prophesy unto you a false vision and divination, and a thing of nought, and the deceit of their heart. ¹⁵Therefore thus saith the LORD concerning the prophets that prophesy in my name, and I sent them not, yet they say, Sword and famine shall not be in this land; By sword and famine shall those prophets be consumed."

Jeremiah 23:9-32 "⁹Mine heart within me is broken because of the prophets; all my bones shake; I am like a drunken man, and like a man whom wine hath overcome, because of the LORD, and because of the words of his holiness. ¹⁰For the land is full of adulterers; for because of swearing the land mourneth; the pleasant places of the wilderness are dried up, and their course is evil, and their force is not right. ¹¹For both prophet and priest are profane; yea, in my house have I found their wickedness, saith the LORD. ¹²Wherefore their way shall be unto them as slippery ways in the darkness: they shall be driven on, and fall therein: for I will bring evil upon them, even the year of their visitation, saith the LORD. ¹³And I have seen folly in the prophets of Samaria; they prophesied in Baal, and caused my people Israel to err. ¹⁴I have seen also in the prophets of Jerusalem an horrible thing: they commit adultery, and walk in lies: they strengthen also the hands of evildoers, that none doth return from his wickedness: they are all of them unto me as Sodom, and the inhabitants thereof as Gomorrah. ¹⁵Therefore thus saith the LORD of hosts concerning the prophets; Behold, I will feed them with wormwood, and make them drink the water of gall: for from the prophets of Jerusalem is profaneness gone forth into all the land. ¹⁶Thus saith the LORD of hosts, Hearken not unto the words of the prophets that prophesy unto you: they make you vain: they speak a vision of their own heart, and not out of the mouth of the LORD. ¹⁷They say still unto them that despise me, The LORD hath said, Ye shall have peace; and they say unto every one that walketh after the imagination of his own heart, No evil shall come upon you. ¹⁸For who hath stood in the counsel of the LORD, and hath perceived and heard his word? who hath marked his word, and heard it? ¹⁹Behold, a whirlwind of the LORD is gone forth in fury, even a grievous whirlwind: it shall fall grievously upon the head of the wicked. ²⁰The anger of the LORD shall not return, until he have executed, and till he have performed the thoughts of his heart: in the latter days ye shall consider it perfectly. ²¹I have not sent these prophets, yet they ran: I have not spoken to them, yet they prophesied. ²²But if they had stood in my counsel, and had caused my people to hear my words, then they should have turned them from their evil way, and from the evil of their doings. ²³Am I a God at hand, saith the LORD, and not a God afar off? ²⁴Can any hide himself in secret places that I shall not see him? saith the LORD. Do not I fill heaven and earth? saith the LORD. ²⁵I have heard what the prophets said, that prophesy lies in my name, saying, I have dreamed, I have dreamed. ²⁶How long shall this be in the heart of the prophets that prophesy lies? yea, they are prophets of the deceit of their own heart; ²⁷Which think to cause my people to forget my name by their dreams which they tell every man to his neighbour, as their fathers have forgotten my name for Baal. ²⁸The prophet that hath a dream, let him tell a dream; and he that hath my word, let him speak my word faithfully. What is the chaff to the wheat? saith the LORD. ²⁹Is not my word like as a fire? saith the LORD; and like a hammer that breaketh the rock in pieces? ³⁰Therefore, behold, I am against the prophets, saith the LORD, that steal my words every one from his neighbour. ³¹Behold, I am against the prophets, saith the LORD, that use their tongues, and say, He saith. ³²Behold, I am against them that prophesy false dreams, saith the LORD, and do tell them, and cause my people to err by their lies, and by their lightness; yet I sent them not, nor commanded them: therefore they shall not profit this people at all, saith the LORD."

Jeremiah 28:1-15 "¹And it came to pass the same year, in the beginning of the reign of Zedekiah king of Judah, in the fourth year, and in the fifth month, that Hananiah the son of Azur the prophet, which was of Gibeon, spake unto me in the house of the LORD, in the presence of the priests and of all the people, saying, ²Thus speaketh the LORD of hosts, the God of Israel, saying, I have broken the yoke of the king of Babylon. ³Within two full years will I bring again into this place all the vessels of the LORD's house, that Nebuchadnezzar king of Babylon took away from this place, and carried them to Babylon: ⁴And I will bring again to this place Jeconiah the son of Jehoiakim king of Judah, with all the captives of Judah, that went into Babylon, saith the LORD: for I will break the yoke of the king of Babylon. ⁵Then the prophet Jeremiah said unto the prophet Hananiah in the presence of the priests, and in the presence of all the people that stood in the house of the LORD, ⁶Even the prophet Jeremiah said, Amen: the LORD do so: the LORD perform thy words which thou hast prophesied, to bring again the vessels of the LORD's house, and all that is carried away captive, from Babylon into this place. ⁷Nevertheless hear thou now this word that I speak in thine ears, and in the ears of all the people; ⁸The prophets that have been before me and before thee of old prophesied both against many countries, and against great kingdoms, of war, and of evil, and of pestilence. ⁹The prophet which prophesieth of peace, when the word of the prophet shall come to pass, then shall the prophet be known, that the LORD hath truly sent him. ¹⁰Then Hananiah the prophet took the yoke from off the prophet Jeremiah's neck, and brake it. ¹¹And Hananiah spake in the presence of all the people, saying, Thus saith the LORD; Even so will I break the yoke of Nebuchadnezzar king of Babylon from the neck of all nations within the space of two full years. And the prophet Jeremiah went his way. ¹²Then the word of the LORD came unto Jeremiah the prophet, after that Hananiah the prophet had broken the yoke from off the neck of the prophet Jeremiah, saying, ¹³Go and tell Hananiah, saying, Thus saith the LORD; Thou hast broken the yokes of wood; but thou shalt make for them yokes of iron. ¹⁴For thus saith the

LORD of hosts, the God of Israel; I have put a yoke of iron upon the neck of all these nations, that they may serve Nebuchadnezzar king of Babylon; and they shall serve him: and I have given him the beasts of the field also. ¹⁵Then said the prophet Jeremiah unto Hananiah the prophet, Hear now, Hananiah; The LORD hath not sent thee; but thou makest this people to trust in a lie."

Jeremiah 29:8-9 "⁸For thus saith the LORD of hosts, the God of Israel; Let not your prophets and your diviners, that be in the midst of you, deceive you, neither hearken to your dreams which ye cause to be dreamed. ⁹For they prophesy falsely unto you in my name: I have not sent them, saith the LORD."

Ezekiel 13:3-6 "³Thus saith the Lord GOD; Woe unto the foolish prophets, that follow their own spirit, and have seen nothing! ⁴O Israel, thy prophets are like the foxes in the deserts. ⁵Ye have not gone up into the gaps, neither made up the hedge for the house of Israel to stand in the battle in the day of the LORD. ⁶They have seen vanity and lying divination, saying, The LORD saith: and the LORD hath not sent them: and they have made others to hope that they would confirm the word."

Who The Lord Sent

Genesis 19:1-13 "¹And there came two angels to Sodom at even; and Lot sat in the gate of Sodom: and Lot seeing them rose up to meet them; and he bowed himself with his face toward the ground; ²And he said, Behold now, my lords, turn in, I pray you, into your servant's house, and tarry all night, and wash your feet, and ye shall rise up early, and go on your ways. And they said, Nay; but we will abide in the street all night. ³And he pressed upon them greatly; and they turned in unto him, and entered into his house; and he made them a feast, and did bake unleavened bread, and they did eat. ⁴But before they lay down, the men of the city, even the meXn of Sodom, compassed the house round, both old and young, all the people from every quarter: ⁵And they called unto Lot, and said unto him, Where are the men which came in to thee this night? bring them out unto us, that we may know them. ⁶And Lot went out at the door unto them, and shut the door after him, ⁷And said, I pray you, brethren, do not so wickedly. ⁸Behold now, I have two daughters which have not known man; let me, I pray you, bring them out unto you, and do ye to them as is good in your eyes: only unto these men do nothing; for therefore came they under the shadow of my roof. [9]And they said, Stand back. And they said again, This one fellow came in to sojourn, and he will needs be a judge: now will we deal worse with thee, than with them. And they pressed sore upon the man, even Lot, and came near to break the door. [10]But the men put forth their hand, and pulled Lot into the house to them, and shut to the door. [11]And they smote the men that were at the door of the house with blindness, both small and great: so that they wearied themselves to find the door. [12]And the men said unto Lot, Hast thou here any besides? son in law, and thy sons, and thy daughters, and whatsoever thou hast in the city, bring them out of this place: [13]For we will destroy this place, because the cry of them is waxen great before the face of the LORD; and the LORD hath sent us to destroy it."

Exodus 3:13-14 "[13]And Moses said unto God, Behold, when I come unto the children of Israel, and shall say unto them, The God of your fathers hath sent me unto you; and they shall say to me, What is his name? what shall I say unto them? [14]And God said unto Moses, I AM THAT I AM: and he said, Thus shalt thou say unto the children of Israel, I AM hath sent me unto you."

Exodus 7:14-16 "[14]And the LORD said unto Moses, Pharaoh's heart is hardened, he refuseth to let the people go. [15]Get thee unto Pharaoh in the morning; lo, he goeth out unto the water; and thou shalt stand by the river's brink against he come; and the rod which was turned to a serpent shalt thou take in thine hand. [16]And thou shalt say unto him, The LORD God of the Hebrews hath sent me unto thee, saying, Let my people go, that they may serve me in the wilderness: and, behold, hitherto thou wouldest not hear."

Exodus 23:20-25 "[20]Behold, I send an Angel before thee, to keep thee in the way, and to bring thee into the place which I have prepared. [21]Beware of him, and obey his voice, provoke him not; for he will not pardon your transgressions: for my name is in him. [22]But if thou shalt indeed obey his voice, and do all that I speak; then I will be an enemy unto thine enemies, and an adversary unto thine adversaries. [23]For mine Angel shall go before thee,

and bring thee in unto the Amorites, and the Hittites, and the Perizzites, and the Canaanites, and the Hivites, and the Jebusites: and I will cut them off. [24]Thou shalt not bow down to their gods, nor serve them, nor do after their works: but thou shalt utterly overthrow them, and quite break down their images. [25]And ye shall serve the LORD your God, and he shall bless thy bread, and thy water; and I will take sickness away from the midst of thee."

Numbers 16:28 "And Moses said, Hereby ye shall know that the LORD hath sent me to do all these works; for I have not done them of mine own mind."

2 Kings 17:13 "Yet the LORD testified against Israel, and against Judah, by all the prophets, and by all the seers, saying, Turn ye from your evil ways, and keep my commandments and my statutes, according to all the law which I commanded your fathers, and which I sent to you by my servants the prophets."

Isaiah 48:12-16 "[12]Hearken unto me, O Jacob and Israel, my called; I am he; I am the first, I also am the last. [13]Mine hand also hath laid the foundation of the earth, and my right hand hath spanned the heavens: when I call unto them, they stand up together. [14]All ye, assemble yourselves, and hear; which among them hath declared these things? The LORD hath loved him: he will do his pleasure on Babylon, and his arm shall be on the Chaldeans. [15]I, even I, have spoken; yea, I have called him: I have brought him, and he shall make his way prosperous. [16]Come ye near unto me, hear ye this; I have not spoken in secret from the beginning; from the time that it was, there am I: and now the Lord GOD, and his Spirit, hath sent me."

Jeremiah 16:14-16 "[14]Therefore, behold, the days come, saith the LORD, that it shall no more be said, The LORD liveth, that brought up the children of Israel out of the land of Egypt; [15]But, The LORD liveth, that brought up the children of Israel from the land of the north, and from all the lands whither he had driven them: and I will bring them again into their land that I gave unto their fathers. [16]Behold, I will send for many fishers, saith the LORD, and they shall fish them; and after will I send for many hunters, and they shall hunt them from every mountain, and from every hill, and out of the holes of the rocks."

Jeremiah 19:14 "Then came Jeremiah from Tophet, whither the LORD had sent him to prophesy; and he stood in the court of the LORD's house; and said to all the people."

Jeremiah 25:4 "And the LORD hath sent unto you all his servants the prophets, rising early and sending them; but ye have not hearkened, nor inclined your ear to hear."

Jeremiah 26:12 "Then spake Jeremiah unto all the princes and to all the people, saying, The LORD sent me to prophesy against this house and against this city all the words that ye have heard."

Jeremiah 28:9 "The prophet which prophesieth of peace, when the word of the prophet shall come to pass, then shall the prophet be known, that the LORD hath truly sent him."

Daniel 3:28 "Then Nebuchadnezzar spake, and said, Blessed be the God of Shadrach, Meshach, and Abed-nego, who hath sent his angel, and delivered his servants that trusted in him, and have changed the king's word, and yielded their bodies, that they might not serve nor worship any god, except their own God."

Zechariah 7:12 "Yea, they made their hearts as an adamant stone, lest they should hear the law, and the words which the LORD of hosts hath sent in his spirit by the former prophets: therefore came a great wrath from the LORD of hosts."

Malachi 3:1 "Behold, I will send my messenger, and he shall prepare the way before me: and the Lord, whom ye seek, shall suddenly come to his temple, even the messenger of the covenant, whom ye delight in: behold, he shall come, saith the LORD of hosts."

Matthew 10:5-16 "⁵These twelve Jesus sent forth, and commanded them, saying, Go not into the way of the Gentiles, and into any city of the Samaritans enter ye not: ⁶But go rather to the lost sheep of the house of Israel. ⁷And as ye go, preach, saying, The kingdom of heaven is at hand. ⁸Heal the sick, cleanse the lepers, raise the dead, cast out devils: freely ye have received, freely give. ⁹Provide neither gold, nor silver, nor brass in your purses, ¹⁰Nor scrip for your journey, neither two coats, neither shoes, nor yet staves: for the workman is worthy of his meat. ¹¹And into whatsoever city or town ye shall enter, inquire who in it is worthy; and there abide till ye go thence. ¹²And when ye come into an house, salute it. ¹³And if the house be worthy, let your peace come upon it: but if it be not worthy, let your peace return to you. ¹⁴And whosoever shall not receive you, nor hear your words, when ye depart out of that house or city, shake off the dust of your feet. ¹⁵Verily I say unto you, It shall be more tolerable for the land of Sodom and Gomorrha in the day of judgment, than for that city. ¹⁶Behold, I send you forth as sheep in the midst of wolves: be ye therefore wise as serpents, and harmless as doves."

Matthew 11:7-11 "⁷And as they departed, Jesus began to say unto the multitudes concerning John, What went ye out into the wilderness to see? A reed shaken with the wind? ⁸But what went ye out for to see? A man clothed in soft raiment? behold, they that wear soft clothing are in kings' houses. ⁹But what went ye out for to see? A prophet? yea, I say unto you, and more than a prophet. ¹⁰For this is he, of whom it is written, Behold, I send my messenger before thy face, which shall prepare thy way before thee. ¹¹Verily I say unto you, Among them that are born of women there hath not risen a greater than John the Baptist: notwithstanding he that is least in the kingdom of heaven is greater than he."

Matthew 13:41 "The Son of man shall send forth his angels, and they shall gather out of his kingdom all things that offend, and them which do iniquity."

Matthew 23:33-34 "³³Ye serpents, ye generation of vipers, how can ye escape the damnation of hell? ³⁴Wherefore, behold, I send unto you prophets, and wise men, and scribes: and some of them ye shall kill and crucify; and some of them shall ye scourge in your synagogues, and persecute them from city to city."

Matthew 28:16-20 "¹⁶Then the eleven disciples went away into Galilee, into a mountain where Jesus had appointed them. ¹⁷And when they saw him, they worshipped him: but some doubted. ¹⁸And Jesus came and spake unto them, saying, All power is given unto me in heaven and in earth. ¹⁹Go ye therefore, and teach all nations, baptizing them in the name of the Father, and of the Son, and of the Holy Ghost: [20]Teaching them to observe all things whatsoever I have commanded you: and, lo, I am with you alway, even unto the end of the world. Amen."

Mark 6:4-7 "[4]But Jesus said unto them, A prophet is not without honour, but in his own country, and among his own kin, and in his own house. [5]And he could there do no mighty work, save that he laid his hands upon a few sick folk, and healed them. [6]And he marvelled because of their unbelief. And he went round about the villages, teaching. [7]And he called unto him the twelve, and began to send them forth by two and two; and gave them power over unclean spirits."

Mark 16:9-20 "[9]Now when Jesus was risen early the first day of the week, he appeared first to Mary Magdalene, out of whom he had cast seven devils. [10]And she went and told them that had been with him, as they mourned and wept. [11]And they, when they had heard that he was alive, and had been seen of her, believed not. [12]After that he appeared in another form unto two of them, as they walked, and went into the country. [13]And they went and told it unto the residue: neither believed they them. [14]Afterward he appeared unto the eleven as they sat at meat, and upbraided them with their unbelief and hardness of heart, because they believed not them which had seen him after he was risen. [15]And he said unto them, Go ye into all the world, and preach the gospel to every creature. [16]He that believeth and is baptized shall be saved; but he that believeth not shall be damned. [17]And these signs shall follow them that believe; In my name shall they cast out devils; they shall speak with new tongues; [18]They shall take up serpents; and if they drink any deadly thing, it shall not hurt them; they shall lay hands on the sick, and they shall recover. [19]So then after the Lord had spoken unto them, he was received up into heaven, and sat on the right hand of God. [20]And they went forth, and preached everywhere, the Lord working with them, and confirming the word with signs following. Amen."

Luke 7:22-28 "[22]Then Jesus answering said unto them, Go your way, and tell John what things ye have seen and heard; how that the blind see, the lame walk, the lepers are cleansed, the deaf hear, the dead are raised, to the poor the gospel is preached. [23]And blessed is he, whosoever shall not be offended in me. [24]And when the messengers of John were departed, he began to speak unto the people concerning John, What went ye out into the wilderness for to see? A reed shaken with the wind? [25]But what went ye out for to see? A man clothed in soft raiment? Behold, they which are gorgeously apparelled, and live delicately, are in kings' courts. [26]But what went ye out for to see? A prophet? Yea, I say unto you, and much more than a prophet. [27]This is he, of whom it is written, Behold, I send my messenger before thy face, which shall prepare thy way before thee. [28]For I say unto you, Among those that are born of women there is not a greater prophet than John the Baptist: but he that is least in the kingdom of God is greater than he."

Luke 9:1-2 "[1]Then he called his twelve disciples together, and gave them power and authority over all devils, and to cure diseases. [2]And he sent them to preach the kingdom of God, and to heal the sick."

Luke 10:1-16 "[1]After these things the Lord appointed other seventy also, and sent them two and two before his face into every city and place, whither he himself would come. [2]Therefore said he unto them, The harvest truly is great, but the labourers are few: pray ye therefore the Lord of the harvest, that he would send forth labourers into his harvest. [3]Go your ways: behold, I send you forth as lambs among wolves. [4]Carry neither purse, nor scrip, nor shoes: and salute no man by the way. [5]And into whatsoever house ye enter, first say, Peace be to this house. [6]And if the son of peace be there, your peace shall rest upon it: if not, it shall turn to you again. [7]And in the same house remain, eating and drinking such things as they give: for the labourer is worthy of his hire. Go not from house to house. [8]And into whatsoever city ye enter, and they receive you, eat such things as are set before you: [9]And heal the sick that are therein, and say unto them, The kingdom of God is come nigh unto you. [10]But into whatsoever city ye enter, and they receive you not, go your ways out into the streets of the same, and say, [11]Even the very dust of your city, which cleaveth on us, we do wipe off against you: notwithstanding be ye sure of this, that the kingdom of God is come nigh unto you. [12]But I say unto you, that it shall be more tolerable in that day for Sodom, than for that city. ¹³Woe unto thee, Chorazin! woe unto thee, Bethsaida! for if the mighty works had been done in Tyre and Sidon, which have been done in you, they had a great while ago repented, sitting in sackcloth and ashes. ¹⁴But it shall be more tolerable for Tyre and Sidon at the judgment, than for you. ¹⁵And thou, Capernaum, which art exalted to heaven, shalt be thrust down to hell. ¹⁶He that heareth you heareth me; and he that despiseth you despiseth me; and he that despiseth me despiseth him that sent me."

John 1:6-8 "⁶There was a man sent from God, whose name was John. ⁷The same came for a witness, to bear witness of the Light, that all men through him might believe. ⁸He was not that Light, but was sent to bear witness of that Light."

John 1:32-34 "³²And John bare record, saying, I saw the Spirit descending from heaven like a dove, and it abode upon him. ³³And I knew him not: but he that sent me to baptize with water, the same said unto me, Upon whom thou shalt see the Spirit descending, and remaining on him, the same is he which baptizeth with the Holy Ghost. ³⁴And I saw, and bare record that this is the Son of God."

John 3:27-28 "²⁷John answered and said, A man can receive nothing, except it be given him from heaven. ²⁸Ye yourselves bear me witness, that I said, I am not the Christ, but that I am sent before him."

John 17:1-18 "¹These words spake Jesus, and lifted up his eyes to heaven, and said, Father, the hour is come; glorify thy Son, that thy Son also may glorify thee: ²As thou hast given him power over all flesh, that he should give eternal life to as many as thou hast given him. ³And this is life eternal, that they might know thee the only true God, and Jesus Christ, whom thou hast sent. ⁴I have glorified thee on the earth: I have finished the work which thou gavest me to do. ⁵And now, O Father, glorify thou me with thine own self with the glory which I had with thee before the world was. ⁶I have manifested thy name unto the men which thou gavest me out of the world: thine they were, and thou gavest them me; and they have kept thy word. ⁷Now they have known that all things whatsoever thou hast given me are of

thee. ⁸For I have given unto them the words which thou gavest me; and they have received them, and have known surely that I came out from thee, and they have believed that thou didst send me. ⁹I pray for them: I pray not for the world, but for them which thou hast given me; for they are thine. ¹⁰And all mine are thine, and thine are mine; and I am glorified in them. ¹¹And now I am no more in the world, but these are in the world, and I come to thee. Holy Father, keep through thine own name those whom thou hast given me, that they may be one, as we are. ¹²While I was with them in the world, I kept them in thy name: those that thou gavest me I have kept, and none of them is lost, but the son of perdition; that the scripture might be fulfilled. ¹³And now come I to thee; and these things I speak in the world, that they might have my joy fulfilled in themselves. ¹⁴I have given them thy word; and the world hath hated them, because they are not of the world, even as I am not of the world. ¹⁵I pray not that thou shouldest take them out of the world, but that thou shouldest keep them from the evil. ¹⁶They are not of the world, even as I am not of the world. ¹⁷Sanctify them through thy truth: thy word is truth. ¹⁸As thou hast sent me into the world, even so have I also sent them into the world."

John 20:21-22 "²¹Then said Jesus to them again, Peace be unto you: as my Father hath sent me, even so send I you. ²²And when he had said this, he breathed on them, and saith unto them, Receive ye the Holy Ghost."

Acts 9:1-6 "¹And Saul, yet breathing out threatenings and slaughter against the disciples of the Lord, went unto the high priest, ²And desired of him letters to Damascus to the synagogues, that if he found any of this way, whether they were men or women, he might bring them bound unto Jerusalem. ³And as he journeyed, he came near Damascus: and suddenly there shined round about him a light from heaven: ⁴And he fell to the earth, and heard a voice saying unto him, Saul, Saul, why persecutest thou me? ⁵And he said, Who art thou, Lord? And the Lord said, I am Jesus whom thou persecutest: it is hard for thee to kick against the pricks. ⁶And he trembling and astonished said, Lord, what wilt thou have me to do? And the Lord said unto him, Arise, and go into the city, and it shall be told thee what thou must do."

Acts 22:6-10 "⁶And it came to pass, that, as I made my journey, and was come nigh unto Damascus about noon, suddenly there shone from heaven a great light round about me. ⁷And I fell unto the ground, and heard a voice saying unto me, Saul, Saul, why persecutest thou me? ⁸And I answered, Who art thou, Lord? And he said unto me, I am Jesus of Nazareth, whom thou persecutest. ⁹And they that were with me saw indeed the light, and were afraid; but they heard not the voice of him that spake to me. ¹⁰And I said, What shall I do, Lord? And the Lord said unto me, Arise, and go into Damascus; and there it shall be told thee of all things which are appointed for thee to do."

Acts 26:12-17 "¹²Whereupon as I went to Damascus with authority and commission from the chief priests, ¹³At midday, O king, I saw in the way a light from heaven, above the brightness of the sun, shining round about me and them which journeyed with me. ¹⁴And when we were all fallen to the earth, I heard a voice speaking unto me, and saying in the Hebrew tongue, Saul, Saul, why persecutest thou me? it is hard for thee to kick against the pricks. ¹⁵And I said, Who art thou, Lord? And he said, I am Jesus whom thou persecutest. ¹⁶But rise, and stand upon thy feet: for I have appeared unto thee for this purpose, to make thee a minister and a witness both of these things which thou hast seen, and of those things in the which I will appear unto thee; ¹⁷Delivering thee from the people, and from the Gentiles, unto whom now I send thee."

1 Corinthians 1:12-17 "¹²Now this I say, that every one of you saith, I am of Paul; and I of Apollos; and I of Cephas; and I of Christ. ¹³Is Christ divided? was Paul crucified for you? or were ye baptized in the name of Paul? ¹⁴I thank God that I baptized none of you, but Crispus and Gaius; ¹⁵Lest any should say that I had baptized in mine own name. ¹⁶And I baptized also the household of Stephanas: besides, I know not whether I baptized any other. ¹⁷For Christ sent me not to baptize, but to preach the gospel: not with wisdom of words, lest the cross of Christ should be made of none effect."

Revelation 1:1 "The Revelation of Jesus Christ, which God gave unto him, to shew unto his servants things which must shortly come to pass; and he sent and signified it by his angel unto his servant John."

Revelation 22:6 "And he said unto me, These sayings are faithful and true: and the Lord God of the holy prophets sent his angel to shew unto his servants the things which must shortly be done."

Revelation 22:16 "I Jesus have sent mine angel to testify unto you these things in the churches. I am the root and the offspring of David, and the bright and morning star."

SEPARATION

Israel Being Separate From All Other People

Leviticus 20:22-26 "²²Ye shall therefore keep all my statutes, and all my judgments, and do them: that the land, whither I bring you to dwell therein, spue you not out. ²³And ye shall not walk in the manners of the nation, which I cast out before you: for they committed all these things, and therefore I abhorred them. ²⁴But I have said unto you, Ye shall inherit their land, and I will give it unto you to possess it, a land that floweth with milk and honey: I am the LORD your God, which have separated you from other people. ²⁵Ye shall therefore put difference between clean beasts and unclean, and between unclean fowls and clean: and ye shall not make your souls abominable by beast, or by fowl, or by any manner of living thing that creepeth on the ground, which I have separated from you as unclean. ²⁶And ye shall be holy unto me: for I the LORD am holy, and have severed you from other people, that ye should be mine."

1 Kings 8:51-53 "⁵¹For they be thy people, and thine inheritance, which thou broughtest forth out of Egypt, from the midst of the furnace of iron: ⁵²That thine eyes may be open unto the supplication of thy servant, and unto the supplication of thy people Israel, to hearken unto them in all that they call for unto thee. ⁵³For thou didst separate them from among all the people of the earth, to be thine inheritance, as thou spakest by the hand of Moses thy servant, when thou broughtest our fathers out of Egypt, O Lord GOD."

Nothing Being Able To Separate You From The Love Of God

Romans 8:39 "Nor height, nor depth, nor any other creature, shall be able to separate us from the love of God, which is in Christ Jesus our Lord."

Separating Yourself From Unclean Things

Isaiah 52:11 "Depart ye, depart ye, go ye out from thence, touch no unclean thing; go ye out of the midst of her; be ye clean, that bear the vessels of the LORD."

2 Corinthians 6:14-18 "¹⁴Be ye not unequally yoked together with unbelievers: for what fellowship hath righteousness with unrighteousness? and what communion hath light with darkness? ¹⁵And what concord hath Christ with Belial? or what part hath he that believeth with an infidel? ¹⁶And what agreement hath the temple of God with idols? for ye are the temple of the living God; as God hath said, I will dwell in them, and walk in them; and I will be their God, and they shall be my people. ¹⁷Wherefore come out from among them, and be ye separate, saith the Lord, and touch not the unclean thing; and I will receive you, ¹⁸And will be a Father unto you, and ye shall be my sons and daughters, saith the Lord Almighty."

Revelation 18:4 "And I heard another voice from heaven, saying, Come out of her, my people, that ye be not partakers of her sins, and that ye receive not of her plagues."

What Separates You From God

Isaiah 59:1-2 "¹Behold, the LORD's hand is not shortened, that it cannot save; neither his ear heavy, that it cannot hear: ²But your iniquities have separated between you and your God, and your sins have hid his face from you, that he will not hear."

Who The Lord Will Separate

Deuteronomy 29:19-21 "¹⁹And it come to pass, when he heareth the words of this curse, that he bless himself in his heart, saying, I shall have peace, though I walk in the imagination of mine heart, to add drunkenness to thirst: ²⁰The LORD will not spare him, but then the anger of the LORD and his jealousy shall smoke against that man, and all the curses that are written in this book shall lie upon him, and the LORD shall blot out his name from under heaven. ²¹And the LORD shall separate him unto evil out of all the tribes of Israel, according to all the curses of the covenant that are written in this book of the law."

Matthew 13:24-50 "²⁴Another parable put he forth unto them, saying, The kingdom of heaven is likened unto a man which sowed good seed in his field: ²⁵But while men slept, his enemy came and sowed tares among the wheat, and went his way. ²⁶But when the blade was sprung up, and brought forth fruit, then appeared the tares also. ²⁷So the servants of the householder came and said unto him, Sir, didst not thou sow good seed in thy field? from whence then hath it tares? ²⁸He said unto them, An enemy hath done this. The servants said unto him, Wilt thou then that we go and gather them up? ²⁹But he said, Nay; lest while ye gather up the tares, ye root up also the wheat with them. ³⁰Let both grow together until the harvest: and in the time of harvest I will say to the reapers, Gather ye together first the tares, and bind them in bundles to burn them: but gather the wheat into my barn. ³¹Another parable put he forth unto them, saying, The kingdom of heaven is like to a grain of mustard seed, which a man took, and sowed in his field: ³²Which indeed is the least of all seeds: but when it is grown, it is the greatest among herbs, and becometh a tree, so that the birds of the air come and lodge in the branches thereof. ³³Another parable spake he unto them; The kingdom of heaven is like unto leaven, which a woman took, and hid in three measures of meal, till the whole was leavened. ³⁴All these things spake Jesus unto the multitude in parables; and without a parable spake he not unto them: ³⁵That it might be fulfilled which was spoken by the prophet, saying, I will open my mouth in parables; I will utter things which have been kept secret from the foundation of the world. ³⁶Then Jesus sent the multitude away, and went into the house: and his disciples came unto him, saying, Declare unto us the parable of the tares of the field. ³⁷He answered and said unto them, He that soweth the good seed is the Son of man; ³⁸The field is the world; the good seed are the children of the kingdom; but the tares are the children of the wicked one; ³⁹The enemy that sowed them is the devil; the harvest is the end of the world; and the reapers are the angels. ⁴⁰As therefore the tares are gathered and burned in the fire; so shall it be in the end of this world. ⁴¹The Son of man shall send forth his angels, and they shall gather out of his kingdom all things that offend, and them which do iniquity; ⁴²And shall cast them into a furnace of fire: there shall be wailing and gnashing of teeth. ⁴³Then shall the righteous shine forth as the sun in the kingdom of their Father. Who hath ears to hear, let him hear. ⁴⁴Again, the kingdom of heaven is like unto treasure hid in a field; the which when a man hath found, he hideth, and for joy thereof goeth and selleth all that he hath, and buyeth that field. ⁴⁵Again, the kingdom of heaven is like unto a merchant man, seeking goodly pearls: ⁴⁶Who, when he had found one pearl of great price, went and sold all that he had, and bought it. ⁴⁷Again, the kingdom of heaven is like unto a net, that was cast into the sea, and gathered of every kind: ⁴⁸Which, when it was full, they drew to shore, and sat down, and gathered the good into vessels, but cast the bad away. ⁴⁹So shall it be at the end of the world: the angels shall come forth, and sever the wicked from among the just, ⁵⁰And shall cast them into the furnace of fire: there shall be wailing and gnashing of teeth."

Matthew 25:31-46 "³¹When the Son of man shall come in his glory, and all the holy angels with him, then shall he sit upon the throne of his glory: ³²And before him shall be gathered all nations: and he shall separate them one from another, as a shepherd divideth his sheep from the goats: ³³And he shall set the sheep on his right hand, but the goats on the left. ³⁴Then shall the King say unto them on his right hand, Come, ye blessed of my Father, inherit the kingdom prepared for you from the foundation of the world: ³⁵For I was an hungred, and ye gave me meat: I was thirsty, and ye gave me drink: I was a stranger, and ye took me in: ³⁶Naked, and ye clothed me: I was sick, and ye visited me: I was in prison, and ye came unto me. ³⁷Then shall the righteous answer him, saying, Lord, when saw we thee an hungred, and fed thee? or thirsty, and gave thee drink? ³⁸When saw we thee a stranger, and took thee in? or naked, and clothed thee? ³⁹Or when saw we thee sick, or in prison, and came unto thee? ⁴⁰And the King shall answer and say unto them, Verily I say unto you, Inasmuch as ye have done it unto one of the least of these my brethren, ye have done it unto me. ⁴¹Then shall he say also unto them on the left hand, Depart from me, ye cursed, into everlasting fire, prepared for the devil and his angels: ⁴²For I was an hungred, and ye gave me no meat: I was thirsty, and ye gave me no drink: ⁴³I was a stranger, and ye took me not in: naked, and ye clothed me not: sick, and in prison, and ye visited me not. ⁴⁴Then shall they also answer him,

saying, Lord, when saw we thee an hungred, or athirst, or a stranger, or naked, or sick, or in prison, and did not minister unto thee? ⁴⁵Then shall he answer them, saying, Verily I say unto you, Inasmuch as ye did it not to one of the least of these, ye did it not to me. ⁴⁶And these shall go away into everlasting punishment: but the righteous into life eternal."

SERVANTS

Faithful Servants

Matthew 24:42-47 "⁴²Watch therefore: for ye know not what hour your Lord doth come. ⁴³But know this, that if the goodman of the house had known in what watch the thief would come, he would have watched, and would not have suffered his house to be broken up. ⁴⁴Therefore be ye also ready: for in such an hour as ye think not the Son of man cometh. ⁴⁵Who then is a faithful and wise servant, whom his lord hath made ruler over his household, to give them meat in due season? ⁴⁶Blessed is that servant, whom his lord when he cometh shall find so doing. ⁴⁷Verily I say unto you, That he shall make him ruler over all his goods."

Luke 12:35-40 "³⁵Let your loins be girded about, and your lights burning; ³⁶And ye yourselves like unto men that wait for their lord, when he will return from the wedding; that when he cometh and knocketh, they may open unto him immediately. ³⁷Blessed are those servants, whom the lord when he cometh shall find watching: verily I say unto you, that he shall gird himself, and make them to sit down to meat, and will come forth and serve them. ³⁸And if he shall come in the second watch, or come in the third watch, and find them so, blessed are those servants. ³⁹And this know, that if the goodman of the house had known what hour the thief would come, he would have watched, and not have suffered his house to be broken through. ⁴⁰Be ye therefore ready also: for the Son of man cometh at an hour when ye think not."

Luke 19:12-19 "¹²He said therefore, A certain nobleman went into a far country to receive for himself a kingdom, and to return. ¹³And he called his ten servants, and delivered them ten pounds, and said unto them, Occupy till I come. ¹⁴But his citizens hated him, and sent a message after him, saying, We will not have this man to reign over us.

¹⁵And it came to pass, that when he was returned, having received the kingdom, then he commanded these servants to be called unto him, to whom he had given the money, that he might know how much every man had gained by trading. ¹⁶Then came the first, saying, Lord, thy pound hath gained ten pounds. ¹⁷And he said unto him, Well, thou good servant: because thou hast been faithful in a very little, have thou authority over ten cities. ¹⁸And the second came, saying, Lord, thy pound hath gained five pounds. ¹⁹And he said likewise to him, Be thou also over five cities."

Jesus Christ Taking The Form Of A Servant
Luke 22:22-27 "²²And truly the Son of man goeth, as it was determined: but woe unto that man by whom he is betrayed! ²³And they began to inquire among themselves, which of them it was that should do this thing. ²⁴And there was also a strife among them, which of them should be accounted the greatest. ²⁵And he said unto them, The kings of the Gentiles exercise lordship over them; and they that exercise authority upon them are called benefactors. ²⁶But ye shall not be so: but he that is greatest among you, let him be as the younger; and he that is chief, as he that doth serve. ²⁷For whether is greater, he that sitteth at meat, or he that serveth? is not he that sitteth at meat? but I am among you as he that serveth."

Philippians 2:5-8 "⁵Let this mind be in you, which was also in Christ Jesus: ⁶Who, being in the form of God, thought it not robbery to be equal with God: ⁷But made himself of no reputation, and took upon him the form of a servant, and was made in the likeness of men: ⁸And being found in fashion as a man, he humbled himself, and became obedient unto death, even the death of the cross."

Servants Not Being Able To Serve Two Masters
Matthew 6:24 "No man can serve two masters: for either he will hate the one, and love the other; or else he will hold to the one, and despise the other. Ye cannot serve God and mammon."

Luke 16:13 "No servant can serve two masters: for either he will hate the one, and love the other; or else he will hold to the one, and despise the other. Ye cannot serve God and mammon."

1 Corinthians 10:20-22 "²⁰But I say, that the things which the Gentiles sacrifice, they sacrifice to devils, and not to God: and I would not that ye should have fellowship with devils. ²¹Ye cannot drink the cup of the Lord, and the cup of devils: ye cannot be partakers of the Lord's table, and of the table of devils. ²²Do we provoke the Lord to jealousy? are we stronger than he?"

2 Corinthians 6:14-16 "¹⁴Be ye not unequally yoked together with unbelievers: for what fellowship hath righteousness with unrighteousness? and what communion hath light with darkness? ¹⁵And what concord hath Christ with Belial? or what part hath he that believeth with an infidel? ¹⁶And what agreement hath the temple of God with idols? for ye are the temple of the living God; as God hath said, I will dwell in them, and walk in them; and I will be their God, and they shall be my people."

James 3:9-12 "⁹Therewith bless we God, even the Father; and therewith curse we men, which are made after the similitude of God. ¹⁰Out of the same mouth proceedeth blessing and cursing. My brethren, these things ought not so to be. ¹¹Doth a fountain send forth at the same place sweet water and bitter? ¹²Can the fig tree, my brethren, bear olive berries? either a vine, figs? so can no fountain both yield salt water and fresh."

Servants Not Being Greater Than Their Masters
Matthew 10:24-25 "²⁴The disciple is not above his master, nor the servant above his lord. ²⁵It is enough for the disciple that he be as his master, and the servant as his lord. If they have called the master of the house Beelzebub, how much more shall they call them of his household?"

John 13:16 "Verily, verily, I say unto you, The servant is not greater than his lord; neither he that is sent greater than he that sent him."

John 15:20 "Remember the word that I said unto you, The servant is not greater than his lord. If they have persecuted me, they will also persecute you; if they have kept my saying, they will keep yours also."

The Servant Of The Lord
Isaiah 42:1-7 "¹Behold my servant, whom I uphold; mine elect, in whom my soul delighteth; I have put my spirit upon him: he shall bring forth judgment to the Gentiles. ²He shall not cry, nor lift up, nor cause his voice to be heard in the street.

³A bruised reed shall he not break, and the smoking flax shall he not quench: he shall bring forth judgment unto truth. ⁴He shall not fail nor be discouraged, till he have set judgment in the earth: and the isles shall wait for his law. ⁵Thus saith God the LORD, he that created the heavens, and stretched them out; he that spread forth the earth, and that which cometh out of it; he that giveth breath unto the people upon it, and spirit to them that walk therein: ⁶I the LORD have called thee in righteousness, and will hold thine hand, and will keep thee, and give thee for a covenant of the people, for a light of the Gentiles; ⁷To open the blind eyes, to bring out the prisoners from the prison, and them that sit in darkness out of the prison house."

Isaiah 50:4-10 "⁴The Lord GOD hath given me the tongue of the learned, that I should know how to speak a word in season to him that is weary: he wakeneth morning by morning, he wakeneth mine ear to hear as the learned. ⁵The Lord GOD hath opened mine ear, and I was not rebellious, neither turned away back. ⁶I gave my back to the smiters, and my cheeks to them that plucked off the hair: I hid not my face from shame and spitting. ⁷For the Lord GOD will help me; therefore shall I not be confounded: therefore have I set my face like a flint, and I know that I shall not be ashamed. ⁸He is near that justifieth me; who will contend with me? let us stand together: who is mine adversary? let him come near to me. ⁹Behold, the Lord GOD will help me; who is he that shall condemn me? lo, they all shall wax old as a garment; the moth shall eat them up. ¹⁰Who is among you that feareth the LORD, that obeyeth the voice of his servant, that walketh in darkness, and hath no light? let him trust in the name of the LORD, and stay upon his God."

Isaiah 52:12-15 "¹²For ye shall not go out with haste, nor go by flight: for the LORD will go before you; and the God of Israel will be your rereward. ¹³Behold, my servant shall deal prudently, he shall be exalted and extolled, and be very high. ¹⁴As many were astonied at thee; his visage was so marred more than any man, and his form more than the sons of men: ¹⁵So shall he sprinkle many nations; the kings shall shut their mouths at him: for that which had not been told them shall they see; and that which they had not heard shall they consider."

Isaiah 53:1-12 "¹Who hath believed our report? and to whom is the arm of the LORD revealed? ²For he shall grow up before him as a tender plant, and as a root out of a dry ground: he hath no form nor comeliness; and when we shall see him, there is no beauty that we should desire him. ³He is despised and rejected of men; a man of sorrows, and acquainted with grief: and we hid as it were our faces from him; he was despised, and we esteemed him not. ⁴Surely he hath borne our griefs, and carried our sorrows: yet we did esteem him stricken, smitten of God, and afflicted. ⁵But he was wounded for our transgressions, he was bruised for our iniquities: the chastisement of our peace was upon him; and with his stripes we are healed. ⁶All we like sheep have gone astray; we have turned every one to his own way; and the LORD hath laid on him the iniquity of us all. ⁷He was oppressed, and he was afflicted, yet he opened not his mouth: he is brought as a lamb to the slaughter, and as a sheep before her shearers is dumb, so he openeth not his mouth. ⁸He was taken from prison and from judgment: and who shall declare his generation? for he was cut off out of the land of the living: for the transgression of my people was he stricken. ⁹And he made his grave with the wicked, and with the rich in his death; because he had done no violence, neither was any deceit in his mouth. ¹⁰Yet it pleased the LORD to bruise him; he hath put him to grief: when thou shalt make his soul an offering for sin, he shall see his seed, he shall prolong his days, and the pleasure of the LORD shall prosper in his hand. ¹¹He shall see of the travail of his soul, and shall be satisfied: by his knowledge shall my righteous servant justify many; for he shall bear their iniquities. ¹²Therefore will I divide him a portion with the great, and he shall divide the spoil with the strong; because he hath poured out his soul unto death: and he was numbered with the transgressors; and he bare the sin of many, and made intercession for the transgressors."

The Servants Of The Lord

Deuteronomy 32:36-43 "³⁶For the LORD shall judge his people, and repent himself for his servants, when he seeth that their power is gone, and there is none shut up, or left. ³⁷And he shall say, Where are their gods, their rock in whom they trusted, ³⁸Which did eat the fat of their sacrifices, and drank the wine of their drink offerings? let them rise up and help you, and be your protection. ³⁹See now that I, even I, am he, and there is no god with me: I kill, and I make alive; I wound, and I heal: neither is there any that can deliver out of my hand. ⁴⁰For I lift up my hand to heaven, and say, I live for ever. ⁴¹If I whet my glittering sword, and mine hand take hold on judgment; I will render vengeance to mine enemies, and will reward them that hate me. ⁴²I will make mine arrows drunk with blood, and my sword shall devour flesh; and that with the blood of the slain and of the captives, from the beginning of revenges upon the enemy. ⁴³Rejoice, O ye nations, with his people: for he will avenge the blood of his servants, and will render vengeance to his adversaries, and will be merciful unto his land, and to his people."

1 Kings 8:23 "And he said, LORD God of Israel, there is no God like thee, in heaven above, or on earth beneath, who keepest covenant and mercy with thy servants that walk before thee with all their heart."

2 Chronicles 6:14 "And said, O LORD God of Israel, there is no God like thee in the heaven, nor in the earth; which keepest covenant, and shewest mercy unto thy servants, that walk before thee with all their hearts."

Psalm 19:9-11 "⁹The fear of the LORD is clean, enduring for ever: the judgments of the LORD are true and righteous altogether. ¹⁰More to be desired are they than gold, yea, than much fine gold: sweeter also than honey and the honeycomb. ¹¹Moreover by them is thy servant warned: and in keeping of them there is great reward."

Psalm 34:22 "The LORD redeemeth the soul of his servants: and none of them that trust in him shall be desolate."

Isaiah 54:17 "No weapon that is formed against thee shall prosper; and every tongue that shall rise against thee in judgment thou shalt condemn. This is the heritage of the servants of the LORD, and their righteousness is of me, saith the LORD."

Isaiah 56:6-7 "⁶Also the sons of the stranger, that join themselves to the LORD, to serve him, and to love the name of the LORD, to be his servants, every one that keepeth the sabbath from polluting

it, and taketh hold of my covenant; ⁷Even them will I bring to my holy mountain, and make them joyful in my house of prayer: their burnt offerings and their sacrifices shall be accepted upon mine altar; for mine house shall be called an house of prayer for all people."

Isaiah 65:8-10 "⁸Thus saith the LORD, As the new wine is found in the cluster, and one saith, Destroy it not; for a blessing is in it: so will I do for my servants' sakes, that I may not destroy them all. ⁹And I will bring forth a seed out of Jacob, and out of Judah an inheritor of my mountains: and mine elect shall inherit it, and my servants shall dwell there. ¹⁰And Sharon shall be a fold of flocks, and the valley of Achor a place for the herds to lie down in, for my people that have sought me."

Isaiah 65:13-15 "¹³Therefore thus saith the Lord GOD, Behold, my servants shall eat, but ye shall be hungry: behold, my servants shall drink, but ye shall be thirsty: behold, my servants shall rejoice, but ye shall be ashamed: ¹⁴Behold, my servants shall sing for joy of heart, but ye shall cry for sorrow of heart, and shall howl for vexation of spirit. ¹⁵And ye shall leave your name for a curse unto my chosen: for the Lord GOD shall slay thee, and call his servants by another name."

Isaiah 66:14 "And when ye see this, your heart shall rejoice, and your bones shall flourish like an herb: and the hand of the LORD shall be known toward his servants, and his indignation toward his enemies."

Daniel 3:28 "Then Nebuchadnezzar spake, and said, Blessed be the God of Shadrach, Meshach, and Abed-nego, who hath sent his angel, and delivered his servants that trusted in him, and have changed the king's word, and yielded their bodies, that they might not serve nor worship any god, except their own God."

John 12:23-26 "²³And Jesus answered them, saying, The hour is come, that the Son of man should be glorified. ²⁴Verily, verily, I say unto you, Except a corn of wheat fall into the ground and die, it abideth alone: but if it die, it bringeth forth much fruit. ²⁵He that loveth his life shall lose it; and he that hateth his life in this world shall keep it unto life eternal. ²⁶If any man serve me, let him follow me; and where I am, there shall also my servant be: if any man serve me, him will my Father honour."

Romans 14:16-18 "[16]Let not then your good be evil spoken of: [17]For the kingdom of God is not meat and drink; but righteousness, and peace, and joy in the Holy Ghost. [18]For he that in these things serveth Christ is acceptable to God, and approved of men."

1 Corinthians 7:21-22 "[21]Art thou called being a servant? care not for it: but if thou mayest be made free, use it rather. [22]For he that is called in the Lord, being a servant, is the Lord's freeman: likewise also he that is called, being free, is Christ's servant."

Revelation 7:1-4 "[1]And after these things I saw four angels standing on the four corners of the earth, holding the four winds of the earth, that the wind should not blow on the earth, nor on the sea, nor on any tree. [2]And I saw another angel ascending from the east, having the seal of the living God: and he cried with a loud voice to the four angels, to whom it was given to hurt the earth and the sea, [3]Saying, Hurt not the earth, neither the sea, nor the trees, till we have sealed the servants of our God in their foreheads. [4]And I heard the number of them which were sealed: and there were sealed an hundred and forty and four thousand of all the tribes of the children of Israel."

Revelation 19:1-2 "[1]And after these things I heard a great voice of much people in heaven, saying, Alleluia; Salvation, and glory, and honour, and power, unto the Lord our God: [2]For true and righteous are his judgments: for he hath judged the great whore, which did corrupt the earth with her fornication, and hath avenged the blood of his servants at her hand."

Revelation 22:1-6 "[1]And he shewed me a pure river of water of life, clear as crystal, proceeding out of the throne of God and of the Lamb. [2]In the midst of the street of it, and on either side of the river, was there the tree of life, which bare twelve manner of fruits, and yielded her fruit every month: and the leaves of the tree were for the healing of the nations. [3]And there shall be no more curse: but the throne of God and of the Lamb shall be in it; and his servants shall serve him: [4]And they shall see his face; and his name shall be in their foreheads. [5]And there shall be no night there; and they need no candle, neither light of the sun; for the Lord God giveth them light: and they shall reign for ever and ever. [6]And he said unto me, These sayings are faithful and true: and the Lord God of the holy prophets sent his angel to shew unto his servants the things which must shortly be done."

Unfaithful Servants

Matthew 24:42-51 "[42]Watch therefore: for ye know not what hour your Lord doth come. [43]But know this, that if the goodman of the house had known in what watch the thief would come, he would have watched, and would not have suffered his house to be broken up. [44]Therefore be ye also ready: for in such an hour as ye think not the Son of man cometh. [45]Who then is a faithful and wise servant, whom his lord hath made ruler over his household, to give them meat in due season? [46]Blessed is that servant, whom his lord when he cometh shall find so doing. [47]Verily I say unto you, That he shall make him ruler over all his goods. [48]But and if that evil servant shall say in his heart, My lord delayeth his coming; [49]And shall begin to smite his fellowservants, and to eat and drink with the drunken; [50]The lord of that servant shall come in a day when he looketh not for him, and in an hour that he is not aware of, [51]And shall cut him asunder, and appoint him his portion with the hypocrites: there shall be weeping and gnashing of teeth."

Luke 19:12-27 "[12]He said therefore, A certain nobleman went into a far country to receive for himself a kingdom, and to return. [13]And he called his ten servants, and delivered them ten pounds, and said unto them, Occupy till I come. [14]But his citizens hated him, and sent a message after him, saying, We will not have this man to reign over us. [15]And it came to pass, that when he was returned, having received the kingdom, then he commanded these servants to be called unto him, to whom he had given the money, that he might know how much every man had gained by trading. [16]Then came the first, saying, Lord, thy pound hath gained ten pounds. [17]And he said unto him, Well, thou good servant: because thou hast been faithful in a very little, have thou authority over ten cities. [18]And the second came, saying, Lord, thy pound hath gained five pounds. [19]And he said likewise to him, Be thou also over five cities. ²⁰And another came, saying, Lord, behold, here is thy pound, which I have kept laid up in a napkin: ²¹For I feared thee, because thou art an austere man: thou takest up that thou layedst not down, and reapest that thou didst not sow. ²²And he saith unto him, Out of thine own mouth will I judge thee, thou wicked servant. Thou knewest that I was an austere man, taking up that I laid not down, and reaping that I did not sow: ²³Wherefore then gavest not thou my money into the bank, that at my coming I might have required mine own with usury? ²⁴And he said unto them that stood by, Take from him the pound, and give it to him that hath ten pounds. ²⁵(And they said unto him, Lord, he hath ten pounds.) ²⁶For I say unto you, That unto every one which hath shall be given; and from him that hath not, even that he hath shall be taken away from him. ²⁷But those mine enemies, which would not that I should reign over them, bring hither, and slay them before me."

What Servants Should Do

Ephesians 6:5-8 "⁵Servants, be obedient to them that are your masters according to the flesh, with fear and trembling, in singleness of your heart, as unto Christ; ⁶Not with eyeservice, as menpleasers; but as the servants of Christ, doing the will of God from the heart; ⁷With good will doing service, as to the Lord, and not to men: ⁸Knowing that whatsoever good thing any man doeth, the same shall he receive of the Lord, whether he be bond or free."

Colossians 3:22-23 "²²Servants, obey in all things your masters according to the flesh; not with eyeservice, as menpleasers; but in singleness of heart, fearing God: ²³And whatsoever ye do, do it heartily, as to the Lord, and not unto men."

1 Timothy 6:1-2 "¹Let as many servants as are under the yoke count their own masters worthy of all honour, that the name of God and his doctrine be not blasphemed. ²And they that have believing masters, let them not despise them, because they are brethren; but rather do them service, because they are faithful and beloved, partakers of the benefit. These things teach and exhort."

Titus 2:9 "Exhort servants to be obedient unto their own masters, and to please them well in all things; not answering again."

Who Are The Servants Of Corruption

2 Peter 2:1-19 "¹But there were false prophets also among the people, even as there shall be false teachers among you, who privily shall bring in damnable heresies, even denying the Lord that bought them, and bring upon themselves swift destruction. ²And many shall follow their pernicious ways; by reason of whom the way of truth shall be evil spoken of. ³And through covetousness shall they with feigned words make merchandise of you: whose judgment now of a long time lingereth not, and their damnation slumbereth not. ⁴For if God spared not the angels that sinned, but cast them down to hell, and delivered them into chains of darkness, to be reserved unto judgment; ⁵And spared not the old world, but saved Noah the eighth person, a preacher of righteousness, bringing in the flood upon the world of the ungodly; ⁶And turning the cities of Sodom and Gomorrha into ashes condemned them with an overthrow, making them an ensample unto those that after should live ungodly; ⁷And delivered just Lot, vexed with the filthy conversation of the wicked: ⁸(For that righteous man dwelling among them, in seeing and hearing, vexed his righteous soul from day to day with their unlawful deeds;) ⁹The Lord knoweth how to deliver the godly out of temptations, and to reserve the unjust unto the day of judgment to be punished: ¹⁰But chiefly them that walk after the flesh in the lust of uncleanness, and despise government. Presumptuous are they, selfwilled, they are not afraid to speak evil of dignities. ¹¹Whereas angels, which are greater in power and might, bring not railing accusation against them before the Lord. ¹²But these, as natural brute beasts, made to be taken and destroyed, speak evil of the things that they understand not; and shall utterly perish in their own corruption; ¹³And shall receive the reward of unrighteousness, as they that count it pleasure to riot in the day time. Spots they are and blemishes, sporting themselves with their own deceivings while they feast with you; ¹⁴Having eyes full of adultery, and that cannot cease from sin; beguiling unstable souls: an heart they have exercised with covetous practices; cursed children: ¹⁵Which have forsaken the right way, and are gone astray, following the way of Balaam the son of Bosor, who loved the wages of unrighteousness; ¹⁶But was rebuked for his iniquity: the dumb ass speaking with man's voice forbad the madness of the prophet. [17]These are wells without water, clouds that are carried with a tempest; to whom the mist of darkness is reserved for ever. [18]For when they speak great swelling words of vanity, they allure through the lusts of the flesh, through much wantonness, those that were clean escaped from them who live in error. [19]While they promise them liberty, they themselves are the servants of corruption: for of whom a man is overcome, of the same is he brought in bondage."

Who Is A Servant Of The Lord

Leviticus 25:55 "For unto me the children of Israel are servants; they are my servants whom I brought forth out of the land of Egypt: I am the LORD your God."

Joshua 1:1-2 "[1]Now after the death of Moses the servant of the LORD it came to pass, that the LORD spake unto Joshua the son of Nun, Moses' minister, saying, [2]Moses my servant is dead; now therefore arise, go over this Jordan, thou, and all this people, unto the land which I do give to them, even to the children of Israel."

Joshua 22:5 "But take diligent heed to do the commandment and the law, which Moses the servant of the LORD charged you, to love the LORD your God, and to walk in all his ways, and to keep his commandments, and to cleave unto him, and to serve him with all your heart and with all your soul."

1 Kings 8:51-53 "[51]For they be thy people, and thine inheritance, which thou broughtest forth out of Egypt, from the midst of the furnace of iron: [52]That thine eyes may be open unto the supplication of thy servant, and unto the supplication of thy people Israel, to hearken unto them in all that they call for unto thee. [53]For thou didst separate them from among all the people of the earth, to be thine inheritance, as thou spakest by the hand of Moses thy servant, when thou broughtest our fathers out of Egypt, O Lord GOD."

2 Kings 21:10 "And the LORD spake by his servants the prophets, saying."

1 Chronicles 16:11-13 "[11]Seek the LORD and his strength, seek his face continually. [12]Remember his marvellous works that he hath done, his wonders, and the judgments of his mouth; [13]O ye seed of Israel his servant, ye children of Jacob, his chosen ones."

Nehemiah 1:5-8 "[5]And said, I beseech thee, O LORD God of heaven, the great and terrible God, that keepeth covenant and mercy for them that love him and observe his commandments: [6]Let thine ear now be attentive, and thine eyes open, that thou mayest hear the prayer of thy servant, which I pray before thee now, day and night, for the children of Israel thy servants, and confess the sins of the children of Israel, which we have sinned against thee: both I and my father's house have sinned. [7]We have dealt very corruptly against thee, and have not kept the commandments, nor the statutes, nor the judgments, which thou commandedst thy servant Moses. [8]Remember, I beseech thee, the word that thou commandedst thy servant Moses, saying, If ye transgress, I will scatter you abroad among the nations."

Nehemiah 9:7-14 "[7]Thou art the LORD the God, who didst choose Abram, and broughtest him forth out of Ur of the Chaldees, and gavest him the name of Abraham; [8]And foundest his heart faithful before thee, and madest a covenant with him to give the land of the Canaanites, the Hittites, the Amorites, and the Perizzites, and the Jebusites, and the Girgashites, to give it, I say, to his seed, and hast performed thy words; for thou art righteous: [9]And didst see the affliction of our fathers in Egypt, and heardest their cry by the Red sea; [10]And shewedst signs and wonders upon Pharaoh, and on all his servants, and on all the people of his land: for thou knewest that they dealt proudly against them. So didst thou get thee a name, as it is this day. [11]And thou didst divide the sea before them, so that they went through the midst of the sea on the dry land; and their persecutors thou threwest into the deeps, as a stone into the mighty waters. [12]Moreover thou leddest them in the day by a cloudy pillar; and in the night by a pillar of fire, to give them light in the way wherein they should go. [13]Thou camest down also upon mount Sinai, and spakest with them from heaven, and gavest them right judgments, and true laws, good statutes and commandments: [14]And madest known unto them thy holy sabbath, and commandedst them precepts, statutes, and laws, by the hand of Moses thy servant."

Psalm 89:19-26 "[19]Then thou spakest in vision to thy holy one, and saidst, I have laid help upon one that is mighty; I have exalted one chosen out of the people. [20]I have found David my servant; with my holy oil have I anointed him: [21]With whom my hand shall be established: mine arm also shall strengthen him. [22]The enemy shall not exact upon him; nor the son of wickedness afflict him. [23]And I will beat down his foes before his face, and plague them that hate him. [24]But my faithfulness and my mercy shall be with him: and in my name shall his horn be exalted. [25]I will set his hand also in the sea, and his right hand in the rivers. [26]He shall cry unto me, Thou art my father, my God, and the rock of my salvation."

Psalm 105:4-6 "[4]Seek the LORD, and his strength: seek his face evermore. [5]Remember his marvellous works that he hath done; his wonders, and the judgments of his mouth; [6]O ye seed of Abraham his servant, ye children of Jacob his chosen."

Psalm 136:3-22 "[3]O give thanks to the Lord of lords: for his mercy endureth for ever. [4]To him who alone doeth great wonders: for his mercy endureth for ever. [5]To him that by wisdom made the heavens: for his mercy endureth for ever. [6]To him that stretched out the earth above the waters: for his mercy endureth for ever. [7]To him that made great lights: for his mercy endureth for ever: [8]The sun to rule by day: for his mercy endureth for ever: [9]The moon and stars to rule by night: for his mercy endureth for ever. [10]To him that smote Egypt in their firstborn: for his mercy endureth for ever: [11]And brought out Israel from among them: for his mercy endureth for ever: [12]With a strong hand, and with a stretched out arm: for his mercy endureth for ever. [13]To him which divided the Red sea into parts: for his mercy endureth for ever: [14]And made Israel to pass through the midst of it: for his mercy endureth for ever: [15]But overthrew Pharaoh and his host in the Red sea: for his mercy endureth for ever. [16]To him which led his people through the wilderness: for his mercy endureth for ever. [17]To him which smote great kings: for his mercy endureth for ever: [18]And slew famous kings: for his mercy endureth for ever: [19]Sihon king of the Amorites: for his mercy endureth for ever: [20]And Og the king of Bashan: for his mercy endureth for ever: [21]And gave their land for an heritage: for his mercy endureth for ever: [22]Even an heritage unto Israel his servant: for his mercy endureth for ever."

Isaiah 41:8-10 "[8]But thou, Israel, art my servant, Jacob whom I have chosen, the seed of Abraham my friend. [9]Thou whom I have taken from the ends of the earth, and called thee from the chief men thereof, and said unto thee, Thou art my servant; I have chosen thee, and not cast thee away. [10]Fear thou not; for I am with thee: be not dismayed; for I am thy God: I will strengthen thee; yea, I will help thee; yea, I will uphold thee with the right hand of my righteousness."

Isaiah 43:3-10 "[3]For I am the LORD thy God, the Holy One of Israel, thy Saviour: I gave Egypt for thy ransom, Ethiopia and Seba for thee. [4]Since thou wast precious in my sight, thou hast been honourable, and I have loved thee: therefore will I give men for thee, and people for thy life. [5]Fear not: for I am with thee: I will bring thy seed from the east, and gather thee from the west; [6]I will say to the north, Give up; and to the south, Keep not back: bring my sons from far, and my daughters from the ends of the earth; [7]Even every one that is called by my name: for I have created him for my glory, I have formed him; yea, I have made him. [8]Bring forth the blind people that have eyes, and the deaf that have ears. [9]Let all the nations be gathered together, and let the people be assembled: who among them can declare this, and shew us former things? let them bring forth their witnesses, that they may be justified: or let them hear, and say, It is truth. [10]Ye are my witnesses, saith the LORD, and my servant whom I have chosen: that ye may know and believe me, and understand that I am he: before me there was no God formed, neither shall there be after me."

Isaiah 44:1-2 "[1]Yet now hear, O Jacob my servant; and Israel, whom I have chosen: [2]Thus saith the LORD that made thee, and formed thee from the womb, which will help thee; Fear not, O Jacob, my servant; and thou, Jesurun, whom I have chosen."

Isaiah 45:3-4 "[3]And I will give thee the treasures of darkness, and hidden riches of secret places, that thou mayest know that I, the LORD, which call thee by thy name, am the God of Israel. [4]For Jacob my servant's sake, and Israel mine elect, I have even called thee by thy name: I have surnamed thee, though thou hast not known me."

Isaiah 48:20 "Go ye forth of Babylon, flee ye from the Chaldeans, with a voice of singing declare ye, tell this, utter it even to the end of the earth; say ye, The LORD hath redeemed his servant Jacob."

Isaiah 49:1-5 "¹Listen, O isles, unto me; and hearken, ye people, from far; The LORD hath called me from the womb; from the bowels of my mother hath he made mention of my name. ²And he hath made my mouth like a sharp sword; in the shadow of his hand hath he hid me, and made me a polished shaft; in his quiver hath he hid me; ³And said unto me, Thou art my servant, O Israel, in whom I will be glorified. ⁴Then I said, I have laboured in vain, I have spent my strength for nought, and in vain: yet surely my judgment is with the LORD, and my work with my God. ⁵And now, saith the LORD that formed me from the womb to be his servant, to bring Jacob again to him, Though Israel be not gathered, yet shall I be glorious in the eyes of the LORD, and my God shall be my strength."

Jeremiah 25:4-9 "⁴And the LORD hath sent unto you all his servants the prophets, rising early and sending them; but ye have not hearkened, nor inclined your ear to hear. ⁵They said, Turn ye again now every one from his evil way, and from the evil of your doings, and dwell in the land that the LORD hath given unto you and to your fathers for ever and ever: ⁶And go not after other gods to serve them, and to worship them, and provoke me not to anger with the works of your hands; and I will do you no hurt. ⁷Yet ye have not hearkened unto me, saith the LORD; that ye might provoke me to anger with the works of your hands to your own hurt. ⁸Therefore thus saith the LORD of hosts; Because ye have not heard my words, ⁹Behold, I will send and take all the families of the north, saith the LORD, and Nebuchadrezzar the king of Babylon, my servant, and will bring them against this land, and against the inhabitants thereof, and against all these nations round about, and will utterly destroy them, and make them an astonishment, and an hissing, and perpetual desolations."

Jeremiah 27:4-6 "⁴And command them to say unto their masters, Thus saith the LORD of hosts, the God of Israel; Thus shall ye say unto your masters; ⁵I have made the earth, the man and the beast that are upon the ground, by my great power and by my outstretched arm, and have given it unto whom it seemed meet unto me. ⁶And now have I given all these lands unto the hand of Nebuchadnezzar the king of Babylon, my servant; and the beasts of the field have I given him also to serve him."

Jeremiah 30:10 "Therefore fear thou not, O my servant Jacob, saith the LORD; neither be dismayed, O Israel: for, lo, I will save thee from afar, and thy seed from the land of their captivity; and Jacob shall return, and shall be in rest, and be quiet, and none shall make him afraid."

Jeremiah 46:28 "Fear thou not, O Jacob my servant, saith the LORD: for I am with thee; for I will make a full end of all the nations whither I have driven thee: but I will not make a full end of thee, but correct thee in measure; yet will I not leave thee wholly unpunished."

Ezekiel 28:25 "Thus saith the Lord GOD; When I shall have gathered the house of Israel from the people among whom they are scattered, and shall be sanctified in them in the sight of the heathen, then shall they dwell in their land that I have given to my servant Jacob."

Daniel 9:4-6 "⁴And I prayed unto the LORD my God, and made my confession, and said, O Lord, the great and dreadful God, keeping the covenant and mercy to them that love him, and to them that keep his commandments; ⁵We have sinned, and have committed iniquity, and have done wickedly, and have rebelled, even by departing from thy precepts and from thy judgments: ⁶Neither have we hearkened unto thy servants the prophets, which spake in thy name to our kings, our princes, and our fathers, and to all the people of the land."

Daniel 9:10-11 "¹⁰Neither have we obeyed the voice of the LORD our God, to walk in his laws, which he set before us by his servants the prophets. ¹¹Yea, all Israel have transgressed thy law, even by departing, that they might not obey thy voice; therefore the curse is poured upon us, and the oath that is written in the law of Moses the servant of God, because we have sinned against him."

Zechariah 1:4-6 "⁴Be ye not as your fathers, unto whom the former prophets have cried, saying, Thus saith the LORD of hosts; Turn ye now from your evil ways, and from your evil doings: but they did not hear, nor hearken unto me, saith the

LORD. ⁵Your fathers, where are they? and the prophets, do they live for ever? ⁶But my words and my statutes, which I commanded my servants the prophets, did they not take hold of your fathers? and they returned and said, Like as the LORD of hosts thought to do unto us, according to our ways, and according to our doings, so hath he dealt with us."

Luke 1:68-69 "⁶⁸Blessed be the Lord God of Israel; for he hath visited and redeemed his people, ⁶⁹And hath raised up an horn of salvation for us in the house of his servant David."

Romans 6:15-22 "¹⁵What then? shall we sin, because we are not under the law, but under grace? God forbid. ¹⁶Know ye not, that to whom ye yield yourselves servants to obey, his servants ye are to whom ye obey; whether of sin unto death, or of obedience unto righteousness? ¹⁷But God be thanked, that ye were the servants of sin, but ye have obeyed from the heart that form of doctrine which was delivered you. ¹⁸Being then made free from sin, ye became the servants of righteousness. ¹⁹I speak after the manner of men because of the infirmity of your flesh: for as ye have yielded your members servants to uncleanness and to iniquity unto iniquity; even so now yield your members servants to righteousness unto holiness. ²⁰For when ye were the servants of sin, ye were free from righteousness. ²¹What fruit had ye then in those things whereof ye are now ashamed? for the end of those things is death. ²²But now being made free from sin, and become servants to God, ye have your fruit unto holiness, and the end everlasting life."

1 Corinthians 7:21-22 "²¹Art thou called being a servant? care not for it: but if thou mayest be made free, use it rather. ²²For he that is called in the Lord, being a servant, is the Lord's freeman: likewise also he that is called, being free, is Christ's servant."

2 Corinthians 4:1-5 "¹Therefore seeing we have this ministry, as we have received mercy, we faint not; ²But have renounced the hidden things of dishonesty, not walking in craftiness, nor handling the word of God deceitfully; but by manifestation of the truth commending ourselves to every man's conscience in the sight of God. ³But if our gospel be hid, it is hid to them that are lost: ⁴In whom the god of this world hath blinded the minds of them which believe not, lest the light of the glorious gospel of Christ, who is the image of God, should shine unto them. ⁵For we preach not ourselves, but Christ Jesus the Lord; and ourselves your servants for Jesus' sake."

Revelation 15:3 "And they sing the song of Moses the servant of God, and the song of the Lamb, saying, Great and marvellous are thy works, Lord God Almighty; just and true are thy ways, thou King of saints."

Who Is Not A Mere Servant

John 15:1-15 "¹I am the true vine, and my Father is the husbandman. ²Every branch in me that beareth not fruit he taketh away: and every branch that beareth fruit, he purgeth it, that it may bring forth more fruit. ³Now ye are clean through the word which I have spoken unto you. ⁴Abide in me, and I in you. As the branch cannot bear fruit of itself, except it abide in the vine; no more can ye, except ye abide in me. ⁵I am the vine, ye are the branches: He that abideth in me, and I in him, the same bringeth forth much fruit: for without me ye can do nothing. ⁶If a man abide not in me, he is cast forth as a branch, and is withered; and men gather them, and cast them into the fire, and they are burned. ⁷If ye abide in me, and my words abide in you, ye shall ask what ye will, and it shall be done unto you. ⁸Herein is my Father glorified, that ye bear much fruit; so shall ye be my disciples. ⁹As the Father hath loved me, so have I loved you: continue ye in my love. ¹⁰If ye keep my commandments, ye shall abide in my love; even as I have kept my Father's commandments, and abide in his love. ¹¹These things have I spoken unto you, that my joy might remain in you, and that your joy might be full. ¹²This is my commandment, That ye love one another, as I have loved you. ¹³Greater love hath no man than this, that a man lay down his life for his friends. ¹⁴Ye are my friends, if ye do whatsoever I command you. ¹⁵Henceforth I call you not servants; for the servant knoweth not what his lord doeth: but I have called you friends; for all things that I have heard of my Father I have made known unto you."

Galatians 4:6-7 "⁶And because ye are sons, God hath sent forth the Spirit of his Son into your hearts, crying, Abba, Father. ⁷Wherefore thou art no more a servant, but a son; and if a son, then an heir of God through Christ."

Who Is Not The Servant Of Christ

Galatians 1:6-10 "6I marvel that ye are so soon removed from him that called you into the grace of Christ unto another gospel: 7Which is not another; but there be some that trouble you, and would pervert the gospel of Christ. 8But though we, or an angel from heaven, preach any other gospel unto you than that which we have preached unto you, let him be accursed. 9As we said before, so say I now again, If any man preach any other gospel unto you than that ye have received, let him be accursed. 10For do I now persuade men, or God? or do I seek to please men? for if I yet pleased men, I should not be the servant of Christ."

Who Is The Servant Of Sin

John 8:34-35 "34Jesus answered them, Verily, verily, I say unto you, Whosoever committeth sin is the servant of sin. 35And the servant abideth not in the house for ever: but the Son abideth ever."

Romans 6:15-20 "15What then? shall we sin, because we are not under the law, but under grace? God forbid. 16Know ye not, that to whom ye yield yourselves servants to obey, his servants ye are to whom ye obey; whether of sin unto death, or of obedience unto righteousness? 17But God be thanked, that ye were the servants of sin, but ye have obeyed from the heart that form of doctrine which was delivered you. 18Being then made free from sin, ye became the servants of righteousness. 19I speak after the manner of men because of the infirmity of your flesh: for as ye have yielded your members servants to uncleanness and to iniquity unto iniquity; even so now yield your members servants to righteousness unto holiness. 20For when ye were the servants of sin, ye were free from righteousness."

Who Not To Be The Servant Of

1 Corinthians 7:23-24 "23Ye are bought with a price; be not ye the servants of men. 24Brethren, let every man, wherein he is called, therein abide with God."

Who Shall Be Servant Of All

Matthew 23:8-11 "8But be not ye called Rabbi: for one is your Master, even Christ; and all ye are brethren. 9And call no man your father upon the earth: for one is your Father, which is in heaven. 10Neither be ye called masters: for one is your Master, even Christ. 11But he that is greatest among you shall be your servant."

Mark 9:35 "And he sat down, and called the twelve, and saith unto them, If any man desire to be first, the same shall be last of all, and servant of all."

Mark 10:42-44 "42But Jesus called them to him, and saith unto them, Ye know that they which are accounted to rule over the Gentiles exercise lordship over them; and their great ones exercise authority upon them. 43But so shall it not be among you: but whosoever will be great among you, shall be your minister: 44And whosoever of you will be the chiefest, shall be servant of all."

Who Shall Be Servant To The Wise Of Heart

Proverbs 11:29 "He that troubleth his own house shall inherit the wind: and the fool shall be servant to the wise of heart."

Whose Servants Are Wicked

Proverbs 29:12 "If a ruler hearken to lies, all his servants are wicked."

Wise Servants

Proverbs 14:35 "The king's favour is toward a wise servant: but his wrath is against him that causeth shame."

Proverbs 17:2 "A wise servant shall have rule over a son that causeth shame, and shall have part of the inheritance among the brethren."

SERVICE

How To Serve The Lord

Psalm 2:11 "Serve the LORD with fear, and rejoice with trembling."

Psalm 100:2 "Serve the LORD with gladness: come before his presence with singing."

Zephaniah 3:9 "For then will I turn to the people a pure language, that they may all call upon the name of the LORD, to serve him with one consent."

Romans 7:4-6 "4Wherefore, my brethren, ye also are become dead to the law by the body of Christ; that ye should be married to another, even to him who is raised from the dead, that we should bring forth fruit unto God. ⁵For when we were in the flesh, the motions of sins, which were by the law, did work in our members to bring forth fruit unto death. ⁶But now we are delivered from the law, that being dead wherein we were held; that we should serve in newness of spirit, and not in the oldness of the letter."

Serving The Lord
Exodus 23:25 "And ye shall serve the LORD your God, and he shall bless thy bread, and thy water; and I will take sickness away from the midst of thee."

Deuteronomy 6:13 "Thou shalt fear the LORD thy God, and serve him, and shalt swear by his name."

Deuteronomy 10:12 "And now, Israel, what doth the LORD thy God require of thee, but to fear the LORD thy God, to walk in all his ways, and to love him, and to serve the LORD thy God with all thy heart and with all thy soul."

Deuteronomy 10:20 "Thou shalt fear the LORD thy God; him shalt thou serve, and to him shalt thou cleave, and swear by his name."

Deuteronomy 13:4 "Ye shall walk after the LORD your God, and fear him, and keep his commandments, and obey his voice, and ye shall serve him, and cleave unto him."

Joshua 22:5 "But take diligent heed to do the commandment and the law, which Moses the servant of the LORD charged you, to love the LORD your God, and to walk in all his ways, and to keep his commandments, and to cleave unto him, and to serve him with all your heart and with all your soul."

Joshua 24:14-15 "¹⁴Now therefore fear the LORD, and serve him in sincerity and in truth: and put away the gods which your fathers served on the other side of the flood, and in Egypt; and serve ye the LORD. ¹⁵And if it seem evil unto you to serve the LORD, choose you this day whom ye will serve; whether the gods which your fathers served that were on the other side of the flood, or the gods of the Amorites, in whose land ye dwell: but as for me and my house, we will serve the LORD."

1 Samuel 12:24 "Only fear the LORD, and serve him in truth with all your heart: for consider how great things he hath done for you."

2 Kings 17:35-38 "³⁵With whom the LORD had made a covenant, and charged them saying, Ye shall not fear other gods, nor bow yourselves to them, nor serve them, nor sacrifice to them: ³⁶But the LORD, who brought you up out of the land of Egypt with great power and a stretched out arm, him shall ye fear, and him shall ye worship, and to him shall ye do sacrifice. ³⁷And the statutes, and the ordinances, and the law, and the commandment, which he wrote for you, ye shall observe to do for evermore; and ye shall not fear other gods. ³⁸And the covenant that I have made with you ye shall not forget; neither shall ye fear other gods."

1 Chronicles 28:9 "And thou, Solomon my son, know thou the God of thy father, and serve him with a perfect heart and with a willing mind: for the LORD searcheth all hearts, and understandeth all the imaginations of the thoughts: if thou seek him, he will be found of thee; but if thou forsake him, he will cast thee off for ever."

2 Chronicles 30:8 "Now be ye not stiffnecked, as your fathers were, but yield yourselves unto the LORD, and enter into his sanctuary, which he hath sanctified for ever: and serve the LORD your God, that the fierceness of his wrath may turn away from you."

Psalm 2:11 "Serve the LORD with fear, and rejoice with trembling."

Psalm 100:2 "Serve the LORD with gladness: come before his presence with singing."

Matthew 4:10 "Then saith Jesus unto him, Get thee hence, Satan: for it is written, Thou shalt worship the Lord thy God, and him only shalt thou serve."

Luke 4:8 "And Jesus answered and said unto him, Get thee behind me, Satan: for it is written, Thou shalt worship the Lord thy God, and him only shalt thou serve."

Romans 12:10-11 "¹⁰Be kindly affectioned one to another with brotherly love; in honour preferring one another; ¹¹Not slothful in business; fervent in spirit; serving the Lord."

The Reward For Not Serving The Lord
Deuteronomy 28:47-48 "⁴⁷Because thou servedst not the LORD thy God with joyfulness, and with

gladness of heart, for the abundance of all things; [48]Therefore shalt thou serve thine enemies which the LORD shall send against thee, in hunger, and in thirst, and in nakedness, and in want of all things: and he shall put a yoke of iron upon thy neck, until he have destroyed thee."

The Reward For Serving Idols

Exodus 23:31-33 "[31]And I will set thy bounds from the Red sea even unto the sea of the Philistines, and from the desert unto the river: for I will deliver the inhabitants of the land into your hand; and thou shalt drive them out before thee. [32]Thou shalt make no covenant with them, nor with their gods. [33]They shall not dwell in thy land, lest they make thee sin against me: for if thou serve their gods, it will surely be a snare unto thee."

Deuteronomy 8:19-20 "[19]And it shall be, if thou do at all forget the LORD thy God, and walk after other gods, and serve them, and worship them, I testify against you this day that ye shall surely perish. [20]As the nations which the LORD destroyeth before your face, so shall ye perish; because ye would not be obedient unto the voice of the LORD your God."

Deuteronomy 11:16-18 "[16]Take heed to yourselves, that your heart be not deceived, and ye turn aside, and serve other gods, and worship them; [17]And then the LORD's wrath be kindled against you, and he shut up the heaven, that there be no rain, and that the land yield not her fruit; and lest ye perish quickly from off the good land which the LORD giveth you. [18]Therefore shall ye lay up these my words in your heart and in your soul, and bind them for a sign upon your hand, that they may be as frontlets between your eyes."

Deuteronomy 11:26-28 "[26]Behold, I set before you this day a blessing and a curse; [27]A blessing, if ye obey the commandments of the LORD your God, which I command you this day: [28]And a curse, if ye will not obey the commandments of the LORD your God, but turn aside out of the way which I command you this day, to go after other gods, which ye have not known."

Deuteronomy 29:17-29 "[17]And ye have seen their abominations, and their idols, wood and stone, silver and gold, which were among them:) [18]Lest there should be among you man, or woman, or family, or tribe, whose heart turneth away this day from the LORD our God, to go and serve the gods of these nations; lest there should be among you a root that beareth gall and wormwood; [19]And it come to pass, when he heareth the words of this curse, that he bless himself in his heart, saying, I shall have peace, though I walk in the imagination of mine heart, to add drunkenness to thirst: [20]The LORD will not spare him, but then the anger of the LORD and his jealousy shall smoke against that man, and all the curses that are written in this book shall lie upon him, and the LORD shall blot out his name from under heaven. [21]And the LORD shall separate him unto evil out of all the tribes of Israel, according to all the curses of the covenant that are written in this book of the law: [22]So that the generation to come of your children that shall rise up after you, and the stranger that shall come from a far land, shall say, when they see the plagues of that land, and the sicknesses which the LORD hath laid upon it; [23]And that the whole land thereof is brimstone, and salt, and burning, that it is not sown, nor beareth, nor any grass groweth therein, like the overthrow of Sodom, and Gomorrah, Admah, and Zeboim, which the LORD overthrew in his anger, and in his wrath: [24]Even all nations shall say, Wherefore hath the LORD done thus unto this land? what meaneth the heat of this great anger? [25]Then men shall say, Because they have forsaken the covenant of the LORD God of their fathers, which he made with them when he brought them forth out of the land of Egypt: [26]For they went and served other gods, and worshipped them, gods whom they knew not, and whom he had not given unto them: [27]And the anger of the LORD was kindled against this land, to bring upon it all the curses that are written in this book: [28]And the LORD rooted them out of their land in anger, and in wrath, and in great indignation, and cast them into another land, as it is this day. [29]The secret things belong unto the LORD our God: but those things which are revealed belong unto us and to our children for ever, that we may do all the words of this law."

Deuteronomy 30:15-18 "[15]See, I have set before thee this day life and good, and death and evil; [16]In that I command thee this day to love the LORD thy God, to walk in his ways, and to keep his commandments and his statutes and his judgments, that thou mayest live and multiply: and the LORD thy God shall bless thee in the land whither thou goest to possess it. [17]But if thine heart turn away, so that thou wilt not hear, but shalt be drawn away, and worship other gods, and serve them; [18]I denounce unto you this day, that ye shall surely perish, and that ye shall not prolong your days upon the land, whither thou passest over Jordan to go to possess it."

Deuteronomy 31:16-18 "[16]And the LORD said unto Moses, Behold, thou shalt sleep with thy fathers; and this people will rise up, and go a whoring after the gods of the strangers of the land, whither they go to be among them, and will forsake me, and break my covenant which I have made with them. [17]Then my anger shall be kindled against them in that day, and I will forsake them, and I will hide my face from them, and they shall be devoured, and many evils and troubles shall befall them; so that they will say in that day. Are not these evils come upon us, because our God is not among us? [18]And I will surely hide my face in that day for all the evils which they shall have wrought, in that they are turned unto other gods."

Joshua 23:15-16 "[15]Therefore it shall come to pass, that as all good things are come upon you, which the LORD your God promised you; so shall the LORD bring upon you all evil things, until he have destroyed you from off this good land which the LORD your God hath given you. [16]When ye have transgressed the covenant of the LORD your God, which he commanded you, and have gone and served other gods, and bowed yourselves to them; then shall the anger of the LORD be kindled against you, and ye shall perish quickly from off the good land which he hath given unto you."

Joshua 24:20 "If ye forsake the LORD, and serve strange gods, then he will turn and do you hurt, and consume you, after that he hath done you good."

Judges 2:19 "And it came to pass, when the judge was dead, that they returned, and corrupted themselves more than their fathers, in following other gods to serve them, and to bow down unto them; they ceased not from their own doings, nor from their stubborn way."

Judges 10:11-14 "[11]And the LORD said unto the children of Israel, Did not I deliver you from the Egyptians, and from the Amorites, from the children of Ammon, and from the Philistines? [12]The Zidonians also, and the Amalekites, and the Maonites, did oppress you; and ye cried to me, and I delivered you out of their hand. [13]Yet ye have forsaken me, and served other gods: wherefore I will deliver you no more. [14]Go and cry unto the gods which ye have chosen; let them deliver you in the time of your tribulation."

1 Samuel 8:4-18 "[4]Then all the elders of Israel gathered themselves together, and came to Samuel unto Ramah, [5]And said unto him, Behold, thou art old, and thy sons walk not in thy ways: now make us a king to judge us like all the nations. [6]But the thing displeased Samuel, when they said, Give us a king to judge us. And Samuel prayed unto the LORD. [7]And the LORD said unto Samuel, Hearken unto the voice of the people in all that they say unto thee: for they have not rejected thee, but they have rejected me, that I should not reign over them. [8]According to all the works which they have done since the day that I brought them up out of Egypt even unto this day, wherewith they have forsaken me, and served other gods, so do they also unto thee. [9]Now therefore hearken unto their voice: howbeit yet protest solemnly unto them, and shew them the manner of the king that shall reign over them. [10]And Samuel told all the words of the LORD unto the people that asked of him a king. [11]And he said, This will be the manner of the king that shall reign over you: He will take your sons, and appoint them for himself, for his chariots, and to be his horsemen; and some shall run before his chariots. [12]And he will appoint him captains over thousands, and captains over fifties; and will set them to ear his ground, and to reap his harvest, and to make his instruments of war, and instruments of his chariots. [13]And he will take your daughters to be confectionaries, and to be cooks, and to be bakers. [14]And he will take your fields, and your vineyards, and your oliveyards, even the best of them, and give them to his servants. [15]And he will take the tenth of your seed, and of your vineyards, and give to his officers, and to his servants. [16]And he will take your menservants, and your maidservants, and your goodliest young men, and your asses, and put them to his work. [17]He will take the tenth of your sheep: and ye shall be his servants. [18]And ye shall cry out in that day because of your king which ye shall have chosen you; and the LORD will not hear you in that day."

1 Kings 9:6-9 "⁶But if ye shall at all turn from following me, ye or your children, and will not keep my commandments and my statutes which I have set before you, but go and serve other gods, and worship them: ⁷Then will I cut off Israel out of the land which I have given them; and this house, which I have hallowed for my name, will I cast out of my sight; and Israel shall be a proverb and a byword among all people: ⁸And at this house, which is high, every one that passeth by it shall be astonished, and shall hiss; and they shall say, Why hath the LORD done thus unto this land, and to this house? ⁹And they shall answer, Because they forsook the LORD their God, who brought forth their fathers out of the land of Egypt, and have taken hold upon other gods, and have worshipped them, and served them: therefore hath the LORD brought upon them all this evil."

2 Kings 22:16-17 "¹⁶Thus saith the LORD, Behold, I will bring evil upon this place, and upon the inhabitants thereof, even all the words of the book which the king of Judah hath read: ¹⁷Because they have forsaken me, and have burned incense unto other gods, that they might provoke me to anger with all the works of their hands; therefore my wrath shall be kindled against this place, and shall not be quenched."

2 Chronicles 34:24-25 "²⁴Thus saith the LORD, Behold, I will bring evil upon this place, and upon the inhabitants thereof, even all the curses that are written in the book which they have read before the king of Judah: ²⁵Because they have forsaken me, and have burned incense unto other gods, that they might provoke me to anger with all the works of their hands; therefore my wrath shall be poured out upon this place, and shall not be quenched."

Psalm 106:35-36 "³⁵But were mingled among the heathen, and learned their works. ³⁶And they served their idols: which were a snare unto them."

Jeremiah 5:18-19 "¹⁸Nevertheless in those days, saith the LORD, I will not make a full end with you. ¹⁹And it shall come to pass, when ye shall say, Wherefore doeth the LORD our God all these things unto us? then shalt thou answer them, Like

as ye have forsaken me, and served strange gods in your land, so shall ye serve strangers in a land that is not yours."

Jeremiah 16:11-13 "¹¹Then shalt thou say unto them, Because your fathers have forsaken me, saith the LORD, and have walked after other gods, and have served them, and have worshipped them, and have forsaken me, and have not kept my law; ¹²And ye have done worse than your fathers; for, behold, ye walk every one after the imagination of his evil heart, that they may not hearken unto me: ¹³Therefore will I cast you out of this land into a land that ye know not, neither ye nor your fathers; and there shall ye serve other gods day and night; where I will not shew you favour."

Jeremiah 22:8-9 "⁸And many nations shall pass by this city, and they shall say every man to his neighbour, Wherefore hath the LORD done thus unto this great city? ⁹Then they shall answer, Because they have forsaken the covenant of the LORD their God, and worshipped other gods, and served them."

Jeremiah 25:4-6 "⁴And the LORD hath sent unto you all his servants the prophets, rising early and sending them; but ye have not hearkened, nor inclined your ear to hear. ⁵They said, Turn ye again now every one from his evil way, and from the evil of your doings, and dwell in the land that the LORD hath given unto you and to your fathers for ever and ever: ⁶And go not after other gods to serve them, and to worship them, and provoke me not to anger with the works of your hands; and I will do you no hurt."

The Reward For Serving The Lord

Exodus 23:25-27 "²⁵And ye shall serve the LORD your God, and he shall bless thy bread, and thy water; and I will take sickness away from the midst of thee. ²⁶There shall nothing cast their young, nor be barren, in thy land: the number of thy days I will fulfil. ²⁷I will send my fear before thee, and will destroy all the people to whom thou shalt come, and I will make all thine enemies turn their backs unto thee."

Deuteronomy 11:13-15 "¹³And it shall come to pass, if ye shall hearken diligently unto my commandments which I command you this day, to love the LORD your God, and to serve him with all your heart and with all your soul, [14]That I will give you the rain of your land in his due season, the first rain and the latter rain, that thou mayest gather in thy corn, and thy wine, and thine oil. [15]And I will send grass in thy fields for thy cattle, that thou mayest eat and be full."

1 Samuel 7:3 "And Samuel spake unto all the house of Israel, saying, If ye do return unto the LORD with all your hearts, then put away the strange gods and Ashtaroth from among you, and prepare your hearts unto the LORD, and serve him only: and he will deliver you out of the hand of the Philistines."

1 Samuel 12:14 "If ye will fear the LORD, and serve him, and obey his voice, and not rebel against the commandment of the LORD, then shall both ye and also the king that reigneth over you continue following the LORD your God."

2 Chronicles 30:8 "Now be ye not stiffnecked, as your fathers were, but yield yourselves unto the LORD, and enter into his sanctuary, which he hath sanctified for ever: and serve the LORD your God, that the fierceness of his wrath may turn away from you."

Job 36:5-11 "[5]Behold, God is mighty, and despiseth not any: he is mighty in strength and wisdom. [6]He preserveth not the life of the wicked: but giveth right to the poor. [7]He withdraweth not his eyes from the righteous: but with kings are they on the throne; yea, he doth establish them for ever, and they are exalted. [8]And if they be bound in fetters, and be holden in cords of affliction; [9]Then he sheweth them their work, and their transgressions that they have exceeded. [10]He openeth also their ear to discipline, and commandeth that they return from iniquity. [11]If they obey and serve him, they shall spend their days in prosperity, and their years in pleasures."

What Cannot Be Served Together

Matthew 6:24 "No man can serve two masters: for either he will hate the one, and love the other; or else he will hold to the one, and despise the other. Ye cannot serve God and mammon."

Luke 16:13 "No servant can serve two masters: for either he will hate the one, and love the other; or else he will hold to the one, and despise the other. Ye cannot serve God and mammon."

1 Corinthians 10:20-22 "[20]But I say, that the things which the Gentiles sacrifice, they sacrifice to devils, and not to God: and I would not that ye should have fellowship with devils. [21]Ye cannot drink the cup of the Lord, and the cup of devils: ye cannot be partakers of the Lord's table, and of the table of devils. [22]Do we provoke the Lord to jealousy? are we stronger than he?"

2 Corinthians 6:14-16 "[14]Be ye not unequally yoked together with unbelievers: for what fellowship hath righteousness with unrighteousness? and what communion hath light with darkness? [15]And what concord hath Christ with Belial? or what part hath he that believeth with an infidel? [16]And what agreement hath the temple of God with idols? for ye are the temple of the living God; as God hath said, I will dwell in them, and walk in them; and I will be their God, and they shall be my people."

What Not To Serve

Exodus 20:2-5 "[2]I am the LORD thy God, which have brought thee out of the land of Egypt, out of the house of bondage. [3]Thou shalt have no other gods before me. [4]Thou shalt not make unto thee any graven image, or any likeness of any thing that is in heaven above, or that is in the earth beneath, or that is in the water under the earth: [5]Thou shalt not bow down thyself to them, nor serve them: for I the LORD thy God am a jealous God, visiting the iniquity of the fathers upon the children unto the third and fourth generation of them that hate me."

Exodus 23:24 "Thou shalt not bow down to their gods, nor serve them, nor do after their works: but thou shalt utterly overthrow them, and quite break down their images."

Deuteronomy 5:6-9 "[6]I am the LORD thy God, which brought thee out of the land of Egypt, from the house of bondage. [7]Thou shalt have none other gods before me. [8]Thou shalt not make thee any graven image, or any likeness of any thing that is in heaven above, or that is in the earth beneath, or that is in the waters beneath the earth: [9]Thou shalt not bow down thyself unto them, nor serve them: for I the LORD thy God am a jealous God, visiting the iniquity of the fathers upon the children unto the third and fourth generation of them that hate me."

Deuteronomy 7:16 "And thou shalt consume all the people which the LORD thy God shall deliver thee; thine eye shall have no pity upon them: neither shalt thou serve their gods; for that will be a snare unto thee."

Deuteronomy 28:14 "And thou shalt not go aside from any of the words which I command thee this day, to the right hand, or to the left, to go after other gods to serve them."

Joshua 23:6-7 "⁶Be ye therefore very courageous to keep and to do all that is written in the book of the law of Moses, that ye turn not aside therefrom to the right hand or to the left; ⁷That ye come not among these nations, these that remain among you; neither make mention of the name of their gods, nor cause to swear by them, neither serve them, nor bow yourselves unto them."

2 Kings 17:35-38 "³⁵With whom the LORD had made a covenant, and charged them saying, Ye shall not fear other gods, nor bow yourselves to them, nor serve them, nor sacrifice to them: ³⁶But the LORD, who brought you up out of the land of Egypt with great power and a stretched out arm, him shall ye fear, and him shall ye worship, and to him shall ye do sacrifice. ³⁷And the statutes, and the ordinances, and the law, and the commandment, which he wrote for you, ye shall observe to do for evermore; and ye shall not fear other gods. ³⁸And the covenant that I have made with you ye shall not forget; neither shall ye fear other gods."

Jeremiah 25:4-6 "⁴And the LORD hath sent unto you all his servants the prophets, rising early and sending them; but ye have not hearkened, nor inclined your ear to hear. ⁵They said, Turn ye again now every one from his evil way, and from the evil of your doings, and dwell in the land that the LORD hath given unto you and to your fathers for ever and ever: ⁶And go not after other gods to serve them, and to worship them, and provoke me not to anger with the works of your hands; and I will do you no hurt."

Romans 6:3-7 "³Know ye not, that so many of us as were baptized into Jesus Christ were baptized into his death? ⁴Therefore we are buried with him by baptism into death: that like as Christ was raised up from the dead by the glory of the Father, even so we also should walk in newness of life. ⁵For if we have been planted together in the like-

ness of his death, we shall be also in the likeness of his resurrection: ⁶Knowing this, that our old man is crucified with him, that the body of sin might be destroyed, that henceforth we should not serve sin. ⁷For he that is dead is freed from sin."

1 Corinthians 7:23 "Ye are bought with a price; be not ye the servants of men."

Who Served The Creature More Than The Creator

Romans 1:18-25 "¹⁸For the wrath of God is revealed from heaven against all ungodliness and unrighteousness of men, who hold the truth in unrighteousness; ¹⁹Because that which may be known of God is manifest in them; for God hath shewed it unto them. ²⁰For the invisible things of him from the creation of the world are clearly seen, being understood by the things that are made, even his eternal power and Godhead; so that they are without excuse: ²¹Because that, when they knew God, they glorified him not as God, neither were thankful; but became vain in their imaginations, and their foolish heart was darkened. ²²Professing themselves to be wise, they became fools, ²³And changed the glory of the uncorruptible God into an image made like to corruptible man, and to birds, and fourfooted beasts, and creeping things. ²⁴Wherefore God also gave them up to uncleanness through the lusts of their own hearts, to dishonour their own bodies between themselves: ²⁵Who changed the truth of God into a lie, and worshipped and served the creature more than the Creator, who is blessed for ever. Amen."

Who Serves God

Revelation 7:9-15 "⁹After this I beheld, and, lo, a great multitude, which no man could number, of all nations, and kindreds, and people, and tongues, stood before the throne, and before the Lamb, clothed with white robes, and palms in their hands; ¹⁰And cried with a loud voice, saying, Salvation to our God which sitteth upon the throne, and unto the Lamb. ¹¹And all the angels stood round about the throne, and about the elders and the four beasts, and fell before the throne on their faces, and worshipped God, ¹²Saying, Amen: Blessing, and glory, and wisdom, and thanksgiving, and honour, and power, and might, be unto our God for ever and ever. Amen. ¹³And one of the elders answered, saying unto me, What are these which are arrayed in white robes? and whence came they? ¹⁴And I said unto him, Sir, thou knowest. And he said to me, These are they which came out of great tribulation, and have washed their robes, and made them white in the blood of the Lamb. ¹⁵Therefore are they before the throne of God, and serve him day and night in his temple: and he that sitteth on the throne shall dwell among them."

Who Shall Serve The Lord

Daniel 7:13-14 "¹³I saw in the night visions, and, behold, one like the Son of man came with the clouds of heaven, and came to the Ancient of days, and they brought him near before him. ¹⁴And there was given him dominion, and glory, and a kingdom, that all people, nations, and languages, should serve him: his dominion is an everlasting dominion, which shall not pass away, and his kingdom that which shall not be destroyed."

Daniel 7:27 "And the kingdom and dominion, and the greatness of the kingdom under the whole heaven, shall be given to the people of the saints of the most High, whose kingdom is an everlasting kingdom, and all dominions shall serve and obey him."

SEXUAL ACTIVITIES

Avoiding Fornication

1 Corinthians 6:13-20 "¹³Meats for the belly, and the belly for meats: but God shall destroy both it and them. Now the body is not for fornication, but for the Lord; and the Lord for the body. ¹⁴And God hath both raised up the Lord, and will also raise up us by his own power. ¹⁵Know ye not that your bodies are the members of Christ? shall I then take the members of Christ, and make them the members of an harlot? God forbid. ¹⁶What? know ye not that he which is joined to an harlot is one body? for two, saith he, shall be one flesh. ¹⁷But he that is joined unto the Lord is one spirit. ¹⁸Flee fornication. Every sin that a man doeth is without the body; but he that committeth fornication sinneth against his own body. ¹⁹What? know ye not that your body is the temple of the Holy Ghost which is in you, which ye have of God, and ye are not your own? ²⁰For ye are bought with a price: therefore glorify God in your body, and in your spirit, which are God's."

1 Corinthians 7:1-9 "¹Now concerning the things whereof ye wrote unto me: It is good for a man not to touch a woman. ²Nevertheless, to avoid fornication, let every man have his own wife, and let every woman have her own husband. ³Let the husband render unto the wife due benevolence: and likewise also the wife unto the husband. ⁴The wife hath not power of her own body, but the husband: and likewise also the husband hath not power of his own body, but the wife. ⁵Defraud ye not one the other, except it be with consent for a time, that ye may give yourselves to fasting and prayer; and come together again, that Satan tempt you not for your incontinency. ⁶But I speak this by permission, and not of commandment. ⁷For I would that all men were even as I myself. But every man hath his proper gift of God, one after this manner, and another after that. ⁸I say therefore to the unmarried and widows, It is good for them if they abide even as I. ⁹But if they cannot contain, let them marry: for it is better to marry than to burn."

The Reward For Sexual Sins

Genesis 19:4-14 "⁴But before they lay down, the men of the city, even the men of Sodom, compassed the house round, both old and young, all the people from every quarter: ⁵And they called unto Lot, and said unto him, Where are the men which came in to thee this night? bring them out unto us, that we may know them. ⁶And Lot went out at the door unto them, and shut the door after him, ⁷And said, I pray you, brethren, do not so wickedly. ⁸Behold now, I have two daughters which have not known man; let me, I pray you, bring them out unto you, and do ye to them as is good in your eyes: only unto these men do nothing; for therefore came they under the shadow of my roof. ⁹And they said, Stand back. And they said again, This one fellow came in to sojourn, and he will needs be a judge: now will we deal worse with thee, than with them. And they pressed sore upon the man, even Lot, and came near to break the door. ¹⁰But the men put forth their hand, and pulled Lot into the house to them, and shut to the door. ¹¹And they smote the men that were at the door of the house with blindness, both small and great: so that they wearied themselves to find the door. ¹²And the men said unto Lot, Hast thou here any besides? son in law, and thy sons, and thy daughters, and whatsoever thou hast in the city, bring them out of this place: ¹³For we will destroy this place, because the cry of them is waxen great before the face of the LORD; and the LORD hath sent us to destroy it. [14]And Lot went out, and spake unto his sons in law, which married his daughters, and said, Up, get you out of this place; for the LORD will destroy this city. But he seemed as one that mocked unto his sons in law."

Ezekiel 16:23-26 "[23]And it came to pass after all thy wickedness, (woe, woe unto thee! saith the Lord GOD;) [24]That thou hast also built unto thee an eminent place, and hast made thee an high place in every street. [25]Thou hast built thy high place at every head of the way, and hast made thy beauty to be abhorred, and hast opened thy feet to every one that passed by, and multiplied thy whoredoms. [26]Thou hast also committed fornication with the Egyptians thy neighbours, great of flesh; and hast increased thy whoredoms, to provoke me to anger."

1 Corinthians 10:8 "Neither let us commit fornication, as some of them committed, and fell in one day three and twenty thousand."

Ephesians 5:5-7 "[5]For this ye know, that no whoremonger, nor unclean person, nor covetous man, who is an idolater, hath any inheritance in the kingdom of Christ and of God. [6]Let no man deceive you with vain words: for because of these things cometh the wrath of God upon the children of disobedience. [7]Be not ye therefore partakers with them."

Colossians 3:5-6 "[5]Mortify therefore your members which are upon the earth; fornication, uncleanness, inordinate affection, evil concupiscence, and covetousness, which is idolatry: [6]For which things' sake the wrath of God cometh on the children of disobedience."

Those That Commit Bestiality

Exodus 22:19 "Whosoever lieth with a beast shall surely be put to death."

Leviticus 20:15-16 "[15]And if a man lie with a beast, he shall surely be put to death: and ye shall slay the beast. [16]And if a woman approach unto any beast, and lie down thereto, thou shalt kill the woman, and the beast: they shall surely be put to death; their blood shall be upon them."

Deuteronomy 27:21 "Cursed be he that lieth with any manner of beast. And all the people shall say, Amen."

Those That Commit Fornication

1 Corinthians 6:18 "Flee fornication. Every sin that a man doeth is without the body; but he that committeth fornication sinneth against his own body."

Jude 7-16 "[7]Even as Sodom and Gomorrha, and the cities about them in like manner, giving themselves over to fornication, and going after strange flesh, are set forth for an example, suffering the vengeance of eternal fire. [8]Likewise also these filthy dreamers defile the flesh, despise dominion, and speak evil of dignities. [9]Yet Michael the archangel, when contending with the devil he disputed about the body of Moses, durst not bring against him a railing accusation, but said, The Lord rebuke thee. [10]But these speak evil of those things which they know not: but what they know naturally, as brute beasts, in those things they corrupt themselves. [11]Woe unto them! for they have gone in the way of Cain, and ran greedily after the error of Balaam for reward, and perished in the gainsaying of Core. [12]These are spots in your feasts of charity, when they feast with you, feeding themselves without fear: clouds they are without water, carried about of winds; trees whose fruit withereth, without fruit, twice dead, plucked up by the roots; [13]Raging waves of the sea, foaming out their own shame; wandering stars, to whom is reserved the blackness of darkness for ever. [14]And Enoch also, the seventh from Adam, prophesied of these, saying, Behold, the Lord cometh with ten thousands of his saints, [15]To execute judgment upon all, and to convince all that are ungodly among them of all their ungodly deeds which they have ungodly committed, and of all their hard speeches which ungodly sinners have spoken against him. [16]These are murmurers, complainers, walking after their own lusts; and their mouth speaketh great swelling words, having men's persons in admiration because of advantage."

Those That Commit Incest

Leviticus 20:11-12 "[11]And the man that lieth with his father's wife hath uncovered his father's nakedness: both of them shall surely be put to death; their blood shall be upon them. [12]And if a man lie with his daughter in law, both of them shall surely be put to death: they have wrought confusion; their blood shall be upon them."

Leviticus 20:14 "And if a man take a wife and her mother, it is wickedness: they shall be burnt with fire, both he and they; that there be no wickedness among you."

Leviticus 20:17 "And if a man shall take his sister, his father's daughter, or his mother's daughter, and see her nakedness, and she see his nakedness; it is a wicked thing; and they shall be cut off in the sight of their people: he hath uncovered his sister's nakedness; he shall bear his iniquity."

Leviticus 20:19-21 "¹⁹And thou shalt not uncover the nakedness of thy mother's sister, nor of thy father's sister: for he uncovereth his near kin: they shall bear their iniquity. ²⁰And if a man shall lie with his uncle's wife, he hath uncovered his uncle's nakedness: they shall bear their sin; they shall die childless. ²¹And if a man shall take his brother's wife, it is an unclean thing: he hath uncovered his brother's nakedness; they shall be childless."

Deuteronomy 27:20 "Cursed be he that lieth with his father's wife; because he uncovereth his father's skirt. And all the people shall say, Amen."

Deuteronomy 27:22-23 "²²Cursed be he that lieth with his sister, the daughter of his father, or the daughter of his mother. And all the people shall say, Amen. ²³Cursed be he that lieth with his mother in law. And all the people shall say, Amen."

Those That Have Homosexual Relations
Leviticus 20:13 "If a man also lie with mankind, as he lieth with a woman, both of them have committed an abomination: they shall surely be put to death; their blood shall be upon them."

1 Timothy 1:8-10 "⁸But we know that the law is good, if a man use it lawfully; ⁹Knowing this, that the law is not made for a righteous man, but for the lawless and disobedient, for the ungodly and for sinners, for unholy and profane, for murderers of fathers and murderers of mothers, for manslayers, ¹⁰For whoremongers, for them that defile themselves with mankind, for menstealers, for liars, for perjured persons, and if there be any other thing that is contrary to sound doctrine."

Jude 7-16 "⁷Even as Sodom and Gomorrha, and the cities about them in like manner, giving themselves over to fornication, and going after strange flesh, are set forth for an example, suffering the vengeance of eternal fire. ⁸Likewise also these filthy dreamers defile the flesh, despise dominion, and speak evil of dignities. ⁹Yet Michael the archangel, when contending with the devil he disputed about the body of Moses, durst not bring against him a railing accusation, but said, The Lord rebuke thee. ¹⁰But these speak evil of those things which they know not: but what they know naturally, as brute beasts, in those things they corrupt themselves. ¹¹Woe unto them! for they have gone in the way of Cain, and ran greedily after the error of Balaam for reward, and perished in the gainsaying of Core. ¹²These are spots in your feasts of charity, when they feast with you, feeding themselves without fear: clouds they are without water, carried about of winds; trees whose fruit withereth, without fruit, twice dead, plucked up by the roots; ¹³Raging waves of the sea, foaming out their own shame; wandering stars, to whom is reserved the blackness of darkness for ever. ¹⁴And Enoch also, the seventh from Adam, prophesied of these, saying, Behold, the Lord cometh with ten thousands of his saints, ¹⁵To execute judgment upon all, and to convince all that are ungodly among them of all their ungodly deeds which they have ungodly committed, and of all their hard speeches which ungodly sinners have spoken against him. ¹⁶These are murmurers, complainers, walking after their own lusts; and their mouth speaketh great swelling words, having men's persons in admiration because of advantage."

Those That Have Sex With A Woman Who Is Menstruating
Leviticus 15:19-24 "¹⁹And if a woman have an issue, and her issue in her flesh be blood, she shall be put apart seven days: and whosoever toucheth her shall be unclean until the even. ²⁰And every thing that she lieth upon in her separation shall be unclean: every thing also that she sitteth upon shall be unclean. ²¹And whosoever toucheth her bed shall wash his clothes, and bathe himself in water, and be unclean until the even. ²²And whosoever toucheth any thing that she sat upon shall wash his clothes, and bathe himself in water, and be unclean until the even. ²³And if it be on her bed, or on any thing whereon she sitteth, when he toucheth it, he shall be unclean until the even. ²⁴And if any man lie with her at all, and her flowers be upon him, he shall be unclean seven days; and all the bed whereon he lieth shall be unclean."

Leviticus 20:18 "And if a man shall lie with a woman having her sickness, and shall uncover her nakedness; he hath discovered her fountain, and she hath uncovered the fountain of her blood: and both of them shall be cut off from among their people."

Those That Have Sex
With Someone Who Is Betrothed
Leviticus 19:20 "And whosoever lieth carnally with a woman, that is a bondmaid, betrothed to an husband, and not at all redeemed, nor freedom given her; she shall be scourged; they shall not be put to death, because she was not free."

Deuteronomy 22:23-24 "²³If a damsel that is a virgin be betrothed unto an husband, and a man find her in the city, and lie with her; ²⁴Then ye shall bring them both out unto the gate of that city, and ye shall stone them with stones that they die; the damsel, because she cried not, being in the city; and the man, because he hath humbled his neighbour's wife: so thou shalt put away evil from among you."

Those That Have Sex
With Someone Who Is Not Betrothed
Exodus 22:16-17 "¹⁶And if a man entice a maid that is not betrothed, and lie with her, he shall surely endow her to be his wife. ¹⁷If her father utterly refuse to give her unto him, he shall pay money according to the dowry of virgins."

Deuteronomy 22:28-29 "²⁸If a man find a damsel that is a virgin, which is not betrothed, and lay hold on her, and lie with her, and they be found; ²⁹Then the man that lay with her shall give unto the damsel's father fifty shekels of silver, and she shall be his wife; because he hath humbled her, he may not put her away all his days."

Those That Rape Women
Deuteronomy 22:25-27 "²⁵But if a man find a betrothed damsel in the field, and the man force her, and lie with her: then the man only that lay with her shall die: ²⁶But unto the damsel thou shalt do nothing; there is in the damsel no sin worthy of death: for as when a man riseth against his neighbour, and slayeth him, even so is this matter: ²⁷For he found her in the field, and the betrothed damsel cried, and there was none to save her."

What Sexual Activities Are Forbidden
Leviticus 18:6-20 "⁶None of you shall approach to any that is near of kin to him, to uncover their nakedness: I am the LORD. ⁷The nakedness of thy father, or the nakedness of thy mother, shalt thou not uncover: she is thy mother; thou shalt not uncover her nakedness. ⁸The nakedness of thy father's wife shalt thou not uncover: it is thy father's nakedness. ⁹The nakedness of thy sister, the daughter of thy father, or daughter of thy mother, whether she be born at home, or born abroad, even their nakedness thou shalt not uncover. ¹⁰The nakedness of thy son's daughter, or of thy daughter's daughter, even their nakedness thou shalt not uncover: for theirs is thine own nakedness. ¹¹The nakedness of thy father's wife's daughter, begotten of thy father, she is thy sister, thou shalt not uncover her nakedness. ¹²Thou shalt not uncover the nakedness of thy father's sister: she is thy father's near kinswoman. ¹³Thou shalt not uncover the nakedness of thy mother's sister: for she is thy mother's near kinswoman. ¹⁴Thou shalt not uncover the nakedness of thy father's brother, thou shalt not approach to his wife: she is thine aunt. ¹⁵Thou shalt not uncover the nakedness of thy daughter in law: she is thy son's wife; thou shalt not uncover her nakedness. ¹⁶Thou shalt not uncover the nakedness of thy brother's wife: it is thy brother's nakedness. ¹⁷Thou shalt not uncover the nakedness of a woman and her daughter, neither shalt thou take her son's daughter, or her daughter's daughter, to uncover her nakedness; for they are her near kinswomen: it is wickedness. ¹⁸Neither shalt thou take a wife to her sister, to vex her, to uncover her nakedness, beside the other in her life time. ¹⁹Also thou shalt not approach unto a woman to uncover her nakedness, as long as she is put apart for her uncleanness. ²⁰Moreover thou shalt not lie carnally with thy neighbour's wife, to defile thyself with her."

Leviticus 18:22-23 "²²Thou shalt not lie with mankind, as with womankind: it is abomination. ²³Neither shalt thou lie with any beast to defile thyself therewith: neither shall any woman stand before a beast to lie down thereto: it is confusion."

Leviticus 20:19 "And thou shalt not uncover the nakedness of thy mother's sister, nor of thy father's sister: for he uncovereth his near kin: they shall bear their iniquity."

Deuteronomy 22:30 "A man shall not take his father's wife, nor discover his father's skirt."

Deuteronomy 23:17-18 "17There shall be no whore of the daughters of Israel, nor a sodomite of the sons of Israel. 18Thou shalt not bring the hire of a whore, or the price of a dog, into the house of the LORD thy God for any vow: for even both these are abomination unto the LORD thy God."

1 Corinthians 10:8 "Neither let us commit fornication, as some of them committed, and fell in one day three and twenty thousand."

Ephesians 5:3 "But fornication, and all uncleanness, or covetousness, let it not be once named among you, as becometh saints."

1 Thessalonians 4:3-5 "3For this is the will of God, even your sanctification, that ye should abstain from fornication: 4That every one of you should know how to possess his vessel in sanctification and honour; 5Not in the lust of concupiscence, even as the Gentiles which know not God."

Why People Partake In
Inappropriate Sexual Behavior

Psalm 81:10-12 "10I am the LORD thy God, which brought thee out of the land of Egypt: open thy mouth wide, and I will fill it. 11But my people would not hearken to my voice; and Israel would none of me. 12So I gave them up unto their own hearts' lust: and they walked in their own counsels."

Romans 1:21-32 "21Because that, when they knew God, they glorified him not as God, neither were thankful; but became vain in their imaginations, and their foolish heart was darkened. 22Professing themselves to be wise, they became fools, 23And changed the glory of the uncorruptible God into an image made like to corruptible man, and to birds, and fourfooted beasts, and creeping things. 24Wherefore God also gave them up to uncleanness through the lusts of their own hearts, to dishonour their own bodies between themselves: 25Who changed the truth of God into a lie, and worshipped and served the creature more than the Creator, who is blessed for ever. Amen. 26For this cause God gave them up unto vile affections: for even their women did change the natural use into that which is against nature: 27And likewise also the men, leaving the natural use of the woman, burned in their lust one toward another; men with men working that which is unseemly, and receiving in themselves that recompence of their error which was meet. 28And even as they did not like to retain God in their knowledge, God gave them over to a reprobate mind, to do those things which are not convenient; 29Being filled with all unrighteousness, fornication, wickedness, covetousness, maliciousness; full of envy, murder, debate, deceit, malignity; whisperers, 30Backbiters, haters of God, despiteful, proud, boasters, inventors of evil things, disobedient to parents, 31Without understanding, covenantbreakers, without natural affection, implacable, unmerciful: 32Who knowing the judgment of God, that they which commit such things are worthy of death, not only do the same, but have pleasure in them that do them."

SHAME

Those That Are Ashamed
Of Jesus Christ

Mark 8:31-38 "31And he began to teach them, that the Son of man must suffer many things, and be rejected of the elders, and of the chief priests, and scribes, and be killed, and after three days rise again. 32And he spake that saying openly. And Peter took him, and began to rebuke him. 33But when he had turned about and looked on his disciples, he rebuked Peter, saying, Get thee behind me, Satan: for thou savourest not the things that be of God, but the things that be of men. 34And when he had called the people unto him with his disciples also, he said unto them, Whosoever will come after me, let him deny himself, and take up his cross, and follow me. 35For whosoever will save his life shall lose it; but whosoever shall lose his life for my sake and the gospel's, the same shall save it. 36For what shall it profit a man, if he shall gain the whole world, and lose his own soul? 37Or what shall a man give in exchange for his soul? 38Whosoever therefore shall be ashamed of me and of my words in this adulterous and sinful generation; of him also shall the Son of man be ashamed, when he cometh in the glory of his Father with the holy angels."

Luke 9:22-27 "22Saying, The Son of man must suffer many things, and be rejected of the elders and chief priests and scribes, and be slain, and be raised the third day. 23And he said to them all, If any man will come after me, let him deny himself, and take up his cross daily, and follow me. [24]For whosoever will save his life shall lose it: but whosoever will lose his life for my sake, the same shall save it. [25]For what is a man advantaged, if he gain the whole world, and lose himself, or be cast away? [26]For whosoever shall be ashamed of me and of my words, of him shall the Son of man be ashamed, when he shall come in his own glory, and in his Father's, and of the holy angels. [27]But I tell you of a truth, there be some standing here, which shall not taste of death, till they see the kingdom of God."

Those That Cause Shame
Proverbs 14:35 "The king's favour is toward a wise servant: but his wrath is against him that causeth shame."

Proverbs 17:2 "A wise servant shall have rule over a son that causeth shame, and shall have part of the inheritance among the brethren."

What Brings Shame
Proverbs 11:2 "When pride cometh, then cometh shame: but with the lowly is wisdom."

What Is Shame
Proverbs 18:13 "He that answereth a matter before he heareth it, it is folly and shame unto him."

Who Causes Shame
Proverbs 10:5 "He that gathereth in summer is a wise son: but he that sleepeth in harvest is a son that causeth shame."

Proverbs 19:26 "He that wasteth his father, and chaseth away his mother, is a son that causeth shame, and bringeth reproach."

Proverbs 28:7 "Whoso keepeth the law is a wise son: but he that is a companion of riotous men shameth his father."

Proverbs 29:15 "The rod and reproof give wisdom: but a child left to himself bringeth his mother to shame."

Who Covers Shame
Proverbs 12:16 "A fool's wrath is presently known: but a prudent man covereth shame."

Who Jesus Christ Will Be Ashamed Of
Mark 8:31-38 "[31]And he began to teach them, that the Son of man must suffer many things, and be rejected of the elders, and of the chief priests, and scribes, and be killed, and after three days rise again. [32]And he spake that saying openly. And Peter took him, and began to rebuke him. [33]But when he had turned about and looked on his disciples, he rebuked Peter, saying, Get thee behind me, Satan: for thou savourest not the things that be of God, but the things that be of men. [34]And when he had called the people unto him with his disciples also, he said unto them, Whosoever will come after me, let him deny himself, and take up his cross, and follow me. [35]For whosoever will save his life shall lose it; but whosoever shall lose his life for my sake and the gospel's, the same shall save it. [36]For what shall it profit a man, if he shall gain the whole world, and lose his own soul? [37]Or what shall a man give in exchange for his soul? [38]Whosoever therefore shall be ashamed of me and of my words in this adulterous and sinful generation; of him also shall the Son of man be ashamed, when he cometh in the glory of his Father with the holy angels."

Luke 9:22-27 "[22]Saying, The Son of man must suffer many things, and be rejected of the elders and chief priests and scribes, and be slain, and be raised the third day. [23]And he said to them all, If any man will come after me, let him deny himself, and take up his cross daily, and follow me. [24]For whosoever will save his life shall lose it: but whosoever will lose his life for my sake, the same shall save it. [25]For what is a man advantaged, if he gain the whole world, and lose himself, or be cast away? [26]For whosoever shall be ashamed of me and of my words, of him shall the Son of man be ashamed, when he shall come in his own glory, and in his Father's, and of the holy angels. [27]But I tell you of a truth, there be some standing here, which shall not taste of death, till they see the kingdom of God."

Who Knows No Shame
Zephaniah 3:5 "The just LORD is in the midst thereof; he will not do iniquity: every morning doth he bring his judgment to light, he faileth not; but the unjust knoweth no shame."

Who Shall Be Ashamed
Job 8:20-22 "[20]Behold, God will not cast away a perfect man, neither will he help the evil doers: [21]Till he fill thy mouth with laughing, and thy lips

with rejoicing. 22They that hate thee shall be clothed with shame; and the dwelling place of the wicked shall come to nought."

Psalm 31:17 "Let me not be ashamed, O LORD; for I have called upon thee: let the wicked be ashamed, and let them be silent in the grave."

Proverbs 3:35 "The wise shall inherit glory: but shame shall be the promotion of fools."

Proverbs 9:7 "He that reproveth a scorner getteth to himself shame: and he that rebuketh a wicked man getteth himself a blot."

Proverbs 13:5 "A righteous man hateth lying: but a wicked man is loathsome, and cometh to shame."

Proverbs 13:18 "Poverty and shame shall be to him that refuseth instruction: but he that regardeth reproof shall be honoured."

Isaiah 42:17 "They shall be turned back, they shall be greatly ashamed, that trust in graven images, that say to the molten images, Ye are our gods."

Isaiah 65:11-13 "11But ye are they that forsake the LORD, that forget my holy mountain, that prepare a table for that troop, and that furnish the drink offering unto that number. 12Therefore will I number you to the sword, and ye shall all bow down to the slaughter: because when I called, ye did not answer; when I spake, ye did not hear; but did evil before mine eyes, and did choose that wherein I delighted not. 13Therefore thus saith the Lord GOD, Behold, my servants shall eat, but ye shall be hungry: behold, my servants shall drink, but ye shall be thirsty: behold, my servants shall rejoice, but ye shall be ashamed."

Jeremiah 3:24-25 "24For shame hath devoured the labour of our fathers from our youth; their flocks and their herds, their sons and their daughters. 25We lie down in our shame, and our confusion covereth us: for we have sinned against the LORD our God, we and our fathers, from our youth even unto this day, and have not obeyed the voice of the LORD our God."

Jeremiah 17:13 "O LORD, the hope of Israel, all that forsake thee shall be ashamed, and they that depart from me shall be written in the earth, because they have forsaken the LORD, the fountain of living waters."

Who Shall Not Be Ashamed

Psalm 31:17 "Let me not be ashamed, O LORD; for I have called upon thee: let the wicked be ashamed, and let them be silent in the grave."

Psalm 37:18-19 "18The LORD knoweth the days of the upright: and their inheritance shall be for ever. 19They shall not be ashamed in the evil time: and in the days of famine they shall be satisfied."

Psalm 119:1-6 "1Blessed are the undefiled in the way, who walk in the law of the LORD. 2Blessed are they that keep his testimonies, and that seek him with the whole heart. 3They also do no iniquity: they walk in his ways. 4Thou hast commanded us to keep thy precepts diligently. 5O that my ways were directed to keep thy statutes! 6Then shall I not be ashamed, when I have respect unto all thy commandments."

Isaiah 28:16 "Therefore thus saith the Lord GOD, Behold, I lay in Zion for a foundation a stone, a tried stone, a precious corner stone, a sure foundation: he that believeth shall not make haste."

Isaiah 49:23 "And kings shall be thy nursing fathers, and their queens thy nursing mothers: they shall bow down to thee with their face toward the earth, and lick up the dust of thy feet; and thou shalt know that I am the LORD: for they shall not be ashamed that wait for me."

Joel 2:23-27 "23Be glad then, ye children of Zion, and rejoice in the LORD your God: for he hath given you the former rain moderately, and he will cause to come down for you the rain, the former rain, and the latter rain in the first month. 24And the floors shall be full of wheat, and the fats shall overflow with wine and oil. 25And I will restore to you the years that the locust hath eaten, the cankerworm, and the caterpiller, and the palmerworm, my great army which I sent among you. 26And ye shall eat in plenty, and be satisfied, and praise the name of the LORD your God, that hath dealt wondrously with you: and my people shall never be ashamed. 27And ye shall know that I am in the midst of Israel, and that I am the LORD your God, and none else: and my people shall never be ashamed."

Romans 10:9-11 "9That if thou shalt confess with thy mouth the Lord Jesus, and shalt believe in thine heart that God hath raised him from the dead, thou shalt be saved. [10]For with the heart man believeth unto righteousness; and with the mouth confession is made unto salvation. [11]For the scripture saith, Whosoever believeth on him shall not be ashamed."

Whose Glory Becomes Shame

Hosea 4:6-7 "[6]My people are destroyed for lack of knowledge: because thou hast rejected knowledge, I will also reject thee, that thou shalt be no priest to me: seeing thou hast forgotten the law of thy God, I will also forget thy children. [7]As they were increased, so they sinned against me: therefore will I change their glory into shame."

Habakkuk 2:6-16 "[6]Shall not all these take up a parable against him, and a taunting proverb against him, and say, Woe to him that increaseth that which is not his! how long? and to him that ladeth himself with thick clay! [7]Shall they not rise up suddenly that shall bite thee, and awake that shall vex thee, and thou shalt be for booties unto them? [8]Because thou hast spoiled many nations, all the remnant of the people shall spoil thee; because of men's blood, and for the violence of the land, of the city, and of all that dwell therein. [9]Woe to him that coveteth an evil covetousness to his house, that he may set his nest on high, that he may be delivered from the power of evil! [10]Thou hast consulted shame to thy house by cutting off many people, and hast sinned against thy soul. [11]For the stone shall cry out of the wall, and the beam out of the timber shall answer it. [12]Woe to him that buildeth a town with blood, and stablisheth a city by iniquity! [13]Behold, is it not of the LORD of hosts that the people shall labour in the very fire, and the people shall weary themselves for very vanity? [14]For the earth shall be filled with the knowledge of the glory of the LORD, as the waters cover the sea. [15]Woe unto him that giveth his neighbour drink, that puttest thy bottle to him, and makest him drunken also, that thou mayest look on their nakedness! [16]Thou art filled with shame for glory: drink thou also, and let thy foreskin be uncovered: the cup of the LORD's right hand shall be turned unto thee, and shameful spewing shall be on thy glory."

Whose Glory Is In Their Shame

Philippians 3:18-19 "[18](For many walk, of whom I have told you often, and now tell you even weeping, that they are the enemies of the cross of Christ: [19]Whose end is destruction, whose God is their belly, and whose glory is in their shame, who mind earthly things.)"

SHEPHERDS/PASTORS

False Shepherds/Pastors

Jeremiah 10:21 "For the pastors are become brutish, and have not sought the LORD: therefore they shall not prosper, and all their flocks shall be scattered."

Jeremiah 12:10-12 "[10]Many pastors have destroyed my vineyard, they have trodden my portion under foot, they have made my pleasant portion a desolate wilderness. [11]They have made it desolate, and being desolate it mourneth unto me; the whole land is made desolate, because no man layeth it to heart. [12]The spoilers are come upon all high places through the wilderness: for the sword of the LORD shall devour from the one end of the land even to the other end of the land: no flesh shall have peace."

Jeremiah 23:1-4 "[1]Woe be unto the pastors that destroy and scatter the sheep of my pasture! saith the LORD. [2]Therefore thus saith the LORD God of Israel against the pastors that feed my people; Ye have scattered my flock, and driven them away, and have not visited them: behold, I will visit upon you the evil of your doings, saith the LORD. [3]And I will gather the remnant of my flock out of all countries whither I have driven them, and will bring them again to their folds; and they shall be fruitful and increase. [4]And I will set up shepherds over them which shall feed them: and they shall fear no more, nor be dismayed, neither shall they be lacking, saith the LORD."

Jeremiah 50:4-6 "[4]In those days, and in that time, saith the LORD, the children of Israel shall come, they and the children of Judah together, going and weeping: they shall go, and seek the LORD their God. [5]They shall ask the way to Zion with their faces thitherward, saying, Come, and let us join ourselves to the LORD in a perpetual covenant that shall not be forgotten. [6]My people hath been lost sheep: their shepherds have caused them to go astray, they have turned them away on the mountains: they have gone from mountain to hill, they have forgotten their restingplace."

Ezekiel 34:1-10 "¹And the word of the LORD came unto me, saying, ²Son of man, prophesy against the shepherds of Israel, prophesy, and say unto them, Thus saith the Lord GOD unto the shepherds; Woe be to the shepherds of Israel that do feed themselves! should not the shepherds feed the flocks? ³Ye eat the fat, and ye clothe you with the wool, ye kill them that are fed: but ye feed not the flock. ⁴The diseased have ye not strengthened, neither have ye healed that which was sick, neither have ye bound up that which was broken, neither have ye brought again that which was driven away, neither have ye sought that which was lost; but with force and with cruelty have ye ruled them. ⁵And they were scattered, because there is no shepherd: and they became meat to all the beasts of the field, when they were scattered. ⁶My sheep wandered through all the mountains, and upon every high hill: yea, my flock was scattered upon all the face of the earth, and none did search or seek after them. ⁷Therefore, ye shepherds, hear the word of the LORD; ⁸As I live, saith the Lord GOD, surely because my flock became a prey, and my flock became meat to every beast of the field, because there was no shepherd, neither did my shepherds search for my flock, but the shepherds fed themselves, and fed not my flock; ⁹Therefore, O ye shepherds, hear the word of the LORD; ¹⁰Thus saith the Lord GOD; Behold, I am against the shepherds; and I will require my flock at their hand, and cause them to cease from feeding the flock; neither shall the shepherds feed themselves any more; for I will deliver my flock from their mouth, that they may not be meat for them."

Zechariah 11:16-17 "¹⁶For, lo, I will raise up a shepherd in the land, which shall not visit those that be cut off, neither shall seek the young one, nor heal that that is broken, nor feed that that standeth still: but he shall eat the flesh of the fat, and tear their claws in pieces. ¹⁷Woe to the idol shepherd that leaveth the flock! the sword shall be upon his arm, and upon his right eye: his arm shall be clean dried up, and his right eye shall be utterly darkened."

John 10:12-13 "¹²But he that is an hireling, and not the shepherd, whose own the sheep are not, seeth the wolf coming, and leaveth the sheep, and fleeth: and the wolf catcheth them, and scattereth the sheep. ¹³The hireling fleeth, because he is an hireling, and careth not for the sheep."

The Lord Being A Shepherd

Genesis 49:24 "But his bow abode in strength, and the arms of his hands were made strong by the hands of the mighty God of Jacob; (from thence is the shepherd, the stone of Israel:)"

Psalm 23:1-4 "¹The LORD is my shepherd; I shall not want. ²He maketh me to lie down in green pastures: he leadeth me beside the still waters. ³He restoreth my soul: he leadeth me in the paths of righteousness for his name's sake. ⁴Yea, though I walk through the valley of the shadow of death, I will fear no evil: for thou art with me; thy rod and thy staff they comfort me."

Psalm 95:7 "For he is our God; and we are the people of his pasture, and the sheep of his hand. To day if ye will hear his voice."

Isaiah 40:10-11 "¹⁰Behold, the Lord GOD will come with strong hand, and his arm shall rule for him: behold, his reward is with him, and his work before him. ¹¹He shall feed his flock like a shepherd: he shall gather the lambs with his arm, and carry them in his bosom, and shall gently lead those that are with young."

Jeremiah 31:10 "Hear the word of the LORD, O ye nations, and declare it in the isles afar off, and say, He that scattered Israel will gather him, and keep him, as a shepherd doth his flock."

Ezekiel 34:11-24 "¹¹For thus saith the Lord GOD; Behold, I, even I, will both search my sheep, and seek them out. ¹²As a shepherd seeketh out his flock in the day that he is among his sheep that are scattered; so will I seek out my sheep, and will deliver them out of all places where they have been scattered in the cloudy and dark day. ¹³And I will bring them out from the people, and gather them from the countries, and will bring them to their own land, and feed them upon the mountains of Israel by the rivers, and in all the inhabited places of the country. ¹⁴I will feed them in a good pasture, and upon the high mountains of Israel shall their fold be: there shall they lie in a good fold, and in a fat pasture shall they feed upon the mountains of Israel. ¹⁵I will feed my flock, and I will cause them to lie down, saith the Lord GOD. ¹⁶I will seek that which was lost, and bring again that which was driven away, and will bind up that which was broken, and will strengthen that which was sick: but I will destroy the fat and the strong; I will feed them with judgment. ¹⁷And as for you, O my flock, thus saith the Lord GOD; Behold, I judge between cattle and cattle, between the rams and the he goats. ¹⁸Seemeth it a small thing unto you to have eaten up the good pasture, but ye must tread down with your feet the residue of your pastures? and to have drunk of the deep waters, but ye must foul the residue with your feet? ¹⁹And as for my flock, they eat that which ye have trodden with your feet; and they drink that which ye have fouled with your feet. ²⁰Therefore thus saith the Lord GOD unto them; Behold, I, even I, will judge between the fat cattle and between the lean cattle. ²¹Because ye have thrust with side and with shoulder, and pushed all the diseased with your horns, till ye have scattered them abroad; ²²Therefore will I save my flock, and they shall no more be a prey; and I will judge between cattle and cattle. ²³And I will set up one shepherd over them, and he shall feed them, even my servant David; he shall feed them, and he shall be their shepherd. ²⁴And I the LORD will be their God, and my servant David a prince among them; I the LORD have spoken it."

John 10:1-18 "¹Verily, verily, I say unto you, He that entereth not by the door into the sheepfold, but climbeth up some other way, the same is a thief and a robber. ²But he that entereth in by the door is the shepherd of the sheep. ³To him the porter openeth; and the sheep hear his voice: and he calleth his own sheep by name, and leadeth them out. ⁴And when he putteth forth his own sheep, he goeth before them, and the sheep follow him: for they know his voice. ⁵And a stranger will they not follow, but will flee from him: for they know not the voice of strangers. ⁶This parable spake Jesus unto them: but they understood not what things they were which he spake unto them. ⁷Then said Jesus unto them again, Verily, verily, I say unto you, I am the door of the sheep. ⁸All that ever came before me are thieves and robbers: but the sheep did not hear them. ⁹I am the door: by me if any man enter in, he shall be saved, and

shall go in and out, and find pasture. ¹⁰The thief cometh not, but for to steal, and to kill, and to destroy: I am come that they might have life, and that they might have it more abundantly. ¹¹I am the good shepherd: the good shepherd giveth his life for the sheep. ¹²But he that is an hireling, and not the shepherd, whose own the sheep are not, seeth the wolf coming, and leaveth the sheep, and fleeth: and the wolf catcheth them, and scattereth the sheep. ¹³The hireling fleeth, because he is an hireling, and careth not for the sheep. ¹⁴I am the good shepherd, and know my sheep, and am known of mine. ¹⁵As the Father knoweth me, even so know I the Father: and I lay down my life for the sheep. ¹⁶And other sheep I have, which are not of this fold: them also I must bring, and they shall hear my voice; and there shall be one fold, and one shepherd. ¹⁷Therefore doth my Father love me, because I lay down my life, that I might take it again. ¹⁸No man taketh it from me, but I lay it down of myself. I have power to lay it down, and I have power to take it again. This commandment have I received of my Father."

1 Peter 2:21-25 "²¹For even hereunto were ye called: because Christ also suffered for us, leaving us an example, that ye should follow his steps: ²²Who did no sin, neither was guile found in his mouth: ²³Who, when he was reviled, reviled not again; when he suffered, he threatened not; but committed himself to him that judgeth righteously: ²⁴Who his own self bare our sins in his own body on the tree, that we, being dead to sins, should live unto righteousness: by whose stripes ye were healed. ²⁵For ye were as sheep going astray; but are now returned unto the Shepherd and Bishop of your souls."

Revelation 7:17 "For the Lamb which is in the midst of the throne shall feed them, and shall lead them unto living fountains of waters: and God shall wipe away all tears from their eyes."

What Pastors Are For
Jeremiah 3:14-15 "¹⁴Turn, O backsliding children, saith the LORD; for I am married unto you: and I will take you one of a city, and two of a family, and I will bring you to Zion: ¹⁵And I will give you pastors according to mine heart, which shall feed you with knowledge and understanding."

Ephesians 4:11-14 "[11]And he gave some, apostles; and some, prophets; and some, evangelists; and some, pastors and teachers; [12]For the perfecting of the saints, for the work of the ministry, for the edifying of the body of Christ: [13]Till we all come in the unity of the faith, and of the knowledge of the Son of God, unto a perfect man, unto the measure of the stature of the fulness of Christ: [14]That we henceforth be no more children, tossed to and fro, and carried about with every wind of doctrine, by the sleight of men, and cunning craftiness, whereby they lie in wait to deceive."

SIMPLICITY

The Simple
Psalm 19:7 "The law of the LORD is perfect, converting the soul: the testimony of the LORD is sure, making wise the simple."

Psalm 116:6 "The LORD preserveth the simple: I was brought low, and he helped me."

Psalm 119:126-130 "[126]It is time for thee, LORD, to work: for they have made void thy law. [127]Therefore I love thy commandments above gold; yea, above fine gold. [128]Therefore I esteem all thy precepts concerning all things to be right; and I hate every false way. [129]Thy testimonies are wonderful: therefore doth my soul keep them. [130]The entrance of thy words giveth light; it giveth understanding unto the simple."

Proverbs 1:22 "How long, ye simple ones, will ye love simplicity? and the scorners delight in their scorning, and fools hate knowledge?"

Proverbs 14:15 "The simple believeth every word: but the prudent man looketh well to his going."

Proverbs 14:18 "The simple inherit folly: but the prudent are crowned with knowledge."

Proverbs 19:25 "Smite a scorner, and the simple will beware: and reprove one that hath understanding, and he will understand knowledge."

Proverbs 21:11 "When the scorner is punished, the simple is made wise: and when the wise is instructed, he receiveth knowledge."

Proverbs 22:3 "A prudent man foreseeth the evil, and hideth himself: but the simple pass on, and are punished."

Proverbs 27:12 "A prudent man foreseeth the evil, and hideth himself; but the simple pass on, and are punished."

SIN

How Sin Entered Into The World
Genesis 3:1-19 "[1]Now the serpent was more subtil than any beast of the field which the LORD God had made. And he said unto the woman, Yea, hath God said, Ye shall not eat of every tree of the garden? [2]And the woman said unto the serpent, We may eat of the fruit of the trees of the garden: [3]But of the fruit of the tree which is in the midst of the garden, God hath said, Ye shall not eat of it, neither shall ye touch it, lest ye die. [4]And the serpent said unto the woman, Ye shall not surely die: [5]For God doth know that in the day ye eat thereof, then your eyes shall be opened, and ye shall be as gods, knowing good and evil. [6]And when the woman saw that the tree was good for food, and that it was pleasant to the eyes, and a tree to be desired to make one wise, she took of the fruit thereof, and did eat, and gave also unto her husband with her; and he did eat. [7]And the eyes of them both were opened, and they knew that they were naked; and they sewed fig leaves together, and made themselves aprons. [8]And they heard the voice of the LORD God walking in the garden in the cool of the day: and Adam and his wife hid themselves from the presence of the LORD God amongst the trees of the garden. [9]And the LORD God called unto Adam, and said unto him, Where art thou? [10]And he said, I heard thy voice in the garden, and I was afraid, because I was naked; and I hid myself. [11]And he said, Who told thee that thou wast naked? Hast thou eaten of the tree, whereof I commanded thee that thou shouldest not eat? [12]And the man said, The woman whom thou gavest to be with me, she gave me of the tree, and I did eat. [13]And the LORD God said unto the woman, What is this that thou hast done? And the woman said, The serpent beguiled me, and I did eat. [14]And the LORD God said unto the serpent, Because thou hast done this, thou art cursed above all cattle, and above every beast of the field; upon thy belly shalt thou go, and dust shalt thou eat all the days of thy life: [15]And I will put enmity between thee and the woman, and between thy seed and her seed; it shall bruise thy

head, and thou shalt bruise his heel. [16]Unto the woman he said, I will greatly multiply thy sorrow and thy conception; in sorrow thou shalt bring forth children; and thy desire shall be to thy husband, and he shall rule over thee. [17]And unto Adam he said, Because thou hast hearkened unto the voice of thy wife, and hast eaten of the tree, of which I commanded thee, saying, Thou shalt not eat of it: cursed is the ground for thy sake; in sorrow shalt thou eat of it all the days of thy life; [18]Thorns also and thistles shall it bring forth to thee; and thou shalt eat the herb of the field; [19]In the sweat of thy face shalt thou eat bread, till thou return unto the ground; for out of it wast thou taken: for dust thou art, and unto dust shalt thou return."

Romans 5:12-21 "[12]Wherefore, as by one man sin entered into the world, and death by sin; and so death passed upon all men, for that all have sinned: [13](For until the law sin was in the world: but sin is not imputed when there is no law. [14]Nevertheless death reigned from Adam to Moses, even over them that had not sinned after the similitude of Adam's transgression, who is the figure of him that was to come. [15]But not as the offence, so also is the free gift. For if through the offence of one many be dead, much more the grace of God, and the gift by grace, which is by one man, Jesus Christ, hath abounded unto many. [16]And not as it was by one that sinned, so is the gift: for the judgment was by one to condemnation, but the free gift is of many offences unto justification. [17]For if by one man's offence death reigned by one; much more they which receive abundance of grace and of the gift of righteousness shall reign in life by one, Jesus Christ.) [18]Therefore as by the offence of one judgment came upon all men to condemnation; even so by the righteousness of one the free gift came upon all men unto justification of life. [19]For as by one man's disobedience many were made sinners, so by the obedience of one shall many be made righteous. [20]Moreover the law entered, that the offence might abound. But where sin abounded, grace did much more abound: [21]That as sin hath reigned unto death, even so might grace reign through righteousness unto eternal life by Jesus Christ our Lord."

1 Corinthians 15:20-28 "[20]But now is Christ risen from the dead, and become the firstfruits of them that slept. [21]For since by man came death, by man came also the resurrection of the dead. [22]For as in Adam all die, even so in Christ shall all be made alive. [23]But every man in his own order: Christ the firstfruits; afterward they that are Christ's at his coming. [24]Then cometh the end, when he shall have delivered up the kingdom to God, even the Father; when he shall have put down all rule and all authority and power. [25]For he must reign, till he hath put all enemies under his feet. [26]The last enemy that shall be destroyed is death. [27]For he hath put all things under his feet. But when he saith, all things are put under him, it is manifest that he is excepted, which did put all things under him. [28]And when all things shall be subdued unto him, then shall the Son also himself be subject unto him that put all things under him, that God may be all in all."

Mankind Being Sinful In Nature

Job 14:1-4 "[1]Man that is born of a woman is of few days, and full of trouble. [2]He cometh forth like a flower, and is cut down: he fleeth also as a shadow, and continueth not. [3]And dost thou open thine eyes upon such an one, and bringest me into judgment with thee? [4]Who can bring a clean thing out of an unclean? not one."

Psalm 51:1-5 "[1]Have mercy upon me, O God, according to thy lovingkindness: according unto the multitude of thy tender mercies blot out my transgressions. [2]Wash me throughly from mine iniquity, and cleanse me from my sin. [3]For I acknowledge my transgressions: and my sin is ever before me. [4]Against thee, thee only, have I sinned, and done this evil in thy sight: that thou mightest be justified when thou speakest, and be clear when thou judgest. [5]Behold, I was shapen in iniquity; and in sin did my mother conceive me."

Psalm 58:1-3 "[1]Do ye indeed speak righteousness, O congregation? do ye judge uprightly, O ye sons of men? [2]Yea, in heart ye work wickedness; ye weigh the violence of your hands in the earth. [3]The wicked are estranged from the womb: they go astray as soon as they be born, speaking lies."

Isaiah 48:8 "Yea, thou heardest not; yea, thou knewest not; yea, from that time that thine ear was not opened: for I knew that thou wouldest deal very treacherously, and wast called a transgressor from the womb."

Ephesians 2:1-3 "¹And you hath he quickened, who were dead in trespasses and sins; ²Wherein in time past ye walked according to the course of this world, according to the prince of the power of the air, the spirit that now worketh in the children of disobedience: ³Among whom also we all had our conversation in times past in the lusts of our flesh, fulfilling the desires of the flesh and of the mind; and were by nature the children of wrath, even as others."

Not Sinning

John 5:14 "Afterward Jesus findeth him in the temple, and said unto him, Behold, thou art made whole: sin no more, lest a worse thing come unto thee."

John 8:10-11 "¹⁰When Jesus had lifted up himself, and saw none but the woman, he said unto her, Woman, where are those thine accusers? hath no man condemned thee? ¹¹She said, No man, Lord. And Jesus said unto her, Neither do I condemn thee: go, and sin no more."

Romans 6:12-13 "¹²Let not sin therefore reign in your mortal body, that ye should obey it in the lusts thereof. ¹³Neither yield ye your members as instruments of unrighteousness unto sin: but yield yourselves unto God, as those that are alive from the dead, and your members as instruments of righteousness unto God."

1 Corinthians 15:34 "Awake to righteousness, and sin not; for some have not the knowledge of God: I speak this to your shame."

Ephesians 4:26 "Be ye angry, and sin not: let not the sun go down upon your wrath."

1 Timothy 5:22 "Lay hands suddenly on no man, neither be partaker of other men's sins: keep thyself pure."

1 John 2:1 "My little children, these things write I unto you, that ye sin not. And if any man sin, we have an advocate with the Father, Jesus Christ the righteous."

Sinners

Job 24:19-20 "¹⁹Drought and heat consume the snow waters: so doth the grave those which have sinned. ²⁰The womb shall forget him; the worm shall feed sweetly on him; he shall be no more

remembered; and wickedness shall be broken as a tree."

Psalm 1:4-5 "⁴The ungodly are not so: but are like the chaff which the wind driveth away. ⁵Therefore the ungodly shall not stand in the judgment, nor sinners in the congregation of the righteous."

Psalm 25:8 "Good and upright is the LORD: therefore will he teach sinners in the way."

Psalm 104:35 "Let the sinners be consumed out of the earth, and let the wicked be no more. Bless thou the LORD, O my soul. Praise ye the LORD."

Proverbs 8:32-36 "³²Now therefore hearken unto me, O ye children: for blessed are they that keep my ways. ³³Hear instruction, and be wise, and refuse it not. ³⁴Blessed is the man that heareth me, watching daily at my gates, waiting at the posts of my doors. ³⁵For whoso findeth me findeth life, and shall obtain favour of the LORD. ³⁶But he that sinneth against me wrongeth his own soul: all they that hate me love death."

Proverbs 11:31 "Behold, the righteous shall be recompensed in the earth: much more the wicked and the sinner."

Proverbs 13:6 "Righteousness keepeth him that is upright in the way: but wickedness overthroweth the sinner."

Proverbs 13:21-22 "²¹Evil pursueth sinners: but to the righteous good shall be repayed. ²²A good man leaveth an inheritance to his children's children: and the wealth of the sinner is laid up for the just."

Ecclesiastes 2:24-26 "²⁴There is nothing better for a man, than that he should eat and drink, and that he should make his soul enjoy good in his labour. This also I saw, that it was from the hand of God. ²⁵For who can eat, or who else can hasten hereunto, more than I? ²⁶For God giveth to a man that is good in his sight wisdom, and knowledge, and joy: but to the sinner he giveth travail, to gather and to heap up, that he may give to him that is good before God. This also is vanity and vexation of spirit."

Ecclesiastes 7:26 "And I find more bitter than death the woman, whose heart is snares and nets, and her hands as bands: whoso pleaseth God shall escape from her; but the sinner shall be taken by her."

Ecclesiastes 9:18 "Wisdom is better than weapons of war: but one sinner destroyeth much good."

Isaiah 13:9 "Behold, the day of the LORD cometh, cruel both with wrath and fierce anger, to lay the land desolate: and he shall destroy the sinners thereof out of it."

Isaiah 33:14 "The sinners in Zion are afraid; fearfulness hath surprised the hypocrites. Who among us shall dwell with the devouring fire? who among us shall dwell with everlasting burnings?"

Ezekiel 18:4 "Behold, all souls are mine; as the soul of the father, so also the soul of the son is mine: the soul that sinneth, it shall die."

Ezekiel 18:20 "The soul that sinneth, it shall die. The son shall not bear the iniquity of the father, neither shall the father bear the iniquity of the son: the righteousness of the righteous shall be upon him, and the wickedness of the wicked shall be upon him."

Amos 9:10 "All the sinners of my people shall die by the sword, which say, The evil shall not overtake nor prevent us."

John 8:34-35 "34Jesus answered them, Verily, verily, I say unto you, Whosoever committeth sin is the servant of sin. 35And the servant abideth not in the house for ever: but the Son abideth ever."

1 Timothy 1:8-9 "8But we know that the law is good, if a man use it lawfully; 9Knowing this, that the law is not made for a righteous man, but for the lawless and disobedient, for the ungodly and for sinners, for unholy and profane, for murderers of fathers and murderers of mothers, for manslayers."

James 4:8 "Draw nigh to God, and he will draw nigh to you. Cleanse your hands, ye sinners; and purify your hearts, ye double minded."

1 John 3:1-6 "1Behold, what manner of love the Father hath bestowed upon us, that we should be called the sons of God: therefore the world knoweth us not, because it knew him not. 2Beloved, now are we the sons of God, and it doth not yet appear what we shall be: but we know that, when he shall appear, we shall be like him; for we shall see him as he is. 3And every man that hath this hope in him purifieth himself, even as he is pure. 4Whosoever committeth sin transgresseth also the law: for sin is the transgression of the law. 5And ye know that he was manifested to take away our sins; and in him is no sin. 6Whosoever abideth in him sinneth not: whosoever sinneth hath not seen him, neither known him."

1 John 3:8 "He that committeth sin is of the devil; for the devil sinneth from the beginning. For this purpose the Son of God was manifested, that he might destroy the works of the devil."

The Reward For Sin
1 Kings 8:28-36 "28Yet have thou respect unto the prayer of thy servant, and to his supplication, O LORD my God, to hearken unto the cry and to the prayer, which thy servant prayeth before thee to day: 29That thine eyes may be open toward this house night and day, even toward the place of which thou hast said, My name shall be there: that thou mayest hearken unto the prayer which thy servant shall make toward this place. 30And hearken thou to the supplication of thy servant, and of thy people Israel, when they shall pray toward this place: and hear thou in heaven thy dwelling place: and when thou hearest, forgive. 31If any man trespass against his neighbour, and an oath be laid upon him to cause him to swear, and the oath come before thine altar in this house: 32Then hear thou in heaven, and do, and judge thy servants, condemning the wicked, to bring his way upon his head; and justifying the righteous, to give him according to his righteousness. 33When thy people Israel be smitten down before the enemy, because they have sinned against thee, and shall turn again to thee, and confess thy name, and pray, and make supplication unto thee in this house: 34Then hear thou in heaven, and forgive the sin of thy people Israel, and bring them again unto the land which thou gavest unto their fathers. 35When heaven is shut up, and there is no rain, because they have sinned against thee; if they pray toward this place, and confess thy name, and turn from their sin, when thou afflictest them: 36Then hear thou in heaven, and forgive the sin of thy servants, and of thy people Israel, that thou teach them the good way wherein they should walk, and give rain upon thy land, which thou hast given to thy people for an inheritance."

1 Kings 8:43-46 "43Hear thou in heaven thy dwelling place, and do according to all that the stranger calleth to thee for: that all people of the earth may know thy name, to fear thee, as do thy people Israel; and that they may know that this house, which I have builded, is called by thy name. ⁴⁴If thy people go out to battle against their enemy, whithersoever thou shalt send them, and shall pray unto the LORD toward the city which thou hast chosen, and toward the house that I have built for thy name: ⁴⁵Then hear thou in heaven their prayer and their supplication, and maintain their cause. ⁴⁶If they sin against thee, (for there is no man that sinneth not,) and thou be angry with them, and deliver them to the enemy, so that they carry them away captives unto the land of the enemy, far or near."

1 Kings 14:15-16 "¹⁵For the LORD shall smite Israel, as a reed is shaken in the water, and he shall root up Israel out of this good land, which he gave to their fathers, and shall scatter them beyond the river, because they have made their groves, provoking the LORD to anger. ¹⁶And he shall give Israel up because of the sins of Jeroboam, who did sin, and who made Israel to sin."

2 Chronicles 6:19-26 "¹⁹Have respect therefore to the prayer of thy servant, and to his supplication, O LORD my God, to hearken unto the cry and the prayer which thy servant prayeth before thee: ²⁰That thine eyes may be open upon this house day and night, upon the place whereof thou hast said that thou wouldest put thy name there; to hearken unto the prayer which thy servant prayeth toward this place. ²¹Hearken therefore unto the supplications of thy servant, and of thy people Israel, which they shall make toward this place: hear thou from thy dwelling place, even from heaven; and when thou hearest, forgive. ²²If a man sin against his neighbour, and an oath be laid upon him to make him swear, and the oath come before thine altar in this house; ²³Then hear thou from heaven, and do, and judge thy servants, by requiting the wicked, by recompensing his way upon his own head; and by justifying the righteous, by giving him according to his righteousness. ²⁴And if thy people Israel be put to the worse before the enemy, because they have sinned against thee; and shall return and confess thy name, and pray and make supplication before thee in this house; ²⁵Then hear thou from the heavens, and forgive the sin of thy people Israel, and bring

them again unto the land which thou gavest to them and to their fathers. ²⁶When the heaven is shut up, and there is no rain, because they have sinned against thee; yet if they pray toward this place, and confess thy name, and turn from their sin, when thou dost afflict them."

Ezra 9:15 "O LORD God of Israel, thou art righteous: for we remain yet escaped, as it is this day: behold, we are before thee in our trespasses: for we cannot stand before thee because of this."

Nehemiah 9:29-31 "²⁹And testifiedst against them, that thou mightest bring them again unto thy law: yet they dealt proudly, and hearkened not unto thy commandments, but sinned against thy judgments, (which if a man do, he shall live in them;) and withdrew the shoulder, and hardened their neck, and would not hear. ³⁰Yet many years didst thou forbear them, and testifiedst against them by thy spirit in thy prophets: yet would they not give ear: therefore gavest thou them into the hand of the people of the lands. ³¹Nevertheless for thy great mercies' sake thou didst not utterly consume them, nor forsake them; for thou art a gracious and merciful God."

Psalm 78:17-34 "¹⁷And they sinned yet more against him by provoking the most High in the wilderness. ¹⁸And they tempted God in their heart by asking meat for their lust. ¹⁹Yea, they spake against God; they said, Can God furnish a table in the wilderness? ²⁰Behold, he smote the rock, that the waters gushed out, and the streams overflowed; can he give bread also? can he provide flesh for his people? ²¹Therefore the LORD heard this, and was wroth: so a fire was kindled against Jacob, and anger also came up against Israel; ²²Because they believed not in God, and trusted not in his salvation: ²³Though he had commanded the clouds from above, and opened the doors of heaven, ²⁴And had rained down manna upon them to eat, and had given them of the corn of heaven. ²⁵Man did eat angels' food: he sent them meat to the full. ²⁶He caused an east wind to blow in the heaven: and by his power he brought in the south wind. ²⁷He rained flesh also upon them as dust, and feathered fowls like as the sand of the sea: ²⁸And he let it fall in the midst of their camp, round about their habitations. ²⁹So they did eat, and were well filled: for he gave them their own desire; ³⁰They were not estranged from their lust.

But while their meat was yet in their mouths, [31]The wrath of God came upon them, and slew the fattest of them, and smote down the chosen men of Israel. [32]For all this they sinned still, and believed not for his wondrous works. [33]Therefore their days did he consume in vanity, and their years in trouble. [34]When he slew them, then they sought him: and they returned and inquired early after God."

Psalm 106:19-43 "[19]They made a calf in Horeb, and worshipped the molten image. [20]Thus they changed their glory into the similitude of an ox that eateth grass. [21]They forgat God their saviour, which had done great things in Egypt; [22]Wondrous works in the land of Ham, and terrible things by the Red sea. [23]Therefore he said that he would destroy them, had not Moses his chosen stood before him in the breach, to turn away his wrath, lest he should destroy them. [24]Yea, they despised the pleasant land, they believed not his word: [25]But murmured in their tents, and hearkened not unto the voice of the LORD. [26]Therefore he lifted up his hand against them, to overthrow them in the wilderness: [27]To overthrow their seed also among the nations, and to scatter them in the lands. [28]They joined themselves also unto Baalpeor, and ate the sacrifices of the dead. [29]Thus they provoked him to anger with their inventions: and the plague brake in upon them. [30]Then stood up Phinehas, and executed judgment: and so the plague was stayed. [31]And that was counted unto him for righteousness unto all generations for evermore. [32]They angered him also at the waters of strife, so that it went ill with Moses for their sakes: [33]Because they provoked his spirit, so that he spake unadvisedly with his lips. [34]They did not destroy the nations, concerning whom the LORD commanded them: [35]But were mingled among the heathen, and learned their works. [36]And they served their idols: which were a snare unto them. [37]Yea, they sacrificed their sons and their daughters unto devils, [38]And shed innocent blood, even the blood of their sons and of their daughters, whom they sacrificed unto the idols of Canaan: and the land was polluted with blood. [39]Thus were they defiled with their own works, and went a whoring with their own inventions. [40]Therefore was the wrath of the LORD kindled against his people, insomuch that he abhorred his own inher-itance. [41]And he gave them into the hand of the heathen; and they that hated them ruled over them. [42]Their enemies also oppressed them, and they were brought into subjection under their hand. [43]Many times did he deliver them; but they provoked him with their counsel, and were brought low for their iniquity."

Isaiah 64:4-5 "[4]For since the beginning of the world men have not heard, nor perceived by the ear, neither hath the eye seen, O God, beside thee, what he hath prepared for him that waiteth for him. [5]Thou meetest him that rejoiceth and wor-keth righteousness, those that remember thee in thy ways: behold, thou art wroth; for we have sinned: in those is continuance, and we shall be saved."

Jeremiah 3:24-25 "[24]For shame hath devoured the labour of our fathers from our youth; their flocks and their herds, their sons and their daughters. [25]We lie down in our shame, and our confusion covereth us: for we have sinned against the LORD our God, we and our fathers, from our youth even unto this day, and have not obeyed the voice of the LORD our God."

Jeremiah 8:14 "Why do we sit still? assemble yourselves, and let us enter into the defenced cities, and let us be silent there: for the LORD our God hath put us to silence, and given us water of gall to drink, because we have sinned against the LORD."

Jeremiah 16:16-18 "[16]Behold, I will send for many fishers, saith the LORD, and they shall fish them; and after will I send for many hunters, and they shall hunt them from every mountain, and from every hill, and out of the holes of the rocks. [17]For mine eyes are upon all their ways: they are not hid from my face, neither is their iniquity hid from mine eyes. [18]And first I will recompense their iniquity and their sin double; because they have defiled my land, they have filled mine inheritance with the carcases of their detestable and abom-inable things."

Jeremiah 30:12-15 "[12]For thus saith the LORD, Thy bruise is incurable, and thy wound is grievous. [13]There is none to plead thy cause, that thou mayest be bound up: thou hast no healing medi-cines. [14]All thy lovers have forgotten thee; they seek thee not; for I have wounded thee with the wound of an enemy, with the chastisement of a cruel one, for the multitude of thine iniquity; because thy sins were increased. ¹⁵Why criest thou for thine affliction? thy sorrow is incurable for the multitude of thine iniquity: because thy sins were increased, I have done these things unto thee."

Ezekiel 28:12-19 "¹²Son of man, take up a lamentation upon the king of Tyrus, and say unto him, Thus saith the Lord GOD; Thou sealest up the sum, full of wisdom, and perfect in beauty. ¹³Thou hast been in Eden the garden of God; every precious stone was thy covering, the sardius, topaz, and the diamond, the beryl, the onyx, and the jasper, the sapphire, the emerald, and the carbuncle, and gold: the workmanship of thy tabrets and of thy pipes was prepared in thee in the day that thou wast created. ¹⁴Thou art the anointed cherub that covereth; and I have set thee so: thou wast upon the holy mountain of God; thou hast walked up and down in the midst of the stones of fire. ¹⁵Thou wast perfect in thy ways from the day that thou wast created, till iniquity was found in thee. ¹⁶By the multitude of thy merchandise they have filled the midst of thee with violence, and thou hast sinned: therefore I will cast thee as profane out of the mountain of God: and I will destroy thee, O covering cherub, from the midst of the stones of fire. ¹⁷Thine heart was lifted up because of thy beauty, thou hast corrupted thy wisdom by reason of thy brightness: I will cast thee to the ground, I will lay thee before kings, that they may behold thee. ¹⁸Thou hast defiled thy sanctuaries by the multitude of thine iniquities, by the iniquity of thy traffick; therefore will I bring forth a fire from the midst of thee, it shall devour thee, and I will bring thee to ashes upon the earth in the sight of all them that behold thee. ¹⁹All they that know thee among the people shall be astonished at thee: thou shalt be a terror, and never shalt thou be any more."

Daniel 9:4-14 "⁴And I prayed unto the LORD my God, and made my confession, and said, O Lord, the great and dreadful God, keeping the covenant and mercy to them that love him, and to them that keep his commandments; ⁵We have sinned, and have committed iniquity, and have done wickedly, and have rebelled, even by departing from thy precepts and from thy judgments: ⁶Neither have we hearkened unto thy servants the prophets, which spake in thy name to our kings, our princes, and our fathers, and to all the people of the land. ⁷O Lord, righteousness belongeth unto thee, but unto us confusion of faces, as at this day; to the men of Judah, and to the inhabitants of Jerusalem, and unto all Israel, that are near, and that are far off, through all the countries whither thou hast driven them, because of their trespass that they have trespassed against thee. ⁸O Lord, to us belongeth confusion of face, to our kings, to our princes, and to our fathers, because we have sinned against thee. ⁹To the Lord our God belong mercies and forgivenesses, though we have rebelled against him; ¹⁰Neither have we obeyed the voice of the LORD our God, to walk in his laws, which he set before us by his servants the prophets. ¹¹Yea, all Israel have transgressed thy law, even by departing, that they might not obey thy voice; therefore the curse is poured upon us, and the oath that is written in the law of Moses the servant of God, because we have sinned against him. ¹²And he hath confirmed his words, which he spake against us, and against our judges that judged us, by bringing upon us a great evil: for under the whole heaven hath not been done as hath been done upon Jerusalem. ¹³As it is written in the law of Moses, all this evil is come upon us: yet made we not our prayer before the LORD our God, that we might turn from our iniquities, and understand thy truth. ¹⁴Therefore hath the LORD watched upon the evil, and brought it upon us: for the LORD our God is righteous in all his works which he doeth: for we obeyed not his voice."

Micah 6:9-16 "⁹The LORD's voice crieth unto the city, and the man of wisdom shall see thy name: hear ye the rod, and who hath appointed it. ¹⁰Are there yet the treasures of wickedness in the house of the wicked, and the scant measure that is abominable? ¹¹Shall I count them pure with the wicked balances, and with the bag of deceitful weights? ¹²For the rich men thereof are full of violence, and the inhabitants thereof have spoken lies, and their tongue is deceitful in their mouth. ¹³Therefore also will I make thee sick in smiting thee, in making thee desolate because of thy sins. ¹⁴Thou shalt eat, but not be satisfied; and thy casting down shall be in the midst of thee; and thou shalt take hold, but shalt not deliver; and that which thou deliverest will I give up to the sword. [15]Thou shalt sow, but thou shalt not reap; thou shalt tread the olives, but thou shalt not anoint thee with oil; and sweet wine, but shalt not drink wine. [16]For the statutes of Omri are kept, and all the works of the house of Ahab, and ye walk in their counsels; that I should make thee a desolation, and the inhabitants thereof an hissing: therefore ye shall bear the reproach of my people."

Micah 7:9 "I will bear the indignation of the LORD, because I have sinned against him, until he plead my cause, and execute judgment for me: he will bring me forth to the light, and I shall behold his righteousness."

Zephaniah 1:17-18 "[17]And I will bring distress upon men, that they shall walk like blind men, because they have sinned against the LORD: and their blood shall be poured out as dust, and their flesh as the dung. [18]Neither their silver nor their gold shall be able to deliver them in the day of the LORD's wrath; but the whole land shall be devoured by the fire of his jealousy: for he shall make even a speedy riddance of all them that dwell in the land."

Hebrews 10:26-30 "[26]For if we sin wilfully after that we have received the knowledge of the truth, there remaineth no more sacrifice for sins, [27]But a certain fearful looking for of judgment and fiery indignation, which shall devour the adversaries. [28]He that despised Moses' law died without mercy under two or three witnesses: [29]Of how much sorer punishment, suppose ye, shall he be thought worthy, who hath trodden under foot the Son of God, and hath counted the blood of the covenant, wherewith he was sanctified, an unholy thing, and hath done despite unto the Spirit of grace? [30]For we know him that hath said, Vengeance belongeth unto me, I will recompense, saith the Lord. And again, The Lord shall judge his people."

The Strength Of Sin
1 Corinthians 15:56 "The sting of death is sin; and the strength of sin is the law."

The Wages Of Sin
Romans 6:23 "For the wages of sin is death; but the gift of God is eternal life through Jesus Christ our Lord."

There Not Being A Single Person Who Does Not Sin
1 Kings 8:46 "If they sin against thee, (for there is no man that sinneth not,) and thou be angry with them, and deliver them to the enemy, so that they carry them away captives unto the land of the enemy, far or near."

2 Chronicles 6:36 "If they sin against thee, (for there is no man which sinneth not,) and thou be angry with them, and deliver them over before their enemies, and they carry them away captives unto a land far off or near."

Psalm 14:1-4 "[1]The fool hath said in his heart, There is no God. They are corrupt, they have done abominable works, there is none that doeth good. [2]The LORD looked down from heaven upon the children of men, to see if there were any that did understand, and seek God. [3]They are all gone aside, they are all together become filthy: there is none that doeth good, no, not one. [4]Have all the workers of iniquity no knowledge? who eat up my people as they eat bread, and call not upon the LORD."

Psalm 53:1 "The fool hath said in his heart, There is no God. Corrupt are they, and have done abominable iniquity: there is none that doeth good."

Proverbs 20:9 "Who can say, I have made my heart clean, I am pure from my sin?"

Ecclesiastes 7:20 "For there is not a just man upon earth, that doeth good, and sinneth not."

Isaiah 64:4-7 "[4]For since the beginning of the world men have not heard, nor perceived by the ear, neither hath the eye seen, O God, beside thee, what he hath prepared for him that waiteth for him. [5]Thou meetest him that rejoiceth and worketh righteousness, those that remember thee in thy ways: behold, thou art wroth; for we have sinned: in those is continuance, and we shall be saved. [6]But we are all as an unclean thing, and all our righteousnesses are as filthy rags; and we all do fade as a leaf; and our iniquities, like the wind, have taken us away. [7]And there is none that calleth upon thy name, that stirreth up himself to take hold of thee: for thou hast hid thy face from us, and hast consumed us, because of our iniquities."

Matthew 19:16-17 "[16]And, behold, one came and said unto him, Good Master, what good thing shall I do, that I may have eternal life? [17]And he said unto him, Why callest thou me good? there is none good but one, that is, God: but if thou wilt enter into life, keep the commandments."

Romans 3:9-12 "[9]What then? are we better than they? No, in no wise: for we have before proved both Jews and Gentiles, that they are all under sin; [10]As it is written, There is none righteous, no, not one: [11]There is none that understandeth, there is none that seeketh after God. [12]They are all gone out of the way, they are together become unprofitable; there is none that doeth good, no, not one."

Romans 3:23 "For all have sinned, and come short of the glory of God."

Romans 5:12 "Wherefore, as by one man sin entered into the world, and death by sin; and so death passed upon all men, for that all have sinned."

Those That Have Sinned In The Law
Romans 2:12-13 "[12]For as many as have sinned without law shall also perish without law: and as many as have sinned in the law shall be judged by the law; [13](For not the hearers of the law are just before God, but the doers of the law shall be justified."

Those That Have Sinned Without Law
Romans 2:12-13 "[12]For as many as have sinned without law shall also perish without law: and as many as have sinned in the law shall be judged by the law; [13](For not the hearers of the law are just before God, but the doers of the law shall be justified."

Those That Say They Have No Sin
1 John 1:7-10 "[7]But if we walk in the light, as he is in the light, we have fellowship one with another, and the blood of Jesus Christ his Son cleanseth us from all sin. [8]If we say that we have no sin, we deceive ourselves, and the truth is not in us. [9]If we confess our sins, he is faithful and just to forgive us our sins, and to cleanse us from all unrighteousness. [10]If we say that we have not sinned, we make him a liar, and his word is not in us."

Those That Cover Sin
Proverbs 28:13 "He that covereth his sins shall not prosper: but whoso confesseth and forsaketh them shall have mercy."

Those That Sin Against Another
1 Samuel 2:24-25 "[24]Nay, my sons; for it is no good report that I hear: ye make the LORD's people to transgress. [25]If one man sin against another, the judge shall judge him: but if a man sin against the LORD, who shall intreat for him? Notwithstanding they hearkened not unto the voice of their father, because the LORD would slay them."

Those That Sin Against The Lord
1 Samuel 2:24-25 "[24]Nay, my sons; for it is no good report that I hear: ye make the LORD's people to transgress. [25]If one man sin against another, the judge shall judge him: but if a man sin against the LORD, who shall intreat for him? Notwithstanding they hearkened not unto the voice of their father, because the LORD would slay them."

Those Whose Sins Are Covered
Psalm 32:1-2 "[1]Blessed is he whose transgression is forgiven, whose sin is covered. [2]Blessed is the man unto whom the LORD imputeth not iniquity, and in whose spirit there is no guile."

Romans 4:6-7 "[6]Even as David also describeth the blessedness of the man, unto whom God imputeth righteousness without works, [7]Saying, Blessed are they whose iniquities are forgiven, and whose sins are covered."

What Cannot Take Away Sins
Hebrews 10:4 "For it is not possible that the blood of bulls and of goats should take away sins."

What Brings Forth Sin
James 1:15 "Then when lust hath conceived, it bringeth forth sin: and sin, when it is finished, bringeth forth death."

What Covers All Sins
Proverbs 10:12 "Hatred stirreth up strifes: but love covereth all sins."

What Is Sin
Deuteronomy 23:21 "When thou shalt vow a vow unto the LORD thy God, thou shalt not slack to pay it: for the LORD thy God will surely require it of thee; and it would be sin in thee."

Proverbs 21:4 "An high look, and a proud heart, and the plowing of the wicked, is sin."

Proverbs 24:9 "The thought of foolishness is sin: and the scorner is an abomination to men."

Romans 14:22-23 "²²Hast thou faith? have it to thyself before God. Happy is he that condemneth not himself in that thing which he alloweth. ²³And he that doubteth is damned if he eat, because he eateth not of faith: for whatsoever is not of faith is sin."

1 Corinthians 15:56 "The sting of death is sin; and the strength of sin is the law."

James 4:17 "Therefore to him that knoweth to do good, and doeth it not, to him it is sin."

1 John 5:17 "All unrighteousness is sin: and there is a sin not unto death."

What Sin Does

Isaiah 59:1-2 "¹Behold, the LORD's hand is not shortened, that it cannot save; neither his ear heavy, that it cannot hear: ²But your iniquities have separated between you and your God, and your sins have hid his face from you, that he will not hear."

Jeremiah 5:23-25 "²³But this people hath a revolting and a rebellious heart; they are revolted and gone. ²⁴Neither say they in their heart, Let us now fear the LORD our God, that giveth rain, both the former and the latter, in his season: he reserveth unto us the appointed weeks of the harvest. ²⁵Your iniquities have turned away these things, and your sins have withholden good things from you."

James 1:15 "Then when lust hath conceived, it bringeth forth sin: and sin, when it is finished, bringeth forth death."

What Sin Is

Proverbs 14:34 "Righteousness exalteth a nation: but sin is a reproach to any people."

1 John 3:4 "Whosoever committeth sin transgresseth also the law: for sin is the transgression of the law."

What Sin Is Unforgivable

Matthew 12:31-32 "³¹Wherefore I say unto you, All manner of sin and blasphemy shall be forgiven unto men: but the blasphemy against the Holy Ghost shall not be forgiven unto men. ³²And whosoever speaketh a word against the Son of man, it shall be forgiven him: but whosoever speaketh against the Holy Ghost, it shall not be forgiven him, neither in this world, neither in the world to come."

Mark 3:28-29 "²⁸Verily I say unto you, All sins shall be forgiven unto the sons of men, and blasphemies wherewith soever they shall blaspheme: ²⁹But he that shall blaspheme against the Holy Ghost hath never forgiveness, but is in danger of eternal damnation."

Luke 12:10 "And whosoever shall speak a word against the Son of man, it shall be forgiven him: but unto him that blasphemeth against the Holy Ghost it shall not be forgiven."

Hebrews 6:4-8 "⁴For it is impossible for those who were once enlightened, and have tasted of the heavenly gift, and were made partakers of the Holy Ghost, ⁵And have tasted the good word of God, and the powers of the world to come, ⁶If they shall fall away, to renew them again unto repentance; seeing they crucify to themselves the Son of God afresh, and put him to an open shame. ⁷For the earth which drinketh in the rain that cometh oft upon it, and bringeth forth herbs meet for them by whom it is dressed, receiveth blessing from God: ⁸But that which beareth thorns and briers is rejected, and is nigh unto cursing; whose end is to be burned."

Hebrews 10:26-29 "²⁶For if we sin wilfully after that we have received the knowledge of the truth, there remaineth no more sacrifice for sins, ²⁷But a certain fearful looking for of judgment and fiery indignation, which shall devour the adversaries. ²⁸He that despised Moses' law died without mercy under two or three witnesses: ²⁹Of how much sorer punishment, suppose ye, shall he be thought worthy, who hath trodden under foot the Son of God, and hath counted the blood of the covenant, wherewith he was sanctified, an unholy thing, and hath done despite unto the Spirit of grace?"

1 John 5:16-17 "¹⁶If any man see his brother sin a sin which is not unto death, he shall ask, and he shall give him life for them that sin not unto death. There is a sin unto death: I do not say that he shall pray for it. ¹⁷All unrighteousness is sin: and there is a sin not unto death."

Where Sin Dwells

Romans 7:17-23 "¹⁷Now then it is no more I that do it, but sin that dwelleth in me. ¹⁸For I know that in me (that is, in my flesh,) dwelleth no good thing: for to will is present with me; but how to perform that which is good I find not. ¹⁹For the good that I would I do not: but the evil which I would not, that I do. [20]Now if I do that I would not, it is no more I that do it, but sin that dwelleth in me. [21]I find then a law, that, when I would do good, evil is present with me. [22]For I delight in the law of God after the inward man: [23]But I see another law in my members, warring against the law of my mind, and bringing me into captivity to the law of sin which is in my members."

Who Does Not Sin

1 John 3:1-6 "[1]Behold, what manner of love the Father hath bestowed upon us, that we should be called the sons of God: therefore the world knoweth us not, because it knew him not. [2]Beloved, now are we the sons of God, and it doth not yet appear what we shall be: but we know that, when he shall appear, we shall be like him; for we shall see him as he is. [3]And every man that hath this hope in him purifieth himself, even as he is pure. [4]Whosoever committeth sin transgresseth also the law: for sin is the transgression of the law. [5]And ye know that he was manifested to take away our sins; and in him is no sin. [6]Whosoever abideth in him sinneth not: whosoever sinneth hath not seen him, neither known him."

1 John 3:9 "Whosoever is born of God doth not commit sin; for his seed remaineth in him: and he cannot sin, because he is born of God."

1 John 5:18 "We know that whosoever is born of God sinneth not; but he that is begotten of God keepeth himself, and that wicked one toucheth him not."

Who Is A Sinner

Proverbs 14:21 "He that despiseth his neighbour sinneth: but he that hath mercy on the poor, happy is he."

Proverbs 19:2 "Also, that the soul be without knowledge, it is not good; and he that hasteth with his feet sinneth."

Romans 3:9-12 "[9]What then? are we better than they? No, in no wise: for we have before proved both Jews and Gentiles, that they are all under sin; [10]As it is written, There is none righteous, no, not one: [11]There is none that understandeth, there is none that seeketh after God. [12]They are all gone out of the way, they are together become unprofitable; there is none that doeth good, no, not one."

James 2:9 "But if ye have respect to persons, ye commit sin, and are convinced of the law as transgressors."

1 John 3:8 "He that committeth sin is of the devil; for the devil sinneth from the beginning. For this purpose the Son of God was manifested, that he might destroy the works of the devil."

Who Is Freed From Sin

Romans 6:1-7 "[1]What shall we say then? Shall we continue in sin, that grace may abound? [2]God forbid. How shall we, that are dead to sin, live any longer therein? [3]Know ye not, that so many of us as were baptized into Jesus Christ were baptized into his death? [4]Therefore we are buried with him by baptism into death: that like as Christ was raised up from the dead by the glory of the Father, even so we also should walk in newness of life. [5]For if we have been planted together in the likeness of his death, we shall be also in the likeness of his resurrection: [6]Knowing this, that our old man is crucified with him, that the body of sin might be destroyed, that henceforth we should not serve sin. [7]For he that is dead is freed from sin."

Who Is The Servant Of Sin

John 8:34-35 "[34]Jesus answered them, Verily, verily, I say unto you, Whosoever committeth sin is the servant of sin. [35]And the servant abideth not in the house for ever: but the Son abideth ever."

Romans 6:15-20 "[15]What then? shall we sin, because we are not under the law, but under grace? God forbid. [16]Know ye not, that to whom ye yield yourselves servants to obey, his servants ye are to whom ye obey; whether of sin unto death, or of obedience unto righteousness? [17]But God be thanked, that ye were the servants of sin, but ye have obeyed from the heart that form of doctrine which was delivered you. [18]Being then made free from sin, ye became the servants of righteousness. [19]I speak after the manner of men because of the infirmity of your flesh: for as ye have yielded your members servants to uncleanness and to iniquity unto iniquity; even so now yield your members servants to righteousness unto holiness. [20]For when ye were the servants of sin, ye were free from righteousness."

Who Makes A Mock At Sin

Proverbs 14:9 "Fools make a mock at sin: but among the righteous there is favour."

Who Sins Against Their Own Body

1 Corinthians 6:18 "Flee fornication. Every sin that a man doeth is without the body; but he that committeth fornication sinneth against his own body."

Why People Sin

Romans 1:28-32 "²⁸And even as they did not like to retain God in their knowledge, God gave them over to a reprobate mind, to do those things which are not convenient; ²⁹Being filled with all unrighteousness, fornication, wickedness, covetousness, maliciousness; full of envy, murder, debate, deceit, malignity; whisperers, ³⁰Backbiters, haters of God, despiteful, proud, boasters, inventors of evil things, disobedient to parents, ³¹Without understanding, covenantbreakers, without natural affection, implacable, unmerciful: ³²Who knowing the judgment of God, that they which commit such things are worthy of death, not only do the same, but have pleasure in them that do them."

Why Sin Does Not Have Dominion Over You

Romans 6:1-14 "¹What shall we say then? Shall we continue in sin, that grace may abound? ²God forbid. How shall we, that are dead to sin, live any longer therein? ³Know ye not, that so many of us as were baptized into Jesus Christ were baptized into his death? ⁴Therefore we are buried with him by baptism into death: that like as Christ was raised up from the dead by the glory of the Father, even so we also should walk in newness of life. ⁵For if we have been planted together in the likeness of his death, we shall be also in the likeness of his resurrection: ⁶Knowing this, that our old man is crucified with him, that the body of sin might be destroyed, that henceforth we should not serve sin. ⁷For he that is dead is freed from sin. ⁸Now if we be dead with Christ, we believe that we shall also live with him: ⁹Knowing that Christ being raised from the dead dieth no more; death hath no more dominion over him. ¹⁰For in that he died, he died unto sin once: but in that he liveth, he liveth unto God. ¹¹Likewise reckon ye also yourselves to be dead indeed unto sin, but alive unto God through Jesus Christ our Lord. ¹²Let not sin therefore reign in your mortal body, that ye should obey it in the lusts thereof. ¹³Neither yield ye your members as instruments of unrighteousness unto sin: but yield yourselves unto God, as those that are alive from the dead, and your members as instruments of righteousness unto God. ¹⁴For sin shall not have dominion over you: for ye are not under the law, but under grace."

Why You Have No Cloak For Your Sin

John 15:1-22 "¹I am the true vine, and my Father is the husbandman. ²Every branch in me that beareth not fruit he taketh away: and every branch that beareth fruit, he purgeth it, that it may bring forth more fruit. ³Now ye are clean through the word which I have spoken unto you. ⁴Abide in me, and I in you. As the branch cannot bear fruit of itself, except it abide in the vine; no more can ye, except ye abide in me. ⁵I am the vine, ye are the branches: He that abideth in me, and I in him, the same bringeth forth much fruit: for without me ye can do nothing. ⁶If a man abide not in me, he is cast forth as a branch, and is withered; and men gather them, and cast them into the fire, and they are burned. ⁷If ye abide in me, and my words abide in you, ye shall ask what ye will, and it shall be done unto you. ⁸Herein is my Father glorified, that ye bear much fruit; so shall ye be my disciples. ⁹As the Father hath loved me, so have I loved you: continue ye in my love. ¹⁰If ye keep my commandments, ye shall abide in my love; even as I have kept my Father's commandments, and abide in his love. ¹¹These things have I spoken unto you, that my joy might remain in you, and that your joy might be full. ¹²This is my commandment, That ye love one another, as I have loved you. ¹³Greater love hath no man than this, that a man lay down his life for his friends. ¹⁴Ye are my friends, if ye do whatsoever I command you. ¹⁵Henceforth I call you not servants; for the servant knoweth not what his lord doeth: but I have called you friends; for all things that I have heard of my Father I have made known unto you. ¹⁶Ye have not chosen me, but I have chosen you, and ordained you, that ye should go and bring forth fruit, and that your fruit should remain: that whatsoever ye shall ask of the Father in my name, he may give it you. ¹⁷These things I command you, that ye love one another. ¹⁸If the world hate you, ye know that it hated me before it hated you. ¹⁹If ye were of the world, the world would love his own: but because ye are not of the world, but I have chosen you out of the world, therefore the world hateth you. ²⁰Remember the word that I said unto you, The servant is not greater than his lord. If they have persecuted me, they will also persecute you; if they have kept my saying, they will keep yours also. [21]But all these things will they do unto you for my name's sake, because they know not him that sent me. [22]If I had not come and spoken unto them, they had not had sin: but now they have no cloke for their sin."

SNARES

Not Being Snared
Deuteronomy 12:29-30 "[29]When the LORD thy God shall cut off the nations from before thee, whither thou goest to possess them, and thou succeedest them, and dwellest in their land; [30]Take heed to thyself that thou be not snared by following them, after that they be destroyed from before thee; and that thou inquire not after their gods, saying, How did these nations serve their gods? even so will I do likewise."

The Lord Plucking You Out Of Nets
Psalm 25:15 "Mine eyes are ever toward the LORD; for he shall pluck my feet out of the net."

What Brings A Snare
Proverbs 29:25 "The fear of man bringeth a snare: but whoso putteth his trust in the LORD shall be safe."

What Is A Snare
Exodus 23:31-33 "[31]And I will set thy bounds from the Red sea even unto the sea of the Philistines, and from the desert unto the river: for I will deliver the inhabitants of the land into your hand; and thou shalt drive them out before thee. [32]Thou shalt make no covenant with them, nor with their gods. [33]They shall not dwell in thy land, lest they make thee sin against me: for if thou serve their gods, it will surely be a snare unto thee."

Exodus 34:11-12 "[11]Observe thou that which I command thee this day: behold, I drive out before thee the Amorite, and the Canaanite, and the Hittite, and the Perizzite, and the Hivite, and the Jebusite. [12]Take heed to thyself, lest thou make a covenant with the inhabitants of the land whither thou goest, lest it be for a snare in the midst of thee."

Deuteronomy 7:16 "And thou shalt consume all the people which the LORD thy God shall deliver thee; thine eye shall have no pity upon them: neither shalt thou serve their gods; for that will be a snare unto thee."

Deuteronomy 7:25 "The graven images of their gods shall ye burn with fire: thou shalt not desire the silver or gold that is on them, nor take it unto thee, lest thou be snared therein: for it is an abomination to the LORD thy God."

Joshua 23:11-13 "[11]Take good heed therefore unto yourselves, that ye love the LORD your God. [12]Else if ye do in any wise go back, and cleave unto the remnant of these nations, even these that remain among you, and shall make marriages with them, and go in unto them, and they to you: [13]Know for a certainty that the LORD your God will no more drive out any of these nations from before you; but they shall be snares and traps unto you, and scourges in your sides, and thorns in your eyes, until ye perish from off this good land which the LORD your God hath given you."

Judges 2:1-3 "[1]And an angel of the LORD came up from Gilgal to Bochim, and said, I made you to go up out of Egypt, and have brought you unto the land which I sware unto your fathers; and I said, I will never break my covenant with you. [2]And ye shall make no league with the inhabitants of this land; ye shall throw down their altars: but ye have not obeyed my voice: why have ye done this? [3]Wherefore I also said, I will not drive them out from before you; but they shall be as thorns in your sides, and their gods shall be a snare unto you."

Psalm 106:35-36 "[35]But were mingled among the heathen, and learned their works. [36]And they served their idols: which were a snare unto them."

Proverbs 18:6-7 "[6]A fool's lips enter into contention, and his mouth calleth for strokes. [7]A fool's mouth is his destruction, and his lips are the snare of his soul."

Proverbs 20:25 "It is a snare to the man who devoureth that which is holy, and after vows to make inquiry."

Who Becomes Snared
Psalm 9:16 "The LORD is known by the judgment which he executeth: the wicked is snared in the work of his own hands. Higgaion. Selah."

Proverbs 12:13 "The wicked is snared by the transgression of his lips: but the just shall come out of trouble."

Proverbs 22:24-25 "24Make no friendship with an angry man; and with a furious man thou shalt not go: 25Lest thou learn his ways, and get a snare to thy soul."

Ecclesiastes 7:26 "And I find more bitter than death the woman, whose heart is snares and nets, and her hands as bands: whoso pleaseth God shall escape from her; but the sinner shall be taken by her."

1 Timothy 6:9 "But they that will be rich fall into temptation and a snare, and into many foolish and hurtful lusts, which drown men in destruction and perdition."

Who Brings A City Into A Snare
Proverbs 29:8 "Scornful men bring a city into a snare: but wise men turn away wrath."

Who Has Snares In Their Way
Job 18:5-10 "5Yea, the light of the wicked shall be put out, and the spark of his fire shall not shine. 6The light shall be dark in his tabernacle, and his candle shall be put out with him. 7The steps of his strength shall be straitened, and his own counsel shall cast him down. 8For he is cast into a net by his own feet, and he walketh upon a snare. 9The gin shall take him by the heel, and the robber shall prevail against him. 10The snare is laid for him in the ground, and a trap for him in the way."

Proverbs 22:5 "Thorns and snares are in the way of the froward: he that doth keep his soul shall be far from them."

Who Sets Snares
Proverbs 29:5-6 "5A man that flattereth his neighbour spreadeth a net for his feet. 6In the transgression of an evil man there is a snare: but the righteous doth sing and rejoice."

Ecclesiastes 7:26 "And I find more bitter than death the woman, whose heart is snares and nets, and her hands as bands: whoso pleaseth God shall escape from her; but the sinner shall be taken by her."

Jeremiah 5:26-28 "26For among my people are found wicked men: they lay wait, as he that setteth snares; they set a trap, they catch men. 27As a cage is full of birds, so are their houses full of deceit: therefore they are become great, and waxen rich. 28They are waxen fat, they shine: yea, they overpass the deeds of the wicked: they judge not the cause, the cause of the fatherless, yet they prosper; and the right of the needy do they not judge."

Who Shall Have The Snare Upon Them
Jeremiah 48:42-43 "42And Moab shall be destroyed from being a people, because he hath magnified himself against the LORD. 43Fear, and the pit, and the snare, shall be upon thee, O inhabitant of Moab, saith the LORD."

SOBRIETY

Being Sober
Proverbs 23:31 "Look not thou upon the wine when it is red, when it giveth his colour in the cup, when it moveth itself aright."

Romans 12:3 "For I say, through the grace given unto me, to every man that is among you, not to think of himself more highly than he ought to think; but to think soberly, according as God hath dealt to every man the measure of faith."

Romans 13:13 "Let us walk honestly, as in the day; not in rioting and drunkenness, not in chambering and wantonness, not in strife and envying."

Ephesians 5:18 "And be not drunk with wine, wherein is excess; but be filled with the Spirit."

1 Thessalonians 5:1-8 "1But of the times and the seasons, brethren, ye have no need that I write unto you. 2For yourselves know perfectly that the day of the Lord so cometh as a thief in the night. 3For when they shall say, Peace and safety; then sudden destruction cometh upon them, as travail upon a woman with child; and they shall not escape. 4But ye, brethren, are not in darkness, that that day should overtake you as a thief. 5Ye are all the children of light, and the children of the day: we are not of the night, nor of darkness. 6Therefore let us not sleep, as do others; but let us watch and be sober. 7For they that sleep sleep in the night; and they that be drunken are drunken in the night. 8But let us, who are of the day, be sober, putting on the breastplate of faith and love; and for an helmet, the hope of salvation."

Titus 2:11-12 "[11]For the grace of God that bringeth salvation hath appeared to all men, [12]Teaching us that, denying ungodliness and worldly lusts, we should live soberly, righteously, and godly, in this present world."

1 Peter 1:13 "Wherefore gird up the loins of your mind, be sober, and hope to the end for the grace that is to be brought unto you at the revelation of Jesus Christ."

1 Peter 4:7 "But the end of all things is at hand: be ye therefore sober, and watch unto prayer."

1 Peter 5:8 "Be sober, be vigilant; because your adversary the devil, as a roaring lion, walketh about, seeking whom he may devour."

Who Should Be Sober
Proverbs 31:4-7 "[4]It is not for kings, O Lemuel, it is not for kings to drink wine; nor for princes strong drink: [5]Lest they drink, and forget the law, and pervert the judgment of any of the afflicted. [6]Give strong drink unto him that is ready to perish, and wine unto those that be of heavy hearts. [7]Let him drink, and forget his poverty, and remember his misery no more."

1 Timothy 3:1-11 "[1]This is a true saying, If a man desire the office of a bishop, he desireth a good work. [2]A bishop then must be blameless, the husband of one wife, vigilant, sober, of good behaviour, given to hospitality, apt to teach; [3]Not given to wine, no striker, not greedy of filthy lucre; but patient, not a brawler, not covetous; [4]One that ruleth well his own house, having his children in subjection with all gravity; [5](For if a man know not how to rule his own house, how shall he take care of the church of God?) [6]Not a novice, lest being lifted up with pride he fall into the condemnation of the devil. [7]Moreover he must have a good report of them which are without; lest he fall into reproach and the snare of the devil. [8]Likewise must the deacons be grave, not doubletongued, not given to much wine, not greedy of filthy lucre; [9]Holding the mystery of the faith in a pure conscience. [10]And let these also first be proved; then let them use the office of a deacon, being found blameless. [11]Even so must their wives be grave, not slanderers, sober, faithful in all things."

Titus 2:1-12 "[1]But speak thou the things which become sound doctrine: [2]That the aged men be sober, grave, temperate, sound in faith, in charity, in patience. [3]The aged women likewise, that they be in behaviour as becometh holiness, not false accusers, not given to much wine, teachers of good things; [4]That they may teach the young women to be sober, to love their husbands, to love their children, [5]To be discreet, chaste, keepers at home, good, obedient to their own husbands, that the word of God be not blasphemed. [6]Young men likewise exhort to be sober minded. [7]In all things shewing thyself a pattern of good works: in doctrine shewing uncorruptness, gravity, sincerity, [8]Sound speech, that cannot be condemned; that he that is of the contrary part may be ashamed, having no evil thing to say of you. [9]Exhort servants to be obedient unto their own masters, and to please them well in all things; not answering again; [10]Not purloining, but shewing all good fidelity; that they may adorn the doctrine of God our Saviour in all things. [11]For the grace of God that bringeth salvation hath appeared to all men, [12]Teaching us that, denying ungodliness and worldly lusts, we should live soberly, righteously, and godly, in this present world."

SORROW

Godly Sorrow
2 Corinthians 7:10 "For godly sorrow worketh repentance to salvation not to be repented of: but the sorrow of the world worketh death."

Sorrow Of The Heart
Proverbs 15:13 "A merry heart maketh a cheerful countenance: but by sorrow of the heart the spirit is broken."

The Lord Wiping Away Tears
Psalm 30:10-11 "[10]Hear, O LORD, and have mercy upon me: LORD, be thou my helper. [11]Thou hast turned for me my mourning into dancing: thou hast put off my sackcloth, and girded me with gladness."

Psalm 116:3-8 "[3]The sorrows of death compassed me, and the pains of hell gat hold upon me: I found trouble and sorrow. [4]Then called I upon the name of the LORD; O LORD, I beseech thee, deliver my soul. [5]Gracious is the LORD, and righteous; yea, our God is merciful. [6]The LORD preserveth the simple: I was brought low, and he helped me. [7]Return unto thy rest, O my soul; for the LORD hath dealt bountifully with thee. ⁸For thou hast delivered my soul from death, mine eyes from tears, and my feet from falling."

Isaiah 25:8-9 "⁸He will swallow up death in victory; and the Lord GOD will wipe away tears from off all faces; and the rebuke of his people shall he take away from off all the earth: for the LORD hath spoken it. ⁹And it shall be said in that day, Lo, this is our God; we have waited for him, and he will save us: this is the LORD; we have waited for him, we will be glad and rejoice in his salvation."

Isaiah 65:17-25 "¹⁷For, behold, I create new heavens and a new earth: and the former shall not be remembered, nor come into mind. ¹⁸But be ye glad and rejoice for ever in that which I create: for, behold, I create Jerusalem a rejoicing, and her people a joy. ¹⁹And I will rejoice in Jerusalem, and joy in my people: and the voice of weeping shall be no more heard in her, nor the voice of crying. ²⁰There shall be no more thence an infant of days, nor an old man that hath not filled his days: for the child shall die an hundred years old; but the sinner being an hundred years old shall be accursed. ²¹And they shall build houses, and inhabit them; and they shall plant vineyards, and eat the fruit of them. ²²They shall not build, and another inhabit; they shall not plant, and another eat: for as the days of a tree are the days of my people, and mine elect shall long enjoy the work of their hands. ²³They shall not labour in vain, nor bring forth for trouble; for they are the seed of the blessed of the LORD, and their offspring with them. ²⁴And it shall come to pass, that before they call, I will answer; and while they are yet speaking, I will hear. ²⁵The wolf and the lamb shall feed together, and the lion shall eat straw like the bullock: and dust shall be the serpent's meat. They shall not hurt nor destroy in all my holy mountain, saith the LORD."

Jeremiah 31:13-14 "¹³Then shall the virgin rejoice in the dance, both young men and old together: for I will turn their mourning into joy, and will comfort them, and make them rejoice from their sorrow. ¹⁴And I will satiate the soul of the priests with fatness, and my people shall be satisfied with my goodness, saith the LORD."

Revelation 7:17 "For the Lamb which is in the midst of the throne shall feed them, and shall lead them unto living fountains of waters: and God shall wipe away all tears from their eyes."

Revelation 21:1-4 "¹And I saw a new heaven and a new earth: for the first heaven and the first earth were passed away; and there was no more sea. ²And I John saw the holy city, new Jerusalem, coming down from God out of heaven, prepared as a bride adorned for her husband. ³And I heard a great voice out of heaven saying, Behold, the tabernacle of God is with men, and he will dwell with them, and they shall be his people, and God himself shall be with them, and be their God. ⁴And God shall wipe away all tears from their eyes; and there shall be no more death, neither sorrow, nor crying, neither shall there be any more pain: for the former things are passed away."

The Sorrow Of The World
2 Corinthians 7:10 "For godly sorrow worketh repentance to salvation not to be repented of: but the sorrow of the world worketh death."

What Has No Sorrow
Proverbs 10:22 "The blessing of the LORD, it maketh rich, and he addeth no sorrow with it."

What Sorrow Is
Ecclesiastes 7:3-4 "³Sorrow is better than laughter: for by the sadness of the countenance the heart is made better. ⁴The heart of the wise is in the house of mourning; but the heart of fools is in the house of mirth."

Who Causes Sorrow
Proverbs 10:10 "He that winketh with the eye causeth sorrow: but a prating fool shall fall."

Who Increases Sorrow
Ecclesiastes 1:18 "For in much wisdom is much grief: and he that increaseth knowledge increaseth sorrow."

Who Shall Have Sorrow
Psalm 32:10 "Many sorrows shall be to the wicked: but he that trusteth in the LORD, mercy shall compass him about."

Proverbs 17:21 "He that begetteth a fool doeth it to his sorrow: and the father of a fool hath no joy."

Proverbs 23:29-30 "²⁹Who hath woe? who hath sorrow? who hath contentions? who hath babbling? who hath wounds without cause? who hath redness of eyes? ³⁰They that tarry long at the wine; they that go to seek mixed wine."

Isaiah 50:4-11 "⁴The Lord GOD hath given me the tongue of the learned, that I should know how to speak a word in season to him that is weary: he wakeneth morning by morning, he wakeneth mine ear to hear as the learned. ⁵The Lord GOD hath opened mine ear, and I was not rebellious, neither turned away back. ⁶I gave my back to the smiters, and my cheeks to them that plucked off the hair: I hid not my face from shame and spitting. ⁷For the Lord GOD will help me; therefore shall I not be confounded: therefore have I set my face like a flint, and I know that I shall not be ashamed. ⁸He is near that justifieth me; who will contend with me? let us stand together: who is mine adversary? let him come near to me. ⁹Behold, the Lord GOD will help me; who is he that shall condemn me? lo, they all shall wax old as a garment; the moth shall eat them up. ¹⁰Who is among you that feareth the LORD, that obeyeth the voice of his servant, that walketh in darkness, and hath no light? let him trust in the name of the LORD, and stay upon his God. ¹¹Behold, all ye that kindle a fire, that compass yourselves about with sparks: walk in the light of your fire, and in the sparks that ye have kindled. This shall ye have of mine hand; ye shall lie down in sorrow."

Isaiah 65:11-14 "¹¹But ye are they that forsake the LORD, that forget my holy mountain, that prepare a table for that troop, and that furnish the drink offering unto that number. ¹²Therefore will I number you to the sword, and ye shall all bow down to the slaughter: because when I called, ye did not answer; when I spake, ye did not hear; but did evil before mine eyes, and did choose that wherein I delighted not. ¹³Therefore thus saith the Lord GOD, Behold, my servants shall eat, but ye shall be hungry: behold, my servants shall drink, but ye shall be thirsty: behold, my servants shall rejoice, but ye shall be ashamed: ¹⁴Behold, my servants shall sing for joy of heart, but ye shall cry for sorrow of heart, and shall howl for vexation of spirit."

1 Timothy 6:10 "For the love of money is the root of all evil: which while some coveted after, they have erred from the faith, and pierced themselves through with many sorrows."

Who Sorrow Shall Flee From
Isaiah 35:10 "And the ransomed of the LORD shall return, and come to Zion with songs and everlasting joy upon their heads: they shall obtain joy and gladness, and sorrow and sighing shall flee away."

Isaiah 51:11 "Therefore the redeemed of the LORD shall return, and come with singing unto Zion; and everlasting joy shall be upon their head: they shall obtain gladness and joy; and sorrow and mourning shall flee away."

SPEECH/COMMUNICATION

Backbiting Tongues
Proverbs 25:23 "The north wind driveth away rain: so doth an angry countenance a backbiting tongue."

Being Slow To Speak
James 1:19 "Wherefore, my beloved brethren, let every man be swift to hear, slow to speak, slow to wrath."

Bridling Your Tongue
Psalm 39:1 "I said, I will take heed to my ways, that I sin not with my tongue: I will keep my mouth with a bridle, while the wicked is before me."

James 3:1-5 "¹My brethren, be not many masters, knowing that we shall receive the greater condemnation. ²For in many things we offend all. If any man offend not in word, the same is a perfect man, and able also to bridle the whole body. ³Behold, we put bits in the horses' mouths, that they may obey us; and we turn about their whole body. ⁴Behold also the ships, which though they be so great, and are driven of fierce winds, yet are they turned about with a very small helm, whithersoever the governor listeth. ⁵Even so the tongue is a little member, and boasteth great things. Behold, how great a matter a little fire kindleth!"

Burning Lips
Proverbs 26:23 "Burning lips and a wicked heart are like a potsherd covered with silver dross."

Evil Communications
1 Corinthians 15:33 "Be not deceived: evil communications corrupt good manners."

Excellent Speech
Proverbs 17:7 "Excellent speech becometh not a fool: much less do lying lips a prince."

Fitly Spoken Words

Proverbs 15:23 "A man hath joy by the answer of his mouth: and a word spoken in due season, how good is it!"

Proverbs 25:11 "A word fitly spoken is like apples of gold in pictures of silver."

Flattering Mouths

Proverbs 26:28 "A lying tongue hateth those that are afflicted by it; and a flattering mouth worketh ruin."

Good Words

Proverbs 12:25 "Heaviness in the heart of man maketh it stoop: but a good word maketh it glad."

Proverbs 15:30 "The light of the eyes rejoiceth the heart: and a good report maketh the bones fat."

Grievous Words

Proverbs 15:1 "A soft answer turneth away wrath: but grievous words stir up anger."

How God Spoke In Past Times
And How He Speaks Now

Hebrews 1:1-2 "[1]God, who at sundry times and in divers manners spake in time past unto the fathers by the prophets, [2]Hath in these last days spoken unto us by his Son, whom he hath appointed heir of all things, by whom also he made the worlds."

How Not To Answer A Fool

Proverbs 26:4-5 "[4]Answer not a fool according to his folly, lest thou also be like unto him. [5]Answer a fool according to his folly, lest he be wise in his own conceit."

How Not To Speak

Leviticus 19:16 "Thou shalt not go up and down as a talebearer among thy people: neither shalt thou stand against the blood of thy neighbour: I am the LORD."

1 Samuel 2:3 "Talk no more so exceeding proudly; let not arrogancy come out of your mouth: for the LORD is a God of knowledge, and by him actions are weighed."

Ecclesiastes 5:1-2 "[1]Keep thy foot when thou goest to the house of God, and be more ready to hear, than to give the sacrifice of fools: for they consider not that they do evil. [2]Be not rash with thy mouth, and let not thine heart be hasty to utter any thing before God: for God is in heaven, and thou upon earth: therefore let thy words be few."

How To Speak

Matthew 5:33-37 "[33]Again, ye have heard that it hath been said by them of old time, Thou shalt not forswear thyself, but shalt perform unto the Lord thine oaths: [34]But I say unto you, Swear not at all; neither by heaven; for it is God's throne: [35]Nor by the earth; for it is his footstool: neither by Jerusalem; for it is the city of the great King. [36]Neither shalt thou swear by thy head, because thou canst not make one hair white or black. [37]But let your communication be, Yea, yea; Nay, nay: for whatsoever is more than these cometh of evil."

Colossians 4:6 "Let your speech be alway with grace, seasoned with salt, that ye may know how ye ought to answer every man."

Titus 2:7-8 "[7]In all things shewing thyself a pattern of good works: in doctrine shewing uncorruptness, gravity, sincerity, [8]Sound speech, that cannot be condemned; that he that is of the contrary part may be ashamed, having no evil thing to say of you."

Hebrews 13:5 "Let your conversation be without covetousness; and be content with such things as ye have: for he hath said, I will never leave thee, nor forsake thee."

James 5:12 "But above all things, my brethren, swear not, neither by heaven, neither by the earth, neither by any other oath: but let your yea be yea; and your nay, nay; lest ye fall into condemnation."

1 Peter 4:11 "If any man speak, let him speak as the oracles of God; if any man minister, let him do it as of the ability which God giveth: that God in all things may be glorified through Jesus Christ, to whom be praise and dominion for ever and ever. Amen."

Perverseness Within The Tongue

Proverbs 15:4 "A wholesome tongue is a tree of life: but perverseness therein is a breach in the spirit."

Righteous Lips

Proverbs 16:13 "Righteous lips are the delight of kings; and they love him that speaketh right."

Soft Words

Proverbs 15:1 "A soft answer turneth away wrath: but grievous words stir up anger."

Proverbs 16:24 "Pleasant words are as an honeycomb, sweet to the soul, and health to the bones."

Proverbs 25:15 "By long forbearing is a prince persuaded, and a soft tongue breaketh the bone."

Talebearers
Proverbs 11:13 "A talebearer revealeth secrets: but he that is of a faithful spirit concealeth the matter."

Proverbs 18:8 "The words of a talebearer are as wounds, and they go down into the innermost parts of the belly."

Proverbs 20:19 "He that goeth about as a talebearer revealeth secrets: therefore meddle not with him that flattereth with his lips."

Proverbs 26:20-22 "20Where no wood is, there the fire goeth out: so where there is no talebearer, the strife ceaseth. 21As coals are to burning coals, and wood to fire; so is a contentious man to kindle strife. 22The words of a talebearer are as wounds, and they go down into the innermost parts of the belly."

The Froward Mouth
Proverbs 8:12-13 "12I wisdom dwell with prudence, and find out knowledge of witty inventions. 13The fear of the LORD is to hate evil: pride, and arrogancy, and the evil way, and the froward mouth, do I hate."

Proverbs 10:31 "The mouth of the just bringeth forth wisdom: but the froward tongue shall be cut out."

The Fruit Of The Mouth
Proverbs 12:14 "A man shall be satisfied with good by the fruit of his mouth: and the recompence of a man's hands shall be rendered unto him."

Proverbs 13:2 "A man shall eat good by the fruit of his mouth: but the soul of the transgressors shall eat violence."

Proverbs 18:20 "A man's belly shall be satisfied with the fruit of his mouth; and with the increase of his lips shall he be filled."

The Holy Spirit Speaking Through People
Isaiah 50:4-5 "4The Lord GOD hath given me the tongue of the learned, that I should know how to speak a word in season to him that is weary: he wakeneth morning by morning, he wakeneth mine ear to hear as the learned. 5The Lord GOD hath opened mine ear, and I was not rebellious, neither turned away back."

Isaiah 51:15-16 "15But I am the LORD thy God, that divided the sea, whose waves roared: The LORD of hosts is his name. 16And I have put my words in thy mouth, and I have covered thee in the shadow of mine hand, that I may plant the heavens, and lay the foundations of the earth, and say unto Zion, Thou art my people."

Isaiah 59:21 "As for me, this is my covenant with them, saith the LORD; My spirit that is upon thee, and my words which I have put in thy mouth, shall not depart out of thy mouth, nor out of the mouth of thy seed, nor out of the mouth of thy seed's seed, saith the LORD, from henceforth and for ever."

Matthew 10:19-20 "19But when they deliver you up, take no thought how or what ye shall speak: for it shall be given you in that same hour what ye shall speak. 20For it is not ye that speak, but the Spirit of your Father which speaketh in you."

Mark 13:11 "But when they shall lead you, and deliver you up, take no thought beforehand what ye shall speak, neither do ye premeditate: but whatsoever shall be given you in that hour, that speak ye: for it is not ye that speak, but the Holy Ghost."

Luke 12:11-12 "11And when they bring you unto the synagogues, and unto magistrates, and powers, take ye no thought how or what thing ye shall answer, or what ye shall say: 12For the Holy Ghost shall teach you in the same hour what ye ought to say."

Luke 21:12-15 "12But before all these, they shall lay their hands on you, and persecute you, delivering you up to the synagogues, and into prisons, being brought before kings and rulers for my name's sake. 13And it shall turn to you for a testimony. 14Settle it therefore in your hearts, not to meditate before what ye shall answer: 15For I will give you a mouth and wisdom, which all your adversaries shall not be able to gainsay nor resist."

Acts 2:4 "And they were all filled with the Holy Ghost, and began to speak with other tongues, as the Spirit gave them utterance."

1 Corinthians 12:3 "Wherefore I give you to understand, that no man speaking by the Spirit of God calleth Jesus accursed: and that no man can say that Jesus is the Lord, but by the Holy Ghost."

2 Peter 1:19-21 "¹⁹We have also a more sure word of prophecy; whereunto ye do well that ye take heed, as unto a light that shineth in a dark place, until the day dawn, and the day star arise in your hearts: ²⁰Knowing this first, that no prophecy of the scripture is of any private interpretation. ²¹For the prophecy came not in old time by the will of man: but holy men of God spake as they were moved by the Holy Ghost."

The Lip Of Truth
Proverbs 12:19 "The lip of truth shall be established for ever: but a lying tongue is but for a moment."

The Lips Of Knowledge
Proverbs 20:15 "There is gold, and a multitude of rubies: but the lips of knowledge are a precious jewel."

The Lips Of The Ungodly
Proverbs 16:27 "An ungodly man diggeth up evil: and in his lips there is as a burning fire."

The Mouth Of A Fool
Proverbs 10:14 "Wise men lay up knowledge: but the mouth of the foolish is near destruction."

Proverbs 12:23 "A prudent man concealeth knowledge: but the heart of fools proclaimeth foolishness."

Proverbs 14:3 "In the mouth of the foolish is a rod of pride: but the lips of the wise shall preserve them."

Proverbs 15:2 "The tongue of the wise useth knowledge aright: but the mouth of fools poureth out foolishness."

Proverbs 15:7 "The lips of the wise disperse knowledge: but the heart of the foolish doeth not so."

Proverbs 15:14 "The heart of him that hath understanding seeketh knowledge: but the mouth of fools feedeth on foolishness."

Proverbs 18:6-7 "⁶A fool's lips enter into contention, and his mouth calleth for strokes. ⁷A fool's mouth is his destruction, and his lips are the snare of his soul."

Proverbs 26:7 "The legs of the lame are not equal: so is a parable in the mouth of fools."

Proverbs 26:9 "As a thorn goeth up into the hand of a drunkard, so is a parable in the mouth of fools."

Ecclesiastes 5:3 "For a dream cometh through the multitude of business; and a fool's voice is known by multitude of words."

Ecclesiastes 10:12-14 "¹²The words of a wise man's mouth are gracious; but the lips of a fool will swallow up himself. ¹³The beginning of the words of his mouth is foolishness: and the end of his talk is mischievous madness. ¹⁴A fool also is full of words: a man cannot tell what shall be; and what shall be after him, who can tell him?"

The Mouth Of The Just
Proverbs 10:20 "The tongue of the just is as choice silver: the heart of the wicked is little worth."

Proverbs 10:31 "The mouth of the just bringeth forth wisdom: but the froward tongue shall be cut out."

The Mouth Of The Righteous
Psalm 37:30 "The mouth of the righteous speaketh wisdom, and his tongue talketh of judgment."

Proverbs 10:11 "The mouth of a righteous man is a well of life: but violence covereth the mouth of the wicked."

Proverbs 10:21 "The lips of the righteous feed many: but fools die for want of wisdom."

Proverbs 10:32 "The lips of the righteous know what is acceptable: but the mouth of the wicked speaketh frowardness."

The Mouth Of The Upright

Proverbs 12:6 "The words of the wicked are to lie in wait for blood: but the mouth of the upright shall deliver them."

The Mouth Of The Wicked
Proverbs 10:6 "Blessings are upon the head of the just: but violence covereth the mouth of the wicked."

Proverbs 10:11 "The mouth of a righteous man is a well of life: but violence covereth the mouth of the wicked."

Proverbs 10:32 "The lips of the righteous know what is acceptable: but the mouth of the wicked speaketh frowardness."

Proverbs 11:11 "By the blessing of the upright the city is exalted: but it is overthrown by the mouth of the wicked."

Proverbs 12:6 "The words of the wicked are to lie in wait for blood: but the mouth of the upright shall deliver them."

Proverbs 15:28 "The heart of the righteous studieth to answer: but the mouth of the wicked poureth out evil things."

Proverbs 19:28 "An ungodly witness scorneth judgment: and the mouth of the wicked devoureth iniquity."

The Multitude Of Words
Proverbs 10:19 "In the multitude of words there wanteth not sin: but he that refraineth his lips is wise."

Proverbs 14:23 "In all labour there is profit: but the talk of the lips tendeth only to penury."

Ecclesiastes 5:3 "For a dream cometh through the multitude of business; and a fool's voice is known by multitude of words."

Ecclesiastes 5:6-7 "⁶Suffer not thy mouth to cause thy flesh to sin; neither say thou before the angel, that it was an error: wherefore should God be angry at thy voice, and destroy the work of thine hands? ⁷For in the multitude of dreams and many words there are also divers vanities: but fear thou God."

The Sweetness Of The Lips
Proverbs 16:21 "The wise in heart shall be called prudent: and the sweetness of the lips increaseth learning."

The Things Which Proceed
Out Of The Mouth
Matthew 15:10-11 "¹⁰And he called the multitude, and said unto them, Hear, and understand: ¹¹Not that which goeth into the mouth defileth a man; but that which cometh out of the mouth, this defileth a man."

Matthew 15:18-19 "¹⁸But those things which proceed out of the mouth come forth from the heart; and they defile the man. ¹⁹For out of the heart proceed evil thoughts, murders, adulteries, fornications, thefts, false witness, blasphemies."

Mark 7:14-16 "¹⁴And when he had called all the people unto him, he said unto them, Hearken unto me every one of you, and understand: ¹⁵There is nothing from without a man, that entering into him can defile him: but the things which come out of him, those are they that defile the man. ¹⁶If any man have ears to hear, let him hear."

The Tongue
Proverbs 18:21 "Death and life are in the power of the tongue: and they that love it shall eat the fruit thereof."

James 3:2-12 "²For in many things we offend all. If any man offend not in word, the same is a perfect man, and able also to bridle the whole body. ³Behold, we put bits in the horses' mouths, that they may obey us; and we turn about their whole body. ⁴Behold also the ships, which though they be so great, and are driven of fierce winds, yet are they turned about with a very small helm, whithersoever the governor listeth. ⁵Even so the tongue is a little member, and boasteth great things. Behold, how great a matter a little fire kindleth! ⁶And the tongue is a fire, a world of iniquity: so is the tongue among our members, that it defileth the whole body, and setteth on fire the course of nature; and it is set on fire of hell. ⁷For every kind of beasts, and of birds, and of serpents, and of things in the sea, is tamed, and hath been tamed of mankind: ⁸But the tongue can no man tame; it is an unruly evil, full of deadly poison. ⁹Therewith bless we God, even the Father; and therewith curse we men, which are made after the similitude of God. ¹⁰Out of the same mouth proceedeth blessing and cursing. My brethren, these things ought not so to be. ¹¹Doth a fountain send forth at the same place sweet water and bitter? ¹²Can the fig tree, my brethren, bear olive berries? either a vine, figs? so can no fountain both yield salt water and fresh."

The Tongue Of The Wise
Proverbs 10:13 "In the lips of him that hath understanding wisdom is found: but a rod is for the back of him that is void of understanding."

Proverbs 12:18 "There is that speaketh like the piercings of a sword: but the tongue of the wise is health."

Proverbs 14:3 "In the mouth of the foolish is a rod of pride: but the lips of the wise shall preserve them."

Proverbs 15:2 "The tongue of the wise useth knowledge aright: but the mouth of fools poureth out foolishness."

Proverbs 15:7 "The lips of the wise disperse knowledge: but the heart of the foolish doeth not so."

Proverbs 29:11 "A fool uttereth all his mind: but a wise man keepeth it in till afterwards."

The Words That Men Speak

Matthew 12:36-37 "[36]But I say unto you, That every idle word that men shall speak, they shall give account thereof in the day of judgment. [37]For by thy words thou shalt be justified, and by thy words thou shalt be condemned."

The Words Of The Pure

Proverbs 15:26 "The thoughts of the wicked are an abomination to the LORD: but the words of the pure are pleasant words."

The Words Of The Wise

Proverbs 18:4 "The words of a man's mouth are as deep waters, and the wellspring of wisdom as a flowing brook."

Ecclesiastes 9:17 "The words of wise men are heard in quiet more than the cry of him that ruleth among fools."

Ecclesiastes 10:12 "The words of a wise man's mouth are gracious; but the lips of a fool will swallow up himself."

Ecclesiastes 12:11 "The words of the wise are as goads, and as nails fastened by the masters of assemblies, which are given from one shepherd."

Those That Are Hasty In Their Words

Proverbs 29:20 "Seest thou a man that is hasty in his words? there is more hope of a fool than of him."

Those That Do Not Keep Their Tongue

Proverbs 13:3 "He that keepeth his mouth keepeth his life: but he that openeth wide his lips shall have destruction."

James 1:26 "If any man among you seem to be religious, and bridleth not his tongue, but deceiveth his own heart, this man's religion is vain."

Those That Do Not Speak Maliciously

Psalm 15:1-5 "[1]LORD, who shall abide in thy tabernacle? who shall dwell in thy holy hill? [2]He that walketh uprightly, and worketh righteousness, and speaketh the truth in his heart. [3]He that backbiteth not with his tongue, nor doeth evil to his neighbour, nor taketh up a reproach against his neighbour. [4]In whose eyes a vile person is contemned; but he honoureth them that fear the LORD. He that sweareth to his own hurt, and changeth not. [5]He that putteth not out his money to usury, nor taketh reward against the innocent. He that doeth these things shall never be moved."

Those That Flatter With The Tongue

Proverbs 20:19 "He that goeth about as a talebearer revealeth secrets: therefore meddle not with him that flattereth with his lips."

Proverbs 28:23 "He that rebuketh a man afterwards shall find more favour than he that flattereth with the tongue."

Proverbs 29:5 "A man that flattereth his neighbour spreadeth a net for his feet."

Those That Have A Perverse Tongue

Proverbs 17:20 "He that hath a froward heart findeth no good: and he that hath a perverse tongue falleth into mischief."

Proverbs 19:1 "Better is the poor that walketh in his integrity, than he that is perverse in his lips, and is a fool."

Those That Keep Their Tongue

Proverbs 10:19 "In the multitude of words there wanteth not sin: but he that refraineth his lips is wise."

Proverbs 13:3 "He that keepeth his mouth keepeth his life: but he that openeth wide his lips shall have destruction."

Proverbs 17:28 "Even a fool, when he holdeth his peace, is counted wise: and he that shutteth his lips is esteemed a man of understanding."

Proverbs 21:23 "Whoso keepeth his mouth and his tongue keepeth his soul from troubles."

Those That Repeat A Matter

Proverbs 17:9 "He that covereth a transgression seeketh love; but he that repeateth a matter separateth very friends."

Those That Speak By The Spirit Of God

1 Corinthians 12:3 "Wherefore I give you to understand, that no man speaking by the Spirit of

God calleth Jesus accursed: and that no man can say that Jesus is the Lord, but by the Holy Ghost."

Those That Speak Deceitfully
Psalm 52:1-7 "¹Why boastest thou thyself in mischief, O mighty man? the goodness of God endureth continually. ²Thy tongue deviseth mischiefs; like a sharp rasor, working deceitfully. ³Thou lovest evil more than good; and lying rather than to speak righteousness. Selah. ⁴Thou lovest all devouring words, O thou deceitful tongue. ⁵God shall likewise destroy thee for ever, he shall take thee away, and pluck thee out of thy dwelling place, and root thee out of the land of the living. Selah. ⁶The righteous also shall see, and fear, and shall laugh at him: ⁷Lo, this is the man that made not God his strength; but trusted in the abundance of his riches, and strengthened himself in his wickedness."

Those That Speak Evil Of Others
James 4:11-12 "¹¹Speak not evil one of another, brethren. He that speaketh evil of his brother, and judgeth his brother, speaketh evil of the law, and judgeth the law: but if thou judge the law, thou art not a doer of the law, but a judge. ¹²There is one lawgiver, who is able to save and to destroy: who art thou that judgest another?"

Those That Speak Right
Proverbs 16:13 "Righteous lips are the delight of kings; and they love him that speaketh right."

Those That Speak The Truth
Psalm 15:1-5 "¹LORD, who shall abide in thy tabernacle? who shall dwell in thy holy hill? ²He that walketh uprightly, and worketh righteousness, and speaketh the truth in his heart. ³He that backbiteth not with his tongue, nor doeth evil to his neighbour, nor taketh up a reproach against his neighbour. ⁴In whose eyes a vile person is contemned; but he honoureth them that fear the LORD. He that sweareth to his own hurt, and changeth not. ⁵He that putteth not out his money to usury, nor taketh reward against the innocent. He that doeth these things shall never be moved."

Proverbs 12:17 "He that speaketh truth sheweth forth righteousness: but a false witness deceit."

Those That Speak Uprightly
Isaiah 33:15-16 "¹⁵He that walketh righteously, and speaketh uprightly; he that despiseth the gain of oppressions, that shaketh his hands from holding of bribes, that stoppeth his ears from hearing of blood, and shutteth his eyes from seeing evil; ¹⁶He shall dwell on high: his place of defence shall be the munitions of rocks: bread shall be given him; his waters shall be sure."

Those That Utter A Slander
Proverbs 10:18 "He that hideth hatred with lying lips, and he that uttereth a slander, is a fool."

What Should Not Proceed Out Of Your Mouth
Exodus 23:13 "And in all things that I have said unto you be circumspect: and make no mention of the name of other gods, neither let it be heard out of thy mouth."

Joshua 23:6-7 "⁶Be ye therefore very courageous to keep and to do all that is written in the book of the law of Moses, that ye turn not aside therefrom to the right hand or to the left; ⁷That ye come not among these nations, these that remain among you; neither make mention of the name of their gods, nor cause to swear by them, neither serve them, nor bow yourselves unto them."

1 Samuel 2:3 "Talk no more so exceeding proudly; let not arrogancy come out of your mouth: for the LORD is a God of knowledge, and by him actions are weighed."

Psalm 34:13 "Keep thy tongue from evil, and thy lips from speaking guile."

Proverbs 4:24 "Put away from thee a froward mouth, and perverse lips put far from thee."

Romans 15:17-18 "¹⁷I have therefore whereof I may glory through Jesus Christ in those things which pertain to God. ¹⁸For I will not dare to speak of any of those things which Christ hath not wrought by me, to make the Gentiles obedient, by word and deed."

Ephesians 4:29-31 "²⁹Let no corrupt communication proceed out of your mouth, but that which is good to the use of edifying, that it may minister grace unto the hearers. ³⁰And grieve not the holy Spirit of God, whereby ye are sealed unto the day of redemption. ³¹Let all bitterness, and wrath, and anger, and clamour, and evil speaking, be put away from you, with all malice."

Ephesians 5:3-4 "³But fornication, and all uncleanness, or covetousness, let it not be once named among you, as becometh saints; [4]Neither filthiness, nor foolish talking, nor jesting, which are not convenient: but rather giving of thanks."

Titus 3:1-2 "[1]Put them in mind to be subject to principalities and powers, to obey magistrates, to be ready to every good work, [2]To speak evil of no man, to be no brawlers, but gentle, shewing all meekness unto all men."

James 4:11 "Speak not evil one of another, brethren. He that speaketh evil of his brother, and judgeth his brother, speaketh evil of the law, and judgeth the law: but if thou judge the law, thou art not a doer of the law, but a judge."

1 Peter 2:1 "Wherefore laying aside all malice, and all guile, and hypocrisies, and envies, and all evil speakings."

1 Peter 3:10 "For he that will love life, and see good days, let him refrain his tongue from evil, and his lips that they speak no guile."

What Should Proceed Out Of Your Mouth
Zechariah 8:16 "These are the things that ye shall do; Speak ye every man the truth to his neighbour; execute the judgment of truth and peace in your gates."

Ephesians 4:25 "Wherefore putting away lying, speak every man truth with his neighbour: for we are members one of another."

Ephesians 4:29 "Let no corrupt communication proceed out of your mouth, but that which is good to the use of edifying, that it may minister grace unto the hearers."

Titus 2:1-15 "[1]But speak thou the things which become sound doctrine: [2]That the aged men be sober, grave, temperate, sound in faith, in charity, in patience. [3]The aged women likewise, that they be in behaviour as becometh holiness, not false accusers, not given to much wine, teachers of good things; [4]That they may teach the young women to be sober, to love their husbands, to love their children, [5]To be discreet, chaste, keepers at home, good, obedient to their own husbands, that the word of God be not blasphemed. [6]Young men likewise exhort to be sober minded. [7]In all things shewing thyself a pattern of good works: in doctrine shewing uncorruptness, gravity, sincerity, [8]Sound speech, that cannot be condemned; that he that is of the contrary part

may be ashamed, having no evil thing to say of you. [9]Exhort servants to be obedient unto their own masters, and to please them well in all things; not answering again; [10]Not purloining, but shewing all good fidelity; that they may adorn the doctrine of God our Saviour in all things. [11]For the grace of God that bringeth salvation hath appeared to all men, [12]Teaching us that, denying ungodliness and worldly lusts, we should live soberly, righteously, and godly, in this present world; [13]Looking for that blessed hope, and the glorious appearing of the great God and our Saviour Jesus Christ; [14]Who gave himself for us, that he might redeem us from all iniquity, and purify unto himself a peculiar people, zealous of good works. [15]These things speak, and exhort, and rebuke with all authority. Let no man despise thee."

What The Lord Speaks
Isaiah 45:19 "I have not spoken in secret, in a dark place of the earth: I said not unto the seed of Jacob, Seek ye me in vain: I the LORD speak righteousness, I declare things that are right."

Whisperers (Gossipers)
Proverbs 16:28 "A froward man soweth strife: and a whisperer separateth chief friends."

Who Holds Their Tongue
Proverbs 10:14 "Wise men lay up knowledge: but the mouth of the foolish is near destruction."

Proverbs 11:12 "He that is void of wisdom despiseth his neighbour: but a man of understanding holdeth his peace."

Proverbs 17:27 "He that hath knowledge spareth his words: and a man of understanding is of an excellent spirit."

Proverbs 29:11 "A fool uttereth all his mind: but a wise man keepeth it in till afterwards."

Who Is Full Of Words
Proverbs 29:11 "A fool uttereth all his mind: but a wise man keepeth it in till afterwards."

Ecclesiastes 5:3 "For a dream cometh through the multitude of business; and a fool's voice is known by multitude of words."

Ecclesiastes 10:12-14 "[12]The words of a wise man's mouth are gracious; but the lips of a fool will swallow up himself. [13]The beginning of the words of his mouth is foolishness: and the end of his talk is mischievous madness. [14]A fool also is full of words: a man cannot tell what shall be; and what shall be after him, who can tell him?"

Who Speaks Evil
Psalm 50:16-20 "¹⁶But unto the wicked God saith, What hast thou to do to declare my statutes, or that thou shouldest take my covenant in thy mouth? ¹⁷Seeing thou hatest instruction, and castest my words behind thee. ¹⁸When thou sawest a thief, then thou consentedst with him, and hast been partaker with adulterers. ¹⁹Thou givest thy mouth to evil, and thy tongue frameth deceit. ²⁰Thou sittest and speakest against thy brother; thou slanderest thine own mother's son."

Proverbs 15:28 "The heart of the righteous studieth to answer: but the mouth of the wicked poureth out evil things."

2 Peter 2:1-12 "¹But there were false prophets also among the people, even as there shall be false teachers among you, who privily shall bring in damnable heresies, even denying the Lord that bought them, and bring upon themselves swift destruction. ²And many shall follow their pernicious ways; by reason of whom the way of truth shall be evil spoken of. ³And through covetousness shall they with feigned words make merchandise of you: whose judgment now of a long time lingereth not, and their damnation slumbereth not. ⁴For if God spared not the angels that sinned, but cast them down to hell, and delivered them into chains of darkness, to be reserved unto judgment; ⁵And spared not the old world, but saved Noah the eighth person, a preacher of righteousness, bringing in the flood upon the world of the ungodly; ⁶And turning the cities of Sodom and Gomorrha into ashes condemned them with an overthrow, making them an ensample unto those that after should live ungodly; ⁷And delivered just Lot, vexed with the filthy conversation of the wicked: ⁸(For that righteous man dwelling among them, in seeing and hearing, vexed his righteous soul from day to day with their unlawful deeds;) ⁹The Lord knoweth how to deliver the godly out of temptations, and to reserve the unjust unto the day of judgment to be punished: ¹⁰But chiefly them that walk after the flesh in the lust of uncleanness, and despise government. Presumptuous are they, selfwilled, they are not afraid to speak evil of dignities. ¹¹Whereas angels, which are greater in power and might, bring not railing accusation against them before the Lord.

¹²But these, as natural brute beasts, made to be taken and destroyed, speak evil of the things that they understand not; and shall utterly perish in their own corruption."

Jude 7-10 "⁷Even as Sodom and Gomorrha, and the cities about them in like manner, giving themselves over to fornication, and going after strange flesh, are set forth for an example, suffering the vengeance of eternal fire. ⁸Likewise also these filthy dreamers defile the flesh, despise dominion, and speak evil of dignities. ⁹Yet Michael the archangel, when contending with the devil he disputed about the body of Moses, durst not bring against him a railing accusation, but said, The Lord rebuke thee. ¹⁰But these speak evil of those things which they know not: but what they know naturally, as brute beasts, in those things they corrupt themselves."

Who Speaks Frowardness
Proverbs 2:11-14 "¹¹Discretion shall preserve thee, understanding shall keep thee: ¹²To deliver thee from the way of the evil man, from the man that speaketh froward things; ¹³Who leave the paths of uprightness, to walk in the ways of darkness; ¹⁴Who rejoice to do evil, and delight in the frowardness of the wicked."

Proverbs 10:32 "The lips of the righteous know what is acceptable: but the mouth of the wicked speaketh frowardness."

Proverbs 16:29-30 "²⁹A violent man enticeth his neighbour, and leadeth him into the way that is not good. ³⁰He shutteth his eyes to devise froward things: moving his lips he bringeth evil to pass."

Who Speaks Perverseness
Isaiah 59:1-3 "¹Behold, the LORD's hand is not shortened, that it cannot save; neither his ear heavy, that it cannot hear: ²But your iniquities have separated between you and your God, and your sins have hid his face from you, that he will not hear. ³For your hands are defiled with blood, and your fingers with iniquity; your lips have spoken lies, your tongue hath muttered perverseness."

Who Speaks Vanity
Psalm 144:7-11 "⁷Send thine hand from above; rid me, and deliver me out of great waters, from the hand of strange children; ⁸Whose mouth speaketh vanity, and their right hand is a right hand of

falsehood. ⁹I will sing a new song unto thee, O God: upon a psaltery and an instrument of ten strings will I sing praises unto thee. ¹⁰It is he that giveth salvation unto kings: who delivereth David his servant from the hurtful sword. ¹¹Rid me, and deliver me from the hand of strange children, whose mouth speaketh vanity, and their right hand is a right hand of falsehood."

Ezekiel 13:3-10 "³Thus saith the Lord GOD; Woe unto the foolish prophets, that follow their own spirit, and have seen nothing! ⁴O Israel, thy prophets are like the foxes in the deserts. ⁵Ye have not gone up into the gaps, neither made up the hedge for the house of Israel to stand in the battle in the day of the LORD. ⁶They have seen vanity and lying divination, saying, The LORD saith: and the LORD hath not sent them: and they have made others to hope that they would confirm the word. ⁷Have ye not seen a vain vision, and have ye not spoken a lying divination, whereas ye say, The LORD saith it; albeit I have not spoken? ⁸Therefore thus saith the Lord GOD; Because ye have spoken vanity, and seen lies, therefore, behold, I am against you, saith the Lord GOD. ⁹And mine hand shall be upon the prophets that see vanity, and that divine lies: they shall not be in the assembly of my people, neither shall they be written in the writing of the house of Israel, neither shall they enter into the land of Israel; and ye shall know that I am the Lord GOD. ¹⁰Because, even because they have seduced my people, saying, Peace; and there was no peace; and one built up a wall, and, lo, others daubed it with untempered morter."

Zechariah 10:2 "For the idols have spoken vanity, and the diviners have seen a lie, and have told false dreams; they comfort in vain: therefore they went their way as a flock, they were troubled, because there was no shepherd."

2 Peter 2:1-18 "¹But there were false prophets also among the people, even as there shall be false teachers among you, who privily shall bring in damnable heresies, even denying the Lord that bought them, and bring upon themselves swift destruction. ²And many shall follow their pernicious ways; by reason of whom the way of truth shall be evil spoken of. ³And through covetousness shall they with feigned words make merchandise of you: whose judgment now of a long time lingereth not, and their damnation slum-

bereth not. ⁴For if God spared not the angels that sinned, but cast them down to hell, and delivered them into chains of darkness, to be reserved unto judgment; ⁵And spared not the old world, but saved Noah the eighth person, a preacher of righteousness, bringing in the flood upon the world of the ungodly; ⁶And turning the cities of Sodom and Gomorrha into ashes condemned them with an overthrow, making them an ensample unto those that after should live ungodly; ⁷And delivered just Lot, vexed with the filthy conversation of the wicked: ⁸(For that righteous man dwelling among them, in seeing and hearing, vexed his righteous soul from day to day with their unlawful deeds;) ⁹The Lord knoweth how to deliver the godly out of temptations, and to reserve the unjust unto the day of judgment to be punished: ¹⁰But chiefly them that walk after the flesh in the lust of uncleanness, and despise government. Presumptuous are they, selfwilled, they are not afraid to speak evil of dignities. ¹¹Whereas angels, which are greater in power and might, bring not railing accusation against them before the Lord. ¹²But these, as natural brute beasts, made to be taken and destroyed, speak evil of the things that they understand not; and shall utterly perish in their own corruption; ¹³And shall receive the reward of unrighteousness, as they that count it pleasure to riot in the day time. Spots they are and blemishes, sporting themselves with their own deceivings while they feast with you; ¹⁴Having eyes full of adultery, and that cannot cease from sin; beguiling unstable souls: an heart they have exercised with covetous practices; cursed children: ¹⁵Which have forsaken the right way, and are gone astray, following the way of Balaam the son of Bosor, who loved the wages of unrighteousness; ¹⁶But was rebuked for his iniquity: the dumb ass speaking with man's voice forbad the madness of the prophet. ¹⁷These are wells without water, clouds that are carried with a tempest; to whom the mist of darkness is reserved for ever. ¹⁸For when they speak great swelling words of vanity, they allure through the lusts of the flesh, through much wantonness, those that were clean escaped from them who live in error."

Who Speaks Visions Of Their Own Heart
Jeremiah 23:16-17 "¹⁶Thus saith the LORD of hosts, Hearken not unto the words of the prophets that

prophesy unto you: they make you vain: they speak a vision of their own heart, and not out of the mouth of the LORD. ¹⁷They say still unto them that despise me, The LORD hath said, Ye shall have peace; and they say unto every one that walketh after the imagination of his own heart, No evil shall come upon you."

Jeremiah 23:25-28 "²⁵I have heard what the prophets said, that prophesy lies in my name, saying, I have dreamed, I have dreamed. ²⁶How long shall this be in the heart of the prophets that prophesy lies? yea, they are prophets of the deceit of their own heart; ²⁷Which think to cause my people to forget my name by their dreams which they tell every man to his neighbour, as their fathers have forgotten my name for Baal. ²⁸The prophet that hath a dream, let him tell a dream; and he that hath my word, let him speak my word faithfully. What is the chaff to the wheat? saith the LORD."

Ezekiel 13:3-7 "³Thus saith the Lord GOD; Woe unto the foolish prophets, that follow their own spirit, and have seen nothing! ⁴O Israel, thy prophets are like the foxes in the deserts. ⁵Ye have not gone up into the gaps, neither made up the hedge for the house of Israel to stand in the battle in the day of the LORD. ⁶They have seen vanity and lying divination, saying, The LORD saith: and the LORD hath not sent them: and they have made others to hope that they would confirm the word. ⁷Have ye not seen a vain vision, and have ye not spoken a lying divination, whereas ye say, The LORD saith it; albeit I have not spoken?"

Ezekiel 13:17-23 "¹⁷Likewise, thou son of man, set thy face against the daughters of thy people, which prophesy out of their own heart; and prophesy thou against them, ¹⁸And say, Thus saith the Lord GOD; Woe to the women that sew pillows to all armholes, and make kerchiefs upon the head of every stature to hunt souls! Will ye hunt the souls of my people, and will ye save the souls alive that come unto you? ¹⁹And will ye pollute me among my people for handfuls of barley and for pieces of bread, to slay the souls that should not die, and to save the souls alive that should not live, by your lying to my people that hear your lies? ²⁰Wherefore thus saith the Lord GOD; Behold, I am against your pillows, wherewith ye there hunt the souls to make them fly, and I will

tear them from your arms, and will let the souls go, even the souls that ye hunt to make them fly. ²¹Your kerchiefs also will I tear, and deliver my people out of your hand, and they shall be no more in your hand to be hunted; and ye shall know that I am the LORD. ²²Because with lies ye have made the heart of the righteous sad, whom I have not made sad; and strengthened the hands of the wicked, that he should not return from his wicked way, by promising him life: ²³Therefore ye shall see no more vanity, nor divine divinations: for I will deliver my people out of your hand: and ye shall know that I am the LORD."

Who Speaks Wisdom

Psalm 37:30 "The mouth of the righteous speaketh wisdom, and his tongue talketh of judgment."

Proverbs 10:31 "The mouth of the just bringeth forth wisdom: but the froward tongue shall be cut out."

Proverbs 31:10-26 "¹⁰Who can find a virtuous woman? for her price is far above rubies. ¹¹The heart of her husband doth safely trust in her, so that he shall have no need of spoil. ¹²She will do him good and not evil all the days of her life. ¹³She seeketh wool, and flax, and worketh willingly with her hands. ¹⁴She is like the merchants' ships; she bringeth her food from afar. ¹⁵She riseth also while it is yet night, and giveth meat to her household, and a portion to her maidens. ¹⁶She considereth a field, and buyeth it: with the fruit of her hands she planteth a vineyard. ¹⁷She girdeth her loins with strength, and strengtheneth her arms. ¹⁸She perceiveth that her merchandise is good: her candle goeth not out by night. ¹⁹She layeth her hands to the spindle, and her hands hold the distaff. ²⁰She stretcheth out her hand to the poor; yea, she reacheth forth her hands to the needy. ²¹She is not afraid of the snow for her household: for all her household are clothed with scarlet. ²²She maketh herself coverings of tapestry; her clothing is silk and purple. ²³Her husband is known in the gates, when he sitteth among the elders of the land. ²⁴She maketh fine linen, and selleth it; and delivereth girdles unto the merchant. ²⁵Strength and honour are her clothing; and she shall rejoice in time to come. ²⁶She openeth her mouth with wisdom; and in her tongue is the law of kindness."

Who Teaches Their Mouth
Proverbs 16:23 "The heart of the wise teacheth his mouth, and addeth learning to his lips."

Wholesome Tongues
Proverbs 15:4 "A wholesome tongue is a tree of life: but perverseness therein is a breach in the spirit."

Whose Lips Talk Of Mischief
Proverbs 24:1-2 "¹Be not thou envious against evil men, neither desire to be with them. ²For their heart studieth destruction, and their lips talk of mischief."

Why You Should Not Speak To A Fool
Proverbs 23:9 "Speak not in the ears of a fool: for he will despise the wisdom of thy words."

SPIRIT/SOULS

Broken Spirits
Proverbs 15:13 "A merry heart maketh a cheerful countenance: but by sorrow of the heart the spirit is broken."

Proverbs 17:22 "A merry heart doeth good like a medicine: but a broken spirit drieth the bones."

Full Souls
Proverbs 27:7 "The full soul loatheth an honeycomb; but to the hungry soul every bitter thing is sweet."

Hungry Souls
Psalm 107:8-9 "⁸Oh that men would praise the LORD for his goodness, and for his wonderful works to the children of men! ⁹For he satisfieth the longing soul, and filleth the hungry soul with goodness."

Proverbs 27:7 "The full soul loatheth an honeycomb; but to the hungry soul every bitter thing is sweet."

The Lord Weighing The Spirits
Proverbs 16:2 "All the ways of a man are clean in his own eyes; but the LORD weigheth the spirits."

Proverbs 21:2 "Every way of a man is right in his own eyes: but the LORD pondereth the hearts."

The Reward For Being Spiritually Minded
Romans 8:6 "For to be carnally minded is death; but to be spiritually minded is life and peace."

The Spirit
Matthew 26:41 "Watch and pray, that ye enter not into temptation: the spirit indeed is willing, but the flesh is weak."

Mark 14:38 "Watch ye and pray, lest ye enter into temptation. The spirit truly is ready, but the flesh is weak."

James 4:5 "Do ye think that the scripture saith in vain, The spirit that dwelleth in us lusteth to envy?"

The Spirit Of Man
Proverbs 18:14 "The spirit of a man will sustain his infirmity; but a wounded spirit who can bear?"

Proverbs 20:27 "The spirit of man is the candle of the LORD, searching all the inward parts of the belly."

Ecclesiastes 12:7 "Then shall the dust return to the earth as it was: and the spirit shall return unto God who gave it."

1 Corinthians 6:19-20 "¹⁹What? know ye not that your body is the temple of the Holy Ghost which is in you, which ye have of God, and ye are not your own? ²⁰For ye are bought with a price: therefore glorify God in your body, and in your spirit, which are God's."

There Being No Man That Has Power Over The Spirit
Ecclesiastes 8:8 "There is no man that hath power over the spirit to retain the spirit; neither hath he power in the day of death: and there is no discharge in that war; neither shall wickedness deliver those that are given to it."

Those That Are Spiritual
1 Corinthians 2:15 "But he that is spiritual judgeth all things, yet he himself is judged of no man."

What Is Spirit/Spiritual
John 3:6 "That which is born of the flesh is flesh; and that which is born of the Spirit is spirit."

John 6:63-64 "⁶³It is the spirit that quickeneth; the flesh profiteth nothing: the words that I speak unto you, they are spirit, and they are life. ⁶⁴But there are some of you that believe not. For Jesus knew from the beginning who they were that believed not, and who should betray him."

Romans 7:14 "For we know that the law is spiritual: but I am carnal, sold under sin."

What Wars Against The Soul
1 Peter 2:11 "Dearly beloved, I beseech you as strangers and pilgrims, abstain from fleshly lusts, which war against the soul."

Wounded Spirits
Proverbs 18:14 "The spirit of a man will sustain his infirmity; but a wounded spirit who can bear?"

STEADFASTNESS

God Being Steadfast
Daniel 6:26 "I make a decree, That in every dominion of my kingdom men tremble and fear before the God of Daniel: for he is the living God, and stedfast for ever, and his kingdom that which shall not be destroyed, and his dominion shall be even unto the end."

Remaining Steadfast
1 Corinthians 15:58 "Therefore, my beloved brethren, be ye stedfast, unmoveable, always abounding in the work of the Lord, forasmuch as ye know that your labour is not in vain in the Lord."

2 Thessalonians 2:15 "Therefore, brethren, stand fast, and hold the traditions which ye have been taught, whether by word, or our epistle."

Who Shall Not Be Moved
Psalm 15:1-5 "¹LORD, who shall abide in thy tabernacle? who shall dwell in thy holy hill? ²He that walketh uprightly, and worketh righteousness, and speaketh the truth in his heart. ³He that backbiteth not with his tongue, nor doeth evil to his neighbour, nor taketh up a reproach against his neighbour. ⁴In whose eyes a vile person is contemned; but he honoureth them that fear the LORD. He that sweareth to his own hurt, and changeth not. ⁵He that putteth not out his money to usury, nor taketh reward against the innocent. He that doeth these things shall never be moved."

Psalm 21:7 "For the king trusteth in the LORD, and through the mercy of the most High he shall not be moved."

Psalm 55:22 "Cast thy burden upon the LORD, and he shall sustain thee: he shall never suffer the righteous to be moved."

Psalm 62:1-2 "¹Truly my soul waiteth upon God: from him cometh my salvation. ²He only is my rock and my salvation; he is my defence; I shall not be greatly moved."

STRANGERS

How Not To Treat Strangers
Exodus 22:21 "Thou shalt neither vex a stranger, nor oppress him: for ye were strangers in the land of Egypt."

Exodus 23:9 "Also thou shalt not oppress a stranger: for ye know the heart of a stranger, seeing ye were strangers in the land of Egypt."

Leviticus 19:33 "And if a stranger sojourn with thee in your land, ye shall not vex him."

Deuteronomy 24:14 "Thou shalt not oppress an hired servant that is poor and needy, whether he be of thy brethren, or of thy strangers that are in thy land within thy gates."

Deuteronomy 24:17 "Thou shalt not pervert the judgment of the stranger, nor of the fatherless; nor take a widow's raiment to pledge."

Zechariah 7:9-10 "⁹Thus speaketh the LORD of hosts, saying, Execute true judgment, and shew mercy and compassions every man to his brother: ¹⁰And oppress not the widow, nor the fatherless, the stranger, nor the poor; and let none of you imagine evil against his brother in your heart."

How To Treat Strangers
Leviticus 19:33-34 "³³And if a stranger sojourn with thee in your land, ye shall not vex him. ³⁴But the stranger that dwelleth with you shall be unto you as one born among you, and thou shalt love him as thyself; for ye were strangers in the land of Egypt: I am the LORD your God."

Deuteronomy 10:17-19 "¹⁷For the LORD your God is God of gods, and Lord of lords, a great God, a mighty, and a terrible, which regardeth not persons, nor taketh reward: ¹⁸He doth execute the judgment of the fatherless and widow, and loveth the stranger, in giving him food and raiment. ¹⁹Love ye therefore the stranger: for ye were strangers in the land of Egypt."

Hebrews 13:1-2 "¹Let brotherly love continue. ²Be not forgetful to entertain strangers: for thereby some have entertained angels unawares."

Strangers That Are Joined To The Lord

Isaiah 56:1-8 "¹Thus saith the LORD, Keep ye judgment, and do justice: for my salvation is near to come, and my righteousness to be revealed. ²Blessed is the man that doeth this, and the son of man that layeth hold on it; that keepeth the sabbath from polluting it, and keepeth his hand from doing any evil. ³Neither let the son of the stranger, that hath joined himself to the LORD, speak, saying, The LORD hath utterly separated me from his people: neither let the eunuch say, Behold, I am a dry tree. ⁴For thus saith the LORD unto the eunuchs that keep my sabbaths, and choose the things that please me, and take hold of my covenant; ⁵Even unto them will I give in mine house and within my walls a place and a name better than of sons and of daughters: I will give them an everlasting name, that shall not be cut off. ⁶Also the sons of the stranger, that join themselves to the LORD, to serve him, and to love the name of the LORD, to be his servants, every one that keepeth the sabbath from polluting it, and taketh hold of my covenant; ⁷Even them will I bring to my holy mountain, and make them joyful in my house of prayer: their burnt offerings and their sacrifices shall be accepted upon mine altar; for mine house shall be called an house of prayer for all people. ⁸The Lord GOD which gathereth the outcasts of Israel saith, Yet will I gather others to him, beside those that are gathered unto him."

STRAYING

Those That Cause Others To Go Astray

Deuteronomy 27:18 "Cursed be he that maketh the blind to wander out of the way. And all the people shall say, Amen."

Proverbs 28:10 "Whoso causeth the righteous to go astray in an evil way, he shall fall himself into his own pit: but the upright shall have good things in possession."

Those That Go Astray

Psalm 119:113-118 "¹¹³I hate vain thoughts: but thy law do I love. ¹¹⁴Thou art my hiding place and my shield: I hope in thy word. ¹¹⁵Depart from me, ye evildoers: for I will keep the commandments of my God. ¹¹⁶Uphold me according unto thy word, that I may live: and let me not be ashamed of my hope. ¹¹⁷Hold thou me up, and I shall be safe: and I will have respect unto thy statutes continually. ¹¹⁸Thou hast trodden down all them that err from thy statutes: for their deceit is falsehood."

Proverbs 21:16 "The man that wandereth out of the way of understanding shall remain in the congregation of the dead."

Proverbs 27:8 "As a bird that wandereth from her nest, so is a man that wandereth from his place."

Jeremiah 14:10 "Thus saith the LORD unto this people, Thus have they loved to wander, they have not refrained their feet, therefore the LORD doth not accept them; he will now remember their iniquity, and visit their sins."

Who Strays From The Right Path

Job 24:13-18 "¹³They are of those that rebel against the light; they know not the ways thereof, nor abide in the paths thereof. ¹⁴The murderer rising with the light killeth the poor and needy, and in the night is as a thief. ¹⁵The eye also of the adulterer waiteth for the twilight, saying, No eye shall see me: and disguiseth his face. ¹⁶In the dark they dig through houses, which they had marked for themselves in the daytime: they know not the light. ¹⁷For the morning is to them even as the shadow of death: if one know them, they are in the terrors of the shadow of death. ¹⁸He is swift as the waters; their portion is cursed in the earth: he beholdeth not the way of the vineyards."

Proverbs 2:11-19 "¹¹Discretion shall preserve thee, understanding shall keep thee: ¹²To deliver thee from the way of the evil man, from the man that speaketh froward things; ¹³Who leave the paths of uprightness, to walk in the ways of darkness; ¹⁴Who rejoice to do evil, and delight in the frowardness of the wicked; ¹⁵Whose ways are crooked, and they froward in their paths: ¹⁶To deliver thee from the strange woman, even from the stranger which flattereth with her words; ¹⁷Which forsaketh the guide of her youth, and forgetteth the covenant of her God. ¹⁸For her house inclineth unto death, and her paths unto the dead. ¹⁹None that go unto her return again, neither take they hold of the paths of life."

Proverbs 5:21-23 "²¹For the ways of man are before the eyes of the LORD, and he pondereth all his goings. ²²His own iniquities shall take the wicked himself, and he shall be holden with the cords of his sins. [23]He shall die without instruction; and in the greatness of his folly he shall go astray."

2 Peter 2:1-19 "[1]But there were false prophets also among the people, even as there shall be false teachers among you, who privily shall bring in damnable heresies, even denying the Lord that bought them, and bring upon themselves swift destruction. [2]And many shall follow their pernicious ways; by reason of whom the way of truth shall be evil spoken of. [3]And through covetousness shall they with feigned words make merchandise of you: whose judgment now of a long time lingereth not, and their damnation slumbereth not. [4]For if God spared not the angels that sinned, but cast them down to hell, and delivered them into chains of darkness, to be reserved unto judgment; [5]And spared not the old world, but saved Noah the eighth person, a preacher of righteousness, bringing in the flood upon the world of the ungodly; [6]And turning the cities of Sodom and Gomorrha into ashes condemned them with an overthrow, making them an ensample unto those that after should live ungodly; [7]And delivered just Lot, vexed with the filthy conversation of the wicked: [8](For that righteous man dwelling among them, in seeing and hearing, vexed his righteous soul from day to day with their unlawful deeds;) [9]The Lord knoweth how to deliver the godly out of temptations, and to reserve the unjust unto the day of judgment to be punished: [10]But chiefly them that walk after the flesh in the lust of uncleanness, and despise government. Presumptuous are they, selfwilled, they are not afraid to speak evil of dignities. [11]Whereas angels, which are greater in power and might, bring not railing accusation against them before the Lord. [12]But these, as natural brute beasts, made to be taken and destroyed, speak evil of the things that they understand not; and shall utterly perish in their own corruption; [13]And shall receive the reward of unrighteousness, as they that count it pleasure to riot in the day time. Spots they are and blemishes, sporting themselves with their own deceivings while they feast with you; [14]Having eyes full of adultery, and that cannot cease from sin; beguiling unstable souls: an heart they have exercised with covetous practices; cursed children: [15]Which have forsaken the right way, and are gone astray, following the way of Balaam the son of Bosor, who loved the wages of unrighteousness; [16]But was rebuked for his iniquity: the dumb ass speaking with man's voice forbad the madness of the prophet. [17]These are wells without water, clouds that are carried with a tempest; to whom the mist of darkness is reserved for ever. [18]For when they speak great swelling words of vanity, they allure through the lusts of the flesh, through much wantonness, those that were clean escaped from them who live in error. [19]While they promise them liberty, they themselves are the servants of corruption: for of whom a man is overcome, of the same is he brought in bondage."

STRENGTH

Being Strong

Deuteronomy 31:6-7 "[6]Be strong and of a good courage, fear not, nor be afraid of them: for the LORD thy God, he it is that doth go with thee; he will not fail thee, nor forsake thee. [7]And Moses called unto Joshua, and said unto him in the sight of all Israel, Be strong and of a good courage: for thou must go with this people unto the land which the LORD hath sworn unto their fathers to give them; and thou shalt cause them to inherit it."

Joshua 1:6-9 "[6]Be strong and of a good courage: for unto this people shalt thou divide for an inheritance the land, which I sware unto their fathers to give them. [7]Only be thou strong and very courageous, that thou mayest observe to do according to all the law, which Moses my servant commanded thee: turn not from it to the right hand or to the left, that thou mayest prosper whithersoever thou goest. [8]This book of the law shall not depart out of thy mouth; but thou shalt meditate therein day and night, that thou mayest observe to do according to all that is written therein: for then thou shalt make thy way prosperous, and then thou shalt have good success. [9]Have not I commanded thee? Be strong and of a good courage; be not afraid, neither be thou dismayed: for the LORD thy God is with thee whithersoever thou goest."

Joshua 23:6 "Be ye therefore very courageous to keep and to do all that is written in the book of the law of Moses, that ye turn not aside therefrom to the right hand or to the left."

1 Kings 2:1-2 "[1]Now the days of David drew nigh that he should die; and he charged Solomon his son, saying, ²I go the way of all the earth: be thou strong therefore, and shew thyself a man."

1 Chronicles 22:13 "Then shalt thou prosper, if thou takest heed to fulfil the statutes and judgments which the LORD charged Moses with concerning Israel: be strong, and of good courage; dread not, nor be dismayed."

2 Chronicles 32:6-7 "⁶And he set captains of war over the people, and gathered them together to him in the street of the gate of the city, and spake comfortably to them, saying, ⁷Be strong and courageous, be not afraid nor dismayed for the king of Assyria, nor for all the multitude that is with him: for there be more with us than with him."

Daniel 10:18-19 "¹⁸Then there came again and touched me one like the appearance of a man, and he strengthened me, ¹⁹And said, O man greatly beloved, fear not: peace be unto thee, be strong, yea, be strong. And when he had spoken unto me, I was strengthened, and said, Let my lord speak; for thou hast strengthened me."

1 Corinthians 16:13 "Watch ye, stand fast in the faith, quit you like men, be strong."

Ephesians 6:10 "Finally, my brethren, be strong in the Lord, and in the power of his might."

Strength Belonging To God
1 Chronicles 29:11-12 "¹¹Thine, O LORD, is the greatness, and the power, and the glory, and the victory, and the majesty: for all that is in the heaven and in the earth is thine; thine is the kingdom, O LORD, and thou art exalted as head above all. ¹²Both riches and honour come of thee, and thou reignest over all; and in thine hand is power and might; and in thine hand it is to make great, and to give strength unto all."

Daniel 2:20 "Daniel answered and said, Blessed be the name of God for ever and ever: for wisdom and might are his."

Strong People
Proverbs 11:16 "A gracious woman retaineth honour: and strong men retain riches."

Isaiah 25:1-3 "¹O LORD, thou art my God; I will exalt thee, I will praise thy name; for thou hast done wonderful things; thy counsels of old are

faithfulness and truth. ²For thou hast made of a city an heap; of a defenced city a ruin: a palace of strangers to be no city; it shall never be built. ³Therefore shall the strong people glorify thee, the city of the terrible nations shall fear thee."

The Lord Being Strong
Deuteronomy 10:17 "For the LORD your God is God of gods, and Lord of lords, a great God, a mighty, and a terrible, which regardeth not persons, nor taketh reward."

Joshua 4:24 "That all the people of the earth might know the hand of the LORD, that it is mighty: that ye might fear the LORD your God for ever."

Nehemiah 9:32 "Now therefore, our God, the great, the mighty, and the terrible God, who keepest covenant and mercy, let not all the trouble seem little before thee, that hath come upon us, on our kings, on our princes, and on our priests, and on our prophets, and on our fathers, and on all thy people, since the time of the kings of Assyria unto this day."

Job 36:5 "Behold, God is mighty, and despiseth not any: he is mighty in strength and wisdom."

Psalm 93:1-4 "¹The LORD reigneth, he is clothed with majesty; the LORD is clothed with strength, wherewith he hath girded himself: the world also is stablished, that it cannot be moved. ²Thy throne is established of old: thou art from everlasting. ³The floods have lifted up, O LORD, the floods have lifted up their voice; the floods lift up their waves. ⁴The LORD on high is mightier than the noise of many waters, yea, than the mighty waves of the sea."

Proverbs 18:10 "The name of the LORD is a strong tower: the righteous runneth into it, and is safe."

Isaiah 26:4 "Trust ye in the LORD for ever: for in the LORD JEHOVAH is everlasting strength."

Jeremiah 10:6 "Forasmuch as there is none like unto thee, O LORD; thou art great, and thy name is great in might."

Jeremiah 32:18-19 "¹⁸Thou shewest lovingkindness unto thousands, and recompensest the iniquity of the fathers into the bosom of their children after them: the Great, the Mighty God, the LORD of hosts, is his name, [19]Great in counsel, and mighty in work: for thine eyes are open upon all the ways of the sons of men: to give every one according to his ways, and according to the fruit of his doings."

Jeremiah 50:34 "Their Redeemer is strong; the LORD of hosts is his name: he shall throughly plead their cause, that he may give rest to the land, and disquiet the inhabitants of Babylon."

Revelation 18:8 "Therefore shall her plagues come in one day, death, and mourning, and famine; and she shall be utterly burned with fire: for strong is the Lord God who judgeth her."

The Lord Being The Source Of Strength

Exodus 15:2 "The LORD is my strength and song, and he is become my salvation: he is my God, and I will prepare him an habitation; my father's God, and I will exalt him."

2 Samuel 22:33-40 "[33]God is my strength and power: and he maketh my way perfect. [34]He maketh my feet like hinds' feet: and setteth me upon my high places. [35]He teacheth my hands to war; so that a bow of steel is broken by mine arms. [36]Thou hast also given me the shield of thy salvation: and thy gentleness hath made me great. [37]Thou hast enlarged my steps under me; so that my feet did not slip. [38]I have pursued mine enemies, and destroyed them; and turned not again until I had consumed them. [39]And I have consumed them, and wounded them, that they could not arise: yea, they are fallen under my feet. [40]For thou hast girded me with strength to battle: them that rose up against me hast thou subdued under me."

1 Chronicles 29:11-12 "[11]Thine, O LORD, is the greatness, and the power, and the glory, and the victory, and the majesty: for all that is in the heaven and in the earth is thine; thine is the kingdom, O LORD, and thou art exalted as head above all. [12]Both riches and honour come of thee, and thou reignest over all; and in thine hand is power and might; and in thine hand it is to make great, and to give strength unto all."

Psalm 18:2 "The LORD is my rock, and my fortress, and my deliverer; my God, my strength, in whom I will trust; my buckler, and the horn of my salvation, and my high tower."

Psalm 18:32 "It is God that girdeth me with strength, and maketh my way perfect."

Psalm 27:1 "The LORD is my light and my salvation; whom shall I fear? the LORD is the strength of my life; of whom shall I be afraid?"

Psalm 28:7-8 "[7]The LORD is my strength and my shield; my heart trusted in him, and I am helped: therefore my heart greatly rejoiceth; and with my song will I praise him. [8]The LORD is their strength, and he is the saving strength of his anointed."

Psalm 31:1-4 "[1]In thee, O LORD, do I put my trust; let me never be ashamed: deliver me in thy righteousness. [2]Bow down thine ear to me; deliver me speedily: be thou my strong rock, for an house of defence to save me. [3]For thou art my rock and my fortress; therefore for thy name's sake lead me, and guide me. [4]Pull me out of the net that they have laid privily for me: for thou art my strength."

Psalm 37:39 "But the salvation of the righteous is of the LORD: he is their strength in the time of trouble."

Psalm 46:1-11 "[1]God is our refuge and strength, a very present help in trouble. [2]Therefore will not we fear, though the earth be removed, and though the mountains be carried into the midst of the sea; [3]Though the waters thereof roar and be troubled, though the mountains shake with the swelling thereof. Selah. [4]There is a river, the streams whereof shall make glad the city of God, the holy place of the tabernacles of the most High. [5]God is in the midst of her; she shall not be moved: God shall help her, and that right early. [6]The heathen raged, the kingdoms were moved: he uttered his voice, the earth melted. [7]The LORD of hosts is with us; the God of Jacob is our refuge. Selah. [8]Come, behold the works of the LORD, what desolations he hath made in the earth. [9]He maketh wars to cease unto the end of the earth; he breaketh the bow, and cutteth the spear in sunder; he burneth the chariot in the fire. [10]Be still, and know that I am God: I will be exalted among the heathen, I will be exalted in the earth. [11]The LORD of hosts is with us; the God of Jacob is our refuge. Selah."

Psalm 59:16-17 "[16]But I will sing of thy power; yea, I will sing aloud of thy mercy in the morning:

for thou hast been my defence and refuge in the day of my trouble. ¹⁷Unto thee, O my strength, will I sing: for God is my defence, and the God of my mercy."

Psalm 62:6-7 "⁶He only is my rock and my salvation: he is my defence; I shall not be moved. ⁷In God is my salvation and my glory: the rock of my strength, and my refuge, is in God."

Psalm 68:35 "O God, thou art terrible out of thy holy places: the God of Israel is he that giveth strength and power unto his people. Blessed be God."

Psalm 73:26 "My flesh and my heart faileth: but God is the strength of my heart, and my portion for ever."

Psalm 118:14 "The LORD is my strength and song, and is become my salvation."

Psalm 138:3-4 "³In the day when I cried thou answeredst me, and strengthenedst me with strength in my soul. ⁴All the kings of the earth shall praise thee, O LORD, when they hear the words of thy mouth."

Psalm 144:1 "Blessed be the LORD my strength, which teacheth my hands to war, and my fingers to fight."

Isaiah 12:2 "Behold, God is my salvation; I will trust, and not be afraid: for the LORD JEHOVAH is my strength and my song; he also is become my salvation."

Isaiah 25:1-4 "¹O LORD, thou art my God; I will exalt thee, I will praise thy name; for thou hast done wonderful things; thy counsels of old are faithfulness and truth. ²For thou hast made of a city an heap; of a defenced city a ruin: a palace of strangers to be no city; it shall never be built. ³Therefore shall the strong people glorify thee, the city of the terrible nations shall fear thee. ⁴For thou hast been a strength to the poor, a strength to the needy in his distress, a refuge from the storm, a shadow from the heat, when the blast of the terrible ones is as a storm against the wall."

Isaiah 49:5 "And now, saith the LORD that formed me from the womb to be his servant, to bring Jacob again to him, Though Israel be not gathered, yet shall I be glorious in the eyes of the LORD, and my God shall be my strength."

Jeremiah 16:19 "O LORD, my strength, and my fortress, and my refuge in the day of affliction, the Gentiles shall come unto thee from the ends of the earth, and shall say, Surely our fathers have inherited lies, vanity, and things wherein there is no profit."

Joel 3:16 "The LORD also shall roar out of Zion, and utter his voice from Jerusalem; and the heavens and the earth shall shake: but the LORD will be the hope of his people, and the strength of the children of Israel."

Habakkuk 3:19 "The LORD God is my strength, and he will make my feet like hinds' feet, and he will make me to walk upon mine high places. To the chief singer on my stringed instruments."

Ephesians 3:14-16 "¹⁴For this cause I bow my knees unto the Father of our Lord Jesus Christ, ¹⁵Of whom the whole family in heaven and earth is named, ¹⁶That he would grant you, according to the riches of his glory, to be strengthened with might by his Spirit in the inner man."

Philippians 4:13 "I can do all things through Christ which strengtheneth me."

1 Peter 5:10 "But the God of all grace, who hath called us unto his eternal glory by Christ Jesus, after that ye have suffered a while, make you perfect, stablish, strengthen, settle you."

The Strength Of The Lord

Psalm 59:8-9 "⁸But thou, O LORD, shalt laugh at them; thou shalt have all the heathen in derision. ⁹Because of his strength will I wait upon thee: for God is my defence."

Psalm 68:34 "Ascribe ye strength unto God: his excellency is over Israel, and his strength is in the clouds."

2 Corinthians 12:8-10 "⁸For this thing I besought the Lord thrice, that it might depart from me. ⁹And he said unto me, My grace is sufficient for thee: for my strength is made perfect in weakness. Most gladly therefore will I rather glory in my infirmities, that the power of Christ may rest upon me. ¹⁰Therefore I take pleasure in infirmities, in reproaches, in necessities, in persecutions, in distresses for Christ's sake: for when I am weak, then am I strong."

Those That Do Not Make God Their Strength

Psalm 52:1-7 "¹Why boastest thou thyself in mischief, O mighty man? the goodness of God endureth continually. ²Thy tongue deviseth mischiefs; like a sharp rasor, working deceitfully. ³Thou lovest evil more than good; and lying rather than to speak righteousness. Selah. ⁴Thou lovest all devouring words, O thou deceitful tongue. ⁵God shall likewise destroy thee for ever, he shall take thee away, and pluck thee out of thy dwelling place, and root thee out of the land of the living. Selah. ⁶The righteous also shall see, and fear, and shall laugh at him: ⁷Lo, this is the man that made not God his strength; but trusted in the abundance of his riches, and strengthened himself in his wickedness."

What Is Better Than Strength

Ecclesiastes 9:16 "Then said I, Wisdom is better than strength: nevertheless the poor man's wisdom is despised, and his words are not heard."

What Has Strength

Proverbs 8:12-14 "¹²I wisdom dwell with prudence, and find out knowledge of witty inventions. ¹³The fear of the LORD is to hate evil: pride, and arrogancy, and the evil way, and the froward mouth, do I hate. ¹⁴Counsel is mine, and sound wisdom: I am understanding; I have strength."

What Is Strength

Nehemiah 8:10 "Then he said unto them, Go your way, eat the fat, and drink the sweet, and send portions unto them for whom nothing is prepared: for this day is holy unto our Lord: neither be ye sorry; for the joy of the LORD is your strength."

Proverbs 10:29 "The way of the LORD is strength to the upright: but destruction shall be to the workers of iniquity."

What Strengthens The Wise

Ecclesiastes 7:19 "Wisdom strengtheneth the wise more than ten mighty men which are in the city."

What The Mighty Should Not Do

Jeremiah 9:23 "Thus saith the LORD, Let not the wise man glory in his wisdom, neither let the mighty man glory in his might, let not the rich man glory in his riches."

Where Strength Is

1 Chronicles 16:26-27 "²⁶For all the gods of the people are idols: but the LORD made the heavens. ²⁷Glory and honour are in his presence; strength and gladness are in his place."

Job 12:9-16 "⁹Who knoweth not in all these that the hand of the LORD hath wrought this? ¹⁰In whose hand is the soul of every living thing, and the breath of all mankind. ¹¹Doth not the ear try words? and the mouth taste his meat? ¹²With the ancient is wisdom; and in length of days understanding. ¹³With him is wisdom and strength, he hath counsel and understanding. ¹⁴Behold, he breaketh down, and it cannot be built again: he shutteth up a man, and there can be no opening. ¹⁵Behold, he withholdeth the waters, and they dry up: also he sendeth them out, and they overturn the earth. ¹⁶With him is strength and wisdom: the deceived and the deceiver are his."

Who Is Strong

Proverbs 24:5 "A wise man is strong; yea, a man of knowledge increaseth strength."

1 Corinthians 4:8-10 "⁸Now ye are full, now ye are rich, ye have reigned as kings without us: and I would to God ye did reign, that we also might reign with you. ⁹For I think that God hath set forth us the apostles last, as it were appointed to death: for we are made a spectacle unto the world, and to angels, and to men. ¹⁰We are fools for Christ's sake, but ye are wise in Christ; we are weak, but ye are strong; ye are honourable, but we are despised."

2 Corinthians 12:8-10 "⁸For this thing I besought the Lord thrice, that it might depart from me. ⁹And he said unto me, My grace is sufficient for thee: for my strength is made perfect in weakness. Most gladly therefore will I rather glory in my infirmities, that the power of Christ may rest upon me. ¹⁰Therefore I take pleasure in infirmities, in reproaches, in necessities, in persecutions, in distresses for Christ's sake: for when I am weak, then am I strong."

2 Corinthians 13:3-5 "³Since ye seek a proof of Christ speaking in me, which to you-ward is not weak, but is mighty in you. ⁴For though he was crucified through weakness, yet he liveth by the power of God. For we also are weak in him, but we shall live with him by the power of God toward you. ⁵Examine yourselves, whether ye be in the faith; prove your own selves. Know ye not your own selves, how that Jesus Christ is in you, except ye be reprobates?"

1 John 2:13-14 "[13]I write unto you, fathers, because ye have known him that is from the beginning. I write unto you, young men, because ye have overcome the wicked one. I write unto you, little children, because ye have known the Father. [14]I have written unto you, fathers, because ye have known him that is from the beginning. I have written unto you, young men, because ye are strong, and the word of God abideth in you, and ye have overcome the wicked one."

Who The Lord Strengthens

1 Samuel 2:10 "The adversaries of the LORD shall be broken to pieces; out of heaven shall he thunder upon them: the LORD shall judge the ends of the earth; and he shall give strength unto his king, and exalt the horn of his anointed."

Psalm 27:14 "Wait on the LORD: be of good courage, and he shall strengthen thine heart: wait, I say, on the LORD."

Psalm 29:11 "The LORD will give strength unto his people; the LORD will bless his people with peace."

Psalm 31:24 "Be of good courage, and he shall strengthen your heart, all ye that hope in the LORD."

Isaiah 40:28-29 "[28]Hast thou not known? hast thou not heard, that the everlasting God, the LORD, the Creator of the ends of the earth, fainteth not, neither is weary? there is no searching of his understanding. [29]He giveth power to the faint; and to them that have no might he increaseth strength."

Isaiah 41:8-10 "[8]But thou, Israel, art my servant, Jacob whom I have chosen, the seed of Abraham my friend. [9]Thou whom I have taken from the ends of the earth, and called thee from the chief men thereof, and said unto thee, Thou art my servant; I have chosen thee, and not cast thee away. [10]Fear thou not; for I am with thee: be not dismayed; for I am thy God: I will strengthen thee; yea, I will help thee; yea, I will uphold thee with the right hand of my righteousness."

Ezekiel 34:11-16 "[11]For thus saith the Lord GOD; Behold, I, even I, will both search my sheep, and seek them out. [12]As a shepherd seeketh out his flock in the day that he is among his sheep that are scattered; so will I seek out my sheep, and will deliver them out of all places where they have been scattered in the cloudy and dark day. [13]And I will bring them out from the people, and gather them from the countries, and will bring them to their own land, and feed them upon the mountains of Israel by the rivers, and in all the inhabited places of the country. [14]I will feed them in a good pasture, and upon the high mountains of Israel shall their fold be: there shall they lie in a good fold, and in a fat pasture shall they feed upon the mountains of Israel. [15]I will feed my flock, and I will cause them to lie down, saith the Lord GOD. [16]I will seek that which was lost, and bring again that which was driven away, and will bind up that which was broken, and will strengthen that which was sick: but I will destroy the fat and the strong; I will feed them with judgment."

Whose Strength Is Small

Proverbs 24:10 "If thou faint in the day of adversity, thy strength is small."

STRIFE

Avoiding Strife

Proverbs 3:30 "Strive not with a man without cause, if he have done thee no harm."

Proverbs 17:14 "The beginning of strife is as when one letteth out water: therefore leave off contention, before it be meddled with."

Proverbs 20:3 "It is an honour for a man to cease from strife: but every fool will be meddling."

Proverbs 25:8-10 "[8]Go not forth hastily to strive, lest thou know not what to do in the end thereof, when thy neighbour hath put thee to shame. [9]Debate thy cause with thy neighbour himself; and discover not a secret to another: [10]Lest he that heareth it put thee to shame, and thine infamy turn not away."

Romans 13:13 "Let us walk honestly, as in the day; not in rioting and drunkenness, not in chambering and wantonness, not in strife and envying."

Philippians 2:3 "Let nothing be done through strife or vainglory; but in lowliness of mind let each esteem other better than themselves."

How To Rid Strife

Proverbs 22:10 "Cast out the scorner, and contention shall go out; yea, strife and reproach shall cease."

The Beginning Of Strife
Proverbs 17:14 "The beginning of strife is as when one letteth out water: therefore leave off contention, before it be meddled with."

The Place Where Strife Exists
James 3:13-16 "13Who is a wise man and endued with knowledge among you? let him shew out of a good conversation his works with meekness of wisdom. 14But if ye have bitter envying and strife in your hearts, glory not, and lie not against the truth. 15This wisdom descendeth not from above, but is earthly, sensual, devilish. 16For where envying and strife is, there is confusion and every evil work."

Those That Love Strife
Proverbs 17:19 "He loveth transgression that loveth strife: and he that exalteth his gate seeketh destruction."

Those That Meddle With Strife
Proverbs 26:17 "He that passeth by, and meddleth with strife belonging not to him, is like one that taketh a dog by the ears."

What Brings Forth Strife
Proverbs 30:33 "Surely the churning of milk bringeth forth butter, and the wringing of the nose bringeth forth blood: so the forcing of wrath bringeth forth strife."

What Stirs Up Strifes
Proverbs 10:12 "Hatred stirreth up strifes: but love covereth all sins."

Where Strife Ceases
Proverbs 26:20 "Where no wood is, there the fire goeth out: so where there is no talebearer, the strife ceaseth."

Who Appeases Strife
Proverbs 15:18 "A wrathful man stirreth up strife: but he that is slow to anger appeaseth strife."

Who Has Strife Among Them
1 Corinthians 3:3 "For ye are yet carnal: for whereas there is among you envying, and strife, and divisions, are ye not carnal, and walk as men?"

Who Kindles Strife
Proverbs 26:20-21 "20Where no wood is, there the fire goeth out: so where there is no talebearer, the strife ceaseth. 21As coals are to burning coals, and wood to fire; so is a contentious man to kindle strife."

Who Sows Strife
Proverbs 16:28 "A froward man soweth strife: and a whisperer separateth chief friends."

Who Stirs Up Strife
Proverbs 15:18 "A wrathful man stirreth up strife: but he that is slow to anger appeaseth strife."

Proverbs 28:25 "He that is of a proud heart stirreth up strife: but he that putteth his trust in the LORD shall be made fat."

Proverbs 29:22 "An angry man stirreth up strife, and a furious man aboundeth in transgression."

Why You Should Avoid Strife
Proverbs 25:8-10 "8Go not forth hastily to strive, lest thou know not what to do in the end thereof, when thy neighbour hath put thee to shame. 9Debate thy cause with thy neighbour himself; and discover not a secret to another: 10Lest he that heareth it put thee to shame, and thine infamy turn not away."

STRIVING

Those That Strive For The Mastery
1 Corinthians 9:24-25 "24Know ye not that they which run in a race run all, but one receiveth the prize? So run, that ye may obtain. 25And every man that striveth for the mastery is temperate in all things. Now they do it to obtain a corruptible crown; but we an incorruptible."

What To Strive For
Luke 13:23-24 "23Then said one unto him, Lord, are there few that be saved? And he said unto them, 24Strive to enter in at the strait gate: for many, I say unto you, will seek to enter in, and shall not be able."

1 Corinthians 9:24 "Know ye not that they which run in a race run all, but one receiveth the prize? So run, that ye may obtain."

Philippians 3:14 "I press toward the mark for the prize of the high calling of God in Christ Jesus."

STUBBORNNESS

What Stubbornness Is
1 Samuel 15:23 "For rebellion is as the sin of witchcraft, and stubbornness is as iniquity and idolatry. Because thou hast rejected the word of

the LORD, he hath also rejected thee from being king."

STUMBLING/SLIPPING

Not Casting Stumblingblocks

Leviticus 19:14 "Thou shalt not curse the deaf, nor put a stumblingblock before the blind, but shalt fear thy God: I am the LORD."

Romans 14:10-23 "¹⁰But why dost thou judge thy brother? or why dost thou set at nought thy brother? for we shall all stand before the judgment seat of Christ. ¹¹For it is written, As I live, saith the Lord, every knee shall bow to me, and every tongue shall confess to God. ¹²So then every one of us shall give account of himself to God. ¹³Let us not therefore judge one another any more: but judge this rather, that no man put a stumblingblock or an occasion to fall in his brother's way. ¹⁴I know, and am persuaded by the Lord Jesus, that there is nothing unclean of itself: but to him that esteemeth any thing to be unclean, to him it is unclean. ¹⁵But if thy brother be grieved with thy meat, now walkest thou not charitably. Destroy not him with thy meat, for whom Christ died. ¹⁶Let not then your good be evil spoken of: ¹⁷For the kingdom of God is not meat and drink; but righteousness, and peace, and joy in the Holy Ghost. ¹⁸For he that in these things serveth Christ is acceptable to God, and approved of men. ¹⁹Let us therefore follow after the things which make for peace, and things wherewith one may edify another. ²⁰For meat destroy not the work of God. All things indeed are pure; but it is evil for that man who eateth with offence. ²¹It is good neither to eat flesh, nor to drink wine, nor any thing whereby thy brother stumbleth, or is offended, or is made weak. ²²Hast thou faith? have it to thyself before God. Happy is he that condemneth not himself in that thing which he alloweth. ²³And he that doubteth is damned if he eat, because he eateth not of faith: for whatsoever is not of faith is sin."

1 Corinthians 8:1-13 "¹Now as touching things offered unto idols, we know that we all have knowledge. Knowledge puffeth up, but charity edifieth. ²And if any man think that he knoweth any thing, he knoweth nothing yet as he ought to know. ³But if any man love God, the same is known of him. ⁴As concerning therefore the eating of those things that are offered in sacrifice unto idols, we know that an idol is nothing in the world, and that there is none other God but one. ⁵For though there be that are called gods, whether in heaven or in earth, (as there be gods many, and lords many,) ⁶But to us there is but one God, the Father, of whom are all things, and we in him; and one Lord Jesus Christ, by whom are all things, and we by him. ⁷Howbeit there is not in every man that knowledge: for some with conscience of the idol unto this hour eat it as a thing offered unto an idol; and their conscience being weak is defiled. ⁸But meat commendeth us not to God: for neither, if we eat, are we the better; neither, if we eat not, are we the worse. ⁹But take heed lest by any means this liberty of yours become a stumblingblock to them that are weak. ¹⁰For if any man see thee which hast knowledge sit at meat in the idol's temple, shall not the conscience of him which is weak be emboldened to eat those things which are offered to idols; ¹¹And through thy knowledge shall the weak brother perish, for whom Christ died? ¹²But when ye sin so against the brethren, and wound their weak conscience, ye sin against Christ. ¹³Wherefore, if meat make my brother to offend, I will eat no flesh while the world standeth, lest I make my brother to offend."

1 Corinthians 10:23-33 "²³All things are lawful for me, but all things are not expedient: all things are lawful for me, but all things edify not. ²⁴Let no man seek his own, but every man another's wealth. ²⁵Whatsoever is sold in the shambles, that eat, asking no question for conscience sake: ²⁶For the earth is the Lord's, and the fulness thereof. ²⁷If any of them that believe not bid you to a feast, and ye be disposed to go; whatsoever is set before you, eat, asking no question for conscience sake. ²⁸But if any man say unto you, This is offered in sacrifice unto idols, eat not for his sake that shewed it, and for conscience sake: for the earth is the Lord's, and the fulness thereof: ²⁹Conscience, I say, not thine own, but of the other: for why is my liberty judged of another man's conscience? ³⁰For if I by grace be a partaker, why am I evil spoken of for that for which I give thanks? ³¹Whether therefore ye eat, or drink, or whatsoever ye do, do all to the glory of God. ³²Give none offence, neither to the Jews, nor to the Gentiles, nor to the church of

God: ³³Even as I please all men in all things, not seeking mine own profit, but the profit of many, that they may be saved."

The Lord Preventing You From Slipping
2 Samuel 22:33-37 "³³God is my strength and power: and he maketh my way perfect. ³⁴He maketh my feet like hinds' feet: and setteth me upon my high places. ³⁵He teacheth my hands to war; so that a bow of steel is broken by mine arms. ³⁶Thou hast also given me the shield of thy salvation: and thy gentleness hath made me great. ³⁷Thou hast enlarged my steps under me; so that my feet did not slip."

Psalm 18:31-36 "³¹For who is God save the LORD? or who is a rock save our God? ³²It is God that girdeth me with strength, and maketh my way perfect. ³³He maketh my feet like hinds' feet, and setteth me upon my high places. ³⁴He teacheth my hands to war, so that a bow of steel is broken by mine arms. ³⁵Thou hast also given me the shield of thy salvation: and thy right hand hath holden me up, and thy gentleness hath made me great. ³⁶Thou hast enlarged my steps under me, that my feet did not slip."

Psalm 55:22 "Cast thy burden upon the LORD, and he shall sustain thee: he shall never suffer the righteous to be moved."

Psalm 66:8-9 "⁸O bless our God, ye people, and make the voice of his praise to be heard: ⁹Which holdeth our soul in life, and suffereth not our feet to be moved."

Psalm 94:18 "When I said, My foot slippeth; thy mercy, O LORD, held me up."

Jude 24-25 "²⁴Now unto him that is able to keep you from falling, and to present you faultless before the presence of his glory with exceeding joy, ²⁵To the only wise God our Saviour, be glory and majesty, dominion and power, both now and ever. Amen."

The Stumblingstone
Isaiah 8:13-15 "¹³Sanctify the LORD of hosts himself; and let him be your fear, and let him be your dread. ¹⁴And he shall be for a sanctuary; but for a stone of stumbling and for a rock of offence to both the houses of Israel, for a gin and for a snare to the inhabitants of Jerusalem. ¹⁵And many

among them shall stumble, and fall, and be broken, and be snared, and be taken."

Romans 9:30-33 "³⁰What shall we say then? That the Gentiles, which followed not after righteousness, have attained to righteousness, even the righteousness which is of faith. ³¹But Israel, which followed after the law of righteousness, hath not attained to the law of righteousness. ³²Wherefore? Because they sought it not by faith, but as it were by the works of the law. For they stumbled at that stumblingstone; ³³As it is written, Behold, I lay in Sion a stumblingstone and rock of offence: and whosoever believeth on him shall not be ashamed."

1 Peter 2:4-8 "⁴To whom coming, as unto a living stone, disallowed indeed of men, but chosen of God, and precious, ⁵Ye also, as lively stones, are built up a spiritual house, an holy priesthood, to offer up spiritual sacrifices, acceptable to God by Jesus Christ. ⁶Wherefore also it is contained in the scripture, Behold, I lay in Sion a chief corner stone, elect, precious: and he that believeth on him shall not be confounded. ⁷Unto you therefore which believe he is precious: but unto them which be disobedient, the stone which the builders disallowed, the same is made the head of the corner, ⁸And a stone of stumbling, and a rock of offence, even to them which stumble at the word, being disobedient: whereunto also they were appointed."

What Is A Stumblingblock To Jews
1 Corinthians 1:22-23 "²²For the Jews require a sign, and the Greeks seek after wisdom: ²³But we preach Christ crucified, unto the Jews a stumblingblock, and unto the Greeks foolishness."

Who Shall Not Stumble
Psalm 26:1 "Judge me, O LORD; for I have walked in mine integrity: I have trusted also in the LORD; therefore I shall not slide."

Psalm 37:30-31 "³⁰The mouth of the righteous speaketh wisdom, and his tongue talketh of judgment. ³¹The law of his God is in his heart; none of his steps shall slide."

Psalm 55:22 "Cast thy burden upon the LORD, and he shall sustain thee: he shall never suffer the righteous to be moved."

John 11:9 "Jesus answered, Are there not twelve hours in the day? If any man walk in the day, he stumbleth not, because he seeth the light of this world."

2 Peter 1:1-10 "¹Simon Peter, a servant and an apostle of Jesus Christ, to them that have obtained like precious faith with us through the righteousness of God and our Saviour Jesus Christ: ²Grace and peace be multiplied unto you through the knowledge of God, and of Jesus our Lord, ³According as his divine power hath given unto us all things that pertain unto life and godliness, through the knowledge of him that hath called us to glory and virtue: ⁴Whereby are given unto us exceeding great and precious promises: that by these ye might be partakers of the divine nature, having escaped the corruption that is in the world through lust. ⁵And beside this, giving all diligence, add to your faith virtue; and to virtue knowledge; ⁶And to knowledge temperance; and to temperance patience; and to patience godliness; ⁷And to godliness brotherly kindness; and to brotherly kindness charity. ⁸For if these things be in you, and abound, they make you that ye shall neither be barren nor unfruitful in the knowledge of our Lord Jesus Christ. ⁹But he that lacketh these things is blind, and cannot see afar off, and hath forgotten that he was purged from his old sins. ¹⁰Wherefore the rather, brethren, give diligence to make your calling and election sure: for if ye do these things, ye shall never fall."

1 John 2:10 "He that loveth his brother abideth in the light, and there is none occasion of stumbling in him."

Who Stumbles

Deuteronomy 32:31-35 "³¹For their rock is not as our Rock, even our enemies themselves being judges. ³²For their vine is of the vine of Sodom, and of the fields of Gomorrah: their grapes are grapes of gall, their clusters are bitter: ³³Their wine is the poison of dragons, and the cruel venom of asps. ³⁴Is not this laid up in store with me, and sealed up among my treasures? ³⁵To me belongeth vengeance, and recompence; their foot shall slide in due time: for the day of their calamity is at hand, and the things that shall come upon them make haste."

Proverbs 4:19 "The way of the wicked is as darkness: they know not at what they stumble."

John 11:9-10 "⁹Jesus answered, Are there not twelve hours in the day? If any man walk in the day, he stumbleth not, because he seeth the light of this world. ¹⁰But if a man walk in the night, he stumbleth, because there is no light in him."

John 12:35-36 "³⁵Then Jesus said unto them, Yet a little while is the light with you. Walk while ye have the light, lest darkness come upon you: for he that walketh in darkness knoweth not whither he goeth. ³⁶While ye have light, believe in the light, that ye may be the children of light. These things spake Jesus, and departed, and did hide himself from them."

Romans 11:1-11 "¹I say then, Hath God cast away his people? God forbid. For I also am an Israelite, of the seed of Abraham, of the tribe of Benjamin. ²God hath not cast away his people which he foreknew. Wot ye not what the scripture saith of Elias? how he maketh intercession to God against Israel, saying, ³Lord, they have killed thy prophets, and digged down thine altars; and I am left alone, and they seek my life. ⁴But what saith the answer of God unto him? I have reserved to myself seven thousand men, who have not bowed the knee to the image of Baal. ⁵Even so then at this present time also there is a remnant according to the election of grace. ⁶And if by grace, then is it no more of works: otherwise grace is no more grace. But if it be of works, then is it no more grace: otherwise work is no more work. ⁷What then? Israel hath not obtained that which he seeketh for; but the election hath obtained it, and the rest were blinded ⁸(According as it is written, God hath given them the spirit of slumber, eyes that they should not see, and ears that they should not hear;) unto this day. ⁹And David saith, Let their table be made a snare, and a trap, and a stumbling block, and a recompence unto them: ¹⁰Let their eyes be darkened, that they may not see, and bow down their back alway. ¹¹I say then, Have they stumbled that they should fall? God forbid: but rather through their fall salvation is come unto the Gentiles, for to provoke them to jealousy."

SUBMISSION

Submitting Yourself To The Lord

2 Chronicles 30:8 "Now be ye not stiffnecked, as your fathers were, but yield yourselves unto the

L ORD, and enter into his sanctuary, which he hath sanctified for ever: and serve the L ORD your God, that the fierceness of his wrath may turn away from you."

James 4:7 "Submit yourselves therefore to God. Resist the devil, and he will flee from you."

Who To Submit To
Romans 13:1 "Let every soul be subject unto the higher powers. For there is no power but of God: the powers that be are ordained of God."

Ephesians 5:21-22 "²¹Submitting yourselves one to another in the fear of God. ²²Wives, submit yourselves unto your own husbands, as unto the Lord."

Colossians 3:18 "Wives, submit yourselves unto your own husbands, as it is fit in the Lord."

Hebrews 13:17 "Obey them that have the rule over you, and submit yourselves: for they watch for your souls, as they that must give account, that they may do it with joy, and not with grief: for that is unprofitable for you."

1 Peter 2:13-15 "¹³Submit yourselves to every ordinance of man for the Lord's sake: whether it be to the king, as supreme; ¹⁴Or unto governors, as unto them that are sent by him for the punishment of evildoers, and for the praise of them that do well. ¹⁵For so is the will of God, that with well doing ye may put to silence the ignorance of foolish men."

1 Peter 5:5 "Likewise, ye younger, submit yourselves unto the elder. Yea, all of you be subject one to another, and be clothed with humility: for God resisteth the proud, and giveth grace to the humble."

SUBSTANCE

The Substance Of Things Hoped For
Hebrews 11:1-3 "¹Now faith is the substance of things hoped for, the evidence of things not seen. ²For by it the elders obtained a good report. ³Through faith we understand that the worlds were framed by the word of God, so that things which are seen were not made of things which do appear."

Who Inherits Substance
Proverbs 8:12-21 "¹²I wisdom dwell with prudence, and find out knowledge of witty inventions. ¹³The

fear of the L ORD is to hate evil: pride, and arrogancy, and the evil way, and the froward mouth, do I hate. ¹⁴Counsel is mine, and sound wisdom: I am understanding; I have strength. ¹⁵By me kings reign, and princes decree justice. ¹⁶By me princes rule, and nobles, even all the judges of the earth. ¹⁷I love them that love me; and those that seek me early shall find me. ¹⁸Riches and honour are with me; yea, durable riches and righteousness. ¹⁹My fruit is better than gold, yea, than fine gold; and my revenue than choice silver. ²⁰I lead in the way of righteousness, in the midst of the paths of judgment: ²¹That I may cause those that love me to inherit substance; and I will fill their treasures."

SUFFERING

Jesus Christ Suffering
Isaiah 50:4-10 "⁴The Lord G OD hath given me the tongue of the learned, that I should know how to speak a word in season to him that is weary: he wakeneth morning by morning, he wakeneth mine ear to hear as the learned. ⁵The Lord G OD hath opened mine ear, and I was not rebellious, neither turned away back. ⁶I gave my back to the smiters, and my cheeks to them that plucked off the hair: I hid not my face from shame and spitting. ⁷For the Lord G OD will help me; therefore shall I not be confounded: therefore have I set my face like a flint, and I know that I shall not be ashamed. ⁸He is near that justifieth me; who will contend with me? let us stand together: who is mine adversary? let him come near to me. ⁹Behold, the Lord G OD will help me; who is he that shall condemn me? lo, they all shall wax old as a garment; the moth shall eat them up. ¹⁰Who is among you that feareth the L ORD, that obeyeth the voice of his servant, that walketh in darkness, and hath no light? let him trust in the name of the L ORD, and stay upon his God."

Isaiah 52:12-15 "¹²For ye shall not go out with haste, nor go by flight: for the L ORD will go before you; and the God of Israel will be your rereward. ¹³Behold, my servant shall deal prudently, he shall be exalted and extolled, and be very high. ¹⁴As many were astonied at thee; his visage was so marred more than any man, and his form more than the sons of men: ¹⁵So shall he sprinkle many nations; the kings shall shut their mouths at him:

for that which had not been told them shall they see; and that which they had not heard shall they consider."

Isaiah 53:1-12 "¹Who hath believed our report? and to whom is the arm of the LORD revealed? ²For he shall grow up before him as a tender plant, and as a root out of a dry ground: he hath no form nor comeliness; and when we shall see him, there is no beauty that we should desire him. ³He is despised and rejected of men; a man of sorrows, and acquainted with grief: and we hid as it were our faces from him; he was despised, and we esteemed him not. ⁴Surely he hath borne our griefs, and carried our sorrows: yet we did esteem him stricken, smitten of God, and afflicted. ⁵But he was wounded for our transgressions, he was bruised for our iniquities: the chastisement of our peace was upon him; and with his stripes we are healed. ⁶All we like sheep have gone astray; we have turned every one to his own way; and the LORD hath laid on him the iniquity of us all. ⁷He was oppressed, and he was afflicted, yet he opened not his mouth: he is brought as a lamb to the slaughter, and as a sheep before her shearers is dumb, so he openeth not his mouth. ⁸He was taken from prison and from judgment: and who shall declare his generation? for he was cut off out of the land of the living: for the transgression of my people was he stricken. ⁹And he made his grave with the wicked, and with the rich in his death; because he had done no violence, neither was any deceit in his mouth. ¹⁰Yet it pleased the LORD to bruise him; he hath put him to grief: when thou shalt make his soul an offering for sin, he shall see his seed, he shall prolong his days, and the pleasure of the LORD shall prosper in his hand. ¹¹He shall see of the travail of his soul, and shall be satisfied: by his knowledge shall my righteous servant justify many; for he shall bear their iniquities. ¹²Therefore will I divide him a portion with the great, and he shall divide the spoil with the strong; because he hath poured out his soul unto death: and he was numbered with the transgressors; and he bare the sin of many, and made intercession for the transgressors."

Psalm 22:1-21 "¹My God, my God, why hast thou forsaken me? why art thou so far from helping me, and from the words of my roaring? ²O my God, I cry in the daytime, but thou hearest not; and in the night season, and am not silent. ³But thou art holy, O thou that inhabitest the praises of Israel. ⁴Our fathers trusted in thee: they trusted, and thou didst deliver them. ⁵They cried unto thee, and were delivered: they trusted in thee, and were not confounded. ⁶But I am a worm, and no man; a reproach of men, and despised of the people. ⁷All they that see me laugh me to scorn: they shoot out the lip, they shake the head saying, ⁸He trusted on the LORD that he would deliver him: let him deliver him, seeing he delighted in him. ⁹But thou art he that took me out of the womb: thou didst make me hope when I was upon my mother's breasts. ¹⁰I was cast upon thee from the womb: thou art my God from my mother's belly. ¹¹Be not far from me; for trouble is near; for there is none to help. ¹²Many bulls have compassed me: strong bulls of Bashan have beset me round. ¹³They gaped upon me with their mouths, as a ravening and a roaring lion. ¹⁴I am poured out like water, and all my bones are out of joint: my heart is like wax; it is melted in the midst of my bowels. ¹⁵My strength is dried up like a potsherd; and my tongue cleaveth to my jaws; and thou hast brought me into the dust of death. ¹⁶For dogs have compassed me: the assembly of the wicked have inclosed me: they pierced my hands and my feet. ¹⁷I may tell all my bones: they look and stare upon me. ¹⁸They part my garments among them, and cast lots upon my vesture. ¹⁹But be not thou far from me, O LORD: O my strength, haste thee to help me. ²⁰Deliver my soul from the sword; my darling from the power of the dog. ²¹Save me from the lion's mouth: for thou hast heard me from the horns of the unicorns."

Matthew 16:21 "From that time forth began Jesus to shew unto his disciples, how that he must go unto Jerusalem, and suffer many things of the elders and chief priests and scribes, and be killed, and be raised again the third day."

Matthew 17:22-23 "²²And while they abode in Galilee, Jesus said unto them, The Son of man shall be betrayed into the hands of men: ²³And they shall kill him, and the third day he shall be raised again. And they were exceeding sorry."

Matthew 20:18-19 "¹⁸Behold, we go up to Jerusalem; and the Son of man shall be betrayed unto the chief priests and unto the scribes, and they shall condemn him to death, 19And shall deliver him to the Gentiles to mock, and to scourge, and to crucify him: and the third day he shall rise again."

Mark 8:31 "And he began to teach them, that the Son of man must suffer many things, and be rejected of the elders, and of the chief priests, and scribes, and be killed, and after three days rise again."

Luke 9:22 "Saying, The Son of man must suffer many things, and be rejected of the elders and chief priests and scribes, and be slain, and be raised the third day."

Luke 17:24-25 "24For as the lightning, that lighteneth out of the one part under heaven, shineth unto the other part under heaven; so shall also the Son of man be in his day. 25But first must he suffer many things, and be rejected of this generation."

Luke 18:31-33 "31Then he took unto him the twelve, and said unto them, Behold, we go up to Jerusalem, and all things that are written by the prophets concerning the Son of man shall be accomplished. 32For he shall be delivered unto the Gentiles, and shall be mocked, and spitefully entreated, and spitted on: 33And they shall scourge him, and put him to death: and the third day he shall rise again."

Luke 24:25-26 "25Then he said unto them, O fools, and slow of heart to believe all that the prophets have spoken: 26Ought not Christ to have suffered these things, and to enter into his glory?"

Luke 24:44-46 "44And he said unto them, These are the words which I spake unto you, while I was yet with you, that all things must be fulfilled, which were written in the law of Moses, and in the prophets, and in the psalms, concerning me. 45Then opened he their understanding, that they might understand the scriptures, 46And said unto them, Thus it is written, and thus it behoved Christ to suffer, and to rise from the dead the third day."

John 7:16-19 "16Jesus answered them, and said, My doctrine is not mine, but his that sent me. 17If any man will do his will, he shall know of the doctrine, whether it be of God, or whether I speak of myself. 18He that speaketh of himself seeketh his

own glory: but he that seeketh his glory that sent him, the same is true, and no unrighteousness is in him. 19Did not Moses give you the law, and yet none of you keepeth the law? Why go ye about to kill me?"

John 8:37-40 "37I know that ye are Abraham's seed; but ye seek to kill me, because my word hath no place in you. 38I speak that which I have seen with my Father: and ye do that which ye have seen with your father. 39They answered and said unto him, Abraham is our father. Jesus saith unto them, If ye were Abraham's children, ye would do the works of Abraham. 40But now ye seek to kill me, a man that hath told you the truth, which I have heard of God: this did not Abraham."

Acts 3:13-18 "13The God of Abraham, and of Isaac, and of Jacob, the God of our fathers, hath glorified his Son Jesus; whom ye delivered up, and denied him in the presence of Pilate, when he was determined to let him go. 14But ye denied the Holy One and the Just, and desired a murderer to be granted unto you; 15And killed the Prince of life, whom God hath raised from the dead; whereof we are witnesses. 16And his name through faith in his name hath made this man strong, whom ye see and know: yea, the faith which is by him hath given him this perfect soundness in the presence of you all. 17And now, brethren, I wot that through ignorance ye did it, as did also your rulers. 18But those things, which God before had shewed by the mouth of all his prophets, that Christ should suffer, he hath so fulfilled."

Acts 17:3 "Opening and alleging, that Christ must needs have suffered, and risen again from the dead; and that this Jesus, whom I preach unto you, is Christ."

Acts 26:23 "That Christ should suffer, and that he should be the first that should rise from the dead, and should shew light unto the people, and to the Gentiles."

Hebrews 2:9-18 "9But we see Jesus, who was made a little lower than the angels for the suffering of death, crowned with glory and honour; that he by the grace of God should taste death for every man. 10For it became him, for whom are all things, and by whom are all things, in bringing many sons unto glory, to make the captain of their salvation perfect through sufferings. 11For both he that sanctifieth and they who are sanctified are all of one: for which cause he is not ashamed to call them brethren, 12Saying, I will declare thy name unto my brethren, in the midst of the church will I sing praise unto thee. 13And again, I will put my trust in him. And again, Behold I and the children which God hath given me. 14Forasmuch then as the children are partakers of flesh and blood, he also himself likewise took part of the same; that through death he might destroy him that had the power of death, that is, the devil; 15And deliver them who through fear of death were all their lifetime subject to bondage. 16For verily he took not on him the nature of angels; but he took on him the seed of Abraham. 17Wherefore in all things it behoved him to be made like unto his brethren, that he might be a merciful and faithful high priest in things pertaining to God, to make reconciliation for the sins of the people. 18For in that he himself hath suffered being tempted, he is able to succour them that are tempted."

Hebrews 5:5-8 "5So also Christ glorified not himself to be made an high priest; but he that said unto him, Thou art my Son, to day have I begotten thee. 6As he saith also in another place, Thou art a priest for ever after the order of Melchisedec. 7Who in the days of his flesh, when he had offered up prayers and supplications with strong crying and tears unto him that was able to save him from death, and was heard in that he feared; 8Though he were a Son, yet learned he obedience by the things which he suffered."

Hebrews 13:12 "Wherefore Jesus also, that he might sanctify the people with his own blood, suffered without the gate."

1 Peter 1:10-11 "10Of which salvation the prophets have inquired and searched diligently, who prophesied of the grace that should come unto you: 11Searching what, or what manner of time the Spirit of Christ which was in them did signify, when it testified beforehand the sufferings of Christ, and the glory that should follow."

1 Peter 2:21-24 "21For even hereunto were ye called: because Christ also suffered for us, leaving us an example, that ye should follow his steps: 22Who did no sin, neither was guile found in his mouth: 23Who, when he was reviled, reviled not again; when he suffered, he threatened not; but

committed himself to him that judgeth righteously: 24Who his own self bare our sins in his own body on the tree, that we, being dead to sins, should live unto righteousness: by whose stripes ye were healed."

1 Peter 3:18 "For Christ also hath once suffered for sins, the just for the unjust, that he might bring us to God, being put to death in the flesh, but quickened by the Spirit."

1 Peter 4:1 "Forasmuch then as Christ hath suffered for us in the flesh, arm yourselves likewise with the same mind: for he that hath suffered in the flesh hath ceased from sin."

Suffering For Jesus Christ
Philippians 1:29 "For unto you it is given in the behalf of Christ, not only to believe on him, but also to suffer for his sake."

1 Peter 4:1 "Forasmuch then as Christ hath suffered for us in the flesh, arm yourselves likewise with the same mind: for he that hath suffered in the flesh hath ceased from sin."

The Sufferings Of This Present Time
Romans 8:18-23 "18For I reckon that the sufferings of this present time are not worthy to be compared with the glory which shall be revealed in us. 19For the earnest expectation of the creature waiteth for the manifestation of the sons of God. 20For the creature was made subject to vanity, not willingly, but by reason of him who hath subjected the same in hope, 21Because the creature itself also shall be delivered from the bondage of corruption into the glorious liberty of the children of God. 22For we know that the whole creation groaneth and travaileth in pain together until now. 23And not only they, but ourselves also, which have the firstfruits of the Spirit, even we ourselves groan within ourselves, waiting for the adoption, to wit, the redemption of our body."

Those That Suffer For Jesus Christ
Romans 8:14-17 "14For as many as are led by the Spirit of God, they are the sons of God. 15For ye have not received the spirit of bondage again to fear; but ye have received the Spirit of adoption, whereby we cry, Abba, Father. 16The Spirit itself beareth witness with our spirit, that we are the children of God: 17And if children, then heirs; heirs of God, and joint-heirs with Christ; if so be

that we suffer with him, that we may be also glorified together."

2 Corinthians 1:5 "For as the sufferings of Christ abound in us, so our consolation also aboundeth by Christ."

Philippians 3:7-10 "⁷But what things were gain to me, those I counted loss for Christ. ⁸Yea doubtless, and I count all things but loss for the excellency of the knowledge of Christ Jesus my Lord: for whom I have suffered the loss of all things, and do count them but dung, that I may win Christ, ⁹And be found in him, not having mine own righteousness, which is of the law, but that which is through the faith of Christ, the righteousness which is of God by faith: ¹⁰That I may know him, and the power of his resurrection, and the fellowship of his sufferings, being made conformable unto his death."

2 Timothy 2:10-12 "¹⁰Therefore I endure all things for the elect's sakes, that they may also obtain the salvation which is in Christ Jesus with eternal glory. ¹¹It is a faithful saying: For if we be dead with him, we shall also live with him: ¹²If we suffer, we shall also reign with him: if we deny him, he also will deny us."

1 Peter 3:12-17 "¹²For the eyes of the Lord are over the righteous, and his ears are open unto their prayers: but the face of the Lord is against them that do evil. ¹³And who is he that will harm you, if ye be followers of that which is good? ¹⁴But and if ye suffer for righteousness' sake, happy are ye: and be not afraid of their terror, neither be troubled; ¹⁵But sanctify the Lord God in your hearts: and be ready always to give an answer to every man that asketh you a reason of the hope that is in you with meekness and fear: ¹⁶Having a good conscience; that, whereas they speak evil of you, as of evildoers, they may be ashamed that falsely accuse your good conversation in Christ. ¹⁷For it is better, if the will of God be so, that ye suffer for well doing, than for evil doing."

1 Peter 4:1 "Forasmuch then as Christ hath suffered for us in the flesh, arm yourselves likewise with the same mind: for he that hath suffered in the flesh hath ceased from sin."

1 Peter 4:12-19 "¹²Beloved, think it not strange concerning the fiery trial which is to try you, as though some strange thing happened unto you: ¹³But rejoice, inasmuch as ye are partakers of Christ's sufferings; that, when his glory shall be revealed, ye may be glad also with exceeding joy. ¹⁴If ye be reproached for the name of Christ, happy are ye; for the spirit of glory and of God resteth upon you: on their part he is evil spoken of, but on your part he is glorified. ¹⁵But let none of you suffer as a murderer, or as a thief, or as an evildoer, or as a busybody in other men's matters. ¹⁶Yet if any man suffer as a Christian, let him not be ashamed; but let him glorify God on this behalf. ¹⁷For the time is come that judgment must begin at the house of God: and if it first begin at us, what shall the end be of them that obey not the gospel of God? ¹⁸And if the righteous scarcely be saved, where shall the ungodly and the sinner appear? ¹⁹Wherefore let them that suffer according to the will of God commit the keeping of their souls to him in well doing, as unto a faithful Creator."

Revelation 2:8-10 "⁸And unto the angel of the church in Smyrna write; These things saith the first and the last, which was dead, and is alive; ⁹I know thy works, and tribulation, and poverty, (but thou art rich) and I know the blasphemy of them which say they are Jews, and are not, but are the synagogue of Satan. ¹⁰Fear none of those things which thou shalt suffer: behold, the devil shall cast some of you into prison, that ye may be tried; and ye shall have tribulation ten days: be thou faithful unto death, and I will give thee a crown of life."

Revelation 20:4-6 "⁴And I saw thrones, and they sat upon them, and judgment was given unto them: and I saw the souls of them that were beheaded for the witness of Jesus, and for the word of God, and which had not worshipped the beast, neither his image, neither had received his mark upon their foreheads, or in their hands; and they lived and reigned with Christ a thousand years. ⁵But the rest of the dead lived not again until the thousand years were finished. This is the first resurrection. ⁶Blessed and holy is he that hath part in the first resurrection: on such the second death hath no power, but they shall be priests of God and of Christ, and shall reign with him a thousand years."

Walking With Longsuffering

Ephesians 4:1-3 "¹I therefore, the prisoner of the Lord, beseech you that ye walk worthy of the vocation wherewith ye are called, [2]With all lowliness and meekness, with longsuffering, forbearing one another in love; [3]Endeavouring to keep the unity of the Spirit in the bond of peace."

Who Shall Suffer Persecution

1 Corinthians 4:9-13 "[9]For I think that God hath set forth us the apostles last, as it were appointed to death: for we are made a spectacle unto the world, and to angels, and to men. [10]We are fools for Christ's sake, but ye are wise in Christ; we are weak, but ye are strong; ye are honourable, but we are despised. [11]Even unto this present hour we both hunger, and thirst, and are naked, and are buffeted, and have no certain dwellingplace; [12]And labour, working with our own hands: being reviled, we bless; being persecuted, we suffer it: [13]Being defamed, we intreat: we are made as the filth of the world, and are the offscouring of all things unto this day."

2 Timothy 3:12 "Yea, and all that will live godly in Christ Jesus shall suffer persecution."

1 Peter 5:8-10 "[8]Be sober, be vigilant; because your adversary the devil, as a roaring lion, walketh about, seeking whom he may devour: [9]Whom resist stedfast in the faith, knowing that the same afflictions are accomplished in your brethren that are in the world. [10]But the God of all grace, who hath called us unto his eternal glory by Christ Jesus, after that ye have suffered a while, make you perfect, stablish, strengthen, settle you."

Why God's People Suffer

2 Thessalonians 1:3-5 "[3]We are bound to thank God always for you, brethren, as it is meet, because that your faith groweth exceedingly, and the charity of every one of you all toward each other aboundeth; [4]So that we ourselves glory in you in the churches of God for your patience and faith in all your persecutions and tribulations that ye endure: [5]Which is a manifest token of the righteous judgment of God, that ye may be counted worthy of the kingdom of God, for which ye also suffer."

SURETY

Jesus Christ Being Surety

Isaiah 28:16 "Therefore thus saith the Lord GOD, Behold, I lay in Zion for a foundation a stone, a tried stone, a precious corner stone, a sure foundation: he that believeth shall not make haste."

Hebrews 7:15-22 "[15]And it is yet far more evident: for that after the similitude of Melchisedec there ariseth another priest, [16]Who is made, not after the law of a carnal commandment, but after the power of an endless life. [17]For he testifieth, Thou art a priest for ever after the order of Melchisedec. [18]For there is verily a disannulling of the commandment going before for the weakness and unprofitableness thereof. [19]For the law made nothing perfect, but the bringing in of a better hope did; by the which we draw nigh unto God. [20]And inasmuch as not without an oath he was made priest: [21](For those priests were made without an oath; but this with an oath by him that said unto him, The Lord sware and will not repent, Thou art a priest for ever after the order of Melchisedec:) [22]By so much was Jesus made a surety of a better testament."

Those That Are Surety For A Stranger

Proverbs 11:15 "He that is surety for a stranger shall smart for it: and he that hateth suretiship is sure."

Those That Hate Suretyship

Proverbs 11:15 "He that is surety for a stranger shall smart for it: and he that hateth suretiship is sure."

What Is Sure

Psalm 19:7 "The law of the LORD is perfect, converting the soul: the testimony of the LORD is sure, making wise the simple."

Psalm 93:1-5 "[1]The LORD reigneth, he is clothed with majesty; the LORD is clothed with strength, wherewith he hath girded himself: the world also is stablished, that it cannot be moved. [2]Thy throne is established of old: thou art from everlasting. [3]The floods have lifted up, O LORD, the floods have lifted up their voice; the floods lift up their waves. [4]The LORD on high is mightier than the noise of many waters, yea, than the mighty waves of the sea. [5]Thy testimonies are very sure: holiness becometh thine house, O LORD, for ever."

Psalm 111:2-7 "[2]The works of the LORD are great, sought out of all them that have pleasure therein. [3]His work is honourable and glorious: and his righteousness endureth for ever. [4]He hath made his wonderful works to be remembered: the LORD is gracious and full of compassion. [5]He hath given meat unto them that fear him: he will ever be mindful of his covenant. [6]He hath shewed his people the power of his works, that he may give them the heritage of the heathen. [7]The works of his hands are verity and judgment; all his commandments are sure."

Daniel 2:31-45 "[31]Thou, O king, sawest, and behold a great image. This great image, whose brightness was excellent, stood before thee; and the form thereof was terrible. [32]This image's head was of fine gold, his breast and his arms of silver, his belly and his thighs of brass, [33]His legs of iron, his feet part of iron and part of clay. [34]Thou sawest till that a stone was cut out without hands, which smote the image upon his feet that were of iron and clay, and brake them to pieces. [35]Then was the iron, the clay, the brass, the silver, and the gold, broken to pieces together, and became like the chaff of the summer threshingfloors; and the wind carried them away, that no place was found for them: and the stone that smote the image became a great mountain, and filled the whole earth. [36]This is the dream; and we will tell the interpretation thereof before the king. [37]Thou, O king, art a king of kings: for the God of heaven hath given thee a kingdom, power, and strength, and glory. [38]And wheresoever the children of men dwell, the beasts of the field and the fowls of the heaven hath he given into thine hand, and hath made thee ruler over them all. Thou art this head of gold. [39]And after thee shall arise another kingdom inferior to thee, and another third kingdom of brass, which shall bear rule over all the earth. [40]And the fourth kingdom shall be strong as iron: forasmuch as iron breaketh in pieces and subdueth all things: and as iron that breaketh all these, shall it break in pieces and bruise. [41]And whereas thou sawest the feet and toes, part of potters' clay, and part of iron, the kingdom shall be divided; but there shall be in it of the strength of the iron, forasmuch as thou sawest the iron mixed with miry clay. [42]And as the toes of the feet were part of iron, and part of clay, so the kingdom shall be partly strong, and partly broken. [43]And whereas thou sawest iron mixed with miry clay, they shall mingle themselves with the seed of men: but they shall not cleave one to another, even as iron is not

mixed with clay. [44]And in the days of these kings shall the God of heaven set up a kingdom, which shall never be destroyed: and the kingdom shall not be left to other people, but it shall break in pieces and consume all these kingdoms, and it shall stand for ever. [45]Forasmuch as thou sawest that the stone was cut out of the mountain without hands, and that it brake in pieces the iron, the brass, the clay, the silver, and the gold; the great God hath made known to the king what shall come to pass hereafter: and the dream is certain, and the interpretation thereof sure."

2 Timothy 2:19 "Nevertheless the foundation of God standeth sure, having this seal, The Lord knoweth them that are his. And, Let every one that nameth the name of Christ depart from iniquity."

2 Peter 1:19-21 "[19]We have also a more sure word of prophecy; whereunto ye do well that ye take heed, as unto a light that shineth in a dark place, until the day dawn, and the day star arise in your hearts: [20]Knowing this first, that no prophecy of the scripture is of any private interpretation. [21]For the prophecy came not in old time by the will of man: but holy men of God spake as they were moved by the Holy Ghost."

Who Is Sure
Proverbs 11:15 "He that is surety for a stranger shall smart for it: and he that hateth suretiship is sure."

Isaiah 33:15-16 "[15]He that walketh righteously, and speaketh uprightly; he that despiseth the gain of oppressions, that shaketh his hands from holding of bribes, that stoppeth his ears from hearing of blood, and shutteth his eyes from seeing evil; [16]He shall dwell on high: his place of defence shall be the munitions of rocks: bread shall be given him; his waters shall be sure."

SWEARING/VOWING

Not Breaking Your Vows To The Lord
Numbers 30:2 "If a man vow a vow unto the LORD, or swear an oath to bind his soul with a bond; he shall not break his word, he shall do according to all that proceedeth out of his mouth."

Deuteronomy 23:21-23 "[21]When thou shalt vow a vow unto the LORD thy God, thou shalt not slack to pay it: for the LORD thy God will surely require it of thee; and it would be sin in thee. ²²But if thou shalt forbear to vow, it shall be no sin in thee. ²³That which is gone out of thy lips thou shalt keep and perform; even a freewill offering, according as thou hast vowed unto the LORD thy God, which thou hast promised with thy mouth."

Psalm 76:11 "Vow, and pay unto the LORD your God: let all that be round about him bring presents unto him that ought to be feared."

Ecclesiastes 5:4 "When thou vowest a vow unto God, defer not to pay it; for he hath no pleasure in fools: pay that which thou hast vowed."

Not Swearing Or Vowing At All
Ecclesiastes 5:4-6 "⁴When thou vowest a vow unto God, defer not to pay it; for he hath no pleasure in fools: pay that which thou hast vowed. ⁵Better is it that thou shouldest not vow, than that thou shouldest vow and not pay. ⁶Suffer not thy mouth to cause thy flesh to sin; neither say thou before the angel, that it was an error: wherefore should God be angry at thy voice, and destroy the work of thine hands?"

Matthew 5:33-37 "³³Again, ye have heard that it hath been said by them of old time, Thou shalt not forswear thyself, but shalt perform unto the Lord thine oaths: ³⁴But I say unto you, Swear not at all; neither by heaven; for it is God's throne: ³⁵Nor by the earth; for it is his footstool: neither by Jerusalem; for it is the city of the great King. ³⁶Neither shalt thou swear by thy head, because thou canst not make one hair white or black. ³⁷But let your communication be, Yea, yea; Nay, nay: for whatsoever is more than these cometh of evil."

James 5:12 "But above all things, my brethren, swear not, neither by heaven, neither by the earth, neither by any other oath: but let your yea be yea; and your nay, nay; lest ye fall into condemnation."

The Reward For Not Vowing
Deuteronomy 23:21-22 "²¹When thou shalt vow a vow unto the LORD thy God, thou shalt not slack to pay it: for the LORD thy God will surely require it of thee; and it would be sin in thee. ²²But if thou shalt forbear to vow, it shall be no sin in thee."

Those That Keep Their Vows
Even Though They May Be Harmed
Psalm 15:1-5 "¹LORD, who shall abide in thy tabernacle? who shall dwell in thy holy hill? ²He that walketh uprightly, and worketh righteousness, and speaketh the truth in his heart. ³He that backbiteth not with his tongue, nor doeth evil to his neighbour, nor taketh up a reproach against his neighbour. ⁴In whose eyes a vile person is contemned; but he honoureth them that fear the LORD. He that sweareth to his own hurt, and changeth not. ⁵He that putteth not out his money to usury, nor taketh reward against the innocent. He that doeth these things shall never be moved."

Those That Swear By Idols
Amos 8:14 "They that swear by the sin of Samaria, and say, Thy god, O Dan, liveth; and, The manner of Beer-sheba liveth; even they shall fall, and never rise up again."

T*t*

TEACHING

False Teachers

2 Peter 2:1-22 "¹But there were false prophets also among the people, even as there shall be false teachers among you, who privily shall bring in damnable heresies, even denying the Lord that bought them, and bring upon themselves swift destruction. ²And many shall follow their pernicious ways; by reason of whom the way of truth shall be evil spoken of. ³And through covetousness shall they with feigned words make merchandise of you: whose judgment now of a long time lingereth not, and their damnation slumbereth not. ⁴For if God spared not the angels that sinned, but cast them down to hell, and delivered them into chains of darkness, to be reserved unto judgment; ⁵And spared not the old world, but saved Noah the eighth person, a preacher of righteousness, bringing in the flood upon the world of the ungodly; ⁶And turning the cities of Sodom and Gomorrha into ashes condemned them with an overthrow, making them an ensample unto those that after should live ungodly; ⁷And delivered just Lot, vexed with the filthy conversation of the wicked: ⁸(For that righteous man dwelling among them, in seeing and hearing, vexed his righteous soul from day to day with their unlawful deeds;) ⁹The Lord knoweth how to deliver the godly out of temptations, and to reserve the unjust unto the day of judgment to be punished: ¹⁰But chiefly them that walk after the flesh in the lust of uncleanness, and despise government. Presumptuous are they, selfwilled, they are not afraid to speak evil of dignities. ¹¹Whereas angels, which are greater in power and might, bring not railing accusation against them before the Lord. ¹²But these, as natural brute beasts, made to be taken and destroyed, speak evil of the things that they understand not; and shall utterly perish in their own corruption; ¹³And shall receive the reward of unrighteousness, as they that count it pleasure to riot in the day time. Spots they are and blemishes, sporting themselves with their own deceivings while they feast with you; ¹⁴Having eyes full of adultery, and that cannot cease from sin; beguiling unstable souls: an heart they have exercised with covetous practices; cursed children: ¹⁵Which have forsaken the right way, and are gone astray, following the way of Balaam the son of Bosor, who loved the wages of unrighteousness; ¹⁶But was rebuked for his iniquity: the dumb ass speaking with man's voice forbad the madness of the prophet. ¹⁷These are wells without water, clouds that are carried with a tempest; to whom the mist of darkness is reserved for ever. ¹⁸For when they speak great swelling words of vanity, they allure through the lusts of the flesh, through much wantonness, those that were clean escaped from them who live in error. ¹⁹While they promise them liberty, they themselves are the servants of corruption: for of whom a man is overcome, of the same is he brought in bondage. ²⁰For if after they have escaped the pollutions of the world through the knowledge of the Lord and Saviour Jesus Christ, they are again entangled therein, and overcome, the latter end is worse with them than the beginning. ²¹For it had been better for them not to have known the way of righteousness, than, after they have known it, to turn from the holy commandment delivered unto them. ²²But it is happened unto them according to the true proverb, The dog is turned to his own vomit again; and the sow that was washed to her wallowing in the mire."

Teaching Others

Colossians 1:26-28 "²⁶Even the mystery which hath been hid from ages and from generations, but now is made manifest to his saints: ²⁷To whom God would make known what is the riches of the glory of this mystery among the Gentiles; which is Christ in you, the hope of glory: ²⁸Whom we preach, warning every man, and teaching every man in all wisdom; that we may present every man perfect in Christ Jesus:"

Colossians 3:16 "Let the word of Christ dwell in you richly in all wisdom; teaching and admonishing one another in psalms and hymns and spiritual songs, singing with grace in your hearts to the Lord."

The Lord Teaching

2 Samuel 22:33-35 "³³God is my strength and power: and he maketh my way perfect. ³⁴He maketh my feet like hinds' feet: and setteth me upon my high places. ³⁵He teacheth my hands to war; so that a bow of steel is broken by mine arms."

Nehemiah 9:16-20 "[16]But they and our fathers dealt proudly, and hardened their necks, and hearkened not to thy commandments, [17]And re-0fused to obey, neither were mindful of thy wonders that thou didst among them; but hardened their necks, and in their rebellion appointed a captain to return to their bondage: but thou art a God ready to pardon, gracious and merciful, slow to anger, and of great kindness, and forsookest them not. [18]Yea, when they had made them a molten calf, and said, This is thy God that brought thee up out of Egypt, and had wrought great provocations; [19]Yet thou in thy manifold mercies forsookest them not in the wilderness: the pillar of the cloud departed not from them by day, to lead them in the way; neither the pillar of fire by night, to shew them light, and the way wherein they should go. [20]Thou gavest also thy good spirit to instruct them, and withheldest not thy manna from their mouth, and gavest them water for their thirst."

Job 35:10-11 "[10]But none saith, Where is God my maker, who giveth songs in the night; [11]Who teacheth us more than the beasts of the earth, and maketh us wiser than the fowls of heaven?"

Psalm 18:31-34 "[31]For who is God save the LORD? or who is a rock save our God? [32]It is God that girdeth me with strength, and maketh my way perfect. [33]He maketh my feet like hinds' feet, and setteth me upon my high places. [34]He teacheth my hands to war, so that a bow of steel is broken by mine arms."

Psalm 25:5 "Lead me in thy truth, and teach me: for thou art the God of my salvation; on thee do I wait all the day."

Psalm 25:8 "Good and upright is the LORD: therefore will he teach sinners in the way."

Psalm 71:17 "O God, thou hast taught me from my youth: and hitherto have I declared thy wondrous works."

Psalm 94:10-11 "[10]He that chastiseth the heathen, shall not he correct? he that teacheth man knowledge, shall not he know? [11]The LORD knoweth the thoughts of man, that they are vanity."

Psalm 119:65-68 "[65]Thou hast dealt well with thy servant, O LORD, according unto thy word. [66]Teach me good judgment and knowledge: for I have believed thy commandments. [67]Before I was afflicted I went astray: but now have I kept thy word. [68]Thou art good, and doest good; teach me thy statutes."

Psalm 119:89-102 "[89]For ever, O LORD, thy word is settled in heaven. [90]Thy faithfulness is unto all generations: thou hast established the earth, and it abideth. [91]They continue this day according to thine ordinances: for all are thy servants. [92]Unless thy law had been my delights, I should then have perished in mine affliction. [93]I will never forget thy precepts: for with them thou hast quickened me. [94]I am thine, save me; for I have sought thy precepts. [95]The wicked have waited for me to destroy me: but I will consider thy testimonies. [96]I have seen an end of all perfection: but thy commandment is exceeding broad. [97]O how love I thy law! it is my meditation all the day. [98]Thou through thy commandments hast made me wiser than mine enemies: for they are ever with me. [99]I have more understanding than all my teachers: for thy testimonies are my meditation. [100]I understand more than the ancients, because I keep thy precepts. [101]I have refrained my feet from every evil way, that I might keep thy word. [102]I have not departed from thy judgments: for thou hast taught me."

Psalm 143:10 "Teach me to do thy will; for thou art my God: thy spirit is good; lead me into the land of uprightness."

Psalm 144:1 "Blessed be the LORD my strength, which teacheth my hands to war, and my fingers to fight:"

Isaiah 2:1-3 "[1]the word that Isaiah the son of Amoz saw concerning Judah and Jerusalem. [2]And it shall come to pass in the last days, that the mountain of the LORD's house shall be established in the top of the mountains, and shall be exalted above the hills; and all nations shall flow unto it. [3]And many people shall go and say, Come ye, and let us go up to the mountain of the LORD, to the house of the God of Jacob; and he will teach us of his ways, and we will walk in his paths: for out of Zion shall go forth the law, and the word of the LORD from Jerusalem."

Isaiah 48:17 "Thus saith the LORD, thy Redeemer, the Holy One of Israel; I am the LORD thy God which teacheth thee to profit, which leadeth thee by the way that thou shouldest go."

Isaiah 50:4-5 "⁴The Lord GOD hath given me the tongue of the learned, that I should know how to speak a word in season to him that is weary: he wakeneth morning by morning, he wakeneth mine ear to hear as the learned. ⁵The Lord GOD hath opened mine ear, and I was not rebellious, neither turned away back."

Jeremiah 32:33-36 "³³And they have turned unto me the back, and not the face: though I taught them, rising up early and teaching them, yet they have not hearkened to receive instruction. ³⁴But they set their abominations in the house, which is called by my name, to defile it. ³⁵And they built the high places of Baal, which are in the valley of the son of Hinnom, to cause their sons and their daughters to pass through the fire unto Molech; which I commanded them not, neither came it into my mind, that they should do this abomination, to cause Judah to sin. ³⁶And now therefore thus saith the LORD, the God of Israel, concerning this city, whereof ye say, It shall be delivered into the hand of the king of Babylon by the sword, and by the famine, and by the pestilence;"

Micah 4:1-2 "¹But in the last days it shall come to pass, that the mountain of the house of the LORD shall be established in the top of the mountains, and it shall be exalted above the hills; and people shall flow unto it. ²And many nations shall come, and say, Come, and let us go up to the mountain of the LORD, and to the house of the God of Jacob; and he will teach us of his ways, and we will walk in his paths: for the law shall go forth of Zion, and the word of the LORD from Jerusalem."

Matthew 22:16 "And they sent out unto him their disciples with the Herodians, saying, Master, we know that thou art true, and teachest the way of God in truth, neither carest thou for any man: for thou regardest not the person of men."

Mark 12:14 "And when they were come, they say unto him, Master, we know that thou art true, and carest for no man: for thou regardest not the person of men, but teachest the way of God in truth: Is it lawful to give tribute to Caesar, or not?"

Luke 12:11-12 "¹¹And when they bring you unto the synagogues, and unto magistrates, and powers, take ye no thought how or what thing ye shall answer, or what ye shall say: ¹²For the Holy Ghost shall teach you in the same hour what ye ought to say."

Luke 20:21 "And they asked him, saying, Master, we know that thou sayest and teachest rightly, neither acceptest thou the person of any, but teachest the way of God truly:"

John 14:23-26 "²³Jesus answered and said unto him, If a man love me, he will keep my words: and my Father will love him, and we will come unto him, and make our abode with him. ²⁴He that loveth me not keepeth not my sayings: and the word which ye hear is not mine, but the Father's which sent me. ²⁵These things have I spoken unto you, being yet present with you. ²⁶But the Comforter, which is the Holy Ghost, whom the Father will send in my name, he shall teach you all things, and bring all things to your remembrance, whatsoever I have said unto you."

John 16:13-14 "¹³Howbeit when he, the Spirit of truth, is come, he will guide you into all truth: for he shall not speak of himself; but whatsoever he shall hear, that shall he speak: and he will shew you things to come. ¹⁴He shall glorify me: for he shall receive of mine, and shall shew it unto you."

1 Corinthians 2:12-14 "¹²Now we have received, not the spirit of the world, but the spirit which is of God; that we might know the things that are freely given to us of God. ¹³Which things also we speak, not in the words which man's wisdom teacheth, but which the Holy Ghost teacheth; comparing spiritual things with spiritual. ¹⁴But the natural man receiveth not the things of the Spirit of God: for they are foolishness unto him: neither can he know them, because they are spiritually discerned."

The Reward For Teaching A Child The Right Way
Proverbs 22:6 "Train up a child in the way he should go: and when he is old, he will not depart from it."

The Reward For Teaching A Just Man
Proverbs 9:9 "Give instruction to a wise man, and he will be yet wiser: teach a just man, and he will increase in learning."

The Reward For Teaching
Rebellion Against The Lord

Jeremiah 28:16-17 "[16]Therefore thus saith the LORD; Behold, I will cast thee from off the face of the earth: this year thou shalt die, because thou hast taught rebellion against the LORD. [17]So Hananiah the prophet died the same year in the seventh month."

Those That Teach Doctrines
Contrary To Christ's

1 Timothy 1:3-7 "[3]As I besought thee to abide still at Ephesus, when I went into Macedonia, that thou mightest charge some that they teach no other doctrine, [4]Neither give heed to fables and endless genealogies, which minister questions, rather than godly edifying which is in faith: so do. [5]Now the end of the commandment is charity out of a pure heart, and of a good conscience, and of faith unfeigned: [6]From which some having swerved have turned aside unto vain jangling; [7]Desiring to be teachers of the law; understanding neither what they say, nor whereof they affirm."

1 Timothy 6:3-5 "[3]If any man teach otherwise, and consent not to wholesome words, even the words of our Lord Jesus Christ, and to the doctrine which is according to godliness; [4]He is proud, knowing nothing, but doting about questions and strifes of words, whereof cometh envy, strife, railings, evil surmisings, [5]Perverse disputings of men of corrupt minds, and destitute of the truth, supposing that gain is godliness: from such withdraw thyself."

Titus 1:10-16 "[10]For there are many unruly and vain talkers and deceivers, specially they of the circumcision: [11]Whose mouths must be stopped, who subvert whole houses, teaching things which they ought not, for filthy lucre's sake. [12]One of themselves, even a prophet of their own, said, The Cretians are alway liars, evil beasts, slow bellies. [13]This witness is true. Wherefore rebuke them sharply, that they may be sound in the faith; [14]Not giving heed to Jewish fables, and commandments of men, that turn from the truth. [15]Unto the pure all things are pure: but unto them that are defiled and unbelieving is nothing pure; but even their mind and conscience is defiled. [16]They profess that they know God; but in works they deny him, being abominable, and disobedient, and unto every good work reprobate."

Those That Teach Others
To Break The Commandments

Matthew 5:19 "Whosoever therefore shall break one of these least commandments, and shall teach men so, he shall be called the least in the kingdom of heaven: but whosoever shall do and teach them, the same shall be called great in the kingdom of heaven."

Revelation 2:12-16 "[12]And to the angel of the church in Pergamos write; These things saith he which hath the sharp sword with two edges; [13]I know thy works, and where thou dwellest, even where Satan's seat is: and thou holdest fast my name, and hast not denied my faith, even in those days wherein Antipas was my faithful martyr, who was slain among you, where Satan dwelleth. [14]But I have a few things against thee, because thou hast there them that hold the doctrine of Balaam, who taught Balac to cast a stumblingblock before the children of Israel, to eat things sacrificed unto idols, and to commit fornication. [15]So hast thou also them that hold the doctrine of the Nicolaitans, which thing I hate. [16]Repent; or else I will come unto thee quickly, and will fight against them with the sword of my mouth."

Revelation 2:18-23 "[18]And unto the angel of the church in Thyatira write; These things saith the Son of God, who hath his eyes like unto a flame of fire, and his feet are like fine brass; [19]I know thy works, and charity, and service, and faith, and thy patience, and thy works; and the last to be more than the first. [20]Notwithstanding I have a few things against thee, because thou sufferest that woman Jezebel, which calleth herself a prophetess, to teach and to seduce my servants to commit fornication, and to eat things sacrificed unto idols. [21]And I gave her space to repent of her fornication; and she repented not. [22]Behold, I will cast her into a bed, and them that commit adultery with her into great tribulation, except they repent of their deeds. [23]And I will kill her children with death; and all the churches shall know that I am he which searcheth the reins and hearts: and I will give unto every one of you according to your works."

Those That Teach Others
To Keep The Commandments

Matthew 5:19 "Whosoever therefore shall break one of these least commandments, and shall teach men so, he shall be called the least in the kingdom of heaven: but whosoever shall do and teach them, the same shall be called great in the kingdom of heaven."

What Teachers Are For

Ephesians 4:11-14 "[11]And he gave some, apostles; and some, prophets; and some, evangelists; and some, pastors and teachers; [12]For the perfecting of the saints, for the work of the ministry, for the edifying of the body of Christ: [13]Till we all come in the unity of the faith, and of the knowledge of the Son of God, unto a perfect man, unto the measure of the stature of the fulness of Christ: [14]That we henceforth be no more children, tossed to and fro, and carried about with every wind of doctrine, by the sleight of men, and cunning craftiness, whereby they lie in wait to deceive;"

What Teaches

Psalm 119:65-71 "[65]Thou hast dealt well with thy servant, O LORD, according unto thy word. [66]Teach me good judgment and knowledge: for I have believed thy commandments. [67]Before I was afflicted I went astray: but now have I kept thy word. [68]Thou art good, and doest good; teach me thy statutes. [69]The proud have forged a lie against me: but I will keep thy precepts with my whole heart. [70]Their heart is as fat as grease; but I delight in thy law. [71]It is good for me that I have been afflicted; that I might learn thy statutes."

Romans 15:1-4 "[1]We then that are strong ought to bear the infirmities of the weak, and not to please ourselves. [2]Let every one of us please his neighbour for his good to edification. [3]For even Christ pleased not himself; but, as it is written, The reproaches of them that reproached thee fell on me. [4]For whatsoever things were written aforetime were written for our learning, that we through patience and comfort of the scriptures might have hope."

2 Timothy 3:14-17 "[14]But continue thou in the things which thou hast learned and hast been assured of, knowing of whom thou hast learned them; [15]And that from a child thou hast known the holy scriptures, which are able to make thee wise unto salvation through faith which is in Christ Jesus. [16]All scripture is given by inspiration of God, and is profitable for doctrine, for reproof, for correction, for instruction in righteousness:

[17]That the man of God may be perfect, throughly furnished unto all good works."

Titus 2:11-12 "[11]For the grace of God that bringeth salvation hath appeared to all men, [12]Teaching us that, denying ungodliness and worldly lusts, we should live soberly, righteously, and godly, in this present world;"

1 John 2:22-27 "[22]Who is a liar but he that denieth that Jesus is the Christ? He is antichrist, that denieth the Father and the Son. [23]Whosoever denieth the Son, the same hath not the Father: (but) he that acknowledgeth the Son hath the Father also. [24]Let that therefore abide in you, which ye have heard from the beginning. If that which ye have heard from the beginning shall remain in you, ye also shall continue in the Son, and in the Father. [25]And this is the promise that he hath promised us, even eternal life. [26]These things have I written unto you concerning them that seduce you. [27]But the anointing which ye have received of him abideth in you, and ye need not that any man teach you: but as the same anointing teacheth you of all things, and is truth, and is no lie, and even as it hath taught you, ye shall abide in him."

What To Teach

Deuteronomy 4:9-10 "[9]Only take heed to thyself, and keep thy soul diligently, lest thou forget the things which thine eyes have seen, and lest they depart from thy heart all the days of thy life: but teach them thy sons, and thy sons' sons; [10]Specially the day that thou stoodest before the LORD thy God in Horeb, when the LORD said unto me, Gather me the people together, and I will make them hear my words, that they may learn to fear me all the days that they shall live upon the earth, and that they may teach their children."

Deuteronomy 4:14 "And the LORD commanded me at that time to teach you statutes and judgments, that ye might do them in the land whither ye go over to possess it."

Deuteronomy 6:1-9 "[1]Now these are the commandments, the statutes, and the judgments, which the LORD your God commanded to teach you, that ye might do them in the land whither ye go to possess it: [2]That thou mightest fear the LORD thy God, to keep all his statutes and his commandments, which I command thee, thou, and thy son, and thy son's son, all the days of thy life; and that thy days may be prolonged. ³Hear therefore, O Israel, and observe to do it; that it may be well with thee, and that ye may increase mightily, as the LORD God of thy fathers hath promised thee, in the land that floweth with milk and honey. ⁴Hear, O Israel: The LORD our God is one LORD: ⁵And thou shalt love the LORD thy God with all thine heart, and with all thy soul, and with all thy might. ⁶And these words, which I command thee this day, shall be in thine heart: ⁷And thou shalt teach them diligently unto thy children, and shalt talk of them when thou sittest in thine house, and when thou walkest by the way, and when thou liest down, and when thou risest up. ⁸And thou shalt bind them for a sign upon thine hand, and they shall be as frontlets between thine eyes. ⁹And thou shalt write them upon the posts of thy house, and on thy gates."

Deuteronomy 6:20-25 "²⁰And when thy son asketh thee in time to come, saying, What mean the testimonies, and the statutes, and the judgments, which the LORD our God hath commanded you? ²¹Then thou shalt say unto thy son, We were Pharaoh's bondmen in Egypt; and the LORD brought us out of Egypt with a mighty hand: ²²And the LORD shewed signs and wonders, great and sore, upon Egypt, upon Pharaoh, and upon all his household, before our eyes: ²³And he brought us out from thence, that he might bring us in, to give us the land which he sware unto our fathers. ²⁴And the LORD commanded us to do all these statutes, to fear the LORD our God, for our good always, that he might preserve us alive, as it is at this day. ²⁵And it shall be our righteousness, if we observe to do all these commandments before the LORD our God, as he hath commanded us."

Deuteronomy 11:13-21 "¹³And it shall come to pass, if ye shall hearken diligently unto my commandments which I command you this day, to love the LORD your God, and to serve him with all your heart and with all your soul, ¹⁴That I will give you the rain of your land in his due season, the first rain and the latter rain, that thou mayest gather in thy corn, and thy wine, and thine oil. ¹⁵And I will send grass in thy fields for thy cattle, that thou mayest eat and be full. ¹⁶Take heed to yourselves, that your heart be not deceived, and ye turn aside, and serve other gods, and worship them; ¹⁷And then the LORD's wrath be kindled

against you, and he shut up the heaven, that there be no rain, and that the land yield not her fruit; and lest ye perish quickly from off the good land which the LORD giveth you. ¹⁸Therefore shall ye lay up these my words in your heart and in your soul, and bind them for a sign upon your hand, that they may be as frontlets between your eyes. ¹⁹And ye shall teach them your children, speaking of them when thou sittest in thine house, and when thou walkest by the way, when thou liest down, and when thou risest up. ²⁰And thou shalt write them upon the door posts of thine house, and upon thy gates: ²¹That your days may be multiplied, and the days of your children, in the land which the LORD sware unto your fathers to give them, as the days of heaven upon the earth."

Deuteronomy 32:45-46 "⁴⁵And Moses made an end of speaking all these words to all Israel: ⁴⁶And he said unto them, Set your hearts unto all the words which I testify among you this day, which ye shall command your children to observe to do, all the words of this law."

Matthew 28:18-20 "¹⁸And Jesus came and spake unto them, saying, All power is given unto me in heaven and in earth. ¹⁹Go ye therefore, and teach all nations, baptizing them in the name of the Father, and of the Son, and of the Holy Ghost: ²⁰Teaching them to observe all things whatsoever I have commanded you: and, lo, I am with you alway, even unto the end of the world. Amen."

Who Teaches The Doctrine Of Men

Isaiah 29:13-14 "¹³Wherefore the Lord said, Forasmuch as this people draw near me with their mouth, and with their lips do honour me, but have removed their heart far from me, and their fear toward me is taught by the precept of men: ¹⁴Therefore, behold, I will proceed to do a marvellous work among this people, even a marvellous work and a wonder: for the wisdom of their wise men shall perish, and the understanding of their prudent men shall be hid."

Mark 7:6-13 "⁶He answered and said unto them, Well hath Esaias prophesied of you hypocrites, as it is written, This people honoureth me with their lips, but their heart is far from me. ⁷Howbeit in vain do they worship me, teaching for doctrines the commandments of men. ⁸For laying aside the commandment of God, ye hold the tradition of men, as the washing of pots and cups: and many other such like things ye do. ⁹And he said unto them, Full well ye reject the commandment of God, that ye may keep your own tradition. ¹⁰For Moses said, Honour thy father and thy mother; and, Whoso curseth father or mother, let him die the death: ¹¹But ye say, If a man shall say to his father or mother, It is Corban, that is to say, a gift, by whatsoever thou mightest be profited by me; he shall be free. ¹²And ye suffer him no more to do ought for his father or his mother; ¹³Making the word of God of none effect through your tradition, which ye have delivered: and many such like things do ye."

Who The Lord Teaches
Psalm 25:8-9 "⁸Good and upright is the LORD: therefore will he teach sinners in the way. ⁹The meek will he guide in judgment: and the meek will he teach his way."

1 Thessalonians 4:2-9 "²For ye know what commandments we gave you by the Lord Jesus. ³For this is the will of God, even your sanctification, that ye should abstain from fornication: ⁴That every one of you should know how to possess his vessel in sanctification and honour; ⁵Not in the lust of concupiscence, even as the Gentiles which know not God: ⁶That no man go beyond and defraud his brother in any matter: because that the Lord is the avenger of all such, as we also have forewarned you and testified. ⁷For God hath not called us unto uncleanness, but unto holiness. ⁸He therefore that despiseth, despiseth not man, but God, who hath also given unto us his holy Spirit. ⁹But as touching brotherly love ye need not that I write unto you: for ye yourselves are taught of God to love one another."

TEMPERANCE

Those That Are Not Temperate
Proverbs 25:28 "He that hath no rule over his own spirit is like a city that is broken down, and without walls."

2 Peter 1:1-9 "¹Simon Peter, a servant and an apostle of Jesus Christ, to them that have obtained like precious faith with us through the righteousness of God and our Saviour Jesus Christ: ²Grace and peace be multiplied unto you through the

knowledge of God, and of Jesus our Lord, ³According as his divine power hath given unto us all things that pertain unto life and godliness, through the knowledge of him that hath called us to glory and virtue: ⁴Whereby are given unto us exceeding great and precious promises: that by these ye might be partakers of the divine nature, having escaped the corruption that is in the world through lust. ⁵And beside this, giving all diligence, add to your faith virtue; and to virtue knowledge; ⁶And to knowledge temperance; and to temperance patience; and to patience godliness; ⁷And to godliness brotherly kindness; and to brotherly kindness charity. ⁸For if these things be in you, and abound, they make you that ye shall neither be barren nor unfruitful in the knowledge of our Lord Jesus Christ. ⁹But he that lacketh these things is blind, and cannot see afar off, and hath forgotten that he was purged from his old sins."

Those That Are Temperate
Proverbs 16:32 "He that is slow to anger is better than the mighty; and he that ruleth his spirit than he that taketh a city."

2 Peter 1:1-11 "¹Simon Peter, a servant and an apostle of Jesus Christ, to them that have obtained like precious faith with us through the righteousness of God and our Saviour Jesus Christ: ²Grace and peace be multiplied unto you through the knowledge of God, and of Jesus our Lord, ³According as his divine power hath given unto us all things that pertain unto life and godliness, through the knowledge of him that hath called us to glory and virtue: ⁴Whereby are given unto us exceeding great and precious promises: that by these ye might be partakers of the divine nature, having escaped the corruption that is in the world through lust. ⁵And beside this, giving all diligence, add to your faith virtue; and to virtue knowledge; ⁶And to knowledge temperance; and to temperance patience; and to patience godliness; ⁷And to godliness brotherly kindness; and to brotherly kindness charity. ⁸For if these things be in you, and abound, they make you that ye shall neither be barren nor unfruitful in the knowledge of our Lord Jesus Christ. ⁹But he that lacketh these things is blind, and cannot see afar off, and hath forgotten that he was purged from his old sins. ¹⁰Wherefore the rather, brethren, give diligence to make your calling and election sure: for if ye do these things, ye shall never fall: [11]For so an entrance shall be ministered unto you abundantly into the everlasting kingdom of our Lord and Saviour Jesus Christ."

Who Is Temperate
1 Corinthians 9:24-25 "[24]Know ye not that they which run in a race run all, but one receiveth the prize? So run, that ye may obtain. [25]And every man that striveth for the mastery is temperate in all things. Now they do it to obtain a corruptible crown; but we an incorruptible."

Who Should Be Temperate
Titus 2:1-2 "[1]But speak thou the things which become sound doctrine: [2]That the aged men be sober, grave, temperate, sound in faith, in charity, in patience."

TEMPTATION

Alertness And Prayer Preventing Temptation
Matthew 26:41 "Watch and pray, that ye enter not into temptation: the spirit indeed is willing, but the flesh is weak."

Mark 14:38 "Watch ye and pray, lest ye enter into temptation. The spirit truly is ready, but the flesh is weak."

Luke 22:40 "And when he was at the place, he said unto them, Pray that ye enter not into temptation."

Luke 22:46 "And said unto them, Why sleep ye? rise and pray, lest ye enter into temptation."

God Limiting Temptation
1 Corinthians 10:13 "There hath no temptation taken you but such as is common to man: but God is faithful, who will not suffer you to be tempted above that ye are able; but will with the temptation also make a way to escape, that ye may be able to bear it."

God Not Tempting Anyone
James 1:13 "Let no man say when he is tempted, I am tempted of God: for God cannot be tempted with evil, neither tempteth he any man:"

Jesus Christ Being Tempted
Matthew 4:1 "Then was Jesus led up of the Spirit into the wilderness to be tempted of the devil."

Luke 22:22-28 "[22]And truly the Son of man goeth, as it was determined: but woe unto that man by whom he is betrayed! [23]And they began to inquire among themselves, which of them it was that should do this thing. [24]And there was also a strife among them, which of them should be accounted the greatest. [25]And he said unto them, The kings of the Gentiles exercise lordship over them; and they that exercise authority upon them are called benefactors. [26]But ye shall not be so: but he that is greatest among you, let him be as the younger; and he that is chief, as he that doth serve. [27]For whether is greater, he that sitteth at meat, or he that serveth? is not he that sitteth at meat? but I am among you as he that serveth. [28]Ye are they which have continued with me in my temptations."

Hebrews 2:9-18 "[9]But we see Jesus, who was made a little lower than the angels for the suffering of death, crowned with glory and honour; that he by the grace of God should taste death for every man. [10]For it became him, for whom are all things, and by whom are all things, in bringing many sons unto glory, to make the captain of their salvation perfect through sufferings. [11]For both he that sanctifieth and they who are sanctified are all of one: for which cause he is not ashamed to call them brethren, [12]Saying, I will declare thy name unto my brethren, in the midst of the church will I sing praise unto thee. [13]And again, I will put my trust in him. And again, Behold I and the children which God hath given me. [14]Forasmuch then as the children are partakers of flesh and blood, he also himself likewise took part of the same; that through death he might destroy him that had the power of death, that is, the devil; [15]And deliver them who through fear of death were all their lifetime subject to bondage. [16]For verily he took not on him the nature of angels; but he took on him the seed of Abraham. [17]Wherefore in all things it behoved him to be made like unto his brethren, that he might be a merciful and faithful high priest in things pertaining to God, to make reconciliation for the sins of the people. [18]For in that he himself hath suffered being tempted, he is able to succour them that are tempted."

Hebrews 4:14-15 "[14]Seeing then that we have a great high priest, that is passed into the heavens, Jesus the Son of God, let us hold fast our profession. [15]For we have not an high priest which cannot be touched with the feeling of our infirmities; but was in all points tempted like as we are, yet without sin."

Not Tempting The Lord
Deuteronomy 6:16 "Ye shall not tempt the LORD your God, as ye tempted him in Massah."

Matthew 4:7 "Jesus said unto him, It is written again, Thou shalt not tempt the Lord thy God."

1 Corinthians 10:9 "Neither let us tempt Christ, as some of them also tempted, and were destroyed of serpents."

The Lord Knowing How To Deliver The Godly Out Of Temptations
2 Peter 2:9 "The Lord knoweth how to deliver the godly out of temptations, and to reserve the unjust unto the day of judgment to be punished:"

The Reward For Tempting The Lord
1 Corinthians 10:9 "Neither let us tempt Christ, as some of them also tempted, and were destroyed of serpents."

When People Are Tempted
James 1:13-14 "¹³Let no man say when he is tempted, I am tempted of God: for God cannot be tempted with evil, neither tempteth he any man: ¹⁴But every man is tempted, when he is drawn away of his own lust, and enticed."

Who Falls Into Temptation
1 Timothy 6:9 "But they that will be rich fall into temptation and a snare, and into many foolish and hurtful lusts, which drown men in destruction and perdition."

THANKFULNESS

Being Thankful
Colossians 3:15 "And let the peace of God rule in your hearts, to the which also ye are called in one body; and be ye thankful."

1 Thessalonians 5:17-18 "¹⁷Pray without ceasing. ¹⁸In every thing give thanks: for this is the will of God in Christ Jesus concerning you."

Giving Thanks To The Lord
2 Samuel 22:50 "Therefore I will give thanks unto thee, O LORD, among the heathen, and I will sing praises unto thy name."

1 Chronicles 16:8-9 "⁸Give thanks unto the LORD, call upon his name, make known his deeds among the people. ⁹Sing unto him, sing psalms unto him, talk ye of all his wondrous works."

1 Chronicles 16:34 "O give thanks unto the LORD; for he is good; for his mercy endureth for ever."

Psalm 18:46-49 "⁴⁶The LORD liveth; and blessed be my rock; and let the God of my salvation be exalted. ⁴⁷It is God that avengeth me, and subdueth the people under me. ⁴⁸He delivereth me from mine enemies: yea, thou liftest me up above those that rise up against me: thou hast delivered me from the violent man. ⁴⁹Therefore will I give thanks unto thee, O LORD, among the heathen, and sing praises unto thy name."

Psalm 30:4 "Sing unto the LORD, O ye saints of his, and give thanks at the remembrance of his holiness."

Psalm 35:17-18 "¹⁷Lord, how long wilt thou look on? rescue my soul from their destructions, my darling from the lions. ¹⁸I will give thee thanks in the great congregation: I will praise thee among much people."

Psalm 92:1 "It is a good thing to give thanks unto the LORD, and to sing praises unto thy name, O most High:"

Psalm 97:12 "Rejoice in the LORD, ye righteous; and give thanks at the remembrance of his holiness."

Psalm 100:4-5 "⁴Enter into his gates with thanksgiving, and into his courts with praise: be thankful unto him, and bless his name. ⁵For the LORD is good; his mercy is everlasting; and his truth endureth to all generations."

Psalm 105:1-2 "¹O give thanks unto the LORD; call upon his name: make known his deeds among the people. ²Sing unto him, sing psalms unto him: talk ye of all his wondrous works."

Psalm 107:1 "O give thanks unto the LORD, for he is good: for his mercy endureth for ever."

Psalm 118:1 "O give thanks unto the LORD; for he is good: because his mercy endureth for ever."

Psalm 118:29 "O give thanks unto the LORD; for he is good: for his mercy endureth for ever."

Psalm 136:1-26 "¹O give thanks unto the Lord; for he is good: for his mercy endureth for ever. ²O give thanks unto the God of gods: for his mercy endureth for ever. ³O give thanks to the Lord of lords: for his mercy endureth for ever. ⁴To him who alone doeth great wonders: for his mercy endureth for ever. ⁵To him that by wisdom made the heavens: for his mercy endureth for ever. ⁶To him that stretched out the earth above the waters: for his mercy endureth for ever. ⁷To him that made great lights: for his mercy endureth for ever: ⁸The sun to rule by day: for his mercy endureth for ever: ⁹The moon and stars to rule by night: for his mercy endureth for ever. ¹⁰To him that smote Egypt in their firstborn: for his mercy endureth for ever: ¹¹And brought out Israel from among them: for his mercy endureth for ever: ¹²With a strong hand, and with a stretched out arm: for his mercy endureth for ever. ¹³To him which divided the Red sea into parts: for his mercy endureth for ever: ¹⁴And made Israel to pass through the midst of it: for his mercy endureth for ever: ¹⁵But overthrew Pharaoh and his host in the Red sea: for his mercy endureth for ever. ¹⁶To him which led his people through the wilderness: for his mercy endureth for ever. ¹⁷To him which smote great kings: for his mercy endureth for ever: ¹⁸ And slew famous kings: for his mercy endureth for ever: ¹⁹Sihon king of the Amorites: for his mercy endureth for ever: ²⁰And Og the king of Bashan: for his mercy endureth for ever: ²¹And gave their land for an heritage: for his mercy endureth for ever: ²²Even an heritage unto Israel his servant: for his mercy endureth for ever. ²³Who remembered us in our low estate: for his mercy endureth for ever: ²⁴And hath redeemed us from our enemies: for his mercy endureth for ever. ²⁵Who giveth food to all flesh: for his mercy endureth for ever. ²⁶O give thanks unto the God of heaven: for his mercy endureth for ever."

Romans 7:25 "I thank God through Jesus Christ our Lord. So then with the mind I myself serve the law of God; but with the flesh the law of sin."

Ephesians 5:20 "Giving thanks always for all things unto God and the Father in the name of our Lord Jesus Christ;"

Colossians 1:9-12 "⁹For this cause we also, since the day we heard it, do not cease to pray for you, and to desire that ye might be filled with the knowledge of his will in all wisdom and spiritual understanding; ¹⁰That ye might walk worthy of the Lord unto all pleasing, being fruitful in every good work, and increasing in the knowledge of God; ¹¹Strengthened with all might, according to his glorious power, unto all patience and longsuffering with joyfulness; ¹²Giving thanks unto the Father, which hath made us meet to be partakers of the inheritance of the saints in light:"

Colossians 3:17 "And whatsoever ye do in word or deed, do all in the name of the Lord Jesus, giving thanks to God and the Father by him."

1 Thessalonians 2:13 "For this cause also thank we God without ceasing, because, when ye received the word of God which ye heard of us, ye received it not as the word of men, but as it is in truth, the word of God, which effectually worketh also in you that believe."

Hebrews 13:12-15 "¹²Wherefore Jesus also, that he might sanctify the people with his own blood, suffered without the gate. ¹³Let us go forth therefore unto him without the camp, bearing his reproach. ¹⁴For here have we no continuing city, but we seek one to come. ¹⁵By him therefore let us offer the sacrifice of praise to God continually, that is, the fruit of our lips giving thanks to his name."

Who Shall Give Thanks
To The Name Of The Lord
Psalm 140:12-13 "¹²I know that the Lord will maintain the cause of the afflicted, and the right of the poor. ¹³Surely the righteous shall give thanks unto thy name: the upright shall dwell in thy presence."

THEFT

Not Stealing
Exodus 20:15 "Thou shalt not steal."

Leviticus 19:11 "Ye shall not steal, neither deal falsely, neither lie one to another."

Leviticus 19:13 "Thou shalt not defraud thy neighbour, neither rob him: the wages of him that is hired shall not abide with thee all night until the morning."

Deuteronomy 5:19 "Neither shalt thou steal."

Proverbs 22:22 "Rob not the poor, because he is poor: neither oppress the afflicted in the gate:"

Matthew 19:18 "He saith unto him, Which? Jesus said, Thou shalt do no murder, Thou shalt not commit adultery, Thou shalt not steal, Thou shalt not bear false witness,"

Romans 13:8-9 "⁸Owe no man any thing, but to love one another: for he that loveth another hath fulfilled the law. ⁹For this, Thou shalt not commit adultery, Thou shalt not kill, Thou shalt not steal, Thou shalt not bear false witness, Thou shalt not covet; and if there be any other commandment, it is briefly comprehended in this saying, namely, Thou shalt love thy neighbour as thyself."

Ephesians 4:28 "Let him that stole steal no more: but rather let him labour, working with his hands the thing which is good, that he may have to give to him that needeth."

Restoring What You Stole
Leviticus 6:1-5 "¹And the LORD spake unto Moses, saying, ²If a soul sin, and commit a trespass against the LORD, and lie unto his neighbour in that which was delivered him to keep, or in fellowship, or in a thing taken away by violence, or hath deceived his neighbour; ³Or have found that which was lost, and lieth concerning it, and sweareth falsely; in any of all these that a man doeth, sinning therein: ⁴Then it shall be, because he hath sinned, and is guilty, that he shall restore that which he took violently away, or the thing which he hath deceitfully gotten, or that which was delivered him to keep, or the lost thing which he found, ⁵Or all that about which he hath sworn falsely; he shall even restore it in the principal, and shall add the fifth part more thereto, and give it unto him to whom it appertaineth, in the day of his trespass offering."

Proverbs 6:30-31 "³⁰Men do not despise a thief, if he steal to satisfy his soul when he is hungry; ³¹But if he be found, he shall restore sevenfold; he shall give all the substance of his house."

The Reward For Stealing
Hosea 4:1-3 "¹Hear the word of the LORD, ye children of Israel: for the LORD hath a controversy with the inhabitants of the land, because there is no truth, nor mercy, nor knowledge of God in the land. ²By swearing, and lying, and killing, and stealing, and committing adultery, they break out, and blood toucheth blood. ³Therefore shall the land mourn, and every one that dwelleth therein shall languish, with the beasts of the field, and with the fowls of heaven; yea, the fishes of the sea also shall be taken away."

Thieves
Exodus 21:16 "And he that stealeth a man, and selleth him, or if he be found in his hand, he shall surely be put to death."

Proverbs 1:10-19 "¹⁰My son, if sinners entice thee, consent thou not. ¹¹If they say, Come with us, let us lay wait for blood, let us lurk privily for the innocent without cause: ¹²Let us swallow them up alive as the grave; and whole, as those that go down into the pit: ¹³We shall find all precious substance, we shall fill our houses with spoil: ¹⁴Cast in thy lot among us; let us all have one purse: ¹⁵My son, walk not thou in the way with them; refrain thy foot from their path: ¹⁶For their feet run to evil, and make haste to shed blood. ¹⁷Surely in vain the net is spread in the sight of any bird. ¹⁸And they lay wait for their own blood; they lurk privily for their own lives. ¹⁹So are the ways of every one that is greedy of gain; which taketh away the life of the owners thereof."

Proverbs 28:24 "Whoso robbeth his father or his mother, and saith, It is no transgression; the same is the companion of a destroyer."

Those That Partner With Thieves
Proverbs 29:24 "Whoso is partner with a thief hateth his own soul: he heareth cursing, and bewrayeth it not."

Who Made The House Of The Lord
A Den Of Thieves
Matthew 21:12-13 "¹²And Jesus went into the temple of God, and cast out all them that sold and bought in the temple, and overthrew the tables of the moneychangers, and the seats of them that sold doves, ¹³And said unto them, It is written, My house shall be called the house of prayer; but ye have made it a den of thieves."

Mark 11:15-17 "¹⁵And they come to Jerusalem: and Jesus went into the temple, and began to cast out them that sold and bought in the temple, and overthrew the tables of the moneychangers, and the seats of them that sold doves; ¹⁶And would not suffer that any man should carry any vessel through the temple. ¹⁷And he taught, saying unto them, Is it not written, My house shall be called of all nations the house of prayer? but ye have made it a den of thieves."

Luke 19:45-46 "⁴⁵And he went into the temple, and began to cast out them that sold therein, and them that bought; ⁴⁶Saying unto them, It is written, My house is the house of prayer: but ye have made it a den of thieves."

John 2:13-16 "¹³And the Jews' passover was at hand, and Jesus went up to Jerusalem, ¹⁴And found in the temple those that sold oxen and sheep and doves, and the changers of money sitting: ¹⁵And when he had made a scourge of small cords, he drove them all out of the temple, and the sheep, and the oxen; and poured out the changers' money, and overthrew the tables; ¹⁶And said unto them that sold doves, Take these things hence; make not my Father's house an house of merchandise."

THIRST

Thirsting For God

Psalm 42:2 "My soul thirsteth for God, for the living God: when shall I come and appear before God?"

Psalm 63:1 "O God, thou art my God; early will I seek thee: my soul thirsteth for thee, my flesh longeth for thee in a dry and thirsty land, where no water is;"

Those That Thirst After Righteousness

Isaiah 44:1-3 "¹Yet now hear, O Jacob my servant; and Israel, whom I have chosen: ²Thus saith the LORD that made thee, and formed thee from the womb, which will help thee; Fear not, O Jacob, my servant; and thou, Jesurun, whom I have chosen. ³For I will pour water upon him that is thirsty, and floods upon the dry ground: I will pour my spirit upon thy seed, and my blessing upon thine offspring:"

Isaiah 55:1-3 "¹Ho, every one that thirsteth, come ye to the waters, and he that hath no money; come ye, buy, and eat; yea, come, buy wine and milk without money and without price. ²Wherefore do ye spend money for that which is not bread? and your labour for that which satisfieth not? hearken diligently unto me, and eat ye that which is good,

and let your soul delight itself in fatness. ³Incline your ear, and come unto me: hear, and your soul shall live; and I will make an everlasting covenant with you, even the sure mercies of David."

Matthew 5:6 "Blessed are they which do hunger and thirst after righteousness: for they shall be filled."

John 7:37-38 "³⁷In the last day, that great day of the feast, Jesus stood and cried, saying, If any man thirst, let him come unto me, and drink. ³⁸He that believeth on me, as the scripture hath said, out of his belly shall flow rivers of living water."

Revelation 21:6 "And he said unto me, It is done. I am Alpha and Omega, the beginning and the end. I will give unto him that is athirst of the fountain of the water of life freely."

Revelation 22:17 "And the Spirit and the bride say, Come. And let him that heareth say, Come. And let him that is athirst come. And whosoever will, let him take the water of life freely."

Who Shall Not Thirst

Isaiah 65:13 "Therefore thus saith the Lord GOD, Behold, my servants shall eat, but ye shall be hungry: behold, my servants shall drink, but ye shall be thirsty: behold, my servants shall rejoice, but ye shall be ashamed:"

John 4:13-14 "¹³Jesus answered and said unto her, Whosoever drinketh of this water shall thirst again: ¹⁴But whosoever drinketh of the water that I shall give him shall never thirst; but the water that I shall give him shall be in him a well of water springing up into everlasting life."

John 6:35 "And Jesus said unto them, I am the bread of life: he that cometh to me shall never hunger; and he that believeth on me shall never thirst."

Revelation 7:9-17 "⁹After this I beheld, and, lo, a great multitude, which no man could number, of all nations, and kindreds, and people, and tongues, stood before the throne, and before the Lamb, clothed with white robes, and palms in their hands; ¹⁰And cried with a loud voice, saying, Salvation to our God which sitteth upon the throne, and unto the Lamb. ¹¹And all the angels stood round about the throne, and about the elders and the four beasts, and fell before the throne on their faces, and worshipped God, ¹²Saying, Amen: Blessing, and glory, and wisdom, and thanksgiving, and honour, and power, and might, be unto our God for ever and ever. Amen. [13]And one of the elders answered, saying unto me, What are these which are arrayed in white robes? and whence came they? [14]And I said unto him, Sir, thou knowest. And he said to me, These are they which came out of great tribulation, and have washed their robes, and made them white in the blood of the Lamb. [15]Therefore are they before the throne of God, and serve him day and night in his temple: and he that sitteth on the throne shall dwell among them. [16]They shall hunger no more, neither thirst any more; neither shall the sun light on them, nor any heat. [17]For the Lamb which is in the midst of the throne shall feed them, and shall lead them unto living fountains of waters: and God shall wipe away all tears from their eyes."

Who Shall Thirst
Isaiah 65:11-13 "[11]But ye are they that forsake the LORD, that forget my holy mountain, that prepare a table for that troop, and that furnish the drink offering unto that number. [12]Therefore will I number you to the sword, and ye shall all bow down to the slaughter: because when I called, ye did not answer; when I spake, ye did not hear; but did evil before mine eyes, and did choose that wherein I delighted not. [13]Therefore thus saith the Lord GOD, Behold, my servants shall eat, but ye shall be hungry: behold, my servants shall drink, but ye shall be thirsty: behold, my servants shall rejoice, but ye shall be ashamed:"

John 4:11-13 "[11]The woman saith unto him, Sir, thou hast nothing to draw with, and the well is deep: from whence then hast thou that living water? [12]Art thou greater than our father Jacob, which gave us the well, and drank thereof himself, and his children, and his cattle? [13]Jesus answered and said unto her, Whosoever drinketh of this water shall thirst again:"

THRONE

God The Father Giving
Jesus Christ The Throne Of David
Luke 1:31-33 "[31]And, behold, thou shalt conceive in thy womb, and bring forth a son, and shalt call his name JESUS. [32]He shall be great, and shall be called the Son of the Highest: and the Lord God

shall give unto him the throne of his father David: [33]And he shall reign over the house of Jacob for ever; and of his kingdom there shall be no end."

The Throne Of The Lord
Psalm 9:7 "But the LORD shall endure for ever: he hath prepared his throne for judgment."

Psalm 11:4 "The LORD is in his holy temple, the LORD's throne is in heaven: his eyes behold, his eyelids try, the children of men."

Psalm 45:6 "Thy throne, O God, is for ever and ever: the sceptre of thy kingdom is a right sceptre."

Psalm 93:1-2 "[1]The LORD reigneth, he is clothed with majesty; the LORD is clothed with strength, wherewith he hath girded himself: the world also is stablished, that it cannot be moved. [2]Thy throne is established of old: thou art from everlasting."

Psalm 103:19 "The LORD hath prepared his throne in the heavens; and his kingdom ruleth over all."

Lamentations 5:19 "Thou, O LORD, remainest for ever; thy throne from generation to generation."

Daniel 7:9 "I beheld till the thrones were cast down, and the Ancient of days did sit, whose garment was white as snow, and the hair of his head like the pure wool: his throne was like the fiery flame, and his wheels as burning fire."

Hebrews 1:8 "But unto the Son he saith, Thy throne, O God, is for ever and ever: a sceptre of righteousness is the sceptre of thy kingdom."

What Is The Lord's Throne
Isaiah 66:1 "Thus saith the LORD, The heaven is my throne, and the earth is my footstool: where is the house that ye build unto me? and where is the place of my rest?"

Jeremiah 3:17 "At that time they shall call Jerusalem the throne of the LORD; and all the nations shall be gathered unto it, to the name of the LORD, to Jerusalem: neither shall they walk any more after the imagination of their evil heart."

Matthew 5:34-35 "[34]But I say unto you, Swear not at all; neither by heaven; for it is God's throne: [35]Nor by the earth; for it is his footstool: neither by Jerusalem; for it is the city of the great King."

What The Throne Is Established By

Proverbs 16:12 "It is an abomination to kings to commit wickedness: for the throne is established by righteousness."

Who Shall Sit With Christ
On His Throne

Revelation 3:14-21 "14And unto the angel of the church of the Laodiceans write; These things saith the Amen, the faithful and true witness, the beginning of the creation of God; 15I know thy works, that thou art neither cold nor hot: I would thou wert cold or hot. 16So then because thou art lukewarm, and neither cold nor hot, I will spue thee out of my mouth. 17Because thou sayest, I am rich, and increased with goods, and have need of nothing; and knowest not that thou art wretched, and miserable, and poor, and blind, and naked: 18I counsel thee to buy of me gold tried in the fire, that thou mayest be rich; and white raiment, that thou mayest be clothed, and that the shame of thy nakedness do not appear; and anoint thine eyes with eyesalve, that thou mayest see. 19As many as I love, I rebuke and chasten: be zealous therefore, and repent. 20Behold, I stand at the door, and knock: if any man hear my voice, and open the door, I will come in to him, and will sup with him, and he with me. 21To him that overcometh will I grant to sit with me in my throne, even as I also overcame, and am set down with my Father in his throne."

Whose Throne Shall Be Established

2 Samuel 7:8-16 "8Now therefore so shalt thou say unto my servant David, Thus saith the LORD of hosts, I took thee from the sheepcote, from following the sheep, to be ruler over my people, over Israel: 9And I was with thee whithersoever thou wentest, and have cut off all thine enemies out of thy sight, and have made thee a great name, like unto the name of the great men that are in the earth. 10Moreover I will appoint a place for my people Israel, and will plant them, that they may dwell in a place of their own, and move no more; neither shall the children of wickedness afflict them any more, as beforetime, 11And as since the time that I commanded judges to be over my people Israel, and have caused thee to rest from all thine enemies. Also the LORD telleth thee that he will make thee an house. 12And when thy days be fulfilled, and thou shalt sleep with thy fathers, I will set up thy seed after thee, which shall proceed out of thy bowels, and I will establish his kingdom. 13He shall

build an house for my name, and I will stablish the throne of his kingdom for ever. 14I will be his father, and he shall be my son. If he commit iniquity, I will chasten him with the rod of men, and with the stripes of the children of men: 15But my mercy shall not depart away from him, as I took it from Saul, whom I put away before thee. 16And thine house and thy kingdom shall be established for ever before thee: thy throne shall be established for ever."

1 Chronicles 28:2-7 "2Then David the king stood up upon his feet, and said, Hear me, my brethren, and my people: As for me, I had in mine heart to build an house of rest for the ark of the covenant of the LORD, and for the footstool of our God, and had made ready for the building: 3But God said unto me, Thou shalt not build an house for my name, because thou hast been a man of war, and hast shed blood. 4Howbeit the LORD God of Israel chose me before all the house of my father to be king over Israel for ever: for he hath chosen Judah to be the ruler; and of the house of Judah, the house of my father; and among the sons of my father he liked me to make me king over all Israel: 5And of all my sons, (for the LORD hath given me many sons,) he hath chosen Solomon my son to sit upon the throne of the kingdom of the LORD over Israel. 6And he said unto me, Solomon thy son, he shall build my house and my courts: for I have chosen him to be my son, and I will be his father. 7Moreover I will establish his kingdom for ever, if he be constant to do my commandments and my judgments, as at this day."

Job 36:5-7 "5Behold, God is mighty, and despiseth not any: he is mighty in strength and wisdom. 6He preserveth not the life of the wicked: but giveth right to the poor. 7He withdraweth not his eyes from the righteous: but with kings are they on the throne; yea, he doth establish them for ever, and they are exalted."

Psalm 89:19-37 "19Then thou spakest in vision to thy holy one, and saidst, I have laid help upon one that is mighty; I have exalted one chosen out of the people. 20I have found David my servant; with my holy oil have I anointed him: 21With whom my hand shall be established: mine arm also shall strengthen him. 22The enemy shall not exact upon him; nor the son of wickedness afflict him. 23And I will beat down his foes before his face, and plague them that hate him. [24]But my faithfulness and my mercy shall be with him: and in my name shall his horn be exalted. [25]I will set his hand also in the sea, and his right hand in the rivers. [26]He shall cry unto me, Thou art my father, my God, and the rock of my salvation. [27]Also I will make him my firstborn, higher than the kings of the earth. [28]My mercy will I keep for him for evermore, and my covenant shall stand fast with him. [29]His seed also will I make to endure for ever, and his throne as the days of heaven. [30]If his children forsake my law, and walk not in my judgments; [31]If they break my statutes, and keep not my commandments; [32]Then will I visit their transgression with the rod, and their iniquity with stripes. [33]Nevertheless my lovingkindness will I not utterly take from him, nor suffer my faithfulness to fail. [34]My covenant will I not break, nor alter the thing that is gone out of my lips. [35]Once have I sworn by my holiness that I will not lie unto David. [36]His seed shall endure forever, and his throne as the sun before me. [37]It shall be established for ever as the moon, and as a faithful witness in heaven. Selah."

Proverbs 25:4-5 "[4]Take away the dross from the silver, and there shall come forth a vessel for the finer. [5]Take away the wicked from before the king, and his throne shall be established in righteousness."

Proverbs 29:14 "The king that faithfully judgeth the poor, his throne shall be established for ever."

TIME

The Difference Between
The Lord's Time And Our Time
Psalm 90:1-4 "[1]LORD, thou hast been our dwelling place in all generations. [2]Before the mountains were brought forth, or ever thou hadst formed the earth and the world, even from everlasting to everlasting, thou art God. [3]Thou turnest man to destruction; and sayest, Return, ye children of men. [4]For a thousand years in thy sight are but as yesterday when it is past, and as a watch in the night."

2 Peter 3:8 "But, beloved, be not ignorant of this one thing, that one day is with the Lord as a thousand years, and a thousand years as one day."

The Lord's Years
Job 36:26 "Behold, God is great, and we know him not, neither can the number of his years be searched out."

Psalm 102:24-27 "[24]I said, O my God, take me not away in the midst of my days: thy years are throughout all generations. [25]Of old hast thou laid the foundation of the earth: and the heavens are the work of thy hands. [26]They shall perish, but thou shalt endure: yea, all of them shall wax old like a garment; as a vesture shalt thou change them, and they shall be changed: [27]But thou art the same, and thy years shall have no end."

Hebrews 1:10-12 "[10]And, Thou, Lord, in the beginning hast laid the foundation of the earth; and the heavens are the works of thine hands: [11]They shall perish; but thou remainest; and they all shall wax old as doth a garment; [12]And as a vesture shalt thou fold them up, and they shall be changed: but thou art the same, and thy years shall not fail."

There Being A Time For Every Purpose
Ecclesiastes 3:1-9 "[1]To every thing there is a season, and a time to every purpose under the heaven: [2]A time to be born, and a time to die; a time to plant, and a time to pluck up that which is planted; [3]A time to kill, and a time to heal; a time to break down, and a time to build up; [4]A time to weep, and a time to laugh; a time to mourn, and a time to dance; [5]A time to cast away stones, and a time to gather stones together; a time to embrace, and a time to refrain from embracing; [6]A time to get, and a time to lose; a time to keep, and a time to cast away; [7]A time to rend, and a time to sew; a time to keep silence, and a time to speak; [8]A time to love, and a time to hate; a time of war, and a time of peace. [9]What profit hath he that worketh in that wherein he laboureth?"

Ecclesiastes 3:16-17 "[16]And moreover I saw under the sun the place of judgment, that wickedness was there; and the place of righteousness, that iniquity was there. [17]I said in mine heart, God shall judge the righteous and the wicked: for there is a time there for every purpose and for every work."

Ecclesiastes 8:6 "Because to every purpose there is time and judgment, therefore the misery of man is great upon him."

TITHE

The Amount To Be Tithed
Genesis 28:20-22 "²⁰And Jacob vowed a vow, saying, If God will be with me, and will keep me in this way that I go, and will give me bread to eat, and raiment to put on, ²¹So that I come again to my father's house in peace; then shall the LORD be my God: ²²And this stone, which I have set for a pillar, shall be God's house: and of all that thou shalt give me I will surely give the tenth unto thee."

Numbers 18:20-21 "²⁰And the LORD spake unto Aaron, Thou shalt have no inheritance in their land, neither shalt thou have any part among them: I am thy part and thine inheritance among the children of Israel. ²¹And, behold, I have given the children of Levi all the tenth in Israel for an inheritance, for their service which they serve, even the service of the tabernacle of the congregation."

The Tithe Belonging To The Lord
Leviticus 27:30 "And all the tithe of the land, whether of the seed of the land, or of the fruit of the tree, is the LORD's: it is holy unto the LORD."

Tithing Your Increase
Deuteronomy 14:22-29 "²²Thou shalt truly tithe all the increase of thy seed, that the field bringeth forth year by year. ²³And thou shalt eat before the LORD thy God, in the place which he shall choose to place his name there, the tithe of thy corn, of thy wine, and of thine oil, and the firstlings of thy herds and of thy flocks; that thou mayest learn to fear the LORD thy God always. ²⁴And if the way be too long for thee, so that thou art not able to carry it; or if the place be too far from thee, which the LORD thy God shall choose to set his name there, when the LORD thy God hath blessed thee: ²⁵Then shalt thou turn it into money, and bind up the money in thine hand, and shalt go unto the place which the LORD thy God shall choose: ²⁶And thou shalt bestow that money for whatsoever thy soul lusteth after, for oxen, or for sheep, or for wine, or for strong drink, or for whatsoever thy soul desireth: and thou shalt eat there before the LORD thy God, and thou shalt rejoice, thou, and thine household, ²⁷And the Levite that is within thy gates; thou shalt not forsake him; for he hath no part nor inheritance with thee. ²⁸At the end of three years thou shalt bring forth all the tithe of thine increase the same year, and shalt lay it up

within thy gates: ²⁹And the Levite, (because he hath no part nor inheritance with thee,) and the stranger, and the fatherless, and the widow, which are within thy gates, shall come, and shall eat and be satisfied; that the LORD thy God may bless thee in all the work of thine hand which thou doest."

Who Pays Their Tithe, But Does Not Do Weightier Matters Of The Law
Matthew 23:23 "Woe unto you, scribes and Pharisees, hypocrites! for ye pay tithe of mint and anise and cummin, and have omitted the weightier matters of the law, judgment, mercy, and faith: these ought ye to have done, and not to leave the other undone."

Luke 11:42 "But woe unto you, Pharisees! for ye tithe mint and rue and all manner of herbs, and pass over judgment and the love of God: these ought ye to have done, and not to leave the other undone."

Luke 18:9-12 "⁹And he spake this parable unto certain which trusted in themselves that they were righteous, and despised others: ¹⁰Two men went up into the temple to pray; the one a Pharisee, and the other a publican. ¹¹The Pharisee stood and prayed thus with himself, God, I thank thee, that I am not as other men are, extortioners, unjust, adulterers, or even as this publican. ¹²I fast twice in the week, I give tithes of all that I possess."

TONGUES

Those That Speak In An Unknown Tongue
1 Corinthians 14:1-5 "¹Follow after charity, and desire spiritual gifts, but rather that ye may prophesy. ²For he that speaketh in an unknown tongue speaketh not unto men, but unto God: for no man understandeth him; howbeit in the spirit he speaketh mysteries. ³But he that prophesieth speaketh unto men to edification, and exhortation, and comfort. ⁴He that speaketh in an unknown tongue edifieth himself; but he that prophesieth edifieth the church. ⁵I would that ye all spake with tongues, but rather that ye prophesied: for greater is he that prophesieth than he that speaketh with tongues, except he interpret, that the church may receive edifying."

1 Corinthians 14:13 "Wherefore let him that speaketh in an unknown tongue pray that he may interpret."

1 Corinthians 14:27 "If any man speak in an unknown tongue, let it be by two, or at the most by three, and that by course; and let one interpret."

Tongues Vs. Prophesying

1 Corinthians 14:1-40 "[1]Follow after charity, and desire spiritual gifts, but rather that ye may prophesy. [2]For he that speaketh in an unknown tongue speaketh not unto men, but unto God: for no man understandeth him; howbeit in the spirit he speaketh mysteries. [3]But he that prophesieth speaketh unto men to edification, and exhortation, and comfort. [4]He that speaketh in an unknown tongue edifieth himself; but he that prophesieth edifieth the church. [5]I would that ye all spake with tongues, but rather that ye prophesied: for greater is he that prophesieth than he that speaketh with tongues, except he interpret, that the church may receive edifying. [6]Now, brethren, if I come unto you speaking with tongues, what shall I profit you, except I shall speak to you either by revelation, or by knowledge, or by prophesying, or by doctrine? [7]And even things without life giving sound, whether pipe or harp, except they give a distinction in the sounds, how shall it be known what is piped or harped? [8]For if the trumpet give an uncertain sound, who shall prepare himself to the battle? [9]So likewise ye, except ye utter by the tongue words easy to be understood, how shall it be known what is spoken? for ye shall speak into the air. [10]There are, it may be, so many kinds of voices in the world, and none of them is without signification. [11]Therefore if I know not the meaning of the voice, I shall be unto him that speaketh a barbarian, and he that speaketh shall be a barbarian unto me. [12]Even so ye, forasmuch as ye are zealous of spiritual gifts, seek that ye may excel to the edifying of the church. [13]Wherefore let him that speaketh in an unknown tongue pray that he may interpret. [14]For if I pray in an unknown tongue, my spirit prayeth, but my understanding is unfruitful. [15]What is it then? I will pray with the spirit, and I will pray with the understanding also: I will sing with the spirit, and I will sing with the understanding also. [16]Else when thou shalt bless with the spirit, how shall he that occupieth the room of the unlearned say Amen at thy giving of thanks, seeing he understandeth not what thou sayest? [17]For thou verily givest thanks well, but the other is not edified. [18]I thank my God, I speak with tongues more than ye all: [19]Yet in the church I had rather speak five words with my understanding, that by my voice I might teach others also, than ten thousand words in an unknown tongue. [20]Brethren, be not children in understanding: howbeit in malice be ye children, but in understanding be men. [21]In the law it is written, With men of other tongues and other lips will I speak unto this people; and yet for all that will they not hear me, saith the Lord. [22]Wherefore tongues are for a sign, not to them that believe, but to them that believe not: but prophesying serveth not for them that believe not, but for them which believe. [23]If therefore the whole church be come together into one place, and all speak with tongues, and there come in those that are unlearned, or unbelievers, will they not say that ye are mad? [24]But if all prophesy, and there come in one that believeth not, or one unlearned, he is convinced of all, he is judged of all: [25]And thus are the secrets of his heart made manifest; and so falling down on his face he will worship God, and report that God is in you of a truth. [26]How is it then, brethren? when ye come together, everyone of you hath a psalm, hath a doctrine, hath a tongue, hath a revelation, hath an interpretation. Let all things be done unto edifying. [27]If any man speak in an unknown tongue, let it be by two, or at the most by three, and that by course; and let one interpret. [28]But if there be no interpreter, let him keep silence in the church; and let him speak to himself, and to God. [29]Let the prophets speak two or three, and let the other judge. [30]If any thing be revealed to another that sitteth by, let the first hold his peace. [31]For ye may all prophesy one by one, that all may learn, and all may be comforted. [32]And the spirits of the prophets are subject to the prophets. [33]For God is not the author of confusion, but of peace, as in all churches of the saints. [34]Let your women keep silence in the churches: for it is not permitted unto them to speak; but they are commanded to be under obedience, as also saith the law. [35]And if they will learn any thing, let them ask their husbands at home: for it is a shame for women to speak in the church. [36]What? came the word of God out from you? or came it unto you only?

³⁷If any man think himself to be a prophet, or spiritual, let him acknowledge that the things that I write unto you are the commandments of the Lord. ³⁸But if any man be ignorant, let him be ignorant. ³⁹Wherefore, brethren, covet to prophesy, and forbid not to speak with tongues. ⁴⁰Let all things be done decently and in order."

What Tongues Are For
1 Corinthians 14:22 "Wherefore tongues are for a sign, not to them that believe, but to them that believe not: but prophesying serveth not for them that believe not, but for them which believe."

Who Shall Speak With New Tongues
Mark 16:16-19 "¹⁶He that believeth and is baptized shall be saved; but he that believeth not shall be damned. ¹⁷And these signs shall follow them that believe; In my name shall they cast out devils; they shall speak with new tongues; ¹⁸They shall take up serpents; and if they drink any deadly thing, it shall not hurt them; they shall lay hands on the sick, and they shall recover. ¹⁹So then after the Lord had spoken unto them, he was received up into heaven, and sat on the right hand of God."

Acts 2:1-13 "¹And when the day of Pentecost was fully come, they were all with one accord in one place. ²And suddenly there came a sound from heaven as of a rushing mighty wind, and it filled all the house where they were sitting. ³And there appeared unto them cloven tongues like as of fire, and it sat upon each of them. ⁴And they were all filled with the Holy Ghost, and began to speak with other tongues, as the Spirit gave them utterance. ⁵And there were dwelling at Jerusalem Jews, devout men, out of every nation under heaven. ⁶Now when this was noised abroad, the multitude came together, and were confounded, because that every man heard them speak in his own language. ⁷And they were all amazed and marvelled, saying one to another, Behold, are not all these which speak Galilaeans? ⁸And how hear we every man in our own tongue, wherein we were born? ⁹Parthians, and Medes, and Elamites, and the dwellers in Mesopotamia, and in Judaea, and Cappadocia, in Pontus, and Asia, ¹⁰Phrygia, and Pamphylia, in Egypt, and in the parts of Libya about Cyrene, and strangers of Rome, Jews and proselytes, ¹¹Cretes and Arabians, we do hear them speak in our tongues the wonderful works of God. ¹²And they were all amazed, and were in doubt, saying one to another, What meaneth this? ¹³Others mocking said, These men are full of new wine."

TRADITION

Who Makes The Word Of God Ineffective Through The Keeping Of Tradition
Isaiah 29:13 "Wherefore the Lord said, Forasmuch as this people draw near me with their mouth, and with their lips do honour me, but have removed their heart far from me, and their fear toward me is taught by the precept of men:"

Mark 7:6-13 "⁶He answered and said unto them, Well hath Esaias prophesied of you hypocrites, as it is written, This people honoureth me with their lips, but their heart is far from me. ⁷Howbeit in vain do they worship me, teaching for doctrines the commandments of men. ⁸For laying aside the commandment of God, ye hold the tradition of men, as the washing of pots and cups: and many other such like things ye do. ⁹And he said unto them, Full well ye reject the commandment of God, that ye may keep your own tradition. ¹⁰For Moses said, Honour thy father and thy mother; and, Whoso curseth father or mother, let him die the death: ¹¹But ye say, If a man shall say to his father or mother, It is Corban, that is to say, a gift, by whatsoever thou mightest be profited by me; he shall be free. ¹²And ye suffer him no more to do ought for his father or his mother; ¹³Making the word of God of none effect through your tradition, which ye have delivered: and many such like things do ye."

TRANSGRESSION

Casting Away Your Transgressions
Ezekiel 18:31 "Cast away from you all your transgressions, whereby ye have transgressed; and make you a new heart and a new spirit: for why will ye die, O house of Israel?"

The Lord Purging Transgressions
Psalm 65:1-3 "¹Praise waiteth for thee, O God, in Sion: and unto thee shall the vow be performed. ²O thou that hearest prayer, unto thee shall all flesh come. ³Iniquities prevail against me: as for our transgressions, thou shalt purge them away."

Psalm 103:8-12 "⁸The LORD is merciful and gracious, slow to anger, and plenteous in mercy. ⁹He will not always chide: neither will he keep his anger for ever. ¹⁰He hath not dealt with us after our sins; nor rewarded us according to our iniquities. ¹¹For as the heaven is high above the earth, so great is his mercy toward them that fear him. ¹²As far as the east is from the west, so far hath he removed our transgressions from us."

Isaiah 43:16-26 "¹⁶Thus saith the LORD, which maketh a way in the sea, and a path in the mighty waters; ¹⁷Which bringeth forth the chariot and horse, the army and the power; they shall lie down together, they shall not rise: they are extinct, they are quenched as tow. ¹⁸Remember ye not the former things, neither consider the things of old. ¹⁹Behold, I will do a new thing; now it shall spring forth; shall ye not know it? I will even make a way in the wilderness, and rivers in the desert. ²⁰The beast of the field shall honour me, the dragons and the owls: because I give waters in the wilderness, and rivers in the desert, to give drink to my people, my chosen. ²¹This people have I formed for myself; they shall shew forth my praise. ²²But thou hast not called upon me, O Jacob; but thou hast been weary of me, O Israel. ²³Thou hast not brought me the small cattle of thy burnt offerings; neither hast thou honoured me with thy sacrifices. I have not caused thee to serve with an offering, nor wearied thee with incense. ²⁴Thou hast bought me no sweet cane with money, neither hast thou filled me with the fat of thy sacrifices: but thou hast made me to serve with thy sins, thou hast wearied me with thine iniquities. ²⁵I, even I, am he that blotteth out thy transgressions for mine own sake, and will not remember thy sins. ²⁶Put me in remembrance: let us plead together: declare thou, that thou mayest be justified."

Micah 7:18-20 "¹⁸Who is a God like unto thee, that pardoneth iniquity, and passeth by the transgression of the remnant of his heritage? he retaineth not his anger for ever, because he delighteth in mercy. ¹⁹He will turn again, he will have compassion upon us; he will subdue our iniquities; and thou wilt cast all their sins into the depths of the sea. ²⁰Thou wilt perform the truth to Jacob, and the mercy to Abraham, which thou hast sworn unto our fathers from the days of old."

The Reward For Transgression

Psalm 107:17 "Fools because of their transgression, and because of their iniquities, are afflicted."

Proverbs 28:1-2 "¹The wicked flee when no man pursueth: but the righteous are bold as a lion. ²For the transgression of a land many are the princes thereof: but by a man of understanding and knowledge the state thereof shall be prolonged."

Isaiah 43:16-28 "¹⁶Thus saith the LORD, which maketh a way in the sea, and a path in the mighty waters; ¹⁷Which bringeth forth the chariot and horse, the army and the power; they shall lie down together, they shall not rise: they are extinct, they are quenched as tow. ¹⁸Remember ye not the former things, neither consider the things of old. ¹⁹Behold, I will do a new thing; now it shall spring forth; shall ye not know it? I will even make a way in the wilderness, and rivers in the desert. ²⁰The beast of the field shall honour me, the dragons and the owls: because I give waters in the wilderness, and rivers in the desert, to give drink to my people, my chosen. ²¹This people have I formed for myself; they shall shew forth my praise. ²²But thou hast not called upon me, O Jacob; but thou hast been weary of me, O Israel. ²³Thou hast not brought me the small cattle of thy burnt offerings; neither hast thou honoured me with thy sacrifices. I have not caused thee to serve with an offering, nor wearied thee with incense. ²⁴Thou hast bought me no sweet cane with money, neither hast thou filled me with the fat of thy sacrifices: but thou hast made me to serve with thy sins, thou hast wearied me with thine iniquities. ²⁵I, even I, am he that blotteth out thy transgressions for mine own sake, and will not remember thy sins. ²⁶Put me in remembrance: let us plead together: declare thou, that thou mayest be justified. ²⁷Thy first father hath sinned, and thy teachers have transgressed against me. ²⁸Therefore I have profaned the princes of the sanctuary, and have given Jacob to the curse, and Israel to reproaches."

Daniel 9:4-14 "⁴And I prayed unto the LORD my God, and made my confession, and said, O Lord, the great and dreadful God, keeping the covenant and mercy to them that love him, and to them that keep his commandments; ⁵We have sinned, and have committed iniquity, and have done wickedly, and have rebelled, even by departing from thy precepts and from thy judgments: ⁶Neither have we hearkened unto thy servants the prophets, which spake in thy name to our kings, our princes, and our fathers, and to all the people of the land. ⁷O Lord, righteousness belongeth unto thee, but unto us confusion of faces, as at this day; to the men of Judah, and to the inhabitants of Jerusalem, and unto all Israel, that are near, and that are far off, through all the countries whither thou hast driven them, because of their trespass that they have trespassed against thee. ⁸O Lord, to us belongeth confusion of face, to our kings, to our princes, and to our fathers, because we have sinned against thee. ⁹To the Lord our God belong mercies and forgivenesses, though we have rebelled against him; ¹⁰Neither have we obeyed the voice of the Lord our God, to walk in his laws, which he set before us by his servants the prophets. ¹¹Yea, all Israel have transgressed thy law, even by departing, that they might not obey thy voice; therefore the curse is poured upon us, and the oath that is written in the law of Moses the servant of God, because we have sinned against him. ¹²And he hath confirmed his words, which he spake against us, and against our judges that judged us, by bringing upon us a great evil: for under the whole heaven hath not been done as hath been done upon Jerusalem. ¹³As it is written in the law of Moses, all this evil is come upon us: yet made we not our prayer before the Lord our God, that we might turn from our iniquities, and understand thy truth. ¹⁴Therefore hath the Lord watched upon the evil, and brought it upon us: for the Lord our God is righteous in all his works which he doeth: for we obeyed not his voice."

Transgressors
Psalm 37:38 "But the transgressors shall be destroyed together: the end of the wicked shall be cut off."

Proverbs 2:21-22 "²¹For the upright shall dwell in the land, and the perfect shall remain in it. ²²But the wicked shall be cut off from the earth, and the transgressors shall be rooted out of it."

Proverbs 11:3 "The integrity of the upright shall guide them: but the perverseness of transgressors shall destroy them."

Proverbs 11:6 "The righteousness of the upright shall deliver them: but transgressors shall be taken in their own naughtiness."

Proverbs 13:2 "A man shall eat good by the fruit of his mouth: but the soul of the transgressors shall eat violence."

Proverbs 13:15 "Good understanding giveth favour: but the way of transgressors is hard."

Proverbs 21:18 "The wicked shall be a ransom for the righteous, and the transgressor for the upright."

Proverbs 22:12 "The eyes of the Lord preserve knowledge, and he overthroweth the words of the transgressor."

Proverbs 26:10 "The great God that formed all things both rewardeth the fool, and rewardeth transgressors."

Isaiah 66:23-24 "²³And it shall come to pass, that from one new moon to another, and from one sabbath to another, shall all flesh come to worship before me, saith the Lord. ²⁴And they shall go forth, and look upon the carcases of the men that have transgressed against me: for their worm shall not die, neither shall their fire be quenched; and they shall be an abhorring unto all flesh."

2 John 9 "Whosoever transgresseth, and abideth not in the doctrine of Christ, hath not God. He that abideth in the doctrine of Christ, he hath both the Father and the Son."

What Is The Transgression Of The Law
1 John 3:4 "Whosoever committeth sin transgresseth also the law: for sin is the transgression of the law."

When Transgression Increases
Proverbs 29:16 "When the wicked are multiplied, transgression increaseth: but the righteous shall see their fall."

Who Abounds In Transgression
Proverbs 29:22 "An angry man stirreth up strife, and a furious man aboundeth in transgression."

Who Loves Transgression
Proverbs 17:19 "He loveth transgression that loveth strife: and he that exalteth his gate seeketh destruction."

Who Transgresses The Law
James 2:9 "But if ye have respect to persons, ye commit sin, and are convinced of the law as transgressors."

James 2:11 "For he that said, Do not commit adultery, said also, Do not kill. Now if thou commit no adultery, yet if thou kill, thou art become a transgressor of the law."

1 John 3:4 "Whosoever committeth sin transgresseth also the law: for sin is the transgression of the law."

TREACHERY

The Reward For Dealing Treacherously Against The Lord
Hosea 5:7 "They have dealt treacherously against the LORD: for they have begotten strange children: now shall a month devour them with their portions."

TREE OF LIFE

What Is A Tree Of Life
Proverbs 11:30 "The fruit of the righteous is a tree of life; and he that winneth souls is wise."

Proverbs 13:12 "Hope deferred maketh the heart sick: but when the desire cometh, it is a tree of life."

Proverbs 15:4 "A wholesome tongue is a tree of life: but perverseness therein is a breach in the spirit."

Where The Tree Of Life Is
Genesis 2:9 "And out of the ground made the LORD God to grow every tree that is pleasant to the sight, and good for food; the tree of life also in the midst of the garden, and the tree of knowledge of good and evil."

Revelation 2:7 "He that hath an ear, let him hear what the Spirit saith unto the churches; To him that overcometh will I give to eat of the tree of life, which is in the midst of the paradise of God."

Revelation 22:1-2 "¹And he shewed me a pure river of water of life, clear as crystal, proceeding out of the throne of God and of the Lamb. ²In the midst of the street of it, and on either side of the river, was there the tree of life, which bare twelve manner of fruits, and yielded her fruit every month: and the leaves of the tree were for the healing of the nations."

Who Shall Have Access To The Tree Of Life
Revelation 2:7 "He that hath an ear, let him hear what the Spirit saith unto the churches; To him that overcometh will I give to eat of the tree of life, which is in the midst of the paradise of God."

Revelation 22:13-14 "¹³I am Alpha and Omega, the beginning and the end, the first and the last. ¹⁴Blessed are they that do his commandments, that they may have right to the tree of life, and may enter in through the gates into the city."

TRIAL

The Lord Trying
1 Chronicles 29:17 "I know also, my God, that thou triest the heart, and hast pleasure in uprightness. As for me, in the uprightness of mine heart I have willingly offered all these things: and now have I seen with joy thy people, which are present here, to offer willingly unto thee."

Psalm 7:9 "Oh let the wickedness of the wicked come to an end; but establish the just: for the righteous God trieth the hearts and reins."

Psalm 11:4-5 "⁴The LORD is in his holy temple, the LORD's throne is in heaven: his eyes behold, his eyelids try, the children of men. ⁵The LORD trieth the righteous: but the wicked and him that loveth violence his soul hateth."

Psalm 26:2 "Examine me, O LORD, and prove me; try my reins and my heart."

Proverbs 17:3 "The fining pot is for silver, and the furnace for gold: but the LORD trieth the hearts."

Jeremiah 17:9-10 "⁹The heart is deceitful above all things, and desperately wicked: who can know it? ¹⁰I the LORD search the heart, I try the reins, even to give every man according to his ways, and according to the fruit of his doings."

Zechariah 13:9 "And I will bring the third part through the fire, and will refine them as silver is refined, and will try them as gold is tried: they shall call on my name, and I will hear them: I will say, It is my people: and they shall say, The LORD is my God."

The Trying Of Your Faith
James 1:2-3 "[2]My brethren, count it all joy when ye fall into divers temptations; [3]Knowing this, that the trying of your faith worketh patience."

1 Peter 1:6-9 "[6]Wherein ye greatly rejoice, though now for a season, if need be, ye are in heaviness through manifold temptations: [7]That the trial of your faith, being much more precious than of gold that perisheth, though it be tried with fire, might be found unto praise and honour and glory at the appearing of Jesus Christ: [8]Whom having not seen, ye love; in whom, though now ye see him not, yet believing, ye rejoice with joy unspeakable and full of glory: [9]Receiving the end of your faith, even the salvation of your souls."

What Is Tried
2 Samuel 22:31 "As for God, his way is perfect; the word of the LORD is tried: he is a buckler to all them that trust in him."

Psalm 12:6 "The words of the LORD are pure words: as silver tried in a furnace of earth, purified seven times."

Psalm 18:30 "As for God, his way is perfect: the word of the LORD is tried: he is a buckler to all those that trust in him."

What Shall Be Tried
1 Corinthians 3:13-15 "[13]Every man's work shall be made manifest: for the day shall declare it, because it shall be revealed by fire; and the fire shall try every man's work of what sort it is. [14]If any man's work abide which he hath built thereupon, he shall receive a reward. [15]If any man's work shall be burned, he shall suffer loss: but he himself shall be saved; yet so as by fire."

Revelation 3:7-10 "[7]And to the angel of the church in Philadelphia write; These things saith he that is holy, he that is true, he that hath the key of David, he that openeth, and no man shutteth; and shutteth, and no man openeth; [8]I know thy works: behold, I have set before thee an open door, and no man can shut it: for thou hast a little strength, and hast kept my word, and hast not denied my name. [9]Behold, I will make them of the synagogue of Satan, which say they are Jews, and are not, but do lie; behold, I will make them to come and worship before thy feet, and to know that I have loved thee. [10]Because thou hast kept the word of my patience, I also will keep thee from the hour of temptation, which shall come upon all the world, to try them that dwell upon the earth."

What To Try
Lamentations 3:39-40 "[39]Wherefore doth a living man complain, a man for the punishment of his sins? [40]Let us search and try our ways, and turn again to the LORD."

1 John 4:1-3 "[1]Beloved, believe not every spirit, but try the spirits whether they are of God: because many false prophets are gone out into the world. [2]Hereby know ye the Spirit of God: Every spirit that confesseth that Jesus Christ is come in the flesh is of God: [3]And every spirit that confesseth not that Jesus Christ is come in the flesh is not of God: and this is that spirit of antichrist, whereof ye have heard that it should come; and even now already is it in the world."

What Tries Words
Job 34:2-3 "[2]Hear my words, O ye wise men; and give ear unto me, ye that have knowledge. [3]For the ear trieth words, as the mouth tasteth meat."

Who The Lord Tries
Psalm 11:5 "The LORD trieth the righteous: but the wicked and him that loveth violence his soul hateth."

TRIBULATION

There Being Tribulation In The World
John 16:31-33 "[31]Jesus answered them, Do ye now believe? [32]Behold, the hour cometh, yea, is now come, that ye shall be scattered, every man to his own, and shall leave me alone: and yet I am not alone, because the Father is with me. [33]These things I have spoken unto you, that in me ye might have peace. In the world ye shall have tribulation: but be of good cheer; I have overcome the world."

Those Which Came Out Of Great Tribulation
Revelation 7:9-17 "[9]After this I beheld, and, lo, a great multitude, which no man could number, of all nations, and kindreds, and people, and tongues, stood before the throne, and before the Lamb, clothed with white robes, and palms in

their hands; [10]And cried with a loud voice, saying, Salvation to our God which sitteth upon the throne, and unto the Lamb. [11]And all the angels stood round about the throne, and about the elders and the four beasts, and fell before the throne on their faces, and worshipped God, [12]Saying, Amen: Blessing, and glory, and wisdom, and thanksgiving, and honour, and power, and might, be unto our God for ever and ever. Amen. [13]And one of the elders answered, saying unto me, What are these which are arrayed in white robes? and whence came they? [14]And I said unto him, Sir, thou knowest. And he said to me, These are they which came out of great tribulation, and have washed their robes, and made them white in the blood of the Lamb. [15]Therefore are they before the throne of God, and serve him day and night in his temple: and he that sitteth on the throne shall dwell among them. [16]They shall hunger no more, neither thirst any more; neither shall the sun light on them, nor any heat. [17]For the Lamb which is in the midst of the throne shall feed them, and shall lead them unto living fountains of waters: and God shall wipe away all tears from their eyes."

What Tribulation Does
Romans 5:3-4 "[3]And not only so, but we glory in tribulations also: knowing that tribulation worketh patience; [4]And patience, experience; and experience, hope:"

When There Will Be Great Tribulation
Matthew 24:1-22 "[1]And Jesus went out, and departed from the temple: and his disciples came to him for to shew him the buildings of the temple. [2]And Jesus said unto them, See ye not all these things? verily I say unto you, There shall not be left here one stone upon another, that shall not be thrown down. [3]And as he sat upon the mount of Olives, the disciples came unto him privately, saying, Tell us, when shall these things be? and what shall be the sign of thy coming, and of the end of the world? [4]And Jesus answered and said unto them, Take heed that no man deceive you. [5]For many shall come in my name, saying, I am Christ; and shall deceive many. [6]And ye shall hear of wars and rumours of wars: see that ye be not troubled: for all these things must come to pass, but the end is not yet. [7]For nation shall rise against nation, and kingdom against kingdom: and there shall be famines, and pestilences, and earthquakes, in divers places. [8]All these are the beginning of sorrows. [9]Then shall they deliver you up to be afflicted, and shall kill you: and ye shall be hated of all nations for my name's sake. [10]And then shall many be offended, and shall betray one another, and shall hate one another. [11]And many false prophets shall rise, and shall deceive many. [12]And because iniquity shall abound, the love of many shall wax cold. [13]But he that shall endure unto the end, the same shall be saved. [14]And this gospel of the kingdom shall be preached in all the world for a witness unto all nations; and then shall the end come. [15]When ye therefore shall see the abomination of desolation, spoken of by Daniel the prophet, stand in the holy place, (whoso readeth, let him understand:) [16]Then let them which be in Judaea flee into the mountains: [17]Let him which is on the housetop not come down to take any thing out of his house: [18]Neither let him which is in the field return back to take his clothes. [19]And woe unto them that are with child, and to them that give suck in those days! [20]But pray ye that your flight be not in the winter, neither on the sabbath day: [21]For then shall be great tribulation, such as was not since the beginning of the world to this time, no, nor ever shall be. [22]And except those days should be shortened, there should no flesh be saved: but for the elect's sake those days shall be shortened."

Mark 13:1-20 "[1]And as he went out of the temple, one of his disciples saith unto him, Master, see what manner of stones and what buildings are here! [2]And Jesus answering said unto him, Seest thou these great buildings? there shall not be left one stone upon another, that shall not be thrown down. [3]And as he sat upon the mount of Olives over against the temple, Peter and James and John and Andrew asked him privately, [4]Tell us, when shall these things be? and what shall be the sign when all these things shall be fulfilled? [5]And Jesus answering them began to say, Take heed lest any man deceive you: [6]For many shall come in my name, saying, I am Christ; and shall deceive many. [7]And when ye shall hear of wars and rumours of wars, be ye not troubled: for such things must needs be; but the end shall not be yet.

[8]For nation shall rise against nation, and kingdom against kingdom: and there shall be earthquakes in divers places, and there shall be famines and troubles: these are the beginnings of sorrows. [9]But take heed to yourselves: for they shall deliver you up to councils; and in the synagogues ye shall be beaten: and ye shall be brought before rulers and kings for my sake, for a testimony against them. [10]And the gospel must first be published among all nations. [11]But when they shall lead you, and deliver you up, take no thought beforehand what ye shall speak, neither do ye premeditate: but whatsoever shall be given you in that hour, that speak ye: for it is not ye that speak, but the Holy Ghost. [12]Now the brother shall betray the brother to death, and the father the son; and children shall rise up against their parents, and shall cause them to be put to death. [13]And ye shall be hated of all men for my name's sake: but he that shall endure unto the end, the same shall be saved. [14]But when ye shall see the abomination of desolation, spoken of by Daniel the prophet, standing where it ought not, (let him that readeth understand,) then let them that be in Judaea flee to the mountains: [15]And let him that is on the housetop not go down into the house, neither enter therein, to take any thing out of his house: [16]And let him that is in the field not turn back again for to take up his garment. [17]But woe to them that are with child, and to them that give suck in those days! [18]And pray ye that your flight be not in the winter. [19]For in those days shall be affliction, such as was not from the beginning of the creation which God created unto this time, neither shall be. [20]And except that the Lord had shortened those days, no flesh should be saved: but for the elect's sake, whom he hath chosen, he hath shortened the days."

Who Will Have Tribulation

Romans 2:9 "Tribulation and anguish, upon every soul of man that doeth evil, of the Jew first, and also of the Gentile;"

Revelation 2:18-22 "[18]And unto the angel of the church in Thyatira write; These things saith the Son of God, who hath his eyes like unto a flame of fire, and his feet are like fine brass; [19]I know thy works, and charity, and service, and faith, and thy patience, and thy works; and the last to be more than the first. [20]Notwithstanding I have a few things against thee, because thou sufferest that woman Jezebel, which calleth herself a prophetess, to teach and to seduce my servants to commit fornication, and to eat things sacrificed unto idols. [21]And I gave her space to repent of her fornication; and she repented not. [22]Behold, I will cast her into a bed, and them that commit adultery with her into great tribulation, except they repent of their deeds."

TRIBUTE

Rendering Tribute

Matthew 22:16-21 "[16]And they sent out unto him their disciples with the Herodians, saying, Master, we know that thou art true, and teachest the way of God in truth, neither carest thou for any man: for thou regardest not the person of men. [17]Tell us therefore, What thinkest thou? Is it lawful to give tribute unto Caesar, or not? [18]But Jesus perceived their wickedness, and said, Why tempt ye me, ye hypocrites? [19]Shew me the tribute money. And they brought unto him a penny. [20]And he saith unto them, Whose is this image and superscription? [21]They say unto him, Caesar's. Then saith he unto them, Render therefore unto Caesar the things which are Caesar's; and unto God the things that are God's."

Mark 12:14-17 "[14]And when they were come, they say unto him, Master, we know that thou art true, and carest for no man: for thou regardest not the person of men, but teachest the way of God in truth: Is it lawful to give tribute to Caesar, or not? [15]Shall we give, or shall we not give? But he, knowing their hypocrisy, said unto them, Why tempt ye me? bring me a penny, that I may see it. [16]And they brought it. And he saith unto them, Whose is this image and superscription? And they said unto him, Caesar's. [17]And Jesus answering said unto them, Render to Caesar the things that are Caesar's, and to God the things that are God's. And they marvelled at him."

Luke 20:21-25 "[21]And they asked him, saying, Master, we know that thou sayest and teachest rightly, neither acceptest thou the person of any, but teachest the way of God truly: [22]Is it lawful for us to give tribute unto Caesar, or no? [23]But he perceived their craftiness, and said unto them, Why tempt ye me? [24]Shew me a penny. Whose image and superscription hath it? They answered and said, Caesar's. [25]And he said unto them, Render therefore unto Caesar the things which be Caesar's, and unto God the things which be God's."

Romans 13:1-7 "[1]Let every soul be subject unto the higher powers. For there is no power but of God: the powers that be are ordained of God. [2]Whosoever therefore resisteth the power, resisteth the ordinance of God: and they that resist shall receive to themselves damnation. [3]For rulers are not a terror to good works, but to the evil. Wilt thou then not be afraid of the power? do that which is good, and thou shalt have praise of the same: [4]For he is the minister of God to thee for good. But if thou do that which is evil, be afraid; for he beareth not the sword in vain: for he is the minister of God, a revenger to execute wrath upon him that doeth evil. [5]Wherefore ye must needs be subject, not only for wrath, but also for conscience sake. [6]For for this cause pay ye tribute also: for they are God's ministers, attending continually upon this very thing. [7]Render therefore to all their dues: tribute to whom tribute is due; custom to whom custom; fear to whom fear; honour to whom honour."

Who Shall Be Under Tribute
Proverbs 12:24 "The hand of the diligent shall bear rule: but the slothful shall be under tribute."

Why You Should Pay Tribute
Romans 13:1-6 "[1]Let every soul be subject unto the higher powers. For there is no power but of God: the powers that be are ordained of God. [2]Whosoever therefore resisteth the power, resisteth the ordinance of God: and they that resist shall receive to themselves damnation. [3]For rulers are not a terror to good works, but to the evil. Wilt thou then not be afraid of the power? do that which is good, and thou shalt have praise of the same: [4]For he is the minister of God to thee for good. But if thou do that which is evil, be afraid; for he beareth not the sword in vain: for he is the minister of God, a revenger to execute wrath upon him that doeth evil. [5]Wherefore ye must needs be subject, not only for wrath, but also for conscience sake. [6]For for this cause pay ye

tribute also: for they are God's ministers, attending continually upon this very thing."

TROUBLE

Not Being Troubled
John 14:23-27 "[23]Jesus answered and said unto him, If a man love me, he will keep my words: and my Father will love him, and we will come unto him, and make our abode with him. [24]He that loveth me not keepeth not my sayings: and the word which ye hear is not mine, but the Father's which sent me. [25]These things have I spoken unto you, being yet present with you. [26]But the Comforter, which is the Holy Ghost, whom the Father will send in my name, he shall teach you all things, and bring all things to your remembrance, whatsoever I have said unto you. [27]Peace I leave with you, my peace I give unto you: not as the world giveth, give I unto you. Let not your heart be troubled, neither let it be afraid."

John 16:31-33 "[31]Jesus answered them, Do ye now believe? [32]Behold, the hour cometh, yea, is now come, that ye shall be scattered, every man to his own, and shall leave me alone: and yet I am not alone, because the Father is with me. [33]These things I have spoken unto you, that in me ye might have peace. In the world ye shall have tribulation: but be of good cheer; I have overcome the world."

The Lord Bringing You Out Of Trouble
Psalm 143:11 "Quicken me, O LORD, for thy name's sake: for thy righteousness' sake bring my soul out of trouble."

Those That Are Troubled
2 Thessalonians 1:7 "And to you who are troubled rest with us, when the Lord Jesus shall be revealed from heaven with his mighty angels,"

Where Trouble Is
Proverbs 15:6 "In the house of the righteous is much treasure: but in the revenues of the wicked is trouble."

Who Is Born Into Trouble
Job 5:7 "Yet man is born unto trouble, as the sparks fly upward."

Job 14:1-2 "[1]Man that is born of a woman is of few days, and full of trouble. [2]He cometh forth like a flower, and is cut down: he fleeth also as a shadow, and continueth not."

Who Keeps Their Soul From Troubles
Proverbs 21:23 "Whoso keepeth his mouth and his tongue keepeth his soul from troubles."

Who Shall Come Out Of Trouble
Proverbs 11:8 "The righteous is delivered out of trouble, and the wicked cometh in his stead."

Proverbs 12:13 "The wicked is snared by the transgression of his lips: but the just shall come out of trouble."

Who Troubles Their Own House
Proverbs 15:27 "He that is greedy of gain troubleth his own house; but he that hateth gifts shall live."

Why People Have Trouble
Psalm 78:32-37 "32For all this they sinned still, and believed not for his wondrous works. 33Therefore their days did he consume in vanity, and their years in trouble. 34When he slew them, then they sought him: and they returned and inquired early after God. 35And they remembered that God was their rock, and the high God their redeemer. 36Nevertheless they did flatter him with their mouth, and they lied unto him with their tongues. 37For their heart was not right with him, neither were they stedfast in his covenant."

Zechariah 10:1-2 "1Ask ye of the LORD rain in the time of the latter rain; so the LORD shall make bright clouds, and give them showers of rain, to every one grass in the field. 2For the idols have spoken vanity, and the diviners have seen a lie, and have told false dreams; they comfort in vain: therefore they went their way as a flock, they were troubled, because there was no shepherd."

TRUST

The Lord Being Your Trust
Psalm 71:4-5 "4Deliver me, O my God, out of the hand of the wicked, out of the hand of the unrighteous and cruel man. 5For thou art my hope, O Lord GOD: thou art my trust from my youth."

The Reward For Not Trusting In The Lord
Psalm 78:21-31 "21Therefore the LORD heard this, and was wroth: so a fire was kindled against Jacob, and anger also came up against Israel; 22Because they believed not in God, and trusted not in his salvation: 23Though he had commanded the clouds from above, and opened the doors of heaven, 24And had rained down manna upon them to eat, and had given them of the corn of heaven. 25Man did eat angels' food: he sent them meat to the full. 26He caused an east wind to blow in the heaven: and by his power he brought in the south wind. 27He rained flesh also upon them as dust, and feathered fowls like as the sand of the sea: 28And he let it fall in the midst of their camp, round about their habitations. 29So they did eat, and were well filled: for he gave them their own desire; 30They were not estranged from their lust. But while their meat was yet in their mouths, 31The wrath of God came upon them, and slew the fattest of them, and smote down the chosen men of Israel."

The Reward For Trusting In Man
Hosea 10:13-15 "13Ye have plowed wickedness, ye have reaped iniquity; ye have eaten the fruit of lies: because thou didst trust in thy way, in the multitude of thy mighty men. 14Therefore shall a tumult arise among thy people, and all thy fortresses shall be spoiled, as Shalman spoiled Beth-arbel in the day of battle: the mother was dashed in pieces upon her children. 15So shall Bethel do unto you because of your great wickedness: in a morning shall the king of Israel utterly be cut off."

The Reward For Trusting In Oppression And Perverseness
Isaiah 30:12-17 "12Wherefore thus saith the Holy One of Israel, Because ye despise this word, and trust in oppression and perverseness, and stay thereon: 13Therefore this iniquity shall be to you as a breach ready to fall, swelling out in a high wall, whose breaking cometh suddenly at an instant. 14And he shall break it as the breaking of the potters' vessel that is broken in pieces; he shall not spare: so that there shall not be found in the bursting of it a sherd to take fire from the hearth, or to take water withal out of the pit. 15For thus saith the Lord GOD, the Holy One of Israel; In returning and rest shall ye be saved; in quietness and in confidence shall be your strength: and ye would not. 16But ye said, No; for we will flee upon horses; therefore shall ye flee: and, We will ride

upon the swift; therefore shall they that pursue you be swift. [17]One thousand shall flee at the rebuke of one; at the rebuke of five shall ye flee: till ye be left as a beacon upon the top of a mountain, and as an ensign on an hill."

The Reward For Trusting In The Lord

Psalm 33:20-21 "[20]Our soul waiteth for the LORD: he is our help and our shield. [21]For our heart shall rejoice in him, because we have trusted in his holy name."

Psalm 37:3 "Trust in the LORD, and do good; so shalt thou dwell in the land, and verily thou shalt be fed."

Psalm 37:40 "And the LORD shall help them and deliver them: he shall deliver them from the wicked, and save them, because they trust in him."

The Reward For Trusting In Wickedness

Isaiah 47:10-11 "[10]For thou hast trusted in thy wickedness: thou hast said, None seeth me. Thy wisdom and thy knowledge, it hath perverted thee; and thou hast said in thine heart, I am, and none else beside me. [11]Therefore shall evil come upon thee; thou shalt not know from whence it riseth: and mischief shall fall upon thee; thou shalt not be able to put it off: and desolation shall come upon thee suddenly, which thou shalt not know."

Those That Do Not Trust In The Lord

Isaiah 31:1-3 "[1]Woe to them that go down to Egypt for help; and stay on horses, and trust in chariots, because they are many; and in horsemen, because they are very strong; but they look not unto the Holy One of Israel, neither seek the LORD! [2]Yet he also is wise, and will bring evil, and will not call back his words: but will arise against the house of the evildoers, and against the help of them that work iniquity. [3]Now the Egyptians are men, and not God; and their horses flesh, and not spirit. When the LORD shall stretch out his hand, both he that helpeth shall fall, and he that is holpen shall fall down, and they all shall fail together."

Zephaniah 3:1-2 "[1]Woe to her that is filthy and polluted, to the oppressing city! [2]She obeyed not the voice; she received not correction; she trusted not in the LORD; she drew not near to her God."

Those That Trust In Idols

Psalm 115:4-8 "[4]Their idols are silver and gold, the work of men's hands. [5]They have mouths, but they speak not: eyes have they, but they see not: [6]They have ears, but they hear not: noses have they, but they smell not: [7]They have hands, but they handle not: feet have they, but they walk not: neither speak they through their throat. [8]They that make them are like unto them; so is every one that trusteth in them."

Psalm 135:15-18 "[15]The idols of the heathen are silver and gold, the work of men's hands. [16]They have mouths, but they speak not; eyes have they, but they see not; [17]They have ears, but they hear not; neither is there any breath in their mouths. [18]They that make them are like unto them: so is every one that trusteth in them."

Isaiah 42:17 "They shall be turned back, they shall be greatly ashamed, that trust in graven images, that say to the molten images, Ye are our gods."

Habakkuk 2:18-19 "[18]What profiteth the graven image that the maker thereof hath graven it; the molten image, and a teacher of lies, that the maker of his work trusteth therein, to make dumb idols? [19]Woe unto him that saith to the wood, Awake; to the dumb stone, Arise, it shall teach! Behold, it is laid over with gold and silver, and there is no breath at all in the midst of it."

Those That Trust In Man

Isaiah 31:1-3 "[1]Woe to them that go down to Egypt for help; and stay on horses, and trust in chariots, because they are many; and in horsemen, because they are very strong; but they look not unto the Holy One of Israel, neither seek the LORD! [2]Yet he also is wise, and will bring evil, and will not call back his words: but will arise against the house of the evildoers, and against the help of them that work iniquity. [3]Now the Egyptians are men, and not God; and their horses flesh, and not spirit. When the LORD shall stretch out his hand, both he that helpeth shall fall, and he that is holpen shall fall down, and they all shall fail together."

Jeremiah 17:5-6 "[5]Thus saith the LORD; Cursed be the man that trusteth in man, and maketh flesh his arm, and whose heart departeth from the LORD. [6]For he shall be like the heath in the desert, and shall not see when good cometh; but shall inhabit the parched places in the wilderness, in a salt land and not inhabited."

Those That Trust In The Lord

2 Samuel 22:31 "As for God, his way is perfect; the word of the LORD is tried: he is a buckler to all them that trust in him."

2 Kings 18:5-8 "⁵He trusted in the LORD God of Israel; so that after him was none like him among all the kings of Judah, nor any that were before him. ⁶For he clave to the LORD, and departed not from following him, but kept his commandments, which the LORD commanded Moses. ⁷And the LORD was with him; and he prospered whithersoever he went forth: and he rebelled against the king of Assyria, and served him not. ⁸He smote the Philistines, even unto Gaza, and the borders thereof, from the tower of the watchmen to the fenced city."

Psalm 2:11-12 "¹¹Serve the LORD with fear, and rejoice with trembling. ¹²Kiss the Son, lest he be angry, and ye perish from the way, when his wrath is kindled but a little. Blessed are all they that put their trust in him."

Psalm 17:6-7 "⁶I have called upon thee, for thou wilt hear me, O God: incline thine ear unto me, and hear my speech. ⁷Shew thy marvellous lovingkindness, O thou that savest by thy right hand them which put their trust in thee from those that rise up against them."

Psalm 18:30 "As for God, his way is perfect: the word of the LORD is tried: he is a buckler to all those that trust in him."

Psalm 21:7 "For the king trusteth in the LORD, and through the mercy of the most High he shall not be moved."

Psalm 26:1 "Judge me, O LORD; for I have walked in mine integrity: I have trusted also in the LORD; therefore I shall not slide."

Psalm 32:10 "Many sorrows shall be to the wicked: but he that trusteth in the LORD, mercy shall compass him about."

Psalm 34:8 "O taste and see that the LORD is good: blessed is the man that trusteth in him."

Psalm 34:22 "The LORD redeemeth the soul of his servants: and none of them that trust in him shall be desolate."

Psalm 40:4 "Blessed is that man that maketh the LORD his trust, and respecteth not the proud, nor such as turn aside to lies."

Psalm 84:12 "O LORD of hosts, blessed is the man that trusteth in thee."

Psalm 119:41-45 "⁴¹Let thy mercies come also unto me, O LORD, even thy salvation, according to thy word. ⁴²So shall I have wherewith to answer him that reproacheth me: for I trust in thy word. ⁴³And take not the word of truth utterly out of my mouth; for I have hoped in thy judgments. ⁴⁴So shall I keep thy law continually for ever and ever. ⁴⁵And I will walk at liberty: for I seek thy precepts."

Psalm 125:1 "They that trust in the LORD shall be as mount Zion, which cannot be removed, but abideth for ever."

Proverbs 16:20 "He that handleth a matter wisely shall find good: and whoso trusteth in the LORD, happy is he."

Proverbs 28:25 "He that is of a proud heart stirreth up strife: but he that putteth his trust in the LORD shall be made fat."

Proverbs 29:25 "The fear of man bringeth a snare: but whoso putteth his trust in the LORD shall be safe."

Proverbs 30:5 "Every word of God is pure: he is a shield unto them that put their trust in him."

Isaiah 57:13-15 "¹³When thou criest, let thy companies deliver thee; but the wind shall carry them all away; vanity shall take them: but he that putteth his trust in me shall possess the land, and shall inherit my holy mountain; ¹⁴And shall say, Cast ye up, cast ye up, prepare the way, take up the stumblingblock out of the way of my people. ¹⁵For thus saith the high and lofty One that inhabiteth eternity, whose name is Holy; I dwell in the high and holy place, with him also that is of a contrite and humble spirit, to revive the spirit of the humble, and to revive the heart of the contrite ones."

Jeremiah 17:7-8 "⁷Blessed is the man that trusteth in the LORD, and whose hope the LORD is. ⁸For he shall be as a tree planted by the waters, and that spreadeth out her roots by the river, and shall not see when heat cometh, but her leaf shall be green; and shall not be careful in the year of drought, neither shall cease from yielding fruit."

Daniel 3:28 "Then Nebuchadnezzar spake, and said, Blessed be the God of Shadrach, Meshach, and Abed-nego, who hath sent his angel, and delivered his servants that trusted in him, and have changed the king's word, and yielded their bodies, that they might not serve nor worship any god, except their own God."

Nahum 1:7 "The LORD is good, a strong hold in the day of trouble; and he knoweth them that trust in him."

Those That Trust In Their Own Heart
Proverbs 28:26 "He that trusteth in his own heart is a fool: but whoso walketh wisely, he shall be delivered."

Those That Trust In Wealth
Psalm 49:6-20 "6They that trust in their wealth, and boast themselves in the multitude of their riches; 7None of them can by any means redeem his brother, nor give to God a ransom for him: 8(For the redemption of their soul is precious, and it ceaseth for ever:) 9That he should still live for ever, and not see corruption. 10For he seeth that wise men die, likewise the fool and the brutish person perish, and leave their wealth to others. 11Their inward thought is, that their houses shall continue for ever, and their dwelling places to all generations; they call their lands after their own names. 12Nevertheless man being in honour abideth not: he is like the beasts that perish. 13This their way is their folly: yet their posterity approve their sayings. Selah. 14Like sheep they are laid in the grave; death shall feed on them; and the upright shall have dominion over them in the morning; and their beauty shall consume in the grave from their dwelling. 15But God will redeem my soul from the power of the grave: for he shall receive me. Selah. 16Be not thou afraid when one is made rich, when the glory of his house is increased; 17For when he dieth he shall carry nothing away: his glory shall not descend after him. 18Though while he lived he blessed his soul: and men will praise thee, when thou doest well to thyself. 19He shall go to the generation of his fathers; they shall never see light. 20Man that is in honour, and understandeth not, is like the beasts that perish."

Psalm 52:1-7 "1Why boastest thou thyself in mischief, O mighty man? the goodness of God endureth continually. 2Thy tongue deviseth mischiefs; like a sharp rasor, working deceitfully. 3Thou lovest evil more than good; and lying rather than to speak righteousness. Selah. 4Thou lovest all devouring words, O thou deceitful tongue. 5God shall likewise destroy thee for ever, he shall take thee away, and pluck thee out of thy dwelling place, and root thee out of the land of the living. Selah. 6The righteous also shall see, and fear, and shall laugh at him: 7Lo, this is the man that made not God his strength; but trusted in the abundance of his riches, and strengthened himself in his wickedness."

Proverbs 11:28 "He that trusteth in his riches shall fall: but the righteous shall flourish as a branch."

Matthew 19:23-26 "23Then said Jesus unto his disciples, Verily I say unto you, That a rich man shall hardly enter into the kingdom of heaven. 24And again I say unto you, It is easier for a camel to go through the eye of a needle, than for a rich man to enter into the kingdom of God. 25When his disciples heard it, they were exceedingly amazed, saying, Who then can be saved? 26But Jesus beheld them, and said unto them, With men this is impossible; but with God all things are possible."

Mark 10:23-27 "23And Jesus looked round about, and saith unto his disciples, How hardly shall they that have riches enter into the kingdom of God! 24And the disciples were astonished at his words. But Jesus answereth again, and saith unto them, Children, how hard is it for them that trust in riches to enter into the kingdom of God! 25It is easier for a camel to go through the eye of a needle, than for a rich man to enter into the kingdom of God. 26And they were astonished out of measure, saying among themselves, Who then can be saved? 27And Jesus looking upon them saith, With men it is impossible, but not with God: for with God all things are possible."

Luke 18:24-27 "24And when Jesus saw that he was very sorrowful, he said, How hardly shall they that have riches enter into the kingdom of God! 25For it is easier for a camel to go through a needle's eye, than for a rich man to enter into the kingdom of God. 26And they that heard it said, Who then can be saved? 27And he said, The things which are impossible with men are possible with God."

Trusting In The Lord

2 Samuel 22:3 "The God of my rock; in him will I trust: he is my shield, and the horn of my salvation, my high tower, and my refuge, my saviour; thou savest me from violence."

Job 13:15-16 "[15]Though he slay me, yet will I trust in him: but I will maintain mine own ways before him. [16]He also shall be my salvation: for an hypocrite shall not come before him."

Psalm 4:5 "Offer the sacrifices of righteousness, and put your trust in the LORD."

Psalm 11:1 "In the LORD put I my trust: How say ye to my soul, Flee as a bird to your mountain?"

Psalm 13:5-6 "[5]But I have trusted in thy mercy; my heart shall rejoice in thy salvation. [6]I will sing unto the LORD, because he hath dealt bountifully with me."

Psalm 16:1 "Preserve me, O God: for in thee do I put my trust."

Psalm 18:2 "The LORD is my rock, and my fortress, and my deliverer; my God, my strength, in whom I will trust; my buckler, and the horn of my salvation, and my high tower."

Psalm 20:6-7 "[6]Now know I that the LORD saveth his anointed; he will hear him from his holy heaven with the saving strength of his right hand. [7]Some trust in chariots, and some in horses: but we will remember the name of the LORD our God."

Psalm 25:1-2 "[1]Unto thee, O LORD, do I lift up my soul. [2]O my God, I trust in thee: let me not be ashamed, let not mine enemies triumph over me."

Psalm 25:15-20 "[15]Mine eyes are ever toward the LORD; for he shall pluck my feet out of the net. [16]Turn thee unto me, and have mercy upon me; for I am desolate and afflicted. [17]The troubles of my heart are enlarged: O bring thou me out of my distresses. [18]Look upon mine affliction and my pain; and forgive all my sins. [19]Consider mine enemies; for they are many; and they hate me with cruel hatred. [20]O keep my soul, and deliver me: let me not be ashamed; for I put my trust in thee."

Psalm 28:7 "The LORD is my strength and my shield; my heart trusted in him, and I am helped: therefore my heart greatly rejoiceth; and with my song will I praise him."

Psalm 31:1 "In thee, O LORD, do I put my trust; let me never be ashamed: deliver me in thy righteousness."

Psalm 31:6 "I have hated them that regard lying vanities: but I trust in the LORD."

Psalm 31:14 "But I trusted in thee, O LORD: I said, Thou art my God."

Psalm 37:3 "Trust in the LORD, and do good; so shalt thou dwell in the land, and verily thou shalt be fed."

Psalm 37:5 "Commit thy way unto the LORD; trust also in him; and he shall bring it to pass."

Psalm 52:8 "But I am like a green olive tree in the house of God: I trust in the mercy of God for ever and ever."

Psalm 55:23 "But thou, O God, shalt bring them down into the pit of destruction: bloody and deceitful men shall not live out half their days; but I will trust in thee."

Psalm 56:4 "In God I will praise his word, in God I have put my trust; I will not fear what flesh can do unto me."

Psalm 56:11 "In God have I put my trust: I will not be afraid what man can do unto me."

Psalm 57:1 "Be merciful unto me, O God, be merciful unto me: for my soul trusteth in thee: yea, in the shadow of thy wings will I make my refuge, until these calamities be overpast."

Psalm 61:1-4 "[1]Hear my cry, O God; attend unto my prayer. [2]From the end of the earth will I cry unto thee, when my heart is overwhelmed: lead me to the rock that is higher than I. [3]For thou hast been a shelter for me, and a strong tower from the enemy. [4]I will abide in thy tabernacle for ever: I will trust in the covert of thy wings. Selah."

Psalm 62:7-8 "[7]In God is my salvation and my glory: the rock of my strength, and my refuge, is in God. [8]Trust in him at all times; ye people, pour out your heart before him: God is a refuge for us. Selah."

Psalm 71:1 "In thee, O LORD, do I put my trust: let me never be put to confusion."

Psalm 73:28 "But it is good for me to draw near to God: I have put my trust in the Lord GOD, that I may declare all thy works."

Psalm 91:2 "I will say of the LORD, He is my refuge and my fortress: my God; in him will I trust."

Psalm 115:9-11 "⁹O Israel, trust thou in the LORD: he is their help and their shield. ¹⁰O house of Aaron, trust in the LORD: he is their help and their shield. ¹¹Ye that fear the LORD, trust in the LORD: he is their help and their shield."

Psalm 118:8-9 "⁸It is better to trust in the LORD than to put confidence in man. ⁹It is better to trust in the LORD than to put confidence in princes."

Psalm 141:8 "But mine eyes are unto thee, O GOD the Lord: in thee is my trust; leave not my soul destitute."

Psalm 143:7-8 "⁷Hear me speedily, O LORD: my spirit faileth: hide not thy face from me, lest I be like unto them that go down into the pit. ⁸Cause me to hear thy lovingkindness in the morning; for in thee do I trust: cause me to know the way wherein I should walk; for I lift up my soul unto thee."

Psalm 144:1-2 "¹Blessed be the LORD my strength, which teacheth my hands to war, and my fingers to fight: ²My goodness, and my fortress; my high tower, and my deliverer; my shield, and he in whom I trust; who subdueth my people under me."

Proverbs 3:5 "Trust in the LORD with all thine heart; and lean not unto thine own understanding."

Isaiah 12:2 "Behold, God is my salvation; I will trust, and not be afraid: for the LORD JEHOVAH is my strength and my song; he also is become my salvation."

Isaiah 26:4 "Trust ye in the LORD for ever: for in the LORD JEHOVAH is everlasting strength:"

Isaiah 50:10 "Who is among you that feareth the LORD, that obeyeth the voice of his servant, that walketh in darkness, and hath no light? let him trust in the name of the LORD, and stay upon his God."

2 Corinthians 1:9 "But we had the sentence of death in ourselves, that we should not trust in ourselves, but in God which raiseth the dead:"

Colossians 2:6 "As ye have therefore received Christ Jesus the Lord, so walk ye in him:"

1 Timothy 6:17 "Charge them that are rich in this world, that they be not highminded, nor trust in uncertain riches, but in the living God, who giveth us richly all things to enjoy;"

Hebrews 2:9-13 "⁹But we see Jesus, who was made a little lower than the angels for the suffering of death, crowned with glory and honour; that he by the grace of God should taste death for every man. ¹⁰For it became him, for whom are all things, and by whom are all things, in bringing many sons unto glory, to make the captain of their salvation perfect through sufferings. ¹¹For both he that sanctifieth and they who are sanctified are all of one: for which cause he is not ashamed to call them brethren, ¹²Saying, I will declare thy name unto my brethren, in the midst of the church will I sing praise unto thee. ¹³And again, I will put my trust in him. And again, Behold I and the children which God hath given me."

What Not To Trust In
Job 15:31 "Let not him that is deceived trust in vanity: for vanity shall be his recompence."

Psalm 62:10 "Trust not in oppression, and become not vain in robbery: if riches increase, set not your heart upon them."

1 Timothy 6:17 "Charge them that are rich in this world, that they be not highminded, nor trust in uncertain riches, but in the living God, who giveth us richly all things to enjoy;"

Who Not To Trust In
Psalm 118:8-9 "⁸It is better to trust in the LORD than to put confidence in man. ⁹It is better to trust in the LORD than to put confidence in princes."

Psalm 146:3 "Put not your trust in princes, nor in the son of man, in whom there is no help."

Jeremiah 9:4-6 "[4]Take ye heed every one of his neighbour, and trust ye not in any brother: for every brother will utterly supplant, and every neighbour will walk with slanders. [5]And they will deceive every one his neighbour, and will not speak the truth: they have taught their tongue to speak lies, and weary themselves to commit iniquity. [6]Thine habitation is in the midst of deceit; through deceit they refuse to know me, saith the LORD."

Micah 7:1-6 "[1]Woe is me! for I am as when they have gathered the summer fruits, as the grape-gleanings of the vintage: there is no cluster to eat: my soul desired the firstripe fruit. [2]The good man is perished out of the earth: and there is none upright among men: they all lie in wait for blood; they hunt every man his brother with a net. [3]That they may do evil with both hands earnestly, the prince asketh, and the judge asketh for a reward; and the great man, he uttereth his mischievous desire: so they wrap it up. [4]The best of them is as a brier: the most upright is sharper than a thorn hedge: the day of thy watchmen and thy visitation cometh; now shall be their perplexity. [5]Trust ye not in a friend, put ye not confidence in a guide: keep the doors of thy mouth from her that lieth in thy bosom. [6]For the son dishonoureth the father, the daughter riseth up against her mother, the daughter in law against her mother in law; a man's enemies are the men of his own house."

2 Corinthians 1:9 "But we had the sentence of death in ourselves, that we should not trust in ourselves, but in God which raiseth the dead:"

Who Trusts In The Lord
Psalm 9:9-10 "[9]The LORD also will be a refuge for the oppressed, a refuge in times of trouble. [10]And they that know thy name will put their trust in thee: for thou, LORD, hast not forsaken them that seek thee."

Psalm 36:7 "How excellent is thy lovingkindness, O God! therefore the children of men put their trust under the shadow of thy wings."

Psalm 64:10 "The righteous shall be glad in the LORD, and shall trust in him; and all the upright in heart shall glory."

Psalm 112:6-7 "[6]Surely he shall not be moved for ever: the righteous shall be in everlasting remembrance. [7]He shall not be afraid of evil tidings: his heart is fixed, trusting in the LORD."

Who Trusts In Vanity
Isaiah 59:1-4 "[1]Behold, the LORD's hand is not shortened, that it cannot save; neither his ear heavy, that it cannot hear: [2]But your iniquities have separated between you and your God, and your sins have hid his face from you, that he will not hear. [3]For your hands are defiled with blood, and your fingers with iniquity; your lips have spoken lies, your tongue hath muttered perverseness. [4]None calleth for justice, nor any pleadeth for truth: they trust in vanity, and speak lies; they conceive mischief, and bring forth iniquity."

TRUTH

Buying The Truth
Proverbs 23:23 "Buy the truth, and sell it not; also wisdom, and instruction, and understanding."

How To Recognize The Spirit Of Truth
1 John 4:6 "We are of God: he that knoweth God heareth us; he that is not of God heareth not us. Hereby know we the spirit of truth, and the spirit of error."

Speaking The Truth
Zechariah 8:16 "These are the things that ye shall do; Speak ye every man the truth to his neighbour; execute the judgment of truth and peace in your gates:"

Ephesians 4:25 "Wherefore putting away lying, speak every man truth with his neighbour: for we are members one of another."

The Lip Of Truth
Proverbs 12:19 "The lip of truth shall be established for ever: but a lying tongue is but for a moment."

The Lord Being True
Exodus 34:6 "And the LORD passed by before him, and proclaimed, The LORD, The LORD God, merciful and gracious, longsuffering, and abundant in goodness and truth,"

Deuteronomy 32:4 "He is the Rock, his work is perfect: for all his ways are judgment: a God of truth and without iniquity, just and right is he."

Psalm 31:5 "Into thine hand I commit my spirit: thou hast redeemed me, O LORD God of truth."

Psalm 86:15 "But thou, O Lord, art a God full of compassion, and gracious, longsuffering, and plenteous in mercy and truth."

Jeremiah 10:10 "But the LORD is the true God, he is the living God, and an everlasting king: at his wrath the earth shall tremble, and the nations shall not be able to abide his indignation."

Matthew 22:16 "And they sent out unto him their disciples with the Herodians, saying, Master, we know that thou art true, and teachest the way of God in truth, neither carest thou for any man: for thou regardest not the person of men."

Mark 12:14 "And when they were come, they say unto him, Master, we know that thou art true, and carest for no man: for thou regardest not the person of men, but teachest the way of God in truth: Is it lawful to give tribute to Caesar, or not?"

Luke 20:21 "And they asked him, saying, Master, we know that thou sayest and teachest rightly, neither acceptest thou the person of any, but teachest the way of God truly:"

John 3:33 "He that hath received his testimony hath set to his seal that God is true."

John 7:28 "Then cried Jesus in the temple as he taught, saying, Ye both know me, and ye know whence I am: and I am not come of myself, but he that sent me is true, whom ye know not."

John 8:25-26 "25Then said they unto him, Who art thou? And Jesus saith unto them, Even the same that I said unto you from the beginning. 26I have many things to say and to judge of you: but he that sent me is true; and I speak to the world those things which I have heard of him."

John 14:6 "Jesus saith unto him, I am the way, the truth, and the life: no man cometh unto the Father, but by me."

1 Thessalonians 1:9 "For they themselves shew of us what manner of entering in we had unto you, and how ye turned to God from idols to serve the living and true God;"

1 John 5:20 "And we know that the Son of God is come, and hath given us an understanding, that we may know him that is true, and we are in him that is true, even in his Son Jesus Christ. This is the true God, and eternal life."

Revelation 3:7 "And to the angel of the church in Philadelphia write; These things saith he that is holy, he that is true, he that hath the key of David, he that openeth, and no man shutteth; and shutteth, and no man openeth;"

God Keeping Truth For Ever
Psalm 146:5-6 "5Happy is he that hath the God of Jacob for his help, whose hope is in the LORD his God: 6Which made heaven, and earth, the sea, and all that therein is: which keepeth truth for ever:"

The Reward For Lacking Truth
Hosea 4:1 "Hear the word of the LORD, ye children of Israel: for the LORD hath a controversy with the inhabitants of the land, because there is no truth, nor mercy, nor knowledge of God in the land."

The Spirit Of Truth
John 14:16-19 "16And I will pray the Father, and he shall give you another Comforter, that he may abide with you for ever; 17Even the Spirit of truth; whom the world cannot receive, because it seeth him not, neither knoweth him: but ye know him; for he dwelleth with you, and shall be in you. 18I will not leave you comfortless: I will come to you. 19Yet a little while, and the world seeth me no more; but ye see me: because I live, ye shall live also."

John 15:1-27 "1I am the true vine, and my Father is the husbandman. 2Every branch in me that beareth not fruit he taketh away: and every branch that beareth fruit, he purgeth it, that it may bring forth more fruit. 3Now ye are clean through the word which I have spoken unto you. 4Abide in me, and I in you. As the branch cannot bear fruit of itself, except it abide in the vine; no more can ye, except ye abide in me. 5I am the vine, ye are the branches: He that abideth in me, and I in him, the same bringeth forth much fruit: for without me ye can do nothing. 6If a man abide not in me, he is cast forth as a branch, and is withered; and men gather them, and cast them into the fire, and they are burned. 7If ye abide in me, and my words abide in you, ye shall ask what ye will, and it shall be done unto you. 8Herein is my Father glorified, that ye bear much fruit; so shall ye be my disciples. 9As the Father hath loved me, so have I loved you: continue ye in my love. ¹⁰If ye keep my commandments, ye shall abide in my love; even as I have kept my Father's commandments, and abide in his love. ¹¹These things have I spoken unto you, that my joy might remain in you, and that your joy might be full. ¹²This is my commandment, That ye love one another, as I have loved you. ¹³Greater love hath no man than this, that a man lay down his life for his friends. ¹⁴Ye are my friends, if ye do whatsoever I command you. ¹⁵Henceforth I call you not servants; for the servant knoweth not what his lord doeth: but I have called you friends; for all things that I have heard of my Father I have made known unto you. ¹⁶Ye have not chosen me, but I have chosen you, and ordained you, that ye should go and bring forth fruit, and that your fruit should remain: that whatsoever ye shall ask of the Father in my name, he may give it you. ¹⁷These things I command you, that ye love one another. ¹⁸If the world hate you, ye know that it hated me before it hated you. ¹⁹If ye were of the world, the world would love his own: but because ye are not of the world, but I have chosen you out of the world, therefore the world hateth you. ²⁰Remember the word that I said unto you, The servant is not greater than his lord. If they have persecuted me, they will also persecute you; if they have kept my saying, they will keep yours also. ²¹But all these things will they do unto you for my name's sake, because they know not him that sent me. ²²If I had not come and spoken unto them, they had not had sin: but now they have no cloke for their sin. ²³He that hateth me hateth my Father also. ²⁴If I had not done among them the works which none other man did, they had not had sin: but now have they both seen and hated both me and my Father. ²⁵But this cometh to pass, that the word might be fulfilled that is written in their law, They hated me without a cause. ²⁶But when the Comforter is come, whom I will send unto you from the Father, even the Spirit of truth, which proceedeth from the Father, he shall testify of me: ²⁷And ye also shall bear witness, because ye have been with me from the beginning."

John 16:5-13 "⁵But now I go my way to him that sent me; and none of you asketh me, Whither goest thou? ⁶But because I have said these things unto you, sorrow hath filled your heart. ⁷Nevertheless I tell you the truth; It is expedient for you that I go away: for if I go not away, the Comforter will not come unto you; but if I depart, I will send him unto you. ⁸And when he is come, he will reprove the world of sin, and of righteousness, and of judgment: ⁹Of sin, because they believe not on me; ¹⁰Of righteousness, because I go to my Father, and ye see me no more; ¹¹Of judgment, because the prince of this world is judged. ¹²I have yet many things to say unto you, but ye cannot bear them now. ¹³Howbeit when he, the Spirit of truth, is come, he will guide you into all truth: for he shall not speak of himself; but whatsoever he shall hear, that shall he speak: and he will shew you things to come."

The Truth Coming By Jesus Christ
John 1:17 "For the law was given by Moses, but grace and truth came by Jesus Christ."

John 18:37 "Pilate therefore said unto him, Art thou a king then? Jesus answered, Thou sayest that I am a king. To this end was I born, and for this cause came I into the world, that I should bear witness unto the truth. Every one that is of the truth heareth my voice."

The Truth Of The Lord
Psalm 91:2-4 "²I will say of the LORD, He is my refuge and my fortress: my God; in him will I trust. ³Surely he shall deliver thee from the snare of the fowler, and from the noisome pestilence. ⁴He shall cover thee with his feathers, and under his wings shalt thou trust: his truth shall be thy shield and buckler."

Psalm 100:5 "For the LORD is good; his mercy is everlasting; and his truth endureth to all generations."

Psalm 108:3-4 "³I will praise thee, O LORD, among the people: and I will sing praises unto thee among the nations. ⁴For thy mercy is great above the heavens: and thy truth reacheth unto the clouds."

Psalm 117:2 "For his merciful kindness is great toward us: and the truth of the LORD endureth for ever. Praise ye the LORD."

Those That Are Of The Truth
John 18:37 "Pilate therefore said unto him, Art thou a king then? Jesus answered, Thou sayest that I am a king. To this end was I born, and for this

cause came I into the world, that I should bear witness unto the truth. Every one that is of the truth heareth my voice."

Those That Deal Truly
Proverbs 12:22 "Lying lips are abomination to the LORD: but they that deal truly are his delight."

John 3:21 "But he that doeth truth cometh to the light, that his deeds may be made manifest, that they are wrought in God."

Those That Hold The Truth
In Unrighteousness
Romans 1:18 "For the wrath of God is revealed from heaven against all ungodliness and unrighteousness of men, who hold the truth in unrighteousness;"

Those That Speak The Truth
Psalm 15:1-5 "¹LORD, who shall abide in thy tabernacle? who shall dwell in thy holy hill? ²He that walketh uprightly, and worketh righteousness, and speaketh the truth in his heart. ³He that backbiteth not with his tongue, nor doeth evil to his neighbour, nor taketh up a reproach against his neighbour. ⁴In whose eyes a vile person is contemned; but he honoureth them that fear the LORD. He that sweareth to his own hurt, and changeth not. ⁵He that putteth not out his money to usury, nor taketh reward against the innocent. He that doeth these things shall never be moved."

Proverbs 12:17 "He that speaketh truth sheweth forth righteousness: but a false witness deceit."

What Is Done In Truth
Psalm 33:4 "For the word of the LORD is right; and all his works are done in truth."

Psalm 111:4-8 "⁴He hath made his wonderful works to be remembered: the LORD is gracious and full of compassion. ⁵He hath given meat unto them that fear him: he will ever be mindful of his covenant. ⁶He hath shewed his people the power of his works, that he may give them the heritage of the heathen. ⁷The works of his hands are verity and judgment; all his commandments are sure. ⁸They stand fast for ever and ever, and are done in truth and uprightness."

What Is Truth
Psalm 25:10 "All the paths of the LORD are mercy and truth unto such as keep his covenant and his testimonies."

Psalm 119:137-142 "¹³⁷Righteous art thou, O LORD, and upright are thy judgments. ¹³⁸Thy testimonies that thou hast commanded are righteous and very faithful. ¹³⁹My zeal hath consumed me, because mine enemies have forgotten thy words. ¹⁴⁰Thy word is very pure: therefore thy servant loveth it. ¹⁴¹I am small and despised: yet do not I forget thy precepts. ¹⁴²Thy righteousness is an everlasting righteousness, and thy law is the truth."

Psalm 119:151 "Thou art near, O LORD; and all thy commandments are truth."

Psalm 119:159-160 "¹⁵⁹Consider how I love thy precepts: quicken me, O LORD, according to thy lovingkindness. ¹⁶⁰Thy word is true from the beginning: and every one of thy righteous judgments endureth for ever."

Isaiah 25:1 "O LORD, thou art my God; I will exalt thee, I will praise thy name; for thou hast done wonderful things; thy counsels of old are faithfulness and truth."

Daniel 4:37 "Now I Nebuchadnezzar praise and extol and honour the King of heaven, all whose works are truth, and his ways judgment: and those that walk in pride he is able to abase."

John 8:13-14 "¹³The Pharisees therefore said unto him, Thou bearest record of thyself; thy record is not true. ¹⁴Jesus answered and said unto them, Though I bear record of myself, yet my record is true: for I know whence I came, and whither I go; but ye cannot tell whence I come, and whither I go."

John 17:1-17 "¹These words spake Jesus, and lifted up his eyes to heaven, and said, Father, the hour is come; glorify thy Son, that thy Son also may glorify thee: ²As thou hast given him power over all flesh, that he should give eternal life to as many as thou hast given him. ³And this is life eternal, that they might know thee the only true God, and Jesus Christ, whom thou hast sent. ⁴I have glorified thee on the earth: I have finished the work which thou gavest me to do. ⁵And now, O Father, glorify thou me with thine own self with the glory which I had with thee before the world was. ⁶I have manifested thy name unto the men which thou gavest me out of the world: thine they were, and thou gavest them me; and they have kept thy word. 7Now they have known that all things whatsoever thou hast given me are of thee. 8For I have given unto them the words which thou gavest me; and they have received them, and have known surely that I came out from thee, and they have believed that thou didst send me. 9I pray for them: I pray not for the world, but for them which thou hast given me; for they are thine. 10And all mine are thine, and thine are mine; and I am glorified in them. 11And now I am no more in the world, but these are in the world, and I come to thee. Holy Father, keep through thine own name those whom thou hast given me, that they may be one, as we are. 12While I was with them in the world, I kept them in thy name: those that thou gavest me I have kept, and none of them is lost, but the son of perdition; that the scripture might be fulfilled. 13And now come I to thee; and these things I speak in the world, that they might have my joy fulfilled in themselves. 14I have given them thy word; and the world hath hated them, because they are not of the world, even as I am not of the world. 15I pray not that thou shouldest take them out of the world, but that thou shouldest keep them from the evil. 16They are not of the world, even as I am not of the world. 17Sanctify them through thy truth: thy word is truth."

1 Thessalonians 2:13 "For this cause also thank we God without ceasing, because, when ye received the word of God which ye heard of us, ye received it not as the word of men, but as it is in truth, the word of God, which effectually worketh also in you that believe."

1 Timothy 3:14-15 "14These things write I unto thee, hoping to come unto thee shortly: 15But if I tarry long, that thou mayest know how thou oughtest to behave thyself in the house of God, which is the church of the living God, the pillar and ground of the truth."

1 John 2:24-27 "24Let that therefore abide in you, which ye have heard from the beginning. If that which ye have heard from the beginning shall remain in you, ye also shall continue in the Son, and in the Father. 25And this is the promise that he hath promised us, even eternal life. 26These

things have I written unto you concerning them that seduce you. 27But the anointing which ye have received of him abideth in you, and ye need not that any man teach you: but as the same anointing teacheth you of all things, and is truth, and is no lie, and even as it hath taught you, ye shall abide in him."

1 John 5:6 "This is he that came by water and blood, even Jesus Christ; not by water only, but by water and blood. And it is the Spirit that beareth witness, because the Spirit is truth."

Revelation 15:3 "And they sing the song of Moses the servant of God, and the song of the Lamb, saying, Great and marvellous are thy works, Lord God Almighty; just and true are thy ways, thou King of saints."

Revelation 16:7 "And I heard another out of the altar say, Even so, Lord God Almighty, true and righteous are thy judgments."

Revelation 19:1-2 "1And after these things I heard a great voice of much people in heaven, saying, Alleluia; Salvation, and glory, and honour, and power, unto the Lord our God: 2For true and righteous are his judgments: for he hath judged the great whore, which did corrupt the earth with her fornication, and hath avenged the blood of his servants at her hand."

Revelation 22:1-6 "1And he shewed me a pure river of water of life, clear as crystal, proceeding out of the throne of God and of the Lamb. 2In the midst of the street of it, and on either side of the river, was there the tree of life, which bare twelve manner of fruits, and yielded her fruit every month: and the leaves of the tree were for the healing of the nations. 3And there shall be no more curse: but the throne of God and of the Lamb shall be in it; and his servants shall serve him: 4And they shall see his face; and his name shall be in their foreheads. 5And there shall be no night there; and they need no candle, neither light of the sun; for the Lord God giveth them light: and they shall reign for ever and ever. 6And he said unto me, These sayings are faithful and true: and the Lord God of the holy prophets sent his angel to shew unto his servants the things which must shortly be done."

What Truth Does
Psalm 61:5-7 "[5]For thou, O God, hast heard my vows: thou hast given me the heritage of those that fear thy name. [6]Thou wilt prolong the king's life: and his years as many generations. [7]He shall abide before God for ever: O prepare mercy and truth, which may preserve him."

Proverbs 16:6 "By mercy and truth iniquity is purged: and by the fear of the LORD men depart from evil."

Proverbs 20:28 "Mercy and truth preserve the king: and his throne is upholden by mercy."

John 8:32 "And ye shall know the truth, and the truth shall make you free."

Where The Truth Dwells
2 John 1-2 "[1]The elder unto the elect lady and her children, whom I love in the truth; and not I only, but also all they that have known the truth; [2]For the truth's sake, which dwelleth in us, and shall be with us for ever."

Who Is True
John 7:16-18 "[16]Jesus answered them, and said, My doctrine is not mine, but his that sent me. [17]If any man will do his will, he shall know of the doctrine, whether it be of God, or whether I speak of myself. [18]He that speaketh of himself seeketh his own glory: but he that seeketh his glory that sent him, the same is true, and no unrighteousness is in him."

1 John 3:17-21 "[17]But whoso hath this world's good, and seeth his brother have need, and shutteth up his bowels of compassion from him, how dwelleth the love of God in him? [18]My little children, let us not love in word, neither in tongue; but in deed and in truth. [19]And hereby we know that we are of the truth, and shall assure our hearts before him. [20]For if our heart condemn us, God is greater than our heart, and knoweth all things. [21]Beloved, if our heart condemn us not, then have we confidence toward God."

1 John 4:1-2 "[1]Beloved, believe not every spirit, but try the spirits whether they are of God: because many false prophets are gone out into the world. [2]Hereby know ye the Spirit of God: Every spirit that confesseth that Jesus Christ is come in the flesh is of God:"

Who Shall Have Truth
Psalm 25:10 "All the paths of the LORD are mercy and truth unto such as keep his covenant and his testimonies."

Proverbs 14:22 "Do they not err that devise evil? but mercy and truth shall be to them that devise good."

Who The Truth Is Not In
John 8:42-44 "[42]Jesus said unto them, If God were your Father, ye would love me: for I proceeded forth and came from God; neither came I of myself, but he sent me. [43]Why do ye not understand my speech? even because ye cannot hear my word. [44]Ye are of your father the devil, and the lusts of your father ye will do. He was a murderer from the beginning, and abode not in the truth, because there is no truth in him. When he speaketh a lie, he speaketh of his own: for he is a liar, and the father of it."

1 John 1:5-6 "[5]This then is the message which we have heard of him, and declare unto you, that God is light, and in him is no darkness at all. [6]If we say that we have fellowship with him, and walk in darkness, we lie, and do not the truth:"

1 John 1:8 "If we say that we have no sin, we deceive ourselves, and the truth is not in us."

1 John 2:1-4 "[1]My little children, these things write I unto you, that ye sin not. And if any man sin, we have an advocate with the Father, Jesus Christ the righteous: [2]And he is the propitiation for our sins: and not for ours only, but also for the sins of the whole world. [3]And hereby we do know that we know him, if we keep his commandments. [4]He that saith, I know him, and keepeth not his commandments, is a liar, and the truth is not in him."

1 John 4:1-3 "[1]Beloved, believe not every spirit, but try the spirits whether they are of God: because many false prophets are gone out into the world. [2]Hereby know ye the Spirit of God: Every spirit that confesseth that Jesus Christ is come in the flesh is of God: [3]And every spirit that confesseth not that Jesus Christ is come in the flesh is not of God: and this is that spirit of antichrist, whereof ye have heard that it should come; and even now already is it in the world."

TURNING

The Reward For Turning From Evil

2 Chronicles 7:12-14 "¹²And the LORD appeared to Solomon by night, and said unto him, I have heard thy prayer, and have chosen this place to myself for an house of sacrifice. ¹³If I shut up heaven that there be no rain, or if I command the locusts to devour the land, or if I send pestilence among my people; ¹⁴If my people, which are called by my name, shall humble themselves, and pray, and seek my face, and turn from their wicked ways; then will I hear from heaven, and will forgive their sin, and will heal their land."

Jeremiah 18:5-8 "⁵Then the word of the LORD came to me, saying, ⁶O house of Israel, cannot I do with you as this potter? saith the LORD. Behold, as the clay is in the potter's hand, so are ye in mine hand, O house of Israel. ⁷At what instant I shall speak concerning a nation, and concerning a kingdom, to pluck up, and to pull down, and to destroy it; ⁸If that nation, against whom I have pronounced, turn from their evil, I will repent of the evil that I thought to do unto them."

The Reward For Turning From The Lord

Numbers 14:43 "For the Amalekites and the Canaanites are there before you, and ye shall fall by the sword: because ye are turned away from the LORD, therefore the LORD will not be with you."

Deuteronomy 11:16-18 "¹⁶Take heed to yourselves, that your heart be not deceived, and ye turn aside, and serve other gods, and worship them; ¹⁷And then the LORD's wrath be kindled against you, and he shut up the heaven, that there be no rain, and that the land yield not her fruit; and lest ye perish quickly from off the good land which the LORD giveth you. ¹⁸Therefore shall ye lay up these my words in your heart and in your soul, and bind them for a sign upon your hand, that they may be as frontlets between your eyes."

Deuteronomy 29:17-29 "¹⁷And ye have seen their abominations, and their idols, wood and stone, silver and gold, which were among them:) ¹⁸Lest there should be among you man, or woman, or family, or tribe, whose heart turneth away this day from the LORD our God, to go and serve the gods of these nations; lest there should be among you a root that beareth gall and wormwood;

¹⁹And it come to pass, when he heareth the words of this curse, that he bless himself in his heart, saying, I shall have peace, though I walk in the imagination of mine heart, to add drunkenness to thirst: ²⁰The LORD will not spare him, but then the anger of the LORD and his jealousy shall smoke against that man, and all the curses that are written in this book shall lie upon him, and the LORD shall blot out his name from under heaven. ²¹And the LORD shall separate him unto evil out of all the tribes of Israel, according to all the curses of the covenant that are written in this book of the law: ²²So that the generation to come of your children that shall rise up after you, and the stranger that shall come from a far land, shall say, when they see the plagues of that land, and the sicknesses which the LORD hath laid upon it; ²³And that the whole land thereof is brimstone, and salt, and burning, that it is not sown, nor beareth, nor any grass groweth therein, like the overthrow of Sodom, and Gomorrah, Admah, and Zeboim, which the LORD overthrew in his anger, and in his wrath: ²⁴Even all nations shall say, Wherefore hath the LORD done thus unto this land? what meaneth the heat of this great anger? ²⁵Then men shall say, Because they have forsaken the covenant of the LORD God of their fathers, which he made with them when he brought them forth out of the land of Egypt: ²⁶For they went and served other gods, and worshipped them, gods whom they knew not, and whom he had not given unto them: ²⁷And the anger of the LORD was kindled against this land, to bring upon it all the curses that are written in this book: ²⁸And the LORD rooted them out of their land in anger, and in wrath, and in great indignation, and cast them into another land, as it is this day. ²⁹The secret things belong unto the LORD our God: but those things which are revealed belong unto us and to our children for ever, that we may do all the words of this law."

Deuteronomy 30:15-18 "¹⁵See, I have set before thee this day life and good, and death and evil; ¹⁶In that I command thee this day to love the LORD thy God, to walk in his ways, and to keep his commandments and his statutes and his judgments, that thou mayest live and multiply: and the LORD thy God shall bless thee in the land

whither thou goest to possess it. ¹⁷But if thine heart turn away, so that thou wilt not hear, but shalt be drawn away, and worship other gods, and serve them; ¹⁸I denounce unto you this day, that ye shall surely perish, and that ye shall not prolong your days upon the land, whither thou passest over Jordan to go to possess it."

Deuteronomy 31:29 "For I know that after my death ye will utterly corrupt yourselves, and turn aside from the way which I have commanded you; and evil will befall you in the latter days; because ye will do evil in the sight of the LORD, to provoke him to anger through the work of your hands."

1 Kings 9:6-9 "⁶But if ye shall at all turn from following me, ye or your children, and will not keep my commandments and my statutes which I have set before you, but go and serve other gods, and worship them: ⁷Then will I cut off Israel out of the land which I have given them; and this house, which I have hallowed for my name, will I cast out of my sight; and Israel shall be a proverb and a byword among all people: ⁸And at this house, which is high, every one that passeth by it shall be astonished, and shall hiss; and they shall say, Why hath the LORD done thus unto this land, and to this house? ⁹And they shall answer, Because they forsook the LORD their God, who brought forth their fathers out of the land of Egypt, and have taken hold upon other gods, and have worshipped them, and served them: therefore hath the LORD brought upon them all this evil."

2 Chronicles 29:6-9 "⁶For our fathers have trespassed, and done that which was evil in the eyes of the LORD our God, and have forsaken him, and have turned away their faces from the habitation of the LORD, and turned their backs. ⁷Also they have shut up the doors of the porch, and put out the lamps, and have not burned incense nor offered burnt offerings in the holy place unto the God of Israel. ⁸Wherefore the wrath of the LORD was upon Judah and Jerusalem, and he hath delivered them to trouble, to astonishment, and to hissing, as ye see with your eyes. ⁹For, lo, our fathers have fallen by the sword, and our sons and our daughters and our wives are in captivity for this."

Job 34:23-28 "²³For he will not lay upon man more than right; that he should enter into judgment with God. ²⁴He shall break in pieces mighty men without number, and set others in their stead. ²⁵Therefore he knoweth their works, and he overturneth them in the night, so that they are destroyed. ²⁶He striketh them as wicked men in the open sight of others; ²⁷Because they turned back from him, and would not consider any of his ways: ²⁸So that they cause the cry of the poor to come unto him, and he heareth the cry of the afflicted."

Amos 4:9-12 "⁹I have smitten you with blasting and mildew: when your gardens and your vineyards and your fig trees and your olive trees increased, the palmerworm devoured them: yet have ye not returned unto me, saith the LORD. ¹⁰I have sent among you the pestilence after the manner of Egypt: your young men have I slain with the sword, and have taken away your horses; and I have made the stink of your camps to come up unto your nostrils: yet have ye not returned unto me, saith the LORD. ¹¹I have overthrown some of you, as God overthrew Sodom and Gomorrah, and ye were as a firebrand plucked out of the burning: yet have ye not returned unto me, saith the LORD. ¹²Therefore thus will I do unto thee, O Israel: and because I will do this unto thee, prepare to meet thy God, O Israel."

The Reward For
Turning To The Lord

Deuteronomy 4:29-31 "²⁹But if from thence thou shalt seek the LORD thy God, thou shalt find him, if thou seek him with all thy heart and with all thy soul. ³⁰When thou art in tribulation, and all these things are come upon thee, even in the latter days, if thou turn to the LORD thy God, and shalt be obedient unto his voice; ³¹(For the LORD thy God is a merciful God;) he will not forsake thee, neither destroy thee, nor forget the covenant of thy fathers which he sware unto them."

Deuteronomy 30:8-10 "⁸And thou shalt return and obey the voice of the LORD, and do all his commandments which I command thee this day. ⁹And the LORD thy God will make thee plenteous in every work of thine hand, in the fruit of thy body, and in the fruit of thy cattle, and in the fruit of thy land, for good: for the LORD will again rejoice over thee for good, as he rejoiced over thy fathers: [10]If thou shalt hearken unto the voice of the LORD thy God, to keep his commandments and his statutes which are written in this book of the law, and if thou turn unto the LORD thy God with all thine heart, and with all thy soul."

1 Samuel 7:3 "And Samuel spake unto all the house of Israel, saying, If ye do return unto the LORD with all your hearts, then put away the strange gods and Ashtaroth from among you, and prepare your hearts unto the LORD, and serve him only: and he will deliver you out of the hand of the Philistines."

1 Kings 8:28-36 "[28]Yet have thou respect unto the prayer of thy servant, and to his supplication, O LORD my God, to hearken unto the cry and to the prayer, which thy servant prayeth before thee to day: [29]That thine eyes may be open toward this house night and day, even toward the place of which thou hast said, My name shall be there: that thou mayest hearken unto the prayer which thy servant shall make toward this place. [30]And hearken thou to the supplication of thy servant, and of thy people Israel, when they shall pray toward this place: and hear thou in heaven thy dwelling place: and when thou hearest, forgive. [31]If any man trespass against his neighbour, and an oath be laid upon him to cause him to swear, and the oath come before thine altar in this house: [32]Then hear thou in heaven, and do, and judge thy servants, condemning the wicked, to bring his way upon his head; and justifying the righteous, to give him according to his righteousness. [33]When thy people Israel be smitten down before the enemy, because they have sinned against thee, and shall turn again to thee, and confess thy name, and pray, and make supplication unto thee in this house: [34]Then hear thou in heaven, and forgive the sin of thy people Israel, and bring them again unto the land which thou gavest unto their fathers. [35]When heaven is shut up, and there is no rain, because they have sinned against thee; if they pray toward this place, and confess thy name, and turn from their sin, when thou afflictest them: [36]Then hear thou in heaven, and forgive the sin of thy servants, and of thy people Israel, that thou teach them the good way wherein they should walk, and give rain upon thy land, which thou hast given to thy people for an inheritance."

1 Kings 8:44-50 "[44]If thy people go out to battle against their enemy, whithersoever thou shalt send them, and shall pray unto the LORD toward the city which thou hast chosen, and toward the house that I have built for thy name: [45]Then hear thou in heaven their prayer and their supplication, and maintain their cause. [46]If they sin against thee, (for there is no man that sinneth not,) and thou be angry with them, and deliver them to the enemy, so that they carry them away captives unto the land of the enemy, far or near; [47]Yet if they shall bethink themselves in the land whither they were carried captives, and repent, and make supplication unto thee in the land of them that carried them captives, saying, We have sinned, and have done perversely, we have committed wickedness; [48]And so return unto thee with all their heart, and with all their soul, in the land of their enemies, which led them away captive, and pray unto thee toward their land, which thou gavest unto their fathers, the city which thou hast chosen, and the house which I have built for thy name: [49]Then hear thou their prayer and their supplication in heaven thy dwelling place, and maintain their cause, [50]And forgive thy people that have sinned against thee and all their transgressions wherein they have transgressed against thee, and give them compassion before them who carried them captive, that they may have compassion on them:"

2 Chronicles 6:19-39 "[19]Have respect therefore to the prayer of thy servant, and to his supplication, O LORD my God, to hearken unto the cry and the prayer which thy servant prayeth before thee: [20]That thine eyes may be open upon this house day and night, upon the place whereof thou hast said that thou wouldest put thy name there; to hearken unto the prayer which thy servant prayeth toward this place. [21]Hearken therefore unto the supplications of thy servant, and of thy people Israel, which they shall make toward this place: hear thou from thy dwelling place, even from heaven; and when thou hearest, forgive. [22]If a man sin against his neighbour, and an oath be laid upon him to make him swear, and the oath come before thine altar in this house; [23]Then hear thou from heaven, and do, and judge thy servants, by requiting the wicked, by recompensing his way upon his own head; and by justifying the righteous, by giving him according to his righteousness. 24And if thy people Israel be put to the worse before the enemy, because they have sinned against thee; and shall return and confess thy name, and pray and make supplication before thee in this house; 25Then hear thou from the heavens, and forgive the sin of thy people Israel, and bring them again unto the land which thou gavest to them and to their fathers. 26When the heaven is shut up, and there is no rain, because they have sinned against thee; yet if they pray toward this place, and confess thy name, and turn from their sin, when thou dost afflict them; 27Then hear thou from heaven, and forgive the sin of thy servants, and of thy people Israel, when thou hast taught them the good way, wherein they should walk; and send rain upon thy land, which thou hast given unto thy people for an inheritance. 28If there be dearth in the land, if there be pestilence, if there be blasting, or mildew, locusts, or caterpillers; if their enemies besiege them in the cities of their land; whatsoever sore or whatsoever sickness there be: 29Then what prayer or what supplication soever shall be made of any man, or of all thy people Israel, when every one shall know his own sore and his own grief, and shall spread forth his hands in this house: 30Then hear thou from heaven thy dwelling place, and forgive, and render unto every man according unto all his ways, whose heart thou knowest; (for thou only knowest the hearts of the children of men:) 31That they may fear thee, to walk in thy ways, so long as they live in the land which thou gavest unto our fathers. 32Moreover concerning the stranger, which is not of thy people Israel, but is come from a far country for thy great name's sake, and thy mighty hand, and thy stretched out arm; if they come and pray in this house; 33Then hear thou from the heavens, even from thy dwelling place, and do according to all that the stranger calleth to thee for; that all people of the earth may know thy name, and fear thee, as doth thy people Israel, and may know that this house which I have built is called by thy name. 34If thy people go out to war against their enemies by the way that thou shalt send them, and they pray unto thee toward this city which thou hast chosen, and the house which I have built for thy name; 35Then hear thou from the heavens their prayer and their supplication, and maintain their

cause. 36If they sin against thee, (for there is no man which sinneth not,) and thou be angry with them, and deliver them over before their enemies, and they carry them away captives unto a land far off or near; 37Yet if they bethink themselves in the land whither they are carried captive, and turn and pray unto thee in the land of their captivity, saying, We have sinned, we have done amiss, and have dealt wickedly; 38If they return to thee with all their heart and with all their soul in the land of their captivity, whither they have carried them captives, and pray toward their land, which thou gavest unto their fathers, and toward the city which thou hast chosen, and toward the house which I have built for thy name: 39Then hear thou from the heavens, even from thy dwelling place, their prayer and their supplications, and maintain their cause, and forgive thy people which have sinned against thee."

2 Chronicles 30:9 "For if ye turn again unto the LORD, your brethren and your children shall find compassion before them that lead them captive, so that they shall come again into this land: for the LORD your God is gracious and merciful, and will not turn away his face from you, if ye return unto him."

Nehemiah 1:5-9 "5And said, I beseech thee, O LORD God of heaven, the great and terrible God, that keepeth covenant and mercy for them that love him and observe his commandments: 6Let thine ear now be attentive, and thine eyes open, that thou mayest hear the prayer of thy servant, which I pray before thee now, day and night, for the children of Israel thy servants, and confess the sins of the children of Israel, which we have sinned against thee: both I and my father's house have sinned. 7We have dealt very corruptly against thee, and have not kept the commandments, nor the statutes, nor the judgments, which thou commandedst thy servant Moses. 8Remember, I beseech thee, the word that thou commandedst thy servant Moses, saying, If ye transgress, I will scatter you abroad among the nations: 9But if ye turn unto me, and keep my commandments, and do them; though there were of you cast out unto the uttermost part of the heaven, yet will I gather them from thence, and will bring them unto the place that I have chosen to set my name there."

Isaiah 30:15 "For thus saith the Lord GOD, the Holy One of Israel; In returning and rest shall ye be saved; in quietness and in confidence shall be your strength: and ye would not."

Isaiah 55:7 "Let the wicked forsake his way, and the unrighteous man his thoughts: and let him return unto the LORD, and he will have mercy upon him; and to our God, for he will abundantly pardon."

Jeremiah 3:11-15 "¹¹And the LORD said unto me, The backsliding Israel hath justified herself more than treacherous Judah. ¹²Go and proclaim these words toward the north, and say, Return, thou backsliding Israel, saith the LORD; and I will not cause mine anger to fall upon you: for I am merciful, saith the LORD, and I will not keep anger for ever. ¹³Only acknowledge thine iniquity, that thou hast transgressed against the LORD thy God, and hast scattered thy ways to the strangers under every green tree, and ye have not obeyed my voice, saith the LORD. ¹⁴Turn, O backsliding children, saith the LORD; for I am married unto you: and I will take you one of a city, and two of a family, and I will bring you to Zion: ¹⁵And I will give you pastors according to mine heart, which shall feed you with knowledge and understanding."

Jeremiah 3:21-22 "²¹A voice was heard upon the high places, weeping and supplications of the children of Israel: for they have perverted their way, and they have forgotten the LORD their God. ²²Return, ye backsliding children, and I will heal your backslidings. Behold, we come unto thee; for thou art the LORD our God."

Jeremiah 4:1-2 "¹If thou wilt return, O Israel, saith the LORD, return unto me: and if thou wilt put away thine abominations out of my sight, then shalt thou not remove. ²And thou shalt swear, The LORD liveth, in truth, in judgment, and in righteousness; and the nations shall bless themselves in him, and in him shall they glory."

Zechariah 1:3 "Therefore say thou unto them, Thus saith the LORD of hosts; Turn ye unto me, saith the LORD of hosts, and I will turn unto you, saith the LORD of hosts."

Malachi 3:7 "Even from the days of your fathers ye are gone away from mine ordinances, and have not kept them. Return unto me, and I will return unto you, saith the LORD of hosts. But ye said, Wherein shall we return?"

Those That Turn From Righteousness

Ezekiel 3:20-21 "²⁰Again, When a righteous man doth turn from his righteousness, and commit iniquity, and I lay a stumblingblock before him, he shall die: because thou hast not given him warning, he shall die in his sin, and his righteousness which he hath done shall not be remembered; but his blood will I require at thine hand. ²¹Nevertheless if thou warn the righteous man, that the righteous sin not, and he doth not sin, he shall surely live, because he is warned; also thou hast delivered thy soul."

Ezekiel 18:24-26 "²⁴But when the righteous turneth away from his righteousness, and committeth iniquity, and doeth according to all the abominations that the wicked man doeth, shall he live? All his righteousness that he hath done shall not be mentioned: in his trespass that he hath trespassed, and in his sin that he hath sinned, in them shall he die. ²⁵Yet ye say, The way of the Lord is not equal. Hear now, O house of Israel; Is not my way equal? are not your ways unequal? ²⁶When a righteous man turneth away from his righteousness, and committeth iniquity, and dieth in them; for his iniquity that he hath done shall he die."

Ezekiel 33:11-20 "¹¹Say unto them, As I live, saith the Lord GOD, I have no pleasure in the death of the wicked; but that the wicked turn from his way and live: turn ye, turn ye from your evil ways; for why will ye die, O house of Israel? ¹²Therefore, thou son of man, say unto the children of thy people, The righteousness of the righteous shall not deliver him in the day of his transgression: as for the wickedness of the wicked, he shall not fall thereby in the day that he turneth from his wickedness; neither shall the righteous be able to live for his righteousness in the day that he sinneth. ¹³When I shall say to the righteous, that he shall surely live; if he trust to his own righteousness, and commit iniquity, all his righteousnesses shall not be remembered; but for his iniquity that he hath committed, he shall die for it. ¹⁴Again, when I say unto the wicked, Thou shalt surely die; if he turn from his sin, and do that which is lawful and right; ¹⁵If the wicked restore the pledge, give again that he had robbed, walk in the statutes of life, without committing iniquity; he shall surely live, he shall not die. ¹⁶None of his sins that he hath committed shall be mentioned unto him: he hath done that which is lawful and right; he shall surely live. ¹⁷Yet the children of thy people say, The way of the Lord is not equal: but as for them, their way is not equal. ¹⁸When the righteous turneth from his righteousness, and committeth iniquity, he shall even die thereby. ¹⁹But if the wicked turn from his wickedness, and do that which is lawful and right, he shall live thereby. ²⁰Yet ye say, The way of the Lord is not equal. O ye house of Israel, I will judge you every one after his ways."

Those That Turn From Wickedness

Ezekiel 18:21-23 "²¹But if the wicked will turn from all his sins that he hath committed, and keep all my statutes, and do that which is lawful and right, he shall surely live, he shall not die. ²²All his transgressions that he hath committed, they shall not be mentioned unto him: in his righteousness that he hath done he shall live. ²³Have I any pleasure at all that the wicked should die? saith the Lord GOD: and not that he should return from his ways, and live?"

Ezekiel 18:27-28 "²⁷Again, when the wicked man turneth away from his wickedness that he hath committed, and doeth that which is lawful and right, he shall save his soul alive. ²⁸Because he considereth, and turneth away from all his transgressions that he hath committed, he shall surely live, he shall not die."

Ezekiel 33:11-20 "¹¹Say unto them, As I live, saith the Lord GOD, I have no pleasure in the death of the wicked; but that the wicked turn from his way and live: turn ye, turn ye from your evil ways; for why will ye die, O house of Israel? ¹²Therefore, thou son of man, say unto the children of thy people, The righteousness of the righteous shall not deliver him in the day of his transgression: as for the wickedness of the wicked, he shall not fall thereby in the day that he turneth from his wickedness; neither shall the righteous be able to live for his righteousness in the day that he sinneth. ¹³When I shall say to the righteous, that he shall surely live; if he trust to his own righteousness, and

commit iniquity, all his righteousnesses shall not be remembered; but for his iniquity that he hath committed, he shall die for it. ¹⁴Again, when I say unto the wicked, Thou shalt surely die; if he turn from his sin, and do that which is lawful and right; ¹⁵If the wicked restore the pledge, give again that he had robbed, walk in the statutes of life, without committing iniquity; he shall surely live, he shall not die. ¹⁶None of his sins that he hath committed shall be mentioned unto him: he hath done that which is lawful and right; he shall surely live. ¹⁷Yet the children of thy people say, The way of the Lord is not equal: but as for them, their way is not equal. ¹⁸When the righteous turneth from his righteousness, and committeth iniquity, he shall even die thereby. ¹⁹But if the wicked turn from his wickedness, and do that which is lawful and right, he shall live thereby. ²⁰Yet ye say, The way of the Lord is not equal. O ye house of Israel, I will judge you every one after his ways."

Turning To The Lord

Jeremiah 3:1 "They say, If a man put away his wife, and she go from him, and become another man's, shall he return unto her again? shall not that land be greatly polluted? but thou hast played the harlot with many lovers; yet return again to me, saith the LORD."

Jeremiah 3:14 "Turn, O backsliding children, saith the LORD; for I am married unto you: and I will take you one of a city, and two of a family, and I will bring you to Zion:"

Jeremiah 3:22 "Return, ye backsliding children, and I will heal your backslidings. Behold, we come unto thee; for thou art the LORD our God."

Lamentations 3:39-40 "³⁹Wherefore doth a living man complain, a man for the punishment of his sins? ⁴⁰Let us search and try our ways, and turn again to the LORD."

Hosea 12:6 "Therefore turn thou to thy God: keep mercy and judgment, and wait on thy God continually."

Joel 2:12-13 "¹²Therefore also now, saith the LORD, turn ye even to me with all your heart, and with fasting, and with weeping, and with mourning: ¹³And rend your heart, and not your garments, and turn unto the LORD your God: for he is gracious and merciful, slow to anger, and of great kindness, and repenteth him of the evil."

Acts 14:8-15 "⁸And there sat a certain man at Lystra, impotent in his feet, being a cripple from his mother's womb, who never had walked: ⁹The same heard Paul speak: who stedfastly beholding him, and perceiving that he had faith to be healed, ¹⁰Said with a loud voice, Stand upright on thy feet. And he leaped and walked. ¹¹And when the people saw what Paul had done, they lifted up their voices, saying in the speech of Lycaonia, The gods are come down to us in the likeness of men. ¹²And they called Barnabas, Jupiter; and Paul, Mercurius, because he was the chief speaker. ¹³Then the priest of Jupiter, which was before their city, brought oxen and garlands unto the gates, and would have done sacrifice with the people. ¹⁴Which when the apostles, Barnabas and Paul, heard of, they rent their clothes, and ran in among the people, crying out, ¹⁵And saying, Sirs, why do ye these things? We also are men of like passions with you, and preach unto you that ye should turn from these vanities unto the living God, which made heaven, and earth, and the sea, and all things that are therein:"

What Not To Turn From
Deuteronomy 5:32-33 "³²Ye shall observe to do therefore as the LORD your God hath commanded you: ye shall not turn aside to the right hand or to the left. ³³Ye shall walk in all the ways which the LORD your God hath commanded you, that ye may live, and that it may be well with you, and that ye may prolong your days in the land which ye shall possess."

Joshua 1:7 "Only be thou strong and very courageous, that thou mayest observe to do according to all the law, which Moses my servant commanded thee: turn not from it to the right hand or to the left, that thou mayest prosper whithersoever thou goest."

Joshua 23:6 "Be ye therefore very courageous to keep and to do all that is written in the book of the law of Moses, that ye turn not aside therefrom to the right hand or to the left;"

What Not To Turn To
Leviticus 19:4 "Turn ye not unto idols, nor make to yourselves molten gods: I am the LORD your God."

What To Turn From
2 Kings 17:13 "Yet the LORD testified against Israel, and against Judah, by all the prophets, and by all the seers, saying, Turn ye from your evil ways, and keep my commandments and my statutes, according to all the law which I commanded your fathers, and which I sent to you by my servants the prophets."

Proverbs 4:14-15 "¹⁴Enter not into the path of the wicked, and go not in the way of evil men. ¹⁵Avoid it, pass not by it, turn from it, and pass away."

Ezekiel 18:29-30 "²⁹Yet saith the house of Israel, The way of the Lord is not equal. O house of Israel, are not my ways equal? are not your ways unequal? ³⁰Therefore I will judge you, O house of Israel, every one according to his ways, saith the Lord GOD. Repent, and turn yourselves from all your transgressions; so iniquity shall not be your ruin."

Zechariah 1:4 "Be ye not as your fathers, unto whom the former prophets have cried, saying, Thus saith the LORD of hosts; Turn ye now from your evil ways, and from your evil doings: but they did not hear, nor hearken unto me, saith the LORD."

Acts 14:8-15 "⁸And there sat a certain man at Lystra, impotent in his feet, being a cripple from his mother's womb, who never had walked: ⁹The same heard Paul speak: who stedfastly beholding him, and perceiving that he had faith to be healed, ¹⁰Said with a loud voice, Stand upright on thy feet. And he leaped and walked. ¹¹And when the people saw what Paul had done, they lifted up their voices, saying in the speech of Lycaonia, The gods are come down to us in the likeness of men. ¹²And they called Barnabas, Jupiter; and Paul, Mercurius, because he was the chief speaker. ¹³Then the priest of Jupiter, which was before their city, brought oxen and garlands unto the gates, and would have done sacrifice with the people. ¹⁴Which when the apostles, Barnabas and Paul, heard of, they rent their clothes, and ran in among the people, crying out, ¹⁵And saying, Sirs, why do ye these things? We also are men of like passions with you, and preach unto you that ye should turn from these vanities unto the living God, which made heaven, and earth, and the sea, and all things that are therein:"

Who To Turn From

2 Timothy 3:1-5 "¹This know also, that in the last days perilous times shall come. ²For men shall be lovers of their own selves, covetous, boasters, proud, blasphemers, disobedient to parents, unthankful, unholy, ³Without natural affection, trucebreakers, false accusers, incontinent, fierce, despisers of those that are good, ⁴Traitors, heady, highminded, lovers of pleasures more than lovers of God; ⁵Having a form of godliness, but denying the power thereof: from such turn away."

Uu

UNBELIEF

The Reward For Not Believing The Lord

2 Kings 17:13-23 "¹³Yet the LORD testified against Israel, and against Judah, by all the prophets, and by all the seers, saying, Turn ye from your evil ways, and keep my commandments and my statutes, according to all the law which I commanded your fathers, and which I sent to you by my servants the prophets. ¹⁴Notwithstanding they would not hear, but hardened their necks, like to the neck of their fathers, that did not believe in the LORD their God. ¹⁵And they rejected his statutes, and his covenant that he made with their fathers, and his testimonies which he testified against them; and they followed vanity, and became vain, and went after the heathen that were round about them, concerning whom the LORD had charged them, that they should not do like them. ¹⁶And they left all the commandments of the LORD their God, and made them molten images, even two calves, and made a grove, and worshipped all the host of heaven, and served Baal. ¹⁷And they caused their sons and their daughters to pass through the fire, and used divination and enchantments, and sold themselves to do evil in the sight of the LORD, to provoke him to anger. ¹⁸Therefore the LORD was very angry with Israel, and removed them out of his sight: there was none left but the tribe of Judah only. ¹⁹Also Judah kept not the commandments of the LORD their God, but walked in the statutes of Israel which they made. ²⁰And the LORD rejected all the seed of Israel, and afflicted them, and delivered them into the hand of spoilers, until he had cast them out of his sight. ²¹For he rent Israel from the house of David; and they made Jeroboam the son of Nebat king: and Jeroboam drave Israel from following the LORD, and made them sin a great sin. ²²For the children of Israel walked in all the sins of Jeroboam which he did; they departed not from them; ²³Until the LORD removed Israel out of his sight, as he had said by all his servants the prophets. So was Israel carried away out of their own land to Assyria unto this day."

Psalm 78:17-34 "¹⁷And they sinned yet more against him by provoking the most High in the wilderness. ¹⁸And they tempted God in their heart by asking meat for their lust. ¹⁹Yea, they spake against God; they said, Can God furnish a table in the wilderness? ²⁰Behold, he smote the rock, that the waters gushed out, and the streams overflowed; can he give bread also? can he provide flesh for his people? ²¹Therefore the LORD heard this, and was wroth: so a fire was kindled against Jacob, and anger also came up against Israel; ²²Because they believed not in God, and trusted not in his salvation: ²³Though he had commanded the clouds from above, and opened the doors of heaven, ²⁴And had rained down manna upon them to eat, and had given them of the corn of heaven. ²⁵Man did eat angels' food: he sent them meat to the full. ²⁶He caused an east wind to blow in the heaven: and by his power he brought in the south wind. ²⁷He rained flesh also upon them as dust, and feathered fowls like as the sand of the sea: ²⁸And he let it fall in the midst of their camp, round about their habitations. ²⁹So they did eat, and were well filled: for he gave them their own desire; ³⁰They were not estranged from their lust. But while their meat was yet in their mouths, ³¹The wrath of God came upon them, and slew the fattest of them, and smote down the chosen men of Israel. ³²For all this they sinned still, and believed not for his wondrous works. ³³Therefore their days did he consume in vanity, and their years in trouble. ³⁴When he slew them, then they sought him: and they returned and inquired early after God."

Psalm 106:21-27 "²¹They forgat God their saviour, which had done great things in Egypt; ²²Wondrous works in the land of Ham, and terrible things by the Red sea. ²³Therefore he said that he would destroy them, had not Moses his chosen stood before him in the breach, to turn away his wrath, lest he should destroy them. ²⁴Yea, they despised the pleasant land, they believed not his word: ²⁵But murmured in their tents, and hearkened not unto the voice of the LORD. ²⁶Therefore he lifted up his hand against them, to overthrow them in the wilderness: ²⁷To overthrow their seed also among the nations, and to scatter them in the lands."

Matthew 17:19-20 "¹⁹Then came the disciples to Jesus apart, and said, Why could not we cast him out? ²⁰And Jesus said unto them, Because of your unbelief: for verily I say unto you, If ye have faith as a grain of mustard seed, ye shall say unto this mountain, Remove hence to yonder place; and it shall remove; and nothing shall be impossible unto you."

Romans 11:20-21 "²⁰Well; because of unbelief they were broken off, and thou standest by faith. Be not highminded, but fear: ²¹For if God spared not the natural branches, take heed lest he also spare not thee."

Those That Are Defiled And Unbelieving

Titus 1:15-16 "¹⁵Unto the pure all things are pure: but unto them that are defiled and unbelieving is nothing pure; but even their mind and conscience is defiled. ¹⁶They profess that they know God; but in works they deny him, being abominable, and disobedient, and unto every good work reprobate."

Those That Do Not Believe In The Lord

Mark 16:16-19 "¹⁶He that believeth and is baptized shall be saved; but he that believeth not shall be damned. ¹⁷And these signs shall follow them that believe; In my name shall they cast out devils; they shall speak with new tongues; ¹⁸They shall take up serpents; and if they drink any deadly thing, it shall not hurt them; they shall lay hands on the sick, and they shall recover. ¹⁹So then after the Lord had spoken unto them, he was received up into heaven, and sat on the right hand of God."

John 3:17-18 "¹⁷For God sent not his Son into the world to condemn the world; but that the world through him might be saved. ¹⁸He that believeth on him is not condemned: but he that believeth not is condemned already, because he hath not believed in the name of the only begotten Son of God."

John 3:36 "He that believeth on the Son hath everlasting life: and he that believeth not the Son shall not see life; but the wrath of God abideth on him."

John 6:63-65 "⁶³It is the spirit that quickeneth; the flesh profiteth nothing: the words that I speak unto you, they are spirit, and they are life. ⁶⁴But

there are some of you that believe not. For Jesus knew from the beginning who they were that believed not, and who should betray him. ⁶⁵And he said, Therefore said I unto you, that no man can come unto me, except it were given unto him of my Father."

John 8:21-24 "²¹Then said Jesus again unto them, I go my way, and ye shall seek me, and shall die in your sins: whither I go, ye cannot come. ²²Then said the Jews, Will he kill himself? because he saith, Whither I go, ye cannot come. ²³And he said unto them, Ye are from beneath; I am from above: ye are of this world; I am not of this world. ²⁴I said therefore unto you, that ye shall die in your sins: for if ye believe not that I am he, ye shall die in your sins."

John 12:44-48 "⁴⁴Jesus cried and said, He that believeth on me, believeth not on me, but on him that sent me. ⁴⁵And he that seeth me seeth him that sent me. ⁴⁶I am come a light into the world, that whosoever believeth on me should not abide in darkness. ⁴⁷And if any man hear my words, and believe not, I judge him not: for I came not to judge the world, but to save the world. ⁴⁸He that rejecteth me, and receiveth not my words, hath one that judgeth him: the word that I have spoken, the same shall judge him in the last day."

1 Corinthians 14:22 "Wherefore tongues are for a sign, not to them that believe, but to them that believe not: but prophesying serveth not for them that believe not, but for them which believe."

2 Corinthians 4:3-4 "³But if our gospel be hid, it is hid to them that are lost: ⁴In whom the god of this world hath blinded the minds of them which believe not, lest the light of the glorious gospel of Christ, who is the image of God, should shine unto them."

2 Thessalonians 2:8-12 "⁸And then shall that Wicked be revealed, whom the Lord shall consume with the spirit of his mouth, and shall destroy with the brightness of his coming: ⁹Even him, whose coming is after the working of Satan with all power and signs and lying wonders, ¹⁰And with all deceivableness of unrighteousness in them that perish; because they received not the love of the truth, that they might be saved. ¹¹And for this cause God shall send them strong delusion, that they should believe a lie: [12]That they all might be damned who believed not the truth, but had pleasure in unrighteousness."

1 John 5:10 "He that believeth on the Son of God hath the witness in himself: he that believeth not God hath made him a liar; because he believeth not the record that God gave of his Son."

Revelation 21:6-8 "[6]And he said unto me, It is done. I am Alpha and Omega, the beginning and the end. I will give unto him that is athirst of the fountain of the water of life freely. [7]He that overcometh shall inherit all things; and I will be his God, and he shall be my son. [8]But the fearful, and unbelieving, and the abominable, and murderers, and whoremongers, and sorcerers, and idolaters, and all liars, shall have their part in the lake which burneth with fire and brimstone: which is the second death."

Why Some Do Not Believe The Lord

John 3:10-12 "[10]Jesus answered and said unto him, Art thou a master of Israel, and knowest not these things? [11]Verily, verily, I say unto thee, We speak that we do know, and testify that we have seen; and ye receive not our witness. [12]If I have told you earthly things, and ye believe not, how shall ye believe, if I tell you of heavenly things?"

John 8:37-47 "[37]I know that ye are Abraham's seed; but ye seek to kill me, because my word hath no place in you. [38]I speak that which I have seen with my Father: and ye do that which ye have seen with your father. [39]They answered and said unto him, Abraham is our father. Jesus saith unto them, If ye were Abraham's children, ye would do the works of Abraham. [40]But now ye seek to kill me, a man that hath told you the truth, which I have heard of God: this did not Abraham. [41]Ye do the deeds of your father. Then said they to him, We be not born of fornication; we have one Father, even God. [42]Jesus said unto them, If God were your Father, ye would love me: for I proceeded forth and came from God; neither came I of myself, but he sent me. [43]Why do ye not understand my speech? even because ye cannot hear my word. [44]Ye are of your father the devil, and the lusts of your father ye will do. He was a murderer from the beginning, and abode not in the truth, because there is no truth in him.

When he speaketh a lie, he speaketh of his own: for he is a liar, and the father of it. [45]And because I tell you the truth, ye believe me not. [46]Which of you convinceth me of sin? And if I say the truth, why do ye not believe me? [47]He that is of God heareth God's words: ye therefore hear them not, because ye are not of God."

John 10:25-30 "[25]Jesus answered them, I told you, and ye believed not: the works that I do in my Father's name, they bear witness of me. [26]But ye believe not, because ye are not of my sheep, as I said unto you. [27]My sheep hear my voice, and I know them, and they follow me: [28]And I give unto them eternal life; and they shall never perish, neither shall any man pluck them out of my hand. [29]My Father, which gave them me, is greater than all; and no man is able to pluck them out of my Father's hand. [30]I and my Father are one."

John 12:35-43 "[35]Then Jesus said unto them, Yet a little while is the light with you. Walk while ye have the light, lest darkness come upon you: for he that walketh in darkness knoweth not whither he goeth. [36]While ye have light, believe in the light, that ye may be the children of light. These things spake Jesus, and departed, and did hide himself from them. [37]But though he had done so many miracles before them, yet they believed not on him: [38]That the saying of Esaias the prophet might be fulfilled, which he spake, Lord, who hath believed our report? and to whom hath the arm of the Lord been revealed? [39]Therefore they could not believe, because that Esaias said again, [40]He hath blinded their eyes, and hardened their heart; that they should not see with their eyes, nor understand with their heart, and be converted, and I should heal them. [41]These things said Esaias, when he saw his glory, and spake of him. [42]Nevertheless among the chief rulers also many believed on him; but because of the Pharisees they did not confess him, lest they should be put out of the synagogue: [43]For they loved the praise of men more than the praise of God."

UNCLEANNESS

God Not Calling Us To Uncleanness

1 Thessalonians 4:7 "For God hath not called us unto uncleanness, but unto holiness."

Not Being Unclean

Ephesians 5:3-4 "³But fornication, and all uncleanness, or covetousness, let it not be once named among you, as becometh saints; ⁴Neither filthiness, nor foolish talking, nor jesting, which are not convenient: but rather giving of thanks."

The Reward For Being Unclean

Ephesians 5:5-7 "⁵For this ye know, that no whoremonger, nor unclean person, nor covetous man, who is an idolater, hath any inheritance in the kingdom of Christ and of God. ⁶Let no man deceive you with vain words: for because of these things cometh the wrath of God upon the children of disobedience. ⁷Be not ye therefore partakers with them."

Colossians 3:5-6 "⁵Mortify therefore your members which are upon the earth; fornication, uncleanness, inordinate affection, evil concupiscence, and covetousness, which is idolatry: ⁶For which things' sake the wrath of God cometh on the children of disobedience:"

There Being Nothing Unclean Of Itself

Romans 14:14 "I know, and am persuaded by the Lord Jesus, that there is nothing unclean of itself: but to him that esteemeth any thing to be unclean, to him it is unclean."

Unclean People

Ephesians 5:5 "For this ye know, that no whoremonger, nor unclean person, nor covetous man, who is an idolater, hath any inheritance in the kingdom of Christ and of God."

Unclean Spirits

Mark 3:7-11 "⁷But Jesus withdrew himself with his disciples to the sea: and a great multitude from Galilee followed him, and from Judaea, ⁸And from Jerusalem, and from Idumaea, and from beyond Jordan; and they about Tyre and Sidon, a great multitude, when they had heard what great things he did, came unto him. ⁹And he spake to his disciples, that a small ship should wait on him because of the multitude, lest they should throng him. ¹⁰For he had healed many; insomuch that they pressed upon him for to touch him, as many as had plagues. ¹¹And unclean spirits, when they saw him, fell down before him, and cried, saying, Thou art the Son of God."

Luke 4:31-36 "³¹And came down to Capernaum, a city of Galilee, and taught them on the sabbath days. ³²And they were astonished at his doctrine: for his word was with power. ³³And in the synagogue there was a man, which had a spirit of an unclean devil, and cried out with a loud voice, ³⁴Saying, Let us alone; what have we to do with thee, thou Jesus of Nazareth? art thou come to destroy us? I know thee who thou art; the Holy One of God. ³⁵And Jesus rebuked him, saying, Hold thy peace, and come out of him. And when the devil had thrown him in the midst, he came out of him, and hurt him not. ³⁶And they were all amazed, and spake among themselves, saying, What a word is this! for with authority and power he commandeth the unclean spirits, and they come out."

Luke 4:40-41 "⁴⁰Now when the sun was setting, all they that had any sick with divers diseases brought them unto him; and he laid his hands on every one of them, and healed them. ⁴¹And devils also came out of many, crying out, and saying, Thou art Christ the Son of God. And he rebuking them suffered them not to speak: for they knew that he was Christ."

What Animals Are Unclean

Exodus 22:31 "And ye shall be holy men unto me: neither shall ye eat any flesh that is torn of beasts in the field; ye shall cast it to the dogs."

Leviticus 11:4-44 "⁴Nevertheless these shall ye not eat of them that chew the cud, or of them that divide the hoof: as the camel, because he cheweth the cud, but divideth not the hoof; he is unclean unto you. ⁵And the coney, because he cheweth the cud, but divideth not the hoof; he is unclean unto you. ⁶And the hare, because he cheweth the cud, but divideth not the hoof; he is unclean unto you. ⁷And the swine, though he divide the hoof, and be clovenfooted, yet he cheweth not the cud; he is unclean to you. ⁸Of their flesh shall ye not eat, and their carcase shall ye not touch; they are unclean to you. ⁹These shall ye eat of all that are in the waters: whatsoever hath fins and scales in the waters, in the seas, and in the rivers, them shall ye eat. ¹⁰And all that have not fins and scales in the seas, and in the rivers, of all that move in the waters, and of any living thing which is in the waters, they shall be an abomination unto you: [11]They shall be even an abomination unto you; ye shall not eat of their flesh, but ye shall have their carcases in abomination. [12]Whatsoever hath no fins nor scales in the waters, that shall be an abomination unto you. [13]And these are they which ye shall have in abomination among the fowls; they shall not be eaten, they are an abomination: the eagle, and the ossifrage, and the ospray, [14]And the vulture, and the kite after his kind; [15]Every raven after his kind; [16]And the owl, and the night hawk, and the cuckow, and the hawk after his kind, [17]And the little owl, and the cormorant, and the great owl, [18]And the swan, and the pelican, and the gier eagle [19]And the stork, the heron after her kind, and the lapwing, and the bat. [20]All fowls that creep, going upon all four, shall be an abomination unto you. [21]Yet these may ye eat of every flying creeping thing that goeth upon all four, which have legs above their feet, to leap withal upon the earth; [22]Even these of them ye may eat; the locust after his kind, and the bald locust after his kind, and the beetle after his kind, and the grasshopper after his kind. [23]But all other flying creeping things, which have four feet, shall be an abomination unto you. [24]And for these ye shall be unclean: whosoever toucheth the carcase of them shall be unclean until the even. [25]And whosoever beareth ought of the carcase of them shall wash his clothes, and be unclean until the even. [26]The carcases of every beast which divideth the hoof, and is not cloven-footed, nor cheweth the cud, are unclean unto you: every one that toucheth them shall be unclean. [27]And whatsoever goeth upon his paws, among all manner of beasts that go on all four, those are unclean unto you: whoso toucheth their carcase shall be unclean until the even. [28]And he that beareth the carcase of them shall wash his clothes, and be unclean until the even: they are unclean unto you. [29]These also shall be unclean unto you among the creeping things that creep upon the earth; the weasel, and the mouse, and the tortoise after his kind, [30]And the ferret, and the chameleon, and the lizard, and the snail, and the mole. [31]These are unclean to you among all that creep: whosoever doth touch them, when they be dead, shall be unclean until the even. [32]And upon whatsoever any of them, when they

are dead, doth fall, it shall be unclean; whether it be any vessel of wood, or raiment, or skin, or sack, whatsoever vessel it be, wherein any work is done, it must be put into water, and it shall be unclean until the even; so it shall be cleansed. [33]And every earthen vessel, whereinto any of them falleth, whatsoever is in it shall be unclean; and ye shall break it. [34]Of all meat which may be eaten, that on which such water cometh shall be unclean: and all drink that may be drunk in every such vessel shall be unclean. [35]And every thing whereupon any part of their carcase falleth shall be unclean; whether it be oven, or ranges for pots, they shall be broken down: for they are unclean, and shall be unclean unto you. [36]Nevertheless a fountain or pit, wherein there is plenty of water, shall be clean: but that which toucheth their carcase shall be unclean. [37]And if any part of their carcase fall upon any sowing seed which is to be sown, it shall be clean. [38]But if any water be put upon the seed, and any part of their carcase fall thereon, it shall be unclean unto you. [39]And if any beast, of which ye may eat, die; he that toucheth the carcase thereof shall be unclean until the even. [40]And he that eateth of the carcase of it shall wash his clothes, and be unclean until the even: he also that beareth the carcase of it shall wash his clothes, and be unclean until the even. [41]And every creeping thing that creepeth upon the earth shall be an abomination; it shall not be eaten. [42]Whatsoever goeth upon the belly, and whatsoever goeth upon all four, or whatsoever hath more feet among all creeping things that creep upon the earth, them ye shall not eat; for they are an abomination. [43]Ye shall not make yourselves abominable with any creeping thing that creepeth, neither shall ye make yourselves unclean with them, that ye should be defiled thereby. [44]For I am the LORD your God: ye shall therefore sanctify yourselves, and ye shall be holy; for I am holy: neither shall ye defile yourselves with any manner of creeping thing that creepeth upon the earth."

Leviticus 20:25 "Ye shall therefore put difference between clean beasts and unclean, and between unclean fowls and clean: and ye shall not make your souls abominable by beast, or by fowl, or by any manner of living thing that creepeth on the ground, which I have separated from you as unclean."

Deuteronomy 14:7-21 "⁷Nevertheless these ye shall not eat of them that chew the cud, or of them that divide the cloven hoof; as the camel, and the hare, and the coney: for they chew the cud, but divide not the hoof; therefore they are unclean unto you. ⁸And the swine, because it divideth the hoof, yet cheweth not the cud, it is unclean unto you: ye shall not eat of their flesh, nor touch their dead carcase. ⁹These ye shall eat of all that are in the waters: all that have fins and scales shall ye eat: ¹⁰And whatsoever hath not fins and scales ye may not eat; it is unclean unto you. ¹¹Of all clean birds ye shall eat. ¹²But these are they of which ye shall not eat: the eagle, and ossifrage, and the ospray, ¹³And the glede, and the kite, and the vulture after his kind, ¹⁴And every raven after his kind, ¹⁵And the owl, and the night hawk, and the cuckow, and the hawk after his kind, ¹⁶The little owl, and the great owl, and the swan, ¹⁷And the pelican, and the gier eagle, and the cormorant, ¹⁸And the stork, and the heron after her kind, and the lapwing, and the bat. ¹⁹And every creeping thing that flieth is unclean unto you: they shall not be eaten. ²⁰But of all clean fowls ye may eat. ²¹Ye shall not eat of any thing that dieth of itself: thou shalt give it unto the stranger that is in thy gates, that he may eat it; or thou mayest sell it unto an alien: for thou art an holy people unto the LORD thy God. Thou shalt not seethe a kid in his mother's milk."

Who Is Unclean

Leviticus 12:1-8 "¹And the LORD spake unto Moses, saying, ²Speak unto the children of Israel, saying, If a woman have conceived seed, and born a man child: then she shall be unclean seven days; according to the days of the separation for her infirmity shall she be unclean. ³And in the eighth day the flesh of his foreskin shall be circumcised. ⁴And she shall then continue in the blood of her purifying three and thirty days; she shall touch no hallowed thing, nor come into the sanctuary, until the days of her purifying be fulfilled. ⁵But if she bear a maid child, then she shall be unclean two weeks, as in her separation: and she shall continue in the blood of her purifying threescore and six days. ⁶And when the days of her purifying are fulfilled, for a son, or for a daughter, she shall

bring a lamb of the first year for a burnt offering, and a young pigeon, or a turtledove, for a sin offering, unto the door of the tabernacle of the congregation, unto the priest: ⁷Who shall offer it before the LORD, and make an atonement for her; and she shall be cleansed from the issue of her blood. This is the law for her that hath born a male or a female. ⁸And if she be not able to bring a lamb, then she shall bring two turtles, or two young pigeons; the one for the burnt offering, and the other for a sin offering: and the priest shall make an atonement for her, and she shall be clean."

Leviticus 15:1-33 "¹And the LORD spake unto Moses and to Aaron, saying, ²Speak unto the children of Israel, and say unto them, When any man hath a running issue out of his flesh, because of his issue he is unclean. ³And this shall be his uncleanness in his issue: whether his flesh run with his issue, or his flesh be stopped from his issue, it is his uncleanness. ⁴Every bed, whereon he lieth that hath the issue, is unclean: and every thing, whereon he sitteth, shall be unclean. ⁵And whosoever toucheth his bed shall wash his clothes, and bathe himself in water, and be unclean until the even. ⁶And he that sitteth on any thing whereon he sat that hath the issue shall wash his clothes, and bathe himself in water, and be unclean until the even. ⁷And he that toucheth the flesh of him that hath the issue shall wash his clothes, and bathe himself in water, and be unclean until the even. ⁸And if he that hath the issue spit upon him that is clean; then he shall wash his clothes, and bathe himself in water, and be unclean until the even. ⁹And what saddle soever he rideth upon that hath the issue shall be unclean. ¹⁰And whosoever toucheth any thing that was under him shall be unclean until the even: and he that beareth any of those things shall wash his clothes, and bathe himself in water, and be unclean until the even. ¹¹And whomsoever he toucheth that hath the issue, and hath not rinsed his hands in water, he shall wash his clothes, and bathe himself in water, and be unclean until the even. ¹²And the vessel of earth, that he toucheth which hath the issue, shall be broken: and every vessel of wood shall be rinsed in water. ¹³And when he that hath an issue is cleansed of his issue; then he shall number to himself seven days for his cleansing, and wash his clothes, and bathe his flesh in running water, and shall be clean. [14]And on the eighth day he shall take to him two turtledoves, or two young pigeons, and come before the LORD unto the door of the tabernacle of the congregation, and give them unto the priest: [15]And the priest shall offer them, the one for a sin offering, and the other for a burnt offering; and the priest shall make an atonement for him before the LORD for his issue. [16]And if any man's seed of copulation go out from him, then he shall wash all his flesh in water, and be unclean until the even. [17]And every garment, and every skin, whereon is the seed of copulation, shall be washed with water, and be unclean until the even. [18]The woman also with whom man shall lie with seed of copulation, they shall both bathe themselves in water, and be unclean until the even. [19]And if a woman have an issue, and her issue in her flesh be blood, she shall be put apart seven days: and whosoever toucheth her shall be unclean until the even. [20]And every thing that she lieth upon in her separation shall be unclean: every thing also that she sitteth upon shall be unclean. [21]And whosoever toucheth her bed shall wash his clothes, and bathe himself in water, and be unclean until the even. [22]And whosoever toucheth any thing that she sat upon shall wash his clothes, and bathe himself in water, and be unclean until the even. [23]And if it be on her bed, or on any thing whereon she sitteth, when he toucheth it, he shall be unclean until the even. [24]And if any man lie with her at all, and her flowers be upon him, he shall be unclean seven days; and all the bed whereon he lieth shall be unclean. [25]And if a woman have an issue of her blood many days out of the time of her separation, or if it run beyond the time of her separation; all the days of the issue of her uncleanness shall be as the days of her separation: she shall be unclean. [26]Every bed whereon she lieth all the days of her issue shall be unto her as the bed of her separation: and whatsoever she sitteth upon shall be unclean, as the uncleanness of her separation. [27]And whosoever toucheth those things shall be unclean, and shall wash his clothes, and bathe himself in water, and be unclean until the even. [28]But if she be cleansed of her issue, then she shall number to herself seven days, and after that she shall be clean. [29]And on the eighth day she shall take unto her two turtles, or two young pigeons, and bring them unto the priest, to the door of the tabernacle of the congregation. [30]And the priest shall offer the one for a sin offering, and the other for a burnt offering; and the priest shall make an atonement for her before the LORD for the issue of her uncleanness. [31]Thus shall ye separate the children of Israel from their uncleanness; that they die not in their uncleanness, when they defile my tabernacle that is among them. [32]This is the law of him that hath an issue, and of him whose seed goeth from him, and is defiled therewith; [33]And of her that is sick of her flowers, and of him that hath an issue, of the man, and of the woman, and of him that lieth with her that is unclean."

Whose Life Is Among The Unclean
Job 36:13-14 "[13]But the hypocrites in heart heap up wrath: they cry not when he bindeth them. [14]They die in youth, and their life is among the unclean."

Why God Let People Go Into Uncleanness
Psalm 81:10-12 "[10]I am the LORD thy God, which brought thee out of the land of Egypt: open thy mouth wide, and I will fill it. [11]But my people would not hearken to my voice; and Israel would none of me. [12]So I gave them up unto their own hearts' lust: and they walked in their own counsels."

Romans 1:21-24 "[21]Because that, when they knew God, they glorified him not as God, neither were thankful; but became vain in their imaginations, and their foolish heart was darkened. [22]Professing themselves to be wise, they became fools, [23]And changed the glory of the uncorruptible God into an image made like to corruptible man, and to birds, and fourfooted beasts, and creeping things. [24]Wherefore God also gave them up to uncleanness through the lusts of their own hearts, to dishonour their own bodies between themselves:"

UNDEFILEMENT

The Undefiled
Psalm 119:1-3 "[1]Blessed are the undefiled in the way, who walk in the law of the LORD. [2]Blessed are they that keep his testimonies, and that seek him with the whole heart. [3]They also do no iniquity: they walk in his ways."

Revelation 3:1-5 "¹And unto the angel of the church in Sardis write; These things saith he that hath the seven Spirits of God, and the seven stars; I know thy works, that thou hast a name that thou livest, and art dead. ²Be watchful, and strengthen the things which remain, that are ready to die: for I have not found thy works perfect before God. ³Remember therefore how thou hast received and heard, and hold fast, and repent. If therefore thou shalt not watch, I will come on thee as a thief, and thou shalt not know what hour I will come upon thee. ⁴Thou hast a few names even in Sardis which have not defiled their garments; and they shall walk with me in white: for they are worthy. ⁵He that overcometh, the same shall be clothed in white raiment; and I will not blot out his name out of the book of life, but I will confess his name before my Father, and before his angels."

UNDERSTANDING

Acquiring Understanding
Proverbs 4:7 "Wisdom is the principal thing; therefore get wisdom: and with all thy getting get understanding."

Proverbs 23:23 "Buy the truth, and sell it not; also wisdom, and instruction, and understanding."

Good Understanding
Proverbs 13:15 "Good understanding giveth favour: but the way of transgressors is hard."

How Understanding Is Acquired
Psalm 119:89-104 "⁸⁹For ever, O LORD, thy word is settled in heaven. ⁹⁰Thy faithfulness is unto all generations: thou hast established the earth, and it abideth. ⁹¹They continue this day according to thine ordinances: for all are thy servants. ⁹²Unless thy law had been my delights, I should then have perished in mine affliction. ⁹³I will never forget thy precepts: for with them thou hast quickened me. ⁹⁴I am thine, save me; for I have sought thy precepts. ⁹⁵The wicked have waited for me to destroy me: but I will consider thy testimonies. ⁹⁶I have seen an end of all perfection: but thy commandment is exceeding broad. ⁹⁷O how love I thy law! it is my meditation all the day. ⁹⁸Thou through thy commandments hast made me wiser than mine enemies: for they are ever with me. ⁹⁹I have more understanding than all my teachers: for thy testimonies are my meditation. ¹⁰⁰I understand more than the ancients, because I keep thy precepts. ¹⁰¹I have refrained my feet from every evil way, that I might keep thy word. ¹⁰²I have not departed from thy judgments: for thou hast taught me. ¹⁰³How sweet are thy words unto my taste! yea, sweeter than honey to my mouth! ¹⁰⁴Through thy precepts I get understanding: therefore I hate every false way."

Hebrews 11:3 "Through faith we understand that the worlds were framed by the word of God, so that things which are seen were not made of things which do appear."

Not Leaning To Your Own Understanding
Proverbs 3:5 "Trust in the LORD with all thine heart; and lean not unto thine own understanding."

The Lord Giving Understanding
1 Chronicles 22:12 "Only the LORD give thee wisdom and understanding, and give thee charge concerning Israel, that thou mayest keep the law of the LORD thy God."

Job 32:8 "But there is a spirit in man: and the inspiration of the Almighty giveth them understanding."

Psalm 119:73-75 "⁷³Thy hands have made me and fashioned me: give me understanding, that I may learn thy commandments. ⁷⁴They that fear thee will be glad when they see me; because I have hoped in thy word. ⁷⁵I know, O LORD, that thy judgments are right, and that thou in faithfulness hast afflicted me."

Psalm 119:126-130 "¹²⁶It is time for thee, LORD, to work: for they have made void thy law. ¹²⁷Therefore I love thy commandments above gold; yea, above fine gold. ¹²⁸Therefore I esteem all thy precepts concerning all things to be right; and I hate every false way. ¹²⁹Thy testimonies are wonderful: therefore doth my soul keep them. ¹³⁰The entrance of thy words giveth light; it giveth understanding unto the simple."

Luke 24:44-47 "⁴⁴And he said unto them, These are the words which I spake unto you, while I was yet with you, that all things must be fulfilled, which were written in the law of Moses, and in the prophets, and in the psalms, concerning me.

[45]Then opened he their understanding, that they might understand the scriptures, [46]And said unto them, Thus it is written, and thus it behoved Christ to suffer, and to rise from the dead the third day: [47]And that repentance and remission of sins should be preached in his name among all nations, beginning at Jerusalem."

1 John 5:20 "And we know that the Son of God is come, and hath given us an understanding, that we may know him that is true, and we are in him that is true, even in his Son Jesus Christ. This is the true God, and eternal life."

The Understanding Of The Lord

Psalm 147:5 "Great is our Lord, and of great power: his understanding is infinite."

Isaiah 40:28 "Hast thou not known? hast thou not heard, that the everlasting God, the LORD, the Creator of the ends of the earth, fainteth not, neither is weary? there is no searching of his understanding."

There Being No Understanding Against The Lord

Proverbs 21:30 "There is no wisdom nor understanding nor counsel against the LORD."

Those That Are Void Of Understanding

Proverbs 10:13 "In the lips of him that hath understanding wisdom is found: but a rod is for the back of him that is void of understanding."

Proverbs 17:18 "A man void of understanding striketh hands, and becometh surety in the presence of his friend."

Proverbs 24:30-34 "[30]I went by the field of the slothful, and by the vineyard of the man void of understanding; [31]And, lo, it was all grown over with thorns, and nettles had covered the face thereof, and the stone wall thereof was broken down. [32]Then I saw, and considered it well: I looked upon it, and received instruction. [33]Yet a little sleep, a little slumber, a little folding of the hands to sleep: [34]So shall thy poverty come as one that travelleth; and thy want as an armed man."

Jeremiah 5:20-21 "[20]Declare this in the house of Jacob, and publish it in Judah, saying, [21]Hear now this, O foolish people, and without understanding; which have eyes, and see not; which have ears, and hear not:"

Those That Understand

Proverbs 3:13 "Happy is the man that findeth wisdom, and the man that getteth understanding."

Proverbs 8:1-9 "[1]Doth not wisdom cry? and understanding put forth her voice? [2]She standeth in the top of high places, by the way in the places of the paths. [3]She crieth at the gates, at the entry of the city, at the coming in at the doors. [4]Unto you, O men, I call; and my voice is to the sons of man. [5]O ye simple, understand wisdom: and, ye fools, be ye of an understanding heart. [6]Hear; for I will speak of excellent things; and the opening of my lips shall be right things. [7]For my mouth shall speak truth; and wickedness is an abomination to my lips. [8]All the words of my mouth are in righteousness; there is nothing froward or perverse in them. [9]They are all plain to him that understandeth, and right to them that find knowledge."

Proverbs 10:13 "In the lips of him that hath understanding wisdom is found: but a rod is for the back of him that is void of understanding."

Proverbs 10:23 "It is as sport to a fool to do mischief: but a man of understanding hath wisdom."

Proverbs 11:12 "He that is void of wisdom despiseth his neighbour: but a man of understanding holdeth his peace."

Proverbs 14:6 "A scorner seeketh wisdom, and findeth it not: but knowledge is easy unto him that understandeth."

Proverbs 14:33 "Wisdom resteth in the heart of him that hath understanding: but that which is in the midst of fools is made known."

Proverbs 15:14 "The heart of him that hath understanding seeketh knowledge: but the mouth of fools feedeth on foolishness."

Proverbs 15:21 "Folly is joy to him that is destitute of wisdom: but a man of understanding walketh uprightly."

Proverbs 16:22 "Understanding is a wellspring of life unto him that hath it: but the instruction of fools is folly."

Proverbs 17:24 "Wisdom is before him that hath understanding; but the eyes of a fool are in the ends of the earth."

Proverbs 17:27 "He that hath knowledge spareth his words: and a man of understanding is of an excellent spirit."

Proverbs 19:8 "He that getteth wisdom loveth his own soul: he that keepeth understanding shall find good."

Proverbs 19:25 "Smite a scorner, and the simple will beware: and reprove one that hath understanding, and he will understand knowledge."

Proverbs 20:5 "Counsel in the heart of man is like deep water; but a man of understanding will draw it out."

Proverbs 28:2 "For the transgression of a land many are the princes thereof: but by a man of understanding and knowledge the state thereof shall be prolonged."

Proverbs 28:11 "The rich man is wise in his own conceit; but the poor that hath understanding searcheth him out."

Daniel 2:20-21 "20Daniel answered and said, Blessed be the name of God for ever and ever: for wisdom and might are his: 21And he changeth the times and the seasons: he removeth kings, and setteth up kings: he giveth wisdom unto the wise, and knowledge to them that know understanding:"

What Fools Do Not Understand
Psalm 92:5-6 "5O LORD, how great are thy works! and thy thoughts are very deep. 6A brutish man knoweth not; neither doth a fool understand this."

What Is Understanding
Deuteronomy 4:5-6 "5Behold, I have taught you statutes and judgments, even as the LORD my God commanded me, that ye should do so in the land whither ye go to possess it. 6Keep therefore and do them; for this is your wisdom and your understanding in the sight of the nations, which shall hear all these statutes, and say, Surely this great nation is a wise and understanding people."

Job 28:28 "And unto man he said, Behold, the fear of the Lord, that is wisdom; and to depart from evil is understanding."

Proverbs 8:12-14 "12I wisdom dwell with prudence, and find out knowledge of witty inventions. 13The fear of the LORD is to hate evil: pride, and arrogancy, and the evil way, and the froward mouth, do I hate. 14Counsel is mine, and sound wisdom: I am understanding; I have strength."

Proverbs 9:10 "The fear of the LORD is the beginning of wisdom: and the knowledge of the holy is understanding."

What Is Understood By The Things That Are Made By God
Romans 1:18-20 "18For the wrath of God is revealed from heaven against all ungodliness and unrighteousness of men, who hold the truth in unrighteousness; 19Because that which may be known of God is manifest in them; for God hath shewed it unto them. 20For the invisible things of him from the creation of the world are clearly seen, being understood by the things that are made, even his eternal power and Godhead; so that they are without excuse:"

What Passes All Understanding
Ephesians 3:19 "And to know the love of Christ, which passeth knowledge, that ye might be filled with all the fulness of God."

Philippians 4:7 "And the peace of God, which passeth all understanding, shall keep your hearts and minds through Christ Jesus."

What To Call Understanding
Proverbs 7:4 "Say unto wisdom, Thou art my sister; and call understanding thy kinswoman:"

What Understanding Does
Proverbs 2:10-20 "10When wisdom entereth into thine heart, and knowledge is pleasant unto thy soul; 11Discretion shall preserve thee, understanding shall keep thee: 12To deliver thee from the way of the evil man, from the man that speaketh froward things; 13Who leave the paths of uprightness, to walk in the ways of darkness; 14Who rejoice to do evil, and delight in the frowardness of the wicked; 15Whose ways are crooked, and they froward in their paths: 16To deliver thee from the strange woman, even from the stranger which flattereth with her words; 17Which forsaketh the guide of her youth, and forgetteth the covenant of her God. 18For her house inclineth unto death, and her paths unto the dead. 19None that go unto her return again, neither take they hold of the paths of life. 20That thou mayest walk

in the way of good men, and keep the paths of the righteous."

Proverbs 24:3 "Through wisdom is an house builded; and by understanding it is established:"

What Understanding Is
Proverbs 16:22 "Understanding is a wellspring of life unto him that hath it: but the instruction of fools is folly."

What Understanding Is Better Than
Proverbs 16:16 "How much better is it to get wisdom than gold! and to get understanding rather to be chosen than silver!"

What Was Established By Understanding
Proverbs 3:19 "The LORD by wisdom hath founded the earth; by understanding hath he established the heavens."

What You Should Try To Understand
Ephesians 5:17 "Wherefore be ye not unwise, but understanding what the will of the Lord is."

Where Understanding Comes From
Proverbs 2:6 "For the LORD giveth wisdom: out of his mouth cometh knowledge and understanding."

Who Has No Delight In Understanding
Proverbs 18:2 "A fool hath no delight in understanding, but that his heart may discover itself."

Who Is Void Of Understanding
Isaiah 44:9-19 "[9]They that make a graven image are all of them vanity; and their delectable things shall not profit; and they are their own witnesses; they see not, nor know; that they may be ashamed. [10]Who hath formed a god, or molten a graven image that is profitable for nothing? [11]Behold, all his fellows shall be ashamed: and the workmen, they are of men: let them all be gathered together, let them stand up; yet they shall fear, and they shall be ashamed together. [12]The smith with the tongs both worketh in the coals, and fashioneth it with hammers, and worketh it with the strength of his arms: yea, he is hungry, and his strength faileth: he drinketh no water, and is faint. [13]The carpenter stretcheth out his rule; he marketh it out with a line; he fitteth it with planes, and he marketh it out with the compass, and maketh it after the figure of a man, according to the beauty of a man; that it may remain in the house. [14]He heweth him down

cedars, and taketh the cypress and the oak, which he strengtheneth for himself among the trees of the forest: he planteth an ash, and the rain doth nourish it. [15]Then shall it be for a man to burn: for he will take thereof, and warm himself; yea, he kindleth it, and baketh bread; yea, he maketh a god, and worshippeth it; he maketh it a graven image, and falleth down thereto. [16]He burneth part thereof in the fire; with part thereof he eateth flesh; he roasteth roast, and is satisfied: yea, he warmeth himself, and saith, Aha, I am warm, I have seen the fire: [17]And the residue thereof he maketh a god, even his graven image: he falleth down unto it, and worshippeth it, and prayeth unto it, and saith, Deliver me; for thou art my god. [18]They have not known nor understood: for he hath shut their eyes, that they cannot see; and their hearts, that they cannot understand. [19]And none considereth in his heart, neither is there knowledge nor understanding to say, I have burned part of it in the fire; yea, also I have baked bread upon the coals thereof; I have roasted flesh, and eaten it: and shall I make the residue thereof an abomination? shall I fall down to the stock of a tree?"

Proverbs 6:32 "But whoso committeth adultery with a woman lacketh understanding: he that doeth it destroyeth his own soul."

Proverbs 12:11 "He that tilleth his land shall be satisfied with bread: but he that followeth vain persons is void of understanding."

Proverbs 28:5 "Evil men understand not judgment: but they that seek the LORD understand all things."

Daniel 12:10 "Many shall be purified, and made white, and tried; but the wicked shall do wickedly: and none of the wicked shall understand; but the wise shall understand."

Romans 1:21-23 "[21]Because that, when they knew God, they glorified him not as God, neither were thankful; but became vain in their imaginations, and their foolish heart was darkened. [22]Professing themselves to be wise, they became fools, [23]And changed the glory of the uncorruptible God into an image made like to corruptible man, and to birds, and fourfooted beasts, and creeping things."

Ephesians 4:17-19 "[17]This I say therefore, and testify in the Lord, that ye henceforth walk not as other Gentiles walk, in the vanity of their mind, [18]Having the understanding darkened, being alienated from the life of God through the ignorance that is in them, because of the blindness of their heart: [19]Who being past feeling have given themselves over unto lasciviousness, to work all uncleanness with greediness."

Who Understands

Psalm 111:10 "The fear of the LORD is the beginning of wisdom: a good understanding have all they that do his commandments: his praise endureth for ever."

Psalm 119:89-100 "[89]For ever, O LORD, thy word is settled in heaven. [90]Thy faithfulness is unto all generations: thou hast established the earth, and it abideth. [91]They continue this day according to thine ordinances: for all are thy servants. [92]Unless thy law had been my delights, I should then have perished in mine affliction. [93]I will never forget thy precepts: for with them thou hast quickened me. [94]I am thine, save me; for I have sought thy precepts. [95]The wicked have waited for me to destroy me: but I will consider thy testimonies. [96]I have seen an end of all perfection: but thy commandment is exceeding broad. [97]O how love I thy law! it is my meditation all the day. [98]Thou through thy commandments hast made me wiser than mine enemies: for they are ever with me. [99]I have more understanding than all my teachers: for thy testimonies are my meditation. [100]I understand more than the ancients, because I keep thy precepts."

Proverbs 2:1-9 "[1]My son, if thou wilt receive my words, and hide my commandments with thee; [2]So that thou incline thine ear unto wisdom, and apply thine heart to understanding; [3]Yea, if thou criest after knowledge, and liftest up thy voice for understanding; [4]If thou seekest her as silver, and searchest for her as for hid treasures; [5]Then shalt thou understand the fear of the LORD, and find the knowledge of God. [6]For the LORD giveth wisdom: out of his mouth cometh knowledge and understanding. [7]He layeth up sound wisdom for the righteous: he is a buckler to them that walk uprightly. [8]He keepeth the paths of judgment, and preserveth the way of his saints. [9]Then shalt thou understand righteousness, and judgment, and equity; yea, every good path."

Proverbs 14:29 "He that is slow to wrath is of great understanding: but he that is hasty of spirit exalteth folly."

Proverbs 15:32 "He that refuseth instruction despiseth his own soul: but he that heareth reproof getteth understanding."

Proverbs 17:28 "Even a fool, when he holdeth his peace, is counted wise: and he that shutteth his lips is esteemed a man of understanding."

Proverbs 19:25 "Smite a scorner, and the simple will beware: and reprove one that hath understanding, and he will understand knowledge."

Proverbs 28:5 "Evil men understand not judgment: but they that seek the LORD understand all things."

Daniel 12:10 "Many shall be purified, and made white, and tried; but the wicked shall do wickedly: and none of the wicked shall understand; but the wise shall understand."

Why Some People
Do Not Understand The Lord

Deuteronomy 29:4 "Yet the LORD hath not given you an heart to perceive, and eyes to see, and ears to hear, unto this day."

Isaiah 6:8-10 "[8]Also I heard the voice of the Lord, saying, Whom shall I send, and who will go for us? Then said I, Here am I; send me. [9]And he said, Go, and tell this people, Hear ye indeed, but understand not; and see ye indeed, but perceive not. [10]Make the heart of this people fat, and make their ears heavy, and shut their eyes; lest they see with their eyes, and hear with their ears, and understand with their heart, and convert, and be healed."

Isaiah 28:9-13 "[9]Whom shall he teach knowledge? and whom shall he make to understand doctrine? them that are weaned from the milk, and drawn from the breasts. [10]For precept must be upon precept, precept upon precept; line upon line, line upon line; here a little, and there a little: [11]For with stammering lips and another tongue will he speak to this people. [12]To whom he said, This is the rest wherewith ye may cause the weary to rest; and this is the refreshing: yet they would not hear. [13]But the word of the LORD was unto them precept upon precept, precept upon precept; line upon line, line upon line; here a little, and there a little; that they might go, and fall backward, and be broken, and snared, and taken."

Isaiah 29:9-12 "⁹Stay yourselves, and wonder; cry ye out, and cry: they are drunken, but not with wine; they stagger, but not with strong drink. ¹⁰For the LORD hath poured out upon you the spirit of deep sleep, and hath closed your eyes: the prophets and your rulers, the seers hath he covered. ¹¹And the vision of all is become unto you as the words of a book that is sealed, which men deliver to one that is learned, saying, Read this, I pray thee: and he saith, I cannot; for it is sealed: ¹²And the book is delivered to him that is not learned, saying, Read this, I pray thee: and he saith, I am not learned."

Isaiah 44:7-18 "⁷And who, as I, shall call, and shall declare it, and set it in order for me, since I appointed the ancient people? and the things that are coming, and shall come, let them shew unto them. ⁸Fear ye not, neither be afraid: have not I told thee from that time, and have declared it? ye are even my witnesses. Is there a God beside me? yea, there is no God; I know not any. ⁹They that make a graven image are all of them vanity; and their delectable things shall not profit; and they are their own witnesses; they see not, nor know; that they may be ashamed. ¹⁰Who hath formed a god, or molten a graven image that is profitable for nothing? ¹¹Behold, all his fellows shall be ashamed: and the workmen, they are of men: let them all be gathered together, let them stand up; yet they shall fear, and they shall be ashamed together. ¹²The smith with the tongs both worketh in the coals, and fashioneth it with hammers, and worketh it with the strength of his arms: yea, he is hungry, and his strength faileth: he drinketh no water, and is faint. ¹³The carpenter stretcheth out his rule; he marketh it out with a line; he fitteth it with planes, and he marketh it out with the compass, and maketh it after the figure of a man, according to the beauty of a man; that it may remain in the house. ¹⁴He heweth him down cedars, and taketh the cypress and the oak, which he strengtheneth for himself among the trees of the forest: he planteth an ash, and the rain doth nourish it. ¹⁵Then shall it be for a man to burn: for he will take thereof, and warm himself; yea, he kindleth it, and baketh bread; yea, he

maketh a god, and worshippeth it; he maketh it a graven image, and falleth down thereto. ¹⁶He burneth part thereof in the fire; with part thereof he eateth flesh; he roasteth roast, and is satisfied: yea, he warmeth himself, and saith, Aha, I am warm, I have seen the fire: ¹⁷And the residue thereof he maketh a god, even his graven image: he falleth down unto it, and worshippeth it, and prayeth unto it, and saith, Deliver me; for thou art my god. ¹⁸They have not known nor understood: for he hath shut their eyes, that they cannot see; and their hearts, that they cannot understand."

Jeremiah 5:20-21 "²⁰Declare this in the house of Jacob, and publish it in Judah, saying, ²¹Hear now this, O foolish people, and without understanding; which have eyes, and see not; which have ears, and hear not:"

Jeremiah 6:10 "To whom shall I speak, and give warning, that they may hear? behold, their ear is uncircumcised, and they cannot hearken: behold, the word of the LORD is unto them a reproach; they have no delight in it."

Ezekiel 12:1-2 "¹The word of the LORD also came unto me, saying, ²Son of man, thou dwellest in the midst of a rebellious house, which have eyes to see, and see not; they have ears to hear, and hear not: for they are a rebellious house."

Matthew 13:10-17 "¹⁰And the disciples came, and said unto him, Why speakest thou unto them in parables? ¹¹He answered and said unto them, Because it is given unto you to know the mysteries of the kingdom of heaven, but to them it is not given. ¹²For whosoever hath, to him shall be given, and he shall have more abundance: but whosoever hath not, from him shall be taken away even that he hath. ¹³Therefore speak I to them in parables: because they seeing see not; and hearing they hear not, neither do they understand. ¹⁴And in them is fulfilled the prophecy of Esaias, which saith, By hearing ye shall hear, and shall not understand; and seeing ye shall see, and shall not perceive: ¹⁵For this people's heart is waxed gross, and their ears are dull of hearing, and their eyes they have closed; lest at any time they should see with their eyes, and hear with their ears, and should understand with their heart, and should be converted, and I should heal them. ¹⁶But blessed are your eyes, for they see:

and your ears, for they hear. [17]For verily I say unto you, That many prophets and righteous men have desired to see those things which ye see, and have not seen them; and to hear those things which ye hear, and have not heard them."

Mark 4:9-12 "[9]And he said unto them, He that hath ears to hear, let him hear. [10]And when he was alone, they that were about him with the twelve asked of him the parable. [11]And he said unto them, Unto you it is given to know the mystery of the kingdom of God: but unto them that are without, all these things are done in parables: [12]That seeing they may see, and not perceive; and hearing they may hear, and not understand; lest at any time they should be converted, and their sins should be forgiven them."

Luke 8:9-10 "[9]And his disciples asked him, saying, What might this parable be? [10]And he said, Unto you it is given to know the mysteries of the kingdom of God: but to others in parables; that seeing they might not see, and hearing they might not understand."

John 8:37-47 "[37]I know that ye are Abraham's seed; but ye seek to kill me, because my word hath no place in you. [38]I speak that which I have seen with my Father: and ye do that which ye have seen with your father. [39]They answered and said unto him, Abraham is our father. Jesus saith unto them, If ye were Abraham's children, ye would do the works of Abraham. [40]But now ye seek to kill me, a man that hath told you the truth, which I have heard of God: this did not Abraham. [41]Ye do the deeds of your father. Then said they to him, We be not born of fornication; we have one Father, even God. [42]Jesus said unto them, If God were your Father, ye would love me: for I proceeded forth and came from God; neither came I of myself, but he sent me. [43]Why do ye not understand my speech? even because ye cannot hear my word. [44]Ye are of your father the devil, and the lusts of your father ye will do. He was a murderer from the beginning, and abode not in the truth, because there is no truth in him. When he speaketh a lie, he speaketh of his own: for he is a liar, and the father of it. [45]And because I tell you the truth, ye believe me not. [46]Which of you convinceth me of sin? And if I say the truth, why do ye not believe me? [47]He that is of God

heareth God's words: ye therefore hear them not, because ye are not of God."

John 12:35-43 "[35]Then Jesus said unto them, Yet a little while is the light with you. Walk while ye have the light, lest darkness come upon you: for he that walketh in darkness knoweth not whither he goeth. [36]While ye have light, believe in the light, that ye may be the children of light. These things spake Jesus, and departed, and did hide himself from them. [37]But though he had done so many miracles before them, yet they believed not on him: [38]That the saying of Esaias the prophet might be fulfilled, which he spake, Lord, who hath believed our report? and to whom hath the arm of the Lord been revealed? [39]Therefore they could not believe, because that Esaias said again, [40]He hath blinded their eyes, and hardened their heart; that they should not see with their eyes, nor understand with their heart, and be converted, and I should heal them. [41]These things said Esaias, when he saw his glory, and spake of him. [42]Nevertheless among the chief rulers also many believed on him; but because of the Pharisees they did not confess him, lest they should be put out of the synagogue: [43]For they loved the praise of men more than the praise of God."

John 14:9-17 "[9]Jesus saith unto him, Have I been so long time with you, and yet hast thou not known me, Philip? he that hath seen me hath seen the Father; and how sayest thou then, Shew us the Father? [10]Believest thou not that I am in the Father, and the Father in me? the words that I speak unto you I speak not of myself: but the Father that dwelleth in me, he doeth the works. [11]Believe me that I am in the Father, and the Father in me: or else believe me for the very works' sake. [12]Verily, verily, I say unto you, He that believeth on me, the works that I do shall he do also; and greater works than these shall he do; because I go unto my Father. [13]And whatsoever ye shall ask in my name, that will I do, that the Father may be glorified in the Son. [14]If ye shall ask any thing in my name, I will do it. [15]If ye love me, keep my commandments. [16]And I will pray the Father, and he shall give you another Comforter, that he may abide with you for ever; [17]Even the Spirit of truth; whom the world cannot receive, because it seeth him not, neither knoweth him: but ye know him; for he dwelleth with you, and shall be in you."

Acts 28:25-28 "²⁵And when they agreed not among themselves, they departed, after that Paul had spoken one word, Well spake the Holy Ghost by Esaias the prophet unto our fathers, ²⁶Saying, Go unto this people, and say, Hearing ye shall hear, and shall not understand; and seeing ye shall see, and not perceive: ²⁷For the heart of this people is waxed gross, and their ears are dull of hearing, and their eyes have they closed; lest they should see with their eyes, and hear with their ears, and understand with their heart, and should be converted, and I should heal them. ²⁸Be it known therefore unto you, that the salvation of God is sent unto the Gentiles, and that they will hear it."

Romans 11:7-8 "⁷What then? Israel hath not obtained that which he seeketh for; but the election hath obtained it, and the rest were blinded ⁸(According as it is written, God hath given them the spirit of slumber, eyes that they should not see, and ears that they should not hear;) unto this day."

1 Corinthians 2:12-16 "¹²Now we have received, not the spirit of the world, but the spirit which is of God; that we might know the things that are freely given to us of God. ¹³Which things also we speak, not in the words which man's wisdom teacheth, but which the Holy Ghost teacheth; comparing spiritual things with spiritual. ¹⁴But the natural man receiveth not the things of the Spirit of God: for they are foolishness unto him: neither can he know them, because they are spiritually discerned. ¹⁵But he that is spiritual judgeth all things, yet he himself is judged of no man. ¹⁶For who hath known the mind of the Lord, that he may instruct him? But we have the mind of Christ."

1 Corinthians 14:1-21 "¹Follow after charity, and desire spiritual gifts, but rather that ye may prophesy. ²For he that speaketh in an unknown tongue speaketh not unto men, but unto God: for no man understandeth him; howbeit in the spirit he speaketh mysteries. ³But he that prophesieth speaketh unto men to edification, and exhortation, and comfort. ⁴He that speaketh in an unknown tongue edifieth himself; but he that prophesieth edifieth the church. ⁵I would that ye all spake with tongues, but rather that ye prophesied: for greater is he that prophesieth than he that speaketh with tongues, except he interpret, that the church may receive edifying. ⁶Now, brethren, if I come unto you speaking with tongues, what shall I profit you, except I shall speak to you either by revelation, or by knowledge, or by prophesying, or by doctrine? ⁷And even things without life giving sound, whether pipe or harp, except they give a distinction in the sounds, how shall it be known what is piped or harped? ⁸For if the trumpet give an uncertain sound, who shall prepare himself to the battle? ⁹So likewise ye, except ye utter by the tongue words easy to be understood, how shall it be known what is spoken? for ye shall speak into the air. ¹⁰There are, it may be, so many kinds of voices in the world, and none of them is without signification. ¹¹Therefore if I know not the meaning of the voice, I shall be unto him that speaketh a barbarian, and he that speaketh shall be a barbarian unto me. ¹²Even so ye, forasmuch as ye are zealous of spiritual gifts, seek that ye may excel to the edifying of the church. ¹³Wherefore let him that speaketh in an unknown tongue pray that he may interpret. ¹⁴For if I pray in an unknown tongue, my spirit prayeth, but my understanding is unfruitful. ¹⁵What is it then? I will pray with the spirit, and I will pray with the understanding also: I will sing with the spirit, and I will sing with the understanding also. ¹⁶Else when thou shalt bless with the spirit, how shall he that occupieth the room of the unlearned say Amen at thy giving of thanks, seeing he understandeth not what thou sayest? ¹⁷For thou verily givest thanks well, but the other is not edified. ¹⁸I thank my God, I speak with tongues more than ye all: ¹⁹Yet in the church I had rather speak five words with my understanding, that by my voice I might teach others also, than ten thousand words in an unknown tongue. ²⁰Brethren, be not children in understanding: howbeit in malice be ye children, but in understanding be men. ²¹In the law it is written, With men of other tongues and other lips will I speak unto this people; and yet for all that will they not hear me, saith the Lord."

2 Corinthians 3:14-15 "¹⁴But their minds were blinded: for until this day remaineth the same vail untaken away in the reading of the old testament; which vail is done away in Christ. ¹⁵But even unto this day, when Moses is read, the vail is upon their heart."

Ephesians 4:17-18 "¹⁷This I say therefore, and testify in the Lord, that ye henceforth walk not as other Gentiles walk, in the vanity of their mind, [18]Having the understanding darkened, being alienated from the life of God through the ignorance that is in them, because of the blindness of their heart:"

Hebrews 5:11-12 "[11]Of whom we have many things to say, and hard to be uttered, seeing ye are dull of hearing. [12]For when for the time ye ought to be teachers, ye have need that one teach you again which be the first principles of the oracles of God; and are become such as have need of milk, and not of strong meat."

1 John 3:1 "Behold, what manner of love the Father hath bestowed upon us, that we should be called the sons of God: therefore the world knoweth us not, because it knew him not."

UNGODLINESS

The Ungodly

Psalm 1:1-6 "[1]Blessed is the man that walketh not in the counsel of the ungodly, nor standeth in the way of sinners, nor sitteth in the seat of the scornful. [2]But his delight is in the law of the LORD; and in his law doth he meditate day and night. [3]And he shall be like a tree planted by the rivers of water, that bringeth forth his fruit in his season; his leaf also shall not wither; and whatsoever he doeth shall prosper. [4]The ungodly are not so: but are like the chaff which the wind driveth away. [5]Therefore the ungodly shall not stand in the judgment, nor sinners in the congregation of the righteous. [6]For the LORD knoweth the way of the righteous: but the way of the ungodly shall perish."

Proverbs 16:27 "An ungodly man diggeth up evil: and in his lips there is as a burning fire."

Proverbs 19:28 "An ungodly witness scorneth judgment: and the mouth of the wicked devoureth iniquity."

Romans 1:18 "For the wrath of God is revealed from heaven against all ungodliness and unrighteousness of men, who hold the truth in unrighteousness;"

1 Timothy 1:8-9 "[8]But we know that the law is good, if a man use it lawfully; [9]Knowing this, that the law is not made for a righteous man, but for the lawless and disobedient, for the ungodly and

for sinners, for unholy and profane, for murderers of fathers and murderers of mothers, for manslayers,"

2 Peter 1:1-9 "[1]Simon Peter, a servant and an apostle of Jesus Christ, to them that have obtained like precious faith with us through the righteousness of God and our Saviour Jesus Christ: [2]Grace and peace be multiplied unto you through the knowledge of God, and of Jesus our Lord, [3]According as his divine power hath given unto us all things that pertain unto life and godliness, through the knowledge of him that hath called us to glory and virtue: [4]Whereby are given unto us exceeding great and precious promises: that by these ye might be partakers of the divine nature, having escaped the corruption that is in the world through lust. [5]And beside this, giving all diligence, add to your faith virtue; and to virtue knowledge; [6]And to knowledge temperance; and to temperance patience; and to patience godliness; [7]And to godliness brotherly kindness; and to brotherly kindness charity. [8]For if these things be in you, and abound, they make you that ye shall neither be barren nor unfruitful in the knowledge of our Lord Jesus Christ. [9]But he that lacketh these things is blind, and cannot see afar off, and hath forgotten that he was purged from his old sins."

UNITY

Jesus Christ Uniting People

John 10:6-16 "[6]This parable spake Jesus unto them: but they understood not what things they were which he spake unto them. [7]Then said Jesus unto them again, Verily, verily, I say unto you, I am the door of the sheep. [8]All that ever came before me are thieves and robbers: but the sheep did not hear them. [9]I am the door: by me if any man enter in, he shall be saved, and shall go in and out, and find pasture. [10]The thief cometh not, but for to steal, and to kill, and to destroy: I am come that they might have life, and that they might have it more abundantly. [11]I am the good shepherd: the good shepherd giveth his life for the sheep. [12]But he that is an hireling, and not the shepherd, whose own the sheep are not, seeth the wolf coming, and leaveth the sheep, and fleeth: and the wolf catcheth them, and scattereth the sheep. [13]The hireling fleeth, because he is an hireling, and careth not for the sheep. [14]I am the good shepherd, and know my sheep, and am known of mine. [15]As the Father knoweth me, even so know I the Father: and I lay down my life for the sheep. [16]And other sheep I have, which are not of this fold: them also I must bring, and they shall hear my voice; and there shall be one fold, and one shepherd."

Ephesians 2:13-18 "[13]But now in Christ Jesus ye who sometimes were far off are made nigh by the blood of Christ. [14]For he is our peace, who hath made both one, and hath broken down the middle wall of partition between us; [15]Having abolished in his flesh the enmity, even the law of commandments contained in ordinances; for to make in himself of twain one new man, so making peace; [16]And that he might reconcile both unto God in one body by the cross, having slain the enmity thereby: [17]And came and preached peace to you which were afar off, and to them that were nigh. [18]For through him we both have access by one Spirit unto the Father."

The Community Of The Believers
Acts 2:44-47 "[44]And all that believed were together, and had all things common; [45]And sold their possessions and goods, and parted them to all men, as every man had need. [46]And they, continuing daily with one accord in the temple, and breaking bread from house to house, did eat their meat with gladness and singleness of heart, [47]Praising God, and having favour with all the people. And the Lord added to the church daily such as should be saved."

Unity Being Good
Psalm 133:1 "Behold, how good and how pleasant it is for brethren to dwell together in unity!"

Who Is United In Christ
John 17:1-23 "[1]These words spake Jesus, and lifted up his eyes to heaven, and said, Father, the hour is come; glorify thy Son, that thy Son also may glorify thee: [2]As thou hast given him power over all flesh, that he should give eternal life to as many as thou hast given him. [3]And this is life eternal, that they might know thee the only true God, and Jesus Christ, whom thou hast sent. [4]I have glorified thee on the earth: I have finished the work which thou gavest me to do. [5]And now, O Father, glorify thou me with thine own self

with the glory which I had with thee before the world was. [6]I have manifested thy name unto the men which thou gavest me out of the world: thine they were, and thou gavest them me; and they have kept thy word. [7]Now they have known that all things whatsoever thou hast given me are of thee. [8]For I have given unto them the words which thou gavest me; and they have received them, and have known surely that I came out from thee, and they have believed that thou didst send me. [9]I pray for them: I pray not for the world, but for them which thou hast given me; for they are thine. [10]And all mine are thine, and thine are mine; and I am glorified in them. [11]And now I am no more in the world, but these are in the world, and I come to thee. Holy Father, keep through thine own name those whom thou hast given me, that they may be one, as we are. [12]While I was with them in the world, I kept them in thy name: those that thou gavest me I have kept, and none of them is lost, but the son of perdition; that the scripture might be fulfilled. [13]And now come I to thee; and these things I speak in the world, that they might have my joy fulfilled in themselves. [14]I have given them thy word; and the world hath hated them, because they are not of the world, even as I am not of the world. [15]I pray not that thou shouldest take them out of the world, but that thou shouldest keep them from the evil. [16]They are not of the world, even as I am not of the world. [17]Sanctify them through thy truth: thy word is truth. [18]As thou hast sent me into the world, even so have I also sent them into the world. [19]And for their sakes I sanctify myself, that they also might be sanctified through the truth. [20]Neither pray I for these alone, but for them also which shall believe on me through their word; [21]That they all may be one; as thou, Father, art in me, and I in thee, that they also may be one in us: that the world may believe that thou hast sent me. [22]And the glory which thou gavest me I have given them; that they may be one, even as we are one: [23]I in them, and thou in me, that they may be made perfect in one; and that the world may know that thou hast sent me, and hast loved them, as thou hast loved me."

1 Corinthians 12:12-13 "[12]For as the body is one, and hath many members, and all the members of that one body, being many, are one body: so also is

Christ. ¹³For by one Spirit are we all baptized into one body, whether we be Jews or Gentiles, whether we be bond or free; and have been all made to drink into one Spirit."

Galatians 3:27-29 "²⁷For as many of you as have been baptized into Christ have put on Christ. ²⁸There is neither Jew nor Greek, there is neither bond nor free, there is neither male nor female: for ye are all one in Christ Jesus. ²⁹And if ye be Christ's, then are ye Abraham's seed, and heirs according to the promise."

UNJUSTNESS

The Unjust
Proverbs 11:7 "When a wicked man dieth, his expectation shall perish: and the hope of unjust men perisheth."

Proverbs 29:27 "An unjust man is an abomination to the just: and he that is upright in the way is abomination to the wicked."

Zephaniah 3:1-5 "¹Woe to her that is filthy and polluted, to the oppressing city! ²She obeyed not the voice; she received not correction; she trusted not in the LORD; she drew not near to her God. ³Her princes within her are roaring lions; her judges are evening wolves; they gnaw not the bones till the morrow. ⁴Her prophets are light and treacherous persons: her priests have polluted the sanctuary, they have done violence to the law. ⁵The just LORD is in the midst thereof; he will not do iniquity: every morning doth he bring his judgment to light, he faileth not; but the unjust knoweth no shame."

Matthew 5:45 "That ye may be the children of your Father which is in heaven: for he maketh his sun to rise on the evil and on the good, and sendeth rain on the just and on the unjust."

Luke 16:10-12 "¹⁰He that is faithful in that which is least is faithful also in much: and he that is unjust in the least is unjust also in much. ¹¹If therefore ye have not been faithful in the unrighteous mammon, who will commit to your trust the true riches? ¹²And if ye have not been faithful in that which is another man's, who shall give you that which is your own?"

Who Is Unjust
Luke 16:10-12 "¹⁰He that is faithful in that which is least is faithful also in much: and he that is unjust in the least is unjust also in much. ¹¹If therefore ye have not been faithful in the unrighteous mammon, who will commit to your trust the true riches? ¹²And if ye have not been faithful in that which is another man's, who shall give you that which is your own?"

UNRIGHTEOUSNESS

The Lord Having No Unrighteousness
Psalm 92:15 "To shew that the LORD is upright: he is my rock, and there is no unrighteousness in him."

The Unrighteous
Jeremiah 22:13 "Woe unto him that buildeth his house by unrighteousness, and his chambers by wrong; that useth his neighbour's service without wages, and giveth him not for his work;"

Romans 1:18 "For the wrath of God is revealed from heaven against all ungodliness and unrighteousness of men, who hold the truth in unrighteousness;"

Romans 2:8 "But unto them that are contentious, and do not obey the truth, but obey unrighteousness, indignation and wrath,"

1 Corinthians 6:9-11 "⁹Know ye not that the unrighteous shall not inherit the kingdom of God? Be not deceived: neither fornicators, nor idolaters, nor adulterers, nor effeminate, nor abusers of themselves with mankind, ¹⁰Nor thieves, nor covetous, nor drunkards, nor revilers, nor extortioners, shall inherit the kingdom of God. ¹¹And such were some of you: but ye are washed, but ye are sanctified, but ye are justified in the name of the Lord Jesus, and by the Spirit of our God."

2 Thessalonians 2:8-12 "⁸And then shall that Wicked be revealed, whom the Lord shall consume with the spirit of his mouth, and shall destroy with the brightness of his coming: ⁹Even him, whose coming is after the working of Satan with all power and signs and lying wonders, ¹⁰And with all deceivableness of unrighteousness in them that perish; because they received not the love of the truth, that they might be saved. [11]And for this cause God shall send them strong delusion, that they should believe a lie: [12]That they all might be damned who believed not the truth, but had pleasure in unrighteousness."

2 Peter 2:12-15 "[12]But these, as natural brute beasts, made to be taken and destroyed, speak evil of the things that they understand not; and shall utterly perish in their own corruption; [13]And shall receive the reward of unrighteousness, as they that count it pleasure to riot in the day time. Spots they are and blemishes, sporting themselves with their own deceivings while they feast with you; [14]Having eyes full of adultery, and that cannot cease from sin; beguiling unstable souls: an heart they have exercised with covetous practices; cursed children: [15]Which have forsaken the right way, and are gone astray, following the way of Balaam the son of Bosor, who loved the wages of unrighteousness;"

What Unrighteousness Is
1 John 5:17 "All unrighteousness is sin: and there is a sin not unto death."

UPHOLDMENT

The Lord Holding People Up
Psalm 18:31-36 "[31]For who is God save the LORD? or who is a rock save our God? [32]It is God that girdeth me with strength, and maketh my way perfect. [33]He maketh my feet like hinds' feet, and setteth me upon my high places. [34]He teacheth my hands to war, so that a bow of steel is broken by mine arms. [35]Thou hast also given me the shield of thy salvation: and thy right hand hath holden me up, and thy gentleness hath made me great. [36]Thou hast enlarged my steps under me, that my feet did not slip."

Psalm 71:4-6 "[4]Deliver me, O my God, out of the hand of the wicked, out of the hand of the unrighteous and cruel man. [5]For thou art my hope, O Lord GOD: thou art my trust from my youth. [6]By thee have I been holden up from the womb: thou art he that took me out of my mother's bowels: my praise shall be continually of thee."

Psalm 94:18 "When I said, My foot slippeth; thy mercy, O LORD, held me up."

What Upholds
Proverbs 20:28 "Mercy and truth preserve the king: and his throne is upholden by mercy."

Proverbs 29:23 "A man's pride shall bring him low: but honour shall uphold the humble in spirit."

Who The Lord Upholds
Psalm 37:17 "For the arms of the wicked shall be broken: but the LORD upholdeth the righteous."

Psalm 37:23-24 "[23]The steps of a good man are ordered by the LORD: and he delighteth in his way. [24]Though he fall, he shall not be utterly cast down: for the LORD upholdeth him with his hand."

Psalm 145:14 "The LORD upholdeth all that fall, and raiseth up all those that be bowed down."

Isaiah 41:8-10 "[8]But thou, Israel, art my servant, Jacob whom I have chosen, the seed of Abraham my friend. [9]Thou whom I have taken from the ends of the earth, and called thee from the chief men thereof, and said unto thee, Thou art my servant; I have chosen thee, and not cast thee away. [10]Fear thou not; for I am with thee: be not dismayed; for I am thy God: I will strengthen thee; yea, I will help thee; yea, I will uphold thee with the right hand of my righteousness."

UPLIFT

The Lord Lifting People Up
1 Samuel 2:7 "The LORD maketh poor, and maketh rich: he bringeth low, and lifteth up."

Psalm 3:3 "But thou, O LORD, art a shield for me; my glory, and the lifter up of mine head."

Psalm 40:1-2 "[1]I waited patiently for the LORD; and he inclined unto me, and heard my cry. [2]He brought me up also out of an horrible pit, out of the miry clay, and set my feet upon a rock, and established my goings."

Who The Lord Lifts Up
1 Samuel 2:7-8 "[7]The LORD maketh poor, and maketh rich: he bringeth low, and lifteth up. [8]He

raiseth up the poor out of the dust, and lifteth up the beggar from the dunghill, to set them among princes, and to make them inherit the throne of glory: for the pillars of the earth are the LORD's, and he hath set the world upon them."

Job 5:8-11 "⁸I would seek unto God, and unto God would I commit my cause: ⁹Which doeth great things and unsearchable; marvellous things without number: ¹⁰Who giveth rain upon the earth, and sendeth waters upon the fields: ¹¹To set up on high those that be low; that those which mourn may be exalted to safety."

Psalm 113:5-8 "⁵Who is like unto the LORD our God, who dwelleth on high, ⁶Who humbleth himself to behold the things that are in heaven, and in the earth! ⁷He raiseth up the poor out of the dust, and lifteth the needy out of the dunghill; ⁸That he may set him with princes, even with the princes of his people."

Psalm 145:14 "The LORD upholdeth all that fall, and raiseth up all those that be bowed down."

Psalm 146:8 "The LORD openeth the eyes of the blind: the LORD raiseth them that are bowed down: the LORD loveth the righteous:"

Psalm 147:6 "The LORD lifteth up the meek: he casteth the wicked down to the ground."

James 4:10 "Humble yourselves in the sight of the Lord, and he shall lift you up."

1 Peter 5:6 "Humble yourselves therefore under the mighty hand of God, that he may exalt you in due time:"

UPRIGHTNESS

The Lord Being Upright
Psalm 25:8 "Good and upright is the LORD: therefore will he teach sinners in the way."

Psalm 92:15 "To shew that the LORD is upright: he is my rock, and there is no unrighteousness in him."

Isaiah 26:4-7 "⁴Trust ye in the LORD for ever: for in the LORD JEHOVAH is everlasting strength: ⁵For he bringeth down them that dwell on high; the lofty city, he layeth it low; he layeth it low,

even to the ground; he bringeth it even to the dust. ⁶The foot shall tread it down, even the feet of the poor, and the steps of the needy. ⁷The way of the just is uprightness: thou, most upright, dost weigh the path of the just."

The Lord Having Pleasure In Uprightness
1 Chronicles 29:17 "I know also, my God, that thou triest the heart, and hast pleasure in uprightness. As for me, in the uprightness of mine heart I have willingly offered all these things: and now have I seen with joy thy people, which are present here, to offer willingly unto thee."

The Reward For Being Upright
2 Samuel 22:21-26 "²¹The LORD rewarded me according to my righteousness: according to the cleanness of my hands hath he recompensed me. ²²For I have kept the ways of the LORD, and have not wickedly departed from my God. ²³For all his judgments were before me: and as for his statutes, I did not depart from them. ²⁴I was also upright before him, and have kept myself from mine iniquity. ²⁵Therefore the LORD hath recompensed me according to my righteousness; according to my cleanness in his eye sight. ²⁶With the merciful thou wilt shew thyself merciful, and with the upright man thou wilt shew thyself upright."

Psalm 18:20-25 "²⁰The LORD rewarded me according to my righteousness; according to the cleanness of my hands hath he recompensed me. ²¹For I have kept the ways of the LORD, and have not wickedly departed from my God. ²²For all his judgments were before me, and I did not put away his statutes from me. ²³I was also upright before him, and I kept myself from mine iniquity. ²⁴Therefore hath the LORD recompensed me according to my righteousness, according to the cleanness of my hands in his eyesight. ²⁵With the merciful thou wilt shew thyself merciful; with an upright man thou wilt shew thyself upright;"

The Upright
2 Samuel 22:21-26 "²¹The LORD rewarded me according to my righteousness: according to the cleanness of my hands hath he recompensed me. ²²For I have kept the ways of the LORD, and have not wickedly departed from my God. ²³For all his judgments were before me: and as for his statutes, I did not depart from them. ²⁴I was also upright before him, and have kept myself from mine

iniquity. [25]Therefore the LORD hath recompensed me according to my righteousness; according to my cleanness in his eye sight. [26]With the merciful thou wilt shew thyself merciful, and with the upright man thou wilt shew thyself upright."

Job 1:6-10 "[6]Now there was a day when the sons of God came to present themselves before the LORD, and Satan came also among them. [7]And the LORD said unto Satan, Whence comest thou? Then Satan answered the LORD, and said, From going to and fro in the earth, and from walking up and down in it. [8]And the LORD said unto Satan, Hast thou considered my servant Job, that there is none like him in the earth, a perfect and an upright man, one that feareth God, and escheweth evil? [9]Then Satan answered the LORD, and said, Doth Job fear God for nought? [10]Hast not thou made an hedge about him, and about his house, and about all that he hath on every side? thou hast blessed the work of his hands, and his substance is increased in the land."

Psalm 7:10 "My defence is of God, which saveth the upright in heart."

Psalm 11:7 "For the righteous LORD loveth righteousness; his countenance doth behold the upright."

Psalm 15:1-5 "[1]LORD, who shall abide in thy tabernacle? who shall dwell in thy holy hill? [2]He that walketh uprightly, and worketh righteousness, and speaketh the truth in his heart. [3]He that backbiteth not with his tongue, nor doeth evil to his neighbour, nor taketh up a reproach against his neighbour. [4]In whose eyes a vile person is contemned; but he honoureth them that fear the LORD. He that sweareth to his own hurt, and changeth not. [5]He that putteth not out his money to usury, nor taketh reward against the innocent. He that doeth these things shall never be moved."

Psalm 18:24-25 "[24]Therefore hath the LORD recompensed me according to my righteousness, according to the cleanness of my hands in his eyesight. [25]With the merciful thou wilt shew thyself merciful; with an upright man thou wilt shew thyself upright;"

Psalm 32:11 "Be glad in the LORD, and rejoice, ye righteous: and shout for joy, all ye that are upright in heart."

Psalm 37:18-19 "[18]The LORD knoweth the days of the upright: and their inheritance shall be for ever. [19]They shall not be ashamed in the evil time: and in the days of famine they shall be satisfied."

Psalm 37:37 "Mark the perfect man, and behold the upright: for the end of that man is peace."

Psalm 49:6-14 "[6]They that trust in their wealth, and boast themselves in the multitude of their riches; [7]None of them can by any means redeem his brother, nor give to God a ransom for him: [8](For the redemption of their soul is precious, and it ceaseth for ever:) [9]That he should still live for ever, and not see corruption. [10]For he seeth that wise men die, likewise the fool and the brutish person perish, and leave their wealth to others. [11]Their inward thought is, that their houses shall continue for ever, and their dwelling places to all generations; they call their lands after their own names. [12]Nevertheless man being in honour abideth not: he is like the beasts that perish. [13]This their way is their folly: yet their posterity approve their sayings. Selah. [14]Like sheep they are laid in the grave; death shall feed on them; and the upright shall have dominion over them in the morning; and their beauty shall consume in the grave from their dwelling."

Psalm 64:10 "The righteous shall be glad in the LORD, and shall trust in him; and all the upright in heart shall glory."

Psalm 84:11 "For the LORD God is a sun and shield: the LORD will give grace and glory: no good thing will he withhold from them that walk uprightly."

Psalm 112:1-4 "[1]Praise ye the LORD. Blessed is the man that feareth the LORD, that delighteth greatly in his commandments. [2]His seed shall be mighty upon earth: the generation of the upright shall be blessed. [3]Wealth and riches shall be in his house: and his righteousness endureth for ever. [4]Unto the upright there ariseth light in the darkness: he is gracious, and full of compassion, and righteous."

Psalm 140:12-13 "[12]I know that the LORD will maintain the cause of the afflicted, and the right of the poor. [13]Surely the righteous shall give thanks unto thy name: the upright shall dwell in thy presence."

Proverbs 2:6-7 "⁶For the Lord giveth wisdom: out of his mouth cometh knowledge and understanding. ⁷He layeth up sound wisdom for the righteous: he is a buckler to them that walk uprightly."

Proverbs 2:21 "For the upright shall dwell in the land, and the perfect shall remain in it."

Proverbs 10:9 "He that walketh uprightly walketh surely: but he that perverteth his ways shall be known."

Proverbs 10:29 "The way of the Lord is strength to the upright: but destruction shall be to the workers of iniquity."

Proverbs 11:3 "The integrity of the upright shall guide them: but the perverseness of transgressors shall destroy them."

Proverbs 11:11 "By the blessing of the upright the city is exalted: but it is overthrown by the mouth of the wicked."

Proverbs 11:20 "They that are of a froward heart are abomination to the Lord: but such as are upright in their way are his delight."

Proverbs 12:6 "The words of the wicked are to lie in wait for blood: but the mouth of the upright shall deliver them."

Proverbs 13:6 "Righteousness keepeth him that is upright in the way: but wickedness overthroweth the sinner."

Proverbs 14:2 "He that walketh in his uprightness feareth the Lord: but he that is perverse in his ways despiseth him."

Proverbs 14:11 "The house of the wicked shall be overthrown: but the tabernacle of the upright shall flourish."

Proverbs 15:8 "The sacrifice of the wicked is an abomination to the Lord: but the prayer of the upright is his delight."

Proverbs 16:17 "The highway of the upright is to depart from evil: he that keepeth his way preserveth his soul."

Proverbs 21:29 "A wicked man hardeneth his face: but as for the upright, he directeth his way."

Proverbs 28:6 "Better is the poor that walketh in his uprightness, than he that is perverse in his ways, though he be rich."

Proverbs 28:10 "Whoso causeth the righteous to go astray in an evil way, he shall fall himself into his own pit: but the upright shall have good things in possession."

Proverbs 28:18 "Whoso walketh uprightly shall be saved: but he that is perverse in his ways shall fall at once."

Proverbs 29:10 "The bloodthirsty hate the upright: but the just seek his soul."

Proverbs 29:27 "An unjust man is an abomination to the just: and he that is upright in the way is abomination to the wicked."

Isaiah 33:15-16 "¹⁵He that walketh righteously, and speaketh uprightly; he that despiseth the gain of oppressions, that shaketh his hands from holding of bribes, that stoppeth his ears from hearing of blood, and shutteth his eyes from seeing evil; ¹⁶He shall dwell on high: his place of defence shall be the munitions of rocks: bread shall be given him; his waters shall be sure."

What Is Done In Uprightness
Psalm 111:4-8 "⁴He hath made his wonderful works to be remembered: the Lord is gracious and full of compassion. ⁵He hath given meat unto them that fear him: he will ever be mindful of his covenant. ⁶He hath shewed his people the power of his works, that he may give them the heritage of the heathen. ⁷The works of his hands are verity and judgment; all his commandments are sure. ⁸They stand fast for ever and ever, and are done in truth and uprightness."

What Is Upright
Psalm 119:137 "Righteous art thou, O Lord, and upright are thy judgments."

Isaiah 26:7 "The way of the just is uprightness: thou, most upright, dost weigh the path of the just."

Who The Lord Shows Himself Upright Toward
2 Samuel 22:21-26 "²¹The Lord rewarded me according to my righteousness: according to the cleanness of my hands hath he recompensed me. ²²For I have kept the ways of the Lord, and have

not wickedly departed from my God. [23]For all his judgments were before me: and as for his statutes, I did not depart from them. [24]I was also upright before him, and have kept myself from mine iniquity. [25]Therefore the LORD hath recompensed me according to my righteousness; according to my cleanness in his eye sight. [26]With the merciful thou wilt shew thyself merciful, and with the upright man thou wilt shew thyself upright."

Psalm 18:24-25 "[24]Therefore hath the LORD recompensed me according to my righteousness, according to the cleanness of my hands in his eyesight. [25]With the merciful thou wilt shew thyself merciful; with an upright man thou wilt shew thyself upright;"

Who Walks Uprightly
Proverbs 15:21 "Folly is joy to him that is destitute of wisdom: but a man of understanding walketh uprightly."

Isaiah 57:1-2 "[1]The righteous perisheth, and no man layeth it to heart: and merciful men are taken away, none considering that the righteous is taken away from the evil to come. [2]He shall enter into peace: they shall rest in their beds, each one walking in his uprightness."

USURY

Not Laying Usury Upon Your Brother
Exodus 22:25 "If thou lend money to any of my people that is poor by thee, thou shalt not be to him as an usurer, neither shalt thou lay upon him usury."

Leviticus 25:35-38 "[35]And if thy brother be waxen poor, and fallen in decay with thee; then thou shalt relieve him: yea, though he be a stranger, or a sojourner; that he may live with thee. [36]Take thou no usury of him, or increase: but fear thy God; that thy brother may live with thee. [37]Thou shalt not give him thy money upon usury, nor lend him thy victuals for increase. [38]I am the LORD your God, which brought you forth out of the land of Egypt, to give you the land of Canaan, and to be your God."

Deuteronomy 23:19-20 "[19]Thou shalt not lend upon usury to thy brother; usury of money, usury of victuals, usury of any thing that is lent upon usury: [20]Unto a stranger thou mayest lend upon usury; but unto thy brother thou shalt not lend upon usury: that the LORD thy God may bless thee in all that thou settest thine hand to in the land whither thou goest to possess it."

Those That Do Not Lay Usury Upon Others
Psalm 15:1-5 "[1]LORD, who shall abide in thy tabernacle? who shall dwell in thy holy hill? [2]He that walketh uprightly, and worketh righteousness, and speaketh the truth in his heart. [3]He that backbiteth not with his tongue, nor doeth evil to his neighbour, nor taketh up a reproach against his neighbour. [4]In whose eyes a vile person is contemned; but he honoureth them that fear the LORD. He that sweareth to his own hurt, and changeth not. [5]He that putteth not out his money to usury, nor taketh reward against the innocent. He that doeth these things shall never be moved."

Ezekiel 18:5-9 "[5]But if a man be just, and do that which is lawful and right, [6]And hath not eaten upon the mountains, neither hath lifted up his eyes to the idols of the house of Israel, neither hath defiled his neighbour's wife, neither hath come near to a menstruous woman, [7]And hath not oppressed any, but hath restored to the debtor his pledge, hath spoiled none by violence, hath given his bread to the hungry, and hath covered the naked with a garment; [8]He that hath not given forth upon usury, neither hath taken any increase, that hath withdrawn his hand from iniquity, hath executed true judgment between man and man, [9]Hath walked in my statutes, and hath kept my judgments, to deal truly; he is just, he shall surely live, saith the Lord GOD."

V*v*

VAINGLORY

Not Desiring Vainglory
Galatians 5:26 "Let us not be desirous of vain glory, provoking one another, envying one another."

Not Doing Anything Through Vainglory
Philippians 2:3 "Let nothing be done through strife or vainglory; but in lowliness of mind let each esteem other better than themselves."

VANISHING

What Vanishes Away
Psalm 103:15-16 "15As for man, his days are as grass: as a flower of the field, so he flourisheth. 16For the wind passeth over it, and it is gone; and the place thereof shall know it no more."

Isaiah 40:6-8 "6The voice said, Cry. And he said, What shall I cry? All flesh is grass, and all the goodliness thereof is as the flower of the field: 7The grass withereth, the flower fadeth: because the spirit of the LORD bloweth upon it: surely the people is grass. 8The grass withereth, the flower fadeth: but the word of our God shall stand for ever."

James 4:14 "Whereas ye know not what shall be on the morrow. For what is your life? It is even a vapour, that appeareth for a little time, and then vanisheth away."

1 Peter 1:24 "For all flesh is as grass, and all the glory of man as the flower of grass. The grass withereth, and the flower thereof falleth away:"

VANITY

God Not Hearing Or Regarding Vanity
Job 35:13 "Surely God will not hear vanity, neither will the Almighty regard it."

The Reward For Following Vanity
2 Kings 17:7-23 "7For so it was, that the children of Israel had sinned against the LORD their God, which had brought them up out of the land of Egypt, from under the hand of Pharoah king of Egypt, and had feared other gods, 8And walked in the statutes of the heathen, whom the LORD cast out from before the children of Israel, and of the kings of Israel, which they had made. 9And the children of Israel did secretly those things that were not right against the LORD their God, and they built them high places in all their cities, from the tower of the watchmen to the fenced city. 10And they set them up images and groves in every high hill, and under every green tree: 11And there they burnt incense in all the high places, as did the heathen whom the LORD carried away before them; and wrought wicked things to provoke the LORD to anger: 12For they served idols, whereof the LORD had said unto them, Ye shall not do this thing. 13Yet the LORD testified against Israel, and against Judah, by all the prophets, and by all the seers, saying, Turn ye from your evil ways, and keep my commandments and my statutes, according to all the law which I commanded your fathers, and which I sent to you by my servants the prophets. 14Notwithstanding they would not hear, but hardened their necks, like to the neck of their fathers, that did not believe in the LORD their God. 15And they rejected his statutes, and his covenant that he made with their fathers, and his testimonies which he testified against them; and they followed vanity, and became vain, and went after the heathen that were round about them, concerning whom the LORD had charged them, that they should not do like them. 16And they left all the commandments of the LORD their God, and made them molten images, even two calves, and made a grove, and worshipped all the host of heaven, and served Baal. 17And they caused their sons and their daughters to pass through the fire, and used divination and enchantments, and sold themselves to do evil in the sight of the LORD, to provoke him to anger: 18Therefore the LORD was very angry with Israel, and removed them out of his sight: there was none left but the tribe of Judah only. 19Also Judah kept not the commandments of the LORD their God, but walked in the statutes of Israel which they made. 20And the LORD rejected all the seed of Israel, and afflicted them, and delivered them into the hand of spoilers, until he had cast them out of his sight. 21For he rent Israel from the house of David; and they made Jeroboam the son of Nebat king: and Jeroboam drave Israel from following the LORD, and made

them sin a great sin. ²²For the children of Israel walked in all the sins of Jeroboam which he did; they departed not from them; ²³Until the LORD removed Israel out of his sight, as he had said by all his servants the prophets. So was Israel carried away out of their own land to Assyria unto this day."

Job 15:31 "Let not him that is deceived trust in vanity: for vanity shall be his recompence."

Jeremiah 18:13-17 "¹³Therefore thus saith the LORD; Ask ye now among the heathen, who hath heard such things: the virgin of Israel hath done a very horrible thing. ¹⁴Will a man leave the snow of Lebanon which cometh from the rock of the field? or shall the cold flowing waters that come from another place be forsaken? ¹⁵Because my people hath forgotten me, they have burned incense to vanity, and they have caused them to stumble in their ways from the ancient paths, to walk in paths, in a way not cast up; ¹⁶To make their land desolate, and a perpetual hissing; every one that passeth thereby shall be astonished, and wag his head. ¹⁷I will scatter them as with an east wind before the enemy; I will shew them the back, and not the face, in the day of their calamity."

Vain Men
Job 11:7-12 "⁷Canst thou by searching find out God? canst thou find out the Almighty unto perfection? ⁸It is as high as heaven; what canst thou do? deeper than hell; what canst thou know? ⁹The measure thereof is longer than the earth, and broader than the sea. ¹⁰If he cut off, and shut up, or gather together, then who can hinder him? ¹¹For he knoweth vain men: he seeth wickedness also; will he not then consider it? ¹²For vain man would be wise, though man be born like a wild ass's colt."

James 2:20-22 "²⁰But wilt thou know, O vain man, that faith without works is dead? ²¹Was not Abraham our father justified by works, when he had offered Isaac his son upon the altar? ²²Seest thou how faith wrought with his works, and by works was faith made perfect?"

Wealth Gotten By Vanity
Proverbs 13:11 "Wealth gotten by vanity shall be diminished: but he that gathereth by labour shall increase."

What Is Not Vain
Deuteronomy 32:45-47 "⁴⁵And Moses made an end of speaking all these words to all Israel: ⁴⁶And he said unto them, Set your hearts unto all the words which I testify among you this day, which ye shall command your children to observe to do, all the words of this law. ⁴⁷For it is not a vain thing for you; because it is your life: and through this thing ye shall prolong your days in the land, whither ye go over Jordan to possess it."

What Is Vanity
Psalm 39:5 "Behold, thou hast made my days as an handbreadth; and mine age is as nothing before thee: verily every man at his best state is altogether vanity. Selah."

Psalm 60:11-12 "¹¹Give us help from trouble: for vain is the help of man. ¹²Through God we shall do valiantly: for he it is that shall tread down our enemies."

Psalm 94:11 "The LORD knoweth the thoughts of man, that they are vanity."

Psalm 108:12-13 "¹²Give us help from trouble: for vain is the help of man. ¹³Through God we shall do valiantly: for he it is that shall tread down our enemies."

Psalm 144:3-4 "³LORD, what is man, that thou takest knowledge of him! or the son of man, that thou makest account of him! ⁴Man is like to vanity: his days are as a shadow that passeth away."

Proverbs 21:6 "The getting of treasures by a lying tongue is a vanity tossed to and fro of them that seek death."

Proverbs 31:30 "Favour is deceitful, and beauty is vain: but a woman that feareth the LORD, she shall be praised."

Ecclesiastes 1:1-2 "¹The words of the Preacher, the son of David, king in Jerusalem. ²Vanity of vanities, saith the Preacher, vanity of vanities; all is vanity."

Ecclesiastes 1:12-14 "¹²I the Preacher was king over Israel in Jerusalem. ¹³And I gave my heart to seek and search out by wisdom concerning all things that are done under heaven: this sore travail hath God given to the sons of man to be exercised therewith. [14]I have seen all the works that are done under the sun; and, behold, all is vanity and vexation of spirit."

Ecclesiastes 2:1 "I said in mine heart, Go to now, I will prove thee with mirth, therefore enjoy pleasure: and, behold, this also is vanity."

Ecclesiastes 2:15 "Then said I in my heart, As it happeneth to the fool, so it happeneth even to me; and why was I then more wise? Then I said in my heart, that this also is vanity."

Ecclesiastes 2:17 "Therefore I hated life; because the work that is wrought under the sun is grievous unto me: for all is vanity and vexation of spirit."

Ecclesiastes 2:18-19 "[18]Yea, I hated all my labour which I had taken under the sun: because I should leave it unto the man that shall be after me. [19]And who knoweth whether he shall be a wise man or a fool? yet shall he have rule over all my labour wherein I have laboured, and wherein I have shewed myself wise under the sun. This is also vanity."

Ecclesiastes 2:20-23 "[20]Therefore I went about to cause my heart to despair of all the labour which I took under the sun. [21]For there is a man whose labour is in wisdom, and in knowledge, and in equity; yet to a man that hath not laboured therein shall he leave it for his portion. This also is vanity and a great evil. [22]For what hath man of all his labour, and of the vexation of his heart, wherein he hath laboured under the sun? [23]For all his days are sorrows, and his travail grief; yea, his heart taketh not rest in the night. This is also vanity."

Ecclesiastes 2:24-26 "[24]There is nothing better for a man, than that he should eat and drink, and that he should make his soul enjoy good in his labour. This also I saw, that it was from the hand of God. [25]For who can eat, or who else can hasten hereunto, more than I? [26]For God giveth to a man that is good in his sight wisdom, and knowledge, and joy: but to the sinner he giveth travail, to gather and to heap up, that he may give to him that is good before God. This also is vanity and vexation of spirit."

Ecclesiastes 3:18-19 "[18]I said in mine heart concerning the estate of the sons of men, that God

might manifest them, and that they might see that they themselves are beasts. [19]For that which befalleth the sons of men befalleth beasts; even one thing befalleth them: as the one dieth, so dieth the other; yea, they have all one breath; so that a man hath no preeminence above a beast: for all is vanity."

Ecclesiastes 4:4 "Again, I considered all travail, and every right work, that for this a man is envied of his neighbour. This is also vanity and vexation of spirit."

Ecclesiastes 4:7-8 "[7]Then I returned, and I saw vanity under the sun. [8]There is one alone, and there is not a second; yea, he hath neither child nor brother: yet is there no end of all his labour; neither is his eye satisfied with riches; neither saith he, For whom do I labour, and bereave my soul of good? This is also vanity, yea, it is a sore travail."

Ecclesiastes 4:13-16 "[13]Better is a poor and a wise child than an old and foolish king, who will no more be admonished. [14]For out of prison he cometh to reign; whereas also he that is born in his kingdom becometh poor. [15]I considered all the living which walk under the sun, with the second child that shall stand up in his stead. [16]There is no end of all the people, even of all that have been before them: they also that come after shall not rejoice in him. Surely this also is vanity and vexation of spirit."

Ecclesiastes 5:6-7 "[6]Suffer not thy mouth to cause thy flesh to sin; neither say thou before the angel, that it was an error: wherefore should God be angry at thy voice, and destroy the work of thine hands? [7]For in the multitude of dreams and many words there are also divers vanities: but fear thou God."

Ecclesiastes 5:10 "He that loveth silver shall not be satisfied with silver; nor he that loveth abundance with increase: this is also vanity."

Ecclesiastes 6:9 "Better is the sight of the eyes than the wandering of the desire: this is also vanity and vexation of spirit."

Ecclesiastes 7:5-6 "[5]It is better to hear the rebuke of the wise, than for a man to hear the song of fools. [6]For as the crackling of thorns under a pot, so is the laughter of the fool: this also is vanity."

Ecclesiastes 8:9-10 "⁹All this have I seen, and applied my heart unto every work that is done under the sun: there is a time wherein one man ruleth over another to his own hurt. ¹⁰And so I saw the wicked buried, who had come and gone from the place of the holy, and they were forgotten in the city where they had so done: this is also vanity."

Ecclesiastes 8:14 "There is a vanity which is done upon the earth; that there be just men, unto whom it happeneth according to the work of the wicked; again, there be wicked men, to whom it happeneth according to the work of the righteous: I said that this also is vanity."

Ecclesiastes 11:8-10 "⁸But if a man live many years, and rejoice in them all; yet let him remember the days of darkness; for they shall be many. All that cometh is vanity. ⁹Rejoice, O young man, in thy youth; and let thy heart cheer thee in the days of thy youth, and walk in the ways of thine heart, and in the sight of thine eyes: but know thou, that for all these things God will bring thee into judgment. ¹⁰Therefore remove sorrow from thy heart, and put away evil from thy flesh: for childhood and youth are vanity."

Ecclesiastes 12:7-8 "⁷Then shall the dust return to the earth as it was: and the spirit shall return unto God who gave it. ⁸Vanity of vanities, saith the preacher; all is vanity."

Isaiah 41:29 "Behold, they are all vanity; their works are nothing: their molten images are wind and confusion."

Isaiah 44:9 "They that make a graven image are all of them vanity; and their delectable things shall not profit; and they are their own witnesses; they see not, nor know; that they may be ashamed."

Isaiah 57:3-13 "³But draw near hither, ye sons of the sorceress, the seed of the adulterer and the whore. ⁴Against whom do ye sport yourselves? against whom make ye a wide mouth, and draw out the tongue? are ye not children of transgression, a seed of falsehood, ⁵Enflaming yourselves with idols under every green tree, slaying the children in the valleys under the clifts of the rocks? ⁶Among the smooth stones of the stream is thy portion; they, they are thy lot: even to them hast thou poured a drink offering, thou hast offered a meat offering. Should I receive comfort in these? ⁷Upon a lofty and high mountain hast thou set thy bed: even thither wentest thou up to offer sacrifice. ⁸Behind the doors also and the posts hast thou set up thy remembrance: for thou hast discovered thyself to another than me, and art gone up; thou hast enlarged thy bed, and made thee a covenant with them; thou lovedst their bed where thou sawest it. ⁹And thou wentest to the king with ointment, and didst increase thy perfumes, and didst send thy messengers far off, and didst debase thyself even unto hell. ¹⁰Thou art wearied in the greatness of thy way; yet saidst thou not, There is no hope: thou hast found the life of thine hand; therefore thou wast not grieved. ¹¹And of whom hast thou been afraid or feared, that thou hast lied, and hast not remembered me, nor laid it to thy heart? have not I held my peace even of old, and thou fearest me not? ¹²I will declare thy righteousness, and thy works; for they shall not profit thee. ¹³When thou criest, let thy companies deliver thee; but the wind shall carry them all away; vanity shall take them: but he that putteth his trust in me shall possess the land, and shall inherit my holy mountain;"

Jeremiah 3:23 "Truly in vain is salvation hoped for from the hills, and from the multitude of mountains: truly in the LORD our God is the salvation of Israel."

Jeremiah 10:2-5 "²Thus saith the LORD, Learn not the way of the heathen, and be not dismayed at the signs of heaven; for the heathen are dismayed at them. ³For the customs of the people are vain: for one cutteth a tree out of the forest, the work of the hands of the workman, with the axe. ⁴They deck it with silver and with gold; they fasten it with nails and with hammers, that it move not. ⁵They are upright as the palm tree, but speak not: they must needs be borne, because they cannot go. Be not afraid of them; for they cannot do evil, neither also is it in them to do good."

Jeremiah 10:14-15 "¹⁴Every man is brutish in his knowledge: every founder is confounded by the graven image: for his molten image is falsehood, and there is no breath in them. ¹⁵They are vanity, and the work of errors: in the time of their visitation they shall perish."

Jeremiah 16:19-20 "¹⁹O LORD, my strength, and my fortress, and my refuge in the day of affliction, the Gentiles shall come unto thee from the ends of the earth, and shall say, Surely our fathers have inherited lies, vanity, and things wherein there is no profit. ²⁰Shall a man make gods unto himself, and they are no gods?"

Jeremiah 51:17-18 "¹⁷Every man is brutish by his knowledge; every founder is confounded by the graven image: for his molten image is falsehood, and there is no breath in them. ¹⁸They are vanity, the work of errors: in the time of their visitation they shall perish."

Acts 14:8-15 "⁸And there sat a certain man at Lystra, impotent in his feet, being a cripple from his mother's womb, who never had walked: ⁹The same heard Paul speak: who stedfastly beholding him, and perceiving that he had faith to be healed, ¹⁰Said with a loud voice, Stand upright on thy feet. And he leaped and walked. ¹¹And when the people saw what Paul had done, they lifted up their voices, saying in the speech of Lycaonia, The gods are come down to us in the likeness of men. ¹²And they called Barnabas, Jupiter; and Paul, Mercurius, because he was the chief speaker. ¹³Then the priest of Jupiter, which was before their city, brought oxen and garlands unto the gates, and would have done sacrifice with the people. ¹⁴Which when the apostles, Barnabas and Paul, heard of, they rent their clothes, and ran in among the people, crying out, ¹⁵And saying, Sirs, why do ye these things? We also are men of like passions with you, and preach unto you that ye should turn from these vanities unto the living God, which made heaven, and earth, and the sea, and all things that are therein:"

1 Corinthians 3:20-21 "²⁰And again, The Lord knoweth the thoughts of the wise, that they are vain. ²¹Therefore let no man glory in men. For all things are yours;"

James 1:26 "If any man among you seem to be religious, and bridleth not his tongue, but deceiveth his own heart, this man's religion is vain."

What Was Made Subject To Vanity
Romans 8:18-21 "¹⁸For I reckon that the sufferings of this present time are not worthy to be compared with the glory which shall be revealed in us. ¹⁹For the earnest expectation of the creature waiteth for the manifestation of the sons of God.

²⁰For the creature was made subject to vanity, not willingly, but by reason of him who hath subjected the same in hope, ²¹Because the creature itself also shall be delivered from the bondage of corruption into the glorious liberty of the children of God."

Who Became Vain
Romans 1:18-23 "¹⁸For the wrath of God is revealed from heaven against all ungodliness and unrighteousness of men, who hold the truth in unrighteousness; ¹⁹Because that which may be known of God is manifest in them; for God hath shewed it unto them. ²⁰For the invisible things of him from the creation of the world are clearly seen, being understood by the things that are made, even his eternal power and Godhead; so that they are without excuse: ²¹Because that, when they knew God, they glorified him not as God, neither were thankful; but became vain in their imaginations, and their foolish heart was darkened. ²²Professing themselves to be wise, they became fools, ²³And changed the glory of the uncorruptible God into an image made like to corruptible man, and to birds, and fourfooted beasts, and creeping things."

Ephesians 4:17-19 "¹⁷This I say therefore, and testify in the Lord, that ye henceforth walk not as other Gentiles walk, in the vanity of their mind, ¹⁸Having the understanding darkened, being alienated from the life of God through the ignorance that is in them, because of the blindness of their heart: ¹⁹Who being past feeling have given themselves over unto lasciviousness, to work all uncleanness with greediness."

Who Shall Reap Vanity
Proverbs 22:8 "He that soweth iniquity shall reap vanity: and the rod of his anger shall fail."

VENGEANCE

Not Avenging
Leviticus 19:18 "Thou shalt not avenge, nor bear any grudge against the children of thy people, but thou shalt love thy neighbour as thyself: I am the LORD."

Proverbs 20:22 "Say not thou, I will recompense evil; but wait on the LORD, and he shall save thee."

Proverbs 24:28-29 "²⁸Be not a witness against thy neighbour without cause; and deceive not with thy lips. ²⁹Say not, I will do so to him as he hath done to me: I will render to the man according to his work."

Matthew 5:38-42 "³⁸Ye have heard that it hath been said, An eye for an eye, and a tooth for a tooth: ³⁹But I say unto you, That ye resist not evil: but whosoever shall smite thee on thy right cheek, turn to him the other also. ⁴⁰And if any man will sue thee at the law, and take away thy coat, let him have thy cloke also. ⁴¹And whosoever shall compel thee to go a mile, go with him twain. ⁴²Give to him that asketh thee, and from him that would borrow of thee turn not thou away."

Luke 6:27-30 "²⁷But I say unto you which hear, Love your enemies, do good to them which hate you, ²⁸Bless them that curse you, and pray for them which despitefully use you. ²⁹And unto him that smiteth thee on the one cheek offer also the other; and him that taketh away thy cloke forbid not to take thy coat also. ³⁰Give to every man that asketh of thee; and of him that taketh away thy goods ask them not again."

Romans 12:17-21 "¹⁷Recompense to no man evil for evil. Provide things honest in the sight of all men. ¹⁸If it be possible, as much as lieth in you, live peaceably with all men. ¹⁹Dearly beloved, avenge not yourselves, but rather give place unto wrath: for it is written, Vengeance is mine; I will repay, saith the Lord. ²⁰Therefore if thine enemy hunger, feed him; if he thirst, give him drink: for in so doing thou shalt heap coals of fire on his head. ²¹Be not overcome of evil, but overcome evil with good."

1 Thessalonians 5:15 "See that none render evil for evil unto any man; but ever follow that which is good, both among yourselves, and to all men."

1 Peter 3:8-9 "⁸Finally, be ye all of one mind, having compassion one of another, love as brethren, be pitiful, be courteous: ⁹Not rendering evil for evil, or railing for railing: but contrariwise blessing; knowing that ye are thereunto called, that ye should inherit a blessing."

The Lord Avenging
2 Samuel 22:48 "It is God that avengeth me, and that bringeth down the people under me,"

Psalm 18:47 "It is God that avengeth me, and subdueth the people under me."

Nahum 1:2 "God is jealous, and the LORD revengeth; the LORD revengeth, and is furious; the LORD will take vengeance on his adversaries, and he reserveth wrath for his enemies."

Romans 12:19 "Dearly beloved, avenge not yourselves, but rather give place unto wrath: for it is written, Vengeance is mine; I will repay, saith the Lord."

Hebrews 10:30 "For we know him that hath said, Vengeance belongeth unto me, I will recompense, saith the Lord. And again, The Lord shall judge his people."

Vengeance Belonging To The Lord
Deuteronomy 32:35-36 "³⁵To me belongeth vengeance, and recompence; their foot shall slide in due time: for the day of their calamity is at hand, and the things that shall come upon them make haste. ³⁶For the LORD shall judge his people, and repent himself for his servants, when he seeth that their power is gone, and there is none shut up, or left."

Psalm 94:1 "O LORD God, to whom vengeance belongeth; O God, to whom vengeance belongeth, shew thyself."

Romans 12:19 "Dearly beloved, avenge not yourselves, but rather give place unto wrath: for it is written, Vengeance is mine; I will repay, saith the Lord."

Hebrews 10:30 "For we know him that hath said, Vengeance belongeth unto me, I will recompense, saith the Lord. And again, The Lord shall judge his people."

Who The Lord Shall Avenge
Deuteronomy 32:36-43 "³⁶For the LORD shall judge his people, and repent himself for his servants, when he seeth that their power is gone, and there is none shut up, or left. ³⁷And he shall say, Where are their gods, their rock in whom they trusted, ³⁸Which did eat the fat of their sacrifices, and drank the wine of their drink offerings? let them rise up and help you, and be your protection. ³⁹See now that I, even I, am he, and there is no god with me: I kill, and I make alive; I wound, and I heal: neither is there any that can deliver

out of my hand. [40]For I lift up my hand to heaven, and say, I live for ever. [41]If I whet my glittering sword, and mine hand take hold on judgment; I will render vengeance to mine enemies, and will reward them that hate me. [42]I will make mine arrows drunk with blood, and my sword shall devour flesh; and that with the blood of the slain and of the captives, from the beginning of revenges upon the enemy. [43]Rejoice, O ye nations, with his people: for he will avenge the blood of his servants, and will render vengeance to his adversaries, and will be merciful unto his land, and to his people."

Luke 18:7-8 "[7]And shall not God avenge his own elect, which cry day and night unto him, though he bear long with them? [8]I tell you that he will avenge them speedily. Nevertheless when the Son of man cometh, shall he find faith on the earth?"

Revelation 6:9-11 "[9]And when he had opened the fifth seal, I saw under the altar the souls of them that were slain for the word of God, and for the testimony which they held: [10]And they cried with a loud voice, saying, How long, O Lord, holy and true, dost thou not judge and avenge our blood on them that dwell on the earth? [11]And white robes were given unto every one of them; and it was said unto them, that they should rest yet for a little season, until their fellowservants also and their brethren, that should be killed as they were, should be fulfilled."

Revelation 18:20 "Rejoice over her, thou heaven, and ye holy apostles and prophets; for God hath avenged you on her."

Revelation 19:1-2 "[1]And after these things I heard a great voice of much people in heaven, saying, Alleluia; Salvation, and glory, and honour, and power, unto the Lord our God: [2]For true and righteous are his judgments: for he hath judged the great whore, which did corrupt the earth with her fornication, and hath avenged the blood of his servants at her hand."

Who The Lord Shall Take Vengeance Upon
Deuteronomy 32:36-43 "[36]For the LORD shall judge his people, and repent himself for his servants, when he seeth that their power is gone, and there is none shut up, or left. [37]And he shall say, Where are their gods, their rock in whom they trusted, [38]Which did eat the fat of their sacrifices, and drank the wine of their drink offerings? let them rise up and help you, and be your protection. [39]See now that I, even I, am he, and there is no god with me: I kill, and I make alive; I wound, and I heal: neither is there any that can deliver out of my hand. [40]For I lift up my hand to heaven, and say, I live for ever. [41]If I whet my glittering sword, and mine hand take hold on judgment; I will render vengeance to mine enemies, and will reward them that hate me. [42]I will make mine arrows drunk with blood, and my sword shall devour flesh; and that with the blood of the slain and of the captives, from the beginning of revenges upon the enemy. [43]Rejoice, O ye nations, with his people: for he will avenge the blood of his servants, and will render vengeance to his adversaries, and will be merciful unto his land, and to his people."

Jeremiah 5:26-29 "[26]For among my people are found wicked men: they lay wait, as he that setteth snares; they set a trap, they catch men. [27]As a cage is full of birds, so are their houses full of deceit: therefore they are become great, and waxen rich. [28]They are waxen fat, they shine: yea, they overpass the deeds of the wicked: they judge not the cause, the cause of the fatherless, yet they prosper; and the right of the needy do they not judge. [29]Shall I not visit for these things? saith the LORD: shall not my soul be avenged on such a nation as this?"

Nahum 1:2 "God is jealous, and the LORD revengeth; the LORD revengeth, and is furious; the LORD will take vengeance on his adversaries, and he reserveth wrath for his enemies."

1 Thessalonians 4:3-6 "[3]For this is the will of God, even your sanctification, that ye should abstain from fornication: [4]That every one of you should know how to possess his vessel in sanctification and honour; [5]Not in the lust of concupiscence, even as the Gentiles which know not God: [6]That no man go beyond and defraud his brother in any matter: because that the Lord is the avenger of all such, as we also have forewarned you and testified."

2 Thessalonians 1:7-9 "[7]And to you who are troubled rest with us, when the Lord Jesus shall be revealed from heaven with his mighty angels, [8]In flaming fire taking vengeance on them that know not God, and that obey not the gospel of our Lord Jesus Christ: [9]Who shall be punished with everlasting destruction from the presence of the Lord, and from the glory of his power;"

Jude 7 "Even as Sodom and Gomorrha, and the cities about them in like manner, giving themselves over to fornication, and going after strange flesh, are set forth for an example, suffering the vengeance of eternal fire."

Revelation 19:1-2 "[1]And after these things I heard a great voice of much people in heaven, saying, Alleluia; Salvation, and glory, and honour, and power, unto the Lord our God: [2]For true and righteous are his judgments: for he hath judged the great whore, which did corrupt the earth with her fornication, and hath avenged the blood of his servants at her hand."

VICTORY/OVERCOMING

God Giving Victory Through Jesus Christ
1 Corinthians 15:57-58 "[57]But thanks be to God, which giveth us the victory through our Lord Jesus Christ. [58]Therefore, my beloved brethren, be ye stedfast, unmoveable, always abounding in the work of the Lord, forasmuch as ye know that your labour is not in vain in the Lord."

2 Corinthians 2:14 "Now thanks be unto God, which always causeth us to triumph in Christ, and maketh manifest the savour of his knowledge by us in every place."

The Lord Triumphing
Exodus 15:1 "Then sang Moses and the children of Israel this song unto the LORD, and spake, saying, I will sing unto the LORD, for he hath triumphed gloriously: the horse and his rider hath he thrown into the sea."

Psalm 98:1 "O sing unto the LORD a new song; for he hath done marvellous things: his right hand, and his holy arm, hath gotten him the victory."

Isaiah 42:13 "The LORD shall go forth as a mighty man, he shall stir up jealousy like a man of war: he shall cry, yea, roar; he shall prevail against his enemies."

John 16:31-33 "[31]Jesus answered them, Do ye now believe? [32]Behold, the hour cometh, yea, is now come, that ye shall be scattered, every man to his own, and shall leave me alone: and yet I am not alone, because the Father is with me. [33]These things I have spoken unto you, that in me ye might have peace. In the world ye shall have tribulation: but be of good cheer; I have overcome the world."

Colossians 2:8-15 "[8]Beware lest any man spoil you through philosophy and vain deceit, after the tradition of men, after the rudiments of the world, and not after Christ. [9]For in him dwelleth all the fulness of the Godhead bodily. [10]And ye are complete in him, which is the head of all principality and power: [11]In whom also ye are circumcised with the circumcision made without hands, in putting off the body of the sins of the flesh by the circumcision of Christ: [12]Buried with him in baptism, wherein also ye are risen with him through the faith of the operation of God, who hath raised him from the dead. [13]And you, being dead in your sins and the uncircumcision of your flesh, hath he quickened together with him, having forgiven you all trespasses; [14]Blotting out the handwriting of ordinances that was against us, which was contrary to us, and took it out of the way, nailing it to his cross; [15]And having spoiled principalities and powers, he made a shew of them openly, triumphing over them in it."

Revelation 3:14-21 "[14]And unto the angel of the church of the Laodiceans write; These things saith the Amen, the faithful and true witness, the beginning of the creation of God; [15]I know thy works, that thou art neither cold nor hot: I would thou wert cold or hot. [16]So then because thou art lukewarm, and neither cold nor hot, I will spue thee out of my mouth. [17]Because thou sayest, I am rich, and increased with goods, and have need of nothing; and knowest not that thou art wretched, and miserable, and poor, and blind, and naked: [18]I counsel thee to buy of me gold tried in the fire, that thou mayest be rich; and white raiment, that thou mayest be clothed, and that the shame of thy nakedness do not appear; and anoint thine eyes with eyesalve, that thou mayest see. [19]As many as I love, I rebuke and chasten: be zealous therefore, and repent. [20]Behold, I stand at the door, and knock: if any man hear my voice, and open the door, I will come in to him, and will sup with him, and he with me. [21]To him that overcometh will I grant to sit with me in my throne, even as I also overcame, and am set down with my Father in his throne."

Revelation 5:5 "And one of the elders saith unto me, Weep not: behold, the Lion of the tribe of Juda, the Root of David, hath prevailed to open the book, and to loose the seven seals thereof."

Revelation 17:12-14 "[12]And the ten horns which thou sawest are ten kings, which have received no kingdom as yet; but receive power as kings one hour with the beast. [13]These have one mind, and shall give their power and strength unto the beast. [14]These shall make war with the Lamb, and the Lamb shall overcome them: for he is Lord of lords, and King of kings: and they that are with him are called, and chosen, and faithful."

The Triumphing Of The Wicked
Job 20:1-5 "[1]Then answered Zophar the Naamathite, and said, [2]Therefore do my thoughts cause me to answer, and for this I make haste. [3]I have heard the check of my reproach, and the spirit of my understanding causeth me to answer. [4]Knowest thou not this of old, since man was placed upon earth, [5]That the triumphing of the wicked is short, and the joy of the hypocrite but for a moment?"

The Victory Belonging To The Lord
1 Chronicles 29:11 "Thine, O LORD, is the greatness, and the power, and the glory, and the victory, and the majesty: for all that is in the heaven and in the earth is thine; thine is the kingdom, O LORD, and thou art exalted as head above all."

Those That Overcome (Are Victorious)
Revelation 2:7 "He that hath an ear, let him hear what the Spirit saith unto the churches; To him that overcometh will I give to eat of the tree of life, which is in the midst of the paradise of God."

Revelation 2:11 "He that hath an ear, let him hear what the Spirit saith unto the churches; He that overcometh shall not be hurt of the second death."

Revelation 2:17 "He that hath an ear, let him hear what the Spirit saith unto the churches; To him that overcometh will I give to eat of the hidden manna, and will give him a white stone, and in the stone a new name written, which no man knoweth saving he that receiveth it."

Revelation 2:26-28 "[26]And he that overcometh, and keepeth my works unto the end, to him will I give power over the nations: [27]And he shall rule them with a rod of iron; as the vessels of a potter shall they be broken to shivers: even as I received of my Father. [28]And I will give him the morning star."

Revelation 3:5 "He that overcometh, the same shall be clothed in white raiment; and I will not blot out his name out of the book of life, but I will confess his name before my Father, and before his angels."

Revelation 3:12 "Him that overcometh will I make a pillar in the temple of my God, and he shall go no more out: and I will write upon him the name of my God, and the name of the city of my God, which is new Jerusalem, which cometh down out of heaven from my God: and I will write upon him my new name."

Revelation 3:21 "To him that overcometh will I grant to sit with me in my throne, even as I also overcame, and am set down with my Father in his throne."

Revelation 21:7 "He that overcometh shall inherit all things; and I will be his God, and he shall be my son."

What Will Be Swallowed Up In Victory
Isaiah 25:8-9 "[8]He will swallow up death in victory; and the Lord GOD will wipe away tears from off all faces; and the rebuke of his people shall he take away from off all the earth: for the LORD hath spoken it. [9]And it shall be said in that day, Lo, this is our God; we have waited for him, and he will save us: this is the LORD; we have waited for him, we will be glad and rejoice in his salvation."

1 Corinthians 15:25-28 "[25]For he must reign, till he hath put all enemies under his feet. [26]The last enemy that shall be destroyed is death. [27]For he hath put all things under his feet. But when he saith, all things are put under him, it is manifest that he is excepted, which did put all things under him. [28]And when all things shall be subdued unto him, then shall the Son also himself be subject unto him that put all things under him, that God may be all in all."

1 Corinthians 15:50-56 "⁵⁰Now this I say, brethren, that flesh and blood cannot inherit the kingdom of God; neither doth corruption inherit incorruption. ⁵¹Behold, I shew you a mystery; We shall not all sleep, but we shall all be changed, ⁵²In a moment, in the twinkling of an eye, at the last trump: for the trumpet shall sound, and the dead shall be raised incorruptible, and we shall be changed. ⁵³For this corruptible must put on incorruption, and this mortal must put on immortality. ⁵⁴So when this corruptible shall have put on incorruption, and this mortal shall have put on immortality, then shall be brought to pass the saying that is written, Death is swallowed up in victory. ⁵⁵O death, where is thy sting? O grave, where is thy victory? ⁵⁶The sting of death is sin; and the strength of sin is the law."

Who Overcomes The Wicked

1 John 2:13-14 "¹³I write unto you, fathers, because ye have known him that is from the beginning. I write unto you, young men, because ye have overcome the wicked one. I write unto you, little children, because ye have known the Father. ¹⁴I have written unto you, fathers, because ye have known him that is from the beginning. I have written unto you, young men, because ye are strong, and the word of God abideth in you, and ye have overcome the wicked one."

1 John 4:1-4 "¹Beloved, believe not every spirit, but try the spirits whether they are of God: because many false prophets are gone out into the world. ²Hereby know ye the Spirit of God: Every spirit that confesseth that Jesus Christ is come in the flesh is of God: ³And every spirit that confesseth not that Jesus Christ is come in the flesh is not of God: and this is that spirit of antichrist, whereof ye have heard that it should come; and even now already is it in the world. ⁴Ye are of God, little children, and have overcome them: because greater is he that is in you, than he that is in the world."

Who Overcomes The World

1 John 5:4-5 "⁴For whatsoever is born of God overcometh the world: and this is the victory that overcometh the world, even our faith. ⁵Who is he that overcometh the world, but he that believeth that Jesus is the Son of God?"

VIOLENCE

Not Performing Violence

Exodus 20:13 "Thou shalt not kill."

Deuteronomy 5:17 "Thou shalt not kill."

Proverbs 1:10-15 "¹⁰My son, if sinners entice thee, consent thou not. ¹¹If they say, Come with us, let us lay wait for blood, let us lurk privily for the innocent without cause: ¹²Let us swallow them up alive as the grave; and whole, as those that go down into the pit: ¹³We shall find all precious substance, we shall fill our houses with spoil: ¹⁴Cast in thy lot among us; let us all have one purse: ¹⁵My son, walk not thou in the way with them; refrain thy foot from their path:"

Matthew 19:18 "He saith unto him, Which? Jesus said, Thou shalt do no murder, Thou shalt not commit adultery, Thou shalt not steal, Thou shalt not bear false witness,"

Luke 3:14 "And the soldiers likewise demanded of him, saying, And what shall we do? And he said unto them, Do violence to no man, neither accuse any falsely; and be content with your wages."

Romans 13:8-9 "⁸Owe no man any thing, but to love one another: for he that loveth another hath fulfilled the law. ⁹For this, Thou shalt not commit adultery, Thou shalt not kill, Thou shalt not steal, Thou shalt not bear false witness, Thou shalt not covet; and if there be any other commandment, it is briefly comprehended in this saying, namely, Thou shalt love thy neighbour as thyself."

Romans 13:13 "Let us walk honestly, as in the day; not in rioting and drunkenness, not in chambering and wantonness, not in strife and envying."

Titus 3:1-2 "¹Put them in mind to be subject to principalities and powers, to obey magistrates, to be ready to every good work, ²To speak evil of no man, to be no brawlers, but gentle, shewing all meekness unto all men."

James 2:11 "For he that said, Do not commit adultery, said also, Do not kill. Now if thou commit no adultery, yet if thou kill, thou art become a transgressor of the law."

The Lord Hating Violence

Psalm 11:5 "The LORD trieth the righteous: but the wicked and him that loveth violence his soul hateth."

Proverbs 6:16-19 "16These six things doth the LORD hate: yea, seven are an abomination unto him: 17A proud look, a lying tongue, and hands that shed innocent blood, 18An heart that deviseth wicked imaginations, feet that be swift in running to mischief, 19A false witness that speaketh lies, and he that soweth discord among brethren."

The Reward For Violence

Genesis 6:11-13 "11The earth also was corrupt before God, and the earth was filled with violence. 12And God looked upon the earth, and, behold, it was corrupt; for all flesh had corrupted his way upon the earth. 13And God said unto Noah, The end of all flesh is come before me; for the earth is filled with violence through them; and, behold, I will destroy them with the earth."

Psalm 106:37-43 "37Yea, they sacrificed their sons and their daughters unto devils, 38And shed innocent blood, even the blood of their sons and of their daughters, whom they sacrificed unto the idols of Canaan: and the land was polluted with blood. 39Thus were they defiled with their own works, and went a whoring with their own inventions. 40Therefore was the wrath of the LORD kindled against his people, insomuch that he abhorred his own inheritance. 41And he gave them into the hand of the heathen; and they that hated them ruled over them. 42Their enemies also oppressed them, and they were brought into subjection under their hand. 43Many times did he deliver them; but they provoked him with their counsel, and were brought low for their iniquity."

Jeremiah 19:3-15 "3And say, Hear ye the word of the LORD, O kings of Judah, and inhabitants of Jerusalem; Thus saith the LORD of hosts, the God of Israel; Behold, I will bring evil upon this place, the which whosoever heareth, his ears shall tingle. 4Because they have forsaken me, and have estranged this place, and have burned incense in it unto other gods, whom neither they nor their fathers have known, nor the kings of Judah, and have filled this place with the blood of innocents; 5They have built also the high places of Baal, to burn their sons with fire for burnt offerings unto Baal, which I commanded not, nor spake it, neither came it into my mind: 6Therefore, behold, the days come, saith the LORD, that this place shall no more be called Tophet, nor The valley of the son of Hinnom, but The valley of slaughter. 7And I will make void the counsel of Judah and Jerusalem in this place; and I will cause them to fall by the sword before their enemies, and by the hands of them that seek their lives: and their carcases will I give to be meat for the fowls of the heaven, and for the beasts of the earth. 8And I will make this city desolate, and an hissing; every one that passeth thereby shall be astonished and hiss because of all the plagues thereof. 9And I will cause them to eat the flesh of their sons and the flesh of their daughters, and they shall eat every one the flesh of his friend in the siege and straitness, wherewith their enemies, and they that seek their lives, shall straiten them. 10Then shalt thou break the bottle in the sight of the men that go with thee, 11And shalt say unto them, Thus saith the LORD of hosts; Even so will I break this people and this city, as one breaketh a potter's vessel, that cannot be made whole again: and they shall bury them in Tophet, till there be no place to bury. 12Thus will I do unto this place, saith the LORD, and to the inhabitants thereof, and even make this city as Tophet: 13And the houses of Jerusalem, and the houses of the kings of Judah, shall be defiled as the place of Tophet, because of all the houses upon whose roofs they have burned incense unto all the host of heaven, and have poured out drink offerings unto other gods. 14Then came Jeremiah from Tophet, whither the LORD had sent him to prophesy; and he stood in the court of the LORD's house; and said to all the people, 15Thus saith the LORD of hosts, the God of Israel; Behold, I will bring upon this city and upon all her towns all the evil that I have pronounced against it, because they have hardened their necks, that they might not hear my words."

Hosea 4:1-3 "1Hear the word of the LORD, ye children of Israel: for the LORD hath a controversy with the inhabitants of the land, because there is no truth, nor mercy, nor knowledge of God in the land. 2By swearing, and lying, and killing, and stealing, and committing adultery, they break out, and blood toucheth blood. 3Therefore shall the land mourn, and every one that dwelleth therein shall languish, with the beasts of the field, and with the fowls of heaven; yea, the fishes of the sea also shall be taken away."

Joel 3:19 "Egypt shall be a desolation, and Edom shall be a desolate wilderness, for the violence against the children of Judah, because they have shed innocent blood in their land."

Violent People

Genesis 9:5-6 "⁵And surely your blood of your lives will I require; at the hand of every beast will I require it, and at the hand of man; at the hand of every man's brother will I require the life of man. ⁶Whoso sheddeth man's blood, by man shall his blood be shed: for in the image of God made he man."

Exodus 21:12-15 "¹²He that smiteth a man, so that he die, shall be surely put to death. ¹³And if a man lie not in wait, but God deliver him into his hand; then I will appoint thee a place whither he shall flee. ¹⁴But if a man come presumptuously upon his neighbour, to slay him with guile; thou shalt take him from mine altar, that he may die. ¹⁵And he that smiteth his father, or his mother, shall be surely put to death."

Leviticus 24:17 "And he that killeth any man shall surely be put to death."

Leviticus 24:21 "And he that killeth a beast, he shall restore it: and he that killeth a man, he shall be put to death."

Numbers 35:30-33 "³⁰Whoso killeth any person, the murderer shall be put to death by the mouth of witnesses: but one witness shall not testify against any person to cause him to die. ³¹Moreover ye shall take no satisfaction for the life of a murderer, which is guilty of death: but he shall be surely put to death. ³²And ye shall take no satisfaction for him that is fled to the city of his refuge, that he should come again to dwell in the land, until the death of the priest. ³³So ye shall not pollute the land wherein ye are: for blood it defileth the land: and the land cannot be cleansed of the blood that is shed therein, but by the blood of him that shed it."

Deuteronomy 27:24-25 "²⁴Cursed be he that smiteth his neighbour secretly. And all the people shall say, Amen. ²⁵Cursed be he that taketh reward to slay

an innocent person. And all the people shall say, Amen."

2 Kings 21:16 "Moreover Manasseh shed innocent blood very much, till he had filled Jerusalem from one end to another; beside his sin wherewith he made Judah to sin, in doing that which was evil in the sight of the LORD."

Psalm 55:23 "But thou, O God, shalt bring them down into the pit of destruction: bloody and deceitful men shall not live out half their days; but I will trust in thee."

Psalm 92:5-6 "⁵O LORD, how great are thy works! and thy thoughts are very deep. ⁶A brutish man knoweth not; neither doth a fool understand this."

Proverbs 1:10-19 "¹⁰My son, if sinners entice thee, consent thou not. ¹¹If they say, Come with us, let us lay wait for blood, let us lurk privily for the innocent without cause: ¹²Let us swallow them up alive as the grave; and whole, as those that go down into the pit: ¹³We shall find all precious substance, we shall fill our houses with spoil: ¹⁴Cast in thy lot among us; let us all have one purse: ¹⁵My son, walk not thou in the way with them; refrain thy foot from their path: ¹⁶For their feet run to evil, and make haste to shed blood. ¹⁷Surely in vain the net is spread in the sight of any bird. ¹⁸And they lay wait for their own blood; they lurk privily for their own lives. ¹⁹So are the ways of every one that is greedy of gain; which taketh away the life of the owners thereof."

Proverbs 16:29-30 "²⁹A violent man enticeth his neighbour, and leadeth him into the way that is not good. ³⁰He shutteth his eyes to devise froward things: moving his lips he bringeth evil to pass."

Proverbs 28:17 "A man that doeth violence to the blood of any person shall flee to the pit; let no man stay him."

Proverbs 29:10 "The bloodthirsty hate the upright: but the just seek his soul."

Ezekiel 18:1-13 "¹The word of the LORD came unto me again, saying, ²What mean ye, that ye use this proverb concerning the land of Israel, saying, The fathers have eaten sour grapes, and the children's teeth are set on edge? ³As I live, saith the Lord GOD, ye shall not have occasion any more to use this proverb in Israel. ⁴Behold, all souls are mine; as the soul of the father, so also the soul of the son is mine: the soul that sinneth, it shall die. ⁵But if a man be just, and do that which is lawful and right, ⁶And hath not eaten upon the mountains, neither hath lifted up his eyes to the idols of the house of Israel, neither hath defiled his neighbour's wife, neither hath come near to a menstruous woman, ⁷And hath not oppressed any, but hath restored to the debtor his pledge, hath spoiled none by violence, hath given his bread to the hungry, and hath covered the naked with a garment; ⁸He that hath not given forth upon usury, neither hath taken any increase, that hath withdrawn his hand from iniquity, hath executed true judgment between man and man, ⁹Hath walked in my statutes, and hath kept my judgments, to deal truly; he is just, he shall surely live, saith the Lord GOD. ¹⁰If he beget a son that is a robber, a shedder of blood, and that doeth the like to any one of these things, ¹¹And that doeth not any of those duties, but even hath eaten upon the mountains, and defiled his neighbour's wife, ¹²Hath oppressed the poor and needy, hath spoiled by violence, hath not restored the pledge, and hath lifted up his eyes to the idols, hath committed abomination, ¹³Hath given forth upon usury, and hath taken increase: shall he then live? he shall not live: he hath done all these abominations; he shall surely die; his blood shall be upon him."

Habakkuk 2:6-17 "⁶Shall not all these take up a parable against him, and a taunting proverb against him, and say, Woe to him that increaseth that which is not his! how long? and to him that ladeth himself with thick clay! ⁷Shall they not rise up suddenly that shall bite thee, and awake that shall vex thee, and thou shalt be for booties unto them? ⁸Because thou hast spoiled many nations, all the remnant of the people shall spoil thee; because of men's blood, and for the violence of the land, of the city, and of all that dwell therein. ⁹Woe to him that coveteth an evil covetousness to his house, that he may set his nest on high, that he may be delivered from the power of evil! ¹⁰Thou hast consulted shame to thy house by cutting off many people, and hast sinned against thy soul. ¹¹For the stone shall cry out of the wall, and the beam out of the timber shall answer it. ¹²Woe to him that buildeth a town with blood, and stablisheth a city by iniquity! ¹³Behold, is it not of the LORD of hosts that the people shall labour in the very fire, and the people shall weary themselves for very vanity? ¹⁴For the earth shall be filled with the knowledge of the glory of the LORD, as the waters cover the sea. ¹⁵Woe unto him that giveth his neighbour drink, that puttest thy bottle to him, and makest him drunken also, that thou mayest look on their nakedness! ¹⁶Thou art filled with shame for glory: drink thou also, and let thy foreskin be uncovered: the cup of the LORD's right hand shall be turned unto thee, and shameful spewing shall be on thy glory. ¹⁷For the violence of Lebanon shall cover thee, and the spoil of beasts, which made them afraid, because of men's blood, and for the violence of the land, of the city, and of all that dwell therein."

Matthew 26:52 "Then said Jesus unto him, Put up again thy sword into his place: for all they that take the sword shall perish with the sword."

1 Timothy 1:8-9 "⁸But we know that the law is good, if a man use it lawfully; ⁹Knowing this, that the law is not made for a righteous man, but for the lawless and disobedient, for the ungodly and for sinners, for unholy and profane, for murderers of fathers and murderers of mothers, for manslayers,"

James 2:11 "For he that said, Do not commit adultery, said also, Do not kill. Now if thou commit no adultery, yet if thou kill, thou art become a transgressor of the law."

1 John 3:15 "Whosoever hateth his brother is a murderer: and ye know that no murderer hath eternal life abiding in him."

Revelation 13:10 "He that leadeth into captivity shall go into captivity: he that killeth with the sword must be killed with the sword. Here is the patience and the faith of the saints."

Revelation 21:8 "But the fearful, and unbelieving, and the abominable, and murderers, and whoremongers, and sorcerers, and idolaters, and all liars, shall have their part in the lake which burneth with fire and brimstone: which is the second death."

Revelation 22:13-15 "¹³I am Alpha and Omega, the beginning and the end, the first and the last.

[14]Blessed are they that do his commandments, that they may have right to the tree of life, and may enter in through the gates into the city. [15]For without are dogs, and sorcerers, and whoremongers, and murderers, and idolaters, and whosoever loveth and maketh a lie."

What Violence Does
Numbers 35:33 "So ye shall not pollute the land wherein ye are: for blood it defileth the land: and the land cannot be cleansed of the blood that is shed therein, but by the blood of him that shed it."

Who Is Violent
Psalm 139:19-20 "[19]Surely thou wilt slay the wicked, O God: depart from me therefore, ye bloody men. [20]For they speak against thee wickedly, and thine enemies take thy name in vain."

Proverbs 10:6 "Blessings are upon the head of the just: but violence covereth the mouth of the wicked."

Proverbs 10:11 "The mouth of a righteous man is a well of life: but violence covereth the mouth of the wicked."

Isaiah 59:1-7 "[1]Behold, the LORD's hand is not shortened, that it cannot save; neither his ear heavy, that it cannot hear: [2]But your iniquities have separated between you and your God, and your sins have hid his face from you, that he will not hear. [3]For your hands are defiled with blood, and your fingers with iniquity; your lips have spoken lies, your tongue hath muttered perverseness. [4]None calleth for justice, nor any pleadeth for truth: they trust in vanity, and speak lies; they conceive mischief, and bring forth iniquity. [5]They hatch cockatrice' eggs, and weave the spider's web: he that eateth of their eggs dieth, and that which is crushed breaketh out into a viper. [6]Their webs shall not become garments, neither shall they cover themselves with their works: their works are works of iniquity, and the act of violence is in their hands. [7]Their feet run to evil, and they make hast to shed innocent blood: their thoughts are thoughts of iniquity; wasting and destruction are in their paths."

Micah 6:10-12 "[10]Are there yet the treasures of wickedness in the house of the wicked, and the scant measure that is abominable? [11]Shall I count them pure with the wicked balances, and with the bag of deceitful weights? [12]For the rich men thereof are full of violence, and the inhabitants thereof have spoken lies, and their tongue is deceitful in their mouth."

1 John 3:15 "Whosoever hateth his brother is a murderer: and ye know that no murderer hath eternal life abiding in him."

Who Shall Eat Violence
Proverbs 13:2 "A man shall eat good by the fruit of his mouth: but the soul of the transgressors shall eat violence."

VIRTUE

The Virtuous
Proverbs 12:4 "A virtuous woman is a crown to her husband: but she that maketh ashamed is as rottenness in his bones."

Proverbs 31:10-31 "[10]Who can find a virtuous woman? for her price is far above rubies. [11]The heart of her husband doth safely trust in her, so that he shall have no need of spoil. [12]She will do him good and not evil all the days of her life. [13]She seeketh wool, and flax, and worketh willingly with her hands. [14]She is like the merchants' ships; she bringeth her food from afar. [15]She riseth also while it is yet night, and giveth meat to her household, and a portion to her maidens. [16]She considereth a field, and buyeth it: with the fruit of her hands she planteth a vineyard. [17]She girdeth her loins with strength, and strengtheneth her arms. [18]She perceiveth that her merchandise is good: her candle goeth not out by night. [19]She layeth her hands to the spindle, and her hands hold the distaff. [20]She stretcheth out her hand to the poor; yea, she reacheth forth her hands to the needy. [21]She is not afraid of the snow for her household: for all her household are clothed with scarlet. [22]She maketh herself coverings of tapestry; her clothing is silk and purple. [23]Her husband is known in the gates, when he sitteth among the elders of the land. [24]She maketh fine linen, and selleth it; and delivereth girdles unto the merchant. [25]Strength and honour are her clothing; and she shall rejoice in time to come. [26]She openeth her mouth with wisdom; and in her tongue is the law of kindness. ²⁷She looketh well to the ways of her household, and eateth not the bread of idleness. ²⁸Her children arise up, and call her blessed; her husband also, and he praiseth her. ²⁹Many daughters have done virtuously, but thou excellest them all. ³⁰Favour is deceitful, and beauty is vain: but a woman that feareth the LORD, she shall be praised. ³¹Give her of the fruit of her hands; and let her own works praise her in the gates."

2 Peter 1:1-11 "¹Simon Peter, a servant and an apostle of Jesus Christ, to them that have obtained like precious faith with us through the righteousness of God and our Saviour Jesus Christ: ²Grace and peace be multiplied unto you through the knowledge of God, and of Jesus our Lord, ³According as his divine power hath given unto us all things that pertain unto life and godliness, through the knowledge of him that hath called us to glory and virtue: ⁴Whereby are given unto us exceeding great and precious promises: that by these ye might be partakers of the divine nature, having escaped the corruption that is in the world through lust. ⁵And beside this, giving all diligence, add to your faith virtue; and to virtue knowledge; ⁶And to knowledge temperance; and to temperance patience; and to patience godliness; ⁷And to godliness brotherly kindness; and to brotherly kindness charity. ⁸For if these things be in you, and abound, they make you that ye shall neither be barren nor unfruitful in the knowledge of our Lord Jesus Christ. ⁹But he that lacketh these things is blind, and cannot see afar off, and hath forgotten that he was purged from his old sins. ¹⁰Wherefore the rather, brethren, give diligence to make your calling and election sure: for if ye do these things, ye shall never fall: ¹¹For so an entrance shall be ministered unto you abundantly into the everlasting kingdom of our Lord and Saviour Jesus Christ."

Those That Lack Virtue

2 Peter 1:1-9 "¹Simon Peter, a servant and an apostle of Jesus Christ, to them that have obtained like precious faith with us through the righteousness of God and our Saviour Jesus Christ: ²Grace and peace be multiplied unto you through the knowledge of God, and of Jesus our Lord, ³According as his divine power hath given unto us all things that pertain unto life and godliness, through the knowledge of him that hath called us to glory and virtue: ⁴Whereby are given unto us exceeding great and precious promises: that by these ye might be partakers of the divine nature, having escaped the corruption that is in the world through lust. ⁵And beside this, giving all diligence, add to your faith virtue; and to virtue knowledge; ⁶And to knowledge temperance; and to temperance patience; and to patience godliness; ⁷And to godliness brotherly kindness; and to brotherly kindness charity. ⁸For if these things be in you, and abound, they make you that ye shall neither be barren nor unfruitful in the knowledge of our Lord Jesus Christ. ⁹But he that lacketh these things is blind, and cannot see afar off, and hath forgotten that he was purged from his old sins."

WAITING

The Reward For Waiting On The Lord

Psalm 27:14 "Wait on the LORD: be of good courage, and he shall strengthen thine heart: wait, I say, on the LORD."

Psalm 37:34 "Wait on the LORD, and keep his way, and he shall exalt thee to inherit the land: when the wicked are cut off, thou shalt see it."

Psalm 40:1 "I waited patiently for the LORD; and he inclined unto me, and heard my cry."

Proverbs 20:22 "Say not thou, I will recompense evil; but wait on the LORD, and he shall save thee."

Isaiah 25:8-9 "⁸He will swallow up death in victory; and the Lord GOD will wipe away tears from off all faces; and the rebuke of his people shall he take away from off all the earth: for the LORD hath spoken it. ⁹And it shall be said in that day, Lo, this is our God; we have waited for him, and he will save us: this is the LORD; we have waited for him, we will be glad and rejoice in his salvation."

Those That Wait On The Lord

Psalm 37:9 "For evildoers shall be cut off: but those that wait upon the LORD, they shall inherit the earth."

Isaiah 30:18 "And therefore will the LORD wait, that he may be gracious unto you, and therefore will he be exalted, that he may have mercy upon you: for the LORD is a God of judgment: blessed are all they that wait for him."

Isaiah 33:2 "O LORD, be gracious unto us; we have waited for thee: be thou their arm every morning, our salvation also in the time of trouble."

Isaiah 40:30-31 "³⁰Even the youths shall faint and be weary, and the young men shall utterly fall: ³¹But they that wait upon the LORD shall renew their strength; they shall mount up with wings as eagles; they shall run, and not be weary; and they shall walk, and not faint."

Isaiah 49:23 "And kings shall be thy nursing fathers, and their queens thy nursing mothers: they shall bow down to thee with their face toward the earth, and lick up the dust of thy feet; and thou shalt know that I am the LORD: for they shall not be ashamed that wait for me."

Isaiah 64:4 "For since the beginning of the world men have not heard, nor perceived by the ear, neither hath the eye seen, O God, beside thee, what he hath prepared for him that waiteth for him."

Lamentations 3:25 "The LORD is good unto them that wait for him, to the soul that seeketh him."

Matthew 24:45-51 "⁴⁵Who then is a faithful and wise servant, whom his lord hath made ruler over his household, to give them meat in due season? ⁴⁶Blessed is that servant, whom his lord when he cometh shall find so doing. ⁴⁷Verily I say unto you, That he shall make him ruler over all his goods. ⁴⁸But and if that evil servant shall say in his heart, My lord delayeth his coming; ⁴⁹And shall begin to smite his fellowservants, and to eat and drink with the drunken; ⁵⁰The lord of that servant shall come in a day when he looketh not for him, and in an hour that he is not aware of, ⁵¹And shall cut him asunder, and appoint him his portion with the hypocrites: there shall be weeping and gnashing of teeth."

Luke 12:35-40 "³⁵Let your loins be girded about, and your lights burning; ³⁶And ye yourselves like unto men that wait for their lord, when he will return from the wedding; that when he cometh and knocketh, they may open unto him immediately. ³⁷Blessed are those servants, whom the lord when he cometh shall find watching: verily I say unto you, that he shall gird himself, and make them to sit down to meat, and will come forth and serve them. ³⁸And if he shall come in the second watch, or come in the third watch, and find them so, blessed are those servants. ³⁹And this know, that if the goodman of the house had known what hour the thief would come, he would have watched, and not have suffered his house to be broken through. ⁴⁰Be ye therefore ready also: for the Son of man cometh at an hour when ye think not."

1 Corinthians 2:9 "But as it is written, Eye hath not seen, nor ear heard, neither have entered into the heart of man, the things which God hath prepared for them that love him."

Waiting On The Lord

Psalm 25:5 "Lead me in thy truth, and teach me: for thou art the God of my salvation; on thee do I wait all the day."

Psalm 25:15-21 "[15]Mine eyes are ever toward the LORD; for he shall pluck my feet out of the net. [16]Turn thee unto me, and have mercy upon me; for I am desolate and afflicted. [17]The troubles of my heart are enlarged: O bring thou me out of my distresses. [18]Look upon mine affliction and my pain; and forgive all my sins. [19]Consider mine enemies; for they are many; and they hate me with cruel hatred. [20]O keep my soul, and deliver me: let me not be ashamed; for I put my trust in thee. [21]Let integrity and uprightness preserve me; for I wait on thee."

Psalm 27:14 "Wait on the LORD: be of good courage, and he shall strengthen thine heart: wait, I say, on the LORD."

Psalm 33:20 "Our soul waiteth for the LORD: he is our help and our shield."

Psalm 37:7 "Rest in the LORD, and wait patiently for him: fret not thyself because of him who prospereth in his way, because of the man who bringeth wicked devices to pass."

Psalm 37:34 "Wait on the LORD, and keep his way, and he shall exalt thee to inherit the land: when the wicked are cut off, thou shalt see it."

Psalm 52:8-9 "[8]But I am like a green olive tree in the house of God: I trust in the mercy of God for ever and ever. [9]I will praise thee for ever, because thou hast done it: and I will wait on thy name; for it is good before thy saints."

Psalm 59:9 "Because of his strength will I wait upon thee: for God is my defence."

Psalm 130:5-6 "[5]I wait for the LORD, my soul doth wait, and in his word do I hope. [6]My soul waiteth for the Lord more than they that watch for the morning: I say, more than they that watch for the morning."

Proverbs 20:22 "Say not thou, I will recompense evil; but wait on the LORD, and he shall save thee."

Isaiah 8:16-17 "[16]Bind up the testimony, seal the law among my disciples. [17]And I will wait upon the LORD, that hideth his face from the house of Jacob, and I will look for him."

Isaiah 26:8 "Yea, in the way of thy judgments, O LORD, have we waited for thee; the desire of our soul is to thy name, and to the remembrance of thee."

Jeremiah 14:22 "Are there any among the vanities of the Gentiles that can cause rain? or can the heavens give showers? art not thou he, O LORD our God? therefore we will wait upon thee: for thou hast made all these things."

Lamentations 3:26 "It is good that a man should both hope and quietly wait for the salvation of the LORD."

Hosea 12:6 "Therefore turn thou to thy God: keep mercy and judgment, and wait on thy God continually."

Micah 7:7 "Therefore I will look unto the LORD; I will wait for the God of my salvation: my God will hear me."

Zephaniah 3:8 "Therefore wait ye upon me, saith the LORD, until the day that I rise up to the prey: for my determination is to gather the nations, that I may assemble the kingdoms, to pour upon them mine indignation, even all my fierce anger: for all the earth shall be devoured with the fire of my jealousy."

Who Waits For The Lord

Romans 8:18-23 "[18]For I reckon that the sufferings of this present time are not worthy to be compared with the glory which shall be revealed in us. [19]For the earnest expectation of the creature waiteth for the manifestation of the sons of God. [20]For the creature was made subject to vanity, not willingly, but by reason of him who hath subjected the same in hope, [21]Because the creature itself also shall be delivered from the bondage of corruption into the glorious liberty of the children of God. [22]For we know that the whole creation groaneth and travaileth in pain together until now. [23]And not only they, but ourselves also, which have the firstfruits of the Spirit, even we ourselves groan within ourselves, waiting for the adoption, to wit, the redemption of our body."

Galatians 5:1-6 "¹Stand fast therefore in the liberty wherewith Christ hath made us free, and be not entangled again with the yoke of bondage. ²Behold, I Paul say unto you, that if ye be circumcised, Christ shall profit you nothing. ³For I testify again to every man that is circumcised, that he is a debtor to do the whole law. ⁴Christ is become of no effect unto you, whosoever of you are justified by the law; ye are fallen from grace. ⁵For we through the Spirit wait for the hope of righteousness by faith. ⁶For in Jesus Christ neither circumcision availeth anything, nor uncircumcision; but faith which worketh by love."

WANTONNESS

Not Walking In Wantonness
Romans 13:13 "Let us walk honestly, as in the day; not in rioting and drunkenness, not in chambering and wantonness, not in strife and envying."

WAR/WEAPONS

Fighting The Good Fight
1 Timothy 1:18-19 "¹⁸This charge I commit unto thee, son Timothy, according to the prophecies which went before on thee, that thou by them mightest war a good warfare; ¹⁹Holding faith, and a good conscience; which some having put away concerning faith have made shipwreck:"

1 Timothy 6:12 "Fight the good fight of faith, lay hold on eternal life, whereunto thou art also called, and hast professed a good profession before many witnesses."

2 Timothy 4:7 "I have fought a good fight, I have finished my course, I have kept the faith:"

Jesus Christ Coming To Send Us A Sword
Matthew 10:33-34 "³³But whosoever shall deny me before men, him will I also deny before my Father which is in heaven. ³⁴Think not that I am come to send peace on earth: I came not to send peace, but a sword."

Nations Not Warring Against
Each Other Anymore
Isaiah 2:1-4 "¹the word that Isaiah the son of Amoz saw concerning Judah and Jerusalem. ²And it shall come to pass in the last days, that the mountain of the LORD's house shall be established in the top of the mountains, and shall be exalted above the hills; and all nations shall flow unto it. ³And many people shall go and say, Come ye, and let us go up to the mountain of the LORD, to the house of the God of Jacob; and he will teach us of his ways, and we will walk in his paths: for out of Zion shall go forth the law, and the word of the LORD from Jerusalem. ⁴And he shall judge among the nations, and shall rebuke many people: and they shall beat their swords into plowshares, and their spears into pruninghooks: nation shall not lift up sword against nation, neither shall they learn war any more."

Micah 4:1-5 "¹But in the last days it shall come to pass, that the mountain of the house of the LORD shall be established in the top of the mountains, and it shall be exalted above the hills; and people shall flow unto it. ²And many nations shall come, and say, Come, and let us go up to the mountain of the LORD, and to the house of the God of Jacob; and he will teach us of his ways, and we will walk in his paths: for the law shall go forth of Zion, and the word of the LORD from Jerusalem. ³And he shall judge among many people, and rebuke strong nations afar off; and they shall beat their swords into plowshares, and their spears into pruninghooks: nation shall not lift up a sword against nation, neither shall they learn war any more. ⁴But they shall sit every man under his vine and under his fig tree; and none shall make them afraid: for the mouth of the LORD of hosts hath spoken it. ⁵For all people will walk every one in the name of his god, and we will walk in the name of the LORD our God for ever and ever."

The Lord Being A Warrior
Exodus 15:3 "The LORD is a man of war: the LORD is his name."

Isaiah 42:13 "The LORD shall go forth as a mighty man, he shall stir up jealousy like a man of war: he shall cry, yea, roar; he shall prevail against his enemies."

Revelation 19:11 "And I saw heaven opened, and behold a white horse; and he that sat upon him was called Faithful and True, and in righteousness he doth judge and make war."

The Lord Teaching You How To War

2 Samuel 22:33-35 "³³God is my strength and power: and he maketh my way perfect. ³⁴He maketh my feet like hinds' feet: and setteth me upon my high places. ³⁵He teacheth my hands to war; so that a bow of steel is broken by mine arms."

Psalm 18:31-34 "³¹For who is God save the LORD? or who is a rock save our God? ³²It is God that girdeth me with strength, and maketh my way perfect. ³³He maketh my feet like hinds' feet, and setteth me upon my high places. ³⁴He teacheth my hands to war, so that a bow of steel is broken by mine arms."

Psalm 144:1 "Blessed be the LORD my strength, which teacheth my hands to war, and my fingers to fight:"

The Weapons Of A Spiritual War

2 Corinthians 10:3-6 "³For though we walk in the flesh, we do not war after the flesh: ⁴(For the weapons of our warfare are not carnal, but mighty through God to the pulling down of strong holds;) ⁵Casting down imaginations, and every high thing that exalteth itself against the knowledge of God, and bringing into captivity every thought to the obedience of Christ; ⁶And having in a readiness to revenge all disobedience, when your obedience is fulfilled."

Ephesians 6:10-17 "¹⁰Finally, my brethren, be strong in the Lord, and in the power of his might. ¹¹Put on the whole armour of God, that ye may be able to stand against the wiles of the devil. ¹²For we wrestle not against flesh and blood, but against principalities, against powers, against the rulers of the darkness of this world, against spiritual wickedness in high places. ¹³Wherefore take unto you the whole armour of God, that ye may be able to withstand in the evil day, and having done all, to stand. ¹⁴Stand therefore, having your loins girt about with truth, and having on the breastplate of righteousness; ¹⁵And your feet shod with the preparation of the gospel of peace; ¹⁶Above all, taking the shield of faith, wherewith ye shall be able to quench all the fiery darts of the wicked. ¹⁷And take the helmet of salvation, and the sword of the Spirit, which is the word of God:"

The Word Of God Being A Sword

Isaiah 11:1-4 "¹And there shall come forth a rod out of the stem of Jesse, and a Branch shall grow out of his roots: ²And the spirit of the LORD shall rest upon him, the spirit of wisdom and understanding, the spirit of counsel and might, the spirit of knowledge and of the fear of the LORD; ³And shall make him of quick understanding in the fear of the LORD: and he shall not judge after the sight of his eyes, neither reprove after the hearing of his ears: ⁴But with righteousness shall he judge the poor, and reprove with equity for the meek of the earth: and he shall smite the earth with the rod of his mouth, and with the breath of his lips shall he slay the wicked."

Isaiah 49:1-2 "¹Listen, O isles, unto me; and hearken, ye people, from far; The LORD hath called me from the womb; from the bowels of my mother hath he made mention of my name. ²And he hath made my mouth like a sharp sword; in the shadow of his hand hath he hid me, and made me a polished shaft; in his quiver hath he hid me;"

Hosea 6:1-5 "¹Come, and let us return unto the LORD: for he hath torn, and he will heal us; he hath smitten, and he will bind us up. ²After two days will he revive us: in the third day he will raise us up, and we shall live in his sight. ³Then shall we know, if we follow on to know the LORD: his going forth is prepared as the morning; and he shall come unto us as the rain, as the latter and former rain unto the earth. ⁴O Ephraim, what shall I do unto thee? O Judah, what shall I do unto thee? for your goodness is as a morning cloud, and as the early dew it goeth away. ⁵Therefore have I hewed them by the prophets; I have slain them by the words of my mouth: and thy judgments are as the light that goeth forth."

Ephesians 6:17 "And take the helmet of salvation, and the sword of the Spirit, which is the word of God:"

Hebrews 4:12 "For the word of God is quick, and powerful, and sharper than any twoedged sword, piercing even to the dividing asunder of soul and spirit, and of the joints and marrow, and is a discerner of the thoughts and intents of the heart."

Revelation 1:14-17 "[14]His head and his hairs were white like wool, as white as snow; and his eyes were as a flame of fire; [15]And his feet like unto fine brass, as if they burned in a furnace; and his voice as the sound of many waters. [16]And he had in his right hand seven stars: and out of his mouth went a sharp twoedged sword: and his countenance was as the sun shineth in his strength. [17]And when I saw him, I fell at his feet as dead. And he laid his right hand upon me, saying unto me, Fear not; I am the first and the last:"

Revelation 2:12-16 "[12]And to the angel of the church in Pergamos write; These things saith he which hath the sharp sword with two edges; [13]I know thy works, and where thou dwellest, even where Satan's seat is: and thou holdest fast my name, and hast not denied my faith, even in those days wherein Antipas was my faithful martyr, who was slain among you, where Satan dwelleth. [14]But I have a few things against thee, because thou hast there them that hold the doctrine of Balaam, who taught Balac to cast a stumblingblock before the children of Israel, to eat things sacrificed unto idols, and to commit fornication. [15]So hast thou also them that hold the doctrine of the Nicolaitans, which thing I hate. [16]Repent; or else I will come unto thee quickly, and will fight against them with the sword of my mouth."

Revelation 19:11-21 "[11]And I saw heaven opened, and behold a white horse; and he that sat upon him was called Faithful and True, and in righteousness he doth judge and make war. [12]His eyes were as a flame of fire, and on his head were many crowns; and he had a name written, that no man knew, but he himself. [13]And he was clothed with a vesture dipped in blood: and his name is called The Word of God. [14]And the armies which were in heaven followed him upon white horses, clothed in fine linen, white and clean. [15]And out of his mouth goeth a sharp sword, that with it he should smite the nations: and he shall rule them with a rod of iron: and he treadeth the winepress of the fierceness and wrath of Almighty God. [16]And he hath on his vesture and on his thigh a name written, KING OF KINGS, AND LORD OF LORDS. [17]And I saw an angel standing in the sun; and he cried with a loud voice, saying to all the fowls that fly in the midst of heaven, Come and gather yourselves together unto the supper of the great God; [18]That ye may eat the flesh of kings, and the flesh of captains, and the flesh of mighty men, and the flesh of horses, and of them that sit on them, and the flesh of all men, both free and bond, both small and great. [19]And I saw the beast, and the kings of the earth, and their armies, gathered together to make war against him that sat on the horse, and against his army. [20]And the beast was taken, and with him the false prophet that wrought miracles before him, with which he deceived them that had received the mark of the beast, and them that worshipped his image. These both were cast alive into a lake of fire burning with brimstone. [21]And the remnant were slain with the sword of him that sat upon the horse, which sword proceeded out of his mouth: and all the fowls were filled with their flesh."

There Being A Time For War
Ecclesiastes 3:1-9 "[1]To every thing there is a season, and a time to every purpose under the heaven: [2]A time to be born, and a time to die; a time to plant, and a time to pluck up that which is planted; [3]A time to kill, and a time to heal; a time to break down, and a time to build up; [4]A time to weep, and a time to laugh; a time to mourn, and a time to dance; [5]A time to cast away stones, and a time to gather stones together; a time to embrace, and a time to refrain from embracing; [6]A time to get, and a time to lose; a time to keep, and a time to cast away; [7]A time to rend, and a time to sew; a time to keep silence, and a time to speak; [8]A time to love, and a time to hate; a time of war, and a time of peace. [9]What profit hath he that worketh in that wherein he laboureth?"

What Believers Do Not War After
2 Corinthians 10:1-3 "[1]Now I Paul myself beseech you by the meekness and gentleness of Christ, who in presence am base among you, but being absent am bold toward you: [2]But I beseech you, that I may not be bold when I am present with that confidence, wherewith I think to be bold against some, which think of us as if we walked according to the flesh. [3]For though we walk in the flesh, we do not war after the flesh:"

What Believers Do Not War Against

Ephesians 6:10-12 "¹⁰Finally, my brethren, be strong in the Lord, and in the power of his might. ¹¹Put on the whole armour of God, that ye may be able to stand against the wiles of the devil. ¹²For we wrestle not against flesh and blood, but against principalities, against powers, against the rulers of the darkness of this world, against spiritual wickedness in high places."

What Believers War Against

Ephesians 6:10-12 "¹⁰Finally, my brethren, be strong in the Lord, and in the power of his might. ¹¹Put on the whole armour of God, that ye may be able to stand against the wiles of the devil. ¹²For we wrestle not against flesh and blood, but against principalities, against powers, against the rulers of the darkness of this world, against spiritual wickedness in high places."

What Is Better Than Weapons Of War

Ecclesiastes 9:18 "Wisdom is better than weapons of war: but one sinner destroyeth much good."

What Wars Against The Mind

Romans 7:21-25 "²¹I find then a law, that, when I would do good, evil is present with me. ²²For I delight in the law of God after the inward man: ²³But I see another law in my members, warring against the law of my mind, and bringing me into captivity to the law of sin which is in my members. ²⁴O wretched man that I am! who shall deliver me from the body of this death? ²⁵I thank God through Jesus Christ our Lord. So then with the mind I myself serve the law of God; but with the flesh the law of sin."

What Wars Against The Spirit

Galatians 5:16-18 "¹⁶This I say then, Walk in the Spirit, and ye shall not fulfil the lust of the flesh. ¹⁷For the flesh lusteth against the Spirit, and the Spirit against the flesh: and these are contrary the one to the other: so that ye cannot do the things that ye would. ¹⁸But if ye be led of the Spirit, ye are not under the law."

1 Peter 2:11 "Dearly beloved, I beseech you as strangers and pilgrims, abstain from fleshly lusts, which war against the soul;"

Where Wars Come From

James 4:1-3 "¹From whence come wars and fightings among you? come they not hence, even of your lusts that war in your members? ²Ye lust, and have not: ye kill, and desire to have, and cannot obtain: ye fight and war, yet ye have not, because ye ask not. ³Ye ask, and receive not, because ye ask amiss, that ye may consume it upon your lusts."

Who Will Attempt To Make War With Jesus Christ And His Saints

Daniel 8:17-26 "¹⁷So he came near where I stood: and when he came, I was afraid, and fell upon my face: but he said unto me, Understand, O son of man: for at the time of the end shall be the vision. ¹⁸Now as he was speaking with me, I was in a deep sleep on my face toward the ground: but he touched me, and set me upright. ¹⁹And he said, Behold, I will make thee know what shall be in the last end of the indignation: for at the time appointed the end shall be. ²⁰The ram which thou sawest having two horns are the kings of Media and Persia. ²¹And the rough goat is the king of Grecia: and the great horn that is between his eyes is the first king. ²²Now that being broken, whereas four stood up for it, four kingdoms shall stand up out of the nation, but not in his power. ²³And in the latter time of their kingdom, when the transgressors are come to the full, a king of fierce countenance, and understanding dark sentences, shall stand up. ²⁴And his power shall be mighty, but not by his own power: and he shall destroy wonderfully, and shall prosper, and practise, and shall destroy the mighty and the holy people. ²⁵And through his policy also he shall cause craft to prosper in his hand; and he shall magnify himself in his heart, and by peace shall destroy many: he shall also stand up against the Prince of princes; but he shall be broken without hand. ²⁶And the vision of the evening and the morning which was told is true: wherefore shut thou up the vision; for it shall be for many days."

Revelation 11:1-7 "¹And there was given me a reed like unto a rod: and the angel stood, saying, Rise, and measure the temple of God, and the altar, and them that worship therein. ²But the court which is without the temple leave out, and measure it not; for it is given unto the Gentiles: and the holy city shall they tread under foot forty and two months. ³And I will give power unto my two witnesses, and they shall prophesy a thousand two hundred and threescore days, clothed in sackcloth. [4]These are the two olive trees, and the two candlesticks standing before the God of the earth. [5]And if any man will hurt them, fire proceedeth out of their mouth, and devoureth their enemies: and if any man will hurt them, he must in this manner be killed. [6]These have power to shut heaven, that it rain not in the days of their prophecy: and have power over waters to turn them to blood, and to smite the earth with all plagues, as often as they will. [7]And when they shall have finished their testimony, the beast that ascendeth out of the bottomless pit shall make war against them, and shall overcome them, and kill them."

Revelation 12:1-17 "[1]And there appeared a great wonder in heaven; a woman clothed with the sun, and the moon under her feet, and upon her head a crown of twelve stars: [2]And she being with child cried, travailing in birth, and pained to be delivered. [3]And there appeared another wonder in heaven; and behold a great red dragon, having seven heads and ten horns, and seven crowns upon his heads. [4]And his tail drew the third part of the stars of heaven, and did cast them to the earth: and the dragon stood before the woman which was ready to be delivered, for to devour her child as soon as it was born. [5]And she brought forth a man child, who was to rule all nations with a rod of iron: and her child was caught up unto God, and to his throne. [6]And the woman fled into the wilderness, where she hath a place prepared of God, that they should feed her there a thousand two hundred and threescore days. [7]And there was war in heaven: Michael and his angels fought against the dragon; and the dragon fought and his angels, [8]And prevailed not; neither was their place found any more in heaven. [9]And the great dragon was cast out, that old serpent, called the Devil, and Satan, which deceiveth the whole world: he was cast out into the earth, and his angels were cast out with him. [10]And I heard a loud voice saying in heaven, Now is come salvation, and strength, and the kingdom of our God, and the power of his Christ: for the accuser of our brethren is cast down, which accused them before our God day and night. [11]And they overcame him by the blood of the Lamb, and by the word of their testimony; and they loved not their lives unto the death. [12]Therefore rejoice, ye heavens, and ye that dwell in them. Woe to the inhabiters of the earth and of the sea! for the devil is come down unto you, having great wrath, because he knoweth that he hath but a short time. [13]And when the dragon saw that he was cast unto the earth, he persecuted the woman which brought forth the man child. [14]And to the woman were given two wings of a great eagle, that she might fly into the wilderness, into her place, where she is nourished for a time, and times, and half a time, from the face of the serpent. [15]And the serpent cast out of his mouth water as a flood after the woman, that he might cause her to be carried away of the flood. [16]And the earth helped the woman, and the earth opened her mouth, and swallowed up the flood which the dragon cast out of his mouth. [17]And the dragon was wroth with the woman, and went to make war with the remnant of her seed, which keep the commandments of God, and have the testimony of Jesus Christ."

Revelation 13:1-7 "[1]And I stood upon the sand of the sea, and saw a beast rise up out of the sea, having seven heads and ten horns, and upon his horns ten crowns, and upon his heads the name of blasphemy. [2]And the beast which I saw was like unto a leopard, and his feet were as the feet of a bear, and his mouth as the mouth of a lion: and the dragon gave him his power, and his seat, and great authority. [3]And I saw one of his heads as it were wounded to death; and his deadly wound was healed: and all the world wondered after the beast. [4]And they worshipped the dragon which gave power unto the beast: and they worshipped the beast, saying, Who is like unto the beast? who is able to make war with him? [5]And there was given unto him a mouth speaking great things and blasphemies; and power was given unto him to continue forty and two months. [6]And he opened his mouth in blasphemy against God, to blaspheme his name, and his tabernacle, and them that dwell in heaven. [7]And it was given unto him to make war with the saints, and to overcome them: and power was given him over all kindreds, and tongues, and nations."

Revelation 16:12-21 "[12]And the sixth angel poured out his vial upon the great river Euphrates; and the water thereof was dried up, that the way of the kings of the east might be prepared. [13]And I saw three unclean spirits like frogs come out of the mouth of the dragon, and out of the mouth of the beast, and out of the mouth of the false prophet. [14]For they are the spirits of devils, working miracles, which go forth unto the kings of the earth and of the whole world, to gather them to the battle of that great day of God Almighty. [15]Behold, I come as a thief. Blessed is he that watcheth, and keepeth his garments, lest he walk naked, and they see his shame. [16]And he gathered them together into a place called in the Hebrew tongue Armageddon. [17]And the seventh angel poured out his vial into the air; and there came a great voice out of the temple of heaven, from the throne, saying, It is done. [18]And there were voices, and thunders, and lightnings; and there was a great earthquake, such as was not since men were upon the earth, so mighty an earthquake, and so great. [19]And the great city was divided into three parts, and the cities of the nations fell: and great Babylon came in remembrance before God, to give unto her the cup of the wine of the fierceness of his wrath. [20]And every island fled away, and the mountains were not found. [21]And there fell upon men a great hail out of heaven, every stone about the weight of a talent: and men blasphemed God because of the plague of the hail; for the plague thereof was exceeding great."

Revelation 17:12-14 "[12]And the ten horns which thou sawest are ten kings, which have received no kingdom as yet; but receive power as kings one hour with the beast. [13]These have one mind, and shall give their power and strength unto the beast. [14]These shall make war with the Lamb, and the Lamb shall overcome them: for he is Lord of lords, and King of kings: and they that are with him are called, and chosen, and faithful."

Revelation 19:11-19 "[11]And I saw heaven opened, and behold a white horse; and he that sat upon him was called Faithful and True, and in righteousness he doth judge and make war. [12]His eyes were as a flame of fire, and on his head were many crowns; and he had a name written, that no man knew, but he himself. [13]And he was clothed with a vesture dipped in blood: and his name is called The Word of God. [14]And the armies which were in heaven followed him upon white horses, clothed in fine linen, white and clean. [15]And out of his mouth goeth a sharp sword, that with it he

should smite the nations: and he shall rule them with a rod of iron: and he treadeth the winepress of the fierceness and wrath of Almighty God. [16]And he hath on his vesture and on his thigh a name written, KING OF KINGS, AND LORD OF LORDS. [17]And I saw an angel standing in the sun; and he cried with a loud voice, saying to all the fowls that fly in the midst of heaven, Come and gather yourselves together unto the supper of the great God; [18]That ye may eat the flesh of kings, and the flesh of captains, and the flesh of mighty men, and the flesh of horses, and of them that sit on them, and the flesh of all men, both free and bond, both small and great. [19]And I saw the beast, and the kings of the earth, and their armies, gathered together to make war against him that sat on the horse, and against his army."

Revelation 20:7-10 "[7]And when the thousand years are expired, Satan shall be loosed out of his prison, [8]And shall go out to deceive the nations which are in the four quarters of the earth, Gog and Magog, to gather them together to battle: the number of whom is as the sand of the sea. [9]And they went up on the breadth of the earth, and compassed the camp of the saints about, and the beloved city: and fire came down from God out of heaven, and devoured them. [10]And the devil that deceived them was cast into the lake of fire and brimstone, where the beast and the false prophet are, and shall be tormented day and night for ever and ever."

WARNING

The Reward For Not Warning Others
Ezekiel 3:16-18 "[16]And it came to pass at the end of seven days, that the word of the LORD came unto me, saying, [17]Son of man, I have made thee a watchman unto the house of Israel: therefore hear the word at my mouth, and give them warning from me. [18]When I say unto the wicked, Thou shalt surely die; and thou givest him not warning, nor speakest to warn the wicked from his wicked way, to save his life; the same wicked man shall die in his iniquity; but his blood will I require at thine hand."

Ezekiel 3:20 "Again, When a righteous man doth turn from his righteousness, and commit iniquity, and I lay a stumblingblock before him, he shall die: because thou hast not given him warning, he shall die in his sin, and his righteousness which he hath done shall not be remembered; but his blood will I require at thine hand."

Ezekiel 33:1-8 "¹Again the word of the LORD came unto me, saying, ²Son of man, speak to the children of thy people, and say unto them, When I bring the sword upon a land, if the people of the land take a man of their coasts, and set him for their watchman: ³If when he seeth the sword come upon the land, he blow the trumpet, and warn the people; ⁴Then whosoever heareth the sound of the trumpet, and taketh not warning; if the sword come, and take him away, his blood shall be upon his own head. ⁵He heard the sound of the trumpet, and took not warning; his blood shall be upon him. But he that taketh warning shall deliver his soul. ⁶But if the watchman see the sword come, and blow not the trumpet, and the people be not warned; if the sword come, and take any person from among them, he is taken away in his iniquity; but his blood will I require at the watchman's hand. ⁷So thou, O son of man, I have set thee a watchman unto the house of Israel; therefore thou shalt hear the word at my mouth, and warn them from me. ⁸When I say unto the wicked, O wicked man, thou shalt surely die; if thou dost not speak to warn the wicked from his way, that wicked man shall die in his iniquity; but his blood will I require at thine hand."

The Reward For Warning Others
Ezekiel 3:19 "Yet if thou warn the wicked, and he turn not from his wickedness, nor from his wicked way, he shall die in his iniquity; but thou hast delivered thy soul."

Ezekiel 3:21 "Nevertheless if thou warn the righteous man, that the righteous sin not, and he doth not sin, he shall surely live, because he is warned; also thou hast delivered thy soul."

Ezekiel 33:9 "Nevertheless, if thou warn the wicked of his way to turn from it; if he do not turn from his way, he shall die in his iniquity; but thou hast delivered thy soul."

Warning Others
Colossians 1:26-28 "²⁶Even the mystery which hath been hid from ages and from generations, but now is made manifest to his saints: ²⁷To whom God would make known what is the riches of the glory of this mystery among the Gentiles; which is Christ in you, the hope of glory: ²⁸Whom we preach, warning every man, and teaching every man in all wisdom; that we may present every man perfect in Christ Jesus:"

Who To Warn
1 Thessalonians 5:14 "Now we exhort you, brethren, warn them that are unruly, comfort the feebleminded, support the weak, be patient toward all men."

WAVERING

Not Wavering
Hebrews 10:23 "Let us hold fast the profession of our faith without wavering; (for he is faithful that promised;)"

James 1:5-6 "⁵If any of you lack wisdom, let him ask of God, that giveth to all men liberally, and upbraideth not; and it shall be given him. ⁶But let him ask in faith, nothing wavering. For he that wavereth is like a wave of the sea driven with the wind and tossed."

Those That Waver
James 1:5-8 "⁵If any of you lack wisdom, let him ask of God, that giveth to all men liberally, and upbraideth not; and it shall be given him. ⁶But let him ask in faith, nothing wavering. For he that wavereth is like a wave of the sea driven with the wind and tossed. ⁷For let not that man think that he shall receive any thing of the Lord. ⁸A double minded man is unstable in all his ways."

WAYS

The Way Of Life
Proverbs 15:24 "The way of life is above to the wise, that he may depart from hell beneath."

The Way Of Righteousness
Proverbs 12:28 "In the way of righteousness is life; and in the pathway thereof there is no death."

The Way Of The Righteous
Psalm 1:6 "For the LORD knoweth the way of the righteous: but the way of the ungodly shall perish."

The Way Of The Ungodly
Psalm 1:6 "For the LORD knoweth the way of the righteous: but the way of the ungodly shall perish."

The Way Of The Wicked
Proverbs 4:19 "The way of the wicked is as darkness: they know not at what they stumble."

The Way That Leads To Destruction
Matthew 7:13 "Enter ye in at the strait gate: for wide is the gate, and broad is the way, that leadeth to destruction, and many there be which go in thereat:"

The Ways Of Man
Proverbs 5:21 "For the ways of man are before the eyes of the LORD, and he pondereth all his goings."

Proverbs 16:2 "All the ways of a man are clean in his own eyes; but the LORD weigheth the spirits."

Proverbs 21:2 "Every way of a man is right in his own eyes: but the LORD pondereth the hearts."

Proverbs 21:8 "The way of man is froward and strange: but as for the pure, his work is right."

Isaiah 55:7-9 "[7]Let the wicked forsake his way, and the unrighteous man his thoughts: and let him return unto the LORD, and he will have mercy upon him; and to our God, for he will abundantly pardon. [8]For my thoughts are not your thoughts, neither are your ways my ways, saith the LORD. [9]For as the heavens are higher than the earth, so are my ways higher than your ways, and my thoughts than your thoughts."

Jeremiah 10:23 "O LORD, I know that the way of man is not in himself: it is not in man that walketh to direct his steps."

Ezekiel 18:25-30 "[25]Yet ye say, The way of the Lord is not equal. Hear now, O house of Israel; Is not my way equal? are not your ways unequal? [26]When a righteous man turneth away from his righteousness, and committeth iniquity, and dieth in them; for his iniquity that he hath done shall he die. [27]Again, when the wicked man turneth away from his wickedness that he hath committed, and doeth that which is lawful and right, he shall save his soul alive. [28]Because he considereth, and turneth away from all his transgressions that he hath committed, he shall surely live, he shall not die. [29]Yet saith the house of Israel, The way of the Lord is not equal. O house of Israel, are not my ways equal? are not your ways unequal? [30]Therefore I will judge you, O house of Israel, every one according to his ways, saith the Lord GOD. Repent, and turn yourselves from all your transgressions; so iniquity shall not be your ruin."

Ezekiel 33:17-20 "[17]Yet the children of thy people say, The way of the Lord is not equal: but as for them, their way is not equal. [18]When the righteous turneth from his righteousness, and committeth iniquity, he shall even die thereby. [19]But if the wicked turn from his wickedness, and do that which is lawful and right, he shall live thereby. [20]Yet ye say, The way of the Lord is not equal. O ye house of Israel, I will judge you every one after his ways."

The Ways Of The Lord
Deuteronomy 32:4 "He is the Rock, his work is perfect: for all his ways are judgment: a God of truth and without iniquity, just and right is he."

2 Samuel 22:31 "As for God, his way is perfect; the word of the LORD is tried: he is a buckler to all them that trust in him."

Psalm 18:30 "As for God, his way is perfect: the word of the LORD is tried: he is a buckler to all those that trust in him."

Psalm 103:6-7 "[6]The LORD executeth righteousness and judgment for all that are oppressed. [7]He made known his ways unto Moses, his acts unto the children of Israel."

Proverbs 10:29 "The way of the LORD is strength to the upright: but destruction shall be to the workers of iniquity."

Isaiah 55:7-9 "[7]Let the wicked forsake his way, and the unrighteous man his thoughts: and let him return unto the LORD, and he will have mercy upon him; and to our God, for he will abundantly pardon. [8]For my thoughts are not your thoughts, neither are your ways my ways, saith the LORD. [9]For as the heavens are higher than the earth, so are my ways higher than your ways, and my thoughts than your thoughts."

Ezekiel 18:25-30 "[25]Yet ye say, The way of the Lord is not equal. Hear now, O house of Israel; Is not my way equal? are not your ways unequal? [26]When a righteous man turneth away from his righteousness, and committeth iniquity, and dieth in them; for his iniquity that he hath done shall he die. [27]Again, when the wicked man turneth away from his wickedness that he hath committed, and doeth that which is lawful and right, he shall save his soul alive. [28]Because he considereth, and turneth away from all his transgressions that he hath committed, he shall surely live, he shall not die. [29]Yet saith the house of Israel, The way of the Lord is not equal. O house of Israel, are not my ways equal? are not your ways unequal? [30]Therefore I will judge you, O house of Israel, every one according to his ways, saith the Lord God. Repent, and turn yourselves from all your transgressions; so iniquity shall not be your ruin."

Ezekiel 33:17-20 "[17]Yet the children of thy people say, The way of the Lord is not equal: but as for them, their way is not equal. [18]When the righteous turneth from his righteousness, and committeth iniquity, he shall even die thereby. [19]But if the wicked turn from his wickedness, and do that which is lawful and right, he shall live thereby. [20]Yet ye say, The way of the Lord is not equal. O ye house of Israel, I will judge you every one after his ways."

Daniel 4:37 "Now I Nebuchadnezzar praise and extol and honour the King of heaven, all whose works are truth, and his ways judgment: and those that walk in pride he is able to abase."

Hosea 14:9 "Who is wise, and he shall understand these things? prudent, and he shall know them? for the ways of the LORD are right, and the just shall walk in them: but the transgressors shall fall therein."

Romans 11:33-36 "[33]O the depth of the riches both of the wisdom and knowledge of God! how unsearchable are his judgments, and his ways past finding out! [34]For who hath known the mind of the Lord? or who hath been his counsellor? [35]Or who hath first given to him, and it shall be recompensed unto him again? [36]For of him, and through him, and to him, are all things: to whom be glory for ever. Amen."

Revelation 15:3 "And they sing the song of Moses the servant of God, and the song of the Lamb, saying, Great and marvellous are thy works, Lord God Almighty; just and true are thy ways, thou King of saints."

There Being A Way
That Seems Right To A Man
Proverbs 14:12 "There is a way which seemeth right unto a man, but the end thereof are the ways of death."

Proverbs 16:25 "There is a way that seemeth right unto a man, but the end thereof are the ways of death."

What Is The Way Of Life
Proverbs 6:23 "For the commandment is a lamp; and the law is light; and reproofs of instruction are the way of life:"

Who Is In The Way Of Life
Proverbs 10:17 "He is in the way of life that keepeth instruction: but he that refuseth reproof erreth."

Whose Ways Are Crooked
Proverbs 2:11-15 "[11]Discretion shall preserve thee, understanding shall keep thee: [12]To deliver thee from the way of the evil man, from the man that speaketh froward things; [13]Who leave the paths of uprightness, to walk in the ways of darkness; [14]Who rejoice to do evil, and delight in the frowardness of the wicked; [15]Whose ways are crooked, and they froward in their paths:"

WEALTH

A Man's Life Not Consisting In Wealth
Luke 12:13-15 "[13]And one of the company said unto him, Master, speak to my brother, that he divide the inheritance with me. [14]And he said unto him, Man, who made me a judge or a divider over you? [15]And he said unto them, Take heed, and beware of covetousness: for a man's life consisteth not in the abundance of the things which he possesseth."

House And Riches
Proverbs 19:14 "House and riches are the inheritance of fathers and a prudent wife is from the LORD."

Not Laboring To Be Rich
Proverbs 23:4 "Labour not to be rich: cease from thine own wisdom."

Not Setting Your Heart Upon Riches

Psalm 62:10 "Trust not in oppression, and become not vain in robbery: if riches increase, set not your heart upon them."

Riches Disappearing

Proverbs 23:5 "Wilt thou set thine eyes upon that which is not? for riches certainly make themselves wings; they fly away as an eagle toward heaven."

Proverbs 27:23-24 "²³Be thou diligent to know the state of thy flocks, and look well to thy herds. ²⁴For riches are not for ever: and doth the crown endure to every generation?"

The Acquisition Of Treasures By Lying

Proverbs 21:6 "The getting of treasures by a lying tongue is a vanity tossed to and fro of them that seek death."

The Lord Being The Maker Of The Wealthy

Deuteronomy 8:17-18 "¹⁷And thou say in thine heart, My power and the might of mine hand hath gotten me this wealth. ¹⁸But thou shalt remember the LORD thy God: for it is he that giveth thee power to get wealth, that he may establish his covenant which he sware unto thy fathers, as it is this day."

1 Samuel 2:7 "The LORD maketh poor, and maketh rich: he bringeth low, and lifteth up."

1 Chronicles 29:11-12 "¹¹Thine, O LORD, is the greatness, and the power, and the glory, and the victory, and the majesty: for all that is in the heaven and in the earth is thine; thine is the kingdom, O LORD, and thou art exalted as head above all. ¹²Both riches and honour come of thee, and thou reignest over all; and in thine hand is power and might; and in thine hand it is to make great, and to give strength unto all."

Job 1:20-21 "²⁰Then Job arose, and rent his mantle, and shaved his head, and fell down upon the ground, and worshipped, ²¹And said, Naked came I out of my mother's womb, and naked shall I return thither: the LORD gave, and the LORD hath taken away; blessed be the name of the LORD."

Job 34:12-19 "¹²Yea, surely God will not do wickedly, neither will the Almighty pervert judgment. ¹³Who hath given him a charge over the earth? or who hath disposed the whole world? ¹⁴If he set his heart upon man, if he gather unto himself his spirit and his breath; ¹⁵All flesh shall perish together, and man shall turn again unto dust. ¹⁶If now thou hast understanding, hear this: hearken to the voice of my words. ¹⁷Shall even he that hateth right govern? and wilt thou condemn him that is most just? ¹⁸Is it fit to say to a king, Thou art wicked? and to princes, Ye are ungodly? ¹⁹How much less to him that accepteth not the persons of princes, nor regardeth the rich more than the poor? for they all are the work of his hands."

Proverbs 22:2 "The rich and poor meet together: the LORD is the maker of them all."

The Love Of Money

1 Timothy 6:10 "For the love of money is the root of all evil: which while some coveted after, they have erred from the faith, and pierced themselves through with many sorrows."

The Rich

Proverbs 10:15 "The rich man's wealth is his strong city: the destruction of the poor is their poverty."

Proverbs 14:20 "The poor is hated even of his own neighbour: but the rich hath many friends."

Proverbs 18:11 "The rich man's wealth is his strong city, and as an high wall in his own conceit."

Proverbs 18:23 "The poor useth intreaties; but the rich answereth roughly."

Proverbs 22:7 "The rich ruleth over the poor, and the borrower is servant to the lender."

Proverbs 28:11 "The rich man is wise in his own conceit; but the poor that hath understanding searcheth him out."

Ecclesiastes 5:12 "The sleep of a labouring man is sweet, whether he eat little or much: but the abundance of the rich will not suffer him to sleep."

Matthew 19:23-26 "²³Then said Jesus unto his disciples, Verily I say unto you, That a rich man shall hardly enter into the kingdom of heaven. ²⁴And again I say unto you, It is easier for a camel to go through the eye of a needle, than for a rich man to enter into the kingdom of God. ²⁵When his disciples heard it, they were exceedingly amazed, saying, Who then can be saved? ²⁶But Jesus beheld them, and said unto them, With men this is impossible; but with God all things are possible."

Mark 10:23-27 "²³And Jesus looked round about, and saith unto his disciples, How hardly shall they that have riches enter into the kingdom of God! ²⁴And the disciples were astonished at his words. But Jesus answereth again, and saith unto them, Children, how hard is it for them that trust in riches to enter into the kingdom of God! ²⁵It is easier for a camel to go through the eye of a needle, than for a rich man to enter into the kingdom of God. ²⁶And they were astonished out of measure, saying among themselves, Who then can be saved? ²⁷And Jesus looking upon them saith, With men it is impossible, but not with God: for with God all things are possible."

Luke 6:24-26 "²⁴But woe unto you that are rich! for ye have received your consolation. ²⁵Woe unto you that are full! for ye shall hunger. Woe unto you that laugh now! for ye shall mourn and weep. ²⁶Woe unto you, when all men shall speak well of you! for so did their fathers to the false prophets."

Luke 16:19-31 "¹⁹There was a certain rich man, which was clothed in purple and fine linen, and fared sumptuously every day: ²⁰And there was a certain beggar named Lazarus, which was laid at his gate, full of sores, ²¹And desiring to be fed with the crumbs which fell from the rich man's table: moreover the dogs came and licked his sores. ²²And it came to pass, that the beggar died, and was carried by the angels into Abraham's bosom: the rich man also died, and was buried; ²³And in hell he lift up his eyes, being in torments, and seeth Abraham afar off, and Lazarus in his bosom. ²⁴And he cried and said, Father Abraham, have mercy on me, and send Lazarus, that he may dip the tip of his finger in water, and cool my tongue; for I am tormented in this flame. ²⁵But Abraham said, Son, remember that thou in thy lifetime receivedst thy good things, and likewise Lazarus evil things: but now he is comforted, and thou art tormented. ²⁶And beside all this, between us and you there is a great gulf fixed: so that they which would pass from hence to you cannot; neither can they pass to us, that would come from thence. ²⁷Then he said, I pray thee therefore, father, that thou wouldest send him to my father's house: ²⁸For I have five brethren; that he may testify unto them, lest they also come into this place of torment. ²⁹Abraham saith unto him, They have Moses and the prophets; let them hear them. ³⁰And he said, Nay, father Abraham: but if one went unto them from the dead, they will repent. ³¹And he said unto him, If they hear not Moses and the prophets, neither will they be persuaded, though one rose from the dead."

Luke 18:24-27 "²⁴And when Jesus saw that he was very sorrowful, he said, How hardly shall they that have riches enter into the kingdom of God! ²⁵For it is easier for a camel to go through a needle's eye, than for a rich man to enter into the kingdom of God. ²⁶And they that heard it said, Who then can be saved? ²⁷And he said, The things which are impossible with men are possible with God."

1 Timothy 6:7-9 "⁷For we brought nothing into this world, and it is certain we can carry nothing out. ⁸And having food and raiment let us be therewith content. ⁹But they that will be rich fall into temptation and a snare, and into many foolish and hurtful lusts, which drown men in destruction and perdition."

James 5:1-6 "¹Go to now, ye rich men, weep and howl for your miseries that shall come upon you. ²Your riches are corrupted, and your garments are motheaten. ³Your gold and silver is cankered; and the rust of them shall be a witness against you, and shall eat your flesh as it were fire. Ye have heaped treasure together for the last days. ⁴Behold, the hire of the labourers who have reaped down your fields, which is of you kept back by fraud, crieth: and the cries of them which have reaped are entered into the ears of the Lord of sabaoth. ⁵Ye have lived in pleasure on the earth, and been wanton; ye have nourished your hearts, as in a day of slaughter. ⁶Ye have condemned and killed the just; and he doth not resist you."

The Riches Of The Lord
Psalm 104:24 "O LORD, how manifold are thy works! in wisdom hast thou made them all: the earth is full of thy riches."

The Wealth Of The Sinner
Proverbs 13:22 "A good man leaveth an inheritance to his children's children: and the wealth of the sinner is laid up for the just."

Those That Acquire Riches Unjustly
Proverbs 22:16 "He that oppresseth the poor to increase his riches, and he that giveth to the rich, shall surely come to want."

Proverbs 28:8 "He that by usury and unjust gain increaseth his substance, he shall gather it for him that will pity the poor."

Jeremiah 17:11 "As the partridge sitteth on eggs, and hatcheth them not; so he that getteth riches, and not by right, shall leave them in the midst of his days, and at his end shall be a fool."

Habakkuk 2:6-17 "⁶Shall not all these take up a parable against him, and a taunting proverb against him, and say, Woe to him that increaseth that which is not his! how long? and to him that ladeth himself with thick clay! ⁷Shall they not rise up suddenly that shall bite thee, and awake that shall vex thee, and thou shalt be for booties unto them? ⁸Because thou hast spoiled many nations, all the remnant of the people shall spoil thee; because of men's blood, and for the violence of the land, of the city, and of all that dwell therein. ⁹Woe to him that coveteth an evil covetousness to his house, that he may set his nest on high, that he may be delivered from the power of evil! ¹⁰Thou hast consulted shame to thy house by cutting off many people, and hast sinned against thy soul. ¹¹For the stone shall cry out of the wall, and the beam out of the timber shall answer it. ¹²Woe to him that buildeth a town with blood, and stablisheth a city by iniquity! ¹³Behold, is it not of the LORD of hosts that the people shall labour in the very fire, and the people shall weary themselves for very vanity? ¹⁴For the earth shall be filled with the knowledge of the glory of the LORD, as the waters cover the sea. ¹⁵Woe unto him that giveth his neighbour drink, that puttest thy bottle to him, and makest him drunken also, that thou mayest look on their nakedness! ¹⁶Thou art filled with shame for glory: drink thou also, and let thy foreskin be uncovered: the cup of the LORD's right hand shall be turned unto thee, and shameful spewing shall be on thy glory. ¹⁷For the violence of Lebanon shall cover thee, and the spoil of beasts, which made them afraid, because of men's blood, and for the violence of the land, of the city, and of all that dwell therein."

Those That Love Wealth
Proverbs 21:17 "He that loveth pleasure shall be a poor man: he that loveth wine and oil shall not be rich."

Ecclesiastes 5:10 "He that loveth silver shall not be satisfied with silver; nor he that loveth abundance with increase: this is also vanity."

Those That Rush To Be Rich
Proverbs 28:20 "A faithful man shall abound with blessings: but he that maketh haste to be rich shall not be innocent."

Proverbs 28:22 "He that hasteth to be rich hath an evil eye, and considereth not that poverty shall come upon him."

Those That Trust In Wealth
Psalm 49:6-20 "⁶They that trust in their wealth, and boast themselves in the multitude of their riches; ⁷None of them can by any means redeem his brother, nor give to God a ransom for him: ⁸(For the redemption of their soul is precious, and it ceaseth for ever:) ⁹That he should still live for ever, and not see corruption. ¹⁰For he seeth that wise men die, likewise the fool and the brutish person perish, and leave their wealth to others. ¹¹Their inward thought is, that their houses shall continue for ever, and their dwelling places to all generations; they call their lands after their own names. ¹²Nevertheless man being in honour abideth not: he is like the beasts that perish. ¹³This their way is their folly: yet their posterity approve their sayings. Selah. ¹⁴Like sheep they are laid in the grave; death shall feed on them; and the upright shall have dominion over them in the morning; and their beauty shall consume in the grave from their dwelling. ¹⁵But God will redeem my soul from the power of the grave: for he shall receive me. Selah. ¹⁶Be not thou afraid when one is made rich, when the glory of his house is increased; ¹⁷For when he dieth he shall carry nothing away: his glory shall not descend after him. ¹⁸Though while he lived he blessed his soul: and men will praise thee, when thou doest well to thyself. ¹⁹He shall go to the generation of his fathers; they shall never see light. ²⁰Man that

is in honour, and understandeth not, is like the beasts that perish."

Psalm 52:1-7 "¹Why boastest thou thyself in mischief, O mighty man? the goodness of God endureth continually. ²Thy tongue deviseth mischiefs; like a sharp rasor, working deceitfully. ³Thou lovest evil more than good; and lying rather than to speak righteousness. Selah. ⁴Thou lovest all devouring words, O thou deceitful tongue. ⁵God shall likewise destroy thee for ever, he shall take thee away, and pluck thee out of thy dwelling place, and root thee out of the land of the living. Selah. ⁶The righteous also shall see, and fear, and shall laugh at him: ⁷Lo, this is the man that made not God his strength; but trusted in the abundance of his riches, and strengthened himself in his wickedness."

Proverbs 11:28 "He that trusteth in his riches shall fall: but the righteous shall flourish as a branch."

Matthew 19:23-26 "²³Then said Jesus unto his disciples, Verily I say unto you, That a rich man shall hardly enter into the kingdom of heaven. ²⁴And again I say unto you, It is easier for a camel to go through the eye of a needle, than for a rich man to enter into the kingdom of God. ²⁵When his disciples heard it, they were exceedingly amazed, saying, Who then can be saved? ²⁶But Jesus beheld them, and said unto them, With men this is impossible; but with God all things are possible."

Mark 10:23-27 "²³And Jesus looked round about, and saith unto his disciples, How hardly shall they that have riches enter into the kingdom of God! ²⁴And the disciples were astonished at his words. But Jesus answereth again, and saith unto them, Children, how hard is it for them that trust in riches to enter into the kingdom of God! ²⁵It is easier for a camel to go through the eye of a needle, than for a rich man to enter into the kingdom of God. ²⁶And they were astonished out of measure, saying among themselves, Who then can be saved? ²⁷And Jesus looking upon them saith, With men it is impossible, but not with God: for with God all things are possible."

Luke 18:24-27 "²⁴And when Jesus saw that he was very sorrowful, he said, How hardly shall they that have riches enter into the kingdom of God!

²⁵For it is easier for a camel to go through a needle's eye, than for a rich man to enter into the kingdom of God. ²⁶And they that heard it said, Who then can be saved? ²⁷And he said, The things which are impossible with men are possible with God."

Treasures Of Wickedness
Psalm 37:16 "A little that a righteous man hath is better than the riches of many wicked."

Proverbs 10:2 "Treasures of wickedness profit nothing: but righteousness delivereth from death."

Micah 6:10-12 "¹⁰Are there yet the treasures of wickedness in the house of the wicked, and the scant measure that is abominable? ¹¹Shall I count them pure with the wicked balances, and with the bag of deceitful weights? ¹²For the rich men thereof are full of violence, and the inhabitants thereof have spoken lies, and their tongue is deceitful in their mouth."

Wealth Gotten By Vanity
Proverbs 13:11 "Wealth gotten by vanity shall be diminished: but he that gathereth by labour shall increase."

What Cannot Be Purchased With Money
Psalm 49:6-10 "⁶They that trust in their wealth, and boast themselves in the multitude of their riches; ⁷None of them can by any means redeem his brother, nor give to God a ransom for him: ⁸(For the redemption of their soul is precious, and it ceaseth for ever:) ⁹That he should still live for ever, and not see corruption. ¹⁰For he seeth that wise men die, likewise the fool and the brutish person perish, and leave their wealth to others."

Acts 8:20 "But Peter said unto him, Thy money perish with thee, because thou hast thought that the gift of God may be purchased with money."

What Is Better Than Monetary Riches
Psalm 19:9-10 "⁹The fear of the LORD is clean, enduring for ever: the judgments of the LORD are true and righteous altogether. ¹⁰More to be desired are they than gold, yea, than much fine gold: sweeter also than honey and the honeycomb."

Psalm 37:16 "A little that a righteous man hath is better than the riches of many wicked."

Psalm 119:65-72 "⁶⁵Thou hast dealt well with thy servant, O LORD, according unto thy word. ⁶⁶Teach me good judgment and knowledge: for I have believed thy commandments. ⁶⁷Before I was afflicted I went astray: but now have I kept thy word. ⁶⁸Thou art good, and doest good; teach me thy statutes. ⁶⁹The proud have forged a lie against me: but I will keep thy precepts with my whole heart. ⁷⁰Their heart is as fat as grease; but I delight in thy law. ⁷¹It is good for me that I have been afflicted; that I might learn thy statutes. ⁷²The law of thy mouth is better unto me than thousands of gold and silver."

Proverbs 8:10-19 "¹⁰Receive my instruction, and not silver; and knowledge rather than choice gold. ¹¹For wisdom is better than rubies; and all the things that may be desired are not to be compared to it. ¹²I wisdom dwell with prudence, and find out knowledge of witty inventions. ¹³The fear of the LORD is to hate evil: pride, and arrogancy, and the evil way, and the froward mouth, do I hate. ¹⁴Counsel is mine, and sound wisdom: I am understanding; I have strength. ¹⁵By me kings reign, and princes decree justice. ¹⁶By me princes rule, and nobles, even all the judges of the earth. ¹⁷I love them that love me; and those that seek me early shall find me. ¹⁸Riches and honour are with me; yea, durable riches and righteousness. ¹⁹My fruit is better than gold, yea, than fine gold; and my revenue than choice silver."

Proverbs 15:16 "Better is little with the fear of the LORD than great treasure and trouble therewith."

Proverbs 16:8 "Better is a little with righteousness than great revenues without right."

Proverbs 22:1 "A good name is rather to be chosen than great riches, and loving favour rather than silver and gold."

Proverbs 28:6 "Better is the poor that walketh in his uprightness, than he that is perverse in his ways, though he be rich."

Ecclesiastes 7:1 "A good name is better than precious ointment; and the day of death than the day of one's birth."

What Makes You Rich
Proverbs 10:4 "He becometh poor that dealeth with a slack hand: but the hand of the diligent maketh rich."

Proverbs 10:22 "The blessing of the LORD, it maketh rich, and he addeth no sorrow with it."

Proverbs 22:4 "By humility and the fear of the LORD are riches, and honour, and life."

2 Corinthians 8:9 "For ye know the grace of our Lord Jesus Christ, that, though he was rich, yet for your sakes he became poor, that ye through his poverty might be rich."

What Money Is
Ecclesiastes 7:12 "For wisdom is a defence, and money is a defence: but the excellency of knowledge is, that wisdom giveth life to them that have it."

What The Rich Should Do
1 Timothy 6:17-19 "¹⁷Charge them that are rich in this world, that they be not highminded, nor trust in uncertain riches, but in the living God, who giveth us richly all things to enjoy; ¹⁸That they do good, that they be rich in good works, ready to distribute, willing to communicate; ¹⁹Laying up in store for themselves a good foundation against the time to come, that they may lay hold on eternal life."

What The Rich Should Not Do
Jeremiah 9:23 "Thus saith the LORD, Let not the wise man glory in his wisdom, neither let the mighty man glory in his might, let not the rich man glory in his riches:"

1 Timothy 6:17 "Charge them that are rich in this world, that they be not highminded, nor trust in uncertain riches, but in the living God, who giveth us richly all things to enjoy;"

What Wealth Does
Proverbs 19:4 "Wealth maketh many friends; but the poor is separated from his neighbour."

Proverbs 23:5 "Wilt thou set thine eyes upon that which is not? for riches certainly make themselves wings; they fly away as an eagle toward heaven."

Where Riches Will Not Profit
Proverbs 11:4 "Riches profit not in the day of wrath: but righteousness delivereth from death."

Zephaniah 1:18 "Neither their silver nor their gold shall be able to deliver them in the day of the LORD's wrath; but the whole land shall be devoured by the fire of his jealousy: for he shall make even a speedy riddance of all them that dwell in the land."

Who Retains Riches
Proverbs 11:16 "A gracious woman retaineth honour: and strong men retain riches."

Who Shall Have Wealth
Psalm 112:1-3 "¹Praise ye the LORD. Blessed is the man that feareth the LORD, that delighteth greatly in his commandments. ²His seed shall be mighty upon earth: the generation of the upright shall be blessed. ³Wealth and riches shall be in his house: and his righteousness endureth for ever."

Proverbs 8:12-21 "¹²I wisdom dwell with prudence, and find out knowledge of witty inventions. ¹³The fear of the LORD is to hate evil: pride, and arrogancy, and the evil way, and the froward mouth, do I hate. ¹⁴Counsel is mine, and sound wisdom: I am understanding; I have strength. ¹⁵By me kings reign, and princes decree justice. ¹⁶By me princes rule, and nobles, even all the judges of the earth. ¹⁷I love them that love me; and those that seek me early shall find me. ¹⁸Riches and honour are with me; yea, durable riches and righteousness. ¹⁹My fruit is better than gold, yea, than fine gold; and my revenue than choice silver. ²⁰I lead in the way of righteousness, in the midst of the paths of judgment: ²¹That I may cause those that love me to inherit substance; and I will fill their treasures."

Who Shall Not Be Rich
Proverbs 21:17 "He that loveth pleasure shall be a poor man: he that loveth wine and oil shall not be rich."

WHOLENESS

What Makes You Whole
Matthew 9:22 "But Jesus turned him about, and when he saw her, he said, Daughter, be of good comfort; thy faith hath made thee whole. And the woman was made whole from that hour."

Mark 5:34 "And he said unto her, Daughter, thy faith hath made thee whole; go in peace, and be whole of thy plague."

Mark 10:52 "And Jesus said unto him, Go thy way; thy faith hath made thee whole. And immediately he received his sight, and followed Jesus in the way."

Luke 7:50 "And he said to the woman, Thy faith hath saved thee; go in peace."

Luke 8:48 "And he said unto her, Daughter, be of good comfort: thy faith hath made thee whole; go in peace."

Luke 17:19 "And he said unto him, Arise, go thy way: thy faith hath made thee whole."

Luke 18:42 "And Jesus said unto him, Receive thy sight: thy faith hath saved thee."

Acts 4:9-10 "⁹If we this day be examined of the good deed done to the impotent man, by what means he is made whole; ¹⁰Be it known unto you all, and to all the people of Israel, that by the name of Jesus Christ of Nazareth, whom ye crucified, whom God raised from the dead, even by him doth this man stand here before you whole."

WHOREDOM

Avoiding Harlots
Proverbs 5:1-14 "¹My son, attend unto my wisdom, and bow thine ear to my understanding: ²That thou mayest regard discretion, and that thy lips may keep knowledge. ³For the lips of a strange woman drop as an honeycomb, and her mouth is smoother than oil: ⁴But her end is bitter as wormwood, sharp as a twoedged sword. ⁵Her feet go down to death; her steps take hold on hell. ⁶Lest thou shouldest ponder the path of life, her ways are moveable, that thou canst not know them. ⁷Hear me now therefore, O ye children, and depart not from the words of my mouth. ⁸Remove thy way far from her, and come not nigh the door of her house: ⁹Lest thou give thine honour unto others, and thy years unto the cruel: ¹⁰Lest strangers be filled with thy wealth; and thy labours be in the house of a stranger; ¹¹And thou mourn at the last, when thy flesh and thy body are consumed, ¹²And say, How have I hated instruction, and my heart despised reproof; ¹³And have not obeyed the voice of my teachers, nor inclined mine ear to them that instructed me! ¹⁴I was almost in all evil in the midst of the congregation and assembly."

Proverbs 6:24-25 "24To keep thee from the evil woman, from the flattery of the tongue of a strange woman. 25Lust not after her beauty in thine heart; neither let her take thee with her eyelids."

Proverbs 7:4-27 "4Say unto wisdom, Thou art my sister; and call understanding thy kinswoman: 5That they may keep thee from the strange woman, from the stranger which flattereth with her words. 6For at the window of my house I looked through my casement, 7And beheld among the simple ones, I discerned among the youths, a young man void of understanding, 8Passing through the street near her corner; and he went the way to her house, 9In the twilight, in the evening, in the black and dark night: 10And, behold, there met him a woman with the attire of an harlot, and subtil of heart. 11(She is loud and stubborn; her feet abide not in her house: 12Now is she without, now in the streets, and lieth in wait at every corner.) 13So she caught him, and kissed him, and with an impudent face said unto him, 14I have peace offerings with me; this day have I payed my vows. 15Therefore came I forth to meet thee, diligently to seek thy face, and I have found thee. 16I have decked my bed with coverings of tapestry, with carved works, with fine linen of Egypt. 17I have perfumed my bed with myrrh, aloes, and cinnamon. 18Come, let us take our fill of love until the morning: let us solace ourselves with loves. 19For the goodman is not at home, he is gone a long journey: 20He hath taken a bag of money with him, and will come home at the day appointed. 21With her much fair speech she caused him to yield, with the flattering of her lips she forced him. 22He goeth after her straightway, as an ox goeth to the slaughter, or as a fool to the correction of the stocks; 23Till a dart strike through his liver; as a bird hasteth to the snare, and knoweth not that it is for his life. 24Hearken unto me now therefore, O ye children, and attend to the words of my mouth. 25Let not thine heart decline to her ways, go not astray in her paths. 26For she hath cast down many wounded: yea, many strong men have been slain by her. 27Her house is the way to hell, going down to the chambers of death."

Not Contributing To Whoredom

Leviticus 19:29 "Do not prostitute thy daughter, to cause her to be a whore; lest the land fall to whoredom, and the land become full of wickedness."

Deuteronomy 23:17-18 "17There shall be no whore of the daughters of Israel, nor a sodomite of the sons of Israel. 18Thou shalt not bring the hire of a whore, or the price of a dog, into the house of the LORD thy God for any vow: for even both these are abomination unto the LORD thy God."

Proverbs 5:15-20 "15Drink waters out of thine own cistern, and running waters out of thine own well. 16Let thy fountains be dispersed abroad, and rivers of waters in the streets. 17Let them be only thine own, and not strangers' with thee. 18Let thy fountain be blessed: and rejoice with the wife of thy youth. 19Let her be as the loving hind and pleasant roe; let her breasts satisfy thee at all times; and be thou ravished always with her love. 20And why wilt thou, my son, be ravished with a strange woman, and embrace the bosom of a stranger?"

The Reward For Whoredom

Leviticus 19:29 "Do not prostitute thy daughter, to cause her to be a whore; lest the land fall to whoredom, and the land become full of wickedness."

Proverbs 5:1-14 "1My son, attend unto my wisdom, and bow thine ear to my understanding: 2That thou mayest regard discretion, and that thy lips may keep knowledge. 3For the lips of a strange woman drop as an honeycomb, and her mouth is smoother than oil: 4But her end is bitter as wormwood, sharp as a twoedged sword. 5Her feet go down to death; her steps take hold on hell. 6Lest thou shouldest ponder the path of life, her ways are moveable, that thou canst not know them. 7Hear me now therefore, O ye children, and depart not from the words of my mouth. 8Remove thy way far from her, and come not nigh the door of her house: 9Lest thou give thine honour unto others, and thy years unto the cruel: 10Lest strangers be filled with thy wealth; and thy labours be in the house of a stranger; 11And thou mourn at the last, when thy flesh and thy body are consumed, 12And say, How have I hated instruction, and my heart despised reproof; 13And have not obeyed the voice of my teachers, nor inclined mine ear to them that instructed me! 14I was almost in all evil in the midst of the congregation and assembly."

Proverbs 6:26-28 "²⁶For by means of a whorish woman a man is brought to a piece of bread: and the adulteress will hunt for the precious life. ²⁷Can a man take fire in his bosom, and his clothes not be burned? ²⁸Can one go upon hot coals, and his feet not be burned?"

Jeremiah 3:1-3 "¹They say, If a man put away his wife, and she go from him, and become another man's, shall he return unto her again? shall not that land be greatly polluted? but thou hast played the harlot with many lovers; yet return again to me, saith the LORD. ²Lift up thine eyes unto the high places, and see where thou hast not been lien with. In the ways hast thou sat for them, as the Arabian in the wilderness; and thou hast polluted the land with thy whoredoms and with thy wickedness. ³Therefore the showers have been withholden, and there hath been no latter rain; and thou hadst a whore's forehead, thou refusedst to be ashamed."

Ezekiel 16:23-44 "²³And it came to pass after all thy wickedness, (woe, woe unto thee! saith the Lord GOD;) ²⁴That thou hast also built unto thee an eminent place, and hast made thee an high place in every street. ²⁵Thou hast built thy high place at every head of the way, and hast made thy beauty to be abhorred, and hast opened thy feet to every one that passed by, and multiplied thy whoredoms. ²⁶Thou hast also committed fornication with the Egyptians thy neighbours, great of flesh; and hast increased thy whoredoms, to provoke me to anger. ²⁷Behold, therefore I have stretched out my hand over thee, and have diminished thine ordinary food, and delivered thee unto the will of them that hate thee, the daughters of the Philistines, which are ashamed of thy lewd way. ²⁸Thou hast played the whore also with the Assyrians, because thou wast unsatiable; yea, thou hast played the harlot with them, and yet couldest not be satisfied. ²⁹Thou hast moreover multiplied thy fornication in the land of Canaan unto Chaldea; and yet thou wast not satisfied herewith. ³⁰How weak is thine heart, saith the Lord GOD, seeing thou doest all these things, the work of an imperious whorish woman; ³¹In that thou buildest thine eminent place in the head of every way, and makest thine high place in every street; and hast not been as an harlot, in that thou scornest hire; ³²But as a wife that committeth adultery, which taketh strangers instead of her husband! ³³They give gifts to all whores: but thou givest thy gifts to all thy lovers, and hirest them, that they may come unto thee on every side for thy whoredom. ³⁴And the contrary is in thee from other women in thy whoredoms, whereas none followeth thee to commit whoredoms: and in that thou givest a reward, and no reward is given unto thee, therefore thou art contrary. ³⁵Wherefore, O harlot, hear the word of the LORD: ³⁶Thus saith the Lord GOD; Because thy filthiness was poured out, and thy nakedness discovered through thy whoredoms with thy lovers, and with all the idols of thy abominations, and by the blood of thy children, which thou didst give unto them; ³⁷Behold, therefore I will gather all thy lovers, with whom thou hast taken pleasure, and all them that thou hast loved, with all them that thou hast hated; I will even gather them round about against thee, and will discover thy nakedness unto them, that they may see all thy nakedness. ³⁸And I will judge thee, as women that break wedlock and shed blood are judged; and I will give thee blood in fury and jealousy. ³⁹And I will also give thee into their hand, and they shall throw down thine eminent place, and shall break down thy high places: they shall strip thee also of thy clothes, and shall take thy fair jewels, and leave thee naked and bare. ⁴⁰They shall also bring up a company against thee, and they shall stone thee with stones, and thrust thee through with their swords. ⁴¹And they shall burn thine houses with fire, and execute judgments upon thee in the sight of many women: and I will cause thee to cease from playing the harlot, and thou also shalt give no hire any more. ⁴²So will I make my fury toward thee to rest, and my jealousy shall depart from thee, and I will be quiet, and will be no more angry. ⁴³Because thou hast not remembered the days of thy youth, but hast fretted me in all these things; behold, therefore I also will recompense thy way upon thine head, saith the Lord GOD: and thou shalt not commit this lewdness above all thine abominations. ⁴⁴Behold, every one that useth proverbs shall use this proverb against thee, saying, As is the mother, so is her daughter."

Hosea 4:11-12 "¹¹Whoredom and wine and new wine take away the heart. ¹²My people ask counsel at their stocks, and their staff declareth unto them: for the spirit of whoredoms hath caused them to err, and they have gone a whoring from under their God."

Nahum 3:4-7 "⁴Because of the multitude of the whoredoms of the wellfavoured harlot, the mistress of witchcrafts, that selleth nations through her whoredoms, and families through her witchcrafts. ⁵Behold, I am against thee, saith the LORD of hosts; and I will discover thy skirts upon thy face, and I will shew the nations thy nakedness, and the kingdoms thy shame. ⁶And I will cast abominable filth upon thee, and make thee vile, and will set thee as a gazingstock. ⁷And it shall come to pass, that all they that look upon thee shall flee from thee, and say, Nineveh is laid waste: who will bemoan her? whence shall I seek comforters for thee?"

Those That Are Joined To A Harlot

1 Corinthians 6:13-20 "¹³Meats for the belly, and the belly for meats: but God shall destroy both it and them. Now the body is not for fornication, but for the Lord; and the Lord for the body. ¹⁴And God hath both raised up the Lord, and will also raise up us by his own power. ¹⁵Know ye not that your bodies are the members of Christ? shall I then take the members of Christ, and make them the members of an harlot? God forbid. ¹⁶What? know ye not that he which is joined to an harlot is one body? for two, saith he, shall be one flesh. ¹⁷But he that is joined unto the Lord is one spirit. ¹⁸Flee fornication. Every sin that a man doeth is without the body; but he that committeth fornication sinneth against his own body. ¹⁹What? know ye not that your body is the temple of the Holy Ghost which is in you, which ye have of God, and ye are not your own? ²⁰For ye are bought with a price: therefore glorify God in your body, and in your spirit, which are God's."

What Keeps You Away From Whores

Proverbs 7:4-5 "⁴Say unto wisdom, Thou art my sister; and call understanding thy kinswoman: ⁵That they may keep thee from the strange woman, from the stranger which flattereth with her words."

What Should Be Done To Whores
According To The Law

Deuteronomy 22:13-21 "¹³If any man take a wife, and go in unto her, and hate her, ¹⁴And give occasions of speech against her, and bring up an evil

name upon her, and say, I took this woman, and when I came to her, I found her not a maid: ¹⁵Then shall the father of the damsel, and her mother, take and bring forth the tokens of the damsel's virginity unto the elders of the city in the gate: ¹⁶And the damsel's father shall say unto the elders, I gave my daughter unto this man to wife, and he hateth her; ¹⁷And, lo, he hath given occasions of speech against her, saying, I found not thy daughter a maid; and yet these are the tokens of my daughter's virginity. And they shall spread the cloth before the elders of the city. ¹⁸And the elders of that city shall take that man and chastise him; ¹⁹And they shall amerce him in an hundred shekels of silver, and give them unto the father of the damsel, because he hath brought up an evil name upon a virgin of Israel: and she shall be his wife; he may not put her away all his days. ²⁰But if this thing be true, and the tokens of virginity be not found for the damsel: ²¹Then they shall bring out the damsel to the door of her father's house, and the men of her city shall stone her with stones that she die: because she hath wrought folly in Israel, to play the whore in her father's house: so shalt thou put evil away from among you."

Who Falls Victim To Whores

Proverbs 7:4-26 "⁴Say unto wisdom, Thou art my sister; and call understanding thy kinswoman: ⁵That they may keep thee from the strange woman, from the stranger which flattereth with her words. ⁶For at the window of my house I looked through my casement, ⁷And beheld among the simple ones, I discerned among the youths, a young man void of understanding, ⁸Passing through the street near her corner; and he went the way to her house, ⁹In the twilight, in the evening, in the black and dark night: ¹⁰And, behold, there met him a woman with the attire of an harlot, and subtil of heart. ¹¹(She is loud and stubborn; her feet abide not in her house: ¹²Now is she without, now in the streets, and lieth in wait at every corner.) ¹³So she caught him, and kissed him, and with an impudent face said unto him, ¹⁴I have peace offerings with me; this day have I payed my vows. ¹⁵Therefore came I forth to meet thee, diligently to seek thy face, and I have found thee. ¹⁶I have decked my bed with coverings of tapestry, with carved works, with fine linen of Egypt. ¹⁷I have perfumed my bed with myrrh, aloes, and cinnamon. ¹⁸Come, let us take our fill of love until the morning: let us solace ourselves with loves. ¹⁹For the goodman is not at home, he is gone a long journey: ²⁰He hath taken a bag of money with him, and will come home at the day appointed. ²¹With her much fair speech she caused him to yield, with the flattering of her lips she forced him. ²²He goeth after her straightway, as an ox goeth to the slaughter, or as a fool to the correction of the stocks; ²³Till a dart strike through his liver; as a bird hasteth to the snare, and knoweth not that it is for his life. ²⁴Hearken unto me now therefore, O ye children, and attend to the words of my mouth. ²⁵Let not thine heart decline to her ways, go not astray in her paths. ²⁶For she hath cast down many wounded: yea, many strong men have been slain by her."

Proverbs 22:14 "The mouth of strange women is a deep pit: he that is abhorred of the LORD shall fall therein."

Ecclesiastes 7:26 "And I find more bitter than death the woman, whose heart is snares and nets, and her hands as bands: whoso pleaseth God shall escape from her; but the sinner shall be taken by her."

Who Shall Escape From Whores
Ecclesiastes 7:26 "And I find more bitter than death the woman, whose heart is snares and nets, and her hands as bands: whoso pleaseth God shall escape from her; but the sinner shall be taken by her."

Whoremongers
Proverbs 2:16-19 "¹⁶To deliver thee from the strange woman, even from the stranger which flattereth with her words; ¹⁷Which forsaketh the guide of her youth, and forgetteth the covenant of her God. ¹⁸For her house inclineth unto death, and her paths unto the dead. ¹⁹None that go unto her return again, neither take they hold of the paths of life."

Proverbs 7:4-23 "⁴Say unto wisdom, Thou art my sister; and call understanding thy kinswoman: ⁵That they may keep thee from the strange woman, from the stranger which flattereth with her words. ⁶For at the window of my house I looked through my casement, ⁷And beheld among the simple ones, I discerned among the youths, a young man void of understanding, ⁸Passing through the street near her corner; and he went the way to her house, ⁹In the twilight, in the evening, in the black and dark night: ¹⁰And, behold, there met him a woman with the attire of an harlot, and subtil of heart. ¹¹(She is loud and stubborn; her feet abide not in her house: ¹²Now is she without, now in the streets, and lieth in wait at every corner.) ¹³So she caught him, and kissed him, and with an impudent face said unto him, ¹⁴I have peace offerings with me; this day have I payed my vows. ¹⁵Therefore came I forth to meet thee, diligently to seek thy face, and I have found thee. ¹⁶I have decked my bed with coverings of tapestry, with carved works, with fine linen of Egypt. ¹⁷I have perfumed my bed with myrrh, aloes, and cinnamon. ¹⁸Come, let us take our fill of love until the morning: let us solace ourselves with loves. ¹⁹For the goodman is not at home, he is gone a long journey: ²⁰He hath taken a bag of money with him, and will come home at the day appointed. ²¹With her much fair speech she caused him to yield, with the flattering of her lips she forced him. ²²He goeth after her straightway, as an ox goeth to the slaughter, or as a fool to the correction of the stocks; ²³Till a dart strike through his liver; as a bird hasteth to the snare, and knoweth not that it is for his life."

Proverbs 29:3 "Whoso loveth wisdom rejoiceth his father: but he that keepeth company with harlots spendeth his substance."

Ephesians 5:5-7 "⁵For this ye know, that no whoremonger, nor unclean person, nor covetous man, who is an idolater, hath any inheritance in the kingdom of Christ and of God. ⁶Let no man deceive you with vain words: for because of these things cometh the wrath of God upon the children of disobedience. ⁷Be not ye therefore partakers with them."

1 Timothy 1:8-10 "⁸But we know that the law is good, if a man use it lawfully; ⁹Knowing this, that the law is not made for a righteous man, but for the lawless and disobedient, for the ungodly and for sinners, for unholy and profane, for murderers of fathers and murderers of mothers, for manslayers, ¹⁰For whoremongers, for them that defile themselves with mankind, for menstealers, for liars, for perjured persons, and if there be any other thing that is contrary to sound doctrine;"

Hebrews 13:4 "Marriage is honourable in all, and the bed undefiled: but whoremongers and adulterers God will judge."

Revelation 21:8 "But the fearful, and unbelieving, and the abominable, and murderers, and whoremongers, and sorcerers, and idolaters, and all liars, shall have their part in the lake which burneth with fire and brimstone: which is the second death."

Revelation 22:13-15 "[13]I am Alpha and Omega, the beginning and the end, the first and the last. [14]Blessed are they that do his commandments, that they may have right to the tree of life, and may enter in through the gates into the city. [15]For without are dogs, and sorcerers, and whoremongers, and murderers, and idolaters, and whosoever loveth and maketh a lie."

Whores
Proverbs 2:16-19 "[16]To deliver thee from the strange woman, even from the stranger which flattereth with her words; [17]Which forsaketh the guide of her youth, and forgetteth the covenant of her God. [18]For her house inclineth unto death, and her paths unto the dead. [19]None that go unto her return again, neither take they hold of the paths of life."

Proverbs 5:1-6 "[1]My son, attend unto my wisdom, and bow thine ear to my understanding: [2]That thou mayest regard discretion, and that thy lips may keep knowledge. [3]For the lips of a strange woman drop as an honeycomb, and her mouth is smoother than oil: [4]But her end is bitter as wormwood, sharp as a twoedged sword. [5]Her feet go down to death; her steps take hold on hell. [6]Lest thou shouldest ponder the path of life, her ways are moveable, that thou canst not know them."

Proverbs 7:4-27 "[4]Say unto wisdom, Thou art my sister; and call understanding thy kinswoman: [5]That they may keep thee from the strange woman, from the stranger which flattereth with her words. [6]For at the window of my house I looked through my casement, [7]And beheld among the simple ones, I discerned among the youths, a young man void of understanding, [8]Passing through the street near her corner; and he went the way to her house, [9]In the twilight, in the evening, in the black and dark night: [10]And, behold, there met him a woman with the attire of an harlot, and subtil of heart. [11](She is loud and stubborn; her feet abide not in her house: [12]Now is she without, now in the streets, and lieth in wait at every corner.) [13]So she caught him, and kissed him, and with an impudent face said unto him, [14]I have peace offerings with me; this day have I payed my vows. [15]Therefore came I forth to meet thee, diligently to seek thy face, and I have found thee. [16]I have decked my bed with coverings of tapestry, with carved works, with fine linen of Egypt. [17]I have perfumed my bed with myrrh, aloes, and cinnamon. [18]Come, let us take our fill of love until the morning: let us solace ourselves with loves. [19]For the goodman is not at home, he is gone a long journey: [20]He hath taken a bag of money with him, and will come home at the day appointed. [21]With her much fair speech she caused him to yield, with the flattering of her lips she forced him. [22]He goeth after her straightway, as an ox goeth to the slaughter, or as a fool to the correction of the stocks; [23]Till a dart strike through his liver; as a bird hasteth to the snare, and knoweth not that it is for his life. [24]Hearken unto me now therefore, O ye children, and attend to the words of my mouth. [25]Let not thine heart decline to her ways, go not astray in her paths. [26]For she hath cast down many wounded: yea, many strong men have been slain by her. [27]Her house is the way to hell, going down to the chambers of death."

Proverbs 22:14 "The mouth of strange women is a deep pit: he that is abhorred of the L ORD shall fall therein."

Proverbs 23:27-28 "[27]For a whore is a deep ditch; and a strange woman is a narrow pit. [28]She also lieth in wait as for a prey, and increaseth the transgressors among men."

Ecclesiastes 7:26 "And I find more bitter than death the woman, whose heart is snares and nets, and her hands as bands: whoso pleaseth God shall escape from her; but the sinner shall be taken by her."

WICKEDNESS

How The Land Becomes Full Of Wickedness
Leviticus 19:29 "Do not prostitute thy daughter, to cause her to be a whore; lest the land fall

to whoredom, and the land become full of wickedness."

Little With Right Being
Better Than Much With Wickedness
Psalm 37:16 "A little that a righteous man hath is better than the riches of many wicked."

Psalm 84:10 "For a day in thy courts is better than a thousand. I had rather be a doorkeeper in the house of my God, than to dwell in the tents of wickedness."

Nobody Being Established By Wickedness
Proverbs 12:3 "A man shall not be established by wickedness: but the root of the righteous shall not be moved."

The Lord Hating Wickedness
Psalm 11:5 "The LORD trieth the righteous: but the wicked and him that loveth violence his soul hateth."

The Plowing Of The Wicked
Proverbs 21:4 "An high look, and a proud heart, and the plowing of the wicked, is sin."

The Reward For Wickedness
Deuteronomy 28:20 "The LORD shall send upon thee cursing, vexation, and rebuke, in all that thou settest thine hand unto for to do, until thou be destroyed, and until thou perish quickly; because of the wickedness of thy doings, whereby thou hast forsaken me."

1 Samuel 12:24-25 "24Only fear the LORD, and serve him in truth with all your heart: for consider how great things he hath done for you. 25But if ye shall still do wickedly, ye shall be consumed, both ye and your king."

2 Kings 21:6 "And he made his son pass through the fire, and observed times, and used enchantments, and dealt with familiar spirits and wizards: he wrought much wickedness in the sight of the LORD, to provoke him to anger."

2 Kings 21:10-16 "10And the LORD spake by his servants the prophets, saying, 11Because Manasseh king of Judah hath done these abominations, and hath done wickedly above all that the Amorites did, which were before him, and hath made Judah also to sin with his idols: 12Therefore thus saith the LORD God of Israel, Behold, I am bring-

ing such evil upon Jerusalem and Judah, that whosoever heareth of it, both his ears shall tingle. 13And I will stretch over Jerusalem the line of Samaria, and the plummet of the house of Ahab: and I will wipe Jerusalem as a man wipeth a dish, wiping it, and turning it upside down. 14And I will forsake the remnant of mine inheritance, and deliver them into the hand of their enemies; and they shall become a prey and a spoil to all their enemies; 15Because they have done that which was evil in my sight, and have provoked me to anger, since the day their fathers came forth out of Egypt, even unto this day. 16Moreover Manasseh shed innocent blood very much, till he had filled Jerusalem from one end to another; beside his sin wherewith he made Judah to sin, in doing that which was evil in the sight of the LORD."

2 Chronicles 33:6 "And he caused his children to pass through the fire in the valley of the son of Hinnom: also he observed times, and used enchantments, and used witchcraft, and dealt with a familiar spirit, and with wizards: he wrought much evil in the sight of the LORD, to provoke him to anger."

Proverbs 21:12 "The righteous man wisely considereth the house of the wicked: but God overthroweth the wicked for their wickedness."

Isaiah 47:10-11 "10For thou hast trusted in thy wickedness: thou hast said, None seeth me. Thy wisdom and thy knowledge, it hath perverted thee; and thou hast said in thine heart, I am, and none else beside me. 11Therefore shall evil come upon thee; thou shalt not know from whence it riseth: and mischief shall fall upon thee; thou shalt not be able to put it off: and desolation shall come upon thee suddenly, which thou shalt not know."

Jeremiah 3:1-3 "1They say, If a man put away his wife, and she go from him, and become another man's, shall he return unto her again? shall not that land be greatly polluted? but thou hast played the harlot with many lovers; yet return again to me, saith the LORD. 2Lift up thine eyes unto the high places, and see where thou hast not been lien with. In the ways hast thou sat for them, as the Arabian in the wilderness; and thou hast polluted the land with thy whoredoms and with thy wickedness. 3Therefore the showers have been withholden, and there hath been no latter rain;

and thou hadst a whore's forehead, thou refusedst to be ashamed."

Hosea 10:13-15 "¹³Ye have plowed wickedness, ye have reaped iniquity; ye have eaten the fruit of lies: because thou didst trust in thy way, in the multitude of thy mighty men. ¹⁴Therefore shall a tumult arise among thy people, and all thy fortresses shall be spoiled, as Shalman spoiled Beth-arbel in the day of battle: the mother was dashed in pieces upon her children. ¹⁵So shall Bethel do unto you because of your great wickedness: in a morning shall the king of Israel utterly be cut off."

Micah 6:9-16 "⁹The LORD's voice crieth unto the city, and the man of wisdom shall see thy name: hear ye the rod, and who hath appointed it. ¹⁰Are there yet the treasures of wickedness in the house of the wicked, and the scant measure that is abominable? ¹¹Shall I count them pure with the wicked balances, and with the bag of deceitful weights? ¹²For the rich men thereof are full of violence, and the inhabitants thereof have spoken lies, and their tongue is deceitful in their mouth. ¹³Therefore also will I make thee sick in smiting thee, in making thee desolate because of thy sins. ¹⁴Thou shalt eat, but not be satisfied; and thy casting down shall be in the midst of thee; and thou shalt take hold, but shalt not deliver; and that which thou deliverest will I give up to the sword. ¹⁵Thou shalt sow, but thou shalt not reap; thou shalt tread the olives, but thou shalt not anoint thee with oil; and sweet wine, but shalt not drink wine. ¹⁶For the statutes of Omri are kept, and all the works of the house of Ahab, and ye walk in their counsels; that I should make thee a desolation, and the inhabitants thereof an hissing: therefore ye shall bear the reproach of my people."

The Time When The Wicked Rise
Proverbs 28:12 "When righteous men do rejoice, there is great glory: but when the wicked rise, a man is hidden."

Proverbs 28:28 "When the wicked rise, men hide themselves: but when they perish, the righteous increase."

The Wicked
Exodus 23:7 "Keep thee far from a false matter; and the innocent and righteous slay thou not: for I will not justify the wicked."

1 Samuel 2:8-9 "⁸He raiseth up the poor out of the dust, and lifteth up the beggar from the dunghill, to set them among princes, and to make them inherit the throne of glory: for the pillars of the earth are the LORD's, and he hath set the world upon them. ⁹He will keep the feet of his saints, and the wicked shall be silent in darkness; for by strength shall no man prevail."

Job 4:8 "Even as I have seen, they that plow iniquity, and sow wickedness, reap the same."

Job 8:20-22 "²⁰Behold, God will not cast away a perfect man, neither will he help the evil doers: ²¹Till he fill thy mouth with laughing, and thy lips with rejoicing. ²²They that hate thee shall be clothed with shame; and the dwelling place of the wicked shall come to nought."

Job 15:20-35 "²⁰The wicked man travaileth with pain all his days, and the number of years is hidden to the oppressor. ²¹A dreadful sound is in his ears: in prosperity the destroyer shall come upon him. ²²He believeth not that he shall return out of darkness, and he is waited for of the sword. ²³He wandereth abroad for bread, saying, Where is it? he knoweth that the day of darkness is ready at his hand. ²⁴Trouble and anguish shall make him afraid; they shall prevail against him, as a king ready to the battle. ²⁵For he stretcheth out his hand against God, and strengtheneth himself against the Almighty. ²⁶He runneth upon him, even on his neck, upon the thick bosses of his bucklers: ²⁷Because he covereth his face with his fatness, and maketh collops of fat on his flanks. ²⁸And he dwelleth in desolate cities, and in houses which no man inhabiteth, which are ready to become heaps. ²⁹He shall not be rich, neither shall his substance continue, neither shall he prolong the perfection thereof upon the earth. ³⁰He shall not depart out of darkness; the flame shall dry up his branches, and by the breath of his mouth shall he go away. ³¹Let not him that is deceived trust in vanity: for vanity shall be his recompence. ³²It shall be accomplished before his time, and his branch shall not be green. ³³He shall shake off his unripe grape as the vine, and shall cast off his flower as the olive. ³⁴For the congregation of hypocrites shall be desolate, and fire shall consume the tabernacles of bribery. ³⁵They conceive mischief, and bring forth vanity, and their belly prepareth deceit."

Job 18:5-21 "⁵Yea, the light of the wicked shall be put out, and the spark of his fire shall not shine. ⁶The light shall be dark in his tabernacle, and his candle shall be put out with him. ⁷The steps of his strength shall be straitened, and his own counsel shall cast him down. ⁸For he is cast into a net by his own feet, and he walketh upon a snare. ⁹The gin shall take him by the heel, and the robber shall prevail against him. ¹⁰The snare is laid for him in the ground, and a trap for him in the way. ¹¹Terrors shall make him afraid on every side, and shall drive him to his feet. ¹²His strength shall be hungerbitten, and destruction shall be ready at his side. ¹³It shall devour the strength of his skin: even the firstborn of death shall devour his strength. ¹⁴His confidence shall be rooted out of his tabernacle, and it shall bring him to the king of terrors. ¹⁵It shall dwell in his tabernacle, because it is none of his: brimstone shall be scattered upon his habitation. ¹⁶His roots shall be dried up beneath, and above shall his branch be cut off. ¹⁷His remembrance shall perish from the earth, and he shall have no name in the street. ¹⁸He shall be driven from light into darkness, and chased out of the world. ¹⁹He shall neither have son nor nephew among his people, nor any remaining in his dwellings. ²⁰They that come after him shall be astonied at his day, as they that went before were affrighted. ²¹Surely such are the dwellings of the wicked, and this is the place of him that knoweth not God."

Job 20:1-19 "¹Then answered Zophar the Naamathite, and said, ²Therefore do my thoughts cause me to answer, and for this I make haste. ³I have heard the check of my reproach, and the spirit of my understanding causeth me to answer. ⁴Knowest thou not this of old, since man was placed upon earth, ⁵That the triumphing of the wicked is short, and the joy of the hypocrite but for a moment? ⁶Though his excellency mount up to the heavens, and his head reach unto the clouds; ⁷Yet he shall perish for ever like his own dung: they which have seen him shall say, Where is he? ⁸He shall fly away as a dream, and shall not be found: yea, he shall be chased away as a vision of the night. ⁹The eye also which saw him shall see him no more; neither shall his place any more behold him. ¹⁰His children shall seek to please the poor, and his hands shall restore their goods.

¹¹His bones are full of the sin of his youth, which shall lie down with him in the dust. ¹²Though wickedness be sweet in his mouth, though he hide it under his tongue; ¹³Though he spare it, and forsake it not; but keep it still within his mouth: ¹⁴Yet his meat in his bowels is turned, it is the gall of asps within him. ¹⁵He hath swallowed down riches, and he shall vomit them up again: God shall cast them out of his belly. ¹⁶He shall suck the poison of asps: the viper's tongue shall slay him. ¹⁷He shall not see the rivers, the floods, the brooks of honey and butter. ¹⁸That which he laboured for shall he restore, and shall not swallow it down: according to his substance shall the restitution be, and he shall not rejoice therein. ¹⁹Because he hath oppressed and hath forsaken the poor; because he hath violently taken away an house which he builded not;"

Job 21:7-30 "⁷Wherefore do the wicked live, become old, yea, are mighty in power? ⁸Their seed is established in their sight with them, and their offspring before their eyes. ⁹Their houses are safe from fear, neither is the rod of God upon them. ¹⁰Their bull gendereth, and faileth not; their cow calveth, and casteth not her calf. ¹¹They send forth their little ones like a flock, and their children dance. ¹²They take the timbrel and harp, and rejoice at the sound of the organ. ¹³They spend their days in wealth, and in a moment go down to the grave. ¹⁴Therefore they say unto God, Depart from us; for we desire not the knowledge of thy ways. ¹⁵What is the Almighty, that we should serve him? and what profit should we have, if we pray unto him? ¹⁶Lo, their good is not in their hand: the counsel of the wicked is far from me. ¹⁷How oft is the candle of the wicked put out! and how oft cometh their destruction upon them! God distributeth sorrows in his anger. ¹⁸They are as stubble before the wind, and as chaff that the storm carrieth away. ¹⁹God layeth up his iniquity for his children: he rewardeth him, and he shall know it. ²⁰His eyes shall see his destruction, and he shall drink of the wrath of the Almighty. ²¹For what pleasure hath he in his house after him, when the number of his months is cut off in the midst? ²²Shall any teach God knowledge? seeing he judgeth those that are high. ²³One dieth in his full strength, being wholly at ease and quiet. ²⁴His breasts are full of milk, and his bones are moistened with marrow. [25]And another dieth in the bitterness of his soul, and never eateth with pleasure. [26]They shall lie down alike in the dust, and the worms shall cover them. [27]Behold, I know your thoughts, and the devices which ye wrongfully imagine against me. [28]For ye say, Where is the house of the prince? and where are the dwelling places of the wicked? [29]Have ye not asked them that go by the way? and do ye not know their tokens, [30]That the wicked is reserved to the day of destruction? they shall be brought forth to the day of wrath."

Job 24:13-21 "[13]They are of those that rebel against the light; they know not the ways thereof, nor abide in the paths thereof. [14]The murderer rising with the light killeth the poor and needy, and in the night is as a thief. [15]The eye also of the adulterer waiteth for the twilight, saying, No eye shall see me: and disguiseth his face. [16]In the dark they dig through houses, which they had marked for themselves in the daytime: they know not the light. [17]For the morning is to them even as the shadow of death: if one know them, they are in the terrors of the shadow of death. [18]He is swift as the waters; their portion is cursed in the earth: he beholdeth not the way of the vineyards. [19]Drought and heat consume the snow waters: so doth the grave those which have sinned. [20]The womb shall forget him; the worm shall feed sweetly on him; he shall be no more remembered; and wickedness shall be broken as a tree. [21]He evil entreateth the barren that beareth not: and doeth not good to the widow."

Job 36:5-6 "[5]Behold, God is mighty, and despiseth not any: he is mighty in strength and wisdom. [6]He preserveth not the life of the wicked: but giveth right to the poor."

Psalm 7:11 "God judgeth the righteous, and God is angry with the wicked every day."

Psalm 9:16-17 "[16]The LORD is known by the judgment which he executeth: the wicked is snared in the work of his own hands. Higgaion. Selah. [17]The wicked shall be turned into hell, and all the nations that forget God."

Psalm 10:2-4 "[2]The wicked in his pride doth persecute the poor: let them be taken in the devices that they have imagined. [3]For the wicked boasteth of his heart's desire, and blesseth the covetous, whom the LORD abhorreth. [4]The wicked, through the pride of his countenance, will not seek after God: God is not in all his thoughts."

Psalm 11:2 "For, lo, the wicked bend their bow, they make ready their arrow upon the string, that they may privily shoot at the upright in heart."

Psalm 11:5-6 "[5]The LORD trieth the righteous: but the wicked and him that loveth violence his soul hateth. [6]Upon the wicked he shall rain snares, fire and brimstone, and an horrible tempest: this shall be the portion of their cup."

Psalm 28:3-5 "[3]Draw me not away with the wicked, and with the workers of iniquity, which speak peace to their neighbours, but mischief is in their hearts. [4]Give them according to their deeds, and according to the wickedness of their endeavours: give them after the work of their hands; render to them their desert. [5]Because they regard not the works of the LORD, nor the operation of his hands, he shall destroy them, and not build them up."

Psalm 31:17 "Let me not be ashamed, O LORD; for I have called upon thee: let the wicked be ashamed, and let them be silent in the grave."

Psalm 32:10 "Many sorrows shall be to the wicked: but he that trusteth in the LORD, mercy shall compass him about."

Psalm 34:21 "Evil shall slay the wicked: and they that hate the righteous shall be desolate."

Psalm 37:9-10 "[9]For evildoers shall be cut off: but those that wait upon the LORD, they shall inherit the earth. [10]For yet a little while, and the wicked shall not be: yea, thou shalt diligently consider his place, and it shall not be."

Psalm 37:16-17 "[16]A little that a righteous man hath is better than the riches of many wicked. [17]For the arms of the wicked shall be broken: but the LORD upholdeth the righteous."

Psalm 37:20-21 "[20]But the wicked shall perish, and the enemies of the LORD shall be as the fat of lambs: they shall consume; into smoke shall they consume away. [21]The wicked borroweth, and payeth not again: but the righteous sheweth mercy, and giveth."

Psalm 37:28 "For the LORD loveth judgment, and forsaketh not his saints; they are preserved for ever: but the seed of the wicked shall be cut off."

Psalm 37:38 "But the transgressors shall be destroyed together: the end of the wicked shall be cut off."

Psalm 50:16-21 "16But unto the wicked God saith, What hast thou to do to declare my statutes, or that thou shouldest take my covenant in thy mouth? 17Seeing thou hatest instruction, and castest my words behind thee. 18When thou sawest a thief, then thou consentedst with him, and hast been partaker with adulterers. 19Thou givest thy mouth to evil, and thy tongue frameth deceit. 20Thou sittest and speakest against thy brother; thou slanderest thine own mother's son. 21These things hast thou done, and I kept silence; thou thoughtest that I was altogether such an one as thyself: but I will reprove thee, and set them in order before thine eyes."

Psalm 52:1-7 "1Why boastest thou thyself in mischief, O mighty man? the goodness of God endureth continually. 2Thy tongue deviseth mischiefs; like a sharp rasor, working deceitfully. 3Thou lovest evil more than good; and lying rather than to speak righteousness. Selah. 4Thou lovest all devouring words, O thou deceitful tongue. 5God shall likewise destroy thee for ever, he shall take thee away, and pluck thee out of thy dwelling place, and root thee out of the land of the living. Selah. 6The righteous also shall see, and fear, and shall laugh at him: 7Lo, this is the man that made not God his strength; but trusted in the abundance of his riches, and strengthened himself in his wickedness."

Psalm 58:3-5 "3The wicked are estranged from the womb: they go astray as soon as they be born, speaking lies. 4Their poison is like the poison of a serpent: they are like the deaf adder that stoppeth her ear; 5Which will not hearken to the voice of charmers, charming never so wisely."

Psalm 75:7-10 "7But God is the judge: he putteth down one, and setteth up another. 8For in the hand of the LORD there is a cup, and the wine is red; it is full of mixture; and he poureth out of the same: but the dregs thereof, all the wicked of the earth shall wring them out, and drink them. 9But I will declare for ever; I will sing praises to the God of Jacob. 10All the horns of the wicked also will I cut off; but the horns of the righteous shall be exalted."

Psalm 94:3-7 "3LORD, how long shall the wicked, how long shall the wicked triumph? 4How long shall they utter and speak hard things? and all the workers of iniquity boast themselves? 5They break in pieces thy people, O LORD, and afflict thine heritage. 6They slay the widow and the stranger, and murder the fatherless. 7Yet they say, The LORD shall not see, neither shall the God of Jacob regard it."

Psalm 104:35 "Let the sinners be consumed out of the earth, and let the wicked be no more. Bless thou the LORD, O my soul. Praise ye the LORD."

Psalm 112:6-10 "6Surely he shall not be moved for ever: the righteous shall be in everlasting remembrance. 7He shall not be afraid of evil tidings: his heart is fixed, trusting in the LORD. 8His heart is established, he shall not be afraid, until he see his desire upon his enemies. 9He hath dispersed, he hath given to the poor; his righteousness endureth for ever; his horn shall be exalted with honour. 10The wicked shall see it, and be grieved; he shall gnash with his teeth, and melt away: the desire of the wicked shall perish."

Psalm 119:113-119 "113I hate vain thoughts: but thy law do I love. 114Thou art my hiding place and my shield: I hope in thy word. 115Depart from me, ye evildoers: for I will keep the commandments of my God. 116Uphold me according unto thy word, that I may live: and let me not be ashamed of my hope. 117Hold thou me up, and I shall be safe: and I will have respect unto thy statutes continually. 118Thou hast trodden down all them that err from thy statutes: for their deceit is falsehood. 119Thou puttest away all the wicked of the earth like dross: therefore I love thy testimonies."

Psalm 119:155 "Salvation is far from the wicked: for they seek not thy statutes."

Psalm 125:3 "For the rod of the wicked shall not rest upon the lot of the righteous; lest the righteous put forth their hands unto iniquity."

Psalm 139:19-20 "[19]Surely thou wilt slay the wicked, O God: depart from me therefore, ye bloody men. [20]For they speak against thee wickedly, and thine enemies take thy name in vain."

Psalm 145:20 "The LORD preserveth all them that love him: but all the wicked will he destroy."

Psalm 146:9 "The LORD preserveth the strangers; he relieveth the fatherless and widow: but the way of the wicked he turneth upside down."

Psalm 147:6 "The LORD lifteth up the meek: he casteth the wicked down to the ground."

Proverbs 2:21-22 "[21]For the upright shall dwell in the land, and the perfect shall remain in it. [22]But the wicked shall be cut off from the earth, and the transgressors shall be rooted out of it."

Proverbs 3:33 "The curse of the LORD is in the house of the wicked: but he blesseth the habitation of the just."

Proverbs 4:19 "The way of the wicked is as darkness: they know not at what they stumble."

Proverbs 5:21-23 "[21]For the ways of man are before the eyes of the LORD, and he pondereth all his goings. [22]His own iniquities shall take the wicked himself, and he shall be holden with the cords of his sins. [23]He shall die without instruction; and in the greatness of his folly he shall go astray."

Proverbs 10:3 "The LORD will not suffer the soul of the righteous to famish: but he casteth away the substance of the wicked."

Proverbs 10:6-7 "[6]Blessings are upon the head of the just: but violence covereth the mouth of the wicked. [7]The memory of the just is blessed: but the name of the wicked shall rot."

Proverbs 10:11 "The mouth of a righteous man is a well of life: but violence covereth the mouth of the wicked."

Proverbs 10:16 "The labour of the righteous tendeth to life: the fruit of the wicked to sin."

Proverbs 10:20 "The tongue of the just is as choice silver: the heart of the wicked is little worth."

Proverbs 10:24-25 "[24]The fear of the wicked, it shall come upon him: but the desire of the righteous shall be granted. [25]As the whirlwind passeth, so is the wicked no more: but the righteous is an everlasting foundation."

Proverbs 10:27-28 "[27]The fear of the LORD prolongeth days: but the years of the wicked shall be shortened. [28]The hope of the righteous shall be gladness: but the expectation of the wicked shall perish."

Proverbs 10:30 "The righteous shall never be removed: but the wicked shall not inhabit the earth."

Proverbs 10:32 "The lips of the righteous know what is acceptable: but the mouth of the wicked speaketh frowardness."

Proverbs 11:5 "The righteousness of the perfect shall direct his way: but the wicked shall fall by his own wickedness."

Proverbs 11:7-8 "[7]When a wicked man dieth, his expectation shall perish: and the hope of unjust men perisheth. [8]The righteous is delivered out of trouble, and the wicked cometh in his stead."

Proverbs 11:10-11 "[10]When it goeth well with the righteous, the city rejoiceth: and when the wicked perish, there is shouting. [11]By the blessing of the upright the city is exalted: but it is overthrown by the mouth of the wicked."

Proverbs 11:18 "The wicked worketh a deceitful work: but to him that soweth righteousness shall be a sure reward."

Proverbs 11:21 "Though hand join in hand, the wicked shall not be unpunished: but the seed of the righteous shall be delivered."

Proverbs 11:23 "The desire of the righteous is only good: but the expectation of the wicked is wrath."

Proverbs 11:31 "Behold, the righteous shall be recompensed in the earth: much more the wicked and the sinner."

Proverbs 12:2 "A good man obtaineth favour of the LORD: but a man of wicked devices will he condemn."

Proverbs 12:5-7 "[5]The thoughts of the righteous are right: but the counsels of the wicked are deceit. [6]The words of the wicked are to lie in wait for blood: but the mouth of the upright shall deliver them. [7]The wicked are overthrown, and are not: but the house of the righteous shall stand."

Proverbs 12:10 "A righteous man regardeth the life of his beast: but the tender mercies of the wicked are cruel."

Proverbs 12:12-13 "[12]The wicked desireth the net of evil men: but the root of the righteous yieldeth fruit. [13]The wicked is snared by the transgression of his lips: but the just shall come out of trouble."

Proverbs 12:21 "There shall no evil happen to the just: but the wicked shall be filled with mischief."

Proverbs 12:26 "The righteous is more excellent than his neighbour: but the way of the wicked seduceth them."

Proverbs 13:5 "A righteous man hateth lying: but a wicked man is loathsome, and cometh to shame."

Proverbs 13:9 "The light of the righteous rejoiceth: but the lamp of the wicked shall be put out."

Proverbs 13:17 "A wicked messenger falleth into mischief: but a faithful ambassador is health."

Proverbs 13:25 "The righteous eateth to the satisfying of his soul: but the belly of the wicked shall want."

Proverbs 14:11 "The house of the wicked shall be overthrown: but the tabernacle of the upright shall flourish."

Proverbs 14:17-19 "[17]He that is soon angry dealeth foolishly: and a man of wicked devices is hated. [18]The simple inherit folly: but the prudent are crowned with knowledge. [19]The evil bow before the good; and the wicked at the gates of the righteous."

Proverbs 14:32 "The wicked is driven away in his wickedness: but the righteous hath hope in his death."

Proverbs 15:6-9 "[6]In the house of the righteous is much treasure: but in the revenues of the wicked is trouble. [7]The lips of the wise disperse knowledge: but the heart of the foolish doeth not so. [8]The sacrifice of the wicked is an abomination to the LORD:

but the prayer of the upright is his delight. [9]The way of the wicked is an abomination unto the LORD: but he loveth him that followeth after righteousness."

Proverbs 15:26 "The thoughts of the wicked are an abomination to the LORD: but the words of the pure are pleasant words."

Proverbs 15:28-29 "[28]The heart of the righteous studieth to answer: but the mouth of the wicked poureth out evil things. [29]The LORD is far from the wicked: but he heareth the prayer of the righteous."

Proverbs 16:4 "The LORD hath made all things for himself: yea, even the wicked for the day of evil."

Proverbs 17:4 "A wicked doer giveth heed to false lips; and a liar giveth ear to a naughty tongue."

Proverbs 17:23 "A wicked man taketh a gift out of the bosom to pervert the ways of judgment."

Proverbs 18:3 "When the wicked cometh, then cometh also contempt, and with ignominy reproach."

Proverbs 19:28 "An ungodly witness scorneth judgment: and the mouth of the wicked devoureth iniquity."

Proverbs 21:7 "The robbery of the wicked shall destroy them; because they refuse to do judgment."

Proverbs 21:10 "The soul of the wicked desireth evil: his neighbour findeth no favour in his eyes."

Proverbs 21:12 "The righteous man wisely considereth the house of the wicked: but God overthroweth the wicked for their wickedness."

Proverbs 21:18 "The wicked shall be a ransom for the righteous, and the transgressor for the upright."

Proverbs 21:29 "A wicked man hardeneth his face: but as for the upright, he directeth his way."

Proverbs 24:16 "For a just man falleth seven times, and riseth up again: but the wicked shall fall into mischief."

Proverbs 24:20 "For there shall be no reward to the evil man; the candle of the wicked shall be put out."

Proverbs 28:1 "The wicked flee when no man pursueth: but the righteous are bold as a lion."

Proverbs 28:12 "When righteous men do rejoice, there is great glory: but when the wicked rise, a man is hidden."

Proverbs 28:28 "When the wicked rise, men hide themselves: but when they perish, the righteous increase."

Proverbs 29:2 "When the righteous are in authority, the people rejoice: but when the wicked beareth rule, the people mourn."

Proverbs 29:7 "The righteous considereth the cause of the poor: but the wicked regardeth not to know it."

Proverbs 29:16 "When the wicked are multiplied, transgression increaseth: but the righteous shall see their fall."

Proverbs 29:27 "An unjust man is an abomination to the just: and he that is upright in the way is abomination to the wicked."

Ecclesiastes 3:17 "I said in mine heart, God shall judge the righteous and the wicked: for there is a time there for every purpose and for every work."

Isaiah 3:11 "Woe unto the wicked! it shall be ill with him: for the reward of his hands shall be given him."

Isaiah 13:9-11 "⁹Behold, the day of the LORD cometh, cruel both with wrath and fierce anger, to lay the land desolate: and he shall destroy the sinners thereof out of it. ¹⁰For the stars of heaven and the constellations thereof shall not give their light: the sun shall be darkened in his going forth, and the moon shall not cause her light to shine. ¹¹And I will punish the world for their evil, and the wicked for their iniquity; and I will cause the arrogancy of the proud to cease, and will lay low the haughtiness of the terrible."

Isaiah 48:22 "There is no peace, saith the LORD, unto the wicked."

Isaiah 57:20-21 "²⁰But the wicked are like the troubled sea, when it cannot rest, whose waters cast up mire and dirt. ²¹There is no peace, saith my God, to the wicked."

Jeremiah 5:26-29 "²⁶For among my people are found wicked men: they lay wait, as he that setteth snares; they set a trap, they catch men. ²⁷As a cage is full of birds, so are their houses full of deceit: therefore they are become great, and waxen rich. ²⁸They are waxen fat, they shine: yea, they overpass the deeds of the wicked: they judge not the cause, the cause of the fatherless, yet they prosper; and the right of the needy do they not judge. ²⁹Shall I not visit for these things? saith the LORD: shall not my soul be avenged on such a nation as this?"

Jeremiah 23:19 "Behold, a whirlwind of the LORD is gone forth in fury, even a grievous whirlwind: it shall fall grievously upon the head of the wicked."

Jeremiah 30:23 "Behold, the whirlwind of the LORD goeth forth with fury, a continuing whirlwind: it shall fall with pain upon the head of the wicked."

Daniel 12:10 "Many shall be purified, and made white, and tried; but the wicked shall do wickedly: and none of the wicked shall understand; but the wise shall understand."

Micah 6:10-12 "¹⁰Are there yet the treasures of wickedness in the house of the wicked, and the scant measure that is abominable? ¹¹Shall I count them pure with the wicked balances, and with the bag of deceitful weights? ¹²For the rich men thereof are full of violence, and the inhabitants thereof have spoken lies, and their tongue is deceitful in their mouth."

Nahum 1:3 "The LORD is slow to anger, and great in power, and will not at all acquit the wicked: the LORD hath his way in the whirlwind and in the storm, and the clouds are the dust of his feet."

Nahum 1:14-15 "¹⁴And the LORD hath given a commandment concerning thee, that no more of thy name be sown: out of the house of thy gods will I cut off the graven image and the molten image: I will make thy grave; for thou art vile. ¹⁵Behold upon the mountains the feet of him that bringeth good tidings, that publisheth peace! O Judah, keep thy solemn feasts, perform thy vows: for the wicked shall no more pass through thee; he is utterly cut off."

Malachi 4:1 "For, behold, the day cometh, that shall burn as an oven; and all the proud, yea, and all that do wickedly, shall be stubble: and the day that cometh shall burn them up, saith the LORD of hosts, that it shall leave them neither root nor branch."

Treasures Of Wickedness
Psalm 37:16 "A little that a righteous man hath is better than the riches of many wicked."

Proverbs 10:2 "Treasures of wickedness profit nothing: but righteousness delivereth from death."

Micah 6:10-12 "¹⁰Are there yet the treasures of wickedness in the house of the wicked, and the scant measure that is abominable? ¹¹Shall I count them pure with the wicked balances, and with the bag of deceitful weights? ¹²For the rich men thereof are full of violence, and the inhabitants thereof have spoken lies, and their tongue is deceitful in their mouth."

What Is Wicked
Leviticus 18:17 "Thou shalt not uncover the nakedness of a woman and her daughter, neither shalt thou take her son's daughter, or her daughter's daughter, to uncover her nakedness; for they are her near kinswomen: it is wickedness."

Leviticus 20:14 "And if a man take a wife and her mother, it is wickedness: they shall be burnt with fire, both he and they; that there be no wickedness among you."

Leviticus 20:17 "And if a man shall take his sister, his father's daughter, or his mother's daughter, and see her nakedness, and she see his nakedness; it is a wicked thing; and they shall be cut off in the sight of their people: he hath uncovered his sister's nakedness; he shall bear his iniquity."

Jeremiah 17:9-10 "⁹The heart is deceitful above all things, and desperately wicked: who can know it? ¹⁰I the LORD search the heart, I try the reins, even to give every man according to his ways, and according to the fruit of his doings."

What Lies In Wickedness
1 John 5:19 "And we know that we are of God, and the whole world lieth in wickedness."

What Wickedness Cannot Do
Ecclesiastes 8:8 "There is no man that hath power over the spirit to retain the spirit; neither hath he power in the day of death: and there is no discharge in that war; neither shall wickedness deliver those that are given to it."

What Wickedness Does
Job 35:8 "Thy wickedness may hurt a man as thou art; and thy righteousness may profit the son of man."

Proverbs 13:6 "Righteousness keepeth him that is upright in the way: but wickedness overthroweth the sinner."

Isaiah 9:18 "For wickedness burneth as the fire: it shall devour the briers and thorns, and shall kindle in the thickets of the forest, and they shall mount up like the lifting up of smoke."

Jeremiah 2:19 "Thine own wickedness shall correct thee, and thy backslidings shall reprove thee: know therefore and see that it is an evil thing and bitter, that thou hast forsaken the LORD thy God, and that my fear is not in thee, saith the Lord GOD of hosts."

WILL OF GOD

Jesus Christ Doing
The Will Of God The Father
Psalm 40:7-9 "⁷Then said I, Lo, I come: in the volume of the book it is written of me, ⁸I delight to do thy will, O my God: yea, thy law is within my heart. ⁹I have preached righteousness in the great congregation: lo, I have not refrained my lips, O LORD, thou knowest."

John 4:34 "Jesus saith unto them, My meat is to do the will of him that sent me, and to finish his work."

John 5:17-20 "¹⁷But Jesus answered them, My Father worketh hitherto, and I work. ¹⁸Therefore the Jews sought the more to kill him, because he not only had broken the sabbath, but said also that God was his Father, making himself equal with God. ¹⁹Then answered Jesus and said unto them, Verily, verily, I say unto you, The Son can do nothing of himself, but what he seeth the Father do: for what things soever he doeth, these also doeth the Son likewise. ²⁰For the Father loveth the Son, and sheweth him all things that himself doeth: and he will shew him greater works than these, that ye may marvel."

John 5:23-30 "²³That all men should honour the Son, even as they honour the Father. He that honoureth not the Son honoureth not the Father which hath sent him. ²⁴Verily, verily, I say unto you, He that heareth my word, and believeth on him that sent me, hath everlasting life, and shall not come into condemnation; but is passed from death unto life. ²⁵Verily, verily, I say unto you, The hour is coming, and now is, when the dead shall hear the voice of the Son of God: and they that hear shall live. ²⁶For as the Father hath life in himself; so hath he given to the Son to have life in himself; ²⁷And hath given him authority to execute judgment also, because he is the Son of man. ²⁸Marvel not at this: for the hour is coming, in the which all that are in the graves shall hear his voice ²⁹And shall come forth; they that have done good, unto the resurrection of life; and they that have done evil, unto the resurrection of damnation. ³⁰I can of mine own self do nothing: as I hear, I judge: and my judgment is just; because I seek not mine own will, but the will of the Father which hath sent me."

John 6:35-38 "³⁵And Jesus said unto them, I am the bread of life: he that cometh to me shall never hunger; and he that believeth on me shall never thirst. ³⁶But I said unto you, That ye also have seen me, and believe not. ³⁷All that the Father giveth me shall come to me; and him that cometh to me I will in no wise cast out. ³⁸For I came down from heaven, not to do mine own will, but the will of him that sent me."

John 8:25-29 "²⁵Then said they unto him, Who art thou? And Jesus saith unto them, Even the same that I said unto you from the beginning. ²⁶I have many things to say and to judge of you: but he that sent me is true; and I speak to the world those things which I have heard of him. ²⁷They understood not that he spake to them of the Father. ²⁸Then said Jesus unto them, When ye have lifted up the Son of man, then shall ye know that I am he, and that I do nothing of myself; but as my Father hath taught me, I speak these things. ²⁹And he that sent me is with me: the Father hath not left me alone; for I do always those things that please him."

John 9:3-4 "³Jesus answered, Neither hath this man sinned, nor his parents: but that the works of God should be made manifest in him. ⁴I must work the works of him that sent me, while it is day: the night cometh, when no man can work."

John 14:23-31 "²³Jesus answered and said unto him, If a man love me, he will keep my words: and my Father will love him, and we will come unto him, and make our abode with him. ²⁴He that loveth me not keepeth not my sayings: and the word which ye hear is not mine, but the Father's which sent me. ²⁵These things have I spoken unto you, being yet present with you. ²⁶But the Comforter, which is the Holy Ghost, whom the Father will send in my name, he shall teach you all things, and bring all things to your remembrance, whatsoever I have said unto you. ²⁷Peace I leave with you, my peace I give unto you: not as the world giveth, give I unto you. Let not your heart be troubled, neither let it be afraid. ²⁸Ye have heard how I said unto you, I go away, and come again unto you. If ye loved me, ye would rejoice, because I said, I go unto the Father: for my Father is greater than I. ²⁹And now I have told you before it come to pass, that, when it is come to pass, ye might believe. ³⁰Hereafter I will not talk much with you: for the prince of this world cometh, and hath nothing in me. ³¹But that the world may know that I love the Father; and as the Father gave me commandment, even so I do. Arise, let us go hence."

John 17:1-4 "¹These words spake Jesus, and lifted up his eyes to heaven, and said, Father, the hour is come; glorify thy Son, that thy Son also may glorify thee: ²As thou hast given him power over all flesh, that he should give eternal life to as many as thou hast given him. ³And this is life eternal, that they might know thee the only true God, and Jesus Christ, whom thou hast sent. ⁴I have glorified thee on the earth: I have finished the work which thou gavest me to do."

Hebrews 10:4-10 "⁴For it is not possible that the blood of bulls and of goats should take away sins. ⁵Wherefore when he cometh into the world, he saith, Sacrifice and offering thou wouldest not, but a body hast thou prepared me: ⁶In burnt offerings and sacrifices for sin thou hast had no pleasure. ⁷Then said I, Lo, I come (in the volume of the book it is written of me,) to do thy will, O God. ⁸Above when he said, Sacrifice and offering and burnt offerings and offering for sin thou wouldest not, neither hadst pleasure therein; which are offered by the law; [9]Then said he, Lo, I come to do thy will, O God. He taketh away the first, that he may establish the second. [10]By the which will we are sanctified through the offering of the body of Jesus Christ once for all."

Those That Do The Will Of God
Matthew 7:21 "Not every one that saith unto me, Lord, Lord, shall enter into the kingdom of heaven; but he that doeth the will of my Father which is in heaven."

Matthew 12:46-50 "[46]While he yet talked to the people, behold, his mother and his brethren stood without, desiring to speak with him. [47]Then one said unto him, Behold, thy mother and thy brethren stand without, desiring to speak with thee. [48]But he answered and said unto him that told him, Who is my mother? and who are my brethren? [49]And he stretched forth his hand toward his disciples, and said, Behold my mother and my brethren! [50]For whosoever shall do the will of my Father which is in heaven, the same is my brother, and sister, and mother."

Mark 3:31-35 "[31]There came then his brethren and his mother, and, standing without, sent unto him, calling him. [32]And the multitude sat about him, and they said unto him, Behold, thy mother and thy brethren without seek for thee. [33]And he answered them, saying, Who is my mother, or my brethren? [34]And he looked round about on them which sat about him, and said, Behold my mother and my brethren! [35]For whosoever shall do the will of God, the same is my brother, and my sister, and mother."

John 7:16-17 "[16]Jesus answered them, and said, My doctrine is not mine, but his that sent me. [17]If any man will do his will, he shall know of the doctrine, whether it be of God, or whether I speak of myself."

1 John 2:17 "And the world passeth away, and the lust thereof: but he that doeth the will of God abideth for ever."

Trying To Understand The Will Of God
Ephesians 5:17 "Wherefore be ye not unwise, but understanding what the will of the Lord is."

What Is In Accordance With The Will Of God
Romans 8:26-27 "[26]Likewise the Spirit also helpeth our infirmities: for we know not what we should pray for as we ought: but the Spirit itself maketh intercession for us with groanings which cannot be uttered. [27]And he that searcheth the hearts knoweth what is the mind of the Spirit, because he maketh intercession for the saints according to the will of God."

Galatians 1:3-4 "[3]Grace be to you and peace from God the Father, and from our Lord Jesus Christ, [4]Who gave himself for our sins, that he might deliver us from this present evil world, according to the will of God and our Father:"

Ephesians 1:3-11 "[3]Blessed be the God and Father of our Lord Jesus Christ, who hath blessed us with all spiritual blessings in heavenly places in Christ: [4]According as he hath chosen us in him before the foundation of the world, that we should be holy and without blame before him in love: [5]Having predestinated us unto the adoption of children by Jesus Christ to himself, according to the good pleasure of his will, [6]To the praise of the glory of his grace, wherein he hath made us accepted in the beloved. [7]In whom we have redemption through his blood, the forgiveness of sins, according to the riches of his grace; [8]Wherein he hath abounded toward us in all wisdom and prudence; [9]Having made known unto us the mystery of his will, according to his good pleasure which he hath purposed in himself: [10]That in the dispensation of the fulness of times he might gather together in one all things in Christ, both which are in heaven, and which are on earth; even in him: [11]In whom also we have obtained an inheritance, being predestinated according to the purpose of him who worketh all things after the counsel of his own will:"

What Is Not The Will Of God
Matthew 18:11-14 "[11]For the Son of man is come to save that which was lost. [12]How think ye? if a man have an hundred sheep, and one of them be gone astray, doth he not leave the ninety and nine, and goeth into the mountains, and seeketh that which is gone astray? [13]And if so be that he find it, verily I say unto you, he rejoiceth more of that sheep, than of the ninety and nine which went not astray. [14]Even so it is not the will of your Father which is in heaven, that one of these little ones should perish."

2 Peter 3:9 "The Lord is not slack concerning his promise, as some men count slackness; but is longsuffering to us-ward, not willing that any should perish, but that all should come to repentance."

What Is The Will Of God

John 6:35-40 "[35]And Jesus said unto them, I am the bread of life: he that cometh to me shall never hunger; and he that believeth on me shall never thirst. [36]But I said unto you, That ye also have seen me, and believe not. [37]All that the Father giveth me shall come to me; and him that cometh to me I will in no wise cast out. [38]For I came down from heaven, not to do mine own will, but the will of him that sent me. [39]And this is the Father's will which hath sent me, that of all which he hath given me I should lose nothing, but should raise it up again at the last day. [40]And this is the will of him that sent me, that every one which seeth the Son, and believeth on him, may have everlasting life: and I will raise him up at the last day."

1 Thessalonians 4:2-7 "[2]For ye know what commandments we gave you by the Lord Jesus. [3]For this is the will of God, even your sanctification, that ye should abstain from fornication: [4]That every one of you should know how to possess his vessel in sanctification and honour; [5]Not in the lust of concupiscence, even as the Gentiles which know not God: [6]That no man go beyond and defraud his brother in any matter: because that the Lord is the avenger of all such, as we also have forewarned you and testified. [7]For God hath not called us unto uncleanness, but unto holiness."

1 Thessalonians 5:14-18 "[14]Now we exhort you, brethren, warn them that are unruly, comfort the feebleminded, support the weak, be patient toward all men. [15]See that none render evil for evil unto any man; but ever follow that which is good, both among yourselves, and to all men. [16]Rejoice evermore. [17]Pray without ceasing. [18]In every thing give thanks: for this is the will of God in Christ Jesus concerning you."

1 Peter 2:13-15 "[13]Submit yourselves to every ordinance of man for the Lord's sake: whether it be to the king, as supreme; [14]Or unto governors, as unto them that are sent by him for the punishment of evildoers, and for the praise of them that do well. [15]For so is the will of God, that with well doing ye may put to silence the ignorance of foolish men:"

2 Peter 3:9 "The Lord is not slack concerning his promise, as some men count slackness; but is longsuffering to us-ward, not willing that any should perish, but that all should come to repentance."

WISDOM

Being Wise

Proverbs 8:33 "Hear instruction, and be wise, and refuse it not."

Proverbs 27:11 "My son, be wise, and make my heart glad, that I may answer him that reproacheth me."

Ephesians 5:15 "See then that ye walk circumspectly, not as fools, but as wise,"

Bonding With Wisdom

Proverbs 7:4 "Say unto wisdom, Thou art my sister; and call understanding thy kinswoman:"

Ceasing From Your Own Wisdom

Proverbs 23:4 "Labour not to be rich: cease from thine own wisdom."

Not Being Wise In Your Own Eyes

Proverbs 3:7 "Be not wise in thine own eyes: fear the LORD, and depart from evil."

Romans 12:16 "Be of the same mind one toward another. Mind not high things, but condescend to men of low estate. Be not wise in your own conceits."

Not Making Yourself Over Wise

Ecclesiastes 7:16 "Be not righteous over much; neither make thyself over wise: why shouldest thou destroy thyself?"

Getting Wisdom

Proverbs 4:7 "Wisdom is the principal thing; therefore get wisdom: and with all thy getting get understanding."

Proverbs 23:23 "Buy the truth, and sell it not; also wisdom, and instruction, and understanding."

God Being Mighty In Wisdom

Job 36:5 "Behold, God is mighty, and despiseth not any: he is mighty in strength and wisdom."

The Attributes Of Wisdom

Proverbs 8:1-31 "[1]Doth not wisdom cry? and understanding put forth her voice? [2]She standeth in the top of high places, by the way in the places of the paths. [3]She crieth at the gates, at the entry of the city, at the coming in at the doors. [4]Unto you, O men, I call; and my voice is to the sons of man. 5O ye simple, understand wisdom: and, ye fools, be ye of an understanding heart. 6Hear; for I will speak of excellent things; and the opening of my lips shall be right things. 7For my mouth shall speak truth; and wickedness is an abomination to my lips. 8All the words of my mouth are in righteousness; there is nothing froward or perverse in them. 9They are all plain to him that understandeth, and right to them that find knowledge. 10Receive my instruction, and not silver; and knowledge rather than choice gold. 11For wisdom is better than rubies; and all the things that may be desired are not to be compared to it. 12I wisdom dwell with prudence, and find out knowledge of witty inventions. 13The fear of the LORD is to hate evil: pride, and arrogancy, and the evil way, and the froward mouth, do I hate. 14Counsel is mine, and sound wisdom: I am understanding; I have strength. 15By me kings reign, and princes decree justice. 16By me princes rule, and nobles, even all the judges of the earth. 17I love them that love me; and those that seek me early shall find me. 18Riches and honour are with me; yea, durable riches and righteousness. 19My fruit is better than gold, yea, than fine gold; and my revenue than choice silver. 20I lead in the way of righteousness, in the midst of the paths of judgment: 21That I may cause those that love me to inherit substance; and I will fill their treasures. 22The LORD possessed me in the beginning of his way, before his works of old. 23I was set up from everlasting, from the beginning, or ever the earth was. 24When there were no depths, I was brought forth; when there were no fountains abounding with water. 25Before the mountains were settled, before the hills was I brought forth: 26While as yet he had not made the earth, nor the fields, nor the highest part of the dust of the world. 27When he prepared the heavens, I was there: when he set a compass upon the face of the depth: 28When he established the clouds above: when he strengthened the fountains of the deep: 29When he gave to the sea his decree, that the waters should not pass his commandment: when he appointed the foundations of the earth: 30Then I was by him, as one brought up with him: and I was daily his delight, rejoicing always before him; 31Rejoicing in the habitable part of his earth; and my delights were with the sons of men."

The Lord Creating Everything By Wisdom

Psalm 136:3-9 "3O give thanks to the Lord of lords: for his mercy endureth for ever. 4To him who alone doeth great wonders: for his mercy endureth for ever. 5To him that by wisdom made the heavens: for his mercy endureth for ever. 6To him that stretched out the earth above the waters: for his mercy endureth for ever. 7To him that made great lights: for his mercy endureth for ever: 8The sun to rule by day: for his mercy endureth for ever: 9The moon and stars to rule by night: for his mercy endureth for ever."

Proverbs 3:19 "The LORD by wisdom hath founded the earth; by understanding hath he established the heavens."

Jeremiah 10:10-12 "10But the LORD is the true God, he is the living God, and an everlasting king: at his wrath the earth shall tremble, and the nations shall not be able to abide his indignation. 11Thus shall ye say unto them, The gods that have not made the heavens and the earth, even they shall perish from the earth, and from under these heavens. 12He hath made the earth by his power, he hath established the world by his wisdom, and hath stretched out the heavens by his discretion."

The Lord Giving Wisdom

1 Chronicles 22:12 "Only the LORD give thee wisdom and understanding, and give thee charge concerning Israel, that thou mayest keep the law of the LORD thy God."

Proverbs 2:1-22 "1My son, if thou wilt receive my words, and hide my commandments with thee; 2So that thou incline thine ear unto wisdom, and apply thine heart to understanding; 3Yea, if thou criest after knowledge, and liftest up thy voice for understanding; 4If thou seekest her as silver, and searchest for her as for hid treasures; 5Then shalt thou understand the fear of the LORD, and find the knowledge of God. 6For the LORD giveth wisdom: out of his mouth cometh knowledge and understanding. 7He layeth up sound wisdom for the righteous: he is a buckler to them that walk uprightly. 8He keepeth the paths of judgment, and preserveth the way of his saints. 9Then shalt thou understand righteousness, and judgment, and equity; yea, every good path. 10When wisdom entereth into thine heart, and knowledge is pleasant unto thy soul; [11]Discretion shall preserve thee, understanding shall keep thee: [12]To deliver thee from the way of the evil man, from the man that speaketh froward things; [13]Who leave the paths of uprightness, to walk in the ways of darkness; [14]Who rejoice to do evil, and delight in the frowardness of the wicked; [15]Whose ways are crooked, and they froward in their paths: [16]To deliver thee from the strange woman, even from the stranger which flattereth with her words; [17]Which forsaketh the guide of her youth, and forgetteth the covenant of her God. [18]For her house inclineth unto death, and her paths unto the dead. [19]None that go unto her return again, neither take they hold of the paths of life. [20]That thou mayest walk in the way of good men, and keep the paths of the righteous. [21]For the upright shall dwell in the land, and the perfect shall remain in it. [22]But the wicked shall be cut off from the earth, and the transgressors shall be rooted out of it."

Ecclesiastes 2:24-26 "[24]There is nothing better for a man, than that he should eat and drink, and that he should make his soul enjoy good in his labour. This also I saw, that it was from the hand of God. [25]For who can eat, or who else can hasten hereunto, more than I? [26]For God giveth to a man that is good in his sight wisdom, and knowledge, and joy: but to the sinner he giveth travail, to gather and to heap up, that he may give to him that is good before God. This also is vanity and vexation of spirit."

Daniel 1:17 "As for these four children, God gave them knowledge and skill in all learning and wisdom: and Daniel had understanding in all visions and dreams."

Daniel 2:20-21 "[20]Daniel answered and said, Blessed be the name of God for ever and ever: for wisdom and might are his: [21]And he changeth the times and the seasons: he removeth kings, and setteth up kings: he giveth wisdom unto the wise, and knowledge to them that know understanding:"

1 Corinthians 2:6-16 "[6]Howbeit we speak wisdom among them that are perfect: yet not the wisdom of this world, nor of the princes of this world, that come to nought: [7]But we speak the wisdom of God in a mystery, even the hidden wisdom, which God ordained before the world unto our glory: [8]Which none of the princes of this world knew: for had they known it, they would not have crucified the Lord of glory. [9]But as it is written, Eye hath not seen, nor ear heard, neither have entered into the heart of man, the things which God hath prepared for them that love him. [10]But God hath revealed them unto us by his Spirit: for the Spirit searcheth all things, yea, the deep things of God. [11]For what man knoweth the things of a man, save the spirit of man which is in him? even so the things of God knoweth no man, but the Spirit of God. [12]Now we have received, not the spirit of the world, but the spirit which is of God; that we might know the things that are freely given to us of God. [13]Which things also we speak, not in the words which man's wisdom teacheth, but which the Holy Ghost teacheth; comparing spiritual things with spiritual. [14]But the natural man receiveth not the things of the Spirit of God: for they are foolishness unto him: neither can he know them, because they are spiritually discerned. [15]But he that is spiritual judgeth all things, yet he himself is judged of no man. [16]For who hath known the mind of the Lord, that he may instruct him? But we have the mind of Christ."

The Price Of Wisdom

Job 28:12-19 "[12]But where shall wisdom be found? and where is the place of understanding? [13]Man knoweth not the price thereof; neither is it found in the land of the living. [14]The depth saith, It is not in me: and the sea saith, It is not with me. [15]It cannot be gotten for gold, neither shall silver be weighed for the price thereof. [16]It cannot be valued with the gold of Ophir, with the precious onyx, or the sapphire. [17]The gold and the crystal cannot equal it: and the exchange of it shall not be for jewels of fine gold. [18]No mention shall be made of coral, or of pearls: for the price of wisdom is above rubies. [19]The topaz of Ethiopia shall not equal it, neither shall it be valued with pure gold."

The Revenue Of Wisdom

Proverbs 8:12-19 "[12]I wisdom dwell with prudence, and find out knowledge of witty inventions. [13]The fear of the LORD is to hate evil: pride, and arrogancy, and the evil way, and the froward mouth, do I hate. [14]Counsel is mine, and sound wisdom: I am understanding; I have strength. [15]By me kings reign, and princes decree justice. [16]By me princes rule, and nobles, even all the judges of the earth. [17]I love them that love me; and those that seek me early shall find me. [18]Riches and honour are with me; yea, durable riches and righteousness. [19]My fruit is better than gold, yea, than fine gold; and my revenue than choice silver."

The Reward For Despising Wisdom

Proverbs 1:20-32 "[20]Wisdom crieth without; she uttereth her voice in the streets: [21]She crieth in the chief place of concourse, in the openings of the gates: in the city she uttereth her words, saying, [22]How long, ye simple ones, will ye love simplicity? and the scorners delight in their scorning, and fools hate knowledge? [23]Turn you at my reproof: behold, I will pour out my spirit unto you, I will make known my words unto you. [24]Because I have called, and ye refused; I have stretched out my hand, and no man regarded; [25]But ye have set at nought all my counsel, and would none of my reproof: [26]I also will laugh at your calamity; I will mock when your fear cometh; [27]When your fear cometh as desolation, and your destruction cometh as a whirlwind; when distress and anguish cometh upon you. [28]Then shall they call upon me, but I will not answer; they shall seek me early, but they shall not find me: [29]For that they hated knowledge, and did not choose the fear of the LORD: [30]They would none of my counsel: they despised all my reproof. [31]Therefore shall they eat of the fruit of their own way, and be filled with their own devices. [32]For the turning away of the simple shall slay them, and the prosperity of fools shall destroy them."

The Reward For Trusting In Your Own Wisdom

Isaiah 47:10-11 "[10]For thou hast trusted in thy wickedness: thou hast said, None seeth me. Thy wisdom and thy knowledge, it hath perverted thee; and thou hast said in thine heart, I am, and none else beside me. [11]Therefore shall evil come upon thee; thou shalt not know from whence it riseth: and mischief shall fall upon thee; thou shalt not be able to put it off: and desolation shall come upon thee suddenly, which thou shalt not know."

The Time When Wisdom Enters Into Your Heart

Proverbs 2:10-20 "[10]When wisdom entereth into thine heart, and knowledge is pleasant unto thy soul; [11]Discretion shall preserve thee, understanding shall keep thee: [12]To deliver thee from the way of the evil man, from the man that speaketh froward things; [13]Who leave the paths of uprightness, to walk in the ways of darkness; [14]Who rejoice to do evil, and delight in the frowardness of the wicked; [15]Whose ways are crooked, and they froward in their paths: [16]To deliver thee from the strange woman, even from the stranger which flattereth with her words; [17]Which forsaketh the guide of her youth, and forgetteth the covenant of her God. [18]For her house inclineth unto death, and her paths unto the dead. [19]None that go unto her return again, neither take they hold of the paths of life. [20]That thou mayest walk in the way of good men, and keep the paths of the righteous."

The Wellspring Of Wisdom

Proverbs 18:4 "The words of a man's mouth are as deep waters, and the wellspring of wisdom as a flowing brook."

The Wisdom Of The Lord

Romans 11:33-36 "[33]O the depth of the riches both of the wisdom and knowledge of God! how unsearchable are his judgments, and his ways past finding out! [34]For who hath known the mind of the Lord? or who hath been his counseller? [35]Or who hath first given to him, and it shall be recompensed unto him again? [36]For of him, and through him, and to him, are all things: to whom be glory for ever. Amen."

1 Corinthians 1:20-25 "[20]Where is the wise? where is the scribe? where is the disputer of this world? hath not God made foolish the wisdom of this world? [21]For after that in the wisdom of God the world by wisdom knew not God, it pleased God by the foolishness of preaching to save them that believe. [22]For the Jews require a sign, and the Greeks seek after wisdom: [23]But we preach Christ crucified, unto the Jews a stumblingblock, and unto the Greeks foolishness; [24]But unto them which are called, both Jews and Greeks, Christ the power of God, and the wisdom of God. [25]Because the foolishness of God is wiser than men; and the weakness of God is stronger than men."

1 Corinthians 2:6-8 "⁶Howbeit we speak wisdom among them that are perfect: yet not the wisdom of this world, nor of the princes of this world, that come to nought: ⁷But we speak the wisdom of God in a mystery, even the hidden wisdom, which God ordained before the world unto our glory: ⁸Which none of the princes of this world knew: for had they known it, they would not have crucified the Lord of glory."

James 3:17 "But the wisdom that is from above is first pure, then peaceable, gentle, and easy to be intreated, full of mercy and good fruits, without partiality, and without hypocrisy."

The Wisdom Of The Prudent
Proverbs 14:8 "The wisdom of the prudent is to understand his way: but the folly of fools is deceit."

The Wisdom Of The World
Psalm 94:11 "The LORD knoweth the thoughts of man, that they are vanity."

Isaiah 29:13-14 "¹³Wherefore the Lord said, Forasmuch as this people draw near me with their mouth, and with their lips do honour me, but have removed their heart far from me, and their fear toward me is taught by the precept of men: ¹⁴Therefore, behold, I will proceed to do a marvellous work among this people, even a marvellous work and a wonder: for the wisdom of their wise men shall perish, and the understanding of their prudent men shall be hid."

1 Corinthians 1:18-20 "¹⁸For the preaching of the cross is to them that perish foolishness; but unto us which are saved it is the power of God. ¹⁹For it is written, I will destroy the wisdom of the wise, and will bring to nothing the understanding of the prudent. ²⁰Where is the wise? where is the scribe? where is the disputer of this world? hath not God made foolish the wisdom of this world?"

1 Corinthians 2:6 "Howbeit we speak wisdom among them that are perfect: yet not the wisdom of this world, nor of the princes of this world, that come to nought:"

1 Corinthians 3:18-23 "¹⁸Let no man deceive himself. If any man among you seemeth to be wise in this world, let him become a fool, that he may be wise. ¹⁹For the wisdom of this world is foolishness with God. For it is written, He taketh the wise in their own craftiness. ²⁰And again, The Lord knoweth the thoughts of the wise, that they are vain. ²¹Therefore let no man glory in men. For all things are yours; ²²Whether Paul, or Apollos, or Cephas, or the world, or life, or death, or things present, or things to come; all are yours; ²³And ye are Christ's; and Christ is God's."

James 3:13-16 "¹³Who is a wise man and endued with knowledge among you? let him shew out of a good conversation his works with meekness of wisdom. ¹⁴But if ye have bitter envying and strife in your hearts, glory not, and lie not against the truth. ¹⁵This wisdom descendeth not from above, but is earthly, sensual, devilish. ¹⁶For where envying and strife is, there is confusion and every evil work."

The Wise
Proverbs 3:35 "The wise shall inherit glory: but shame shall be the promotion of fools."

Proverbs 9:9 "Give instruction to a wise man, and he will be yet wiser: teach a just man, and he will increase in learning."

Proverbs 10:1 "The proverbs of Solomon. A wise son maketh a glad father: but a foolish son is the heaviness of his mother."

Proverbs 10:8 "The wise in heart will receive commandments: but a prating fool shall fall."

Proverbs 10:13-14 "¹³In the lips of him that hath understanding wisdom is found: but a rod is for the back of him that is void of understanding. ¹⁴Wise men lay up knowledge: but the mouth of the foolish is near destruction."

Proverbs 12:18 "There is that speaketh like the piercings of a sword: but the tongue of the wise is health."

Proverbs 13:1 "A wise son heareth his father's instruction: but a scorner heareth not rebuke."

Proverbs 14:1 "Every wise woman buildeth her house: but the foolish plucketh it down with her hands."

Proverbs 14:3 "In the mouth of the foolish is a rod of pride: but the lips of the wise shall preserve them."

Proverbs 14:16 "A wise man feareth, and departeth from evil: but the fool rageth, and is confident."

Proverbs 14:24 "The crown of the wise is their riches: but the foolishness of fools is folly."

Proverbs 15:2 "The tongue of the wise useth knowledge aright: but the mouth of fools poureth out foolishness."

Proverbs 15:7 "The lips of the wise disperse knowledge: but the heart of the foolish doeth not so."

Proverbs 15:20 "A wise son maketh a glad father: but a foolish man despiseth his mother."

Proverbs 15:24 "The way of life is above to the wise, that he may depart from hell beneath."

Proverbs 16:14 "The wrath of a king is as messengers of death: but a wise man will pacify it."

Proverbs 16:20-23 "20He that handleth a matter wisely shall find good: and whoso trusteth in the LORD, happy is he. 21The wise in heart shall be called prudent: and the sweetness of the lips increaseth learning. 22Understanding is a wellspring of life unto him that hath it: but the instruction of fools is folly. 23The heart of the wise teacheth his mouth, and addeth learning to his lips."

Proverbs 17:10 "A reproof entereth more into a wise man than an hundred stripes into a fool."

Proverbs 18:15 "The heart of the prudent getteth knowledge; and the ear of the wise seeketh knowledge."

Proverbs 21:20 "There is treasure to be desired and oil in the dwelling of the wise; but a foolish man spendeth it up."

Proverbs 21:22 "A wise man scaleth the city of the mighty, and casteth down the strength of the confidence thereof."

Proverbs 24:5 "A wise man is strong; yea, a man of knowledge increaseth strength."

Proverbs 28:26 "He that trusteth in his own heart is a fool: but whoso walketh wisely, he shall be delivered."

Proverbs 29:8 "Scornful men bring a city into a snare: but wise men turn away wrath."

Proverbs 29:11 "A fool uttereth all his mind: but a wise man keepeth it in till afterwards."

Ecclesiastes 2:14 "The wise man's eyes are in his head; but the fool walketh in darkness: and I myself perceived also that one event happeneth to them all."

Ecclesiastes 4:13-14 "13Better is a poor and a wise child than an old and foolish king, who will no more be admonished. 14For out of prison he cometh to reign; whereas also he that is born in his kingdom becometh poor."

Ecclesiastes 7:4 "The heart of the wise is in the house of mourning; but the heart of fools is in the house of mirth."

Ecclesiastes 7:7 "Surely oppression maketh a wise man mad; and a gift destroyeth the heart."

Ecclesiastes 7:12 "For wisdom is a defence, and money is a defence: but the excellency of knowledge is, that wisdom giveth life to them that have it."

Ecclesiastes 7:19 "Wisdom strengtheneth the wise more than ten mighty men which are in the city."

Ecclesiastes 8:2-5 "2I counsel thee to keep the king's commandment, and that in regard of the oath of God. 3Be not hasty to go out of his sight: stand not in an evil thing; for he doeth whatsoever pleaseth him. 4Where the word of a king is, there is power: and who may say unto him, What doest thou? 5Whoso keepeth the commandment shall feel no evil thing: and a wise man's heart discerneth both time and judgment."

Ecclesiastes 9:17 "The words of wise men are heard in quiet more than the cry of him that ruleth among fools."

Ecclesiastes 10:2 "A wise man's heart is at his right hand; but a fool's heart at his left."

Ecclesiastes 10:12 "The words of a wise man's mouth are gracious; but the lips of a fool will swallow up himself."

Ecclesiastes 12:11 "The words of the wise are as goads, and as nails fastened by the masters of assemblies, which are given from one shepherd."

Daniel 2:20-21 "20Daniel answered and said, Blessed be the name of God for ever and ever: for wisdom and might are his: 21And he changeth the times and the seasons: he removeth kings, and setteth up kings: he giveth wisdom unto the wise, and knowledge to them that know understanding:"

Daniel 12:3 "And they that be wise shall shine as the brightness of the firmament; and they that turn many to righteousness as the stars for ever and ever."

Daniel 12:10 "Many shall be purified, and made white, and tried; but the wicked shall do wickedly: and none of the wicked shall understand; but the wise shall understand."

There Being No Wisdom Against The Lord
Proverbs 21:30 "There is no wisdom nor understanding nor counsel against the LORD."

Those That Are Wise According To The World
Job 37:23-24 "23Touching the Almighty, we cannot find him out: he is excellent in power, and in judgment, and in plenty of justice: he will not afflict. 24Men do therefore fear him: he respecteth not any that are wise of heart."

Isaiah 44:24-25 "24Thus saith the LORD, thy redeemer, and he that formed thee from the womb, I am the LORD that maketh all things; that stretcheth forth the heavens alone; that spreadeth abroad the earth by myself; 25That frustrateth the tokens of the liars, and maketh diviners mad; that turneth wise men backward, and maketh their knowledge foolish;"

Romans 1:21-22 "21Because that, when they knew God, they glorified him not as God, neither were thankful; but became vain in their imaginations, and their foolish heart was darkened. 22Professing themselves to be wise, they became fools,"

1 Corinthians 3:18 "Let no man deceive himself. If any man among you seemeth to be wise in this world, let him become a fool, that he may be wise."

Those That Are Wise In Their Own Eyes
Proverbs 26:12 "Seest thou a man wise in his own conceit? there is more hope of a fool than of him."

Isaiah 5:21 "Woe unto them that are wise in their own eyes, and prudent in their own sight!"

Those That Find Wisdom
Proverbs 3:13 "Happy is the man that findeth wisdom, and the man that getteth understanding."

Proverbs 8:32-35 "32Now therefore hearken unto me, O ye children: for blessed are they that keep my ways. 33Hear instruction, and be wise, and refuse it not. 34Blessed is the man that heareth me, watching daily at my gates, waiting at the posts of my doors. 35For whoso findeth me findeth life, and shall obtain favour of the LORD."

Those That Get Wisdom
Proverbs 19:8 "He that getteth wisdom loveth his own soul: he that keepeth understanding shall find good."

Those That Hear Wisdom
Proverbs 1:20-33 "20Wisdom crieth without; she uttereth her voice in the streets: 21She crieth in the chief place of concourse, in the openings of the gates: in the city she uttereth her words, saying, 22How long, ye simple ones, will ye love simplicity? and the scorners delight in their scorning, and fools hate knowledge? 23Turn you at my reproof: behold, I will pour out my spirit unto you, I will make known my words unto you. 24Because I have called, and ye refused; I have stretched out my hand, and no man regarded; 25But ye have set at nought all my counsel, and would none of my reproof: 26I also will laugh at your calamity; I will mock when your fear cometh; 27When your fear cometh as desolation, and your destruction cometh as a whirlwind; when distress and anguish cometh upon you. 28Then shall they call upon me, but I will not answer; they shall seek me early, but they shall not find me: 29For that they hated knowledge, and did not choose the fear of the LORD: 30They would none of my counsel: they despised all my reproof. 31Therefore shall they eat of the fruit of their own way, and be filled with their own devices. 32For the turning away of the simple shall slay them, and the prosperity of fools shall destroy them. 33But whoso hearkeneth unto me shall dwell safely, and shall be quiet from fear of evil."

Proverbs 8:32-34 "32Now therefore hearken unto me, O ye children: for blessed are they that keep my ways. 33Hear instruction, and be wise, and refuse it not. 34Blessed is the man that heareth me, watching daily at my gates, waiting at the posts of my doors."

Those That Lack Wisdom
Proverbs 11:12 "He that is void of wisdom despiseth his neighbour: but a man of understanding holdeth his peace."

Proverbs 15:21 "Folly is joy to him that is destitute of wisdom: but a man of understanding walketh uprightly."

Those That Love Wisdom

Proverbs 8:12-21 "[12]I wisdom dwell with prudence, and find out knowledge of witty inventions. [13]The fear of the LORD is to hate evil: pride, and arrogancy, and the evil way, and the froward mouth, do I hate. [14]Counsel is mine, and sound wisdom: I am understanding; I have strength. [15]By me kings reign, and princes decree justice. [16]By me princes rule, and nobles, even all the judges of the earth. [17]I love them that love me; and those that seek me early shall find me. [18]Riches and honour are with me; yea, durable riches and righteousness. [19]My fruit is better than gold, yea, than fine gold; and my revenue than choice silver. [20]I lead in the way of righteousness, in the midst of the paths of judgment: [21]That I may cause those that love me to inherit substance; and I will fill their treasures."

Proverbs 29:3 "Whoso loveth wisdom rejoiceth his father: but he that keepeth company with harlots spendeth his substance."

What Accompanies Wisdom

Proverbs 8:12 "I wisdom dwell with prudence, and find out knowledge of witty inventions."

Ecclesiastes 1:18 "For in much wisdom is much grief: and he that increaseth knowledge increaseth sorrow."

What Gives Wisdom

Proverbs 29:15 "The rod and reproof give wisdom: but a child left to himself bringeth his mother to shame."

What Is Able To Make You Wise

Psalm 19:7 "The law of the LORD is perfect, converting the soul: the testimony of the LORD is sure, making wise the simple."

Psalm 119:89-98 "[89]For ever, O LORD, thy word is settled in heaven. [90]Thy faithfulness is unto all generations: thou hast established the earth, and it abideth. [91]They continue this day according to thine ordinances: for all are thy servants. [92]Unless thy law had been my delights, I should then have perished in mine affliction. [93]I will never forget thy precepts: for with them thou hast quickened me. [94]I am thine, save me; for I have sought thy precepts. [95]The wicked have waited for me to destroy me: but I will consider thy testimonies. [96]I have seen an end of all perfection: but thy commandment is exceeding broad. [97]O how love I thy law! it is my meditation all the day. [98]Thou through thy commandments hast made me wiser than mine enemies: for they are ever with me."

Psalm 119:126-130 "[126]It is time for thee, LORD, to work: for they have made void thy law. [127]Therefore I love thy commandments above gold; yea, above fine gold. [128]Therefore I esteem all thy precepts concerning all things to be right; and I hate every false way. [129]Thy testimonies are wonderful: therefore doth my soul keep them. [130]The entrance of thy words giveth light; it giveth understanding unto the simple."

2 Timothy 3:14-15 "[14]But continue thou in the things which thou hast learned and hast been assured of, knowing of whom thou hast learned them; [15]And that from a child thou hast known the holy scriptures, which are able to make thee wise unto salvation through faith which is in Christ Jesus."

What Is Wisdom

Deuteronomy 4:5-6 "[5]Behold, I have taught you statutes and judgments, even as the LORD my God commanded me, that ye should do so in the land whither ye go to possess it. [6]Keep therefore and do them; for this is your wisdom and your understanding in the sight of the nations, which shall hear all these statutes, and say, Surely this great nation is a wise and understanding people."

Job 28:28 "And unto man he said, Behold, the fear of the Lord, that is wisdom; and to depart from evil is understanding."

Psalm 111:10 "The fear of the LORD is the beginning of wisdom: a good understanding have all they that do his commandments: his praise endureth for ever."

Proverbs 1:7 "The fear of the LORD is the beginning of knowledge: but fools despise wisdom and instruction."

Proverbs 9:10 "The fear of the LORD is the beginning of wisdom: and the knowledge of the holy is understanding."

Proverbs 15:33 "The fear of the LORD is the instruction of wisdom; and before honour is humility."

What The Wise Should Not Do
Jeremiah 9:23 "Thus saith the LORD, Let not the wise man glory in his wisdom, neither let the mighty man glory in his might, let not the rich man glory in his riches:"

What Wisdom Does
Proverbs 1:20-23 "20Wisdom crieth without; she uttereth her voice in the streets: 21She crieth in the chief place of concourse, in the openings of the gates: in the city she uttereth her words, saying, 22How long, ye simple ones, will ye love simplicity? and the scorners delight in their scorning, and fools hate knowledge? 23Turn you at my reproof: behold, I will pour out my spirit unto you, I will make known my words unto you."

Proverbs 24:3 "Through wisdom is an house builded; and by understanding it is established:"

Ecclesiastes 7:12 "For wisdom is a defence, and money is a defence: but the excellency of knowledge is, that wisdom giveth life to them that have it."

Ecclesiastes 7:19 "Wisdom strengtheneth the wise more than ten mighty men which are in the city."

What Wisdom Is
Proverbs 4:7 "Wisdom is the principal thing; therefore get wisdom: and with all thy getting get understanding."

Proverbs 8:11-14 "11For wisdom is better than rubies; and all the things that may be desired are not to be compared to it. 12I wisdom dwell with prudence, and find out knowledge of witty inventions. 13The fear of the LORD is to hate evil: pride, and arrogancy, and the evil way, and the froward mouth, do I hate. 14Counsel is mine, and sound wisdom: I am understanding; I have strength."

Proverbs 17:24 "Wisdom is before him that hath understanding; but the eyes of a fool are in the ends of the earth."

Proverbs 24:7 "Wisdom is too high for a fool: he openeth not his mouth in the gate."

Proverbs 24:13-14 "13My son, eat thou honey, because it is good; and the honeycomb, which is sweet to thy taste: 14So shall the knowledge of wisdom be unto thy soul: when thou hast found it, then there shall be a reward, and thy expectation shall not be cut off."

Ecclesiastes 7:11-12 "11Wisdom is good with an inheritance: and by it there is profit to them that see the sun. 12For wisdom is a defence, and money is a defence: but the excellency of knowledge is, that wisdom giveth life to them that have it."

Ecclesiastes 9:16 "Then said I, Wisdom is better than strength: nevertheless the poor man's wisdom is despised, and his words are not heard."

Ecclesiastes 9:18 "Wisdom is better than weapons of war: but one sinner destroyeth much good."

Ecclesiastes 10:10 "If the iron be blunt, and he do not whet the edge, then must he put to more strength: but wisdom is profitable to direct."

Where Wisdom Is Found
Job 12:9-16 "9Who knoweth not in all these that the hand of the LORD hath wrought this? 10In whose hand is the soul of every living thing, and the breath of all mankind. 11Doth not the ear try words? and the mouth taste his meat? 12With the ancient is wisdom; and in length of days understanding. 13With him is wisdom and strength, he hath counsel and understanding. 14Behold, he breaketh down, and it cannot be built again: he shutteth up a man, and there can be no opening. 15Behold, he withholdeth the waters, and they dry up: also he sendeth them out, and they overturn the earth. 16With him is strength and wisdom: the deceived and the deceiver are his."

Job 28:20-28 "20Whence then cometh wisdom? and where is the place of understanding? 21Seeing it is hid from the eyes of all living, and kept close from the fowls of the air. 22Destruction and death say, We have heard the fame thereof with our ears. 23God understandeth the way thereof, and he knoweth the place thereof. 24For he looketh to the ends of the earth, and seeth under the whole heaven; 25To make the weight for the winds; and he weigheth the waters by measure. 26When he made a decree for the rain, and a way for the lightning of the thunder: 27Then did he see it, and declare it; he prepared it, yea, and searched it out. 28And unto man he said, Behold, the fear of the

Lord, that is wisdom; and to depart from evil is understanding."

Proverbs 10:13 "In the lips of him that hath understanding wisdom is found: but a rod is for the back of him that is void of understanding."

Proverbs 14:33 "Wisdom resteth in the heart of him that hath understanding: but that which is in the midst of fools is made known."

Who Despises Wisdom
Proverbs 1:7 "The fear of the LORD is the beginning of knowledge: but fools despise wisdom and instruction."

Proverbs 1:22 "How long, ye simple ones, will ye love simplicity? and the scorners delight in their scorning, and fools hate knowledge?"

Proverbs 15:5 "A fool despiseth his father's instruction: but he that regardeth reproof is prudent."

Proverbs 23:9 "Speak not in the ears of a fool: for he will despise the wisdom of thy words."

Who Does Not Find Wisdom
Proverbs 14:6 "A scorner seeketh wisdom, and findeth it not: but knowledge is easy unto him that understandeth."

Who God Gives Wisdom To
Ecclesiastes 2:24-26 "24There is nothing better for a man, than that he should eat and drink, and that he should make his soul enjoy good in his labour. This also I saw, that it was from the hand of God. 25For who can eat, or who else can hasten hereunto, more than I? 26For God giveth to a man that is good in his sight wisdom, and knowledge, and joy: but to the sinner he giveth travail, to gather and to heap up, that he may give to him that is good before God. This also is vanity and vexation of spirit."

Daniel 1:8-17 "8But Daniel purposed in his heart that he would not defile himself with the portion of the king's meat, nor with the wine which he drank: therefore he requested of the prince of the eunuchs that he might not defile himself. 9Now God had brought Daniel into favour and tender love with the prince of the eunuchs. 10And the prince of the eunuchs said unto Daniel, I fear my lord the king, who hath appointed your meat and your drink: for why should he see your faces worse liking than the children which are of your sort? then shall ye make me endanger my head to the king. 11Then said Daniel to Melzar, whom the prince of the eunuchs had set over Daniel, Hananiah, Mishael, and Azariah, 12Prove thy servants, I beseech thee, ten days; and let them give us pulse to eat, and water to drink. 13Then let our countenances be looked upon before thee, and the countenance of the children that eat of the portion of the king's meat: and as thou seest, deal with thy servants. 14So he consented to them in this matter, and proved them ten days. 15And at the end of ten days their countenances appeared fairer and fatter in flesh than all the children which did eat the portion of the king's meat. 16Thus Melzar took away the portion of their meat, and the wine that they should drink; and gave them pulse. 17As for these four children, God gave them knowledge and skill in all learning and wisdom: and Daniel had understanding in all visions and dreams."

Daniel 2:20-21 "20Daniel answered and said, Blessed be the name of God for ever and ever: for wisdom and might are his: 21And he changeth the times and the seasons: he removeth kings, and setteth up kings: he giveth wisdom unto the wise, and knowledge to them that know understanding:"

Who Is Not Always Wise
Job 32:9 "Great men are not always wise: neither do the aged understand judgment."

Who Is Not Wise
Proverbs 20:1 "Wine is a mocker, strong drink is raging: and whosoever is deceived thereby is not wise."

Who Is Wise
Proverbs 10:5 "He that gathereth in summer is a wise son: but he that sleepeth in harvest is a son that causeth shame."

Proverbs 10:19 "In the multitude of words there wanteth not sin: but he that refraineth his lips is wise."

Proverbs 10:23 "It is as sport to a fool to do mischief: but a man of understanding hath wisdom."

Proverbs 11:2 "When pride cometh, then cometh shame: but with the lowly is wisdom."

Proverbs 11:30 "The fruit of the righteous is a tree of life; and he that winneth souls is wise."

Proverbs 12:15 "The way of a fool is right in his own eyes: but he that hearkeneth unto counsel is wise."

Proverbs 13:10 "Only by pride cometh contention: but with the well advised is wisdom."

Proverbs 13:20 "He that walketh with wise men shall be wise: but a companion of fools shall be destroyed."

Proverbs 14:33 "Wisdom resteth in the heart of him that hath understanding: but that which is in the midst of fools is made known."

Proverbs 17:28 "Even a fool, when he holdeth his peace, is counted wise: and he that shutteth his lips is esteemed a man of understanding."

1 Corinthians 4:9-10 "⁹For I think that God hath set forth us the apostles last, as it were appointed to death: for we are made a spectacle unto the world, and to angels, and to men. ¹⁰We are fools for Christ's sake, but ye are wise in Christ; we are weak, but ye are strong; ye are honourable, but we are despised."

Who Is Wise In Their Own Conceit
Proverbs 26:16 "The sluggard is wiser in his own conceit than seven men that can render a reason."

Proverbs 28:11 "The rich man is wise in his own conceit; but the poor that hath understanding searcheth him out."

Wisdom Being Better Than Wealth
Proverbs 8:10-19 "¹⁰Receive my instruction, and not silver; and knowledge rather than choice gold. ¹¹For wisdom is better than rubies; and all the things that may be desired are not to be compared to it. ¹²I wisdom dwell with prudence, and find out knowledge of witty inventions. ¹³The fear of the LORD is to hate evil: pride, and arrogancy, and the evil way, and the froward mouth, do I hate. ¹⁴Counsel is mine, and sound wisdom: I am understanding; I have strength. ¹⁵By me kings reign, and princes decree justice. ¹⁶By me princes rule, and nobles, even all the judges of the earth. ¹⁷I love them that love me; and those that seek me early shall find me. ¹⁸Riches and honour are with me; yea, durable riches and righteousness. ¹⁹My fruit is better than gold, yea, than fine gold; and my revenue than choice silver."

Proverbs 16:16 "How much better is it to get wisdom than gold! and to get understanding rather to be chosen than silver!"

Wisdom Belonging To God
Daniel 2:20 "Daniel answered and said, Blessed be the name of God for ever and ever: for wisdom and might are his:"

WITNESS

Faithful Witnesses
Proverbs 14:5 "A faithful witness will not lie: but a false witness will utter lies."

Proverbs 14:25 "A true witness delivereth souls: but a deceitful witness speaketh lies."

False Witnesses
Proverbs 12:17 "He that speaketh truth sheweth forth righteousness: but a false witness deceit."

Proverbs 14:5 "A faithful witness will not lie: but a false witness will utter lies."

Proverbs 14:25 "A true witness delivereth souls: but a deceitful witness speaketh lies."

Proverbs 19:5 "A false witness shall not be unpunished, and he that speaketh lies shall not escape."

Proverbs 19:9 "A false witness shall not be unpunished, and he that speaketh lies shall perish."

Proverbs 21:28 "A false witness shall perish: but the man that heareth speaketh constantly."

Proverbs 25:18 "A man that beareth false witness against his neighbour is a maul, and a sword, and a sharp arrow."

God The Father Giving Witness To Jesus Christ
Matthew 17:4-5 "⁴Then answered Peter, and said unto Jesus, Lord, it is good for us to be here: if thou wilt, let us make here three tabernacles; one for thee, aånd one for Moses, and one for Elias. ⁵While he yet spake, behold, a bright cloud overshadowed them: and behold a voice out of the cloud, which said, This is my beloved Son, in whom I am well pleased; hear ye him."

Mark 9:5-7 "⁵And Peter answered and said to Jesus, Master, it is good for us to be here: and let us make three tabernacles; one for thee, and one for Moses, and one for Elias. ⁶For he wist not what to say; for they were sore afraid. ⁷And there was a cloud that overshadowed them: and a voice came out of the cloud, saying, This is my beloved Son: hear him."

Luke 9:33-35 "³³And it came to pass, as they departed from him, Peter said unto Jesus, Master, it is good for us to be here: and let us make three tabernacles; one for thee, and one for Moses, and one for Elias: not knowing what he said. ³⁴While he thus spake, there came a cloud, and overshadowed them: and they feared as they entered into the cloud. ³⁵And there came a voice out of the cloud, saying, This is my beloved Son: hear him."

John 5:23-38 "²³That all men should honour the Son, even as they honour the Father. He that honoureth not the Son honoureth not the Father which hath sent him. ²⁴Verily, verily, I say unto you, He that heareth my word, and believeth on him that sent me, hath everlasting life, and shall not come into condemnation; but is passed from death unto life. ²⁵Verily, verily, I say unto you, The hour is coming, and now is, when the dead shall hear the voice of the Son of God: and they that hear shall live. ²⁶For as the Father hath life in himself; so hath he given to the Son to have life in himself; ²⁷And hath given him authority to execute judgment also, because he is the Son of man. ²⁸Marvel not at this: for the hour is coming, in the which all that are in the graves shall hear his voice, ²⁹And shall come forth; they that have done good, unto the resurrection of life; and they that have done evil, unto the resurrection of damnation. ³⁰I can of mine own self do nothing: as I hear, I judge: and my judgment is just; because I seek not mine own will, but the will of the Father which hath sent me. ³¹If I bear witness of myself, my witness is not true. ³²There is another that beareth witness of me; and I know that the witness which he witnesseth of me is true. ³³Ye sent unto John, and he bare witness unto the truth. ³⁴But I receive not testimony from man: but these things I say, that ye might be saved. ³⁵He was a burning and a shining light: and ye were willing for a season to rejoice in his light. ³⁶But I have greater witness than that of John: for the works which the Father hath given me to finish, the same works that I do, bear witness of me, that the Father hath sent me. ³⁷And the Father himself, which hath sent me, hath borne witness of me. Ye have neither heard his voice at any time, nor seen his shape. ³⁸And ye have not his word abiding in you: for whom he hath sent, him ye believe not."

John 8:13-18 "¹³The Pharisees therefore said unto him, Thou bearest record of thyself; thy record is not true. ¹⁴Jesus answered and said unto them, Though I bear record of myself, yet my record is true: for I know whence I came, and whither I go; but ye cannot tell whence I come, and whither I go. ¹⁵Ye judge after the flesh; I judge no man. ¹⁶And yet if I judge, my judgment is true: for I am not alone, but I and the Father that sent me. ¹⁷It is also written in your law, that the testimony of two men is true. ¹⁸I am one that bear witness of myself, and the Father that sent me beareth witness of me."

John 10:25-38 "²⁵Jesus answered them, I told you, and ye believed not: the works that I do in my Father's name, they bear witness of me. ²⁶But ye believe not, because ye are not of my sheep, as I said unto you. ²⁷My sheep hear my voice, and I know them, and they follow me: ²⁸And I give unto them eternal life; and they shall never perish, neither shall any man pluck them out of my hand. ²⁹My Father, which gave them me, is greater than all; and no man is able to pluck them out of my Father's hand. ³⁰I and my Father are one. ³¹Then the Jews took up stones again to stone him. ³²Jesus answered them, Many good works have I shewed you from my Father; for which of those works do ye stone me? ³³The Jews answered him, saying, For a good work we stone thee not; but for blasphemy; and because that thou, being a man, makest thyself God. ³⁴Jesus answered them, Is it not written in your law, I said, Ye are gods? ³⁵If he called them gods, unto whom the word of God came, and the scripture cannot be broken; ³⁶Say ye of him, whom the Father hath sanctified, and sent into the world, Thou blasphemest; because I said, I am the Son of God? ³⁷If I do not the works of my Father, believe me not. ³⁸But if I do, though ye believe not me, believe the works: that ye may know, and believe, that the Father is in me, and I in him."

John 12:23-30 "²³And Jesus answered them, saying, The hour is come, that the Son of man should be glorified. ²⁴Verily, verily, I say unto you, Except a corn of wheat fall into the ground and die, it abideth alone: but if it die, it bringeth forth much fruit. ²⁵He that loveth his life shall lose it; and he that hateth his life in this world shall keep it unto life eternal. ²⁶If any man serve me, let him follow me; and where I am, there shall also my servant be: if any man serve me, him will my Father honour. ²⁷Now is my soul troubled; and what shall I say? Father, save me from this hour: but for this cause came I unto this hour. ²⁸Father, glorify thy name. Then came there a voice from heaven, saying, I have both glorified it, and will glorify it again. ²⁹The people therefore, that stood by, and heard it, said that it thundered: others said, An angel spake to him. ³⁰Jesus answered and said, This voice came not because of me, but for your sakes."

Acts 2:22 "Ye men of Israel, hear these words; Jesus of Nazareth, a man approved of God among you by miracles and wonders and signs, which God did by him in the midst of you, as ye yourselves also know:"

2 Peter 1:16-18 "¹⁶For we have not followed cunningly devised fables, when we made known unto you the power and coming of our Lord Jesus Christ, but were eyewitnesses of his majesty. ¹⁷For he received from God the Father honour and glory, when there came such a voice to him from the excellent glory, This is my beloved Son, in whom I am well pleased. ¹⁸And this voice which came from heaven we heard, when we were with him in the holy mount."

1 John 5:5-9 "⁵Who is he that overcometh the world, but he that believeth that Jesus is the Son of God? ⁶This is he that came by water and blood, even Jesus Christ; not by water only, but by water and blood. And it is the Spirit that beareth witness, because the Spirit is truth. ⁷For there are three that bear record in heaven, the Father, the Word, and the Holy Ghost: and these three are one. ⁸And there are three that bear witness in earth, the spirit, and the water, and the blood: and these three agree in one. ⁹If we receive the witness of men, the witness of God is greater: for this is the witness of God which he hath testified of his Son."

Jesus Christ Being The Faithful And True Witness

Revelation 1:4-5 "⁴John to the seven churches which are in Asia: Grace be unto you, and peace, from him which is, and which was, and which is to come; and from the seven Spirits which are before his throne; ⁵And from Jesus Christ, who is the faithful witness, and the first begotten of the dead, and the prince of the kings of the earth. Unto him that loved us, and washed us from our sins in his own blood,"

Revelation 3:14 "And unto the angel of the church of the Laodiceans write; These things saith the Amen, the faithful and true witness, the beginning of the creation of God;"

Jesus Christ Coming To Bear Witness To The Truth

John 18:37 "Pilate therefore said unto him, Art thou a king then? Jesus answered, Thou sayest that I am a king. To this end was I born, and for this cause came I into the world, that I should bear witness unto the truth. Every one that is of the truth heareth my voice."

Not Bearing False Witness

Exodus 20:16 "Thou shalt not bear false witness against thy neighbour."

Exodus 23:1 "Thou shalt not raise a false report: put not thine hand with the wicked to be an unrighteous witness."

Exodus 23:7 "Keep thee far from a false matter; and the innocent and righteous slay thou not: for I will not justify the wicked."

Deuteronomy 5:20 "Neither shalt thou bear false witness against thy neighbour."

Proverbs 24:28-29 "²⁸Be not a witness against thy neighbour without cause; and deceive not with thy lips. ²⁹Say not, I will do so to him as he hath done to me: I will render to the man according to his work."

Matthew 19:18 "He saith unto him, Which? Jesus said, Thou shalt do no murder, Thou shalt not commit adultery, Thou shalt not steal, Thou shalt not bear false witness,"

Luke 3:14 "And the soldiers likewise demanded of him, saying, And what shall we do? And he said unto them, Do violence to no man, neither accuse any falsely; and be content with your wages."

Romans 13:8-9 "⁸Owe no man any thing, but to love one another: for he that loveth another hath fulfilled the law. ⁹For this, Thou shalt not commit adultery, Thou shalt not kill, Thou shalt not steal, Thou shalt not bear false witness, Thou shalt not covet; and if there be any other commandment, it is briefly comprehended in this saying, namely, Thou shalt love thy neighbour as thyself."

The Holy Spirit Witnessing

John 15:1-27 "¹I am the true vine, and my Father is the husbandman. ²Every branch in me that beareth not fruit he taketh away: and every branch that beareth fruit, he purgeth it, that it may bring forth more fruit. ³Now ye are clean through the word which I have spoken unto you. ⁴Abide in me, and I in you. As the branch cannot bear fruit of itself, except it abide in the vine; no more can ye, except ye abide in me. ⁵I am the vine, ye are the branches: He that abideth in me, and I in him, the same bringeth forth much fruit: for without me ye can do nothing. ⁶If a man abide not in me, he is cast forth as a branch, and is withered; and men gather them, and cast them into the fire, and they are burned. ⁷If ye abide in me, and my words abide in you, ye shall ask what ye will, and it shall be done unto you. ⁸Herein is my Father glorified, that ye bear much fruit; so shall ye be my disciples. ⁹As the Father hath loved me, so have I loved you: continue ye in my love. ¹⁰If ye keep my commandments, ye shall abide in my love; even as I have kept my Father's commandments, and abide in his love. ¹¹These things have I spoken unto you, that my joy might remain in you, and that your joy might be full. ¹²This is my commandment, That ye love one another, as I have loved you. ¹³Greater love hath no man than this, that a man lay down his life for his friends. ¹⁴Ye are my friends, if ye do whatsoever I command you. ¹⁵Henceforth I call you not servants; for the servant knoweth not what his lord doeth: but I have called you friends; for all things that I have heard of my Father I have made known unto you. ¹⁶Ye have not chosen me, but I have chosen you, and ordained you, that ye should go and bring forth fruit, and that your fruit should remain: that whatsoever ye shall ask of the Father in my name, he may give it you. ¹⁷These things I command you, that ye love one another. ¹⁸If the world hate you, ye know that it hated me before it hated you. ¹⁹If ye were of the world, the world would love his own: but because ye are not of the world, but I have chosen you out of the world, therefore the world hateth you. ²⁰Remember the word that I said unto you, The servant is not greater than his lord. If they have persecuted me, they will also persecute you; if they have kept my saying, they will keep yours also. ²¹But all these things will they do unto you for my name's sake, because they know not him that sent me. ²²If I had not come and spoken unto them, they had not had sin: but now they have no cloke for their sin. ²³He that hateth me hateth my Father also. ²⁴If I had not done among them the works which none other man did, they had not had sin: but now have they both seen and hated both me and my Father. ²⁵But this cometh to pass, that the word might be fulfilled that is written in their law, They hated me without a cause. ²⁶But when the Comforter is come, whom I will send unto you from the Father, even the Spirit of truth, which proceedeth from the Father, he shall testify of me: ²⁷And ye also shall bear witness, because ye have been with me from the beginning."

Acts 5:30-32 "³⁰The God of our fathers raised up Jesus, whom ye slew and hanged on a tree. ³¹Him hath God exalted with his right hand to be a Prince and a Saviour, for to give repentance to Israel, and forgiveness of sins. ³²And we are his witnesses of these things; and so is also the Holy Ghost, whom God hath given to them that obey him."

Acts 20:22-23 "²²And now, behold, I go bound in the spirit unto Jerusalem, not knowing the things that shall befall me there: ²³Save that the Holy Ghost witnesseth in every city, saying that bonds and afflictions abide me."

Romans 8:16 "The Spirit itself beareth witness with our spirit, that we are the children of God:"

Ephesians 3:1-5 "¹For this cause I Paul, the prisoner of Jesus Christ for you Gentiles, ²If ye have heard of the dispensation of the grace of God which is given me to youward: ³How that by revelation he made known unto me the mystery; (as I wrote afore in few words, ⁴Whereby, when ye read, ye may understand my knowledge in the mystery of Christ) ⁵Which in other ages was not made known unto the sons of men, as it is now revealed unto his holy apostles and prophets by the Spirit;"

Hebrews 10:15 "Whereof the Holy Ghost also is a witness to us: for after that he had said before,"

1 John 5:5-7 "⁵Who is he that overcometh the world, but he that believeth that Jesus is the Son of God? ⁶This is he that came by water and blood, even Jesus Christ; not by water only, but by water and blood. And it is the Spirit that beareth witness, because the Spirit is truth. ⁷For there are three that bear record in heaven, the Father, the Word, and the Holy Ghost: and these three are one."

The Necessity Of More Than One Witness For Anything To Be Established

Numbers 35:30 "Whoso killeth any person, the murderer shall be put to death by the mouth of witnesses: but one witness shall not testify against any person to cause him to die."

Deuteronomy 17:6 "At the mouth of two witnesses, or three witnesses, shall he that is worthy of death be put to death; but at the mouth of one witness he shall not be put to death."

Deuteronomy 19:15-21 "¹⁵One witness shall not rise up against a man for any iniquity, or for any sin, in any sin that he sinneth: at the mouth of two witnesses, or at the mouth of three witnesses, shall the matter be established. ¹⁶If a false witness rise up against any man to testify against him that which is wrong; ¹⁷Then both the men, between whom the controversy is, shall stand before the LORD, before the priests and the judges, which shall be in those days; ¹⁸And the judges shall make diligent inquisition: and, behold, if the witness be a false witness, and hath testified falsely against his brother; ¹⁹Then shall ye do unto him, as he had thought to have done unto his brother: so shalt thou put the evil away from among you. ²⁰And those which remain shall hear, and fear, and shall henceforth commit no more any such evil among you. ²¹And thine eye shall not pity; but life shall go for life, eye for eye, tooth for tooth, hand for hand, foot for foot."

Matthew 18:15-16 "¹⁵Moreover if thy brother shall trespass against thee, go and tell him his fault between thee and him alone: if he shall hear thee, thou hast gained thy brother. ¹⁶But if he will not hear thee, then take with thee one or two more, that in the mouth of two or three witnesses every word may be established."

John 8:13-19 "¹³The Pharisees therefore said unto him, Thou bearest record of thyself; thy record is not true. ¹⁴Jesus answered and said unto them, Though I bear record of myself, yet my record is true: for I know whence I came, and whither I go; but ye cannot tell whence I come, and whither I go. ¹⁵Ye judge after the flesh; I judge no man. ¹⁶And yet if I judge, my judgment is true: for I am not alone, but I and the Father that sent me. ¹⁷It is also written in your law, that the testimony of two men is true. ¹⁸I am one that bear witness of myself, and the Father that sent me beareth witness of me. ¹⁹Then said they unto him, Where is thy Father? Jesus answered, Ye neither know me, nor my Father: if ye had known me, ye should have known my Father also."

2 Corinthians 13:1 "This is the third time I am coming to you. In the mouth of two or three witnesses shall every word be established."

Hebrews 10:28 "He that despised Moses' law died without mercy under two or three witnesses:"

The Testimonies Of The Lord

Psalm 19:7 "The law of the LORD is perfect, converting the soul: the testimony of the LORD is sure, making wise the simple."

Psalm 93:1-5 "¹The LORD reigneth, he is clothed with majesty; the LORD is clothed with strength, wherewith he hath girded himself: the world also is stablished, that it cannot be moved. ²Thy throne is established of old: thou art from everlasting. ³The floods have lifted up, O LORD, the floods have lifted up their voice; the floods lift up their waves. ⁴The LORD on high is mightier than the noise of many waters, yea, than the mighty waves of the sea. ⁵Thy testimonies are very sure: holiness becometh thine house, O LORD, for ever."

Psalm 119:126-129 "¹²⁶It is time for thee, LORD, to work: for they have made void thy law. ¹²⁷Therefore I love thy commandments above gold; yea, above fine gold. [128]Therefore I esteem all thy precepts concerning all things to be right; and I hate every false way. [129]Thy testimonies are wonderful: therefore doth my soul keep them."

Psalm 119:137-138 "[137]Righteous art thou, O LORD, and upright are thy judgments. [138]Thy testimonies that thou hast commanded are righteous and very faithful."

1 John 5:7-9 "[7]For there are three that bear record in heaven, the Father, the Word, and the Holy Ghost: and these three are one. [8]And there are three that bear witness in earth, the spirit, and the water, and the blood: and these three agree in one. [9]If we receive the witness of men, the witness of God is greater: for this is the witness of God which he hath testified of his Son."

Revelation 19:10 "And I fell at his feet to worship him. And he said unto me, See thou do it not: I am thy fellowservant, and of thy brethren that have the testimony of Jesus: worship God: for the testimony of Jesus is the spirit of prophecy."

The Two Witnesses
Revelation 11:1-14 "[1]And there was given me a reed like unto a rod: and the angel stood, saying, Rise, and measure the temple of God, and the altar, and them that worship therein. [2]But the court which is without the temple leave out, and measure it not; for it is given unto the Gentiles: and the holy city shall they tread under foot forty and two months. [3]And I will give power unto my two witnesses, and they shall prophesy a thousand two hundred and threescore days, clothed in sackcloth. [4]These are the two olive trees, and the two candlesticks standing before the God of the earth. [5]And if any man will hurt them, fire proceedeth out of their mouth, and devoureth their enemies: and if any man will hurt them, he must in this manner be killed. [6]These have power to shut heaven, that it rain not in the days of their prophecy: and have power over waters to turn them to blood, and to smite the earth with all plagues, as often as they will. [7]And when they shall have finished their testimony, the beast that ascendeth out of the bottomless pit shall make war against them, and shall overcome them, and kill them. [8]And their dead bodies shall lie in the street of the great city, which spiritually is called Sodom and Egypt, where also our Lord was crucified. [9]And they of the people and kindreds and tongues and nations shall see their dead bodies three days and an half, and shall not suffer their dead bodies to be put in graves. [10]And they that dwell upon the earth shall rejoice over them, and make merry, and shall send gifts one to another; because these two prophets tormented them that dwelt on the earth. [11]And after three days and an half the Spirit of life from God entered into them, and they stood upon their feet; and great fear fell upon them which saw them. [12]And they heard a great voice from heaven saying unto them, Come up hither. And they ascended up to heaven in a cloud; and their enemies beheld them. [13]And the same hour was there a great earthquake, and the tenth part of the city fell, and in the earthquake were slain of men seven thousand: and the remnant were affrighted, and gave glory to the God of heaven. [14]The second woe is past; and, behold, the third woe cometh quickly."

There Being Three That Bear Record In Heaven
1 John 5:5-10 "[5]Who is he that overcometh the world, but he that believeth that Jesus is the Son of God? [6]This is he that came by water and blood, even Jesus Christ; not by water only, but by water and blood. And it is the Spirit that beareth witness, because the Spirit is truth. [7]For there are three that bear record in heaven, the Father, the Word, and the Holy Ghost: and these three are one. [8]And there are three that bear witness in earth, the spirit, and the water, and the blood: and these three agree in one. [9]If we receive the witness of men, the witness of God is greater: for this is the witness of God which he hath testified of his Son. [10]He that believeth on the Son of God hath the witness in himself: he that believeth not God hath made him a liar; because he believeth not the record that God gave of his Son."

Ungodly Witnesses
Proverbs 19:28 "An ungodly witness scorneth judgment: and the mouth of the wicked devoureth iniquity."

What Bears Witness Against You
Isaiah 3:9 "The shew of their countenance doth witness against them; and they declare their sin as Sodom, they hide it not. Woe unto their soul! for they have rewarded evil unto themselves."

Romans 2:14-15 "¹⁴For when the Gentiles, which have not the law, do by nature the things contained in the law, these, having not the law, are a law unto themselves: ¹⁵Which shew the work of the law written in their hearts, their conscience also bearing witness, and their thoughts the mean while accusing or else excusing one another;)"

What Testifies Of Jesus Christ

John 5:23-39 "²³That all men should honour the Son, even as they honour the Father. He that honoureth not the Son honoureth not the Father which hath sent him. ²⁴Verily, verily, I say unto you, He that heareth my word, and believeth on him that sent me, hath everlasting life, and shall not come into condemnation; but is passed from death unto life. ²⁵Verily, verily, I say unto you, The hour is coming, and now is, when the dead shall hear the voice of the Son of God: and they that hear shall live. ²⁶For as the Father hath life in himself; so hath he given to the Son to have life in himself; ²⁷And hath given him authority to execute judgment also, because he is the Son of man. ²⁸Marvel not at this: for the hour is coming, in the which all that are in the graves shall hear his voice, ²⁹And shall come forth; they that have done good, unto the resurrection of life; and they that have done evil, unto the resurrection of damnation. ³⁰I can of mine own self do nothing: as I hear, I judge: and my judgment is just; because I seek not mine own will, but the will of the Father which hath sent me. ³¹If I bear witness of myself, my witness is not true. ³²There is another that beareth witness of me; and I know that the witness which he witnesseth of me is true. ³³Ye sent unto John, and he bare witness unto the truth. ³⁴But I receive not testimony from man: but these things I say, that ye might be saved. ³⁵He was a burning and a shining light: and ye were willing for a season to rejoice in his light. ³⁶But I have greater witness than that of John: for the works which the Father hath given me to finish, the same works that I do, bear witness of me, that the Father hath sent me. ³⁷And the Father himself, which hath sent me, hath borne witness of me. Ye have neither heard his voice at any time, nor seen his shape. ³⁸And ye have not his word abiding in you: for whom he hath sent, him ye believe not. ³⁹Search the scriptures; for in them ye think ye have eternal life: and they are they which testify of me."

Who Is A Witness Of The Lord

Isaiah 43:3-12 "³For I am the LORD thy God, the Holy One of Israel, thy Saviour: I gave Egypt for thy ransom, Ethiopia and Seba for thee. ⁴Since thou wast precious in my sight, thou hast been honourable, and I have loved thee: therefore will I give men for thee, and people for thy life. ⁵Fear not: for I am with thee: I will bring thy seed from the east, and gather thee from the west; ⁶I will say to the north, Give up; and to the south, Keep not back: bring my sons from far, and my daughters from the ends of the earth; ⁷Even every one that is called by my name: for I have created him for my glory, I have formed him; yea, I have made him. ⁸Bring forth the blind people that have eyes, and the deaf that have ears. ⁹Let all the nations be gathered together, and let the people be assembled: who among them can declare this, and shew us former things? let them bring forth their witnesses, that they may be justified: or let them hear, and say, It is truth. ¹⁰Ye are my witnesses, saith the LORD, and my servant whom I have chosen: that ye may know and believe me, and understand that I am he: before me there was no God formed, neither shall there be after me. ¹¹I, even I, am the LORD; and beside me there is no saviour. ¹²I have declared, and have saved, and I have shewed, when there was no strange god among you: therefore ye are my witnesses, saith the LORD, that I am God."

Isaiah 44:1-8 "¹Yet now hear, O Jacob my servant; and Israel, whom I have chosen: ²Thus saith the LORD that made thee, and formed thee from the womb, which will help thee; Fear not, O Jacob, my servant; and thou, Jesurun, whom I have chosen. ³For I will pour water upon him that is thirsty, and floods upon the dry ground: I will pour my spirit upon thy seed, and my blessing upon thine offspring: ⁴And they shall spring up as among the grass, as willows by the water courses. ⁵One shall say, I am the LORD's; and another shall call himself by the name of Jacob; and another shall subscribe with his hand unto the LORD, and surname himself by the name of Israel. ⁶Thus saith the LORD the King of Israel, and his redeemer the LORD of hosts; I am the first, and I am the last; and beside me there is no God. ⁷And who, as I, shall call, and shall declare it, and set it in order for me, since I appointed the ancient people? and the things that are coming, and shall come, let them shew unto them. ⁸Fear ye not, neither be afraid: have not I told thee from that time, and have declared it? ye are even my witnesses. Is there a God beside me? yea, there is no God; I know not any."

John 1:6-15 "⁶There was a man sent from God, whose name was John. ⁷The same came for a witness, to bear witness of the Light, that all men through him might believe. ⁸He was not that Light, but was sent to bear witness of that Light. ⁹That was the true Light, which lighteth every man that cometh into the world. ¹⁰He was in the world, and the world was made by him, and the world knew him not. ¹¹He came unto his own, and his own received him not. ¹²But as many as received him, to them gave he power to become the sons of God, even to them that believe on his name: ¹³Which were born, not of blood, nor of the will of the flesh, nor of the will of man, but of God. ¹⁴And the Word was made flesh, and dwelt among us, (and we beheld his glory, the glory as of the only begotten of the Father,) full of grace and truth. ¹⁵John bare witness of him, and cried, saying, This was he of whom I spake, He that cometh after me is preferred before me: for he was before me."

John 5:23-47 "²³That all men should honour the Son, even as they honour the Father. He that honoureth not the Son honoureth not the Father which hath sent him. ²⁴Verily, verily, I say unto you, He that heareth my word, and believeth on him that sent me, hath everlasting life, and shall not come into condemnation; but is passed from death unto life. ²⁵Verily, verily, I say unto you, The hour is coming, and now is, when the dead shall hear the voice of the Son of God: and they that hear shall live. ²⁶For as the Father hath life in himself; so hath he given to the Son to have life in himself; ²⁷And hath given him authority to execute judgment also, because he is the Son of man. ²⁸Marvel not at this: for the hour is coming, in the which all that are in the graves shall hear his voice, ²⁹And shall come forth; they that have done good, unto the resurrection of life; and they that have done evil, unto the resurrection of damnation. ³⁰I

can of mine own self do nothing: as I hear, I judge: and my judgment is just; because I seek not mine own will, but the will of the Father which hath sent me. ³¹If I bear witness of myself, my witness is not true. ³²There is another that beareth witness of me; and I know that the witness which he witnesseth of me is true. ³³Ye sent unto John, and he bare witness unto the truth. ³⁴But I receive not testimony from man: but these things I say, that ye might be saved. ³⁵He was a burning and a shining light: and ye were willing for a season to rejoice in his light. ³⁶But I have greater witness than that of John: for the works which the Father hath given me to finish, the same works that I do, bear witness of me, that the Father hath sent me. ³⁷And the Father himself, which hath sent me, hath borne witness of me. Ye have neither heard his voice at any time, nor seen his shape. ³⁸And ye have not his word abiding in you: for whom he hath sent, him ye believe not. ³⁹Search the scriptures; for in them ye think ye have eternal life: and they are they which testify of me. ⁴⁰And ye will not come to me, that ye might have life. ⁴¹I receive not honour from men. ⁴²But I know you, that ye have not the love of God in you. ⁴³I am come in my Father's name, and ye receive me not: if another shall come in his own name, him ye will receive. ⁴⁴How can ye believe, which receive honour one of another, and seek not the honour that cometh from God only? ⁴⁵Do not think that I will accuse you to the Father: there is one that accuseth you, even Moses, in whom ye trust. ⁴⁶For had ye believed Moses, ye would have believed me: for he wrote of me. ⁴⁷But if ye believe not his writings, how shall ye believe my words?"

Acts 1:6-11 "⁶When they therefore were come together, they asked of him, saying, Lord, wilt thou at this time restore again the kingdom to Israel? ⁷And he said unto them, It is not for you to know the times or the seasons, which the Father hath put in his own power. ⁸But ye shall receive power, after that the Holy Ghost is come upon you: and ye shall be witnesses unto me both in Jerusalem, and in all Judaea, and in Samaria, and unto the uttermost part of the earth. ⁹And when he had spoken these things, while they beheld, he was taken up; and a cloud received him out of their sight. ¹⁰And while they looked stedfastly toward heaven as he went up, behold, two men stood by them in white apparel; ¹¹Which also said, Ye men of Galilee, why stand ye gazing up into heaven? this same Jesus, which is taken up from you into heaven, shall so come in like manner as ye have seen him go into heaven."

Acts 3:11-15 "¹¹And as the lame man which was healed held Peter and John, all the people ran together unto them in the porch that is called Solomon's, greatly wondering. ¹²And when Peter saw it, he answered unto the people, Ye men of Israel, why marvel ye at this? or why look ye so earnestly on us, as though by our own power or holiness we had made this man to walk? ¹³The God of Abraham, and of Isaac, and of Jacob, the God of our fathers, hath glorified his Son Jesus; whom ye delivered up, and denied him in the presence of Pilate, when he was determined to let him go. ¹⁴But ye denied the Holy One and the Just, and desired a murderer to be granted unto you; ¹⁵And killed the Prince of life, whom God hath raised from the dead; whereof we are witnesses."

Acts 5:29-32 "²⁹Then Peter and the other apostles answered and said, We ought to obey God rather than men. ³⁰The God of our fathers raised up Jesus, whom ye slew and hanged on a tree. ³¹Him hath God exalted with his right hand to be a Prince and a Saviour, for to give repentance to Israel, and forgiveness of sins. ³²And we are his witnesses of these things; and so is also the Holy Ghost, whom God hath given to them that obey him."

Acts 10:37-43 "³⁷That word, I say, ye know, which was published throughout all Judaea, and began from Galilee, after the baptism which John preached; ³⁸How God anointed Jesus of Nazareth with the Holy Ghost and with power: who went about doing good, and healing all that were oppressed of the devil; for God was with him. ³⁹And we are witnesses of all things which he did both in the land of the Jews, and in Jerusalem; whom they slew and hanged on a tree: ⁴⁰Him God raised up the third day, and shewed him openly; ⁴¹Not to all the people, but unto witnesses chosen before of God, even to us, who did eat and drink with him after he rose from the dead. ⁴²And he commanded us to preach unto the people, and

to testify that it is he which was ordained of God to be the Judge of quick and dead. ⁴³To him give all the prophets witness, that through his name whosoever believeth in him shall receive remission of sins."

2 Peter 1:1-16 "¹Simon Peter, a servant and an apostle of Jesus Christ, to them that have obtained like precious faith with us through the righteousness of God and our Saviour Jesus Christ: ²Grace and peace be multiplied unto you through the knowledge of God, and of Jesus our Lord, ³According as his divine power hath given unto us all things that pertain unto life and godliness, through the knowledge of him that hath called us to glory and virtue: ⁴Whereby are given unto us exceeding great and precious promises: that by these ye might be partakers of the divine nature, having escaped the corruption that is in the world through lust. ⁵And beside this, giving all diligence, add to your faith virtue; and to virtue knowledge; ⁶And to knowledge temperance; and to temperance patience; and to patience godliness; ⁷And to godliness brotherly kindness; and to brotherly kindness charity. ⁸For if these things be in you, and abound, they make you that ye shall neither be barren nor unfruitful in the knowledge of our Lord Jesus Christ. ⁹But he that lacketh these things is blind, and cannot see afar off, and hath forgotten that he was purged from his old sins. ¹⁰Wherefore the rather, brethren, give diligence to make your calling and election sure: for if ye do these things, ye shall never fall: ¹¹For so an entrance shall be ministered unto you abundantly into the everlasting kingdom of our Lord and Saviour Jesus Christ. ¹²Wherefore I will not be negligent to put you always in remembrance of these things, though ye know them, and be established in the present truth. ¹³Yea, I think it meet, as long as I am in this tabernacle, to stir you up by putting you in remembrance; ¹⁴Knowing that shortly I must put off this my tabernacle, even as our Lord Jesus Christ hath shewed me. ¹⁵Moreover I will endeavour that ye may be able after my decease to have these things always in remembrance. ¹⁶For we have not followed cunningly devised fables, when we made known unto you the power and coming of our Lord Jesus Christ, but were eyewitnesses of his majesty."

1 John 1:1-3 "[1]That which was from the beginning, which we have heard, which we have seen with our eyes, which we have looked upon, and our hands have handled, of the Word of life; [2](For the life was manifested, and we have seen it, and bear witness, and shew unto you that eternal life, which was with the Father, and was manifested unto us;) [3]That which we have seen and heard declare we unto you, that ye also may have fellowship with us: and truly our fellowship is with the Father, and with his Son Jesus Christ."

Revelation 1:1-2 "[1]The Revelation of Jesus Christ, which God gave unto him, to shew unto his servants things which must shortly come to pass; and he sent and signified it by his angel unto his servant John: [2]Who bare record of the word of God, and of the testimony of Jesus Christ, and of all things that he saw."

WOMEN

Contentious Women

Proverbs 19:13 "A foolish son is the calamity of his father: and the contentions of a wife are a continual dropping."

Proverbs 27:15-16 "[15]A continual dropping in a very rainy day and a contentious woman are alike. [16]Whosoever hideth her hideth the wind, and the ointment of his right hand, which bewrayeth itself."

Dwelling With A Contentious Woman

Proverbs 21:9 "It is better to dwell in a corner of the housetop, than with a brawling woman in a wide house."

Proverbs 21:19 "It is better to dwell in the wilderness, than with a contentious and an angry woman."

Proverbs 25:24 "It is better to dwell in the corner of the housetop, than with a brawling woman and in a wide house."

Foolish Women

Proverbs 14:1 "Every wise woman buildeth her house: but the foolish plucketh it down with her hands."

Gracious Women

Proverbs 11:16 "A gracious woman retaineth honour: and strong men retain riches."

The Curse On Women

Genesis 3:16 "Unto the woman he said, I will greatly multiply thy sorrow and thy conception; in sorrow thou shalt bring forth children; and thy desire shall be to thy husband, and he shall rule over thee."

Virtuous Women

Proverbs 12:4 "A virtuous woman is a crown to her husband: but she that maketh ashamed is as rottenness in his bones."

Proverbs 31:10-31 "[10]Who can find a virtuous woman? for her price is far above rubies. [11]The heart of her husband doth safely trust in her, so that he shall have no need of spoil. [12]She will do him good and not evil all the days of her life. [13]She seeketh wool, and flax, and worketh willingly with her hands. [14]She is like the merchants' ships; she bringeth her food from afar. [15]She riseth also while it is yet night, and giveth meat to her household, and a portion to her maidens. [16]She considereth a field, and buyeth it: with the fruit of her hands she planteth a vineyard. [17]She girdeth her loins with strength, and strengtheneth her arms. [18]She perceiveth that her merchandise is good: her candle goeth not out by night. [19]She layeth her hands to the spindle, and her hands hold the distaff. [20]She stretcheth out her hand to the poor; yea, she reacheth forth her hands to the needy. [21]She is not afraid of the snow for her household: for all her household are clothed with scarlet. [22]She maketh herself coverings of tapestry; her clothing is silk and purple. [23]Her husband is known in the gates, when he sitteth among the elders of the land. [24]She maketh fine linen, and selleth it; and delivereth girdles unto the merchant. [25]Strength and honour are her clothing; and she shall rejoice in time to come. [26]She openeth her mouth with wisdom; and in her tongue is the law of kindness. [27]She looketh well to the ways of her household, and eateth not the bread of idleness. [28]Her children arise up, and call her blessed; her husband also, and he praiseth her. [29]Many daughters have done virtuously, but thou excellest them all. [30]Favour is deceitful, and beauty is vain: but a woman that feareth the LORD, she shall be praised. [31]Give her of the fruit of her hands; and let her own works praise her in the gates."

What Women Should Do

1 Corinthians 11:2-16 "²Now I praise you, brethren, that ye remember me in all things, and keep the ordinances, as I delivered them to you. ³But I would have you know, that the head of every man is Christ; and the head of the woman is the man; and the head of Christ is God. ⁴Every man praying or prophesying, having his head covered, dishonoureth his head. ⁵But every woman that prayeth or prophesieth with her head uncovered dishonoureth her head: for that is even all one as if she were shaven. ⁶For if the woman be not covered, let her also be shorn: but if it be a shame for a woman to be shorn or shaven, let her be covered. ⁷For a man indeed ought not to cover his head, forasmuch as he is the image and glory of God: but the woman is the glory of the man. ⁸For the man is not of the woman; but the woman of the man. ⁹Neither was the man created for the woman; but the woman for the man. ¹⁰For this cause ought the woman to have power on her head because of the angels. ¹¹Nevertheless neither is the man without the woman, neither the woman without the man, in the Lord. ¹²For as the woman is of the man, even so is the man also by the woman; but all things of God. ¹³Judge in yourselves: is it comely that a woman pray unto God uncovered? ¹⁴Doth not even nature itself teach you, that, if a man have long hair, it is a shame unto him? ¹⁵But if a woman have long hair, it is a glory to her: for her hair is given her for a covering. ¹⁶But if any man seem to be contentious, we have no such custom, neither the churches of God."

1 Timothy 2:8-11 "⁸I will therefore that men pray every where, lifting up holy hands, without wrath and doubting. ⁹In like manner also, that women adorn themselves in modest apparel, with shamefacedness and sobriety; not with broided hair, or gold, or pearls, or costly array; ¹⁰But (which becometh women professing godliness) with good works. ¹¹Let the woman learn in silence with all subjection."

What Women Should Not Do

Deuteronomy 22:5 "The woman shall not wear that which pertaineth unto a man, neither shall a man put on a woman's garment: for all that do so are abomination unto the LORD thy God."

1 Corinthians 14:34-35 "³⁴Let your women keep silence in the churches: for it is not permitted unto them to speak; but they are commanded to be under obedience, as also saith the law. ³⁵And if they will learn any thing, let them ask their husbands at home: for it is a shame for women to speak in the church."

1 Timothy 2:12 "But I suffer not a woman to teach, nor to usurp authority over the man, but to be in silence."

Where Women Originate From

Genesis 2:23 "And Adam said, This is now bone of my bones, and flesh of my flesh: she shall be called Woman, because she was taken out of Man."

1 Corinthians 11:8 "For the man is not of the woman; but the woman of the man."

1 Corinthians 11:11-12 "¹¹Nevertheless neither is the man without the woman, neither the woman without the man, in the Lord. ¹²For as the woman is of the man, even so is the man also by the woman; but all things of God."

Women Being Equal To Men In Christ

Galatians 3:27-29 "²⁷For as many of you as have been baptized into Christ have put on Christ. ²⁸There is neither Jew nor Greek, there is neither bond nor free, there is neither male nor female: for ye are all one in Christ Jesus. ²⁹And if ye be Christ's, then are ye Abraham's seed, and heirs according to the promise."

Women That Cause Shame

Proverbs 12:4 "A virtuous woman is a crown to her husband: but she that maketh ashamed is as rottenness in his bones."

Women That Fear The Lord

Proverbs 31:30 "Favour is deceitful, and beauty is vain: but a woman that feareth the LORD, she shall be praised."

Who Is The Head Of A Woman

Genesis 3:16 "Unto the woman he said, I will greatly multiply thy sorrow and thy conception; in sorrow thou shalt bring forth children; and thy desire shall be to thy husband, and he shall rule over thee."

1 Corinthians 11:2-3 "²Now I praise you, brethren, that ye remember me in all things, and keep the ordinances, as I delivered them to you. ³But I would have you know, that the head of every man is Christ; and the head of the woman is the man; and the head of Christ is God."

Ephesians 5:22-23 "²²Wives, submit yourselves unto your own husbands, as unto the Lord. ²³For the husband is the head of the wife, even as Christ is the head of the church: and he is the saviour of the body."

Why Women Should Not Have Authority Over Men

Genesis 3:1-16 "¹Now the serpent was more subtil than any beast of the field which the LORD God had made. And he said unto the woman, Yea, hath God said, Ye shall not eat of every tree of the garden? ²And the woman said unto the serpent, We may eat of the fruit of the trees of the garden: ³But of the fruit of the tree which is in the midst of the garden, God hath said, Ye shall not eat of it, neither shall ye touch it, lest ye die. ⁴And the serpent said unto the woman, Ye shall not surely die: ⁵For God doth know that in the day ye eat thereof, then your eyes shall be opened, and ye shall be as gods, knowing good and evil. ⁶And when the woman saw that the tree was good for food, and that it was pleasant to the eyes, and a tree to be desired to make one wise, she took of the fruit thereof, and did eat, and gave also unto her husband with her; and he did eat. ⁷And the eyes of them both were opened, and they knew that they were naked; and they sewed fig leaves together, and made themselves aprons. ⁸And they heard the voice of the LORD God walking in the garden in the cool of the day: and Adam and his wife hid themselves from the presence of the LORD God amongst the trees of the garden. ⁹And the LORD God called unto Adam, and said unto him, Where art thou? ¹⁰And he said, I heard thy voice in the garden, and I was afraid, because I was naked; and I hid myself. ¹¹And he said, Who told thee that thou wast naked? Hast thou eaten of the tree, whereof I commanded thee that thou shouldest not eat? ¹²And the man said, The woman whom thou gavest to be with me, she gave me of the tree, and I did eat. ¹³And the LORD God said unto the woman, What is this that thou hast done? And the woman said, The serpent beguiled me, and I did eat. ¹⁴And the LORD God said unto the serpent, Because thou

hast done this, thou art cursed above all cattle, and above every beast of the field; upon thy belly shalt thou go, and dust shalt thou eat all the days of thy life: ¹⁵And I will put enmity between thee and the woman, and between thy seed and her seed; it shall bruise thy head, and thou shalt bruise his heel. ¹⁶Unto the woman he said, I will greatly multiply thy sorrow and thy conception; in sorrow thou shalt bring forth children; and thy desire shall be to thy husband, and he shall rule over thee."

1 Timothy 2:12-15 "¹²But I suffer not a woman to teach, nor to usurp authority over the man, but to be in silence. ¹³For Adam was first formed, then Eve. ¹⁴And Adam was not deceived, but the woman being deceived was in the transgression. ¹⁵Notwithstanding she shall be saved in childbearing, if they continue in faith and charity and holiness with sobriety."

Wise Women

Proverbs 14:1 "Every wise woman buildeth her house: but the foolish plucketh it down with her hands."

Women Needing Men

1 Corinthians 11:11-12 "¹¹Nevertheless neither is the man without the woman, neither the woman without the man, in the Lord. ¹²For as the woman is of the man, even so is the man also by the woman; but all things of God."

WORD OF GOD

Jesus Christ Being The Word Of God

John 1:1-18 "¹In the beginning was the Word, and the Word was with God, and the Word was God. ²The same was in the beginning with God. ³All things were made by him; and without him was not any thing made that was made. ⁴In him was life; and the life was the light of men. ⁵And the light shineth in darkness; and the darkness comprehended it not. ⁶There was a man sent from God, whose name was John. ⁷The same came for a witness, to bear witness of the Light, that all men through him might believe. ⁸He was not that Light, but was sent to bear witness of that Light. ⁹That was the true Light, which lighteth every man that cometh into the world. ¹⁰He was in the world, and the world was made by him, and the world knew him not. [11]He came unto his own, and his own received him not. [12]But as many as received him, to them gave he power to become the sons of God, even to them that believe on his name: [13]Which were born, not of blood, nor of the will of the flesh, nor of the will of man, but of God. [14]And the Word was made flesh, and dwelt among us, (and we beheld his glory, the glory as of the only begotten of the Father,) full of grace and truth. [15]John bare witness of him, and cried, saying, This was he of whom I spake, He that cometh after me is preferred before me: for he was before me. [16]And of his fulness have all we received, and grace for grace. [17]For the law was given by Moses, but grace and truth came by Jesus Christ. [18]No man hath seen God at any time; the only begotten Son, which is in the bosom of the Father, he hath declared him."

1 John 1:1-3 "[1]That which was from the beginning, which we have heard, which we have seen with our eyes, which we have looked upon, and our hands have handled, of the Word of life; [2](For the life was manifested, and we have seen it, and bear witness, and shew unto you that eternal life, which was with the Father, and was manifested unto us;) [3]That which we have seen and heard declare we unto you, that ye also may have fellowship with us: and truly our fellowship is with the Father, and with his Son Jesus Christ."

Revelation 19:11-15 "[11]And I saw heaven opened, and behold a white horse; and he that sat upon him was called Faithful and True, and in righteousness he doth judge and make war. [12]His eyes were as a flame of fire, and on his head were many crowns; and he had a name written, that no man knew, but he himself. [13]And he was clothed with a vesture dipped in blood: and his name is called The Word of God. [14]And the armies which were in heaven followed him upon white horses, clothed in fine linen, white and clean. [15]And out of his mouth goeth a sharp sword, that with it he should smite the nations: and he shall rule them with a rod of iron: and he treadeth the winepress of the fierceness and wrath of Almighty God."

Letting The Word Of God Dwell Within You
Colossians 3:16 "Let the word of Christ dwell in you richly in all wisdom; teaching and admonishing one another in psalms and hymns and spiritual songs, singing with grace in your hearts to the Lord."

Man Living By The Word Of God
Deuteronomy 8:3 "And he humbled thee, and suffered thee to hunger, and fed thee with manna, which thou knewest not, neither did thy fathers know; that he might make thee know that man doth not live by bread only, but by every word that proceedeth out of the mouth of the LORD doth man live."

Matthew 4:4 "But he answered and said, It is written, Man shall not live by bread alone, but by every word that proceedeth out of the mouth of God."

Luke 4:4 "And Jesus answered him, saying, It is written, That man shall not live by bread alone, but by every word of God."

Not Adding To Or Diminishing From The Word Of God
Deuteronomy 4:2 "Ye shall not add unto the word which I command you, neither shall ye diminish ought from it, that ye may keep the commandments of the LORD your God which I command you."

Deuteronomy 12:31-32 "[31]Thou shalt not do so unto the LORD thy God: for every abomination to the LORD, which he hateth, have they done unto their gods; for even their sons and their daughters they have burnt in the fire to their gods. [32]What thing soever I command you, observe to do it: thou shalt not add thereto, nor diminish from it."

Proverbs 30:5-6 "[5]Every word of God is pure: he is a shield unto them that put their trust in him. [6]Add thou not unto his words, lest he reprove thee, and thou be found a liar."

The Reward For Despising The Word Of God
Numbers 15:30-31 "[30]But the soul that doeth ought presumptuously, whether he be born in the land, or a stranger, the same reproacheth the LORD; and that soul shall be cut off from among his people. [31]Because he hath despised the word of the LORD, and hath broken his commandment, that soul shall utterly be cut off; his iniquity shall be upon him."

2 Chronicles 36:16 "But they mocked the messengers of God, and despised his words, and misused his prophets, until the wrath of the LORD arose against his people, till there was no remedy."

Isaiah 5:24 "Therefore as the fire devoureth the stubble, and the flame consumeth the chaff, so their root shall be as rottenness, and their blossom shall go up as dust: because they have cast away the law of the LORD of hosts, and despised the word of the Holy One of Israel."

Isaiah 30:8-17 "⁸Now go, write it before them in a table, and note it in a book, that it may be for the time to come for ever and ever: ⁹That this is a rebellious people, lying children, children that will not hear the law of the LORD: ¹⁰Which say to the seers, See not; and to the prophets, Prophesy not unto us right things, speak unto us smooth things, prophesy deceits: ¹¹Get you out of the way, turn aside out of the path, cause the Holy One of Israel to cease from before us. ¹²Wherefore thus saith the Holy One of Israel, Because ye despise this word, and trust in oppression and perverseness, and stay thereon: ¹³Therefore this iniquity shall be to you as a breach ready to fall, swelling out in a high wall, whose breaking cometh suddenly at an instant. ¹⁴And he shall break it as the breaking of the potters' vessel that is broken in pieces; he shall not spare: so that there shall not be found in the bursting of it a sherd to take fire from the hearth, or to take water withal out of the pit. ¹⁵For thus saith the Lord GOD, the Holy One of Israel; In returning and rest shall ye be saved; in quietness and in confidence shall be your strength: and ye would not. ¹⁶But ye said, No; for we will flee upon horses; therefore shall ye flee: and, We will ride upon the swift; therefore shall they that pursue you be swift. ¹⁷One thousand shall flee at the rebuke of one; at the rebuke of five shall ye flee: till ye be left as a beacon upon the top of a mountain, and as an ensign on an hill."

Amos 2:4-5 "⁴Thus saith the LORD; For three transgressions of Judah, and for four, I will not turn away the punishment thereof; because they have despised the law of the LORD, and have not kept his commandments, and their lies caused them to err, after the which their fathers have walked: ⁵But I will send a fire upon Judah, and it shall devour the palaces of Jerusalem."

The Sowing Of God's Word

Matthew 13:3-9 "³And he spake many things unto them in parables, saying, Behold, a sower went forth to sow; ⁴And when he sowed, some seeds fell by the way side, and the fowls came and devoured them up: ⁵Some fell upon stony places, where they had not much earth: and forthwith they sprung up, because they had no deepness of earth: ⁶And when

the sun was up, they were scorched; and because they had no root, they withered away. ⁷And some fell among thorns; and the thorns sprung up, and choked them: ⁸But other fell into good ground, and brought forth fruit, some an hundredfold, some sixtyfold, some thirtyfold. ⁹Who hath ears to hear, let him hear."

Matthew 13:18-23 "¹⁸Hear ye therefore the parable of the sower. ¹⁹When any one heareth the word of the kingdom, and understandeth it not, then cometh the wicked one, and catcheth away that which was sown in his heart. This is he which received seed by the way side. ²⁰But he that received the seed into stony places, the same is he that heareth the word, and anon with joy receiveth it; ²¹Yet hath he not root in himself, but dureth for a while: for when tribulation or persecution ariseth because of the word, by and by he is offended. ²²He also that received seed among the thorns is he that heareth the word; and the care of this world, and the deceitfulness of riches, choke the word, and he becometh unfruitful. ²³But he that received seed into the good ground is he that heareth the word, and understandeth it; which also beareth fruit, and bringeth forth, some an hundredfold, some sixty, some thirty."

Mark 4:1-20 "¹And he began again to teach by the sea side: and there was gathered unto him a great multitude, so that he entered into a ship, and sat in the sea; and the whole multitude was by the sea on the land. ²And he taught them many things by parables, and said unto them in his doctrine, ³Hearken; Behold, there went out a sower to sow: ⁴And it came to pass, as he sowed, some fell by the way side, and the fowls of the air came and devoured it up. ⁵And some fell on stony ground, where it had not much earth; and immediately it sprang up, because it had no depth of earth: ⁶But when the sun was up, it was scorched; and because it had no root, it withered away. ⁷And some fell among thorns, and the thorns grew up, and choked it, and it yielded no fruit. ⁸And other fell on good ground, and did yield fruit that sprang up and increased; and brought forth, some thirty, and some sixty, and some an hundred. ⁹And he said unto them, He that hath ears to hear, let him hear. ¹⁰And when he was alone, they that were about him with the twelve asked of him the parable. ¹¹And he said unto them, Unto you it is given to know the mystery of the kingdom of God: but unto them that are without, all these things are done in parables: [12]That seeing they may see, and not perceive; and hearing they may hear, and not understand; lest at any time they should be converted, and their sins should be forgiven them. [13]And he said unto them, Know ye not this parable? and how then will ye know all parables? [14]The sower soweth the word. [15]And these are they by the way side, where the word is sown; but when they have heard, Satan cometh immediately, and taketh away the word that was sown in their hearts. [16]And these are they likewise which are sown on stony ground; who, when they have heard the word, immediately receive it with gladness; [17]And have no root in themselves, and so endure but for a time: afterward, when affliction or persecution ariseth for the word's sake, immediately they are offended. [18]And these are they which are sown among thorns; such as hear the word, [19]And the cares of this world, and the deceitfulness of riches, and the lusts of other things entering in, choke the word, and it becometh unfruitful. [20]And these are they which are sown on good ground; such as hear the word, and receive it, and bring forth fruit, some thirtyfold, some sixty, and some an hundred."

Luke 8:4-15 "[4]And when much people were gathered together, and were come to him out of every city, he spake by a parable: [5]A sower went out to sow his seed: and as he sowed, some fell by the way side; and it was trodden down, and the fowls of the air devoured it. [6]And some fell upon a rock; and as soon as it was sprung up, it withered away, because it lacked moisture. [7]And some fell among thorns; and the thorns sprang up with it, and choked it. [8]And other fell on good ground, and sprang up, and bare fruit an hundredfold. And when he had said these things, he cried, He that hath ears to hear, let him hear. [9]And his disciples asked him, saying, What might this parable be? [10]And he said, Unto you it is given to know the mysteries of the kingdom of God: but to others in parables; that seeing they might not see, and hearing they might not understand. [11]Now the parable is this: The seed is the word of God. [12]Those by the way side are they that hear; then cometh the devil, and taketh away the word out of their hearts, lest they should believe and be saved. [13]They on the rock are they, which, when they hear, receive the word with joy; and these have no root, which for a while believe, and in time of temptation fall away. [14]And that which fell among thorns are they, which, when they have heard, go forth, and are choked with cares and riches and pleasures of this life, and bring no fruit to perfection. [15]But that on the good ground are they, which in an honest and good heart, having heard the word, keep it, and bring forth fruit with patience."

The Time When There Is A Word Of God Famine
Amos 8:11-14 "[11]Behold, the days come, saith the Lord GOD, that I will send a famine in the land, not a famine of bread, nor a thirst for water, but of hearing the words of the LORD: [12]And they shall wander from sea to sea, and from the north even to the east, they shall run to and fro to seek the word of the LORD, and shall not find it. [13]In that day shall the fair virgins and young men faint for thirst. [14]They that swear by the sin of Samaria, and say, Thy god, O Dan, liveth; and, The manner of Beersheba liveth; even they shall fall, and never rise up again."

The Word Of God Enduring Forever
Isaiah 40:8 "The grass withereth, the flower fadeth: but the word of our God shall stand for ever."

Matthew 24:35 "Heaven and earth shall pass away, but my words shall not pass away."

Mark 13:31 "Heaven and earth shall pass away: but my words shall not pass away."

Luke 21:33 "Heaven and earth shall pass away: but my words shall not pass away."

1 Peter 1:22-23 "[22]Seeing ye have purified your souls in obeying the truth through the Spirit unto unfeigned love of the brethren, see that ye love one another with a pure heart fervently: [23]Being born again, not of corruptible seed, but of incorruptible, by the word of God, which liveth and abideth for ever."

1 Peter 1:25 "But the word of the Lord endureth for ever. And this is the word which by the gospel is preached unto you."

Those That Despise The Word Of God
Proverbs 13:13 "Whoso despiseth the word shall be destroyed: but he that feareth the commandment shall be rewarded."

What Comes By The Word Of God
Romans 10:17 "So then faith cometh by hearing, and hearing by the word of God."

What Is The Word Of God

Ephesians 6:17 "And take the helmet of salvation, and the sword of the Spirit, which is the word of God:"

What The Word Of God Does

Acts 20:32 "And now, brethren, I commend you to God, and to the word of his grace, which is able to build you up, and to give you an inheritance among all them which are sanctified."

What The Word Of God Is

2 Samuel 22:31 "As for God, his way is perfect; the word of the LORD is tried: he is a buckler to all them that trust in him."

Psalm 12:6 "The words of the LORD are pure words: as silver tried in a furnace of earth, purified seven times."

Psalm 18:30 "As for God, his way is perfect: the word of the LORD is tried: he is a buckler to all those that trust in him."

Psalm 33:4 "For the word of the LORD is right; and all his works are done in truth."

Psalm 119:89-103 "[89]For ever, O LORD, thy word is settled in heaven. [90]Thy faithfulness is unto all generations: thou hast established the earth, and it abideth. [91]They continue this day according to thine ordinances: for all are thy servants. [92]Unless thy law had been my delights, I should then have perished in mine affliction. [93]I will never forget thy precepts: for with them thou hast quickened me. [94]I am thine, save me; for I have sought thy precepts. [95]The wicked have waited for me to destroy me: but I will consider thy testimonies. [96]I have seen an end of all perfection: but thy commandment is exceeding broad. [97]O how love I thy law! it is my meditation all the day. [98]Thou through thy commandments hast made me wiser than mine enemies: for they are ever with me. [99]I have more understanding than all my teachers: for thy testimonies are my meditation. [100]I understand more than the ancients, because I keep thy precepts. [101]I have refrained my feet from every evil way, that I might keep thy word. [102]I have not departed from thy judgments: for thou hast taught me. [103]How sweet are thy words unto my taste! yea, sweeter than honey to my mouth!"

Psalm 119:137-140 "[137]Righteous art thou, O LORD, and upright are thy judgments. [138]Thy testimonies that thou hast commanded are righteous and very faithful. [139]My zeal hath consumed me, because mine enemies have forgotten thy words. [140]Thy word is very pure: therefore thy servant loveth it."

Psalm 119:159-160 "[159]Consider how I love thy precepts: quicken me, O LORD, according to thy lovingkindness. [160]Thy word is true from the beginning: and every one of thy righteous judgments endureth for ever."

Proverbs 30:5-6 "[5]Every word of God is pure: he is a shield unto them that put their trust in him. [6]Add thou not unto his words, lest he reprove thee, and thou be found a liar."

Isaiah 39:8 "Then said Hezekiah to Isaiah, Good is the word of the LORD which thou hast spoken. He said moreover, For there shall be peace and truth in my days."

Jeremiah 23:29 "Is not my word like as a fire? saith the LORD; and like a hammer that breaketh the rock in pieces?"

John 6:63-64 "[63]It is the spirit that quickeneth; the flesh profiteth nothing: the words that I speak unto you, they are spirit, and they are life. [64]But there are some of you that believe not. For Jesus knew from the beginning who they were that believed not, and who should betray him."

John 17:1-17 "[1]These words spake Jesus, and lifted up his eyes to heaven, and said, Father, the hour is come; glorify thy Son, that thy Son also may glorify thee: [2]As thou hast given him power over all flesh, that he should give eternal life to as many as thou hast given him. [3]And this is life eternal, that they might know thee the only true God, and Jesus Christ, whom thou hast sent. [4]I have glorified thee on the earth: I have finished the work which thou gavest me to do. [5]And now, O Father, glorify thou me with thine own self with the glory which I had with thee before the world was. [6]I have manifested thy name unto the men which thou gavest me out of the world: thine they were, and thou gavest them me; and they have kept thy word. [7]Now they have known that all things whatsoever thou hast given me are of thee. [8]For I have given unto them the words which thou gavest me; and they have received them, and have known surely that I came out from thee, and they have believed that thou didst send me. ⁹I pray for them: I pray not for the world, but for them which thou hast given me; for they are thine. ¹⁰And all mine are thine, and thine are mine; and I am glorified in them. ¹¹And now I am no more in the world, but these are in the world, and I come to thee. Holy Father, keep through thine own name those whom thou hast given me, that they may be one, as we are. ¹²While I was with them in the world, I kept them in thy name: those that thou gavest me I have kept, and none of them is lost, but the son of perdition; that the scripture might be fulfilled. ¹³And now come I to thee; and these things I speak in the world, that they might have my joy fulfilled in themselves. ¹⁴I have given them thy word; and the world hath hated them, because they are not of the world, even as I am not of the world. ¹⁵I pray not that thou shouldest take them out of the world, but that thou shouldest keep them from the evil. ¹⁶They are not of the world, even as I am not of the world. ¹⁷Sanctify them through thy truth: thy word is truth."

1 Thessalonians 2:13 "For this cause also thank we God without ceasing, because, when ye received the word of God which ye heard of us, ye received it not as the word of men, but as it is in truth, the word of God, which effectually worketh also in you that believe."

Hebrews 4:12 "For the word of God is quick, and powerful, and sharper than any twoedged sword, piercing even to the dividing asunder of soul and spirit, and of the joints and marrow, and is a discerner of the thoughts and intents of the heart."

Where The Word Of God Shall Go Forth From
Isaiah 2:1-3 "¹the word that Isaiah the son of Amoz saw concerning Judah and Jerusalem. ²And it shall come to pass in the last days, that the mountain of the LORD's house shall be established in the top of the mountains, and shall be exalted above the hills; and all nations shall flow unto it. ³And many people shall go and say, Come ye, and let us go up to the mountain of the LORD, to the house of the God of Jacob; and he will teach us of his ways, and we will walk in his paths: for out of Zion shall go forth the law, and the word of the LORD from Jerusalem."

Micah 4:1-2 "¹But in the last days it shall come to pass, that the mountain of the house of the LORD shall be established in the top of the mountains, and it shall be exalted above the hills; and people shall flow unto it. ²And many nations shall come, and say, Come, and let us go up to the mountain of the LORD, and to the house of the God of Jacob; and he will teach us of his ways, and we will walk in his paths: for the law shall go forth of Zion, and the word of the LORD from Jerusalem."

Who Does Not Have
The Word Of God In Them
1 John 1:7-10 "⁷But if we walk in the light, as he is in the light, we have fellowship one with another, and the blood of Jesus Christ his Son cleanseth us from all sin. ⁸If we say that we have no sin, we deceive ourselves, and the truth is not in us. ⁹If we confess our sins, he is faithful and just to forgive us our sins, and to cleanse us from all unrighteousness. ¹⁰If we say that we have not sinned, we make him a liar, and his word is not in us."

Who Jesus Christ Gives The Word Of God To
John 17:1-14 "¹These words spake Jesus, and lifted up his eyes to heaven, and said, Father, the hour is come; glorify thy Son, that thy Son also may glorify thee: ²As thou hast given him power over all flesh, that he should give eternal life to as many as thou hast given him. ³And this is life eternal, that they might know thee the only true God, and Jesus Christ, whom thou hast sent. ⁴I have glorified thee on the earth: I have finished the work which thou gavest me to do. ⁵And now, O Father, glorify thou me with thine own self with the glory which I had with thee before the world was. ⁶I have manifested thy name unto the men which thou gavest me out of the world: thine they were, and thou gavest them me; and they have kept thy word. ⁷Now they have known that all things whatsoever thou hast given me are of thee. ⁸For I have given unto them the words which thou gavest me; and they have received them, and have known surely that I came out from thee, and they have believed that thou didst send me. ⁹I pray for them: I pray not for the world, but for them which thou hast given me; for they are thine. ¹⁰And all mine are thine, and thine are mine; and I am glorified in them. ¹¹And now I am no more in the world, but these are in the world, and I come to thee. Holy Father, keep through thine own name those whom thou hast given me, that

they may be one, as we are. [12]While I was with them in the world, I kept them in thy name: those that thou gavest me I have kept, and none of them is lost, but the son of perdition; that the scripture might be fulfilled. [13]And now come I to thee; and these things I speak in the world, that they might have my joy fulfilled in themselves. [14]I have given them thy word; and the world hath hated them, because they are not of the world, even as I am not of the world."

Who The Word Of God Works In

1 Thessalonians 2:13 "For this cause also thank we God without ceasing, because, when ye received the word of God which ye heard of us, ye received it not as the word of men, but as it is in truth, the word of God, which effectually worketh also in you that believe."

WORLD

The Lord Creating The World

Psalm 89:8-11 "[8]O LORD God of hosts, who is a strong LORD like unto thee? or to thy faithfulness round about thee? [9]Thou rulest the raging of the sea: when the waves thereof arise, thou stillest them. [10]Thou hast broken Rahab in pieces, as one that is slain; thou hast scattered thine enemies with thy strong arm. [11]The heavens are thine, the earth also is thine: as for the world and the fulness thereof, thou hast founded them."

Psalm 90:2 "Before the mountains were brought forth, or ever thou hadst formed the earth and the world, even from everlasting to everlasting, thou art God."

Jeremiah 10:10-12 "[10]But the LORD is the true God, he is the living God, and an everlasting king: at his wrath the earth shall tremble, and the nations shall not be able to abide his indignation. [11]Thus shall ye say unto them, The gods that have not made the heavens and the earth, even they shall perish from the earth, and from under these heavens. [12]He hath made the earth by his power, he hath established the world by his wisdom, and hath stretched out the heavens by his discretion."

John 1:1-10 "[1]In the beginning was the Word, and the Word was with God, and the Word was God. [2]The same was in the beginning with God. [3]All things were made by him; and without him was not any thing made that was made. [4]In him was life; and the life was the light of men. [5]And the light shineth in darkness; and the darkness comprehended it not. [6]There was a man sent from God, whose name was John. [7]The same came for a witness, to bear witness of the Light, that all men through him might believe. [8]He was not that Light, but was sent to bear witness of that Light. [9]That was the true Light, which lighteth every man that cometh into the world. [10]He was in the world, and the world was made by him, and the world knew him not."

Acts 17:23-25 "[23]For as I passed by, and beheld your devotions, I found an altar with this inscription, TO THE UNKNOWN GOD. Whom therefore ye ignorantly worship, him declare I unto you. [24]God that made the world and all things therein, seeing that he is Lord of heaven and earth, dwelleth not in temples made with hands; [25]Neither is worshipped with men's hands, as though he needed any thing, seeing he giveth to all life, and breath, and all things;"

Hebrews 1:1-2 "[1]God, who at sundry times and in divers manners spake in time past unto the fathers by the prophets, [2]Hath in these last days spoken unto us by his Son, whom he hath appointed heir of all things, by whom also he made the worlds;"

Hebrews 11:3 "Through faith we understand that the worlds were framed by the word of God, so that things which are seen were not made of things which do appear."

The Lord Judging The World

Psalm 96:13 "Before the LORD: for he cometh, for he cometh to judge the earth: he shall judge the world with righteousness, and the people with his truth."

John 12:23-31 "[23]And Jesus answered them, saying, The hour is come, that the Son of man should be glorified. [24]Verily, verily, I say unto you, Except a corn of wheat fall into the ground and die, it abideth alone: but if it die, it bringeth forth much fruit. [25]He that loveth his life shall lose it; and he that hateth his life in this world shall keep it unto life eternal. [26]If any man serve me, let him follow me; and where I am, there shall also my servant be: if any man serve me, him will my Father honour. [27]Now is my soul troubled; and what shall I say? Father, save me from this hour: but for this cause came I unto this hour. [28]Father, glorify thy name. Then came there a voice from heaven, saying, I have both glorified it, and will glorify it again. ²⁹The people therefore, that stood by, and heard it, said that it thundered: others said, An angel spake to him. ³⁰Jesus answered and said, This voice came not because of me, but for your sakes. ³¹Now is the judgment of this world: now shall the prince of this world be cast out."

Acts 17:30-31 "³⁰And the times of this ignorance God winked at; but now commandeth all men every where to repent: ³¹Because he hath appointed a day, in the which he will judge the world in righteousness by that man whom he hath ordained; whereof he hath given assurance unto all men, in that he hath raised him from the dead."

2 Peter 3:3-8 "³Knowing this first, that there shall come in the last days scoffers, walking after their own lusts, ⁴And saying, Where is the promise of his coming? for since the fathers fell asleep, all things continue as they were from the beginning of the creation. ⁵For this they willingly are ignorant of, that by the word of God the heavens were of old, and the earth standing out of the water and in the water: ⁶Whereby the world that then was, being overflowed with water, perished: ⁷But the heavens and the earth, which are now, by the same word are kept in store, reserved unto fire against the day of judgment and perdition of ungodly men. ⁸But, beloved, be not ignorant of this one thing, that one day is with the Lord as a thousand years, and a thousand years as one day."

The Lord Punishing The World
Isaiah 13:9-16 "⁹Behold, the day of the LORD cometh, cruel both with wrath and fierce anger, to lay the land desolate: and he shall destroy the sinners thereof out of it. ¹⁰For the stars of heaven and the constellations thereof shall not give their light: the sun shall be darkened in his going forth, and the moon shall not cause her light to shine. ¹¹And I will punish the world for their evil, and the wicked for their iniquity; and I will cause the arrogancy of the proud to cease, and will lay low the haughtiness of the terrible. ¹²I will make a man more precious than fine gold; even a man than the golden wedge of Ophir. ¹³Therefore I will shake the heavens, and the earth shall remove out of her place, in the wrath of the LORD of hosts, and in the day of his fierce anger. ¹⁴And it shall be as the chased roe, and as

a sheep that no man taketh up: they shall every man turn to his own people, and flee every one into his own land. ¹⁵Every one that is found shall be thrust through; and every one that is joined unto them shall fall by the sword. ¹⁶Their children also shall be dashed to pieces before their eyes; their houses shall be spoiled, and their wives ravished."

Isaiah 66:15-17 "¹⁵For, behold, the LORD will come with fire, and with his chariots like a whirlwind, to render his anger with fury, and his rebuke with flames of fire. ¹⁶For by fire and by his sword will the LORD plead with all flesh: and the slain of the LORD shall be many. ¹⁷They that sanctify themselves, and purify themselves in the gardens behind one tree in the midst, eating swine's flesh, and the abomination, and the mouse, shall be consumed together, saith the LORD."

The World Hating Jesus Christ
John 7:6-8 "⁶Then Jesus said unto them, My time is not yet come: but your time is alway ready. ⁷The world cannot hate you; but me it hateth, because I testify of it, that the works thereof are evil. ⁸Go ye up unto this feast: I go not up yet unto this feast; for my time is not yet full come."

John 15:1-25 "¹I am the true vine, and my Father is the husbandman. ²Every branch in me that beareth not fruit he taketh away: and every branch that beareth fruit, he purgeth it, that it may bring forth more fruit. ³Now ye are clean through the word which I have spoken unto you. ⁴Abide in me, and I in you. As the branch cannot bear fruit of itself, except it abide in the vine; no more can ye, except ye abide in me. ⁵I am the vine, ye are the branches: He that abideth in me, and I in him, the same bringeth forth much fruit: for without me ye can do nothing. ⁶If a man abide not in me, he is cast forth as a branch, and is withered; and men gather them, and cast them into the fire, and they are burned. ⁷If ye abide in me, and my words abide in you, ye shall ask what ye will, and it shall be done unto you. ⁸Herein is my Father glorified, that ye bear much fruit; so shall ye be my disciples. ⁹As the Father hath loved me, so have I loved you: continue ye in my love. ¹⁰If ye keep my commandments, ye shall abide in my love; even as I have kept my Father's commandments, and abide in his love. [11]These things have I spoken unto you, that my joy might remain in you, and that your joy might be full. [12]This is my commandment, That ye love one another, as I have loved you. [13]Greater love hath no man than this, that a man lay down his life for his friends. [14]Ye are my friends, if ye do whatsoever I command you. [15]Henceforth I call you not servants; for the servant knoweth not what his lord doeth: but I have called you friends; for all things that I have heard of my Father I have made known unto you. [16]Ye have not chosen me, but I have chosen you, and ordained you, that ye should go and bring forth fruit, and that your fruit should remain: that whatsoever ye shall ask of the Father in my name, he may give it you. [17]These things I command you, that ye love one another. [18]If the world hate you, ye know that it hated me before it hated you. [19]If ye were of the world, the world would love his own: but because ye are not of the world, but I have chosen you out of the world, therefore the world hateth you. [20]Remember the word that I said unto you, The servant is not greater than his lord. If they have persecuted me, they will also persecute you; if they have kept my saying, they will keep yours also. [21]But all these things will they do unto you for my name's sake, because they know not him that sent me. [22]If I had not come and spoken unto them, they had not had sin: but now they have no cloke for their sin. [23]He that hateth me hateth my Father also. [24]If I had not done among them the works which none other man did, they had not had sin: but now have they both seen and hated both me and my Father. [25]But this cometh to pass, that the word might be fulfilled that is written in their law, They hated me without a cause."

The World Lying In Wickedness
1 John 5:19 "And we know that we are of God, and the whole world lieth in wickedness."

The World Not Knowing God The Father
John 17:25 "O righteous Father, the world hath not known thee: but I have known thee, and these have known that thou hast sent me."

The World Passing Away
1 John 2:15-17 "[15]Love not the world, neither the things that are in the world. If any man love the world, the love of the Father is not in him. [16]For all that is in the world, the lust of the flesh, and the lust of the eyes, and the pride of life, is not of the Father, but is of the world. [17]And the world passeth away, and the lust thereof: but he that doeth the will of God abideth for ever."

The World That Exists Now
2 Peter 3:3-8 "[3]Knowing this first, that there shall come in the last days scoffers, walking after their own lusts, [4]And saying, Where is the promise of his coming? for since the fathers fell asleep, all things continue as they were from the beginning of the creation. [5]For this they willingly are ignorant of, that by the word of God the heavens were of old, and the earth standing out of the water and in the water: [6]Whereby the world that then was, being overflowed with water, perished: [7]But the heavens and the earth, which are now, by the same word are kept in store, reserved unto fire against the day of judgment and perdition of ungodly men. [8]But, beloved, be not ignorant of this one thing, that one day is with the Lord as a thousand years, and a thousand years as one day."

Those That Love The World
1 John 2:15 "Love not the world, neither the things that are in the world. If any man love the world, the love of the Father is not in him."

What Happened To The Old World
Genesis 6:17 "And, behold, I, even I, do bring a flood of waters upon the earth, to destroy all flesh, wherein is the breath of life, from under heaven; and every thing that is in the earth shall die."

Genesis 7:4 "For yet seven days, and I will cause it to rain upon the earth forty days and forty nights; and every living substance that I have made will I destroy from off the face of the earth."

Genesis 7:10-12 "[10]And it came to pass after seven days, that the waters of the flood were upon the earth. [11]In the six hundredth year of Noah's life, in the second month, the seventeenth day of the month, the same day were all the fountains of the great deep broken up, and the windows of heaven were opened. [12]And the rain was upon the earth forty days and forty nights."

Genesis 7:21-24 "[21]And all flesh died that moved upon the earth, both of fowl, and of cattle, and of beast, and of every creeping thing that creepeth upon the earth, and every man: 22All in whose nostrils was the breath of life, of all that was in the dry land, died. 23And every living substance was destroyed which was upon the face of the ground, both man, and cattle, and the creeping things, and the fowl of the heaven; and they were destroyed from the earth: and Noah only remained alive, and they that were with him in the ark. 24And the waters prevailed upon the earth an hundred and fifty days."

2 Peter 2:4-5 "4For if God spared not the angels that sinned, but cast them down to hell, and delivered them into chains of darkness, to be reserved unto judgment; 5And spared not the old world, but saved Noah the eighth person, a preacher of righteousness, bringing in the flood upon the world of the ungodly;"

2 Peter 3:3-6 "3Knowing this first, that there shall come in the last days scoffers, walking after their own lusts, 4And saying, Where is the promise of his coming? for since the fathers fell asleep, all things continue as they were from the beginning of the creation. 5For this they willingly are ignorant of, that by the word of God the heavens were of old, and the earth standing out of the water and in the water: 6Whereby the world that then was, being overflowed with water, perished:"

What Is Not Of The World
John 18:35-36 "35Pilate answered, Am I a Jew? Thine own nation and the chief priests have delivered thee unto me: what hast thou done? 36Jesus answered, My kingdom is not of this world: if my kingdom were of this world, then would my servants fight, that I should not be delivered to the Jews: but now is my kingdom not from hence."

What Is Of The World
2 Peter 1:4 "Whereby are given unto us exceeding great and precious promises: that by these ye might be partakers of the divine nature, having escaped the corruption that is in the world through lust."

1 John 2:16 "For all that is in the world, the lust of the flesh, and the lust of the eyes, and the pride of life, is not of the Father, but is of the world."

Who The World Hates
Matthew 10:16-22 "16Behold, I send you forth as sheep in the midst of wolves: be ye therefore wise as serpents, and harmless as doves. 17But beware of men: for they will deliver you up to the councils, and they will scourge you in their synagogues; 18And ye shall be brought before governors and kings for my sake, for a testimony against them and the Gentiles. 19But when they deliver you up, take no thought how or what ye shall speak: for it shall be given you in that same hour what ye shall speak. 20For it is not ye that speak, but the Spirit of your Father which speaketh in you. 21And the brother shall deliver up the brother to death, and the father the child: and the children shall rise up against their parents, and cause them to be put to death. 22And ye shall be hated of all men for my name's sake: but he that endureth to the end shall be saved."

Matthew 24:1-9 "1And Jesus went out, and departed from the temple: and his disciples came to him for to shew him the buildings of the temple. 2And Jesus said unto them, See ye not all these things? verily I say unto you, There shall not be left here one stone upon another, that shall not be thrown down. 3And as he sat upon the mount of Olives, the disciples came unto him privately, saying, Tell us, when shall these things be? and what shall be the sign of thy coming, and of the end of the world? 4And Jesus answered and said unto them, Take heed that no man deceive you. 5For many shall come in my name, saying, I am Christ; and shall deceive many. 6And ye shall hear of wars and rumours of wars: see that ye be not troubled: for all these things must come to pass, but the end is not yet. 7For nation shall rise against nation, and kingdom against kingdom: and there shall be famines, and pestilences, and earthquakes, in divers places. 8All these are the beginning of sorrows. 9Then shall they deliver you up to be afflicted, and shall kill you: and ye shall be hated of all nations for my name's sake."

Mark 13:1-13 "1And as he went out of the temple, one of his disciples saith unto him, Master, see what manner of stones and what buildings are here! 2And Jesus answering said unto him, Seest thou these great buildings? there shall not be left one stone upon another, that shall not be thrown down. 3And as he sat upon the mount of Olives over against the temple, Peter and James and John and Andrew asked him privately, 4Tell us, when shall these things be? and what shall be the sign when all these things shall be fulfilled? 5And

Jesus answering them began to say, Take heed lest any man deceive you: [6]For many shall come in my name, saying, I am Christ; and shall deceive many. [7]And when ye shall hear of wars and rumours of wars, be ye not troubled: for such things must needs be; but the end shall not be yet. [8]For nation shall rise against nation, and kingdom against kingdom: and there shall be earthquakes in divers places, and there shall be famines and troubles: these are the beginnings of sorrows. [9]But take heed to yourselves: for they shall deliver you up to councils; and in the synagogues ye shall be beaten: and ye shall be brought before rulers and kings for my sake, for a testimony against them. [10]And the gospel must first be published among all nations. [11]But when they shall lead you, and deliver you up, take no thought beforehand what ye shall speak, neither do ye premeditate: but whatsoever shall be given you in that hour, that speak ye: for it is not ye that speak, but the Holy Ghost. [12]Now the brother shall betray the brother to death, and the father the son; and children shall rise up against their parents, and shall cause them to be put to death. [13]And ye shall be hated of all men for my name's sake: but he that shall endure unto the end, the same shall be saved."

Luke 21:5-17 "[5]And as some spake of the temple, how it was adorned with goodly stones and gifts, he said, [6]As for these things which ye behold, the days will come, in the which there shall not be left one stone upon another, that shall not be thrown down. [7]And they asked him, saying, Master, but when shall these things be? and what sign will there be when these things shall come to pass? [8]And he said, Take heed that ye be not deceived: for many shall come in my name, saying, I am Christ; and the time draweth near: go ye not therefore after them. [9]But when ye shall hear of wars and commotions, be not terrified: for these things must first come to pass; but the end is not by and by. [10]Then said he unto them, Nation shall rise against nation, and kingdom against kingdom: [11]And great earthquakes shall be in divers places, and famines, and pestilences; and fearful sights and great signs shall there be from heaven. [12]But before all these, they shall lay their hands on you, and persecute you, delivering you up to the synagogues, and into prisons, being brought before kings and rulers for my name's sake.

[13]And it shall turn to you for a testimony. [14]Settle it therefore in your hearts, not to meditate before what ye shall answer: [15]For I will give you a mouth and wisdom, which all your adversaries shall not be able to gainsay nor resist. [16]And ye shall be betrayed both by parents, and brethren, and kinsfolks, and friends; and some of you shall they cause to be put to death. [17]And ye shall be hated of all men for my name's sake."

John 15:1-19 "[1]I am the true vine, and my Father is the husbandman. [2]Every branch in me that beareth not fruit he taketh away: and every branch that beareth fruit, he purgeth it, that it may bring forth more fruit. [3]Now ye are clean through the word which I have spoken unto you. [4]Abide in me, and I in you. As the branch cannot bear fruit of itself, except it abide in the vine; no more can ye, except ye abide in me. [5]I am the vine, ye are the branches: He that abideth in me, and I in him, the same bringeth forth much fruit: for without me ye can do nothing. [6]If a man abide not in me, he is cast forth as a branch, and is withered; and men gather them, and cast them into the fire, and they are burned. [7]If ye abide in me, and my words abide in you, ye shall ask what ye will, and it shall be done unto you. [8]Herein is my Father glorified, that ye bear much fruit; so shall ye be my disciples. [9]As the Father hath loved me, so have I loved you: continue ye in my love. [10]If ye keep my commandments, ye shall abide in my love; even as I have kept my Father's commandments, and abide in his love. [11]These things have I spoken unto you, that my joy might remain in you, and that your joy might be full. [12]This is my commandment, That ye love one another, as I have loved you. [13]Greater love hath no man than this, that a man lay down his life for his friends. [14]Ye are my friends, if ye do whatsoever I command you. [15]Henceforth I call you not servants; for the servant knoweth not what his lord doeth: but I have called you friends; for all things that I have heard of my Father I have made known unto you. [16]Ye have not chosen me, but I have chosen you, and ordained you, that ye should go and bring forth fruit, and that your fruit should remain: that whatsoever ye shall ask of the Father in my name, he may give it you. [17]These things I command you, that ye love one another. [18]If the world hate you, ye know that it hated me before it hated you. ¹⁹If ye were of the world, the world would love his own: but because ye are not of the world, but I have chosen you out of the world, therefore the world hateth you."

John 17:1-14 "¹These words spake Jesus, and lifted up his eyes to heaven, and said, Father, the hour is come; glorify thy Son, that thy Son also may glorify thee: ²As thou hast given him power over all flesh, that he should give eternal life to as many as thou hast given him. And this is life eternal, that they might know thee the only true God, and Jesus Christ, whom thou hast sent. ⁴I have glorified thee on the earth: I have finished the work which thou gavest me to do. ⁵And now, O Father, glorify thou me with thine own self with the glory which I had with thee before the world was. ⁶I have manifested thy name unto the men which thou gavest me out of the world: thine they were, and thou gavest them me; and they have kept thy word. ⁷Now they have known that all things whatsoever thou hast given me are of thee. ⁸For I have given unto them the words which thou gavest me; and they have received them, and have known surely that I came out from thee, and they have believed that thou didst send me. ⁹I pray for them: I pray not for the world, but for them which thou hast given me; for they are thine. ¹⁰And all mine are thine, and thine are mine; and I am glorified in them. ¹¹And now I am no more in the world, but these are in the world, and I come to thee. Holy Father, keep through thine own name those whom thou hast given me, that they may be one, as we are. ¹²While I was with them in the world, I kept them in thy name: those that thou gavest me I have kept, and none of them is lost, but the son of perdition; that the scripture might be fulfilled. ¹³And now come I to thee; and these things I speak in the world, that they might have my joy fulfilled in themselves. ¹⁴I have given them thy word; and the world hath hated them, because they are not of the world, even as I am not of the world."

1 John 3:11-13 "¹¹For this is the message that ye heard from the beginning, that we should love one another. ¹²Not as Cain, who was of that wicked one, and slew his brother. And wherefore slew he him? Because his own works were evil, and his

brother's righteous. ¹³Marvel not, my brethren, if the world hate you."

Who The World Hears
1 John 4:1-5 "¹Beloved, believe not every spirit, but try the spirits whether they are of God: because many false prophets are gone out into the world. ²Hereby know ye the Spirit of God: Every spirit that confesseth that Jesus Christ is come in the flesh is of God: ³And every spirit that confesseth not that Jesus Christ is come in the flesh is not of God: and this is that spirit of antichrist, whereof ye have heard that it should come; and even now already is it in the world. ⁴Ye are of God, little children, and have overcome them: because greater is he that is in you, than he that is in the world. ⁵They are of the world: therefore speak they of the world, and the world heareth them."

Who Is Of The World
1 John 4:1-5 "¹Beloved, believe not every spirit, but try the spirits whether they are of God: because many false prophets are gone out into the world. ²Hereby know ye the Spirit of God: Every spirit that confesseth that Jesus Christ is come in the flesh is of God: ³And every spirit that confesseth not that Jesus Christ is come in the flesh is not of God: and this is that spirit of antichrist, whereof ye have heard that it should come; and even now already is it in the world. ⁴Ye are of God, little children, and have overcome them: because greater is he that is in you, than he that is in the world. ⁵They are of the world: therefore speak they of the world, and the world heareth them."

Why The World Has Woes
Matthew 18:7 "Woe unto the world because of offences! for it must needs be that offences come; but woe to that man by whom the offence cometh!"

Why The World Hates Jesus Christ
And Those That Believe In Him
John 7:6-7 "⁶Then Jesus said unto them, My time is not yet come: but your time is alway ready. ⁷The world cannot hate you; but me it hateth, because I testify of it, that the works thereof are evil."

John 15:1-19 "¹I am the true vine, and my Father is the husbandman. ²Every branch in me that beareth not fruit he taketh away: and every branch that beareth fruit, he purgeth it, that it may bring forth more fruit. [3]Now ye are clean through the word which I have spoken unto you. [4]Abide in me, and I in you. As the branch cannot bear fruit of itself, except it abide in the vine; no more can ye, except ye abide in me. [5]I am the vine, ye are the branches: He that abideth in me, and I in him, the same bringeth forth much fruit: for without me ye can do nothing. [6]If a man abide not in me, he is cast forth as a branch, and is withered; and men gather them, and cast them into the fire, and they are burned. [7]If ye abide in me, and my words abide in you, ye shall ask what ye will, and it shall be done unto you. [8]Herein is my Father glorified, that ye bear much fruit; so shall ye be my disciples. [9]As the Father hath loved me, so have I loved you: continue ye in my love. [10]If ye keep my commandments, ye shall abide in my love; even as I have kept my Father's commandments, and abide in his love. [11]These things have I spoken unto you, that my joy might remain in you, and that your joy might be full. [12]This is my commandment, That ye love one another, as I have loved you. [13]Greater love hath no man than this, that a man lay down his life for his friends. [14]Ye are my friends, if ye do whatsoever I command you. [15]Henceforth I call you not servants; for the servant knoweth not what his lord doeth: but I have called you friends; for all things that I have heard of my Father I have made known unto you. [16]Ye have not chosen me, but I have chosen you, and ordained you, that ye should go and bring forth fruit, and that your fruit should remain: that whatsoever ye shall ask of the Father in my name, he may give it you. [17]These things I command you, that ye love one another. [18]If the world hate you, ye know that it hated me before it hated you. [19]If ye were of the world, the world would love his own: but because ye are not of the world, but I have chosen you out of the world, therefore the world hateth you."

John 17:1-16 "[1]These words spake Jesus, and lifted up his eyes to heaven, and said, Father, the hour is come; glorify thy Son, that thy Son also may glorify thee: [2]As thou hast given him power over all flesh, that he should give eternal life to as many as thou hast given him. [3]And this is life eternal, that they might know thee the only true God, and Jesus Christ, whom thou hast sent. [4]I have glorified thee on the earth: I have finished the work which thou gavest me to do. [5]And now, O Father, glorify thou me with thine own self with the glory which I had with thee before the world was. [6]I have manifested thy name unto the men which thou gavest me out of the world: thine they were, and thou gavest them me; and they have kept thy word. [7]Now they have known that all things whatsoever thou hast given me are of thee. [8]For I have given unto them the words which thou gavest me; and they have received them, and have known surely that I came out from thee, and they have believed that thou didst send me. [9]I pray for them: I pray not for the world, but for them which thou hast given me; for they are thine. [10]And all mine are thine, and thine are mine; and I am glorified in them. [11]And now I am no more in the world, but these are in the world, and I come to thee. Holy Father, keep through thine own name those whom thou hast given me, that they may be one, as we are. [12]While I was with them in the world, I kept them in thy name: those that thou gavest me I have kept, and none of them is lost, but the son of perdition; that the scripture might be fulfilled. [13]And now come I to thee; and these things I speak in the world, that they might have my joy fulfilled in themselves. [14]I have given them thy word; and the world hath hated them, because they are not of the world, even as I am not of the world. [15]I pray not that thou shouldest take them out of the world, but that thou shouldest keep them from the evil. [16]They are not of the world, even as I am not of the world."

Worldly Men

Psalm 17:13-14 "[13]Arise, O LORD, disappoint him, cast him down: deliver my soul from the wicked, which is thy sword: [14]From men which are thy hand, O LORD, from men of the world, which have their portion in this life, and whose belly thou fillest with thy hid treasure: they are full of children, and leave the rest of their substance to their babes."

1 Corinthians 2:6-8 "[6]Howbeit we speak wisdom among them that are perfect: yet not the wisdom of this world, nor of the princes of this world, that come to nought: [7]But we speak the wisdom of God in a mystery, even the hidden wisdom, which God ordained before the world unto our glory: [8]Which none of the princes of this world knew: for had they known it, they would not have crucified the Lord of glory."

WORSHIP

All The Earth Worshipping The Lord
Psalm 22:27-29 "[27]All the ends of the world shall remember and turn unto the LORD: and all the kindreds of the nations shall worship before thee. [28]For the kingdom is the LORD's: and he is the governor among the nations. [29]All they that be fat upon earth shall eat and worship: all they that go down to the dust shall bow before him: and none can keep alive his own soul."

Psalm 66:3-4 "[3]Say unto God, How terrible art thou in thy works! through the greatness of thy power shall thine enemies submit themselves unto thee. [4]All the earth shall worship thee, and shall sing unto thee; they shall sing to thy name. Selah."

Isaiah 66:23 "And it shall come to pass, that from one new moon to another, and from one sabbath to another, shall all flesh come to worship before me, saith the LORD."

Zephaniah 2:11 "The LORD will be terrible unto them: for he will famish all the gods of the earth; and men shall worship him, every one from his place, even all the isles of the heathen."

Revelation 15:4 "Who shall not fear thee, O Lord, and glorify thy name? for thou only art holy: for all nations shall come and worship before thee; for thy judgments are made manifest."

How God Should Not Be Worshipped
Acts 17:22-25 "[22]Then Paul stood in the midst of Mars' hill, and said, Ye men of Athens, I perceive that in all things ye are too superstitious. [23]For as I passed by, and beheld your devotions, I found an altar with this inscription, TO THE UNKNOWN GOD. Whom therefore ye ignorantly worship, him declare I unto you. [24]God that made the world and all things therein, seeing that he is Lord of heaven and earth, dwelleth not in temples made with hands; [25]Neither is worshipped with men's hands, as though he needed any thing, seeing he giveth to all life, and breath, and all things;"

The Reward For Worshipping Idols
Exodus 32:7-8 "[7]And the LORD said unto Moses, Go, get thee down; for thy people, which thou broughtest out of the land of Egypt, have corrupted themselves: [8]They have turned aside quickly out of the way which I commanded them: they have made them a molten calf, and have worshipped it, and have sacrificed thereunto, and said, These be thy gods, O Israel, which have brought thee up out of the land of Egypt."

Deuteronomy 8:19-20 "[19]And it shall be, if thou do at all forget the LORD thy God, and walk after other gods, and serve them, and worship them, I testify against you this day that ye shall surely perish. [20]As the nations which the LORD destroyeth before your face, so shall ye perish; because ye would not be obedient unto the voice of the LORD your God."

Deuteronomy 11:16-18 "[16]Take heed to yourselves, that your heart be not deceived, and ye turn aside, and serve other gods, and worship them; [17]And then the LORD's wrath be kindled against you, and he shut up the heaven, that there be no rain, and that the land yield not her fruit; and lest ye perish quickly from off the good land which the LORD giveth you. [18]Therefore shall ye lay up these my words in your heart and in your soul, and bind them for a sign upon your hand, that they may be as frontlets between your eyes."

Deuteronomy 29:17-29 "[17]And ye have seen their abominations, and their idols, wood and stone, silver and gold, which were among them:) [18]Lest there should be among you man, or woman, or family, or tribe, whose heart turneth away this day from the LORD our God, to go and serve the gods of these nations; lest there should be among you a root that beareth gall and wormwood; [19]And it come to pass, when he heareth the words of this curse, that he bless himself in his heart, saying, I shall have peace, though I walk in the imagination of mine heart, to add drunkenness to thirst: [20]The LORD will not spare him, but then the anger of the LORD and his jealousy shall smoke against that man, and all the curses that are written in this book shall lie upon him, and the LORD shall blot out his name from under heaven. [21]And the LORD shall separate him unto evil out of all the tribes of Israel, according to all the curses of the covenant that are written in this book of the law: ²²So that the generation to come of your children that shall rise up after you, and the stranger that shall come from a far land, shall say, when they see the plagues of that land, and the sicknesses which the LORD hath laid upon it; ²³And that the whole land thereof is brimstone, and salt, and burning, that it is not sown, nor beareth, nor any grass groweth therein, like the overthrow of Sodom, and Gomorrah, Admah, and Zeboim, which the LORD overthrew in his anger, and in his wrath: ²⁴Even all nations shall say, Wherefore hath the LORD done thus unto this land? what meaneth the heat of this great anger? ²⁵Then men shall say, Because they have forsaken the covenant of the LORD God of their fathers, which he made with them when he brought them forth out of the land of Egypt: ²⁶For they went and served other gods, and worshipped them, gods whom they knew not, and whom he had not given unto them: ²⁷And the anger of the LORD was kindled against this land, to bring upon it all the curses that are written in this book: ²⁸And the LORD rooted them out of their land in anger, and in wrath, and in great indignation, and cast them into another land, as it is this day. ²⁹The secret things belong unto the LORD our God: but those things which are revealed belong unto us and to our children for ever, that we may do all the words of this law."

Deuteronomy 30:15-18 "¹⁵See, I have set before thee this day life and good, and death and evil; ¹⁶In that I command thee this day to love the LORD thy God, to walk in his ways, and to keep his commandments and his statutes and his judgments, that thou mayest live and multiply: and the LORD thy God shall bless thee in the land whither thou goest to possess it. ¹⁷But if thine heart turn away, so that thou wilt not hear, but shalt be drawn away, and worship other gods, and serve them; ¹⁸I denounce unto you this day, that ye shall surely perish, and that ye shall not prolong your days upon the land, whither thou passest over Jordan to go to possess it."

Deuteronomy 32:17-24 "¹⁷They sacrificed unto devils, not to God; to gods whom they knew not, to new gods that came newly up, whom your fathers feared not. ¹⁸Of the Rock that begat thee

thou art unmindful, and hast forgotten God that formed thee. ¹⁹And when the LORD saw it, he abhorred them, because of the provoking of his sons, and of his daughters. ²⁰And he said, I will hide my face from them, I will see what their end shall be: for they are a very froward generation, children in whom is no faith. ²¹They have moved me to jealousy with that which is not God; they have provoked me to anger with their vanities: and I will move them to jealousy with those which are not a people; I will provoke them to anger with a foolish nation. ²²For a fire is kindled in mine anger, and shall burn unto the lowest hell, and shall consume the earth with her increase, and set on fire the foundations of the mountains. ²³I will heap mischiefs upon them; I will spend mine arrows upon them. ²⁴They shall be burnt with hunger, and devoured with burning heat, and with bitter destruction: I will also send the teeth of beasts upon them, with the poison of serpents of the dust."

1 Kings 9:6-9 "⁶But if ye shall at all turn from following me, ye or your children, and will not keep my commandments and my statutes which I have set before you, but go and serve other gods, and worship them: ⁷Then will I cut off Israel out of the land which I have given them; and this house, which I have hallowed for my name, will I cast out of my sight; and Israel shall be a proverb and a byword among all people: ⁸And at this house, which is high, every one that passeth by it shall be astonished, and shall hiss; and they shall say, Why hath the LORD done thus unto this land, and to this house? ⁹And they shall answer, Because they forsook the LORD their God, who brought forth their fathers out of the land of Egypt, and have taken hold upon other gods, and have worshipped them, and served them: therefore hath the LORD brought upon them all this evil."

1 Kings 11:31-37 "³¹And he said to Jeroboam, Take thee ten pieces: for thus saith the LORD, the God of Israel, Behold, I will rend the kingdom out of the hand of Solomon, and will give ten tribes to thee: ³²(But he shall have one tribe for my servant David's sake, and for Jerusalem's sake, the city which I have chosen out of all the tribes of Israel:) ³³Because that they have forsaken me, and have worshipped Ashtoreth the goddess of the Zidonians, Chemosh the god of the Moabites, and Milcom the god of the children of Ammon, and have not walked in my ways, to do that which is right in mine eyes, and to keep my statutes and my judgments, as did David his father. ³⁴Howbeit I will not take the whole kingdom out of his hand: but I will make him prince all the days of his life for David my servant's sake, whom I chose, because he kept my commandments and my statutes: ³⁵But I will take the kingdom out of his son's hand, and will give it unto thee, even ten tribes. ³⁶And unto his son will I give one tribe, that David my servant may have a light alway before me in Jerusalem, the city which I have chosen me to put my name there. ³⁷And I will take thee, and thou shalt reign according to all that thy soul desireth, and shalt be king over Israel."

2 Kings 17:7-23 "⁷For so it was, that the children of Israel had sinned against the LORD their God, which had brought them up out of the land of Egypt, from under the hand of Pharoah king of Egypt, and had feared other gods, ⁸And walked in the statutes of the heathen, whom the LORD cast out from before the children of Israel, and of the kings of Israel, which they had made. ⁹And the children of Israel did secretly those things that were not right against the LORD their God, and they built them high places in all their cities, from the tower of the watchmen to the fenced city. ¹⁰And they set them up images and groves in every high hill, and under every green tree: ¹¹And there they burnt incense in all the high places, as did the heathen whom the LORD carried away before them; and wrought wicked things to provoke the LORD to anger: ¹²For they served idols, whereof the LORD had said unto them, Ye shall not do this thing. ¹³Yet the LORD testified against Israel, and against Judah, by all the prophets, and by all the seers, saying, Turn ye from your evil ways, and keep my commandments and my statutes, according to all the law which I commanded your fathers, and which I sent to you by my servants the prophets. ¹⁴Notwithstanding they would not hear, but hardened their necks, like to the neck of their fathers, that did not believe in the LORD their God. ¹⁵And they rejected his statutes, and his covenant that he made with their fathers, and his testimonies which he testified

against them; and they followed vanity, and became vain, and went after the heathen that were round about them, concerning whom the LORD had charged them, that they should not do like them. ¹⁶And they left all the commandments of the LORD their God, and made them molten images, even two calves, and made a grove, and worshipped all the host of heaven, and served Baal. ¹⁷And they caused their sons and their daughters to pass through the fire, and used divination and enchantments, and sold themselves to do evil in the sight of the LORD, to provoke him to anger. ¹⁸Therefore the LORD was very angry with Israel, and removed them out of his sight: there was none left but the tribe of Judah only. ¹⁹Also Judah kept not the commandments of the LORD their God, but walked in the statutes of Israel which they made. ²⁰And the LORD rejected all the seed of Israel, and afflicted them, and delivered them into the hand of spoilers, until he had cast them out of his sight. ²¹For he rent Israel from the house of David; and they made Jeroboam the son of Nebat king: and Jeroboam drave Israel from following the LORD, and made them sin a great sin. ²²For the children of Israel walked in all the sins of Jeroboam which he did; they departed not from them; ²³Until the LORD removed Israel out of his sight, as he had said by all his servants the prophets. So was Israel carried away out of their own land to Assyria unto this day."

2 Kings 22:16-17 "¹⁶Thus saith the LORD, Behold, I will bring evil upon this place, and upon the inhabitants thereof, even all the words of the book which the king of Judah hath read: ¹⁷Because they have forsaken me, and have burned incense unto other gods, that they might provoke me to anger with all the works of their hands; therefore my wrath shall be kindled against this place, and shall not be quenched."

2 Chronicles 34:24-25 "²⁴Thus saith the LORD, Behold, I will bring evil upon this place, and upon the inhabitants thereof, even all the curses that are written in the book which they have read before the king of Judah: ²⁵Because they have forsaken me, and have burned incense unto other gods, that they might provoke me to anger with all the works of their hands; therefore my wrath shall be poured out upon this place, and shall not be quenched."

Psalm 106:19-23 "¹⁹They made a calf in Horeb, and worshipped the molten image. ²⁰Thus they changed their glory into the similitude of an ox that eateth grass. ²¹They forgat God their saviour, which had done great things in Egypt; ²²Wondrous works in the land of Ham, and terrible things by the Red sea. ²³Therefore he said that he would destroy them, had not Moses his chosen stood before him in the breach, to turn away his wrath, lest he should destroy them."

Jeremiah 11:17 "For the LORD of hosts, that planted thee, hath pronounced evil against thee, for the evil of the house of Israel and of the house of Judah, which they have done against themselves to provoke me to anger in offering incense unto Baal."

Jeremiah 16:11-13 "¹¹Then shalt thou say unto them, Because your fathers have forsaken me, saith the LORD, and have walked after other gods, and have served them, and have worshipped them, and have forsaken me, and have not kept my law; ¹²And ye have done worse than your fathers; for, behold, ye walk every one after the imagination of his evil heart, that they may not hearken unto me: ¹³Therefore will I cast you out of this land into a land that ye know not, neither ye nor your fathers; and there shall ye serve other gods day and night; where I will not shew you favour."

Jeremiah 18:13-17 "¹³Therefore thus saith the LORD; Ask ye now among the heathen, who hath heard such things: the virgin of Israel hath done a very horrible thing. ¹⁴Will a man leave the snow of Lebanon which cometh from the rock of the field? or shall the cold flowing waters that come from another place be forsaken? ¹⁵Because my people hath forgotten me, they have burned incense to vanity, and they have caused them to stumble in their ways from the ancient paths, to walk in paths, in a way not cast up; ¹⁶To make their land desolate, and a perpetual hissing; every one that passeth thereby shall be astonished, and wag his head. ¹⁷I will scatter them as with an east wind before the enemy; I will shew them the back, and not the face, in the day of their calamity."

Jeremiah 22:8-9 "⁸And many nations shall pass by this city, and they shall say every man to his neighbour, Wherefore hath the LORD done thus unto this great city? ⁹Then they shall answer, Because they have forsaken the covenant of the LORD their God, and worshipped other gods, and served them."

Jeremiah 25:4-14 "⁴And the LORD hath sent unto you all his servants the prophets, rising early and sending them; but ye have not hearkened, nor inclined your ear to hear. ⁵They said, Turn ye again now every one from his evil way, and from the evil of your doings, and dwell in the land that the LORD hath given unto you and to your fathers for ever and ever: ⁶And go not after other gods to serve them, and to worship them, and provoke me not to anger with the works of your hands; and I will do you no hurt. ⁷Yet ye have not hearkened unto me, saith the LORD; that ye might provoke me to anger with the works of your hands to your own hurt. ⁸Therefore thus saith the LORD of hosts; Because ye have not heard my words, ⁹Behold, I will send and take all the families of the north, saith the LORD, and Nebuchadrezzar the king of Babylon, my servant, and will bring them against this land, and against the inhabitants thereof, and against all these nations round about, and will utterly destroy them, and make them an astonishment, and an hissing, and perpetual desolations. ¹⁰Moreover I will take from them the voice of mirth, and the voice of gladness, the voice of the bridegroom, and the voice of the bride, the sound of the millstones, and the light of the candle. ¹¹And this whole land shall be a desolation, and an astonishment; and these nations shall serve the king of Babylon seventy years. ¹²And it shall come to pass, when seventy years are accomplished, that I will punish the king of Babylon, and that nation, saith the LORD, for their iniquity, and the land of the Chaldeans, and will make it perpetual desolations. ¹³And I will bring upon that land all my words which I have pronounced against it, even all that is written in this book, which Jeremiah hath prophesied against all the nations. ¹⁴For many nations and great kings shall serve themselves of them also: and I will recompense them according to their deeds, and according to the works of their own hands."

Acts 7:42-43 "⁴²Then God turned, and gave them up to worship the host of heaven; as it is written in the book of the prophets, O ye house of Israel, have ye offered to me slain beasts and sacrifices by the space of forty years in the wilderness? ⁴³Yea, ye took up the tabernacle of Moloch, and the star of your god Remphan, figures which ye made to worship them: and I will carry you away beyond Babylon."

Those That Do Not Worship The Beast

Revelation 20:4-6 "⁴And I saw thrones, and they sat upon them, and judgment was given unto them: and I saw the souls of them that were beheaded for the witness of Jesus, and for the word of God, and which had not worshipped the beast, neither his image, neither had received his mark upon their foreheads, or in their hands; and they lived and reigned with Christ a thousand years. ⁵But the rest of the dead lived not again until the thousand years were finished. This is the first resurrection. ⁶Blessed and holy is he that hath part in the first resurrection: on such the second death hath no power, but they shall be priests of God and of Christ, and shall reign with him a thousand years."

Those That Worship Idols

Psalm 73:26-27 "²⁶My flesh and my heart faileth: but God is the strength of my heart, and my portion for ever. ²⁷For, lo, they that are far from thee shall perish: thou hast destroyed all them that go a whoring from thee."

Isaiah 44:9-19 "⁹They that make a graven image are all of them vanity; and their delectable things shall not profit; and they are their own witnesses; they see not, nor know; that they may be ashamed. ¹⁰Who hath formed a god, or molten a graven image that is profitable for nothing? ¹¹Behold, all his fellows shall be ashamed: and the workmen, they are of men: let them all be gathered together, let them stand up; yet they shall fear, and they shall be ashamed together. ¹²The smith with the tongs both worketh in the coals, and fashioneth it with hammers, and worketh it with the strength of his arms: yea, he is hungry, and his strength faileth: he drinketh no water, and is faint. ¹³The carpenter stretcheth out his rule; he marketh it out with a line; he fitteth it with planes, and he marketh it out with the compass, and maketh it after the fig-

ure of a man, according to the beauty of a man; that it may remain in the house. ¹⁴He heweth him down cedars, and taketh the cypress and the oak, which he strengtheneth for himself among the trees of the forest: he planteth an ash, and the rain doth nourish it. ¹⁵Then shall it be for a man to burn: for he will take thereof, and warm himself; yea, he kindleth it, and baketh bread; yea, he maketh a god, and worshippeth it; he maketh it a graven image, and falleth down thereto. ¹⁶He burneth part thereof in the fire; with part thereof he eateth flesh; he roasteth roast, and is satisfied: yea, he warmeth himself, and saith, Aha, I am warm, I have seen the fire: ¹⁷And the residue thereof he maketh a god, even his graven image: he falleth down unto it, and worshippeth it, and prayeth unto it, and saith, Deliver me; for thou art my god. ¹⁸They have not known nor understood: for he hath shut their eyes, that they cannot see; and their hearts, that they cannot understand. ¹⁹And none considereth in his heart, neither is there knowledge nor understanding to say, I have burned part of it in the fire; yea, also I have baked bread upon the coals thereof; I have roasted flesh, and eaten it: and shall I make the residue thereof an abomination? shall I fall down to the stock of a tree?"

Jeremiah 13:9-10 "⁹Thus saith the LORD, After this manner will I mar the pride of Judah, and the great pride of Jerusalem. ¹⁰This evil people, which refuse to hear my words, which walk in the imagination of their heart, and walk after other gods, to serve them, and to worship them, shall even be as this girdle, which is good for nothing."

Those That Worship The Beast

Revelation 14:9-11 "⁹And the third angel followed them, saying with a loud voice, If any man worship the beast and his image, and receive his mark in his forehead, or in his hand, ¹⁰The same shall drink of the wine of the wrath of God, which is poured out without mixture into the cup of his indignation; and he shall be tormented with fire and brimstone in the presence of the holy angels, and in the presence of the Lamb: ¹¹And the smoke of their torment ascendeth up for ever and ever: and they have no rest day nor night, who worship the beast and his image, and whosoever receiveth the mark of his name."

Revelation 16:1-2 "¹And I heard a great voice out of the temple saying to the seven angels, Go your ways, and pour out the vials of the wrath of God upon the earth. ²And the first went, and poured out his vial upon the earth; and there fell a noisome and grievous sore upon the men which had the mark of the beast, and upon them which worshipped his image."

Revelation 19:19-21 "¹⁹And I saw the beast, and the kings of the earth, and their armies, gathered together to make war against him that sat on the horse, and against his army. ²⁰And the beast was taken, and with him the false prophet that wrought miracles before him, with which he deceived them that had received the mark of the beast, and them that worshipped his image. These both were cast alive into a lake of fire burning with brimstone. ²¹And the remnant were slain with the sword of him that sat upon the horse, which sword proceeded out of his mouth: and all the fowls were filled with their flesh."

What Not To Worship

Exodus 20:2-5 "²I am the LORD thy God, which have brought thee out of the land of Egypt, out of the house of bondage. ³Thou shalt have no other gods before me. ⁴Thou shalt not make unto thee any graven image, or any likeness of any thing that is in heaven above, or that is in the earth beneath, or that is in the water under the earth: ⁵Thou shalt not bow down thyself to them, nor serve them: for I the LORD thy God am a jealous God, visiting the iniquity of the fathers upon the children unto the third and fourth generation of them that hate me;"

Exodus 34:14 "For thou shalt worship no other god: for the LORD, whose name is Jealous, is a jealous God:"

Deuteronomy 5:6-9 "⁶I am the LORD thy God, which brought thee out of the land of Egypt, from the house of bondage. ⁷Thou shalt have none other gods before me. ⁸Thou shalt not make thee any graven image, or any likeness of any thing that is in heaven above, or that is in the earth beneath, or that is in the waters beneath the earth: ⁹Thou shalt not bow down thyself unto them, nor serve them: for I the LORD thy God am a jealous God, visiting the iniquity of the fathers

upon the children unto the third and fourth generation of them that hate me,"

2 Kings 17:35-38 "³⁵With whom the LORD had made a covenant, and charged them saying, Ye shall not fear other gods, nor bow yourselves to them, nor serve them, nor sacrifice to them: ³⁶But the LORD, who brought you up out of the land of Egypt with great power and a stretched out arm, him shall ye fear, and him shall ye worship, and to him shall ye do sacrifice. ³⁷And the statutes, and the ordinances, and the law, and the commandment, which he wrote for you, ye shall observe to do for evermore; and ye shall not fear other gods. ³⁸And the covenant that I have made with you ye shall not forget; neither shall ye fear other gods."

Psalm 81:9 "There shall no strange god be in thee; neither shalt thou worship any strange god."

Jeremiah 25:4-6 "⁴And the LORD hath sent unto you all his servants the prophets, rising early and sending them; but ye have not hearkened, nor inclined your ear to hear. ⁵They said, Turn ye again now every one from his evil way, and from the evil of your doings, and dwell in the land that the LORD hath given unto you and to your fathers for ever and ever: ⁶And go not after other gods to serve them, and to worship them, and provoke me not to anger with the works of your hands; and I will do you no hurt."

Hosea 13:4 "Yet I am the LORD thy God from the land of Egypt, and thou shalt know no god but me: for there is no saviour beside me."

Acts 10:25-26 "²⁵And as Peter was coming in, Cornelius met him, and fell down at his feet, and worshipped him. ²⁶But Peter took him up, saying, Stand up; I myself also am a man."

Acts 14:8-18 "⁸And there sat a certain man at Lystra, impotent in his feet, being a cripple from his mother's womb, who never had walked: ⁹The same heard Paul speak: who stedfastly beholding him, and perceiving that he had faith to be healed, ¹⁰Said with a loud voice, Stand upright on thy feet. And he leaped and walked. ¹¹And when the people saw what Paul had done, they lifted up their voices, saying in the speech of Lycaonia, The gods are come down to us in the likeness of men. ¹²And they called Barnabas, Jupiter; and Paul,

Mercurius, because he was the chief speaker. [13]Then the priest of Jupiter, which was before their city, brought oxen and garlands unto the gates, and would have done sacrifice with the people. [14]Which when the apostles, Barnabas and Paul, heard of, they rent their clothes, and ran in among the people, crying out, [15]And saying, Sirs, why do ye these things? We also are men of like passions with you, and preach unto you that ye should turn from these vanities unto the living God, which made heaven, and earth, and the sea, and all things that are therein: [16]Who in times past suffered all nations to walk in their own ways. [17]Nevertheless he left not himself without witness, in that he did good, and gave us rain from heaven, and fruitful seasons, filling our hearts with food and gladness. [18]And with these sayings scarce restrained they the people, that they had not done sacrifice unto them."

Revelation 19:10 "And I fell at his feet to worship him. And he said unto me, See thou do it not: I am thy fellowservant, and of thy brethren that have the testimony of Jesus: worship God: for the testimony of Jesus is the spirit of prophecy."

Revelation 22:8-9 "[8]And I John saw these things, and heard them. And when I had heard and seen, I fell down to worship before the feet of the angel which shewed me these things. [9]Then saith he unto me, See thou do it not: for I am thy fellowservant, and of thy brethren the prophets, and of them which keep the sayings of this book: worship God."

What Those That
Worship God Must Do
John 4:23-24 "[23]But the hour cometh, and now is, when the true worshippers shall worship the Father in spirit and in truth: for the Father seeketh such to worship him. [24]God is a Spirit: and they that worship him must worship him in spirit and in truth."

Who Shall Worship The Beast
Revelation 13:1-8 "[1]And I stood upon the sand of the sea, and saw a beast rise up out of the sea, having seven heads and ten horns, and upon his horns ten crowns, and upon his heads the name of blasphemy. [2]And the beast which I saw was like unto a leopard, and his feet were as the feet of a bear, and his mouth as the mouth of a lion: and the dragon gave him his power, and his seat,

and great authority. [3]And I saw one of his heads as it were wounded to death; and his deadly wound was healed: and all the world wondered after the beast. [4]And they worshipped the dragon which gave power unto the beast: and they worshipped the beast, saying, Who is like unto the beast? who is able to make war with him? [5]And there was given unto him a mouth speaking great things and blasphemies; and power was given unto him to continue forty and two months. [6]And he opened his mouth in blasphemy against God, to blaspheme his name, and his tabernacle, and them that dwell in heaven. [7]And it was given unto him to make war with the saints, and to overcome them: and power was given him over all kindreds, and tongues, and nations. [8]And all that dwell upon the earth shall worship him, whose names are not written in the book of life of the Lamb slain from the foundation of the world."

Who Worships God In The Spirit
Philippians 3:3 "For we are the circumcision, which worship God in the spirit, and rejoice in Christ Jesus, and have no confidence in the flesh."

Who Worships The Creature
More Than The Creator
Romans 1:18-25 "[18]For the wrath of God is revealed from heaven against all ungodliness and unrighteousness of men, who hold the truth in unrighteousness; [19]Because that which may be known of God is manifest in them; for God hath shewed it unto them. [20]For the invisible things of him from the creation of the world are clearly seen, being understood by the things that are made, even his eternal power and Godhead; so that they are without excuse: [21]Because that, when they knew God, they glorified him not as God, neither were thankful; but became vain in their imaginations, and their foolish heart was darkened. [22]Professing themselves to be wise, they became fools, [23]And changed the glory of the uncorruptible God into an image made like to corruptible man, and to birds, and fourfooted beasts, and creeping things. [24]Wherefore God also gave them up to uncleanness through the lusts of their own hearts, to dishonour their own bodies between themselves: [25]Who changed the truth of God into a lie, and worshipped and served the creature more than the Creator, who is blessed for ever. Amen."

Who Worships The Lord

Nehemiah 9:6 "Thou, even thou, art LORD alone; thou hast made heaven, the heaven of heavens, with all their host, the earth, and all things that are therein, the seas, and all that is therein, and thou preservest them all; and the host of heaven worshippeth thee."

Who Worships The Lord In Vain

Isaiah 29:13 "Wherefore the Lord said, Forasmuch as this people draw near me with their mouth, and with their lips do honour me, but have removed their heart far from me, and their fear toward me is taught by the precept of men:"

Ezekiel 33:30-32 "30Also, thou son of man, the children of thy people still are talking against thee by the walls and in the doors of the houses, and speak one to another, every one to his brother, saying, Come, I pray you, and hear what is the word that cometh forth from the LORD. 31And they come unto thee as the people cometh, and they sit before thee as my people, and they hear thy words, but they will not do them: for with their mouth they shew much love, but their heart goeth after their covetousness. 32And, lo, thou art unto them as a very lovely song of one that hath a pleasant voice, and can play well on an instrument: for they hear thy words, but they do them not."

Mark 7:6-13 "6He answered and said unto them, Well hath Esaias prophesied of you hypocrites, as it is written, This people honoureth me with their lips, but their heart is far from me. 7Howbeit in vain do they worship me, teaching for doctrines the commandments of men. 8For laying aside the commandment of God, ye hold the tradition of men, as the washing of pots and cups: and many other such like things ye do. 9And he said unto them, Full well ye reject the commandment of God, that ye may keep your own tradition. 10For Moses said, Honour thy father and thy mother; and, Whoso curseth father or mother, let him die the death: 11But ye say, If a man shall say to his father or mother, It is Corban, that is to say, a gift, by whatsoever thou mightest be profited by me; he shall be free. 12And ye suffer him no more to do ought for his father or his mother; 13Making the word of God of none effect through your tradition, which ye have delivered: and many such like things do ye."

Worshipping The Lord

2 Kings 17:35-36 "35With whom the LORD had made a covenant, and charged them saying, Ye shall not fear other gods, nor bow yourselves to them, nor serve them, nor sacrifice to them: 36But the LORD, who brought you up out of the land of Egypt with great power and a stretched out arm, him shall ye fear, and him shall ye worship, and to him shall ye do sacrifice."

1 Chronicles 16:28-29 "28Give unto the LORD, ye kindreds of the people, give unto the LORD glory and strength. 29Give unto the LORD the glory due unto his name: bring an offering, and come before him: worship the LORD in the beauty of holiness."

Psalm 29:2 "Give unto the LORD the glory due unto his name; worship the LORD in the beauty of holiness."

Psalm 63:1-4 "1O God, thou art my God; early will I seek thee: my soul thirsteth for thee, my flesh longeth for thee in a dry and thirsty land, where no water is; 2To see thy power and thy glory, so as I have seen thee in the sanctuary. 3Because thy lovingkindness is better than life, my lips shall praise thee. 4Thus will I bless thee while I live: I will lift up my hands in thy name."

Psalm 95:6 "O come, let us worship and bow down: let us kneel before the LORD our maker."

Psalm 99:5 "Exalt ye the LORD our God, and worship at his footstool; for he is holy."

Psalm 99:9 "Exalt the LORD our God, and worship at his holy hill; for the LORD our God is holy."

Matthew 4:10 "Then saith Jesus unto him, Get thee hence, Satan: for it is written, Thou shalt worship the Lord thy God, and him only shalt thou serve."

Luke 4:8 "And Jesus answered and said unto him, Get thee behind me, Satan: for it is written, Thou shalt worship the Lord thy God, and him only shalt thou serve."

Revelation 14:7 "Saying with a loud voice, Fear God, and give glory to him; for the hour of his judgment is come: and worship him that made heaven, and earth, and the sea, and the fountains of waters."

Revelation 19:10 "And I fell at his feet to worship him. And he said unto me, See thou do it not: I am thy fellowservant, and of thy brethren that have the testimony of Jesus: worship God: for the testimony of Jesus is the spirit of prophecy."

Revelation 22:8-9 "⁸And 1 John saw these things, and heard them. And when I had heard and seen, I fell down to worship before the feet of the angel which shewed me these things. ⁹Then saith he unto me, See thou do it not: for I am thy fellowservant, and of thy brethren the prophets, and of them which keep the sayings of this book: worship God."

WRATH

A Fool's Wrath
Proverbs 12:16 "A fool's wrath is presently known: but a prudent man covereth shame."

Proverbs 27:3 "A stone is heavy, and the sand weighty; but a fool's wrath is heavier than them both."

Being Slow To Wrath
James 1:19 "Wherefore, my beloved brethren, let every man be swift to hear, slow to speak, slow to wrath:"

Forsaking Wrath
Psalm 37:8 "Cease from anger, and forsake wrath: fret not thyself in any wise to do evil."

Ephesians 4:31 "Let all bitterness, and wrath, and anger, and clamour, and evil speaking, be put away from you, with all malice:"

The Forcing Of Wrath
Proverbs 30:33 "Surely the churning of milk bringeth forth butter, and the wringing of the nose bringeth forth blood: so the forcing of wrath bringeth forth strife."

The King's Wrath
Proverbs 14:35 "The king's favour is toward a wise servant: but his wrath is against him that causeth shame."

Proverbs 16:14 "The wrath of a king is as messengers of death: but a wise man will pacify it."

Proverbs 19:12 "The king's wrath is as the roaring of a lion; but his favour is as dew upon the grass."

The Seven Vials Of Wrath
Revelation 15:1-8 "¹And I saw another sign in heaven, great and marvellous, seven angels having the seven last plagues; for in them is filled up the wrath of God. ²And I saw as it were a sea of glass mingled with fire: and them that had gotten the victory over the beast, and over his image, and over his mark, and over the number of his name, stand on the sea of glass, having the harps of God. ³And they sing the song of Moses the servant of God, and the song of the Lamb, saying, Great and marvellous are thy works, Lord God Almighty; just and true are thy ways, thou King of saints. ⁴Who shall not fear thee, O Lord, and glorify thy name? for thou only art holy: for all nations shall come and worship before thee; for thy judgments are made manifest. ⁵And after that I looked, and, behold, the temple of the tabernacle of the testimony in heaven was opened: ⁶And the seven angels came out of the temple, having the seven plagues, clothed in pure and white linen, and having their breasts girded with golden girdles. ⁷And one of the four beasts gave unto the seven angels seven golden vials full of the wrath of God, who liveth for ever and ever. ⁸And the temple was filled with smoke from the glory of God, and from his power; and no man was able to enter into the temple, till the seven plagues of the seven angels were fulfilled."

Revelation 16:1-21 "¹And I heard a great voice out of the temple saying to the seven angels, Go your ways, and pour out the vials of the wrath of God upon the earth. ²And the first went, and poured out his vial upon the earth; and there fell a noisome and grievous sore upon the men which had the mark of the beast, and upon them which worshipped his image. ³And the second angel poured out his vial upon the sea; and it became as the blood of a dead man: and every living soul died in the sea. ⁴And the third angel poured out his vial upon the rivers and fountains of waters; and they became blood. ⁵And I heard the angel of the waters say, Thou art righteous, O Lord, which art, and wast, and shalt be, because thou hast judged thus. ⁶For they have shed the blood of saints and prophets, and thou hast given them blood to drink; for they are worthy. ⁷And I heard another out of the altar say, Even so, Lord God Almighty, true and righteous are thy judgments.

8And the fourth angel poured out his vial upon the sun; and power was given unto him to scorch men with fire. 9And men were scorched with great heat, and blasphemed the name of God, which hath power over these plagues: and they repented not to give him glory. 10And the fifth angel poured out his vial upon the seat of the beast; and his kingdom was full of darkness; and they gnawed their tongues for pain, 11And blasphemed the God of heaven because of their pains and their sores, and repented not of their deeds. 12And the sixth angel poured out his vial upon the great river Euphrates; and the water thereof was dried up, that the way of the kings of the east might be prepared. 13And I saw three unclean spirits like frogs come out of the mouth of the dragon, and out of the mouth of the beast, and out of the mouth of the false prophet. 14For they are the spirits of devils, working miracles, which go forth unto the kings of the earth and of the whole world, to gather them to the battle of that great day of God Almighty. 15Behold, I come as a thief. Blessed is he that watcheth, and keepeth his garments, lest he walk naked, and they see his shame. 16And he gathered them together into a place called in the Hebrew tongue Armageddon. 17And the seventh angel poured out his vial into the air; and there came a great voice out of the temple of heaven, from the throne, saying, It is done. 18And there were voices, and thunders, and lightnings; and there was a great earthquake, such as was not since men were upon the earth, so mighty an earthquake, and so great. 19And the great city was divided into three parts, and the cities of the nations fell: and great Babylon came in remembrance before God, to give unto her the cup of the wine of the fierceness of his wrath. 20And every island fled away, and the mountains were not found. 21And there fell upon men a great hail out of heaven, every stone about the weight of a talent: and men blasphemed God because of the plague of the hail; for the plague thereof was exceeding great."

The Wrath Of Man
James 1:19-21 "19Wherefore, my beloved brethren, let every man be swift to hear, slow to speak, slow to wrath: 20For the wrath of man worketh not the righteousness of God. 21Wherefore lay apart all filthiness and superfluity of naughtiness, and receive with meekness the engrafted word, which is able to save your souls."

The Wrath Of The Lord
Isaiah 9:19-21 "19Through the wrath of the LORD of hosts is the land darkened, and the people shall be as the fuel of the fire: no man shall spare his brother. 20And he shall snatch on the right hand, and be hungry; and he shall eat on the left hand, and they shall not be satisfied: they shall eat every man the flesh of his own arm: 21Manasseh, Ephraim; and Ephraim, Manasseh: and they together shall be against Judah. For all this his anger is not turned away, but his hand is stretched out still."

Jeremiah 10:10 "But the LORD is the true God, he is the living God, and an everlasting king: at his wrath the earth shall tremble, and the nations shall not be able to abide his indignation."

Romans 1:18-20 "18For the wrath of God is revealed from heaven against all ungodliness and unrighteousness of men, who hold the truth in unrighteousness; 19Because that which may be known of God is manifest in them; for God hath shewed it unto them. 20For the invisible things of him from the creation of the world are clearly seen, being understood by the things that are made, even his eternal power and Godhead; so that they are without excuse:"

Revelation 19:11-15 "11And I saw heaven opened, and behold a white horse; and he that sat upon him was called Faithful and True, and in righteousness he doth judge and make war. 12His eyes were as a flame of fire, and on his head were many crowns; and he had a name written, that no man knew, but he himself. 13And he was clothed with a vesture dipped in blood: and his name is called The Word of God. 14And the armies which were in heaven followed him upon white horses, clothed in fine linen, white and clean. 15And out of his mouth goeth a sharp sword, that with it he should smite the nations: and he shall rule them with a rod of iron: and he treadeth the winepress of the fierceness and wrath of Almighty God."

Those That Are Slow To Wrath
Proverbs 14:29 "He that is slow to wrath is of great understanding: but he that is hasty of spirit exalteth folly."

Proverbs 15:18 "A wrathful man stirreth up strife: but he that is slow to anger appeaseth strife."

Proverbs 16:32 "He that is slow to anger is better than the mighty; and he that ruleth his spirit than he that taketh a city."

What Shall Not Profit In The Day Of Wrath

Proverbs 11:4 "Riches profit not in the day of wrath: but righteousness delivereth from death."

Zephaniah 1:18 "Neither their silver nor their gold shall be able to deliver them in the day of the LORD's wrath; but the whole land shall be devoured by the fire of his jealousy: for he shall make even a speedy riddance of all them that dwell in the land."

What Turns Away Wrath

Proverbs 15:1 "A soft answer turneth away wrath: but grievous words stir up anger."

What Wrath Does

Job 5:1-2 "¹Call now, if there be any that will answer thee; and to which of the saints wilt thou turn? ²For wrath killeth the foolish man, and envy slayeth the silly one."

What Wrath Is

Proverbs 27:4 "Wrath is cruel, and anger is outrageous; but who is able to stand before envy?"

Who Can Expect Wrath

Proverbs 11:23 "The desire of the righteous is only good: but the expectation of the wicked is wrath."

Who Is Not Appointed To Wrath

Isaiah 57:1-2 "¹The righteous perisheth, and no man layeth it to heart: and merciful men are taken away, none considering that the righteous is taken away from the evil to come. ²He shall enter into peace: they shall rest in their beds, each one walking in his uprightness."

Micah 7:1-2 "¹Woe is me! for I am as when they have gathered the summer fruits, as the grape-gleanings of the vintage: there is no cluster to eat: my soul desired the firstripe fruit. ²The good man is perished out of the earth: and there is none upright among men: they all lie in wait for blood; they hunt every man his brother with a net."

Romans 5:6-9 "⁶For when we were yet without strength, in due time Christ died for the ungodly. ⁷For scarcely for a righteous man will one die: yet peradventure for a good man some would even dare to die. ⁸But God commendeth his love toward us, in that, while we were yet sinners, Christ died for us. ⁹Much more then, being now justified by his blood, we shall be saved from wrath through him."

1 Thessalonians 1:6-10 "⁶And ye became followers of us, and of the Lord, having received the word in much affliction, with joy of the Holy Ghost: ⁷So that ye were ensamples to all that believe in Macedonia and Achaia. ⁸For from you sounded out the word of the Lord not only in Macedonia and Achaia, but also in every place your faith to Godward is spread abroad; so that we need not to speak any thing. ⁹For they themselves shew of us what manner of entering in we had unto you, and how ye turned to God from idols to serve the living and true God; ¹⁰And to wait for his Son from heaven, whom he raised from the dead, even Jesus, which delivered us from the wrath to come."

1 Thessalonians 5:5-11 "⁵Ye are all the children of light, and the children of the day: we are not of the night, nor of darkness. ⁶Therefore let us not sleep, as do others; but let us watch and be sober. ⁷For they that sleep sleep in the night; and they that be drunken are drunken in the night. ⁸But let us, who are of the day, be sober, putting on the breastplate of faith and love; and for an helmet, the hope of salvation. ⁹For God hath not appointed us to wrath, but to obtain salvation by our Lord Jesus Christ, ¹⁰Who died for us, that, whether we wake or sleep, we should live together with him. ¹¹Wherefore comfort yourselves together, and edify one another, even as also ye do."

Who Shall Have The Wrath Of God Upon Them

Exodus 22:20-24 "²⁰He that sacrificeth unto any god, save unto the LORD only, he shall be utterly destroyed. ²¹Thou shalt neither vex a stranger, nor oppress him: for ye were strangers in the land of Egypt. ²²Ye shall not afflict any widow, or fatherless child. ²³If thou afflict them in any wise, and they cry at all unto me, I will surely hear their cry; ²⁴And my wrath shall wax hot, and I will kill you with the sword; and your wives shall be widows, and your children fatherless."

Exodus 32:7-10 "⁷And the LORD said unto Moses, Go, get thee down; for thy people, which thou broughtest out of the land of Egypt, have cor-rupted themselves: [8]They have turned aside quickly out of the way which I commanded them: they have made them a molten calf, and have worshipped it, and have sacrificed there-unto, and said, These be thy gods, O Israel, which have brought thee up out of the land of Egypt. [9]And the LORD said unto Moses, I have seen this people, and, behold, it is a stiffnecked people: [10]Now therefore let me alone, that my wrath may wax hot against them, and that I may consume them: and I will make of thee a great nation."

Deuteronomy 11:16-17 "[16]Take heed to yourselves, that your heart be not deceived, and ye turn aside, and serve other gods, and worship them; [17]And then the LORD's wrath be kindled against you, and he shut up the heaven, that there be no rain, and that the land yield not her fruit; and lest ye perish quickly from off the good land which the LORD giveth you."

2 Kings 22:13 "Go ye, inquire of the LORD for me, and for the people, and for all Judah, concerning the words of this book that is found: for great is the wrath of the LORD that is kindled against us, because our fathers have not hearkened unto the words of this book, to do according unto all that which is written concerning us."

2 Kings 22:16-17 "[16]Thus saith the LORD, Behold, I will bring evil upon this place, and upon the inhabitants thereof, even all the words of the book which the king of Judah hath read: [17]Be-cause they have forsaken me, and have burned incense unto other gods, that they might provoke me to anger with all the works of their hands; therefore my wrath shall be kindled against this place, and shall not be quenched."

2 Chronicles 29:6-9 "[6]For our fathers have tres-passed, and done that which was evil in the eyes of the LORD our God, and have forsaken him, and have turned away their faces from the habitation of the LORD, and turned their backs. [7]Also they have shut up the doors of the porch, and put out the lamps, and have not burned incense nor offered burnt offerings in the holy place unto the God of Israel. [8]Wherefore the wrath of the LORD was upon Judah and Jerusalem, and he hath deliv-ered them to trouble, to astonishment, and to hiss-ing, as ye see with your eyes. [9]For, lo, our fathers

have fallen by the sword, and our sons and our daughters and our wives are in captivity for this."

2 Chronicles 34:21 "Go, inquire of the LORD for me, and for them that are left in Israel and in Judah, concerning the words of the book that is found: for great is the wrath of the LORD that is poured out upon us, because our fathers have not kept the word of the LORD, to do after all that is written in this book."

2 Chronicles 34:24-25 "[24]Thus saith the LORD, Behold, I will bring evil upon this place, and upon the inhabitants thereof, even all the curses that are written in the book which they have read before the king of Judah: [25]Because they have forsaken me, and have burned incense unto other gods, that they might provoke me to anger with all the works of their hands; therefore my wrath shall be poured out upon this place, and shall not be quenched."

2 Chronicles 36:16 "But they mocked the messen-gers of God, and despised his words, and misused his prophets, until the wrath of the LORD arose against his people, till there was no remedy."

Ezra 8:22 "For I was ashamed to require of the king a band of soldiers and horsemen to help us against the enemy in the way: because we had spoken unto the king, saying, The hand of our God is upon all them for good that seek him; but his power and his wrath is against all them that forsake him."

Job 21:17-20 "[17]How oft is the candle of the wicked put out! and how oft cometh their destruction upon them! God distributeth sorrows in his anger. [18]They are as stubble before the wind, and as chaff that the storm carrieth away. [19]God layeth up his iniquity for his children: he rewardeth him, and he shall know it. [20]His eyes shall see his destruction, and he shall drink of the wrath of the Almighty."

Job 36:5-14 "[5]Behold, God is mighty, and despiseth not any: he is mighty in strength and wisdom. [6] He preserveth not the life of the wicked: but giveth right to the poor. [7]He withdraweth not his eyes from the righteous: but with kings are they on the throne; yea, he doth establish them for ever, and they are exalted. [8]And if they be bound in fetters, and be holden in cords of affliction; ⁹Then he sheweth them their work, and their transgressions that they have exceeded. ¹⁰He openeth also their ear to discipline, and commandeth that they return from iniquity. ¹¹If they obey and serve him, they shall spend their days in prosperity, and their years in pleasures. ¹²But if they obey not, they shall perish by the sword, and they shall die without knowledge. ¹³But the hypocrites in heart heap up wrath: they cry not when he bindeth them. ¹⁴They die in youth, and their life is among the unclean."

Psalm 2:1-12 "¹Why do the heathen rage, and the people imagine a vain thing? ²The kings of the earth set themselves, and the rulers take counsel together, against the LORD, and against his anointed, saying, ³Let us break their bands asunder, and cast away their cords from us. ⁴He that sitteth in the heavens shall laugh: the Lord shall have them in derision. ⁵Then shall he speak unto them in his wrath, and vex them in his sore displeasure. ⁶Yet have I set my king upon my holy hill of Zion. ⁷I will declare the decree: the LORD hath said unto me, Thou art my Son; this day have I begotten thee. ⁸Ask of me, and I shall give thee the heathen for thine inheritance, and the uttermost parts of the earth for thy possession. ⁹Thou shalt break them with a rod of iron; thou shalt dash them in pieces like a potter's vessel. ¹⁰Be wise now therefore, O ye kings: be instructed, ye judges of the earth. ¹¹Serve the LORD with fear, and rejoice with trembling. ¹²Kiss the Son, lest he be angry, and ye perish from the way, when his wrath is kindled but a little. Blessed are all they that put their trust in him."

Psalm 21:7-9 "⁷For the king trusteth in the LORD, and through the mercy of the most High he shall not be moved. ⁸Thine hand shall find out all thine enemies: thy right hand shall find out those that hate thee. ⁹Thou shalt make them as a fiery oven in the time of thine anger: the LORD shall swallow them up in his wrath, and the fire shall devour them."

Psalm 78:17-31 "¹⁷And they sinned yet more against him by provoking the most High in the wilderness. ¹⁸And they tempted God in their heart by asking meat for their lust. ¹⁹Yea, they spake against God; they said, Can God furnish a table in the wilderness? ²⁰Behold, he smote the rock, that the waters gushed out, and the streams overflowed; can he give bread also? can he provide flesh for his people? ²¹Therefore the LORD heard this, and was wroth: so a fire was kindled against Jacob, and anger also came up against Israel; ²²Because they believed not in God, and trusted not in his salvation: ²³Though he had commanded the clouds from above, and opened the doors of heaven, ²⁴And had rained down manna upon them to eat, and had given them of the corn of heaven. ²⁵Man did eat angels' food: he sent them meat to the full. ²⁶He caused an east wind to blow in the heaven: and by his power he brought in the south wind. ²⁷He rained flesh also upon them as dust, and feathered fowls like as the sand of the sea: ²⁸And he let it fall in the midst of their camp, round about their habitations. ²⁹So they did eat, and were well filled: for he gave them their own desire; ³⁰They were not estranged from their lust. But while their meat was yet in their mouths, ³¹The wrath of God came upon them, and slew the fattest of them, and smote down the chosen men of Israel."

Jeremiah 4:3-4 "³For thus saith the LORD to the men of Judah and Jerusalem, Break up your fallow ground, and sow not among thorns. ⁴Circumcise yourselves to the LORD, and take away the foreskins of your heart, ye men of Judah and inhabitants of Jerusalem: lest my fury come forth like fire, and burn that none can quench it, because of the evil of your doings."

Jeremiah 10:24-25 "²⁴O LORD, correct me, but with judgment; not in thine anger, lest thou bring me to nothing. ²⁵Pour out thy fury upon the heathen that know thee not, and upon the families that call not on thy name: for they have eaten up Jacob, and devoured him, and consumed him, and have made his habitation desolate."

Nahum 1:2 "God is jealous, and the LORD revengeth; the LORD revengeth, and is furious; the LORD will take vengeance on his adversaries, and he reserveth wrath for his enemies."

John 3:36 "He that believeth on the Son hath everlasting life: and he that believeth not the Son shall not see life; but the wrath of God abideth on him."

Romans 2:1-8 "¹Therefore thou art inexcusable, O man, whosoever thou art that judgest: for wherein thou judgest another, thou condemnest thyself; for thou that judgest doest the same things. ²But we are sure that the judgment of God is according to truth against them which commit such things. ³And thinkest thou this, O man, that judgest them which do such things, and doest the same, that thou shalt escape the judgment of God? ⁴Or despisest thou the riches of his goodness and forbearance and longsuffering; not knowing that the goodness of God leadeth thee to repentance? ⁵But after thy hardness and impenitent heart treasurest up unto thyself wrath against the day of wrath and revelation of the righteous judgment of God; ⁶Who will render to every man according to his deeds: ⁷To them who by patient continuance in well doing seek for glory and honour and immortality, eternal life: ⁸But unto them that are contentious, and do not obey the truth, but obey unrighteousness, indignation and wrath,"

Ephesians 5:5-7 "⁵For this ye know, that no whoremonger, nor unclean person, nor covetous man, who is an idolater, hath any inheritance in the kingdom of Christ and of God. ⁶Let no man deceive you with vain words: for because of these things cometh the wrath of God upon the children of disobedience. ⁷Be not ye therefore partakers with them."

Colossians 3:5-6 "⁵Mortify therefore your members which are upon the earth; fornication, uncleanness, inordinate affection, evil concupiscence, and covetousness, which is idolatry: ⁶For which things' sake the wrath of God cometh on the children of disobedience:"

Revelation 11:15-18 "¹⁵And the seventh angel sounded; and there were great voices in heaven, saying, The kingdoms of this world are become the kingdoms of our Lord, and of his Christ; and he shall reign for ever and ever. ¹⁶And the four and twenty elders, which sat before God on their seats, fell upon their faces, and worshipped God, ¹⁷Saying, We give thee thanks, O Lord God Almighty, which art, and wast, and art to come; because thou hast taken to thee thy great power, and hast reigned. ¹⁸And the nations were angry, and thy wrath is come, and the time of the dead, that they should be judged, and that thou shouldest give reward unto thy servants the prophets, and to the saints, and them that fear thy name, small and great; and shouldest destroy them which destroy the earth."

Revelation 14:9-11 "⁹And the third angel followed them, saying with a loud voice, If any man worship the beast and his image, and receive his mark in his forehead, or in his hand, ¹⁰The same shall drink of the wine of the wrath of God, which is poured out without mixture into the cup of his indignation; and he shall be tormented with fire and brimstone in the presence of the holy angels, and in the presence of the Lamb: ¹¹And the smoke of their torment ascendeth up for ever and ever: and they have no rest day nor night, who worship the beast and his image, and whosoever receiveth the mark of his name."

Who The Wrath Of The Lord Will Turn Away From

2 Chronicles 30:8 "Now be ye not stiffnecked, as your fathers were, but yield yourselves unto the LORD, and enter into his sanctuary, which he hath sanctified for ever: and serve the LORD your God, that the fierceness of his wrath may turn away from you."

Who Turns Away Wrath

Proverbs 29:8 "Scornful men bring a city into a snare: but wise men turn away wrath."

Wrathful Men

Proverbs 15:18 "A wrathful man stirreth up strife: but he that is slow to anger appeaseth strife."

Proverbs 19:19 "A man of great wrath shall suffer punishment: for if thou deliver him, yet thou must do it again."

Proverbs 29:22 "An angry man stirreth up strife, and a furious man aboundeth in transgression."

YOKE

Not Being Entangled With The Yoke Of Bondage

Acts 15:10 "Now therefore why tempt ye God, to put a yoke upon the neck of the disciples, which neither our fathers nor we were able to bear?"

Galatians 5:1 "Stand fast therefore in the liberty wherewith Christ hath made us free, and be not entangled again with the yoke of bondage."

The Lord Breaking Yokes

Leviticus 26:11-13 "¹¹And I will set my tabernacle among you: and my soul shall not abhor you. ¹²And I will walk among you, and will be your God, and ye shall be my people. ¹³I am the LORD your God, which brought you forth out of the land of Egypt, that ye should not be their bondmen; and I have broken the bands of your yoke, and made you go upright."

Ezekiel 34:27-29 "²⁷And the tree of the field shall yield her fruit, and the earth shall yield her increase, and they shall be safe in their land, and shall know that I am the LORD, when I have broken the bands of their yoke, and delivered them out of the hand of those that served themselves of them. ²⁸And they shall no more be a prey to the heathen, neither shall the beast of the land devour them; but they shall dwell safely, and none shall make them afraid. ²⁹And I will raise up for them a plant of renown, and they shall be no more consumed with hunger in the land, neither bear the shame of the heathen any more."

The Yoke Of Jesus Christ

Matthew 11:25-30 "²⁵At that time Jesus answered and said, I thank thee, O Father, Lord of heaven and earth, because thou hast hid these things from the wise and prudent, and hast revealed them unto babes. ²⁶Even so, Father: for so it seemed good in thy sight. ²⁷All things are delivered unto me of my Father: and no man knoweth the Son, but the Father; neither knoweth any man the Father, save the Son, and he to whomsoever the Son will reveal him. ²⁸Come unto me, all ye that labour and are heavy laden, and I will give you rest. ²⁹Take my yoke upon you, and learn of me; for I am meek and lowly in heart: and ye shall find rest unto your souls. ³⁰For my yoke is easy, and my burden is light."

Who Not To Be Equally Yoked With

2 Corinthians 6:14-18 "¹⁴Be ye not unequally yoked together with unbelievers: for what fellowship hath righteousness with unrighteousness? and what communion hath light with darkness? ¹⁵And what concord hath Christ with Belial? or what part hath he that believeth with an infidel? ¹⁶And what agreement hath the temple of God with idols? for ye are the temple of the living God; as God hath said, I will dwell in them, and walk in them; and I will be their God, and they shall be my people. ¹⁷Wherefore come out from among them, and be ye separate, saith the Lord, and touch not the unclean thing; and I will receive you, ¹⁸And will be a Father unto you, and ye shall be my sons and daughters, saith the Lord Almighty."